S0-BAM-894

S. Pub.111-14

2009-2010

OFFICIAL CONGRESSIONAL DIRECTORY

111TH CONGRESS

CONVENED JANUARY 6, 2009

JOINT COMMITTEE ON PRINTING
UNITED STATES CONGRESS

UNITED STATES GOVERNMENT PRINTING OFFICE
WASHINGTON, DC

Front Cover

Located beneath the East Front Plaza, the Capitol Visitor Center was opened to the public on December 2, 2008. The newest edition to the U.S. Capitol, the 580,000 square foot facility houses an exhibition hall, restaurant, orientation theaters, and other visitor amenities. Photo by the Architect of the Capitol.

U.S. GOVERNMENT OFFICIAL EDITION NOTICE

Use of ISBN Prefix

This is the Official U.S. Government edition of this publication and is herein identified to certify its authenticity. Use of the 0-16 ISBN prefix is for U.S. Government Printing Office Official Editions only. The Superintendent of Documents of the U.S. Government Printing Office requests that any reprinted edition clearly be labeled as a copy of the authentic work with a new ISBN.

Printed by BERNAN
A wholly owned subsidiary of The Rowman & Littlefield Publishing Group, Inc.
4501 Forbes Boulevard, Suite 200, Lanham, Maryland 20706
http://www.bernan.com 800-865-3457; info@bernan.com

ISBN: 978-1-60175-809-5 (paperback)
ISBN: 978-1-60175-810-1 (casebound)

NOTES

Closing date for compilation of the Congressional Directory was October 2, 2009.

[Democrats in roman, Republicans in *italic*.]

The following changes have occurred in the membership of the 111th Congress since the election of November 4, 2008:

Name	Resigned or [Died]	Successor	Elected or [Appointed]	Sworn in
SENATORS				
Roland Burris, IL [1]			[Dec. 31, 2008]	Jan. 15, 2009
Joseph R. Biden, Jr., DE [2]	Jan. 15, 2009	Edward E. Kaufman	[Jan. 15, 2009]	Jan. 16, 2009
Hillary Rodham Clinton, NY [3]	Jan. 21, 2009	Kirsten E. Gillibrand	[Jan. 23, 2009]	Jan. 27, 2009 [4]
Ken Salazar, CO [5]	Jan. 21, 2009	Michael F. Bennet	[Jan. 21, 2009]	Jan. 22, 2009
Arlen Specter, PA [6]				
Al Franken, MN			Nov. 4, 2008	July 7, 2009 [7]
Edward M. Kennedy, MA	[Aug. 25, 2009]	Paul G. Kirk, Jr. [8]	[Sept. 24, 2009]	Sept. 25, 2009
Mel Martinez, FL	Sept. 9, 2009	*George S. LeMieux*	[Sept. 9, 2009]	Sept. 10, 2009
REPRESENTATIVES				
Rahm Emanuel, 5th IL [9]	Jan. 6, 2009	Mike Quigley	Apr. 7, 2009	Apr. 21, 2009
Kirsten E. Gillibrand, 20th NY [10]	Jan. 26, 2009	Scott Murphy	Mar. 31, 2009	Apr. 29, 2009
Hilda Solis, 32d CA [11]	Feb. 24, 2009	Judy Chu	July 14, 2009	July 16, 2009
Ellen O. Tauscher, 10th CA [12]	June 26, 2009			
John M. McHugh, 23d NY [13]	Sept. 21, 2009			

[1] Appointed to fill the vacancy at the end of the 110th Congress; however, because his credentials were not immediately accepted by the Senate, he was not sworn-in until after the 111th Congress had already begun.
[2] Resigned having been elected Vice President of the United States.
[3] Resigned to become Secretary of State.
[4] Appointed January 23, 2009 to fill the vacancy caused by the resignation of Hillary Clinton; appointment took effect upon her resignation from the House of Representatives on January 26, 2009, took the oath of office on January 27, 2009.
[5] Resigned to become Secretary of the Interior.
[6] Senator Specter changed party affiliation from Republican to Democrat on April 30, 2009.
[7] Contested election resolved June 30, 2009.
[8] Appointed to fill this seat until a special election is held on January 19, 2010, the winner of which will complete the term ending January 3, 2013.
[9] Representative-elect Emanuel did not take his seat (effective January 3, 2009) in anticipation of becoming White House Chief of Staff.
[10] Resigned.
[11] Resigned.
[12] Resigned.
[13] Resigned.

[Democrats in roman, Republicans in *italic*.]

The following changes occurred in the membership of the 110th Congress after the election of November 7, 2006:

Name	Resigned or [Died]	Successor	Elected or [Appointed]	Sworn in
SENATORS				
Craig Thomas, WY	[June 4, 2007]	*John Barrasso*	[June 22, 2007]	June 25, 2007
Trent Lott, MS	Dec. 18, 2007	*Roger F. Wicker*	[Dec. 31, 2007]	Dec. 31, 2007
Barack Obama, IL [1]	Nov. 16, 2008	Roland Burris	[Dec. 31, 2008]	Jan. 15, 2009 [2]
REPRESENTATIVES				
Charlie Norwood, 10th GA	[Feb. 13, 2007]	*Paul C. Broun*	July 17, 2007	July 25, 2007
Juanita Millender-McDonald, 37th CA	[Apr. 22, 2007]	Laura Richardson	Aug. 21, 2007	Sept. 4, 2007

Name	Resigned or [Died]	Successor	Elected or [Appointed]	Sworn in
Martin T. Meehan, 5th MA	July 1, 2007	Niki Tsongas	Oct. 16, 2007 ...	Oct. 18, 2007
Paul Gillmor, 5th OH	[Sept. 5, 2007] ..	*Robert E. Latta*	Dec. 11, 2007 ..	Dec. 13, 2007
Jo Ann Davis, 1st VA	[Oct. 6, 2007] ...	*Robert J. Wittman*	Dec. 11, 2007 ..	Dec. 13, 2007
J. Dennis Hastert, 14th IL	Nov. 26, 2007 ...	Bill Foster	Mar. 8, 2008	Mar. 11, 2008
Julia Carson, 7th IN	[Dec. 15, 2007]	André Carson	Mar. 11, 2008 ..	Mar. 13, 2008
Roger F. Wicker, 1st MS [3]	Dec. 31, 2007 ...	Travis W. Childers	May 13, 2008 ..	May 20, 2008
Bobby Jindal, 1st LA [4]	Jan. 14 2008	*Steve Scalise*	May 3, 2008	May 7, 2008
Richard H. Baker, 6th LA	Feb. 2, 2008	Donald J. Cazayoux, Jr.	May 3, 2008	May 6, 2008
Tom Lantos, 12th CA	[Feb. 11, 2008]	Jackie Speier	Apr. 8, 2008	Apr. 10, 2008
Albert Russell Wynn, 4th MD	May 31, 2008 ...	Donna F. Edwards	June 17, 2008 ..	June 19, 2008
Stephanie Tubbs Jones, 11th OH	[Aug. 20, 2008]	Marcia L. Fudge	Nov. 18, 2008 ..	Nov. 19, 2008
Tom Davis, 11th VA	Nov. 24, 2008 ...	....	....	

[1] Resigned having been elected President of the United States.

[2] Was appointed during, but after the *sine die* adjournment of, the 110th Congress; however, his credentials were not accepted by the Senate until after the 111th Congress convened.

[3] Resigned to accept appointment to the United States Senate.

[4] Resigned having been elected Governor of Louisiana.

FOREWORD

The *Congressional Directory* is one of the oldest working handbooks within the United States Government. While there were unofficial directories for Congress in one form or another beginning with the 1st Congress in 1789, the Congressional Directory published in 1847 for the 30th Congress is considered by scholars and historians to be the first official edition because it was the first to be ordered and paid for by Congress. With the addition of biographical sketches of legislators in 1867, the Congressional Directory attained its modern format.

The Congressional Directory is published by the United States Congress in partnership with the Government Printing Office, at the direction of the Joint Committee on Printing under the authority of Title 44, Section 721 of the U.S. Code.

JOINT COMMITTEE ON PRINTING

Charles E. Schumer, Senator from New York, *Chair.*

Robert A. Brady, Representative from Pennsylvania, *Vice Chair.*

Senate

Patty Murray, of Washington.
Tom Udall, of New Mexico.
Robert F. Bennett, of Utah.
Saxby Chambliss, of Georgia.

House

Michael E. Capuano, of Massachusetts.
Susan A. Davis, of California.
Daniel E. Lungren, of California.
Kevin McCarthy, of California.

The 2009–2010 Congressional Directory was compiled by the Government Printing Office, under the direction of the Joint Committee on Printing by:

Project Manager.—Evangeline Brown.

Editors: Farnsworth Alston; Mary Ann Carter; Sarah Randolph.

Typographer.—Michael Colbert.

Proofreader.—Margaret Ross-Smith.

Special Assistance.—Peter Byrd, former Congressional Staff.

State District Maps.—Election Data Services, Inc.

Representatives' Zip Codes.—House Office of Mailing Services / U.S. Postal Service.

For sale by the Superintendent of Documents, U.S. Government Printing Office

Internet: bookstore.gpo.gov; Phone: toll free (866) 512–1800; DC area (202) 512–1800

Fax: (202) 512–2250; Mail: Stop SSOP, Washington, DC 20402–0001

Paper Cover ISBN–978–0–16–083727–2

Casebound ISBN–978–0–16–083728–9

CONTENTS

Name Index on page 1117

111th Congress*

THE VICE PRESIDENT

JOSEPH R. BIDEN, JR., Democrat, of Wilmington, DE; born in Scranton, PA, November 20, 1942; education: St. Helena's School, Wilmington, DE; Archmere Academy, Claymont, DE; A.B., history and political science, University of Delaware; J.D., Syracuse University College of Law; married: Jill Tracy Biden; children: Joseph R. Biden III, Robert Hunter Biden, and Ashley Blazer Biden; admitted to the bar, December 1968, Wilmington, DE; engaged in private practice until 1972; served on New Castle County Council, 1970–72; elected to the U.S. Senate on November 7, 1972; reelected to each succeeding Senate term; served on committees: chair, Foreign Relations; Judiciary; elected as 47th Vice President of the United States on November 4, 2008; took the oath of office on January 20, 2009.

The Ceremonial Office of the Vice President is S–212 in the Capitol. The Vice President has offices in the Dirksen Senate Office Building, the Eisenhower Executive Office Building (EEOB) and the White House (West Wing).

Chief of Staff to the Vice President.—Ron Klain, EEOB, room 202, 456–2423.
Deputy Chief of Staff to the Vice President.—Alan Hoffman, EEOB, room 202, 456–2423.
Counsel to the Vice President.—Cynthia Hogan, EEOB, room 246, 456–3241.
Director of Communications to the Vice President.—Jay Carney, EEOB, room 284, 456–5249.
Press Secretary to the Vice President.—Elizabeth Alexander, EEOB, room 284, 456–5249.
Assistant to the Vice President for—
Domestic Policy.—Terrell McSweeny, EEOB, room 222, 456–3071.
Economic Policy.—Jared Bernstein, EEOB, room 222, 456–3071.
National Security Advisor.—Tony Blinken, EEOB, room 246, 456–2646.
Chief of Staff to Dr. Jill Biden.—Cathy Russell, EEOB, room 200, 456–6773.
Director of Scheduling to the Vice President.—Elisabeth Hire, EEOB, room 239, 456–6773.
Director of Advance to the Vice President.—Vacant, EEOB, room 241, 456–6773.
Executive Assistants to the Vice President: Nancy Orloff, Michele Smith, West Wing.
Director of Correspondence.—Daniel Griffin, EEOB, room 233, 456–6770.

*Biographies are based on information furnished or authorized by the respective Senators and Representatives.

ALABAMA

(Population 2000, 4,447,100)

SENATORS

RICHARD C. SHELBY, Republican, of Tuscaloosa, AL; born in Birmingham, AL, May 6, 1934; education: attended the public schools; B.A., University of Alabama, 1957; LL.B., University of Alabama School of Law, 1963; professional: attorney; admitted to the Alabama bar in 1961 and commenced practice in Tuscaloosa; member, Alabama State Senate, 1970–78; law clerk, Supreme Court of Alabama, 1961–62; city prosecutor, Tuscaloosa, 1963–71; U.S. Magistrate, Northern District of Alabama, 1966–70; special assistant Attorney General, State of Alabama, 1969–71; chairman, legislative council of the Alabama Legislature, 1977–78; former president, Tuscaloosa County Mental Health Association; member of Alabama Code Revision Committee, 1971–75; member: Phi Alpha Delta legal fraternity, Tuscaloosa County; Alabama and American bar associations; First Presbyterian Church of Tuscaloosa; Exchange Club; American Judicature Society; Alabama Law Institute; married: the former Annette Nevin in 1960; children: Richard C., Jr., and Claude Nevin; committees: ranking member, Banking, Housing, and Urban Affairs; Appropriations; Special Committee on Aging; elected to the 96th Congress on November 7, 1978; reelected to the three succeeding Congresses; elected to the U.S. Senate on November 4, 1986; reelected to each succeeding Senate term.

Office Listings

http://shelby.senate.gov

304 Russell Senate Office Building, Washington, DC 20510 .... (202) 224–5744
Chief of Staff.—Alan Hanson. FAX: 224–3416
Personal Secretary / Appointments.—Anne Caldwell.
Press Secretary.—Jonathan Graffeo.
The Federal Building, 1118 Greensboro Avenue #240, Tuscaloosa, AL 35403 .... (205) 759–5047
Vance Federal Building, Room 321, 1800 5th Avenue North, Birmingham, AL 35203 .... (205) 731–1384
John A. Campbell Federal Courthouse, 113 St. Joseph Street, Mobile, AL 36602 ... (251) 694–4164
Frank M. Johnson Federal Courthouse, Suite 445, 15 Lee Street, Montgomery, AL 36104 .... (334) 223–7303
Huntsville International Airport, 1000 Glenn Hearn Boulevard, Box 20127, Huntsville, AL 35824 .... (256) 772–0460

* * *

JEFF SESSIONS, Republican, of Mobile, AL; born in Hybart, AL, December 24, 1946; education: graduated Wilcox County High School, Camden, AL; B.A., Huntingdon College, Montgomery, AL, 1969; J.D., University of Alabama, Tuscaloosa, 1973; professional: U.S. Army Reserves, captain, 1973–86; attorney; admitted to the Alabama bar in 1973 and commenced practice for Guin, Bouldin and Porch in Russellville, 1973–75; Assistant U.S. Attorney, South District of Alabama, 1975–77; attorney for Stockman & Bedsole, 1977–81; U.S. Attorney, South District of Alabama, 1981–93; attorney for Stockman, Bedsole and Sessions, 1993–94; Attorney General, State of Alabama, 1994–96; member: Huntingdon College Board of Trustees; Samford University, Board of Overseers; delegate, General Conference, United Methodist Church; Montgomery Lions Club; Mobile United Methodist Inner City Mission; American Bar Association; Ashland Place United Methodist Church; married: the former Mary Blackshear, 1969; children: Ruth, Mary Abigail, and Samuel; International Narcotics Control Caucus; committees: Armed Services; Budget; Energy and Natural Resources; Judiciary; elected to the U.S. Senate on November 5, 1996; reelected to each succeeding Senate term.

Office Listings

http://sessions.senate.gov

335 Russell Senate Office Building, Washington, DC 20510 .... (202) 224–4124
Chief of Staff.—Rick Dearborn. FAX: 224–3149
Scheduler.—Kate Hollis.
Executive Assistant.—Peggi Hanrahan.
Communications Director.—Stephen Boyd.
341 Vance Federal Building, 1800 Fifth Avenue North, Birmingham, AL 35203 .... (205) 731–1500
Field Representative.—Lindsay Davis.
Colonial Bank Centre, Suite 2300–A, 41 West I–65 Service Road North, Mobile, AL 36608 .... (251) 414–3083
Field Representative.—Valerie Day.
200 Clinton Avenue, NW., Suite 802, Huntsville, AL 35801 .... (256) 533–0979

Field Representative.—Lisa Montgomery.
7550 Halcyon Summit Drive, Suite 150, Montgomery, AL 36117 .... (334) 244–7017
State Director.—Chuck Spurlock.

REPRESENTATIVES

FIRST DISTRICT

JO BONNER, Republican, of Mobile, AL; born in Selma, AL, November 19, 1959; education: B.A., in Journalism, University of Alabama, 1982; organizations: Rotary Club; Mobile Area Chamber of Commerce; University of Alabama Alumni Association; Leadership Mobile; Junior League of Mobile; International Committee for the Mobile Tricentennial; professional: congressional aide to Representative Sonny Callahan, serving as Press Secretary, 1985–89, and Chief of Staff, 1989–2002; married: Janee; children: Jennifer Lee and Josiah Robins, III; committees: Appropriations; Standards of Official Conduct; elected to the 108th Congress on November 5, 2002; reelected to each succeeding Congress.

Office Listings

http://bonner.house.gov

2236 Rayburn House Office Building, Washington, DC 20515 .... (202) 225–4931
Chief of Staff.—Alan Spencer. FAX: 225–0562
Legislative Director.—Kelle Strickland.
Scheduler.—Suzanna Weeks.
11 North Water Street, Suite 15290, Mobile, AL 36602 .... (251) 690–2811
(800) 288–8721
1302 North McKenzie Street, Foley, AL 36535 .... (251) 943–2073

Counties: BALDWIN, CLARKE (part), ESCAMBIA, MOBILE, MONROE, WASHINGTON. Population (2000), 635,300.

ZIP Codes: 36420, 36425–27, 36432, 36436, 36439, 36441, 36444–46, 36451, 36456–58, 36460–62, 36470–71, 36475, 36480–83, 36502–05, 36507, 36509, 36511–13, 36515, 36518, 36521–30, 36532–33, 36535–36, 36538–39, 36541–45, 36547–51, 36553, 36555–56, 36558–62, 36564, 36567–69, 36571–72, 36575–85, 36587, 36590, 36601–13, 36615–19, 36621–22, 36628, 36633, 36640, 36652, 36660, 36663, 36670–71, 36685, 36688–89, 36691, 36693, 36695, 36720–23, 36726, 36728, 36741, 36751, 36762, 36768–69, 36784

* * *

SECOND DISTRICT

BOBBY BRIGHT, Democrat, of Montgomery, AL; born in Midland City, AL, July 21, 1952; education: B.S., Auburn University, Auburn, AL; M.A., Troy University, Troy, AL; J.D., Thomas Goode Jones School of Law, Montgomery, AL; professional: corrections officer; attorney; financial advisor; Mayor of Montgomery; awards: Alabama Tourism Advocate of the Year; Government Tourism Advocate of the Year; Director, Alabama Baptist Board; married: Lynn Clardy Bright; children: Neal, Lisa, and Katie; committees: Agriculture; Armed Services; Small Business; elected to the 111th Congress on November 4, 2008.

Office Listings

http://bright.house.gov

1205 Longworth House Office Building, Washington, DC 20515 .... (202) 225–2901
Chief of Staff.—Meg Joseph. FAX: 225–8913
Legislative Director.—Juan Hinojosa.
Communications Director.—Lewis Lowe.
Director of Scheduling.—Jenny Selzer.
22 Monroe Street, Suite B, Montgomery, AL 36104 .... (334) 277–9113
256 Honeysuckle Road, Suite #15, Dothan, AL 36305 .... (334) 794–9680
101 North Main Street, Opp, AL 35467.
275 North Union Avenue, Ozark, AL 36360.

Counties: AUTAUGA, BARBOUR, BULLOCK, BUTLER, COFFEE, CONECUH, COVINGTON, CRENSHAW, DALE, ELMORE, GENEVA, HENRY, HOUSTON, LOWNDES, MONTGOMERY (part), PIKE. Population (2000), 635,300.

ZIP Codes: 35010, 36003, 36005–06, 36008–10, 36015–17, 36020, 36022, 36024–43, 36046–49, 36051–54, 36061–62, 36064–69, 36071–72, 36078–82, 36089, 36091–93, 36101–18, 36120–21, 36123–25, 36130, 36132, 36135, 36140–42, 36177, 36191, 36301–05, 36310–14, 36316–23, 36330–31, 36340, 36343–46, 36349–53, 36360–62, 36370–71, 36373–76, 36401, 36420, 36426, 36429, 36432, 36442, 36449, 36453–56, 36467, 36471, 36473–77, 36483, 36502, 36524, 36703, 36749, 36752, 36758, 36761, 36775, 36785

* * *

THIRD DISTRICT

MIKE ROGERS, Republican, of Saks, AL; born in Hammond, IN, July 16, 1958; education: B.A., Jacksonville State University, 1981; M.P.A., Jacksonville State University, 1984; J.D., Birmingham School of Law, 1991; professional: attorney; awards: Anniston Star Citizen of the Year, 1998; public service: Calhoun County Commissioner, 1987–91; Alabama House of Representatives, 1994–2002; family: married to Beth; children: Emily, Evan, and Elliot; committees: Agriculture; Armed Services; Homeland Security; elected to the 108th Congress on November 5, 2002; reelected to each succeeding Congress.

Office Listings

http://www/house.gov/mike-rogers

324 Cannon House Office Building, Washington, DC 20515 .... (202) 225–3261
Chief of Staff.—Marshall Macomber. FAX: 226–8485
Deputy Chief of Staff.—Chris Brinson.
Press Secretary.—Shea Snider.
Scheduler.—Laura Hooper.
1129 Noble Street, 104 Federal Building, Anniston, AL 36201 .... (256) 236–5655
District Director.—Sheri Rollins.
1819 Pepperell Parkway, Suite 203, Opelika, AL 36801 .... (334) 745–6222
Field Representative.—Cheryl Cunningham.
7550 Halcyon Summit Drive, Montgomery, AL 36117 .... (334) 277–4210
Field Representative.—Alvin Lewis.

Counties: CALHOUN, CHAMBERS, CHEROKEE, CLAY, CLEBURNE, COOSA (part), LEE, MACON, MONTGOMERY (part), RANDOLPH, RUSSELL, TALLADEGA, TALLAPOOSA. Population (2000), 635,300.

ZIP Codes: 35010, 35014, 35032, 35044, 35078, 35082, 35089, 35096, 35136, 35160, 35183, 35960, 35973, 35983, 36013, 36023, 36026, 36036, 36039, 36043, 36046–47, 36052, 36057–58, 36064–65, 36069–70, 36075, 36088, 36101–21, 36123–25, 36201, 36215, 36252–63, 36265–76, 36278–80, 36766, 36801–04, 36825, 36830, 36850, 36853–55, 36858–65, 36867–79, 36959

* * *

FOURTH DISTRICT

ROBERT B. ADERHOLT, Republican, of Haleyville, AL; born in Haleyville, July 22, 1965; education: graduate, Birmingham Southern University; J.D., Cumberland School of Law, Samford University; professional: attorney; assistant legal advisor to Governor Fob James, 1995–96; Haleyville municipal judge, 1992–96; George Bush delegate, Republican National Convention, 1992; Republican nominee for the 17th District, Alabama House of Representatives, 1990; married: Caroline McDonald; children: Mary Elliott and Robert Hayes; committees: Appropriations; Budget; elected to the 105th Congress; reelected to each succeeding Congress.

Office Listings

http://www.aderholt.house.gov

1433 Longworth House Office Building, Washington, DC 20515 .... (202) 225–4876
Chief of Staff.—Mark Busching. FAX: 225–5587
Legislative Director.—Mark Dawson.
Communications Director / Press Secretary.—Darrell Jordan.
Executive Assistant.—Tiffany Noel.
247 Carl Elliott Building, 1710 Alabama Avenue, Room 247, Jasper, AL 35501 .... (205) 221–2310
District Field Director.—Paul Housel.
205 Fourth Avenue, NE., Suite 104, Cullman, AL 35055 .... (256) 734–6043
Director of Constituent Services.—Jennifer Taylor.
107 Federal Building, 600 Broad Street, Gadsden, AL 35901 .... (256) 546–0201
Field Representative.—Jason Harper.
Morgan County Courthouse, P.O. Box 668, Decatur, AL 35602 .... (256) 350–4093
Field Representative.—Daniel Tidwell.

Counties: BLOUNT, CULLMAN, DEKALB, ETOWAH, FAYETTE, FRANKLIN, LAMAR, MARION, MARSHALL, MORGAN (part), PICKENS (part), ST. CLAIR (part), WALKER, WINSTON. Population (2000), 635,300.

ZIP Codes: 35006, 35013, 35016, 35019, 35031, 35033, 35038, 35049, 35053, 35055–58, 35062–63, 35070, 35077, 35079, 35083, 35087, 35097–98, 35121, 35126, 35130–31, 35133, 35146, 35148, 35172, 35175, 35179–80, 35205–07, 35212–13, 35215, 35441, 35447, 35461, 35466, 35481, 35501–04, 35540–46, 35548–55, 35559–60, 35563–65, 35570–82, 35584–87, 35592–94, 35601, 35603, 35619, 35621–22, 35640, 35651, 35653–54, 35670, 35672–73, 35747, 35754–55, 35760, 35765, 35769, 35771, 35775–76, 35901–07, 35950–54, 35956–57, 35959–64, 35966–68, 35971–76, 35978–81, 35983–84, 35986–90, 36064, 36117, 36271–72, 36275

* * *

FIFTH DISTRICT

PARKER GRIFFITH, Democrat, of Huntsville, AL; born in Shreveport, LA, June 6, 1942; education: graduated, B.S., Louisiana State University, 1966; M.D., Louisiana State University Medical School, 1970; professional: captain; radiation oncologist, Huntsville, AL, 1975–1992; VA Army Reserve, 1970–73; small business owner 1975 to present; elected Alabama State Senate, 2006; retired physician; teacher; religion: Episcopalian; married: Virginia; children: five; committees: Science and Technology, Small Business; Transportation and Infrastructure; elected to the 111th Congress on November 4, 2008.

Office Listings

dr.griffith@mail.house.gov

417 Cannon House Office Building, Washington, DC 20515 .... (202) 225–4801
Chief of Staff.—Sharon Wheeler. FAX: 225–4392
Legislative Director.—Megan Swearingen.
Scheduler.—Leigh Pettis.
2101 Clinton Avenue, West Suite 302, Huntsville, AL 35805 .... (256) 551–0190
District Director.—Jim McCamy.
Morgan County Courthouse, 5th Floor, Decatur, AL 35602 .... (256) 355–9400
Caseworker.—Peggy Towns.
The Bevill Center.
1011 George Wallace Boulevard, Tuscumbia, AL 35674 .... (256) 381–3450
Field Directory.—Gene Tackett.

Counties: COLBERT, JACKSON, LAUDERDALE, LAWRENCE, LIMESTONE, MADISON, MORGAN (part). Population (2000), 635,300.

ZIP Codes: 35016, 35205–06, 35209–10, 35212, 35215, 35540, 35582, 35601–03, 35609–20, 35630–34, 35640, 35643, 35645–54, 35660–62, 35671–74, 35677, 35699, 35739–42, 35744–46, 35748–52, 35755–69, 35771–74, 35776, 35801–16, 35824, 35893–96, 35898–99, 35958, 35966, 35978–79, 36104

* * *

SIXTH DISTRICT

SPENCER BACHUS, Republican, of Vestavia Hills, AL; born in Birmingham, AL, December 28, 1947; education: B.A., Auburn University, 1969; J.D., University of Alabama, 1972; professional: law firm, Bachus, Dempsey, Carson, and Steed, senior partner; member: Hunter Street Baptist Church; Alabama State Representative and Senator; school board; Republican Party Chair; children: Warren, Stuart, Elliott, Candace, and Lisa; committees: ranking member, Financial Services; elected to the 103rd Congress, November 3, 1992; reelected to each succeeding Congress.

Office Listings

http://www.house.gov/bachus

2246 Rayburn House Office Building, Washington, DC 20515 .... (202) 225–4921
Chief of Staff.—Michael Staley. FAX: 225–2082
Press Secretary.—Tim Johnson.
Legislative Director.—Clint Shouppe.
1900 International Park Drive, Suite 107, Birmingham, AL 35243 .... (205) 969–2296
703 Second Avenue, North, P.O. Box 502, Clanton, AL 35046 .... (205) 280–0704
Scheduler.—Sarah Riser.

Counties: BIBB, CHILTON, COOSA (part), JEFFERSON (part), SHELBY, ST. CLAIR (part), TUSCALOOSA (part). CITIES AND TOWNSHIPS: Adamsville, Alabaster, Argo, Brookside, Brookwood, Calera, Cardiff, Clanton, Columbiana, County Line, Fultondale, Gardendale, Graysville, Harpersville, Helena, Homewood, Hoover, Hueytown, Irondale, Jemison, Kimberly, Leeds, Maytown, Montevallo, Morris, Mountain Brook, Mulga, North Johns, Northport, Pelham, Pell City, Pleasant Grove, Ragland, Sumiton, Sylvan Springs, Thorsby, Trafford, Trussville, Vestavia Hills, Vincent, Warrior, West Jefferson, Wilsonville, Wilton, and portions of Bessemer, Birmingham, Tarrant, Tuscaloosa, and West Blocton. Population (2000), 635,300.

ZIP Codes: 35004–07, 35015, 35022–23, 35035, 35040, 35043, 35046, 35048, 35051–52, 35054, 35060, 35062–63, 35068, 35071, 35073–74, 35078–80, 35085, 35091, 35094, 35096, 35111–12, 35114–20, 35123–28, 35130–31, 35133, 35135, 35137, 35139, 35142–44, 35146–48, 35151, 35171–73, 35175–76, 35178, 35180–88, 35201–03, 35205–07, 35209–10, 35212–17, 35219, 35222–26, 35230, 35233, 35235–37, 35240, 35242–46, 35249, 35253–55, 35259–61, 35266, 35277–83, 35285, 35287–99, 35402–03, 35406–07, 35444, 35446, 35452, 35456–58, 35466, 35468, 35473, 35475–76, 35480, 35482, 35490, 35546, 35579, 35953, 35987, 36006, 36051, 36064, 36091, 36750, 36758, 36790, 36792–93

* * *

SEVENTH DISTRICT

ARTUR DAVIS, Democrat, of Birmingham, AL; born in Montgomery, AL, October 9, 1967; education: graduated from Jefferson Davis High School, Montgomery, AL; B.A., *magna cum laude,* Harvard University, Cambridge, MA, 1990; J.D., *cum laude,* Harvard Law School, Cambridge, MA, 1993; professional: Attorney; public service: interned with U.S. Senator Howell Heflin (D–AL); interned with the Southern Poverty Law Center; clerked for Federal Judge Myron Thompson; served as an Assistant U.S. Attorney for the Middle District of Alabama, 1994–98; attorney in private practice, 1998–2002; memberships and boards: Board of Trustees, Tuskegee University; Board of Advisors, Harvard Law and Policy Review; Board of Directors, Alabama Center for Law and Civic Government; Board of Directors, The Salvation Army, Jefferson County Alabama; religion: Lutheran; committees: House Administration; Ways and Means; elected to the 108th Congress on November 5, 2002; reelected to each succeeding Congress.

Office Listings

http://www.house.gov/arturdavis

208 Cannon House Office Building, Washington, DC 20515 .... (202) 225–2665
Chief of Staff.—Chanelle Hardy. FAX: 226–9567
Executive Assistant / Scheduler.—Allyson Freeman.
Legislative Director.—Alison O'Donnell.
Press Secretary.—Addie Whisenant.
2 20th Street, North, Suite 1130, Birmingham, AL 35203 .... (205) 254–1960
District Director.—Frank Adams.
908 Alabama Avenue, Federal Building, Suite 112, Selma, AL 36701 .... (334) 877–4414
Deputy District Director.—Tammy Maul.
102 East Washington Street, Suite F, Demopolis, AL 36732 .... (334) 287–0860
205 North Washington Street, UWA Station 40, Suites 236–237, Livingston, AL 35470 .... (205) 652–5834
1118 Greensboro Avenue, Suite 336, Tuscaloosa, AL 35401 .... (205) 752–5380

Counties: CHOCTAW, CLARKE (part), DALLAS, GREENE, HALE, JEFFERSON (part), MARENGO, PERRY, PICKENS (part), SUMTER, TUSCALOOSA (part), WILCOX. Population (2000), 635,300.

ZIP Codes: 35005–06, 35020–23, 35034, 35036, 35041–42, 35061, 35064, 35068, 35071, 35073–74, 35079, 35111, 35117, 35126–27, 35173, 35175, 35184, 35188, 35203–15, 35217–18, 35221–22, 35224, 35228–29, 35233–35, 35238, 35243, 35401, 35404–06, 35440–44, 35446–49, 35452–53, 35456, 35459–60, 35462–64, 35466, 35469–71, 35473–78, 35480–81, 35485–87, 35490–91, 35546, 35601, 35603, 35640, 35754, 36030, 36032, 36040, 36064, 36105, 36435–36, 36451, 36482, 36524, 36540, 36545, 36558, 36701–03, 36720, 36722–23, 36726–28, 36732, 36736, 36738, 36740–42, 36744–45, 36748–54, 36756, 36758–59, 36761–69, 36773, 36775–76, 36782–86, 36790, 36792–93, 36901, 36904, 36906–08, 36910, 36912–13, 36915–16, 36919, 36921–22, 36925

ALASKA

(Population 2000, 626,932)

SENATORS

LISA MURKOWSKI, Republican, of Anchorage, AK; born in Ketchikan, AK, May 22, 1957; education: Willamette University, 1975–77; Georgetown University, 1978–80, B.A., Economics; Willamette College of Law, 1982–85, J.D.; professional: attorney; private law practice; Alaska and Anchorage Bar Associations: First Bank Board of Directors; organizations: Catholic Social Services; YWCA; Alaskans for Drug-Free Youth; Alaska Federation of Republican Women; Arctic Power; public service: Anchorage Equal Rights Commission; Anchorage District Court Attorney, 1987–89; Task Force on the Homeless, 1990–91; Alaska State Representative, 1998–2002; family: married to Verne Martell; children: Nicholas and Matthew; committees: Appropriations; Energy and Natural Resources; Health, Education, Labor and Pensions; Indian Affairs; appointed to the U.S. Senate on December 20, 2002; elected to the 109th Congress for a full Senate term on November 2, 2004.

Office Listings

http://murkowski.senate.gov

709 Hart Senate Office Building, Washington, DC 20510 .... (202) 224–6665
Chief of Staff.—Karen Y. Knutson. FAX: 224–5301
Legislative Director.—Edward Hild.
Scheduler.—Kristen Nothdurft.
Communications Director.—Michael Brumas.
510 L Street, #550, Anchorage, AK 99501 .... (907) 271–3735
101 12th Avenue, Room 216, Fairbanks, AK 99701 .... (907) 456–0233
4079 Tongass Avenue; Suite 204, Ketchikan, AK 99901 .... (907) 225–6880
851 East Westpoint Drive, Wasilla, AK 99654 .... (907) 376–7665

* * *

MARK BEGICH, Democrat, of Anchorage, AK; born in Anchorage, March 31, 1962; education: Stellar High School, 1981; professional: Small Business Owner; Real Estate and Property Management; Alaska Student Loan Corporation 1995–02, chair 1996–02; Alaska Commission of Post-Secondary Education 1995–02, chair 1996–98; University of Alaska Board of Regents 2001–02; public service: Anchorage Assembly Member, 1988–98; Mayor of Anchorage, 2003–09; member: Boys & Girls Club; Association of the United States Army; Air Force Association; family: married to Deborah Bonito; children: Jacob Begich; committees: Armed Services; Commerce, Science, and Transportation; Veterans' Affairs; elected to U.S. Senate on November 4, 2008.

Office Listings

http://begich.senate.gov

825 Hart Senate Office Building, Washington, DC 20510 .... (202) 224–3004
Chief of Staff.—David Ramseur. FAX: 228–3205
Legislative Director.—John Richards.
Administrative Director.—Matt Payne-Funk.
Scheduling Director.—John Vezina.
222 West Seventh Avenue, No. 2, Anchorage, AK 99513 .... (907) 271–5915
101 12th Avenue, Room 206, Fairbanks, AK 99701 .... (907) 456–0261

REPRESENTATIVE

AT LARGE

DON YOUNG, Republican, of Fort Yukon, AK; born in Meridian, CA, June 9, 1933; education: A.A., Yuba Junior College; B.A., Chico State College, Chico, CA; Honorary Doctorate of Laws, University of Alaska, Fairbanks; State House of Representatives, 1966–70; U.S. Army, 41st Tank Battalion, 1955–57; elected member of the State Senate, 1970–73; served on the Fort Yukon City Council for six years, serving four years as mayor; educator for nine years; river boat captain; member: National Education Association, Elks, Lions, Jaycees; married: Lula Fredson of Fort Yukon; children: Joni and Dawn; committees: ranking member, Natural Resources; Transportation and Infrastructure; elected to the 93rd Congress in a special election, March 6, 1973, to fill the vacancy created by the death of Congressman Nick Begich; reelected to each succeeding Congress.

Office Listings

http://www.house.gov/donyoung

2111 Rayburn House Office Building, Washington, DC 20515 .... (202) 225–5765
Administrative Assistant.—Michael Anderson. FAX: 225–0425
Press Secretary.—Meredith Kenny.
Executive Assistant / Office Manager.—Paul Milotte.
Legislative Director.—Pamela Day.
510 L Street, Suite 580, Anchorage, AK 99501 .... (907) 271–5978
101 12th Avenue, Box 10, Fairbanks, AK 99701 .... (907) 456–0210
971 Federal Building, Box 21247, Juneau, AK 99802 .... (907) 586–7400
540 Water Street, Ketchikan, AK 99901 .... (907) 225–6880
130 Trading Bay Road, Suite 350, Kenai, AK 99611 .... (907) 283–5808
851 East Westpoint Drive, #307, Wasilla, AK 99654 .... (907) 376–7665

Population (2000), 626,932.

ZIP Codes: 99501–24, 99540, 99546–59, 99561, 99563–69, 99571–81, 99583–91, 99599, 99602–15, 99619–22, 99624–41, 99643–45, 99647–72, 99674–95, 99697, 99701–12, 99714, 99716, 99720–27, 99729–30, 99732–34, 99736–86, 99788–89, 99791, 99801–03, 99811, 99820–21, 99824–27, 99829–30, 99832–33, 99835–36, 99840–41, 99850, 99901, 99903, 99918–19, 99921–23, 99925–29, 99950

ARIZONA

(Population 2000, 5,140,683)

SENATORS

JOHN McCAIN, Republican, of Phoenix, AZ; born in the Panama Canal Zone, August 29, 1936; education: graduated Episcopal High School, Alexandria, VA, 1954; graduated, U.S. Naval Academy, Annapolis, MD, 1958; National War College, Washington, DC, 1973; retired captain (pilot), U.S. Navy, 1958–81; military awards: Silver Star, Bronze Star, Legion of Merit, Purple Heart, and Distinguished Flying Cross; chair, International Republican Institute; married to the former Cindy Hensley; seven children: Doug, Andy, Sidney, Meghan, Jack, Jim, and Bridget; committees: ranking member, Armed Services; Energy and Natural Resources; Health, Education, Labor and Pensions; Homeland Security and Governmental Affairs; Indian Affairs; elected to the 98th Congress in November, 1982; reelected to the 99th Congress in November, 1984; elected to the U.S. Senate in November, 1986; reelected to each succeeding Senate term.

Office Listings

http://mccain.senate.gov

241 Russell Senate Office Building, Washington, DC 20510 .... (202) 224–2235
Chief of Staff.—Mark Buse. TDD: 224–7132
Legislative Director.—Ann Begeman.
Communications Director.—Brooke Buchanan.
Scheduler.—Ellen Cahill.
5353 N. 16th Street, Suite 105, Phoenix, AZ 85016 .... (602) 952–2410
TDD: 952–0170
4703 S. Lakeshore Drive, Suite 1, Tempe, AZ 85282 .... (480) 897–6289
407 West Congress Street, Suite 103, Tucson, AZ 85701 .... (602) 670–6334

* * *

JON KYL, Republican, of Phoenix, AZ; born in Oakland, NE, April 25, 1942; education: graduated Bloomfield High School, Bloomfield, IA, 1960; B.A., University of Arizona, Tucson, 1964 (Phi Beta Kappa, Phi Kappa Phi); LL.B., University of Arizona, 1966; professional: editor-in-chief, *Arizona Law Review*; attorney, admitted to the Arizona State bar, 1966; former partner in Phoenix law firm of Jennings, Strouss and Salmon, 1966–86; chairman, Phoenix Chamber of Commerce (1984–85); married: the former Caryll Louise Collins; children: Kristine and John; committees: Finance; Judiciary; elected to the 100th Congress on November 4, 1986; reelected to each succeeding Congress; elected to the U.S. Senate in November, 1994; reelected to each succeeding Senate term.

Office Listings

http://kyl.senate.gov

730 Hart Senate Office Building, Washington, DC 20515 .... (202) 224–4521
Chief of Staff.—Tim Glazewski. FAX: 224–2207
Legislative Director.—Elizabeth Maier.
Office Director.—Celeste Gold.
Scheduler.—Kelicia Wright.
Suite 120, 2200 East Camelback Road, Phoenix, AZ 85016 .... (602) 840–1891
Suite 150, 6840 North Oracle Road, Tucson, AZ 85704 .... (520) 575–8633

REPRESENTATIVES

FIRST DISTRICT

ANN KIRKPATRICK, Democrat, of Flagstaff, AZ; born in McNary, AZ, March 24, 1950; education: graduated, Blue Ridge High School; B.A., Asian Studies and Secondary Education, University of Arizona, 1972; J.D., University of Arizona College of Law, 1979; served as Coconino County's first female Deputy County Attorney; served as Sedona City Attorney; taught Business Law and Ethics at Coconino Community College; Arizona State House of Representatives, 2004–08; former president of United Way of Northern Arizona and Flagstaff Symphony Association; served on the Board of Directors of Big Sisters, Flagstaff Library Foundation, and Lowell Observatory; children: Whitney and Ashley; committees: Homeland Security; Small Business; Veterans' Affairs; elected to the 111th Congress on November 4, 2008.

Office Listings

http://kirkpatrick.house.gov

1123 Longworth House Office Building, Washington, DC 20515 .... (202) 225–2315
Chief of Staff.—Michael Frias. FAX: 226–9739
Legislative Director.—Betsy Quilligan.
Scheduler / Press Assistant.—Kyle McNally.
240 South Montezuma Street, #101, Prescott, AZ 86303 .... (928) 445–3434
District Director.—Virginia Turner. FAX: 445–4160
Deputy District Director.—Carmen Gallus.

Counties: APACHE, COCONINO, GILA, GRAHAM, GREENLEE, NAVAJO (part), PINAL (part), YAVAPAI. CITIES AND TOWNSHIPS: Flagstaff, Prescott, Casa Grande, Sedona, Show Low, Payson, Florence, Coolidge, Eloy, Kearny, Hayden, San Manuel, Mammoth, Oracle, Winkelman, Superior, Globe, Miami, Bylas, Safford, Thatcher, Clifton, Morenci, Duncan, Window Rock, St. Johns, Springerville, Pinetop-Lakeside, McNary, Winslow, Holbrook, Page, Tuba City, Prescott Valley, Chino Valley, Skull Valley, Williams, Seligman, Mayer, Dewey-Humboldt, Cottonwood, Verde Valley. Population (2000), 641,329.

ZIP Codes: 85218, 85221–23, 85228, 85230–32, 85235, 85237–38, 85241, 85245, 85272–73, 85291–94, 85324, 85332, 85362, 85390, 85501–02, 85530–36, 85539–48, 85550–54, 85618, 85623, 85631, 85643, 85653, 85658, 85739, 85901–02, 85911–12, 85920, 85922–42, 86001–04, 86011, 86015–18, 86020, 86022–25, 86028–29, 86031–33, 86035–36, 86038, 86040, 86045–47, 86052–54, 86301–05, 86312–15, 86320–27, 86329–43, 86351, 86502–08, 86510–12, 86514–15, 86520, 86535, 86538, 86540, 86544–45, 86547, 86556

* * *

SECOND DISTRICT

TRENT FRANKS, Republican, of Phoenix, AZ; born in Uravan, CO, June 19, 1957; education: attended Ottawa University; graduate of the Center for Constitutional Studies; professional: small business owner; oil field and drilling engineer; Executive Director, Arizona Family Research Institute; conservative writer, and former radio commentator, with Family Life Radio and NBC affiliate KTKP 1280 AM; public service: Arizona House of Representatives, 1985–87; appointed in 1987 to head the Arizona Governor's Office for Children; awards: True Blue award, Family Research Council; Spirit of Enterprise award, U.S. Chamber of Commerce; Taxpayer Hero, Council for Citizens Against Government Waste; Friend of Education award, Education Freedom Coalition; religion: Baptist; member, North Phoenix Baptist Church; married: Josephine; committees: Armed Services; Judiciary; elected to the 108th Congress on November 5, 2002; reelected to each succeeding Congress.

Office Listings

http://www.house.gov/franks

2435 Rayburn House Office Building, Washington, DC 20515 .... (202) 225–4576
Chief of Staff.—Tom Stallings. FAX: 225–6328
Legislative Director.—Jeff Choudhry.
Scheduler.—Lisa Teschler.
7121 W. Bell Road, Suite 200, Glendale, AZ 85308 .... (623) 776–7911

Counties: COCONINO (part), LAPAZ (part), MARICOPA (part), MOHAVE, NAVAJO (part), YAVAPAI (part). Population (2000), 641,329.

ZIP Codes: 85029, 85037, 85051, 85098, 85301–10, 85312, 85318, 85320, 85326, 85335, 85338, 85340, 85342, 85345, 85351, 85355, 85358, 85360–61, 85363, 85372–76, 85378–83, 85385, 85387, 85390, 86021, 86030, 86034, 86039, 86042–43, 86401–06, 86411–13, 86426–27, 86429–46

* * *

THIRD DISTRICT

JOHN B. SHADEGG, Republican, of Phoenix, AZ; born in Phoenix, October 22, 1949; education: graduated Camelback High School; B.A., University of Arizona, Tucson, 1972; J.D., University of Arizona, 1975; professional: Air National Guard, 1969–75; admitted to the Arizona bar, 1976; law offices of John Shadegg; special counsel, Arizona House Republican Caucus, 1991–92; special assistant attorney general, 1983–90; advisor, U.S. Sentencing Commission; founding director/executive committee member, Goldwater Institute for Public Policy; member/former president, Crime Victim Foundation; chairman, Arizona Juvenile Justice Advisory Council; advisory board, Salvation Army; vestry, Christ Church of the Ascension Episcopal, 1989–91; member, Law Society, ASU College of Law; chairman, Arizona Republican Caucus, 1985–87; chairman, Proposition 108—Two-Thirds Tax Limitation Initiative,

1992; member, Fiscal Accountability and Reform Efforts (FARE) Committee, 1991–92; counsel, Arizonans for Wildlife Conservation (no on Proposition 200), 1992; Victims Bill of Rights Task Force, 1989–90; member, Growing Smarter Committee, (yes on Proposition 303), 1998; married: Shirley; children: Courtney and Stephen; assistant whip; committees: Energy and Commerce; Select Committee on Energy Independence and Global Warming; elected to the 104th Congress; reelected to each succeeding Congress.

Office Listings

http://johnshadegg.house.gov

436 Cannon House Office Building, Washington, DC 20515 .... (202) 225–3361
Chief of Staff.—Kristin Thompson. FAX: 225–3462
Scheduler.—Elissa Scannell.
Press Secretary.—Steven Miller.
2400 East Arizona Biltmore Circle, Suite 1290, Phoenix, AZ 85016 .... (602) 263–5300
Deputy District Director.—James Ashley.

Counties: MARICOPA (part). CITIES AND TOWNSHIPS: Carefree, Cave Creek, Paradise Valley, and Phoenix (part). Population (2000), 641,329.

ZIP Codes: 85012–24, 85027–29, 85032, 85046, 85050–51, 85053–54, 85060, 85071, 85075, 85078–80, 85082, 85098–99, 85250–51, 85253–54, 85262, 85308, 85310, 85327, 85331, 85377

* * *

FOURTH DISTRICT

ED PASTOR, Democrat, of Phoenix, AZ; born in Claypool, AZ, June 28, 1943; education: attended public schools in Miami, AZ; graduate of Arizona State University; B.A., chemistry, 1966; J.D., Arizona University, 1974; professional: member, Governor Raul Castro's staff; taught chemistry, North High School; former deputy director of Guadalupe Organization, Inc.; elected supervisor, board of supervisors, Maricopa County; served board of directors for the National Association of Counties; vice chairman, Employment Steering Committee; president, Arizona County Supervisors Association; member, executive committee of the Arizona Association of Counties; resigned, May, 1991; board of directors, Neighborhood Housing Services of America; National Association of Latino Elected Officials; served as director at large, ASU Alumni Association; founding board member, ASU Los Diablos Alumni Association; served on board of directors of the National Council of La Raza; Arizona Joint Partnership Training Council; National Conference of Christians and Jews; Friendly House; Chicanos Por La Causa; Phoenix Economic Growth Corporation; Sun Angel Foundation; vice president, Valley of the Sun United Way; advisory member, Boys Club of Metropolitan Phoenix; married: Verma; two daughters: Yvonne and Laura; appointed a Chief Deputy Minority Whip; committees: Appropriations; elected by special election on September 24, 1991, to fill the vacancy caused by the resignation of Morris K. Udall; elected in November, 1992, to the 103rd Congress; reelected to each succeeding Congress.

Office Listings

http://www.house.gov/pastor

2465 Rayburn House Office Building, Washington, DC 20515 .... (202) 225–4065
Executive Assistant.—Laura Campos. FAX: 225–1655
411 North Central Avenue, Suite 150, Phoenix, AZ 85004 .... (602) 256–0551
District Director.—Elisa de la Vara.

Counties: MARICOPA (part). Population (2000), 641,329.

ZIP Codes: 85001–09, 85012–19, 85025–26, 85030–31, 85033–36, 85038, 85040–44, 85051, 85061–64, 85066–69, 85072–74, 85076, 85082, 85099, 85283, 85301, 85303, 85309, 85311, 85339, 86045, 86329, 86337

* * *

FIFTH DISTRICT

HARRY E. MITCHELL, Democrat, of Tempe, AZ; born in Phoenix, AZ, July 18, 1940; education: graduated from Tempe High School, Tempe, AZ; B.S. in political science, Arizona State University, 1962; master's degree in public administration, Arizona State University, 1980; professional: taught American government and economics, Tempe High School, 1964–92; former Mayor and Councilman, Tempe, AZ; former member, Arizona State Senate; former chairman,

Arizona Democratic Party; to honor his success as Mayor, the City of Tempe erected a 35-foot statute of Harry in downtown Tempe and renamed the city's government center the Harry E. Mitchell Government Complex; served as an adjunct professor at his alma mater, ASU; family: married to Marianne; two children; five grandchildren; committees: Science and Technology; Transportation and Infrastructure; Veterans' Affairs; elected to the 110th Congress on November 7, 2006; reelected to the 111th Congress.

Office Listings

http://mitchell.house.gov

1410 Longworth House Office Building, Washington, DC 20515 .... (202) 225–2190
Chief of Staff.—Alexis Tameron. FAX: 225–3263
Executive Assistant.—Chris Quigley.
Legislative Assistants: Carrie Solomon, Paul Swanson, Matthew Weisman.
Special Assistant / Tour Coordinator.—Caitlyn Cardineau.
Communications Director.—Adam Bozzi.
7201 East Camelback Road, Suite 335, Scottsdale, AZ 85251 .... (480) 946–2411

Counties: MARICOPA (part). CITIES AND TOWNSHIPS: Chandler, Fountain Hills, Mesa, Phoenix, Rio Verde, Scottsdale, Tempe. Ahwatukee, the Salt River Pima Indian Reservation, and the Fort McDowell Yavapai Apache Indian Reservation. Population (2000), 641,329.

ZIP Codes: 85008, 85018, 85044–45, 05048, 85070, 85076, 85201–03, 85210, 85215, 85224–26, 85250–64, 85267–69, 85274, 85287, 85331, 85281, 85283

* * *

SIXTH DISTRICT

JEFF FLAKE, Republican, of Mesa, AZ; born in Snowflake, AZ, December 31, 1962; education: Brigham Young University; B.A., International Relations; M.A., Political Science; religion: Mormon; served a mission in South Africa and Zimbabwe; professional: businessman; Shipley, Smoak & Henry (public affairs firm); Executive Director, Foundation for Democracy; Executive Director, Goldwater Institute; married: Cheryl; children: Ryan, Alexis, Austin, Tanner, and Dallin; committees: Foreign Affairs; Natural Resources; Oversight and Government Reform; elected to the 107th Congress on November 7, 2000; reelected to each succeeding Congress.

Office Listings

http://www.house.gov/flake

240 Cannon House Office Building, Washington, DC 20515 .... (202) 225–2635
Chief of Staff.—Margaret Klessig. FAX: 226–4386
Scheduler.—Nikki Bullock.
Press Secretary.—Matthew Specht.
1640 South Stapley, Suite 215, Mesa, AZ 85204 .... (480) 833–0092

Counties: MARICOPA (part), PINAL (part). CITIES AND TOWNSHIPS: Apache Junction, Chandler, Gilbert, Mesa, and Queen Creek. Population (2000), 641,329.

ZIP Codes: 85201, 85203–08, 85210–20, 85224–25, 85227, 85233–34, 85236, 85242, 85244, 85246, 85248–49, 85254, 85275, 85277–78, 85290, 85296–97, 85299

* * *

SEVENTH DISTRICT

RAÚL M. GRIJALVA, Democrat, of Tucson, AZ; born in Tucson, February 19, 1948; education: Sunnyside High School, Tucson, AZ; B.A., University of Arizona; professional: former Assistant Dean for Hispanic Student Affairs, University of Arizona; former Director of the El Pueblo Neighborhood Center; public service: Tucson Unified School District Governing Board, 1974–86; Pima County Board of Supervisors, 1989–2002; family: married to Ramona; three daughters; committees: Education and Labor; Natural Resources; elected to the 108th Congress on November 5, 2002; reelected to each succeeding Congress.

Office Listings

http://www.house.gov/grijalva

1440 Longworth House Office Building, Washington, DC 20515 .... (202) 225–2435
Chief of Staff.—Gloria Montaño. FAX: 225–1541
Legislative Director.—Chris Kaumo.
Press Liaison / Scheduler.—Natalie Luna.
Scheduler.—Kelsey Mishkin.
810 East 22nd Street, Suite 102, Tucson, AZ 85713 .... (520) 622–6788
1455 South 4th Avenue, Suite 4, Yuma, AZ 85364 .... (928) 343–7933

Counties: LA PAZ (part), MARICOPA (part), PIMA (part), PINAL (part), SANTA CRUZ (part), YUMA. Population (2000), 641,329.

ZIP Codes: 85033, 85035, 85037, 85043, 85221–22, 85226, 85228, 85232, 85239, 85242, 85248–49, 85273, 85321–23, 85325–26, 85328–29, 85333–34, 85336–37, 85339–41, 85343–44, 85346–50, 85352–54, 85356–57, 85359, 85364–67, 85369, 85371, 85601, 85621, 85628, 85631, 85633–34, 85639–40, 85648, 85653, 85662, 85701–03, 85705–06, 85711, 85713–14, 85716–17, 85719, 85721–26, 85733–36, 85743, 85745–46, 85754

* * *

EIGHTH DISTRICT

GABRIELLE GIFFORDS, Democrat, of Tucson, AZ; born in Tucson, June 8, 1970; education: B.A., Scripps College, Claremont, CA, 1993; William Fulbright Scholarship, study abroad Chihuahua, Mexico; M.A. in regional planning, Cornell University, NY, 1996; president, Atlantic Association of Young Political Leaders; represents the National Committee on China–U.S. Relations as a Young Leader's Forum Fellow; German Marshall Fund Manfred-Worner Fellow; selected for the inaugural two-year class of the Aspen-Rodel Fellowships in Public Leadership, 2005; Arizona State House of Representatives, 2001–03; Arizona State Senator, 2003–05; religion: Jewish; married: Mark Kelly, Captain United States Navy; committees: Armed Services; Foreign Affairs; Science and Technology; elected to the 110th Congress on November 7, 2006; relected to the 111th Congress on November 4, 2008.

Office Listings

http://giffords.house.gov/

1728 Longworth House Office Building, Washington, DC 20515 .... (202) 225–2542
Chief of Staff.—Pia Carusone. FAX: 225–0378
Scheduler.—Jennifer Cox.
1661 North Swan, Suite 112, Tucson, AZ 85712 .... (520) 881–3588
District Director.—Ron Barber.
77 Calle Portal, Suite B–160, Sierra Vista, AZ 85635 .... (520) 459–3115

Counties: COCHISE, PIMA (part), PINAL (part), SANTA CRUZ (part). Population (2000), 641,329.

ZIP Codes: 85602–03, 85605–11, 85613–17, 85619–20, 85622, 85624–27, 85629–30, 85632, 85635–38, 85641, 85643–46, 85650, 85652–55, 85670, 85704–16, 85718–19, 85728, 85730–32, 85736–45, 85747–52

ARKANSAS

(Population 2000, 2,673,400)

SENATORS

BLANCHE L. LINCOLN, Democrat, of Helena, AR; born in Helena, September 30, 1960; education: graduate of Helena Central High School; daughter of the late Jordan Bennett Lambert, Jr., and Martha Kelly Lambert; B.S., in biology, at Randolph Macon Woman's College, Lynchburg, VA, 1982; also attended the University of Arkansas, Fayetteville; member, Chi Omega sorority; American Red Cross volunteer; married to Dr. Stephen R. Lincoln; mother of twin boys, Bennett and Reece; committees: chair, Agriculture, Nutrition, and Forestry; Energy and Natural Resources; Finance; Special Committee on Aging; elected to the U.S. House of Representatives for the 103rd and 104th Congresses; elected to the U.S. Senate on November 3, 1998; reelected to each succeeding Senate term.

Office Listings

http://lincoln.senate.gov

355 Dirksen Senate Office Building, Washington, DC 20510 .... (202) 224–4843
Chief of Staff.—Elizabeth Burks. FAX: 228–1371
Legislative Director.—Jim Stowers.
Press Secretary.—Katie Laning.
Scheduler.—Liz Thompson.
912 West Fourth Street, Little Rock, AR 72201 .... (501) 375–2993
4 South College Avenue, #205, Fayetteville, AR 72701 .... (479) 251–1224
Federal Building, Suite 315, 615 South Main, Jonesboro, AR 72401 .... (870) 910–6896
101 East Waterman, Dumas, AR 71693 .... (870) 382–1023
Miller County Courthouse, 400 Laurel Street, #101, Texarkana, AR 71854 .... (870) 774–3106

* * *

MARK L. PRYOR, Democrat, of Little Rock, AR; born in Fayetteville, AR, January 10, 1963; education: B.A., University of Arkansas, 1985; J.D., University of Arkansas, 1988; professional: attorney; Wright, Lindsey & Jennings (law firm); public service: elected, Arkansas House of Representatives, 1990; elected, Arkansas Attorney General, 1998; family: married to Jill; children: Adams and Porter; his father, David Pryor, was a former Governor and U.S. Senator from Arkansas; committees: Appropriations; Commerce, Science, and Transportation; Homeland Security and Governmental Affairs; Rules and Administration; Small Business and Entrepreneurship; Select Committee on Ethics; elected to the U.S. Senate on November 5, 2002; reelected to each succeeding Senate term.

Office Listings

http://pryor.senate.gov

255 Dirksen Senate Office Building, Washington, DC 20510 .... (202) 224–2353
Chief of Staff.—Bob Russell. FAX: 228–0908
Legislative Director.—Andy York.
Communications Director.—Michael Teague.
Office Manager.—Patrice Bolling.
500 Clinton Avenue, Suite 401, Little Rock, AR 72201 .... (501) 324–6336

REPRESENTATIVES

FIRST DISTRICT

MARION BERRY, Democrat, of Gillett, AR; born in Stuttgart, AR, August 27, 1942; education: graduated, DeWitt High School; B.S., pharmacy, University of Arkansas, 1965; professional: Gillett, Arkansas city council, 1976–80; Arkansas Soil and Water Conservation Commission, 1964–86; White House Domestic Policy Council, 1993–96; special assistant to President William Clinton for Agricultural Trade and Food Assistance, 1993; member, Domestic Policy Council, The White House, 1993–96; member, Arkansas Soil and Water Conservation Commission, 1986–94, serving as chairman in 1992; Gillett City Councilman, 1976–80; married: the former Carolyn Lowe in 1962; children: Ann Coggin and Mitchell; co-chairman, Democratic Blue Dog Coalition's Health Care Task Force; co-chair, House Affordable Medicines Task Force; Congressional Methamphetamine Caucus; Congressional Missing and

Exploited Children's Caucus; Congressional Rural Caucus; Congressional Silk Road Caucus; co-chair, Congressional Soybean Caucus; Congressional Steel Caucus; House Renewable Energy and Energy Efficiency Caucus; New Democrat Coalition; Rural Health Care Coalition; Brain Injury Caucus; Rural Working Group; committees: Appropriations; Budget; elected to the 105th Congress; reelected to each succeeding Congress.

Office Listings

http://www.house.gov/berry

2305 Rayburn House Office Building, Washington, DC 20515 .... (202) 225–4076
Chief of Staff.—Chad Causey. FAX: 225–5602
Press Secretary.—Angela Guyadeen.
Legislative Director.—Chris Wallace.
116 North First Street, Suite C–1, Cabot, AR 72023 .... (501) 843–3043
108 East Huntington Avenue, Jonesboro, AR 72401 .... (800) 866–2701
1 East 7th Street, Suite 200, Mountain Home, AR 72653 .... (870) 425–3511

Counties: ARKANSAS, BAXTER, CLAY, CLEBURNE, CRAIGHEAD, CRITTENDEN, CROSS, FULTON, GREENE, INDEPENDENCE, IZARD, JACKSON, LAWRENCE, LEE, LONOKE, MISSISSIPPI, MONROE, PHILLIPS, POINSETT, PRAIRIE, RANDOLPH, ST. FRANCIS, SEARCY, SHARP, STONE, WOODRUFF. Population (2000), 668,360.

ZIP Codes: 72003, 72005–07, 72014, 72017, 72020–21, 72023–24, 72026, 72029, 72031, 72036–38, 72040–44, 72046, 72048, 72051, 72055, 72059–60, 72064, 72067, 72069, 72072–76, 72083, 72086, 72101–02, 72108, 72112, 72121, 72123, 72130–31, 72134, 72137, 72139–40, 72142–43, 72153, 72160, 72165–66, 72169–70, 72175–76, 72179, 72189, 72301, 72303, 72310–13, 72315–16, 72319–22, 72324–33, 72335–36, 72338–42, 72346–48, 72350–55, 72358–60, 72364–70, 72372–74, 72376–77, 72383–84, 72386–87, 72389–92, 72394–96, 72401–04, 72410–17, 72419, 72421–22, 72424–45, 72447, 72449–51, 72453–62, 72464–67, 72469–76, 72478–79, 72482, 72501, 72503, 72512–13, 72515, 72517, 72519–34, 72536–40, 72542–46, 72550, 72553–56, 72560–62, 72564–69, 72571–73, 72575–79, 72581, 72583–85, 72587, 72610, 72613, 72617, 72623, 72626, 72629, 72631, 72633, 72635–36, 72639, 72642, 72645, 72650–51, 72653–54, 72658, 72663, 72669, 72675, 72679–80, 72685–86

* * *

SECOND DISTRICT

VIC SNYDER, Democrat, of Little Rock, AR; born in Medford, OR, September 27, 1947; education: graduated from Medford High School, 1965; corporal, U.S. Marine Corps, 1967–69, including one year in Vietnam with Headquarters Company, First Marine Division; B.A., chemistry, 1975, Willamette University, Salem, OR; M.D., 1979, University of Oregon Health Sciences Center, Portland; family practice residency, 1979–82, University of Arkansas for Medical Sciences; family practice physician in central Arkansas, 1982–96; medical missions to Cambodian refugee camps in Thailand, El Salvadoran refugee camps in Honduras, a West African mission hospital in Sierra Leone, and an Ethiopian refugee camp in Sudan; J.D., 1988, University of Arkansas at Little Rock School of Law; Arkansas State Senator, 1991–96; committees: Armed Services; Veterans' Affairs; elected to the 105th Congress; reelected to each succeeding Congress.

Office Listings

http://www.house.gov/snyder

2210 Rayburn House Office Building, Washington, DC 20515 .... (202) 225–2506
Chief of Staff.—David Boling. FAX: 225–5903
Press Secretary.—Betsy Barrett.
Legislative Director.—James Savage.
1501 N. University, Suite 150, Little Rock, AR 72207 .... (501) 324–5941
District Director.—Amanda Nixon White.

Counties: CONWAY, FAULKNER, PERRY, PULASKI, SALINE, VAN BUREN, WHITE, YELL. Population (2000), 668,176.

ZIP Codes: 71772, 71909, 72001–02, 72010–13, 72015–18, 72020, 72022–23, 72025, 72027–28, 72030–35, 72039, 72045–47, 72052–53, 72057–61, 72063, 72065–68, 72070, 72076, 72078–82, 72085, 72087–89, 72099, 72102–04, 72106–08, 72110–11, 72113–22, 72124–27, 72131, 72135–37, 72139, 72141–43, 72145, 72149, 72153, 72156–57, 72164, 72167, 72173, 72178, 72180–81, 72183, 72190, 72199, 72201–07, 72209–12, 72214–17, 72219, 72221–23, 72225, 72227, 72231, 72260, 72295, 72419, 72568, 72629, 72645, 72679, 72823–24, 72827–29, 72833–34, 72838, 72841–42, 72853, 72857, 72860, 72943

* * *

THIRD DISTRICT

JOHN BOOZMAN, Republican, of Rogers, AR; born in Shreveport, LA, December 10, 1950; education: Northside High School, Fort Smith, AR; University of Arkansas, completing his pre-optometry requirements; graduated, Southern College of Optometry, 1977; professional: optometrist; entered private practice as a co-founder of the Boozman-Hof Eye Clinic; community service: volunteer optometrist at the Arkansas School for the Blind, and at area clinics; public service: Rogers School Board, serving two terms; member: state and local cattlemen's associations; Benton County Fair Board; Fellowship of Christian Athletes; Arkansas Athletes Outreach Board; religion: Baptist; married: the former Cathy Marley; three daughters; committees: Foreign Affairs; Transportation and Infrastructure; Veterans' Affairs; elected to the 107th Congress, by special election, on November 20, 2001; reelected to each succeeding Congress.

Office Listings

http://www.house.gov/boozman

1519 Longworth House Office Building, Washington, DC 20515 .... (202) 225–4301
Chief of Staff.—Matthew Sagely. FAX: 225–5713
Communications Director.—Sara Lasure.
Scheduler.—Lesley Parker.
4943 Old Greenwood, Suite 1, Fort Smith, AR 72903 .... (479) 782–7787
303 N. Main, Suite 102, Harrison, AR 72601 .... (870) 741–6900
213 W. Monroe, Suite K, Lowell, AR 72745 .... (479) 725–0400
Deputy Chief of Staff.—Stacey McClure.

Counties: BENTON, BOONE, CARROLL, CRAWFORD, FRANKLIN, JOHNSON, MADISON, MARION, NEWTON, POPE, SEBASTIAN, WASHINGTON. Population (2000), 668,479.

ZIP Codes: 71937, 71944–45, 71953, 71972–73, 72063, 72080, 72601–02, 72611, 72613, 72615–16, 72619, 72624, 72628, 72630–34, 72638–41, 72644–45, 72648, 72653, 72655, 72660–63, 72666, 72668, 72670, 72672, 72675, 72677, 72679, 72682–83, 72685–87, 72701–04, 72711–12, 72714–19, 72721–22, 72727–30, 72732–42, 72744–45, 72747, 72749, 72751–53, 72756–58, 72760–62, 72764–66, 72768–70, 72773–74, 72776, 72801–02, 72811–12, 72820–21, 72823, 72830, 72832, 72837–43, 72845–47, 72852, 72854, 72856–58, 72860, 72901–06, 72908, 72913–14, 72916–19, 72921, 72923, 72927–28, 72930, 72932–38, 72940–41, 72944–49, 72951–52, 72955–57, 72959

* * *

FOURTH DISTRICT

MIKE ROSS, Democrat, of Prescott, AR; born in Texarkana, AR, August 2, 1961; education: Hope High School; B.A., University of Arkansas at Little Rock, 1987; professional: former small businessman; former owner of Ross Pharmacy, Inc., in Prescott, AR; public service: Chief of Staff to Arkansas Lt. Governor Winston Bryant, 1985–89; three term State Senator, 1991–2000; organizations: Executive Director, Arkansas Youth Suicide Prevention Commission, 1985–89; First United Methodist Church in Prescott, AR; awards: Advocates for Community and Rural Education's ''Champion of Rural Arkansas'' award, 2008; Arkansas Hospital Association's ''Statesman of the Year'' award, 2008; Blue Dog Coalition's ''Spirit of Freedom'' award, 2008; NAACP Pine Bluff Chapter's ''Shining Star'' award, 2008; 60 Plus Association's ''Cyber Security Crusader'' award, 2008; married: Holly; children: Alex and Sydney Beth; committees: Energy and Commerce; Foreign Affairs; elected to the 107th Congress on November 7, 2000; reelected to each succeeding Congress.

Office Listings

http://ross.house.gov

2436 Rayburn House Office Building, Washington, DC 20515 .... (202) 225–3772
Chief of Staff.—Drew Goesl. FAX: 225–1314
Legislative Director.—Laura Abshire.
Communications Director.—Brad Howard.
District Director.—Jeff Weaver.
221 West Main Street, Prescott, AR 71857 .... (870) 887–6787
George Howard Jr. Federal Building, 100 East 8th Avenue, Room 2521 Pine Bluff, AR 71601 .... (870) 536–3376
300 Exchange Street, Suite A, Hot Springs, AR 71901 .... (501) 520–5892
Union County Courthouse, Suite 406, 101 North Washington Street, El Dorado, AR 71730 .... (870) 881–0681

Counties: ASHLEY, BRADLEY, CALHOUN, CHICOT, CLARK, CLEVELAND, COLUMBIA, DALLAS, DESHA, DREW, GARLAND, GRANT, HEMPSTEAD, HOT SPRING, HOWARD, JEFFERSON, LAFAYETTE, LINCOLN, LITTLE RIVER, LOGAN, MILLER, MONTGOMERY, NEVADA, OUACHITA, PIKE, POLK, SCOTT, SEVIER, UNION. Population (2000), 668,385.

ZIP Codes: 71601–03, 71611–13, 71630–31, 71635, 71638–40, 71642–44, 71646–47, 71651–63, 71665–67, 71670–71, 71674–78, 71701, 71711, 71720–22, 71724–26, 71728, 71730–31, 71740, 71742–45, 71747–54, 71758–59,

71762–66, 71768, 71770, 71772, 71801–02, 71820, 71822–23, 71825–28, 71831–42, 71844–47, 71851–55, 71857–62, 71864–66, 71901–03, 71909–10, 71913–14, 71920–23, 71929, 71932–33, 71935, 71937, 71940–45, 71949–50, 71952–53, 71956–62, 71964–65, 71968–73, 71998–99, 72004, 72015, 72046, 72055, 72057, 72065, 72072–73, 72079, 72084, 72087, 72104–05, 72128–29, 72132–33, 72150, 72152, 72160, 72167–68, 72175, 72182, 72379, 72826–27, 72833–35, 72838, 72841–42, 72851, 72855, 72863, 72865, 72924, 72926–28, 72933, 72943–44, 72949–51, 72958

CALIFORNIA

(Population 2000, 33,871,648)

SENATORS

DIANNE FEINSTEIN, Democrat, of San Francisco, CA; born in San Francisco, June 22, 1933; education: B.A., Stanford University, 1955; elected to San Francisco Board of Supervisors, 1970–78; president of Board of Supervisors: 1970–71, 1974–75, 1978; mayor of San Francisco, 1978–88; candidate for governor of California, 1990; recipient: Distinguished Woman Award, *San Francisco Examiner;* Achievement Award, Business and Professional Women's Club, 1970; Golden Gate University, California, LL.D. (hon.), 1979; SCOPUS Award for Outstanding Public Service, American Friends of the Hebrew University of Jerusalem; University of Santa Clara, D.P.S. (hon.); University of Manila, D.P.A. (hon.), 1981; Antioch University, LL.D. (hon.), 1983; Los Angeles Anti-Defamation League of B'nai B'rith's Distinguished Service Award, 1984; French Legion d'Honneur from President Mitterand, 1984; Mills College, LL.D. (hon.), 1985; U.S. Army's Commander's Award for Public Service, 1986; Brotherhood/Sisterhood Award, National Conference of Christians and Jews, 1986; Paulist Fathers Award, 1987; Episcopal Church Award for Service, 1987; U.S. Navy Distinguished Civilian Award, 1987; Silver Spur Award for Outstanding Public Service, San Francisco Planning and Urban Renewal Association, 1987; All Pro Management Team Award for No. 1 Mayor, *City and State* Magazine, 1987; Community Service Award Honoree for Public Service, 1987; American Jewish Congress, 1987; President's Award, St. Ignatius High School, San Francisco, 1988; Coro Investment in Leadership Award, 1988; President's Medal, University of California at San Francisco, 1988; University of San Francisco, D.H.L. (hon.), 1988; member: Coro Foundation, Fellowship, 1955–56; California Women's Board of Terms and Parole, 1960–66, executive committee; U.S. Conference of Mayors, 1983–88; Mayor's Commission on Crime, San Francisco; Bank of California, director, 1988–89; San Francisco Education Fund's Permanent Fund, 1988–89; Japan Society of Northern California, 1988–89; Inter-American Dialogue, 1988–present; Publius Award from the Center for the Study of the Presidency and Congress, 2009; chair, U.S. Senate Caucus on International Narcotics Control; married: Dr. Bertram Feinstein (dec.); married on January 20, 1980, to Richard C. Blum; children: one child; three stepchildren; religion: Jewish; committees: chair, Select Committee on Intelligence; Appropriations; Judiciary; Rules and Administration; elected to the U.S. Senate, by special election, on November 3, 1992, to fill the vacancy caused by the resignation of Senator Pete Wilson; reelected to each succeeding Senate term.

Office Listings

http://feinstein.senate.gov

331 Hart Senate Office Building, Washington, DC 20510 .... (202) 224–3841
Chief of Staff.—Chris Thompson. FAX: 228–3954
Legislative Director.—John Watts.
Director of Communications.—Gil Duran.
750 B Street, Suite 1030, San Diego, CA 92101 .... (619) 231–9712
2500 Tulare Street, Suite 4290, Fresno, CA 93721 .... (559) 485–7430
One Post Street, Suite 2450, San Francisco, CA 94104 .... (415) 393–0707
11111 San Monica Boulevard, Suite 915, Los Angeles, CA 90025 .... (310) 914–7300

* * *

BARBARA BOXER, Democrat, of Rancho Mirage, CA; born in Brooklyn, NY, November 11, 1940; education: B.A. in economics, Brooklyn College, 1962; professional: stockbroker and economic researcher with securities firms on Wall Street, 1962–65; journalist and associate editor, *Pacific Sun* newspaper, 1972–74; congressional aide, Fifth Congressional District, California, 1974–76; elected Marin County Board of Supervisors, 1976–82; first woman president, Marin County Board of Supervisors; Edgar Wayburn award, Sierra Club, 1997; Policy Leadership award, Family Violence Prevention Fund, 2000; Circle of Courage award, Afghan Women Association International and the Women's Intercultural Network, 2003; Children's Champion award, California Head Start Association, 2003; married: Stewart Boxer, 1962; children: Doug and Nicole; committees: chair, Environment and Public Works; chair, Select Committee on Ethics; Commerce, Science, and Transportation; Foreign Relations; elected November 2, 1982 to 98th Congress; reelected to the 99th–102nd Congresses; elected to the U.S. Senate on November 3, 1992; reelected to each succeeding Senate term.

Office Listings

http://boxer.senate.gov

112 Hart Senate Office Building, Washington, DC 20510 .... (202) 224–3553

Chief of Staff.—Laura Schiller. FAX: 228–2382
Legislative Director.—Sean Moore.
Communications Director.—Natalie Ravitz.
1700 Montgomery Street, Suite 240, San Francisco, CA 94111 .... (415) 403–0100
312 North Spring Street, Suite 1748, Los Angeles, CA 90012 .... (213) 894–5000
501 I Street, Suite 7–600, Sacramento, CA 95814 .... (916) 448–2787
201North E Street, Suite 210, San Bernardino, CA 92401 .... (909) 888–8525
600 B Street, Suite 2240, San Diego, CA 92101 .... (619) 239–3884
2500 Tulare Street, Suite 5290, Fresno, CA 93721 .... (209) 497–5109

REPRESENTATIVES

FIRST DISTRICT

MIKE THOMPSON, Democrat, of Napa Valley, CA; born in St. Helena, CA, January 24, 1951; education: graduated, St. Helena High School, St. Helena, CA; U.S. Army, 1969–72; Purple Heart; B.A., Chico State University, 1982; M.A., Chico State University, 1996; teacher at San Francisco State University, and Chico State University; elected to the California State Senate, 2nd District, 1990–98; former chairman of the California State Senate Budget Committee; married to Janet; two children: Christopher and Jon; committees: Ways and Means; Permanent Select Committee on Intelligence; elected to the 106th Congress; reelected to each succeeding Congress.

Office Listings

http://mikethompson.house.gov http://www.house.gov/writerep

231 Cannon House Office Building, Washington, DC 20515 .... (202) 225–3311
Chief of Staff.—Charles Jefferson. FAX: 225–4335
Legislative Director.—Jonathan Birdsong.
Communication Director.—Laurel Brown.
1040 Main Street, Suite 101, Napa, CA 94559 .... (707) 226–9898
317 Third Street, Suite 1, Eureka, CA 95501 .... (707) 269–9595
Post Office Box 2208, Fort Bragg, CA 95437 .... (707) 962–0933
712 Main Street, Suite 1, Woodland, CA 95695 .... (530) 662–5272

Counties: DEL NORTE COUNTY. CITIES AND TOWNSHIPS: Crescent City, Fortdeck, Gasquet, Klamath, Prison, Smith River. HUMBOLDT COUNTY. CITIES AND TOWNSHIPS: Alderpoint, Areata, Bayside, Blocksburg, Blue Lake, Burcka, Carlotta, Eureka, Ferndale, Fortuna, Garberville, Hoopa, Hydseville, Kneeland, Korbel, Loleta, McKinlayville, Myers Flat, Orick, Petrolia, Redcrest, Redway, Rio Del, Scotia, Trinidad, Whitehorn, Willow Creek. LAKE COUNTY. CITIES AND TOWNSHIPS: Clearlake, Clearlake Oaks, Clearlake Park, Cobb, Glenhaven, Kelseyville, Lakeport, Lower Lake, Lucerne, Middletown, Nice, Upper Lake. MENDOCINO COUNTY. CITIES AND TOWNSHIPS: Albion, Boonville, Calpella, Compiche, Covelo, Elk, Finley, Fort Bragg, Gualala, Hopland, Laytonville, Little River, Manchester, Mendocino, Philo, Piercy, Point Arena, Potter Valley, Redwood Valley, Talmage, Ukiah, Willits, Yorkville. NAPA COUNTY. CITIES AND TOWNSHIPS: American Canyon, Angwin, Aetna Springs, Calistoga, Deer Park, Oakville, Pope Valley, Rutherford, St. Helena. SONOMA COUNTY (part). CITIES AND TOWNSHIPS: Alexander Valley, Cloverdale, Geyserville, Healdsburg, Mark West, Santa Rosa, Sonoma, Windsor. YOLO COUNTY (part). CITIES AND TOWNSHIPS: Davis, West Sacramento, Winters, and Woodland. Population (2000), 639,087.

ZIP Codes: 94503, 94508, 94515, 94558–59, 94562, 94567, 94573–74, 94576, 94581, 94589–90, 94599, 95403–04, 95409–10, 95415–18, 95420, 95422–29, 95432–33, 95435, 95437, 95441–43, 95445, 95448–49, 95451–54, 95456–61, 95463–64, 95466, 95468–70, 95476, 95481–82, 95485, 95487–88, 95490, 95492–94, 95501–03, 95511, 95514, 95518–19, 95521, 95524–26, 95528, 95531–32, 95534, 95536–38, 95540, 95542–43, 95545–51, 95553–56, 95558–60, 95562, 95564–65, 95567, 95569–71, 95573, 95585, 95587, 95589, 95605, 95612, 95615–16, 95618, 95691, 95694–95, 95776, 95798–99, 95899

* * *

SECOND DISTRICT

WALLY HERGER, Republican, of Marysville, CA; born in Sutter County, CA, May 20, 1945; education: graduated East Nicolaus High School; attended California State University, Sacramento, CA; professional: cattle rancher; small businessman; East Nicolaus High School Board of Trustees, 1977–80; California State Assemblyman, 1980–86; member: National Federation of Independent Business; Sutter County Taxpayers Association; Yuba-Sutter Farm Bureau; California Cattlemen's Association; California Chamber of Commerce; Big Brothers/Big Sisters Board of Directors; South Yuba Rotary Club; married: the former Pamela Sargent; children: eight; committees: Ways and Means; elected to the 100th Congress, November 4, 1986; reelected to each succeeding Congress.

Office Listings

242 Cannon House Office Building, Washington, DC 20515 .... (202) 225–3076
Administrative Assistant.—Derek Harley. FAX: 226–0852
Legislative Director.—Darin Thacker.
Press Secretary.—Matt Lavoie.
Executive Assistant / Scheduler.—Adriana Dotson.
2635 Forest Avenue, Suite 100, Chico, CA 95928 .... (530) 893–8363
District Director.—Fran Peace.
410 Hemsted Drive, Suite 115, Redding, CA 96002 .... (530) 223–5898

Counties: BUTTE (part), COLUSA, GLENN, SHASTA, SISKIYOU, SUTTER, TEHAMA, TRINITY, YOLO (part), YUBA. Population (2000), 639,087.

ZIP Codes: 95526–27, 95552, 95563, 95568, 95595, 95606–07, 95627, 95637, 95645, 95653, 95659, 95668, 95674, 95676, 95679, 95692, 95697–98, 95837, 95901, 95903, 95912–14, 95917–20, 95922, 95925–29, 95932, 95935–39, 95941–43, 95947–48, 95950–51, 95953–55, 95957–58, 95960–63, 95967, 95969–74, 95976–79, 95981–82, 95987–88, 95991–93, 96001–03, 96007–08, 96010–11, 96013–14, 96016–17, 96019, 96021–25, 96027–29, 96031–35, 96037–41, 96044, 96046–52, 96055–59, 96061–65, 96067, 96069–71, 96073–76, 96078–80, 96084–97, 96099, 96101, 96103–04, 96114, 96118, 96122, 96124, 96134, 96137, 96161

* * *

THIRD DISTRICT

DANIEL E. LUNGREN, Republican, of Gold River, CA; born in Long Beach, CA, September 22, 1946; education: St. Anthony's High School, Long Beach, CA, 1964; B.A., English, University of Notre Dame, 1968 (with honors); attended University of Southern California Law Center, 1968–69; J.D., Georgetown University Law Center, 1971; professional: attorney, associate and partner, Ball, Hunt, Brown & Baerwitz (law firm), 1973–78; U.S. House of Representatives, 1979–89; elected California Attorney General, 1990, served two terms; Republican nominee for Governor of California, 1998; radio talk show host; consultant; private law practice, 1999–2004; religion: Catholic; married: the former Barbara (Bobbi) Knolls, 1969; children: Jeff, Kelly, and Kathleen; committees: ranking member, House Administration; Homeland Security; Judiciary; elected to the 109th Congress on November 2, 2004; reelected to each succeeding Congress.

Office Listings

http://www.house.gov/lungren

2448 Rayburn House Office Building, Washington, DC 20515 .... (202) 225–5716
Chief of Staff.—Peter Tateishi. FAX: 226–1298
Communications Director.—Brian Kaveney.
Scheduler.—Dominic Storelli.
2339 Gold Medal Way, Suite 220, Gold River, CA 95670 .... (916) 859–9906

Counties: ALPINE, AMADOR, CALAVERAS, SACRAMENTO (part), SOLANO (part). CITIES AND TOWNSHIPS: Amador, Arden-Arcade, Carmichael, Citrus Heights, Elk Grove, Fair Oaks, Folsom, Foothill Farms, Galt, Gold River, Ione, Jackson, Laguna, Laguna West, LaRiviera, North Highland, Rancho Cordova, Rancho Murieta, Rio Linda, Rio Vista, Roseville, Sacramento, Vineyard, and Wilton. Population (2000), 639,088.

ZIP Codes: 94571, 94585, 95221–26, 95228–30, 95232–33, 95236, 95245–52, 95254–55, 95257, 95601, 95608, 95610–11, 95615, 95620–21, 95624, 95626, 95628–30, 95632, 95638–40, 95642, 95646, 95652, 95654–55, 95660, 95662, 95665–66, 95668–71, 95673, 95675, 95683, 95685, 95688–90, 95693–94, 95699, 95742, 95758–59, 95763, 95821, 95825–30, 95832, 95835–37, 95841–43, 95864, 96021–22, 96029, 96035, 96055, 96061, 96080, 96120

* * *

FOURTH DISTRICT

TOM McCLINTOCK, Republican, of Granite Bay, CA; born in Bronxville, NY, July 10, 1956; education: B.A., *Cum Laude* political science, UCLA, Los Angeles, CA; 1978; married: Lori; two children; committees: Education and Labor; Natural Resources; elected to the 111th Congress on November 4, 2008.

Office Listings

http://www.mcclintock.house.gov

508 Cannon House Office Building, Washington, DC 20515 .... (202) 225–2511

Chief of Staff.—Igor Birman. FAX: 225–5444
Legislative Director.—Kristen Glenn.
Scheduler / Staff Assistant.—Kim Unitt-Zupkus.
Legislative Correspondent.—Will Dunham.
Legislative Aide.—Tyler Eure.
4230 Douglas Boulevard, Suite 200, Granite Bay, CA 95746 .... (916) 859–9906
District Director.—Dan Brennan.

Counties: BUTTE (part), EL DORADO, LASSEN, MODOC, NEVADA, PLACER, PLUMAS, SACRAMENTO (part), SIERRA. Population (2000), 639,088.

ZIP Codes: 95602–04, 95609, 95613–14, 95617, 95619, 95623, 95626, 95628–31, 95633–36, 95648, 95650–51, 95656, 95658, 95661–64, 95667–68, 95672, 95677–78, 95681–82, 95684, 95701, 95703, 95709, 95712–15, 95717, 95720–22, 95724, 95726, 95728, 95735–36, 95741, 95746–47, 95762, 95765, 95816, 95910, 95915–16, 95922–24, 95930, 95934, 95940–41, 95944–47, 95949, 95956, 95959–60, 95965–66, 95968, 95971, 95975, 95977, 95980, 95983–84, 95986, 96006, 96009, 96015, 96020, 96054, 96056, 96068, 96101, 96103–30, 96132–33, 96135–37, 96140–43, 96145–46, 96148, 96150–52, 96154–56, 96158, 96160–62

* * *

FIFTH DISTRICT

DORIS OKADA MATSUI, Democrat, of Sacramento, CA; born in Posten, AZ, September 25, 1944; education: B.A., University of California, Berkeley, CA, 1966; professional: staff, White House, 1992–98; private advocate; organizations: Meridian International Center Board of Trustees; Woodrow Wilson Center Board of Trustees; California Institute Board of Directors; married: Robert Matsui, 1966; children: Brian Robert; committees: Energy and Commerce; Rules; elected by special election on March 8, 2005 to the 109th Congress, to fill the vacancy caused by the death of her husband, Representative Robert Matsui; reelected to each succeeding Congress.

Office Listings

http://www.house.gov/matsui

222 Cannon House Office Building, Washington, DC 20515 .... (202) 225–7163
Chief of Staff.—Julie Eddy. FAX: 225–0566
Executive Assistant.—Erin Robbins.
Legislative Director.—Gabe Horwitz.
Communications Director.—Alexis Marks.
Press Secretary.—Mara Lee.
501 I Street, 12–600, Sacramento, CA 95814 .... (916) 498–5600
District Director.—Nathan Dietrich.

County: SACRAMENTO COUNTY (part). CITY: Sacramento. Population (2000), 639,088.

ZIP Codes: 94204–09, 94211, 94229–30, 94232, 94234–37, 94239–40, 94244, 94246–49, 94252, 94254, 94256–59, 94261–63, 94267–69, 94271, 94273–74, 94277–80, 94282, 94284–91, 94293–99, 95660, 95670, 95758, 95812–20, 95822–29, 95831–35, 95838, 95840–43, 95851–53, 95860, 95864–67, 95887, 95894

* * *

SIXTH DISTRICT

LYNN C. WOOLSEY, Democrat, of Petaluma, CA; born in Seattle, WA, November 3, 1937; education: graduated from Lincoln High School, Seattle; B.S., University of San Francisco, 1981; president and founder, Woolsey Personnel Service, 1980–92; human resources manager, Harris Digital Telephone Systems, 1969–80; elected member, Petaluma City Council, 1984–92; vice mayor, 1989 and 1992; member and chair, Sonoma County National Women's Political Caucus; chair, Sonoma County Commission on the Status of Women; Business and Professional Women; National Organization for Women; Sierra Club; chair, Sonoma County Hazardous Materials Management Commission; Association of Bay Area Governments, Regional Hazardous Materials Representative; advisory committee, CAL Energy Commission; co-chair, Education Task Force of the California Delegation Bipartisan Caucus; the Renewable Energy Caucus; the Congressional Human Rights Caucus; the Missing and Exploited Children's Caucus (founding member); the Congressional Task Force on Health and Tobacco; the Internet Caucus; the Congressional Task Force on International HIV/AIDS; the Congressional Friends of Animals; and the Livable Communities Task Force; chair of the Children's Task Force; co-chair of the Democratic Caucus Task Force on Welfare Reform; co-chair of the Progressive Caucus; four children, and four grandchildren; committees: Education and Labor; Science and Technology; elected on November 3, 1992 to the 103rd Congress; reelected to each succeeding Congress.

Office Listings

http://www.house.gov/woolsey

2263 Rayburn House Office Building, Washington, DC 20515 .... (202) 225–5161
Chief of Staff.—Nora Matus. FAX: 225–5163
Press Secretary.—Christopher Shields.
1101 College Avenue, Suite 200, Santa Rosa, CA 95404 .... (707) 542–7182
District Director.—Wendy Friefeld.
1050 Northgate Drive, Suite 354, San Rafael, CA 94903 .... (415) 507–9554

Counties: MARIN, SONOMA (part). CITIES AND TOWNSHIPS: Santa Rosa, Sebastapol, Cotati, Petaluma, and Sonoma to Golden Gate Bridge. Population (2000), 639,087.

ZIP Codes: 94901, 94903–04, 94912–15, 94920, 94922–31, 94933, 94937–42, 94945–57, 94960, 94963–66, 94970–79, 94998–99, 95401–07, 95409, 95412, 95419, 95421, 95430–31, 95436, 95439, 95441–42, 95444, 95446, 95448, 95450, 95452, 95462, 95465, 95471–73, 95476, 95480, 95486, 95492, 95497

* * *

SEVENTH DISTRICT

GEORGE MILLER, Democrat, of Martinez, CA; born in Richmond, CA, May 17, 1945; education: attended Martinez public schools; Diablo Valley College; graduated, San Francisco State College, 1968; J.D., University of California at Davis School of Law, 1972; member: California State bar; Davis Law School Alumni Association; served five years as legislative aide to Senate majority leader, California State Legislature; past chairman and member of Contra Costa County Democratic Central Committee; past president of Martinez Democratic Club; married: the former Cynthia Caccavo; children: George and Stephen; four grandchildren; committees: chair, Education and Labor; Natural Resources; elected to the 94th Congress, November 5, 1974; reelected to each succeeding Congress.

Office Listings

http://www.house.gov/georgemiller george.miller@mail.house.gov

2205 Rayburn House Office Building, Washington, DC 20515 .... (202) 225–2095
Chief of Staff/Press Secretary.—Daniel Weiss. FAX: 225–5609
Personal Secretary.—Sylvia Arthur.
1333 Willow Pass Road, Suite 203, Concord, CA 94520 .... (925) 602–1880
District Director.—Barbara Johnson.
Room 281, 3220 Blume Drive, Richmond, CA 94806 .... (510) 262–6500
Field Representative.—Latressa Alford.
375 G Street, Suite 1, Vallejo, CA 94592 .... (707) 645–1888
Field Representative.—Kathy Hoffman.

Counties: CONTRA COSTA (part), SOLANO (part). CITIES AND TOWNSHIPS: Benicia, Clayton, Concord, Crockett, El Sobrante, Green Valley, Hercules, Martinez, Pinole, Pittsburg, Port Costa, Richmond, Rodeo, San Pablo, Sulsun Valley, Vacaville, and Vallejo. Population (2000), 639,088.

ZIP Codes: 94503, 94510, 94517, 94519–25, 94527, 94529, 94533–34, 94547, 94553, 94564–65, 94569, 94572, 94585, 94589–92, 94801–08, 94820, 94875, 95687–88, 95696

* * *

EIGHTH DISTRICT

NANCY PELOSI, Democrat, of San Francisco, CA; born in Baltimore, MD, March 26, 1940; daughter of the late Representative Thomas D'Alesandro, Jr., of MD; education: graduated, Institute of Notre Dame High School, 1958; B.A., Trinity College, Washington, DC (major, political science; minor, history), 1962; northern chair, California Democratic Party, 1977–81; state chair, California Democratic Party, 1981–83; chair, 1984 Democratic National Convention Host Committee; finance chair, Democratic Senatorial Campaign Committee, 1985–86; member: Democratic National Committee; California Democratic Party Executive Committee; San Francisco Library Commission; Board of Trustees, LSB Leakey Foundation; married: Paul F. Pelosi, 1963; children: Nancy Corinne, Christine, Jacqueline, Paul, Jr., and Alexandra; 8 grandchildren; elected by special election, June 2, 1987, to the 100th Congress to fill the vacancy caused by the death of Sala Burton; elected Minority Whip in the 108th Congress; Minority Leader in the 109th Congress and Speaker of the House in the 110th and 111th Congresses.

Office Listings

http://www.house.gov/pelosi sf.nancy@mail.house.gov

235 Cannon House Office Building, Washington, DC 20515 .... (202) 225–4965
Chief of Staff.—Terri McCullough. FAX: 225–8259
Office Manager.—Paula Short.
90 7th Street, Suite 2–8000, San Francisco, CA 94103 .... (415) 556–4862
District Director.—Dan Bernal.

County: SAN FRANCISCO COUNTY (part). CITY: San Francisco. Population (2000), 639,088.

ZIP Codes: 94101–12, 94114–15, 94117–26, 94128–47, 94150–52, 94155–56, 94158–66, 94168, 94170, 94172, 94175, 94177, 94188, 94199

* * *

NINTH DISTRICT

BARBARA LEE, Democrat, of Oakland, CA; born in El Paso, TX, July 16, 1946; education: graduated, San Fernando High School; B.A., Mills College, 1973; MSW, University of California, Berkeley, 1975; congressional aide and public servant; senior advisor and chief of staff to Congressman Ronald V. Dellums in Washington, DC, and Oakland, CA, 1975–87; California State Assembly, 1990–96; California State Senate, 1996–98; Assembly committees: Housing and Land Use; Appropriations; Business and Professions; Industrial Relations; Judiciary; Revenue and Taxation; board member, California State Coastal Conservancy, District Export Council, and California Defense Conversion Council; committees: Appropriations; elected to the 105th Congress on April 7, 1998, by special election, to fill the remaining term of retiring Representative Ronald V. Dellums; reelected to each succeeding Congress.

Office Listings

http://www.house.gov/lee

2444 Rayburn House Office Building, Washington, DC 20515 .... (202) 225–2661
Chief of Staff.—Julie Nickson. FAX: 225–9817
Scheduler.—Tatyana Kalinga.
Communications Director.—Nicole Williams.
Legislative Director.—Christos Tsentas.
1301 Clay Street, Suite 1000–N, Oakland, CA 94612 .... (510) 763–0370

Counties: ALAMEDA COUNTY. CITIES: Alameda, Albany, Berkeley, Emeryville, Kensington, Piedmont. OAKLAND COUNTY (part). Population (2000), 639,088.

ZIP Codes: 94541–42, 94546, 94552, 94577–80, 94588, 94601–13, 94615, 94617–26, 94643, 94649, 94659–62, 94666, 94701–10, 94712, 94720

* * *

TENTH DISTRICT

VACANT

Counties: CONTRA COSTA (part), ALAMEDA (part), SACRAMENTO (part), SOLANO (part). CITIES AND TOWNSHIPS: Alamo, Antioch, Blackhawk, Bethel Island, Brentwood, Byron, Clayton, Concord, Danville, Diablo, Dublin, Fairfield, Lafayette, Livermore, Moraga, Oakley, Orinda, Pleasant Hill, and Walnut Creek. Population (2000), 639,088.

ZIP Codes: 94507, 94509–12, 94516, 94518, 94520–21, 94523, 94530–31, 94533–35, 94548–51, 94556, 94561, 94563, 94570–71, 94575, 94585, 94588, 94595–98, 94706–08, 94803, 95377, 95391, 95620, 95625, 95641, 95680, 95690

* * *

ELEVENTH DISTRICT

JERRY MCNERNEY, Democrat, of Pleasanton, CA; born in Albuquerque, NM, June 18, 1951; attended the U.S. Military Academy, West Point, NY, 1969–71; A.S., University of New

Mexico, Albuquerque, NM, 1973; M.S., University of New Mexico, NM, 1975; Ph.D. in Mathematics, University of New Mexico, 1981; professional: wind engineer; entrepreneur; business owner; married: Mary; children: Michael, Windy and Greg; committees: Energy and Commerce; Veterans' Affairs; elected to the 110th Congress on November 7, 2006; reelected to the 111th Congress.

Office Listings

http://www.house.gov

312 Cannon House Office Building, Washington, DC 20515 .... (202) 225–1947
Chief of Staff.—Nick Holder. FAX: 225–4060
Executive Assistant.—Teresa Frison.
Communications Director.—Sarah Hersh.
Legislative Director.—Andrew Horowitz.
5776 Stoneridge Mall Road, #175, Pleasanton, CA 94588 .... (925) 737–0727
District Director.—Nicole Damasco Alioto.
2222 Grand Canal Boulevard, #7, Stockton, CA 95207 .... (209) 476–8552

Counties: ALAMEDA (part), CONTRA COSTA (part), SAN JOAQUIN (part), SANTA CLARA (part). CITIES AND TOWNSHIPS: Blackhawk, Brentwood, Byron, Clements, Danville, Diablo, Discovery Bay, Dublin, Escalon, Farmington, Linden, Lockeford, Lodi, Manteca, Morada, Morgan Hill, Pleasanton, Ripon, San Ramon, Stockton, Sunol, Tracy, and Woodbridge. Population (2000), 639,088.

ZIP Codes: 94506–07, 94509, 94513–14, 94526, 94528, 94539, 94550, 94566, 94568, 94583, 94586, 94588, 95020, 95023, 95037–38, 95046, 95127, 95132, 95135, 95138, 95140, 95204, 95207, 95209–12, 95215, 95219–20, 95227, 95230, 95234, 95236–37, 95240–42, 95253, 95258, 95267, 95297, 95304, 95320, 95336–37, 95361, 95366, 95376–77, 95391, 95686

* * *

TWELFTH DISTRICT

JACKIE SPEIER, Democrat, of Hillsborough, CA; born in San Francisco, CA, May 14, 1950; education: B.A., University of California at Davis; J.D., University of California, Hastings College of the Law, 1976; legislative council, Congressman Leo J. Ryan; member, San Mateo County Board of Supervisors; member, California State Assembly; senator, California State Senate; married: Barry Dennis; two children: Jackson Sierra and Stephanie Sierra; committees: Financial Services, Oversight and Government Reform, Select Committee on Energy Independence and Global Warming; elected to the 111th Congress on November 4, 2008.

Office Listings

http://speier.house.gov

211 Cannon House Office Building, Washington, DC 20515 .... (202) 225–3531
Administrative Assistant.—Gina Gribow. FAX: 226–4183
Legislative Director.—Erin Ryan.
400 South El Camino Real, Suite 410, San Mateo, CA 94402 .... (650) 342–0300
District Representative.—Margo Rosen.

Counties: SAN MATEO COUNTY (part). CITIES: Brisbane, Burlingame, Colma, Daly City, Foster City, Hillsborough, Millbrae, Montara, Moss Beach, Pacifica, Redwood City, San Bruno, San Carlos, San Mateo, South San Francisco. SAN FRANCISCO COUNTY (part). CITIES: San Francisco. Population (2000), 639,088.

ZIP Codes: 94005, 94010–11, 94013–17, 94021, 94030, 94037–38, 94044, 94061–63, 94065–66, 94070, 94080, 94083, 94099, 94112, 94116–17, 94122, 94127–28, 94131–32, 94143, 94401–09, 94497

* * *

THIRTEENTH DISTRICT

FORTNEY PETE STARK, Democrat, of Fremont, CA; born in Milwaukee, WI, November 11, 1931; education: graduated, Wauwatosa, WI, High School, 1949; B.S., Massachusetts Institute of Technology, 1953; M.B.A., University of California, Berkeley, 1960; G.E.D., East Bay Skills Center, Oakland, 1972 (honorary); served in U.S. Air Force, 1955–57, first lieutenant; banker, founder, and president, Security National Bank, Walnut Creek, CA, 1963–72; trustee, California Democratic Council; chairman, board of trustees, Starr King School of Ministry, Berkeley; trustee, Graduate Theological Union, Berkeley; sponsor, Northern California American Civil Liberties Union; board member, Housing Development Corporation and Council for

Civic Unity; director, Common Cause, 1971–72; married: Deborah Roderick; children: Jeffrey Peter, Beatrice Stark Winslow, Thekla Stark Wainwright, Sarah Stark Ramirez, Fortney Stark III, Hannah and Andrew; committees: Ways and Means; elected to the 93rd Congress, November 7, 1972; reelected to each succeeding Congress.

Office Listings

239 Cannon House Office Building, Washington, DC 20515 .... (202) 225–5065
Chief of Staff.—Debbie Curtis. FAX: 226–3805
Personal Assistant.—Rebecca Slater.
39300 Civic Center Drive, Fremont, CA 94538 .... (510) 494–1388
District Administrator.—Jo Cazenave.

Counties: ALAMEDA COUNTY (part). CITIES AND TOWNSHIPS: Alameda, Castro Valley, Fremont, Hayward, Newark, Oakland, San Leandro, San Lorenzo, Sunol, and Union City. Population (2000), 639,088.

ZIP Codes: 94501–02, 94536, 94538–39, 94541–42, 94544–06, 94552, 94560, 94566, 94588, 94577–80, 94586–87, 94603, 94614, 94557

* * *

FOURTEENTH DISTRICT

ANNA G. ESHOO, Democrat, of Menlo Park, CA; born in New Britain, CT, December 13, 1942; education: attended Canada College; San Mateo supervisor, 1983–92; served on the House Committees on Science, Space, and Technology, and Merchant Marine and Fisheries; selected to co-chair the House Medical Technology Caucus, 1994; committees: Energy and Commerce; Permanent Select Committee on Intelligence; elected on November 3, 1992, to the 103rd Congress; reelected to each succeeding Congress.

Office Listings

http://www-eshoo.house.gov

205 Cannon House Office Building, Washington, DC 20515 .... (202) 225–8104
Chief of Staff.—Jason Mahler. FAX: 225–8890
Executive Assistant.—Jena Gross.
698 Emerson Street, Palo Alto, CA 94301 .... (650) 323–2984
Chief of Staff.—Karen Chapman.

Counties: SAN MATEO (part), SANTA CLARA (part), SANTA CRUZ (part). CITIES AND TOWNSHIPS: Amesti, Aptos, Atherton, Belmont, Ben Lomond, Bonny Doon, Boulder Creek, Brookdale, Corralitos, Davenport, East Palo Alto, Felton, Half Moon Bay, Interlaken, La Honda, Los Altos, Los Altos Hills, Menlo Park, Monte Sereno, Mountain View, Palo Alto, Portola Valley, Redwood City, San Carlos, Scotts Valley, Stanford, Sunnyvale, and Woodside. Population (2000), 639,088.

ZIP Codes: 94002, 94018–28, 94035, 94039–43, 94060–64, 94074, 94085–89, 94301–06, 94309, 95003, 95005–08, 95014, 95017–18, 95030, 95033, 95041, 95051, 95060, 95065–67, 95070–71, 95073, 95076, 95130

* * *

FIFTEENTH DISTRICT

MICHAEL M. HONDA, Democrat, of San Jose, CA; born in Walnut Creek, CA, June 27, 1941; education: San Jose State University, received degrees in Biological Sciences and Spanish, and a Masters Degree in Education; awards: California Federation of Teachers Legislator of the Year; Outreach Paratransit Services Humanitarian Award; AEA Legislator of the Year; Service Employees International Union Home Care Champion Award; Asian Law Alliance Community Impact Award; AFL–CIO Distinguished Friend of Labor Award; chair, Congressional Asian Pacific American Caucus; chair, Ethiopia and Ethiopian American Caucus; public service: Peace Corps; San Jose Planning Commission; San Jose Unified School Board; Santa Clara County Board of Supervisors; California State Assemblyman; married: Jeanne; children: Mark and Michelle; committees: Appropriations; vice chair, Democratic National Committee; senior Majority Whip; elected to the 107th Congress on November 7, 2000; reelected to each succeeding Congress.

Office Listings

http://www.house.gov/honda

1713 Longworth House Office Building, Washington, DC 20515 .... (202) 225–2631

Chief of Staff.—Jennifer Van der Heide Escobar. FAX: 225–2699
Legislative Director.—Eric Werwa.
Senior Legislative Counsel.—Gloria Chan.
Communications Director.—Michael Shank.
1999 South Bascom Avenue, Suite 815, Campbell, CA 95008 .... (408) 558–8085
District Director.—Meri Maben.

Counties: SANTA CLARA COUNTY (part). CITIES AND TOWNSHIPS: Campbell, Cambrian Park, Cupertino, Fruitdale, Gilroy, Lexington Hill, Los Gatos, Milpitas, San Jose, and Santa Clara. Population (2000), 639,088.

ZIP Codes: 94024, 94087, 95002, 95008–09, 95011, 95014–15, 95020–21, 95026, 95030–33, 95035–37, 95044, 95050–56, 95070, 95101, 95112, 95117–18, 95120, 95123–34, 95150, 95153–55, 95157, 95160–61, 95170

* * *

SIXTEENTH DISTRICT

ZOE LOFGREN, Democrat, of San Jose, CA; born in San Mateo, CA, December 21, 1947; education: graduated Gunn High School, 1966; B.A., Stanford University, Stanford, CA, 1970; J.D., Santa Clara Law School, Santa Clara, CA, 1975; admitted to the California bar, 1975; District of Columbia bar, 1981; Supreme Court, 1986; member: board of trustees, San Jose Evergreen Community College District, 1979–81; board of supervisors, Santa Clara County, CA, 1981–94; married: John Marshall Collins, 1978; children: Sheila and John; committees: chair, Standards of Official Conduct; Homeland Security; House Administration; Judiciary; elected to the 104th Congress; reelected to each succeeding Congress.

Office Listings

http://www.house.gov/lofgren

102 Cannon House Office Building, Washington, DC 20515 .... (202) 225–3072
Chief of Staff.—Stacey Leavandosky. FAX: 225–3336
Communications Director.—Kyra Jennings.
Executive Assistant / Scheduler.—Haley Smith.
635 North First Street, Suite B, San Jose, CA 95112 .... (408) 271–8700
Chief of Staff.—Sandra Soto.

Counties: SANTA CLARA COUNTY (part). CITIES AND TOWNSHIPS: San Jose, San Martin, and unincorporated portions of southern Santa Clara County. Population (2000), 639,088.

ZIP Codes: 95008, 95013, 95020, 95035, 95037, 95042, 95046, 95103, 95106, 95108–13, 95115–16, 95118–28, 95131–36, 95138–40, 95148, 95151–52, 95156, 95158–59, 95164, 95172–73, 95190–94, 95196

* * *

SEVENTEENTH DISTRICT

SAM FARR, Democrat, of Carmel, CA; born in San Francisco, CA, July 4, 1941; education: attended Carmel, CA, public schools; B.S., biology, Willamette University, Salem, OR; studied at the Monterey Institute of International Studies; served in the Peace Corps for two years in Colombia, South America; worked as a consultant and employee of the California Assembly; elected to the California Assembly, 1980–93; former member of California Assembly's Committees on Education, Insurance, and Natural Resources; married to Shary Baldwin; one daughter: Jessica; committees: Appropriations; elected on June 8, 1993, by special election, to fill the vacancy caused by the resignation of Representative Leon Panetta; reelected to each succeeding Congress.

Office Listings

http://www.farr.house.gov

1126 Longworth House Office Building, Washington, DC 20515 .... (202) 225–2861
Administrative Assistant.—Rochelle Dornatt.
Legislative Director.—Debbie Merrill.
Press Secretary.—Jessica Schafer.
701 Ocean Avenue, Santa Cruz, CA 95060 .... (831) 429–1976
100 West Alisal Street, Salinas, CA 93901 .... (831) 424–2229

Counties: MONTEREY, SAN BENITO, SANTA CRUZ (southern half). Population (2000), 639,088.

ZIP Codes: 93426, 93450–51, 93901–02, 93905–08, 93912, 93915, 93920–28, 93930, 93932–33, 93940, 93942–44, 93950, 93953–55, 93960, 93962, 95001, 95003–04, 95010, 95012, 95019, 95023–24, 95039, 95043, 95045, 95060–65, 95073, 95075–77

* * *

EIGHTEENTH DISTRICT

DENNIS A. CARDOZA, Democrat, of Atwater, CA; born in Merced, CA, March 31, 1959; education: B.A., University of Maryland, 1982; professional: businessman; public service: Atwater City Council, 1984–87; California State Assembly, 1996–2002; awards: California State Sheriff's Association Legislator of the Year; Small Business Roundtable Legislator of the Year; Small Business Association Legislator of the Year; and University of California Legislator of the Year, for his work on behalf of U.C. Merced; religion: Catholic; family: married to Dr. Kathleen McLoughlin; children: Joey, Brittany, and Elaina; committees: Agriculture; Rules; elected to the 108th Congress on November 5, 2002; reelected to each succeeding Congress.

Office Listings

http://www.house.gov/cardoza

1224 Longworth House Office Building, Washington, DC 20515 .... (202) 225–6131
Chief of Staff.—Jennifer Walsh. FAX: 225–0819
Legislative Director.—Jason Lumia.
1010 10th Street, Suite 5800, Modesto, CA 95354 .... (209) 527–1914
District Director.—Lisa Mantarro Moore.

Counties: FRESNO (part), MADERA (part), MERCED, SAN JOAQUIN (part), STANISLAUS (part). CITIES AND TOWNSHIPS: Atwater, Ceres, Dos Palos, Gustine, Lathrop, Livingston, Los Banos, Modesto, Newman, Patterson, and Stockton. Population (2000), 639,088.

ZIP Codes: 93606, 93610, 93620, 93622, 93630, 93635, 93637, 93661, 93665, 93706, 93722, 95201–08, 95210, 95213, 95215, 95231, 95269, 95296, 95301, 95303–04, 95307, 95312–13, 95315, 95317, 95319, 95322, 95324, 95326, 95330, 95333–34, 95336–37, 95340–41, 95344, 95348, 95350–54, 95357–58, 95360, 95363, 95365, 95369, 95374, 95380, 95385, 95387–88, 95397

* * *

NINETEENTH DISTRICT

GEORGE RADANOVICH, Republican, of Mariposa, CA; born in Mariposa, June 20, 1955; education: graduated, Mariposa County High School; B.A., California State Polytechnic University, 1978; assistant manager, Yosemite Bank, 1980–83; opened Mariposa County's first winery, 1986; charter member and president of the Mariposa Wine Grape Growers Association; founder, Mariposa Creek Parkway, 1985; treasurer, Mariposa Historical Society, 1982–83; member: Wine Institute; California Farm Bureau; California Association of Wine Grape Growers; Chambers of Commerce; California Ag Leadership, class XXI; chairman: Mariposa County Board of Supervisors; Mariposa County Planning Commission; executive director of the California State Mining and Mineral Museum Association; former chairman, Western Caucus, 106th Congress; founding member of the Wine Caucus; committees: Energy and Commerce; elected to the 104th Congress; reelected to each succeeding Congress.

Office Listings

http://www.radanovich.house.gov

2410 Rayburn House Office Building, Washington, DC 20515 .... (202) 225–4540
Chief of Staff.—Ted Maness. FAX: 225–3402
Scheduler.—Jennifer Han.
1040 East Herndon, Suite 201, Fresno, CA 93720 .... (559) 449–2490
District Director.—Darren Rose.
3509 Coffee Road, Suite D3, Madesto, CA 95355 .... (209) 579–5438

Counties: FRESNO (part), MADERA (part), MARIPOSA (part), STANISLAUS (part), TUOLUMNE. CITIES AND TOWNSHIPS: Ahwahnee, Auberry, Bass Lake, Big Oak Flat, Cathey's Valley, Ceres, Chinese Camp, Chowchilla, Coarsegold, Columbia, Coleville, Coulterville, Crows Landing, Dardanelle, Denair, El Portal, Farmington, Firebaugh, Fish Camp, Fresno, Groveland, Hickman, Hornitos, Hughson, Kerman, Keyes, La Grange, Long Barn, Madera, Mariposa, Mendota, Midpines, Mi Wuk Village, Moccasin, Modesto, North Fork, Oakdale, Oakhurst, O'Neals, Pinecrest, Raymond, Riverbank, Salida, San Joaquin, Snelling, Sonora, Soulsbyville, Standard, Strawberry, Tranquillity, Tuolumne, Turlock, Twain Harte, Vernalis, Waterford, Wishon, and Yosemite National Park. Population (2000), 639,088.

ZIP Codes: 93601–02, 93604, 93610, 93614, 93622–23, 93626, 93630, 93637–40, 93643–45, 93650, 93653, 93660, 93668–69, 93703–06, 93710–11, 93720, 93722, 93726, 93728–29, 93741, 93755, 93765, 93780, 93784, 93790–94, 95230, 95305–07, 95309–11, 95313–14, 95316, 95318, 95321, 95323, 95325–29, 95335, 95338, 95345–47, 95350, 95355–58, 95361, 95364, 95367–69, 95370, 95372–73, 95375, 95379–83, 95385–86, 95389–90, 96107

* * *

TWENTIETH DISTRICT

JIM COSTA, Democrat, of Fresno, CA; born in Fresno, April 13, 1952; education: B.A., California State University, Fresno, CA, 1974; professional: Chief Executive Officer Costa Group, 2002–present; employee, Costa Brothers Dairy, 1959–74; Senator California State Senate, 1994–2002; assembly member, California State Assembly, 1978–94; administrative assistant, California Assemblyman Richard Lehman, 1976–78; special assistant, Congressman John Krebs, 1975–76; member of the California State Assembly, 1978–94; member of the California State Senate, 1994–2002; private advocate; member: Fact Steering Committee, Fresno County Farm Board; religion: Catholic; committees: Agriculture; Foreign Affairs; Natural Resources; elected to the 109th Congress on November 2, 2004; reelected to each succeeding Congress.

Office Listings

http://www.house.gov/costa

1314 Longworth House Office Building, Washington, DC 20515 .... (202) 225–3341
Chief of Staff.—Scott Nishioki. FAX: 225–9308
Deputy Chief of Staff / Scheduler.—Juan Lopez.
2300 Tulare Street, #315, Fresno, CA 93721 .... (559) 495–1620
District Director.—Vacant.

Counties: FRESNO (part), KERN (part), KINGS. Population (2000), 639,088.

ZIP Codes: 93202–04, 93206, 93210, 93212, 93215–16, 93220, 93230, 93232, 93234, 93239, 93241–42, 93245–46, 93249–50, 93263, 93266, 93280, 93282, 93301, 93305, 93307, 93383, 93387, 93518, 93607–09, 93616, 93620, 93622, 93624–25, 93627, 93631, 93640, 93648, 93652, 93656–57, 93660, 93662, 93668, 93701–09, 93712, 93714–18, 93721–22, 93724–25, 93727–28, 93744–45, 93750, 93760–62, 93764, 93771–79, 93786, 93844, 93888

* * *

TWENTY-FIRST DISTRICT

DEVIN NUNES, Republican, of Tulare, CA; born in Tulare County, CA, October 1, 1973; education: A.A., College of the Sequoias; B.S., Agricultural Business, and a Masters Degree in Agriculture, from California Polytechnic State University, San Luis Obispo; graduate, California Agriculture Leadership Fellowship Program; professional: farmer and businessman; elected, College of the Sequoias Board of Trustees, 1996; reelected, 2000; appointed by President George W. Bush to serve as California State Director of the U.S. Department of Agriculture Rural Development Office, 2001; religion: Catholic; married: the former Elizabeth Tamariz, 2003; one child; committees: Budget; Ways and Means; elected to the 108th Congress on November 5, 2002; reelected to each succeeding Congress.

Office Listings

http://www.nunes.house.gov

1013 Longworth House Office Building, Washington, DC 20515 .... (202) 225–2523
Chief of Staff.—Johnny Amaral. FAX: 225–3404
Legislative Director.—Damon Nelson.
Communications Director.—Andrew House.
Executive Assistant.—Jennifer Buckley.
113 North Church Street, Suite 208, Visalia, CA 93291 .... (559) 733–3861
264 Clovis Avenue, Suite 206, Clovis, CA 93612 .... (559) 323–5235

Counties: TULARE, FRESNO (part). Population (2000), 639,088.

ZIP Codes: 93201, 93207–08, 93212, 93215, 93218–19, 93221, 93223, 93227, 93235, 93237, 93242, 93244, 93247, 93256–58, 93260–62, 93265, 93267, 93270–72, 93274–75, 93277–79, 93286, 93290–92, 93602–03, 93605, 93609, 93611–13, 93615–16, 93618, 93621, 93625–26, 93628, 93631, 93633–34, 93641–42, 93646–49, 93651, 93654, 93656–57, 93662, 93664, 93666–67, 93670, 93673, 93675, 93703, 93710, 93720, 93726–27, 93740, 93747

* * *

TWENTY-SECOND DISTRICT

KEVIN McCARTHY, Republican, of Bakersfield, CA; born in Bakersfield, January 26, 1965; education: graduated, Bakersfield High School, 1983; B.S., Business Administration,

CSU–Bakersfield, 1989; M.B.A., CSU–Bakersfield, 1994; professional: intern, worked up to District Director for U.S. Congressman Bill Thomas, 1987–2002; served as Trustee, Kern Community College District, 2000–02; served in the California State Assembly, 2002–06; elected, California Assembly Republican Leader, 2003–06; married to the former Judy Wages, 1992; two children: Connor and Meghan; committees: Financial Services; House Administration; elected to the 110th Congress on November 7, 2006; reelected to the 111th Congress.

Office Listings

http://www.kevinmccarthy.house.gov

1523 Longworth House Office Building, Washington, DC 20515 .... (202) 225–2915
Chief of Staff.—James Min. FAX: 225–2908
Scheduler.—Kristin Thomson.
Legislative Director.—Shelby Hagenauer.
Press Secretary.—Nick Bouknight.
4100 Empire Drive, Suite 150, Bakersfield, CA 93309 .... (661) 327–3611
District Administrator.—Robin Lake Foster.
5805 Capistrano Avenue, Suite C, Atascadero, CA 93422 .... (805) 461–1034

Counties: KERN COUNTY (part). CITIES AND TOWNSHIPS: Arvin, Bakersfield, Bodfish, Boron, Caliente, California City, Cantil, China Lake, Edison, Edwards, Fellows, Frazier Park, Glennville, Havilah, Inyokern, Keene, Kernville, Lake Isabella, Lebec, Maricopa, McKittrick, Mojave, Monolith, North Edwards, Onyx, Randsberg, Ridgecrest, Rosamond, Taft, Tehachapi, Tupman, Weldon, Willow Springs, Wofford Heights, Woody. SAN LUIS OBISPO COUNTY (part). CITIES AND TOWNSHIPS: Arroyo Grande, Paso Robles, San Miguel, Atascadero, Shandon, Templeton, San Luis Obispo, Nipomo. LOS ANGELES COUNTY (part). CITIES AND TOWNSHIPS: Lancaster. Population (2000) 639,088.

ZIP Codes: 91390, 92832, 92834, 93203, 93205–06, 93215, 93222, 93224–26, 93238, 93240–41, 93243, 93249–52, 93255, 93263, 93268, 93276, 93283, 93285, 93287, 93301–09, 93311–14, 93380, 93384–86, 93388–90, 93401–02, 93405, 93407, 93409–10, 93420, 93422–23, 93426, 93428, 93430, 93432, 93442, 93444, 93446–47, 93451, 93453–54, 93461, 93465, 93501–02, 93504–05, 93516, 93518–19, 93522–24, 93527–28, 93531–32, 93534–36, 93539, 93554–56, 93558, 93560–61, 93581, 93584, 93596

* * *

TWENTY-THIRD DISTRICT

LOIS CAPPS, Democrat, of Santa Barbara, CA; born in Ladysmith, WI, January 10, 1938; education: graduated Flathead County High School, Kalispell, MT, 1955; B.S. in Nursing, Pacific Lutheran University, 1959; M.A. in Religion, Yale University, 1964; M.A. in Education, University of California at Santa Barbara, 1990; professional: head nurse, Yale New Haven Hospital; staff nurse, Visiting Nurses Association, Hamden, CT; elementary district nurse, Santa Barbara School District; director, Teenage Pregnancy and Parenting Project, Santa Barbara County; director, Santa Barbara School District Parent and Child Education Center; instructor of early childhood education, Santa Barbara City College; board member: American Red Cross, American Heart Association, Family Service Agency, Santa Barbara Women's Political Committee; married: Walter Capps, 1960; children: Lisa, Todd, and Laura; committees: Energy and Commerce; Natural Resources; elected by special election on March 10, 1998, to the 105th Congress, to fill the vacancy caused by the death of her husband Rep. Walter Capps; reelected to each succeeding Congress.

Office Listings

http://www.house.gov/capps

1110 Longworth House Office Building, Washington, DC 20515 .... (202) 225–3601
Chief of Staff.—Randolph Harrison. FAX: 225–5632
Legislative Director.—Jonathan Levenshus.
Press Secretary.—Emily Kryder.
Executive Assistant.—Sarah Ethington.
1411 Marsh Street, Suite 205, San Luis Obispo, CA 93401 .... (805) 546–8348
District Representatives: Betsy Umhofer, Greg Haas.
301 East Carrillo Street, Suite A, Santa Barbara, CA 93101 .... (805) 730–1710
District Director.—Sharon Siegel.
2675 North Ventura Road, Suite 104, Port Hueneme, CA 93041 .... (805) 985–6807
District Representative.—Vanessa Hernandez.

Counties: SAN LUIS OBISPO COUNTY (part). CITIES AND TOWNSHIPS: Baywood-Los Osos, Cambria, Cayucos, Grover Beach, Morro Bay, Nipomo, Oceano, Pismo Beach, San Luis Obispo. SANTA BARBARA COUNTY (part). CITIES AND TOWNSHIPS: Carpinteria, Goleta, Guadalupe, Isla Vista, Mission Canyon, Montecito, Santa Barbara, Santa Maria, Summerland, Toro Canyon. VENTURA COUNTY (part). CITIES AND TOWNSHIPS: Channel Island, El Rio, Oxnard, Port Hueneme, and San Buenaventura. Population (2000), 639,088.

ZIP Codes: 92832, 93001, 93003, 93013–14, 93030–36, 93041, 93043–44, 93067, 93101–03, 93105–11, 93116–18, 93120–21, 93130, 93140, 93150, 93160, 93190, 93199, 93401–03, 93405–06, 93408, 93412, 93420–21, 93424, 93428, 93430, 93433–35, 93442–45, 93448–49, 93452, 93454–56, 93458, 93483

* * *

TWENTY-FOURTH DISTRICT

ELTON GALLEGLY, Republican, of Simi Valley, CA; born in Huntington Park, CA, March 7, 1944; education: graduated Huntington Park High School, 1962; attended Los Angeles State College; businessman; member, Simi Valley City Council, 1979; mayor, city of Simi Valley, 1980–86; former vice-chairman and chairman, Ventura County Association of Governments; former member, board of directors, Moorpark College Foundation; delegate to 1988 Republican National Convention; married: the former Janice L. Shrader, 1974; children: Shawn G., Shawn P., Kevin, and Shannon; committees: Foreign Affairs; Judiciary; Natural Resources; Permanent Select Committee on Intelligence; elected to the 100th Congress on November 4, 1986; re-elected to each succeeding Congress.

Office Listings

2309 Rayburn House Office Building, Washington, DC 20515 .... (202) 225–5811
Chief of Staff.—Joel D. Kassiday. FAX: 225–1100
Executive Assistant.—Marianne Brant.
Press Secretary.—Tom Pfeifer.
2829 Townsgate Road, Suite 315, Thousand Oaks, CA 91361 .... (805) 497–2224
District Chief of Staff.—Brian Miller. (800) 423–0023

Counties: VENTURA COUNTY (part). CITIES AND TOWNSHIPS: Bell Canyon, Camarillo, Fillmore, Moorpark, Newbury Park, Oak Park, Oak View, Ojai, Piru, Santa Paula, Simi Valley, Somis, Thousand Oaks, Ventura, Westlake Village. SANTA BARBARA COUNTY (part). CITIES AND TOWNSHIPS: Buellton, Lompoc, Los Alamos, Los Olivos, Orcutt, Santa Barbara, Santa Ynez, and Solvang. Population (2000), 639,088.

ZIP Codes: 91301, 91304, 91307, 91311, 91319–20, 91358–62, 91377, 91406, 91413, 93001, 93003–07, 93009–13, 93015–16, 93020–24, 93030, 93033, 93036, 93040–42, 93060–66, 93094, 93099, 93105, 93111, 93117, 93225, 93252, 93254, 93427, 93429, 93436–38, 93440–41, 93454–55, 93457–58, 93460, 93463–64

* * *

TWENTY-FIFTH DISTRICT

HOWARD P. ''BUCK'' MCKEON, Republican, of Santa Clarita, CA; born in Los Angeles, CA, September 9, 1938; education: graduated, Verdugo Hills High School, Tujunga, CA; B.S., Brigham Young University; owner, Howard and Phil's Western Wear; mayor and city councilman, Santa Clarita, 1987–92; member: board of directors, Canyon Country Chamber of Commerce; California Republican State Central Committee; advisory council, Boy Scouts of America; president and trustee, William S. Hart School District, 1979–87; chairman and director, Henry Mayo Newhall Memorial Hospital, 1983–87; chairman and founding director, Valencia National Bank, 1987–92; honorary chairman, Red Cross Community Support Campaign, 1992; honorary chairman, Leukemia Society Celebrity Program, 1990 and 1994; president, Republican Freshman Class of the 103rd Congress; married: to the former Patricia Kunz, 1962; children: Tamara, Howard D., John Matthew, Kimberly, David Owen, and Tricia; committees: Armed Services; Education and Labor; elected on November 3, 1992, to the 103rd Congress; reelected to each succeeding Congress.

Office Listings

http://www.house.gov/mckeon

2184 Rayburn House Office Building, Washington, DC 20515 .... (202) 225–1956
Chief of Staff.—Bob Cochran. FAX: 226–0683
Executive Assistant / Appointments.—Candace Dodge.
District Director.—Bob Haueter.
26650 The Old Road, Suite 203, Santa Clarita, CA 91355 .... (661) 254–2111
1008 West Avenue, M–14, Suite E1, Palmdale, CA 93551 .... (661) 274–9688

Counties: INYO, LOS ANGELES (part), MONO, SAN BERNARDINO (part). CITIES AND TOWNSHIPS: Acton, Adelanto, Baker, Barstow, Benton, Big Pine, Bishop, Bridgeport, Castaic, Canyon Country, Coleville, Death Valley, Edwards, Ft. Irwin, Helendale, Hesperia, Hinkley, Independence, Inyokern, June Lake, Keeler, La Crescenta, Lancaster, Littlerock, Little Lake, Little Vinning, Llano, Lone Pine, Mammoth Lakes, Newberry Springs, Newhall, Nipton, Olancha, Oro Grande, Palmdale, Pearblossom, Phelan, Pinon Hills, Ridgecrest, Santa Clarita, Shoshone, Stevenson Ranch, Sunland, Sylmar, Tecopa, Topaz, Trona, Tujunga, Valencia, Valyerno, Victorville, and Yermo. Population (2000), 639,087.

ZIP Codes: 91042, 91214, 91310, 91321–22, 91350–51, 91354–55, 91380–81, 91383–87, 91390, 92301, 92309–12, 92328, 92342, 92345, 92347, 92364–65, 92368, 92371–72, 92384, 92389, 92392–94, 92398, 92832, 93510, 93512–17, 93524, 93526–27, 93529–30, 93534–35, 93541–46, 93549–53, 93560, 93562, 93586, 93590–92, 93599, 96107, 96133

* * *

TWENTY-SIXTH DISTRICT

DAVID DREIER, Republican, of San Dimas, CA; born in Kansas City, MO, July 5, 1952; education: B.A. (*cum laude*) in political science, Claremont McKenna College, 1975; M.A., American Government, Claremont Graduate School, 1976; Winston S. Churchill Fellow; Phi Sigma Alpha; professional: director, corporate relations, Claremont McKenna College, 1975–78; member: board of governors, James Madison Society; Republican State Central Committee of California; Los Angeles Town Hall; named Outstanding Young Man of America and Outstanding Young Californian, 1976 and 1978; director, marketing and government affairs, Industrial Hydrocarbons, 1979–80; vice president, Dreier Development, 1985–present; author of congressional reform package incorporated into the House Rules; committees: Rules; elected to the 97th Congress on November 4, 1980; reelected to each succeeding Congress.

Office Listings

http://www.house.gov/dreier

233 Cannon House Office Building, Washington, DC 20515 .... (202) 225–2305
Chief of Staff.—Bradley W. Smith. FAX: 225–7018
Executive Assistant.—Melissa Gould.
Legislative Director.—Alisa Do.
510 East Foothill Boulevard, Suite 201, San Dimas, CA 91773 .... (909) 575–6226

Counties: LOS ANGELES (part). CITIES: Altadena, Arcadia, Bradbury, Claremont, Covina, Glendora, La Canada Flintridge, La Crescenta, La Verne, Monrovia, Montrose, Pasadena, San Antonio Heights, San Dimas, San Gabriel, San Marino, Sierra Madre, Walnut. SAN BERNARDINO (part). CITIES: Montclair, Rancho Cucamonga, Upland, and Wrightwood. Population (2000), 639,088.

ZIP Codes: 91001, 91006–07, 91010–12, 91016–17, 91020–21, 91023–25, 91066, 91077, 91104, 91107–08, 91118, 91131, 91185, 91187, 91191, 91214, 91390, 91410, 91701, 91711, 91730, 91737, 91739–41, 91750, 91759, 91763, 91773, 91775, 91784, 91786, 91789, 92329, 92336, 92345, 92358, 92371–72, 92397, 92407

* * *

TWENTY-SEVENTH DISTRICT

BRAD SHERMAN, Democrat, of Sherman Oaks, CA; born in Los Angeles, CA, October 24, 1954; education: B.A., *summa cum laude,* UCLA, 1974; J.D., *magna cum laude,* Harvard Law School, 1979; professional: admitted to the California bar in 1979 and began practice in Los Angeles; attorney, CPA, certified tax law specialist; elected to the California State Board of Equalization, 1990, serving as chairman, 1991–95; committees: Financial Services; Foreign Affairs; Judiciary; elected to the 105th Congress; reelected to each succeeding Congress.

Office Listings

2242 Rayburn House Office Building, Washington, DC 20515 .... (202) 225–5911
Administrative Assistant.—Bradford Cheney. FAX: 225–5879
Legislative Director.—Gary Goldberg.
Communications Director.—Matt Farrauto.
Legislative Correspondent.—Matt Dicker.
5000 Van Nuys Boulevard, Suite 420, Sherman Oaks, CA 91403 .... (818) 501–9200
District Director.—Matthew Dababneh.

Counties: LOS ANGELES COUNTY (part). Population (2000), 639,088.

ZIP Codes: 91040–41, 91043, 91303–06, 91309, 91311–12, 91316, 91324–30, 91335, 91337, 91342–46, 91352, 91356–57, 91364, 91367, 91371, 91394–96, 91401, 91403, 91405–06, 91409, 91411, 91416, 91423, 91426, 91436, 91470, 91482, 91495–96, 91504–07, 91510, 91601, 91605–06

* * *

TWENTY-EIGHTH DISTRICT

HOWARD L. BERMAN, Democrat, of Van Nuys, CA; born in Los Angeles, CA, April 15, 1941; education: B.A. in international relations, UCLA, 1962; LL.B., UCLA School of Law, 1965; California Assembly Fellowship Program, 1965–70; Vista volunteer, 1966–67; admitted to the California bar, 1966; practiced law until election to California Assembly in

1972; named assembly majority leader in first term; served as chair of the Assembly Democratic Caucus and policy research management committee; member: regional board of the Anti-Defamation League; past president, California Federation of Young Democrats; married: Janis; children: Brinley and Lindsey; committees: chair, Foreign Affairs; Judiciary; elected to the 98th Congress on November 2, 1982; reelected to each succeeding Congress.

Office Listings

http://www.house.gov/berman

2221 Rayburn House Office Building, Washington, DC 20515 .... (202) 225–4695
Chief of Staff / Legislative Director.—Julia Massimino. FAX: 225–3196
Executive Assistant/Appointments.—Deanne Samuels.
14546 Hamlin Street, Suite 202, Van Nuys, CA 91411 .... (818) 994–7200
District Director.—Gene Smith.

Counties: LOS ANGELES COUNTY (part). Portions of the city of Los Angeles, including all or part of the communities of Arleta, Encino, North Hollywood, North Hills, Pacoima, Panorama City, San Fernando, Sherman Oaks, Studio City, Valley Village, and Van Nuys. Population (2000), 639,087.

ZIP Codes: 90028, 90046, 90049, 90068, 91316, 91331, 91333–34, 91340–43, 91345, 91352–53, 91356, 91388, 91392–93, 91401–08, 91411–12, 91423, 91436, 91497, 91499, 91505, 91601–12, 91614–18

* * *

TWENTY-NINTH DISTRICT

ADAM B. SCHIFF, Democrat, of Burbank, CA; born in Framingham, MA, June 20, 1960; education: B.A., Stanford University, 1982; J.D., Harvard University, 1985; professional: Attorney; U.S. Attorney's Office, served as a criminal prosecutor; chosen by the Dept. of Justice to assist the Czechoslovakian government in reforming their criminal justice system; public service: elected to the California State Senate, 1996; involved in numerous community service activities; awards: Dept. of Justice Special Achievement Award; Council of State Governments Toll Fellowship; California League of High Schools Legislator of the Year; family: married: Eve; children: Alexa and Elijah; committees: Appropriations; Judiciary; Permanent Select Committee on Intelligence; elected to the 107th Congress on November 7, 2000; reelected to each succeeding Congress.

Office Listings

http://www.house.gov/schiff

2447 Rayburn House Office Building, Washington, DC 20515 .... (202) 225–4176
Chief of Staff.—Timothy Bergreen. FAX: 225–5828
Communications Director.—Sean Oblack.
Executive Assistant.—Christopher Hoven.
87 North Raymond Avenue, Suite 800, Pasadena, CA 91103 .... (626) 304–2727
District Director.—Ann Peifer.

Counties: LOS ANGELES COUNTY (part). CITIES: Alhambra, Altadena, Burbank, Glendale, Griffith Park, Monterey Park, Pasadena, San Gabriel, South Pasadena, and Temple City. Population (2000), 639,088.

ZIP Codes: 90004–06, 90010, 90020, 90026–27, 90029, 90035–36, 90038–39, 90046, 90048, 90064, 90068, 91001, 91003, 91007, 91011, 91030–31, 91046, 91101–10, 91114–17, 91121, 91123–26, 91129, 91175, 91182, 91184, 91186, 91188–89, 91201–10, 91214, 91221–22, 91224–26, 91501–06, 91508, 91521–23, 91775–76, 91780, 91801, 91803–04

* * *

THIRTIETH DISTRICT

HENRY A. WAXMAN, Democrat, of Los Angeles, CA; born in Los Angeles, September 12, 1939; education: B.A., political science, UCLA, 1961; J.D., School of Law; admitted to the California State bar, 1965; served three terms as California State Assemblyman; former chairman, California Assembly Health Committee; Select Committee on Medical Malpractice; and Committee on Elections and Reapportionment; president, California Federation of Young Democrats, 1965–67; member: Guardians of the Jewish Home for the Aged; American Jewish Congress; Sierra Club; married: the former Janet Kessler, 1971; children: Carol Lynn and Michael David; committees: chair, Energy and Commerce; elected to the 94th Congress on November 5, 1974; reelected to each succeeding Congress.

Office Listings

http://www.house.gov/waxman

2204 Rayburn House Office Building, Washington, DC 20515 .... (202) 225–3976
Chief of Staff.—Pat Delgado. FAX: 225–4099
8436 West Third Street, Suite 600, Los Angeles, CA 90048 .... (323) 651–1040
District Director.—Lisa Pinto.

Counties: LOS ANGELES COUNTY (part). CITIES AND TOWNSHIPS: Agoura Hills, Bel-Air, Beverly Hills, Brentwood, Calabasas, Canoga Park, Century City, Chatsworth, Hidden Hills, Malibu, Northridge, Pacific Palisades, Pico-Robertson, Santa Monica, Tarzana, Topanga, West Hills, West Hollywood, Westlake Village, West Los Angeles, Westwood, and Woodland Hills. Population (2000), 639,088.

ZIP Codes: 90024–25, 90027–29, 90032, 90034–36, 90038–39, 90046, 90048–49, 90057, 90063–64, 90067–69, 90072–73, 90075–77, 90095, 90209–13, 90263–65, 90272, 90290–91, 90401–11, 91301–04, 91307–08, 91311, 91313, 91324, 91356, 91361–65, 91367, 91372, 91376, 91399

* * *

THIRTY-FIRST DISTRICT

XAVIER BECERRA, Democrat, of Los Angeles, CA; born in Sacramento, CA, January 26, 1958; education: graduated, McClatchy High School, Sacramento, 1976; B.A., Stanford University, 1980; J.D., Stanford Law School, 1984; admitted to California bar, 1985; attended Universidad de Salamanca, 1978–79; staff attorney, ''Reggie Fellow,'' Legal Assistance Corporation of Central Massachusetts, 1984–85; administrative assistant for State Senator Art Torres, California State Legislature, 1986; Deputy Attorney General, Office of the Attorney General, State of California, 1987–90; Assemblyman, California State Legislature, 1990–92; member: Mexican American State Legislators Policy Institute; Mexican American Bar Association; chairperson: Hispanic Employee Advisory Committee to the State Attorney General, 1989; honorary member: Association of California State Attorneys and Administrative Law Judges; former member: steering committee, Greater Eastside Voter Registration Project; Construction and General Laborers Union, Local 185 (Sacramento); Pitzer College Board of Trustees; National Association of Latino's Electoral and appointed to the Official Board of Directors; vice chair, Democrat Caucus of the 111th Congress; married to Dr. Carolina Reyes; children: Clarisa, Olivia, Natalia; committees: Budget; Ways and Means; appointed Assistant to the Speaker of the House for the 110th Congress; elected on November 3, 1992, to the 103rd Congress; reelected to each succeeding Congress.

Office Listings

http://www.house.gov/becerra

1119 Longworth House Office Building, Washington, DC 20515 .... (202) 225–6235
Chief of Staff.—Debra Dixon. FAX: 225–2202
Legislative Director.—Sean McClusk.
Scheduler.—Stephanie Venegas.
1910 Sunset Boulevard, Suite 810, Los Angeles, CA 90026 .... (213) 483–1425
District Director.—Laura Arciniega.

Counties: LOS ANGELES COUNTY (part). CITIES: Los Angeles. Population (2000), 639,088.

ZIP Codes: 90004–07, 90011–12, 90015, 90018, 90020–22, 90026, 90028–29, 90031–32, 90037–39, 90041–42, 90048, 90057–58, 90065, 90072

* * *

THIRTY-SECOND DISTRICT

JUDY M. CHU, Democrat, of El Monte, CA; born in Los Angeles, CA, July 7, 1953; education: B.A. in math from UCLA, Los Angeles, CA, 1974; Ph.D. in psychology from the California School of Professional Psychology, 1979; professional: Garvey School District Board member, 1985–88; Monterey Park City Council and Mayor, 1988–2001; California State Assembly, 2001–2006; California State Board of Equalization, 2006–2009; first Chinese American woman elected to Congress; family: married to Assembly member Mike Eng in 1978; committees: Education and Labor; elected to the 111th Congress on July 14, 2009, by special election to fill the vacancy caused by the resignation of United States Representative Hilda Solis.

Office Listings

http://www.chu.house.gov

2421 Rayburn House Office Building, Washington, DC 20515 .... (202) 225–5464

Chief of Staff.—Amelia Wang. FAX: 225–5467
Legislative Director.—Allison Rose.
Legislative Corespondent / System Administrator.—Eric Stecklow.
Staff Assistant.—Lisa Strumwasser.
4401 Santa Anita Avenue, Suite 211, El Monte, CA 91731 .... (626) 448–1271
Field Deputy / Case Worker.—Rachael Hsin. FAX: 448–8062
Deputy Press Secretary.—Fred Ortega.
District Scheduler.—Erika Lopez.
District Manager.—Bryan Urais.

Counties: LOS ANGELES COUNTY (part). CITIES: Azusa, Baldwin Park, Covina, Duarte, El Monte, South El Monte, Irwindale, Monterey Park, Rosemead, San Gabriel, South San Gabriel, and portions of East Los Angeles, Citrus CDP, Glendora, Industry City, Los Angeles, Temple City, Vincent CDP, and West Covina. Population (2000), 639,087.

ZIP Codes: 90022, 90032, 90034–36, 90044–45, 90047–48, 90063–64, 90066–67, 90089, 91009–10, 91016, 91702, 91706, 91722–24, 91731–33, 91740, 91754–55, 91770, 91790–93

* * *

THIRTY-THIRD DISTRICT

DIANE E. WATSON, Democrat, of Los Angeles, CA; born in Los Angeles, November 12, 1933; education: B.A. in Education, University of California, Los Angeles; M.S. in School Psychology, California State University, Los Angeles; attended the John F. Kennedy School of Government at Harvard University and earned a Ph.D., in Educational Administration from the Claremont Graduate University; professional: served as an elementary school teacher, acting principal, assistant superintendent of child welfare and attendance, and school psychologist; served on the faculty at both California State University, Los Angeles, and Long Beach; Health Occupations Specialist, California Department of Education; awards: named Legislator of the Year by numerous California universities, associations, and organizations; public service: Los Angeles Unified School District Board Member; served as California State Senator, 1979–99; served as U.S. Ambassador to the Federated States of Micronesia, 1999–2001; committees: Foreign Affairs; Oversight and Government Reform; elected to the 107th Congress, by special election, on June 5, 2001; reelected to each succeeding Congress.

Office Listings

2430 Rayburn Office Building, Washington, DC 20515 .... (202) 225–7084
Chief of Staff.—Richard Butcher. FAX: 225–2422
Legislative Director.—Abdul Henderson.
Scheduler / Special Assistant.—Alice Holmes-McKoy.
Communications Director.—Dorinda White.
4322 Wilshire Boulevard, Suite 302, Los Angeles, CA 90010 .... (323) 965–1422
District Director.—Paullette Starks.

Counties: LOS ANGELES COUNTY (part). CITIES: Culver City, Los Angeles City, communities of Ladera Heights and View Park-Windsor Hills. Population (2000), 639,088.

ZIP Codes: 90004–08, 90010–11, 90016, 90018–20, 90022, 90026–29, 90033–39, 90043–45, 90047–48, 90053, 90056–58, 90062–64, 90066, 90068, 90070, 90078, 90083, 90093, 90099, 90103, 90230–33

* * *

THIRTY-FOURTH DISTRICT

LUCILLE ROYBAL-ALLARD, Democrat, of Los Angeles, CA; born in Los Angeles, June 12, 1941; education: B.A., California State University, Los Angeles, 1965; served in the California State Assembly, 1987–92; the first woman to serve as the chair of the California Democratic Congressional Delegation in the 105th Congress; in the 106th Congress, she became the first woman to chair the Congressional Hispanic Caucus, and the first Latina in history to be appointed to the House Appropriations Committee; married: Edward T. Allard III; two children: Lisa Marie and Ricardo; two stepchildren: Angela and Guy Mark; committees: Appropriations; the first Mexican-American woman elected to Congress on November 3, 1992 to the 103rd Congress; reelected to each succeeding Congress.

Office Listings

http://www.house.gov/roybal-allard

2330 Rayburn House Office Building, Washington, DC 20515–0534 .... (202) 225–1766

Chief of Staff.—Paul Cunningham. FAX: 226–0350
Legislative Director.—Victor G. Castillo.
Executive Assistant.—Christine C. Ochoa.
255 East Temple Street, Suite 1860, Los Angeles, CA 90012–3334 .... (213) 628–9230
District Director.—Ana Figueroa.

Counties: LOS ANGELES COUNTY (part). CITIES: Bell, Belflower, Bell Gardens, Boyle Heights, Chinatown, Commerce, Cudahy, Downey, Downtown Los Angeles, East Los Angeles, Florence, Huntington Park, Little Tokyo, Maywood, Pico Union, South Park, Vernon, and Westlake. Population (2000), 639,088.

ZIP Codes: 90001, 90005–7, 90011–15, 90017, 90020–23, 90026, 90033, 90040, 90057–58, 90063, 90071, 90201, 90255, 90270, 90241–42, 90706

* * *

THIRTY-FIFTH DISTRICT

MAXINE WATERS, Democrat, of Los Angeles, CA; born in St. Louis, MO, August 15, 1938; education: B.A., California State University; honorary degrees: Harris-Stowe State College, St. Louis, MO, and Central State University, Wilberforce, OH, Spelman College, Atlanta, GA, North Carolina A&T State University, Howard University, Central State University, Bishop College, Morgan State University; elected to California State Assembly, 1976; reelected every two years thereafter; member: Assembly Democratic Caucus, Board of TransAfrica Foundation, National Women's Political Caucus; chair, Democratic Caucus Special Committee on Election Reform; chair, Ways and Means Subcommittee on State Administration; chair, Joint Committee on Public Pension Fund Investments; founding member, National Commission for Economic Conversion and Disarmament; member of the board, Center for National Policy; Clara Elizabeth Jackson Carter Foundation (Spelman College); Minority AIDS Project; married to Sidney Williams, former U.S. Ambassador to the Commonwealth of the Bahamas; two children: Karen and Edward; committees: Financial Services; Judiciary; Chief Deputy Majority Whip; elected to the 102nd Congress on November 6, 1990; reelected to each succeeding Congress.

Office Listings

2344 Rayburn House Office Building, Washington, DC 20515 .... (202) 225–2201
Chief of Staff.—Mikael Moore. FAX: 225–7854
Legislative Director.—Andrea Martin.
10124 South Broadway, Suite 1, Los Angeles, CA 90003 .... (323) 757–8900
District Director.—Blanca Jimenez.

Counties: LOS ANGELES COUNTY (part). CITIES: Gardena, Hawthorne, Inglewood, Lawndale, Los Angeles, Playa Del Ray, and Torrance. Population (2000), 639,088.

ZIP Codes: 90001–03, 90007, 90009, 90037, 90044–45, 90047, 90052, 90056, 90059, 90061, 90066, 90082, 90094, 90189, 90247–51, 90260–61, 90293, 90301–13, 90397–98, 90504, 90506

* * *

THIRTY-SIXTH DISTRICT

JANE HARMAN, Democrat, of Venice, CA; born in New York, NY, June 28, 1945; education: University High School, Los Angeles, CA, 1962; B.A., Smith College, Northampton, MA, 1966; J.D., Harvard University Law School, Cambridge, MA, 1969; professional: attorney; admitted to the District of Columbia Bar, 1969; counsel for Jones, Day, Reavis and Pogue (law firm); Director and General Counsel for Harman International Industries; Special Counsel, Department of Defense, 1979; Regents' Professor at UCLA, 1999; organizations: L.A. County High Technology Committee; South Bay Alliance for Choice; Center for National Policy; International Human Rights Law Group; member of the Visiting Committee of the John F. Kennedy School of Government, Harvard University; National Commission on Terrorism; family: married to Sidney Harman, 1980; children: Brian Lakes Frank, Hilary Lakes Frank, Daniel Geier Harman, and Justine Leigh Harman; committees: Energy and Commerce; Homeland Security; elected to the 103rd, 104th, and 105th Congresses; candidate for Governor of California, 1998; elected to the 107th Congress on November 7, 2000; reelected to each succeeding Congress.

Office Listings

http://www.house.gov/harman

2400 Rayburn House Office Building, Washington, DC 20515 .... (202) 225–8220

Chief of Staff.—John Hess. FAX: 226–7290
Legislative Director.—Jay Hulings.
Scheduler.—Janaki Dighe.
2321 East Rosecrans Boulevard, Suite 3270, El Segundo, CA 90245 .... (310) 643–3636
544 North Avalon Boulevard, Suite 307, Wilmington, CA 90744 .... (310) 549–8282

Counties: LOS ANGELES COUNTY (part). CITIES: El Segundo, Harbor City, Hermosa Beach, Lawndale, Lennox, Los Angeles, Manhattan Beach, Marina Del Rey, Playa Del Rey, Redondo Beach, San Pedro, Torrance, Venice, Westchester, West Carson, and Wilmington. Population (2000), 639,087.

ZIP Codes: 90009, 90025, 90034, 90039, 90045, 90064, 90066, 90080, 90245, 90248, 90254, 90266–67, 90277–78, 90291–92, 90294–96, 90304, 90404–05, 90501–10, 90710, 90717, 90731–34, 90744, 90748

* * *

THIRTY-SEVENTH DISTRICT

LAURA RICHARDSON, Democrat of Long Beach, CA; born in Los Angeles, CA, April 14, 1962; education: B.A., political science, University of California, Los Angeles, CA, 1984; M.B.A., business administration, University of Southern California, Los Angeles, CA, 1996; professional: businesswoman, Fortune 40 Company Xerox Corporation; staff, United States Representative Juanita Millender-McDonald of California, 1996–98; member, Long Beach, CA, City Council, 2000–06; staff, Lieutenant Governor Cruz Bustamante of California, 2001–06; member, California State Assembly, 2006–07; served as the assistant speaker Pro Tempore in the California State Legislature; religion: Christian-Non-Denominational; committees: Homeland Security; Transportation and Infrastructure; elected to the 110th Congress, by special election on August 21, 2007, to fill the vacancy caused by the death of United States Representative Juanita Millender-McDonald; elected to a full term in the 111th Congress on November 4, 2008.

Office Listings

http://www.richardson.house.gov

1725 Longworth House Office Building, Washington, DC 20515 .... (202) 225–7924
Chief of Staff.—Shirley Cooks.
Legislative Director.—Matt Chiller.
Legislative Counsel.—Gregory Berry.
Press Secretary.—Michael J. Eagle.
Scheduler.—Stephanie Albanese.
100 West Broadway, West Tower, Suite 600, Long Beach, CA 90802 .... (562) 436–3828
District Director.—Eric Boyd.
Scheduler.—Daysha Austin.

Counties: LOS ANGELES COUNTY (part). CITIES: Carson, Compton, and Long Beach, Signal Hill, South Los Angeles, Watts and Willowbrook. Population (2000), 639,088.

ZIP Codes: 90002–03, 90044, 90059, 90061, 90220–24, 90247, 90501–02, 90713, 90723, 90745–47, 90749, 90755, 90801–10, 90813–15, 90822, 90842, 90844–48, 90888, 90899

* * *

THIRTY-EIGHTH DISTRICT

GRACE F. NAPOLITANO, Democrat, of Los Angeles, CA; born in Brownsville, TX, December 4, 1936; maiden name: Flores; education: Brownsville High School, Brownsville, TX; Cerritos College, Norwalk, CA; Texas Southmost College, Brownsville, TX; professional: Transportation Coordinator, Ford Motor Company; elected to Norwalk, CA, City Council, 1986; became mayor of Norwalk, CA, 1989; elected to the California Assembly, 58th District, 1992–98; married: Frank Napolitano; children: Yolanda Dyer, Fred Musquiz, Edward Musquiz, Michael Musquiz, and Cynthia Dowling; organizations: Norwalk Lions Club; Veterans of Foreign Wars (auxiliary); American Legion (auxiliary); Soroptimist International; past director, Cerritos College Foundation; director, Community Family Guidance Center; League of United Latin American Citizens; director, Los Angeles County Sanitation District; director, Los Angeles County Vector Control (Southeast District); director, Southeast Los Angeles Private Industry Council; director, Los Angeles County Sheriff's Authority; National Women's Political Caucus; past national board secretary, United States-Mexico Sister Cities Association; member, Congressional Hispanic Caucus; co-chair, Congressional Mental Health Caucus; committees: Natural Resources; Transportation and Infrastructure; elected to the 106th Congress; reelected to each succeeding Congress.

Office Listings

http://www.house.gov/napolitano

1610 Longworth House Office Building, Washington, DC 20515 .... (202) 225–5256
Chief of Staff.—Daniel Chao. FAX: 225–0027
Legislative Director.—Joe Sheehy.
Press Secretary.—Christopher Honey.
Scheduler.—Elizabeth Decker.
11627 East Telegraph Road, Suite 100, Santa Fe Springs, CA 90670 .... (562) 801–2134
District Director.—Ben Cardenas.

Counties: LOS ANGELES COUNTY (part). Population (2000), 639,088.

ZIP Codes: 90601, 90605–06, 90640, 90650–52, 90659–62, 90665, 90670, 90703, 90731, 90806, 91715–16, 91744–47, 91766–70, 91789–90, 91792, 91795

* * *

THIRTY-NINTH DISTRICT

LINDA T. SÁNCHEZ, Democrat, of Lakewood, CA; born in Orange, CA, January 28, 1969; education: B.A., University of California, Berkeley; J.D., U.C.L.A. Law School; passed bar exam in 1995; professional: attorney; has practiced in the areas of appellate, civil rights, and employment law; International Brotherhood of Electrical Workers Local 441; National Electrical Contractors Association; and Orange County Central Labor Council Executive Secretary, AFL–CIO; organizations: National Women's Political Caucus; Women in Leadership; religion: Catholic; committees: Judiciary; Ways and Means; elected to the 108th Congress on November 5, 2002; reelected to each succeeding Congress.

Office Listings

http://www.house.gov/lindasanchez

1222 Longworth House Office Building, Washington, DC 20515 .... (202) 225–6676
Chief of Staff.—Meghan Johnson. FAX: 226–1012
Legislative Director.—Celeste Drake.
Communications Director.—Marsha Catron.
Scheduler.—Ruth Carnegie.
17906 Crusader Avenue, Suite 100, Cerritos, CA 90703 .... (562) 860–5050
District Director.—Bill Grady.

Counties: LOS ANGELES COUNTY (part). Population (2000), 639,088.

ZIP Codes: 90001–02, 90059, 90255, 90262, 90280, 90601–06, 90608–10, 90637–39, 90670, 90701–03, 90706, 90711–16, 90723, 90805, 90807–08

* * *

FORTIETH DISTRICT

EDWARD R. ROYCE, Republican, of Fullerton, CA; born in Los Angeles, CA, October 12, 1951; education: B.A., California State University, Fullerton, 1977; professional: small business owner; controller; corporate tax manager; California State Senate, 1982–92; member: Fullerton Chamber of Commerce; board member, Literacy Volunteers of America; California Interscholastic Athletic Foundation board of advisers; married: Marie Therese Porter, 1985; committees: Financial Services; Foreign Affairs; elected on November 3, 1992 to the 103rd Congress; reelected to each succeeding Congress.

Office Listings

http://www.royce.house.gov

2185 Rayburn House Office Building, Washington, DC 20515 .... (202) 225–4111
Chief of Staff / Legislative Director.—Amy Porter. FAX: 226–0335
Press Secretary.—Gregory Keeley.
1110 East Chapman Avenue, Suite 207, Orange, CA 92866 .... (714) 744–4130
District Director.—Sara Catalan.

Counties: ORANGE COUNTY. The north and west part including the cities of Anaheim, Buena Park, Cypress, Fullerton, Garden Grove, La Palma, Los Alamitos, Orange, Placentia, Rossmoor, Stanton, Villa Park, and Westminster. Population (2000), 639,088.

ZIP Codes: 90620–24, 90630–31, 90638, 90680, 90720–21, 90740, 90808, 92647, 92683–84, 92705–06, 92801–02, 92804–07, 92821, 92831–38, 92840–41, 92844–46, 92856–57, 92859, 92861, 92863, 92865–71

* * *

FORTY-FIRST DISTRICT

JERRY LEWIS, Republican, of Redlands, CA; born in Seattle, WA, October 21, 1934; education: graduated, San Bernardino High School, 1952; B.A., UCLA, 1956; graduate intern in public affairs, Coro Foundation; life underwriter; former member, San Bernardino School Board; served in California State Assembly, 1968–78; insurance executive, 1959–78; married to Arlene Willis; seven children; committees: ranking member Appropriations; elected to the 96th Congress, November 7, 1978; reelected to each succeeding Congress.

Office Listings

http://www.house.gov/jerrylewis

2112 Rayburn House Office Building, Washington, DC 20515 .... (202) 225–5861
Administrative Assistant.—Arlene Willis. FAX: 225–6498
Deputy Chief of Staff / Communications Director.—Jim Specht.
1150 Brookside Avenue, No. J5, Redlands, CA 92373 .... (909) 862–6030
District Representative.—Tara Clarke.

Counties: RIVERSIDE (part), SAN BERNARDINO (part). CITIES AND TOWNSHIPS: Adelanto, Amboy, Angelus Oaks, Apple Valley, Argus, Arrowbear Lake, Banning, Beaumont, Big Bear City, Big Bear Lake, Blue Jay, Bryn Mawr, Big River, Cabazon, Cadiz, Calimesa, Cedar Glen, Cedar Pines Park, Cherry Valley, Cima, Colton, Crestline, Crest Park, Daggett, Desert Hot Springs, Earp, East Highlands, Essex, Fawnskin, Forest Falls, Grand Terrace, Green Valley Lake, Havasu Lake, Hesperia, Highland, Joshua Tree, Kelso, Lake Arrowhead, Landers, Loma Linda, Lucerne Valley, Ludlow, Mentone, Morongo Valley, Mountain Pass, Needles, Newberry Springs, Nipton, Oro Grande, Parker Dam, Redlands, Rim Forest, Running Springs, San Bernardino, San Jacinto, Sky Forest, Spring Valley Lake, Sugarloaf, Twentynine Palms, Twin Peaks, Valle Vista, Vidal, Yucaipa, and Yucca Valley. Population (2000), 639,088.

ZIP Codes: 92220, 92223, 92230, 92240–42, 92252, 92256, 92258, 92267–68, 92277–78, 92280, 92282, 92284–86, 92304–05, 92307–08, 92311, 92313–15, 92317–18, 92320–27, 92332–33, 92338–42, 92345–46, 92350, 92352, 92354, 92356–57, 92359, 92363–66, 92368–69, 92371, 92373–75, 92378, 92382, 92385–86, 92391–92, 92399, 92404–05, 92407–08, 92410, 92424, 92427, 92544, 92555, 92557, 92581–83

* * *

FORTY-SECOND DISTRICT

GARY G. MILLER, Republican, of Diamond Bar, CA; born in Huntsville, AR, October 16, 1948; education: Loma Vista Elementary School, Whittier, CA; California High School, Whittier, CA; Lowell High School, LaHabra, CA; Mount San Antonio College, Walnut, CA; military service: private, U.S. Army, 1967; professional: developer; owner, G. Miller Development Company; public service: Diamond Bar, CA, City Council, 1989–95; Mayor, 1992; California State Assembly, 1995–98; married: Cathy Miller; children: Brian, Elizabeth, Loren, and Matthew; committees: Financial Services; Transportation and Infrastructure; elected to the 106th Congress; reelected to each succeeding Congress.

Office Listings

http://www.house.gov/garymiller

2349 Rayburn House Office Building, Washington, DC 20515 .... (202) 225–3201
Chief of Staff.—John Rothrock. FAX: 226–6962
Legislative Director / Senior Policy Advisor.—Sandra Bitter.
Executive Director.—Kevin McKee.
1800 East Lambert Road, Suite 150, Brea, CA 92821 .... (714) 257–1142
District Director.—Steven Thornton.

Counties: LOS ANGELES (part), ORANGE (part), and SAN BERNARDINO (part). CITIES AND TOWNSHIPS: Anaheim, Brea, Chino, Chino Hills, Diamond Bar, La Habra, La Habra Heights, Las Flores, Mission Viejo, Placentia, Rancho Santa Margarita, Rowland Heights, Yorba Linda and Whittier. Population (2000), 639,088.

ZIP Codes: 90601–05, 90607, 90631–33, 91708–10, 91729, 91743, 91748, 91758, 91765, 92676, 92679, 92688, 92691–92, 92807–08, 92821–23, 92833, 92885–87

* * *

FORTY-THIRD DISTRICT

JOE BACA, Democrat, of San Bernardino County, CA; born in Belen, NM, January 23, 1947; education: graduated from California State University, Los Angeles, with a bachelor's degree in Sociology; professional: GTE Corp. (community relations); Interstate World Travel (owner); military service: Army; public service: elected to the California State Assembly, 1992, and served as Assistant Speaker Pro Tempore, and the Speaker's Federal Government Liaison, 1997–98; elected to the California State Senate, 1998; awards: American Legion California Legislator of the Year; VFW Outstanding Legislator; League of Women Voters Citizen of Distinction; San Bernardino Kiwanis Club Kiwanian of the Year; Boy Scouts of America Distinguished Citizen; 2004 National Farmers Union Presidential Award; U.S. Department of Agriculture Coalition of Minority Employees Award of Excellence; U.S. Hispanic Chamber of Commerce President's Achievement Award; Democratic Caucus Task Force on Homeland Security; Democratic Caucus Task Force on Immigration; past chair, Congressional Hispanic Caucus; co-chair, Congressional Sex and Violence in the Media Caucus; House Army Caucus; Congressional Diabetes Caucus; Cancer Caucus; Military/Veterans Caucus; U.S.-Mexico Caucus; Blue Dog Coalition, the Nursing Caucus, Native American Caucus; Armenian Caucus; Good Movement Caucus and Out of Poverty Caucus; chair, CHC Corporate America Task Force; married: Barbara; four children: Joe Jr., Jeremy, Natalie, and Jennifer; committees: Agriculture; Financial Services; Natural Resources; elected to the 106th Congress on November 16, 1999, by special election; reelected to each succeeding Congress.

Office Listings

2245 Rayburn House Office Building, Washington, DC 20515 .... (202) 225–6161
Chief of Staff.—Linda Macias. FAX: 225–8671
Executive Assistant.—M. Lena Beery.
Press Secretary.—John Lowrey.
201 North E Street, Suite 102, San Bernardino, CA 92401 .... (909) 885–2222
District Director.—Sam Garcia.

Counties: SAN BERNARDINO COUNTY (part). CITIES: Colton, Fontana, Ontario, Redlands, Rialto, and San Bernardino. Population (2000), 639,087.

ZIP Codes: 91758, 91761–62, 91764, 92316, 92324, 92334–37, 92346, 92376–77, 92401–08, 92410–13, 92415, 92418, 92423

* * *

FORTY-FOURTH DISTRICT

KEN CALVERT, Republican, of Corona, CA; born in Corona, June 8, 1953; education: A.A., Chaffey College, CA, 1973; B.A. in economics, San Diego State University, 1975; professional: congressional aide to Rep. Victor V. Veysey, CA; general manager, Jolly Fox Restaurant, Corona, 1975–79; Marcus W. Meairs Co., Corona, 1979–81; president and general manager, Ken Calvert Real Properties, 1981–92; County Youth Chairman, Rep. Veysey's District, 1970, then 43rd District, 1972; Corona/Norco Youth Chairman for Nixon, 1968 and 1972; Reagan-Bush campaign worker, 1980; co-chair, Wilson for Senate Campaign, 1982; chairman Riverside Republican Party, 1984–88; co-chairman, George Deukmejian election, 1978, 1982 and 1986; co-chairman, George Bush election, 1988; co-chairman, Pete Wilson Senate elections, 1982 and 1988; co-chairman, Pete Wilson for Governor election, 1990; charter member, Riverside County Republican Winners Circle; former vice president, Corona/Norco Republican Assembly; chairman and charter member, Lincoln Club of Riverside County, 1986–90; president, Corona Rotary Club, 1991; past president, Corona Elks; Navy League of Corona/Norco; Corona Chamber of Commerce, 1990; past chairman, Norco Chamber of Commerce; County of Riverside Asset Leasing; past chairman, Corona/Norco Board of Realtors; Monday Morning Group; Corona Group; executive board, Economic Development Partnership; charter member, Corona Community Hospital Corporate 200 Club; Silver Eagles (March AFB Support Group); co-chair, Corona Airport Advisory Commission; Generic Drug Equity Caucus; co-chair, Caucus to Fight and Control Methamphetamine; co-chair, Manufactured Housing Caucus; Defense Study Group; Hellenic Caucus; Fire Caucus; National Guard & Reserve Caucus; Human Rights Caucus; Baltic Caucus; Travel and Tourism Caucus; Coalition for Autism Research and Education; Diabetes Caucus; Missing and Exploited Children's Caucus; Zero Capital Gains Tax Caucus; Medical Technology Caucus; Law Enforcement Caucus; Correctional Officers Caucus; Western Caucus; Sportsman's Caucus; Native American Caucus; Coastal Caucus; Beef Caucus; Boating Caucus;

Canada Caucus; Goods Movement Caucus; Hydrogen Caucus; International Conservation Caucus; Congressional Internet Caucus; Real Estate Caucus; Renewable Energy and Energy Efficiency Caucus; Specialty Crop. Caucus; Suburban Agenda; Wine Caucus; Armenian Caucus; India Caucus; International Anti-Piracy Caucus; Moroccan Caucus; 2015 Caucus (House Cancer Caucus); Electronic Warfare Caucus; Modeling & Simulation Training Caucus; Navy-Marine Corps Caucus; Shipbuilding Caucus; Special Operations Forces Caucus; STEM Caucus; Immigration Reform Caucus; Congressional Border Caucus; Fetal Alcohol Syndrome Caucus; Congressional Alzheimer's Taskforce; Heart and Stroke Coalition; Cystic Fibrosis Caucus; committees: Appropriations; elected on November 3, 1992 to the 103rd Congress; reelected to each succeeding Congress.

Office Listings

2201 Rayburn House Office Building, Washington, DC 20515 .... (202) 225–1986
Chief of Staff.—Dave Ramey. FAX: 225–2004
Legislative Director.—Maria Bowie.
Press Secretary.—Rebecca Rudman.
3400 Central Avenue, Suite 200, Riverside, CA 92506 .... (951) 784–4300
District Manager.—Jolyn Murphy.

Counties: ORANGE COUNTY (part). CITIES AND TOWNSHIPS: Coto d'Casa, Ledera Ranch, Margarita, Rancho Santa, San Clemente, San Juan Capistrano. RIVERSIDE COUNTY (part). CITIES AND TOWNSHIPS: Corona, March AFB, Mira Loma, Norco, Perris, and Riverside. Population (2000), 639,088.

ZIP Codes: 92501–09, 92513–18, 92521–22, 92532, 92557, 92570, 92596, 92672–75, 92679, 92694, 92860, 92879–83

* * *

FORTY-FIFTH DISTRICT

MARY BONO MACK, Republican, of Palm Springs, CA; born in Cleveland, OH, October 24, 1961; daughter of Clay Whitaker, retired physician and surgeon, and Karen, retired chemist; Bachelor of Fine Arts in Art History, University of Southern California, 1984; Woman of the Year, 1993, San Gorgonio Chapter of the Girl Scouts of America for her assistance to victims of a tragic Girl Scout bus crash in Palm Springs; board member: Palm Springs International Film Festival; first lady of Palm Springs and active in a wide range of community charities and service organizations; leadership role in support of the D.A.R.E. program, Olive Crest Home for Abused Children, Tiempos de Los Ninos; certified personal fitness instructor in martial arts (Karate, Tae Kwan Do); accomplished gymnast with Gymnastics Olympica; appointed chair, Congressional Salton Sea Task Force; married Sonny Bono, 1986; two children: Chesare Elan and Chianna Maria; committees: Energy and Commerce; elected by special election on April 7, 1998 to the 105th Congress, to fill the vacancy caused by the death of her husband Rep. Sonny Bono; reelected to each succeeding Congress.

Office Listings

http://www.house.gov/bono

104 Cannon House Office Building, Washington, DC 20515 .... (202) 225–5330
Chief of Staff.—Frank Cullen. FAX: 225–2961
Legislative Director.—Chris Foster.
Communications Director.—Jennifer May.
Scheduler / Executive Assistant.—Petrina Pyle.
707 East Tahquitz Canyon Way, Suite 9, Palm Springs, CA 92262 .... (760) 320–1076
District Director.—Marc Troast.
1600 E. Florida Avenue, Suite 301, Hemet, CA 92544 .... (951) 658–2312

Counties: RIVERSIDE COUNTY (part). CITIES AND TOWNSHIPS: Bermuda Dunes, Blythe, Cathedral City, Coachella, East Blythe, East Hemet, Hemet, Idyllwild-Pine, Indian Wells, Indio, La Quinta, Mecca, Moreno Valley, Murrieta, Palm Desert, Palm Springs, Rancho Mirage, Thousand Palms, and Winchester. Population (2000), 639,088.

ZIP Codes: 92201, 92203, 92210–11, 92220, 92225–26, 92234–36, 92239–41, 92253–55, 92260–64, 92270, 92274, 92276, 92282, 92536, 92539, 92543–46, 92548–49, 92551–57, 92561–64, 92567, 92571, 92584–86, 92590–92, 92595–96

* * *

FORTY-SIXTH DISTRICT

DANA ROHRABACHER, Republican, of Huntington Beach, CA; born in Coronado, CA, June 21, 1947; education: graduated Palos Verdes High School, CA, 1965; attended Los Angeles Harbor College, Wilmington, CA, 1965–67; B.A., Long Beach State College, CA, 1969; M.A., University of Southern California, Los Angeles, 1975; writer/journalist; speechwriter and special assistant to the President, The White House, Washington, DC, 1981–88; assistant press secretary, Reagan/Bush Committee, 1980; reporter, City News Service/Radio News West, and editorial writer, *Orange County Register*, 1972–80; committees: Foreign Affairs; Science and Technology; elected on November 8, 1988, to the 101st Congress; reelected to each succeeding Congress.

Office Listings

http://www.house.gov/rohrabacher

2300 Rayburn House Office Building, Washington, DC 20515 .... (202) 225–2415
Chief of Staff/Legislative Director.—Richard T. ''Rick'' Dykema. FAX: 225–0145
Communications Director.—Tara Setmayer.
101 Main Street, Suite 380, Huntington Beach, CA 92648 .... (714) 960–6483
District Director.—Kathleen M. Hollingsworth.

Counties: ORANGE COUNTY (part). Communities of Fountain Valley, Huntington Beach, Costa Mesa, Westminster, Seal Beach, Santa Ana, Midway City, Garden Grove, Newport Beach, Sunset Beach, Surfside. LOS ANGELES COUNTY (part). COMMUNITIES OF: Avalon, Long Beach, Palos Verdes, Palos Verdes Estates, Rancho Palos Verdes, Rolling Hills, Rolling Hills Estates, and San Pedro. Population (2000), 639,088.

ZIP Codes: 90274–75, 90704, 90731–32, 90740, 90742–44, 90802–04, 90808, 90813–15, 90822, 90831–35, 90840, 90853, 92626–28, 92646–49, 92655, 92683, 92702, 92708, 92711–12, 92725, 92735, 92799, 92841, 92843–44

* * *

FORTY-SEVENTH DISTRICT

LORETTA SANCHEZ, Democrat, of Anaheim, CA; born in Lynwood, CA, January 7, 1960; education: graduate of Chapman University; M.B.A., American University; specializes in assisting public agencies with finance matters; member, Blue Dog Coalition; Law Enforcement Caucus; Congressional Women's Caucus; committees: Armed Services; Homeland Security; elected to the 105th Congress; reelected to each succeeding Congress.

Office Listings

http://www.house.gov/sanchez

1114 Longworth House Office Building, Washington, DC 20515 .... (202) 225–2965
Chief of Staff.—Adrienne Elrod. FAX: 225–5859
Legislative Director.—Kate Riley.
Legislative Assistants: Jessica Fernendez, Eduardo Lerna, Annie Yea.
Communications Director.—Paula Negrete.
12397 Lewis Street, Suite 101, Garden Grove, CA 92840 .... (714) 621–0102
District Director.—Paula Negrete.
Press Assistant.—Caroline Hogan.

Counties: ORANGE COUNTY (part). CITIES: Anaheim (west and north-south of the Anaheim Stadium-Disneyland corridor), Fullerton, Garden Grove, Orange, and Santa Ana. Population (2000), 639,087.

ZIP Codes: 90680, 92609, 92616, 92619, 92623, 92650, 92652, 92654, 92658, 92679, 92697–98, 92701–04, 92706–07, 92735, 92781, 92801–02, 92804–05, 92812, 92815–17, 92825, 92832–33, 92840–41, 92843–44, 92850, 92868

* * *

FORTY-EIGHTH DISTRICT

JOHN CAMPBELL, Republican, of Irvine, CA; born in Los Angeles, CA, July 19, 1955; education: B.A., University of California, Los Angeles, CA; M.A., University of Southern California, Los Angeles, CA; professional: certified public accountant; member of the California state senate; married: Catherine; children: two sons; committees: Budget; Financial Services; Joint Economic Committee; elected to the 109th Congress by special election to fill the vacancy caused by the resignation of United States Representative Christopher Cox; elected to the 110th Congress; reelected to the 111th Congress on November 4, 2008.

Office Listings

http://www.house.gov/campbell

1507 Longworth House Office Building, Washington, DC 20515 .... (202) 225–5611

Chief of Staff.—Muffy Lewis. FAX: 225–9177
Executive Assistant.—Carolyn Noble.
Legislative Director.—David Malech.
Press Secretary.—Brent Hall.
610 Newport Center Drive, Suite 330, Newport Beach, CA 92660 .... (949) 756–2244

Counties: ORANGE COUNTY (part). CITIES: Aliso Viejo, Corona del Mar, Dana Point, Foothill Ranch, Irvine, Laguna Beach, Laguna Hills, Laguna Niguel, Laguna Woods, Lake Forest, Newport Beach, Orange, San Juan Capistrano, Santa Ana, and Tustin. Population (2000), 639,089.

ZIP Codes: 92602–04, 92606–07, 92610, 92612, 92614, 92618, 92620, 92624–25, 92629–30, 92651, 92653, 92656–57, 92660–63, 92674–75, 92677–79, 92690, 92693, 92705, 92780, 92782

* * *

FORTY-NINTH DISTRICT

DARRELL E. ISSA, Republican, of Vista, CA; born in Cleveland, OH, November 1, 1953; education: Siena Heights College; military service: U.S. Army; attended college on an ROTC scholarship; professional: Businessman; founder and CEO of Directed Electronics, Inc.; past Chairman, Consumer Electronics Association; Board of Directors, Electronics Industry Association; public service: Co-Chairman of the campaign to pass the California Civil Rights Initiative (Proposition 209); Chairman of the Volunteer Committee for the 1996 Republican National Convention; Chairman of the San Diego County Lincoln Club; candidate for the U.S. Senate in 1998; architect of 2003 California recall campaign of former Governor Gray Davis; married: Kathy; children: William; committees: ranking member, Oversight and Government Reform; Judiciary; elected to the 107th Congress on November 7, 2000; reelected to each succeeding Congress.

Office Listings

http://www.house.gov/issa

2347 Rayburn House Office Building, Washington, DC 20515 .... (202) 225–3906
Chief of Staff.—Dale Neugebauer. FAX: 225–3303
Legislative Director.—Jason Scism.
Press Secretary.—Kurt Bardella.
Scheduler.—Mary Pritschau.
1800 Thibodo Road, #310, Vista, CA 92081 .... (760) 599–5000

Counties: RIVERSIDE (part), SAN DIEGO (part). Population (2000), 639,087

ZIP Codes: 92003, 92025–28, 92036, 92049, 92051–52, 92054–61, 92065–66, 92068–70, 92081–86, 92088, 92128, 92530, 92532, 92548, 92562–63, 92567, 92570–72, 92584–87, 92589–93, 92595–96, 92599

* * *

FIFTIETH DISTRICT

BRIAN P. BILBRAY, Republican, of San Diego, CA; born in Coronado, CA, January 28, 1951; education: graduated Mar Vista High School; attended South Western College; professional: tax consultant; city council; Imperial Beach, CA; 1976–78; mayor, Imperial Beach, CA, 1978–85; San Diego County Board of Supervisors, 1985–95; married: Karen; five children; committees: Oversight and Government Reform; Science and Technology; Veterans' Affairs; elected to the 104th Congress and to the two succeeding Congresses (January 3, 1995–2001); unsuccessful candidate for reelection to the 107th Congress; elected by special election, to fill the vacancy caused by the resignation of United States Representative Randall ''Duke'' Cunningham and reelected to each succeeding Congress.

Office Listings

http://www.house.gov/bilbray

2348 Rayburn House Office Building, Washington, DC 20515 .... (202) 225–0508
Chief of Staff.—Steve Danon. FAX: 225–2558
Legislative Director.—Lorissa Bounds.
Scheduler.—Jennifer Polk.
Press Secretary.—Fritz Chaleff.
462 Stevens Avenue, Suite 107, Solana Beach, CA 92075 .... (858) 350–1150

Counties: SAN DIEGO COUNTY (part). Population (2000), 639,087.

ZIP Codes: 92007–09, 92013–14, 92018, 92023–27, 92029–30, 92033, 92037, 92046, 92067, 92069, 92075, 92078–79, 92081–84, 92091, 92096, 92109–11, 92117, 92121–22, 92126–30, 92145, 92172, 92177, 92191, 92196, 92198

* * *

FIFTY-FIRST DISTRICT

BOB FILNER, Democrat, of San Diego, CA; born in Pittsburgh, PA, September 4, 1942; education: B.A., Cornell University, Ithaca, NY, 1963; M.A., University of Delaware, 1969; Ph.D., Cornell University, 1973; professor, San Diego State University, 1970–92; San Diego Board of Education, 1979–83 (president, 1982); San Diego City Council, 1987–92 (deputy mayor, 1990); member: Sierra Club, NAACP, Navy League, Gray Panthers, Economic Conversion Council, Common Cause, ACLU, ADL, NWPC, MAPA; married: Jane Merrill Filner, 1985; children: Erin and Adam; committees: chair, Veterans' Affairs; Transportation and Infrastructure; elected on November 3, 1992 to the 103rd Congress; reelected to each succeeding Congress.

Office Listings

http://www.house.gov/filner

2428 Rayburn House Office Building, Washington, DC 20515 .... (202) 225–8045
Chief of Staff.—Tony Buckles. FAX: 225–9073
Executive Assistant.—Kim Messineo.
Legislative Director.—Sharon Wagener.
Senior Legislative Assistant.—Sharon Schultze.
333 F Street, Suite A, Chula Vista, CA 91910 .... (619) 422–5963
1101 Airport Road, Suite D, Imperial, CA 92251 .... (760) 355–8800

Counties: SAN DIEGO COUNTY (part), IMPERIAL COUNTY. CITIES: Brawley, Calexico, Calipatria, Chula Vista, El Centro, Holtville, Imperial, National City, San Diego, San Ysidro, and Westmorland. Population (2000), 639,087.

ZIP Codes: 91902, 91905–06, 91908–15, 91917, 91921, 91934, 91945, 91947, 91950, 91963, 91977, 91980, 92102, 92105, 92113–15, 92136, 92139, 92143, 92149, 92153–54, 92173, 92179, 92222, 92227, 92231–33, 92243–44, 92249–51, 92257, 92259, 92266, 92273–75, 92281, 92283

* * *

FIFTY-SECOND DISTRICT

DUNCAN HUNTER, Republican, of Lakeside, CA; born in San Diego, CA, December 7, 1976; education: graduated from Granite Hills High School; B.S., Business Administration, San Diego State University, San Diego, CA, 2001; professional: business analyst; military: captain, United States Marine Corps, 2002–05; United States Marine Corps Reserves, 2005–08; religion: Protestant; married: Margaret; children: Duncan, Elizabeth, and Sarah; committees: Armed Services; Education and Labor; elected to the 111th Congress on November 4, 2008.

Office Listings

http://www.hunter.house.gov

1429 Longworth House Office Building, Washington, DC 20515 .... (202) 225–5672
Chief of Staff.—Victoria Middleton. FAX: 225–0235
Scheduler/Office Manager.—Blaire Bartlett.
Communications Director.—Joe Kasper.
1870 Cordell Court, Suite 206, El Cajon, CA 92020 .... (619) 448–5201

Counties: SAN DIEGO COUNTY (part). CITIES AND TOWNSHIPS: Alpine, Barona I.R., Borrego Springs, Boulder Park, Boulevard, Campo, Descanso, Dulzura, El Cajon, Guatay, Indian Res., Jacumba, Jamul, Lakeside, La Mesa, Lemon Grove, Mount Laguna, Pine Valley, Potrero, Poway, Ramona, San Diego, Santee, Spring Valley, Tecate, and Palo Verde. Population (2000), 639,087.

ZIP Codes: 91901, 91903, 91905–06, 91915–17, 91931, 91935, 91941–45, 91948, 91962, 91976–79, 92004, 92019–22, 92025, 92036, 92040, 92064–66, 92071–72, 92074, 92090, 92108, 92111, 92115, 92119–20, 92123–24, 92126, 92128–29, 92131, 92142, 92145, 92150, 92158–60, 92190, 92193–94, 92199

* * *

FIFTY-THIRD DISTRICT

SUSAN A. DAVIS, Democrat, of San Diego, CA; born in Cambridge, MA, April 13, 1944; education: B.S., University of California at Berkeley; M.A., University of North Carolina; public service: served three terms in the California State Assembly; served nine years on the San Diego City School Board; former President of the League of Women Voters of San Diego; awards: California School Boards Association Legislator of the Year; League of Middle Schools Legislator of the Year; family: married to Steve; children: Jeffrey and Benjamin; grandson: Henry; granddaughter: Jane; committees: Armed Services; Education and Labor; House Administration; elected to the 107th Congress on November 7, 2000; reelected to each succeeding Congress.

Office Listings

http://www.house.gov/susandavis

1526 Longworth House Office Building, Washington DC 20515 .... (202) 225–2040
Chief of Staff.—Lisa Sherman. FAX: 225–2948
Press Secretary.—Aaron Hunter.
Scheduler.—Cynthia Patton.
4305 University Avenue, Suite 515, San Diego, CA 92105 .... (619) 280–5353
District Director.—Jessica Poole.

Counties: SAN DIEGO COUNTY (part). Population (2000), 639,087.

ZIP Codes: 91932–33, 91945–46, 91977, 92037–39, 92092–93, 92101–18, 92120–23, 92132–38, 92140, 92147, 92152, 92155, 92161, 92163–71, 92175–76, 92178, 92182, 92184, 92186–87, 92192, 92195

COLORADO

(Population 2000, 4,301,261)

SENATORS

MARK UDALL, Democrat, of Eldorado Springs, CO; born in Tucson, AZ, July 18, 1950; B.A., Williams College, Williamstown, MA, 1972; field coordinator, Morris K. Udall for President, 1974; executive director, Colorado Outward Bound School, 1985–95; member of the Colorado State House of Representatives, 1996–98; member of the U.S. House of Representatives, 1999–2008; married: Maggie Fox; two children; committees: Armed Services; Energy and Natural Resources; Special Committee on Aging; elected to the U.S. Senate on November 4, 2008.

Office Listings

http://markudall.senate.gov

SH–317 Hart Senate Office Building, Washington, DC 20510 .... (202) 224–5941
Chief of Staff.—Michael Sozan. FAX: 224–6471
Legislative Director / Senior Legislative Counsel.—Heather Urban.
Press Secretary.—Tara Trujillo.
Scheduler.—Lisa Carpenter.
999 18th Street, Suite N1525, Denver, CO 80202 .... (303) 650–7820

* * *

MICHAEL F. BENNET, Democrat, of Denver, CO; born in New Delhi, India, November 28, 1964; education: B.A., Wesleyan University, 1987; J.D., Yale Law School, 1993; editor-in-chief of the *Yale Law Journal;* counsel to U.S. Deputy Attorney General, 1995–97; special assistant, U.S. Attorney, CT, 1997; managing director, Anschutz Investment Co., 1997–2003; chief of staff to mayor of Denver, CO, 2003–05; superintendent, Denver Public Schools, 2005–09; married: Susan D. Dagget; children: Caroline, Halina, and Anne; committees: Agriculture, Nutrition, and Forestry; Banking, Housing, and Urban Affairs; Health, Education, Labor and Pensions; Special Committee on Aging; appointed January 21, 2009, to the 111th United States Senate for the term ending January 3, 2011, to fill the vacancy caused by the resignation of Kenneth L. Salazar, took the oath of office on January 22, 2009.

Office Listings

http://bennet.senate.gov

702 Hart Senate Office Building, Washington, DC 20510–0606 .... (202) 224–5852
Chief of Staff.—Jeff Lane. FAX: 228–5036
Legislative Director.—Ayth Elhassani.
Communications Director.—Deirdre Murray.
Scheduler.—Karin Ballman.
2300 15th Street, Suite 450, Denver, CO 80202 .... (303) 455–3358
FAX: 455–8851
129 West B Street, Pueblo, CO 81003 .... (719) 542–7550
FAX: 542–7555
609 Main Street, Suite 110, Alamosa, CO 81101 .... (719) 587–0096
FAX: 587–0098
409 North Tejon, Suite 107, Colorado Springs, CO 80903 .... (719) 328–1100
FAX: 328–1129
1200 South College Avenue, Suite 211, Fort Collins, CO 80524 .... (970) 224–2200
FAX: 224–2205
109 East Railroad Avenue, #4, Fort Morgan, CO 80701 .... (970) 542–9446
FAX: 542–3088
225 North 5th Street, Suite 511, Grand Junction, CO 81501 .... (970) 241–6631
FAX: 241–8313
835 East 2nd Avenue, Suite 203, Durango, CO 81301 .... (970) 259–1710
FAX: 259–9789

REPRESENTATIVES

FIRST DISTRICT

DIANA DEGETTE, Democrat, of Denver, CO; born in Tachikowa, Japan, July 29, 1957; education: B.A., political science, *magna cum laude*, The Colorado College, 1979; J.D., New York University School of Law, 1982 (Root Tilden Scholar); professional: attorney with

McDermott, Hansen, and Reilly; Colorado Deputy State Public Defender, Appellate Division, 1982–84; Colorado House of Representatives, 1992–96; board of directors, Planned Parenthood, Rocky Mountain Chapter; member and formerly on board of governors, Colorado Bar Association; member, Colorado Women's Bar Association; past memberships: board of trustees, The Colorado College; Denver Women's Commission; board of directors, Colorado Trial Lawyers Association; former editor, *Trial Talk* magazine; listed in 1994–96 edition of *Who's Who in America*; Chief Deputy Whip; committees: vice chair, Energy and Commerce; Natural Resources; elected to the 105th Congress; reelected to each succeeding Congress.

Office Listings

http://degette.house.gov

2335 Rayburn House Office Building, Washington, DC 20515 .... (202) 225–4431
Chief of Staff.—Lisa B. Cohen. FAX: 225–5657
Scheduler.—Isra Pananon.
Communications Director.—Kristofer Eisenla.
600 Grant Street, Suite 202, Denver, CO 80203 .... (303) 844–4988
District Administrator.—Christopher Arend.

Counties: ADAMS (part), ARAPAHOE (part), DENVER, JEFFERSON (part). Population (2000), 614,465.

ZIP Codes: 80110–11, 80113, 80121, 80123, 80127, 80150–51, 80155, 80201–12, 80214–24, 80226–32, 80235–39, 80243–44, 80246–52, 80255–57, 80259, 80261–62, 80264–66, 80270–71, 80273–75, 80279, 80281, 80285, 80290–95, 80299

* * *

SECOND DISTRICT

JARED POLIS, Democrat, of Boulder, CO; born in Boulder, CO, May 12, 1975; education: B.A., political science, Princeton University, Princeton, NJ, 1996; professional: internet entrepreneur; founder of New America Schools; chair, Colorado State Board of Education; House Democratic Steering and Policy Committee; religion: Jewish; committees: Education and Labor; Rules; elected to the 111th Congress on November 4, 2008.

Office Listings

http://www.polis.house.gov

501 Cannon House Office Building, Washington, DC 20515 .... (202) 225–2161
Chief of Staff.—Brian Branton.
Legislative Director.—Rosalyn Kumar.
Press Secretary.—Lara Cottingham.
Scheduler.—Lisa Kaufmann.
4770 Baseline Road, Suite 220, Boulder, CO 80303 .... (303) 484–9596
1200 East 78th Avenue, Suite 10, Thornton, CO 80303 .... (303) 287–4159
101 West Main Street, P.O. Box 1453, Suite 101D, Frisco, CO 80443 .... (970) 668–3240

Counties: ADAMS (part), BOULDER (part), BROOMFIELD, CLEAR CREEK, EAGLE, GILPIN, GRAND, JEFFERSON (part), SUMMIT, WELD (part). Population (2000), 614,465.

ZIP Codes: 80003, 80005, 80007, 80020–21, 80025–28, 80030–31, 80035–36, 80038, 80212, 80221, 80229, 80233–34, 80241, 80260, 80263, 80301–10, 80314, 80321–23, 80328–29, 80403, 80422–24, 80426–28, 80435–36, 80438–39, 80442–44, 80446–47, 80451–52, 80455, 80459, 80463, 80466, 80468, 80471, 80474, 80476–78, 80481–82, 80497–98, 80503–04, 80510, 80514, 80516, 80520, 80530, 80540, 80544, 80602, 80614, 80640, 81620–21, 81623, 81631–32, 81637, 81645, 81649, 81655, 81657–58

* * *

THIRD DISTRICT

JOHN T. SALAZAR, Democrat, of Manassas, CO; born in Alamosa, CO, July 21, 1953; education: B.S., Adams State College, Alamosa, CO, 1981; graduated from the Colorado Agricultural Leadership Forum, 1992; professional: served in the U.S. Army, 1973–76; farmer; rancher; business owner; public service: Governor's Economic Development Advisory Board; the state Agricultural Commission; board of directors of the Rio Grande Water Conservation District; board of directors of the Colorado Agricultural Leadership Forum; Colorado Agricultural Commission, 1999–2002; Colorado State House of Representatives, 2003–04; married: Mary Lou Salazar; children: Jesus, Esteban, and Miguel; committees: Appropriations; Select

Committee on Energy Independence and Global Warming; elected to the 109th Congress on November 2, 2004; reelected to each succeeding Congress.

Office Listings

http://www.house.gov/salazar

326 Cannon House Office Building, Washington, DC 20515 .... (202) 225–4761
Chief of Staff.—Ronnie Carleton. FAX: 226–9669
Legislative Director.—Eric Wortman.
Scheduler.—Annie Fetcher.
134 West B Street, Pueblo, CO 81003 .... (719) 543–8200
225 North 5th Street, Suite 702, Grand Junction, CO 81501 .... (970) 245–7107
609 Main Street, #6, Alamosa, CO 81101 .... (719) 587–5105
813 Main Avenue, Suite 300, Durango, CO 81301 .... (970) 259–1012

Counties: ALAMOSA, ARCHULETA, CONEJOS, COSTILLA, CUSTER, DELTA, DOLORES, GARFIELD, GUNNISON, HINSDALE, HUERFANO, JACKSON, LA PLATA, LAS ANIMAS, MESA, MINERAL, MOFFAT, MONTEZUMA, MONTROSE, OTERO (part), OURAY, PITKIN, PUEBLO, RIO BLANCO, RIO GRANDE, ROUTT, SAGUACHE, SAN JUAN, SAN MIGUEL. Population (2000), 614,467.

ZIP Codes: 80423–24, 80428, 80430, 80434–35, 80443, 80446–47, 80456, 80459, 80463, 80467, 80469, 80473, 80479–80, 80483, 80487–88, 80498, 81001–12, 81019–20, 81022–25, 81027, 81029, 81033, 81039–41, 81043–44, 81046, 81049–50, 81054–55, 81058–59, 81062, 81064, 81067, 81069, 81077, 81081–82, 81089, 81091, 81101–02, 81120–38, 81140–41, 81143–44, 81146–49, 81151–55, 81157, 81201, 81210–12, 81215, 81220–26, 81228, 81230–33, 81235–37, 81239–41, 81243, 81248, 81251–53, 81301–03, 81320–21, 81323–32, 81334–35, 81401–02, 81410–11, 81413–16, 81418–20, 81422–35, 81501–06, 81520–27, 81601–02, 81610–12, 81615, 81621, 81623–26, 81630, 81633, 81635–36, 81638–43, 81646–48, 81650, 81652–56

* * *

FOURTH DISTRICT

BETSY MARKEY, Democrat, of Fort Collins, CO; born in Cresskill, NJ, April 27, 1956; education: B.S., political science, University of Florida, Gainesville, FL, 1978; M.P.A., Public Administration, American University, Washington, DC; professional: small business owner; awards: Presidential Management Fellow; National Association of Female Executives; National Association of Women Business Owners; Pi Alpha Alpha (the National Honor Society for Public Administrators); religion: Catholic; married: Jim Kelly; three children; caucuses: Sustainable Energy and Environment Coalition; Sportsmen's, Rural Education; Green Schools, Middle Class, Rural Health Care Coalition; Fire Services, Ports to Plains, Military Veterans; committees: Agriculture; Transportation and Infrastructure; elected to the 111th Congress on November 4, 2008.

Office Listings

http://www.betsymarkey.house.gov

1229 Longworth House Office Building, Washington, DC 20515 .... (202) 225–4676
Chief of Staff.—Anne Caprara. FAX: 225–5870
Legislative Director.—Brad Mollet.
Communications Director.—Ben Marter.
Director of Scheduling.—Jeannette Cleland.
123 North College Avenue, Suite 220, Ft. Collins, CO 80524 .... (970) 221–7110
FAX: 221–7240
822 7th Street, #9, Greeley, CO 80631 .... (970) 351–6007
FAX: 351–6068
301 South 5th Street, Lamar, CO 81052 .... (719) 931–4003
FAX: 931–4005
109½ South Third Street, Sterling, CO 80721 .... (970) 522–0203
FAX: 522–1783

Counties: BACA, BOULDER (part), BENT, CHEYENNE, CROWLEY, KIOWA, KIT CARSON, LARIMER, LINCOLN, LOGAN, MORGAN, PHILLIPS, PROWERS, OTERO (part), SEDGEWICK, WASHINGTON, WELD (part), YUMA. Population (2000), 614,466.

ZIP Codes: 80501–04, 80510–13, 80515, 80517, 80521–28, 80530, 80532–43, 80545–47, 80549–51, 80553, 80603, 80610–12, 80615, 80620–24, 80631–34, 80638–39, 80642–46, 80648–54, 80701, 80705, 80720–23, 80726–29, 80731–37, 80740–47, 80749–51, 80754–55, 80757–59, 80801–02, 80804–05, 80807, 80810, 80812, 80815, 80818, 80821–26, 80828, 80830, 80832–34, 80836, 80861–62, 81021, 81024, 81027, 81029–30, 81033–34, 81036, 81038, 81041, 81043–47, 81049–50, 81052, 81054, 81057, 81059, 81062–64, 81071, 81073, 81076, 81084, 81087, 81090, 81092

* * *

FIFTH DISTRICT

DOUG LAMBORN, Republican, of Colorado Springs, CO; born in Leavenworth, KS, May 24, 1954; education: B.S., University of Kansas Lawrence, 1978; J.D., University of Kansas Lawrence, 1985; lawyer, private practice (business and real estate); Colorado State House of Representatives 1995–98; Colorado State Senate, 1998–2006; married: Jeanie; five children; committees: Armed Services; Natural Resources; Veterans' Affairs; elected to the 110th Congress on November 7, 2006; reelected to the 111th Congress on November 4, 2008.

Office Listings

http://www.house.gov/lamborn

437 Cannon House Office Building, Washington, DC 20515 .... (202) 225–4422
Chief of Staff.—Robert McCreary. FAX: 226–2638
Deputy Chief of Staff/Legislative Director.—Craig Rushing.
Director of Communications.—Catherine Mortenson.
Scheduler/Executive Assistant.—Abby Gunderson.
1271 Kelly Johnson Boulevard, Suite 110, Colorado Springs, CO 80920 .... (719) 520–0055

Counties: CHAFFEE, EL PASO, FREMONT, LAKE, PARK (part), TELLER. Population (2000), 614,467.

ZIP Codes: 80104, 80106, 80132–33, 80135, 80420, 80432, 80438, 80440, 80443, 80448–49, 80456, 80461, 80475, 80808–09, 80813–14, 80816–17, 80819–20, 80827, 80829–33, 80835, 80840–41, 80860, 80863–64, 80866, 80901, 80903–22, 80925–26, 80928–37, 80940–47, 80949–50, 80960, 80962, 80970, 80977, 80995, 80997, 81008, 81154, 81201, 81211–12, 81221, 81223, 81226–28, 81233, 81236, 81240–42, 81244, 81251, 81253

* * *

SIXTH DISTRICT

MIKE COFFMAN, Republican, of Aurora, CO; born in Fort Leonard Wood, MO, March 19, 1955; education: attended, Aurora Central High School; B.A., University of Colorado, Boulder, CO, 1979; military: United States Army, 1972–74; United States Army Reserve, 1975–78; United States Marine Corps, 1979–82; United States Marine Corps Reserve, 1983–94, and 2005–06; professional: business owner; elected to the Colorado State House of Representatives, 1989–94; elected to the Colorado State Senate, 1994–98; Colorado State Treasurer, 1999–2007; Colorado Secretary of State, 2007–08; religion: Methodist; married: Cynthia; committees: Armed Service; Natural Resources; Small Business; elected to the 111th Congress on November 4, 2008.

Office Listings

http://www.coffman.house.gov

1508 Longworth House Office Building, Washington, DC 20515 .... (202) 225–7882
Chief of Staff.—Jacque Ponder. FAX: 226–4623
Scheduler.—Ashling Thurmond.
9220 Kimmer Drive, Suite 200, Lone Tree, CO 80124 .... (720) 283–9772

Counties: ARAPAHOE (part), DOUGLAS, ELBERT, JEFFERSON (part), PARK (part). Population (2000), 614,466.

ZIP Codes: 80013–16, 80018, 80046, 80101–09, 80111–12, 80116–18, 80120–31, 80134–38, 80160–63, 80165–66, 80225, 80231, 80235–36, 80247, 80401, 80403, 80421, 80425, 80433, 80437, 80439, 80453–54, 80457, 80465, 80470, 80808, 80828, 80830–33, 80835

* * *

SEVENTH DISTRICT

ED PERLMUTTER, Democrat, of Golden, CO; born in Denver, CO, May 1, 1953; education: B.A., University of Colorado, 1975; J.D., University of Colorado, 1978; professional: served as a member of the Board of Governors of the Colorado Bar Association; served on the Board of Trustees and Judicial Performance Commission for the First Judicial District; Trustee, Midwest Research Institute, the primary operator of the National Renewable Energy Laboratory; board member, National Jewish Medical and Research Center; elected to two four-year terms to represent central Jefferson County as a Colorado State Senator, 1995–2003; served on numerous committees in the State Senate, including Water, Finance, Judiciary, Child Welfare, Telecommunication, Transportation, Legal Services, and Oil and Gas; also served as chair of the Public Policy and Planning Committee, chair of the Bi-Partisan Renewable Energy Caucus, and President Pro Tem (2001–02 session); divorced; three children; committees: Financial Services; Rules; elected to the 110th Congress on November 7, 2006; reelected to the 111th Congress.

Office Listings

http://perlmutter.house.gov/

415 Cannon House Office Building, Washington, DC 20515 .... (202) 225–2645
Chief of Staff.—Danielle Radovich Piper. FAX: 225–5278
Legislative Director.—Matt Henken.
Scheduler / Executive Assistant.—Alison Inderforth.
Staff Assistant.—Haley Nicholson.
12600 West Colfax Avenue, Suite B400, Lakewood, CO 80215 .... (303) 274–7944

Counties: ADAMS (part), ARAPAHOE (part), JEFFERSON (part). CITIES AND TOWNSHIPS: Arvada, Aurora, Bennett, Brighton, Commerce City, Edgewater, Golden, Lakewood, and Wheat Ridge. Population (2000), 614,465.

ZIP Codes: 80001–07, 80010–14, 80017–19, 80021–22, 80030, 80033–34, 80040–42, 80044–45, 80047, 80102–03, 80105, 80123, 80127, 80136–37, 80212, 80214–16, 80221, 80226–35, 80241, 80247, 80401–03, 80419, 80465, 80601–03, 80640, 80642–43, 80654

CONNECTICUT

(Population 2000, 3,405,565)

SENATORS

CHRISTOPHER J. DODD, Democrat, of East Haddam, CT; born in Willimantic, CT, May 27, 1944; son of Thomas J. and Grace Murphy Dodd; education: graduated, Georgetown Preparatory School, 1962; B.A., English Literature, Providence College, 1966; J.D., University of Louisville School of Law, 1972; admitted to Connecticut bar, 1973; served in Army National Gaurd and U.S. Army Reserves, 1969–75; Peace Corps volunteer, Dominican Republic, 1966–68; married to Jackie Clegg; two children, Grace and Christina; founded the Senate Children's Caucus; co-chair, Senate India Caucus; House committees: served on the Rules Committee, Judiciary Committee, and Science and Technology Committee; appointed to the Select Committee on the Outer Continental Shelf and the Select Committee on Assassinations; appointed to the Commission on Security and Cooperation in Europe; committees: chair, Banking, Housing, and Urban Affairs; Foreign Relations; Health, Education, Labor, and Pensions; Rules and Administration; Joint Committee on the Library of Congress; elected to the 94th Congress, November 5, 1974; reelected to the 95th and 96th Congresses; elected to the U.S. Senate, November 4, 1980; reelected to each succeeding Senate term.

Office Listings

http://dodd.senate.gov

448 Russell Senate Office Building, Washington, DC 20510 .... (202) 224–2823
Chief of Staff.—Miles Lackey. FAX: 224–1083
Legislative Director.—Jim Fenton.
30 Lewis Street, Hartford, CT 06103 .... (860) 258–6940
State Director.—Ed Mann.

* * *

JOSEPH I. LIEBERMAN, Independent Democrat, of New Haven, CT; born in Stamford, CT, February 24, 1942; education: attended Stamford public schools; B.A., Yale University, 1964; law degree, Yale Law School, 1967; Connecticut State Senate, 1970–80; majority leader, 1974–80; honorary degrees: Yeshiva University, University of Hartford; Connecticut's 21st attorney general, 1983; reelected in 1986; author of "The Power-Broker" (Houghton Mifflin Company, 1966), a biography of late Democratic Party chairman John M. Bailey; "The Scorpion and the Tarantula" (Houghton Mifflin Company, 1970), a study of early efforts to control nuclear proliferation; "The Legacy" (Spoonwood Press, 1981), a history of Connecticut politics from 1930–80; "Child Support in America" (Yale University Press, 1986); "In Praise of Public Life" (Simon and Schuster, 2000); and "An Amazing Adventure" (Simon and Schuster, 2003); married: Hadassah Lieberman; children: Matthew, Rebecca, Ethan, and Hana; member, Democratic Leadership Council; Democratic candidate for Vice President, 2000; committees: chair, Homeland Security and Governmental Affairs; Armed Services; Small Business and Entrepreneurship; elected on November 8, 1988, to the U.S. Senate; reelected to each succeeding Senate term.

Office Listings

http://lieberman.senate.gov

706 Hart Senate Office Building, Washington, DC 20510 .... (202) 224–4041
Chief of Staff.—Clarine Nardi Riddle. FAX: 224–9750
Executive Assistant.—Rayanne Bostick.
Legislative Director.—Todd Stein.
One Constitution Plaza, 7th Floor, Hartford, CT 06103 .... (860) 549–8463
State Director.—Sherry Brown.

REPRESENTATIVES

FIRST DISTRICT

JOHN B. LARSON, Democrat, of East Hartford, CT; born in Hartford, CT, July 22, 1948; education: Mayberry Elementary School, East Hartford, CT; East Hartford High School; B.A., Central Connecticut State University; Senior Fellow, Yale University, Bush Center for Child Development and Social Policy; professional: high school teacher, 1972–77; insurance broker,

1978–98; president, Larson and Lyork; public service: Connecticut State Senate, 12 years, President Pro Tempore, 8 years; married: Leslie Larson; children: Carolyn, Laura, and Raymond; committees: Ways and Means; Select Committee on Energy Independence and Global Warming; elected to the 106th Congress; reelected to each succeeding Congress.

Office Listings

http://www.house.gov/larson

106 Cannon House Office Building, Washington, DC 20515 .... (202) 225–2265
Chief of Staff.—Amy O'Donnell. FAX: 225–1031
Press Secretary.—Emily Barocas.
Scheduler.—Liz Malerba.
221 Main Street, Hartford, CT 06106–1864 .... (860) 278–8888

Counties: HARTFORD (part), LITCHFIELD (part), MIDDLESEX (part). Population (2000), 681,113.

ZIP Codes: 06002, 06006, 06010–11, 06016, 06021, 06023, 06025–28, 06033, 06035, 06037, 06040–41, 06045, 06057, 06060–61, 06063–65, 06067, 06073–74, 06088, 06090–91, 06094–96, 06098, 06101–12, 06114–15, 06117–20, 06123, 06126–29, 06131–34, 06137–38, 06140–47, 06150–56, 06160–61, 06176, 06180, 06183, 06199, 06416, 06422, 06444, 06457, 06467, 06479–80, 06489, 06759, 06790

* * *

SECOND DISTRICT

JOE COURTNEY, Democrat, of Vernon, CT; born in Hartford, CT, April 6, 1953; education: B.A., Tufts University, 1971–75; University of Connecticut Law School, 1975–78; public service: Connecticut State Representative, 1987–94; Vernon Town Attorney, 2003–06; professional: attorney, Courtney, Boyan, and Foran, LLC, 1978–2006; religion: Roman Catholic; married: Audrey Courtney; children: Robert and Elizabeth; committees: Armed Services; Education and Labor; elected to the 110th Congress on November 7, 2006; reelected to the 111th Congress on November 4, 2008.

Office Listings

http://www.house.gov/courtney

215 Cannon House Office Building, Washington, DC 20515 .... (202) 225–2076
Chief of Staff.—Jason Gross. FAX: 225–4977
Deputy Chief of Staff / Communications Director.—Brian Farber.
Scheduler.—Tracy Roberts.
Legislative Director.—Neil McKiernan.
2 Courthouse Square, Norwich, CT 06360 .... (860) 886–0139
District Director.—Jenny Contois.

Counties: HARTFORD (part), MIDDLESEX (part), NEW LONDON, TOLLAND, WINDHAM. Population (2000), 681,113.

ZIP Codes: 06029, 06033, 06040, 06043, 06066, 06071–73, 06075–78, 06080, 06082–84, 06093, 06226, 06230–35, 06237–39, 06241–51, 06254–56, 06258–60, 06262–69, 06277–82, 06320, 06330–40, 06349–51, 06353–55, 06357, 06359–60, 06365, 06370–80, 06382–85, 06387–89, 06409, 06412–15, 06417, 06419–20, 06422–24, 06426, 06438–39, 06441–43, 06447, 06456–57, 06459, 06469, 06474–75, 06498

* * *

THIRD DISTRICT

ROSA L. DELAURO, Democrat, of New Haven, CT; born in New Haven, March 2, 1943; education: graduated, Lauralton Hall High School; attended London School of Economics, Queen Mary College, London, 1962–63; B.A., *cum laude*, history and political science, Marymount College, NY, 1964; M.A., international politics, Columbia University, NY, 1966; professional: executive assistant to Mayor Frank Logue, city of New Haven, 1976–77; executive assistant/development administrator, city of New Haven, 1977–78; chief of staff, Senator Christopher Dodd, 1980–87; executive director, Countdown '87, 1987–88; executive director, Emily's List, 1989–90; married: Stanley Greenberg; children: Anna, Kathryn, and Jonathan; committees: Appropriations; Budget; elected to the 102nd Congress on November 6, 1990; reelected to each succeeding Congress.

Office Listings

http://www.delauro.house.gov

2413 Rayburn House Office Building, Washington, DC 20515 .... (202) 225–3661
Chief of Staff.—Kevin Brennan. FAX: 225–4890
Legislative Director.—Leticia Mederos.
Executive Assistant.—Tiavalya Jefferson.
59 Elm Street, New Haven, CT 06510 .... (203) 562–3718
District Director.—Jennifer Lamb.

Counties: FAIRFIELD (part), MIDDLESEX (part), NEW HAVEN (part). CITIES AND TOWNSHIPS: Ansonia, Beacon Falls, Bethany, Branford, Derby, Durham, East Haven, Guilford, Hamden, Middlefield, Middletown, Milford, Naugatuck, New Haven, North Branford, North Haven, Orange, Prospect, Seymour, Shelton, Stratford, Wallingford, Waterbury, West Haven, and Woodbridge. Population (2000), 681,113.

ZIP Codes: 06401, 06403, 06405, 06410, 06418, 06422, 06437, 06450, 06455, 06457, 06460, 06471–73, 06477, 06481, 06483–84, 06492–94, 06501–21, 06524–25, 06530–38, 06540, 06607, 06614–15, 06706, 06708, 06712, 06762, 06770

* * *

FOURTH DISTRICT

JAMES A. HIMES, Democrat, of Cos Cob, CT; born in Lima, Peru to American parents, July 5, 1966; education: B.A., Harvard University, Cambridge, MA, 1988; M.Phil, Oxford University, Oxford, England, 1990; professional: vice president, Goldman Sachs & Co., 1990–2002; vice president, Enterprise Community Partners, 2002–2007; Commissioner, Greenwich Housing Authority; chair, Greenwich Democratic Town Committee; married: Mary Himes, 1994; children: Emma and Linley; committees: Financial Services; Homeland Security; elected to the 111th Congress on November 4, 2008.

Office Listings

http://www.himes.house.gov

214 Cannon House Office Building, Washington, DC 20515 .... (202) 225–5541
Chief of Staff.—Jason Cole. FAX: 225–9629
Executive Assistant.—Caitlin Donohue.
888 Washington Boulevard, Stamford, CT 06901–2927 .... (866) 453–0028
211 State Street, 2nd Floor, Bridgeport, CT 06604–4223 .... (866) 453–0028
District Director.—Kathleen Warner.

Counties: FAIRFIELD (part), NEW HAVEN (part). CITIES AND TOWNSHIPS: Bridgeport, Darien, Easton, Fairfield, Greenwich, Monroe, New Canaan, Norwalk, Oxford, Redding, Ridgefield, Shelton, Stamford, Trumbull Weston, Westport, and Wilton. Population (2000), 681,113.

ZIP Codes: 06468, 06478, 06483–84, 06491, 06601–02, 06604–08, 06610–12, 06673, 06699, 06807, 06820, 06824–25, 06828–31, 06836, 06838, 06840, 06850–58, 06860, 06870, 06875–81, 06883, 06888–90, 06896–97, 06901–07, 06910–14, 06920–22, 06925–28

* * *

FIFTH DISTRICT

CHRISTOPHER S. MURPHY, Democrat, of Cheshire, CT; born August 3, 1973; grew up in Connecticut; graduated with honors, double major in history and political science, Williams College, MA; graduated, University of Connecticut Law School, Hartford, CT, 2002; former member, Southington Planning and Zoning Commission; served for eight years in the Connecticut General Assembly; in 2005, succeeding in passing Connecticut's landmark Stem Cell Investment Act; committees: Energy and Commerce; Oversight and Government Reform; elected to the 110th Congress on November 7, 2006; reelected to the 111th Congress.

Office Listings

http://www.chrismurphy.house.gov

412 Cannon House Office Building, Washington, DC 20515 .... (202) 225–4476
Chief of Staff.—Francis Creighton. FAX: 225–5933
Communications Director.—Kristen Bossi.
Scheduler/Executive Assistant.—Jessica Elledge.
114 West Main Street, Suite 206, New Britain, CT 06053 .... (860) 223–8412
District Director.—Robert Michalik.

Counties: FAIRFIELD (part), HARTFORD (part), LITCHFIELD, NEW HAVEN (part). CITIES: Danbury, Meriden, New Britain, Torrington, and Waterbury. Population (2000), 681,113.

ZIP Codes: 06001, 06013, 06018–20, 06022, 06024, 06030–32, 06034, 06039, 06050–53, 06058–59, 06062, 06068–70, 06079, 06081, 06085, 06087, 06089, 06092, 06107, 06404, 06408, 06410–11, 06440, 06450–51, 06454, 06470, 06482, 06487–88, 06701–06, 06708, 06710, 06716, 06720–26, 06749–59, 06762–63, 06776–79, 06781–87, 06790–91, 06793–96, 06798, 06801, 06804, 06810–14, 06816–17

DELAWARE

(Population 2000, 783,600)

SENATORS

THOMAS R. CARPER, Democrat, of Wilmington, DE; born in Beckley, WV, January 23, 1947; education: B.A., Ohio State University, 1968; M.B.A., University of Delaware, 1975; military service: U.S. Navy, served during Vietnam War; public service: Delaware State Treasurer, 1977–83; U.S. House of Representatives, 1983–93; Governor of Delaware, 1993–2001; organizations: National Governors' Association; Democratic Leadership Council; religion: Presbyterian; family: married to the former Martha Ann Stacy; children: Ben and Christopher; committees: Environment and Public Works; Finance; Homeland Security and Governmental Affairs; elected to the U.S. Senate on November 7, 2000; reelected to each succeeding Senate term.

Office Listings

http://carper.senate.gov

513 Hart Senate Office Building, Washington, DC 20510 .... (202) 224–2441
Chief of Staff.—Jim Reilly. FAX: 228–2190
Legislative Director.—Bill Ghent.
Administrative Director.—Madge Farooq.
2215 Federal Building, 300 South New Street, Dover, DE 19904 .... (302) 674–3308
301 North Walnut Street, Suite 102 L–1, Wilmington, DE 19801 .... (302) 573–6291
12 The Circle, Georgetown, DE 19947 .... (302) 856–7690

* * *

EDWARD E. KAUFMAN, Democrat, of Wilmington, DE; born in Philadelphia, PA, March 15, 1939; education: B.S., Duke University, 1960; M.B.A., Wharton School of the University of Pennsylvania, 1966; professional: DuPont Company, 1966–73; State Director, Senator Joe Biden, 1973–76; Chief of Staff, Senator Joe Biden, 1976–95; Duke Law School Center for the Study of Congress, Senior Lecturing Fellow, 1991–present, co-chair, 1995–99; Broadcasting Board of Governors (BBG), Board member, 1995–2008; religion: Roman Catholic; married: Lynne; children: Kelly Murry and Meg; committees: Foreign Relations; Judiciary; appointed on January 15, 2009 to the United States Senate to fill the vacancy caused by the resignation of Joseph R. Biden, Jr., and took the oath of office on January 16, 2009.

Office Listings

http://kaufman.senate.gov

383 Russell Senate Office Building, Washington, DC 20510 .... (202) 224–5042
Chief of Staff.—Jeff Connaughton. FAX: 228–3075
Legislative Director.—Jane Woodfin.
Press Secretary.—Alex Snyder-Mackler.
Office Manager.—Trinity Hall.
1105 North Market Street, Suite 2000, Wilmington, DE 19801–1233 .... (302) 573–6345
State Director.—John DiEleuterio.
24 Northwest Front Street, Windsor Building, Suite 101, Milford, DE 19963 .... (302) 424–8090

REPRESENTATIVE

AT LARGE

MICHAEL N. CASTLE, Republican, of Wilmington, DE; born in Wilmington, July 2, 1939; education: graduate of Tower Hill School, 1957; B.S. in economics, Hamilton College, Clinton, NY, 1961; J.D., Georgetown University Law School, 1964; professional: attorney; admitted to the District of Columbia and Delaware bars, 1964; commenced practice in Wilmington; Delaware House of Representatives, 1966–67; Delaware Senate, 1968–76; Lieutenant Governor of Delaware, 1981–85; Governor, 1985–92; awarded honorary degrees: Wesley College, 1986; Widener College, 1986; Delaware State University, 1986; Hamilton College, 1991; Jefferson Medical College, Philadelphia, PA, 1992; active in the National Governors Association, serving three years as chairman of the Human Resources Committee; co-vice chairman for NGA's Task Force on Health Care with President Clinton; past president of the Council of State Governments; past chairman of the Southern Governors Association; chaired the Republican Governors

Association, 1988; American Diabetes Association's C. Everett Koop Award for Health Promotion and Awareness, 1992; member: Delaware Bar Association, American Bar Association; former member: National Governors Association, Republican Governors Association, National Assessment Governing Board, Council of State Governors, Southern Governors Association; honorary board of directors, Delaware Greenways; task forces: co-chairman, Congressional Task Force to the National Campaign to Reduce Teen Pregnancy; House Tobacco Task Force; co-chair, House Diabetes Caucus; co-chair, Biomedical Research Caucus; co-chair, Passenger Rail Caucus; co-chair, Community College Caucus; married: Jane DiSabatino, 1992; committees: Education and Labor; Financial Services; elected to the 103rd Congress on November 3, 1992; reelected to each succeeding Congress.

Office Listings

http://www.castle.house.gov

1233 Longworth House Office Building, Washington, DC 20515 .... (202) 225–4165
Chief of Staff.—Mike Quaranta. FAX: 225–2291
Assistant Press Secretary.—Stephanie Fitzpatrick.
Legislative Director.—Kate Dickens.
Scheduler.—Kristy Huxhold.
201 North Walnut Street, Suite 107, Wilmington, DE 19801 .... (302) 428–1902
Office Director.—Jeff Dayton. FAX: 428–1905
J. Allen Frear Federal Building, 300 South New Street, Dover, DE 19904 .... (302) 736–1666

Counties: KENT, NEW CASTLE, SUSSEX. CITIES AND TOWNSHIPS: Brookside, Camden, Claymont, Delaware City, Dover, Edgemoor, Elsmere, Georgetown, Harrington, Highland, Acres, Kent Acres, Laurel, Lewes, Middletown, Milford, Millsboro, New Castle, Newark, Pike Creek, Rising Sun-Lebanon, Rodney Village, Seaford, Smyrna, Stanton, Talleyville, Wilmington, Wilmington Minor, and Woodside East. Population (2000), 783,600.

ZIP Codes: 19701–03, 19706–18, 19720–21, 19725–26, 19730–36, 19801–10, 19850, 19880, 19884–87, 19890–99, 19901–06, 19930–31, 19933–34, 19936, 19938–41, 19943–47, 19950–56, 19958, 19960–64, 19966–71, 19973, 19975, 19977, 19979–80

FLORIDA

(Population 2000, 15,982,378)

SENATORS

BILL NELSON, Democrat, of Orlando, FL, born in Miami, FL, September 29, 1942; education: Melbourne High School, 1960; B.A., Yale University, 1965; J.D. University of Virginia School of Law, 1968; professional: attorney; admitted to the Florida Bar, 1968; captain, U.S. Army Reserve, 1965–71; active duty, 1968–70; public service: Florida State House of Representatives, 1973–79; U.S. House of Representatives, 1979–91; Florida Treasurer, Insurance Commissioner, and State Fire Marshal, 1995–2001; Astronaut: payload specialist on the space shuttle *Columbia*, January, 1986; married: the former Grace Cavert; children: Bill Jr. and Nan Ellen; committees: Armed Services; Budget; Commerce, Science, and Transportation; Finance; Select Committee on Intelligence; Special Committee on Aging; elected to the U.S. Senate on November 7, 2000; reelected to each succeeding Senate term.

Office Listings

http://billnelson.senate.gov

716 Hart Senate Office Building, Washington, DC 20510 .... (202) 224–5274
Chief of Staff.—Pete Mitchell. FAX: 228–2183
Deputy Chief of Staff, Communications.—Dan McLaughlin.
Deputy Chief of Staff, Administration.—Brenda Strickland.
Legislative Director.—Neal Higgins.
U.S. Courthouse Annex, 111 North Adams Street, Tallahassee, FL 32301 .... (850) 942–8415
Chief of Staff.—Pete Mitchell.
801 North Florida Avenue, 4th Floor, Tampa, FL 33602 .... (813) 225–7040
2925 Salzedo Street, Coral Gables, FL 33134 .... (305) 536–5999
3416 University Drive, Ft. Lauderdale, FL 33328 .... (954) 693–4851
500 Australian Avenue, Suite 125, West Palm Beach, FL 33401 .... (561) 514–0189
225 East Robinson Street, Suite 410, Orlando, FL 32801 .... (407) 872–7161
1301 Riverplace Boulevard, Suite 2281, Jacksonville, FL 32207 .... (904) 346–4500
2000 Main Street, Suite 801, Ft. Myers, FL 33901 .... (239) 334–7760

* * *

GEORGE S. LEMIEUX, Republican, of Tallahassee, FL; born in Broward County, FL, May 21, 1969; education: B.A., political science, Emory University, Atlanta, GA, 1991; J.D., Georgetown University School of Law, Washington, DC, 1994; professional: elected Chairman of the Broward County Republican Party, 2000; served as Florida's Deputy Attorney General and Chief of Staff to the Attorney General's Office, 2003; served as the Executive Director of the Crist/Kottkamp transition team, 2007, and led the Executive Office of the Governor as the Governor's Chief of Staff, 2007; in 2008, rejoined the Gunster, Yoakley firm and was selected to lead Gunster, Yoakley as Chairman of the firm; married: Meike; children: Max, Taylor, and Chase; committees: Armed Services; Commerce, Science, and Transportation; Special Committee on Aging; appointed to the 111th U.S. Senate on September 9, 2009, to fill the vacancy caused by the resignation of Melquiades R. Martinez; took the oath of office and began service on September 10, 2009.

Office Listings

http://lemieux.senate.gov

356 Russell Senate Office Building, Washington, DC 20510 .... (202) 224–3041
Chief of Staff.—Kerry Feehery. FAX: 228–5171
Legislative Director.—Michael Zehr.
201 South Orange Avenue, Suite 350, Orlando, FL 32801 .... (407) 254–2573
1650 Prudential Drive, Suite 220, Jacksonville, FL 32207 .... (904) 398–8586
2120 Main Street, Suite 200, Fort Myers, FL 33901 .... (239) 332–3898
1 North Palafox Street, Suite 159, Pensacola, FL 32502 .... (850) 433–2603
3802 Spectrum Boulevard, Suite 106, Tampa, FL 33612 .... (813) 977–6450
8669 Northwest 36th Street, Suite 110, Miami, FL 33166 .... (305) 444–8332
642 North Federal Highway, Fort Lauderdale, FL 33304 .... (866) 630–7106

REPRESENTATIVES

FIRST DISTRICT

JEFF MILLER, Republican, of Chumuckla, FL; born in St. Petersburg, FL, June 27, 1959; education: B.A., University of Florida, 1984; professional: real estate broker; public service: Executive Assistant to the Commissioner of Agriculture, 1984–88; Environmental Land Management Study Commission, 1992; Santa Rosa County Planning Board Vice Chairman, 1996–98; elected to the Florida House of Representatives in 1998; reelected in 2000; served as House Majority Whip: organizations: Kiwanis Club of Milton; Florida Historical Society; Santa Rosa County United Way; Milton Pregnancy Resource Center Advisory Board; Gulf Coast Council of Boy Scouts; Florida FFA Foundation; religion: Methodist; married: Vicki Griswold; children: Scott and Clint; committees: Armed Services; Veterans' Affairs; Permanent Select Committee on Intelligence; elected to the 107th Congress, by special election, on October 16, 2001; reelected to each succeeding Congress.

Office Listings

2439 Rayburn House Office Building, Washington, DC 20515 .... (202) 225–4136
Chief of Staff.—Dan McFaul. FAX: 225–3414
Legislative Director.—Pete Giambastiani.
Scheduler.—Diane Cihota.
4300 Bayou Boulevard, Suite 13, Pensacola, FL 32503 .... (850) 479–1183
District Director.—Sheilah Bowman.
348 Southwest Miracle Strip Parkway, Unit 24, Ft. Walton Beach, FL 32548 .... (850) 664–1266

Counties: ESCAMBIA, HOLMES, OKALOOSA (part), SANTA ROSA, WALTON (part), WASHINGTON. CITIES AND TOWNSHIPS: Bonifay, Carryville, Crestview, DeFuniak Springs, Destin, Fountain, Freeport, Ft. Walton Beach, Gulf Breeze, Jay, Laurel Hill, Lynn Haven, Milton, Noma, Pace, Paxton, Pensacola, Sunnyside, Westville, and Youngstown. Population (2000), 639,295.

ZIP Codes: 32501–09, 32511–14, 32516, 32520–24, 32526, 32530–31, 32533–42, 32544, 32547–49, 32559–72, 32577–79, 32580, 32583, 32588, 32591, 32598

* * *

SECOND DISTRICT

ALLEN BOYD, Democrat, of Monticello, FL; born in Valdosta, GA, June 6, 1945; education: graduated, Jefferson County High School, Monticello, 1963; B.S., Florida State University, 1969; professional: partner and general manager, F.A. Boyd and Sons, Inc., family farm corporation; first lieutenant, U.S. Army 101st Airborne Division, Vietnam, 1969–71, receiving the CIB and other decorations; Florida House of Representatives, 1989–96; elected majority whip; chaired Governmental Operations Committee (1992–94) and House Democratic Conservative Caucus (Blue Dogs); member: Peanut Producers Association; Farm Bureau; Cattlemen's Association; local historical association; Chamber of Commerce; and Kiwanis; board member, National Cotton Council; member, First United Methodist Church; married: the former Stephannie Ann Roush, 1970; children: Fred Allen Boyd III (d), Suzanne, John, and David; committees: Appropriations; Budget; elected to the 105th Congress; reelected to each succeeding Congress.

Office Listings

http:/www.house.gov/boyd

1227 Longworth House Office Building, Washington, DC 20515 .... (202) 225–5235
Chief of Staff.—Melanie Morris. FAX: 225–5615
Legislative Director.—Kara Stencel.
Legislative Assistants: William Bridgemohan, Clint Cates, Josh Gifford.
Executive Assistant/Scheduler.—Renata Middleton.
1650 Summit Lake Drive, Suite 103, Tallahassee, FL 32317 .... (850) 561–3979
District Director.—Jerry Smithwick.
30 West Government Street, Panama City, FL 32401 .... (850) 785–0812
District Representative.—Carter Johnson.

Counties: BAY, CALHOUN, DIXIE, FRANKLIN, GADSDEN, GULF, JACKSON, JEFFERSON (part), LAFEYETTE, LEON (part), LIBERTY, OKALOOSA (part), SUWANNE, TAYLOR, WALKULLA, WALTON (part). Population (2000), 639,295.

ZIP Codes: 32008, 32013, 32024, 32038, 32055, 32060, 32062, 32064, 32066, 32071, 32094, 32096, 32126, 32140, 32170, 32175, 32267, 32301–18, 32320–24, 32326–34, 32336, 32343–44, 32346–48, 32351–53, 32355–62, 32395, 32399,

32401–13, 32417, 32420–21, 32423–24, 32426, 32428, 32430–32, 32437–38, 32440, 32442–49, 32454, 32456–57, 32459–61, 32465–66, 32541, 32550, 32578, 32628, 32648, 32680, 32692

* * *

THIRD DISTRICT

CORRINE BROWN, Democrat, of Jacksonville, FL; born in Jacksonville, November 11, 1946; education: B.S., Florida A&M University, 1969; master's degree, Florida A&M University, 1971; education specialist degree, University of Florida; honorary doctor of law, Edward Waters College; faculty member: Florida Community College in Jacksonville; University of Florida; and Edward Waters College; served in the Florida House of Representatives for 10 years; first woman elected chairperson of the Duval County Legislative Delegation; served as a consultant to the Governor's Committee on Aging; member: Congressional Black Caucus; Women's Caucus; and Progressive Caucus; Human Rights Caucus; Missing and Exploited Children's Caucus; Diabetes Caucus; Duma Study Group; Community College Caucus; Older Americans Caucus; one child: Shantrel; committees: Transportation and Infrastructure; Veterans' Affairs; elected on November 3, 1992, to the 103rd Congress; reelected to each succeeding Congress.

Office Listings

http://www.house.gov/corrinebrown

2336 Rayburn House Office Building, Washington, DC 20515 .... (202) 225–0123
Chief of Staff.—E. Ronnie Simmons. FAX: 225–2256
Executive Assistant/Scheduler.—Darla E. Smallwood.
Legislative Director.—Nick Martinelli.
Communications Director.—David Simon.
101 East Union Street, Suite 202, Jacksonville, FL 32202 .... (904) 354–1652
219 Lime Avenue, Orlando, FL 32802 .... (407) 872–0656

Counties: ALACHUA (part), CLAY (part), DUVAL (part), LAKE (part), MARION (part), ORANGE (part), PUTNAM (part), SEMINOLE (part), VOLUSIA (part). Population (2000), 639,295.

ZIP Codes: 32003, 32007, 32043, 32066, 32073, 32102, 32105, 32112–13, 32130–31, 32134, 32138, 32140, 32147–49, 32160, 32177, 32179–80, 32182, 32185, 32190, 32201–11, 32215–16, 32218–19, 32231–32, 32234, 32236, 32238–39, 32244, 32247, 32254, 32277, 32601–04, 32627, 32631, 32640–41, 32653–54, 32662, 32666–67, 32681, 32702–03, 32712–13, 32720–24, 32736, 32751, 32757, 32763, 32767–68, 32771–73, 32776, 32789, 32798, 32801, 32804–05, 32808–11, 32818–19, 32835, 32839, 32855, 32858, 32861, 32868, 33142, 33160–61, 33179, 34488, 34761

* * *

FOURTH DISTRICT

ANDER CRENSHAW, Republican, of Jacksonville, FL; born in Jacksonville, September 1, 1944; education: B.A., University of Georgia, 1966; J.D., University of Florida, 1969; professional: investment banker; religion: Episcopal; public service: former member of the Florida House of Representatives and the Florida State Senate; served as President of the Florida State Senate; married: Kitty; children: Sarah and Alex; committees: Appropriations; elected to the 107th Congress on November 7, 2000; reelected to each succeeding Congress.

Office Listings

http://www.crenshaw.house.gov

440 Cannon House Office Building, Washington, DC 20515 .... (202) 225–2501
Chief of Staff.—John Ariale. FAX: 225–2504
Legislative Director.—Erica Striebel.
Communications Director.—Barbara Riley.
1061 Riverside Avenue, Suite 100, Jacksonville, FL 32204 .... (904) 598–0481
District Director.—Jacqueline Smith.
212 North Marion Avenue, Suite 209, Lake City, FL 32055 .... (386) 365–3316

Counties: BAKER, COLUMBIA, DUVAL (part), HAMILTON, JEFFERSON (part), LEON (part), MADISON, NASSAU, UNION. CITIES AND TOWNSHIPS: Greenville, Hilliard, Jacksonville, Jacksonville Beach, Jasper, Jennings, Lake Butler, Lake City, Lee, Macclenny, Madison, Monticello, Nassau Village-Ratliff, Palm Valley, Tallahassee, White Springs, and Yulee. Population (2000), 639,295.

ZIP Codes: 32009, 32011, 32024–26, 32034–35, 32038, 32040–41, 32046, 32052–56, 32058–59, 32061, 32063, 32072, 32083, 32087, 32094, 32096–97, 32204–05, 32207, 32210–12, 32214, 32216–18, 32223–29, 32233–35, 32237, 32240–

41, 32244–46, 32250, 32255–58, 32266, 32277, 32301, 32311, 32317, 32331, 32336–37, 32340–41, 32344–45, 32350, 32643, 32697, 33142

* * *

FIFTH DISTRICT

GINNY BROWN-WAITE, Republican, of Brooksville, FL; born in Albany, NY, October 5, 1943; education: B.S., State University of New York, 1976; Russell Sage College, 1984; Labor Studies Program Certification, Cornell University; professional: served as a Legislative Director in the New York State Senate for almost 18 years; public service: Hernando County, FL, Commissioner; Florida State Senate, 1992–2002; served as Senate Majority Whip, and President Pro Tempore; recipient of numerous awards for community service; widow; children: three daughters; committees: Ways and Means; elected to the 108th Congress on November 5, 2002; reelected to each succeeding Congress.

Office Listings

http://www.house.gov/brown-waite

414 Cannon House Office Building, Washington, DC 20515 .... (202) 225–1002
Chief of Staff.—Pete Meachum. FAX: 226–6559
Executive Assistant.—Courtney Cannon.
Legislative Director.—Justin Grabelle.
Press Secretary.—Lindsay Gilbride.
16224 Spring Hill Drive, Brooksville, FL 34604 .... (352) 799–8354
15000 Citrus County Drive, Unit 100, Dade City Business Center, Dade City, FL 33523 .... (352) 567–6707

Counties: CITRUS, HERNANDO, LAKE (part), LEVY (part), MARION (part), PASCO (part), POLK (part), SUMTER. CITIES AND TOWNSHIPS: Brooksville, Dade City, and Clermont. Population (2000), 639,295.

ZIP Codes: 32159, 32162, 32621, 32625–26, 32635, 32639, 32644, 32658, 32668, 32683, 32696, 32778, 32825, 33513–14, 33521, 33523–26, 33537–38, 33540–44, 33548–49, 33556, 33558–59, 33574, 33576, 33585, 33593, 33597, 33809–10, 33849, 33868, 34218, 34220, 34423, 34428–34, 34436, 34442, 34445–53, 34460–61, 34464–65, 34481–82, 34484, 34487, 34498, 34601–11, 34613–14, 34636, 34639, 34653–55, 34661, 34667, 34669, 34711–13, 34731, 34736–37, 34748, 34753, 34755, 34762, 34785, 34787–89, 34797

* * *

SIXTH DISTRICT

CLIFF STEARNS, Republican, of Ocala, FL; born in Washington, DC, April 16, 1941; education: graduated, Woodrow Wilson High, Washington, DC, 1959; B.S., electrical engineering, George Washington University, Washington, DC, 1963; Air Force ROTC Distinguished Military Graduate; graduate work, University of California, Los Angeles, 1965; served, U.S. Air Force (captain), 1963–67; businessman; past president: Silver Springs Kiwanis; member: Marion County/Ocala Energy Task Force, Tourist Development Council, Ocala Board of Realtors, American Hotel/Motel Association in Florida, American Hotel/Motel Association of the United States, Grace Presbyterian Church; board of directors, Boys Club of Ocala; trustee: Munroe Regional Hospital; married: the former Joan Moore; children: Douglas, Bundy, and Scott; committees: Energy and Commerce; Veterans' Affairs; elected November 8, 1988, to the 101st Congress; reelected to each succeeding Congress.

Office Listings

http://www.house.gov/stearns

2370 Rayburn House Office Building, Washington, DC 20515 .... (202) 225–5744
Chief of Staff.—Jack Seum. FAX: 225–3973
Legislative Director.—Matt Mandel.
Scheduler / Office Manager.—Joan Smutko.
115 Southeast 25th Avenue, Ocala, FL 34471 .... (352) 351–8777
District Manager.—John Konkus.
5700 S.W. 34th Street, #425, Gainesville, FL 32608 .... (352) 337–0003
1726 Kinglsey Avenue S.E., Suite 8, Orange Park, FL 32073 .... (904) 269–3203

Counties: ALACHUA (part), BRADFORD, CLAY (part), DUVAL (part), GILCHREST, LAKE (part), LEVY (part), MARION (part). CITIES AND TOWNSHIPS: Ocala, Gainesville, Leesburg, Orange Park, Middleburg, and Jacksonville. Population (2000), 639,295.

ZIP Codes: 32003, 32006, 32008, 32030, 32042–44, 32050, 32054, 32058, 32065, 32067–68, 32073, 32079, 32083, 32091, 32099, 32111, 32113, 32133, 32140, 32158–59, 32162, 32179, 32183, 32195, 32205, 32210, 32215, 32219–22, 32234,

32244, 32254, 32276, 32601, 32603, 32605–12, 32614–16, 32618–19, 32621–22, 32631, 32633–34, 32643, 32653, 32655–56, 32658, 32663–64, 32666–69, 32681, 32686, 32693–94, 32696, 33142, 33160–61, 34420–21, 34432, 34436, 34470–76, 34478, 34480–83, 34491–92, 34731, 34748–49

* * *

SEVENTH DISTRICT

JOHN L. MICA, Republican, of Winter Park, FL; born in Binghamton, NY, January 27, 1943; education: graduated, Miami-Edison High School, Miami, FL; B.A., University of Florida, 1967; professional: president, MK Development; managing general partner, Cellular Communications; former government affairs consultant, Mica, Dudinsky and Associates; executive director, Local Government Study Commissions, Palm Beach County, 1970–72; executive director, Orange County Local Government Study Commission, 1972–74; Florida State House of Representatives, 1976–80; administrative assistant, U.S. Senator Paula Hawkins, 1980–85; Florida State Good Government Award, 1973; one of five Florida Jaycees Outstanding Young Men of America, 1978; member: Kiwanis, U.S. Capitol Preservation Commission, Tiger Bay Club, co-chairman, Speaker's Task Force for a Drug Free America, Florida Blue Key; U.S. Capitol Preservation Commission; brother of former Congressman Daniel A. Mica; married: the former Patricia Szymanek, 1972; children: D'Anne Leigh and John Clark; committees: Oversight and Government Reform; Transportation and Infrastructure; elected on November 3, 1992 to the 103rd Congress; reelected to each succeeding Congress.

Office Listings

http://www.house.gov/mica

2313 Rayburn House Office Building, Washington, DC 20515 .... (202) 225–4035
Chief of Staff.—Russell L. Roberts. FAX: 226–0821
Executive Assistant / Scheduler.—Alicia Melvin.
Legislative Director / Press Secretary.—Brian Waldrip.
100 East Sybelia Avenue, #340, Maitland, FL 32751 .... (407) 657–8080
840 Deltona Boulevard, Suite G, Deltona, FL 32725 .... (386) 860–1499
770 West Granada Boulevard, Suite 315, Ormond Beach, FL 32174 .... (386) 676–7750
3000 North Ponce de Leon Boulevard, Suite 1, St. Augustine, FL 32084 .... (904) 810–5048
2509 Crill Avenue, #200, Palatka, FL 32177 .... (386) 328–1622
1 Florida Park Drive South, Suite 100, Palm Coast, FL 32137 .... (386) 246–6042

Counties: ORANGE COUNTY (part). CITIES AND TOWNSHIPS: Maitland, Winter Park. SEMINOLE COUNTY. CITIES AND TOWNSHIPS: Altamonte Springs, Casselberry, Heathrow, Lake Mary, Longwood, Sanford, Winter Springs. VOLUSIA COUNTY (part). CITIES AND TOWNSHIPS: Daytona Beach, Debary, Deland, Deltona, Holly Hill, Lake Helen, Orange City, Ormond Beach, Pierson. FLAGLER COUNTY. CITIES AND TOWNSHIPS: Beverly Beach, Bunnell, Flagler Beach, Marineland, Palm Coast. ST. JOHNS COUNTY. CITIES AND TOWNSHIPS: Hastings, Ponte Vedra Beach, St. Augustine, St. Augustine Beach. PUTNAM COUNTY (part). CITIES AND TOWNSHIPS: Crescent City, Palatka, Pomona Park, and Welaka. Population, (2000), 639,295.

ZIP Codes: 32004, 32033, 32080, 32082, 32084–86, 32092, 32095, 32110, 32112, 32114–22, 32125, 32130–31, 32135–37, 32139, 32142, 32145, 32151, 32157, 32164, 32173–78, 32180–81, 32187, 32189, 32193, 32198, 32259–60, 32701, 32706–08, 32713–15, 32718, 32720, 32724–25, 32728, 32730, 32738, 32744, 32746–47, 32750–53, 32763–64, 32771, 32773–74, 32779, 32789, 32791–92, 32795, 32799

* * *

EIGHTH DISTRICT

ALAN GRAYSON, Democrat, of Orlando, FL; born in Bronx, NY, March 13, 1958; education: graduated from Bronx High School of Science, Bronx, NY; A.B., Harvard University, Cambridge, MA, 1978; M.P.P., Harvard University, Cambridge, MA, 1983; J.D., Harvard University, Cambridge, MA, 1983; professional: assistant, U.S. Circuit Court of Appeals, Washington, DC; President of IDT Corporation; co-founder of the Alliance for Aging Research, attorney; partner in the law firm of Grayson and Kubli; married: Lolita Grayson; children: Skye, Star, Sage, Storm, and Stone; committees: Financial Services; Science and Technology; elected to the 111th Congress on November 4, 2008.

Office Listings

http://www.grayson.house.gov

1605 Longworth House Office Building, Washington, DC 20515 .... (202) 225–2176
Chief of Staff.—Julie Tagen. FAX: 225–0999
Deputy Chief of Staff.—Aysha Moshi.
445 North Garland Avenue, Suite 402, Orlando, FL 32801 .... (407) 841–1757
FAX: 841–1754

416 West Main Street, Tavares, FL 32778 .... (407) 841–1757
FAX: 841–1754

Counties: ORANGE (part), OSCEOLA (part), MARION (part), LAKE (part). CITIES AND TOWNSHIPS: Astatula, Azalea, Bay Hill, Bay Lake, Belle Isle, Belleview, Celebration, Conway, Doctor Phillips, Edgewood, Eustis, Fairview Shores, Howey-in-the-Hills, Holden Heights, Leesburg, Meadow Wood, Mid Florida Lakes, Montverde, Oakland, Ocala Part, Ocoee, Orlando, Silver Springs Shores, Sky Lakes, Tavares, Umatilla, Union Park, Williamsburg, Windermere, Winter Garden, and Winter Park. Population (2000), 639,295.

ZIP Codes: 32113, 32179, 32192, 32617, 32702–03, 32710, 32726–27, 32735–36, 32756–57, 32777–78, 32784, 32789, 32792, 32801–07, 32809–12, 32814, 32817–19, 32821–22, 32824–25, 32827, 32829–30, 32835–37, 32839, 32853–54, 32856–57, 32859–60, 32862, 32867, 32869, 32872, 32877, 32885–87, 32890–91, 32893, 32896–98, 33030, 33032–33, 33161, 33186, 34470–72, 34475, 34479–80, 34488–89, 34705, 34711, 34729, 34734, 34740, 34746–47, 34756, 34760–61, 34777–78, 34786–88

* * *

NINTH DISTRICT

GUS M. BILIRAKIS, Republican, of Palm Harbor, FL; born in Gainesville, FL, February 8, 1963; raised in Tarpon Springs, FL; education: B.A., University of Florida, 1986; J.D., Stetson University, 1989; son of former Representative Michael Bilirakis (1983–2006); volunteered on his father's congressional campaigns; interned for President Ronald Reagan and the National Republican Congressional Committee; worked for former Representative Don Sundquist (R–TN); ran the Bilirakis Law Group, specializing in wills, trusts, and estate planning, Holiday, FL; taught government classes, St. Petersburg College; member of the Florida House of Representatives, 1998–2006; chaired several prominent panels in the State House, including Crime Prevention, Public Safety Appropriations, and the Economic Development, Trade, and Banking Committee; married: Eva; children: Michael, Teddy, Manuel, and Nicholas; Senior Republican Freshman Whip; committees: Foreign Affairs; Homeland Security; Veterans' Affairs; elected to the 110th Congress on November 7, 2006; reelected to the 111th Congress.

Office Listings

http://bilirakis.house.gov

1124 Longworth House Office Building, Washington, DC 20515 .... (202) 225–5755
Chief of Staff.—Terry Carmack. FAX: 225–4085
Press Secretary.—David Peluso.
Executive Assistant.—Jennifer Dombrowski.
Palm Harbor Professional Center, 35111 U.S. Highway 19 North, Suite 301, Palm Harbor, FL 34684 .... (727) 773–2871
District Director.—Shawn Foster.
10941 North 56th Street, Temple Terrace, FL 33617 .... (813) 985–8541

Counties: HILLSBOROUGH (part), PASCO (part), PINELLAS (part). CITIES AND TOWNSHIPS: Bearss, Bloomingdale, Brandon, Carrollwood Village, Citrus Park, Clearwater, Countryside, Crystal Springs, Dale Mabry, Eastlake Woodlands, Elfers, Fishhawk, Holiday, Hudson, Hunters Green, Lutz, New Port Richey, Odessa, Oldsmar, Palm Harbor, Plant City, Safety Harbor, Seffner, Seven Springs, Tarpon Springs, Temple Terrace, Thonotosassa, Trinity, Valrico, and Veterans Village. Population (2000), 639,296.

ZIP Codes: 33511, 33527, 33530, 33539–40, 33542, 33547–49, 33556, 33558–59, 33563, 33565–67, 33569, 33583–84, 33587, 33592, 33594–95, 33598, 33612–13, 33617–18, 33624–26, 33637, 33647, 33688, 33755–59, 33761, 33763–66, 33769, 33810, 34652–56, 34667–69, 34673–74, 34677, 34679–80, 34683–85, 34688–91, 34695

* * *

TENTH DISTRICT

C. W. BILL YOUNG, Republican, of Indian Shores, FL; born in Harmarville, PA, December 16, 1930; elected Florida's only Republican State Senator in 1960; reelected 1964, 1966, 1967 (special election), and 1968, serving as minority leader from 1963 to 1970; national committeeman, Florida Young Republicans, 1957–59; state chairman, Florida Young Republicans, 1959–61; member, Florida Constitution Revision Commission, 1965–67; dean of the Florida Republican delegation; the senior Republican in the Congress; married: Beverly; children: three sons; committees: Appropriations; elected to the 92nd Congress, November 3, 1970; reelected to each succeeding Congress.

Office Listings

2407 Rayburn House Office Building, Washington, DC 20515 .... (202) 225–5961
Chief of Staff.—Harry Glenn. FAX: 225–9764
Legislative Director.—Brad Stine.
Defense Appropriations.—Tom Rice.
360 Central Avenue, Suite 1480, St. Petersburg, FL 33701 .... (727) 893–3191
9210 113th Street, Seminole, FL 33772 .... (727) 394–6950

Counties: PINELLAS COUNTY (part). Population (2000), 639,295.

ZIP Codes: 33701–16, 33729, 33731–32, 33734, 33736–38, 33740–44, 33755–56, 33760–65, 33767, 33770–82, 33784–86, 34660, 34681–84, 34697–98

* * *

ELEVENTH DISTRICT

KATHY CASTOR, Democrat, of Tampa, FL; born in Miami, FL, August 20, 1966; education: B.A., Political Science, Emory University, 1988; J.D., Florida State University, 1991; professional: Assistant General Counsel, State of Florida, Department of Community Affairs, 1991–94; attorney, Icard Merrill, 1994–95; partner, Broad and Cassel, 1995–2000; ran for Florida State Senate, 2000; Hillsborough County Commissioner, 2002–06; religion: member of Palma Ceia Presbyterian Church; married: William Lewis; children: two; committees: Energy and Commerce; Standards of Official Conduct; elected to the 110th Congress on November 7, 2006; reelected to the 111th Congress.

Office Listings

http://castor.house.gov

317 Cannon House Office Building, Washington, DC 20515 .... (202) 225–3376
Chief of Staff.—Clay Phillips. FAX: 225–5652
Legislative Director.—Courtney Christian.
Scheduler.—Lara Hopkins.
4144 North Armenia Avenue, Suite 300, Tampa, FL 33607 .... (813) 871–2817
District Director.—Chloe Coney.
Press Secretary.—Ellen Gedalius.

Counties: HILLSBOROUGH (part), MANATEE (part), PINELLAS (part). CITIES: Apollo Beach, Bradenton, Carrollwood, Carrollwood Village, Citrus Park, Ellenton, Gibsonton, Gulfport, Lutz, Northdale, Oldsmar, Palmetto, Riverview, Ruskin, St. Petersburg, Tampa, Temple Terrace, and Town 'N' Country, Ybor City. Population (2000), 639,295.

ZIP Codes: 33534, 33549, 33559, 33569–70, 33572, 33586, 33601–19, 33621–26, 33629–31, 33634–35, 33637, 33647, 33650–51, 33655, 33663–64, 33672–75, 33677, 33679–82, 33684–87, 33690, 33694, 33697, 33701, 33705, 33707, 33710–13, 33730, 33733, 33747, 33784, 34205, 34208, 34221–22, 34677

* * *

TWELFTH DISTRICT

ADAM H. PUTNAM, Republican, of Bartow, FL; born in Bartow, FL, July 31, 1974; education: Bartow High School; University of Florida, B.S., Food and Resource Economics; professional: farmer; rancher; awards: Outstanding Male Graduate of the University of Florida; Who's Who in American Politics; organizations: Florida 4–H Foundation; Sheriff's Youth Villa Board of Associates; Chamber of Commerce; Polk County Farm Bureau; public service: Florida House of Representatives, 1996–2000; married: Melissa; committees: Financial Services; elected to the 107th Congress on November 7, 2000; reelected to each succeeding Congress.

Office Listings

http://www.house.gov/putnam

442 Cannon House Office Building, Washington, DC 20515 .... (202) 225–1252
Chief of Staff / Director of Communications.—Charles Cooper. FAX: 226–0585
Executive Assistant.—Kristene Henkelman.
Legislative Director.—Karen Williams.
650 East Davidson Street, Bartow, FL 33830 .... (863) 534–3530
District Director.—Cheryl Fulford.

Counties: HILLSBOROUGH (part), OSCEOLA (part), POLK (part). CITIES AND TOWNSHIPS: Apollo Beach, Auburndale, Babson Park, Bartow, Brandon, Davenport, Dundee, Eagle Lake, Fort Meade, Frostproof, Gibsonton, Haines City, Highland

City, Hillcrest Heights, Indian Lake Estates, Lakeland, Lake Alfred, Lake Hamilton, Lake Wales, Mulberry, Plant City, Poinciana, Polk City, Riverview, Ruskin, Seffner, Sun City Center, Tampa, Temple Terrace, Thonotosassa, Wimauma, and Winter Haven. Population (2000), 639,296.

ZIP Codes: 33030, 33033, 33170, 33183, 33186, 33503, 33508–11, 33527, 33534, 33547, 33550, 33563–64, 33566–73, 33575, 33584, 33592, 33594, 33598, 33610, 33617, 33619, 33637, 33689, 33801–07, 33809–11, 33813, 33815, 33820, 33823, 33825, 33827, 33830–31, 33834–41, 33843–47, 33850–51, 33853–56, 33859–60, 33863, 33867–68, 33877, 33880–85, 33888, 33896–98, 34758–59

* * *

THIRTEENTH DISTRICT

VERN BUCHANAN, Republican, of Longboat Key, FL; born in Detroit, MI, May 8, 1951; education: B.B.A., Business Administration, Cleary University; M.B.A., University of Detroit; honorary degree: Doctorate of Science in Business Administration, Cleary University; professional: founder and chairman, Buchanan Enterprises; founder and chairman, Buchanan Automotive Group, 1992; operations include Sarasota Ford and 18 auto franchises in the southeastern United States; experience in real estate including home building and property development and management; awards: One of America's Ten Outstanding Young Men, U.S. Jaycees; Entrepreneur of the Year, Inc. Magazine and Arthur Young; Entrepreneur of the Year, Harvard Business School, Club of Detroit; One of Michigan's Five Outstanding Young Men, Michigan Jaycees; President's Award, Ford Motor Company; Certified Retailer Award, J.D. Power and Associates; Outstanding Citizen Award, United Negro College Fund; Outstanding Philanthropic Corporation Award, National Society of Fund Raising Executives; Freedom Award for Business and Industry, NAACP; The American Jewish Committee Civic Achievement Award; Tampa Bay Business Hall of Fame Award; married: Sandy Buchanan; children: James and Matt; committees: Small Business; Transportation and Infrastructure; Veterans' Affairs; elected to the 110th Congress on November 7, 2006; reelected to the 111th Congress.

Office Listings

http://www.buchanan.house.gov

218 Cannon House Office Building, Washington, DC 20515 .... (202) 225–5015
Chief of Staff.—Dave Karvelas. FAX: 226–0828
Deputy Chief of Staff.—Don Green.
Legislative Director.—Shane Lieberman.
Scheduler.—Sydney Gruters.
235 North Orange Avenue, Suite 201, Sarasota, FL 34236 .... (941) 951–6643
District Director.—Sally Tibbetts.
2424 Manatee Avenue West, Suite 104, Bradenton, FL 34205 .... (941) 747–9081

Counties: CHARLOTTE (part), DESOTO, HARDEE, MANATEE (part), SARASOTA. Population (2000), 639,295.

ZIP Codes: 33138, 33160–61, 33598, 33834, 33865, 33873, 33890, 33946–47, 34201–12, 34215–19, 34221–24, 34228–43, 34250–51, 34260, 34264–70, 34272, 34274–78, 34280–82, 34284–89, 34292–93, 34295

* * *

FOURTEENTH DISTRICT

CONNIE MACK, Republican, of Fort Myers, FL; born in Fort Myers, August 12, 1967; education: B.S., University of Florida, Gainesville, FL, 1993; professional: marketing executive; member, Florida state House of Representatives, 2000–03; son of U.S. Senator Connie Mack III, step-great-grandson of Senator Tom Connally, great-grandson of Senator Morris Sheppard, and great-great-grandson of Congressman John Levi Sheppard; married: U.S. Representative Mary Bono Mack; children: Addison and Connie; committees: Budget; Foreign Affairs; Transportation and Infrastructure; elected to the 109th Congress on November 2, 2004; reelected to each succeeding Congress.

Office Listings

http://mack.house.gov

115 Cannon House Office Building, Washington, DC 20515 .... (202) 225–2536
Chief of Staff.—Jeff Cohen. FAX: 226–0439
Legislative Director.—Francis Gibbs.
Press Secretary.—Stephanie DuBois.
Executive Assistant.—Mackenzie Miles.
804 Nicholas Parkway East, Suite 1, Cape Coral, FL 33990 .... (239) 573–5837

3301 Tamiami Trail E, Building F, First Floor, Naples, FL 34112 .... (239) 252–6225

Counties: CHARLOTTE (part), COLLIER (part), LEE. Population (2000), 639,295.

ZIP Codes: 33030, 33033, 33160, 33186, 33189, 33901–22, 33924, 33927–28, 33931–32, 33936, 33945–46, 33948, 33953–57, 33965, 33970–72, 33981, 33990–91, 33993–94, 34101–10, 34112–14, 34116, 34119, 34133–36, 34140, 34142, 34145–46, 34224

* * *

FIFTEENTH DISTRICT

BILL POSEY, Republican, of Rockledge, FL; born in Washington, DC, December 18, 1947; education: graduated Cocoa High School, 1966; A.A., Brevard Community College, Cocoa, FL; National Legislator of the Year by the American Legislative Exchange Council; married: Katie Posey; children: Pamela and Catherine; member, House Aerospace Caucus, Republican Study Committee; committees: Financial Services; elected to the 111th Congress on November 4, 2008.

Office Listings

http://www.posey.house.gov

132 Cannon House Office Building, Washington, DC 20515 .... (202) 225–3671
Chief of Staff.—Dana Gartzke. FAX: 225–3516
Deputy Chief of Staff.—Stuart Burns.
Scheduler.—Jessie Rager.
2725 Judge Fran Jamieson Way Building C, Melbourne, FL 32940 .... (321) 632–1776
District Director.—Kathryn Rudloff.

Counties: BREVARD (part), INDIAN RIVER, OSCEOLA (part), POLK (part). Population (2000), 639,295.

ZIP Codes: 32815, 32899, 32901–12, 32919–20, 32922–26, 32931–32, 32934–37, 32940–41, 32948–53, 32955–58, 32960–71, 32976, 32978, 33837, 33848, 33858, 33868, 33896–98, 34739, 34741–47, 34758–59, 34769–73, 34972

* * *

SIXTEENTH DISTRICT

THOMAS J. ROONEY, Republican, of Tequesta, FL; born in Philadelphia, PA, November 21, 1970; education: B.A., Washington and Jefferson, Washington, PA; M.A., University of Florida, Gainesville, FL; J.D., University of Miami, Coral Gables, FL; member, Roman Catholic Church; married: Tara; children: Tommy, Sean, and Seamus; committees: Armed Services; Judiciary; elected to the 111th Congress on November 4, 2008.

Office Listings

http://www.rooney.house.gov

1529 Longworth House Office Building, Washington, DC 20515 .... (202) 225–5792
Chief of Staff.—Brian Crawford. FAX: 225–3132
Communications Director.—Jeffrey Ostermayer.
335 South East Ocean Boulevard, Stuart, FL 34994 .... (772) 288–4668
226 Taylor Street, Suite 200, Punta Gorda, FL 33950 .... (941) 575–9101

Counties: CHARLOTTE (part), GLADES, HENDRY (part), HIGHLANDS, MARTIN (part), OKEECHOBEE, PALM BEACH (part), ST. LUCIE (part). Population (2000), 639,295.

ZIP Codes: 33138, 33160–61, 33170, 33186, 33410–12, 33414, 33418, 33421, 33440, 33455, 33458, 33467, 33469–71, 33475, 33477–78, 33825–26, 33852, 33857, 33862, 33870–72, 33875–76, 33917, 33920, 33930, 33935, 33938, 33944, 33948–55, 33960, 33972, 33975, 33980, 33982–83, 34142, 34945–47, 34949–53, 34956–58, 34972–74, 34981–88, 34990–92, 34994–97

* * *

SEVENTEENTH DISTRICT

KENDRICK B. MEEK, Democrat, of Miami, FL; born in Miami, September 6, 1966; education: B.S., Florida A&M University, 1989; organizations: NAACP; 100 Black Men of

America, Inc.; Greater Miami Service Corps; Omega Psi Phi Fraternity; awards: Mothers Against Drunk Driving Outstanding Service Award; Ebony Magazine's 50 Leaders of Tomorrow; Adams-Powell Civil Rights Award; public service: Florida House of Representatives, 1994–98; Florida State Senate, 1998–2002; married: Leslie Dixon; children: Lauren and Kendrick B., Jr.; son of former Florida U.S. Representative Carrie P. Meek; committees: Ways and Means; elected to the 108th Congress on November 5, 2002; reelected to each succeeding Congress.

Office Listings

http://www.house.gov/kenmeek

1039 Longworth House Office Building, Washington, DC 20515 .... (202) 225–4506
Chief of Staff.—John Schelble. FAX: 226–0777
Senior Advisor.—Tasha Cole.
Legislative Director.—Clarence Williams.
Scheduler.—Portia Hickson.
111 N.W. 183rd Street, Suite 315, Miami Gardens, FL 33169 .... (305) 690–5905
District Office Director.—Joyce Postell.
10100 Pines Boulevard, 3rd Floor, Building B, Pembroke Pines, FL 33026 .... (954) 450–6767

Counties: DADE (part), BROWARD (part). Population (2000), 639,296.

ZIP Codes: 33008–09, 33013, 33020–25, 33054–56, 33081, 33083, 33090, 33092, 33101, 33110, 33127, 33136–38, 33142, 33147, 33150–51, 33156, 33160–62, 33164, 33167–69, 33179–81, 33197, 33238, 33242, 33247, 33256, 33261

* * *

EIGHTEENTH DISTRICT

ILEANA ROS-LEHTINEN, Republican, of Miami, FL; born in Havana, Cuba, July 15, 1952; education: B.A., English, Florida International University; M.S., educational leadership, Florida International University; Ed.D, University of Miami, 2004; certified Florida school teacher; founder and former owner, Eastern Academy; elected to Florida House of Representatives, 1982; elected to Florida State Senate, 1986; former president, Bilingual Private School Association; regular contributor to leading Spanish-language newspaper; during House tenure, married then-State Representative Dexter Lehtinen; children: Amanda Michelle and Patricia Marie; committees: Foreign Affairs; elected on August 29, 1989 to the 101st Congress; reelected to each succeeding Congress.

Office Listings

2470 Rayburn House Office Building, Washington, DC 20515 .... (202) 225–3931
Chief of Staff.—Arthur Estopinan. FAX: 225–5620
Deputy Director.—Christine del Portillo.
Legislative Director.—Sara Gamino.
Press Secretary.—Alex Cruz.
4960 S.W. 72nd Avenue, Suite 208, Miami, FL 33155 .... (305) 668–2285

Counties: DADE (part), MONROE (part). CITIES AND TOWNSHIPS: Coral Gables, Florida City, Homestead, Key Biscayne, Miami, Miami Beach, South Miami, and West Miami. Population (2000), 639,295.

ZIP Codes: 33001, 33030, 33032–34, 33036–37, 33039–45, 33050–52, 33070, 33109, 33111–12, 33114, 33119, 33121, 33124–36, 33139–46, 33149, 33154–59, 33165, 33170, 33174, 33176, 33186, 33189–90, 33195, 33197, 33199, 33231, 33233–34, 33239, 33243, 33245, 33255, 33257, 33265, 33296, 33299

* * *

NINETEENTH DISTRICT

ROBERT WEXLER, Democrat, of Boca Raton, FL; born in Queens, NY, January 2, 1961; education: graduate of Hollywood Hills High School; University of Florida, 1982; George Washington University Law School, 1985; admitted to the Florida bar in 1985; attorney; Florida State Senator, 1990–96; member: Palm Beach Planning and Zoning Commission, 1989–90, Palm Beach County Democratic Executive Committee, 1989–92, Palm Beach County Affordable Housing Committee, 1990–91, Florida Bar Association, South Palm Beach County Jewish Federation, Palm Beach County Anti-Defamation League; married to the former Laurie Cohen; three children; committees: Foreign Affairs; Judiciary; elected to the 105th Congress; reelected to each succeeding Congress.

Office Listings

2241 Rayburn House Office Building, Washington, DC 20515 .... (202) 225–3001
Chief of Staff.—Eric Johnson. FAX: 225–5974
Deputy Chief of Staff / Communications Director.—Joshua Rugin.
2500 North Military Trail, Suite 490, Boca Raton, FL 33431 .... (561) 988–6302
District Director.—Wendi Lipsich.
5790 Margate Boulevard, Margate, FL 33063 .... (954) 972–6454

Counties: BROWARD (part), PALM BEACH (part). CITIES AND TOWNSHIPS: Atlantis, Boca Raton, Boynton Beach, Coconut Creek, Coral Springs, Deerfield Beach, Delray Beach, Greenacres, Lake Worth, Lantana, Margate, Pompano Beach, and Tamarac. Population (2000) 639,295.

ZIP Codes: 33063–66, 33068–69, 33071, 33073, 33075–77, 33093, 33321, 33406, 33411, 33413–15, 33417, 33426, 33428, 33431, 33433–34, 33436–37, 33441–42, 33445–46, 33448, 33454, 33461–63, 33466–67, 33481–82, 33484, 33486–88, 33496–99

* * *

TWENTIETH DISTRICT

DEBBIE WASSERMAN SCHULTZ, Democrat, of Weston, FL; born in Forest Hills, Queens County, NY, September 27, 1966; education: B.A., University of Florida, Gainesville, FL, 1988; M.A., University of Florida, FL, 1990; professional: Public Policy Curriculum Specialist, Nova Southeastern University; Adjunct Instructor, Political Science, Broward Community College; aide to United States Representative Peter Deutsch, 1989–92; member, Florida State House of Representatives, 1992–2000; member, Florida State Senate, 2000–04; organizations: Board of Trustees, Westside Regional Medical Center; Outstanding Freshman Legislator, Florida Women's Political Caucus; Secretary; Board of Directors, American Jewish Congress; Member, Broward National Organization for Women; Board of Directors, National Safety Council, South Florida Chapter; religion: Jewish; married: Steve; children: Rebecca, Jake, Shelby; Senior Democratic Whip; committees: Appropriations; Judiciary; elected to the 109th Congress on November 2, 2004; reelected to each succeeding Congress.

Office Listings

http://www.house.gov/wasserman-schultz

118 Cannon House Office Building, Washington, DC 20515 .... (202) 225–7931
Chief of Staff.—Tracie Pough. FAX: 226–2052
Communications Director.—Jonathon Beeton.
Legislative Director.—Coby Dolan.
Office Manager.—Kate Houghton.
10100 Pines Boulevard, Pembroke Pines, FL 33026 .... (954) 437–3926
19200 West Country Club Drive, Third Floor, Aventura, FL 33180 .... (305) 936–5724

Counties: BROWARD COUNTY (PART). CITIES: Dania Beach, Davie, Lazy Lake, Plantation, Wilton Manors, Weston. DADE COUNTY (part). CITIES: Bay Harbor Island, North Bay Village, and Sunny Isles. MIAMI-DADE COUNTY (part). CITIES: Davie, Fort Lauderdale, Hollywood, Miami Beach, North Miami, Sunrise. Population (2000), 639,295.

ZIP Codes: 33004, 33009, 33019–21, 33024, 33026, 33030, 33033, 33084, 33137, 33139–41, 33147, 33154, 33156, 33160–61, 33170, 33180–81, 33301, 33304–05, 33309, 33311–15, 33317–19, 33321–32, 33334, 33336, 33338, 33345, 33351, 33355, 33394

* * *

TWENTY-FIRST DISTRICT

LINCOLN DIAZ-BALART, Republican, of Miami, FL; born in Havana, Cuba, August 13, 1954; education: graduated, American School of Madrid, Spain, 1972; B.A., New College of the University of South Florida, Sarasota, 1976; J.D., Case Western Reserve University Law School, 1979; professional: attorney; admitted to the Florida bar, 1979; partner, Fowler, White, Burnett, Hurley, Banick and Strickroot, P.A., Miami; Florida State House, 1986–89; Florida State Senate, 1989–92; founding member, Miami-Westchester Lions Club; member, Organization for Retarded Citizens; married the former Cristina Fernandez, 1976; two children: Lincoln Gabriel and Daniel; Assistant Republican Whip; Congressional Human Rights Caucus; committees: Rules; elected on November 3, 1992 to the 103rd Congress; reelected to each succeeding Congress.

Office Listings

http://diaz-balart.house.gov

2244 Rayburn House Office Building, Washington, DC 20515 .... (202) 225–4211
Chief of Staff.—Ana M. Carbonell. FAX: 225–8576
Administrative Assistant.—Towner French.
Legislative Director.—Cesar Gonzalez.
Press Secretary.—Andres Gonzalez.
8525 NW., 53 Terrace, Suite 102, Miami, FL 33166 .... (305) 470–8555
District Director.—Victoria Martinez.

Counties: BROWARD COUNTY (part), DADE COUNTY (part). CITIES AND TOWNSHIPS: Central Kendall, Doral, Fontainebleau, Hialeah, Miami Lakes, Miami Springs, Miramar, Pembroke Pines, Richmond Heights, Sweetwater, Virginia Gardens, and Westchester. Population (2000), 639,295.

ZIP Codes: 33002, 33010–17, 33027–29, 33054–55, 33082, 33102, 33107, 33116, 33122, 33126, 33143, 33148, 33152, 33155–58, 33165–66, 33172–74, 33176, 33178, 33186, 33188, 33266, 33283

* * *

TWENTY-SECOND DISTRICT

RON KLEIN, Democrat, of Boca Raton, FL; born in Cleveland, OH, July 7, 1957; education: graduated, Cleveland Heights High School, 1975; B.A., The Ohio State University, 1979; J.D., Case Western Reserve University Law School, 1982; professional: attorney; admitted to the Florida State Bar, 1986; former partner, Sachs, Sax & Klein, P.A.; elected to the Florida House of Representatives, District 90, 1992; reelected, 1994; elected to the Florida Senate, District 30, 1996; reelected in 2000, 2004; married to the former Dori Dragin, 1982; children: Brian and Lauren; committees: Financial Services; Foreign Affairs; elected to the 110th Congress on November 7, 2006; reelected to the 111th Congress.

Office Listings

http://www.klein.house.gov

313 Cannon House Office Building, Washington, DC 20515 .... (202) 225–3026
Chief of Staff.—Garrett Donovan. FAX: 225–8398
Legislative Director.—Mira Kogen Resnick.
Press Secretary.—Melissa Silverman.
Scheduler.—Jeff Champagne.
1900 Glades Road, Suite 260, Boca Raton, FL 33431 .... (561) 544–6910
District Director.—Felicia Goldstein.

Counties: BROWARD (part), PALM BEACH (part). CITIES: Aventura, Bal Harbour, Bay Harbor Islands, Biscayne Park, Boca Raton, Boynton Beach, Bring Breezes, Cloud Lake, Dania, Deerfield Beach, Delray Beach, Fort Lauderdale, Glen Ridge, Golden Beach, Gulf Stream, Hallandale, Highland Beach, Hillsboro Beach, Hollywood, Hypoluxo, Indian Creek, Juno Beach, Lake Park, Lake Worth, Lantana, Lauderdale by the Sea, Lazy Lake, Lighthouse Point, Manalapan, North Bay Village, North Palm Beach, Oakland Park, Ocean Ridge, Palm Beach, Palm Beach Gardens, Palm Beach Shores, Pembroke Park, Pompano Beach, Rivera Beach, Sea Ranch Lakes, South Palm Beach, Surfside, West Palm Beach, and Wilton Manors. Population (2000), 639,295.

ZIP Codes: 33004, 33009, 33015, 33033, 33060–62, 33064–65, 33067, 33071–74, 33076, 33097, 33128, 33153, 33155–56, 33161, 33163, 33165, 33179, 33186, 33189, 33280, 33301, 33303–09, 33312, 33314–17, 33324, 33328, 33334–35, 33339, 33346, 33348, 33401, 33403–08, 33410–12, 33415, 33418–20, 33424, 33426–27, 33429, 33431–36, 33441–45, 33458, 33460–64, 33468, 33477–78, 33480, 33483, 33486–87

* * *

TWENTY-THIRD DISTRICT

ALCEE L. HASTINGS, Democrat, of Miramar, FL; born in Altamonte Springs, FL, September 5, 1936; education: graduated, Crooms Academy, Sanford, FL, 1954; B.A., Fisk University, Nashville, TN, 1958; Howard University, Washington, DC; J.D., Florida A&M University, Tallahassee, 1963; attorney; admitted to the Florida bar, 1963; circuit judge, U.S. District Court for the Southern District of Florida; member: African Methodist Episcopal Church, NAACP, Miami-Dade Chamber of Commerce, Family Christian Association, ACLU, Southern Poverty Law Center, National Organization for Women, Planned Parenthood, Women and Children First, Inc., Sierra Club, Cousteau Society, Broward County Democratic Executive Committee, Dade County Democratic Executive Committee, Lauderhill Democratic Club, Hollywood Hills Democratic Club, Pembroke Pines Democratic Club, Urban League, National Bar Association, Florida Chapter of the National Bar Association, T.J. Reddick Bar Association, National Conference of Black Lawyers, Simon Wiesenthal Center, The Furtivist Society; Progressive Black Police Officers Club, International Black Firefighters Association; co-chair, Florida Delegation; co-chair, Helsinki Commission; three children: Alcee Lamar II, Chelsea, and Leigh; committees: vice chair, Permanent Select Committee on Intelligence; Rules; Senior Democratic Whip; elected on November 3, 1992, to the 103rd Congress; reelected to each succeeding Congress.

Office Listings

http://www.house.gov/alceehastings

2353 Rayburn House Office Building, Washington, DC 20515 .... (202) 225–1313
Chief of Staff.—David Goldenberg. FAX: 225–1171
Legislative Assistants: Eve Lieberman, Audrey Nicoleau.
Office Manager / Scheduler.—Barbara Harper.
2701 West Oakland Park Boulevard, Suite 200, Ft. Lauderdale, FL 33311 .... (954) 733–2800
Chief of Staff.—Arthur W. Kennedy.
Mangonia Park Town Hall, 1755 East Tiffany Drive, Mangonia Park, FL 33407 .... (561) 881–9618

Counties: BROWARD (part), HENDRY (part), MARTIN (part), PALM BEACH (part), ST. LUCIE (part). Population (2000), 639,295.

ZIP Codes: 33025, 33027–28, 33033, 33060, 33064, 33066, 33068–69, 33142, 33155–56, 33158, 33160–61, 33179, 33269, 33301–02, 33304–05, 33309–13, 33315, 33317, 33319–22, 33330–32, 33334, 33340, 33349, 33351, 33359, 33401–09, 33411, 33413–17, 33425, 33430, 33435, 33437–41, 33444–45, 33447, 33459–62, 33465, 33467, 33470, 33476, 33483, 33493, 34945–48, 34950–51, 34954, 34956, 34972, 34974, 34979, 34981, 34986–87

* * *

TWENTY-FOURTH DISTRICT

SUZANNE M. KOSMAS, Democrat of New Smyrna Beach, FL; born in Arlington, VA, February 25, 1944; education: B.S., Stetson University, DeLand, FL, 1998; professional: former owner of Prestige Properties Real Estate; public service: Florida House of Representatives, 1997–2004; chair, Board of United Way of Volusia County; Executive Board Member at United Way of Women's Initiative, the Atlantic Center for the Arts; Friends of Spruce Creek Preserve, and Southeast Volusia Habitat for Humanity, Vice President of Volusia / Flagler Boys & Girls Club; religion: Methodist; children: Paul, Michael, David, and Kristen; committees: Financial Services, Science and Technology; elected to the 111th Congress on November 4, 2008.

Office Listings

http://www.kosmas.house.gov

238 Cannon House Office Building, Washington, DC 20515 .... (202) 225–2706
Chief of Staff.—Leslie Pollner. FAX: 226–6299
Deputy Chief of Staff / Legislative Director.—Chris Matthiesen.
Scheduler.—Kristen Tilley.
12424 Research Parkway, Suite 135, Orlando, FL 32826 .... (407) 208–1106
1000 City Center Circle, 2nd Floor, Port Orange, FL 32129 .... (386) 756–9798

Counties: BREVARD (part), ORANGE (part), SEMINOLE (part), VOLUSIA (part). Population (2000), 639,295.

ZIP Codes: 32114, 32118–19, 32123–24, 32127–29, 32132, 32141, 32168–70, 32701, 32703–04, 32707–09, 32712, 32714, 32716, 32719, 32732–33, 32738–39, 32751, 32754, 32757, 32759, 32762, 32764–66, 32775, 32779–83, 32789–90, 32792–94, 32796, 32798, 32810, 32816–17, 32820, 32824–29, 32831–33, 32878, 32922, 32926–27, 32953–54, 32959, 33313, 33319, 33337, 33388

* * *

TWENTY-FIFTH DISTRICT

MARIO DIAZ-BALART, Republican, of Miami, FL; born in Ft. Lauderdale, FL, September 25, 1961; education: University of South Florida; professional: President, Gordon Diaz-Balart and Partners (public relations and marketing business); religion: Catholic; public service: Administrative Assistant to the Mayor of Miami, 1985–88; Florida House of Representatives, 1988–92, and 2000–02; Florida State Senate, 1992–2000; committees: Budget; Science and Technology; Transportation and Infrastructure; elected to the 108th Congress on November 5, 2002; reelected to each succeeding Congress.

Office Listings

http://www.house.gov/mariodiaz-balart

328 Cannon House Office Building, Washington, DC 20515 .... (202) 225–2778
Chief of Staff.—Nilda Pedrosa. FAX: 226–0346
Legislative Director.—Lauren Robitaille.
12851 SW 42nd Street, Suite 131, Miami, FL 33175 .... (305) 225–6866
District Director.—Miguel Otero.
4715 Golden Gate Parkway, Suite 1, Naples, FL 34116 .... (239) 348–1620
District Representative.—George Barton.

Counties: COLLIER (part), DADE (part). Population (2000), 639,295.

ZIP Codes: 33015–16, 33018, 33030–35, 33157, 33166, 33170, 33175–78, 33182–87, 33189–90, 33193–94, 33196, 34113–14, 34116–17, 34120, 34137–39, 34141–43

GEORGIA

(Population 2000, 8,186,453)

SENATORS

SAXBY CHAMBLISS, Republican, of Moultrie, GA; born in Warrenton, NC, November 10, 1943; education: graduated, C.E. Byrd High School, Shreveport, LA, 1962; B.B.A., University of Georgia, 1966; J.D., University of Tennessee College of Law, 1968; professional: served on the state bar of Georgia's Disciplinary Review Panel, 1969; member: Moultrie-Colquitt County Economic Development Authority; Colquitt County Economic Development Corporation; married: the former Julianne Frohbert, 1966; children: Lia Chambliss Baker, and C. Saxby (Bo), Jr.; committees: ranking member, Agriculture, Nutrition, and Forestry; Armed Services; Rules and Administration; Joint Committee on Printing; Select Committee on Intelligence; Special Committee on Aging; elected to the 104th Congress; reelected to each succeeding Congress; elected to the U.S. Senate on November 5, 2002; reelected to the U.S. Senate on November 4, 2008.

Office Listings

http://chambliss.senate.gov

416 Russell Senate Office Building, Washington, DC 20510 .... (202) 224–3521 FAX: 224–0103
Chief of Staff.—Charlie Harman.
Office Manager.—Kate Vickers.
Executive Assistant.—Teresa Ervin.
Legislative Director.—Monty Philpot.
Communications Director.—Bronwyn Lance Chester.
100 Galleria Parkway, Suite 1340, Atlanta, GA 30339 .... (770) 763–9090
State Director.—Steven Meeks.
419–A South Main Street, P.O. Box 3217, Moultrie, GA 31776 .... (229) 985–2112
Field Representative.—Debbie Cannon.
P.O. Box 13832, Savannah, GA 31416 .... (800) 234–4208
Field Representative.—Kathryn Murph.
1054 Claussen Road, Suite 313, Augusta, GA 30907 .... (706) 738–0302
Field Representative.—Jim Hussey.
300 Mulberry Street, Suite 502, Macon, GA 31201 .... (478) 741–1417 FAX: 471–1437

* * *

JOHNNY ISAKSON, Republican, of Marietta GA; born in Fulton County, GA, December 28, 1944; education: University of Georgia; professional: real estate executive; president, Northside Realty; public service: Georgia State House of Representatives, 1976–90; Georgia State Senate, 1992–96; appointed chairman of the Georgia Board of Election, 1996; awards: Republican National Committee ''Best Legislator in America,'' 1989; organizations: chairman of the board, Georgian Club; trustee, Kennesaw State University; board of directors, Metro Atlanta and Georgia Chambers of Commerce; past president, Cobb Chamber of Commerce; executive committee, National Association of Realtors; president, Realty Alliance; advisory board, Federal National Mortgage Association; married: Dianne; children: John, Kevin, and Julie; religion: Methodist; election to the 106th Congress on February 23, 1999, by special election; reelected to each succeeding Congress; committees: vice chair, Select Committee on Ethics; Commerce, Science, and Transportation; Foreign Relations; Health, Education, Labor, and Pensions; Small Business and Entrepreneurship; Veterans' Affairs; elected to the U.S. Senate on November 2, 2004.

Office Listings

http://isakson.senate.gov

120 Russell Senate Office Building, Washington, DC 20510 .... (202) 224–3643 FAX: 228–0724
Chief of Staff.—Chris Carr.
Deputy Chief of Staff / Communications Director.—Joan Kirchner.
Scheduler.—Molly Manning.
One Overton Park, 3625 Cumberland Boulevard, Suite 970, Atlanta, GA 30339 ..... (770) 661–0999

REPRESENTATIVES

FIRST DISTRICT

JACK KINGSTON, Republican, of Savannah, GA; born in Bryan, TX, April, 24, 1955; education: Michigan State University, 1973–74; University of Georgia, 1974–78; insurance salesman; vice president, Palmer and Cay/Carswell; Georgia State Legislature, 1984–92; member: Savannah Health Mission, Isle of Hope Community Association, Christ Church; married: Elizabeth Morris Kingston, 1979; children: Betsy, John, Ann, and Jim; committees: Appropriations; elected on November 3, 1992 to the 103rd Congress; reelected to each succeeding Congress.

Office Listings

http://www.house.gov/kingston

2368 Rayburn House Office Building, Washington, DC 20515 .... (202) 225–5831
Chief of Staff.—Jerr Rosenbaum. FAX: 226–2269
Legislative Director.—Merritt Myers.
Legislative Assistants.—Norah Bel, Meg Gilley.
Legislative Correspondent.—Allison Thigpen.
Communications Director.—Chris Crawford.
One Diamond Causeway, Suite 7, Savannah, GA 31406 .... (912) 352–0101
Casework Manager.—Trish DePriest.
Caseworker.—Bruce Bazemore.
Field Representative.—Alexandra Tabarrok.
Staff Assistant.—Myrlene Free.
P.O. Box 40, Baxley, GA 31515 .... (912) 367–7403
District Director.—Shiela Elliott.
Caseworker / Field Representative.—Brooke Floyd.
Brunswick Federal Building, 805 Gloucester Street, Room 304, Brunswick, GA 31520 .... (912) 265–9010
Caseworker / Field Representatives.—Tim Wessinger, Charles Wilson.
P.O. Box 5264, Valdosta, GA 31603 .... (229) 247–9188
Caseworker / Field Representative.—Christan Varner.
Ag Liaison / Field Representative.—Shae Walden.

Counties: APPLING, ATKINSON, BACON, BERRIEN, BRANTLEY, BRYAN, CAMDEN, CHARLTON, CHATHAM (part), CLINCH, COFFEE, COOK, ECHOLS, GLYNN, JEFF DAVIS, LANIER, LIBERTY, LONG, LOWNDES (part), MCINTOSH, PIERCE, TELFAIR, WARE, WAYNE, WHEELER. POPULATION (2005), 629,727.

ZIP Codes: 30411, 30427–28, 31037, 31055, 31060, 31077, 31083, 31300–01, 31305, 31308–09, 31313–16, 31319–21, 31323–24, 31327–28, 31331–33, 31404, 31406, 31410–11, 31419, 31500–31602, 31605–24, 31627, 31630–32, 31634–36, 31637, 31639–42, 31645–99, 31749, 31794, 31798

* * *

SECOND DISTRICT

SANFORD D. BISHOP, JR., Democrat, of Albany, GA; born in Mobile, AL, February 4, 1947; education: attended Mobile County public schools; B.A., Morehouse College, 1968; J.D., Emory University, 1971; professional: attorney; admitted to the Georgia and Alabama bars; Georgia House of Representatives, 1977–91; Georgia Senate, 1991–93; former member: Executive Board, Boy Scouts of America; YMCA; Sigma Pi Phi Fraternity; Kappa Alpha Psi Fraternity; 32nd Degree Mason, Shriner; member: Mt. Zion Baptist Church, Albany, GA; married: Vivian Creighton Bishop; child: Aeysha Reese; committees: Appropriations; elected to the 103rd Congress; reelected to each succeeding Congress.

Office Listings

http://www.bishop.house.gov

2429 Rayburn House Office Building, Washington, DC 20515 .... (202) 225–3631
Chief of Staff.—Phyllis Hallmon. FAX: 225–2203
Press Secretary.—Jennie Gibson.
Office Manager / Scheduler.—Martina Morgan.
Albany Towers, 235 W. Roosevelt Avenue, Suite 114, Albany, GA 31701 .... (229) 439–8067
District Director.—Kenneth Cutts.
137 East Jackson Street, Thomasville, GA 31792 .... (229) 226–7789
Field Representative.—Michael Bryant.
18 Ninth Street, Suite 201, Columbus, GA 31901 .... (706) 320–9477
Field Representatives: Elaine Gillespie, Wallace Sholar.

Counties: BAKER, BROOKS, CALHOUN, CHATTAHOOCHEE, CLAY, CRAWFORD, CRISP, DECATUR, DOOLY, DOUGHERTY, EARLY, GRADY, LEE, LOWNDES, MACON, MARION, MILLER, MITCHELL, MUSCOGEE, PEACH, QUITMAN, RANDOLPH, SCHLEY, SEMINOLE, STEWART, SUMTER, TALBOT, TAYLOR, TERRELL, THOMAS, WEBSTER, WORTH. Population (2000), 629,735.

ZIP Codes: 30150, 30290, 31010, 31015, 31039, 31068–69, 31072, 31092, 31201, 31204, 31211, 31217, 31328, 31601–03, 31605–06, 31625–26, 31629, 31636–38, 31641, 31643, 31698, 31701–12, 31714, 31716, 31719–22, 31727, 31730, 31733, 31735, 31738–39, 31743–44, 31747, 31749, 31753, 31756–58, 31763–65, 31768, 31771–72, 31775–76, 31778–84, 31787–96, 31799, 31803, 31805, 31814–15, 31821, 31824–25, 31832, 31901–07, 31914, 31995, 31997–99, 39813, 39815, 39817–19, 39823–29, 39832, 39834, 39836–37, 39840–42, 39845–46, 39851–52, 39854, 39859, 39861–62, 39866–67, 39870, 39877, 39885–86, 39897

* * *

THIRD DISTRICT

LYNN A. WESTMORELAND, Republican, of Sharpsburg, GA; born in Atlanta, GA, April 2, 1950; education: graduated from Therrell High School, Atlanta, GA; attended Georgia State University, Atlanta, GA, 1969–71; member of the Georgia State University, 1993–2004; professional: real estate developer; public service: Minority Leader, Georgia State House, 2000–04; Representative, Georgia State House, 1992–2004; religion: Baptist; organizations: Fayette Board of Realtors; Fayette County Safe Kids Council; Georgia Homebuilders; National Board of Realtors; National Rifle Association; married: Joan; children: Heather, Marcy, and Trae; committees: Oversight and Government Reform; Small Business; Transportation and Infrastructure; elected to the 109th Congress on November 2, 2004; reelected to each succeeding Congress.

Office Listings

http://www.house.gov/westmoreland

1118 Longworth House Office Building, Washington, DC 20515 .... (202) 225–5901
Chief of Staff.—Chip Lake. FAX: 225–2515
Deputy Chief of Staff / Communications Director.—Brian Robinson.
Legislative Director.—Joe Lillis.
Office Manager.—Claire Ouiment.
2753 East Highway 34, Suite 3, Newnan, GA 30265 .... (770) 683–2033

Counties: BIBB COUNTY (part). CITIES AND TOWNSHIPS: Macon, Payne. BUTTS COUNTY (part). CITIES AND TOWNSHIPS: Flovilla, Jackson, Jenkinsburg. CARROLL COUNTY (part). CITIES AND TOWNSHIPS: Bowdon, Carrollton, Mount Zion, Roopville, Temple, Villa Rica, Whitesburg. COWETA COUNTY (part). CITIES AND TOWNSHIPS: Grantville, Haralson, Lone Oak (also Meriwether), Luthersville, Moreland, Newnan, Palmetto, Senoia, Sharpsburg, Turin. DOUGLAS COUNTY (part). CITIES AND TOWNSHIPS: Austell, Douglasville, Lithia Springs, Winston. FAYETTE COUNTY. CITIES AND TOWNSHIPS: Brooks, Fayetteville, Peachtree City, Tyrone, Woolsey. HARRIS COUNTY (part). CITIES AND TOWNSHIPS: Cataula, Ellerslie, Fortson, Hamilton, Midland, Pine Mountain, Pine Mountain Valley, Shiloh, Waverly Hall, West Point. HENRY COUNTY (part). CITIES AND TOWNSHIPS: Hampton, Locust Grove, McDonough, Stockbridge. JASPER COUNTY (part). CITIES AND TOWNSHIPS: Monticello, Shady Dale. JONES COUNTY (part). CITIES AND TOWNSHIPS: Gray, Haddcock. LAMAR COUNTY. CITIES AND TOWNSHIPS: Aldora, Barnesville, Milner. MUSCOGEE COUNTY (part). CITIES AND TOWNSHIPS: Bibb City, Columbus. NEWTON COUNTY (part). CITIES AND TOWNSHIPS: Covington, Mansfield, Newborn, Oxford, Porterdale. PIKE COUNTY. CITIES AND TOWNSHIPS: Concord, Meansville, Molena, Williamson, Zebulon. ROCKDALE COUNTY (part). CITIES AND TOWNSHIPS: Conyers. SPALDING COUNTY (part). CITIES AND TOWNSHIPS: Griffin, Orchard Hill, Sunny Side. TROUP COUNTY (part). CITIES AND TOWNSHIPS: Hogansville, LaGrange. UPSON COUNTY (part). CITIES AND TOWNSHIPS: Thomaston, and Yatesville. Population (2000), 629,700.

ZIP Codes: 30013–14, 30016, 30055–56, 30094, 30108, 30110, 30116–17, 30122, 30133–35, 30154, 30170, 30179–80, 30185, 30187, 30204–06, 30213–17, 30220, 30223–24, 30228–30, 30233–34, 30236, 30238, 30240–41, 30248, 30252–53, 30256–59, 30263–66, 30268–69, 30271, 30273, 30275–77, 30281, 30284–86, 30289–90, 30292, 30295, 30904, 31002, 31004, 31016, 31024, 31029, 31032, 31038, 31046, 31064, 31066, 31085, 31097, 31204, 31210–11, 31220–21, 31602, 31632, 31801, 31804, 31807–08, 31811, 31820, 31822–23, 31826, 31829–31, 31833, 31904, 31907–09, 31993

* * *

FOURTH DISTRICT

HENRY C. ''HANK'' JOHNSON, JR., Democrat, of Lithonia, GA; born in Washington, DC, October 2, 1954; B.A., Clark College (Clark Atlanta University), Atlanta, GA, 1976; J.D., Thurgood Marshall School of Law, Texas Southern University, Houston, TX, 1979; professional: partner, Johnson & Johnson Law Group LLC, 1980–2007; judge, Magistrate Court, 1989–2001; associate, Dekalb County Commissioner, 2001–06; married: Mereda, 1979; two children: Randi and Alex; committees: Armed Services; Judiciary; elected to the 110th Congress on November 7, 2006; reelected to the 111th Congress.

Office Listings

http://www.hankjohnson.house.gov

1133 Longworth House Office Building, Washington, DC 20515 .... (202) 225–1605

Chief of Staff.—Daraka Satcher. FAX: 226–0691
Legislative Director.—Sean Foertsch.
Communications Director.—Richard A. Phelan.
Office Manager / Scheduler.—Loretta Davis.
5700 Hillandale Drive, Suite 110, Lithonia, GA 30058 .... (770) 987–2291
District Director.—Kathy Register.
3469 Lawrenceville Highway, Suite 205, Tucker, GA 30084 .... (770) 939–2016
Office Manager / Constituent Services Representative.—Katie Dailey.

Counties: DEKALB (part), GWINNETT (part). CITIES: Avondale Estates, Chamblee, Conyers, Clarkston, Decatur, Doraville, Lilburn, Lithonia, Pine Lake, Norcross and Stone Mountain. Population (2000), 629,726.

ZIP Codes: 30002–03, 30012–13, 30021, 30030–38, 30039, 30047, 30052, 30058, 30071, 30079, 30083–88, 30093–94, 30096, 30316–17, 30319, 30329, 30340–41, 30345

* * *

FIFTH DISTRICT

JOHN LEWIS, Democrat, of Atlanta, GA; born in Pike County, AL, February 21, 1940; education: graduated Pike County Training School, Brundidge, AL, 1957; B.A., American Baptist Theological Seminary, Nashville, TN, 1961; B.A., Fisk University, Nashville, TN, 1963; civil rights leader; Atlanta City Council, 1982–86; member: Martin Luther King Center for Social Change, African American Institute, Robert F. Kennedy Memorial; married the former Lillian Miles in 1968; one child, John Miles Lewis; committees: Ways and Means; appointed Senior Chief Deputy Democratic Whip for the 109th Congress; elected to the 100th Congress on November 4, 1986; reelected to each succeeding Congress.

Office Listings

http://www.house.gov/johnlewis

343 Cannon House Office Building, Washington, DC 20515 .... (202) 225–3801
Chief of Staff.—Michael Collins. FAX: 225–0351
Officer Manager / Scheduler.—Jacob Gillison.
Director of Communications.—Brenda Jones.
Legislative Director.—Michaeleen Crowell.
100 Peachtree Street, NW., Suite 1920, Atlanta, GA 30303 .... (404) 659–0116
District Director.—Tharon Johnson.

Counties: CLAYTON (part), COBB (part), DEKALB (part), FULTON (part). Population (2000), 629,727.

ZIP Codes: 30030, 30032–34, 30297, 30303–19, 30322, 30324, 30326–29, 30331, 30336–39, 30342, 30344–45, 30349, 30354

* * *

SIXTH DISTRICT

TOM PRICE, Republican, of Roswell, GA; born in Lansing, MI, October 8, 1954; education: B.A., University of Michigan, 1976; M.D., University of Michigan, 1979; professional: physician; member of the Georgia state senate, 1997–2004; member: Cobb Chamber of Commerce; Civil Air Patrol; Advisory Board, Georgia Partnership for Excellence in Education; religion: Presbyterian; married: Elizabeth; one child, Robert; committees: Education and Labor; Financial Services; elected to the 109th Congress on November 2, 2004; reelected to each succeeding Congress.

Office Listings

http://www.house.gov/tomprice

424 Cannon House Office Building, Washington, DC 20515 .... (202) 225–4501
Chief of Staff.—Matt McGinley. FAX: 225–4656
District Director.—Jeff Hamling.
3730 Roswell Road, Suite 50, Marietta, GA 30062 .... (770) 565–4990
100 North Street, Suite 150, Canton, GA 30114 .... (678) 493–6176

Counties: CHEROKEE (part), COBB (part), FULTON (part). CITIES AND TOWNSHIPS: Dunwoody, Marietta, Roswell, Sandy Springs, and Smyrna. Population (2000), 629,725.

ZIP Codes: 30004–07, 30009–10, 30022–24, 30041, 30060, 30062, 30064–68, 30075–77, 30092, 30096–97, 30101–02, 30106, 30115, 30127, 30141, 30144, 30152, 30156, 30160, 30168, 30188–89, 30327–28, 30339, 30342, 30350, 31032, 31146, 31150, 31156, 31602, 31632

* * *

SEVENTH DISTRICT

JOHN LINDER, Republican, of Duluth, GA; born in Deer River, MN, September 9, 1942; education: graduate, Deer River High School, 1957; B.S., 1963, and D.D.S., University of Minnesota, 1967; captain, U.S. Air Force, 1967–69; former dentist; president, Linder Financial Corporation; Georgia State Representative, 1975–80, 1983–90; member: Georgia GOP, Rotary Club, American Legion; married: Lynne Peterson Linder, 1963; children: Matt and Kristine; committees: Ways and Means; elected on November 3, 1992, to the 103rd Congress; reelected to each succeeding Congress.

Office Listings

http://linder.house.gov

1026 Longworth House Office Building, Washington, DC 20515 .... (202) 225–4272
Chief of Staff.—Rob Woodall. FAX: 225–4696
Legislative Director.—Valentina Valenta.
Scheduler.—Kelley Kurtz.
75 Langley Drive, Lawrenceville, GA 30045–6935 .... (770) 232–3005

Counties: BARROW, FORSYTH (part), GWINNETT (part), NEWTON, WALTON. Population (2000), 629,725.

ZIP Codes: 30004–05, 30012, 30017, 30019, 30024, 30039–47, 30049, 30052, 30071, 30078, 30087, 30092, 30095–97, 30101–03, 30107, 30114–15, 30120–21, 30123, 30127, 30132, 30134, 30137, 30141–43, 30145–46, 30153, 30157, 30168–69, 30178–80, 30183–84, 30188–89, 30515, 30518–19, 31139

* * *

EIGHTH DISTRICT

JIM MARSHALL, Democrat, of Macon, GA; born in Ithaca, NY, March 31, 1948; education: graduated high school, Mobile, AL, 1966; graduated, B.A., Princeton University, 1972 (National Merit Scholarship); graduated, J.D., Boston University Law School, 1977; military service: U.S. Army; infantry combat in Vietnam; served as an Airborne-Ranger reconnaissance platoon sergeant; decorated for heroism; received Purple Heart and two Bronze Stars; professional: joined the Mercer University Law School faculty in 1979; public service: participates in numerous community service activities; elected Mayor of Macon, GA, 1995; married: Camille; children: Mary and Robert; committees: Agriculture; Armed Services; elected to the 108th Congress on November 5, 2002; reelected to each succeeding Congress.

Office Listings

http://jimmarshall.house.gov

515 Cannon House Office Building, Washington, DC 20515 .... (202) 225–6531
Chief of Staff.—Doug Moore. FAX: 225–3013
Communications Director.—Doug Moore.
Legislative Director.—Tim Nelson.
682 Cherry Street, Suite 300, Macon, GA 31201 .... (478) 464–0255
District Director.—Hobby Stripling.
503 Bellevue Avenue, Suite C, Dublin, GA 31021 .... (478) 296–2023

Counties: BALDWIN (part), BEN HILL, BIBB, BLECKLEY, BUTTS, COLQUITT, DODGE, HOUSTON, JASPER, JONES, IRWIN, LAURENS, MONROE, NEWTON (part), PULASKI, TIFT, TURNER, TWIGGS, WILCOX, WILKINSON, WORTH (part). Population (2000), 629,748.

ZIP Codes: 30013–16, 30025, 30052, 30054–56, 30070, 30094, 30204, 30216, 30223–24, 30233–34, 30248, 30252, 30411, 30428, 30454, 30457, 31001–05, 31008–09, 31011–15, 31017, 31019–25, 31027–34, 31036–38, 31040, 31042, 31044, 31046–47, 31052, 31054, 31059–62, 31064–66, 31069, 31071–72, 31075, 31077, 31079, 31084–88, 31090–93, 31095–99, 31201–13, 31216–17, 31220–21, 31295–97, 31622, 31637, 31705, 31712, 31714, 31722, 31727, 31733–34, 31738, 31744, 31747, 31753, 31756, 31765, 31768–69, 31771–73, 31775–76, 31778, 31781, 31783–84, 31788–91, 31793–96, 31798

* * *

NINTH DISTRICT

NATHAN DEAL, Republican, of Clermont, GA; born in Millen, GA, August 25, 1942; education: graduated, Washington County High School, Sandersville, 1960; B.A., Mercer University, Macon, GA, 1964; J.D., Mercer University, Walter F. George School of Law, Macon, GA, 1966; admitted to the Georgia bar, 1966; captain, U.S. Army, 1966–68; Georgia State Senate, 1981–92; president pro tempore, 1991–92; married: the former Emilie Sandra Dunagan, 1966; children: Jason, Mary Emily, Carrie, and Katie; committees: Energy and Commerce; elected on November 3, 1992, to the 103rd Congress; reelected to each succeeding Congress.

Office Listings

http://www.house.gov/deal

2133 Rayburn House Office Building, Washington, DC 20515 .... (202) 225–5211
Chief of Staff.—Chris Riley. FAX: 225–8272
Press Secretaries: Chris Riley, Todd Smith.
108 West Lafayette Square, Suite 102, Lafayette, GA 30728 .... (706) 638–7042
P.O. Box 1015, Gainesville, GA 30503 .... (770) 535–2592
415 East Walnut Avenue, Suite 108, Dalton, GA 30721 .... (706) 226–5320

Counties: CATOOSA, DADE, DAWSON, FANNIN, FORSYTH (part), GILMER, GORDON, HALL, LUMPKIN, MURRAY, PICKENS, UNION, WALKER, WHITE, AND WHITFIELD. CITIES AND TOWNSHIPS: Blairsville, Blue Ridge, Calhoun, Chatsworth, Chickamauga, Cisco, Clermont, Cleveland, Cohutta, Conyers, Cumming, Dacula, Dahlonega, Dalton, Dawsonville, East Ellijay, Ellijay, Eton, Fairmount, Flowery Branch, Fort Oglethorpe, Gainesville, Gillsville, Grayson, Helen, Jasper, LaFayette, Lawrenceville, Loganville, Lookout Mountain, Lula, McCaysville, Morgantown, Oakwood, Plainville, Ranger, Rest Haven, Resaca, Ringgold, Rossville, Sautee Nacoochee, Talking Rock, Trenton, Tunnel Hill, and Varnell. Population (2000), 629,702.

ZIP Codes: 30004–05, 30024, 30028, 30040–41, 30097, 30103, 30107, 30139, 30143, 30148, 30171, 30175, 30177, 30501–07, 30510, 30512–14, 30517–19, 30522, 30527–28, 30533–34, 30536, 30539, 30541–43, 30545, 30548, 30554–55, 30559–60, 30564, 30566–67, 30571–72, 30575, 30582, 30597, 30635, 30641, 30701, 30703, 30707–08, 30710–11, 30719–22, 30724–28, 30731–42, 30747, 30750–51, 30753, 30755–57

* * *

TENTH DISTRICT

PAUL C. BROUN, Republican, of Fulton, GA; born in Clarke County, GA, May 14, 1946; education: B.S. in Chemistry, University of Georgia, Athens, GA, 1967; M.D., Medical College of Georgia, Augusta, GA, 1971; professional: physician; served, U.S. Marine Corps Reserves, 1964–67; member: Rotary Club; Athens-Clarke County Chamber of Commerce; Prince Avenue Baptist Church; religion: Southern Baptist; married: Nancy ''Niki'' Bronson Broun; children: Carly, Collins, Lucy; grandchildren: Lucile, Tillman; committees: Homeland Security; Natural Resources; Science and Technology; elected by special election to the 110th Congress on July 17, 2007; reelected to the 111th Congress.

Office Listings

http://www.house.gov/broun

2104 Rayburn House Office Building, Washington, DC 20515 .... (202) 225–4101
Chief of Staff.—Aloysius Hogan. FAX: 226–0776
Office Manager / Scheduler.—Teddie Norton.

Counties: BANKS, COLUMBIA, CLARKE, ELBERT, FRANKLIN, GREENE, HABERSHAM, HART, JACKSON, LINCOLN, MCDUFFIE, MADISON, MORGAN, OCONEE, OGLETHORPE, PUTNAM, RABUN, RICHMOND (part), STEPHENS, TOWNS, WILKES. Population (2000), 629,762.

ZIP Codes: 30025, 30055–56, 30510–11, 30516–17, 30520–21, 30523, 30525, 30529–31, 30535, 30537–38, 30543–44, 30546–49, 30552–54, 30557–58, 30562–63, 30565, 30567–68, 30571, 30573, 30575–77, 30580–82, 30596, 30598–99, 30601–09, 30612, 30619, 30621–31, 30633–35, 30638–39, 30641–43, 30645–50, 30660, 30662–69, 30671, 30673, 30677–78, 30683, 30802, 30805–06, 30808–09, 30813–14, 30817, 30824, 30901, 30903–07, 30909, 30911–14, 30916–17, 30919, 31024, 31026, 31061

* * *

ELEVENTH DISTRICT

PHIL GINGREY, Republican, of Marietta, GA; born in Augusta, GA, July 10, 1942; education: B.S., Georgia Tech, 1965; M.D., Medical College of Georgia, 1969; professional: Physician; set up a pro-life OB-GYN practice; organizations: Cobb County Medical Society; Medical Association of Georgia; American Medical Association; Georgia OB-GYN Society; public service: Marietta School Board, 1993–97; Georgia State Senate, 1999–2002; House Policy Committee; married: Billie Ayers; children: Billy, Gannon, Phyllis, and Laura; committees: Energy and Commerce; elected to the 108th Congress on November 5, 2002; reelected to each succeeding Congress.

Office Listings

http://www.house.gov/gingrey

119 Cannon House Office Building, Washington, DC 20515 .... (202) 225–2931
Chief of Staff.—David Sours. FAX: 225–2944
Legislative Director.—Joshua Waller.
Executive Assistant / Director of Operations.—Catherine Morvis.
219 Roswell Street, Marietta, GA 30060 .... (770) 429–1776
600 East 1st Street, Suite 301, Rome, GA 30161 .... (706) 290–1776

Counties: BARTOW, CARROLL (part), CHATTOOGA, COBB (part), DOUGLAS, FLOYD, HARALSON, GORDON (part), PAULDING, POLK. Population (2000) 629,730.

ZIP Codes: 30008, 30060–64, 30066–67, 30069, 30080–81, 30090, 30101–05, 30108–13, 30116–27, 30129, 30132, 30134, 30137–41, 30144–45, 30147, 30149–50, 30152–53, 30161–65, 30176, 30178–80, 30182

* * *

TWELFTH DISTRICT

JOHN BARROW, Democrat, of Savannah, GA; born in Athens, October 31, 1955; education: graduated from Clarke Central High School, Athens-Clarke County, GA, 1973; B.A., University of Georgia, Athens, GA, 1976; J.D., Harvard University, Cambridge, MA, 1979; professional: law clerk for Judge, Savannah, GA; law clerk for Judge, Fiftieth Circuit Court of Appeals; founding member, Wilburn, Lewis, Barrow and Stotz, PC.; county commissioner; lawyer, private practice; Athens-Clarke, GA, city-county commissioner, 1990–2004; religion: Baptist; children: James and Ruth; committees: Energy and Commerce; elected to the 109th Congress on November 2, 2004; reelected to each succeeding Congress.

Office Listings

http://www.barrow.house.gov

213 Cannon House Office Building, Washington, DC 20515 .... (202) 225–2823
Chief of Staff.—Ashley Jones. FAX: 225–3377
Deputy Chief of Staff.—Ashley Jones.
Legislative Director.—Hill Thomas.
Communications Director.—Jane Brodsky.
925 Laney Walker Boulevard, Suite 300, Augusta, GA 30901 .... (706) 722–4494
450 Mall Boulevard, Suite A, Savannah, GA 31406 .... (912) 354–7282
City Hall, 141 West Haynes Street, P.O. Box 1017, Sandersville, GA 31082 .... (478) 553–1923
Vidalia Community Center, 107 Old Airport Road, Suite A, Vidalia, GA .... (912) 537–9301

Counties: BALDWIN (part), BULLOCH, BURKE, CANDLER, CHATHAM (part), EFFINGHAM, EMANUEL, EVANS, GLASCOCK, HANCOCK, JEFFERSON, JENKINS, JOHNSON, MONTGOMERY, RICHMOND (part), SCREVEN, TALIAFERRO, TATTNALL, TOOMBS, TREUTLEN, WARREN, WASHINGTON. CITIES AND TOWNSHIPS: Augusta, Milledgeville, Savannah, Statesboro, Vidalia. Population (2000) 629,727.

ZIP Codes: 30400–01, 30410, 30412–15, 30417, 30420–21, 30423, 30425–27, 30429, 30436, 30438–39, 30441–42, 30445–48, 30456, 30452–53, 30455–58, 30461, 30464, 30467, 30470–71, 30473–74, 30477, 30631, 30664, 30669, 30678, 30803, 30805, 30807, 30810, 30815–16, 30818, 30820–24, 30828, 30830, 30833, 30901, 30904, 30906, 30909, 30934, 31002, 31018, 31033–35, 31045, 31049, 31061, 31067, 31082, 31087, 31089, 31094, 31096, 31302–03, 31307–08, 31312, 31318, 31321–22, 31326, 31329, 31401, 31404–08, 31410, 31415, 31419

* * *

THIRTEENTH DISTRICT

DAVID SCOTT, Democrat, of Atlanta, GA; born in Aynor, SC, June 27, 1945; education: Florida A&M University, graduated with honors, 1967; M.B.A., graduated with honors, University of Pennsylvania Wharton School of Finance, 1969; professional: businessman; owner and CEO, Dayn-Mark Advertising; public service: Georgia House of Representatives, 1974–82; Georgia State Senate, 1983–2002; married: Alfredia Aaron, 1969; children: Dayna and Marcye; committees: Agriculture; Financial Services; Foreign Affairs; elected to the 108th Congress on November 5, 2002; reelected to each succeeding Congress.

Office Listings

http://davidscott.house.gov

225 Cannon House Office Building, Washington, DC 20515 .... (202) 225–2939
Chief of Staff.—Michael Andel. FAX: 225–4628
Deputy Chief of Staff for Administration.—Angie Borja.
Legislative Director.—Gary Woodward.
173 North Main Street, Jonesboro, GA 30236 .... (770) 210–5073
888 Concord Road, Suite 100, Smyra, GA 30080 .... (770) 432–5405

Counties: CLAYTON, COBB, DEKALB, DOUGLAS, FULTON, HENRY. POPULATION (2000) 629,732.

ZIP Codes: 30008, 30034, 30060, 30064, 30067, 30080, 30081–82, 30106, 30111, 30122, 30126–27, 30133–35, 30141, 30154, 30168, 30187, 30213, 30215, 30228, 30236–38, 30250, 30253, 30260, 30268, 30272–74, 30281, 30287–88, 30291, 30294, 30296–97, 30331, 30337, 30339, 30344, 30349, 31192

HAWAII

(Population 2000, 1,211,537)

SENATORS

DANIEL K. INOUYE, Democrat, of Honolulu, HI; born in Honolulu, September 7, 1924; education: A.B., government and economics, University of Hawaii, 1950; J.D., George Washington University Law School, 1952; majority leader, Territorial House of Representatives, 1954–58; Territorial Senate, 1958–59; enlisted as private, 442nd Infantry Regimental Combat Team, 1943; second lieutenant, battlefield commission, 1944; served in France and Italy; retired captain, U.S. Army; Senate Democratic Steering and Coordination; religion: Methodist; married: Irene Hirano, first wife the former Margaret Shinobu Awamura of Honolulu died in 2006; one son: Daniel Ken Inouye, Jr.; committees: chair, Appropriations; Commerce, Science and Transportation; Indian Affairs; Rules and Administration; elected on July 28, 1959, to the 86th Congress; reelected to the 87th Congress; elected to the U.S. Senate on November 6, 1962; reelected to each succeeding Senate term.

Office Listings

http://inouye.senate.gov

722 Hart Senate Office Building, Washington, DC 20510 .... (202) 224–3934
Administrative Assistant.—Patrick H. DeLeon. FAX: 224–6747
Office Manager.—Beverly MacDonald. TDD: 224–1233
Personal Secretary.—Jessica Lee.
Legislative Director.—Marie Blanco.
300 Ala Moana Boulevard, Suite 7–212, Honolulu, HI 96850 .... (808) 541–2542
Hilo Auxiliary Office, 101 Aupuni Street, No. 205, Hilo, HI 96720 .... (808) 935–0844

* * *

DANIEL K. AKAKA, Democrat, of Honolulu, HI; born in Honolulu, September 11, 1924; education: graduated, Kamehameha High School, 1942; University of Hawaii, 1948–66, bachelor of education, professional certificate, master of education; served in the U.S. Army, 1945–47; teacher, 1953–60; vice principal, 1960; principal, 1963–71; program specialist, 1968–71; director, 1971–74; director and special assistant in human resources, 1975–76; board of directors, Hanahauoli School; Act 4 Educational Advisory Commission; Library Advisory Council; Na Hookama O Pauahi Scholarship Committee, Kamehameha Schools; commissioner, Manpower and Full Employment Commission; member and Minister of Music, Kawaiahao Church; married: the former Mary Mildred Chong (deceased, 2006); children: Millannie, Daniel, Jr., Gerard, Alan, and Nicholas; committees: chair, Veterans' Affairs; Armed Services; Banking, Housing, and Urban Affairs; Homeland Security and Governmental Affairs; Indian Affairs; elected to the 95th Congress in November, 1976; reelected to each succeeding Congress; appointed to the U.S. Senate in April, 1990, to fill the vacancy caused by the death of Senator Spark Matsunaga; elected to complete the unexpired term in November, 1990; reelected to each succeeding Senate term.

Office Listings

http://akaka.senate.gov

141 Hart Senate Office Building, Washington, DC 20510 .... (202) 224–6361
Legislative Director/Counsel.—Jennifer L. Tyree. FAX: 224–6747
Fiscal Office Secretary.—Patricia L. Hill.
Prince Kuhio Federal Building, 300 Ala Moana Boulevard, Room 3–106, P.O. Box 50144, Honolulu, HI 96850 .... (808) 522–8970
Chief of Staff.—Joan Ohashi Akai.
101 Aupuni Street, Suite 213, Hilo, HI 96720 .... (808) 935–1114

REPRESENTATIVES

FIRST DISTRICT

NEIL ABERCROMBIE, Democrat, of Honolulu, HI; born in Buffalo, NY, June 26, 1938; education: graduated from Williamsville High School, Williamsville, NY; B.A., Union College, 1959; Ph.D., University of Hawaii, 1974; professional: candidate for election to the U.S. Senate, 1970; Hawaii House of Representatives, 1974–78; Hawaii State Senate, 1978–86; Honolulu City

Council, 1988–90; married: Nancie Caraway; committees: Armed Services; Natural Resources; elected to the U.S. House of Representatives on September 20, 1986, to fill the vacancy caused by the resignation of Cecil Heftel; elected to the 102nd Congress, November 6, 1990; reelected to each succeeding Congress.

Office Listings

http://www.house.gov/abercrombie

1502 Longworth House Office Building, Washington, DC 20515 .... (202) 225–2726
Legislative Director.—Wendy Clerinx. FAX: 225–4580
Deputy Chief of Staff.—Kathleen Chapman.
Press Secretary.—Dave Helfert.
300 Ala Moana Boulevard, Room 4–104, Honolulu, HI 96850 .... (808) 541–2570
Chief of Staff.—Amy Asselbaye.

Counties: HONOLULU COUNTY (part). CITIES AND TOWNSHIPS: Aiea Pearl City, Ewa Beach, Honolulu, Mililani, and Waipahu. Population (2000), 606,718.

ZIP Codes: 96701, 96706, 96782, 96789, 96797, 96801–28, 96830, 96835–44, 96846–50, 96853, 96858–61

* * *

SECOND DISTRICT

MAZIE K. HIRONO, Democrat, of Hawaii; born in Fukushima, Japan, November 3, 1947; naturalized U.S. citizen in 1959; education: Kaimuki High School, 1966; Phi Beta Kappa, University of Hawaii at Manoa, 1970; Georgetown University Law Center, 1978; Deputy Attorney General, Anti-Trust Division, State of Hawaii, 1978–80; Shim, Tam, Kirimitsu, Kitamura and Chang (law firm), 1984–88; State Representative, Hawaii State Legislature, 1980–94; Lt. Governor, State of Hawaii, 1994–2002; candidate for Governor, State of Hawaii, 2002; married to Leighton Kim Oshima; committees: Education and Labor; Transportation and Infrastructure; elected to the 110th Congress on November 7, 2006; reelected to the 111th Congress.

Office Listings

http://hirono.house.gov/ mazie.hirono@mail.house.gov

1229 Longworth House Office Building, Washington, DC 20515 .... (202) 225–4906
Chief of Staff (Honolulu).—Carl Takamura. FAX: 225–4987
Director.—Francis Nakamoto.
Deputy Chief of Staff.—Susan Kodani.
Prince Kuhio Federal Building, Room 5104, Honolulu, HI 96850 .... (808) 541–1986
District Director.—Yvonne Lau.

Counties: HAWAI'I COUNTY. CITIES: Hawi, Hilo, Honoka'a, Kailua-Kona, Na'alehu, Kealakekua, Pahoa, Ocean View, Volcano, Waimea, Waikoloa. MAUI COUNTY. CITIES: Hana, Kahului, Kaunakakai, Lahaina, Lana'i City, Makawao, Wailuku. KALAWAO COUNTY. CITY: Kalaupapa. HONOLULU COUNTY (part). CITIES: Hale'iwa, Honolulu, Kailua, Kane'ohe, Kapolei, La'ie, Makakilo, Nanakuli, Wahiawa, Waialua, Wai'anae, Waimanalo. KAUA'I COUNTY. CITIES: Hanalei, Hanapepe, Kalaheo, Kapa'a, Kekaha, Kilauea, Koloa, Lihue, Waimea. NORTHWESTERN HAWAIIAN ISLANDS. ISLANDS OF: Becker, French Frigate Shoals, Gardener Pinnacles, Hermes and Kure Atolls, Laysan, Lisianski, Maro Reef, Nihoa, and Pearl. Population (2000), 604,819.

ZIP Codes: 96703–05, 96707–10, 96712–22, 96725–34, 96737–57, 96759–74, 96776–81, 96783–86, 96788–93, 96795–97, 96854, 96857, 96862–63

IDAHO

(Population 2000, 1,293,953)

SENATORS

MIKE CRAPO, Republican, of Idaho Falls, ID; born in Idaho Falls, May 20, 1951; education: graduated, Idaho Falls High School, 1969; B.A., Brigham Young University, Provo, UT, 1973; J.D., Harvard University Law School, Cambridge, MA, 1977; professional: attorney; admitted to the California bar, 1977; admitted to the Idaho bar, 1979; law clerk, Hon. James M. Carter, Judge of the U.S. Court of Appeals for the Ninth Circuit, San Diego, CA, 1977–78; associate attorney, Gibson, Dunn, and Crutcher, San Diego, 1978–79; attorney, Holden, Kidwell, Hahn and Crapo, 1979–92; partner, 1983–92; Idaho State Senate, 1984–92, assistant majority leader, 1987–89, president pro tempore, 1989–92; member: American Bar Association, Boy Scouts of America, Idaho Falls Rotary Club, 1984–88; married: the former Susan Diane Hasleton, 1974; children: Michelle, Brian, Stephanie, Lara, and Paul; co-chair, Western Water Caucus; co-chair, Sportsman Caucus; co-chair, COPD Caucus; committees: Banking, Housing, and Urban Affairs; Budget; Environment and Public Works; Finance; Indian Affairs; elected on November 3, 1992, to the 103rd Congress; reelected to each succeeding Congress; elected to the U.S. Senate on November 3, 1998; reelected to each succeeding Senate term.

Office Listings

http://crapo.senate.gov

239 Dirksen Senate Office Building, Washington, DC 20510 .... (202) 224–6142
Chief of Staff.—Peter Fischer. FAX: 228–1375
Communications Director.—Susan Wheeler.
Legislative Director.—Ken Flanz.
251 East Front Street, Suite 205, Boise, ID 83702 .... (208) 334–1776
Chief of Staff.—John Hoehne.
610 Hubbard Street, Suite 209, Coeur d'Alene, ID 83814 .... (208) 664–5490
Director.—Karen Roetter.
313 D Street, Suite 105, Lewiston, ID 83501 .... (208) 743–1492
Director.—Peter Stegner.
275 South 5th Avenue, Suite 225, Pocatello, ID 83201 .... (208) 236–6775
Director.—Farhanna Hibbert.
524 East Cleveland, Suite 220, Caldwell, ID 83605 .... (208) 455–0360
Director.—Bryan Ricker.
410 Memorial Drive, Suite 204, Idaho Falls, ID 83402 .... (208) 522–9779
Director.—Leslie Huddleston.
202 Falls Avenue, Suite 2, Twin Falls, ID 83301 .... (208) 734–2515
Director.—A.J. Church.

* * *

JAMES E. RISCH, Republican, of Boise, ID; born in Milwaukee, WI, May 3, 1943; education: St. Johns Cathedral High School, Milwaukee, WI; B.S., forestry, University of Idaho, Moscow, ID, 1965; J.D., University of Idaho, Moscow, ID, 1968, Law Review, College of Law Advisory Committee; professional: Ada County Prosecuting Attorney, 1970–74; president, Idaho Prosecuting Attorneys Association, 1973; Idaho State Senate, 1974–88, 1995–2003; Assistant Majority Leader, 1996; Majority Leader, 1997–82, 1997–2002; President Pro Tempore, 1983–1988; Lieutenant Governor of Idaho, 2003–06, 2007–09; Governor of Idaho, 2006; small business owner; ranch/farmer; former partner Risch, Goss, Insinger, Gustavel law firm; member, National Cattle Association; Idaho Cattle Association; American, Idaho and Boise Valley Angus Association; National Rifle Association; Ducks Unlimited; Rocky Mountain Elk Foundation; married: Vicki; children: James, Jason, and Jordan, 2 daughters-in-law; 6 grandchildren; Congressional Youth Leadership Council; Impact Aid Coalition; Senate Rural Health Caucus; Rural Education Caucus; WMD/Terrorism Caucus; National Guard Caucus; Western Caucus, Sportsman Caucus, Recycling Caucus, Republican High Tech Task Force; committees: Energy and Natural Resources; Foreign Relations; Small Business and Entrepreneurship; Select Committee on Ethics; Select Committee on Intelligence; Joint Economic Committee; elected to the U.S. Senate on November 4, 2008.

Office Listings

http://risch.senate.gov

483 Russell Senate Office Building, Washington, DC 20510 .... (202) 224–2752

Chief of Staff.—John Sandy. FAX: 224–2573
Communications Director.—Brad Hoaglun.
Executive Assistant / Scheduler.—Vanessa Kermick.
Legislative Director.—Corey McDaniel.
350 North Ninth Street, Suite 302, Boise, ID 83702 .... (208) 342–7985
610 Hubbard, Suite 121, Coeur d'Alene, ID 83814 .... (208) 667–6130
490 Memorial Drive, Suite 101, Idaho Falls, ID 83402 .... (208) 523–5541
313 D Street, Suite 106, Lewiston, ID 83501 .... (208) 743–0792
275 South Fifth Avenue, Suite 290, Pocatello, ID 83201 .... (208) 236–6817
560 Filer Avenue, Suite A, Twin Falls, ID 83301 .... (208) 734–6780

REPRESENTATIVES

FIRST DISTRICT

WALT MINNICK, Democrat, of Boise, ID; born in Walla Walla, WA, September 20, 1942; education: undergraduate, Whitman College, Walla Walla, WA, 1964; M.B.A., Harvard Business School, Cambridge, MA, 1966; law degree, Harvard Law School, Cambridge, MA, 1969; professional: Pentagon, OMB; White House; former CEO of Trus Joist and Summerwinds Garden Center; religion: Unitarian Universalist; married: A.K. Leinhart-Minnick, Blue Dog Coalition; four children; three grandchildren; committees: Agriculture; Financial Services; elected to the 111th Congress on November 4, 2008.

Office Listings

http://minnick.house.gov/

1517 Longworth House Office Building, Washington, DC 20515 .... (202) 225–6611
Chief of Staff.—Kate Haas. FAX: 225–3029
Legislative Director.—Rob Ellsworth.
Scheduler.—Sabrina Kirkwood.
33 Broadway Avenue, Suite 251, Meridian, ID 83642 .... (208) 888–3188
1900 Northwest Boulevard, Suite 106, Coeur d'Alene, ID 83814 .... (208) 667–0127
310 Main St. Lewiston, ID 83501 .... (208) 743–1388

Counties: ADA (part), ADAMS, BENEWAH, BOISE, BONNER, BOUNDARY, CANYON, CLEARWATER, GEM, IDAHO, KOOTENAI, LATAH, LEWIS, NEZ PERCE, OWYHEE, PAYETTE, SHOSHONE, VALLEY, WASHINGTON. Population (2000), 648,774.

ZIP Codes: 83501, 83520, 83522–26, 83530–31, 83533, 83535–37, 83539–49, 83552–55, 83602, 83604–07, 83610–12, 83615–17, 83619, 83622, 83624, 83626–32, 83634–39, 83641–45, 83647, 83650–57, 83660–61, 83666, 83669–72, 83676–77, 83680, 83686–87, 83702, 83704–06, 83708–09, 83711, 83713–14, 83716, 83719, 83799, 83801–06, 83808–16, 83821–27, 83830, 83832–37, 83839–58, 83860–61, 83864–74, 83876–77

* * *

SECOND DISTRICT

MICHAEL K. SIMPSON, Republican, of Blackfoot, ID; born in Burley, ID, September 8, 1950; education: graduated, Blackfoot High School, 1968; Utah State University, 1972; Washington University School of Dental Medicine, 1977; professional: dentist, private practice; Blackfoot, ID, City Council, 1981–85; Idaho State Legislature, 1985–98; Idaho Speaker of the House 1992–98; married: Kathy Simpson; committees: Appropriations; Budget; elected to the 106th Congress; reelected to each succeeding Congress.

Office Listings

http://www.house.gov/simpson mike.simpson@mail.house.gov

1339 Longworth House Office Building, Washington, DC 20515 .... (202) 225–5531
Chief of Staff.—Lindsay Slater. FAX: 225–8216
Scheduler.—Kaylyn Peterson.
Legislative Director.—Malisah Small.
Press Secretary.—Nikki Watts.
802 West Bannock, Suite 600, Boise, ID 83702 .... (208) 334–1953
1341 Fillmore, #202, Twin Falls, ID 83301 .... (208) 734–7219
490 Memorial Drive, Suite 103, Idaho Falls, ID 83402 .... (208) 523–6701
275 South Fifth Avenue, #275, Pocatello, ID 83201 .... (208) 478–4160

Counties: ADA (part), BANNOCK, BEAR LAKE, BINGHAM, BLAINE, BONNEVILLE, BUTTE, CAMAS, CARIBOU, CASSIA, CLARK, CUSTER, ELMORE, FRANKLIN, FREMONT, GOODING, JEFFERSON, JEROME, LEMHI, LINCOLN, MADISON, MINIDOKA, ONEIDA, POWER, TETON, TWIN FALLS. Population (2000), 645,179.

ZIP Codes: 83201–06, 83209–15, 83217–18, 83220–21, 83223, 83226–30, 83232–39, 83241, 83243–46, 83250–56, 83261–63, 83271–72, 83274, 83276–78, 83281, 83283, 83285–87, 83301–03, 83311–14, 83316, 83318, 83320–25, 83327–28, 83330, 83332–38, 83340–44, 83346–50, 83352–55, 83401–06, 83415, 83420–25, 83427–29, 83431, 83433–36, 83438, 83440–46, 83448–52, 83454–55, 83460, 83462–69, 83601–02, 83604, 83623–24, 83627, 83633–34, 83647–48, 83701–09, 83712, 83714–17, 83720–33, 83735, 83744, 83756

ILLINOIS

(Population, 2000 12,419,293)

SENATORS

RICHARD DURBIN, Democrat, of Springfield, IL; born in East St. Louis, IL, November 21, 1944; son of William and Ann Durbin; education: graduated, Assumption High School, East St. Louis; B.S., foreign service and economics, Georgetown University, Washington, DC, 1966; J.D., Georgetown University Law Center, 1969; professional: attorney, admitted to the Illinois bar in 1969; began practice in Springfield; legal counsel to Lieutenant Governor Paul Simon, 1969–72; legal counsel to Illinois Senate Judiciary Committee, 1972–82; parliamentarian, Illinois Senate, 1969–82; president, New Members Democratic Caucus, 98th Congress; associate professor of medical humanities, Southern Illinois University School of Medicine; elected as Assistant Democratic Leader, 2004; elected as Assistant Majority Leader, 2006; married: the former Loretta Schaefer, 1967; children: Christine, Paul, and Jennifer; committees: Appropriations; Judiciary; Rules and Administration; Joint Committee on the Library; elected to the 98th Congress, November 2, 1982; reelected to each succeeding Congress; elected to the U.S. Senate on November 5, 1996; reelected to each succeeding Senate term.

Office Listings

http://durbin.senate.gov

309 Hart Senate Office Building, Washington, DC 20510	(202) 224–2152
Chief of Staff.—Patrick Souders.	FAX: 228–0400
Legislative Director.—Dena Morris.	TTY: 224–8180
Director of Scheduling.—Claire Dickhut.	
230 South Dearborn, Kluczynski Building 38th Floor, Chicago, IL 60604	(312) 353–4952
Chief of Staff.—Mike Daly.	
525 South Eighth Street, Springfield, IL 62703	(217) 492–4062
Director.—Bill Houlihan.	
701 North Court Street, Marion, IL 62959	(618) 998–8812

* * *

ROLAND W. BURRIS, Democrat, of Chicago, IL; born in Centralia, IL, August 3, 1937; education: B.A., political science, Southern Illinois University in Carbondale, IL, 1959; J.D., Howard University School of Law, 1963; professional: National Bank Examiner for the Comptroller of the Currency U.S. Treasury Department 1963–64; Vice President of the Continental Illinois National Bank, 1964–73, Director of the Department of Central Management Services, 1973–77; National Executive Director and Chief Operating Officer for Operation PUSH January–October, 1977; Comptroller of Illinois, 1979–99, Illinois Attorney General, 1991–95; Chairman / CEO of Burris & Lebed Consulting, LLC, 2002–08; married: Dr. Berlean M. Burris, Ph.D.; children: Roland and Rolanda; Congressional Black Caucus; committees: Armed Services Committee; Veterans Affairs Committee; Homeland Security and Governmental Affairs; appointed December 31, 2008, to the United States Senate for the term ending January 3, 2011, to fill the vacancy caused by the resignation of Barack Obama, took the oath of office on January 15, 2009.

Office Listings

http://burris.senate.gov

387 Russell Senate Office Building, Washington, DC 20510	(202) 224–2854
Chief of Staff.—Brady King.	FAX: 228–3333
Legislative Director.—Ken Montoya.	TDD: 228–4480
Director of Communications.—Jim O'Connor.	
Scheduler.—Robin Nichols.	
230 South Dearborn Street, Suite 3900, Chicago, IL 60604	(312) 886–3506
607 East Adams Street, Suite 1520, Springfield, IL 62701	(217) 492–5089
701 North Court Street, Marion, IL 62959	(618) 997–2402
1911 Fifty-Second Avenue, Moline, IL 61265	(309) 736–1217

REPRESENTATIVES

FIRST DISTRICT

BOBBY L. RUSH, Democrat, of Chicago, IL; born in Albany, GA; November 23, 1946; education: attended Marshall High School, Marshall, IL; B.A., Roosevelt University, Chicago,

IL, 1974; M.A., University of Illinois, Chicago, IL, 1994; M.A., McCormick Theological Seminary, Chicago, IL, 1998; professional: United States Army, 1963–68; insurance agent; alderman, Chicago, Illinois, city council, 1983–93; deputy chairman, Illinois Democratic Party, 1990; unsuccessful candidate for mayor of Chicago, IL, 1999; minister; married: Carolyn; five children; committees: Energy and Commerce; elected on Novmeber 3, 1992 to the 103rd Congress; reelected to each succeeding Congress.

Office Listings

http://www.house.gov/rush

2416 Rayburn House Office Building, Washington, DC 20515 .... (202) 225–4372
Chief of Staff.—Rev. Stanley Watkins. FAX: 226–0333
Legislative Director.—Christopher Brown.
Executive Assistant/Scheduler.—N. Lenette Myers.
Communications Director / Press Secretary.—Sharon Jenkins.
Deputy Communications Director / Press Secretary.—Stephanie Gadlin.
700–706 East 79th Street, Chicago, IL 60619 .... (773) 224–6500
District Director.—Rev. Stanley Watkins.
3235 West 147th Street, Midlothian, IL 60445 .... (708) 385–9550
Suburban Director.—Younus Suleman.

Counties: COOK COUNTY (part). CITIES AND TOWNSHIPS: Alsip, Blue Island, Chicago, Country Club Hills, Evergreen Park, Homewood, Midlothian, Oak Forest, Orland Hills, Orland Park, Palos Heights, Posen, Robbins, and Tinley Park. Population (2000), 653,647.

ZIP Codes: 60406, 60445, 60452, 60456, 60462–63, 60469, 60472, 60477–78, 60482, 60615–16, 60619–21, 60636–37, 60643, 60652–53, 60803, 60805

* * *

SECOND DISTRICT

JESSE L. JACKSON, JR., Democrat, of Chicago, IL; born in Greenville, SC, March 11, 1965; education: B.S. in business management, *magna cum laude,* North Carolina A&T State University, 1987; M.A., Chicago Theological Seminary, 1989; J.D., University of Illinois College of Law, 1993; member, Congressional Black Caucus, Congressional Progressive Caucus; elected Secretary of the Democratic National Committee's Black Caucus; national field director, National Rainbow Coalition, 1993–95; member, Rainbow/Push Action Network; married: Sandi; two children; committees: Appropriations; elected to the 104th Congress (special election); reelected to each succeeding Congress.

Office Listings

http://www.house.gov/jackson

2419 Rayburn House Office Building, Washington, DC 20515 .... (202) 225–0773
Chief of Staff.—Kenneth Edmonds. FAX: 225–0899
Legislative Director.—Charles Dujon.
Legislative Assistant.—Megan Moore.
Executive Assistant/Scheduler.—DeBorah Posey.
17926 South Halsted, Homewood, IL 60430 .... (708) 798–6000
District Director.—Rick Bryant.
7121 South Yates Boulevard, Chicago, IL 60649 .... (773) 734–9660

Counties: COOK (part), WILL (part). CITIES AND TOWNSHIPS: Blue Island, Burnham, Calumet City, Calumet Park, Chicago, Chicago Heights, Country Club Hills Crestwood, Dixmoor, Dolton, East Hazel Crest, Flossmoor, Ford Heights, Glenwood, Harvey, Hazel Crest, Homewood, Lansing, Lynwood, Markham, Matteson, Midlothian, Monee, Oak Forest, Olympia Fields, Park Forest, Phoenix, Posen, Richton Park, Riverdale, Robbins, Sauk Village, South Chicago Heights, South Holland, Steger, Tinley Park, Thornton, and University Park. Population (2000), 653,647.

ZIP Codes: 60406, 60409, 60411–12, 60417, 60419, 60422–23, 60425–26, 60429–30, 60438, 60443, 60445, 60449, 60452, 60461, 60466, 60471, 60473, 60475–78, 60615, 60617, 60620, 60628, 60633, 60636–37, 60643, 60649, 60827

* * *

THIRD DISTRICT

DANIEL LIPINSKI, Democrat, of Chicago, IL; born in Chicago, July 15, 1966; son of former Congressman William Lipinski, 1983–2004; education: B.S., Mechanical Engineering, *magna cum laude,* Northwestern University, 1988; M.S., Engineering-Economic Systems, Stanford University, 1989; Ph.D., political science, Duke University, 1998; professional: aide to United States Representative George Sangmeister, 1993–94; aide to United States Representative Jerry Costello, 1995–96; aide to United States Representative Rod Blagojevich, 1999–2000; professor, James Madison University Washington Program, Washington, DC, 2000; professor, University of Notre Dame, South Bend, IN, 2000–01; professor, University of Tennessee, Knoxville, TN, 2001–04; married: Judy; committees: Science and Technology; Small Business; Transportation and Infrastructure; elected to the 109th Congress on November 2, 2004; reelected to each succeeding Congress.

Office Listings

http://www.lipinski.house.gov

1717 Longworth House Office Building, Washington, DC 20515 .... (202) 225–5701
Chief of Staff.—Jason Tai. FAX: 225–1012
Office Administrative.—Jennifer Sypolt.
Legislative Director.—Eric Lausten.
Senior Legislative Assistant.—John Veysey.
6245 South Archer Avenue, Chicago, IL 60638 .... (312) 886–0481
Chief of Staff.—Jerry Hurckes.
19 West Hillgrove Avenue, LaGrange, IL 60525 .... (708) 352–0524
5309 West 95th Street, Oak Lawn, IL 60453 .... (708) 424–0853

Counties: COOK COUNTY (part). CITIES AND TOWNSHIPS: Alsip, Argo, Bedford Park, Berwyn, Bridgeview, Burr Ridge, Chicago, Chicago Ridge, Cicero, Countryside, Hickory Hills, Hinsdale, Hometown, Hodgkins, Indian Head Park, Justice Burbank, LaGrange, Lyons, McCook, North Riverside, Oak Lawn, Oak Park, Palos Hills, Palos Park, Proviso, Riverside, Stickney, Summit Brookfield, Western Springs, Willow Springs, and Worth. Population (2000), 653,647

ZIP Codes: 60126, 60130, 60154, 60162, 60402, 60415, 60426, 60430, 60453–59, 60463–65, 60477, 60480, 60482, 60499, 60501, 60513, 60521, 60525–27, 60534, 60546, 60558, 60570, 60608–09, 60616, 60620, 60623, 60629, 60632, 60636, 60638, 60643, 60652, 60655, 60803–05

* * *

FOURTH DISTRICT

LUIS V. GUTIERREZ, Democrat, of Chicago, IL; born in Chicago, December 10, 1953; education: B.A., Northeastern Illinois University, DeKalb, Ill., 1974; professional: teacher; social worker, Illinois; state department of children and family services; administrative assistant, Chicago, Ill., mayor's office subcommittee on infrastructure, 1984–85; co-founder, West Town-26th Ward Independent Political Organization, 1985; alderman, Chicago, Ill., city council, 1986–93, president pro tem, 1989–92; Democratic National Committee, 1984; married: Soraida Arocho; children: Omaira and Jessica; committees: Financial Services; Judiciary; elected on November 3, 1992, to the 103rd Congress; reelected to each succeeding Congress.

Office Listings

http://www.house.gov/gutierrez

2266 Rayburn House Office Building, Washington, DC 20515 .... (202) 225–8203
Chief of Staff.—Jennice Fuentes. FAX: 225–7810
Legislative Director.—Susan Collins.
Communications Director.—Scott Frotman.
2201 West North Avenue, Chicago, IL 60647 .... (773) 342–0774
FAX: 342–0776

Counties: COOK COUNTY (part). CITIES: Berkeley, Brookfield, Chicago, Ciero, Elmwood Park, Forest Park, Hillside, Maywood, Melrose Park, Northlake, Oak Park, Stickney, Stone Park, and Westchester. Population (2000), 653,647.

ZIP Codes: 60130, 60141, 60153–55, 60160, 60162–65, 60304–05, 60402, 60443, 60446, 60473, 60513, 60526, 60542, 60546, 60608–09, 60612, 60614, 60616, 60618, 60622–23, 60625, 60629, 60632, 60639, 60641, 60644, 60647, 60651, 60707, 60804

* * *

FIFTH DISTRICT

MIKE QUIGLEY, Democrat, of Chicago, IL; born in Indianapolis, October 17, 1958; education: B.A., political science, Roosevelt University, 1981; M.P.P., University of Chicago, 1985; J.D., Loyola University, 1989; professional: Cook County aldermanic aide, 1983–89; Practicing Attorney, 1990–present; Cook County Commissioner, 1998–2009; Adjunct Professor, Roosevelt University, 2006–07; Adjunct Professor, Loyola University, 2002–09; married: Barbara; children: Meghan and Alyson; committees: Oversight and Government Reform, Judiciary; elected to the 111th Congress on April 7, 2009.

Office Listings

http://www.quigley.house.gov

1319 Longworth House Office Building, Washington, DC 20515 .... (202) 225–4061
Chief of Staff.—Sean O'Brien. FAX: 225–5603
Communications Director.—Aviva Gibbs.
Scheduler.—Monica Foskett.
Legislative Director.—Lindsey Matese.
3742 West Irving Park Road, Chicago, IL 60618 .... (773) 267–5926

Counties: COOK COUNTY (part). Population (2007), 652,430.

ZIP Codes: 60018, 60106, 60131, 60153, 60160–61, 60164–65, 60171, 60176, 60504, 60525, 60613–14, 60618, 60625, 60630–31, 60634, 60639–41, 60646, 60656–57, 60659–60, 60677, 60706–07, 60712, 60714

* * *

SIXTH DISTRICT

PETER J. ROSKAM, Republican, of Wheaton, IL; born in Hinsdale, IL, September 13, 1961; education: B.A., University of Illinois, Urbana-Champaign, IL, 1983; J.D., Illinois Institute of Technology Chicago-Kent College of Law, Chicago, IL, 1989; professional: lawyer, private practice; staff, United States Representative Tom DeLay of Texas, 1985–86; United States Representative Henry Hyde of Illinois, 1986–87; teacher; businessman; member, Illinois house of representatives, 1993–99; member, Illinois senate, 2000–06; married: Elizabeth; children: four; committees: Ways and Means; elected to the 110th Congress on November 7, 2006; reelected to the 111th Congress.

Office Listings

http://www.house.gov/roskam

507 Cannon House Office Building, Washington, DC 20515 .... (202) 225–4561
Chief of Staff.—Steven Moore. FAX: 225–1166
Scheduler.—Mike Dankler.
Legislative Director.—David Mork.
Press Secretary.—Matt Vriesema.
150 South Bloomingdale Road, Suite 200, Bloomingdale, IL 60108 .... (630) 893–9670

Counties: COOK (part), DUPAGE (part). CITIES AND TOWNSHIPS: Addison, Arlington Heights, Bensenville, Bloomingdale, Carol Stream, Des Plaines, Elk Grove, Elk Grove Village, Elmhurst, Glen Ellyn, Glendale Heights, Hanover Park Streamwood, Itasca, Leyden Proviso, Lombard, Maine, Milton, Oak Brook, Oak Brook Terrace, Roselle, Villa Park, Wayne, Westchester, Westmont, Wheaton, Winfield, and York. Population (2000), 615,419.

ZIP Codes: 60005, 60007–09, 60016–18, 60056, 60067, 60101, 60103, 60105–08, 60116–17, 60120, 60125–26, 60128, 60131–33, 60137–39, 60143, 60148, 60157, 60172–73, 60176, 60181, 60185, 60187–95, 60197, 60199, 60399, 60515, 60523, 60532, 60559, 60563, 60666, 60688, 60701

* * *

SEVENTH DISTRICT

DANNY K. DAVIS, Democrat, of Chicago, IL; born in Parkdale, AR, September 6, 1941; education: B.A., Arkansas AM&N College, 1961; M.A., Chicago State University; Ph.D., Union Institute, Cincinnati, OH; educator and health planner-administrator; board of directors, National Housing Partnership; Cook County Board of Commissioners, 1990–96; former alderman of the Chicago City Council's 29th ward, receiving the Independent Voters of Illinois ''Best Alderman Award'' for 1980–81, 1981–82, and 1989–90; co-chair, Clinton-Gore-Braun '92; founder and past president, Westside Association for Community Action; past president, National Association of Community Health Centers; 1987 recipient of the Leon M. Despres Award; married to Vera G. Davis; two sons: Jonathan and Stacey; committees: Oversight and Government Reform; Ways and Means; elected to the 105th Congress; reelected to each succeeding Congress.

Office Listings

http://www.davis.house.gov

2159 Rayburn House Office Building, Washington, DC 20515 .... (202) 225–5006

Chief of Staff.—Yul Edwards. FAX: 225–5641
Legislative Director.—Jill Hunter-Williams.
Director of Issues and Communications.—Ira Cohen.
3333 West Arthington Street, Suite 130, Chicago, IL 60624 .... (773) 533–7520
2301 Roosevelt Road, Broadview, IL 60155 .... (708) 345–6857

Counties: COOK COUNTY (part). CITIES AND TOWNSHIPS: Bellwood, Berkley, Broadview, Chicago, Forest Park, Hillside, Maywood, Oak Park, River Forest, and Westchester. Population (2000), 653,647.

ZIP Codes: 60104, 60130, 60141, 60153–55, 60160, 60162–63, 60301–05, 60546, 60601–12, 60614–16, 60621–24, 60636–37, 60639, 60644, 60651, 60653–54, 60661, 60663–65, 60667–75, 60678–81, 60683–88, 60690–91, 60693–97, 60707, 60804

* * *

EIGHTH DISTRICT

MELISSA L. BEAN, Democrat, of Chicago, IL; born in Chicago, January 22, 1962; education: graduated, Maine East High School, Park Ridge, IL, 1980; A.A., Oakton Community College, Des Plaines, IL, 1982; B.A., Roosevelt University, Chicago, IL, 2002; professional: president, sales; Resources Incorporated, 1995–present; vice president, sales, Dataflex Corporation, 1994–95; area manager, UDS/Motorola, 1989–91; branch manager, MTI Systems Incorporated/Arrow Electronics, 1985–89; district sales manager, DJC Corporation 1982–85; Palatine Chamber of Commerce; Barrington area Professional Women; National Association of Women Business Owners; president of Deer Lake Homeowners Association; boards of Barrington Children's Choir and the Lines Elementary parent-teacher organization; religion: Serbian Orthodox; married: Alan; children: Victoria, Michelle; committees: Financial Services; Small Business; elected to the 109th Congress on November 2, 2004; reelected to each succeeding Congress.

Office Listings

http://www.house.gov/bean

432 Cannon House Office Building, Washington, DC 20515 .... (202) 225–3711
Chief of Staff.—Elizabeth Hart. FAX: 225–7830
Legislative Director.—J.D. Grom.
1701 East Woodfield Road, Schaumburg, IL 60173 .... (847) 517–2927
District Director.—Nick Jordan.

Counties: COOK COUNTY (part). TOWNSHIPS: Barrington, Hanover, Palatine, and Schaumburg. LAKE COUNTY (part). TOWNSHIPS: Antioch, Avon, Bentor, Cuba, Ela, Fremont, Grant, Lake Villa, Libertyville, Newport, Warren, Wauconda, and Zion. MCHENRY COUNTY (part). CITIES: Burton, Dorr, Greenwood, Hebron, McHenry, Nunda, and Richmond. Population (2000), 653,647.

ZIP Codes: 60002, 60004–05, 60007–08, 60010–14, 60020–21, 60030–31, 60033–34, 60038, 60041–42, 60046–51, 60060–61, 60067, 60071–75, 60081, 60083–85, 60087, 60095–99, 60103, 60107, 60120, 60133, 60159, 60168, 60172–73, 60179, 60192–96

* * *

NINTH DISTRICT

JANICE D. SCHAKOWSKY, Democrat, of Evanston, IL; born in Chicago, IL, May 26, 1944; education: B.A., University of Illinois, 1965; consumer advocate; program director, Illinois Public Action; executive director, Illinois State Council of Senior Citizens, 1985–90; State Representative, 18th District, Illinois General Assembly, 1991–99; served on Labor and Commerce, Human Service Appropriations, Health Care, and Electric Deregulation Committees; religion: Jewish; married: Robert Creamer; children: Ian, Mary, and Lauren; committees: Energy and Commerce; Permanent Select Committee on Intelligence; elected to the 106th Congress; reelected to each succeeding Congress.

Office Listings

http://www.house.gov/schakowsky

2367 Rayburn House Office Building, Washington, DC 20515 .... (202) 225–2111
Chief of Staff.—Cathy Hurwit. FAX: 226–6890
Communications Director.—Trevor Kincaid.
Legislative Director.—Isaac Brown.
Appointments Secretary.—Kim Muzeroll.
5533 Broadway, Chicago, IL 60640 .... (773) 506–7100

District Director.—Leslie Combs.
820 Davis Street, Suite 105, Evanston, IL 60201 .... (847) 328–3409

Counties: COOK COUNTY (part). CITIES: Chicago, Evanston, Glenview, Golf, Lincolnwood, Morton Grove, Niles, and Skokie. Population (2000), 653,647.

ZIP Codes: 60016, 60018–19, 60025, 60029, 60053, 60056, 60068, 60076–77, 60091, 60176, 60201–04, 60208, 60611, 60613, 60626, 60630–31, 60640, 60645–46, 60656–57, 60659–60, 60706, 60712, 60714

* * *

TENTH DISTRICT

MARK STEVEN KIRK, Republican, of Highland Park, IL; born in Champaign, IL, September 15, 1959; education: New Trier East High School, Winnetka, IL, 1977; B.A., Cornell University, 1981; J.D., Georgetown University, 1992; professional: attorney; military service: Lt. Commander, U.S. Navy Reserve; Administrative Assistant to Rep. John Porter (R–IL), 1984–90; World Bank, served as an International Finance Corp. officer; Dept. of State, served as Special Assistant to the Assistant Secretary for Inter-American Affairs; Baker & McKenzie (law firm); served as Counsel on the House Committee on International Relations; committees: Appropriations; elected to the 107th Congress on November 7, 2000; reelected to each succeeding Congress.

Office Listings

http://www.house.gov/kirk

1030 Longworth House Office Building, Washington, DC 20515 .... (202) 225–4835
Chief of Staff.—Lester Munson. FAX: 225–0837
Legislative Director.—Patrick Magnuson.
707 Skokie Boulevard, Suite 350, Northbrook, IL 60062 .... (847) 940–0202
Press Secretary.—Eric Elk.

Counties: COOK (part), LAKE (part). Population (2000), 653,647.

ZIP Codes: 60004–06, 60008, 60010, 60015–16, 60022, 60025–26, 60030–31, 60035, 60037, 60040, 60043–45, 60047–48, 60056, 60060–62, 60064–65, 60067, 60069–70, 60074, 60078–79, 60082–83, 60085–93, 60173, 60195, 60201

* * *

ELEVENTH DISTRICT

DEBORAH L. HALVORSON, Democrat, of Crete, IL; born in Chicago Heights, IL, March 1, 1958; education: graduated, Bloom High School, 1976; A.G.S., Prairie State College, 1998; B.A., Governors State University, 2001; M.A., Governors State University, 2003; professional: Crete Township Clerk, 1993–96; Illinois State Senator, 1996–2008; Illinois State Senate Majority Leader, 2005–2008; religion: Lutheran; married: Jim Bush; four children; four grandchildren; New Democrat Caucus; co-chair, New Democrat Energy Task Force; Democratic Steering and Policy Committee; committee: Agriculture; Small Business; Veterans' Affairs; elected to the 111th Congress on November 4, 2008.

Office Listings

http://www.halvorson.house.gov

1541 Longworth House Office Building, Washington, DC 20515 .... (202) 225–3635
Chief of Staff.—Gideon Blustein. FAX: 225–3521
Executive Assistant.—Erica Bordador.
Deputy Chief of Staff / Legislative Director.—Corey Tellez.
116 North Chicago Street, Suite 401, Joliet, IL 60432 .... (815) 726–4998
District Manager.—Marylin Turner.
Director of Communications.—Roxane Geraci.

Counties: BUREAU (part), GRUNDY, KANKAKEE, LA SALLE, LIVINGSTON (part), MCLEAN (part), WILL (part), and WOODFORD (part). Population (2000), 653,658.

ZIP Codes: 60401, 60407–11, 60416–17, 60420–21, 60423–24, 60430–37, 60442, 60444–45, 60447–51, 60466, 60468, 60470, 60474–75, 60477, 60479, 60481, 60504, 60518, 60531, 60541, 60544, 60548–49, 60551–52, 60557, 60625, 60640, 60646, 60660, 60901–02, 60910, 60912–15, 60917, 60919, 60922, 60935, 60940–41, 60944, 60950, 60954,

60961, 60964, 61238, 61240–41, 61254, 61262, 61273, 61301, 61312, 61314–17, 61320–23, 61325–26, 61328–30, 61332, 61334, 61337–38, 61341–42, 61344–45, 61348–50, 61354, 61356, 61358–62, 61364, 61368, 61370–74, 61376–77, 61379, 61701–02, 61704, 61725, 61732, 61736, 61744–45, 61748, 61752, 61754, 61760–61, 61772, 61774, 61790

* * *

TWELFTH DISTRICT

JERRY F. COSTELLO, Democrat, of Belleville, IL; born in East St. Louis, IL, September 25, 1949; education: graduated, Assumption High, East St. Louis, IL, 1968; A.A., Belleville Area College, IL, 1970; B.A., Maryville College of the Sacred Heart, St. Louis, MO, 1973; professional: county bailiff, Illinois 20th judicial circuit; deputy sheriff, St. Clair County, IL; director of court services and probation, Illinois 20th judicial district; chief investigator, Illinois state attorney's office, St. Clair County, IL; elected board chair, St. Clair County, IL, 1980–88; married: the former Georgia Jean Cockrum, 1968; children: Jerry II, Gina Costello, and John; committees: Science and Technology; Transportation and Infrastructure; elected to the 100th Congress by special election to fill the vacancy caused by the death of United States Representative Charles Melvin Price; reelected to each succeeding Congress.

Office Listings

http://www.house.gov/costello

2408 Rayburn House Office Building, Washington, DC 20515 .... (202) 225–5661
Chief of Staff.—David Gillies. FAX: 225–0285
Scheduler.—Karl Britton.
Legislative Director.—Sarah Blackwood.
Press Secretary.—David Gillies.
2060 Delmar Avenue, Suite B, Granite City, IL 62040 .... (618) 451–7065
8787 State Street, Suite 102, East Saint Louis, IL 62203 .... (618) 397–8833
144 Lincoln Place Court, Suite 4, Belleville, IL 62221 .... (618) 233–8026
201 East Nolen Street, West Frankfort, IL 62896 .... (618) 937–6402
250 West Cherry Street, Carbondale, IL 62901 .... (618) 529–3791
1330 Swanwick Street, Chester, IL 62233 .... (618) 826–3043

Counties: ALEXANDER, FRANKLIN, JACKSON, MADISON (part), MONROE, PERRY, PULASKI, RANDOLPH, ST. CLAIR, UNION, WILLIAMSON (part). Population (2000), 653,647.

ZIP Codes: 62002, 62010, 62018, 62024–25, 62035, 62040, 62048, 62059–60, 62071, 62084, 62087, 62090, 62095, 62201–08, 62217, 62220–26, 62232–34, 62236–44, 62246, 62248, 62254–61, 62263–65, 62268–69, 62272, 62274, 62277–80, 62282, 62284–86, 62288–89, 62292–95, 62297–98, 62812, 62819, 62822, 62831–32, 62836, 62840, 62846, 62859–60, 62865, 62883–84, 62888, 62890, 62896–97, 62901–03, 62905–07, 62912, 62914–18, 62920, 62922–24, 62926–27, 62932–33, 62939–42, 62948–52, 62956–59, 62961–64, 62966, 62969–71, 62973–76, 62983, 62987–88, 62990, 62992–94, 62996–99

* * *

THIRTEENTH DISTRICT

JUDY BIGGERT, Republican, of Hinsdale, IL; born in Chicago, IL, August 15, 1937; education: graduated from New Trier High School, 1955; B.A., Stanford University, 1959; J.D., Northwestern University School of Law, 1963; professional: attorney, 1975–99; Illinois House of Representatives (81st District), 1993–98; Assistant House Republican Leader, 1995–99; has served on numerous local civic and community organizations and groups; religion: Episcopalian; married: Rody P. Biggert; children: Courtney, Alison, Rody, and Adrienne; committees: Education and Labor; Financial Services; Science and Technology; elected to the 106th Congress; reelected to each succeeding Congress.

Office Listings

1034 Longworth House Office Building, Washington, DC 20515 .... (202) 225–3515
Chief of Staff.—Kathy Lydon. FAX: 225–9420
Press Secretary.—Zachary Cikanek.
Legislative Director.—Cade Clurman.
Scheduler.—Jackie Abba.
6262 South Route 83, Suite 305, Willowbrook, IL 60527 .... (630) 655–2052

Counties: COOK (part), DUPAGE (part), WILL (part). Population (2000), 653,647.

ZIP Codes: 60181, 60403, 60432, 60435, 60439, 60440–41, 60446, 60448, 60462–64, 60467, 60477, 60483, 60487, 60490–91, 60502–04, 60514–17, 60519, 60521–23, 60527, 60532, 60540, 60543–44, 60555, 60559, 60561, 60563–67, 60572, 60585–86, 60597, 60599

* * *

FOURTEENTH DISTRICT

BILL FOSTER, Democrat of Batavia, IL; born in Madison, WI, October 7, 1955; education: graduated, B.S., University of Wisconsin-Madison, 1976; Ph.D., Harvard University, 1983; elected Fellow of the American Physical Society, received the Rossi Prize for Cosmic Ray Physics for the discovery of the neutrino burse from Supernova SN1987a, received the Particle Accelerator Technology Prize from the Institute of Electrical and Electronic Engineers; award: Energy Conservation award from the U.S. Department of Energy for his invention and application of permanent magnets for Fermilab's accelerator; married: Aesook Byon, 2008; children: Billy and Christine; committees: Financial Services; Oversight and Government Reform; elected to the 110th Congress in a special election on March 8, 2008; reelected to the 111th Congress.

Office Listings

http://foster.house.gov

1339 Longworth House Office Building, Washington, DC 20515 .... (202) 225–2976
Chief of Staff.—Jason Linde. FAX: 225–0697
Communications Director.—Shannon O'Brien.
Legislative Director.—Sandy Sussman.
Scheduler.—Daisy Tomaselli.
27 North River Street, Batavia, IL 60510 .... (630) 406–1114
District Director.—Sue Klinkhamer.
Scheduler.—Caroline Merkel.
119 West First Street, Dixon, IL 61021 .... (815) 288–0680

Counties: BUREAU (part), DEKALB (part), DUPAGE (part), HENRY (part), KANE, KENDALL, LEE, WHITESIDE (part). CITIES AND TOWNSHIPS: Amboy, Ashton, Aurora, Barrington Hills, Bartlett, Batavia, Big Rock, Bristol, Burlington, Carol Stream, Carpentersville, Clare, Compton, Cornell, Cortland, DeKalb, Dixon, Dundee, East and West, Earlville, Elburn, Elgin, Esmond, Forreston, Franklin Grove, Geneva, Genoa, Gilberts, Hampshire, Harmon, Hinckley, Kaneville, Kingston, Kirkland, Lee, Leland, Malta, Maple Park, Mendota, Millbrook, Millington, Minooka, Montgomery, Mooseheart, Nelson, Newark, North Aurora, Oswego, Paw Paw, Plano, Plato Center, St. Charles, Sandwich, Shabbona, Sleepy Hollow, Somonauk, South Elgin, Steward, Sublette, Sugar Grove, Sycamore, Virgil, Warrenville, Wasco, Waterman, Wayne, West Brooklyn, West Chicago, Wheaton, Winfield, and Yorkville. Population (2000), 653,647.

ZIP Codes: 60010, 60102–03, 60109–10, 60112, 60115, 60118–23, 60134, 60136, 60140, 60142, 60144, 60147, 60150–52, 60170, 60174–75, 60177–78, 60183–87, 60190, 60431, 60447, 60450, 60504–06, 60510–12, 60518, 60520, 60530–31, 60536–39, 60541–45, 60548, 60550, 60552–56, 60560, 60563, 60568, 60640, 60660, 61006, 61021, 61031, 61042, 61057–58, 61068, 61071, 61081, 61234–35, 61238, 61240–41, 61243, 61250, 61254, 61258, 61270, 61273–74, 61277, 61283, 61310, 61318, 61324, 61330–31, 61342, 61344, 61346, 61349, 61353, 61367, 61376, 61378, 61434, 61443

* * *

FIFTEENTH DISTRICT

TIMOTHY V. JOHNSON, Republican, of Sidney, IL; born in Champaign, IL, July 23, 1946; education: B.A., University of Illinois, Phi Beta Kappa; J.D., University of Illinois College of Law, graduated with high honors; professional: attorney; public service: Urbana, IL, City Council, 1971–75; Illinois House of Representatives, 1976–2000; Deputy Majority Leader; Champaign County, IL, Republican Party Chair, 1990–96; committees: Agriculture; Transportation and Infrastructure; elected to the 107th Congress on November 7, 2000; reelected to each succeeding Congress.

Office Listings

http://www.timjohnson.house.gov

1207 Longworth House Office Building, Washington, DC 20515 .... (202) 225–2371
Chief of Staff.—Jerome T. Clarke. FAX: 226–0791
Legislative Director.—Stephen Borg.
2004 Fox Drive, Champaign, IL 61820 .... (217) 403–4690

Counties: CHAMPAIGN, CLARK, COLES, CRAWFORD, CUMBERLAND, DEWITT, DOUGLAS, EDGAR, EDWARDS (part), FORD, GALLATIN (part), IROQUOIS, LAWRENCE (part), LIVINGSTON (part), MACON (part), MCLEAN (part), MOULTRIE, PIATT, SALINE (part), VERMILION, WABASH (part), WHITE (part). CITIES AND TOWNSHIPS: Bloomington-Normal, Champaign-Urbana, Charleston-Mattoon, Danville, Decatur, Mount Carmel, and Pontiac. Population (2000), 653,647.

ZIP Codes: 60420, 60423, 60437, 60449, 60460, 60518, 60531, 60551–52, 60901–02, 60911–14, 60917–22, 60924, 60926–34, 60936, 60938–42, 60945–46, 60948–49, 60951–53, 60955–57, 60959–64, 60966–70, 60973–74, 61252, 61270, 61311, 61313, 61319, 61321, 61333, 61364, 61401, 61434, 61448–49, 61530, 61701–02, 61704, 61709–10, 61720, 61722, 61724, 61726–28, 61730–31, 61735, 61737, 61739–41, 61743, 61748–50, 61752–53, 61758, 61761, 61764, 61769–70, 61772–73, 61775–78, 61791, 61799, 61801–03, 61810–18, 61820–22, 61824–26, 61830–34, 61839–59,

61862–66, 61870–78, 61880, 61882–84, 61910–14, 61917, 61919–20, 61924–25, 61928–33, 61936–38, 61940–44, 61949, 61951, 61953, 61955–56, 62401, 62410, 62413, 62420–21, 62423, 62427–28, 62432–33, 62435–36, 62439–42, 62445, 62447, 62449, 62451, 62454, 62460, 62462, 62466–69, 62474, 62477–78, 62481, 62521–22, 62526, 62532, 62544, 62549–50, 62701–03, 62821, 62827, 62844, 62863, 62867, 62869, 62871, 62930, 62934, 62946, 62984

* * *

SIXTEENTH DISTRICT

DONALD A. MANZULLO, Republican, of Egan, IL; born in Rockford, IL, March 24, 1944; education: B.A., American University, Washington, DC, 1987; J.D., Marquette University Law School, Milwaukee, WI, 1970; admitted to Illinois bar, 1970; president, Ogle County Bar Association, 1971, 1973; advisor, Oregon Ambulance Corporation; founder, Oregon Youth, Inc.; member: State of Illinois and City of Oregon chambers of commerce; Friends of Severson Dells; Natural Land Institute; Ogle County Historic Society; Northern Illinois Alliance for the Arts; Aircraft Owners and Pilots Association; Ogle County Pilots Association; Kiwanis International; Illinois Farm Bureau; Ogle County Farm Bureau; National Federation of Independent Business; Citizens Against Government Waste; married: Freda Teslik, 1982; children: Niel, Noel, and Katherine; committees: Financial Services; Foreign Affairs; elected on November 3, 1992, to the 103rd Congress; reelected to each succeeding Congress.

Office Listings

http://www.manzullo.house.gov

2228 Rayburn House Office Building, Washington, DC 20515 .... (202) 225–5676
Chief of Staff.—Adam Magary FAX: 225–5284
Legislative Director.—Phil Eskeland.
Scheduler.—Kelli Nelson.
Communications Director (Rockford).—Rich Carter.
415 South Mulford Road, Rockford, IL 61108 .... (815) 394–1231
District Director.—Pam Sexton.
101 North Virginia Street, Suite 170, Crystal Lake, IL 60014 .... (815) 356–9800
Caseworker.—Kathleen Davis.

Counties: BOONE, CARROLL, DEKALB (part), JO DAVIESS, MCHENRY (part), OGLE, STEPHENSON, WHITESIDE (part), WINNEBAGO. Population (2000), 653,647.

ZIP Codes: 60001, 60010, 60012–14, 60021, 60033–34, 60039, 60042, 60050–51, 60098, 60102, 60111, 60113, 60115, 60129, 60135, 60140, 60142, 60145–46, 60150, 60152, 60156, 60178, 60180, 60530, 61001, 61006–08, 61010–16, 61018–21, 61024–25, 61027–28, 61030–32, 61036, 61038–39, 61041, 61043–44, 61046–54, 61059–65, 61067–68, 61070–75, 61077–81, 61084–85, 61087–89, 61091, 61101–12, 61114–15, 61125–26, 61130–32, 61230, 61250–52, 61261, 61266, 61270, 61285

* * *

SEVENTEENTH DISTRICT

PHIL HARE, Democrat, of Rock Island, IL; born in Galesburg, IL, February 21, 1949; education: graduated, Alleman High School, 1969; attended Blackhawk College, Moline, IL; tailor of men's suits for 13 years at Seaford Clothing Factory; served as union leader and as president of UNITE HERE, Local 617; served in the U.S. Army Reserves for six years; District Director for U.S. Congressman Lane Evans (D–IL), 1983–2006; married: Beckie; children: Lou and Amy; committees: Education and Labor; Transportation and Infrastructure; Senior Whip; elected on November 7, 2006 to the 110th Congress; reelected to the 111th Congress.

Office Listings

428 Cannon House Office Building, Washington, DC 20515 .... (202) 225–5905
Administrative Assistant.—Tom O'Donnell. FAX: 225–5396
Office Manager.—Eda Robinson.
Press Secretary.—Tim Schlittner.
2001 52nd Avenue, #5, Moline, IL 61265 .... (309) 793–5760
District Representative.—Pat O'Brien.
261 North Broad, Suite 5, Galesburg, IL 61401 .... (309) 342–4411
236 North Water, Suite 765, Decatur, IL 62523 .... (217) 422–9150
210 North Broad Street, Carlinville, IL 62626 .... (217) 854–2290

Counties: ADAMS (part), CALHOUN, CHRISTIAN (part), FAYETTE (part), FULTON, GREENE (part), HANCOCK, HENDERSON, HENRY (part), JERSEY (part), KNOX (part), MACON (part), MACOUPIN, MADISON (part), MCDONOUGH, MERCER, MONTGOMERY (part), PIKE (part), ROCK ISLAND, SANGAMON (part), SHELBY (part), WARREN, WHITESIDE (part). Population (2000), 653,647.

ZIP Codes: 61037, 61071, 61081, 61201, 61204, 61230–33, 61236–37, 61239–42, 61244, 61251, 61256–57, 61259–65, 61272, 61275–76, 61278–79, 61281–82, 61284, 61299, 61318, 61342, 61364, 61401–02, 61410–20, 61422–23, 61425, 61427, 61430–43, 61447–48, 61450, 61452–55, 61458–60, 61462, 61465–78, 61480, 61482, 61484, 61486, 61488–90, 61501, 61519–20, 61524, 61531, 61533, 61542–44, 61553, 61560, 61563, 61569, 61572, 61611, 61701, 61761, 62001–02, 62006, 62009, 62011–14, 62017, 62019, 62021, 62023, 62027, 62031–33, 62036–37, 62044–45, 62047, 62049–53, 62056, 62058, 62063, 62065, 62069–70, 62074–75, 62077–79, 62082, 62085–86, 62088–89, 62091–94, 62097–98, 62262, 62301, 62305–06, 62311, 62313, 62316, 62320–21, 62326, 62329–30, 62334, 62336, 62338, 62341, 62343, 62345, 62348, 62351, 62354–56, 62358, 62360–61, 62366–67, 62370, 62373–74, 62376, 62379–80, 62431, 62513–15, 62520–23, 62525–26, 62537, 62539, 62544, 62549–51, 62557, 62560–61, 62572, 62615, 62624, 62626, 62629–30, 62640, 62644, 62649, 62661, 62667, 62670, 62672, 62674, 62683, 62685, 62690, 62692, 62701–05, 62707–08, 62713, 62781, 62794, 62796

* * *

EIGHTEENTH DISTRICT

AARON SCHOCK, Republican, of Peoria, IL; born in Morris, MN, May 28, 1981; B.S. in Finance, Bradley University, Peoria, IL, 2002; professional: President of Peoria Board of Education, youngest school board president in history; Illinois House of Representatives 2005–09, Director of Development for Petersen Companies of Peoria, 2007; awards: named one of Peoria's *40 Leaders Under 40*, 2004; Peoria Jaycees Good Government Award, 2004; Richard Mautino Excellence in Government Award, 2005; Community Workshop and Training Center Advocacy Award, 2005; Guardian Angels Arc-Angel Award, 2005; Illinois Healthcare Association's Legislator of the Year, 2005–07; Illinois Long Term Care Association's Legislator of the Year Award, 2006; Life Services Network Legislator of the Year, 2006; Illinois Committee for Honest Government Outstanding Legislative and Constituent Service Award, 2007; religion: Christian; Deputy Republican Whip; Animal Protection Caucus; Community College Caucus; House Diversity and Innovation Caucus; House Rural Education Caucus; Congressional Hunger Caucus; Congressional Fire Services Caucus; Congressional Services Caucus; House Recycling Caucus; Republican Study Group, Tuesday Group; committees: Oversight and Government Reform; Small Business; Transportation and Infrastructure; elected to the 111th Congress on November 4, 2008.

Office Listings

http://www.schock.house.gov

509 Cannon House Office Building, Washington, DC 20515 .... (202) 225–6201
Chief of Staff.—Steven Shearer. FAX: 225–9249
Deputy Chief of Staff.—Pamela Mattox.
Legislative Director.—Aaron Smith.
Communications Director.—Dave Natonski.
Legislative Assistants.—Margie Almanza, Mark Roman.
Legislative Correspondent.—Josh Baggett.
Staff Assistant.—Mike Pasko.
100 Northeast Monroe Street, Room 100, Peoria, IL 61602 .... (309) 671–7027
FAX: 671–7309
209 West State Street, Jacksonville, IL 62650 .... (217) 245–1431
FAX: 243–6852
235 South 6th Street, Springfield, IL 62701 .... (217) 670–1653
FAX: 670–1806

Counties: ADAMS (part), BROWN, BUREAU (part), CASS, KNOX (part), LOGAN, MACON (part), MARSHALL, MASON, MCLEAN, MENARD, MORGAN, PEORIA, PIKE (part), PUTNAM, SANGAMON (part), SCHUYLER, SCOTT, STARK, TAZEWELL, WOODFORD (part). Population (2000), 653,647.

ZIP Codes: 61314, 61320–21, 61326–27, 61330, 61334–36, 61340, 61345, 61349, 61362–63, 61369–70, 61375, 61377, 61401, 61410, 61414, 61421, 61424, 61426, 61428, 61434, 61436, 61440, 61443, 61448–49, 61451–52, 61455, 61458, 61467, 61472, 61479, 61483–85, 61488–89, 61491, 61501, 61516–17, 61523, 61525–26, 61528–37, 61539–42, 61545–48, 61550, 61552, 61554–55, 61558–62, 61564–65, 61567–72, 61601–07, 61610–12, 61614–16, 61625, 61628–30, 61632–41, 61643–44, 61650–56, 61704, 61721, 61723, 61729, 61733–34, 61738, 61742, 61747, 61749, 61751, 61755–56, 61759–61, 61771, 61774, 61778, 61830, 62305, 62311–12, 62314, 62319–20, 62323–25, 62338–40, 62344, 62346–47, 62349, 62352–53, 62357, 62359–60, 62362–63, 62365, 62367, 62375, 62378, 62501, 62512, 62515, 62518–22, 62524, 62526, 62535, 62539, 62541, 62543, 62548, 62551, 62554, 62561, 62573, 62601, 62610–13, 62615, 62617–18, 62621–22, 62624–25, 62627–29, 62631, 62633–35, 62638–39, 62642–44, 62650–51, 62655–56, 62660–68, 62670–71, 62673, 62675, 62677, 62681–82, 62684, 62688, 62690–95, 62701–07, 62713, 62715, 62719, 62721–22, 62726, 62736, 62739, 62746, 62756–57, 62761, 62765, 62767, 62769, 62776–77, 62781, 62786, 62791, 62796

* * *

NINETEENTH DISTRICT

JOHN SHIMKUS, Republican, of Collinsville, IL; born in Collinsville, February 21, 1958; education: graduated from Collinsville High School; B.S., West Point Military Academy, West

Point, NY, 1980; teaching certificate, Christ College, Irvine, CA, 1990; M.B.A., Southern Illinois University, Edwardsville, 1997; U.S. Army Reserves, 1980–85; government and history teacher, Metro East Lutheran High School, Edwardsville, IL; Collinsville township trustee, 1989; Madison county treasurer, 1990–96; married: the former Karen Muth, 1987; children: David, Daniel, and Joshua; committees: Energy and Commerce; elected to the 105th Congress; reelected to each succeeding Congress.

Office Listings

http://www.shimkus.house.gov

2452 Rayburn House Office Building, Washington, DC 20515 .... (202) 225–5271
Chief of Staff.—Craig Roberts. FAX: 225–5880
Legislative Director.—Ryan Tracy.
240 Regency Centre, Collinsville, IL 62234 .... (618) 344–3065
3130 Chatham Road, Suite C, Springfield, IL 62704 .... (217) 492–5090
District Director.—Deb Detmers.
221 East Broadway, Suite 102, Centralia, IL 62801 .... (618) 532–9676
120 South Fair, Olney, IL 62450 .... (618) 392–7737
110 East Locust Street, Room 12, Harrisburg, IL 62946 .... (618) 252–8271

Counties: BOND, CHRISTIAN (part), CLAY, CLINTON, EDWARDS (part), EFFINGHAM, FAYETTE (part), GALLATIN (part), GREENE (part), HAMILTON, HARDIN, JASPER, JEFFERSON, JERSEY (part), JOHNSON, LAWRENCE (part), MADISON (part), MARION, MASSAC, MONTGOMERY (part), POPE, RICHLAND, SALINE (part), SANGAMON (part), SHELBY (part), WABASH (part), WASHINGTON, WAYNE, WHITE (part), WILLIAMSON (part). Population (2000), 653,647.

ZIP Codes: 61957, 62001–02, 62010, 62012, 62015–17, 62019, 62021–22, 62024–26, 62028, 62030, 62034–35, 62040, 62044, 62046, 62049, 62051–52, 62054, 62056, 62061–62, 62067, 62074–76, 62080–81, 62083, 62086, 62088, 62094, 62097, 62214–16, 62218–19, 62230–31, 62234, 62237, 62245–47, 62249–50, 62252–55, 62257–58, 62262–63, 62265–66, 62268–69, 62271, 62273, 62275, 62281, 62284, 62293–94, 62338, 62401, 62410–11, 62413–14, 62417–28, 62431–36, 62438–52, 62454, 62458–69, 62471, 62473–81, 62510, 62513, 62515, 62517, 62520–22, 62526, 62530–31, 62533–34, 62536, 62538–40, 62545–48, 62550, 62553, 62555–58, 62560, 62563, 62565, 62567–68, 62570–72, 62615, 62629, 62689–90, 62703–04, 62707, 62716, 62723, 62762–64, 62766, 62791, 62801, 62803, 62805–12, 62814–25, 62827–31, 62833–44, 62846, 62848–72, 62874–87, 62889–99, 62908–10, 62912, 62917, 62919, 62921–23, 62926, 62928, 62930–31, 62934–35, 62938–39, 62941, 62943, 62946–47, 62953–56, 62959–60, 62965, 62967, 62972, 62977, 62979, 62982–85, 62987, 62991, 62995

INDIANA

(Population 2000, 6,080,485)

SENATORS

RICHARD G. LUGAR, Republican, of Indianapolis, IN; born in Indianapolis, April 14, 1932; education: graduated, Shortridge High School, valedictorian, 1950; B.A., Denison University, Granville, OH, valedictorian, 1954; Rhodes Scholar, B.A., M.A., Pembroke College, Oxford, England, 1956; professional: served in the U.S. Navy, 1957–60; businessman; president and treasurer, Lugar Stock Farms, Inc., a livestock and grain operation; vice president and treasurer, Thomas L. Green and Co., manufacturers of food production machinery, 1960–67; member, Indianapolis Board of School Commissioners, 1964–67; mayor of Indianapolis, 1968–75; member, advisory board, U.S. Conference of Mayors, 1969–75; National League of Cities, advisory council, 1972–75, president, 1971; Advisory Commission on Intergovernmental Relations, 1969–75, vice chairman, 1971–75; board of trustees, Denison University; Phi Beta Kappa; 41 honorary degrees; recipient of Fiorello LaGuardia Award, 1975; member, St. Luke's Methodist Church; married the former Charlene Smeltzer, 1956; four sons and thirteen grandchildren; committees: Agriculture, Nutrition, and Forestry; Foreign Relations; elected to the U.S. Senate on November 2, 1976, sworn in on January 3, 1977 as the 1,705th Senator; reelected to each succeeding Senate term.

Office Listings

http://lugar.senate.gov

306 Hart Senate Office Building, Washington, DC 20510 .... (202) 224–4814
Administrative Assistant.—Martin W. Morris. FAX: 228–0360
Legislative Director.—Chris Geeslin.
Press Secretary.—Andy Fisher.
Scheduler.—Brad McKinney.
10 West Market Street, Room 1180, Indianapolis, IN 46204 .... (317) 226–5555
Federal Building, Room 122, 101 Northwest Martin Luther King Boulevard, Evansville, IN 47708 .... (812) 465–6313
6384–A West Jefferson Boulevard, Fort Wayne, IN 46804 .... (260) 422–1505
175 West Lincolnway, Suite G–1, Valparaiso, IN 46383 .... (219) 548–8035

* * *

EVAN BAYH, Democrat, of Indianapolis, IN; born in Shirkieville, IN, December 26, 1955; education: graduated St. Albans School, Washington, DC, 1974; B.A. with honors in business economics, Indiana University, 1978; J.D., University of Virginia Law School, 1982; professional: admitted to the District of Columbia and Indiana bars, 1984; law clerk for the Southern District of Indiana court, 1982–83; attorney with Hogan and Hartson, Washington, 1983–84; attorney for Bayh, Tabbert and Capehart, Washington, 1985; attorney for Bingham Summers, Welsh and Spilman, Indianapolis, 1986; elected as Secretary of State of Indiana, 1986–89; elected Governor of Indiana, 1988; reelected, 1992; chairman, Democratic Governors' Association, 1994; chairman, National Education Goals Panel, 1995; chairman, Education Commission of the States, 1995; Above and Beyond Award, Indiana Black Expo, 1995; Breaking the Glass Ceiling Award from Women Executives in State Government, 1996; keynote speaker, National Democratic Convention, 1996; member of the executive committee on the National Governors' Association, 1996; Red Poling Chair, business economics at Indiana University, 1997; chairman, Democratic Leadership Council; married: Susan Breshears, April 13, 1985; twin sons, Birch Evans IV, and Nicholas Harrison; committees: Armed Services; Banking, Housing and Urban Affairs; Energy and Natural Resources; Small Business and Entrepreneurship; Special Committee on Aging; Select Committee on Intelligence; elected to the U.S. Senate on November 3, 1998; reelected to each succeeding Senate term.

Office Listings

http://bayh.senate.gov

131 Russell Senate Office Building, Washington, DC 20510 .... (202) 224–5623
Chief of Staff.—Charlie Salem. FAX: 228–1377
Executive Assistant.—Val Nosler.
Legislative Director.—Jayme Roth.
Scheduler.—Doug Landry.
130 South Main Street, Suite 110, South Bend, IN 44601 .... (574) 236–8302
1650 Market Tower, 10 West Market Street, Indianapolis, IN 46204 .... (317) 554–0750
101 Martin Luther King, Jr. Boulevard, Evansville, IN 47708 .... (812) 465–6500
1300 South Harrison Street, Room 3161, Ft. Wayne, IL 36802 .... (260) 426–3151

1201 East 10th Street, Suite 106, Jeffersonville, IN 47130 .... (812) 218–2317
Hammond Courthouse, 5400 Federal Plaza, Suite 3200, Hammond, IL 46320 .... (219) 852–2763

REPRESENTATIVES

FIRST DISTRICT

PETER J. VISCLOSKY, Democrat, of Merrillville, IN; born in Gary, IN, August 13, 1949; education: graduated, Andrean High School, Merrillville, 1967; B.S., accounting, Indiana University Northwest, Gary, 1970; J.D., University of Notre Dame Law School, Notre Dame, IN, 1973; LL.M., international and comparative law, Georgetown University Law Center, Washington, DC, 1982; professional: attorney; admitted to the Indiana state bar, 1974, the District of Columbia bar, 1978, and the U.S. Supreme Court bar, 1980; associate staff, U.S. House of Representatives, Committee on Appropriations, 1977–80, Committee on the Budget, 1980–82; practicing attorney, Merrillville law firm, 1983–84; wife: Joanne Royce; children: John Daniel and Timothy Patrick; committees: Appropriations; elected to the 99th Congress on November 6, 1984; reelected to each succeeding Congress.

Office Listings

http://www.house.gov/visclosky

2256 Rayburn House Office Building, Washington, DC 20515 .... (202) 225–2461
Chief of Staff.—Charles Brimmer. FAX: 225–2493
Appropriations Director.—Shari Davenport.
Executive Assistant.—Korry Baack.
Communications Director.—Jacob Ritvo.
7895 Broadway, Suite A, Merrillville, IN 46410 .... (219) 795–1844
District Director.—Mark Lopez. FAX: 795–1850
(888) 423–7383

Counties: BENTON, JASPER, LAKE, NEWTON, PORTER (part). Population (2000), 675,767.

ZIP Codes: 46301–04, 46307–08, 46310–12, 46319–25, 46327, 46341–42, 46345, 46347–49, 46355–56, 46360, 46366, 46368, 46372–73, 46375–77, 46379–85, 46390, 46392–94, 46401–11, 47917, 47921–22, 47942–44, 47948, 47951, 47963–64, 47970–71, 47977–78, 47984, 47986, 47995

* * *

SECOND DISTRICT

JOE DONNELLY, Democrat, of Granger, IN; born in Massapequa, NY, September 29, 1955; education: B.A., major: government, the University of Notre Dame, 1977; J.D., the University of Notre Dame, 1981; member: Law Firm of Nemeth, Feeny and Masters, in South Bend, IN; small business owner in Mishawaka; served on Indiana State Election Board, 1988–89; member of the Mishawaka Marian High School Board, 1997–2001, served as president; 2000–01; married to Jill; children: Molly and Joseph Jr.; committees: Financial Services; Veterans' Affairs; elected to the 110th Congress on November 7, 2006; reelected to the 111th Congress.

Office Listings

http://donnelly.house.gov

1530 Longworth House Office Building, Washington, DC 20515 .... (202) 225–3915
Chief of Staff.—Joel Elliott. FAX: 225–6798
Legislative Director.—Nathan Fenstermacher.
Scheduler.—Jessica McEwen.
Press Secretary.—Samantha Slater.
207 West Colfax Avenue, South Bend, IN 46601–1601 .... (574) 288–2780

Counties: CARROLL, CASS, ELKHART (part), FULTON, LAPORTE, MARSHALL, PORTER (part), PULASKI, ST. JOSEPH, STARKE, WHITE (part). CITIES: Elkhart, Kokomo, LaPorte, Logansport, Monticello, Mishawaka, Plymouth, Rochester, South Bend, and Westville. Population (2000), 675,767.

ZIP Codes: 46041, 46051, 46056, 46065, 46143, 46301, 46304, 46340–42, 46345–46, 46348, 46350, 46352, 46360–61, 46365–66, 46371, 46374, 46382–83, 46390–91, 46501, 46504, 46506, 46511, 46513–17, 46524, 46526, 46528, 46530–32, 46534, 46536–37, 46539, 46544–46, 46550, 46552, 46554, 46556, 46561, 46563, 46570, 46572, 46574, 46595, 46601, 46604, 46613–17, 46619–20, 46624, 46626, 46628–29, 46634–35, 46637, 46660, 46680, 46699, 46901–02, 46910, 46912–13, 46915–17, 46920, 46922–23, 46926, 46929, 46931–32, 46939, 46942, 46945, 46947, 46950–51, 46960–61, 46967–68, 46970, 46975, 46977–79, 46982, 46985, 46988, 46994, 46996, 46998, 47920, 47923, 47925–26, 47946, 47950, 47957, 47959, 47960, 47997

* * *

THIRD DISTRICT

MARK E. SOUDER, Republican, of Fort Wayne, IN; born in Grabill, IN, July 18, 1950; education: graduated from Leo High School, 1968; B.S., Indiana University, Fort Wayne, 1972; M.B.A., University of Notre Dame Graduate School of Business, 1974; professional: partner, Historic Souder's of Grabill; majority owner of Souder's General Store; vice president, Our Country Home, fixture manufacturing business; attends Emmanuel Community Church; served as economic development liaison for then-Representative Dan Coats (IN–4th District); appointed Republican staff director of the House Select Committee on Children, Youth and Families, 1984; legislative director and deputy chief of staff for former Senator Coats; member: Grabill Chamber of Commerce; former head of Congressional Action Committee of Ft. Wayne Chamber of Commerce; married: the former Diane Zimmer, 1974; children: Brooke, Nathan, and Zachary; committees: Education and Labor; Homeland Security; Oversight and Government Reform; elected to the 104th Congress; reelected to each succeeding Congress.

Office Listings

http://www.house.gov/souder

2231 Rayburn House Office Building, Washington, DC 20515 .... (202) 225–4436
Chief of Staff.—Renee Howell. FAX: 225–3479
Scheduler.—Kari Amstutz.
1300 South Harrison, Room 3105, Fort Wayne, IN 46802 .... (260) 424–3041
District Director.—Derek Pillie.
320 North Chicago Avenue, Suite 9B, Goshen, IN 46528 .... (574) 533–5802
700 Park Avenue, The Boathouse, Suite D, Winona Lake, IN 46590 .... (574) 269–1940

Counties: ALLEN (part), DEKALB, ELKHART (part), KOSCIUSKO, LAGRANGE, NOBLE, STEUBEN, WHITLEY. Population (2000), 675,617.

ZIP Codes: 46502, 46504, 46506–08, 46510, 46516, 46524, 46526–28, 46538–40, 46542–43, 46550, 46553, 46555, 46562, 46565–67, 46571, 46573, 46580–82, 46590, 46701, 46703–06, 46710, 46721, 46723, 46725, 46730, 46732, 46737–38, 46741–43, 46746–48, 46750, 46755, 46760–61, 46763–65, 46767, 46771, 46773–74, 46776–77, 46779, 46783–89, 46793–99, 46801–09, 46814–16, 46818–19, 46825, 46835, 46845, 46850–69, 46885, 46895–99, 46910, 46962, 46975, 46982

* * *

FOURTH DISTRICT

STEVE BUYER, Republican, of Monticello, IN; born in Rensselaer, IN, November 26, 1958; education: graduated, North White High School, 1976; B.S., business administration, The Citadel, 1980; J.D., Valparaiso University School of Law, 1984; admitted to the Virginia and Indiana bars; professional: U.S. Army Judge Advocate General Corps, 1984–87; assigned Deputy to the Attorney General of Indiana, 1987–88; family law practice, 1988–92; U.S. Army Reserves, 1980–present (major); legal counsel, 22nd Theatre Army in Operations Desert Shield and Desert Storm; married: to the former Joni Lynn Geyer; children: Colleen and Ryan; co-chair, National Guard and Reserve Components Caucus; committees: ranking member, Veterans' Affairs; Energy and Commerce; elected to the 103rd Congress, November 3, 1992; reelected to each succeeding Congress.

Office Listings

http://www.house.gov/buyer

2230 Rayburn House Office Building, Washington, DC 20515 .... (202) 225–5037
Chief of Staff.—Mike Copher.
Executive Assistant.—Tasha Sotomayor.
Legislative Director.—Tim Welter.
Press Secretary.—Anjulen Anderson.
2680 East Main Street, Suite 332, Plainfield, IN 46168 .... (317) 838–0404
District Director.—Jim Huston.
100 South Main Street, Monticello, IN 47960 .... (574) 583–9819
1801 I Street, Bedford, IN 47421 .... (812) 277–9590

Counties: BOONE, CLINTON, FOUNTAIN (part), HENDRICKS, JOHNSON (part), LAWRENCE (part), MARION (part), MONROE (part), MONTGOMERY, MORGAN, TIPPECANOE, WHITE (part). Population (2000), 675,617.

ZIP Codes: 46035, 46039, 46041, 46049–50, 46052, 46057–58, 46060, 46065, 46067, 46069, 46071, 46075, 46077, 46102–03, 46106, 46111–13, 46118, 46120–23, 46125, 46131, 46142–43, 46147, 46149, 46151, 46157–58, 46160, 46165–

68, 46172, 46175, 46180–81, 46183–84, 46214, 46221, 46224, 46231, 46234, 46241, 46254, 46268, 46278, 46920, 46923, 46979, 47108, 47260, 47264, 47403–04, 47420–21, 47429–30, 47433, 47436–37, 47446, 47451, 47456, 47460, 47462–64, 47467, 47470, 47901–07, 47909, 47916, 47918, 47920, 47923–24, 47929–30, 47932–41, 47944, 47949, 47952, 47954–55, 47958–60, 47962, 47965, 47967–68, 47970–71, 47978, 47980–81, 47983, 47987–90, 47992, 47994–96

* * *

FIFTH DISTRICT

DAN BURTON, Republican, of Indianapolis, IN; born in Indianapolis, June 21, 1938; education: graduated, Shortridge High School, 1956; Indiana University, 1956–57; Cincinnati Bible Seminary, 1958–60; served in the U.S. Army, 1957–58; U.S. Army Reserves, 1958–64; businessman, insurance and real estate firm owner since 1968; served, Indiana House of Representatives, 1967–68 and 1977–80; Indiana State Senate, 1969–70 and 1981–82; president: Volunteers of America, Indiana Christian Benevolent Association, Committee for Constitutional Government, and Family Support Center; member, Jaycees; 33rd degree Mason, Scottish rite division; married the former Barbara Jean Logan, 1959 (deceased, 2002); three children: Kelly, Danielle Lee, and Danny Lee II; remarried: Dr. Samia Tawil, 2006; committees: Foreign Affairs; Oversight and Government Reform; elected on November 2, 1982, to the 98th Congress; reelected to each succeeding Congress.

Office Listings

http://www.burton.house.gov

2308 Rayburn House Office Building, Washington, DC 20515 .... (202) 225–2276
Chief of Staff.—Mark Walker. FAX: 225–0016
Scheduler / Office Manager.—Diane Menorca.
Press Secretary.—John Donnelly.
8900 Keystone at the Crossing, Suite 1050, Indianapolis, IN 46240 .... (317) 848–0201
District Director.—Rick Wilson.
209 South Washington Street, Marion, IN 46952 .... (765) 662–6770

Counties: GRANT, HAMILTON, HANCOCK, HOWARD (part), HUNTINGTON, JOHNSON (part), MARION (part), MIAMI, SHELBY, TIPTON, WABASH. Population (2000), 675,794.

ZIP Codes: 46030–34, 46036, 46038, 46040, 46045, 46047, 46049, 46055, 46060–61, 46064, 46068–70, 46072, 46074, 46076–77, 46082, 46110, 46115, 46117, 46124, 46126, 46129–31, 46140, 46143, 46148, 46150, 46154, 46161–63, 46176, 46182, 46184, 46186, 46217, 46220, 46226–27, 46229, 46236–37, 46239–40, 46250, 46256, 46259–60, 46280, 46290, 46307, 46347, 46355, 46379–80, 46702, 46713–14, 46725, 46750, 46766, 46770, 46783, 46787, 46792, 46901–04, 46910–11, 46914, 46919, 46921, 46926, 46928–30, 46932–33, 46936–38, 46940–41, 46943, 46946, 46951–53, 46957–59, 46962, 46965, 46970–71, 46974–75, 46979–80, 46982, 46984, 46986–87, 46989–92, 46995, 47234, 47246, 47272, 47342, 47384

* * *

SIXTH DISTRICT

MIKE PENCE, Republican, of Columbus, IN; born in Columbus, June 7, 1959; education: Hanover College, 1981; J.D., Indiana University School of Law, 1986; professional: former Republican nominee for the U.S. House of Representatives in the 2nd District in 1988 and 1990; President, Indiana Policy Review Foundation, 1991–93; radio broadcaster: the Mike Pence Show, syndicated statewide in Indiana; married: Karen; children: Michael, Charlotte, and Audrey; committees: Foreign Affairs; elected to the 107th Congress on November 7, 2000; reelected to each succeeding Congress.

Office Listings

http://mikepence.house.gov

1431 Longworth House Office Building, Washington, DC 20515 .... (202) 225–3021
Chief of Staff.—Bill Smith. FAX: 225–3382
Legislative Director.—Nathaniel Milazzo.
Press Secretary.—Daniel Son.
Executive Assistant.—Jennifer Pavlik.
1134 Meridian Street, Anderson, IN 46016 .... (765) 640–2919
District Director.—Lani Czarniecki.

Counties: ALLEN (part), ADAMS, BARTHOLOMEW (part), BLACKFORD, DEARBORN (part), DECATUR, DELAWARE, FAYETTE, FRANKLIN, HENRY, JAY, JOHNSON (part), MADISON, RANDOLPH, RUSH, SHELBY (part), UNION, WAYNE, WELLS. Population (2000), 675,669.

ZIP Codes: 46001, 46011–18, 46036, 46040, 46044, 46048, 46051, 46056, 46063–64, 46070, 46104, 46110, 46115, 46124, 46126–27, 46131, 46133, 46140, 46142, 46144, 46146, 46148, 46150–51, 46155–56, 46160–62, 46164, 46173, 46176,

46181–82, 46186, 46711, 46714, 46731, 46733, 46740, 46745, 46750, 46759, 46766, 46769–70, 46772–73, 46777–78, 46780–83, 46791–92, 46797–98, 46809, 46816, 46819, 46928, 46952–53, 46989, 46991, 47003, 47006, 47010, 47012, 47016, 47022, 47024–25, 47030, 47035–37, 47060, 47201, 47203, 47225–26, 47234, 47240, 47244, 47246, 47261, 47263, 47265, 47272, 47280, 47283, 47302–08, 47320, 47322, 47324–27, 47330–31, 47334–42, 47344–46, 47348, 47351–62, 47366–71, 47373–75, 47380–88, 47390, 47392–94, 47396, 47448

* * *

SEVENTH DISTRICT

ANDRÉ CARSON, Democrat, of Indianapolis, IN; born in Indianapolis, October 16, 1974; graduated Arsenal Technical High School, Indianapolis, IN; education: B.A. in Criminal Justice Management, Concordia University Wisconsin, Mequon, WI; M.B.A, Indiana Wesleyan University, Marion, IN; professional: Investigative Officer for the Indiana State Excise Police, 1997–2006; Indiana Department of Homeland Security's Intelligence Fusion Center, 2006; City County Councilor, Marion County, 2007; religion: Muslim; married: Mariama; children: Salimah; committees: Financial Services; elected to the 110th Congress on March 11, 2008, by special election, to fill the vacancy caused by the death of United States Representative Julia Carson; elected to the 111th Congress on November 4, 2008.

Office Listings

http://www.carson.house.gov

425 Cannon House Office Building, Washington, DC 20515 .... (202) 225–4011
Deputy Chief of Staff / Counsel.—Ken Nealy. FAX: 225–5633
Legislative Director.—Erin Rosenberg.
Legislative Assistants: Umar Ahmed, Nathan Bennett, Nida Zaman.
Scheduler.—Kasey Kendrick.
300 East Fall Creek Parkway North Drive, Suite 300, Indianapolis, IN 46205 .... (317) 283–6516
Chief of Staff.—Ellen Quigley. FAX: 283–6567
Press Secretary / Director of Intergovernmental Relations.—Justin Ohlemiller.

Counties: MARION. City of Indianapolis, township of Center, parts of the townships of Decatur, Lawrence, Perry, Pike, Warren, Washington, and Wayne, included are the cities of Beech Grove and Lawrence. Population (2000), 675,456.

ZIP Codes: 46107, 46160, 46201–09, 46211, 46214, 46216–22, 46224–31, 46234–35, 46237, 46239–42, 46244, 46247, 46249, 46251, 46253–55, 46260, 46266, 46268, 46274–75, 46277–78, 46282–83, 46285, 46291, 46295–96, 46298

* * *

EIGHTH DISTRICT

BRAD ELLSWORTH, Democrat, of Evansville, IN; born in Jasper, IN, September 11, 1958; graduated from William Henry Harrison High School, Evansville, IN, 1979; bachelor's degree in Sociology, Indiana State University–Evansville, 1981; M.B.A. in Criminology, Indiana State University, 1993; sheriff, Vanderburgh County Sheriff's Department, 1999–2006; married the former Beth Wannamueller; one daughter, Andrea; committees: Agriculture; Armed Services; Small Business; elected to the 110th Congress on November 7, 2006; reelected to the 111th Congress on November 4, 2008.

Office Listings

http://www.house.gov/ellsworth

513 Cannon House Office Building, Washington, DC 20515 .... (202) 225–4636
Chief of Staff.—Cori Smith. FAX: 225–3284
Press Secretary.—Liz Farrar.
Legislative Director.—Jed D'Ercole.
Executive Assistant.—Megan Giles.
101 Northwest Martin Luther King, Jr. Boulevard, Room 124, Evansville, IN 47708 .... (812) 465–6484
District Director.—Patrick Scates.
901 Wabash Avenue, Suite 140, Terre Haute, IN 47807 .... (812) 232–0523

Counties: CLAY, DAVIESS, FOUNTAIN (part), GIBSON, GREENE, PARKE, PIKE, POSEY, PUTNAM, SULLIVAN, VANDERBURGH, VERMILLION, VIGO, WARREN, WARRICK. Population (2000), 675,564.

ZIP Codes: 46105, 46120–21, 46128, 46135, 46165–66, 46170–72, 46175, 47403–04, 47424, 47427, 47429, 47431–33, 47438–39, 47441, 47443, 47445–46, 47449, 47453, 47455–57, 47459–60, 47462, 47465, 47469–71, 47501, 47512, 47516, 47519, 47522–24, 47527–29, 47535, 47537, 47541–42, 47553, 47557–58, 47561–62, 47564, 47567–68, 47573, 47578, 47581, 47584–85, 47590–91, 47596–98, 47601, 47610–14, 47616, 47618–20, 47629–31, 47633, 47637–40,

47647–49, 47654, 47660, 47665–66, 47670, 47683, 47701–06, 47708, 47710–16, 47719–22, 47724–25, 47727–28, 47730–37, 47739–41, 47744, 47747, 47750, 47801–05, 47807–09, 47811–12, 47830–34, 47836–38, 47840–42, 47845–66, 47868–72, 47874–76, 47878–82, 47884–85, 47917–18, 47921, 47928, 47932, 47952, 47966, 47969–70, 47974–75, 47982, 47987, 47989, 47991–93

* * *

NINTH DISTRICT

BARON P. HILL, Democrat, of Seymour, IN; born in Seymour, June 23, 1953; education: graduated, Seymour High School; B.A. in history, Furman University, Greenville, SC, 1975; professional: ran an insurance and real estate business in Seymour; Indiana House of Representatives, 1982–90; Executive Director to the Indiana Student Assistance Commission, 1992; financial analyst with Merrill Lynch; named to the Indiana Basketball Hall of Fame, 2000; participated in the Elks Club, American Red Cross, and Seymour Chamber of Commerce; former president, Seymour Jaycees; former Communications Co-Chair, Blue Dog Coalition; former member, New Democrat Coalition; named Chief Deputy Whip, 108th Congress; member: First United Methodist Church, Seymour, IN; married: Betty Schepman Hill; children: Jennifer, Cara and Elizabeth; committees: Energy and Commerce; Science and Technology; Joint Economic Committee; elected to the 106th Congress in November, 1998; reelected to the 107th and 108th Congresses; elected to the 110th Congress on November 7, 2006; reelected to the 111th Congress on November 4, 2008.

Office Listings

http://www.baronhill.house.gov

223 Cannon House Office Building, Washington, DC 20515 .... (202) 225–5315
Chief of Staff.—John Zody. FAX: 226–6866
Scheduler.—Joel Riethmiller.
Press Secretary.—Katie Moreau.
Legislative Director.—Lori Pepper.
279 Quartermaster Drive, Jeffersonville, IN 47130 .... (812) 288–3999
District Director.—John Zody.
320 West 8th Street, Suite 114, Bloomington, IN 47404 .... (812) 336–3000

Counties: BARTHOLOMEW (part), BROWN, CLARK, CRAWFORD, DEARBORN (part), DUBOIS, FLOYD, HARRISON, JACKSON, JEFFERSON, MONROE (part), OHIO, ORANGE, PERRY, RIPLEY, SCOTT, SPENCER, SWITZERLAND, WASHINGTON. Population (2000), 675,599.

ZIP Codes: 46151, 46160, 46164, 46181, 47001, 47006, 47011, 47017–23, 47025, 47031–34, 47037–43, 47102, 47104, 47106–08, 47110–12, 47114–20, 47122–26, 47129–47, 47150–51, 47160–67, 47170, 47172, 47174, 47177, 47199, 47201–03, 47220, 47223–24, 47227–32, 47235–36, 47240, 47243–45, 47247, 47249–50, 47260, 47264–65, 47270, 47273–74, 47281–83, 47401–08, 47426, 47432, 47434–36, 47448, 47452, 47454, 47458, 47462, 47468–69, 47513–15, 47520–21, 47523, 47525, 47527, 47531–32, 47536–37, 47541–42, 47545–47, 47549–52, 47556, 47564, 47574–77, 47579–81, 47586, 47588, 47590, 47601, 47611, 47615, 47617, 47634–35, 47637

IOWA

(Population 2000, 2,926,324)

SENATORS

CHUCK GRASSLEY, Republican, of Cedar Falls, IA; born in New Hartford, IA, September 17, 1933; education: graduated, New Hartford Community High School, 1951; B.A., University of Northern Iowa, 1955; M.A., University of Northern Iowa, 1956; doctoral studies, University of Iowa, 1957–58; professional: farmer; member: Iowa State Legislature, 1959–74; Farm Bureau; State and County Historical Society; Masons; Baptist Church; and International Association of Machinists, 1962–71; co-chair, International Narcotics Control Caucus; married: the former Barbara Ann Speicher, 1954; children: Lee, Wendy, Robin Lynn, Michele Marie; committees: ranking member, Finance; Agriculture, Nutrition, and Forestry; Budget; Judiciary; Joint Committee on Taxation; elected to the 94th Congress, November 5, 1974; reelected to the 95th and 96th Congresses; elected to the U.S. Senate, November 4, 1980; reelected to each succeeding Senate term.

Office Listings

http://grassley.senate.gov

135 Hart Senate Office Building, Washington, DC 20510 .... (202) 224–3744
Chief of Staff.—David Young. FAX: 224–6020
Director of Communications.—Jill Kozeny.
Legislative Director.—Kolan Davis.
721 Federal Building, 210 Walnut Street, Des Moines, IA 50309 .... (515) 288–1145
State Administrator.—Robert Renaud.
150 1st Avenue, NE., Suite 325, Cedar Rapids, IA 52401 .... (319) 363–6832
120 Federal Courthouse Building, 320 Sixth Street, Sioux City, IA 51101 .... (712) 233–1860
210 Waterloo Building, 531 Commercial Street, Waterloo, IA 50701 .... (319) 232–6657
131 West 3rd Street, Suite 180, Davenport, IA 52801 .... (319) 322–4331
307 Federal Building, 8 South Sixth Street, Council Bluffs, IA 51501 .... (712) 322–7103

* * *

TOM HARKIN, Democrat, of Cumming, IA; born in Cumming, November 19, 1939; education: graduated, Dowling Catholic High School, Des Moines, IA; B.S., Iowa State University, Ames, 1962; U.S. Navy, 1962–67; military service: LCDR, U.S. Naval Reserves; LL.B., Catholic University of America, Washington, DC, 1972; admitted to the bar, Des Moines, IA, 1972; married: the former Ruth Raduenz, 1968; children: Amy and Jenny; committees: chair, Health, Education, Labor, and Pensions; Agriculture, Nutrition, and Forestry; Appropriations; Small Business and Entrepreneurship; elected to the 94th Congress on November 5, 1974; reelected to four succeeding Congresses; elected to the U.S. Senate on November 6, 1984; reelected to each succeeding Senate term.

Office Listings

http://harkin.senate.gov

731 Hart Senate Office Building, Washington, DC 20510 .... (202) 224–3254
Chief of Staff.—Brian Ahlberg. FAX: 224–9369
Communications Director.—Kate Cyrul.
Federal Building, 210 Walnut Street, Room 733, Des Moines, IA 50309 .... (515) 284–4574
150 First Avenue, NE., Suite 370, Cedar Rapids, IA 52401 .... (319) 365–4504
1606 Brady Street, Suite 323, Davenport, IA 52801 .... (563) 322–1338
Federal Building, 320 Sixth Street, Room 110, Sioux City, IA 51101 .... (712) 252–1550
Federal Building, 350 West Sixth Street, Room 315, Dubuque, IA 52001 .... (563) 582–2130

REPRESENTATIVES

FIRST DISTRICT

BRUCE L. BRALEY, Democrat, of Waterloo, IA; born in Grinnell, IA, October 30, 1957; education: B.A., Iowa State University, Ames, IA, 1980; J.D., University of Iowa Law School, Iowa City, IA, 1983; professional: attorney, Dulton, Braun, Staack & Hellman, 1983–2006; married: Carolyn; children: Lisa, David and Paul; chair, Populist Caucus; committees: Energy and Commerce; elected to the 110th Congress on November 7, 2006; reelected to the 111th Congress.

Office Listings

http://www.house.gov/braley

1019 Longworth House Office Building, Washington, DC 20515 .... (202) 225–2911
Chief of Staff.—Sarah Benzing. FAX: 226–0757
501 Sycamore Street, Suite 610, Waterloo, IA 50703 .... (319) 287–3233
District Director.—Karen Erickson.
350 West Sixth Street, Suite 222, Dubuque, IA 52001 .... (563) 557–7789
209 West Fourth Street, Davenport, IA 52801 .... (563) 323–5988
District Director.—Pete DeKock.

Counties: BLACK HAWK, BREMER, BUCHANAN, BUTLER, CLAYTON, CLINTON, DELAWARE, DUBUQUE, FAYETTE, JACKSON, JONES, SCOTT. Population (2000), 585,302.

ZIP Codes: 50601–02, 50604–08, 50611, 50613–14, 50619, 50622–23, 50625–26, 50629, 50631, 50634, 50636, 50641, 50643–44, 50647–51, 50654–55, 50660, 50662, 50664–68, 50670–71, 50674, 50676–77, 50681–82, 50701–04, 50706–07, 50799, 52001–04, 52030–33, 52035–50, 52052–54, 52056–57, 52060, 52064–66, 52068–79, 52099, 52135, 52141–42, 52147, 52156–59, 52164, 52166, 52169, 52171, 52175, 52205, 52207, 52210, 52212, 52223, 52226, 52237, 52252, 52254, 52305, 52309–10, 52312, 52320–21, 52323, 52326, 52329–30, 52362, 52701, 52722, 52726–33, 52736, 52742, 52745–48, 52750–51, 52753, 52756–58, 52765, 52767–68, 52771, 52773–74, 52777, 52801–09

* * *

SECOND DISTRICT

DAVID LOEBSACK, Democrat, of Mt. Vernon, IA; born in Sioux City, IA, December 23, 1952; education: graduated, East High School, 1970; B.A., Iowa State University, 1974; M.A., Iowa State University, 1976; Ph.D., Political Science, University of California, Davis, 1985; professional: professor, Political Science, Cornell College, 1982–2006; married: Teresa Loebsack; four children; committees: Armed Services; Education and Labor; elected to the 110th Congress on November 7, 2006; reelected to the 111th Congress.

Office Listings

http://www.loebsack.house.gov

1221 Longworth House Office Building, Washington, DC 20515 .... (202) 225–6576
Chief of Staff.—Eric Witte.
Office Manager / Scheduler.—Heidi Hotopp.
150 First Avenue, NE., Suite 375, Cedar Rapids, IA 52401 .... (319) 364–2288
District Director.—Rob Sueppel. FAX: 226–0757
125 South Dubuque Street, Iowa City, IA 52240–4003 .... (319) 351–0789

Counties: APPANOOSE, CEDAR, DAVIS, DES MOINES, HENRY, JEFFERSON, JOHNSON, LEE, LINN, LOUISA, MUSCATINE, VAN BUREN, WAPELLO, WASHINGTON, WAYNE. Population (2000), 585,241.

ZIP Codes: 50008, 50052, 50060, 50123, 50147, 50165, 50238, 52201–02, 52213–14, 52216, 52218–19, 52227–28, 52233, 52235, 52240–48, 52253, 52255, 52302, 52305–06, 52314, 52317, 52319–20, 52322–24, 52327–28, 52333, 52336–38, 52340–41, 52344, 52350, 52352–53, 52356, 52358–59, 52401–11, 52497–99, 52501, 52530–31, 52533, 52535–38, 52540, 52542, 52544, 52548–49, 52551, 52553–57, 52560, 52565–67, 52570–74, 52580–81, 52583–84, 52588, 52590, 52593–94, 52601, 52619–21, 52623–27, 52630–32, 52635, 52637–42, 52644–56, 52658–60, 52720–21, 52731, 52737–39, 52747, 52749, 52752, 52754–55, 52759–61, 52766, 52769, 52772, 52776, 52778

* * *

THIRD DISTRICT

LEONARD L. BOSWELL, Democrat, of Des Moines, IA; born in Harrison County, MO, January 10, 1934; education: graduated, Lamoni High School, 1952; B.A., Graceland College, Lamoni, IA, 1969; military service: lieutenant colonel, U.S. Army, 1956–76; awards: two Distinguished Flying Crosses, two Bronze Stars, Soldier's Medal; Iowa State Senate, 1984–96; Iowa State Senate President, 1992–96; lay minister, RLDS Church; member: American Legion, Disabled American Veterans of Foreign Wars, Iowa Farm Bureau, Iowa Cattlemen's Association, Graceland College Board of Trustees; Farmer's Co-op Grain and Seed Board of Directors, 1979–93 (president for 13 years); The Coalition (Blue Dogs); co-chair and member emeritus, Mississippi River Caucus; co-chair, Methamphetamine Caucus; married: Darlene (Dody) Votava Boswell, 1955; children: Cindy, Diana, and Joe; committees: Agriculture; Transportation and Infrastructure; elected to the 105th Congress; reelected to each succeeding Congress.

Office Listings

http://boswell.house.gov

1427 Longworth House Office Building, Washington, DC 20515 .... (202) 225–3806
Chief of Staff / Communications Director.—Susan McAvoy. FAX: 225–5608
Legislative Director.—Ross Maradian.
Executive Assistant.—Sandy Carter.
300 East Locust Street, Suite 320, Des Moines, IA 50309 .... (515) 282–1909
District Director.—Sally Bowzer.

Counties: BENTON, GRUNDY, IOWA, JASPER, KEOKUK, LUCAS, MAHASKA, MARION, MONROE, POLK, POWESHIEK, TAMA. Population (2000), 585,305.

ZIP Codes: 50007, 50009, 50015, 50021, 50027–28, 50032, 50035, 50044, 50047, 50049, 50054, 50057, 50061–62, 50068, 50073, 50104, 50109, 50111–12, 50116, 50119, 50127, 50131, 50135–39, 50143, 50148, 50150–51, 50153, 50156–58, 50163, 50168–71, 50173, 50206–08, 50214, 50219, 50222, 50225–26, 50228, 50232, 50237–38, 50240, 50242–43, 50251–52, 50255–58, 50265–66, 50268, 50272, 50301–23, 50325, 50327–36, 50338–40, 50347, 50350, 50359–64, 50367–69, 50380–81, 50391–96, 50398, 50601, 50604, 50609, 50612–13, 50621, 50624, 50627, 50632, 50635, 50638, 50642–43, 50651–52, 50657, 50660, 50665, 50669, 50672–73, 50675, 50680, 50936, 50940, 50947, 50950, 50980–81, 52203–04, 52206, 52208–09, 52211, 52213, 52215, 52217, 52220–22, 52224–25, 52228–29, 52231–32, 52236, 52248–49, 52251, 52257, 52301, 52307–08, 52313, 52315–16, 52318, 52322, 52324–25, 52332, 52334–35, 52339, 52342, 52345–49, 52351, 52354–55, 52361, 52404, 52531, 52534, 52543, 52550, 52552, 52561–63, 52568–69, 52576–77, 52585–86, 52591, 52595

* * *

FOURTH DISTRICT

TOM LATHAM, Republican, of Ames, IA; born in Hampton, IA, July 14, 1948; education: attended Alexander Community School; graduated Cal (Latimer) Community College, 1966; attended Wartburg College, 1966–67; Iowa State University, 1976–70; agriculture business major; professional: marketing representative, independent insurance agent, bank teller and bookkeeper; member and past president, Nazareth Lutheran Church; past chairman, Franklin County Extension Council; secretary, Republican Party of Iowa; 5th District representative, Republican State Central Committee; co-chairman, Franklin County Republican Central Committee; Iowa delegation whip; member: 1992 Republican National Convention, Iowa Farm Bureau Federation, Iowa Soybean Association, American Seed Trade Association, Iowa Corn Growers Association, Iowa Seed Association, Agribusiness Association of Iowa, I.S.U. Extension Citizens Advisory Council; married: Mary Katherine (Kathy), 1975; children: Justin, Jennifer, and Jill; committees: Appropriations; elected to the 104th Congress; reelected to each succeeding Congress.

Office Listings

http://www.house.gov/latham

2217 Rayburn House Office Building, Washington, DC 20515 .... (202) 225–5476
Chief of Staff.—James Carstensen. FAX: 225–3301
Press Secretary.—Fred Love.
Scheduler.—Amanda McDonnell.
1421 South Bell Avenue, Ames, IA 50010 .... (515) 232–2885
District Director.—Clarke Scanlon.
812 Highway 18 East, P.O. Box 532, Clear Lake, IA 50428 .... (641) 357–5225
Regional Representative.—Lois Clark.
1426 Central Avenue, Suite A, Fort Dodge, IA 50501 .... (515) 573–2738
Regional Representative.—Jim Oberhelman.

Counties: ALLAMAKEE, BOONE, CALHOUN, CERRO GORDO, CHICKASAW, DALLAS, EMMET, FLOYD, FRANKLIN, GREENE, HAMILTON, HANCOCK, HARDIN, HOWARD, HUMBOLDT, KOSSUTH, MADISON, MARSHALL, MITCHELL, PALO ALTO, POCAHONTAS, STORY, WARREN, WEBSTER, WINNEBAGO, WINNESHIEK, WORTH, WRIGHT. Population (2000), 585,305.

ZIP Codes: 50001, 50003, 50005–06, 50010–14, 50028, 50031, 50033–34, 50036–41, 50046–47, 50050–51, 50055–56, 50058–59, 50061, 50063–64, 50066, 50069–72, 50075, 50078, 50101–02, 50105–07, 50109, 50118, 50120, 50122, 50124–26, 50129–30, 50132, 50134, 50139, 50141–42, 50145–46, 50148–49, 50151–52, 50154–56, 50158, 50160–62, 50166–67, 50201, 50206, 50210–13, 50217–18, 50220, 50222–23, 50225, 50227, 50229–31, 50233–36, 50239–41, 50244, 50246–49, 50252, 50257–59, 50261, 50263, 50266, 50269, 50271, 50273, 50276, 50278, 50320, 50323, 50325, 50401–02, 50420–21, 50423–24, 50426–28, 50430–36, 50438–41, 50444, 50446–61, 50464–73, 50475–84, 50501, 50510–11, 50514–33, 50536, 50538–46, 50548, 50551–52, 50554, 50556–63, 50566, 50568–71, 50573–75, 50577–79, 50581–83, 50586, 50590–91, 50593–95, 50597–99, 50601, 50603, 50605, 50609, 50616, 50619–21, 50625, 50627–28, 50630, 50632–33, 50635–36, 50645, 50653, 50658–59, 50661, 50672, 50674, 50680, 51334, 51342, 51344, 51358, 51364–65, 51433, 51443, 51449, 51453, 51462, 51510, 52101, 52132–34, 52136, 52140, 52144, 52146, 52149, 52151, 52154–56, 52159–63, 52165, 52168, 52170–72

* * *

FIFTH DISTRICT

STEVE KING, Republican, of Odebolt, IA; born in Storm Lake, IA, May 28, 1949; education: graduated, Denison Community High School; attended Northwest Missouri State University, Maryville, MO, 1967–70; professional: agri-businessman; owner and operator of King Construction Company; public service: Iowa State Senate, 1996–2002; religion: Catholic; family: married to Marilyn; children: David, Michael, and Jeff; committees: Agriculture; Judiciary; Small Business; elected to the 108th Congress on November 5, 2002; reelected to each succeeding Congress.

Office Listings

http://www.steveking.house.gov

1131 Longworth House Office Building, Washington, DC 20515 .... (202) 225–4426
Chief of Staff.—Brenna Findley. FAX: 225–3193
Legislative Director.—Bentley Graves.
Scheduler / Executive Assistant.—Rachel Simonin.
Communications Director.—Samantha Barrett.
Press Secretary.—Matt Lahr.
526 Nebraska Street, Sioux City, IA 51101 .... (712) 224–4692
40 Pearl Street, Council Bluffs, IA 51503 .... (712) 325–1404
208 West Taylor Street, Creston, IA 50801 .... (641) 782–2495
306 North Grand Avenue, Spencer, IA 51301 .... (712) 580–7754
800 Oneida Street, Suite A, Storm Lake, IA 50588 .... (712) 732–4197

Counties: ADAIR, ADAMS, AUDUBON, BUENA VISTA, CARROLL, CASS, CHEROKEE, CLARKE, CLAY, CRAWFORD, DECATUR, DICKINSON, FREMONT, GUTHRIE, HARRISON, IDA, LYON, MILLS, MONONA, MONTGOMERY, O'BRIEN, OSCEOLA, PAGE, PLYMOUTH, POTTAWATTAMIE, RINGGOLD, SAC, SHELBY, SIOUX, TAYLOR, UNION, WOODBURY. Population (2000), 584,967.

ZIP Codes: 50002, 50020, 50022, 50025–26, 50029, 50042, 50048, 50058, 50065, 50067, 50070, 50074, 50076, 50103, 50108, 50110, 50115, 50117, 50119, 50123, 50128, 50133, 50140, 50144, 50146, 50149, 50151, 50155, 50164, 50174, 50210, 50213, 50216, 50222, 50233, 50250, 50254, 50257, 50262, 50264, 50273–77, 50510, 50535, 50565, 50567–68, 50576, 50583, 50585, 50588, 50592, 50801, 50830–31, 50833, 50835–37, 50839–43, 50845–49, 50851, 50853–54, 50857–64, 51001–12, 51014–16, 51018–20, 51022–31, 51033–41, 51044–56, 51058–63, 51101–06, 51108–09, 51111, 51201, 51230–32, 51234–35, 51237–50, 51301, 51331, 51333, 51338, 51340–41, 51343, 51345–47, 51350–51, 51354–55, 51357, 51360, 51363–64, 51366, 51401, 51430–33, 51436, 51439–52, 51454–55, 51458–61, 51463, 51465–67, 51501–03, 51510, 51520–21, 51523, 51525–37, 51540–46, 51548–49, 51551–66, 51570–73, 51575–79, 51591, 51593, 51601–03, 51630–32, 51636–40, 51645–54, 51656

KANSAS

(Population 2000, 2,688,418)

SENATORS

SAM BROWNBACK, Republican, of Topeka, KS; born in Garrett, KS, September 12, 1956; education: graduated from Prairie View High School, 1974; B.S., with honors, Kansas State University, Manhattan, KS, 1978; J.D., University of Kansas, Lawrence, 1982; professional: Kansas Bar; attorney, broadcaster, teacher; U.S. House of Representatives, 1994–96; State Secretary of Agriculture, 1986–93; White House Fellow, Office of the U.S. Trade Representative, 1990–91; member: Topeka Fellowship Council, Kansas Bar Association, Kansas State University and Kansas University alumni associations; married: the former Mary Stauffer, 1982; children: Abby, Andy, Liz, Mark and Jenna; commision on Security and Cooperation in Europe; committees: ranking member, Joint Economic Committee; Appropriations; Commerce, Science, and Transportation; Energy and Natural Resources; Special Committee on Aging; elected to the U.S. Senate in November, 1996, to fill the remainder of the vacancy caused by the resignation of Senator Bob Dole; reelected to each succeeding Senate term.

Office Listings

http://brownback.senate.gov

303 Hart Senate Office Building, Washington, DC 20510 .... (202) 224–6521
Chief of Staff.—Glen Chambers. FAX: 228–1265
Legislative Director.—Landon Fulmer.
Scheduler.—Devon Gallagher.
Communications Director.—Brian Hart.
612 South Kansas, Topeka, KS 66603 .... (785) 233–2503
Kansas Scheduler.—Denise Coatney.
1001–C North Broadway, Pittsburg, KS 66762 .... (316) 231–6040
Grant Director.—Anne Emerson.
245 North Waco, Suite 240, Wichita, KS 67202 .... (620) 264–8066
State Director.—Chuck Alderson.
11111 West 95th, Suite 245, Overland Park, KS 66214 .... (913) 492–6378
Deputy Chief of Staff.—George Stafford.
811 North Main, Suite A, Garden City, KS 67846 .... (620) 275–1124
Regional Director.—Dennis Mesa.

* * *

PAT ROBERTS, Republican, of Dodge City, KS; born in Topeka, KS, April 20, 1936; education: graduated, Holton High School, Holton, KS, 1954; B.S., journalism, Kansas State University, Manhattan, KS, 1958; professional: captain, U.S. Marine Corps, 1958–62; editor and reporter, Arizona newspapers, 1962–67; aide to Senator Frank Carlson, 1967–68; aide to Representative Keith Sebelius, 1969–80; U.S. House of Representatives, 1980–96; founding member: bipartisan Caucus on Unfunded Mandates, House Rural Health Care Coalition; shepherded the 1996 Freedom to Farm Act through the House and Senate; awards: honorary American Farmer, Future Farmers of America; 1993 Wheat Man of the Year, Kansas Association of Wheat Growers; Golden Carrot Award, Public Voice; Golden Bulldog Award, Watchdogs of the Treasury; numerous Guardian of Small Business awards, National Federation of Independent Business; 1995 Dwight D. Eisenhower Medal, Eisenhower Exchange Fellowship; 2001 U.S. Marine Corps Semper Fidelis Award; married: the former Franki Fann, 1969; children: David, Ashleigh, and Anne-Wesley; committees: Agriculture, Nutrition, and Forestry; Finance; Health Education, Labor, and Pensions; Rules and Administration; Select Committee on Ethics; elected to the U.S. Senate in November, 1996; reelected to each succeeding Senate term.

Office Listings

http://roberts.senate.gov

109 Hart Senate Office Building, Washington, DC 20510 .... (202) 224–4774
Chief of Staff.—Jackie Cottrell. FAX: 224–3514
Legislative Director.—Mike Seyfert.
Scheduler.—Rebecca Mank.
Communications Director.—Sarah Little.
100 Military Plaza, P.O. Box 550, Dodge City, KS 67801 .... (620) 227–2244
District Director.—Debbie Pugh.
155 North Market Street, Suite 120, Wichita, KS 67202 .... (316) 263–0416
District Director.—Karin Wisdom.
Frank Carlson Federal Building, 444 SE Quincy, Room 392, Topeka, KS 66683 .... (785) 295–2745

District Director.—Gilda Lintz.
11900 College Boulevard, Suite 203, Overland Park, KS 66210 .... (913) 451–9343
State Director.—Chad Tenpenny.

REPRESENTATIVES

FIRST DISTRICT

JERRY MORAN, Republican, of Hays, KS; born in Great Bend, KS, May 29, 1954; education: B.S., economics, 1976; J.D., University of Kansas, 1981; M.B.A. candidate, Fort Hays State University; partner, Jeter and Moran, Attorneys at Law, Hays, KS; former bank officer and university instructor; represented 37th District in Kansas Senate, 1989–97, serving as vice president in 1993–95 and majority leader in 1995–97; Special Assistant Attorney General, State of Kansas, 1982–85; Deputy Attorney, Rooks County, 1987–95; governor, board of governors, University of Kansas School of Law, 1990 (vice president, 1993–94; president, 1994–95); member: board of directors, Kansas Chamber of Commerce and Industry, 1996–97; Hays Chamber of Commerce; Northwest Kansas and Ellis County bar associations; Phi Alpha Delta legal fraternity; Rotary Club; Lions International; board of trustees, Fort Hays State University Endowment Association; founding co-chair, Congressional Rural Caucus; co-chair, Dwight D. Eisenhower Memorial Commission; married: Robba Moran; children: Kelsey and Alex; committees: Agriculture; Transportation and Infrastructure; Veterans' Affairs; elected to the 105th Congress; reelected to each succeeding Congress.

Office Listings

http://www.jerrymoran.house.gov

2202 Rayburn House Office Building, Washington, DC 20515 .... (202) 225–2715
Chief of Staff.—Todd Novascore. FAX: 225–5124
Legislative Director.—Alex Richard.
Press Secretary.—Brecke Latham.
Office Manager—Mark Colwell.
1200 Main Street, Suite 402, P.O. Box 249, Hays KS 67601–0249 .... (785) 628–6401
1 North Main, Suite 525, P.O. Box 1128, Hutchinson, KS 67504–1128 .... (620) 665–6138
119 West Iron Avenue, Suite 403, P.O. Box 766, Salina, KS 67401 .... (785) 309–0572

Counties: BARBER, BARTON, CHASE, CHEYENNE, CLARK, CLAY, CLOUD, COMANCHE, DECATUR, DICKINSON, EDWARDS, ELLIS, ELLSWORTH, FINNEY, FORD, GEARY (part), GOVE, GRAHAM, GRANT, GRAY, GREELEY, GREENWOOD (part), HAMILTON, HASKELL, HODGEMAN, JEWELL, KEARNY, KIOWA, LANE, LINCOLN, LOGAN, LYON, MCPHERSON, MARION (part), MARSHALL, MEADE, MITCHELL, MORRIS, MORTON, NEMAHA (part), NESS, NORTON, OSBORNE, OTTAWA, PAWNEE, PHILLIPS, PRATT, RAWLINS, RENO, REPUBLIC, RICE, ROOKS, RUSH, RUSSELL, SALINE, SCOTT, SEWARD, SHERIDAN, SHERMAN, SMITH, STAFFORD, STANTON, STEVENS, THOMAS, TREGO, WABAUNSEE, WALLACE, WASHINGTON, WICHITA. Population (2000), 672,105.

ZIP Codes: 66401, 66403–04, 66406–08, 66411–13, 66423, 66427, 66431, 66438, 66441, 66501–02, 66507–08, 66514, 66518, 66523, 66526, 66534, 66536, 66538, 66541, 66544, 66547–48, 66610, 66614–15, 66801, 66830, 66833–35, 66838, 66840, 66843, 66845–46, 66849–51, 66853–54, 66858–62, 66864–66, 66868–70, 66872–73, 66901, 66930, 66932–33, 66935–46, 66948–49, 66951–53, 66955–56, 66958–64, 66966–68, 66970, 67009, 67020–21, 67028–29, 67035, 67053–54, 67057, 67059, 67061–63, 67065–66, 67068, 67070, 67073, 67104, 67107–09, 67112, 67114, 67124, 67127, 67134, 67138, 67143, 67151, 67155, 67335, 67401–02, 67410, 67416–18, 67420, 67422–23, 67425, 67427–28, 67430–32, 67436–39, 67441–52, 67454–60, 67464, 67466–68, 67470, 67473–76, 67478, 67480–85, 67487, 67490–92, 67501–02, 67504–05, 67510–16, 67518–26, 67529–30, 67543–48, 67550, 67552–54, 67556–57, 67559–61, 67563–68, 67570, 67572–76, 67578–79, 67581, 67583–85, 67601, 67621–23, 67625–29, 67631–32, 67634–35, 67637–40, 67642–51, 67653–61, 67663–65, 67667, 67669, 67671–75, 67701, 67730–41, 67743–45, 67748–49, 67751–53, 67756–58, 67761–62, 67764, 67801, 67831, 67834–42, 67844, 67846, 67849–51, 67853–55, 67857, 67859–65, 67867, 67869–71, 67876–80, 67882, 67901, 67905, 67950–54

* * *

SECOND DISTRICT

LYNN JENKINS, Republican, of Topeka, KS; born in Topeka, KS, June 10, 1963; education: A.A., Kansas State University, Manhattan, KS, 1985; B.S., accounting / economics, Weber State College, Ogden, UT, 1985; professional: Certified Public Accountant; Accountant, Braunsdorf, Carson, and Clinkinbeard; Accountant, Baird, Kurtz and Dobson; Certified Public Accountant, Public Accounting, Specialty Taxation, 1985–present; Representative, Kansas State House of Representatives, 1999–2000; Senator, Kansas State Senate, 2001–02; Treasurer, State of Kansas, 2003–08; children: Hayley and Hayden; Community Pharmacy Caucus; House Army Caucus; Military Veterans Caucus; Nuclear Issues Working Group; Cystic Fibrosis Caucus; committees: Financial Services; elected to the 111th Congress on November 4, 2008.

Office Listings

http://lynnjenkins.house.gov

130 Cannon House Office Building, Washington, DC 20515 .... (202) 225–6601
Chief of Staff.—Pat Leopold. FAX: 225–7986
Legislative Director.—Eric Schmutz.
Scheduler.—April Moore.
Press Aide.—Mary Geiger.
510 Southwest 10th Avenue, Topeka, KS 66612 .... (785) 234–5966
701 North Broadway, Pittsburgh, KS 66762 .... (620) 231–5966

Counties: ALLEN, ANDERSON, ATCHISON, BOURBON, BROWN, CHEROKEE, COFFEY, CRAWFORD, DONIPHAN, DOUGLAS (part), FRANKLIN, GEARY, JACKSON, JEFFERSON, LABETE, LEAVENWORTH, LINN, MIAMI, NEMAHA (part), NEOSHO, OSAGE, POTTAWATOMIE, RILEY, SHAWNEE, WILSON, WOODSON. Population (2000), 672,102.

ZIP Codes: 66002, 66006–08, 66010, 66012–17, 66020–21, 66023–27, 66032–33, 66035–36, 66039–50, 66052–54, 66056, 66058, 66060, 66064, 66066–67, 66070–73, 66075–80, 66083, 66086–88, 66090–91, 66093–95, 66097, 66109, 66112, 66401–04, 66407, 66409, 66413–20, 66422, 66424–29, 66431–32, 66434, 66436, 66439–40, 66442, 66449, 66451, 66502–03, 66505–06, 66509–10, 66512, 66515–17, 66520–24, 66527–28, 66531–40, 66542–44, 66546–50, 66552, 66554, 66601, 66603–12, 66614–22, 66624–26, 66628–29, 66636–37, 66642, 66647, 66652–53, 66667, 66675, 66683, 66692, 66699, 66701, 66710–14, 66716–17, 66720, 66724–25, 66728, 66732–36, 66738–43, 66746, 66748–49, 66751, 66753–63, 66767, 66769–73, 66775–83, 66834, 66839, 66849, 66852, 66854, 66856–57, 66864, 66868, 66870–71, 66933, 67047, 67330, 67332, 67335–37, 67341–42, 67351, 67354, 67356–57

* * *

THIRD DISTRICT

DENNIS MOORE, Democrat, of Lenexa, KS; born in Anthony, KS, November 8, 1945; education: Jefferson Elementary School, and Charles Curtis Intermediate School, Wichita, KS; B.A., University of Kansas, 1967; J.D., Washburn University of Law, 1970; professional: attorney; admitted to Kansas Bar, 1970, first practiced in Topeka, KS; Assistant Attorney General of Kansas, 1971–73; Johnson County District Attorney, 1977–89; Johnson County Community College Board of Trustees, 1993–99; member, American Legion; married: Stephene Moore; seven children: Todd, Scott, Andrew, Felicia Barge, Valerie Swearingen, Nathan Hansen, and Adam Hansen; military: U.S. Army, 2nd Lieutenant, 1970; U.S. Army Reserves, Captain, 1970–73; committees: Financial Services; Small Business; elected to the 106th Congress; reelected to each succeeding Congress.

Office Listings

http://www.house.gov/moore

1727 Longworth House Office Building, Washington, DC 20515 .... (202) 225–2865
Chief of Staff.—Howard Bauleke. FAX: 225–2807
Scheduler.—Ray Wittlinger.
Communications Director.—Rebecca Black.
8417 Santa Fe Drive, Room 101, Overland Park, KS 66212 .... (913) 383–2013
District Director.—Kevin Albrecht.
500 State Avenue, Room 176, Kansas City, KS 66101 .... (913) 621–0832
901 Kentucky Street, #205, Lawrence, KS 66044 .... (785) 842–9313
Constituent Services Director.—Becky Fast.

Counties: DOUGLAS (part), JOHNSON, WYANDOTTE. Population (2000), 672,124.

ZIP Codes: 66006–07, 66012–13, 66018–19, 66026, 66030–31, 66035–36, 66044–47, 66049–51, 66053, 66061–64, 66071, 66077, 66083, 66085, 66092, 66101–06, 66109–13, 66115, 66117–19, 66160, 66201–27, 66250–51, 66276, 66282–83, 66285–86

* * *

FOURTH DISTRICT

TODD TIAHRT, Republican, of Goddard, KS; born in Vermillion, SD, June 15, 1951; education: attended South Dakota School of Mines and Technology; B.A., Evangel College, Springfield, MO, 1975; M.B.A., Southwest Missouri State, 1989; professional: Dean of the Kansas House Congressional Delegation; proposal manager, The Boeing Company; married: the former Vicki Holland, 1976; children: Jessica, John, and Luke; committees: Appropriations; elected to the 104th Congress; reelected to each succeeding Congress.

Office Listings

http://www.house.gov/tiahrt

2441 Rayburn House Office Building, Washington, DC 20515 .... (202) 225–6216
Administrative Assistant.—Jeff Kahrs. FAX: 225–3489
Deputy Chief of Staff / Legislative Director.—Amy Claire Brusch.
Scheduler.—Melissa James.
Communications Director.—Sam Sackett.
155 North Market Street, Suite 400, Wichita, KS 67202 .... (316) 262–8992
District Director.—Robert Noland.

Counties: BUTLER, CHAUTAUQUA, COWLEY, ELK, GRENWOOD (part), HARPER, HARVEY, KINGMAN, MONTGOMERY, SEDGWICK, SUMNER. Population (2000), 672,101.

ZIP Codes: 66840, 66842, 66853, 66863, 66866, 66870, 67001–05, 67008–10, 67012–13, 67016–20, 67022–26, 67030–31, 67035–39, 67041–42, 67045, 67047, 67049–52, 67055–56, 67058, 67060–62, 67067–68, 67070, 67072, 67074, 67101, 67103, 67105–08, 67110–12, 67114, 67117–20, 67122–23, 67131–33, 67135, 67137–38, 67140, 67142, 67144, 67146–47, 67149–52, 67154, 67156, 67159, 67201–21, 67226, 67230, 67235, 67260, 67275–78, 67301, 67333–35, 67337, 67340, 67344–47, 67349, 67351–53, 67355, 67360–61, 67363–64, 67522, 67543

KENTUCKY

(Population 2000, 4,041,769)

SENATORS

MITCH McCONNELL, Republican, of Louisville, KY; born in Colbert County, AL, February 20, 1942; education: graduated Manual High School, Louisville, 1960, president of the student body; B.A. with honors, University of Louisville, 1964, president of the student council, president of the student body of the College of Arts and Sciences; J.D., University of Kentucky Law School, 1967, president of student bar association, outstanding oral advocate; professional: attorney, admitted to the Kentucky bar, 1967; chief legislative assistant to U.S. Senator Marlow Cook, 1968–70; Deputy Assistant U.S. Attorney General, 1974–75; Judge/Executive of Jefferson County, KY, 1978–84; chairman, National Republican Senatorial Committee, 1997–2000; chairman, Joint Congressional Committee on Inaugural Ceremonies, 1999–2001; Senate Majority Whip, 2002–06; Senate Republican Leader, 2007–present; married to Elaine Chao on February 6, 1993; children: Elly, Claire and Porter; committees: Agriculture, Nutrition, and Forestry; Appropriations; Rules and Administration; elected to the U.S. Senate on November 6, 1984; reelected to each succeeding Senate term.

Office Listings

http://mcconnell.senate.gov

361A Russell Senate Office Building, Washington, DC 20510 .... (202) 224–2541
Chief of Staff.—William H. Piper. FAX: 224–2499
Scheduler.—Stefanie Hagar.
Legislative Director.—Scott Raab.
Press Secretary.—Robert Steurer.
601 West Broadway, Suite 630, Louisville, KY 40202 .... (502) 582–6304
State Director.—Larry Cox.
1885 Dixie Highway, Suite 345, Fort Wright, KY 41011 .... (606) 578–0188
300 South Main Street, Suite 310, London, KY 40741 .... (606) 864–2026
Professional Arts Building, Suite 100, 2320 Broadway, Paducah, KY 42001 .... (270) 442–4554
771 Corporate Drive, Suite 108, Lexington, KY 40503 .... (606) 224–8286
Federal Building, Room 102, 241 Main Street, Bowling Green, KY 42101 .... (270) 781–1673

* * *

JIM BUNNING, Republican, of Southgate, KY; born in Southgate, October 23, 1931; education: graduated, St. Xavier High School, Cincinnati, OH, 1949; B.S., Xavier University, Cincinnati, OH, 1953; professional: baseball player, Hall of Fame; investment broker and agent; president, Jim Bunning Agency, Inc.; member of Kentucky State Senate (minority floor leader), 1979–83; member: Ft. Thomas City Council, 1977–79; appointed member, Ohio, Kentucky, and Indiana Regional Council of Governments, Cincinnati, OH; National Committeeman, Republican National Committee, 1983–92; appointed member, President's National Advisory Board on International Education Programs, 1984–88; member: board of directors of Kentucky Special Olympics, Ft. Thomas (KY) Lions Club, Brighton Street Center Community Action Group; married: the former Mary Catherine Theis, 1952; children: Barbara, Jim, Joan, Cathy, Bill, Bridgett, Mark, David and Amy; committees: Banking, Housing, and Urban Affairs; Budget; Energy and Natural Resources; Finance; elected to the 100th Congress, November 4, 1986; reelected to each succeeding Congress; elected to the U.S. Senate in November, 1998; reelected to each succeeding Senate term.

Office Listings

http://bunning.senate.gov

316 Hart Senate Office Building, Washington, DC 20515 .... (202) 224–4343
Personnel Assistant / Scheduler.—Kara Kirtley. FAX: 228–1373
Chief of Staff.—Kim Taylor Dean.
Legislative Director.—William Henderson.
Press Secretary.—Michael Reynard.
Scheduler.—Anna Sohriakoff.
1717 Dixie Highway, Suite 220, Fort Wright, KY 41011 .... (859) 219–2239
State Director.—Debbie McKinney.
The Federal Building, 423 Frederica Street, Room 305, Owensboro, KY 42301 ..... (270) 689–9085
717 Corporate Drive, Lexington, KY 40503 .... (859) 219–2239
1100 South Main Street, Suite 12, Hopkinsville, KY 42240 .... (270) 885–1212

REPRESENTATIVES

FIRST DISTRICT

ED WHITFIELD, Republican, of Hopkinsville, KY; born in Hopkinsville, May 25, 1943; education: graduated, Madisonville High School, Madisonville, KY; B.S., University of Kentucky, Lexington, 1965; J.D., University of Kentucky, 1969; attended American University's Wesley Theological Seminary, Washington, DC; military service: first lieutenant, U.S. Army Reserves, 1967–73; professional: attorney, private practice, 1970–79; vice president, CSX Corporation, 1979–90; admitted to bar: Kentucky, 1970, and Florida, 1993; began practice in 1970 in Hopkinsville, KY; member, Kentucky House, 1973, one term; married: Constance Harriman Whitfield; children: Kate; committees: Energy and Commerce; elected to the 104th Congress; reelected to each succeeding Congress.

Office Listings

2411 Rayburn House Office Building, Washington, DC 20515 .... (202) 225–3115
Chief of Staff.—John Sparkman. FAX: 225–3547
Scheduler / Office Manager.—Elizabeth Leasure.
Legislative Director.—Cory Hicks.
1403 South Main Street, Hopkinsville, KY 42240 .... (270) 885–8079
District Director.—Michael Pape.
200 North Main, Suite F, Tompkinsville, KY 42167 .... (270) 487–9509
Field Representative.—Sandy Simpson.
222 First Street, Suite 224, Henderson, KY 42420 .... (270) 826–4180
Field Representative.—Ed West.
100 Fountain Avenue, Room 104, Paducah, KY 42001 .... (270) 442–6901
Field Representative.—Janece Everett.

Counties: ADAIR, ALLEN, BALLARD, BUTLER, CALDWELL, CALLOWAY, CARLISLE, CASEY, CHRISTIAN, CLINTON, CRITTENDEN, CUMBERLAND, FULTON, GRAVES, HENDERSON, HICKMAN, HOPKINS, LINCOLN (part), LIVINGSTON, LOGAN, LYON, MARSHALL, MCCRACKEN, MCLEAN, METCALF, MONROE, MUHLENBERG, OHIO (part), RUSSELL, SIMPSON, TODD, TRIGG, UNION, WEBSTER. Population (2000), 673,629.

ZIP Codes: 40009, 40328, 40437, 40442, 40448, 40464, 40484, 40489, 42001–03, 42020–25, 42027–29, 42031–33, 42035–41, 42044–45, 42047–51, 42053–56, 42058, 42060–61, 42063–64, 42066, 42069–71, 42076, 42078–79, 42081–88, 42101, 42104, 42120, 42122–24, 42129, 42133–35, 42140–41, 42150–51, 42153–54, 42164, 42166–67, 42170, 42201–04, 42206, 42209–211, 42214–17, 42219–21, 42223, 42232, 42234, 42236, 42240–41, 42251–52, 42254, 42256, 42261–62, 42265–67, 42273–74, 42276, 42280, 42283, 42286–88, 42301, 42320–28, 42330, 42332–34, 42337, 42339, 42344–45, 42347, 42349–50, 42352, 42354, 42356, 42367–69, 42371–72, 42374–76, 42402–04, 42406, 42408–11, 42413, 42419–20, 42431, 42436–37, 42440–42, 42444–45, 42450–53, 42455–64, 42516, 42528, 42539, 42541, 42544, 42565–67, 42602–03, 42629, 42642, 42711, 42715, 42717, 42720–21, 42728, 42731, 42733, 42735, 42740–43, 42746, 42749, 42753, 42759, 42786

* * *

SECOND DISTRICT

BRETT GUTHRIE, Republican, of Bowling Green, KY; born in Florence, AL, February 18, 1964; education: B.S., United States Military Academy, West Point, NY, 1987; M.P.M., Yale University, New Haven, CT, 1997; military service: U.S. Army, Field Artillery Office, 101st Airborne Division, 1987–90; professional: Vice President, Trace Die Cast, 1991–2009; member: Kentucky Senate, 1998–2009; married: Beth; children: Caroline, Robby, and Elizabeth; committees: Education and Labor; Transportation and Infrastructure; elected to the 111th Congress on November 4, 2008.

Office Listings

http://www.guthrie.house.gov

510 Cannon House Office Building, Washington, DC 20515 .... (202) 225–3501
Chief of Staff.—Eric Bergren.
Legislative Director.—Megan Spindel.
Communications Director.—Nate Hudson.
Scheduler.—Jennifer Beil.
1001 Center Street, Suite 300, Bowling Green, KY 42101 .... (270) 842–9896
District Director.—Mark Lord.

Counties: BARREN, BRECKINRIDGE, BULLITT, DAVIESS, EDMONSON, GRAYSON, GREEN, HANCOCK, HARDIN, HART, JEFFERSON (part), LARUE, MARION, MEADE, NELSON, OHIO (part), SHELBY, SPENCER, TAYLOR, WARREN, WASHINGTON. Population (2000), 673,244.

ZIP Codes: 40003–04, 40008–09, 40012–13, 40018–20, 40022–23, 40033, 40037, 40040, 40046–49, 40051–52, 40057, 40060–63, 40065–69, 40071, 40076, 40078, 40104, 40107–11, 40115, 40117–19, 40121, 40129, 40140, 40142–46,

40150, 40152–53, 40155, 40157, 40159–62, 40164–65, 40170–71, 40175–78, 40219, 40229, 40245, 40272, 40291, 40299, 40328, 40330, 40342, 40448, 40468, 40601, 42101–04, 42122–23, 42127–31, 42133, 42141–42, 42152, 42156–57, 42159–60, 42163, 42166, 42170–71, 42201, 42206–07, 42210, 42251, 42257, 42259, 42270, 42274–75, 42283, 42285, 42301–04, 42320, 42327, 42333–34, 42338, 42343, 42347–49, 42351–52, 42355–56, 42361, 42364, 42366, 42368, 42370, 42375–78, 42701–02, 42712–13, 42716, 42718–19, 42721–22, 42724, 42726, 42728–29, 42732–33, 42740, 42743, 42746, 42748–49, 42754–55, 42757–58, 42762, 42764–65, 42776, 42782–84, 42788

* * *

THIRD DISTRICT

JOHN A. YARMUTH, Democrat, of Louisville, KY; born in Louisville, November 4, 1947; education: graduated, Atherton High School, Louisville, 1965; graduated, Yale University, New Haven, CT, 1969; professional: Legislative Aide for Kentucky Senator Marlow Cook 1971–74; publisher, *Louisville Today Magazine*, 1976–82; Associate Vice President of University Relations at the University of Louisville, 1983–86; Vice President of a local healthcare firm 1986–90; founder, editor and writer *LEO Newsweekly*, 1990–2005; Television host and commentator, 2003–05; awards: 2007 Spirit of Enterprise Award; Louisville Alzheimer's Association Person of the Year; named Outstanding New Member of Congress by the Committee for Education and Funding; 16 Metro Louisville Journalism Awards for editorial and column writing; married: Cathy Yarmuth, 1981; child: Aaron; committees: Budget; Ways and Means; elected to the 110th Congress on November 7, 2006.

Office Listings

http://www.yarmuth.house.gov

435 Cannon House Office Building, Washington, DC 20515 .... (202) 225–5401
Chief of Staff.—Julie Carr. FAX: 225–5776
Legislative Director.—Ashley Bromagen.
Press Secretary.—Trey Pollard.
Scheduler.—Keidra King.
600 Martin Luther King, Jr. Place, Suite 216, Louisville, KY 40202 .... (502) 582–5129
District Director.—Carolyn Tandy.

Counties: JEFFERSON COUNTY. Population (2000), 674,032.

ZIP Codes: 40018, 40023, 40025, 40027, 40041, 40059, 40109, 40118, 40201–25, 40228–29, 40231–33, 40241–43, 40245, 40250–53, 40255–59, 40261, 40266, 40268–70, 40272, 40280–83, 40285, 40287, 40289–99

* * *

FOURTH DISTRICT

GEOFF DAVIS, Republican, of Hebron, KY; born October 26, 1958; education: attended public schools, West Pittsburgh, PA; B.S., U.S. Military Academy, West Point, NY, 1981; professional: U.S. Army, 1976–87; Assault Helicopter Flight Commander, 82nd Airborne Division; Army Ranger and Senior Parachutist; manufacturing consultant; founder, Republic Consulting, formerly known as Capstone, Incorporated, 1992–present; organizations: 82nd Airborne Association; American Legion volunteer chaplain; National Rifle Association; Northern Kentucky Chamber of Commerce; married: Pat; six children; committees: Ways and Means; elected to the 109th Congress on November 2, 2004; reelected to each succeeding Congress.

Office Listings

http://www.geoffdavis.house.gov

1108 Longworth House Office Building, Washington, DC 20515 .... (202) 225–3465
Chief of Staff.—Armstrong Robinson. FAX: 225–0003
Scheduler / Office Manager.—Rebecca Hobbs.
Communications Director.—Alexandra Haynes.
300 Buttermilk Pike, Suite 314, KY 41017 .... (859) 426–0080
1405 Greenup Avenue, Suite 236, Ashland, KY 41101 .... (606) 324–9898
108 West Jefferson Street, La Grange, KY 40031 .... (502) 222–2233
201 Government Street, Kenton Commonwealth Center, Suite 102, Maysville, KY 41056 .... (606) 564–6004
400 North Main Street, City Building, Suite 145, Williamstown, KY 41097 .... (859) 824–3320

Counties: BATH (part), BOONE, BOYD, BRACKEN, CAMPBELL, CARROLL, CARTER, ELLIOTT, FLEMING, GALLATIN, GRANT, GREENUP, HARRISON, HENRY, KENTON, LEWIS, MASON, NICHOLAS, OLDHAM, OWEN, PENDLETON, ROBERTSON, SCOTT (part), TRIMBLE. Population (2000), 673,588.

ZIP Codes: 40006–07, 40010–11, 40014, 40019, 40026, 40031–32, 40036, 40045, 40050, 40055–59, 40068, 40070, 40075, 40077, 40241, 40245, 40311, 40324, 40346, 40350–51, 40353, 40355, 40358–61, 40363, 40366, 40370–71, 40374,

40379, 40601, 41001–08, 41010–12, 41014–19, 41022, 41030–31, 41033–35, 41037, 41039–46, 41048–49, 41051–56, 41059, 41061–65, 41071–76, 41080–81, 41083, 41085–86, 41091–99, 41101–02, 41105, 41121, 41128–29, 41132, 41135, 41139, 41141–44, 41146, 41149, 41164, 41166, 41168–69, 41171, 41173–75, 41179–81, 41183, 41189, 41472, 45275, 45277, 45298, 45999

* * *

FIFTH DISTRICT

HAROLD ROGERS, Republican, of Somerset, KY; born in Barrier, KY, December 31, 1937; education: graduated, Wayne County High School, 1955; attended Western Kentucky University, 1956–57; A.B., University of Kentucky, 1962; LL.B., University of Kentucky Law School, 1964; professional: lawyer, admitted to the Kentucky State bar, 1964; commenced practice in Somerset; member, North Carolina and Kentucky National Guard, 1957–64; associate, Smith and Blackburn, 1964–67; private practice, 1967–69; Commonwealth Attorney, Pulaski and Rockcastle Counties, KY, 1969–80; delegate, Republican National Convention, 1972, 1976, 1980, 1984, and 1988; Republican nominee for Lieutenant Governor, KY, 1979; past president, Kentucky Commonwealth Attorneys Association; member and past president, Somerset-Pulaski County Chamber of Commerce and Pulaski County Industrial Foundation; founder, Southern Kentucky Economic Development Council, 1986; member, Chowder and Marching Society, 1981–present; member, Republican Steering Committee; married the former Shirley McDowell, 1957; three children: Anthony, Allison, and John Marshall; committees: Appropriations; elected to the 97th Congress, November 4, 1980; reelected to each succeeding Congress.

Office Listings

http://www.house.gov/rogers

2406 Rayburn House Office Building, Washington, DC 20515 .... (202) 225–4601
Administrative Assistant.—Will Smith. FAX: 225–0940
Office Manager.—Julia Casey.
Communications Director.—Stefani Zimmerman.
551 Clifty Street, Somerset, KY 42501 .... (606) 679–8346
District Administrator.—Robert L. Mitchell.
601 Main Street, Hazard, KY 41701 .... (606) 439–0794
100 Resource Drive, Suite A, Prestonsburg, KY 41653 .... (606) 886–0844

Counties: BATH (part), BELL, BREATHITT, CLAY, FLOYD, HARLAN, JACKSON, JOHNSON, KNOTT, KNOX, LAUREL, LAWRENCE, LEE, LESLIE, LETCHER, MAGOFFIN, MARTIN, MCCREARY, MENIFEE, MORGAN, OWSLEY, PERRY, PIKE, PULASKI, ROCKCASTLE, ROWAN, WAYNE, WHITLEY, WOLFE. Population (2000), 673,670.

ZIP Codes: 40313, 40316–17, 40319, 40322, 40329, 40336–37, 40346, 40351, 40358, 40360, 40371, 40387, 40402–03, 40409, 40419, 40421, 40434, 40445, 40447, 40456, 40460, 40467, 40481, 40486, 40488, 40492, 40701–02, 40724, 40729–30, 40734, 40737, 40740–45, 40751, 40754–55, 40759, 40763, 40769, 40771, 40801, 40803, 40806–08, 40810, 40813, 40815–16, 40818–20, 40823–24, 40826–31, 40840, 40843–45, 40847, 40849, 40854–56, 40858, 40862–63, 40865, 40868, 40870, 40873–74, 40902–03, 40906, 40913–15, 40921, 40923, 40927, 40930, 40932, 40935, 40939–41, 40943–44, 40946, 40949, 40951, 40953, 40955, 40958, 40962, 40964–65, 40972, 40977, 40979, 40981–83, 40988, 40995, 40997, 40999, 41124, 41129, 41132, 41159–60, 41164, 41168, 41180, 41201, 41203–04, 41214, 41216, 41219, 41222, 41224, 41226, 41230–32, 41234, 41238, 41240, 41250, 41254–57, 41260, 41262–65, 41267–68, 41271, 41274, 41301, 41307, 41310–11, 41313–14, 41317, 41332–33, 41338–39, 41342, 41344, 41347–48, 41351–52, 41360, 41362, 41364–68, 41385–86, 41390, 41397, 41408, 41410, 41413, 41419, 41421–22, 41425–26, 41433, 41451, 41459, 41464–65, 41472, 41477, 41501–03, 41512–14, 41517, 41519–20, 41522, 41524, 41526–28, 41531, 41534–35, 41537–40, 41542–44, 41546–49, 41553–55, 41557–64, 41566–68, 41571–72, 41601–07, 41612, 41615–16, 41619, 41621–22, 41630–32, 41635–36, 41640, 41642–43, 41645, 41647, 41649–51, 41653, 41655, 41659–60, 41663, 41666–67, 41669, 41701–02, 41712–14, 41719, 41721–23, 41725, 41727, 41729, 41731, 41735–36, 41739–40, 41743, 41745–47, 41749, 41751, 41754, 41759–60, 41762–64, 41766, 41772–78, 41804, 41810, 41812, 41815, 41817, 41819, 41821–22, 41824–26, 41828, 41831–40, 41843–45, 41847–49, 41855, 41858–59, 41861–62, 42501–03, 42518–19, 42533, 42544, 42553, 42558, 42564, 42567, 42603, 42631, 42633–35, 42638, 42642, 42647, 42649, 42653

* * *

SIXTH DISTRICT

BEN CHANDLER, Democrat, of Woodford County, KY; born in Versailles, KY, September 12, 1959; education: B.A., History, University of Kentucky; J.D., University of Kentucky College of Law; public service: elected Kentucky State Auditor, 1991; elected Kentucky Attorney General, 1995; reelected in 1999; Democratic nominee for Governor, 2003; religion: member of Pisgah Presbyterian Church; family: married to Jennifer; children: Lucie, Albert IV, and Branham; committees: Appropriations; Science and Technology; Standards of Official Conduct; elected to the 108th Congress, by special election, on February 17, 2004; reelected to each succeeding Congress.

Office Listings

http://www.chandler.house.gov

1504 Longworth House Office Building, Washington, DC 20515 .... (202) 225–4706
Chief of Staff.—Denis Fleming, Jr. FAX: 225–2122
Legislative Director.—Jim Creevy.
Communications Director.—Jennifer Krimm.
1010 Monarch Street, Suite 310, Lexington, KY 40503 .... (859) 219–1366

Counties: ANDERSON, BOURBON, BOYLE, CLARK, ESTILL, FAYETTE, FRANKLIN, GARRARD, JESSAMINE, LINCOLN (part), MADISON, MERCER, MONTGOMERY, POWELL, SCOTT (part), WOODFORD. Population (2000), 673,626.

ZIP Codes: 40003, 40046, 40076, 40078, 40310–12, 40320, 40324, 40328, 40330, 40334, 40336–37, 40339–40, 40342, 40346–48, 40353, 40355–57, 40361–62, 40370, 40372, 40374, 40376, 40379–80, 40383–86, 40390–92, 40403–05, 40409–10, 40419, 40422–23, 40437, 40440, 40444–47, 40452, 40461, 40464, 40468, 40472–73, 40475–76, 40484, 40489, 40495, 40502–17, 40522–24, 40526, 40533, 40536, 40544, 40546, 40550, 40555, 40574–83, 40588, 40591, 40598, 40601–04, 40618–22, 41031, 41901–06, 42567

LOUISIANA

(Population 2000, 4,468,976)

SENATORS

MARY L. LANDRIEU, Democrat, of New Orleans, LA; born in Alexandria, VA, November 23, 1955; education: B.A., Louisiana State University, 1977; real estate broker, specializing in townhouse development; represented New Orleans House District 90 in Louisiana Legislature, 1979–87; State Treasurer, 1987–95; vice chair, Louisiana Council on Child Abuse; member, Business and Professional Women; majority council member, Emily's List; past national president, Women's Legislative Network; past vice president, Women Executives in State Government; delegate to every Democratic National Convention since 1980; married: E. Frank Snellings; children: Connor, and Mary Shannon; committees: chair, Small Business and Entrepreneurship; Appropriations; Energy and Natural Resources; Homeland Security and Governmental Affairs; elected to the U.S. Senate on November 5, 1996; reelected to each succeeding Senate term.

Office Listings

http://landrieu.senate.gov

328 Hart Senate Office Building, Washington, DC 20510 .... (202) 224–5824
Chief of Staff.—Jane Campbell. FAX: 224–9735
Scheduler.—Kate Nicolai.
Communications Director.—Stephanie Allen.
Legislative Director.—Tom Michels.
Hale Boggs Federal Building, 500 Poydras Street, Room 1005, New Orleans, LA 70130 .... (504) 589–2427
U.S. Courthouse, 300 Fannin Street, Room 2240, Shreveport, LA 71101–3086 .... (318) 676–3085
U.S. Federal Court House, 707 Florida Street, Room 326, Baton Rouge, LA 70801 .. (225) 389–0395
Hibernia Tower, One Lakeshore Drive, Suite 1260, Lake Charles, LA 70629 .... (337) 436–6650

* * *

DAVID VITTER, Republican, of Metairie, LA; born in Metairie, May 3, 1961; education: Harvard University; Oxford University Rhodes Scholar; Tulane University School of Law; professional: attorney; adjunct law professor, Tulane and Loyola Universities; religion: Catholic; public service: Louisiana House of Representatives, 1992–99; U.S. House of Representatives, 1999–2005; awards: Alliance for Good Government ''Legislator of the Year''; Victims and Citizens Against Crime ''Outstanding Legislator'' and ''Lifetime Achievement Award''; married: Wendy Baldwin Vitter; children: Sophie, Lise, Airey, and Jack; committees: Armed Services; Banking, Housing, and Uran Affairs; Commerce, Science, and Transportation; Environment and Public Works; Small Business and Entrepreneurship; elected to the U.S. Senate on November 2, 2004.

Office Listings

http://vitter.senate.gov

516 Hart Senate Office Building, Washington, DC 20510 .... (202) 224–4623
Chief of Staff.—Kyle Ruckert. FAX: 228–5061
Deputy Chief of Staff.—Tonya Newman.
2800 Veterans Boulevard, Suite 201, Metairie, LA 70002 .... (504) 589–2753
858 Convention Street, Baton Rouge, LA 70801 .... (225) 383–0331
1217 North 19th Street, Monroe, LA 71201 .... (318) 325–8120
2230 South MacArthur Street, Suite 4, Alexandria, LA 71301 .... (318) 448–0169
920 Pierremont Road, Suite 113, Shreveport, LA 71106 .... (318) 861–0437
3221 Ryan Street, Suite E, Lake Charles, LA 70601 .... (337) 436–0453
800 Lafayette Street, Suite 1200, Lafayette, LA 70501 .... (337) 262–6898

REPRESENTATIVES

FIRST DISTRICT

STEVE SCALISE, Republican, of Jefferson, LA; born in New Orleans, LA, October 6, 1965; education: B.S., Louisiana State University, Baton Rouge, LA, 1983; professional: Computer Programmer for technology company; Louisiana House of Representatives, 1995–2007, Louisiana Senate, 2007–2008; awards: Spirit of Enterprise, U.S. Chamber of Commerce; religion:

Catholic; married: former Jennifer LeTulle; children: Madison; committees: Energy and Commerce; elected to 110th Congress on May 4, 2008 in special election; reelected to the 111th Congress on November 4, 2008.

Office Listings

http://www.scalise.house.gov

429 Cannon House Office Building, Washington, DC 20515 .... (202) 225–3015
Chief of Staff.—Lynnel Ruckert. FAX: 226–0386
Legislative Director.—Megan Bel.
Scheduler.—Caitlin Songy.
Communications Director.—Luke Bolar.
110 Veterans Memorial Boulevard, Suite 500, Metaire, LA 70005 .... (504) 837–1259
District Director.—Charles Henry.
21454 Koop Drive, Suite 1E, Mandeville, LA 70471 .... (985) 893–9064
112 South Cypress Street, Hammond, LA 70403 .... (985) 340–2185

Parishes: JEFFERSON (part), ORLEANS (part), ST. CHARLES (part), ST. TAMMANY, TANGIPAHOA, WASHINGTON. Population (2000), 638,355.

ZIP Codes: 70001–06, 70009–11, 70033, 70047, 70053, 70055–56, 70058, 70060, 70062, 70064–65, 70072, 70087, 70094, 70115, 70118–19, 70121–24, 70160, 70181, 70183–84, 70401–04, 70420, 70422, 70426–27, 70429, 70431, 70433–38, 70442–48, 70450–52, 70454–67, 70469–71

* * *

SECOND DISTRICT

ANH ''JOSEPH'' CAO, Republican, of New Orleans, LA; born in Saigon, Vietnam, March 13, 1967; B.S., physics, Baylor University, Waco, TX, 1990; M.A., philosophy, Fordham University, New York, NY, 1995; J.D., Loyola University, New Orleans, LA, 2000; professional: Jesuit seminarian; admitted to the bar, New Orleans, LA; Legal Counsel, Boat People SOS; attorney, Waltzer & Associates; attorney, the Law Office of Anh Quang Cao; member, the Orleans Parish Board of Election Supervisors; member, the National Advisory Council of the U.S. Conference of Catholic Bishops; religion: Catholic: married: Hieu ''Kate''; children: Betsy and Sophia; committees: Transportation and Infrastructure; Homeland Security; elected to the 111th Congress on November 4, 2008.

Office Listings

http://www.josephcao.house.gov

2113 Rayburn House Office Building, Washington, DC 20515 .... (202) 225–6636
Chief of Staff.—Clayton Hall. FAX: 225–1988
Office Manager / Scheduler.—Cheyenne Steel.
Legislative Director.—A. Brooke Bennett.
Communications Director.—Princella Smith.
4640 South Carrollton Avenue, Suite 120, New Orleans, LA 70119 .... (504) 483–2335
District Office Manager.—Murray Nelson.
Deputy Chief of Staff.—Rosalind Peychaud.
200 Derbigny Street, Gretna, LA 70053.
624 Williams Boulevard, Kenner, LA 70062.

Parishes: JEFFERSON, ORLEANS. Population (2000), 638,562.

ZIP Codes: 70001, 70003, 70053, 70056, 70058, 70062, 70065, 70094, 70112–19, 70121–23, 70125–31, 70163

* * *

THIRD DISTRICT

CHARLIE MELANCON, Democrat, of Lafayette, LA; born in Napoleonville, LA, October 3, 1947; education: B.S., University of Southwestern Louisiana, Lafayette, LA, 1971; professional: businessman; chairman, Louisiana State University Agricultural Development Council; member, Louisiana State House of Representatives, 1987–93; awards: named Outstanding Legislator by the Louisiana Municipal Association; received the Distinguished Service Award from the Louisiana Restaurant Association; member: UL–Lafayette Alumni Association; Ducks Unlimited; Kappa Sigma Alumni Association; married: Peachy; children: Charles Joseph, Claire; committees: Budget; Energy and Commerce; elected to the 109th Congress on November 2, 2004; reelected to each succeeding Congress.

Office Listings

http://www.house.gov/melancon

404 Cannon House Office Building, Washington, DC 20515 .... (202) 225–4031
Chief of Staff.—Joe Bonfiglio. FAX: 226–3944
Legislative Director.—Chris Debosier.
Scheduler.—Jody Stacoffe.
1201 South Purpera, Sutie 601, Gonzales, LA 70737 .... (225) 621–8490
District Director.—Luke Theriot.
423 Lafayette Street, Suite 107, Houma, LA 70360 .... (985) 876–3033
124 East Main Street, Suite 100, New Iberia, LA 70560 .... (337) 367–8231
8201 West Judge Perez Drive, Chalmette, LA 70043 .... (504) 271–1707

Parishes: ASCENSION (part), ASSUMPTION, IBERIA, JEFFERSON (part), LAFOURCHE, PLAQUEMINES, ST. BERNARD, ST. CHARLES (part), ST. JAMES, ST. JOHN THE BAPTIST, ST. MARTIN, ST. MARY, TERREBONNE. Population (2000), 638,322.

ZIP Codes: 70030–32, 70036–41, 70043–44, 70047, 70049–52, 70056–58, 70067–72, 70075–76, 70078–87, 70090–92, 70301–02, 70310, 70339–46, 70353–54, 70356–61, 70363–64, 70371–75, 70377, 70380–81, 70390–95, 70397, 70512–14, 70517–19, 70521–23, 70528, 70538, 70540, 70544, 70552, 70560, 70562–63, 70569, 70582, 70592, 70723, 70725, 70734, 70737, 70743, 70763, 70778, 70792

* * *

FOURTH DISTRICT

JOHN FLEMING, Republican, of Minden, LA; born in Meridian, MS, July 5, 1951; education: B.S., University of Mississippi, Oxford, MS, 1973; M.D., University of Mississippi, Oxford, MS, 1976; professional: family physician and businessman; military: Lieutenant Commander, U.S. Navy; awards: Louisiana Family Doctor of the Year, 2007; religion: Southern Baptist; married: Cindy; four children; committees: Armed Services; Natural Resources; elected to the 111th Congress on November 4, 2008.

Office Listings

http://www.fleming.house.gov

1023 Longworth House Office Building, Washington, DC 20515 .... (202) 225–2777
Chief of Staff.—Lee Fletcher. FAX: 225–8039
Legislative Director.—Ben Schultz.
Scheduler.—LeAnn Russell.
Communications.—Amy Jones.
6425 Youree Drive, Suite 350, Shreveport, LA 71105 .... (318) 798–2254
District Director.—Rebecca Turner Wilson.
1606 South Fifth Street, Leesville, LA 71446 .... (337) 238–0778
District Director.—Lee Turner.
700 Benton Road, Bossier City, LA 71111 .... (318) 549–1712

Parishes: ALLEN, BEAUREGARD, BIENVILLE, BOSSIER, CADDO, CLAIBORNE, DESOTO, GRANT, NATCHITOCHES, RED RIVER, SABINE, VERNON, WEBSTER. Population (2000), 638,466.

ZIP Codes: 70633–34, 70637–39, 70644, 70648, 70651–57, 70659–60, 70662, 71001–04, 71006–09, 71016, 71018–19, 71021, 71023–25, 71027–34, 71036–40, 71043–52, 71055, 71058, 71060–61, 71063–73, 71075, 71078–80, 71082, 71101–13, 71115, 71118–20, 71129–30, 71133–38, 71148–49, 71151–54, 71156, 71161–66, 71171–72, 71222, 71235, 71251, 71256, 71268, 71275, 71360, 71403–04, 71406–07, 71411, 71414, 71416–17, 71419, 71423, 71426–29, 71432, 71434, 71438–39, 71443, 71446–47, 71449–50, 71452, 71454–63, 71467–69, 71474–75, 71486, 71496–97

* * *

FIFTH DISTRICT

RODNEY ALEXANDER, Republican, of Quitman, LA; born in Bienville, LA, December 5, 1946; education: attended Louisiana Tech University; professional: businessman, with a background in the insurance and construction industries; organizations: member, Louisiana Farm Bureau and the National Rifle Association; public service: Jackson Parish Police Jury, 1970–85; served as President during the last seven years of his tenure; Louisiana House of Representatives, 1987–2002; U.S. Air Force Reserves, 1965–71; religion: Baptist; married: Nancy; three children; committees: Appropriations; elected to the 108th Congress on December 7, 2002; reelected to each succeeding Congress.

Office Listings

http://www.house.gov/alexander

316 Cannon House Office Building, Washington, DC 20515 .... (202) 225–8490

Chief of Staff.—Adam Terry. FAX: 225–5639
Press Secretary.—Jamie Hanks.
Scheduler.—BeBe Terrell.
1900 Stubbs Avenue, Suite B, Monroe, LA 71201 .... (318) 322–3500
1412 Centre Court, Suite 402, Alexandria, LA 71301 .... (318) 445–0818

Parishes: ALLEN (part), AVOYELLES, CALDWELL, CATAHOULA, CONCORDIA, EVANGELINE (part), EAST CARROLL, FRANKLIN, IBERVILLE (part), JACKSON, LASALLE, LINCOLN, MADISON, MOREHOUSE, OUACHITA, POINT COUPEE (part), RAPIDES, RICHLAND, TENSAS, UNION, WEST CARROLL, WINN. Population (2000), 638,517.

ZIP Codes: 70532, 70554, 70576, 70585–86, 70655–57, 70759–60, 70764–65, 70772, 70781, 70783, 71001, 71031, 71201–03, 71207–13, 71218–23, 71225–27, 71229–30, 71232–35, 71237–38, 71240–43, 71245, 71247, 71249–51, 71253–54, 71256, 71259–61, 71263–64, 71266, 71268–70, 71272–73, 71275–77, 71279–82, 71284, 71286, 71291–92, 71294–95, 71301–03, 71306–07, 71309, 71315–16, 71320, 71322–31, 71333–34, 71336, 71339–43, 71346, 71348, 71350–51, 71354–57, 71360–63, 71365–69, 71371, 71373, 71375, 71377–78, 71401, 71404–05, 71407, 71409–10, 71415, 71417–18, 71422–25, 71427, 71430–33, 71435, 71438, 71440–41, 71447–48, 71454–55, 71457, 71463, 71465–67, 71471–73, 71477, 71479–80, 71483, 71485

* * *

SIXTH DISTRICT

BILL CASSIDY, Republican, of Baton Rouge, LA; born in Highland Park, IL, September 28, 1957; education: graduated, Tara High School; B.S., Louisiana State University, Baton Rouge, LA, 1979; M.D., Louisiana State University Medical School, New Orleans, LA, 1983; professional: Medical Doctor; Associate Professor, Baton Rouge; Medical Doctor, founder, Associate Professor of Medicine with LSU Health Science Center; member of the Louisiana State Senate; married: Laura Layden Cassidy, M.D.; children: Will, Meg, and Kate; committees: Agriculture; Education and Labor; Natural Resources; elected to the 111th Congress on November 4, 2008.

Office Listings

http//:www.cassidy.house.gov

506 Cannon House Office Building, Washington, DC 20515 .... (202) 225–3901
Chief of Staff.—Josh Robinson. FAX: 225–7313
Office Manager / Scheduler.—Mary Stundebeck.
5555 Hilton Avenue, Suite 100, Baton Rouge, LA 70808 .... (225) 929–7711
29261 Frost Road, Livingston, LA 70753 .... (225) 686–4413

Parishes: ASCENSION, EAST BATON ROUGE, EAST FELICIANA, IBERVILLE, Livingston, Pointe Coupee, St. Helena, West Baton Rouge, West Feliciana. Population (2000), 638,324.

ZIP Codes: 70403, 70422, 70436, 70441, 70443–44, 70449, 70453, 70462, 70466, 70586, 70704, 70706–07, 70710–12, 70714–15, 70718–19, 70721–22, 70726–30, 70732–34, 70736–40, 70744, 70747–49, 70752–57, 70759–62, 70764, 70767, 70769–70, 70772–78, 70780, 70782–89, 70791, 70801–23, 70826, 70831, 70833, 70835–37, 70874, 70879, 70883–84, 70892–96, 70898

* * *

SEVENTH DISTRICT

CHARLES W. BOUSTANY, JR., Republican, of Lafayette, LA; born in New Orleans, LA, February 21, 1956; education: graduated Cathedral Carmel High School, Lafayette, LA; B.S., University of Southwestern Louisiana, Lafayette, LA, 1978; M.D., Louisiana State University School of Medicine, New Orleans, LA, 1982; professional: surgeon; public service: served on the Louisiana Organ Procurement Agency Tissue Advisory Board; board of directors for the Greater Lafayette Chamber of Commerce, 2001; Chamber of Commerce as Vice President for Government Affairs, 2002; president of the Lafayette Parish Medical Society; chaired the American Heart Association's Gala; Healthcare Division of the UL-Lafayette Centennial Fundraiser, which provided $75 million of university endowed chairs, professorships and scholarships; member of Leadership Lafayette Class IIIXX, 2002; member, Lafayette Parish Republican Executive Committee, 1996–2001; Republican Policy Committee; vice-chairman of the Bush/Cheney Victory 2000 Campaign for Lafayette Parish; board of directors for Lafayette General Medical Center; married: the former Bridget Edwards; children: Erik and Ashley; committees: Ways and Means; elected to the 109th Congress on December 4, 2004; reelected to each succeeding Congress.

Office Listings

http://www.house.gov/boustany

1117 Longworth House Office Building, Washington, DC 20515 .... (202) 225–2031
Chief of Staff.—Jeff Dobrozsi. FAX: 225–5724
Legislative Director.—Terry Fish.
Scheduler.—Hunter Pickels.
800 Lafayette Street, Suite 1400, Lafayette, LA 70501 .... (337) 235–6322
700 Ryan Street, Lake Charles, LA 70601 .... (337) 433–1747

Parishes: ACADIA, CALCASIEU, CAMERON, EVANGELINE, JEFFERSON DAVIS, LAFAYETTE, ST. LANDRY, VERMILION. Population (2000), 638,430.

ZIP Codes: 70501–12, 70515–18, 70520, 70524–29, 70531–35, 70537, 70541–43, 70546, 70548–51, 70554–56, 70558–59, 70570–71, 70575, 70577–78, 70580–81, 70583–84, 70586, 70589, 70591–92, 70596, 70598, 70601–02, 70605–07, 70609, 70611–12, 70615–16, 70630–33, 70640, 70643, 70645–48, 70650, 70655, 70658, 70661, 70663–65, 70668–69, 70750, 71322, 71345, 71353, 71356, 71358, 71362

MAINE

(Population, 2000 1,274,923)

SENATORS

OLYMPIA J. SNOWE, Republican, of Auburn, ME; born in Augusta, ME, February 21, 1947; education: graduated from Edward Little High School, Auburn, ME, 1965; B.A., University of Maine, Orono, 1969; member, Holy Trinity Greek Orthodox Church of Lewiston-Auburn; active member of civic and community organizations; elected to the Maine House of Representatives, 1973, to the seat vacated by the death of her first husband, the late Peter Snowe; reelected for a full two-year term in 1974; elected to the Maine Senate, 1976; chaired the Joint Standing Committee on Health and Institutional Services; elected to the 96th Congress on November 7, 1978—the youngest Republican woman, and first Greek-American woman elected; reelected to the 97th through 103rd Congresses; past member: House Budget Committee; House Foreign Affairs Committee; leading member of the former House Select Committee on Aging, ranking Republican on its Subcommittee on Human Services; married to former Maine Governor John R. McKernan, Jr.; committees: ranking member, Small Business and Entrepreneurship; Commerce, Science, and Transportation; Finance; Select Committee on Intelligence; elected to the U.S. Senate on November 8, 1994; reelected to each succeeding Senate term.

Office Listings

http://snowe.senate.gov

154 Russell Senate Office Building, Washington, DC 20510 .... (202) 224–5344
Chief of Staff.—John Richter. FAX: 224–1946
Executive Assistant.—Anna Levin.
Communications Director.—David Snepp.
2 Great Falls Plaza, Suite 7B, Auburn, ME 04210 .... (207) 786–2451
Regional Representative.—Diane Jackson.
40 Western Avenue, Suite 408C, Augusta, ME 04330 .... (207) 622–8292
Regional Representative.—Deb McNeil.
One Cumberland Place, Suite 306, Bangor, ME 04401 .... (207) 945–0432
State Director.—Gail Kelly.
231 Main Street, P.O. Box 215, Biddeford, ME 04005 .... (207) 282–4144
Regional Representative.—Peter Morin.
3 Canal Plaza, Suite 601, P.O. Box 188, Portland, ME 04112 .... (207) 874–0883
Regional Representative.—Cheryl Leeman.
169 Academy Street, Suite 3, Presque Isle, ME 04769 .... (207) 764–5124
Regional Representative.—Sharon Campbell.

* * *

SUSAN M. COLLINS, Republican, of Bangor, ME; born in Caribou, ME, December 7, 1952; education: graduated, Caribou High School, 1971; B.A., *magna cum laude,* Phi Beta Kappa, St. Lawrence University, Canton, NY; Outstanding Alumni Award, St. Lawrence University, 1992; staff director, Senate Subcommittee on the Oversight of Government Management, 1981–87; for 12 years, principal advisor on business issues to former Senator William S. Cohen; Commissioner of Professional and Financial Regulation for Maine Governor John R. McKernan, Jr., 1987; New England administrator, Small Business Administration, 1992–93; appointed Deputy Treasurer of Massachusetts, 1993; executive director, Husson College Center for Family Business, 1994–96; committees: ranking member, Homeland Security and Governmental Affairs; Appropriations; Armed Services; Special Committee on Aging; elected to the U.S. Senate on November 5, 1996; reelected to each succeeding Senate term.

Office Listings

http://collins.senate.gov

413 Dirksen Senate Office Building, Washington, DC 20510 .... (202) 224–2523
Chief of Staff.—Steven Abbott. FAX: 224–2693
Communications Director.—Kevin Kelley.
Legislative Director.—Rob Epplin.
P.O. Box 655, 202 Harlow Street, Room 204, Bangor, ME 04402 .... (207) 945–0417
State Representative.—Carol Woodcock.
68 Sewall Street, Room 507, Augusta, ME 04330 .... (207) 622–8414
State Representative.—Bobby Reynolds.
160 Main Street, Biddeford, ME 04005 .... (207) 283–1101
State Representative.—Bobby Reynolds.
11 Lisbon Street, Lewiston, ME 04240 .... (207) 784–6969

State Representative.—Peter Rogers.
25 Sweden Street, Suite A, Caribou, ME 04736 .... (207) 493–5873
State Representative.—Philip Bosse.
1 Canal Plaza, Suite 802, Portland, ME 04101 .... (207) 780–3575
State Representative.—Jennifer Duddy.

REPRESENTATIVES

FIRST DISTRICT

CHELLIE PINGREE, Democrat, of North Haven, ME; born in Minneapolis, MN, April 2, 1955; education: B.A., College of the Atlantic, Bar Harbor, ME, 1979; professional: farmer; businesswoman; religion: Lutheran; divorced: three children; House Oceans Caucus; Progressive Caucus, Women's Caucus; Sustainable Energy and Environment Coalition; National Guard and Reserve Component Caucus; Humanities Caucus; Bicycle Caucus; Philanthropy Caucus; House Trade Working Group; committees: Armed Services; Rules; elected to the 111th Congress on November 4, 2008.

Office Listings

http://pingree.house.gov

1037 Longworth House Office Building, Washington, DC 20515 .... (202) 225–6116
Chief of Staff.—Lisa Prosienski. FAX: 225–5590
Legislative Director.—Claire Benjamin.
Scheduler.—Avery Ash.
57 Exchange Street, Suite 302, Portland, ME 04101 .... (207) 774–5019

Counties: CUMBERLAND, KENNEBEC (part), KNOX, LINCOLN, SAGADAHOC, YORK. Population (2000), 637,461.

ZIP Codes: 03901–11, 04001–11, 04013–15, 04017, 04019–21, 04024, 04027–30, 04032–34, 04038–40, 04042–43, 04046–50, 04053–57, 04061–64, 04066, 04069–79, 04082–87, 04090–98, 04101–10, 04112, 04116, 04122–24, 04259–60, 04265, 04284, 04287, 04330, 04332–33, 04336, 04338, 04341–55, 04357–60, 04363–64, 04530, 04535–39, 04541, 04543–44, 04547–48, 04551, 04553–56, 04558, 04562–65, 04567–68, 04570–76, 04578–79, 04841, 04843, 04846–56, 04858–65, 04901, 04910, 04917–18, 04922, 04926–27, 04935, 04937, 04941, 04949, 04952, 04962–63, 04973, 04987–89, 04992

* * *

SECOND DISTRICT

MICHAEL H. MICHAUD, Democrat, of East Millinocket, ME; born on January 18, 1955; grew up in Medway, ME; education: graduate, Harvard University John F. Kennedy School of Government Program for Senior Executives in State and Local Government; professional: mill worker; community service: actively involved in a variety of local, regional, and statewide civic and economic development organizations; public service: Maine House of Representatives, 1980–94; Maine State Senate, 1994–2002; religion: Catholic; committees: Small Business; Transportation and Infrastructure; Veterans' Affairs; elected to the 108th Congress on November 5, 2002; reelected to each succeeding Congress.

Office Listings

http://www.house.gov/michaud

1724 Longworth Office Building, Washington, DC 20515 .... (202) 225–6306
Chief of Staff.—Peter Chandler. FAX: 225–2943
Legislative Director.—Kim Glas.
Scheduler.—Diane Smith.
Press Secretary.—Ed Gilman.
6 State Street, Bangor, ME 04401 .... (207) 942–6935
179 Lisbon Street, Ground Floor, Lewiston, ME 04240 .... (207) 782–3704
445 Main Street, Presque Isle, ME 04769 .... (207) 764–1036
16 Common Street, Waterville, ME 04901 .... (207) 873–5713

Counties: ANDROSCOGGIN, AROOSTOOK, FRANKLIN, HANCOCK, KENNEBEC (part), OXFORD, PENOBSCOT, PISCATAQUIS, SOMERSET, WALDO, WASHINGTON. Population (2000), 637,461.

ZIP Codes: 04010, 04016, 04022, 04037, 04041, 04051, 04068, 04088, 04210–12, 04216–17, 04219–28, 04230–31, 04234, 04236–41, 04243, 04250, 04252–58, 04261–63, 04266–68, 04270–71, 04274–76, 04278, 04280–83, 04285–86, 04288–92, 04294, 04354, 04401–02, 04406, 04408, 04410–24, 04426–31, 04434–35, 04438, 04441–44, 04448–51, 04453–

57, 04459–64, 04467–69, 04471–76, 04478–79, 04481, 04485, 04487–93, 04495–97, 04549, 04605–07, 04609, 04611–17, 04619, 04622–31, 04634–35, 04637, 04640, 04642–46, 04648–50, 04652–58, 04660, 04662, 04664, 04666–69, 04671–77, 04679–81, 04683–86, 04691, 04693–94, 04730, 04732–47, 04750–51, 04756–66, 04768–70, 04772–77, 04779–81, 04783, 04785–88, 04848–51, 04857, 04903, 04911–12, 04915, 04920–25, 04928–30, 04932–33, 04936–45, 04947, 04949–58, 04961, 04964–67, 04969–76, 04978–79, 04981–88, 04992

MARYLAND

(Population 2000, 5,296,486)

SENATORS

BARBARA A. MIKULSKI, Democrat, of Baltimore, MD; born in Baltimore, July 20, 1936; education: B.A., Mount St. Agnes College, 1958; M.S.W., University of Maryland School of Social Work, 1965; former social worker for Catholic Charities and city of Baltimore; served as an adjunct professor, Department of Sociology, Loyola College; elected to the Baltimore City Council, 1971; Democratic nominee for the U.S. Senate in 1974, winning 43 percent of vote; elected to the U.S. House of Representatives in November, 1976; first woman appointed to the Energy and Commerce Committee; also served on the Merchant Marine and Fisheries Committee; became the first woman representing the Democratic Party to be elected to a Senate seat not previously held by her husband, and the first Democratic woman ever to serve in both houses of Congress; Secretary, Democratic Conference; first woman to be elected to a leadership post; committees: Appropriations; Health, Education, Labor, and Pensions; Select Committee on Intelligence; elected to the U.S. Senate in November, 1986; reelected to each succeeding Senate term.

Office Listings

http://mikulski.senate.gov

503 Hart Senate Office Building, Washington, DC 20510 .... (202) 224–4654
Chief of Staff.—Julia Frifield. FAX: 224–8858
Legislative Director.—Christie Dawson.
1629 Thames Street, Suite 400, Baltimore, MD 21231 .... (410) 962–4510
State Director.—Sally Wingo (acting).
60 West Street, Suite 302, Annapolis, MD 21401 .... (410) 263–1805
6404 Ivy Lane, Suite 406, Greenbelt, MD 20770 .... (301) 345–5517
32 West Washington Street, Suite 203, Hagerstown, MD 21740 .... (301) 797–2826
The Gallery Plaza Building, 212 Main Street, Suite 200, Salisbury, MD 21801 ...... (410) 546–7711

* * *

BENJAMIN L. CARDIN, Democrat, of Baltimore, MD; born in Baltimore, October 5, 1943; education: graduated, City College High School, 1961; B.A., *cum laude*, University of Pittsburgh, 1964; L.L.B., 1st in class, University of Maryland School of Law, 1967; professional: attorney, Rosen and Esterson, 1967–78; elected to Maryland House of Delegates in November 1966, served from 1967–87; Speaker of the House of Delegates, youngest Speaker at the time, 1979–87; elected to U.S. House of Representatives in November 1986, Maryland 3rd Congressional District, served from 1987–2007; member: Associated Jewish Charities and Welfare Fund, 1985–89; Trustee, St. Mary's College, 1988–99; Lifetime Member, NAACP, since 1990; Board of Visitors, University of Maryland Law School, 1991–present; President's Board of Visitors, UMBC, 1998–present; Board of Visitors, U.S. Naval Academy, 2007–present; awards: Congressional Award, Small Business Council of America, 1993, 1999, 2005; Public Sector Distinguished Award, Tax Foundation, 2003; Congressional Voice for Children Award, National PTA, 2009; Commissioner, Commission for Security and Cooperation in Europe (CSCE), since 1993; co-chair, CSCE, 2003–06; chair, Commission for Security and Cooperation in Europe, 2009–present; Vice President, Organization for Security and Cooperation in Europe Parliamentary Assembly, 2006–present; religion: Jewish; married: Myrna Edelman of Baltimore, 1964; two children, (one deceased); two grandchildren; committees: Budget; Environment and Public Works; Foreign Relations; Judiciary; Small Business and Entrepreneurship; elected to the U.S. Senate on November 7, 2006.

Office Listings

http://cardin.senate.gov

509 Hart Senate Office Building, Washington, DC 20510 .... (202) 224–4524
Chief of Staff.—Chris Lynch. FAX: 224–1651
Policy Director.—Priscilla Ross. TDD: 224–3452
Appointments Secretary.—Debbie Yamada.
100 South Charles Street, Tower I, Suite 1710, Baltimore, MD 21201 .... (410) 962–4436
State Director.—Bailey Fine. FAX: 962–4256
10201 Martin Luther King, Jr. Highway, Suite 210, Bowie, MD 20720 .... (301) 860–0414
129 East Main Street, Suite 115, P.O. Box 11, Salisbury, MD 21803 .... (410) 546–4250
13 Canal Street, Room 305, Cumberland, MD 21502 .... (301) 777–2957

REPRESENTATIVES

FIRST DISTRICT

FRANK KRATOVIL, Jr., Democrat of Stevensville, MD; born in Lanham, MD, May 29, 1968; graduated from Queen Anne High School, 1986; B.A., Western Maryland College, Westminster, MD, 1990; J.D., University of Baltimore School of Law, Baltimore, MD, 1994; professional: law clerk, Prince George's County Circuit Court, 1995–97; Assistant State's Attorney, Prince George's County, MD, 1995–97; Assistant State's Attorney, Queen Anne's County, MD, 1997–2001; appointed as Deputy State's Attorney, Kent County, MD; State's Attorney, Queen Anne County, MD, 2003–2008; religion: Protestant; married: Kimberly; children: Frankie, Cole, Jackson, and Nate; member, Blue Dog Coalition; New Democrat Coalition; Chesapeake Bay Caucus; committees: Agriculture; Armed Services; Natural Resources; elected to the 111th Congress on November 4, 2008.

Office Listings

http://kratovil.house.gov

314 Cannon House Office Building, Washington, DC 20515 .... (202) 225–5311
Chief of Staff.—Tim McCann. FAX: 225–0254
Office Manager / Scheduler.—Donna Frohn.
Legislative Director.—Ben Abrams.
Press Secretary.—Kevin Lawlor.
102 Turpins Lane, Centreville, MD 21617 .... (443) 262–9136
District Office Manager.—Karen Willis.
One Plaza East, Suite 103, East Main Street, Salisbury, MD 21801 .... (410) 334–3072
District Office Manager.—Tamara Lee-Brooks.
202 South Main Street, Bel Air, MD 21014 .... (410) 420–8822
District Office Manager.—Justin Hayes.

Counties: Anne Arundel (part), Baltimore (part), Caroline, Cecil, Dorchester, Harford (part), Kent, Queen Anne's, Somerset, Talbot, Wicomico, Worcester. Population (2000), 662,062.

ZIP Codes: 21001, 21009, 21012–15, 21018, 21023, 21028, 21030–32, 21034, 21047, 21050–51, 21054, 21057, 21078, 21082, 21084–85, 21087, 21092–93, 21108, 21111, 21113, 21122, 21128, 21131, 21136, 21144, 21146, 21156, 21162, 21206, 21225–26, 21234, 21236, 21240, 21286, 21401–05, 21411–12, 21601, 21606–07, 21609–10, 21612–13, 21617, 21619–20, 21622–29, 21631–32, 21634–36, 21638–41, 21643–45, 21647–73, 21675–79, 21681–85, 21687, 21690, 21801–04, 21810–11, 21813–14, 21817, 21821–22, 21824, 21826, 21829–30, 21835–38, 21840–43, 21849–53, 21856–57, 21861–67, 21869, 21871–72, 21874–75, 21890, 21901–04, 21911–22, 21930

* * *

SECOND DISTRICT

C. A. DUTCH RUPPERSBERGER, Democrat, of Cockeysville, MD; born in Baltimore, MD, January 31, 1946; education: Baltimore City College; University of Maryland, College Park; J.D., University of Baltimore Law School, 1970; professional: attorney; partner, Ruppersberger, Clark, and Mister (law firm); public service: Baltimore County Assistant State's Attorney; Baltimore County Council; Baltimore County Executive, 1994–2002; married: the former Kay Murphy; children: Cory and Jill; committees: Appropriations; Permanent Select Committee on Intelligence; elected to the 108th Congress on November 5, 2002; reelected to each succeeding Congress.

Office Listings

http://dutch.house.gov

2453 Rayburn House Office Building, Washington, DC 20515 .... (202) 225–3061
Chief of Staff.—Tara Oursler. FAX: 225–3094
Deputy Chief of Staff /Press Secretary.—Heather Molino.
Senior Policy Advisor.—Walter Gonzales.
Legislative Director.—Steve Jost.
The Atrium, 375 West Padonia Road, Suite 200, Timonium, MD 21093 .... (410) 628–2701
District Office Manager / Scheduler.—Carol Merkel.
Deputy Office Manager / Casework Supervisor.—Cori Duggins.

Counties: Anne Arundel (part), Baltimore City (part), Baltimore County (part), Harford (part). Population (2000), 662,060.

ZIP Codes: 20755, 21001, 21005, 21009–10, 21017, 21022, 21027, 21030–31, 21034, 21040, 21047, 21050–52, 21056–57, 21060–62, 21065, 21071, 21076–78, 21085, 21087, 21090, 21093–94, 21104, 21111, 21113, 21117, 21122–23,

21130, 21133, 21136, 21144, 21162–63, 21204, 21206, 21208, 21212–14, 21219–22, 21224–27, 21230, 21234, 21236–37, 21239, 21244, 21252, 21284–86

* * *

THIRD DISTRICT

JOHN P. SARBANES, Democrat, of Baltimore, MD; born in Baltimore, May 22, 1962; education: A.B., *cum laude*, Woodrow Wilson School of Public and International Affairs, Princeton University, 1984; Fulbright Scholar, Greece, 1985; J.D., Harvard University School of Law, 1988; professional: law clerk to Judge J. Frederick Motz, U.S. District Court for the District of Maryland, 1988–89; admitted to Maryland Bar, 1988; member: American Bar Association; Maryland State Bar Association; attorney, Venable, LLP, 1989–2006 (chair, health care practice); founding member, Board of Trustees, Dunbar Project, 1990–94; Board of Directors, Public Justice Center, 1991–2006 (president, 1994–97); Institute for Christian and Jewish Studies, 1991-present (past chair, membership committee); Special Assistant to State Superintendent of Schools, State Department of Education, 1998–2005; awards: Unsung Hero Award, Maryland Chapter of the Association of Fundraising Professionals, 2006; Arthur W. Machen, Jr., Award, Maryland Legal Services Corp., 2006; married to Dina Sarbanes; three children; committees: Energy and Commerce; Natural Resources; elected to the 110th Congress on November 7, 2006; relected to the 111th Congress on November 4, 2008.

Office Listings

http://www.sarbanes.house.gov

426 Cannon House Office Building, Washington, DC 20510 .... (202) 225–4016
Chief of Staff.—Jason Gleason. FAX: 225–9219
Press Secretary.—Pia Carusone.
Communications Director.—Makeda Scott.
600 Baltimore Avenue, Suite 303, Towson, MD 21204 .... (410) 832–8890

Counties: ANNE ARUNDEL (part), BALTIMORE (part), HOWARD (part), BALTIMORE CITY (part). TOWNS: Arbutus, Crofton, Ellicott City, Elkridge, Glen Burnie, Halethrope, Lansdowne, Linthicum, Maryland City, Odenton, Owings Mills, Parkville, Pikesville, Reisterstown, Russett City, Severn, and Towson. Population (2000), 662,062.

ZIP Codes: 20701, 20723–24, 20755, 20759, 20794, 21022, 21029, 21032, 21035, 21037, 21043–46, 21054, 21060–61, 21071, 21075, 21090, 21093, 21108, 21113–14, 21117, 21122–23, 21136, 21144, 21146, 21153, 21201–02, 21204–06, 21208–15, 21218, 21222, 21227–31, 21234, 21236–37, 21239, 21252, 21281–82, 21285–86, 21401–05, 21411–12

* * *

FOURTH DISTRICT

DONNA F. EDWARDS, Democrat, of Fort Washington, MD; born in Yanceyville, NC, June 28, 1959; education: B.A., Wake Forest University, Winston-Salem, NC, 1980; J.D., Franklin Pierce Law Center, Concord, NH, 1989; professional: executive director, Arca Foundation, 2000–08; Founder and executive director, National Network to End Domestic Violence, 1996–99; executive director, Center for New Democracy, 1994–96; member: board of directors, National Network to End Domestic Violence; Citizens for Responsibility and Ethics in Washington; League of Conservation Voters, Common Cause; Tom Lantos Human Rights Commission; committees: Science and Technology; Transportation and Infrastructure; elected by special election on June 17, 2008, to fill the vacancy caused by the resignation of U.S. Representative Albert Russell Wynn, and elected to a full term in the 111th Congress on November 4, 2008.

Office Listings

http://www.donnaedwards.house.gov

318 Cannon House Office Building, Washington, DC 20515 .... (202) 225–8699
Chief of Staff.—Adrienne Christian. FAX: 225–8714
Legislative Director.—Terra Sabag.
Communications Director.—Dan Weber.
5001 Silver Hill Road, Suite 106, Suitland, MD 20746 .... (301) 516–7601
8730 Georgia Avenue, Suite 209, Silver Spring, MD 20910 .... (301) 562–7960

Counties: MONTGOMERY (part), PRINCE GEORGE'S (part). CITIES AND TOWNSHIPS: Bladensburg, Brentwood, Brookeville, Capitol Heights, Cheverly, Colmar Manor, Cottage City, District Heights, Edmonston, Fairmount Heights, Glenarden, Landover Hills, Largo, Laytonsville, Morningside, Mount Rainier, New Carrollton, North Brentwood, Olney, Riverdale, Rockville, Seat Pleasant, University Park, and Upper Marlboro. Population (2000), 662,062.

ZIP Codes: 20703, 20706–07, 20710, 20720–21, 20731, 20735, 20737, 20743–48, 20750, 20752–53, 20757, 20762, 20769, 20772, 20774–75, 20777, 20781–85, 20788, 20790–92, 20797, 20799, 20830, 20832–33, 20841, 20853, 20855, 20860–62, 20866, 20868, 20871–72, 20874, 20876–77, 20879, 20882, 20886, 20901, 20903–06, 20910–12, 21771, 21797

* * *

FIFTH DISTRICT

STENY H. HOYER, Democrat, of Mechanicsville, MD; born in New York, NY, June 14, 1939; education: graduated Suitland High School; B.S., University of Maryland, 1963; J.D., Georgetown University Law Center, 1966; Honorary Doctor of Public Service, University of Maryland, 1988; admitted to the Maryland Bar Association, 1966; professional: practicing attorney, 1966–90; Maryland State Senate, 1967–79; vice chairman, Prince George's County, MD, Senate delegation, 1967–69; chairman, Prince George's County, MD, Senate delegation, 1969–75; president, Maryland State Senate, 1975–79; member, State Board for Higher Education, 1978–81; married: Judith Pickett, deceased, February 6, 1997; children: Susan, Stefany, and Anne; Democratic Steering Committee; House Majority Leader, 110th Congress; elected to the 97th Congress on May 19, 1981, by special election; reelected to each succeeding Congress.

Office Listings

http://www.hoyer.house.gov

1705 Longworth House Office Building, Washington, DC 20515	(202) 225–4131
Chief of Staff.—Terry Lierman.	FAX: 226–0663
Administrative Assistant.—Jim Wood.	
U.S. Federal Courthouse, Suite 310, 6500 Cherrywood Lane, Greenbelt, MD 20770	(301) 474–0119
401 Post Office Road, Suite 202, Waldorf, MD 20602	(301) 843–1577

Counties: ANNE ARUNDEL (part), CALVERT, CHARLES, PRINCE GEORGE'S (part), ST. MARY'S. Population (2000), 662,060.

ZIP Codes: 20601–04, 20606–13, 20615–30, 20632, 20634–37, 20639–40, 20643, 20645–46, 20650, 20653, 20656–62, 20664, 20667, 20670, 20674–78, 20680, 20682, 20684–90, 20692–93, 20695, 20697, 20704–09, 20711, 20714–21, 20725–26, 20732–33, 20735–38, 20740–42, 20744, 20748–49, 20751, 20754, 20758, 20764–65, 20768–74, 20776, 20778–79, 20781–84, 20904, 21035, 21037, 21054, 21106, 21113, 21140

* * *

SIXTH DISTRICT

ROSCOE G. BARTLETT, Republican, of Frederick, MD; born in Moreland, KY, June 3, 1926; education: B.A., Columbia Union College, 1947; M.A., 1948, and Ph.D., University of Maryland, 1952; still an active farmer, prior to his election to Congress, he had retired after owning and operating a small business for 10 years; awards: awarded 20 patents for inventions during his scientific career as a professor and research engineer; Jeffries Aerospace Medicine and Life Sciences Research Award, 1999; held positions at Loma Linda University, the Navy's School of Aviation Medicine, John Hopkins Applied Physics Laboratory, and at IBM; married to Ellen; 10 children; committees: Armed Services; Science and Technology; Small Business; elected to the 103rd Congress; reelected to each succeeding Congress.

Office Listings

http://www.bartlett.house.gov

2412 Rayburn House Office Building, Washington, DC 20515	(202) 225–2721
Chief of Staff / Legislative Director.—Bud Otis.	FAX: 225–2193
Office Manager / Scheduler.—Barb Calligan.	
11377 Robinwood Drive, Hagerstown, MD 21742	(301) 797–6043
7360 Guilford Drive, Suite 101, Frederick, MD 21704	(301) 694–3030
15 Main Street, Suite 110, Westminster, MD 21157	(410) 857–1115
1 Frederick Street, Cumberland, MD 21502	(301) 724–3105

Counties: ALLEGANY, BALTIMORE (part), CARROLL, FREDERICK, GARRETT, HARFORD (part), MONTGOMERY (part), WASHINGTON. CITIES AND TOWNSHIPS: Baltimore, Boonsboro, Cumberland, Emmitsburg, Frederick, Frostburg, Funkstown, Hagerstown, Hancock, Middletown, Mount Airy, Oakland, Reisterstown, Sharpsburg, Smithburg, Thurmont, Timonium, Walkersville, Westminster, Williamsport, Woodsboro. Also includes Antietam National Battlefield and Camp David. Population (2000), 662,060.

ZIP Codes: 20842, 20871–72, 20876, 20882, 21014, 21020, 21029–30, 21034, 21036, 21041–43, 21047–48, 21050, 21053, 21074–75, 21084, 21088, 21102, 21104–05, 21111, 21120, 21131–32, 21136, 21152, 21154–55, 21157–58,

21160–61, 21163, 21501–05, 21520–24, 21528–32, 21536, 21538–43, 21545, 21550, 21555–57, 21560–62, 21701–05, 21709–11, 21713–23, 21727, 21733–34, 21740–42, 21746–50, 21754–59, 21762, 21766–67, 21769–71, 21773–84, 21787–88, 21790–91, 21793, 21795, 21797–98

* * *

SEVENTH DISTRICT

ELIJAH E. CUMMINGS, Democrat, of Baltimore, MD; born in Baltimore, January 18, 1951; education: graduated, Baltimore City College High School, 1969; B.S., political science, Phi Beta Kappa, Howard University, Washington, DC, 1973; J.D., University of Maryland Law School, 1976; professional: attorney; admitted to the Maryland bar in 1976; delegate, Maryland State Legislature, 1982–96; chairman, Maryland Legislative Black Caucus, 1984; speaker pro tempore, Maryland General Assembly, 1995–96; vice chairman, Constitutional and Administrative Law Committee; vice chairman, Economic Matters Committee; president, sophomore class, student government treasurer and student government president at Howard University; member: Governor's Commission on Black Males; New Psalmist Baptist Church, Baltimore, MD; active in civic affairs, and recipient of numerous community awards; co-chair of the House AIDS Working Group; Task Force on Health Care Reform; committees: Oversight and Government Reform; Transportation and Infrastructure; Joint Economic Committee; elected to the 104th Congress by special election in April, 1996; reelected to each succeeding Congress.

Office Listings

http://www.house.gov/cummings

2235 Rayburn House Office Building, Washington, DC 20515 .... (202) 225–4741
Chief of Staff.—Vernon Simms. FAX: 225–3178
Legislative Director.—Nikki Jones.
Legislative Assistants: Kim Johnson, Lucinda Lessley, Martin Levine.
Press Secretary.—Jennifer Kohl.
1010 Park Avenue, Suite 105, Baltimore, MD 21201 .... (410) 685–9199
754 Frederick Road, Catonsville, MD 21228 .... (410) 719–8777
8267 Main Street, Room 102, Ellicott City, MD 21043 .... (410) 465–8259

Counties: BALTIMORE (part), HOWARD (part), BALTIMORE CITY (part). Population (2000), 662,060.

ZIP Codes: 20701, 20723, 20759, 20763, 20777, 20794, 20833, 21029, 21036, 21042–45, 21075, 21104, 21117, 21133, 21163, 21201–03, 21205–18, 21223–24, 21227–31, 21233, 21235, 21239, 21241, 21244, 21250–51, 21263–65, 21268, 21270, 21273–75, 21278–80, 21283, 21287–90, 21297–98, 21723, 21737–38, 21765, 21771, 21784, 21794, 21797

* * *

EIGHTH DISTRICT

CHRIS VAN HOLLEN, Democrat, of Kensington, MD; born in Karachi, Pakistan, January 10, 1959; education: B.A., Swarthmore College, 1982; Masters in Public Policy, Harvard University, 1985; J.D., Georgetown University, 1990; professional: attorney; legislative assistant to former Maryland U.S. Senator Charles McC. Mathias, Jr.; staff member, U.S. Senate Committee on Foreign Relations; senior legislative advisor to former Maryland Governor William Donald Schaefer; public service: elected, Maryland House of Delegates, 1990; elected, Maryland State Senate, 1994; married: Katherine; children: Anna, Nicholas, and Alexander; committees: Oversight and Government Reform; Ways and Means; elected to the 108th Congress on November 5, 2002; reelected to each succeeding Congress.

Office Listings

http://www.house.gov/vanhollen

1707 Longworth House Office Building, Washington, DC 20515 .... (202) 225–5341
Chief of Staff.—David Weaver. FAX: 225–0375
Legislative Director.—Bill Parsons.
Press Secretary.—Bridgett Frey.
51 Monroe Street, Suite 507, Rockville, MD 20850 .... (301) 424–3501
District Director.—Joan Kleinman.

Counties: MONTGOMERY (part), PRINCE GEORGES (part). Population (2000), 662,060.

ZIP Codes: 20712, 20722, 20782–83, 20787, 20810–18, 20824–25, 20827, 20837–39, 20841–42, 20847–55, 20857, 20859, 20871, 20874–80, 20883–86, 20889, 20891–92, 20894–99, 20901–08, 20910, 20912–16, 20918, 20997

MASSACHUSETTS

(Population 2000, 6,349,097)

SENATORS

JOHN F. KERRY, Democrat, of Boston, MA; born in Denver, CO, December 11, 1943; education: graduated, St. Paul's School, Concord, NH, 1962; B.A., Yale University, New Haven, CT, 1966; J.D., Boston College Law School, Boston, MA, 1976; served, U.S. Navy, discharged with rank of lieutenant; decorations: Silver Star, Bronze Star with Combat ''V'', three Purple Hearts, various theatre campaign decorations; attorney, admitted to Massachusetts bar, 1976; appointed first assistant district attorney, Middlesex County, 1977; elected lieutenant governor, Massachusetts, 1982; married: Teresa Heinz; committees: chair, Foreign Relations; Commerce, Science, and Transportation; Finance; Small Business and Entrepreneurship; appointed to Democratic Leadership for 104th and 105th Congresses; elected to the U.S. Senate on November 6, 1984; reelected to each succeeding Senate term.

Office Listings

http://kerry.senate.gov

218 Russell Senate Office Building, Washington, DC 20510 .... (202) 224–2742
Chief of Staff.—David McKean. FAX: 224–8525
Legislative Director.—John Phillips.
Personal Secretary.—Kaaren Hinck.
One Bowdoin Square, 10th Floor, Boston, MA 02114 .... (617) 565–8519
Suite 311, 222 Milliken Place, Fall River, MA 02722 .... (508) 677–0522
One Financial Plaza, Springfield, MA 01103 .... (413) 747–3942

* * *

PAUL G. KIRK, Jr., Democrat, of Marstons Mills, MA; born in Boston, MA, January 18, 1938; education: graduated, St. Sebastian's School, Newton, MA, 1956; B.A., Harvard College, Cambridge, MA, 1960; J.D., Harvard Law School, Cambridge, MA, 1964; professional: served, United States Army (ROTC) 1961–68; attorney, admitted to Massachusetts bar, 1965; served as Assistant District Attorney, Middlesex County, 1965; Special Assistant, U.S. Senator Edward M. Kennedy, 1969–77; law partner, Sullivan and Worcester LLP, Boston, MA, 1977–90; Chairman, Democratic National Committee, 1985–89; Chairman, National Democratic Institute of International Affairs, 1992–2001; CEO and Chairman, Kirk & Associates, 1990–2009; Chairman, John F. Kennedy Library Foundation, 1992–2009; Co-Chairman, Commission on Presidential Debates, 1987–2009; Director, Edward M., Kennedy Institute for the United States Senate, 2009; married: Gail L. Kirk; committees: Armed Services; Homeland Security and Government Affairs; appointed to the U.S. Senate on September 24, 2009 by Massachusetts Governor Deval Patrick to serve as interim Senator until the special election to fill out the term of the late Senator Edward M. Kennedy.

Office Listings

188 Russell Senate Office Building, Washington, DC 20510 .... (202) 224–4543
Chief of Staff.—Eric Mogilnicki. FAX: 224–2417
Legislative Director.—Carey Parker.
Personal Secretary.—Lauren Janes.
JFK Federal Building, Suite 2400, Boston, MA 02203 .... (617) 565–3170
State Director.—Barbara Souliotis.

REPRESENTATIVES

FIRST DISTRICT

JOHN W. OLVER, Democrat, of Amherst, MA; born in Honesdale, PA, September 3, 1936; education: B.S., Rensselaer Polytechnic Institute, 1955; M.A., Tufts University, 1956; taught for 2 years at Franklin Technical Institute, Boston, MA; Ph.D., Massachusetts Institute of Technology, 1961; professional: chemistry professor, University of Massachusetts-Amherst; Massachusetts House, 1968–72; Massachusetts Senate, 1972–91; became first Democrat since the Spanish-American War to represent the First Congressional District, 1991; elected by special election on June 4, 1991, to fill the vacancy caused by the death of Silvio Conte; married: Rose Olver; children: Martha; committees: Appropriations; elected on June 4, 1991, by special election, to the 102nd Congress; reelected to each succeeding Congress.

Office Listings

http://www.house.gov/olver

1111 Longworth House Office Building, Washington, DC 20515 .... (202) 225–5335
Chief of Staff.—Hunter Ridgway. FAX: 226–1224
Press Secretary.—Sara Merriam.
Scheduler.—Jason Powers.
Legislative Director.—Lisa Wiehl.
463 Main Street, Fitchburg, MA 01420 .... (978) 342–8722
Office Manager.—Peggy Kane.
57 Suffolk Street, Suite 310, Holyoke, MA 01040 .... (413) 532–7010
District Director.—Jon Niedzielski.
78 Center Street, Pittsfield, MA 01201 .... (413) 442–0946
Office Manager.—Cindy Clark.

Counties: BERKSHIRE, FRANKLIN, HAMPDEN (part), HAMPSHIRE (part), MIDDLESEX (part), WORCESTER (part). Population (2000), 634,479.

ZIP Codes: 01002–05, 01007–08, 01011–12, 01026–27, 01029, 01031–34, 01037–41, 01050, 01054, 01059, 01066, 01068–75, 01077, 01080–82, 01084–86, 01088–90, 01093–94, 01096–98, 01102, 01107, 01201–03, 01220, 01222–27, 01229–30, 01235–38, 01240, 01242–45, 01247, 01252–60, 01262–64, 01266–67, 01270, 01301–02, 01330–31, 01337–44, 01346–47, 01349–51, 01355, 01360, 01364, 01366–68, 01370, 01373, 01375–76, 01378–80, 01420, 01430–31, 01436, 01438, 01440–41, 01452–53, 01462–63, 01468–69, 01473–75, 01477, 01531, 01564, 01585

* * *

SECOND DISTRICT

RICHARD E. NEAL, Democrat, of Springfield, MA; born in Springfield, February 14, 1949; education: graduated, Springfield Technical High School, 1968; B.A., American International College, Springfield, 1972; M.A., University of Hartford Barney School of Business and Public Administration, West Hartford, CT, 1976; instructor and lecturer; assistant to mayor of Springfield, 1973–78; Springfield City Council, 1978–84; mayor, City of Springfield, 1983–89; member: Massachusetts Mayors Association; Adult Education Council; American International College Alumni Association; Boys Club Alumni Association; Emily Bill Athletic Association; Cancer Crusade; John Boyle O'Reilly Club; United States Conference of Mayors; Valley Press Club; Solid Waste Advisory Committee for the State of Massachusetts; Committee on Leadership and Government; Mass Jobs Council; trustee: Springfield Libraries and Museums Association, Springfield Red Cross, Springfield YMCA; married: Maureen; four children: Rory Christopher, Brendan Conway, Maura Katherine, and Sean Richard; committees: Ways and Means; elected on November 8, 1988 to the 101st Congress; reelected to each succeeding Congress.

Office Listings

http://www.house.gov/neal

2208 Rayburn House Office Building, Washington, DC 20515 .... (202) 225–5601
Administrative Assistant.—Ann Jablon. FAX: 225–8112
Executive Assistant.—Sarah Bontempo.
Press Secretary.—Bill Tranghese.
Federal Building, Room 309, 1550 Main Street, Springfield, MA 01103 .... (413) 785–0325
District Manager.—James Leydon.
4 Congress Street, Milford, MA 01757 .... (508) 634–8198
Office Manager.—Virginia Purcell.

Counties: HAMPDEN (part), HAMPSHIRE (part), NORFOLK (part), WORCESTER (part). Population (2000), 634,444.

ZIP Codes: 01001, 01009–10, 01013–14, 01020–22, 01027–28, 01030, 01035–36, 01053, 01056–57, 01060–63, 01069, 01075, 01079–81, 01083, 01092, 01095, 01101–09, 01111, 01115–16, 01118–19, 01128–29, 01133, 01138–39, 01144, 01151–52, 01199, 01504, 01506–09, 01515–16, 01518–19, 01521, 01524–27, 01529, 01534–38, 01540, 01542, 01550, 01560, 01562, 01566, 01568–71, 01585–86, 01588, 01590, 01607, 01611, 01747, 01756–57

* * *

THIRD DISTRICT

JAMES P. McGOVERN, Democrat, of Worcester, MA; born in Worcester, November 20, 1959; education: B.A., M.P.A., American University; legislative director and senior aide to Congressman Joe Moakley (D–South Boston); led the 1989 investigation into the murders of six Jesuit priests and two lay women in El Salvador; managed George McGovern's (D–SD) 1984 presidential campaign in Massachusetts and delivered his nomination speech at the Democratic National Convention; board of directors, Jesuit International Volunteers; former volunteer, Mt. Carmel House, an emergency shelter for battered and abused women; married: Lisa Murray McGovern; committees: Budget; Rules; elected to the 105th Congress; reelected to each succeeding Congress.

Office Listings

http://www.house.gov/mcgovern

438 Cannon House Office Building, Washington, DC 20515 .... (202) 225–6101
Chief of Staff.—Christopher Philbin. FAX: 225–5759
Legislative Director.—Cindy Buhl.
Press Secretary.—Michael Mershon.
34 Mechanic Street, Worcester, MA 01608 .... (508) 831–7356
District Director.—Joe O'Brien.
8 North Main Street, Room 200, Attleboro, MA 02703 .... (508) 431–8025
District Representative.—Lisa Nelson.
218 South Main Street, Room 204, Fall River, MA 02721 .... (508) 677–0140
District Representative.—Patrick Norton.
255 Main Street, Room 104, Marlborough, MA 01752 .... (508) 460–9292
District Representative.—Mary Pat Gibbons.

Counties: BRISTOL (part), MIDDLESEX (part), NORFOLK (part), WORCESTER (part). CITIES AND TOWNSHIPS: Ashland, Attleborough, Auburn, Boylston, Clinton, Fall River, Franklin, Holden, Holliston, Hopkinton, Marlborough, Medway, North Attleborough, Northborough, Paxton, Plainville, Princeton, Rehoboth, Rutland, Seekonk, Shrewsbury, Somerset, Southborough, Swansea, West Boylston, Westborough, Worcester, and Wrentham. Population (2000), 634,585.

ZIP Codes: 01501, 01505, 01510, 01517, 01520, 01522, 01527, 01532, 01541, 01543, 01545–46, 01580–83, 01601–15, 01653–55, 01721, 01745–46, 01748–49, 01752, 01772, 01784, 02038, 02053, 02070, 02093, 02703, 02720–21, 02723–26, 02760–63, 02769, 02771, 02777

* * *

FOURTH DISTRICT

BARNEY FRANK, Democrat, of Newton, MA; born in Bayonne, NJ, March 31, 1940; education: graduated, Bayonne High School, 1957; B.A., Harvard College, 1962; graduate student in political science, Harvard University, 1962–67; teaching fellow in government, Harvard College, 1963–66; J.D., Harvard University, 1977; admitted to the Massachusetts bar, 1979; executive assistant to Mayor Kevin White of Boston, 1968–71; administrative assistant to U.S. Congressman Michael F. Harrington, 1971–72; member, Massachusetts Legislature, 1973–80; Senior Whip; co-chair, Democratic Parliamentary Group; committees: chair, Financial Services; elected to the 97th Congress, November 4, 1980; reelected to each succeeding Congress.

Office Listings

http://www.house.gov/frank

2252 Rayburn House Office Building, Washington, DC 20515 .... (202) 225–5931
Chief of Staff.—Peter Kovar. FAX: 225–0182
Deputy Chief of Staff / Scheduler.—Maria Giesta.
Assistant to the Chief of Staff.—Marisa Greenwald.
29 Crafts Street, Suite 375, Newton, MA 02458 .... (617) 332–3920
District Director.—Dorothy Reichard.
558 Pleasant Street, Room 309, New Bedford, MA 02740 .... (508) 999–6462
Office Manager.—Lisa Lowney.
The Jones Building, Suite 310, 29 Broadway, Taunton, MA 02780 .... (508) 822–4796
Office Manager.—Garth Patterson.

Counties: BRISTOL (part), MIDDLESEX (part), NORFOLK (part), PLYMOUTH (part). CITIES AND TOWNSHIPS: Acushnet, Berkley, Brookline, Dartmouth, Dighton, Dover, Fairhaven, Fall River, Foxboro, Freetown, Halifax, Lakeville, Mansfield, Marion, Mattapoisett, Middleborough, Millis, New Bedford, Newton, Norfolk, Norton, Raynham, Rochester, Sharon, Sherborn, Taunton, Wareham, Wellesley, and Westport. Population (2000), 634,624.

ZIP Codes: 02021, 02030, 02032, 02035, 02048, 02053–54, 02056, 02067, 02130, 02135, 02215, 02330, 02333, 02338, 02344, 02346–47, 02349, 02360, 02367, 02445–47, 02456–62, 02464–68, 02472, 02476, 02481–82, 02492–93, 02495, 02532, 02538, 02558, 02571, 02576, 02702, 02712, 02714–15, 02717–23, 02738–48, 02764, 02766–70, 02779–80, 02783, 02790–91

* * *

FIFTH DISTRICT

NIKI TSONGAS, Democrat, of Lowell, MA; born in Chico, CA, April 26, 1946; graduated from Narimasu American High School, Japan, 1964; B.A., Smith College, Northampton, MA,

1968; J.D., Boston University, Boston, MA, 1988; professional: social worker; lawyer, Middlesex Community College's dean of external affairs; widowed: Paul Tsongas; children: Ashley Tsongas, Katina Tsongas, and Molly Tsongas; committees: Armed Services; Budget; Natural Resources; elected to 110th Congress, by special election, to fill the vacancy caused by the resignation of Representative Martin Meehan; reelected to the 111th Congress on November 4, 2008.

Office Listings

http://www.tsongas.house.gov

1607 Longworth House Office Building, Washington, DC 20515 .... (202) 225–3411
Chief of Staff.—Katie Elbert. FAX: 226–0771
Legislative Director.—Michael Brownlie.
Scheduler.—Jen Gannon.
492 Main Street, Acton, MA 01720 .... (978) 263–1951
District Director.—Jane Adams.
305 Essex Street, 4th Floor, Lawrence, MA 01840 .... (978) 681–6200
District Director.—June Black.
11 Kearney Square, 3rd Floor, Lowell, MA 01852 .... (978) 459–0101
District Director.—Brian Martin.

Counties: ESSEX COUNTY, MIDDLESEX COUNTY, WORCESTER COUNTY. Population (2000), 635,326.

ZIP Codes: 01432, 01450–51, 01460, 01464, 01503, 01523, 01718–20, 01740–42, 01749, 01754, 01775–76, 01778, 01810, 01821, 01824, 01826–27, 01830, 01840–44, 01850–54, 01862–63, 01876, 01879, 01886

* * *

SIXTH DISTRICT

JOHN F. TIERNEY, Democrat, of Salem, MA; born in Salem, September 18, 1951; education: graduated, Salem High School; B.A., political science, Salem State College, 1973; J.D., Suffolk University, 1976; professional: attorney, admitted to the Massachusetts bar in 1976; sole practitioner, 1976–80; partner, Tierney, Kalis and Lucas, 1981–96; member: Salem Chamber of Commerce, 1976–96 (president, 1995); trustee, Salem State College, 1992–97; married: Patrice M., 1997; committees: Education and Labor; Oversight and Government Reform; Permanent Select Committee on Intelligence; elected to the 105th Congress; reelected to each succeeding Congress.

Office Listings

http://www.house.gov/tierney

2238 Rayburn House Office Building, Washington, DC 20515 .... (202) 225–8020
Chief of Staff.—Betsy Arnold. FAX: 225–5915
Legislative Director.—Kevin McDermott.
Executive Assistant.—Katrina Economou.
17 Peabody Square, Peabody, MA 01960 .... (978) 531–1669
District Director.—Gary Barrett.
Room 105, Lynn City Hall, Lynn, MA 01902 .... (781) 595–7375

Counties: ESSEX, MIDDLESEX. CITIES AND TOWNSHIPS: Amesbury, Bedford, Beverly, Boxford, Burlington, Danvers, Essex, Georgetown, Gloucester, Groveland, Hamilton, Ipswich, Lynn, Lynnfield, Manchester by the Sea, Marblehead, Merrimac, Middletown, Nahant, Newbury, Newburyport, North Andover, North Reading, Peabody, Reading, Rockport, Rowley, Salem, Salisbury, Saugus, Swampscott, Topsfield, Wenham, West Newbury, Wakefield, and Wilmington. Population (2000), 636,554.

ZIP Codes: 01730–31, 01801, 01803, 01805, 01810, 01821, 01833–34, 01845, 01860, 01864, 01867, 01880, 01885, 01887, 01889, 01901–08, 01910, 01913, 01915, 01921–23, 01929–31, 01936–38, 01940, 01944–45, 01949–52, 01960–61, 01965–66, 01969–71, 01982–85

* * *

SEVENTH DISTRICT

EDWARD J. MARKEY, Democrat, of Malden, MA; born in Malden, July 11, 1946; graduated from Malden Catholic High School, Malden, MA, 1964; B.A., Boston College, Chestnut Hill, MA, 1968; J.D., Boston College Law School, Chestnut Hill, MA, 1972; professional: lawyer, private practice; member, Massachusetts State House of Representatives, 1973–76; military: United States Army Reserve, 1968–73; Commission on Security and Cooperation in

Europe; married: Dr. Susan Blumenthal; committees: chair, Select Committee on Energy Independence and Global Warming; Energy and Commerce; Natural Resources; elected to the 94th Congress, November 2, 1976, to fill the vacancy caused by the death of Representative Torbert H. Macdonald; at the same time elected to the 95th Congress; reelected to each succeeding Congress.

Office Listings

http://www.house.gov/markey

2108 Rayburn House Office Building, Washington, DC 20515 .... (202) 225–2836
Chief of Staff.—Jeff Duncan. FAX: 226–0092
Scheduler.—Nancy Morrissey.
5 High Street, Suite 101, Medford, MA 02155 .... (781) 396–2900
188 Concord Street, Suite 102, Framingham, MA 01701 .... (508) 875–2900

Counties: MIDDLESEX (part), SUFFOLK (part). CITIES AND TOWNSHIPS: Arlington, Belmont, Everett, Framingham, Lexington, Lincoln, Malden, Medford, Melrose, Natick, Revere, Stoneham, Waltham, Watertown, Wayland, Weston, Winchester, Winthrop, and Woburn. Population (2000), 634,287.

ZIP Codes: 01701–02, 01760, 01773, 01778, 01801, 01890, 02148–49, 02151–52, 02155, 02176, 02180, 02420–21, 02451–54, 02472, 02474–76, 02478, 02493

* * *

EIGHTH DISTRICT

MICHAEL E. CAPUANO, Democrat, of Somerville, MA; born in Somerville, January 9, 1952; education: graduated, Somerville High School, 1969; B.A., Dartmouth College, 1973; J.D., Boston College Law School, 1977; professional: admitted to the Massachusetts Bar, 1977; Alderman in Somerville, MA, 1977–79; Alderman-at-Large, 1985–89; elected Mayor for five terms, 1990 to January, 1999, when he resigned to be sworn in as a U.S. Representative; Democratic Regional Whip; chair, Organizational, Study, and Review Committee, Democratic Caucus; married: Barbara Teebagy of Somerville, MA, in 1974; children: Michael and Joseph; committees: Financial Services; House Administration; Transportation and Infrastructure; Joint Committee on Printing; elected to the 106th Congress; reelected to each succeeding Congress.

Office Listings

http://www.house.gov/capuano

1414 Longworth House Office Building, Washington, DC 20515 .... (202) 225–5111
Chief of Staff.—Robert Primus. FAX: 225–9322
Office Manager / Scheduler.—Mary Doherty.
Senior Legislative Assistant.—Noelle Melton.
110 First Street, Cambridge, MA 02141 .... (617) 621–6208
District Director.—Jon Lenicheck.

Counties: MIDDLESEX (part), SUFFOLK (part). CITIES AND TOWNSHIPS: Boston, Cambridge, Chelsea, and Somerville. Population (2000), 634,835.

ZIP Codes: 02108–11, 02113–22, 02124–26, 02128–31, 02133–36, 02138–45, 02150–51, 02155, 02163, 02199, 02215–17, 02228, 02238–39, 02295, 02297, 02446, 02458, 02467, 02472, 02478

* * *

NINTH DISTRICT

STEPHEN F. LYNCH, Democrat, of South Boston, MA; born in South Boston, March 31, 1955; education: South Boston High School, 1973; B.S., Wentworth Institute of Technology; J.D., Boston College Law School; Master in Public Administration, JFK School of Government, Harvard University; professional: attorney; former President of Ironworkers Local #7; organizations: South Boston Boys and Girls Club; Boston Children's Museum; Colonel Daniel Marr Boys and Girls Club; Chinatown Trust Fund; South Boston Harbor Academy Charter School; Friends for Children; public service: elected to the Massachusetts House of Representatives in 1994, and the State Senate in 1996; family: married to Margaret; two children: Victoria and Crystal; committees: Financial Services; Oversight and Government Reform; elected to the 107th Congress, by special election, on October 16, 2001; reelected to each succeeding Congress.

Office Listings

http://www.house.gov/lynch

221 Cannon House Office Building, Washington, DC 20515 .... (202) 225–8273
Chief of Staff.—Kevin Ryan. FAX: 225–3984
Legislative Director.—Caroline Powers.
Executive Assistant.—Greta Hebert.
88 Black Falcon Avenue, Suite 340, Boston, MA 02210 .... (617) 428–2000
166 Main Street, Brockton, MA 02401 .... (508) 586–5555

Counties: BRISTOL (part), NORFOLK (part), PLYMOUTH (part), SUFFOLK (part). Population (2000), 634,062.

ZIP Codes: 02021, 02026–27, 02032, 02052, 02062, 02071–72, 02081, 02090, 02101–10, 02112, 02114, 02116, 02122, 02124–27, 02130–32, 02136–37, 02151, 02169–71, 02184–87, 02196, 02201–12, 02222, 02241, 02266, 02283–84, 02293, 02297, 02301–05, 02322, 02324–25, 02333–34, 02337, 02341, 02343, 02350, 02356–57, 02368, 02375, 02379, 02382, 02467, 02481, 02492, 02494

* * *

TENTH DISTRICT

BILL DELAHUNT, Democrat, of Quincy, MA; born in Boston, MA, July 18, 1941; education: B.A., political science, Middlebury College, VT; M.A., J.D., Boston College Law School, 1967; U.S. Coast Guard Reserves, 1963–71; professional: admitted to the Massachusetts Bar in 1967 and began practice in Boston; assistant majority leader, Massachusetts House of Representatives, 1973–75; Norfolk County District Attorney, 1975–96; president, Massachusetts District Attorneys Association, 1985; member, Council of Young American Political Leaders fact-finding mission to Poland, 1979; named citizen of the Year by South Shore Coalition for Human Rights, 1983; delegate, Human Rights Project fact-finding mission to Cuba, 1988; member, Anti-Defamation League of B'nai B'rith fact-finding mission to Israel, 1990; chairman, Development Committee, South Shore Association for Retarded Citizens; Democratic State Committeeman, Norfolk District; advisory board member, Jane Doe Safety Fund; honoree of the Boston Area Rape Crisis Center for contribution to preventing sexual assault, 1993; New England Region honoree, Anti-Defamation League, 1994; Massachusetts Bar Association Public Service Award, 1994; member, Board of Directors, RYKA Rose Foundation; co-chair, Coast Guard Caucus; Older Americans Caucus; Democratic Task Force on Crime; Law Enforcement Caucus; Congressional Human Rights Caucus; Democratic Steering Committee; two daughters: Kirsten and Kara; committees: Foreign Affairs; Judiciary; elected to the 105th Congress; reelected to each succeeding Congress.

Office Listings

http://www.house.gov/delahunt

2454 Rayburn House Office Building, Washington, DC 20515 .... (202) 225–3111
Chief of Staff.—Mark Forrest. FAX: 225–5658
146 Main Street, Hyannis, MA 02601 .... (508) 771–0666
District Scheduler.—Laune Burnett.
1250 Hancock Street, Suite 802N, Quincy, MA 02169 .... (617) 770–3700
Regional Representative.—Kim Arouca.

Counties: BARNSTABLE, DUKES, NANTUCKET, NORFOLK (part), PLYMOUTH (part). Population (2000), 635,901.

ZIP Codes: 02018, 02020, 02025, 02035, 02040–41, 02043–45, 02047, 02050–51, 02055, 02059–61, 02065–66, 02169–71, 02184, 02186, 02188–91, 02269, 02327, 02330–32, 02339–41, 02345, 02351, 02355, 02358–62, 02364, 02366–67, 02370, 02381, 02532, 02534–37, 02539–43, 02552–54, 02556–57, 02559, 02561–65, 02568, 02573–75, 02584, 02601, 02630–35, 02637–39, 02641–53, 02655, 02657, 02659–64, 02666–73, 02675, 02713

MICHIGAN

(Population 2000, 9,938,444)

SENATORS

CARL LEVIN, Democrat, of Detroit, MI; born in Detroit, June 28, 1934; education: graduated, Central High School, Detroit, 1952; Swarthmore College, Swarthmore, PA, 1956; Harvard Law School, Boston, MA, 1959; admitted to the Michigan bar in 1959; professional: lawyer; Grossman, Hyman and Grossman, Detroit, 1959–64; assistant attorney general and general counsel for Michigan Civil Rights Commission, 1964–67; chief appellate defender for city of Detroit, 1968–69; counsel, Schlussel, Lifton, Simon, Rands and Kaufman, 1971–73; counsel, Jaffe, Snider, Raitt, Garratt and Heuer, 1978–79; member, City Council of Detroit, 1969–77 (president, 1974–77); member: Congregation T'Chiyah; American, Michigan and Detroit bar associations; former instructor at Wayne State University and the University of Detroit; married: the former Barbara Halpern, 1961; children: Kate, Laura, and Erica; committees: chair, Armed Services; Homeland Security and Governmental Affairs; Small Business and Entrepreneurship; Select Committee on Intelligence; elected to the U.S. Senate on November 7, 1978; reelected to each succeeding Senate term.

Office Listings

http://levin.senate.gov

269 Russell Senate Office Building, Washington, DC 20510 .... (202) 224–6221
Chief of Staff.—David Lyles. FAX: 224–1388
Legislative Director.—Jack Danielson.
Scheduler.—Alison Warner.
Press Secretary.—Tara Andringa.
477 Michigan Avenue, McNamara Building, Room 1860, Detroit, MI 48226 .... (313) 226–6020
Federal Building, Room 720, 110 Michigan Street, NW, Grand Rapids, MI 49503.. (616) 456–2531
1810 Michigan National Tower, 124 West Allegan Street, Suite 1810, Lansing, MI 48933 .... (517) 377–1508
524 Ludington Street, Suite LL103, Escanaba, MI 49829 .... (906) 789–0052
515 North Washington, Suite 402, Saginaw, MI 48607 .... (989) 754–2494
30500 VanDyke, Suite 206, Warren, MI 48093 .... (586) 573–9145
107 Cass Street, Suite E, Traverse City, MI 49684 .... (616) 947–9569

* * *

DEBBIE STABENOW, Democrat, of Lansing, MI; born in Gladwin, MI, April 29, 1950; education: Clare High School; B.A., Michigan State University, 1972; M.S.W., Michigan State University, 1975; public service: Ingham County, MI, Commissioner, 1975–78, chairperson for two years; Michigan State House of Representatives, 1979–90; Michigan State Senate, 1991–94; religion: Methodist; married to Thomas Athans; children: Todd and Michelle; committees: Agriculture, Nutrition, and Forestry; Budget; Finance; Energy and Natural Resources; elected to the U.S. House of Representatives in 1996 and 1998; elected to the U.S. Senate on November 7, 2000; reelected to each succeeding Senate term.

Office Listings

http://stabenow.senate.gov

133 Hart Senate Office Building, Washington, DC 20510 .... (202) 224–4822
Chief of Staff.—Amanda Renteria. FAX: 228–0325
Legislative Director.—Tim Love.
Deputy Chief of Staff.—Brent Colburn.
Scheduler.—Anne Stanski.
221 West Lake Lansing Road, Suite 100, East Lansing, MI 48823 .... (517) 203–1760
Marquette Building, 243 West Congress, Suite 550, Detroit, MI 48226 .... (313) 961–4330
432 North Saginaw, Suite 301, Flint, MI 48502 .... (810) 720–4172
3335 South Airport Road West, Suite 6B, Traverse City, MI 49684 .... (231) 929–1031
3280 Beltline Court, Suite 400, Grand Rapids, MI 49525 .... (616) 975–0052
1901 West Ridge, Suite 7, Marquette, MI 49855 .... (906) 228–8756

REPRESENTATIVES

FIRST DISTRICT

BART STUPAK, Democrat, of Menominee, MI; born in Milwaukee, WI, February 29, 1952; education: graduated, Gladstone High School, Gladstone, MI, 1970; B.S., Saginaw Valley State

College, 1977; J.D., Thomas Cooley Law School, 1981; professional: attorney; admitted to the Michigan bar, 1981; Michigan State House of Representatives, 1989–90; member: Elks Club; State Employees Retirement Association; Sons of the American Legion; Wildlife Unlimited; National Rifle Association; Knights of Columbus; national committeeman, Boy Scouts of America; co-chairman, Law Enforcement Caucus; co-chairman, Northern Border Caucus; married: the former Laurie Ann Olsen; children: Ken and Bart, Jr. (deceased); committees: Energy and Commerce; elected on November 3, 1992, to the 103rd Congress; reelected to each succeeding Congress.

Office Listings

http://www.house.gov/stupak

2268 Rayburn House Office Building, Washington, DC 20515 .... (202) 225–4735
Chief of Staff.—Scott Schloegel. FAX: 225–4744
Press Secretary.—Michelle Begnoche.
Legislative Director.—Nick Choate.
Scheduler / Executive Assistant.—Rachel Stevenson.
District Director.—Tom Baldini.
575 Court Street, West Branch, MI 48661 .... (989) 345–2258
902 Ludington Street, Escanaba, MI 49829 .... (906) 786–4504
1229 West Washington, Marquette, MI 49855 .... (906) 228–3700
111 East Chisholm, Alpena, MI 49707 .... (989) 356–0690
2 South 6th Street, Suite 3, Crystal Falls, MI 49920 .... (906) 875–3751
616 Sheldon Avenue, Room 213, Houghton, MI 49931 .... (906) 482–1371
200 Division Street, Petoskey, MI 49770 .... (231) 348–0657

Counties: ALCONA, ALGER, ALPENA, ANTRIM, ARENAC, BARAGA, BAY (part), CHARLEVOIX, CHEBOYGAN, CHIPPEWA, CRAWFORD, DELTA, DICKINSON, EMMET, GLADWIN, GOGEBIC, HOUGHTON, IOSEO, IRON, KEWEENAW, LUCE, MACKINAC, MARQUETTE, MENOMINEE, MONTMORENCY, OGEMAW, ONTONAGON, OSCODA, OTSEGO, PRESQUE ISLE, SCHOOLCRAFT. Population (2000), 662,563.

ZIP Codes: 48610–13, 48618–19, 48621, 48623–24, 48628, 48631, 48634–36, 48642, 48647, 48650, 48652–54, 48658–59, 48661, 48703, 48705–06, 48721, 48728, 48730, 48737–40, 48742–43, 48745, 48748–50, 48756, 48761–66, 48770, 49611–12, 49615, 49622, 49627, 49629, 49648, 49659, 49676, 49701, 49705–07, 49709–13, 49715–30, 49733–40, 49743–49, 49751–53, 49755–57, 49759–62, 49764–66, 49768–70, 49774–77, 49779–85, 49788, 49790–93, 49795–97, 49799, 49801–02, 49805–08, 49812, 49814–22, 49825–27, 49829, 49831, 49833–41, 49845, 49847–49, 49852–55, 49858, 49861–64, 49866, 49868, 49870–74, 49876–81, 49883–87, 49891–96, 49901–03, 49905, 49908, 49910–13, 49915–22, 49925, 49927, 49929–31, 49934–35, 49938, 49945–48, 49950, 49952–53, 49955, 49958–65, 49967–71

* * *

SECOND DISTRICT

PETER HOEKSTRA, Republican, of Holland, MI; born in Groningen, the Netherlands, October 30, 1953; education: graduated, Holland Christian High School; B.A., Hope College, Holland, 1975; M.B.A., University of Michigan, 1977; professional: vice president for product management, Herman Miller, Inc.; married: the former Diane Johnson; children: Erin, Allison, and Bryan; committees: Education and Labor; Permanent Select Committee on Intelligence; elected on November 3, 1992, to the 103rd Congress; reelected to each succeeding Congress.

Office Listings

http://hoekstra.house.gov

2234 Rayburn House Office Building, Washington, DC 20515 .... (202) 225–4401
Chief of Staff / Legislative Director.—Justin Wormmeester. FAX: 226–0779
Scheduler / Executive Assistant.—Leah Scott.
District Director of Policy.—Jon DeWitte.
184 South River, Holland, MI 49423 .... (616) 395–0030
900 Third Street, Suite 203, Muskegon, MI 49440 .... (231) 722–8386
210½ North Mitchell Street, Cadillac, MI 49601 .... (231) 775–0050

Counties: ALLEGAN (part), BENZIE, KENT (part), LAKE, MANISTEE, MASON, MUSKEGON, NEWAYGO, OCEANA, OTTAWA, WEXFORD. Population (2000), 662,563.

ZIP Codes: 49010, 49078, 49080, 49303–04, 49307, 49309, 49312, 49314–15, 49318–19, 49321, 49323, 49327–30, 49333, 49336–38, 49343, 49345–46, 49348–49, 49401–06, 49408–13, 49415, 49417–31, 49434–37, 49440–46, 49448–49, 49451–61, 49463–64, 49544, 49601, 49613–14, 49616–20, 49623, 49625–26, 49628, 49630, 49633–35, 49638, 49640, 49642–45, 49649–50, 49655–56, 49660, 49663, 49668, 49675, 49677, 49683, 49688–89

* * *

THIRD DISTRICT

VERNON J. EHLERS, Republican, of Grand Rapids, MI; born in Pipestone, MN, February 6, 1934; educated at home by his parents; attended Calvin College; undergraduate degree in physics and Ph.D. in nuclear physics, University of California at Berkeley; taught and did research at Berkeley for 6 years; returned to Calvin College; taught physics and became chairman, Physics Department; served on various boards and commissions; member, Michigan House and Senate; first research physicist in Congress; while on Science Committee in 1997–98, was selected to rewrite the Nation's science policy; introduced National Science Education Acts aimed at reforming K–12 science, mathematics, engineering, and technology education; as a member of the House Administration Committee, guided the program to revamp the House computer system, connect it to the Internet, and allow all citizens to access House documents; member and former elder, Eastern Avenue Christian Reformed Church, Grand Rapids, MI; married: the former Johanna Meulink; four adult children: Heidi, Brian, Marla, and Todd; three grandchildren; one great-grandchild; committees: Education and Labor; Science and Technology; Transportation and Infrastructure; elected to the 103rd Congress by special election, on December 7, 1993; reelected to each succeeding Congress.

Office Listings

http://www.house.gov/ehlers

2182 Rayburn House Office Building, Washington, DC 20515 .... (202) 225–3831
Chief of Staff.—Bill McBride. FAX: 225–5144
Legislative Director.—Rachel Fenton.
Executive Assistant / Scheduler.—Alysha Chadderdon.
Press Secretary.—Kevan Chapman.
110 Michigan Street, NW., Suite 166, Grand Rapids, MI 49503 .... (616) 451–8383
Community Services Director.—Rick Treur.

Counties: BARRY, IONIA, KENT (part). CITIES: Belding, Cedar Springs, East Grand Rapids, Grand Rapids, Grandville, Hastings, Ionia, Kentwood, Lowell, Portland, Rockford, Walker, and Wyoming. Population (2000), 662,563.

ZIP Codes: 48809, 48815, 48834, 48837–38, 48845–46, 48849, 48851, 48860–61, 48865, 48870–71, 48873, 48875, 48881, 48887, 48890, 48897, 49017, 49021, 49035, 49046, 49050, 49058, 49060, 49073, 49080, 49083, 49301–02, 49306, 49315–17, 49319, 49321, 49325–26, 49331, 49333, 49341, 49343–45, 49347–48, 49351, 49355–57, 49418, 49468, 49501–10, 49512, 49514–16, 49518, 49523, 49525, 49530, 49544, 49546, 49548, 49550, 49555, 49560, 49588, 49599

* * *

FOURTH DISTRICT

DAVE CAMP, Republican, of Midland, MI; born in Midland, July 9, 1953; education: graduated, H.H. Dow High School, Midland, 1971; B.A., *magna cum laude*, Albion College, Albion, MI, 1975; J.D., University of San Diego, 1978; attorney; member: State Bar of Michigan; State Bar of California; District of Columbia bar, U.S. Supreme Court; U.S. District Court, Eastern District of Michigan and Southern District of California; Midland County Bar Association; law practice, Midland, 1979–91; Special Assistant Attorney General, 1980–84; administrative assistant to Congressman Bill Schuette, Michigan's 10th Congressional District, 1985–87; State Representative, Michigan's 102nd district, 1989–91; chairman, Corrections Day Advisory Group; Deputy Minority Whip; Executive Committee, National Republican Congressional Committee; Rural Health Care Coalition; 1998 Adoption Hall of Fame Inductee; American Farm Bureau Federation 1998 Golden Plow award recipient; married: attorney Nancy Keil of Midland, 1994; three children; committees: ranking member, Ways and Means; Joint Committee on Taxation; elected to Congress on November 6, 1990; reelected to each succeeding Congress.

Office Listings

http://www.house.gov/camp

137 Cannon House Office Building, Washington, DC 20515 .... (202) 225–3561
Chief of Staff.—Jim Brandell. FAX: 225–9679
Communications Director.—Sage Eastman.
Legislative Director.—Brian Sutter.
Scheduler.—Allie Judson.
135 Ashman Street, Midland, MI, 48640 .... (989) 631–2552
121 East Front Street, Suite 202, Traverse City, MI 49684 .... (231) 929–4711

Counties: CLARE COUNTY. CITIES: Clare, Farwell, Harrison, Lake, Lake George. GRAND TRAVERSE COUNTY. CITIES: Acme, Fife Lake, Grawn, Interlochen, Kingsley, Mayfield, Old Mission, Traverse City, Williamsburg. GRATIOT COUNTY. CITIES:

Alma, Ashley, Bannister, Breckenridge, Elm Hall, Elwell, Ithaca, Middleton, North Star, Perrinton, Pompeii, Riverdale, Sumner, St. Louis, Wheeler. ISABELLA COUNTY. CITIES: Blanchard, Millbrook, Mt. Pleasant, Rosebush, Shepherd, Weidman, Winn. KALKASKA COUNTY. CITIES: Kalkaska, Rapid City, South Boardman. LEELANAU COUNTY. CITIES: Cedar, Empire, Glen Arbor, Lake Leelanau, Leland, Maple City, Northport, Omena, Suttons Bay. MECOSTA COUNTY. CITIES: Barryton, Big Rapids, Canadian Lakes, Chippewa Lakes, Mecosta, Morley, Paris, Remus, Stanwood. MIDLAND COUNTY. CITIES: Coleman, Edenville, Hope, Laporte, Midland, North Bradley, Poseyville, Sanford. MISSAUKEE COUNTY. CITIES: Falmouth, Lake City, McBain, Merritt, Moorestown. MONTCALM COUNTY. CITIES: Alger, Butternut, Carson City, Cedar Lake, Coral, Crystal, Edmore, Entrican, Fenwick, Gowen, Greenville, Howard City, Lakeview, Langston, Maple Hill, McBride, Pierson, Sand Lake, Sheridan, Sidney, Six Lakes, Stanton, Trufant, Vestaburg, Vickeryville. OSCEOLA COUNTY. CITIES: Evart, Hersey, LeRoy, Marion, Reed City, Sears, Tustin. ROSCOMMON COUNTY. CITIES: Higgins Lake, Houghton Lake, Houghton Lake Heights, Prudenville, Roscommon, St. Helen. SAGINAW COUNTY (part). CITIES: Birch Run, Brant, Bridgeport, Burt, Carrolton, Chesaning, Fosters, Freeland, Fremont, Hemlock, Merrill, Oakley, Richland, Saginaw, Shields, Spalding, St. Charles, University Center. SHIAWASSEE COUNTY (part). CITIES: Bancroft, Caledonia, Chapin, Corunna, Henderson, Laingsburg, Morrice, New Haven, New Lothrup, Owosso, Perry, Shaftsburg, Venice, and Vernon. Population (2000), 662,563.

ZIP Codes: 48415, 48417, 48429, 48433, 48436, 48449, 48457, 48460, 48476, 48601–04, 48608–09, 48614–18, 48620, 48622–30, 48632–33, 48637, 48640–42, 48649, 48651–53, 48655–57, 48662, 48667, 48670, 48674, 48686, 48706, 48722, 48724, 48801–02, 48804, 48806–07, 48809, 48811–12, 48817–18, 48829–32, 48834, 48837–38, 48841, 48845, 48847, 48850, 48852–53, 48856, 48858–59, 48862, 48866–67, 48874–75, 48877–80, 48883–86, 48888–89, 48891, 48893, 48896, 49305, 49307, 49310, 49320, 49322–23, 49326, 49328–29, 49332, 49336–40, 49342–43, 49346–47, 49601, 49610, 49612, 49620–21, 49630–33, 49636–37, 49639–40, 49643, 49646, 49649, 49651, 49653–55, 49657, 49659, 49663–67, 49670, 49673–74, 49676–77, 49679–80, 49682–86, 49688, 49690, 49696, 49738

* * *

FIFTH DISTRICT

DALE E. KILDEE, Democrat, of Flint, MI; born in Flint, September 16, 1929; education: graduated, St. Mary High School, 1947; B.A., Sacred Heart Seminary, Detroit, 1952; M.A., University of Michigan, Ann Arbor, 1961; graduate studies in history and political science, University of Peshawar, Pakistan, under Rotary Foundation Fellowship; professional: teacher, University of Detroit High School, 1954–56; Flint Central High School, 1956–64; served as State Representative, 1965–74; State Senator, 1975–77; member: Optimists, Urban League, Knights of Columbus, Phi Delta Kappa national honorary fraternity, American Federation of Teachers; life member, National Association for the Advancement of Colored People; married: the former Gayle Heyn, 1965; children: David, Laura, and Paul; six grandchildren; committees: Education and Labor; Natural Resources; elected to the 95th Congress, November 2, 1976; reelected to each succeeding Congress.

Office Listings

2107 Rayburn House Office Building, Washington, DC 20515 .... (202) 225–3611
Chief of Staff.—Callie Coffman. FAX: 225–6393
Legislative Director.—Peter Karafotas.
Executive Assistant.—Evita Mendiola.
432 North Saginaw, Suite 410, Flint, MI 48502 .... (810) 239–1437
District Director, all Districts.—Tiffany Anderson-Flynn. (800) 662–2685
515 North Washington Avenue, Suite 401, Saginaw, MI 48607 .... (989) 755–8904
916 Washington Avenue, Suite 205, Bay City, MI 48708 .... (989) 891–0990

Counties: BAY (part), GENESEE, SAGINAW (part), TUSCOLA. Population (2000), 662,563.

ZIP Codes: 48411, 48415, 48417–18, 48420–21, 48423, 48426, 48429–30, 48433, 48435–39, 48449, 48451, 48453, 48457–58, 48460, 48462–64, 48473, 48501–07, 48509, 48519, 48529, 48531–32, 48550–57, 48601–07, 48623, 48631, 48663, 48701, 48706–08, 48710, 48722–23, 48726–27, 48729, 48732–36, 48741, 48744, 48746–47, 48757–60, 48767–69, 48787

* * *

SIXTH DISTRICT

FRED UPTON, Republican, of St. Joseph, MI; born in St. Joseph, April 23, 1953; education: graduated, Shattuck School, Fairbault, MN, 1971; B.A., journalism, University of Michigan, Ann Arbor, 1975; professional: field manager, Dave Stockman Campaign, 1976; staff member, Congressman Dave Stockman, 1976–80; legislative assistant, Office of Management and Budget, 1981–83; deputy director of Legislative Affairs, 1983–84; director of Legislative Affairs, 1984–85; member: First Congregational Church, Emil Verbin Society; married: the former Amey Rulon-Miller; committees: Energy and Commerce; elected to the 100th Congress on November 4, 1986; reelected to each succeeding Congress.

Office Listings

http://www.tellupton@mail.house.gov

2183 Rayburn House Office Building, Washington, DC 20515 .... (202) 225–3761
Chief of Staff.—Joan Hillebrands. FAX: 225–4986
Executive Assistant.—Bits Thomas.
800 Centre, Suite 106, 800 Ship Street, St. Joseph, MI 49085 .... (269) 982–1986
157 South Kalamazoo Mall, Suite 180, Kalamazoo, MI 49006 .... (269) 385–0039

Counties: ALLEGAN (part), BERRIEN, CALHOUN (part), CASS, KALAMAZOO, ST. JOSEPH, VAN BUREN. CITIES AND TOWNSHIPS: Allegan, Augusta, Bangor, Baroda, Benton Harbor, Berrien Springs, Berrien Center, Bloomingdale, Breedsville, Bridgman, Buchanan, Burr Oak, Cassopolis, Centreville, Climax, Coloma, Colon, Comstock, Constantine, Covert, Decatur, Delton, Dowagiac, Eau Claire, Edwardsburg, Fulton, Galesburg, Galien, Gobles, Grand Junction, Hagar Shores, Harbert, Hartford, Hickory Corners, Jones, Kalamazoo, Kendall, Lacota, Lakeside, Lawrence, Lawton, Leonidas, Marcellus, Mattawan, Mendon, Nazareth, New Troy, New Buffalo, Niles, Nottawa, Oshtemo, Otsego, Paw Paw, Plainwell, Portage, Pullman, Richland, Riverside, Sawyer, Schoolcraft, Scotts, Sodus, South Haven, St. Joseph, Stevensville, Sturgis, Three Oaks, Three Rivers, Union Pier, Union, Vandalia, Vicksburg, Watervliet, and White Pigeon. Population (2000), 662,563.

ZIP Codes: 48867, 49001–15, 49017, 49019, 49022–24, 49026–27, 49030–32, 49034, 49038–43, 49045, 49047–48, 49051–53, 49055–57, 49060–67, 49070–72, 49074–75, 49077–81, 49083–85, 49087–88, 49090–91, 49093, 49095, 49097–99, 49101–04, 49106–07, 49111–13, 49115–17, 49119–21, 49125–30, 49311, 49315–16, 49323, 49328, 49333, 49335, 49344, 49348, 49408, 49416, 49450

* * *

SEVENTH DISTRICT

MARK H. SCHAUER, Democrat, of Battle Creek, MI; born in Howell, MI, October 2, 1961; education: B.S., Albion College, 1984; M.A., Western Michigan University, 1986; M.A., Michigan State University, 1995; professional: Urban Planner, Calhoun County Planning Department; Executive Director, Community Action Agency of South Central Michigan; Coordinator, Calhoun County Human Services Coordinating Council; member, Michigan House of Representatives; Democratic Floor Leader and Democratic Leader, Michigan Senate; religion: Methodist; married: Christine; children: three stepchildren; Battle Creek City Commissioner; New Democrat Coalition Caucus; committees: Agriculture; Transportation and Infrastructure; elected to the 111th Congress on November 4, 2008.

Office Listings

http://www.schauer.house.gov

1408 Longworth House Office Building, Washington, DC 20515 .... (202) 225–6276
Chief of Staff.—Ken Brock. FAX: 225–6281
Washington Director.—B.J. Neidhardt.
Legislative Director.—John Mulcrone.
Press Secretary.—Zack Pohl.
800 West Ganson Avenue, Jackson, MI 49202 .... (517) 780–9075
(877) 737–6407

Counties: BRANCH, CALHOUN (part), EATON, HILLSDALE, JACKSON, LENAWEE, WASHTENAW (part). Population (2000), 662,563.

ZIP Codes: 48103, 48105, 48115, 48118, 48130, 48158, 48160, 48167, 48170, 48175–76, 48178, 48189, 48601, 48813, 48821, 48827, 48837, 48849, 48861, 48876, 48890, 48906, 48908, 48911, 48917, 49011, 49014–18, 49020–21, 49028–30, 49033, 49036, 49040, 49051–52, 49058, 49068–69, 49073, 49076, 49082, 49089, 49092, 49094, 49096, 49201–04, 49220–21, 49224, 49227–30, 49232–42, 49245–59, 49261–69, 49271–72, 49274–77, 49279, 49281–89

* * *

EIGHTH DISTRICT

MIKE ROGERS, Republican, of Brighton, MI; born in Livingston County, MI, June 2, 1963; education: B.S., Adrian College; also attended the University of Michigan as an Army ROTC member; military service: U.S. Army, 1st Lieutenant, served in a rapid deployment unit as a Company Commander; professional: FBI Special Agent, assigned to public corruption and organized crime units; businessman; co-founder of E.B.I. Builders, Inc.; organizations: American Heart Association; Women's Resource Center; Brighton Rotary Club; Society of Former Special Agents of the FBI; religion: Methodist; married: Diane; children: Erin and Jonathan; committees: Energy and Commerce; Permanent Select Committee on Intelligence; elected to the 107th Congress on November 7, 2000; reelected to each succeeding Congress.

Office Listings

http://www.house.gov/mikerogers

133 Cannon House Office Building, Washington, DC 20515 .... (202) 225–4872
Chief of Staff.—Andy Keiser. FAX: 225–5820
Legislative Director.—Mike Ward.
Scheduler.—Margarita Valdez.
Press Secretary.—Sylvia Warner.
1000 West St. Joseph, Lansing, MI 48915 .... (517) 702–8000

Counties: CLINTON, INGHAM, LIVINGSTON, OAKLAND (part), SHIAWASSE (part). Population (2000), 662,563.

ZIP Codes: 48114, 48116, 48137, 48139, 48143, 48169, 48178, 48189, 48329, 48346–48, 48350, 48353, 48356–57, 48359–62, 48366–67, 48370–71, 48380, 48386, 48414, 48418, 48428–30, 48436, 48438–39, 48442, 48451, 48455, 48462, 48504, 48507, 48805, 48807–08, 48816–17, 48819–27, 48831, 48833, 48835–37, 48840, 48842–45, 48848, 48854–55, 48857, 48863–64, 48866–67, 48872–73, 48875, 48879, 48882, 48892, 48894–95, 48901, 48906, 48909–13, 48915–19, 48921–22, 48924, 48929–30, 48933, 48937, 48950–51, 48956, 48980, 49078, 49080, 49251, 49264, 49285

* * *

NINTH DISTRICT

GARY C. PETERS, Democrat, of Bloomfield Township, MI; born in Pontiac, MI, December 1, 1958; education: B.A., Alma College, Alma, MI, 1980; M.B.A., University of Detroit, Detroit, MI, 1984; J.D., Wayne State University, Detroit, MI, 1989; M.A., Michigan State University, East Lansing, MI, 2007; professional: Assistant Vice President, Merrill Lynch, 1980–89; Vice President, UBS / Paine Webber, 1989–2003; City Council, Rochester Hills, MI, 1991–93; Lt. Commander, Navy Reserve, 1993–2005; Michigan Senate, 1995–2002; Chief Administrative Officer for the Bureau of Investments, State of Michigan, 2003; Lottery Commissioner, State of Michigan, 2003–07; Griffin Endowed Chair in American Government, Central Michigan University, 2007–08; religion: Episcopalian; married: Colleen Ochoa Peters; three children: Gary Jr., Madeline, and Alana; Armenian Caucus; Congressional Automotive Caucus; Congressional Caucus on India and Indian Americans; Congressional Fire Services Caucus; Congressional Pakistan Caucus; House Bangladesh Caucus; House Manufacturing Caucus; Law Enforcement Caucus; LGBT Equality Caucus; National Guard & Reserve Component Caucus; New Democrat Coalition; Pro-Choice Caucus; committees: Financial Services; Science and Technology; elected to the 111th Congress on November 4, 2008.

Office Listings

http://www.peters.house.gov

1130 Longworth House Office Building, Washington, DC 20515 .... (202) 225–5802
Chief of Staff.—Eric Feldman. FAX: 226–2356
Legislative Director.—Jonathan Smith.
Press Secretary.—Cullen Schwarz.
560 Kirts Boulevard, #105, Troy, MI 48084 .... (248) 273–4227
District Office Director.—Dianna McBroom.

Counties: OAKLAND (part). CITIES AND TOWNSHIPS: Auburn Hills, Berkley, Beverly Hills, Bingham Farms, Birmingham, Bloomfield Hills, Bloomfield, Clawson, Farmington, Farmington Hills, Franklin, Keego Harbor, Lake Angelus, Oakland, Orchard Lake, Orion, Pontiac, Rochester, Rochester Hills, Royal Oak, Southfield, Sylvan Lake, Troy, Waterford, and West Bloomfield. Population (2000), 662,563.

ZIP Codes: 48007, 48009, 48012, 48017, 48025, 48067–68, 48072–73, 48083–85, 48098–99, 48167, 48301–04, 48306–09, 48320–36, 48340–43, 48346, 48359–60, 48362–63, 48367, 48370, 48382, 48387, 48390, 48398

* * *

TENTH DISTRICT

CANDICE S. MILLER, Republican, of Harrison Township, MI; born in St. Clair Shores, MI, May 7, 1954; education: attended Macomb Community College and Northwood University; public service: Harrison Township Board of Trustees, 1979; Harrison Township Supervisor, 1980–92; Macomb County Treasurer, 1992–94; Michigan Secretary of State, 1994–2002; professional: worked in a family-owned marina business before she became involved in public service; religion: Presbyterian; married: Macomb County Circuit Court Judge Donald Miller; children: Wendy; committees: Homeland Security; Transportation and Infrastructure; Select Committee on Energy Independence and Global Warming; elected to the 108th Congress on November 5, 2002; reelected to each succeeding Congress.

Office Listings

http://candicemiller.house.gov

228 Cannon House Office Building, Washington, DC 20515 .... (202) 225–2106
Chief of Staff.—Jamie Roe. FAX: 226–1169
Deputy Chief of Staff.—Sean Moran.
Legislative Director.—Caleb Overdorff.
Scheduler.—Paul Anstine.
Press Secretary.—Phaedra Dugan.
48653 Van Dyke Avenue, Shelby Township, MI 48317 .... (586) 997–5010

Counties: HURON, LAPEER, MACOMB (part), SAINT CLAIR, SANILAC. Population (2000), 662,562.

ZIP Codes: 48001–06, 48014, 48022–23, 48027–28, 48032, 48039–42, 48044–45, 48047–51, 48054, 48059–65, 48074, 48079, 48094–97, 48306, 48310–18, 48371, 48401, 48410, 48412–13, 48416, 48419, 48421–23, 48426–28, 48432, 48434–35, 48438, 48440–41, 48444–46, 48450, 48453–56, 48461–72, 48475, 48720, 48725–27, 48729, 48731, 48735, 48741, 48744, 48754–55, 48759–60, 48767

* * *

ELEVENTH DISTRICT

THADDEUS G. MCCOTTER, Republican, of Livonia, MI; born in Detroit, MI, August 22, 1965; education: B.A., University of Detroit, 1987; J.D., University of Detroit Law School, 1990; professional: attorney; public service: elected to the Schoolcraft Community College Trustees, 1989; elected to the Wayne County Commission, 1992; elected to the Michigan State Senate, 1998; awards: Michigan Jaycees Outstanding Michigander, 2001; Police Officers Association of Michigan Legislator of the Year, 2002; chair, Republican House Policy Committee; religion: Catholic; married: Rita; children: George, Timothy, and Emilia; committees: Financial Services; elected to the 108th Congress on November 5, 2002; reelected to each succeeding Congress.

Office Listings

http://www.house.gov/mccotter

1632 Longworth House Office Building, Washington, DC 20515 .... (202) 225–8171
Chief of Staff.—Andrew Anuzis. FAX: 225–2667
Scheduler.—Natalie Rose.
Legislative Director.—Paul Blocher.
Press Secretary.—Jameson Cunningham.
17197 North Laurel Park Drive, Suite 216, Livonia, MI 48152 .... (734) 632–0314
213 West Huron, Milford, MI 48381 .... (248) 685–9495

Counties: WAYNE COUNTY. CITIES: Livonia, Canton Township, Plymouth City, Plymouth Township, Northville City, Northville Township, Belleville, Van Buren Township, Wayne, Westland, Garden City, Redford Township, Dearborn Heights. OAKLAND COUNTY. CITIES: Novi, South Lyon, Lyon Township, Milford, Wixom, Walled Lake, Commerce Township, White Lake, Highland, and Waterford. Population (2000), 662,563.

ZIP Codes: 48111–12, 48127, 48135–36, 48141, 48150–54, 48165, 48167, 48170, 48174, 48178, 48184–88, 48239–40, 48327, 48329, 48346, 48356–57, 48374–77, 48380–83, 48386–87, 48390–91, 48393

* * *

TWELFTH DISTRICT

SANDER M. LEVIN, Democrat, of Royal Oak, MI; born in Detroit, MI, September 6, 1931; education: graduated, Central High School, Detroit, 1949; B.A., University of Chicago, 1952; M.A., Columbia University, New York, NY, 1954; LL.B., Harvard University, Cambridge, MA, 1957; professional: attorney, admitted to the Michigan bar in 1958 and commenced practice in Detroit, MI; member: Oakland Board of Supervisors, 1961–64; Michigan Senate, 1965–70; Democratic floor leader in State Senate; served on the Advisory Committee on the Education of Handicapped Children in the Department of Health, Education, and Welfare, 1965–68; chairman, Michigan Democratic Party, 1968–69; Democratic candidate for governor, 1970 and 1974; fellow, Kennedy School of Government, Institute of Politics, Harvard University, 1975; assistant administrator, Agency for International Development, 1977–81; married: the former Victoria Schlafer (deceased); children: Jennifer, Andrew, Madeleine, and Matthew; committees: Ways and Means; Joint Committee on Taxation; elected on November 2, 1982, to the 98th Congress; reelected to each succeeding Congress.

Office Listings

http://www.house.gov/levin

1236 Longworth Office House Building, Washington, DC 20515 .... (202) 225–4961
Chief of Staff.—Hilarie Chambers. FAX: 226–1033
Scheduler.—Monica Chrzaszcz.
27085 Gratiot Avenue, Roseville, MI 48066 .... (586) 498–7122
District Administrator.—Rudy Hobbs.

Counties: MACOMB (part), OAKLAND (part). CITIES: Center Line, Clinton Township, Eastpointe, Ferndale, Fraser, Hazel Park, Huntington Woods, Lake Township, Lathrup Village, Madison Heights, Mt. Clemens, Oak Park, Pleasant Ridge, Roseville, Royal Oak, Royal Oak Township, Southfield, St. Clair Shores, Sterling Heights, and Warren. Population (2000), 662,563.

ZIP Codes: 48015, 48021, 48025–26, 48030, 48034–38, 48043, 48046, 48066–67, 48069–71, 48075–76, 48080–82, 48086, 48088–93, 48220, 48236–37, 48310, 48312, 48397

* * *

THIRTEENTH DISTRICT

CAROLYN C. KILPATRICK, Democrat, of Detroit, MI; born in Detroit, June 25, 1945; education: attended Ferris State University, Big Rapids, MI, 1968–70; graduated, B.S. in education, Western Michigan University, Kalamazoo, MI, 1972; M.S., education administration, University of Michigan, Ann Arbor, MI, 1977; Honorary Doctorate of Public Service, Ferris State University, 2008; professional: teacher; served in Michigan House of Representatives, 1979–96; member, Detroit Substance Abuse Advisory Council; participated in first-of-its-kind African Trade Mission; delegate, U.N. International Women's Conference; led Michigan Department of Agriculture delegation to the International Agriculture Show, Nairobi, Kenya; awards: Anthony Wayne Award for Leadership, Wayne State University; Burton-Abercrombie Award, 13th Congressional District; Distinguished Legislator Award, University of Michigan; named Woman of the Year by Gentlemen of Wall Street, Inc.; listed in *Who's Who in Black America, Who's Who in Black Detroit,* and *Who's Who in American Politics*; Women of Achievement and Courage Award; U.S. Air Force Academy Board; Presidential Distinguished Service Award; Gift of Life Legislator of the Year Award; American Society of Transplantation; chair, Congressional Black Caucus, 2007–08; former chair, Michigan Legislative Black Caucus; Canda-United States Inter-Parliamentary Group; two children: Kwame and Ayanna; committees: Appropriations; elected to the 105th Congress; reelected to each succeeding Congress.

Office Listings

http://www.house.gov/kilpatrick

2264 Rayburn House Office Building, Washington, DC 20515 .... (202) 225–2261
Chief of Staff.—Kimberly S. Rudolph. FAX: 225–5730
Executive Assistant.—Roxanne Scott.
Legislative Director.—James M. Williams.
1274 Library Street, Suite 1B, Detroit, MI 48226 .... (313) 965–9004
District Director.—Duron V. Marshall.
Communications Director.—Tracy A. Walker.
10600 West Jefferson, Room 203, River Rouge, MI 48218 .... (313) 297–6951

Counties: WAYNE COUNTY. Population (2000), 628,363.

ZIP Codes: 48146, 48192, 48201–02, 48204–18, 48224–26, 48229–30, 48234, 48236

* * *

FOURTEENTH DISTRICT

JOHN CONYERS, JR., Democrat, of Detroit, MI; born in Detroit, May 16, 1929; son of John and Lucille Conyers; education: B.A., Wayne State University, 1957; LL.B., Wayne State Law School, June 1958; served as officer in the U.S. Army Corps of Engineers, one year in Korea; awarded combat and merit citations; engaged in many civil rights and labor activities; legislative assistant to Congressman John D. Dingell, December 1958 to May 1961; appointed Referee for the Workmen's Compensation Department, State of Michigan, by Governor John B. Swainson in October 1961; former vice chairman of Americans for Democratic Action; vice chairman of the National Advisory Council of the ACLU; member: Kappa Alpha Psi; Wolverine Bar; NAACP; Tuskegee Airmen, Inc.; organizations: Congressional Black Caucus; Progressive Caucus; married: Monica Conyers; children: John III, and Carl; committees: chair, Judiciary; elected to the 89th Congress on November 3, 1964; reelected to each succeeding Congress.

Office Listings

http://www.house.gov/conyers

2426 Rayburn House Office Building, Washington, DC 20515 .... (202) 225–5126
Chief of Staff.—Cynthia Martin. FAX: 225–0072
Scheduler.—Rinia Shelby.
Federal Courthouse, Suite 669, 231 West Lafayette, Detroit, MI 48226 .... (313) 961–5670
District Director.—Vacant.
2615 West Jefferson, Trenton, MI 48183 .... (734) 675–4084
FAX: 675–4218

Counties: WAYNE COUNTY (part). CITIES AND TOWNSHIPS: Allen Park, Detroit, Dearborn, Gibraltar, Grosse Ile, Hamtramack, Highland Park, Melvindale, Riverview, Southgate, and Trenton. Population (2000), 662,563.

ZIP Codes: 48101–02, 48120–22, 48124, 48126–27, 48138, 48173, 48180, 48183, 48192, 48195, 48203–04, 48206, 48210–12, 48219, 48221, 48223, 48227–28, 48235, 48238–40

* * *

FIFTEENTH DISTRICT

JOHN D. DINGELL, Democrat, of Dearborn, MI; born in Colorado Springs, CO, July 8, 1926; education: B.S., Georgetown University, 1949; J.D., Georgetown University Law School, 1952; professional: World War II veteran; assistant Wayne County prosecutor, 1953–55; member: Migratory Bird Conservation Commission; married: the former Deborah Insley; committees: chair, Energy and Commerce; elected to the 84th Congress in a special election to fill the vacant seat of his late father, the Honorable John D. Dingell, December 13, 1955; reelected to the 85th and each succeeding Congress.

Office Listings

http://www.house.gov/dingell

2328 Rayburn House Office Building, Washington, DC 20515 .... (202) 225–4071
Chief of Staff.—Michael Robbins.
Legislative Director.—Katie Murtha.
Scheduler.—Beth Siniawski.
Press Secretary.—Adam Benson.
19855 West Outer Drive, Suite 103–E, Dearborn, MI 48124 .... (313) 278–2936
District Administrator.—Andy LaBarre.
23 East Front Street, Suite 103, Monroe, MI 48161 .... (734) 243–1849
301 West Michigan Avenue, Ypsilanti, MI 48197 .... (734) 481–1100

Counties: WAYNE COUNTY (part). CITIES AND TOWNSHIPS: Brownstown Township, Dearborn, Dearborn Heights, Flat Rock, Gibraltar, Rockwood, Romulus, Taylor, Woodhaven. MONROE COUNTY. CITIES AND TOWNSHIPS: Azalia, Carleton, Dundee, Erie, Ida, Lambertville, LaSalle, Luna Pier, Maybee, Milan, Monroe, Newport, Ottawa Lake, Petersburg, Samaria, S. Rockwood, Temperance. WASHTENAW COUNTY (part). CITIES AND TOWNSHIPS: Ann Arbor, Pittsfield Township, York Township, Superior Township, Ypsilanti, and Ypsilanti Township. Population (2000), 662,563.

ZIP Codes: 48103–11, 48113, 48117, 48123–28, 48131, 48133–34, 48140–41, 48144–45, 48157, 48159–62, 48164, 48166, 48170, 48173–74, 48176–77, 48179–80, 48182–84, 48186, 48190–92, 48197–98, 48228, 48239, 49228–29, 49238, 49267, 49270, 49276

MINNESOTA

(Population 2000, 4,919,479)

SENATORS

AMY KLOBUCHAR, Democrat, of Minneapolis, MN; born in Plymouth, MN, May 25, 1960; education: B.A., *magna cum laude*, Yale University, 1982; J.D., *magna cum laude*, University of Chicago Law School, 1985; professional: Attorney at law firm Dorsey & Whitney, 1985–93, Partner in 1993; Partner at law firm Gray, Plant, Mooty, Mooty & Bennett, 1993–98; religion: Congregationalist; public service: City of Minneapolis prosecutor, 1988; elected Hennepin County Attorney, 1998, reelected, 2002; married: John; child: Abigail; committees: Agriculture, Nutrition, and Forestry; Commerce, Science, and Transportation, Environment and Public Works; Judiciary; Joint Economic Committee; elected to the U.S. Senate on November 7, 2006.

Office Listings

http://klobuchar.senate.gov

302 Hart Senate Office Building, Washington, DC 20510 .... (202) 224–3244
Chief of Staff.—Marjorie Duske.
Legislative Director.—Vacant.
Deputy Chief of Staff.—John Davis.
Press Secretary.—Linden Zakula.
Scheduler.—Lauren Mandelker.
1200 Washington Avenue, South, Suite 250, Minneapolis, MN 55111 .... (612) 727–5220
State Director.—Zach Rodvold.

* * *

AL FRANKEN, Democrat, of Minneapolis, MN; raised in St. Louis Park, MN, born May 21, 1951; education: Harvard, Cambridge, MA, 1973; professional: comedy writer, author, and radio talk show host; has taken part in seven USO tours, visiting our troops overseas in Germany, Bosnia, Kosovo and Uzbekistan—as well as visiting Iraq, Afghanistan, and Kuwait four times; married: Franni Franken for 34 years; two children; committees: Health, Education, Labor, and Pension; Judiciary; Indian Affairs; Special Committee on Aging; elected to the 111th U.S. Senate on November 4, 2008.

Office Listings

info@franken.senate.gov

320 Hart Senate Office Building, Washington, DC 20510 .... (202) 224–5641
Chief of Staff.—Drew Littman. FAX: 224–0044
State Director.—Alana Petersen.
Legislative Director.—Ben Olinksy.
Scheduler.—Jamie Drogin.
Communications Director.—Casey Aden-Wansbury.
Press Secretary.—Jess McIntosh.
Gerald W. Heaney Federal Building and U.S. Courthouse, 316 North Robert Street, Suite 615, St. Paul, MN 55101 .... (651) 221–1016
FAX: 221–1078

REPRESENTATIVES

FIRST DISTRICT

TIMOTHY J. WALZ, Democrat, of Mankato, MN; born in West Point, NE, April 6, 1964; education: B.S., Chadron State College, Chadron, NE; M.S., St. Mary's University, Winona, MN; professional: high school teacher; military: Command Sergeant Major, Minnesota's 1st/ 34th Division of the Army National Guard, 1981–2005; awards: 2002 Minnesota Ethics in Education award winner, 2003 Mankato Teacher of the Year, and the 2003 Minnesota Teacher of Excellence; married: Gwen Whipple Walz, 1994; children: Hope and Gus; committees: Agriculture; Transportation and Infrastructure; Veterans' Affairs; elected to the 110th Congress on November 7, 2006; reelected to the 111th Congress.

Office Listings

http://www.walz.house.gov

1722 Longworth House Office Building, Washington, DC 20515 .... (202) 225–2472

Chief of Staff.—Josh Syrjamaki. FAX: 225–3433
Legislative Director.—Chris Schmitter.
Senior Policy Advisor.—Jeff Lomonaco.
Scheduler.—Andrea Fetherston.
227 East Main Street, Suite 220, Mankato, MN 56001 .... (507) 388–2149
1134 Seventh Street, NW., Rochester, MN 55901 .... (507) 206–0643

Counties: BLUE EARTH COUNTY. CITIES: Amboy, Eagle Lake, Garden City, Good Thunder, Lake Crystal, Madison Lake, Mankato, Mapleton, Pemberton, St. Clair, Vernon Center. BROWN COUNTY. CITIES: Comfrey, Hanska, New Ulm, Sleepy Eye, Springfield. COTTONWOOD COUNTY. CITIES: Mountain Lake, Storedon, Westbrook. DODGE COUNTY. CITIES: Claremont, Dodge Center, Hayfield, Kasson, Mantorville, West Concord, Windom. FARIBAULT COUNTY. CITIES: Blue Earth, Bricelyn, Delavan, Easton, Elmore, Frost, Huntley, Kiester, Minnesota Lake, Walters, Wells, Winnebago. FILLMORE COUNTY. CITIES: Canton, Chatfield, Fountain, Harmony, Lanesboro, Mabel, Ostrander, Peterson, Preston, Rushford, Spring Valley, Whalan, Wykoff. FREEBORN COUNTY. CITIES: Albert Lea, Alden, Clarks Grove, Conger, Emmons, Freeborn, Geneva, Glenville, Hartland, Hayward, Hollandale, London, Manchester, Myrtle, Oakland, Twin Lakes. HOUSTON COUNTY. CITIES: Brownsville, Caledonia, Eitzen, Hokah, Houston, La Crescent, Spring Grove. JACKSON COUNTY. CITIES: Heron, Jackson, Lake Field. MARTIN COUNTY. CITY: Fairmont. MOWER COUNTY. CITIES: Adams, Austin, Brownsdale, Dexter, Elkton, Grand Meadow, Lansing, LeRoy, Lyle, Rose Creek, Sargeant, Taopi, Waltham. MURRAY COUNTY. CITIES: Fulda, Slayton. NICOLLET COUNTY. CITIES: North Mankato, St. Peter. NOBLES COUNTY. CITIES: Adrian, Worthington. OLMSTED COUNTY. CITIES: Byron, Dover, Eyota, Oronoco, Rochester, Stewartville, Viola. PIPESTONE COUNTY. CITIES: Edgerton, Jasper, Pipestone Ruthton. ROCK COUNTY. CITY: Lurverne. STEELE COUNTY. CITIES: Blooming Prairie, Ellendale, Hope, Medford, Meriden, Owatonna. WABASHA COUNTY. CITIES: Elgin, Hammond, Kellogg, Lake City, Mazeppa, Milleville, Plainview, Reads Landing, Theilman, Wabasha. WASECA COUNTY. CITIES: Janesville, New Richland, Otisco, Waldorf, Waseca. WATONWAN COUNTY. CITIES: Madelia, St. James. WINONA COUNTY. CITIES: Altura, Dakota, Goodview, Homer, Lewiston, Minnesota City, Rollingstone, St. Charles, Stockton, Utica, and Winona. Population (2000), 614,935.

ZIP Codes: 55021, 55027, 55041, 55049, 55052, 55060, 55901–06, 55909–10, 55912, 55917–27, 55929, 55931–36, 55939–47, 55949–57, 55959–65, 55967–77, 55979, 55981–83, 55985, 55987–88, 55990–92, 56001–03, 56006–07, 56009–11, 56013–14, 56016, 56019–21, 56023–29, 56031, 56033–34, 56036–37, 56039, 56041–43, 56045–48, 56050–51, 56054–55, 56058, 56060, 56062–63, 56065, 56068, 56072–74, 56078, 56080–83, 56085, 56087–91, 56093, 56096–98, 56101, 56110–11, 56114–23, 56125, 56127–29, 56131, 56134, 56136–41, 56143–47, 56149–53, 56155–56, 56158–62, 56164–68, 56170–74, 56176–77, 56180–81, 56183, 56185–87, 56266

* * *

SECOND DISTRICT

JOHN KLINE, Republican, of Lakeville, MN; born in Allentown, PA, September 6, 1947; education: B.A., Rice University, 1969; M.P.A., Shippensburg University, 1988; military service: U.S. Marine Corps, 1969–94; retired at the rank of Colonel; organizations: Boy Scouts of America; Marine Corps League; Veterans of Foreign Wars; Marine Corps Association; American Legion; Retired Officers Association; past president, Marine Corps Coordinating Council of Minnesota; religion: Methodist; family: married to Vicky; children: Kathy and Dan; committees: ranking member, Education and Labor; Armed Services; elected to the 108th Congress on November 5, 2002; reelected to each succeeding Congress.

Office Listings

http://www.house.gov/kline

1210 Longworth House Office Building, Washington, DC 20515 .... (202) 225–2271
Chief of Staff.—Jean Hinz. FAX: 225–2595
Legislative Director.—Yelena Vaynberg.
Executive Assistant.—Brooke Dorobiala.
Press Secretary.—Troy Young.
Scheduler.—Clair Silliman.
101 West Burnsville Parkway, Suite 201, Burnsville, MN 55337 .... (952) 808–1213

Counties: CARVER COUNTY. CITIES: Chanhassen, Chaska, Waconia, Victoria. DAKOTA COUNTY (part). CITIES: Apple Valley, Burnsville, Eagan, Farmington, Hastings, Inver Grove Heights. GOODHUE COUNTY. CITIES: Cannon Falls, Pine Island, Red Wing, Zumbrota. LE SUEUR COUNTY. CITIES: Le Sueur, Le Center, Montgomery. RICE COUNTY. CITIES: Faribault, Northfield. SCOTT COUNTY. CITIES: Shakopee, Savage, Prior Lake, New Prague, Jordan, Belle Plaine. WASHINGTON COUNTY (part). CITIES: Woodbury, and Cottage Grove. Population (2000), 614,934.

ZIP Codes: 55001, 55009–10, 55016, 55018–21, 55024, 55026–27, 55031, 55033, 55041, 55044, 55046, 55049, 55052–55, 55057, 55065–66, 55068, 55071, 55075–77, 55085, 55087–89, 55118, 55120–25, 55129, 55306, 55315, 55317–18, 55322, 55328, 55331, 55337, 55339, 55346–47, 55352, 55360, 55367–68, 55372, 55375, 55378–79, 55386–88, 55397, 55946, 55956, 55963, 55983, 55985, 55992, 56011, 56017, 56028, 56050, 56052, 56057–58, 56063, 56069, 56071, 56082, 56096

* * *

THIRD DISTRICT

ERIK PAULSEN, Republican, of Eden Prairie, MN; born in Bakersfield, CA, May 14, 1965; education: B.A., St. Olaf College, Northfield, MN, 1987; Med Tech Caucus; National Guard

Caucus; Diabetes Caucus; Law Enforcement Caucus; Financial Literacy Caucus; Sportsman's Caucus; Nuclear Issues Working; U.S. China Working Group; Renewable Energy Caucus; religion: Lutheran; married: Kelly; children: four daughters; committees: Financial Services; elected to the 111th Congress on November 4, 2008.

Office Listings

http://www.paulsen.house.gov

126 Cannon House Office Building, Washington, DC 20515 .... (202) 225–2871
Chief of Staff.—Laurie Esau.' FAX: 225–6351
Legislative Director.—Noah Jacobson.
Press Secretary.—Andrew Foxwell.
Scheduler.—Kayla Priehs.
250 Prairie Center Drive, Suite 230, Eden Prairie, MN 55344 .... (952) 405–8510
FAX: 405–8514

Counties: ANOKA (part), HENNEPIN (part). CITIES AND TOWNSHIPS: Bloomington, Brooklyn Center, Brooklyn Park, Champlin, Coon Rapids, Corcoran, Dayton, Deephaven, Eden Prarie, Edina, Excelsior, Greenwood, Hassan, Hopkins, Independence, Long Lake, Loretto, Maple Grove, Maple Plain, Medicine Lake, Medina, Minnetonka Beach, Minnetonka, Minnetrista, Mound, Orono, Osseo, Plymouth, Rogers, Saint Bonifacius, Shorewood, Spring Park, Tonka Bay, Wayzata, and Woodland. Population (2000), 614,935.

ZIP Codes: 55304–05, 55311, 55316, 55323, 55327, 55331, 55340–41, 55343–48, 55356–57, 55359, 55361, 55364, 55369, 55373–75, 55378, 55384, 55387–88, 55391–92, 55410, 55416, 55420, 55422–26, 55428–31, 55433, 55435–39, 55441–48, 55569–72, 55574, 55576–79, 55592–93, 55595–99

* * *

FOURTH DISTRICT

BETTY McCOLLUM, Democrat-Farmer-Labor, of St. Paul, MN; born in Minneapolis, MN, July 12, 1954; education: A.A., Inver Hills Community College; B.S., College of St. Catherine; professional: teacher and sales manager; single; children: Sean and Katie; public service: North St. Paul City Council, 1986–92; Minnesota House of Representatives, 1992–2000; organizations: Girl Scouts of America; VFW Ladies' Auxiliary; and American Legion Ladies' Auxiliary; awards: Friend of the National Parks Award, National Parks Conservation Association, 2005; Friend of College Access Award, National Association for College Admission Counseling, 2006; Congressional Leadership Award, InterAction, 2006; Congressional Arts Leadership Award, Americans for the Arts, 2007; founder, Congressional Global Health Caucus; Senior Democratic Whip; appointments: National Council on the Arts; committees: Appropriations; Budget; elected to the 107th Congress on November 7, 2000; reelected to each succeeding Congress.

Office Listings

http://www.house.gov/mccollum

1714 Longworth House Office Building, Washington, DC 20515 .... (202) 225–6631
Chief of Staff.—Bill Harper. FAX: 225–1968
Legislative Director.—Peter Frosch.
Office Director.—Tod Herskovitz.
165 Western Avenue North, Suite 17, St. Paul, MN 55102 .... (651) 224–9191
Communications / District Director.—Joshua Straka.

Counties: DAKOTA (part), RAMSEY, WASHINGTON (part). Population (2000), 614,935.

ZIP Codes: 55016, 55042, 55055, 55071, 55075–77, 55090, 55101–10, 55112–20, 55125–29, 55133, 55144, 55146, 55150, 55155, 55161, 55164–66, 55168–70, 55172, 55175, 55177, 55182, 55187–88, 55190–91, 55199, 55421, 55432, 55449

* * *

FIFTH DISTRICT

KEITH ELLISON, Democrat-Farmer-Labor, of Minneapolis, MN; born in Detroit, MI, August 4, 1963; education: University of Detroit Jesuit High School and Academy, 1981; Wayne State University, 1987; University of Minnesota Law School, 1990; professional: The Law Office of Lindquist & Vennum, 1990–93; Executive Director of the nonprofit Legal Rights Center in Minneapolis, 1993–98; Hassan & Reed Ltd., 1998–2001; Ellison Law Offices, 2003–06; served in Minnesota State Legislature District 58B, 2003–06; married, four children; commissions: Center for Strategic and International Studies Commission on Global Health; House Democracy Assistance Commission; Tom Lantos Human Rights Commission; caucuses: founder, Consumer Justice Caucus; vice-chair, Progressive Caucus; vice-chair, LBT, Caucus; Congressional Black Caucus; Populist Caucus; Pro-choice Caucus; Green Jobs Caucus; committees: Financial Services; Foreign Affairs; elected to the 110th Congress on November 7, 2006; reelected to the 111th Congress.

Office Listings

http://ellison.house.gov

1122 Longworth House Office Building, Washington, DC 20515 .... (202) 225–4755
Chief of Staff.—Kari Moe. FAX: 225–4886
Legislative Director.—Minh Ta.
Communications Director.—Rick Jauert.
2100 Plymouth Avenue, Minneapolis, MN 55411 .... (612) 522–1212
District Director.—Brian Elliott.

Counties: ANOKA (part), HENNEPIN (part), RAMSEY (part). CITIES: Columbia Heights, Crystal, Ft. Snelling, Fridley, Golden Valley, Hilltop, Hopkins, Minneapolis, New Hope, Richfield, Robbinsdale, St. Anthony, St. Louis Park, and Spring Lake Park, Population (2000), 614,935.

ZIP Codes: 55111–12, 55305, 55343, 55401–30, 55432–33, 55440–41, 55450, 55454–55, 55458–60, 55470, 55472, 55474, 55479–80, 55483–88

* * *

SIXTH DISTRICT

MICHELE BACHMANN, Republican, of Stillwater, MN; born in Waterloo, IA, April 6, 1956; education: B.A., Winona State University, Winona, MN, 1978; J.D., Coburn School of Law, Oral Roberts University, Tulsa, OK; LL.M. in tax law at the College of William and Mary, Williamsburg, VA; professional: federal tax litigation attorney; served six years in the Minnesota State Senate; organizations: New Heights Charter School; married: Marcus; children: Lucas, Harrison, Elisa, Caroline, and Sophia; committees: Financial Services; elected to the 110th Congress on November 7, 2006; reelected to the 111th Congress on November 4, 2008.

Office Listings

http://www.bachmann.house.gov

107 Cannon House Office Building, Washington, DC 20515 .... (202) 225–2331
Chief of Staff.—Michelle Marston. FAX: 225–6475
Legislative Director.—Jessica Perry.
Scheduler.—Kim Rubin.
Press Secretary.—Debbee Keller.
6043 Hudson Road, Suite 330, Woodbury, MN 55125 .... (651) 731–5400
110 2nd Street South, Suite 232, Waite Park, MN 56387 .... (320) 253–5931
FAX: 240–6905

Counties: ANOKA (part), BENTON, SHERBURNE, STEARNS (part), WASHINGTON (part), WRIGHT. CITIES: Andover, Anoka, Blaine, Elk River, Forest Lake, Lino Lakes, St. Cloud, Stillwater, Ramsey, and Woodbury. Population (2000), 614,935.

ZIP Codes: 55001, 55003, 55005–06, 55011, 55014, 55025, 55031, 55038, 55042–43, 55047, 55070, 55073, 55079, 55082–83, 55092, 55110, 55112, 55115, 55125, 55128–29, 55301–04, 55308–09, 55313, 55319–21, 55328–30, 55341, 55349, 55353, 55358–59, 55362–63, 55365, 55371, 55373–74, 55376, 55380–82, 55388–90, 55395, 55398, 55412–13, 55417–18, 55429–30, 55432, 55434, 55448–49, 56301, 56303–04, 56307, 56310, 56314, 56320, 56329–31, 56340, 56352, 56357, 56362, 56367–68, 56373–75, 56377, 56379, 56387–88, 56393, 56395–99

* * *

SEVENTH DISTRICT

COLLIN C. PETERSON, Democrat, of Detroit Lakes, MN; born in Fargo, ND, June 29, 1944; education: graduated from Glyndon (MN) High School, 1962; B.A. in business administration and accounting, Moorhead State University, 1966; U.S. Army National Guard, 1963–69; CPA, owner and partner; Minnesota State Senator, 1976–86; member: AOPA, Safari Club, Ducks Unlimited, American Legion, Sea Plane Pilots Association, Pheasants Forever, Benevolent Protective Order of Elks, Cormorant Lakes Sportsmen Club; three children: Sean, Jason, and Elliott; committees: chair, Agriculture; elected to the 102nd Congress, November 6, 1990; reelected to each succeeding Congress.

Office Listings

http://collinpeterson.house.gov

2211 Rayburn House Office Building, Washington, DC 20515 .... (202) 225–2165
Chief of Staff.—Mark Brownell.
Legislative Director.—Robin Goracke.
Executive Assistant.—Cherie Slayton.
Assistants: Matt Forbes, Chris Iacaruso, Sara Kloek.
Lake Avenue Plaza Building, Suite 107, 714 Lake Avenue, Detroit Lakes, MN 56501 .... (218) 847–5056
Minnesota Wheat Growers Building, 2603 Wheat Drive, Red Lake, MN 56750 ..... (218) 253–4356
320 Southwest Fourth Street, Centre Point Mall, Willmar, MN 56201 .... (320) 235–1061

Counties: BECKER, BELTRAMI (part), BIG STONE, CHIPPEWA, CLAY, CLEARWATER, DOUGLAS, GRANT, KANDIYOHI, KITTSON, LAC QUI PARLE, LAKE OF THE WOODS, LINCOLN, LYON, MAHNOMEN, MARSHALL, MCLEOD, MEEKER, NORMAN, OTTER TAIL, PENNINGTON, POLK, POPE, RED LAKE, REDWOOD, RENVILLE, ROSEAU, SIBLEY, STEARNS (part), STEVENS, SWIFT, TODD, TRAVERSE, WILKIN, YELLOW MEDICINE. Population (2000) 614,935.

ZIP Codes: 55307, 55310, 55312, 55314, 55321, 55324–25, 55329, 55332–36, 55338–39, 55342, 55350, 55353–55, 55366, 55368, 55370, 55381–82, 55385, 55389, 55395–96, 55409, 55970, 56011, 56044, 56054, 56058, 56083, 56085, 56087, 56113, 56115, 56129, 56132, 56136, 56142, 56149, 56152, 56157, 56164, 56166, 56169–70, 56175, 56178, 56180, 56201, 56207–12, 56214–16, 56218–32, 56235–37, 56239–41, 56243–45, 56248–49, 56251–53, 56255–58, 56260, 56262–67, 56270–71, 56273–74, 56276–85, 56287–89, 56291–97, 56301–04, 56307–12, 56314–16, 56318–21, 56323–24, 56326–27, 56329, 56331–32, 56334, 56336, 56339–40, 56343, 56345, 56347, 56349, 56352, 56354–55, 56360–62, 56368, 56372–74, 56377–79, 56381–82, 56385, 56387, 56393, 56395–99, 56433–34, 56436–38, 56440, 56443, 56446, 56453, 56458, 56461, 56464, 56466–67, 56470, 56475, 56477–79, 56481–82, 56501–02, 56510–11, 56514–25, 56527–29, 56531, 56533–38, 56540–54, 56556–57, 56560–63, 56565–81, 56583–94, 56601, 56619, 56621, 56623, 56633–34, 56644, 56646–47, 56650–52, 56661, 56663, 56666–67, 56670–71, 56673, 56676, 56678, 56682–87, 56701, 56710–11, 56713–16, 56720–29, 56731–38, 56740–42, 56744, 56748, 56750–51, 56754–63

* * *

EIGHTH DISTRICT

JAMES L. OBERSTAR, Democrat, of Chisholm, MN; born in Chisholm, September 10, 1934; education: graduated, Chisholm High School, 1952; B.A., *summa cum laude*, French and political science, College of St. Thomas, St. Paul, MN, 1956; M.A., European area studies, College of Europe, Bruges, Belgium, 1957; Laval University, Canada; Georgetown University, former teacher of English, French, and Creole; served as administrative assistant to the late Congressman John A. Blatnik, 1963–74; administrator of the House Public Works Committee, 1971–74; co-chair, Congressional Travel and Tourism Caucus; Democratic Study Group; Great Lakes Task Force; National Water Alliance; Northeast Midwest Congressional Coalition; Steel Caucus; chairman, Conference of Great Lakes Congressmen; married: Jean Kurth, 1993; children: Thomas Edward, Katherine Noelle, Anne-Therese, Monica Rose, Charlie, and Lindy; committees: chair, Transportation and Infrastructure; elected to the 94th Congress, November 5, 1974; reelected to each succeeding Congress.

Office Listings

http://www.house.gov/oberstar

2365 Rayburn House Office Building, Washington, DC 20515 .... (202) 225–6211
Administrative Assistant.—William Richard.
Office Manager.—Marianne Buckley.
Legislative Director.—Chip Gardiner.
Communications Director.—John Schadl.
231 Federal Building, Duluth, MN 55802 .... (218) 727–7474
District Manager.—Jackie Morris.
Chisholm City Hall, 316 West Lake Street, Chisholm, MN 55719 .... (218) 254–5761
District Representative.—Peter Makowski.
Brainerd City Hall, 501 Laurel Street, Brainerd, MN 56401 .... (218) 828–4400
District Representative.—Ken Hasskamp.
38625 14th Avenue, Suite 300B, North Branch, MN 55056 .... (651) 277–1234
District Representative.—Alana Petersen.

Counties: AITKIN, BELTRAMI (part), CARLTON, CASS, CHISAGO, COOK, CROW WING, HUBBARD, ISANTI, ITASCA, KANABEC, KOOCHICHING, LAKE, MILLE LACS, MORRISON, PINE, ST. LOUIS, WADENA. CITIES: Brainerd, Chisholm, Cloquet, Duluth, Grand Rapids, Hibbing, International Falls, and Little Falls. Population (2000), 614,935.

ZIP Codes: 55002, 55005–08, 55012–13, 55017, 55025, 55029–30, 55032, 55036–37, 55040, 55045, 55051, 55056, 55063, 55067, 55069–70, 55072–74, 55078–80, 55084, 55092, 55330–31, 55362, 55371, 55377, 55398, 55408, 55601–07, 55609, 55612–16, 55701–13, 55716–26, 55730–36, 55738, 55741–42, 55744–46, 55748–53, 55756–58, 55760, 55763–69, 55771–72, 55775, 55777, 55779–87, 55790–93, 55795–98, 55801–08, 55810–12, 55814–16, 56028, 56058, 56304, 56307, 56309–11, 56313–15, 56317–19, 56323, 56325–33, 56335–36, 56338–45, 56347, 56350, 56353–61, 56363–64, 56367–69, 56371, 56373, 56376–77, 56381–82, 56384, 56386, 56389, 56401, 56425, 56430–31, 56433–35, 56437,

56441–44, 56446–50, 56452–53, 56455–56, 56458–59, 56461, 56464–70, 56472–75, 56477, 56479, 56481–82, 56484, 56601, 56623, 56626–31, 56633, 56636–37, 56639, 56641, 56647, 56649, 56653–55, 56657–63, 56668–69, 56672, 56678–81, 56683, 56688

MISSISSIPPI

(Population 2000, 2,844,658)

SENATORS

THAD COCHRAN, Republican, of Jackson, MS; born in Pontotoc, MS, December 7, 1937; education: B.A., University of Mississippi, 1959; J.D., University of Mississippi Law School, 1965; received a Rotary Foundation Fellowship and studied international law and jurisprudence at Trinity College, University of Dublin, Ireland, 1963–64; military service: served in U.S. Navy, 1959–61; professional: admitted to Mississippi bar in 1965; board of directors, Jackson Rotary Club, 1970–71; Outstanding Young Man of the Year Award, Junior Chamber of Commerce in Mississippi, 1971; president, young lawyers section of Mississippi State Bar, 1972–73; married: the former Rose Clayton of New Albany, MS, 1964; two children and three grandchildren; committees: ranking member, Appropriations; Agriculture, Nutrition, and Forestry; Rules and Administration; Joint Committee on the Library; elected to the 93rd Congress, November 7, 1972; reelected to 94th and 95th Congresses; chairman of the Senate Republican Conference, 1990–96; elected to the U.S. Senate, November 7, 1978, for the six-year term beginning January 3, 1979; subsequently appointed by the governor, December 27, 1978, to fill the vacancy caused by the resignation of Senator James O. Eastland; reelected to each succeeding Senate term.

Office Listings

http://cochran.senate.gov

113 Dirksen Senate Office Building, Washington, DC 20510 .... (202) 224–5054
Chief of Staff.—T.A. Hawks.
Legislative Director.—Steven Wall.
Press Secretary.—Chris Gallegos.
Scheduler.—Doris Wagley.
190 East Capitol Street, Suite 550, Jackson, MS 39201 .... (601) 965–4459
911 East Jackson Avenue, Suite 249, Oxford, MS 38655 .... (662) 236–1018
2012 15th Street, Suite 451, Gulfport, MS 39501 .... (228) 867–9710

* * *

ROGER F. WICKER, Republican, of Tupelo, MS; born in Pontotoc, MS, July 5, 1951; education: graduated Pontotoc High School; University of Mississippi: B.A., 1973; J.D., 1975; president, Associated Student Body, 1972–73; *Mississippi Law Journal,* 1973–75; Air Force ROTC; U.S. Air Force, 1976–80; U.S. Air Force Reserve, 1980–2004 (retired with rank of lieutenant colonel); U.S. House of Representatives Rules Committee staff for Representative Trent Lott, 1980–82; private law practice, 1982–94; Lee County Public Defender, 1984–87; Tupelo City Judge pro tempore, 1986–87; Mississippi State Senate, 1988–94, chairman: Elections Committee (1992), Public Health and Welfare Committee (1993–94); member: Lions Club, University of Mississippi Hall of Fame, Sigma Nu Fraternity Hall of Fame, Omicron Delta Kappa, Phi Delta Phi; religion: Southern Baptist, deacon, adult choir of First Baptist Church, Tupelo, MS; married: Gayle Long Wicker; children: Margaret (Manning) McPhillips, Caroline (Kirk) Sims, and McDaniel; committees: Armed Services; Commerce, Science and Transportation; Foreign Relations; Small Business and Entrepreneurship; Veterans' Affairs; elected to the 104th Congress, November 8, 1994; president, Republican freshman class, 1995; reelected to each succeeding Congress; appointed by the governor, December 31, 2007, to fill the vacancy caused by the resignation of Senator Trent Lott; elected to the U.S. Senate on November 4, 2008.

Office Listings

http://wicker.senate.gov

555 Dirksen Senate Office Building, Washington, DC 20510 .... (202) 224–6253
Chief of Staff.—Michelle Barlow. FAX: 228–0378
Legislative Director.—Susan Sweat.
Scheduler.—Hardy Lott.
Communications Director.—Jordan Stoick.
245 East Capitol Street, Suite 226, Jackson, MS 39201 .... (601) 965–4644
FAX: 695–4007
452 Courthouse Road, Suite F, Gulfport, MS 39507 .... (228) 604–2383
FAX: 896–4359
3118 Pascagoula Street, Suite 179, Pascagoula, MS 39567 .... (228) 762–5400
FAX: 762–0137
2801 West Main Street, Tupelo, MS 38801 .... (662) 844–5010
FAX: 844–5030

321 Losher Street, P.O. Box 385, Hernando, MS 38632 .... (662) 429–1002
FAX: 429–6002

REPRESENTATIVES

FIRST DISTRICT

TRAVIS W. CHILDERS, Democrat, of Booneville, MS; born in Booneville, March 29, 1958; education: graduated, Booneville High School; B.B.A., University of Mississippi, 1980; professional: Chancery Clerk, 1991–2007; President of Chancery Clerks Association, 2001–02; co-chair, Rural Caucus; Sportsmen Caucus; Blue Dog Coalition; religion: Southern Baptist; married: Tami Childers; children: Dustin and Lauren; committees: Agriculture; Financial Services; elected to the 110th Congress by special election on May 13, 2008, to fill the vacancy caused by United States Representative Roger Wicker; reelected to the 111th Congress on November 4, 2008.

Office Listings

http://www.childers.house.gov

1708 Longworth House Office Building, Washington, DC 20515 .... (202) 225–4306
Chief of Staff.—Brad Morris. FAX: 225–3549
Legislative Director.—Benjamin Lincoln.
Press Secretary.—Dana Edelstein.
Scheduler.—Richard Davidson.
337 East Main Street, Suite A, Tupelo, MS 38804 .... (662) 841–8808
523 Main Street, P.O. Box 1072, Columbus, MS 39703 .... (662) 327–0748
2564 Highway 51 South, Hernando, MS 38632 .... (662) 449–3090

Counties: ALCORN, BENTON, CALHOUN, CHICKASAW, CHOCTAW, CLAY, DESOTO, GRENADA, ITTAWAMBA, LAFAYETTE, LEE, LOWNDES, MARSHALL, MONROE, PANOLA, PONTOTOC, PRENTISS, TATE, TIPPAH, TISHIMINGO, UNION, WEBSTER (part), WINSTON (part), YALOBUSHA. Population (2000), 711,160.

ZIP Codes: 38601–03, 38606, 38610–11, 38618–21, 38625, 38627, 38629, 38632–35, 38637–38, 38641–42, 38647, 38649–52, 38654–55, 38658–59, 38661, 38663, 38665–66, 38668, 38670–74, 38677, 38679–80, 38683, 38685–86, 38801–04, 38820–21, 38824–29, 38833–35, 38838–39, 38841, 38843–44, 38846–52, 38854–60, 38862–66, 38868–71, 38873–80, 38901–02, 38913–16, 38920, 38922, 38925–27, 38929, 38940, 38948–49, 38951, 38953, 38955, 38960–61, 38965, 39108, 39339, 39701–05, 39710, 39730, 39735–37, 39740–41, 39743–46, 39750–56, 39759, 39766–67, 39769, 39771–73, 39776

* * *

SECOND DISTRICT

BENNIE G. THOMPSON, Democrat, of Bolton, MS; born in Bolton, January 28, 1948; education: graduated, Hinds County Agriculture High School; B.A., Tougaloo College, 1968; M.S., Jackson State University, 1972; professional: teacher; Bolton Board of Aldermen, 1969–73; mayor of Bolton, 1973–79; Hinds County Board of Supervisors, 1980–93; Congressional Black Caucus; Sunbelt Caucus; Rural Caucus; Progressive Caucus; Housing Assistance Council; NAACP 100 Black Men of Jackson, MS; Southern Regional Council; Kappa Alpha Psi Fraternity; married to the former London Johnson, Ph.D.; one daughter: BendaLonne; committees: chair, Homeland Security; elected to the 103rd Congress in a special election; reelected to each succeeding Congress.

Office Listings

http://www.house.gov/thompson

2432 Rayburn House Office Building, Washington, DC 20515 .... (202) 225–5876
Administrative Assistant.—Marsha G. McCraven. FAX: 225–5898
Communications Director.—Lanier Avant.
Legislative Director.—Karis Gutter.
107 West Madison Street, P.O. Box 610, Bolton, MS 39041–0610 .... (601) 866–9003
District Director.—Charlie Horhn.
3607 Medgar Evers Boulevard, Jackson, MS 39213 .... (601) 982–8582
263 East Main Street, Marks, MS 38646 .... (662) 326–9003
Mound Bayou City Hall, Room 134, 106 West Green Street, Mound Bayou, MS 38762 .... (662) 741–9003
509 Highway 82 West, Greenwood, MS 38930 .... (662) 455–9003
910 Courthouse Lane, Greenville, MS 38701 .... (662) 335–9003

Counties: ATTALA, BOLIVAR, CARROLL, CLAIBORNE, COAHOMA, COPIAH, HINDS (part), HOLMES, HUMPHREYS, ISSAQUENA, JEFFERSON, LEAKE (part), LEFLORE, MADISON (part), MONTGOMERY, QUITMAN, SHARKEY, SUNFLOWER, TALLAHATCHIE, TUNICA, WARREN, WASHINGTON, YAZOO. Population (2000), 711,164.

ZIP Codes: 38606, 38609, 38614, 38617, 38621–23, 38626, 38628, 38630–31, 38639, 38643–46, 38664–65, 38669–70, 38676, 38701–04, 38720–23, 38725–26, 38730–33, 38736–40, 38744–46, 38748–49, 38751, 38753–54, 38756, 38758–62, 38764–65, 38767–69, 38771–74, 38776, 38778, 38780–82, 38901, 38912, 38917, 38920–21, 38923–25, 38927–28, 38930, 38935, 38940–41, 38943–48, 38950, 38952–54, 38957–59, 38961–64, 38966–67, 39038–41, 39045–46, 39051, 39054, 39056, 39058–61, 39063, 39066–67, 39069, 39071–72, 39077–79, 39083, 39086, 39088, 39090, 39095–97, 39107–08, 39110, 39113, 39115, 39120, 39144, 39146, 39150, 39154, 39156–57, 39159–60, 39162–63, 39166, 39169–71, 39173–77, 39179–83, 39191–92, 39194, 39201–07, 39209–10, 39212–13, 39215–17, 39225, 39235, 39269, 39271–72, 39282–84, 39286, 39289, 39296, 39653, 39661, 39668, 39745, 39747, 39767

* * *

THIRD DISTRICT

GREGG HARPER, Republican, of Pearl, MS; born in Jackson, MS, June 1, 1956; education: graduated from Pearl High School, Pearl, MS, 1974; B.S., Mississippi College, Clinton, MS, 1978; J.D., University of Mississippi, Oxford, MS, 1981; professional: prosecuting attorney; member, Pearl Chamber of Commerce, Rankin County Chamber of Commerce; Republican Steering Committee; religion: Southern Baptist; married: the former Sidney Carol Hancock; children: Livingston and Maggie; committees: Budget; House Administration; Judiciary; Standards of Official Conduct; Joint Committee on the Library; elected to the 111th Congress on November 4, 2008.

Office Listings

http://www.harper.house.gov

307 Cannon House Office Building, Washington, DC 20515 .... (202) 225–5031
Chief of Staff.—Michael Cravens. FAX: 225–5797
Policy Director.—Scot Malvaney.
Communications Director.—Adam Buckalew.
Scheduler.—Marcy Scoggins.
2507–A Old Brandon Road, Pearl, MS 39208 .... (601) 932–2410
District Director.—Chip Reynolds.
823 22nd Avenue, Meridian, MS 39301 .... (601) 693–6681
Special Assistants: Lynne Compton, Sally Wilkinson.
1 Research Boulevard, Suite 206, Starkville, MS 39759 .... (662) 324–0007
Special Assistant.—Henry Moseley.
230 South Whitworth Street, Brookhaven, MS 39601 .... (601) 823–3400
District Field Representative.—Evan Gardner.

Counties: ADANS, AMITE, COVINGTON, FRANKLIN, HINDS (part), JASPER (part), JEFF DAVIS, JONES (part), KEMPER, LAUDERDALE, LAWRENCE, LEAKE (part), LINCOLN, MADISON (part), MARION (part), NESHOBA, NEWTON, NOXUBEE, OKTIBBEHA, PIKE, RANKIN, SCOTT, SIMPSON, SMITH, WALTHALL, WEBSTER (part), WILKINSON, WINSTON. Population (2000), 711,164.

ZIP Codes: 39041–44, 39046–47, 39051, 39057, 39062, 39069, 39071, 39073–74, 39078, 39080, 39082–83, 39087, 39090, 39092, 39094, 39098, 39108–12, 39114, 39116–17, 39119–22, 39130, 39140, 39145, 39148–49, 39151–53, 39157–58, 39161, 39165, 39167–68, 39189–91, 39193, 39202, 39206, 39208–09, 39211, 39213, 39216, 39218, 39232, 39236, 39288, 39298, 39301–05, 39307, 39309, 39320, 39323, 39325–28, 39332, 39335–39, 39341–42, 39345–46, 39350, 39352, 39354, 39358–59, 39361, 39364–65, 39402, 39421–22, 39427–29, 39439, 39443, 39460, 39474, 39478–80, 39482–83, 39601–03, 39629–33, 39635, 39638, 39641, 39643, 39645, 39647–49, 39652–54, 39656–57, 39661–69, 39701, 39735, 39739, 39743, 39750, 39755, 39759–60, 39762, 39769

* * *

FOURTH DISTRICT

GENE TAYLOR, Democrat, of Bay St. Louis, MS; born in New Orleans, LA, September 17, 1953; education: graduated from De LaSalle High School, New Orleans, LA, 1971; B.A., Tulane University, New Orleans, LA, 1974; graduate studies in business and economics, University of Southern Mississippi, August 1978–April 1980; U.S. Coast Guard Reserves, 1971–84, first class petty officer, search and rescue boat skipper; sales representative, Stone Container Corporation, 1977–89; city councilman, Bay St. Louis, 1981–83; State Senator, 1983–89; member: American Legion; Rotary; Boys and Girls Club of the Gulf Coast; married the former Margaret Gordon, 1978; children: Sarah, Emily, Gary; committees: Armed Services; Transportation and Infrastructure; elected to the 101st Congress, by special election, on October 17, 1989, to fill the vacancy caused by the death of Larkin Smith; reelected to each succeeding Congress.

Office Listings

http://www.taylor.house.gov

2269 Rayburn House Office Building, Washington, DC 20515 .... (202) 225–5772
Chief of Staff.—Stephen Peranich. FAX: 225–7074
Legislative Director.—Ethan Rabin.
Executive Assistant.—Elizabeth Harris.
2424 Fourteenth Street, Gulfport, MS 39501 .... (228) 864–7670
District Manager.—Beau Gex.
215 Federal Building, 701 Main Street, Hattiesburg, MS 39401 .... (601) 582–3246
2900–B Government Street, Ocean Springs, MS 39564 .... (228) 872–7950
527 Central Avenue, Laurel, MS 39440 .... (601) 425–3905

Counties: CLARKE, FORREST, GEORGE, GREENE, HANCOCK, HARRISON, JACKSON, JASPER (part), JONES, LAMAR, MARION (part), PEARL RIVER, PERRY, STONE, WAYNE. CITIES AND TOWNSHIPS: Biloxi, Gulfport, Hattiesburg, Laurel, and Pascagoula. Population (2000), 711,170.

ZIP Codes: 39301, 39307, 39322, 39324, 39330, 39332, 39347–48, 39355–56, 39360, 39362–63, 39366–67, 39401–04, 39406, 39422–23, 39425–26, 39429, 39436–37, 39439–43, 39451–52, 39455–57, 39459, 39461–66, 39470, 39475–78, 39480–82, 39501–03, 39505–07, 39520–22, 39525, 39529–35, 39540, 39552–53, 39555–56, 39558, 39560–69, 39571–74, 39576–77, 39581, 39595

MISSOURI

(Population 2000, 5,595,211)

SENATORS

CHRISTOPHER S. BOND, Republican, of Mexico, MO; born in St. Louis, MO, March 6, 1939; education: B.A., *cum laude*, Woodrow Wilson School of Public and International Affairs of Princeton University, 1960; J.D., valedictorian, University of Virginia, 1963; held a clerkship with the U.S. Court of Appeals for the Fifth Circuit, 1964; practiced law in Washington, DC, and returned to Missouri, 1967; assistant attorney general of Missouri, 1969; state auditor, 1970; Governor of Missouri, 1973–77, 1981–85; married: the former Linda Holwick; children: Samuel Reid Bond; committees: vice chair, Select Committee on Intelligence; Appropriations; Environment and Public Works; Small Business and Entrepreneurship; elected to the U.S. Senate on November 4, 1986; reelected to each succeeding Senate term.

Office Listings

http://bond.senate.gov

274 Russell Senate Office Building, Washington, DC 20510 .... (202) 224–5721
Chief of Staff.—Brian Klippenstein. FAX: 224–8149
Deputy Chief of Staff / Legislative Director.—Kara Smith.
Legal Counsel.—John Stoody.
Scheduling Secretary.—Courtney Ellis.
1001 Cherry Street, Suite 204, Columbia, MO 65201 .... (573) 442–8151
911 Main Street, Suite 2224, Kansas City, MO 64105 .... (816) 471–7141
7700 Bonhomme, Suite 615, Clayton, MO 63105 .... (314) 725–4484
300 South Jefferson, Suite 401, Springfield, MO 65806 .... (417) 864–8258
Rush H. Limbaugh Sr., U.S. Courthouse, 555 Independence Street, Suite 1500, Cape Girardeau, MO 63703 .... (573) 334–7044
FAX: 334–7352
308 East High, Suite 202, Jefferson City, MO 65101 .... (573) 634–2488

* * *

CLAIRE McCASKILL, Democrat of Kirkwood, MO; born in Rolla, MO, July 24, 1953; raised in Lebanon, MO and Columbia, MO; education: B.A., University of Missouri-Columbia, 1975; J.D., University of Missouri-Columbia School of Law, 1978; professional: clerk with the Missouri Court of Appeals, Western District in Kansas City, 1978; assistant prosecutor, Jackson County prosecutor's office, 1979–83; Missouri state representative, 1983–88; practiced law in Kansas City, MO, 1983–92; Jackson County Legislator-At-Large, 1991–93; Jackson County Prosecutor, 1993–99; Missouri state auditor, 1999–2006; married: Joseph Shephard, 2002; together, they have seven children: Benjamin, Carl, Marilyn, Michael, Austin, Maddie, Lily; appointed deputy whip for the majority, 2007; committees: Armed Services; Commerce, Science, and Transportation; Homeland Security and Governmental Affairs; Special Committee on Aging; elected to the U.S. Senate of the 110th Congress on November 7, 2006.

Office Listings

http://mccaskill.senate.gov

717 Hart Senate Office Building, Washington, DC 20510 .... (202) 224–6154
Chief of Staff.—Julie Dwyer. FAX: 228–6326
Deputy Chief of Staff.—Tod Martin.
Legislative Director.—Stephen Hedger.
Communications Director.—Adrianne Marsh.
5850 Delmar Boulevard, Suite A, St. Louis, MO 63112 .... (314) 367–1364
Regional Director.—Michelle Sherod.
4141 Pennsylvania Avenue, Suite 101, Kansas City, MO 64111 .... (816) 421–1639
Regional Director.—Corey Dillon.
555 Independence Avenue, Room 1600, Cape Girardeau, MO 63703 .... (573) 651–0964
District Director.—Christy Ferrell.
915 East Ash Street, Columbia, MO 65201 .... (573) 442–7130
Regional Director.—Cindy Hall.
324 Park Central West, Suite 101, Springfield, MO 65806 .... (417) 868–8745

REPRESENTATIVES

FIRST DISTRICT

WM. LACY CLAY, Democrat, of St. Louis, MO; born in St. Louis, July 27, 1956; education: Springbrook High School, Silver Spring, MD, 1974; B.S., University of Maryland, 1983, with a degree in government and politics, and a certificate in paralegal studies; public service: Missouri House of Representatives, 1983–91; Missouri State Senate, 1991–2000; nonprofit organizations: St. Louis Gateway Classic Sports Foundation; Mary Ryder Homes; William L. Clay Scholarship and Research Fund; married: Ivie Lewellen Clay; children: Carol, and William III; committees: Financial Services; Oversight and Government Reform; elected to the 107th Congress on November 7, 2000; reelected to each succeeding Congress.

Office Listings

http://www.lacyclay.house.gov

2418 Rayburn House Office Building, Washington, DC 20515 .... (202) 225–2406
Legislative Director / Administrative Assistant.—Michele Bogdanovich.
Scheduler.—Karyn Long.
Senior Policy Advisor.—Frank Davis.
Legislative Assistants.—Richard Pecantee, Marvin Steele.
625 North Euclid Avenue, Suite 326, St. Louis, MO 63108 .... (314) 367–1970
8021 West Florissant, St. Louis, MO 63136 .... (314) 890–0349
Press Secretary.—Steven Engelhardt.

Counties: ST. LOUIS (part). Population (2000), 621,690.

ZIP Codes: 63031–34, 63042–44, 63074, 63101–08, 63110, 63112–15, 63117, 63119–22, 63124, 63130–38, 63141, 63145–47, 63150, 63155–56, 63160, 63164, 63166–67, 63169, 63171, 63177–80, 63182, 63188, 63190, 63195–99

* * *

SECOND DISTRICT

W. TODD AKIN, Republican, of St. Louis, MO; born in New York, NY, July 5, 1947; education: B.S., Worcester Polytechnic Institute, 1971; military service: Officer, U.S. Army Engineers; professional: engineer and businessman; IBM; Laclede Steel; taught International Marketing, undergraduate level; public service: appointed to the Bicentennial Commission of the U.S. Constitution, 1987; Missouri House of Representatives, 1988–2000; organizations: Boy Scouts of America; Missouri Right to Life; Mission Gate Prison Ministry; family: married to Lulli; children: Wynn, Perry, Micah, Ezra, Hannah and Abigail; committees: Armed Services; Science and Technology; Small Business; elected to the 107th Congress on November 7, 2000; reelected to each succeeding Congress.

Office Listings

http://www.house.gov/akin

117 Cannon House Office Building, Washington, DC 20515 .... (202) 225–2561
Chief of Staff.—Paul Protic. FAX: 225–2563
Scheduler.—Tressa Merola.
301 Sovereign Court, Suite 201, St. Louis, MO 63011 .... (314) 590–0029
District Director.—Patrick Werner.

Counties: LINCOLN, ST. CHARLES (part), ST. LOUIS (part). Population (2000), 621,690.

ZIP Codes: 63001, 63005–06, 63011, 63017, 63021–22, 63024–26, 63038, 63040, 63043, 63049, 63069, 63088, 63099, 63110, 63114, 63117, 63119, 63122–29, 63131, 63134, 63141, 63144–46, 63301–04, 63333–34, 63338, 63343–44, 63346–49, 63359, 63362, 63366–67, 63369–70, 63373, 63376–77, 63379, 63381, 63383, 63385–87, 63389–90

* * *

THIRD DISTRICT

RUSS CARNAHAN, Democrat, of St. Louis, MO; born in Columbia, MO, July 10, 1958; education: B.S., Public Administration, University of Missouri-Columbia, 1979; J.D., University of Missouri-Columbia School of Law, 1983; professional: Missouri State Representative, 2001–

04; BJC Healthcare, 1995–2004; private law practice; organizations: United Way of Greater St. Louis; Louis Regional Commerce and Growth Association; FOCUS Leadership St. Louis, Class of 1997–98; State Historical Society of Missouri; Landmarks Association of St. Louis; Compton Heights Neighborhood Association; Missouri Bar Association; Bar Association of Metropolitan St. Louis; Boy Scouts, Eagle Scout recipient; Friends of Tower Grove Park, Missouri Botanical Gardens and DeMenil Mansion; awards: St. Louis Regional Chamber of Commerce and Growth Association Lewis and Clark Statesman Award; St. Louis Business Journal 2002 Legislative Award and the Missouri Bar 2002 Legislative Award; married: Debra Carnahan; children: Austin and Andrew; committees: Foreign Affairs; Science and Technology; Transportation and Infrastructure; elected to the 109th Congress on November 2, 2004; reelected to each succeeding Congress.

Office Listings

http://russcarnahan.house.gov

1710 Longworth House Office Building, Washington, DC 20515 .... (202) 225–2671
Chief of Staff.—Caroline Pelot Battles. FAX: 225–7452
Legislative Director.—Jeremy Haldeman.
Communications Director.—Jim Hubbard.
Scheduler.—Rachel Hines.
8764 Manchester Road, Suite 203, St. Louis, MO 63144 .... (314) 962–1523
Communications Director.—Glen Campbell.

Counties: JEFFERSON, SAINTE GENEVIEVE, ST. LOUIS, ST. LOUIS CITY. CITIES: St. Louis. Population (2000), 621,690.

ZIP Codes: 63010, 63012, 63015–16, 63019–20, 63023, 63025–26, 63028, 63030, 63036, 63041, 63047–53, 63057, 63060, 63065–66, 63069–72, 63087, 63102, 63104–05, 63109–11, 63116–19, 63122–30, 63132, 63139, 63143–44, 63151, 63157–58, 63163, 63627–28, 63640, 63645, 63661, 63670, 63673

* * *

FOURTH DISTRICT

IKE SKELTON, Democrat, of Lexington, MO; born in Lexington, December 20, 1931; education: graduated, Lexington High School, 1949; attended Wentworth Military Academy, Lexington; A.B., 1953, LL.B., 1956, University of Missouri; attended University of Edinburgh (Scotland), 1953; professional: lawyer; admitted to the Missouri bar in 1956 and commenced practice in Lexington; prosecuting attorney, Lafayette County, 1957–60; special assistant attorney general, 1961–63; elected, State Senate, 1970; reelected, 1974; member: Phi Beta Kappa honor society, Missouri Bar Association, Lions, Elks, Masons, Boy Scouts, First Christian Church; married the late Susan B. Anding, 1961; three children: Ike, James, and Page; committees: chair, Armed Services; elected to the 95th Congress on November 2, 1976; reelected to each succeeding Congress.

Office Listings

http://www.house.gov/skelton

2206 Rayburn House Office Building, Washington, DC 20515 .... (202) 225–2876
Chief of Staff.—Robert Hagedorn.
Deputy Chief of Staff.—Whitney Frost.
Legislative Director.—Dana O'Brien.
Press Secretary.—Rebecca Loving.
514–B Northwest 7 Highway, Blue Springs, MO 64014 .... (816) 228–4242
Chief of Staff.—Robert Hagedorn.
908 Thompson Boulevard, Sedalia, MO 65301 .... (660) 826–2675
1401 Southwest Boulevard, Jefferson City, MO 65109 .... (573) 635–3499
219 North Adams, Lebanon, MO 65536 .... (417) 532–7964

Counties: BARTON, BATES, BENTON, CAMDEN (part), CASS (part), CEDAR, COLE, DADE, DALLAS, HENRY, HICKORY, JACKSON (part), JOHNSON, LACLEDE, LAFAYETTE, MONITEAU, MORGAN, PETTIS, POLK (part), PULASKI, RAY, SALINE, ST. CLAIR, VERNON, WEBSTER. Population (2000), 621,690.

ZIP Codes: 64001, 64011, 64013–14, 64016–17, 64019–22, 64024, 64029, 64034–37, 64040, 64058, 64061–62, 64067, 64071, 64074–77, 64080, 64082, 64084–86, 64088, 64090, 64093, 64096–97, 64624, 64637, 64668, 64670–71, 64701, 64720, 64722–26, 64728, 64730, 64733, 64735, 64738–48, 64750, 64752, 64755–56, 64759, 64761–63, 64765, 64767, 64769–72, 64776, 64778–81, 64783–84, 64788, 64790, 64832, 64855, 65011, 65018, 65020, 65023, 65025–26, 65032, 65034, 65037–38, 65040, 65042, 65046, 65049–50, 65052–53, 65055, 65065, 65072, 65074, 65076, 65078–79, 65081, 65084, 65101–11, 65287, 65301–02, 65305, 65320–21, 65323–27, 65329–30, 65332–40, 65344–45, 65347–51, 65354–55, 65360, 65452, 65457, 65459, 65461, 65463, 65470, 65473, 65534, 65536, 65543, 65550, 65552, 65556–67, 65572, 65583–84, 65590–91, 65601, 65603–04, 65607, 65632, 65634–36, 65640, 65644, 65646, 65648–50, 65652, 65661–62, 65668, 65674, 65682, 65685, 65706, 65713, 65722, 65724, 65727, 65732, 65735, 65742, 65746, 65752, 65757, 65764, 65767, 65774, 65779, 65783, 65785–87

* * *

FIFTH DISTRICT

EMANUEL CLEAVER II, Democrat, of Kansas City, MO; born in Waxahachie, TX, October 27, 1944; education: M. Div., Saint Paul School of Theology, MO, 1974; B.S., Prairie View A&M University, TX, 1972; professional: Senior Pastor, St. James United Methodist Church; City Councilman, Kansas City, MO, 5th District, 1979–91; founder, Harmony in a World of Difference, 1991; founder, Southern Christian Leadership Conference, Kansas City Chapter; Mayor of Kansas City, MO, 1991–99; member, President-elect Bill Clinton's Transitional Team, 1992; host, Under the Clock, KCUR radio, 1999–2004; first vice chair of the Congressional Black Caucus; married: Dianne; four children; three grandchildren; committees: Financial Services; Homeland Security; Select Committee on Energy Independence and Global Warming; elected to the 109th Congress on November 2, 2004; reelected to each succeeding Congress.

Office Listings

http://www.house.gov/cleaver

1027 Longworth House Office Building, Washington, DC 20515 .... (202) 225–4535
Legislative Director / Chief of Staff.—Leslie Woolley. FAX: 225–4403
Communications Director.—Danny Rotert.
Scheduler.—Brad Benton.
101 West 31st Street, Kansas City, MO 64108 .... (816) 842–4545
District Director.—Geoff Jolley.
211 Maple Avenue, Independence, MO 64050 .... (816) 833–4545

Counties: CASS COUNTY (part), JACKSON COUNTY (part). CITIES AND TOWNSHIPS: Belton, Grandview, Greenwood, Independence, Kansas City, Lee's Summit, Peculiar, Raymore, Raytown, and Sugar Creek. Population (2000), 621,691.

ZIP Codes: 64012, 64014–15, 64029–30, 64034, 64050–58, 64061, 64063–65, 64070, 64075, 64078, 64080–83, 64086, 64101–02, 64105–06, 64108–14, 64120–21, 64123–34, 64136–39, 64141, 64145–49, 64170–71, 64179–80, 64184–85, 64187–88, 64191–94, 64196–99, 64701, 64734, 64944, 64999

* * *

SIXTH DISTRICT

SAM GRAVES, Republican, of Tarkio, MO; born in Fairfax, MO, November 7, 1963; education: B.S., University of Missouri-Columbia, 1986; professional: farmer; organizations: Missouri Farm Bureau; Northwest Missouri State University Agriculture Advisory Committee; University Extension Council; Rotary Club; awards: Associated Industries Voice of Missouri Business Award; Tom Henderson Award; Tarkio Community Betterment Award; Missouri Physical Therapy Association Award; Outstanding Young Farmer Award, 1997; Hero of the Taxpayer Award; NFIB Guardian of Small Business Award; public service: elected to the Missouri House of Representatives, 1992; and the Missouri State Senate, 1994; religion: Baptist; married: Lesley; children: Megan, Emily, and Sam III; committees: ranking member; Small Business; Agriculture; Transportation and Infrastructure; elected to the 107th Congress on November 7, 2000; reelected to each succeeding Congress.

Office Listings

http://www.house.gov/graves

1415 Longworth House Office Building, Washington, DC 20515 .... (202) 225–7041
Chief of Staff.—Tom Brown. FAX: 225–8221
Press Secretary.—Jason Klindt.
201 South Eighth Street, Room 330, St. Joseph, MO 64501 .... (816) 233–9818
113 Blue Jay Drive, Suite 100, Liberty, MO 64068 .... (816) 792–3976

Counties: ANDREW, ATCHISON, BUCHANAN, CALDWELL, CARROLL, CHARITON, CLAY, CLINTON, COOPER, DAVIESS, DEKALB, GENTRY, GRUNDY, HARRISON, HOLT, HOWARD, JACKSON (part), LINN, LIVINGSTON, MERCER, NODAWAY, PLATTE, PUTNAM, SCHUYLER, SULLIVAN, WORTH. Population (2000), 621,690.

ZIP Codes: 63535–36, 63541, 63544–46, 63548, 63551, 63556–57, 63560–61, 63565–67, 64013–16, 64018, 64024, 64028–29, 64048, 64056–58, 64060, 64062, 64064, 64066, 64068–69, 64072–75, 64077, 64079, 64085–88, 64092, 64098, 64116–19, 64144, 64150–58, 64161, 64163–68, 64188, 64190, 64193, 64195, 64243, 64401–02, 64420–24, 64426–34, 64436–49, 64451, 64453–59, 64461, 64463, 64465–71, 64473–77, 64479–94, 64496–99, 64501–08, 64601, 64620, 64622–25, 64628, 64630–33, 64635–61, 64664, 64667–68, 64670–74, 64676, 64679, 64681–83, 64686, 64688–89, 65018, 65025, 65046, 65068, 65081, 65230, 65233, 65236–37, 65246, 65248, 65250, 65254, 65256–57, 65261, 65274, 65276, 65279, 65281, 65286–87, 65301, 65322, 65347–48, 65354

* * *

SEVENTH DISTRICT

ROY BLUNT, Republican, of Springfield, MO; born in Niangua, MO, January 10, 1950; education: B.A. in history, Southwest Baptist University, 1970; M.A. in history, Missouri State University (then Southwest Missouri State University), 1972; professional: president of Southwest Baptist University, 1993–96; author; two-term Missouri Secretary of State; clerk and chief election officer, Greene County, MO; past chair: Missouri Housing Development Commission, Governor's Council on Literacy; past co-chairman, Missouri Opportunity 2000 Commission; past member, Project Democracy Commission for Voter Participation in the United States; board member, American Council of Young Political Leaders; served as first chairman of the Missouri Prison Fellowship; named one of the Ten Outstanding Young Americans, 1986; member, the Travel-Tourism Caucus; married to Abigail Blunt; children: Matt, former Governor of the state of Missouri and Naval reserve officer; Amy, a lawyer in the Kansas City area; Andy, an attorney in Jefferson City; and Charlie, who is four, lives at home with his parents; committees: deputy ranking member, Energy and Commerce; Permanent Select Committee on Intelligence; elected to the 105th Congress; reelected to each succeeding Congress.

Office Listings

http://www.gopwhip.gov http://www.blunt.house.gov

2229 Rayburn House Office Building, Washington, DC 20515 .... (202) 225–6536
Chief of Staff.—Amy Poe. FAX: 225–5604
Deputy Chief of Staff.—Burson Taylor Snyder.
Director of Scheduling.—Richard Eddings.
Legislative Director.—Brain Diffell.
Legislative Assistant.—Kristina Weger.
Legislative Aides: Eric Gustafson, Marshall Kinne.
Assistant Press Secretary.—Meggie Lyzenga.
Staff Assistant.—Tom Brandt.
2740–B East Sunshine, Springfield, MO 65804 .... (417) 889–1800
District Director.—Sharon Nahon.
101 Range Line Road, Box 20, Joplin, MO 64801 .... (417) 781–1041

Counties: BARRY, CHRISTIAN, GREENE, JASPER, LAWRENCE, MCDONALD, NEWTON, POLK (part), STONE, TANEY (part). Population (2000), 621,690.

ZIP Codes: 64748, 64755–56, 64766, 64769, 64801–04, 64830–36, 64840–44, 64847–50, 64853–59, 64861–70, 64873–74, 65603–05, 65608–20, 65622–27, 65629–31, 65633, 65635, 65637–38, 65640–41, 65645–50, 65652–58, 65661, 65663–64, 65666, 65669, 65672–76, 65680–82, 65686, 65702, 65705, 65707–08, 65710, 65712, 65714–15, 65720–21, 65723, 65725–30, 65733–34, 65737–42, 65744–45, 65747, 65752–57, 65759–62, 65765–73, 65781, 65784–85, 65801–10, 65814, 65817, 65890, 65898–99

* * *

EIGHTH DISTRICT

JO ANN EMERSON, Republican, of Cape Girardeau, MO; born in Washington, DC, September 16, 1950; education: B.A., political science, Ohio Wesleyan University, Delaware, OH, 1972; Senior Vice President of Public Affairs, American Insurance Association; director, State Relations and Grassroots Programs, National Restaurant Association; deputy communications director, National Republican Congressional Committee; member: board of directors, Bread for the World; co-chair, board of directors, Congressional Hunger Caucus; PEO Women's Service Group, Cape Girardeau, MO; Copper Dome Society, Southeast Missouri State University; advisory committee, Children's Inn, National Institutes of Health; advisory board, Arneson Institute for Practical Politics and Public Affairs, Ohio Weslyan University; married: Ron Gladney, 2000; children: Victoria and Katharine; six stepchildren: Elizabeth, Abigail, Victoria, Stephanie, Alison, Jessica, and Sam; committees: Appropriations; elected on November 5, 1996, by special election, to the 104th Congress; reelected to each succeeding Congress.

Office Listings

http://www.house.gov/emerson

2440 Rayburn House Office Building, Washington, DC 20515 .... (202) 225–4404
Chief of Staff.—Jeffrey Connor. FAX: 226–0326
Executive Assistant / Scheduler.—Atalie Ebersole.
555 Independence, Suite 1400, Cape Girardeau, MO 63703 .... (573) 335–0101
Chief of Staff.—Josh Haynes.
1301 Kingshighway, Rolla, MO 65401 .... (573) 364–2455

35 Court Square, Suite 300, West Plains, MO 65775 .... (417) 255–1515
22 East Columbia, Farmington, MO 63640 .... (573) 756–9755

Counties: BOLLINGER, BUTLER, CAPE GIRARDEAU, CARTER, CRAWFORD, DENT, DOUGLAS, DUNKLIN, HOWELL, IRON, MADISON, MISSISSIPPI, NEW MADRID, OREGON, OZARK, PEMISCOT, PERRY, PHELPS, REYNOLDS, RIPLEY, ST. FRANÇOIS, SCOTT, SHANNON, STODDARD, TANEY (part), TEXAS, WASHINGTON, WAYNE, WRIGHT. Population (2000), 621,690.

ZIP Codes: 63028, 63030, 63036, 63071, 63080, 63087, 63601, 63620–26, 63628–33, 63636–38, 63640, 63648, 63650–51, 63653–56, 63660, 63662–66, 63674–75, 63701–03, 63730, 63732, 63735–40, 63742–48, 63750–52, 63755, 63758, 63760, 63763–64, 63766–67, 63769–72, 63774–76, 63779–85, 63787, 63801, 63820–30, 63833–34, 63837, 63839–41, 63845–53, 63855, 63857, 63860, 63862–63, 63866–70, 63873–82, 63901–02, 63931–45, 63950–57, 63960–67, 65401–02, 65409, 65436, 65438–41, 65444, 65446, 65449, 65453, 65456, 65459, 65461–62, 65464, 65466, 65468, 65479, 65483–84, 65501, 65529, 65532, 65541–42, 65546, 65548, 65550, 65552, 65555, 65557, 65564–66, 65570–71, 65586, 65588–89, 65606, 65608–09, 65614, 65616, 65618, 65620, 65626–27, 65629, 65637–38, 65652–53, 65655, 65660, 65662, 65666–67, 65676, 65679–80, 65688–90, 65692, 65701–02, 65704, 65711, 65713, 65715, 65717, 65720, 65729, 65731, 65733, 65740–41, 65744, 65746, 65753, 65755, 65759–62, 65766, 65768, 65773, 65775, 65777–78, 65784, 65788–91, 65793

* * *

NINTH DISTRICT

BLAINE LUETKEMEYER, Republican, of St. Elizabeth, MO; born in Jefferson City, MO, May 7, 1952; education: graduate of Lincoln University, Jefferson City, MO, 1974; where he earned a degree with distinction in political science and a minor in business administration, 1999–2005; professional: served as Missouri State Representative and after leaving office was appointed by the governor to serve as the Director of the Missouri Division of Tourism; lifelong member of St. Elizabeth Catholic Church; married: Jackie; committees: Agriculture; Oversight and Government Reform; Small Business; elected to the 111th Congress on November 4, 2008.

Office Listings

http://luetkemeyer.house.gov

1118 Longworth House Office Building, Washington, DC 20515 .... (202) 225–2956
Chief of Staff.—Seth Appleton. FAX: 225–5712
Legislative Assistants: Dan Burgess, Chris Brown, Ali Gabel.
Deputy Press Secretary.—Keith Beardslee.
Office Manager.—Erin Houg.
Staff Assistant.—Laura Hardecke.
3610 Buttonwood Drive, Suite 200, Columbia, MO 65201 .... (573) 886–8929
District Director.—Gary Marble FAX: 886–8901
Press Secretary.—Paul Sloca.
Director of Constituent Affairs.—Keri Dozier.
Caseworkers: Amy Blair, Jessica Hoskins.
516 Jefferson Street, Washington, MO 63090 .... (636) 239–2276
Deputy District Director.—Dan Engemann. FAX 239–0478
201 North Third Street, Suite 120, Hannibal, MO 63401 .... (573) 231–1012
Field Representative.—Tanner Smith. FAX: 231–1014

Counties: ADAIR, AUDRAIN, BOONE, CALLAWAY, CAMDEN (part), CLARK, CRAWFORD, FRANKLIN, GASCONADE, KNOX, LEWIS, MACON, MARIES, MARION, MILLER, MONROE, MONTGOMERY, OSAGE, PIKE, RALLS, RANDOLPH, ST. CHARLES (part), SCOTLAND, SHELBY, WARREN. Population (2000), 621,690.

ZIP Codes: 63005, 63013–15, 63037, 63039, 63041, 63055–56, 63060, 63068–69, 63072–73, 63077, 63079–80, 63084, 63089–91, 63303–04, 63330, 63332–34, 63336, 63339, 63341–42, 63344–45, 63348–53, 63357, 63359, 63361, 63363, 63365–67, 63376, 63378, 63381–85, 63388, 63390, 63401, 63430–43, 63445–48, 63450–54, 63456–69, 63471–74, 63501, 63530–34, 63536–40, 63543–44, 63546–47, 63549, 63552, 63555, 63557–59, 63563, 64631, 64658, 64856, 65001, 65010, 65013–14, 65016–17, 65024, 65026, 65031–32, 65035–36, 65039–41, 65043, 65047–49, 65051, 65054, 65058–59, 65061–67, 65069, 65072, 65074–77, 65080, 65082–83, 65085, 65101, 65201–03, 65205, 65211–12, 65215–18, 65230–32, 65239–40, 65243–44, 65247, 65251, 65255–60, 65262–65, 65270, 65275, 65278–85, 65299, 65337, 65441, 65443, 65446, 65449, 65452–53, 65456, 65459, 65486, 65535, 65559–60, 65565, 65580, 65582, 65586, 65591

MONTANA

(Population 2000, 902,195)

SENATORS

MAX BAUCUS, Democrat, of Helena, MT; born in Helena, December 11, 1941; education: graduated, Helena High School, 1959; B.A. in economics, Stanford University, 1964; LL.B., Stanford University Law School, 1967; attorney, Civil Aeronautics Board, 1967–71; attorney, George and Baucus law firm, Missoula, MT; member, Montana and District of Columbia bar associations; served in Montana House of Representatives, 1973–74; one child, Zeno; committees: chair, Finance; vice chair, Joint Committee on Taxation; Agriculture, Nutrition, and Forestry; Environment and Public Works; elected to the 94th Congress, November 5, 1974; reelected to the 95th Congress; elected to the U.S. Senate, November 7, 1978, for the six-year term beginning January 3, 1979; subsequently appointed on December 15, 1978, to fill the vacancy caused by the resignation of Senator Paul Hatfield; reelected to each succeeding Senate term.

Office Listings

http://baucus.senate.gov

511 Hart Senate Office Building, Washington, DC 20510 .... (202) 224–2651
Chief of Staff.—Jon Selib. FAX: 224–0515
Legislative Director.—Paul Wilkins.
Press Secretary.—Ty Matsdorf.
DC Scheduler.—Lisa Stark.
222 North 32nd Street, Suite 100, Billings, MT 59101 .... (406) 657–6790
32 East Babcock, Room 114, Bozeman, MT 59715 .... (406) 586–6104
125 West Granite, Butte, MT 59701 .... (406) 782–8700
113 3rd Street North, Great Falls, MT 59401 .... (406) 761–1574
30 West 14th Street, Helena, MT 59601 .... (406) 449–5480
8 Third Street East, Kalispell, MT 59901 .... (406) 756–1150
280 East Front Street, Missoula, MT 59801 .... (406) 329–3123
122 West Town Street, Glendive, MT 59330 .... (406) 365–7002
State Chief of Staff.—Barrett Kaiser. (800) 332–6106

* * *

JON TESTER, Democrat, of Big Sandy, MT; born in Havre, MT, August 21, 1956; education: graduated, Big Sandy High School, 1974; B.S. in Music, University of Great Falls, 1978; professional: farmer, T-Bone Farms, Big Sandy, 1978–present; teacher, Big Sandy School District, 1978–80; member, Big Sandy Soil Conservation Service Committee, 1980–83; chairman, Big Sandy School Board of Trustees, 1983–92; Past Master, Treasure Lodge #95 of the Masons; member, Chouteau County Agricultural Stabilization and Conservation Service Committee, 1990–95; member, Organic Crop Improvement Association, 1996–97; served in Montana Senate, 1999–2007; Montana Senate Democratic Whip, 2001–03; Montana Senate Democratic Leader, 2003–05; Montana Senate President, 2005–07; vice chair, Congressional Sportsmen's Caucus; married: the former Sharla Bitz; two children: Christine and Shon; committees: Appropriations; Banking, Housing, and Urban Affairs; Homeland Security and Governmental Affairs; Indian Affairs; Veterans' Affairs; elected to the U.S. Senate on November 7, 2006.

Office Listings

http://tester.senate.gov

204 Russell Senate Office Building, Washington, DC 20510 .... (202) 224–2644
Chief of Staff.—Stephanie Schriock. FAX: 224–8594
Deputy Chief of Staff.—Bridget Walsh
Deputy Legislative Director.—James Wise.
Communications Director.—Matt McKenna.
Director of Scheduling.—Gina Ormand.
Granite Tower, 222 North 32nd Street, Suite 101, Billings, MT 59101 .... (406) 252–0550
211 Haggerty Lane, Bozeman, MT 59715 .... (406) 586–4450
Silver Bow Center, 125 West Granite, Suite 200, Butte, MT 59701 .... (406) 723–3277
122 West Towne, Glendine, MT 59330 .... (406) 365–2391
321 First Avenue North, Great Falls, MT 59401 .... (406) 452–9585
Capital One Center, 208 North Montana Avenue, Suite 202, Helena, MT 59601 .... (406) 449–5401
State Director.—Bill Lombardi.
1845 Highway 93 South, Suite 210, Kalispell, MT 59901 .... (406) 257–3360
116 West Front Street, Missoula, MT 59801 .... (406) 728–3003
Deputy State Director.—Dayna Swanson.

REPRESENTATIVE

AT LARGE

DENNY REHBERG, Republican, of Billings, MT; born in Billings, October 5, 1955; education: B.A., Washington State University, 1977; professional: rancher; public service: interned in the Montana State Senate, 1977–79; legislative assistant to Rep. Ron Marlenee (R–MT), 1979–82; elected to the Montana House of Representatives, 1984; appointed Lt. Governor of Montana in 1991; elected Lt. Governor in 1992; chairman, Drought Advisory Committee; Worker's Compensation Task Force; and the Montana Rural Development Council; Republican nominee for the U.S. Senate, 1996; married: Janice; children: A.J., Katie, and Elsie; committees: Appropriations; elected to the 107th Congress on November 7, 2000; reelected to each succeeding Congress.

Office Listings

http://www.rehberg.house.gov

2448 Rayburn House Office Building, Washington, DC 20515 .... (202) 225–3211
Chief of Staff.—Jay Martin. FAX: 225–5687
Communications Director.—Jed Link.
1201 Grand Avenue, Suite 101, Billings, MT 59102 .... (406) 256–1019
District Director.—Dustin Frost.
105 Smelter Avenue, NE., Suite 116, Great Falls, MT 59404 .... (406) 454–1066
950 North Montana Avenue, Helena, MT 59601 .... (406) 443–7878
301 East Broadway, Suite 2, Missoula, MT 59802 .... (406) 543–9550

Counties: BEAVERHEAD, BIG HORN, BLAINE, BROADWATER, CARBON, CARTER, CASCADE, CHOUTEAU, CUSTER, DANIELS, DAWSON, DEER LODGE, FALLON, FERGUS, FLATHEAD, GALLATIN, GARFIELD, GLACIER, GOLDEN VALLEY, GRANITE, HILL, JEFFERSON, JUDITH BASIN, LAKE, LEWIS AND CLARK, LIBERTY, LINCOLN, MADISON, MCCONE, MEAGHER, MINERAL, MISSOULA, MUSSELLSHELL PARK, PETROLEUM, PHILLIPS, PONDERA, POWDER RIVER, POWELL, PRAIRIE, RAVALLI, RICHLAND, ROOSEVELT, ROSEBUD, SANDERS, SHERIDAN, SILVER BOW, STILLWATER, SWEET GRASS, TETON, TOOLE, TREASURE, VALLEY, WHEATLAND, WIBAUX, YELLOWSTONE. Population (2000), 902,195.

ZIP Codes: 59001–04, 59006–08, 59010–16, 59018–20, 59022, 59024–39, 59041, 59043–44, 59046–47, 59050, 59052–55, 59057–59, 59061–72, 59074–79, 59081–89, 59101–08, 59201, 59211–15, 59217–19, 59221–23, 59225–26, 59230–31, 59240–44, 59247–48, 59250, 59252–63, 59270, 59273–76, 59301, 59311–19, 59322–24, 59326–27, 59330, 59332–33, 59336–39, 59341, 59343–45, 59347, 59349, 59351, 59353–54, 59401–06, 59410–12, 59414, 59416–22, 59424–25, 59427, 59430, 59432–36, 59440–48, 59450–54, 59456–57, 59460–69, 59471–72, 59474, 59477, 59479–80, 59482–87, 59489, 59501, 59520–32, 59535, 59537–38, 59540, 59542, 59544–47, 59601–02, 59604, 59620, 59623–24, 59626, 59631–36, 59638–45, 59647–48, 59701–03, 59710–11, 59713–22, 59724–25, 59727–33, 59735–36, 59739–41, 59743, 59745–52, 59754–56, 59758–62, 59771–73, 59801–04, 59806–08, 59812, 59820–21, 59823–35, 59837, 59840–48, 59851, 59853–56, 59858–60, 59863–68, 59870–75, 59901, 59903–04, 59910–23, 59925–37

NEBRASKA

(Population 2000, 1,711,263)

SENATORS

BEN NELSON, Democrat, of Omaha, NE; born in McCook, NE, May 17, 1941; education: B.A., 1963, M.A., 1965, J.D., 1970, University of Nebraska, Lincoln, NE; honorary degrees, Creighton University, 1992; Peru State College, 1993; College of Saint Mary, 1995; Midland Lutheran College, 1998; Dana College, 1999; professional: attorney; Director, Nebraska Department of Insurance; President and CEO of the Central National Insurance Group; Executive Vice President and Chief of Staff of the National Association of Insurance Commissioners; Kennedy, Holland, DeLacy, and Svoboda (law firm); Governor of Nebraska, 1991–99; awards: American Legislative Exchange Council, Thomas Jefferson Freedom Award; National Guard, Charles Dick Medal of Merit; American Legion, Nebraska Chapter, Outstanding Service and Assistance to Veterans; Business Industry Political Action Committee, Adam Smith Award; U.S. Chamber of Commerce, Spirit of Enterprise Awards; National Association of Manufacturers, Award for Manufacturing Legislative Excellence; Independent Bankers Association, Hon. Horst G. Denk Congressional Award; Small Business Survival Committee Award; National Association of Mutual Insurance Companies, Benjamin Franklin Public Policy Award; Coalition for Medicare Choices, Leadership Award; American Hospital Association, Appreciation for Distinguished Leadership; National Rural Health Association, Rural Health Champion Award; Nebraska Rural Health Association, President's Award; Madonna Rehabilitation Hospital, Madonna Spirit Award; American Network of Community Options and Resources, Congressional Award; American Association of Community Colleges' Council for Resource Development, Congressional Award; Nebraska Investment Finance Authority, Housing Champion Award; National Council for Adaption, Hall of Fame Award; Indian American Friendship Council, Recognition of Service Award; Pheasants Forever, Conservation Service Award; Renewable Energy Alliance, Renewable Energy Leadership Award; American Farm Bureau, Friend of Farm Bureau Award; National Farmers Union, Presidential Award for Leadership and Golden Triangle Awards; Agricultural Retailers Association, Legislator of the Year; Nebraska Wheat Growers Association; Man of the Year Award; Water Systems Council, Wellcare Leadership Award; University of Nebraska Alumni Association, Founders Medallion Award; George W. Norris Award; Nebraska Broadcasters Association, Friend of Nebraska Broadcasters Award; Governors' Ethanol Coalition Award; Nebraska Groundwater Foundation Achievement Award; National Insurance Regulatory Examiners Society, Schrader-Nelson Award; National Eagle Scout Association, Distinguished Eagle Award; married: Diane; four children; committees: Agriculture, Nutrition, and Forestry; Appropriations; Armed Services; Rules and Administration; elected to the U.S. Senate on November 7, 2000; reelected to each succeeding Senate term.

Office Listings

http://bennelson.senate.gov

720 Hart Senate Office Building, Washington, DC 20510	(202) 224–6551
Chief of Staff.—Tim Becker.	FAX: 228–0012
Communications Director.—Jake Thompson.	
Scheduler.—Melanie Rogge.	
Legislative Director.—Christina Gallagher.	
440 North Eighth Street, Suite 120, Lincoln, NE 68508	(402) 441–4600
7602 Pacific Street, Suite 205, Omaha, NE 68114	(402) 391–3411
P.O. Box 1472, Scottsbluff, NE 69361	(308) 631–7614
P.O. Box 2105, Kearney, NE 68848	(308) 293–5818
P.O. Box 791, South Sioux City, NE 68776	(402) 209–3595

* * *

MIKE JOHANNS, Republican, of Omaha, NE; born in Osage, IA, June 18, 1950; education: B.A., St. Mary's College, Winona, MN, 1971; J.D., Creighton University, Omaha, NE, 1974; professional: Lancaster County Board, 1983–87; Lincoln City Council, 1989–91; Mayor of Lincoln, 1991–98; Nebraska Governor, 1999–2005; Secretary of Agriculture, 2005–2007; Senate Community College Caucus, Senate Impact Aid Coalition, Rural Health Caucus, Congressional Heart and Stroke Coalition, Parkinson's Action Network, Army Caucus, Air Force Caucus, Senate Cultural Caucus; Congressional Vision Caucus; Farmer Cooperative Caucus; religion: Catholic; married: Stephanie Johanns; two children, five grandchildren; committees: Agriculture, Nutrition, and Forestry; Banking, Housing, and Urban Affairs; Commerce, Science and Transportation; Indian Affairs; Veterans' Affairs; elected to the U.S. Senate on November 4, 2008.

Office Listings

http://johanns.senate.gov

404 Russell Senate Office Building, Washington, DC 20510 .... (202) 224–4224
Chief of Staff.—Terri Moore. FAX: 224–0436
Legislative Director.—Terry Van Doren.
Press Secretary.—Sarah Pompei.
Administrative Director.—Cherri Carpenter.
294 Federal Building, 100 Centennial Mall, North, Lincoln, NE 68508 .... (402) 476–1400
State Director.—Nancy Johner.
9900 Nicholas Street, Suite 325, Omaha, NE 68114 .... (402) 758–8981
4111 Fourth Avenue, Suite 26, Kearney, NE 68845 .... (308) 236–7473
115 Railway Street, Suite C102, Scottsbluff, NE 69361 .... (308) 632–6032

REPRESENTATIVES

FIRST DISTRICT

JEFF FORTENBERRY, Republican, of Lincoln, NE; born in Baton Rouge, LA, December 27, 1960; education: B.A., Louisiana State University, 1978; M.P.P., Georgetown University, Washington, DC, 1986; M. Div., Franciscan University, Steubenville, Ohio, 1996; professional: Lincoln City Council, 1997–2001; publishing executive; worked as economist; managed a public relations firm; congressional aide for the Senate Subcommittee on Intergovernmental Relations; family: married to Celeste Gregory; children: five; committees: Agriculture; Foreign Affairs; Oversight and Government Reform; elected to the 109th Congress on November 2, 2004; reelected to each succeeding Congress.

Office Listings

http://www.fortenberry.house.gov

1535 Longworth House Office Building, Washington, DC 20515 .... (202) 225–4806
Chief of Staff.—Kelly Lungren-McCollum. FAX: 225–5686
Legislative Director.—Alan Feyerherm.
Press Secretary.—Josh Moenning.
Scheduler.—Andrea Ahrens.
301 South 13th Street, Suite 100, Lincoln, NE 68508 .... (402) 438–1598
629 North Broad Street, P.O. Box 377, Fremont, NE 68025 .... (402) 727–0888
125 South 4th Street, Suite 101, Norfolk, NE 68701 .... (402) 379–2064

Counties: BURT, BUTLER, CASS, CEDAR (part), COLFAX, CUMING, DAKOTA, DIXON, DODGE, GAGE, JOHNSON, LANCASTER, MADISON, NEMAHA, OTOE, PAWNEE, RICHARDSON, SARPY (part), THURSTON, WASHINGTON, WAYNE. Population (2000), 570,421.

ZIP Codes: 68001–04, 68007–09, 68014–20, 68023, 68025–26, 68028–31, 68033–34, 68036–42, 68044–48, 68050, 68055, 68057–59, 68061–68, 68070–73, 68112, 68122–23, 68133, 68136, 68138, 68142, 68144, 68152, 68301, 68304–05, 68307, 68309–10, 68313–14, 68316–21, 68323–24, 68328–33, 68336–37, 68339, 68341–49, 68351, 68355, 68357–60, 68364, 68366–68, 68371–72, 68376, 68378, 68380–82, 68401–05, 68407, 68409–10, 68413–15, 68417–24, 68428, 68430–31, 68433–34, 68437–39, 68441–43, 68445–48, 68450, 68452–58, 68460–67, 68501–10, 68512, 68514, 68516, 68520–24, 68526, 68528–29, 68532, 68542, 68583, 68588, 68601, 68621, 68624, 68626, 68629, 68631–33, 68635, 68641–44, 68648–49, 68658–59, 68661–62, 68666–67, 68669, 68701–02, 68710, 68715–17, 68723–24, 68727–28, 68731–33, 68739–41, 68743, 68745, 68747–49, 68751–52, 68757–58, 68767–68, 68770–71, 68776, 68779, 68781, 68784–85, 68787–88, 68790–92

* * *

SECOND DISTRICT

LEE TERRY, Republican, of Omaha, NE; born in Omaha, January 29, 1962; education: B.A., University of Nebraska, 1984; J.D., Creighton Law School, 1987; attorney; elected to the Omaha, NE, City Council, 1990–98; served as vice president and president, and on the audit, legislative, and cable television committees; religion: Christian; married: Robyn; children: Nolan, Ryan, and Jack; committees: Energy and Commerce; elected to the 106th Congress; reelected to each succeeding Congress.

Office Listings

http://www.leeterry.house.gov

2331 Rayburn House Office Building, Washington, DC 20515 .... (202) 225–4155

Chief of Staff.—Eric Hultman. FAX: 226–5452
Legislative Director.—Brad Schweer.
Appointment Secretary.—Sarah Tuma.
Press Secretary.—Lisa Ellis.
11717 Burt Street, Suite 106, Omaha, NE 68154 .... (402) 397–9944
District Director.—Molly Koozer-Lloyd.

Counties: DOUGLAS, SARPY (part). CITIES: Bellevue, Bennington, Boys Town, Elkhorn, Gretna, La Vista, Omaha, Offutt AFB, Papillion, Plattsmouth, Ralston, Springfield, Valley, and Waterloo. Population (2007), 620,000.

ZIP Codes: 68005, 68007, 68010, 68022, 68028, 68046, 68056, 68064, 68069, 68101–14, 68116–20, 68122–24, 68127–28, 68130–35, 68137–39, 68142, 68144–45, 68147, 68152, 68154–55, 68157, 68164, 68175–76, 68178–80, 68182–83, 68197–98

* * *

THIRD DISTRICT

ADRIAN SMITH, Republican, of Gering, NE; born in Scotts Bluff, NE, December 19, 1970; education: graduated from Gering High School, Gering, NE, 1989; attended Liberty University, Lynchburg, VA; 1989–90; B.S., University of Nebraska, 1993; professional: business owner; teacher; Gering, NE, city council, 1994–98; member of the Nebraska state legislature, 1999–2007; committees: Agriculture; Natural Resources; Science and Technology; elected to the 110th Congress on November 7, 2006; reelected to the 111th Congress on November 4, 2008.

Office Listings

http://adriansmith.house.gov

503 Cannon House Office Building, Washington, DC 20515 .... (202) 225–6435
Chief of Staff.—Jeff Shapiro. FAX: 225–0207
Legislative Director.—Monica Jirik.
Press Secretary.—Charles Isom.
Scheduler.—Jena Hoehne.
416 Valley View Drive, Suite 600, Scottsbluff, NE 69361 .... (308) 633–6333
1811 West Second Street, Suite 105, Grand Island, NE 68803 .... (308) 384–3900

Counties: ADAMS, ANTELOPE, ARTHUR, BANNER, BLAINE, BOONE, BOX BUTTE, BOYD, BROWN, BUFFALO, CEDAR (part), CHASE, CHERRY, CHEYENNE, CLAY, CUSTER, DAWES, DAWSON, DEUEL, DUNDY, FILLMORE, FRANKLIN, FRONTIER, FURNAS, GARDEN, GARFIELD, GOSPER, GRANT, GREELEY, HALL, HAMILTON, HARLAN, HAYES, HITCHCOCK, HOLT, HOOKER, HOWARD, JEFFERSON, KEARNEY, KEITH, KEYA PAHA, KIMBALL, KNOX, LINCOLN, LOGAN, LOUP, MCPHERSON, MERRICK, MORRILL, NANCE, NUCKOLLS, PERKINS, PHELPS, PIERCE, PLATTE, POLK, RED WILLOW, ROCK, SALINE, SCOTTS BLUFF, SHERIDAN, SHERMAN, SIOUX, THAYER, THOMAS, VALLEY, WEBSTER, WHEELER, YORK. Population (2000), 570,421.

ZIP Codes: 68303, 68310, 68313, 68315–16, 68319, 68322, 68325–27, 68333, 68335, 68338–43, 68350–52, 68354, 68359, 68361–62, 68365, 68367, 68370–71, 68375, 68377, 68401, 68405–06, 68416, 68423–24, 68429, 68436, 68440, 68444–45, 68452–53, 68460, 68464–65, 68467, 68601–02, 68620–23, 68627–28, 68631, 68634, 68636–38, 68640, 68642–44, 68647, 68651–55, 68658, 68660, 68662–66, 68701, 68711, 68713–14, 68717–20, 68722–27, 68729–30, 68734–36, 68738–39, 68742, 68746–48, 68752–53, 68755–56, 68758–61, 68763–67, 68769, 68771, 68773–74, 68777–78, 68780–81, 68783, 68786, 68789, 68792, 68801–03, 68810, 68812–18, 68820–28, 68831–38, 68840–50, 68852–56, 68858–66, 68869–76, 68878–79, 68881–83, 68901–02, 68920, 68922–30, 68932–50, 68952, 68954–61, 68964, 68966–67, 68969–82, 69001, 69020–30, 69032–34, 69036–46, 69101, 69103, 69120–23, 69125, 69127–35, 69138, 69140–57, 69160–63, 69165–71, 69190, 69201, 69210–12, 69214, 69216–21, 69301, 69331, 69333–37, 69339–41, 69343, 69345–48, 69350–58, 69360–61, 69363, 69365–67

NEVADA

(Population 2000, 1,998,257)

SENATORS

HARRY REID, Democrat, of Searchlight, NV; born in Searchlight, December 2, 1939; education: graduated, Basic High School, Henderson, NV, 1957; associate degree in science, Southern Utah State College, 1959; B.S., Utah State University, Phi Kappa Phi, 1961; J.D., George Washington School of Law, Washington, DC, 1964; admitted to the Nevada State bar in 1963, a year before graduating from law school; while attending law school, worked as a U.S. Capitol police officer; city attorney, Henderson, 1964–66; member and chairman, South Nevada Memorial Hospital Board of Trustees, 1967–69; elected: Nevada State Assembly, 1969–70; Lieutenant Governor, State of Nevada, 1970–74; served, executive committee, National Conference of Lieutenant Governors; chairman, Nevada Gaming Commission, 1977–81; member: Nevada State, Clark County and American bar associations; married the former Landra Gould in 1959; five children: Lana, Rory, Leif, Josh, and Key; elected to the 98th Congress on November 2, 1982, and reelected to the 99th Congress; Assistant Democratic Leader, 1998–2004; elected Democratic leader for the 109th Congress, and Majority leader for the 110th Congress; elected to the U.S. Senate on November 4, 1986; reelected to each succeeding Senate term.

Office Listings

http://reid.senate.gov

522 Hart Senate Office Building, Washington, DC 20510 .... (202) 224–3542
Chief of Staff.—Gary Myrick. FAX: 224–7327
Deputy Chief of Staff: David McCallum.
Executive Assistant.—Janice Shelton.
Legislative Director.—Dayle Cristinzio.
600 East Williams Street, Room 302, Carson City, NV 89701 .... (775) 882–7343
Office Director.—Yolanda Garcia.
333 Las Vegas Boulevard South, Suite 8016, Las Vegas, NV 89101 .... (702) 388–5020
Office Director.—Shannon Raborn.
400 S. Virginia Street, Suite 902, Reno, NV 89501 .... (775) 686–5750
District Manager.—Mary Conelly.

* * *

JOHN ENSIGN, Republican, of Las Vegas, NV; born in Roseville, CA, March 25, 1958; education: E.W. Clark High School, Las Vegas, NV, 1976; B.S., University of Nevada at Las Vegas, 1976–79; Oregon State University, 1981; Colorado State University, 1985; professional: veterinarian; organizations: Las Vegas Southwest Rotary; Las Vegas Chamber of Commerce; Sigma Chi (fraternal organization); Meadows Christian Fellowship; married: Darlene Ensign, 1987; children: Trevor, Siena, and Michael; committees: Budget; Commerce, Science, and Transportation; Finance; Homeland Seurity and Governmental Affairs; Rules and Administration; elected to the U.S. House of Representatives in 1994; reelected in 1996; elected to the U.S. Senate on November 7, 2000; reelected to each succeeding Senate term.

Office Listings

http://ensign.senate.gov

119 Russell Senate Office Building, Washington, DC 20510 .... (202) 224–6244
Chief of Staff.—Aaron Cohen. FAX: 228–2193
Scheduler.—Rachel Roberts.
Legislative Director.—Pam Thiessen.
Communications Director.—Rebeca Fisher.
333 Las Vegas Boulevard South, Suite 8203, Las Vegas, NV 89101 .... (702) 388–6605
State Director.—Sonja Joya.
600 East William Street, Suite 304, Carson City, NV 89701 .... (775) 885–9111
Rural Coordinator.—Kevin Kirkeby.
400 South Virginia Street, Suite 738, Reno, NV 89501 .... (775) 686–5770

REPRESENTATIVES

FIRST DISTRICT

SHELLEY BERKLEY, Democrat, of Las Vegas, NV; born in New York, NY, January 20, 1951; education: graduate of Clark County, NV, public school system; B.A., University of

Nevada at Las Vegas, 1972; J.D., University of San Diego School of Law, 1976; professional: attorney; Nevada State Assembly, 1982–84; former deputy director, Nevada State Commerce Department; hotel executive; vice-chair, Nevada University and Community College System Board of Regents, 1990–98; has served on numerous civic, business, and professional organizations; married: Larry Lehrner; children: Max Berkley and Sam Berkley; committees: Foreign Affairs; Ways and Means; elected to the 106h Congress; reelected to each succeeding Congress.

Office Listings

http://www.house.gov/berkley

405 Cannon House Office Building, Washington, DC 20515 .... (202) 225–5965
Chief of Staff.—Richard Urey. FAX: 225–3119
Legislative Director.—Bryan George.
Communications Director.—David Cherry.
Scheduler.—Joanne Jensen.
2340 Paseo Del Prado, Suite D–106, Las Vegas, NV 89102 .... (702) 220–9823
District Director.—Tod Story.

Counties: CLARK COUNTY (part). CITIES: Las Vegas, and North Las Vegas. Population (2000), 666,088.

ZIP Codes: 89030–33, 89036, 89084, 89086, 89101–04, 89106–10, 89114–17, 89119, 89121–22, 89125–35, 89137, 89142–46, 89149–56, 89160, 89170, 89177, 89185, 89193

* * *

SECOND DISTRICT

DEAN HELLER, Republican, of Carson City, NV; born in Castro Valley, CA, May 10, 1960; education: B.B.A., specializing in finance and securities analysis, University of Southern California, 1985; institutional stockbroker and broker/trader on the Pacific Stock Exchange; Chief Deputy State Treasurer, Public Funds Representative; Nevada State Assemblyman, 1990–94; Secretary of State, 1994–2002; Founding Board Member of the Boys and Girls Club of Western Nevada and the Western Nevada Community College Foundation; Advisory Board Member for Nevada's Foster Grandparent program; married: Lynne Heller; children: Hilary, Harris, Drew and Emmy; committees: Ways and Means; elected to the 110th Congress on November 7, 2006; reelected to the 111th Congress on November 4, 2008.

Office Listings

125 Cannon House Office Building, Washington, DC 20515 .... (202) 225–6155
Chief of Staff.—Mac Abrams. FAX: 225–5679
Legislative Director.—Greg Facchiano.
Press Secretary.—Stewart Bybee.
Scheduler.—Mari Naskashima.
400 South Virginia Street, Suite 502, Reno, NV 89501 .... (775) 686–5760
District Director.—Ashley Carrigan.
600 Las Vegas Boulevard South, Suite 680, Las Vegas, NV 89101 .... (702) 255–1651
405 Idaho Street, Suite 502, Elko, NV 89801 .... (775) 777–7920

Counties: CARSON CITY, CHURCHILL, CLARK (part), DOUGLAS, ELKO, ESMERALDA, EUREKA, HUMBOLDT, LANDER, LINCOLN, LYON, MINERAL, NYE, PERSHING, STOREY, WASHOE, WHITE PINE. Population (2000), 666,087.

ZIP Codes: 89001, 89003, 89008, 89010, 89013, 89017, 89019–24, 89026–27, 89030–31, 89041–43, 89045, 89047–49, 89052, 89060–61, 89115, 89124, 89137, 89139, 89141, 89156, 89191, 89301, 89310–11, 89314–19, 89402–15, 89418–36, 89438–40, 89442, 89444–52, 89460, 89496, 89501–07, 89509–13, 89515, 89520–21, 89523, 89533, 89557, 89570, 89701–06, 89711–14, 89721, 89801–03, 89815, 89820–26, 89828, 89830–32, 89834–35, 89883

* * *

THIRD DISTRICT

DINA TITUS, Democrat, of Las Vegas, NV; born in Thomasville, GA, May 23, 1950; education: B.A., College of William and Mary, 1970; M.A., University of Georgia, 1973; Ph.D., Florida State University, 1976; professional: professor, University of Nevada, Las Vegas; public service: Nevada State Senator, 1989–2008; Minority Leader, 1993–2008; religion: Greek Orthodox; married: Thomas C. Wright, Ph.D.; committees: Education and Labor; Homeland Security; Transportation and Infrastructure; elected to the 111th Congress on November 4, 2008.

Office Listings

http://www.titus.house.gov

319 Cannon House Office Building, Washington, DC 20515 .... (202) 225–3252
Chief of Staff.—Jay Gertsema. FAX: 225–2185
Legislative Director.—Karen Agostisi.
Communications Director.—Andrew Stoddard.
Scheduler.—Megan Chambers.
8215 South Eastern Avenue, Suite 205, Las Vegas, NV 89123 .... (702) 387–4941
District Director.—Dan Giraldo.

Counties: CLARK COUNTY (part). Population (2000), 666,082.

ZIP Codes: 89004–05, 89007, 89009, 89011–12, 89014–16, 89018, 89025, 89028–30, 89039–40, 89046, 89052–53, 89070, 89074, 89077, 89101–4, 89108–11, 89113, 89117–24, 89128–29, 89134–36, 89138–39, 89141–42, 89146–49, 89156, 89159, 89162–63, 89170, 89173, 89177, 89180, 89185, 89191, 89193, 89195, 89199

NEW HAMPSHIRE

(Population 2000, 1,235,786)

SENATORS

JUDD GREGG, Republican, of Rye, NH; born in Nashua, NH, February 14, 1947; education: graduated Phillips Exeter Academy, 1965; A.B., Columbia University, New York City, 1969; J.D., 1972, and LL.M., 1975, Boston University; professional: attorney; admitted to the New Hampshire bar, 1972; commenced practice in Nashua, NH; practiced law, 1975–80; member, Governor's Executive Council, 1978–80; elected Governor of New Hampshire, 1988–92; married to the former Kathleen MacLellan, 1973; three children: Molly, Sarah, and Joshua; committees: ranking member, Budget; Appropriations; Banking, Housing, and Urban Affairs; Health, Education, Labor, and Pensions; elected to the 97th Congress, November 4, 1980, and reelected to the 98th–100th Congresses; elected to the U.S. Senate on November 3, 1992; reelected to each succeeding Senate term.

Office Listings

http://gregg.senate.gov

393 Russell Senate Office Building, Washington, DC 20510 .... (202) 224–3324
Chief of Staff.—Alyssa Shooshan. FAX: 224–4952
Administrative Assistant.—Christopher Gahan.
Communications Director.—Andrea Wuebker.
Scheduler.—Erin Wall.
125 North Main Street, Concord, NH 03301 .... (603) 225–7115
41 Hooksett Road, Unit #2, Manchester, NH 03104 .... (603) 622–7979
16 Pease Boulevard, Portsmouth, NH 03801 .... (603) 431–2171
60 Pleasant Street, Berlin, NH 03570 .... (603) 752–2604

* * *

JEANNE SHAHEEN, Democrat, of Madbury, NH; born in Saint Charles, MO, January 28, 1947; education: graduated, Selinsgrove Area High School, Selinsgrove, PA, 1965; B.A., Shippensburg University, Shippensburg, PA, 1969; M.S.S., University of Mississippi, 1973; professional: high school teacher; co-owner of a small retail business; consultant; New Hampshire State Senator; Governor of New Hampshire; Director of Harvard's Institute of Politics; married: William Shaheen; three children: Stefany, Stacey, and Molly; Commission on Security and Cooperation in Europe; committees: Foreign Relations; Energy and Natural Resources; Small Business and Entrepreneurship; elected to the 111th U.S. Senate on November 4, 2008.

Office Listings

http://shaheen.senate.gov

520 Hart Senate Office Building, Washington, DC 20510 .... (202) 224–2841
Chief of Staff.—Maura Keefe.
Deputy Chief of Staff.—Jessie Lyons.
Legislative Director.—Michael Yudin.
Communications Director.—Colleen Murray.
Scheduler.—Justin Burkhardt.
Counsel.—Judy Reardon.
1589 Elm Street, Suite 3, Manchester, NH 03101 .... (603) 647–7500
60 Main Street, Nashua, NH 03060 .... (603) 883–0196
340 Central Avenue, Suite 205, Dover, NH 03820 .... (603) 750–3004
50 Opera House Square, Claremont, NH 03743 .... (603) 542–4872

REPRESENTATIVES

FIRST DISTRICT

CAROL SHEA-PORTER, Democrat, of Rochester, NH; born in New York City, NY; December, 1952; education: graduated from Oyster River High School, Durham, NH, 1971; B.A., University of New Hampshire, Durham, NH, 1975; M.P.A., University of New Hampshire, Durham, NH, 1979; professional: social worker; professor; married: Gene; two children; committees: Armed Services; Education and Labor; Natural Resources; elected to the 110th Congress on November 7, 2006; reelected to the 111th Congress on November 4, 2008.

Office Listings

http://www.shea-porter.house.gov

1330 Longworth House Office Building, Washington, DC 20515 .... (202) 225–5456
FAX: 225–5822
Chief of Staff.—Mike Brown.
Legislative Director.—Robert Mollen.
Communications Director.—Jamie Radice.
Scheduler.—Naomi Andrews.
33 Lowell Street, Manchester, NH, 03101 .... (603) 641–9536
104 Washington Street, Dover, NH, 03820 .... (603) 743–4813

Counties: BELKNAP (part), CARROLL, HILLSBOROUGH (part), ROCKINGHAM, STAFFORD. CITIES: Bedford, Conway, Derry, Dover, Exeter, Goffstown, Laconia, Londonderry, Manchester, Merrimack, Portsmouth, and Rochester. Population (2000), 617,575.

ZIP Codes: 03032, 03034, 03036–38, 03040–42, 03044–45, 03053–54, 03077, 03101–06, 03108–11, 03218, 03220, 03225–27, 03237, 03246–47, 03249, 03253–54, 03256, 03259, 03261, 03263, 03269, 03290–91, 03298–99, 03307, 03801–05, 03809–10, 03812–22, 03824–27, 03830, 03832–33, 03835–60, 03862, 03864–75, 03878, 03882–87, 03890, 03894, 03896–97

* * *

SECOND DISTRICT

PAUL W. HODES, Democrat, of Concord, NH; born in New York City, NY, on March 21, 1951; education: B.A., Dartmouth College, Hanover, NH, 1972; J.D., Boston College, Chestnut Hill, MA, 1978; professional: assistant attorney general of New Hampshire, 1979–82; special prosecutor for the state of New Hampshire, 1992; lawyer, private practice; professional entertainer; married: Peggo Horstmann Hodes; children: Max and Ariana; committees: Financial Services; Oversight and Government Reform; unsuccessful candidate for election to 109th Congress in 2004; elected to the 110th Congress on November 7, 2006; reelected to the 111th Congress.

Office Listings

http://www.house.gov/hodes

1317 Longworth House Office Building, Washington, DC 20515 .... (202) 225–5206
FAX: 225–2946
Chief of Staff.—Matt Robison.
Scheduler.—Jesse Mayer.
Legislative Director.—Lauren Oppenheimer.
Press Secretary.—Mark Bergman.
18 North Main Street, Suite 400, Concord, NH 03301 .... (603) 223–9814
FAX: 223–9819
221 Main Street, Suite 201, Nashua, NH 03060 .... (603) 579–6913
FAX: 579–6916
29 Center Street, Keene, NH 03431 .... (603) 358–1023
FAX: 358–1025
32 Main Street, Room 110, Littleton, NH 03561 .... (603) 444–8967
151 Main Street, Suite 2, Berlin, NH 03570 .... (603) 752–4680

Counties: BELKNAP (part), CHESHIRE, COOS, GRAFTON, HILLSBOROUGH (part), MERRIMACK (part), ROCKINGHAM (part), SULLIVAN. Population (2000), 618,211.

ZIP Codes: 03031, 03033, 03037, 03043, 03045–49, 03051–52, 03055, 03057, 03060–64, 03070–71, 03073, 03076, 03079, 03082, 03084, 03086–87, 03215–17, 03220–24, 03226, 03229–31, 03233–35, 03238, 03240–45, 03251–52, 03255, 03257–58, 03260–64, 03266, 03268–69, 03272–76, 03278–82, 03284, 03287, 03289, 03293, 03301–05, 03307, 03431, 03435, 03440–52, 03455–58, 03461–62, 03464–70, 03561, 03570, 03574–76, 03579–85, 03587–90, 03592–93, 03595, 03597–98, 03601–05, 03607–09, 03740–41, 03743, 03745–46, 03748–56, 03765–66, 03768–71, 03773–74, 03777, 03779–82, 03784–85, 03811

NEW JERSEY

(Population 2000 8,414,350)

SENATORS

FRANK R. LAUTENBERG, Democrat, of Cliffside Park, NJ; born in Paterson, NJ, January 23, 1924; education: Nutley High School, Nutley, NJ, 1941; B.S., Economics, Columbia University School of Business, New York, NY, 1949; professional: U.S. Army Signal Corps, 1942–46; data processing firm founder, and CEO, 1952–82; commissioner, Port Authority of New York and New Jersey, 1978–82; commissioner, New Jersey Economic Development Authority; member: U.S. Holocaust Memorial Council; Advisory Council of the Graduate School of Business, Columbia University; appointed by the Governor on December 27, 1982, to complete the unexpired term of Senator Nicholas F. Brady; elected to the U.S. Senate on November 2, 1982; reelected in 1988 and 1994; not a candidate for reelection in 2000; replaced Senator Robert Torricelli as the Democratic candidate for the U.S. Senate in October 2002; four children: Ellen, Nan, Lisa and Joshua; committees: Appropriations; Commerce, Science, and Transportation; Environment and Public Works; elected to the U.S. Senate on November 5, 2002; reelected to the U.S. Senate on November 4, 2008.

Office Listings

http://lautenberg.senate.gov

324 Hart Senate Office Building, Washington, DC 20510 .... (202) 224–3224
Chief of Staff.—Dan Katz. FAX: 228–4054
Chief Counsel.—Doug Mehan.
Legislative Director.—Michelle Schwartz.
Press Secretary.—Michael Pagan.
One Gateway Center, Suite 102, Newark, NJ 07102 .... (973) 639–8700
One Port Center, Suite 505, 2 Riverside Drive, Camden, NJ 08101 .... (856) 338–8922
FAX: 338–8936

* * *

ROBERT MENENDEZ, Democrat, of Hoboken, NJ; born in New York City, NY, January 1, 1954; education: graduated, Union Hill High School, 1972; B.A., St. Peter's College, Jersey City, NJ, 1976; J.D., Rutgers Law School, Newark, NJ, 1979; professional: attorney; elected to the Union City Board of Education, 1974–78; admitted to the New Jersey bar, 1980; mayor of Union City, 1986–92; member: New Jersey Assembly, 1987–91; New Jersey State Senate, 1991–92; chair, New Jersey Hispanic Leadership Program; New Jersey Hispanic Elected Officials Organization; New Jersey Majors Coalition; president and co-founder, Alliance Civic Association; U.S. House of Representatives 1993–2006; vice chair, Democratic Caucus, 1998–2002; chair, Democratic Caucus, 2002–06; chair, Democratic Senatorial Campaign Committee, 2009–present; children: Alicia and Robert; committees: Banking, Housing and Urban Affairs; Budget; Energy and Natural Resources; Finance; Foreign Relations; elected on November 3, 1992 to the 103rd Congress; reelected to each succeeding Congress; appointed to the U.S. Senate on January 17, 2006 by Governor Jon S. Corzine; elected to the 110th Congress for a full Senate term on November 7, 2006.

Office Listings

http://menendez.senate.gov

528 Hart Senate Office Building, Washington, DC 20510 .... (202) 224–4744
Chief of Staff.—Danny O'Brien. FAX: 228–2197
Press Secretary.—Afshin Mohamadi.
Office Manager.—Margaret Wetherald.
One Gateway Center, 11th Floor, Newark, NJ 07102 .... (973) 645–3030
208 Whitehorse Pike, Suite 18, Barrington, NJ 08007–1322 .... (856) 757–5353

REPRESENTATIVES

FIRST DISTRICT

ROBERT E. ANDREWS, Democrat, of Haddon Heights, NJ; born in Camden, NJ, August 4, 1957; education: graduated, Triton High School, Runnemede, NJ, 1975; B.S., political science, Bucknell University, *summa cum laude*, Phi Beta Kappa, Lewisburg, PA, 1979; J.D., *magna cum laude*, Cornell Law School, Cornell Law Review, Ithaca, NY, 1982; Camden County Freeholder, 1986–90; Camden County Freeholder Director, 1988–90; married: Camille Spinello; children: Jacquelyn and Josi; committees: Armed Services; Budget; Education and Labor; election on November 6, 1990, to the 101st Congress, to fill the vacancy caused by the resignation of James Florio; elected at the same time to the 102nd Congress; reelected to each succeeding Congress.

Office Listings

http://www.house.gov/andrews

2265 Rayburn House Office Building, Washington, DC 20515 .... (202) 225–6501
Chief of Staff.—Matt Walker. FAX: 225–6583
Scheduler.—Frank Zywicki.
Legislative Director.—Mike Gaffin.
Press Secretary.—Fran Tagmire.
515 Grove Street, Suite 3C, Haddon Heights, NJ 08035 .... (856) 546–5100
District Director.—Amanda Caruso.
63 North Broad Street, Woodbury, NJ 08096 .... (856) 848–3900

Counties: BURLINGTON COUNTY. CITIES AND TOWNSHIPS: Maple Shade, Palmyra, Riverton. CAMDEN COUNTY. CITIES AND TOWNSHIPS: Audubon, Audubon Park, Barrington, Bellmawr, Berlin, Berlin Township, Brooklawn, Camden, Chesilhurst, Clementon, Collingswood, Gibbsboro, Gloucester City, Gloucester Township, Haddon Heights, Haddon Township, Hi-Nella, Laurel Springs, Lawnside, Lindenwold, Magnolia, Mt. Ephraim, Oaklyn, Pennsauken, Pine Hill, Pine Valley, Runnemede, Somerdale, Stratford, Tavistock, Voorhees, Winslow, Woodlynne. GLOUCESTER COUNTY. CITIES AND TOWNSHIPS: Deptford, E. Greenwich, Greenwich, Logan Township, Mantua, Monroe, National Park, Paulsboro, Washington Township, and Wenonah. Population (2000), 647,258.

ZIP Codes: 08002–04, 08007, 08009, 08012, 08014, 08018, 08020–21, 08026–33, 08035, 08037, 08043, 08045, 08049, 08051–52, 08056, 08059, 08061–63, 08065–66, 08071, 08076–80, 08081, 08083–86, 08089–91, 08093–97, 08099, 08101–10

* * *

SECOND DISTRICT

FRANK A. LoBIONDO, Republican, of Ventnor, NJ; born in Bridgeton, NJ, May 12, 1946; education: graduated, B.S., St. Joseph's University, Philadelphia, PA, 1968; professional: operations manager, LoBiondo Brothers Motor Express, 1968–94; Cumberland County Freeholder, 1985–87; New Jersey General Assembly, 1988–94; awards and honors: honorary Coast Guard Chief Petty Officer; Board of Directors, Young Men's Christian Association; Honorary Rotarian; Taxpayer Hero Award; Watchdog of the Treasury Award; Veterans Foreign Wars ''Outstanding Federal Legislator of the Year'' Award; Humane Society of the United States-Humane Champion Award; National Association of Community Health Centers—Distinguished Community Health Superhero; Super Friend of Seniors Award; two-time winner of the Friend of the National Parks Award; March of Dimes FDR Award for community service; 2001 President's Award, Literacy Volunteers of America, NJ, Inc.; committees: Armed Services; Transportation and Infrastructure; elected to the 104th Congress; reelected to each succeeding Congress.

Office Listings

http://www.house.gov/lobiondo

2427 Rayburn House Office Building, Washington, DC 20515 .... (202) 225–6572
Chief of Staff.—Mary Annie Harper. FAX: 225–3318
Executive Assistant.—JoBeth Banas.
5914 Main Street, Mays Landing, NJ 08330 .... (609) 625–5008
District Director.—Linda Hinckley.

Counties: BURLINGTON (part). CITIES AND TOWNSHIPS: Shamong, Washington. CAMDEN COUNTY (part). ATLANTIC COUNTY. CITIES AND TOWNSHIPS: Absecon, Atlantic City, Brigantine, Buena, Cardiff, Collings Lake, Cologne, Corbin City, Dorothy, Egg Harbor, Estell Manor, Galloway, Hammonton, Landisville, Leeds Point, Linwood, Longport, Margate, Mays Landing, Milmay, Minotola, Mizpah, Newtonville, Northfield, Oceanville, Pleasantville, Pomona, Port Republic, Richland, Somers Point, Ventnor. CAPE MAY COUNTY. CITIES AND TOWNSHIPS: Avalon, Bargaintown, Beesley's, Belleplain, Burleigh, Cape May, Cape May C.H., Cape May Point, Cold Springs, Del Haven, Dennisville, Dias Creek, Eldora, Erma, Fishing Creek, Goshen, Green Creek, Greenfield, Marmora, Ocean City, Ocean View, Rio Grande, Sea Isle, South Dennis, South Seaville, Stone Harbor, Strathmere, Tuckahoe, Villas, Whitesboro, Wildwood, Woodbine. CUMBERLAND COUNTY. CITIES AND TOWNSHIPS: Bridgeton, Cedarville, Centerton, Deerfield, Delmont, Dividing Creek, Dorchester, Elwood, Fairton, Fortescue, Greenwich, Heislerville, Hopewell, Leesburg, Mauricetown, Millville, Newport, Port Elizabeth, Port Norris, Rosenhayn, Shiloh, Vineland. GLOUCESTER COUNTY (part). CITIES AND TOWNSHIPS: Clayton, Ewan, Franklinville, Glassboro, Harrisonville, Malaga, Mantua, Mickleton, Mullica Hill, Newfield, Pitman, Richwood, Sewell, Swedesboro, Williamstown, Woodbury. SALEM COUNTY. CITIES AND TOWNSHIPS: Alloway, Carney's Point, Daretown, Deepwater, Elmer, Elsinboro, Hancocks Bridge, Monroeville, Norma, Pedricktown, Penns Grove, Pennsville, Quinton, Salem, and Woodstown. Population (2000), 647,258.

ZIP Codes: 08001, 08004, 08009, 08019–20, 08023, 08025, 08028, 08037–39, 08051, 08056, 08061–62, 08067, 08069–72, 08074, 08079–80, 08085, 08088–89, 08094, 08098, 08201–05, 08210, 08212–15, 08217–21, 08223, 08225–26, 08230–32, 08234, 08240–48, 08250–52, 08260, 08270, 08302, 08310–24, 08326–30, 08332, 08340–50, 08352–53, 08360–62, 08401–04, 08406

* * *

THIRD DISTRICT

JOHN H. ADLER, Democrat, of Cherry Hill, NJ; born in Philadelphia, PA, August 23, 1959; education: B.A., Harvard University, Cambridge, MA, 1981; J.D., Harvard University, Cambridge, MA, 1984; professional: attorney, 1984–2008; New Jersey State Senate 1991–2008; religion: Jewish; married: Shelley; children: Jeffrey, Alex, Andrew, and Oliver; committees: Financial Services; Veterans' Affairs; elected to the 111th Congress on November 4, 2008.

Office Listings

http://www.adler.house.gov

1223 Longworth House Office Building, Washington, DC 20515	(202) 225–4765
Chief of Staff.—Jill Greco.	FAX: 225–0778
247 Main Street, Toms River, NJ 08753	(732) 608–7235
District Representative.—Mary Campbell.	FAX: 608–7268
28 North Maple Avenue, Marlton, NJ 08053	(856) 985–2777
	FAX: 985–2788

Counties: BURLINGTON (part), CAMDEN (part), OCEAN (part). Population (2000), 647,257.

ZIP Codes: 08002–06, 08008–11, 08015–16, 08019, 08034, 08036, 08043, 08046, 08048, 08050, 08053–55, 08057, 08060, 08064–65, 08068, 08073, 08075, 08077, 08087–88, 08092, 08094, 08109, 08215, 08224, 08352, 08501, 08511, 08562, 08618, 08640–41, 08690, 08721–23, 08731–32, 08734–36, 08739–41, 08751–59

* * *

FOURTH DISTRICT

CHRISTOPHER H. SMITH, Republican, of Robbinsville, NJ; born in Rahway, NJ, March 4, 1953; attended Worcester College, England, 1974; B.A., Trenton State College, 1975; businessman; executive director, New Jersey Right to Life Committee, Inc., 1976–78; religion: Catholic; married to the former Marie Hahn, 1976; four adult children; one grandchild; co-chair, Commission on Security and Cooperation in Europe; co-chair, Congressional Pro-Life Caucus; committees: Foreign Affairs; elected to the 97th Congress, November 4, 1980; reelected to each succeeding Congress.

Office Listings

http://www.house.gov/chrissmith

2373 Rayburn House Office Building, Washington, DC 20515	(202) 225–3765
Chief of Staff.—Mary McDermott Noonan.	FAX: 225–7768
1540 Kuser Road, Suite A9, Hamilton, NJ 08619	(609) 585–7878
108 Lacey Road, Suite 38A, Whiting, NJ 08759	(732) 350–2300

Counties: BURLINGTON COUNTY. MUNICIPALITIES: Bordentown City, Bordentown Township, Burlington City, Burlington Township, Chesterfield, Fieldsboro, Florence, Mansfield, Springfield. MERCER COUNTY. MUNICIPALITIES: East Windsor, Hamilton, Highstown, Trenton, Washington Township. MONMOUTH COUNTY. MUNICIPALITIES: Allentown, Brielle, Colts Neck, Farmingdale, Freehold, Freehold Borough, Howell, Manasquan, Millstone Township, Roosevelt, Sea Girt, Spring Lake Heights, Upper Freehold, Wall. OCEAN COUNTY. MUNICIPALITIES: Bay Head, Brick, Jackson, Lakehurst, Lakewood, Manchester, Mantoloking, Plumstead, Pt. Pleasant, and Pt. Pleasant Beach. Population (2000), 647,258.

ZIP Codes: 07710, 07715, 07719, 07722, 07726–28, 07731, 07753, 07762, 08010, 08016, 08022, 08041–42, 08060, 08068, 08075, 08501, 08505, 08510, 08512, 08514–15, 08518, 08520, 08526–27, 08533, 08535, 08554–55, 08561, 08601–07, 08609–11, 08619–20, 08625, 08629, 08638, 08645–48, 08650, 08666, 08690–91, 08695, 08701, 08720, 08723–24, 08730, 08733, 08736, 08738, 08742, 08750, 08753, 08757, 08759

* * *

FIFTH DISTRICT

SCOTT GARRETT, Republican, of Wantage Township, NJ; born in Englewood, NJ, July 7, 1959; education: High Point Regional High School, 1977; B.A., Montclair State University,

1981; J.D., Rutgers University Law School, 1984; professional: attorney; counsel attorney with law firm of Sellar Richardson; organizations: Big Brothers, Big Sisters; Sussex County Chamber of Commerce; Sussex County Board of Agriculture; New Jersey State Assemblyman, 1990–2002; family: married to Mary Ellen; children: Jennifer and Brittany; committees: Budget; Financial Services; elected to the 108th Congress on November 5, 2002; reelected to each succeeding Congress.

Office Listings

http://www.house.gov/garrett

137 Cannon House Office Building, Washington, DC 20515 .... (202) 225–4465
Chief of Staff.—Amy Smith. FAX: 225–9048
Legislative Director.—Chris Russell.
Communications Director.—Erica Elliott.
266 Harristown Road, Suite 104, Glen Rock, NJ 07452 .... (201)444–5454
District Director.—Tatiana Glavan.
93 Main Street, Newton, NJ 07860 .... (973) 300–2000

Counties: BERGEN (part), PASSAIC (part), SUSSEX, WARREN. Population (2000), 647,257.

ZIP Codes: 07401, 07403, 07416–23, 07428, 07430, 07432, 07435–36, 07438–39, 07446, 07450–52, 07456, 07458, 07460–63, 07465, 07480–81, 07495, 07498, 07620–21, 07624, 07626–28, 07630, 07640–42, 07645–49, 07652–53, 07656, 07661–62, 07670, 07675–77, 07820–23, 07825–27, 07829, 07831–33, 07838–40, 07844, 07846, 07848, 07851, 07855, 07860, 07863, 07865, 07871, 07875, 07877, 07879–82, 07890, 08802, 08804, 08808, 08865–86

* * *

SIXTH DISTRICT

FRANK PALLONE, JR., Democrat, of Long Branch, NJ; born in Long Branch, October 30, 1951; education: B.A., Middlebury College, Middlebury, VT, 1973; M.A., Fletcher School of Law and Diplomacy, 1974; J.D., Rutgers University School of Law, 1978; member of the bar: Florida, New York, Pennsylvania, and New Jersey; attorney, Marine Advisory Service; assistant professor, Cook College, Rutgers University Sea Grant Extension Program; counsel, Monmouth County, NJ, Protective Services for the Elderly; instructor, Monmouth College; Long Branch City Council, 1982–88; New Jersey State Senate, 1983–88; married the former Sarah Hospodor, 1992; committees: Energy and Commerce; Natural Resources; elected to the 100th Congress, by special election, on November 8, 1988, to fill the vacancy caused by the death of James J. Howard; reelected to each succeeding Congress.

Office Listings

http://www.house.gov/pallone

237 Cannon House Office Building, Washington, DC 20515 .... (202) 225–4671
Chief of Staff.—Jeff Carroll. FAX: 225–9665
Legislative Director.—Tim Delmonico.
Communications Director.—Rich McGrath.
District Director.—Janice Fuller.
504 Broadway, Long Branch, NJ 07740 .... (732) 571–1140
67/69 Church Street, Kilmer Square, New Brunswick, NJ 08901–1242 .... (732) 249–8892

Counties: MONMOUTH COUNTY. CITIES AND TOWNSHIPS: Aberdeen, Allenhurst, Asbury Park, Atlantic Highlands, Avon-by-the-Sea, Belmar, Bradley Beach, Deal, Hazlet, Highlands, Interlaken, Keansburg, Keyport, Loch Arbour, Long Branch, Manalapan, Marlboro, Matawan, Middletown, Monmouth Beach, Neptune City, Neptune Twp., Ocean, Red Bank, Sea Birght, South Belmar, Union Beach, West Long Branch. MIDDLESEX COUNTY. CITIES AND TOWNSHIPS: Dunellen, Edison, Highland Park, Metuchen, Middlesex, New Brunswick, Old Bridge, Piscataway, Sayerville, South Amboy. SOMERSET COUNTY. CITIES: Franklin. UNION COUNTY. CITIES: Plainfield. Population (2000), 647,257.

ZIP Codes: 07060–63, 07080, 07701–02, 07704, 07709–12, 07715–21, 07723–24, 07726, 07730, 07732, 07734–35, 07737, 07740, 07746–48, 07750–56, 07758, 07760, 07764, 08812, 08816–18, 08820, 08830–31, 08837, 08840, 08846, 08854–55, 08857, 08859, 08871–73, 08877–79, 08899, 08901, 08903–04, 08906, 08922, 08933, 08988–89

* * *

SEVENTH DISTRICT

LEONARD LANCE, Republican, of Clinton Township, NJ; born in Easton, PA, June 25, 1952; education: B.A., Lehigh University Bethlehem, PA, 1974; J.D., Vanderbilt University Law School, Memphis, TN, 1977; M.P.A., Woodrow Wilson School of Public and International Affairs at Princeton University, Princeton, NJ, 1982; professional: judicial clerk; lawyer, private practice; member, New Jersey state assembly, 1991–2002; member, New Jersey state senate, 2002–09; minority leader, New Jersey state senate, 2004–08; Congressional Diabetes Caucus; Congressional Wildlife Caucus; co-chair, House Republican Israel Caucus; House Cancer Care Working Group; Passenger Rail Caucus; religion: Roman Catholic; committees: Financial Services; elected to the 111th Congress on November 4, 2008.

Office Listings

http://www.lance.house.gov

114 Cannon House Office Building, Washington, DC 20515 .... (202) 225–5361
Chief of Staff.—Todd Mitchell. FAX: 225–9460
Legislative Director.—Jon Taets.
Scheduler.—Sarah Armstrong.
Communications Director.—Angie Lundberg.
425 North Avenue, East, Westfield, NJ 07090 .... (908) 518–7733
23 Royal Road, Suite 101, Flemington, NJ 08822 .... (908) 789–6900
District Director.—Jeanne Ashmore.
Deputy Chief of Staff.—Amanda Woloshen.

Counties: MIDDLESEX COUNTY. MUNICIPALITIES: Edison, South Plainfield, Woodbridge. UNION COUNTY. MUNICIPALITIES: Berkeley Heights, Clark, Cranford, Fanwood, Garwood, Kenilworth, Linden, Mountainside, New Providence, Roselle Park, Scotch Plains, Springfield, Summit, Union, Westfield, Winfield. HUNTERDON COUNTY. MUNICIPALITIES: Alexandria, Bethlehem, Bloomsbury, Califon, Clinton Township, Clinton, Flemington, Glen Gardner, Hampton, High Bridge, Holland, Lebanon, Lebanon Township, Milford, Oldwick, Raritan, Readington, Tewksbury, Union. SOMERSET COUNTY. MUNICIPALITIES: Bedminster, Bernardsville, Bound Brook, Branchburg, Bridgewater, Far Hills, Green Brook, Hillsborough, Manville, Montgomery Township, Millstone, North Plainfield, Peapack-Gladstone, Rocky Hill, South Bound Brook, Warren, and Watchung. Population (2000), 647,257.

ZIP Codes: 07001, 07008, 07016, 07023, 07027, 07033, 07036, 07040, 07059–60, 07062–64, 07066–67, 07069, 07076, 07080–81, 07083, 07090–92, 07095, 07204, 07830, 07901–02, 07921–22, 07924, 07931, 07934, 07974, 07977–79, 08502, 08504, 08540, 08551, 08553, 08558, 08801–02, 08804–05, 08807, 08809, 08812, 08820–22, 08825–27, 08829–30, 08832–37, 08840, 08844, 08848, 08853, 08858, 08863, 08867, 08870, 08876, 08880, 08885, 08887–89

* * *

EIGHTH DISTRICT

BILL PASCRELL, JR., Democrat, of Paterson, NJ; born in Paterson, January 25, 1937; education: B.A., journalism, and M.A., philosophy, Fordham University; veteran, U.S. Army and Army Reserves; professional: educator; elected Minority Leader Pro Tempore, New Jersey General Assembly, 1988–96; mayor of Paterson, 1990–96; named Mayor of the Year by bipartisan NJ Conference of Mayors, 1996; started Paterson's first Economic Development Corporation; married the former Elsie Marie Botto; three children: William III, Glenn, and David; committees: Homeland Security; Ways and Means; elected to the 105th Congress; reelected to each succeeding Congress.

Office Listings

http://www.pascrell.house.gov

2464 Rayburn House Office Building, Washington, DC 20515 .... (202) 225–5751
Chief of Staff.—Ben Rich. FAX: 225–5782
Legislative Director.—Assad Akhter.
Economic Policy Advisor.—Jamine Vasquez.
Health Policy Advisor.—Mandy Spears.
Legislative Assistant.—Arthur Mandel.
Legislative Correspondent / Scheduler.—Kristen Molloy.
Staff Assistant.—Jessica Abraham.
200 Federal Plaza, Suite 500, Paterson, NJ 07505 .... (201) 523–5152
Communications Director.—Paul Brubaker.

Counties: ESSEX COUNTY. CITIES: Belleville, Bloomfield, Cedar Grove. Glen Ridge, Livingston, Montclair, Nutley, South Orange, Verona, West Orange. PASSAIC COUNTY. CITIES: Clifton, Haledon, Little Falls, North Haledon, Passaic, Paterson, Pompton Lakes, Prospect Park, Totowa, Wayne, and West Paterson. Population (2000), 647,258

ZIP Codes: 07003–04, 07009, 07011–15, 07028, 07039, 07042–44, 07052, 07055, 07079, 07107, 07109–10, 07424, 07442, 07470, 07474, 07477, 07501–14, 07522, 07524, 07533, 07538, 07543–44

* * *

NINTH DISTRICT

STEVEN R. ROTHMAN, Democrat, of Fair Lawn, NJ; born in Englewood, NJ, October 14, 1952; education: graduate, Tenafly High School, 1970; B.A., Syracuse University, Syracuse,

NY, 1974; J.D., Washington University School of Law, St. Louis, MO, 1977; professional: attorney; two-term mayor of Englewood, NJ, spearheaded business growth and installed a fiscally conservative management team, transforming Englewood's bond rating from one of the worst to the best in Bergen County; Judge, Bergen County Surrogate Court, 1993–96; founding member, New Democratic Coalition; authored the Secure Our Schools Act; married to Jennifer; two children and three step children; committees: Appropriations; Science and Technology; elected to the 105th Congress; reelected to each succeeding Congress.

Office Listings

http://www.rothman.house.gov

2303 Rayburn House Office Building, Washington, DC 20515 .... (202) 225–5061
Chief of Staff.—Bob Decheine. FAX: 225–5851
Executive Assistant / Scheduler.—Caherine Collentine.
Legislative Director.—Marc Cevasco.
Communications Director.—Carrie Giddins.
25 Main Street, Court Plaza, Hackensack, NJ 07601–7089 .... (201) 646–0808
District Director.—Kevin Donnelly.
130 Central Avenue, Jersey City, NJ 07306–2118 .... (201) 798–1366
Office Director.—Al Zampella.

Counties: BERGEN COUNTY. CITIES AND TOWNS: Bogota, Carlstadt, Cliffside Park, East Rutherford, Edgewater, Elmwood Park, Englewood, Englewood Cliffs, Fair Lawn, Fairview, Fort Lee, Garfield, Hackensack, Hasbrouck Heights, Leonia, Little Ferry, Lodi, Lyndhurst, Maywood, Moonachie, New Milford, North Arlington, Palisades Park, Ridgefield, Ridgefield Park, Rutherford, Saddle Brook, South Hackensack, Teaneck, Teterboro, Wallington, Wood Ridge. HUDSON COUNTY. CITIES AND TOWNS: Kearny (ward 1: districts 1, 2, and 6; ward 3; and ward 4: districts 5–7), Secaucus, North Bergen, Jersey City. PASSAIC COUNTY (part). BOROUGH: Hawthorne. Population (2000), 647,258.

ZIP Codes: 07010, 07020, 07022, 07024, 07026, 07031–32, 07042, 07047, 07057, 07070–75, 07094, 07096–97, 07099, 07306–08, 07407, 07410, 07601–08, 07631–32, 07643–44, 07646, 07650, 07657, 07660, 07663, 07666, 07670

* * *

TENTH DISTRICT

DONALD M. PAYNE, Democrat, of Newark, NJ; born in Newark, July 16, 1934; education: graduated, Barringer High School, Newark, 1952; B.A., Seton Hall University, South Orange, NJ, 1957; professional: businessman; president, YMCA of the USA, 1970–73; elected to the Essex County Board of Chosen Freeholders, 1972–78; elected to the Newark Municipal Council, 1982–88; member: NAACP; Council on Foreign Relations; serves on the advisory council of the U.S. Committee for UNICEF; Advisory Commission on Intergovernmental Relations; former chairman, Congressional Black Caucus; board of directors: Congressional Black Caucus Foundation, National Endowment for Democracy; Bethlehem Baptist Church; family: widower; three children; committees: Education and Labor; Foreign Affairs; elected on November 8, 1988, to the 101st Congress; reelected to each succeeding Congress.

Office Listings

2310 Rayburn House Office Building, Washington, DC 20515 .... (202) 225–3436
Chief of Staff.—Maxine James. FAX: 225–4160
Legislative Director / Press Secretary.—Kerry McKenney.
50 Walnut Street, Room 1016, Newark, NJ 07102 .... (973) 645–3213
333 North Broad Street, Elizabeth, NJ 07202 .... (908) 629–0222
253 Martin Luther King Drive, Jersey City, NJ 07305 .... (201) 369–0392

Counties: ESSEX, HUDSON, SHORT HILLS, UNION. CITIES AND TOWNSHIPS: Bayonne, East Orange, Elizabeth, Hillside, Irvington, Jersey City, Linden, Maplewood Millburn, Montclair, Newark, Orange, Rahway, Roselle, South Orange, Union, and West Orange. Population (2000), 647,258.

ZIP Codes: 07002, 07017–19, 07028, 07036, 07040–42, 07044, 07050–52, 07065, 07078–79, 07083, 07088, 07101–03, 07105–08, 07111–12, 07114–75, 07184, 07188–89, 07191–95, 07197–99, 07201–03, 07205–08, 07304–05

* * *

ELEVENTH DISTRICT

RODNEY P. FRELINGHUYSEN, Republican, of Morristown, NJ; born in New York, NY, April 29, 1946; education: graduated Hobart College, NY, 1969; attended graduate school in Connecticut; served, U.S. Army, 93rd Engineer Battalion; honorably discharged, 1971; Morris County state and federal aid coordinator and administrative assistant, 1972; member, Morris

County Board of Chosen Freeholders, 1974–83 (director, 1980); served on: Welfare and Mental Health boards; Human Services and Private Industry councils; New Jersey General Assembly, 1983–94; chairman, Assembly Appropriations Committee, 1988–89 and 1992–94; member: American Legion, and Veterans of Foreign Wars; named Legislator of the Year by the Veterans of Foreign Wars, the New Jersey Association of Mental Health Agencies, and the New Jersey Association of Retarded Citizens; honored by numerous organizations; married: Virginia Frelinghuysen; children: Louisine and Sarah; committees: Appropriations; elected to the 104th Congress in November, 1994; reelected to each succeeding Congress.

Office Listings

http://www.frelinghuysen.house.gov

2442 Rayburn House Office Building, Washington, DC 20515 .... (202) 225–5034
Chief of Staff.—Nancy Fox. FAX: 225–3186
Press Secretary.—Steve Wilson.
Legislative Director.—Steve Wilson.
Scheduler.—Tina Wei.
30 Schuyler Place, 2nd Floor, Morristown, NJ 07960 .... (973) 984–0711

Counties: ESSEX COUNTY. CITIES AND TOWNSHIPS: Caldwell, Essex Fells, Fairfield Township, Livingston, Millburn, North Caldwell, Roseland, West Caldwell. MORRIS COUNTY. CITIES AND TOWNSHIPS: Bernardsville, municipalities of Boonton Town, Boonton Township, Brookside, Budd Lake, Butler, Califon, Cedar Knolls, Chatham Borough, Chatham Township, Chester Borough, Chester Township, Convent Station, Denville, Dover Town, East Hanover, Flanders, Florham Park, Gillette, Green Pond, Green Village, Hanover, Harding, Hibernia, Ironia, Jefferson, Kenvill, Kinnelon, Lake Hiawatha, Lake Hopatcong, Landing, Ledgewood, Lincoln Park, Long Valley, Madison, Mendham Borough, Mendham Township, Millington, Mine Hill, Montville, Morris Plains, Morris Township, Morristown, Mount Arlington, Mountain Lakes, Mount Olive, Mount Tabor, Netcong, Newfoundland, New Vernon, Oak Ridge, Parsippany-Troy Hills, Passaic Township, Pequannock, Picatinny, Pine Brook, Randolph, Riverdale, Rockaway Borough, Rockaway Township, Roxbury, Schooley's Mountain, Stanhope, Stirling, Succasunna, Towaco, Victory Gardens, Washington Township, Wharton, and Whippany. PASSAIC COUNTY. CITIES: Bloomingdale. SOMERSET COUNTY. CITIES AND TOWNSHIPS: Bernards Township, Bridgewater, Raritan Borough, and Somerville. SUSSEX COUNTY. CITIES AND TOWNSHIPS: Byram, Hopatcong, Sparta, and Stanhope. Population (2000), 647,258.

ZIP Codes: 07004–07, 07021, 07034–35, 07039, 07041, 07045–46, 07054, 07058, 07068, 07078, 07082, 07405, 07438, 07440, 07444, 07457, 07801–03, 07806, 07821, 07828, 07830, 07834, 07836–37, 07840, 07842–43, 07845, 07847, 07849–50, 07852–53, 07856–57, 07866, 07869–71, 07874, 07876, 07878, 07885, 07920, 07926–28, 07930, 07932–36, 07938–40, 07945–46, 07950, 07960–63, 07970, 07976, 07980–81, 07983, 07999, 08807, 08869, 08876, 08896

* * *

TWELFTH DISTRICT

RUSH D. HOLT, Democrat, of Hopewell Township, NJ; born in Weston, WV, October 15, 1948; son of the youngest person ever to be elected to the U.S. Senate; education: B.A., Carleton College, 1970; M.S. and Ph.D., physics, New York University, 1981; physicist; New York City Environmental Protection Administration, 1972–74; teaching fellow, New York University, 1974–80; Congressional Science Fellow, U.S. House of Representatives, Office of Representative Bob Edgar, 1982–83; professor, Swarthmore College, 1980–88; acting chief, Nuclear & Scientific Division, Office of Strategic Forces, U.S. Department of State, 1987–89; assistant director, Princeton Plasma Physics Laboratory, Princeton, NJ, 1989–97; Protestant; married: Margaret Lancefield; children: Michael, Dejan, and Rachel; chair, Select Intelligence Oversight Panel; committees: Education and Labor; Natural Resources; Permanent Select Committee on Intelligence; elected to the 106th Congress; reelected to each succeeding Congress.

Office Listings

http://holt.house.gov

1214 Longworth House Office Building, Washington, DC 20515 .... (202) 225–5801
Chief of Staff.—Christopher Hartmann. FAX: 225–6025
Legislative Director.—Christopher Gaston.
Communications Director.—Zachary Goldberg.
Executive Assistant.—Nicole Williams.
50 Washington Road, West Windsor, NJ 08550 .... (609) 750–9365
District Director.—Leslie Potter.

Counties: HUNTERDON COUNTY. CITIES AND TOWNSHIPS: Delaware, East Amwell, Franklin, Frenchtown, Kingwood, Lambertville, Stockton, West Amwell. MERCER COUNTY. CITIES AND TOWNSHIPS: Ewing, Hopewell Borough, Hopewell Township, Lawrence, Pennington, Princeton Borough, Princeton Township, Trenton, West Windsor. MIDDLESEX COUNTY. CITIES AND TOWNSHIPS: Cranbury, East Brunswick, Helmetta, Jamesburg, Milltown, Monroe, North Brunswick, Old Bridge, Plainsboro Township, South River, Spotswood, South Brunswick. MONMOUTH COUNTY. CITIES AND TOWNSHIPS: Eatontown, Englishtown, Fair Haven, Freehold Township, Holmdel, Little Silver, Manalapan, Marlboro, Middletown, Oceanport, Rumson, Shrewsbury Borough, Shrewsbury Township, Tinton Falls. SOMERSET COUNTY. CITIES AND TOWNSHIPS: Franklin Township. Population (2000), 647,258.

ZIP Codes: 07701–04, 07712, 07724, 07726, 07728, 07733, 07738–39, 07746, 07748, 07751, 07753, 07757, 07760, 07763, 07765, 07777, 07799, 08512, 08525, 08528, 08530, 08534, 08536, 08540–44, 08550–51, 08556–57, 08559–60, 08570, 08608–09, 08611, 08618–19, 08628, 08638, 08648, 08690, 08801, 08803, 08809–10, 08816, 08822–25, 08828, 08831, 08844, 08850, 08852, 08857, 08859, 08867–68, 08873, 08875, 08882, 08884, 08890, 08901–02, 08905, 08922

* * *

THIRTEENTH DISTRICT

ALBIO SIRES, Democrat, of West New York, NJ; born in Bejucal, Provincia de la Habana, Cuba, January 26, 1951; education: graduated, Memorial High School; B.A., St. Peter's College, 1974; M.A., Middlebury College, Middlebury, VT, 1985; studied Spanish in Madrid, Spain; professional: businessman, teacher; part-owner, A.M. Title Agency, Union Township; mayor, West New York, NJ, 1995–2006; member: New Jersey House, 1999–2006; speaker, New Jersey House, 2002–2005; family: wife, Adrienne; stepdaughter, Tara Kole; committees: Foreign Affairs; Transportation and Infrastructure; elected to the 109th Congress by special election to fill the vacancy caused by the resignation of Robert Menendez; elected to the 110th Congress; reelected to the 111th Congress on November 4, 2008.

Office Listings

http://www.sires.house.gov

1024 Longworth House Office Building, Washington, DC 20515 .... (202) 225–7919
Chief of Staff.—Gene Martorony. FAX: 226–0792
Administrative Director / Scheduler.—Judi Wolford.
Legislative Director.—Kate Fink.
Communications Director.—Erica Daughtrey.
35 Journal Square, Suite 906, Jersey City, NJ 07306 .... (201) 222–2828
Bayonne City Hall, 630 Avenue C, Room 4, Bayonne, NJ 07002 .... (201) 823–2900
5500 Palisades Avenue, Suite A, West New York, NJ 07093 .... (201) 558–0800
100 Cooke Avenue, Second Floor, Carteret, NJ 07008 .... (732) 969–9160
Perth Amboy City Hall, First Floor, Perth Amboy, NJ 08861 .... (732) 442–0610

Counties: ESSEX (part), HUDSON (part), MIDDLESEX (part), UNION (part). CITIES AND TOWNSHIPS: Bayonne, Carteret, East Newark, Elizabeth, Guttenberg, Harrison Township, Hoboken, Jersey City, Kearny, Linden, Newark, North Bergen, Port Reading, Perth Amboy, Sewaren, Union City, Weehawken, West New York, and Woodbridge. Population (2000), 647,258.

ZIP Codes: 07002–03, 07008, 07029–30, 07036, 07047, 07064, 07077, 07086–87, 07093, 07095, 07102–05, 07107, 07114, 07201–02, 07206, 07302–11, 08861–62

NEW MEXICO

(Population 2000, 1,819,046)

SENATORS

JEFF BINGAMAN, Democrat, of Santa Fe, NM; born in El Paso, TX, October 3, 1943; raised in Silver City, NM; graduate of Western High (now Silver High), 1961; B.A., government, Harvard University, 1965; J.D., Stanford Law School, 1968; U.S. Army Reserves, 1968–74; Assistant New Mexico Attorney General, 1969, as counsel to the State constitutional convention; private practice, 1970–78; New Mexico Attorney General, 1979–83; member: Methodist Church; married: the former Anne Kovacovich; one son, John; committees: chair, Energy and Natural Resources; Finance; Health, Education, Labor, and Pensions; Joint Economic Committee; elected to the U.S. Senate on November 2, 1982; reelected to each succeeding Senate term.

Office Listings

http://bingaman.senate.gov

703 Hart Senate Office Building, Washington, DC 20510 .... (202) 224–5521
Administrative Assistant.—Stephen Ward. TDD: 224–1792
Legislative Director.—Trudy Vincent.
Press Secretary.—Jude McCartin.
Personal Assistant.—Virginia White.
Loretto Town Centre, Suite 148, 505 South Main, Las Cruces, NM 88001 .... (505) 523–6561
625 Silver Avenue SW., Suite 130, Albuquerque, NM 87102 .... (505) 346–6601
105 West Third Street, Suite 409, Roswell, NM 88201 .... (505) 622–7113
119 East Marcy, Suite 101, Santa Fe, NM 87501 .... (505) 988–6647
106–B West Main, Farmington, NM 87102 .... (505) 325–5030

* * *

TOM UDALL, Democrat, of Santa Fe, NM; born in Tucson, AZ, May 18, 1948; education: graduate of McLean High School, 1966; B.A., Prescott College, Prescott, AZ, 1970; LL.B., Cambridge University, Cambridge, England, 1975; J.D., University of New Mexico, Albuquerque, NM, 1977; professional: admitted to New Mexico Bar, 1978; served as New Mexico Attorney General, 1990–98; served as U.S. Representative for New Mexico's Third Congressional District, 1998–2008; married: Jill Z. Cooper; children: Amanda; member of the Commission on Security and Cooperation in Europe; committees: Commerce, Science and Transportation; Environment and Public Works, Indian Affairs; Rules and Administration; Joint Committee on Printing; elected to the U.S. Senate on November 4, 2008.

Office Listings

http://tomudall.senate.gov

110 Hart Senate Office Building, Washington, DC 20510 .... (202) 224–6621
Chief of Staff.—Tom Nagle. FAX: 228–3261
Legislative Director.—Michael Collins.
Communications Director.—Marissa Padilla.
Executive Assistant.—Donda Morgan.
219 Central Avenue, NW., Suite 210, Albuquerque, NM 87102 .... (505) 346–6791
Loretto Town Centre, 505 South Main, Suite 118, Las Cruces, NM 88001 .... (575) 526–5475
120 South Federal Place, Suite 302, Santa Fe, NM 87501 .... (505) 988–6511

REPRESENTATIVES

FIRST DISTRICT

MARTIN HEINRICH, Democrat, of Albuquerque, NM; born in Fallon, NV, October 17, 1971; B.S., University of Missouri, 1995; Albuquerque City Council, 2003–07, including one term as president, 2005–06; trustee, New Mexico State Natural Resources; married: Julie Heinrich; children: Carter and Micah Heinrich; committees: Armed Services; Natural Resources; elected to the 111th Congress on November 4, 2008.

Office Listings

http://www.heinrich.house.gov

1505 Longworth House Office Building, Washington, DC 20515 .... (202) 225–6316

Chief of Staff.—Steve Haro. FAX: 225–4975
Legislative Director.—John Blair.
Executive Assistant.—Amelia Thomas.
20 First Plaza, NW., Suite 603, Albuquerque, NM 87102 .... (505) 346–6781

Counties: BERNALILLO (part), SANDOVAL (part), SANTA FE (part), TORRANCE, VALENCIA (part). CITIES AND TOWNSHIPS: Albuquerque, Belen, Estancia, Los Lunas, Moriarty, Mountainair, and Rio Rancho. Population (2000), 606,391.

ZIP Codes: 87001–02, 87004, 87008–09, 87015–16, 87031–32, 87035–36, 87042–43, 87047–48, 87059–61, 87063, 87068, 87070, 87101–25, 87131, 87151, 87153–54, 87158, 87176, 87181, 87184–85, 87187, 87190–99, 88301, 88321

* * *

SECOND DISTRICT

HARRY TEAGUE, Democrat, of Hobbs, NM; born in Gracemont, OK, June 29, 1949; professional: businessman; owner, Teaco; religion: Baptist; married: Nancy; children: Troy and Kristy; committees: Transportation and Infrastructure; Veterans' Affairs; elected to the 111th Congress on Novmeber 4, 2008.

Office Listings

http://www.teague.house.gov

1007 Longworth House Office Building, Washington, DC 20515 .... (202) 225–2365
Chief of Staff.—Adrian Saenz. FAX: 225–9599
Press Secretary.—Sara Schreiber.
Scheduler.—John Gomez.
Legislative Aides: Vivek Gopalan, Art Terrazas.
Legislative Correspondent.—Kate Alexander.
Staff Assistant.—Cristal Jones.
135 West Griggs, Las Cruces, NM 88001 .... (575) 522–3908
3445 Lambros Loop NE, Los Lunas, NM 87031 .... (505) 865–7802
200 East Broadway, Suite 200, Hobbs, NM 88240 .... (575) 393–0510
111 School of Mines Road, Socorro, NM 87801 .... (575) 835–8919
102 East 4th Street, Roswell, NM 88201 .... (575) 622–4178

Counties: BERNALILLO (part), CATRON, CHAVES, CIBOLA, DEBACA, DONA ANA, EDDY, GRANT, GUADALUPE, HIDALGO, LEA, LINCOLN, LUNA, MCKINLEY (part), OTERO, SIERRA, SOCORRO, VALENCIA (part). Population (2000), 606,406.

ZIP Codes: 87002, 87005–07, 87011, 87014, 87020–23, 87026, 87028, 87031, 87034, 87038, 87040, 87045, 87049, 87051, 87062, 87068, 87105, 87121, 87315, 87321, 87327, 87357, 87711, 87724, 87801, 87820–21, 87823–25, 87827–32, 87901, 87930–31, 87933, 87935–37, 87939–43, 88001–09, 88011–12, 88020–21, 88023–34, 88036, 88038–49, 88051–56, 88058, 88061–63, 88065, 88072, 88081, 88114, 88116, 88119, 88134, 88136, 88201–03, 88210–11, 88220–21, 88230–32, 88240–42, 88244, 88250, 88252–56, 88260, 88262–65, 88267–68, 88301, 88310–12, 88314, 88316–18, 88323–25, 88330, 88336–55, 88417, 88431, 88435

* * *

THIRD DISTRICT

BEN RAY LUJÁN, Democrat, of Santa Fe, NM; born in Nambe, NM; June 7, 1972; education: New Mexico Highland University; Business Administration, Highlands University, Las Vegas, NM; professional: elected to the New Mexico Public Regulation Commission, 2005–08; member of the Hispanic Caucus; Native American Caucus; Sustainable Energy and Environment Coalition; committees: Homeland Security; Science and Technology; elected to the 111th Congress on November 4, 2008.

Office Listings

http://www.lujan.house.gov

502 Cannon House Office Building, Washington, DC 20515 .... (202) 225–6190
Chief of Staff.—Angela Ramirez. FAX: 226–1331
Legislative Director.—Andrew Jones.
Press Secretary.—Mark Nicastre.
Executive Assistant / Scheduler.—Chris Garcia.
811 St. Michaels Drive, Suite 104, Santa Fe, NM 87505 .... (505) 984–8950
District Director.—Jennifer Conn Catechis.
800 Municipal Drive, Farmington, NM 87401 .... (505) 324–1005
Constituent Services Representative / Veterans Liaison.—Pete Valencia.
110 West Aztec, Suite 102, Gallup, NM 87301 .... (505) 863–0582
Native American Outreach.—Gertrude Lee.
Highlands University, P.O. Box 1368, Las Vegas, NM 87701 .... (505) 454–3038

Chamber of Commerce, 404 West Route 66 Boulevard, Tucumcari, NM 88401 ..... (575) 461–3029
City Hall, 3200 Civic Center Circle, NE., #330, Rio Rancho, NM 87144 .... (505) 994–0499
Deputy Director.—Chris Neubauer.

Counties: BERNALILLO (part), NAVAJO NATION, COLFAX, CURRY, HARDING; LOS ALAMOS, MCKINLEY (part), MORA, QUAY, RIO, ROOSEVELT, SANDOVAL (part), SAN JUAN, SAN MIGUEL, SANTA FE, TAOS, UNION. Population (2000), 606,249.

ZIP Codes: 87001, 87004, 87010, 87012–13, 87015, 87017–18, 87024–25, 87027, 87029, 87037, 87041, 87044–48, 87052–53, 87056, 87064, 87072, 87083, 87114, 87120, 87123–24, 87144, 87174, 87301–02, 87305, 87310–13, 87316–17, 87319–23, 87325–26, 87328, 87347, 87364–65, 87375, 87401–02, 87410, 87412–13, 87415–21, 87455, 87461, 87499, 87501–25, 87527–33, 87535, 87537–40, 87543–45, 87548–49, 87551–54, 87556–58, 87560, 87562, 87564–67, 87569, 87571, 87573–83, 87592, 87594, 87701, 87710, 87712–15, 87718, 87722–23, 87728–36, 87740, 87742–43, 87745–47, 87749–50, 87752–53, 88101–03, 88112–13, 88115–16, 88118, 88120–26, 88130, 88132–35, 88401, 88410–11, 88414–16, 88418–19, 88421–22, 88424, 88426–27, 88430, 88433–34, 88436–37, 88439

NEW YORK

(Population 2000, 18,976,457)

SENATORS

CHARLES E. SCHUMER, Democrat, of Brooklyn and Queens, NY; born in Brooklyn, November 23, 1950; education: graduated valedictorian, Madison High School; Harvard University, *magna cum laude*, 1971; J.D. with honors, Harvard Law School, 1974; professional: admitted to the New York State Bar in 1975; elected to the New York State Assembly, 1974; served on Judiciary, Health, Education, and Cities committees; chairman, subcommittee on City Management and Governance, 1977; chairman, Committee on Oversight and Investigation, 1979; reelected to each succeeding legislative session until December 1980; married: Iris Weinshall, 1980; children: Jessica Emily and Alison Emma; committees: chair, Rules and Administration; chair, Joint Committee on Printing; vice chair, Joint Committee on the Library; vice chair, Joint Economic Committee; Banking, Housing, and Urban Affairs; Finance; Judiciary; elected to the 97th Congress on November 4, 1980; reelected to each succeeding Congress; elected to the U.S. Senate on November 3, 1998; reelected to each succeeding Senate term.

Office Listings

http://schumer.senate.gov

313 Hart Senate Office Building, Washington, DC 20510 .... (202) 224–6542
Chief of Staff.—Mike Lynch. FAX: 228–3027
Communications Director.—Brian Fallon.
Executive Assistant.—Emily Umhoefer.
757 Third Avenue, Suite 17–02, New York, NY 10017 .... (212) 486–4430
Leo O'Brien Building, 1 Clinton Square, Room 420, Albany, NY 12207 .... (518) 431–4070
130 South Elmwood Avenue, #660, Buffalo, NY 14202 .... (716) 846–4111
100 State Street, Room 3040, Rochester, NY 14614 .... (585) 263–5866
100 South Clinton, Room 841, Syracuse, NY 13261–7318 .... (315) 423–5471
Federal Office Building, 15 Henry Street, #B6, Binghamton, NY 13901 .... (607) 772–8109
Two Greenway Plaza, 145 Pine Lawn Road, #300, Melville, NY 11747 .... (631) 753–0978
One Park Place, Suite 100, Peekskill, NY 10566 .... (914) 734–1532

* * *

KIRSTEN E. GILLIBRAND, Democrat, of Greenport, NY; born in Albany, NY, December 9, 1966; education: B.A., Dartmouth College, Hanover, NH, 1988; J.D., UCLA, Los Angeles, CA, 1991; professional: attorney; Special Counsel to the U.S. Secretary of Housing and Urban Development Andrew Cuomo; private legal practice; religion: Catholic; married: Jonathan Gillibrand 2001; two sons: Theodore 2004, Henry 2008; committees: Agriculture, Nutrition, and Forestry; Environment and Public Works; Foreign Relations; Special Committee on Aging; appointed to the 111th Congress on January 23, 2009, to fill the vacancy caused by the resignation of Hillary Clinton.

Office Listings

http://gillibrand.senate.gov

478 Russell Senate Office Building, Washington, DC 20510 .... (202) 224–4451
Chief of Staff.—Jess Fassler. FAX: 228–0282
Legislative Director.—Brooke Jamison.
Communications Director.—Matt Canter.
Scheduler.—Maeve Kelly.
780 Third Avenue, Suite 2601, New York, NY 10017 .... (212) 688–6262
Federal Office Building, 1 Clinton Square, Room 821, Albany, NY 12207 .... (518) 431–0128
Larkin at Exchange, 726 Exchange Street, Suite 511, Buffalo, NY 14210 .... (716) 854–9731
155 Pinelawn Road, Suite 250 North, Melville, NY 11747 .... (631) 249–2825
P.O. Box 884, Nyack, NY 10960 .... (845) 875–4585
P.O. Box 273, Lowville, NY 13367 .... (315) 376–6118
Federal Office Building, 100 State Street, Room 4195, Rochester, NY 14614 .... (585) 263–6250
Federal Office Building, 100 South Clinton Street, Room 1470, P.O. Box 7378, Syracuse, NY 13261 .... (315) 448–0468
Westchester County Office .... (914) 725–9294

REPRESENTATIVES

FIRST DISTRICT

TIMOTHY H. BISHOP, Democrat, of Southampton, NY; born in Southampton, June 1, 1950; education: Southampton High School, 1968; A.B., in history, from Holy Cross College; M.P.A., Long Island University, 1981; professional: educator; Provost of Southampton College, 1986–2002; community service: Southampton Rotary Club Scholarship Committee; Southampton Town Board of Ethics; Eastern Long Island Coastal Conservation Alliance; Bridgehampton Childcare and Recreation Center; religion: Catholic; married: Kathryn; children: Molly and Meghan; committees: Budget; Education and Labor; Transportation and Infrastructure; elected to the 108th Congress on November 5, 2002; reelected to each succeeding Congress.

Office Listings

http:/www.house.gov/timbishop

306 Cannon House Office Building, Washington, DC 20515 .... (202) 225–3826
Chief of Staff.—Pete Spiro. FAX: 225–3143
Legislative Director.—Mark Copeland.
Scheduler / Staff Assistant.—Hannah Shedrick.
District Director / Communications Director.—Jon Schneider.
3680 Route 112, Suite C, Coram, NY 11727 .... (631) 696–6500
137 Hampton Road, Southampton, NY 11968 .... (631) 259–8450

Counties: SUFFOLK COUNTY (part). CITIES: Brookhaven, Smithtown, Southampton, and Montauk. Population (2000), 654,360.

ZIP Codes: 00501, 00544, 11713, 11715, 11719–20, 11727, 11733, 11738, 11741–42, 11745, 11754–55, 11763–64, 11766–68, 11772, 11776–80, 11784, 11786–90, 11792, 11794, 11901, 11930–35, 11937, 11939–42, 11944, 11946–65, 11967–73, 11975–78, 11980

* * *

SECOND DISTRICT

STEVE ISRAEL, Democrat, of Huntington, NY; born in Brooklyn, NY, May 30, 1958; education: B.A., George Washington University, 1982; professional: public relations and marketing executive; public service: Legislative Assistant for Rep. Richard Ottinger (D–NY), 1980–83; Suffolk County Executive for Intergovernmental Relations, 1988–91; elected to the Huntington Town Board, 1993; reelected two times; organizations: Institute on the Holocaust; Touro Law Center; Nature Conservancy; Audubon Society; awards: Child Care Council of Suffolk Leadership Award; Anti-Defamation League and Sons of Italy Purple Aster Award; committees: Appropriations; elected to the 107th Congress on November 7, 2000; reelected to each succeeding Congress.

Office Listings

http://www.house.gov/israel

2457 Rayburn House Office Building, Washington, DC 20515 .... (202) 225–3335
Chief of Staff.—Jack Pratt. FAX: 225–4669
Communications Director.—Lindsay Hamilton.
Legislative Director.—Mike Ryan.
150 Motor Parkway, Suite 108, Hauppauge, NY 11788 .... (631) 951–2210
District Director.—Tracie Holmberg. (516) 505–1448

Counties: NASSAU COUNTY (part), SUFFOLK COUNTY (part). CITIES: Asharoken, Bay Shore, Bayport, Bohemia, Brentwood, Brightwaters, Centerport, Central Islip, Cold Springs Harbor, Commack, Copiague, Deer Park, Dix Hills, East Farmingdale, East Northport, Eaton's Neck, Elwood, Fort Salonga, Great River, Greenlawn, Halesite, Hauppauge, Holbrook, Huntington, Huntington Station, Islandia, Islip, Islip Terrace, Jericho, King's Park, Lindenhurst, Lloyd Harbor, Melville, North Amityville, Northport, Oakdale, Ocean Beach, Old Bethpage, Plainview, Ronkonkoma, Sayville, Smithtown, South Huntington, Syosset, West Babylon, West Hills, West Islip, West Sayville, Wheatley Heights, Woodbury and Wyandanch. Population (2000), 654,360.

ZIP Codes: 11701, 11703–06, 11714–18, 11721–22, 11724–26, 11729–31, 11735, 11737, 11739–43, 11746–47, 11749–54, 11757, 11760, 11767–70, 11772, 11775, 11779, 11782, 11787–88, 11791, 11796–98, 11801, 11803–04

* * *

THIRD DISTRICT

PETER T. KING, Republican, of Seaford, NY; born in Manhattan, NY, April 5, 1944; education: B.A., St. Francis College, NY, 1965; J.D., University of Notre Dame Law School,

IN, 1968; military service: served, U.S. Army Reserve National Guard, specialist 5, 1968–73; admitted to New York bar, 1968; professional: attorney; Deputy Nassau County Attorney, 1972–74, executive assistant to the Nassau County Executive, 1974–76; general counsel, Nassau Off-Track Betting Corporation, 1977; Hempstead Town Councilman, 1978–81; Nassau County Comptroller, 1981–92; member: Ancient Order of Hiberians, Long Island Committee for Soviet Jewry, Sons of Italy, Knights of Columbus, 69th Infantry Veterans Corps, American Legion; married: Rosemary Wiedl King, 1967; children: Sean and Erin; grandson, Jack; committees: Financial Services; Homeland Security; Permanent Select Committee on Intelligence; elected on November 3, 1992 to the 103rd Congress; reelected to each succeeding Congress.

Office Listings

http://www.house.gov/king

339 Cannon House Office Building, Washington, DC 20515 .... (202) 225–7896
Chief of Staff / Press Secretary.—Kevin Fogarty. FAX: 226–2279
Legislative Director.—Kerryann Watkins.
1003 Park Boulevard, Massapequa Park, NY 11762 .... (516) 541–4225
District Director.—Anne Rosenfeld.
Suffolk County .... (631) 541–4225

Counties: NASSAU (part), SUFFOLK (part). CITIES AND TOWNSHIPS: Amityville, Babylon, Baldwin, Bayshore, Bayville, Bellmore, Bethpage, Brightwaters, Brookville, Cedar Beach, Centre Island, Copiague, Cove Neck, East Islip, East Norwich, Farmingdale, Freeport, Gilgo Beach, Glen Cove, Glen Head, Glenwood Landing, Greenvale, Harbor Isle, Hicksville, Island Park, Islip, Jericho, Lattingtown, Laurel Hollow, Levittown, Lido Beach, Lindenhurst, Locust Grove, Locust Valley, Long Beach, Massapequa, Massapequa Park, Matinecock, Merrick, Mill Neck, Muttontown, North Babylon, North Bellmore, North Lindenhurst, Oak Beach, Oceanside, Old Bethpage, Old Brookville, Old Westbury, Oyster Bay, Oyster Bay Cove, Plainview, Point Lookout, Sea Cliff, Seaford, Syosset, Wantagh, West Babylon, West Bayshore, Westbury, West Islip, and Woodbury. Population (2000), 654,361.

ZIP Codes: 11510, 11520, 11542, 11545, 11547–48, 11558, 11560–61, 11566, 11568–69, 11572, 11576, 11579, 11590, 11599, 11701–04, 11706, 11709–10, 11714, 11718, 11724, 11726, 11730, 11732, 11735–37, 11751, 11753, 11756–58, 11762, 11765, 11771, 11773–74, 11783, 11791, 11793, 11795, 11797, 11801–04, 11815, 11819, 11854–55

* * *

FOURTH DISTRICT

CAROLYN McCARTHY, Democrat, of Mineola, NY; born in Brooklyn, NY, January 5, 1944; education: graduated, Mineola High School, 1962; graduated, nursing school, 1964; professonal: licensed practical nurse in ICU Section, Glen Cove Hospital; married: Dennis McCarthy, 1967; widowed on December 7, 1993, when her husband was killed and her only son, Kevin, severely wounded in the Long Island Railroad Massacre; turned personal nightmare into a crusade against violence—speaking out with other families of the Long Island tragedy, not just to the victims of the shooting but to crime victims across the country; committees: Education and Labor; Financial Services; elected to the 105th Congress; reelected to each succeeding Congress.

Office Listings

http://www.house.gov/carolynmccarthy

2346 Rayburn House Office Building, Washington, DC 20515 .... (202) 225–5516
Chief of Staff.—Mike Spira. FAX: 225–5758
District Director.—Christopher Chaffee.
Executive Assistant.—Ellen McNamara.
Communications Director.—Ray Zaccaro.
300 Garden City Plaza, Suite 200, Garden City, NY 11530 .... (516) 739–3008

Counties: NASSAU (part). CITIES AND TOWNSHIPS: Atlantic Beach, Baldwin, Bellerose, Carle Place, Cedarhurst, East Meadow, East Rockaway, East Williston, Elmont, Floral Park, Franklin Square, Freeport, Garden City, Garden City Park, Hempstead, Hewlett, Inwood, Lakeview, Lawrence, Lynbrook, Malverne, Merrick, Mineola, New Cassel, New Hyde Park, North Bellmore, North New Hyde Park, Oceanside, Rockville Centre, Roosevelt, Salisbury, Stewart Manor, South Floral Park, South Valley Stream, Uniondale, Valley Stream, West Hempstead, Westbury, Williston Park, Woodmere, and Woodsburgh. Population (2000) 654,360.

ZIP Codes: 11001–03, 11010, 11040, 11096, 11501, 11509–10, 11514, 11516, 11518, 11520, 11530, 11540, 11549–57, 11559, 11561, 11563–66, 11568, 11570–72, 11575, 11577, 11580–83, 11588, 11590, 11592–99, 11710, 11793

* * *

FIFTH DISTRICT

GARY L. ACKERMAN, Democrat, of Queens, NY; born in Brooklyn, NY, November 19, 1942; education: graduate, Queens College, Flushing, NY; attended St. John's University, Jamaica, NY; professional: public school teacher; newspaper editor; businessman; New York State Senate, 1979–83; married: the former Rita Tewel; children: Lauren, Corey, and Ari; committees: Financial Services; Foreign Affairs; elected by special election on March 1, 1983, to the 98th Congress, to fill the vacancy caused by the death of Representative Benjamin Rosenthal; reelected to each succeeding Congress.

Office Listings

http://www.house.gov/ackerman

2243 Rayburn House Office Building, Washington, DC 20515 .... (202) 225–2601
Chief of Staff.—Jedd Moskowitz. FAX: 225–1589
Scheduler.—Brenda Connolly.
Legislative Director.—Steven Boms.
Press Secretary.—Jordan Goldes.
218–14 Northern Boulevard, Bayside, NY 11361 .... (718) 423–2154
District Office Administrator.—Moya Berry.

Counties: NASSAU (part), QUEENS (part). CITIES AND TOWNSHIPS: Auburndale, Bay Terrace, Bayside, Bell Park Gardens, Bell Park Manor, Centre Island, Clearview, Corona, Deepdale, Douglaston, Douglaston Manor, East Elmhurst, East Hills, Flushing, Fresh Meadows, Glen Oaks, Great Neck, Great Neck Estates, Great Neck Gardens, Great Neck Plaza, Greenvale, Herricks, Hillcrest, Hollis Court Gardens, Hollis Hills, Jackson Heights, Jamaica Estates, Kensington, Kew Gardens Hills, Kings Point, Lake Success, Lefrak City, Linden Hill, Little Neck, Malba, Manor Haven, North Shore Towers, Oakland Gardens, Pomonok, Port Washington, Port Washington North, Queensboro Hill, Roslyn, Roslyn Estates, Roslyn Harbor, Roslyn Heights, Russell Gardens, Saddle Rock, Saddle Rock Estates, Sands Point, Searington, Thomaston, University Gardens, West Neck, and Windsor Park. Population (2000), 654,361.

ZIP Codes: 11004–05, 11020–24, 11030, 11040, 11042, 11050–55, 11351–52, 11354–58, 11360–66, 11368–69, 11372–73, 11375, 11379, 11423, 11426–27, 11432, 11507, 11542, 11548, 11560, 11568, 11576–77, 11596

* * *

SIXTH DISTRICT

GREGORY W. MEEKS, Democrat, of Southern Queens, NY; born in Harlem, NY, September 25, 1953; education: P.S. 183; Robert F. Wagner Junior High School; Julia Richman High School, New York, NY; bachelor degree, Adelphi University, 1971–75; J.D., Howard University School of Law, 1975–78; professional: lawyer, admitted to bar, 1979; Queens District Attorney's Office, 1978–83, Assistant Specialist Narcotic Prosecutor, 1981–83; Assistant Counsel to State Investigation Commission, 1983–85; serving as Assistant District Attorney; Supervising Judge, New York State Workers' Compensation Board; public service: New York State Assemblyman, 1992–97; organizations: Alpha Phi Alpha Fraternity; Council of Black-Elected Democrats; National Bar Association; Task Force on Financial Services; co-chair of the Congressional Services Caucus; co-chair of the Organizations of American States; active member of the Congressional Black Caucus; married: Simone-Marie Meeks, 1997; children: Aja, Ebony, and Nia-Ayana; committees: Financial Services; Foreign Affairs; elected to the 105th Congress on February 3, 1998; reelected to each succeeding Congress.

Office Listings

http://www.house.gov/meeks

2342 Rayburn House Office Building, Washington, DC 20515 .... (202) 225–3461
Chief of Staff.—Sophia King. FAX: 226–4169
Legislative Director.—Samuel ''Tre'' Riddle.
Office Manager / Scheduler.—Patricia Fisher.
153–01 Jamaica Avenue, Jamaica, NY 11432 .... (718) 725–6000
Chief of Staff.—Robert Simmons.
1931 Mott Avenue, Room 305, Far Rockaway, NY 11691 .... (718) 327–9791
Community Liaison.—Joan McCroud.

Counties: QUEENS COUNTY (part). CITIES AND TOWNSHIPS: Arverne, Cambria Heights, Edgemere, Far Rockaway, Floral Park, Glen Oaks, Hammels, Hollis, Howard Beach, Jamaica, Jamaica Estates, Kew Gardens, Laurelton, New Hyde Park, Ozone Park, Queens Village, Richmond Hill, Rosedale, St. Albans, South Jamaica, South Ozone Park, Springfield Gardens, and Woodhaven. Population (2000), 654,361.

ZIP Codes: 11001, 11004, 11040, 11405, 11411–20, 11422–23, 11425–36, 11439, 11451, 11484, 11690–93

* * *

SEVENTH DISTRICT

JOSEPH CROWLEY, Democrat, of Elmhurst, Queens, NY; born in Woodside, NY, March 16, 1962; education: graduated, Power Memorial High School, 1981; B.A., political science communicatios, Queens College (City University of New York), Flushing, NY, 1985; professional: elected to the New York State Assembly, 1986–98; Assembly Committees: Racing and Wagering; Banking, Consumer Affairs, and Protection; Election Law; Labor and Housing; serving in the leadership of the U.S. House of Representatives as the Chief Deputy Whip; chair, New Democrats Coalition Caucus; Founder and current chair of the Bangladesh Caucus; Founder and co-chair of the Congressional Musicians Caucus; religion: Roman Catholic; married: Kasey Nilson; children: Cullen, Kenzie and Liam; committees: Foreign Affairs; Ways and Means; elected to the 106th Congress; reelected to each succeeding Congress.

Office Listings

http://house.gov/crowley

2404 Rayburn House Office Building, Washington, DC 20510 .... (202) 225–3965
Chief of Staff.—Kate Winkler. FAX: 225–1909
Office Manager.—Merle Eisenberg.
Legislative Director.—Gregg Sheiowitz.
2800 Bruckner Boulevard, Suite 301, Bronx, NY 10465 .... (718) 931–1400
177 Dreiser Loop, Room 3, Bronx, NY 10475 .... (718) 320–2314
74–09 37th Avenue, Suite 306–B, Jackson Heights, NY 11372 .... (718) 779–1400

Counties: BRONX (part), QUEENS (part). Population (2000), 654,360.

ZIP Codes: 10458, 10460–62, 10464–67, 10469, 10472–75, 10805, 11103–04, 11354, 11356, 11368–73, 11377–78, 11380

* * *

EIGHTH DISTRICT

JERROLD NADLER, Democrat, of New York, NY; born in Brooklyn, NY, June 13, 1947; education: graduated from Stuyvesant High School, 1965; B.A., Columbia University, 1970; J.D., Fordham University, 1978; professional: New York State Assembly, 1977–92; member: ACLU; NARAL Pro-Choice America; AIPAC; National Organization for Women; Assistant Whip; married: 1976; one child; committees: Judiciary; Transportation and Infrastructure; elected to the 102nd Congress on November 3, 1992, to fill the vacancy caused by the death of Representative Ted Weiss; at the same time elected to the 103rd Congress; reelected to each succeeding Congress.

Office Listings

http://www.house.gov/nadler

2334 Rayburn House Office Building, Washington, DC 20515 .... (202) 225–5635
Director.—John Doty. FAX: 225–6923
201 Varick Street, Suite 669, New York, NY 10014 .... (212) 367–7350
Chief of Staff.—Amy Rutkin.
445 Neptune Avenue, Brooklyn, NY 11224 .... (718) 373–3198

Counties: KINGS (part), NEW YORK (part). Population (2000), 654,360.

ZIP Codes: 10001–08, 10010–14, 10016, 10018–20, 10023–24, 10036, 10038, 10041, 10043, 10047–48, 10069, 10072, 10080–81, 10101–02, 10108–09, 10113–14, 10116–17, 10119–24, 10129, 10132–33, 10149, 10199, 10209, 10213, 10242, 10249, 10256, 10260, 10265, 10268–70, 10272–82, 10285–86, 10292, 11204, 11214–15, 11218–20, 11223–24, 11228, 11230–32, 11235

* * *

NINTH DISTRICT

ANTHONY D. WEINER, Democrat, of Brooklyn, NY; born in Brooklyn, September 4, 1964; education: graduated, Brooklyn Tech High School; B.A., State University of New York at Plattsburgh, 1985; professional: served in the New York City Council, 1992–98; selected to serve as Freshman Whip, 106th Congress; committees: Energy and Commerce; Judiciary; elected to the 106th Congress; reelected to each succeeding Congress.

Office Listings

http://www.weiner.house.gov

2104 Rayburn House Office Building, Washington, DC 20515 .... (202) 225–6616
Chief of Staff.—Marie Ternes. FAX: 226–7253
Legislative Director.—Joe Dunn.
Scheduler.—Beth Chrusciel.
80–02 Kew Gardens Road, Suite 5000, Kew Gardens, NY 11415 .... (718) 520–9001
District Director.—Glen Caplin.
90–16 Rockaway Beach Boulevard, Rockaway, NY 11693 .... (718) 318–9255
1800 Sheepshead Bay Road, Brooklyn, NY 11235 .... (718) 743–0441

Counties: KINGS COUNTY (part). CITIES AND TOWNSHIPS: Bergen Beach, Brighton Beach, Canasie, Flatbush, Flatlands, Gerritsen Beach, Georgetowne, Kensington, Manhattan Beach, Marine Park, Midwood, Mill Basin, Park Slope, Parkville, Sheepshead Bay, Windsor Terrace. QUEENS COUNTY (part). CITIES AND TOWNSHIPS: Belle Harbor, Breezy Point, Briarwood, Broad Channel, Corona, Elmhurst, Far Rockaway, Forest Hills, Glendale, Hamilton Beach, Howard Beach, Kew Gardens, Lindenwood, Middle Village, Neponsit, Ozone Park, Rego Park, Richmond Hill, Ridgewood, Rockway Point, Roxbury, West Lawrence, and Woodhaven. Population (2000), 654,360.

ZIP Codes: 11204, 11208, 11210, 11218, 11223, 11229–30, 11234–36, 11358, 11361, 11364–67, 11373–75, 11378–79, 11381, 11385, 11414–18, 11421, 11424, 11427, 11432, 11435, 11693–95, 11697

* * *

TENTH DISTRICT

EDOLPHUS TOWNS, Democrat, of Brooklyn, NY; born in Chadbourn, NC, July 21, 1934; graduated, West Side High School, Chadbourn, 1952; B.S., North Carolina A&T State University, Greensboro, 1956; master's degree in social work, Adelphi University, Garden City, NY, 1973; U.S. Army, 1956–58; teacher, Medgar Evers College, Brookyln, NY, and for the New York City public school system; deputy hospital administrator, 1965–71; deputy president, Borough of Brooklyn, 1976–82; member: Kiwanis, Boy Scouts Advisory Council, Salvation Army, Phi Beta Sigma Fraternity; married the former Gwendolyn Forbes in 1960; two children: Darryl and Deidra; committees: chair, Oversight and Government Reform; elected on November 2, 1982, to the 98th Congress; reelected to each succeeding Congress.

Office Listings

http://www.house.gov/towns

2232 Rayburn House Office Building, Washington, DC 20515 .... (202) 225–5936
Senior Political and Policy Advisor.—Lars Hydle. FAX: 225–1018
Deputy Chief of Staff.—Roberta Hopkins.
Executive Assistant / Scheduler.—Sonjiah Davis.
186 Joralemon Street, Suite 1102, Brooklyn, NY 11201 .... (718) 855–8018
Chief of Staff.—Albert Wiltshire.
District Director.—Jennifer James.
104–08 Flatlands Avenue, Brooklyn, NY 11236 .... (718) 272–1175

Counties: KINGS COUNTY (part). Population (2000), 654,361.

ZIP Codes: 11201–03, 11205–08, 11210–13, 11216–17, 11221, 11230, 11233–34, 11236, 11238–39, 11245, 11247–48, 11251, 11256

* * *

ELEVENTH DISTRICT

YVETTE D. CLARKE, Democrat, of Brooklyn, NY; born in Brooklyn, November 21, 1964; education: attended Edward R. Murrow High School; attended Oberlin College; professional: Legislative Aide to New York State Senator Velmanette Montgomery; Executive Assistant to NY Assemblywoman Barbara Clark; Staff Assistant, NY Compensation Board Chair Barbara Patton; Director of Youth Programs, Hospital League / Local 1199 Training and Upgrading Fund; Director of Business Development for the Bronx Empowerment Zone (BOEDC); member of City Council of New York, 2001–06; committees: Education and Labor; Homeland Security; Small Business; elected to the 110th Congress on November 7, 2006; reelected to the 111th Congress on November 4, 2008.

Office Listings

http://clarke.house.gov

1029 Longworth House Office Building, Washington, DC 20515 .... (202) 225–6231

Chief of Staff.—Nigel Stephens. FAX: 226–0112
Legislative Director.—Algene Sajery.
123 Linden Boulevard, 4th Floor, Brooklyn, NY 11226 .... (718) 287–1142

Counties: KINGS COUNTY (part). Population (2000), 654,361.

ZIP Codes: 11201, 11203, 11210, 11212–13, 11215–18, 11225–26, 11230–31, 11233–34, 11236, 11238, 11241–42

* * *

TWELFTH DISTRICT

NYDIA M. VELÁZQUEZ, Democrat, of New York, NY; born in Yabucoa, Puerto Rico, March 28, 1953; education: B.A. in political science, University of Puerto Rico, 1974; M.A. in political science, New York University, 1976; professional: faculty member, University of Puerto Rico, 1976–81; adjunct professor, Hunter College of the City University of New York, 1981–83; special assistant to Congressman Ed Towns, 1983; member, City Council of New York, 1984–86; national director of Migration Division Office, Department of Labor and Human Resources of Puerto Rico, 1986–89; director, Department of Puerto Rican Community Affairs in the United States, 1989–92; committees: chair, Small Business; Financial Services; elected on November 3, 1992, to the 103rd Congress; reelected to each succeeding Congress.

Office Listings

http://www.house.gov/velazquez

2466 Rayburn House Office Building, Washington, DC 20515 .... (202) 225–2361
Chief of Staff.—Michael Day. FAX: 226–0327
Press Secretary.—Gail O'Connor.
Scheduler.—Erika Lopez.
Legislative Director.—Sean Huges.
268 Broadway, Sutie 201, Brooklyn, NY 11211 .... (718) 599–3658
16 Court Street, Suite 1006, Brooklyn, NY 11241 .... (718) 222–5819
173 Avenue B, New York, NY 10009 .... (212) 673–3997

Counties: KINGS (part), NEW YORK (part), QUEENS (part). Population (2000), 654,360.

ZIP Codes: 10002, 10009, 10012–13, 10038, 11104, 11201, 11205–08, 11211, 11215, 11219–22, 11231–32, 11237, 11251, 11377–78, 11385, 11416, 11421

* * *

THIRTEENTH DISTRICT

MICHAEL E. MCMAHON, Democrat, of Staten Island, NY; born in Staten Island, September 12, 1957; education: St. Joseph Hill Academy; Monsignor Farrell High School; B.A., New York University, 1980; University of Heidelberg, 1982; J.D., New York Law School, 1985; professional: lawyer; counsel, New York State Assemblymen Eric Vitaliano and Elizabeth Connelly, 1987–2000; partner, O'Leary, McMahon and Spero, 1983–2008; member, New York City Council, 2001–08; religion; Roman Catholic; married: Judith (nee Novellino); children: Joseph and Julia; Freshmen Class Whip; New Democrat Coalition; committees: Foreign Affairs; Transportation and Infrastructure; elected to the 111th Congress on November 4, 2008.

Office Listings

http://www.mcmahon.house.gov

323 Cannon House Office Building, Washington, DC 20515 .... (202) 225–3371
Chief of Staff.—Chris McCannell. FAX: 226–1272
Legislative Director.—Jeffrey Siegel.
Communications Director.—Lauren Amendolara.
Scheduler.—Peter Rocco.
265 New Dorp Lane, 2nd Floor, Staten Island, NY 10306 .... (718) 351–1062
District Director.—Patrick Hyland. FAX: 980–0768
District Scheduler.—Mary Alice Tait.
8505 4th Avenue, Brooklyn, NY 11209 .... (718) 630–5277
Brooklyn Director.—Jonathan Yedin. FAX: 630–5388

Counties: KINGS (part), RICHMOND. Population (2000), 654,361.

ZIP Codes: 10301–10, 10312–14, 11204, 11209, 11214, 11219–20, 11223, 11228, 11252

* * *

FOURTEENTH DISTRICT

CAROLYN B. MALONEY, Democrat, of New York City, NY; born in Greensboro, NC, February 19, 1946; education: B.A., Greensboro College, Greensboro, NC, 1968; professional: various positions, New York City Board of Education, 1970–77; legislative aide, New York State Assembly, senior program analyst, 1977–79; executive director of advisory council, 1979–82; director of special projects, New York State Senate Office of the Minority Leader; New York City council member, 1982–93; chairperson, New York City Council Committee on Contracts; member: Council Committee on Aging, National Organization of Women, Common Cause, Sierra Club, Americans for Democratic Action, New York City Council Committee on Housing and Buildings, Citizens Union, Grand Central Business Improvement District, Harlem Urban Development Corporation (1982–91), Commission on Early Childhood Development Programs, Council of Senior Citizen Centers of New York City (1982–87); married: Clifton H.W. Maloney, 1976; children: Virginia Marshall Maloney and Christina Paul Maloney; committees: Financial Services; Oversight and Government Reform; chair, Joint Economic Committee; elected on November 3, 1992, to the 103rd Congress; reelected to each succeeding Congress.

Office Listings

http://www.maloney.house.gov

2332 Rayburn House Office Building, Washington, DC 20515 .... (202) 225–7944
Administrative Assistant.—Ben Chevat. FAX: 225–4709
Legislative Director.—Orly Isaacson.
1651 Third Avenue, Suite 311, New York, NY 10128 .... (212) 860–0606
28–11 Astoria Boulevard, Astoria, NY 11102 .... (718) 932–1804

Counties: NEW YORK (part), QUEENS (part). CITIES AND TOWNSHIPS: Astoria, Manhattan, Queens, Long Island City, Roosevelt Island, Sunnyside, and Woodside. Population (2000), 654,361.

ZIP Codes: 10012, 10016–24, 10026, 10028–29, 10036, 10044, 10055, 10103–07, 10110–12, 10126, 10128, 10138, 10150–60, 10162–79, 11101–06, 11375, 11377

* * *

FIFTEENTH DISTRICT

CHARLES B. RANGEL, Democrat-Liberal, of New York, NY; born in Harlem, NY, June 11, 1930; attended DeWitt Clinton High School; served in U.S. Army, 1948–52; awarded the Purple Heart, Bronze Star for Valor, U.S. and Korean presidential citations, and three battle stars while serving in combat with the Second Infantry Division in Korea; honorably discharged with rank of staff sergeant; after military duty, completed high school, 1953; graduated from New York University School of Commerce, student under the G.I. bill; 1957 dean's list; graduated from St. John's University School of Law, dean's list student under a full three-year scholarship, 1960; lawyer; admitted to practice in the courts of the State of New York, U.S. Federal Court, Southern District of New York, and U.S. Customs Court; appointed assistant U.S. attorney, Southern District of New York, 1961; legal counsel, New York City Housing and Redevelopment Board, Neighborhood Conservation Bureau; general counsel, National Advisory Commission on Selective Service, 1966; served two terms in the New York State Assembly, 1966–70; active in 369th Veterans Association; Community Education Program; and Martin Luther King, Jr., Democratic Club; married: Alma Carter; two children: Steven and Alicia; committees: chair, Ways and Means; chair, Joint Committee on Taxation; elected to the 92nd Congress, November 3, 1970; reelected to each succeeding Congress.

Office Listings

http://www.house.gov/rangel

2354 Rayburn House Office Building, Washington, DC 20515 .... (202) 225–4365
Counsel / Chief of Staff.—George Henry. FAX: 225–0816
163 West 125th Street, Room 737, New York, NY 10027 .... (212) 663–3900
District Administrator.—Vivian E. Jones.

Counties: BRONX (part), NEW YORK (part), QUEENS (part). Population (2000), 654,361.

ZIP Codes: 10023–27, 10029–35, 10037, 10039–40, 10115–16, 10169, 10463, 11105

* * *

SIXTEENTH DISTRICT

JOSÉ E. SERRANO, Democrat, of Bronx, NY; born in Mayagüez, PR, October 24, 1943; education: Dodge Vocational High School, Bronx, NY; attended Lehman College, City University of New York, NY; served with the U.S. Army Medical Corps, 1964–66; employed by the Manufacturers Hanover Bank, 1961–69; Community School District 7, 1969–74; New York State Assemblyman, 1974–90; chairman, Consumer Affairs Committee, 1979–83; chairman, Education Committee, 1983–90; five children: Lisa, Jose Marco, Justine, Jonathan and Benjamin; committees: Appropriations; elected to the 101st Congress, by special election, March 28, 1990, to fill the vacancy caused by the resignation of Robert Garcia; reelected to each succeeding Congress.

Office Listings

http://serrano.house.gov

2227 Rayburn House Office Building, Washington, DC 20515 .... (202) 225–4361
Executive Assistant.—Pichy Marty. FAX: 225–6001
Legislative Director.—Nadine Berg.
Scheduler.—Elisa Howie.
903 Dawson Street, Bronx, NY 10459 .... (718) 620–0084
Chief of Staff.—Paul Lipson.

Counties: BRONX COUNTY (part). CITIES AND TOWNSHIPS: Bronx. Population (2000), 654,360.

ZIP Codes: 10451–60, 10463, 10468, 10472–74

* * *

SEVENTEENTH DISTRICT

ELIOT L. ENGEL, Democrat, of Bronx, NY; born in Bronx, February 18, 1947; education: B.A., Hunter-Lehman College, 1969; M.A., City University of New York, 1973; J.D., New York Law School, 1987; professional: teacher and counselor in the New York City public school system, 1969–77; elected to the New York legislature, 1977–88; chaired the Assembly Committee on Alcoholism and Substance Abuse and subcommittee on Mitchell-Lama Housing (twelve years prior to his election to Congress); member: Congressional Human Rights Caucus; Democratic Study Group on Health; Long Island Sound Caucus; co-chairman, Albanian Issues Caucus; board member, Congressional Ad Hoc Committee on Irish Affairs; married: Patricia Ennis, 1980; children: Julia, Jonathan, and Philip; committees: Energy and Commerce; Foreign Affairs; elected on November 8, 1988, to the 101st Congress; reelected to each succeeding Congress.

Office Listings

http://www.engel.house.gov

2161 Rayburn House Office Building, Washington, DC 20515 .... (202) 225–2464
Administrative Assistant.—E.H. ''Ned'' Michalek. FAX: 225–5513
Office Manager.—Brittany Starr.
3655 Johnson Avenue, Bronx, NY 10463 .... (718) 796–9700
Chief of Staff.—William Weitz.
6 Gramatan Avenue, Suite 205, Mt. Vernon, NY 10550 .... (914) 699–4100
261 West Nyack Road, West Nyack, NY 10994 .... (845) 358–7800

Counties: BRONX (part), WESTCHESTER (part). CITIES AND TOWNSHIPS: Parts of Bronx, Mount Vernon, Yonkers. ROCKLAND COUNTY. TOWNSHIPS: Clarkstown, Orangetown, Ramapo, Population (2000), 654,360.

ZIP Codes: 10458, 10463, 10466–71, 10475, 10522, 10533, 10550–52, 10557–58, 10591, 10701, 10704–06, 10708, 10901, 10913, 10920, 10931, 10952, 10954, 10956, 10960, 10962, 10964–65, 10968, 10970, 10974, 10976–77, 10983, 10989, 10994

* * *

EIGHTEENTH DISTRICT

NITA M. LOWEY, Democrat, of Harrison, NY; born in New York, NY, July 5, 1937; education: graduated, Bronx High School of Science, 1955; B.A., Mount Holyoke College,

1959; assistant to Secretary of State for Economic Development and Neighborhood Preservation, and deputy director, Division of Economic Opportunity, 1975–85; Assistant Secretary of State, 1985–87; member: boards of directors, Close-Up Foundation; Effective Parenting Information for Children; Windward School, Downstate (New York Region); Westchester Jewish Conference; Westchester Opportunity Program; National Committee of the Police Corps; Women's Network of the YWCA; Legal Awareness for Women; National Women's Political Caucus of Westchester; American Jewish Committee of Westchester; married: Stephen Lowey, 1961; children: Dana, Jacqueline, and Douglas; committees: Appropriations; elected on November 8, 1988, to the 101st Congress; reelected to each succeeding Congress.

Office Listings

http://www.house.gov/lowey

2329 Rayburn House Office Building, Washington, DC 20515 .... (202) 225–6506
Chief of Staff.—Elizabeth Stanley. FAX: 225–0546
Executive Assistant.—Jennifer Sacks.
Legislative Director.—Jean Doyle.
Communications Director.—Matt Dennis.
Suite 310, 222 Mamaroneck Avenue, White Plains, NY 10605 .... (914) 428–1707
District Administrator.—Patricia Keegan.

Counties: ROCKLAND (part), WESTCHESTER (part). CITIES AND TOWNSHIPS: Ardsley, Ardsley on the Hundson, Briarcliff Manor; Bronxville, Chappaqua, Congers, Crestwood, Dobbs Ferry, Eastchester, Elmsford, Harrison, Hartsdale, Hasting-on-Hudson, Haverstraw, Hawthorne, Irvington, Larchmont, Mamaroneck, Maryknoll, Millwood, Mt. Kisco, New City, New Rochelle, North Castle, Ossining, Pelham, Pleasantville, Port Chester, Purchase, Rye, Rye Brook, Scarsdale, Sleepy Hollow, Tarrytown, Thornwood, Tuckahoe, Valhalla, Valley Cottage, West Harrison, West Haverstraw, White Plains, and Yonkers. Population (2000), 654,360.

ZIP Codes: 10502, 10504, 10506, 10510, 10514, 10522–23, 10528, 10530, 10532–33, 10538, 10543, 10546, 10549, 10562, 10570, 10573, 10577, 10580, 10583, 10591, 10594–95, 10601–07, 10610, 10650, 10701–10, 10801–05, 10920, 10923, 10927, 10956, 10989, 10993–94

* * *

NINETEENTH DISTRICT

JOHN J. HALL, Democrat, of Dover Plains, NY; born in Baltimore, MD, July 23, 1948; a three-time National Science Foundation scholar in High School; studied physics at Notre Dame University and transferred to Loyola College; professional: musician and co-founder of the band Orleans; served one term on Ulster County Legislature; served two terms on the Saugerties School Board; married: Pamela Bingham Hall; one daughter; committees: Transportation and Infrastructure; Veterans' Affairs; Select Committee on Energy Independence and Global Warming; elected to the 110th Congress on November 7, 2006; reelected to the 111th Congress.

Office Listings

http://www.johnhall.house.gov

1217 Longworth House Office Building, Washington, DC 20515 .... (202) 225–5441
Chief of Staff.—Susan Spear. FAX: 225–3289
Legislative Director.—Jim Bradley.
Orange County Government Center, 255 Main Street, Room 3232G, Goshen, NY 10924 .... (845) 291–4100
Putnam County Office Building, 40 Gleneida Avenue, 3rd Floor, Carmel, NY 10512 .... (845) 225–3641
District Director.—Frank Giancamilli. EXT: 49371

Counties: DUTCHESS COUNTY (part). CITIES AND TOWNSHIPS: Beacon, Castle Point, Chelsea, Dover Plains, Fishkill, Glenham, Holmes, Hopewell Junction, Hughsonville, Pawling, Poughkeepsie, Poughquag, Stormville, Wappingers Falls, Wingdale. ORANGE COUNTY (part). CITIES AND TOWNSHIPS: Amity, Arden, Bear Mountain, Bellvale, Blooming Grove, Burnside, Campbell Hall, Central Valley, Chester, Cornwall, Cornwall-on-Hudson, Craigville, Cuddebackville, Durlandville, Eagle Valley, Edenville, Finchville, Finnegan's Corner, Firthcliff, Florida, Fort Montgomery, Gardnerville, Goddefroy, Goshen, Greenwood Lake, Guymard, Harriman, Highland Falls, Highland Mills, Huguenot, Johnson, Kiryas Joel, Little Britain, Little York, Maybrook, Middletown, Monroe, Montgomery, Mountainville, New Hampton, New Milford, New Vernon, New Windsor, Newburgh, Otisville, Oxford Depot, Phillipsburg, Pine Island, Port Jervis, Ridgebury, Rock Tavern, Salisbury Mills, Slate Hill, Sloatsburg, Southfields, Sparrowbush, Sterling Forest, Stony Ford, Suffern, Sugarloaf, Tuxedo, Tuxedo Park, Unionville, Vails Gate, Wallkill, Warwick, Washingtonville, West Point, Westbrookville, Westtown, Wickham Village. PUTNAM COUNTY. CITIES AND TOWNSHIPS: Baldwin Place, Brewster, Carmel, Cold Spring, Garrison, Kent, Lake Peekskill, Mahopac, Mahopac Falls, Patterson, Putnam Valley. ROCKLAND COUNTY. CITIES AND TOWNSHIPS: Garnerville, Haverstraw, Pomona, Stony Point, Thiells, Tomkins Cove. WESTCHESTER COUNTY. CITIES AND TOWNSHIPS: Amawalk, Baldwin Place, Bedford, Bedford Hills, Buchanan, Cortlandt Manor, Crompound, Cross River, Croton Falls, Croton-on-Hudson, Golden's Bridge, Jefferson Valley, Katonah, Lincolndale, Mohegan Lake, Montrose, Mt. Kisco, North Salem, Peekskill, Pound Ridge, Purdys, Shenorock, Shrub Oak, Somers, South Salem, Verplanck, Waccabuc, and Yorktown Heights. Population (2000), 654,361.

ZIP Codes: 10501, 10504–07, 10509, 10511–12, 10516–21, 10524, 10526–27, 10530, 10535–37, 10540–42, 10545, 10547–49, 10551, 10558, 10560, 10562, 10566–67, 10571–72, 10576, 10578–79, 10587–90, 10596–98, 10602, 10911, 10916–18, 10921–26, 10928, 10930, 10940–41, 10943, 10950, 10953, 10958, 10963, 10969–70, 10973, 10975, 10979–80, 10984, 10986–87, 10990, 10992, 10996–98, 11518, 11542, 11568, 11572, 11701–02, 11704, 11706–09, 11721, 11724, 11730–31, 11740, 11757, 11768, 11797, 12508, 12510–12, 12518, 12520, 12522, 12524, 12527, 12531, 12533, 12537–38, 12540, 12543, 12549, 12552–53, 12555, 12563–64, 12570, 12575, 12577–78, 12582, 12584, 12590, 12592, 12594, 12601–04, 12729, 12746, 12771, 12780, 12785

* * *

TWENTIETH DISTRICT

SCOTT MURPHY, Democrat, of Glens Falls, NY; born in Columbia, MO, January 26, 1970; education: graduated from David H. Hickman High School, Columbia, MO, 1988; A.B., Harvard University, Cambridge, MA, 1992; professional: businessman; married: Jen Hogan; children: Simone, Lux, and Duke; committees: Agriculture; Armed Services; elected to the 111th Congress on March 31, 2009 by special election to fill the vacancy caused by the resignation of United States Representative Kirsten Gillibrand.

Office Listings

http://www.scottmurphy.house.gov

120 Cannon House Office Building, Washington, DC 20515 .... (202) 225–5614
Chief of Staff.—Todd Schulte. FAX: 225–1168
Legislative Director.—Andrew Lattanner.
Communications Director.—Maggie McKeon.
623 Warren Street, Hudson, NY 12534 .... (518) 828–3109
136 Glen Street, Glens Falls, NY 12801 .... (518) 743–0964
487 Broadway, Saratoga Springs, NY 12866 .... (518) 581–8247
District Director.—Rob Scholz.

Counties: COLUMBIA, DELAWARE (part), DUTCHESS (part), ESSEX (part), GREENE, RENSSELAER (part), SARATOGA (part), OTSEGO (part), WARREN, and WASHINGTON. Population (2000), 654,360.

ZIP Codes: 12010, 12015, 12017–20, 12022, 12024–25, 12027–29, 12033, 12037, 12040, 12042, 12046, 12050–52, 12057–60, 12062, 12065, 12074–76, 12083, 12086–87, 12089–90, 12093–94, 12106, 12115, 12118, 12123–25, 12130, 12132–34, 12136, 12138, 12140, 12143, 12148, 12151, 12153–56, 12165, 12167–70, 12172–74, 12176, 12180, 12182, 12184–85, 12192, 12195–96, 12198, 12405–07, 12413–14, 12418, 12421–24, 12427, 12430–31, 12434, 12438–39, 12442, 12444, 12450–51, 12454–55, 12459–60, 12463, 12468–70, 12473–74, 12480, 12482, 12485, 12492, 12496, 12501–03, 12507, 12513–14, 12516–17, 12521–23, 12526, 12529, 12533–34, 12538, 12540, 12545–46, 12565, 12567, 12569–72, 12578, 12580–81, 12583, 12585, 12590, 12592, 12594, 12601, 12603, 12776, 12801, 12803–04, 12808–11, 12814–17, 12819–24, 12827–28, 12831–39, 12841, 12843–46, 12848–50, 12853–56, 12859–63, 12865–66, 12870–74, 12878, 12883–87, 12942–43, 12946, 12977, 12983, 13326, 13450, 13488, 13731, 13739–40, 13750, 13752–53, 13755, 13757, 13775, 13782, 13786, 13788, 13804, 13806–07, 13820, 13838, 13842, 13846, 13849, 13856, 13860

* * *

TWENTY-FIRST DISTRICT

PAUL D. TONKO, Democrat, of Amsterdam, NY; born in Amsterdam, NY, June 18, 1949; education: graduated Amsterdam High School, Amsterdam, NY, in 1967; B.S. Degree, mechanical and industrial engineering, Clarkson University, Potsdam, NY, 1971; professional: Engineer, NYS Department of Transportation; Engineer, NYS Department of Public Service; Montgomery County Board of Supervisors, 1976–83; chairman, Montgomery County Board of Supervisors, 1981–83; NYS Assembly, 1983–2007; chairman, NYS Assembly Standing Committee on Energy, 1992–2007; President & CEO, NYS Energy Research and Development Authority, 2007–08; caucuses: vice-chair, Sustainable Energy and Environment Coalition; committees: Education and Labor, Science and Technology; elected to the 111th Congress on November 4, 2008.

Office Listings

http://www.tonko.house.gov

128 Cannon House Office Building, Washington, DC 20515 .... (202) 225–5076
Chief of Staff.—Michael Lehman. FAX: 225–5077
Press Secretary.—Deau Duffy.
Legislative Director.—Joseph Eaves.
Leo W. O'Brein Federal Building, 1 Clinton Square, Albany, NY 12207 .... (518) 465–0700
105 Jay Street, (Schenetady City Hall), Room 15, Schenectady, NY 12305 .... (518) 374–4547
61 Church Street, (Amsterdam City Hall), Room 309, Amsterdam, NY 12010 .... (518) 843–3400

Counties: ALBANY, FULTON (part), MONTGOMERY, RENSSELAER (part), SARATOGA (part), SCHOHARIE, and SCHENECTADY. Population (2000), 654,361.

ZIP Codes: 12007–10, 12016, 12019, 12027, 12031, 12033, 12035–36, 12041, 12043, 12045–47, 12053–54, 12056, 12061, 12063–64, 12066–73, 12077–78, 12082–87, 12092–93, 12095, 12107, 12110, 12116, 12120–23, 12128, 12131, 12137, 12141, 12143–44, 12147, 12149–50, 12157–61, 12166–67, 12175, 12177, 12179–83, 12186–89, 12193–94, 12197–98, 12201–12, 12214, 12220, 12222–40, 12242–50, 12252, 12255–57, 12260–61, 12288, 12301–09, 12325, 12345, 12434, 12469, 13317, 13320, 13339, 13410, 13428, 13452, 13459

* * *

TWENTY-SECOND DISTRICT

MAURICE D. HINCHEY, Democrat, of Hurley, NY; born in New York, NY, October 27, 1938; education: graduated, Saugerties High School, 1956; B.S., State College, New Paltz, NY, 1968; M.A., State College, New Paltz, 1969; professional: Seaman First Class, U.S. Navy, 1956–59; teacher; public administrator; elected to the New York State Assembly, 1975–92; member: New York Council of State Governments; National Conference of State Legislatures; married: Allison Lee Hinchey, 2006; three children: Maurice Scott, Josef, and Michelle Rebecca; committees: Appropriations; Natural Resources; Joint Economic Committee; elected on November 3, 1992 to the 103rd Congress; reelected to each succeeding Congress.

Office Listings

http://www.house.gov/hinchey

2431 Rayburn House Office Building, Washington, DC 20515 .... (202) 225–6335
Chief of Staff.—Dan Ahouse. FAX: 226–0774
Legislative Director.—Michael Iger.
Communications Director.—Jeff Lieberson.
291 Wall Street, Kingston, NY 12401 .... (845) 331–4466
100A Federal Building, Binghamton, NY 13901 .... (607) 773–2768
123 South Cayuga Street, Suite 201, Ithaca, NY 14850 .... (607) 273–1388
City Hall, Third Floor, 16 James Street, Middletown, NY 10940 .... (845) 344–3211

Counties: BROOME COUNTY (part); CITIES AND TOWNS OF: Binghamton, Conklin, Kirkwood, Sanford, Union (includes villages of Endicott and Johnson City), Vestal, and Windsor. DELAWARE COUNTY (part); TOWNS OF: Deposit, Hancock, and Tompkins. DUTCHESS COUNTY (part). CITIES: Poughkeepsie. ORANGE COUNTY (part); CITIES AND TOWNS OF: Crawford, Middletown, Montgomery (includes village of Walden), Newburgh, and Wallkill. SULLIVAN COUNTY; CITIES AND TOWNS OF: Bethel, Callicoon, Cochecton, Delaware, Fallsburg, Forestburgh, Fremont, Highland, Liberty, Lumberland, Mamakating, Neversink, Rockland, Thompson, and Tusten. TIOGA COUNTY (part). CITIES AND TOWNS: Barton, Nichols, Owego, and Spencer. TOMPKINS COUNTY (part). CITIES AND TOWNS: Danby, and Ithaca. ULSTER COUNTY. CITIES AND TOWNS: Denning, Esopus, Gardiner, Hardenburgh, Hurley, Kingston, Lloyd, Marbletown, Marlborough, New Paltz, Olive, Plattekill, Rochester, Rosendale, Saugerties, Shandaken, Shawangunk, Ulster, Wawarsing (includes village of Ellenville), and Woodstock. Population (2000), 654,361.

ZIP Codes: 10915, 10919, 10932, 10940–41, 10985, 12401–02, 12404, 12406, 12409–12, 12416, 12419–20, 12428–29, 12432–33, 12435–36, 12440–41, 12443, 12446, 12448–49, 12451–53, 12455–58, 12461, 12464–66, 12469, 12471–72, 12475, 12477, 12480–81, 12483–84, 12486–87, 12489–91, 12493–95, 12498, 12504, 12506, 12515, 12525, 12528, 12530, 12541–44, 12547–51, 12561, 12566, 12568, 12574–75, 12583, 12586, 12588–89, 12601, 12603, 12701, 12719–27, 12729, 12732–34, 12736–38, 12740–43, 12745, 12747–52, 12754, 12758–60, 12762–70, 12775–84, 12786–92, 12814, 12853, 12857–58, 12879, 12883, 12928, 12983, 13068, 13501, 13730, 13732, 13734, 13737, 13743, 13748–49, 13754, 13756, 13760, 13774, 13783, 13790, 13795, 13811–13, 13820, 13826, 13850, 13856, 13864–65, 13901–05, 14817, 14850–51, 14853, 14859, 14867, 14883, 14889, 14892

* * *

TWENTY-THIRD DISTRICT

VACANT

Counties: CLINTON, ESSEX (part), FRANKLIN, FULTON (part), HAMILTON, JEFFERSON, LEWIS, MADISON, ONEIDA (part), OSWEGO, ST. LAWRENCE. Population (2000), 654,361.

ZIP Codes: 12010, 12023, 12025, 12032, 12036, 12070, 12078, 12086, 12095, 12108, 12117, 12134, 12139, 12164, 12167, 12190, 12812, 12842, 12847, 12851–52, 12857, 12864, 12883, 12901, 12903, 12910–24, 12926–30, 12932–37, 12939, 12941, 12944–46, 12949–50, 12952–53, 12955–62, 12964–67, 12969–70, 12972–76, 12978–81, 12983, 12985–87, 12989, 12992–93, 12996–98, 13028, 13030, 13032–33, 13035–37, 13042–44, 13052, 13061, 13064, 13069, 13072, 13074, 13076, 13082–83, 13093, 13103–04, 13107, 13111, 13114–15, 13121–23, 13126, 13131–32, 13134–36, 13142, 13144–45, 13156, 13158, 13163, 13167, 13301–04, 13308–10, 13313–16, 13318–19, 13321–23, 13325–29, 13332–35, 13337–43, 13345–46, 13348, 13350, 13352, 13354–55, 13357, 13360–65, 13367–68, 13401–03, 13406–11, 13413, 13415, 13417–18, 13421, 13424–25, 13428, 13431, 13433, 13435–41, 13449–50, 13452, 13455–57, 13460–61, 13465, 13468–69, 13471, 13473, 13475, 13477–80, 13482–86, 13488–95, 13501–05, 13599, 13601–03, 13605–08, 13611–28, 13630–43, 13645–52, 13654–62, 13664–85, 13687–88, 13690–97, 13699

* * *

TWENTY-FOURTH DISTRICT

MICHAEL A. ARCURI, Democrat, of Utica, NY; born in Utica, June 11, 1959; education: graduated, Proctor High School; B.A., SUNY Albany, 1981; J.D., New York Law School, 1984; professional: private practice attorney, 1988–94; counsel, New Hartford Central School District Board of Education; elected Oneida County District Attorney, 1993; President, New York District Attorney's Association, 2003; two children; committees: Rules; Transportation and Infrastructure; elected to the 110th Congress on November 7, 2006; reelected to the 111th Congress.

Office Listings

http://www.arcuri.house.gov/

127 Cannon House Office Building, Washington, DC 20515 .... (202) 225–3665
Chief of Staff.—Sam Marchio. FAX: 225–1891
Executive Assistant.—Mark Cornell.
Alexander Pirnie Federal Office Building, 10 Broad Street, Room 330, Utica, NY 13501 .... (313) 793–8146
District Director.—Joe Johnson.
16 Church Street, Carriage House Right, Cortland, NY 13045 .... (607) 756–2470
17 East Genesee Street, Auburn, NY 13021 .... (315) 252–2777

Counties: BROOME (part), CAYUGA (part), CHENANGO, CORTLAND, HERKIMER (part), ONEIDA (part), ONTARIO (part), OTSEGO (part), SENECA, TIOGA (part), TOMPKINS (part). Population (2000), 654,361.

ZIP Codes: 13021–22, 13024, 13026, 13032–34, 13040, 13042, 13045, 13052–54, 13056, 13062, 13065, 13068, 13071–74, 13077, 13080–81, 13083, 13087, 13092, 13101–02, 13117–18, 13124, 13136, 13139–41, 13147–48, 13152, 13155, 13157–60, 13162, 13165–66, 13302–05, 13308–09, 13312, 13315, 13317–20, 13322–29, 13331–33, 13335, 13337–40, 13342–43, 13345, 13348, 13350, 13353–54, 13357, 13360–61, 13363, 13365, 13367–68, 13403–04, 13406–07, 13411, 13413, 13415–17, 13420–21, 13424–26, 13431, 13433, 13436–42, 13452, 13454, 13456, 13460–61, 13464, 13468–73, 13475–78, 13480, 13485–86, 13489–93, 13495, 13501–02, 13601, 13603, 13605–08, 13611–26, 13628, 13630, 13632–43, 13645–52, 13654–56, 13658–62, 13664–69, 13672–85, 13687, 13690–97, 13699, 13730, 13733–34, 13736, 13738, 13743–47, 13752–54, 13758, 13760, 13776–78, 13780, 13784, 13787, 13790, 13794, 13796–97, 13801–03, 13807–11, 13813–15, 13820, 13825–27, 13830, 13832–33, 13835, 13838, 13840–41, 13843–45, 13848–49, 13856, 13859, 13861–64, 14433, 14443, 14456, 14468–69, 14489, 14504, 14521, 14532, 14541, 14548, 14571, 14588, 14817, 14841, 14847, 14850–52, 14854, 14860, 14867, 14881–83, 14886

* * *

TWENTY-FIFTH DISTRICT

DANIEL B. MAFFEI, Democrat, of DeWitt, NY; born in Syracuse, NY; July 4, 1968; bachelor's Degree in history from Brown University, Providence, RI, 1990; masters of journalism from Columbia University's Graduate School of Journalism, 1991; masters of public policy from Harvard University's John F. Kennedy School of Government, 1995; religion: Catholic; married: Abby Davidson-Maffei; committees: Financial Services; Judiciary; elected to the 111th Congress on November 4, 2008.

Office Listings

http://www.walsh.house.govh

1630 Longworth House Office Building, Washington, DC 20515 .... (202) 225–3701
Chief of Staff.—Jill Allen Murray. FAX: 225–4042
Executive Assistant.—Kaii Torrence.
1000 South Clinton Street, Room 1340, P.O. Box 7306, Syracuse, NY 13216 .... (315) 423–5657
Chief of Staff.—Michael Whyland. .... FAX: 423–5669
1280 Titus Avenue, Rochester, NY 14617 .... (585) 336–7291
FAX: 336–7274

Counties: CAYUGA (part), MONROE (part), ONONDAGA, and WAYNE. CITIES AND TOWNSHIPS: Arcadia, Butler, Camillus, Cato, Cicero, Clay, Conquest, DeWitt, Elbridge, Fabius, Galen, Geddes, Huron, Ira, Irondequoit, LaFayette, Lyons, Lysander, Macedon, Manlius, Marcellus, Marion, Onondaga, Ontario, Otisco, Palmyra, Penfield, Pompey, Rose, Salina, Savannah, Skaneateles, Sodus, Spafford, Sterling, Syracuse, Tully, Van Buren, Victory, Walworth, Webster, Williamson, and Wolcott. Population (2000), 654,361.

ZIP Codes: 13020–21, 13027, 13029–31, 13033, 13035, 13037, 13039–41, 13051–53, 13057, 13060, 13063–64, 13066, 13068–69, 13077–78, 13080, 13082, 13084, 13088, 13090, 13104, 13108, 13110–13, 13116–17, 13119–20, 13122, 13126, 13135, 13137–38, 13140–41, 13143, 13146, 13148, 13152–54, 13156, 13159, 13164–66, 13201–12, 13214–15, 13217–21, 13224–25, 13235, 13244, 13250–52, 13261, 13290, 14413, 14432–33, 14449–50, 14489, 14502, 14505, 14513, 14516, 14519–20, 14522, 14526, 14537–38, 14542, 14551, 14555, 14563–64, 14568, 14580, 14589–90, 14609, 14617, 14621–22, 14625

* * *

TWENTY-SIXTH DISTRICT

CHRISTOPHER JOHN LEE, Republican, of Clarence, NY; born in Kenmore, NY, April 1, 1964; education: B.A., University of Rochester, NY, 1987; M.B.A., Chapman University, Orange, CA, 1997; professional: Pacific Rim Sales Manager, Enidine Inc., 1995–97; Director, International Sales and Marketing, Enidine Inc., 2000–02; General Manager, Enidine Inc., 2003–04; President, Automation Group, Enidine Inc., 2005–07; Deputy Republican Whip; married: Michele; children: Johnathan; committees: Financial Services; elected to the 111th Congress on November 4, 2008.

Office Listings

http://www.chrislee.house.gov

1711 Longworth House Office Building, Washington, DC 20515 .... (202) 225–5265
Chief of Staff.—Brian Schubert. FAX: 225–5910
Executive Assistant.—Laura Ringdahl.
Communications Director.—Michael Ricci.
Legislative Director.—Kelly Dixon.
Press Secretary.—Andrea Bozek.
325 Essjay Road, Suite 405, Williamsville, NY 14221 .... (716) 634–2324
1577 West Ridge Road, Greece, NY 14615 .... (585) 663–5570

Counties: ERIE (part), GENESEE, LIVINGSTON, MONROE (part), NIAGARA (part), ORLEANS (part), WYOMING. Population (2000), 654,361.

ZIP Codes: 14001, 14004–05, 14008–09, 14011–13, 14020–21, 14024, 14026, 14030–32, 14036, 14038–39, 14043, 14051, 14054, 14056, 14058–59, 14066–68, 14082–83, 14086, 14094–95, 14098, 14103, 14105, 14113, 14120, 14125, 14130–32, 14139, 14143, 14145, 14167, 14215, 14221, 14224–26, 14228, 14231, 14260, 14304, 14410–11, 14414, 14416, 14420, 14422–23, 14427–30, 14435, 14437, 14452, 14454, 14462, 14464, 14466, 14468, 14470–72, 14476–77, 14479–82, 14485–88, 14510–12, 14514–15, 14517, 14525, 14530, 14533, 14536, 14539, 14545–46, 14549–50, 14556–60, 14569, 14571–72, 14591–92, 14606, 14612, 14615–16, 14624, 14626, 14822, 14836, 14846

* * *

TWENTY-SEVENTH DISTRICT

BRIAN HIGGINS, Democrat, of Buffalo, NY; born in Buffalo, October 6, 1959; education: B.A., Buffalo State College, NY, 1984; M.A., Buffalo State College, 1985; M.P.A., Harvard University, Cambridge, MA, 1996; professional: lecturer, Buffalo State College; member of the Buffalo Common Council, 1988–94; member of the New York state assembly, 1999–2004; married: Mary Jane Hannon; two children: John and Maeve; committees: Ways and Means; elected to the 109th Congress on November 2, 2004; reelected to each succeeding Congress.

Office Listings

http://www.higgins.house.gov

431 Cannon House Office Building, Washington, DC 20515 .... (202) 225–3306
Chief of Staff.—Andy Tantillo. FAX: 226–0347
Communications Director.—Theresa Kennedy.
Legislative Director.—Andy Tantillo.
Larkin Building, 726 Exchange Street, Suite 601, Buffalo, NY 14210 .... (716) 852–3501
Fenton Building, 2 East 2nd Street, Suite 300, Jamestown, NY 14701 .... (716) 484–0729

Counties: CHAUTAUQUA, ERIE (part). CITIES AND TOWNSHIPS: Boston, Brant, Buffalo, Cheektowaga, Colden, Concord, Collins, East Aurora, Eden, Elma, Evans, Hamburg, Holland, Lackawanna, North Boston, North Collins, Orchard Park, Sardinia, and Seneca. Population (2000), 654,361.

ZIP Codes: 14004, 14006, 14010, 14025–27, 14030, 14033–35, 14037, 14040, 14043, 14047–48, 14052, 14055, 14057, 14059, 14061–63, 14069–70, 14075, 14080–81, 14085–86, 14091, 14102, 14110–12, 14127, 14134–36, 14138–41, 14145, 14166, 14169–70, 14201–03, 14206–16, 14218–22, 14224–27, 14233, 14240–41, 14264–65, 14267, 14269, 14272, 14276, 14280, 14504, 14701–04, 14710, 14712, 14716, 14718, 14720, 14722–24, 14726, 14728, 14732–33, 14736, 14738, 14740, 14742, 14747, 14750, 14752, 14756–58, 14767, 14769, 14775, 14781–82, 14784–85, 14787

* * *

TWENTY-EIGHTH DISTRICT

LOUISE McINTOSH SLAUGHTER, Democrat, of Fairport, NY; born in Harlan County, KY, August 14, 1929; education: B.S. in microbiology (1951) and M.S. in public health

(1953), University of Kentucky; elected to Monroe County legislature, two terms, 1976–79; elected to New York State Assembly, two terms, 1982–86; Distinguished Public Health Legislation Award, American Public Health Association, 1998; married: Robert Slaughter; three daughters; seven grandchildren; committees: chair, Rules; elected to the 100th Congress on November 4, 1986; reelected to each succeeding Congress.

Office Listings

http://www.louise.house.gov

2469 Rayburn House Office Building, Washington, DC 20515 .... (202) 225–3615
Chief of Staff.—Greg Regan. FAX: 225–7822
Legislative Director.—John Monsif.
Communications Director.—Vince Morris.
Scheduler.—Kelsey Hornbach
3120 Federal Building, 100 State Street, Rochester, NY 14614 .... (585) 232–4850
465 Main Street, Suite 105, Buffalo, NY 14203 .... (716) 853–5813
1910 Pine Avenue, Niagara Falls, NY 14301 .... (716) 282–1274

Counties: Erie (part), Monroe (part), Niagara (part), Orleans (part). CITIES AND TOWNSHIPS: Appleton, Barker, Brighton, Buffalo, Burt, East Rochester, Fairport, Grand Island, Greece, Hamlin, Hilton, Irondequoit, Kendall, Kent, Lewiston, Lyndonville, Model City, Morton, Newfane, Niagara Falls, Olcott, Penfield, Perinton, Ransomville, Rochester, Sanborn, Stella Niagara, Tonawanda, Waterport, Wilson and Youngstown. Population (2000), 654,361.

ZIP Codes: 14008, 14012, 14028, 14067, 14072, 14092, 14094, 14098, 14107–09, 14126, 14131–32, 14144, 14150–51, 14172, 14174, 14202–03, 14205–12, 14214–15, 14217, 14222–23, 14225–26, 14263, 14270, 14273, 14301–05, 14411, 14420, 14445, 14450, 14464, 14468, 14470, 14476–77, 14508, 14526, 14534, 14571, 14602–25, 14627, 14638–39, 14642–47, 14649–53, 14660, 14664, 14673

* * *

TWENTY-NINTH DISTRICT

ERIC J. J. MASSA, Democrat, of Corning, NY; born in Charleston, SC, September 16, 1959; education: graduated, B.S., U.S. Naval Academy, Annapolis, MD, 1981; military: U.S. Navy Commander, 1981–2001; Senior Aide to the Supreme Allied Commander of NATO, General Wesley K. Clark; professional: staffer at the U.S. House of Representatives Armed Services Committee; Business Consultant; Corning Inc., Senior Project Manager; awards: Legion of Merit, Defense Meritorious Service Medal; Meritorious Service Medal; Navy Commendation Medal (3); Navy Achievement Medal (4); member of Populist Caucus; Universal Healthcare Reform Caucus; Wine Caucus; committees: Agriculture; Armed Services; Homeland Security; elected to the 111th Congress on November 4, 2008.

Office Listings

http://www.massa.house.gov

1208 Longworth House Office Building, Washington, DC 20515 .... (202) 225–3161
Chief of Staff.—Joe Racalto. FAX: 226–6599
Legislative Director.—Ronald Hikel.
Communications Director.—Jared Smith.
District Director.—David Marion.
89 West Market Street, Corning, NY 14830 .... (607) 654–7566
317 North Union Street, Olean, NY 14760 .... (716) 372–2090
1 Grove Street, Suite 101, Pittsford, NY 14534 .... (585) 218–0040

Counties: ALLEGANY, CATTARAUGUS, CHEMUNG, MONROE (part), ONTARIO (part), SCHUYLER, STEUBEN, YATES. Population (2000), 654,361.

ZIP Codes: 14009, 14024, 14029–30, 14041–42, 14060, 14065, 14070, 14081, 14101, 14129, 14133, 14138, 14141, 14168, 14171, 14173, 14414–15, 14418, 14423–25, 14428, 14432, 14437, 14441, 14445, 14450, 14453, 14456, 14461, 14463, 14466–67, 14469, 14471–72, 14475, 14478, 14482, 14485, 14487, 14489, 14502, 14504, 14506–07, 14512–14, 14518, 14522, 14526–27, 14529, 14532, 14534, 14536, 14543–44, 14546–48, 14559–61, 14564, 14572, 14585–86, 14606, 14610, 14618, 14620, 14623–25, 14706–09, 14711, 14714–15, 14717, 14719, 14721, 14726–27, 14729–31, 14735, 14737–39, 14741, 14743–45, 14747–48, 14751, 14753–55, 14760, 14766, 14770, 14772, 14774, 14777–79, 14783, 14786, 14788, 14801–10, 14812–16, 14818–27, 14830–31, 14836–46, 14855–59, 14861, 14863–65, 14867, 14869–74, 14876–80, 14884–87, 14889, 14891–95, 14897–98, 14901–05, 14925

NORTH CAROLINA

(Population 2000, 8,049,313)

SENATORS

RICHARD BURR, Republican, of Winston-Salem, NC; born in Charlottesville, VA, November 30, 1955; education: R.J. Reynolds High School, Winston-Salem, NC, 1974; B.A., Communications, Wake Forest University, Winston-Salem, NC, 1978; professional: sales manager, Carswell Distributing; member: Reynolds Rotary Club; board member, Brenner Children's Hospital; public service: U.S. House of Representatives, 1995–2005; served as vice-chairman of the Energy and Commerce Committee; married: Brooke Fauth, 1984; children: two sons; committees: ranking member, Veterans' Affairs; Armed Services; Energy and Natural Resources; Health, Education, Labor, and Pensions; Select Committee on Intelligence; elected to the U.S. Senate on November 2, 2004.

Office Listings

http://burr.senate.gov

217 Russell Senate Office Building, Washington, DC 20510 .... (202) 224–3154
Chief of Staff.—Chris Joyner. FAX: 228–2981
Legislative Director.—Natasha Hickman.
2000 West First Street, Suite 508, Winston-Salem, NC 27104 .... (336) 631–5125
State Director.—Dean Myers.

* * *

KAY R. HAGAN, Democrat, of Greensboro, NC; born in Shelby, NC, May 26, 1953; education: B.A., Florida State University, 1975; J.D., Wake Forest University School of Law, 1978; professional: attorney and vice president of the Estate and Trust Division, NCNB, 1978–88; public service: North Carolina State Senator, 1999–2009; religion: Presbyterian; married: Chip Hagan; children: two daughters, one son; committees: Armed Services; Health, Education, Labor, and Pensions; Small Business and Entrepreneurship; elected to the U.S. Senate on November 4, 2008.

Office Listings

htttp://hagan.senate.gov

521 Dirksen Senate Office Building, Washington, DC 20510 .... (202) 224–6342
Chief of Staff.—Crystal King. FAX: 228–2563
Legislative Director.—Mike Harney.
Communications Director.—Stephanie Allen.
State Director.—Melissa Midgett.
310 New Bern Avenue, Suite 122, Raleigh, NC 27601 .... (919) 856–4630
701 Green Valley Road, Suite 201, Greensboro, NC 27408 .... (336) 333–5311
1520 South Boulevard, Charlotte, NC 28203 .... (704) 334–2448

REPRESENTATIVES

FIRST DISTRICT

G. K. BUTTERFIELD, Democrat, of Wilson County, NC; born, April 27, 1947; education: North Carolina Central University, graduated in 1971, with degrees in Sociology and Political Science; North Carolina Central University School of Law, graduated in 1974, with a Juris Doctor degree; military service: U.S. Army, 1968–1970; served as a Personnel Specialist; discharged with the rank of Specialist E–4; professional: attorney; private practice, 1974–1988; public service: elected to the North Carolina Superior Court bench in November, 1988; appointed on February 8, 2001, by Governor Michael F. Easley to the North Carolina Supreme Court; after leaving the Supreme Court, following the 2002 election, Governor Easley appointed Justice Butterfield as a Special Superior Court Judge; served until his retirement on May 7, 2004; organizations: North Carolina Bar Association; North Carolina Association of Black Lawyers; Wilson Opportunities Industrialization Center; religion: Baptist; appointed Chief Deputy Whip, 110th Congress; committees: Energy and Commerce; Standards of Official Conduct; elected to the 108th Congress, by special election, on July 20, 2004; elected to the 109th Congress on November 2, 2004; reelected to each succeeding Congress.

Office Listings

http://www.butterfield.house.gov

413 Cannon House Office Building, Washington, DC 20515 .... (202) 225–3101
Chief of Staff.—Tonya Williams. FAX: 225–3354
Communications Director.—Ken Willis.
Legislative Director.—Jerome Murray.
Scheduler.—Darnise Nelson.
415 East Boulevard, Suite 100, Williamston, NC 27892 .... (252) 789–4939
216 West Nash Street, Suite B, Wilson, NC 27893 .... (252) 237–9816

Counties: BEAUFORT (part), BERTIE, CHOWAN, CRAVEN (part), EDGECOMBE, GATES, GRANVILLE VANCE (part), GREENE, HALIFAX, HARTFORD, JONES (part), MARTIN, NORTHAMPTON, PASQUOTANK, PERQUIMANS, PITT (part), WARREN, WASHINGTON, WAYNE (part), WILSON (part). Population (2000), 619,178.

ZIP Codes: 27507, 27530–31, 27533–34, 27536–37, 27551, 27553, 27556, 27563, 27565, 27570, 27584, 27586, 27589, 27594, 27801, 27803–06, 27809, 27811–14, 27817–23, 27825, 27827–29, 27831–35, 27837, 27839–47, 27849–50, 27852–55, 27857–58, 27860–64, 27866–67, 27869–74, 27876–77, 27879, 27881, 27883–84, 27886–95, 27897, 27906–07, 27909–10, 27919, 27922, 27924, 27926, 27928, 27930, 27932, 27935, 27937–38, 27942, 27944, 27946, 27957, 27962, 27967, 27969–70, 27979–80, 27983, 27985–86, 28216, 28226, 28502–04, 28513, 28523, 28526, 28530, 28538, 28551, 28554–55, 28560–63, 28573, 28580, 28585–86, 28590, 28645

* * *

SECOND DISTRICT

BOB ETHERIDGE, Democrat, of Lillington, NC; born in Sampson County, NC, August 7, 1941; B.S., business administration, Campbell University, NC, 1965; graduate studies in economics, North Carolina State University, 1967; U.S. Army, 1965–67; businessman, bank director, licensed realtor; North Carolina General Assembly, 1978–88; North Carolina Superintendent of Public Instruction, 1988–96; Harnett County commissioner, 1972–76, serving as chairman of the board in 1974–76; past member: National Council of Chief State School Officers; Governor's Executive Cabinet; advisory board, Mathematics / Science Education Network; Board of the North Carolina Council on Economic Education; board of trustees, North Carolina Symphony; board of trustees, University of North Carolina Center for Public Television; Harnett County Mental Health Board; North Carolina Law and Order Commission; member and past president, Occoneechee Boy Scout Council; received Lillington Jaycees Distinguished Service Award and Lillington Community Service Award; elder, Presbyterian Church; married: former Faye Cameron, 1965; three children: Brian, Catherine, and David; committees: Budget; Ways and Means; elected to the 105th Congress; reelected to each succeeding Congress.

Office Listings

http://www.house.gov/etheridge

1533 Longworth House Office Building, Washington, DC 20515 .... (202) 225–4531
Chief of Staff.—Russ Swindell. FAX: 225–5662
Legislative Director.—David Weinreich.
Press Secretary.—Don Owens.
Scheduler.—Julia Cava.
609 North First Street, Lillington, NC 27564 .... (910) 814–0335
333 Fayetteville Street, Raleigh, NC 27601 .... (919) 829–9122

Counties: CHATHAM, CUMBERLAND, FRANKLIN, HARNETT, JOHNSTON, LEE, NASH, SAMPSON (part), VANCE, and WAKE (part). Population (2000), 619,178.

ZIP Codes: 27207–08, 27213, 27237, 27252, 27256, 27298, 27312, 27325, 27330–32, 27344, 27349, 27355, 27405, 27501, 27504–06, 27508, 27520–21, 27524–26, 27529, 27536–37, 27540, 27542–44, 27546, 27549, 27552, 27555, 27557, 27559, 27562, 27564, 27568–70, 27576–77, 27589, 27591–93, 27596–97, 27601–03, 27605–07, 27610, 27614, 27625, 27698, 27801–04, 27807, 27809, 27816, 27822, 27829, 27850, 27856, 27863, 27878, 27880, 27882, 27891, 27893–94, 27896, 28301, 28303, 28307–08, 28310–11, 28314, 28323, 28326, 28328, 28334–35, 28339, 28341, 28355–56, 28365–66, 28368, 28382, 28385, 28390, 28393, 28441, 28444, 28447, 28453, 28458, 28466, 28478

* * *

THIRD DISTRICT

WALTER B. JONES, Republican, of Farmville, NC; born in Farmville, February 10, 1943; education: graduated Hargrave Military Academy, Chatham, VA, 1961; B.A., Atlantic Christian College, Wilson, NC, 1966; served in North Carolina National Guard; self-employed, sales; member: North Carolina House of Representatives, 1983–92; married: Joe Anne Whitehurst

Jones; one child, Ashley Elizabeth Jones; committees: Armed Services; Financial Services; elected to the 104th Congress; reelected to each succeeding Congress.

Office Listings

2333 Rayburn House Office Building, Washington, DC 20515 .... (202) 225–3415
Chief of Staff.—Glen Downs. FAX: 225–3286
Office Manager.—Molly Norton.
Press Secretary.—Kathleen Joyce.
1105–C Corporate Drive, Greenville, NC 27858 .... (252) 931–1003
District Office Manager.—Millicent A. Lilley.

Counties: BEAUFORT (part), CAMDEN, CARTERET, CRAVEN (part), CURRITUCK, DARE, DUPLIN (part), HYDE, JONES (part), LENOIR (part), MARTIN (part), ONSLOW (part), PAMLICO, PENDER (part), PITT (part), SAMPSON, TYRRELL and WAYNE (part). CITIES: Atlantic Beach, Ayden, Beaufort, Belhaven, Burgaw, Clinton, Emerald Isle, Fremont, Goldsboro, Greenville, Havelock, Jacksonville, Kill Devil Hills, Kinston, Kitty Hawk, Morehead City, Mount Olive, Nags Head, New Bern, Newport, River Bend, Trent Woods, Wallace, Washington, and Winterville. Population (2000), 619,178.

ZIP Codes: 27530–32, 27534, 27542, 27557, 27569, 27803–04, 27807–10, 27814, 27817, 27822, 27824, 27826, 27828–30, 27834, 27836–37, 27851–52, 27856, 27858, 27860, 27863, 27865, 27868, 27871, 27875, 27879, 27880, 27882–83, 27885, 27888–89, 27892–93, 27896, 27909, 27915–17, 27920–21, 27923, 27925, 27927–29, 27936, 27939, 27941, 27943, 27947–50, 27953–54, 27956, 27958–60, 27962, 27964–66, 27968, 27972–74, 27976, 27978, 27981–82, 28333, 28341, 28445, 28454, 28460, 28501, 28504, 28508–13, 28515–16, 28518–22, 28524–29, 28531–33, 28537, 28539–47, 28551–53, 28555–57, 28560, 28562, 28564, 28570–72, 28574–75, 28577–87, 28589–90, 28594

* * *

FOURTH DISTRICT

DAVID E. PRICE, Democrat, of Chapel Hill, NC; born in Erwin, TN, August 17, 1940; education: B.A., Morehead Scholar, University of North Carolina; Bachelor of Divinity, 1964, and Ph.D., political science, 1969, Yale University; professional: professor of political science and public policy, Duke University; author of four books on Congress and the American political system; served North Carolina's Fourth District in the U.S. House of Representatives, 1987–94; in the 102nd Congress, wrote and pushed to passage the Scientific and Advanced Technology Bill and sponsored the Home Ownership Assistance Act; past chairman and executive director, North Carolina Democratic Party; Hubert Humphrey Public Service Award, American Political Science Association, 1990; member, North Carolina's Transit 2001 Commission; past chairman of the board and Sunday School teacher, Binkley Memorial Baptist Church; married: Lisa Price; children: Karen and Michael; committees: Appropriations; elected to the 100th–103rd Congresses; elected to the 105th Congress; reelected to each succeeding Congress.

Office Listings

http://www.house.gov/price

2162 Rayburn House Office Building, Washington, DC 20515 .... (202) 225–1784
Chief of Staff.—Jean-Louise Beard. FAX: 225–2014
Legislative Director/Deputy Chief of Staff.—Asher Hildebrand.
Executive Assistant.—Teresa Saunders.
Systems Manager.—Jackson Tufts.
5400 Trinity Place, Suite 205, Raleigh, NC 27607 .... (919) 859–5999
District Director.—Rose Auman.
88 Vilcom Center, Suite 140, Chapel Hill, NC 27514 .... (919) 967–7924
411 West Chapel Hill Street, Durham, NC 27701 .... (919) 688–3004

Counties: CHATHAM (part), DURHAM, ORANGE, WAKE (part). Population (2000), 619,178.

ZIP Codes: 27228, 27231, 27243, 27278, 27302, 27312, 27330, 27501–03, 27510–17, 27519, 27523, 27526, 27529, 27539–41, 27560, 27562, 27572, 27583, 27592, 27599, 27603, 27606–07, 27610, 27612–15, 27617, 27623–24, 27656, 27675–76, 27690, 27695, 27699, 27701–05, 27707–13, 27715, 27717, 27722

* * *

FIFTH DISTRICT

VIRGINIA FOXX, Republican, of Banner Elk, NC; born in New York, NY, June 29, 1943; education: B.A., University of North Carolina, Chapel Hill, NC, 1968; M.A.C.T., University of North Carolina, Chapel Hill, NC, 1972; Ed.D., University of North Carolina, Greensboro, NC, 1985; professional: professor, Caldwell Community College, Hudson, NC; professor, Appalachian State University, Boone, NC; Assistant Dean, Appalachian State University, Boone, NC;

president, Mayland Community College, Spruce Pine, NC, 1987–94; nursery operator; deputy secretary for management, North Carolina Department of Administration; organizations: member, Watauga County board of education, 1967–88; member, North Carolina State Senate, 1994–2004; Executive Committee of North Carolina Citizens for Business and Industry; Z. Smith Reynolds Foundation Advisory Panel; National Advisory Council for Women's Educational Programs; Board of Directors of the NC Center for Public Research; UNC–Chapel Hill Board of Visitors; National Conference of State Legislatures' Blue Ribbon Advisory Panel on Child Care; Foscoe-Grandfather Community Center Board; family: married to Tom Foxx; one daughter; committees: Rules; elected to the 109th Congress on November 2, 2004; reelected to each succeeding Congress.

Office Listings

http://www.house.gov/foxx

1230 Longworth House Office Building, Washington, DC 20515 .... (202) 225–2071
Chief of Staff.—Todd Poole. FAX: 225–2995
Legislative Director.—Brandon Renz.
Press Secretary.—Aaron Groen.
6000 Meadowbrook Mall, Suite 3, Clemmons, NC 27012 .... (336) 778–0211
240 Highway 105 Extension, Suite 200, Boone, NC 28607 .... (828) 265–0240

Counties: ALEXANDER COUNTY. CITIES: Bethlehem, Hiddenite, Stony Point, Taylorsville. ALLEGANY COUNTY. CITIES: Ennice, Glade Valley, Laurel Springs, Sparta. ASHE COUNTY. CITIES: Crumpler, Glendale Springs, Grassy Creek, Jefferson, Lansing, Scottville, Todd, Warrensville, West Jefferson. DAVIE COUNTY. CITIES: Advance, Cooleemee, Mocksville. FORSYTH COUNTY (part). CITIES: Bethania, Clemmons, Kernersville, King, Lewisville, Pfafftown, Rural Hall, Tobaccoville, Walkertown, Winston-Salem. IREDELL COUNTY (part). CITIES: Harmony, Love Valley, Mooresville, Olin, Statesville, Turnersburg, Troutman. ROCKINGHAM COUNTY (part). CITIES: Madison, Stokesdale. STOKES COUNTY. CITIES: Danbury, Germanton, Lawsonville, King, Pine Hall, Pinnacle, Sandy Ridge, and Walnut Cove. SURRY COUNTY. CITIES: Ararat, Dobson, Elkin, Flat Rock, Mount Airy, Pilot Mountain, Siloam, Toast, Westfield, White Plains. WATAUGA COUNTY. CITIES: Beech Mountain, Blowing Rock, Boone, Deep Gap, Seven Devils, Sugar Grove, Triplett, Vilas, Zionville. WILKES COUNTY. CITIES: Boomer, Cricket, Hays, Fairplains, Ferguson, Millers Creek, Moravian Falls, Mulberry, N. Wilkesboro, Olin, Pleasant Hill, Roaring River, Ronda, Thurmond, Traphill, Wilkesboro. YADKIN COUNTY. CITIES: Arlington, Booneville, East Bend, Hamptonville, Jonesville, Turnersburg, and Yadkinville. Population (2000), 619,178.

ZIP Codes: 27006–07, 27009–14, 27016–25, 27028, 27030, 27040–43, 27045–47, 27049–53, 27055, 27094, 27098–99, 27101–09, 27111, 27113–17, 27120, 27127, 27130, 27150–51, 27155–57, 27199, 27201–02, 27235, 27244, 27265, 27284–85, 27305, 27314–15, 27320, 27326, 27343, 27357–58, 27360, 27379, 27565, 27582, 27893, 28115, 28125, 28166, 28601, 28604–08, 28615, 28617–18, 28621–27, 28629–31, 28634–36, 28640, 28642–45, 28649, 28651, 28654, 28656, 28659–60, 28663, 28665, 28668–70, 28672, 28675–79, 28681, 28683–85, 28688–89, 28691–94, 28697–99

* * *

SIXTH DISTRICT

HOWARD COBLE, Republican, of Greensboro, NC; born in Greensboro, March 18, 1931; education: Appalachian State University, Boone, NC, 1949–50; A.B., history, Guilford College, Greensboro, NC, 1958; J.D., University of North Carolina School of Law, Chapel Hill, 1962; military service: U.S. Coast Guard as a seaman recruit, 1952; active duty, 1952–56 and 1977–78; reserve duty, 1960–82; retired with rank of captain; last reserve duty assignment, commanding officer, U.S. Coast Guard Reserve Unit, Wilmington, NC; professional: attorney; admitted to North Carolina bar, 1966; field claim representative and superintendent, auto insurance, 1961–67; elected to North Carolina House of Representatives, 1969; assistant U.S. attorney, Middle District of North Carolina, 1969–73; commissioner (secretary), North Carolina Department of Revenue, 1973–77; North Carolina House of Representatives, 1979–83; practiced law with law firm of Turner, Enochs and Sparrow, Greensboro, NC, 1979–84; member: Alamance Presbyterian Church, American Legion, Veterans of Foreign Wars of the United States, Lions Club, Greensboro Bar Association, North Carolina Bar Association, North Carolina State Bar; North Carolina State co-chairman, American Legislative Exchange Council, 1983–84; committees: Judiciary; Transportation and Infrastructure; elected to the 99th Congress on November 6, 1984; reelected to each succeeding Congress.

Office Listings

http://www.house.gov/coble

2468 Rayburn House Office Building, Washington, DC 20515 .... (202) 225–3065
Chief of Staff / Press Secretary.—Ed McDonald. FAX: 225–8611
Executive Assistant.—Jennifer Brooks.
2102 North Elm Street, Suite B, Greensboro, NC 27408–5100 .... (336) 333–5005
Office Manager.—Chris Beaman.
1634 North Main Street, Suite 101, High Point, NC 27262–7723 .... (336) 886–5106
District Representative.—Nancy Mazza.
241 Sunset Avenue, Suite 101, Asheboro, NC 27203–5658 .... (336) 626–3060
District Representative.—Rebecca Redding.
P.O. Box 807, Granite Quarry, NC 28027–0807 .... (704) 209–0426

District Representative.—Terri Welch.
124 West Elm Street, P.O. Box 812, Graham, NC 27253–0812 .... (336) 229–0159
District Representative.—Janine Osborne.

Counties: ALAMANCE (part), DAVIDSON (part), GUILFORD (part), MOORE, RANDOLPH, ROWAN (part). Population (2000), 620,590.

ZIP Codes: 27201–05, 27208–09, 27214–17, 27220, 27230, 27233, 27235, 27239, 27242, 27244, 27248–49, 27252–53, 27258–65, 27281–84, 27288–89, 27292, 27295, 27298–99, 27301–02, 27310, 27312–13, 27316–17, 27325, 27330, 27340–42, 27344, 27349–50, 27355–61, 27370–71, 27373–74, 27376–77, 27401–10, 27415–17, 27419–20, 27425, 27427, 27429, 27435, 27438, 27455, 27495, 27498–99, 27607, 27612–13, 27640, 27803–04, 28023, 28041, 28071–72, 28081, 28083, 28088, 28125, 28127, 28137–38, 28144, 28146–47, 28315, 28326–27, 28347, 28350, 28370, 28373–74, 28387–88, 28394

* * *

SEVENTH DISTRICT

MIKE McINTYRE, Democrat, of Lumberton, NC; born in Robeson County, August 6, 1956; education: B.A., Phi Beta Kappa Morehead Scholar, 1978, and J.D., 1981, University of North Carolina; upon graduation, received the Algernon Sydney Sullivan Award for ''unselfish interest in the welfare of his fellow man''; professional: attorney; past president, Lumberton Economic Advancement for Dowtown; formerly on board of directors of Lumberton Rotary Club, Chamber of Commerce and a local group home for the mentally handicapped; active in the Boy Scouts of America, and Lumberton PTA; married: the former Dee Strickland; two children; committees: Agriculture; Armed Services; elected to the 105th Congress; reelected to each succeeding Congress.

Office Listings

http://www.house.gov/mcintyre

2437 Rayburn House Office Building, Washington, DC 20515 .... (202) 225–2731
Chief of Staff/Press Secretary.—Dean Mitchell. FAX: 225–5773
Deputy Chief of Staff.—Audrey Lesesne.
Chief of Constituent Services.—Vivian Lipford.
Legislative Director.—Blair Miligan.
Federal Building, 301 Green Street, Room 218, Fayetteville, NC 28401 .... (910) 323–0260
201 North Front Street, Suite 410, Wilmington, NC 28401 .... (910) 815–4959
500 North Cedar Street, Lumberton, NC 28358 .... (910) 735–0610
District Chief of Staff.—Marie Thompson.

Counties: BLADEN, BRUNSWICK, COLUMBUS, CUMBERLAND (part), DUPLIN (part), NEW HANOVER, PENDER, ROBESON, SAMPSON (part). Population (2000), 619,178.

ZIP Codes: 28301–06, 28309, 28311–12, 28318–20, 28325, 28328, 28331–32, 28334, 28337, 28340–42, 28344, 28348–49, 28356–60, 28362, 28364–66, 28369, 28371–72, 28375, 28377–78, 28383–86, 28390–93, 28395, 28398–99, 28401–12, 28420–25, 28428–36, 28438–39, 28441–59, 28461–70, 28472, 28478–80, 28513, 28518, 28521, 28572, 28574

* * *

EIGHTH DISTRICT

LARRY KISSELL, Democrat, of Biscoe, NC; born in Biscoe, January 31, 1951; education: B.A. in economics, Wake Forest University, 1973; professional: textile mill worker, 27 years at Russell Hosiery Mill; seven years as a high school teacher at East Montgomery High School; married: Tina; children: Jenny and Aspen; committee: Agriculture, Armed Services; elected to the 111th Congress on November 4, 2008.

Office Listings

http://www.kissell.house.gov

512 Cannon House Office Building, Washington, DC 20515 .... (202) 225–3715
Chief of Staff.—Leanne Powell. FAX: 225–4036
Legislative Director.—Bryan Mitchell.
Executive Assistant.—Elena DiTraglia.
325 McGill Avenue, Suite 500, Concord, NC 28027 .... (704) 786–1612
Chief of Staff.—Leanne Powell.
230 East Franklin Street, Rockingham, NC 28379 .... (910) 997–2070
District Director.—Thomas Thacker.
6257 Raeford Road, Suite 2, Fayetteville, NC 28304 .... (910) 920–2070

Counties: ANSON, CABARRUS (part), CUMBERLAND (part), HOKE, MECKLENBURG (part), MONTGOMERY, RICHMOND, SCOTLAND (part), STANLY, UNION (part). Population (2000), 619,178.

ZIP Codes: 27209, 27215, 27229, 27247, 27253, 27281, 27284, 27306, 27312, 27320, 27341, 27356, 27358, 27371, 27405, 27534, 27803–04, 27893, 28001–02, 28007, 28009, 28025–27, 28036, 28071, 28075, 28081–83, 28091, 28097, 28102–04, 28107–12, 28119, 28124, 28127–29, 28133, 28135, 28137–38, 28159, 28163, 28167, 28170, 28174, 28204–05, 28209–13, 28215, 28217–18, 28220, 28223, 28227, 28229, 28262, 28270, 28278, 28301, 28303–06, 28308, 28311, 28314–15, 28325, 28329–30, 28338, 28343, 28345, 28347, 28349, 28351–53, 28357, 28361, 28363–64, 28367, 28371, 28376–77, 28379–80, 28382, 28386, 28396

* * *

NINTH DISTRICT

SUE WILKINS MYRICK, Republican, of Charlotte, NC; born in Tiffin, OH, August 1, 1941; education: graduated Port Clinton High School, Port Clinton, OH; attended Heidelberg College; professional: former president and CEO, Myrick Advertising and Myrick Enterprises; mayor of Charlotte, NC, 1987–91; Charlotte City Council, 1983–85; active with the National League of Cities and the U.S. Conference of Mayors; served on former President Bush's Affordable Housing Commission; member: Charlotte Chamber of Commerce; Muscular Dystrophy Association; March of Dimes; Elks Auxiliary; PTA; Cub Scout den mother; United Methodist Church; founder, Charitable Outreach Society; married: Ed Myrick, 1977; five children; committees: Energy and Commerce; Permanent Select Committee on Intelligence; elected to the 104th Congress; reelected to each succeeding Congress.

Office Listings

http://www.myrick.house.gov

230 Cannon House Office Building, Washington, DC 20515 .... (202) 225–1976
Administrative Assistant.—Sarah Hale. FAX: 225–3389
Executive Assistant.—Hollie Arnold.
6525 Morrison Boulevard, Suite 100, Charlotte, NC 28211 .... (704) 362–1060
197 West Main Avenue, Gastonia, NC 28052 .... (704) 861–1976

Counties: GASTON (part), MECKLENBURG (part), UNION (part). Population (2000), 619,178.

ZIP Codes: 28006, 28012, 28016–17, 28031–34, 28036, 28042, 28052–56, 28070, 28077–80, 28086, 28092–93, 28098, 28101, 28103–07, 28110, 28112, 28114, 28120, 28126, 28130, 28134, 28136, 28150–52, 28164, 28169, 28173–74, 28201, 28203–04, 28206–11, 28213–17, 28222, 28226–27, 28241, 28247, 28250, 28253, 28261–62, 28269–71, 28273–74, 28277–78, 28287

* * *

TENTH DISTRICT

PATRICK T. MCHENRY, Republican, of Cherryville, NC; born in Gastonia, NC, October 22, 1975; education: graduated Ashbrook High School, Gastonia, NC; attended North Carolina State University, Raleigh, NC; B.A., Belmont Abbey College, Belmont, NC, 1999; professional: realtor; media executive; appointed special assistant to the U.S. Secretary of Labor by President George W. Bush in 2001; member, North Carolina House of Representatives, 2002–04; organizations: Gaston Chamber of Commerce, Gastonia Rotary Club, the National Rifle Association, Saint Michael Church; board of directors, United Way's Success by Six Youth Program; committees: Budget; Financial Services; Oversight and Government Reform; elected to the 109th Congress on November 2, 2004; reelected to each succeeding Congress.

Office Listings

http://www.house.gov/mchenry

224 Cannon House Office Building, Washington, DC 20515 .... (202) 225–2576
Chief of Staff.—Parker Poling. FAX: 225–0316
Legislative Director.—Jennifer Mundy.
Communications Director.—Brock McCleary.
Scheduler.—Sarah Jones.
87 Fourth Street, NW., Suite A, P.O. Box 1830, Hickory, NC 28603 .... (828) 327–6100

Counties: AVERY, BURKE, CALDWELL, CATAWBA, CLEVELAND, GASTON (part), IREDELL (part), LINCOLN, MITCHELL, and RUTHERFORD (part). CITIES AND TOWNSHIPS: Hickory, Lenoir, Morganton, Shelby, and Mooresville. Population (2000), 619,178.

ZIP Codes: 28006, 28010, 28016–21, 28024, 28033, 28036–38, 28040, 28042–43, 28052, 28073–74, 28076, 28080, 28086, 28089–90, 28092, 28114–15, 28117, 28139, 28150, 28152, 28164, 28166–69, 28601–07, 28609–13, 28616, 28619,

28621–22, 28624–25, 28628–30, 28633, 28635–38, 28641, 28645–47, 28650, 28652–55, 28657–58, 28661–62, 28664, 28666–67, 28671, 28673, 28676–78, 28680–82, 28687, 28690, 28699, 28705, 28720, 28740, 28746, 28752, 28761, 28765, 28777

* * *

ELEVENTH DISTRICT

HEATH SHULER, Democrat, of Waynesville, NC; born in Bryson City, NC, December 31, 1971; graduated from Swain County High School; B.A., University of Tennessee, 2001; entrepreneur; married to the former Nikol Davis; two children: Navy and Island; committees: Small Business; Transportation and Infrastructure; elected to the 110th Congress on November 7, 2006; reelected to the 111th Congress on November 4, 2008.

Office Listings

http://www.shuler.house.gov

422 Cannon House Office Building, Washington, DC 20515 .... (202) 225–6401
Chief of Staff.—Hayden Rogers. FAX: 226–6422
Legislative Director.—Jed Bhuta.
Scheduler.—Julie Fishman.
356 Biltmore Avenue, Suite 400, Asheville, NC 28801 .... (828) 252–1651
Director of Constituent Services.—Myrna Campbell.

Counties: BUNCOMBE, CHEROKEE, CLAY, GRAHAM, HAYWOOD, HENDERSON, JACKSON, MCDOWELL, MACON, MADISON, POLK, RUTHERFORD (part), SWAIN, TRANSYLVANIA, YANCEY. Population (2000), 619,177.

ZIP Codes: 28043, 28074, 28114, 28139, 28160, 28647, 28655, 28701–02, 28704, 28707–19, 28721–45, 28747–58, 28760–63, 28766, 28768, 28770–79, 28781–93, 28801–06, 28810, 28813–16, 28901–06, 28909

* * *

TWELFTH DISTRICT

MELVIN L. WATT, Democrat, of Charlotte, NC; born in Charlotte, August 26, 1945; education: graduated, York Road High School, Charlotte, 1963; B.S., business adminisration, University of North Carolina, Chapel Hill, 1967; J.D., Yale University Law School, New Haven, CT, 1970; professional: attorney; admitted to the District of Columbia bar, 1970, admitted to the North Carolina bar, 1971; began practice with Chambers, Stein, Ferguson and Becton, 1971–92; North Carolina State Senate, 1985–86; life member, NAACP; member, Mount Olive Presbyterian Church; past president, Mecklenburg County Bar Association, Johnson C. Smith University Board of Visitors; Central Piedmont Community College Foundation; North Carolina Association of Black Lawyers; North Carolina Association of Trial Lawyers; Legal Aid of Southern Piedmont; NationsBank Community Development Corporation; Charlotte Chamber of Commerce; Sports Action Council; Auditorium-Coliseum-Civic Center Authority; United Way; Mint Museum; Inroads, Inc.; Family Housing Services; Public Education Forum; Dilworth Community Development Association; Cities in Schools; West Charlotte Business Incubator; Housing Authority Scholarship Board; Morehead Scholarship Selection Committee, Forsyth Region; married: the former Eulada Paysour, 1968; children: Brian and Jason; committees: Financial Services; Judiciary; elected on November 3, 1992, to the 103rd Congress; reelected to each succeeding Congress.

Office Listings

http://www.house.gov/watt

2304 Rayburn House Office Building, Washington, DC 20515 .... (202) 225–1510
Chief of Staff.—Danielle Owen. FAX: 225–1512
1230 West Morehead Street, Suite 306, Charlotte, NC 28208 .... (704) 344–9950
301 South Greene Street, Suite 210, Greensboro, NC 27401 .... (336) 275–9950
District Director.—Torre Jessup.

Counties: CABARRUS COUNTY (part). DAVIDSON COUNTY (part). CITIES AND TOWNSHIPS: Lexington, and Thomasville. FORSYTH COUNTY (part). CITIES AND TOWNSHIPS: Winston-Salem. GUILFORD COUNTY (part). CITIES AND TOWNSHIPS: High Point, Greensboro. MECKLENBURG COUNTY. CITIES AND TOWNSHIPS: Charlotte. ROWAN COUNTY. CITIES: Salisbury. Population (2000), 619,178.

ZIP Codes: 27010, 27012–13, 27019, 27040, 27045, 27051, 27054, 27101, 27103–07, 27110, 27127, 27214, 27260, 27262–63, 27265, 27282, 27284, 27292–95, 27299, 27310, 27320, 27351, 27360, 27401, 27403, 27405–11, 27534, 27803–04, 27893, 28023, 28027, 28035–36, 28039, 28078, 28081, 28115, 28123, 28125, 28134, 28144–47, 28159,

28202–17, 28219, 28221, 28224, 28226–28, 28230–37, 28240, 28242–43, 28254–56, 28258, 28260, 28262, 28265–66, 28269–70, 28272–73, 28275, 28278, 28280–82, 28284–85, 28289–90, 28296–97

* * *

THIRTEENTH DISTRICT

BRAD MILLER, Democrat, of Raleigh, NC; born in Fayetteville, NC, May 19, 1953; education: B.A., Political Science, University of North Carolina, 1975; Master's Degree, Political Science, London School of Economics, 1978; J.D., Columbia University Law School, 1979; professional: attorney; law clerk to Circuit Court of Appeals Judge J. Dickson Phillips, Jr., 1979–80; has practiced law in Raleigh since 1980, and has been in private practice since 1991; public service: North Carolina House of Representatives, 1992–94; North Carolina State Senate, 1996–2002; religion: Episcopal; family: married to Esther Hall; committees: Financial Services; Foreign Affairs; Science and Technology; elected to the 108th Congress on November 5, 2002; reelected to each succeeding Congress.

Office Listings

http://www.house.gov/bradmiller

1722 Longworth House Office Building, Washington, DC 20515 .... (202) 225–3032
Chief of Staff.—Mark Harkins. FAX: 225–0181
Deputy Chief of Staff / Legislative Director.—Ryan Hedgepeth.
Communications Director.—LuAnn Canipe.
Scheduler.—Anna Rose.
1300 St. Mary's Street, Suite 504, Raleigh, NC 27605 .... (919) 836–1313
125 South Elm Street, Suite 504, Greensboro, NC 27401 .... (336) 574–2909

Counties: ALAMANCE (part), CASWELL, GRANVILLE (part), GUILFORD (part), PERSON, ROCKINGHAM (part), WAKE (part). Population (2000), 619,178.

ZIP Codes: 27025, 27027, 27048, 27212, 27214–17, 27231, 27244, 27249, 27253, 27258, 27288–89, 27291, 27301–02, 27305, 27311, 27320, 27323, 27326, 27343, 27375, 27379, 27401, 27403, 27403–10, 27412–13, 27415, 27419, 27455, 27495, 27497, 27507, 27509, 27511–12, 27522, 27525, 27541, 27544–45, 27564–65, 27571–74, 27581–83, 27587–88, 27591, 27596–97, 27601, 27603–10, 27612–17, 27619–20, 27622, 27625, 27627–29, 27635–36, 27640, 27658, 27661, 27668, 27690, 27698

NORTH DAKOTA

(Population 2000, 642,200)

SENATORS

KENT CONRAD, Democrat, of Bismarck, ND; born in Bismarck, March 12, 1948; education: graduated from Wheelus High School, Tripoli, Libya, 1966; attended the University of Missouri, Columbia, 1967; B.A., Stanford University, CA, 1971; M.B.A., George Washington University, Washington, DC, 1975; professional: assistant to the Tax Commissioner, Bismarck, 1974–80; director, Management Planning and Personnel, North Dakota Tax Department, March–December 1980; Tax Commissioner, State of North Dakota, 1981–86; married Lucy Calautti, February 1987; one child by former marriage: Jessamyn Abigail; committees: chair, Budget; Agriculture, Nutrition, and Forestry; Finance; Indian Affairs; Joint Committee on Taxation; elected to the U.S. Senate on November 4, 1986; was not a candidate for a second term to Senate seat he had won in 1986; subsequently elected by special election on December 4, 1992, to fill the vacancy caused by the death of Senator Quentin Burdick, whose term would have expired on January 3, 1995; took the oath of office on December 14, 1992; reelected to each succeeding Senate term.

Office Listings

http://conrad.senate.gov

530 Hart Senate Office Building, Washington, DC 20510 .... (202) 224–2043
Chief of Staff.—Sara Garland. FAX: 224–7776
Legislative Director.—Tom Mahr.
220 East Rosser Avenue, Room 228, Bismarck, ND 58501 .... (701) 258–4648
State Director (West Region).—Marty Boeckel.
657 Second Avenue North, Room 306, Fargo, ND 58102 .... (701) 232–8030
State Director (East Region).—Scott Stofferahn. TDD: 232–2139
102 North Fourth Street, Suite 104, Grand Forks, ND 58203 .... (701) 775–9601
100 First Street, SW., Room 105, Minot, ND 58701 .... (701) 852–0703

* * *

BYRON L. DORGAN, Democrat, of Bismarck, ND; born in Dickinson, ND, May 14, 1942; education: graduated, Regent High School, 1961; B.S., University of North Dakota, 1965; M.B.A., University of Denver, 1966; professional: North Dakota State Tax Commissioner, 1969–80, the only elected state tax commissioner in the nation; received 80 percent of the vote in 1976 tax commissioner reelection bid; chairman, Multi-State Tax Commission, 1972–74; executive committee member, National Association of Tax Administrators, 1972–75; selected by the *Washington Monthly* as one of the outstanding state officials in the United States, 1975; chosen by one of North Dakota's leading newspapers as the individual with the greatest influence on State government, 1977; elected to Congress, 1980; elected president of Democratic freshman class during first term; reelected, 1982, with 72 percent of the vote; reelected to Congress in 1984 with 78.5 percent of the vote, setting three election records in North Dakota—largest vote ever received by a statewide candidate, largest vote by a U.S. House candidate, and largest majority by a U.S. House candidate; his 242,000 votes in 1984 were the most received anywhere in the nation by an opposed House candidate; reelected to each succeeding Congress; served on three congressional committees during first term in Congress: Agriculture, Small Business, and Veterans' Affairs; named to the Ways and Means Committee, January 1983; called the real successor to Bill Langer and the State's most exciting office holder in generations, by the 1983 *Book of America*; 1990 *New York Times* editorial said, ''Mr. Dorgan sets an example for political statesmanship''; named to Select Committee on Hunger in 1985; chairman, International Task Force on Select Committee on Hunger; chairman, Democratic Policy Committee, 106th thru 109th Congresses; assistant Democratic Leader for Policy, 106th and 107th Congresses; assistant Democratic Floor Leader, 104th and 105th Congresses; assistant Democratic Floor Leader, ex officio, 106th and 107th Congresses; married: Kim Dorgan; children: Scott, Shelly (deceased), Brendon, and Haley; committees: chair, Indian Affairs; Appropriations; Commerce, Science, and Transportation; Energy and Natural Resources; elected to the U.S. Senate on November 3, 1992; first sworn in on December 15, 1992, to fill the remainder of the term in North Dakota's open Senate seat, then sworn in January 5, 1993, for 6-year term; reelected to each succeeding Senate term.

Office Listings

http://dorgan.senate.gov

322 Hart Senate Office Building, Washington, DC 20510 .... (202) 224–2551
Chief of Staff.—Elizabeth Gore. FAX: 224–1193
Communications Director.—Justin Kitsch.
Office Manager.—Brandon Hirsch.
State Director.—Pam Gulleson.
220 East Rosser Avenue, Room 312, Bismarck, ND 58502 .... (701) 250–4618
1802 32nd Avenue South, Suite B, P.O. Box 9060, Fargo, ND 58106 .... (701) 239–5389
102 North Fourth Street, Room 108, Grand Forks, ND 58201 .... (701) 746–8972
100 First Street SW., Suite 105, Minot, ND 58701 .... (701) 852–0703

REPRESENTATIVE

AT LARGE

EARL POMEROY, Democrat-NPL, of Valley City, ND; born in Valley City, September 2, 1952; education: B.A. and J.D., University of North Dakota, Grand Forks, 1974, 1979; graduate research in legal history, University of Durham, England, 1975–76; professional: attorney; admitted to North Dakota bar, 1979; North Dakota House of Representatives, 1980–84; Insurance Commissioner of North Dakota, 1985–92; president, National Association of Insurance Commissioners, 1990; married: Mary Pomeroy; children: Kathryn and Scott; committees: Agriculture; Ways and Means; elected to the 103rd Congress on November 3, 1992; reelected to each succeeding Congress.

Office Listings

http://www.house.gov/pomeroy

1501 Longworth House Office Building, Washington, DC 20515 .... (202) 225–2611
Chief of Staff.—Bob Siggins. FAX: 226–0893
Legislative Directors: Melanie Rhinehart, Van Tassell.
Press Secretary.—Sandra Salstrom.
Federal Building, 220 East Rosser Avenue, Room 328, Bismarck, ND 58501 .... (701) 224–0355
3003 32nd Avenue South, Suite 6, Fargo, ND 58103 .... (701) 235–9760
State Director.—Ross Keys.

Population (2000), 642,200.

ZIP Codes: 58001–02, 58004–09, 58011–13, 58015–18, 58021, 58027, 58029, 58030–33, 58035–36, 58038, 58040–43, 58045–49, 58051–54, 58056–65, 58067–69, 58071–72, 58074–79, 58081, 58102–09, 58121–22, 58124–26, 58201–06, 58208, 58210, 58212, 58214, 58216, 58218–20, 58222–25, 58227–31, 58233, 58235–41, 58243–44, 58249–51, 58254–62, 58265–67, 58269–78, 58281–82, 58301, 58310–11, 58313, 58316–19, 58321, 58323–25, 58327, 58329–32, 58335, 58338–39, 58341, 58343–46, 58348, 58351–53, 58355–57, 58359, 58361–63, 58365–70, 58372, 58374, 58377, 58379–82, 58384–86, 58401–02, 58405, 58413, 58415–16, 58418, 58420–26, 58428–31, 58433, 58436, 58438–45, 58448, 58451–52, 58454–56, 58458, 58460–61, 58463–64, 58466–67, 58472, 58474–84, 58486–88, 58490, 58492, 58494–97, 58501–07, 58520–21, 58523–24, 58528–33, 58535, 58538, 58540–42, 58544–45, 58549, 58552, 58554, 58558–66, 58568–73, 58575–77, 58579–81, 58601–02, 58620–23, 58625–27, 58630–32, 58634, 58636, 58638–47, 58649–56, 58701–05, 58707, 58710–13, 58716, 58718, 58721–23, 58725, 58727, 58730–31, 58733–37, 58740–41, 58744, 58746–48, 58750, 58752, 58755–63, 58765, 58768–73, 58775–76, 58778–79, 58781–85, 58787–90, 58792–95, 58801–02, 58830–31, 58833, 58835, 58838, 58843–45, 58847, 58849, 58852–54, 58856

OHIO

(Population 2000, 11,353,140)

SENATORS

GEORGE V. VOINOVICH, Republican, of Cleveland, OH; born in Cleveland, July 15, 1936; B.A., Ohio University, 1958; J.D., College of Law, Ohio State University, 1961; Honorary Doctorate of Law, Ohio University, 1981; Honorary Doctorate of Public Administration, Findlay University, 1993; public service: Assistant Attorney General, Ohio, 1963; member, Ohio House of Representatives, 1967–71; Cuyahoga County Auditor, 1971–76; Cuyahoga County Commissioner, 1977–78; Lieutenant Governor, Ohio, 1979; Mayor, Cleveland, OH, 1979–86; 65th Governor of Ohio, 1990–98; President, National League of Cities, 1985; chairman, National Governor's Association, 1997–98; Catholic; married: Janet Voinovich; three children: George, Betsy, and Peter; committees: Appropriations; Environment and Public Works; Homeland Security and Governmental Affairs; elected to the U.S. Senate on November 3, 1998; reelected to each succeeding Senate term.

Office Listings

http://voinovich.senate.gov

524 Hart Senate Office Building, Washington, DC 20510 .... (202) 224–3353
Chief of Staff.—Phil Park. FAX: 228–1382
Communication Director.—Garrette Silverman.
Director of Operations.—Laurel Edmondson.
1240 East Ninth Street, Suite 2955, Cleveland, OH 44199 .... (216) 522–7095
Regional Representative.—Diane Downing.
37 West Broad Street, Suite 310, Columbus, OH 43215 .... (614) 469–6697
37 West Broad Street, Suite 300, Columbus, OH 43215 .... (614) 469–6774
State Director.—Beth Hansen.
36 East 7th Street, Room 2615, Cincinnati, OH 45202 .... (513) 684–3265
District Representative.—Nan Cahall.
420 Madison Avenue, Room 1210, Toledo, OH 43604 .... (419) 259–3895
District Representative.—Wes Fahrbach.
Constituent Services Director.—Michael Dustman.
78 West Washington Street, Nelsonville, OH 45764 .... (740) 441–6410
District Representative.—Brandon Kern.

* * *

SHERROD BROWN, Democrat, of Avon Lake, OH; born in Mansfield, OH, November 9, 1952; education: B.A., Yale University, New Haven, CT, 1974; M.A., Education, Ohio State University, Columbus, OH, 1979; M.A., Public Administration, Ohio State University, Columbus, OH, 1981; professional: Ohio House of Representatives, 1975–83; Ohio Secretary of State, 1983–91; U.S. House of Representatives, 1992–2006; member: Eagle Scouts of America; married: Connie Schultz; children: Emily, Elizabeth, Andrew and Caitlin; committees: Agriculture, Nutrition, and Forestry; Banking, Housing, and Urban Affairs; Health, Education, Labor, and Pensions; Veterans' Affairs; Select Committee on Ethics; elected to the 103rd Congress on November 3, 1992; reelected to each succeeding Congress; elected to the U.S. Senate on November 7, 2006.

Office Listings

http://brown.senate.gov

713 Hart Senate Office Building, Washington, DC 20510 .... (202) 224–2315
Chief of Staff.—Mark Powden. FAX: 228–6321
Legislative Director.—Eleanor Dehoney.
Communications Director.—Joanna Kuebler.
Press Secretary.—Meghan Dubyak.
1301 East Ninth Street, Suite 1710, Cleveland, OH 44114 .... (216) 522–7272
State Director.—John Ryan.
Deputy State Director.—Beth Thames.
425 Walnut Street, Suite 2310, Cincinnati, OH 45202 .... (513) 684–1021
200 North High Street, Room 614, Columbus, OH 43215 .... (614) 469–2083
205 West 20th Street, Suite M280, Lorain, OH 44052 .... (440) 242–4100

REPRESENTATIVES

FIRST DISTRICT

STEVE DRIEHAUS, Democrat, of Cincinnati, OH; born in Cincinnati, June 24, 1966; education: graduated Elder High School, Cincinnati, OH, 1984; B.A., Miami University, Oxford, OH, 1988; M.P.A., Indiana University, Bloomington, IN, 1995; professional: Ohio House of Representatives, 2001–09; Ohio House Minority Whip, 2005–08; Peace Corps volunteer, Senegal, 1988–90; married: Lucienne Driehaus, 1991; children: Alex, Claire, and Jack; committees: Financial Services, Oversight and Government Reform; elected to the 111th Congress on November 4, 2008.

Office Listings

http://www.driehaus.house.gov

408 Cannon House Office Building, Washington, DC 20515 .... (202) 225–2216
Chief of Staff.—Greg Mecher. FAX: 225–3012
Legislative Director.—Sarah Curtis.
Press Secretary.—Tim Mulvey.
Scheduler / Executive Assistant.—Heidi Black.
Carew Tower, 441 Vine Street, Room 3003, Cincinnati, OH 45202 .... (513) 684–2723
District Director.—Steve Brinker. FAX: 421–8722

Counties: BUTLER (part), HAMILTON (part). Population (2000), 630,730.

ZIP Codes: 45001–02, 45013–14, 45030, 45033, 45040–41, 45051–54, 45056, 45070, 45201–21, 45223–25, 45229, 45231–34, 45236–41, 45246–48, 45250–53, 45258, 45262–64, 45267–71, 45273–74, 45277, 45280, 45296, 45298–99

* * *

SECOND DISTRICT

JEAN SCHMIDT, Republican, of Miami Township; born in Cincinnati, OH, November 29th; education: B.A., University of Cincinnati, 1974; professional: Miami Township Trustee, 1989–2000; Ohio House of Representatives, 2000–04; president, Right to Life of Greater Cincinnati, 2004–05; religion: Catholic; married: Peter; children: Emilie; co-chair, Congressional Pro-Life Women's Caucus; committees: Agriculture; Transportation and Infrastructure; elected to the 109th Congress by special election on August 5, 2005; reelected to each succeeding Congress.

Office Listings

http://www.house.gov/schmidt

418 Cannon House Office Building, Washington, DC 20515 .... (202) 225–3164
Chief of Staff.—Barry Bennett. FAX: 225–1992
Legislative Director.—Joe Jansen.
Communications Director.—Bruce Pfaff.
Scheduler.—Jennifer Pielsticker.
8044 Montgomery Road, Suite 170, Cincinnati, OH 45236 .... (513) 791–0381
District Director.—Gertrud Whitaker.
601 Chillicothe Street, Portsmouth, OH 45662 .... (740) 354–1440

Counties: ADAMS, BROWN, CLERMONT, HAMILTON (part), PIKE, SCIOTO (part), WARREN (part). Population (2000), 630,730.

ZIP Codes: 45034, 45036, 45039–40, 45054, 45065, 45068, 45101–03, 45105–07, 45111–13, 45115, 45118–22, 45130–31, 45133, 45140, 45142, 45144–45, 45147–48, 45150, 45152–54, 45156–58, 45160, 45162, 45167–68, 45171, 45174, 45176, 45202, 45206–09, 45212–13, 45222, 45226–27, 45230, 45235–37, 45241–46, 45249, 45254–55, 45601, 45612–13, 45616, 45618, 45624, 45630, 45642, 45646, 45648, 45650, 45652, 45657, 45660–63, 45671, 45679, 45683–84, 45687, 45690, 45693, 45697

* * *

THIRD DISTRICT

MICHAEL R. TURNER, Republican, of Dayton, OH; born in Dayton, January 11, 1960; education: B.A., Ohio Northern University, 1982; J.D., Case Western Reserve University Law School, 1985; M.B.A., University of Dayton, 1992; professional: attorney; president, JMD Development (real estate company); corporate counsel, MTC International (holding company); organizations: Ohio Bar Association; California Bar Association; public service: Mayor of Dayton, 1994–2002; married to Lori; children: Jessica and Carolyn; committees: Armed Services; Oversight and Government Reform; elected to the 108th Congress on November 5, 2002; reelected to each succeeding Congress.

Office Listings

http://www.turner.house.gov

1740 Longworth House Office Building, Washington, DC 20515 .... (202) 225–6465
Chief of Staff.—Stacy Palmer-Barton. FAX: 225–6754
Legislative Director.—Joseph Heaton.
120 West Third Street, Suite 305, Dayton, OH 45402 .... (937) 225–2843
61 East Main Street, Suite 1, Wilmington, OH 45177 .... (937) 383–8931

Counties: CLINTON, HIGHLAND, MONTGOMERY (part), WARREN (part). Population (2000), 630,730.

ZIP Codes: 45005, 45032, 45036, 45040, 45042, 45044, 45054, 45066, 45068, 45107, 45110, 45113–14, 45118, 45123, 45132–33, 45135, 45138, 45140, 45142, 45146, 45148, 45155, 45159, 45164, 45166, 45169, 45177, 45206, 45240–41, 45309, 45315, 45322, 45325, 45327, 45335, 45338, 45342–45, 45354, 45371, 45377, 45381, 45401–10, 45412–20, 45422, 45426–29, 45431–32, 45437, 45439–41, 45448–49, 45454, 45458–59, 45463, 45469–70, 45475, 45479, 45481–82, 45490, 45612, 45660, 45679, 45697

* * *

FOURTH DISTRICT

JAMES D. ''JIM'' JORDAN, Republican, of Urbana, OH; born in Troy, OH, February 17, 1964; education: graduated, Graham High School, St. Paris, OH, 1982; B.S. in economics, University of Wisconsin, Madison, WI, 1986; M.A. in education, The Ohio State University, Columbus, OH, 1991; J.D., Capital University School of Law, Columbus, OH, 2001; professional: assistant wrestling coach, The Ohio State University, 1987–95; State Representative, Ohio House of Representatives, 85th District, 1995–2001; State Senator, Ohio State Senate, 12th District, 2001–07; awards: four-time high school wrestling champion (Ohio), 1979–82; two-time NCAA Division 1 National Wrestling Champion, 1985–86; three-time All American, 1984–86; Wisconsin Badgers Hall of Fame; third place, Olympic Trials in Wrestling, 1988; Friend of the Taxpayer, Americans for the Tax Reform, 1997; Leadership in Government Award from the Ohio Roundtable and Freedom forum, 2001; awards from the United Conservatives of Ohio: Outstanding Freshman Legislator Award, 1996; Watchdog of the Treasury, 1996, 2000, 2004; Pro-Life Legislator of the Year, 1998; Outstanding Legislator Award, 2004; activities: Grace Bible Church, Springfield; Local and National Right to Life organizations; Champaign County Republican Executive Committee; married: Polly (Stickley) Jordan; parents: John and Shirley Jordan; children: Rachel, Benjamin, Jessie, and Issac; committees: Budget, Oversight and Government Reform; Judiciary; elected to the 110th Congress on November 7, 2006; reelected to the Congress.

Office Listings

http://www.jordan.house.gov

515 Cannon House Office Building, Washington, DC 20515 .... (202) 225–2676
Chief of Staff.—Ray Yonkura. FAX: 226–0577
Legislative Director.—George Poulios.
Executive Assistant / Scheduler.—Melissa Evans.
3121 West Elm Plaza, Lima, OH 45805–2516 .... (419) 999–6455
100 East Main Cross Street, Suite 201, Findlay, OH 45840–3311 .... (419) 423–3210
24 West Third Street, Room 314, Mansfield, OH 44902–1299 .... (419) 522–5757
District Director.—Fred Shimp.

Counties: ALLEN, AUGLAIZE, CHAMPAIGN, HANCOCK, HARDIN, LOGAN, MARION, MORROW, RICHLAND, SHELBY, WYANDOT (part). Population (2000), 630,730.

ZIP Codes: 43003, 43009, 43011, 43019, 43044–45, 43047, 43050, 43060, 43067, 43070, 43072, 43074, 43078, 43083–84, 43301–02, 43306, 43310–11, 43314–26, 43330–38, 43340–51, 43356–60, 43516, 44802, 44804–05, 44813, 44817, 44822, 44827, 44830, 44833, 44837, 44843, 44849, 44862, 44864–65, 44875, 44878, 44901–07, 44999, 45013, 45302, 45306, 45312, 45317, 45326, 45333–34, 45336, 45340, 45344, 45353, 45356, 45360, 45363, 45365, 45380, 45388–89, 45404, 45414, 45420, 45424, 45431–32, 45502, 45801–02, 45804–10, 45812, 45814, 45816–17, 45819–20, 45822, 45830, 45833, 45835–36, 45839–41, 45843–45, 45850, 45854, 45856, 45858–59, 45862, 45865, 45867–72, 45877, 45881, 45884–85, 45887–90, 45894–97

* * *

FIFTH DISTRICT

ROBERT E. ''BOB'' LATTA, of Bowling Green, OH; born in Bluffton, OH, April 18, 1956; Graduated, Bowling Green High School, Bowling Green, OH, 1974; Bowling Green State University, Bowling Green, OH, 1978; B.A., history, University of Toledo School of Law, Toledo, OH, 1981; J.D., Legislator, Lawyer; awards: Ohio Farm Bureau ''Friend of Farm Bureau'' Award, 2008; the United States Chamber of Commerce ''Spirit of Enterprise'' Award, 2008; and the American Conservative Union ''ACU Conservative'' Award, 2008; United Conservatives of Ohio ''Watchdog of the Treasury'' in 1998, 2000, and 2005; The U.S. Sportsmen's Alliance, ''Patriot Award'', 2002, Ohio National Guard ''Major General Charles Dick Award for Legislative Excellence'', 1999; ''President's Award'', 2006; religion: Roman Catholic; Wife, Marcia ''Sloan'' Latta; Daughters, Elizabeth and Maria Latta; member, Bowling Green Noon Kiwanis, Bowling Green Chamber of Commerce, Wood County Farm Bureau; committees: Agriculture; Budget; Transportation and Infrastructure; elected to the 111th Congress on November 4, 2008.

Office Listings

http://latta.house.gov

1531 Longworth House Office Building, Washington, DC 20515 .... (202) 225–6405
Chief of Staff.—Ryan Walker. FAX: 225–1985
Legislative Director.—Allison Witt.
Press Secretary.—David Popp.
Executive Assistant / Scheduler.—Hillary Solt.
1045 North Main Street, Suite 6, Bowling Green, OH 43402 .... (419) 354–8700
101 Clinton Street, Suite 1200, Defiance, OH 43512 .... (419) 782–1996
11 East Main Street, Norwalk, OH 44857 .... (419) 668–0206

Counties: ASHLAND (part), CRAWFORD, DEFIANCE, FULTON, HENRY, HURON, LUCAS (part), MERCER (part), PAULDING, PUTNAM, SANDUSKY, SENECA, VAN WERT, WILLIAMS, WOOD, WYANDOT (part). Population (2000), 630,730.

ZIP Codes: 43302, 43314, 43316, 43323, 43337, 43351, 43402–03, 43406–07, 43410, 43413–14, 43416, 43420, 43430–31, 43435, 43437, 43441–43, 43447, 43449–51, 43457, 43460, 43462–67, 43469, 43501–02, 43504–06, 4351012, 43515–27, 43529–36, 43540–43, 43545, 43547–58, 43565–67, 43569–71, 43605, 43619, 43654, 44035, 44235, 44287, 44802, 44805, 44807, 44809, 44811, 44815, 44817–18, 44820, 44825–28, 44830, 44833, 44836–37, 44841, 44844–51, 44853–57, 44859–61, 44865–67, 44874–75, 44878, 44880–83, 44887–90, 45813, 45815, 45817, 45821–22, 45827–28, 45830–33, 45837–38, 45844, 45846, 45848–49, 45851, 45853, 45855–56, 45858, 45861–64, 45868, 45872–77, 45879–80, 45882, 45886–87, 45889, 45891, 45893–94, 45898–99

* * *

SIXTH DISTRICT

CHARLES A. WILSON, Democrat, of St. Clairsville, OH; born in Martins Ferry, OH, January 18, 1943; raised in Dillonvale, OH; education: B.A., Ohio University; degree from the Cincinnati College of Mortuary Science; professional: director, Wilson Furniture and Funeral Company; served in the Ohio Legislative; 1997–2003, and Ohio Senate, 2004–05; family: four sons and eight grandchildren; committees: Financial Services; Science and Technology; elected to the 110th Congress on November 7, 2006; reelected to the 111th Congress on November 4, 2008.

Office Listings

226 Cannon House Office Building, Washington, DC 20515 .... (202) 225–5705
Chief of Staff.—Candace Bryan Abbey. FAX: 225–5907
Legislative Director.—Joan Gregory.
Communications Director.—Hillary Viers.
Scheduler.—Lloyd Patashnick.
800 Main Street, Bridgeport, OH 43912 .... (740) 633–5705
District Director.—Chris Gagin.
4137 Boardman-Canfield Road, Canfield, OH 44406 .... (330) 533–7250
258 Front Street, Marietta, OH 45750 .... (740) 376–0868
1200 Main Street, Wellsville, OH 43968 .... (330) 532–3740
202 Park Avenue, Suite C, Ironton, OH 45638 .... (740) 533–9423

Counties: ATHENS (part), BELMONT, COLUMBIANA, GALLIA, JEFFERSON, LAWRENCE, MAHONING (part), MEIGS, MONROE, NOBLE, SCIOTO (part), WASHINGTON. Population (2000), 630,730.

ZIP Codes: 43711, 43713, 4371619, 43724, 43728, 43732, 43747, 43752, 43754, 43757, 43759, 43772–73, 43778–80, 43786–89, 43793, 43901–03, 43905–10, 43912–17, 43920, 43925–26, 43930–35, 43937–48, 43950–53, 43961–64, 43967–

68, 43970–71, 43973, 43977, 43983, 43985, 44401, 44406, 44408, 44412–13, 44415–16, 44422–23, 44427, 44429, 44431–32, 44441–45, 44449, 44451–52, 44454–55, 44460, 44481, 44490, 44492–93, 44502, 44507, 44511–15, 44601, 44609, 44619, 44625, 44634, 44657, 44665, 44672, 45014, 45040, 45054, 45065, 45067–68, 45107, 45110, 45113–14, 45123, 45132–33, 45135, 45138, 45140, 45142, 45146, 45148, 45155, 45159, 45162, 45164, 45166, 45172, 45177, 45419, 45614, 45619–20, 45623, 45629, 45631, 45636, 45638, 45643, 45645, 45648, 45653, 45656, 45658–59, 45662, 45669, 45674–75, 45677–78, 45680, 45682, 45685–86, 45688, 45694, 45696, 45699, 45701, 45710–15, 45720–21, 45723–24, 45727, 45729, 45732, 45734–35, 45739, 45741–46, 45750, 45760–61, 45764, 45766–73, 45775–80, 45783–84, 45786–89

* * *

SEVENTH DISTRICT

STEVE AUSTRIA, Republican, of Beavercreek, OH; born in Xenia, OH, October 12, 1958; education: B.A., Marquette University, Milwaukee, WI, 1982; Freshman Class President, 2008–10; religion: Catholic; committees: Budget; Homeland Security; elected to the 111th Congress on November 4, 2008.

Office Listings

http://www.austria.house.gov

1641 Longworth House Office Building, Washington, DC 20515 .... (202) 225–4324
Chief of Staff.—Wayne Struble.
Press Secretary.—Courtney Whetstone.
Legislative Assistant.—Courtney Temple.
Executive Assistant.—Steven Gilleland.
Legislative Correspondent.—Christin O'Brien.
5 West North Street, Suite 200, Springfield, OH 45504 .... (937) 325–9188
District Director.—Scott Corbitt.
207 South Broad Street, Lancaster, OH 43130 .... (740) 654–7825

Counties: CLARK, FAIRFIELD, FAYETTE, FRANKLIN (part), GREENE, PERRY, PICKAWAY, ROSS (part). Population (2000), 630,730.

ZIP Codes: 43009–10, 43044, 43046, 43062, 43068, 43076, 43078, 43102–03, 43105–07, 43109–10, 43112–13, 43115–17, 43125, 43128, 43130, 43135–38, 43140, 43142–43, 43145–48, 43150, 43153–57, 43160, 43163–64, 43199, 43207, 43213, 43217, 43227, 43232, 43314, 43730–31, 43739, 43748, 43758, 43760–61, 43764, 43766, 43777, 43782–83, 45123, 45135, 45169, 45301, 45305, 45307, 45314, 45316, 45319, 45323–24, 45335, 45341, 45344, 45349, 45368–70, 45372, 45384–85, 45387, 45424, 45430–35, 45440, 45458–59, 45501–06, 45601, 45628, 45644, 45671, 45732

* * *

EIGHTH DISTRICT

JOHN A. BOEHNER, Republican, of West Chester, OH; born in Reading, OH, November 17, 1949; education: graduated, Moeller High School, Cincinnati, OH, 1968; B.S., Xavier University, 1977; president, Nucite Sales, Inc.; Ohio House of Representatives, 1984–90; ranking Republican member, Commerce and Labor Committee; Energy and Environment Committee; Judiciary and Criminal Justice; elected, Union Township Trustees, 1981; elected, president, Union Township Board of Trustees, 1984; member: St. John Catholic Church; Ohio Farm Bureau; Lakota Hills Homeowners Association; Knights of Columbus, Pope John XXIII; Union Chamber of Commerce; American Heart Association Board; Butler County Mental Health Association; YMCA Capital Campaign; Union Elementary School PTA; Middletown Chamber of Commerce; American Legion Post 218 of Middletown Butler County Trustees and Clerks Association; married the former Deborah Gunlack, 1973; two children: Lindsay, Tricia; committees: Republican Leader; elected to the 102nd Congress; reelected to each succeeding Congress.

Office Listings

http://johnboehner.house.gov

1011 Longworth House Office Building, Washington, DC 20515 .... (202) 225–6205
Chief of Staff.—Mick Krieger. FAX: 225–5117
Press Secretary.—Jessica R. Towhey.
7969 Cincinnati-Dayton road, Suite B, West Chester, OH 45069 .... (513) 779–5400
12 South Plum Street, Troy, Ohio 45373 .... (937) 339–1524

Counties: BUTLER (part), DARKE, MERCER (part), MIAMI, MONTGOMERY (part), PREBLE. Population (2000), 630,730.

ZIP Codes: 45003–05, 45011–15, 45018, 45025–26, 45036, 45042–44, 45050, 45055–56, 45061–64, 45067, 45069, 45071, 45073, 45099, 45241, 45246, 45303–04, 45308–12, 45317–18, 45320–22, 45325–28, 45330–32, 45337–39, 45344, 45346–48, 45350–52, 45356, 45358–59, 45361–62, 45365, 45371, 45373–74, 45378, 45380–83, 45388, 45390, 45402–04, 45406, 45414, 45424, 45431–32, 45822, 45826, 45828, 45845–46, 45860, 45865–66, 45869, 45883, 45885

* * *

NINTH DISTRICT

MARCY KAPTUR, Democrat, of Toledo, OH; born in Toledo, June 17, 1946; education: graduated, St. Ursula Academy, Toledo, 1964; B.A., University of Wisconsin, Madison, 1968; Master of Urban Planning, University of Michigan, Ann Arbor, 1974; attended University of Manchester, England, 1974; professional: urban planner; assistant director for urban affairs, domestic policy staff, White House, 1977–79; American Planning Association and American Institute of Certified Planners Fellow; member: National Center for Urban Ethnic Affairs advisory committee; University of Michigan Urban Planning Alumni Association; NAACP Urban League; Polish Museum; Polish American Historical Association; Lucas County Democratic Party Executive Committee; Democratic Women's Campaign Association; Little Flower Parish Church; House Auto Parts Task Force; co-chair, Ukrainian and 4–H Caucuses; religion: Roman Catholic; committees: Appropriations; Budget; Oversight and Government Reform; elected on November 2, 1982, to the 98th Congress; reelected to each succeeding Congress.

Office Listings

http://www.kaptur.house.gov

2186 Rayburn House Office Building, Washington, DC 20515 .... (202) 225–4146
Chief of Staff.—Steve Katich.
Deputy Chief of Staff.—Nathan Facey. FAX: 225–7711
Office Manager / Scheduler.—Norma Olsen.
One Maritime Plaza, Suite 600, Toledo, OH 43604 .... (419) 259–7500
Administrative Assistant.—Steve Katich.

Counties: ERIE COUNTY. CITIES AND TOWNSHIPS: Bellevue, Berlin Heights, Berlinville, Birmingham, Bloomingville, Bronson, Castalia, Chatham, Clarksfield, Collins, East Townsend, Fitchville, Hartland, Huron, Kimball, Litchfield, Milan, Mitiwanga, Monroeville, New London, Norwalk, Nova, Olena, Ridgefield, River Corners, Ruggles, Ruggles Beach, Sandusky, Shinrock, Spencer, Steuben, Sullivan, Wakeman, West Clarksfield. LORAIN COUNTY. CITIES AND TOWNSHIPS: Amherst, Beaver Park, Belden, Beulah Beach, Brownhelm, Columbia Station, Elyria, Grafton, Henrietta, Kipton, Lagrange, Linwood Park, Lorain, North Eaton, Oberlin, Ridgeville, Rochester, South Amherst, Vermilion, Wellington. LUCAS COUNTY (part). CITIES AND TOWNSHIPS: Berkey, Curtice, Gypsum, Harbor View, Holland, Maumee, Monclova, Northwood, Oregon, Swanton, Sylvania, Toledo, Waterville, Whitehouse, Woodville. OTTAWA COUNTY. CITIES AND TOWNSHIPS: Bay Shore, Bono, Catawba Island, Clay Center, Danbury, Eagle Beach, Elliston, Elmore, Gem Beach, Genoa, Graytown, Hessville, Isle St. George, Kelleys Island, Lacarne, Lakeside, Lindsey, Marblehead, Martin, Oak Harbor, Port Clinton, Portage, Put-in-Bay, Rocky Ridge, Springbrook, Vickery, Washington, Wayne, Whites Landing, and Williston. Population (2000), 630,730.

ZIP Codes: 43408, 43412, 43416, 43430, 43432–34, 43436, 43438–40, 43442, 43445–47, 43449, 43452, 43456, 43458, 43464, 43468–69, 43504, 43528, 43537, 43542, 43558, 43560, 43566, 43571, 43601–18, 43620, 43623–24, 43635, 43652, 43656–57, 43659–61, 43666–67, 43681–82, 43697, 43699, 44001, 44028, 44035, 44044, 44049–50, 44053, 44074, 44089–90, 44253, 44256, 44275, 44280, 44811, 44814, 44816, 44824, 44826, 44839, 44846–47, 44851, 44857, 44859, 44870–71, 44880, 44889

* * *

TENTH DISTRICT

DENNIS J. KUCINICH, Democrat, of Cleveland, OH; born in Cleveland, October 8, 1946; B.A., and M.A. in speech and communications, Case Western Reserve University, 1974; editor, professor; Cleveland City Councilman, 1969–75; Clerk of the Municipal Court, 1975–77; Mayor of Cleveland, 1977–79; Ohio Senate, 1994–96; named Outstanding Ohio Senator by National Association of Social Workers for his work on health and social welfare issues; one child, Jackie; committees: Education and Labor; Oversight and Government Reform; elected to the 105th Congress; reelected to each succeeding Congress.

Office Listings

http://kucinich.house.gov

2445 Rayburn House Office Building, Washington, DC 20515 .... (202) 225–5871
Chief of Staff.—Jaron Bourke. FAX: 225–5745
Legislative Director.—Vic Edgerton.
14400 Detroit Avenue, Lakewood, OH 44107 .... (216) 228–8850

Counties: CUYAHOGA COUNTY (part). CITIES AND TOWNSHIPS: Bay Village, Berea, Brooklyn, Brooklyn Heights, Cleveland, Cuyahaga Heights, Fairview Park, Lakewood, Newberg Heights, North Olmsted, Olmsted Falls, Olmsted Township, Parma, Rocky River, Seven Hills, Strongsville, and Westlake. Population (2000), 630,730.

ZIP Codes: 44017, 44070, 44102, 44105, 44107, 44109, 44111, 44113, 44115–16, 44125–27, 44129–31, 44134–42, 44144–46, 44149, 44181

* * *

ELEVENTH DISTRICT

MARCIA L. FUDGE, Democrat, of Cleveland, OH; born in Shaker Heights, OH, October 29, 1952; B.S., Ohio State University, 1975; J.D., Cleveland Marshall College of Law, 1983; professional: Director of Budget and Finance, Cuyahoga County Prosecutor's Office; Chief Administrator for Cuyahoga County Prosecutor Stephanie Tubbs Jones; Mayor of Warrensville Heights, OH; committees: Education and Labor; Science and Technology; elected to the 110th Congress, by special election, to fill the vacancy caused by the death of United States Representative Stephanie Tubbs Jones; reelected to the 111th Congress on November 4, 2008.

Office Listings

http://www.fudge.house.gov

1513 Longworth House Office Building, Washington, DC 20515 .... (202) 225–7032
Legislative Director.—Brandon Garrett.
Legislative Counsels: LaDavia Drane, Maheen Siddiqui.
Press Secretary.—Aketa Simmons.
Legislative Correspondent.—Eric Hammond.
Staff Assistant.—Clifton Williams.
Military Fellow.—Heidi Brodmarkle.
Scheduler / Office Manager.—Erin Finley.
4834 Richmond Road, Suite 150, Warrensville Heights, OH 44128 .... (216) 522–4900
Healthcare / Senior Citizen Liaison.—Beverly R. Charles.
Assistant / Media / Government Liaison.—Lloyd Brown.
Staff Assistant / Hispanic Community Liaison.—Fiol Smith.
Scheduler / Staff Assistant.—Linda R. Matthews.
Staff Assistant / Economic Development Liaison.—Daniel Fellenbaum.
Staff Assistant / Faith Based Liaision.—Stephen Caviness.
Staff Assistant / Jewish Community Liaison.—Janice Bilchik.
Youth Liaison / Staff Assistant.—Thione Niang.

Counties: CUYAHOGA COUNTY (part). CITIES: Beachwood, Bedford, Bedford Heights, Brahtenahl Village, Cleveland, Cleveland Heights, East Cleveland, Euclid, Garfield Heights, Highland Hills Village, Lyndhurst, Maple Heights, Mayfield Heights, North Randall Village, Oakwood Village, Orange Village, Pepper Pike, Richmond Heights, Shaker Heights, South Euclid, University Heights, Warrensville Heights, and Woodmere Village. Population (2000), 630,730.

ZIP Codes: 44101–15, 44118–44130, 44132, 44135, 44137, 44143–44, 44146, 44178, 44181, 44185, 44188–95, 44197–99

* * *

TWELFTH DISTRICT

PATRICK J. TIBERI, Republican, of Columbus, OH; born in Columbus, October 21, 1962; education: B.A., Ohio State University, 1985; professional: real estate agent; assistant to U.S. Representative John Kasich (R–OH); public service: served as Majority Leader, Ohio House of Representatives, 1992–2000; organizations: Westerville Chamber of Commerce; Columbus Board of Realtors; Military Veterans and Community Service Commission; Sons of Italy; awards: Fraternal Order of Police Outstanding Legislator; Watchdog of the Treasury Award; American Red Cross Volunteer Service Award; married: Denice; committees: Ways and Means; elected to the 107th Congress on November 7, 2000; reelected to each succeeding Congress.

Office Listings

http://www.house.gov/tiberi

113 Cannon House Office Building, Washington, DC 20515 .... (202) 225–5355
Chief of Staff.—Chris Zeigler. FAX: 226–4523
Legislative Director.—Adam Francis.
Communications Director.—Breann Gonzalez.
3000 Corporate Drive, Suite 310, Columbus, OH 43231 .... (614) 523–2555
District Director.—Mark Bell.

Counties: DELAWARE, FRANKLIN (part), LICKING (part). Population (2000), 630,730.

ZIP Codes: 43001–04, 43011, 43013, 43015–18, 43021, 43023, 43025–27, 43031–33, 43035, 43040, 43046, 43054–56, 43061–62, 43064–66, 43068, 43071, 43073–74, 43080–82, 43085–86, 43105, 43147, 43201, 43203, 43205–07, 43209, 43211, 43213–15, 43218–19, 43224, 43226–27, 43229–32, 43235–36, 43240, 43334, 43342, 43344, 43356

* * *

THIRTEENTH DISTRICT

BETTY SUTTON, Democrat, of Copley, OH; born in Barberton, OH, July 31, 1963; education: B.A., Kent State University, Kent, OH, 1985; J.D., University of Akron, Akron, OH, 1990; professional: lawyer, private practice; city council, Barberton, OH, 1991–92; member, Ohio House of Representatives, state of Ohio, 1993–2000; married: Doug Corwon; committees: Energy and Commerce; elected to the 110th Congress on November 7, 2006; reelected to the 111th Congress on November 4, 2008.

Office Listings

http://www.sutton.house.gov

1721 Longworth House Office Building, Washington, DC 20515 .... (202) 225–3401
Chief of Staff.—Nichole Francis Reynolds. FAX: 225–2266
Legislative Director.—Christine Corcoran.
Scheduler.—Elizabeth Walters.
205 West Twentieth Street, M–230, Lorain, OH 44052 .... (440) 245–5350
39 East Market Street, LL #1, Akron, OH 44308 .... (330) 865–8450

Counties: CUYAHOGA (part), LORAIN (part), MEDINA (part), SUMMIT (part). CITIES AND TOWNSHIPS: Akron, Lorain, Elyria, N. Ridgeville, Brunswick, Strongsville, and N. Royalton. Population (2000), 630,730.

ZIP Codes: 44001, 44011–12, 44028, 44035–36, 44039, 44044, 44052–55, 44133, 44136, 44141, 44147, 44149, 44203, 44210, 44212, 44216, 44221–24, 44230, 44233, 44253, 44256, 44264, 44280–81, 44286, 44301–04, 44306–14, 44317, 44319–22, 44325–26, 44328, 44333–34, 44372, 44393, 44398–99, 44614, 44645, 44685, 44720

* * *

FOURTEENTH DISTRICT

STEVEN C. LATOURETTE, Republican, of Bainbridge Township, OH; born in Cleveland, OH, July 22, 1954; education: graduated, Cleveland Heights High School, 1972; B.A., University of Michigan, 1976; J.D., Cleveland State University, 1979; professional: assistant public defender, Lake County, OH, Public Defender's Office, 1980–83; associated with Painesville firm of Cannon, Stern, Aveni and Krivok, 1983–86; Baker, Hackenberg and Collins, 1986–88; prosecuting attorney, Lake County, OH, 1988–94; served on the Lake County Budget Commission; executive board of the Lake County Narcotics Agency; chairman, County Task Force on Domestic Violence; trustee, Cleveland Policy Historical Society; director, Regional Forensic Laboratory; member: Lake County Association of Police Chiefs, Ohio Prosecuting Attorneys Association, and National District Attorneys Association; appointed to serve as a fellow of the American College of Prosecuting Attorneys; married: Jennifer; children: Sarah, Sam, Clare, Amy, and Emma; committees: Appropriations; elected to the 104th Congress; reelected to each succeeding Congress.

Office Listings

http://www.latourette.house.gov

2371 Rayburn House Office Building, Washington, DC 20515 .... (202) 225–5731
Chief of Staff.—Joe Guzzo. FAX: 225–3307
Communications Director.—Deborah Setliff.
Executive Assistant / Scheduler.—Kathy Kato.
Legislative Director.—Kate Ostrander.
1 Victoria Place, Room 320, Painesville, OH 44077 .... (440) 352–3939
Twinsburg Government Center, 10075 Ravenna Road, Twinsburg, OH 44087 .... (330) 425–9291

Counties: ASHTABULA, CUYAHOGA (part), GEAUGA, LAKE, PORTAGE (part), SUMMIT (part), TRUMBULL (part). Population (2000), 630,730.

ZIP Codes: 44003–05, 44010, 44021–24, 44026, 44030, 44032–33, 44040–41, 44045–48, 44056–57, 44060–62, 44064–65, 44067–68, 44072–73, 44076–77, 44080–82, 44084–88, 44092–97, 44099, 44124, 44139, 44141, 44143, 44202, 44221, 44223–24, 44231, 44234, 44236–37, 44240, 44255, 44262, 44264, 44278, 44404, 44410, 44417–18, 44428, 44439, 44450, 44470, 44491

* * *

FIFTEENTH DISTRICT

MARY JO KILROY, Democrat, of Columbus, OH; born in Cleveland, OH; April 30, 1949; education: B.A., Cleveland State University, Cleveland, OH, 1977; J.D., Ohio State University Law School, Columbus, OH, 1980; professional: attorney; admitted to the Ohio Bar, 1981; Columbus Board of Education, 1992–2000; vice-president of Columbus Board of Education, 1993, and 1998; president, Columbus Board of Education, 1999; Franklin County Commission, 2001–08; president, Franklin County Board of Commissioners, 2005, and 2007; awards: Public Official of the Year by the Central Ohio Chapter of the National Association of Social Workers, 1996; Kaleidoscope Youth Coalition Community Award, 1998; Community Leadership Award, 1998; Central Ohio Clean Fuels Coalition Outstanding Official, 2004; Community Shelter Board Mel Schottenstein Leadership Award, 2004; Goodman Guild Outstanding Commitment to Adult Education, 2007; Shamrock Club of Columbus Presidents Award, 2008; Mercy for Animals Compassionate Leadership Award, 2008; Hometown Heroes Award for Legislator Who Supports Service Members, 2009; Amvets Post 300 Honorary Member of the Year, 2009; member, Investment Advisory Board EMA MORPC; Franklin County Planning Commission; married: Robert Handelman; children: Julia and Rosa; committees: Financial Services; Homeland Security; elected to the 111th Congress on November 4, 2008.

Office Listings

http://www.kilroy.house.gov

1237 Longworth House Office Building, Washington, DC 20515 .... (202) 225–2015
Chief of Staff.—Randy Borntrager. FAX: 225–3529
Scheduler.—Ashley Senn.
Legislative Director.—Jennifer Keaton.
Communications Director.—Paul Tencher.
1299 Olentangy River Road, Suite 200, Columbus, OH 43212 .... (614) 294–2196
FAX: 294–2384

Counties: FRANKLIN (part), MADISON, UNION. Population (2000), 630,730.

ZIP Codes: 43016–17, 43026, 43029, 43036, 43040–41, 43045, 43060, 43064–65, 43067, 43077, 43085, 43119, 43123, 43125, 43137, 43140, 43143, 43146, 43151, 43153, 43162, 43201–06, 43207, 43210–12, 43214–15, 43220–21, 43223–24, 43228–29, 43235, 43344, 43358

* * *

SIXTEENTH DISTRICT

JOHN BOCCIERI, Democrat, of Alliance, OH; born in Youngstown, OH, October 5, 1969; education: B.S., St. Bonaventure University, St. Bonaventure, NY, 1992; M.A., public administration, Webster University, St. Louis, MO, 1996; M.B.A., Webster University, St. Louis, MO, 1996; military service: Major, Air Force Reserve C–130 pilot, 1994–present; professional: United States Air Force; Tours in Iraq and Afghanistan including Operation Iraqi Freedom; Operation Enduring Freedom; Ohio House of Representatives, 2000–06; Ohio Senate, 2007–08; married: Stacey Kennedy-Boccieri; 4 children; committees: Agriculture; Transportation and Infrastructure; elected to the 111th Congress on November 4, 2008.

Office Listings

http://www.boccieri.house.gov

1516 Longworth House Office Building, Washington, DC 20515 .... (202) 225–3876
Chief of Staff.—Anthony Trevena. FAX: 225–3059
Press Secretary.—Jessica Kershaw.
DC Scheduler.—Kelly Misselwitz.
Legislative Director.—Chad Tanner.
300 West Tuscarawas Street, Suite 716, Canton, OH 44702 .... (330) 489–4414
District Staff Director.—Anthony Trevena.
District Scheduler.—Katie Jones.

Counties: ASHLAND (part), MEDINA (part), STARK, WAYNE. Population (2000), 630,730.

ZIP Codes: 44090, 44201, 44203, 44214–17, 44230, 44233, 44235, 44251, 44253–54, 44256, 44258, 44260, 44270, 44273–76, 44280–82, 44287, 44321, 44333, 44601, 44606, 44608, 44611–14, 44618, 44624, 44626–27, 44630, 44632, 44634, 44636, 44638, 44640–41, 44643, 44645–48, 44650, 44652, 44657, 44659, 44662, 44666–67, 44669–70, 44676–77,

44680, 44685, 44688–89, 44691, 44701–12, 44714, 44718, 44720–21, 44730, 44735, 44750, 44760, 44767, 44799, 44805, 44822, 44838, 44840, 44842–43, 44864, 44866, 44878, 44880, 44903

* * *

SEVENTEENTH DISTRICT

TIM RYAN, Democrat, of Niles, OH; born in Niles, July 16, 1973; education: B.S., Bowling Green University, 1995; J.D., Franklin Pierce Law Center, 2000; awarded a National Italian American Foundation Scholarship; professional: attorney; internship, Trumbull County Prosecutor's Office; also worked as a congressional legislative aide in Washington, DC; organizations: former president, Trumbull County Young Democrats; former chairman, Earning by Learning Program in Warren, OH; public service: Ohio State Senate, 2000–02; religion: Catholic; committees: Appropriations; elected to the 108th Congress on November 5, 2002; reelected to each succeeding Congress.

Office Listings

http://timryan.house.gov

1421 Longworth House Office Building, Washington, DC 20515 .... (202) 225–5261
Chief of Staff.—Ron Grimes. FAX: 225–3719
Scheduler.—Erin Isenberg.
Legislative Director.—Ryan Keating.
197 West Market Street, Warren, OH 44481 .... (330) 373–0074
241 Federal Plaza West, Youngstown, OH 44503 .... (330) 740–0193

Counties: MAHONING (part), PORTAGE (part), SUMMIT (part), TRUMBULL (part). Population (2000), 630,730.

ZIP Codes: 44201, 44211, 44221, 44223–24, 44231–32, 44236, 44240–43, 44250, 44255, 44260, 44265–66, 44272, 44278, 44285, 44288, 44302–06, 44308, 44310–13, 44315–16, 44319, 44402–06, 44410–12, 44417–18, 44420, 44424–25, 44429–30, 44436–38, 44440, 44444, 44446, 44449–50, 44453, 44470–71, 44473, 44481–86, 44488, 44491, 44501–07, 44509–12, 44514–15, 44555, 44599, 44632, 44685, 44720

* * *

EIGHTEENTH DISTRICT

ZACHARY T. SPACE, Democrat, of Dover, OH; born in Dover, OH, January 27, 1961; education: graduated from Dover High School, Dover, OH, 1979; B.A., Kenyon College, Gambier, OH, 1983; J.D., The Ohio State University, 1986; professional: lawyer, private practice; Dover, Law Director, 2000–06; married: Mary Space; children: Gina and Nicholas; committees: Energy and Commerce; Veterans' Affairs; elected to the 110th Congress on November 7, 2006; reelected to the 111th Congress.

Office Listings

http://www.space.house.gov

315 Cannon House Office Building, Washington, DC 20515 .... (202) 225–6265
Chief of Staff.—Stuart Chapman. FAX: 225–3394
Scheduler.—Lauren Lapolla.
Senior Legislative Assistants: Jillian Carroll, Dan Farmer.
Communications Director.—Andrew Ricci.
137 East Iron Avenue, Dover, OH 44622 .... (330) 364–4300
Toll-free (866) 910–7577
District Director.—Ken Engstrom.
17 North Fourth Street, Suite A, Zanesville, OH 43701 .... (740) 452–6339
14 South Paint Street, Suite 6, Chillicothe, OH 45601 .... (740) 779–1636

Counties: ATHENS (part), BELMONT (PART), CARROLL, COSHOCTON, GUERNSEY, HARRISON, HOCKING, HOLMES, JACKSON, KNOX, LICKING (part), MORGAN, MUSKINGUM, ROSS (part), TUSCARAWAS, VINTON. Population (2000), 630,730.

ZIP Codes: 43005–06, 43008, 43011, 43014, 43019, 43022–23, 43025, 43028, 43030, 43037, 43048, 43050, 43055–56, 43058, 43071, 43076, 43080, 43093, 43098, 43101–02, 43107, 43111, 43127, 43130, 43135, 43138, 43144, 43149, 43152, 43155, 43158, 43160, 43701–02, 43718, 43720–25, 43727–28, 43730–36, 43738–40, 43746, 43749–50, 43755–56, 43758, 43760, 43762, 43766–68, 43771–73, 43777–78, 43780, 43787, 43791, 43802–05, 43811–12, 43821–22, 43824, 43828, 43830, 43832, 43836–37, 43840, 43842–45, 43901, 43903, 43906–08, 43910, 43927–28, 43933, 43945, 43950, 43972–74, 43976–77, 43981, 43983–84, 43986, 43988, 44427, 44607–08, 44610–12, 44615, 44617, 44620–22, 44624–29, 44631, 44633, 44637–39, 44643–44, 44651, 44653–54, 44656–57, 44660–61, 44663, 44671, 44675–76, 44678–83, 44687–90, 44693, 44695, 44697, 44699, 44730, 44813, 44822, 44842, 45123, 45601, 45612–13, 45617, 45621–22, 45628, 45633–34, 45640, 45644, 45647, 45651, 45653–54, 45656, 45672–73, 45681–82, 45685, 45690, 45692, 45695, 45698, 45701, 45710–11, 45715–16, 45719, 45732, 45740–41, 45761, 45764, 45766, 45780, 45782, 45786

OKLAHOMA

(Population 2000, 3,450,654)

SENATORS

JAMES M. INHOFE, Republican, of Tulsa, OK; born in Des Moines, IA, November 17, 1934; education: graduated Central High School, Tulsa, OK, 1953; B.A., University of Tulsa, OK, 1959; military service: served in the U.S. Army, private first class, 1957–58; professional: businessman; active pilot; president, Quaker Life Insurance Company; Oklahoma House of Representatives, 1967–69; Oklahoma State Senate, 1969–77; Mayor of Tulsa, OK, 1978–84; religion: member, First Presbyterian Church of Tulsa; married: Kay Kirkpatrick; children: Jim, Perry, Molly, and Katy; twelve grandchildren; committees: ranking member, Environment and Public Works; Armed Services; Foreign Relations; elected to the 100th Congress on November 4, 1986; reelected to each succeeding Congress; elected to the U.S. Senate on November 8, 1994, finishing the unexpired term of Senator David Boren; reelected to each succeeding Senate term.

Office Listings

http://inhofe.senate.gov

453 Russell Senate Office Building, Washington, DC 20510 .... (202) 224–4721
Chief of Staff.—Ryan Thompson. FAX: 228–0380
Legislative Director.—Ryan Jackson.
Press Secretary.—Jared Young.
Scheduler.—Wendi Price.
1924 South Utica, Suite 530, Tulsa, OK 74104–6511 .... (918) 748–5111
1900 Northwest Expressway, Suite 1210, Oklahoma City, OK 73118 .... (405) 608–4381
302 North Independence, Suite 104, Enid, OK 73701 .... (580) 234–5101
215 East Choctaw, Suite 106, McAlester, OK 74501 .... (918) 426–0933

* * *

TOM COBURN, Republican, of Muskogee, OK; born in Casper, WY, March 14, 1948; education: Central High School, Muskogee, OK, 1966; B.S., Oklahoma State University, 1970; Oklahoma University Medical School, 1983; professional: manufacturing manager, Coburn Ophthalmic Division, Coburn Optical Industries, 1970–78; family physician, 1983–present; member, American Medical Association, Oklahoma State Medical Association, East Central County Medical Society, American Academy of Family Practice; religion: First Baptist Church, ordained deacon; member, Promise Keepers; public service: U.S. House of Representatives, 1995–2001; married: Carolyn Denton Coburn, 1968; children: Callie, Katie, and Sarah; committees: Health, Education, Labor, and Pensions; Homeland Security and Government Affairs; Indian Affairs; Judiciary; Select Committee on Intelligence; elected to the U.S. Senate on November 2, 2004.

Office Listings

http://coburn.senate.gov

172 Russell Hart Senate Office Building, Washington, DC 20510 .... (202) 224–5754
Chief of Staff.—Michael Schwartz. FAX: 224–6008
Legislative Director.—Roland Foster.
Communications Director.—John Hart.
Scheduler.—Courtney Shadegg.
1800 South Baltimore, Suite 800, Tulsa, OK 74119 .... (918) 581–7651
100 North Broadway, Suite 1820, Oklahoma City, OK 73102 .... (405) 231–4941

REPRESENTATIVES

FIRST DISTRICT

JOHN SULLIVAN, Republican, of Tulsa, OK; born in Tulsa, January 1, 1965; education: B.B.A., Northeastern State University, 1992; professional: fuel sales, Love's Country Stores; Real Estate, McGraw, Davison, Stewart; public service: Oklahoma House of Representatives, 1995–2002; organizations: member, St. Mary's Church; member, National Rifle Association; member, Tulsa County Republican Men's Club; U.S. House of Representatives Assistant Majority Whip; family: married to Judy; children: Thomas, Meredith, Sydney, Daniel; committees:

Energy and Commerce; Select Committee on Energy Independence and Global Warming; elected to the 107th Congress, by special election, on January 8, 2002; reelected to each succeeding Congress.

Office Listings

http://sullivan.house.gov

434 Cannon House Office Building, Washington, DC 20510 .... (202) 225–2211
Chief of Staff.—Elizabeth Bartheld. FAX: 225–9187
Executive Assistant.—John Senger.
5727 South Lewis, Suite 520, Tulsa, OK 74105 .... (918) 749–0014
District Director.—Richard Hedgecock.

Counties: CREEK (part), ROGERS (part), TULSA, WAGONER, WASHINGTON. Population (2000), 690,131.

ZIP Codes: 74003–06, 74008, 74011–14, 74021–22, 74029, 74033, 74037, 74039, 74041, 74043, 74047–48, 74050–51, 74053, 74055, 74061, 74063, 74066, 74070, 74073, 74080, 74082–83, 74101–08, 74110, 74112, 74114–17, 74119–21, 74126–30, 74132–37, 74141, 74145–50, 74152–53, 74155–59, 74169–72, 74182–84, 74186–87, 74189, 74192–94, 74337, 74352, 74403, 74429, 74434, 74436, 74446, 74454, 74458, 74467, 74477

* * *

SECOND DISTRICT

DAN BOREN, Democrat, of Muskogee, OK; born in Shawnee, OK, August 2, 1973; education: B.S., Texas Christian University, Fort Worth, TX, 1997; M.B.A., University of Oklahoma, 2001; professional: president, Seminole State College Educational Foundation; vice-president, Robbins Energy Corporation; loan processor, Banc First Corporation; staff for United States Representative Wesley Watkins; education administrator; bank teller; aide, Oklahoma Corporation Commission; member of the Oklahoma State House of Representatives, 2002–04; organizations: Big Brothers Big Sisters Board; The Jasmine Moran Children's Museum Board; KIPP Foundation Board Member; married: Andrea; children: Janna; committees: Armed Services; Natural Resources; Permanent Select Committee on Intelligence; elected to the 109th Congress on November 2, 2004; reelected to each succeeding Congress.

Office Listings

http://www.house.gov/boren

216 Cannon House Office Building, Washington, DC 20515 .... (202) 225–2701
Chief of Staff.—Jason Buckner. FAX: 225–3038
Legislative Director.—Wendy Kirchoff.
Press Secretary.—Cole Perryman.
Scheduler.—Erica Rixen.
431 West Broadway, Muskogee, OK 74401 .... (918) 687–2533
District Coordinator.—Ben Robinson.
309 West 1st Street, Claremore, OK 74017 .... (918) 341–9336
321 South Third, Suite 4, McAlester, OK 74501 .... (918) 423–5951
112 North 12th Avenue, Durant, OK 74701 .... (580) 931–0333

Counties: ADAIR, ATOKA, BRYAN, CANADIAN, CHEROKEE, CHOCTAW, COAL, CRAIG, CREEK, DELAWARE, HASKELL, HUGHES, JOHNSTON, LATIMER, LEFLORE, MAYES, MCCURTAIN, MCINTOSH, MUSKOGEE, NOWATA, OKFUSKEE, OTTAWA, PAWNEE, PITTSBURG, PUSHMATAHA, ROGERS, SEMINOLE, SEQUOYAH. Population (2000), 690,130.

ZIP Codes: 73014, 73036, 73064, 73078, 73085, 73090, 73447, 73449–50, 73455, 73460–62, 74010, 74015–16, 74018, 74020, 74027–28, 74030–31, 74034, 74036, 74038–39, 74041–42, 74044–45, 74047–49, 74052–53, 74058, 74067–68, 74071–72, 74080–81, 74083, 74085, 74101, 74103, 74301, 74330–33, 74335, 74337–40, 74343–44, 74346–47, 74349–50, 74352, 74355, 74358–63, 74365–67, 74369–70, 74401–02, 74421–23, 74425–26, 74428, 74430–32, 74434–38, 74441–42, 74445, 74447, 74450, 74455, 74459, 74461–64, 74468–70, 74472, 74502, 74521–23, 74525, 74530–31, 74533–34, 74536, 74538, 74546–47, 74552–54, 74556, 74560–63, 74565, 74569–72, 74576, 74578, 74650, 74701, 74720, 74723, 74726–30, 74733, 74735–36, 74740–41, 74743, 74745, 74747–48, 74750, 74756, 74759, 74764, 74766, 74829–30, 74833, 74837, 74839, 74845, 74848–50, 74856, 74859–60, 74867–68, 74880, 74883–85, 74901–02, 74930, 74932, 74935–37, 74940–42, 74944–46, 74948, 74951, 74953–56, 74959–60, 74962, 74964–66

* * *

THIRD DISTRICT

FRANK D. LUCAS, Republican, of Cheyenne, OK; born in Cheyenne, January 6, 1960; education: B.S., Agricultural Economics, Oklahoma State University, 1982; professional: rancher and farmer; served in Oklahoma State House of Representatives, 1989–94; secretary, Oklahoma

House Republican Caucus, 1991–94; member: Oklahoma Farm Bureau, Oklahoma Cattlemen's Association, and Oklahoma Shorthorn Association; married: Lynda Bradshaw Lucas; children: Jessica, Ashlea, and Grant; committees: Agriculture; Financial Services; Science and Technology; elected to the 103rd Congress, by special election, in May 1994; reelected to each succeeding Congress.

Office Listings

http://www.house.gov/lucas

2311 Rayburn House Office Building, Washington, DC 20515 .... (202) 225–5565
Legislative Director.—Courtney Box. FAX: 225–8698
Communications Director.—Leslie Shedd.
Scheduler / Office Manager.—Brianna Jett.
Legislative Assistants: Alex Browning, Larry Calhoun, Graves Englund.
10952 Northwest Expressway, Suite B, Yukon, OK 73099 .... (405) 373–1958
Chief of Staff.—Stacey Glasscock.
720 South Husband, Suite 7, Stillwater, OK 74075 .... (405) 624–6407
Field Representative.—Tyler Laughlin.
2728 Williams Avenue, Suite F, Woodward, OK 73801 .... (580) 256–5752
Field Representative.—Troy White.

Counties: ALFALFA, BEAVER, BECKHAM, BLAINE, CADDO, CANADIAN (part), CIMARRON, CREEK (part), CUSTER, DEWEY, ELLIS, GARFIELD, GRANT, GREER, HARMON, HARPER, JACKSON, KINGFISHER, KAY, KIOWA, LINCOLN, LOGAN, MAJOR, NOBLE, OSAGE, PAWNEE, PAYNE, ROGER MILLS, TEXAS, WASHITA, WOODS, AND WOODWARD. CITIES: Altus, Clinton, El Reno, Elk City, Enid, Guthrie, Guymon, Oklahoma City, Perry, Ponce City, Sapulpa, Stillwater, Tulsa, Weatherford, Woodward and Yukon. Population (2000), 690,131.

ZIP Codes: 73001, 73003, 73005–07, 73009, 73014–17, 73021–22, 73024, 73027–29, 73033–34, 73036, 73038, 73040–45, 73047–48, 73050, 73053–54, 73056, 73058–59, 73061–64, 73073, 73077–79, 73085, 73090, 73092, 73094, 73096–97, 73099, 73127, 73437, 73501, 73521–23, 73526, 73532, 73537, 73539, 73544, 73547, 73549–50, 73554, 73556, 73559–60, 73564, 73566, 73571, 73601, 73620, 73622, 73624–28, 73632, 73638–39, 73641–42, 73644–48, 73650–51, 73654–55, 73658–64, 73666–69, 73673, 73701–03, 73705–06, 73716–20, 73722, 73724, 73726–31, 73733–39, 73741–44, 73746–47, 73749–50, 73753–64, 73766, 73768, 73770–73, 73801–02, 73832, 73834–35, 73838, 73840–44, 73847–48, 73851–53, 73855, 73857–60, 73901, 73931–33, 73937–39, 73942, 73944–47, 73949–51, 74001–03, 74010, 74020, 74022–23, 74026, 74028, 74030, 74032, 74034–35, 74038–39, 74044–47, 74051–52, 74054, 74056, 74058–60, 74062–63, 74066–68, 74070–71, 74073–79, 74081, 74084–85, 74106, 74126–27, 74131–32, 74601–02, 74604, 74630–33, 74636–37, 74640–41, 74643–44, 74646–47, 74650–53, 74824, 74832, 74834, 74851, 74855, 74859, 74864, 74869, 74875, 74881

* * *

FOURTH DISTRICT

TOM COLE, Republican, of Moore, OK; born in Shreveport, LA, April 28, 1949; education: B.A., Grinnell College, 1971; M.A. Yale University, 1974; Ph.D., University of Oklahoma, 1984; Watson Fellow, 1971–72; and a Fulbright Fellow, 1977–78; professional: former college professor of history and politics; President, Cole Hargrave Snodgrass & Associates (political consulting firm); public service: Oklahoma State Senate, 1988–91; Oklahoma Secretary of State, 1995–99; has served as Chairman, and Executive Director, of the Oklahoma Republican Party; former Chairman of the National Republican Congressional Committee; and Chief of Staff of the Republican National Committee; family: married to Ellen; one child: Mason; religion: United Methodist; committees: Appropriations; elected to the 108th Congress on November 5, 2002; reelected to each succeeding Congress.

Office Listings

http://www.house.gov/cole

2458 Rayburn House Office Building, Washington, DC 20515 .... (202) 225–6165
Chief of Staff.—Sean Murphy. FAX: 225–3512
Deputy Chief of Staff / Legislative Director.—Chris Caron.
Press Secretary.—Liz Eddy.
2420 Springer Drive, Suite 120, Norman, OK 73069 .... (405) 329–6500
711 Southwest, D Avenue, Suite 201, Lawton, OK 73501 .... (580) 357–2131
104 East 12th, Ada, OK 74820 .... (580) 436–5375

Counties: CANADIAN (part), CARTER, CLEVELAND, COMANCHE, COTTON, GARVIN, GRADY, JEFFERSON, LOVE, MARSHALL, MCCLAIN, MURRAY, OKLAHOMA (part), PONTOTOC, STEPHENS, TILLMAN. Population (2000), 690,131.

ZIP Codes: 73002, 73004, 73006, 73010–11, 73017–20, 73023, 73026, 73030–32, 73036, 73051–52, 73055, 73057, 73059, 73064–65, 73067–72, 73074–75, 73079–80, 73082, 73086, 73089, 73092–93, 73095, 73098–99, 73110, 73115, 73127–30, 73135, 73139–40, 73145, 73149–50, 73153, 73159–60, 73165, 73169–70, 73173, 73179, 73189, 73401–03, 73425, 73430, 73433–44, 73446, 73448, 73453, 73456, 73458–59, 73463, 73476, 73481, 73487–88, 73491, 73501–03, 73505–07, 73520, 73527–31, 73533–34, 73536, 73538, 73540–43, 73546, 73548, 73551–53, 73555, 73557, 73559, 73561–62, 73564–70, 73572–73, 74820–21, 74825, 74831, 74842–44, 74851, 74857, 74865, 74871–72

* * *

FIFTH DISTRICT

MARY FALLIN, Republican, of Oklahoma City, OK; born in Warrensburg, MO, December 9, 1954; education: attended Oklahoma Baptist University, Shawnee, OK, 1973–75; B.S., Oklahoma State University, Stillwater, OK, 1977; attended, University of Central Oklahoma, Edmond, OK, 1979–81; professional: hotel management; member of the Oklahoma State House of Representatives, 1990–94; Oklahoma Lieutenant Governor, 1995–2007; children: Christina and Price; committees: Armed Services; Small Business; Transportation and Infrastructure; elected to the 110th Congress on November 7, 2006; reelected to the 111th Congress.

Office Listings

http://www.fallin.house.gov

1432 Longworth House Office Building, Washington, DC 20515 .... (202) 225–2132
Chief of Staff.—Nate Webb. FAX: 226–1463
Washington Chief of Staff.—Patrick Lyden.
Scheduler.—Dana Wolpert.
Communications Director.—Katie Bruns.
120 North Robinson Avenue, Suite 100, Oklahoma City, OK 73102 .... (405) 234–9900
20 East 9th Street, Suite 137, Shawnee, OK 74801 .... (405) 273–1733

Counties: OKLAHOMA (part), POTTAWATOMIE, and SEMINOLE. CITIES: Arcadia, Asher, Aydelotte, Bethany, Bethel Acres, Bowlegs, Brooksville, Choctaw, Cromwell, Del City, Earlsboro, Edmond, Forrest Park, Harrah, Johnson, Jones, Konawa, Lake Aluma, Lima, Luther, Macomb, Maud, McLoud, Midwest City, Newalla, Nichols Hills, Nicoma Park, Oklahoma City, Pink, Sasakwa, Seminole, Shawnee, Smith Village, Spencer, St. Louis, Tecumesh, The Village, Tribbey, Valley Brook, Wanette, Warr Acres, Wewoka, and Woodlawn Park. Population (2000), 690,131.

ZIP Codes: 73003, 73007–08, 73013, 73020, 73034, 73045, 73049, 73054, 73066, 73078, 73083–84, 73097, 73099, 73101–32, 73134–37, 73139, 73141–49, 73151–52, 73154–57, 73159–60, 73162, 73164, 73169, 73172–73, 73178–79, 73184–85, 73190, 73194–96, 73198, 74587, 74801–02, 74804, 74818, 74826, 74830, 74837, 74840, 74849, 74851–52, 74854–55, 74857, 74859, 74866–68, 74873, 74878, 74884

OREGON

(Population 2000, 3,421,399)

SENATORS

RON WYDEN, Democrat, of Portland, OR; born in Wichita, KS, May 3, 1949; education: graduated from Palo Alto High School, 1967; B.A. in political science, with distinction, Stanford University, 1971; J.D., University of Oregon Law School, 1974; professional: attorney; member, American Bar Association; former director, Oregon Legal Services for the Elderly; former public member, Oregon State Board of Examiners of Nursing Home Administrators; co-founder and codirector, Oregon Gray Panthers, 1974–80; married: Nancy Bass Wyden; children: Adam David, Lilly Anne, Ava Rose, and William Peter; committees: Budget; Energy and Natural Resources; Finance; Special Committee on Aging; Select Committee on Intelligence; elected to the 97th Congress, November 4, 1980; reelected to each succeeding Congress; elected to the U.S. Senate on February 6, 1996, to fill the unexpired term of Senator Bob Packwood; reelected to each succeeding Senate term.

Office Listings

http://wyden.senate.gov

223 Dirksen Senate Office Building, Washington, DC 20510 .... (202) 224–5244
Chief of Staff.—Josh Kardon. FAX: 228–2717
Legislative Aides: Jeff Michels, Joshua Sheinkman.
Communications Director.—Jennifer Hoelzer.
Schedulers: Sallie Derr, Wayne Binkley.
1220 Southwest Third Avenue, Suite 585, Portland, OR 97204 .... (503) 326–7525
405 East Eighth Avenue, Suite 2020, Eugene, OR 97401 .... (541) 431–0229
The Federal Courthouse, 310 West Sixth Street, Room 118, Medford, OR 97501 ... (541) 858–5122
The Jamison Building, 131 Northwest Hawthorne Avenue, Suite 107, Bend, OR 97701 .... (541) 330–9142
SAC Annex Building, 105 Fir Street, Suite 201, LaGrande, OR 97850 .... (541) 962–7691
707 Thirteenth Street, SE., Suite 285, Salem, OR 97310 .... (503) 589–4555

* * *

JEFF MERKLEY, Democrat, of East Multhnomah County, OR; born in Myrtle Creek, OR; October 24, 1956; education: graduated from David Douglas High School, B.A., international relations, Stanford University, 1979; M.P.P., Woodrow Wilson School, Princeton University, 1982; professional: Presidential Fellow at the Office of the Secretary of Defense, 1982–85; Policy Analyst at the Congressional Budget Office, 1985–89; Executive Director of Portland Habitat for Humanity, 1991–94; Director of Housing Development at Human Solutions, 1995–96; President of World Affairs Council of Oregon, 1996–2003; elected to Oregon House of Representatives, 1999; Democratic Leader of the Oregon House of Representatives, 2003; elected Speaker of the Oregon House of Representatives, 2007; married: Mary Sorteberg; children: Brynne and Jonathan; committees: Banking, Housing, and Urban Affairs; Budget; Environment and Public Works; Health, Education, Labor, and Pensions; elected to U.S. Senate on November 4, 2008.

Office Listings

http://merkley.senate.gov

107 Russell Senate Office Building, Washington, DC 20510 .... (202) 224–3753
Chief of Staff.—Michael Zamore. FAX: 228–3997
Legislative Director.—Tamara Fucile.
Director of Administration.—Jennifer Piorkowski.
Communications Director.—Julie Edwards.
1400 One World Trade Center, 121 Southwest Salmon, Portland, OR 97204 .... (503) 326–3386
Jamison Building, 131 Northwest Hawthorne, Suite 208, Bend, OR 97701 .... (541) 318–1298
Wayne Morse Federal Courthouse, 405 East 8th, Suite 2010, Eugene, OR 97401 ... (541) 465–6750
10 South Bartlett Street, Suite 201, Medford, OR 97501 .... (541) 608–9102
495 State Street, Suite 330, Salem, OR 97301 .... (503) 362–8102
310 Southeast Second Street, Suite 105, Pendleton, OR 97801 .... (541) 278–1129

REPRESENTATIVES

FIRST DISTRICT

DAVID WU, Democrat, of Portland, OR; born in Taiwan, April 8, 1955; moved to the United States, with his family, in October, 1961; education: B.S., Stanford University, 1977; attended, Harvard University Medical School; J.D., Yale University, 1982; professional: lawyer; co-founder of Cohen & Wu (law firm), 1988; first Chinese American member of the U.S. House of Representatives; past chair, Congressional Asian Pacific American Caucus; member, New Democrat Coalition; married: Michelle; two children: Matthew and Sarah; committees: Education and Labor; Science and Technology; elected to the 106th Congress; reelected to each succeeding Congress.

Office Listings

http://www.house.gov/wu

2338 Rayburn House Office Building, Washington, DC 20515 .... (202) 225–0855
Chief of Staff.—Julie Tippens. FAX: 225–9497
Scheduler / Executive Assistant.—Erin Devaney.
Communications Director.—Julia Louise Krahe.
620 Southwest Main Street, Suite 606, Portland, OR 97205 .... (503) 326–2901

Counties: CLATSOP, COLUMBIA, MULTNOMAH (part), WASHINGTON, YAMHILL. Population (2000), 684,277.

ZIP Codes: 97005–08, 97016, 97018, 97035, 97048, 97051, 97053–54, 97056, 97062, 97064, 97070, 97075–78, 97101–03, 97106, 97109–11, 97113–17, 97119, 97121, 97123–25, 97127–28, 97132–33, 97138, 97140, 97144–46, 97148, 97201, 97204–05, 97207–10, 97219, 97221, 97223–25, 97228–29, 97231, 97239–40, 97251, 97253–55, 97258, 97272, 97280–81, 97291, 97296, 97298, 97378, 97396, 97498

* * *

SECOND DISTRICT

GREG WALDEN, Republican, of Hood River, OR; born in The Dalles, OR, January 10, 1957; education: B.S., Journalism, University of Oregon, 1981; member: Associated Oregon Industries; Oregon Health Sciences Foundation; Hood River Rotary Club; Hood River Elk's Club; National Federation of Independent Business; Hood River Chamber of Commerce; Hood River Memorial Hospital; Columbia Bancorp; Oregon State House of Representatives, 1989–95, and Majority Leader, 1991–93; Assistant Majority Leader, Oregon State Senate, 1995–97; awards: Oregon Jaycees Outstanding Young Oregonian, 1991; National Republican Legislators Association Legislator of the Year, 1993; married: Mylene Walden; one child: Anthony David Walden; committees: Energy and Commerce; elected to the 106th Congress on November 3, 1998; reelected to each succeeding Congress.

Office Listings

http://www.walden.house.gov

2352 Rayburn House Office Building, Washington, DC 20515 .... (202) 225–6730
Chief of Staff.—Brian MacDonald. (800) 533–3303
Senior Policy Advisors: Valerie Henry, Colby Marshall. FAX: 225–5774
Executive Assistant.—Blair Larkens.
Press Secretary.—Andrew Whelan.
843 East Main Street, Suite 400, Medford, OR 97504 .... (541) 776–4646
District Director.—John Snider. (800) 533–3303
1211 Washington Avenue, LaGrande, OR 97850 .... (541) 389–4408
1051 Northwest Bond Street, Suite 400, Bend, OR 97701 .... (541) 624–2400
FAX: 624–2402

Counties: BAKER, CROOK, DESCHUTES, GILLIAM, GRANT, HARNEY, HOOD RIVER, JACKSON, JEFFERSON, JOSEPHINE (part), KLAMATH, LAKE, MALHEUR, MORROW, SHERMAN, UMATILLA, UNION, WALLOWA, WASCO, WHEELER. Population (2000), 684,280.

ZIP Codes: 97001, 97014, 97021, 97029, 97031, 97033, 97037, 97039–41, 97044, 97050, 97057–58, 97063, 97065, 97116, 97425, 97501–04, 97520, 97522, 97524–28, 97530, 97533, 97535–37, 97539–41, 97544, 97601–04, 97620–27, 97630, 97632–41, 97701–02, 97707–12, 97720–22, 97730–39, 97741, 97750–54, 97756, 97758–61, 97801, 97810, 97812–14, 97817–20, 97823–28, 97830, 97833–46, 97848, 97850, 97856–57, 97859, 97861–62, 97864–65, 97867–70, 97873–77, 97880, 97882–86, 97901–11, 97913–14, 97917–18, 97920

* * *

THIRD DISTRICT

EARL BLUMENAUER, Democrat, of Portland, OR; born in Portland, August 16, 1948; education: graduated from Centennial High School; B.A., Lewis and Clark College; J.D., Northwestern School of Law; professional: assistant to the president, Portland State University; served in Oregon State Legislature 1973–78; chaired Revenue and School Finance Committee; Multnomah County Commissioner, 1978–85; Portland City Commissioner 1986–96; served on Governor's Commission on Higher Education; National League of Cities Transportation Committee; National Civic League Board of Directors; Oregon Environmental Council; Oregon Public Broadcasting; married: Margaret Kirkpatrick; children: Jon and Anne; committees: Budget; Ways and Means; Select Committee on Energy Independence and Global Warming; elected to the U.S. House of Representatives on May 21, 1996, to fill the vacancy created by Representative Ron Wyden's election to the U.S. Senate; reelected to each succeeding Congress.

Office Listings

http://blumenauer.house.gov

2267 Rayburn House Office Building, Washington, DC 20515 .... (202) 225–4811
Deputy Chief of Staff.—James Koski. FAX: 225–8941
Scheduler.—Michael Harold.
Communications Director.—Sahar Wali.
Legislative Director.—Janine Benner.
729 Northeast Oregon Street, Suite 115, Portland, OR 97232 .... (503) 231–2300
District Director.—Julia Pomeroy.

Counties: MULTNOMAH (part), CLAKAMUS (part). Population (2000), 684,279.

ZIP Codes: 97004, 97009, 97011, 97014–15, 97017, 97019, 97022–24, 97028, 97030, 97035, 97045, 97049, 97055, 97060, 97067, 97080, 97124, 97133, 97202–03, 97206, 97210–18, 97220, 97222, 97227, 97229–33, 97236, 97238, 97242, 97256, 97266–67, 97269, 97282–83, 97286, 97290, 97292–94, 97299

* * *

FOURTH DISTRICT

PETER A. DEFAZIO, Democrat, of Springfield, OR; born in Needham, MA, May 27, 1947; B.A., Tufts University, 1969; M.S., University of Oregon, 1977; professional: aide to Representative Jim Weaver, 1977–82; commissioner, Lane County, 1983–86; married: Myrnie Daut; committees: Homeland Security; Natural Resources; Transportation and Infrastructure; elected to the 100th Congress, November 4, 1986; reelected to each succeeding Congress.

Office Listings

http://www.house.gov/defazio

2134 Rayburn House Office Building, Washington, DC 20515 .... (202) 225–6416
Chief of Staff.—Penny Dodge. FAX: 225–0032
Legislative Director.—Auke Mahar-Piersma.
Scheduler.—Jamie Harrell.
405 East Eighth Avenue, Suite 2030, Eugene, OR 97401 .... (541) 465–6732
District Director.—Karmen Fore.
125 Central Avenue, Room 350, Coos Bay, OR 97420 .... (541) 269–2609
612 Southeast Jackson Street, Room 9, Roseburg, OR 97470 .... (541) 440–3523

Counties: BENTON (part), COOS, CURRY, DOUGLAS, JOSEPHINE (part), LANE, LINN. CITIES: Eugene, Roseburg, and Coos Bay. Population (2000), 684,280.

ZIP Codes: 97321–22, 97324, 97326–27, 97329–30, 97333, 97335–36, 97345–46, 97348, 97350, 97352, 97355, 97358, 97360–61, 97370, 97374, 97377, 97383, 97386, 97389, 97401–17, 97419–20, 97423–24, 97426–32, 97434–44, 97446–59, 97461–67, 97469–70, 97472–73, 97476–82, 97484, 97486–99, 97523, 97526–27, 97530–34, 97537–38, 97543–44

* * *

FIFTH DISTRICT

KURT SCHRADER, Democrat, of Canby, OR; born in Bridgeport, CT, October 19, 1951; education; B.A., Cornell University, 1973, D.V.M. University, IL, 1977; professional: small business owner, veterinarian; past member; Oregon State Senate, Oregon House of Representatives, Canby Planning Commission; religion: Episcopalian; married: Martha Schrader; children: Clare, Maren, Steven, Travis, and R.J.; committees; Agriculture; Budget; Small Business; elected to the 111th Congress on November 4, 2008.

Office Listings

http://schrader.house.gov

1419 Longworth House Office Building, Washington, DC 20515 .... (202) 225–5711
Chief of Staff.—Paul Gage. FAX: 225–5699
Legislative Director.—Chris Huckleberry.
Executive Assistant / Scheduler.—Anne Marie Feeney.
494 State Street, Suite 210, Salem, OR 97301 .... (503) 588–9100
112 8th Street, Oregon City, OR 97045 .... (503) 557–1324
District Director.—Suzanne Kunse

Counties: BENTON (part); CLACKAMAS (part); LINCOLN; MARION; MULTNOMAH (part); POLK; TILLAMOOK. CITIES: Corvallis, Portland, Salem, and Tillamook. Population (2000), 684,333.

ZIP Codes: 97002, 97004, 97010, 97013, 97015, 97017, 97020, 97023, 97026–27, 97032, 97034–36, 97038, 97042, 97045, 97062, 97068, 97070–71, 97101, 97107–08, 97112, 97118, 97122, 97130–31, 97134–37, 97140–41, 97143, 97147, 97149, 97201, 97219, 97222, 97239, 97267–68, 97301–14, 97321, 97324–25, 97330–31, 97333, 97338–39, 97341–44, 97346–47, 97350–52, 97357–62, 97364–73, 97375–76, 97380–81, 97383–85, 97388, 97390–92, 97394, 97396, 97498

PENNSYLVANIA

(Population 2000, 12,281,054)

SENATORS

ARLEN SPECTER, Democrat, of Philadelphia, PA; born in Wichita, KS, February 12, 1930; education: graduated, Russell High School, Russell, KS, 1947; B.A., international relations, Phi Beta Kappa, University of Pennsylvania, 1951; LL.B., Yale Law School, 1956; board of editors, *Law Journal*; military service: served in U.S. Air Force, 1951–53, attaining rank of first lieutenant; professional: member, law firm of Dechert, Price and Rhoads before and after serving two terms as district attorney of Philadelphia, 1966–74; married: former Joan Levy, who was elected to the city council of Philadelphia in 1979; children: Shanin and Stephen; served as assistant counsel to the Warren Commission, 1964; served on Pennsylvania's State Planning Board, The White House Conference on Youth, The National Commission on Criminal Justice, and the Peace Corps National Advisory Council; committees: Appropriations; Environment and Public Works; Judiciary; Veterans' Affairs; Special Committee on Aging; elected to the U.S. Senate on November 4, 1980; reelected to each succeeding Senate term.

Office Listings

http://specter.senate.gov

711 Hart Senate Office Building, Washington, DC 20510 .... (202) 224–4254
Chief of Staff.—Scott Hoeflich. FAX: 228–1229
Legislative Director.—Christoper Bradish.
Administrative Director.—Kate Schramm.
600 Arch Street, Suite 9400, Philadelphia, PA 19106 .... (215) 597–7200
Regional Enterprise Tower, 425 Sixth Avenue, Suite 1450, Pittsburgh, PA 15219–1837 .... (412) 644–3400
Federal Building, 17 South Park Row, Suite B–120, Erie, PA 16501 .... (814) 453–3010
Federal Building, 228 Walnut Street, Room 1104, Harrisburg, PA 17101 .... (717) 782–3951
Federal Building, 504 West Hamilton Street, Suite 3814, Allentown, PA 18101 .... (610) 434–1444
310 Spruce Street, Suite 201, Scranton, PA 18503 .... (570) 346–2006
7 North Wilkes Barre Boulevard, Stegmaier Building, Room 377M, Wilkes Barre, PA 18702 .... (570) 826–6265

* * *

ROBERT P. CASEY, JR., Democrat, of Scranton, PA; born in Scranton, April 13, 1960; education: A.B., English, College of the Holy Cross, 1982; J.D., Catholic University of America, 1988; professional: lawyer; Pennsylvania State Auditor General, 1997–2005; Pennsylvania State Treasurer, 2005–07; married: Terese; four daughters: Elyse, Caroline, Julia, and Marena; committees: Agriculture, Nutrition, and Forestry; Health, Education, Labor, and Pension; Foreign Relations; Joint Economic Committee; Special Committee on Aging; elected to the 110th Congress on November 7, 2006; reelected to the 111th Congress.

Office Listings

http://casey.senate.gov

393 Russell Senate Office Building, Washington, DC 20510 .... (202) 224–6324
(866) 802–2833
Chief of Staff.—James W. Brown. FAX: 228–0604
Legislative Director.—Richard D. Spiegelman.
Communications Director.—Larry Smar.
22 South Third Street, Suite 6A, Harrisburg, PA 17101 .... (717) 231–7540
(866) 461–9159
FAX: 231–7542
2000 Market Street, Suite 1870, Philadelphia, PA 19103 .... (215) 405–9660
FAX: 405–9669
Regional Enterprise Tower, 425 Sixth Avenue, Suite 2490, Pittsburgh, PA 15219 .. (412) 803–7370
FAX: 803–7379
409 Lackawanna Avenue, Suite 301, Scranton, PA 18503 .... (570) 941–0930
FAX: 941–0937
817 East Bishop Street, Suite C, Bellefonte, PA 16823 .... (814) 357–0314
FAX: 375–0318
17 South Park Row, Suite B–150, Erie, PA 16501 .... (814) 874–5080
FAX: 874–5084
840 Hamilton Street, Suite 301, Allentown, PA 18101 .... (610) 782–9470
FAX: 782–9474

REPRESENTATIVES

FIRST DISTRICT

ROBERT A. BRADY, Democrat, of Philadelphia, PA; born in Philadelphia, April 7, 1945; education: graduated from St. Thomas More High School; professional: carpenter; union official; assistant Sergeant-At-Arms, Philadelphia City Council, 1975–83; Deputy Mayor for Labor, W. Wilson Goode Administration; consultant to Pennsylvania State Senate; Pennsylvania Turnpike Commissioner; board of directors, Philadelphia Redevelopment Authority; Democratic Party Executive; ward leader; chairman, Philadelphia Democratic Party; member of Pennsylvania Democratic State Committee, and Democratic National Committee; religion: Catholic; married: Debra Brady; children: Robert and Kimberly; committees: chair, House Administration; Armed Services; elected to the 105th Congress on May 21, 1998, to fill the unexpired term of Representative Tom Foglietta; reelected to each succeeding Congress.

Office Listings

http://www.house.gov/robertbrady

206 Cannon House Office Building, Washington, DC 20515 .... (202) 225–4731
Chief of Staff.—Stan White. FAX: 225–0088
Appointments Secretary.—Bianca Lacey.
Press Secretary.—Karen Warrington.
1907–09 South Broad Street, Philadelphia, PA 19148 .... (215) 389–4627
The Colony Building, 511–13 Welsh Street, 1st Floor, Chester, PA 19103 .... (610) 874–7094
2637 East Clearfield Street, Philadelphia, PA 19134 .... (267) 519–2252
2630 Memphis St. Philadelphia, PA 19121 .... (215) 426–4616

Counties: PHILADELPHIA (part). CITIES AND TOWNSHIPS: Chester City, Chester Township, Eddystone Borough, Colwyn Borough, Ridley Township, Tinicum Township, Darby Township, and Yeadon Borough. Population (2000), 630,730.

ZIP Codes: 19012–16, 19018, 19022–23, 19029, 19032, 19036, 19050, 19078–79, 19086, 19092–93, 19101, 19105–09, 19111–13, 19120, 19122–26, 19130–34, 19137–51, 19153–54, 19160–62, 19170–73, 19175, 19177–78, 19181–82, 19185, 19187–88

* * *

SECOND DISTRICT

CHAKA FATTAH, Democrat, of Philadelphia, PA; born in Philadelphia, November 21, 1956; education: attended Overbrook High School, Community College of Philadelphia, University of Pennsylvania's Wharton School; M.A., University of Pennsylvania's Fels School of State and Local Government, 1986; completed Senior Executive Program for State Officials at Harvard University's John F. Kennedy School of Government; Pennsylvania State House of Representatives, 1982–88; Pennsylvania State Senate, 1988–94; author, *Gaining Early Awareness and Readiness for Undergraduate Programs* (GEAR-UP), enacted in 1998 offering college readiness preparation and scholarships for low-income students; founded Graduate Opportunities Conference, 1987; now called the Fattah Conference on Higher Education; founded Philadelphia College Opportunity Resources for Education (CORE Philly) scholarship program; founded the American Cities Foundation; former trustee, Temple University, Pennsylvania State University, Lincoln University and Community College of Philadelphia; past chair, Executive Board, Pennsylvania Higher Education Assistance Agency; recognized for outstanding leadership in *Time* magazine, and in *Ebony* magazine as one of 50 Future Leaders; member, Mt. Carmel Baptist Church; chair, Congressional Urban Caucus; married: the former Renée Chenault; four children; committees: Appropriations; elected to the 104th Congress on November 8, 1994; reelected to each succeeding Congress.

Office Listings

http://www.fattah.house.gov

2301 Rayburn House Office Building, Washington, DC 20515 .... (202) 225–4001
Chief of Staff.—Michelle Anderson Lee. FAX: 225–5392
Legislative Director.—Nuku Ofori.
Communications Director.—Debra Anderson.
4104 Walnut Street, Philadelphia, PA 19104 .... (215) 387–6404
6632 Germantown Avenue, Philadelphia, PA 19119 .... (215) 848–9386

Counties: MONTGOMERY (part), PHILADELPHIA. Population (2000), 630,730.

ZIP Codes: 19004, 19012, 19027, 19038, 19046, 19093, 19095, 19101–04, 19107, 19109–11, 19118–24, 19126–32, 19138–41, 19143–48, 19150, 19161–62, 19170–71, 19173, 19178, 19184, 19187, 19191–93, 19196–97

* * *

THIRD DISTRICT

KATHLEEN A. DAHLKEMPER, Democrat, of Erie, PA; born in Erie, December 10, 1957; education: B.S., dietetics, Edinboro University, Edinboro, PA, 1982; professional: business owner, Dahlkemper Landscaping & Design; Director, Lake Erie Arboretum Dietitician, 25 years; married: Dan Dahlkemper; 5 children; committees: Agriculture; Science and Technology; Small Business; elected to the 111th Congress on November 4, 2008.

Office Listings

http://www.house.gov/english

516 Cannon House Office Building, Washington, DC 20515 .... (202) 225–5406
Chief of Staff.—Tina Mengine. FAX: 225–3103
Legislative Director.—Ivana Alexander.
Senior Policy Advisor / Counselor.—Dan Hill.
Legislative Aide.—Melissa Sidman.
Press Secretary.—Zac Petkanas.
Scheduler.—Kate Regan.
208 East Bayfront Parkway, Suite 102, Erie, PA 16507 .... (814) 456–2038
District Director.—Amy Cuzzola-Kern.

Counties: ARMSTRONG (part), BUTLER (part), CRAWFORD (part), ERIE, MERCER (part), VENANGO (part), WARREN (part). Population (2000), 630,730.

ZIP Codes: 16001–03, 16016–18, 16020, 16022–23, 16025, 16027–30, 16033–35, 16037–41, 16045–46, 16048–53, 16055–57, 16059, 16061, 16110–11, 16113–14, 16124–25, 16127, 16130–31, 16133–34, 16137, 16142–43, 16145–46, 16148, 16150–51, 16153–54, 16156, 16159, 16201, 16210, 16218, 16222–24, 16226, 16229, 16232, 16242, 16244–45, 16249–50, 16253, 16259, 16261–63, 16311–12, 16314, 16316–17, 16319, 16323, 16327, 16329, 16335, 16340, 16342, 16345, 16350–51, 16354, 16360, 16362, 16365–69, 16371–74, 16388, 16401–07, 16410–13, 16415, 16417, 16420–24, 16426–28, 16430, 16432–36, 16438, 16440–44, 16475, 16501–12, 16514–15, 16522, 16530–34, 16538, 16541, 16544, 16546, 16550, 16553–54, 16563, 16565

* * *

FOURTH DISTRICT

JASON ALTMIRE, Democrat, of McCandless, PA; born in Lower Burrell, PA, March 7, 1968; B.S., Florida State University, Tallahassee, FL, 1990; M.H.S.A., George Washington University, Washington, DC, 1998; professional: Acting Vice President for Government Relations and Community Health Services for University of Pittsburgh Medical Center; Director of Federal Government Relations, Federation of American Hospitals; Legislative Assistant to Congressman Pete Peterson (D-FL); married: Kelly Altmire; two children; committees: Education and Labor; Small Business; Transportation and Infrastructure; elected to the 110th Congress on November 7, 2006; reelected to the 111th Congress on November 4, 2008.

Office Listings

http://www.altmire.house.gov

332 Cannon House Office Building, Washington, DC 20515 .... (202) 225–2565
Chief of Staff.—Sharon Werner. FAX: 226–2274
Legislative Director.—Dori Friedberg.
Scheduler.—Cody Lundquist.
2110 McLean Street, Aliquippa, PA 15001 .... (724) 378–0928
District Director.—Michelle Dorothy.
2124 Freeport Road, Natrona Heights, PA 15065 .... (724) 226–1304

Counties: ALLEGHENY (part), BEAVER, BUTLER (part), LAWRENCE, MERCER (part), WESTMORELAND (part). Population (2000), 630,730.

ZIP Codes: 15001, 15003, 15005–07, 15009–10, 15014–15, 15024, 15026–27, 15030, 15032, 15042–44, 15046, 15049–52, 15056, 15059, 15061, 15065–66, 15068–69, 15074, 15076–77, 15081, 15084–86, 15090–91, 15095–96, 15101, 15108, 15116, 15127, 15139, 15143–44, 15146, 15202, 15209, 15212, 15214–15, 15223, 15229, 15235, 15237–39, 15601, 15626, 15632, 15650, 15668, 16002, 16024–25, 16033, 16037, 16040, 16046, 16051–52, 16055–57, 16059, 16061, 16063, 16066, 16101–03, 16105, 16107–08, 16112, 16115–17, 16120–21, 16123, 16127, 16132, 16136, 16140–43, 16148, 16155–57, 16159–61, 16172, 16229

* * *

FIFTH DISTRICT

GLENN THOMPSON, Republican, of Howard Township, PA; born in Bellefonte, PA, July 27, 1959; education: B.S., therapeutic recreation, Pennsylvania State University, 1981; M.Ed., health science/therapeutic recreation, Temple University, 1998; NHA/L, Nursing Home Administrator, Marywood University, 2006; professional: Rehabilitation Services Manager for Susquehanna Health Services, Adjunct Faculty for Cambria County Community College; Chief, Recreational Therapist for the Williamsport Hospital; Residential Services Aid for Hope Enterprises, Orderly for Centre Crest Nursing Home; Organization/Awards: Past President/Fire Fighter/EMT/Rescue Technician for Howard VFD; former, Howard Boy Scout Master; former, President and Senior VP for Juniata Valley Boy Scout Council; International Advisory Council Member for the Accreditation of Rehabilitation Facilities Commission; Board member/vice chair of Private Industry Council of Central Corridors; political career: Centre County Republican chair, PA Republican State Committee, alternate delegate for the Republican National Convention; candidate for the PA House of Representatives, 1998 and 2000; member, Bald Eagle Area School District Board of Education; religion: Protestant; married to Penny Ammerman-Thompson; three sons, Parker, Logan and Kale; committees: Agriculture; Education and Labor; Small Business; elected to the 111th Congress on November 4, 2008.

Office Listings

http://thompson.house.gov

124 Cannon House Office Building, Washington, DC 20515 .... (202) 225–5121
Chief of Staff.—Jordan Clark. FAX: 225–5796
Legislative Director.—Matthew Brennan.
Scheduler.—Darrell Owens.
Communications Director.—Tina Kreisher.
127 West Spring Street, Suite C, Titusville, PA 16354 .... (814) 827–3985
District Director.—Peter Winkler.
3555 Benner Pike, Suite 101, Bellefonte, PA 16823 .... (814) 353–0215

Counties: CAMERON, CENTRE, CLARION, CLEARFIELD (part), CLINTON, CRAWFORD (part), ELK, FOREST, JEFFERSON, JUNIATA (part), LYCOMING (part), MCKEAN, MIFFLIN (part), POTTER, TIOGA, VENANGO (part), WARREN (part). Population (2000), 630,730.

ZIP Codes: 15711, 15715, 15730, 15733, 15744, 15753, 15757, 15764, 15767, 15770, 15772, 15776, 15778, 15780–81, 15784, 15801, 15821, 15823–25, 15827–29, 15831–32, 15834, 15840–41, 15845–49, 15851, 15853, 15856–57, 15860–61, 15863–66, 15868, 15870, 16028, 16036, 16049, 16054, 16058, 16153, 16213–14, 16217, 16220–22, 16224–26, 16230, 16232–35, 16239–40, 16242, 16248, 16254–58, 16260, 16301, 16311, 16313–14, 16317, 16319, 16321–23, 16326–29, 16331–34, 16340–47, 16351–54, 16361–62, 16364–65, 16370–71, 16373–75, 16404, 16416, 16434, 16620, 16627, 16645, 16651, 16661, 16663, 16666–77, 16681, 16686, 16701, 16720, 16724–35, 16738, 16740, 16743–46, 16748–50, 16801–05, 16820–23, 16825–30, 16832–41, 16843–45, 16847–56, 16858–61, 16863–66, 16868, 16870–79, 16881–82, 16901, 16911–12, 16914–15, 16917–18, 16920–23, 16927–30, 16932–33, 16935–40, 16942–43, 16946–48, 16950, 17004, 17009, 17029, 17044, 17051, 17063, 17084, 17099, 17701–02, 17720–21, 17723–24, 17726–27, 17729, 17738–40, 17744–45, 17747–48, 17750–52, 17754, 17759–60, 17764–65, 17767, 17769, 17773, 17776–79, 17810, 17841

* * *

SIXTH DISTRICT

JIM GERLACH, Republican, of Chester Spings, PA; born in Ellwood City, PA, February 25, 1955; education: B.A., Dickinson College, 1977; J.D., Dickinson School of Law, 1980; professional: attorney; former special counsel to the regional law firm of Fox, Rothschild, O'Brien & Frankel; community service: board of directors, MECA (Mission for Educating Children with Autism); Dickinson College Board of Trustees; Chester County Agricultural Development Council; public service: Pennsylvania House of Representatives, 1991–94; Pennsylvania State Senate, 1995–2002; children: Katie, Jimmy, and Robby; committees: Financial Services; Transportation and Infrastructure; elected to the 108th Congress on November 5, 2002; reelected to each succeeding Congress.

Office Listings

http://www.gerlach.house.gov

308 Cannon House Office Building, Washington, DC 20515 .... (202) 225–4315
Chief of Staff.—Bill Tighe. FAX: 225–8440
Legislative Director.—Annie Fultz.
Communications Director.—Kori Walter.
111 East Uwchlan Avenue, Exton, PA 19341 .... (610) 594–1415
840 North Park Road, Wyomissing, PA 19610 .... (610) 376–7630
580 Main Street, Suite #4, Trappe, PA 19426 .... (610) 409–2780

Counties: BERKS (part), CHESTER (part), LEHIGH (part), MONTGOMERY (part). Population (2000), 630,730.

ZIP Codes: 17527, 17555, 17569, 18011, 18031, 18041, 18056, 18062, 18070, 18092, 19003–04, 19010, 19025, 19031, 19034–35, 19041, 19066, 19072, 19085, 19087, 19096, 19131, 19151, 19301, 19310, 19312, 19316, 19320, 19333,

19335, 19341, 19343–45, 19353–55, 19358, 19365–67, 19369, 19371–72, 19376, 19380, 19382, 19401, 19403–04, 19409, 19421, 19423, 19425–26, 19428, 19430, 19432, 19438, 19442, 19444, 19446, 19457, 19460, 19462, 19464–65, 19468, 19470, 19473–75, 19480–85, 19490, 19493–96, 19503–05, 19508, 19511–12, 19518–20, 19522–23, 19525, 19530, 19535, 19538–40, 19542–43, 19545, 19547–48, 19562, 19565, 19601–02, 19604–12

* * *

SEVENTH DISTRICT

JOE SESTAK, Democrat, of Edgmont, PA; born in Secane, PA, December 12, 1951; education: B.S., United States Naval Academy, Annapolis, MD, 1974; Masters of Public Administration, Harvard University, Cambridge, MA, 1980; Ph.D., Political Economy and Government, Harvard University, Cambridge, MA, 1984; professional: Director for Defense Policy, National Security Council, 1994–97; Director of Deep Blue, the Navy's anti-terrorism group, United States Navy, 2001–02; Deputy Chief of Naval Operations, Warfare Requirements and Programs, United States Navy, 2005; military: Commander of the USS *George Washington* aircraft carrier battle group in combat in Afghanistan and Iraq, 2002–03; awards: Vice Admiral, United States Navy, 2005; married to Susan Leslie Clark-Sestak; father of Alexandra Megan Sestak; committees: Armed Services; Education and Labor; Small Business; elected to the 110th Congress on November 7, 2006; reelected to the 111th Congress on November 4, 2008.

Office Listings

http://sestak.house.gov

1022 Longworth House Office Building, Washington, DC 20515 .... (202) 225–2011
Chief of Staff.—Bibiana Boerio. FAX: 226–0280
600 North Jackson Street, Suite 203, Media, PA 19063 .... (610) 892–8623
District Director.—Bill Walsh.

Counties: CHESTER (part), DELAWARE (part), MONTGOMERY (part). Population (2000), 630,730.

ZIP Codes: 19008, 19010, 19014–15, 19017–18, 19022–23, 19026, 19028–29, 19032–33, 19036–37, 19039, 19041, 19043, 19050, 19052, 19061, 19063–65, 19070, 19073–74, 19076, 19078–79, 19081–83, 19085–87, 19094, 19312, 19317, 19319, 19331, 19333, 19339–40, 19342, 19355, 19373, 19380, 19382, 19395, 19403, 19405–06, 19426, 19428, 19468

* * *

EIGHTH DISTRICT

PATRICK MURPHY, Democrat, of Bristol, PA; born in Philadelphia, PA, October 19, 1973; education: attended Bucks County Community College, 1991–92; B.S., psychology and human resources, King's College, Wilkes-Barre, PA, 1996; J.D., Widener University School of Law, Harrisburg, PA, 1999; military service: Army, 1996–2004; Army Reserve, deployed to Bosnia, 2002, and as a paratrooper with the 82nd Airborne Division, Baghdad, Iraq, 2003–04; military awards: Bronze Star; Presidential Unit citation; professional: Harrisburg Civil Law Clinic; practiced law at Cozen O'Connor; religion: Roman Catholic; married: Jenni (Safford) Murphy; one daughter, Margaret (Maggie); Blue Dog Coalition Caucus; New Democrat Coalition Caucus; committees: Armed Services; Permanent Select Committee on Intelligence; elected to the 110th Congress on November 7, 2006; reelected to the 111th Congress.

Office Listings

http://patrickmurphy.house.gov/

1609 Longworth House Office Building, Washington, DC 20515 .... (202) 225–4276
Chief of Staff.—Scott Fairchild. FAX: 225–9511
Legislative Director.—Seth Frotman.
414 Mill Street, Bristol, PA 19007 .... (215) 826–1963
District Director.—Nat Binns.
72 North Main Street, Doylestown, PA 18901 .... (215) 348–1194
Outreach Coordinator.—Larry Glick.

Counties: BUCKS, MONTGOMERY (part), PHILADELPHIA (part). Population (2000), 630,730.

ZIP Codes: 18036, 18039, 18041–42, 18054–55, 18073, 18077, 18081, 18901, 18910–17, 18920–23, 18925–35, 18938, 18940, 18942–44, 18946–47, 18949–51, 18953–56, 18960, 18962–64, 18966, 18968–70, 18972, 18974, 18976–77, 18980–81, 18991, 19001–02, 19006–08, 19020–21, 19025, 19030, 19034, 19038, 19040, 19044, 19047–49, 19053–59, 19067, 19075, 19090, 19114, 19116, 19154–55, 19440, 19454

* * *

NINTH DISTRICT

BILL SHUSTER, Republican, of Hollidaysburg, PA; born in McKeesport, PA, January 10, 1961; education: Everett High School, Bedford County, PA; B.A., Dickinson College; M.B.A., American University; professional: businessman; Goodyear Tire & Rubber Corp.; Bandag, Inc.; President and General Manager, Shuster Chrysler; organizations: member, Zion Lutheran Church; National Federation of Independent Business; National Rifle Association; Y.M.C.A.; Precious Life, Inc.; Rotary Club; Board of Directors, Pennsylvania Automotive Association; Board of Trustees, Homewood Home Retirement Community; Sigma Chi Fraternity; family: married to Rebecca; two children: Ali and Garrett; committees: Armed Services; Natural Resources; Transportation and Infrastructure; elected to the 107th Congress, by special election, on May 15, 2001; reelected to each succeeding Congress.

Office Listings

http://www.house.gov/shuster

204 Cannon House Office Building, Washington, DC 20515	(202) 225–2431
Chief of Staff.—Jeff Loveng.	FAX: 225–2486
Legislative Director.—Stephen Martinko.	
Scheduler.—Kelley Halliwell.	
310 Penn Street, Suite 200, Hollidaysburg, PA 16648	(814) 696–6318
100 Lincoln Way East, Suite B, Chambersburg, PA 17201	(717) 264–8308
827 Water Street, #3, Indiana, PA 15701	(724) 463–0516
118 West Main Street, Suite 302, Somerset, PA 15501	(814) 443–3918

Counties: BEDFORD, BLAIR, CAMBRIA (part), CLEARFIELD (part), CUMBERLAND (part), FAYETTE (part), FRANKLIN, FULTON, HUNTINGDON, INDIANA (part), JUNIATA, MIFFLIN, PERRY (part), SOMERSET (part), WESTMORELAND (part). Population (2000), 630,730.

ZIP Codes: 15411, 15416, 15421, 15424–25, 15431, 15436–37, 15440, 15445, 15451, 15459, 15462, 15464–65, 15469–70, 15478–79, 15501, 15510, 15521–22, 15530, 15532–42, 15545, 15549–54, 15557–60, 15562–65, 15681, 15701, 15712–14, 15716–17, 15720–25, 15727–29, 15731–32, 15734, 15738–39, 15741–42, 15746–48, 15750, 15752–54, 15756–59, 15763, 15765, 15767, 15771–72, 15774–75, 15777, 15783, 15840, 15920, 15924, 15926, 15929, 15931, 15936, 15940, 15944, 15946, 15949, 15954, 15961, 15963, 16211, 16222, 16246, 16256, 16601–03, 16611, 16613, 16616–17, 16619, 16621–25, 16627, 16629–31, 16633–41, 16644, 16646–48, 16650–52, 16654–57, 16659–62, 16664–65, 16667–75, 16678–80, 16682–86, 16689, 16691–95, 16823, 16833, 16844, 16861, 16865, 16871, 16877, 17002, 17004, 17006, 17013–14, 17021, 17024, 17035, 17037, 17040, 17044–45, 17047, 17049, 17051–54, 17056, 17058–60, 17062, 17065–66, 17068, 17071, 17074–76, 17081–82, 17086, 17090, 17094, 17201, 17210–15, 17217, 17219–25, 17228–29, 17231–33, 17235–41, 17243–44, 17246–47, 17249–57, 17260–68, 17270–72, 17307, 17324

* * *

TENTH DISTRICT

CHRISTOPHER P. CARNEY, Democrat, of Dimock, PA, born in Cedar Rapids, IA, March 2, 1959; education: B.S.S., Cornell College, 1981; M.A., University of Wyoming, 1983; Ph.D., University of Nebraska, 1993; professional: Associate Professor of Political Science, Penn State University, Scranton; United States Navy Reserves; Senior Counterterrorism Advisor (Civilian); Special Advisor on Counterterrorism to Deputy Secretary of Defense; married: Jennifer, 1987; five children: Ryne, Sean, Seth, Keeley, and Brett; committees: Homeland Security; Transportation and Infrastructure; elected to the 110th Congress on November 7, 2006; reelected to the 111th Congress on November 4, 2008.

Office Listings

http://www.carney.house.gov

416 Cannon House Office Building, Washington, DC 20515	(202) 225–3731
Chief of Staff.—April Metwalli.	FAX: 225–9594
Legislative Director.—Aaron Davis.	
Communications Director.—Vincent Rongione.	
Scheduler.—Kim Henry.	
233 Northern Boulevard, Suite 4, Lackawanna County, PA 18411	(570) 585–9988
District Director.—Paul Macknosky.	
175 Pine Street, Suite 103, Lycoming County, PA 17701	(570) 327–1902
521 Franklin Street, Sahmokin, PA 17872	(570) 644–1682
	FAX: 644–1684

Counties: BRADFORD, LACKAWANNA (part), LUZERNE (part), LYCOMING (part), MONTOUR, NORTHUMBERLAND, PIKE, SNYDER, SULLIVAN, SUSQUEHANNA, TIOGA (part), UNION, WAYNE, WYOMING. Population (2000), 630,730.

ZIP Codes: 16910, 16914, 16925–26, 16930, 16932, 16936, 16945, 16947, 17017, 17045, 17063, 17086, 17701, 17703, 17705, 17724, 17728, 17730, 17731, 17735, 17737, 17742, 17749, 17756, 17758, 17762–63, 17765, 17768, 17771–72, 17774, 17777, 17801, 17810, 17812–15, 17820–24, 17827, 17829–37, 17840–42, 17844–45, 17847, 17850–51, 17853, 17855–57, 17860–62, 17864–68, 17870, 17872, 17876–77, 17880–87, 17889, 18301, 18324–26, 18328, 18336–37, 18340, 18371, 18403, 18405, 18407, 18410–11, 18413–17, 18419–21, 18424–28, 18430–31, 18433–41, 18443–49, 18451–65, 18469–73, 18512, 18612, 18614–16, 18618–19, 18622–23, 18625–30, 18632, 18636, 18640–41, 18653–54, 18656–57, 18704, 18708, 18801, 18810, 18812–18, 18820–34, 18837, 18840, 18842–48, 18850–51, 18853–54

* * *

ELEVENTH DISTRICT

PAUL E. KANJORSKI, Democrat, of Nanticoke, PA; born in Nanticoke, April 2, 1937; U.S. Capitol Page School, Washington, DC, 1954; attended: Wyoming Seminary, Kingston, PA; Temple University, Philadelphia, PA; Dickinson School of Law, Carlisle, PA; served in U.S. Army, private, 1960–61; attorney, admitted to Pennsylvania State Bar, 1966; began practice in Wilkes Barre, PA, November 7, 1966; married to the former Nancy Marie Hickerson; one daughter, Nancy; committees: Financial Services; Oversight and Government Reform; elected to the 99th Congress on November 6, 1984; reelected to each succeeding Congress.

Office Listings

http://kanjorski.house.gov

2188 Rayburn House Office Building, Washington, DC 20515 .... (202) 225–6511
Chief of Staff.—Karen Feather. FAX: 225–0764
Legislative Director.—Kate McMahon.
Executive Assistant.—Donna Giobbi.
Press Secretary.—Abigail E. McDonough.
The Stegmaier Building, 7 North Wilkes Barre Boulevard, Suite 400–M, Wilkes Barre, PA 18702–5283 .... (570) 825–2200
546 Spruce Street, Scranton, PA 18503 .... (570) 496–1011

Counties: CARBON, COLUMBIA, LACKAWANNA (part), LUZERNE (part), MONROE. Population (2000), 630,730.

ZIP Codes: 17814–15, 17820–21, 17824, 17839, 17846, 17858–59, 17878, 17888, 17920, 17985, 18012, 18030, 18058, 18071, 18201–02, 18210–12, 18216, 18219, 18221–25, 18229–30, 18232, 18234–35, 18237, 18239–41, 18244, 18246–47, 18249–51, 18254–56, 18301–02, 18320–23, 18325–27, 18330–35, 18341–42, 18344, 18346–50, 18352–57, 18360, 18370, 18372, 18434, 18447–48, 18452, 18466, 18501–05, 18507–10, 18512, 18514–15, 18517–19, 18601–03, 18610–12, 18617, 18621–22, 18624, 18631, 18634–35, 18640–44, 18651, 18655, 18660–61, 18690, 18701–11, 18761–67, 18769, 18773

* * *

TWELFTH DISTRICT

JOHN P. MURTHA, Democrat, of Johnstown, PA; born in New Martinsville, WV, June 17, 1932; graduated, Ramsey High School, Mount Pleasant, PA; Kiskiminetas Spring School; B.A. in economics, University of Pittsburgh; graduate study at Indiana University of Pennsylvania; served in Marine Corps as an enlisted Marine commissioned as an officer; discharged as a first lieutenant; maintained active reserve officer status; volunteered for one year of active duty in Vietnam as a major; served with 1st Marines, a Marine infantry regiment, 1966–67, south of Danang; awarded Bronze Star Medal with combat ''V'', two Purple Heart medals, Vietnamese Cross of Gallantry, and service medals; retired colonel, U.S. Marine Corps Reserves; elected to Pennsylvania House of Representatives in 1969, served continuously until elected to U.S. House of Representatives; recipient of Pennsylvania Distinguished Service Medal and Pennsylvania Meritorious Service Medal (the commonwealth's two highest honors); first Vietnam veteran to be elected to Congress; received 9 honorary doctorate degrees from colleges and universities; married Joyce Bell; three children: Donna Sue and twin sons, John and Patrick; committees: Appropriations; elected to the 93rd Congress, February 5, 1974; reelected to each succeeding Congress.

Office Listings

http://www.murtha.house.gov

2423 Rayburn House Office Building, Washington, DC 20515 .... (202) 225–2065
Chief of Staff.—John Hugya.
Office Coordinator.—Michael Mathis.
Schedule Coordinator.—Jane Phipps.
Legislative Director.—Whitney Morton.
Communications Director.—Matthew Mazonkey.
Appropriations Staff.—Patrick Alwine, Charles Horner.
647 Main Street, Suite 401, Johnstown, PA 15901 .... (814) 535–2642

District Director.—Mark Critz.

Counties: ALLEGHENY COUNTY (part). CITIES AND TOWNSHIPS: East Deer, and Tarentum; ARMSTRONG COUNTY (part). CITIES AND TOWNSHIPS: Apollo, Bethel, Burrell, Elderton, Ford City, Ford Cliff, Freeport, Gilpin, Kiskiminetas, Kittanning, Leechburg, Manor, Manorville, North Apollo, North Buffalo, Parks, Plumcreek, South Bend, and South Buffalo; CAMBRIA COUNTY (part). CITIES AND TOWNSHIPS: Adams, Barr, Blacklick, Brownstown, Cambria, Carrolltown, Cassandra, Conemaugh, Cresson, Croyle, Daisytown, Dale, East Carroll, East Conemaugh, East Taylor, Ebensburg, Ehrenfeld, Ferndale, Franklin, Geistown, Jackson, Johnstown, Lilly, Lorain, Lower Yoder, Middle Taylor, Munster, Nanty Glo, Portage, Richland, Sankertown, Scalp Level, South Fork, Southmonth, Stonycreek, Summerhill, Susquehanna, Upper Yoder, Vintondale, Washington, Westmont, West Carroll, West Taylor, Wilmore. FAYETTE COUNTY (part). CITIES AND TOWNSHIPS: Belle Vernon, Brownsville, Bullskin, Connellsville, Dawson, Dunbar, Everson, Fayette City, Franklin, Georges, German, Jefferson, Lower Tyrone, Luzerne, Masontown, Menallen, Newell, Nicholson, North Union, Perry, Perryopolis, Point Marion, Redstone, Saltlick, South Union, Springhill, Upper Tyrone, Uniontown, Vanderbilt, Washington. GREENE COUNTY, INDIANA COUNTY (part). CITIES AND TOWNSHIPS: Cherryhill, Clymer, Indiana, Pine, White. SOMERSET COUNTY (part). CITIES AND TOWNSHIPS: Benson, Boswell, Conemaugh, Hooversville, Jefferson, Jenner, Jennerstown, Lincoln, Middlecreek, Paint, Quemahoning, Seven Springs, Stoystown, Windber. WASHINGTON COUNTY (part). CITIES AND TOWNSHIPS: Allenport, Beallsville, Bentleyville, California, Canonsburg, Canton, Carroll, Centerville, Charleroi, Chartier, Coal Center, Cokeburg, Deemston, Donora, Dunlevy, East Bethlehem, East Washington, Elco, Ellsworth, Fallowfield, Finleyville, Houston, Long Branch, Marianna, Monongahela, New Eagle, North Bethlehem, North Charleroi, North Strabane, Roscoe, Somerset, South Strabane, Speers, Stockdale, Twilight, Union, Washington, West Bethlehem, West Brownsville, West Pike Run. WESTMORELAND COUNTY (part). CITIES AND TOWNSHIPS: Allegheny, Arnold, Avonmore, Bell, Bessemer, Bolivar, Bovard, Bridgeport, Crabtree, Derry, Dorothy, Duncan, East Herminie, East Huntingdon, East Vandergrift, Fairfield, Hannastown, Heccla, Hempfield, Hugus, Hyde Park, Jacobs Creek, Latrobe, Laurel Run, Lloydsville, Lowber, Lower Burrell, Loyalhanna, Luxor, Mammoth, Mechlings, Mineral, Monessen, Mount Pleasant, New Alexandria, New Florence, New Kensington, North Belle Vernon, North Washington, Oklahoma, Paulton, Port Royal, Rillton, Rostraver, Salem, Scottdale, Seward, Sewickley, Smithton, South Huntingdon, Spring Garden, St. Clair, United, Unity, Upper Burrell, Vandergrift, Washington, Wayne, Westmoreland, West Herminie, West Leechburg, West Newton, Wyano, and Yukon. Population (2000), 630,730.

ZIP Codes: 15012, 15022, 15030, 15033, 15038, 15062–63, 15067–68, 15072, 15083, 15087, 15089, 15301, 15310, 15313–17, 15320, 15322, 15324–25, 15327, 15329–34, 15336–38, 15341–42, 15344–49, 15351–54, 15357–60, 15362–64, 15366, 15368, 15370, 15377, 15380, 15401, 15410–13, 15415, 15417, 15419–20, 15422–25, 15427–36, 15438, 15442–44, 15446–47, 15449–51, 15454–56, 15458, 15460, 15463, 15466–68, 15472–77, 15479–80, 15482–86, 15488–90, 15492, 15501–02, 15520, 15531, 15541, 15544, 15547–48, 15551, 15555, 15557, 15561, 15563, 15601, 15610, 15613, 15618, 15620–22, 15624–25, 15627, 15629, 15631, 15633, 15635, 15637, 15641–42, 15644, 15646, 15650, 15655–56, 15660–62, 15664, 15666, 15670–71, 15673–74, 15677–78, 15680–90, 15701, 15705, 15710, 15714, 15717, 15722, 15724, 15728, 15732, 15736–37, 15745, 15748, 15760–62, 15765, 15773–74, 15779, 15901–02, 15904–07, 15909, 15921–23, 15925, 15927–28, 15930–31, 15934–38, 15940, 15942–46, 15948, 15951–63, 16055, 16201, 16215, 16226, 16228–29, 16236, 16238, 16240, 16249, 16630, 16641, 16646, 16668–69

* * *

THIRTEENTH DISTRICT

ALLYSON Y. SCHWARTZ, Democrat, of Rydal, PA; born in Queens County, NY, October 3, 1948; education: graduated from the Calhoun School, New York, NY, 1966; B.A., Simmons College, Boston, MA, 1970; M.S.W., Bryn Mawr College, Bryn Mawr, PA, 1972; professional: executive director of the Elizabeth Blackwell Center, 1977–88; Deputy Commissioner of the Philadelphia Department of Human Services, 1988–90; elected to the Pennsylvania State Senate, 1991–2004; member: Pennsylvania State Board of Education; Pennsylvania Council on Higher Education; Education Commission of the States; married: Dr. David Schwartz; children: Daniel and Jordan; committees: Budget; Ways and Means; elected to the 109th Congress on November 2, 2004; reelected to each succeeding Congress.

Office Listings

http://www.house.gov/schwartz

330 Cannon House Office Building, Washington, DC 20515 .... (202) 225–6111
Chief of Staff.—Daniel McElhatton. FAX: 226–0611
Legislative Director.—John Sherry.
Communications Director.—Rachel Magnuson.
706 West Avenue, Jenkintown, PA 19046 .... (215) 517–6572
District Director.—Julie Slavet.
7219 Frankford Avenue, Philadelphia, PA 19135 .... (215) 335–3355

County: MONTGOMERY COUNTY; CITIES AND TOWNSHIPS: Abington Wards, Hatfield, Horsham, Lower Frederick, Lower Gwynedd, Lower Moreland, Lower Salford, Malborough, Montgomery, New Hanover, Plymouth, Springfield, Towamencin, Upper Dublin, Upper Frederick, Upper Gwynedd, Upper Moreland, Upper Salford, Whitemarsh, Whitpain. Boroughs of Ambler, Bryn Athyn, Green Lane, Hatboro, Hatfield, Jenkintown, Lansdale, North Wales, Rockledge, Schwenksville. PHILADELPHIA COUNTY; CITY OF: Philadelphia. Population (2000), 630,730.

ZIP Codes: 18054, 18074, 18914–15, 18932, 18936, 18957–58, 18964, 18969, 18979, 19001–02, 19006, 19009, 19019, 19025, 19027, 19038, 19040, 19044, 19046, 19075, 19090, 19096, 19111, 19114–16, 19118, 19120, 19124, 19128, 19134–37, 19149, 19152, 19154–55, 19244, 19255, 19422, 19424, 19428, 19435–38, 19440–41, 19443–44, 19446, 19450–51, 19454–55, 19462, 19464, 19473, 19477–78, 19486–87, 19489, 19492, 19504, 19512, 19525

* * *

FOURTEENTH DISTRICT

MICHAEL F. DOYLE, Democrat, of Forest Hills, PA; born in Swissvale, PA, August 5, 1953; graduated, Swissvale Area High School, 1971; B.S., Pennsylvania State University, 1975; co-owner, Eastgate Insurance Agency, Inc., 1983; elected and served as finance and recreation chairman, Swissvale Borough Council, 1977–81; member: Leadership Pittsburgh Alumni Association, Lions Club, Ancient Order of the Hibernians, Italian Sons and Daughters of America, and Penn State Alumni Association; member: Democratic Caucus, Democratic Study Group, Pennsylvania Democratic Delegation, Congressional Steel Caucus, Travel and Tourism CMO, Ad Hoc Committee on Irish Affairs, and National Italian-American Foundation; married Susan Beth Doyle, 1975; four children: Michael, David, Kevin, and Alexandra; committees: Energy and Commerce; elected to the 104th Congress, November 8, 1994; reelected to each succeeding Congress.

Office Listings

http://www.house.gov/doyle

401 Cannon House Office Building, Washington, DC 20515 .... (202) 225–2135
Administrative Assistant.—David Lucas. FAX: 225–3084
Legislative Director.—Kenneth DeGraff.
Office Manager / Scheduler.—Ellen Young.
225 Ross Street, 5th Floor, Pittsburgh, PA 15219 .... (412) 261–5091
District Director.—Paul D'Alesandro.
11 Duff Road, Penn Hills, PA 15235 .... (412) 241–6055
627 Lysle Boulevard, McKeesport, PA 15132 .... (412) 664–4049

County: ALLEGHENY COUNTY (part); CITIES AND TOWNSHIPS OF: Avalon, Baldwin Borough, Baldwin Township, Blawnox, Braddock, Braddock Hills, Chalfant, Clairton, Coraopolis, Dravosburg, Duquesne, E. McKeesport, E. Pittsburgh, Edgewood, Elizabeth Borough, Elizabeth Township, Etna, Forest Hills, Glassport, Ingram, Kennedy, Liberty, Lincoln, McKees Rocks, McKeesport, Millvale, Monroeville, Mt. Oliver, Munhall, Neville, North Braddock, North Versailles, O'Hara Township, Penn Hills, Pitcairn, Pittsburgh, Port Vue, Rankin, Reserve, Robinson, Stowe, Swissvale, Sharpsburg, Turtle Creek, Verona, Versailles, Wall, West Homestead, West Mifflin, Whitaker, Wilkins, Wilkinsburg, and Wilmerding. Population (2000), 630,730.

ZIP Codes: 15025, 15034–35, 15037, 15044–45, 15063, 15104, 15106, 15108, 15110, 15112, 15116, 15120, 15122, 15132–37, 15140, 15145–48, 15201–19, 15221–27, 15230, 15232–36, 15238–40, 15242, 15244, 15250–51, 15253, 15255, 15257–62, 15264–65, 15267–68, 15272, 15274, 15278–79, 15281–83, 15285–86, 15290, 15295

* * *

FIFTEENTH DISTRICT

CHARLES W. DENT, Republican, of Allentown, PA, born in Allentown, May 24, 1960; education: B.A., foreign service and international politics, Pennsylvania State University, 1982; M.A., public administration, Lehigh University, 1993; professional: Legislator Development Officer, Lehigh University, 1986–90; sales representative, P.A. Peters, Inc.; Pennsylvania State House, District 132, 1991–98; Representative, Pennsylvania State Senate, 1998–2004; religion: First Presbyterian Church; married: Pamela Jane Serfass; children: Kathryn Elizabeth, William Reed, and Charles John (Jack); committees: Homeland Security; Standards of Official Conduct; Transportation and Infrastructure; elected to the 109th Congress on November 2, 2004; reelected to each succeeding Congress.

Office Listings

http://www.dent.house.gov

1009 Longworth House Office Building, Washington, DC 20515 .... (202) 225–6411
Chief of Staff.—George McElwee. FAX: 226–0778
Legislative Director.—Laura Stevens-Kent.
701 West Broad Street, Suite 200, Bethlehem, PA 18018 .... (610) 861–9734
206 Main Street, East Greenville, PA 18041 .... (215) 541–4106

Counties: BERKS (part), LEHIGH, MONTGOMERY (part), NORTHAMPTON. POPULATION (2000), 630,730.

ZIP Codes: 18001–03, 18010–11, 18013–18, 18020, 18025, 18031–32, 18034–38, 18040–46, 18049–55, 18059–60, 18062–70, 18072–74, 18076–80, 18083–88, 18091–92, 18098–99, 18101–06, 18109, 18175, 18195, 18343, 18351, 18918, 18924, 18951, 18960, 18964, 18969, 18971, 19438, 19440, 19464, 19472, 19504–05, 19512, 19525, 19529–30, 19539

* * *

SIXTEENTH DISTRICT

JOSEPH R. PITTS, Republican, of Kennett Square, PA; born in Lexington, KY, October 10, 1939; education: B.A., philosophy and religion, Asbury College, KY; military service: served in U.S. Air Force, 1963–69, rising from second lieutenant to captain; professional: nursery business owner and operator; math and science teacher, Great Valley High School, Malvern, PA, 1969–72; teacher, Mortonsville Elementary School, Versailles, KY; member: Pennsylvania House of Representatives, 1972–96, serving as chairman of Appropriations Committee, 1989–96, and of Labor Relations Committee, 1981–88; married: the former Virginia M. Pratt in 1961; children: Karen, Carol, and Daniel; committees: Energy and Commerce; elected to the 105th Congress; reelected to each succeeding Congress.

Office Listings

http://www.house.gov/pitts

221 Cannon House Office Building, Washington, DC 20515 .... (202) 225–2411
Chief of Staff.—Gabe Neville. FAX: 225–2013
Legislative Director.—Monica Volante.
Press Secretary.—Andrew Wimer.
P.O. Box 837, Unionville, PA 19375 .... (610) 444–4581
150 North Queen Street, Suite 716, Lancaster, PA 17603 .... (717) 393–0667

Counties: LANCASTER, BERK (part). CITIES AND TOWNSHIPS: Reading, Bern, Lower Heidelberg, South Heidelberg, Spring. BOROUGH OF: Wernersville. CHESTER COUNTY (part). CITIES AND TOWNSHIPS: Birmingham, East Bradford, East Fallowfield, East Marlborough, East Nottingham, Elk, Franklin, Highland, Kennett, London Britain, London Grove, Londonderry, Lower Oxford, New Garden, New London, Newlin, Penn, Pennsbury, Upper Oxford, West Fallowfield, West Marlborough, West Nottingham. BOROUGHS OF: Avondale, Kennett Square, Oxford, Parkesburg, West Chester, and West Grove. Population (2000), 630,730.

ZIP Codes: 17501–09, 17512, 17516–22, 17527–29, 17532–38, 17540, 17543, 17545, 17547, 17549–52, 17554–55, 17557, 17560, 17562–70, 17572–73, 17575–76, 17578–85, 17601–08, 19106, 19310–11, 19317–20, 19330, 19342, 19346–48, 19350–52, 19357, 19360, 19362–63, 19365, 19374–75, 19380–83, 19390, 19395, 19464, 19501, 19540, 19543, 19565, 19601–02, 19604–05, 19608–11

* * *

SEVENTEENTH DISTRICT

TIM HOLDEN, Democrat, of St. Clair, PA; born in Pottsville, PA, March 5, 1957; education: attended St. Clair High School, St. Clair; Fork Union Military Academy; University of Richmond, Richmond, VA; B.A., Bloomsburg State College, 1980; professional: sheriff of Schuylkill County, PA, 1985–93; licensed insurance broker and real estate agent, John J. Holden Insurance Agency and Holden Realty Company, St. Clair; member: Pennsylvania Sheriffs Association; Fraternal Order of Police; St. Clair Fish and Game Association; Benevolent and Protective Order of the Elks Lodge 1533; co-chair, Correctional Officers Caucus; co-chair, House Mining Caucus; co-chair, Northeast Agriculture Caucus; Ad-Hoc Committee for Irish Affairs; Alzheimer's Caucus; Appalachian Region Commission Caucus; Arts Caucus; Autism Caucus; Blue Dog Coalition; Congressional 4–H Caucus; Congressional Beef Caucus; Congressional Caucus on Armenian Issues; Congressional Cement Caucus; Congressional Hellenic Caucus; Diabetes Caucus; Firefighter's Caucus; Friends of Ireland; Home Health Care Working Group; Homeland Security Caucus; House Auto Caucus; House Baltic Caucus; House Commuter Caucus; House Nursing Caucus; Iraq Fallen Heroes Caucus; Law Enforcement Caucus; Mental Health Caucus; National Guard and Reserve Components Caucus; Rural Caucus; Rural Health Care Caucus; Special Operations Forces Caucus; Sportsmens Causus; Steel Caucus; Water Infrastructure Caucus; Wine Caucus; committees: Agriculture; Transportation and Infrastructure; elected to the 103rd Congress; reelected to each succeeding Congress.

Office Listings

2417 Rayburn House Office Building, Washington, DC 20515 .... (202) 225–5546
Chief of Staff.—Trish Reilly. FAX: 226–0996
Legislative Director.—Keith Pemrick.
Projects Director.—Bill Hanley.
Scheduler.—Jason Knecht.
1721 North Front Street, Suite 105, Harrisburg, PA 17102 .... (717) 234–5904
4918 Kutztown Road, Temple, PA 19560 .... (610) 921–3502
758 Cumberland Street, Lebanon, PA 17042 .... (717) 270–1395
101 North Centre Street, Suite 303, Pottsville, PA 17901 .... (570) 622–4212

Counties: BERKS (part), DAUPHIN, LEBANON, PERRY (part), SCHUYLKILL. Population (2000), 630,730.

ZIP Codes: 17003, 17005, 17010, 17016–18, 17020, 17022–24, 17026, 17028, 17030, 17032–34, 17036, 17038–39, 17041–42, 17045–46, 17048, 17053, 17057, 17061–62, 17064, 17067–69, 17073–74, 17077–78, 17080, 17083, 17085, 17087–88, 17097–98, 17101–13, 17120–30, 17140, 17177, 17502, 17830, 17836, 17901, 17921–23, 17925, 17929–36, 17938, 17941–46, 17948–49, 17951–54, 17957, 17959–61, 17963–68, 17970, 17972, 17974, 17976, 17978–83, 17985, 18211, 18214, 18218, 18220, 18231, 18237, 18240–42, 18245, 18248, 18250, 18252, 18255, 19506–07, 19510, 19512, 19516, 19518, 19522, 19526, 19529–30, 19533–34, 19536, 19541, 19544, 19547, 19549–51, 19554–55, 19559–60, 19564–65, 19567, 19601, 19604–06

* * *

EIGHTEENTH DISTRICT

TIM MURPHY, Republican, of Upper St. Clair, PA; born in Cleveland, OH, September 11, 1952; education: B.S., Wheeling Jesuit University, 1974; M.A., Cleveland State University, 1976; Ph.D., University of Pittsburgh, 1979; professional: Psychologist; holds two adjunct faculty positions at the University of Pittsburgh; Associate Professor in the Department of Public Health, and in the Department of Pediatrics; public service: Pennsylvania State Senate, 1996–2002; military: Lieutenant Commander, Medical Service Corps, United States Navy Reserve; religion: Catholic; family: married to Nan Missig; children: Bevin; co-chair, 21st Century Healthcare Caucus; Ad Hoc Congressional Committee for Irish Affairs / Friends of Ireland Caucus; Bipartisan Congressional Down Syndrome Caucus; Bipartisan Congressional Pro-Life Caucus; Congressional Caucus on Hellenic Issues; Congressional Caucus on India and Indian Americans; Congressional Cystic Fibrosis Caucus; Congressional Fire Services Caucus; Congressional Manufacturing Caucus; co-chair, Congressional Men's Health Caucus; co-chair, Congressional Mental Health Caucus; Congressional Multiple Sclerosis Caucus; co-chair, Congressional Natural Gas Caucus; Congressional Services Caucus; Congressional Sportsmen's Caucus; Congressional Steel Caucus; Congressional Study Group on Public Health; House Land Conservation Caucus; House Recycling Caucus; Hydrogen Fuel Cell Caucus; National Guard and Reserve Component Caucus; Northeast Midwest Congressional Coalition / Caucus; Medical and Dental Doctors in Congress Caucus; Middle Class Caucus; Military Veteran Caucus; Nuclear Issues Working Group; Renewable Energy and Energy Efficiency Caucus; Robotics Caucus; Suburban Agenda Caucus; USO Congressional Caucus; committees: Energy and Commerce; elected to the 108th Congress on November 5, 2002; reelected to each succeeding Congress.

Office Listings

http://murphy.house.gov

322 Cannon House Office Building, Washington, DC 20515 .... (202) 225–2301
Chief of Staff.—Susan Mosychuk.
Legislative Director.—Aric Nesbitt.
Scheduler.—Janelle Belland.
Press Secretary.—Mark Carpenter.
504 Washington Road, Pittsburgh, PA 15228 .... (412) 344–5583

Counties: ALLEGHENY (part), WASHINGTON (part), WESTMORELAND (part). CITIES AND TOWNSHIPS: Greensburg, and Jeannette. Population (2000), 630,730.

ZIP Codes: 15001, 15004, 15017–22, 15025–26, 15028, 15031, 15033, 15036–37, 15044, 15046–47, 15053–55, 15057, 15060, 15063–64, 15071, 15075, 15078, 15082–83, 15085, 15088–89, 15102, 15106, 15108, 15126, 15129, 15131, 15136, 15142, 15146, 15205, 15209, 15212, 15215–16, 15220–21, 15226–28, 15231, 15234–36, 15238, 15241, 15243, 15270, 15277, 15301, 15311–12, 15314, 15317, 15321, 15323, 15329–30, 15332, 15339–40, 15342, 15345, 15350, 15361, 15363, 15365, 15367, 15376–79, 15448, 15501, 15601, 15605–06, 15611–12, 15615–17, 15619, 15622–23, 15626, 15628, 15632, 15634, 15636–40, 15642, 15644, 15647, 15650, 15655, 15658, 15663, 15665, 15668, 15672, 15675–76, 15679, 15683, 15687–88, 15691–93, 15695–97

* * *

NINETEENTH DISTRICT

TODD RUSSELL PLATTS, Republican, of York County, PA; born in York County, March 5, 1962; education: York Suburban High School, 1980; B.S. in Public Administration, Shippensburg University of Pennsylvania, 1984; J.D., Pepperdine University School of Law, 1991; professional: Attorney; organizations: York County Transportation Coalition; Statewide Children's Health Insurance Program Advisory Council; York Metropolitan Planning Organization; public service: Pennsylvania House of Representatives, 1992–2000; married: Leslie; children: T.J. and Kelsey; committees: Armed Services; Education and Labor; Transportation and Infrastructure; elected to the 107th Congress on November 7, 2000; reelected to each succeeding Congress.

Office Listings

http://www.house.gov/platts

2455 Rayburn House Office Building, Washington, DC 20515 .... (202) 225–5836
Chief of Staff.—Scott E. Miller. FAX: 226–1000
2209 East Market Street, York, PA 17402 .... (717) 600–1919
Deputy Chief of Staff.—Bob Reilly.
22 Chambersburg Street, Gettysburg, PA 17325 .... (717) 338–1919
59 West Louther Street, Carlisle, PA 17013 .... (717) 249–0190

Counties: ADAMS COUNTY, CUMBERLAND COUNTY (part), YORK COUNTY. Population (2000), 647,065.

ZIP Codes: 17001, 17007, 17011–13, 17015, 17019, 17025, 17027, 17043, 17050, 17053, 17055, 17065, 17070, 17072, 17089–90, 17093, 17214, 17222, 17257, 17301–04, 17306–07, 17309–25, 17327, 17329, 17331–33, 17337, 17339–40, 17342–45, 17347, 17349–50, 17352–56, 17358, 17360–66, 17368, 17370–72, 17375, 17401–08, 17415

RHODE ISLAND

(Population 2000, 1,048,319)

SENATORS

JACK REED, Democrat, of Jamestown, RI; born in Providence, RI, November 12, 1949; graduated, La Salle Academy, Providence, RI, 1967; B.S., U.S. Military Academy, West Point, NY, 1971; M.P.P., Kennedy School of Government, Harvard University, 1973; J.D., Harvard Law School, 1982; professional: served in the U.S. Army, 1967–79; platoon leader, company commander, battalion staff officer, 1973–77; associate professor, Department of Social Sciences, U.S. Military Academy, West Point, NY, 1978–79; 2nd BN (Abn) 504th Infantry, 82nd Airborne Division, Fort Bragg, NC; lawyer, admitted to the Washington, DC bar, 1983; military awards: Army commendation medal with Oak Leaf Cluster, ranger, senior parachutist, jumpmaster, expert infantryman's badge; elected to the Rhode Island State Senate, 1985–90; committees: Appropriations; Armed Services; Banking, Housing, and Urban Affairs; Health, Education, Labor, and Pensions; elected to the 102nd Congress on November 6, 1990; served three terms in the U.S. House of Representatives; elected to the U.S. Senate, November 5, 1996; reelected to each succeeding Senate term.

Office Listings

http://reed.senate.gov

728 Hart Senate Office Building, Washington, DC 20510 .... (202) 224–4642
Chief of Staff.—Neil Campbell. FAX: 224–4680
Deputy Chief of Staff.—Cathy Nagle.
Press Secretary.—Chip Unruh.
1000 Chapel View Boulevard, Suite 290, Cranston, RI 02920 .... (401) 943–3100
Chief of Staff.—Raymond Simone.
U.S. District Courthouse, One Exchange Terrace, Suite 408, Providence, RI 02903 (401) 528–5200

* * *

SHELDON WHITEHOUSE, Democrat, of Newport, RI; born in New York City, NY, October 20, 1955; education: B.A., Yale University, New Haven, CT, 1978; J.D., University of Virginia, Charlottesville, VA, 1982; director, Rhode Island Department of Business Regulation, 1992–94; United States Attorney, 1994–98; Attorney General, Rhode Island state, 1999–2003; committees: Budget; Environment and Public Works; Judiciary; Select Committee on Intelligence; Special Committee on Aging; elected to the U.S. Senate on November 7, 2006.

Office Listings

http://whitehouse.senate.gov

502 Hart Senate Office Building, Washington, DC 20510 .... (202) 224–2921
Chief of Staff.—Mindy Myers. FAX: 228–6362
Legislative Director.—Carlos Angulo.
Communications Director.—Alex Swartsel.
170 Westminster Street, Suite 1100, Providence, RI 02903 .... (401) 453–5294
State Director.—George Carvalho.

REPRESENTATIVES

FIRST DISTRICT

PATRICK J. KENNEDY, Democrat, of Providence, RI; born in Brighton, MA, July 14, 1967; education: graduated, Phillips Academy, Andover, MA; B.A., Providence College, Providence, RI, 1991; public service: Rhode Island State Legislature, 1988–94; member: Rhode Island Special Olympics (board of directors), Rhode Island March of Dimes, Rhode Island Lung Association, Rhode Island Mental Health Association, Rhode Island Chapter of National Committee for the Prevention of Child Abuse; committees: Appropriations; Oversight and Government Reform; elected to the 104th Congress; reelected to each succeeding Congress.

Office Listings

http://www.house.gov/patrickkennedy

407 Cannon House Office Building, Washington, DC 20515 .... (202) 225–4911

Chief of Staff.—Adam Brand. FAX: 225–3290
Deputy Chief of Staff.—Kimber Colton.
Legislative Director.—William Garner.
Executive Assistant.—Terri Alford.
Press Secretary.—Kerrie Bennett.
249 Roosevelt Avenue, Suite 200, Pawtucket, RI 02860 .... (401) 729–5600
District Director.—George Zainyeh.

Counties: BRISTOL, NEWPORT, PROVIDENCE (part). CITIES AND TOWNSHIPS: Barrington, Bristol, Burrillville, Central Falls, Cumberland, East Providence, Jamestown, Lincoln, Little Compton, Middleton, Newport, North Providence, North Smithfield, Providence, Pawtucket, Portsmouth, Smithfield, Tiverton, Warren, and Woonsocket. Population (2000), 524,157.

ZIP Codes: 02801, 02802, 02806, 02809, 02824, 02826, 02828, 02830, 02835, 02837, 02838, 02839, 02840, 02841, 02842, 02858, 02859, 02860, 02861, 02862, 02863, 02864, 02865, 02871, 02872, 02876, 02878, 02885, 02895, 02896, 02903, 02904, 02906, 02908, 02909, 02911, 02912, 02914, 02915, 02916, 02917, 02918, 02940

* * *

SECOND DISTRICT

JAMES R. LANGEVIN, Democrat, of Warwick, RI; born in Providence, RI, April 22, 1964; education: B.A., Political Science / Public Administration, Rhode Island College, 1990; Masters of Public Administration, Harvard University, 1994; community service: American Red Cross; March of Dimes; Lions Club of Warwick; PARI Independent Living Center; Knights of Columbus; public service: secretary, Rhode Island Constitutional Convention, 1986; Rhode Island State Representative, 1989–95; Rhode Island Secretary of State, 1995–2000; committees: Armed Services; Budget; Permanent Select Committee on Intelligence; elected to the 107th Congress; reelected to each succeeding Congress.

Office Listings

http://www.langevin.house.gov

109 Cannon House Office Building, Washington, DC 20515 .... (202) 225–2735
Chief of Staff.—Kristin Nicholson. FAX: 225–5976
Legislative Director.—Rachel Bornstein.
Office Manager.—Stu Rose.
The Summit South, 300 Centerville Road, Suite 200, Warwick, RI 02886 .... (401) 732–9400
District Director.—Ken Wild.

Counties: KENT, PROVIDENCE (part), WASHINGTON. CITIES AND TOWNSHIPS: Charleston, Coventry, Cranston, Exeter, Foster, Glocester, Greenwich (East and West), Hopkinton, Johnston, Kingstown (North and South), Narragansett, New Shoreham, Providence, Richmond, Warwick, West Warwick, Westerly, and Sctuate. Population (2000), 538,032.

ZIP Codes: 02804, 02807–08, 02812–18, 02822–23, 02825, 02827–29, 02831–33, 02836, 02852, 02857, 02873–75, 02877, 02879–83, 02886–89, 02891–94, 02898, 02901–05, 02907–11, 02917, 02919–21

SOUTH CAROLINA

(Population 2000, 4,012,012)

SENATORS

LINDSEY GRAHAM, Republican, of Seneca, SC; born in Seneca, July 9, 1955; education: graduated, Daniel High School, Central, SC; B.A., University of South Carolina, 1977; awarded J.D., 1981; military service: joined the U.S. Air Force, 1982; Base Legal Office and Area Defense Counsel, Rhein Main Air Force Base, Germany, 1984; circuit trial counsel, U.S. Air Forces; Base Staff Judge Advocate, McEntire Air National Guard Base, SC, 1989–1994; presently a Colonel, Air Force Reserves; award: Meritorious Service Medal for Active Duty Tour in Europe; professional: established private law practice, 1988; former member, South Carolina House of Representatives; Assistant County Attorney for Oconee County, 1988–92; City Attorney for Central, SC, 1990–94; member: Walhalla Rotary; American Legion Post 120; appointed to the Judicial Arbitration Commission by the Chief Justice of the Supreme Court; religion: attends Corinth Baptist Church; committees: Armed Services; Budget; Homeland Security and Governmental Affairs; Judiciary; Veterans' Affairs; Select Committee on Aging; elected to the 104th Congress on November 8, 1994; reelected to each succeeding Congress; elected to the U.S. Senate on November 5, 2002.

Office Listings

http://lgraham.senate.gov

290 Russell Senate Office Building, Washington, DC 20510 .... (202) 224–5972
Chief of Staff.—Richard Perry. FAX: 224–3808
Legislative Director.—Jen Olson.
Press Secretary.—Meghan Huges.
Scheduler.—Alice James.
130 South Main Street, Suite 700, Greenville, SC 29601 .... (864) 250–1417
State Director.—Jane Goolsby.
Upstate Regional Director.—Van Cato.
530 Johnnie Dodds Boulevard, Suite 202, Mt. Pleasant, SC 29464 .... (843) 849–3887
Low Country Regional Director.—Bill Tuten.
508 Hampton Street, Suite 202, Columbia, SC 29201 .... (803) 933–0112
Midlands Regional Director.—Rene Ann Tewkesbury.
John L. McMillan Federal Building, 401 West Evans Street, Suite 111, Florence, SC 29501 .... (843) 669–1505
Pee Dee Regional Director.—Celia Urquhart.
140 East Main Street, Suite 110, Rock Hill, SC 29730 .... (803) 366–2828
Piedmont Regional Outreach Director.—Wes Hickman.
124 Exchange Street, Suite A, Pendleton, SC 29670 .... (864) 646–4090
Senior Adviosr.—Denise Bauld.

* * *

JIM DEMINT, Republican, of Greenville, SC; born in Greenville, September 2, 1951; education: West Hampton High School, Greenville, SC, 1969; B.S., University of Tennessee, 1973; M.B.A., Clemson University, 1981; certified management consultant and certified quality trainer; advertising and marketing businessman; started his own company, DeMint Marketing; active in Greenville, SC, business and educational organizations; U.S. House of Representatives, 1999–2005; religion: Presbyterian; family: married to Debbie; four children; committees: Banking, Housing, and Urban Affairs; Commerce, Science, and Transportation; Foreign Relations; Joint Economic Committee; elected to the U.S. Senate on November 2, 2004.

Office Listings

http://demint.senate.gov

340 Russell Senate Office Building, Washington, DC 20510 .... (202) 224–6121
Chief of Staff.—Bret Bernhardt. FAX: 228–5143
Policy Director.—Matt Hoskins.
Senior Administrative Advisor.—Ellen Weaver.
Communications Director.—Wesley Denton.
105 North Spring Street, Suite 109, Greenville, SC 29601 .... (864) 233–5366
112 Custom House, 200 East Bay Street, Charleston, SC 29401 .... (843) 727–4525
1901 Main Street, Suite 1475, Columbia, SC 29201 .... (803) 771–6112

REPRESENTATIVES

FIRST DISTRICT

HENRY E. BROWN, JR., Republican, of Hanahan, SC; born in Lee County, SC, December 20, 1935; education: Berkeley High School; Baptist College; and The Citadel; professional: businessman; Piggly Wiggly Carolina Co., Inc.; helped develop the Lowcountry Investment Corp.; awards: National Republican Legislator of the Year; South Carolina Taxpayers Watchdog Award; South Carolina Association of Realtors Legislator of the Year; honorary degree, Doctor of Business Administration, The Citadel; married: Billye; three children; public service: Hanahan City Council, 1981–85; South Carolina House of Representatives, 1985–2000; committees: Natural Resources; Transportation and Infrastructure; Veterans' Affairs; elected to the 107th Congress on November 7, 2000; reelected to each succeeding Congress.

Office Listings

http://www.house.gov/henrybrown

1124 Longworth House Office Building, Washington, DC 20515 .... (202) 225–3176
Chief of Staff.—Chris Berardini. FAX: 225–3407
Legislative Director.—Ryan Bowley.
Press Secretary.—Katie McKinney.
5900 Core Avenue, Suite 401, North Charleston, SC 29406 .... (843) 747–4175
District Director.—Kathy Crawford.
1800 North Oak Street, Suite C, Myrtle Beach, SC 29577 .... (843) 445–6459

Counties: BERKELEY (part), CHARLESTON (part), DORCHESTER (part), GEORGETOWN (part), HORRY. Population (2000), 668,668.

ZIP Codes: 29401–07, 29410, 29412–14, 29416–20, 29422–25, 29429, 29436, 29439–40, 29442, 29445, 29449, 29451, 29455–58, 29461, 29464–66, 29469–70, 29472, 29474–75, 29482–85, 29487, 29511, 29526–28, 29544–45, 29566, 29568–69, 29572, 29575–79, 29581–82, 29585, 29587–88, 29597–98

* * *

SECOND DISTRICT

JOE WILSON, Republican, of Springdale, SC; born in Charleston, SC, July 31, 1947; education: graduated, B.A., Washington & Lee University, Lexington, VA; J.D., University of South Carolina School of Law; professional: attorney; Kirkland, Wilson, Moore, Taylor & Thomas (law firm); served on the staff of Senator Strom Thurmond and Congressman Floyd Spence; former Deputy General Counsel, U.S. Department of Energy; former Judge of the town of Springdale, SC; military service: U.S. Army Reserves, 1972–75; retired Colonel in the South Carolina Army National Guard as a Staff Judge Advocate for the 218th Mechanized Infantry Brigade, 1975–2003; organizations: Cayce-West Columbia Rotary Club; Sheriff's Department Law Enforcement Advisory Council; Reserve Officers Association; Lexington County Historical Society; Columbia Home Builders Association; County Community and Resource Development Committee; American Heart Association; Mid-Carolina Mental Health Association; Cayce-West Columbia Jaycees; Kidney Foundation; South Carolina Lung Association; Alston-Wilkes Society; Cayce-West Metro Chamber of Commerce; Columbia World Affairs Council; Fellowship of Christian Athletes, Sinclair Lodge 154; Jamil Temple; Woodmen of the World; Sons of Confederate Veterans; Military Order of the World Wars; Lexington, Greater Irmo, Chapin, Columbia, West Metro, and Batesburg-Leesville Chambers of Commerce; West Metro and Dutch Fork Women's Republican Clubs; and Executive Council of the Indian Waters Council, Boy Scouts of America; awards: U.S. Chamber of Commerce Spirit of Enterprise Award; Americans for Tax Reform Friend of the Taxpayer Award; National Taxpayers' Union; Taxpayers' Friend Award; Americans for Prosperity; Friend of the American Motorist Award; public service: South Carolina State Senate, 1984–2001; family: married to Roxanne Dusenbury McCrory; four sons; committees: Armed Services; Education and Labor; Foreign Affairs; Assistant GOP Whip; member, Republican Policy Committee; elected to the 107th Congress, by special election, on December 18, 2001; reelected to each succeeding Congress.

Office Listings

http://joewilson.house.gov

212 Cannon House Office Building, Washington, DC 20515 .... (202) 225–2452
Chief of Staff.—Eric Dell. FAX: 225–2455
Press Secretary.—Ryan Murphy.
Legislative Director.—Melissa Chandler.
903 Port Republic Street, P.O. Box 1538, Beaufort, SC 29901 .... (843) 521–2530
1700 Sunset Boulevard (U.S. 378), Suite 1, West Columbia, SC 29169 .... (803) 939–0041

Counties: AIKEN (part), ALLENDALE, BARNWELL, BEAUFORT, CALHOUN (part), HAMPTON, JASPER, LEXINGTON, ORANGEBURG (part), RICHLAND (part). CITIES AND TOWNSHIPS: Aiken, Allendale, Ballentine, Barnwell, Batesburg, Beaufort, Blackville, Bluffton, Blythewood, Brunson, Cayce, Chapin, Columbia, Coosawhatchie, Cope, Cordova, Crocketville, Daufuskie Island, Early Branch, Elko, Estill, Fairfax, Furman, Garnett, Gaston, Gifford, Gilbert, Hampton, Hardeeville, Hilda, Hilton Head Island, Irmo, Islandston, Kline, Leesville, Lexington, Livingston, Luray, Martin, Miley, Montmorenci, Neeses, North, Norway, Orangeburg, Pelion, Pineland, Port Royal, Ridgeland, Ruffin, Scotia, Springfield, St. Helena Island, St. Matthews, State Park, Swansea, Sycamore, Tillman, Ulmer, Varnville, West Columbia, White Rock, Williams, Williston, Windsor, and Yemassee. Population (2000), 668,668.

ZIP Codes: 29002, 29006, 29016, 29033, 29036, 29045, 29053–54, 29063, 29070–73, 29075, 29078, 29107, 29112–13, 29115–16, 29118, 29123, 29128, 29130, 29135, 29137, 29142, 29146–47, 29160, 29164, 29169–72, 29177, 29180, 29203–07, 29209–10, 29212, 29219, 29221, 29223–24, 29226–27, 29229, 29260, 29290, 29292, 29405, 29412–13, 29436, 29470, 29472, 29801, 29803, 29805, 29810, 29812–13, 29817, 29826–27, 29836, 29839, 29843, 29846, 29849, 29853, 29901–07, 29909–11, 29913–16, 29918, 29920–28, 29932–36, 29938–41, 29943–45

* * *

THIRD DISTRICT

J. GRESHAM BARRETT, Republican, of Westminster, SC; born in Oconee County, SC, February 14, 1961; education: B.S., Business Administration, The Citadel, 1983; military service: U.S. Army, 1983–87; professional: small businessman; organizations: Westminster Rotary Club; Oconee County Boy Scouts; Westminster Chamber of Commerce; Oconee County Red Cross; public service: South Carolina House of Representatives, 1997–2002; religion: Baptist; attends Westminster Baptist Church; married to Natalie; children: Madison, Jeb, and Ross; committees: Financial Services; Foreign Affairs; Standard of Official Conduct; elected to the 108th Congress on November 5, 2002; reelected to each succeeding Congress.

Office Listings

http://www.house.gov/barrett

439 Cannon House Office Building, Washington, DC 20515 .... (202) 225–5301
Chief of Staff.—Darryl Broome. FAX: 225–3216
Legislative Director.—James Miller.
303 West Beltline Boulevard, Anderson, SC 29625 .... (864) 224–7401
115 Enterprise Court, Suite B, Greenwood, SC 29649 .... (864) 223–8251
233 Pendleton Street, NW., Aiken, SC 29801 .... (803) 649–5571

Counties: ABBEVILLE, AIKEN (part), ANDERSON, EDGEFIELD, GREENWOOD, LAURENS (part), MCCORMICK, OCONEE, PICKENS, SALUDA. Population (2000), 668,669.

ZIP Codes: 29006, 29037, 29070, 29105, 29127–29, 29138, 29166, 29178, 29325, 29332, 29334–35, 29351, 29355, 29360, 29370, 29384, 29388, 29406, 29611, 29620–28, 29630–33, 29635, 29638–49, 29653–59, 29661, 29664–67, 29669–73, 29675–79, 29682, 29684–86, 29689, 29691–93, 29695–97, 29801–05, 29808–09, 29816, 29819, 29821–22, 29824, 29828–29, 29831–32, 29834–35, 29838, 29840–42, 29844–45, 29847–48, 29850–51, 29853, 29856, 29860–61

* * *

FOURTH DISTRICT

BOB INGLIS, Republican, of Travelers Rest, SC; born in Savannah, GA, October 11, 1959; native of Bluffton, SC; education: May River Academy, Bluffton, SC, 1977; Duke University, Durham, NC, 1981; University of Virginia Law School, Charlottesville, VA, 1984; professional: attorney; admitted to the South Carolina Bar, 1984; Hunger, Maclean, Exley & Dunn (law firm), 1984–86; Leatherwood, Walker, Todd & Mann (law firm), 1986–92 and 1999–2004; religion: Presbyterian; member, Redeemer Presbyterian Church; married: the former Mary Anne Williams, 1982; five children; U.S. House of Representatives, 1993–98; committees: Foreign Affairs; Science and Technology; elected to the 109th Congress on November 2, 2004; reelected to each succeeding Congress.

Office Listings

http://www.inglis.house.gov

100 Cannon House Office Building, Washington, DC 20515 .... (202) 225–6030
Chief of Staff.—Wayne Roper. FAX: 226–1177
Deputy Chief of Staff/Legislative Director.—Garth Van Meter.
Legislative Assistants: Whitt Hance, Marcus Huskey, Cynthia Lewis, Catrina Rorke, David Weil.
Executive Assistant.—Katie Banks.
105 North Spring Street, Suite 111, Greenville, SC 29601 .... (864) 232–1141
Communications Director.—Price Atkinson.
145 North Church Street, BTC #56, Spartanburg, SC 29306 .... (864) 582–6422

Constituent Liaison: Dwayne Hatchett, Brent Troxell.

Counties: GREENVILLE, LAURENS (part), SPARTANBURG, UNION. Population (2000), 668,669.

ZIP Codes: 29031, 29178, 29301–07, 29316, 29318–24, 29329–31, 29333–36, 29338, 29346, 29348–49, 29353, 29356, 29364–65, 29368–69, 29372–79, 29385–86, 29388, 29390–91, 29395, 29564, 29601–17, 29627, 29635–36, 29644–45, 29650–52, 29654, 29661–62, 29669, 29673, 29680–81, 29683, 29687–88, 29690, 29698

* * *

FIFTH DISTRICT

JOHN M. SPRATT, JR., Democrat, of York, SC; born in Charlotte, NC, November 1, 1942; education: graduated, York High School, 1960; A.B., Davidson College, 1964; president of student body and Phi Beta Kappa, Davidson College; M.A., economics, Oxford University, Corpus Christi College (Marshall Scholar), 1966; LL.B., Yale Law School, 1969; admitted to the South Carolina Bar in 1969; military service: active duty, U.S. Army, 1969–71, discharged as captain; member: Operations Analysis Group, Office of the Assistant Secretary of Defense (Comptroller), received Meritorious Service Medal; professional: private practice of law, Spratt, McKeown and Spratt, York, SC, 1971–82; attorney, York County, 1973–82; president, Bank of Fort Mill, 1973–82; president, Spratt Insurance Agency, Inc.; president, York Chamber of Commerce; chairman, Winthrop College Board of Visitors; chairman, Divine Saviour Hospital Board; board of visitors, Davidson and Coker Colleges; president, Western York County United Fund; board of directors, Piedmont Legal Services; House of Delegates, South Carolina bar; religion: elder, First Presbyterian Church, York; married: Jane Stacy Spratt, 1968; children: Susan, Sarah, and Catherine; committees: chair, Budget; Armed Services; elected to the 98th Congress, November 2, 1982; reelected to each succeeding Congress.

Office Listings

http://www.spratt.house.gov

1401 Longworth House Office Building, Washington, DC 20515 .... (202) 225–5501
Chief of Staff.—Dawn O'Connell. FAX: 225–0464
Deputy Chief of Staff / Communications Director.—Chuck Fant.
P.O. Box 350, Rock Hill, SC 29731 .... (803) 327–1114
District Administrator.—Robert Hopkins.
707 Bultman Drive, Sumter, SC 29150 .... (803) 773–3362
88 Public Square, Darlington, SC 29532–0025 .... (843) 393–3998

Counties: CHEROKEE, CHESTER, CHESTERFIELD, DARLINGTON, DILLON, FAIRFIELD, FLORENCE (part), KERSHAW, LANCASTER, LEE, MARLBORO, NEWBERRY, SUMTER (part), YORK. Population (2000), 668,668.

ZIP Codes: 29009–10, 29014–16, 29020, 29031–32, 29036–37, 29040, 29045, 29055, 29058, 29065, 29067, 29069, 29074–75, 29078–79, 29101–02, 29104, 29106, 29108, 29122, 29126–28, 29130, 29132, 29145, 29150–54, 29161, 29163, 29175–76, 29178, 29180, 29203, 29218, 29307, 29323, 29330, 29332, 29340–42, 29355, 29372, 29501, 29506, 29512, 29516, 29520, 29525, 29532, 29536, 29540, 29543, 29547, 29550–51, 29563, 29565, 29567, 29570, 29573–74, 29581, 29584, 29592–94, 29596, 29654, 29702–04, 29706, 29708–10, 29712, 29714–18, 29720–22, 29724, 29726–32, 29734, 29741–45

* * *

SIXTH DISTRICT

JAMES E. CLYBURN, Democrat, of Columbia, SC; born in Sumter, SC, July 21, 1940; education: graduated, Mather Academy, Camden, SC, 1957; B.S., South Carolina State University, Orangeburg, 1962; attended University of South Carolina Law School, Columbia, 1972–74; professional: South Carolina State Human Affairs Commissioner; assistant to the Governor for Human Resource Development; executive director, South Carolina Commission for Farm Workers, Inc.; director, Neighborhood Youth Corps and New Careers; counselor, South Carolina Employment Security Commission; member: lifetime member, NAACP; Southern Regional Council; Omega Psi Phi Fraternity, Inc.; Arabian Temple, No. 139; Nemiah Lodge No. 51 F&AM; married: the former Emily England; children: Mignon, Jennifer and Angela; elected vice chair, Democratic Caucus, 2002; chair, Democratic Caucus 2006; Majority Whip; elected on November 3, 1992, to the 103rd Congress; reelected to each succeeding Congress.

Office Listings

http://www.clyburn.house.gov

2135 Rayburn House Office Building, Washington, DC 20515 .... (202) 225–3315

Chief of Staff.—Yelberton Watkins. FAX: 225–2313
Deputy Chief of Staff.—Barvetta Singletary.
Legislative Director.—Danny Cromer.
Scheduler.—Jennie Chaplin.

1225 Lady Street, Suite 200, Columbia, SC 29201 .... (803) 799–1100
District Director.—Robert Nance.

181 East Evans Street, Suite 314, Post Office Box 6286, Florence, SC 29502 .... (803) 662–1212

176 Brooks Boulevard, Santee, SC 29142 .... (803) 854–4700

Counties: BAMBERG COUNTY. CITIES AND TOWNSHIPS: Bamberg, Denmark, Erhardt, Olar. BERKELEY COUNTY (part). CITIES AND TOWNSHIPS: Bethera, Cross, Daniel Island, Huger, Jamestown, Pineville, Russellville, Saint Stephen, Wando. CALHOUN COUNTY (part). CITY OF: Cameron, Creston, Fort Motte, St. Matthews. CHARLESTON COUNTY (part). CITIES AND TOWNSHIPS: Adams Run, Charleston, Edisto Island, Hollywood, Johns Island, Ravenel, Wadmalaw Island. CLARENDON COUNTY. CITIES AND TOWNSHIPS: Alcolu, Davis Station, Gable, Manning, New Zion, Rimini, Summerton, Turbeville. COLLETON COUNTY. CITIES AND TOWNSHIPS: Ashton, Cottageville, Green Pond, Hendersonville, Islandton, Jacksonboro, Lodge, Ritter, Round O, Smoaks, Walterboro, Williams. DORCHESTER COUNTY (part). CITIES AND TOWNSHIPS: Dorchester, Harleyville, Reevesville, Ridgeville, Rosinville, Saint George. FLORENCE COUNTY (part). CITIES AND TOWNSHIPS: Coward, Effingham, Florence, Johnsonville, Lake City, Olanta, Pamplico, Quinby, Scranton, Timmonsville. GEORGETOWN COUNTY (part). CITIES AND TOWNSHIPS: Andrews, Outland, Sampit. MARION COUNTY. CITIES AND TOWNSHIPS: Centenary, Gresham, Marion, Mullins, Nichols, Rains, Sellers. LEE COUNTY (part). CITIES AND TOWNSHIPS: Elliott, Lynchburg. ORANGEBURG COUNTY (part). CITIES AND TOWNSHIPS: Bowman, Branchville, Cardova, Cope, Elloree, Eutawville, Holly Hill, Norway, Orangeburg, Rowesville, Santee, Vance. RICHLAND COUNTY (part). CITIES AND TOWNSHIPS: Blythewood, Columbia, Eastover, Gadsden, Hopkins. SUMTER COUNTY (part). CITIES AND TOWNSHIPS: Mayesville, Oswego, Pinewood, Sumter. WILLIAMSBURG COUNTY. CITIES AND TOWNSHIPS: Cades, Greeleyville, Hemingway, Kingstree, Lane, Nesmith, Salters, and Trio. Population (2000), 668,670.

ZIP Codes: 29001, 29003, 29006, 29010, 29018, 29030, 29038–42, 29044–48, 29051–52, 29056, 29059, 29061–62, 29078, 29080–82, 29102, 29104, 29107, 29111, 29113–15, 29117–18, 29125, 29128, 29130, 29133, 29135, 29142–43, 29146, 29148, 29150, 29153–54, 29161–63, 29168, 29201–05, 29208–09, 29211, 29214–17, 29220, 29223, 29225, 29228, 29230, 29240, 29250, 29403, 29405–06, 29409, 29415, 29418, 29426, 29430–38, 29440, 29446–50, 29452–53, 29461, 29466, 29468, 29470–72, 29474–77, 29479, 29481, 29488, 29492–93, 29501–06, 29510, 29518–19, 29530, 29541, 29546, 29554–56, 29560, 29565, 29571, 29574, 29580–81, 29583, 29589–92, 29817, 29843, 29929, 29931, 29945

SOUTH DAKOTA

(Population 2000, 754,844)

SENATORS

TIM JOHNSON, Democrat, of Vermillion, SD, born in Canton, SD, December 28, 1946; education: B.A., Phi Beta Kappa, University of South Dakota, 1969; M.A., political science, University of South Dakota, 1970; post-graduate study in political science, Michigan State University, 1970–71; J.D., University of South Dakota, 1975; budget advisor to the Michigan State Senate Appropriations Committee, 1971–72; admitted to the South Dakota bar in 1975 and began private law practice in Vermillion; elected to the South Dakota House of Representatives, 1978; reelected, 1980; elected to the South Dakota State Senate, 1982; reelected, 1984; served on the Joint Appropriations Committee and the Senate Judiciary Committee; served as Clay County Deputy State's Attorney, 1985; awards: named Outstanding Citizen of Vermillion, 1983; received South Dakota Education Association's ''Friend of Education'' Award, 1983; Billy Sutton Award for Legislative Achievement, 1984; elected to the U.S. House of Representatives, 1986; reelected to each succeeding Congress; delegate, Democratic National Convention, 1988–92; member: President's Export Council, 1999; religion: Lutheran; married: Barbara Brooks, 1969; children: Brooks, Brendan and Kelsey Marie; committees: Appropriations; Banking, Housing, and Urban Affairs; Energy and Natural Resources; Indian Affairs; elected to the U.S. Senate on November 5, 1996; reelected to each succeeding Senate term.

Office Listings

http://johnson.senate.gov

136 Hart Senate Office Building, Washington, DC 20510 .... (202) 224–5842
Chief of Staff.—Drey Samuelson. FAX: 228–5765
Legislative Director.—Todd Stubbendieck.
Communications Director.—Julianne Fisher.
5015 South Bar Oak, Sioux Falls, SD 57108 .... (605) 332–8896
State Director.—Sharon Boysen.
320 South First Street, Suite 103, Aberdeen, SD 57401 .... (605) 226–3440
405 East Omaha Street, Suite B, Rapid City, SD 57701 .... (605) 341–3990

* * *

JOHN THUNE, Republican, of Sioux Falls, SD; born in Pierre, SD, January 7, 1961; education: Jones County High School, 1979; B.S., business administration, Biola University, CA; M.B.A., University of South Dakota, 1984; professional: executive director, South Dakota Municipal League; board of directors, National League of Cities; executive director, South Dakota Republican Party, 1989–91; appointed, State Railroad Director, 1991; former congressional legislative assistant, and deputy staff director; elected, U.S. House of Representatives, 1997–2003; married: Kimberly Weems, 1984; children: Brittany and Larissa; committees: Agriculture, Nutrition, and Forestry; Armed Services; Commerce, Science, and Transportation; Small Business and Entrepreneurship; elected to the U.S. Senate on November 2, 2004.

Office Listings

http://thune.senate.gov

493 Russell Senate Office Building, Washington, DC 20510 .... (202) 224–2321
Chief of Staff.—Matt Zabel. FAX: 228–5429
General Counsel.—Summer Mersinger.
Legislative Director.—Dave Schwietert.
Communications Director.—Andi Fouberg.
320 North Main Avenue, Suite B, Sioux Falls, SD 57104 .... (605) 334–9596
1312 West Main Street, Rapid City, SD 57701 .... (605) 348–7551
320 South First Street, Suite 101, Aberdeen, SD 57401 .... (605) 225–8823

REPRESENTATIVE

AT LARGE

STEPHANIE HERSETH SANDLIN, Democrat, of Brookings, SD; born in Aberdeen, SD, December 3, 1970; education: graduated, Valedictorian, Groton High School; B.A. in Government, Georgetown University, *summa cum laude* and Phi Beta Kappa; J.D., with honors from the Georgetown University Law Center, and was a senior editor of the law review; professional: attorney; member, South Dakota Bar; served on the faculty of Georgetown University Law Center; worked on telecommunications and energy issues for the South Dakota Public Utilities Commission; organized commission meetings with Indian tribal leaders regarding utility regulation on Indian reservations; worked with U.S. District Court Judge Charles B. Kornmann; also served as a law clerk on the U.S. Court of Appeals for the Fourth Circuit; Executive Director, South Dakota Farmers Union Foundation; committees: Agriculture; Natural Resources; Veterans' Affairs; Select Committee on Energy Independence and Global Warming; elected to the 108th Congress by special election, on June 1, 2004; reelected to each succeeding Congress.

Office Listings

http://www.hersethsandlin.house.gov

331 Cannon House Office Building, Washington, DC 20515 .... (202) 225–2801
Chief of Staff.—Tessa Gould. FAX: 225–5823
Deputy Chief of Staff.—Russ Levsen.
Press Secretary.—Betsy Hart.
Legislative Director.—Josh Albert.
Scheduler.—Margaret Sampson.
326 East 8th Street, Suite 108, Sioux Falls, SD 57103 .... (605) 367–8371
Southeast Director.—Steven Dahlmeier.
343 Quincy Street, Sutie 102, Rapid City, SD 57702 .... (605) 394–5280
Western Director.—Kate Kelley.
121 Fourth Avenue, SW., Suite 1, Aberdeen, SD 57401 .... (605) 626–3440
District Director.—Maeve King.

Population (2000), 754,844.

ZIP Codes: 57001–07, 57010, 57012–18, 57020–22, 57024–59, 57061–73, 57075–79, 57101, 57103–10, 57117–18, 57186, 57188–89, 57192–98, 57201, 57212–14, 57216–21, 57223–27, 57231–39, 57241–43, 57245–49, 57251–53, 57255–66, 57268–74, 57276, 57278–79, 57301, 57311–15, 57317, 57319, 57321–26, 57328–32, 57334–35, 57337, 57339–42, 57344–46, 57348–50, 57353–56, 57358–59, 57361–71, 57373–76, 57379–86, 57399, 57401–02, 57420–22, 57424, 57426–30, 57432–42, 57445–46, 57448–52, 57454–57, 57460–61, 57465–77, 57479, 57481, 57501, 57520–23, 57528–29, 57531–34, 57536–38, 57540–44, 57547–48, 57551–53, 57555, 57559–60, 57562–64, 57566–72, 57574, 57576–77, 57579–80, 57584–85, 57601, 57620–23, 57625–26, 57630–34, 57636, 57638–42, 57644–46, 57648–52, 57656–61, 57701–03, 57706, 57709, 57714, 57716–20, 57722, 57724–25, 57730, 57732, 57735, 57737–38, 57741, 57744–45, 57747–48, 57750–52, 57754–56, 57758–64, 57766–67, 57769–70, 57772–73, 57775–77, 57779–80, 57782–83, 57785, 57787–88, 57790–94, 57799

TENNESSEE

(Population 2000, 5,689,283)

SENATORS

LAMAR ALEXANDER, Republican, of Nashville, TN; born in Maryville, TN, July 3, 1940; education: graduated with honors in Latin American history, Phi Beta Kappa, Vanderbilt University; New York University Law School; served as Law Review editor; professional: clerk to Judge John Minor Wisdom, U.S. Court of Appeals in New Orleans; legislative assistant to Senator Howard Baker (R–TN), 1967; executive assistant to Bryce Harlow, counselor to President Nixon, 1969; President, University of Tennessee, 1988–91; co-director, Empower America, 1994–95; helped found a company that is now the nation's largest provider of worksite day care, Bright Horizons; public service: Republican nominee for Governor of Tennessee, 1974; Governor of Tennessee, 1979–87; U.S. Secretary of Education, 1991–93; community service: chairman, Salvation Army Red Shield Family Initiative; chairman, Senate Republican Conference; and the Museum of Appalachia in Norris, TN; received Tennessee Conservation League Conservationist of the Year Award; family: married to Honey Alexander; four children; committees: Appropriations; Budget; Environment and Public Works; Health, Education, Labor, and Pensions; Rules and Administration; elected to the U.S. Senate on November 5, 2002.

Office Listings

http://alexander.senate.gov

455 Dirksen Senate Office Building, Washington, DC 20510 .... (202) 224–4944
Chief of Staff.—David Morgenstern. FAX: 228–3398
Legislative Director.—Matt Sonnesyn.
Press Secretary.—Jim Jeffries.
Executive Assistant / Scheduler.—Bonnie Sansonetti.
3322 West End Avenue, Suite 120, Nashville, TN 37203 .... (615) 736–5129
Howard H. Baker, Jr. U.S. Courthouse; 800 Market Street, Suite 112, Knoxville, TN 37902 .... (865) 545–4253
Federal Building, 167 North Main Street, Suite 1068, Memphis, TN 38103 .... (901) 544–4224
Federal Building, 109 South Highland Street, Suite B–9, Jackson, TN 38301 .... (731) 423–9344
Joel E. Solomon Federal Building, 900 Georgia Avenue, Suite 260, Chattanooga, TN 37402 .... (423) 752–5337
Tri-Cities Regional Airport, Terminal Building, P.O. Box 1113, 2525 Highway 75, Suite 101, Blountville, TN 37617 .... (423) 325–6240

* * *

BOB CORKER, Republican, of Chattanooga, TN; born in Orangeburg, SC, August 24, 1952; education: B.S., Industrial Management, University of Tennessee, Knoxville, TN, 1974; professional: founder of Bencor Corporation, a construction company specializing in retail properties which operated in 18 states, 1978–90; founder of the Corker Group, acquisition, development, and operation of commercial real estate, 1982–2006; honors: named to the University of Tennessee at Chattanooga's ''Entrepreneurial Hall of Fame,'' 2005; community service: founding chair, Chattanooga Neighborhood Enterprise, Inc., a non-profit organization that has helped over 10,000 families secure decent, fit and affordable housing, 1986–92; public service: commissioner, State of Tennessee Department of Finance and Administration, 1995–96; mayor, City of Chattanooga, 2001–05; married: Elizabeth Corker, 1987; two children: Julia and Emily; committees: Banking, Housing, and Urban Affairs; Energy and Natural Resources; Foreign Relations; Special Committee on Aging; elected to the U.S. Senate on November 7, 2006.

Office Listings

http://corker.senate.gov

185 Dirksen Senate Office Building, Washington, DC 20510 .... (202) 224–3344
Chief of Staff.—Todd Womack. FAX: 228–0566
Legislative Director.—Paul Palagyi.
Executive Assistant / Scheduler.—Ramona Lessen.
Press Secretary.—Laura Lefler.
3322 West End Avenue, Suite 610, Nashville, TN 37203 .... (615) 279–8125
100 Peabody Place, Suite 1335, Memphis, TN 38103 .... (901) 683–1910
Howard Baker Federal Building, 800 Market Street, Suite 121, Knoxville, TN 37902 .... (865) 637–4180
Tri-Cities Regional Airport 2525, Highway 75, Suite 126, Blountville, TN 37617 .. (423) 323–1252
10 West Martin Luther King Boulevard, Sixth Floor, Chattanooga, TN 37402 .... (423) 756–2757
Ed Jones Federal Building, 109 South Highland Avenue, Suite B8, Jackson, TN 38301 .... (731) 424–9655

REPRESENTATIVES

FIRST DISTRICT

DAVID "PHIL" ROE, Republican, of Johnson City, TN; born in Clarksville, TN; July 21, 1945; education: B.S., Austin Peay State University Clarksville, TN, 1967; M.D., University of Tennessee, Knoxville, TN, 1970; professional: United States Army Medical Corps, 1970–72; Vice Mayor of Johnson City, 2003–07; Mayor of Johnson City, 2007–09; Physicians' Caucus; Health Caucus; religion: Members of Munsey United Methodist Church; married: Pam; children: David C. Roe, John Roe, and Whitney Larkin: committees: Agriculture; Education and Labor; Veterans Affairs; elected to the 111th Congress.

Office Listings

http://www.roe.house.gov

419 Cannon House Office Building, Washington, DC 20515 .... (202) 225–6356
Chief of Staff.—Andrew Duke. FAX: 225–5714
Communications Director.—Amanda Little.
Scheduler.—Amber Aimar.
Legislative Director.—Matt Meyer.
Staff Assistant.—Tiffany McGuffee.
205 Revere Street, Kingsport, TN 37660 .... (423) 247–8161
FAX: 247–0119
Higher Education Building, P.O. Box 1728, Kingsport, TN 37662.
District Director.—Bill Snodgrass
Field Representative.—John Abe Teague.
Administrative Assistant.—Sheila Houser.
Caseworker.—Carolyn Ferguson.
1609 College Park Drive, Suite 4, Morristown, TN 37813 .... (423) 254–1400
Field Representative.—Danny Roy Price. FAX: 254–1403
Caseworkers: Cheryl Bennett, Ann Reuschel.

Counties: CARTER, COCKE, GREENE, HAMBLEN, HANCOCK, HAWKINS, JEFFERSON, JOHNSON, SEVIER, SULLIVAN, UNICOI, WASHINGTON. Population (2000), 632,143.

ZIP Codes: 37601–02, 37604–05, 37614–18, 37620–21, 37625, 37640–45, 37650, 37656–60, 37662–65, 37680–84, 37686–88, 37690–92, 37694, 37699, 37711, 37713, 37722, 37725, 37727, 37731, 37738, 37743–45, 37752–53, 37760, 37764–65, 37778, 37809–11, 37813–16, 37818, 37821–22, 37843, 37857, 37860, 37862–65, 37868–69, 37873, 37876–77, 37879, 37881, 37890–91

* * *

SECOND DISTRICT

JOHN J. DUNCAN, JR., Republican, of Knoxville, TN; born in Lebanon, TN, July 21, 1947; education: B.S. in journalism, University of Tennessee, 1969; J.D., National Law Center, George Washington University, 1973; served in both the Army National Guard and the U.S. Army Reserves, retiring with the rank of captain; private law practice, Knoxville, 1973–81; appointed State Trial Judge by Governor Lamar Alexander in 1981 and elected to a full eight-year term in 1982 without opposition, receiving the highest number of votes of any candidate on the ballot that year; member: American Legion 40 and 8, Elks, Sertoma Club, Masons, Scottish Rite and Shrine; present or past board member: Red Cross, Girl's Club, YWCA, Sunshine Center for the Mentally Retarded, Beck Black Heritage Center, Knoxville Union Rescue Mission, Senior Citizens Home Aid Service; religion: active elder at Eastminster Presbyterian Church; married: the former Lynn Hawkins; children: Tara, Whitney, John J. III and Zane; committees: Natural Resources; Oversight and Government Reform; Transportation and Infrastructure; elected to both the 100th Congress (special election) and the 101st Congress in separate elections held on November 8, 1988; reelected to each succeeding Congress.

Office Listings

http://www.house.gov/duncan

2207 Rayburn House Office Building, Washington, DC 20515 .... (202) 225–5435
Chief of Staff.—Bob Griffitts. FAX: 225–6440
Deputy Chief of Staff.—Don Walker.
Press Secretary.—Amy Westmoreland.
6 East Madison Avenue, Athens, TN 37303 .... (423) 745–4671
800 Market Street, Suite 100, Knoxville, TN 37902 .... (423) 523–3772
District Director.—Bob Griffitts.
200 East Broadway Avenue, Suite 414, Maryville, TN 37804 .... (423) 984–5464

Counties: BLOUNT, KNOX (part), LOUDON, MCMINN, MONROE. CITIES AND TOWNSHIPS: Alcoa, Athens, Englewood, Etowah, Farragut, Halls (Knox Co.), Knoxville, Lenoir City, Loudon, Madisonville, Maryville, Powell, Seymour, and Sweetwater. Population (2000), 632,144.

ZIP Codes: 37303, 37309, 37311–12, 37314, 37322–23, 37325, 37329, 37331, 37353–54, 37369–71, 37385, 37701, 37709, 37721, 37725, 37737, 37742, 37754, 37764, 37771–72, 37774, 37777, 37779, 37801–04, 37806–07, 37820, 37826, 37830, 37846, 37849, 37853, 37865, 37871, 37874, 37876, 37878, 37880, 37882, 37885–86, 37901–02, 37909, 37912, 37914–24, 37927–33, 37938–40, 37950, 37990, 37995–98

* * *

THIRD DISTRICT

ZACH WAMP, Republican, of Chattanooga, TN; born in Fort Benning, GA, October 28, 1957; graduated, McCallie School, Chattanooga, 1976; attended University of North Carolina at Chapel Hill and University of Tennessee; commercial and industrial real estate broker; named Chattanooga Business Leader of the Year; chairman, Hamilton County Republican Party; regional director, Tennessee Republican Party; awards: received Tennessee Jaycees' Outstanding Young Tennessean Award, 1996; U.S. Chamber of Commerce Spirit of Enterprise Award; Citizens Against Government Waste ''A'' Rating; National Taxpayers Union Friend of the Taxpayers Award; recognized by the Citizens Taxpayers Association of Hamilton County, the National Federation of Independent Business and the Concord Coalition for casting tough votes to reduce spending; member, Red Bank Baptist Church; married: Kimberly Watts Wamp, 1985; two children: Weston and Coty; committees: Appropriations; elected to the 104th Congress; reelected to each succeeding Congress.

Office Listings

http://www.house.gov/wamp

1436 Longworth House Office Building, Washington, DC 20515 .... (202) 225–3271
Chief of Staff.—Helen Hardin. FAX: 225–3494
Legislative Director.—Melissa Chapman.
Scheduler.—Emily Hall.
900 Georgia Avenue, Suite 126, Chattanooga, TN 37402 .... (423) 756–2342
District Director.—Leigh McClure.
Federal Building, 200 Administration Road, Suite 100, Oak Ridge, TN 37830 .... (865) 576–1976
District Director.—Gina McMahon.

Counties: ANDERSON, BRADLEY, CLAIBORNE, GRAINGER, HAMILTON, JEFFERSON (part), MEIGS, POLK, RHEA, ROANE (part), UNION. Population (2000), 632,143.

ZIP Codes: 37302, 37304, 37307–12, 37315–17, 37320–23, 37325–26, 37332–33, 37336–38, 37341, 37343, 37350–51, 37353, 37361–64, 37369, 37373, 37375, 37377, 37379, 37381, 37384, 37391, 37397, 37401–12, 37414–16, 37419, 37421–22, 37424, 37450, 37705, 37707–10, 37715–17, 37719, 37721, 37724–26, 37730, 37752, 37754, 37760, 37763–64, 37769, 37771, 37774, 37779, 37806–07, 37811, 37820–21, 37824–26, 37828, 37830–31, 37840, 37846, 37848–49, 37851, 37861, 37866, 37869–71, 37874, 37876–77, 37879–81, 37888, 37890, 37931, 37938

* * *

FOURTH DISTRICT

LINCOLN DAVIS, Democrat, of Pall Mall, TN; born in Pall Mall, September 13, 1943; education: Alvin C. York Agricultural Institute, 1962; B.S., Agronomy, Tennessee Technological University, 1966; professional: farmer and general contractor; civic organizations: Tennessee State Jaycees; Pickett County Chamber of Commerce; Upper Cumberland Developmental District; Boy Scouts; public service: Mayor of Byrdstown, TN, 1978–82; Tennessee State Representative, 1980–84; Tennessee State Senator, 1996–2002; religion: Baptist; married: Lynda; children: Larissa, Lynn and Libby; committees: Appropriations; Science and Technology; elected to the 108th Congress on November 5, 2002; reelected to each succeeding Congress.

Office Listings

http://www.house.gov/lincolndavis

410 Cannon House Office Building, Washington, DC 20515 .... (202) 225–6831
Chief of Staff.—Beecher Frasier. FAX: 226–5172
Legislative Director.—Brandi Lowell.
Press Secretary.—Tom Hayden.
1064 North Gateway Avenue, Rockwood, TN 37854 .... (865) 354–3323
629 North Main Street, Jamestown, TN 38556 .... (931) 879–2361

1804 Carmack Boulevard, Suite A, Columbia, TN 38401 .... (931) 490–8699
477 North Chancery Street, Suite A–1, McMinnville, TN 37110 .... (931) 473–7251

Counties: BLEDSOE, CAMPBELL, COFFEE, CUMBERLAND, FENTRESS, FRANKLIN, GILES, GRUNDY, HICKMAN (part), LAWRENCE, LEWIS, LINCOLN, MARION, MAURY, MOORE, MORGAN, PICKETT, ROANE (part), SCOTT, SEQUATCHIE, VAN BUREN, WARREN, WHITE, WILLIAMSON (part). Population (2000), 632,143.

ZIP Codes: 37018, 37025–26, 37033, 37037, 37047, 37062, 37064, 37078, 37091, 37096, 37098, 37110–11, 37129–33, 37137, 37144, 37160, 37166, 37171, 37174, 37179, 37183, 37190, 37301, 37305–06, 37313, 37318, 37324, 37327–28, 37330, 37334–35, 37337, 37339–40, 37342, 37345, 37347–49, 37352, 37355–57, 37359–60, 37365–67, 37374–83, 37387–89, 37394, 37396–98, 37419, 37714–15, 37719, 37721, 37723, 37726, 37729, 37732–33, 37748, 37755–57, 37762–63, 37766, 37769–71, 37773, 37778, 37819, 37829, 37840–41, 37845, 37847, 37852, 37854, 37867, 37869–70, 37872, 37880, 37887, 37892, 38370, 38401–02, 38449, 38451, 38453–57, 38459–64, 38468–69, 38472–78, 38481–83, 38486–88, 38504, 38506, 38549–50, 38553, 38555–59, 38565, 38571–72, 38574, 38577–79, 38581, 38583, 38585, 38587, 38589

* * *

FIFTH DISTRICT

JIM COOPER, Democrat, of Nashville, TN; born in Nashville, June 19, 1954; education: B.A., history and economics, University of North Carolina at Chapel Hill, 1975; Rhodes Scholar, Oxford University, 1977; J.D., Harvard Law School, 1980; admitted to Tennessee bar, 1980; professional: attorney; Waller, Lansden, Dortch, and Davis (law firm), 1980–82; Managing Director, Equitable Securities, 1995–99; Adjunct Professor, Vanderbilt University Owen School of Management, 1995–2002; partner, Brentwood Capital Advisors LLC, 1999–2002; married: Martha Hays; children: Mary, Jamie, and Hayes; committees: Armed Services; Oversight and Government Reform; elected to the U.S. House of Representatives, 1982–95; elected to the 108th Congress on November 5, 2002; reelected to each succeeding Congress.

Office Listings

http://www.cooper.house.gov

1536 Longworth House Office Building, Washington, DC 20515 .... (202) 225–4311
Chief of Staff.—Lisa Quigley. FAX: 226–1035
Legislative Director.—James Leuschen.
605 Church Street, Nashville, TN 37219 .... (615) 736–5295

Counties: CHEATHAM (part), DAVIDSON, WILSON (part). Population (2000), 632,143.

ZIP Codes: 37011, 37013, 37015, 37027, 37032, 37034–35, 37064, 37070–72, 37076, 37080, 37082, 37086–88, 37090, 37115–16, 37121–22, 37135, 37138, 37143, 37146, 37189, 37201–22, 37224, 37227–30, 37232, 37234–36, 37238–50

* * *

SIXTH DISTRICT

BART GORDON, Democrat, of Murfreesboro, TN; born in Murfreesboro, January 24, 1949; graduated, Central High School, Murfreesboro, 1967; B.S., *cum laude*, Middle Tennessee State University, Murfreesboro, 1971; J.D., University of Tennessee College of Law, Knoxville, 1973; professional: served in U.S. Army Reserves, 1971–72; admitted to the Tennessee State Bar, 1974; opened private law practice in Murfreesboro, 1974; elected to the Tennessee Democratic Party's executive committee, 1974; appointed executive director of the Tennessee Democratic Party, 1979; elected the first full-time chairman of the Tennessee Democratic Party, 1981; resigned chairmanship, 1983, to successfully seek congressional seat; past chairman: Rutherford County United Givers Fund and Rutherford County Cancer Crusade; board member: Rutherford County Chamber of Commerce, MTSU Foundation; member, St. Mark's Methodist Church, Murfreesboro; married: Leslie Peyton Gordon; child: Peyton Margaret; committees: chair, Science and Technology; Energy and Commerce; elected to the 99th Congress on November 6, 1984; reelected to each succeeding Congress.

Office Listings

http://www.gordon.house.gov

2306 Rayburn House Office Building, Washington, DC 20515 .... (202) 225–4231
Chief of Staff.—Julie Eubank. FAX: 225–6887
Scheduler.—Amy Taylor.
P.O. Box 1986, 305 West Main Street, Murfreesboro, TN 37133 .... (615) 896–1986

District Chief of Staff.—Kent Syler.
P.O. Box 1140, 15 South Jefferson, Cookeville, TN 38501 .... (931) 528–5907
Sumner County Courthouse, Room B–100, Gallatin, TN 37066 .... (615) 451–5174

Counties: BEDFORD, CANNON, CLAY, DEKALB, JACKSON, MACON, MARSHALL, OVERTON, PUTNAM, ROBERTSON, RUTHERFORD, SMITH, SUMNER, TROUSDALE, WILSON (part). CITIES AND TOWNSHIPS: Carthage, Celina, Cookeville, Gainesboro, Gallatin, Hartsville, Lafayette, Lewisburg, Livingston, Murfreesboro, Shelbyville, Smithville, Springfield, Watertown, and Woodbury. Population (2000), 632,143.

ZIP Codes: 37010, 37012, 37014, 37016, 37018–20, 37022, 37026, 37030–32, 37034, 37037, 37046–49, 37057, 37059–60, 37063, 37066, 37072–75, 37077, 37080, 37083, 37085–87, 37090–91, 37095, 37110, 37118–19, 37122, 37127–28, 37135–36, 37141, 37144–46, 37148–53, 37160–62, 37166–67, 37172, 37174, 37180, 37183–84, 37186, 37188, 37190, 37357, 37360, 37388, 38451, 38472, 38501–03, 38505–06, 38541–45, 38547–48, 38551–52, 38554, 38560, 38562–64, 38567–70, 38573–75, 38580–83, 38588–89

* * *

SEVENTH DISTRICT

MARSHA BLACKBURN, Republican, of Franklin, TN; born in Laurel, MS, June 6, 1952; education: B.S., Mississippi State University, 1973; professional: retail marketing; public service: American Council of Young Political Leaders; executive director, Tennessee Film, Entertainment, and Music Commission; chairman, Governor's Prayer Breakfast; Tennessee State Senate, 1998–2002; minority whip; community service: Rotary Club; Chamber of Commerce; Arthritis Foundation; Nashville Symphony Guild Board; Tennessee Biotechnology Association; March of Dimes; American Lung Association; awards: Chi Omega Alumnae Greek Woman of the Year, 1999; Middle Tennessee 100 Most Powerful People, 1999–2002; married: Chuck; children: Mary Morgan Ketchel and Chad; committees: Energy and Commerce; Select Committee on Energy Independence and Global Warming; elected to the 108th Congress on November 5, 2002; reelected to each succeeding Congress.

Office Listings

http://www.house.gov/blackburn

217 Cannon House Office Building, Washington, DC 20515 .... (202) 225–2811
Chief of Staff.—Steve Brophy. FAX: 225–3004
Executive Assistant.—Katie Morgan.
7975 Stage Hill Boulevard, Suite 1, Memphis, TN 38133 .... (901) 382–5811
City Hall Mall, 109 3rd Avenue South, Suite 117, Franklin, TN 37064 .... (615) 591–5161
1850 Memorial Drive, Clarksville, TN 37043 .... (931) 503–0391

Counties: CHEATHAM (part), CHESTER, DAVIDSON (part), DECATUR, FAYETTE, HARDEMAN, HARDIN, HENDERSON, HICKMAN (part), MCNAIRY, MONTGOMERY (part), PERRY, SHELBY (part), WAYNE, WILLIAMSON (part). Population (2000), 632,139.

ZIP Codes: 37010, 37014–15, 37024–25, 37027, 37032–33, 37035–36, 37040–43, 37046, 37052, 37055, 37060, 37062, 37064–65, 37067–69, 37079, 37082, 37096–98, 37101, 37135, 37137, 37140, 37155, 37174, 37179, 37187, 37191, 37211, 37215, 37220–21, 38002, 38004, 38008, 38010–11, 38014, 38016–18, 38027–29, 38036, 38039, 38042, 38044–46, 38048–49, 38052–53, 38057, 38060–61, 38066–69, 38075–76, 38088, 38128, 38133–34, 38138–39, 38141, 38163, 38183–84, 38310–11, 38313, 38315, 38321, 38326–29, 38332, 38334, 38339–41, 38345, 38347, 38351–52, 38356–57, 38359, 38361, 38363, 38365–68, 38370–72, 38374–76, 38379–81, 38388, 38390, 38392–93, 38425, 38450, 38452, 38463, 38471, 38475, 38485–86

* * *

EIGHTH DISTRICT

JOHN S. TANNER, Democrat, of Union City, TN; born at Dyersburg Army Air Base, Halls, TN, September 22, 1944; attended elementary and high school in Union City; B.S., University of Tennessee at Knoxville, 1966; J.D., University of Tennessee at Knoxville, 1968; professional: attorney; admitted to the Tennessee bar, 1968; commenced practice in Union City; served, U.S. Navy, lieutenant, 1968–72; colonel, Tennessee Army National Guard, 1974–2000; member, Elam, Glasgow, Tanner and Acree law firm until 1988; businessman; elected to Tennessee House of Representatives, 1976–88; chairman, House Committee on Commerce, 1987–88; member: Obion County Chamber of Commerce; Obion County Cancer Society; Union City Rotary Club, Paul Harris Fellow; Obion County Bar Association; American Legion; Masons; religion: First Christian Church (Disciples of Christ) of Union City; married: the former Betty Ann Portis; children: Elizabeth Tanner Atkins and John Portis; four grandchildren; member: chair, U.S. delegation to NATO Parliamentary Assembly; current President of the NATO Parliamentary Assembly; Blue Dog Coalition; Congressional Sportsmen's Caucus; committees: Foreign Affairs; Ways and Means; elected to the 101st Congress on November 8, 1988; reelected to each succeeding Congress.

Office Listings

http://www.house.gov/tanner

1226 Longworth House Office Building, Washington, DC 20515 .... (202) 225–4714
Administrative Assistant.—Vickie Walling. FAX: 225–1765
Communications Director.—Randy Ford.
Executive Assistant.—Kathy Becker.
203 West Church Street, Union City, TN 38261 .... (731) 885–7070
District Director.—Brad Thompson.
Federal Building, Room B–7, Jackson, TN 38301 .... (731) 423–4848
8120 Highway 51 North, Suite 3, Millington, TN 38053 .... (901) 873–5690

Counties: BENTON, CARROLL, CROCKETT, DICKSON, DYER, GIBSON, HAYWOOD, HENRY, HOUSTON, HUMPHREYS, LAKE, LAUDERDALE, MADISON, MONTGOMERY (part), OBION, SHELBY (part), STEWART, TIPTON, WEAKLEY. Population (2000), 632,142.

ZIP Codes: 37015, 37023, 37025, 37028–29, 37036, 37040, 37043–44, 37050–52, 37055–56, 37058, 37061–62, 37078–79, 37097, 37101, 37134, 37142, 37165, 37171, 37175, 37178, 37181, 37185, 37187, 38001, 38004, 38006–07, 38011–12, 38015, 38019, 38021, 38023–25, 38030, 38034, 38037, 38040–41, 38047, 38049–50, 38053–55, 38058–59, 38063, 38069–71, 38075, 38077, 38079–80, 38083, 38127–29, 38135, 38201, 38220–26, 38229–33, 38235–38, 38240–42, 38251, 38253–61, 38271, 38281, 38301–03, 38305, 38308, 38313–14, 38316–18, 38320–21, 38324, 38330–31, 38333, 38336–38, 38341–44, 38346, 38348, 38355–56, 38358, 38362, 38366, 38369, 38378, 38380, 38382, 38387, 38389–92

* * *

NINTH DISTRICT

STEPHEN IRA ''STEVE'' COHEN, Democrat, of Memphis, TN; born in Memphis, May 24, 1949 of Dr. Morris D. Cohen and Genevieve Cohen; B.A., Vanderbilt University in Nashville, TN, 1971; J.D., Cecil C. Humphreys School of Law of Memphis State University (renamed University of Memphis), 1973; Legal Advisor for the Memphis Police Department, 1974–77; Delegate to and Vice President of Tennessee Constitutional Convention, 1977; Commissioner on the Shelby County Commission, 1978–80; Tennessee State Senator for District 30, 1982–2006; Delegate at the 1980 and 1992 Democratic National Conventions; Regional Whip; committees: Judiciary; Transportation and Infrastructure; elected to the 110th Congress on November 7, 2006; reelected to the 111th Congress on November 4, 2008.

Office Listings

http://www.cohen.house.gov

1005 Longworth House Office Building, Washington, DC 20515 .... (202) 225–3265
Chief of Staff.—Marilyn Dillihay. FAX: 225–5663
Scheduler.—Craig Dulniak.
Legislative Director.—Reisha Phills.
Communications Director.—Steven Broderick.
167 North Main Street, Suite 369, Memphis, TN 38103 .... (901) 544–4131
FAX: 544–4329

County: SHELBY COUNTY (part). CITY OF: Memphis. Population (2000), 632,143.

ZIP Codes: 37501, 38016–18, 38101, 38103–09, 38111–20, 38122, 38124–28, 38130–37, 38139, 38141–42, 38145–48, 38151–52, 38157, 38159, 38161, 38165–68, 38173–75, 38177, 38181–82, 38186–88, 38190, 38193–95, 38197

TEXAS

(Population 2000, 20,851,820)

SENATORS

KAY BAILEY HUTCHISON, Republican, of Dallas, TX; born in Galveston, TX, July 22, 1943; raised in La Marque, TX; education: graduated, The University of Texas at Austin and The University of Texas School of Law; professional: Texas House of Representatives, 1972–76; appointed vice chair, National Transportation Safety Board, 1976; senior vice president and general counsel, RepublicBank Corporation; co-founded, Fidelity National Bank of Dallas; owned, McCraw Candies, Inc.; political and legal correspondent, KPRC–TV, Houston; member: development boards of SMU and Texas A&M schools of business; trustee, The University of Texas Law School Foundation; elected Texas State Treasurer, 1990; religion: Episcopalian; married: Ray Hutchison; committees: ranking member, Commerce, Science and Transportation; Appropriations; Banking, Housing, and Urban Affairs; Rules and Administration; elected to the U.S. Senate, by special election, on June 5, 1993, to fill the vacancy caused by the resignation of Senator Lloyd Bentsen; reelected to each succeeding Senate term.

Office Listings

http://hutchison.senate.gov

284 Russell Senate Office Building, Washington, DC 20510 .... (202) 224–5922
Deputy Chief of Staff.—James Christoferson.
Legislative Director.—Matthew Acock.
Federal Building, 300 East Eighth Street, Suite 961, Austin, TX 78701 .... (512) 916–5834
10440 North Central Expressway, Suite 1160, LB 606, Dallas, TX 75231 .... (214) 361–3500
1919 Smith Street, Suite 800, Houston, TX 77002 .... (713) 653–3456
1906–G Tyler Street, Harlingen, TX 78550 .... (956) 425–2253
500 Chestnut Street, Suite 1570, Abilene, TX 79602 .... (325) 676–2839
3133 General Hudnell Drive, Suite 120, San Antonio, TX 78226 .... (210) 340–2885

* * *

JOHN CORNYN, Republican, of San Antonio, TX; born in Houston, TX, February 2, 1952; education: graduated, Trinity University, and St. Mary's School of Law, San Antonio, TX; Masters of Law, University of Virginia, Charlottesville, VA; professional: attorney; Bexar County District Court Judge; Presiding Judge, Fourth Administrative Judicial Region; Texas Supreme Court, 1990–97; Texas Attorney General, 1999–2002; community service: Salvation Army Adult Rehabilitation Council; World Affairs Council of San Antonio; Lutheran General Hospital Board; awards: Outstanding Texas Leader Award, 2000; James Madison Award, 2001; chair, National Republican Senatorial Committee; committees: Agriculture, Nutrition, and Forestry; Budget; Finance; Judiciary; elected to the U.S. Senate on November 5, 2002, for the term beginning January 3, 2003; appointed to the Senate on December 2, 2002, to fill the vacancy caused by the resignation of Senator Phil Gramm; reelected to the U.S. Senate on November 4, 2008.

Office Listings

http://cornyn.senate.gov

517 Hart Senate Office Building, Washington, DC 20510 .... (202) 224–2934
Chief of Staff.—Beth Jafari. FAX: 228–2856
Legislative Director.—Russ Thomasson.
5300 Memorial Drive, Houston, TX 77007 .... (713) 572–3337
Providence Tower, 5001 Spring Valley Road, #1125E, Dallas, TX 75244 .... (972) 239–1310
100 East Ferguson Street, Suite 1004, Tyler, TX 75702 .... (903) 593–0902
221 West Sixth Street, Suite 1530, Austin, TX 78701 .... (512) 469–6034
Wells Fargo Center, 1500 Broadway, #1230, Lubbock, TX 79401 .... (806) 472–7533
222 East Van Buren, Suite 404, Harlingen, TX 78550 .... (956) 423–0162
600 Navarro Street, Suite 210, San Antonio, TX 78205 .... (210) 224–7485

REPRESENTATIVES

FIRST DISTRICT

LOUIE GOHMERT, Republican, of Tyler, TX; born in Pittsburg, TX, August 18, 1953; education: B.A., Texas A&M University, 1975; J.D., Baylor University, Waco, TX, 1977; professional: United States Army, 1978–82; district judge, Smith County, 1992–2002; appointed by Governor Rick Perry to complete an unexpired term as Chief Justice of the 12th Court of Appeals, 2002–03; Brigade Commander of the Corps of Cadets, Texas A&M; organizations: President of the South Tyler Rotary Club; Boy Scout District Board of Directors; religion: deacon at Green Acres Baptist Church; director of Leadership Tyler; director of Centrepoint Ministries; married: Kathy; children: Katy, Caroline, Sarah; committees: Judiciary; Natural Resources; Small Business; elected to the 109th Congress on November 2, 2004; reelected to each succeeding Congress.

Office Listings

http://www.gohmert.house.gov

511 Cannon House Office Building, Washington, DC 20515 .... (202) 225–3035
Chief of Staff.—Michael Tomberlin. FAX: 226–1230
Legislative Director.—Scott Lively.
Communications Director.—Laura Mszar.
1121 East Southeast Loop 323, Suite 206, Tyler, TX 75701 .... (903) 561–6349

Counties: ANGELINA, CASS (part), GREGG, HARRISON, MARION, NACOGDOCHES, PANOLA, RUSK, SABINE, SAN AUGUSTINE, SHELBY, SMITH, UPSHUR. Population (2000), 651,619.

ZIP Codes: 75551, 75555, 75562, 75564–65, 75601–08, 75615, 75631, 75633, 75637, 75639–45, 75647, 75650–54, 75657–63, 75666–67, 75669–72, 75680, 75682–85, 75687–89, 75691–94, 75701–13, 75750, 75755, 75757, 75760, 75762, 75771, 75788–89, 75791–92, 75797–99, 75901–04, 75915, 75929–31, 75935, 75937, 75941, 75943–44, 75946–49, 75954, 75958–59, 75961–65, 75968–69, 75972–75, 75978, 75980

* * *

SECOND DISTRICT

TED POE, Republican, of Humble, TX; born in Temple, TX, October 13, 1948; education: B.A., political science, Abilene Christian University, Abilene, TX, 1970; J.D., University of Houston, TX, 1973; professional: United States Air Force, 1970–1976; Felony Court Judge, 1981–2004; Trainer, Federal Bureau of Investigations National Academy; Chief Felony Prosecutor, District Attorney, Harris County, TX; United States Air Force Reserves Instructor, University of Houston; organizations: Board of the National Children's Alliance; Child Abuse Prevention Council; Victim's Rights Caucus; family: married to Carol; children: Kim, Kara, Kurt, and Kellee; committees: Foreign Affairs; Judiciary; elected to the 109th Congress on November 2, 2004; reelected to each succeeding Congress.

Office Listings

http://www.poe.house.gov

430 Cannon House Office Building, Washington, DC 20515 .... (202) 225–6565
Chief of Staff.—Janet Diaz-Brown. FAX: 225–5547
Press Secretary.—DeeAnn Thigpen.
Scheduler.—Elizabeth Steil.
1801 Kingwood Drive, Suite 240, Kingwood, TX 77339 .... (866) 447–0242
505 Orleans, Suite 100, Beaumont, TX 77701 .... (409) 212–1997

Counties: ANGELINA, CHEROKEE, GRIMES, HARDIN, HOUSTON, JASPER, LIBERTY, MONTGOMERY (part), NACOGDOCHES (part), NEWTON, ORANGE, POLK, SABINE, SAN AUGUSTINE, SAN JACINTO, TRINITY, TYLER, WALKER. Population (2000), 651,619.

ZIP Codes: 75757, 75759, 75764, 75766, 75772, 75780, 75784–85, 75789, 75834–35, 75839, 75844–45, 75847, 75849, 75851–52, 75856, 75858, 75862, 75865, 75901–04, 75915, 75925–26, 75928–34, 75936–39, 75941–42, 75944, 75947–49, 75951, 75956, 75959–61, 75965–66, 75968–69, 75972, 75976–80, 77301–03, 77306, 77320, 77326–28, 77331–32, 77334–35, 77340–42, 77350–51, 77354, 77356–60, 77363–64, 77367–69, 77371–72, 77374, 77376, 77378, 77399, 77519, 77533, 77535, 77538, 77561, 77564, 77574–75, 77582, 77585, 77611–12, 77614–17, 77624–26, 77630–32, 77639, 77656–57, 77659, 77660, 77662–64, 77670, 77830–31, 77861, 77868, 77872, 77875–76

* * *

THIRD DISTRICT

SAM JOHNSON, Republican, of Dallas, TX; born in San Antonio, TX, October 11, 1930; education: B.S., business administration, Southern Methodist University, Dallas, TX, 1951; M.A., international affairs, George Washington University, Washington, DC, 1974; military service: served in Air Force, 29 years; Korea and Vietnam (POW in Vietnam, six years, ten months); director, Air Force Fighter Weapons School; flew with Air Force Thunderbirds Precision Flying Demonstration Team; graduate of Armed Services Staff College and National War

College; military awards: two Silver Stars, two Legions of Merit, Distinguished Flying Cross, one Bronze Star with Valor, two Purple Hearts, four Air Medals, and three Outstanding Unit awards; ended career with rank of colonel and Air Division commander; retired, 1979; professional: opened homebuilding company, 1979; served seven years in Texas House of Representatives; Smithsonian Board of Regents; U.S./Russian Joint Commission on POW/MIA; Texas State Society; Congressional Medal of Honor Society; National Patriot Award Recipient, 2009; Rotary International, Paul Hairrs Fellow; founder, Republican Study Committee (formerly Conservative Action Team); chairman of the Board of Directors, Institute of Basic Life Principles; married the former Shirley L. Melton, 1950; three children: Dr. James Robert Johnson, Shirley Virginia (Gini) Mulligan and Beverly Briney; committees: Ways and Means; elected to the 102nd Congress by special election on May 18, 1991, to fill the vacancy caused by the resignation of Steve Bartlett; reelected to each succeeding Congress.

Office Listings

http://www.samjohnson.house.gov

1211 Longworth House Office Building, Washington, DC 20515 .... (202) 225–4201
Chief of Staff.—Dave Heil. FAX: 225–1485
Legislative Director.—Mark Williams.
Executive Assistant.—Lindsey Ray.
2929 North Central Expressway, Suite 240, Richardson, TX 75080 .... (972) 470–0892

Counties: COLLIN (part), DALLAS, (part). CITIES AND TOWNSHIPS: Allen, Dallas, Frisco, Garland, McKinney, Murphy, Parker, Plano, Richardson, Rowlett, and Sachse. Population (2000), 651,620.

ZIP Codes: 75002, 75007, 75009, 75013, 75023–26, 75030, 75034–35, 75040–42, 75044–48, 75069–71, 75074–75, 75078, 75080–82, 75085–86, 75088–89, 75093–94, 75098, 75228, 75238, 75245, 75248, 75252, 75287, 75355, 75367, 75370, 75378, 75382, 75409, 75424, 75442, 75454, 78243

* * *

FOURTH DISTRICT

RALPH M. HALL, Republican, of Rockwall, TX; born in Fate, TX, May 3, 1923; education: graduated, Rockwall High School, 1941; attended, Texas Christian University and the University of Texas; LL.B., Southern Methodist University, 1951; professional: lieutenant, carrier pilot (senior grade), U.S. Navy, 1942–45; lawyer; admitted to the Texas bar, 1951; practiced law in Rockwall; county judge, Rockwall County, 1950–62; former president and chief executive officer, Texas Aluminum Corporation; past general counsel, Texas Extrusion Company, Inc.; past organizer, chairman, board of directors, now chairman of board, Lakeside National Bank of Rockwall (now Lakeside Bancshares, Inc.); past chairman, board of directors, Lakeside News, Inc.; past vice chairman, board of directors, Bank of Crowley; president, North and East Trading Company; vice president, Crowley Holding Co.; member: Texas State Senate, 1962–72; American Legion Post 117; VFW Post 6796; Rockwall Rotary Club; Rotary Clubs International; member: First Methodist Church; married: the former Mary Ellen Murphy, 1944; three sons: Hampton, Brett and Blakeley; committees: Energy and Commerce; Science and Technology; elected to the 97th Congress, November 4, 1980; reelected to each succeeding Congress.

Office Listings

http://www.house.gov/ralphhall

2405 Rayburn House Office Building, Washington, DC 20515 .... (202) 225–6673
Chief of Staff.—Janet Perry Poppleton. FAX: 225–3332
Legislative Director.—Amy Dyer.
104 North San Jacinto Street, Rockwall, TX 75087–2508 .... (972) 771–9118
District Assistant.—Tom Hughes.
101 East Pecan Street, Suite 114, Sherman, TX 75090–5989 .... (903) 892–1112
District Assistant.—Judy Rowton.
U.S. P.O., 320 Church Street, Suite 132, Sulphur Springs, TX 75482–2606 .... (903) 885–8138
District Assistant.—Martha Glover.
Bowie County Courthouse, 710 James Bowie Drive, New Boston, TX 75570–2328 (903) 628–8309
District Assistant.—Eric Cain.
4303 Texas Boulevard, Suite 2, Texarkana, TX 75503–3094 .... (903) 794–4445
District Assistant.—Marjorie Chandler.
Collin County Courts Facility, 1800 North Graves Street, Suite 101, McKinney, TX 75069–3322 .... (214) 726–9949
District Assistant.—Linda Schenck.

Counties: BOWIE COUNTY. CITIES AND TOWNSHIPS: De Kalb, Hooks, Leary, Maud, Nash, New Boston, Red Lick, Redwater, Texarkana, Wake Village. CAMP COUNTY, CITIES AND TOWNSHIPS: Pittsburg, Rocky Mound. CASS COUNTY. CITIES

AND TOWNSHIPS: Atlanta, Avinger, Bloomburg, Domino, Douglassville, Hughes Springs, Linden, Marietta, Queen City. COLLIN COUNTY. CITIES AND TOWNSHIPS: Allen, Anna, Blue Ridge, Celina, Fairview, Farmersville, Frisco, Josephine, Lavon, Lowry Crossing, Lucas, McKinney, Melissa, Nevada, New Hope, Parker, Princeton, Prosper, Royse City, Sachse, St. Paul, Van Alstyne, Westminster, Weston, Wylie, Winfield. DELTA COUNTY. CITIES AND TOWNSHIPS: Cooper, Pecan Gap. FANNIN COUNTY. CITIES AND TOWNSHIPS: Bailey, Bonham, Dodd City, Ector, Honey Grove, Ladonia, Leonard, Pecan Gap, Ravenna, Savoy, Trenton, Whitewright, Windom. FRANKLIN COUNTY. CITIES AND TOWNSHIPS: Mount Vernon, Winnsboro. GRAYSON COUNTY. CITIES AND TOWNSHIPS: Bells, Collinsville, Denison, Dorchester, Gunter, Howe, Knollwood, Pottsboro, Sadler, Sherman, Southmayd, Tioga, Tom Bean, Van Alstyne, Whitesboro, Whitewright. HOPKINS COUNTY. CITIES AND TOWNSHIPS: Como, Cumby, Sulphur Springs, Tira. HUNT COUNTY. CITIES AND TOWNSHIPS: Caddo Mills, Campbell, Celeste, Commerce, Greenville, Hawk Cove, Josephine, Lone Oak, Neylandville, Quinlan, West Tawakoni, Wolfe City. LAMAR COUNTY. CITIES AND TOWNSHIPS: Blossom, Deport, Paris, Reno, Roxton, Sun Valley, Toco. MORRIS COUNTY. CITIES AND TOWNSHIPS: Daingerfield, Hughes Springs, Lone Star, Naples, Omaha. RAINS COUNTY. CITIES AND TOWNSHIPS: Alba, East Tawakoni, Emory, Point. RED RIVER COUNTY. CITIES AND TOWNSHIPS: Annona, Avery, Bogata, Clarksville, Deport, Detroit. ROCKWALL COUNTY. CITIES AND TOWNSHIPS: Fate, Garland, Heath, McLendon-Chisholm, Mobile City, Rockwall, Rowlett, Royse City, Wylie. TITUS COUNTY. CITIES AND TOWNSHIPS: Miller's Cove, Mount Pleasant, Talco.

ZIP Codes: 75002, 75009, 75013, 75019, 75030, 75032, 75034–35, 75040–41, 75058, 75069, 75071, 75074, 75076, 75078, 75087–88, 75090, 75094, 75097–98, 75132, 75135, 75164, 75166, 75173, 75189, 75407, 75409, 75413–14, 75416–18, 75422–24, 75426, 75428–29, 75431–33, 75435–36, 75438–40, 75442, 75446, 75449, 75452–55, 75457, 75459, 75460, 75462, 75469, 75472–73, 75474, 75476, 75477, 75479, 75482, 75486–87, 75489, 75490–95, 75501, 75550–51, 75554, 75556, 75559–61, 75563, 75566–73, 75572, 75630, 75638, 75656, 75668, 75686, 75855, 76233, 76264, 76268, 76271, 76273

* * *

FIFTH DISTRICT

JEB HENSARLING, Republican, of Dallas, TX; born in Stephenville, TX, May 29, 1957; education: B.A., economics, Texas A&M University, 1979; J.D., University of Texas School of Law, 1982; professional: businessman; vice president, Maverick Capital, 1993–96; owner, San Jacinto Ventures, 1996–2002; vice president, Green Mountain Energy Co., 1999–2001; community service: American Cancer Society for the Dallas Metro Area; Children's Education Fund; Habitat for Humanity; religion: Christian; married: Melissa; children: Claire and Travis; committees: Budget; Financial Services; elected to the 108th Congress on November 5, 2002; reelected to each succeeding Congress.

Office Listings

http://www.house.gov/hensarling

129 Cannon House Office Building, Washington, DC 20515 .... (202) 225–3484
Chief of Staff.—Dee Buchanan. FAX: 226–4888
Legislative Director.—Edward Skala.
Press Secretary.—Vacant.
6510 Abrams Road, Suite 243, Dallas, TX 75238 .... (214) 349–9996
702 East Corsicana Street, Athens, TX 77571 .... (903) 675–8288

Counties: ANDERSON, CHEROKEE, DALLAS (part), HENDERSON, KAUFMAN, VAN ZANDT, WOOD. Population (2000), 651,620.

ZIP Codes: 75030, 75032, 75041, 75043, 75047, 75049, 75088, 75103, 75114, 75117–18, 75124, 75126–27, 75140, 75142–43, 75147–50, 75156–61, 75163, 75169, 75180–82, 75185, 75187, 75214, 75218, 75227–28, 75231, 75238, 75243, 75253, 75336, 75355, 75357, 75359, 75374, 75382, 75390, 75393–94, 75410, 75444, 75474, 75480, 75494, 75497, 75751–52, 75754, 75756–59, 75763–66, 75770, 75772–73, 75778–80, 75782–85, 75789–90, 75801–03, 75832, 75839, 75844, 75853, 75861, 75880, 75882, 75884, 75886, 75925, 75976

* * *

SIXTH DISTRICT

JOE BARTON, Republican, of Ennis, TX; born in Waco, TX, September 15, 1949; education: graduated Waco High School, 1968; B.S., industrial engineering, Texas A&M University, College Station, 1972; M.S., industrial administration, Purdue University, West Lafayette, IN, 1973; professional: plant manager, and assistant to the vice president, Ennis Business Forms, Inc., 1973–81; awarded White House Fellowship, 1981–82; served as aide to James B. Edwards, Secretary, Department of Energy; member, Natural Gas Decontrol Task Force in the Office of Planning, Policy and Analysis; worked with the Department of Energy task force in support of the President's Private Sector Survey on Cost Control; natural gas decontrol and project cost control consultant, Atlantic Richfield Company; cofounder, Houston County Volunteer Ambulance Service, 1976; vice president, Houston County Industrial Development Authority, 1980; chairman, Crockett Parks and Recreation Board, 1979–80; vice president, Houston County Chamber of Commerce, 1977–80; member, Dallas Energy Forum; religion: Methodist; married: Terri; son, Jack; children: Brad, Alison and Kristin, from a previous marriage; stepchildren: Lindsay, and Cullen; committees: ranking member, Energy and Commerce; elected to the 99th Congress on November 6, 1984; reelected to each succeeding Congress.

Office Listings

http://www.joebarton.house.gov

2109 Rayburn House Office Building, Washington, DC 20515 .... (202) 225–2002
Chief of Staff.—Ron Wright. FAX: 225–3052
Legislative Director.—Theresa Lavery.
Press Secretary.—Sean Brown.
Scheduler.—Linda Gillespie.
6001 West Ronald Reagan Memorial Highway, Suite 200, Arlington, TX 76017 .... (817) 543–1000
2106A West Ennis Avenue, Ennis, TX 75119 .... (972) 875–8488
303 North 6th Street, Crockett, TX 75835 .... (936) 544–8488

Counties: ELLIS, FREESTONE, HOUSTON, LEON, LIMESTONE, NAVARRO, TARRANT, TRINITY. CITIES AND TOWNSHIPS: Arlington, Bardwell, Buffalo, Centerville, Corsicana, Crockett, Crowley, Dawson, Ennis, Fairfield, Ferris, Fort Worth, Frost, Grapeland, Groveton, Italy, Kerens, Lovelady, Mansfield, Maypearl, Mexia, Midlothian, Milford, Oak Leaf, Palmer, Pecan Hill, Red Oak, Rice, Richland, and Waxahachie. Population (2000), 651,620.

ZIP Codes: 75050, 75052, 75054, 75101–02, 75104–06, 75109–10, 75119–20, 75125, 75144, 75146, 75151–55, 75165, 75167–68, 75831, 75833–35, 75838, 75840, 75844–52, 75855–56, 75858–60, 75862, 75865, 75926, 76001–07, 76010–19, 76028, 76036, 76040–41, 76050, 76055, 76060, 76063–65, 76084, 76094, 76096–97, 76119–20, 76123, 76126, 76132–34, 76140, 76155, 76162–63, 76623, 76626, 76635, 76639, 76641–42, 76651, 76667, 76670, 76679, 76681, 76686, 76693, 77850, 77855, 77865, 77871

* * *

SEVENTH DISTRICT

JOHN ABNEY CULBERSON, Republican, of Harris County, TX; born in Houston, TX, August 24, 1956; education: B.A., Southern Methodist University; J.D., South Texas College of Law; professional: attorney; awards: Citizens for a Sound Economy Friend of the Taxpayer Award; Texas Eagle Forum Freedom and Family Award; Houston Jaycees Outstanding Young Houstonian Award; Champion of Border Security; Ancient Coin Collectors Guild; Friend of Numismatics; Club for Growth's Defender of Economic Freedom; Congressional Management Foundation's Silver Mouse Award; Family Research Canals True Blue Award; Water Advocate ''Friend of the Shareholder'' Recognition; U.S. Chamber of Commerce; Spirit of Enterprise Guardian of Small Business by NFIB; Recognition from the 60 Plus Association; NumbersUSA ''A'' for Consistently Voting for American Workers and the Environment through Immigration Reduction; public service: Texas House of Representatives, 1987–2000; married: Belinda Burney, 1989; child: Caroline; committees: Appropriations; elected to the 107th Congress on November 7, 2000; reelected to each succeeding Congress.

Office Listings

http://www.culberson.house.gov

1514 Longworth House Office Building, Washington, DC 20515 .... (202) 225–2571
Chief of Staff.—Tony Essalih. FAX: 225–4381
Legislative Director.—Jeff Morehouse.
Office Manager.—Jamie Gahun.
10000 Memorial Drive, Suite 620, Houston, TX 77024–3490 .... (713) 682–8828
District Director.—Ellie Essalih.

County: HARRIS COUNTY (part). Population (2000), 651,620.

ZIP Codes: 77002, 77004–08, 77019, 77024–25, 77027, 77030, 77035–36, 77040–43, 77046, 77055–57, 77063–65, 77070, 77074, 77077, 77079–81, 77084, 77086, 77094–96, 77098, 77215, 77218–19, 77224–25, 77227, 77241–44, 77255–57, 77265–66, 77269, 77277, 77279–82, 77284, 77401–02, 77429, 77433

* * *

EIGHTH DISTRICT

KEVIN BRADY, Republican, of The Woodlands, TX; born in Vermillion, SD, April 11, 1955; education: B.S., business, University of South Dakota; professional: served in Texas House of Representatives, 1991–96, the first Republican to capture the 15th District seat since the 1800s; chair, Council of Chambers of Greater Houston; president, East Texas Chamber Executive Association; president, South Montgomery County Woodlands Chamber of Commerce, 1985–present; director, Texas Chamber of Commerce Executives; Rotarian; awards: Achievement Award, Texas Conservative Coalition; Outstanding Young Texan (one of five), Texas Jaycees; Ten Best Legislators for Families and Children, State Bar of Texas; Legislative

Standout, Dallas Morning News; Scholars Achievement Award for Excellence in Public Service, North Harris Montgomery Community College District; Victims Rights Equalizer Award, Texans for Equal Justice Center; Support for Family Issues Award, Texas Extension Homemakers Association; religion: attends Saints Simon and Jude Catholic Church; married: Cathy Brady; committees: ranking member, Joint Economic Committee; Ways and Means; elected to the 105th Congress; reelected to each succeeding Congress.

Office Listings

http://www.house.gov/brady

301 Cannon House Office Building, Washington, DC 20515 .... (202) 225–4901
Chief of Staff.—Doug Centilli. FAX: 225–5524
Press Secretary.—Jessica Peetoom.
Legislative Director.—Kimberly Thompson.
200 River Pointe Drive, Suite 304, Conroe, TX 77304 .... (936) 441–5700
District Director.—Sarah Stephens.
1202 Sam Houston Avenue, Suite 8, Huntsville, TX 77340 .... (936) 439–9542
420 Green Avenue, Orange, TX 77630 .... (409) 883–4197

COUNTIES: HARDIN, JASPER, LIBERTY (part), MONTGOMERY, NEWTON, ORANGE, POLK, SAN JACINTO, TRINTY (part), TYLER, WALKER. CITIES AND TOWNSHIPS: Bevil Oaks, Bridge City, Browndell, Buna, Chester, Coldspring, Conroe, Colmesneil, Corrigan, Cut and Shoot, Dayton Lakes, Deweyville, Evadale, Goodrich, Hardin, Huntsville, Jasper, Kenefick, Kirbyville, Kountze, Lake Livingston, Lumberton, Magnolia, Mauriceville, Montgomery, New Waverly, Newton, Oak Ridge North, Oakhurst, Onalaska, Orange, Palton Village, Panorama Village, Pine Forest, Pinehurst, Pinewood Estates, Point Blank, Porter Heights, Roman Fores, Rose City, Rose Hill Acres, Seven Oaks, Shenandoah, Shepherd, Silshee, Sour Lake, South Toledo Bend, Splendora, Stagecoach, The Woodlands, Trinity, Vidor, West Livingston, West Orange, Willis, Woodbranch, and Woodville. Population (2000), 651,619.

ZIP Codes: 75931, 75951, 75956, 75966, 77318, 77320, 77340–44, 77348–49, 77350–51, 77355, 77359–60, 77364, 77367, 77371, 77378, 77399, 77561, 77611, 77614, 77630–32, 77656, 77659, 77862, 77939

* * *

NINTH DISTRICT

AL GREEN, Democrat, of Houston, TX; born in New Orleans, LA, September 1, 1947; raised in Florida; education: Florida A&M University, Tallahassee, FL, 1966–71; attended Tuskegee University, Tuskegee, AL; J.D., Texas Southern University, Houston, TX, 1974; professional: co-founded and co-managed the law firm of Green, Wilson, Dewberry and Fitch; Justice of the Peace, Precinct 7, Position 2, 1977–2004; organizations: former president of the Houston NAACP; Houston Citizens Chamber of Commerce; awards: Distinguished Service Award, 1978; Black Heritage Society, Outstanding Leadership Award, 1981; American Federation of Teachers, Citation for Service as a ''Courageous Defender of Due Process for Educators,'' 1983; *Ebony* Magazine's 100 Most Influential Black People, 2006; and the NAACP Fort Bend Branch Mickey Leland Humanitarian Award, 2006; Texas Black Democrats' Profiles of Courage Award, 2007; the AFL-CIO MLK Drum Major Award for Service, 2007; committees: Financial Services; Homeland Security; elected to the 109th Congress on November 2, 2004; reelected to each succeeding Congress.

Office Listings

http://www.house.gov/algreen

236 Cannon House Office Building, Washington, DC 20515 .... (202) 225–7508
Chief of Staff.—Jacqueline Ellis. FAX: 225–2947
Legislative Director.—Susie Saavedra.
Senior Legislative Assistant.—Renee Mayo.
Communications Director.—Vacant.
3003 South Loop West, Suite 460, Houston, TX 77054 .... (713) 383–9234
District Director.—Cynthia Baggage.

Counties: FORT BEND, HARRIS. Population (2000), 651,619.

ZIP Codes: 77004–05, 77021, 77025, 77030–31, 77033, 77035–36, 77042, 77045, 77047–48, 77051, 77053–54, 77056–57, 77061, 77063, 77071–72, 77074, 77077, 77081–83, 77085, 77087, 77096, 77099, 77230–31, 77233, 77235–37, 77251, 77254, 77263, 77271–72, 77274, 77401, 77411, 77469, 77477–78, 77489

* * *

TENTH DISTRICT

MICHAEL T. MCCAUL, Republican, of Austin, TX; born in Dallas, TX, January 14, 1962; education: B.S., Trinity University, San Antonio, TX, 1984; J.D., St. Mary's University, San

Antonio, TX, 1987; professional: lawyer, private practice; deputy attorney general, office of Texas State Attorney General; committees: Foreign Affairs; Homeland Security; Science and Technology; elected to the 109th Congress on November 2, 2004; reelected to each succeeding Congress.

Office Listings

http://www.mccaul.house.gov

131 Cannon House Office Builiding, Washington, DC 20515 .... (202) 225–2401
Chief of Staff.—Greg Hill. FAX: 225–5955
Deputy Chief of Staff.—Gene Irisari.
Legislative Director.—Alex Manning.
Scheduler / Office Manager.—Mary Donaldson.
5929 Balcones Drive, Suite 305, Austin, TX 78731 .... (512) 473–2357
Communications Director.—Mike Rosen.
Rosewood Professional Building, 990 Village Square, Suite B, Tomball, TX 77375 (281) 255–8372
1550 Foxlake, Suite 120, Houston, TX 77084 .... (281) 398–1247
2000 South Market Street, Suite 303, Brenham, TX 77833 .... (979) 830–8497

Counties: AUSTIN, BASTROP, BURLESON, HARRIS, LEE, TRAVIS, WALLER, WASHINGTON. Population (2000), 651,619.

ZIP Codes: 77070, 77084, 77094–95, 77218, 77269, 77284, 77375, 77377, 77379, 77383, 77388–89, 77391, 77410, 77413, 77418, 77423, 77426, 77429, 77433, 77445–47, 77449–50, 77452, 77466, 77473–74, 77476, 77484–85, 77491–94, 77833–36, 77838, 77852–53, 77863, 77868, 77878–80, 78602, 78615, 78621, 78650–51, 78653, 78659–60, 78664, 78682–83, 78691, 78703, 78705, 78708, 78710, 78713, 78716, 78718, 78720, 78724, 78727–31, 78733, 78746, 78751–59, 78761, 78763, 78765–66, 78779–80, 78785, 78788–89, 78931–33, 78940, 78942, 78944, 78946–48, 78950

* * *

ELEVENTH DISTRICT

K. MICHAEL CONAWAY, Republican, of Midland, TX; born in Borger, TX, June 11, 1948; education: B.B.A., Texas A&M–Commerce, 1970; professional: Spec 5 United States Army, 1970–72; tax manager, Price Waterhouse & Company, 1972–80; Chief Financial Officer, Keith D. Graham & Lantern Petroleum Company, 1980–81; Chief Financial Officer, Bush Exploration Company, 1982–84; Chief Financial Officer, Spectrum 7 Energy Corporation, 1984–86; Senior Vice President / Chief Financial Officer, United Bank, 1987–90; Senior Vice President, Texas Commerce Bank, 1990–92; owner, K. Conaway CPA, 1993–present; Deputy Republican Whip; religion: Baptist; married: Suzanne; children: Brian, Erin, Kara, and Stephanie; committees: Agriculture; Armed Services; Permanent Select Committee on Intelligence; Standards on Official Conduct; elected to the 109th Congress on November 2, 2004; reelected to each succeeding Congress.

Office Listings

http://www.house.gov/conaway

1527 Longworth House Office Building, Washington, DC 20515 .... (202) 225–3605
Chief of Staff.—Richard Hudson. FAX: 225–1783
Legislative Director.—Scott C. Graves.
Scheduler.—Faith Rodill.
6 Desta Drive, Suite 2000, Midland, TX 79705 .... (432) 687–2390
District Scheduler.—Patsy Bain.
33 East Twohig, Room 307, San Angelo, TX 76903 .... (325) 659–4010
Regional Director.—Joanne Powell.

Counties: ANDREWS, BROWN, BURNET, COKE, COLEMAN, COMANCHE, CONCHO, CRANE, DAWSON, ECTOR, GILLESPIE, MENARD, MIDLAND, MILLS, GLASSCOCK, IRION, KIMBLE, LAMPASAS, LLANO, LOVING, MARTIN, MASON, MCCULLOCH, SUTTON (part), TOM GREEN, UPTON, MITCHELL, NOLAN (part), REAGAN, RUNNELS, SAN SABA, SCHLEICHER, SCURRY, STERLING, WARD, WINKLER. POPULATION (2000), 651,620.

ZIP Codes: 76246, 76432, 76442, 76444, 76455, 76550, 76801–04, 76821, 76823, 76825, 76834, 76837, 76844, 76853, 76856, 76859, 76861, 76864, 76866, 76872–73, 76877, 76901–04, 76932–33, 76935–36, 76941, 76945, 76950–51, 76957, 77381–82, 77393, 78611, 78624, 78643, 78654–69, 79331, 79512, 79532, 79545, 79549–50, 79556, 79565, 79567, 79605–09, 79714, 79760–69, 79701–13, 79739, 79742, 79745, 79756, 79778, 79789

* * *

TWELFTH DISTRICT

KAY GRANGER, Republican, of Fort Worth, TX; born in Greenville, TX, January 18, 1943; education: B.S., *magna cum laude*, 1965, and Honorary Doctorate of Humane Letters, 1992,

Texas Wesleyan University; professional: owner, Kay Granger Insurance Agency, Inc.; former public school teacher; elected Mayor of Fort Worth, 1991, serving three terms; during her tenure, Fort Worth received All-America City Award from the National Civic League; former Fort Worth Councilwoman; past chair, Fort Worth Zoning Commission; past board member: Dallas-Fort Worth International Airport; North Texas Commission; Fort Worth Convention and Visitors Bureau; U.S. Conference of Mayors Advisory Board; Business and Professional Women's Woman of the Year, 1989; three grown children: J.D., Brandon and Chelsea; first woman Republican to represent Texas in the U.S. House; vice chair, Republican Conference; Deputy Republican Whip; committees: Appropriations; elected to the 105th Congress; reelected to each succeeding Congress.

Office Listings

http://www.house.gov/granger

320 Cannon House Office Building, Washington, DC 20515 .... (202) 225–5071
Chief of Staff.—Craig Albright. FAX: 225–5683
Deputy Chief of Staff.—Chelsey Hickman.
Legislative Director.—Amy Tenhouse.
Staff Assistant.—Ashley Hale.
Scheduler.—Nicole Audet.
1701 River Run Road, Suite 407, Fort Worth, TX 76107 .... (817) 338–0909
District Director.—Barbara Ragland. (817) 335–5852

Counties: PARKER, TARRANT (part), WISE. Population (2000), 651,619.

ZIP Codes: 76008, 76020, 76023, 76035–36, 76049, 76052, 76066–68, 76071, 76073, 76078, 76082, 76085–88, 76098, 76101–02, 76104, 76106–11, 76113–18, 76121–23, 76126–27, 76129–37, 76147–48, 76161–64, 76177, 76179–82, 76185, 76191–93, 76195–99, 76225, 76234, 76244, 76246, 76248, 76262, 76267, 76270, 76299, 76426, 76431, 76439, 76462, 76485–87, 76490

* * *

THIRTEENTH DISTRICT

MAC THORNBERRY, Republican, of Clarendon, TX; born in Clarendon, July 15, 1958; education: graduate, Clarendon High School; B.A., Texas Tech University; law degree, University of Texas; professional: rancher; attorney; admitted to the Texas bar, 1983; member: Joint Forces Command Transformation; Republican Study Committee; Proliferation Prevention Forum; Congressional Rural Caucus; Rural Health Care Coalition; Anti-Terrorism Caucus; Interagency Coordination, Western Caucus; married: Sarah Adams, 1986; children: Will and Mary Kemp; committees: Armed Services; Permanent Select Committee on Intelligence; elected to the 104th Congress; reelected to each succeeding Congress.

Office Listings

http://www.house.gov/thornberry

2209 Rayburn House Office Building, Washington, DC 20515 .... (202) 225–3706
Administrative Assistant.—Kelly Buck. FAX: 225–3486
Office Manager.—Kala Weller.
905 South Filmore, Suite 520, Amarillo, TX 79101 .... (806) 371–8844
Chief of Staff.—Bill Harris.
4245 Kemp, Suite 506, Wichita Falls, TX 76308 .... (940) 692–1700

Counties: ARCHER (part), ARMSTRONG, BAYLOR, BRISCOE, CARSON, CHILDRESS, CLAY, COLLINGSWORTH, COOKE (part), COTTLE, CROSBY, DALLAM, DICKENS, DONLEY, FOARD, GRAY, HALL, HANSFORD, HARDEMAN, HARTLEY, HASKELL, HEMPHILL, HUTCHINSON, JACK, JONES, KING, KNOX, LIPSCOMB, MONTAGUE, MOORE, MOTLEY, OCHILTREE, OLDHAM, PALO PINTO, POTTER, RANDALL, ROBERTS, SHERMAN, STONEWALL, SWISHER, THROCKMORTON, WHEELER, WICHITA, WILBARGER. Population (2000), 651,619.

ZIP Codes: 76066, 76067–68, 76228, 76230, 76234, 76238–40, 76250–53, 76255, 76261, 76263, 76265–66, 76270, 76272, 76301–02, 76305–11, 76352, 76354, 76357, 76360, 76363–67, 76369, 76371–73, 76377, 76379–80, 76384–85, 76388–89, 76427, 76430, 76449–50, 76453, 76458–59, 76462–63, 76472, 76475, 76483–84, 76486–87, 76491, 79001–03, 79005, 79007–08, 79010–16, 79018–19, 79022, 79024, 79029, 79033–34, 79036, 79039–40, 79042, 79044, 79046, 79051–52, 79054, 79056–59, 79061–62, 79065–66, 79068, 79070, 79077–81, 79083–84, 79086–88, 79091–97, 79101–11, 79114, 79116–21, 79124, 79159, 79166, 79168, 79172, 79174, 79178, 79185, 79187, 79189, 79201, 79220, 79223, 79225–27, 79229–30, 79233–34, 79236–37, 79239, 79243–45, 79247–48, 79251–52, 79255–57, 79259, 79261, 79322, 79343, 79357, 79370, 79501–03, 79505, 79520–21, 79525, 79529, 79533, 79536, 79539–40, 79544, 79547–48, 79553, 79560, 79601

* * *

FOURTEENTH DISTRICT

RON PAUL, Republican, of Lake Jackson, TX; born in Pittsburgh, PA, August 20, 1935; education: B.A., Gettysburg College, 1957; M.D., Duke College of Medicine, North Carolina, 1961; professional: captain, U.S. Air Force, 1963–68; obstetrician and gynecologist; represented Texas' 22nd District in the U.S. House of Representatives, 1976–77, and 1979–85; married: the former Carol Wells, 1957; children: Ronnie, Lori Pyeatt, Rand, Robert and Joy LeBlanc; committees: Financial Services; Foreign Affairs; elected to the 105th Congress; reelected to each succeeding Congress.

Office Listings

http://www.house.gov/paul

203 Cannon House Office Building, Washington, DC 20515 .... (202) 225–2831
Chief of Staff.—Tom Lizardo.
Legislative Director.—Norman Singleton.
Press Secretary.—Rachel Mills.
1501 East Mockingbird Lane, Suite 229, Victoria, TX 77904 .... (361) 576–1231
122 West Way Street, Suite 301, Lake Jackson, TX 77566 .... (979) 285–0231
601 25 Street, Suite 216, Galveston, TX 77550 .... (409) 766–7013

Counties: ARANSAS, BRAZORIA (part), CALHOUN, CHAMBERS, FORT BEND (part), GALVESTON (part), JACKSON, MATAGORDA, VICTORIA, WHARTON. Population (2000), 651,619.

ZIP Codes: 77082, 77404, 77414–15, 77417, 77419–20, 77422–23, 77428, 77430–32, 77435–37, 77440–41, 77443–44, 77448, 77450–51, 77453–58, 77461, 77463–65, 77467–69, 77471, 77476, 77480, 77482–83, 77485–86, 77488, 77493–94, 77510–12, 77514–18, 77520–21, 77531, 77534–35, 77539, 77541–42, 77546, 77549–55, 77560, 77563, 77565–66, 77568, 77571, 77573–74, 77577–78, 77580–81, 77583–84, 77590–92, 77597, 77617, 77623, 77650, 77661, 77665, 77901–05, 77951, 77957, 77961–62, 77968–71, 77973, 77976–79, 77982–83, 77988, 77991, 77995, 78336, 78358, 78381–82

* * *

FIFTEENTH DISTRICT

RUBÉN HINOJOSA, Democrat, of Mercedes, TX; born in Edcouch, August 20, 1940; education: B.B.A., 1962, and M.B.A., 1980, University of Texas; professional: president and chief financial officer, H&H Foods, Inc.; elected member, Texas State Board of Education, 1975–84; board of directors, National Livestock and Meat Board and Texas Beef Industry Council, 1989–93; past president and chair of the board of directors, Southwestern Meat Packers Association; chair and member, board of trustees, South Texas Community College, 1993–96; past public member, Texas State Bar Board of Directors; former adjunct professor, Pan American University School of Business; past director, Rio Grande Valley Chamber of Commerce; Knapp Memorial Hospital Board of Trustees; Our Lady of Mercy Church Board of Catholic Advisors; past member, board of trustees, Mercedes Independent School District; former U.S. Jaycee Ambassador to Colombia and Ecuador; married: Martha; children: Ruben, Jr., Laura, Iliana, Kaitlin, and Karén; committees: Education and Labor; Financial Services; elected to the 105th Congress; reelected to each succeeding Congress.

Office Listings

http://www.hinojosa.house.gov

2463 Rayburn House Office Building, Washington, DC 20515 .... (202) 225–2531
Chief of Staff.—Connie Humphrey. FAX: 225–5688
Policy Advisor.—Greg Davis.
Communications Director.—Teno Villarreal.
2864 West Trenton Road, Edinburg, TX 78539 .... (956) 682–5545
District Director.—Salomon Torres.
107 South St. Mary's Street, Beeville, TX 78102 .... (361) 358–8400
District Director.—Judy McAda.

Counties: BEE, BROOKS, CAMERON, DEWITT, DUVALL, GOLIAD, HIDALGO (part), JIM WELLS, KARNES, LIVE OAK, NUECES, REFUGIO, SAN PATRICIO. CITIES AND TOWNSHIPS: Alamo, Alice, Beeville, Bishop, Donna, Driscoll, Edcouch, Edinburg, Elroy, Elsa, Goliad, Harlingen, LaVilla, Mathis, McAllen, Mercedes, Mission, Odem, Pharr, San Juan, Sinton, Taft, Three Rivers, and Weslaco. Population: (2000) 651,619.

ZIP Codes: 77905, 77954, 77960, 77963, 77967, 77974, 77989, 77993–94, 78022, 78060, 78071, 78075, 78102, 78104, 78107, 78119, 78125, 78142, 78145–46, 78151, 78162, 78330, 78332, 78335–36, 78343, 78350, 78352–53, 78355,

78359, 78362–64, 78368, 78370, 78372, 78374, 78380, 78383, 78387, 78389–91, 78501–05, 78516, 78537–41, 78543, 78549, 78557–58, 78561–63, 78565, 78569–70, 78572–74, 78577, 78579–80, 78589, 78595–96, 78599

* * *

SIXTEENTH DISTRICT

SILVESTRE REYES, Democrat, of El Paso, TX; born in Canutillo, TX, November 10, 1944; education: graduated, Canutillo High School, 1964; associate degree, El Paso Community College, 1976; attended University of Texas, Austin, 1964–65, and El Paso, 1965–66; served in U.S. Army, 1966–68, Vietnam combat veteran; U.S. Border Patrol, chief patrol agent, 26½ years, retired December 1, 1995; member: Canutillo School Board, 1968–69, 21st Century Democrats, El Paso County Democrats, and Unite El Paso; married: the former Carolina Gaytan, 1968; children: Monica, Rebecca and Silvestre Reyes, Jr.; committees: chair, Permanent Select Committee on Intelligence; Armed Services; elected on November 5, 1996, to the 105th Congress; reelected to each succeeding Congress.

Office Listings

http://www.house.gov/reyes

2433 Rayburn House Office Building, Washington, DC 20515 .... (202) 225–4831
Chief of Staff.—Perry Finney Brody. FAX: 225–2016
Press Secretary.—Vincent Perez.
Scheduler / Office Manager.—Liza Lynch.
Legislative Director.—Kimberley Alton.
310 North Mesa, Suite 400, El Paso, TX 79901 .... (915) 534–4400
Deputy Chief of Staff.—Sal Payan. FAX: 534–7426

Counties: EL PASO (part). CITIES AND TOWNSHIPS: Anthony, Canutillo, El Paso, Fabens, Horizon City, San Elizario, Socorro, Vinton, and Westway. Population (2000), 651,619.

ZIP Codes: 79821, 79835–36, 79838–39, 79849, 79901–08, 79910, 79912–18, 79920, 79922–27, 79929–32, 79934–38, 79940–55, 79958, 79960–61, 79968, 79976, 79978, 79980, 79995–99, 88510–21, 88523–36, 88538–50, 88553–63, 88565–90, 88595

* * *

SEVENTEENTH DISTRICT

CHET EDWARDS, Democrat, of Waco, TX; born in Corpus Christi, TX, November 24, 1951; education: graduated Memorial High School, Houston, TX, 1970; B.A., Texas A&M University, College Station, 1974; M.B.A., Harvard Business School, Boston, MA, 1981; professional: legislative assistant to Texas Congressman Olin ''Tiger'' Teague, 1974–77; marketing representative, Trammell Crow Company, 1981–85; president, Edwards Communications, Inc.; member, Texas State Senate, 1983–90; married: the former Lea Ann Wood; children: John Thomas and Garrison Alexander; committees: Appropriations; Budget; elected to the 102nd Congress, November 6, 1990; reelected to each succeeding Congress.

Office Listings

http://edwards.house.gov

2369 Rayburn House Office Building, Washington, DC 20515 .... (202) 225–6105
Chief of Staff.—Chris Chwastyk. FAX: 225–0350
Press Secretary.—Joshua Taylor.
600 Austin Avenue, Suite 29, Waco, TX 76710 .... (254) 752–9600
District Director.—Sam Murphey.
Wright Plaza, 115 South Main Street, Suite 202, Cleburne, TX 76033 .... (817) 645–4743
Deputy District Director.—Chris Turner.
4001 East 29th Street, Suite 116, Bryan, TX 77802 .... (979) 691–8797
FAX: 691–8939

Counties: BOSQUE, BRAZOS, BURLESON (part), GRIMES (part), HILL, HOOD, JOHNSON, LIMESTONE (part), MADISON, MCLENNAN, ROBERTSON (part), SOMMERVELL. CITIES OF: Anderson, Bryan, Cleburne, College Station, Glen Rose, Granbury, Groesbeck, Hillsboro, Madisonville, Miami, Valley Mills, and Waco. Population (2005), 651,786.

ZIP Codes: 75846, 75852, 76009, 76028, 76031, 76033, 76035–36, 76043–44, 76048–50, 76055, 76058–59, 76061, 76063, 76070, 76077, 76084, 76087, 76093, 76097, 76433, 76439, 76462, 76465, 76467, 76476, 76524, 76557, 76561, 76596, 76621–22, 76624, 76627–31, 76633–38, 76640, 76642–45, 76648–50, 76652–55, 76657, 76660, 76664–66, 76670–71, 76673, 76676, 76678, 76682, 76684, 76687, 76689–92, 76701–08, 76710–12, 76714–16, 76795, 76797–99, 77333, 77356, 77363, 77801–03, 77805–08, 77830–31, 77836–38, 77840–45, 77852, 77856, 77859, 77861–64, 77866–68, 77870, 77872–73, 77875–76, 77878–79, 77881–82

* * *

EIGHTEENTH DISTRICT

SHEILA JACKSON LEE, Democrat, of Houston, TX; born in Queens, NY, January 12, 1950; education: graduated, Jamaica High School; B.A., Yale University, New Haven, CT, 1972; J.D., University of Virginia Law School, 1975; professional: practicing attorney for 12 years; AKA Sorority; Houston Area Urban League; American Bar Association; staff counsel, U.S. House Select Committee on Assassinations, 1977–78; admitted to the Texas bar, 1975; city council (at large), Houston, 1990–94; Houston Municipal Judge, 1987–90; married Dr. Elwyn Cornelius Lee, 1973; two children: Erica Shelwyn and Jason Cornelius Bennett; committees: Foreign Affairs; Homeland Security; Judiciary; elected to the 104th Congress; reelected to each succeeding Congress.

Office Listings

http://www.jacksonlee.house.gov

2160 Rayburn House Office Building, Washington, DC 20515 .... (202) 225–3816
Chief of Staff.—Leon Buck. FAX: 225–3317
Deputy Chief of Staff.—Shashrina Thomas.
Senior Legislative Counsel.—Talib Karim.
Foreign Affairs LA.—Sam Rosmarin.
Legislative Correspondent.—Erin Dominguez.
Scheduler.—Phyllis Khaing.
Staff Assistant.—Sumer Alhinnawi.
1919 Smith Street, Suite 1180, Houston, TX 77002 .... (713) 655–0050
District Director.—Steven James.
District Administrator.—Michael Halpin.
Casework Director.—Carmen Hernandez.
District Liaison / Logistics Director.—Reginald Williams.
Community Liaison.—Anita James.
Executive Assistant.—Janice Weaver.
Special Assistant.—Bronson E. Woods.
Communications Director.—Alex Dailey.
Caseworker.—Yavuz Alavi.
420 West 19th Street, Houston, TX 77008 .... (713) 861–4070
6719 West Montgomery, Suite 204, Houston, Texas 77091 .... (713) 691–4882

Counties: HARRIS COUNTY (part). CITY OF: Houston. Population (2000), 651,620.

ZIP Codes: 77001–10, 77013, 77016, 77018–24, 77026, 77028–30, 77033, 77035, 77038, 77040–41, 77045, 77047–48, 77051–52, 77054–55, 77064, 77066–67, 77076, 77078, 77080, 77086–88, 77091–93, 77097–98, 77201–06, 77208, 77210, 77212, 77216, 77219, 77221, 77226, 77230, 77233, 77238, 77240–41, 77251–53, 77255, 77265–66, 77277, 77288, 77291–93, 77297–99

* * *

NINETEENTH DISTRICT

RANDY NEUGEBAUER, Republican, of Lubbock, TX; born in St. Louis, MO, December 24, 1949; education: Texas Tech University, 1972; professional: small businessman (home building industry); organizations: West Texas Home Builders Association; Land Use and Developers Council; Texas Association of Builders; National Association of Home Builders; Campus Crusade for Christ; public service: Lubbock City Council, 1992–98; served as Mayor Pro Tempore, 1994–96; leader, coalition to create the Ports-to-Plains Trade Corridor; awards: Lubbock Chamber of Commerce Distinguished Service Award; Reese Air Force Base Friend of Reese Award; religion: Baptist; married: Dana; two children; committees: Agriculture; Financial Services; Science and Technology; elected to the 108th Congress, by special election, on June 3, 2003; reelected to each succeeding Congress.

Office Listings

http://www.randy.house.gov

1424 Longworth House Office Building, Washington, DC 20515 .... (202) 225–4005

Chief of Staff.—Janette Whitener. FAX: 225–9615
Communications Director.—Michelle Ozanus.
Legislative Assistant.—Andrew Brandt.
Legislative Director / Policy Advisor.—Kathy Reding Bergren.
Senior Legislative Assistant.—Daniel T. Hilton.
Legislative Assistant / Scheduler.—Michele Rager.
Legislative Assistant / Legislative Correspondent.—Stephanie L. Shafer.
Staff Assistant.—Teresa Morales.
Communications Assistant.—Beth Breeding.
Federal Building, 611 University Avenue, #220, Lubbock, TX 79401 .... (806) 763–1611
District Director.—Brice Foster.

Counties: ARCHER, BAILEY, BORDEN, CALLAHAN, CASTRO, COCHRAN, DEAF SMITH, EASTLAND, FISHER, FLOYD, GAINES, GARZA, HALE, HOCKLEY, HOWARD, KENT, LAMB, LUBBOCK, LYNN, NOLAN, PARMER, SHACKELFORD, STEPHENS, TAYLOR, TERRY, YOAKUM, YOUNG. Population (2000), 651,619.

ZIP Codes: 76302, 76305, 76308, 76310, 76351, 76360, 76366, 76370, 76372, 76374, 76379, 76389, 76424, 76427, 76429–30, 76435, 76437, 76442–43, 76445, 76448, 76450, 76454, 76459–60, 76462–64, 76466, 76469–70, 76475, 76481, 76491, 79009, 79021, 79025, 79027, 79031–32, 79035, 79041, 79043, 79045, 79053, 79063–64, 79072–73, 79082, 79085, 79221, 79231, 79235, 79241, 79250, 79258, 79311–14, 79316, 79320, 79323–26, 79329–30, 79336, 79338–39, 79342, 79344–47, 79350–51, 79353, 79355–56, 79358–60, 79363–64, 79366–67, 79369–73, 79376, 79378–83, 79401–16, 79423–24, 79430, 79452–53, 79457, 79464, 79490–91, 79493, 79499, 79504, 79506, 79508, 79510–11, 79518–20, 79526, 79528, 79530, 79532–37, 79541, 79543, 79545–46, 79549, 79556, 79560–63, 79566–67, 79601–05, 79720–21, 79733, 79738, 79748

* * *

TWENTIETH DISTRICT

CHARLES A. GONZALEZ, Democrat, of San Antonio, TX; born in San Antonio, May 5, 1945; son of former Representative Henry Gonzalez, who served the 20th district from 1961–99; education: Thomas A. Edison High School, 1965; B.A., University of Texas at Austin, 1969; J.D., St. Mary's School of Law, 1972; professional: elementary school teacher; private attorney, 1972–82; Municipal Court Judge; County Court at Law Judge, 1983–87; District Judge, 1989–97; chair, Congressional Hispanic Caucus Civil Rights Task Force; Democratic Senior Whip; committees: Energy and Commerce; House Administration; Judiciary; elected to the 106th Congress; reelected to each succeeding Congress.

Office Listings

http://www.gonzalez.house.gov

303 Cannon House Office Building, Washington, DC 20515 .... (202) 225–3236
Chief of Staff.—Leo Muñoz. FAX: 225–1915
Secheduler.—Jayne Ann Wolsey.
Press Secretary.—Ginette Magaña.
Federal Building, B–124, 727 East Durango Boulevard, San Antonio, TX 78206 ... (210) 472–6195

Counties: BEXAR COUNTY (part). CITIES OF: Alamo Heights, Balcones Heights, Converse, Kirby, Lackland AFB, Leon Valley, and San Antonio. Population (2000), 651,619.

ZIP Codes: 78073, 78109, 78201–19, 78225–31, 78233, 78236–46, 78250, 78252, 78254

* * *

TWENTY-FIRST DISTRICT

LAMAR S. SMITH, Republican, of San Antonio, TX; born in San Antonio, November 19, 1947; education: graduated, Texas Military Institute, San Antonio, 1965; B.A., Yale University, New Haven, CT, 1969; management intern, Small Business Administration, Washington, DC, 1969–70; business and financial writer, *The Christian Science Monitor*, Boston, MA, 1970–72; J.D., Southern Methodist University School of Law, Dallas, TX, 1975; admitted to the State bar of Texas, 1975, and commenced practice in San Antonio with the firm of Maebius and Duncan, Inc.; elected chairman of the Republican Party of Bexar County, TX, 1978 and 1980; elected District 57–F State Representative, 1981; elected Precinct 3 Commissioner of Bexar County, 1982 and 1984; partner, Lamar Seeligson Ranch, Jim Wells County, TX; married: Beth Schaefer; children: Nell Seeligson and Tobin Wells; committees: ranking member, Judiciary; Homeland Security; Science and Technology; elected to the 100th Congress on November 4, 1986; reelected to each succeeding Congress.

Office Listings

http://lamarsmith.house.gov

2409 Rayburn House Office Building, Washington, DC 20515 .... (202) 225–4236
Chief of Staff / Assistant to the Chairman.—Jennifer Brown. FAX: 225–8628
Administrative Assistant / Scheduler.—Katie Comer.
Guaranty Federal Building, 1100 North East Loop 410, Suite 640, San Antonio, TX 78209 .... (210) 821–5024
District Director.—O'Lene Stone.
3536 Bee Cave Road, Suite 212, Austin, TX 78746 .... (512) 306–0439
301 Junction Highway, Suite 346C, Kerrville, TX 78028 .... (830) 896–0154

Counties: BEXAR (part), BLANCO, COMAL, HAYS (part), KERR, REAL, TRAVIS (part). Population (2000), 651,619.

ZIP Codes: 78006, 78015, 78070, 78135, 78148, 78150, 78154, 78163, 78209, 78213, 78216–18, 78239, 78247, 78258–61, 78266, 78270, 78280, 78606, 78610–11, 78613, 78618–20, 78623, 78630–31, 78635–36, 78641, 78645–46, 78652, 78654, 78663, 78666, 78669, 78676, 78726, 78730, 78732–39, 78746, 78749–50, 78759, 78780

* * *

TWENTY-SECOND DISTRICT

PETE OLSON, Republican of Sugar Land, TX; born in Fort Lewis, WA, December 9, 1962; education: B.A., Rice University, Houston, TX, 1985; Law Degree, University of Texas, Austin, TX, 1988; United States Navy, 1988–98; United States Senate, 1998–2007; Naval Aviator wings, 1991; Naval Liaison United States Senate; religion: United Methodist; married: Nancy Olson; children: Kate and Grant; committees: Homeland Security; Science and Technology; Transportation and Infrastructure; elected to the 111th Congress on November 4, 2008.

Office Listings

http://olson.house.gov

514 Cannon House Office Building, Washington, DC 20515 .... (202) 225–5951
Chief of Staff.—John Wyatt. FAX: 225–5241
Legislative Director.—JT Jezierski.
Communications Director.—Melissa Kelly.
Scheduler.—Marjorie Dornette.
1650 Highway 6, Suite 150, Sugarland, TX 77478 .... (281) 494–2690
District Director.—Nathan Cook.
17225 El Camino Real, Suite 447, Houston, TX 77058 .... (281) 486–1095
Deputy District Director.—Tyler Nelson. FAX: 486–1479

Counties: BRAZORIA, FORT BEND, GALVESTON, HARRIS (part), JEFFERSON. CITIES OF: Baytown, Beaumont, Galveston, La Marque, Missouri City, Port Arthur, Pearland, Rosenberg, Stafford, Sugar Land and Texas City. Population (2000), 651,619.

ZIP Codes: 77044, 77049, 77058, 77062, 77089, 77258, 77346, 77362, 77364, 77369, 77435, 77510–11, 77514, 77517–18, 77520–22, 77532, 77535, 77539, 77546, 77549–55, 77560, 77562–63, 77565, 77568, 77573–75, 77580–82, 77590–92, 77597–98, 77613, 77617, 77619, 77622–23, 77625–27, 77629, 77631, 77640–43, 77650–51, 77655, 77659–61, 77663–65, 77701–08, 77710, 77713, 77720, 77725–26

* * *

TWENTY-THIRD DISTRICT

CIRO D. RODRIGUEZ, Democrat, of San Antonio, TX; education: attended San Antonio College; B.A., political science, St. Mary's University; M.S.W., Our Lady of the Lake University; professional: Harlandale Independent School District School Board; served, Texas State House of Representatives, 1987–97; taught undergraduate and graduate courses at Worden School of Social Work; caseworker, Texas Department of Mental Health and Mental Retardation; faculty associate, Our Lady of the Lake University; consultant, Intercultural Development Research Association; married: Carolina Pena; children: one daughter, Xochil Daria; member: Congressional Hispanic Caucus; Congressional Hispanic Caucus Veterans' Taskforce; CHC Agriculture Taskforce; U.S.-Mexico Inter-Parliamentary Group; committees: Appropriations; Veterans' Affairs; elected to the 105th Congress in a special election, reelected to the 106th–108th Congresses; elected to the 110th Congress on November 7, 2006; reelected to the 111th Congress.

Office Listings

http://www.rodriguez.house.gov

2351 Rayburn House Office Building, Washington, DC 20515 .... (202) 225–4511
Chief of Staff.—César Blanco. FAX: 225–2237
Legislative Director.—Rene Muñoz.
Press Secretary.—Rebeca Chapa.
Scheduler / Executive Assistant.—María Campos.
1313 Southeast Military Drive, Suite 101, San Antonio, TX 78214 .... (210) 922–1874
FAX: 923–8447
6363 DeZavala Road, Suite 105, San Antonio, TX 78249 .... (210) 561–9421
FAX: 561–9442
209 East Losoya, Del Rio, TX 78840 .... (830) 774–5500
FAX: 774–2200
100 South Monroe Street, Eagle Pass, TX 78852 .... (830) 757–8398
FAX: 752–1893
103 West Callaghan, Fort Stockton, TX 79735 .... (432) 336–3975
FAX: 336–3961

Counties: BEXAR (part), BREWSTER, CROCKETT, CULBERSON, DIMMIT, EDWARDS, EL PASO (part), HUDSPETH, JEFF DAVIS, KINNEY, MAVERICK, MEDINA, PECOS, PRESIDIO, REEVES, SUTTON (part), TERRELL, UVALDE, VAL VERDE, ZAVALA. POPULATION (2000) 651,619.

ZIP Codes: 76943, 76950, 78002, 78006, 78009, 78015–16, 78023, 78039, 78052, 78054, 78056, 78059, 78066, 78069, 78073, 78112, 78163, 78202–03, 78205, 78210–11, 78214, 78216, 78220–26, 78230–32, 78235, 78240, 78242, 78245, 78248–58, 78260, 78263–64, 78269, 78801–02, 78827–30, 78832, 78834, 78836–43, 78847, 78850–53, 78860–61, 78870–72, 78877, 78880–81, 78884, 78886, 79718, 79730, 79734–35, 79740, 79743–44, 79770, 79772, 79780–81, 79785–86, 79830–32, 79834, 79836–37, 79839, 79842–43, 79845–48, 79851–55, 79927–28, 79938

* * *

TWENTY-FOURTH DISTRICT

KENNY MARCHANT, Republican, of Coppell, TX; born in Bonham, TX, February 23, 1951; education: B.A., Southern Nazarene University, Bethany, OK, 1974; attended Nazarene Theological Seminary, Kansas City, MO, 1975–76; professional: real estate developer; member of the Carrollton, TX, city council, 1980–84; mayor of Carrollton, TX, 1984–87; member of the Texas State House of Representatives, 1987–2004; member, Advisory Board of Children's Medical Center; married: Donna; four children; committees: Financial Services; elected to the 109th Congress on November 2, 2004; reelected to each succeeding Congress.

Office Listings

http://www.house.gov/marchant

227 Cannon House Office Building, Washington, DC 20515 .... (202) 225–6605
Chief of Staff.—Brian Thomas. FAX: 225–0074
Scheduler.—Amanda Buchanan.
9901 East Valley Ranch Parkway, Suite 3035, Irving, TX 75063 .... (972) 556–0162

Counties: DALLAS (part), TARRANT (part). CITIES AND TOWNSHIPS: Bedford, Carrollton, Cedar Hill, Colleyville, Coppell, Dallas, Duncanville, Euless, Farmer's Branch, Fort Worth, Grand Prairie, Irving, and Southlake. Population (2000), 651,619.

ZIP Codes: 75006–07, 75010–11, 75014–17, 75019, 75024, 75027, 75029, 75037, 75038, 75050–54, 75056–57, 75060–63, 75067, 75093, 75099, 75104, 75106, 75116, 75137–38, 75211, 75234, 75236, 75244, 75249, 75261, 75287, 75368, 75370, 75379, 75381, 75387, 75396, 75398, 76005–06, 76011, 76021–22, 76034, 76039, 76040, 76051, 76054, 76092, 76095, 76099, 76155, 76262, 76299

* * *

TWENTY-FIFTH DISTRICT

LLOYD DOGGETT, Democrat, of Austin, TX; born in Austin, October 6, 1946; education: graduated, Austin High School; B.B.A., University of Texas, Austin, 1967; J.D., University of Texas, 1970; president, University of Texas Student Body; associate editor, *Texas Law Review*; Outstanding Young Lawyer, Austin Association of Young Lawyers; president, Texas Consumer Association; religion: member, First United Methodist Church; admitted to the Texas State Bar, 1971; Texas State Senate, 1973–85, elected at age 26; Senate author of 124 state laws and Senate sponsor of 63 House bills enacted into law; elected president pro tempore of Texas Senate; served as acting governor; named Outstanding Young Texan by Texas Jaycees; Arthur B. DeWitty Award for outstanding achievement in human rights, Austin NAACP; honored for work by Austin Rape Crisis Center, Planned Parenthood of Austin; Austin Chapter, American Institute of Architects; Austin Council on Alcoholism; Disabled American Veterans; justice on Texas Supreme Court, 1989–94; chairman, Supreme Court Task Force on Judicial Ethics, 1992–94; Outstanding Judge (Mexican-American Bar of Texas), 1993; adjunct professor, University of Texas School of Law, 1989–94; James Madison Award, Texas Freedom of Information Foundation, 1990; First Amendment Award, National Society of Professional Journalists, 1990; member: co-founder, House Information Technology Roundtable; Democratic Caucus Task Force on Education; Congressional Task Force on Tobacco and Health; Democratic Caucus Task Force on Child Care; married: Libby Belk Doggett, 1969; children: Lisa and Cathy; committees: Budget; Ways and Means; elected to the 104th Congress; reelected to each succeeding Congress.

Office Listings

http://www.house.gov/doggett

201 Cannon House Office Building, Washington, DC 20515 .... (202) 225–4865
Chief of Staff.—Michael J. Mucchetti. FAX: 225–3073
Systems Administrator.—Shant Nahapetian.
Press Secretary.—Sarah Dohl.
Staff Assistant.—Allison Portnoy.
300 East 8th Street, Suite 763, Austin, TX 78701 .... (512) 916–5921
District Director.—Amanda Tyler

Counties: BASTROP, CALDWELL, COLORADO, FAYETTE, GONZALES, HAYS, LAVACA, TRAVIS (part). Population (2000), 651,619.

ZIP Codes: 77434, 77442, 77474, 77954, 77964, 77975, 77984, 77986–87, 77994–95, 78122, 78130, 78140, 78159, 78602, 78604, 78610, 78612, 78614, 78616–17, 78619–23, 78629, 78632, 78638, 78640, 78644, 78648, 78652–53, 78655–56, 78658–59, 78661–63, 78666–67, 78669, 78676–77, 78701–02, 78704–05, 78719, 78721–25, 78734–39, 78741–42, 78744–49, 78751–52, 78760–62, 78932–35, 78938, 78940–43, 78945–46, 78949–54, 78956–57, 78959–63

* * *

TWENTY-SIXTH DISTRICT

MICHAEL C. BURGESS, Republican, of Denton County, TX; born, December 23, 1950; education: Bachelor and Masters degrees in Physiology, North Texas State University, M.D., University of Texas Medical School in Houston; Masters degree in Medical Management, University of Texas in Dallas; completed medical residency programs, Parkland Hospital in Dallas; professional: founder, Private Practice Specialty Group for Obstetrics and Gynecology; former Chief of Staff and Chief of Obstetrics, Lewisville Medical Center; organizations: former president, Denton County Medical Society; Denton County delegate, Texas Medical Association; alternate delegate, American Medical Association; married: Laura; three children; committees: Energy and Commerce; Joint Economic Committee; elected to the 108th Congress on November 5, 2002; reelected to each succeeding Congress.

Office Listings

http://www.burgess.house.gov

229 Cannon House Office Building, Washington, DC 20515 .... (202) 225–7772
Chief of Staff.—Barry Brown. FAX: 225–2919
Legislative Director.—James Paluskiewicz.
Press Secretary.—Lauren Bean.
1660 South Stemmons Freeway, Suite 230, Lewisville, TX 75067 .... (972) 434–9700
1100 Circle Drive, Suite 200, Fort Worth, TX 76119 .... (817) 531–8454

Counties: COOKE (part), DALLAS (part), DENTON (part), TARRANT (part). Population (2000) 651,619.

ZIP Codes: 75009, 75019, 75022, 75028, 75034, 75056–57, 75063, 75067–68, 75077–78, 75261, 76012–13, 76021–22, 76034, 76040, 76051–54, 76092, 76102–05, 7610–12, 76115, 76117–20, 76134, 76140, 76148, 76177, 76180, 76201, 76205, 76207–10, 76226–27, 76233–34, 76240, 76247–49, 76258–59, 76262, 76266, 76272, 76273

* * *

TWENTY-SEVENTH DISTRICT

SOLOMON P. ORTIZ, Democrat, of Corpus Christi, TX; born in Robstown, TX, June 3, 1937; education: attended Robstown High School; attended Del Mar College, Corpus Christi; officers certificate, Institute of Applied Science, Chicago, IL, 1962; officers certificate, National Sheriffs Training Institute, Los Angeles, CA, 1977; served in U.S. Army, Sp4c. 1960–62; professional: insurance agent; Nueces County constable, 1965–68; Nueces County commissioner, 1969–76; Nueces County sheriff, 1977–82; member: Congressional Hispanic Caucus (chairman, 102nd Congress); Congressional Hispanic Caucus Institute (chairman of the board, 102nd Congress); Army Caucus; Depot Caucus; Sheriffs' Association of Texas; National Sheriffs' Association; Corpus Christi Rotary Club; American Red Cross; United Way; honors: *Who's Who Among Hispanic Americans;* Man of the Year, International Order of Foresters (1981); Conservation Legislator of the Year for the Sportsman Clubs of Texas (1986); Boss of the Year by the American Businesswomen Association (1980); National Government Hispanic Business Advocate, U.S. Hispanic Chamber of Commerce (1992); Leadership Award, Latin American Management Association (1991); National Security Leadership Award, American Security Council (1992); Tree of Life Award, Jewish National Fund (1987); Quality of Life Award (USO) 2001; children: Yvette and Solomon, Jr.; committees: Armed Services; Transportation and Infrastructure; elected on November 2, 1982 to the 98th Congress; reelected to each succeeding Congress.

Office Listings

http://www.ortiz.house.gov

2110 Rayburn House Office Building, Washington, DC 20515 .... (202) 225–7742
Chief of Staff.—Denise Blanchard. FAX: 226–1134
Executive Assistant / Scheduling.—Randy Zarate.
Legislative Director.—Mac King.
Press Secretary.—Jose Borjon.
3649 Leopard, Suite 510, Corpus Christi, TX 78408 .... (361) 883–5868
1805 Ruben Torres Boulevard, Suite B–27, Brownsville, TX 78521 .... (956) 541–1242

Counties: CAMERON (part), KENNEDY, KLEBERG, NUECES, SAN PATRICO, (part), WILLACY. Population (2000), 651,619.

ZIP Codes: 78330, 78335–36, 78338–39, 78343, 78347, 78351, 78359, 78362–64, 78373–74, 78379–80, 78383, 78385, 78390, 78401–19, 78426–27, 78460, 78463, 78465–78, 78480, 78520–23, 78526, 78550, 78552, 78559, 78561, 78566–67, 78569, 78575, 78578, 78580, 78583, 78586, 78590, 78592, 78594, 78597–98

* * *

TWENTY-EIGHTH DISTRICT

HENRY CUELLAR, Democrat, of Laredo, TX; born in Laredo, September 19, 1955; education: A.A., political science, Laredo Community College, Laredo, TX, 1976; B.S., foreign service, Georgetown University, Washington, DC, 1978; J.D., University of Texas, 1981; M.B.A., international trade, Texas A&M University, Laredo, TX, 1982; PhD., government, University of Texas, Austin, TX, 1998; professional: lawyer, private practice; attorney, Law Office of Henry Cuellar, 1981–present; instructor, Department of Government, Laredo Community College, Laredo, TX, 1982–86; Licensed United States Customs Broker, 1983–present; adjunct professor, International Commercial Law, Texas A&M International, 1984–86; Representative, Texas State House of Representatives, 1986–2001; Secretary of State, State of Texas, 2001; public and civic organizations: board of directors, Kiwanis Club of Laredo, TX, 1982–83; co-founder/president, Laredo Volunteers Lawyers Program, Inc., 1982–83; board of directors, United Way, 1982–83; co-founder/treasurer, Stop Child Abuse and Neglect, 1982–83, and advisory board member, 1984; president, board of directors, Laredo Legal Aid Society, Inc., 1982–84; president, board of directors, Laredo Young Lawyers Association, 1983–84; sustaining member, Texas Democratic Party, 1984; legal advisor, American GI, local chapter, 1986–87; International Trade Association, Laredo State University, 1988; Texas Delegate, National Democratic Convention, 1992; president, board of directors, International Good Neighbor Council; member, The College of the State Bar of Texas, 1994; Texas Lyceum, 1997; policy board of advisors, Texas Hispanic Journal of Law, University of Texas Law School, 2002; member: American Bar Association; Inter-American Bar Association; Texas Bar Association; Webb/Laredo Bar Association; recipient of various awards; religion: Catholic; married: Imelda; children: Christina Alexandra and Catherine Ann; committees: Agriculture; Homeland Security; Oversight and Government Reform; elected to the 109th Congress on November 2, 2004; reelected to each succeeding Congress.

Office Listings

http://www.cuellar.house.gov

336 Cannon House Office Bulding, Washington, DC 20515 .... (202) 225–1640
Chief of Staff.—Terry Stinson. FAX: 225–1641
Legislative Director.—Alastair Rami.
Scheduler.—Amy Travieso.
615 East Houston Street, Suite 451, San Antonio, TX 78205 .... (210) 271–2851

320 North Main, Suite 221, McAllen, TX 78501 .... (956) 631–4826
602 Calton Road, Suite 2, Laredo, TX 78041 .... (956) 725–0639
100 South Austin, Suite 1, Seguin, TX 78155 .... (830) 401–0457

Counties: ATASCOSA, BEXAR, FRIO, GUADALUPE, HIDALGO, IM HOGG, LA SALLE, MCMULLEN, STARR, WEBB, WILSON, ZAPATA. Population (2000), 651,627.

ZIP Codes: 76272, 78005–08, 78011–12, 78014, 78017, 78019, 78021, 78026, 78040–41, 78043, 78045–46, 78050, 78052, 78057, 78061–62, 78064–65, 78067, 78072, 78076, 78108, 78112–14, 78121, 78123–24, 78143, 78147, 78150, 78152, 78154–55, 78160–61, 78263, 78344, 78360–61, 78369, 78371, 78501, 78503–04, 78536, 78545, 78548, 78557, 78560, 78565, 78572–74, 78576–77, 78582, 78584–85, 78588, 78591, 78595, 78638, 78670

* * *

TWENTY-NINTH DISTRICT

GENE GREEN, Democrat, of Houston, TX; born in Houston, October 17, 1947; education: B.A., University of Houston, 1971; admitted, Texas bar, 1977; professional: business manager; attorney; Texas State Representative, 1973–85; Texas State Senator, 1985–92; member: Houston Bar Association; Texas Bar Association; American Bar Association; Communications Workers of America; Aldine Optimist Club; Gulf Coast Conservation Association; Lindale Lions Club; Texas Historical Society; Texas State Society; co-chair, Democratic Israel Working Group; Traumatic Brain Injury Task Force; Bi-Cameral Congressional Caucus on Parkinson's Disease; Community College Caucus; Congressional Steel Caucus; co-chair, Congressional Urban Healthcare Caucus; Missing and Exploited Children's Caucus; National Marine Sanctuary Caucus; National Wildlife Refuge Caucus; Pell Grant Caucus; Recycling Caucus; Sportsmen's Caucus; Urban Caucus; Victim's Rights Caucus; co-chair, Vision Caucus; Democratic Deputy Whip; married: Helen Albers, January 23, 1970; children: Angela and Christopher; committees: Energy and Commerce; Foreign Affairs; elected on November 3, 1992, to the 103rd Congress; reelected to each succeeding Congress.

Office Listings

http://www.house.gov/green

2372 Rayburn House Office Building, Washington, DC 20515 .... (202) 225–1688
Legislative Director.—Vince Jesaitis. FAX: 225–9903
Press Secretary.—Brenda Arredondo.
Legislative Assistants: Lindsay Mosshart, Abigail Pinkele, Derrick Ramos.
Scheduler.—Tim Merritt.
256 North Sam Houston Parkway East, Suite 29, Houston, TX 77060 .... (281) 999–5879
Chief of Staff / Administrative Assistant.—Rhonda Jackson.
11811 Interstate–10 East, Suite 430, Houston, TX 77029 .... (713) 330–0761
909 Decker Drive, Suite 124, Baytown, TX 77520 .... (281) 420–0502

Counties: HARRIS COUNTY (part). CITIES AND TOWNSHIPS: Baytown, Channelview, Galena Park, Houston, Humble, Jacinto City, La Porte, Pasadena, and South Houston. Population (2000), 651,620.

ZIP Codes: 77003, 77009, 77011–13, 77015–18, 77020–23, 77026, 77029, 77032, 77034, 77037, 77039, 77044, 77049–50, 77060–61, 77075–76, 77087, 77091, 77093, 77205–07, 77213, 77216–17, 77220–23, 77226, 77229, 77234, 77249, 77261–62, 77275, 77287, 77291–93, 77315, 77396, 77501–04, 77506, 77520–22, 77530, 77536, 77547, 77562, 77571–72, 77580, 77587

* * *

THIRTIETH DISTRICT

EDDIE BERNICE JOHNSON, Democrat, of Dallas, TX; born in Waco, TX, December 3, 1935; education: nursing diploma, St. Mary's at Notre Dame, 1955; B.S., nursing, Texas Christian, 1967; M.P.A, Southern Methodist, 1976; proprietor, Eddie Bernice Johnson and Associates consulting and airport concession management; Texas House of Representatives, 1972–77; Carter administration appointee, 1977–81; Texas State Senate, 1986–92; NABTP Mickey Leland Award for Excellence in Diversity, 2000; National Association of School Nurses, Inc., Legislative Award, 2000; The State of Texas Honorary Texan issued by the Governor of Texas, 2000; Links, Inc., Co-Founders Award, 2000; 100 Black Men of America, Inc., Woman of the Year, 2001; National Black Caucus of State Legislators Image Award, 2001; National Conference of Black Mayors, Inc. President's Award, 2001; Alpha Kappa Alpha Trailblazer, 2002; Thurgood Marshall Scholarship Community Leader, 2002; Phi Beta Sigma Fraternity Woman of the Year, 2002; CBCF Outstanding Leadership, 2002; congressional caucuses: Asian-Pacific; Airpower; Army; Arts; Biomedical Research; chair (107th Congress), Congressional Black Caucus; Children's Working Group; co-chair, Task Force on International HIV / AIDS; Fire Services; Human Rights Caucus; Korean Caucus; Livable Communities Task Force; Medical Technology; Oil & Gas Educational Forum; Singapore Caucus; Study Group on Japan; Tex-21 Transportation Caucus; Urban; Womens' Caucus; Women's Issues; member: St. John Baptist Church, Dallas; children: Dawrence Kirk; committees: Science and Technology; Transportation and Infrastructure; elected on November 3, 1992, to the 103rd Congress; reelected to each succeeding Congress.

Office Listings

http://www.ebjohnson.house.gov

1511 Longworth House Office Building, Washington, DC 20515 .... (202) 225–8885
Chief of Staff / Legislative Director.—Murat Gokcigdem. FAX: 226–1477
Scheduler / Executive Assistant.—Nanette Ladell Spencer.
Communications Director.—Phoebe Silag.
Senior Policy Advisor.—Jennifer Stiddard.
Senior Legislative Assistant.—Joye Purser.
Legislative Assistants: Chris Crowe, Trisha Raines.
Special Assistant.—Marcus Paulsen.
3102 Maple Avenue, Suite 600, Dallas, TX 75201 .... (214) 922–8885
District Director.—Rod Givens.

Counties: DALLAS (part). CITIES AND TOWNSHIPS: Cedar Hill, Dallas, De Soto, Duncanville, Glenn Heights, Hutchins, Lancaster, Ovilla, and Wilmer. Population (2000), 651,620.

ZIP Codes: 75104, 75115–16, 75125, 75134, 75137, 75141, 75146, 75149, 75154, 75159, 75172, 75201–04, 75206–10, 75212, 75214–20, 75223–24, 75226–28, 75232–33, 75235–37, 75239, 75241, 75246–47, 75253

* * *

THIRTY-FIRST DISTRICT

JOHN R. CARTER, Republican, of Round Rock, TX; born in Houston, TX, November 6, 1941; education: Texas Tech University, 1964; University of Texas Law School, 1969; professional: attorney; private law practice; public service: appointed and elected a Texas District Court Judge, 1981–2001; awards: recipient and namesake of the Williamson County ''John R. Carter Lifetime Achievement Award''; family: married to Erika Carter; children: Gilianne, John, Theodore, and Erika Danielle; committees: Appropriations; elected to 108th Congress on November 5, 2002; reelected to each succeeding Congress.

Office Listings

http://www.house.gov/carter

409 Cannon House Office Building, Washington, DC 20515 .... (202) 225–3864
Chief of Staff.—John Walker. FAX: 225–5886
Deputy Chief of Staff.—Brendan Belair.
Communications Director.—John Stone.
Scheduler.—Mary Randolph Carpenter.
1717 North IH 35, Round Rock, TX 78664 .... (512) 246–1600
Chief of Staff.—Jonas Miller.
6544B South General Bruce Drive, Temple, TX 76502 .... (254) 933–1392
Regional Director.—Greg Schannep.

Counties: BELL, CORYELL, ERATH, FALLS, HAMILTON, MILIAM, SOUTHERN ROBERTSON, WILLIAMSON. POPULATION (2000), 651,209.

ZIP Codes: 76401, 76436, 76446, 76457, 76501–05, 76508, 76511, 76513, 76518–20, 76522–28, 76530–31, 76533–34, 76537–38, 76540–44, 76547–49, 76554, 76557–59, 76561, 76564–67, 76569–71, 76573–74, 76577–79, 76596–99, 76632, 76656, 76680, 76685, 76689, 77410, 77426, 77466, 77473, 77492, 77805–07, 77834, 77836, 77838, 77841, 77852, 77857, 77862, 77866, 77878–79, 77881, 78363, 78602, 78613, 78615, 78626, 78628, 78634, 78641–42, 78646, 78673–74, 78664, 78681, 78717, 78729, 78931, 78933, 78940, 78942, 78944, 78948, 78950

* * *

THIRTY-SECOND DISTRICT

PETE SESSIONS, Republican, of Dallas, TX; born in Waco, TX, March 22, 1955; education: Bachelor of Science in social sciences, political science, Southwestern University, Georgetown, TX, 1978; professional: worked for Southwestern Bell, and Bell Communications Research (formerly Bell Labs), 1978–94; vice president for public policy, National Center for Policy

Analysis, 1994–95; board member, White Rock YMCA; trustee, Southwestern University; member, National Eagle Scout Association's national committee; advisor to president, Special Olympics Texas; past chairman, East Dallas Chamber of Commerce; awards: Honorary Doctorate, Dallas Baptist University; National Distinguished Eagle Scout Award; Boy Scouts of America; Leadership Award, American College of Emergency Physicians; Spirit of Enterprise Award, U.S. Chamber of Commerce; Best and Brightest, American Conservative Union; Guardian of Small Business Award, National Federation of Independent Business; Taxpayers' Friend Award, National Taxpayers Union; National Leadership Award, National Down Syndrome Society; Champion of Healthcare Innovation Award, Healthcare Leadership Council; Wireless Industry Achievement Award, Cellular Telecommunications and Internet Association; religion: Methodist; married: Juanita Sessions; two children: Bill and Alex; chair, National Republican Congressional Committee; co-chairman, Congressional Down Syndrome Caucus; co-chairman, Congressional Missile Defense Caucus; committees: Rules; elected on November 5, 1996, to the 105th Congress; reelected to each succeeding Congress.

Office Listings

http://www.sessions.house.gov

2233 Rayburn House Office Building, Washington, DC 20515–4332 .... (202) 225–2231
Chief of Staff.—Josh Saltzman. FAX: 225–5878
Communications Director.—Emily Davis.
Legislative Director.—Keagan Lenihan.
Park Central VII, 12750 Merit Drive, Suite 1434, Dallas, TX 75251 .... (972) 392–0505

County: DALLAS (part). CITIES AND TOWNSHIPS: Addison, Cockrell Hill, Dallas, Grand Prairie, Highland Park, Irving, Richardson, and University Park. Population (2000), 651,619.

ZIP Codes: 75001, 75038–39, 75050–51, 75060–63, 75080–81, 75203–06, 75208–09, 75211–12, 75214, 75219–20, 75222, 75224–25, 75229–31, 75233, 75240, 75244, 75248, 75251, 75254, 75262

UTAH

(Population 2000, 2,233,169)

SENATORS

ORRIN G. HATCH, Republican, of Salt Lake City, UT; born in Pittsburgh, PA, March 22, 1934; education: B.S., Brigham Young University, Provo, UT, 1959; J.D., University of Pittsburgh, 1962; practiced law in Salt Lake City, UT, and Pittsburgh, PA; senior partner, Hatch and Plumb law firm, Salt Lake City; worked his way through high school, college, and law school at the metal lathing building trade; holds ''AV'' rating in Martindale-Hubbell Law Directory; member: AFL-CIO, Salt Lake County Bar Association; Utah Bar Association; American Bar Association; Pennsylvania Bar Association; Allegheny County Bar Association and numerous other professional and fraternal organizations; honorary doctorate, University of Maryland; honorary doctor of laws: Pepperdine University; Southern Utah University; Widener University, University of Pittsburgh; honorary national ski patroller and other honorary degrees; Senate Republican High Tech Task Force; Congressional International Anti-Privacy Caucus; author of numerous national publications; member, Church of Jesus Christ of Latter-Day Saints; married: Elaine Hansen of Newton, UT; children: Brent, Marcia, Scott, Kimberly, Alysa, and Jess; committees: Finance; Health, Education, Labor, and Pensions; Judiciary; Joint Committee on Taxation; Select Committee on Intelligence; Special Committee on Aging; elected to the U.S. Senate on November 2, 1976; reelected to each succeeding Senate term.

Office Listings

http://hatch.senate.gov

104 Hart Senate Office Building, Washington, DC 20510	(202) 224–5251
Chief of Staff.—Jace Johnson.	FAX: 224–6331
Legislative Director.—Christopher Campbell.	
Communications Director.—Mark Eddington.	
Scheduler.—Ruth Montoya.	
Federal Building, Suite 8402, Salt Lake City, UT 84138	(801) 524–4380
State Director.—Melanie Bowen.	
Federal Building, 324 25th Street, Suite 1006, Ogden, UT 84401	(801) 625–5672
51 South University Avenue, Suite 320, Provo, UT 84606	(801) 375–7881
197 East Tabernacle, Room 2, St. George, UT 84770	(435) 634–1795
77 North Main Street, Suite 112, Cedar City, UT 84720	(435) 586–8435

* * *

ROBERT F. BENNETT, Republican, of Salt Lake City, UT; born in Salt Lake City, September 18, 1933; education: B.S., University of Utah, 1957; professional: chief executive officer of Franklin Quest, Salt Lake City; chief congressional liaison, U.S. Department of Transportation; awards: ''Entrepreneur of the Year,'' *Inc.* magazine, 1989; High-Tech Legislator of the Year, 2001; Emerging Congressional Leader, 2002; author, *Gaining Control*, 1987; author, *Leap of Faith: Confronting the Origins of the Book of Mormon,* 2009; member, The Church of Jesus Christ of Latter-Day Saints; honorary doctorates: University of Utah, Utah Valley State College, Snow College, Westminster College, Salt Lake Community College; married: Joyce McKay; children: James, Julie, Robert, Wendy, Heather, and Heidi; committees: Appropriations; Energy and Natural Resources; Banking, Housing, and Urban Affairs; Homeland Security and Government Affairs; Rules and Administration; Joint Economic Committee; Joint Committee on the Library; Joint Committee on Printing; elected to the U.S. Senate on November 3, 1992; reelected to each succeeding Senate term.

Office Listings

http://bennett.senate.gov

431 Dirksen Senate Office Building, Washington, DC 20510	(202) 224–5444
Chief of Staff.—Mary Jane Collipriest.	FAX: 228–1168
Deputy Chief of Staff / Legislative Director.—Brian Smith.	
Office Manager.—Sandy Knickman.	
Press Secretary.—Tara DiJulio.	
Wallace F. Bennett Federal Building, Suite 4225, Salt Lake City, UT 84138	(801) 524–5933
State Director.—Tim Sheehan.	
Federal Building, 324 25th Street, Suite 1410, Ogden, UT 84401	(801) 625–5676
51 South University Avenue, Suite 310, Provo, UT 84601–4424	(801) 851–2525
Federal Building, 196 East Tabernacle Street, Room 21, St. George, UT 84770–3474	(435) 628–5514
77 North Main, #113, Cedar City, UT 84720	(435) 865–1335

REPRESENTATIVES

FIRST DISTRICT

ROB BISHOP, Republican, of Brigham City, UT; born in Kaysville, UT, July 13, 1951; education: B.A., Political Science, *magna cum laude,* University of Utah, 1974; professional: high-school teacher; public service: Utah House of Representatives, 1979–94, Speaker of the House his last two years; elected, chair, Utah Republican Party, 1997 (served two terms); religion: Church of Jesus Christ of Latter-day Saints; family: married to Jeralynn Hansen; children: Shule, Jarom, Zenock, Maren, and Jashon; committees: Armed Services; Education and Labor; Natural Resources; elected to the 108th Congress on November 5, 2002; reelected to each succeeding Congress.

Office Listings

http://www.house.gov/robbishop

123 Cannon House Office Building, Washington, DC 20515 .... (202) 225–0453
Chief of Staff.—Scott Parker. FAX: 225–5857
Legislative Assistants: Wayne Bradshaw, Steve Petersen, Cody Stewart.
Scheduler / Deputy Chief of Staff.—Jennifer Griffith.
6 North Main Street, Brigham City, UT 84302 .... (435) 734–2270
FAX: 734–2290
125 South State Street, Suite 5420, Salt Lake City, UT 84138–1102 .... (801) 532–3244
(801) 532–3583
324 25th Street, 1017 Federal Building, Ogden, UT 94401 .... (801) 625–0107

Counties: BOX ELDER, CACHE, DAVIS, JUAB (part), MORGAN, RICH, SALT LAKE (part), SUMMIT, TOOELE, WEBER. Population (2000), 744,389.

ZIP Codes: 84010–11, 84014–18, 84022, 84024–25, 84028–29, 84033–34, 84036–38, 84040–41, 84044, 84050, 84054–56, 84060–61, 84064, 84067–69, 84071, 84074–75, 84080, 84083, 84086–87, 84089, 84098, 84101–06, 84110–11, 84114–16, 84119–20, 84122, 84125–28, 84130–31, 84133–34, 84136, 84138–39, 84141, 84144–45, 84147, 84150–51, 84180, 84189–90, 84199, 84201, 84244, 84301–02, 84304–41, 84401–05, 84407–09, 84412, 84414–15, 84628

* * *

SECOND DISTRICT

JIM MATHESON, Democrat, of Salt Lake City, UT; born in Salt Lake City, March 21, 1960; education: B.A., Harvard University; M.B.A., University of California at Los Angeles (UCLA); professional: energy businessman; Bonneville Pacific; Energy Strategies, Inc.; The Matheson Group; organizations: Environmental Policy Institute; Salt Lake Public Utilities Board; Scott M. Matheson Leadership Forum; religion: Church of Jesus Christ of Latter-Day Saints; married: Amy; children: William and Harris; committees: Energy and Commerce; Science and Technology; elected to the 107th Congress on November 7, 2000; reelected to each succeeding Congress.

Office Listings

http://www.matheson.house.gov

2434 Rayburn House Office Building, Washington, DC 20515 .... (202) 225–3011
Chief of Staff.—Amy Andryszak. FAX: 225–5638
Executive Assistant.—Nicole Christensen.
240 East Morris Avenue, #235, Salt Lake City, UT 84115 .... (801) 486–1236
District Director.—Mike Reberg.
321 North Mall Drive, #E101B, St. George, UT 84790 .... (435) 627–0880
120 East Main Street-LL, Price, UT 84501 .... (435) 636–3722

Counties: CARBON, DAGGETT, DUCHENSNE, EMERY, GARFIELD, GRAND, IRON, KANE, PIUTE, SALT LAKE (part), SAN JUAN, UNITAH, UTAH (part), WASATCH, WASHINGTON, WAYNE. Population (2000), 744,390.

ZIP Codes: 84001–04, 84007–08, 84020–21, 84023, 84026–27, 84031–32, 84035, 84039, 84043, 84046–47, 84049, 84051–53, 84062–63, 84066, 84070, 84072–73, 84076, 84078–79, 84082, 84085, 84090–94, 84102–03, 84105–09, 84112–13, 84115–17, 84119, 84121, 84123–24, 84132, 84143, 84148, 84152, 84157–58, 84165, 84171, 84501, 84510–13, 84515–16, 84518, 84520–23, 84525–26, 84528–37, 84539, 84540, 84542, 84604, 84710, 84712, 84714–23, 84725–26, 84729, 84732–38, 84740–43, 84745–47, 84749–50, 84753, 84755–65, 84767, 84770–76, 84779–84, 84790–91

* * *

THIRD DISTRICT

JASON CHAFFETZ, Republican, of Alpine, UT; born in Los Gatos, CA; March 26, 1967; education: B.A., communications, Brigham Young University, Provo, UT, 1989; professional: business executive; chief of staff, Utah governor John Huntsman, 2004; President, Maxtera Utah, 2005–present; trustee, Utah Valley board of trustees; chair, Utah National Guard Adjutant General Review; Commissioner, Highland City Planning Commission; President, BYU Utah County Cougar Club; Cougar Club (BYU) Board of Directors; awards: starting placekicker, BYU Football Team, 1988–89; Best Run Campaign, General Election, Utah 2004, Huntsman for Governor; Western Athletic Conference Champions, 1989; Cougar Club Academic Athlete Award, 1988–89; Academic All-WAC Football Team, 1989; National All-Bowl Football Team, 1988; religion: Church of Jesus Christ of Latter-day Saints; married: Julie, in 1991; children: Max, Ellis, and Kate; committees: Judiciary; Natural Resources; Oversight and Government Reform; elected to the 111th Congress on November 4, 2008.

Office Listings

http://chaffetz.house.gov

1032 Longworth House Office Building, Washington, DC 20515 .... (202) 225–7751
Chief of Staff.—Justin Harding. FAX: 225–5629
Legislative Director.—Mike Jerman.
Scheduler / Office Manager.—Karilyn Henshaw.
Communications Director / Legislative Aide.—Alisia Essig.
Senior Policy Advisor / Counsel.—Erek Loosli.
Legislative Staff Assistant / Legislative Aide.—Fred Ferguson.
51 South University Avenue, Suite 317, Provo, UT 84601 .... (801) 851–2500
Deputy District Director.—Dell Smith. FAX: 851–2509
3895 West 7800 South, Suite 201, West Jordan, UT 84088 .... (801) 282–5502
District Director.—Jennifer Scott. FAX: 282–6081

Counties: BEAVER, JUAB (part), MILLARD, SALT LAKE (part), SANPETE, SEVIER, UTAH (part). Population (2000), 744,390.

ZIP Codes: 84003, 84006, 84013, 84042–44, 84047, 84057–59, 84062, 84065, 84070, 84084, 84088, 84095, 84097, 84107, 84118–20, 84123, 84128, 84170, 84184, 84199, 84601–06, 84620–24, 84626–27, 84629–40, 84642–57, 84660, 84662–65, 84667, 84701, 84711, 84713, 84724, 84728, 84730–31, 84739, 84744, 84751–52, 84754, 84766

VERMONT

(Population 2000, 608,827)

SENATORS

PATRICK J. LEAHY, Democrat, of Middlesex, VT; born in Montpelier, VT, March 31, 1940, son of Howard and Alba Leahy; education: graduate of St. Michael's High School, Montpelier, 1957; B.A., St. Michael's College, 1961; J.D., Georgetown University, 1964; professional: attorney, admitted to the Vermont bar, 1964; admitted to the District of Columbia bar, 1979; admitted to practice before: the Vermont Supreme Court, 1964; the Federal District Court of Vermont, 1965; the Second Circuit Court of Appeals in New York, 1966; and the U.S. Supreme Court, 1968; State's Attorney, Chittenden County, 1966–74; vice president, National District Attorneys Association, 1971–74; married: the former Marcelle Pomerleau, 1962; children: Kevin, Alicia, and Mark; first Democrat and youngest person in Vermont to be elected to the U.S. Senate; committees: chair, Judiciary; Agriculture, Nutrition, and Forestry; Appropriations; elected to the Senate on November 5, 1974; reelected to each succeeding Senate term.

Office Listings

http://leahy.senate.gov

433 Russell Senate Office Building, Washington, DC 20515 .... (202) 224–4242
Chief of Staff.—Ed Pagano. FAX: 224–3479
Administrative Director.—Ann Berry.
Legislative Director.—John P. Dowd.
Communications Director.—David Carle.
Federal Building, Room 338, Montpelier, VT 05602 .... (802) 229–0569
199 Main Street, Courthouse Plaza, Burlington, VT 05401 .... (802) 863–2525
State Director.—Chuck Ross.

* * *

BERNARD SANDERS, Independent, of Burlington, VT; born in Brooklyn, NY, September 8, 1941; education: graduated, Madison High School, Brooklyn; B.S., political science, University of Chicago, 1964; professional: carpenter; writer; college professor; Mayor of Burlington, VT, 1981–89; married: the former Jane O'Meara, 1988; children: Levi, Heather, Carina and David; committees: Budget; Energy and Natural Resources; Environment and Public Works; Health, Education, Labor, and Pensions; Veterans' Affairs; elected to the 102nd Congress on November 6, 1990; reelected to each succeeding Congress; elected to the U.S. Senate on November 7, 2006.

Office Listings

http://sanders.senate.gov

332 Dirksen Senate Office Building, Washington, DC 20510 .... (202) 224–5141
Chief of Staff.—Stanley ''Huck'' Gutman. FAX: 228–0776
Legislative Director.—Peter Tyler.
Communications Director.—Michael Briggs.
1 Church Street, Second Floor, Burlington, VT 05401 .... (802) 862–0697

REPRESENTATIVE

AT LARGE

PETER WELCH, Democrat, of Hartland, VT; born in Springfield, MA, May 2, 1947; education: Cathedral High School, Springfield, MA, 1969; B.A., *magna cum laude*, College of the Holy Cross, 1969; J.D., University of California at Berkley, 1973; professional: attorney, admitted to VT Bar, 1974; founding partner, Welch, Graham & Manby; served in Vermont State Senate, 1981–89, 2001–07; Minority Leader, 1983–85; President pro tempore, 1985–89, 2003–07; family: wife, Joan Smith (deceased), currently married to Margaret Cheney; five children: Beth, Mary, Bill, John and Michael; three stepchildren; committees: Energy and Commerce; Oversight and Government Reform; Standards of Official Conduct; elected to the 110th Congress on November 7, 2006; reelected to the 111th Congress on November 4, 2008.

Office Listings

http://www.welch.house.gov

1404 Longworth House Office Building, Washington, DC 20515 .... (202) 225–4115

Chief of Staff.—Bob Rogan.
Scheduler / Executive Assistant.—Jake Oster.
Legislative Director.—Andrew Savage.
Communications Director.—Paul Heintz.
30 Main Street, Third Floor, Suite 350, Burlington, VT 05401 .... (802) 652–2450
State Director.—Patricia Coates.

Population (2000), 608,827.

ZIP Codes: 05001, 05009, 05030–43, 05045–56, 05058–62, 05065, 05067–77, 05079, 05081, 05083–86, 05088–89, 05091, 05101, 05141–43, 05146, 05148–56, 05158–59, 05161, 05201, 05250–55, 05257, 05260–62, 05301–04, 05340–46, 05350–63, 05401–07, 05439–66, 05468–74, 05476–79, 05481–83, 05485–92, 05494–95, 05601–04, 05609, 05620, 05633, 05640–41, 05647–58, 05660–67, 05669–82, 05701–02, 05730–48, 05750–51, 05753, 05757–70, 05772–78, 05819–30, 05832–33, 05836–43, 05845–51, 05853, 05855, 05857–63, 05866–68, 05871–75, 05901–07

VIRGINIA

(Population 2000, 7,078,515)

SENATORS

JIM WEBB, Democrat, of Arlington County, VA; born in St. Joseph, MO, February 9, 1946; education: B.S., engineering, U.S. Naval Academy, 1968; J.D., Georgetown University Law Center, 1975; professional: Infantry officer, U.S. Marine Corps, 1968–72 (combat service in Vietnam); counsel, House Committee on Veterans' Affairs, 1977–81; Assistant Secretary of Defense, Reserve Affairs, 1984–87; Secretary of the Navy, 1987–88; broad career as a writer and journalist; literature professor, U.S. Naval Academy; Emmy-Award winning TV journalist; author, six best-selling novels, two non-fiction works, including a history of the Scots-Irish people; screenwriter and producer; business consultant; awards: Military awards: Navy Cross; Silver Star Medal; two Bronze Star Medals with combat ''V''; two Purple Heart Medals; campaign and unit citations; numerous civilian awards including Military Order of the Purple Heart's (MOPH) Special Leadership Award; Military Coalition's Award of Merit; Blinded American Veterans Foundation's George ''Buck'' Gillespie Congressional Award for Meritorious Service; Veterans of Foreign Wars, 2008; Gold Medal and Citation of Merit; American Legion's National Commander's Public Relations Award, 2008; Military Officers Association of America (MOAA) Colonel Arthur T. Marix Congressional Leadership Award, 2009; Department of Defense Distinguished Public Service Medal; Medal of Honor Society's Patriot Award; American Legion National Commander's Public Service Award; Veterans of Foreign Wars Media Service Award; Marine Corps League's Military Order of the Iron Mike Award; John H. Russell Leadership Award; Marine Corps Correspondent Association's Robert L. Denig Distinguished Service Award; married: Hong: Hong Le; children: Amy, James Robert, Sarah, Julia, and Georgia; committees: Armed Services; Foreign Relations; Veterans' Affairs; Joint Economic Committee; elected to the U.S. Senate on November 7, 2006.

Office Listings

http://webb.senate.gov

248 Russell Senate Office Building, Washington, DC 20510 .... (202) 224–4024
Chief of Staff.—Paul Reagan. FAX: 228–6363
Communications Director.—Jessica Smith.
Legislative Director.—David Bonine.
Scheduler.—Melissa Bruns.
State Director.—Conaway Haskins.
222 Central Park Avenue, Suite 120, Virginia Beach, VA 23462 .... (757) 518–1674
507 East Franklin Street, Richmond, VA 23219 .... (804) 771–2221
3140 Chaparral Drive, Building C, Suite 101, Roanoke, VA 24018 .... (540) 772–4236
756 Park Avenue, Norton, VA 24273 ....
TBD, Arlington, VA.
7309 Arlington Boulevard, Suite 316, Falls Church, VA 22042 .... (703) 573–7090
FAX: 573–7098
308 Craghead Street, Suite 102A, Danville, VA 24541 .... (434) 792–0976
FAX: 972–0960

* * *

MARK R. WARNER, Democrat, of Alexandria, VA; born in Indianapolis, IN, December 15, 1954; son of Robert and Marge Warner of Vernon, CT; education: B.A., political science, The George Washington University, 1977, J.D., Harvard Law School, 1980; Governor, Commonwealth of Virginia, 2002–06; chairman of the National Governor's Association, 2004–05; religion: Presbyterian; wife: Lisa Collis; children: Madison, Gillian, Eliza; committees: Banking, Housing, and Urban Affairs; Budget, Commerce, Science, and Transportation; Rules and Administration; Joint Economic Committee; elected to the U.S. Senate on November 4, 2008.

Office Listings

http://warner.senate.gov

SR–459A Russell Senate Office Building, Washington, DC 20510 .... (202) 224–2023
Chief of Staff.—Luke S. Albee. FAX: 224–2530
Communications Director.—Kevin Hall.
Press Assistant.—Riki Parikh.
Scheduler.—Walker Irving.
Policy Advisor / Legislative Director.—Jonathan Davidson.
Legislative Correspondents: Nicholas Devereux, Michelle Maywurm, Leah Ralph.
Projects Coordinator.—Kelly Thomasson.
180 West Main Street, Abingdon, VA 24210 .... (276) 628–8158

FAX: 628–1036

101 West Main Street, Suite 4900, Norfolk, VA 23510 .... (757) 441–3079
FAX: 441–6250

5309 Commonwealth Centre Parkway, Midlothian, VA 23112 .... (804) 739–0247
FAX: 739–3478

129B Salem Avenue, Southwest, Roanoke, VA 24011 .... (540) 857–2676
FAX: 857–2800

REPRESENTATIVES

FIRST DISTRICT

ROBERT J. WITTMAN, Republican, of Montross, VA; born in Washington, DC, February 2, 1959; B.S., Biology Virginia Polytechnic Institute and State University, 1981, M.P.H., Health Policy and Administration University of North Carolina at Chapel Hill, 1989, Ph.D., Virginia Commonwealth University Public Policy and Administration, 1992; professional: Field Director for the Virginia Health Department's Division of Shellfish Sanitation; religion: Episcopalian; Public Service: Montross Town Council, 1986–96, Mayor of Montross, 1992–96; Westmoreland County Board of Supervisors, 1995–2003 and chairman, 2003–05; Virginia House of Delegates, 2005–07; married: Kathryn Wittman; children: Devon and Joshua; committees: Armed Services; Natural Resources; elected to the 110th Congress on December 11, 2007 in a special election; reelected to the 111th Congress.

Office Listings

http://www.wittman.house.gov

1318 Longworth House Office Building, Washington, DC 20515 .... (202) 225–4261
Chief of Staff.—Mary Springer. FAX: 225–4382
Legislative Director.—Jamie Miller.
Press Secretary.—Tom Crosson.
Scheduler/Office Manager.—Whitney Stockett.
4904–B George Washington Memorial Parkway, Yorktown, VA 23692 .... (757) 874–6687
District Director.—Joe Schumacher.
3504 Plank Road, Suite 203 Fredericksburg, VA 22407 .... (540) 548–1086
508 Church Lane, Tappahannock, VA 22560 .... (804) 443–0668

Counties: CAROLINE (part), ESSEX, FAUQUIER (part), GLOUCESTER, JAMES CITY, KING AND QUEEN, KING GEORGE, KING WILLIAM, LANCASTER, MATHEWS, MIDDLESEX, NORTHUMBERLAND, PRINCE WILLIAM (part), RICHMOND, SPOTSYLVANIA (part), STAFFORD, WESTMORELAND, YORK. CITIES AND TOWNSHIPS: Bowling Green, Chancellorsville, Cobbs Creek, Colonial Beach, Dumfries, Falmouth, Fredericksburg, Hampton, Kilmarnock, Lightfoot, Montross, Newport News, Poquoson, Quantico, Saluda, Seaford, Tappahannock, Toano, Triangle, Warsaw, West Point, White Stone, Williamsburg, and Yorktown. Population (2000), 643,514.

ZIP Codes: 20106, 20112, 20115, 20119, 20128, 20138–39, 20181, 20186–87, 22026, 22134–35, 22172, 22191, 22193, 22401–08, 22412, 22427, 22430, 22432, 22435–38, 22442–43, 22446, 22448, 22451, 22454, 22456, 22460, 22463, 22469, 22471–73, 22476, 22480–82, 22485, 22488, 22501, 22503–04, 22507–09, 22511, 22513–14, 22517, 22520, 22523–24, 22526, 22528–30, 22535, 22538–39, 22544–48, 22552–56, 22558, 22560, 22570, 22572, 22576–81, 22639, 22712, 22720, 22728, 22734, 22739, 22742, 23001, 23003, 23009, 23011, 23017–18, 23021, 23023–25, 23031–32, 23035, 23043, 23045, 23050, 23056, 23061–62, 23064, 23066, 23068–72, 23076, 23079, 23081, 23085–86, 23089–92, 23106–10, 23115, 23117, 23119, 23125–28, 23130–31, 23138, 23148–49, 2315356, 23161, 23163, 23168–69, 23175–78, 23180–81, 23183–88, 23190–91, 23354, 23601–03, 23605–06, 23608–09, 23612, 23662–63, 23665–67, 23669–70, 23681, 23690–94, 23696

* * *

SECOND DISTRICT

GLENN C. NYE III, Democrat, of Hampton Roads, VA; born in Philadelphia, PA, September 9, 1974; education: B.S., School of Foreign Service at Georgetown University, Washington, DC, 1996; State Department's Superior Honor Award, 2001; Blue Dog Caucus; committees: Veterans' Affairs; Small Business; elected to the 111th Congress on November 4, 2008.

Office Listings

http://www.nye.house.gov

116 Cannon House Office Building, Washington, DC 20515 .... (202) 225–4215
Chief of Staff.—Angela Kouters. FAX: 225–4218
Communications Director.—Clark Pettig.
Executive Assistant.—Emily Contillo.
4772 Euclid Road, Suite E, Virginia Beach, VA 23462 .... (757) 497–6859

District Director.—Erica Walker Cash.
3386 Front Street, Accomac, VA 23301 .... (757) 326–6201

Counties: ACCOMACK, NORTHAMPTON. CITIES: Hampton, Norfolk, and Virginia Beach. Population (2000), 643,510.

ZIP Codes: 23301–03, 23306–08, 23310, 23313, 23316, 23336–37, 23341, 23345, 23347, 23350, 23354, 23356–59, 23389, 23395, 23398–99, 23401, 23404–05, 23407–10, 23412–23, 23426–27, 23429, 23440–43, 23450–67, 23471, 23479–80, 23482–83, 23486, 23488, 23502–03, 23505–08, 23511–13, 23515, 23518–19, 23521, 23529, 23541, 23551, 23605, 23651, 23661, 23663–66, 23669

* * *

THIRD DISTRICT

ROBERT C. ''BOBBY'' SCOTT, Democrat, of Newport News, VA; born in Washington, DC, April 30, 1947; education: graduated, Groton High School; B.A., Harvard University; J.D., Boston College Law School; professional: served in the Massachusetts National Guard; attorney; admitted to the Virginia bar; Virginia House of Delegates, 1978–83; Senate of Virginia, 1983–92; member: Alpha Phi Alpha Fraternity; March of Dimes Board of Directors; NAACP; Peninsula Chamber of Commerce; Peninsula Legal Aid Center Board of Directors; Sigma Pi Phi Fraternity; committees: Budget; Education and Labor; Judiciary; elected on November 3, 1992 to the 103rd Congress; reelected to each succeeding Congress.

Office Listings

http://www.bobbyscott.house.gov

1201 Longworth House Office Building, Washington, DC 20515 .... (202) 225–8351
Chief of Staff.—Joni L. Ivey. FAX: 225–8354
Executive Assistant.—Randi Petty.
Communications Director.—Larry Dillard.
Legislative Director.—Ilana Brunner.
Legislative Counsel.—Rashage Green.
Legislative Assistants: David Dailey, Christian Haines, Carolyn Hughes.
2600 Washington Avenue, Suite 1010, Newport News, VA 23607 .... (757) 380–1000
District Director.—Gisele Russell.
400 North 8th Street, Suite 430, Richmond, VA 23219 .... (804) 644–4845
District Scheduler.—Nkechi George-Winkler.

Counties: CHARLES CITY, HENRICO (part), NEW KENT, PRINCE GEORGES, SURRY. CITIES: Hampton (part), Newport News (part), Norfolk (part), Portsmouth and Richmond (part). Population (2000), 643,476.

ZIP Codes: 23011, 23030, 23059–60, 23075, 23089, 23111, 23124, 23140–41, 23147, 23150, 23181, 23185, 23218–25, 23227–28, 23230–32, 23234, 23240–41, 23249–50, 23260–61, 23269–70, 23272, 23274–76, 23278–79, 23282, 23284–86, 23290–93, 23295, 23298, 23501–02, 23504–05, 23507–10, 23513–14, 23517–18, 23520, 23523, 23530, 23601–09, 23628, 23630–31, 23653, 23661, 23663–64, 23666–70, 23701–05, 23707–09, 23839, 23842, 23846, 23860, 23875, 23881, 23883, 23888, 23898–99

* * *

FOURTH DISTRICT

J. RANDY FORBES, Republican, of Chesapeake, VA; born in Chesapeake, February 17, 1952; education: B.A., Randolph-Macon College; J.D., University of Virginia School of Law; professional: attorney; religion: Baptist; public service: Virginia House of Delegates, 1990–97; Virginia State Senate, 1997–2001; Republican House Floor Leader, 1994–97; Republican Senate Floor Leader, 1998–2001; Chairman of the Republican Party of Virginia, 1996–2000; married: Shirley; children: Neil, Jamie, Jordan, and Justin; committees: Armed Services; Judiciary; elected to the 107th Congress, by special election, on June 19, 2001; reelected to each succeeding Congress.

Office Listings

2438 Rayburn House Office Building, Washington, DC 20515 .... (202) 225–6365
Chief of Staff.—Dee Gilmore. FAX: 226–1170
Communications Director.—Jessica Mancari.
Legislative Director.—Ryan Kaldahl.
505 Independence Parkway, Lake Center 2, Suite 104, Chesapeake, VA 23322 ...... (757) 382–0080
District Representative.—Curtis Byrd.
2903 Boulevard, Suite B, Colonial Heights, VA 23834 .... (804) 526–4969
District Representative.—Ron White.
425 H. South Main Street, Emporia, VA 23847 .... (434) 634–5575

District Field Representative.—Rick Franklin.

Counties: AMELIA, BRUNSWICK (part), CHESTERFIELD (part), DINWIDDIE, GREENSVILLE, ISLE OF WIGHT (part), NOTTOWAY, POWHATAN, PRINCE GEORGE (part), SOUTHAMPTON, SUSSEX. Population (2000), 643,477.

ZIP Codes: 23002, 23083, 23101, 23105, 23112–14, 23120, 23139, 23234, 23236–37, 23304, 23314–15, 23320–28, 23397, 23424, 23430–39, 23487, 23501, 23801, 23803–06, 23821, 23824, 23827–34, 23836–38, 23840–42, 23844–45, 23847, 23850–51, 23856–57, 23860, 23866–67, 23872–76, 23878–79, 23882, 23884–85, 23887–91, 23894, 23897–98, 23920, 23922, 23930, 23938, 23950, 23955

* * *

FIFTH DISTRICT

TOM PERRIELLO, Democrat, of Ivy, VA; born in Charlottesville, VA, October 9, 1974; education: B.A., Yale University, 1996; J.D., Yale University, New Haven, CT, 2001; professional: national security consultant; international justice advocate; social entrepreneur; committees: Transportation and Infrastructure; Veterans' Affairs; elected to the 111th Congress on November 4, 2008.

Office Listings

http://www.perriello.house.gov

1520 Longworth House Office Building, Washington, DC 20515 .... (202) 225–4711
Chief of Staff.—Lise Clavel. FAX: 225–5681
Scheduler.—Jay Tansey.
Communications Director.—Jessica Barba.
Legislative Director.—Beth Elliott.
313 2nd Street, SE., Suite 112, Charlottesville, VA 22902 .... (434) 293–9631
308 Craghead Street, Suite 102, Danville, VA 24541 .... (434) 791–2596
515 South Main Street, Farmville, VA 23901 .... (434) 392–1997
10 East Church Street, Suite K, Martinsville, VA 24112 .... (276) 656–2291

Counties: ALBEMARLE COUNTY. CITIES AND TOWNSHIPS: Charlotteville, Batesville, Covesville, Esmont, Greenwood, Hatton, Ivy, Keene, Keswick, North Garden, Scottsville. APPOMATTOX COUNTY. CITIES AND TOWNSHIPS: Appomattox, Evergreen, Pamplin, Spout Spring. BEDFORD COUNTY. CITIES AND TOWNSHIPS: Bedford, Big Island, Goodview, Coleman Falls, Forest, Goode, Huddleston, Lowry, Thaxton. BRUNSWICK COUNTY. BUCKINGHAM COUNTY. CITIES AND TOWNSHIPS: Andersonville, Arvonia, Buckingham, Dillwyn, Buckingham, New Canton. CAMPBELL COUNTY. CITIES AND TOWNSHIPS: Altavista, Brookneal, Concord, Evington, Gladys, Long Island, Lynch Station, Naruna, Rustburg. CHARLOTTE COUNTY. CITIES AND TOWNSHIPS: Barnesville, Charlotte Court House, Cullen, Drakes Branch, Keysville, Phenix, Randolph, Red House, Red Oak, Saxe, Wylliesburg. CUMBERLAND COUNTY. CITIES AND TOWNSHIPS: Carterville, Cumberland. DANVILLE CITY: Danville. FLUVANNA COUNTY. CITIES AND TOWNSHIPS: Bremo Bluff, Bybee, Carysbrook, Columbia, Fort Union, Kents Store, Palmyra, Troy. FRANKLIN COUNTY. CITIES AND TOWNSHIPS: Boones Mill, Callaway, Ferrum, Glade Hill, Henry, Redwood, Penhook, Rocky Mount, Union Hall, Waidsboro, Wirtz. GREENE COUNTY. HALIFAX COUNTY. CITIES AND TOWNSHIPS: Alton, Clover, Cluster Springs, Crystal Hall, Denniston, Halifax, Ingram, Lennig, Mayo, Nathalie, Republican Grove, Scottsburg, Turbeville, Vernon Hill, Virgilina. HENRY COUNTY. CITIES AND TOWNSHIPS: Axton, Bassett, Collinsville, Fieldale, Ridgeway, Spencer, Stanleytown. LUNENBURG COUNTY. CITIES AND TOWNSHIPS: Tamworth, Dundas, Fort Mitchell, Kenbridge, Lunenburg, Rehoboth, Victoria. MARTINSVILLE CITY: Martinsville. MECKLENBURG COUNTY. CITIES AND TOWNSHIPS: Baskerville, Blackridge, Boydton, Bracey, Chase City, Clarksville, Forksville, LaCross, Palmer Springs, Skipwith, South Hill, Union Level Buffalo Junction, Nelson. NELSON COUNTY. CITIES AND TOWNSHIPS: Afton, Arrington, Faber, Lovingston, Massies Mill, Nellysford, Montebello, Gladstone, Norwood, Piney River, Roseland, Schuyler, Shipman, Tye River, Tyro, Wingina. PITTSYLVANIA COUNTY. CITIES AND TOWNSHIPS: Blairs, Callands, Cascade, Chatham, Pittsville, Sandy Level, Dry Fork, Gretna, Hurt, Java, Keeling, Ringgold, Sutherlin. PRINCE EDWARD COUNTY. CITIES AND TOWNSHIPS: Green Bay, Farmville, Darlington Heights, Green Bay, Hampden-Sydney, Meherrin, Prospect, Rice, and South Boston. Population (2000), 643,497.

ZIP Codes: 22901–11, 22920, 22922–24, 22931–32, 22935–38, 22940, 22942–43, 22945–47, 22949, 22952, 22954, 22958–59, 22963–65, 22967–69, 22971, 22973–74, 22976, 22987, 23004, 23022, 23027, 23038, 23040, 23055, 23084, 23093, 23123, 23139, 23821, 23824, 23843, 23845, 23856–57, 23868, 23887, 23889, 23893, 23901, 23909, 23915, 23917, 23919–24, 23927, 23934, 23936–39, 23941–44, 23947, 23950, 23952, 23954, 23958–60, 23962–64, 23966–68, 23970, 23974, 23976, 24012, 24053–55, 24059, 24064–65, 24067, 24069, 24076, 24078–79, 24082, 24088–89, 24091–92, 24095, 24101–02, 24104, 24112–15, 24120–22, 24133, 24137, 24139, 24146, 24148, 24151, 24153, 24161, 24168, 24171, 24174, 24176–77, 24179, 24184–85, 24312, 24464, 24483, 24501–02, 24504, 24517, 24520, 24522–23, 24527–31, 24534–35, 24538–41, 24543–44, 24549–51, 24553–54, 24556–58, 24562–63, 24565–66, 24569–71, 24574, 24576–77, 24580–81, 24585–86, 24588–90, 24592–94, 24597–99

* * *

SIXTH DISTRICT

BOB GOODLATTE, Republican, of Roanoke, VA; born in Holyoke, MA, September 22, 1952; education: B.A., Bates College, Lewiston, ME, 1974; J.D., Washington and Lee University, 1977; Massachusetts bar, 1977; Virginia bar, 1978; professional: began practice in Roanoke, VA, 1979; district director for Congressman M. Caldwell Butler, 1977–79; attorney, sole practitioner, 1979–81; partner, 1981–92; chairman of the sixth district Virginia Republican

Committee, 1983–88; member: Civitan Club of Roanoke (president, 1989–90); former member, Building Better Boards Advisory Council; married: Maryellen Flaherty, 1974; children: Jennifer and Robert; deputy Republican whip; committees: Agriculture; Judiciary; elected on November 3, 1992, to the 103rd Congress; reelected to each succeeding Congress.

Office Listings

http://www.goodlatte.house.gov

2240 Rayburn House Office Building, Washington, DC 20515 .... (202) 225–5431
Chief of Staff.—Shelley Husband. FAX: 225–9681
Legislative Counsel.—Branden Ritchie.
Press Secretary.—Kathryn Rexrode.
10 Franklin Road, SE, Suite 540, Roanoke, VA 24011 .... (540) 857–2672
District Director.—Pete Larkin.
916 Main Street, Suite 300, Lynchburg, VA 24504 .... (804) 845–8306
7 Court Square, Staunton, VA 24401 .... (540) 885–3861
2 South Main Street, First Floor, Suite A, Harrisonburg, VA 22801 .... (540) 432–2391

Counties: ALLEGHANY (part), AMHERST, AUGUSTA, BATH, BEDFORD (part), BOTETOURT, HIGHLAND, ROANOKE (part), ROCKBRIDGE, ROCKINGHAM , SHENANDOAH. CITIES: Buena Vista, Covington, Harrisonburg, Lexington, Lynchburg, Roanoke, Salem, Staunton, and Waynesboro. Population (2000), 643,504.

ZIP Codes: 22626, 22641, 22644–45, 22652, 22654, 22657, 22660, 22664, 22801–03, 22807, 22810–12, 22815, 22820–21, 22824, 22827, 22830–34, 22840–48, 22850, 22853, 22920, 22922, 22939, 22952, 22967, 22980, 24001–20, 24022–38, 24040, 24042–44, 24048, 24053, 24059, 24064–66, 24070, 24077, 24079, 24083, 24085, 24087, 24090, 24101, 24121–22, 24130, 24153, 24156, 24174–75, 24178–79, 24401–02, 24411–13, 24415–16, 24421–22, 24426, 24430–33, 24435, 24437–42, 24445, 24450, 24458–60, 24463, 24465, 24467–69, 24471–73, 24476–77, 24479, 24482–87, 24501–06, 24512–15, 24521, 24523, 24526, 24533, 24536, 24550–51, 24553, 24555–56, 24572, 24574, 24578–79, 24595

* * *

SEVENTH DISTRICT

ERIC CANTOR, Republican, of Henrico County, VA; born in Henrico County, June 6, 1963; education: Bachelor's Degree, George Washington University, 1985; Law Degree, College of William and Mary, 1988; Masters Degree, Columbia University, 1989; professional: attorney; organizations: Western Henrico Rotary; Henrico County Republican Committee; President, Virginia-Israel Foundation; Virginia Holocaust Museum Board of Trustees; Elk Hill Farm Board of Trustees; elected to the Virginia House of Delegates, 1991; appointed Chief Deputy Majority Whip, December, 2002; appointed Republican Whip, December, 2008; married: Diana; three children; committees: Ways and Means; elected to the 107th Congress on November 7, 2000; reelected to each succeeding Congress.

Office Listings

http://www.cantor.house.gov

H–307 The Capitol, Washington, DC 20515 .... (202) 225–0197
Chief of Staff.—Steve Stombres.
Policy Director.—Neil Bradley.
329 Cannon House Office Building, Washington, DC 20515 .... (202) 225–2815
Chief of Staff.—Kristi Way. FAX: 225–0011
4201 Dominion Boulevard, Suite 110, Glen Allen, VA 23060 .... (804) 747–4073
763 Madison Road, Suite 207, Culpeper, VA 22701 .... (540) 825–8960

Counties: CAROLINE (part), CHESTERFIELD (part), CULPEPER, GOOCHLAND, HANOVER, HENRICO (part), LOUISIA, MADISON, ORANGE, PAGE, RAPPAHANNOCK, SPOTSYLVANIA (part). CITIES: Richmond. Population (2000), 643,499.

ZIP Codes: 20106, 20119, 20186, 22407, 22433, 22508, 22534, 22542, 22546, 22553, 22565, 22567, 22580, 22610, 22623, 22627, 22630, 22640, 22650, 22701, 22709, 22711, 22713–16, 22718–19, 22721–27, 22729–38, 22740–41, 22743, 22746–49, 22827, 22835, 22849, 22851, 22903, 22923, 22942, 22947–48, 22957, 22960, 22972, 22974, 22989, 23005, 23015, 23024, 23038–39, 23047, 23058–60, 23063, 23065, 23067, 23069, 23084, 23093, 23102–03, 23111–14, 23116–17, 23120, 23124, 23129, 23146, 23153, 23160, 23162, 23170, 23173, 23192, 23221–30, 23233–36, 23242, 23255, 23273, 23280, 23288–89, 23294–95

* * *

EIGHTH DISTRICT

JAMES P. MORAN, Democrat, of Alexandria, VA; born in Buffalo, NY, May 16, 1945; education: B.A., College of Holy Cross; Bernard Baruch Graduate School of Finance—City

University of New York; M.P.A., University of Pittsburgh Graduate School of Public and International Affairs; served on City Council of Alexandria, 1979–82; Vice Mayor, 1982–84; Mayor, 1985–90; founding member of the New Democrat Coalition, a group of more than 75 centrist House Democrats committed to fiscal responsibility, improvements to education, and maintaining America's economic competitiveness; co-chair of the Congressional Prevention Coalition; named as one of two ''High Technology Legislators of the Year'' by the Information Technology Industry Council; in 2000 named to the ''Legislative Hall of Fame'' by the American Electronics Association for his work on technology issues; married: LuAnn; children: James, Patrick, Mary, and Dorothy; committees: Appropriations; elected to the 102nd Congress on November 6, 1990; reelected to each succeeding Congress.

Office Listings

http://moran.house.gov

2239 Rayburn House Office Building, Washington, DC 20515 .... (202) 225–4376
Chief of Staff.—Austin Durrer. FAX: 225–0017
Legislative Director.—Tim Aiken.
333 North Fairfax Street, Suite 201, Alexandria, VA 22314 .... (703) 971–4700
District Director.—Susie Warner.

Counties: ARLINGTON, FAIRFAX (part). CITIES: Alexandria, and Falls Church. Population (2000), 643,503.

ZIP Codes: 20170–71, 20190–91, 20194–96, 20206, 20231, 20301, 20310, 20330, 20350, 20406, 20453, 22003, 22027, 22031, 22037, 22040–44, 22046–47, 22060, 22079, 22101–03, 22107–09, 22122, 22124, 22150–51, 22159, 22180–82, 22201–07, 22209–17, 22219, 22222, 22225–27, 22229–30, 22234, 22240–45, 22301–07, 22310–15, 22320–21, 22331–34, 22336

* * *

NINTH DISTRICT

RICK BOUCHER, Democrat, of Abingdon, VA; born in Washington County, VA, August 1, 1946; education: graduated, Abingdon High School, 1964; B.A., Roanoke College, 1968; J.D., University of Virginia School of Law, 1971; professional: associate, Milbank, Tweed, Hadley and McCloy, New York, NY; partner, Boucher and Boucher, Abingdon, VA; elected to the Virginia State Senate in 1975 and reelected in 1979; former chairman of the Oil and Gas Subcommittee of the Virginia Coal and Energy Commission; former member: Virginia State Crime Commission; Virginia Commission on Interstate Cooperation; Law and Justice Committee of the National Conference of State Legislatures; member: board of directors, First Virginia Bank, Damascus; Abingdon United Methodist Church; Kappa Alpha order; Phi Alpha Delta legal fraternity; American Bar Association; Virginia Bar Association; Association of the Bar of the City of New York; recipient of the Abingdon Jaycees Outstanding Young Businessman Award, 1975; assistant whip; committees: Energy and Commerce; Judiciary; elected to the 98th Congress on November 2, 1982; reelected to each succeeding Congress.

Office Listings

http://www.boucher.house.gov

2187 Rayburn House Office Building, Washington, DC 20515 .... (202) 225–3861
Chief of Staff.—Laura Vaught. FAX: 225–0442
Comunications Director.—Courtney Lamie.
188 East Main Street, Abingdon, VA 24210 .... (540) 628–1145
District Administrator.—Linda Di Yorio.
1 Cloverleaf Square, Suite C–1, Big Stone Gap, VA 24219 .... (540) 523–5450
112 North Washington Avenue, P.O. Box 1268, Pulaski, VA 24301 .... (540) 980–4310

Counties: ALLEGHANY (part), BLAND, BUCHANAN, CARROLL, CRAIG, DICKENSON, FLOYD, GILES, GRAYSON, HENRY (part), LEE, MONTGOMERY, PATRICK, PULASKI, ROANOKE (part), RUSSELL, SCOTT, SMYTH, TAZEWELL, WASHINGTON, WISE, WYTHE. CITIES: Bristol, Covington, Galax, Norton, and Radford. Population (2000), 643,514.

ZIP Codes: 24018–19, 24053, 24055, 24058–64, 24068, 24070, 24072–73, 24076, 24079, 24082, 24084, 24086–87, 24089, 24091, 24093–94, 24104–05, 24111–12, 24120–22, 24124, 24126–29, 24131–34, 24136, 24138, 24141–43, 24147–50, 24153, 24162, 24165, 24167, 24171, 24175, 24177, 24185, 24201–03, 24209–12, 24215–21, 24224–26, 24228, 24230, 24236–37, 24239, 24243–46, 24248, 24250–51, 24256, 24258, 24260, 24263, 24265–66, 24269–73, 24277, 24279–83, 24290, 24292–93, 24301, 24311–19, 24322–28, 24330, 24333, 24340, 24343, 24347–48, 24350–52, 24354, 24360–61, 24363, 24366, 24368, 24370, 24374–75, 24377–78, 24380–82, 24422, 24426, 24448, 24457, 24474, 24502, 24526, 24550–51, 24556, 24601–09, 24612–14, 24618–20, 24622, 24624, 24627–28, 24630–31, 24634–35, 24637, 24639–41, 24646–47, 24649, 24651, 24656–58

* * *

TENTH DISTRICT

FRANK R. WOLF, Republican, of Vienna, VA; born in Philadelphia, PA, January 30, 1939; education: B.A., Pennsylvania State University, 1961; LL.B., Georgetown University Law School, 1965; served in the U.S. Army Signal Corps (Reserves); professional: lawyer, admitted to the Virginia State Bar; legislative assistant for former U.S. Congressman Edward G. Biester, Jr., 1968–71; assistant to Secretary of the Interior Rogers C.B. Morton, 1971–74; Deputy Assistant Secretary for Congressional and Legislative Affairs, Department of the Interior, 1974–75; member, Vienna Presbyterian Church; married: the former Carolyn Stover; children: Frank, Jr., Virginia, Anne, Brenda, and Rebecca; committees: Appropriations; elected to the 97th Congress, November 4, 1980; reelected to each succeeding Congress.

Office Listings

http://www.wolf.house.gov

241 Cannon House Office Building, Washington, DC 20515 .... (202) 225–5136
Chief of Staff / Press Secretary.—Dan Scandling. FAX: 225–0437
Legislative Director.—Janet Shaffron.
13873 Park Center Road, Suite 130, Herndon, VA 20171 .... (703) 709–5800
Director of Constituent Services.—Judy McCary.
110 North Cameron Street, Winchester, VA 22601 .... (540) 667–0900

Counties: CLARKE, FAIRFAX (part), FAUQUIER (part), FREDERICK, LOUDOUN, PRINCE WILLIAM (part), WARREN. CITIES: Manassas, Manassas Park, and Winchester. Population (2000), 643,512.

ZIP Codes: 20101–05, 20107–13, 20115–18, 20120–22, 20129–32, 20134–35, 20137, 20140–44, 20146–49, 20151–53, 20158–60, 20163–67, 20170–72, 20175–78, 20180, 20184–90, 20194, 20197–98, 22026, 22033, 22043–44, 22046, 22066–67, 22101, 22106, 22184–85, 22193, 22207, 22556, 22601–04, 22610–11, 22620, 22622, 22624–25, 22630, 22637, 22639, 22642–43, 22645–46, 22649, 22654–57, 22663

* * *

ELEVENTH DISTRICT

GERALD E. CONNOLLY, Democrat, of Fairfax, VA; born in Boston, MA, March 30, 1950; education: graduated B.A., Maryknoll College; M.A., public administration, Harvard University, 1979; professional: member, Fairfax County Board of Supervisors, 1995–2003, chairman, 2003–07; religion: Roman Catholic; married: Cathy; children: Caitlin; committees: Budget; Foreign Affairs; Oversight and Government Reform; elected to the 111th Congress on November 4, 2008.

Office Listings

http://www.geraldconnolly.house.gov

327 Cannon House Office Building, Washington, DC 20515 .... (202) 225–1492
Chief of Staff.—James Walkinshaw. FAX: 225–3071
Legislative Director.—Dominic Bonaiuto.
Communications Director.—George Burke.
4115 Annandale Road, Annandale, VA 22003 .... (703) 256–3071
District Director.—Sharon Stark.
4308 Ridgewood Center Drive, Woodbridge, VA 22192 .... (703) 670–4989
Prince William Director.—Colin Davenport.

Counties: FAIRFAX (part), PRINCE WILLIAM (part). CITIES: Alexandria, Annandale, Burke, Centreville, Clifton, Fairfax, Fairfax Station, Herndon, Lorton, Manassas, Oakton, Occoquan, Springfield, Vienna, and Woodbridge. Population (2000), 643,509.

ZIP Codes: 20069–70, 20109–10, 20112, 20119–22, 20124, 20136–37, 20155–56, 20168–69, 20171, 20181–82, 22003, 22009, 22015, 22027, 22030–33, 22035, 22038–39, 22044, 22060, 22079, 22081–82, 22102, 22116, 22118–21, 22124–25, 22150–53, 22156, 22158–61, 22180–83, 22185, 22191–95, 22199, 22308–09, 22312

WASHINGTON

(Population 2000, 5,894,121)

SENATORS

PATTY MURRAY, Democrat, of Seattle, WA; born in Seattle, October 11, 1950; education: B.A., Washington State University, 1972; professional: teacher; lobbyist; Shoreline Community College; citizen lobbyist for environmental and educational issues, 1983–88; parent education instructor for Crystal Springs, 1984–87; school board member, 1985–89; elected Board of Directors, Shoreline School District, 1985–89; Washington State Senate, 1988–92; Democratic Whip, 1990–92; State Senate committees: Education; Ways and Means; Commerce and Labor; Domestic Timber Processing Select Committee; Open Government Select Committee; chair, School Transportation Safety Task Force; award: Washington State Legislator of the Year, 1990; married: Rob Murray; children: Randy and Sara; committees: Appropriations; Budget; Health, Education, Labor and Pensions; Rules and Administration; Veterans' Affairs; Joint Committee on Printing; elected to the U.S. Senate on November 3, 1992; reelected to each succeeding Senate term.

Office Listings

http://murray.senate.gov

173 Russell Senate Office Building, Washington, DC 20510 .... (202) 224–2621
Chief of Staff.—Jeff Bjornstad. FAX: 224–0238
Legislative Director.—Evan Schatz. TDD: 224–4430
Communications Director.—Alex Glass.
2988 Jackson Federal Building, 915 Second Avenue, Seattle, WA 98174 .... (206) 553–5545
State Director.—Brian Kristjansson.
The Marshall House, 1323 Officer's Row, Vancouver, WA 98661 .... (360) 696–7797
District Director.—Theresa Wagner.
10 North Post Road, Suite 600, Spokane, WA 99201 .... (509) 624–9515
District Director.—Erin Vincent.
2930 Wetmore Avenue, Suite 903, Everett, WA 98201 .... (425) 259–6515
District Director.—Shawn Bills.
402 East Yakima Avenue, Suite 390, Yakima, WA 98901 .... (509) 453–7462
District Director.—Rebecca Mengelos.
1611 116th Avenue, NW., Suite 214, Bellevue, WA 98004 .... (425) 462–4460
District Director.—Sergio Geva-Flores.
950 Pacific Avenue, Room 650, Tacoma, WA 98402 .... (253) 572–3636
District Director.—Mary McBride.

* * *

MARIA CANTWELL, Democrat, of Edmonds, WA; born in Indianapolis, IN, October 13, 1958; education: B.A., Miami University, Miami, OH, 1980; professional: businesswoman; RealNetworks, Inc.; organizations: South Snohomish County Chamber of Commerce; Alderwood Rotary; Mountlake Terrace Friends of the Library; public service: Washington State House of Representatives, 1987–92; U.S. House of Representatives, 1992–94; religion: Roman Catholic; committees: Commerce, Science, and Transportation; Energy and Natural Resources; Finance; Indian Affairs; Small Business and Entrepreneurship; elected to the U.S. Senate on November 7, 2000; reelected to each succeeding Senate term.

Office Listings

http://cantwell.senate.gov

511 Dirksen Senate Office Building, Washington, DC 20510 .... (202) 224–3441
Chief of Staff.—Katharine Lister. FAX: 228–0514
Deputy Chief of Staff.—Amit Ronen.
Legislative Director.—Mac Campbell.
Office Manager.—Nancy Hadley.
915 Second Avenue, Suite 3206, Seattle, WA 98174 .... (206) 220–6400
The Marshall House, 1313 Officers Row, Vancouver, WA 98661 .... (360) 696–7838
950 Pacific Avenue, Suite 615, Tacoma, WA 98402 .... (253) 572–2281
U.S. Federal Courthouse, West 920 Riverside, Suite 697, Spokane, WA 99201 ...... (509) 353–2507
825 Jadwin Avenue, 204/204A, Richland, WA 99352 .... (509) 946–8106
2930 Wetmore Avenue, Suite 9B, Everett, WA 98201 .... (425) 303–0114

REPRESENTATIVES

FIRST DISTRICT

JAY INSLEE, Democrat, of Bainbridge Island, WA; born in Seattle, WA, February 9, 1951; education: graduated, Ingraham High School, 1969; B.A., University of Washington, 1973; J.D., Willamette School of Law, 1976; professional: attorney, 1976–92; Washington State House of Representatives, 14th Legislative District, 1988–92; served on Appropriations; Housing; Judiciary; and Financial Institutions and Insurance Committees; attorney, 1995–96; Regional Director, U.S. Department of Health and Human Services, 1997–98; married: Trudi; three children: Jack, Connor, and Joe; committees: Energy and Commerce; Natural Resources; Select Committee on Energy Independence and Global Warming; elected to the 103rd Congress to represent the 4th District, November 3, 1992; elected to the 106th Congress to represent the 1st District on November 3, 1998; reelected to each succeeding Congress.

Office Listings

http://www.house.gov/inslee

403 Cannon House Office Building, Washington, DC 20515 .... (202) 225–6311
Chief of Staff.—Brian Bonlender. FAX: 226–1606
Legislative Director.—Beth Osborne.
Press Secretary.—Vacant.
Executive Assistant.—Laura Burgher.
Shoreline Center, 18560 First Avenue, NE., Suite E–800, Shoreline, WA 98155–2150 .... (206) 361–0233
17701 Fjord Drive, NE., Suite A–112, Liberty Bay Marina, Poulsbo, WA 98370 ... (360) 598–2342
District Director.—Sharmila K. Swenson.

Counties: KING (part), KITSAP (part), SNOHOMISH (part). CITIES AND TOWNSHIPS: Bainbridge Island, Bothell, Bremerton, Brier, Duvall, Edmonds, Everett, Hansville, Indianola, Kenmore, Keyport, Kingston, Kirkland, Lake Forest, Lynnwood, Mill Creek, Monroe, Mountlake Terrace, Mukilteo, Port Gamble, Poulsbo, Redmond, Rollingbay, Seabeck, Seattle, Shoreline, Silverdale, Snohomish, Suquamish, and Woodinville. Population (2000), 654,904.

ZIP Codes: 98011–12, 98019–20, 98021, 98026, 98028, 98033–34, 98036–37, 98041, 98043, 98046, 98052, 98061, 98072–74, 98077, 98082–83, 98110, 98133, 98155, 98160, 98177, 98204, 98208, 98272, 98275, 98290, 98296, 98311–12, 98315, 98340, 98342, 98345–46, 98364, 98370, 98380, 98383, 98392–93

* * *

SECOND DISTRICT

RICK LARSEN, Democrat, of Everett, WA; born in Arlington, WA, June 15, 1965; education: B.A., Pacific Lutheran University; M.P.A., University of Minnesota; professional: economic development official at the Port of Everett; Director of Public Affairs for a health provider association; public service: Snohomish County Council; religion: Methodist; married: Tiia Karlen; children: Robert and Per; committees: Armed Services; Transportation and Infrastructure; elected to the 107th Congress on November 7, 2000; reelected to each succeeding Congress.

Office Listings

http:/www.house.gov/larsen

108 Cannon House Office Building, Washington, DC 20515 .... (202) 225–2605
Chief of Staff.—Kimberly Johnston. FAX: 225–4420
Legislative Director.—Jasper MacSlarrow.
Communications Director.—Amanda Mahnke.
2930 Wetmore Avenue, Suite 9F, Everett, WA 98201 .... (425) 252–3188
119 North Commercial Street, Suite 1350, Bellingham, WA 98225 .... (360) 733–5144

Counties: ISLAND, KING (part), SAN JUAN, SKAGIT, SNOHOMISH (part), WHATCOM. CITIES AND TOWNSHIPS: Bellingham, Everett, and Mount Vernon. Population (2000), 654,903.

ZIP Codes: 98201, 98203–08, 98213, 98220–33, 98235–41, 98243–45, 98247–53, 98255–64, 98266–67, 98270–84, 98286–88, 98290–97

* * *

THIRD DISTRICT

BRIAN BAIRD, Democrat, of Vancouver, WA; born in Chama, NM, March 7, 1956; education: B.S., University of Utah, 1977; M.S., University of Wyoming, 1980; Ph.D., University of Wyoming, 1984; professional: licensed clinical psychologist; practiced in Washington State and Oregon; professor and former chair, Department of Psychology at Pacific Lutheran University; has worked in a variety of medical environments prior to election to the U.S. Congress; elected President of the Democratic Freshman Class for the 106th Congress; Congressional Career and Technical Education Caucus (co-founder); Congressional Caucus to Control and Fight Methamphetamine (co-founder); Congressional National Parks Caucus (co-founder); Addiction, Treatment, and Recovery Caucus; Community College Caucus; Community Health Centers Caucus; Congressional Boating Caucus; Congressional Brain Injury Task Force; Congressional Caucus on Intellectual Property Promotion and Piracy Prevention; Congressional China Caucus; Congressional Coast Guard Caucus; Congressional Coastal Caucus; Congressional Diabetes Caucus; Congressional Fire Service Caucus; Congressional Fitness Caucus; Congressional Mental Health Caucus; Congressional Native American Caucus; Congressional Port Security Caucus; Congressional Rural Caucus; Congressional Ski and Snowboard Caucus; Democratic Caucus; Friends of New Zealand Caucus; Hellenic Caucus; House Education Caucus; House Science, Technology, Engineering and Math Education Caucus; International Conservation Caucus; Medical Malpractice Caucus; New Democrat Caucus; Northwest Energy Caucus; Prochoice Caucus Democratic Task Force; Renewable Energy and Energy Efficiency Caucus; U.S. China Working Group; Congressional Law Enforcement Caucus; Mountain West Caucus; Middle East Economic Partnership Caucus; committees: Science and Technology; Transportation and Infrastructure; Democratic Regional Whip; elected to the 106th Congress; reelected to each succeeding Congress.

Office Listings

http://www.house.gov/baird

2350 Rayburn House Office Building, Washington, DC 20515 .... (202) 225–3536
Chief of Staff.—Lisa Austin. FAX: 225–3478
Press Secretary.—Garrett Russo.
Executive Assistant.—Brianne Adderley.
750 Anderson Street, Suite B, Vancouver, WA 98661 .... (360) 695–6292
District Director.—Kelly Love.
120 Union Avenue, Suite 105, Olympia, WA 98501 .... (360) 352–9768

Counties: CLARK COUNTY. CITIES AND TOWNSHIPS: Amboy, Ariel, Battle Ground, Brush Prairie, Camas, Heisson, La Center, Ridgefield, Vancouver, Washougal, Woodland, Yacolt. COWLITZ COUNTY. CITIES AND TOWNSHIPS: Carrolls, Castle Rock, Cougar, Kalama, Kelso, Longview, Ryderwood, Silverlake, Toutle. LEWIS COUNTY. CITIES AND TOWNSHIPS: Adna, Centralia, Chehalis, Cinebar, Curtis, Doty, Ethel, Galvin, Glenoma, Mineral, Morton, Mossyrock, Napavine, Onalaska, Packwood, Pe Ell, Randle, Salkum, Silver Creek, Toledo, Vader, Winlock. PACIFIC COUNTY. CITIES AND TOWNSHIPS: Bay Center, Chinook, Ilwaco, Lebam, Long Beach, Menlo, Nahcotta, Naselle, Ocean Park, Oysterville, Raymond, Seaview, South Bend, Tokeland. PIERCE COUNTY. CITIES AND TOWNSHIPS: Elbe. SKAMANIA COUNTY (part). CITIES AND TOWNSHIPS: Carson, North Bonneville, Stevenson, Underwood. THURSTON COUNTY (part). CITIES AND TOWNSHIPS: Buroda, Littlerock, Olympia, Tenino, and Rochester. WAHKIAKUM COUNTY. CITIES AND TOWNSHIPS: Cathlamet, Grays River, Rosburg, and Skamokawa. Population (2000), 654,898.

ZIP Codes: 98304, 98328, 98330, 98336, 98355–56, 98361, 98377, 98501–09, 98511–13, 98522, 98527, 98531–33, 98537–39, 98541–42, 98544, 98547, 98554, 98556–57, 98559, 98561, 98564–65, 98568, 98570, 98572, 98576–77, 98579, 98581–83, 98585–86, 98589–91, 98593, 98595–97, 98601–04, 98606–07, 98609–12, 98614, 98616, 98621–22, 98624–26, 98628–29, 98631–32, 98635, 98637–45, 98647–51, 98660–66, 98668, 98671–72, 98674–75, 98682–87

* * *

FOURTH DISTRICT

DOC HASTINGS, Republican, of Pasco, WA; born in Spokane, WA, February 7, 1941; education: graduated, Pasco High School, 1959; attended Columbia Basin College and Central Washington State University, Ellensburg, WA; military service: U.S. Army Reserves, 1963–69; professional: president, Columbia Basin Paper and Supply; board of directors, Yakima Federal Savings and Loan; member: Washington State House of Representatives, 1979–87; Republican Caucus chairman, assistant majority leader, and National Platform Committee, 1984; president: Pasco Chamber of Commerce; Pasco Downtown Development Association; Pasco Jaycees (chamber president); chairman, Franklin County Republican Central Committee, 1974–78; delegate, Republican National Convention, 1976–84; married: Claire Hastings, 1967; children: Kirsten, Petrina and Colin; committees: ranking member, Natural Resources; elected to the 104th Congress; reelected to each succeeding Congress.

Office Listings

http://www.house.gov/hastings

1203 Longworth House Office Building, Washington, DC 20515 .... (202) 225–5816
Administrative Assistant.—Jessica Gleason. FAX: 225–3251
Scheduler / Office Manager.—Ilene Clauson.
Press Secretary.—Charlie Keller.
2715 Saint Andrews Loop, Suite D, Pasco, WA 99302 .... (509) 543–9396

402 East Yakima Avenue, Suite 760, WA 98901 .... (509) 452–3243

Counties: ADAMS COUNTY (part). CITIES: Othello. BENTON COUNTY. CITIES AND TOWNSHIPS: Benton City, Kennewick, Paterson, Plymouth, Prosser, Richland, West Richland. CHELAN COUNTY. CITIES AND TOWNSHIPS: Ardenvoir, Cashmere, Chelan, Chelan Falls, Dryden, Entiat, Leavenworth, Malaga, Manson, Monitor, Peshastin, Stehekin, Wenatchee. DOUGLAS COUNTY. CITIES AND TOWNSHIPS: Bridgeport, East Wenatchee, Leahy, Mansfield, Orondo, Palisades, Rock Island, Waterville. FRANKLIN COUNTY. CITIES AND TOWNSHIPS: Basin City, Connell, Eltopia, Kahlotus, Mesa, Pasco, Windust. GRANT COUNTY. CITIES AND TOWNSHIPS: Beverly, Coulee City, Desert Aire, Electric City, Ephrata, George, Grand Coulee, Hartline, Marlin, Mattawa, Moses Lake, Quincy, Royal City, Soap Lake, Stratford, Warden, Wilson Creek. KITTITAS COUNTY. CITIES AND TOWNSHIPS: Cle Elum, Easton, Ellensburg, Hyak, Kittitas, Ronald, Roslyn, Snoqualmic Pass, South Cle Elum, Thorp, Vantage. KLICKITAT COUNTY. CITIES AND TOWNSHIPS: Alderdale, Appleton, Bickleton, Bingen, Centerville, Cook, Dallesport, Glenwood, Goldendale, Husum, Klickitat, Lyle, Roosevelt, Trout Lake, Wahkiacus, White Salmon, Wishram, Wishram Heights. SKAMANIA COUNTY (part), YAKIMA COUNTY. CITIES AND TOWNSHIPS: Brownstown, Buena, Carson, Cowiche, Grandview, Granger, Harrah, Mabton, Moxee, Naches, Outlook, Parker, Selah, Sunnyside, Tieton, Toppenish, Underwood, Wapato, White Swan, Yakima, and Zillah. Population (2000), 654,901.

ZIP Codes: 98068, 98602, 98605, 98610, 98613, 98617, 98619–20, 98623, 98628, 98635, 98648, 98650–51, 98670, 98672–73, 98801–02, 98807, 98811–13, 98815–17, 98819, 98821–24, 98826, 98828–32, 98834, 98836–37, 98843, 98845, 98847–48, 98850–53, 98857–58, 98860, 98901–04, 98907–09, 98920–23, 98925–26, 98929–30, 98932–44, 98946–48, 98950–53, 99103, 99115–16, 99123–24, 99133, 99135, 99155, 99301–02, 99320–22, 99326, 99330, 99335–38, 99343–46, 99349–50, 99352–54, 99356–57

* * *

FIFTH DISTRICT

CATHY McMORRIS RODGERS, Republican, of Spokane, WA; born in Salem, OR, May 22, 1969; education: B.A., Pensacola Christian College, Pensacola, FL, 1990; M.B.A., University of Washington, Seattle, WA, 2002; professional: fruit orchard worker; member, Washington State House of Representatives, 1994–2004; minority leader, 2002–03; organizations: member, Grace Evangelical Free Church; married: Brian Rodgers; children: Cole; committees: Armed Services; Education and Labor; Natural Resources; elected to the 109th Congress on November 2, 2004; reelected to each succeeding Congress.

Office Listings

http://www.house.gov/mcmorris

1323 Longworth House Office Building, Washington, DC 20515 .... (202) 225–2006
Chief of Staff.—Jeremy Deutsch. FAX: 225–3392
Legislative Director.—Kim Betz.
Scheduler.—Jinyoung Lee.
Communications Director.—Destry Henderson.
10 North Post Street, 6th floor, Spokane, WA 99210 .... (509) 353–2374
District Director.—David Condon.
555 South Main Street, Colville, WA 99114 .... (509) 684–3481
29 South Palouse Street, Walla Walla, WA 99362 .... (509) 529–9358

Counties: ADAMS (part), ASOTIN, COLUMBIA, FERRY, GARFIELD, LINCOLN, PEND OREILLE, OKANAGAN, SPOKANE, STEVENS, WALLA WALLA, WHITMAN. Population (2000), 654,901.

ZIP Codes: 98812, 98814, 98819, 98827, 98829, 98832–34, 98840–41, 98844, 98846, 98849, 98855–57, 98859, 98862, 99001, 99003–06, 99008–09, 99011–14, 99016–23, 99025–27, 99029–34, 99036–37, 99039–40, 99101–05, 99107, 99109–11, 99113–14, 99116–19, 99121–22, 99125–26, 99128–31, 99133–41, 99143–44, 99146–61, 99163–67, 99169–71, 99173–74, 99176, 99179–81, 99185, 99201–20, 99223–24, 99228, 99251–52, 99256, 99258, 99260, 99302, 99323–24, 99326, 99328–29, 99333, 99335, 99341, 99344, 99347–48, 99356, 99359–63, 99371, 99401–03

* * *

SIXTH DISTRICT

NORMAN D. DICKS, Democrat, of Bremerton, WA; born in Bremerton, December 16, 1940; education: graduated, West Bremerton High School, 1959; B.A., political science, University of Washington, 1963; J.D., University of Washington School of Law, 1968; admitted to Washington bar, 1968; joined the staff of Senator Warren G. Magnuson in 1968 as legislative assistant and appropriations assistant, named administrative assistant in 1973, and held that post until he resigned to campaign for Congress in February 1976; member: Democratic Caucus; Puget Sound Naval Bases Association; Navy League of the United States; married: the former Suzanne Callison, 1967; children: David and Ryan; committees: Appropriations; elected to the 95th Congress; reelected to each succeeding Congress.

Office Listings

2467 Rayburn House Office Building, Washington, DC 20515 .... (202) 225–5916
Chief of Staff / Press Secretary.—George Behan. FAX: 226–1176
Legislative Director.—Pete Modaff.
Scheduler.—Yodit Tewelde.
1019 Pacific Avenue, Suite 806, Tacoma, WA 98402 .... (253) 593–6536
District Director.—Clark Mather.
Norm Dicks Government Center, 345 Sixth Street, Suite 500, Bremerton, WA 98337 .... (360) 479–4011
Deputy District Director.—Cheri Williams.
322 East Fifth Street, Port Angeles, WA 98362 .... (360) 452–3370
District Representative.—Judith Morris.

Counties: CLALLAM COUNTY. CITIES AND TOWNSHIPS: Forks, Port Angeles, La Push, Sequim, Sekiu, Neah Bay. GRAYS HARBOR COUNTY. CITIES AND TOWNSHIPS: Aberdeen, Hoquiam, Montesano, Ocean City, Ocean Shores, Moclips, Westport. JEFFERSON COUNTY. CITIES AND TOWNSHIPS: Port Townsend, Quilcene. KITSAP COUNTY (part). CITIES AND TOWNSHIPS: Bremerton, Port Orchard, Gorst. MASON COUNTY. CITIES AND TOWNSHIPS: Shelton, Belfair, Allyn, Union. PIERCE COUNTY (part). CITIES AND TOWNSHIPS: Tacoma, Gig Harbor, Lakebay, and Lakewood. Population (2000), 654,902.

ZIP Codes: 98305, 98310–12, 98314, 98320, 98322, 98324–26, 98329, 98331–33, 98335, 98337, 98339, 98343, 98349–51, 98353, 98357–59, 98362–63, 98365–68, 98373, 98376, 98378, 98380–82, 98384, 98386, 98394–95, 98401–09, 98411–13, 98415–16, 98418, 98442, 98444–45, 98464–67, 98471, 98477, 98481, 98492, 98497–99, 98502, 98520, 98524, 98526, 98528, 98535–37, 98541, 98546–48, 98550, 98552, 98555, 98557, 98560, 98562–63, 98566, 98568–69, 98571, 98575, 98584, 98587–88, 98592, 98595

* * *

SEVENTH DISTRICT

JIM McDERMOTT, Democrat, of Seattle, WA; born in Chicago, IL, December 28, 1936; education: B.S., Wheaton College, Wheaton, IL, 1958; M.D., University of Illinois Medical School, Chicago, 1963; residency in adult psychiatry, University of Illinois Hospitals, 1964–66; residency in child psychiatry, University of Washington Hospitals, Seattle, 1966–68; served, U.S. Navy Medical Corps, lieutenant commander, 1968–70; psychiatrist; Washington State House of Representatives, 1971–72; Washington State Senate, 1975–87; Democratic nominee for governor, 1980; regional medical officer, Sub-Saharan Africa, U.S. Foreign Service, 1987–88; practicing psychiatrist and assistant clinical professor of psychiatry, University of Washington, Seattle, 1970–83; member: Washington State Medical Association; King County Medical Society; American Psychiatric Association; religion: St. Mark's Episcopal Church, Seattle; married: Therese M. Hansen; grown children: Katherine and James; grandchildren; committees: Ways and Means; elected on November 8, 1988, to the 101st Congress; reelected to each succeeding Congress.

Office Listings

http://www.house.gov/mcdermott

1035 Longworth House Office Building, Washington, DC 20515 .... (202) 225–3106
Chief of Staff.—Mike DeCesare. FAX: 225–6197
Legislative Director.—Vacant.
Executive Assistant.—Elizabeth Becton.
1809 Seventh Avenue, Suite 1212, Seattle, WA 98101–1313 .... (206) 553–7170
District Administrator.—James Allen.

Counties: KING COUNTY (part). CITIES AND TOWNSHIPS: Burien (part), Lake Forest Park, Vashon Island, Shoreline, SeaTac, Seattle, Tukwila. Population (2000), 654,902.

ZIP Codes: 98013, 98055, 98070, 98101–09, 98111–19, 98121–22, 98124–27, 98129, 98131, 98133–34, 98136, 98139, 98141, 98144–46, 98151, 98154–55, 98161, 98164–66, 98168, 98171, 98174–75, 98177–78, 98181, 98184–85, 98190–91, 98194–95, 98199

* * *

EIGHTH DISTRICT

DAVID G. REICHERT, Republican, of Auburn, WA; born in Detroit Lakes, MI, August 29, 1950; education: graduated, Kent Meridian High School, Renton, WA, 1968; A.A., Concordia Lutheran College, Portland, OR, 1970; professional: U.S. Air Force Reserve, 1971–76; U.S. Air Force, 1976; police officer, King County, WA, 1972–97; sheriff, King County, WA, 1997–2004; member: president, Washington State Sheriff's Association; executive board member, Washington Association of Sheriffs and Police Chiefs; co-chair, Washington State Partners in Crisis; awards: recipient of the 2004 National Sheriff's Association's ''Sheriff of the Year''; two-time Medal of Valor Award Recipient from the King County sheriff's office; Washington Policy Center's Champion of Freedom Award; Families Northwest Public Policy Award; married: Julie; children: Angela, Tabitha, and Daniel; committees: Ways and Means; elected to the 109th Congress on November 2, 2004; reelected to each succeeding Congress.

Office Listings

http://www.reichert.house.gov

1730 Longworth House Office Building, Washington, DC 20515 .... (202) 225–7761
Chief of Staff.—Chris Miller. FAX: 225–4282
Legislative Director.—Jason Edgar.
Executive Assistant / Scheduler.—Nichole Robison.
2737 Seventh-Eighth Avenue, SE., Suite 202, Mercer Island, WA 98040 .... (206) 275–3438
District Director.—Sue Foy.

Counties: KING COUNTY (part). CITIES AND TOWNSHIPS: Auburn, Baring, Beaux Arts Village, Bellevue, Black Diamond, Carnation, Duvall, Enumclaw, Fall City, Issaquah, Kent, Mercer Island, Maple Valley, New Castle, North Bend, Preston, Redmond, Renton, Skykomish, Snoqualmie, Summit, Woodinville. PIERCE COUNTY. CITIES AND TOWNSHIPS: Ashford, Bonney Lake, Buckley, Carbonado, Eatonville, Elbe, Graham, Orting, Roy, South Prairie, Spanaway, and Wilkeson. Population (2000), 654,905.

ZIP Codes: 98002, 98004–10, 98014–15, 98019, 98022, 98024–25, 98027, 98029–31, 98033, 98035, 98038–40, 98042, 98045, 98050–53, 98055–56, 98058–59, 98064–65, 98068, 98074–75, 98077, 98092, 98304, 98321, 98323, 98328, 98330, 98338, 98344, 98348, 98352, 98360, 98372–75, 98385, 98387, 98390, 98396–98, 98446

* * *

NINTH DISTRICT

ADAM SMITH, Democrat, of Tacoma, WA; born in Washington, DC, June 15, 1965; education: graduated, Tyee High School, 1983; graduated, Fordham University, NY, 1987; law degree, University of Washington, 1990; admitted to the Washington bar in 1991; professional: prosecutor for the city of Seattle; Washington State Senate, 1990–96; member: Kent Drinking Driver Task Force; board member, Judson Park Retirement Home; married: Sara Smith, 1993; committees: Armed Services; Permanent Select Committee on Intelligence; elected to the 105th Congress; reelected to each succeeding Congress.

Office Listings

http://www.adamsmith.house.gov

2402 Rayburn House Office Building, Washington, DC 20515 .... (202) 225–8901
Chief of Staff.—Shana Chandler. FAX: 225–5893
Communications Director.—Michael Amato.
2209 Pacific Avenue, Suite B, Tacoma, WA 98402 .... (253) 593–6600
District Director.—Linda Danforth.
Office Manager.—Diane Brazell.

Counties: KING (part), PIERCE (part), THURSTON (part). CITIES: Algona, Auburn, Burien, Des Moines, Dupont, Edgewood, Federal Way, Fife, Kent, Lacey, Lakewood, Milton, Muckleshoot Indian Reservation, Nisqually Indian Reservation, Normandy Park, Olympia, Pacific, Puyallup, Puyallup Indian Reservation, Renton, Roy, SeaTac, Spanaway, Steilacoom, Tacoma, Tukwila, and Yelm. Population (2000), 654,902.

ZIP Codes: 98001–03, 98023, 98030–32, 98047, 98054–55, 98057–58, 98062–63, 98071, 98089, 98092–93, 98131–32, 98138, 98148, 98158, 98166, 98168, 98171, 98178, 98188, 98198, 98303, 98327–28, 98338, 98354, 98371–75, 98387–88, 98390–91, 98402, 98404, 98421–22, 98424, 98430–31, 98433, 98438–39, 98443–46, 98467, 98492–93, 98497–99, 98503, 98506, 98509, 98513, 98516, 98558, 98576, 98580, 98597

WEST VIRGINIA

(Population 2000, 1,808,344)

SENATORS

ROBERT C. BYRD, Democrat, of Sophia, WV; born in North Wilkesboro, NC, November 20, 1917; Baptist; married Erma Ora James (deceased) March 25, 2006; two daughters: Mrs. Mohammad (Mona Byrd) Fatemi and Mrs. Jon (Marjorie Byrd) Moore; six grandchildren: Erik, Darius, Fredrik Fatemi, Michael (deceased), Mona Moore Pearson and Mary Anne Moore Clarkson; six great-grandchildren; committees: Appropriations; Armed Services; Budget; Rules and Administration; sworn in to the U.S. Senate on January 3, 1959; reelected to each succeeding Senate term.

Office Listings

http://byrd.senate.gov

311 Hart Senate Office Building, Washington, DC 20510 .... (202) 224–3954
Chief of Staff.—Barbara Videnieks. FAX: 228–0002
Administrative Assistant.—Elysa Smith.
Press Secretary.—Jesse Jacobs.
300 Virginia Street East, Suite 2630, Charleston, WV 25301 .... (304) 342–5855
State Director.—Anne Barth.
217 West King Street, Room 238, Martinsburg, WV 25401 .... (304) 264–4626

* * *

JOHN D. ROCKEFELLER IV, Democrat, of Charleston, WV; born in New York City, NY, June 18, 1937; education: graduated, Phillips Exeter Academy, Exeter, NH, 1954; A.B., Harvard University, Cambridge, MA, 1961; honorary degrees: J.D., West Virginia University; Marshall University; Davis and Elkins College; Dickinson College; University of Alabama; University of Cincinnati; doctor of humanities, West Virginia Institute of Technology; doctor of public service, Salem College; professional service: Vista volunteer, Emmons, WV, 1964; West Virginia House of Delegates, 1966–68; elected Secretary of State of West Virginia, 1968; president, West Virginia Wesleyan College, 1973–76; Governor of West Virginia, 1976–84; married: the former Sharon Percy; children: John, Valerie, Charles and Justin; committees: chair, Commerce, Science, and Transportation, Finance; Veterans' Affairs; Select Committee on Intelligence; Joint Committee on Taxation; elected to the U.S. Senate on November 6, 1984; reelected to each succeeding Senate term.

Office Listings

http://rockefeller.senate.gov

531 Hart Senate Office Building, Washington, DC 20510 .... (202) 224–6472
Chief of Staff.—Kerry Ates. FAX: 224–7665
Legislative Director.—Chris Schloesser.
Communications Director.—Wendy Morigi.
405 Capitol Street, Suite 508, Charleston, WV 25301 .... (304) 347–5372
220 North Kanawha Street, Suite 1, Beckley, WV 25801 .... (304) 253–9704
118 Adams Street, Suite 301, Fairmont, WV 26554 .... (304) 367–0122
217 West King Street, Suite 307, Martinsburg, WV 25401 .... (304) 262–9285

REPRESENTATIVES

FIRST DISTRICT

ALAN B. MOLLOHAN, Democrat, of Fairmont, WV; born in Fairmont, May 14, 1943; son of former Congressman Robert H. Mollohan and Helen Holt Mollohan; education: graduated, Greenbrier Military School, Lewisburg, WV, 1962; A.B., College of William and Mary, Williamsburg, VA, 1966; J.D., West Virginia University College of Law, Morgantown, 1970; professional: captain, U.S. Army Reserves, 1970–83; attorney; admitted to the West Virginia bar, 1970 (commenced practice in Fairmont); admitted to the District of Columbia bar, 1975; religion: member, First Baptist Church, Fairmont; married: the former Barbara Whiting, 1976; children: Alan, Robert, Andrew, Karl and Mary Kathryn; committees: Appropriations; elected to the 98th Congress on November 2, 1982; reelected to each succeeding Congress.

Office Listings

2302 Rayburn House Office Building, Washington, DC 20515 .... (202) 225–4172
Chief of Staff.—Colleen McCarty. FAX: 225–7564
Scheduler.—Jill Butash.
Legislative Director.—Julie Aaronson.
Press Secretary.—David Herring.
209 Post Office Building, P.O. Box 1400, Clarksburg, WV 26302–1400 .... (304) 623–4422
48 Donley Street, Marina Tower, Suite 504, Morgantown, WV 26501 .... (304) 292–3019
Federal Building, Room 2040, 425 Juliana Street, Parkersburg, WV 26101–0145 ... (304) 428–0493
Federal Building, 1125 Chapline Street, Wheeling, WV 26003–2900 .... (304) 232–5390

Counties: BARBOUR, BROOKE, DODDRIDGE, GILMER, GRANT, HANCOCK, HARRISON, MARION, MARSHALL, MINERAL, MONONGALIA, OHIO, PLEASANTS, PRESTON, RITCHIE, TAYLOR, TUCKER, TYLER, WETZEL, WOOD. CITIES AND TOWNSHIPS: Albright, Alma, Alvy, Anmoore, Arthur, Arthurdate, Auburn, Aurora, Baldwin, Barrackville, Baxter, Bayard, Beech Bottom, Belington, Belleville, Belleville, Bellview, Belmont, Bens Run, Benwood, Berea, Bethany, Big Run, Blacksville, Blandville, Booth, Brandonville, Bretz, Bridgeport, Bristol, Brownton, Bruceton Mills, Burlington, Burnt House, Burton, Cabins, Cairo, Cameron, Carolina, Cassville, Cedarville, Center Point, Central Station, Century, Chester, Clarksburg, Coburn, Colfax, Colliers, Core, Corinth, Cove, Coxs Mills, Cuzzart, Dallas, Davis, Davisville, Dawmont, Dellslow, Dorcas, Eglon, Elk Garden, Ellenboro, Elm Grove, Enterprise, Eureka, Everettville, Fairmont, Fairview, Farmington, Flemington, Flower, Follansbee, Folsom, Fort Ashby, Fort Neal, Four States, Friendly, Galloway, Gilmer, Glen Dale, Glen Easton, Glenville, Goffs, Gormania, Grafton, Grant Town, Granville, Greenwood, Gypsy, Hambleton, Harrisville, Hastings, Haywood, Hazelton, Hebron, Hendricks, Hepzibah, Highland, Hundred, Idamay, Independence, Industrial, Jacksonburg, Jere, Jordan, Junior, Keyser, Kingmont, Kingwood, Knob Fork, Lahmansville, Letter Gap, Lima, Linn, Littleton, Lockney, Lost Creek, Lumberport, MacFarlan, Mahone, Maidsville, Mannington, Masontown, Maysville, McMechen, McWhorter, Meadowbrook, Medley, Metz, Middlebourne, Mineralwells, Moatsville, Monongah, Montana Mines, Morgantown, Moundsville, Mount Clare, Mount Storm, Mountain, New Creek, New Cumberland, New England, New Manchester, New Martinsville, New Milton, Newberne, Newburg, Newell, Normantown, North Parkersburg, Nutter Fort, Osage, Owings, Paden City, Parkersburg, Parsons, Pennsboro, Pentress, Perkins, Petersburg, Petroleum, Philippi, Piedmont, Pine Grove, Porters Falls, Proctor, Pullman, Pursglove, Rachel, Reader, Red Creek, Reedsville, Reynoldsville, Riegeley, Rivesville, Rocket Center, Rockport, Rosedale, Rosemont, Rowlesburg, Saint George, Saint Marys, Salem, Sand Fork, Shinnston, Shirley, Shocks, Short Creek, Simpson, Sistersville, Smithburg, Smithfield, Smithville, Spelter, Stonewood, Stouts Mill, Stumptown, Tanner, Terra Alta, Thomas, Thornton, Toll Gate, Troy, Triadelphia, Tunnelton, Valley Grove, Vienna, Volga, Wadestown, Walker, Wallace, Wana, Warwood, Washington, Watson, Waverly Weirton, Wellsburg, Wendel, West Liberty, West Milford, West Union, Westover, Wheeling Wick, Wilbur, Wiley Ford, Wileyville, Williamstown, Wilson, Wilsonburg, Windsor Heights, Wolf Summit, Worthington, and Wyatt. Population (2000), 602,543.

ZIP Codes: 25258, 25267, 26003, 26030–41, 26047, 26050, 26055–56, 26058–60, 26062, 26070, 26074–75, 26101–06, 26120–21, 26133–34, 26142–43, 26146–50, 26155, 26159, 26161–62, 26164, 26167, 26169–70, 26175, 26178, 26180–81, 26184, 26186–87, 26201, 26238, 26250, 26254, 26260, 26263, 26269, 26271, 26275–76, 26283, 26287, 26289, 26292, 26301–02, 26306, 26320–21, 26323, 26325, 26327, 26330, 26332, 26334–35, 26337, 26339, 26342, 26346–49, 26351, 26354, 26361–62, 26366, 26369, 26374, 26377–78, 26384–86, 26404–05, 26408, 26410–12, 26415–16, 26419, 26421–22, 26424–26, 26430–31, 26434–38, 26440, 26443–44, 26448, 26451, 26456, 26463, 26501–02, 26504–08, 26519–21, 26524–25, 26527, 26529, 26531, 26534, 26537, 26541–44, 26546–47, 26554–55, 26559–63, 26566, 26568, 26570–72, 26574–76, 26578, 26581–82, 26585–88, 26590–91, 26611, 26623, 26636, 26638, 26705, 26710, 26716–17, 26719–20, 26726, 26731, 26734, 26739, 26743, 26750, 26753, 26764, 26767, 26833, 26847, 26852, 26855

* * *

SECOND DISTRICT

SHELLEY MOORE CAPITO, Republican, of Charleston, WV; born in Glen Dale, WV, November 26, 1953; education: B.S., Duke University; M.Ed., University of Virginia; professional: career counselor; West Virginia State College; West Virginia Board of Regents; organizations: Community Council of Kanawha Valley; YWCA; West Virginia Interagency Council for Early Intervention; Habitat for Humanity; public service: elected to the West Virginia House of Delegates, 1996; reelected in 1998; awards: Coalition for a Tobacco-Free West Virginia Legislator of the Year; religion: Presbyterian; married: to Charles L., Jr.; three children; committees: Financial Services; Transportation and Infrastructure; Select Committee on Energy Independence and Global Warming; elected to the 107th Congress on November 7, 2000; reelected to each succeeding Congress.

Office Listings

http://www.house.gov/capito

2443 Rayburn House Office Building, Washington, DC 20515 .... (202) 225–2711
Chief of Staff.—Joel Brubaker. FAX: 225–7856
Office Manager.—Alison Bibbee.
Legislative Director.—Aaron Sporck.
4815 MacCorkle Avenue, Southeast, Charleston, WV 25304 .... (304) 925–5964
300 Foxcroft Avenue, Suite 102, Martinsburg, WV 25401 .... (304) 264–8810

Counties: BERKELEY, BRAXTON, CALHOUN, CLAY, HAMPSHIRE, HARDY, JACKSON, JEFFERSON, KANAWHA, LEWIS, MASON, MORGAN, PENDLETON, PUTNAM, RANDOLPH, ROANE, UPSHUR, WIRT. Population (2000), 602,245.

ZIP Codes: 25002–03, 25005, 25011, 25015, 25019, 25025–26, 25030, 25033, 25035, 25039, 25043, 25045–46, 25054, 25059, 25061, 25063–64, 25067, 25070–71, 25075, 25079, 25081–83, 25085–86, 25088, 25102–03, 25106–07, 25109–

13, 25123–26, 25132–34, 25136, 25139, 25141, 25143, 25147, 25150, 25156, 25159–60, 25162, 25164, 25168, 25177, 25187, 25201–02, 25211, 25213–14, 25231, 25234–35, 25239, 25241, 25243–45, 25247–48, 25251–53, 25259–62, 25264–68, 25270–71, 25275–76, 25279, 25281, 25285–87, 25301–06, 25309, 25311–15, 25317, 25320–39, 25350, 25356–58, 25360–62, 25364–65, 25375, 25392, 25396, 25401–02, 25410–11, 25413–14, 25419–23, 25425, 25427–32, 25434, 25437–38, 25440–44, 25446, 25502–03, 25510, 25515, 25520, 25523, 25526, 25541, 25550, 25560, 25569, 26133, 26136–38, 26141, 26143, 26147, 26151–52, 26160–61, 26164, 26173, 26180, 26201–02, 26205, 26210, 26215, 26218, 26224, 26228–30, 26234, 26236–38, 26241, 26253–54, 26257, 26259, 26261, 26263, 26267–68, 26270, 26273, 26276, 26278, 26280, 26282–83, 26285, 26293–94, 26296, 26321, 26335, 26338, 26342–43, 26351, 26372, 26376, 26378, 26384–85, 26412, 26430, 26443, 26447, 26452, 26546, 26590, 26601, 26610–11, 26615, 26617, 26619, 26621, 26623–24, 26627, 26629, 26631, 26636, 26638–39, 26641, 26651, 26656, 26660, 26662, 26667, 26671, 26675–76, 26678–79, 26681, 26684, 26690–91, 26704–05, 26707, 26710–11, 26714, 26717, 26722, 26731, 26739, 26743, 26750, 26755, 26757, 26761, 26763–64, 26801–02, 26804, 26807–08, 26810, 26812, 26814–15, 26817–18, 26823–24, 26836, 26838, 26845, 26847, 26851–52, 26865–66, 26884, 26886

* * *

THIRD DISTRICT

NICK J. RAHALL II, Democrat, of Beckley, WV; born in Beckley, May 20, 1949; education: graduated, Woodrow Wilson High School, Beckley, 1967; A.B., Duke University, Durham, NC, 1971; graduate work, George Washington University, Washington, DC; colonel, U.S. Air Force Civil Air Patrol; president, West Virginia Society of Washington, DC; business executive; sales representative, WWNR radio station; president, Mountaineer Tour and Travel Agency, 1974; president, West Virginia Broadcasting; awards: Coal Man of the Year, *Coal Industry News,* 1979; Young Democrat of the Year, Young Democrats, 1980; recipient, West Virginia American Legion Distingushed Service Award, 1984; delegate, Democratic National Conventions, 1972, 1976, 1980, 1984; member: Rotary; Elks; Moose; Eagles; NAACP; National Rifle Association; AF & AM; RAM; Mount Hope Commandery; Shrine Club; Benie Kedeem Temple in Charleston; Beckley Presbyterian Church; chairman and founder, Congressional Coal Group; Democratic Leadership Council; Congressional Arts Caucus; Congressional Black Caucus; Congressional Fitness Caucus; International Workers' Rights Caucus; ITS Caucus; Qatar Caucus; Congressional Rural Caucus; Congressional Steel Caucus; Congressional Textile Caucus; Congressional Travel and Tourism Caucus; Congressional Truck Caucus; Wine Caucus; Automobile Task Force; Democratic Congressional Campaign Committee; Democratic Study Group; Energy and Environment Study Conference; married: the former Melinda Ross; children: Rebecca Ashley, Nick Joe III, and Suzanne Nicole; grandchildren: Madison; committees: chair, Natural Resources; vice chair, Transportation and Infrastructure; elected to the 95th Congress, November 2, 1976; reelected to each succeeding Congress.

Office Listings

http://www.house.gov/rahall

2307 Rayburn House Office Building, Washington, DC 20515 .... (202) 225–3452
Administrative Assistant.—Kent Keyser. FAX: 225–9061
Executive Assistant.—Vickie Bandy.
Legislative Director.—Erika Young.
Press Secretary.—Tonya Allen.
815 Fifth Avenue, Huntington, WV 25701 .... (304) 522–6425
301 Prince Street, Beckley, WV 25801 .... (304) 252–5000
220 Dingess Street, Logan, WV 25601 .... (304) 752–4934
1005 Federal Building, Bluefield, WV 24701 .... (304) 325–6222

Counties: BOONE, CABELL, FAYETTE, GREENBRIER, LINCOLN, LOGAN, MCDOWELL, MERCER, MINGO, MONROE, NICHOLAS, POCAHONTAS, RALEIGH, SUMMERS, WAYNE, WEBSTER, WYOMING. Population (2000), 603,556.

ZIP Codes: 24701, 24712, 24714–16, 24719, 24724, 24726, 24729, 24731–33, 24736–40, 24747, 24751, 24801, 24808, 24811, 24813, 24815–18, 24820–31, 24834, 24836, 24839, 24842–57, 24859–62, 24866–74, 24878–82, 24884, 24887–88, 24892, 24894–99, 24901–02, 24910, 24915–18, 24920, 24924–25, 24927, 24931, 24934–36, 24938, 24941, 24943–46, 24950–51, 24954, 24957, 24961–63, 24966, 24970, 24974, 24976–77, 24981, 24983–86, 24991, 24993, 25002–04, 25007–10, 25021–22, 25024, 25028, 25031, 25036, 25040, 25043–44, 25047–49, 25051, 25053, 25057, 25059–60, 25062, 25076, 25081, 25083, 25085, 25090, 25093, 25108, 25114–15, 25118–19, 25121, 25130, 25136, 25139–40, 25142, 25148–49, 25152, 25154, 25161, 25165, 25169, 25173–74, 25180–81, 25183, 25185–86, 25193, 25202–06, 25208–09, 25213, 25501, 25504–08, 25510–12, 25514, 25517, 25520–21, 25523–24, 25526, 25529–30, 25534–35, 25537, 25540–41, 25544–45, 25547, 25555, 25557, 25559, 25562, 25564–65, 25567, 25570–73, 25601, 25606–08, 25611–12, 25614, 25617, 25621, 25624–25, 25628, 25630, 25632, 25634–39, 25644, 25646–47, 25649–54, 25661, 25665–67, 25669–72, 25674, 25676, 25678, 25682, 25685–88, 25690–92, 25694, 25696, 25699, 25701–29, 25755, 25770–79, 25801–02, 25810–13, 25816–18, 25820, 25823, 25825–27, 25831–33, 25836–37, 25839–41, 25843–49, 25851, 25853–57, 25859–60, 25862, 25864–66, 25868, 25870–71, 25873, 25875–76, 25878–80, 25882, 25901–02, 25904, 25906–09, 25911, 25913–22, 25927–28, 25931–32, 25934, 25936, 25938, 25942–43, 25951, 25958, 25961–62, 25965–67, 25969, 25971–72, 25976–79, 25981, 25984–86, 25989, 26202–03, 26205–06, 26208–09, 26217, 26222, 26230, 26234, 26261, 26264, 26266, 26288, 26291, 26294, 26298, 26610, 26617, 26639, 26651, 26656, 26660, 26662, 26674, 26676, 26678–81, 26684, 26690–91

WISCONSIN

(Population 2000, 5,363,675)

SENATORS

HERB KOHL, Democrat, of Milwaukee, WI; born in Milwaukee, February 7, 1935; education: graduated, Washington High School, Milwaukee, 1952; B.A., University of Wisconsin, Madison, 1956; M.B.A., Harvard Graduate School of Business Administration, Cambridge, MA, 1958; LL.D., Cardinal Stritch College, Milwaukee, WI, 1986 (honorary); served, U.S. Army Reserves, 1958–64; businessman; president, Herbert Kohl Investments; owner, Milwaukee Bucks NBA basketball team; past chairman, Milwaukee's United Way Campaign; State Chairman, Democratic Party of Wisconsin, 1975–77; honors and awards: Pen and Mike Club Wisconsin Sports Personality of the Year, 1985; Wisconsin Broadcasters Association Joe Killeen Memorial Sportsman of the Year, 1985; Greater Milwaukee Convention and Visitors Bureau Lamplighter Award, 1986; Wisconsin Parkinson's Association Humanitarian of the Year, 1986; Kiwanis Milwaukee Award, 1987; Madison Magazine's Best Corporate Citizen, 1997; Inducted into the Wisconsin Athletic Hall of Fame, 2007; Working Mothers Magazine Best of Congress Award, 2008; committees: chair, Special Committee on Aging; Appropriations; Banking, Housing and Urban Affairs; Judiciary; elected to the U.S. Senate on November 8, 1988; reelected to each succeeding Senate term.

Office Listings

http://kohl.senate.gov

330 Hart Senate Office Building, Washington, DC 20510 .... (202) 224–5653
Chief of Staff.—Phil Karsting. FAX: 224–9787
Legislative Director.—Chad Metzler.
Communications Director.—Lynn Becker.
Executive Assistant.—Arlene Branca.
310 West Wisconsin Avenue, Suite 950, Milwaukee, WI 53203 .... (414) 297–4451
14 West Mifflin Street, Suite 207, Madison, WI 53703 .... (608) 264–5338
402 Graham Avenue, Suite 206, Eau Claire, WI 54701 .... (715) 832–8424
4321 West College Avenue, Suite 235, Appleton, WI 54914 .... (920) 738–1640
205 5th Avenue, Room 216, LaCrosse, WI 54601 .... (608) 796–0045

* * *

RUSSELL D. FEINGOLD, Democrat, of Middleton, WI; born in Janesville, WI, March 2, 1953; education: graduated, Craig High School, Janesville, WI, 1971; B.A., University of Wisconsin-Madison, 1975; Rhodes Scholar, Oxford University, 1977; J.D., Harvard Law School, 1979; professional: practicing attorney, Foley & Lardner and LaFollette & Sinykin, Madison, WI, 1979–85; Wisconsin State Senate, 1983–93; four children: daughters, Jessica and Ellen; stepsons, Sam Speerschneider and Ted Speerschneider; committees: Budget; Foreign Relations; Judiciary; Select Committee on Intelligence; Democratic Policy Committee; elected to the U.S. Senate on November 3, 1992; reelected to each succeeding Senate term.

Office Listings

http://feingold.senate.gov

506 Hart Senate Office Building, Washington, DC 20510 .... (202) 224–5323
Chief of Staff.—Mary Irvine. FAX: 224–2725
Legislative Director.—Paul Weinberger.
Press Secretary.—Zach Lowe.
517 East Wisconsin Avenue, Room 408, Milwaukee, WI 53202 .... (414) 276–7282
1600 Aspen Commons, Room 100, Middleton, WI 53562 .... (608) 828–1200
State Coordinator.—Jay Robaidek.
401 Fifth Street, Room 410, Wausau, WI 54401 .... (715) 848–5660
425 State Street, Room 225, LaCrosse, WI 54603 .... (608) 782–5585
1640 Main Street, Green Bay, WI 54302 .... (920) 465–7508

REPRESENTATIVES

FIRST DISTRICT

PAUL RYAN, Republican, of Janesville, WI; born in Janesville, January 29, 1970; education: Joseph A. Craig High School; economic and political science degrees, Miami University, Ohio;

professional: marketing consultant, Ryan Inc., Central (construction firm); aide to former U.S. Senator Bob Kasten (R–WI); advisor to former Vice Presidential candidate Jack Kemp, and U.S. Drug Czar Bill Bennett; legislative director, U.S. Senate; organizations: Janesville Bowmen, Inc.; Ducks Unlimited; married: Janna Ryan; three children: daughter, Liza; sons, Charlie and Sam; committees: ranking member, Budget; Ways and Means; elected to the 106th Congress; reelected to each succeeding Congress.

Office Listings

http://www.house.gov/ryan

1113 Longworth House Office Building, Washington, DC 20515	(202) 225–3031
Administrative Assistant.—Joyce Meyer.	FAX: 225–3393
Legislative Director.—Matt Hoffmann.	
Scheduler.—Sarah Peer.	
20 South Main Street, Suite 10, Janesville, WI 53545	(608) 752–4050
5455 Sheridan Road, Suite 125, Kenosha, WI 53140	(262) 654–1901
216 Sixth Street, Racine, WI 53403	(262) 637–0510

Counties: KENOSHA, MILWAUKEE (part), RACINE, ROCK (part), WALWORTH (part), WAUKESHA (part). Population (2000), 670,458.

ZIP Codes: 53101–05, 53108–09, 53114–15, 53119–21, 53125–26, 53128–30, 53132, 53138–44, 53146–54, 53156–59, 53167–68, 53170–72, 53176–77, 53179, 53181–82, 53184–85, 53189–92, 53194–95, 53207, 53219–21, 53228, 53401–08, 53501, 53505, 53511, 53525, 53534, 53538, 53545–48, 53563, 53585

* * *

SECOND DISTRICT

TAMMY BALDWIN, Democrat, of Madison, WI; born in Madison, February 11, 1962; education: graduated from Madison West High School, 1980; A.B., mathematics and government, Smith College, 1984; J.D., University of Wisconsin Law School, 1989; professional: attorney, 1989–92; elected to the Dane County Board of Supervisors, 1986–94; elected to the State Assembly from the 78th district, 1993–99; committees: Energy and Commerce; Judiciary; elected to the 106th Congress; reelected to each succeeding Congress.

Office Listings

http://tammybaldwin.house.gov

2446 Rayburn House Office Building, Washington, DC 20515	(202) 225–2906
Chief of Staff.—Bill Murat.	FAX: 225–6942
Legislative Director.—Elissa Levin.	
Appointment Secretary.—Maureen Hekmat.	
Press Secretary.—Jerilyn Goodman.	(608) 258–9800
10 East Doty Street, Suite 405, Madison, WI 53703	(608) 258–9800
District Director.—Curt Finkelmeyer.	
400 East Grand Avenue, Suite 402, Beloit, WI 53511	(608) 362–2800

Counties: COLUMBIA, DANE, GREEN, JEFFERSON (part), ROCK (part), SAUK (part), WALWORTH (part). Population (2000), 670,457.

ZIP Codes: 53038, 53094, 53098, 53190, 53501–02, 53504, 53508, 53511–12, 53515–17, 53520–23, 53527–29, 53531–32, 53534, 53536–38, 53542, 53544–46, 53548–51, 53555, 53558–63, 53566, 53570–72, 53574–76, 53578, 53581–83, 53589–91, 53593–94, 53596–98, 53701–08, 53711, 53713–19, 53725–26, 53744, 53777–79, 53782–94, 53901, 53911, 53913, 53916, 53923, 53925–26, 53928, 53932–33, 53935, 53951, 53954–57, 53959–60, 53965, 53968–69

* * *

THIRD DISTRICT

RON KIND, Democrat, of La Crosse, WI; born in La Crosse, March 16, 1963; education: B.A., Harvard University, 1985; M.A., London School of Economics, 1986; J.D., University of Minnesota Law School, 1990; admitted to the Wisconsin bar, 1990; state prosecutor, La Crosse County District Attorney's Office; board of directors, La Crosse Boys and Girls Club; Coulee Council on Alcohol and Drug Abuse; Wisconsin Harvard Club; Wisconsin Bar Association; La Crosse County Bar Association; married: Tawni Zappa in 1994; two sons: Jonathan and Matthew; committees: Natural Resources; Ways and Means; elected to the 105th Congress; reelected to each succeeding Congress.

Office Listings

http://www.kind.house.gov

1406 Longworth House Office Building, Washington, DC 20515 .... (202) 225–5506
Chief of Staff.—Erik Olson. FAX: 225–5739
Press Secretary.—Leah Hunter.
Legislative Director.—Travis Robey.
Scheduler.—Steve Sipe.
205 Fifth Avenue South, Suite 400, La Crosse, WI 54601 .... (608) 782–2558
District Director.—Loren Kannenberg.
131 South Barstow Street, Suite 301, Eau Claire, WI 54701 .... (715) 831–9214
Staff Assistant / Case Worker.—Mark Aumann.

Counties: BUFFALO, CLARK (part), CRAWFORD, DUNN, EAU CLAIRE, GRANT, IOWA, JACKSON, JUNEAU, LA CROSSE, LAFAYETTE, MONROE, PEPIN, PIERCE, RICHLAND, SAUK (part), ST. CROIX, TREMPEALEAU, VERNON. Population (2000), 670,462.

ZIP Codes: 53503–04, 53506–07, 53510, 53516–18, 53522, 53526, 53530, 53533, 53535, 53540–41, 53543–44, 53553–54, 53556, 53560, 53565, 53569, 53573, 53577–78, 53580–84, 53586–88, 53595, 53599, 53801–13, 53816–18, 53820–21, 53824–27, 53913, 53924, 53929, 53937, 53940–44, 53948, 53950–51, 53958–59, 53961–62, 53965, 53968, 54001–05, 54007, 54009–11, 54013–17, 54020–28, 54082, 54420, 54436–37, 54446, 54449, 54456–57, 54460, 54466, 54479, 54488, 54493, 54601–03, 54610–12, 54614–16, 54618–32, 54634–46, 54648–62, 54664–67, 54669–70, 54701–03, 54720–30, 54733–43, 54746–47, 54749–51, 54754–65, 54767–73

* * *

FOURTH DISTRICT

GWEN MOORE, Democrat, of Milwaukee, WI; born in Racine, WI, April 18, 1951; education: graduated North Division High School, Milwaukee; B.A., Political Science, Marquette University, Milwaukee, WI, 1978; professional: Program and Planning Analyst for the State of Wisconsin Services; housing officer, Wisconsin Housing and Development Authority; member: Wisconsin state assembly, 1989–92; Wisconsin state senate, 1993–2004; president pro tempore, 1997–98; three children; committees: Budget; Financial Services; elected to the 109th Congress on November 2, 2004; reelected to the each succeeding Congress.

Office Listings

http://www.house.gov/moore

1239 Longworth House Office Building, Washington, DC 20515 .... (202) 225–4572
Chief of Staff.—Win Boerckel. FAX: 225–8135
219 North Milwaukee Street, Suite 3A, Milwaukee, WI 53202 .... (414) 297–1140
District Administrator.—Lois O'Keefe.

Counties: MILWAUKEE (part). CITIES AND TOWNSHIPS: Milwaukee, Cudahy, South Milwaukee, St. Francis, West Allis, and West Milwaukee. Population (2000), 670,458.

ZIP Codes: 53110, 53154, 53172, 53201–28, 53233–35, 53237, 53268, 53270, 53277–78, 53280–81, 53284–85, 53288, 53290, 53293, 53295

* * *

FIFTH DISTRICT

F. JAMES SENSENBRENNER, JR., Republican, of Menomonee Falls, WI; born in Chicago, IL, June 14, 1943; education: graduated, Milwaukee Country Day School, 1961; A.B., Stanford University, 1965; J.D., University of Wisconsin Law School, 1968; admitted to the Wisconsin bar, 1968; commenced practice in Cedarburg, WI; admitted to practice before the U.S. Supreme Court in 1972; professional: attorney; staff member of former U.S. Congressman J. Arthur Younger of California, 1965; elected to the Wisconsin Assembly, 1968, reelected in 1970, 1972, and 1974; elected to Wisconsin Senate in a special election, 1975, reelected in 1976 (assistant minority leader); member: Waukesha County Republican Party; Wisconsin Bar Association; Friends of Museums; American Philatelic Society; married: the former Cheryl Warren, 1977; children: Frank James III and Robert Alan; committees: ranking member, Select Committee on Energy Independence and Global Warming; Judiciary; Science and Technology; elected to the 96th Congress, November 7, 1978; reelected to each succeeding Congress.

Office Listings

http://www.sensenbrenner.house.gov

2449 Rayburn House Office Building, Washington, DC 20515 .... (202) 225–5101

Chief of Staff.—Tom Schreibel.
Press Secretary.—Wendy Riemann.
Scheduler / Office Manager.—Todd Washam.
120 Bishops Way, Room 154, Brookfield, WI 53005 .... (262) 784–1111
Chief of Staff.—Tom Schreibel.

Counties: JEFFERSON (part), MILWAUKEE (part), OZAUKEE, WASHINGTON, WAUKESHA (part). Population (2000), 670,458.

ZIP Codes: 53002, 53004–05, 53007–08, 53012–13, 53017–18, 53021–22, 53024, 53027, 53029, 53033, 53037–38, 53040, 53045–46, 53051–52, 53056, 53058, 53060, 53064, 53066, 53069, 53072, 53074, 53076, 53080, 53085–86, 53089–90, 53092, 53095, 53097–98, 53118, 53122, 53127, 53137, 53146, 53151, 53156, 53178, 53183, 53186–90, 53208–14, 53217, 53219, 53222–23, 53225–28, 53263, 53538, 53549

* * *

SIXTH DISTRICT

THOMAS E. PETRI, Republican, of Fond du Lac, WI; born in Marinette, WI, May 28, 1940; education: graduated, Lowell P. Goodrich High School, 1958; B.A., Harvard University, Cambridge, MA, 1962; J.D., Harvard Law School, 1965; professional: admitted to the Wisconsin State and Fond du Lac County Bar Associations, 1965; lawyer; law clerk to Federal Judge James Doyle, 1965; Peace Corps volunteer, 1966–67; White House aide, 1969; commenced law practice in Fond du Lac, 1970; elected to the Wisconsin State Senate in 1972; reelected in 1976, and served until April, 1979; married; one daughter; committees: Education and Labor; Transportation and Infrastructure; elected to the 96th Congress, by special election, on April 3, 1979, to fill the vacancy caused by the death of William A. Steiger; reelected to each succeeding Congress.

Office Listings

http://www.petri.house.gov

2462 Rayburn House Office Building, Washington, DC 20515 .... (202) 225–2476
Chief of Staff / Legislative Director.—Debra Gebhardt. FAX: 225–2356
Communications Director.—Niel Wright.
Office Manager.—Linda Towse.
490 West Rolling Meadows Drive, Suite B, Fond du Lac, WI 54937 .... (920) 922–1180
District Director.—David G. Anderson.
2390 State Road 44, Suite B, Oshkosh, WI 54904 .... (920) 231–6333

Counties: ADAMS, CALUMET (part), DODGE, FOND DU LAC, GREEN LAKE, JEFFERSON (part), MANITOWOC, MARQUETTE, OUTAGAMIE (part), SHEBOYGAN, WAUSHARA, WINNEBAGO. Population (2000), 670,459.

ZIP Codes: 53001, 53003, 53006, 53010–11, 53013–16, 53019–21, 53023, 53026–27, 53031–32, 53034–36, 53039, 53042, 53044, 53047–50, 53057, 53059, 53061–63, 53065–66, 53070, 53073, 53075, 53078–79, 53081–83, 53085, 53088, 53091, 53093–94, 53098–99, 53137, 53205, 53207, 53215, 53221, 53557, 53579, 53594, 53901, 53910, 53916–17, 53919–20, 53922–23, 53925–27, 53930–34, 53936, 53939, 53946–47, 53949–50, 53952–54, 53956, 53963–65, 53968, 54110, 54115, 54123, 54126, 54129–30, 54136, 54140, 54160, 54169, 54207–08, 54214–16, 54220–21, 54227–28, 54230, 54232, 54240–41, 54245, 54247, 54413, 54457, 54486, 54494, 54499, 54613, 54619, 54638, 54648, 54660, 54755, 54901–04, 54906, 54909, 54911, 54913–15, 54921–23, 54927, 54930, 54932–37, 54941, 54943–44, 54947, 54950, 54952, 54956–57, 54960, 54963–68, 54970–71, 54974, 54976, 54979–86

* * *

SEVENTH DISTRICT

DAVID R. OBEY, Democrat, of Wausau, WI; born in Okmulgee, OK, October 3, 1938; education: graduated Wausau High School, 1956; M.A. in political science, University of Wisconsin, 1960 (graduate work in Russian government and foreign policy); elected to the Wisconsin Legislature from Marathon County's 2nd District at the age of 24; reelected three times; assistant Democratic floor leader; married: Joan Lepinski of Wausau, WI, 1962; children: Craig David and Douglas David; committees: chair, Appropriations; elected to the 91st Congress, by special election, on April 1, 1969, to fill the vacancy created by the resignation of Melvin R. Laird; reelected to each succeeding Congress.

Office Listings

http://www.obey.house.gov

2314 Rayburn House Office Building, Washington, DC 20515 .... (202) 225–3365
Chief of Staff.—Christina Hamilton.
Scheduler.—Carly M. Burns.
Press Secretary.—Ellis Brachman.
401 Fifth Street, Suite 406A, Wausau, WI 54403 .... (715) 842–5606

District Representative.—Doug Hill.
1401 Tower Avenue, Suite 307, Superior, WI 54880 .... (715) 398–4426

Counties: ASHLAND, BARRON, BAYFIELD, BURNETT, CHIPPEWA, CLARK (part), DOUGLAS, IRON, LANGLADE (part), LINCOLN, MARATHON, ONEIDA (part), POLK, PORTAGE, PRICE, RUSK, SAWYER, TAYLOR, WASHBURN, WOOD. Population (2000), 670,462.

ZIP Codes: 54001, 54004–07, 54009, 54017, 54020, 54024, 54026, 54401–12, 54414–15, 54417–18, 54420–29, 54432–35, 54437, 54439–43, 54447–49, 54451–52, 54454–55, 54457–60, 54462–63, 54466–67, 54469–76, 54479–81, 54484–85, 54487–90, 54492, 54494–95, 54498–99, 54501, 54513–15, 54517, 54524–27, 54529–32, 54534, 54536–38, 54545–47, 54550, 54552, 54555–56, 54559, 54563–65, 54703, 54724, 54726–33, 54739, 54745, 54748, 54757, 54762–63, 54766, 54768, 54771, 54774, 54801, 54805–06, 54810, 54812–14, 54816–22, 54824, 54826–30, 54832, 54834–50, 54853–59, 54861–62, 54864–65, 54867–68, 54870–76, 54880, 54888–91, 54893, 54895–96, 54909, 54921, 54945, 54966, 54977, 54981

* * *

EIGHTH DISTRICT

STEVE KAGEN, Democrat, of Appleton, WI; born in Appleton, WI, December 12, 1949; education: B.S., University of Wisconsin, Madison, WI, 1972; M.D., University of Wisconsin, Madison, WI, 1976; professional: physician; married: Gayle; committees: Agriculture; Transportation and Infrastructure; elected to the 110th Congress on November 7, 2006; reelected to the 111th Congress on November 4, 2008.

Office Listings

http://www.kagen.house.gov

1232 Longworth House Office Building, Washington, DC 20515 .... (202) 225–5665
Chief of Staff.—David Williams. FAX: 225–5729
Legislative Director.—Rob Mosher.
Scheduler.—Katie Tilley.
Press Secretary.—Jake Rubi.
700 East Walnut Street, Green Bay, WI 54301 .... (920) 437–1954
Deputy District Director.—Bambi Yingst.
333 West College Avenue, Appleton, WI 54911 .... (920) 380–0061
District Director.—Craig Moser.

Counties: BROWN, CALUMET (part), DOOR, FLORENCE, FOREST, KEWAUNEE, LANGLADE (part), MARINETTE, MENOMINEE, OCONTO, ONEIDA (part), OUTAGAMIE (part), SHAWANO, VILAS, WAUPACA. Population (2000), 670,461.

ZIP Codes: 54101–04, 54106–07, 54110–15, 54119–21, 54124–28, 54130–31, 54135, 54137–41, 54143, 54149–57, 54159, 54161–62, 54165–66, 54169–71, 54173–75, 54177, 54180, 54182, 54201–02, 54204–05, 54208–13, 54216–17, 54226–27, 54229–30, 54234–35, 54241, 54246, 54301–08, 54311, 54313, 54324, 54344, 54408–09, 54414, 54416, 54418, 54424, 54427–28, 54430, 54435, 54450, 54452, 54462–65, 54485–87, 54491, 54499, 54501, 54511–12, 54519–21, 54529, 54531, 54538–43, 54545, 54548, 54554, 54557–58, 54560–62, 54564, 54566, 54568, 54911–15, 54919, 54922, 54926, 54928–29, 54931, 54933, 54940, 54942, 54944–50, 54952, 54956, 54961–62, 54965, 54969, 54975, 54977–78, 54981, 54983, 54990

WYOMING

(Population 2000, 493,782)

SENATORS

MICHAEL B. ENZI, Republican, of Gillette, WY; born in Bremerton, WA, February 1, 1944; education: B.S., accounting, George Washington University, 1966; M.B.A., Denver University, 1968; professional: served in Wyoming National Guard, 1967–73; accounting manager and computer programmer, Dunbar Well Service, 1985–97; director, Black Hills Corporation, a New York Stock Exchange company, 1992–96; member, founding board of directors, First Wyoming Bank of Gillette, 1978–88; owner, with wife, of NZ Shoes; served in Wyoming House of Representatives, 1987–91, and in Wyoming State Senate, 1991–96; Mayor of Gillette, 1975–82; commissioner, Western Interstate Commission for Higher Education, 1995–96; served on the Education Commission of the States, 1989–93; president, Wyoming Association of Municipalities, 1980–82; president, Wyoming Jaycees, 1973–74; member: Lions Club; elder, Presbyterian Church; Eagle Scout; married: Diana Buckley, 1969; children: Amy, Brad, and Emily; committees: ranking member, Health, Education, Labor and Pensions; Budget; Finance; Small Business and Entrepreneurship; elected to the U.S. Senate in November, 1996; reelected to each succeeding Senate term.

Office Listings

http://enzi.senate.gov

379–A Russell Senate Office Building, Washington, DC 20510 .... (202) 224–3424
Chief of Staff.—Flip McConnaughey. FAX: 228–0359
Legislative Director.—Randi Reid.
Press Secretary.—Elly Pickett.
Office Manager.—Christen Thompson.
Federal Center, Suite 2007, 2120 Capitol Avenue, Cheyenne, WY 82001 .... (307) 772–2477
400 South Kendrick, Suite 303, Gillette, WY 82716 .... (307) 682–6268
100 East B Street, Room 3201, P.O. Box 33201, Casper, WY 82602 .... (307) 261–6572
P.O. Box 12470, Jackson, WY 83002 .... (307) 739–9507

* * *

JOHN BARRASSO, Republican, of Casper, WY; born in Reading, PA, July 21, 1952; education: B.S., Georgetown University, Washington, DC, 1974; M.D., Georgetown University, Washington, DC, 1978; professional: Casper Orthopaedic Associates, 1983–2007; Chief of Staff, Wyoming Medical Center, 2003–05; President, Wyoming Medical Society; President, National Association of Physician Broadcasters, 1988–89; member, Wyoming State Senate, 2002–06; wife: Bobbi; children: Peter, Emma and Hadley; committees: vice chair, Indian Affairs; Energy and Natural Resources; Environment and Public Works; Foreign Relations; sworn in by Vice President Cheney on June 25, 2007 to the 110th Congress to fill the vacancy caused by the death of Senator Craig Thomas; elected to the U.S. Senate on November 4, 2008.

Office Listings

http://barrasso.senate.gov

307 Dirksen Senate Office Building, Washington, DC 20510 .... (202) 224–6441
Chief of Staff.—Shawn Whitman. FAX: 224–1724
Legislative Director.—Bryn Stewart.
Communications Director.—Gregory Keeley.
Office Manager.—Amber Moyerman.
2201 Federal Building, Casper, WY 82601 .... (307) 261–6413
2120 Capitol Avenue, Suite 2013, Cheyenne, WY 82001 .... (307) 772–2451
2632 Foothills Boulevard, Suite 101, Rock Springs, WY 82901 .... (307) 362–5012
325 West Main, Suite F, Riverton, WY 82501 .... (307) 856–6642
2 North Main Street, Suite 206, Sheridan, WY 82801 .... (307) 672–6456

REPRESENTATIVE

AT LARGE

CYNTHIA M. LUMMIS, Republican, of Cheyenne, WY; born in Cheyenne, WY, September 10, 1954; education: graduated, B.S., animal science, University of Wyoming, 1976; B.S., biology, University of Wyoming, 1978; J.D., University of Wyoming, 1985; professional: Attorney at Law, 1986–present; rancher, 1976–present; Representative, Wyoming State House of Representatives, 1979–82; clerk, Wyoming Supreme Court, 1985; Representative, Wyoming State House of Representatives, 1985–93; Senator, Wyoming State Legislature, 1993–94; Interim Director of State Lands, State of Wyoming, 1997–98; General Counsel, Office of the Governor, 1995–97; State Treasurer, State of Wyoming, 1998–2006; chair, Western State Treasurer's Association; Advisory Board, Center for the Rocky Mountain West at the University of Montana; Board of Member, American Women's Financial Education Foundation; Director, Cheyenne Frontier Days; member, Cheyenne's Vision 2020; member, Laramie Foundation and its Wyoming Women's History House; member, Leadership Wyoming Board; Advisory Board, Ruckelshaus Institute for Environment and Natural Resources at the University of Wyoming; member, Trinity Lutheran Church; member, Wyoming Business Alliance; member, Wyoming Stock Growers Agricultural Land Trust, married: Al Wiederspahn; children: Annaliese; committees: Agriculture; Budget; Natural Resources; elected to the 111th Congress on November 4, 2008.

Office Listings

http://lummis.house.gov

1004 Longworth House Office Building, Washington, DC 20515 .... (202) 225–2311
Chief of Staff.—Tom Wiblemo. FAX: 225–3057
Legislative Director.—Rick Axthelm.
Press Secretary.—Ryan Taylor.
100 East B Street, Suite 4003, Casper, WY 82602 .... (307) 261–6595
District Representatives: Jackie King, Ryan McConnaughey.
2120 Capitol Avenue, Suite 2015, Cheyenne, WY 82001 .... (307) 772–2595
Chief of Staff.—Tucker Fagan. FAX: 772–2597
Scheduler.—Christie Clark.
District Representative.—Johnnie Burton.
45 East Loucks, Suite 300F, Sheridan, WY 82801 .... (307) 673–4608
District Representative.—Matt Jones. FAX: 673–4982
404 N Street, Suite 204, Rock Springs, WY 82901 .... (307) 362–4095
District Representatives: Pat Aullman, Bonnie Cannon. FAX: 362–4097

Population (2000), 493,782.

ZIP Codes: 82001, 82003, 82005–10, 82050–55, 82058–61, 82063, 82070–73, 82081–84, 82190, 82201, 82210, 82212–15, 82217–19, 82221–25, 82227, 82229, 82240, 82242–44, 82301, 82310, 82321–25, 82327, 82329, 82331–32, 82334–36, 82401, 82410–12, 82414, 82420–23, 82426, 82428, 82430–35, 82440–43, 82450, 82501, 82510, 82512–16, 82520, 82523–24, 82601–02, 82604–05, 82609, 82615, 82620, 82630, 82633, 82635–40, 82642–44, 82646, 82648–49, 82701, 82710–12, 82714–18, 82720–21, 82723, 82725, 82727, 82729–32, 82801, 82831–40, 82842, 82844–45, 82901–02, 82922–23, 82925, 82929–39, 82941–45, 83001–02, 83011–14, 83025, 83101, 83110–16, 83118–24, 83126–28

AMERICAN SAMOA

(Population 2000, 57,291)

DELEGATE

ENI F. H. FALEOMAVAEGA, Democrat, of Vailoatai, AS; born in Vailoatai, August 15, 1943; education: graduate of Kahuku High School, Hawaii, 1962; B.A., Brigham Young University, 1966; J.D., University of Houston Law School, 1972; LL.M., University of California, Berkeley, 1973; admitted to U.S. Supreme Court and American Samoa bars; military service: enlisted, U.S. Army, 1966–69; Vietnam veteran; captain, USAR, Judge Advocate General Corps, 1982–92; professional: administrative assistant to American Samoa's Delegate to Washington, 1973–75; staff counsel, Committee on Interior and Insular Affairs, 1975–81; deputy attorney general, American Samoa, 1981–84; elected Lieutenant Governor, American Samoa, 1984–89; member: Democratic Study Group; National American Indian Prayer Breakfast Group; National Association of Secretaries of State; National Conference of Lieutenant Governors; Navy League of the United States; Pago Pago Lions Club; Veterans of Foreign Wars; Congressional Arts Caucus; Congressional Hispanic Caucus; Congressional Human Rights Caucus; Congressional Travel and Tourism Caucus; married: Hinanui Bambridge Cave of Tahiti; five children; committees: Foreign Affairs; Natural Resources; elected to the 101st Congress on November 8, 1988; reelected to each succeeding Congress.

Office Listings

http://www.house.gov/faleomavaega

2422 Rayburn House Office Building, Washington, DC 20515 .... (202) 225–8577
Chief of Staff.—Lisa Williams. FAX: 225–8757
Scheduler / Office Manager.—Hana Atuatasi.
Legislative Director.—David Richmond.
P.O. Drawer X, Pago Pago, AS 96799 .... (684) 633–1372

ZIP Codes: 96799

* * *

DISTRICT OF COLUMBIA

(Population 2000, 572,059)

DELEGATE

ELEANOR HOLMES NORTON, Democrat, of Washington, DC; born in Washington, DC, June 13, 1937; education: graduated, Dunbar High School, 1955; B.A., Antioch College, 1960; M.A., Yale Graduate School, 1963; J.D., Yale Law School, 1964; honorary degrees: Cedar Crest College, 1969; Bard College, 1971; Princeton University, 1973; Marymount College, 1974; City College of New York, 1975; Georgetown University, 1977; New York University, 1978; Howard University, 1978; Brown University, 1978; Wilberforce University, 1978; Wayne State University, 1980; Gallaudet College, 1980; Denison University, 1980; Syracuse University, 1981; Yeshiva University, 1981; Lawrence University, 1981; Emanuel College, 1981; Spelman College, 1982; University of Massachusetts, 1983; Smith College, 1983; Medical College of Pennsylvania, 1983; Tufts University, 1984; Bowdoin College, 1985; Antioch College, 1985; Haverford College, 1986; Lesley College, 1986; New Haven University, 1986; University of San Diego, 1986; Sojourner-Douglas College, 1987; Salem State College, 1987; Rutgers University, 1988; St. Joseph's College, 1988; University of Lowell, 1988; Colgate University, 1989; Drury College, 1989; Florida International University, 1989; St. Lawrence University, 1989; University of Wisconsin, 1989; University of Hartford, 1990; Ohio Wesleyan University, 1990; Wake Forest University, 1990; Fisk University, 1991; Tougalvo University, 1992; University of Southern Connecticut, 1992; professional: professor of law, Georgetown University, 1982–90; past / present member: chair, New York Commission on Human Rights, 1970–76; chair, Equal Employment Opportunity Commission, 1977–81; Community Foundation of Greater Washington, board; Yale Corporation, 1982–88; trustee, Rockefeller Foundation, 1982–90; executive assistant to the mayor of New York City (concurrent appointment); law clerk, Judge A. Leon Higginbotham, Federal District Court, 3rd Circuit; attorney, admitted to practice by examination in the District of Columbia, Pennsylvania and in the U.S. Supreme Court; Council on Foreign Relations; Overseas Development Council; U.S. Committee to Monitor the Helsinki accords; Carter Center, Atlanta, Georgia; boards of Martin Luther King, Jr. Center for Social Change and Environmental Law Institute; Workplace Health Fund; honors awards: Harper Fellow, Yale Law School, 1976, (for "a person . . . who has made a distinguished contribution to the public life of the nation . . ."); Yale Law School Association Citation of Merit Medal to the Outstanding Alumnus of the Law School, 1980; Chancellor's Distinguished Lecturer, University of California Law School (Boalt Hall), Berkeley, 1981; Visiting Fellow, Harvard University, John F. Kennedy School of Government, spring 1984; Visiting Phi Beta Kappa Scholar, 1985; Distinguished Public Service Award, Center for National Policy, 1985; Ralph E. Shikes Bicentennial Fellow, Harvard Law School, 1987; One Hundred Most Important Women (*Ladies Home Journal*, 1988); One Hundred Most Powerful Women in Washington (The *Washingtonian* magazine, September 1989); divorced; two children: John and Katherine; committees: Homeland Security; Oversight and Government Reform; Transportation and Infrastructure; elected to the 102nd Congress on November 6, 1990; reelected to each succeeding Congress.

Office Listings

http://www.norton.house.gov

2136 Rayburn House Office Building, Washington, DC 20515 .... (202) 225–8050
Chief of Staff.—Sheila Bunn. FAX: 225–3002
Legislative Director.—Bradley Truding.
Executive Assistant.—Raven Roddey.
Communications Director.—Sonsyrea Tate Montgomery.

ZIP Codes: 20001–13, 20015–20, 20024, 20026–27, 20029–30, 20032–33, 20035–45, 20047, 20049–53, 20055–71, 20073–77, 20080, 20088, 20090–91, 20099, 20201–04, 20206–08, 20210–13, 20215–24, 20226–33, 20235, 20237, 20239–42, 20244–45, 20250, 20254, 20260, 20268, 20270, 20277, 20289, 20301, 20303, 20306–07, 20310, 20314–15, 20317–19, 20330, 20340, 20350, 20370, 20372–76, 20380, 20388–95, 20398, 20401–16, 20418–29, 20431, 20433–37, 20439–42, 20444, 20447, 20451, 20453, 20456, 20460, 20463, 20469, 20472, 20500, 20503–10, 20515, 20520–27, 20530–36, 20538–44, 20546–49, 20551–55, 20557, 20559–60, 20565–66, 20570–73, 20575–77, 20579–81, 20585–86, 20590–91, 20593–94, 20597, 20599

* * *

GUAM

(Population 2000, 154,805)

DELEGATE

MADELEINE Z. BORDALLO, Democrat, of Tamuning, Guam, born on May 31, 1933; education: Associate Degree in Music, St. Catherine's College, St. Paul, MN, 1953; professional: First Lady of Guam, 1975–78, and 1983–86; Guam Senator, 1981–82, and 1987–94 (five terms); Lt. Governor of Guam, 1995–2002 (two terms); National Committee Chair for the National Democratic Party, 1964–2004; family: Ricardo J. Bordallo (deceased); daughter, Deborah; granddaughter, Nicole; committees: Armed Services; Natural Resources; elected to the 108th Congress on November 5, 2002; reelected to each succeeding Congress.

Office Listings

http://www.house.gov/bordallo

427 Cannon House Office Building, Washington, DC 20515 .... (202) 225–1188
Chief of Staff.—John Whitt. FAX: 226–0341
Legislative Director.—Matthew Herrmann.
Press Secretary.—Matthew Mateo.
Scheduler.—Rosanne Meno.
120 Father Duenas Avenue, Suite 107, Hagåtña, GU 96910 .... (671) 477–4272

ZIP Codes: 96910, 96912–13, 96915–17, 96919, 96921, 96923, 96926, 96928–29, 96931–32

NORTHERN MARIANA ISLANDS

(Population 2000, 69,221)

DELEGATE

GREGORIO KILILI CAMACHO SABLAN, Democrat, of Saipan, MP; born in Saipan, MP, January 19, 1955; education: University of Hawaii, Manoa Honolulu, HI; 1989–90; professional: member, Northern Mariana Islands Commonwealth Legislature, 1982–86 (2 terms); Special Assistant to Senator Daniel Inouye; Special Assistant to Northern Mariana Islands Governor Pedro P. Tenorio; Executive Director of the Commonwealth Election Commission; family: married Andrea C. Sablan, son Jesse, daughter Patricia; caucuses: Congressional Asian Pacific American Caucus; Congressional Hispanic Caucus; American Citizens Abroad Caucus; Bi-Partisan Disabilities Caucus; Democratic Caucus; Community College Caucus; National Marine Sanctuary Caucus; Friends of New Zealand Caucus; International Conservation Caucus; committees: Natural Resources; Education and Labor; elected to the 111th Congress on November 4, 2008.

Office Listings

http://www.sablan.house.gov

423 Cannon House Office Building, Washington, DC 20515 .... (202) 225–2646
Chief of Staff.—Robert J. Schwalbach. FAX: 226–4249
Scheduler.—Chai Cruz.
JCT II Building, Susupe, P.O. Box 504879, Saipan, MP 96950 .... (670) 323–2647
District Officer Director.—Mike Tenorio. FAX: 323–2649

ZIP Codes: 96950, 96951, 96952

* * *

PUERTO RICO

(Population 2000, 3,808,610)

RESIDENT COMMISSIONER

PEDRO R. PIERLUISI, Democratic, of Guaynabo, PR; born in San Juan, PR, April 26, 1959; education: Contemporary U.S. History, Tulane University, New Orleans, LA, 1981; Juris Doctor, George Washington University, Washington, DC, 1984; professional: Verner & LipfertAssoc., Washington, DC, 1984–85; Cole, Corette & Abrutyn, Washington, DC, 1985–88; Pierluisi & Pierluisi, San Juan, PR, 1990–92; Attorney General of Puerto Rico, 1993–96; O'Neill & Borges, San Jaun, PR, 1997–2007; religion: Catholic; married: Maria Elena Carrión; family: four children; committees: Education and Labor; Natural Resources, Judiciary; elected to the 111th Congress on November 4, 2008.

Office Listings

http://www.pierluisi.house.gov

1218 Longworth House Office Building, Washington, DC 20515 .... (202) 225–2615
Chief of Staff.—Carmen M. Feliciano. FAX: 225–2154
Communications Director.—Dennise Pérez.
Legislative Director.—John Laufer.
Legislative Counsel.—Jonathan Thessin.
Legislative Assistant.—María Teresa Carro.
Legislative Correspondents: Anina Caso, Eduardo Hilera, Geenae Rivera.
Staff Assistant.—Sonia García.
Administrative Assistant.—Odette Santini.
250 Calle Fortaleza, Old San Juan, PR 00901 .... (787) 723–6333
District Office Director.—Rosemarie ''Maí'' Vizcarrondo. FAX: 729–7738
Office Manager.—Aimée Irlanda.
Constituent Liaison.—Carlos Cátala.
Press Aide.—Sylvia Escoto.
Staff Assistant (Public Relation & Web Master).—Eda Delucca.
Senior Case Worker.—Luis Ortíz.
Social Security Case Worker.—Cristina Sierra.
Immigration Case Worker.—Jacqueline Rodríguez.
Veteran's Case Worker.—Segundo J. Ferro.

ZIP Codes: 00601–06, 00610–14, 00616–17, 00622–25, 00627, 00631, 00636–38, 00641, 00646–48, 00650, 00652–62, 00664, 00667, 00669–70, 00674, 00676–78, 00680–83, 00685, 00687–88, 00690, 00692–94, 00698, 00701, 00703–

05, 00707, 00714–21, 00723, 00725–42, 00744–45, 00751, 00754, 00757, 00765–69, 00771–73, 00775, 00777–78, 00780, 00782–86, 00791–92, 00794–95, 00901–36, 00938, 00940, 00949–63, 00965–66, 00968–71, 00975–79, 00981–88

* * *

VIRGIN ISLANDS

(Population 2000, 108,612)

DELEGATE

DONNA M. CHRISTENSEN, Democrat, of St. Croix, VI; born in Teaneck, NJ, September 19, 1945; B.S., St. Mary's College, Notre Dame, IN, 1966; M.D., George Washington University School of Medicine, 1970; physician, family medicine; Acting Commissioner of Health, 1994–95; medical director, St. Croix Hospital, 1987–88; founding member and vice president, Virgin Islands Medical Institute; trustee, National Medical Association; past secretary and two-time past president, Virgin Islands Medical Society; founding member and trustee, Caribbean Youth Organization; member: Democratic National Committee; Virgin Islands Democratic Territorial Committee (past vice chair); Substance Abuse Coalition; St. Dunstan's Episcopal School Board of Directors; Caribbean Studies Association; Women's Coalition of St. Croix; St. Croix Environmental Association; past chair, Christian Education Committee; Friedensthal Moravian Church; past member: Virgin Islands Board of Education; Democratic Platform Committee; cohost, Straight Up TV interview program, 1993; married: Chris Christensen; children: two daughters: Rabiah Layla and Karida Yasmeen; member: Congressional Black Caucus; Congressional Women's Caucus; committees: Energy and Commerce; Natural Resources; elected to the 105th Congress; reelected to each succeeding Congress.

Office Listings

http://www.donnachristensen.house.gov

1510 Longworth House Office Building, Washington, DC 20515 .... (202) 225–1790
Chief of Staff.—Monique Clendinen Watson. FAX: 225–5517
Executive Assistant / Scheduler.—Shelley Thomas.
Nisky Center, 2nd Floor, Suite 207, St. Thomas, VI 00802 .... (340) 774–4408
Office Assistant.—Joyce Jackson.
Office Manager.—Eddie Delagarde.
Sunny Isle Shopping Center, Space No. 25, P.O. Box 5980, St. Croix, VI 00823 ... (340) 778–5900
Office Manager.—Luz Belardo-Webster.

ZIP Codes: 00801–05, 00820–24, 00830–31, 00840–41, 00850–51

STATE DELEGATIONS

Number before names designates Congressional district. Democrats in roman; Republicans in *italic*; Independent in SMALL CAPS; Independent Democrat in *SMALL CAPS ITALIC;* Resident Commissioner and Delegates in **boldface**.

ALABAMA

SENATORS
Richard C. Shelby
Jeff Sessions

REPRESENTATIVES
[Democrats 3, Republicans 4]

1. *Jo Bonner*
2. Bobby Bright
3. *Mike Rogers*
4. *Robert B. Aderholt*
5. Parker Griffith
6. *Spencer Bachus*
7. Artur Davis

ALASKA

SENATORS
Lisa Murkowski
Mark Begich

REPRESENTATIVE
[Republican 1]
At Large - *Don Young*

ARIZONA

SENATORS
John McCain
Jon Kyl

REPRESENTATIVES
[Democrats 5, Republicans 3]

1. Ann Kirkpatrick
2. *Trent Franks*
3. *John B. Shadegg*
4. Ed Pastor
5. Harry E. Mitchell
6. *Jeff Flake*
7. Raúl M. Grijalva
8. Gabrielle Giffords

ARKANSAS

SENATORS
Blanche L. Lincoln
Mark L. Pryor

REPRESENTATIVES
[Democrats 3, Republicans 1]

1. Marion Berry
2. Vic Snyder
3. *John Boozman*
4. Mike Ross

CALIFORNIA

SENATORS
Dianne Feinstein
Barbara Boxer

REPRESENTATIVES
[Democrats 33, Republicans 19, Vacant 1]

1. Mike Thompson
2. *Wally Herger*
3. *Daniel E. Lungren*
4. *Tom McClintock*
5. Doris O. Matsui
6. Lynn C. Woolsey

7. George Miller
8. Nancy Pelosi
9. Barbara Lee
10. ——[1]
11. Jerry McNerney
12. Jackie Speier
13. Fortney Pete Stark
14. Anna G. Eshoo
15. Michael M. Honda
16. Zoe Lofgren
17. Sam Farr
18. Dennis A. Cardoza
19. *George Radanovich*
20. Jim Costa
21. *Devin Nunes*
22. *Kevin McCarthy*
23. Lois Capps
24. *Elton Gallegly*
25. *Howard P. "Buck" McKeon*
26. *David Dreier*
27. Brad Sherman
28. Howard L. Berman
29. Adam B. Schiff
30. Henry A. Waxman
31. Xavier Becerra
32. Judy Chu
33. Diane E. Watson
34. Lucille Roybal-Allard
35. Maxine Waters
36. Jane Harman
37. Laura Richardson
38. Grace F. Napolitano
39. Linda T. Sánchez
40. *Edward R. Royce*
41. *Jerry Lewis*
42. *Gary G. Miller*
43. Joe Baca
44. *Ken Calvert*
45. *Mary Bono Mack*
46. *Dana Rohrabacher*
47. Loretta Sanchez
48. *John Campbell*
49. *Darrell E. Issa*
50. *Brian P. Bilbray*
51. Bob Filner
52. *Duncan Hunter*
53. Susan A. Davis

COLORADO

SENATORS
Mark Udall
Michael F. Bennet

REPRESENTATIVES
[Democrats 5, Republicans 2]

1. Diana DeGette
2. Jared Polis
3. John T. Salazar
4. Betsy Markey
5. *Doug Lamborn*
6. *Mike Coffman*
7. Ed Perlmutter

CONNECTICUT

SENATORS
Christopher J. Dodd
*JOSEPH I. LIEBERMAN***

REPRESENTATIVES
[Democrats 5]

1. John B. Larson
2. Joe Courtney
3. Rosa L. DeLauro
4. James A. Himes
5. Christopher S. Murphy

DELAWARE

SENATORS
Thomas R. Carper
Edward E. Kaufman

REPRESENTATIVE
[Republican 1]

At Large - *Michael N. Castle*

FLORIDA

SENATORS
Bill Nelson
George S. LeMieux

REPRESENTATIVES
[Democrats 10, Republicans 15]

1. *Jeff Miller*
2. Allen Boyd
3. Corrine Brown
4. *Ander Crenshaw*
5. *Ginny Brown-Waite*
6. *Cliff Stearns*
7. *John L. Mica*
8. Alan Grayson
9. *Gus M. Bilirakis*
10. *C. W. Bill Young*
11. Kathy Castor
12. *Adam H. Putnam*

13. *Vern Buchanan*
14. *Connie Mack*
15. *Bill Posey*
16. *Thomas J. Rooney*
17. Kendrick B. Meek
18. *Ileana Ros-Lehtinen*
19. Robert Wexler
20. Debbie Wasserman Schultz
21. *Lincoln Diaz-Balart*
22. Ron Klein
23. Alcee L. Hastings
24. Suzanne M. Kosmas
25. *Mario Diaz-Balart*

GEORGIA

SENATORS
Saxby Chambliss
Johnny Isakson

REPRESENTATIVES
[Democrats 6, Republicans 7]

1. *Jack Kingston*
2. Sanford D. Bishop, Jr.
3. *Lynn A. Westmoreland*
4. Henry C. ''Hank'' Johnson, Jr.
5. John Lewis
6. *Tom Price*
7. *John Linder*
8. Jim Marshall
9. *Nathan Deal*
10. *Paul C. Broun*
11. *Phil Gingrey*
12. John Barrow
13. David Scott

HAWAII

SENATORS
Daniel K. Inouye
Daniel K. Akaka

REPRESENTATIVES
[Democrats 2]

1. Neil Abercrombie
2. Mazie K. Hirono

IDAHO

SENATORS
Mike Crapo
James E. Risch

REPRESENTATIVES
[Democrats 1, Republicans 1]

1. Walt Minnick
2. *Michael K. Simpson*

ILLINOIS

SENATORS
Richard Durbin
Roland W. Burris

REPRESENTATIVES
[Democrats 12, Republicans 7]

1. Bobby L. Rush
2. Jesse L. Jackson, Jr.
3. Daniel Lipinski
4. Luis V. Gutierrez
5. Mike Quigley
6. *Peter J. Roskam*
7. Danny K. Davis
8. Melissa L. Bean
9. Janice D. Schakowsky
10. *Mark Steven Kirk*
11. Deborah L. Halvorson
12. Jerry F. Costello
13. *Judy Biggert*
14. Bill Foster
15. *Timothy V. Johnson*
16. *Donald A. Manzullo*
17. Phil Hare
18. *Aaron Schock*
19. *John Shimkus*

INDIANA

SENATORS
Richard G. Lugar
Evan Bayh

REPRESENTATIVES
[Democrats 5, Republicans 4]

1. Peter J. Visclosky
2. Joe Donnelly
3. *Mark E. Souder*
4. *Steve Buyer*
5. *Dan Burton*
6. *Mike Pence*
7. André Carson
8. Brad Ellsworth
9. Baron P. Hill

IOWA

SENATORS
Chuck Grassley
Tom Harkin

REPRESENTATIVES
[Democrats 3, Republicans 2]

1. Bruce L. Braley
2. David Loebsack
3. Leonard L. Boswell
4. *Tom Latham*
5. *Steve King*

KANSAS

SENATORS
Sam Brownback
Pat Roberts

REPRESENTATIVES
[Democrats 1, Republicans 3]

1. *Jerry Moran*
2. *Lynn Jenkins*
3. Dennis Moore
4. *Todd Tiahrt*

KENTUCKY

SENATORS
Mitch McConnell
Jim Bunning

REPRESENTATIVES
[Democrats 2, Republicans 4]

1. *Ed Whitfield*
2. *Brett Guthrie*
3. John A. Yarmuth
4. *Geoff Davis*
5. *Harold Rogers*
6. Ben Chandler

LOUISIANA

SENATORS
Mary L. Landrieu
David Vitter

REPRESENTATIVES
[Democrats 1, Republicans 6]

1. *Steve Scalise*
2. *Anh "Joseph" Cao*
3. Charlie Melancon
4. *John Fleming*
5. *Rodney Alexander*
6. *Bill Cassidy*
7. *Charles W. Boustany, Jr.*

MAINE

SENATORS
Olympia J. Snowe
Susan M. Collins

REPRESENTATIVES
[Democrats 2]

1. Chellie Pingree
2. Michael H. Michaud

MARYLAND

SENATORS
Barbara A. Mikulski
Benjamin L. Cardin

REPRESENTATIVES
[Democrats 7, Republicans 1]

1. Frank Kratovil, Jr.
2. C. A. Dutch Ruppersberger
3. John P. Sarbanes
4. Donna F. Edwards
5. Steny H. Hoyer
6. *Roscoe G. Bartlett*
7. Elijah E. Cummings
8. Chris Van Hollen

MASSACHUSETTS

SENATORS
John F. Kerry
Paul G. Kirk, Jr

REPRESENTATIVES
[Democrats 10]

1. John W. Olver
2. Richard E. Neal
3. James P. McGovern
4. Barney Frank
5. Niki Tsongas
6. John F. Tierney
7. Edward J. Markey
8. Michael E. Capuano
9. Stephen F. Lynch
10. Bill Delahunt

MICHIGAN

SENATORS
Carl Levin
Debbie Stabenow

REPRESENTATIVES
[Democrats 8, Republicans 7]

1. Bart Stupak
2. *Peter Hoekstra*
3. *Vernon J. Ehlers*
4. *Dave Camp*
5. Dale E. Kildee
6. *Fred Upton*
7. Mark H. Schauer
8. *Mike Rogers*
9. Gary C. Peters
10. *Candice S. Miller*
11. *Thaddeus G. McCotter*
12. Sander M. Levin
13. Carolyn C. Kilpatrick
14. John Conyers, Jr.
15. John D. Dingell

MINNESOTA

SENATORS
Amy Klobuchar
Al Franken

REPRESENTATIVES
[Democrats 5, Republicans 3]

1. Timothy J. Walz
2. *John Kline*
3. *Erik Paulsen*
4. Betty McCollum
5. Keith Ellison
6. *Michele Bachmann*
7. Collin C. Peterson
8. James L. Oberstar

MISSISSIPPI

SENATORS
Thad Cochran
Roger F. Wicker

REPRESENTATIVES
[Democrats 3, Republicans 1]

1. Travis W. Childers
2. Bennie G. Thompson
3. *Gregg Harper*
4. Gene Taylor

MISSOURI

SENATORS
Christopher S. Bond
Claire McCaskill

REPRESENTATIVES
[Democrats 4, Republicans 5]

1. Wm. Lacy Clay
2. *W. Todd Akin*
3. Russ Carnahan
4. Ike Skelton
5. Emanuel Cleaver
6. *Sam Graves*
7. *Roy Blunt*
8. *Jo Ann Emerson*
9. *Blaine Luetkemeyer*

MONTANA

SENATORS
Max Baucus
Jon Tester

REPRESENTATIVE
[Republican 1]

At Large - *Denny Rehberg*

NEBRASKA

SENATORS
Ben Nelson
Mike Johanns

REPRESENTATIVES
[Republicans 3]

1. *Jeff Fortenberry*
2. *Lee Terry*
3. *Adrian Smith*

NEVADA

SENATORS
Harry Reid
John Ensign

REPRESENTATIVES
[Democrats 2, Republicans 1]

1. Shelley Berkley
2. *Dean Heller*
3. Dina Titus

NEW HAMPSHIRE

SENATORS
Judd Gregg
Jeanne Shaheen

REPRESENTATIVES
[Democrats 2]

1. Carol Shea-Porter
2. Paul W. Hodes

NEW JERSEY

SENATORS
Frank R. Lautenberg
Robert Menendez

REPRESENTATIVES
[Democrats 8, Republicans 5]

1. Robert E. Andrews
2. *Frank A. LoBiondo*
3. John H. Adler
4. *Christopher H. Smith*
5. *Scott Garrett*
6. Frank Pallone, Jr.
7. *Leonard Lance*
8. Bill Pascrell, Jr.
9. Steven R. Rothman
10. Donald M. Payne
11. *Rodney P. Frelinghuysen*
12. Rush D. Holt
13. Albio Sires

NEW MEXICO

SENATORS
Jeff Bingaman
Tom Udall

REPRESENTATIVES
[Democrats 3]

1. Martin Heinrich
2. Harry Teague
3. Ben Ray Luján

NEW YORK

SENATORS
Charles E. Schumer
Kirsten E. Gillibrand

REPRESENTATIVES
[Democrats 26, Republicans 2, Vacant 1]

1. Timothy H. Bishop
2. Steve Israel
3. *Peter T. King*
4. Carolyn McCarthy
5. Gary L. Ackerman
6. Gregory W. Meeks
7. Joseph Crowley
8. Jerrold Nadler
9. Anthony D. Weiner
10. Edolphus Towns
11. Yvette D. Clarke
12. Nydia M. Velázquez

13. Michael E. McMahon
14. Carolyn B. Maloney
15. Charles B. Rangel
16. José E. Serrano
17. Eliot L. Engel
18. Nita M. Lowey
19. John J. Hall
20. Scott Murphy
21. Paul Tonko
22. Maurice D. Hinchey
23. ——[2]
24. Michael A. Arcuri
25. Daniel B. Maffei
26. *Christopher John Lee*
27. Brian Higgins
28. Louise McIntosh Slaughter
29. Eric J. J. Massa

NORTH CAROLINA

SENATORS
Richard Burr
Kay R. Hagan

REPRESENTATIVES
[Democrats 8, Republicans 5]

1. G. K. Butterfield
2. Bob Etheridge
3. *Walter B. Jones*
4. David E. Price
5. *Virginia Foxx*
6. *Howard Coble*
7. Mike McIntyre
8. Larry Kissell
9. *Sue Wilkins Myrick*
10. *Patrick T. McHenry*
11. Heath Shuler
12. Melvin L. Watt
13. Brad Miller

NORTH DAKOTA

SENATORS
Kent Conrad
Byron L. Dorgan

REPRESENTATIVE
[Democrat 1]

At Large - Earl Pomeroy

OHIO

SENATORS
George V. Voinovich
Sherrod Brown

REPRESENTATIVES
[Democrats 10, Republicans 8]

1. Steve Driehaus
2. *Jean Schmidt*
3. *Michael R. Turner*
4. *Jim Jordan*
5. *Robert E. Latta*
6. Charles A. Wilson
7. *Steve Austria*
8. *John A. Boehner*
9. Marcy Kaptur
10. Dennis J. Kucinich
11. Marcia L. Fudge
12. *Patrick J. Tiberi*
13. Betty Sutton
14. *Steven C. LaTourette*
15. Mary Jo Kilroy
16. John A. Boccieri
17. Tim Ryan
18. Zachary T. Space

OKLAHOMA

SENATORS
James M. Inhofe
Tom Coburn

REPRESENTATIVES
[Democrats 1, Republicans 4]

1. *John Sullivan*
2. Dan Boren
3. *Frank D. Lucas*
4. *Tom Cole*
5. *Mary Fallin*

OREGON

SENATORS
Ron Wyden
Jeff Merkley

REPRESENTATIVES
[Democrats 4, Republicans 1]

1. David Wu

2. *Greg Walden*
3. Earl Blumenauer
4. Peter A. DeFazio
5. Kurt Schrader

PENNSYLVANIA

SENATORS
Arlen Specter
Robert P. Casey, Jr.

REPRESENTATIVES
[Democrats 12, Republicans 7]

1. Robert A. Brady
2. Chaka Fattah
3. Kathleen A. Dahlkemper
4. Jason Altmire
5. *Glenn Thompson*
6. *Jim Gerlach*
7. Joe Sestak
8. Patrick J. Murphy
9. *Bill Shuster*
10. Christopher P. Carney
11. Paul E. Kanjorski
12. John P. Murtha
13. Allyson Y. Schwartz
14. Michael F. Doyle
15. *Charles W. Dent*
16. *Joseph R. Pitts*
17. Tim Holden
18. *Tim Murphy*
19. *Todd Russell Platts*

RHODE ISLAND

SENATORS
Jack Reed
Sheldon Whitehouse

REPRESENTATIVES
[Democrats 2]

1. Patrick J. Kennedy
2. James R. Langevin

SOUTH CAROLINA

SENATORS
Lindsey Graham
Jim DeMint

REPRESENTATIVES
[Democrats 2, Republicans 4]

1. *Henry E. Brown, Jr.*
2. *Joe Wilson*
3. *J. Gresham Barrett*
4. *Bob Inglis*
5. John M. Spratt, Jr.
6. James E. Clyburn

SOUTH DAKOTA

SENATORS
Tim Johnson
John Thune

REPRESENTATIVE
[Democrat 1]

At Large - Stephanie Herseth Sandlin

TENNESSEE

SENATORS
Lamar Alexander
Bob Corker

REPRESENTATIVES
[Democrats 5, Republicans 4]

1. *David P. Roe*
2. *John J. Duncan, Jr.*
3. *Zach Wamp*
4. Lincoln Davis
5. Jim Cooper
6. Bart Gordon
7. *Marsha Blackburn*
8. John S. Tanner
9. Steve Cohen

TEXAS

SENATORS
Kay Bailey Hutchison
John Cornyn

REPRESENTATIVES
[Democrats 12, Republicans 20]

1. *Louie Gohmert*
2. *Ted Poe*
3. *Sam Johnson*
4. *Ralph M. Hall*
5. *Jeb Hensarling*
6. *Joe Barton*
7. *John Abney Culberson*
8. *Kevin Brady*
9. Al Green
10. *Michael T. McCaul*
11. *K. Michael Conaway*
12. *Kay Granger*
13. *Mac Thornberry*
14. *Ron Paul*
15. Rubén Hinojosa
16. Silvestre Reyes
17. Chet Edwards
18. Sheila Jackson-Lee
19. *Randy Neugebauer*
20. Charles A. Gonzalez
21. *Lamar Smith*
22. *Pete Olson*
23. Ciro D. Rodriguez
24. *Kenny Marchant*
25. Lloyd Doggett
26. *Michael C. Burgess*
27. Solomon P. Ortiz
28. Henry Cuellar
29. Gene Green
30. Eddie Bernice Johnson
31. *John R. Carter*
32. *Pete Sessions*

UTAH

SENATORS
Orrin G. Hatch
Robert F. Bennett

REPRESENTATIVES
[Democrats 1, Republicans 2]

1. *Rob Bishop*
2. Jim Matheson
3. *Jason Chaffetz*

VERMONT

SENATORS
Patrick J. Leahy
BERNARD SANDERS*

REPRESENTATIVE
[Democrat 1]

At Large - Peter Welch

VIRGINIA

SENATORS
Jim Webb
Mark R. Warner

REPRESENTATIVES
[Democrats 6, Republicans 5]

1. *Robert J. Wittman*
2. Glenn C. Nye
3. Robert C. "Bobby" Scott
4. *J. Randy Forbes*
5. Thomas S. P. Perriello
6. *Bob Goodlatte*
7. *Eric Cantor*
8. James P. Moran
9. Rick Boucher
10. *Frank R. Wolf*
11. Gerald E. Connolly

WASHINGTON

SENATORS
Patty Murray
Maria Cantwell

REPRESENTATIVES
[Democrats 6, Republicans 3]

1. Jay Inslee
2. Rick Larsen
3. Brian Baird
4. *Doc Hastings*
5. *Cathy McMorris Rodgers*
6. Norman D. Dicks
7. Jim McDermott
8. *David G. Reichert*
9. Adam Smith

WEST VIRGINIA

SENATORS
Robert C. Byrd
John D. Rockefeller IV

REPRESENTATIVES
[Democrats 2, Republicans 1]

1. Alan B. Mollohan
2. *Shelley Moore Capito*
3. Nick J. Rahall II

WISCONSIN

SENATORS
Herb Kohl
Russell D. Feingold

REPRESENTATIVES
[Democrats 5, Republicans 3]

1. *Paul Ryan*
2. Tammy Baldwin
3. Ron Kind
4. Gwen Moore
5. *F. James Sensenbrenner, Jr.*
6. *Thomas E. Petri*
7. David R. Obey
8. Steve Kagen

WYOMING

SENATORS
Michael B. Enzi
John Barrasso

REPRESENTATIVE
[Republican 1]
At Large - *Cynthia M. Lummis*

AMERICAN SAMOA

DELEGATE
[Democrat 1]
Eni F. H. Faleomavaega

DISTRICT OF COLUMBIA

DELEGATE
[Democrat 1]
Eleanor Holmes Norton

GUAM

DELEGATE
[Democrat 1]
Madeleine Z. Bordallo

NORTHERN MARIANA ISLANDS

DELEGATE
[Democrat 1]
Gregorio Kilili Camacho Sablan

PUERTO RICO

RESIDENT COMMISSIONER
[Democrat 1]
Pedro R. Pierluisi

VIRGIN ISLANDS

DELEGATE
[Democrat 1]
Donna M. Christensen

*Independent
**Independent Democrat
[1] Vacancy due to the resignation of Ellen O. Tauscher, effective June 26, 2009.
[2] Vacancy due to the resignation of John M. McHugh, September 21, 2009.

ALPHABETICAL LIST

SENATORS

Alphabetical list of Senators, Representatives, Delegates, and Resident Commissioner. Democrats in roman (58); Republicans in *italic* (40); Independent in SMALL CAPS (1); Independent Democrat in *SMALL CAPS ITALIC* (1).

Akaka, Daniel K., HI
Alexander, Lamar, TN
*Barrasso, John,*WY
Baucus, Max, MT
Bayh, Evan, IN
Begich, Mark, AK
Bennet, Michael F., CO
Bennett, Robert F., UT
Bingaman, Jeff, NM
Bond, Christopher S., MO
Boxer, Barbara, CA
Brown, Sherrod, OH
Brownback, Sam, KS
Bunning, Jim, KY
Burr, Richard, NC
Burris, Roland W., IL
Byrd, Robert C., WV
Cantwell, Maria, WA
Cardin, Benjamin L., MD
Carper, Thomas R., DE
Casey, Robert P., Jr., PA
Chambliss, Saxby, GA
Coburn, Tom, OK
Cochran, Thad, MS
Collins, Susan M., ME
Conrad, Kent, ND
Corker, Bob, TN
Cornyn, John, TX
Crapo, Mike, ID
DeMint, Jim, SC
Dodd, Christopher J., CT
Dorgan, Byron L., ND
Durbin, Richard, IL
Ensign, John, NV
Enzi, Michael B., WY
Feingold, Russell D., WI
Feinstein, Dianne, CA
Franken, Al, MN
Gillibrand, Kirsten E., NY
Graham, Lindsey, SC
Grassley, Chuck, IA
Gregg, Judd, NH
Hagan, Kay R., NC
Harkin, Tom, IA
Hatch, Orrin G., UT
Hutchison, Kay Bailey, TX
Inhofe, James M., OK
Inouye, Daniel K., HI
Isakson, Johnny, GA
Johanns, Mike, NE
Johnson, Tim, SD
Kaufman, Edward E., DE
Kerry, John F., MA
Kirk, Paul G., Jr., MA
Klobuchar, Amy, MN
Kohl, Herb, WI
Kyl, Jon, AZ
Landrieu, Mary L., LA
Lautenberg, Frank R., NJ
Leahy, Patrick J., VT
LeMieux, George S., FL
Levin, Carl, MI
LIEBERMAN, JOSEPH I., CT
Lincoln, Blanche L., AR
Lugar, Richard G., IN
McCain, John, AZ
McCaskill, Claire, MO
McConnell, Mitch, KY
Menendez, Robert, NJ
Mikulski, Barbara A., MD
Murkowski, Lisa, AK
Murray, Patty, WA
Nelson, Ben, NE
Nelson, Bill, FL
Pryor, Mark L., AR
Reed, Jack, RI
Reid, Harry, NV
Risch, James E., ID
Roberts, Pat, KS
Rockefeller, John D., IV, WV
SANDERS, BERNARD, VT
Schumer, Charles E., NY
Sessions, Jeff, AL
Shaheen, Jeanne, NH
Shelby, Richard C., AL
Snowe, Olympia J., ME
Specter, Arlen, PA
Stabenow, Debbie, MI
Tester, Jon, MT
Thune, John, SD
Udall, Mark, CO
Udall, Tom, NM
Vitter, David, LA
Voinovich, George V., OH
Warner, Mark R., VA
Webb, Jim, VA
Whitehouse, Sheldon, RI
Wicker, Roger F., MS
Wyden, Ron, OR

REPRESENTATIVES, RESIDENT COMMISSIONER, AND DELEGATES

Democrats in roman (256); Republicans in *italic* (177); Vacancies (2); Resident Commissioner and Delegates in **boldface** (6); total, 441.

Abercrombie, Neil, HI (1st)
Ackerman, Gary L., NY (5th)
Aderholt, Robert B., AL (4th)
Adler, John H., NJ (3d)
Akin, W. Todd, MO (2d)
Alexander, Rodney, LA (5th)
Altmire, Jason, PA (4th)
Andrews, Robert E., NJ (1st)
Arcuri, Michael A., NY (24th)
Austria, Steve, OH (7th)
Baca, Joe, CA (43d)
Bachmann, Michele, MN (6th)
Bachus, Spencer, AL (6th)
Baird, Brian, WA (3d)
Baldwin, Tammy, WI (2d)
Barrett, J. Gresham, SC (3d)
Barrow, John, GA (12th)
Bartlett, Roscoe G., MD (6th)
Barton, Joe, TX (6th)
Bean, Melissa L., IL (8th)
Becerra, Xavier, CA (31st)
Berkley, Shelley, NV (1st)
Berman, Howard L., CA (28th)
Berry, Marion, AR (1st)
Biggert, Judy, IL (13th)
Bilbray, Brian P., CA (50th)
Bilirakis, Gus M., FL (9th)
Bishop, Rob, UT (1st)
Bishop, Sanford D., Jr., GA (2d)
Bishop, Timothy H., NY (1st)
Blackburn, Marsha, TN (7th)
Blumenauer, Earl, OR (3d)
Blunt, Roy, MO (7th)
Boccieri, John A., OH (16th)
Boehner, John A., OH (8th)
Bonner, Jo, AL (1st)
Bono Mack, Mary, CA (45th)
Boozman, John, AR (3d)
Boren, Dan, OK (2d)
Boswell, Leonard L., IA (3d)
Boucher, Rick, VA (9th)
Boustany, Charles W., Jr., LA (7th)
Boyd, Allen, FL (2d)
Brady, Kevin, TX (8th)
Brady, Robert A., PA (1st)
Braley, Bruce L., IA (1st)
Bright, Bobby, AL (2d)
Broun, Paul C., GA (10th)
Brown, Corrine, FL (3d)
Brown, Henry E., Jr., SC (1st)
Brown-Waite, Ginny, FL (5th)
Buchanan, Vern, FL (13th)
Burgess, Michael C., TX (26th)
Burton, Dan, IN (5th)
Butterfield, G. K., NC (1st)
Buyer, Steve, IN (4th)
Calvert, Ken, CA (44th)
Camp, Dave, MI (4th)
Campbell, John, CA (48th)
Cantor, Eric, VA (7th)
Cao, Anh "Joseph", LA (2d)
Capito, Shelley Moore, WV (2d)
Capps, Lois, CA (23d)
Capuano, Michael E., MA (8th)
Cardoza, Dennis A., CA (18th)
Carnahan, Russ, MO (3d)
Carney, Christopher P., PA (10th)
Carson, André, IN (7th)
Carter, John R., TX (31st)
Cassidy, Bill, LA (6th)
Castle, Michael N., DE (At Large)
Castor, Kathy, FL (11th)
Chaffetz, Jason, UT (3d)
Chandler, Ben, KY (6th)
Childers, Travis W., MS (1st)
Chu, Judy, CA (32d)
Clarke, Yvette D., NY (11th)
Clay, Wm. Lacy, MO (1st)
Cleaver, Emanuel, MO (5th)
Clyburn, James E., SC (6th)
Coble, Howard, NC (6th)
Coffman, Mike, CO (6th)
Cohen, Steve, TN (9th)
Cole, Tom, OK (4th)
Conaway, K. Michael, TX (11th)
Connolly, Gerald E., VA (11th)
Conyers, John, Jr., MI (14th)
Cooper, Jim, TN (5th)
Costa, Jim, CA (20th)
Costello, Jerry F., IL (12th)
Courtney, Joe, CT (2d)
Crenshaw, Ander, FL (4th)
Crowley, Joseph, NY (7th)
Cuellar, Henry, TX (28th)
Culberson, John Abney, TX (7th)
Cummings, Elijah E., MD (7th)
Dahlkemper, Kathleen A., PA (3d)
Davis, Artur, AL (7th)
Davis, Danny K., IL (7th)
Davis, Geoff, KY (4th)
Davis, Lincoln, TN (4th)
Davis, Susan A., CA (53d)
Deal, Nathan, GA (9th)
DeFazio, Peter A., OR (4th)
DeGette, Diana, CO (1st)
Delahunt, Bill, MA (10th)
DeLauro, Rosa L., CT (3d)
Dent, Charles W., PA (15th)
Diaz-Balart, Lincoln, FL (21st)
Diaz-Balart, Mario, FL (25th)
Dicks, Norman D., WA (6th)
Dingell, John D., MI (15th)
Doggett, Lloyd, TX (25th)
Donnelly, Joe, IN (2d)
Doyle, Michael F., PA (14th)
Dreier, David, CA (26th)
Driehaus, Steve, OH (1st)
Duncan, John J., Jr., TN (2d)

Edwards, Chet, TX (17th)
Edwards, Donna F., MD (4th)
Ehlers, Vernon J., MI (3d)
Ellison, Keith, MN (5th)
Ellsworth, Brad, IN (8th)
Emerson, Jo Ann, MO (8th)
Engel, Eliot L., NY (17th)
Eshoo, Anna G., CA (14th)
Etheridge, Bob, NC (2d)
Fallin, Mary, OK (5th)
Farr, Sam, CA (17th)
Fattah, Chaka, PA (2d)
Filner, Bob, CA (51st)
Flake, Jeff, AZ (6th)
Fleming, John, LA (4th)
Forbes, J. Randy, VA (4th)
Fortenberry, Jeff, NE (1st)
Foster, Bill, IL (14th)
Foxx, Virginia, NC (5th)
Frank, Barney, MA (4th)
Franks, Trent, AZ (2d)
Frelinghuysen, Rodney P., NJ (11th)
Fudge, Marcia L., OH (11th)
Gallegly, Elton, CA (24th)
Garrett, Scott, NJ (5th)
Gerlach, Jim, PA (6th)
Giffords, Gabrielle, AZ (8th)
Gingrey, Phil, GA (11th)
Gohmert, Louie, TX (1st)
Gonzalez, Charles A., TX (20th)
Goodlatte, Bob, VA (6th)
Gordon, Bart, TN (6th)
Granger, Kay, TX (12th)
Graves, Sam, MO (6th)
Grayson, Alan, FL (8th)
Green, Al, TX (9th)
Green, Gene, TX (29th)
Griffith, Parker, AL (5th)
Grijalva, Raúl M., AZ (7th)
Guthrie, Brett, KY (2d)
Gutierrez, Luis V., IL (4th)
Hall, John J., NY (19th)
Hall, Ralph M., TX (4th)
Halvorson, Deborah L., IL (11th)
Hare, Phil, IL (17th)
Harman, Jane, CA (36th)
Harper, Gregg, MS (3d)
Hastings, Alcee L., FL (23d)
Hastings, Doc, WA (4th)
Heinrich, Martin, NM (1st)
Heller, Dean, NV (2d)
Hensarling, Jeb, TX (5th)
Herger, Wally, CA (2d)
Herseth Sandlin, Stephanie, SD (At Large)
Higgins, Brian, NY (27th)
Hill, Baron P., IN (9th)
Himes, James A., CT (4th)
Hinchey, Maurice D., NY (22d)
Hinojosa, Rubén, TX (15th)
Hirono, Mazie K., HI (2d)
Hodes, Paul W., NH (2d)
Hoekstra, Peter, MI (2d)
Holden, Tim, PA (17th)
Holt, Rush D., NJ (12th)
Honda, Michael M., CA (15th)
Hoyer, Steny H., MD (5th)
Hunter, Duncan, CA (52d)
Inglis, Bob, SC (4th)
Inslee, Jay, WA (1st)
Israel, Steve, NY (2d)
Issa, Darrell E., CA (49th)
Jackson, Jesse L., Jr., IL (2d)
Jackson-Lee, Sheila, TX (18th)
Jenkins, Lynn, KS (2d)
Johnson, Eddie Bernice, TX (30th)
Johnson, Henry C. "Hank", Jr., GA (4th)
Johnson, Sam, TX (3d)
Johnson, Timothy V., IL (15th)
Jones, Walter B., NC (3d)
Jordan, Jim, OH (4th)
Kagen, Steve, WI (8th)
Kanjorski, Paul E., PA (11th)
Kaptur, Marcy, OH (9th)
Kennedy, Patrick J., RI (1st)
Kildee, Dale E., MI (5th)
Kilpatrick, Carolyn C., MI (13th)
Kilroy, Mary Jo, OH (15th)
Kind, Ron, WI (3d)
King, Peter T., NY (3d)
King, Steve, IA (5th)
Kingston, Jack, GA (1st)
Kirk, Mark Steven, IL (10th)
Kirkpatrick, Ann, AZ (1st)
Kissell, Larry, NC (8th)
Klein, Ron, FL (22d)
Kline, John, MN (2d)
Kosmas, Suzanne M., FL (24th)
Kratovil, Frank, Jr., MD (1st)
Kucinich, Dennis J., OH (10th)
Lamborn, Doug, CO (5th)
Lance, Leonard, NJ (7th)
Langevin, James R., RI (2d)
Larsen, Rick, WA (2d)
Larson, John B., CT (1st)
Latham, Tom, IA (4th)
LaTourette, Steven C., OH (14th)
Latta, Robert E., OH (5th)
Lee, Barbara, CA (9th)
Lee, Christopher John, NY (26th)
Levin, Sander M., MI (12th)
Lewis, Jerry, CA (41st)
Lewis, John, GA (5th)
Linder, John, GA (7th)
Lipinski, Daniel, IL (3d)
LoBiondo, Frank A., NJ (2d)
Loebsack, David, IA (2d)
Lofgren, Zoe, CA (16th)
Lowey, Nita M., NY (18th)
Lucas, Frank D., OK (3d)
Luetkemeyer, Blaine, MO (9th)
Luján, Ben Ray, NM (3d)
Lummis, Cynthia M., WY (At Large)
Lungren, Daniel E., CA (3d)
Lynch, Stephen F., MA (9th)
McCarthy, Carolyn, NY (4th)
McCarthy, Kevin, CA (22d)
McCaul, Michael, T., TX (10th)
McClintock, Tom, CA (4th)
McCollum, Betty, MN (4th)
McCotter, Thaddeus G., MI (11th)
McDermott, Jim, WA (7th)
McGovern, James P., MA (3d)

McHenry, Patrick T., NC (10th)
McIntyre, Mike, NC (7th)
McKeon, Howard P. ''Buck'', CA (25th)
McMahon, Michael E., NY (13th)
McMorris Rodgers, Cathy, WA (5th)
McNerney, Jerry, CA (11th)
Mack, Connie, FL (14th)
Maffei, Daniel B., NY (25th)
Maloney, Carolyn B., NY (14th)
Manzullo, Donald A., IL (16th)
Marchant, Kenny, TX (24th)
Markey, Betsy, CO (4th)
Markey, Edward J., MA (7th)
Marshall, Jim, GA (8th)
Massa, Eric J. J., NY (29th)
Matheson, Jim, UT (2d)
Matsui, Doris O., CA (5th)
Meek, Kendrick B., FL (17th)
Meeks, Gregory W., NY (6th)
Melancon, Charlie, LA (3d)
Mica, John L., FL (7th)
Michaud, Michael H., ME (2d)
Miller, Brad, NC (13th)
Miller, Candice S., MI (10th)
Miller, Gary G., CA (42d)
Miller, George, CA (7th)
Miller, Jeff, FL (1st)
Minnick, Walt, ID (1st)
Mitchell, Harry E., AZ (5th)
Mollohan, Alan B., WV (1st)
Moore, Dennis, KS (3d)
Moore, Gwen, WI (4th)
Moran, James P., VA (8th)
Moran, Jerry, KS (1st)
Murphy, Christopher S., CT (5th)
Murphy, Patrick J., PA (8th)
Murphy, Scott, NY (20th)
Murphy, Tim, PA (18th)
Murtha, John P., PA (12th)
Myrick, Sue Wilkins, NC (9th)
Nadler, Jerrold, NY (8th)
Napolitano, Grace F., CA (38th)
Neal, Richard E., MA (2d)
Neugebauer, Randy, TX (19th)
Nunes, Devin, CA (21st)
Nye, Glenn C., VA (2d)
Oberstar, James L., MN (8th)
Obey, David R., WI (7th)
Olson, Pete, TX (22d)
Olver, John W., MA (1st)
Ortiz, Solomon P., TX (27th)
Pallone, Frank, Jr., NJ (6th)
Pascrell, Bill, Jr., NJ (8th)
Pastor, Ed, AZ (4th)
Paul, Ron, TX (14th)
Paulsen, Erik, MN (3d)
Payne, Donald M., NJ (10th)
Pelosi, Nancy, CA (8th)
Pence, Mike, IN (6th)
Perlmutter, Ed, CO (7th)
Perriello, Thomas S.P., VA (5th)
Peters, Gary C., MI (9th)
Peterson, Collin C., MN (7th)
Petri, Thomas E., WI (6th)
Pingree, Chellie, ME (1st)
Pitts, Joseph R., PA (16th)
Platts, Todd Russell, PA (19th)
Poe, Ted, TX (2d)
Polis, Jared, CO (2d)
Pomeroy, Earl, ND (At Large)
Posey, Bill, FL (15th)
Price, David E., NC (4th)
Price, Tom, GA (6th)
Putnam, Adam H., FL (12th)
Quigley, Mike, IL (5th)
Radanovich, George, CA (19th)
Rahall, Nick J. II, WV (3d)
Rangel, Charles B., NY (15th)
Rehberg, Denny, MT (At Large)
Reichert, David G., WA (8th)
Reyes, Silvestre, TX (16th)
Richardson, Laura, CA (37th)
Rodriguez, Ciro D., TX (23d)
Roe, David P., TN (1st)
Rogers, Harold, KY (5th)
Rogers, Mike, AL (3d)
Rogers, Mike, MI (8th)
Rohrabacher, Dana, CA (46th)
Rooney, Thomas J., FL (16th)
Roskam, Peter J., IL (6th)
Ros-Lehtinen, Ileana, FL (18th)
Ross, Mike, AR (4th)
Rothman, Steven R., NJ (9th)
Roybal-Allard, Lucille, CA (34th)
Royce, Edward R., CA (40th)
Ruppersberger, C. A. Dutch, MD (2d)
Rush, Bobby L., IL (1st)
Ryan, Paul, WI (1st)
Ryan, Tim, OH (17th)
Salazar, John T., CO (3d)
Sánchez, Linda T., CA (39th)
Sanchez, Loretta, CA (47th)
Sarbanes, John P., MD (3d)
Scalise, Steve, LA (1st)
Schakowsky, Janice D., IL (9th)
Schauer, Mark H., MI (7th)
Schiff, Adam B., CA (29th)
Schmidt, Jean, OH (2d)
Schock, Aaron, IL (18th)
Schrader, Kurt, OR (5th)
Schwartz, Allyson Y., PA (13th)
Scott, David, GA (13th)
Scott, Robert C. ''Bobby'', VA (3d)
Sensenbrenner, F. James, Jr., WI (5th)
Serrano, José E., NY (16th)
Sessions, Pete, TX (32d)
Sestak, Joe, PA (7th)
Shadegg, John B., AZ (3d)
Shea-Porter, Carol, NH (1st)
Sherman, Brad, CA (27th)
Shimkus, John, IL (19th)
Shuler, Heath, NC (11th)
Shuster, Bill, PA (9th)
Simpson, Michael K., ID (2d)
Sires, Albio, NJ (13th)
Skelton, Ike, MO (4th)
Slaughter, Louise McIntosh, NY (28th)
Smith, Adam, WA (9th)
Smith, Adrian, NE (3d)
Smith, Christopher H., NJ (4th)
Smith, Lamar, TX (21st)
Snyder, Vic, AR (2d)

Souder, Mark E., IN (3d)
Space, Zachary T., OH (18th)
Speier, Jackie, CA (12th)
Spratt, John M., Jr., SC (5th)
Stark, Fortney Pete, CA (13th)
Stearns, Cliff, FL (6th)
Stupak, Bart, MI (1st)
Sullivan, John, OK (1st)
Sutton, Betty, OH (13th)
Tanner, John S., TN (8th)
Taylor, Gene, MS (4th)
Teague, Harry, NM (2d)
Terry, Lee, NE (2d)
Thompson, Bennie G., MS (2d)
Thompson, Glenn, PA (5th)
Thompson, Mike, CA (1st)
Thornberry, Mac, TX (13th)
Tiahrt, Todd, KS (4th)
Tiberi, Patrick J., OH (12th)
Tierney, John F., MA (6th)
Titus, Dina, NV (3d)
Tonko, Paul, NY (21st)
Towns, Edolphus, NY (10th)
Tsongas, Niki, MA (5th)
Turner, Michael R., OH (3d)
Upton, Fred, MI (6th)
Van Hollen, Chris, MD (8th)
Velázquez, Nydia M., NY (12th)
Visclosky, Peter J., IN (1st)
Walden, Greg, OR (2d)
Walz, Timothy J., MN (1st)
Wamp, Zach, TN (3d)
Wasserman Schultz, Debbie, FL (20th)
Waters, Maxine, CA (35th)
Watson, Diane E., CA (33d)
Watt, Melvin L., NC (12th)
Waxman, Henry A., CA (30th)
Weiner, Anthony D., NY (9th)
Welch, Peter, VT (At Large)
Westmoreland, Lynn A. GA (3d)
Wexler, Robert, FL (19th)
Whitfield, Ed, KY (1st)
Wilson, Charles A., OH (6th)
Wilson, Joe, SC (2d)
Wittman, Robert J., VA (1st)
Wolf, Frank R., VA (10th)
Woolsey, Lynn C., CA (6th)
Wu, David, OR (1st)
Yarmuth, John A., KY (3d)
Young, C. W. Bill, FL (10th)
Young, Don, AK (At Large)

DELEGATES
Bordallo, Madeleine Z., GU
Christensen, Donna M., VI
Faleomavaega, Eni F. H., AS
Sablan, Gregorio Kilili Camacho, MP
Norton, Eleanor Holmes, DC

RESIDENT COMISSIONER
Pierluisi, Pedro R., PR

111th Congress
Nine-Digit Postal ZIP Codes

Senate Post Office (20510): The four-digit numbers in these tables were assigned by the Senate Committee on Rules and Administration. Mail to all Senate offices is delivered by the main Post Office in the Dirksen Senate Office Building.

Senate Committees

Committee on Agriculture, Nutrition, and Forestry .... –6000
Committee on Appropriations .... –6025
Committee on Armed Services .... –6050
Committee on Banking, Housing, and Urban Affairs .... –6075
Committee on the Budget .... –6100
Committee on Commerce, Science, and Transportation .... –6125
Committee on Energy and Natural Resources .... –6150
Committee on Environment and Public Works .... –6175
Committee on Finance .... –6200
Committee on Foreign Relations .... –6225
Committee on Health, Education, Labor and Pensions .... –6300
Committee on Homeland Security and Governmental Affairs .... –6250
Committee on Indian Affairs .... –6450
Committee on the Judiciary .... –6275
Committee on Rules and Administration .... –6325
Committee on Small Business and Entrepreneurship .... –6350
Committee on Veterans' Affairs .... –6375
Committee on Aging (Special) .... –6400
Committee on Ethics (Select) .... –6425
Committee on Intelligence (Select) .... –6475

Joint Committee Offices, Senate Side

Joint Economic Committee .... –6602
Joint Committee on the Library .... –6625
Joint Committee on Printing .... –6650
Joint Committee on Taxation .... –6675

Senate Leadership Offices

President Pro Tempore .... –7000
Chaplain .... –7002
Majority Leader .... –7010
Assistant Majority Leader .... –7012
Secretary for the Majority .... –7014
Minority Leader .... –7020
Assistant Minority Leader .... –7022
Secretary for the Minority .... –7024
Democratic Policy Committee .... –7050
Republican Conference .... –7060
Secretary to the Republican Conference .... –7062
Republican Policy Committee .... –7064
Republican Steering Committee .... –7066
National Security Working Group .... –7070

Senate Officers

Secretary of the Senate .... –7100
- Curator .... –7102
- Disbursing Office .... –7104
- Printing and Document Service .... –7106
- Historical Office .... –7108
- Human Resources .... –7109
- Interparliamentary Services .... –7110
- Senate Library .... –7112
- Office of Senate Security .... –7114
- Office of Public Records .... –7116
- Office of Official Reporters of Debates .... –7117
- Stationery Room .... –7118
- U.S. Capitol Preservation Commission .... –7122
- Office of Conservation and Preservation .... –7124
- Information Systems .... –7125
- Web Technology Office .... –7126
- Legislative Systems .... –7127
- Senate Gift Shop .... –7128
- Senate Legal Counsel .... –7130
- Emergency Terror Response (COOP) .... –7131
- Chief Counsel for Employment .... –7132

Senate Sergeant at Arms .... –7200
- General Counsel .... –7201
- Finance Division .... –7205
- Budget .... –7205
- Accouting .... –7205
- Hair Care Services .... –7206
- Procurement .... –7207
- Capitol Guide Service .... –7209
- Employee Assistance Program Office .... –7211
- Human Resources .... –7212
- Safety Program .... –7212
- Health Promotion / Seminars .... –7213
- Placement Office .... –7214
- Workman's Compensation .... –7214
- Joint Office of Education and Training .... –7215
- Capitol Police .... –7218
- Congressional Special Services Office .... –7228
- Office of Security and Emergency Preparedness .... –7229

Office Support Services .... –7230
- Customer Support .... –7231
- IT Request Processing .... –7232
- Chief Information Officer .... –7233
- State Liaison .... –7285
- Police Liaison and Operations .... –7235
- Periodical Press Gallery .... –7234
- Press Gallery .... –7238
- Press Photo Gallery .... –7242
- Radio and TV Gallery .... –7246
- Webster Hall .... –7248

Other Offices on the Senate Side

Senate Legal Counsel .... –7250
Central Operations—Administration .... –7260
- Parking / ID .... –7262
- Printing Graphics and Direct Mail—PSQ 7264
- Printing Graphics and Driect Mail—Capitol Hill .... –7266
- Facilities .... –7204
- Furniture Shop .... –7204
- Framing Shop .... –7204
- Cabinet Shop .... –7204
- Photo Studio .... –7216
- Post Office .... –7220
- Recording Studio .... –7220
- Senate Legislative Counsel .... –7275

Program Management .... –7276
IT Support Services—Administration .... –7280
- Telecom Support .... –7281

Equipment Services	–7282	Amtrak Ticket Office	–9010
Desktop/Lan Support	–7284	Airlines Ticket Office (CATO)	–9014
IT Research/Deployment	–7292	Child Care Center	–9022
Technology Development-Administration	–7290	Credit Union	–9026
Systems Architecture	–7277	Veterans' Liaison	–9054
Information Security	–7278	Social Security Liaison	–9064
Applications Development	–7291	Caucus of Internationa Narcotics Control	–9070
Network Engineering and Management	–7293	Army Liaison	–9082
Enterprise IT Systems	–7294	Air Force Liaison	–9083
Inter/Intranet Services	–7296	Coast Guard Liaison	–9084
Architect of the Capitol	–8000	Navy Liaison	–9085
Superintendent of Senate Buildings	–8002	Marine Liaison	–9087
Restaurant	–8050		

House Post Office (20515): Mail to all House offices is delivered by the main Post Office in the Longworth House Office Building.

House Committees Leadership

U.S. House of Representatives	–0001	Committee on House Administration	–6157
Cannon House Office Building	–0002	Committee on the Judiciary	–6216
Rayburn House Office Building	–0003	Committee on Natural Resources	–6201
Longworth House Office Building	–0004	Committee on Oversight and Government Reform	–6143
Ford House Office Building	–0006	Committee on Rules	–6269
The Capitol	–0007	Committee on Science and Technology	–6301
Committee on Agriculture	–6001	Committee on Small Business	–6315
Committee on Appropriations	–6015	Committee on Standards of Official Conduct	–6328
Committee on Armed Services	–6035	Committee on Transportation and Infrastructure	–6256
Committee on the Budget	–6065	Committee on Veterans' Affairs	–6335
Committee on Education and Labor	–6100	Committee on Ways and Means	–6348
Committee on Energy and Commerce	–6115	Select Committee on Energy Independence and Global Warming	–6482
Committee on Financial Services	–6050	Permanent Select Committee on Intelligence	–6415
Committee on Foreign Affairs	–6128		
Committee on Homeland Security	–6480		

Joint Committee Offices, House Side

Joint Economic Committee	–6432	Joint Committee on Printing	–6446
Joint Committee on the Library	–6439	Joint Committee on Taxation	–6453

House Leadership Offices

Office of the Speaker	–6501	Office of the Republican Leader	–6537
Office of the Majority Leader	–6502	Office of the Republican Whip	–6538
Office of the Majority Whip	–6503	House Republican Conference	–6544
Democratic Caucus	–6524	Legislative Digest (Republican Conference)	–6546
Democratic Congressional Campaign Committee	–6525	Republican Congressional Committee, National	–6547
Democratic Steering and Policy Committee	–6527	Republican Policy Committee	–6549
Democratic Cloakroom	–6528	Republican Cloakroom	–6650

House Officers

Office of the Clerk	–6601	HIR Information Systems Security	–6165
Office of History and Preservation	–6612	Outplacement Services	–9920
Office of Employment and Counsel	–6622	Office of Employee Assistance	–6619
House Page School	–9996	ADA Services	–6860
House Page Dorm	–6606	Personnel and Benefits	–9980
Legislative Computer Systems	–6618	Child Care Center	–0001
Office of Legislative Operations	–6602	Payroll	–6604
Legislative Resource Center	–6612	Members' Services	–9970
Official Reporters	–6615	Office Supply Service	–6860
Office of Publication Services	–6611	House Gift Shop	–6860
Office of Interparliamentary Affairs	–6579	Mail List/Processing	–6860
Office of the Chaplain	–6655	Mailing Services	–6860
Office of the House Historian	–6701	Contractor Management	–6860
Office of the Parliamentarian	–6731	Photography	–6623
Chief Administrative Officer	–6860	House Recording Studio	–6613
First Call	–6660	Furniture Support Services	–6610
Administrative Counsel	–6660	House Office Service Center	–6860
Periodical Press Gallery	–6624	Budget	–6604
Press Gallery	–6625	Financial Counseling	–6604
Radio/TV Correspondents' Gallery	–6627	Procurement Desktop Help	–9940
HIR Call Center	–6165	Office of the Sergeant at Arms	–6634

House Commissions and Offices

Congressional Executive Commission on China	–6481
Commission on Security and Cooperation in Europe	–6460
Commission on Congressional Mailing Standards	–6461
Office of the Law Revision Counsel	–6711
Office of Emergency Planning, Preparedness and Operations	–6462
Office of the Legislative Counsel	–6721
General Counsel	–6532
Architect of the Capitol	–6906
Attending Physician	–6907
Congressional Budget Office	–6925

Liaison Offices

Air Force	–6854
Army	–6855
Coast Guard	–6856
Navy	–6857
Office of Personnel Management	–6858
Veterans' Administration	–6859

TERMS OF SERVICE

EXPIRATION OF THE TERMS OF SENATORS

CLASS I.—SENATORS WHOSE TERMS OF SERVICE EXPIRE IN 2013

[33 Senators in this group: Democrats, 22; Republicans, 9; Independent, 1; Independent Democrat, 1]

Name	Party	Residence
Akaka, Daniel K.[1]	D.	Honolulu, HI.
Barrasso, John[2]	R.	Casper, WY.
Bingaman, Jeff	D.	Santa Fe, NM.
Brown, Sherrod	D.	Avon, OH.
Byrd, Robert C.	D.	Sophia, WV.
Cantwell, Maria	D.	Edmonds, WA.
Cardin, Benjamin L.	D.	Baltimore, MD.
Carper, Thomas R.	D.	Wilmington, DE.
Casey, Robert P., Jr.	D.	Scranton, PA.
Conrad, Kent[3]	D.	Bismarck, ND.
Corker, Bob	R.	Chattanooga, TN.
Ensign, John	R.	Las Vegas, NV.
Feinstein, Dianne[4]	D.	San Francisco, CA.
Gillibrand, Kirsten E.[5]	D.	Hudson, NY.
Hatch, Orrin G.	R.	Salt Lake City, UT.
Hutchison, Kay Bailey[6]	R.	Dallas, TX.
Kirk, Paul G., Jr.[7]	D.	Marstons Mills, MA.
Klobuchar, Amy	D.	Minneapolis, MN.
Kohl, Herb	D.	Milwaukee, WI.
Kyl, Jon	R.	Phoenix, AZ.
Lieberman, Joseph I.	I.D.	New Haven, CT.
Lugar, Richard G.	R.	Indianapolis, IN.
McCaskill, Claire	D.	Kirkwood, MO.
Menendez, Robert[8]	D.	Hoboken, NJ.
Nelson, Ben	D.	Omaha, NE.
Nelson, Bill	D.	Orlando, FL.
Sanders, Bernard	I.	Burlington, VT.
Snowe, Olympia J.	R.	Auburn, ME.
Stabenow, Debbie	D.	Lansing, MI.
Tester, Jon	D.	Big Sandy, MT.
Webb, Jim	D.	Arlington, VA.
Whitehouse, Sheldon	D.	Providence, RI.
Wicker, Roger F.[9]	R.	Tupelo, MS.

[1] Senator Akaka was appointed April 28, 1990, to fill the vacancy caused by the death of Senator Spark M. Matsunaga, and took the oath of office on May 16, 1990; subsequently elected in a special election on November 6, 1990, for the remainder of the unexpired term; subsequently elected to a full term in 1994.

[2] Senator Barrasso was appointed on June 22, 2007, to fill the vacancy caused by the death of Senator Craig Thomas, and took the oath of office on June 25, 2007.

[3] Senator Conrad resigned his term from Class III after winning a special election on December 4, 1992, to fill the vacancy caused by the death of Senator Quentin Burdick. Senator Conrad's seniority in the Senate continues without a break in service. He took the oath of office on December 15, 1992.

[4] Senator Feinstein won the special election held on November 3, 1992, to fill the vacancy caused by the resignation of Senator Pete Wilson. She took the oath of office on November 10, 1992. She won the seat from Senator John Seymour who had been appointed on January 7, 1991. She was elected to a full term in 1994.

[5] Senator Gillibrand was appointed on January 23, 2009, to fill the vacancy caused by the resignation of Hillary Rodham Clinton. She took the oath of office on January 27, 2009.

[6] Senator Hutchison won the special election held on June 5, 1993, to fill remainder of the term of Senator Lloyd Bentsen. She took the oath of office on June 14, 1993. She won the seat from Senator Bob Krueger, who had been appointed on January 21, 1993. She was elected to a full term in 1994.

[7] Senator Kirk was appointed on September 24, 2009, to fill the vacancy caused by the death of Edward M. Kennedy. He took the oath of office on September 25, 2009.

[8] Senator Menendez was appointed on January 17, 2006, to fill the vacancy caused by the resignation of Senator Jon S. Corzine; subsequently elected to a full term in November 2006.

[9] Senator Wicker was appointed on December 31, 2007, to fill the vacancy caused by the seat left vacant by the resignation of Trett Lott. He took the oath of office on December 31, 2007; subsequently elected in a special election on November 4, 2008.

Class II.—SENATORS WHOSE TERMS OF SERVICE EXPIRE IN 2015

[33 Senators in this group: Democrats, 20; Republicans, 13]

Name	Party	Residence
Alexander, Lamar	R.	Nashville, TN.
Baucus, Max	D.	Helena, MT.
Begich, Mark	D.	Anchorage, AK.
Chambliss, Saxby	R.	Moultrie, GA.
Cochran, Thad	R.	Jackson, MS.
Collins, Susan M.	R.	Bangor, ME.
Cornyn, John	R.	San Antonio, TX.
Durbin, Richard	D.	Springfield, IL.
Franken, Al [1]	D.	Minneapolis, MN.
Enzi, Michael B.	R.	Gillette, WY.
Graham, Lindsey	R.	Seneca, SC.
Hagan, Kay R.	D.	Greensboro, NC.
Harkin, Tom	D.	Cumming, IA.
Inhofe, James M.[2]	R.	Tulsa, OK.
Johanns, Mike	R.	Omaha, NE.
Johnson, Tim	D.	Vermillion, SD.
Kaufman, Edward E.[3]	D.	Greenville, DE.
Kerry, John F.	D.	Boston, MA.
Landrieu, Mary L.	D.	New Orleans, LA.
Lautenberg, Frank R.[4]	D.	Cliffside Park, NJ.
Levin, Carl	D.	Detroit, MI.
McConnell, Mitch	R.	Louisville, KY.
Merkley, Jeff	D.	Portland, OR.
Pryor, Mark L.	D.	Little Rock, AR.
Risch, James E.	R.	Boise, ID.
Reed, Jack	D.	Jamestown, RI.
Roberts, Pat	R.	Dodge City, KS.
Rockefeller, John D., IV	D.	Charleston, WV.
Shaheen, Jeanne	D.	Madbury, NH.
Sessions, Jeff	R.	Mobile, AL.
Udall, Mark	D.	Eldorado Springs, CO.
Udall, Tom	D.	Santa Fe, NM.
Warner, Mark R.	D.	Alexandria, VA.

[1] Contested election was resolved June 30, 2009; Senator Franken was sworn into office on July 7, 2009.

[2] Senator Inhofe won the special election held on November 8, 1994, to fill the remainder of the term of Senator David Boren, and took the oath of office on November 17, 1994. He was elected to a full term in 1996.

[3] Senator Kaufman was appointed on January 15, 2009, to fill the vacancy caused by the resignation of Joseph R. Biden, Jr. and took the oath of office on January 16, 2009.

[4] Senator Lautenberg replaced Senator Robert Torricelli as the Democratic candidate for the U.S. Senate in October 2002.

CLASS III.—SENATORS WHOSE TERMS OF SERVICE EXPIRE IN 2011

[34 Senators in this group: Democrats, 16; Republicans, 18]

Name	Party	Residence
Bayh, Evan	D.	Indianapolis, IN.
Bennet, Michael F.[1]	D.	Denver, CO.
Bennett, Robert F.	R.	Salt Lake City, UT.
Bond, Christopher S.	R.	Mexico, MO.
Boxer, Barbara	D.	Palm Springs, CA.
Brownback, Sam[2]	R.	Topeka, KS.
Bunning, Jim	R.	Southgate, KY.
Burr, Richard	R.	Winston-Salem, NC.
Burris, Roland W.[3]	D.	Chatham, IL.
Coburn, Tom	R.	Muskogee, OK.
Crapo, Mike	R.	Idaho Falls, ID.
DeMint, Jim	R.	Greenville, SC.
Dodd, Christopher J.	D.	East Haddam, CT.
Dorgan, Byron L.[4]	D.	Bismarck, ND.
Feingold, Russell D.	D.	Middleton, WI.
Grassley, Chuck	R.	Cedar Falls, IA.
Gregg, Judd	R.	Greenfield, NH.
Inouye, Daniel K.	D.	Honolulu, HI.
Isakson, Johnny	R.	Marietta, GA.
Leahy, Patrick J.	D.	Middlesex, VT.
LeMieux, George S.[5]	R.	Tallahassee, FL.
Lincoln, Blanche L.	D.	Helena, AR.
McCain, John	R.	Phoenix, AZ.
Mikulski, Barbara A.	D.	Baltimore, MD.
Murkowski, Lisa[6]	R.	Anchorage, AK.
Murray, Patty	D.	Seattle, WA.
Reid, Harry	D.	Searchlight, NV.
Schumer, Charles E.	D.	Brooklyn, NY.
Shelby, Richard C.[7]	R.	Tuscaloosa, AL.
Specter, Arlen[8]	D.	Philadelphia, PA.
Thune, John	R.	Sioux Falls, SD.
Vitter, David	R	Metairie, LA.
Voinovich, George V.	R.	Cleveland, OH.
Wyden, Ron[9]	D.	Portland, OR.

[1] Senator Bennet was appointed on January 21, 2009, to fill the vacancy caused by the resignation of Kenneth L. Salazar. He took the oath of office on January 22, 2009.

[2] Senator Brownback was elected on November 5, 1996, to fill the remainder of the term of Senator Bob Dole. He took the oath of office on November 27, 1996; his service was made retroactive to November 7, 1996, when his Senate service began. He won the seat from Senator Sheila Frahm, who was appointed on June 11, 1996.

[3] Senator Burris was appointed on December 31, 2008, to fill the vacancy caused by the resignation of Barack H. Obama, his credentials were found in order on January 12, 2009, and he took the oath of office on January 15, 2009.

[4] Senator Dorgan was elected to a 6-year term on November 3, 1992, and subsequently was appointed December 14, 1992 to fill the vacancy caused by the resignation of Senator Kent Conrad.

[5] Senator LeMieux was appointed on September 9, 2009, to fill the vacancy caused by the resignation of Mel Martinez. He took the oath of office on September 10, 2009.

[6] Senator Murkowski was appointed on December 20, 2002, to fill the vacancy caused by the resignation of her father, Senator Frank Murkowski. She was elected to a full term in 2004.

[7] Senator Shelby changed party affiliation from Democrat to Republican on November 5, 1994.

[8] Senator Specter changed party affiliation from Republican to Democrat on April 30, 2009.

[9] Senator Wyden won a special election on January 30, 1996, to fill the vacancy caused by the resignation of Senator Robert Packwood, and began service on February 6, 1996. He was reelected to a full term in 1998.

CONTINUOUS SERVICE OF SENATORS

[Democrats in roman (58); Republicans in *italic* (40); Independent in SMALL CAPS (1); Independent Democrat in *SMALL CAPS ITALIC* (1); total, 100]

Rank	Name	State	Beginning of present service
1	Byrd, Robert C.†	West Virginia	Jan. 3, 1959.
2	Inouye, Daniel K.†	Hawaii	Jan. 3, 1963.
3	Leahy, Patrick J.	Vermont	Jan. 3, 1975.
4	*Hatch, Orrin G.*	Utah	Jan. 3, 1977.
	Lugar, Richard G.	Indiana	
5	Baucus, Max † [1]	Montana	Dec. 15, 1978.
6	*Cochran, Thad* † [2]	Mississippi	Dec. 27, 1978.
7	Levin, Carl	Michigan	Jan. 3, 1979.
8	Dodd, Christopher J.†	Connecticut	Jan. 3, 1981.
	Grassley, Chuck †	Iowa	
	Specter, Arlen [3]	Pennsylvania	
9	Bingaman, Jeff	New Mexico	Jan. 3, 1983.
10	Kerry, John F.[4]	Massachusetts	Jan. 2, 1985.
11	Harkin, Tom †	Iowa	Jan. 3, 1985
	McConnell, Mitch	Kentucky	
12	Rockefeller, John D., IV [5]	West Virginia	Jan. 15, 1985.
13	*Bond, Christopher S.*	Missouri	Jan. 3, 1987.
	Conrad, Kent	North Dakota	
	McCain, John †	Arizona	
	Mikulski, Barbara A.†	Maryland	
	Reid, Harry †	Nevada	
	Shelby, Richard C.†	Alabama	
14	Kohl, Herb	Wisconsin	Jan. 3, 1989.
	LIEBERMAN, JOSEPH I.	Connecticut	
15	Akaka, Daniel K.† [6]	Hawaii	May 16, 1990.
16	Feinstein, Dianne [7]	California	Nov. 10, 1992.‡
17	Dorgan, Byron L.† [8]	North Dakota	Dec. 14, 1992.
18	*Bennett, Robert F.*	Utah	Jan. 3, 1993.
	Boxer, Barbara †	California	
	Feingold, Russell D.	Wisconsin	
	Gregg, Judd †	New Hampshire	
	Murray, Patty	Washington	
19	*Hutchison, Kay Bailey* [9]	Texas	June 14, 1993.
20	*Inhofe, James M.* † [10]	Oklahoma	Nov. 17, 1994. ‡
21	*Kyl, Jon* †	Arizona	Jan. 3, 1995.
	Snowe, Olympia J.†	Maine	
22	Wyden, Ron † [11]	Oregon	Feb. 6, 1996. ‡
23	*Brownback, Sam* † [12]	Kansas	Nov. 7, 1996. ‡
24	*Collins, Susan M.*	Maine	Jan. 3, 1997.
	Durbin, Richard †	Illinois	
	Enzi, Michael B.	Wyoming	
	Johnson, Tim †	South Dakota	
	Landrieu, Mary L.	Louisiana	
	Reed, Jack †	Rhode Island	
	Roberts, Pat †	Kansas	
	Sessions, Jeff	Alabama	
25	Bayh, Evan	Indiana	Jan. 3, 1999.
	Bunning, Jim †	Kentucky	
	Crapo, Mike †	Idaho	
	Lincoln, Blanche L. †	Arkansas	
	Schumer, Charles E. †	New York	
	Voinovich, George V.	Ohio	
26	Cantwell, Maria †	Washington	Jan. 3, 2001.

CONTINUOUS SERVICE OF SENATORS—CONTINUED

[Democrats in roman (58); Republicans in *italic* (40); Independent in SMALL CAPS (1); Independent Democrat in *SMALL CAPS ITALIC* (1); total, 100]

Rank	Name	State	Beginning of present service
	Carper, Thomas R.†	Delaware	
	Ensign, John †	Nevada	
	Nelson, Bill †	Florida	
	Nelson, Ben	Nebraska	
	Stabenow, Debbie †	Michigan	
27	*Cornyn, John* [13]	Texas	Dec. 2, 2002.
28	*Murkowski, Lisa* [14]	Alaska	Dec. 20, 2002.
29	*Alexander, Lamar*	Tennessee	Jan. 3, 2003.
	Chambliss, Saxby †	Georgia	
	Graham, Lindsey †	South Carolina	
	Lautenberg, Frank R. [15]	New Jersey	
	Pryor, Mark L.	Arkansas	
30	*Burr, Richard* †	North Carolina	Jan. 3, 2005.
	Coburn, Tom †	Oklahoma	
	DeMint, Jim †	South Carolina	
	Isakson, Johnny †	Georgia	
	Thune, John †	South Dakota	
	Vitter, David †	Louisiana	
31	Menendez, Robert † [16]	New Jersey	Jan. 18, 2006.
32	Brown, Sherrod †	Ohio	Jan. 3, 2007.
	Cardin, Benjamin L. †	Maryland	
	Casey, Robert P., Jr.	Pennsylvania	
	Corker, Bob	Tennessee	
	Klobuchar, Amy	Minnesota	
	McCaskill, Claire	Missouri	
	SANDERS, BERNARD †	Vermont	
	Tester, Jon	Montana	
	Webb, Jim	Vermont	
	Whitehouse, Sheldon	Rhode Island	
33	Barrasso, John [17]	Wyoming	June 22, 2007.
34	Wicker, Roger F.† [18]	Mississippi	Dec. 31, 2007.
35	Begich, Mark	Alaska	Jan. 3, 2009.
	Hagan, Kay R.	North Carolina	
	Johanns, Mike	Nebraska	
	Merkley, Jeff	Oregon	
	Risch, James E.	Idaho	
	Shaheen, Jeanne	New Hampshire	
	Udall, Mark†	Colorado	
	Udall, Tom†	New Mexico	
	Warner, Mark R.	Virginia	
36	Burris, Roland W.[19]	Illinois	Jan. 12, 2009.
37	Kaufman, Edward E.	Delaware	Jan 15, 2009.
38	Bennet, Michael F. [20]	Colorado	Jan. 21, 2009.
39	Gillibrand, Kirsten E.† [21]	New York	Jan. 27, 2009.
40	Franken, Al [22]	Minnesota	July 7, 2009.
41	*LeMieux, George S.* [23]	Florida	Sept. 10, 2009.
42	Kirk, Paul G., Jr.[24]	Massachusetts	Sept. 24, 2009.

† Served in the House of Representatives previous to service in the Senate.

‡ Senators elected to complete unexpired terms typically begin their terms on the day following the election, but individual cases may vary.

[1] Senator Baucus was elected November 7, 1978, for the 6-year term commencing January 3, 1979; subsequently appointed December 15, 1978, to fill the vacancy caused by the resignation of Senator Paul Hatfield.

[2] Senator Cochran was elected November 6, 1978, for the 6-year term commencing January 3, 1979; subsequently appointed December 27, 1978, to fill the vacancy caused by the resignation of Senator James Eastland.

[3] Senator Specter changed party affiliation from Republican to Democrat on April 30, 2009.

[4] Senator Kerry was elected November 6, 1984, for the 6-year term commencing January 3, 1985; subsequently appointed January 2, 1985, to fill the vacancy caused by the resignation of Senator Paul E. Tsongas.

[5] Senator Rockefeller was elected November 6, 1984, for the 6-year term commencing January 3, 1985; did not take his seat until January 15, 1985.

[6] Senator Akaka was appointed April 28, 1990, to fill the vacancy caused by the death of Senator Spark M. Matsunaga, and took the oath of office on May 16, 1990; subsequently elected in a special election on November 6, 1990, for the remainder of the unexpired term.

[7] Senator Feinstein was elected on November 3, 1992, to fill the vacancy caused by the resignation of Senator Pete Wilson. She replaced appointed Senator John Seymour when she took the oath of office on November 10, 1992.

[8] Senator Dorgan was elected to a 6-year term on November 3, 1992, and subsequently was appointed December 14, 1992 to complete the unexpired term of Senator Kent Conrad.

[9] Senator Hutchison won a special election on June 5, 1993, to fill the vacancy caused by the resignation of Senator Lloyd Bentsen. She won the seat from Senator Bob Krueger, who had been appointed on January 21, 1993.

[10] Senator Inhofe won the special election held on November 8, 1994, to fill the remainder of the term of Senator David Boren, and took the oath of office on November 17, 1994. He was elected to a full term in 1996.

[11] Senator Wyden won a special election on January 30, 1996, to fill the vacancy caused by the resignation of Senator Bob Packwood. He was reelected to a full term in 1998.

[12] Senator Brownback was elected on November 5, 1996, to fill the vacancy caused by the resignation of Senator Bob Dole. He replaced appointed Senator Sheila Frahm when he took the oath of office on November 27, 1996. His seat was made retroactive to November 7, 1996 when his Senate service began.

[13] Senator Cornyn was elected on November 5, 2002, for a 6-year term commencing January 3, 2003; subsequently appointed on December 2, 2002, to fill the vacancy caused by the resignation of Senator Phil Gramm.

[14] Senator Murkowski was appointed on December 20, 2002, to fill the vacancy caused by the resignation of her father, Senator Frank Murkowski. She was elected to a full term in 2004.

[15] Senator Lautenberg previously served in the Senate from December 27, 1982, until January 3, 2001.

[16] Senator Menendez was appointed on January 17, 2006, to fill the vacancy caused by the resignation of Senator Jon S. Corzine; subsequently elected to a full term in November 2006.

[17] Senator Barrasso was appointed on June 22, 2007, to fill the vacancy caused by the death of Senator Craig Thomas, and took the oath of office on June 25, 2007; subsequently elected in a special election on November 2008.

[18] Senator Wicker was appointed on December 31, 2007, to fill the vacancy caused by the resignation of Trent Lott; subsequently elected in a special election on November 4, 2008.

[19] Senator Burris was appointed on December 31, 2008, to fill the vacancy caused by the resignation of Barack H. Obama, his credentials were found in order on January 12, 2009, and he took the oath of office on January 15, 2009.

[20] Senator Bennet was appointed on January 21, 2009, to fill the vacancy caused by the resignation of Ken Salazar, and took the oath of office on January 22, 2009.

[21] Senator Gillibrand was appointed on January 23, 2009, to fill the vacancy caused by the resignation of Senator Hillary Clinton, and took the oath of office on January 27, 2009.

[22] The contested election case between Senator Franken and Senator Coleman was resolved by Minnesota's Supreme Court on June 30, 2009. Franken was sworn into office on July 7, 2009. The Senate seat had remained vacant from January 3 until July 6.

[23] Senator LeMieux was appointed on September 9, 2009, to fill the vacancy due to the resignation of Senator Mel Martinez, and took the oath of office on September 10, 2009.

[24] Senator Kirk was appointed on September 24, 2009, to fill the vacancy caused by the death of Edward M. Kennedy. He took the oath of office on September 25, 2009.

CONGRESSES IN WHICH REPRESENTATIVES, RESIDENT COMMISSIONER, AND DELEGATES HAVE SERVED WITH BEGINNING OF PRESENT SERVICE

[* Elected to fill a vacancy; Democrats in roman (256); Republicans in *italic* (177); Vacancies (2); Resident Commissioner and Delegates in **boldface** (6); total, 441]

Name	State	Congresses (inclusive)	Beginning of present service
28 terms, consecutive			
Dingell, John D.	MI	*84th to 111th	Dec. 13, 1955
23 terms, consecutive			
Conyers, John, Jr.	MI	89th to 111th	Jan. 3, 1965
21 terms, consecutive			
Obey, David R.	WI	*91st to 111th	Apr. 1, 1969
20 terms, consecutive			
Rangel, Charles B.	NY	92d to 111th	Jan. 3, 1971
Young, C. W. Bill	FL	92d to 111th	Jan. 3, 1971
19 terms, consecutive			
Murtha, John P.	PA	*93d to 111th	Feb. 5, 1974
Stark, Fortney Pete	CA	93d to 111th	Jan. 3, 1973
Young, Don	AK	*93d to 111th	Mar. 6, 1973
18 terms, consecutive			
Markey, Edward J.	MA	*94th to 111th	Nov. 2, 1976
Miller, George	CA	94th to 111th	Jan. 3, 1975
Oberstar, James L.	MN	94th to 111th	Jan. 3, 1975
Waxman, Henry A.	CA	94th to 111th	Jan. 3, 1975
17 terms, consecutive			
Dicks, Norman D.	WA	95th to 111th	Jan. 3, 1977
Kildee, Dale E.	MI	95th to 111th	Jan. 3, 1977
Rahall, Nick J., II	WV	95th to 111th	Jan. 3, 1977
Skelton, Ike	MO	95th to 111th	Jan. 3, 1977
16 terms, consecutive			
Lewis, Jerry	CA	96th to 111th	Jan. 3, 1979
Petri, Thomas E.	WI	*96th to 111th	Apr. 3, 1979
Sensenbrenner, F. James, Jr.	WI	96th to 111th	Jan. 3, 1979
15 terms, consecutive			
Dreier, David	CA	97th to 111th	Jan. 3, 1981
Frank, Barney	MA	97th to 111th	Jan. 3, 1981
Hall, Ralph M.	TX	97th to 111th	Jan. 3, 1981
Hoyer, Steny H.	MD	*97th to 111th	May 19, 1981
Rogers, Harold	KY	97th to 111th	Jan. 3, 1981
Smith, Christopher H.	NJ	97th to 111th	Jan. 3, 1981
Wolf, Frank R.	VA	97th to 111th	Jan. 3, 1981
14 terms, consecutive			
Ackerman, Gary L.	NY	*98th to 111th	Mar. 1, 1983
Berman, Howard L.	CA	98th to 111th	Jan. 3, 1983
Boucher, Rick	VA	98th to 111th	Jan. 3, 1983

CONGRESSES IN WHICH REPRESENTATIVES, RESIDENT COMMISSIONER, AND DELEGATES HAVE SERVED WITH BEGINNING OF PRESENT SERVICE—CONTINUED

[* Elected to fill a vacancy; Democrats in roman (256); Republicans in *italic* (177); Vacancies (2); Resident Commissioner and Delegates in **boldface** (6); total, 441]

Name	State	Congresses (inclusive)	Beginning of present service
Burton, Dan	IN	98th to 111th	Jan. 3, 1983
Kaptur, Marcy	OH	98th to 111th	Jan. 3, 1983
Levin, Sander M.	MI	98th to 111th	Jan. 3, 1983
Mollohan, Alan B.	WV	98th to 111th	Jan. 3, 1983
Ortiz, Solomon P.	TX	98th to 111th	Jan. 3, 1983
Spratt, John M., Jr.	SC	98th to 111th	Jan. 3, 1983
Towns, Edolphus	NY	98th to 111th	Jan. 3, 1983
13 terms, consecutive			
Barton, Joe	TX	99th to 111th	Jan. 3, 1985
Coble, Howard	NC	99th to 111th	Jan. 3, 1985
Gordon, Bart	TN	99th to 111th	Jan. 3, 1985
Kanjorski, Paul E.	PA	99th to 111th	Jan. 3, 1985
Visclosky, Peter J.	IN	99th to 111th	Jan. 3, 1985
12 terms, consecutive			
Costello, Jerry F.	IL	*100th to 111th	Aug. 9, 1988
DeFazio, Peter A.	OR	100th to 111th	Jan. 3, 1987
Duncan, John J., Jr.	TN	*100th to 111th	Nov. 8, 1988
Gallegly, Elton	CA	100th to 111th	Jan. 3, 1987
Herger, Wally	CA	100th to 111th	Jan. 3, 1987
Lewis, John	GA	100th to 111th	Jan. 3, 1987
Pallone, Frank, Jr.	NJ	*100th to 111th	Nov. 8, 1988
Pelosi, Nancy	CA	*100th to 111th	June 2, 1987
Slaughter, Louise McIntosh	NY	100th to 111th	Jan. 3, 1987
Smith, Lamar	TX	100th to 111th	Jan. 3, 1987
Upton, Fred	MI	100th to 111th	Jan. 3, 1987
11 terms, consecutive			
Andrews, Robert E.	NJ	*101st to 111th	Nov. 6, 1990
Engel, Eliot L.	NY	101st to 111th	Jan. 3, 1989
Lowey, Nita M.	NY	101st to 111th	Jan. 3, 1989
McDermott, Jim	WA	101st to 111th	Jan. 3, 1989
Neal, Richard E.	MA	101st to 111th	Jan. 3, 1989
Payne, Donald M.	NJ	101st to 111th	Jan. 3, 1989
Rohrabacher, Dana	CA	101st to 111th	Jan. 3, 1989
Ros-Lehtinen, Ileana	FL	*101st to 111th	Aug. 29, 1989
Serrano, José E.	NY	*101st to 111th	Mar. 20, 1990
Stearns, Cliff	FL	101st to 111th	Jan. 3, 1989
Tanner, John S.	TN	101st to 111th	Jan. 3, 1989
Taylor, Gene	MS	*101st to 111th	Oct. 17, 1989
11 terms, not consecutive			
Abercrombie, Neil	HI	*99th, 102d to 111th.	Jan. 3, 1991
Paul, Ron	TX	94th, 96th to 98th, 105th to 111th.	Jan. 3, 1997
Price, David E.	NC	100th to 103d, 105th to 111th.	Jan 3. 1997

CONGRESSES IN WHICH REPRESENTATIVES, RESIDENT COMMISSIONER, AND DELEGATES HAVE SERVED WITH BEGINNING OF PRESENT SERVICE—CONTINUED

[* Elected to fill a vacancy; Democrats in roman (256); Republicans in *italic* (177); Vacancies (2); Resident Commissioner and Delegates in **boldface** (6); total, 441]

Name	State	Congresses (inclusive)	Beginning of present service
10 terms, consecutive			
Boehner, John A.	OH	102d to 111th	Jan. 3, 1991
Camp, Dave	MI	102d to 111th	Jan. 3, 1991
DeLauro, Rosa L.	CT	102d to 111th	Jan. 3, 1991
Edwards, Chet	TX	102d to 111th	Jan. 3, 1991
Johnson, Sam	TX	*102d to 111th	May 8, 1991
Moran, James P.	VA	102d to 111th	Jan. 3, 1991
Nadler, Jerrold	NY	*102d to 111th	Nov. 3, 1992
Olver, John W.	MA	*102d to 111th	June 4, 1991
Pastor, Ed	AZ	*102d to 111th	Sep. 24, 1991
Peterson, Collin C.	MN	102d to 111th	Jan. 3, 1991
Waters, Maxine	CA	102d to 111th	Jan. 3, 1991
10 terms, not consecutive			
Cooper, Jim	TN	98th to 103d and 108th to 111th.	Jan. 3, 2003
9 terms, consecutive			
Bachus, Spencer	AL	103d to 111th	Jan. 3, 1993
Bartlett, Roscoe G.	MD	103d to 111th	Jan. 3, 1993
Becerra, Xavier	CA	103d to 111th	Jan. 3, 1993
Bishop, Sanford D., Jr.	GA	103d to 111th	Jan. 3, 1993
Brown, Corrine	FL	103d to 111th	Jan. 3, 1993
Buyer, Steve	IN	103d to 111th	Jan. 3, 1993
Calvert, Ken	CA	103d to 111th	Jan. 3, 1993
Castle, Michael N.	DE	103d to 111th	Jan. 3, 1993
Clyburn, James E.	SC	103d to 111th	Jan. 3, 1993
Deal, Nathan	GA	103d to 111th	Jan. 3, 1993
Diaz-Balart, Lincoln	FL	103d to 111th	Jan. 3, 1993
Ehlers, Vernon J.	MI	103d to 111th	Dec. 7, 1993
Eshoo, Anna G.	CA	103d to 111th	Jan. 3, 1993
Farr, Sam	CA	*103d to 111th	June 8, 1993
Filner, Bob	CA	103d to 111th	Jan. 3, 1993
Goodlatte, Bob	VA	103d to 111th	Jan. 3, 1993
Green, Gene	TX	103d to 111th	Jan. 3, 1993
Gutierrez, Luis V.	IL	103d to 111th	Jan. 3, 1993
Hastings, Alcee L.	FL	103d to 111th	Jan. 3, 1993
Hinchey, Maurice D.	NY	103d to 111th	Jan. 3, 1993
Hoekstra, Peter	MI	103d to 111th	Jan. 3, 1993
Holden, Tim	PA	103d to 111th	Jan. 3, 1993
Johnson, Eddie Bernice	TX	103d to 111th	Jan. 3, 1993
King, Peter T.	NY	103d to 111th	Jan. 3, 1993
Kingston, Jack	GA	103d to 111th	Jan. 3, 1993
Linder, John	GA	103d to 111th	Jan. 3, 1993
Lucas, Frank D.	OK	*103d to 111th	May 10, 1994
McKeon, Howard P. ''Buck''	CA	103d to 111th	Jan. 3, 1993
Maloney, Carolyn B.	NY	103d to 111th	Jan. 3, 1993
Manzullo, Donald A.	IL	103d to 111th	Jan. 3, 1993
Mica, John L.	FL	103d to 111th	Jan. 3, 1993
Pomeroy, Earl	ND	103d to 111th	Jan. 3, 1993
Roybal-Allard, Lucille	CA	103d to 111th	Jan. 3, 1993

CONGRESSES IN WHICH REPRESENTATIVES, RESIDENT COMMISSIONER, AND DELEGATES HAVE SERVED WITH BEGINNING OF PRESENT SERVICE—CONTINUED

[* Elected to fill a vacancy; Democrats in roman (256); Republicans in *italic* (177); Vacancies (2); Resident Commissioner and Delegates in **boldface** (6); total, 441]

Name	State	Congresses (inclusive)	Beginning of present service
Royce, Edward R.	CA	103d to 111th	Jan. 3, 1993
Rush, Bobby L.	IL	103d to 111th	Jan. 3, 1993
Scott, Robert C. ''Bobby''	VA	103d to 111th	Jan. 3, 1993
Stupak, Bart	MI	103d to 111th	Jan. 3, 1993
Thompson, Bennie G.	MS	*103d to 111th	Apr. 13, 1993
Velázquez, Nydia M.	NY	103d to 111th	Jan. 3, 1993
Watt, Melvin L.	NC	103d to 111th	Jan. 3, 1993
Woolsey, Lynn C.	CA	103d to 111th	Jan. 3, 1993
8 terms, consecutive			
Blumenauer, Earl	OR	*104th to 111th	May 21, 1996
Cummings, Elijah E.	MD	*104th to 111th	Apr. 16, 1996
Doggett, Lloyd	TX	104th to 111th	Jan. 3, 1995
Doyle, Michael F.	PA	104th to 111th	Jan. 3, 1995
Emerson, Jo Ann	MO	*104th to 111th	Nov. 5, 1996
Fattah, Chaka	PA	104th to 111th	Jan. 3, 1995
Frelinghuysen, Rodney P.	NJ	104th to 111th	Jan. 3, 1995
Hastings, Doc	WA	104th to 111th	Jan. 3, 1995
Jackson-Lee, Sheila	TX	104th to 111th	Jan. 3, 1995
Jackson, Jesse L., Jr.	IL	*104th to 111th	Dec. 12, 1995
Jones, Walter B.	NC	104th to 111th	Jan. 3, 1995
Kennedy, Patrick J.	RI	104th to 111th	Jan. 3, 1995
Latham, Tom	IA	104th to 111th	Jan. 3, 1995
LaTourette, Steven C.	OH	104th to 111th	Jan. 3, 1995
LoBiondo, Frank A.	NJ	104th to 111th	Jan. 3, 1995
Lofgren, Zoe	CA	104th to 111th	Jan. 3, 1995
Myrick, Sue Wilkins	NC	104th to 111th	Jan. 3, 1995
Radanovich, George	CA	104th to 111th	Jan. 3, 1995
Shadegg, John B.	AZ	104th to 111th	Jan. 3, 1995
Souder, Mark E.	IN	104th to 111th	Jan. 3, 1995
Thornberry, Mac	TX	104th to 111th	Jan. 3, 1995
Tiahrt, Todd	KS	104th to 111th	Jan. 3, 1995
Wamp, Zach	TN	104th to 111th	Jan. 3, 1995
Whitfield, Ed	KY	104th to 111th	Jan. 3, 1995
8 terms, not consecutive			
Harman, Jane	CA	103d to 105th and 107th to 111th.	Jan. 3, 2001
Lungren, Daniel E.	CA	96th to 100th and 109th to 111th.	Jan. 3, 2005
7 terms			
Aderholt, Robert B.	AL	105th to 111th	Jan. 3, 1997
Berry, Marion	AR	105th to 111th	Jan. 3, 1997
Blunt, Roy	MO	105th to 111th	Jan. 3, 1997
Bono Mack, Mary	CA	*105th to 111th	Apr. 7, 1998
Boswell, Leonard L.	IA	105th to 111th	Jan. 3, 1997
Boyd, Allen	FL	105th to 111th	Jan. 3, 1997
Brady, Kevin	TX	105th to 111th	Jan. 3, 1997
Brady, Robert A.	PA	*105th to 111th	May 19, 1998

CONGRESSES IN WHICH REPRESENTATIVES, RESIDENT COMMISSIONER, AND DELEGATES HAVE SERVED WITH BEGINNING OF PRESENT SERVICE—CONTINUED

[*Elected to fill a vacancy; Democrats in roman (256); Republicans in *italic* (177); Vacancies (2); Resident Commissioner and Delegates in **boldface** (6); total, 441]

Name	State	Congresses (inclusive)	Beginning of present service
Capps, Lois	CA	*105th to 111th	Mar. 10, 1998
Davis, Danny K.	IL	105th to 111th	Jan. 3, 1997
DeGette, Diana	CO	105th to 111th	Jan. 3, 1997
Delahunt, Bill.	MA	105th to 111th	Jan. 3, 1997
Etheridge, Bob	NC	105th to 111th	Jan. 3, 1997
Granger, Kay	TX	105th to 111th	Jan. 3, 1997
Hinojosa, Rubén	TX	105th to 111th	Jan. 3, 1997
Kilpatrick, Carolyn C.	MI	105th to 111th	Jan. 3, 1997
Kind, Ron	WI	105th to 111th	Jan. 3, 1997
Kucinich, Dennis J.	OH	105th to 111th	Jan. 3, 1997
Lee, Barbara	CA	*105th to 111th	Apr. 7, 1998
McCarthy, Carolyn	NY	105th to 111th	Jan. 3, 1997
McGovern, James P.	MA	105th to 111th	Jan. 3, 1997
McIntyre, Mike	NC	105th to 111th	Jan. 3, 1997
Meeks, Gregory W.	NY	*105th to 111th	Feb. 3, 1998
Moran, Jerry	KS	105th to 111th	Jan. 3, 1997
Pascrell, Bill, Jr.	NJ	105th to 111th	Jan. 3, 1997
Pitts, Joseph R.	PA	105th to 111th	Jan. 3, 1997
Reyes, Silvestre	TX	105th to 111th	Jan. 3, 1997
Rothman, Steven R.	NJ	105th to 111th	Jan. 3, 1997
Sanchez, Loretta	CA	105th to 111th	Jan. 3, 1997
Sessions, Pete	TX	105th to 111th	Jan. 3, 1997
Sherman, Brad	CA	105th to 111th	Jan. 3, 1997
Shimkus, John	IL	105th to 111th	Jan. 3, 1997
Smith, Adam	WA	105th to 111th	Jan. 3, 1997
Snyder, Vic	AR	105th to 111th	Jan. 3, 1997
Tierney, John F.	MA	105th to 111th	Jan. 3, 1997
Wexler, Robert	FL	105th to 111th	Jan. 3, 1997
7 terms, not consecutive			
Inslee, Jay	WA	*103d, 106th to 111th.	Jan. 3, 1999
6 terms			
Baca, Joe	CA	*106th to 111th	Nov. 16, 1999
Baird, Brian	WA	106th to 111th	Jan. 3, 1999
Baldwin, Tammy	WI	106th to 111th	Jan. 3, 1999
Berkley, Shelley	NV	106th to 111th	Jan. 3, 1999
Biggert, Judy	IL	106th to 111th	Jan. 3, 1999
Capuano, Michael E.	MA	106th to 111th	Jan. 3, 1999
Crowley, Joseph	NY	106th to 111th	Jan. 3, 1999
Gonzalez, Charles A.	TX	106th to 111th	Jan. 3, 1999
Holt, Rush D.	NJ	106th to 111th	Jan. 3, 1999
Larson, John B.	CT	106th to 111th	Jan. 3, 1999
Miller, Gary G.	CA	106th to 111th	Jan. 3, 1999
Moore, Dennis	KS	106th to 111th	Jan. 3, 1999
Napolitano, Grace F.	CA	106th to 111th	Jan. 3, 1999
Ryan, Paul	WI	106th to 111th	Jan. 3, 1999
Schakowsky, Janice D.	IL	106th to 111th	Jan. 3, 1999
Simpson, Michael K.	ID	106th to 111th	Jan. 3, 1999

CONGRESSES IN WHICH REPRESENTATIVES, RESIDENT COMMISSIONER, AND DELEGATES HAVE SERVED WITH BEGINNING OF PRESENT SERVICE—CONTINUED

[* Elected to fill a vacancy; Democrats in roman (256); Republicans in *italic* (177); Vacancies (2); Resident Commissioner and Delegates in **boldface** (6); total, 441]

Name	State	Congresses (inclusive)	Beginning of present service
Terry, Lee	NE	106th to 111th	Jan. 3, 1999
Thompson, Mike	CA	106th to 111th	Jan. 3, 1999
Walden, Greg	OR	106th to 111th	Jan. 3, 1999
Weiner, Anthony D.	NY	106th to 111th	Jan. 3, 1999
Wu, David	OR	106th to 111th	Jan. 3, 1999
6 terms, not consecutive			
Bilbray, Brian P.	CA	104th to 106th and *109th to 111th.	June 6, 2006
Inglis, Bob	SC	103d to 105th and 109th to 111th.	Jan. 3, 2005
Rodriguez, Ciro D.	TX	105th to 108th and 111th.	Jan. 3, 2007
5 terms			
Akin, W. Todd	MO	107th to 111th	Jan. 3, 2001
Boozman, John	AR	*107th to 111th	Nov. 20, 2001
Brown, Henry E., Jr.	SC	107th to 111th	Jan. 3, 2001
Cantor, Eric	VA	107th to 111th	Jan. 3, 2001
Capito, Shelley Moore	WV	107th to 111th	Jan. 3, 2001
Clay, Wm. Lacy	MO	107th to 111th	Jan. 3, 2001
Crenshaw, Ander	FL	107th to 111th	Jan. 3, 2001
Culberson, John Abney	TX	107th to 111th	Jan. 3, 2001
Davis, Susan A.	CA	107th to 111th	Jan. 3, 2001
Flake, Jeff	AZ	107th to 111th	Jan. 3, 2001
Forbes, J. Randy	VA	*107th to 111th	June 19, 2001
Graves, Sam	MO	107th to 111th	Jan. 3, 2001
Honda, Michael M.	CA	107th to 111th	Jan. 3, 2001
Israel, Steve	NY	107th to 111th	Jan. 3, 2001
Issa, Darrell E.	CA	107th to 111th	Jan. 3, 2001
Johnson, Timothy V.	IL	107th to 111th	Jan. 3, 2001
Kirk, Mark Steven	IL	107th to 111th	Jan. 3, 2001
Langevin, James R.	RI	107th to 111th	Jan. 3, 2001
Larsen, Rick	WA	107th to 111th	Jan. 3, 2001
Lynch, Stephen F.	MA	*107th to 111th	Oct. 16, 2001
McCollum, Betty	MN	107th to 111th	Jan. 3, 2001
Matheson, Jim	UT	107th to 111th	Jan. 3, 2001
Miller, Jeff	FL	*107th to 111th	Oct. 16, 2001
Pence, Mike	IN	107th to 111th	Jan. 3, 2001
Platts, Todd Russell	PA	107th to 111th	Jan. 3, 2001
Putnam, Adam H.	FL	107th to 111th	Jan. 3, 2001
Rehberg, Denny	MT	107th to 111th	Jan. 3, 2001
Rogers, Mike	MI	107th to 111th	Jan. 3, 2001
Ross, Mike	AR	107th to 111th	Jan. 3, 2001
Schiff, Adam B.	CA	107th to 111th	Jan. 3, 2001
Shuster, Bill	PA	*107th to 111th	May 15, 2001
Sullivan, John	OK	*107th to 111th	Feb. 15, 2002
Tiberi, Patrick J.	OH	107th to 111th	Jan. 3, 2001
Watson, Diane E.	CA	*107th to 111th	June 5, 2001
Wilson, Joe	SC	*107th to 111th	Dec. 18, 2001

CONGRESSES IN WHICH REPRESENTATIVES, RESIDENT COMMISSIONER, AND DELEGATES HAVE SERVED WITH BEGINNING OF PRESENT SERVICE—CONTINUED

[* Elected to fill a vacancy; Democrats in roman (256); Republicans in *italic* (177); Vacancies (2); Resident Commissioner and Delegates in **boldface** (6); total, 441]

Name	State	Congresses (inclusive)	Beginning of present service
5 terms, not consecutive			
Hill, Baron P.	IN	106th to 108th and 110th to 111th.	Jan. 3, 2007
4 terms			
Alexander, Rodney	LA	108th to 111th	Jan. 3, 2003
Barrett, J. Gresham	SC	108th to 111th	Jan. 3, 2003
Bishop, Rob	UT	108th to 111th	Jan. 3, 2003
Bishop, Timothy H.	NY	108th to 111th	Jan. 3, 2003
Blackburn, Marsha	TN	108th to 111th	Jan. 3, 2003
Bonner, Jo	AL	108th to 111th	Jan. 3, 2003
Brown-Waite, Ginny	FL	108th to 111th	Jan. 3, 2003
Burgess, Michael C.	TX	108th to 111th	Jan. 3, 2003
Butterfield, G. K.	NC	* 108th to 111th	July 20, 2004
Cardoza, Dennis A.	CA	108th to 111th	Jan. 3, 2003
Carter, John R.	TX	108th to 111th	Jan. 3, 2003
Chandler, Ben	KY	* 108th to 111th	Feb. 17, 2004
Davis, Artur	AL	108th to 111th	Jan. 3, 2003
Davis, Lincoln	TN	108th to 111th	Jan. 3, 2003
Diaz-Balart, Mario	FL	108th to 111th	Jan. 3, 2003
Franks, Trent	AZ	108th to 111th	Jan. 3, 2003
Garrett, Scott	NJ	108th to 111th	Jan. 3, 2003
Gerlach, Jim	PA	108th to 111th	Jan. 3, 2003
Gingrey, Phil	GA	108th to 111th	Jan. 3, 2003
Grijalva, Raúl M.	AZ	108th to 111th	Jan. 3, 2003
Hensarling, Jeb	TX	108th to 111th	Jan. 3, 2003
Herseth Sandlin, Stephanie	SD	* 108th to 111th	June 1, 2004
King, Steve	IA	108th to 111th	Jan. 3, 2003
Kline, John	MN	108th to 111th	Jan. 3, 2003
Marshall, Jim	GA	108th to 111th	Jan. 3, 2003
McCotter, Thaddeus G.	MI	108th to 111th	Jan. 3, 2003
Meek, Kendrick B.	FL	108th to 111th	Jan. 3, 2003
Michaud, Michael H.	ME	108th to 111th	Jan. 3, 2003
Miller, Brad	NC	108th to 111th	Jan. 3, 2003
Miller, Candice S.	MI	108th to 111th	Jan. 3, 2003
Murphy, Tim	PA	108th to 111th	Jan. 3, 2003
Neugebauer, Randy	TX	*108th to 111th	June 3, 2003
Nunes, Devin	CA	108th to 111th	Jan. 3, 2003
Rogers, Mike	AL	108th to 111th	Jan. 3, 2003
Ruppersberger, C. A. Dutch	MD	108th to 111th	Jan. 3, 2003
Ryan, Tim	OH	108th to 111th	Jan. 3, 2003
Sánchez, Linda T.	CA	108th to 111th	Jan. 3, 2003
Scott, David	GA	108th to 111th	Jan. 3, 2003
Turner, Michael R.	OH	108th to 111th	Jan. 3, 2003
Van Hollen, Chris	MD	108th to 111th	Jan. 3, 2003
3 terms			
Barrow, John	GA	109th and 111th	Jan. 3, 2005
Bean, Melissa L.	IL	109th and 111th	Jan. 3, 2005
Boren, Dan	OK	109th and 111th	Jan. 3, 2005

CONGRESSES IN WHICH REPRESENTATIVES, RESIDENT COMMISSIONER, AND DELEGATES HAVE SERVED WITH BEGINNING OF PRESENT SERVICE—CONTINUED

[* Elected to fill a vacancy; Democrats in roman (256); Republicans in *italic* (177); Vacancies (2); Resident Commissioner and Delegates in **boldface** (6); total, 441]

Name	State	Congresses (inclusive)	Beginning of present service
Boustany, Charles W., Jr.	LA	109th and 111th	Jan. 3, 2005
Campbell, John	CA	109th and 111th	Dec. 6, 2005
Carnahan, Russ	MO	109th and 111th	Jan. 3, 2005
Cleaver, Emanuel	MO	109th and 111th	Jan. 3, 2005
Conaway, K. Michael	TX	109th and 111th	Jan. 3, 2005
Costa, Jim	CA	109th and 111th	Jan. 3, 2005
Cuellar, Henry	TX	109th and 111th	Jan. 3, 2005
Davis, Geoff	KY	109th and 111th	Jan. 3, 2005
Dent, Charles W.	PA	109th and 111th	Jan. 3, 2005
Fortenberry, Jeff	NE	109th and 111th	Jan. 3, 2005
Foxx, Virginia	NC	109th and 111th	Jan. 3, 2005
Gohmert, Louie	TX	109th and 111th	Jan. 3, 2005
Green, Al	TX	109th and 111th	Jan. 3, 2005
Higgins, Brian	NY	109th and 111th	Jan. 3, 2005
Lipinski, Daniel	IL	109th and 111th	Jan. 3, 2005
McCaul, Michael T.	TX	109th and 111th	Jan. 3, 2005
McHenry, Patrick T.	NC	109th and 111th	Jan. 3, 2005
McMorris Rodgers, Cathy	WA	109th and 111th	Jan. 3, 2005
Mack, Connie	FL	109th and 111th	Jan. 3, 2005
Marchant, Kenny	TX	109th and 111th	Jan. 3, 2005
Matsui, Doris O.	CA	109th and 111th	Mar. 8, 2005
Melancon, Charlie	LA	109th and 111th	Jan. 3, 2005
Moore, Gwen	WI	109th and 111th	Jan. 3, 2005
Poe, Ted	TX	109th and 111th	Jan. 3, 2005
Price, Tom	GA	109th and 111th	Jan. 3, 2005
Reichert, David G.	WA	109th and 111th	Jan. 3, 2005
Salazar, John T.	CO	109th and 111th	Jan. 3, 2005
Schwartz, Allyson Y.	PA	109th and 111th	Jan. 3, 2005
Schmidt, Jean	OH	109th and 111th	Aug. 2, 2005
Sires, Albio	NJ	109th and 111th	Nov. 13, 2006
Wasserman Schultz, Debbie	FL	109th and 111th	Jan. 3, 2005
Westmoreland, Lynn A.	GA	109th and 111th	Jan. 3, 2005
2 terms			
Altmire, Jason	PA	110th to 111th	Jan. 3, 2007
Arcuri, Michael A.	NY	110th to 111th	Jan. 3, 2007
Bachmann, Michele	MN	110th to 111th	Jan. 3, 2007
Bilirakis, Gus M.	FL	110th to 111th	Jan. 3, 2007
Braley, Bruce L.	IA	110th to 111th	Jan. 3, 2007
Broun, Paul C.	GA	*110th to 111th	July 17, 2007
Buchanan, Vern	FL	110th to 111th	Jan. 3, 2007
Carney, Christopher P.	PA	110th to 111th	Jan. 3, 2007
Carson, André	IN	*110th to 111th	Mar. 11, 2008
Castor, Kathy	FL	110th to 111th	Jan. 3, 2007
Childers, Travis W.	MS	*110th to 111th	May 13, 2008
Clarke, Yvette D.	NY	110th to 111th	Jan. 3, 2007
Cohen, Steve	TN	110th to 111th	Jan. 3, 2007
Courtney, Joe	CT	110th to 111th	Jan. 3, 2007
Donnelly, Joe	IN	110th to 111th	Jan. 3, 2007

CONGRESSES IN WHICH REPRESENTATIVES, RESIDENT COMMISSIONER, AND DELEGATES HAVE SERVED WITH BEGINNING OF PRESENT SERVICE—CONTINUED

[* Elected to fill a vacancy; Democrats in roman (256); Republicans in *italic* (177); Vacancies (2); Resident Commissioner and Delegates in **boldface** (6); total, 441]

Name	State	Congresses (inclusive)	Beginning of present service
Edwards, Donna F.	MD	*110th to 111th	June 17, 2008
Ellison, Keith	MN	110th to 111th	Jan. 3, 2007
Ellsworth, Brad	ID	110th to 111th	Jan. 3, 2007
Fallin, Mary	OK	110th to 111th	Jan. 3, 2007
Foster, Bill	IL	*110th to 111th	Mar. 8, 2008
Fudge, Marcia L.	OH	*110th to 111th	Nov. 18, 2008
Giffords, Gabrielle	AZ	110th to 111th	Jan. 3, 2007
Hall, John J.	NY	110th to 111th	Jan. 3, 2007
Hare, Phil	IL	110th to 111th	Jan. 3, 2007
Heller, Dean	NV	110th to 111th	Jan. 3, 2007
Hirono, Mazie K.	HI	110th to 111th	Jan. 3, 2007
Hodes, Paul W.	NH	110th to 111th	Jan. 3, 2007
Johnson, Henry C. ''Hank'', Jr.	GA	110th to 111th	Jan. 3, 2007
Jordan, Jim	OH	110th to 111th	Jan. 3, 2007
Kagen, Steve	WI	110th to 111th	Jan. 3, 2007
Klein, Ron	FL	110th to 111th	Jan. 3, 2007
Lamborn, Doug	CO	110th to 111th	Jan. 3, 2007
Latta, Robert E.	OH	*110th to 111th	Dec. 11, 2007
Loebsack, David	IA	110th to 111th	Jan. 3, 2007
McCarthy, Kevin	CA	110th to 111th	Jan. 3, 2007
McNerney, Jerry	CA	110th to 111th	Jan. 3, 2007
Mitchell, Harry E.	AZ	110th to 111th	Jan. 3, 2007
Murphy, Christopher S.	CT	110th to 111th	Jan. 3, 2007
Murphy, Patrick J.	PA	110th to 111th	Jan. 3, 2007
Perlmutter, Ed	CO	110th to 111th	Jan. 3, 2007
Richardson, Laura	CA	*110th to 111th	Aug. 21, 2007
Roskam, Peter J.	IL	110th to 111th	Jan. 3, 2007
Sarbanes, John P.	MD	110th to 111th	Jan. 3, 2007
Scalise, Steve	LA	*110th to 111th	May 3, 2008
Sestak, Joe	PA	110th to 111th	Jan. 3, 2007
Shea-Porter, Carol	NH	110th to 111th	Jan. 3, 2007
Shuler, Heath	NC	110th to 111th	Jan. 3, 2007
Smith, Adrian	NE	110th to 111th	Jan. 3, 2007
Space, Zackary T.	OH	110th to 111th	Jan. 3, 2007
Speier, Jackie	CA	*110th to 111th	Apr. 8, 2008
Sutton, Betty	OH	110th to 111th	Jan. 3, 2007
Tsongas, Niki	MA	*110th to 111th	Oct. 16, 2007
Walz, Timothy J.	MN	110th to 111th	Jan. 3, 2007
Welch, Peter	VT	110th to 111th	Jan. 3, 2007
Wilson, Charles A.	OH	110th to 111th	Jan. 3, 2007
Wittman, Robert J.	VA	*110th to 111th	Dec. 11, 2007
Yarmuth, John A.	KY	110th to 111th	Jan. 3, 2007
1 term			
Adler, John H.	NJ	111th	Jan. 3, 2009
Austria, Steve	OH	111th	Jan. 3, 2009

CONGRESSES IN WHICH REPRESENTATIVES, RESIDENT COMMISSIONER, AND DELEGATES HAVE SERVED WITH BEGINNING OF PRESENT SERVICE—CONTINUED

[* Elected to fill a vacancy; Democrats in roman (256); Republicans in *italic* (177); Vacancies (2); Resident Commissioner and Delegates in **boldface** (6); total, 441]

Name	State	Congresses (inclusive)	Beginning of present service
Boccieri, John A.	OH	111th	Jan. 3, 2009
Bright, Bobby	AL	111th	Jan. 3, 2009
Cao, Anh "Joseph"	LA	111th	Jan. 3, 2009
Cassidy, Bill	LA	111th	Jan. 3, 2009
Chaffetz, Jason	UT	111th	Jan. 3, 2009
Chu, Judy	CA	*111th	July 16, 2009
Coffman, Mike	CO	111th	Jan. 3, 2009
Connolly, Gerald E.	VA	111th	Jan. 3, 2009
Dahlkemper, Kathleen A.	PA	111th	Jan. 3, 2009
Driehaus, Steve	OH	111th	Jan. 3, 2009
Fleming, John	LA	111th	Jan. 3, 2009
Grayson, Alan	FL	111th	Jan. 3, 2009
Griffith, Parker	AL	111th	Jan. 3, 2009
Guthrie, Brett	KY	111th	Jan. 3, 2009
Halvorson, Deborah L.	IL	111th	Jan. 3, 2009
Harper, Gregg	MS	111th	Jan. 3, 2009
Heinrich, Martin	NM	111th	Jan. 3, 2009
Himes, James A.	CT	111th	Jan. 3, 2009
Hunter, Duncan	CA	111th	Jan. 3, 2009
Jenkins, Lynn	KS	111th	Jan. 3, 2009
Kilroy, Mary Jo	OH	111th	Jan. 3, 2009
Kirkpatrick, Ann	AZ	111th	Jan. 3, 2009
Kissell, Larry	NC	111th	Jan. 3, 2009
Kosmas, Suzanne M.	FL	111th	Jan. 3, 2009
Kratovil, Frank, Jr.	MD	111th	Jan. 3, 2009
Lance, Leonard	NJ	111th	Jan. 3, 2009
Lee, Christopher John	NY	111th	Jan. 3, 2009
Luetkemeyer, Blaine	MO	111th	Jan. 3, 2009
Luján, Ben Ray	NM	111th	Jan. 3, 2009
Lummis, Cynthia M.	WY	111th	Jan. 3, 2009
McClintock, Tom	CA	111th	Jan. 3, 2009
McMahon, Michael E.	NY	111th	Jan. 3, 2009
Maffei, Daniel B.	NY	111th	Jan. 3, 2009
Markey, Betsy	CO	111th	Jan. 3, 2009
Massa, Eric J. J.	NY	111th	Jan. 3, 2009
Minnick, Walt	ID	111th	Jan. 3, 2009
Murphy, Scott	NY	*111th	Mar. 31, 2009
Nye, Glenn C.	VA	111th	Jan. 3, 2009
Olson, Pete	TX	111th	Jan. 3, 2009
Paulsen, Erik	MN	111th	Jan. 3, 2009
Perriello, Thomas S. P.	VA	111th	Jan. 3, 2009
Peters, Gary C.	MI	111th	Jan. 3, 2009
Pingree, Chellie	ME	111th	Jan. 3, 2009
Polis, Jared	CO	111th	Jan. 3, 2009
Posey, Bill	FL	111th	Jan. 3, 2009
Quigley, Mike	IL	*111th	Apr. 7, 2009

CONGRESSES IN WHICH REPRESENTATIVES, RESIDENT COMMISSIONER, AND DELEGATES HAVE SERVED WITH BEGINNING OF PRESENT SERVICE—CONTINUED

[* Elected to fill a vacancy; Democrats in roman (256); Republicans in *italic* (177); Vacancies (2); Resident Commissioner and Delegates in **boldface** (6); total, 441]

Name	State	Congresses (inclusive)	Beginning of present service
Roe, David P.	TN	111th	Jan. 3, 2009
Rooney, Thomas J.	FL	111th	Jan. 3, 2009
Schauer, Mark H.	MI	111th	Jan. 3, 2009
Schock, Aaron	IL	111th	Jan. 3, 2009
Schrader, Kurt	OR	111th	Jan. 3, 2009
Teague, Harry	NM	111th	Jan. 3, 2009
Thompson, Glenn	PA	111th	Jan. 3, 2009
Titus, Dina	NV	111th	Jan. 3, 2009
Tonko, Paul	NY	111th	Jan. 3, 2009
RESIDENT COMMISSIONER			
Pierluisi, Pedro R.	PR	111th	Jan. 3, 2009
DELEGATES			
Faleomavaega, Eni F. H.	AS	101st to 111th	Jan. 3, 1989
Norton, Eleanor Holmes	DC	102d to 111th	Jan. 3, 1991
Christensen, Donna M.	VI	105th to 111th	Jan. 3, 1997
Bordallo, Madeleine Z.	GU	108th to 111th	Jan. 3, 2003
Sablan, Gregorio Kilili Camacho	MP	111th	Jan. 3, 2009

NOTE: Members elected by special election are considered to begin service on the date of the election, except for those elected after a sine die adjournment. If elected after the Congress has adjourned for the session, Members are considered to begin their service on the day after the election.

STANDING COMMITTEES OF THE SENATE

[Democrats in roman; Republicans in *italic*; Independent in SMALL CAPS; Independent Democrat in *SMALL CAPS ITALIC*]

[Room numbers beginning with SD are in the Dirksen Building, SH in the Hart Building, SR in the Russell Building, and S in The Capitol]

Agriculture, Nutrition, and Forestry

328A Russell Senate Office Building 20510–6000

phone 224–2035, fax 224–1725, TTY / TDD 224–2587

http://agriculture.senate.gov

meets first and third Wednesdays of each month

Blanche L. Lincoln, of Arkansas, *Chair*

Tom Harkin, of Iowa.
Patrick J. Leahy, of Vermont.
Kent Conrad, of North Dakota.
Max Baucus, of Montana.
Debbie Stabenow, of Michigan.
Ben Nelson, of Nebraska.
Sherrod Brown, of Ohio.
Robert P. Casey, Jr., of Pennsylvania.
Amy Klobuchar, of Minnesota.
Michael F. Bennet, of Colorado.
Kirsten E. Gillibrand, of New York.

Saxby Chambliss, of Georgia.
Richard G. Lugar, of Indiana.
Thad Cochran, of Mississippi.
Mitch McConnell, of Kentucky.
Pat Roberts, of Kansas.
Mike Johanns, of Nebraska.
Chuck Grassley, of Iowa.
John Thune, of South Dakota.
John Cornyn, of Texas.

SUBCOMMITTEES

[The chairman and ranking minority member are ex officio (non-voting) members of all subcommittees on which they do not serve.]

Domestic and Foreign Marketing, Inspection, and Plant and Animal Health

Kirsten E. Gillibrand, of New York, *Chair*

Kent Conrad, of North Dakota.
Max Baucus, of Montana.
Ben Nelson, of Nebraska.
Amy Klobuchar, of Minnesota.

Mike Johanns, of Nebraska.
Richard G. Lugar, of Indiana.
Mitch McConnell, of Kentucky.
Pat Roberts, of Kansas.

Energy, Science and Technology

Debbie Stabenow, of Michigan, *Chair*

Kent Conrad, of North Dakota.
Ben Nelson, of Nebraska.
Sherrod Brown, of Ohio.
Amy Klobuchar, of Minnesota.
Michael F. Bennet, of Colorado.
Kirsten E. Gillibrand, of New York.

John Thune, of South Dakota.
Richard G. Lugar, of Indiana.
Pat Roberts, of Kansas.
Mike Johanns, of Nebraska.
Chuck Grassley, of Iowa.
John Cornyn, of Texas.

Hunger, Nutrition and Family Farms

Sherrod Brown, of Ohio, *Chair*

Patrick J. Leahy, of Vermont.
Max Baucus, of Montana.
Blanche L. Lincoln, of Arkansas.
Debbie Stabenow, of Michigan.
Robert P. Casey, Jr., of Pennsylvania.
Amy Klobuchar, of Minnesota.
Michael F. Bennet, of Colorado.
Kirsten E. Gillibrand, of New York.

Richard G. Lugar, of Indiana.
Thad Cochran, of Mississippi.
Mitch McConnell, of Kentucky.
John Cornyn, of Texas.

Production, Income Protection and Price Support

Robert P. Casey, Jr., of Pennsylvania, *Chair*

Patrick J. Leahy, of Vermont.
Kent Conrad, of North Dakota.
Max Baucus, of Montana.
Blanche L. Lincoln, of Arkansas.
Sherrod Brown, of Ohio.

Pat Roberts, of Kansas.
Thad Cochran, of Mississippi.
Mike Johanns, of Nebraska.
Chuck Grassley, of Iowa.
John Thune, of South Dakota.

Rural Revitalization, Conservation, Forestry and Credit

Blanche L. Lincoln, of Arkansas, *Chair*

Patrick J. Leahy, of Vermont.
Debbie Stabenow, of Michigan.
Ben Nelson, of Nebraska.
Robert P. Casey, Jr., of Pennsylvania.
Michael F. Bennet, of Colorado.

John Cornyn, of Texas.
Thad Cochran, of Mississippi.
Mitch McConnell, of Kentucky.
Chuck Grassley, of Iowa.
John Thune, of South Dakota.

STAFF

Committee on Agriculture, Nutrition, and Forestry (SR–328A), 224–2035, fax 224–1725.
Majority Staff Director.—Mark Halverson.
Senior Professional Staff: Richard Bender, Eldon Boes.
Senior Counsels: Phil Buchan, Amy Lowenthal.
Press Secretary.—Grant Gustafson.
Chief Counsel.—Susan Keith.
Professional Staff: Todd Batta, Dan Christenson, Cory Claussen, Veronica McBeth, Derek Miller, Karla Thieman.
Chief Economist.—Stephanie Mercier.
Executive Assistant.—Mindy VanWoerkom.
Minority Staff Director.—Martha Scott Poindexter.
Legislative Correspondent.—Carlisle Clarke.
Senior Professional Staff: Kate Coler, Dawn Stump.
Press Secretary.—Erin Hamm.
Chief Economist.—Hayden Milberg.
Professional Staff: Brandon Beshears, Betsy Croker, Jane Anna Harris, Christy Seyfert.
Non-designated:
Staff Assistant.—Nyka Aukstuolis.
IT.—Jacob Chaney.
Archivist.—Katie Salay.
GPO Detailee.—Micah Wortham.
Chief Clerk.—Jessie Williams.
Legislative Correspondents: Hillary Caron, David Howard.

Appropriations

S–128 The Capitol 20510–6025, phone 224–7363

http://appropriations.senate.gov

meets upon call of the chair

Daniel K. Inouye, of Hawaii, *Chair*

Robert C. Byrd, of West Virginia.
Patrick J. Leahy, of Vermont.
Tom Harkin, of Iowa.
Barbara A. Mikulski, of Maryland.
Herb Kohl, of Wisconsin.
Patty Murray, of Washington.
Byron L. Dorgan, of North Dakota.
Dianne Feinstein, of California.
Richard Durbin, of Illinois.
Tim Johnson, of South Dakota.
Mary L. Landrieu, of Louisiana.
Jack Reed, of Rhode Island.
Frank R. Lautenberg, of New Jersey.
Ben Nelson, of Nebraska.
Mark L. Pryor, of Arkansas.
Jon Tester, of Montana.
Arlen Specter, of Pennsylvania.

Thad Cochran, of Mississippi.
Christopher S. Bond, of Missouri.
Mitch McConnell, of Kentucky.
Richard C. Shelby, of Alabama.
Judd Gregg, of New Hampshire.
Robert F. Bennett, of Utah.
Kay Bailey Hutchison, of Texas.
Sam Brownback, of Kansas.
Lamar Alexander, of Tennessee.
Susan M. Collins, of Maine.
George V. Voinovich, of Ohio.
Lisa Murkowski, of Alaska.

SUBCOMMITTEES

[The chairman and ranking minority member are ex officio members of all subcommittees on which they do not serve.]

Agriculture, Rural Development, Food and Drug Administration, and Related Agencies

Herb Kohl, of Wisconsin, *Chair*

Tom Harkin, of Iowa.
Byron L. Dorgan, of North Dakota.
Dianne Feinstein, of California.
Richard Durbin, of Illinois.
Tim Johnson, of South Dakota.
Ben Nelson, of Nebraska.
Jack Reed, of Rhode Island.
Mark L. Pryor, of Arkansas.
Arlen Specter, of Pennsylvania.

Sam Brownback, of Kansas.
Robert F. Bennett, of Utah.
Thad Cochran, of Mississippi.
Christopher S. Bond, of Missouri.
Mitch McConnell, of Kentucky.
Susan M. Collins, of Maine.

Commerce, Justice, Science, and Related Agencies

Barbara A. Mikulski, of Maryland, *Chair*

Daniel K. Inouye, of Hawaii.
Patrick J. Leahy, of Vermont.
Herb Kohl, of Wisconsin.
Byron L. Dorgan, of North Dakota.
Dianne Feinstein, of California.
Jack Reed, of Rhode Island.
Frank R. Lautenberg, of New Jersey.
Ben Nelson, of Nebraska.
Mark L. Pryor, of Arkansas.

Richard C. Shelby, of Alabama.
Judd Gregg, of New Hampshire.
Mitch McConnell, of Kentucky.
Kay Bailey Hutchison, of Texas.
Lamar Alexander, of Tennessee.
George V. Voinovich, of Ohio.
Lisa Murkowski, of Alaska.

Defense

Daniel K. Inouye, of Hawaii, *Chair*

Robert C. Byrd, of West Virginia.
Patrick J. Leahy, of Vermont.
Tom Harkin, of Iowa.
Byron L. Dorgan, of North Dakota.
Richard Durbin, of Illinois.
Dianne Feinstein, of California.
Barbara A. Mikulski, of Maryland.
Herb Kohl, of Wisconsin.
Patty Murray, of Washington.
Arlen Specter, of Pennsylvania.

Thad Cochran, of Mississippi.
Christopher S. Bond, of Missouri.
Mitch McConnell, of Kentucky.
Richard C. Shelby, of Alabama.
Judd Gregg, of New Hampshire.
Kay Bailey Hutchison, of Texas.
Robert F. Bennett, of Utah.
Sam Brownback, of Kansas.

Energy and Water Development

Byron L. Dorgan, of North Dakota, *Chair*

Robert C. Byrd, of West Virginia.
Patty Murray, of Washington.
Dianne Feinstein, of California.
Tim Johnson, of South Dakota.
Mary L. Landrieu, of Louisiana.
Jack Reed, of Rhode Island.
Frank R. Lautenberg, of New Jersey.
Tom Harkin, of Iowa.
Jon Tester, of Montana.

Robert F. Bennett, of Utah.
Thad Cochran, of Mississippi.
Mitch McConnell, of Kentucky.
Christopher S. Bond, of Missouri.
Kay Bailey Hutchison, of Texas.
Richard C. Shelby, of Alabama.
Lamar Alexander, of Tennessee.
George V. Voinovich, of Ohio.

Financial Services and General Government

Richard Durbin, of Illinois, *Chair*

Mary L. Landrieu, of Louisiana.
Frank R. Lautenberg, of New Jersey.
Ben Nelson, of Nebraska.
Jon Tester, of Montana.

Susan M. Collins, of Maine.
Christopher S. Bond, of Missouri.
Lamar Alexander, of Tennessee.

Homeland Security

Robert C. Byrd, of West Virginia, *Chair*

Daniel K. Inouye, of Hawaii.
Patrick J. Leahy, of Vermont.
Barbara A. Mikulski, of Maryland.
Patty Murray, of Washington.
Mary L. Landrieu, of Louisiana.
Frank R. Lautenberg, of New Jersey.
Jon Tester, of Montana.
Arlen Specter, of Pennsylvania.

George V. Voinovich, of Ohio.
Thad Cochran, of Mississippi.
Judd Gregg, of New Hampshire.
Richard C. Shelby, of Alabama.
Sam Brownback, of Kansas.
Lisa Murkowski, of Alaska.

Interior, Environment, and Related Agencies

Dianne Feinstein, of California, *Chair*

Robert C. Byrd, of West Virginia.
Patrick J. Leahy, of Vermont.
Byron L. Dorgan, of North Dakota.
Barbara A. Mikulski, of Maryland.
Herb Kohl, of Wisconsin.
Tim Johnson, of South Dakota.
Jack Reed, of Rhode Island.
Ben Nelson, of Nebraska.
Jon Tester, of Montana.

Lamar Alexander, of Tennessee.
Thad Cochran, of Mississippi.
Robert F. Bennett, of Utah.
Judd Gregg, of New Hampshire.
Lisa Murkowski, of Alaska.
Susan M. Collins, of Maine.

Labor, Health and Human Services, Education, and Related Agencies

Tom Harkin, of Iowa, *Chair*

Daniel K. Inouye, of Hawaii.
Herb Kohl, of Wisconsin.
Patty Murray, of Washington.
Mary L. Landrieu, of Louisiana.
Richard Durbin, of Illinois.
Jack Reed, of Rhode Island.
Mark L. Pryor, of Arkansas.
Arlen Specter, of Pennsylvania.

Thad Cochran, of Mississippi.
Judd Gregg, of New Hampshire.
Kay Bailey Hutchison, of Texas.
Richard C. Shelby, of Alabama.
Lamar Alexander, of Tennessee.

Legislative Branch

Ben Nelson, of Nebraska, *Chair*

Mark L. Pryor, of Arkansas.
Jon Tester, of Montana.

Lisa Murkowski, of Alaska.

Military Construction and Veterans Affairs, and Related Agencies

Tim Johnson, of South Dakota, *Chair*

Daniel K. Inouye, of Hawaii.
Mary L. Landrieu, of Louisiana.
Robert C. Byrd, of West Virginia.
Patty Murray, of Washington.
Jack Reed, of Rhode Island.
Ben Nelson, of Nebraska.
Mark L. Pryor, of Arkansas.

Kay Bailey Hutchison, of Texas.
Sam Brownback, of Kansas.
Mitch McConnell, of Kentucky.
Susan M. Collins, of Maine.
Lisa Murkowski, of Alaska.

State, Foreign Operations, and Related Programs

Patrick J. Leahy, of Vermont, *Chair*

Daniel K. Inouye, of Hawaii.
Tom Harkin, of Iowa.
Barbara A. Mikulski, of Maryland.
Richard Durbin, of Illinois.
Tim Johnson, of South Dakota.
Mary L. Landrieu, of Louisiana.
Frank R. Lautenberg, of New Jersey.
Arlen Specter, of Pennsylvania.

Judd Gregg, of New Hampshire.
Mitch McConnell, of Kentucky.
Robert F. Bennett, of Utah.
Christopher S. Bond, of Missouri.
Sam Brownback, of Kansas.
George V. Voinovich, of Ohio.

Transportation and Housing and Urban Development, and Related Agencies

Patty Murray, of Washington, *Chair*

Robert C. Byrd, of West Virginia.
Barbara A. Mikulski, of Maryland.
Herb Kohl, of Wisconsin.
Richard Durbin, of Illinois.
Byron L. Dorgan, of North Dakota.
Patrick J. Leahy, of Vermont.
Tom Harkin, of Iowa.
Dianne Feinstein, of California.
Tim Johnson, of South Dakota.
Frank R. Lautenberg, of New Jersey.
Arlen Specter, of Pennsylvania.

Christopher S. Bond, of Missouri.
Richard C. Shelby, of Alabama.
Robert F. Bennett, of Utah.
Kay Bailey Hutchison, of Texas.
Sam Brownback, of Kansas.
Lamar Alexander, of Tennessee.
Susan M. Collins, of Maine.
George V. Voinovich, of Ohio.

STAFF

Committee on Appropriations (S–128), 224–7363.

Majority Staff Director.—Charles J. Houy (S–128).
Deputy Staff Director.—Margaret Cummisky (S–128).
Chief Clerk.—Robert W. Putnam (SD–114).
Deputy Chief Clerk.—Bridget Zarate (S–122).
Communications Director.—Rob Blumenthal (S–128).
Deputy Communications Director.—John Bray (S–128).
Professional Staff: John J. Conway (SD–114); Lila Helms (S–128); Colleen Gaydos (S–128); Fernanda Motta (SD–114).
Assistant to the Chairman.—Ericka Rojas (S–128).
Technical Systems Manager.—Hong Nguyen (SD–114).
Minority Staff Director.—Bruce Evans (S–146A), 4–7257.
Communications Director.—Chris Gallegos (S–113).
Professional Staff.—Carolyn E. Apostolou (S–146A).
Staff Assistant.—Sarah Wilson (S–146A).

Subcommittee on Agriculture, Rural Development, Food and Drug Administration and Related Agencies (SD–129), 4–8090.
Majority Clerk.—Galen Fountain (SD–129).
Professional Staff: Jessica Arden Frederick, Dianne Nellor (SD–129).
Staff Assistant.—Molly Barackman (SD–184).
Minority Clerk.—Fitz Elder (SD–190), 4–5270.
Professional Staff: Stacy McBride (SD–190).

Subcommittee on Commerce, Justice, Science, and Related Agencies (SD–142), 4–5202.
Majority Clerk.—Gabrielle Batkin (SD–142).
Professional Staff: Jessica M. Berry (SD–142); Jeremy Weirich (SD–142).
Staff Assistant.—Michael Bain (SD–142).
Minority Clerk.—Art Cameron (SH–123), 4–7277.
Professional Staff: Allen Cutler (SH–125); Goodloe Sutton (SH–125).
Staff Assistant.—Katie Batte (SD–125).

Subcommittee on Defense (SD–122), 4–6688.
Majority Clerk.—Charles J. Houy (SD–122).
Professional Staff: Nicole Di Resta (SD–122); Kate Fitzpatrick (SD–122); Katy Hagan (SD–122); Kate Kaufer (SD–122), Ellen Maldonado (SD–122); Erik Raven (SD–122); Gary Reese (SD–122); Betsy Schmid (SD–122); Bridget Zarate (SD–122).
Staff Assistant.—Rachel Meyer (SD–122).
Minority Clerk.—Stewart Holmes (SD–117), 4–7255.
Professional Staff: Alycia Farrell (SD–115); Brian Potts (SD–115); Brian Wilson (SD–115).

Subcommittee on Energy and Water, and Development (SD–184), 4–8119.
Majority Clerk.—Doug Clapp (SD–184).
Professional Staff: Roger Cockrell (SD–184); Fanz Wuerfmannsdobler (SD–184).
Staff Assistant.—Molly Barackman (SD–184).
Minority Clerk.—Scott O'Malia (SD–188), 4–7260.
Professional Staff.—Brad Fuller (SD–188).

Subcommittee on Financial Services and General Government (SD–184), 4–1133.
Majority Clerk.—Marianne Upton (SD–184).
Professional Staff: Diana Gourlay Hamilton (SD–184); Melissa Z. Petersen (SD–184).
Staff Assistant.—Molly Barackman (SD–184).
Minority Clerk.—Mary Dietrich (SD–125), 4–2104.
Professional Staff.—Rachel Jones (SD–125).
Staff Assistant.—LaShawnda Smith (SD–125).

Subcommittee on Homeland Security (SD–135), 4–8244.
Majority Clerk.—Charles Kieffer (SD–135).
Professional Staff: Chip Walgren (SD–135); Scott Nance (SD–135); Christa Thompson (SD–135); Suzanne Bentzel (SD–135).
Staff Assistant.—Michael Bain (SD–142).
Minority Clerk.—Rebecca Davies (SH–125), 4–4319.
Professional Staff.—Carol Cribbs (SH–125).
Staff Assistant.—Katie Batte (SH–125).

Subcommittee on Interior, Environment, and Related Agencies (SD–131), 8–0774.
Majority Clerk.—Peter Keifhaber (SD–131).
Professional Staff: Ginny James (SD–131); Rachael Taylor (SD–131); Scott Dalzell (SD–131); Chris Watkins (SD–131).
Staff Assistant.—Teri Curtin (SD–131).
Minority Clerk.—Leif Fonnesbeck (SH–125), 4–7233.
Professional Staff: Rebecca Benn (SH–125); Rachelle Schroeder (SD–125).
Staff Assistant.—Katie Batte (SH–125).

Subcommittee on Departments of Labor, Health and Human Services, and Education, and Related Agencies (SD–131), 4–9145.
Majority Clerk.—Ellen Murray (SD–131).
Professional Staff: Erik Fatemi (SD–131); Mark Laisch (SD–131); Adrienne Hallett (SD–131); Lisa Bernhardt (SD–131).
Staff Assistant.—Teri Curtin (SD–131).
Minority Clerk.—Bettilou Taylor (SD–156), 4–7230.
Professional Staff: Dale Cabaniss (SD–156); Sara Lover Swaney (SD–156).
Staff Assistant.—Jeff Kratz (SD–156).
Subcommittee on Legislative Branch (SD–135) 4–3477.
Majority Clerk.—Nancy Oklewicz (SD–135).
Staff Assistant.—Teri Curtin (SD–131).
Minority Clerk.—Carolyn E. Apostolou (S–146A), 4–7238.
Staff Assistant.—Sarah Wilson (S–146A).
Subcommittee on Military Construction and Veterans Affairs, and Related Agencies (SD–125), 4–8224.
Majority Clerk.—Christina Evans (SD–125).
Professional Staff: Chad Schulken (SD–125); Andrew Vanlandingham (SD–125).
Staff Assistant.—Rachel Meyer (SD–122).
Minority Clerk.—Dennis Balkham (SH–125), 4–5245.
Professional Staff.—Ben Hammond (SH–125).
Staff Assistant.—Katie Batte (SH–125).
Subcommittee on State, Foreign Operations, and Related Programs (SD–127), 4–7284.
Majority Clerk.—Tim Rieser (SD–127).
Professional Staff: Nikole Manatt (SD–127); Janett Stormes (SD–127).
Staff Assistant.—Rachel Meyer (SD–122).
Minority Clerk.—Paul Grove (SH–125), 4–2104.
Professional Staff.—Michele Wymer (SH–125).
Staff Assistant.—LaShawnda Smith, (SH–125).
Subcommittee on Transportation and Housing and Urban Development, and Related Agencies (SD–142), 4–7281.
Majority Clerk.—Alex Keenan (SD–142).
Professional Staff: Meaghan L. McCarthy (SD–142); Rachel Milberg (SD–142).
Staff Assistant.—Michael Bain (SD–142).
Minority Clerk.—Jon Kamarck (SD–128), 4–5310.
Professional Staff: Matthew McCardle (SD–128); Ellen Beares (SD–128).
Editorial and Printing (SD–126): Richard L. Larson, 4–7265; Doris Jackson (GPO), 4–7217; Mark Moore (GPO), 4–7266; Reginald Stewart (GPO), 4–7267; Celina Inman (GPO), 4–7217.
Clerical Assistant.—George Castro (SD–120), 4–5433.

Armed Services

228 Russell Senate Office Building 20510–6050

phone 224–3871, http://www.senate.gov/~armed_services

meets every Tuesday and Thursday

Carl Levin, of Michigan, *Chair*

Robert C. Byrd, of West Virginia.
JOSEPH I. LIEBERMAN, of Connecticut.
Jack Reed, of Rhode Island.
Daniel K. Akaka, of Hawaii.
Bill Nelson, of Florida.
Ben Nelson, of Nebraska.
Evan Bayh, of Indiana.
Jim Webb, of Virginia.
Claire McCaskill, of Missouri.
Mark Udall, of Colorado.
Kay R. Hagan, of North Carolina.
Mark Begich, of Alaska.
Roland W. Burris, of Illinois.
Paul G. Kirk, Jr., of Massachusetts.

John McCain, of Arizona.
James M. Inhofe, of Oklahoma.
Jeff Sessions, of Alabama.
Saxby Chambliss, of Georgia.
Lindsey Graham, of South Carolina.
John Thune, of South Dakota.
Roger F. Wicker, of Mississippi.
George S. LeMieux, of Florida.
Richard Burr, of North Carolina.
David Vitter, of Louisiana.
Susan M. Collins, of Maine.

SUBCOMMITTEES

[The chairman and the ranking minority member are ex officio (non-voting) members of all subcommittees on which they do not serve.]

Airland

JOSEPH I. LIEBERMAN, of Connecticut, *Chair*

Evan Bayh, of Indiana.
Jim Webb, of Virginia.
Claire McCaskill, of Missouri.
Kay R. Hagan, of North Carolina.
Mark Begich, of Alaska.
Roland W. Burris, of Illinois.

John Thune, of South Dakota.
James M. Inhofe, of Oklahoma.
Jeff Sessions, of Alabama.
Saxby Chambliss, of Georgia.
Richard Burr, of North Carolina.

Emerging Threats and Capabilities

Bill Nelson, of Florida, *Chair*

Robert C. Byrd, of West Virginia.
Jack Reed, of Rhode Island.
Ben Nelson, of Nebraska.
Evan Bayh, of Indiana.
Mark Udall, of Colorado.
Paul G. Kirk, Jr., of Massachusetts.

George S. LeMieux, of Florida.
Lindsey Graham, of South Carolina.
Roger F. Wicker, of Mississippi.
Richard Burr, of North Carolina.
Susan M. Collins, of Maine.

Personnel

Jim Webb, of Virginia, *Chair*

JOSEPH I. LIEBERMAN, of Connecticut.
Daniel K. Akaka, of Hawaii.
Ben Nelson, of Nebraska.
Claire McCaskill, of Missouri.
Kay R. Hagan, of North Carolina.
Mark Begich, of Alaska.
Roland W. Burris, of Illinois.
Paul G. Kirk, Jr., of Massachusetts.

Lindsey Graham, of South Carolina.
Saxby Chambliss, of Georgia.
John Thune, of South Dakota.
Roger F. Wicker, of Mississippi.
George S. LeMieux, of Florida.
David Vitter, of Louisiana.
Susan M. Collins, of Maine.

Readiness and Management Support

Evan Bayh, of Indiana, *Chair*

Robert C. Byrd, of West Virginia.
Daniel K. Akaka, of Hawaii.
Claire McCaskill, of Missouri.
Mark Udall, of Colorado.
Roland W. Burris, of Illinois.

Richard Burr, of North Carolina.
James M. Inhofe, of Oklahoma.
Saxby Chambliss, of Georgia.
John Thune, of South Dakota.

Seapower

Jack Reed, of Rhode Island, *Chair*

JOSEPH I. LIEBERMAN, of Connecticut.
Daniel K. Akaka, of Hawaii.
Bill Nelson, of Florida.
Jim Webb, of Virginia.
Kay R. Hagan, of North Carolina.
Paul G. Kirk, Jr., of Massachusetts.

Roger F. Wicker, of Mississippi.
Jeff Sessions, of Alabama.
George S. LeMieux, of Florida.
David Vitter, of Louisiana.
Susan M. Collins, of Maine.

Strategic Forces

Ben Nelson, of Nebraska, *Chair*

Robert C. Byrd, of West Virginia.
Jack Reed, of Rhode Island.
Bill Nelson, of Florida.
Mark Udall, of Colorado.
Mark Begich, of Alaska.

David Vitter, of Louisiana.
Jeff Sessions, of Alabama.
James M. Inhofe, of Oklahoma.
Lindsey Graham, of South Carolina.

STAFF

Committee on Armed Services (SR–228), 224–3871.
Majority Staff Director.—Richard D. DeBobes.
Chief Clerk.—Christine E. Cowart.
General Counsel.—Peter K. Levine.
Counsels: Jonathan D. Clark, Ilona R. Cohen, Madelyn R. Creedon, Gabriella Eisen, Howard H. Hoege III, Gerald J. Leeling, William G.P. Monahan, Russell L. Shaffer.
Professional Staff Members: Joseph M. Bryan, Creighton Greene, Richard W. Fieldhouse, Michael J. Kuiken, Terence K. Laughlin, Thomas K. McConnell, Michael J. Noblet, Roy F. Phillips, John H. Quirk V, Arun A. Seraphin, William K. Sutey.
Research Assistant.—Jessica L. Kingston.
Assistant Chief Clerk and Security Manager.—Cindy Pearson.
Nominations and Hearings Clerk.—Leah C. Brewer.
Systems Administrator.—Gary J. Howard.
Printing and Documents Clerk.—June M. Borawski.
Security Clerk.—Jennifer L. Stoker.
Legislative Clerk.—Mary J. Kyle.
Special Assistant.—Travis E. Smith.
Staff Assistants: Kevin A. Cronin, Christine G. Lang, Paul J. Hubbard, Jennifer R. Knowles, Brian F. Sebold, Breon N. Wells.
Republican Staff Director.—Joseph W. Bowab.
Deputy Minority Staff Director.—Richard H. Fontaine.
Executive Assistant for the Minority.—Greg R. Lilly.
Minority Counsels: David M. Morriss, Richard F. Walsh.
Investigative Counsel.—Pablo E. Carrillo.
Professional Staff Members: Adam J. Barker, Church Hutton, Michael V. Kostiw, Daniel A. Lerner, Lucian L. Niemeyer, Christopher J. Paul, Diana G. Tabler, Dana W. White.
Subcommittee on Airland:
Majority Professional Staff Members: William K. Sutey (Lead), Creighton Greene, Michael J. Kuiken.
Minority Professional Staff Members: Christopher J. Paul (Lead), Pablo E. Carrillo, Church Hutton, David M. Morriss.

Staff Assistant.—Brian F. Sebold.

Subcommittee on Emerging Threats and Capabilities:

Majority Professional Staff Members: Richard W. Fieldhouse (Lead), Madelyn R. Creedon, Michael J. Kuiken, William G.P. Monahan, Michael J. Noblet, Arun A. Seraphin, Russell L. Shaffer.

Minority Professional Staff Members: Michael V. Kostiw (Lead), Adam J. Barker, Dana W. White, Church Hutton.

Staff Assistant.—Paul J. Hubbard.

Subcommittee on Personnel:

Majority Professional Staff Members: Gerald J. Leeling (Lead), Jonathan D. Clark, Gabriella Eisen.

Minority Professional Staff Members: Richard F. Walsh (Co-lead), Diana G. Tabler (Co-lead).

Staff Assistant.—Vacant.

Subcommittee on Readiness and Management Support:

Majority Professional Staff Members: Peter K. Levine (Lead), Terence K. Laughlin, John H. Quirk V, Russell L. Shaffer.

Minority Professional Staff Members: Lucian L. Niemeyer (Lead), Adam J. Barker, Pablo E. Carrillo, David M. Morriss, Christopher J. Paul.

Staff Assistant.—Breon N. Wells.

Subcommittee on Seapower:

Majority Professional Staff Members: Creighton Greene (Lead), Thomas K. McConnell.

Minority Professional Staff Members: Christopher J. Paul (Lead), Pablo E. Carrillo, David M. Morriss.

Staff Assistant.—Brian F. Sebold.

Subcommittee on Strategic Forces:

Majority Professional Staff Members: Madelyn R. Creedon (Lead), Richard W. Fieldhouse, Creighton Greene, Thomas K. McConnell.

Minority Professional Staff Members: Daniel A. Lerner (Lead), Christopher J. Paul, Dana W. White.

Staff Assistant.—Kevin A. Cronin.

Majority Professional Staff for—

Acquisition Policy.—Peter K. Levine.

Acquisition Workforce.—Peter K. Levine.

Ammunition.—John H. Quirk V.

Arms Control/Non-proliferation: Madelyn R. Creedon, Richard W. Fieldhouse.

Aviation Systems: Madelyn R. Creedon, Creighton Greene.

Base Realignment and Closure (BRAC).—Terence K. Laughlin.

Buy America.—Peter K. Levine.

Chemical-Biological Defense.—Richard W. Fieldhouse.

Chemical Demilitarization.—Richard W. Fieldhouse.

Civilian Nominations.—Peter K. Levine.

Civilian Personnel Policy: Gabriella Eisen, Gerald J. Leeling, Peter K. Levine.

Combatant Commands.—

AFRICOM.—Michael J. Kuiken.

CENTCOM.—William G.P. Monahan, Michael J. Kuiken, William K. Sutey.

EUCOM.—William G.P. Monahan.

JFCOM.—John H. Quirk V, Arun A. Seraphin.

NORTHCOM.—Richard W. Fieldhouse.

PACOM.—Russell L. Shaffer.

SOCOM.—Michael J. Noblet.

SOUTHCOM.—Michael J. Kuiken.

STRATCOM.—Madelyn R. Creedon.

TRANSCOM.—Creighton Greene.

Combating Terrorism: Michael J. Kuiken, William G.P. Monahan, Michael J. Noblet, Russell L. Shaffer.

Competition Policy/Mergers and Acquisitions.—Peter K. Levine.

Competitive Sourcing/A–76.—Peter K. Levine.

Contracting (including service contracts).—Peter K. Levine.

Construction, Housing, Global Basing, and Land Use.—Terence K. Laughlin.

Cooperative Threat Reduction Programs.—Madelyn R. Creedon.

Counterdrug Programs.—Michael J. Kuiken.

Defense Energy Use/Alternative Energy Issues.—John H. Quirk V.

Defense Laboratory Management: Peter K. Levine, Arun A. Seraphin.

Defense Security Assistance: Michael J. Kuiken, William G.P. Monahan, Russell L. Shaffer.

Defense Spending and Supplementals.—Roy F. Phillips.

Department of Defense Schools: Gabriella Eisen, Gerald J. Leeling.
Department of Energy Issues.—Madelyn R. Creedon.
Depot Maintenance.—John H. Quirk V.
Detainee Policy: Peter K. Levine, William G.P. Monahan.
Domestic Preparedness.—Richard W. Fieldhouse.
Environmental Issues.—Peter K. Levine, Russell L. Shaffer.
Export Controls.—Peter K. Levine.
Financial Management.—Peter K. Levine.
Force Readiness/Training.—John H. Quirk V.
Foreign Language Policy.—Creighton Greene.
Foreign Policy/Geographical Region.—
Afghanistan.—William G.P. Monahan.
Africa.—Michael J. Kuiken.
Asia/Pacific Region.—Russell L. Shaffer.
Europe/Russia: Madelyn R. Creedon, William G.P. Monahan.
Iraq.—William K. Sutey.
Middle East.—Michael J. Kuiken.
South and Central America.—Michael J. Kuiken.
Ground Systems.—
Army: Michael J. Kuiken, William K. Sutey.
Marine Corps.—Thomas K. McConnell.
Homeland Defense/Security: Richard W. Fieldhouse, Gary Leeling.
Humanitarian and Civic Assistance: Michael J. Kuiken, William G.P. Monahan.
Information Assurance/Cyber Security: Creighton Greene, Thomas K. McConnell, Arun A. Seraphin.
Information Management: Creighton Greene, Peter K. Levine.
Information Technology Systems.—
Business Systems.—Peter K. Levine, Arun A. Seraphin.
Tactical Systems: Creighton Greene, Arun A. Seraphin.
Intelligence Issues: Creighton Greene, Thomas K. McConnell.
Interagency Reform/Goldwater-Nichols II.—Thomas K. McConnell.
International Defense Cooperation: Peter K. Levine, William G.P. Monahan.
Inventory Management: Peter K. Levine, John H. Quirk V.
Investigations: Joseph M. Bryan, Ilona R. Cohen, Howard H. Hoege III.
Military Personnel Issues: Jonathan D. Clark, Gabriella Eisen, Gerald J. Leeling.
End Strength: Jonathan D. Clark, Gerald J. Leeling.
Health Care: Gabriella Eisen, Gerald J. Leeling.
Homosexual Conduct Policy: Jonathan D. Clark, Gerald J. Leeling.
Military Family Policy: Gabriella Eisen, Gerald J. Leeling.
Military Personnel Policy: Jonathan D. Clark, Gerald J. Leeling.
Military Nominations.—Gerald J. Leeling.
Military Space.—Madelyn R. Creedon.
Military Strategy.—William K. Sutey.
Missile Defense.—Richard W. Fieldhouse.
Morale, Welfare and Recreation/Commissaries/Exchanges: Gabriella Eisen, Gerald J. Leeling.
National Defense Stockpile.—John H. Quirk V.
Nuclear Weapons Stockpile.—Madelyn R. Creedon.
Pay and Benefits: Jonathan D. Clark, Gerald J. Leeling.
Peacekeeping.—Michael J. Kuiken, William G.P. Monahan.
POW/MIA Issues.—Jonathan D. Clark.
Personnel Protective Items.—John H. Quirk V.
Quadrennial Defense Review (QDR).—William K. Sutey.
Readiness/O&M.—John H. Quirk V.
Reprogramming.—Roy F. Phillips.
Science and Technology.—Arun A. Seraphin.
Sexual Harassment/Sexual Assault Policy: Gerald J. Leeling, Gabriella Eisen.
Shipbuilding Programs.—Creighton Greene.
Small Business: Peter K. Levine, Arun A. Seraphin.
Special Operations Forces.—Michael J. Noblet.
Stability Operations: Michael J. Kuiken, William G.P. Monahan.
Strategic Programs.—Madelyn R. Creedon.
Test and Evaluation: Peter K. Levine, Arun A. Seraphin.
Transportation and Logistics Policy.—Creighton Greene.
Unmanned Aircraft Systems: Creighton Greene, Thomas K. McConnell.
Working Capital Fund.—John H. Quirk V.
Women in Combat: Jonathan D. Clark, Gerald J. Leeling.

Wounded Warrior Issues.— Gerald J. Leeling, Gabriella Eisen.

Minority Professional Staff Members for—

Acquisition and Contracting Policy: Pablo E. Carrillo, Christopher J. Paul.

Air Force Programs, Readiness, and Operations and Maintenance: Pablo E. Carrillo, Christopher J. Paul.

Arms Control and Non-proliferation.—Dana W. White.

Army Programs, Readiness, and Operations and Maintenance.—Adam J. Barker.

Budget and Reprogramming.—Lucian L. Niemeyer.

Chemical-Biological Defense.—Adam J. Barker.

Chemical-Demilitarization.—Dana W. White.

Civilian Personnel.—Diana G. Tabler.

Combatant Commands.—

AFRICOM.—Dana W. White.

CENTCOM.—Michael V. Kostiw.

EUCOM.—Dana W. White.

JFCOM.—Church Hutton.

NORTHCOM.—Adam J. Barker.

PACOM.—Dana W. White.

SOCOM.—Adam J. Barker.

SOUTHCOM.—Dana W. White.

STRATCOM.—Daniel A. Lerner.

TRANSCOM.—Christopher J. Paul.

Counterdrug Programs.—Dana W. White.

Defense Security Assistance.—Dana W. White.

Depot Maintenance.—Lucian L. Niemeyer.

Detainees and Military Commissions: Pablo E. Carrillo, Richard Fontaine, David M. Morriss, Christopher J. Paul.

Department of Energy National Security Programs.—Daniel A. Lerner.

Environmental Issues.—David M. Morriss.

Export Controls.—Dana W. White.

Health Care.—Diana G. Tabler.

Homeland Defense—Adam J. Barker.

Information Assurance and Cyber Security.—Church Hutton.

Information Technology.—Church Hutton.

Intelligence Programs.—Michael V. Kostiw.

Laboratories.—Church Hutton.

Marine Corps Programs, Readiness, and Operations and Maintenance.—David M. Morriss.

Military Construction and BRAC.—Lucian L. Niemeyer.

Military Personnel and Family Benefits: Diana G. Tabler, Richard F. Walsh.

Missile Defense.—Daniel A. Lerner.

National Military Strategy.—Richard H. Fontaine.

Navy Programs, Readiness, and Operations and Maintenance: Pablo E. Carrillo, Christopher J. Paul.

Nominations.—Richard F. Walsh.

Oversight Investigations: Pablo E. Carrillo, Christopher J. Paul.

Science and Technology.—Church Hutton.

Space Programs.—Daniel A. Lerner.

Special Operations Forces.—Adam J. Barker.

Test and Evaluation.—Church Hutton.

Banking, Housing, and Urban Affairs

534 Dirksen Senate Office Building 20510

phone 224–7391, http://banking.senate.gov

Christopher J. Dodd, of Connecticut, *Chair*

Tim Johnson, of South Dakota.
Jack Reed, of Rhode Island.
Charles E. Schumer, of New York.
Evan Bayh, of Indiana.
Robert Menendez, of New Jersey.
Daniel K. Akaka, of Hawaii.
Sherrod Brown, of Ohio.
Jon Tester, of Montana.
Herb Kohl, of Wisconsin.
Mark R. Warner, of Virginia.
Jeff Merkley, of Oregon.
Michael F. Bennet, of Colorado.

Richard C. Shelby, of Alabama.
Robert F. Bennett, of Utah.
Jim Bunning, of Kentucky.
Mike Crapo, of Idaho.
Bob Corker, of Tennessee.
Jim DeMint, of South Carolina.
David Vitter, of Louisiana.
Mike Johanns, of Nebraska.
Kay Bailey Hutchison, of Texas.
Judd Gregg, of New Hampshire.

SUBCOMMITTEES

[The chairman and ranking minority member are ex officio members of all subcommittees.]

Economic Policy

Sherrod Brown, of Ohio, *Chair*

Jon Tester, of Montana.
Jeff Merkley, of Oregon.
Christopher J. Dodd, of Connecticut.

Jim DeMint, of South Carolina.

Financial Institutions

Tim Johnson, of South Dakota, *Chair*

Jack Reed, of Rhode Island.
Charles E. Schumer, of New York.
Evan Bayh, of Indiana.
Robert Menendez, of New Jersey.
Daniel K. Akaka, of Hawaii.
Jon Tester, of Montana.
Herb Kohl, of Wisconsin.
Jeff Merkley, of Oregon.
Michael F. Bennet, of Colorado.

Mike Crapo, of Idaho.
Robert F. Bennett, of Utah.
Kay Bailey Hutchison, of Texas.
Jim Bunning, of Kentucky.
Bob Corker, of Tennessee.
Jim DeMint, of South Carolina.

Housing, Transportation, and Community Development

Robert Menendez, of New Jersey, *Chair*

Tim Johnson, of South Dakota.
Jack Reed, of Rhode Island.
Charles E. Schumer, of New York.
Daniel K. Akaka, of Hawaii.
Sherrod Brown, of Ohio.
Jon Tester, of Montana.
Herb Kohl, of Wisconsin.
Mark R. Warner, of Virginia.
Jeff Merkley, of Oregon.

David Vitter, of Louisiana.
Kay Bailey Hutchison, of Texas.
Robert F. Bennett, of Utah.
Mike Johanns, of Nebraska.
Mike Crapo, of Idaho.
Jim DeMint, of South Carolina.

Securities, Insurance, and Investment

Jack Reed, of Rhode Island, *Chair*

Tim Johnson, of South Dakota.
Charles E. Schumer, of New York.
Evan Bayh, of Indiana.
Robert Menendez, of New Jersey.
Daniel K. Akaka, of Hawaii.
Sherrod Brown, of Ohio.
Mark R. Warner, of Virginia.
Michael F. Bennet, of Colorado.
Christopher J. Dodd, of Connecticut.

Jim Bunning, of Kentucky.
Robert F. Bennett, of Utah.
Mike Crapo, of Idaho.
David Vitter, of Louisiana.
Mike Johanns, of Nebraska.
Bob Corker, of Tennessee.

Security and International Trade and Finance

Evan Bayh, of Indiana, *Chair*

Herb Kohl, of Wisconsin.
Mark R. Warner, of Virginia.
Michael F. Bennet, of Colorado.
Christopher J. Dodd, of Connecticut.

Bob Corker, of Tennessee.
Mike Johanns, of Nebraska.

STAFF

Committee on Banking, Housing, and Urban Affairs (SD–534), 224–7391.
Majority Staff Director.—Edward Silverman.
Chief Counsel.—Amy Friend.
Senior Counsel.—Dean Shahinian.
Counsels: Catherine Galicia, Lynsey Graham Rea.
Research Director.—Peter Bondi.
Senior Policy Advisors: Julie Chon, Charles Yi, Mitch Warren.
Legislative Assistants: Drew Colbert, Brian Filipowich, Lisa Frumin, Misha Mintz-Roth.
Professional Staff Members: Beth Cooper, Joe Hepp, Colin McGinnis, Jonathan Miller, Neal Orringer.
Communications Director.—Kirstin Brost.
Press Secretary.—Justine Sessions.
Chief Economist.—Marc Jarsulic.
FTA Fellow.—Bonnie Graves.
FDIC Detailee.—Matthew Green.
CRS Detailee.—Mark Jickling.
OCC Detailee.—Deborah Katz.
Subcommittee Staff Directors:
Economic Policy.—Chris Slevin.
Financial Institutions.—Laura Swanson.
Housing, Transportation, and Community Development.—Michael Passante.
Securities, Insurance, and Investment.—Kara Stein.
Security and International Trade and Finance.—Ellen Chube.
Minority Staff Director and Chief Counsel.—William Duhnke.
Minority Deputy Staff Director and Chief Counsel.—Mark Oesterle.
Senior Counsel.—Andrew Olmem, Hester Peirce.
Counsels: Jim Johnson, Jeff Stoltzfoos.
Special Counsel.—Heath Tarbert.
Senior Investigative Counsel.—John O'Hara.
Senior Economist.—Mike Piwowar.
Chief Economist.—Jeff Wrase.
Professional Staff Members: Chad Davis, Shannon Hines, Rhyse Nance, Mike Nielsen, Emily Pereira.
Chief Clerk.—Dawn L. Ratliff.
Hearing Clerk.—Devin Hartley.
IT Director.—Shelvin Simmons.
Staff Assistant.—Pamela Streeter.
Editorial Assistant.—Jim Crowell.

Budget

624 Dirksen Senate Office Building 20510–6100

phone 224–0642, http://budget.senate.gov

meets first Thursday of each month

Kent Conrad, of North Dakota, *Chair*

Patty Murray, of Washington.
Ron Wyden, of Oregon.
Russell D. Feingold, of Wisconsin.
Robert C. Byrd, of West Virginia.
Bill Nelson, of Florida.
Debbie Stabenow, of Michigan.
Robert Menendez, of New Jersey.
Benjamin L. Cardin, of Maryland.
BERNARD SANDERS, of Vermont.
Sheldon Whitehouse, of Rhode Island.
Mark R. Warner, of Virginia.
Jeff Merkley, of Oregon.

Judd Gregg, of New Hampshire.
Chuck Grassley, of Iowa.
Michael B. Enzi, of Wyoming.
Jeff Sessions, of Alabama.
Jim Bunning, of Kentucky.
Mike Crapo, of Idaho.
John Ensign, of Nevada.
John Cornyn, of Texas.
Lindsey Graham, of South Carolina.
Lamar Alexander, of Tennessee.

(No Subcommittees)

STAFF

Committee on Budget (SD–624), 224–0642.
Majority Staff Director.—Mary Naylor, 4–0862.
Deputy Staff Directors: Joel Friedman, 4–0538; John Righter, 4–0544.
General Counsel.—Joe Gaeta, 4–2757.
Senior Analyst for—
Revenues.—Steve Bailey, 4–2835.
Analyst for—
Budget: Robyn Hiestand, 4–9731; Mah Mohning, 4–0061; John Fuher, 4–9484.
Health Care.—Purva Rawal, 4–5369.
Income Security, Medicaid.—Jim Esquea, 4–5811.
Justice, Homeland Security, Community, and Regional Development.—Mike Jones, 4–0833.
National Security and International Affairs, National Security.—Russell Rumbaugh, 4–0872.
Social Security and Medicare.—Sarah Kuehl, 4–0559.
Executive Assistant.—Anne Page, 4–0533.
Communications Director.—Stu Nagurka, 4–7436.
Deputy Communications Director.—Steve Posner, 4–7925.
Graphics Production Coordinator.—Kobye Noel, 4–3728.
Chief Economist.—Jim Klumpner, Matt Salomon, 4–6588.
Staff Assistants: Josh Ryan, 4–0581; Ben Soskin, 4–0547; Ronald Storhaug, 4–0837.
Minority Staff Director.—Cheri Reidy, 4–0557.
Deputy Staff Director.—Denzel McGuire, 8–5846.
Counsel.—Allison Parent, 4–0857.
Communications Director.—Betsy Holahan, 4–6011.
Chief Economist.—Jim Carter, 4–0536.
Executive Assistant.—Kim Proctor, 4–8695.
Director for—
Federal Programs and Budget Process.—Jim Hearn, 4–2370.
Health Policy.—David Fisher, 2–6988.
Professional Staff: Winnie Chang, 4–1602; Nicole Foltz, 4–0838; Matt Giroux, 4–8583; Jeff Gonzalez, 4–2586; Giovanni Gutierrez, 4–0865; Gordon Gray, 4–5846; Mike Lofgren, 4–9373; David Myers, 4–0843; Elizabeth Wore, 4–6744.
Senior Analyst for—
Budget Review.—Rodger Mahan, 4–0564.
Analyst for—
Energy, Natural Resources, and Agriculture.—Adam Hechavarria, 4–4471.
Science and Technology.—Greg McNeill, 4–3023.

Non-designated:
Chief Clerk.—Lynne Seymour, 4–0191.
Computer Systems Administrator.—George Woodall, 4–6576.
Publications Department.—Letitia Fletcher, 4–0855.
Staff Assistants: Samuel Armocido, 4–0796; Dylan Morris, 4–0565.

Commerce, Science, and Transportation

508 Dirksen Senate Office Building 20510–6125

phone 224–5115, TTY / TDD 224–8418 http://commerce.senate.gov

meets first and third Tuesdays of each month

John D. Rockefeller IV, of West Virginia, *Chair*

Daniel K. Inouye, of Hawaii.
John F. Kerry, of Massachusetts.
Byron L. Dorgan, of North Dakota.
Barbara Boxer, of California.
Bill Nelson, of Florida.
Maria Cantwell, of Washington.
Frank R. Lautenberg, of New Jersey.
Mark L. Pryor, of Arkansas.
Claire McCaskill, of Missouri.
Amy Klobuchar, of Minnesota.
Tom Udall, of New Mexico.
Mark R. Warner, of Virginia.
Mark Begich, of Alaska.

Kay Bailey Hutchison, of Texas.
Olympia J. Snowe, of Maine.
John Ensign, of Nevada.
Jim DeMint, of South Carolina.
John Thune, of South Dakota.
Roger F. Wicker, of Mississippi.
George S. LeMieux, of Florida.
Johnny Isakson, of Georgia.
David Vitter, of Louisiana.
Sam Brownback, of Kansas.
Mike Johanns, of Nebraska.

SUBCOMMITTEES

[The chair and the vice chair are ex officio members of all subcommittees.]

Aviation Operations, Safety, and Security

Byron L. Dorgan, of North Dakota, *Chair*

Daniel K. Inouye, of Hawaii.
John F. Kerry, of Massachusetts.
Barbara Boxer, of California.
Bill Nelson, of Florida.
Maria Cantwell, of Washington.
Frank R. Lautenberg, of New Jersey.
Mark L. Pryor, of Arkansas.
Claire McCaskill, of Missouri.
Amy Klobuchar, of Minnesota.
Mark R. Warner, of Virginia.
Mark Begich, of Alaska.

Jim DeMint, of South Carolina.
Olympia J. Snowe, of Maine.
John Ensign, of Nevada.
John Thune, of South Dakota.
Roger F. Wicker, of Mississippi.
George S. LeMieux, of Florida.
Johnny Isakson, of Georgia.
David Vitter, of Louisiana.
Sam Brownback, of Kansas.
Mike Johanns, of Nebraska.

Communications and Technology, and the Internet

John F. Kerry, of Massachusetts, *Chair*

Daniel K. Inouye, of Hawaii.
Byron L. Dorgan, of North Dakota.
Bill Nelson, of Florida.
Maria Cantwell, of Washington.
Frank R. Lautenberg, of New Jersey.
Mark L. Pryor, of Arkansas.
Claire McCaskill, of Missouri.
Amy Klobuchar, of Minnesota.
Tom Udall, of New Mexico.
Mark R. Warner, of Virginia.
Mark Begich, of Alaska.

John Ensign, of Nevada.
Olympia J. Snowe, of Maine.
Jim DeMint, of South Carolina.
John Thune, of South Dakota.
Roger F. Wicker, of Mississippi.
George S. LeMieux, of Florida.
Johnny Isakson, of Georgia.
David Vitter, of Louisiana.
Sam Brownback, of Kansas.
Mike Johanns, of Nebraska.

Competitiveness, Innovation, and Export Promotion

Amy Klobuchar, of Minnesota, *Chair*

John F. Kerry, of Massachusetts.
Byron L. Dorgan, of North Dakota.
Claire McCaskill, of Missouri.
Tom Udall, of New Mexico.
Mark R. Warner, of Virginia.
Mark Begich, of Alaska.

George S. LeMieux, of Florida.
John Ensign, of Nevada.
Jim DeMint, of South Carolina.
John Thune, of South Dakota.
Sam Brownback, of Kansas.
Mike Johanns, of Nebraska.

Consumer Protection, Product Safety, and Insurance

Mark L. Pryor, of Arkansas, *Chair*

Byron L. Dorgan, of North Dakota.
Barbara Boxer, of California.
Bill Nelson, of Florida.
Claire McCaskill, of Missouri.
Amy Klobuchar, of Minnesota.
Tom Udall, of New Mexico.

Roger F. Wicker, of Mississippi.
Olympia J. Snowe, of Maine.
Jim DeMint, of South Carolina.
John Thune, of South Dakota.
Johnny Isakson, of Georgia.
David Vitter, of Louisiana.

Oceans, Atmosphere, Fisheries, and Coast Guard

Maria Cantwell, of Washington, *Chair*

Daniel K. Inouye, of Hawaii.
John F. Kerry, of Massachusetts.
Barbara Boxer, of California.
Frank R. Lautenberg, of New Jersey.
Mark Begich, of Alaska.

Olympia J. Snowe, of Maine.
Roger F. Wicker, of Mississippi.
George S. LeMieux, of Florida.
Johnny Isakson, of Georgia.
David Vitter, of Louisiana.

Science and Space

Bill Nelson, of Florida, *Chair*

Daniel K. Inouye, of Hawaii.
John F. Kerry, of Massachusetts.
Barbara Boxer, of California.
Mark L. Pryor, of Arkansas.
Tom Udall, of New Mexico.
Mark R. Warner, of Virginia.

David Vitter, of Louisiana.
Olympia J. Snowe, of Maine.
John Ensign, of Nevada.
John Thune, of South Dakota.
Johnny Isakson, of Georgia.
Mike Johanns, of Nebraska.

Surface Transportation and Merchant Marine Infrastructure, Safety, and Security

Frank R. Lautenberg, of New Jersey, *Chair*

Daniel K. Inouye, of Hawaii.
John F. Kerry, of Massachusetts.
Byron L. Dorgan, of North Dakota.
Barbara Boxer, of California.
Maria Cantwell, of Washington.
Mark L. Pryor, of Arkansas.
Tom Udall, of New Mexico.
Mark R. Warner, of Virginia.
Mark Begich, of Alaska.

John Thune, of South Dakota.
Olympia J. Snowe, of Maine.
John Ensign, of Nevada.
Jim DeMint, of South Carolina.
Roger F. Wicker, of Mississippi.
Johnny Isakson, of Georgia.
David Vitter, of Louisiana.
Sam Brownback, of Kansas.
Mike Johanns, of Nebraska.

STAFF

Committee on Commerce, Science, and Transportation (SD–508), 224–5115.
Majority Staff Director.—Ellen Doneski.
Deputy Staff Director.—James Reid.
General Counsel.—Bruce Andrews.
Senior Climate Advisor.—Tom Dower.
Communications Director.—Jamie Smith.
Deputy Communications Director.—Jena Longo.

Press Assistant.—Charles Stewart.
Director of Operations, Special Assistant.—Vanessa Jones.
Staff Assistants: Tyler Roth, Taylor Woods.
Oversight and Investigations Office:
Chief Investigator.—John Williams.
Counsel.—Erik Jones.
Professional Staff.—Jeff Zubricki.
Investigator.—Jackson Eaton.
Staff Assistant.—Anna Crane.
FTC Detailee.—Lisa Hone.
Minority Staff Director.—Ann Begeman (acting).
Chief Counsel.—Brian Hendricks.
Communications Director.—Joe Brenckle.
Executive Assistant.—Theresa Eugene.
Senior Counsel.—Todd Bertoson.
Nominations Clerk.—Becky Hooks.
TSA Detailee.—Pamela Friedmann.
Aviation Operations, Safety, and Security Staff
Majority Senior Professional Staff.—Gael Sullivan.
Professional Staff Member.—Rich Swayze.
FAA Detailee.—Jim Conneely.
Staff Assistant.—Adam Duffy.
Minority Senior Professional Staff.—Jarrod Thompson.
Professional Staff.—Tom Jones.
Staff Assistant.—Dan Neumann.
Communications, Technology, and the Internet Staff
Majority Senior Counsel.—Jessica Rosenworcel.
Counsel.—Alex Hoehn-Saric.
Staff Assistant.—Danielle Rodman.
Minority Counsel.—Brian Hendricks.
Professional Staff Member.—David Quinalty.
Competitiveness, Innovation, and Export Promotion Staff
Majority Senior Counsel.—David Strickland.
Counsels: Christian Fjeld, Matthew Morrissey.
Professional Staff.—Jared Bomberg.
Staff Assistant.—Natasha Mbabazi.
Minority Professional Staff.—Brian Carr.
Consumer Protection, Product Safety, and Insurance Staff
Majority Senior Counsel.—David Strickland.
Counsels: Christian Fjeld, Matthew Morrissey.
Professional Staff.—Jared Bomberg.
Staff Assistant.—Natasha Mbabazi.
Minority Professional Staff: Hugh Carroll, Becky Hooks.
Oceans, Atmosphere, Fisheries, and Coast Guard Staff
Majority Professional Staff.—Kris Sarri.
Counsel.—Jeff Lewis.
Staff Assistant.—Julie Hrdlicka.
Coast Guard Detailee.—Mike Sim.
Sea Grant Fellow.—Anne Cooper.
Minority Professional Staff.—Mike Conathan.
Staff Assistant.—Sara Gibson.
Coast Guard Fellow.—Paul Mehler.
Sea Grant Fellow.—Mark Gleason.
Science and Space Staff
Majority Professional Staff: Chan Lieu, Ann Zulkosky.
Staff Assistant.—Elizabeth Bacon.
AAAS Fellow.—Matt McMahon.
Minority Senior Advisor.—Jeff Bingham.
Professional Staff.—H.J. Derr.
Surface Transportation and Merchant Marine Infrastructure, Safety, and Security Staff
Majority Professional Staff: John Drake, Dabney Hegg.
Counsel.—Melissa Porter.
Staff Assistant.—Shira Bergstein.
MARAD Detailee.—Christopher Moore.
GAO Detailee.—Nancy Lueke.
Minority Professional Staff: Ann Begeman, Mary Phillips.
Staff Assistant.—Dan Neumann.

Bipartisan Staff:
Chief Clerk.—Anne Willis Hill.
Hearing Clerk.—Naomi Eskin.
Director, Information Technology.—Jonathan Bowen.
Editor.—Rebecca Kojm.
GPO Detailee.—Jacqueline Washington.
Bipartisan Staff, Legislative Counsel's Office:
Legislative Counsel.—Lloyd Ator.
Staff Assistant.—Christopher Knox.
Bipartisan Staff, Public Information Office:
Professional Staff.—Robert Foster.
Public Information Staff.—Yvonne Gowdy.
Staff Assistant.—Stephanie Lieu.

Energy and Natural Resources

304 Dirksen Senate Office Building 20510

phone 224–4971, fax 224–6163, http://energy.senate.gov

meets upon call of the chair

Jeff Bingaman, of New Mexico, *Chair*

Byron L. Dorgan, of North Dakota.
Ron Wyden, of Oregon.
Tim Johnson, of South Dakota.
Mary L. Landrieu, of Louisiana.
Maria Cantwell, of Washington.
Robert Menendez, of New Jersey.
Blanche L. Lincoln, of Arkansas.
BERNARD SANDERS, of Vermont.
Evan Bayh, of Indiana.
Debbie Stabenow, of Michigan.
Mark Udall, of Colorado.
Jeanne Shaheen, of New Hampshire.

Lisa Murkowski, of Alaska.
Richard Burr, of North Carolina.
John Barrasso, of Wyoming.
Sam Brownback, of Kansas.
James E. Risch, of Idaho.
John McCain, of Arizona.
Robert F. Bennett, of Utah.
Jim Bunning, of Kentucky.
Jeff Sessions, of Alabama.
Bob Corker, of Tennessee.

SUBCOMMITTEES

[The chairman and the ranking minority member are ex officio members of all subcommittees.]

Energy

Maria Cantwell, of Washington, *Chair*

Byron L. Dorgan, of North Dakota.
Ron Wyden, of Oregon.
Mary L. Landrieu, of Louisiana.
Robert Menendez, of New Jersey.
BERNARD SANDERS, of Vermont.
Evan Bayh, of Indiana.
Debbie Stabenow, of Michigan.
Mark Udall, of Colorado.
Jeanne Shaheen, of New Hampshire.

James E. Risch, of Idaho.
Richard Burr, of North Carolina.
John Barrasso, of Wyoming.
Sam Brownback, of Kansas.
Robert F. Bennett, of Utah.
Jim Bunning, of Kentucky.
Jeff Sessions, of Alabama.
Bob Corker, of Tennessee.

National Parks

Mark Udall, of Colorado, *Chair*

Byron L. Dorgan, of North Dakota.
Mary L. Landrieu, of Louisiana.
Robert Menendez, of New Jersey.
Blanche L. Lincoln, of Arkansas.
BERNARD SANDERS, of Vermont.
Evan Bayh, of Indiana.
Debbie Stabenow, of Michigan.

Richard Burr, of North Carolina.
John Barrasso, of Wyoming.
Sam Brownback, of Kansas.
John McCain, of Arizona.
Jim Bunning, of Kentucky.
Bob Corker, of Tennessee.

Public Lands and Forests

Ron Wyden, of Oregon, *Chair*

Tim Johnson, of South Dakota.
Mary L. Landrieu, of Louisiana.
Maria Cantwell, of Washington.
Robert Menendez, of New Jersey.
Blanche L. Lincoln, of Arkansas.
Mark Udall, of Colorado.
Jeanne Shaheen, of New Hampshire.

John Barrasso, of Wyoming.
James E. Risch, of Idaho.
John McCain, of Arizona.
Robert F. Bennett, of Utah.
Jeff Sessions, of Alabama.
Bob Corker, of Tennessee.

Water and Power

Debbie Stabenow, of Michigan, *Chair*

Byron L. Dorgan, of North Dakota.
Tim Johnson, of South Dakota.
Maria Cantwell, of Washington.
Blanche L. Lincoln, of Arkansas.
BERNARD SANDERS, of Vermont.
Evan Bayh, of Indiana.
Jeanne Shaheen, of New Hampshire.
Sam Brownback, of Kansas.
James E. Risch, of Idaho.
John McCain, of Arizona.
Robert F. Bennett, of Utah.
Jim Bunning, of Kentucky.
Jeff Sessions, of Alabama.

STAFF

Committee on Energy and Natural Resources (SD–304), 224–4971, fax 224–6163.
Majority Staff Director.—Bob Simon.
Administrator Director.—Nancy Hall.
Chief Counsel.—Sam Fowler.
Senior Counsels: Patty Beneke, David Brooks, Deborah Estes, Linda Lance.
Counsels: Michael Carr, Scott Miller, Tanya Trujillo.
Chief Clerk.—Mia Bennett.
Executive Assistant.—Amanda Kelly.
Systems Administrator.—Dawson Foard.
Communications Director.—Bill Wicker.
Press Secretary.—David Marks.
Professional Staff: Allyson Anderson, Tara Billingsley, Jonathan Black, Jonathan Epstein, Alicia Jackson, Leon Lowery, Kevin Rennert, Al Stayman, Sara Tucker.
Legislative Aide.—Jorge Silva-Banuelos.
Staff Assistants: Rosemarie Calabro, Abigail Campbell, Allison Seyferth, Gina Weinstock.
Calendar Clerk.—Amber Passmore.
Printer/Editors: Monica Chestnut, Wanda Green.
Receptionist.—Meagan Gins.
Minority Staff Director.—McKie Campbell.
Chief Counsel.—Karen Billups.
Deputy Chief Counsel.—Kellie Donnelly.
Counsels: Isaac Edwards, Kaleb Froehlich, Kevin Simpson.
Executive Assistant.—Megan Hermann.
Communications Director.—Robert Dillon.
Press Secretary.—Anne Johnson.
Professional Staff: Frank Gladics, Colin Hayes, Josh Johnson, Chuck Kleeschulte.
Legislative Aides: Whitney Drew, Brian Hughes.
Staff Assistant.—Kari Smith.

Environment and Public Works

410 Dirksen Senate Office Building 20510–6175

phone 224–6176, www.senate.gov/~epw

meets first and third Thursdays of each month

Barbara Boxer, of California, *Chair*

Max Baucus, of Montana.
Thomas R. Carper, of Delaware.
Frank R. Lautenberg, of New Jersey.
Benjamin L. Cardin, of Maryland.
BERNARD SANDERS, of Vermont.
Amy Klobuchar, of Minnesota.
Sheldon Whitehouse, of Rhode Island.
Tom Udall, of New Mexico.
Jeff Merkley, of Oregon.
Kirsten E. Gillibrand, of New York.
Arlen Specter, of Pennsylvania.

James M. Inhofe, of Oklahoma.
George V. Voinovich, of Ohio.
David Vitter, of Louisiana.
John Barrasso, of Wyoming.
Mike Crapo, of Idaho.
Christopher S. Bond, of Missouri.
Lamar Alexander, of Tennessee.

SUBCOMMITTEES

[The chairman and the ranking minority member are ex officio (non-voting) members of all subcommittees on which they do not serve.]

Children's Health

Amy Klobuchar, of Minnesota, *Chair*

Tom Udall, of New Mexico.
Jeff Merkley, of Oregon.
Arlen Specter, of Pennsylvania.

Lamar Alexander, of Tennessee.
David Vitter, of Louisiana.

Clean Air and Nuclear Safety

Thomas R. Carper, of Delaware, *Chair*

Max Baucus, of Montana.
Benjamin L. Cardin, of Maryland.
BERNARD SANDERS, of Vermont.
Jeff Merkley, of Oregon.

David Vitter, of Louisiana.
George V. Voinovich, of Ohio.
Christopher S. Bond, of Missouri.

Green Jobs and the New Economy

BERNARD SANDERS, of Vermont, *Chair*

Thomas R. Carper, of Delaware.
Kirsten E. Gillibrand, of New York.

Christopher S. Bond, of Missouri.
George V. Voinovich, of Ohio.

Oversight

Sheldon Whitehouse, of Rhode Island, *Chair*

Tom Udall, of New Mexico.
Kirsten E. Gillibrand, of New York.

John Barrasso, of Wyoming.
David Vitter, of Louisiana.

Superfund, Toxics and Environmental Health

Frank R. Lautenberg, of New Jersey, *Chair*

Max Baucus, of Montana.
Amy Klobuchar, of Minnesota.
Sheldon Whitehouse, of Rhode Island.
Kirsten E. Gillibrand, of New York.
Arlen Specter, of Pennsylvania.
David Vitter, of Louisiana.
George V. Voinovich, of Ohio.
Christopher S. Bond, of Missouri.

Transportation and Infrastructure

Max Baucus, of Montana, *Chair*

Thomas R. Carper, of Delaware.
Frank R. Lautenberg, of New Jersey.
Benjamin L. Cardin, of Maryland.
BERNARD SANDERS, of Vermont.
Amy Klobuchar, of Minnesota.
Arlen Specter, of Pennsylvania.
George V. Voinovich, of Ohio.
David Vitter, of Louisiana.
John Barrasso, of Wyoming.
Mike Crapo, of Idaho.

Water and Wildlife

Benjamin L. Cardin, of Maryland, *Chair*

Frank R. Lautenberg, of New Jersey.
Sheldon Whitehouse, of Rhode Island.
Tom Udall, of New Mexico.
Jeff Merkley, of Oregon.
Mike Crapo, of Idaho.
John Barrasso, of Wyoming.
Lamar Alexander, of Tennessee.

STAFF

Committee on Environment and Public Works (SD–410), phone 224–8832; Majority fax (SD–410), 224–1273; (SH–508), 228–0574.
Majority Staff Director/Chief Counsel.—Bettina Poirier.
Majority Senior Counsels: Grant Cope, Thomas Fox, Joe Goffman, Jessica Holliday, James Wrathall.
Counsels: Alyson Cooke, Tyler Rushforth.
Majority Senior Policy Advisor.—Susan Binder.
Majority Senior Policy Director for Transportation.—Katherine Dedrick.
Office Manager.—Carolyn Mack.
Chief Clerk.—Alicia Gordon.
System Administrator.—Rae Ann Phipps.
Communications Director.—Peter Rafle.
Professional Staff Members: Jason Albritton, Eric Thu.
Editorial Director.—Stephen Chapman.
GPO Detailees: LaVern Finks, Brenda Samuels.
Staff Assistants: Javier Gamboa, Heather Majors, Nathan McCray.
Majority Press Assistant.—Anne Collesano.
Majority Special Assistant.—Paul Ordal.
Majority Press Secretary.—Kate Gilman.
Detailees: Lea Anderson, Katie Umekubo.
Majority Senior Investigator.—Robert Tanner.
Research Assistant.—Ashley Harvard.
Majority Intern.—Katie Lee.
Minority fax (SD–456), 224–1273; (SH–508), 228–0574.
Minority Staff Director.—Ruth Van Mark.
Deputy Staff Director.—Mike Catanzaro.
Communications Director.— Matt Dempsey.
Executive/Research Assistant.—Elizabeth Fox.
Counsels: George Sugiyama, Tom Hassenboehler, Matthew Hite, Adcock Rebeckah.
Senior Economist.—James O'Keeffe.
Professional Staff Members: Dan Barron, Annie Caputo, Alex Herrgott, Angelina Giancarlo.
Minority Deputy Press Secretary.—David Lungren.
Research Assistants: Alex Renjel, Scott Smith, Dimitri Karakitsos.
Staff Assistant.—Jonathan Hackett.

Finance

219 Dirksen Senate Office Building 20510

phone 224–4515, fax 224–0554, http://finance.senate.gov

meets second and fourth Tuesdays of each month

Max Baucus, of Montana, *Chair*

John D. Rockefeller IV, of West Virginia.
Kent Conrad, of North Dakota.
Jeff Bingaman, of New Mexico.
John F. Kerry, of Massachusetts.
Blanche L. Lincoln, of Arkansas.
Ron Wyden, of Oregon.
Charles E. Schumer, of New York.
Debbie Stabenow, of Michigan.
Maria Cantwell, of Washington.
Bill Nelson, of Florida.
Robert Menendez, of New Jersey.
Thomas R. Carper, of Delaware.

Chuck Grassley, of Iowa.
Orrin G. Hatch, of Utah.
Olympia J. Snowe, of Maine.
Jon Kyl, of Arizona.
Jim Bunning, of Kentucky.
Mike Crapo, of Idaho.
Pat Roberts, of Kansas.
John Ensign, of Nevada.
Michael B. Enzi, of Wyoming.
John Cornyn, of Texas.

SUBCOMMITTEES

[The chairman and the ranking minority member are ex officio (non-voting) members of all subcommittees on which they do not serve.]

Energy, Natural Resources, and Infrastructure

Jeff Bingaman, of New Mexico, *Chair*

Kent Conrad, of North Dakota.
John F. Kerry, of Massachusetts.
Blanche L. Lincoln, of Arkansas.
Debbie Stabenow, of Michigan.
Maria Cantwell, of Washington.
Bill Nelson, of Florida.
Thomas R. Carper, of Delaware.

Jim Bunning, of Kentucky.
Mike Crapo, of Idaho.
John Cornyn, of Texas.
Orrin G. Hatch, of Utah.
Michael B. Enzi, of Wyoming.

Health Care

John D. Rockefeller IV, of West Virginia, *Chair*

Jeff Bingaman, of New Mexico.
John F. Kerry, of Massachusetts.
Blanche L. Lincoln, of Arkansas.
Ron Wyden, of Oregon.
Charles E. Schumer, of New York.
Debbie Stabenow, of Michigan.
Maria Cantwell, of Washington.
Bill Nelson, of Florida.
Robert Menendez, of New Jersey.
Thomas R. Carper, of Delaware.

Orrin G. Hatch, of Utah.
Olympia J. Snowe, of Maine.
John Ensign, of Nevada.
Michael B. Enzi, of Wyoming.
John Cornyn, of Texas.
Jon Kyl, of Arizona.
Jim Bunning, of Kentucky.
Mike Crapo, of Idaho.

International Trade, and Global Competitiveness

Ron Wyden, of Oregon, *Chair*

John D. Rockefeller IV, of West Virginia.
Jeff Bingaman, of New Mexico.
John F. Kerry, of Massachusetts.
Debbie Stabenow, of Michigan.
Maria Cantwell, of Washington.
Robert Menendez, of New Jersey.

Mike Crapo, of Idaho.
Olympia J. Snowe, of Maine.
Jim Bunning, of Kentucky.
Pat Roberts, of Kansas.

Social Security, Pensions, and Family Policy

Blanche L. Lincoln, of Arkansas, *Chair*

John D. Rockefeller IV, of West Virginia.
Kent Conrad, of North Dakota.
Charles E. Schumer, of New York.
Bill Nelson, of Florida.

Pat Roberts, of Kansas.
Jon Kyl, of Arizona.
John Ensign, of Nevada.

Taxation and IRS Oversight and Long-Term Growth

Kent Conrad, of North Dakota, *Chair*

Max Baucus, of Montana.
John D. Rockefeller IV, of West Virginia.
Ron Wyden, of Oregon.
Charles E. Schumer, of New York.
Debbie Stabenow, of Michigan.
Maria Cantwell, of Washington.
Robert Menendez, of New Jersey.
Thomas R. Carper, of Delaware.

Jon Kyl, of Arizona.
Orrin G. Hatch, of Utah.
Olympia J. Snowe, of Maine.
Pat Roberts, of Kansas.
John Ensign, of Nevada.
Michael B. Enzi, of Wyoming.
John Cornyn, of Texas.

STAFF

Committee on Finance (SD–219), 224–4515, fax 228–0554.
Majority Staff Director.—Russ Sullivan.
Chief Counsel.—Bill Dauster.
Senior Advisor.—John Angell.
Counsel and Senior Advisor for Indian Affairs.—Richard Litsey.
Chief Tax.—Cathy Koch.
Tax Counsel.—Tiffany Smith.
Professional Staff: Shawn Bishop, Chris Dawe, Neleen Eisinger, Yvette Fontenot, Deidra Henry-Spires, Holly Porter, Chelsea Thomas.
Health Policy Advisor.—Kelly Whitener.
Health Counsel.—David Schwartz.
Senior Benefits Counsel.—Thomas Reeder.
Natural Resource Advisor.—Pat Bousliman.
Tax Research Assistant.—Kelcy Poulson.
Research Assistant.—Kerra Melvin.
Economic Development Advisor.—Joseph Adams.
Senior Business and Accounting Advisor.—David Hughes.
Investigator.—Christopher Law.
Tax Detailee.—Mary Baker.
Senior Counsel to Chairman and Chief Health Counsel.—Elizabeth Fowler.
Health Research Assistant.—Andrew Hu.
Chief International Trade Counsel.—Arnber Cottle.
Trade Counsels: Ayesha Khanna, Michael Smart.
International Trade Analyst.—Rory Murphy, Hun Quach.
International Trade Advisor.—Darci Vetter.
Trade Detailee.—Vacant.
Senior Budget Analyst.—Alan Cohen.
Professional Staff Social Security.—Tom Klouda.
Detailee.—Jason Carver.
Fellows: Scott Berkowitz, Hanada Miki, Laura Hoffmeister, Toni Miles.
Assistant to the Staff Director.—Jim Frisk.
Senior Advisor and Counsel.—Scott Mulhauser.
Press Secretaries: Erin Shields, Dan Virkstis.
Press Assistant.—Jennifer Donohue.
Press Detailees: Sarah Allen, Scott Allen.
Legislative Correspondent.—Matthew Slonaker.
Chief Editor.—Robert Merulla.
Editor.—Tim Danowski.
Chief Clerk.—Carla Martin.
Deputy Chief Clerk and Historian.—Josh Levasseur.
Deputy Clerk.—Mark Blair.
Hearing Clerk.—Jewel Harper.

Staff Assistants: Matt Schmechel, Challee Stefani, Erin Windauer.
IT Director.—Joe Carnucci.
Archivist.—Athena Schritz.
Minority Staff Director and Chief Counsel.—Kolan Davis.
Deputy Staff Director/Chief Tax Counsel.—Mark Prater.
Tax Counsels: Tony Coughlan, James Lyons, Theresa Pattara.
Tax and Benefits Counsel.—Christopher Condeluci.
Tax and Nomination Professional Staff.—Nick Wyatt.
Research Assistant.—Chris Colin.
Special Counsel and Chief Investigator.—Emilia DiSanto.
Senior Investigative Counsel.—Jason Foster.
Senior Health Investigative Counsel.—Angela Choy.
Investigators: Chris Armstrong, Melvin Feuerberg, Paul Thacker.
Investigative Assistant.—Brian Downey.
Health Policy Director and Chief Health Counsel.—Mark Hayes.
Health Policy Advisors: Michael Park, Becky Shipp, Susan Walden, Rodney Whitlock, Andrew Mckechnie.
Health Staff Assistant.—Kevin Courtois.
Chief International Trade Counsel.—Stephen Schaefer.
International Trade Counsel.—David Johanson, David Ross.
International Trade Policy Advisor.—Claudia Poteet.
Chief Social Security Analyst.—Steve Robinson.
Communications Director.—Jill Kozeny.
Press Secretary.—Jill Gerber.
Detailees: Sean Barnett, Kyle Burns, Randoe Dice, Chantal Matin, Preston Rutledge.
Fellows: Carolyn Coda, Terri Postma.

Foreign Relations

450 Dirksen Senate Office Building 20510–6225

phone 224–4651, http://foreign.senate.gov

meets each Tuesday

John F. Kerry, of Massachusetts, *Chair*

Christopher J. Dodd, of Connecticut.
Russell D. Feingold, of Wisconsin.
Barbara Boxer, of California.
Robert Menendez, of New Jersey.
Benjamin L. Cardin, of Maryland.
Robert P. Casey, Jr., of Pennsylvania.
Jim Webb, of Virginia.
Jeanne Shaheen, of New Hampshire.
Edward E. Kaufman, of Delaware.
Kirsten E. Gillibrand, of New York.

Richard G. Lugar, of Indiana.
Bob Corker, of Tennessee.
Johnny Isakson, of Georgia.
James E. Risch, of Idaho.
Jim DeMint, of South Carolina.
John Barrasso, of Wyoming.
Roger F. Wicker, of Mississippi.
James M. Inhofe, of Oklahoma.

SUBCOMMITTEES

[The chairman and ranking minority member are ex officio (non-voting) members of all subcommittees on which they do not serve.]

African Affairs

Russell D. Feingold, of Wisconsin, *Chair*

Benjamin L. Cardin, of Maryland.
Jim Webb, of Virginia.
Edward E. Kaufman, of Delaware.
Jeanne Shaheen, of New Hampshire.

Johnny Isakson, of Georgia.
Jim DeMint, of South Carolina.
Bob Corker, of Tennessee.
James M. Inhofe, of Oklahoma.

East Asian and Pacific Affairs

Jim Webb, of Virginia, *Chair*

Christopher J. Dodd, of Connecticut.
Russell D. Feingold, of Wisconsin.
Barbara Boxer, of California.
Robert P. Casey, Jr., of Pennsylvania.
Kirsten E. Gillibrand, of New York.

James M. Inhofe, of Oklahoma.
Johnny Isakson, of Georgia.
John Barrasso, of Wyoming.
Roger F. Wicker, of Mississippi.

European Affairs

Jeanne Shaheen, of New Hampshire, *Chair*

Christopher J. Dodd, of Connecticut.
Robert Menendez, of New Jersey.
Robert P. Casey, Jr., of Pennsylvania.
Jim Webb, of Virginia.
Edward E. Kaufman, of Delaware.

Jim DeMint, of South Carolina.
James E. Risch, of Idaho.
Bob Corker, of Tennessee.
Roger F. Wicker, of Mississippi.

International Development and Foreign Assistance, Economic Affairs and International Environmental Protection

Robert Menendez, of New Jersey, *Chair*

Barbara Boxer, of California.
Benjamin L. Cardin, of Maryland.
Robert P. Casey, Jr., of Pennsylvania.
Jeanne Shaheen, of New Hampshire.
Kirsten E. Gillibrand, of New York.

Bob Corker, of Tennessee.
Roger F. Wicker, of Mississippi.
Jim DeMint, of South Carolina.
James E. Risch, of Idaho.

International Operations and Organizations, Human Rights, Democracy and Global Women's Issues

Barbara Boxer, of California, *Chair*

Russell D. Feingold, of Wisconsin.
Robert Menendez, of New Jersey.
Edward E. Kaufman, of Delaware.
Jeanne Shaheen, of New Hampshire.
Kirsten E. Gillibrand, of New York.
Roger F. Wicker, of Mississippi.
Jim DeMint, of South Carolina.
John Barrasso, of Wyoming.
James M. Inhofe, of Oklahoma.

Near Eastern and South and Central Asian Affairs

Robert P. Casey, Jr., of Pennsylvania, *Chair*

Christopher J. Dodd, of Connecticut.
Russell D. Feingold, of Wisconsin.
Barbara Boxer, of California.
Benjamin L. Cardin, of Maryland.
Edward E. Kaufman, of Delaware.
James E. Risch, of Idaho.
Bob Corker, of Tennessee.
John Barrasso, of Wyoming.
Johnny Isakson, of Georgia.

Western Hemisphere, Peace Corps, and Global Narcotics Affairs

Christopher J. Dodd, of Connecticut, *Chair*

Robert Menendez, of New Jersey.
Benjamin L. Cardin, of Maryland.
Jim Webb, of Virginia.
Kirsten E. Gillibrand, of New York.
John Barrasso, of Wyoming.
Johnny Isakson, of Georgia.
James E. Risch, of Idaho.
James M. Inhofe, of Oklahoma.

STAFF

Committee on Foreign Relations (SD–446), 224–4651.
Majority Staff Director.—David McKean.
Deputy Staff Director and Chief Counsel.—Frank Lowenstein.
Counsel.—Robin Lerner.
Special Assistant.—Laura Sullivan.
Legislative Assistant.—Dillon Guthrie.
Legislative Research Assistant.—Andrew Imbrie.
Staff Assistants: Emily Mendrala, David Nibert, Andrew Winetroub.
Press Secretary.—Frederick Jones.
Deputy Press Secretary.—Tomeika Bowden.
Professional Staff: Fulton Armstrong, Daniel Benaim, Jonah Blank, Perry Cammack, Heidi Crebo-Rediker, Steven Feldstein, Kathleen Frangione, Douglas Frantz, Frank Jannuzi, John Kiriakou, Edward Levine, Nicholas Ma, Melanie Nakagawa, Shannon Smith, Fatema Sumar, Atman Trivedi, Anthony Wier, Laura Winthrop.
Minority Staff Director.—Kenneth A. Myers, Jr. 224–6797.
Deputy Staff Director.—Daniel C. Diller.
Press Secretary.—Andrew J. Fisher.
Minority Chief Counsel.—Michael Mattler.
Professional Staff: Jay Branegan, Shellie Bressler, Neil Brown, Paul Foldi, Patrick Garvey, Mark Helmke, Garrett Johnson, Keith Luse, Carl Meacham, Thomas Moore, Michael Phelan, Nilmini Rubin, Marik String, Connie Veillette, David Willkie.
Legislative Assistant.—Katie Lee, Kezia McKeague.
Staff Assistant.—Cory Gill.
Non-Designated Committee Staff (SD–446), 224–4651.
Office Manager.—Samantha Hamilton.
Chief Clerk.—Susan Oursler.
Deputy Chief Clerk.—Megan Moyerman.
Executive/Legislative Clerk.—Gail Coppage.
Director of Protocol/Foreign Travel.—Meg Murphy.
Hearing Coordinator.—Bertie H. Bowman.
Systems Administrator.—James Carter.
Staff Assistants: Barbara Allem, Matt Dixson, Brittney Opacak.
Archivist Research Assistant.—Deborah M. Johnson.
Printing Clerks: Betty Acton, Michael W. Bennett.

Health, Education, Labor, and Pensions

428 Dirksen Senate Office Building 20510–6300

phone 224–5375, http://help.senate.gov

meets second and fourth Wednesdays of each month

Tom Harkin, of Iowa, *Chair*

Christopher J. Dodd, of Connecticut.
Barbara A. Mikulski, of Maryland.
Jeff Bingaman, of New Mexico.
Patty Murray, of Washington.
Jack Reed, of Rhode Island.
BERNARD SANDERS, of Vermont.
Sherrod Brown, of Ohio.
Robert P. Casey, Jr., of Pennsylvania.
Kay R. Hagan, of North Carolina.
Jeff Merkley, of Oregon.
Al Franken, of Minnesota.
Michael F. Bennet, of Colorado.

Michael B. Enzi, of Wyoming.
Judd Gregg, of New Hampshire.
Lamar Alexander, of Tennessee.
Richard Burr, of North Carolina.
Johnny Isakson, of Georgia.
John McCain, of Arizona.
Orrin G. Hatch, of Utah.
Lisa Murkowski, of Alaska.
Tom Coburn, of Oklahoma.
Pat Roberts, of Kansas.

SUBCOMMITTEES

[The chairman and ranking minority member are ex officio members of all subcommittees on which they do not serve.]

* Children and Families [1]

Christopher J. Dodd, of Connecticut, *Chair*

Jeff Bingaman, of New Mexico.
Patty Murray, of Washington.
Jack Reed, of Rhode Island.
BERNARD SANDERS, of Vermont.
Sherrod Brown, of Ohio.
Robert P. Casey, Jr., of Pennsylvania.
Kay R. Hagan, of North Carolina.
Jeff Merkley, of Oregon.

Lamar Alexander, of Tennessee.
Judd Gregg, of New Hampshire.
John McCain, of Arizona.
Orrin G. Hatch, of Utah.
Lisa Murkowski, of Alaska.
Tom Coburn, of Oklahoma.
Pat Roberts, of Kansas.

Employment and Workplace Safety

Patty Murray, of Washington, *Chair*

Christopher J. Dodd, of Connecticut.
Tom Harkin, of Iowa.
Barbara A. Mikulski, of Maryland.
Sherrod Brown, of Ohio.
Kay R. Hagan, of North Carolina.
Jeff Merkley, of Oregon.
Al Franken, of Minnesota.

Johnny Isakson, of Georgia.
Judd Gregg, of New Hampshire.
Richard Burr, of North Carolina.
John McCain, of Arizona.
Orrin G. Hatch, of Utah.
Lisa Murkowski, of Alaska.

Retirement and Aging [1]

Barbara A. Mikulski, of Maryland, *Chair*

Tom Harkin, of Iowa.
Jeff Bingaman, of New Mexico.
Jack Reed, of Rhode Island.
BERNARD SANDERS, of Vermont.
Robert P. Casey, Jr., of Pennsylvania.
Al Franken, of Minnesota.

Richard Burr, of North Carolina.
Judd Gregg, of New Hampshire.
Lamar Alexander, of Tennessee.
Johnny Isakson, of Georgia.
Tom Coburn, of Oklahoma.

STAFF

Committee on Health, Education, Labor, and Pensions (SH–644), 224–0767, fax 224–6510, TDD 224–1975.

Staff Director/Chief Counsel.—Michael Myers, SD–644, 4–3961.

Chief Counsel on Policy.—Jeffrey Teitz, SD–644, 4–4781.

Policy Director for Disability and Special Needs Policy.—Connie Garner, SD–644, 4–6390.

Director, Economic Development.—Ron Carlton, SH–632, 4–2613.

Professional Staff Member.—Rick Alley, SH–527, 4–5094.

Senior Staff Assistant.—Shawn Daugherty, SD–644, 4–7751.

Executive Assistant to the Committee.—Terri Roney, SD–644, 4–5510.

Health Policy Office (4–7675)

Staff Director for Health.—David Bowen, SH–527, 4–5406.

Detailee.—Stacey Sachs, SD–644, 4–2236.

Staff Assistant for Health.—Andrea Harris, SH–527, 4–6065.

Senior Advisor on National Health Reform.—John McDonough, SH–527, 4–6840.

Deputy Staff Director for Health.—Tom Kraus, SH–527, 4–9154.

Deputy Staff Director for Health.—Topher Spiro, SH–527, 4–6064.

Health Policy Advisor.—Craig Martinez, SH–527, 4–9154.

Staff Assistant.—Andrew Garrett, SH–527, 4–6858.

Health Fellows: Caroline Fichtenberg, SH–527, 4–5307; Stephanie Hammonds, SH–527, 4–6366; Joe Hutter, SH–527, 4–5362; Taryn Morrissey, SH–527, 4–9157.

Detailee.—William McConagha, SH–527, 4–8409.

Education Policy Office 4–5501

Research Assistant.—Thomas Showalter, SH–615, 4–6061.

Staff Assistant.—Sarah Whitton, SH–615, 8–6685.

Education Policy Advisor.—Robin Juliano, SH–615, 4–2009.

Chief Education Counsel.—Bethany Little, SH–615, 4–9866.

Senior Education Policy Advisors: David Johns, SH–615, 8–6708; Luke Swarthout, SH–615, 4–9508.

Labor Policy Office 4–5441

Legislative Assistant.—Carmen Torres, SH–632, 4–5363.

Senior Labor and Employment Counsels: Livia Lam, SH–632, 4–6368; Lauren McFerran, SH–632, 4–2775.

Detaillee.—Debra Ford, SH–632, 4–1379.

General Counsel/Labor Policy Director.—Portia Wu, SH–632, 4–6572.

Subcommittee on Employment and Workplace Safety 4–2621 (personal office)

Subcommittee Staff Director.—Vacant, SH–143, 4–4925.

Professional Staff Members: Crystal Bridgeman, SH–143, 4–6695; Michael Waske, 4–2570.

Subcommittee on Children and Families 4–2623 (personal office)

Subcommittee Staff Director.—Jim Fenton, SH–404, 4–2823

Professional Staff Members: Tamar Magarik Haro, SH–404, 4–5484; Averi Pakulis, SH–404, 4–2831; Jeremy Sharp, SH–404, 4–0584.

Legislative Assistant.—Madeline Gitomer, SH–404, 4–0207.

Fellows: Joe Caldwell, SH–404, 4–6403; Monica Feit, SH–404, 4–8914.

Subcommittee on Retirement and Aging 4–9243

Subcommittee Staff Director.—Peter Ruben, SD–424, 4–7962.

Professional Staff Member.—Mona Shah, SD–424, 4–1493.

Disability 4–3254 (personal office)

Disability Counsel.—Lee Perselay, SH–607, 4–6201.

Legislative Assistant.—Jenelle Krishnomoorhty, Sara Selgrade, SH–607, 4–3254.

Judiciary Office 4–7229

Senior Counsels: Janice Kaguyutan, SH–632, 4–1897; Christine Leonard, SH–632, 4–7959.

Staff Assistant.—Sara Kingsley, SH–632, 4–5146.

---

[1] On January 31, 2007, the Committee was polled and agreed that the name of the Subcommittee on Education and Early Childhood Development would be changed to the Subcommittee on Children and Families, the Subcommittee on Retirement Security and Aging would be changed to the Subcommittee on Retirement and Aging, and that the Committee would discontinue the Subcommittee on Bioterrorism and Public Health Preparedness.

* Minority Subcommittee Member order corrected March 2007.

Homeland Security and Governmental Affairs

340 Dirksen Senate Office Building 20510

phone 224–2627, fax 228–3792, http://hsgac.senate.gov

Hearing Room—SD–342 Dirksen Senate Office Building

meets first Wednesday of each month

Joseph I. Lieberman, of Connecticut, *Chair*

Carl Levin, of Michigan.
Daniel K. Akaka, of Hawaii.
Thomas R. Carper, of Delaware.
Mark L. Pryor, of Arkansas.
Mary L. Landrieu, of Louisiana.
Claire McCaskill, of Missouri.
Jon Tester, of Montana.
Roland W. Burris, of Illinois.
Paul G. Kirk, Jr., of Massachusetts.

Susan M. Collins, of Maine.
Tom Coburn, of Oklahoma.
John McCain, of Arizona.
George V. Voinovich, of Ohio.
John Ensign, of Nevada.
Lindsey Graham, of South Carolina.
Robert F. Bennett, of Utah.

SUBCOMMITTEES

[The chairman and the ranking minority member are ex officio members of all subcommittees.]

Federal Financial Management, Government Information, Federal Services, and International Security (FFM)

Thomas R. Carper, of Delaware, *Chair*

Carl Levin, of Michigan.
Daniel K. Akaka, of Hawaii.
Mark L. Pryor, of Arkansas.
Claire McCaskill, of Missouri.
Roland W. Burris, of Illinois.

John McCain, of Arizona.
Tom Coburn, of Oklahoma.
George V. Voinovich, of Ohio.
John Ensign, of Nevada.

Oversight of Government Management, the Federal Workforce, and the District of Columbia (OGM)

Daniel K. Akaka, of Hawaii, *Chair*

Carl Levin, of Michigan.
Mary L. Landrieu, of Louisiana.
Roland W. Burris, of Illinois.
Paul G. Kirk, Jr., of Massachusetts.

George V. Voinovich, of Ohio.
Lindsey Graham, of South Carolina.
Robert F. Bennett, of Utah.

Permanent Subcommittee on Investigations (PSI)

Carl Levin, of Michigan, *Chair*

Thomas R. Carper, of Delaware.
Mark L. Pryor, of Arkansas.
Claire McCaskill, of Missouri.
Jon Tester, of Montana.
Paul G. Kirk, Jr., of Massachusetts.

Tom Coburn, of Oklahoma.
Susan M. Collins, of Maine.
John McCain, of Arizona.
John Ensign, of Nevada.

Ad Hoc Subcommittee on State, Local, and Private Sector Preparedness and Integration (SLPSPI)

Mark L. Pryor, of Arkansas, *Chair*

Daniel K. Akaka, of Hawaii.
Mary L. Landrieu, of Louisiana.
Jon Tester, of Montana.
John Ensign, of Nevada.
George V. Voinovich, of Ohio.
Lindsey Graham, of South Carolina.

Ad Hoc Subcommittee on Contracting Oversight (SCO)

Claire McCaskill, of Missouri, *Chair*

Carl Levin, of Michigan.
Thomas R. Carper, of Delaware.
Mark L. Pryor, of Arkansas.
Jon Tester, of Montana.
Paul G. Kirk, Jr., of Massachusetts.
Robert F. Bennett, of Utah.
Susan M. Collins, of Maine.
Tom Coburn, of Oklahoma.
John McCain, of Arizona.
Lindsey Graham, of South Carolina.

Ad Hoc Subcommittee on Disaster Recovery (SDR)

Mary L. Landrieu, of Louisiana, *Chair*

Claire McCaskill, of Missouri.
Roland W. Burris, of Illinois.
Lindsey Graham, of South Carolina.
Robert F. Bennett, of Utah.

STAFF

Committee on Homeland Security and Governmental Affairs (SD–340), 224–2627.
Majority Staff Director.—Michael Alexander.
Chief Counsel.—Kevin Landy.
Chief Clerk.—Trina Driessnack Tyrer.
Senior Counsels: Beth Grossman, Larry Novey.
Counsels: Troy Cribb, Jeff Greene, Holly Idelson, Jonathan Kraden, Gordon Lederman, Mary Beth Schultz, Kenya Wiley.
Professional Staff: Jason Barnosky, Christian Beckner, Aaron Firoved, Elyse Greenwald, Seamus Hughes, Kristine Lam, Jim McGee, Blas Nunez-Neto, Deborah Parkinson, Adam Sedgewick, Jason Yanussi.
Communications Director.—Leslie Phillips.
Communications Advisor.—Scott Campbell.
Deputy Press Secretary.—Sara Lonardo.
Executive Assistant / Office Manager.—Janet Burrell.
Staff Assistants: Anun Malik, Nicole Martinez, Carly Steier, Naomi Wilson.
Detailees: Jeannette Hanna-Ruiz, Paula Haurilesko.
Publications Clerk / Detailee.—Pat Hogan.
Financial Clerk.—John Gleason.
Archivist / Librarian.—Elisabeth Butler.
Systems Administrator / Web Master.—Dan Muchow.
Minority Staff Director / Chief Counsel.—Brandon Milhorn (SD–344), 224–4751.
Deputy Staff Director.—Mary Beth Carozza.
General Counsel.—Andy Weis.
Deputy General Counsel.—Molly Wilkinson.
Director of Homeland Security Affairs.—Rob Strayer.
Director of Governmental Affairs.—Amanda Wood.
Senior Counsels: Ivy Johnson, Asha Mathew.
Counsels: John Grant, Mark LeDuc, Lisa Nieman, Jen Tarr.
Professional Staff: Jenn Capriola, Brooke Hayes, Adam Killian, Devin O'Brien.
Communications Director.—Jeannine Guttman.
Office Manager.—Chris Keach.
Staff Assistants: Doug Campbell, Josh Lortie.
Research Assistant.—Neil Cutter.
Detailees: Eric Cho, John Dettleff, Mathew Hanna, Jim Huse, Teresa Neven.
Subcommittee on Federal Financial Management, Government Information, Federal Services, and International Security (FFM) (SH–432), 224–7155.
Majority Staff Director.—John Kilvington.
Clerk.—Deirdre Armstrong.

Counsel.—Velvet Johnson.
Professional Staff: Wendy Anderson, Brad Belzak, Erik Hopkins, Peter Tyler.
Legislative Aide.—John Collins.
Minority Staff Director/General Counsel.—Bryan Parker (SH–439), 224–2254.
Senior Policy Advisor.—Alice Joe.
Professional Staff: Alan Elias, Justin Stevens.
Research Assistant.—Adam Kim.
Subcommittee on Oversight of Government Management, the Federal Workforce, and the District of Columbia (OGM) (SH–605), 224–4551.
Majority Staff Director.—Lisa Powell.
Clerk.—Benjamin Rhodeside.
Counsels: Christine Khim, Bryan Polisuk.
Professional Staff: Evan Cash, Jessica Nagasako, Kata Sybenga, Joel Spangenberg.
Fellow.—Shelley Finlayson.
Minority Staff Director.—Jennifer Hemingway (SH–604), 224–3682.
Counsels: Charles Abernathy, Tara Shaw.
Professional Staff.—Thomas Bishop.
Legislative Aide.—Sean Stiff.
Permanent Subcommittee on Investigations (PSI) (SR–199), 224–9505.
Majority Staff Director/Chief Counsel.—Elise Bean.
Clerk.—Mary Robertson.
Counsel/Chief Investigator.—Robert Roach.
Counsels: Daniel Goshorn, David Katz, Ross Kirschner, Alison Murphy, Zachary Schram, Laura Stuber.
Detailees: Jennifer Auchterlone, Nina Horowitz, Jason Medica.
Fellow.—Marcelle Johns.
Minority Staff Director.—Chris Barkley (SR–199), 224–3721.
Counsels: Anthony Cotto, Timothy Terry.
Chief Investigator.—Keith Ashdown.
Senior Investigator.—Justin Rood.
Professional Staff.—David Cole.
Ad Hoc Subcommittee on State, Local, and Private Sector Preparedness and Integration (SLPSPI) (SH–613B), 224–4462.
Majority Staff Director.—Vacant.
Clerk.—Kelsey Stroud.
Professional Staff: Jason Bockenstedt, Shannon Lovejoy.
Minority Staff Director.—Mike McBride (SH–613B), 224–4462.
Ad Hoc Subcommittee on Contracting Oversight (SCO) (SR–102), 228–3862.
Majority Staff Director.—Margaret Daum.
Clerk.—Kelsey Stroud.
Counsel.—Alan Kahn.
Detailee.—Margaret Chan.
Minority Staff Director.—Molly Wilkinson.
Detailees: Jim Huse, Teresa Neven.
Ad Hoc Subcommittee on Disaster Recovery (SDR) (SH–613B), 224–4462.
Majority Staff Director.—Ben Billings.
Clerk.—Kelsey Stroud.
Professional Staff.—Melinda Glazer.
Research Assistant.—Rachel Brown.
Minority Staff Director.—Andy Olson (SH–613B), 224–4462.

Judiciary

224 Dirksen Senate Office Building 20510–6275

phone 224–7703, fax 224–9516, http://www.senate.gov/~judiciary

meets upon call of the chair

Patrick J. Leahy, of Vermont, *Chair*

Herb Kohl, of Wisconsin.
Dianne Feinstein, of California.
Russell D. Feingold, of Wisconsin.
Charles E. Schumer, of New York.
Richard Durbin, of Illinois.
Benjamin L. Cardin, of Maryland.
Sheldon Whitehouse, of Rhode Island.
Amy Klobuchar, of Minnesota.
Edward E. Kaufman, of Delaware.
Arlen Specter, of Pennsylvania.
Al Franken, of Minnesota.

Jeff Sessions, of Alabama.
Orrin G. Hatch, of Utah.
Chuck Grassley, of Iowa.
Jon Kyl, of Arizona.
Lindsey Graham, of South Carolina.
John Cornyn, of Texas.
Tom Coburn, of Oklahoma.

SUBCOMMITTEES

Administrative Oversight and the Courts

Sheldon Whitehouse, of Rhode Island, *Chair*

Dianne Feinstein, of California.
Russell D. Feingold, of Wisconsin.
Charles E. Schumer, of New York.
Benjamin L. Cardin, of Maryland.
Edward E. Kaufman, of Delaware.
Al Franken, of Minnesota.

Jeff Sessions, of Alabama.
Chuck Grassley, of Iowa.
Jon Kyl, of Arizona.
Lindsey Graham, of South Carolina.

Antitrust, Competition Policy and Consumer Rights

Herb Kohl, of Wisconsin, *Chair*

Charles E. Schumer, of New York.
Sheldon Whitehouse, of Rhode Island.
Amy Klobuchar, of Minnesota.
Edward E. Kaufman, of Delaware.
Arlen Specter, of Pennsylvania.
Al Franken, of Minnesota.

Orrin G. Hatch, of Utah.
Chuck Grassley, of Iowa.
John Cornyn, of Texas.

Crime and Drugs

Arlen Specter, of Pennsylvania, *Chair*

Herb Kohl, of Wisconsin.
Dianne Feinstein, of California.
Russell D. Feingold, of Wisconsin.
Charles E. Schumer, of New York.
Richard Durbin, of Illinois.
Benjamin L. Cardin, of Maryland.
Amy Klobuchar, of Minnesota.
Edward E. Kaufman, of Delaware.

Lindsey Graham, of South Carolina.
Orrin G. Hatch, of Utah.
Chuck Grassley, of Iowa.
Jeff Sessions, of Alabama.
Tom Coburn, of Oklahoma.

Human Rights and the Law

Richard Durbin, of Illinois, *Chair*

Russell D. Feingold, of Wisconsin.
Benjamin L. Cardin, of Maryland.
Edward E. Kaufman, of Delaware.
Arlen Specter, of Pennsylvania.
Al Franken, of Minnesota.

Tom Coburn, of Oklahoma.
John Cornyn, of Texas.
Lindsey Graham, of South Carolina.

Immigration, Refugees and Border Security

Charles E. Schumer, of New York, *Chair*

Patrick J. Leahy, of Vermont.
Dianne Feinstein, of California.
Richard Durbin, of Illinois.
Sheldon Whitehouse, of Rhode Island.
John Cornyn, of Texas.
Chuck Grassley, of Iowa.
Jon Kyl, of Arizona.
Jeff Sessions, of Alabama.

Terrorism, Technology and Homeland Security

Benjamin L. Cardin, of Maryland, *Chair*

Herb Kohl, of Wisconsin.
Dianne Feinstein, of California.
Charles E. Schumer, of New York.
Richard Durbin, of Illinois.
Edward E. Kaufman, of Delaware.
Jon Kyl, of Arizona.
Orrin G. Hatch, of Utah.
Jeff Sessions, of Alabama.
John Cornyn, of Texas.
Tom Coburn, of Oklahoma.

The Constitution

Russell D. Feingold, of Wisconsin, *Chair*

Dianne Feinstein, of California.
Richard Durbin, of Illinois.
Benjamin L. Cardin, of Maryland.
Sheldon Whitehouse, of Rhode Island.
Arlen Specter, of Pennsylvania.
Tom Coburn, of Oklahoma.
Jon Kyl, of Arizona.
John Cornyn, of Texas.
Lindsey Graham, of South Carolina.

STAFF

Committee on the Judiciary (SD–224), 224–7703, fax 224–9516.
Majority Staff Director/Chief Counsel.—Bruce Cohen.
Legislative Staff Assistant to the Chief Counsel.—Elise Burditt.
Deputy Staff Director/General Counsel for Civil Justice.—Kristine Lucius.
Chief Counsel for Nominations and Oversight.—Jeremy Paris.
Chief Counsel for Privacy and Information Policy.—Lydia Griggsby.
Chief Counsel for Criminal Justice.—Noah Bookbinder.
Senior Counsel for National Security.—Zulima Espinel.
Senior Counsel, I.P. and Antitrust.—Aaron Cooper.
Senior Counsels: Roscoe Jones, Tara Magner, Matthew Virkstis.
Investigative Counsel.—Margaret Whitney.
Nominations Counsel.—Shanna Singh Hughey.
Counsels: Curtis Legeyt, Anya McMurray, Juan Valdivieso.
Professional Staff Member.—Adrienne Wojeciechowski.
Detailee.—Chan Park.
Press Secretary.—Erica Chabot.
Press Assistant.—Patrick Sheahan.
Chief Clerk.—Roslyne Turner.
Assistant to Chief Clerk.—Erin O'Neill.
Nominations Clerk.—Sarah Hackett.
Hearings Clerk.—Julia Gagne.
Law Librarian.—Charles Papirmeister.
Archivist.—Michael Donaghue.
Legislative Calendar Clerk.—Alberta Easter.
Systems Administrator.—Brian Hockin.
Legislative Staff Assistants: Bree Bang-Jenson, Kelsey Kobelt, Matthew Smith, David Stebbins, Joseph Thomas, Laura Trainor, Scott Wilson.
Staff Assistants: Kiera Flynn, Sarah Hasazi.
Court Reporter.—Lisa Dennis.
GPO Printer.—Cecilia Morcombe.
Minority Staff Director.—Brian Benczkowski.
Professional Staff Member and Assistant to Staff Director.—Michael Drummond.
Deputy Staff Director.—Matthew Miner.
Chief Counsel.—William Smith.
General Counsel.—Joe Matal.
Counsels: William Hall, Theodore Lehman, Mark Patton, Seth Wood.

Counsel for Nominations.—Danielle Cutrona.
Professional Staff Member for Nominations.—Lauren Pastarnack.
Legislative Counsel.—Kimberly Kilpatrick.
Professional Staff Member.—Barbara Ledeen.
Press Secretary.—Stephen Miller.
Press Assistant.—Andrew Logan.
Staff Assistants: Andrew Bennion, Allison Busbee, Kate Laborde, Sarah Thompson.
Archivist.—Stuart Paine.
Director of Information Systems.—Steve Kirkland.

Subcommittee on Administrative Oversight and the Courts (SD–161), 224–8352.
Majority Chief Counsel.—Sam Goodstein.
Counsels: Darell Brown, Stephen Lilley, Suzanne Renaud.
Legislative Correspondent.—Bill Hoffman.
Minority Deputy Chief Counsel.—Bradley Hayes (SD–G66), 224–7572.
Legislative Counsel.—John Ellis.
Detailee.—Sam Ramer.
Fellow.—Jeffrey Boobar.

Subcommittee on Antitrust, Competition Policy and Consumer Rights (SD–308), 224–3406.
Majority Chief Counsel.—Caroline Holland.
Senior Counsel.—Seth Bloom.
Counsels: Marni Karlin, Kristen Kreple.
Legislative Aide.—Nicole Silver.
Minority Chief of Staff.—Jace Johnson, 224–5251.
Counsels: William Castle, Matthew Bryan Hickman, Thomas Jipping, Matthew Sangren,

Subcommittee on the Constitution (SH–807), 224–5573.
Majority Chief Counsel.—Bob Schiff.
Counsels: Lara Flint, Susan Rohol.
Judiciary Clerk.—Elizabeth Hill.
Legislative Aide.—Margaret Whiting.
Minority Chief Counsel.—Brooke Bacak (SD–153), 224–4280.
General Counsel.—Elizabeth Hays.
Counsel.—Sarah Beth Groshart.

Subcommittee on Crime and Drugs (SH–305), 224–0558.
Majority Chief Counsel.—Hannibal Kemerer.
Counsels: Danielle Edwards, Matt Weiner.
Detailee.—Linda Hoffa.
Minority Chief Counsel.—Walt Kuhn (SH–202B), 224–5972.
Professional Staffer.—Leigh Ellen Lybrand.
Special Counsel.—John Patrick.

Subcommittee on Human Rights and the Law (SD–524), 224–1158.
Majority Chief Counsel.—Joseph Zogby.
Senior Counsel.—Michael Zubrensky.
Counsels: Heloisa Griggs, Daniel Swanson.
Detailee.—Lara Quint.
Minority (SD–153), 224–4280.

Subcommittee on Immigration, Border Security and Refugees (SD–520), 224–8352.
Majority Chief Counsel.—Stephanie Martz.
Counsels: Leon Fresco, Rebecca Kelly.
Immigration Detailee.—Jessica Owens.
Legislative Correspondent.—Rachel Yemini.
Legislative Assistant.—Marco DeLeon.
Minority Chief Counsel.—Matthew Johnson (SD–141), 224–7840.
Legislative Director.—Russ Thomasson.
Legal Assistant.—Valera Vollor.
Counsels: Gustav Eyler, Holt Lackey.

Subcommittee on Terrorism, Technology and Homeland Security (SH–815), 228–3177.
Majority Chief Counsel.—Bill Van Horne.
Counsel.—Danielle Solomon.
Legislative Correspondent.—Andrew Remo.
Fellow.—Troy Ware.
Minority Chief Counsel.—Stephen Higgins (SH–325), 224–6791.
Counsel.—Ryan Myers.
Legislative Correspondent.—Eva Arlia.

Senator Feinstein Judiciary Staff (SD–524), 224–3841.
Chief Counsel.—Neil Quinter.
Counsels: Carole Angel, Helen Lane Dilg.
Legislative Aide.—Caitlin Doyle.

Senator Klobuchar Judiciary Staff (SH–302), 224–3244.
Chief Counsel.—Jonathan Becker.
Counsel.—Paige Herwig.
Senator Kaufman Judiciary Staff (SR–383), 224–5042.
Chief Counsel.—Hugh Geoffrey Moulton.
Senator Franken Judiciary Staff (SH–320), 224–5641.
Legislative Assistant.—Alvaro Bedoya.
Legislative Aide.—Natalie Volin.
Senator Grassley Judiciary Staff (SD–159), 224–5564.
Chief Counsel.—Rita Lari Jochum.
Counsel.—Nick Podsiadly.

Rules and Administration

305 Russell Senate Office Building 20510–6325

phone 224–6352, http://rules.senate.gov

[Legislative Reorganization Act of 1946]

meets second and fourth Wednesday of each month

Charles E. Schumer, of New York, *Chair*

Robert C. Byrd, of West Virginia.
Daniel K. Inouye, of Hawaii.
Christopher J. Dodd, of Connecticut.
Dianne Feinstein, of California.
Richard Durbin, of Illinois.
Ben Nelson, of Nebraska.
Patty Murray, of Washington.
Mark L. Pryor, of Arkansas.
Tom Udall, of New Mexico.
Mark R. Warner, of Virginia.

Robert F. Bennett, of Utah.
Mitch McConnell, of Kentucky.
Thad Cochran, of Mississippi.
Kay Bailey Hutchison, of Texas.
Saxby Chambliss, of Georgia.
Lamar Alexander, of Tennessee.
John Ensign, of Nevada.
Pat Roberts, of Kansas.

(No Subcommittees)

STAFF

Committee on Rules and Administration (SR–305), 224–6352.
Majority Staff Director.—Jean Parvin Bordewich.
Deputy Staff Director.—Jennifer Griffith.
Chief Counsel.—Jason Abel.
Counsels: Adam Ambrogi, Sonia Gill, Julia Richardson.
Elections Counsel.—Veronica Gillespie.
Administrative Assistant to Democratic Staff Director.—Carole Blessington.
Professional Staff: Josh Brekenfeld, Lauryn Bruck.
Minority Staff Director.—Mary Suit Jones.
Deputy Staff Director.—Shaun Parkin.
Chief Counsel.—Paul Vinovich.
Elections Counsel.—Michael Merrell.
Professional Staff: Rachel Creviston, Trish Kent, Abbie Platt.
Non-Designated Staff:
Director for Administration and Policy.—Chris Shunk.
Chief Clerk.—Lynden Armstrong.
Professional Staff.—Matthew McGowan, 4–0281.
Staff Assistants: Scott Levin, Justin Perkins.
Auditors: Leann Alwood, Joanne Yi.

Small Business and Entrepreneurship

428A Russell Senate Office Building 20510

phone 224–5175, fax 224–5619, http://sbc.senate.gov/

[Created pursuant to S. Res. 58, 81st Congress]

meets first Wednesday of each month

Mary L. Landrieu, of Louisiana, *Chair*

John F. Kerry, of Massachusetts.
Carl Levin, of Michigan.
Tom Harkin, of Iowa.
JOSEPH I. LIEBERMAN, of Connecticut.
Maria Cantwell, of Washington.
Evan Bayh, of Indiana.
Mark L. Pryor, of Arkansas.
Benjamin L. Cardin, of Maryland.
Jeanne Shaheen, of New Hampshire.
Kay R. Hagan, of North Carolina.

Olympia J. Snowe, of Maine.
Christopher S. Bond, of Missouri.
David Vitter, of Louisiana.
John Thune, of South Dakota.
Michael B. Enzi, of Wyoming.
Johnny Isakson, of Georgia.
Roger F. Wicker, of Mississippi.
James E. Risch, of Idaho.

(No Subcommittees)

STAFF

Committee on Small Business and Entrepreneurship (SR–428A), 224–5175, fax 224–6619.
Majority Staff Director.—Donald Cravins, Jr.
Deputy Staff Director.—Kevin Wheeler.
Assistant to the Staff Director.—Amber Gorman.
Social Security and Tax Counsel.—Kathy Kerrigan.
Counsels: Barry La Sala, Greg Willis.
Legislative Correspondent.—Oriel Feldman Hall.
Legislative Assistant.—Brian Rice.
Professional Staff Member.—John Phillips.
Press Secretary.—Kathryn Seck.
Research Analyst.—Karen Radermacher.
Chief Clerk.—Lena Postanowicz.
Staff Assistant.—Kelly Aschliman.
Minority Staff Director.—Wally Hsueh.
Deputy Staff Director and Counsel.—Matthew Walker.
Chief Counsel and Regulatory Counsel.—Alex Hecht.
Tax and Finance Advisor.—Kathleen Black.
Economist and Press Secretary.—Matthew Berger.
Counsel.—Chris Lucas.
Professional Staff Members: Diane Dietz, Meredith West.
Research Assistants: Chris Averill, Adam Reece.
Staff Assistant.—Tara Crumb.

Veterans' Affairs

SR–412 Russell Senate Office Building

phone 224–9126, http://veterans.senate.gov

meets first Wednesday of each month

Daniel K. Akaka, of Hawaii, *Chair*

John D. Rockefeller IV, of West Virginia.
Patty Murray, of Washington.
BERNARD SANDERS, of Vermont.
Sherrod Brown, of Ohio.
Jim Webb, of Virginia.
Jon Tester, of Montana.
Mark Begich, of Alaska.
Roland W. Burris, of Illinois.
Arlen Specter, of Pennsylvania.

Richard Burr, of North Carolina.
Johnny Isakson, of Georgia.
Roger F. Wicker, of Mississippi.
Mike Johanns, of Nebraska.
Lindsey Graham, of South Carolina.

(No Subcommittees)

STAFF

Committee on Veterans' Affairs (SR–412), 224–9126, fax 224–9575.
Majority Staff Director.—William E. Brew.
Deputy Staff Director.—Kim Lipsky.
Chief Benefits Counsel.—Dahlia Melendrez.
Counsels: Justin Constantine, Nancy Hogan.
Professional Staff Member.—Babette Polzer.
Special Projects Counsel.—Mary Ellen McCarthy.
Legislative Assistants: Ryan Pettit, Preethi Raghavan.
Director of Correspondence.—Jenny McCarthy.
Communications Director/Legislative Assistant.—Kawika Riley.
Executive Assistant.—Lexi Simpson.
Staff Assistants: Melissa Sullivan, Kathryn Monet.
Minority Staff Director.—Lupe Wissel (825–A Hart), 224–2074, fax 224–8908.
Office Manager.—Hilda Graham.
General Counsel.—Amanda Meredith.
Senior Advisor.—Jonathan Towers.
Professional Staff Member.—Mindi Walker.
Deputy Press Secretary.—Mary Sarah Kinner.
Investigators: Walter Zaykowsky, John McDonald.
Research Assistant.—Victoria Lee.
Staff Assistant.—Caroline Cain.
Non-Designated:
Chief Clerk.—Kelly Fado.
Hearing Clerk/Systems Administrator.—Matt Lawrence.

SELECT AND SPECIAL COMMITTEES OF THE SENATE

Committee on Indian Affairs

838 Hart Senate Office Building 20510–6450

phone 224–2251, http://indian.senate.gov

[Created pursuant to S. Res. 4, 95th Congress; amended by S. Res. 71, 103d Congress]

meets every Thursday of each month

Byron L. Dorgan, of North Dakota, *Chair*

John Barrasso, of Wyoming, *Vice Chair*

Daniel K. Inouye, of Hawaii.
Kent Conrad, of North Dakota.
Daniel K. Akaka, of Hawaii.
Tim Johnson, of South Dakota.
Maria Cantwell, of Washington.
Jon Tester, of Montana.
Tom Udall, of New Mexico.
Al Franken, of Minnesota.

John McCain, of Arizona.
Lisa Murkowski, of Alaska.
Tom Coburn, of Oklahoma.
Mike Crapo, of Idaho.
Mike Johanns, of Nebraska.

(No Subcommittees)

STAFF

Majority Staff Director / Chief Counsel.—Allison Binney.
Senior Counsel.—Rollie Wilson.
Counsel.—Tracy Hartzler-Toon.
Policy Director.—John Harte.
Deputy Policy Director.—Eamon Walsh.
Senior Policy Advisor.—Brenda Shore.
Health Policy Advisor.—Erin Bailey.
Communications Director.—Barry Aàtt.
Minority Staff Director / Chief Counsel.—David A. Mullon, Jr.
Deputy Chief Counsel.—Rhonda Harjo.
Senior Counsel.—James Hall.
Staff Assistant.—Ken Degenfelder.
Counsel.—Justin Memmott.

Select Committee on Ethics

220 Hart Senate Office Building 20510, phone 224–2981, fax 224–7416

[Created pursuant to S. Res. 338, 88th Congress; amended by S. Res. 110, 95th Congress]

Barbara Boxer, of California, *Chair*

Johnny Isakson, of Georgia, *Vice Chair*

Mark L. Pryor, of Arkansas.
Sherrod Brown, of Ohio.

Pat Roberts, of Kansas.
James E. Risch, of Idaho.

STAFF

Staff Director/Chief Counsel.—John C. Sassaman.
Deputy Staff Director.—Annette Gillis.
Counsel and Director of Education and Training.—Matthew Mesmer.
Counsels: Audra Bayes, Tremayne Bunaugh, William Corcoran, Rochelle Ford, Daniel A. Schwager, Lynn Tran.
Professional Staff.—John Lewter.
Systems Administrator.—Danny Remington.
Staff Assistants: Emily Chucovich, Daniel Donahue, Chelsey Simonovich, Julian Wolfson.

Select Committee on Intelligence

211 Hart Senate Office Building 20510–6475, phone 224–1700

http://www.senate.gov/~intelligence

[Created pursuant to S. Res. 400, 94th Congress]

Dianne Feinstein, of California, *Chair*

Christopher S. Bond, of Missouri, *Vice Chair*

John D. Rockefeller IV, of West Virginia.
Ron Wyden, of Oregon.
Evan Bayh, of Indiana.
Barbara A. Mikulski, of Maryland.
Russell D. Feingold, of Wisconsin.
Bill Nelson, of Florida.
Sheldon Whitehouse, of Rhode Island.

Orrin G. Hatch, of Utah.
Olympia J. Snowe, of Maine.
Saxby Chambliss, of Georgia.
Richard Burr, of North Carolina.
Tom Coburn, of Oklahoma.
James E. Risch, of Idaho.

Ex Officio

Harry Reid, of Nevada.
Carl Levin, of Michigan.

Mitch McConnell, of Kentucky.
John McCain, of Arizona.

STAFF

Majority Staff Director.—David Grannis.
Minority Staff Director.—Louis B. Tucker.
Chief Clerk.—Kathleen P. McGhee.

Special Committee on Aging

G–31 Dirksen Senate Office Building 20510, phone 224–5364

http://aging.senate.gov

[Reauthorized pursuant to S. Res. 4, 95th Congress]

Herb Kohl, of Wisconsin, *Chair*

Ron Wyden, of Oregon.
Blanche L. Lincoln, of Arkansas.
Evan Bayh, of Indiana.
Bill Nelson, of Florida.
Robert P. Casey, Jr., of Pennsylvania.
Claire McCaskill, of Missouri.
Sheldon Whitehouse, of Rhode Island.
Mark Udall, of Colorado.
Michael F. Bennet, of Colorado.
Kirsten E. Gillibrand, of New York.
Arlen Specter, of Pennsylvania.
Al Franken, of Minnesota.

Bob Corker, of Tennessee.
Richard C. Shelby, of Alabama.
Susan M. Collins, of Maine.
Orrin G. Hatch, of Utah.
George S. LeMieux, of Florida.
Sam Brownback, of Kansas.
Lindsey Graham, of South Carolina.
Saxby Chambliss, of Georgia.

STAFF

Majority Staff Director.—Debra Whitman.
Policy Advisor.—Cara Goldstein.
Press Secretary.—Ashley Glacel.
Chief of Oversight and Investigations.—Jack Mitchell.
Senior Policy Advisors: Anne Montgomery, Stacy Stordahl, Nicole Brown, Jeff Cruz.
Chief Counsel.—Kristine Blackwood.
Staff Assistants: Evan Hellman, Kristin Rzeczkowski.
Minority Staff (SH–628), 224–5364, fax 224–9926.
Staff Director.—Michael Bassett.
Senior Legislative Assistant.—Alicia Hennie.
Communications Director.—Chuck Harper.
Legislative Assistant.—Clay Brockman.
Senior Investigator.—Marco Villagrana.
Professional Staff Member.—Martin Schuh.

National Republican Senatorial Committee

425 Second Street, NE., 20002, phone 675–6000, fax 675–6058

John Cornyn, of Texas, *Chair*

STAFF

Executive Director.—Rob Jesmer.
Director of:
Administration.—Vacant.
Communications.—Brian Walsh.
Finance.—Dorinda Moss.
Legal Counsel.—Sean Cairncross.
Political Director.—Randy Bumps.
Research.—Victoria Newton.

Senate Republican Policy Committee

347 Russell Senate Office Building, phone 224–2946
fax 224–1235, http://rpc.senate.gov

John Thune, of South Dakota, *Chair*

STAFF

Staff Director.—Matt Zabel.
Deputy Staff Director.—Doug Schwartz.
Communications Director.—Kyle Downey.
Administrative Director.—Craig Cheney.
Analysts:
Chief Economist and Budget.—Jon Lieber.
Health Policy Counsel.—Andy Chasin.
Commerce, Transportation, Banking and Housing.—Mike O'Rielly.
Education and Welfare.—Amanda Farris.
Energy, Environment, Agriculture and Labor.—Derrick Morgan.
Foreign and Defense Affairs.—Michael Stransky.
Judiciary and Homeland Security.—Gregg Nunziata.
Professional Staff:
Editor.—John Mitchell.
System Administrator/RVA Analyst.—Thomas Pulju.
Station Manager/Special Projects.—Carolyn Laird.
Station Operator/Project Assistant.—Paul McKernan.

Senate Republican Conference

405 Hart Senate Office Building, phone 224–2764
http://src.senate.gov

Chair.—Lamar Alexander, of Tennessee.
Vice Chair.—Lisa Murkowski, of Alaska.

STAFF

Conference of the Majority (SH–405), 224–2764.
Staff Director.—Ryan Loskarn.
Deputy Staff Director for Policy.—Matt Sonnesyn.
Senior Writer.—Mary Katherine Ascik.
Press Secretary.—Nick Simpson.
Office Manager.—Misty Marshall.
Spanish News Coordinator.—Carlos Gonzalez.
Media Services Director.—Dave Hodgdon.
Production Manager.—Cyrus Pearson.
Videographer/Editor.—Lane Marshall.
Senior Graphics Designer.—Chris Angrisani.
Graphics Designer.—Laura Gill.
Systems Engineer.—Nate Green.
Communications Assistant.—Emily Hill.
Internal Communications Director.—Kim Allen.
Audio/Video Producer.—Andrea Turnbough.
Online Communications Advisor.—Sean Hackburth.
Web Developer.—Judson Blewett.
Floor Monitor.—Ryan Wrasse.
Member and Guest Relations.—Robbie Champion.

Democratic Policy Committee

419 Hart Senate Office Building, phone 224–3232

Byron L. Dorgan, of North Dakota, *Chair*

Evan Bayh, of Indiana, Regional Chair.
Jack Reed, of Rhode Island, Regional Chair.
Mary L. Landrieu, of Louisiana, Regional Chair.
Harry Reid, of Nevada.
John D. Rockefeller IV, of West Virginia.
Daniel K. Akaka, of Hawaii.
Russell D. Feingold, of Wisconsin.
JOSEPH I. LIEBERMAN, of Connecticut.
Dianne Feinstein, of California.
Ron Wyden, of Oregon.
Tim Johnson, of South Dakota.
Charles E. Schumer, of New York.
Blanche L. Lincoln, of Arkansas.
Bill Nelson, of Florida.
Thomas R. Carper, of Delaware.
Barbara A. Mikulski, of Maryland.
Frank R. Lautenberg, of New Jersey.
Sherrod Brown, of Ohio.
Richard Durbin, of Illinois, ex officio, (as Assistant Democratic Leader).
Patty Murray, of Washington, ex officio, (as Secretary of the Conference).

STAFF

Staff Director.—Chuck Cooper.
Assistant to the Staff Director.—Jesse Comart.
Research Director.—Tim Gaffaney.
Policy Advisors: Joi Chaney, Kristin Devine, Jacqueline Lampert, Ryan Mulvenon, Erika Moritsugu.
New Policy Director.—Doug Steiger.
Oversight and Legal Team, Counsel.—Leslie Gross-Davis.
Policy Analyst.—Holly Teliska.
Senior Vote Analyst.—Doug Connolly.
Communications Director.—Barry Piatt.

Press Assistant.—Kati Card.

Steering and Outreach Committee

712 Hart Senate Office Building, phone 224–9048

Debbie Stabenow, of Michigan *Chair*

John F. Kerry, of Massachusetts.
Daniel K. Inouye, of Hawaii.
Robert C. Byrd, of West Virginia.
John D. Rockefeller IV, of West Virginia.
Patrick J. Leahy, of Vermont.
Christopher J. Dodd, of Connecticut.
Tom Harkin, of Iowa.
Max Baucus, of Montana.
Kent Conrad, of North Dakota.
Carl Levin, of Michigan.
Herb Kohl, of Wisconsin.
Barbara Boxer, of California.
Jeff Bingaman, of New Mexico.
Harry Reid, of Nevada.
Richard Durbin, of Illinois.
Mark L. Pryor, of Arkansas.

STAFF

Staff Director.—Kriston Alford McIntosh.
Deputy Director.—Nicole Sawran.
Director of Outreach Communications.—LaVenia LaVelle.
Associate Directors: Marcus Fleming, Eloy Martinez, Courtney Rowe.
Staff Assistant.—Blake Kelly.

Senate Democratic Multimedia Center

619 Hart Senate Office Building, phone 224–1430

Harry Reid, of Nevada, *Chair*

STAFF

Communications Director.—Rodell Mollineau.
Director of Broadcast Operations.—Brian Jones.
Director of New Media.—Aaron Myers.
Deputy Director of New Media.—Erin Skinner Cochran.
Editors: Ike Blake, Toby Hayman, Alice Liu, Kerry Sullivan.
Engineer.—Aaron Gillespy.
Event Coordinator.—Matt Jorgenson.
Graphic Design Specialist.—Perisha Gates.
New Media Creative Director.—Jordan Higgins.
Multimedia Specialist.—Ian Shifrin.
Press Assistant.—Jason Botelho.
Producer.—Nicole Boxer.
Radio Producer.—Jose Ozoria.
Videographers: Clare Flood, Kevin Kelleher.

Senate Democratic Conference

173 Russell Senate Office Building, phone 224–2621, fax 224–0238

Secretary.—Patty Murray, of Washington State.
Leadership Staff Director.—Mike Spahn.
Floor and Communication Aide.—Stacy Rich.

Democratic Senatorial Campaign Committee

120 Maryland Avenue, NE., 20002, phone 224–2447

Robert Menendez, of New Jersey, *Chair*

Amy Klobuchar, of Minnesota, *Vice Chair*

Harry Reid, of Nevada, *Democratic Leader*

Vacant, *Outreach and Policy Chair*

STAFF

Executive Director.—J.B. Poersch.

Communications Director.—Eric Schultz.

Political Director.—Martha McKenna.

Finance Director.—Liz Lowery.

Comptroller.—Darlene Setter.

Legal Counsel.—Mark Elias.

OFFICERS AND OFFICIALS OF THE SENATE

Capitol Telephone Directory, 224–3121

Senate room prefixes:

Capitol—S, Russell Senate Office Building—SR

Dirksen Senate Office Building—SD, Hart Senate Office Building—SH

PRESIDENT OF THE SENATE

Vice President of the United States and President of the Senate.—Joseph R. Biden, Jr.

The Ceremonial Office of the Vice President is S–212 in the Capitol. The Vice President has offices in the Dirksen Senate Office Building, the Eisenhower Executive Office Building (EEOB) and the White House (West Wing).

Chief of Staff to the Vice President and Counsel.—Ronald Klain, EEOB, room 202, 456–9000.
Deputy Chief of Staff.—Alan Hoffman, EEOB, room 204, 456–9000.
Counsel to the Vice President.—Cynthia Hogan, EEOB, room 245, 456–9590.
Assistant to the Vice President for—
Communications.—Jay Carney, EEOB, room 288, 456–0373.
Domestic Policy.—Terrell McSweeney, EEOB, room 218, 456–2728.
Legislative Affairs.—Sudafi Henry, EEOB, room 243, 456–1540.
National Security Affairs.—Tony Blinken, EEOB, room 246A, 456–9501.
Executive Assistant to the Vice President.—Michele Smith, West Wing, 456–7000.
Chief of Staff to Dr. Biden.—Cathy Russell, EEOB, room 201, 456–7458.
Deputy Assistant to the Vice President and Director of Scheduling.—Elisabeth Hire, EEOB, room 239, 456–6773.

PRESIDENT PRO TEMPORE

S–126 The Capitol, phone 224–2848

President Pro Tempore of the Senate.—Robert C. Byrd.
Executive Assistant.—Betsy Dietz, 224–2848.

MAJORITY LEADER

S–221 The Capitol, phone 224–2158, fax 224–7362

Majority Leader.—Harry Reid.
Chief of Staff.—Gary Myrick.
Deputy Chief of Staff.—David McCallum.
Executive Assistant.—Janice Shelton.
Scheduler.—Robin McCain.
Policy Director.—Randy Devalk.
Legislative Director.—Dayle Cristinzio.
Communications Staff Director.—Rodell Mollineau.
Speechwriter.—Stephen Krupin.
Legal Counsels: Mike Castellano, Serena Hoy.
Assistant to the Chief of Staff.—Danica Daneshforouz.
Assistant Scheduler.—Krysta Juris.

ASSISTANT MAJORITY LEADER

S–321 The Capitol, phone 224–9447

Assistant Democratic Leader.—Richard Durbin.
Chief of Staff.—Pat Souders.
Director of Operations.—Sally Brown-Shaklee.
Director of Scheduling.—Claire Reuschel.
Communications Director.—Joe Shoemaker.
National Press Secretary.—Max Gleischman.
Illinois Press Secretary.—Christina Mulka.
Press Assistant.—Ben Garmisa.
Speechwriter.—Molly Rowley.
Director of Floor Operations/Counsel.—Anne Wall.
Floor Counsel.—Reema Dodin.
Special Assistant.—Amanda Agosti.
Staff Assistant.—Sarah Ryan.

REPUBLICAN LEADER

S–230 The Capitol, phone 224–3135, fax 228–1264

Republican Leader.—Mitch McConnell.
Chief of Staff.—Kyle Simmons.
Deputy Chief of Staff.—Sharon Soderstrom.
Scheduler.—Stefanie Hagar.
Assistant Scheduler.—Rebecca Winnett.
Director of Administration.—Julie Adams.
Policy Advisor and Counsel.—Brandi Wilson White.
Domestic Policy Director.—Rohit Kumar.
Policy Advisors: Megan Hauck, Libby Jarvis, Derek Kan, Malloy McDaniel, Dan Schneider, Lanier Swann.
Legal Counsels: John Abegg, Brian Lewis.
National Security Advisor.—Tom Hawkins.
Communications Director.—Don Stewart.
Speechwriter.—Brian McGuire.
Press Secretary.—Jennifer Morris.
Press Assistant.—Rachel Ball.
Communications Advisor.—David Meyers.
Systems Administrator.—Elmamoun Sulfab.
Staff Assistants: Emily Adelman, Amanda Hendricks, Lindsey Waldman.

REPUBLICAN COMMUNICATIONS CENTER

S–230 The Capitol, phone 228–6397

Staff Director.—Josh Holmes
Press Secretary.—John Ashbrook.
Deputy Press Secretary.—Allison Moore.
Analyst.—Matt Kenney.
Communications Advisor, New Media.—David Hauptmann.
Communications Advisor.—Webber Steinhoff.

OFFICE OF THE REPUBLICAN WHIP

S–208 The Capitol, phone 224–2708, fax 228–1507

Republican Whip.—Jon Kyl.
Chief of Staff.—Lisa Wolski.
Deputy Chief of Staff.—Denzel McGuire.
Whip Liaisons: Danielle Burr, Ryan Peebles.
Floor Assistant.—Conner Collins.
Policy Council.—Jon Gans.
Speech Writer.—Rachel Currie.
Scheduler.—Kelicia Wright.

Executive Assistant to the Chief of Staff.—Lauren Bellman.

OFFICE OF THE SECRETARY

S–312 The Capitol, phone 224–3622

NANCY ERICKSON, Secretary of the Senate; elected and sworn in as the 32nd Secretary of the Senate on January 4, 2007; native of South Dakota; B.A. in government and history from Augustana College, Sioux Falls, SD; M.A. in public policy from American University, Washington, DC; Democratic Representative, Senate Sergeant at Arms (SAA); Deputy Chief of Staff, Senator Tom Daschle; General Accounting Office.

Secretary of the Senate.—Nancy Erickson (S–312), 224–3622.
Chief of Staff.—Robert W. Paxton (S–333), 224–5636.
Deputy Chief of Staff.—Beth Provenzano (S–312), 224–6254.
Capitol Offices Liaison.—Gerald Thompson (SB–36), 224–1483.
Assistant Secretary of the Senate.—Sheila M. Dwyer (S–414C), 224–2114.
General Counsel.—Adam Bramwell (S–333), 224–8789.
Executive Accounts Administrator.—Zoraida Torres (S–414B), 224–7099.
Director (LIS Project Office).—Marsha Misenhimer (SD–B44A), 224–2500.
Bill Clerk.—Mary Anne Clarkson (S–123), 224–2120.
Director of:
Captioning Services.—JoEllen R. Dicken (ST–54), 224–4321.
Conservation and Preservation.—Carl Fritter, (S–416), 224–4550.
Curator.—Diane Skvarla (S–411), 224–2955.
Daily Digest, Editor.—Elizabeth Brown (S–421 and S–421A), 224–2658.
Assistant Editor.—Joseph Johnston, 224–2658.
Disbursing Office, Financial Clerk.—Chris J. Doby (SH–127), 224–3205.
Assistant Financial Clerk.—Ileana Garcia, 224–3208.
Enrolling Clerk.—Margarida Curtis (S–139), 224–8427.
Assistant Enrolling Clerk.—Cassandra Byrd, 224–7108.
Executive Clerk.—Michelle Haynes (S–138), 224–4341.
Assistant Executive Clerk.—Brian Malloy, 224–1918.
Historian.—Donald A. Ritchie (SH–201), 224–6900.
Associate Historian.—Betty K. Koed, 224–0753.
Human Resources, Director.—Patricia Richter (SH–231B), 224–3625.
Information Systems, Systems Administrator.—Dan Kulnis (S–422), 224–4883.
Webmaster.—Arin Shapiro, 224–2020.
Interparliamentary Services, Director.—Sally Walsh (SH–808), 224–3047.
Journal Clerk.—Scott Sanborn (S–135), 224–4650.
Legislative Clerk.—Kathleen Alvarez (S–134), 224–4350.
Assistant Legislative Clerk.—John Merlino, 224–3630.
Librarian.—Leona Faust (acting), (SR–B15), 224–3313.
Official Reporters of Debates, Chief Reporter.—Jerald D. Linell (S–410A), 224–7525.
Coordinator of the Record.—Petie Gallacher, 224–1238.
Morning Business Editor.—Jack Hickman (S–123), 224–3079.
Parliamentarian.—Alan S. Frumin (S–133), 224–6128.
Senior Assistant Parliamentarians: Elizabeth MacDonough, 224–6128; Peter Robinson, 224–5133.
Printing and Document Services, Director.—Karen Moore (SH–B04), 224–0205.
Assistant to the Director.—Bud Johnson, 224–2555.
Public Records, Superintendent.—Pamela B. Gavin (SH–232), 224–0762.
Assistant Superintendent.—Dana McCallum, 224–0329.
Information Specialist for—
Campaign Finance.—Raymond Davis, 224–0761.
Ethics and Disclosure.—April Judd, 224–0763.
Lobbying and Foreign Travel.—Erica Omorogieva, 224–0758.
Senate Chief Counsel for Employment.—Jean Manning (SH–103), 224–5424.
Senate Gift Shop, Director.—Ernie LePire (SDG–42), 224–7308.
Senate Page School, Principal.—Kathryn S. Weeden, 224–3926.
Senate Security, Director.—Michael P. DiSilvestro (S–407), 224–5632.
Deputy Director.—Margaret Garland, 224–5632.
Stationery, Keeper of the Stationery.—Michael V. McNeal, 224–3381.
Assistant Keeper of the Stationery.—Tony Super, 224–4846.
Joint Office of Education and Training, Director.—Peggy Greenberg (SH–121), 224–5969.

OFFICE OF THE CHAPLAIN

S–332 The Capitol, phone 224–2510, fax 224–9686

BARRY C. BLACK, Chaplain, U.S. Senate; born in Baltimore, MD, on November 1, 1948; education: Bachelor of Arts, Theology, Oakwood College, 1970; Master of Divinity, Andrews Theological Seminary, 1973; Master of Arts, Counseling, North Carolina Central University, 1978; Doctor of Ministry, Theology, Eastern Baptist Seminary, 1982; Master of Arts, Management, Salve Regina University, 1989; Doctor of Philosophy, Psychology, United States International University, 1996; military service: U.S. Navy, 1976–2003; rising to the rank of Rear Admiral; Chief of Navy Chaplains, 2000–2003; awards: Navy Distingusihed Service Medal; Legion of Merit Medal; Defense Meritorious Service Medal; Meritorious Service Medals (two awards); Navy and Marine Corps Commendation Medals (two awards); 1995 NAACP Renowned Service Award; family: married to Brenda; three children: Barry II, Brendan, and Bradford.

Chaplain of the Senate.—Barry C. Black.
Chief of Staff.—Alan N. Keiran, 224–7456.
Communications Director.—Lisa Schultz, 224–3894.
Staff Scheduler / Executive Assistant.—Jody Spraggins-Scott, 224–2048.

OFFICE OF THE SERGEANT AT ARMS

S–151 The Capitol, phone 224–2341, fax 224–7690

TERRANCE W. GAINER, Sergeant at Arms, U.S. Senate; elected and sworn in as the 38th Sergeant at Arms on January 4, 2007; education: B.A., sociology from St. Benedict's College; M.S., management and public service; J.D. from DePaul University of Chicago; Military service: Decorated veteran who served in the Vietnam War and as a Captain in the U.S. Naval Reserve until 2000; professional: Law enforcement career began in Chicago, IL, 1968; rose through the ranks serving as Deputy IG of Illinois, Deputy Director of Illinois State Police and U.S. Department of Transportation; appointed Director of Illinois State Police in March, 1991; Gainer went on to serve as second in command of the Metropolitan Police Department of the District of Columbia beginning in May, 1998 and Chief of the U.S. Capitol Police from 2002–06; Until his appointment as Sergeant at Arms; Gainer served the private sector focusing on emergency preparedness issues and law enforcement programs supporting Army and Marine operations in Iraq and Afghanistan; family: married, with 6 children and 12 grandchildren.

Sergeant at Arms.—Terrance W. Gainer.
Deputy Sergeant at Arms.—Drew Willison.
Administrative Assistant.—Rick Edwards, SB–8.
Senior Assistant Sergeant at Arms for Police Operations, Security and Emergency Preparedness.—Michael Heidingsfield, SVC 305, 224–2976.
Assistant Sergeant at Arms for Police Operations.—Richard Majauskas, SDG–10, 224–7052.
Assistant Sergeant at Arms for Operations.—Bret Swanson, SD–150, 224–7747.
Assistant Sergeant at Arms and Chief Information Officer.—Kimball Win, (Postal Square), 224–0459.
Assistant Sergeant at Arms for Security and Emergency Prepardness.—Richard Majauskas, SVC 305, 224–1404.

EXECUTIVE OFFICE

Appointment Desk Manager.—Joy Ogden, North Door Capitol Building, 1st Floor, 224–6304.
Capitol Information Officer.—Laura Parker, S–151, 224–2341.
Doorkeeper Supervisor.—Myron J. Fleming, SB–6, 224–1879.
Employee Assistance Program Administrator.—Christy Prietsch, Hart Senate Office Building, 228–3902.
Protocol Officer.—Becky Daugherty, S–151, 224–2341.

CAPITOL FACILITIES

Capitol Facilities Manager.—Skip Rouse, ST–62, 224–4171.

CENTRAL OPERATIONS

Director of Central Operations.—Mike Brown (acting), SD–G61A, 224–8587.
Administrative Services Manager.—Joann Soults, SD–G84, 224–4716.
Hair Care Manager.—Kimberly Johnson, SR–B70, 224–4560.
Parking Manager.—Juanita Rilling, SD–G58, 224–8888.
Photo Studio Manager.—Bill Allen, SD–G85, 224–6000.
Printing, Graphics and Direct Mail Manager.—Juanita Rilling, SD–G82, 224–5981.

FINANCIAL MANAGEMENT

Chief Financial Officer.—Christopher Dey (Postal Square), 224–6292.
Accounting and Budget Manager.—Peter DuBois, 224–1499.
Accounts Payable Manager.—Roy McElwee, 224–6074.
Financial Analysis Manager.—David Salem, 224–8844.
Procurement Manager.—David Baker, 224–2547.

HUMAN RESOURCES

Director of Human Resources.—Patrick Murphy, SH–142, 224–2889.
SAA Safety Office Officer.—Irvin Queja, 228–0823.
Senate Placement Officer Manager.—Brian Bean, 224–9167.
Workers' Compensation Office Manager.—Catherine Modeste Brooks, 224–3796.

IT SUPPORT SERVICES

Director of IT Support Services.—Vicki Sinnet (Postal Square), 224–0459.
Desktop/LAN Support Manager.—Tim Dean, 224–3564.
Office Equipment Services Manager.—Win Grayson, 224–6779.
Telecom Services Manager.—Rick Kauffman, 224–9293.

MEDIA GALLERIES

Director of the Daily Press Gallery.—S. Joseph Keenan, S–316, 224–0241.
Director of the Periodical Press Gallery.—Edward V. Pesce, S–320, 224–0265.
Director of the Press Photographers Gallery.—Jeff Kent, S–317, 224–6548.
Director of the Radio and Television Gallery.—Michael Mastrian, S–325, 224–7610.

OFFICE OF EDUCATION AND TRAINING

Director of the Office of Education and Training.—Peggy Greenberg, SH–121, 224–5969.

OFFICE OF POLICE OPERATIONS, SECURITY AND EMERGENCY PREPARDNESS

Deputy Assistant Sergeant at Arms for Contingency and Emergency Preparedness Operations.—Michael Johnson (Postal Square), 224–1969.
Deputy Assistant Sergeant at Arms for LESO.—Dick Attridge, SVC 305, 224–3691.
Director for Security Policy and Planning (Postal Square).—Michael Chandler, 228–6737.

OFFICE SUPPORT SERVICES

Administrative Services Executive Manager.—Barbara Graybill (Postal Square), 224–5402.
Customer Support Manager.—Dave Cape, SD–180, 224–0310.
State Office Liaison.—Jeanne Tessieri (Postal Square), 224–5409.

PAGE PROGRAM

Director of the Page Program.—Elizabeth Roach (Webster Hall), 228–1291.

POLICE OPERATIONS

Chief of Staff, Operations.—Dan O'Sullivan, SDG–10, 224–8794.

PROCESS MANAGEMENT & INNOVATION

Director of Process Management & Innovation.—Ed Jankus (Postal Square), 224–7780.
IT Research & Deployment Manager.—Steve Walker, 224–1768.
Program Management Manager.—Joe Eckert, 224–2982.

RECORDING STUDIO

Recording Studio Manager.—Dave Bass, ST–29, 224–4979.

SENATE POST OFFICE

Senate Postmaster.—Joe Collins, SD–B23, 224–5675.
Superintendent of Mails.—Alan Stone, SD–B28, 224–1060.

TECHNOLOGY DEVELOPMENT

Director of Technology Development.—Tracy Williams (Postal Square), 224–8157.
Enterprise IT Operations Manager.—Karlos Davis, 224–3322.
Information Technology Security Manager.—Paul Grabow, 224–4966.
Research Services Branch.—Tom Meenan, 224–8620.
Network Engineering and Management Manager.—Wes Gardner, 224–9269.
Systems Development Services Manager.—Jay Moore, 224–0092.

OFFICE OF THE SECRETARY FOR THE MAJORITY

S–309 The Capitol, phone 224–3735

Secretary for the Majority.—Lula Johnson Davis.
Assistant Secretary for the Majority.—Tim Mitchell (S–118), 224–5551.
Administrative Assistant to the Secretary.—Nancy Iacomini.
Executive Assistant to the Secretary.—Amber Huus.

S–225 Majority Cloakroom, phone 224–4691

Cloakroom Assistants: Brandon Durflinger, Emma Fulkerson, Esteban Galvan, Meredith Mellody.

OFFICE OF THE SECRETARY FOR THE MINORITY

S–337 The Capitol, phone 224–3835, fax 224–2860

Secretary for the Minority.—David J. Schiappa (S–337).
Assistant Secretary for the Minority.—Laura Dove (S–335).
Administrative Assistant.—Noelle Busk Ringel (S–337).
Floor Assistant.—Jody Hernandez (S–335), phone 224–6191.

S–226 Minority Cloakroom, phone 224–6191

Cloakroom Assistants: Robert Duncan, Ashley Messick, Loren Streit, Patrick Kilcur.

S–335 Republican Legislative Scheduling, phone 224–5456

OFFICE OF THE LEGISLATIVE COUNSEL

668 Dirksen Senate Office Building, phone 224–6461, fax 224–0567

Legislative Counsel.—James W. Fransen.
Deputy Legislative Counsel.—William F. Jensen III.
Senior Counsels: Anthony C. Coe, Polly W. Craighill, Gary L. Endicott, Mark J. Mathiesen.

Assistant Counsels: Charles E. Armstrong, Laura M. Ayoud, John W. Baggaley, William R. Baird, Heather L. Burnham, Colin D. Campbell, Jr., Darcie E. Chan, Kevin M. Davis, Stephanie Easley, Ruth A. Ernst, Amy E. Gaynor, John A. Goetcheus, Robert A. Grant, John A. Henderson, Michelle L. Johnson-Weider, Stacy E. Kern-Scheerer, Elizabeth Aldridge King, Mark S. Koster, Heather A. Lowell, Kelly J. Malone, Matthew D. McGhie, Mark M. McGunagle, Allison M. Otto, Kristin K. Romero, Margaret A. Roth-Warren.

Staff Attorneys: Kimberly D. Albrecht-Taylor, Vincent J. Gaiani, Kimberly A. Whitaker, Alison J. Wright.

Systems Integrator.—Thomas E. Cole.

Office Manager.—Donna L. Pasqualino.

Senior Staff Assistants: Kimberly Bourne-Goldring, Diane E. Nesmeyer.

Staff Assistants: Lauren M. DeLaCruz, Daniela A. Gonzalez, Rebekah J. Musgrove, Patricia H. Olsavsky.

OFFICE OF SENATE LEGAL COUNSEL

642 Hart Senate Office Building, phone 224–4435, fax 224–3391

Senate Legal Counsel.—Morgan J. Frankel.

Deputy Senate Legal Counsel.—Patricia Mack Bryan.

Assistant Senate Legal Counsels: Thomas E. Caballero, Grant R. Vinik.

Systems Administrator / Legal Assistant.—Sara Fox Jones.

Administrative Assistant.—Kathleen M. Parker.

STANDING COMMITTEES OF THE HOUSE

[Democrats in roman; Republicans in *italic*; Resident Commissioner and Delegates in **boldface**]

[Room numbers beginning with H are in the Capitol, with CHOB in the Cannon House Office Building, with LHOB in the Longworth House Office Building, with RHOB in the Rayburn House Office Building, with H1 in O'Neill House Office Building, and with H2 in the Ford House Office Building]

Agriculture

1301 Longworth House Office Building, phone 225–2171, fax 225–8510

http://agriculture.house.gov

meets first Wednesday of each month

Collin C. Peterson, of Minnesota, *Chair*

Tim Holden, of Pennsylvania.
Mike McIntyre, of North Carolina.
Leonard L. Boswell, of Iowa.
Joe Baca, of California.
Dennis A. Cardoza, of California.
David Scott, of Georgia.
Jim Marshall, of Georgia.
Stephanie Herseth Sandlin, of South Dakota.
Henry Cuellar, of Texas.
Jim Costa, of California.
Brad Ellsworth, of Indiana.
Timothy J. Walz, of Minnesota.
Steve Kagen, of Wisconsin.
Kurt Schrader, of Oregon.
Deborah L. Halvorson, of Illinois.
Kathleen A. Dahlkemper, of Pennsylvania.
Eric J. J. Massa, of New York.
Bobby Bright, of Alabama.
Betsy Markey, of Colorado.
Frank Kratovil, Jr., of Maryland.
Mark H. Schauer, of Michigan.
Larry Kissell, of North Carolina.
John A. Boccieri, of Ohio.
Scott Murphy, of New York.
Earl Pomeroy, of North Dakota.
Travis W. Childers, of Mississippi.
Walt Minnick, of Idaho.

Frank D. Lucas, of Oklahoma.
Bob Goodlatte, of Virginia.
Jerry Moran, of Kansas.
Timothy V. Johnson, of Illinois.
Sam Graves, of Missouri.
Mike Rogers, of Alabama.
Steve King, of Iowa.
Randy Neugebauer, of Texas.
K. Michael Conaway, of Texas.
Jeff Fortenberry, of Nebraska.
Jean Schmidt, of Ohio.
Adrian Smith, of Nebraska.
Robert E. Latta, of Ohio.
David P. Roe, of Tennessee.
Blaine Luetkemeyer, of Missouri.
Glenn Thompson, of Pennsylvania.
Bill Cassidy, of Louisiana.
Cynthia M. Lummis, of Wyoming.

SUBCOMMITTEES

[The chairman and ranking minority member are ex officio (voting) members of all subcommittees on which they do not serve.]

Conservation, Credit, Energy, and Research

Tim Holden, of Pennsylvania, *Chair*

Stephanie Herseth Sandlin, of South Dakota.
Deborah L. Halvorson, of Illinois.
Kathleen A. Dahlkemper, of Pennsylvania.
Betsy Markey, of Colorado.
Mark H. Schauer, of Michigan.
Larry Kissell, of North Carolina.
John A. Boccieri, of Ohio.
Mike McIntyre, of North Carolina.
Jim Costa, of California.
Brad Ellsworth, of Indiana.
Timothy J. Walz, of Minnesota.
Eric J. J. Massa, of New York.
Bobby Bright, of Alabama.
Frank Kratovil, Jr., of Maryland.
Scott Murphy, of New York.
Walt Minnick, of Idaho.
Earl Pomeroy, of North Dakota.

Bob Goodlatte, of Virginia.
Jerry Moran, of Kansas.
Sam Graves, of Missouri.
Mike Rogers, of Alabama.
Steve King, of Iowa.
Randy Neugebauer, of Texas.
Jean Schmidt, of Ohio.
Adrian Smith, of Nebraska.
Robert E. Latta, of Ohio.
Blaine Luetkemeyer, of Missouri.
Glenn Thompson, of Pennsylvania.
Bill Cassidy, of Louisiana.

Department Operations, Oversight, Nutrition, and Forestry

Joe Baca, of California, *Chair*

Henry Cuellar, of Texas.
Steve Kagen, of Wisconsin.
Kurt Schrader, of Oregon.
Kathleen A. Dahlkemper, of Pennsylvania.
Travis W. Childers, of Mississippi.

Jeff Fortenberry, of Nebraska.
Steve King, of Iowa.
Jean Schmidt, of Ohio.
Cynthia M. Lummis, of Wyoming.

General Farm Commodities and Risk Management

Leonard L. Boswell, of Iowa, *Chair*

Jim Marshall, of Georgia.
Brad Ellsworth, of Indiana.
Timothy J. Walz, of Minnesota.
Kurt Schrader, of Oregon.
Stephanie Herseth Sandlin, of South Dakota.
Betsy Markey, of Colorado.
Larry Kissell, of North Carolina.
Deborah L. Halvorson, of Illinois.
Earl Pomeroy, of North Dakota.
Travis W. Childers, of Mississippi.

Jerry Moran, of Kansas.
Timothy V. Johnson, of Illinois.
Sam Graves, of Missouri.
Steve King, of Iowa.
K. Michael Conaway, of Texas.
Robert E. Latta, of Ohio.
Blaine Luetkemeyer, of Missouri.

Horticulture and Organic Agriculture

Dennis A. Cardoza, of California, *Chair*

Eric J. J. Massa, of New York.
Jim Costa, of California.
Kurt Schrader, of Oregon.
Frank Kratovil, Jr., of Maryland.
Scott Murphy, of New York.

Jean Schmidt, of Ohio.
Jerry Moran, of Kansas.
Timothy V. Johnson, of Illinois.
Cynthia M. Lummis, of Wyoming.

Livestock, Dairy, and Poultry

David Scott, of Georgia, *Chair*

Jim Costa, of California.
Steve Kagen, of Wisconsin.
Frank Kratovil, Jr., of Maryland.
Tim Holden, of Pennsylvania.
Leonard L. Boswell, of Iowa.
Joe Baca, of California.
Dennis A. Cardoza, of California.
Betsy Markey, of Colorado.
Scott Murphy, of New York.
Walt Minnick, of Idaho.
Randy Neugebauer, of Texas.
Bob Goodlatte, of Virginia.
Mike Rogers, of Alabama.
Steve King, of Iowa.
K. Michael Conaway, of Texas.
Adrian Smith, of Nebraska.
David P. Roe, of Tennessee.

Rural Development, Biotechnology, Specialty Crops, and Foreign Agriculture

Mike McIntyre, of North Carolina, *Chair*

Bobby Bright, of Alabama.
Jim Marshall, of Georgia.
Henry Cuellar, of Texas.
Larry Kissell, of North Carolina.
Walt Minnick, of Idaho.
K. Michael Conaway, of Texas.
David P. Roe, of Tennessee.
Glenn Thompson, of Pennsylvania.
Bill Cassidy, of Louisiana.

STAFF

Committee on Agriculture (1301 LHOB), 225–2171, fax 225–0917.
Majority Staff Director.—Rob Larew.
Assistant Clerk.—Sangina Wright (1304 LHOB), 5–4668.
Financial Administrator.—Wynn Bott (1340–A LHOB), 5–4963.
Deputy Executive Assistant.—Martha Josephson, 5–0421.
Director, Information Technology.—Merrick Munday, (1306 LHOB), 5–0172.
Chief Counsel.—Andy Baker (1304 LHOB), 5–3069.
Counsel.—Christy Birdsong (1304 LHOB), 5–4453; Nathan Fretz (1303 LHOB), 5–2183; Tony Jackson (1304 LHOB), 5–4927.
Communications Director.—April Demert Slayton (1301–A LHOB), 5–6872.
Chief Economist.—Craig Jagger (1407–A LHOB), 5–1130.
Executive Assistant.—Cherie Slayton.
Hearing Clerk.—Jamie Mitchell (1303 LHOB), 5–3329.
Information Technology Assistant.—John Konya (1301–A), 5–1198.
Office Manager.—Faye Smith, 5–6878.
Senior Professional Staff.—Jeremy Bratt, 5–1564; Crain Claiborn, (1336 LHOB), 5–4652; Anne Simmons (1534 LHOB), 5–1494.
Press Assistant.—James Ryder (1301–A), 5–0020.
Professional Staff.—Scott Kuschmider (1301–A LHOB), 5–1496.
Legislative Assistant.—Alejandra Gonzalez-Arias (1336 LHOB), 5–4962; Tyler Jameson (1407 LHOB), 5–4982; Rebekah Solem, 5–2171.
Legislative Clerk.—Debbie Smith (1304 LHOB), 5–9384.
Staff Assistant.—Shannon Juhnke.
Subcommittee Staff Directors:
Conservation, Credit, Rural Development and Research.—Nona Darrell (1336 LHOB), 5–0420.
Department Operations, Oversight, Nutrition and Forestry.—Lisa Shelton (1407 LHOB), 5–6395.
General Farm Commodities and Risk Management.—Clark Ogilvie (1407 LHOB), 5–0720.
Horticulture and Organic Agriculture.—Keith Jones (1336 LHOB), 5–6238.
Livestock, Dairy, and Poultry.—Chandler Goule (1336 LHOB), 5–8407.
Rural Development, Biotechnology, Specialty Crops, and Foreign Agriculture.—Aleta Botts (1407 LHOB), 5–8248.
Minority Chief of Staff.—Nicole Scott (1305 LHOB), 5–0029.
Chief Counsel.—Kevin Kramp.
Deputy Staff Director.—Josh Mathis.
Communications Director.—Tamara Hinton.
Counsel.—Patricia Barr.
Legislative Assistants: Brent Blevins, Mike Dunlap.

Policy Director.—Bill O'Conner.
Professional Staff: Josh Maxwell, Ben Veghte.
Senior Professional Staff: John Goldberg, Pam Miller, Pelham Straughn, Pete Thomson.
Staff Assistant.—Mary Nowak.

Appropriations

H–218 The Capitol, phone 225–2771

http://www.house.gov/appropriations

David R. Obey, of Wisconsin, *Chair*

John P. Murtha, of Pennsylvania.
Norman D. Dicks, of Washington.
Alan B. Mollohan, of West Virginia.
Marcy Kaptur, of Ohio.
Peter J. Visclosky, of Indiana.
Nita M. Lowey, of New York.
José E. Serrano, of New York.
Rosa L. DeLauro, of Connecticut.
James P. Moran, of Virginia.
John W. Olver, of Massachusetts.
Ed Pastor, of Arizona.
David E. Price, of North Carolina.
Chet Edwards, of Texas.
Patrick J. Kennedy, of Rhode Island.
Maurice D. Hinchey, of New York.
Lucille Roybal-Allard, of California.
Sam Farr, of California.
Jesse L. Jackson, Jr., of Illinois.
Carolyn C. Kilpatrick, of Michigan.
Allen Boyd, of Florida.
Chaka Fattah, of Pennsylvania.
Steven R. Rothman, of New Jersey.
Sanford D. Bishop, Jr., of Georgia.
Marion Berry, of Arkansas.
Barbara Lee, of California.
Adam B. Schiff, of California.
Michael M. Honda, of California.
Betty McCollum, of Minnesota.
Steve Israel, of New York.
Tim Ryan, of Ohio.
C. A. Dutch Ruppersberger, of Maryland.
Ben Chandler, of Kentucky.
Debbie Wasserman Schultz, of Florida.
Ciro D. Rodriguez, of Texas.
Lincoln Davis, of Tennessee.
John T. Salazar, of Colorado.

Jerry Lewis, of California.
C. W. Bill Young, of Florida.
Harold Rogers, of Kentucky.
Frank R. Wolf, of Virginia.
Jack Kingston, of Georgia.
Rodney P. Frelinghuysen, of New Jersey.
Todd Tiahrt, of Kansas.
Zach Wamp, of Tennessee.
Tom Latham, of Iowa.
Robert B. Aderholt, of Alabama.
Jo Ann Emerson, of Missouri.
Kay Granger, of Texas.
Michael K. Simpson, of Idaho.
John Abney Culberson, of Texas.
Mark Steven Kirk, of Illinois.
Ander Crenshaw, of Florida.
Denny Rehberg, of Montana.
John R. Carter, of Texas.
Rodney Alexander, of Louisiana.
Ken Calvert, of California.
Jo Bonner, of Alabama.
Steven C. LaTourette, of Ohio.
Tom Cole, of Oklahoma.

SUBCOMMITTEES

[The chairman and ranking minority member are ex officio (voting) members of all subcommittees on which they do not serve.]

Agriculture, Rural Development, Food and Drug Administration, and Related Agencies

Rosa L. DeLauro, of Connecticut, *Chair*

Sam Farr, of California.
Allen Boyd, of Florida.
Sanford D. Bishop, Jr., of Georgia.
Lincoln Davis, of Tennessee.
Marcy Kaptur, of Ohio.
Maurice D. Hinchey, of New York.
Jesse L. Jackson, Jr., of Illinois.

Jack Kingston, of Georgia.
Tom Latham, of Iowa.
Jo Ann Emerson, of Missouri.
Rodney Alexander, of Louisiana.

Commerce, Justice, Science, and Related Agencies

Alan B. Mollohan, of West Virginia, *Chair*

Patrick J. Kennedy, of Rhode Island.
Chaka Fattah, of Pennsylvania.
Adam B. Schiff, of California.
Michael M. Honda, of California.
C. A. Dutch Ruppersberger, of Maryland.
Peter J. Visclosky, of Indiana.
José E. Serrano, of New York.

Frank R. Wolf, of Virginia.
John Abney Culberson, of Texas.
Robert B. Aderholt, of Alabama.
Jo Bonner, of Alabama.

Defense

John P. Murtha, of Pennsylvania, *Chair*

Norman D. Dicks, of Washington.
Peter J. Visclosky, of Indiana.
James P. Moran, of Virginia.
Marcy Kaptur, of Ohio.
Allen Boyd, of Florida.
Steven R. Rothman, of New Jersey.
Sanford D. Bishop, Jr., of Georgia.
Maurice D. Hinchey, of New York.
Carolyn C. Kilpatrick, of Michigan.

C. W. Bill Young, of Florida.
Rodney P. Frelinghuysen, of New Jersey.
Todd Tiahrt, of Kansas.
Jack Kingston, of Georgia.
Kay Granger, of Texas.
Harold Rogers, of Kentucky.

Energy and Water Development, and Related Agencies

Peter J. Visclosky, of Indiana, *Chair*

Chet Edwards, of Texas.
Ed Pastor, of Arizona.
Marion Berry, of Arkansas.
Chaka Fattah, of Pennsylvania.
Steve Israel, of New York.
Tim Ryan, of Ohio.
John W. Olver, of Massachusetts.
Lincoln Davis, of Tennessee.
John T. Salazar, of Colorado.

Rodney P. Frelinghuysen, of New Jersey.
Zach Wamp, of Tennessee.
Michael K. Simpson, of Idaho.
Denny Rehberg, of Montana.
Ken Calvert, of California.
Rodney Alexander, of Louisiana.

Financial Services and General Government

José E. Serrano, of New York, *Chair*

Debbie Wasserman Schultz, of Florida.
Rosa L. DeLauro, of Connecticut.
Chet Edwards, of Texas.
Allen Boyd, of Florida.
Chaka Fattah, of Pennsylvania.
Barbara Lee, of California.
Adam B. Schiff, of California.

Jo Ann Emerson, of Missouri.
John Abney Culberson, of Texas.
Mark Steven Kirk, of Illinois.
Ander Crenshaw, of Florida.

Homeland Security

David E. Price, of North Carolina, *Chair*

José E. Serrano, of New York.
Ciro D. Rodriguez, of Texas.
C. A. Dutch Ruppersberger, of Maryland.
Alan B. Mollohan, of West Virginia.
Nita M. Lowey, of New York.
Lucille Roybal-Allard, of California.
Sam Farr, of California.
Steven R. Rothman, of New Jersey.

Harold Rogers, of Kentucky.
John R. Carter, of Texas.
John Abney Culberson, of Texas.
Mark Steven Kirk, of Illinois.
Ken Calvert, of California.

Interior, Environment, and Related Agencies

Norman D. Dicks, of Washington, *Chair*

James P. Moran, of Virginia.
Alan B. Mollohan, of West Virginia.
Ben Chandler, of Kentucky.
Maurice D. Hinchey, of New York.
John W. Olver, of Massachusetts.
Ed Pastor, of Arizona.
David E. Price, of North Carolina.
Michael K. Simpson, of Idaho.
Ken Calvert, of California.
Steven C. LaTourette, of Ohio.
Tom Cole, of Oklahoma.

Labor, Health and Human Services, Education, and Related Agencies

David R. Obey, of Wisconsin, *Chair*

Nita M. Lowey, of New York.
Rosa L. DeLauro, of Connecticut.
Jesse L. Jackson, Jr., of Illinois.
Patrick J. Kennedy, of Rhode Island.
Lucille Roybal-Allard, of California.
Barbara Lee, of California.
Michael M. Honda, of California.
Betty McCollum, of Minnesota.
Tim Ryan, of Ohio.
James P. Moran, of Virginia.
Todd Tiahrt, of Kansas.
Denny Rehberg, of Montana.
Rodney Alexander, of Louisiana.
Jo Bonner, of Alabama.
Tom Cole, of Oklahoma.

Legislative Branch

Debbie Wasserman Schultz, of Florida, *Chair*

Michael M. Honda, of California.
Betty McCollum, of Minnesota.
Tim Ryan, of Ohio.
C. A. Dutch Ruppersberger, of Maryland.
Ciro D. Rodriguez, of Texas.
Robert B. Aderholt, of Alabama.
Steven C. LaTourette, of Ohio.
Tom Cole, of Oklahoma.

Military Construction, Veterans' Affairs, and Related Agencies

Chet Edwards, of Texas, *Chair*

Sam Farr, of California.
John T. Salazar, of Colorado.
Norman D. Dicks, of Washington.
Patrick J. Kennedy, of Rhode Island.
Sanford D. Bishop, Jr., of Georgia.
Marion Berry, of Arkansas.
Steve Israel, of New York.
Zach Wamp, of Tennessee.
Ander Crenshaw, of Florida.
C. W. Bill Young, of Florida.
John R. Carter, of Texas.

State, Foreign Operations, and Related Programs

Nita M. Lowey, of New York, *Chair*

Jesse L. Jackson, Jr., of Illinois.
Adam B. Schiff, of California.
Steve Israel, of New York.
Ben Chandler, of Kentucky.
Steven R. Rothman, of New Jersey.
Barbara Lee, of California.
Betty McCollum, of Minnesota.
Kay Granger, of Texas.
Mark Steven Kirk, of Illinois.
Ander Crenshaw, of Florida.
Denny Rehberg, of Montana.

Transportation, Housing and Urban Development, and Related Agencies

John W. Olver, of Massachusetts, *Chair*

Ed Pastor, of Arizona.
Ciro D. Rodriguez, of Texas.
Marcy Kaptur, of Ohio.
David E. Price, of North Carolina.
Lucille Roybal-Allard, of California.
Marion Berry, of Arkansas.
Carolyn C. Kilpatrick, of Michigan.

Tom Latham, of Iowa.
Frank R. Wolf, of Virginia.
John R. Carter, of Texas.
Steven C. LaTourette, of Ohio.

STAFF

Committee on Appropriations (H–218), 225–2771.
Majority Clerk and Staff Director.—Beverly Aimaro Pheto.
Administrative Assistant.—Sandy Farrow.
Office Assistant.—Theodore Powell.
Staff Assistants: Michelle Burkett, Joseph Carlile, Rebecca Motley, Ryan Nickel, Lesley Turner, Matthew Washington.
Communications Director.—Ellis Brachman.
Deputy Press Secretary.—Jenilee Keefe Singer.
Editors: Larry Boarman, Cathy Edwards (B–301A RHOB), 5–2851.
Computer Operations: Vernon Hammett, Cathy Little, Linda Muir, Chauncey Powell, Jay Sivulich (B–305 RHOB), 5–2718.
Minority Staff Director.—Jeff Schockey (1016 LHOB), 5–3481.
Minority Deputy Staff Director.—Dave LesStrang.
Administrative Aides: Jenny Mummert, Kelly Shea.
Subcommittee on Agriculture, Rural Development, Food and Drug Administration, and Related Agencies (2362–A RHOB), 5–2638.
Staff Assistants: Leslie Barrack, Martha Foley, Clifford Isenberg.
Administrative Aide.—Matthew Smith.
Minority Staff Assistants.—David Gibbons, Stephanie Myers (1016 LHOB), 5–3481.
Subcommittee on Commerce, Justice, Science and Related Agencies (H–309), 5–3351.
Staff Assistants: John Blazey, Dixon Butler, Adrienne Simonson, Diana Simpson, Darek Newby.
Administrative Aide.—Tracy LaTurner.
Minority Staff Assistants: John Martens, Mike Ringler (1016 LHOB), 5–3481.
Subcommittee on Defense (H–149), 5–2847.
Staff Assistants: Brooke Boyer, Adam Harris, Celes Hughes, Kevin Jones, Paul Juola, Greg Lankler, Kris Mallard, Linda Pagelsen, Tim Prince, Adrienne Ramsay, Ann Reese, Paul Terry, Christopher White, B.G. Wright, Sarah Young.
Administrative Aide.—Sherry Young.
Minority Staff Assistants: Tom McLemore, Jennifer Miller (1016 LHOB), 5–3481.
Subcommittee on Energy and Water Development, and Related Agencies (2362–B RHOB), 5–3421.
Staff Assistants: Taunja Berquam, Robert Sherman, Joe Levin, James Windle.
Administrative Aide.—Casey Pearce.
Minority Staff Assistants: Rob Blair, Kevin Jones (1016 LHOB), 5–3481.
Subcommittee on Financial Services (1040A LHOB), 5–7245.
Staff Assistants: Bob Bonner, Lee Price, David Reich.
Administrative Aide.—Ariana Sarar.
Minority Staff Assistants: Dena Baron, Alice Hogans, John Martens (1016 LHOB), 5–3481.
Subcommittee on Homeland Security (B–307 RHOB), 5–5834.
Staff Assistants: Jeff Ashford, Stephanie Gupta, Jim Holm, Karyn Kendall, Will Painter.
Administrative Aide.—Michael Birsic.
Minority Staff Assistants: Allison Deters, Ben Nicholson (1016 LHOB), 5–3481.
Subcommittee on Interior, Environment, and Related Agencies (B–308 RHOB), 5–3081.
Staff Assistants: Julie Falkner, Greg Knadle, Delia Scott, Christopher Topik.
Administrative Aide.—Beth Houser.
Minority Staff Assistants: Darren Benjamin, Dave LesStrang (1016 LHOB), 5–3481.
Subcommittee on Labor, Health and Human Services, Education, and Related Agencies (2358 RHOB), 5–3508.
Staff Assistants: Nicole Kunko, Sue Quantius, Donna Shahbaz, Cheryl Smith, Stephen Steigleder.

Administrative Aide.—Albert Lee.
Minority Staff Assistants: Steve Crane, Stephanie Myers (1016 LHOB), 5–3481.
Subcommittee on Legislative Branch (H–147), 6–7252.
Staff Assistants: Michael Stephens, Shalanda Young.
Minority Staff Assistant.—Liz Dawson.
Minority Administrative Aide.—Jennifer Kisiah.
Subcommittee on Military Construction, Veterans' Affairs, and Related Agencies (H–143), 5–3047.
Staff Assistants: Walter Hearne, Carol Murphy, Tim Peterson.
Administrative Aide.—Mary Arnold.
Minority Staff Assistants: Liz Dawson, Martin Delgado (1016 LHOB), 5–3481.
Minority Administrative Aide.—Kelly Shea.
Subcommittee on State and Foreign Operations (HB–26), 5–2401.
Staff Assistants: Nisha Desai, Craig Higgins, Steve Marchese, Michele Sumilas.
Administrative Aide.—Clelia Alvarado.
Minority Staff Assistants: Anne Marie Chotvacs, Alice Hogans, Mike Ringler (1016 LHOB), 5–3481.
Subcommittee on Transportation, HUD and Independent Agencies (2358 RHOB), 5–2141.
Staff Assistants: Kate Hallahan, Laura Hogshead, David Napoliello, Sylvia Garcia.
Administrative Aide.—Alex Gillen.
Minority Staff Assistants: Dena Baron, Allison Deters, Dave Gibbons (1016 LHOB), 5–3481.

Armed Services

2120 Rayburn House Office Building, phone 225–4151, fax 225–9077
http://www.house.gov/hasc

Ike Skelton, of Missouri, *Chair*

John M. Spratt, Jr., of South Carolina.
Solomon P. Ortiz, of Texas.
Gene Taylor, of Mississippi.
Neil Abercrombie, of Hawaii.
Silvestre Reyes, of Texas.
Vic Snyder, of Arkansas.
Adam Smith, of Washington.
Loretta Sanchez, of California.
Mike McIntyre, of North Carolina.
Robert A. Brady, of Pennsylvania.
Robert E. Andrews, of New Jersey.
Susan A. Davis, of California.
James R. Langevin, of Rhode Island.
Rick Larsen, of Washington.
Jim Cooper, of Tennessee.
Jim Marshall, of Georgia.
Madeleine Z. Bordallo, of Guam.
Brad Ellsworth, of Indiana.
Patrick J. Murphy, of Pennsylvania.
Henry C. ''Hank'' Johnson, Jr., of Georgia.
Carol Shea-Porter, of New Hampshire.
Joe Courtney, of Connecticut.
David Loebsack, of Iowa.
Joe Sestak, of Pennsylvania.
Gabrielle Giffords, of Arizona.
Niki Tsongas, of Massachusetts.
Glenn C. Nye, of Virginia.
Chellie Pingree, of Maine.
Larry Kissell, of North Carolina.
Martin Heinrich, of New Mexico.
Frank Kratovil, Jr., of Maryland.
Eric J. J. Massa, of New York.
Bobby Bright, of Alabama.
Scott Murphy, of New York.
Dan Boren, of Oklahoma.
Vacant.

Howard P. ''Buck'' McKeon, of California.
Roscoe G. Bartlett, of Maryland.
Mac Thornberry, of Texas.
Walter B. Jones, of North Carolina.
W. Todd Akin, of Missouri.
J. Randy Forbes, of Virginia.
Jeff Miller, of Florida.
Joe Wilson, of South Carolina.
Frank A. LoBiondo, of New Jersey.
Rob Bishop, of Utah.
Michael R. Turner, of Ohio.
John Kline, of Minnesota.
Mike Rogers, of Alabama.
Trent Franks, of Arizona.
Bill Shuster, of Pennsylvania.
Cathy McMorris Rodgers, of Washington.
K. Michael Conaway, of Texas.
Doug Lamborn, of Colorado.
Robert J. Wittman, of Virginia.
Mary Fallin, of Oklahoma.
Duncan Hunter, of California.
John Fleming, of Louisiana.
Mike Coffman, of Colorado.
Thomas J. Rooney, of Florida.
Todd Russell Platts, of Pennsylvania.

SUBCOMMITTEES

Air and Land Forces

Neil Abercrombie, of Hawaii, *Chair*

John M. Spratt, Jr., of South Carolina.
Silvestre Reyes, of Texas.
Adam Smith, of Washington.
Mike McIntyre, of North Carolina.
Robert A. Brady, of Pennsylvania.
Jim Cooper, of Tennessee.
Jim Marshall, of Georgia.
Joe Sestak, of Pennsylvania.
Gabrielle Giffords, of Arizona.
Niki Tsongas, of Massachusetts.
Larry Kissell, of North Carolina.
Frank Kratovil, Jr., of Maryland.
Eric J. J. Massa, of New York.
Bobby Bright, of Alabama.
Dan Boren, of Oklahoma.
Vacant.

Roscoe G. Bartlett, of Maryland.
Cathy McMorris Rodgers, of Washington.
Mary Fallin, of Oklahoma.
Duncan Hunter, of California.
John Fleming, of Louisiana.
Mike Coffman, of Colorado.
W. Todd Akin, of Missouri.
Jeff Miller, of Florida.
Joe Wilson, of South Carolina.
Frank A. LoBiondo, of New Jersey.
Rob Bishop, of Utah.
Michael R. Turner, of Ohio.
Todd Russell Platts, of Pennsylvania.

Military Personnel

Susan A. Davis, of California, *Chair*

Vic Snyder, of Arkansas.
Loretta Sanchez, of California.
Madeleine Z. Bordallo, of Guam.
Patrick J. Murphy, of Pennsylvania.
Henry C. ''Hank'' Johnson, Jr., of Georgia.
Carol Shea-Porter, of New Hampshire.
David Loebsack, of Iowa.
Niki Tsongas, of Massachusetts.

Joe Wilson, of South Carolina.
Walter B. Jones, of North Carolina.
John Kline, of Minnesota.
Thomas J. Rooney, of Florida.
Mary Fallin, of Oklahoma.
John Fleming, of Louisiana.

Oversight and Investigations

Vic Snyder, of Arkansas, *Chair*

John M. Spratt, Jr., of South Carolina.
Loretta Sanchez, of California.
Susan A. Davis, of California.
Jim Cooper, of Tennessee.
Joe Sestak, of Pennsylvania.
Glenn C. Nye, of Virginia.
Chellie Pingree, of Maine.
Vacant.

Robert J. Wittman, of Virginia.
Walter B. Jones, of North Carolina.
Mike Rogers, of Alabama.
Trent Franks, of Arizona.
Cathy McMorris Rodgers, of Washington.
Doug Lamborn, of Colorado.
Todd Russell Platts, of Pennsylvania.

Readiness

Solomon P. Ortiz, of Texas, *Chair*

Gene Taylor, of Mississippi.
Neil Abercrombie, of Hawaii.
Silvestre Reyes, of Texas.
Jim Marshall, of Georgia.
Madeleine Z. Bordallo, of Guam.
Henry C. ''Hank'' Johnson, Jr., of Georgia.
Carol Shea-Porter, of New Hampshire.
Joe Courtney, of Connecticut.
David Loebsack, of Iowa.
Gabrielle Giffords, of Arizona.
Glenn C. Nye, of Virginia.
Larry Kissell, of North Carolina.
Martin Heinrich, of New Mexico.
Frank Kratovil, Jr., of Maryland.
Bobby Bright, of Alabama.
Dan Boren, of Oklahoma.

J. Randy Forbes, of Virginia.
Rob Bishop, of Utah.
Mike Rogers, of Alabama.
Trent Franks, of Arizona.
Bill Shuster, of Pennsylvania.
K. Michael Conaway, of Texas.
Doug Lamborn, of Colorado.
Robert J. Wittman, of Virginia.
Mary Fallin, of Oklahoma.
John Fleming, of Louisiana.
Frank A. LoBiondo, of New Jersey.
Michael R. Turner, of Ohio.

Seapower and Expeditionary Forces

Gene Taylor, of Mississippi, *Chair*

Solomon P. Ortiz, of Texas.
James R. Langevin, of Rhode Island.
Rick Larsen, of Washington.
Brad Ellsworth, of Indiana.
Joe Courtney, of Connecticut.
Joe Sestak, of Pennsylvania.
Glenn C. Nye, of Virginia.
Chellie Pingree, of Maine.
Eric J. J. Massa, of New York.

W. Todd Akin, of Missouri.
Robert J. Wittman, of Virginia.
Roscoe G. Bartlett, of Maryland.
J. Randy Forbes, of Virginia.
Duncan Hunter, of California.
Mike Coffman, of Colorado.
Thomas J. Rooney, of Florida.

Strategic Forces

James R. Langevin, of Rhode Island, *Chair*

John M. Spratt, Jr., of South Carolina.
Loretta Sanchez, of California.
Robert E. Andrews, of New Jersey.
Rick Larsen, of Washington.
Martin Heinrich, of New Mexico.
Scott Murphy, of New York.
Vacant.

Michael R. Turner, of Ohio.
Mac Thornberry, of Texas.
Trent Franks, of Arizona.
Doug Lamborn, of Colorado.
Mike Rogers, of Alabama.

Terrorism, Unconventional Threats and Capabilities

Adam Smith, of Washington, *Chair*

Mike McIntyre, of North Carolina.
Robert E. Andrews, of New Jersey.
James R. Langevin, of Rhode Island.
Jim Cooper, of Tennessee.
Jim Marshall, of Georgia.
Brad Ellsworth, of Indiana.
Patrick J. Murphy, of Pennsylvania.
Bobby Bright, of Alabama.
Scott Murphy, of New York.

Jeff Miller, of Florida.
Frank A. LoBiondo, of New Jersey.
John Kline, of Minnesota.
Bill Shuster, of Pennsylvania.
K. Michael Conaway, of Texas.
Thomas J. Rooney, of Florida.
Mac Thornberry, of Texas.

STAFF

Committee on Armed Services (2120 RHOB), 225–4151, fax 225–9077.
Staff Director.—Erin C. Conaton.
Deputy Staff Director.—Paul Arcangeli.
General Counsel.—Paul Oostburg Sanz.
Counsels: William Johnson, Suzanne McKenna, Julie Unmacht, Roger Zakheim.
Professional Staff: Aileen Alexander, John D. Chapla, Rudy Barnes, Kari Bingen, Heath Bope, Douglas Bush, Michael Casey, Coleman Everett, William Ebbs, Bob DeGrasse, Lorry Fenner, Cathy Garman, Kevin Gates, Craig Green, Thomas E. Hawley, Michael R. Higgins, Joshua Holly, Andrew Hunter, Jeanette S. James, Dave Kildee, John Kruse, Alex Kugajevsky, Mark R. Lewis, Timothy McClees, Phil MacNaughton, Vickie Plunkett, Douglas C. Roach, Eryn Robinson, Rebecca Ross, Jack Schuler, David Sienicki, Jenness Simler, Robert L. Simmons, John F. Sullivan, Jesse Tolleson, Debra S. Wada, Nancy M. Warner, John Wason, Lynn Williams.
Press Secretaries: Lara Battles, Jennifer Kohl.
Legislative Operations Director.—Joe Hicken.
Staff Assistants: Katy Bloomberg, Scott Bousum, Mary Kate Cunningham, Liz Drummond, Betty B. Gray, Cyndi Howard, Trey Howard, J.J. Johnson, Kathleen Kelly, Rosellen Kim, Zach Steacy, Andrew Tabler.
Printing Clerk.—Linda M. Burnette.

Budget

309 Cannon House Office Building 20515–6065, phone 226–7270, fax 226–7174

http://www.budget.house.gov

John M. Spratt, Jr., of South Carolina, *Chair*

Allyson Y. Schwartz, of Pennsylvania.
Marcy Kaptur, of Ohio.
Xavier Becerra, of California.
Lloyd Doggett, of Texas.
Earl Blumenauer, of Oregon.
Marion Berry, of Arkansas.
Allen Boyd, of Florida.
James P. McGovern, of Massachusetts.
Niki Tsongas, of Massachusetts.
Bob Etheridge, of North Carolina.
Betty McCollum, of Minnesota.
Charlie Melancon, of Louisiana.
John A. Yarmuth, of Kentucky.
Robert E. Andrews, of New Jersey.
Rosa L. DeLauro, of Connecticut.
Chet Edwards, of Texas.
Robert C. ''Bobby'' Scott, of Virginia.
James R. Langevin, of Rhode Island.
Rick Larsen, of Washington.
Timothy H. Bishop, of New York.
Gwen Moore, of Wisconsin.
Gerald E. Connolly, of Virginia.
Kurt Schrader, of Oregon.

Paul Ryan, of Wisconsin.
Scott Garrett, of New Jersey.
Mario Diaz-Balart, of Florida.
Jeb Hensarling, of Texas.
Michael K. Simpson, of Idaho.
Patrick T. McHenry, of North Carolina.
Connie Mack, of Florida.
John Campbell, of California.
Jim Jordan, of Ohio.
Devin Nunes, of California.
Robert B. Aderholt, of Alabama.
Cynthia M. Lummis, of Wyoming.
Steve Austria, of Ohio.
Gregg Harper, of Mississippi.
Robert E. Latta, of Ohio.

(No Subcommittees)

Committee on Budget (207 CHOB), 226–7200, fax 225–9905.
Majority Staff Director.—Tom Kahn.
Deputy Staff Director.—Arthur Burris.
Chief Counsel.—Gail Millar.
Parliamentary Counsel.—Lisa Venus.
Counsel.—Naomi S. Stern.
Chief Economist.—Adam Carasso.
Senior Policy Coordinator.—Sarah Abernathy.
Policy Assistant.—Andrew Fieldhouse.
Budget Review Director.—Kimberly Overbeek.
Senior Budget Review Specialist.—Ellen J. Balis.
Budget Analysts: Stephen G. Elmore, Jason Freihage, Diana Meredith, Morna Miller, Scott R. Russell, Greg R. Waring, Andrea R. Weathers.
Chief Administrator.—Marsha Douglas.
Office Manager.—Sheila A. McDowell.
Senior Staff Assistant.—Linda M. Bywaters.
Systems Administrator.—Jose Guillen.
Committee Printer.—Richard E. Magee.
Staff Assistant.—Marcus D. Stephens, 6–1887.
Minority Chief of Staff.—Austin Smythe, (B71 Cannon), 226–7270, fax 226–7174.
Deputy Staff Director.—Chauncey Goss.
Executive Assistant and Budget Analyst.—Jonathan Romito.
Policy Director.—Pat Knudsen.
Director of Communications.—Angela Kuck.
Special Assistant and Budget Analyst.—John Gray.
Appropriations / Budget Analyst.—Stephen Sepp.
Budget Analysts: Courtney Reinhard, Jim Herz, Ted McCann, Dana Wade.
Chief Counsel / Budget Analyst.—Paul Restuccia.
Counsel / Budget Analyst.—Charlotte Ivancic.
Chief Economist.—Timothy Flynn.

Education and Labor

2181 Rayburn House Office Building, phone 225–3725, fax 226–5398

http://edlabor.house.gov

George Miller, of California, *Chair*

Dale E. Kildee, of Michigan.
Donald M. Payne, of New Jersey.
Robert E. Andrews, of New Jersey.
Robert C. "Bobby" Scott, of Virginia.
Lynn C. Woolsey, of California.
Rubén Hinojosa, of Texas.
Carolyn McCarthy, of New York.
John F. Tierney, of Massachusetts.
Dennis J. Kucinich, of Ohio.
David Wu, of Oregon.
Rush D. Holt, of New Jersey.
Susan A. Davis, of California.
Raúl M. Grijalva, of Arizona.
Timothy H. Bishop, of New York.
Joe Sestak, of Pennsylvania.
David Loebsack, of Iowa.
Mazie K. Hirono, of Hawaii.
Jason Altmire, of Pennsylvania.
Phil Hare, of Illinois.
Yvette D. Clarke, of New York.
Joe Courtney, of Connecticut.
Carol Shea-Porter, of New Hampshire.
Marcia L. Fudge, of Ohio.
Jared Polis, of Colorado.
Paul Tonko, of New York.
Pedro R. Pierluisi, of Puerto Rico.
Gregorio Kilili Camacho Sablan, of Northern Mariana Islands.
Dina Titus, of Nevada.
Judy Chu, of California.

John Kline, of Minnesota.
Thomas E. Petri, of Wisconsin.
Howard P. "Buck" McKeon, of California.
Peter Hoekstra, of Michigan.
Michael N. Castle, of Delaware.
Mark E. Souder, of Indiana.
Vernon J. Ehlers, of Michigan.
Judy Biggert, of Illinois.
Todd Russell Platts, of Pennsylvania.
Joe Wilson, of South Carolina.
Cathy McMorris Rodgers, of Washington.
Tom Price, of Georgia.
Rob Bishop, of Utah.
Brett Guthrie, of Kentucky.
Bill Cassidy, of Louisiana.
Tom McClintock, of California.
Duncan Hunter, of California.
David P. Roe, of Tennessee.
Glenn Thompson, of Pennsylvania.

SUBCOMMITTEES

[The chairman and ranking minority member are ex officio (non-voting) members of all subcommittees on which they do not serve.]

Early Childhood, Elementary and Secondary Education

Dale E. Kildee, of Michigan, *Chair*

Donald M. Payne, of New Jersey.
Robert C. "Bobby" Scott, of Virginia.
Rush D. Holt, of New Jersey.
Susan A. Davis, of California.
Raúl M. Grijalva, of Arizona.
Joe Sestak, of Pennsylvania.
David Loebsack, of Iowa.
Mazie K. Hirono, of Hawaii.
Jared Polis, of Colorado.
Pedro R. Pierluisi, of Puerto Rico.
Gregorio Kilili Camacho Sablan, of Northern Mariana Islands.
Lynn C. Woolsey, of California.
Rubén Hinojosa, of Texas.
Dennis J. Kucinich, of Ohio.
Jason Altmire, of Pennsylvania.
Dina Titus, of Nevada.
Judy Chu, of California.

Michael N. Castle, of Delaware.
Thomas E. Petri, of Wisconsin.
Peter Hoekstra, of Michigan.
Mark E. Souder, of Indiana.
Vernon J. Ehlers, of Michigan.
Judy Biggert, of Illinois.
Todd Russell Platts, of Pennsylvania.
Cathy McMorris Rodgers, of Washington.
Rob Bishop, of Utah.
Bill Cassidy, of Louisiana.
Tom McClintock, of California.
Duncan Hunter, of California.

Healthy Families and Communities

Carolyn McCarthy, of New York, *Chair*

Yvette D. Clarke, of New York.
Robert C. "Bobby" Scott, of Virginia.
Carol Shea-Porter, of New Hampshire.
Paul Tonko, of New York.
Jared Polis, of Colorado.
George Miller, of California.
Judy Chu, of California.

Todd Russell Platts, of Pennsylvania.
Howard P. "Buck" McKeon, of California.
Brett Guthrie, of Kentucky.
David P. Roe, of Tennessee.
Glenn Thompson, of Pennsylvania.

Higher Education, Lifelong Learning, and Competitiveness

Rubén Hinojosa, of Texas, *Chair*

Timothy H. Bishop, of New York.
Jason Altmire, of Pennsylvania.
Joe Courtney, of Connecticut.
Paul Tonko, of New York.
Dina Titus, of Nevada.
Robert E. Andrews, of New Jersey.
John F. Tierney, of Massachusetts.
David Wu, of Oregon.
Susan A. Davis, of California.
Mazie K. Hirono, of Hawaii.
Marcia L. Fudge, of Ohio.
Jared Polis, of Colorado.
Pedro R. Pierluisi, of Puerto Rico.

Brett Guthrie, of Kentucky.
John Kline, of Minnesota.
Michael N. Castle, of Delaware.
Mark E. Souder, of Indiana.
Vernon J. Ehlers, of Michigan.
Judy Biggert, of Illinois.
Bill Cassidy, of Louisiana.
David P. Roe, of Tennessee.
Glenn Thompson, of Pennsylvania.

Health, Employment, Labor, and Pensions

Robert E. Andrews, of New Jersey, *Chair*

David Wu, of Oregon.
Phil Hare, of Illinois.
John F. Tierney, of Massachusetts.
Dennis J. Kucinich, of Ohio.
Marcia L. Fudge, of Ohio.
Dale E. Kildee, of Michigan.
Carolyn McCarthy, of New York.
Rush D. Holt, of New Jersey.
Joe Sestak, of Pennsylvania.
David Loebsack, of Iowa.
Yvette D. Clarke, of New York.
Joe Courtney, of Connecticut.

Tom Price, of Georgia.
John Kline, of Minnesota.
Howard P. "Buck" McKeon, of California.
Joe Wilson, of South Carolina.
Brett Guthrie, of Kentucky.
Tom McClintock, of California.
Duncan Hunter, of California.
David P. Roe, of Tennessee.

Workforce Protections

Lynn C. Woolsey, of California, *Chair*

Carol Shea-Porter, of New Hampshire.
Donald M. Payne, of New Jersey.
Raúl M. Grijalva, of Arizona.
Timothy H. Bishop, of New York.
Phil Hare, of Illinois.
Gregorio Kilili Camacho Sablan, of Northern Mariana Islands.

Cathy McMorris Rodgers, of Washington.
Peter Hoekstra, of Michigan.
Joe Wilson, of South Carolina.
Tom Price, of Georgia.

STAFF

Committee on Education and Labor (2181 RHOB), 225–3725.
Majority Staff Director.—Mark Zuckerman.
Deputy Staff Director.—Alex Nock.
Special Assistant to the Chair.—Daniel Weiss.
Special Assistant to Staff Director/Deputy Staff Director.—Liz Hollis.

General Counsels: Jody Calemine, Stephanie Moore.
Chief Clerk.—Joe Novotny.
Education Policy Director.—Denise Forte.
Senior Education Policy Advisors:
Early Childhood.—Ruth Friedman.
K–12.—Alice Johnson Cain.
Higher Education: Julie Radocchia, Jeffrey Appel.
Education Policy Advisors: Adrienne Dubar, Ajita Talwalker.
Senior Disability Policy Advisor.—Sharon Lewis.
Policy Advisors for Subcommittee on:
Early Childhood.—Lloyd Horwich.
Higher Education.—Ricardo Martinez.
Healthy Families.—Kim Zarish-Becknell.
Special Assistant to the Education Policy Director.—Vacant.
Legislative Fellow, Education.—Lisa Pugh.
Staff Assistants, Education: Fred A. Jones, Jr., Margaret Young.
Labor Policy Director.—Michele Varnhagen.
Deputy Labor Policy Director.—Vacant.
Senior Labor Policy Advisors: Lynn Dondis, Richard Miller.
Labor Policy Advisors: Tico Almeida, Carlos Fenwick, Celine McNicholas, Megan O'Reilly.
Junior Legislative Associates, Labor: Meredith Regine, James Schroll.
Senior Budget/Appropriations Advisor.—Vacant.
Chief Investigative Counsel.—Michael Zola.
Investigative Counsel.—Patrick Findlay.
Senior Investigator.—Ryan Holden.
Investigative Associate.—Vacant.
Staff Attorney.—Fran-Victoria Cox.
Communications Director.—Rachel Racusen.
Press Secretary.—Aaron Albright.
Research and Outreach Director.—Betsy Miller Kittredge.
Online Outreach Specialist.—Mike Kruger.
Hearing Clerk.—Tylease Fitzgerald-Alli.
Staff Assistants: Al Falahi, Broderick Johnson, Helen Pajcic, Alexandria Ruiz.
Financial Administrator.—Daisy Minter.
Financial Staff Assistant.—Marjorie Hamilton.
Senior Systems Administrator.—Dray Thorne.
Systems Administrator.—David Hartzler.
Printer.—Richard McGee.

Minority Staff Director.—Barrett Karr, (2101 RHOB), 5–4527.
General Counsel.—Kirk Boyle.
Chief Clerk/Assistant to the General Counsel.—Linda Stevens.
Executive Assistant.—Angela Jones.
Director of Education and Human Services.—Susan Ross.
Deputy Director of Education and Human Services.—James Bergeron.
Education Policy Counsel.—Mandy Schaumburg.
Director of Workforce Policy.—Ed Gilroy.
Deputy Director of Workforce Policy.—Molly Salmi.
Workforce Policy Counsel.—Jim Paretti.
Senior Legislative Assistant.—Robert Gregg.
Legislative Assistant.—Stephanie Arras.
Professional Staff Members: Richard Hoar, Amy Jones, Kenneth Serafin, Loren Sweatt.
Systems Administrator.—Thomas Benjamin.
Financial and Administrative Officer.—Dianna Ruskowsky.
Communications Director.—Alexa Marrero.
Press Secretary.—Ryan Murphy.
Receptionist/Administrative Assistant.—Theresa Gambo.
Director of Internal Communications.—Angelyn Shapiro.
Coalitions and Member Services Coordinator.—Casey Buboltz.

Energy and Commerce

2125 Rayburn House Office Building, phone 225–2927

http://www.house.gov/commerce

meets fourth Tuesday of each month

Henry A. Waxman, of California, *Chair*

John D. Dingell, of Michigan.
Edward J. Markey, of Massachusetts.
Rick Boucher, of Virginia.
Frank Pallone, Jr., of New Jersey.
Bart Gordon, of Tennessee.
Bobby L. Rush, of Illinois.
Anna G. Eshoo, of California.
Bart Stupak, of Michigan.
Eliot L. Engel, of New York.
Gene Green, of Texas.
Diana DeGette, of Colorado.
Lois Capps, of California.
Michael F. Doyle, of Pennsylvania.
Jane Harman, of California.
Janice D. Schakowsky, of Illinois.
Charles A. Gonzalez, of Texas.
Jay Inslee, of Washington.
Tammy Baldwin, of Wisconsin.
Mike Ross, of Arkansas.
Anthony D. Weiner, of New York.
Jim Matheson, of Utah.
G. K. Butterfield, of North Carolina.
Charlie Melancon, of Louisiana.
John Barrow, of Georgia.
Baron P. Hill, of Indiana.
Doris O. Matsui, of California.
Donna M. Christensen, of Virgin Islands.
Kathy Castor, of Florida.
John P. Sarbanes, of Maryland.
Christopher S. Murphy, of Connecticut.
Zachary T. Space, of Ohio.
Jerry McNerney, of California.
Betty Sutton, of Ohio.
Bruce L. Braley, of Iowa.
Peter Welch, of Vermont.

Joe Barton, of Texas.
Ralph M. Hall, of Texas.
Fred Upton, of Michigan.
Cliff Stearns, of Florida.
Nathan Deal, of Georgia.
Ed Whitfield, of Kentucky.
John Shimkus, of Illinois.
John B. Shadegg, of Arizona.
Roy Blunt, of Missouri.
Steve Buyer, of Indiana.
George Radanovich, of California.
Joseph R. Pitts, of Pennsylvania.
Mary Bono Mack, of California.
Greg Walden, of Oregon.
Lee Terry, of Nebraska.
Mike Rogers, of Michigan.
Sue Wilkins Myrick, of North Carolina.
John Sullivan, of Oklahoma.
Tim Murphy, of Pennsylvania.
Michael C. Burgess, of Texas.
Marsha Blackburn, of Tennessee.
Phil Gingrey, of Georgia.
Steve Scalise, of Louisiana.

SUBCOMMITTEES

[The chairman and ranking minority member are ex officio (voting) members of all subcommittees on which they do not serve.]

Commerce, Trade, and Consumer Protection

Bobby L. Rush, of Illinois, *Chair*

Janice D. Schakowsky, of Illinois.
John P. Sarbanes, of Maryland.
Betty Sutton, of Ohio.
Frank Pallone, Jr., of New Jersey.
Bart Gordon, of Tennessee.
Bart Stupak, of Michigan.
Gene Green, of Texas.
Charles A. Gonzalez, of Texas.
Anthony D. Weiner, of New York.
Jim Matheson, of Utah.
G. K. Butterfield, of North Carolina.
John Barrow, of Georgia.
Doris O. Matsui, of California.
Kathy Castor, of Florida.
Zachary T. Space, of Ohio.
Bruce L. Braley, of Iowa.
Diana DeGette, of Colorado.

George Radanovich, of California.
Cliff Stearns, of Florida.
Ed Whitfield, of Kentucky.
Joseph R. Pitts, of Pennsylvania.
Mary Bono Mack, of California.
Lee Terry, of Nebraska.
Sue Wilkins Myrick, of North Carolina.
John Sullivan, of Oklahoma.
Tim Murphy, of Pennsylvania.
Phil Gingrey, of Georgia.
Steve Scalise, of Louisiana.

Communications, Technology, and the Internet

Rick Boucher, of Virginia, *Chair*

Edward J. Markey, of Massachusetts.
Bart Gordon, of Tennessee.
Bobby L. Rush, of Illinois.
Anna G. Eshoo, of California.
Bart Stupak, of Michigan.
Diana DeGette, of Colorado.
Michael F. Doyle, of Pennsylvania.
Jay Inslee, of Washington.
Anthony D. Weiner, of New York.
G. K. Butterfield, of North Carolina.
Charlie Melancon, of Louisiana.
Baron P. Hill, of Indiana.
Doris O. Matsui, of California.
Donna M. Christensen, of Virgin Islands.
Kathy Castor, of Florida.
Christopher S. Murphy, of Connecticut.
Zachary T. Space, of Ohio.
Jerry McNerney, of California.
Peter Welch, of Vermont.
John D. Dingell, of Michigan.

Cliff Stearns, of Florida.
Fred Upton, of Michigan.
Nathan Deal, of Georgia.
John Shimkus, of Illinois.
John B. Shadegg, of Arizona.
Roy Blunt, of Missouri.
Steve Buyer, of Indiana.
George Radanovich, of California.
Mary Bono Mack, of California.
Greg Walden, of Oregon.
Lee Terry, of Nebraska.
Mike Rogers, of Michigan.
Marsha Blackburn, of Tennessee.

Energy and Environment

Edward J. Markey, of Massachusetts, *Chair*

Michael F. Doyle, of Pennsylvania.
Jay Inslee, of Washington.
G. K. Butterfield, of North Carolina.
Charlie Melancon, of Louisiana.
Baron P. Hill, of Indiana.
Doris O. Matsui, of California.
Jerry McNerney, of California.
Peter Welch, of Vermont.
John D. Dingell, of Michigan.
Rick Boucher, of Virginia.
Frank Pallone, Jr., of New Jersey.
Eliot L. Engel, of New York.
Gene Green, of Texas.
Lois Capps, of California.
Jane Harman, of California.
Charles A. Gonzalez, of Texas.
Tammy Baldwin, of Wisconsin.
Mike Ross, of Arkansas.
Jim Matheson, of Utah.
John Barrow, of Georgia.

Fred Upton, of Michigan.
Ralph M. Hall, of Texas.
Cliff Stearns, of Florida.
Ed Whitfield, of Kentucky.
John Shimkus, of Illinois.
John B. Shadegg, of Arizona.
Roy Blunt, of Missouri.
Joseph R. Pitts, of Pennsylvania.
Mary Bono Mack, of California.
Greg Walden, of Oregon.
John Sullivan, of Oklahoma.
Michael C. Burgess, of Texas.
Steve Scalise, of Louisiana.

Health

Frank Pallone, Jr., of New Jersey, *Chair*

John D. Dingell, of Michigan.
Bart Gordon, of Tennessee.
Anna G. Eshoo, of California.
Eliot L. Engel, of New York.
Gene Green, of Texas.
Diana DeGette, of Colorado.
Lois Capps, of California., Vice Chair
Janice D. Schakowsky, of Illinois.
Tammy Baldwin, of Wisconsin.
Mike Ross, of Arkansas.
Anthony D. Weiner, of New York.
Jim Matheson, of Utah.
Jane Harman, of California.
Charles A. Gonzalez, of Texas.
John Barrow, of Georgia.
Donna M. Christensen, of Virgin Islands.
Kathy Castor, of Florida.
John P. Sarbanes, of Maryland.
Christopher S. Murphy, of Connecticut.
Zachary T. Space, of Ohio.
Betty Sutton, of Ohio.
Bruce L. Braley, of Iowa.

Nathan Deal, of Georgia.
Ralph M. Hall, of Texas.
Ed Whitfield, of Kentucky.
John Shimkus, of Illinois.
John B. Shadegg, of Arizona.
Roy Blunt, of Missouri.
Steve Buyer, of Indiana.
Joseph R. Pitts, of Pennsylvania.
Mike Rogers, of Michigan.
Sue Wilkins Myrick, of North Carolina.
Tim Murphy, of Pennsylvania.
Michael C. Burgess, of Texas.
Marsha Blackburn, of Tennessee.
Phil Gingrey, of Georgia.

Oversight and Investigations

Bart Stupak, of Michigan, *Chair*

Bruce L. Braley, of Iowa.
Edward J. Markey, of Massachusetts.
Diana DeGette, of Colorado.
Michael F. Doyle, of Pennsylvania.
Janice D. Schakowsky, of Illinois.
Mike Ross, of Arkansas.
Donna M. Christensen, of Virgin Islands.
Peter Welch, of Vermont.
Gene Green, of Texas.
Betty Sutton, of Ohio.

Greg Walden, of Oregon.
Nathan Deal, of Georgia.
George Radanovich, of California.
John Sullivan, of Oklahoma.
Michael C. Burgess, of Texas.
Marsha Blackburn, of Tennessee.
Phil Gingrey, of Georgia.

STAFF

Committee on Energy and Commerce (2125 RHOB), 225–2927, fax 225–2525.
Majority Staff Director.—Phil Barnett.
Deputy Committee Staff Director for Health.—Karen Nelson.
Chief Counsel.—Kristin Amerling.
Communications Director, Senior Policy Advisor.—Karen Lightfoot.
Policy Director, Communications, Technology and the Internet.—Pat Delgado.
Chief Clerk.—Earley T. Green.
Chief Legislative Clerk.—Sharon E. Davis.
Office Manager/Executive Assistant to Staff Director.—Sheila Klein.
Chief Counsels:
Commerce, Trade, and Consumer Protection.—Michelle Ash.
Communications, Technology, and the Internet.—Roger Sherman.
Environment and Energy.—Greg Dotson.
Health.—Andy Schneider.
Oversight.—David Leviss.
Investigative.—Michael Gordon.
Public Health.—Ruth Katz.
Senior Advisor.—Bruce Wolpe.
Senior Advisor on Health Policy.—Jack Ebeler.
Senior Investigator and Policy Advisor.—Brian Cohen.
Senior Counsels for Environment and Energy: John Jimison, Lorie Schmidt, Alexandra Teitz.
Counsels:
Commerce, Trade, and Consumer Protection.—Robin Appleberry.
Communications, Trade, and the Internet: Shawn Chang, Tim Powderly.
Energy and Environment: Jeff Baran, Jacqueline Cohen.
Health.—Sarah Despres, Purvee Kempf, Naomi Seiler, Rachel Sher.
Oversight and Investigations.—Tiffany Benjamine, Stacia Cardille, Molly Gaston, Anne Tindall.
Professional Staff Members:
Commerce, Trade, and Consumer Protection.—Anna Laitin.
Energy and Environment.—Alex Barron, Melissa Bez, Alison Cassady.
Health.—Stephen Cha, Tim Gronniger, Anne Morris.
Oversight and Investigations.—Alexandra Golden.
Policy Analyst, Energy and Environment.—Rob Cobbs.
Investigator.—Jennifer Owens.
Special Advisors/Counsels to Subcommittee Chairs:
Commerce, Trade, and Consumer Protection: Timothy Robinson, Angelle Kwemo.
Communications, Technology, and the Internet.—Amy Levine, Laura Vaughn.
Energy and Environment.—Joel Beauvais, Michael Goo.
Health.—Robert Clark, Elana Leventhal.
Oversight and Investigations.—Scott Schloegel, Erika Smith.
Professional Staff Members to Chairman Emeritus: Virgil Miller, Katie Campbell.
Deputy Clerk.—Jennifer Berenholz.
Financial Administrator.—Elizabeth B. Ertel.
Assistant Clerk.—Sean Corcoran.
Press Secretary.—David Kohn.
Press Assistant.—Lindsay Vidal.
Information Technology:
Chief Information Officer.—J.R. Deng.
Deputy Information Officer.—Jeffrey Wease.
Director of New Media.—Mark Noble.
Printer.—Chris Wells.
Special Assistants:
Full Committee: Miriam Edelman, Matthew D. Eisenberg, Mitchell Smiley.
Press.—Elizabeth Letter.
Commerce, Trade, and Consumer Protection.—William Cusey.
Communications, Technology, and the Internet.—Sarah Fisher.
Energy and Environment.—Caitlin Haberman, Peter Ketcham-Colwil.
Health.—Alvin Banks, Alison Corr.
Oversight and Investigations.—Alison Neubaue.
Staff Assistants.—Byron Gwinn, Justine Italiano.
Minority Chief of Staff.—David L. Cavicke (2332A RHOB), 225–3641.
General Counsel.—Lance Kotschwar.
Deputy Chief of Staff, Communications.—Lawrence A. Neal.

Deputy Chief of Staff.—Heather Couri.
Chief Economist.—James ''Ike'' Brannon.
Chief Counsel, Oversight.—Alan M. Slobodin.
Chief Counsel, Health.—Ryan Long.
Senior Professional Staff Member and Chief Financial Officer.—Brian McCullough.
Counsels: Clayton Alspach, Melissa Bartlett, Karen E. Christian, Aaron Cutler, Neil Fried, Sean Hayes, Amanda Mertens Campbell, Mary Neumayr, Krista Rosenthall, Aarti Shah, Shannon M. Weinberg.
Professional Staff: William R.D. Carty, Brandon J. Clark, Gerald S. Couri II, Marie Fishpaw, Peter Spencer, Andrea Spring.
Communications Director.—Lisa Miller.
Administrative and Human Resources Coordinator.—Linda L. Walker.
Legislative Analysts: Sam Costello, Garrett Golding, Chad Grant, Peter E. Kielty.
Director, Information Technology.—Jean M. Woodrow.
Research Analyst.—Jeanne Neal.
Special Assistant.—Kevin Kohl.
Staff Assistant.—Nathan Crow.

Financial Services

2129 Rayburn House Office Building, phone 225–4247

http://www.house.gov/financialservices

meets first Tuesday of each month

Barney Frank, of Massachusetts, *Chair*

Paul E. Kanjorski, of Pennsylvania.
Maxine Waters, of California.
Carolyn B. Maloney, of New York.
Luis V. Gutierrez, of Illinois.
Nydia M. Velázquez, of New York.
Melvin L. Watt, of North Carolina.
Gary L. Ackerman, of New York.
Brad Sherman, of California.
Gregory W. Meeks, of New York.
Dennis Moore, of Kansas.
Michael E. Capuano, of Massachusetts.
Rubén Hinojosa, of Texas.
Wm. Lacy Clay, of Missouri.
Carolyn McCarthy, of New York.
Joe Baca, of California.
Stephen F. Lynch, of Massachusetts.
Brad Miller, of North Carolina.
David Scott, of Georgia.
Al Green, of Texas.
Emanuel Cleaver, of Missouri.
Melissa L. Bean, of Illinois.
Gwen Moore, of Wisconsin.
Paul W. Hodes, of New Hampshire.
Keith Ellison, of Minnesota.
Ron Klein, of Florida.
Charles A. Wilson, of Ohio.
Ed Perlmutter, of Colorado.
Joe Donnelly, of Indiana.
Bill Foster, of Illinois.
André Carson, of Indiana.
Jackie Speier, of California.
Travis W. Childers, of Mississippi.
Walt Minnick, of Idaho.
John H. Adler, of New Jersey.
Mary Jo Kilroy, of Ohio.
Steve Driehaus, of Ohio.
Suzanne M. Kosmas, of Florida.
Alan Grayson, of Florida.
James A. Himes, of Connecticut.
Gary C. Peters, of Michigan.
Daniel B. Maffei, of New York.

Spencer Bachus, of Alabama.
Michael N. Castle, of Delaware.
Peter T. King, of New York.
Edward R. Royce, of California.
Frank D. Lucas, of Oklahoma.
Ron Paul, of Texas.
Donald A. Manzullo, of Illinois.
Walter B. Jones, of North Carolina.
Judy Biggert, of Illinois.
Gary G. Miller, of California.
Shelley Moore Capito, of West Virginia.
Jeb Hensarling, of Texas.
Scott Garrett, of New Jersey.
J. Gresham Barrett, of South Carolina.
Jim Gerlach, of Pennsylvania.
Randy Neugebauer, of Texas.
Tom Price, of Georgia.
Patrick T. McHenry, of North Carolina.
John Campbell, of California.
Adam H. Putnam, of Florida.
Michele Bachmann, of Minnesota.
Kenny Marchant, of Texas.
Thaddeus G. McCotter, of Michigan.
Kevin McCarthy, of California.
Bill Posey, of Florida.
Lynn Jenkins, of Kansas.
Christopher John Lee, of New York.
Erik Paulsen, of Minnesota.
Leonard Lance, of New Jersey.

SUBCOMMITTEES

[The chairman and ranking minority member are ex officio (voting) members of all subcommittees on which they do not serve.]

Capital Markets, Insurance, and Government-Sponsored Enterprises

Paul E. Kanjorski, of Pennsylvania, *Chair*

Gary L. Ackerman, of New York.
Brad Sherman, of California.
Michael E. Capuano, of Massachusetts.
Rubén Hinojosa, of Texas.
Carolyn McCarthy, of New York.
Joe Baca, of California.
Stephen F. Lynch, of Massachusetts.
Brad Miller, of North Carolina.
David Scott, of Georgia.
Nydia M. Velázquez, of New York.
Carolyn B. Maloney, of New York.
Melissa L. Bean, of Illinois.
Gwen Moore, of Wisconsin.
Paul W. Hodes, of New Hampshire.
Ron Klein, of Florida.
Ed Perlmutter, of Colorado.
Joe Donnelly, of Indiana.
André Carson, of Indiana.
Jackie Speier, of California.
Travis W. Childers, of Mississippi.
Charles A. Wilson, of Ohio.
Bill Foster, of Illinois.
Walt Minnick, of Idaho.
John H. Adler, of New Jersey.
Mary Jo Kilroy, of Ohio.
Suzanne M. Kosmas, of Florida.
Alan Grayson, of Florida.
James A. Himes, of Connecticut.
Gary C. Peters, of Michigan.

Scott Garrett, of New Jersey.
Tom Price, of Georgia.
Michael N. Castle, of Delaware.
Peter T. King, of New York.
Frank D. Lucas, of Oklahoma.
Donald A. Manzullo, of Illinois.
Edward R. Royce, of California.
Judy Biggert, of Illinois.
Shelley Moore Capito, of West Virginia.
Jeb Hensarling, of Texas.
Adam H. Putnam, of Florida.
J. Gresham Barrett, of South Carolina.
Jim Gerlach, of Pennsylvania.
John Campbell, of California.
Michele Bachmann, of Minnesota.
Thaddeus G. McCotter, of Michigan.
Randy Neugebauer, of Texas.
Kevin McCarthy, of California.
Bill Posey, of Florida.
Lynn Jenkins, of Kansas.

Domestic Monetary Policy and Technology

Melvin L. Watt, of North Carolina, *Chair*

Carolyn B. Maloney, of New York.
Gregory W. Meeks, of New York.
Wm. Lacy Clay, of Missouri.
Brad Sherman, of California.
Al Green, of Texas.
Emanuel Cleaver, of Missouri.
Keith Ellison, of Minnesota.
John H. Adler, of New Jersey.
Suzanne M. Kosmas, of Florida.

Ron Paul, of Texas.
Michael N. Castle, of Delaware.
Frank D. Lucas, of Oklahoma.
Jim Gerlach, of Pennsylvania.
Tom Price, of Georgia.
Bill Posey, of Florida.
Leonard Lance, of New Jersey.

Financial Institutions and Consumer Credit

Luis V. Gutierrez, of Illinois, *Chair*

Carolyn B. Maloney, of New York.
Melvin L. Watt, of North Carolina.
Gary L. Ackerman, of New York.
Brad Sherman, of California.
Dennis Moore, of Kansas.
Paul E. Kanjorski, of Pennsylvania.
Maxine Waters, of California.
Rubén Hinojosa, of Texas.
Carolyn McCarthy, of New York.
Joe Baca, of California.
Al Green, of Texas.
Wm. Lacy Clay, of Missouri.
Brad Miller, of North Carolina.
David Scott, of Georgia.
Emanuel Cleaver, of Missouri.
Melissa L. Bean, of Illinois.
Paul W. Hodes, of New Hampshire.
Keith Ellison, of Minnesota.
Ron Klein, of Florida.
Charles A. Wilson, of Ohio.
Gregory W. Meeks, of New York.
Bill Foster, of Illinois.
Ed Perlmutter, of Colorado.
Jackie Speier, of California.
Travis W. Childers, of Mississippi.
Walt Minnick, of Idaho.

Jeb Hensarling, of Texas.
J. Gresham Barrett, of South Carolina.
Michael N. Castle, of Delaware.
Peter T. King, of New York.
Edward R. Royce, of California.
Walter B. Jones, of North Carolina.
Shelley Moore Capito, of West Virginia.
Scott Garrett, of New Jersey.
Jim Gerlach, of Pennsylvania.
Randy Neugebauer, of Texas.
Tom Price, of Georgia.
Patrick T. McHenry, of North Carolina.
John Campbell, of California.
Kevin McCarthy, of California.
Kenny Marchant, of Texas.
Christopher John Lee, of New York.
Erik Paulsen, of Minnesota.
Leonard Lance, of New Jersey.

Housing and Community Opportunity

Maxine Waters, of California, *Chair*

Nydia M. Velázquez, of New York.
Stephen F. Lynch, of Massachusetts.
Emanuel Cleaver, of Missouri.
Al Green, of Texas.
Wm. Lacy Clay, of Missouri.
Keith Ellison, of Minnesota.
Joe Donnelly, of Indiana.
Michael E. Capuano, of Massachusetts.
Paul E. Kanjorski, of Pennsylvania.
Luis V. Gutierrez, of Illinois.
Steve Driehaus, of Ohio.
Mary Jo Kilroy, of Ohio.
James A. Himes, of Connecticut.
Daniel B. Maffei, of New York.

Shelley Moore Capito, of West Virginia.
Thaddeus G. McCotter, of Michigan.
Judy Biggert, of Illinois.
Gary G. Miller, of California.
Randy Neugebauer, of Texas.
Walter B. Jones, of North Carolina.
Adam H. Putnam, of Florida.
Kenny Marchant, of Texas.
Lynn Jenkins, of Kansas.
Christopher John Lee, of New York.

International Monetary Policy and Trade

Gregory W. Meeks, of New York, *Chair*

Luis V. Gutierrez, of Illinois.
Maxine Waters, of California.
Melvin L. Watt, of North Carolina.
Gwen Moore, of Wisconsin.
André Carson, of Indiana.
Steve Driehaus, of Ohio.
Gary C. Peters, of Michigan.
Daniel B. Maffei, of New York.

Gary G. Miller, of California.
Edward R. Royce, of California.
Ron Paul, of Texas.
Donald A. Manzullo, of Illinois.
Michele Bachmann, of Minnesota.
Erik Paulsen, of Minnesota.

Oversight and Investigations

Dennis Moore, of Kansas, *Chair*

Stephen F. Lynch, of Massachusetts.
Ron Klein, of Florida.
Jackie Speier, of California.
Gwen Moore, of Wisconsin.
John H. Adler, of New Jersey.
Mary Jo Kilroy, of Ohio.
Steve Driehaus, of Ohio.
Alan Grayson, of Florida.

Judy Biggert, of Illinois.
Patrick T. McHenry, of North Carolina.
Ron Paul, of Texas.
Michele Bachmann, of Minnesota.
Christopher John Lee, of New York.
Erik Paulsen, of Minnesota.

STAFF

Committee on Financial Services (2129 RHOB), 225–4247.
Majority Staff Director/Chief Counsel.—Jeanne Roslanowick.
General Counsel.—Tom Duncan.
Deputy Chief Counsels: Gail Laster, Lawranne Stewart.
Chief Economist.—David A. Smith.
Senior Policy Director.—Michael Beresik.
Senior Counsels: Andrew Miller, Jeffrey Riley.
Counsels: Sanders Adu, Keo Chea, Cassandra Duhaney, Thomas Glassic, Erika Jeffers, Kellie Larkin, Dominique McCoy, Katharine Marks, Daniel Meade, Adrianne Threatt, Kathleen Mellody, Charla Ouertatani, Jason Pitcock, Sabahat Qamar.
Director of Legislative Affairs.—Richard Maurano.
Senior Professional Staff: Todd Harper, Daniel McGlinchey, Peter Roberson, Dennis Shaul, Bill Zavarello.
Professional Staff Members: Meredith Connelly, Amanda Fischer, Karl Haddeland, Todd Harper, Stephane LeBouder, Patricia Lord, Jonathan Obee, Charla Ouertatani, Glen Sears, Brendan Woodbury.
Policy Director, Housing.—Scott Olson.
Senior Policy Advisor.—Katheryn Rosen.
Communications Director.—Steven Adamske.
Press Secretary.—Elizabeth Esfahani.
Clerk.—Lois Richerson.
Staff Associates: Jean Carroll, Marcus Goodman, Marcos Manosalvas, Kirk Schwarzbach, Garett Rose.
Systems Administrator.—Alfred Forman.
Assistant Systems Administrator.—Steve Arauz.
Editor.—Terisa Allison.
Minority Chief of Staff.—Larry Lavender, B–371A Rayburn, 5–7502.
Deputy Chief of Staff.—Warren Tryon.
Deputy Staff Director/Communications.—Vince Randazzo.
Chief Counsel.—Jim Clinger.
General Counsel.—Clinton Jones.
Senior Counsels: James Clinger, Kevin Edgar, Frank Medina, Jason Spence.
Counsels: Michael Borden, Jason Goggins, Adam Trost.
Senior Professional Staff: Cindy Chetti, Tallman Johnson.
Professional Staff: Anthony Cimino, David Oxner, Joe Pinder, Eric Thompson.
Policy Analyst.—Gisele Roget.
Communications Director.—Marisol Garibay.
Assistant Communications Director.—Vacant.
Administrative Assistant.—Angela Gambo.
Executive Staff Assistant.—Rosemary Keech.
System Administrator.—Kim Trimble.
Staff Assistant.—James Ratliff, Anna Wright.

Foreign Affairs

2170 Rayburn House Office Building, phone 225–5021

http://www.foreignaffairs.house.gov

meets first Tuesday of each month

Howard L. Berman, of California, *Chair*

Gary L. Ackerman, of New York.
Eni F. H. Faleomavaega, of American Samoa.
Donald M. Payne, of New Jersey.
Brad Sherman, of California.
Robert Wexler, of Florida.
Eliot L. Engel, of New York.
Bill Delahunt, of Massachusetts.
Gregory W. Meeks, of New York.
Diane E. Watson, of California.
Russ Carnahan, of Missouri.
Albio Sires, of New Jersey.
Gerald E. Connolly, of Virginia.
Michael E. McMahon, of New York.
John S. Tanner, of Tennessee.
Gene Green, of Texas.
Lynn C. Woolsey, of California.
Sheila Jackson-Lee, of Texas.
Barbara Lee, of California.
Shelley Berkley, of Nevada.
Joseph Crowley, of New York.
Mike Ross, of Arkansas.
Brad Miller, of North Carolina.
David Scott, of Georgia.
Jim Costa, of California.
Keith Ellison, of Minnesota.
Gabrielle Giffords, of Arizona.
Ron Klein, of Florida.

Ileana Ros-Lehtinen, of Florida.
Christopher H. Smith, of New Jersey.
Dan Burton, of Indiana.
Elton Gallegly, of California.
Dana Rohrabacher, of California.
Donald A. Manzullo, of Illinois.
Edward R. Royce, of California.
Ron Paul, of Texas.
Jeff Flake, of Arizona.
Mike Pence, of Indiana.
Joe Wilson, of South Carolina.
John Boozman, of Arkansas.
J. Gresham Barrett, of South Carolina.
Connie Mack, of Florida.
Jeff Fortenberry, of Nebraska.
Michael T. McCaul, of Texas.
Ted Poe, of Texas.
Bob Inglis, of South Carolina.
Gus M. Bilirakis, of Florida.

SUBCOMMITTEES

[The chairman and ranking minority member are ex officio (non-voting) members of all subcommittees on which they do not serve.]

Africa and Global Health

Donald M. Payne, of New Jersey, *Chair*

Diane E. Watson, of California.
Barbara Lee, of California.
Brad Miller, of North Carolina.
Gregory W. Meeks, of New York.
Sheila Jackson-Lee, of Texas.
Lynn C. Woolsey, of California.

Christopher H. Smith, of New Jersey.
Jeff Flake, of Arizona.
John Boozman, of Arkansas.
Jeff Fortenberry, of Nebraska.

Asia, the Pacific, and the Global Environment

Eni F. H. Faleomavaega, of American Samoa, *Chair*

Gary L. Ackerman, of New York.
Diane E. Watson, of California.
Mike Ross, of Arkansas.
Brad Sherman, of California.
Eliot L. Engel, of New York.
Gregory W. Meeks, of New York.

Donald A. Manzullo, of Illinois.
Bob Inglis, of South Carolina.
Dana Rohrabacher, of California.
Edward R. Royce, of California.
Jeff Flake, of Arizona.

Europe

Robert Wexler, of Florida, *Chair*

John S. Tanner, of Tennessee.
Bill Delahunt, of Massachusetts.
Albio Sires, of New Jersey.
Michael E. McMahon, of New York.
Shelley Berkley, of Nevada.
Brad Miller, of North Carolina.
David Scott, of Georgia.
Jim Costa, of California.

Elton Gallegly, of California.
Gus M. Bilirakis, of Florida.
Joe Wilson, of South Carolina.
Ted Poe, of Texas.
John Boozman, of Arkansas.
Bob Inglis, of South Carolina.
J. Gresham Barrett, of South Carolina.

International Organizations, Human Rights, and Oversight

Bill Delahunt, of Massachusetts, *Chair*

Russ Carnahan, of Missouri.
Keith Ellison, of Minnesota.
Donald M. Payne, of New Jersey.
Robert Wexler, of Florida.

Dana Rohrabacher, of California.
Ron Paul, of Texas.
Ted Poe, of Texas.

Middle East and South Asia

Gary L. Ackerman, of New York, *Chair*

Russ Carnahan, of Missouri.
Michael E. McMahon, of New York.
Sheila Jackson-Lee, of Texas.
Shelley Berkley, of Nevada.
Joseph Crowley, of New York.
Mike Ross, of Arkansas.
Jim Costa, of California.
Keith Ellison, of Minnesota.
Ron Klein, of Florida.
Brad Sherman, of California.
Robert Wexler, of Florida.
Eliot L. Engel, of New York.
Gerald E. Connolly, of Virginia.
Gene Green, of Texas.

Dan Burton, of Indiana.
Joe Wilson, of South Carolina.
J. Gresham Barrett, of South Carolina.
Jeff Fortenberry, of Nebraska.
Michael T. McCaul, of Texas.
Bob Inglis, of South Carolina.
Gus M. Bilirakis, of Florida.
Dana Rohrabacher, of California.
Edward R. Royce, of California.

Terrorism, Nonproliferation, and Trade

Brad Sherman, of California, *Chair*

Gerald E. Connolly, of Virginia.
David Scott, of Georgia.
Diane E. Watson, of California.
Michael E. McMahon, of New York.
Sheila Jackson-Lee, of Texas.
Ron Klein, of Florida.

Edward R. Royce, of California.
Ted Poe, of Texas.
Donald A. Manzullo, of Illinois.
John Boozman, of Arkansas.
J. Gresham Barrett, of South Carolina.

The Western Hemisphere

Eliot L. Engel, of New York, *Chair*

Gregory W. Meeks, of New York.
Albio Sires, of New Jersey.
Gene Green, of Texas.
Gabrielle Giffords, of Arizona.
Eni F. H. Faleomavaega, of American Samoa.
Donald M. Payne, of New Jersey.
John S. Tanner, of Tennessee.
Barbara Lee, of California.
Joseph Crowley, of New York.
Ron Klein, of Florida.

Connie Mack, of Florida.
Michael T. McCaul, of Texas.
Christopher H. Smith, of New Jersey.
Dan Burton, of Indiana.
Elton Gallegly, of California.
Ron Paul, of Texas.
Jeff Fortenberry, of Nebraska.
Gus M. Bilirakis, of Florida.

STAFF

Committee on Foreign Affairs (2170 RHOB), 225–5021.
Majority Staff Director.—Richard J. Kessler.
Deputy Staff Director.—Douglas J. Campbell.
Chief Counsel.—David S. Abramowitz.
Deputy Chief Counsel.—Kristin Wells.
Senior Policy Advisor/Counsel.—Shanna Winters.
Counsel.—Daniel Silverberg.
Senior Professional Staff: David Fite, Hans Hogrefe, Alan Makovsky, Pearl Alice Marsh, Diana L. Ohlbaum, Peter Quilter, Edmund B. Rice.
Professional Staff: Jasmeet Ahuja, Marissa Doran, Daniel Harsha, Jessica Lee, John Lis, Margarita Seminario, Amanda Sloat, Brent Woolfork.
Professional Staff/Interparliamentary Affairs.—Melissa Adamson.
Communications Director.—Lynne Weil.
Professional Staff/Clerk.—Laura Rush.
Executive Assistant/Travel Coordinator.—Guillermina Garcia.
Financial Administrator.—Jim Farr.
Information Resource Manager.—Vlad Cerga.
Office Manager.—Marilyn Owen.
Deputy Clerk.—Riley Moore.
Press Assistant/Staff Associate.—David Barnes.
Staff Associates: Samantha Goldstein, Mary McVeigh.
Printing Manager/Web Assistant.—Shirley Alexander.
Senior Staff Associate/Hearing Coordinator.—Genell Brown.
Assistant Systems Administrator.—Danny Marca.
Minority Staff Director.—Yleem Poblete (B–360 RHOB), 226–8467.
Senior Policy Advisor and Director of Eurasian Affairs.—Mark Gage.
Chief Counsel.—Doug Anderson.
Senior Professional Staff: Dennis Halpin, Jamie McCormick, Doug Seay.
Professional Staff: Joan Condon, Alan Goldsmith, Gene Gurevich, Greg McCarthy, Sarah Preisser, Robyn Wapner, Matt Zweig.
Communications Director.—Brad Goehner.
Policy Analyst/Administrative Director.—Sarah Kiko.
Special Assistant.—Amber Garlock.
Subcommittee on Africa and Global Health (259A FHOB), 6–7812.
Staff Director.—Noelle Lusane.
Professional Staff.—Vacant.
Minority Professional Staff.—Sheri Rickert.
Staff Associate.—Antonina King.
Subcommittee on Asia, the Pacific and Global Environment (2401A RHOB), 6–7825.
Staff Director.—Lisa Williams.
Professional Staff.—Daniel Bob.
Minority Professional Staff.—Nien Su.
Staff Associate.—Vili Lei.
Subcommittee on Europe (257 FHOB) 6–7820.
Staff Director.—Jonathan Katz.
Professional Staff.—Joshua Rogin.
Minority Professional Staff.—Richard Mereu.
Staff Associate.—Mariana Maguire.
Subcommittee on International Organizations, Human Rights and Oversight (256 FHOB), 6–6434.
Staff Director.—Clifford A. Stammerman.
Professional Staff.—Tracy Jacobson.
Minority Professional Staff.—Paul Berkowitz.
Staff Associate.—Brian Forni.
Subcommittee on the Middle East and South Asia (B358 RHOB), 5–3345.
Staff Director.—Howard Diamond.
Professional Staff.—Vacant.
Minority Professional Staff.—Mark Walker.
Staff Associate.—Dalis Adler.
Subcommittee on Terrorism, Nonproliferation and Trade (253 FHOB), 6–1500.
Staff Director.—Don MacDonald.
Professional Staff.—John Brodtke.
Minority Professional Staff.—Tom Sheehy.
Staff Associate.—Isidro Mariscal.
Subcommittee on the Western Hemisphere (255 FHOB), 6–9980.

Staff Director.—Jason Steinbaum.
Professional Staff.—Eric Jacobstein.
Minority Professional Staff.—Frederick Ratliff.
Staff Associate.—Julie Schoenthaler.

Homeland Security

phone 226–8417, fax 226–3399

Bennie G. Thompson, of Mississippi, *Chair*

Loretta Sanchez, of California.
Jane Harman, of California.
Peter A. DeFazio, of Oregon.
Eleanor Holmes Norton, of District of Columbia.
Zoe Lofgren, of California.
Sheila Jackson-Lee, of Texas.
Henry Cuellar, of Texas.
Christopher P. Carney, of Pennsylvania.
Yvette D. Clarke, of New York.
Laura Richardson, of California.
Ann Kirkpatrick, of Arizona.
Ben Ray Luján, of New Mexico.
Bill Pascrell, Jr., of New Jersey.
Emanuel Cleaver, of Missouri.
Al Green, of Texas.
James A. Himes, of Connecticut.
Mary Jo Kilroy, of Ohio.
Eric J. J. Massa, of New York.
Dina Titus, of Nevada.
Vacant.

Peter T. King, of New York.
Lamar Smith, of Texas.
Mark E. Souder, of Indiana.
Daniel E. Lungren, of California.
Mike Rogers, of Alabama.
Michael T. McCaul, of Texas.
Charles W. Dent, of Pennsylvania.
Gus M. Bilirakis, of Florida.
Paul C. Broun, of Georgia.
Candice S. Miller, of Michigan.
Pete Olson, of Texas.
Anh ''Joseph'' Cao, of Louisiana.
Steve Austria, of Ohio.

SUBCOMMITTEES

[The chairman and ranking minority member are ex officio (voting) members of all subcommittees on which they do not serve.]

Border, Maritime, and Global Counterterrorism

Loretta Sanchez, of California, *Chair*

Jane Harman, of California.
Zoe Lofgren, of California.
Sheila Jackson-Lee, of Texas.
Henry Cuellar, of Texas.
Ann Kirkpatrick, of Arizona.
Bill Pascrell, Jr., of New Jersey.
Al Green, of Texas.
Eric J. J. Massa, of New York.

Mark E. Souder, of Indiana.
Michael T. McCaul, of Texas.
Gus M. Bilirakis, of Florida.
Mike Rogers, of Alabama.
Candice S. Miller, of Michigan.

Emergency Communications, Preparedness, and Response

Henry Cuellar, of Texas, *Chair*

Eleanor Holmes Norton, of District of Columbia.
Laura Richardson, of California.
Bill Pascrell, Jr., of New Jersey.
Emanuel Cleaver, of Missouri.
Dina Titus, of Nevada.
Vacant.

Mike Rogers, of Alabama.
Pete Olson, of Texas.
Anh ''Joseph'' Cao, of Louisiana.
Michael T. McCaul, of Texas.

Emerging Threats, Cybersecurity, and Science and Technology

Yvette D. Clarke, of New York, *Chair*

Loretta Sanchez, of California.
Laura Richardson, of California.
Ben Ray Luján, of New Mexico.
Mary Jo Kilroy, of Ohio.

Daniel E. Lungren, of California.
Paul C. Broun, of Georgia.
Steve Austria, of Ohio.

Intelligence, Information Sharing, and Terrorism Risk Assessment

Jane Harman, of California, *Chair*

Christopher P. Carney, of Pennsylvania.
Yvette D. Clarke, of New York.
Ann Kirkpatrick, of Arizona.
Al Green, of Texas.
James A. Himes, of Connecticut.
Vacant.

Michael T. McCaul, of Texas.
Charles W. Dent, of Pennsylvania.
Paul C. Broun, of Georgia.
Mark E. Souder, of Indiana.

Management, Investigations, and Oversight

Christopher P. Carney, of Pennsylvania, *Chair*

Peter A. DeFazio, of Oregon.
Bill Pascrell, Jr., of New Jersey.
Al Green, of Texas.
Mary Jo Kilroy, of Ohio.

Gus M. Bilirakis, of Florida.
Anh "Joseph" Cao, of Louisiana.
Daniel E. Lungren, of California.

Transportation Security and Infrastructure Protection

Sheila Jackson-Lee, of Texas, *Chair*

Peter A. DeFazio, of Oregon.
Eleanor Holmes Norton, of District of Columbia.
Ann Kirkpatrick, of Arizona.
Ben Ray Luján, of New Mexico.
Emanuel Cleaver, of Missouri.
James A. Himes, of Connecticut.
Eric J. J. Massa, of New York.
Dina Titus, of Nevada.

Charles W. Dent, of Pennsylvania.
Daniel E. Lungren, of California.
Pete Olson, of Texas.
Candice S. Miller, of Michigan.
Steve Austria, of Ohio.

STAFF

Committee on Homeland Security (H2–176 Ford House Office Building) phone 226–2616, fax 226–4499.

Staff Director.—I. Lanier Avant, FHOB / H2–176, (202) 226–2616.
Chief Counsel.—Rosaline Cohen.
Deputy Chief Counsel.—D. Michael Stroud.
Chief Oversight Counsel.—Cherri L. Branson.
Deputy Oversight Counsel.—Arianne Callender.
Communications Director.—Dena Graziano.
Subcommittee Directors: Michael Beland, Michael Blinde, Alison Northrup, Jacob Olcott, Tamla Scott.
Senior Policy Advisor and Counsel.—Angela Rye.
Outreach Coordinator.—Pizza Ashby.
Senior Advisor for Science and Technology.—Christopher A. Beck.
Investigator.—Jill Butler.
Senior Professional Staff Members: Asha George, Todd Levett.
Professional Staff Members / Counsels: Hope Goins, Stephen Vina.
Professional Staff Members: Holly Canevari, Mario Cantu, Paula Delcambre, Thomas McDaniels, Tyrik McKeiver, Erin Murphy, Marisela Salayandia, Alan Snyder, Elizabeth Studdard, Nicole Tisdale, Patricia Zavala.
Press Secretary.—Adam Comis.
Chief Financial Officer.—Dawn M. Criste.
Chief Clerk.—Michael S. Twinchek.
Deputy Chief Clerk.—Natalie Nixon.
Clerks: Ryan Caldwell, Nikki Hadder.
Parliamentarian.—Brian Turbyfill.
Office Manager.—Nicole Wade Johnson.
Printers: Heather Crowell, Diane Norman.
Legislative Assistants: Galen Bean, Cory Horton, Carla Zamudio-Dolan.
Executive Assistant.—Cordie Aziz.
Staff Assistant.—Andrew Newhart.
Minority (Republican) Chief Counsel.—Michael J. Russell, FHOB / H2–117 (202) 226–8417.

Minority (Republican) Senior Counsel.—Coley O'Brien.
Minority (Republican) Counsels: Jennifer Arangio, Kerry Kinirons, Will Rubens.
Minority (Republican) Communications Director.—Shane Wolfe.
Minority (Republican) Press Secretary.—Stephanie Genco.
Minority (Republican) Senior Professional Staff: Richard Balzano, Mandy L. Bowers, Kevin Gundersen, Sterling Marchand, Joseph Vealencis.
Minority (Republican) Legislative Assistants: Amanda Halpern, Lauren Wenger.
Minority (Republican) Staff Assistant.—Joseph Dickey.
Minority (Republican) Professional Staff Detailee-AAAS Congressional Science Fellow.—Ellen Carlin.
Minority (Republican) Professional Staff Detailee-ASME Congressional Fellow.—Matthew Allen.
Minority (Republican) Professional Staff Detailee-Immigration and Customs Enforcement.—James DeBoer.
Minority (Republican) Professional Staff Detailee-U.S. Coast Guard.—Jeremy Obenchain.

House Administration

1309 Longworth House Office Building, phone 226–2061, fax 225–2774

http://cha.house.gov/

Robert A. Brady, of Pennsylvania, *Chair*

Zoe Lofgren, of California, *Vice Chair*

Michael E. Capuano, of Massachusetts.
Charles A. Gonzalez, of Texas.
Susan A. Davis, of California.
Artur Davis, of Alabama.

Daniel E. Lungren, of California.
Kevin McCarthy, of California.
Gregg Harper, of Mississippi.

SUBCOMMITTEES

Capitol Security

Michael E. Capuano, of Massachusetts, *Chair*

Robert A. Brady, of Pennsylvania.

Daniel E. Lungren, of California.

Elections

Zoe Lofgren, of California, *Chair*

Charles A. Gonzalez, of Texas, *Vice Chair*

Susan A. Davis, of California.
Artur Davis, of Alabama.

Kevin McCarthy, of California.
Gregg Harper, of Mississippi.

STAFF

Committee on House Administration (1309 LHOB), 5–2061.
Staff Director.—Jamie P.D. Fleet II.
Chief Counsel.—Charles T. Howell.
Deputy Chief Counsel.—Teri A. Morgan.
Senior Elections Counsel.—Thomas Hicks.
Elections Counsels: Jennifer Daehn, Janelle Hu.
Legislative Assistant / Elections.—Daniel D. Favarulo.
Technology Director.—Sterling D. Spriggs.
IT Systems Manager.—Reggie Jackson.
Legislative Clerk.—Joseph Wallace.
Senior Special Projects Director.—Janice R. Crump.
Communications Director.—Kyle Anderson.
Operations Director.—Eddie Flaherty.
Financial Director.—Kim Stevens.
Professional Staff: Greg Abbott, Khalil Abbuod, Michael L. Harrison, Robert Henline, Ellen A. McCarthy, Kristie Muchnok, Kevin F. Peterson, Matthew Pinkus, Darrell O'Connor, Diana Rodriguez.
Staff Assistants: Matthew DeFreitas, Shervan Sebastian.
Minority Staff Director.—Victor Arnold-Bik (1313 LHOB), 5–8281.
Legislative Counsels: Karin Moore, Peter Schalestock.
Professional Staff: Matt Field, Mary Sue Englund, Katie Ryan.
Director, Member and Committee Services.—George Hadijski.
Communications Director.—Salley Collins.
Communications and Outreach Manager.—Josiah Prendergast.
Director, House Oversight.—Andi Snow.

Commission on Congressional Mailing Standards (1216 LHOB), 5–9337.
Majority Staff Director.—Ellen A. McCarthy.
Professional Staff: Connie D. Goode, Brian M. McCue, Mary E. McHugh.
Minority Staff Director.—Jack Dail (1216A LHOB), 6–0647.
Professional Staff.—Sean Evins.

Judiciary

2138 Rayburn House Office Building, phone 225–3951

http://www.house.gov/judiciary

meets every Wednesday

John Conyers, Jr., of Michigan, *Chair*

Howard L. Berman, of California.
Rick Boucher, of Virginia.
Jerrold Nadler, of New York.
Robert C. ''Bobby'' Scott, of Virginia.
Melvin L. Watt, of North Carolina.
Zoe Lofgren, of California.
Sheila Jackson-Lee, of Texas.
Maxine Waters, of California.
Bill Delahunt, of Massachusetts.
Robert Wexler, of Florida.
Steve Cohen, of Tennessee.
Henry C. ''Hank'' Johnson, Jr., of Georgia.
Pedro R. Pierluisi, of Puerto Rico.
Mike Quigley, of Illinois.
Judy Chu, of California.
Luis V. Gutierrez, of Illinois.
Brad Sherman, of California.
Tammy Baldwin, of Wisconsin.
Charles A. Gonzalez, of Texas.
Anthony D. Weiner, of New York.
Adam B. Schiff, of California.
Linda T. Sánchez, of California.
Debbie Wasserman Schultz, of Florida.
Daniel B. Maffei, of New York.

Lamar Smith, of Texas.
F. James Sensenbrenner, Jr., of Wisconsin.
Howard Coble, of North Carolina.
Elton Gallegly, of California.
Bob Goodlatte, of Virginia.
Daniel E. Lungren, of California.
Darrell E. Issa, of California.
J. Randy Forbes, of Virginia.
Steve King, of Iowa.
Trent Franks, of Arizona.
Louie Gohmert, of Texas.
Jim Jordan, of Ohio.
Ted Poe, of Texas.
Jason Chaffetz, of Utah.
Thomas J. Rooney, of Florida.
Gregg Harper, of Mississippi.

SUBCOMMITTEES

[The chairman and the ranking minority member are ex officio (non-voting) members of all subcommittees on which they do not serve.]

Commercial and Administrative Law

Steve Cohen, of Tennessee, *Chair*

Bill Delahunt, of Massachusetts.
Melvin L. Watt, of North Carolina.
Brad Sherman, of California.
Daniel B. Maffei, of New York.
Zoe Lofgren, of California.
Henry C. ''Hank'' Johnson, Jr., of Georgia.
Robert C. ''Bobby'' Scott, of Virginia.
John Conyers, Jr., of Michigan.

Trent Franks, of Arizona.
Jim Jordan, of Ohio.
Howard Coble, of North Carolina.
Darrell E. Issa, of California.
J. Randy Forbes, of Virginia.
Steve King, of Iowa.
Judy Chu, of California.

Constitution, Civil Rights, and Civil Liberties

Jerrold Nadler, of New York, *Chair*

Melvin L. Watt, of North Carolina.
Robert C. ''Bobby'' Scott, of Virginia.
Bill Delahunt, of Massachusetts.
Henry C. ''Hank'' Johnson, Jr., of Georgia.
Tammy Baldwin, of Wisconsin.
John Conyers, Jr., of Michigan.
Steve Cohen, of Tennessee.
Brad Sherman, of California.
Sheila Jackson-Lee, of Texas.
Judy Chu, of California.

F. James Sensenbrenner, Jr., of Wisconsin.
Thomas J. Rooney, of Florida.
Steve King, of Iowa.
Trent Franks, of Arizona.
Louie Gohmert, of Texas.
Jim Jordan, of Ohio.

Courts and Competition Policy

Henry C. ''Hank'' Johnson, Jr., of Georgia, *Chair*

John Conyers, Jr., of Michigan.
Rick Boucher, of Virginia.
Robert Wexler, of Florida.
Charles A. Gonzalez, of Texas.
Sheila Jackson-Lee, of Texas.
Melvin L. Watt, of North Carolina.
Brad Sherman, of California.
Mike Quigley, of Illinois.

Howard Coble, of North Carolina.
Jason Chaffetz, of Utah.
F. James Sensenbrenner, Jr., of Wisconsin.
Bob Goodlatte, of Virginia.
Darrell E. Issa, of California.
Gregg Harper, of Mississippi.

Crime, Terrorism, and Homeland Security

Robert C. ''Bobby'' Scott, of Virginia, *Chair*

Pedro R. Pierluisi, of Puerto Rico.
Jerrold Nadler, of New York.
Zoe Lofgren, of California.
Sheila Jackson-Lee, of Texas.
Maxine Waters, of California.
Steve Cohen, of Tennessee.
Anthony D. Weiner, of New York.
Debbie Wasserman Schultz, of Florida.
Mike Quigley, of Illinois.

Louie Gohmert, of Texas.
Ted Poe, of Texas.
Bob Goodlatte, of Virginia.
Daniel E. Lungren, of California.
J. Randy Forbes, of Virginia.
Thomas J. Rooney, of Florida.

Immigration, Citizenship, Refugees, Border Security, and International Law

Zoe Lofgren, of California, *Chair*

Howard L. Berman, of California.
Sheila Jackson-Lee, of Texas.
Maxine Waters, of California.
Pedro R. Pierluisi, of Puerto Rico.
Luis V. Gutierrez, of Illinois.
Linda T. Sánchez, of California.
Anthony D. Weiner, of New York.
Charles A. Gonzalez, of Texas.
Bill Delahunt, of Massachusetts.
Judy Chu, of California.

Steve King, of Iowa.
Gregg Harper, of Mississippi.
Elton Gallegly, of California.
Daniel E. Lungren, of California.
Ted Poe, of Texas.
Jason Chaffetz, of Utah.

STAFF

Committee on the Judiciary (2138 RHOB), 225–3951.
Majority Chief Counsel/Staff Director.—Perry H. Apelbaum.
General Counsel/Deputy Staff Director.—Ted Kalo.
Legislative Counsel/Parliamentarian.—George Slover.
Chief Oversight Counsel.—Elliot Mincberg.
Chief Copyright Counsel.—Stacey Dansky.
Chief Administrative Officer.—Anita L. Johnson.
Assistant to the Deputy Staff Director.—Andrea Culebras.
Counsels: Sam Broderick-Sokol, Danielle Brown, Jason Everett, Aaron Hiller, Susan Jensen, Elizabeth Kendall, Michelle Millben, Diana Oo, Eric Tamarkin.
Communications Director.—Jonathan Godfrey.
Information Systems Manager.—Kerli Philippe.
Information Systems Specialists: Seth Ciango, Dwight Sullivan.
Chief Clerk/Office Manager.—Teresa Vest.
Calendar Clerk.—Jennifer Noll.
Publications Clerk.—Timothy Pearson.
Printing Clerk.—Douglas Alexander.
Professional Staff Members: Benjamin Staub, Renata Strause.
Press/Staff Assistant.—Nicole Triplett.
Staff Assistants: Reuben Goetzl, Brandon Johns.
Republican Chief of Staff/General Counsel.—Sean McLaughlin (2142 RHOB), 6–0002.
Legislative Assistant/Legislative Clerk.—Kelsey Whitlock.

Republican Deputy Chief of Staff/Parliamentarian.—Allison Halataei.
Republican Deputy Chief of Staff/Policy Director.—Richard Hertling.
Republican Chief Oversight Counsel.—Crystal Roberts Jezierski.
Communications Director.—Kim Smith.
Deputy Press Secretary.—Charlotte Sellmyer.
Senior Policy Advisor.—Jamie Zuieback.
Professional Staff Member.—Karas Pattison.
Staff Assistant.—Jennifer Lackey.
Antitrust Counsel.—Stewart Jeffries.
Counsels: Justin Long, Zachary Somers.
Finance Clerk/Office Manager.—Diane Hill.

Subcommittee on Commercial and Administrative Law (H2–362 FHOB), 6–7680.
Majority Chief Counsel.—Michone Johnson.
Counsels: Carol Chodroff, James Park, Norberto Salinas.
Professional Staff.—Adam Russell.
Republican Chief Counsel.—Daniel Flores (B–351 RHOB), 5–6906.

Subcommittee on the Constitution, Civil Rights, and Civil Liberties (B–353 RHOB), 5–2825.
Majority Chief of Staff.—David Lachmann.
Counsels: Kanya Bennett, Keenan Keller, Heather Sawyer.
Professional Staff.—Matthew Morgan.
Republican Chief Counsel.—Paul Taylor (H2–347 FHOB), 5–7157.

Subcommittee on Courts and Competition Policy (B–352 RHOB), 5–5741.
Majority Chief Counsel.—Christal Sheppard.
Counsels: George Elliott, Eric Garduño, Anant Raut, Elisabeth Stein.
Professional Staff.—Rosalind Jackson.
Republican Chief Counsel.—Blaine Merritt (B–336 RHOB), 5–2022.
Counsel.—David Whitney.

Subcommittee on Crime, Terrorism, and Homeland Security (B–370 RHOB), 5–5727.
Majority Chief Counsel.—Bobby Vassar.
Counsels.—Joe Graupensperger, Ron LeGrand, Jesselyn McCurdy, Stephanie Pell, Karen Wilkinson.
Professional Staff.—Veronica Eligan.
Republican Chief Counsel.—Caroline Lynch (B–351 RHOB), 5–6906.
Counsel.—Kimani Little.

Subcommittee on Immigration, Citizenship, Refugees, Border Security, and International Law (517 CHOB), 5–3926.
Majority Chief Counsel.—Ur Jaddou (105 CHOB).
Counsels.—Traci Hong, Hammill Hunter, Tom Jawetz, David Shahoulian.
Professional Staff.—Andres Jimenez.
Republican Chief Counsel.—George Fishman (B–351 RHOB), 5–6906.
Counsel.—Andrea Loving.

Natural Resources

1324 Longworth House Office Building, phone 225–6065

http://www.house.gov/resources

meets each Wednesday

Nick J. Rahall II, of West Virginia, *Chair*

Dale E. Kildee, of Michigan.
Eni F. H. Faleomavaega, of American Samoa.
Neil Abercrombie, of Hawaii.
Frank Pallone, Jr., of New Jersey.
Grace F. Napolitano, of California.
Rush D. Holt, of New Jersey.
Raúl M. Grijalva, of Arizona.
Madeleine Z. Bordallo, of Guam.
Jim Costa, of California.
Dan Boren, of Oklahoma.
Gregorio Kilili Camacho Sablan, of Northern Mariana Islands.
Martin Heinrich, of New Mexico.
George Miller, of California.
Edward J. Markey, of Massachusetts.
Peter A. DeFazio, of Oregon.
Maurice D. Hinchey, of New York.
Donna M. Christensen, of Virgin Islands.
Diana DeGette, of Colorado.
Ron Kind, of Wisconsin.
Lois Capps, of California.
Jay Inslee, of Washington.
Joe Baca, of California.
Stephanie Herseth Sandlin, of South Dakota.
John P. Sarbanes, of Maryland.
Carol Shea-Porter, of New Hampshire.
Niki Tsongas, of Massachusetts.
Frank Kratovil, Jr., of Maryland.
Pedro R. Pierluisi, of Puerto Rico.

Doc Hastings, of Washington.
Don Young, of Alaska.
Elton Gallegly, of California.
John J. Duncan, Jr., of Tennessee.
Jeff Flake, of Arizona.
Henry E. Brown, Jr., of South Carolina.
Cathy McMorris Rodgers, of Washington.
Louie Gohmert, of Texas.
Rob Bishop, of Utah.
Bill Shuster, of Pennsylvania.
Doug Lamborn, of Colorado.
Adrian Smith, of Nebraska.
Robert J. Wittman, of Virginia.
Paul C. Broun, of Georgia.
John Fleming, of Louisiana.
Mike Coffman, of Colorado.
Jason Chaffetz, of Utah.
Cynthia M. Lummis, of Wyoming.
Tom McClintock, of California.
Bill Cassidy, of Louisiana.

SUBCOMMITTEES

[The chairman and ranking minority member are ex officio (non-voting) members of all subcommittees on which they do not serve.]

Energy and Mineral Resources

Jim Costa, of California, *Chair*

Eni F. H. Faleomavaega, of American Samoa.
Rush D. Holt, of New Jersey.
Dan Boren, of Oklahoma.
Gregorio Kilili Camacho Sablan, of Northern Mariana Islands.
Martin Heinrich, of New Mexico.
Edward J. Markey, of Massachusetts.
Maurice D. Hinchey, of New York.
John P. Sarbanes, of Maryland.
Niki Tsongas, of Massachusetts.

Doug Lamborn, of Colorado.
Don Young, of Alaska.
Louie Gohmert, of Texas.
John Fleming, of Louisiana.
Jason Chaffetz, of Utah.
Cynthia M. Lummis, of Wyoming.

Insular Affairs, Oceans and Wildlife

Madeleine Z. Bordallo, of Guam, *Chair*

Dale E. Kildee, of Michigan.
Eni F. H. Faleomavaega, of American Samoa.
Neil Abercrombie, of Hawaii.
Frank Pallone, Jr., of New Jersey.
Gregorio Kilili Camacho Sablan, of Northern Mariana Islands.
Donna M. Christensen, of Virgin Islands.
Diana DeGette, of Colorado.
Ron Kind, of Wisconsin.
Lois Capps, of California.
Carol Shea-Porter, of New Hampshire.
Frank Kratovil, Jr., of Maryland.
Pedro R. Pierluisi, of Puerto Rico.
Henry E. Brown, Jr., of South Carolina.
Don Young, of Alaska.
Jeff Flake, of Arizona.
Doug Lamborn, of Colorado.
Robert J. Wittman, of Virginia.
John Fleming, of Louisiana.
Jason Chaffetz, of Utah.
Bill Cassidy, of Louisiana.

National Parks, Forests, and Public Lands

Raúl M. Grijalva, of Arizona, *Chair*

Dale E. Kildee, of Michigan.
Neil Abercrombie, of Hawaii.
Grace F. Napolitano, of California.
Rush D. Holt, of New Jersey.
Madeleine Z. Bordallo, of Guam.
Dan Boren, of Oklahoma.
Martin Heinrich, of New Mexico.
Peter A. DeFazio, of Oregon.
Maurice D. Hinchey, of New York.
Donna M. Christensen, of Virgin Islands.
Diana DeGette, of Colorado.
Ron Kind, of Wisconsin.
Lois Capps, of California.
Jay Inslee, of Washington.
Stephanie Herseth Sandlin, of South Dakota.
John P. Sarbanes, of Maryland.
Carol Shea-Porter, of New Hampshire.
Niki Tsongas, of Massachusetts.
Pedro R. Pierluisi, of Puerto Rico.
Rob Bishop, of Utah.
Don Young, of Alaska.
Elton Gallegly, of California.
John J. Duncan, Jr., of Tennessee.
Jeff Flake, of Arizona.
Henry E. Brown, Jr., of South Carolina.
Louie Gohmert, of Texas.
Bill Shuster, of Pennsylvania.
Robert J. Wittman, of Virginia.
Paul C. Broun, of Georgia.
Mike Coffman, of Colorado.
Cynthia M. Lummis, of Wyoming.
Tom McClintock, of California.

Water and Power

Grace F. Napolitano, of California, *Chair*

George Miller, of California.
Raúl M. Grijalva, of Arizona.
Jim Costa, of California.
Peter A. DeFazio, of Oregon.
Jay Inslee, of Washington.
Joe Baca, of California.
Tom McClintock, of California.
Cathy McMorris Rodgers, of Washington.
Adrian Smith, of Nebraska.
Mike Coffman, of Colorado.

STAFF

Committee on Natural Resources (1324 LHOB), 225–6065.
Majority Chief of Staff.—Jim Zoia
Deputy Chief of Staff.—Ann Adler.
Executive Assistant.—Lisa James.
Staff Assistant.—Kim Le.
Chief Counsel.—Rick Healy.
Legislative Advisor.—Amy Haskell.
Clerk.—Emily Lande.
Chief Financial Officer.—Linda Booth.
Communications Director.—Allyson Groff.
Deputy Communications Director.—Blake Androff.

Press Assistant.—Matthew Spencer.
Chief Administrator.—Linda Livingston.
Deputy Administrator.—Heather Warren.
Chief Clerk.—Nancy Locke.
Calendar Clerk.—Joycelyn Coleman.
Director, Information Technology.—Matt Vaccaro.
Senior IT Engineer.—Ed Van Scoyoc.
Editor/Printer.—Kathy Miller.
Senior Policy Advisor.—Amelia Jenkins.
Minority Chief of Staff.—Todd Young (1329 LHOB), 5–2761.
Chief Counsel.—Lisa Pittman.
Administrator.—Sophia Varnasidis.
Communications Director.—Emily Lawrimore.
Office of Indian Affairs (140 CHOB), 6–9725.
Majority Staff Director.—Marie Howard.
Counsel.—Janet Erickson.
Legislative Staff.—Joshua Pitre.
Clerk.—Teresa Bravo.
Minority Staff Director.—Chris Fluhr.
Subcommittee on Energy and Mineral Resources (1626 LHOB), 225–9297.
Majority Staff Director.—Deborah Lanzone.
Legislative Staff: Steve Feldgus, Wendy Van Asselt.
Clerk.—Marcie Cooperman.
Minority Staff Director.—Tim Charters (H2–186), 6–2311.
Legislative Staff.—Kathy Benedetto.
Subcommittee on Insular Affairs, Oceans and Wildlife (1337 LHOB), 5–0691.
Majority Insular Affairs Staff Director.—Brian Modeste.
Insular Affairs Legislative Staff.—Jed Bullock.
Insular Affairs Clerk.—Rebecca Zepeda.
Subcommittee on Insular Affairs, Oceans and Wildlife (187 FHOB), 6–0200.
Majority Oceans and Wildlife Staff Director.—Jean Flemma.
Oceans and Wildlife Legislative Staff: Julia Hathaway, Karen Hyun, Dave Jansen.
Oceans and Wildlife Clerk/Legislative Advisor.—Katherine Romans.
Sea Grant Fellow.—Joshua Madeira.
Minority Staff Director.—Harry Burroughs (H2–269), 6–2311.
Legislative Staff: Bonnie Bruce, Dave Whaley.
Subcommittee on National Parks, Forests, and Public Lands (1333 LHOB), 226–7736.
Majority Staff Director.—David Watkins.
Legislative Staff: Laurel Angell, Leslie Duncan, Christy Goldfuss.
Clerk.—Domenick Carroll.
NPS Fellow.—Jim Ireland.
Minority Staff Director.—Jim Streeter.
Legislative Staff: Casey Hammond, Jason Knox.
Subcommittee on Water and Power (1522 LHOB), 225–8331.
Majority Staff Director.—David Wegner.
Legislative Staff: Camille Calimlim, Tyler Kruzich.
Clerk.—Marissa Strickfaden.
Minority Staff Director.—Kiel Weaver (186 FHOB), 6–2311.
Legislative Staff.—Nick Strader.
Press Secretary.—Jill Strait.
Staff Assistant.—Neal Kirby.

Oversight and Government Reform

2157 Rayburn House Office Building, phone 225–5051, fax 225–3974, TTY 225–6852

http://oversight.house.gov

Edolphus Towns, of New York, *Chair*

Paul E. Kanjorski, of Pennsylvania.
Carolyn B. Maloney, of New York.
Elijah E. Cummings, of Maryland.
Dennis J. Kucinich, of Ohio.
John F. Tierney, of Massachusetts.
Wm. Lacy Clay, of Missouri.
Diane E. Watson, of California.
Stephen F. Lynch, of Massachusetts.
Jim Cooper, of Tennessee.
Gerald E. Connolly, of Virginia.
Mike Quigley, of Illinois.
Marcy Kaptur, of Ohio.
Eleanor Holmes Norton, of District of Columbia.
Patrick J. Kennedy, of Rhode Island.
Danny K. Davis, of Illinois.
Chris Van Hollen, of Maryland.
Henry Cuellar, of Texas.
Paul W. Hodes, of New Hampshire.
Christopher S. Murphy, of Connecticut.
Peter Welch, of Vermont.
Bill Foster, of Illinois.
Jackie Speier, of California.
Steve Driehaus, of Ohio.
Judy Chu, of California.

Darrell E. Issa, of California.
Dan Burton, of Indiana.
John L. Mica, of Florida.
Mark E. Souder, of Indiana.
John J. Duncan, Jr., of Tennessee.
Michael R. Turner, of Ohio.
Lynn A. Westmoreland, of Georgia.
Patrick T. McHenry, of North Carolina.
Brian P. Bilbray, of California.
Jim Jordan, of Ohio.
Jeff Flake, of Arizona.
Jeff Fortenberry, of Nebraska.
Jason Chaffetz, of Utah.
Aaron Schock, of Illinois.
Blaine Luetkemeyer, of Missouri.
Anh ''Joseph'' Cao, of Louisiana.

SUBCOMMITTEES

[The chairman and ranking minority member are ex officio (voting) members of all subcommittees]

Domestic Policy

Dennis J. Kucinich, of Ohio, *Chair*

Elijah E. Cummings, of Maryland.
John F. Tierney, of Massachusetts.
Diane E. Watson, of California.
Jim Cooper, of Tennessee.
Patrick J. Kennedy, of Rhode Island.
Peter Welch, of Vermont.
Bill Foster, of Illinois.
Marcy Kaptur, of Ohio.

Jim Jordan, of Ohio.
Mark E. Souder, of Indiana.
Dan Burton, of Indiana.
Michael R. Turner, of Ohio.
Jeff Fortenberry, of Nebraska.
Aaron Schock, of Illinois.

Federal Workforce, Postal Service, and the District of Columbia

Stephen F. Lynch, of Massachusetts, *Chair*

Eleanor Holmes Norton, of District of Columbia.
Danny K. Davis, of Illinois.
Elijah E. Cummings, of Maryland.
Dennis J. Kucinich, of Ohio.
Wm. Lacy Clay, of Missouri.
Gerald E. Connolly, of Virginia.

Jason Chaffetz, of Utah.
Mark E. Souder, of Indiana.
Brian P. Bilbray, of California.
Anh ''Joseph'' Cao, of Louisiana.

Government Management, Organization, and Procurement

Diane E. Watson, of California, *Chair*

Paul E. Kanjorski, of Pennsylvania.
Jim Cooper, of Tennessee.
Gerald E. Connolly, of Virginia.
Henry Cuellar, of Texas.
Jackie Speier, of California.
Paul W. Hodes, of New Hampshire.
Christopher S. Murphy, of Connecticut.
Mike Quigley, of Illinois.

Brian P. Bilbray, of California.
Aaron Schock, of Illinois.
John J. Duncan, Jr., of Tennessee.
Jeff Flake, of Arizona.
Blaine Luetkemeyer, of Missouri.

Information Policy, Census, and National Archives

Wm. Lacy Clay, of Missouri, *Chair*

Paul E. Kanjorski, of Pennsylvania.
Carolyn B. Maloney, of New York.
Eleanor Holmes Norton, of District of Columbia.
Danny K. Davis, of Illinois.
Steve Driehaus, of Ohio.
Diane E. Watson, of California.

Patrick T. McHenry, of North Carolina.
Lynn A. Westmoreland, of Georgia.
John L. Mica, of Florida.
Jason Chaffetz, of Utah.

National Security and Foreign Affairs

John F. Tierney, of Massachusetts, *Chair*

Carolyn B. Maloney, of New York.
Patrick J. Kennedy, of Rhode Island.
Chris Van Hollen, of Maryland.
Paul W. Hodes, of New Hampshire.
Christopher S. Murphy, of Connecticut.
Peter Welch, of Vermont.
Bill Foster, of Illinois.
Steve Driehaus, of Ohio.
Stephen F. Lynch, of Massachusetts.
Henry Cuellar, of Texas.
Mike Quigley, of Illinois.

Jeff Flake, of Arizona.
Dan Burton, of Indiana.
John L. Mica, of Florida.
John J. Duncan, Jr., of Tennessee.
Michael R. Turner, of Ohio.
Lynn A. Westmoreland, of Georgia.
Patrick T. McHenry, of North Carolina.
Jim Jordan, of Ohio.
Jeff Fortenberry, of Nebraska.
Blaine Luetkemeyer, of Missouri.

STAFF

Oversight and Government Reform (2157 RHOB), 202–225–5051.

Majority Staff Director.—Ronald Stroman.
Deputy Staff Director.—Michael McCarthy.
Chief Counsel.—John Arlington.
Senior Policy Advisor.—Mark Stephenson.
Senior Investigator/Professional Staff Member.—Chris Knauer.
Senior Investigative Counsels: Joanne Royce, Christopher Staszak.
Senior Counsels: Leah Perry, Steven Rangel.
Senior Policy Advisor/Counsel.—Jason Powell.
Counsels: Krista Boyd, Beverly Britton Fraser, Michael Kubayanda, James Latoff, Julie Rones.
Investigative Counsels: Kevin Barstow, Brian Eiler, Neema Singh Guliani, Bradford Hallmon, Brian Quinn, David Rotman.
Investigators: Lisa Cody, Kwane Drabo, Katherine Graham.
Professional Staff: Craig Fischer, Bill Jusino, Phyllis Love, Ryshelle McCadney, Adam Miles.
Special Assistants: Amy Miller, Gerri Willis.
Professional Staff Members: Christopher Sanders, Alex Wolf.
Director of Communications.—Jenny Rosenberg.
Deputy Director of Communications.—Shrita Sterlin.
Deputy Press Secretary/New Media.—Adam Hodge.

Press Assistant.—Velginy Hernandez.
Chief Clerk.—Carla Hultberg.
Deputy Chief Clerk.—Linda Good.
Assistant Clerks: Marc Johnson, Ophelia Rivas.
Staff Assistants: Aaron Ellias, Peter Fise.
Financial Administrator.—Robin Butler.
Director of Technology.—Eddie Walker.
IT Specialist.—Leneal Scott.
IT Assistant.—Ben Freeman.
Minority Staff Director.—Larry Brady (B–350A RHOB), 5–5074.
Deputy Staff Director.—John Cuaderes.
Communications Director.—Federick Hill.
Press Secretary.—Kurt Bardella.
Deputy Press Secretaries: Benjamin Cole, Seamus Kraft.
General Counsel.—Rob Borden.
Chief Counsel/Policy.—Chas Phillips.
Chief Counsel/Oversight and Investigations.—Jennifer Safavian.
Parliamentarian/Member SVC Coordinator.—Adam Fromm.
Senior Counsels: Tom Alexander, Steve Castor, Howie Denis, Christopher Hixon.
Counsels.—Ashley Callen, Daniel Epstein, Fay Epstein, Hudson Hollister, Marvin Kaplan, Kristina Moore, Jonathan Skladany.
Senior Professional Staff.—Christopher Bright.
Professional Staff Members: Brien Beattie, Molly Boyl, April Canter, Alex Cooper, Meredith Liberty, Mark Marin, John Ohly.
Office Manager.—Donna Harkins.
Executive Assistant.—Sharon Casey.

Subcommittee on Domestic Policy (B–349B RHOB), 225–6427.
Staff Director.—Jaron Bourke.
Counsels: Claire Coleman, Yonatan Zamir.
Professional Staff.—Michael Clark.
Clerk.—Jean Gosa.
Staff Assistant.—Charisma Williams.

Subcommittee on Federal Workforce, Postal Service, and the District of Columbia (B–349A RHOB), 225–5147.
Staff Director.—William Miles.
Professional Staff.—Jill Crissman.
Clerk/Legislative Assistant.—Aisha Elkheshin.
Deputy Clerk/Legislative Assistant.—Dan Zeidman.

Subcommittee on Government Management, Organization, and Procurement (B–372 RHOB), 225–3741.
Staff Director.—Bert Hammond.
Senior Policy Advisor.—Adam Bordes.
Professional Staff.—Deborah Mack.
Clerk.—Valerie VanBuren.

Subcommittee on Information Policy, Census, and National Archives (B–349C RHOB), 225–6751.
Staff Director/Counsel.—Darryl Piggee.
Professional Staff: Anthony Clark, Yvette Cravins, Frank Davis.
Clerk.—Jean Gosa.
Staff Assistant.—Charisma Williams.

Subcommittee on National Security and Foreign Affairs (B–371C RHOB), 225–2548.
Staff Director/Counsel.—Andrew Wright.
Counsels: Talia Dubovi, Scott Lindsay.
Clerk.—Elliot Gillerman.

Rules

H–312 The Capitol, phone 225–9191

http://www.house.gov/rules

meets every Tuesday

Louise McIntosh Slaughter, of New York, *Chair*

James P. McGovern, of Massachusetts.
Alcee L. Hastings, of Florida.
Doris O. Matsui, of California.
Dennis A. Cardoza, of California.
Michael A. Arcuri, of New York.
Ed Perlmutter, of Colorado.
Chellie Pingree, of Maine.
Jared Polis, of Colorado.

David Dreier, of California.
Lincoln Diaz-Balart, of Florida.
Pete Sessions, of Texas.
Virginia Foxx, of North Carolina.

SUBCOMMITTEES

Legislative and Budget Process

Alcee L. Hastings, of Florida, *Chair*

Dennis A. Cardoza, of California.
Chellie Pingree, of Maine.
Jared Polis, of Colorado.
Louise McIntosh Slaughter, of New York.

Lincoln Diaz-Balart, of Florida.
David Dreier, of California.

Rules and Organization of the House

James P. McGovern, of Massachusetts, *Chair*

Doris O. Matsui, of California.
Michael A. Arcuri, of New York.
Ed Perlmutter, of Colorado.
Louise McIntosh Slaughter, of New York.

Pete Sessions, of Texas.
Virginia Foxx, of North Carolina.

STAFF

Committee on Rules (H–312 The Capitol), 225–9091.
Majority Staff Director.—Muftiah McCartin.
Chief Counsel.—Sophie Hayford.
Counsel.—Sampak Garg.
Assistant Counsel.—Liz Pardue.
Legislative Director.—Don Sisson.
Communications Director.—Vincent Morris.
Professional Staff: Tony Abate, Adam Berg, Sonny Sinha, Tim Sheehan, Stefanie Winzeler.
Chief Clerk.—Deb Delaney.
Legislative Clerk.—Sadie Marshall.
Assistant Clerk.—George Agurkis.
Director of Research.—Gary Johnson.
Associate Staff: Claire Benjamin (1037 LHOB); Matthew Henken (415 CHOB); Rosalyn Kumar (501 CHOB); Jason Lumia (Cardoza 1224 LHOB); Nell Maceda (127 CHOB); Lale Mamaux (Hastings 2353 RHOB); Samuel Stefanki (Matsui 222 CHOB); Keith Stern (McGovern 438 CHOB).
Minority Staff Director.—Hugh Halpern (H–152).
Deputy Staff Director.—Adam Jarvis (H–152).
Communications Director.—Jo Maney.
Professional Staff .—Shane Chambers, (1627 LHOB); Jenny Gorski, (1627 LHOB); Rachel Leman (233 CHOB); Celeste West (1627 LHOB).
Clerk.—Luke Hatzis (H–152).
Associate Staff: Brad Smith (Dreier 233 CHOB), Cesar Gonzales (Diaz-Balart 2244 RHOB), Keagan Lenihan (Sessions 1318 LHOB), Brandon Renz (Foxx 1230 LHOB).

Subcommittee on Legislative and Budget Process (2353 LHOB), 5–1313.
Majority Staff Director.—Lale Mamaux (Alcee L. Hastings).
Minority Staff Director.—Cesar Gonzalez (Diaz-Balart).
Subcommittee on Rules and Organization of the House (438 CHOB), 5–6101.
Majority Staff Director.—Keith Stern (McGovern).
Minority Staff Director.—Keagan Lenihan (Sessions).

Science and Technology

2320 Rayburn House Office Building, phone 225–6375, fax 225–3895
http://www.house.gov/science

meets second and fourth Wednesdays of each month

Bart Gordon, of Tennessee, *Chair*
Parker Griffith, of Alabama, *Vice Chair*

Jerry F. Costello, of Illinois.
Eddie Bernice Johnson, of Texas.
Lynn C. Woolsey, of California.
David Wu, of Oregon.
Brian Baird, of Washington.
Brad Miller, of North Carolina.
Daniel Lipinski, of Illinois.
Gabrielle Giffords, of Arizona.
Donna F. Edwards, of Maryland.
Marcia L. Fudge, of Ohio.
Ben Ray Luján, of New Mexico.
Paul Tonko, of New York.
Steven R. Rothman, of New Jersey.
Jim Matheson, of Utah.
Lincoln Davis, of Tennessee.
Ben Chandler, of Kentucky.
Russ Carnahan, of Missouri.
Baron P. Hill, of Indiana.
Harry E. Mitchell, of Arizona.
Charles A. Wilson, of Ohio.
Kathleen A. Dahlkemper, of Pennsylvania.
Alan Grayson, of Florida.
Suzanne M. Kosmas, of Florida.
Gary C. Peters, of Michigan.

Ralph M. Hall, of Texas.
F. James Sensenbrenner, Jr., of Wisconsin.
Lamar Smith, of Texas.
Dana Rohrabacher, of California.
Roscoe G. Bartlett, of Maryland.
Vernon J. Ehlers, of Michigan.
Frank D. Lucas, of Oklahoma.
Judy Biggert, of Illinois.
W. Todd Akin, of Missouri.
Randy Neugebauer, of Texas.
Bob Inglis, of South Carolina.
Michael T. McCaul, of Texas.
Mario Diaz-Balart, of Florida.
Brian P. Bilbray, of California.
Adrian Smith, of Nebraska.
Paul C. Broun, of Georgia.
Pete Olson, of Texas.

SUBCOMMITTEES

[The chairman and ranking minority member are ex officio (voting) members of all subcommittees on which they do not serve.]

Energy and Environment

Brian Baird, of Washington, *Chair*
Paul Tonko, of New York, *Vice Chair*

Jerry F. Costello, of Illinois.
Lynn C. Woolsey, of California.
Donna F. Edwards, of Maryland.
Ben Ray Luján, of New Mexico.
Eddie Bernice Johnson, of Texas.
Daniel Lipinski, of Illinois.
Gabrielle Giffords, of Arizona.
Jim Matheson, of Utah.
Lincoln Davis, of Tennessee.
Ben Chandler, of Kentucky.

Bob Inglis, of South Carolina.
Roscoe G. Bartlett, of Maryland.
Vernon J. Ehlers, of Michigan.
Judy Biggert, of Illinois.
W. Todd Akin, of Missouri.
Randy Neugebauer, of Texas.
Mario Diaz-Balart, of Florida.

Investigations and Oversight

Brad Miller, of North Carolina, *Chair*
Kathleen A. Dahlkemper, of Pennsylvania, *Vice Chair*

Steven R. Rothman, of New Jersey.
Lincoln Davis, of Tennessee.
Charles A. Wilson, of Ohio.
Alan Grayson, of Florida.

Paul C. Broun, of Georgia.
Brian P. Bilbray, of California.

Research and Science Education

Daniel Lipinski, of Illinois, *Chair*

Marcia L. Fudge, of Ohio, *Vice Chair*

Eddie Bernice Johnson, of Texas.
Brian Baird, of Washington.
Parker Griffith, of Alabama.
Paul Tonko, of New York.
Russ Carnahan, of Missouri.

Vernon J. Ehlers, of Michigan.
Randy Neugebauer, of Texas.
Bob Inglis, of South Carolina.
Brian P. Bilbray, of California.

Space and Aeronautics

Gabrielle Giffords, of Arizona, *Chair*

Donna F. Edwards, of Maryland, *Vice Chair*

Marcia L. Fudge, of Ohio.
Parker Griffith, of Alabama.
David Wu, of Oregon.
Steven R. Rothman, of New Jersey.
Baron P. Hill, of Indiana.
Charles A. Wilson, of Ohio.
Alan Grayson, of Florida.
Suzanne M. Kosmas, of Florida.

Pete Olson, of Texas.
F. James Sensenbrenner, Jr., of Wisconsin.
Dana Rohrabacher, of California.
Frank D. Lucas, of Oklahoma.
Michael T. McCaul, of Texas.

Technology and Innovation

David Wu, of Oregon, *Chair*

Ben Ray Luján, of New Mexico, *Vice Chair*

Donna F. Edwards, of Maryland.
Paul Tonko, of New York.
Daniel Lipinski, of Illinois.
Harry E. Mitchell, of Arizona.
Gary C. Peters, of Michigan.

Adrian Smith, of Nebraska.
Judy Biggert, of Illinois.
W. Todd Akin, of Missouri.
Paul C. Broun, of Georgia.

STAFF

Committee on Science (2320 RHOB), 225–6375, fax 225–3895.
Chief of Staff.—Louis Finkel.
Administrative Assistant.—Leigh Ann Brown.
Staff Assistant.—Karly Schledwitz.
Director of Policy and Outreach.—Lori Pepper.
Deputy Communications Director.—Alison Amor.
Financial Administrator.—Dave Laughter.
Counsels: Hilary Cain, John Piazza.
Communications Director.—Alex Dery Snider.
Printer.—Jude Ruckel.
Legislative Clerk.—Deborah Samantar.
Director of Information Technology.—Larry Whittaker.
Minority Staff (395 FHOB), 5–6371, fax 6–0133
Republican Chief of Staff.—Janet Poppleton.
Republican Staff Director.—Leslee Gilbert.
Chief Counsel.—Margaret Caravelli.
Deputy Counsel.—Katy Crooks.
Communications Director.—Zachary Kurz.
Legislative Clerk.—Katie Comer.
Research Assistant.—Alex Matthews.
Staff Assistant.—Aaricka Aldridge.
Press Assistant.—Adrienne Rimmer.
Subcommitte on Energy and Environment (2319 RHOB), 5–8844, fax 5–4439
Majority Staff Director.—Chris King.
Professional Staff: Elaine Phelen, Adam Rosenberg, Shimere Williams.
Research Assistant.—Janie Wise.
Minority Professional Staff: Elizabeth Chapel, Tara Rothschild.

Subcommittee on Technology and Innovation (2321 RHOB), 5–9662, fax 6–6983
Majority Staff Director.—Mike Quear.
Professional Staff: Travis Hite, Meghan Housewright, Holly Logue Prutz.
Research Assistant.—Victoria Johnston.
Minority Professional Staff.—Dan Byers.
Subcommittee on Research and Science Education (2321 RHOB), 5–9662, fax 6–6983
Majority Staff Director.—Dahlia Sokolov.
Professional Staff.—Marcy Gallo.
Research Assistant.—Bess Caughran.
Minority Professional Staff.—Melé Williams.
Subcommittee on Space and Aeronautics (B–374 RHOB), 5–7858, fax 5–6415
Majority Staff Director.—Richard Obermann.
Professional Staff.—Allen Li, Pam Whitney.
Research Assistant.—Devin Bryant.
Minority Professional Staff: Ed Feddeman, Ken Monroe.
Subcommittee on Investigations and Oversight (B–374 RHOB), 5–8772, fax 5–7815
Majority Staff Director.—Dan Pearson.
Counsel, Professional Staff.—Edith Holleman.
Professional Staff: Ken Jacobson, Doug Pasternak, James Paul.
Research Assistant.—Molly O'Rourke.
Minority Professional Staff.—Tom Hammond.

Small Business

2361 Rayburn House Office Building, phone 225–4038, fax 226–5276

http://www.house.gov/smbiz

meets second Thursday of each month

Nydia M. Velázquez, of New York, *Chair*

Dennis Moore, of Kansas.
Heath Shuler, of North Carolina.
Kathleen A. Dahlkemper, of Pennsylvania.
Kurt Schrader, of Oregon.
Ann Kirkpatrick, of Arizona.
Glenn C. Nye, of Virginia.
Michael H. Michaud, of Maine.
Melissa L. Bean, of Illinois.
Daniel Lipinski, of Illinois.
Jason Altmire, of Pennsylvania.
Yvette D. Clarke, of New York.
Brad Ellsworth, of Indiana.
Joe Sestak, of Pennsylvania.
Bobby Bright, of Alabama.
Parker Griffith, of Alabama.
Deborah L. Halvorson, of Illinois.

Sam Graves, of Missouri.
Roscoe G. Bartlett, of Maryland.
W. Todd Akin, of Missouri.
Steve King, of Iowa.
Lynn A. Westmoreland, of Georgia.
Louie Gohmert, of Texas.
Mary Fallin, of Oklahoma.
Vern Buchanan, of Florida.
Blaine Luetkemeyer, of Missouri.
Aaron Schock, of Illinois.
Glenn Thompson, of Pennsylvania.
Mike Coffman, of Colorado.

SUBCOMMITTEES

[The chairman and ranking minority member are ex officio (non-voting) members of all subcommittees on which they do not serve.]

Contracting and Technology

Glenn C. Nye, of Virginia, *Chair*

Yvette D. Clarke, of New York.
Brad Ellsworth, of Indiana.
Kurt Schrader, of Oregon.
Deborah L. Halvorson, of Illinois.
Melissa L. Bean, of Illinois.
Joe Sestak, of Pennsylvania.
Parker Griffith, of Alabama.

Aaron Schock, of Illinois.
Roscoe G. Bartlett, of Maryland.
W. Todd Akin, of Missouri.
Mary Fallin, of Oklahoma.
Glenn Thompson, of Pennsylvania.

Finance and Tax

Kurt Schrader, of Oregon, *Chair*

Dennis Moore, of Kansas.
Ann Kirkpatrick, of Arizona.
Melissa L. Bean, of Illinois.
Joe Sestak, of Pennsylvania.
Deborah L. Halvorson, of Illinois.
Glenn C. Nye, of Virginia.
Michael H. Michaud, of Maine.

Vern Buchanan, of Florida.
Steve King, of Iowa.
W. Todd Akin, of Missouri.
Blaine Luetkemeyer, of Missouri.
Mike Coffman, of Colorado.

Investigations and Oversight

Jason Altmire, of Pennsylvania, *Chair*

Heath Shuler, of North Carolina.
Brad Ellsworth, of Indiana.
Parker Griffith, of Alabama.

Mary Fallin, of Oklahoma.
Louie Gohmert, of Texas.

Regulations and Healthcare

Kathleen A. Dahlkemper, of Pennsylvania, *Chair*

Daniel Lipinski, of Illinois.
Parker Griffith, of Alabama.
Melissa L. Bean, of Illinois.
Jason Altmire, of Pennsylvania.
Joe Sestak, of Pennsylvania.
Bobby Bright, of Alabama.
Lynn A. Westmoreland, of Georgia.
Steve King, of Iowa.
Vern Buchanan, of Florida.
Glenn Thompson, of Pennsylvania.
Mike Coffman, of Colorado.

Rural Development, Entrepreneurship and Trade

Heath Shuler, of North Carolina, *Chair*

Michael H. Michaud, of Maine.
Bobby Bright, of Alabama.
Kathleen A. Dahlkemper, of Pennsylvania.
Ann Kirkpatrick, of Arizona.
Yvette D. Clarke, of New York.
Blaine Luetkemeyer, of Missouri.
Steve King, of Iowa.
Aaron Schock, of Illinois.
Glenn Thompson, of Pennsylvania.

STAFF

Committee on Small Business (2361 RHOB), 225–4038.
Majority Staff Director.—Michael Day.
Deputy Staff Director.—Adam Minehardt.
Chief Counsel.—Timothy Slattery.
Press Secretary.—Duncan Neasham.
Deputy Press Secretary.—Zamir Ahmed.
Banking Counsel.—Andy Jiminez.
General Counsel.—Russell Orban.
Trade Counsel.—Nicole Witenstein.
Office Manager.—Mory Garcia.
Clerk.—Darierre Gutierrez.
Health Counsel.—Tom Dawson.
Technology Counsel.—David Grossman.
Regulations Counsel.—Erik Lieberman.
Agriculture Counsel.—Sarah Gallo.
Staff Assistant.—Xinia Bermudez.
Minority Staff Director.—Karen Haas (B–363 RHOB) 225–5821.
Deputy Staff Director.—Paul Sass.
Chief Counsel.—Barry Pineles.
Chief of Staff to the Member.—Tom Brown.
Counsel.—Jan Oliver.
Press Secretary.—Angela Landers.
Press Assistant.—Kelly Hoffman.
Professional Staff: Lisa Christian, Joe Hartz, Brooke Shupc.

Standards of Official Conduct

HT–2 The Capitol, phone 225–7103, fax 225–7392

Zoe Lofgren, of California, *Chair*

Ben Chandler, of Kentucky.
G. K. Butterfield, of North Carolina.
Kathy Castor, of Florida.
Peter Welch, of Vermont.

Jo Bonner, of Alabama.
K. Michael Conaway, of Texas.
Charles W. Dent, of Pennsylvania.
Gregg Harper, of Mississippi.
Michael T. McCaul, of Texas.

(No Subcommittees)

STAFF

Chief Counsel/Staff Director.—Blake Chisam.
Counsel to the Chair.—Dan Taylor.
Counsel to the Ranking Republican Member.—Todd Ungerecht.
Deputy Chief Counsel.—Morgan Kim.
Director of:
Advice and Education.—Kenyen Brown.
Financial Disclosure Review.—Stan Simpson.
Counsels: Carol E. Dixon, Sheria Clarke, Susan Olson, Peg Perl, Tom Rust, Donald Sherman, Tonia Smith, Clifford Stoddard, Jr.
Staff Assistants: Donna Hayes, Paulicia Larkin.
System Administrator.—Peter Johnson.
Administrative Staff Director.—Joanne White.
Financial Disclosure Advisor.—Deborah Peay.
Investigator.—Frank Davies.
Investigative Clerk.—Amelia Johnson.

OFFICE OF CONGRESSIONAL ETHICS (OCE)

1017 Longworth House Office Building, 20515

phone (202) 225–9739, fax (202) 226–0997, http://oce.house.gov/

Staff Director/Chief Counsel.—Leo J. Wise (202) 225–9739.
Senior Counsel.—Bill Cable.
Administrative Director.—Mary K. Flanagan.
Investigative Counsels: Omar Ashmawy, Elizabeth Horton, Kedric L. Payne, Paul Solis.
Analyst.—Nate Wright.

Board Members:
David Evans Skaggs (Chairman), (202) 225–9739.
Porter J. Goss (Co-Chairman).
Yvonne Brathwaite Burke.
James M. ''Jay'' Eagen III.
Karan L. English.
Allison R. Hayward.
William Eldridge ''Bill'' Frenzel.
Judge Abner J. Mikva.

Transportation and Infrastructure

2165 Rayburn House Office Building, phone 225–4472, fax 225–6782

http://www.house.gov/transportation

meets first Wednesday of each month

James L. Oberstar, of Minnesota, *Chair*

Nick J. Rahall II, of West Virginia, *Vice Chair*

Peter A. DeFazio, of Oregon.
Jerry F. Costello, of Illinois.
Eleanor Holmes Norton, of District of Columbia.
Jerrold Nadler, of New York.
Corrine Brown, of Florida.
Bob Filner, of California.
Eddie Bernice Johnson, of Texas.
Gene Taylor, of Mississippi.
Elijah E. Cummings, of Maryland.
Leonard L. Boswell, of Iowa.
Tim Holden, of Pennsylvania.
Brian Baird, of Washington.
Rick Larsen, of Washington.
Michael E. Capuano, of Massachusetts.
Timothy H. Bishop, of New York.
Michael H. Michaud, of Maine.
Russ Carnahan, of Missouri.
Grace F. Napolitano, of California.
Daniel Lipinski, of Illinois.
Mazie K. Hirono, of Hawaii.
Jason Altmire, of Pennsylvania.
Timothy J. Walz, of Minnesota.
Heath Shuler, of North Carolina.
Michael A. Arcuri, of New York.
Harry E. Mitchell, of Arizona.
Christopher P. Carney, of Pennsylvania.
John J. Hall, of New York.
Steve Kagen, of Wisconsin.
Steve Cohen, of Tennessee.
Laura Richardson, of California.
Albio Sires, of New Jersey.
Donna F. Edwards, of Maryland.
Solomon P. Ortiz, of Texas.
Phil Hare, of Illinois.
John A. Boccieri, of Ohio.
Mark H. Schauer, of Michigan.
Betsy Markey, of Colorado.
Parker Griffith, of Alabama.
Michael E. McMahon, of New York.
Thomas S. P. Perriello, of Virginia.
Dina Titus, of Nevada.
Harry Teague, of New Mexico.
Vacant

John L. Mica, of Florida.
Don Young, of Alaska.
Thomas E. Petri, of Wisconsin.
Howard Coble, of North Carolina.
John J. Duncan, Jr., of Tennessee.
Vernon J. Ehlers, of Michigan.
Frank A. LoBiondo, of New Jersey.
Jerry Moran, of Kansas.
Gary G. Miller, of California.
Henry E. Brown, Jr., of South Carolina.
Timothy V. Johnson, of Illinois.
Todd Russell Platts, of Pennsylvania.
Sam Graves, of Missouri.
Bill Shuster, of Pennsylvania.
John Boozman, of Arkansas.
Shelley Moore Capito, of West Virginia.
Jim Gerlach, of Pennsylvania.
Mario Diaz-Balart, of Florida.
Charles W. Dent, of Pennsylvania.
Connie Mack, of Florida.
Lynn A. Westmoreland, of Georgia.
Jean Schmidt, of Ohio.
Candice S. Miller, of Michigan.
Mary Fallin, of Oklahoma.
Vern Buchanan, of Florida.
Robert E. Latta, of Ohio.
Brett Guthrie, of Kentucky.
Anh ''Joseph'' Cao, of Louisiana.
Aaron Schock, of Illinois.
Pete Olson, of Texas.

SUBCOMMITTEES

[The chairman and ranking minority member are ex officio (voting) members of all subcommittees on which they do not serve.]

Aviation

Jerry F. Costello, of Illinois, *Chair*

Russ Carnahan, of Missouri.
Parker Griffith, of Alabama.
Michael E. McMahon, of New York.
Peter A. DeFazio, of Oregon.
Eleanor Holmes Norton, of District of Columbia.
Bob Filner, of California.
Eddie Bernice Johnson, of Texas.
Leonard L. Boswell, of Iowa.
Tim Holden, of Pennsylvania.
Michael E. Capuano, of Massachusetts.
Daniel Lipinski, of Illinois.
Mazie K. Hirono, of Hawaii.
Harry E. Mitchell, of Arizona.
John J. Hall, of New York.
Steve Cohen, of Tennessee.
Laura Richardson, of California.
John A. Boccieri, of Ohio.
Nick J. Rahall II, of West Virginia.
Corrine Brown, of Florida.
Elijah E. Cummings, of Maryland.
Jason Altmire, of Pennsylvania.
Solomon P. Ortiz, of Texas.
Mark H. Schauer, of Michigan.
Vacant

Thomas E. Petri, of Wisconsin.
Howard Coble, of North Carolina.
John J. Duncan, Jr., of Tennessee.
Vernon J. Ehlers, of Michigan.
Frank A. LoBiondo, of New Jersey.
Jerry Moran, of Kansas.
Sam Graves, of Missouri.
John Boozman, of Arkansas.
Shelley Moore Capito, of West Virginia.
Jim Gerlach, of Pennsylvania.
Charles W. Dent, of Pennsylvania.
Connie Mack, of Florida.
Lynn A. Westmoreland, of Georgia.
Jean Schmidt, of Ohio.
Mary Fallin, of Oklahoma.
Vern Buchanan, of Florida.
Brett Guthrie, of Kentucky.

Coast Guard and Maritime Transportation

Elijah E. Cummings, of Maryland, *Chair*

Corrine Brown, of Florida.
Rick Larsen, of Washington.
Gene Taylor, of Mississippi.
Brian Baird, of Washington.
Timothy H. Bishop, of New York.
Steve Kagen, of Wisconsin.
Michael E. McMahon, of New York.
Laura Richardson, of California.

Frank A. LoBiondo, of New Jersey.
Don Young, of Alaska.
Howard Coble, of North Carolina.
Vernon J. Ehlers, of Michigan.
Todd Russell Platts, of Pennsylvania.
Pete Olson, of Texas.

Economic Development, Public Buildings, and Emergency Management

Eleanor Holmes Norton, of District of Columbia, *Chair*

Betsy Markey, of Colorado.
Michael H. Michaud, of Maine.
Heath Shuler, of North Carolina.
Parker Griffith, of Alabama.
Russ Carnahan, of Missouri.
Timothy J. Walz, of Minnesota.
Michael A. Arcuri, of New York.
Christopher P. Carney, of Pennsylvania.
Donna F. Edwards, of Maryland.
Thomas S. P. Perriello, of Virginia.

Mario Diaz-Balart, of Florida.
Timothy V. Johnson, of Illinois.
Sam Graves, of Missouri.
Shelley Moore Capito, of West Virginia.
Mary Fallin, of Oklahoma.
Brett Guthrie, of Kentucky.
Anh ''Joseph'' Cao, of Louisiana.
Vacant

Highways and Transit

Peter A. DeFazio, of Oregon, *Chair*

Nick J. Rahall II, of West Virginia.
Jerrold Nadler, of New York.
Bob Filner, of California.
Tim Holden, of Pennsylvania.
Brian Baird, of Washington.
Michael E. Capuano, of Massachusetts.
Timothy H. Bishop, of New York.
Michael H. Michaud, of Maine.
Grace F. Napolitano, of California.
Daniel Lipinski, of Illinois.
Mazie K. Hirono, of Hawaii.
Jason Altmire, of Pennsylvania.
Timothy J. Walz, of Minnesota.
Heath Shuler, of North Carolina.
Michael A. Arcuri, of New York.
Harry E. Mitchell, of Arizona.
Christopher P. Carney, of Pennsylvania.
Steve Cohen, of Tennessee.
Laura Richardson, of California.
Albio Sires, of New Jersey.
Donna F. Edwards, of Maryland.
Gene Taylor, of Mississippi.
Leonard L. Boswell, of Iowa.
Rick Larsen, of Washington.
John J. Hall, of New York.
Steve Kagen, of Wisconsin.
Solomon P. Ortiz, of Texas.
Phil Hare, of Illinois.
John A. Boccieri, of Ohio.
Mark H. Schauer, of Michigan.
Vacant

John J. Duncan, Jr., of Tennessee.
Don Young, of Alaska.
Thomas E. Petri, of Wisconsin.
Howard Coble, of North Carolina.
Jerry Moran, of Kansas.
Gary G. Miller, of California.
Henry E. Brown, Jr., of South Carolina.
Timothy V. Johnson, of Illinois.
Todd Russell Platts, of Pennsylvania.
Bill Shuster, of Pennsylvania.
John Boozman, of Arkansas.
Shelley Moore Capito, of West Virginia.
Jim Gerlach, of Pennsylvania.
Mario Diaz-Balart, of Florida.
Charles W. Dent, of Pennsylvania.
Connie Mack, of Florida.
Jean Schmidt, of Ohio.
Candice S. Miller, of Michigan.
Mary Fallin, of Oklahoma.
Vern Buchanan, of Florida.
Robert E. Latta, of Ohio.
Aaron Schock, of Illinois.

Railroads, Pipelines, and Hazardous Materials

Corrine Brown, of Florida, *Chair*

Dina Titus, of Nevada.
Harry Teague, of New Mexico.
Nick J. Rahall II, of West Virginia.
Jerrold Nadler, of New York.
Elijah E. Cummings, of Maryland.
Grace F. Napolitano, of California.
Jason Altmire, of Pennsylvania.
Timothy J. Walz, of Minnesota.
Michael A. Arcuri, of New York.
Christopher P. Carney, of Pennsylvania.
Albio Sires, of New Jersey.
Mark H. Schauer, of Michigan.
Betsy Markey, of Colorado.
Michael E. McMahon, of New York.
Thomas S. P. Perriello, of Virginia.
Peter A. DeFazio, of Oregon.
Jerry F. Costello, of Illinois.
Bob Filner, of California.
Eddie Bernice Johnson, of Texas.
Leonard L. Boswell, of Iowa.
Rick Larsen, of Washington.
Michael H. Michaud, of Maine.
Daniel Lipinski, of Illinois.
Steve Cohen, of Tennessee.
Laura Richardson, of California.

Bill Shuster, of Pennsylvania.
Thomas E. Petri, of Wisconsin.
Jerry Moran, of Kansas.
Gary G. Miller, of California.
Henry E. Brown, Jr., of South Carolina.
Timothy V. Johnson, of Illinois.
Sam Graves, of Missouri.
Jim Gerlach, of Pennsylvania.
Charles W. Dent, of Pennsylvania.
Lynn A. Westmoreland, of Georgia.
Jean Schmidt, of Ohio.
Candice S. Miller, of Michigan.
Vern Buchanan, of Florida.
Robert E. Latta, of Ohio.
Brett Guthrie, of Kentucky.
Aaron Schock, of Illinois.
Anh ''Joseph'' Cao, of Louisiana.
Pete Olson, of Texas.

Water Resources and Environment

Eddie Bernice Johnson, of Texas, *Chair*

Thomas S. P. Perriello, of Virginia.
Jerry F. Costello, of Illinois.
Gene Taylor, of Mississippi.
Brian Baird, of Washington.
Timothy H. Bishop, of New York.
Russ Carnahan, of Missouri.
Steve Kagen, of Wisconsin.
Donna F. Edwards, of Maryland.
Solomon P. Ortiz, of Texas.
Phil Hare, of Illinois.
Dina Titus, of Nevada.
Harry Teague, of New Mexico.
Eleanor Holmes Norton, of District of Columbia.
Michael E. Capuano, of Massachusetts.
Grace F. Napolitano, of California.
Mazie K. Hirono, of Hawaii.
Harry E. Mitchell, of Arizona.
John J. Hall, of New York.
Parker Griffith, of Alabama.
Bob Filner, of California.
Corrine Brown, of Florida.
Vacant

John Boozman, of Arkansas.
Don Young, of Alaska.
John J. Duncan, Jr., of Tennessee.
Vernon J. Ehlers, of Michigan.
Frank A. LoBiondo, of New Jersey.
Gary G. Miller, of California.
Henry E. Brown, Jr., of South Carolina.
Todd Russell Platts, of Pennsylvania.
Bill Shuster, of Pennsylvania.
Mario Diaz-Balart, of Florida.
Connie Mack, of Florida.
Lynn A. Westmoreland, of Georgia.
Candice S. Miller, of Michigan.
Robert E. Latta, of Ohio.
Anh ''Joseph'' Cao, of Louisiana.
Pete Olson, of Texas.

STAFF

Committee on Transportation and Infrastructure (2165 RHOB), 225–4472, fax 225–6782.
Majority Full Committee Staff
Staff Director.—David A. Heymsfeld.
Chief Counsel.—Ward W. McCarragher.
Deputy Chief Counsel.—Stacie Soumbeniotis.
Senior Professional Staff: Sharon Barkeloo, Helena Zyblikewycz.
Administrator.—Dara Schlieker.
Legislative Assistants: Ray Carta, Jennifer Walsh.
Director of Committee Facilities and Operations.—Jimmy Miller.
Staff Assistants: Jonathan Jackson, Kayla Kotila, Bradley Watson.
Minority Full Committee Staff
Chief of Staff.—James W. Coon, (2163 RHOB), 5–9446.
Policy Director.—Amy B. Steinmann.
Counsel.—Suzanne Newhouse.
Legislative Assistant.—Jason W. Rosa.
Staff Assistant.—Jeff Wieand.
Information Systems
Manager of Information Systems.—Keven Sard.
Assistant Systems Administrator.—Scott Putz.
Majority Communications
Director of Communications.—Jim Berard.
Press Secretary.—Mary Kerr.
Communications Assistant.—Julie Carpenter-Lotz.
Minority Communications
Minority Press Secretary.—Justin Harclerode.
Editorial Office
Clerk.—Tracy G. Mosebey.
Printer/Assistant Clerk.—Lindsey S. Collins.
Oversight and Investigations
Majority Staff
Senior Counsels: Trinita Brown, Ken Kopocis.
Senior Professional Staff: H. Clay Foushee, Leila Kahn.
Counsel.—Joseph Wender.
Staff Assistant.—Melanie Harris.
Minority Staff
Legislative Staff Assistant.—Joe Henell.

Subcommittee on Aviation (2251 RHOB), 6–3220, fax 5–4629.
Majority Staff Director.—Giles Giovinazzi.
Professional Staff: Sarah Blackwood, Jana Denning.
Legislative Assistant.—Laurie Bertenthal.
Senior Administrative Staff Assistant.—Pamela Keller.
Minority Staff Director.—Holly E. Woodruff Lyons.
Professional Staff.—Bailey Edwards.
Legislative Staff Assistant.—Ryan Boyce.
Subcommittee on Coast Guard and Maritime Transportation (507 FHOB), 6–3587, fax 6–0922.
Majority Staff Director.—John Cullather.
Senior Professional Staff.—Michael Rodriguez.
Professional Staff.—Lucinda Lessley.
Staff Assistant.—Ianta Summers.
Minority Staff Director.—John Rayfield (505 FHOB), 6–3552, fax 6–2524.
Professional Staff.—Eric Nagel.
Legislative Staff Assistant.—Caroline Califf.
Subcommittee on Economic Development, Public Buildings, and Emergency Management (585 FHOB), 5–9961, fax 6–0922.
Majority Staff Director.—Susan Brita.
Senior Counsel.—Michael Herman.
Counsel.—Elliot Doomes.
Staff Assistant.—Michael Obrock.
Minority Staff Director.—Dan Mathews (592 FHOB), 5–3014, fax 6–1898.
Counsel.—Johanna Hardy.
Legislative Staff Assistant.—Joe Henell.
Subcommittee on Highways and Transit (B–370A RHOB), 5–9989, fax 5–4627.
Majority Staff Director.—Jim Kolb.
Counsel.—Amy Scarton.
Director of Highway Policy.—Todd Kohr.
Professional Staff.—Allison Dane.
Legislative Assistants: Peter Gould, Jackie Schmitz.
Staff Assistant.—Jeff Schnobrich.
Minority Staff Director.—James Tymon (B–375 RHOB), 5–6715, fax 5–4623.
Counsel.—Jennifer Hall.
Professoinal Staff.—Dan Veoni.
Legislative Staff Assistant.—Allison Cullin.
Subcommittee on Railroads, Pipelines, and Hazardous Materials (589 FHOB), 5–3274, fax 6–3475.
Majority Staff Director.—Jennifer Esposito.
Counsel.—Rachel Carr.
Professional Staff.—Nick Martinelli.
Legislative Assistant.—Niels Knutson.
Senior Staff Assistant.—Rose Hamlin.
Minority Staff Director.—Joyce Rose (592 RHOB), 6–0727, fax 6–1898.
Counsel.—Mike Meenan.
Legislative Staff Assistant.—Joe Henell.
Subcommittee on Water Resources and Environment (B–376 RHOB), 5–0060, fax 5–4627.
Majority Staff Director.—Ryan Seiger.
Counsel.—Ted Illston.
Professional Staff: Roderick Hall, Ben Webster.
Legislative Assistant.—Michael Brain.
Staff Assistant.—Jenna Tatum.
Minority Staff Director.—John Anderson (B–375 RHOB), 5–4360, fax 5–5435.
Counsel.—Jonathan Pawlow.
Professional Staff.—Geoff Bowman.
Legislative Staff Assistant.—Allison Cullin.

Veterans' Affairs

335 Cannon House Office Building, phone 225–9756, fax 225–2034

http://www.veterans.house.gov

meets second Wednesday of each month

Bob Filner, of California, *Chair*

Corrine Brown, of Florida.
Vic Snyder, of Arkansas.
Michael H. Michaud, of Maine.
Stephanie Herseth Sandlin, of South Dakota.
Harry E. Mitchell, of Arizona.
John J. Hall, of New York.
Deborah L. Halvorson, of Illinois.
Thomas S. P. Perriello, of Virginia.
Harry Teague, of New Mexico.
Ciro D. Rodriguez, of Texas.
Joe Donnelly, of Indiana.
Jerry McNerney, of California.
Zachary T. Space, of Ohio.
Timothy J. Walz, of Minnesota.
John H. Adler, of New Jersey.
Ann Kirkpatrick, of Arizona.
Glenn C. Nye, of Virginia.

Steve Buyer, of Indiana.
Cliff Stearns, of Florida.
Jerry Moran, of Kansas.
Henry E. Brown, Jr., of South Carolina.
Jeff Miller, of Florida.
John Boozman, of Arkansas.
Brian P. Bilbray, of California.
Doug Lamborn, of Colorado.
Gus M. Bilirakis, of Florida.
Vern Buchanan, of Florida.
David P. Roe, of Tennessee.

SUBCOMMITTEES

Disability Assistance and Memorial Affairs

John J. Hall, of New York, *Chair*

Deborah L. Halvorson, of Illinois.
Joe Donnelly, of Indiana.
Ciro D. Rodriguez, of Texas.
Ann Kirkpatrick, of Arizona.

Doug Lamborn, of Colorado.
Jeff Miller, of Florida.
Brian P. Bilbray, of California.

Economic Opportunity

Stephanie Herseth Sandlin, of South Dakota, *Chair*

Thomas S. P. Perriello, of Virginia.
John H. Adler, of New Jersey.
Ann Kirkpatrick, of Arizona.
Harry Teague, of New Mexico.

John Boozman, of Arkansas.
Jerry Moran, of Kansas.
Gus M. Bilirakis, of Florida.

Health

Michael H. Michaud, of Maine, *Chair*

Corrine Brown, of Florida.
Vic Snyder, of Arkansas.
Harry Teague, of New Mexico.
Ciro D. Rodriguez, of Texas.
Joe Donnelly, of Indiana.
Jerry McNerney, of California.
Glenn C. Nye, of Virginia.
Deborah L. Halvorson, of Illinois.
Thomas S. P. Perriello, of Virginia.

Henry E. Brown, Jr., of South Carolina.
Cliff Stearns, of Florida.
Jerry Moran, of Kansas.
John Boozman, of Arkansas.
Gus M. Bilirakis, of Florida.
Vern Buchanan, of Florida.

Oversight and Investigations

Harry E. Mitchell, of Arizona, *Chair*

Zachary T. Space, of Ohio.
Timothy J. Walz, of Minnesota.
John H. Adler, of New Jersey.
John J. Hall, of New York.
David P. Roe, of Tennessee.
Cliff Stearns, of Florida.
Brian P. Bilbray, of California.

STAFF

Committee on Veterans' Affairs (335 CHOB), 225–9756, fax 225–2034.
Majority Staff Director.—Malcom Shorter.
Chief of Staff.—Tony Buckles.
Chief Counsel.—David Tucker.
Legislative Coordinator.—Debbie Smith.
Communications Director.—Kristal DeKleer.
Financial Manager.—Bernie Dotson.
Office Manager.—Carol Murray.
Committee Clerk.—Shannon Taylor.
Printing Clerk.—Diane Kirkland.
Executive Assistant.—Jian Zapata.
Minority Staff Director/Chief Counsel.—Kimgston Smith (333 CHOB), 225–3527, fax 225–5486.
Deputy Staff Director.—Art Wu.
Executive Assistant.—Sherië Grove.
Legislative Director.—Deborah Collier.
Subcommittee on Disability Assistance and Memorial Affairs (337 CHOB), 225–9164, fax 226–4691.
Majority Staff Director.—Kimberly Ross (acting).
Professional Staff Member.—Jackie Garrick.
Legislative Assistant.—Megan Williams.
Minority Staff Director/Communications Director.—Brian Lawrence.
Executive Assistant.—Sherië Grove.
Subcommittee on Economic Opportunity (335 CHOB), 226–5491, fax 225–2034.
Majority Staff Director/Counsel.—Juan Lara.
Professional Staff Member.—Javier Martinez.
Legislative Assistant.—Orfa Torres.
Minority Staff Director.—Mike Brinck.
Legislative Assistant.—Jon Clark.
Subcommittee on Health (338 CHOB), 225–9154, fax 226–4536.
Majority Staff Director.—Cathy Wiblemo.
Professional Staff Members: Kristy Park, Sharon Schultze.
Legislative Assistant.—Jeff Burdette.
Minority Staff Director.—Dolores Dunn.
Professional Staff Member.—Risa Salsburg.
Legislative Assistant.—Jon Clark.
Subcommittee on Oversight and Investigations (337A CHOB), 225–3569, fax 225–6392.
Majority Staff Director.—Marty Herbert.
Professional Staff Member.—Dion Trahan.
Legislative Assistant.—Todd Chambers.
Minority Staff Director.—Art Wu.
Legislative Director.—Deborah Collier.

Ways and Means

1102 Longworth House Office Building, phone 225–3625

http://waysandmeans.house.gov

Charles B. Rangel, of New York, *Chair*

Fortney Pete Stark, of California.
Sander M. Levin, of Michigan.
Jim McDermott, of Washington.
John Lewis, of Georgia.
Richard E. Neal, of Massachusetts.
John S. Tanner, of Tennessee.
Xavier Becerra, of California.
Lloyd Doggett, of Texas.
Earl Pomeroy, of North Dakota.
Mike Thompson, of California.
John B. Larson, of Connecticut.
Earl Blumenauer, of Oregon.
Ron Kind, of Wisconsin.
Bill Pascrell, Jr., of New Jersey.
Shelley Berkley, of Nevada.
Joseph Crowley, of New York.
Chris Van Hollen, of Maryland.
Kendrick B. Meek, of Florida.
Allyson Y. Schwartz, of Pennsylvania.
Artur Davis, of Alabama.
Danny K. Davis, of Illinois.
Bob Etheridge, of North Carolina.
Linda T. Sánchez, of California.
Brian Higgins, of New York.
John A. Yarmuth, of Kentucky.

Dave Camp, of Michigan.
Wally Herger, of California.
Sam Johnson, of Texas.
Kevin Brady, of Texas.
Paul Ryan, of Wisconsin.
Eric Cantor, of Virginia.
John Linder, of Georgia.
Devin Nunes, of California.
Patrick J. Tiberi, of Ohio.
Ginny Brown-Waite, of Florida.
Geoff Davis, of Kentucky.
David G. Reichert, of Washington.
Charles W. Boustany, Jr., of Louisiana.
Dean Heller, of Nevada.
Peter J. Roskam, of Illinois.

SUBCOMMITTEES

[The chairman and ranking minority member are ex officio (non-voting) members of all subcommittees.]

Health

Fortney Pete Stark, of California, *Chair*

Lloyd Doggett, of Texas.
Mike Thompson, of California.
Xavier Becerra, of California.
Earl Pomeroy, of North Dakota.
Ron Kind, of Wisconsin.
Earl Blumenauer, of Oregon.
Bill Pascrell, Jr., of New Jersey.
Shelley Berkley, of Nevada.

Wally Herger, of California.
Sam Johnson, of Texas.
Paul Ryan, of Wisconsin.
Devin Nunes, of California.
Ginny Brown-Waite, of Florida.

Income Security and Family Support

Jim McDermott, of Washington, *Chair*

Fortney Pete Stark, of California.
Artur Davis, of Alabama.
John Lewis, of Georgia.
Shelley Berkley, of Nevada.
Chris Van Hollen, of Maryland.
Kendrick B. Meek, of Florida.
Sander M. Levin, of Michigan.
Danny K. Davis, of Illinois.

John Linder, of Georgia.
Charles W. Boustany, Jr., of Louisiana.
Dean Heller, of Nevada.
Peter J. Roskam, of Illinois.
Patrick J. Tiberi, of Ohio.

Oversight

John Lewis, of Georgia, *Chair*

Xavier Becerra, of California.
Ron Kind, of Wisconsin.
Bill Pascrell, Jr., of New Jersey.
John B. Larson, of Connecticut.
Artur Davis, of Alabama.
Danny K. Davis, of Illinois.
Bob Etheridge, of North Carolina.
Brian Higgins, of New York.

Charles W. Boustany, Jr., of Louisiana.
David G. Reichert, of Washington.
Peter J. Roskam, of Illinois.
Paul Ryan, of Wisconsin.
John Linder, of Georgia.

Select Revenue Measures

Richard E. Neal, of Massachusetts, *Chair*

Mike Thompson, of California.
John B. Larson, of Connecticut.
Allyson Y. Schwartz, of Pennsylvania.
Earl Blumenauer, of Oregon.
Joseph Crowley, of New York.
Kendrick B. Meek, of Florida.
Brian Higgins, of New York.
John A. Yarmuth, of Kentucky.

Patrick J. Tiberi, of Ohio.
John Linder, of Georgia.
Dean Heller, of Nevada.
Peter J. Roskam, of Illinois.
Geoff Davis, of Kentucky.

Social Security

John S. Tanner, of Tennessee, *Chair*

Earl Pomeroy, of North Dakota.
Allyson Y. Schwartz, of Pennsylvania.
Xavier Becerra, of California.
Lloyd Doggett, of Texas.
Ron Kind, of Wisconsin.
Joseph Crowley, of New York.
Linda T. Sánchez, of California.
John A. Yarmuth, of Kentucky.

Sam Johnson, of Texas.
Kevin Brady, of Texas.
Patrick J. Tiberi, of Ohio.
Ginny Brown-Waite, of Florida.
David G. Reichert, of Washington.

Trade

Sander M. Levin, of Michigan, *Chair*

John S. Tanner, of Tennessee.
Chris Van Hollen, of Maryland.
Jim McDermott, of Washington.
Richard E. Neal, of Massachusetts.
Lloyd Doggett, of Texas.
Earl Pomeroy, of North Dakota.
Bob Etheridge, of North Carolina.
Linda T. Sánchez, of California.

Kevin Brady, of Texas.
Geoff Davis, of Kentucky.
David G. Reichert, of Washington.
Wally Herger, of California.
Devin Nunes, of California.

STAFF

Committee on Ways and Means (1102 LHOB), 225–3625, fax 225–2610.
Majority Chief of Staff.—Janice Mays.
Deputy Staff Director.—Askia Suruma.
Assistant to the Chairman (CBR).—Jon Sheiner.
Professional Staff (CBR).—William Reese.
Assistant to Staff Director.—Kristin Eagan.
Committee Administrator.—Jennifer Gould.
Committee Clerk.—Carrie Breidenbach.
Calendar Clerk.—Carren Turko.
Documents Clerk.—Reggie Greene.
Finance Manager.—Kendra Murray.
Senior Staff Assistant.—Bonie Allen.
Scheduler (CBR).—Holly Biglow.
Staff Assistant.—Dallas Woodrum.

Communications Director and Policy Advisor.—Matthew Beck.
Press Secretary.—Lauren Bloomberg.
IT Manager.—Antoine Walker.
Systems Administrator/Web Administrator.—Wuan Perkins.
Chief Tax Counsel.—John Buckley (1136 LHOB), 225–5522, fax 225–0787.
Select Revenue Measures Staff Director.—Mildeen Worrell.
Oversight Staff Director.—Karen McAfee.
Tax Counsels: Drew Crouch, Kase Jubboori, Aruna Kalyanam.
Professional Staff on Budget and Economy.—Ted Zegers.
Senior Staff Assistant Clerks: Pam Murray, Anthony Tait.
Minority Director of Operations.—Andrew Garber (1139E LHOB), 225–4021.
Staff Assistant.—Kristin Isabelli.
Chief Trade Counsel.—Angela Ellard.
Senior Advisor for Media and Public Affairs.—Sage Eastman.
Communications Director.—Jim Billimoria.
Press Assistant.—Sarah Swinehart.
Staff Director.—Jon Traub.
Legislative Assistants: Justin Hage, Liz Lorenz, Mike Stober.
Trade Economist.—Warren Payne.
Professional Staff: Laura Bozell, Erik Rasmussen, Jill Schmalz, Margo Smith.
Trade Counsel.—Evan Alexander, David Thomas.
Fellow.—Amy Shuart.
Chief Tax Counsel.—Dave Olander.
Tax Counsel.—Aharon Friedman.
Tax Advisor.—Sean Hailey.
Subcommittee on Health (1135 LHOB), 225–3943, fax 226–1765.
Majority Staff Director.—Cybele Bjorklund.
Professional Staff: Chiquita Brooks-LaSure, Debbie Curtis, Jennifer Friedman, Geoffrey Gerhardt.
Senior Staff Assistant/Clerk.—Drew Dawson.
Research/Staff Assistant.—Ruth Brown.
Minority Staff Director.—Dan Elling.
Subcommittee on Income Security (B–317 RHOB), 225–1025, fax 225–9480.
Majority Staff Director.—Nick Gwyn.
Deputy Staff Director.—Sonja Nesbit.
Professional Staff.—Indi Dutta-Gupta.
Staff Assistant/Clerk.—Moyer McCoy.
Subcommittee on Social Security (1129 LHOB), 225–9263, fax 225–5286.
Majority Staff Director.—Kathryn Olson.
Professional Staff.—Joel Najar, Alaine Perry.
Staff Assistant/Clerk.—Jennifer Beeler.
Subcommittee on Trade (1104 LHOB), 226–0158, fax 225–0158.
Majority Staff Director.—Viji Rangaswami.
Trade Counsels: Jason Kearns, Behnaz Kibria, Jennifer McCadney, Alex Perkins, George York.
Senior Staff Assistant/Clerk.—Gwen McFadden.
Legislative Assistant/Clerk.—Annie Minguez.

SELECT AND SPECIAL COMMITTEES OF THE HOUSE

Select Committee on Energy Independence and Global Warming

H2–250 Ford House Office Building, 20515, phone 225–4012, fax 225–4092

[Created pursuant to H. Res. 202, 110th Congress]

Edward J. Markey, of Massachusetts, *Chair*

Earl Blumenauer, of Oregon.
Jay Inslee, of Washington.
John B. Larson, of Connecticut.
Stephanie Herseth Sandlin, of South Dakota.
Emanuel Cleaver, of Missouri.
John J. Hall, of New York.
John T. Salazar, of Colorado.
Jackie Speier, of California.

F. James Sensenbrenner, Jr., of Wisconsin.
John B. Shadegg, of Arizona.
John Sullivan, of Oklahoma.
Marsha Blackburn, of Tennessee.
Brad Miller, of Michigan.
Shelley Moore Capito, of West Virginia.

STAFF

Majority Staff Director and Chief Counsel.—Gerry Waldron.
Deputy Staff Director.—Ana Unruh Cohen.
Counsels: Danielle Baussan, Joel Beauvais, Michael Goo.
Chief Clerk.—Ali Brodsky.
Communications Director.—Eben Burnham-Snyder.
Professional Staff: Jeff Duncan, Michal Freedhoff, Morgan Gray, Jonathan Phillips.
New Media Director.—Jeff Sharp.
Staff Assistant.—Jacqueline Chenault.
Minority Staff Director.—Barton Forsyth.
Communications Director.—Terry Lane.
Distinguished Professional Staff Member.—Harlon Watson.
Professional Staff: Rajesh Bharwani, Tom Schreibel, Andy Zach.

Permanent Select Committee on Intelligence

H–405 The Capitol, phone 225–7690

[Created pursuant to H. Res. 658, 95th Congress]

Silvestre Reyes, of Texas, *Chair*

Alcee L. Hastings, of Florida, *Vice Chair.*

Anna G. Eshoo, of California.
Rush D. Holt, of New Jersey.
C. A. Dutch Ruppersberger, of Maryland.
John F. Tierney, of Massachusetts.
Mike Thompson, of California.
Janice D. Schakowsky, of Illinois.
James R. Langevin, of Rhode Island.
Patrick J. Murphy, of Pennsylvania.
Adam B. Schiff, of California.
Adam Smith, of Washington.
Dan Boren, of Oklahoma.

Peter Hoekstra, of Michigan.
Elton Gallegly, of California.
Mac Thornberry, of Texas.
Mike Rogers, of Michigan.
Sue Wilkins Myrick, of North Carolina.
Roy Blunt, of Missouri.
Jeff Miller, of Florida.
K. Michael Conaway, of Texas.
Peter T. King, of New York.

SUBCOMMITTEES

[The Speaker and Minority Leader are ex officio (non-voting) members of the committee.]

Intelligence Community Management

Anna G. Eshoo, of California, *Chair*
Rush D. Holt, of New Jersey, *Vice Chair*

Alcee L. Hastings, of Florida.
Janice D. Schakowsky, of Illinois.
Patrick J. Murphy, of Pennsylvania.
Sue Wilkins Myrick, of North Carolina.
Roy Blunt, of Missouri.
K. Michael Conaway, of Texas.

Oversight and Investigations

Janice D. Schakowsky, of Illinois, *Chair*
John F. Tierney, of Massachusetts, *Vice Chair*

Patrick J. Murphy, of Pennsylvania.
C. A. Dutch Ruppersberger, of Maryland.
Mike Thompson, of California.
Adam B. Schiff, of California.
Dan Boren, of Oklahoma.
Jeff Miller, of Florida.
Mac Thornberry, of Texas.
Mike Rogers, of Michigan.
Roy Blunt, of Missouri.
Peter T. King, of New York.

Technical and Tactical Intelligence

C. A. Dutch Ruppersberger, of Maryland, *Chair*
Rush D. Holt, of New Jersey, *Vice Chair*

James R. Langevin, of Rhode Island.
Patrick J. Murphy, of Pennsylvania.
Adam B. Schiff, of California.
Adam Smith, of Washington.
Mac Thornberry, of Texas.
Mike Rogers, of Michigan.
Jeff Miller, of Florida.
Peter T. King, of New York.

Terrorism, Human Intelligence, Analysis and Counterintelligence

Mike Thompson, of California, *Chair*
Alcee L. Hastings, of Florida, *Vice Chair*

C. A. Dutch Ruppersberger, of Maryland.
James R. Langevin, of Rhode Island.
Adam B. Schiff, of California.
Adam Smith, of Washington.
Dan Boren, of Oklahoma.
Mike Rogers, of Michigan.
Elton Gallegly, of California.
Sue Wilkins Myrick, of North Carolina.
Jeff Miller, of Florida.
K. Michael Conaway, of Texas.

STAFF

Majority Staff Director.—Michael Delaney.
Deputy Staff Director/General Counsel.—Brian Morrison.
Chief Counsel.—Eric Greenwald.
Chief Clerk.—Courtney Littig.
Executive Assistant.—Stephanie Leaman.
Security Director.—Kristin R. Jepson.
Deputy Security Director.—Kevin Klein.
Systems Administrator.—Brandon Smith.
Budget Director.—Stacey Dixon.
Staff Assistant.—Khizer Syed.
Professional Staff: Iram Ali, Don Campbell, Linda Cohen, Tito Cruz, Stacey Dixon, Mieke Eoyang, Curtis Flood, Larry Hanauer, Jay Hulings, Diane La Voy, Adam Lurie, Robert Minehart, Mary Stone Ross, Mark Young.

Minority Staff Director.—Jim Lewis.
Deputy Minority Staff Director/Chief Counsel.—Chris Donesa.
Minority Staff Assistant.—Ashley Lowry.
Professional Staff: Chelsey Campbell, Meghann Courter, Fred Fleitz, Frank Garcia, Sarah Roland Geffroy, John W. Heath, George Pappas, Kathleen Reilly, Jamal Ware.

House Republican Policy Committee

B–58 Cannon House Office Building, phone, 225–6168

http://republicanhousepolicy.com

meets at the call of the Chair or the Speaker

Thaddeus G. McCotter, of Michigan, *Chair*

Republican Leadership:
Minority Leader.—John A. Boehner, of Ohio.
Minority Whip.—Eric Cantor, of Virginia.
Conference Chair.—Mike Pence, of Indiana.
Conference Vice Chair.—Kay Granger, of Texas.
Conference Secretary.—John R. Carter, of Texas.
NRCC Chair.—Tom Cole, of Oklahoma.

Policy Committee Staff.—B–58 Cannon HOB, 225–6168.
Chief of Staff.—Patrick Rothwell.
Director.—Kristal Quarker, M.P.A.
Policy Analyst.—Paul Blocher.
Policy Research Assistant.—Michael Bars.

Democratic Congressional Campaign Committee

430 South Capitol Street, SE., 20003, phone (202) 863–1500

Executive Committee:
Nancy Pelosi, of California, *Speaker.*
Chris Van Hollen, of Maryland, *Chair.*
Vice Chairs:
Debbie Wasserman Schultz, of Florida, *Incumbent Retention.*
Albio Sires, of New Jersey, *Member Participation and Outreach.*
Bruce Braley, of Iowa, *Candidate Services.*
Joe Crowley, of New York, *Finance.*

STAFF

Executive Director.—Jon Vogel, 485–3419.
Chief Operating Officer.—Kristie Mark, 485–3509.
Political Director.—Robby Mook, 485–3507.
Director of Incumbent Retention.—Jennifer Pihlaja, 485–3454.
Communications Director.—Jennifer Crider, 485–3442.
Chief Financial Officer.—Jackie Forte-Mackay, 485–3401.
Director of:
Candidate Fundraising.—Lauren Dikis, 485–3529.
Candidate Services.—Mark Warren, 485–3420.
Marketing and New Media.—Taryn Rosenkranz, 485–3527.
Member Services.—Beverly Gilyard, 485–3516.
Research.—Nicole Landset, 485–3526.
National Finance Director.—Louisa Whitney, 485–3523.
Press Secretary.—Ryan Rudominer, 485–3430.
National Field Director.—Marlon Marshall, 741–1858.
Policy Director.—Heather McHugh, 485–3531.

Democratic Steering and Policy Committee

H–204 The Capitol, phone 225–0100

Chair.—Nancy Pelosi, Speaker of the House from California.
Co-Chairs:
Steering.—Rosa L. DeLauro, Representative from Connecticut.
Policy.—George Miller, Representative from California.

STAFF

Democratic Steering Committee 225–0100, fax 225–4188.
Steering Advisors: George Kundanis, Jonathan Stivers.

Democratic Policy Committee (H–130), 225–0100, fax 226–0938.
Policy Advisors: George Kundanis, John Lawrence, Amy Rosenbaum.

Democratic Caucus

202A Cannon House Office Building, phone 225–1400, fax 226–4412

ww.dems.gov

John B. Larson, of Connecticut, *Chair*

Xavier Becerra, of California, *Vice Chair*

STAFF

Executive Director.—George Felix Shevlin IV.
Communications Director.—Emily Fabri Barocas.
Communications Advisor.—Elizabeth Ann Bellizzi.
Policy Director.—Catherine Le Tran.
Policy Assistant.—Jehmal Terrence Hudson.
Advisors to the Chair: Christopher Edward Barnes, Shelley Marie Rubino.
Director of Special Projects.—Kimberly Hazel Jaworski.
Staff Assistant.—Salvador Ernan Perez-Gomez.
Assistant to the Chairman.—Srdan Banjac.
Technology and Research Assistant.—Stamatios Stephen Dagadakis.
Legal Fellow.—Justin Andrew Kissinger.
Director of New Media.—Robert M Pierson.
Director of Multimedia.—Antonio Peronace.
Press Assistant.—Alexandra Krasov.
Outreach Assistant.—Elizabeth Roberge Malerba.
Staff Director to the Vice Chair.—Sean Edward McCluskie.
Director of Member Outreach to the Vice Chair.—Melody Star Gonzales.
Research Analyst to the Vice Chair.—James Monroe Gleeson.
Member Outreach Assistants to the Vice Chair: Tonia Nguyen Bui, Eric Louis Delaney, Lorenzo Antonio Rodriguez-Olvera.

National Republican Congressional Committee

320 First Street, SE., 20003, phone 479–7000

Pete Sessions, of Texas, *Chair*

Chair, Executive Committee.—Greg Walden, of Oregon.
Chair of:
Recruitment.—Kevin McCarthy, of California.
Redistricting.—Lynn A. Westmoreland, of Georgia.
Communications.—Mary Fallin, of Oklahoma.
Finance.—Jeb Hensarling, of Texas
Retention.—Mike Rogers, of Michigan.
Coalitions.—David Nunes, of California.

EXECUTIVE COMMITTEE MEMBERS

John A. Boehner, of Ohio.
Eric Cantor, of Virginia.
Mike Pence, of Indiana.
Pete Sessions, of Texas.
Tom Cole, of Oklahoma.
Thaddeus G. McCotter, of Michigan.
John R. Carter, of Texas.
Cathy McMorris Rodgers, of Washington.
David Dreier, of California.
Jo Bonner, of Alabama.
Charles W. Boustany, Jr., of Louisiana.
Michael N. Castle, of Delaware.
Geoff Davis, of Kentucky.
Charles W. Dent, of Pennsylvania.
Lincoln Diaz-Balart, of Florida.
Mary Fallin, of Oklahoma.
Virginia Foxx, of North Carolina.
Gregg Harper, of Mississippi.
Dean Heller, of Nevada.
Jeb Hensarling, of Texas.
Jim Jordan, of Ohio.
Jack Kingston, of Georgia.
Kevin McCarthy, of California.
Jeff Miller, of Florida.
Tim Murphy, of Pennsylvania.
Devin Nunes, of California.
Pete Olson, of Texas.
Tom Price, of Georgia.
Denny Rehberg, of Montana.
Mike Rogers, of Michigan.
Peter J. Roskam, of Illinois.
Edward R. Royce, of California.
Steve Scalise, of Louisiana.
John Shadegg, of Arizona.
Bill Shuster, of Pennsylvania.
Lee Terry, of Nebraska.
Patrick J. Tiberi, of Ohio.
Fred Upton, of Michigan.
Greg Walden, of Oregon.
Lynn A. Westmoreland, of Georgia.

STAFF

Executive Director.—Guy Harrison.
Political Director.—Brian Walsh.
Director of:
Communications.—Ken Spain.
Finance.—Elizabeth Verrill.
Research.—Jon Black.
Counsel.—Jessica Furst.

House Republican Conference

1420 Longworth House Office Building, phone 225–5107, fax 226–0154

Mike Pence, of Indiana, *Chair*

Cathy McMorris Rodgers, of Washington, *Vice Chair*

John R. Carter, of Texas, *Secretary*

STAFF

Chief of Staff.—Mark Short.
Deputy Chief of Staff.—Josh Pitcock.
Director of Operations.—Emily Seidel.
Staff Assistants: Ben Howard, Scott Neale, Ja'Ron K. Smith.
Director of Member Relations.—Katie Strand.
Policy Director.—Russ Vought.
Policy Advisors: Adam Hepburn, Chris Jacobs, Andy Koenig, Sarah Makin, Daris Meeks.
Communications Director.—Matt Lloyd.
Press Secretary.—Mary Vought.
Deputy Press Secretary.—Brian Newell.
Deputy Press Secretary/Deputy of Specialty Media.—Andeliz Castillo.
Director of Coalitions and General Counsel.—Melanie Looney.
Media Coordinator.—Courtney Kolb.
Press Assistant.—Rachel Semmel.
Deputy Directors of Visual Media: Ryan Howell, Bryant Avondoglio.

OFFICERS AND OFFICIALS OF THE HOUSE

OFFICE OF THE SPEAKER

H–232 The Capitol, phone 225–0100, fax 225–4188

http://speaker.house.gov

The Speaker.—Hon. Nancy Pelosi.
Chief of Staff.—John Lawrence, H–232, The Capitol, 225–0100.
Assistant to the Chief of Staff.—Declan Cashman, H–232, The Capitol, 225–0100.
Chief of Staff (CA08 Office).—Terri McCullough, 235 CHOB, 225–4965.
Deputy Chief of Staff.—George Kundanis, H–232, The Capitol, 225–0100.
Senior Advisor.—Diane Dewhirst, H–232, The Capitol, 225–0100.
Counsels to the Speaker: Bernie Raimo, Joe Onek, H–331, The Capitol, 225–0100.
Special Assistant to the Speaker: Stacy Kerr, Kate Knudson, Michael Long, H–232, The Capitol, 225–0100.
Staff Assistants: Geoff Lane, Ricardo Quinto, Veronica Scafaru, H–419, The Capitol, 225–0100.
Staff Assistant (Correspondence).—Stephanie Ueng, 421 CHOB, 225–0100.
Staff Assistant (Mail).—David Silverman, 421 Cannon, 5–0100.
Staff Assistant.—Sam Raymond, H–232, The Capitol, 225–0100.
Director of Scheduling.—Melinda Medlin, H–232, The Capitol, 225–0100.
Deputy Scheduler.—Rebecca Moore, H–232, The Capitol, 225–0100.
Scheduling Assistant.—Mary Kate Barry, H–232, The Capitol, 225–0100.
Policy Directors: Amy Rosenbaum, Dick Meltzer, H–232, The Capitol, 225–0100
Senior Policy Advisors: Wendell Primus, Wyndee Parker, H–419, The Capitol, 5–0100.
Policy Advisors: Scott Boule, Margie Capron, Kit Judge, Lara Levison, Anne MacMillan, Reva Price, Arshi Siddiqui, Erik Stallman, Michael Tecklenburg, Karen Wayland, H–419, The Capitol, 225–0100.
Policy Assistant.—Michael Bloom, H–419, The Capitol, 225–0100.
Director of Strategic Planning.—Ellen Qualls, H–232, The Capitol, 225–0100.
Director of Intergovernmental Affairs.—Cheryl Parker Rose, H–232, The Capitol, 225–0100.
Director Member Services.—Jaime Lizarraga, H–232, The Capitol, 225–0100.
Deputy Director of Member Services: Sydney Jones, Tom Manatos, H–327, The Capitol.
Director of Protocol and Special Events.—Bridget Fallon, H–333, The Capitol, 225–0100.
Deputy Director of Protocol and Special Events.—Bina Surgeon, H–333, The Capitol, 225–0100.
Director of Speechwriting.—Alexandra Veitch, H–334, The Capitol, 225–0100.
Speechwriter.—Jonathan Powell, H–334, The Capitol, 225–0100.
IT Director.—Wil Haynes, HB–13, The Capitol, 225–0100.
Deputy IT Director.—Kamilah Keita, HB–13, The Capitol, 225–0100.
Director of Advance.—Kelly Berens, H–331, The Capitol, 225–0100.
Advance Associate.—Elisa Shyu, H–331, The Capitol, 5–0100.
Outreach Director.—Reva Price, H–419, The Capitol, 225–0100.
Outreach Assistant.—Samantha Smith, H–419, The Capitol, 225–0100.

SPEAKER'S PRESS OFFICE

H–163 The Capitol, phone 225–0100

Communications Director.—Brendan Daly.
Deputy Communications Director.—Nadeam Elshami.
Press Secretary.—Drew Hammill.
Press Assistants: Crystal Chui, Evangeline George, Megan Lassig.
Press Advisors: Stephanie Cherry, Carlos Sanchez

Researcher.—April Greener.
Production Advisor.—Carey Lane.
Director of New Media.—Karina Newton.

SPEAKER'S FLOOR OFFICE

H–209 The Capitol, phone 225–0100

Floor Director.—Jerry Hartz.
Deputy Floor Director.—Catlin O'Neill.
Floor Assistant.—Marisa Harrilchak.

OFFICE OF THE MAJORITY LEADER

H–107 The Capitol, phone 225–3130, fax 226–0663

Majority Leader.—Steny H. Hoyer.
Chief of Staff.—Terry Lierman.
Deputy Chief of Staff.—Stacey Bernards.
Office Manager/Executive Assistant.—Courtney Fry.
Floor Director.—Alexis Covey-Brandt.
Deputy Floor Director.—Austin Burnes.
Floor Assistant.—Michael Eisenberg.
Deputy Director of Member Services.—Rick Palacio.
Legislative Coordinator.—Jessica Lemos.
Deputy Press Secretary.—Katie Grant.
Press and Research Assistant.—Maureen Beach.
Speechwriter.—Rob Goodman.
Senior Policy Advisors: Keith Abouchar, John Hughes, Ed Lorenzen, Elizabeth Murray, Mary Frances Repko, Mariah Sixkiller.
Policy Director.—Michele Stockwell.
Director of Scheduling.—Simone LiTrenta.
Director of External Relations.—Marta David.
Deputy Director of External Relations/Special Assistant.—Troy Clair.
Director of Technology.—Steve Dwyer.
Director of Member Services.—Brian Romick.
System Administrator.—Denis Munoz.
Staff Assistants: Shuwanza Goff, Drew Jacoby, Rosie Krueger.

OFFICE OF THE MAJORITY WHIP

H–329 The Capitol, phone 226–3210

http://democraticwhip.house.gov

Majority Whip.—James E. Clyburn.
Chief of Staff.—Yelberton R. Watkins.
Director of:
Coalitions.—Michael Hacker.
Floor Operations and Counsel.—J. Todd Metcalf.
Member Services.—Wendy Hartman.
Outreach.—Tony Harrison.
Policy.—Barvetta Singletary.
Special Events.—S. Lindy Birch.
Communications Director.—Kristie Greco.
Press Assistant.—Ryan Daniels.
Deputy Floor Directors: Adam Arguelles, Mike Hacker, Allie Neill.
Senior Policy Advisor.—Dave Grimaldi.
Council and Policy Advisor.—Margaret M. Cantrell.

CHIEF DEPUTY MAJORITY WHIPS

Senior Chief Deputy Whip.—John Lewis.

Chief of Staff.—Michael Collins.

Chief Deputy Whips:

Ed Pastor.
John S. Tanner.
Janice D. Schakowsky.
G. K. Butterfield.
Maxine Waters.
Joseph Crowley.
Diana DeGette.
Debbie Wasserman Schultz.

OFFICE OF THE REPUBLICAN LEADER

H–204 The Capitol, phone 225–4000, fax 225–5117

Republican Leader.—John A. Boehner.
Chief of Staff.—Paula Nowakowski.
Deputy Chief of Staff.—Dave Schnittger.
Deputy to the Chief of Staff.—Amy Lozupone.
Executive Assistant.—Kristen Chaplin.
Senior Advisor/Floor Assistant.—Ed Cassidy.
Press Secretary.—Michael Steel.
Press Assistant.—Betsy Andres.
Communications Director.—Kevin Smith.
Deputy Communications Director.—Don Seymour.
Director, Member Services.—Danielle Maurer.
Member Services Manager.—Trevor Kolego.
Outreach Director.—Bill Greene.
Director, Information Technology.—Billy Benjamin.
General Counsel/Director of Floor Operations.—Jo-Marie St. Martin.
Deputy Director of Floor Operations.—Anne Thorsen.
Policy Director.—Mike Sommers.
Counsel/Policy Advisors: Will Kinzel, George Rogers.
Policy Advisors: Jay Cranford, Katherine Haley, Cindy Herrle, Emily Porter, David Stewart.
Policy Analyst.—Jen Stewart.
Financial Assistant.—Karen Paulson.
Floor Assistants: Lydia Calio, Jared Eichhorn, Jay Pierson, Jeff Strunk, Adam Wolf.
Staff Assistants: Patrick Finnegan, Justin Lampert, Grant Saunders.

OFFICE OF THE REPUBLICAN WHIP

H–307 The Capitol, phone 225–0197, fax 226–1115

Republican Whip.—Eric Cantor.
Chief of Staff.—Steve Stombres.
Deputy Chief of Staff.—Rob Collins.
Senior Advisor.—Bill Dolbow.
Director of Policy.—Neil Bradley.
Senior Policy Advisors: Mike Ference, Nicole Gustafson, Cheryl Jaeger, Shimmy Stein.
Director of Floor Operations.—Kyle Nevins.
Floor Assistants: Matt Bravo, John Stipicevic, Chris Vieson.
Communications Director.—John Murray.
Deputy Communications Director.—Matt Lira.
Associate Director of New Media.—Steve Johnston.
Press Secretary.—Brad Dayspring.
Deputy Press Secretary.—Rachel Taylor.
Speechwriter.—David Silverman.
Director of Coalitions.—Jeff Burton.
Deputy Director of Coalitions.—Doug Andres.
Director of Member Services.—Valerie Nelson.
Scheduler.—Amy Barrera.
Assistant Scheduler.—Kathleen O'Connor.
Special Assistant to the Republican Whip.—Richard Cullen.
Staff Assistant.—Austin Tuell.
Researcher.—Matt Hodge.
Strategic Communications.—Brian Patrick.

OFFICE OF THE CHIEF DEPUTY REPUBLICAN WHIP

H–305 The Capitol, phone 225–0197

Chief Deputy Republican Whip.—Kevin McCarthy.
Chief of Staff.—James Min.
Special Assistant.—Freddy Barnes.

OFFICE OF THE CLERK

H–154 The Capitol, phone 225–7000

LORRAINE C. MILLER, Clerk of the House of Representatives; native of Fort Worth, TX; holds an executive master's degree from the Georgetown School of Business; previously served as a senior advisor to Speaker Nancy Pelosi and has nearly two decades of experience working for the House; in addition, has worked for two other Speakers, Jim Wright and Tom Foley, as well as Congressman John Lewis (D–GA); elected president of the Washington, DC Branch NAACP, 2004; member of the historic Shiloh Baptist Church of Washington, DC; member of Shiloh's Henry C. Gregory Family Life Center Foundation Board of Directors; the first African American to serve as an official of the House of Representatives; sworn in as the 35th Clerk of the House of Representatives on February 15, 2007.

Clerk.—Lorraine C. Miller.
Deputy Clerks: Maria A. Lopez, Robert F. Reeves, Deborah M. Spriggs.
Chief of—
Legislative Computer Systems.—Goldey Vansant, 2401 RHOB, 225–1182.
Legislative Operations.—Frances Chiappardi, HT–13, 225–7925.
Legislative Resource Center.—Ronald Dale Thomas, B–106 CHOB, 226–5200.
Office of History and Preservation.—Farar Elliott, B–53 CHOB, 226–1300.
Office of House Employment Counsel.—Gloria Lett, 1036 LHOB, 225–7075.
Office of Publication Services.—Janice Wallace-Hamid, B–28 CHOB, 225–1908.
Official Reporter.—Joe Strickland, 1718 LHOB, 225–2627.
Service Groups—
Congresswoman's Suite.—225–4196.
Members and Family Committee.—225–0622.
Prayer Room.—225–8070.

CHIEF ADMINISTRATIVE OFFICER

HB–30 The Capitol, phone 225–6969

DANIEL P. BEARD, Chief Administrative Officer of the House of Representatives; native of Bellingham, WA; B.A., Western Washington University, 1965; M.A. (1969) and Ph.D. (1973), University of Washington; worked for the Domestic Policy Staff at the White House; Deputy Assistant Secretary for Water and Science, Interior Department; conducted research for the Congressional Research Service at the Library of Congress; Special Assistant to Congressman Sidney R. Yates (D–IL); Administrative Assistant to Senator Max Baucus (D–MT); former Chief Operating Officer and Senior Vice President for Public Policy, National Audubon Society; Staff Director, Committee on Natural Resources, U.S. House of Representatives; Commissioner of the Bureau of Reclamation, Interior Department; senior advisor for the consulting firm Booz Allen Hamilton, Inc.; elected February 15, 2007, as Chief Administrative Officer of the House of Representatives.

Chief Administrative Officer.—Daniel P. Beard.
Deputy Chief Administrative Officers: Walt Edwards, WA–26, RHOB; Ali Qureshi, H2–225, FHOB.
Chief of Staff.—Mel Gipprich, HB–30, The Capitol.
Administrative Counsel.—Tim Blodgett, H2–217, FHOB.
Chief Financial Officer.—Kathy Perdue, H2–330, FHOB.
Human Resources Director.—Jason Hite, H2–105B, FHOB
Chief Information Officer.—Louis Magnotti, H2–631, FHOB.
Director of Communications.—Jeff Ventura, H2–217, FHOB.
Executive Assistant.—Meagan Johns, HB–30, The Capitol.

CHAPLAIN

HB–25 The Capitol, phone 225–2509, fax 226–4928

DANIEL P. COUGHLIN, Chaplain, House of Representatives; residence: Chicago, IL; attended St. Mary of the Lake University, Mundelein, IL, and received a Licentiate Degree in Sacred Theology; ordained a Roman Catholic priest on May 3, 1960, in LaGrange, IL; also attended Loyola University, Chicago, IL, and received a degree in Pastoral Studies; Director of the Office for Divine Worship, Archdiocese of Chicago, under John Cardinal Cody, 1969–84; appointed pastor of St. Francis Xavier Parish in LaGrange, IL, by Joseph Cardinal Bernardin and Director of the Cardinal Stritch Retreat House, Mundelein, IL; Vicar for Priests under Francis Cardinal George, Archbishop of Chicago, 1995–2000; appointed House Chaplain on March 23, 2000.

Chaplain of the House.—Daniel P. Coughlin.
Assistant to the Chaplain.—Elisa Aglieco.
Liaison to Staff.—Karen Bronson.

OFFICE OF THE HOUSE HISTORIAN

B–56 Cannon House Office Building, phone 226–5525

http://historian.house.gov; historian@mail.house.gov

House Historian.—Dr. Robert Remini.
Deputy House Historian.—Dr. Fred L. Beuttler.
Projects Director.—Dr. Thomas J. Rushford.
Research Analyst.—Anthony A. Wallis.
Researcher.—Benjamin Hayes.

OFFICE OF INTERPARLIAMENTARY AFFAIRS

HB–28 Capitol, phone 226–1766

Director.—Dr. Kay King.
Assistant Director.—Janice Robinson.

HOUSE INFORMATION RESOURCES

631 Ford House Office Building, 20515, phone 225–9276, fax 226–6150

CIO and Assistant Chief Administration Officer for House Information Resources.—Louis A. Magnotti III.

OFFICE OF THE ATTENDING PHYSICIAN

H–166 The Capitol, phone 225–5421

(After office hours, call Capitol Operator 224–2145)

Attending Physician.—Dr. Brian P. Monahan.
Chief of Staff.—Christopher R. Picaut.
Deputy Chief of Staff.—Keith Pray.

OFFICE OF INSPECTOR GENERAL

H2–386 Ford House Office Building, phone 226–1250

Inspector General.—James J. Cornell.
Deputy Inspector Generals: Michael E. Benner, Theresa M. Grafenstine.
Director, Information Systems, Quality Assurance and Contract Services.—Steve Johnson.
Administrative Director.—Michael Cronin.

Administrative Assistant.—Deborah E. Jones.

Directors, Performance and Financial Audits and Investigations: Michael E. Benner, Jeffrey Hannahs.

Auditors: Steven Connard, Julie Poole, Andrew Simpson, Andrew Smith.

Director, Information Systems Audits.—Debbie Hunter.

Assistant Director, Information Systems Audits.—Michael Howard.

Auditors: Douglas Carney, Stephen Lockhart, Saad M. Patel.

Directors, Management and Advisory Services: Theresa M. Grafenstine, Michael Ptasienski.

Assistant Directors: Joseph Picolla, Donna Wolfgang.

Process Improvement Specialist.—Rodney T. Upshur.

Management Analysis.—Gregory Roberts.

OFFICE OF THE LAW REVISION COUNSEL

H2–308 Ford House Office Building, 20515–6711, phone 226–2411, fax 225–0010

Law Revision Counsel.—Peter G. LeFevre.

Deputy Counsel.—Ralph V. Seep.

Senior Counsels: Kenneth I. Paretzky, Robert M. Sukol, Timothy D. Trushel.

Assistant Counsels: Sally-Anne Cleveland, Michelle Evans, Katrina M. Hall, Raymond Kaselonis, Katherine L. Lane, Brian Lindsey, Edward T. Mulligan, Michele K. Skarvells, John F. Wagner, Jr., Nicholas Weil.

Staff Assistants: Debra L. Johnson, Monica Thompson.

Printing Editors: Robert E. Belcher, James Cahill.

Senior Systems Engineer.—Eric Loach.

OFFICE OF THE LEGISLATIVE COUNSEL

136 Cannon House Office Building, phone 225–6060

Legislative Counsel.—Sandra L. Strokoff.

Deputy Legislative Counsel.—Edward G. Grossman.

Senior Counsels: Wade Ballou, Douglass Bellis, Timothy Brown, Paul Callen, Sherry Chriss, Ira Forstater, Rosemary Gallagher, James Grossman, Curt Haensel, Jean Harmann, Gregory M. Kostka, Lawrence Johnston, Edward Leong, Hank Savage, Robert Weinhagen, James Wert, Noah Wofsy.

Assistant Counsels: Marshall Barksdale, Philip Bayer, Alison Bell, Hallet Brazelton, Warren Burke, Thomas Cassidy, Henry Christrup, Shawn Conley, Lisa Daly, Thomas Dillon, Mathew Eckstein, Susan Fleishman, Ryan Greenlaw, Kakuti Lin, Molly Lothamer, Michelle Orsi, Christopher Osborne, Scott Probst, Megan Renfrew, Hadley Ross, Anthony Sciascia, Anna Shpak, Jessica Shapiro, Ellen J. Sutherland, Mark Synnes, Sally Walker, Brady Young.

Office Administrator.—Renate Stehr.

Assistant Office Administrator.—Nancy McNeillie.

Systems Administrator.—David Topper.

Senior Systems Analyst.—Peter Szwec.

Director, Information Systems.—Willie Blount.

Publications Coordinator.—Craig Sterkx.

Paralegal.—Kristen Amarosa.

Staff Assistants: Ashley Anderson, Debra Birch, Elonda Blount Pamela Griffiths, Miekl Joyner, Kelly Meryweather, Angelina Patton, Tom Meryweather, Kelly Wike.

OFFICE OF THE PARLIAMENTARIAN

H–209 The Capitol, phone 225–7373

Parliamentarian.—John V. Sullivan.

Deputy Parliamentarian.—Thomas J. Wickham.

Assistant Parliamentarians: Ethan B. Lauer, Jason A. Smith, Max A. Spitzer, Carrie E. Wolf.

Clerk to the Parliamentarian.—Brian C. Cooper.

Assistant Clerks to the Parliamentarian: Lloyd A. Jenkins, Monica Rodriguez.

Precedent Consultant.—Charles W. Johnson III.

Precedent Editors: Deborah W. Khalili, Andrew S. Neal.

Information Technology Manager.—Bryan J. Feldblum.

OFFICE OF THE SERGEANT AT ARMS

H–124 The Capitol, phone 225–2456

WILSON ''BILL'' LIVINGOOD, Sergeant at Arms of the U.S. House of Representatives; born on October 1, 1936 in Philadelphia, PA; B.S., Police Administration, Michigan State University; career record: special agent, U.S. Secret Service's Dallas Field Office, 1961–69; assistant to the special agent in charge of the Presidential Protective Division, 1969; special agent in charge of the Office of Protective Forces, 1970; inspector, Office of Inspection, 1978–82; special agent in charge, Houston Field Office, 1982–86; deputy assistant director, Office of Training, 1986–89; executive assistant to the Director of Secret Service, 1989–95; elected 36th Sergeant at Arms of the U.S. House of Representatives on January 4, 1995, for the 104th Congress; reelected for each succeeding Congress.

Sergeant at Arms.—Wilson ''Bill'' Livingood.
Deputy Sergeant at Arms.—Keni L. Hanley.
Deputy Sergeant at Arms for Police Services and Congressional Relations.—Donald T. Kellaher.
Director, Emergency, Continuity and Preparedness.—Kevin W. Brennan.
Director, Special Events/Protocol.—Ted Daniel.
Assistant to the Sergeant at Arms, Special Events/Protocol.—Kara Boleyn.
Assistant to the Sergeant at Arms, Special Events.—Jack Looney.
Assistant Sergeant at Arms for Administration.—Kathleen Joyce.
Assistant to the Sergeant at Arms.—Stefan J. Bieret.
Assistant to the Sergeant at Arms, Floor Security.—Joyce Hamlett.
Systems Administrators: David Cohen, Bernard Hill.
Staff Assistant.—KaSandra Creenhow.
Counsel to the Sergeant at Arms.—Timothy Blodgett.
Chief Information Officer.—Jim Kaelin.
Director, Office of House Security.—William McFarland.
Assistant Director, Office of House Security.—Dennis Wilson.
Manager, Appointments Desk.—Teresa Johnson.
Director, Chamber Security.—Bill Sims.
Assistant Director, Chamber Security.—Richard Wilson.
Manager, Chamber Support Services.—Andrew Bums.
Director, Identification Services.—Melissa K. Franger.

OFFICE OF EMERGENCY PLANNING, PREPAREDNESS, AND OPERATIONS

H2–192 Ford House Office Building, phone 226–0950

Director.—Curt Coughin.
Deputy Director.—John E. Veatch.
Assistant Director for—
Operations.—Michael P. Susalla.
Preparedness.—Traci L. Brasher.
Special Projects.—W. Lee Trolan.
Executive Assistant.—Linda R. Shealy.
Special Assistant.—Lorraine Foreman.
Program Manager.—Amy R. Rhodes.
Emergency Planning Analyses: P. Dennis LeNard, Jr., Joseph P. Lowry.
Senior Systems/Network Engineer.—Marisa L. Stevenson.

JOINT COMMITTEES

Joint Economic Committee

G01 Dirksen Senate Office Building 20510–6432, phone 224–5171

[Created pursuant to sec. 5(a) of Public Law 304, 79th Congress]

Carolyn B. Maloney, Representative from New York, *Chair*

Charles E. Schumer, Senator from New York, *Vice Chair*

HOUSE

Maurice D. Hinchey, of New York.
Baron P. Hill, of Indiana.
Loretta Sanchez, of California.
Elijah E. Cummings, of Maryland.
Vic Snyder, of Arkansas.

Kevin Brady, of Texas.
Ron Paul, of Texas.
Michael C. Burgess, of Texas.
John Campbell, of California.

SENATE

Jeff Bingaman, of New Mexico.
Amy Klobuchar, of Minnesota.
Robert P. Casey, Jr., of Pennsylvania.
Jim Webb, of Virginia.
Mark R. Warner, of Virginia.

Sam Brownback, of Kansas.
Jim DeMint, of South Carolina.
James E. Risch, of Idaho.
Robert F. Bennett, of Utah.

STAFF

Joint Economic Committee (SDG–01), 224–5171, fax 224–0240.
Majority Staff:
Policy Analyst-Vice Chairman.—Mary O'Dea Ahearn.
Economist.—Paul Chen.
Deputy Staff Director and Chief Economist.—Gail Cohen.
System Administrator.—Barry Dexter.
Senior Economist.—Robert Drago.
Deputy Staff Director/Counsel-Vice Chair.—Stacy Ettinger.
Executive Director.—Nan Gibson.
Economic Policy Advisor-Vice Chair.—Jeff Hamond.
Financial Director.—Colleen Healy.
Senior Policy Analyst.—Elisabeth Jacobs.
Senior Policy Advisor/Counsel-Vice Chair.—Linda Jeng.
Senior Advisor to Vice Chair.—Michael Laskawy.
Senior Economist.—John Marlin.
Policy Analyst.—Michael Neal.
Communications Director.—Barry Nolan.
Press Secretary.—Aaron Rottenstein (acting).
Policy Associate.—Annabelle Tamerjan.
General Counsel.—Andrew Tulloch.
Policy Analyst.—Justin Ungson.
Staff Assistant.—Andrew Wilson.
Minority Staff:
Senior Health Policy Advisor.—Dean Clancy.
Economist.—Rachel Greszler.
Research Assistant.—Lydia Mashburn.

Administrative Assistant.—Jayne McCullough.
Senior Policy Advisor.—Brian Robertson.
Staff Director.—Jeff Schlagenhauf.
Senior Economists: Ted Boll, Gordon Brady, Dan Miller, Robert O'Quinn.
Staff Legislative Policy Director.—Doug Branch.
Executive Assistant.—Connie Foster.

Joint Committee on the Library of Congress

1309 Longworth Building, 20515, phone 225–2061

Robert A. Brady, Representative from Pennsylvania, *Chair*

Charles E. Schumer, Senator from New York, *Vice Chair*

SENATE

Christopher J. Dodd, of Connecticut.
Richard Durbin, of Illinois.
Robert F. Bennett, of Utah.
Thad Cochran, of Mississippi.

HOUSE

Zoe Lofgren, of California.
Debbie Wasserman Schultz, of Florida.
Daniel E. Lungren, of California.
Gregg Harper, of Mississippi

Joint Committee on Printing

SR–305 Russell Senate Office Building, 20515, phone 224–6352

[Created by act of August 3, 1846 (9 Stat. 114); U.S. Code 44, Section 101]

Charles E. Schumer, Senator, New York, *Chair*

Robert A. Brady, Representative, Pennsylvania, *Vice Chair*

SENATE

Patty Murray, of Washington.
Tom Udall, of New Mexico.
Robert F. Bennett, of Utah.
Saxby Chambliss, of Georgia.

HOUSE

Michael E. Capuano, of Massachusetts.
Susan A. Davis, of California.
Daniel E. Lungren, of California.
Kevin McCarthy, of California.

Joint Committee on Taxation

1015 Longworth House Office Building 20515–6453, phone 225–3621

http://www.house.gov/jct

[Created by Public Law 20, 69th Congress]

Charles B. Rangel, Representative from New York, *Chair*

Max Baucus, Senator from Montana, *Vice Chair*

HOUSE

Fortney Pete Stark, of California.
Sander M. Levin, of Michigan.
Dave Camp, of Michigan.
Wally Herger, of California.

SENATE

John D. Rockefeller IV, of West Virginia.
Kent Conrad, of North Dakota.
Chuck Grassley, of Iowa.
Orrin G. Hatch, of Utah.

STAFF

Joint Committee on Taxation (1015 LHOB), 225–3621.
Chief of Staff.—Thomas A. Barthold (1015 LHOB).
Deputy Chief of Staff.—Bernard A. Schmitt (594 FHOB), 226–7575.
Administrative Specialist.—Frank J. Shima (1015 LHOB), 225–3621.
Executive Assistant to the Chief of Staff.—Pamela Williams (1015 LHOB), 225–3621.
Assistant to the Chief of Staff.—Sharon Larimer (1015 LHOB), 225–3621.
Chief Clerk.—John H. Bloyer (1620 LHOB), 225–7377.
Senior Legislation Counsels: Laurie A. Coady (1620 LHOB), 225–7377; Harold E. Hirsch (1620 LHOB), 225–7377; Cecily W. Rock (1620 LHOB), 225–7377; Joseph W. Nega (1620 LHOB), 225–7277.
Legislation Counsels: Gordon M. Clay (G–18 SD), 224–5561; Brion D. Graber (1620 LHOB), 225–7377; Adam Gropper (G–18 SD), 224–5561; Michael Hauswirth (1604 G–18 SD), 224–5561; Marjorie Hoffman (1620 LHOB), 225–7377; Deirdre James (1620 LHOB), 225–7377; Cyndi Lafuente (1604 LHOB), 225–7377; David L. Lenter (1620 LHOB), 225–7377; Rachel Levy (1620 LHOB), 225–7377; Joseph Liker (1604 LHOB), 225–7377; Patrick Nash (1622 LHOB), 225–7377; Kristine Roth (1620 LHOB), 225–7377; Carrie Simons (1604 LHOB), 225–7377; Kashi Way (1620 LHOB), 225–7377; Kristeen Witt (1604 LHOB), 225–7377.
Senior Economists: Nicholas Bull (579A FHOB), 226–7575; James Cilke (593 FHOB), 226–7575; Patrick Driessen (560A FHOB), 226–7575; Robert P. Harvey (561 FHOB), 226–7575; Pamela H. Moomau (595 FHOB), 226–7575; ''Ned'' D.E. Newland (579A FHOB), 6–7575; William T. Sutton (560B FHOB), 6–7575.
Economists: Adam Block (1620 LHOB), 5–7377; Timothy Dowd (578 FHOB), 6–7575; Thomas P. Holtmann (578 FHOB), 6–7575; Julie Marshall (578 FHOB), 6–7575; Jamie McGuire (560 FHOB), 6–7575; John F. Navratil (1620 LHOB), 6–7575; Christopher J. Overend (574B FHOB), 6–7575; Zachary Richards (593 FHOB), 6–7575; Mary Helen Risler (561 FHOB), 6–7575; Karl E. Russo (1620 LHOB), 5–7377; Lori Stuntz (593 FHOB), 6–7575; Kathleen Toma (561 FHOB), 6–7575; Brent Trigg (561 FHOB), 6–7575.
Research Assistant: Andrew Garin (578 FHOB), 6–7575.
Accountants: Kevin Levingston (G–18 SD), 4–5561; Jane Rohrs (G–18 SD), 4–5561.
Senior Refund Counsels: Norman J. Brand (3565 IRS), 622–3580.
Refund Counsels: Chase Gibson (3565 IRS), 622–3580; Robert C. Gotwald (3565 IRS), 622–3580.
Chief Statistical Analyst: Melani M. Houser (596 FHOB), 6–7575.
Statistical Analyst: Tanya Butler, (596 FHOB), 6–7575.
Document Production Specialist: Christine J. Simmons (1620 LHOB), 5–7377.
Tax Resource Specialist: Melissa A. O'Brien (SD–462), 4–0494.

Executive Assistants: B Jean Best (596 LHOB), 6–7575; Jayne Northern (G–18 SD), 4–5561; Lucia J. Rogers (596 FHOB), 6–7575; Patricia C. Smith (1620 LHOB), 5–7377; Sharon Watts (3565 IRS), 622–3580.
Senior Computer Specialist: Hal G. Norman (577 FHOB), 6–7575.
Computer Specialists: Mark High (577 FHOB), 6–7575; Jonathan Newton (577 FHOB), 6–7575; Sandeep Yadav (577 FHOB), 6–7575.
Senior Staff Assistant: Debra L. McMullen (1620 LHOB), 5–2647.
Staff Assistants: Neval E. McMullen (1620 LHOB), 5–2647; Kris Means (1620 LHOB, 5–2647.

ASSIGNMENTS OF SENATORS TO COMMITTEES

[Democrats in roman (58); Republicans in *italic* (40); Independent in SMALL CAPS (1); Independent Democrat in *SMALL CAPS ITALIC* (1); total, 100]

Senator	Committees (Standing, Joint, Special, Select)
Akaka	Veterans' Affairs, *chair.* Armed Services. Banking, Housing, and Urban Affairs. Homeland Security and Governmental Affairs. Indian Affairs.
Alexander	Appropriations. Budget. Environment and Public Works. Health, Education, Labor, and Pensions. Rules and Administration.
Barrasso	Indian Affairs, *vice chair.*. Energy and Natural Resources. Environment and Public Works. Foreign Relations.
Baucus	Finance, *chair.* Joint Committee on Taxation, *vice chair.* Agriculture, Nutrition, and Forestry. Environment and Public Works.
Bayh	Armed Services. Banking, Housing, and Urban Affairs. Energy and Natural Resources. Small Business and Entrepreneurship. Select Committee on Intelligence. Special Committee on Aging.
Begich	Armed Services. Commerce, Science, and Transportation. Veterans' Affairs.
Bennet	Agriculture, Nutrition, and Forestry. Banking, Housing, and Urban Affairs. Health, Education, Labor, and Pensions. Special Committee on Aging.
Bennett	Appropriations. Banking, Housing, and Urban Affairs. Energy and Natural Resources. Homeland Security and Governmental Affairs. Rules and Administration. Joint Committee on the Library. Joint Committee on Printing. Joint Economic Committee.
Bingaman	Energy and Natural Resources, *chair.* Finance. Health, Education, Labor, and Pensions. Joint Economic Committee.
Bond	Select Committee on Intelligence, *vice chair.* Appropriations. Environment and Public Works. Small Business and Entrepreneurship.

Senator	Committees (Standing, Joint, Special, Select)
Boxer	Environment and Public Works, *chair.* Select Committee on Ethics, *chair.* Commerce, Science, and Transportation. Foreign Relations.
Brown	Agriculture, Nutrition, and Forestry. Banking, Housing, and Urban Affairs. Health, Education, Labor, and Pensions. Veterans' Affairs. Select Committee on Ethics.
Brownback	Appropriations. Commerce, Science, and Transportation. Energy and Natural Resources. Joint Economic Committee. Special Committee on Aging.
Bunning	Banking, Housing, and Urban Affairs. Budget. Energy and Natural Resources. Finance.
Burr	Armed Services. Energy and Natural Resources. Health, Education, Labor, and Pensions. Veterans' Affairs. Select Committee on Intelligence.
Burris	Armed Services. Homeland Security and Governmental Affairs. Veterans' Affairs.
Byrd	Appropriations. Armed Services. Budget. Rules and Administration.
Cantwell	Commerce, Science, and Transportation. Energy and Natural Resources. Finance. Indian Affairs. Small Business and Entrepreneurship.
Cardin	Budget. Environment and Public Works. Foreign Relations. Judiciary. Small Business and Entrepreneurship.
Carper	Environment and Public Works. Finance. Homeland Security and Governmental Affairs.
Casey	Agriculture, Nutrition, and Forestry. Foreign Relations. Health, Education, Labor, and Pensions. Joint Economic Committee. Special Committee on Aging.
Chambliss	Agriculture, Nutrition, and Forestry. Armed Services. Rules and Administration. Joint Committee on Printing. Select Committee on Intelligence. Special Committee on Aging.

Senator	Committees (Standing, Joint, Special, Select)
Coburn	Health, Education, Labor, and Pensions. Homeland Security and Governmental Affairs. Indian Affairs. Judiciary. Select Committee on Intelligence.
Cochran	Agriculture, Nutrition, and Forestry. Appropriations. Rules and Administration. Joint Committee on the Library.
Collins	Appropriations. Armed Services. Homeland Security and Governmental Affairs. Special Committee on Aging.
Conrad	Budget, *chair.* Agriculture, Nutrition, and Forestry. Finance. Indian Affairs. Joint Committee on Taxation.
Corker	Banking, Housing, and Urban Affairs. Energy and Natural Resources. Foreign Relations. Special Committee on Aging.
Cornyn	Agriculture, Nutrition, and Forestry. Budget. Finance. Judiciary.
Crapo	Banking, Housing, and Urban Affairs. Budget. Environment and Public Works. Finance. Indian Affairs.
DeMint	Banking, Housing, and Urban Affairs. Commerce, Science, and Transportation. Foreign Relations. Joint Economic Committee.
Dodd	Banking, Housing, and Urban Affairs, *chair.* Foreign Relations. Health, Education, Labor, and Pensions. Rules and Administration. Joint Committee on the Library.
Dorgan	Indian Affairs, *chair.* Appropriations. Commerce, Science, and Transportation. Energy and Natural Resources.
Durbin	Appropriations. Judiciary. Rules and Administration. Joint Committee on the Library.
Ensign	Budget. Commerce, Science, and Transportation. Finance. Homeland Security and Governmental Affairs. Rules and Administration.
Enzi	Budget. Finance. Health, Education, Labor, and Pensions. Small Business and Entrepreneurship.

Senator	Committees (Standing, Joint, Special, Select)
Feingold	Budget. Foreign Relations. Judiciary. Select Committee on Intelligence.
Feinstein	Select Committee on Intelligence, *chair.* Appropriations. Judiciary. Rules and Administration.
Franken	Health, Education, Labor, and Pensions. Indian Affairs. Judiciary. Special Committee on Aging.
Gillibrand	Agriculture, Nutrition, and Forestry. Environment and Public Works. Foreign Relations. Special Committee on Aging.
Graham	Armed Services. Budget. Homeland Security and Governmental Affairs. Judiciary. Veterans' Affairs. Special Committee on Aging.
Grassley	Agriculture, Nutrition, and Forestry. Budget. Finance. Judiciary. Joint Committee on Taxation.
Gregg	Appropriations. Banking, Housing, and Urban Affairs. Budget. Health, Education, Labor, and Pensions.
Hagan	Armed Services. Health, Education, Labor, and Pensions. Small Business and Entrepreneurship.
Harkin	Health, Education, Labor, and Pensions, *chair.* Agriculture, Nutrition, and Forestry. Appropriations. Small Business and Entrepreneurship.
Hatch	Finance. Health, Education, Labor, and Pensions. Judiciary. Joint Committee on Taxation. Select Committee on Intelligence. Special Committee on Aging.
Hutchison	Appropriations. Banking, Housing, and Urban Affairs. Commerce, Science, and Transportation. Rules and Administration.
Inhofe	Armed Services. Environment and Public Works. Foreign Relations.
Inouye	Appropriations, *chair.* Commerce, Science, and Transportation. Indian Affairs. Rules and Administration.

Senator	Committees (Standing, Joint, Special, Select)
Isakson	Select Committee on Ethics, *vice chair.* Commerce, Science, and Transportation. Foreign Relations. Health, Education, Labor, and Pensions. Small Business and Entrepreneurship. Veterans' Affairs.
Johanns	Agriculture, Nutrition, and Forestry. Banking, Housing, and Urban Affairs. Commerce, Science, and Transportation. Indian Affairs. Veterans' Affairs.
Johnson	Appropriations. Banking, Housing, and Urban Affairs. Energy and Natural Resources. Indian Affairs.
Kaufman	Foreign Relations. Judiciary.
Kerry	Foreign Relations, *chair.* Commerce, Science, and Transportation. Finance. Small Business and Entrepreneurship.
Kirk.	Armed Services. Homeland Security and Governmental Affairs.
Klobuchar	Agriculture, Nutrition, and Forestry. Commerce, Science, and Transportation. Environment and Public Works. Judiciary. Joint Economic Committee.
Kohl	Special Committee on Aging, *chair.* Appropriations. Banking, Housing, and Urban Affairs. Judiciary.
Kyl	Finance. Judiciary.
Landrieu	Small Business and Entrepreneurship, *chair.* Appropriations. Energy and Natural Resources. Homeland Security and Governmental Affairs.
Lautenberg	Appropriations. Commerce, Science, and Transportation. Environment and Public Works.
Leahy	Judiciary, *chair.* Agriculture, Nutrition, and Forestry. Appropriations.
LeMieux	Armed Services. Commerce, Science, and Transportation. Special Committee on Aging.
Levin	Armed Services, *chair.* Homeland Security and Governmental Affairs. Small Business and Entrepreneurship. Select Committee on Intelligence.
LIEBERMAN	Homeland Security and Governmental Affairs, *chair.* Armed Services. Small Business and Entrepreneurship.

Senator	Committees (Standing, Joint, Special, Select)
Lincoln	Agriculture, Nutrition, and Forestry *chair.* Energy and Natural Resources. Finance. Special Committee on Aging.
Lugar	Agriculture, Nutrition, and Forestry. Foreign Relations.
McCain	Armed Services. Energy and Natural Resources. Health, Education, Labor, and Pensions. Homeland Security and Governmental Affairs. Indian Affairs. Select Committee on Intelligence.
McCaskill	Armed Services. Commerce, Science, and Transportation. Homeland Security and Governmental Affairs. Special Committee on Aging.
McConnell	Agriculture, Nutrition, and Forestry. Appropriations. Rules and Administration. Select Committee on Intelligence.
Menendez	Banking, Housing, and Urban Affairs. Budget. Energy and Natural Resources. Finance. Foreign Relations.
Merkley	Banking, Housing, and Urban Affairs. Budget. Environment and Public Works. Health, Education, Labor, and Pensions.
Mikulski	Appropriations. Health, Education, Labor, and Pensions. Select Committee on Intelligence.
Murkowski	Appropriations. Energy and Natural Resources. Health, Education, Labor, and Pensions. Indian Affairs.
Murray	Appropriations. Budget. Health, Education, Labor, and Pensions. Rules and Administration. Veterans' Affairs. Joint Committee on Printing.
Nelson, Ben, of Nebraska	Agriculture, Nutrition, and Forestry. Appropriations. Armed Services. Rules and Administration.
Nelson, Bill, of Florida	Armed Services. Budget. Commerce, Science, and Transportation. Finance. Select Committee on Intelligence. Special Committee on Aging.
Pryor	Appropriations. Commerce, Science, and Transportation. Homeland Security and Governmental Affairs. Rules and Administration.

Senator	Committees (Standing, Joint, Special, Select)
	Small Business and Entrepreneurship. Select Committee on Ethics.
Reed	Appropriations. Armed Services. Banking, Housing, and Urban Affairs. Health, Education, Labor, and Pensions.
Reid	Select Committee on Intelligence.
Risch	Energy and Natural Resources. Foreign Relations. Small Business and Entrepreneurship. Joint Economic Committee. Select Committee on Ethics. Select Committee on Intelligence.
Roberts	Agriculture, Nutrition, and Forestry. Finance. Health, Education, Labor, and Pensions. Rules and Administration. Select Committee on Ethics.
Rockefeller	Commerce, Science, and Transportation, *chair.* Finance. Veterans' Affairs. Joint Committee on Taxation. Select Committee on Intelligence.
SANDERS	Budget. Energy and Natural Resources. Environment and Public Works. Health, Education, Labor, and Pensions. Veterans' Affairs.
Schumer	Rules and Administration, *chair.* Joint Committee on Printing, *chair.* Joint Committee on the Library, *vice chair.* Joint Economic Committee, *vice chair.* Banking, Housing, and Urban Affairs. Finance. Judiciary.
Sessions	Armed Services. Budget. Energy and Natural Resources. Judiciary.
Shaheen	Energy and Natural Resources. Foreign Relations. Small Business and Entrepreneurship.
Shelby	Appropriations. Banking, Housing, and Urban Affairs. Special Committee on Aging.
Snowe	Commerce, Science, and Transportation. Finance. Small Business and Entrepreneurship. Select Committee on Intelligence.
Specter	Appropriations. Environment and Public Works. Judiciary. Veterans' Affairs. Special Committee on Aging.

Senator	Committees (Standing, Joint, Special, Select)
Stabenow	Agriculture, Nutrition, and Forestry. Budget. Energy and Natural Resources. Finance.
Tester	Appropriations. Banking, Housing, and Urban Affairs. Homeland Security and Governmental Affairs. Indian Affairs. Veterans' Affairs.
Thune	Agriculture, Nutrition, and Forestry. Armed Services. Commerce, Science, and Transportation. Small Business and Entrepreneurship.
Udall, Mark, of Colorado	Armed Services. Energy and Natural Resources. Special Committee on Aging.
Udall, Tom, of New Mexico	Commerce, Science, and Transportation. Environment and Public Works. Indian Affairs. Rules and Administration. Joint Committee on Printing.
Vitter	Armed Services. Banking, Housing, and Urban Affairs. Commerce, Science, and Transportation. Environment and Public Works. Small Business and Entrepreneurship.
Voinovich	Appropriations. Environment and Public Works. Homeland Security and Governmental Affairs.
Warner	Banking, Housing, and Urban Affairs. Budget. Commerce, Science, and Transportation. Rules and Administration. Joint Economic Committee.
Webb	Armed Services. Foreign Relations. Veterans' Affairs. Joint Economic Committee.
Whitehouse	Budget. Environment and Public Works. Judiciary. Select Committee on Intelligence. Special Committee on Aging.
Wicker	Armed Services. Commerce, Science, and Transportation. Foreign Relations. Small Business and Entrepreneurship. Veterans' Affairs.
Wyden	Budget. Energy and Natural Resources. Finance. Select Committee on Intelligence. Special Committee on Aging.

ASSIGNMENTS OF REPRESENTATIVES, RESIDENT COMMISSIONER, AND DELEGATES TO COMMITTEES

[Democrats in roman (256); Republicans in *italic* (177); Vacancies (2); Resident Commissioner and Delegates in **boldface** (6); total, 441]

Representative	Committees (Standing, Joint, Special, and Select)
Abercrombie	Armed Services. Natural Resources.
Ackerman	Financial Services. Foreign Affairs.
Aderholt	Appropriations. Budget.
Adler, John H., of New Jersey	Armed Services. Veterans' Affairs.
Akin	Armed Services. Science and Technology. Small Business.
Alexander	Appropriations.
Altmire	Education and Labor. Small Business. Transportation and Infrastructure.
Andrews	Armed Services. Budget. Education and Labor.
Arcuri	Rules. Transportation and Infrastructure.
Austria	Budget. Homeland Security.
Baca	Agriculture. Financial Services. Natural Resources.
Bachmann	Financial Services.
Bachus	Financial Services.
Baird	Science and Technology. Transportation and Infrastructure.
Baldwin	Energy and Commerce. Judiciary.
Barrett, J. Gresham, of South Carolina	Armed Services. Foreign Affairs.
Barrow	Energy and Commerce.
Bartlett	Armed Services. Science and Technology. Small Business.

Representative	Committees (Standing, Joint, Special, and Select)
Barton, Joe, of Texas	Energy and Commerce.
Bean	Financial Services. Small Business.
Becerra	Budget. Ways and Means.
Berkley	Foreign Affairs. Ways and Means.
Berman	Foreign Affairs, *chair.* Judiciary.
Berry	Appropriations. Budget.
Biggert	Education and Labor. Financial Services. Science and Technology.
Bilbray	Oversight and Government Reform. Science and Technology. Veterans' Affairs.
Bilirakis	Foreign Affairs. Homeland Security. Veterans' Affairs.
Bishop, Rob, of Utah	Armed Services. Education and Labor. Natural Resources.
Bishop, Sanford D., Jr., of Georgia	Appropriations.
Bishop, Timothy H., of New York	Budget. Education and Labor. Transportation and Infrastructure.
Blackburn	Energy and Commerce. Select Committee on Energy Independence and Global Warming.
Blumenauer	Budget. Ways and Means. Select Committee on Energy Independence and Global Warming.
Blunt	Energy and Commerce. Permanent Select Committee on Intelligence.
Boccieri	Agriculture. Transportation and Infrastructure.
Boehner	Republican Leader.
Bonner	Appropriations. Standards of Official Conduct.
Bono Mack	Energy and Commerce.
Boozman	Foreign Affairs. Transportation and Infrastructure. Veterans' Affairs.
Bordallo	Armed Services. Natural Resources.
Boren	Armed Services. Natural Resources. Permanent Select Committee on Intelligence.

Representative	Committees (Standing, Joint, Special, and Select)
Boswell	Agriculture. Transportation and Infrastructure.
Boucher	Energy and Commerce. Judiciary.
Boustany	Ways and Means.
Boyd	Appropriations. Budget.
Brady, Kevin, of Texas	Ways and Means. Joint Economic Committee.
Brady, Robert A., of Pennsylvania	House Administration, *chair.* Joint Committee on the Library, *chair.* Joint Economic Committee, *chair.* Joint Committee on Printing, *vice chair.* Armed Services.
Braley, Bruce L., of Iowa	Energy and Commerce.
Bright	Agriculture. Armed Services. Small Business.
Broun, Paul C., of Georgia	Homeland Security. Natural Resources. Science and Technology.
Brown, Corrine, of Florida	Transportation and Infrastructure. Veterans' Affairs.
Brown, Henry E., Jr., of South Carolina	Natural Resources. Transportation and Infrastructure. Veterans' Affairs.
Brown-Waite, Ginny, of Florida	Ways and Means.
Buchanan	Small Business. Transportation and Infrastructure. Veterans' Affairs.
Burgess	Energy and Commerce. Joint Economic Committee.
Burton, Dan, of Indiana	Foreign Affairs. Oversight and Government Reform.
Butterfield	Energy and Commerce. Standards of Official Conduct.
Buyer	Energy and Commerce. Veterans' Affairs.
Calvert	Appropriations.
Camp	Ways and Means. Joint Committee on Taxation.
Campbell	Budget. Financial Services. Joint Economic Committee.
Cantor	Ways and Means. Republican Whip.

Representative	Committees (Standing, Joint, Special, and Select)
Cao	Homeland Security. Oversight and Government Reform. Transportation and Infrastructure.
Capito	Financial Services. Transportation and Infrastructure. Select Committee on Energy Independence and Global Warming.
Capps	Energy and Commerce. Natural Resources.
Capuano	Financial Services. House Administration. Transportation and Infrastructure. Joint Committee on Printing.
Cardoza	Agriculture. Rules.
Carnahan	Foreign Affairs. Science and Technology. Transportation and Infrastructure.
Carney	Homeland Security. Transportation and Infrastructure.
Carson, André, of Indiana	Financial Services.
Carter	Appropriations.
Cassidy	Agriculture. Education and Labor. Natural Resources.
Castle	Education and Labor. Financial Services.
Castor, Kathy, of Florida	Energy and Commerce. Standards of Official Conduct.
Chaffetz	Judiciary. Natural Resources. Oversight and Government Reform.
Chandler	Appropriations. Science and Technology. Standards of Official Conduct.
Childers	Agriculture. Financial Services.
Chu	Education and Labor. Oversight and Government Reform. Judiciary.
Christensen	Energy and Commerce. Natural Resources.
Clarke	Education and Labor. Homeland Security. Small Business.
Clay	Financial Services. Oversight and Government Reform.
Cleaver	Financial Services. Homeland Security. Select Committee on Energy Independence and Global Warming.

Representative	Committees (Standing, Joint, Special, and Select)
Clyburn	Majority Whip.
Coble	Judiciary. Transportation and Infrastructure.
Coffman, Mike, of Colorado	Armed Services. Natural Resources. Small Business.
Cohen	Judiciary. Transportation and Infrastructure.
Cole	Appropriations.
Conaway	Agriculture. Armed Services. Standards of Official Conduct. Permanent Select Committee on Intelligence.
Connolly, Gerald E., of Virginia	Budget. Foreign Affairs. Oversight and Government Reform.
Conyers	Judiciary, *chair.*
Cooper	Armed Services. Oversight and Government Reform.
Costa	Agriculture. Foreign Affairs. Natural Resources.
Costello	Science and Technology. Transportation and Infrastructure.
Courtney	Armed Services. Education and Labor.
Crenshaw	Appropriations.
Crowley	Foreign Affairs. Ways and Means.
Cuellar	Agriculture. Homeland Security. Oversight and Government Reform.
Culberson	Appropriations.
Cummings	Oversight and Government Reform. Transportation and Infrastructure. Joint Economic Committee.
Dahlkemper	Agriculture. Science and Technology. Small Business.
Davis, Artur, of Alabama	House Administration. Ways and Means.
Davis, Danny K., of Illinois	Oversight and Government Reform. Ways and Means.
Davis, Geoff, of Kentucky	Ways and Means.
Davis, Lincoln, of Tennessee	Appropriations. Science and Technology.

Representative	Committees (Standing, Joint, Special, and Select)
Davis, Susan A., of California	Armed Services. Education and Labor. House Administration. Joint Committee on Printing.
Deal, Nathan, of Georgia	Energy and Commerce.
DeFazio	Homeland Security. Natural Resources. Transportation and Infrastructure.
DeGette	Energy and Commerce. Natural Resources.
Delahunt	Foreign Affairs. Judiciary.
DeLauro	Appropriations. Budget.
Dent	Homeland Security. Standards of Official Conduct. Transportation and Infrastructure.
Diaz-Balart, Lincoln, of Florida	Rules.
Diaz-Balart, Mario, of Florida	Budget. Science and Technology. Transportation and Infrastructure.
Dicks	Appropriations.
Dingell	Energy and Commerce.
Doggett	Budget. Ways and Means.
Donnelly, Joe, of Indiana	Financial Services. Veterans' Affairs.
Doyle	Energy and Commerce.
Dreier	Rules.
Driehaus	Financial Services. Oversight and Government Reform.
Duncan	Natural Resources. Oversight and Government Reform. Transportation and Infrastructure.
Edwards, Chet, of Texas	Appropriations. Budget.
Edwards, Donna F., of Maryland	Science and Technology. Transportation and Infrastructure.
Ehlers	Education and Labor. Science and Technology. Transportation and Infrastructure.
Ellison	Financial Services. Foreign Affairs.
Ellsworth	Agriculture. Armed Services. Small Business.

Representative	Committees (Standing, Joint, Special, and Select)
Emerson	Appropriations.
Engel	Energy and Commerce. Foreign Affairs.
Eshoo	Energy and Commerce. Permanent Select Committee on Intelligence.
Etheridge	Budget. Ways and Means.
Faleomavaega	Foreign Affairs. Natural Resources.
Fallin	Armed Services. Small Business. Transportation and Infrastructure.
Farr	Appropriations.
Fattah	Appropriations.
Filner	Veterans' Affairs, *chair.* Transportation and Infrastructure.
Flake	Foreign Affairs. Natural Resources. Oversight and Government Reform.
Fleming	Armed Services. Natural Resources.
Forbes	Armed Services. Judiciary.
Fortenberry	Agriculture. Foreign Affairs. Oversight and Government Reform.
Foster	Financial Services. Oversight and Government Reform.
Foxx	Rules.
Frank, Barney, of Massachusetts	Financial Services, *chair.*
Franks, Trent, of Arizona	Armed Services. Judiciary.
Frelinghuysen	Appropriations.
Fudge	Education and Labor. Science and Technology.
Gallegly	Foreign Affairs. Judiciary. Natural Resources. Permanent Select Committee on Intelligence.
Garrett, Scott, of New Jersey	Budget. Financial Services.
Gerlach	Financial Services. Transportation and Infrastructure.
Giffords	Armed Services. Foreign Affairs. Science and Technology.
Gingrey, Phil, of Georgia	Energy and Commerce.

Representative	Committees (Standing, Joint, Special, and Select)
Gohmert	Judiciary. Natural Resources. Small Business.
Gonzalez	Energy and Commerce. House Administration. Judiciary.
Goodlatte	Agriculture. Judiciary.
Gordon, Bart, of Tennessee	Science and Technology, *chair.* Energy and Commerce.
Granger	Appropriations.
Graves	Agriculture. Small Business. Transportation and Infrastructure.
Grayson	Financial Services. Science and Technology.
Green, Al, of Texas	Financial Services. Homeland Security.
Green, Gene, of Texas	Energy and Commerce. Foreign Affairs.
Griffith	Science and Technology. Small Business. Transportation and Infrastructure.
Grijalva	Education and Labor. Natural Resources.
Guthrie	Education and Labor. Transportation and Infrastructure.
Gutierrez	Financial Services. Judiciary.
Hall, John J., of New York	Transportation and Infrastructure. Veterans' Affairs. Select Committee on Energy Independence and Global Warming.
Hall, Ralph M., of Texas	Energy and Commerce. Science and Technology.
Halvorson	Agriculture. Small Business. Veterans' Affairs.
Hare	Education and Labor. Transportation and Infrastructure.
Harman	Energy and Commerce. Homeland Security.
Harper	Budget. House Administration. Judiciary. Standards of Official Conduct. Joint Committee on the Library.
Hastings, Alcee L., of Florida	Permanent Select Committee on Intelligence, *vice chair.* Rules.
Hastings, Doc, of Washington	Natural Resources.

Representative	Committees (Standing, Joint, Special, and Select)
Heinrich	Armed Services. Natural Resources.
Heller	Ways and Means.
Hensarling	Budget. Financial Services.
Herger	Ways and Means. Joint Committee on Taxation.
Herseth	Agriculture. Natural Resources. Veterans' Affairs. Select Committee on Energy Independence and Global Warming.
Higgins	Ways and Means.
Hill	Energy and Commerce. Science and Technology. Joint Economic Committee.
Himes	Financial Services. Homeland Security.
Hinchey	Appropriations. Natural Resources. Joint Economic Committee.
Hinojosa	Education and Labor. Financial Services.
Hirono	Education and Labor. Transportation and Infrastructure.
Hodes	Financial Services. Oversight and Government Reform.
Hoekstra	Education and Labor. Permanent Select Committee on Intelligence.
Holden	Agriculture. Transportation and Infrastructure.
Holt	Education and Labor. Natural Resources. Permanent Select Committee on Intelligence.
Honda	Appropriations.
Hoyer	Majority Leader.
Hunter	Armed Services. Education and Labor.
Inglis	Foreign Affairs. Science and Technology.
Inslee	Energy and Commerce. Natural Resources. Select Committee on Energy Independence and Global Warming.
Israel	Appropriations.
Issa	Judiciary. Oversight and Government Reform.
Jackson, Jesse L., Jr., of Illinois	Appropriations.

Representative	Committees (Standing, Joint, Special, and Select)
Jackson-Lee, Sheila, of Texas	Foreign Affairs. Homeland Security. Judiciary.
Jenkins	Financial Services.
Johnson, Eddie Bernice, of Texas	Science and Technology. Transportation and Infrastructure.
Johnson, Henry C. ''Hank'', Jr., of Georgia	Armed Services. Judiciary.
Johnson, Sam, of Texas	Ways and Means.
Johnson, Timothy V., of Illinois	Agriculture. Transportation and Infrastructure.
Jones	Armed Services. Financial Services.
Jordan, Jim, of Ohio	Budget. Judiciary. Oversight and Government Reform.
Kagen	Agriculture. Transportation and Infrastructure.
Kanjorski	Financial Services. Oversight and Government Reform.
Kaptur	Appropriations. Budget. Oversight and Government Reform.
Kennedy	Appropriations. Oversight and Government Reform. Joint Economic Committee.
Kildee	Education and Labor. Natural Resources.
Kilpatrick, Carolyn C., of Michigan	Appropriations.
Kilroy	Financial Services. Homeland Security.
Kind	Natural Resources. Ways and Means.
King, Peter T., of New York	Financial Services. Homeland Security. Permanent Select Committee on Intelligence.
King, Steve, of Iowa	Agriculture. Judiciary. Small Business.
Kingston	Appropriations.
Kirk	Appropriations.
Kirkpatrick, Ann, of Arizona	Homeland Security. Small Business. Veterans' Affairs.
Kissell	Agriculture. Armed Services.

Representative	Committees (Standing, Joint, Special, and Select)
Klein, Ron, of Florida	Financial Services. Foreign Affairs.
Kline, John, of Minnesota	Armed Services. Education and Labor.
Kosmas	Financial Services. Science and Technology.
Kratovil	Agriculture. Armed Services. Natural Resources.
Kucinich	Education and Labor. Oversight and Government Reform.
Lamborn	Armed Services. Natural Resources. Veterans' Affairs.
Lance	Financial Services.
Langevin	Armed Services. Budget. Permanent Select Committee on Intelligence.
Larsen, Rick, of Washington	Armed Services. Budget. Transportation and Infrastructure.
Larson, John B., of Connecticut	Ways and Means. Select Committee on Energy Independence and Global Warming.
Latham	Appropriations.
LaTourette	Appropriations.
Latta	Agriculture. Budget. Transportation and Infrastructure.
Lee, Barbara, of California	Appropriations. Foreign Affairs.
Lee, Christopher John, of New York	Financial Services.
Levin	Way and Means. Joint Committee on Taxation.
Lewis, Jerry, of California	Appropriations.
Lewis, John, of Georgia	Ways and Means.
Linder	Ways and Means.
Lipinski	Science and Technology. Small Business. Transportation and Infrastructure.
LoBiondo	Armed Services. Transportation and Infrastructure.
Loebsack	Armed Services. Education and Labor.
Lofgren, Zoe, of California	Standards of Official Conduct, *chair.* Homeland Security.

Representative	Committees (Standing, Joint, Special, and Select)
	House Administration. Judiciary. Joint Committee on the Library.
Lowey	Appropriations.
Lucas	Agriculture. Financial Services. Science and Technology.
Luetkemeyer	Agriculture. Oversight and Government Reform. Small Business.
Luján	Homeland Security. Science and Technology.
Lummis	Agriculture. Budget. Natural Resources.
Lungren, Daniel E., of California	Homeland Security. House Administration. Judiciary. Joint Committee on the Library. Joint Committee on Printing.
Lynch	Financial Services. Oversight and Government Reform.
McCarthy, Carolyn, of New York	Education and Labor. Financial Services.
McCarthy, Kevin, of California	Financial Services. House Administration. Joint Committee on Printing.
McCaul	Foreign Affairs. Homeland Security. Science and Technology. Standards of Official Conduct.
McClintock	Education and Labor. Natural Resources.
McCollum	Appropriations. Budget.
McCotter	Financial Services.
McDermott	Ways and Means.
McGovern	Budget. Rules.
McHenry	Budget. Financial Services. Oversight and Government Reform.
McIntyre	Agriculture. Armed Services.
McKeon	Armed Services. Education and Labor.
McMahon	Foreign Affairs. Transportation and Infrastructure.

Representative	Committees (Standing, Joint, Special, and Select)
McMorris Rodgers	Armed Services. Education and Labor. Natural Resources.
McNerney	Energy and Commerce. Veterans' Affairs.
Mack	Budget. Foreign Affairs. Transportation and Infrastructure.
Maffei	Financial Services. Judiciary.
Maloney	Joint Economic Committee, *chair.* Financial Services. Oversight and Government Reform.
Manzullo	Financial Services. Foreign Affairs.
Marchant	Financial Services.
Markey, Betsy, of Colorado	Agriculture. Transportation and Infrastructure.
Markey, Edward J., of Massachusetts	Select Committee on Energy and Independence and Global Warming, *chair.* Energy and Commerce. Natural Resources.
Marshall	Agriculture. Armed Services.
Massa	Agriculture. Armed Services. Homeland Security.
Matheson	Energy and Commerce. Science and Technology.
Matsui	Energy and Commerce. Rules.
Meek, Kendrick B., of Florida	Ways and Means.
Meeks, Gregory W., of New York	Financial Services. Foreign Affairs.
Melancon	Budget. Energy and Commerce.
Mica	Oversight and Government Reform. Transportation and Infrastructure.
Michaud	Small Business. Transportation and Infrastructure. Veterans' Affairs.
Miller, Brad, of North Carolina	Financial Services. Foreign Affairs. Science and Technology.
Miller, Candice S., of Michigan	Homeland Security. Transportation and Infrastructure. Select Committee on Energy Independence and Global Warming.

Representative	Committees (Standing, Joint, Special, and Select)
Miller, Gary G., of California	Financial Services. Transportation and Infrastructure.
Miller, George, of California	Education and Labor, *chair.* Natural Resources.
Miller, Jeff, of Florida	Armed Services. Veterans' Affairs. Permanent Select Committee on Intelligence.
Minnick	Agriculture. Financial Services.
Mitchell	Science and Technology. Transportation and Infrastructure. Veterans' Affairs.
Mollohan	Appropriations.
Moore, Dennis, of Kansas	Financial Services. Small Business.
Moore, Gwen, of Wisconsin	Budget. Financial Services.
Moran, James P., of Virginia	Appropriations.
Moran, Jerry, of Kansas	Agriculture. Transportation and Infrastructure. Veterans' Affairs.
Murphy, Christopher S., of Connecticut	Energy and Commerce. Oversight and Government Reform.
Murphy, Patrick J., of Pennsylvania	Armed Services. Permanent Select Committee on Intelligence.
Murphy, Scott, of New York	Agriculture. Armed Services.
Murphy, Tim, of Pennsylvania	Energy and Commerce.
Murtha	Appropriations.
Myrick	Energy and Commerce. Permanent Select Committee on Intelligence.
Nadler, Jerrold, of New York	Judiciary. Transportation and Infrastructure.
Napolitano	Natural Resources. Transportation and Infrastructure.
Neal, Richard E., of Massachusetts	Ways and Means.
Neugebauer	Agriculture. Financial Services. Science and Technology.
Norton	Homeland Security. Oversight and Government Reform. Transportation and Infrastructure.
Nunes	Budget. Ways and Means.

Representative	Committees (Standing, Joint, Special, and Select)
Nye	Armed Services. Small Business. Veterans' Affairs.
Oberstar	Transportation and Infrastructure, *chair.*
Obey	Appropriations, *chair.*
Olson	Homeland Security. Science and Technology. Transportation and Infrastructure.
Olver	Appropriations.
Ortiz	Armed Services. Transportation and Infrastructure.
Pallone	Energy and Commerce. Natural Resources.
Pascrell	Homeland Security. Ways and Means.
Pastor, Ed, of Arizona	Appropriations.
Paul	Financial Services. Foreign Affairs. Joint Economic Committee.
Paulsen	Financial Services.
Payne	Education and Labor. Foreign Affairs.
Pelosi	The Speaker.
Pence	Foreign Affairs.
Perlmutter	Financial Services. Rules.
Perriello	Transportation and Infrastructure. Veterans' Affairs.
Peters	Financial Services. Science and Technology.
Peterson	Agriculture, *chair.*
Petri	Education and Labor. Transportation and Infrastructure.
Pierluisi	Education and Labor. Judiciary. Natural Resources.
Pingree, Chellie, of Maine	Armed Services. Rules.
Pitts	Energy and Commerce.
Platts	Armed Services. Education and Labor. Transportation and Infrastructure.
Poe, Ted, of Texas	Foreign Affairs. Judiciary.
Polis	Education and Labor. Rules.

Representative	Committees (Standing, Joint, Special, and Select)
Pomeroy	Agriculture. Ways and Means.
Posey	Financial Services.
Price, David E., of North Carolina	Appropriations.
Price, Tom, of Georgia	Education and Labor. Financial Services.
Putnam	Financial Services.
Quigley	Judiciary. Oversight and Government Reform.
Radanovich	Energy and Commerce.
Rahall	Natural Resources, *chair.* Transportation and Infrastructure.
Rangel	Ways and Means, *chair.* Joint Committee on Taxation, *chair.*
Rehberg	Appropriations.
Reichert	Ways and Means.
Reyes	Permanent Select Committee on Intelligence, *chair.* Armed Services.
Richardson	Homeland Security. Transportation and Infrastructure.
Rodriguez	Appropriations. Veterans' Affairs.
Roe, David P., of Tennessee	Agriculture. Education and Labor. Veterans' Affairs.
Rogers, Harold, of Kentucky	Appropriations.
Rogers, Mike, of Alabama	Agriculture. Armed Services. Homeland Security.
Rogers, Mike, of Michigan	Energy and Commerce. Permanent Select Committee on Intelligence.
Rohrabacher	Foreign Affairs. Science and Technology.
Rooney	Armed Services. Judiciary.
Roskam	Ways and Means.
Ros-Lehtinen	Foreign Affairs.
Ross	Energy and Commerce. Foreign Affairs.
Rothman, Steven R., of New Jersey	Appropriations. Science and Technology.
Roybal-Allard	Appropriations.
Royce	Financial Services. Foreign Affairs.

Representative	Committees (Standing, Joint, Special, and Select)
Ruppersberger	Appropriations. Permanent Select Committee on Intelligence.
Rush	Energy and Commerce.
Ryan, Paul, of Wisconsin	Budget. Ways and Means.
Ryan, Tim, of Ohio	Appropriations.
Sablan	Education and Labor. Natural Resources.
Salazar	Appropriations. Select Committee on Energy Independence and Global Warming.
Sánchez, Linda T., of California	Judiciary. Ways and Means.
Sanchez, Loretta, of California	Armed Services. Homeland Security. Joint Economic Committee.
Sarbanes	Energy and Commerce. Natural Resources.
Scalise	Energy and Commerce.
Schakowsky	Energy and Commerce. Permanent Select Committee on Intelligence.
Schauer	Agriculture. Transportation and Infrastructure.
Schiff	Appropriations. Judiciary. Permanent Select Committee on Intelligence.
Schmidt	Agriculture. Transportation and Infrastructure.
Schock	Oversight and Government Reform. Small Business. Transportation and Infrastructure.
Schrader	Agriculture. Budget. Small Business.
Schwartz	Budget. Ways and Means.
Scott, David, of Georgia	Agriculture. Financial Services. Foreign Affairs.
Scott, Robert C. ''Bobby'', of Virginia	Budget. Education and Labor. Judiciary.
Sensenbrenner	Judiciary. Science and Technology. Select Committee on Energy Independence and Global Warming.
Serrano	Appropriations.

Representative	Committees (Standing, Joint, Special, and Select)
Sessions	Rules.
Sestak	Armed Services. Education and Labor. Small Business.
Shadegg	Energy and Commerce. Select Committee on Energy Independence and Global Warming.
Shea-Porter	Armed Services. Education and Labor. Natural Resources.
Sherman	Financial Services. Foreign Affairs. Judiciary.
Shimkus	Energy and Commerce.
Shuler	Small Business. Transportation and Infrastructure.
Shuster	Armed Services. Natural Resources. Transportation and Infrastructure.
Simpson	Appropriations. Budget.
Sires	Foreign Affairs. Transportation and Infrastructure.
Skelton	Armed Services, *chair.*
Slaughter	Rules, *chair.*
Smith, Adam, of Washington	Armed Services. Permanent Select Committee on Intelligence.
Smith, Adrian, of Nebraska	Agriculture. Natural Resources. Science and Technology.
Smith, Christopher H., of New Jersey	Foreign Affairs.
Smith, Lamar, of Texas	Homeland Security. Judiciary. Science and Technology.
Snyder	Armed Services. Veterans' Affairs. Joint Economic Committee.
Souder	Education and Labor. Homeland Security. Oversight and Government Reform.
Space	Energy and Commerce. Veterans' Affairs.
Speier	Financial Services. Oversight and Government Reform. Select Committee on Energy Independence and Global Warming.
Spratt	Budget, *chair.* Armed Services.

Representative	Committees (Standing, Joint, Special, and Select)
Stark	Ways and Means. Joint Committee on Taxation.
Stearns	Energy and Commerce. Veterans' Affairs.
Stupak	Energy and Commerce.
Sullivan	Energy and Commerce. Select Committee on Energy Independence and Global Warming.
Sutton	Energy and Commerce.
Tanner	Foreign Affairs. Ways and Means.
Taylor	Armed Services. Transportation and Infrastructure.
Teague	Transportation and Infrastructure. Veterans' Affairs.
Terry	Energy and Commerce.
Thompson, Bennie G., of Mississippi	Homeland Security, *chair.*
Thompson, Glenn, of Pennsylvania	Agriculture. Education and Labor. Small Business.
Thompson, Mike, of California	Ways and Means. Permanent Select Committee on Intelligence.
Thornberry	Armed Services. Permanent Select Committee on Intelligence.
Tiahrt	Appropriations.
Tiberi	Ways and Means.
Tierney	Education and Labor. Oversight and Government Reform. Permanent Select Committee on Intelligence.
Titus	Education and Labor. Homeland Security. Transportation and Infrastructure.
Tonko	Education and Labor. Science and Technology.
Towns	Oversight and Government Reform, *chair.*
Tsongas	Armed Services. Budget. Natural Resources.
Turner	Armed Services. Oversight and Government Reform.
Upton	Energy and Commerce.
Van Hollen	Oversight and Government Reform. Ways and Means.

Representative	Committees (Standing, Joint, Special, and Select)
Velázquez	Small Business, *chair.* Financial Services.
Visclosky	Appropriations.
Walden	Energy and Commerce.
Walz	Agriculture. Transportation and Infrastructure. Veterans' Affairs.
Wamp	Appropriations.
Wasserman Schultz	Appropriations. Judiciary. Joint Committee on the Library.
Waters	Financial Services. Judiciary.
Watson	Foreign Affairs. Oversight and Government Reform.
Watt	Financial Services. Judiciary.
Waxman	Energy and Commerce, *chair.*
Weiner	Energy and Commerce. Judiciary.
Welch	Energy and Commerce. Oversight and Government Reform. Standards of Official Conduct.
Westmoreland	Oversight and Government Reform. Small Business. Transportation and Infrastructure.
Wexler	Foreign Affairs. Judiciary.
Whitfield	Energy and Commerce.
Wilson, Charles A., of Ohio	Financial Services. Science and Technology.
Wilson, Joe, of South Carolina	Armed Services. Education and Labor. Foreign Affairs.
Wittman	Armed Services. Natural Resources.
Wolf	Appropriations.
Woolsey	Education and Labor. Foreign Affairs. Science and Technology.
Wu	Education and Labor. Science and Technology.
Yarmuth	Budget. Ways and Means.
Young, C. W. Bill, of Florida	Appropriations.
Young, Don, of Alaska	Natural Resources. Transportation and Infrastructure.

CONGRESSIONAL ADVISORY BOARDS, COMMISSIONS, AND GROUPS

BOARD OF VISITORS TO THE AIR FORCE ACADEMY

[Title 10, U.S.C., Section 9355(a)]

Robert F. Bennett, of Utah.
James M. Inhofe, of Oklahoma.
Ben Nelson, of Nebraska.

Doug Lamborn, of Colorado.
Jared Polis, of Colorado.
Loretta Sanchez, of California.
Niki Tsongas, of Massachusetts.

BOARD OF VISITORS TO THE MILITARY ACADEMY

[Title 10, U.S.C., Section 4355(a)]

Jack Reed, of Rhode Island.
Mary L. Landrieu, of Louisiana.
Kay Bailey Hutchison, of Texas.
Richard Burr, of North Carolina.

Maurice D. Hinchey, of New York.
Jim Marshall, of Georgia.
Jerry Lewis, of California.
John Shimkus, of Illinois.
John J. Hall, of New York.

BOARD OF VISITORS TO THE NAVAL ACADEMY

[Title 10, U.S.C., Section 6968(a)]

Barbara A. Mikulski, of Maryland.
John McCain, of Arizona.
Benjamin L. Cardin, of Maryland.
Lisa Murkowski, of Alaska.

Robert J. Wittman, of Virginia.
Elijah E. Cummings, of Maryland.
John Kline, of Minnesota.
Rodney P. Frelinghuysen, of New Jersey.
C. A. Dutch Ruppersberger, of Maryland.

BOARD OF VISITORS TO THE COAST GUARD ACADEMY

[Title 14 U.S.C., Section 194(a)]

John D. Rockefeller IV, of West Virginia.
Maria Cantwell, of Washington.
David Vitter, of Louisiana.
Roger F. Wicker, of Mississippi.

James L. Oberstar, of Minnesota.
Howard Coble, of North Carolina.
John L. Mica, of Florida.
Michael H. Michaud, of Maine.
Joe Courtney, of Connecticut.
Mazie K. Hirono, of Hawaii.

BRITISH-AMERICAN PARLIAMENTARY GROUP

Senate Hart Building, Room 808, phone 224–3047

[Created by Public Law 98–164]

Senate Delegation:
Chair.—Patrick J. Leahy, Senator from Vermont.
Vice Chair.—Thad Cochran, Senator from Mississippi.

House Delegation:
Chair.—Ben Chandler, of Kentucky.
Vice Chair.—John Boozman, of Arkansas.

CANADA–UNITED STATES INTERPARLIAMENTARY GROUP

Senate Hart Building, Room 808, 224–3047

[Created by Public Law 86–42, 22 U.S.C., 1928a–1928d, 276d–276g]

Senate Delegation:
Chair.—Amy Klobuchar, Senator from Minnesota.
Vice Chair.—Mike Crapo, Senator from Idaho.
Director, Interparliamentary Services.—Sally Walsh.

House Delegation:
Paul W. Hodes, of New Hampshire.
James L. Oberstar, of Minnesota.
Michael R. McNulty, of New York.
Peter Welch, of Vermont.

CHINA–UNITED STATES INTERPARLIAMENTARY GROUP

Senate Hart Building, Room 808, phone 224–3047

[Created by Public Law 108–199, Section 153]

Senate Delegation:
Chair.—Patty Murray, Senator from Washington.
Vice Chair.—Vacant.

COMMISSION ON CONGRESSIONAL MAILING STANDARDS

1216 Longworth House Office Building, phone 225–9337

[Created by Public Law 93–191]

Chair.—Susan A. Davis, of California.
Brad Sherman, of California.
Donna F. Edwards, of Maryland.
Daniel E. Lungren, of California.
Tom Price, of Georgia.
Kevin McCarthy, of California.

STAFF

Majority Staff Director.—Ellen McCarthy, 225–9337.
Professional Staff: Matthew A. DeFreitas, Brian M. McCue, Mary McHugh, Connie Thomas.
Counsel.—Charles T. Howell.
Minority Staff Director.—Jack Dail, 226–6044.
Professional Staff: Sean C. Evins, George Hadjiski.

COMMISSION ON SECURITY AND COOPERATION IN EUROPE

234 Ford House Office Building, phone 225–1901, fax 226–4199

http://www.csce.gov

Benjamin L. Cardin, Senator from Maryland, *Chair*

Alcee L. Hastings, Representative from Florida, *Co-Chair*

LEGISLATIVE BRANCH COMMISSIONERS

Senate

Christopher J. Dodd, of Connecticut.
Sheldon Whitehouse, of Rhode Island.
Tom Udall, of New Mexico.
Jeanne Shaheen, of New Hampshire.
Sam Brownback, of Kansas.
Saxby Chambliss, of Georgia.
Richard Burr, of North Carolina.
Roger F. Wicker, of Mississippi.

House

Edward J. Markey, of Massachusetts.
Louise McIntosh Slaughter, of New York.
Mike McIntyre, of North Carolina.
G. K. Butterfield, of North Carolina.
Christopher H. Smith, of New Jersey.
Joseph R. Pitts, of Pennsylvania.
Robert B. Aderholt, of Alabama.
Darrell E. Issa, of California.

EXECUTIVE BRANCH COMMISSIONERS

Department of State.—Vacant.
Department of Defense.—Vacant.
Department of Commerce.—Vacant.

COMMISSION STAFF

Chief of Staff.—Fred L. Turner.
Office Manager.—Daniel Redfield.
Senior Advisor.—Douglas Davidson.
Policy Advisors: Orest Deychakiwsky, Shelly Han, Robert Hand, Janice Helwig, Alex T. Johnson, Ronald J. McNamara, Michael Ochs, Winsome Packer, Kyle Parker, Mischa E. Thompson.
Counsel for International Law.—Erika B. Schlager.
General Counsel.—Marlene Kauffmann.
Policy Director.—Edward P. Joseph.
Communications Director.—Neil H. Simon.
Staff Associate.—Josh Shapiro.

CONGRESSIONAL AWARD FOUNDATION

379 Ford House Office Building, phone (202) 226–0130, fax 226–0131

[Created by Public Law 96–114]

Chair.—Paxton K. Baker, BET J.
Vice Chairs:
Linda Mitchell, Mississippi State University Extension Service (662) 534–7776.
Amb. Roger F. Noriega, Vision Americas, LLC.
Secretary.—Mary Rogers, Pennsylvania.
Treasurer.—Dan Scherder, Scherder & Associates.
Chairman Emeritus.—John Falk, Firecreek Ltd.

Members:

Cliff Akiyama, University of Pennsylvania.
Hon. Max Baucus, United States Senate.
Hon. Gus M. Bilirakis, United States Congress.
Hon. Kwame Brown, DC Councilmember At-Large.
Laurel Call, Assurant Health.
Michael Carozza, Bristol-Myers Squibb Company.
Edward Cohen, Lerner Enterprises.
Kathy Didawick, Blue Cross Blue Shield Association.
Dr. Wiley Dobbs, Idaho.
Mike Esser, Edward Jones.
David Falk, FAME.
Hon. Victor Herbert Fazio, Jr., Akin Gump Strauss Hauer & Feld, LLP.
Michael Flannigan, Rio Tinto.
Jeffrey S. Fried, Washington, DC.
Ron Gillyard, Los Angeles, CA.
Raymond Goulbourne, BET.
George B. Gould, Washington, DC.
J. Steven Hart, Esq., Williams & Jensen, P.C.
Erica Wheelan Heyse, National Director.
David W. Hunt, Esq., White & Case, LLP.
Hon. Johnny Isakson, United States Senate.
Hon. Sheila Jackson-Lee, United States Congress.
Paul Kelly, National Association of Chain Drug Stores.
Annette Lantos, California.
Conrad Lass, Electric Power Supply Association.
Lynn Lyons, Florida.
Marc Monyek, McDonald's Corporation.
Patrick Murphy, Capitol Management.
Major General Robert B. Newman, Jr., The Adjutant General of Virginia.
Kimberly Norman, Affiliated Computer Services, Inc.
Andrew F. Ortiz, Ortiz Leadership Systems.
Jerry Prout, FMC Corporation.
Glenn Reynolds, USTelecom Association.
Adam Ruiz, Kentucky.
Hon. Rodney E. Slater, Patton Boggs, LLP.
David Sutphen, Brunswick Group.
Jeffrey L. Thompson, The Walt Disney Company.
Hon. Jeri Thomson, Former Secretary of the United States Senate.
Joe Watson, Virginia.
Kathryn Weeden, United States Senate Page School.
Jon Wood, Foundation Coal Holdings, Inc.

CONGRESSIONAL CLUB

2001 New Hampshire Avenue, NW., 20009, phone (202) 332–1155, fax 797–0698

President.—Vicki Miller.

Vice Presidents:

(1st) Carolina Reyes.
(2d) Julie Reichert.
(3d) Betty Ann Tanner.
(4th) Freda Manzullo.
(5th) Peggo Horstmann Hodes.
(6th) Virginia Pitts.

Treasurer.—Billie Gingrey.

Recording Secretary.—Peachy Melancon.

Corresponding Secretary.—Judy Istook.

Administrative Assistant.—Lydia de La Vina de Foley.

CONGRESSIONAL EXECUTIVE COMMISSION ON CHINA

242 Ford House Office Building, phone 226–3766, fax 226–3804

[Created by Public Law 106–286]

Byron L. Dorgan, Senator from North Dakota, *Chair.*
Sander M. Levin, Representative from Michigan, *Co-Chair.*

LEGISLATIVE BRANCH COMMISSIONERS

House

Marcy Kaptur, of Ohio.
Michael M. Honda, of California.
Timothy J. Walz, of Minnesota.
David Wu, of Oregon.
Christopher H. Smith, of New Jersey.
Edward R. Royce, of California.
Donald A. Manzullo, of Illinois.
Joseph R. Pitts, of Pennsylvania.

Senate

Max Baucus, of Montana.
Carl Levin, of Michigan.
Dianne Feinstein, of California.
Sherrod Brown of Ohio.
Sam Brownback, of Kansas.
Bob Corker, of Tennessee.
John Barrasso, of Wyoming.

EXECUTIVE BRANCH COMMISSIONERS

To Be Appointed

COMMISSION STAFF

Staff Director.—Charlotte Oldham-Moore.
Co-Chairman's Senior Staff Member.—Douglas Grob.
Director of Administration.—Judy Wright.
Advocacy Director.—Kara Abramson.
Senior Advisors: Anna Brettell, Steve Marshall, Andrea Worden.
Senior Counsels: Lawrence Liu, Sharon Mann.
Senior Research Associate.—Toy Reid.
Manager of Outreach and Special Projects.—Abigail Story.
Printer and Outreach Associate.—Deidre Jackson.

HOUSE DEMOCRACY ASSISTANCE COMMISSION

341 Ford House Office Building, phone 226–1641, fax 226–6062

[Created by H. Res. 5, 111th Congress]

Chair.—David E. Price, of North Carolina.
Ranking Member.—David Dreier, of California.

COMMISSIONERS

Lois Capps, of California.
Rush D. Holt, of New Jersey.
Adam B. Schiff, of California.
Allyson Y. Schwartz, of Pennsylvania.
Donald M. Payne, of New Jersey.
Earl Pomeroy, of North Dakota.
Sam Farr, of California.
Keith Ellison, of Minnesota.
Mazie K. Hirono, of Hawaii.
Lucille Roybal-Allard, of California.
John Boozman, of Arkansas.
Jeff Fortenberry, of Nebraska.
Judy Biggert, of Illinois.
Bill Shuster, of Pennsylvania.
Kay Granger, of Texas.
Charles W. Boustany, Jr., of Louisiana.
Vern Buchanan, of Florida.
K. Michael Conaway, of Texas.

Staff Director.—John J. Lis.
Professional Staff Member.—Margarita R. Seminario.

HOUSE OFFICE BUILDING COMMISSION

H–232 The Capitol, phone 225–0100

[Title 40, U.S.C. 175–176]

Chair.—Nancy Pelosi, Speaker of the House of Representatives.
Steny H. Hoyer, House Majority Leader.
John A. Boehner, House Minority Leader.

HOUSE OF REPRESENTATIVES PAGE BOARD

H–154 The Capitol, phone 225–7000

[Established by House Resolution 611, 97th Congress]

Chair.—Dale E. Kildee, Representative from Michigan.

Members:
Diana DeGette, Representative from Colorado.
Virginia Foxx, Representative from North Carolina.
Rob Bishop, Representative from Utah.
Lorraine C. Miller, Clerk of the House.
Wilson ''Bill'' Livingood, Sergeant at Arms of the House.

Staff Contact:
Maria A. Lopez, Deputy Clerk of the House Page Program.

JAPAN–UNITED STATES FRIENDSHIP COMMISSION

1201 15th Street, NW., Suite 330, phone (202) 653–9800, fax 653–9802

[Created by Public Law 94–118]

Chairman.—Thierry Porte, c / o JC Flowers.
Vice-Chairman.—Dr. Michael J. Green, Japan Chair and Senior Advisor, Center for Strategic and International Studies.
Executive Director.—Eric J. Gangloff.
Assistant Executive Director.—Margaret P. Mihori.
Assistant Executive Director, CULCON.—Pamela L. Fields.
Executive Assistant.—Sylvia L. Dandridge.

Members:
Hon. Kurt N. Campbell, Assistant Secretary of State for East Asian and Pacific Affairs, U.S. Department of State.
Willard G. Clark, Founder, Center for Japanese Art and Culture.
Dr. Robert A. Feldman, Managing Director, Morgan Stanley Japan Securities Co. Ltd.
Ellen H. Hammond, Curator, East Asian Library, Yale University.
Dr. Velina Hasu Hammond, Professor of Theater, School of Theater, University of Southern California.
Hon. Rocco Landesman, Chairman, National Endowment for the Arts.
Hon. James Leach, Chairman, National Endowment for the Humanities.
Hon. James McDermott, U.S. House of Representatives.
Hon. Lisa Murkowski, U.S. Senate.
Dr. David M. O'Brien, Spicer Professor of Politics, University of Virginia.
Hon. Thomas E. Petri, U.S. House of Representatives.
Dr. Susan J. Pharr, Edwin O. Reischauer Professor of Japanese Politics, Harvard University.
Amelia Porges.
Hon. John D. Rockefeller IV, U.S. Senate.

MEXICO–UNITED STATES INTERPARLIAMENTARY GROUP

Senate Hart Building, Room 808, phone 224–3047

[Created by Public Law 82–420, 22 U.S.C. 276h–276k]

Senate Delegation:

Chair.—Christopher J. Dodd, of Connecticut.
Vice Chair.—Vacant.

House Delegation:
Chair.—Ciro D. Rodriguez, of Texas.

MIGRATORY BIRD CONSERVATION COMMISSION

4401 North Fairfax Drive, Room 622, Arlington, VA 22203
phone (703) 358–1716 fax (703) 358–2223

[Created by act of February 18, 1929, 16 U.S.C. 715a]

Chair.—Ken Salazar, Secretary of the Interior.
Blanche L. Lincoln, Senator from Arkansas.
Thad Cochran, Senator from Mississippi.
John D. Dingell, Representative from Michigan.
Robert J. Wittman Representative from Virginia.
Tom Vilsack, Secretary of Agriculture.
Lisa P. Jackson, Administrator of Environmental Protection Agency.
Secretary.—A. Eric Alvarez.

NATO PARLIAMENTARY ASSEMBLY

Headquarters: Place du Petit Sablon 3, B–1000 Brussels, Belgium

[Created by Public Law 84–689, 22 U.S.C., 1928z]

Senate Delegation:
Chair.—Vacant.
Vice Chair.—Vacant.

House Delegation:
Chair.—Kendrick B. Meek, Representative from Florida.

STAFF

Secretary, Senate Delegation.—Julia Hart Reed, Interparliamentary Services, SH–808, 224–3047.
Secretary, House Delegation.—Susan Olsen, 226–8806.

PERMANENT COMMITTEE FOR THE OLIVER WENDELL HOLMES DEVISE FUND

Library of Congress, 20540, phone 707–1082

[Created by act of Congress approved Aug. 5, 1955 (Public Law 246, 84th Congress), to administer Oliver Wendell Holmes Devise Fund, established by same act]

Chairman ex officio.—James H. Billington.
Administrative Officer for the Devise.—James H. Hutson.

UNITED STATES–CHINA ECONOMIC AND SECURITY REVIEW COMMISSION

444 North Capitol Street, NW., phone 624–1407, fax 624–1406

[Created by Public Law 106–398, 114 STAT]

COMMISSIONERS

Chair.—Carolyn Bartholomew.
Vice Chair.—Larry M. Wortzel, Ph.D.

Members:
Daniel A. Blumenthal, Resident Fellow for National Security Affairs.
Peter Brookes, Senior Fellow, National Security Affairs.
Robin Cleveland, Principal Olivet Consulting, LLC.

Jeffrey L. Fiedler, Director Special Projects-Initiatives, International Union of Operating Engineers.
Hon. Patrick A. Mulloy, Adjunct Professor of Public International Law and International Trade Law at Catholic University and George Mason University Law School.
Hon. Dennis C. Shea, Attorney, Government and Public Policy.
Daniel M. Slane, Founder and co-owner of the Slane Company.
Hon. William A. Reinsch, President, National Foreign Trade Council.
Peter Videnieks, Advisor, Foreign Affairs and Energy.
Michael R. Wessel, President, The Wessel Group Inc.

COMMISISON STAFF

Executive Director.—Michael R. Danis.
Associate Director.—Kathleen J. Michels.
Senior Policy Analyst, Trade and Economics.—Paul Magnusson.
Policy Analyst, Trade and Economics: Athanasios Mihalakas, Nargiza Salidjanova.
Senior Policy Analyst, Military and Security Affairs.—Daniel Hartnett.
Policy Analyst, Military and Security Issues.—Robert Sheldon.
Policy Analyst, Foreign Affairs and Energy.—Lee Levkowitz.
Congressional Liaison.—Jonathan Weston.
Research Coordinator.—John Dotson.
Research Assistant.—J.R. Warner.
Budget and Accounting Specialist.—Kathleen Wilson.
Administrative-Program Specialist.—Nicholas Barone.
Executive/Administrative Assistant.—Katherine Koleski.
Human Resources Coordinator.—Douglas Fehrer.
Travel-Procurement Assistant.—Chris Fava.

RUSSIA–UNITED STATES INTERPARLIAMENTARY GROUP

Senate Hart Building, Room 808, phone 224–3047

[Created by Public Law 108–199, Section 154]

Senate Delegation:
Chair.—Ben Nelson, Senator from Nebraska.
Vice Chair.—Judd Gregg, Senator from New Hampshire.

SENATE NATIONAL SECURITY WORKING GROUP

311 Hart Senate Office Building, 20510, phone 228–6425

Administrative Co-Chair.—Robert C. Byrd, Senator from West Virginia.
Administrative Co-Chair.—*Jon Kyl,* Senator from Arizona.
Democratic Leader.—Harry Reid, Senator from Nevada.
Republican Leader.—*Mitch McConnell,* Senator from Kentucky.
Co-Chair.—Carl Levin, Senator from Michigan.
Co-Chair.—*Thad Cochran,* Senator from Mississippi.
Co-Chair.—Frank R. Lautenberg, Senator from New Jersey.
Co-Chair.—John F. Kerry, Senator from Massachusetts.
Co-Chair.—*Lindsey Graham,* Senator from South Carolina.

Members:
Richard Durbin, Senator from Illinois.
Bryon L. Dorgan, Senator from North Dakota.
Bill Nelson, Senator from Florida.
JOSEPH I. LIEBERMAN, Senator from Connecticut.
Benjamin L. Cardin, Senator from Maryland.
Richard G. Lugar, Senator from Indiana.
Jeff Sessions, Senator from Alabama.
Bob Corker, Senator from Tennessee.
George V. Voinovich, Senator from Ohio.
John McCain, Senator from Arizona.
James E. Risch, Senator from Idaho.

STAFF

Democratic Staff Director.—James J. Tuite III, 228–6425.
Republican Staff Director.—Tim Morrison, 224–4521.

U.S. ASSOCIATION OF FORMER MEMBERS OF CONGRESS

1401 K Street, NW., Suite 503, 20005

phone (202) 222–0972, fax 222–0977

The nonpartisan United States Association of Former Members of Congress was founded in 1970 as a nonprofit, educational, research and social organization. It has been chartered by the United States Congress and has approximately 600 members who represented American citizens in both the U.S. Senate and the House of Representatives. The Association promotes improved public understanding of the role of Congress as a unique institution as well as the crucial importance of representative democracy as a system of government, both domestically and internationally.

President.—John J. Rhodes III, of Arizona.
Vice President.—Dennis Hertel, of Michigan.
Treasurer.—Constance A. "Connie" Morella, of Maryland.
Secretary.—Barbara B. Kennelly, of Connecticut.
Immediate Past President.—Jim Slattery, of Kansas.
Honorary Chair.—Walter F. Mondale, of Minnesota.
Executive Director.—Peter M. Weichlein.
Counselors: Dan Glickman, of Kansas; Margaret M. Heckler, of Massachusetts; Matthew F. McHugh, of New York; Mike Parker, of Mississippi; Richard T. Schulze, of Pennsylvania; James W. Symington, of Missouri.

U.S. CAPITOL HISTORICAL SOCIETY

200 Maryland Avenue, NE., 20002, phone (202) 543–8919, fax 544–8244

[Congressional Charter, October 20, 1978, Public Law 95–493, 95th Congress, 92 Stat. 1643]

Chairman of the Board.—Hon. E. Thomas Coleman.
President.—Hon. Ron Sarasin.
Treasurer.—L. Neale Cosby.
General Secretary.—Suzanne C. Dicks.
Vice President of:
Finance and Administration.—Paul E. McGuire.
Membership and Development.—Rebecca A. Evans.
Merchandising.—Diana E. Wailes.
Scholarship and Education.—Donald R. Kennon, Ph.D.

EXECUTIVE COMMITTEE

Donald G. Carlson
Hon. E. Thomas Coleman
L. Neale Cosby
Suzanne C. Dicks
Bryce Larry Harlow
Hon. Richard N. Holwill
Linda Monk
Susan Neely
Hon. Ron Sarasin
Hon. John C. Tuck
(2 Vacancies)

STAFF

Director of:
Education and Outreach.—Felicia Bell.
Marketing.—Mary Hughes.
Manager of:
Accounting Department.—Sheri Williams.
Corporate Giving.—Marilyn Green.
Member Programs.—Diana Friedman Chiu.
Public Programs and Chief Guide.—Steve Livengood.
Associate Historian.—Lauren Borchard
Development Associate.—Maggie McDonald.
Development Coordinator.—Laurent Piereth.
Operations Manager.—Randy Groves.

Receiving Supervisor.—Vince Scott.
Fulfillment Supervisor—Ann McNeil.

U.S. CAPITOL PRESERVATION COMMISSION

[Created pursuant to Public Law 100–696]

Co-Chairs:
Nancy Pelosi, Speaker of the House.
Robert C. Byrd, Senate President Pro Tempore.

House Members:
Steny H. Hoyer, Majority Leader.
John A. Boehner, Republican Leader.
David R. Obey.
Robert A. Brady.
Daniel E. Lungren.
Zach Wamp.
Marcy Kaptur.
Michael E. Capuano.

Senate Members:
Harry Reid, Majority Leader.
Mitch McConnell, Republican Leader.
Charles E. Schumer.
Robert F. Bennett.
Richard Durbin.
Mary L. Landrieu.
Lisa Murkowski.

Architect of the Capitol.—Stephen T. Ayers (acting).

U.S. HOUSE OF REPRESENTATIVES FINE ARTS BOARD

1309 Longworth House Office Building, phone 225–2061

[Created by Public Law 101–696]

Chair.—Robert A. Brady, of Pennsylvania.

Members:
Zoe Lofgren, of California.
Debbie Wasserman Schultz, of Florida.
Daniel E. Lungren, of California.
Gregg Harper, of Mississippi.

U.S. SENATE COMMISSION ON ART

S–411 The Capitol, phone 224–2955

[Created by Public Law 100–696]

Chair.—Harry Reid, of Nevada.
Vice Chair.—Mitch McConnell, of Kentucky.

Members:
Robert C. Byrd, of West Virginia.
Charles E. Schumer, of New York.
Robert F. Bennett, of Utah.

STAFF

Executive Secretary.—Nancy Erickson.
Curator.—Diane K. Skvarla.
Administrator.—Scott M. Strong.
Associate Curator.—Melinda K. Smith.
Collections Manager.—Deborah Wood.
Museum Specialist.—Richard L. Doerner.
Registrar.—Courtney Morfeld.
Collections Specialist.—Theresa Malanum.
Curatorial Assistant.—Amy Burton.
Historical Preservation Officer.—Kelly Steele.

OTHER CONGRESSIONAL OFFICIALS AND SERVICES

ARCHITECT OF THE CAPITOL

ARCHITECT'S OFFICE

SB–15, U.S. Capitol, phone 228–1793, fax 228–1893, http://www.aoc.gov

Architect of the Capitol.—Stephen T. Ayers (acting), AIA.
Assistant to the Architect of the Capitol.—Michael G. Turnbull, 228–1221.
Special Assistant to the Chief Operating Officer.—Frank Tiscione, 228–2124.
Chief Executive Officer for Visitor Services.—Terrie Rouse, 593–1837.
Inspector General.—Carol Bates, 593–0260.
Director of:
Congressional and External Relations.—Mike Culver, 228–1701.
Safety, Fire and Environmental Programs.—Susan Adams, 226–0630.
Chief Administrative Officer.—David Ferguson, 228–1205.
Chief Financial Officer.—Paula Lettice, 228–1819.
Budget Officer.—Lauri Smith, 228–1793.
Communications Officer.—Eva Malecki, 228–1793.
General Counsel.—Peter Kushner, 228–1793.
Executive Officer, U.S. Botanic Garden.—Holly Shimizu, 225–6670.
Curator.—Barbara Wolanin, 228–1222.

U.S. CAPITOL

HT–42, Capitol Superintendent's Service Center, phone 228–8800, fax 225–1957

Superintendent.—Carlos Elias.
Deputy Superintendent.—Larry Brown.
Assistant Superintendent.—Don White, 228–1875.

U.S. CAPITOL VISITOR CENTER

U.S. Capitol Visitor Center, Room SVC–101, 20515, phone 593–1816

Recorded Information 226–8000, Special Services 224–4048, TTY 224–4049

CEO for Visitor Services.—Terrie Rouse.
Director of:
Communications and Marketing.—Tom Fontana.
Exhibits and Education.—Rob Lukens.
Gift Shops.—Susan Sisk.
Restaurant/Special Events.—Miguel Lopez.
Visitor Services.—Beth Plemmons.
Volunteer Coordinator.—Wayne Kehoe.

SENATE OFFICE BUILDINGS

G–45 Dirksen Senate Office Building, phone 224–3141, fax 224–0652

Superintendent.—Robin Morey, 224–6951.
Deputy Superintendent.—Takis Tzamaras, 224–2021.
Assistant Superintendents: Dennis Campbell, Michael Shirven, Marvin Simpson, M. Trent Wolfersberger, 224–5023.

HOUSE OFFICE BUILDINGS

B–341 Rayburn House Office Building, phone 225–4141, fax 225–3003

Superintendent.—William M. Weidemeyer, P.E., CFM, 225–7012.
Deputy Superintendent.—Thomas J. Carroll, 225–4142.
Assistant Superintendents: Daniel Murphy, Mark Reed, Sterling Thomas, Bill Wood, 225–4142.

CAPITOL TELEPHONE EXCHANGE

6110 Postal Square Building, phone 224–3121

Supervisor.—Joan Sartori.

CHILD CARE CENTERS

HOUSE OF REPRESENTATIVES CHILD CARE CENTER

147 Ford House Office Building
Virginia Avenue and 3rd Street, SW., 20515
phone 226–9321, fax 225–6908

Administrative Director.—Monica Barnabae.
Program Director.—Paige Beatty.

SENATE EMPLOYEES' CHILD CARE CENTER

United States Senate, 20510
phone 224–1461, fax 228–3686

Director.—Christine Schoppe Wauls.

COMBINED AIRLINES TICKET OFFICES (CATO)

1800 North Kent Street, Suite 950, Arlington, VA 22209
phone (703) 522–8664, fax 522–0616

General Manager.—Charles A. Dinardo.
Administrative Assistant.—Susan Willis.

B–222 Longworth House Office Building
phone (703) 522–2286, fax (202) 226–5992

Supervisor.—Misty Conner.

B–24 Russell Senate Office Building
phone (703) 522–2286, fax (202) 393–1981

Supervisor.—Cathy Barndhart.

CONGRESSIONAL RECORD DAILY DIGEST

HOUSE SECTION

HT–13 The Capitol, phone 225–2868 (committees), 225–1501 (chamber)

Editors for—
Committee Meetings.—Maura Patricia Kelly.
Chamber Action.—Jenelle Pulis.

SENATE SECTION

S–421 The Capitol, phone 224–2658, fax 224–1220

Editor.—Elizabeth Brown.
Assistant Editor.—Joseph Johnston.

CONGRESSIONAL RECORD INDEX OFFICE

U.S. Government Printing Office, Room C–738

North Capitol and H Streets, NW., 20401, phone 512–0275

Director.—Marcia Thompson, 512–2010, ext. 3–1975.
Deputy Director.—Philip C. Hart, 512–2010, ext. 3–1973.
Historian of Bills.—Barbre A. Brunson, 512–2010, ext. 3–1957.
Editors: Grafton J. Daniels, Jason Parsons.
Indexers: Ytta B. Carr, Joel K. Church, Jennifer E. Jones, Jane M. Wallace.

OFFICE OF CONGRESSIONAL ACCESSIBILITY SERVICES

S–156 Crypt of the Capitol 20510, phone 224–4048, TTY 224–4049

Director.—David Hauck.

LIAISON OFFICES

AIR FORCE

B–322 Rayburn House Office Building

phone 225–6656, 685–4530, DSN 325–4530, BB 386–3012, fax 685–2592

Chief.—Col. Jeffrey ''Tank'' Koch.
Deputy Chief.—Lt. Col. Michael ''Mike'' Madsen.
Liaison Officers: Lt. Col. Heidi Cornell, Maj. William ''Bill'' Denham, Maj. Leland ''Kent'' Leonard.
Budget and Appropriations Liaison Officer.—MAJ Trevor Williams.
Legislative Assistants: Alice Geishecker, MSgt Marvin Tasby.

182 Russell Senate Office Building, phone 224–2481, fax 685–2575

Chief.—Col. John Dolan.
Deputy Chief.—Lt. Col. Darren Hall.
Liaison Officers: Lt. Col. Reginald Bullock, Lt. Col. Kathleen Mikkelson.
Appropriations Liaison Officer.—Lt. Col. Phil Hendrix.

ARMY

B–325 Rayburn House Office Building, phone 225–3853, fax 685–2674

Chief.—COL Scott McBride.
Deputy Chief.—Dr. Dale Jones.
Liaison Officers: LTC Tony Garman, MAJ Louis Kangas, MAJ Jennifer Reynolds, LTC Matt Schwind, MAJ Alex Shaw, MAJ Ca-Asia Shields, MSG Quinton Waterman.
Congressional Caseworkers: Bob Nelson, Gail Warren.

183 Russell Senate Office Building, phone 224–2881, fax 685–2570

Chief.—Vacant.
Deputy Chief.—Larnell Exum.
Liaison Officers: MAJ Colin Brooks, MAJ James Kleager, LTC Ed Larkin, MAJ Jennifer McDonough, LTC Richard Root, MAJ Michael Stella, MSG Olivia Warner.
Congressional Caseworker.—Cynthia Gray.

COAST GUARD

B–320 Rayburn House Office Building, phone 225–4775, fax 426–6081

Director, House Liaison Officer.—CDR Robert Warren.
Deputy, House Liaison Officer.—CDR David Burns.
Assistant House Liaison.—LCDR Stephanie Morrison.

183 Russell Senate Office Building, phone 224–2913, fax 755–1695

Liaison Officer.—CDR Laura Dickey.
Liaison Assistants: CDR Scott Langum, Lee Williams.

NAVY / MARINE CORPS

B–324 Rayburn House Office Building, phone: Navy 225–7126; Marine Corps 225–7124

Director.—CAPT Joe McClain, USN.
Deputy Director.—CDR Brian Elkowitz, USN.
USN Liaison Officers: LT Lauren Baker, USN; LT David Colberg, USN; LT Douglas Robb, USN; LCDR Rogelio Valencia, USN (contracts).
Director USMC.—COL Dave Furness, USMC.
USMC Liaison Officers: MAJ Kaheem Jackson, USMC; MAJ Toby Patterson, USMC.
Office Manager / Administrative Clerk.—SGT Jennifer Evitts, USMC.
House Staff NCO.—GYSGT Darwin Leavell, USMC.

182 Russell Senate Office Building, phone: Navy 685–6003; Marine Corps 685–6010

Director.—CAPT John Nowell, USN.
Deputy Director.—CAPT CJ Cassidy, USN.
USN Liaison Officers: LT Mitch McGuffie, USN; LT Natalie Schultz, USN; LCDR Greg Kausner, USN.
Director, USMC.—COL Phil Skuta, USMC.
USMC Liaison Officers.—MAJ David Walker, USMC; CAPT John O'Brien, USMC.
Assistant Liaison Officers: GYSGT Juan Carrasco, USMC; SGT Megan Cavanaugh, USMC.

GOVERNMENT ACCOUNTABILITY OFFICE

Room 7125, 441 G Street, 20548, phone 512–4400, fax 512–7919 or 512–4641

Managing Director, Congressional Relations.—Ralph Dawn, 512–4544.
Director.—Anne-Marie Lasowski, 512–4146.
Executive Assistant.—Jane Lusby, 512–4378.
Legislative Advisers: Carlos Diz, 512–8256; Rosa Harris, 512–9492; Elizabeth Johnston, 512–6345; Casey Keplinger, 512–9323; Brain Mullins, 512–4384; Elizabeth Sirois, 512–8989; Mary Frances Widner, 512–3804.
Associate Legislative Adviser.—Eden Savino, 512–3613.
Congressional Information Systems Specialist.—Ellen Wedge, 512–6817.
Congressional Correspondence Assistant.—Hazel Baker, 512–5326.
Engagement and Administrative Operations Assistant.—Theodora Guardado-Gallegos, 512–6224.

OFFICE OF PERSONNEL MANAGEMENT

B–332 Rayburn House Office Building, phone 225–4955

Chief.—Charlene E. Luskey.
Senior Civil Service Representative.—Carlos Tingle.
Health Benefits Specialist.—Bob Carr.
Customer Service Specialist.—Doris Daniel.
Administrative Assistant.—Kirk H. Brightman.

SOCIAL SECURITY ADMINISTRATION

G3, L1, Rayburn House Office Building, phone 225–3133, fax 225–3144

Director.—Sharon Wilson.
Congressional Relations Liaisons: LaQuitta Moultrie, Sylvia Taylor-Mackey.

STATE DEPARTMENT LIAISON OFFICE

B–330 Rayburn House Office Building, phone 226–4640, fax 226–4643

Office Director.—Jennifer Schaming-Ronan.
Consular Officer.—Brett Pomainville.
Congressional Relations Specialist.—Janette Brockenborough.

VETERANS' AFFAIRS

B–328 Rayburn House Office Building, phone 225–2280, fax 453–5225

Director.—Patricia J. Covington.
Assistant Director.—Pamela L. Mugg.
Liaison Assistant.—Elaine Waldrop.
Representatives: Tasha Adams, Richard Armstrong, Jr., Gloria Galloway, Stuart A. Weiner.

189 Russell Senate Office Building, phone 224–5351, fax 453–5218

Director.—Patricia J. Covington.
Assistant Director.—Pamela L. Mugg.
Senior Liaison Assistant.—Runako N. Dade.

PAGE SCHOOLS

SENATE

Daniel Webster Senate Page Residence 20510, fax 224–1838

Principal.—Kathryn S. Weeden, 224–3926.
English.—Frances Owens, 228–1024.
Mathematics.—Raymond Cwalina, 228–1018.
Science.—John Malek, 228–1025.
Social Studies.—Michael Bowers, 228–1012.
Secretary.—Kathleen Martin, 224–3927.

HOUSE OF REPRESENTATIVES

LJ–A11 Library of Congress 20540–9996, phone 225–9000, fax 225–9001

Principal/Guidance.—Thomas P. Savannah.
Registrar.—Robin Bridges.
English: Lona Carwile-Klein, John Wilwol.
Languages: Sebastian Hobson, French; Carlton Ashton, Spanish.
Mathematics.—Joshua Dorsey.
Science.—Walter Cuirle.
Social Studies: Dr. Thomas Faith, Dr. Darryl Gonzales.
Technology.—Darryl Gonzalez.
Administrative Assistant.—Robin Bridges.

U.S. CAPITOL POLICE

119 D Street, NE., 20510–7218

Office of the Chief 224–9806, Command Center 224–0908
Communications 224–5151, Emergency 224–0911

U.S. CAPITOL POLICE BOARD

Sergeant at Arms, U.S. Senate.—Terrance W. ''Terry'' Gainer.
Sergeant at Arms, U.S. House of Representatives.—Wilson ''Bill'' Livingood.
Architect of the Capitol.—Stephen T. Ayers (acting), AIA, LEED AP.

OFFICE OF THE CHIEF

Chief of Police.—Phillip D. Morse, Sr.
Executive Officer.—Carol A. Absher.
General Counsel.—Gretchen DeMar.
Deputy Counsel.—James W. Joyce (acting).
Office of:
Directives and Accreditation Division.—Jan E. Jones.
Internal Affairs.—Lt. Kimberly Bolinger.
Public Information.—Sgt. Kimberly A. Schneider.
Chief of Staff.—Richard L. Braddock.

CHIEF OF OPERATIONS

Assistant Chief.—Daniel R. Nichols.
Executive Officer.—Insp. Debra A. Reynolds.

MISSION ASSURANCE BUREAU

Bureau Commander.—Robert Young.
Executive Officer.—Robin Annison.
Command Center: Capt. William Hanny, Insp. Matt K. Perkins, Capt. Jeffery Pickett.
Emergency Management Division.—Director Scott Linsky.
Special Events.—Vacant.

OPERATIONAL SERVICES BUREAU

Bureau Commander.—Insp. Daniel B. Malloy (acting Deputy Chief).
Hazardous Incident Response Division.—Capt. Chad Thomas.
Patrol/Mobile Response Division.—Insp. Lawrence Loughery.

PROTECTIVE SERVICES BUREAU

Bureau Commander.—Deputy Chief Yancey H. Garner.
Investigations Division.—Capt. Eric Waldow.
Dignitary Protection Division.—Insp. Donald Rouiller.

SECURITY SERVICES BUREAU

Bureau Commander.—Robert M. Greeley.
Physical Security Division.—Robert F. Ford.
Technical Countermeasures Division.—Michael Marinucci.
Construction Security Division.—Lt. Mario Bignotti.

UNIFORM SERVICES BUREAU

Bureau Commander.—Deputy Chief Thomas P. Reynolds.
Executive Officer.—Lt. Michael Schmidt.
Capitol Division Commander.—Insp. Sandra D. Coffman.
Senate Division Commander.—Insp. Thomas Loyd.
House Division Commander.—Insp. Fred P. Rogers.
Library Division Commander.—Insp. Allan Morris.

CHIEF ADMINISTRATIVE OFFICER

Chief Administrative Officer.—Gloria Jarmon.
Deputy Chief Administrative Officer.—Vacant.
Director, Office of:
Financial Management.—Steven Haughton.
Human Resources.—Thomas Madigan.
Information Systems.—Norm Farley.
Logistics.—Cathleen English.
Commander, Training Services Bureau.—Deputy Chief Matthew R. Verderosa.

STATISTICAL INFORMATION

VOTES CAST FOR SENATORS IN 2004, 2006, and 2008

[Compiled from official statistics obtained by the Clerk of the House. Figures in the last column, for the 2008 election, may include totals for more candidates than the ones shown.]

State	Vote						Total vote cast in 2008
	2004		2006		2008		
	Republican	Democrat	Democrat	Republican	Democrat	Republican	
Alabama	1,242,200	595,018			752,391	1,305,383	2,060,191
Alaska	149,773	140,424			1,51,767	147,814	317,723
Arizona	1,505,372	404,507	664,141	814,398			
Arkansas	458,036	580,973			804,678		1,011,754
California	4,555,922	6,955,728	5,076,289	2,990,822			
Colorado	980,668	1,081,188			1,230,994	990,755	2,331,621
Connecticut	457,749	945,347	450,844 [1]	109,198			
Delaware			170,567	69,734	257,539	140,595	398,134
Florida	3,672,864	3,590,201	2,890,548	1,826,127			
Georgia	1,864,202	1,287,690			909,923	1,228,033	2,137,956 [2]
Hawaii	87,172	313,629	210,330	126,097			
Idaho	499,796				219,903	371,744	644,780
Illinois	1,390,690	3,597,456			3,615,844	1,520,621	5,329,884
Indiana	903,913	1,496,976		1,171,553			
Iowa	1,038,175	412,365			941,665	560,006	1,502,918
Kansas	780,863	310,337			441,399	727,121	1,210,690
Kentucky	873,507	850,855			847,005	953,816	1,800,821
Louisiana	943,014	877,482			988,298	867,177	1,896,574
Maine			113,131	405,596	279,510	444,300	724,430
Maryland	783,055	1,504,691	965,477	787,182			
Massachusetts			1,500,738	661,532	1,971,974	926,044	3,102,995
Michigan			2,151,278	1,559,597	3,038,386	1,641,070	4,848,620
Minnesota			1,278,849	835,653	1,212,629	1,212,317	2,887,646
Mississippi			213,000	388,399	480,915	1,449,520	2,490,499
Missouri	1,518,089	1,158,261	1,055,255	1,006,941			
Montana			199,845	196,283	348,289	129,369	477,658
Nebraska			378,388	213,928	317,456	455,854	792,511
Nevada	284,640	494,805	238,796	322,501			
New Hampshire	434,847	221,549			358,438	314,403	694,787
New Jersey			58,333	41,998	1,951,218	1,461,025	3,482,445
New Mexico			394,365	163,826	505,128	318,522	823,650
New York	1,625,069	4,384,907	2,698,931	1,212,902			
North Carolina	1,791,450	1,632,527			2,249,311	1,887,510	4,271,970
North Dakota	98,553	212,143	150,146	64,417			
Ohio	3,464,356	1,961,171	2,257,369	1,761,037			
Oklahoma	763,433	596,750			527,736	763,375	1,346,819
Oregon	565,254	1,128,728			864,392	805,159	1,767,504
Pennsylvania	2,925,080	2,334,126	2,392,984	1,684,778			
Rhode Island			206,043	178,950	320,644	116,174	438,812
South Carolina	857,167	704,384			790,621	1,076,534	1,871,431
South Dakota	197,848	193,340			237,889	142,784	380,673
Tennessee			879,976	929,911	767,236	1,579,477	2,424,585
Texas			1,555,202	2,661,789	3,389,365	4,337,469	7,912,075
Utah	626,640	258,955	177,459	356,238			
Vermont	75,398	216,972	[3]	84,924			
Virginia			1,175,606	1,166,277	2,369,327	1,228,830	3,643,294
Washington	1,204,584	1,549,708	1,184,659	832,106			
West Virginia			159,154	47,408	447,560	254,629	702,308
Wisconsin	1,301,183	1,632,697	1,439,214	630,299			
Wyoming			57,671	135,174	126,833	372,109	499,626

[1] Independent Democrat Joseph I. Lieberman was elected on November 7, 2006 with 564,095 votes.

[2] Georgia law requires a majority vote for nomination or election to this office. The recapitulation reflects votes cast in the runoff election held on December 2, 2008.

[3] Independent Bernard Sanders was elected on November 7, 2006 with 171,638 votes.

VOTES CAST FOR REPRESENTATIVES, RESIDENT COMMISSIONER, AND DELEGATES IN 2004, 2006, and 2008

[The figures, compiled from official statistics obtained by the Clerk of the House, show the votes for the Democratic and Republican nominees, except as otherwise indicated. Figures in the last column, for the 2008 election, may include totals for more candidates than the ones shown.]

State and district	Vote cast in 2004		State and district	Vote cast in 2006		State and district	Vote cast in 2008		Total vote cast in 2008
	Repub- lican	Demo- crat		Demo- crat	Repub- lican		Demo- crat	Repub- lican	
AL:			AL:			AL:			
1st	161,067	93,938	1st	52,770	112,944	1st	....	210,660	214,367
2d	70,562	177,086	2d	54,450	124,302	2d	144,368	142,578	287,394
3d	150,411	95,240	3d	63,559	98,257	3d	121,080	142,708	264,120
4th	191,110	64,278	4th	54,382	128,484	4th	66,077	196,741	263,167
5th	74,145	200,999	5th	143,015	....	5th	158,324	147,314	307,282
6th	264,819	....	6th	....	163,514	6th	....	280,902	287,237
7th	61,019	183,408	7th	133,870	....	7th	228,518	....	231,701
AK:			AK:			AK:			
At large	213,216	67,074	At large	93,879	132,743	At large	142,560	158,939	316,978
AZ:			AZ:			AZ:			
1st	148,315	91,776	1st	88,691	105,646	1st	155,791	109,924	278,787
2d	165,260	107,406	2d	89,671	135,150	2d	125,611	200,914	338,023
3d	181,012	....	3d	72,586	112,519	3d	115,759	148,800	275,161
4th	28,238	77,150	4th	56,464	18,627	4th	89,721	26,435	124,427
5th	159,455	102,363	5th	101,838	93,815	5th	149,033	122,165	280,365
6th	202,882	....	6th	....	152,201	6th	115,457	208,582	334,176
7th	59,066	108,868	7th	80,354	46,498	7th	124,304	64,425	196,489
8th	183,363	109,963	8th	137,655	106,790	8th	179,629	140,553	328,266
AR:			AR:			AR:			
1st	81,556	162,388	1st	127,577	56,611	1st	[1]	....	[1]
2d	115,655	160,834	2d	124,871	81,432	2d	212,303	....	277,366
3d	160,629	103,158	3d	75,885	125,039	3d	....	215,196	274,046
4th	....	[1]	4th	128,236	43,360	4th	203,178	....	235,781
CA:			CA:			CA:			
1st	79,970	189,366	1st	144,409	63,194	1st	197,812	67,853	290,472
2d	182,119	90,310	2d	68,234	134,911	2d	118,878	163,459	282,337
3d	177,738	100,025	3d	86,318	135,709	3d	137,971	155,424	314,046
4th	221,926	117,443	4th	126,999	135,818	4th	183,990	185,790	369,780
5th	45,120	138,004	5th	105,676	35,106	5th	164,242	46,002	221,155
6th	85,244	226,423	6th	173,190	64,405	6th	229,672	77,073	320,362
7th	52,446	166,831	7th	118,000	....	7th	170,962	51,166	234,773
8th	31,074	224,017	8th	148,435	19,800	8th	204,996	27,614	285,247
9th	31,278	215,630	9th	167,245	20,786	9th	238,915	26,917	277,600
10th	95,349	182,750	10th	130,859	66,069	10th	192,226	91,877	295,165
11th	163,582	103,587	11th	109,868	96,396	11th	164,500	133,104	297,616
12th	52,593	171,852	12th	138,650	43,674	12th	200,442	49,258	266,853
13th	48,439	144,605	13th	110,756	37,141	13th	166,829	51,447	218,276
14th	69,564	182,712	14th	141,153	48,097	14th	190,301	60,610	272,766
15th	59,953	154,385	15th	115,532	44,186	15th	170,977	55,489	238,589
16th	47,992	129,222	16th	98,929	37,130	16th	146,481	49,399	205,327
17th	65,117	148,958	17th	120,750	35,932	17th	168,907	59,037	228,626
18th	49,973	103,732	18th	71,182	37,531	18th	130,192	....	130,192
19th	155,354	64,047	19th	71,748	110,246	19th	....	179,245	182,101
20th	53,231	61,005	20th	61,120	....	20th	93,023	32,118	125,141
21st	140,721	51,594	21st	42,718	95,214	21st	66,317	143,498	209,815
22d	209,384	....	22d	55,226	133,278	22d	....	224,549	224,549
23d	83,926	153,980	23d	114,661	61,272	23d	171,403	80,385	251,788
24th	178,660	96,397	24th	79,461	129,812	24th	125,560	174,492	300,052
25th	145,575	80,395	25th	55,913	93,987	25th	105,929	144,660	250,589
26th	134,596	107,522	26th	67,878	102,028	26th	108,039	140,615	267,130
27th	66,946	125,296	27th	92,650	42,074	27th	145,812	52,852	212,835
28th	37,868	115,303	28th	79,866	20,629	28th	137,471	....	137,621
29th	62,871	133,670	29th	91,014	39,321	29th	146,198	56,727	212,144
30th	87,465	216,682	30th	151,284	55,904	30th	242,792	....	242,792
31st	22,048	89,363	31st	64,952	....	31st	110,955	....	110,955
32d	....	119,144	32d	76,059	....	32d	130,142	....	130,150
33d	....	166,801	33d	113,715	....	33d	186,924	26,536	213,460
34th	28,175	82,282	34th	57,459	17,359	34th	98,503	29,266	127,769
35th	23,591	125,949	35th	82,498	....	35th	150,778	24,169	182,579
36th	81,666	151,208	36th	105,323	53,068	36th	171,948	78,543	250,491
37th	31,960	118,823	37th	80,716	....	37th	131,342	....	175,252
38th	....	116,851	38th	75,181	24,620	38th	130,211	....	159,324
39th	64,832	100,132	39th	72,149	37,384	39th	125,289	54,533	179,822
40th	147,617	69,684	40th	46,418	100,995	40th	86,772	144,923	231,695
41st	181,605	....	41st	54,235	109,761	41st	99,214	159,486	258,700
42d	167,632	78,393	42d	....	129,720	42d	104,909	158,404	263,313
43d	44,004	86,830	43d	52,791	29,069	43d	108,259	48,312	156,571
44th	138,768	78,796	44th	55,275	89,555	44th	123,890	129,937	253,827
45th	153,523	76,967	45th	64,613	99,638	45th	111,026	155,166	266,192
46th	171,318	90,129	46th	71,573	116,176	46th	122,891	149,818	285,277
47th	43,099	65,684	47th	47,134	28,485	47th	85,878	31,432	123,584
48th	189,004	93,525	48th	74,647	120,130	48th	125,537	171,658	308,702
49th	141,658	79,057	49th	52,227	98,831	49th	90,138	140,300	240,670
50th	169,025	105,590	50th	96,612	118,018	50th	141,635	157,502	313,502
51st	63,526	111,441	51st	78,114	34,931	51st	148,281	49,345	203,825

VOTES CAST FOR REPRESENTATIVES, RESIDENT COMMISSIONER, AND DELEGATES IN 2004, 2006, and 2008—CONTINUED

[The figures, compiled from official statistics obtained by the Clerk of the House, show the votes for the Democratic and Republican nominees, except as otherwise indicated. Figures in the last column, for the 2008 election, may include totals for more candidates than the ones shown.]

State and district	Vote cast in 2004		State and district	Vote cast in 2006		State and district	Vote cast in 2008		Total vote cast in 2008
	Repub- lican	Demo- crat		Demo- crat	Repub- lican		Demo- crat	Repub- lican	
52d	187,799	74,857	52d	61,208	123,696	52d	111,051	160,724	285,138
53d	63,897	146,449	53d	97,541	43,312	53d	161,315	64,658	235,542
CO:			CO:			CO:			
1st	58,659	177,077	1st	129,446	....	1st	203,755	67,345	283,246
2d	94,160	207,900	2d	157,850	65,481	2d	215,571	116,591	344,364
3d	141,376	153,500	3d	146,488	86,930	3d	203,455	126,762	330,217
4th	155,958	136,812	4th	103,748	109,732	4th	187,347	146,028	333,375
5th	193,333	74,098	5th	83,431	123,264	5th	113,025	183,178	305,142
6th	212,778	139,870	6th	108,007	158,806	6th	162,639	250,877	413,516
7th	135,571	106,026	7th	103,918	79,571	7th	173,931	100,055	273,986
CT:			CT:			CT:			
1st	73,601	198,802	1st	154,539	53,010	1st	194,493	76,860	295,557
2d	166,412	140,536	2d	121,248	121,165	2d	198,984	104,574	323,041
3d	69,160	200,638	3d	150,436	44,386	3d	204,761	58,583	297,368
4th	152,493	138,333	4th	99,450	106,510	4th	149,345	146,854	308,776
5th	168,268	107,438	5th	....	94,824	5th	161,178	117,914	302,657
DE:			DE:			DE:			
At large ..	245,978	105,716	At large ..	97,565	143,897	At large ..	146,434	235,437	385,457
FL:			FL:			FL:			
1st	236,604	72,506	1st	62,340	135,786	1st	98,797	232,559	331,356
2d	125,399	201,577	2d	(2)	....	2d	216,804	133,404	350,367
3d	....	172,833	3d	(2)	....	3d	(2)	....	(2)
4th	256,157	....	4th	61,704	141,759	4th	119,330	224,112	343,442
5th	240,315	124,140	5th	108,959	162,421	5th	168,446	265,186	433,632
6th	211,137	116,680	6th	91,528	136,601	6th	146,655	228,302	374,957
7th	(2)	....	7th	87,584	149,656	7th	146,292	238,721	385,013
8th	172,232	112,343	8th	82,526	95,258	8th	172,854	159,490	332,344
9th	284,035	....	9th	96,978	123,016	9th	126,346	216,591	348,378
10th	207,175	91,658	10th	67,950	131,488	10th	118,430	182,781	301,220
11th	....	191,780	11th	97,470	42,454	11th	184,106	72,825	256,931
12th	179,204	96,965	12th	....	124,452	12th	137,465	185,698	323,163
13th	190,477	153,961	13th	118,940	119,309	13th	137,967	204,382	367,996
14th	226,662	108,672	14th	83,920	151,615	14th	93,590	224,602	377,891
15th	210,388	111,538	15th	97,834	125,965	15th	151,951	192,151	361,871
16th	215,563	101,247	16th	115,832	111,415	16th	139,373	209,874	349,247
17th	....	178,690	17th	90,663	....	17th	(2)	....	(2)
18th	143,647	78,281	18th	48,499	79,631	18th	102,372	140,617	242,989
19th	....	(2)	19th	(2)	....	19th	202,465	83,357	306,036
20th	81,213	191,195	20th	(2)	....	20th	202,832	....	261,799
21st	146,507	....	21st	45,522	66,784	21st	99,776	137,226	237,002
22d	192,581	108,258	22d	108,688	100,663	22d	169,041	140,104	309,151
23d	....	(2)	23d	(2)	....	23d	172,835	37,431	210,306
24th	(2)	....	24th	89,863	123,795	24th	211,284	151,863	369,370
25th	(2)	....	25th	43,168	60,765	25th	115,820	130,891	246,711
GA:			GA:			GA:			
1st	188,347	....	1st	43,668	94,961	1st	83,444	165,890	249,334
2d	64,645	129,984	2d	88,662	41,967	2d	158,435	71,351	229,786
3d	80,435	136,273	3d	62,371	130,428	3d	117,522	225,055	342,580
4th	89,509	157,461	4th	106,352	34,778	4th	224,494	....	224,694
5th	....	201,773	5th	122,380	....	5th	231,368	....	231,474
6th	267,542	....	6th	55,294	144,958	6th	106,551	231,520	338,071
7th	258,982	....	7th	53,553	130,561	7th	128,159	209,354	337,513
8th	227,524	73,632	8th	80,660	78,908	8th	157,241	117,446	274,687
9th	197,869	68,462	9th	39,240	128,685	9th	70,537	217,493	288,030
10th	219,136	....	10th	57,032	117,721	10th	114,638	177,265	291,903
11th	120,696	89,591	11th	48,261	118,524	11th	95,220	204,082	299,302
12th	105,132	113,036	12th	71,651	70,787	12th	164,562	84,773	249,335
13th	....	170,657	13th	103,019	45,770	13th	205,919	92,320	298,239
HI:			HI:			HI:			
1st	69,371	128,567	1st	112,904	49,890	1st	154,208	38,115	218,434
2d	79,072	133,317	2d	106,906	68,244	2d	165,748	44,425	237,630
ID:			ID:			ID:			
1st	207,662	90,927	1st	103,935	115,843	1st	175,898	171,687	347,585
2d	193,704	80,133	2d	73,441	132,262	2d	83,878	205,777	290,267
IL:			IL:			IL:			
1st	37,840	212,109	1st	146,623	27,804	1st	233,036	38,361	271,397
2d	....	207,535	2d	146,347	20,395	2d	251,052	29,721	280,776
3d	57,845	167,034	3d	127,768	37,954	3d	172,581	50,336	235,524
4th	15,536	104,761	4th	69,910	11,532	4th	112,529	16,024	139,606
5th	49,530	158,400	5th	114,319	32,250	5th	170,728	50,881	230,892
6th	139,627	110,470	6th	86,572	91,382	6th	109,007	147,906	256,913
7th	35,603	221,133	7th	143,071	21,939	7th	235,343	41,474	276,817
8th	130,601	139,792	8th	93,355	80,720	8th	179,444	116,081	295,525
9th	56,135	175,282	9th	122,852	41,858	9th	181,948	53,593	243,694
10th	177,493	99,218	10th	94,278	107,929	10th	138,176	153,082	291,258
11th	173,057	121,903	11th	88,846	109,009	11th	185,652	109,608	317,895

VOTES CAST FOR REPRESENTATIVES, RESIDENT COMMISSIONER, AND DELEGATES IN 2004, 2006, and 2008—CONTINUED

[The figures, compiled from official statistics obtained by the Clerk of the House, show the votes for the Democratic and Republican nominees, except as otherwise indicated. Figures in the last column, for the 2008 election, may include totals for more candidates than the ones shown.]

State and district	Vote cast in 2004		State and district	Vote cast in 2006		State and district	Vote cast in 2008		Total vote cast in 2008
	Repub-lican	Demo-crat		Demo-crat	Repub-lican		Demo-crat	Repub-lican	
12th	82,677	198,962	12th	157,284	....	12th	212,891	74,382	298,181
13th	200,472	107,836	13th	85,507	119,720	13th	147,430	180,888	337,771
14th	191,618	87,590	14th	79,274	117,870	14th	185,404	135,653	321,057
15th	178,114	113,625	15th	86,025	116,810	15th	104,393	187,121	291,514
16th	204,350	91,452	16th	63,462	125,508	16th	112,648	190,039	312,220
17th	111,680	172,320	17th	115,025	86,161	17th	220,961	....	221,478
18th	216,047	91,548	18th	73,052	150,194	18th	117,642	182,589	310,088
19th	213,451	94,303	19th	92,861	143,491	19th	105,338	203,434	315,589
IN:			IN:			IN:			
1st	82,858	178,406	1st	104,195	40,146	1st	199,954	76,647	282,022
2d	140,496	115,513	2d	103,561	88,300	2d	187,416	84,455	279,346
3d	171,389	76,232	3d	80,357	95,421	3d	112,309	155,693	282,879
4th	190,445	77,574	4th	66,986	111,057	4th	129,038	192,526	321,564
5th	228,718	82,637	5th	64,362	133,118	5th	123,357	234,705	358,062
6th	182,529	85,123	6th	76,812	115,266	6th	94,265	180,608	282,412
7th	97,491	121,303	7th	74,750	64,304	7th	172,650	92,645	265,299
8th	145,576	121,522	8th	131,019	83,704	8th	188,693	102,769	291,462
9th	142,197	140,772	9th	110,454	100,469	9th	181,281	120,529	313,804
IA:			IA:			IA:			
1st	159,993	125,490	1st	114,322	89,729	1st	186,991	102,439	289,430
2d	176,684	117,405	2d	107,683	101,707	2d	175,218	118,778	306,097
3d	136,099	168,007	3d	115,769	103,722	3d	176,904	132,136	313,639
4th	181,294	116,121	4th	90,982	121,650	4th	120,746	185,458	306,204
5th	168,583	97,597	5th	64,181	105,580	5th	99,601	159,430	266,437
KS:			KS:			KS:			
1st	239,776	....	1st	39,781	156,728	1st	34,771	214,549	262,027
2d	165,325	121,532	2d	114,139	106,329	2d	142,013	155,532	307,308
3d	145,542	184,050	3d	153,105	79,824	3d	202,541	142,307	358,858
4th	173,151	81,388	4th	62,166	116,386	4th	90,706	177,617	280,109
KY:			KY:			KY:			
1st	175,972	85,229	1st	83,865	123,618	1st	98,674	178,107	276,786
2d	185,394	87,585	2d	95,415	118,548	2d	143,379	158,936	302,315
3d	197,736	124,040	3d	122,489	116,568	3d	203,843	139,527	343,370
4th	160,982	129,876	4th	88,822	105,845	4th	111,549	190,210	301,759
5th	177,579	....	5th	52,367	147,201	5th	....	177,024	210,468
6th	119,716	175,355	6th	158,765	....	6th	203,764	111,378	315,142
LA:			LA:			LA:			
1st	233,683	54,214	1st	15,944	130,508	1st	98,839	189,168	288,007
2d	46,097	173,510	2d	93,211	13,928	2d	31,318	33,132	66,882
3d	57,042	57,611	3d	79,213	54,950	3d	([3])	....	([3])
4th	([3])	....	4th	40,545	93,727	4th	44,151	44,501	92,572
5th	179,466	58,591	5th	33,233	78,211	5th	....	([3])	([3])
6th	189,106	72,763	6th	....	94,658	6th	125,886	150,332	312,416
7th	75,039	61,493	7th	47,133	113,720	7th	98,280	177,173	286,299
ME:			ME:			ME:			
1st	147,663	219,077	1st	170,949	88,009	1st	205,629	168,930	374,559
2d	135,547	199,303	2d	179,772	75,156	2d	226,274	109,268	335,542
MD:			MD:			MD:			
1st	245,149	77,872	1st	83,738	185,177	1st	177,065	174,213	360,480
2d	75,812	164,751	2d	135,818	60,195	2d	198,578	68,561	276,333
3d	97,008	182,066	3d	150,142	79,174	3d	203,711	87,971	292,448
4th	52,907	196,809	4th	141,897	32,792	4th	258,704	38,739	301,431
5th	87,189	204,867	5th	168,114	....	5th	253,854	82,631	344,691
6th	206,076	90,108	6th	92,030	141,200	6th	128,207	190,926	330,535
7th	60,102	179,189	7th	158,830	....	7th	227,379	53,147	286,020
8th	71,989	215,129	8th	168,872	48,324	8th	229,740	66,351	306,014
MA:			MA:			MA:			
1st	....	229,465	1st	158,057	....	1st	215,696	80,067	309,617
2d	....	217,682	2d	164,939	....	2d	234,369	....	306,820
3d	80,197	192,036	3d	166,973	....	3d	227,619	....	303,315D
4th	....	219,260	4th	176,513	....	4th	203,032	75,571	315,734
5th	88,232	179,652	5th	159,120	....	5th	225,947	....	302,397
6th	91,597	213,458	6th	168,056	72,997	6th	226,216	94,845	338,718
7th	60,334	202,399	7th	171,902	....	7th	212,304	67,978	301,210
8th	....	165,852	8th	125,515	....	8th	185,530	....	244,013
9th	....	218,167	9th	169,420	47,114	9th	242,166	....	317,420
10th	114,879	222,013	10th	171,812	78,439	10th	272,899	....	363,751
MI:			MI:			MI:			
1st	105,706	211,571	1st	180,448	72,753	1st	213,216	107,340	327,836
2d	225,343	94,040	2d	86,950	183,006	2d	119,506	214,100	343,309
3d	214,465	101,395	3d	93,846	171,212	3d	117,961	203,799	333,518
4th	205,274	110,885	4th	100,260	160,041	4th	117,665	204,259	329,764
5th	96,934	208,163	5th	176,171	60,967	5th	221,841	85,017	315,295
6th	197,425	97,978	6th	88,978	142,125	6th	123,257	188,157	319,646
7th	176,053	109,527	7th	112,665	122,348	7th	157,213	149,781	322,286
8th	207,925	125,619	8th	122,107	157,237	8th	145,491	204,408	361,607

VOTES CAST FOR REPRESENTATIVES, RESIDENT COMMISSIONER, AND DELEGATES IN 2004, 2006, and 2008—CONTINUED

[The figures, compiled from official statistics obtained by the Clerk of the House, show the votes for the Democratic and Republican nominees, except as otherwise indicated. Figures in the last column, for the 2008 election, may include totals for more candidates than the ones shown.]

State and district	Vote cast in 2004		State and district	Vote cast in 2006		State and district	Vote cast in 2008		Total vote cast in 2008
	Repub-lican	Demo-crat		Demo-crat	Repub-lican		Demo-crat	Repub-lican	
9th	199,210	134,764	9th	127,620	142,390	9th	183,311	150,035	351,963
10th	227,720	98,029	10th	84,689	179,072	10th	108,354	230,471	347,603
11th	186,431	134,301	11th	114,248	143,658	11th	156,625	177,461	345,182
12th	88,256	210,827	12th	168,494	62,689	12th	225,094	74,565	312,344
13th	40,935	173,246	13th	126,308	....	13th	167,481	43,098	225,922
14th	35,089	213,681	14th	158,755	27,367	14th	227,841	....	246,588
15th	81,828	218,409	15th	181,946	....	15th	231,784	81,802	327,827
MN:			MN:			MN:			
1st	193,132	115,088	1st	141,556	126,486	1st	207,753	109,453	332,400
2d	206,313	147,527	2d	116,343	163,269	2d	164,093	220,924	385,656
3d	231,871	126,665	3d	99,588	184,333	3d	150,787	178,932	369,104
4th	105,467	182,387	4th	172,096	74,797	4th	216,267	98,936	316,018
5th	76,600	218,434	5th	136,060	52,263	5th	228,776	71,020	322,747
6th	203,669	173,309	6th	127,144	151,248	6th	175,786	187,817	404,725
7th	106,349	207,628	7th	179,164	74,557	7th	227,187	87,062	314,680
8th	112,693	228,586	8th	180,670	97,683	8th	241,831	114,871	357,284
MS:			MS:			MS:			
1st	219,328	....	1st	49,174	95,098	1st	185,959	149,818	341,389
2d	107,647	154,626	2d	100,160	55,672	2d	201,606	90,364	291,970
3d	234,874	....	3d	....	125,421	3d	127,698	213,171	340,869
4th	96,740	179,979	4th	110,996	28,117	4th	216,542	73,977	290,519
MO:			MO:			MO:			
1st	64,791	213,658	1st	141,574	47,893	1st	242,570	....	279,277
2d	228,725	115,366	2d	105,242	176,452	2d	132,068	232,276	372,972
3d	125,422	146,894	3d	145,219	70,189	3d	202,470	92,759	305,071
4th	93,334	190,800	4th	159,303	69,254	4th	200,009	103,446	303,455
5th	123,431	161,727	5th	136,149	68,456	5th	197,249	109,166	306,415
6th	196,516	106,987	6th	87,477	150,882	6th	121,894	196,526	330,699
7th	210,080	84,356	7th	72,592	160,942	7th	91,010	219,016	323,212
8th	194,039	71,543	8th	57,557	156,164	8th	72,790	198,798	278,288
9th	193,429	101,343	9th	87,145	149,114	9th	152,956	161,031	322,095
MT:			MT:			MT:			
At large ..	286,076	145,606	At large ..	158,916	239,124	At large ..	155,930	308,470	480,900
NE:			NE:			NE:			
1st	143,756	113,971	1st	86,360	121,015	1st	77,897	184,923	262,820
2d	152,608	90,292	2d	82,504	99,475	2d	131,901	142,473	274,374
3d	218,751	26,434	3d	93,046	113,687	3d	55,087	183,117	238,204
NV:			NV:			NV:			
1st	63,005	133,569	1st	85,025	40,917	1st	154,860	64,837	228,922
2d	195,466	79,978	2d	104,593	117,168	2d	136,548	170,771	329,520
3d	162,240	120,365	3d	98,261	102,232	3d	165,912	147,940	349,812
NH:			NH:			NH:			
1st	204,836	118,226	1st	100,691	95,527	1st	176,435	156,338	340,873
2d	191,188	125,280	2d	108,743	94,088	2d	188,332	138,222	333,675
NJ:			NJ:			NJ:			
1st	66,109	201,163	1st	140,110	....	1st	206,453	74,001	285,157
2d	172,779	86,792	2d	64,277	111,245	2d	110,990	167,701	283,965
3d	195,938	107,034	3d	86,113	122,559	3d	166,390	153,122	319,512
4th	192,671	92,826	4th	62,905	124,482	4th	100,036	202,972	306,551
5th	171,220	122,259	5th	89,503	112,142	5th	131,033	172,653	309,007
6th	70,942	153,981	6th	98,615	43,539	6th	164,077	77,469	245,077
7th	162,597	119,081	7th	95,454	98,399	7th	124,818	148,461	295,628
8th	62,747	152,001	8th	97,568	39,053	8th	159,279	63,107	223,986
9th	68,564	146,038	9th	105,853	40,879	9th	151,182	69,503	223,885
10th	....	155,697	10th	90,264	....	10th	169,945	....	171,793
11th	200,915	91,811	11th	74,414	126,085	11th	113,510	189,696	306,732
12th	115,014	171,691	12th	125,468	65,509	12th	193,732	108,400	306,934
13th	35,288	121,018	13th	77,238	19,284	13th	120,382	34,735	159,753
NM:			NM:			NM:			
1st	147,372	123,339	1st	105,125	105,986	1st	166,271	132,485	298,756
2d	130,498	86,292	2d	63,119	92,620	2d	129,572	101,980	231,552
3d	79,935	175,269	3d	144,880	49,219	3d	161,292	86,618	284,258
NY:			NY:			NY:			
1st	110,786	140,878	1st	92,546	54,044	1st	141,727	100,036	325,670
2d	72,953	147,197	2d	94,100	37,671	2d	143,759	70,145	295,105
3d	151,323	100,737	3d	76,169	86,918	3d	93,481	149,344	320,337
4th	85,505	148,615	4th	93,041	48,121	4th	151,792	84,444	298,708
5th	43,002	114,132	5th	70,033	....	5th	105,836	43,039	205,768
6th	....	125,127	6th	69,405	....	6th	141,180	....	210,336
7th	21,843	100,382	7th	60,266	10,402	7th	113,988	19,373	189,071
8th	35,177	154,098	8th	96,115	17,413	8th	152,153	36,897	253,235
9th	39,648	108,577	9th	67,040	....	9th	106,097	....	203,070
10th	11,099	130,265	10th	72,171	4,666	10th	155,090	8,204	228,761
11th	....	134,175	11th	75,520	6,776	11th	158,235	11,644	230,988
12th	15,697	100,402	12th	55,674	6,143	12th	115,633	12,486	181,916
13th	102,713	72,180	13th	42,229	49,818	13th	107,640	62,441	224,764

VOTES CAST FOR REPRESENTATIVES, RESIDENT COMMISSIONER, AND DELEGATES IN 2004, 2006, and 2008—CONTINUED

[The figures, compiled from official statistics obtained by the Clerk of the House, show the votes for the Democratic and Republican nominees, except as otherwise indicated. Figures in the last column, for the 2008 election, may include totals for more candidates than the ones shown.]

State and district	Vote cast in 2004		State and district	Vote cast in 2006		State and district	Vote cast in 2008		Total vote cast in 2008
	Repub-lican	Demo-crat		Demo-crat	Repub-lican		Demo-crat	Repub-lican	
14th	41,936	175,886	14th	107,095	....	14th	176,426	43,385	274,592
15th	12,355	153,099	15th	93,857	6,592	15th	170,372	15,676	245,159
16th	4,917	106,739	16th	53,179	2,045	16th	123,312	3,941	169,499
17th	40,524	135,344	17th	88,714	22,608	17th	149,676	35,994	243,765
18th	73,975	159,072	18th	119,041	45,472	18th	167,365	73,237	302,028
19th	152,051	87,429	19th	100,119	79,545	19th	141,173	103,813	320,510
20th	163,343	96,630	20th	116,416	94,093	20th	178,996	99,930	334,716
21st	80,121	167,247	21st	139,997	46,752	21st	159,849	85,267	311,931
22d	81,881	148,588	22d	104,423	....	22d	147,238	76,569	290,102
23d	136,222	66,448	23d	58,859	89,482	23d	70,037	120,778	261,238
24th	128,493	85,140	24th	96,093	83,228	24th	121,345	103,379	282,114
25th	155,163	....	25th	100,605	[4]91,187	25th	148,290	106,653	322,180
26th	137,425	116,484	26th	85,145	94,157	26th	109,615	124,845	323,251
27th	125,275	127,267	27th	116,935	36,614	27th	169,196	50,420	293,504
28th	48,981	150,431	28th	98,382	33,361	28th	155,409	42,016	271,887
29th	136,883	104,555	29th	94,609	[4]91,383	29th	131,526	116,137	307,298
NC:			NC:			NC:			
1st	77,508	137,667	1st	82,510	....	1st	192,765	81,506	274,271
2d	87,811	145,079	2d	85,993	43,271	2d	199,730	93,323	298,430
3d	171,863	71,227	3d	45,458	99,519	3d	104,364	201,686	306,050
4th	121,717	217,441	4th	127,340	68,599	4th	265,751	153,947	419,698
5th	167,546	117,271	5th	72,061	96,138	5th	136,103	190,820	326,923
6th	207,470	76,153	6th	44,661	108,433	6th	108,873	221,018	329,891
7th	66,084	180,382	7th	101,787	38,033	7th	215,383	97,472	312,855
8th	125,070	100,101	8th	60,597	60,926	8th	157,185	126,634	283,819
9th	210,783	89,318	9th	53,437	106,206	9th	138,719	241,053	386,483
10th	157,884	88,233	10th	58,214	94,179	10th	126,699	171,774	298,473
11th	159,709	131,188	11th	124,972	107,342	11th	211,112	122,087	340,716
12th	76,898	154,908	12th	71,345	35,127	12th	215,908	85,814	301,722
13th	112,788	160,896	13th	98,540	56,120	13th	221,379	114,383	335,762
ND:			ND:			ND:			
At large	125,684	185,130	At large	142,934	74,687	At large	194,577	119,388	313,965
OH:			OH:			OH:			
1st	173,430	116,235	1st	96,584	105,680	1st	155,455	140,683	296,290
2d	227,102	89,598	2d	117,595	120,112	2d	124,213	148,671	331,624
3d	197,290	119,448	3d	90,650	127,978	3d	115,976	200,204	316,180
4th	167,807	118,538	4th	86,678	129,958	4th	99,499	186,154	285,653
5th	196,649	96,656	5th	98,544	129,813	5th	105,840	188,905	294,745
6th	....	223,842	6th	135,628	82,848	6th	176,330	92,968	283,110
7th	186,534	100,617	7th	89,579	137,899	7th	125,547	174,915	300,462
8th	201,675	90,574	8th	77,640	136,863	8th	95,510	202,063	297,573
9th	95,983	205,149	9th	153,880	55,119	9th	222,054	76,512	298,566
10th	96,463	172,406	10th	138,393	69,996	10th	157,268	107,918	275,809
11th	....	222,371	11th	146,799	29,125	11th	212,667	36,708	249,542
12th	198,912	122,109	12th	108,746	145,943	12th	152,234	197,447	360,388
13th	97,090	201,004	13th	135,639	85,922	13th	192,593	105,050	297,680
14th	201,652	119,714	14th	97,753	144,069	14th	125,214	188,488	323,213
15th	166,520	110,915	15th	109,659	110,714	15th	139,584	137,272	303,838
16th	202,544	101,817	16th	97,955	137,167	16th	169,044	136,293	305,337
17th	62,871	212,800	17th	170,369	41,925	17th	218,896	61,216	280,112
18th	177,600	90,820	18th	129,646	79,259	18th	164,187	110,031	274,218
OK:			OK:			OK:			
1st	187,145	116,731	1st	56,724	116,920	1st	98,890	193,404	292,294
2d	92,963	179,579	2d	122,347	45,861	2d	173,757	72,815	246,572
3d	215,510	....	3d	61,749	128,042	3d	62,297	184,306	264,359
4th	198,985	....	4th	64,775	118,266	4th	79,674	180,080	272,781
5th	180,430	92,719	5th	67,293	108,936	5th	88,996	171,925	260,921
OR:			OR:			OR:			
1st	135,164	203,771	1st	169,409	90,904	1st	237,567	....	332,248
2d	248,461	88,914	2d	82,484	181,529	2d	87,649	236,560	340,379
3d	82,045	245,559	3d	186,380	59,529	3d	254,235	71,063	341,062
4th	140,882	228,611	4th	180,607	109,105	4th	275,143	....	334,146
5th	154,993	184,833	5th	146,973	116,424	5th	181,577	128,297	334,674
PA:			PA:			PA:			
1st	33,266	214,462	1st	137,987	....	1st	242,799	24,714	267,513
2d	34,411	253,226	2d	165,867	17,291	2d	276,870	34,466	311,336
3d	166,580	110,684	3d	85,110	108,525	3d	146,846	139,707	286,553
4th	204,329	116,303	4th	131,847	122,049	4th	186,536	147,411	333,947
5th	192,852	....	5th	76,456	115,126	5th	112,509	155,513	274,177
6th	160,348	153,977	6th	117,892	121,047	6th	164,952	179,423	344,375
7th	196,556	134,932	7th	147,898	114,426	7th	209,955	142,362	352,317
8th	183,229	143,427	8th	125,656	124,138	8th	197,869	145,103	348,515
9th	184,320	80,787	9th	79,610	121,069	9th	98,735	174,951	273,686
10th	191,967	....	10th	110,115	97,862	10th	160,837	124,681	285,518
11th	....	171,147	11th	134,340	51,033	11th	146,379	137,151	283,530

VOTES CAST FOR REPRESENTATIVES, RESIDENT COMMISSIONER, AND DELEGATES IN 2004, 2006, and 2008—CONTINUED

[The figures, compiled from official statistics obtained by the Clerk of the House, show the votes for the Democratic and Republican nominees, except as otherwise indicated. Figures in the last column, for the 2008 election, may include totals for more candidates than the ones shown.]

State and district	Vote cast in 2004		State and district	Vote cast in 2006		State and district	Vote cast in 2008		Total vote cast in 2008
	Republican	Democrat		Democrat	Republican		Democrat	Republican	
12th	....	204,504	12th	123,472	79,612	12th	155,268	113,120	268,388
13th	127,205	171,763	13th	147,368	75,492	13th	196,868	108,271	313,513
14th	....	220,139	14th	161,075	....	14th	242,326	....	265,540
15th	170,634	114,646	15th	86,186	106,153	15th	128,333	181,433	309,766
16th	183,620	98,410	16th	80,915	115,741	16th	120,193	170,329	305,167
17th	113,592	172,412	17th	137,253	75,455	17th	192,699	109,909	302,608
18th	197,894	117,420	18th	105,419	144,632	18th	119,661	213,349	333,010
19th	224,274	....	19th	74,625	142,512	19th	109,533	218,862	328,395
RI:			RI:			RI:			
1st	69,819	124,923	1st	124,634	41,836	1st	145,254	51,340	211,998
2d	43,139	154,392	2d	140,315	....	2d	158,416	67,433	226,234
SC:			SC:			SC:			
1st	186,448	....	1st	....	115,766	1st	163,724	177,540	341,879
2d	181,862	93,249	2d	76,090	127,811	2d	158,627	184,583	343,486
3d	191,052	....	3d	....	111,882	3d	101,724	186,799	288,741
4th	188,795	78,376	4th	57,490	115,553	4th	113,291	184,440	306,928
5th	89,568	152,867	5th	99,669	75,422	5th	188,785	113,282	306,285
6th	75,443	161,987	6th	100,213	53,181	6th	193,378	93,059	286,571
SD:			SD:			SD:			
At large	178,823	207,837	At large	230,468	97,864	At large	256,041	122,966	379,007
TN:			TN:			TN:			
1st	172,543	56,361	1st	65,538	108,336	1st	57,525	168,343	234,381
2d	215,795	52,155	2d	45,025	157,095	2d	63,639	227,120	290,759
3d	166,154	84,295	3d	68,324	130,791	3d	73,059	184,964	266,628
4th	109,993	138,459	4th	123,666	62,449	4th	146,776	94,447	249,805
5th	74,978	168,970	5th	122,919	49,702	5th	181,467	85,471	275,602
6th	87,523	167,448	6th	129,069	60,392	6th	194,264	....	261,028
7th	232,404	....	7th	73,369	152,288	7th	99,549	217,332	316,881
8th	59,853	173,623	8th	129,610	47,492	8th	180,465	....	180,519
9th	41,578	190,648	9th	103,341	31,002	9th	198,798	....	226,282
TX:			TX:			TX:			
1st	157,068	96,281	1st	46,303	104,099	1st	....	189,012	215,826
2d	139,951	108,156	2d	45,080	90,490	2d	....	175,101	196,914
3d	180,099	....	3d	49,529	88,690	3d	108,693	170,742	285,783
4th	182,866	81,585	4th	55,278	106,495	4th	88,067	206,906	300,744
5th	148,816	75,911	5th	50,983	88,478	5th	....	162,894	194,861
6th	168,767	83,609	6th	56,369	91,927	6th	99,919	174,008	280,582
7th	175,440	91,126	7th	64,514	99,318	7th	123,242	162,635	290,934
8th	179,599	77,324	8th	51,393	105,665	8th	70,758	207,128	285,451
9th	42,132	114,462	9th	60,253	....	9th	143,868	....	153,628
10th	182,113	....	10th	71,415	97,726	10th	143,719	179,493	333,083
11th	177,291	50,339	11th	....	107,268	11th	....	189,625	214,676
12th	173,222	66,316	12th	45,676	98,371	12th	82,250	181,662	268,754
13th	189,448	....	13th	33,460	10,107	13th	51,841	180,078	231,919
14th	173,668	....	14th	62,429	94,380	14th	....	191,293	191,293
15th	67,917	96,089	15th	43,236	26,751	15th	107,578	52,303	163,708
16th	49,972	108,577	16th	61,116	....	16th	130,375	16,348	158,723
17th	116,049	125,309	17th	92,478	64,142	17th	134,592	115,581	254,022
18th	....	136,018	18th	65,936	16,448	18th	148,617	39,095	192,198
19th	136,459	93,531	19th	41,676	94,785	19th	58,030	168,501	232,611
20th	54,976	112,480	20th	68,348	....	20th	127,298	44,585	177,055
21st	209,774	121,129	21st	68,312	122,486	21st	....	243,471	304,350
22d	150,386	112,034	22d	76,775	....	22d	140,160	161,996	308,995
23d	170,716	72,480	23d	38,256	32,217	23d	134,090	100,799	240,470
24th	154,435	82,599	24th	52,075	83,835	24th	111,089	151,434	270,495
25th	49,252	108,309	25th	109,911	42,975	25th	191,755	88,693	291,296
26th	180,519	89,809	26th	58,271	94,219	26th	118,167	195,181	324,376
27th	61,955	112,081	27th	62,058	42,538	27th	104,864	69,458	180,951
28th	69,538	106,323	28th	68,372	....	28th	123,494	52,524	179,740
29th	....	78,256	29th	37,174	12,347	29th	79,718	25,512	106,794
30th	....	144,513	30th	81,348	17,850	30th	168,249	32,361	203,976
31st	160,247	80,292	31st	60,293	90,869	31st	106,559	175,563	291,304
32d	109,859	89,030	32d	52,269	71,461	32d	82,406	116,283	203,110
UT:			UT:			UT:			
1st	199,615	85,630	1st	57,922	112,546	1st	92,469	196,799	303,445
2d	147,778	187,250	2d	133,231	84,234	2d	220,666	120,083	348,325
3d	173,010	88,748	3d	53,330	95,455	3d	80,626	187,035	285,069
VT:			VT:			VT:			
At large	[5] 74,271	21,684	At large	139,815	117,023	At large	248,203	....	298,151
VA:			VA:			VA:			
1st	225,071	....	1st	81,083	143,889	1st	150,432	203,839	360,292
2d	132,946	108,180	2d	83,901	88,777	2d	141,857	128,486	270,711
3d	70,194	159,373	3d	133,546	....	3d	239,911	....	247,288
4th	182,444	100,413	4th	....	150,967	4th	135,041	199,075	334,521
5th	172,431	98,237	5th	84,682	125,370	5th	158,810	158,083	317,076
6th	206,560	....	6th	....	153,187	6th	114,367	192,350	312,392

VOTES CAST FOR REPRESENTATIVES, RESIDENT COMMISSIONER, AND DELEGATES IN 2004, 2006, and 2008—CONTINUED

[The figures, compiled from official statistics obtained by the Clerk of the House, show the votes for the Democratic and Republican nominees, except as otherwise indicated. Figures in the last column, for the 2008 election, may include totals for more candidates than the ones shown.]

State and district	Vote cast in 2004		State and district	Vote cast in 2006		State and district	Vote cast in 2008		Total vote cast in 2008
	Republican	Democrat		Democrat	Republican		Democrat	Republican	
7th	230,765	....	7th	88,206	163,706	7th	138,123	233,531	372,337
8th	106,231	171,986	8th	144,700	66,639	8th	222,986	97,425	328,197
9th	98,499	150,039	9th	129,705	61,574	9th	207,306	....	213,570
10th	205,982	116,654	10th	98,769	138,213	10th	147,357	223,140	379,480
11th	186,299	118,305	11th	102,511	130,468	11th	196,598	154,758	359,491
WA:			WA:			WA:			
1st	117,850	204,121	1st	163,832	78,105	1st	233,780	111,240	345,020
2d	106,333	202,383	2d	157,064	87,730	2d	217,416	131,051	348,467
3d	119,027	193,626	3d	147,065	85,915	3d	216,701	121,828	338,529
4th	154,627	92,486	4th	77,054	115,246	4th	99,430	169,940	269,370
5th	179,600	121,333	5th	104,357	134,967	5th	112,382	211,305	323,687
6th	91,228	202,919	6th	158,202	65,883	6th	205,991	102,081	308,072
7th	65,226	272,302	7th	195,462	38,715	7th	291,963	57,054	349,017
8th	173,298	157,148	8th	122,021	129,362	8th	171,358	191,568	362,926
9th	88,304	162,433	9th	119,038	62,082	9th	176,295	93,080	269,375
WV:			WV:			WV:			
1st	79,196	166,583	1st	100,939	55,963	1st	187,734	....	187,864
2d	147,676	106,131	2d	70,470	94,110	2d	110,819	147,334	258,169
3d	76,170	142,682	3d	92,413	40,820	3d	133,522	66,005	199,527
WI:			WI:			WI:			
1st	233,372	116,250	1st	95,761	161,320	1st	125,268	231,009	361,107
2d	145,810	251,637	2d	191,414	113,015	2d	277,914	122,513	400,841
3d	157,866	204,856	3d	163,322	88,523	3d	225,208	122,760	356,400
4th	85,928	212,382	4th	136,735	54,486	4th	222,728	....	254,179
5th	271,153	129,384	5th	112,451	194,669	5th	....	275,271	345,899
6th	238,620	107,209	6th	....	201,367	6th	126,090	221,875	348,264
7th	....	241,306	7th	161,903	91,069	7th	212,666	136,938	349,837
8th	248,070	105,513	8th	141,570	135,622	8th	193,662	164,621	358,647
WY:			WY:			WY:			
At large	132,107	99,989	At large	92,324	93,336	At large	106,758	131,244	249,575

[Table continues on next page]

VOTES CAST FOR REPRESENTATIVES, RESIDENT COMMISSIONER, AND DELEGATES IN 2004, 2006, and 2008—CONTINUED

[The figures, compiled from official statistics obtained by the Clerk of the House, show the votes for the Democratic and Republican nominees, except as otherwise indicated. Figures in the last column, for the 2008 election, may include totals for more candidates than the ones shown.]

Commonwealth of Puerto Rico	Vote						Total vote cast in 2008
	2004		2006		2008		
	New Progressive	Popular Democrat	Popular Democrat	New Progressive	Popular Democrat	New Progressive	
Resident Commissioner (4-year term)	956,828	945,691	....	....	810,093	1,010,285	1,904,366

District of Columbia	Vote						Total vote cast in 2008
	2004		2006		2008		
	Republican	Democrat	Democrat	Republican	Democrat	Republican	
Delegate	18,296	202,027	111,726	....	245,800	17,367	265,853

Guam	Vote						Total vote cast in 2008
	2004		2006		2008		
	Republican	Democrat	Democrat	Republican	Democrat	Write-in	
Delegate	....	31,051	32,677	....	28,247	1,617	29,864

Virgin Islands	Vote						Total vote cast in 2008
	2004		2006		2008		
	Independent	Democrat	Democrat	Republican	Democrat	Write-in	
Delegate	1,512	17,379	19,593	4,447	19,286	69	19,355

American Samoa	Vote						Total vote cast in 2008
	2004		2006		2008		
	Republican	Democrat	Democrat	Republican	Democrat	Republican	
Delegate	5,472	6,656	5,195	4,493	7,499	4,350	12,419

Northern Mariana Islands	Vote		Total vote cast in 2008
	2008		
	Independent	Republican	
Delegate	2,474	2,117	10,161

[1] According to Arkansas law, it is not required to tabulate votes for unopposed candidates.
[2] Under Florida law, the names of those with no opposition are not printed on the ballot.
[3] Under Louisiana law, the names of those with no opposition are not printed on the ballot.
[4] Numbers do not include votes cast for Republican candidate as nominee of other political parties.
[5] The Independent candidate was elected with 186,540 votes.

SESSIONS OF CONGRESS, 1st–111th CONGRESSES, 1789–2009

[Closing date for this table was September 29, 2009.]

MEETING DATES OF CONGRESS: Pursuant to a resolution of the Confederation Congress in 1788, the Constitution went into effect on March 4, 1789. From then until the 20th amendment took effect in January 1934, the term of each Congress began on March 4th of each odd-numbered year; however, Article I, section 4, of the Constitution provided that ''The Congress shall assemble at least once in every Year, and such Meeting shall be on the first Monday in December, unless they shall by law appoint a different day.'' The Congress therefore convened regularly on the first Monday in December until the 20th amendment became effective, which changed the beginning of Congress's term as well as its convening date to January 3rd. So prior to 1934, a new Congress typically would not convene for regular business until 13 months after being elected. One effect of this was that the last session of each Congress was a ''lame duck'' session. After the 20th amendment, the time from the election to the beginning of Congress's term as well as when it convened was reduced to two months. Recognizing that the need might exist for Congress to meet at times other than the regularly scheduled convening date, Article II, section 3 of the Constitution provides that the President ''may, on extraordinary occasions, convene both Houses, or either of them''; hence these sessions occur only if convened by Presidential proclamation. Except as noted, these are separately numbered sessions of a Congress, and are marked by an E in the session column of the table. Until the 20th amendment was adopted, there were also times when special sessions of the Senate were convened, principally for confirming Cabinet and other executive nominations, and occasionally for the ratification of treaties or other executive business. These Senate sessions were also called by Presidential proclamation (typically by the outgoing President, although on occasion by incumbents as well) and are marked by an S in the session column. MEETING PLACES OF CONGRESS: Congress met for the first and second sessions of the First Congress (1789 and 1790) in New York City. From the third session of the First Congress through the first session of the Sixth Congress (1790 to 1800), Philadelphia was the meeting place. Congress has convened in Washington since the second session of the Sixth Congress (1800).

Congress	Session	Convening Date	Adjournment Date	Length in days [1]	Recesses [2]		President pro tempore of the Senate [3]	Speaker of the House of Representatives
					Senate	House of Representatives		
1st	1	Mar. 4, 1789	Sept. 29, 1789	210			John Langdon, of New Hampshire	Frederick A.C. Muhlenberg, of Pennsylvania.
	2	Jan. 4, 1790	Aug. 12, 1790	221			......do.	
	3	Dec. 6, 1790	Mar. 3, 1791	88			......do.	
2d	S	Mar. 4, 1791	Mar. 4, 1791	1			......do.	
	1	Oct. 24, 1791	May 8, 1792	197			Richard Henry Lee, of Virginia	Jonathan Trumbull, of Connecticut.
	2	Nov. 5, 1792	Mar. 2, 1793	119			John Langdon, of New Hampshire.	
3d	S	Mar. 4, 1793	Mar. 4, 1793	1			......do.	
	1	Dec. 2, 1793	June 9, 1794	190			John Langdon, of New Hampshire; Ralph Izard, of South Carolina.	Frederick A.C. Muhlenberg, of Pennsylvania.
	2	Nov. 3, 1794	Mar. 3, 1795	121			Henry Tazewell, of Virginia.	
4th	S	June 8, 1795	June 26, 1795	19			......do.	
	1	Dec. 7, 1795	June 1, 1796	177			Henry Tazewell, of Virginia; Samuel Livermore, of New Hampshire.	Jonathan Dayton, of New Jersey.
	2	Dec. 5, 1796	Mar. 3, 1797	89			William Bingham, of Pennsylvania.	
5th	S	Mar. 4, 1797	Mar. 4, 1797	1				
	1–E	May 15, 1797	July 10, 1797	57			William Bradford, of Rhode Island	Do.
	S	July 17, 1798	July 19, 1798	3				
	2	Nov. 13, 1797	July 16, 1798	246			Jacob Read, of South Carolina; Theodore Sedgwick, of Massachusetts.	
	3	Dec. 3, 1798	Mar. 3, 1799	91			John Laurance, of New York; James Ross, of Pennsylvania.	
6th	1	Dec. 2, 1799	May 14, 1800	164			Samuel Livermore, of New Hampshire; Uriah Tracy, of Connecticut.	Theodore Sedgwick, of Massachusetts.
	2	Nov. 17, 1800	Mar. 3, 1801	107	Dec. 23–Dec. 30, 1800	Dec. 23–Dec. 30, 1800	John E. Howard, of Maryland; James Hillhouse, of Connecticut.	
7th	S	Mar. 4, 1801	Mar. 5, 1801	2				
	1	Dec. 7, 1801	May 3, 1802	148			Abraham Baldwin, of Georgia	Nathaniel Macon, of North Carolina.

	2	Dec. 6, 1802	Mar. 3, 1803	88			Stephen R. Bradley, of Vermont.	
8th	1–E	Oct. 17, 1803	Mar. 27, 1804	163			John Brown, of Kentucky; Jesse Franklin, of North Carolina.	Do.
	2	Nov. 5, 1804	Mar. 3, 1805	119			Joseph Anderson, of Tennessee.	
9th	1	Dec. 2, 1805	Apr. 21, 1806	141			Samuel Smith, of Maryland	Do.
	2	Dec. 1, 1806	Mar. 3, 1807	93			do.	
10th	1–E	Oct. 26, 1807	Apr. 25, 1808	182			do	Joseph B. Varnum, of Massachusetts.
	2	Nov. 7, 1808	Mar. 3, 1809	117			Stephen R. Bradley, of Vermont; John Milledge, of Georgia.	
11th	S	Mar. 4, 1809	Mar. 7, 1809	4				
	1	May 22, 1809	June 28, 1809	38			Andrew Gregg, of Pennsylvania	Do.
	2	Nov. 27, 1809	May 1, 1810	156			John Gaillard, of South Carolina.	
	3	Dec. 3, 1810	Mar. 3, 1811	91			John Pope, of Kentucky.	
12th	1–E	Nov. 4, 1811	July 6, 1812	245			William H. Crawford, of Georgia	Henry Clay, of Kentucky.
	2	Nov. 2, 1812	Mar. 3, 1813	122			do.	
13th	1	May 24, 1813	Aug. 2, 1813	71			do	Do.[4]
	2	Dec. 6, 1813	Apr. 18, 1814	134			Joseph B. Varnum, of Massachusetts; John Gaillard, of South Carolina.	Langdon Cheves, of South Carolina.[4]
	3–E	Sept. 19, 1814	Mar. 3, 1815	166			John Gaillard, of South Carolina.	
14th	1	Dec. 4, 1815	Apr. 30, 1816	148			do	Henry Clay, of Kentucky.
	2	Dec. 2, 1816	Mar. 3, 1817	92			do.	
15th	S	Mar. 4, 1817	Mar. 6, 1817	3			do.	
	1	Dec. 1, 1817	Apr. 20, 1818	141	Dec. 24–Dec. 29, 1817	Dec. 24–Dec. 29, 1817	do	Do.
	2	Nov. 16, 1818	Mar. 3, 1819	108			James Barbour, of Virginia.	
16th	1	Dec. 6, 1819	May 15, 1820	162			James Barbour, of Virginia; John Gaillard, of South Carolina.	Do.[5]
	2	Nov. 13, 1820	Mar. 3, 1821	111			John Gaillard, of South Carolina	John W. Taylor, of New York.[5]
17th	1	Dec. 3, 1821	May 8, 1822	157			do	Philip P. Barbour, of Virginia.
	2	Dec. 2, 1822	Mar. 3, 1823	92			do.	
18th	1	Dec. 1, 1823	May 27, 1824	178			do	Henry Clay, of Kentucky.
	2	Dec. 6, 1824	Mar. 3, 1825	88			do.	
19th	S	Mar. 4, 1825	Mar, 9, 1825	6			do.	
	1	Dec. 5, 1825	May 22, 1826	169			Nathaniel Macon, of North Carolina	John W. Taylor, of New York.
	2	Dec. 4, 1826	Mar. 3, 1827	90			do.	
20th	1	Dec. 3, 1827	May 26, 1828	175			Samuel Smith, of Maryland	Andrew Stevenson, of Virginia.
	2	Dec. 1, 1828	Mar. 3, 1829	93	Dec. 24–Dec. 29, 1828	Dec. 24–Dec. 29, 1828	do.	
21st	S	Mar. 4, 1829	Mar. 17, 1829	14			do.	
	1	Dec. 7, 1829	May 31, 1830	176			do	Do.
	2	Dec. 6, 1830	Mar. 3, 1831	88			do.	
22d	1	Dec. 5, 1831	July 16, 1832	225			Littleton Waller Tazewell, of Virginia	Do.
	2	Dec. 3, 1832	Mar. 2, 1833	91			Hugh Lawson White, of Tennessee.	
23d	1	Dec. 2, 1833	June 30, 1834	211			Hugh Lawson White, of Tennessee; George Poindexter, of Mississippi.	Do.[6]
	2	Dec. 1, 1834	Mar. 3, 1835	93			John Tyler, of Virginia	John Bell, of Tennessee.[6]
24th	1	Dec. 7, 1835	July 4, 1836	211			William R. King, of Alabama	James K. Polk, of Tennessee.
	2	Dec. 5, 1836	Mar. 3, 1837	89			do.	
25th	S	Mar. 4, 1837	Mar. 10, 1837	7			do.	
	1–E	Sept. 4, 1837	Oct. 16, 1837	43			do	Do.
	2	Dec. 4, 1837	July 9, 1838	218			do.	
	3	Dec. 3, 1838	Mar. 3, 1839	91			do.	
26th	1	Dec. 2, 1839	July 21, 1840	233			do	Robert M.T. Hunter, of Virginia.
	2	Dec. 7, 1840	Mar. 3, 1841	87			do.	
27th	S	Mar. 4, 1841	Mar. 15, 1841	12			William R. King, of Alabama; Samuel L. Southard, of New Jersey.	

SESSIONS OF CONGRESS, 1st–111th CONGRESSES, 1789–2009—CONTINUED

[Closing date for this table was September 29, 2009.]

MEETING DATES OF CONGRESS: Pursuant to a resolution of the Confederation Congress in 1788, the Constitution went into effect on March 4, 1789. From then until the 20th amendment took effect in January 1934, the term of each Congress began on March 4th of each odd-numbered year; however, Article I, section 4, of the Constitution provided that ''The Congress shall assemble at least once in every Year, and such Meeting shall be on the first Monday in December, unless they shall by law appoint a different day.'' The Congress therefore convened regularly on the first Monday in December until the 20th amendment became effective, which changed the beginning of Congress's term as well as its convening date to January 3rd. So prior to 1934, a new Congress typically would not convene for regular business until 13 months after being elected. One effect of this was that the last session of each Congress was a ''lame duck'' session. After the 20th amendment, the time from the election to the beginning of Congress's term as well as when it convened was reduced to two months. Recognizing that the need might exist for Congress to meet at times other than the regularly scheduled convening date, Article II, section 3 of the Constitution provides that the President ''may, on extraordinary occasions, convene both Houses, or either of them''; hence these sessions occur only if convened by Presidential proclamation. Except as noted, these are separately numbered sessions of a Congress, and are marked by an E in the session column of the table. Until the 20th amendment was adopted, there were also times when special sessions of the Senate were convened, principally for confirming Cabinet and other executive nominations, and occasionally for the ratification of treaties or other executive business. These Senate sessions were also called by Presidential proclamation (typically by the outgoing President, although on occasion by incumbents as well) and are marked by an S in the session column. MEETING PLACES OF CONGRESS: Congress met for the first and second sessions of the First Congress (1789 and 1790) in New York City. From the third session of the First Congress through the first session of the Sixth Congress (1790 to 1800), Philadelphia was the meeting place. Congress has convened in Washington since the second session of the Sixth Congress (1800).

Congress	Session	Convening Date	Adjournment Date	Length in days [1]	Recesses [2]		President pro tempore of the Senate [3]	Speaker of the House of Representatives
					Senate	House of Representatives		
	1–E	May 31, 1841	Sept. 13, 1841	106			Samuel L. Southard, of New Jersey	John White, of Kentucky.
	2	Dec. 6, 1841	Aug. 31, 1842	269			Willie P. Mangum, of North Carolina.	
	3	Dec. 5, 1842	Mar. 3, 1843	89			do.	
28th	1	Dec. 4, 1843	June 17, 1844	196			do	John W. Jones, of Virginia.
	2	Dec. 2, 1844	Mar. 3, 1845	92			do.	
29th	S	Mar. 4, 1845	Mar. 20, 1845	17				
	1	Dec. 1, 1845	Aug. 10, 1846	253			Ambrose H. Sevier; David R. Atchison, of Missouri.	John W. Davis, of Indiana.
	2	Dec. 7, 1846	Mar. 3, 1847	87			David R. Atchison, of Missouri.	
30th	1	Dec. 6, 1847	Aug. 14, 1848	254			do	Robert C. Winthrop, of Massachusetts.
	2	Dec. 4, 1848	Mar. 3, 1849	90			do.	
31st	S	Mar. 5, 1849	Mar. 23, 1849	19			do.	
	1	Dec. 3, 1849	Sept. 30, 1850	302			William R. King, of Alabama	Howell Cobb, of Georgia.
	2	Dec. 2, 1850	Mar. 3, 1851	92			do.	
32d	S	Mar. 4, 1851	Mar. 13, 1851	10				
	1	Dec. 1, 1851	Aug. 31, 1852	275			do	Linn Boyd, of Kentucky.
	2	Dec. 6, 1852	Mar. 3, 1853	88			David R. Atchison, of Missouri.	
33d	S	Mar. 4, 1853	Apr. 11, 1853	39			do.	
	1	Dec. 5, 1853	Aug. 7, 1854	246			do	Do.
	2	Dec. 4, 1854	Mar. 3, 1855	90			Lewis Cass, of Michigan; Jesse D. Bright, of Indiana.	
34th	1	Dec. 3, 1855	Aug. 18, 1856	260			Charles E. Stuart, of Michigan; Jesse D. Bright, of Indiana.	Nathaniel P. Banks, of Massachusetts.
	2–E	Aug. 21, 1856	Aug. 30, 1856	10			Jesse D. Bright, of Indiana.	
	3	Dec. 1, 1856	Mar. 3, 1857	93			James M. Mason, of Virginia.	
35th	S	Mar. 4, 1857	Mar. 14, 1857	11			James M. Mason, of Virginia; Thomas J. Rusk, of Texas.	
	1	Dec. 7, 1857	June 14, 1858	189	Dec. 23, 1857–Jan. 4, 1858	Dec. 23, 1857–Jan. 4, 1858	Benjamin Fitzpatrick, of Alabama	James L. Orr, of South Carolina.

	S	June 15, 1858	June 16, 1858	2				
	2	Dec. 6, 1858	Mar. 3, 1859	88	Dec. 23, 1858–Jan. 4, 1859	Dec. 23, 1858–Jan. 4, 1859	......do.	
36th	S	Mar. 4, 1859	Mar. 10, 1859	7			......do.	
	1	Dec. 5, 1859	June 25, 1860	202			Benjamin Fitzpatrick, of Alabama; Jesse D. Bright, of Indiana.	William Pennington, of New Jersey.
	S	June 26, 1860	June 28, 1860	3			Benjamin Fitzpatrick, of Alabama.	
	2	Dec. 3, 1860	Mar. 3, 1861	93			Solomon Foot, of Vermont.	
37th	S	Mar. 4, 1861	Mar. 28, 1861	25			......do.	
	1–E	July 4, 1861	Aug. 6, 1861	34			......do	Galusha A. Grow, of Pennsylvania.
	2	Dec. 2, 1861	July 17, 1862	228			......do.	
	3	Dec. 1, 1862	Mar. 3, 1863	93	Dec. 23, 1862–Jan. 5, 1863	Dec. 23, 1862–Jan. 5, 1863	......do.	
38th	S	Mar. 4, 1863	Mar. 14, 1863	11			......do.	
	1	Dec. 7, 1863	July 4, 1864	209	Dec. 23, 1863–Jan. 5, 1864	Dec. 23, 1863–Jan. 5, 1864	Solomon Foot, of Vermont; Daniel Clark, of New Hampshire.	Schuyler Colfax, of Indiana.
	2	Dec. 5, 1864	Mar. 3, 1865	89	Dec. 22, 1864–Jan. 5, 1865	Dec. 22, 1864–Jan. 5, 1865	Daniel Clark, of New Hampshire.	
39th	S	Mar. 4, 1865	Mar. 11, 1865	8			Lafayette S. Foster, of Connecticut.	
	1	Dec. 4, 1865	July 28, 1866	237	Dec. 6–Dec. 11, 1865 Dec. 21, 1865–Jan. 5, 1866	Dec. 6–Dec. 11, 1865 Dec. 21, 1865–Jan. 5, 1866	......do	Do.
	2	Dec. 3, 1866	Mar. 3, 1867	91	Dec. 20, 1866–Jan. 3, 1867	Dec. 20, 1866–Jan. 3, 1867	Benjamin F. Wade, of Ohio.	
40th	1	Mar. 4, 1867	Dec. 1, 1867	273	Mar. 30–July 3, 1867 July 20–Nov. 21, 1867	Mar. 30–July 3, 1867 July 20–Nov. 21, 1867	......do	Do.[7]
	S	Apr. 1, 1867	Apr. 20, 1867	20				
	2	Dec. 2, 1867	Nov. 10, 1868	345	Dec. 20, 1867–Jan. 6, 1868 July 27–Sept. 21, 1868 Sept. 21–Oct. 16, 1868 Oct. 16–Nov. 10, 1868	Dec. 20, 1867–Jan. 6, 1868 July 27–Sept. 21, 1868 Sept. 21–Oct. 16, 1868 Oct. 16–Nov. 10, 1868		
	3	Dec. 7, 1868	Mar. 3, 1869	87	Dec. 21, 1868–Jan. 5, 1869	Dec. 21, 1868–Jan. 5, 1869	......do	Theodore M. Pomeroy, of New York.[7]
41st	1	Mar. 4, 1869	Apr. 10, 1869	38			Henry B. Anthony, of Rhode Island	James G. Blaine, of Maine.
	S	Apr. 12, 1869	Apr. 22, 1869	11				
	2	Dec. 6, 1869	July 15, 1870	222	Dec. 22, 1869–Jan. 10, 1870	Dec. 22, 1869–Jan. 10, 1870	......do.	
	3	Dec. 5, 1870	Mar. 3, 1871	89	Dec. 23, 1870–Jan. 4, 1871	Dec. 22, 1870–Jan. 4, 1871	......do.	
42d	1	Mar. 4, 1871	Apr. 20, 1871	48			......do	Do.
	S	May 10, 1871	May 27, 1871	18			......do.	
	2	Dec. 4, 1871	June 10, 1872	190	Dec. 21, 1871–Jan. 8, 1872	Dec. 21, 1871–Jan. 8, 1872	......do.	
	3	Dec. 2, 1872	Mar. 3, 1873	92	Dec. 20, 1872–Jan. 6, 1873	Dec. 20, 1872–Jan. 6, 1873	......do.	
43d	S	Mar. 4, 1873	Mar. 26, 1873	23			Matthew H. Carpenter, of Wisconsin.	
	1	Dec. 1, 1873	June 23, 1874	204	Dec. 19, 1873–Jan. 5, 1874	Dec. 19, 1873–Jan. 5, 1874	......do	Do.
	2	Dec. 7, 1874	Mar. 3, 1875	87	Dec. 23, 1874–Jan. 5, 1875	Dec. 23, 1874–Jan. 5, 1875	Matthew H. Carpenter, of Wisconsin; Henry B. Anthony, of Rhode Island.	
44th	S	Mar. 5, 1875	Mar. 24, 1875	20			Thomas W. Ferry, of Michigan.	
	1	Dec. 6, 1875	Aug. 15, 1876	254	Dec. 20, 1875–Jan. 5, 1876	Dec. 21, 1875–Jan. 5, 1876	......do	Michael C. Kerr, of Indiana.[8]
	2	Dec. 4, 1876	Mar. 3, 1877	90			......do	Samuel J. Randall, of Pennsylvania.[8]
45th	S	Mar. 5, 1877	Mar. 17, 1877	13			......do.	
	1–E	Oct. 15, 1877	Dec. 3, 1877	50			......do	Do.
	2	Dec. 3, 1877	June 20, 1878	200	Dec. 15, 1877–Jan. 10, 1878	Dec. 15, 1877–Jan. 10, 1878	......do.	
	3	Dec. 2, 1878	Mar. 3, 1879	92	Dec. 20, 1878–Jan. 7, 1879	Dec. 20, 1878–Jan. 7, 1879	......do.	
46th	1–E	Mar. 18, 1879	July 1, 1879	106			Allen G. Thurman, of Ohio	Do.
	2	Dec. 1, 1879	June 16, 1880	199	Dec. 19, 1879–Jan. 6, 1880	Dec. 19, 1879–Jan. 6, 1880	......do.	
	3	Dec. 6, 1880	Mar. 3, 1881	88	Dec. 23, 1880–Jan. 5, 1881	Dec. 23, 1880–Jan. 5, 1881	......do.	
47th	S	Mar. 4, 1881	May. 20, 1881	78				
	S	Oct. 10, 1881	Oct. 29, 1881	20			Thomas F. Bayard, of Delaware; David Davis, of Illinois.	
	1	Dec. 5, 1881	Aug. 8, 1882	247	Dec. 22, 1881–Jan. 5, 1882	Dec. 22, 1881–Jan. 5, 1882	David Davis, of Illinois	J. Warren Keifer, of Ohio.

SESSIONS OF CONGRESS, 1st–111th CONGRESSES, 1789–2009—CONTINUED

[Closing date for this table was September 29, 2009.]

MEETING DATES OF CONGRESS: Pursuant to a resolution of the Confederation Congress in 1788, the Constitution went into effect on March 4, 1789. From then until the 20th amendment took effect in January 1934, the term of each Congress began on March 4th of each odd-numbered year; however, Article I, section 4, of the Constitution provided that ''The Congress shall assemble at least once in every Year, and such Meeting shall be on the first Monday in December, unless they shall by law appoint a different day.'' The Congress therefore convened regularly on the first Monday in December until the 20th amendment became effective, which changed the beginning of Congress's term as well as its convening date to January 3rd. So prior to 1934, a new Congress typically would not convene for regular business until 13 months after being elected. One effect of this was that the last session of each Congress was a ''lame duck'' session. After the 20th amendment, the time from the election to the beginning of Congress's term as well as when it convened was reduced to two months. Recognizing that the need might exist for Congress to meet at times other than the regularly scheduled convening date, Article II, section 3 of the Constitution provides that the President ''may, on extraordinary occasions, convene both Houses, or either of them''; hence these sessions occur only if convened by Presidential proclamation. Except as noted, these are separately numbered sessions of a Congress, and are marked by an E in the session column of the table. Until the 20th amendment was adopted, there were also times when special sessions of the Senate were convened, principally for confirming Cabinet and other executive nominations, and occasionally for the ratification of treaties or other executive business. These Senate sessions were also called by Presidential proclamation (typically by the outgoing President, although on occasion by incumbents as well) and are marked by an S in the session column. MEETING PLACES OF CONGRESS: Congress met for the first and second sessions of the First Congress (1789 and 1790) in New York City. From the third session of the First Congress through the first session of the Sixth Congress (1790 to 1800), Philadelphia was the meeting place. Congress has convened in Washington since the second session of the Sixth Congress (1800).

Congress	Session	Convening Date	Adjournment Date	Length in days[1]	Recesses[2]		President pro tempore of the Senate[3]	Speaker of the House of Representatives
					Senate	House of Representatives		
	2	Dec. 4, 1882	Mar. 3, 1883	90			George F. Edmunds, of Vermont.	J. Warren Keifer, of Ohio.
48th	1	Dec. 3, 1883	July 7, 1884	218	Dec. 24, 1883–Jan. 7, 1884	Dec. 24, 1883–Jan. 7, 1884	......do	John G. Carlisle, of Kentucky.
	2	Dec. 1, 1884	Mar. 3, 1885	93	Dec. 24, 1884–Jan. 5, 1885	Dec. 24, 1884–Jan. 5, 1885	......do.	
49th	S	Mar. 4, 1885	Apr. 2, 1885	30				
	1	Dec. 7, 1885	Aug. 5, 1886	242	Dec. 21, 1885–Jan. 5, 1886	Dec. 21, 1885–Jan. 5, 1886	John Sherman, of Ohio	Do.
	2	Dec. 6, 1886	Mar. 3, 1887	88	Dec. 22, 1886–Jan. 4, 1887	Dec. 22, 1886–Jan. 4, 1887	John J. Ingalls, of Kansas.	
50th	1	Dec. 5, 1887	Oct. 20, 1888	321	Dec. 22, 1887–Jan. 4, 1888	Dec. 22, 1887–Jan. 4, 1888	......do	Do.
	2	Dec. 3, 1888	Mar. 3, 1889	91	Dec. 21, 1888–Jan. 2, 1889	Dec. 21, 1888–Jan. 2, 1889	......do.	
51st	S	Mar. 4, 1889	Apr. 2, 1889	30			......do.	
	1	Dec. 2, 1889	Oct. 1, 1890	304	Dec. 21, 1889–Jan. 6, 1890	Dec. 21, 1889–Jan. 6, 1890	......do	Thomas B. Reed, of Maine.
	2	Dec. 1, 1890	Mar. 3, 1891	93			Charles F. Manderson, of Nebraska.	
52d	1	Dec. 7, 1891	Aug. 5, 1892	251			......do	Charles F. Crisp, of Georgia.
	2	Dec. 5, 1892	Mar. 3, 1893	89	Dec. 22, 1892–Jan. 4, 1893	Dec. 22, 1892–Jan. 4, 1893	......do.	
53d	S	Mar. 4, 1893	Apr. 15, 1893	43			Charles F. Manderson, of Nebraska; Isham G. Harris, of Tennessee.	
	1–E	Aug. 7, 1893	Nov. 3, 1893	89			Isham G. Harris, of Tennessee	Do.
	2	Dec. 4, 1893	Aug. 28, 1894	268		Dec. 21, 1893–Jan. 3, 1894	......do.	
	3	Dec. 3, 1894	Mar. 3, 1895	97		Dec. 23, 1894–Jan. 3, 1895	Matt W. Ransom, of North Carolina; Isham G. Harris, of Tennessee.	
54th	1	Dec. 2, 1895	June 11, 1896	193			William P. Frye, of Maine	Thomas B. Reed, of Maine.
	2	Dec. 7, 1896	Mar. 3, 1897	87	Dec. 22, 1896–Jan. 5, 1897	Dec. 22, 1896–Jan. 5, 1897	......do.	
55th	S	Mar. 4, 1897	Mar. 10, 1897	11			......do.	
	1–E	Mar. 15, 1897	July 24, 1897	131			......do	Do.
	2	Dec. 6, 1897	July 8, 1898	215	Dec. 18, 1897–Jan. 5, 1898	Dec. 18, 1897–Jan. 5, 1898	......do.	
	3	Dec. 5, 1898	Mar. 3, 1899	89	Dec. 21, 1898–Jan. 4, 1899	Dec. 21, 1898–Jan. 4, 1899	......do.	
56th	1	Dec. 4, 1899	June 7, 1900	186	Dec. 20, 1899–Jan. 3, 1900	Dec. 20, 1899–Jan. 3, 1900	......do	David B. Henderson, of Iowa.
	2	Dec. 3, 1900	Mar. 3, 1901	91	Dec. 20, 1900–Jan. 3, 1901	Dec. 21, 1900–Jan. 3, 1901	......do.	
57th	S	Mar. 4, 1901	Mar. 9, 1901	6			......do.	

	1	Dec. 2, 1901	July 1, 1902	212	Dec. 19, 1901–Jan. 6, 1902	Dec. 19, 1901–Jan. 6, 1902	do	Do.
	2	Dec. 1, 1902	Mar. 3, 1903	93	Dec. 20, 1902–Jan. 5, 1903	Dec. 20, 1902–Jan. 5, 1903	do.	
58th	S	Mar. 5, 1903	Mar. 19, 1903	15			do.	
	1–E	Nov. 9, 1903	Dec. 7, 1903	29			do	Joseph G. Cannon, of Illinois.
	2	Dec. 7, 1903	Apr. 28, 1904	144	Dec. 19, 1903–Jan. 4, 1904	Dec. 19, 1903–Jan. 4, 1904	do.	
	3	Dec. 5, 1904	Mar. 3, 1905	89	Dec. 21, 1904–Jan. 4, 1905	Dec. 21, 1904–Jan. 4, 1905	do.	
59th	S	Mar. 4, 1905	Mar. 18, 1905	15			do.	
	1	Dec. 4, 1905	June 30, 1906	209	Dec. 21, 1905–Jan. 4, 1906	Dec. 21, 1905–Jan. 4, 1906	do	Do.
	2	Dec. 3, 1906	Mar. 3, 1907	91	Dec. 20, 1906–Jan. 3, 1907	Dec. 20, 1906–Jan. 3, 1907	do.	
60th	1	Dec. 2, 1907	May 30, 1908	181	Dec. 21, 1907–Jan. 6, 1908	Dec. 21, 1907–Jan. 6, 1908	do	Do.
	2	Dec. 7, 1908	Mar. 3, 1909	87	Dec. 19, 1908–Jan. 4, 1909	Dec. 19, 1908–Jan. 4, 1909	do.	
61st	S	Mar. 4, 1909	Mar. 6, 1909	3			do.	
	1–E	Mar. 15, 1909	Aug. 5, 1909	144			do	Do.
	2	Dec. 6, 1909	June 25, 1910	202	Dec. 21, 1909–Jan. 4, 1910	Dec. 21, 1909–Jan. 4, 1910	do.	
	3	Dec. 5, 1910	Mar. 3, 1911	89	Dec. 21, 1910–Jan. 5, 1911	Dec. 21, 1910–Jan. 5, 1911	do.	
62d	1–E	Apr. 4, 1911	Aug. 22, 1911	141			do.[9]	Champ Clark, of Missouri.
	2	Dec. 4, 1911	Aug. 26, 1912	267	Dec. 21, 1911–Jan. 3, 1912	Dec. 21, 1911–Jan. 3, 1912	Charles Curtis, of Kansas; Augustus O. Bacon, of Georgia; Jacob H. Gallinger, of New Hampshire; Henry Cabot Lodge, of Massachusetts; Frank B. Brandegee, of Connecticut.	
	3	Dec. 2, 1912	Mar. 3, 1913	92	Dec. 19, 1912–Jan. 2, 1913	Dec. 19, 1912–Jan. 2, 1913	Augustus O. Bacon, of Georgia; Jacob H. Gallinger, of New Hampshire.	
63d	S	Mar. 4, 1913	Mar. 17, 1913	14			James P. Clarke, of Arkansas.	
	1–E	Apr. 7, 1913	Dec. 1, 1913	239			do	Do.
	2	Dec. 1, 1913	Oct. 24, 1914	328	Dec. 23, 1913–Jan. 12, 1914	Dec. 23, 1913–Jan. 12, 1914	do.	
	3	Dec. 7, 1914	Mar. 3, 1915	87	Dec. 23–Dec. 28, 1914	Dec. 23–Dec. 28, 1914	do.	
64th	1	Dec. 6, 1915	Sept. 8, 1916	278	Dec. 17, 1915–Jan. 4, 1916	Dec. 17, 1915–Jan. 4, 1916	do[10]	Do.
	2	Dec. 4, 1916	Mar. 3, 1917	90	Dec. 22, 1916–Jan. 2, 1917	Dec. 22, 1916–Jan. 2, 1917	Willard Saulsbury, of Delaware[10]	
65th	S	Mar. 5, 1917	Mar. 16, 1917	12			do.	
	1–E	Apr. 2, 1917	Oct. 6, 1917	188			do	Do.
	2	Dec. 3, 1917	Nov. 21, 1918	354	Dec. 18, 1917–Jan. 3, 1918	Dec. 18, 1917–Jan. 3, 1918	do.	
	3	Dec. 2, 1918	Mar. 3, 1919	92			do.	
66th	1–E	May 19, 1919	Nov. 19, 1919	185	July 1–July 8, 1919	July 1–July 8, 1919	Albert B. Cummins, of Iowa	Frederick H. Gillett, of Massachusetts.
	2	Dec. 1, 1919	June 5, 1920	188	Dec. 20, 1919–Jan. 5, 1920	Dec. 20, 1919–Jan. 5, 1920	do.	
	3	Dec. 6, 1920	Mar. 3, 1921	88			do.	
67th	S	Mar. 4, 1921	Mar. 15, 1921	12			do.	
	1–E	Apr. 11, 1921	Nov. 23, 1921	227	Aug. 24–Sept. 21, 1921	Aug. 24–Sept. 21, 1921	do	Do.
	2	Dec. 5, 1921	Sept. 22, 1922	292	Dec. 22, 1921–Jan. 3, 1922	Dec. 22, 1921–Jan. 3, 1922	do.	
	3–E	Nov. 20, 1922	Dec. 4, 1922	15			do.	
	4	Dec. 4, 1922	Mar. 3, 1923	90			do.	
68th	1	Dec. 3, 1923	June 7, 1924	188	Dec. 20, 1923–Jan. 3, 1924	Dec. 20, 1923–Jan. 3, 1924	do	Do.
	2	Dec. 1, 1924	Mar. 3, 1925	93	Dec. 20–Dec. 29, 1924	Dec. 20–Dec. 29, 1924	do.	
69th	S	Mar. 4, 1925	Mar. 18, 1925	15			Albert B. Cummins, of Iowa; George H. Moses, of New Hampshire.	
	1	Dec. 7, 1925	July 3, 1926	209	Dec. 22, 1925–Jan. 4, 1926	Dec. 22, 1925–Jan. 4, 1926	do	Nicholas Longworth, of Ohio.
	2	Dec. 6, 1926	Mar. 4, 1927	88	Dec. 22, 1926–Jan. 3, 1927	Dec. 22, 1926–Jan. 3, 1927	do.	
70th	1	Dec. 5, 1927	May 29, 1928	177	Dec. 21, 1927–Jan. 4, 1928	Dec. 21, 1927–Jan. 4, 1928	do	Do.
	2	Dec. 3, 1928	Mar. 3, 1929	91	Dec. 22, 1928–Jan. 3, 1929	Dec. 22, 1928–Jan. 3, 1929	do.	
71st	S	Mar. 4, 1929	Mar. 5, 1929	2			do.	
	1–E	Apr. 15, 1929	Nov. 22, 1929	222	June 19–Aug. 19, 1929	June 19–Sept. 23, 1929	do	Do.
	2	Dec. 2, 1929	July 3, 1930	214	Dec. 21, 1929–Jan. 6, 1930	Dec. 21, 1929–Jan. 6, 1930	do.	
	S	July 7, 1930	July 21, 1930	15			do.	

SESSIONS OF CONGRESS, 1st–111th CONGRESSES, 1789–2009—CONTINUED

[Closing date for this table was September 29, 2009.]

MEETING DATES OF CONGRESS: Pursuant to a resolution of the Confederation Congress in 1788, the Constitution went into effect on March 4, 1789. From then until the 20th amendment took effect in January 1934, the term of each Congress began on March 4th of each odd-numbered year; however, Article I, section 4, of the Constitution provided that ''The Congress shall assemble at least once in every Year, and such Meeting shall be on the first Monday in December, unless they shall by law appoint a different day.'' The Congress therefore convened regularly on the first Monday in December until the 20th amendment became effective, which changed the beginning of Congress's term as well as its convening date to January 3rd. So prior to 1934, a new Congress typically would not convene for regular business until 13 months after being elected. One effect of this was that the last session of each Congress was a ''lame duck'' session. After the 20th amendment, the time from the election to the beginning of Congress's term as well as when it convened was reduced to two months. Recognizing that the need might exist for Congress to meet at times other than the regularly scheduled convening date, Article II, section 3 of the Constitution provides that the President ''may, on extraordinary occasions, convene both Houses, or either of them''; hence these sessions occur only if convened by Presidential proclamation. Except as noted, these are separately numbered sessions of a Congress, and are marked by an E in the session column of the table. Until the 20th amendment was adopted, there were also times when special sessions of the Senate were convened, principally for confirming Cabinet and other executive nominations, and occasionally for the ratification of treaties or other executive business. These Senate sessions were also called by Presidential proclamation (typically by the outgoing President, although on occasion by incumbents as well) and are marked by an S in the session column. MEETING PLACES OF CONGRESS: Congress met for the first and second sessions of the First Congress (1789 and 1790) in New York City. From the third session of the First Congress through the first session of the Sixth Congress (1790 to 1800), Philadelphia was the meeting place. Congress has convened in Washington since the second session of the Sixth Congress (1800).

Congress	Session	Convening Date	Adjournment Date	Length in days [1]	Recesses [2]		President pro tempore of the Senate [3]	Speaker of the House of Representatives
					Senate	House of Representatives		
	3	Dec. 1, 1930	Mar. 3, 1931	93	Dec. 20, 1930–Jan. 5, 1931	Dec. 20, 1930–Jan. 5, 1931	George H. Moses, of New Hampshire	Nicholas Longworth, of Ohio.
72d	1	Dec. 7, 1931	July 16, 1932	223	Dec. 22, 1931–Jan. 4, 1932	Dec. 22, 1931–Jan. 4, 1932	......do	John N. Garner, of Texas.
	2	Dec. 5, 1932	Mar. 3, 1933	89			......do.	
73d	S	Mar. 4, 1933	Mar. 6, 1933	3			......do.	
	1–E	Mar. 9, 1933	June 15, 1933	99			Key Pittman, of Nevada	Henry T. Rainey, of Illinois.
	2	Jan. 3, 1934	June 18, 1934	167			......do.	
74th	1	Jan. 3, 1935	Aug. 26, 1935	236			......do	Joseph W. Byrns, of Tennessee.[11]
	2	Jan. 3, 1936	June 20, 1936	170	June 8–June 15, 1936	June 8–June 15, 1936	......do	William B. Bankhead, of Alabama.[11]
75th	1	Jan. 5, 1937	Aug. 21, 1937	229			......do	Do.
	2–E	Nov. 15, 1937	Dec. 21, 1937	37			......do.	
	3	Jan. 3, 1938	June 16, 1938	165			......do.	
76th	1	Jan. 3, 1939	Aug. 5, 1939	215			......do	Do.[12]
	2–E	Sept. 21, 1939	Nov. 3, 1939	44			......do.	
	3	Jan. 3, 1940	Jan. 3, 1941	366	July 11–July 22, 1940	July 11–July 22, 1940	Key Pittman, of Nevada;[13] William H. King, of Utah.[13]	Sam Rayburn, of Texas.[12]
77th	1	Jan. 3, 1941	Jan. 2, 1942	365			Pat Harrison, of Mississippi;[14] Carter Glass, of Virginia.[14]	Do.
	2	Jan. 5, 1942	Dec. 16, 1942	346			Carter Glass, of Virginia.	
78th	1	Jan. 6, 1943	Dec. 21, 1943	350	July 8–Sept. 14, 1943	July 8–Sept. 14, 1943	......do	Do.
	2	Jan. 10, 1944	Dec. 19, 1944	345	Apr. 1–Apr. 12, 1944 June 23–Aug. 1, 1944 Sept. 21–Nov. 14, 1944	Apr. 1–Apr. 12, 1944 June 23–Aug. 1, 1944 Sept. 21–Nov. 14, 1944	......do.	
79th	1	Jan. 3, 1945	Dec. 21, 1945	353	Aug. 1–Sept. 5, 1945	July 21–Sept. 5, 1945	Kenneth McKellar, of Tennessee	Do.
	2	Jan. 14, 1946	Aug. 2, 1946	201		Apr. 18–Apr. 30, 1946	......do.	
80th	[15] 1	Jan. 3, 1947	Dec. 19, 1947	351	July 27–Nov. 17, 1947	July 27–Nov. 17, 1947	Arthur H. Vandenberg, of Michigan	Joseph W. Martin, Jr., of Massachusetts.
	[15] 2	Jan. 6, 1948	Dec. 31, 1948	361	June 20–July 26, 1948 Aug. 7–Dec. 31, 1948	June 20–July 26, 1948 Aug. 7–Dec. 31, 1948	......do.	

81st	1	Jan. 3, 1949	Oct. 19, 1949	290	....	....	Kenneth McKellar, of Tennessee	Sam Rayburn, of Texas.
	2	Jan. 3, 1950	Jan. 2, 1951	365	Sept. 23–Nov. 27–1950	Apr. 6–Apr. 18, 1950 Sept. 23–Nov. 27, 1950	......do.	
82d	1	Jan. 3, 1951	Oct. 20, 1951	291	....	Mar. 22–Apr. 2, 1951 Aug. 23–Sept. 12, 1951	......do	Do.
	2	Jan. 8, 1952	July 7, 1952	182	....	Apr. 10–Apr. 22, 1952	......do.	
83d	1	Jan. 3, 1953	Aug. 3, 1953	213	....	Apr. 2–Apr. 13, 1953	Styles Bridges, of New Hampshire	Joseph W. Martin, Jr., of Massachusetts.
	2	Jan. 6, 1954	Dec. 2, 1954	331	Aug. 20–Nov. 8, 1954 Nov. 18–Nov. 29, 1954	Apr. 15–Apr. 22, 1954 Adjourned sine die Aug. 20, 1954	......do.	
84th	1	Jan. 5, 1955	Aug. 2, 1955	210	Apr. 4–Apr. 13, 1955	Apr. 4–Apr. 13, 1955	Walter F. George, of Georgia	Sam Rayburn, of Texas.
	2	Jan. 3, 1956	July 27, 1956	207	Mar. 29–Apr. 9, 1956	Mar. 29–Apr. 9, 1956	......do.	
85th	1	Jan. 3, 1957	Aug. 30, 1957	239	Apr. 18–Apr. 29, 1957	Apr. 18–Apr. 29, 1957	Carl Hayden, of Arizona	Do.
	2	Jan. 7, 1958	Aug. 24, 1958	230	Apr. 3–Apr. 14, 1958	Apr. 3–Apr. 14, 1958	......do.	
86th	1	Jan. 7, 1959	Sept. 15, 1959	252	Mar. 26–Apr. 7, 1959	Mar. 26–Apr. 7, 1959	......do	Do.
	2	Jan. 6, 1960	Sept. 1, 1960	240	Apr. 14–Apr. 18, 1960 May 27–May 31, 1960 July 3–Aug. 8, 1960	Apr. 14–Apr. 18, 1960 May 27–May 31, 1960 July 3–Aug. 15, 1960	......do.	
87th	1	Jan. 3, 1961	Sept. 27, 1961	268	....	Mar. 30–Apr. 10, 1961	......do	Do.[16]
	2	Jan. 10, 1962	Oct. 13, 1962	277	....	Apr. 19–Apr. 30, 1962	......do	John W. McCormack, of Massachusetts.[16]
88th	1	Jan. 9, 1963	Dec. 30, 1963	356	....	Apr. 11–Apr. 22, 1963	......do	Do.
	2	Jan. 7, 1964	Oct. 3, 1964	270	July 10–July 20, 1964 Aug. 21–Aug. 31, 1964	Mar. 26–Apr. 6, 1964 July 2–July 20, 1964 Aug. 21–Aug. 31, 1964	......do.	
89th	1	Jan. 4, 1965	Oct. 23, 1965	293	....	....	......do	Do.
	2	Jan. 10, 1966	Oct. 22, 1966	286	Apr. 7–Apr. 13, 1966 June 30–July 11, 1966	Apr. 7–Apr. 18, 1966 June 30–July 11, 1966	......do.	
90th	1	Jan. 10, 1967	Dec. 15, 1967	340	Mar. 23–Apr. 3, 1967 June 29–July 10, 1967 Aug. 31–Sept. 11, 1967 Nov. 22–Nov. 27, 1967	Mar. 23–Apr. 3, 1967 June 29–July 10, 1967 Aug. 31–Sept. 11, 1967 Nov. 22–Nov. 27, 1967	......do	Do.
	2	Jan. 15, 1968	Oct. 14, 1968	274	Apr. 11–Apr. 17, 1968 May 29–June 3, 1968 June 3–July 8, 1968 Aug. 2–Sept. 4, 1968	Apr. 11–Apr. 22, 1968 May 29–June 3, 1968 June 3–July 8, 1968 Aug. 2–Sept. 4, 1968	......do.	
91st	1	Jan. 3, 1969	Dec. 23, 1969	355	Feb. 7–Feb. 17, 1969 Apr. 3–Apr. 14, 1969 July 2–July 7, 1969 Aug. 13–Sept. 3, 1969 Nov. 26–Dec. 1, 1969	Feb. 7–Feb. 17, 1969 Apr. 3–Apr. 14, 1969 May 28–June 2, 1969 July 2–July 7, 1969 Aug. 13–Sept. 3, 1969 Nov. 6–Nov. 12, 1969 Nov. 26–Dec. 1, 1969	Richard B. Russell, of Georgia	Do.
	2	Jan. 19, 1970	Jan. 2, 1971	349	Feb. 10–Feb. 16, 1970 Mar. 26–Mar. 31, 1970 Sept. 2–Sept. 8, 1970 Oct. 14–Nov. 16, 1970 Nov. 25–Nov. 30, 1970 Dec. 22–Dec. 28, 1970	Feb. 10–Feb. 16, 1970 Mar. 26–Mar. 31, 1970 May 27–June 1, 1970 July 1–July 6, 1970 Aug. 14–Sept. 9, 1970 Oct. 14–Nov. 16, 1970 Nov. 25–Nov. 30, 1970 Dec. 22–Dec. 29, 1970	......do.	

SESSIONS OF CONGRESS, 1st–111th CONGRESSES, 1789–2009—CONTINUED

[Closing date for this table was September 29, 2009.]

MEETING DATES OF CONGRESS: Pursuant to a resolution of the Confederation Congress in 1788, the Constitution went into effect on March 4, 1789. From then until the 20th amendment took effect in January 1934, the term of each Congress began on March 4th of each odd-numbered year; however, Article I, section 4, of the Constitution provided that ''The Congress shall assemble at least once in every Year, and such Meeting shall be on the first Monday in December, unless they shall by law appoint a different day.'' The Congress therefore convened regularly on the first Monday in December until the 20th amendment became effective, which changed the beginning of Congress's term as well as its convening date to January 3rd. So prior to 1934, a new Congress typically would not convene for regular business until 13 months after being elected. One effect of this was that the last session of each Congress was a ''lame duck'' session. After the 20th amendment, the time from the election to the beginning of Congress's term as well as when it convened was reduced to two months. Recognizing that the need might exist for Congress to meet at times other than the regularly scheduled convening date, Article II, section 3 of the Constitution provides that the President ''may, on extraordinary occasions, convene both Houses, or either of them''; hence these sessions occur only if convened by Presidential proclamation. Except as noted, these are separately numbered sessions of a Congress, and are marked by an E in the session column of the table. Until the 20th amendment was adopted, there were also times when special sessions of the Senate were convened, principally for confirming Cabinet and other executive nominations, and occasionally for the ratification of treaties or other executive business. These Senate sessions were also called by Presidential proclamation (typically by the outgoing President, although on occasion by incumbents as well) and are marked by an S in the session column. MEETING PLACES OF CONGRESS: Congress met for the first and second sessions of the First Congress (1789 and 1790) in New York City. From the third session of the First Congress through the first session of the Sixth Congress (1790 to 1800), Philadelphia was the meeting place. Congress has convened in Washington since the second session of the Sixth Congress (1800).

Congress	Session	Convening Date	Adjournment Date	Length in days [1]	Recesses [2]		President pro tempore of the Senate [3]	Speaker of the House of Representatives
					Senate	House of Representatives		
92d	1	Jan. 21, 1971	Dec. 17, 1971 ...	331	Feb. 11–Feb. 17, 1971 .... Apr. 7–Apr. 14, 1971 May 26–June 1, 1971 June 30–July 6, 1971 Aug. 6–Sept. 8, 1971 Oct. 21–Oct. 26, 1971 Nov. 24–Nov. 29, 1971	Feb. 10–Feb. 17, 1971 .... Apr. 7–Apr. 19, 1971 May 27–June 1, 1971 July 1–July 6, 1971 Aug. 6–Sept. 8, 1971 Oct. 7–Oct. 12, 1971 Oct. 21–Oct. 26, 1971 Nov. 19–Nov. 29, 1971	Richard B. Russell, of Georgia;[17] Allen J. Ellender, of Louisiana.[17]	Carl B. Albert, of Oklahoma.
	2	Jan. 18, 1972	Oct. 18, 1972 ...	275	Feb. 9–Feb. 14, 1972 .... Mar. 30–Apr. 4, 1972 May 25–May 30, 1972 June 30–July 17, 1972 Aug. 18–Sept. 5, 1972	Feb. 9–Feb. 16, 1972 .... Mar. 29–Apr. 10, 1972 May 24–May 30, 1972 June 30–July 17, 1972 Aug. 18–Sept. 5, 1972	Allen J. Ellender, of Louisiana;[18] James O. Eastland, of Mississippi.[18]	
93d	1	Jan. 3, 1973	Dec. 22, 1973 ...	354	Feb. 8–Feb. 15, 1973 .... Apr. 18–Apr. 30, 1973 May 23–May 29, 1973 June 30–July 9, 1973 Aug. 3–Sept. 5, 1973 Oct. 18–Oct. 23, 1973 Nov. 21–Nov. 26, 1973	Feb. 8–Feb. 19, 1973 .... Apr. 19–Apr. 30, 1973 May 24–May 29, 1973 June 30–July 10, 1973 Aug. 3–Sept. 5, 1973 Oct. 4–Oct. 9, 1973 Oct. 18–Oct. 23, 1973 Nov. 15–Nov. 26, 1973	James O. Eastland, of Mississippi	Do.
	2	Jan. 21, 1974	Dec. 20, 1974 ...	334	Feb. 8–Feb. 18, 1974 .... Mar. 13–Mar. 19, 1974 Apr. 11–Apr. 22, 1974 May 23–May 28, 1974 Aug. 22–Sept. 4, 1974 Oct. 17–Nov. 18, 1974 Nov. 26–Dec. 2, 1974	Feb. 7–Feb. 13, 1974 .... Apr. 11–Apr. 22, 1974 May 23–May 28, 1974 Aug. 22–Sept. 11, 1974 Oct. 17–Nov. 18, 1974 Nov. 26–Dec. 3, 1974	......do.	

94th ...	1	Jan. 14, 1975	Dec. 19, 1975 ...	340	Mar. 26–Apr. 7, 1975 .... May 22–June 2, 1975 June 27–July 7, 1975 Aug. 1–Sept. 3, 1975 Oct. 9–Oct. 20, 1975 Oct. 23–Oct. 28, 1975 Nov. 20–Dec. 1, 1975	Mar. 26–Apr. 7, 1975 .... May 22–June 2, 1975 June 26–July 8, 1975 Aug. 1–Sept. 3, 1975 Oct. 9–Oct. 20, 1975 Oct. 23–Oct. 28, 1975 Nov. 20–Dec. 1, 1975	......do	Do.
	2	Jan. 19, 1976	Oct. 1, 1976	257	Feb. 6–Feb. 16, 1976 .... Apr. 14–Apr. 26, 1976 May 28–June 2, 1976 July 2–July 19, 1976 Aug. 10–Aug. 23, 1976 Sept. 1–Sept. 7, 1976	Feb. 11–Feb. 16, 1976 .... Apr. 14–Apr. 26, 1976 May 27–June 1, 1976 July 2–July 19, 1976 Aug. 10–Aug. 23, 1976 Sept. 2–Sept. 8, 1976	......do.	
95th ...	1	Jan. 4, 1977	Dec. 15, 1977 ...	346	Feb. 11–Feb. 21, 1977 .... Apr. 7–Apr. 18, 1977 May 27–June 6, 1977 July 1–July 11, 1977 Aug. 6–Sept. 7, 1977	Feb. 9–Feb. 16, 1977 .... Apr. 6–Apr. 18, 1977 May 26–June 1, 1977 June 30–July 11, 1977 Aug. 5–Sept. 7, 1977 Oct. 6–Oct. 11, 1977	......do	Thomas P. O'Neill, Jr., of Massachusetts.
	2	Jan. 19, 1978	Oct. 15, 1978 ...	270	Feb. 10–Feb. 20, 1978 .... Mar. 23–Apr. 3, 1978 May 26–June 5, 1978 June 29–July 10, 1978 Aug. 25–Sept. 6, 1978	Feb. 9–Feb. 14, 1978 .... Mar. 22–Apr. 3, 1978 May 25–May 31, 1978 June 29–July 10, 1978 Aug. 17–Sept. 6, 1978	......do.	
96th ...	1	Jan. 15, 1979	Jan. 3, 1980	354	Feb. 9–Feb. 19, 1979 .... Apr. 10–Apr. 23, 1979 May 24–June 4, 1979 June 27–July 9, 1979 Aug. 3–Sept. 5, 1979 Nov. 20–Nov. 26, 1979 Adjourned sine die, Dec. 20, 1979	Feb. 8–Feb. 13, 1979 .... Apr. 10–Apr. 23, 1979 May 24–May 30, 1979 June 29–July 9, 1979 Aug. 2–Sept. 5, 1979 Nov. 20–Nov. 26, 1979	Warren G. Magnuson, of Washington ...	Do.
	2	Jan. 3, 1980	Dec. 16, 1980 ...	349	Apr. 3–Apr. 15, 1980 .... May 22–May 28, 1980 July 2–July 21, 1980 Aug. 6–Aug. 18, 1980 Aug. 27–Sept. 3, 1980 Oct. 1–Nov. 12, 1980 Nov. 25–Dec. 1, 1980	Feb. 13–Feb. 19, 1980 .... Apr. 2–Apr. 15, 1980 May 22–May 28, 1980 July 2–July 21, 1980 Aug. 1–Aug. 18, 1980 Aug. 28–Sept. 3, 1980 Oct. 2–Nov. 12, 1980 Nov. 21–Dec. 1, 1980	Warren G. Magnuson, of Washington; Milton Young, of North Dakota;[19] Warren G. Magnuson, of Washington.[19]	
97th ...	1	Jan. 5, 1981	Dec. 16, 1981 ...	347	Feb. 6–Feb. 16, 1981 .... Apr. 10–Apr. 27, 1981 June 25–July 8, 1981 Aug. 3–Sept. 9, 1981 Oct. 7–Oct. 14, 1981 Nov. 24–Nov. 30, 1981	Feb. 6–Feb. 17, 1981 .... Apr. 10–Apr. 27, 1981 June 26–July 8, 1981 Aug. 4–Sept. 9, 1981 Oct. 7–Oct. 13, 1981 Nov. 23–Nov. 30, 1981	Strom Thurmond, of South Carolina	Do.
	2	Jan. 25, 1982	Dec. 23, 1982 ...	333	Feb. 11–Feb. 22, 1982 .... Apr. 1–Apr. 13, 1982 May 27–June 8, 1982 July 1–July 12, 1982 Aug. 20–Sept. 8, 1982 Oct. 1–Nov. 29, 1982	Feb. 10–Feb. 22, 1982 .... Apr. 6–Apr. 20, 1982 May 27–June 2, 1982 July 1–July 12, 1982 Aug. 20–Sept. 8, 1982 Oct. 1–Nov. 29, 1982	......do	

SESSIONS OF CONGRESS, 1st–111th CONGRESSES, 1789–2009—CONTINUED

[Closing date for this table was September 29, 2009.]

MEETING DATES OF CONGRESS: Pursuant to a resolution of the Confederation Congress in 1788, the Constitution went into effect on March 4, 1789. From then until the 20th amendment took effect in January 1934, the term of each Congress began on March 4th of each odd-numbered year; however, Article I, section 4, of the Constitution provided that ''The Congress shall assemble at least once in every Year, and such Meeting shall be on the first Monday in December, unless they shall by law appoint a different day.'' The Congress therefore convened regularly on the first Monday in December until the 20th amendment became effective, which changed the beginning of Congress's term as well as its convening date to January 3rd. So prior to 1934, a new Congress typically would not convene for regular business until 13 months after being elected. One effect of this was that the last session of each Congress was a ''lame duck'' session. After the 20th amendment, the time from the election to the beginning of Congress's term as well as when it convened was reduced to two months. Recognizing that the need might exist for Congress to meet at times other than the regularly scheduled convening date, Article II, section 3 of the Constitution provides that the President ''may, on extraordinary occasions, convene both Houses, or either of them''; hence these sessions occur only if convened by Presidential proclamation. Except as noted, these are separately numbered sessions of a Congress, and are marked by an E in the session column of the table. Until the 20th amendment was adopted, there were also times when special sessions of the Senate were convened, principally for confirming Cabinet and other executive nominations, and occasionally for the ratification of treaties or other executive business. These Senate sessions were also called by Presidential proclamation (typically by the outgoing President, although on occasion by incumbents as well) and are marked by an S in the session column. MEETING PLACES OF CONGRESS: Congress met for the first and second sessions of the First Congress (1789 and 1790) in New York City. From the third session of the First Congress through the first session of the Sixth Congress (1790 to 1800), Philadelphia was the meeting place. Congress has convened in Washington since the second session of the Sixth Congress (1800).

Congress	Session	Convening Date	Adjournment Date	Length in days [1]	Recesses [2]		President pro tempore of the Senate [3]	Speaker of the House of Representatives
					Senate	House of Representatives		
98th ...	1	Jan. 3, 1983	Nov. 18, 1983 ..	320	Jan. 3–Jan. 25, 1983 .... Feb. 3–Feb. 14, 1983 Mar. 24–Apr. 5, 1983 May 26–June 6, 1983 June 29–July 11, 1983 Aug. 4–Sept. 12, 1983 Oct. 7–Oct. 17, 1983	Jan. 6–Jan. 25, 1983 .... Feb. 17–Feb. 22, 1983 Mar. 24–Apr. 5, 1983 May 26–June 1, 1983 June 30–July 11, 1983 Aug. 4–Sept. 12, 1983 Oct. 6–Oct. 17, 1983	Strom Thurmond, of South Carolina	Thomas P. O'Neill, Jr., of Massachusetts.
	2	Jan. 23, 1984	Oct. 12, 1984 ...	264	Feb. 9–Feb. 20, 1984 .... Apr. 12–Apr. 24, 1984 May 24–May 31, 1984 June 29–July 23, 1984 Aug. 10–Sept. 5, 1984	Feb. 9–Feb. 21, 1984 .... Apr. 12–Apr. 24, 1984 May 24–May 30, 1984 June 29–July 23, 1984 Aug. 10–Sept. 5, 1984	......do.	
99th ...	1	Jan. 3, 1985	Dec. 20, 1985 ...	352	Jan. 7–Jan. 21, 1985 .... Feb. 7–Feb. 18, 1985 Apr. 4–Apr. 15, 1985 May 9–May 14, 1985 May 24–June 3, 1985 June 27–July 8, 1985 Aug. 1–Sept. 9, 1985 Nov. 23–Dec. 2, 1985	Jan. 3–Jan. 21, 1985 .... Feb. 7–Feb. 19, 1985 Mar. 7–Mar. 19, 1985 Apr. 4–Apr. 15, 1985 May 23–June 3, 1985 June 27–July 8, 1985 Aug. 1–Sept. 4, 1985 Nov. 21–Dec. 2, 1985	......do	Do.
	2	Jan. 21, 1986	Oct. 18, 1986 ...	278	Feb. 7–Feb. 17, 1986 .... Mar. 27–Apr. 8, 1986 May 21–June 2, 1986 June 26–July 7, 1986 Aug. 15–Sept. 8, 1986	Feb. 6–Feb. 18, 1986 .... Mar. 25–Apr. 8, 1986 May 22–June 3, 1986 June 26–July 14, 1986 Aug. 16–Sept. 8, 1986	......do.	

100th	1	Jan. 6, 1987	Dec. 22, 1987	351	Jan. 6–Jan. 12, 1987 Feb. 5–Feb. 16, 1987 Apr. 10–Apr. 21, 1987 May 21–May 27, 1987 July 1–July 7, 1987 Aug. 7–Sept. 9, 1987 Nov. 20–Nov. 30, 1987	Jan. 8–Jan. 20, 1987 Feb. 11–Feb. 18, 1987 Apr. 9–Apr. 21, 1987 May 21–May 27, 1987 July 1–July 7, 1987 July 15–July 20, 1987 Aug. 7–Sept. 9, 1987 Nov. 10–Nov. 16, 1987 Nov. 20–Nov. 30, 1987	John C. Stennis, of Mississippi	James C. Wright, Jr., of Texas.
	2	Jan. 25, 1988	Oct. 22, 1988	272	Feb. 4–Feb. 15, 1988 Mar. 4– Mar. 14, 1988 Mar. 31–Apr. 11, 1988 Apr. 29–May 9, 1988 May 27–June 6, 1988 June 29–July 6, 1988 July 14–July 25, 1988 Aug. 11–Sept. 7, 1988	Feb. 9–Feb. 16, 1988 Mar. 31–Apr. 11, 1988 May 26–June 1, 1988 June 30–July 7, 1988 July 14–July 26, 1988 Aug. 11–Sept. 7,1988	......do.	
101st	1	Jan. 3, 1989	Nov. 22, 1989	324	Jan. 4–Jan. 20, 1989 Jan. 20–Jan. 25, 1989 Feb. 9–Feb. 21, 1989 Mar. 17–Apr. 4, 1989 Apr. 19–May 1, 1989 May 18–May 31, 1989 June 23–July 11, 1989 Aug. 4–Sept. 6, 1989	Jan. 4–Jan. 19, 1989 Feb. 9–Feb. 21, 1989 Mar. 23–Apr. 3, 1989 Apr. 18–Apr. 25, 1989 May 25–May 31, 1989 June 29–July 10, 1989 Aug. 5–Sept. 6, 1989	Robert C. Byrd, of West Virginia	James C. Wright, Jr., of Texas;[20] Thomas S. Foley, of Washington.[20]
	2	Jan. 23, 1990	Oct. 28, 1990	260	Feb. 8–Feb. 20, 1990 Mar. 9–Mar. 20, 1990 Apr. 5–Apr. 18, 1990 May 24–June 5, 1990 June 28–July 10, 1990 Aug. 4–Sept. 10, 1990	Feb. 7–Feb. 20, 1990 Apr. 4–Apr. 18, 1990 May 25–June 5, 1990 June 28–July 10, 1990 Aug. 4–Sept. 5, 1990	......do.	
102d	1	Jan. 3, 1991	Jan. 3, 1992	366	Feb. 7–Feb. 19, 1991 Mar. 22–Apr. 9, 1991 Apr. 25–May 6, 1991 May 24–June 3, 1991 June 28–July 8, 1991 Aug. 2–Sept. 10, 1991 Nov. 27, 1991–Jan. 3, 1992	Feb. 6–Feb. 19, 1991 Mar. 22–Apr. 9, 1991 May 23–May 29, 1991 June 27–July 9, 1991 Aug. 2–Sept. 11, 1991 Nov. 27, 1991–Jan. 3, 1992	......do	Thomas S. Foley, of Washington.
	2	Jan. 3, 1992	Oct. 9, 1992	281	Jan. 3–Jan. 21, 1992 Feb. 7–Feb. 18, 1992 Apr. 10–Apr. 28, 1992 May 21–June 1, 1992 July 2–July 20, 1992 Aug. 12–Sept. 8, 1992	Jan. 3–Jan. 22, 1992 Apr. 10–Apr. 28, 1992 May 21–May 26, 1992 July 2–July 7, 1992 July 9–July 21, 1992 Aug. 12–Sept. 9, 1992	......do.	

SESSIONS OF CONGRESS, 1st–111th CONGRESSES, 1789–2009—CONTINUED

[Closing date for this table was September 29, 2009.]

MEETING DATES OF CONGRESS: Pursuant to a resolution of the Confederation Congress in 1788, the Constitution went into effect on March 4, 1789. From then until the 20th amendment took effect in January 1934, the term of each Congress began on March 4th of each odd-numbered year; however, Article I, section 4, of the Constitution provided that ''The Congress shall assemble at least once in every Year, and such Meeting shall be on the first Monday in December, unless they shall by law appoint a different day.'' The Congress therefore convened regularly on the first Monday in December until the 20th amendment became effective, which changed the beginning of Congress's term as well as its convening date to January 3rd. So prior to 1934, a new Congress typically would not convene for regular business until 13 months after being elected. One effect of this was that the last session of each Congress was a ''lame duck'' session. After the 20th amendment, the time from the election to the beginning of Congress's term as well as when it convened was reduced to two months. Recognizing that the need might exist for Congress to meet at times other than the regularly scheduled convening date, Article II, section 3 of the Constitution provides that the President ''may, on extraordinary occasions, convene both Houses, or either of them''; hence these sessions occur only if convened by Presidential proclamation. Except as noted, these are separately numbered sessions of a Congress, and are marked by an E in the session column of the table. Until the 20th amendment was adopted, there were also times when special sessions of the Senate were convened, principally for confirming Cabinet and other executive nominations, and occasionally for the ratification of treaties or other executive business. These Senate sessions were also called by Presidential proclamation (typically by the outgoing President, although on occasion by incumbents as well) and are marked by an S in the session column. MEETING PLACES OF CONGRESS: Congress met for the first and second sessions of the First Congress (1789 and 1790) in New York City. From the third session of the First Congress through the first session of the Sixth Congress (1790 to 1800), Philadelphia was the meeting place. Congress has convened in Washington since the second session of the Sixth Congress (1800).

Congress	Session	Convening Date	Adjournment Date	Length in days [1]	Recesses [2]		President pro tempore of the Senate [3]	Speaker of the House of Representatives
					Senate	House of Representatives		
103d	1	Jan. 5, 1993	Nov. 26, 1993	326	Jan. 7–Jan. 20, 1993 Feb. 4–Feb. 16, 1993 Apr. 7–Apr. 19, 1993 May 28–June 7, 1993 July 1–July 13, 1993 Aug. 7–Sept. 7, 1993 Oct. 7–Oct. 13, 1993 Nov. 11–Nov. 16, 1993	Jan. 6–Jan. 20, 1993 Jan. 27–Feb. 2, 1993 Feb. 4–Feb. 16, 1993 Apr. 7–Apr. 19, 1993 May 27–June 8, 1993 July 1–July 13, 1993 Aug. 6–Sept. 8, 1993 Sept. 15–Sept. 21, 1993 Oct. 7–Oct. 12, 1993 Nov. 10–Nov. 15, 1993	Robert C. Byrd, of West Virginia	Thomas S. Foley, of Washington.
	2	Jan. 25, 1994	Dec. 1, 1994	311	Feb. 11–Feb. 22, 1994 Mar. 26–Apr. 11, 1994 May 25–June 7, 1994 July 1–July 11, 1994 Aug. 25–Sept. 12, 1994 Oct. 8–Nov. 30, 1994	Jan. 26–Feb. 1, 1994 Feb. 11–Feb. 22, 1994 Mar. 24–Apr. 12, 1994 May 26–June 8, 1994 June 30–July 12, 1994 Aug. 26–Sept. 12, 1994 Oct. 8–Nov. 29, 1994	......do.	
104th	1	Jan. 4, 1995	Jan. 3, 1996	365	Feb. 16–Feb. 22, 1995 Apr. 7–Apr. 24, 1995 May 26–June 5, 1995 June 30–July 10, 1995 Aug. 11–Sept. 5, 1995 Sept. 29–Oct. 10, 1995 Nov. 20–Nov. 27, 1995	Feb. 16–Feb. 21, 1995 Mar. 16–Mar. 21, 1995 Apr. 7–May 1, 1995 May 3–May 9, 1995 May 25–June 6, 1995 June 30–July 10, 1995 Aug. 4–Sept. 6, 1995 Sept. 29–Oct. 6, 1995 Nov. 20–Nov. 28, 1995	Strom Thurmond, of South Carolina	Newt Gingrich, of Georgia.

	2	Jan. 3, 1996	Oct. 4, 1996	276	Jan. 10–Jan. 22, 1996 Mar. 29–Apr. 15, 1996 May 24–June 3, 1996 June 28–July 8, 1996 Aug. 2–Sept. 3, 1996	Jan. 9–Jan. 22, 1996 Mar. 29–Apr. 15, 1996 May 23–May 29, 1996 June 28–July 8, 1996 Aug. 2–Sept. 4, 1996	......do.	
105th	1	Jan. 7, 1997	Nov. 13, 1997	311	Jan. 9–Jan. 21, 1997 Feb. 13–Feb. 24, 1997 Mar. 21–Apr. 7, 1997 June 27–July 7, 1997 July 31–Sept. 2, 1997 Oct. 9–Oct. 20, 1997	Jan. 9–Jan. 20, 1997 Jan. 21–Feb. 4, 1997 Feb. 13–Feb. 25, 1997 Mar. 21–Apr. 8, 1997 June 26–July 8, 1997 Aug. 1–Sept. 3, 1997 Oct. 9–Oct. 21, 1997	......do	Do.
	2	Jan. 27, 1998	Dec. 19, 1998	327	Feb. 13–Feb. 23, 1998 Apr. 3–Apr. 20, 1998 May 22–June 1, 1998 June 26–July 6, 1998 July 31–Aug. 31, 1998 Adjourned sine die, Oct. 21, 1998.	Jan. 28–Feb. 3, 1998 Feb. 5–Feb. 11, 1998 Feb. 12–Feb. 24, 1998 Apr. 1–Apr. 21, 1998 May 22–June 3, 1998 June 25–July 14, 1998 Aug. 7–Sept. 9, 1998 Oct. 21–Dec. 17, 1998	......do.	
106th	1	Jan. 6, 1999	Nov. 22, 1999	321	Feb. 12–Feb. 22, 1999 Mar. 25–Apr. 12, 1999 May 27–June 7, 1999 July 1–July 12, 1999 Aug. 5–Sept. 8, 1999	Jan. 6–Jan. 19, 1999 Jan. 19–Feb. 2, 1999 Feb. 12–Feb. 23, 1999 Mar. 25–Apr. 12, 1999 May 27–June 7, 1999 July 1–July 12, 1999 Aug. 6–Sept. 8, 1999	......do	J. Dennis Hastert, of Illinois.
	2	Jan. 24, 2000	Dec. 15, 2000	326	Feb. 10–Feb. 22, 2000 Mar. 9–Mar. 20, 2000 Apr. 13–Apr. 25, 2000 May 25–June 6, 2000 June 30–July 10, 2000 July 27–Sept. 5, 2000 Nov. 2–Nov. 14, 2000 Nov. 14–Dec. 5, 2000	Feb. 16–Feb. 29, 2000 Apr. 13–May 2, 2000 May 25–June 6, 2000 June 30–July 10, 2000 July 27–Sept. 6, 2000 Nov. 3–Nov. 13, 2000 Nov. 14–Dec. 4, 2000	......do.	
107th	1	Jan. 3, 2001	Dec. 20, 2001	352	Jan. 8–Jan. 20, 2001 Feb. 15–Feb. 26, 2001 Apr. 6–Apr. 23, 2001 May 26–June 5, 2001 June 29–July 9, 2001 Aug. 3–Sept. 4, 2001 Oct. 18–Oct. 23, 2001 Nov. 16–Nov. 27, 2001	Jan. 6–Jan. 20, 2001 Jan. 20–Jan 30, 2001 Jan. 31–Feb. 6, 2001 Feb. 14–Feb. 26, 2001 Apr. 4–Apr. 24, 2001 May 26–June 5, 2001 June 28–July 10, 2001 Aug. 2–Sept. 5, 2001 Oct. 17–Oct. 23, 2001 Nov. 19–Nov. 27, 2001	Robert C. Byrd, of West Virginia;[21] Strom Thurmond, of South Carolina;[21] Robert C. Byrd, of West Virginia.[21]	Do.
	2	Jan. 23, 2002	Nov. 22, 2002	304	Jan. 29–Feb. 4, 2002 Feb. 15–Feb. 25, 2002 Mar. 22–Apr. 8, 2002 May 23–June 3, 2002 June 28–July 8, 202 Aug. 1–Sept. 3, 2002	Jan. 29–Feb. 4, 2002 Feb. 14–Feb. 26, 2002 Mar. 20–Apr. 9, 2002 May 24–June 4, 2002 June 28–July 8, 2002 July 27–Sept. 4, 2002	Robert C. Byrd, of West Virginia.	

SESSIONS OF CONGRESS, 1st–111th CONGRESSES, 1789–2009—CONTINUED

[Closing date for this table was September 29, 2009.]

MEETING DATES OF CONGRESS: Pursuant to a resolution of the Confederation Congress in 1788, the Constitution went into effect on March 4, 1789. From then until the 20th amendment took effect in January 1934, the term of each Congress began on March 4th of each odd-numbered year; however, Article I, section 4, of the Constitution provided that ''The Congress shall assemble at least once in every Year, and such Meeting shall be on the first Monday in December, unless they shall by law appoint a different day.'' The Congress therefore convened regularly on the first Monday in December until the 20th amendment became effective, which changed the beginning of Congress's term as well as its convening date to January 3rd. So prior to 1934, a new Congress typically would not convene for regular business until 13 months after being elected. One effect of this was that the last session of each Congress was a ''lame duck'' session. After the 20th amendment, the time from the election to the beginning of Congress's term as well as when it convened was reduced to two months. Recognizing that the need might exist for Congress to meet at times other than the regularly scheduled convening date, Article II, section 3 of the Constitution provides that the President ''may, on extraordinary occasions, convene both Houses, or either of them''; hence these sessions occur only if convened by Presidential proclamation. Except as noted, these are separately numbered sessions of a Congress, and are marked by an E in the session column of the table. Until the 20th amendment was adopted, there were also times when special sessions of the Senate were convened, principally for confirming Cabinet and other executive nominations, and occasionally for the ratification of treaties or other executive business. These Senate sessions were also called by Presidential proclamation (typically by the outgoing President, although on occasion by incumbents as well) and are marked by an S in the session column. MEETING PLACES OF CONGRESS: Congress met for the first and second sessions of the First Congress (1789 and 1790) in New York City. From the third session of the First Congress through the first session of the Sixth Congress (1790 to 1800), Philadelphia was the meeting place. Congress has convened in Washington since the second session of the Sixth Congress (1800).

Congress	Session	Convening Date	Adjournment Date	Length in days [1]	Recesses [2]		President pro tempore of the Senate [3]	Speaker of the House of Representatives
					Senate	House of Representatives		
108th	1	Jan. 7, 2003	Dec. 9, 2003	337	Feb. 14–Feb. 24, 2003 Apr. 11–Apr. 28, 2003 May 23–June 2, 2003 June 27–July 7, 2003 Aug. 1–Sept 2, 2003 Oct. 3–Oct. 14, 2003 Nov. 25–Dec. 9, 2003	Jan. 8–Jan. 27, 2003 Feb. 13–Feb. 25, 2003 Apr. 12–Apr. 29, 2003 May 23–June 2, 2003 June 27–July 7, 2003 July 29–Sept. 3, 2003 Nov. 25–Dec. 8, 2003	Ted Stevens, of Alaska	J. Dennis Hastert, of Illinois.
	2	Jan. 20, 2004	Dec. 8, 2004	324	Feb. 12–Feb. 23, 2004 Mar. 12–Mar. 22, 2004 Apr. 8–Apr. 19, 2004 May 21–June 1, 2004 June 9–June 14, 2004 June 25–July 6, 2004 July 22–Sept. 7, 2004 Oct. 11–Nov. 16, 2004 Nov. 24–Dec. 7, 2004	Feb. 11–Feb. 24, 2004 Apr. 2–Apr. 20, 2004 May 20–June 1, 2004 June 9–June 14, 2004 June 25–July 6, 2004 July 22–Sept. 7, 2004 Oct. 9–Nov. 16, 2004 Nov. 24–Dec. 6, 2004	......do.	
109th	1	Jan. 4, 2005	Dec. 22, 2005	353	Jan. 6–Jan. 20, 2005 Jan. 26–Jan. 31, 2005 Feb. 18–Feb. 28, 2005 Mar. 20–Apr. 4, 2005 Apr. 29–May 9, 2005 May 26–June 6, 2005 July 1–July 11, 2005 July 29–Sept. 1, 2005 Sept. 1–Sept. 6, 2005 Oct. 7–Oct. 17, 2005 Nov. 18–Dec. 12, 2005	Jan. 6–Jan. 20, 2005 Jan. 20–Jan. 25, 2005 Jan. 26–Feb. 1, 2005 Feb. 2–Feb. 8, 2005 Feb. 17–Mar. 1, 2005 Mar. 21–Apr. 5, 2005 May 26–June 7, 2005 July 1–July 11, 2005 July 29–Sept. 2, 2005 Oct. 7–Oct. 17, 2005 Nov. 18–Dec. 6, 2005	......do	Do.

	2	Jan. 3, 2006	Dec. 9, 2006	341	Jan. 3–Jan. 18, 2006 .... Feb. 17–Feb. 27, 2006 Mar. 16–Mar. 27, 2006 Apr. 7–Apr. 24, 2006 May 26–June 5, 2006 June 29–July 10, 2006 Aug. 4–Sept. 5, 2006 Sept. 30–Nov. 9, 2006 Nov. 16–Dec. 4, 2006	Jan. 3–Jan. 31, 2006 .... Feb. 1–Feb. 7, 2006 Feb. 8–Feb. 14, 2006 Feb. 16–Feb. 28, 2006 Mar. 16–Mar. 28, 2006 Apr. 6–Apr. 25, 2006 May 25–June 6, 2006 June 29–July 10, 2006 Aug. 2–Sept. 6, 2006 Sept. 30–Nov. 9, 2006 Nov. 15–Dec. 5, 2006	......do.	
110th ..	1	Jan. 4, 2007	Dec. 31, 2007 ...	362	Feb. 17–Feb. 26, 2007 .... Mar. 29–Apr. 10, 2007 May 25–June 4, 2007 June 29–July 9, 2007 Aug. 3–Sept. 4, 2007 Oct. 5–Oct. 15, 2007 Nov. 16–Dec. 3, 2007 Dec. 19–Jan. 3, 2008	Feb. 16–Feb. 27, 2007 .... Mar. 30–Apr. 16, 2007 May 24–June 5, 2007 June 28–July 10, 2007 Aug. 4–Sept. 4, 2007 Nov. 15–Dec. 4, 2007	Robert C. Byrd, of West Virginia	Nancy Pelosi, of California.
	2	Jan. 3, 2008	Jan. 3, 2009	367	Jan. 3–Jan. 22, 2008 .... Feb. 14–Feb. 26, 2008 Mar. 13–Mar. 31, 2008 May 22–June 2, 2008 June 27–July 7, 2008 Aug. 1–Sept. 8, 2008 Oct. 2–Nov. 17, 2008 Nov. 20–Dec. 8, 2008 Dec. 11–Jan. 3, 2009	Jan. 3–Jan. 15, 2008 .... Mar. 14–Mar. 31, 2008 May 22–June 3, 2008 June 26–July 8, 2008 Aug. 1–Sept. 8, 2008 Oct. 3–Nov. 19, 2008 Nov. 20–Dec. 9, 2008 Dec. 10–Jan. 3, 2009	......do.	
111th ..	1	Jan. 6, 2009	....	....	Feb. 13–Feb. 23, 2009 .... Apr. 2–Apr. 20, 2009 May 21–June 1, 2009 June 25–July 6, 2009	Feb. 13–Feb. 23, 2009 .... Apr. 2–Apr. 21, 2009 May 21–June 2, 2009 June 26–July 7, 2009 July 31–Sept. 8, 2009	......do	Do.

[1] For the purposes of this table, a session's ''length in days'' is defined as the total number of calendar days from the convening date to the adjournment date, inclusive. It does not mean the actual number of days that Congress met during that session.

[2] For the purposes of this table, a ''recess'' is defined as any period of three or more complete days, when either the House of Representatives or the Senate is not in session; however, as listed, the recess periods also are inclusive of days only partially in the recess, i.e., the day (or days) when the House and Senate each adjourn to begin the recess, as well as the day (or days) when each body reconvenes at the end of the recess.

[3] The election and role of the President pro tempore has evolved considerably over the Senate's history. ''*Pro tempore* is Latin for 'for the time being'; thus, the post was conceived as a temporary presiding officer. In the eighteenth and nineteenth centuries, the Senate frequently elected several Presidents pro tempore during a single session. Since Vice Presidents presided routinely, the Senate thought it necessary to choose a President pro tempore only for the limited periods when the Vice President might be ill or otherwise absent.'' Since no provision was in place (until the 25th amendment was adopted in 1967) for replacing the Vice President if he died or resigned from office, or if he assumed the Presidency, the President pro tempore would continue under such circumstances to fill the duties of the chair until the next Vice President was elected. Since Mar. 12, 1890, however, Presidents pro tempore have served until ''the Senate otherwise ordered.'' Since 1949, while still elected, the position has gone to the most senior member of the majority party (see footnote 19 for a minority party exception). To gain a more complete understanding of this position, see Robert C. Byrd's *The Senate 1789–1989: Addresses on the History of the United States Senate*, vol. 2, ch. 6 ''The President Pro Tempore,'' pp. 167–183, from which the quotes in this footnote are taken. Also, a complete listing of the dates of election of the Presidents pro tempore is in vol. 4 of the Byrd series (*The Senate 1789–1989: Historical Statistics, 1789–1992*), table 6–2, pp. 647–653.

[4] Henry Clay resigned as Speaker on Jan. 19, 1814. He was succeeded by Langdon Cheves who was elected on that same day.

[5] Henry Clay resigned as Speaker on Oct. 28, 1820, after the sine die adjournment of the first session of the 16th Congress. He was succeeded by John W. Taylor who was elected at the beginning of the second session.

[6] Andrew Stevenson resigned as Speaker on June 2, 1834. He was succeeded by John Bell who was elected on that same day.

[7] Speaker Schuyler Colfax resigned as Speaker on the last day of the 40th Congress, Mar. 3, 1869, in preparation for becoming Vice President of the United States on the following day. Theodore M. Pomeroy was elected Speaker on Mar. 3, and served for only that one day.

[8] Speaker Michael C. Kerr died on Aug. 19, 1876, after the sine die adjournment of the first session of the 44th Congress. Samuel J. Randall was elected Speaker at the beginning of the second session.

[9] William P. Frye resigned as President pro tempore on Apr. 27, 1911.

[10] President pro tempore James P. Clarke died on Oct. 1, 1916, after the sine die adjournment of the first session of the 64th Congress. Willard Saulsbury was elected President pro tempore during the second session.

[11] Speaker Joseph W. Byrns died on June 4, 1936. He was succeeded by William B. Bankhead who was elected Speaker on that same day.

[12] Speaker William B. Bankhead died on Sept. 15, 1940. He was succeeded by Sam Rayburn who was elected Speaker on that same day.

[13] President pro tempore Key Pittman died on Nov. 10, 1940. He was succeeded by William H. King who was elected President pro tempore on Nov. 19, 1940.

[14] President pro tempore Pat Harrison died on June 22, 1941. He was succeeded by Carter Glass who was elected President pro tempore on July 10, 1941.

[15] President Harry S. Truman called the Congress into extraordinary session twice, both times during the 80th Congress. Each time Congress had essentially wrapped up its business for the year, but for technical reasons had not adjourned sine die, so in each case the extraordinary session is considered an extension of the regularly numbered session rather than a separately numbered one. The dates of these extraordinary sessions were Nov. 17 to Dec. 19, 1947, and July 26 to Aug. 7, 1948.

[16] Speaker Sam Rayburn died on Nov. 16, 1961, after the sine die adjournment of the first session of the 87th Congress. John W. McCormack was elected Speaker at the beginning of the second session.

[17] President pro tempore Richard B. Russell died on Jan. 21, 1971. He was succeeded by Allen J. Ellender who was elected to that position on Jan. 22, 1971.

[18] President pro tempore Allen J. Ellender died on July 27, 1972. He was succeeded by James O. Eastland who was elected President pro tempore on July 28, 1972.

[19] Milton Young was elected President pro tempore for one day, Dec. 5, 1980, which was at the end of his 36-year career in the Senate. He was Republican, which was the minority party at that time. Warren G. Magnuson resumed the position of President pro tempore on Dec. 6, 1980.

[20] James C. Wright, Jr., resigned as Speaker on June 6, 1989. He was succeeded by Thomas S. Foley who was elected on that same day.

[21] The 2000 election resulted in an even split in the Senate between Republicans and Democrats. From the date the 107th Congress convened on Jan. 3, 2001, until Inauguration Day on Jan. 20, 2001, Vice President Albert Gore tipped the scale to a Democratic majority, hence Robert C. Byrd served as President pro tempore during this brief period. When Vice President Richard B. Cheney took office on Jan. 20, the Republicans became the majority party, and Strom Thurmond was elected President pro tempore. On June 6, 2001, Republican Senator James Jeffords became an Independent, creating a Democratic majority, and Robert C. Byrd was elected President pro tempore on that day.

CEREMONIAL MEETINGS OF CONGRESS

The following ceremonial meetings of Congress occurred on the following dates, at the designated locations, and for the reasons indicated. Please note that Congress was not in session on these occasions.

-July 16, 1987, 100th Congress, Philadelphia, Pennsylvania, Independence Hall and Congress Hall—In honor of the bicentennial of the Constitution, and in commemoration of the Great Compromise of the Constitutional Convention which was agreed to on July 16, 1787.

-September 6, 2002, 107th Congress, New York City, New York, Federal Hall—In remembrance of the victims and heroes of September 11, 2001, and in recognition of the courage and spirit of the City of New York.

JOINT SESSIONS AND MEETINGS, ADDRESSES TO THE SENATE OR THE HOUSE, AND INAUGURATIONS

1st–111th CONGRESSES, 1789–2009 [1]

The parliamentary difference between a joint session and a joint meeting has evolved over time. In recent years the distinctions have become clearer: a joint session is more formal, and occurs upon the adoption of a concurrent resolution; a joint meeting occurs when each body adopts a unanimous consent agreement to recess to meet with the other legislative body. Joint sessions typically are held to hear an address from the President of the United States or to count electoral votes. Joint meetings typically are held to hear an address from a foreign dignitary or visitors other than the President.

The Speaker of the House of Representatives usually presides over joint sessions and joint meetings; however, the President of the Senate does preside over joint sessions where the electoral votes are counted, as required by the Constitution.

In the earliest years of the Republic, 1789 and 1790, when the national legislature met in New York City, joint gatherings were held in the Senate Chamber in Federal Hall. In Philadelphia, when the legislature met in Congress Hall, such meetings were held in the Senate Chamber, 1790–1793, and in the Hall of the House of Representatives, 1794–1799. Once the Congress moved to the Capitol in Washington in 1800, the Senate Chamber again was used for joint gatherings through 1805. Since 1809, with few exceptions, joint sessions and joint meetings have occurred in the Hall of the House.

Presidential messages on the state of the Union were originally known as the ''Annual Message,'' but since the 80th Congress, in 1947, have been called the ''State of the Union Address.'' After President John Adams's Annual Message on November 22, 1800, these addresses were read by clerks to the individual bodies until President Woodrow Wilson resumed the practice of delivering them to joint sessions on December 2, 1913.

In some instances more than one joint gathering has occurred on the same day. For example, on January 6, 1941, Congress met in joint session to count electoral votes for President and Vice President, and then met again in joint session to receive President Franklin Delano Roosevelt's Annual Message.

Whereas in more recent decades, foreign dignitaries invited to speak before Congress have typically done so at joint meetings, in earlier times (and with several notable exceptions), such visitors were received by the Senate and the House separately, or by one or the other singly, a tradition begun with the visit of General Lafayette of France in 1824. At that time a joint committee decided that each body would honor Lafayette separately, establishing the precedent. (See footnote 7 for more details.) Not all such occasions included formal addresses by such dignitaries (e.g., Lafayette's reception by the Senate in their chamber, at which he did not speak before they adjourned to greet him), hence the ''occasions'' listed in the third column of the table include not only addresses, but also remarks (defined as brief greetings or off-the-cuff comments often requested of the visitor at the last minute) and receptions. Relatively few foreign dignitaries were received by Congress before World War I.

Congress has hosted inaugurations since the first occasion in 1789. They always have been formal joint gatherings, and sometimes they also were joint sessions. Inaugurations were joint sessions when both houses of Congress were in session, and they processed to the ceremony as part of the business of the day. In many cases, however, one or both houses were not in session or were in recess at the time of the ceremony. In this table, inaugurations that were not joint sessions are listed in the second column. Those that were joint sessions are so identified and described in the third column.

JOINT SESSIONS AND MEETINGS, ADDRESSES TO THE SENATE OR THE HOUSE, AND INAUGURATIONS

[See notes at end of table]

Congress & Date	Type	Occasion, topic, or inaugural location	Name and position of dignitary (where applicable)
		NEW YORK CITY	
1st CONGRESS			
Apr. 6, 1789	Joint session	Counting electoral votes	N.A.
Apr. 30, 1789	......do	Inauguration and church service [2]	President George Washington; Right Reverend Samuel Provoost, Senate-appointed Chaplain.
Jan. 8, 1790	......do	Annual Message	President George Washington.
		PHILADELPHIA	
Dec. 8, 1790	......do	......do	Do.
2d CONGRESS			
Oct. 25, 1791	......do	......do	Do.
Nov. 6, 1792	......do	......do	Do.
Feb. 13, 1793	......do	Counting electoral votes	N.A.
3d CONGRESS			
Mar. 4, 1793	Inauguration	Senate Chamber	President George Washington.
Dec. 3, 1793	Joint session	Annual Message	Do.
Nov. 19, 1794	......do	......do	Do.
4th CONGRESS			
Dec. 8, 1795	......do	......do	Do.
Dec. 7, 1796	......do	......do	Do.
Feb. 8, 1797	......do	Counting electoral votes	N.A.
5th CONGRESS			
Mar. 4, 1797	Inauguration	Hall of the House	President John Adams.
May 16, 1797	Joint session	Relations with France	Do.
Nov. 23, 1797	......do	Annual Message	Do.
Dec. 8, 1798	......do	......do	Do.
6th CONGRESS			
Dec. 3, 1799	......do	......do	Do.
Dec. 26, 1799	......do	Funeral procession and oration in memory of George Washington.[3]	Representative Henry Lee.
		WASHINGTON	
Nov. 22, 1800	......do	Annual Message	President John Adams.
Feb. 11, 1801	......do	Counting electoral votes [4]	N.A.
7th CONGRESS			
Mar. 4, 1801	Inauguration	Senate Chamber	President Thomas Jefferson.
8th CONGRESS			
Feb. 13, 1805	Joint session	Counting electoral votes	N.A.
9th CONGRESS			
Mar. 4, 1805	Inauguration	Senate Chamber	President Thomas Jefferson.
10th CONGRESS			
Feb. 8, 1809	Joint session	Counting electoral votes	N.A.
11th CONGRESS			
Mar. 4, 1809	Inauguration	Hall of the House	President James Madison.
12th CONGRESS			
Feb. 10, 1813	Joint session	Counting electoral votes	N.A.
13th CONGRESS			
Mar. 4, 1813	Inauguration	Hall of the House	President James Madison.
14th CONGRESS			
Feb. 12, 1817	Joint session	Counting electoral votes [5]	N.A.
15th CONGRESS			
Mar. 4, 1817	Inauguration	In front of Brick Capitol	President James Monroe.
16th CONGRESS			
Feb. 14, 1821	Joint session	Counting electoral votes [6]	N.A.
17th CONGRESS			
Mar. 5, 1821	Inauguration	Hall of the House	President James Monroe.
18th CONGRESS			
Dec. 9, 1824	Senate	Reception	General Gilbert du Motier, Marquis de Lafayette, of France.
Dec. 10, 1824	House [7]	Address	Speaker Henry Clay; General Gilbert du Motier, Marquis de Lafayette, of France.

JOINT SESSIONS AND MEETINGS, ADDRESSES TO THE SENATE OR THE HOUSE, AND INAUGURATIONS—CONTINUED

[See notes at end of table]

Congress & Date	Type	Occasion, topic, or inaugural location	Name and position of dignitary (where applicable)
Feb. 9, 1825	Joint session	Counting electoral votes [8]	N.A.
19th CONGRESS			
Mar. 4, 1825	Inauguration	Hall of the House	President John Quincy Adams.
20th CONGRESS			
Feb. 11, 1829	Joint session	Counting electoral votes	N.A.
21st CONGRESS			
Mar. 4, 1829	Inauguration	East Portico [9]	President Andrew Jackson.
22d CONGRESS			
Feb. 13, 1833	Joint session	Counting electoral votes	N.A.
23d CONGRESS			
Mar. 4, 1833	Inauguration	Hall of the House [10]	President Andrew Jackson.
Dec. 31, 1834	Joint session	Lafayette eulogy	Representative and former President John Quincy Adams; ceremony attended by President Andrew Jackson.
24th CONGRESS			
Feb. 8, 1837	......do	Counting electoral votes	N.A.
25th CONGRESS			
Mar. 4, 1837	Inauguration	East Portico	President Martin Van Buren.
26th CONGRESS			
Feb. 10, 1841	Joint session	Counting electoral votes	N.A.
27th CONGRESS			
Mar. 4, 1841	Inauguration	East Portico	President William Henry Harrison.
28th CONGRESS			
Feb. 12, 1845	Joint session	Counting electoral votes	N.A.
29th CONGRESS			
Mar. 4, 1845	Inauguration	East Portico	President James Knox Polk.
30th CONGRESS			
Feb. 14, 1849	Joint session	Counting electoral votes	N.A.
31st CONGRESS			
Mar. 5, 1849	Inauguration	East Portico	President Zachary Taylor.
July 10, 1850	Joint session	Oath of office to President Millard Fillmore. [11]	N.A.
32d CONGRESS			
Jan. 5, 1852	Senate	Reception	Louis Kossuth, exiled Governor of Hungary.
Jan. 7, 1852	House	Remarks and Reception	Do.
Feb. 9, 1853	Joint session	Counting electoral votes	N.A.
33d CONGRESS			
Mar. 4, 1853	Inauguration	East Portico	President Franklin Pierce.
34th CONGRESS			
Feb. 11, 1857	Joint session	Counting electoral votes	N.A.
35th CONGRESS			
Mar. 4, 1857	Inauguration	East Portico	President James Buchanan.
36th CONGRESS			
Feb. 13, 1861	Joint session	Counting electoral votes	N.A.
37th CONGRESS			
Mar. 4, 1861	Inauguration	East Portico	President Abraham Lincoln.
Feb. 22, 1862	Joint session	Reading of Washington's farewell address.	John W. Forney, Secretary of the Senate.
38th CONGRESS			
Feb. 8, 1865	......do	Counting electoral votes	N.A.
39th CONGRESS			
Mar. 4, 1865	Inauguration	East Portico	President Abraham Lincoln.
Feb. 12, 1866	Joint session	Memorial to Abraham Lincoln	George Bancroft, historian; ceremony attended by President Andrew Johnson.
40th CONGRESS			
June 9, 1868	House	Address	Anson Burlingame, Envoy to the U.S. from China, and former Representative.

JOINT SESSIONS AND MEETINGS, ADDRESSES TO THE SENATE OR THE HOUSE, AND INAUGURATIONS—CONTINUED

[See notes at end of table]

Congress & Date	Type	Occasion, topic, or inaugural location	Name and position of dignitary (where applicable)
Feb. 10, 1869	Joint session	Counting electoral votes	N.A.
41st CONGRESS			
Mar. 4, 1869	Inauguration	East Portico	President Ulysses S. Grant.
42d CONGRESS			
Mar. 6, 1872	House	Address	Tomomi Iwakura, Ambassador from Japan.
Feb. 12, 1873	Joint session	Counting electoral votes [12]	N.A.
43d CONGRESS			
Mar. 4, 1873	Inauguration	East Portico	President Ulysses S. Grant.
Dec. 18, 1874	Joint meeting	Reception and Remarks	Speaker James G. Blaine; David Kalakaua, King of the Hawaiian Islands.[13]
44th CONGRESS			
Feb. 1, 1877 Feb. 10, 1877 Feb. 12, 1877 Feb. 19, 1877 Feb. 20, 1877 Feb. 21, 1877 Feb. 24, 1877 Feb. 26, 1877 Feb. 28, 1877 Mar. 1, 1877 Mar. 2, 1877	Joint session	Counting electoral votes [14]	N.A.
45th CONGRESS			
Mar. 5, 1877	Inauguration	East Portico	President Rutherford B. Hayes.
46th CONGRESS			
Feb. 2, 1880	House	Address	Charles Stewart Parnell, member of Parliament from Ireland.
Feb. 9, 1881	Joint session	Counting electoral votes	N.A.
47th CONGRESS			
Mar. 4, 1881	Inauguration	East Portico	President James A. Garfield.
Feb. 27, 1882	Joint session	Memorial to James A. Garfield	James G. Blaine, former Speaker, Senator, and Secretary of State; ceremony attended by President Chester A. Arthur.
48th CONGRESS			
Feb. 11, 1885	......do	Counting electoral votes	N.A.
Feb. 21, 1885	......do	Completion of Washington Monument	Representative John D. Long; Representative-elect John W. Daniel,[15] ceremony attended by President Chester A. Arthur.
49th CONGRESS			
Mar. 4, 1885	Inauguration	East Portico	President Grover Cleveland.
50th CONGRESS			
Feb. 13, 1889	Joint session	Counting electoral votes	N.A.
51st CONGRESS			
Mar. 4, 1889	Inauguration	East Portico	President Benjamin Harrison.
Dec. 11, 1889	Joint session	Centennial of George Washington's first inauguration.	Melville W. Fuller, Chief Justice of the United States; ceremony attended by President Benjamin Harrison.
52d CONGRESS			
Feb. 8, 1893	......do	Counting electoral votes	N.A.
53d CONGRESS			
Mar. 4, 1893	Inauguration	East Portico	President Grover Cleveland.
54th CONGRESS			
Feb. 10, 1897	Joint session	Counting electoral votes	N.A.
55th CONGRESS			
Mar. 4, 1897	Inauguration	In front of original Senate Wing of Capitol.	President William McKinley.

JOINT SESSIONS AND MEETINGS, ADDRESSES TO THE SENATE OR THE HOUSE, AND INAUGURATIONS—CONTINUED

[See notes at end of table]

Congress & Date	Type	Occasion, topic, or inaugural location	Name and position of dignitary (where applicable)
56th CONGRESS			
Dec. 12, 1900	Joint meeting	Centennial of the Capital City	Representatives James D. Richardson and Sereno E. Payne, and Senator George F. Hoar; ceremony attended by President William McKinley.
Feb. 13, 1901	Joint session	Counting electoral votes	N.A.
57th CONGRESS			
Mar. 4, 1901	Inauguration	East Portico	President William McKinley.
Feb. 27, 1902	Joint session	Memorial to William McKinley	John Hay, Secretary of State; ceremony attended by President Theodore Roosevelt and Prince Henry of Prussia.
58th CONGRESS			
Feb. 8, 1905	......do	Counting electoral votes	N.A.
59th CONGRESS			
Mar. 4, 1905	Inauguration	East Portico	President Theodore Roosevelt.
60th CONGRESS			
Feb. 10, 1909	Joint session	Counting electoral votes	N.A.
61st CONGRESS			
Mar. 4, 1909	Inauguration	Senate Chamber [16]	President William Howard Taft.
Feb. 9, 1911	House	Address	Count Albert Apponyi, Minister of Education from Hungary.
62d CONGRESS			
Feb. 12, 1913	Joint session	Counting electoral votes	N.A.
Feb. 15, 1913	......do	Memorial for Vice President James S. Sherman.[17]	Senators Elihu Root, Thomas S. Martin, Jacob H. Gallinger, John R. Thornton, Henry Cabot Lodge, John W. Kern, Robert M. LaFollette, John Sharp Williams, Charles Curtis, Albert B. Cummins, George T. Oliver, James A. O'Gorman; Speaker Champ Clark; President William Howard Taft.
63d CONGRESS			
Mar. 4, 1913	Inauguration	East Portico	President Woodrow Wilson.
Apr. 8, 1913	Joint session	Tariff message	Do.
June 23, 1913	......do	Currency and bank reform message	Do.
Aug. 27, 1913	......do	Mexican affairs message	Do.
Dec. 2, 1913	......do	Annual Message	Do.
Jan. 20, 1914	......do	Trusts message	Do.
Mar. 5, 1914	......do	Panama Canal tolls	Do.
Apr. 20, 1914	......do	Mexico message	Do.
Sept. 4, 1914	......do	War tax message	Do.
Dec. 8, 1914	......do	Annual Message	Do.
64th CONGRESS			
Dec. 7, 1915	......do	......do	Do.
Aug. 29, 1916	......do	Railroad message (labor-management dispute).	Do.
Dec. 5, 1916	......do	Annual Message	Do.
Jan. 22, 1917	Senate	Planning ahead for peace	Do.
Feb. 3, 1917	Joint session	Severing diplomatic relations with Germany.	Do.
Feb. 14, 1917	......do	Counting electoral votes	N.A.
Feb. 26, 1917	......do	Arming of merchant ships	President Woodrow Wilson.
65th CONGRESS			
Mar. 5, 1917	Inauguration	East Portico	Do.
Apr. 2, 1917	Joint session	War with Germany	Do.
May 1, 1917	Senate	Address	René Raphaël Viviani, Minister of Justice from France; Jules Jusserand, Ambassador from France; address attended by Marshal Joseph Jacques Césaire Joffre, member of French Commission to U.S.
May 3, 1917	House	......do	Do.
May 5, 1917	......do	......do	Arthur James Balfour, British Secretary of State for Foreign Affairs.
May 8, 1917	Senate	......do	Do.
May 31, 1917	......do	......do	Ferdinando di'Savoia, Prince of Udine, Head of Italian Mission to U.S.
June 2, 1917	House	......do	Ferdinando di'Savoia, Prince of Udine, Head of Italian Mission to U.S.; Guglielmo Marconi, member of Italian Mission to U.S.

JOINT SESSIONS AND MEETINGS, ADDRESSES TO THE SENATE OR THE HOUSE, AND INAUGURATIONS—CONTINUED

[See notes at end of table]

Congress & Date	Type	Occasion, topic, or inaugural location	Name and position of dignitary (where applicable)
June 22, 1917	Senate	Address	Baron Moncheur, Chief of Political Bureau of Belgian Foreign Office at Havre.
June 23, 1917	House	......do	Boris Bakhmetieff, Ambassador from Russia.[18]
June 26, 1917	Senate	......do	Do.
June 27, 1917	House	......do	Baron Moncheur, Chief of Political Bureau of Belgian Foreign Office at Havre.
Aug. 30, 1917	Senate	......do	Kikujirō Ishii, Ambassador from Japan.
Sept. 5, 1917	House	......do	Do.
Dec. 4, 1917	Joint session	Annual Message/War with Austria-Hungary.	President Woodrow Wilson.
Jan. 4, 1918	......do	Federal operation of transportation systems.	Do.
Jan. 5, 1918	Senate	Address	Milenko Vesnic, Head of Serbian War Mission.
Jan. 8, 1918	House	Address	Milenko Vesnic, Head of Serbian War Mission.
Do	Joint session	Program for world's peace	President Woodrow Wilson.
Feb. 11, 1918	......do	Peace message	Do.
May 27, 1918	......do	War finance message	Do.
Sept. 24, 1918	Senate	Address and Reception[19]	Jules Jusserand, Ambassador from France; Vice President Thomas R. Marshall.
Sept. 30 1918	......do	Support of woman suffrage	President Woodrow Wilson.
Nov. 11, 1918	Joint session	Terms of armistice signed by Germany	Do.
Dec. 2, 1918	......do	Annual Message	Do.
Feb. 9, 1919	......do	Memorial to Theodore Roosevelt	Senator Henry Cabot Lodge, Sr.; ceremony attended by former President William Howard Taft.
66th CONGRESS			
June 23, 1919	Senate	Address	Epitácio da Silva Pessoa, President-elect of Brazil.
July 10, 1919	......do	Versailles Treaty	President Woodrow Wilson.
Aug. 8, 1919	Joint session	Cost of living message	Do.
Sept. 18, 1919	......do	Address	President pro tempore Albert B. Cummins; Speaker Frederick H. Gillett; Representative and former Speaker Champ Clark; General John J. Pershing.
Oct. 28, 1919	Senate	......do	Albert I, King of the Belgians.
Do	House	......do	Do.
Feb. 9, 1921	Joint session	Counting electoral votes	N.A.
67th CONGRESS			
Mar. 4, 1921	Inauguration	East Portico	President Warren G. Harding.
Apr. 12, 1921	Joint session	Federal problem message	Do.
July 12, 1921	Senate	Adjusted compensation for veterans of the World War[20].	Do.
Dec. 6, 1921	Joint session	Annual Message	Do.
Feb. 28, 1922	......do	Maintenance of the merchant marine	Do.
Aug. 18, 1922	......do	Coal and railroad message	Do.
Nov. 21, 1922	......do	Promotion of the American merchant marine.	Do.
Dec. 8, 1922	......do	Annual Message[21]	Do.
Feb. 7, 1923	......do	British debt due to the United States	Do.
68th CONGRESS			
Dec. 6, 1923	......do	Annual Message	President Calvin Coolidge.
Feb. 27, 1924	......do	Memorial to Warren G. Harding	Charles Evans Hughes, Secretary of State; ceremony attended by President Calvin Coolidge.
Dec. 15, 1924	......do	Memorial to Woodrow Wilson	Dr. Edwin Anderson Alderman, President of the University of Virginia; ceremony attended by President Calvin Coolidge.
Feb. 11, 1925	......do	Counting electoral votes	N.A.
69th CONGRESS			
Mar. 4, 1925	Inauguration	East Portico	President Calvin Coolidge.
Feb. 22, 1927	Joint session	George Washington birthday message	Do.
70th CONGRESS			
Jan. 25, 1928	House	Reception and Address	William Thomas Cosgrave, President of Executive Council of Ireland.
Feb. 13, 1929	Joint session	Counting electoral votes	N.A.
71st CONGRESS			
Mar. 4, 1929	Inauguration	East Portico	President Herbert Hoover.

JOINT SESSIONS AND MEETINGS, ADDRESSES TO THE SENATE OR THE HOUSE, AND INAUGURATIONS—CONTINUED

[See notes at end of table]

Congress & Date	Type	Occasion, topic, or inaugural location	Name and position of dignitary (where applicable)
Oct. 7, 1929	Senate	Address	James Ramsay MacDonald, Prime Minister of the United Kingdom.
Jan. 13, 1930	......do	Reception	Jan Christiaan Smuts, former Prime Minister of South Africa.
72d CONGRESS			
Feb. 22, 1932	Joint session	Bicentennial of George Washington's birth.	President Herbert Hoover.
May 31, 1932	Senate	Emergency character of economic situation in U.S.	Do.
Feb. 6, 1933	Joint meeting	Memorial to Calyin Coolidge	Arthur Prentice Rugg, Chief Justice of the Supreme Judicial Court of Massachusetts; ceremony attended by President Herbert Hoover.
Feb. 8, 1933	Joint session	Counting electoral votes	N.A.
73d CONGRESS			
Mar. 4, 1933	Inauguration	East Portico	President Franklin Delano Roosevelt.
Jan. 3, 1934	Joint session	Annual Message	President Franklin Delano Roosevelt.
May 20, 1934	......do	100th anniversary, death of Lafayette	André de Laboulaye, Ambassador of France; President Franklin Delano Roosevelt; ceremony attended by Count de Chambrun, great-grandson of Lafayette.
74th CONGRESS			
Jan. 4, 1935	......do	Annual Message	President Franklin Delano Roosevelt.
May 22, 1935	......do	Veto message	Do.
Jan. 3, 1936	......do	Annual Message	Do.
75th CONGRESS			
Jan. 6, 1937	......do	Counting electoral votes	N.A.
Do	......do	Annual Message	President Franklin Delano Roosevelt.
Jan. 20, 1937	Inauguration	East Portico	President Franklin Delano Roosevelt; Vice President John Nance Garner.[22]
Apr. 1, 1937	Senate	Address	John Buchan, Lord Tweedsmuir, Governor General of Canada.
Do	House	......do	Do.
Jan. 3, 1938	Joint session	Annual Message	President Franklin Delano Roosevelt.
76th CONGRESS			
Jan. 4, 1939	......do	......do	Do.
Mar. 4, 1939	......do	Sesquicentennial of the 1st Congress	Do.
May 8, 1939	Senate	Address	Anastasio Somoza Garcia, President of Nicaragua.
Do	House	......do	Do.
June 9, 1939	Joint meeting	Reception[23]	George VI and Elizabeth, King and Queen of the United Kingdom.
Sept. 21, 1939	Joint session	Neutrality address	President Franklin Delano Roosevelt.
Jan. 3, 1940	......do	Annual Message	Do.
May 16, 1940	......do	National defense message	Do.
77th CONGRESS			
Jan. 6, 1941	......do	Counting electoral votes	N.A.
Do	......do	Annual Message	President Franklin Delano Roosevelt.
Jan. 20, 1941	......do	Inauguration, East Portico	President Franklin Delano Roosevelt; Vice President Henry A. Wallace.
Dec. 8, 1941	......do	War with Japan	President Franklin Delano Roosevelt.
Dec. 26, 1941	Joint meeting[24]	Address	Winston Churchill, Prime Minister of the United Kingdom.
Jan. 6, 1942	Joint session	Annual Message	President Franklin Delano Roosevelt.
May 11, 1942	Senate	Address	Manuel Prado, President of Peru.
Do	House	......do	Do.
June 2, 1942	......do	......do	Manuel Luis Quezon, President of the Philippines.[25]
June 4, 1942	Senate	......do	Do.
June 15, 1942	......do	......do	George II, King of Greece.[26]
Do	House	......do	Do.
June 25, 1942	Senate	......do	Peter II, King of Yugoslavia.[26]
Do	House	......do	Do.
Aug. 6, 1942	Senate[27]	......do	Wilhelmina, Queen of the Netherlands.[26]
Nov. 24, 1942	House	......do	Carlos Arroyo del Río, President of Ecuador.
Nov. 25, 1942	Senate	......do	Do.
Dec. 10, 1942	House	......do	Fulgencio Batista, President of Cuba.
78th CONGRESS			
Jan. 7, 1943	Joint session	Annual Message	President Franklin Delano Roosevelt.
Feb. 18, 1943	Senate	Remarks	Madame Chiang Kai-shek, of China.
Do	House	Address	Do.

JOINT SESSIONS AND MEETINGS, ADDRESSES TO THE SENATE OR THE HOUSE, AND INAUGURATIONS—CONTINUED

[See notes at end of table]

Congress & Date	Type	Occasion, topic, or inaugural location	Name and position of dignitary (where applicable)
May 6, 1943	Senate	......do	Enrique Peñaranda, President of Bolivia.
Do	House	......do	Do.
May 13, 1943	Senate	......do	Edvard Beneš, President of Czechoslovakia.[26]
Do	House	......do	Do.
May 19, 1943	Joint meeting	Address	Winston Churchill, Prime Minister of the United Kingdom.
May 27, 1943	Senate	Remarks	Edwin Barclay, President of Liberia.
Do	House	Address	Do.
June 10, 1943	Senate	......do	President Hininio Moríñigo M., President of Paraguay.
Do	House	......do	Do.
Oct. 15, 1943	Senate	......do	Elie Lescot, President of Haiti.
Nov. 18, 1943	Joint meeting	Moscow Conference	Cordell Hull, Secretary of State.
Jan. 20, 1944	Senate	Address	Isaías Medina Angarita, President of Venezuela.
Do	House	......do	Do.
79th CONGRESS			
Jan. 6, 1945	Joint session	Counting electoral votes	N.A.
Jan. 6, 1945	......do	Annual Message	President Roosevelt was not present. His message was read before the Joint Session of Congress.
Jan. 20, 1945	Inauguration	South Portico, The White House[28]	President Franklin Delano Roosevelt; Vice President Harry S. Truman.
Mar. 1, 1945	Joint session	Yalta Conference	President Franklin Delano Roosevelt.
Apr. 16, 1945	......do	Prosecution of the War	President Harry S. Truman.
May 21, 1945	......do	Bestowal of Congressional Medal of Honor on Tech. Sgt. Jake William Lindsey.	General George C. Marshall, Chief of Staff, U.S. Army; President Harry S. Truman.
June 18, 1945	Joint meeting	Address	General Dwight D. Eisenhower, Supreme Commander, Allied Expeditionary Force.
July 2, 1945	Senate	United Nations Charter	President Harry S. Truman.
Oct. 5, 1945	Joint meeting	Address	Admiral Chester W. Nimitz, Commander-in-Chief, Pacific Fleet.
Oct. 23, 1945	Joint session	Universal military training message	President Harry S. Truman.
Nov. 13, 1945	Joint meeting	Address	Clement R. Attlee, Prime Minister of the United Kingdom.
May 25, 1946	Joint session	Railroad strike message	President Harry S. Truman.
July 1, 1946	......do	Memorial to Franklin Delano Roosevelt	John Winant, U.S. Representative on the Economic and Social Council of the United Nations; ceremony attended by President Harry S. Truman and Mrs. Franklin Delano Roosevelt.
80th CONGRESS			
Jan. 6, 1947	......do	State of the Union Address[29]	President Harry S. Truman.
Mar. 12, 1947	......do	Greek-Turkish aid policy	Do.
May 1, 1947	Joint meeting	Address	Miguel Alemán, President of Mexico.
Nov. 17, 1947	Joint session	Aid to Europe message	President Harry S. Truman.
Jan. 7, 1948	......do	State of the Union Address	Do.
Mar. 17, 1948	......do	National security and conditions in Europe.	Do.
Apr. 19, 1948	......do	50th anniversary, liberation of Cuba	President Harry S. Truman; Guillermo Belt, Ambassador of Cuba.
July 27, 1948	......do	Inflation, housing, and civil rights	President Harry S. Truman.
81st CONGRESS			
Jan. 5, 1949	......do	State of the Union Address	Do.
Jan. 6, 1949	......do	Counting electoral votes	N.A.
Jan. 20, 1949	......do	Inauguration, East Portico	President Harry S. Truman; Vice President Alben W. Barkley.
May 19, 1949	Joint meeting	Address	Eurico Gaspar Dutra, President of Brazil.
Aug. 9, 1949	House	......do	Elpidio Quirino, President of the Philippines.
Do	Senate	......do	Do.
Oct. 13, 1949	......do	......do	Jawaharlal Nehru, Prime Minister of India.
Do	House	......do	Do.
Jan. 4, 1950	Joint session	State of the Union Address	President Harry S. Truman.
Apr. 13, 1950	Senate	Address	Gabriel González-Videla, President of Chile.
May 4, 1950	......do	......do	Liaquat Ali Khan, Prime Minister of Pakistan.
Do	House	......do	Do.
May 31, 1950	Joint meeting	Address	Dean Acheson, Secretary of State.
July 28, 1950	Senate	......do	Chōjirō Kuriyama, member of Japanese Diet.

JOINT SESSIONS AND MEETINGS, ADDRESSES TO THE SENATE OR THE HOUSE, AND INAUGURATIONS—CONTINUED

[See notes at end of table]

Congress & Date	Type	Occasion, topic, or inaugural location	Name and position of dignitary (where applicable)
July 31, 1950	House	......do	Tokutarō Kitamura, member of Japanese Diet.
Aug. 1, 1950	......do	......do	Robert Gordon Menzies, Prime Minister of Australia.
Do	Senate	......do	Do.
82d CONGRESS			
Jan. 8, 1951	Joint session	State of the Union Address	President Harry S. Truman.
Feb. 1, 1951	Joint meeting [30]	North Atlantic Treaty Organization	General Dwight D. Eisenhower.
Apr. 2, 1951	Joint meeting	Address	Vincent Auriol, President of France.
Apr. 19, 1951	......do	Return from Pacific Command	General Douglas MacArthur.
June 21, 1951	......do	Address	Galo Plaza, President of Ecuador.
July 2, 1951	Senate	Addresses	Tadao Kuraishi, and Aisuke Okamoto, members of Japanese Diet.
Aug. 23, 1951	......do	Address	Zentarō Kosaka, member of Japanese Diet.
Sept. 24, 1951	Joint meeting	......do	Alcide de Gasperi, Prime Minister of Italy.
Jan. 9, 1952	Joint session	State of the Union Address	President Harry S. Truman.
Jan. 17, 1952	Joint meeting	Address	Winston Churchill, Prime Minister of the United Kingdom.
Apr. 3, 1952	......do	......do	Juliana, Queen of the Netherlands.
May 22, 1952	......do	Korea	General Matthew B. Ridgway.
June 10, 1952	Joint session	Steel industry dispute	President Harry S. Truman.
83d CONGRESS			
Jan. 6, 1953	......do	Counting electoral votes	N.A.
Jan. 20, 1953	......do	Inauguration, East Portico	President Dwight D. Eisenhower; Vice President Richard M. Nixon.
Feb. 2, 1953	......do	State of the Union Address	President Dwight D. Eisenhower.
Jan. 7, 1954	......do	......do	Do.
Jan. 29, 1954	Joint meeting	Address	Celal Bayar, President of Turkey.
May 4, 1954	......do	......do	Vincent Massey, Governor General of Canada.
May 28, 1954	......do	......do	Haile Selassie I, Emperor of Ethiopia.
July 28, 1954	......do	......do	Syngman Rhee, President of South Korea.
Nov. 12, 1954	Senate	Remarks	Shigeru Yoshida, Prime Minister of Japan.
Nov. 17, 1954	......do	Address [31]	Sarvepalli Radhakrishnan, Vice President of India.
Nov. 18, 1954	......do	Remarks	Pierre Mendès-France, Premier of France.
84th CONGRESS			
Jan. 6, 1955	Joint session	State of the Union Address	President Dwight D. Eisenhower.
Jan. 27, 1955	Joint meeting	Address	Paul E. Magliore, President of Haiti.
Mar. 16, 1955	Senate	......do	Robert Gordon Menzies, Prime Minister of Australia.
Do	House	......do	Do.
Mar. 30, 1955	Senate	......do	Mario Scelba, Prime Minister of Italy.
Do	House	......do	Do.
May 4, 1955	Senate	......do	P. Phibunsongkhram, Prime Minister of Thailand.
Do	House	......do	Do.
June 30, 1955	Senate	......do	U Nu, Prime Minister of Burma.
Do	House	......do	Do.
Jan. 5, 1956	Senate	......do	Juscelino Kubitschek de Oliverira, President-elect of Brazil.
Feb. 2, 1956	......do	......do	Anthony Eden, Prime Minister of the United Kingdom.
Do	House	......do	Do.
Feb. 29, 1956	Joint meeting	......do	Giovanni Gronchi, President of Italy.
Mar. 15, 1956	Senate	......do	John Aloysius Costello, Prime Minister of Ireland.
Do	House	......do	Do.
Apr. 30, 1956	Senate	......do	João Goulart, Vice President of Brazil.
May 17, 1956	Joint meeting	......do	Sukarno, President of Indonesia.
85th CONGRESS			
Jan. 5, 1957	Joint session	Middle East message	President Dwight D. Eisenhower.
Jan. 7, 1957	......do	Counting electoral votes	N.A.
Jan. 10, 1957	......do	State of the Union Address	President Dwight D. Eisenhower.
Jan. 21, 1957	......do	Inauguration, East Portico	President Dwight D. Eisenhower; Vice President Richard M. Nixon.
Feb. 27, 1957	House	Address	Guy Mollet, Premier of France.
Do	Senate	......do	Do.
May 9, 1957	Joint meeting	Address	Ngo Dinh Diem, President of Vietnam.
May 28, 1957	House	......do	Konrad Adenauer, Chancellor of West Germany.
Do	Senate	......do	Do.

JOINT SESSIONS AND MEETINGS, ADDRESSES TO THE SENATE OR THE HOUSE, AND INAUGURATIONS—CONTINUED

[See notes at end of table]

Congress & Date	Type	Occasion, topic, or inaugural location	Name and position of dignitary (where applicable)
June 20, 1957	......do	......do	Nobusuke Kishi, Prime Minister of Japan.
Do	House	......do	Do.
July 11, 1957	Senate	......do	Husseyn Shaheed Suhrawardy, Prime Minister of Pakistan.
Jan. 9, 1958	Joint session	State of the Union Address	President Dwight D. Eisenhower.
June 5, 1958	Joint meeting	Address	Theodor Heuss, President of West Germany.
June 10, 1958	Senate	......do	Harold Macmillan, Prime Minister of the United Kingdom.
June 18, 1958	Joint meeting	......do	Carlos F. Garcia, President of the Philippines.
June 25, 1958	House	......do	Muhammad Daoud Khan, Prime Minister of Afghanistan.
Do	Senate	......do	Do.
July 24, 1958	......do	......do	Kwame Nkrumah, Prime Minister of Ghana.
July 25, 1958	House	......do	Do.
July 29, 1958	Senate	......do	Amintore Fanfani, Prime Minister of Italy.
Do	House	......do	Do.
86th CONGRESS			
Jan. 9, 1959	Joint session	State of the Union Address	President Dwight D. Eisenhower.
Jan. 21, 1959	Joint meeting	Address	Arturo Frondizi, President of Argentina.
Feb. 12, 1959	Joint session	Sesquicentennial of Abraham Lincoln's birth.	Fredric March, actor; Carl Sandburg, poet.
Mar. 11, 1959	Joint meeting	Address	Jose Maria Lemus, President of El Salvador.
Mar. 18, 1959	......do	......do	Sean T. O'Kelly, President of Ireland.
May 12, 1959	......do	......do	Baudouin, King of the Belgians.
Jan. 7, 1960	Joint session	State of the Union Address	President Dwight D. Eisenhower.
Mar. 30, 1960	Senate	Address	Harold Macmillan, Prime Minister of the United Kingdom.
Apr. 6, 1960	Joint meeting	......do	Alberto Lleras-Camargo, President of Colombia.
Apr. 25, 1960	......do	......do	Charles de Gaulle, President of France.
Apr. 28, 1960	......do	......do	Mahendra, King of Nepal.
June 29, 1960	......do	......do	Bhumibol Adulyadej, King of Thailand.
87th CONGRESS			
Jan. 6, 1961	Joint session	Counting electoral votes	N.A.
Jan. 20, 1961	......do	Inauguration, East Portico	President John F. Kennedy; Vice President Lyndon B. Johnson.
Jan. 30, 1961	......do	State of the Union Address	President John F. Kennedy.
Apr. 13, 1961	Senate	Remarks	Konrad Adenauer, Chancellor of West Germany.
Apr. 18, 1961	House	Address	Constantine Karamanlis, Prime Minister of Greece.
May 4, 1961	Joint meeting	......do	Habib Bourguiba, President of Tunisia.
May 25, 1961	Joint session	Urgent national needs: foreign aid, defense, civil defense, and outer space.	President John F. Kennedy.
June 22, 1961	Senate	Remarks	Hayato Ikeda, Prime Minister of Japan.
Do	House	Address	Do.
July 12, 1961	Joint meeting	......do	Mohammad Ayub Khan, President of Pakistan.
July 26, 1961	House	......do	Abubakar Tafawa Balewa, Prime Minister of Nigeria.
Sept. 21, 1961	Joint meeting	......do	Manuel Prado, President of Peru.
Jan. 11, 1962	Joint session	State of the Union Address	President John F. Kennedy.
Feb. 26, 1962	Joint meeting	Friendship 7: 1st United States orbital space flight.	Lt. Col. John H. Glenn, Jr., USMC; Friendship 7 astronaut.
Apr. 4, 1962	......do	Address	João Goulart, President of Brazil.
Apr. 12, 1962	......do	......do	Mohammad Reza Shah Pahlavi, Shahanshah of Iran.
88th CONGRESS			
Jan. 14, 1963	Joint session	State of the Union Address	President John F. Kennedy.
May 21, 1963	Joint meeting	Flight of Faith 7 Spacecraft	Maj. Gordon L. Cooper, Jr., USAF, Faith 7 astronaut.
Oct. 2, 1963	Senate	Address	Haile Selassie I, Emperor of Ethiopia.
Nov. 27, 1963	Joint session	Assumption of office	President Lyndon B. Johnson.
Jan. 8, 1964	......do	State of the Union Address	Do.
Jan. 15, 1964	Joint meeting	Address	Antonio Segni, President of Italy.
May 28, 1964	......do	......do	Eamon de Valera, President of Ireland.
89th CONGRESS			
Jan. 4, 1965	Joint session	State of the Union Address	President Lyndon B. Johnson.
Jan. 6, 1965	......do	Counting electoral votes	N.A.
Jan. 20, 1965	Joint session [32]	Inauguration, East Portico	President Lyndon B. Johnson; Vice President Hubert H. Humphrey.

JOINT SESSIONS AND MEETINGS, ADDRESSES TO THE SENATE OR THE HOUSE, AND INAUGURATIONS—CONTINUED

[See notes at end of table]

Congress & Date	Type	Occasion, topic, or inaugural location	Name and position of dignitary (where applicable)
Mar. 15, 1965	Joint session	Voting rights	President Lyndon B. Johnson.
Sept. 14, 1965	Joint meeting	Flight of Gemini 5 Spacecraft	Lt. Col. Gordon L. Cooper, Jr., USAF; and Charles Conrad, Jr., USN; Gemini 5 astronauts.
Jan. 12, 1966	Joint session	State of the Union Address	President Lyndon B. Johnson.
Sept. 15, 1966	Joint meeting	Address	Ferdinand E. Marcos, President of the Philippines.
90th CONGRESS			
Jan. 10, 1967	Joint session	State of the Union Address	President Lyndon B. Johnson.
Apr. 28, 1967	Joint meeting	Vietnam policy	General William C. Westmoreland.
Aug. 16, 1967	Senate	Address	Kurt George Kiesinger, Chancellor of West Germany.
Oct. 27, 1967	Joint meeting	......do	Gustavo Diaz Ordaz, President of Mexico.
Jan. 17, 1968	Joint session	State of the Union Address	President Lyndon B. Johnson.
91st CONGRESS			
Jan. 6, 1969	......do	Counting electoral votes [33]	N.A.
Jan. 9, 1969	Joint meeting	Apollo 8: 1st flight around the moon	Col. Frank Borman, USAF; Capt. James A. Lowell, Jr., USN; Lt. Col. William A. Anders, USAF; Apollo 8 astronauts.
Jan. 14, 1969	Joint session	State of the Union Address	President Lyndon B. Johnson.
Jan. 20, 1969	Joint session [32]	Inauguration, East Portico	President Richard M. Nixon; Vice President Spiro T. Agnew.
Sept. 16, 1969	Joint meeting	Apollo 11: 1st lunar landing	Neil A. Armstrong; Col. Edwin E. Aldrin, Jr., USAF; and Lt. Col. Michael Collins, USAF; Apollo 11 astronauts.
Nov. 13, 1969	House	Executive-Legislative branch relations and Vietnam policy.	President Richard M. Nixon.
Do	Senate	......do	Do.
Jan. 22, 1970	Joint session	State of the Union Address	Do.
Feb. 25, 1970	Joint meeting	Address	Georges Pompidou, President of France.
June 3, 1970	......do	......do	Rafael Caldera, President of Venezuela.
Sept. 22, 1970	......do	Report on prisoners of war	Col. Frank Borman, Representative to the President on Prisoners of War.
92d CONGRESS			
Jan. 22, 1971	Joint session	State of the Union Address	President Richard M. Nixon.
Sept. 9, 1971	......do	Economic policy	Do.
Do	Joint meeting	Apollo 15: lunar mission	Col. David R. Scott, USAF; Col. James B. Irwin, USAF; and Lt. Col. Alfred M. Worden, USAF; Apollo 15 astronauts.
Jan. 20, 1972	Joint session	State of the Union Address	President Richard M. Nixon.
June 1, 1972	......do	European trip report	Do.
June 15, 1972	Joint meeting	Address	Luis Echeverria Alvarez, President of Mexico.
93d CONGRESS			
Jan. 6, 1973	Joint session	Counting electoral votes	N.A.
Jan. 20, 1973	Inauguration	East Portico	President Richard M. Nixon; Vice President Spiro T. Agnew.
Dec. 6, 1973	Joint meeting	Oath of office to, and Address by Vice President Gerald R. Ford.	Vice President Gerald R. Ford; ceremony attended by President Richard M. Nixon.
Do	Senate	Remarks and Reception	Vice President Gerald R. Ford.
Jan. 30 1974	Joint session	State of the Union Address	President Richard M. Nixon.
Aug. 12, 1974	......do	Assumption of office	President Gerald R. Ford.
Oct. 8, 1974	......do	Economy	Do.
Dec. 19, 1974	Senate	Address [34]	Vice President Nelson A. Rockefeller.
94th CONGRESS			
Jan. 15, 1975	Joint session	State of the Union Address	President Gerald R. Ford.
Apr. 10, 1975	......do	State of the World message	Do.
June 17, 1975	Joint meeting	Address	Walter Scheel, President of West Germany.
Nov. 5, 1975	......do	......do	Anwar El Sadat, President of Egypt.
Jan. 19, 1976	Joint session	State of the Union Address	President Gerald R. Ford.
Jan. 28, 1976	Joint meeting	Address	Yitzhak Rabin, Prime Minister of Israel.
Mar. 17, 1976	......do	......do	Liam Cosgrave, Prime Minister of Ireland.
May 18, 1976	Joint meeting	Address	Valery Giscard d'Estaing, President of France.
June 2, 1976	......do	......do	Juan Carlos I, King of Spain.
Sept. 23, 1976	......do	......do	William R. Tolbert, Jr., President of Liberia.

JOINT SESSIONS AND MEETINGS, ADDRESSES TO THE SENATE OR THE HOUSE, AND INAUGURATIONS—CONTINUED

[See notes at end of table]

Congress & Date	Type	Occasion, topic, or inaugural location	Name and position of dignitary (where applicable)
95th CONGRESS			
Jan. 6, 1977	Joint session	Counting electoral votes	N.A.
Jan. 12, 1977	......do	State of the Union Address	President Gerald R. Ford.
Jan. 20, 1977	Inauguration	East Portico	President Jimmy Carter; Vice President Walter F. Mondale.
Feb. 17, 1977	House	Address	José López Portillo, President of Mexico.
Feb. 22, 1977	Joint meeting	Address	Pierre Elliot Trudeau, Prime Minister of Canada.
Apr. 20, 1977	Joint session	Energy	President Jimmy Carter.
Jan. 19, 1978	......do	State of the Union Address	Do.
Sept. 18, 1978	......do	Middle East Peace agreements	President Jimmy Carter; joint session attended by Anwar El Sadat, President of Egypt, and by Menachem Begin, Prime Minister of Israel.
96th CONGRESS			
Jan. 23, 1979	......do	State of the Union Address	Do.
June 18, 1979	......do	Salt II agreements	Do.
Jan. 23, 1980	......do	State of the Union Address	Do.
97th CONGRESS			
Jan. 6, 1981	......do	Counting electoral votes	N.A.
Jan. 20, 1981	Joint session [32]	Inauguration, West Front	President Ronald Reagan; Vice President George Bush.
Feb. 18, 1981	Joint session	Economic recovery	President Ronald Reagan.
Apr. 28, 1981	......do	Economic recovery—inflation	Do.
Jan. 26, 1982	......do	State of the Union Address	Do.
Jan. 28, 1982	Joint meeting	Centennial of birth of Franklin Delano Roosevelt.	Dr. Arthur Schlesinger, historian; Senator Jennings Randolph; Representative Claude Pepper; Averell Harriman, former Governor of New York [35]; former Representative James Roosevelt, son of President Roosevelt.
Apr. 21, 1982	......do	Address	Beatrix, Queen of the Netherlands.
98th CONGRESS			
Jan. 25, 1983	Joint session	State of the Union Address	President Ronald Reagan.
Apr. 27, 1983	......do	Central America	Do.
Oct. 5, 1983	Joint meeting	Address	Karl Carstens, President of West Germany.
Jan. 25, 1984	Joint session	State of the Union Address	President Ronald Reagan.
Mar. 15, 1984	Joint meeting	Address	Dr. Garett FitzGerald, Prime Minister of Ireland.
Mar. 22, 1984	......do	......do	François Mitterand, President of France.
May 8, 1984	......do	Centennial of birth of Harry S. Truman	Representatives Ike Skelton and Alan Wheat; former Senator Stuart Symington; Margaret Truman Daniel, daughter of President Truman; and Senator Mark Hatfield.
May 16, 1984	......do	Address	Miguel de la Madrid, President of Mexico.
99th CONGRESS			
Jan. 7, 1985	Joint session	Counting electoral votes	N.A.
Jan. 21, 1985	Inauguration	Rotunda [36]	President Ronald Reagan; Vice President George Bush.
Feb. 6, 1985	Joint session	State of the Union Address	President Ronald Reagan.
Feb. 20, 1985	Joint meeting	Address	Margaret Thatcher, Prime Minister of the United Kingdom.
Mar. 6, 1985	......do	......do	Bettino Craxi, President of the Council of Ministers of Italy.
Mar. 20, 1985	......do	......do	Raul Alfonsin, President of Argentina.
June 13, 1985	......do	......do	Rajiv Gandhi, Prime Minister of India.
Oct. 9, 1985	......do	......do	Lee Kuan Yew, Prime Minister of Singapore.
Nov. 21, 1985	Joint session	Geneva Summit	President Ronald Reagan.
Feb. 4, 1986	......do	State of the Union Address	Do.
Sept. 11, 1986	Joint meeting	Address	Jose Sarney, President of Brazil.
Sept. 18, 1986	......do	......do	Corazon C. Aquino, President of the Philippines.
100th CONGRESS			
Jan. 27, 1987	Joint session	State of the Union Address	President Ronald Reagan.
Nov. 10, 1987	Joint meeting	Address	Chaim Herzog, President of Israel.
Jan. 25, 1988	Joint session	State of the Union Address	President Ronald Reagan.
Apr. 27, 1988	Joint meeting	Address	Brian Mulroney, Prime Minister of Canada.
June 23, 1988	......do	......do	Robert Hawke, Prime Minister of Australia.

JOINT SESSIONS AND MEETINGS, ADDRESSES TO THE SENATE OR THE HOUSE, AND INAUGURATIONS—CONTINUED

[See notes at end of table]

Congress & Date	Type	Occasion, topic, or inaugural location	Name and position of dignitary (where applicable)
101st CONGRESS			
Jan. 4, 1989	Joint session	Counting electoral votes	N.A.
Jan. 20, 1989	Inauguration	West Front	President George Bush; Vice President Dan Quayle.
Feb. 9, 1989	Joint session	Building a Better America	President George Bush.
Mar. 2, 1989	Joint meeting	Bicentennial of the 1st Congress	President Pro Tempore Robert C. Byrd; Speaker James C. Wright, Jr.; Representatives Lindy Boggs, Thomas S. Foley, and Robert H. Michel; Senators George Mitchell and Robert Dole; Howard Nemerov, Poet Laureate of the United States; David McCullough, historian; Anthony M. Frank, Postmaster General; former Senator Nicholas Brady, Secretary of the Treasury.
Apr. 6, 1989	Senate [37]	Addresses on the 200th anniversary commemoration of Senate's first legislative session.	Former Senators Thomas F. Eagleton and Howard H. Baker, Jr..
June 7, 1989	Joint meeting	Address	Benazir Bhutto, Prime Minister of Pakistan.
Oct. 4, 1989	......do	......do	Carlos Salinas de Gortari, President of Mexico.
Oct. 18, 1989	......do	......do	Roh Tae Woo, President of South Korea.
Nov. 15, 1989	......do	......do	Lech Walesa, chairman of Solidarnosć labor union, Poland.
Jan. 31, 1990	Joint session	State of the Union Address	President George Bush.
Feb. 21, 1990	Joint meeting	Address	Vaclav Hável, President of Czechoslovakia.
Mar. 7, 1990	......do	......do	Giulio Andreotti, President of the Council of Ministers of Italy.
Mar. 27, 1990	......do	Centennial of birth of Dwight D. Eisenhower.	Senator Robert Dole; Walter Cronkite, television journalist; Winston S. Churchill, member of British Parliament and grandson of Prime Minister Churchill; Clark M. Clifford, former Secretary of Defense; James D. Robinson III, chairman of Eisenhower Centennial Foundation; Arnold Palmer, professional golfer; John S.D. Eisenhower, former Ambassador to Belgium and son of President Eisenhower; Representatives Beverly Byron, William F. Goodling, and Pat Roberts.
June 26, 1990	......do	Address	Nelson Mandela, Deputy President of the African National Congress, South Africa.
Sept. 11, 1990	Joint session	Invasion of Kuwait by Iraq	President George Bush.
102d CONGRESS			
Jan. 29, 1991	......do	State of the Union Address	Do.
Mar. 6, 1991	......do	Conclusion of Persian Gulf War	Do.
Apr. 16, 1991	Joint meeting	Address	Violeta B. de Chamorro, President of Nicaragua.
May 8, 1991	House [38]	......do	General H. Norman Schwarzkopf.
May 16, 1991	Joint meeting	Address	Elizabeth II, Queen of the United Kingdom; joint meeting also attended by Prince Philip.
Nov. 14, 1991	......do	......do	Carlos Saul Menem, President of Argentina.
Jan. 28, 1992	Joint session	State of the Union Address	President George Bush.
Apr. 30, 1992	Joint meeting	Address	Richard von Weizsäcker, President of Germany.
June 17, 1992	......do	......do	Boris Yeltsin, President of Russia.
103d CONGRESS			
Jan. 6, 1993	Joint session	Counting electoral votes	N.A.
Jan. 20, 1993	Inauguration	West Front	President William J. Clinton; Vice President Albert Gore.
Feb. 17, 1993	Joint session	Economic Address [39]	President William J. Clinton.
Sept. 22, 1993	......do	Health care reform	Do.
Jan. 25, 1994	......do	State of the Union Address	Do.
May 18, 1994	Joint meeting	Address	Narasimha Rao, Prime Minister of India.
July 26, 1994	......do	Addresses	Hussein I, King of Jordan; Yitzhak Rabin, Prime Minister of Israel.
Oct. 6, 1994	......do	Address	Nelson Mandela, President of South Africa.
104th CONGRESS			
Jan. 24, 1995	Joint session	State of the Union Address	President William J. Clinton.

JOINT SESSIONS AND MEETINGS, ADDRESSES TO THE SENATE OR THE HOUSE, AND INAUGURATIONS—CONTINUED

[See notes at end of table]

Congress & Date	Type	Occasion, topic, or inaugural location	Name and position of dignitary (where applicable)
July 26, 1995	Joint meeting	Address	Kim Yong-sam, President of South Korea.[40]
Oct. 11, 1995	......do	Close of the Commemoration of the 50th Anniversary of World War II.	Speaker Newt Gingrich; Vice President Albert Gore; President Pro Tempore Strom Thurmond; Representatives Henry J. Hyde and G.V. "Sonny" Montgomery; Senators Daniel K. Inouye and Robert Dole; former Representative Robert H. Michel; General Louis H. Wilson (ret.), former Commandant of the Marine Corps.
Dec. 12, 1995	......do	Address	Shimon Peres, Prime Minister of Israel.
Jan. 30, 1996	Joint session	State of the Union Address	President William J. Clinton.
Feb. 1, 1996	Joint meeting	Address	Jacques Chirac, President of France.
July 10, 1996	......do	......do	Benyamin Netanyahu, Prime Minister of Israel.
Sept. 11, 1996	......do	......do	John Bruton, Prime Minister of Ireland.
105th CONGRESS			
Jan. 9, 1997	Joint session	Counting electoral votes	N.A.
Jan. 20, 1997	Inauguration	West Front	President William J. Clinton; Vice President Albert Gore.
Feb. 4, 1997	Joint session	State of the Union Address[41]	President William J. Clinton.
Feb. 27, 1997	Joint meeting	Address	Eduardo Frei, President of Chile.
Jan. 27, 1998	Joint session	State of the Union Address	President William J. Clinton.
June 10, 1998	Joint meeting	Address	Kim Dae-jung, President of South Korea.
July 15, 1998	......do	......do	Emil Constantinescu, President of Romania.
106th CONGRESS			
Jan. 19, 1999	Joint session	State of the Union Address	President William J. Clinton.
Jan. 27, 2000	......do	......do	Do.
Sept. 14, 2000	Joint meeting	Address	Atal Bihari Vajpayee, Prime Minister of India.
107th CONGRESS			
Jan. 6, 2001	Joint session	Counting electoral votes	N.A.
Jan. 20, 2001	Inauguration	West Front	President George W. Bush; Vice President Richard B. Cheney.
Feb. 27, 2001	Joint session	Budget message[39]	President George W. Bush.
Sept. 6, 2001	Joint meeting	Address	Vicente Fox, President of Mexico.
Sept. 20, 2001	Joint session	War on terrorism	President George W. Bush; joint session attended by Tony Blair, Prime Minister of the United Kingdom, by Tom Ridge, Governor of Pennsylvania, by George Pataki, Governor of New York, and by Rudolph Giuliani, Mayor of New York City.
Jan. 29, 2002	......do	State of the Union Address	President George W. Bush; joint session attended by Hamid Karzai, Chairman of the Interim Authority of Afghanistan.
108th CONGRESS			
Jan. 28, 2003	......do	......do	President George W. Bush.
July 17, 2003	Joint meeting	Address	Tony Blair, Prime Minister of the United Kingdom; joint meeting attended by Mrs. George W. Bush.
Jan. 20, 2004	Joint session	State of the Union Address	President George W. Bush.
Feb. 4, 2004	Joint meeting	Address	Jose Maria Aznar, President of the Government of Spain.
June 15, 2004	......do	......do	Hamid Karzai, President of Afghanistan.
Sept. 23, 2004	......do	......do	Ayad Allawi, Interim Prime Minister of Iraq.
109th CONGRESS			
Jan. 6, 2005	Joint session	Counting electoral votes[42]	N.A.
Jan. 20, 2005	Inauguration	West Front	President George W. Bush; Vice President Richard B. Cheney.
Feb. 2, 2005	Joint session	State of the Union Address	President George W. Bush.
Apr. 6, 2005	Joint meeting	Address	Viktor Yushchenko, President of Ukraine.
July 19, 2005	......do	......do	Dr. Manmohan Singh, Prime Minister of India.
Jan. 31, 2006	Joint session	State of the Union Address	President George W. Bush.
Mar. 1, 2006	Joint meeting	Address	Silvio Berlusconi, Prime Minister of Italy.
Mar. 15, 2006	Joint meeting	Address	Ellen Johnson Sirleaf, President of Liberia.
May 24, 2006	......do	......do	Ehud Olmert, Prime Minister of Israel.
June 7, 2006	......do	......do	Dr. Vaira Vike-Freiberga, President of Latvia.
July 26, 2006	......do	......do	Nouri Al-Maliki, Prime Minister of Iraq.
110th CONGRESS			
Jan. 23, 2007	Joint session	State of the Union Address	President George W. Bush.

JOINT SESSIONS AND MEETINGS, ADDRESSES TO THE SENATE OR THE HOUSE, AND INAUGURATIONS—CONTINUED

[See notes at end of table]

Congress & Date	Type	Occasion, topic, or inaugural location	Name and position of dignitary (where applicable)
Mar. 7, 2007	Joint meeting	Address	Abdullah II Ibn Al Hussein, King of Jordan.
Nov. 7, 2007	......do	......do	Nicolas Sarkozy, President of France.
Jan. 28, 2008	Joint session	State of the Union Address	President George W. Bush.
Apr. 30, 2008	Joint meeting	Address	Bertie Ahern, Prime Minister of Ireland.
111th CONGRESS			
Jan. 8, 2009	Joint session	Counting electoral votes	N.A.
Jan. 20, 2009	Inauguration	West Front	President Barack H. Obama; Vice President Joseph R. Biden, Jr.
Feb. 24, 2009	Joint session	Address	President Barack H. Obama.
Mar. 4, 2009	Joint meeting	......do	Gordon Brown, Prime Minister of the United Kingdom.
Sept. 9, 2009	Joint session	Health care reform	President Barack H. Obama.

1 Closing date for this table was September 9, 2009.

2 The oath of office was administered to George Washington outside on the gallery in front of the Senate Chamber, after which the Congress and the President returned to the chamber to hear the inaugural address. They then proceeded to St. Paul's Chapel for the "divine service" performed by the Chaplain of the Congress. Adjournment of the ceremony did not occur until the Congress returned to Federal Hall.

3 Funeral oration was delivered at the German Lutheran Church in Philadelphia.

4 Because of a tie in the electoral vote between Thomas Jefferson and Aaron Burr, the House of Representatives had to decide the election. Thirty-six ballots were required to break the deadlock, with Jefferson's election as President and Burr's as Vice President on February 17. The Twelfth Amendment was added to the Constitution to prevent the 1800 problem from recurring.

5 During most of the period while the Capitol was being reconstructed following the fire of 1814, the Congress met in the "Brick Capitol," constructed on the site of the present Supreme Court building. This joint session took place in the Representatives' chamber on the 2d floor of the building.

6 The joint session to count electoral votes was dissolved because the House and Senate disagreed on Missouri's status regarding statehood. The joint session was reconvened the same day and Missouri's votes were counted.

7 While this occasion has historically been referred to as the first joint meeting of Congress, the Journals of the House and Senate indicate that Lafayette actually addressed the House of Representatives, with some of the Senators present as guests of the House (having been invited at the last minute to attend). Similar occasions, when members of the one body were invited as guests of the other, include the Senate address by Queen Wilhelmina of the Netherlands on Aug. 6, 1942, and the House address by General H. Norman Schwarzkopf on May 8, 1991.

8 Although Andrew Jackson won the popular vote by a substantial amount and had the highest number of electoral votes from among the several candidates, he did not receive the required majority of the electoral votes. The responsibility for choosing the new President therefore devolved upon the House of Representatives. As soon as the Senators left the chamber, the balloting proceeded, and John Quincy Adams was elected on the first ballot.

9 The ceremony was moved outside to accommodate the extraordinarily large crowd of people who had come to Washington to see the inauguration.

10 The ceremony was moved inside because of cold weather.

11 Following the death of President Zachary Taylor, Vice President Millard Fillmore took the Presidential oath of office in a special joint session in the Hall of the House.

12 The joint session to count electoral votes was dissolved three times so that the House and Senate could resolve several electoral disputes.

13 Because of a severe cold and hoarseness, the King could not deliver his speech, which was read by former Representative Elisha Hunt Allen, then serving as Chancellor and Chief Justice of the Hawaiian Islands.

14 The contested election between Rutherford B. Hayes and Samuel J. Tilden created a constitutional crisis. Tilden won the popular vote by a close margin, but disputes concerning the electoral vote returns from four states deadlocked the proceedings of the joint session. Anticipating this development, the Congress had created a special commission of five Senators, five Representatives, and five Supreme Court Justices to resolve such disputes. The Commission met in the Supreme Court Chamber (the present Old Senate Chamber) as each problem arose. In each case, the Commission accepted the Hayes electors, securing his election by one electoral vote. The joint session was convened on 15 occasions, with the last on March 2, just three days before the inauguration.

15 The speech was written by former Speaker and Senator Robert C. Winthrop, who could not attend the ceremony because of ill health.

16 Because of a blizzard, the ceremony was moved inside, where it was held as part of the Senate's special session. President William Howard Taft took the oath of office and gave his inaugural address after Vice President James S. Sherman's inaugural address and the swearing-in of the new senators.

17 Held in the Senate Chamber.

18 Bakhmetieff represented the provisional government of Russia set up after the overthrow of the monarchy in March 1917 and recognized by the United States. The Bolsheviks took over in November 1917.

19 The address and reception were in conjunction with the presentation to the Senate by France of two Sèvres vases in appreciation of the United States' involvement in World War I. The vases are today in the Senate lobby, just off the Senate floor. Two additional Sèvres vases were given without ceremony to the House of Representatives, which today are in the Rayburn Room, not far from the floor of the House.

20 Senators later objected to President Harding's speech (given with no advance notice to most of the Senators) as an unconstitutional effort to interfere with the deliberations of the Senate, and Harding did not repeat visits of this kind.

21 This was the first Annual Message broadcast live on radio.

22 This was the first inauguration held pursuant to the Twentieth Amendment, which changed the date from March 4 to January 20. The Vice Presidential oath, which previously had been given earlier on the same day in the Senate Chamber, was added to the inaugural ceremony as well, but the Vice Presidential inaugural address was discontinued.

23 A joint reception for the King and Queen of the United Kingdom was held in the Rotunda, authorized by Senate Concurrent Resolution 17, 76th Congress. Although the concurrent resolution was structured to establish a joint meeting, the Senate, in fact, adjourned rather than recessed as called for by the resolution.

24 Held in the Senate Chamber.

25 At this time, the Philippines was still a possession of the United States, although it had been made a self-governing commonwealth in 1935, in preparation for full independence in 1946. From 1909 to 1916, Quezon had served in the U.S. House of Representatives as the resident commissioner from the Philippines.

26 In exile.

[27] For this Senate Address by Queen Wilhelmina, the members of the House of Representatives were invited as guests. This occasion has sometimes been mistakenly referred to as a joint meeting.

[28] The oaths of office were taken in simple ceremonies at the White House because the expense and festivity of a Capitol ceremony were thought inappropriate because of the war. The Joint Committee on Arrangements of the Congress was in charge, however, and both the Senate and the House of Representatives were present.

[29] This was the first time the term ''State of the Union Address'' was used for the President's Annual Message. Also, it was the first time the address was shown live on television.

[30] This was an informal meeting in the Coolidge Auditorium of the Library of Congress.

[31] Presentation of new ivory gavel to the Senate.

[32] According to the Congressional Record, the Senate adjourned prior to the inaugural ceremonies, even though the previously adopted resolution had stated the adjournment would come immediately following the inauguration. The Senate Journal records the adjournment as called for in the resolution, hence this listing as a joint session.

[33] The joint session to count electoral votes was dissolved so that the House and Senate could each resolve the dispute regarding a ballot from North Carolina. The joint session was reconvened the same day and the North Carolina vote was counted.

[34] Rockefeller was sworn in as Vice President by Chief Justice Warren E. Burger, after which, by unanimous consent, he was allowed to address the Senate.

[35] Because the Governor had laryngitis, his speech was read by his wife, Pamela.

[36] The ceremony was moved inside because of extremely cold weather.

[37] These commemorative addresses were given in the Old Senate Chamber during a regular legislative session.

[38] For this House Address by General Schwarzkopf, the members of the Senate were invited as guests.

[39] This speech was mislabeled in many sources as a State of the Union Address.

[40] President Kim Yong-sam was in Washington for the dedication of the Korean Veterans' Memorial, held the day after this joint meeting.

[41] This was the first State of the Union Address carried live on the Internet.

[42] The joint session to count electoral votes was dissolved so that the House and Senate could each discuss the dispute regarding the ballots from Ohio. The joint session was reconvened the same day and the Ohio votes were counted.

REPRESENTATIVES UNDER EACH APPORTIONMENT

The original apportionment of Representatives was assigned in 1787 in the Constitution and remained in effect for the 1st and 2d Congresses. Subsequent apportionments based on the censuses over the years have been figured using several different methods approved by Congress, all with the goal of dividing representation among the states as equally as possible. After each census up to and including the thirteenth in 1910, Congress would ènact a law designating the specific changese in the actual number of Representatives as well as the increase in the ratio of persons-per-Representative. After having made no apportionment after the Fourteenth census in 1920, Congress by statute in 1929 fixed the total number of Representatives at 435 (the number attained with the apportionment after the 1910 census), and since that time, only the ratio of persons-per-Representative has continued to increase, in fact, significantly so. Since the total is now fixed, the specific number of Representatives per state is adjusted after each census to reflect its percentage of the entire population. Since the Sixteenth Census in 1940, the "equal proportions" method of apportioning Representatives within the 435 total has been employed. A detailed explanation of the entire apportionment process can be found in *The Historical Atlas of United States Congressional Districts, 1989–1983.* Kenneth C. Martis, The Free Press, New York, 1982.

State	Constitutional apportionment	First Census, 1790	Second Census, 1800	Third Census, 1810	Fourth Census, 1820	Fifth Census, 1830	Sixth Census, 1840	Seventh Census, 1850	Eighth Census, 1860	Ninth Census, 1870	Tenth Census, 1880	Eleventh Census, 1890	Twelfth Census, 1900	Thirteenth Census, 1910	Fifteenth Census, 1930[1]	Sixteenth Census, 1940	Seventeenth Census, 1950	Eighteenth Census, 1960	Nineteenth Census, 1970	Twentieth Census, 1980	Twenty-First Census, 1990	Twenty-Second Census, 2000
AL	......	......	......	[2]	3	5	7	7	6	8	8	9	9	10	9	9	9	8	7	7	7	7
AK	......	......	......	......	......	......	......	......	......	......	......	......	......	......	......	......	[2,3]	1	1	1	1	1
AZ	......	......	......	......	......	......	......	......	......	......	......	......	[2]	[4]1	1	2	2	3	4	5	6	8
AR	......	......	......	......	......	[2]	1	2	3	4	5	6	7	7	7	7	6	4	4	4	4	4
CA	......	......	......	......	......	......	[2]	[4]2	3	4	6	7	8	11	20	23	30	38	43	45	52	53
CO	......	......	......	......	......	......	......	......	......	[2]	1	2	3	4	4	4	4	4	5	6	6	7
CT	5	7	7	7	6	6	4	4	4	4	4	4	5	5	6	6	6	6	6	6	6	5
DE	1	1	1	2	1	1	1	1	1	1	1	1	1	1	1	1	1	1	1	1	1	1
FL	......	......	......	......	......	......	[2]	1	1	2	2	2	3	4	5	6	8	12	15	19	23	25
GA	3	2	4	6	7	9	8	8	7	9	10	11	11	12	10	10	10	10	10	10	11	13
HI	......	......	......	......	......	......	......	......	......	......	......	......	......	......	......	......	[2,3]	2	2	2	2	2
ID	......	......	......	......	......	......	......	......	......	......	[2]	1	1	2	2	2	2	2	2	2	2	2
IL	......	......	......	[2]	1	3	7	9	14	19	20	22	25	27	27	26	25	24	24	22	20	19
IN	......	......	......	[2]	3	7	10	11	11	13	13	13	13	13	12	11	11	11	11	10	10	9
IA	......	......	......	......	......	......	[2]	2	6	9	11	11	11	11	9	8	8	7	6	6	5	5
KS	......	......	......	......	......	......	......	[2]	[4]1	3	7	8	8	8	7	6	6	5	5	5	4	4
KY	[2]	[4]2	6	10	12	13	10	10	9	10	11	11	11	11	9	9	8	7	7	7	6	6
LA	......	......	......	[2]	3	3	4	4	5	6	6	6	7	8	8	8	8	8	8	8	7	7
ME	......	......	......	[5]	7	8	7	6	5	5	4	4	4	4	3	3	3	2	2	2	2	2
MD	6	8	9	9	9	8	6	6	5	6	6	6	6	6	6	6	7	8	8	8	8	8
MA	8	14	17	[5]20	13	12	10	11	10	11	12	13	14	16	15	14	14	12	12	11	10	10
MI	......	......	......	......	......	[2]	3	4	6	9	11	12	12	13	17	17	18	19	19	18	16	15
MN	......	......	......	......	......	......	......	[2]	2	3	5	7	9	10	9	9	9	8	8	8	8	8
MS	......	......	......	[2]	1	2	4	5	5	6	7	7	8	8	7	7	6	5	5	5	5	4
MO	......	......	......	[2]	[4]1	2	5	7	9	13	14	15	16	16	13	13	11	10	10	9	9	9
MT	......	......	......	......	......	......	......	......	......	......	[2]	1	1	2	2	2	2	2	2	2	1	1
NE	......	......	......	......	......	......	......	......	[2]	1	3	6	6	6	5	4	4	3	3	3	3	3
NV	......	......	......	......	......	......	......	......	[2]	1	1	1	1	1	1	1	1	1	1	2	2	3
NH	3	4	5	6	6	5	4	3	3	3	2	2	2	2	2	2	2	2	2	2	2	2
NJ	4	5	6	6	6	6	5	5	5	7	7	8	10	12	14	14	14	15	15	14	13	13
NM	......	......	......	......	......	......	......	......	......	......	......	......	[2]	[4]1	1	2	2	2	2	3	3	3
NY	6	10	17	27	34	40	34	33	31	33	34	34	37	43	45	45	43	41	39	34	31	29
NC	5	10	12	13	13	13	9	8	7	8	9	9	10	10	11	12	12	11	11	11	12	13
ND	......	......	......	......	......	......	......	......	......	......	[2]	1	2	3	2	2	2	2	1	1	1	1
OH	......	......	[2]	6	14	19	21	21	19	20	21	21	21	22	24	23	23	24	23	21	19	18
OK	......	......	......	......	......	......	......	......	......	......	......	......	[2]	8	9	8	6	6	6	6	6	5
OR	......	......	......	......	......	......	......	[2]	1	1	1	2	2	3	3	4	4	4	4	5	5	5
PA	8	13	18	23	26	28	24	25	24	27	28	30	32	36	34	33	30	27	25	23	21	19
RI	1	2	2	2	2	2	2	2	2	2	2	2	2	3	2	2	2	2	2	2	2	2
SC	5	6	8	9	9	9	7	6	4	5	7	7	7	7	6	6	6	6	6	6	6	6
SD	......	......	......	......	......	......	......	......	......	......	[2]	2	2	3	2	2	2	2	2	1	1	1
TN	......	[2]	3	6	9	13	11	10	8	10	10	10	10	10	9	10	9	9	8	9	9	9
TX	......	......	......	......	......	......	[2]	2	4	6	11	13	16	18	21	21	22	23	24	27	30	32
UT	......	......	......	......	......	......	......	......	......	......	......	[2]	1	2	2	2	2	2	2	3	3	3
VT	[2]	[4]2	4	6	5	5	4	3	3	3	2	2	2	2	1	1	1	1	1	1	1	1
VA	10	19	22	23	22	21	15	13	[6]11	9	10	10	10	10	9	9	10	10	10	10	11	11
WA	......	......	......	......	......	......	......	......	......	......	[2]	2	3	5	6	6	7	7	7	8	9	9
WV	......	......	......	......	......	......	......	......	[6]	3	4	4	5	6	6	6	6	5	4	4	3	3
WI	......	......	......	......	......	......	[2]	3	6	8	9	10	11	11	10	10	10	10	9	9	9	8
WY	......	......	......	......	......	......	......	......	......	......	[2]	1	1	1	1	1	1	1	1	1	1	1
Total	65	105	141	181	213	240	223	234	241	292	325	356	386	435	435	435	435	435	435	435	435	435

[1] No apportionment was made after the 1920 census.

[2] The following Representatives were added after the indicated apportionments when these states were admitted in the years listed. The number of these additonal Representatives for each state remained in effect until the next census's apportionment (with the exceptions of California and New Mexico, as explained in footnote 4). They are not included in the total for each column. In reading this table, please remember that the apportionments made after each census took effect with the election two years after the census date. As a result, in the table footnote 2 is placed for several states under the decade preceding the one in which it entered the Union, since the previous decade's apportionment was still in effect at the time of statehood. *Constitutional:* Vermont (1791), 2; Kentucky (1792), 2; *First:* Tennessee (1796), 1; *Second:* Ohio (1803), 1; *Third:* Louisiana (1812), 1; Indiana (1816), 1; Mississippi (1817), 1; Illinois (1818), 1; Alabama (1819), 1; Missouri (1821), 1; *Fifth:* Arkansas (1836), 1; Michigan (1837), 1; *Sixth:* Florida (1845), 1; Texas (1845), 2; Iowa (1846), 2; Wisconsin (1848), 2; California (1850), 2; *Seventh:* Minnesota (1858), 2; Oregon (1859), 1; Kansas (1861), 1; *Eighth:* Nevada (1864), 1; Nebraska (1867), 1; *Ninth:* Colorado (1876), 1; *Tenth:* North Dakota (1889), 1; South Dakota (1889), 2; Montana (1889), 1; Washington (1889), 1; Idaho (1890), 1; Wyoming (1890), 1; *Eleventh:* Utah (1896), 1; *Twelth:* Oklahoma (1907), 5; New Mexico (1912), 2; Arizona (1912), 1; *Seventeenth:* Alaska (1959), 1; Hawaii (1959), 1.

[3] When Alaska and then Hawaii joined the Union in 1959, the law was changed to allow the total membership of the House of Representatives to increase to 436 and then to 437, apportioning one new Representative for each of those states. The total returned to 435 in 1963, when the 1960 census apportionment took effect.

[4] Even though the respective censuses were taken before the following states joined the Union, Representatives for them were apportioned either because of anticipation of statehood or because they had become states in the period between the census and the apportionment, hence they are included in the totals of the respective columns. *First:* Vermont (1791); Kentucky (1792); *Fourth:* Missouri (1821); *Seventh:* California (1850); *Eighth:* Kansas (1861); *Thirteenth:* New Mexico (1912); Arizona (1912). (Please note: These seven states are also included in footnote 2 because they became states while the previous decade's apportionment was still in effect for the House of Representatives.) California's situation was unusual. It was scheduled for inclusion in the figures for the 1850 census apportionment; however, when the apportionment law was passed in 1852, California's census returns were still incomplete so Congress made special provision that the state would retain ''the number of Representatives [two] prescribed by the act of admission * * * into the Union until a new apportionment [i.e., after the 1860 census]'' would be made. The number of Representatives from California actually increased before the next apportionment to three when Congress gave the state an extra Representative during part of the 37th Congress, from 1862 to 1863. Regarding New Mexico, the 1911 apportionment law, passed by the 62d Congress in response to the 1910 census and effective with the 63d Congress in 1913, stated that ''if the Territor[y] of * * * New Mexico shall become [a State] in the Union before the apportionment of Representatives under the next decennial census [it] shall have one Representative * * *.'' When New Mexico became a state in 1912 during the 62d Congress, it was given two Representatives. The number was decreased to one beginning the next year in the 63d.

[5] The ''Maine District'' of Massachusetts became a separate state during the term of the 16th Congress, in 1820. For the remainder of that Congress, Maine was assigned one ''at large'' Representative while Massachusetts continued to have 20 Representatives, the number apportioned to it after the 1810 census. For the 17th Congress (the last before the 1820 census apportionment took effect), seven of Massachusetts's Representatives were reassigned to Maine, leaving Massachusetts with 13.

[6] Of the 11 Representatives apportioned to Virginia after the 1860 census, three were reassigned to West Virginia when that part of Virginia became a separate state in 1863. Since the Virginia seats in the House were vacant at that time because of the Civil War, all of the new Representatives from West Virginia were able to take their seats at once. When Representatives from Virginia reentered the House in 1870, only eight members represented it.

IMPEACHMENT PROCEEDINGS

The provisions of the United States Constitution which apply specifically to impeachments are as follows: Article I, section 2, clause 5; Article I, section 3, clauses 6 and 7; Article II, section 2, clause 1; Article II, section 4; and Article III, section 2, clause 3.

For the officials listed below, the date of impeachment by the House of Representatives is followed by the dates of the Senate trial, with the result of each listed at the end of the entry.

WILLIAM BLOUNT, a Senator of the United States from Tennessee; impeached July 7, 1797; tried Monday, December 17, 1798, to Monday, January 14, 1799; charges dismissed for want of jurisdiction.

JOHN PICKERING, judge of the United States district court for the district of New Hampshire; impeached March 2, 1803; tried Thursday, March 3, 1803, to Monday, March 12, 1804; removed from office.

SAMUEL CHASE, Associate Justice of the Supreme Court of the United States; impeached March 12, 1804; tried Friday, November 30, 1804, to Friday, March 1, 1805; acquitted.

JAMES H. PECK, judge of the United States district court for the district of Missouri; impeached April 24, 1830; tried Monday, April 26, 1830, to Monday, January 31, 1831; acquitted.

WEST H. HUMPHREYS, judge of the United States district court for the middle, eastern, and western districts of Tennessee; impeached May 6, 1862; tried Wednesday, May 7, 1862, to Thursday, June 26, 1862; removed from office and disqualified from future office.

ANDREW JOHNSON, President of the United States; impeached February 24, 1868; tried Tuesday, February 25, 1868, to Tuesday, May 26, 1868; acquitted.

WILLIAM W. BELKNAP, Secretary of War; impeached March 2, 1876; tried Friday, March 3, 1876, to Tuesday, August 1, 1876; acquitted.

CHARLES SWAYNE, judge of the United States district court for the northern district of Florida; impeached December 13, 1904; tried Wednesday, December 14, 1904, to Monday, February 27, 1905; acquitted.

ROBERT W. ARCHBALD, associate judge, United States Commerce Court; impeached July 11, 1912; tried Saturday, July 13, 1912, to Monday, January 13, 1913; removed from office and disqualified from future office.

GEORGE W. ENGLISH, judge of the United States district court for the eastern district of Illinois; impeached April 1, 1926; tried Friday, April 23, 1926, to Monday, December 13, 1926; resigned office Thursday, November 4, 1926; Court of Impeachment adjourned to December 13, 1926, when, on request of House managers, the proceedings were dismissed.

HAROLD LOUDERBACK, judge of the United States district court for the northern district of California; impeached February 24, 1933; tried Monday, May 15, 1933, to Wednesday, May 24, 1933; acquitted.

HALSTED L. RITTER, judge of the United States district court for the southern district of Florida; impeached March 2, 1936; tried Monday, April 6, 1936, to Friday, April 17, 1936; removed from office.

HARRY E. CLAIBORNE, judge of the United States district court of Nevada; impeached July 22, 1986; tried Tuesday, October 7, 1986, to Thursday, October 9, 1986; removed from office.

ALCEE L. HASTINGS, judge of the United States district court for the southern district of Florida; impeached August 3, 1988; tried Wednesday, October 18, 1989, to Friday, October 20, 1989; removed from office.

WALTER L. NIXON, judge of the United States district court for the southern district of Mississippi; impeached May 10, 1989; tried Wednesday, November 1, 1989, to Friday, November 3, 1989; removed from office.

WILLIAM JEFFERSON CLINTON, President of the United States; impeached December 19, 1998; tried Thursday, January 7, 1999, to Friday, February 12, 1999; acquitted.

DELEGATES, REPRESENTATIVES, AND SENATORS SERVING IN THE 1st–111th CONGRESSES [1]

As of July 16, 2009, 11,897 individuals have served: 9,986 only in the House of Representatives, 1,262 only in the Senate, and 649 in both Houses. Total serving in the House of Representatives (including individuals serving in both bodies) is 10,635. Total for the Senate (including individuals serving in both bodies) is 1,911.[2]

State	Date Became Territory	Date Entered Union	Delegates	Representatives Only	Senators Only	Both Houses	Total, Not Including Delegates
Alabama	Mar. 3, 1817	Dec. 14, 1819 (22d)	1	168	24	15	207
Alaska	Aug. 24, 1912	Jan. 3, 1959 (49th)	9	4	7	0	11
Arizona	Feb. 24, 1863	Feb. 14, 1912 (48th)	11	28	7	4	39
Arkansas	Mar. 2, 1819	June 15, 1836 (25th)	3	83	23	9	115
California		Sept. 9, 1850 (31st)		333	32	11	375
Colorado	Feb. 28, 1861	Aug. 1, 1876 (38th)	3	58	25	10	93
Connecticut		Jan. 9, 1788 (5th)		191	28	25	244
Delaware		Dec. 7, 1787 (1st)		47	36	14	97
Florida	Mar. 30, 1822	Mar. 3, 1845 (27th)	5	111	26	6	143
Georgia		Jan. 2, 1788 (4th)		250	37	22	309
Hawaii	June 14, 1900	Aug. 21, 1959 (50th)	10	7	2	3	12
Idaho	Mar. 3, 1863	July 3, 1890 (43d)	9	27	20	6	53
Illinois	Feb. 3, 1809	Dec. 3, 1818 (21st)	3	437	30	22	489
Indiana	May 7, 1800	Dec. 11, 1816 (19th)	3	298	27	17	342
Iowa	June 12, 1838	Dec. 28, 1846 (29th)	2	170	22	11	203
Kansas	May 30, 1854	Jan. 29, 1861 (34th)	2	106	22	9	137
Kentucky		June 1, 1792 (15th)		311	36	29	376
Louisiana	Mar. 24, 1804	Apr. 30, 1812 (18th)	2	149	34	14	197
Maine		Mar. 15, 1820 (23d)		142	18	18	178
Maryland		Apr. 28, 1788 (7th)		254	28	28	310
Massachusetts		Feb. 6, 1788 (6th)		384	20	28	432
Michigan	Jan. 11, 1805	Jan. 26, 1837 (26th)	7	249	24	14	288
Minnesota	Mar. 3, 1849	May 11, 1858 (32d)	3	123	27	11	161
Mississippi	Apr. 17, 1798	Dec. 10, 1817 (20th)	5	110	27	17	154
Missouri	June 4, 1812	Aug. 10, 1821 (24th)	3	292	35	9	336
Montana	May 26, 1864	Nov. 8, 1889 (41st)	5	26	14	6	46
Nebraska	May 30, 1854	Mar. 1, 1867 (37th)	6	87	29	7	123
Nevada	Mar. 2, 1861	Oct. 31, 1864 (36th)	2	27	19	6	52
New Hampshire		June 21, 1788 (9th)		119	36	26	181
New Jersey		Dec. 18, 1787 (3d)		299	48	15	362
New Mexico	Sept. 9, 1850	Jan. 6, 1912 (47th)	13	23	12	4	39
New York		July 26, 1788 (11th)		1,407	36	24	1,467
North Carolina		Nov. 21, 1789 (12th)		307	36	18	361
North Dakota [3]	Mar. 2, 1861	Nov. 2, 1889 (39th)	11	21	15	6	42
Ohio [4]		Mar. 1, 1803 (17th)	2	627	36	19	682
Oklahoma	May 2, 1890	Nov. 16, 1907 (46th)	4	72	11	6	89
Oregon	Aug. 14, 1848	Feb. 14, 1859 (33d)	2	57	32	5	94
Pennsylvania		Dec. 12, 1787 (2d)		1001	33	21	1,054
Rhode Island		May 29, 1790 (13th)		61	37	10	108
South Carolina		May 23, 1788 (8th)		195	39	16	250
South Dakota [3]	Mar. 2, 1861	Nov. 2, 1889 (40th)	11	25	16	10	51
Tennessee		June 1, 1796 (16th)	2	245	40	18	303
Texas		Dec. 29, 1845 (28th)		238	21	10	269
Utah	Sept. 9, 1850	Jan. 4, 1896 (45th)	7	34	12	3	49
Vermont		Mar. 4, 1791 (14th)		80	24	16	120
Virginia		June 25, 1788 (10th)		384	27	26	437
Washington	Mar. 2, 1853	Nov. 11, 1889 (42d)	10	68	13	10	91
West Virginia		June 20, 1863 (35th)		91	22	8	121
Wisconsin	Apr. 20, 1836	May 29, 1848 (30th)	6	171	19	7	197
Wyoming	July 25, 1868	July 10, 1890 (44th)	4	15	18	3	36

[1] March 4, 1789 until July 16, 2009.

[2] Some of the larger states split into smaller states as the country grew westward (e.g., part of Virginia became West Virginia); hence, some individuals represented more than one state in the Congress.

[3] North and South Dakota were formed from a single territory on the same date, and they shared the same delegates before statehood.

[4] The Territory Northwest of the Ohio River was established as a district for purposes of temporary government by the Act of July 13, 1787. Virginia ceded the land beyond the Ohio River, and delegates representing the district first came to the 6th Congress on March 4, 1799.

NOTE: Information was supplied by the Congressional Research Service.

POLITICAL DIVISIONS OF THE SENATE AND HOUSE FROM 1855 TO 2009

[All Figures Reflect Immediate Result of Elections. Figures Supplied by the Clerk of the House]

Congress	Years	SENATE					HOUSE OF REPRESENTATIVES				
		No. of Senators	Democrats	Republicans	Other parties	Vacancies	No. of Representatives	Democrats	Republicans	Other parties	Vacancies
34th	1855–1857	62	42	15	5	....	234	83	108	43	....
35th	1857–1859	64	39	20	5	....	237	131	92	14	....
36th	1859–1861	66	38	26	2	....	237	101	113	23	....
37th	1861–1863	50	11	31	7	1	178	42	106	28	2
38th	1863–1865	51	12	39	....	....	183	80	103	....	....
39th	1865–1867	52	10	42	....	....	191	46	145	....	....
40th	1867–1869	53	11	42	....	....	193	49	143	....	1
41st	1869–1871	74	11	61	....	2	243	73	170	....	....
42d	1871–1873	74	17	57	....	....	243	104	139	....	....
43d	1873–1875	74	19	54	....	1	293	88	203	....	2
44th	1875–1877	76	29	46	....	1	293	181	107	3	2
45th	1877–1879	76	36	39	1	....	293	156	137	....	....
46th	1879–1881	76	43	33	....	....	293	150	128	14	1
47th	1881–1883	76	37	37	2	....	293	130	152	11	....
48th	1883–1885	76	36	40	....	....	325	200	119	6	....
49th	1885–1887	76	34	41	....	1	325	182	140	2	1
50th	1887–1889	76	37	39	....	....	325	170	151	4	....
51st	1889–1891	84	37	47	....	....	330	156	173	1	....
52d	1891–1893	88	39	47	2	....	333	231	88	14	....
53d	1893–1895	88	44	38	3	3	356	220	126	10	....
54th	1895–1897	88	39	44	5	....	357	104	246	7	....
55th	1897–1899	90	34	46	10	....	357	134	206	16	1
56th	1899–1901	90	26	53	11	....	357	163	185	9	....
57th	1901–1903	90	29	56	3	2	357	153	198	5	1
58th	1903–1905	90	32	58	....	....	386	178	207	....	1
59th	1905–1907	90	32	58	....	....	386	136	250	....	....
60th	1907–1909	92	29	61	....	2	386	164	222	....	....
61st	1909–1911	92	32	59	....	1	391	172	219	....	....
62d	1911–1913	92	42	49	....	1	391	228	162	1	....
63d	1913–1915	96	51	44	1	....	435	290	127	18	....
64th	1915–1917	96	56	39	1	....	435	231	193	8	3
65th	1917–1919	96	42	53	1	....	435	[1]210	216	9	....
66th	1919–1921	96	47	48	1	....	435	191	237	7	....
67th	1921–1923	96	37	59	....	....	435	132	300	1	2
68th	1923–1925	96	43	51	2	....	435	207	225	3	....
69th	1925–1927	96	40	54	1	1	435	183	247	5	....
70th	1927–1929	96	47	48	1	....	435	195	237	3	....
71st	1929–1931	96	39	56	1	....	435	163	267	1	4
72d	1931–1933	96	47	48	1	....	435	[2]216	218	1	....
73d	1933–1935	96	59	36	1	....	435	313	117	5	....
74th	1935–1937	96	69	25	2	....	435	322	103	10	....
75th	1937–1939	96	75	17	4	....	435	333	89	13	....
76th	1939–1941	96	69	23	4	....	435	262	169	4	....
77th	1941–1943	96	66	28	2	....	435	267	162	6	....
78th	1943–1945	96	57	38	1	....	435	222	209	4	....
79th	1945–1947	96	57	38	1	....	435	243	190	2	....
80th	1947–1949	96	45	51	....	....	435	188	246	1	....
81st	1949–1951	96	54	42	....	....	435	263	171	1	....
82d	1951–1953	96	48	47	1	....	435	234	199	2	....
83d	1953–1955	96	46	48	2	....	435	213	221	1	....
84th	1955–1957	96	48	47	1	....	435	232	203	....	....
85th	1957–1959	96	49	47	....	....	435	234	201	....	....
86th	1959–1961	98	64	34	....	....	[3]436	283	153	....	....
87th	1961–1963	100	64	36	....	....	[4]437	262	175	....	....
88th	1963–1965	100	67	33	....	....	435	258	176	....	1
89th	1965–1967	100	68	32	....	....	435	295	140	....	....
90th	1967–1969	100	64	36	....	....	435	248	187	....	....
91st	1969–1971	100	58	42	....	....	435	243	192	....	....
92d	1971–1973	100	54	44	2	....	435	255	180	....	....
93d	1973–1975	100	56	42	2	....	435	242	192	1	....
94th	1975–1977	100	60	37	2	....	435	291	144	1	....
95th	1977–1979	100	61	38	1	....	435	292	143	....	....
96th	1979–1981	100	58	41	1	....	435	277	158	....	....
97th	1981–1983	100	46	53	1	....	435	242	192	1	....
98th	1983–1985	100	46	54	....	....	435	269	166	....	....
99th	1985–1987	100	47	53	....	....	435	253	182	....	....
100th	1987–1989	100	55	45	....	....	435	258	177	....	....
101st	1989–1991	100	55	45	....	....	435	260	175	....	....
102d	1991–1993	100	56	44	....	....	435	267	167	1	....
103d	1993–1995	100	57	43	....	....	435	258	176	1	....
104th	1995–1997	100	48	52	....	....	435	204	230	1	....
105th	1997–1999	100	45	55	....	....	435	207	226	2	....
106th	1999–2001	100	45	55	....	....	435	211	223	1	....
107th	2001–2003	100	50	50	....	....	435	212	221	2	....
108th	2003–2005	100	48	51	1	....	435	204	229	1	1
109th	2005–2007	100	44	55	1	....	435	202	232	1	....
110th	2007–2009	100	49	49	2	....	435	233	202	....	....
111th	2009–2011	100	55	41	2	2	435	256	178	....	1

[1] Democrats organized House with help of other parties.

[2] Democrats organized House because of Republican deaths.
[3] Proclamation declaring Alaska a State issued January 3, 1959.
[4] Proclamation declaring Hawaii a State issued August 21, 1959.

GOVERNORS OF THE STATES, COMMONWEALTH, AND TERRITORIES—2009

State, Commonwealth, or Territory	Capital	Governor	Party	Term of service	Expiration of term
				Years	
STATE					
Alabama	Montgomery	Bob Riley	Republican	[c] 4	Jan. 2011
Alaska	Juneau	Sean Parnell	Republican	[f] 4	Dec. 2010
Arizona	Phoenix	Jan Brewer	Republican	[f] 4	Jan. 2011
Arkansas	Little Rock	Mike Beebe	Democrat	[c] 4	Jan. 2011
California	Sacramento	Arnold Schwarzenegger	Republican	[c] 4	Jan. 2011
Colorado	Denver	Bill Ritter	Democratic	[c] 4	Jan. 2011
Connecticut	Hartford	M. Jodi Rell	Republican	[b] 4	Jan. 2011
Delaware	Dover	Jack Markell	Democrat	[c] 4	Jan. 2013
Florida	Tallahassee	Charlie Crist	Republican	[f] 4	Jan. 2011
Georgia	Atlanta	Sonny Perdue	Republican	[f] 4	Jan. 2011
Hawaii	Honolulu	Linda Lingle	Republican	[c] 4	Dec. 2010
Idaho	Boise	C.L. "Butch" Otter	Republican	[b] 4	Jan. 2011
Illinois	Springfield	Pat Quinn	Democrat	[b] 4	Jan. 2011
Indiana	Indianapolis	Mitch Daniels	Republican	[f] 4	Jan. 2013
Iowa	Des Moines	Chet Culver	Democrat	[b] 4	Jan. 2011
Kansas	Topeka	Mark Parkinson	Democrat	[c] 4	Jan. 2011
Kentucky	Frankfort	Steven L. Beshear	Democrat	[c] 4	Dec. 2011
Louisiana	Baton Rouge	Bobby Jindal	Republican	[f] 4	Jan. 2012
Maine	Augusta	John E. Baldacci	Democrat	[f] 4	Jan. 2011
Maryland	Annapolis	Martin O'Malley	Democrat	[f] 4	Jan. 2011
Massachusetts	Boston	Deval Patrick	Democrat	[b] 4	Jan. 2011
Michigan	Lansing	Jennifer M. Granholm	Democrat	[b] 4	Jan. 2011
Minnesota	St. Paul	Tim Pawlenty	Republican	[b] 4	Jan. 2011
Mississippi	Jackson	Haley Barbour	Republican	[c] 4	Jan. 2012
Missouri	Jefferson City	Jay Nixon	Democrat	[c] 4	Jan. 2013
Montana	Helena	Brian Schweitzer	Democrat	[g] 4	Jan. 2013
Nebraska	Lincoln	Dave Heineman	Republican	[c] 4	Jan. 2011
Nevada	Carson City	Jim Gibbons	Republican	[c] 4	Jan. 2011
New Hampshire	Concord	John Lynch	Democrat	[b] 2	Jan. 2011
New Jersey	Trenton	Jon Corzine	Democrat	[c] 4	Jan. 2010
New Mexico	Santa Fe	Bill Richardson	Democrat	[c] 4	Jan. 2011
New York	Albany	David Paterson	Democratic	[b] 4	Jan. 2011
North Carolina	Raleigh	Beverly Perdue	Democrat	[c] 4	Jan. 2013
North Dakota	Bismarck	John Hoeven	Republican	[b] 4	Dec. 2012
Ohio	Columbus	Ted Strickland	Democrat	[c] 4	Jan. 2011
Oklahoma	Oklahoma City	Brad Henry	Democrat	[c] 4	Jan. 2011
Oregon	Salem	Ted Kulongoski	Democrat	[f] 4	Jan. 2011
Pennsylvania	Harrisburg	Edward G. Rendell	Democrat	[c] 4	Jan. 2011
Rhode Island	Providence	Donald Carcieri	Republican	[c] 4	Jan. 2011
South Carolina	Columbia	Mark Sanford	Republican	[c] 4	Jan. 2011
South Dakota	Pierre	Mike Rounds	Republican	[c] 4	Jan. 2011
Tennessee	Nashville	Phil Bredesen	Democrat	[c] 4	Jan. 2011
Texas	Austin	Rick Perry	Republican	[b] 4	Jan. 2011
Utah	Salt Lake City	Jon Huntsman, Jr.	Republican	[b] 4	Jan. 2013
Vermont	Montpelier	Jim Douglas	Republican	[b] 2	Jan. 2011
Virginia	Richmond	Tim Kaine	Democrat	[a] 4	Jan. 2010
Washington	Olympia	Chris Gregoire	Democrat	[d] 4	Jan. 2013
West Virginia	Charleston	Joe Manchin III	Democrat	[c] 4	Jan. 2013
Wisconsin	Madison	Jim Doyle	Democrat	[b] 4	Jan. 2011
Wyoming	Cheyenne	Dave Freudenthal	Democrat	[c] 4	Jan. 2011
COMMONWEALTH OF					
Puerto Rico	San Juan	Luis G. Fortuño	Republican	[b] 4	Jan. 2013
TERRITORIES					
Guam	Agana	Felix P. Camacho	Republican	[c] 4	Jan. 2011
Virgin Islands	Charlotte Amalie	John deJongh, Jr.	Democrat	[c] 4	Jan. 2011
American Samoa	Pago Pago	Togiola T.A. Tulafono	Democrat	[c] 4	Jan. 2013
Northern Mariana Islands.	Saipan	Benigno Fitial	Covenant	[c] 4	Jan. 2010

[a] Cannot succeed himself. [b] No limit. [c] Can serve 2 consecutive terms. [d] Can serve 3 consecutive terms. [e] Can serve 4 consecutive terms. [f] Can serve no more than 8 years in a 12-year period. [g] Can serve no more than 8 years in a 16-year period.

PRESIDENTS AND VICE PRESIDENTS AND THE CONGRESSES COINCIDENT WITH THEIR TERMS [1]

President	Vice President	Service	Congresses
George Washington	John Adams	Apr. 30, 1789–Mar. 3, 1797	1, 2, 3, 4.
John Adams	Thomas Jefferson	Mar. 4, 1797–Mar. 3, 1801	5, 6.
Thomas Jefferson	Aaron Burr	Mar. 4, 1801–Mar. 3, 1805	7, 8.
Do	George Clinton	Mar. 4, 1805–Mar. 3, 1809	9, 10.
James Madison	......do. [2]	Mar. 4, 1809–Mar. 3, 1813	11, 12.
Do	Elbridge Gerry [3]	Mar. 4, 1813–Mar. 3, 1817	13, 14.
James Monroe	Daniel D. Tompkins	Mar. 4, 1817–Mar. 3, 1825	15, 16, 17, 18, 19
John Quincy Adams	John C. Calhoun	Mar. 4, 1825–Mar. 3, 1829	19, 20.
Andrew Jackson	......do. [4]	Mar. 4, 1829–Mar. 3, 1833	21, 22.
Do	Martin Van Buren	Mar. 4, 1833–Mar. 3, 1837	23, 24.
Martin Van Buren	Richard M. Johnson	Mar. 4, 1837–Mar. 3, 1841	25, 26.
William Henry Harrison [5]	John Tyler	Mar. 4, 1841–Apr. 4, 1841	27.
John Tyler		Apr. 6, 1841 –Mar. 3, 1845	27, 28.
James K. Polk	George M. Dallas	Mar. 4, 1845–Mar. 3, 1849	29, 30.
Zachary Taylor [5]	Millard Fillmore	Mar. 5, 1849–July 9, 1850	31.
Millard Fillmore		July 10, 1850–Mar. 3, 1853	31, 32.
Franklin Pierce	William R. King [6]	Mar. 4, 1853–Mar. 3, 1857	33, 34.
James Buchanan	John C. Breckinridge	Mar. 4, 1857–Mar. 3, 1861	35, 36.
Abraham Lincoln	Hannibal Hamlin	Mar. 4, 1861–Mar. 3, 1865	37, 38.
Do.[5]	Andrew Johnson	Mar. 4, 1865–Apr. 15, 1865	39.
Andrew Johnson		Apr. 15, 1865–Mar. 3, 1869	39, 40.
Ulysses S. Grant	Schuyler Colfax	Mar. 4, 1869–Mar. 3, 1873	41, 42.
Do	Henry Wilson [7]	Mar. 4, 1873–Mar. 3, 1877	43, 44.
Rutherford B. Hayes	William A. Wheeler	Mar. 4, 1877–Mar. 3, 1881	45, 46.
James A. Garfield [5]	Chester A. Arthur	Mar. 4, 1881–Sept. 19, 1881	47.
Chester A. Arthur		Sept. 20, 1881–Mar. 3, 1885	47, 48.
Grover Cleveland	Thomas A. Hendricks [8]	Mar. 4, 1885–Mar. 3, 1889	49, 50.
Benjamin Harrison	Levi P. Morton	Mar. 4, 1889–Mar. 3, 1893	51, 52.
Grover Cleveland	Adlai E. Stevenson	Mar. 4, 1893–Mar. 3, 1897	53, 54.
William McKinley	Garret A. Hobart [9]	Mar. 4, 1897–Mar. 3, 1901	55, 56.
Do.[5]	Theodore Roosevelt	Mar. 4, 1901–Sept. 14, 1901	57.
Theodore Roosevelt		Sept. 14, 1901–Mar. 3, 1905	57, 58.
Do	Charles W. Fairbanks	Mar. 4, 1905–Mar. 3, 1909	59, 60.
William H. Taft	James S. Sherman [10]	Mar. 4, 1909–Mar. 3, 1913	61, 62.
Woodrow Wilson	Thomas R. Marshall	Mar. 4, 1913–Mar. 3, 1921	63, 64, 65, 66, 67.
Warren G. Harding [5]	Calvin Coolidge	Mar. 4, 1921–Aug. 2, 1923	67.
Calvin Coolidge		Aug. 3, 1923–Mar. 3, 1925	68.
Do	Charles G. Dawes	Mar. 4, 1925–Mar. 3, 1929	69, 70.
Herbert C. Hoover	Charles Curtis	Mar. 4, 1929–Mar. 3, 1933	71, 72.
Franklin D. Roosevelt	John N. Garner	Mar. 4, 1933–Jan. 20, 1941	73, 74, 75, 76, 77.
Do	Henry A. Wallace	Jan. 20, 1941–Jan. 20, 1945	77, 78, 79.
Do.[5]	Harry S. Truman	Jan. 20, 1945–Apr. 12, 1945	79.
Harry S. Truman		Apr. 12, 1945–Jan. 20, 1949	79, 80, 81.
Do	Alben W. Barkley	Jan. 20, 1949–Jan. 20, 1953	81, 82, 83.
Dwight D. Eisenhower	Richard M. Nixon	Jan. 20, 1953–Jan. 20, 1961	83, 84, 85, 86, 87.
John F. Kennedy [5]	Lyndon B. Johnson	Jan. 20, 1961–Nov. 22, 1963	87, 88, 89.
Lyndon B. Johnson		Nov. 22, 1963–Jan. 20, 1965	88, 89.
Do	Hubert H. Humphrey	Jan. 20, 1965–Jan. 20, 1969	89, 90, 91.
Richard M. Nixon	Spiro T. Agnew [11]	Jan. 20, 1969–Dec. 6, 1973	91, 92, 93.
Do. [13]	Gerald R. Ford [12]	Dec. 6, 1973–Aug. 9, 1974	93.
Gerald R. Ford		Aug. 9, 1974–Dec. 19, 1974	93.
Do	Nelson A. Rockefeller [14]	Dec. 19, 1974–Jan. 20, 1977	93, 94, 95.
James Earl "Jimmy" Carter	Walter F. Mondale	Jan. 20, 1977–Jan. 20, 1981	95, 96, 97.
Ronald Reagan	George Bush	Jan. 20, 1981–Jan. 20, 1989	97, 98, 99, 100, 101.
George Bush	Dan Quayle	Jan. 20, 1989–Jan. 20, 1993	101, 102, 103.
William J. Clinton	Albert Gore	Jan. 20, 1993–Jan. 20, 2001	103, 104, 105, 106, 107.
George W. Bush	Richard B. Cheney	Jan. 20, 2001–Jan. 20, 2009	107, 108, 109, 110, 111.
Barack H. Obama	Joseph R. Biden, Jr.	Jan. 20, 2009–	111.

[1] From 1789 until 1933, the terms of the President and Vice President and the term of the Congress coincided, beginning on March 4 and ending on March 3. This changed when the 20th amendment to the Constitution was adopted in 1933. Beginning in 1934 the convening date for Congress became January 3, and beginning in 1937 the starting date for the Presidential term became January 20. Because of this change, the number of Congresses overlapping with a Presidential term increased from two to three, although the third only overlaps by a few weeks.

[2] Died Apr. 20, 1812.

[3] Died Nov. 23, 1814.

[4] Resigned Dec. 28, 1832, to become a United States Senator from South Carolina.

[5] Died in office.

[6] Died Apr. 18, 1853.

[7] Died Nov. 22, 1875.

[8] Died Nov. 25, 1885.

[9] Died Nov. 21, 1899.

[10] Died Oct. 30, 1912.

[11] Resigned Oct. 10, 1973.

[12] Nominated to be Vice President by President Richard M. Nixon on Oct. 12, 1973; confirmed by the Senate on Nov. 27, 1973; confirmed by the House of Representatives on Dec. 6, 1973; took the oath of office on Dec. 6, 1973 in the Hall of the House of Representatives. This was the first time a Vice President was nominated by the President and confirmed by the Congress pursuant to the 25th amendment to the Constitution.

[13] Resigned from office.

[14] Nominated to be Vice President by President Gerald R. Ford on Aug. 20, 1974; confirmed by the Senate on Dec. 10, 1974; confirmed by the House of Representatives on Dec. 19, 1974; took the oath of office on Dec. 19, 1974, in the Senate Chamber.

CAPITOL BUILDINGS AND GROUNDS

UNITED STATES CAPITOL

Overview of the Building and its Function

The United States Capitol is among the most architecturally impressive and symbolically important buildings in the world. It has housed the chambers of the Senate and the House of Representatives for more than two centuries. Begun in 1793, the Capitol has been built, burnt, rebuilt, extended, and restored; today, it stands as a monument not only to its builders but also to the American people and their government.

As the focal point of the government's legislative branch, the Capitol is the centerpiece of the Capitol complex, which includes the six principal congressional office buildings and three Library of Congress buildings constructed on Capitol Hill in the 19th and 20th centuries.

In addition to its active use by Congress, the Capitol is a museum of American art and history. Each year, it is visited by millions of people from around the world.

A fine example of 19th-century neoclassical architecture, the Capitol combines function with aesthetics. Its design was derived from ancient Greece and Rome and evokes the ideals that guided the nation's founders as they framed their new republic. As the building was expanded from its original design, harmony with the existing portions was carefully maintained.

Today, the Capitol covers a ground area of 175,170 square feet, or about 4 acres, and has a floor area of approximately 16½ acres. Its length, from north to south, is 751 feet 4 inches; its greatest width, including approaches, is 350 feet. Its height above the base line on the east front to the top of the Statue of Freedom is 288 feet; from the basement floor to the top of the dome is an ascent of 365 steps.

The building is divided into five levels. The first, or ground, floor is occupied chiefly by committee rooms and the spaces allocated to various congressional officers. The areas accessible to visitors on this level include the Hall of Columns, the restored Old Supreme Court Chamber, and the Crypt beneath the Rotunda.

The second floor holds the chambers of the House of Representatives (in the south wing) and the Senate (in the north wing). This floor also contains three major public areas. In the center under the dome is the Rotunda, a circular ceremonial space that also serves as a gallery of paintings and sculpture depicting significant people and events in the nation's history. The Rotunda is 96 feet in diameter and rises 180 feet 3 inches to the canopy. The semicircular chamber south of the Rotunda served as the Hall of the House until 1857; now designated National Statuary Hall, it houses part of the Capitol's collection of statues donated by the states in commemoration of notable citizens. The Old Senate Chamber northeast of the Rotunda, which was used by the Senate until 1859, has been returned to its mid-19th-century appearance.

The third floor allows access to the galleries from which visitors to the Capitol may watch the proceedings of the House and the Senate when Congress is in session. The rest of this floor is occupied by offices, committee rooms, and press galleries.

The fourth floor and the basement/terrace level of the Capitol are occupied by offices, machinery rooms, workshops, and other support areas.

Located beneath the East Front plaza, the newest addition to the Capitol is the Capitol Visitor Center (CVC). Preparatory construction activities began in 2002, and the CVC was opened to the public on December 2, 2008. This date was chosen for its significance in the Capitol's history: it was on December 2, 1863, that the Statue of Freedom was placed atop the Capitol to signify completion of the construction of the new dome. The CVC occupies 580,000 square feet of space on three levels and includes an Exhibition Hall, a restaurant, orientation theaters, gift shops, and other visitor amenities as well as office space for the House and Senate.

LOCATION OF THE CAPITOL

The Capitol is located at the eastern end of the Mall on a plateau 88 feet above the level of the Potomac River, commanding a westward view across the Capitol Reflecting Pool to the Washington Monument 1.4 miles away and the Lincoln Memorial 2.2 miles away.

Before 1791, the Federal Government had no permanent site. The early Congresses met in eight different cities: Philadelphia, Baltimore, Lancaster, York, Princeton, Annapolis, Trenton, and New York City. The subject of a permanent capital for the Government of the United States was first raised by Congress in 1783; it was ultimately addressed in Article I, Section 8 of the Constitution (1787), which gave the Congress legislative authority over ''such District (not exceeding ten Miles square) as may, by Cession of Particular States, and the Acceptance of Congress, become the Seat of the Government of the United States. . . .''

In 1788, the State of Maryland ceded to Congress ''any district in this State, not exceeding ten miles square,'' and in 1789 the State of Virginia ceded an equivalent amount of land. In accordance with the ''Residence Act'' passed by Congress in 1790, President Washington in 1791 selected the area that is now the District of Columbia from the land ceded by Maryland (private landowners whose property fell within this area were compensated by a payment of £25 per acre); that ceded by Virginia was not used for the capital and was returned to Virginia in 1846. Also under the provisions of that Act, he selected three commissioners to survey the site and oversee the design and construction of the capital city and its government buildings. The commissioners, in turn, selected the French-American engineer Pierre Charles L'Enfant to plan the new city of Washington. L'Enfant's plan, which was influenced by the gardens at Versailles, arranged the city's streets and avenues in a grid overlaid with baroque diagonals; the result is a functional and aesthetic whole in which government buildings are balanced against public lawns, gardens, squares, and paths. The Capitol itself was located at the elevated east end of the Mall, on the brow of what was then called Jenkins' Hill. The site was, in L'Enfant's words, ''a pedestal waiting for a monument.''

SELECTION OF A PLAN

L'Enfant was expected to design the Capitol and to supervise its construction. However, he refused to produce any drawings for the building, claiming that he carried the design ''in his head''; this fact and his refusal to consider himself subject to the commissioners' authority led to his dismissal in 1792. In March of that year the commissioners announced a competition, suggested by Secretary of State Thomas Jefferson, that would award $500 and a city lot to whoever produced ''the most approved plan'' for the Capitol by mid-July. None of the 17 plans submitted, however, was wholly satisfactory. In October, a letter arrived from Dr. William Thornton, a Scottish-trained physician living in Tortola, British West Indies, requesting an opportunity to present a plan even though the competition had closed. The commissioners granted this request.

Thornton's plan depicted a building composed of three sections. The central section, which was topped by a low dome, was to be flanked on the north and south by two rectangular wings (one for the Senate and one for the House of Representatives). President Washington commended the plan for its ''grandeur, simplicity and convenience,'' and on April 5, 1793, it was accepted by the commissioners; Washington gave his formal approval on July 25.

BRIEF CONSTRUCTION HISTORY

1793–1829

The cornerstone was laid by President Washington in the building's southeast corner on September 18, 1793, with Masonic ceremonies. Work progressed under the direction of three architects in succession. Stephen H. Hallet (an entrant in the earlier competition) and George Hadfield were eventually dismissed by the commissioners because of inappropriate design changes that they tried to impose; James Hoban, the architect of the White House, saw the first phase of the project through to completion.

Construction was a laborious and time-consuming process: the sandstone used for the building had to be ferried on boats from the quarries at Aquia, Virginia; workers had to be induced to leave their homes to come to the relative wilderness of Capitol Hill; and funding was inadequate. By August 1796 the commissioners were forced to focus the entire work effort on the building's north wing so that it at least could be ready for government occupancy as scheduled. Even so, some third-floor rooms were still unfinished when the Congress, the Supreme Court, the Library of Congress, and the courts of the District of Columbia occupied the Capitol in late 1800.

In 1803, Congress allocated funds to resume construction. A year earlier, the office of the Commissioners had been abolished and replaced by a superintendent of the city of Washington. To oversee the renewed construction effort, B. Henry Latrobe was appointed surveyor of public buildings. The first professional architect and engineer to work in America, Latrobe modified Thornton's plan for the south wing to include space for offices and committee rooms; he also introduced alterations to simplify the construction work. Latrobe began work by removing a squat, oval, temporary building known as "the Oven," which had been erected in 1801 as a meeting place for the House of Representatives. By 1807 construction on the south wing was sufficiently advanced that the House was able to occupy its new legislative chamber, and the wing was completed in 1811.

In 1808, as work on the south wing progressed, Latrobe began the rebuilding of the north wing, which had fallen into disrepair. Rather than simply repair the wing, he redesigned the interior of the building to increase its usefulness and durability; among his changes was the addition of a chamber for the Supreme Court. By 1811, he had completed the eastern half of this wing, but funding was being increasingly diverted to preparations for a second war with Great Britain. By 1813, Latrobe had no further work in Washington and so he departed, leaving the north and south wings of the Capitol connected only by a temporary wooden passageway.

The War of 1812 left the Capitol, in Latrobe's later words, "a most magnificent ruin": on August 24, 1814, British troops set fire to the building, and only a sudden rainstorm prevented its complete destruction. Immediately after the fire, Congress met for one session in Blodget's Hotel, which was at Seventh and E Streets, NW. From 1815 to 1819, Congress occupied a building erected for it on First Street, NE, on part of the site now occupied by the Supreme Court Building. This building later came to be known as the Old Brick Capitol.

Latrobe returned to Washington in 1815, when he was rehired to restore the Capitol. In addition to making repairs, he took advantage of this opportunity to make further changes in the building's interior design (for example, an enlargement of the Senate Chamber) and introduce new materials (for example, marble discovered along the upper Potomac). However, he came under increasing pressure because of construction delays (most of which were beyond his control) and cost overruns; finally, he resigned his post in November 1817.

On January 8, 1818, Charles Bulfinch, a prominent Boston architect, was appointed Latrobe's successor. Continuing the restoration of the north and south wings, he was able to make the chambers for the Supreme Court, the House, and the Senate ready for use by 1819. Bulfinch also redesigned and supervised the construction of the Capitol's central section. The copper-covered wooden dome that topped this section was made higher than Bulfinch considered appropriate to the building's size (at the direction of President James Monroe and Secretary of State John Quincy Adams). After completing the last part of the building in 1826, Bulfinch spent the next few years on the Capitol's decoration and landscaping. In 1829, his work was done and his position with the government was terminated. In the 38 years following Bulfinch's tenure, the Capitol was entrusted to the care of the commissioner of public buildings.

1830–1868

The Capitol was by this point already an impressive structure. At ground level, its length was 351 feet 7½ inches and its width was 282 feet 10½ inches. Up to the year 1827—records from later years being incomplete—the project cost was $2,432,851.34. Improvements to the building continued in the years to come (running water in 1832, gas lighting in the 1840s), but by 1850 its size could no longer accommodate the increasing numbers of senators and representatives from newly admitted states. The Senate therefore voted to hold another competition, offering a prize of $500 for the best plan to extend the Capitol. Several suitable plans were submitted, some proposing an eastward extension of the building and others proposing the addition of large north and south wings. However, Congress was unable to decide between these two approaches, and the prize money was divided among five architects. Thus, the tasks of selecting a plan and appointing an architect fell to President Millard Fillmore.

Fillmore's choice was Thomas U. Walter, a Philadelphia architect who had entered the competition. On July 4, 1851, in a ceremony whose principal oration was delivered by Secretary of State Daniel Webster, the president laid the cornerstone in the northeast corner of the House wing. Over the next 14 years, Walter supervised the construction of the extension, ensuring their compatibility with the architectural style of the existing building. However, because the Aquia Creek sandstone used earlier had deteriorated noticeably, he chose to use marble for the exterior. For the veneer, Walter selected marble quarried at Lee, MA, and for the columns he used marble from Cockeysville, MD.

Walter faced several significant challenges during the course of construction. Chief among these was the steady imposition by the government of additional tasks without additional pay. Aside from his work on the Capitol extension, Walter designed the wings of the Patent Office building, extensions to the Treasury and Post Office buildings, and the Marine barracks in Pensacola and Brooklyn. When the Library of Congress in the Capitol's west central section was gutted by a fire in 1851, Walter was commissioned to restore it. He also encountered obstacles in his work on the Capitol extensions. His location of the legislative chambers was changed in 1853 at the direction of President Franklin Pierce, based on the suggestions of the newly appointed supervising engineer, Captain Montgomery C. Meigs. In general, however, the project progressed rapidly: the House of Representatives was able to meet in its new chamber on December 16, 1857, and the Senate first met in its present chamber on January 4, 1859. The old House chamber was later designated National Statuary Hall. In 1861 most construction was suspended because of the Civil War, and the Capitol was used briefly as a military barracks, hospital, and bakery. In 1862 work on the entire building was resumed.

As the new wings were constructed, more than doubling the length of the Capitol, it became apparent that the dome erected by Bulfinch no longer suited the building's proportions. In 1855 Congress voted for its replacement based on Walter's design for a new, fireproof cast-iron dome. The old dome was removed in 1856 and 5,000,000 pounds of new masonry was placed on the existing rotunda walls. Iron used in the dome construction had an aggregate weight of 8,909,200 pounds and was lifted into place by steam-powered derricks.

In 1859, Thomas Crawford's plaster model for the Statue of Freedom, designed for the top of the dome, arrived from the sculptor's studio in Rome. With a height of 19 feet 6 inches, the statue was almost 3 feet taller than specified, and Walter was compelled to make revisions to his design for the dome. When cast in bronze by Clark Mills at his foundry on the outskirts of Washington, it weighed 14,985 pounds. The statue was lifted into place atop the dome in 1863, its final section being installed on December 2 to the accompaniment of gun salutes from the forts around the city.

The work on the dome and the extension was completed under the direction of Edward Clark, who had served as Walter's assistant and was appointed Architect of the Capitol in 1865 after Walter's resignation. In 1866, the Italian-born artist Constantino Brumidi finished the canopy fresco, a monumental painting entitled *The Apotheosis of George Washington*. The Capitol extension was completed in 1868.

1869–1902

Clark continued to hold the post of Architect of the Capitol until his death in 1902. During his tenure, the Capitol underwent considerable modernization. Steam heat was gradually installed in the old Capitol. In 1874 the first elevator was installed, and in the 1880s electric lighting began to replace gas lights.

Between 1884 and 1891, the marble terraces on the north, west, and south sides of the Capitol were constructed. As part of the landscape plan devised by Frederick Law Olmsted, these terraces not only added over 100 rooms to the Capitol but also provided a broader, more substantial visual base for the building.

On November 6, 1898, a gas explosion and fire in the original north wing dramatically illustrated the need for fireproofing. The roofs over the Statuary Hall wing and the original north wing were reconstructed and fireproofed, the work being completed in 1902 by Clark's successor, Elliott Woods. In 1901 the space in the west central front vacated by the Library of Congress was converted to committee rooms.

1903–1970

During the remainder of Woods's service, which ended with his death in 1923, no major structural work was required on the Capitol. The activities performed in the building were limited chiefly to cleaning and refurbishing the interior. David Lynn, the Architect of the Capitol from 1923 until his retirement in 1954, continued these tasks. Between July 1949 and January 1951, the corroded roofs and skylights of both wings and the connecting corridors were replaced with new roofs of concrete and steel, covered with copper. The cast-iron and glass ceilings of the House and Senate chambers were replaced with ceilings of stainless steel and plaster, with a laylight of carved glass and bronze in the middle of each. The House and Senate chambers were completely redecorated, modern lighting was added, and acoustical problems were solved. During this renovation program, the House and Senate vacated their chambers on several occasions so that the work could progress.

The next significant modification made to the Capitol was the east front extension. This project was carried out under the supervision of Architect of the Capitol J. George Stewart, who served from 1954 until his death in 1970. Begun in 1958, it involved the construction of a new east front 32 feet 6 inches east of the old front, faithfully reproducing the sandstone structure in marble. The old sandstone walls were not destroyed; rather, they were left in place to become a part of the interior wall and are now buttressed by the addition. The marble columns of the connecting corridors were also moved and reused. Other elements of this project included repairing the dome, constructing a subway terminal under the Senate steps, reconstructing those steps, cleaning both wings, birdproofing the building, providing furniture and furnishings for 90 new rooms created by the extension, and improving the lighting throughout the building. The project was completed in 1962.

1971–Present

During the nearly 25-year tenure (1971–1995) of Architect of the Capitol George M. White, FAIA, the building was both modernized and restored. Electronic voting equipment was installed in the House chamber in 1973; facilities were added to allow television coverage of the House and Senate debates in 1979 and 1986, respectively; and improved climate control, electronic surveillance systems, and new computer and communications facilities have been added to bring the Capitol up-to-date. The Old Senate Chamber, National Statuary Hall, and the Old Supreme Court Chamber, on the other hand, were restored to their mid-19th-century appearance in the 1970s.

In 1983, work began on the strengthening, renovation, and preservation of the west front of the Capitol. Structural problems had developed over the years because of defects in the original foundations, deterioration of the sandstone facing material, alterations to the basic building fabric (a fourth-floor addition and channeling of the walls to install interior utilities), and damage from the fires of 1814 and 1851 and the 1898 gas explosion.

To strengthen the structure, over one thousand stainless steel tie rods were set into the building's masonry. More than 30 layers of paint were removed, and damaged stonework was repaired or replicated. Ultimately, 40 percent of the sandstone blocks were replaced with limestone. The walls were treated with a special consolidant and then painted to match the marble wings. The entire project was completed in 1987.

A related project, completed in January 1993, effected the repair of the Olmsted terraces, which had been subject to damage from settling, and converted the terrace courtyards into several thousand square feet of meeting space.

As the Capitol enters its third century, restoration and modernization work continues. Alan M. Hantman, FAIA, was appointed in February 1997 to a ten-year term as Architect of the Capitol. Projects under his direction included rehabilitation of the Capitol dome; conservation of murals; improvement of speech-reinforcement, electrical, and fire-protection systems in the Capitol and the Congressional office buildings; work on security improvements within the Capitol complex; restoration of the U.S. Botanic Garden Conservatory; the design and construction of the National Garden adjacent to the Botanic Garden Conservatory; renovation of the building systems in the Dirksen Senate Office Building; publication of the first comprehensive history of the Capitol to appear in a century; and construction of a new Capitol Visitor Center. At the end of Mr. Hantman's term in February 2007, Mr. Stephen T. Ayers, AIA, LEED AP, assumed the position of Acting Architect of the Capitol.

HOUSE OFFICE BUILDINGS

Cannon House Office Building

An increased membership of the Senate and House resulted in a demand for additional rooms for the accommodations of the Senators and Representatives. On March 3, 1903, the Congress authorized the erection of a fireproofed office building for the use of the House. It was designed by the firm of Carrere & Hastings of New York City in the Beaux Arts style. The first brick was laid July 5, 1905, in square No. 690, and formal exercises were held at the laying of the cornerstone on April 14, 1906, in which President Theodore Roosevelt participated. The building was completed and occupied January 10, 1908. A subsequent change in the basis of congressional representation made necessary the building of an additional story in 1913–14. The total cost of the building, including site, furnishings, equipment, and the subway connecting it with the U.S. Capitol, amounted to $4,860,155. This office building contains about 500 rooms, and was considered at the time of its completion fully equipped for all the needs of a modern building for office purposes. A garage was added in the building's courtyard in the 1960s.

Pursuant to authority in the Second Supplemental Appropriations Act, 1955, and subsequent action of the House Office Building Commission, remodeling of the Cannon Building began in 1966. The estimated cost of this work was $5,200,000. Pursuant to the provisions of Public Law 87–453, approved May 21, 1962, the building was named in honor of Joseph G. Cannon of Illinois, who was Speaker at the time the building was constructed.

Longworth House Office Building

Under legislation contained in the Authorization Act of January 10, 1929, and in the urgent deficiency bill of March 4, 1929, provisions were made for an additional House office building, to be located on the west side of New Jersey Avenue (opposite the first House office building). The building was designed by the Allied Architects of Washington in the Neoclassical Revival style.

The cornerstone was laid June 24, 1932, and the building was completed on April 20, 1933. It contains 251 two-room suites and 16 committee rooms. Each suite and committee room is provided with a storeroom. Eight floors are occupied by members. The basement and subbasement contain shops and mechanical areas needed for the maintenance of the building. A cafeteria was added in the building's courtyard in the 1960s. The cost of this building, including site, furnishings, and equipment, was $7,805,705. Pursuant to the provisions of Public Law 87–453, approved May 21, 1962, the building was named in honor of Nicholas Longworth of Ohio, who was Speaker when the second House office building was constructed.

Rayburn House Office Building and Other Related Changes and Improvements

Under legislation contained in the Second Supplemental Appropriations Act, 1955, provision was made for construction of a fireproof office building for the House of Representatives.

All work was carried forward by the Architect of the Capitol under the direction of the House Office Building Commission at a cost totaling $135,279,000.

The Rayburn Building is connected to the Capitol by a subway. Designs for the building were prepared by the firm of Harbeson, Hough, Livingston & Larson of Philadelphia, Associate Architects. The building contains 169 congressional suites; full-committee hearing rooms for 9 standing committees, 16 subcommittee hearing rooms, committee staff rooms and other committee facilities; a large cafeteria and other restaurant facilities; an underground garage; and a variety of liaison offices, press and television facilities, maintenance and equipment shops or rooms, and storage areas. This building has nine stories and a penthouse for machinery.

The cornerstone was laid May 24, 1962, by John W. McCormack, Speaker of the House of Representatives. President John F. Kennedy participated in the cornerstone laying and delivered the address.

A portion of the basement floor was occupied beginning March 12, 1964, by House of Representatives personnel moved from the George Washington Inn property. Full occupancy of the Rayburn Building, under the room-filing regulations, was begun February 23, 1965, and completed April 2, 1965. Pursuant to the provisions of Public Law 87–453, approved May 21, 1962, the building was named in honor of Sam Rayburn of Texas.

House Office Building Annex No. 2, named the ''Gerald R. Ford House of Representatives Office Building,'' was acquired in 1975 from the General Services Administration. The structure, located at Second and D Streets, SW., was built in 1939 for the Federal Bureau of Investigation as a fingerprint file archives. This building has approximately 432,000 square feet of space.

SENATE OFFICE BUILDINGS

Richard Brevard Russell Senate Office Building

In 1891 the Senate provided itself with office space by the purchase of the Maltby Building, then located on the northwest corner of B Street (now Constitution Avenue) and New Jersey

Avenue, NW. When it was condemned as an unsafe structure, Senators needed safer and more commodious office space. Under authorization of the Act of April 28, 1904, square 686 on the northeast corner of Delaware Avenue and B Street, NE. was purchased as a site for the Senate Office Building. The plans for the House Office Building were adapted for the Senate Office Building by the firm of Carrere & Hastings, with the exception that the side of the building fronting on First Street, NE. was temporarily omitted. The cornerstone was laid without special exercises on July 31, 1906, and the building was occupied March 5, 1909. In 1931, the completion of the fourth side of the building was commenced. In 1933 it was completed, together with alterations to the C Street facade, and the construction of terraces, balustrades, and approaches. The cost of the completed building, including the site, furnishings, equipment and the subway connecting it with the United States Capitol, was $8,390,892.

The building was named the ''Richard Brevard Russell Senate Office Building'' by Senate Resolution 296, 92nd Congress, agreed to October 11, 1972, as amended by Senate Resolution 295, 96th Congress, agreed to December 3, 1979.

Everett McKinley Dirksen Senate Office Building

Under legislation contained in the Second Deficiency Appropriations Act, 1948, Public Law 80–785, provision was made for an additional office building for the United States Senate with limits of cost of $1,100,000 for acquisition of the site and $20,600,000 for constructing and equipping the building.

The construction cost limit was subsequently increased to $24,196. All work was carried forward by the Architect of the Capitol under the direction of the Senate Office Building Commission. The New York firm of Eggers & Higgins served as the consulting architect.

The site was acquired and cleared in 1948–49 at a total cost of $1,011,492.

A contract for excavation, concrete footings and mats for the new building was awarded in January 1955, in the amount of $747,200. Groundbreaking ceremonies were held January 26, 1955.

A contract for the superstructure of the new building was awarded September 9, 1955, in the amount of $17,200,000. The cornerstone was laid July 13, 1956.

As a part of this project, a new underground subway system was installed from the Capitol to both the Old and New Senate Office Buildings.

An appropriation of $1,000,000 for furniture and furnishings for the new building was provided in 1958. The building was accepted for beneficial occupancy October 15, 1958.

The building was named the ''Everett McKinley Dirksen Senate Office Building'' by Senate Resolution 296, 92nd Congress, agreed to October 11, 1972, and Senate Resolution 295, 96th Congress, agreed to December 3, 1979.

Philip A. Hart Senate Office Building

Construction as an extension to the Dirksen Senate Office Building was authorized on October 31, 1972; legislation enacted in subsequent years increased the scope of the project and established a total cost ceiling of $137,700,400. The firm of John Carl Warnecke & Associates served as Associate Architect for the project.

Senate Resolution 525, passed August 30, 1976, amended by Senate Resolution 295, 96th Congress, agreed to December 3, 1979, provided that upon completion of the extension it would be named the ''Philip A. Hart Senate Office Building'' to honor the Senator from Michigan.

The contract for clearing of the site, piping for utilities, excavation, and construction of foundation was awarded in December 1975. Groundbreaking took place January 5, 1976. The contract for furnishing and delivery of the exterior stone was awarded in February 1977, and the contract for the superstructure, which included wall and roof systems and the erection of all exterior stonework, was awarded in October 1977. The contract for the first portion of the interior and related work was awarded in December 1978. A contract for interior finishing was awarded in July 1980. The first suite was occupied on November 22, 1982. Alexander Calder's mobile/stabile *Mountains and Clouds* was installed in the building's atrium in November 1986.

CAPITOL POWER PLANT

During the development of the plans for the Cannon and Russell Buildings, the question of heat, light, and power was considered. The Senate and House wings of the Capitol were heated by separate heating plants. The Library of Congress also had a heating plant for that building. It was determined that needs for heating and lighting and electrical power could be met by a central power plant.

A site was selected in Garfield Park. Since this park was a Government reservation, an appropriation was not required to secure title. The determining factors leading to the selection of this site were its proximity to the tracks of what is now the Penn Central Railroad and to the buildings to be served.

The dimensions of the Capitol Power Plant, which was authorized on April 28, 1904, and completed in 1910, were 244 feet 8 inches by 117 feet.

The buildings originally served by the Capitol Power Plant were connected to it by a reinforced-concrete steam tunnel.

In September 1951, when the demand for electrical energy was reaching the maximum capacity of the Capitol Power Plant, arrangements were made to purchase electrical service from the local public utility company and to discontinue electrical generation. The heating and cooling functions of the Capitol Power Plant were expanded in 1935, 1939, 1958, 1973, and 1980. A new refrigeration plant modernization and expansion project was completed in 2007.

U.S. CAPITOL GROUNDS

A Description of the Grounds

Originally a wooded wilderness, the U.S. Capitol Grounds today provide a park-like setting for the Nation's Capitol, offering a picturesque counterpoint to the building's formal architecture. The grounds immediately surrounding the Capitol are bordered by a stone wall and cover an area of 58.8 acres. Their boundaries are Independence Avenue on the south, Constitution Avenue on the north, First Street NE./SE. on the east, and First Street NW./SW. on the west. Over 100 varieties of trees and bushes are planted around the Capitol, and thousands of flowers are used in seasonal displays. In contrast to the building's straight, neoclassical lines, most of the walkways in the grounds are curved. Benches along the paths offer pleasant spots for visitors to appreciate the building, its landscape, and the surrounding areas, most notably the Mall to the west.

The grounds were designed by Frederick Law Olmsted (1822–1903), who planned the landscaping of the area that was performed from 1874 to 1892. Olmsted, who also designed New York's Central Park, is considered the greatest American landscape architect of his day. He was a pioneer in the development of public parks in America, and many of his designs were influenced by his studies of European parks, gardens, and estates. In describing his plan for the Capitol Grounds, Olmsted noted that, ''The ground is in design part of the Capitol, but in all respects subsidiary to the central structure.'' Therefore, he was careful not to group trees or other landscape features in any way that would distract the viewer from the Capitol. The use of sculpture and other ornamentation has also been kept to a minimum.

Many of the trees on the Capitol Grounds have historic or memorial associations. Over 30 states have made symbolic gifts of their state trees to the Capitol Grounds. Many of the trees on the grounds bear plaques that identify their species and their historic significance.

At the East Capitol Street entrance to the Capitol plaza are two large rectangular stone fountains. Six massive red granite lamp piers topped with light fixtures in wrought-iron cages, and 16 smaller bronze light fixtures, line the paved plaza. Three sets of benches are enclosed with wrought-iron railings and grilles; the roofed bench was originally a shelter for streetcar passengers.

The northern part of the grounds offers a shaded walk among trees, flowers, and shrubbery. A small, hexagonal brick structure named the Summer House may be found in the northwest corner of the grounds. This structure contains shaded benches, a central ornamental fountain, and three public drinking fountains. In a small grotto on the eastern side of the Summer House, a stream of water flows and splashes over rocks to create a pleasing sound and cool the summer breezes.

A Brief History of the Grounds Before Olmsted

The land on which the Capitol stands was first occupied by the Manahoacs and the Monacans, who were subtribes of the Algonquin Indians. Early settlers reported that these tribes occasionally held councils not far from the foot of the hill. This land eventually became a part of Cerne Abbey Manor, and at the time of its acquisition by the Federal Government it was owned by Daniel Carroll of Duddington.

The ''Residence Act'' of 1790 provided that the Federal Government should be established in a permanent location by the year 1800. In early March 1791 the commissioners of the city of Washington, who had been appointed by President George Washington, selected the French engineer Pierre Charles L'Enfant to plan the new federal city. L'Enfant decided to locate the Capitol at the elevated east end of the Mall (on what was then called Jenkins' Hill); he described the site as ''a pedestal waiting for a monument.''

At this time the site of the Capitol was a relative wilderness partly overgrown with scrub oak. Oliver Wolcott, a signer of the Declaration of Independence, described the soil as an ''*exceedingly stiff* clay, becoming dust in dry and mortar in rainy weather.''

In 1825, a plan was devised for imposing order on the Capitol Grounds, and it was carried out for almost 15 years. The plan divided the area into flat, rectangular grassy areas bordered by trees, flower beds, and gravel walks. The growth of the trees, however, soon deprived the other plantings of nourishment, and the design became increasingly difficult to maintain in light of sporadic and small appropriations. John Foy, who had charge of the grounds during most of this period, was ''superseded for political reasons,'' and the area was then maintained with little care or forethought. Many rapidly growing but short-lived trees were introduced and soon depleted the soil; a lack of proper pruning and thinning left the majority of the area's vegetation ill-grown, feeble, or dead. Virtually all was removed by the early 1870's, either to make way for building operations during Thomas U. Walter's enlargement of the Capitol or as required by changes in grading to accommodate the new work on the building or the alterations to surrounding streets.

The Olmsted Plan

The mid-19th-century extension of the Capitol, in which the House and Senate wings and the new dome were added, required also that the Capitol Grounds be enlarged, and in 1874 Frederick Law Olmsted was commissioned to plan and oversee the project. As noted above, Olmsted was determined that the grounds should complement the building. In addition, he addressed an architectural problem that had persisted for some years: from the west (the growth of the city had nothing to do with the terraces)—the earthen terraces at the building's base made it seem inadequately supported at the top of the hill. The solution, Olmsted believed, was to construct marble terraces on the north, west, and south sides of the building, thereby causing it to ''gain greatly in the supreme qualities of stability, endurance, and repose.'' He submitted his design for these features in 1875, and after extensive study it was approved.

Work on the grounds began in 1874, concentrating first on the east side and then progressing to the west, north, and south sides. First, the ground was reduced in elevation. Almost 300,000 cubic yards of earth and other material were eventually removed, and over 200 trees were removed. New sewer, gas, and water lines were installed. The soil was then enriched with fertilizers to provide a suitable growth medium for new plantings. Paths and roadways were graded and laid.

By 1876, gas and water service was completed for the entire grounds, and electrical lamp-lighting apparatuses had been installed. Stables and workshops had been removed from the northwest and southwest corners. A streetcar system north and south of the west grounds had been relocated farther from the Capitol, and ornamental shelters were in place at the north and south car-track termini. The granite and bronze lamp piers and ornamental bronze lamps for the east plaza area were completed.

Work accelerated in 1877. By this time, according to Olmsted's report, ''altogether 7,837 plants and trees [had] been set out.'' However, not all had survived: hundreds were stolen or destroyed by vandals, and, as Olmsted explained, ''a large number of cattle [had] been caught trespassing.'' Other work met with less difficulty. Foot-walks were laid with artificial stone, a mixture of cement and sand, and approaches were paved with concrete. An ornamental iron trellis had been installed on the northern east-side walk, and another was under way on the southern walk.

The 1878 appointment of watchmen to patrol the grounds was quite effective in preventing further vandalism, allowing the lawns to be completed and much shrubbery to be added. Also in that year, the roads throughout the grounds were paved.

Most of the work required on the east side of the grounds was completed by 1879, and effort thus shifted largely to the west side. The Pennsylvania Avenue approach was virtually finished, and work on the Maryland Avenue approach had begun. The stone walls on the west side of the grounds were almost finished, and the red granite lamp piers were placed at the eastward entrance from Pennsylvania Avenue.

In the years 1880–82, many features of the grounds were completed. These included the walls and coping around the entire perimeter, the approaches and entrances, and the Summer House. Work on the terraces began in 1882, and most work from this point until 1892 was concentrated on these structures.

In 1885, Olmsted retired from superintendency of the terrace project; he continued to direct the work on the grounds until 1889. Landscaping work was performed to adapt the surrounding areas to the new construction, grading the ground and planting shrubs at the bases of the walls, as the progress of the masonry work allowed. Some trees and other types of vegetation were removed, either because they had decayed or as part of a careful thinning-out process.

In 1888, the wrought-iron lamp frames and railings were placed at the Maryland Avenue entrance, making it the last to be completed. In 1892, the streetcar track that had extended into grounds from Independence Avenue was removed.

The Grounds After Olmsted

In the last years of the 19th century, work on the grounds consisted chiefly of maintenance and repairs as needed. Trees, lawns, and plantings were tended, pruned, and thinned to allow their best growth. This work was quite successful: by 1894, the grounds were so deeply shaded by trees and shrubs that Architect of the Capitol Edward Clark recommended an all-night patrol by watchmen to ensure public safety. A hurricane in September 1896 damaged or destroyed a number of trees, requiring extensive removals in the following year. Also in 1897, electric lighting replaced gas lighting in the grounds.

Between 1910 and 1935, 61.4 acres north of Constitution Avenue were added to the grounds. Approximately 100 acres was added in subsequent years, bringing the total area to 274 acres.

Since 1983, increased security measures have been put into effect, however, the area still functions in many ways as a public park, and visitors are welcome to use the walks to tour the grounds. Demonstrations and ceremonies are often held on the grounds. In the summer, a series of evening concerts by the bands of the Armed Forces is offered free of charge on the west front plaza. On various holidays, concerts by the National Symphony Orchestra are held on the west front lawn.

LEGISLATIVE BRANCH AGENCIES

CONGRESSIONAL BUDGET OFFICE

H2–405 Ford House Office Building, Second and D Streets, SW., 20515
phone (202) 226–2600, http://www.cbo.gov

[Created by Public Law 93–344]

Director.—Doug Elmendorf, 6–2700.
Deputy Director.—Robert A. Sunshine, 6–2702.
General Counsel.—Mark P. Hadley, 6–2633.
Assistant Director for—
Budget Analysis.—Peter H. Fontaine, 6–2800.
Health and Human Resources.—Bruce Vavrichek, 6–2666.
Macroeconomic Analysis.—Robert A. Dennis, 6–2784.
Management, Business and Information Services.—Rod Goodwin, 6–2600.
Microeconomic and Financial Studies.—Joe Kile, 6–2940.
National Security.—J. Michael Gilmore, 6–2900.
Tax Analysis.—G. Thomas Woodward, 6–2687.

GOVERNMENT ACCOUNTABILITY OFFICE

441 G Street, NW., 20548, phone (202) 512–3000
http://www.gao.gov

Comptroller General of the United States.—Gene L. Dodaro (acting), 512–5500, fax 512–5507.
Chief Administrative Officer.—Sallyanne Harper, 512–5800.
General Counsel.—Gary Kepplinger, 512–5400.
Deputy General Counsel and Ethics Counselor.—Dan Gordon, 512–5207.

TEAMS

Acquisition and Sourcing Management.—Katherine Schinasi, 512–4841.
Applied Research and Methods.—Nancy Kingsbury, 512–2700.
Defense Capabilities and Management.—Janet St. Laurent, 512–4300.
Education Workforce and Income Security.—Cindy Fagnoni, 512–7215.
Financial Management and Assurance.—Jeanette M. Franzel, 512–2600.
Financial Markets and Community Investments.—Rick Hillman, 512–8678.
Health Care.—Marjorie Kanof, 512–7114.
Homeland Security and Justice.—Cathleen Berrick, 512–3404.
Information Technology.—Joel Willemssen, 512–6408.
International Affairs and Trade.—Jacquie Williams-Bridgers, 512–3101.
Natural Resources and Environment.—Patricia Dalton, 512–3841.
Physical Infrastructure.—Katherine Siggerud, 512–2834.
Strategic Issues.—J. Christopher Mihm, 512–6806.

SUPPORT FUNCTIONS

Congressional Relations.—Ralph Dawn, 512–4400.
Legislative Advisers: Carlos Diz, 512–8256; Rosa Harris, 512–9492; Elizabeth Johnston, 512–6345; Casey Keplinger, 512–9323; Brian Mullins, 512–4384; Elizabeth Sirius, 512–8989; Mary Frances Widner, 512–3804.
Associate Legislative Adviser.—Sara Schibanoff, 512–4176.
Field Offices.—Denise Hunter (617) 788–0575.

Inspector General.—Frances Garcia, 512–5748.
Opportunity and Inclusiveness.—Carolyn Taylor (acting), 512–2974.
Personnel Appeals Board.—Anne Wagner, 512–3836.
Public Affairs.—Charles "Chuck" Young, 512–3823.
Quality and Continuous Improvement.—Tim Bowling, 512–6100.
Strategic Planning and External Liaison.—Helen Hsing, 512–2639.

MISSION SUPPORT OFFICES

Chief Information Officer.—Joseph Kraus, 512–2898.
Controller.—George H. Strader, 512–5535.
Human Capital Officer.—Cynthia C. Heckmann, 512–6606.
Knowledge Services Officer.—Catherine Teti, 512–9255.
Professional Development Program.—Dave Clark, 512–4126.

U.S. GOVERNMENT PRINTING OFFICE

732 North Capitol Street, NW., 20401

phone (202) 512–0000, http://www.gpo.gov

OFFICE OF THE PUBLIC PRINTER

Public Printer of the United States.—Robert C. Tapella, 512–1000.
Deputy Public Printer.—Paul F. Erickson, 512–1000.
General Counsel.—Drew Spalding (acting), 512–0033.
Deputy General Counsel.—Drew Spalding.
Inspector General.—J. Anthony Ogden, 512–0039.
Chief Technology Officer.—Reynold Schweickhardt, 512–1913.
Director of—
Communications.—Vacant.
Congressional Relations.—Andrew M. Sherman, 512–1991, fax 512–1293.
Equal Employment Opportunity.—Nadine L. Elzy, 512–2014.
Quality Assurance.—Benjamin E. Meyer, 512–1268.

OFFICIAL JOURNALS OF GOVERNMENT

Managing Director.—James C. Bradley, 512–0111.
Director of—
Congressional Publishing Services.—Lyle L. Green, 512–0224.
Congressional Record Index Office.—Marcia Thompson, 512–0275.
Office of Federal Register Publishing Services.—Jeffrey D. MacAfee, 512–2100.

PLANT OPERATIONS

Managing Director.—Olivier A. Girod, 512–0707.
Chief Engineering Officer.—Dennis J. Carey, 512–1018.
Technical Manager, Strategic Planning and Analysis.—Sylvia S.Y. Subt, 512–0707.
Production Manager.—John W. Crawford, 512–0707.
Assistant Production Manager (shift 1).—Marvin A. Verter, 512–0589.
Assistant Production Manager (shift 2).—Richard C. Lewis, 512–0688.
Assistant Production Manager (shift 3).—David N. Boddie, 512–0688.
Superintendent of—
Binding.—Katherine Taylor, 512–0593.
Pre-Press.—Dannie E. Young, 512–0625.
Press.—Barry J. McMahon, 512–0673.
Production Engineering.—David J. Robare, 512–1370.
Production Planning and Control.—Philip J. Markett, Jr., 512–0233.
Manager, Quality Control and Technical Department.—Michael P. Mooney, 512–0766.

OPERATIONS SUPPORT

Director.—J. Michael Brady, 512–0155.

Facilities Manager.—Gary B. Englehart, 512–1042.
Safety Manager.—Reginal N. Johnson, 512–1036.

SECURITY AND INTELLIGENT DOCUMENTS

Managing Director.—Stephen G. LeBlanc, 512–2285.
Operations Manager.—David H. Ford, 512–1194.
Director of—
Business Development.—Gerald Egan, 512–2010.
Product Security.—Kevin P. Kaporch, 512–2285.
Secure Production Manager.—Robert H. Allegar, 512–1485.

AGENCY ACCOUNTS AND MARKETING

Managing Director.—William Kurtz, 512–0086.
Director of—
Creative Services.—Janice E. Sterling, 512–0376.
Digital Media Services.—Sung ''Jeannie'' Lee, 512–1295.
Institute for Federal Printing and Electronic Publishing.—Chris Daniel (acting), 512–1283.
Program Analysis and Research.—Paul J. Giannini, 512–2270.
Sales and Marketing.—Vacant.

PRINT PROCUREMENT

Managing Director.—Ricardo S. Garcia, 512–1269.
Director of—
Agency Publishing Services: Raymond T. Sullivan (acting), 512–2374; Sandra K. MacAfee, 512–0320; David M. Thomas, 512–0327.
Development and Program Support.—Sandra E. Zanko, 512–1400.
Major Acquisitions.—Raymond T. Sullivan, 512–2374.
Procurement Policy and Planning.—Jeffrey R. Dulberg, 512– 0376.
Quality Control for Procured Printing.—Larry P. Vines, 512–0485.

GPO REGIONAL OFFICES

Atlanta.—Gary C. Bush, Manager, 1888 Emery Street, Suite 110, Atlanta, GA 30318–2542 (404) 605–9160, fax 605–9185.
Boston.—Ira L. Fishkin, Manager, John F. Kennedy Federal Building, 15 New Sudbury Street E270, Boston, MA 02203–0002 (617) 565–1370, fax 565–1385.
Charleston Satellite Office.—J. Robert Mann, Manager, 2825 Noisette Boulevard, Charleston, SC 29405–1819 (843) 743–2036, fax 743–2068.
Chicago.—Clint J. Mixon, Assistant Manager, 200 North La Salle Street, Suite 810, Chicago, IL 60601–1055 (312) 353–3916, fax 886–3163.
Columbus.—Steven A. Boortz, Manager, 1335 Dublin Road, Suite 112–B, Columbus, OH 43215–7034 (614) 488–4616, fax 488–4577.
Dallas.—Kelle J. Chatham, Assistant Manager, Federal Office Building, 1100 Commerce Street, Room 731, Dallas, TX 75242–1027 (214) 767–0451, fax 767–4101.
Denver.—Barbara E. Lessans, Manager, 12345 West Alameda Parkway, Suite 208, Lakewood, CO 80228–2824 (303) 236–5292, fax 236–5304.
Hampton, VA.—J. Robert Mann, Manager, 11836 Canon Boulevard, Suite 400, Newport News, VA 23606–2591 (757) 873–2800, fax 873–2805.
New York.—Ira L. Fishkin, Manager, 26 Federal Plaza Room 2930, New York, NY 10278–0004 (212) 264–2252, fax 264–2413.
Oklahoma City Satellite Office.—Barbara E. Lessans, Manager, 3420 D Avenue, Suite 100, Tinker AFB, OK 73145–9188 (405) 610–4146, fax 610–4125.
Philadelphia.—Ira L. Fishkin, Manager, 928 Jaymore Road, Suite A190, Southampton, PA 18966–3820 (215) 364–6465, fax 364–6479.
San Antonio Satellite Office.—Kelle J. Chatham, Assistant Manager, 1531 Connally Street, Suite 2, Lackland AFB, TX 78236–5515 (210) 675–1480, fax 675–2429.
San Diego Satellite Office.—John J. O'Connor, Manager, 8880 Rio San Diego Drive, 8th Floor, San Diego, CA 92108–3609 (619) 209–6178, fax 209–6179.
San Francisco.—John J. O'Connor, Manager, 536 Stone Road, Suite 1, Benicia, CA 94510–1170 (707) 748–1970, fax 748–1980.

Seattle.—David S. Goldberg, Manager, Federal Center South, 4735 East Marginal Way South, Seattle, WA 98134–2397 (206) 764–3726, fax 764–3301.

INFORMATION DISSEMINATION

Superintendent of Documents.—Richard G. Davis (acting), 512–1622.

LIBRARY SERVICES AND CONTENT MANAGEMENT

Director.—Richard G. Davis, 512–1622.
Director of—
Collection Management and Preservation.—Robin L. Haun-mohamed, 512–0052.
Library Planning and Development.—Teddy J. Priebe, 512–2015.
Library Technical Information Services.—Laurie B. Hall, 512–1114.

PUBLICATION AND INFORMATION SALES

Managing Director.—Davita E. Vance-Cooks, 512–0014.
Director of—
Distribution.—Lisa L. Williams, 512–1065.
Sales Planning and Development.—Jeffrey Turner, 512–1055.
Assistant Director of—
Contact Center.—Esther Edmonds, 512–1694
Inventory Acquisition and Analysis.—Alan E. Ptak, 512–2010.

GPO BOOKSTORE

Washington, DC, Metropolitan Area: GPO Bookstore, 710 North Capitol Street, NW., Washington, DC 20401 (202) 512–0132.

TO ORDER PUBLICATIONS:

Phone toll free (866) 512–1800 [DC area: (202) 512–1800, fax (202) 512–2104]. Mail orders to Superintendent of Documents, P.O. Box 371954, Pittsburgh, PA 15250–7954, or order online from http://bookstore.gpo.gov. *GPO Access* technical support: contactcenter@gpo.gov, or toll free (888) 293–6498, [DC area (202) 512–1530].

CHIEF MANAGEMENT OFFICER

Chief Management Officer.—Janet F. Sansone, 512–0005.

ACQUISITIONS

Chief Acquisitions Officer.—Herbert H. Jackson, Jr., 512–0952.
Director of—
Complex Acquisitions.—Arza E. Gardner, 512–1488.
Technology Integration and Transformation.—Bruce O'Dell, 512–1956.
Chief of—
Paper and General Procurements.—Sheree A. Young, 512–2022.
Specialized Procurements.— Larry R. Ferezan, 512–0937.

ENVIRONMENTAL SERVICES

Director.—Vacant.

FINANCE AND ADMINISTRATION

Chief Financial Officer.—Steve Shedd, 512–2073.
Associate CFO—
Agency Controller.—William L. Boesch, Jr.
Operations.—Emily Dean.
Planning, Control and Government Affairs.—William M. Guy.

Controller for—
Customer Service.—Akiko Ward, 512–1684.
Information Dissemination.—William J. Grennon III, 512–2010.

HUMAN CAPITAL

Chief Human Capital Officer.—William T. Harris, 512–1210.
Director of—
Human Capital Operations.—Vicki A. Barber, 512–1124.
Security Services.—Lamont R. Vernon, 512–1103.
Strategic Policy.—Elizabeth A. Shearer, 512–0878.
Workforce Development, Education and Training.—Eve L. Princler, 512–1144.
Chief Medical Officer.—Sheridan B. Easterling, MD, 512–2061.
Manager, Organizational Effectiveness.—Gary R. Musicante, 512–1206.

INFORMATION TECHNOLOGY AND SYSTEMS

Chief Information Officer.—Michael L. Wash, 512–1037.
Chief Strategy and Execution Officer.—Scott A. Stovall, 512–1080.
Director of—
Business Information Systems.—Richard G. Leeds, Jr., 512–0029.
Content and Digital Production Systems.—Layton F. Clay, 512–2001.
End User Support.—Melvin C. Eley, 512–0737.
Enterprise Architecture.—Ida Milner, 512–1313.
Information Security.—John L. Hannan, 512–1021.
IT Operations.—Bartholomew G. Hill, 512–2299.
Quality Assurance.—Manjit Taneja, 512–1445.

LABOR RELATIONS

Director.—T. Michael Frazier, 512–1336.

LIBRARY OF CONGRESS

101 Independence Avenue, SE., 20540, phone (202) 707–5000, fax 707–5844

http://www.loc.gov

OFFICE OF THE LIBRARIAN, LM 608

Librarian of Congress.—James H. Billington, 707–5205.
Confidential Assistant to the Librarian.—Timothy L. Robbins, 707–8174.
Chief Operating Officer.—Jo Ann C. Jenkins, 707–0351.
Director, Office of:
Communications.—Matt Raymond, LM 105, 707–2905.
Editor for—
Calendar of Events.—Erin Allen, 707–2905.
Library of Congress Information Bulletin.—Audrey Fischer, 707–0022.
The Gazette.—Gail Fineberg, 707–9194.
Congressional Relations.—Kathleen Ott, LM 611, 707–3217.
Development.—Susan Siegel, LM 605, 707–1447.
Director of Special Programs.—Larry Stafford, LM 612, 707–5218.
General Counsel.—Elizabeth Pugh, LM 601, 707–6316.
Inspector General.—Karl W. Schornagel, LM 630, 707–6314.
Chief of Contracts and Grants Management.—Debra Murphy, LA 325, 707–2534.

OFFICE OF SECURITY AND EMERGENCY PREPAREDNESS, LM G03

Director.—Kenneth Lopez, 707–8708.

OFFICE OF OPPORTUNITY, INCLUSIVENESS AND COMPLIANCE, LM 624

Director.—Naomi Earp, 707–6024.
Affirmative Action and Special Programs Office.—LM 623, 707–5479.

Dispute Resolution Center.—LM 624, 707–6024.
Equal Employment Opportunity Complaints Office.—LM 626, 707–6024.
Mediation.—707–6024.
ADA.—707–6024.
Interpreting Services.—707–6024.

OFFICE OF THE DIRECTOR FOR HUMAN RESOURCES SERVICES, LM 645

Director.—Dennis Hanratty, LM 645, 707–5659.
Director, Office of:
Strategic Planning and Automation.—John Sigmon, 707–6544.
Workforce Acquisitions.—Susan Frieswyk (acting), 707–6959.
Workforce Management.—Charles Carron, LM 653, 707–6637.
Workforce Performance and Development.—Kimberly Powell, LM 646, 707–8976.
Worklife Services.—Susan Frieswyk, 707–6959.

OFFICE OF THE CHIEF FINANCIAL OFFICER, LM 613

Chief Financial Officer.—Jeffrey Page, LM 613, 707–7350.
Budget Officer.—Mary Klutts, 707–2418.
Disbursing Officer.—Melissa Ladieu, 707–9726.
Financial Reports Officer.—Jay Miller, 707–3548.
Strategic Planning Officer.—Karen Lloyd, 707–6074.
Accouting Operations Officer.—Nicole Broadus, 707–5547.

OFFICE OF THE DIRECTOR FOR INTEGRATED SUPPORT SERVICES, LM 327

Director.—Mary Berghaus Levering, 707–1393.
Chief of:
Facility Services Office.—Neal Graham, 707–7512.
Health Services Officer.—Sandra Charles, LM G40, 707–8035.
Safety Services Officer.—Robert Browne, LM B28, 707–6204.

OFFICE OF STRATEGIC INITIATIVES, LM 637

Associate Librarian for Strategic Initiatives/Chief Information Officer.—Laura E. Campbell, 707–3300.
Deputy Associate Librarian for Strategic Initiatives.—James M. Gallagher, 707–5563.
Executive Program Officer.—George Coulbourne, 707–7856.
Director, Digital Resource Management and Planning.—Molly H. Johnson, 707–0809.
Director, Integration Management.—Elizabeth S. Dulabahn, 707–2369.
Director for Information Technology Services.—Al Banks, LM G51, 707–9562.
Special Assistant to the Director.—Karen Caldwell, 707–3797.

LAW LIBRARY, OFFICE OF THE LAW LIBRARIAN, LM 240

Law Librarian.—Roberta I. Shaffer, 707–9825.
Director, Directorate of Law Library Services.—Donna Scheeder, 707–8939.
Chief, Eastern Law Division.—Peter Roudik, LM 235, 707–9861.
Chief, Public Services.—Robert N. Gee, LM 201, 707–0638.
Chief, Western Law Division.—Kersi B. Shroff, LM 235, 707–7850.

LIBRARY SERVICES, OFFICE OF THE ASSOCIATE LIBRARIAN FOR LIBRARY SERVICES, LM 642

Associate Librarian.—Deanna Marcum, 707–5325.
Deputy Associate Librarian.—Michael Handy, 707–8338.
Director of:
American Folklife Center.—Peggy Bulger, LJ G59, 707–1745.
Veterans History Project.—Robert W. Patrick, LA 143, 707–7308.
Director for Acquisitions and Bibliographic Access.—Beacher Wiggins, 707–5137.

Director, Office for Collections and Services.—Jeremy Adamson, LM 642, 707–7789.
Chief of:
African and Middle Eastern Division.—Mary-Jane Deeb, LJ 220, 707–7937.
Asian Division.—Peter Young, LJ 149, 707–5919.
Children's Literature Center.—Sybille A. Jagusch, LJ 100, 707–5535.
Collections Access, Loan and Management.—Steven J. Herman, LJ G02, 707–7400.
European Division.—Georgette M. Dorn (acting), LJ 250, 707–5414.
Federal Research Division.—David Osborne, LA 5282, 707–3919.
Geography and Map Division.—John R. Hébert, LM B02, 707–8530.
Hispanic Division.—Georgette M. Dorn, LJ 205, 707–5400.
Manuscript Division.—James H. Hutson, LM 102, 707–5383.
Music Division.—Susan H. Vita, LM 113, 707–5503.
Packard Campus of the National Audio-Visual Conservation Center.—Patrick Loughney, 707–7064.
Prints and Photographs Division.—Helena Zinkham (acting), LM 339, 707–5836.
Rare Book and Special Collections Division.—Mark G. Dimunation, LJ Dk B, 707–5434.
Science Technology and Business Division.—Ronald S. Bluestone, LA 5203, 707–0948.
Director, Partnerships and Outreach Programs.—Kathryn Mendenhall, LM 642, 707–5325.
Director, Center for the Book.—John Y. Cole, Jr., LM 650, 707–5221.
Executive Director, Federal Library and Information Center Committee.—Charles V. Stanhope (acting), LA 217, 707–4800.
Interpretive Programs Officer.—William Jacobs, LA G25, 707–3689.
Director, Office of National Library Service for the Blind and Physically Handicapped, TSA.—Frank K. Cylke, 707–5104.
Director, Office of Scholarly Programs.—Carolyn Brown, LJ 120, 707–3302.
Director, Publishing Office.—W. Ralph Eubanks, LM 602, 707–3892.
Visitor Services Officer.—Guilia Adelfio, 707–9779.
Business Enterprises Officer.—Eugene Flanagan, LA 206, 707–8203.
Director for Preservation.—Dianne van der Reyden, 707–7423.

CONGRESSIONAL RESEARCH SERVICE, LM 203

Director.—Daniel P. Mulhollan, 707–5775.
Deputy Director.—Richard C. Ehlke (acting), 707–7087.
Chief Information Officer.—Lisa M. Hoppis, LM 413, 707–2559.
Associate Director, Office of:
Congressional Affairs and Counselor to the Director.—Kent M. Ronhovde, 707–7090.
Finance and Administration.—Edward Jablonski (acting), LM 209, 707–8397.
Legislative Information.—Clifford Cohen, LM 223, 707–1858.
Research.—Roger S. White, LM 203, 707–7844.
Workforce Development.—Bessie E.H. Alkisswani, LM 208, 707–8835.
Assistant Director of:
American Law Division.—Karen L. Lewis, LM 227, 707–7460.
Domestic Social Policy Division.—Laura B. Shrestha (acting), LM 323, 707–7046.
Foreign Affairs, Defense and Trade Division.—Morris Davis, LM 315, 707–8470.
Government and Finance Division.—Collen J. Shogan, LM 303, 707–8321.
Knowledge Services Group.—Robert R. Newlin, LM 215, 707–4313.
Resources, Science and Industry Division.—John L. Moore, LM 423, 707–7232.

U.S. COPYRIGHT OFFICE, LM 403

Register of Copyrights and Associate Librarian for Copyright Services.—Marybeth Peters, 707–8350.
General Counsel.—David Carson, 707–8353.
Deputy General Counsel.—Tanya Sandros, 707–6886.
Chief Operating Officer.—Elizabeth Scheffler, 707–6042.
Associate Register for Registration and Recordation.—Nanette Petruzzelli, 707–8350.
Chief of:
Information and Reference Division.—David Christopher (acting), LM 453, 707–6800.
Receiving and Processing Division.—Melissa Dadant, LM 435, 707–7700.
Copyright Acquisitions Division.—Jewel Player, LM 438C, 707–7125.

UNITED STATES BOTANIC GARDEN

245 First Street, SW., Washington, DC 20024

(202) 225–8333 (information); (202) 226–8333 (receptionist)

http://www.usbg.gov

Director.—Stephen T. Ayers (acting), Architect of the Capitol, 228–1204.
Executive Director.—Holly H. Shimizu, 225–6670.
Administrative Officer.—Elizabeth A. Spar, 225–5002.
Public Programs Manager.—Christine A. Flanagan, 225–1269.
Horticulture Division Manager.—Vacant, 225–6647.
Facility Manager.—John M. Gallagher, 225–6646.

THE CABINET

Vice President of the United States	JOSEPH R. BIDEN, JR.
Secretary of State	HILLARY RODHAM CLINTON.
Secretary of the Treasury	TIMOTHY F. GEITHNER.
Secretary of Defense	ROBERT M. GATES.
Attorney General	ERIC H. HOLDER, JR.
Secretary of the Interior	KENNETH L. SALAZAR.
Secretary of Agriculture	THOMAS J. VILSACK.
Secretary of Commerce	GARY F. LOCKE.
Secretary of Labor	HILDA L. SOLIS.
Secretary of Health and Human Services	KATHLEEN SEBELIUS.
Secretary of Housing and Urban Development	SHAUN L.S. DONOVAN.
Secretary of Transportation	RAYMOND L. LAHOOD.
Secretary of Energy	STEVEN CHU.
Secretary of Education	ARNE DUNCAN.
Secretary of Veterans Affairs	ERIC K. SHINSEKI.
Secretary of Homeland Security	JANET A. NAPOLITANO.
Chief of Staff	RAHM EMANUEL.
Director, Office of Management and Budget	PETER R. ORSZAG.
U.S. Trade Representative	RONALD KIRK.
Administrator, Environmental Protection Agency	LISA P. JACKSON.
Chair, Council of Economic Advisers	CHRISTINA ROMER.
Ambassador, United States Ambassador to the United Nations	SUSAN RICE.

EXECUTIVE BRANCH

THE PRESIDENT

BARACK H. OBAMA, Senator from Illinois and 44th President of the United States; born in Honolulu, Hawaii, August 4, 1961; received a B.A. in 1983 from Columbia University, New York City; worked as a community organizer in Chicago, IL; studied law at Harvard University, where he became the first African American president of the *Harvard Law Review*, and received a J.D. in 1991; practiced law in Chicago, IL; lecturer on constitutional law, University of Chicago; member, Illinois State Senate, 1997–2004; elected as a Democrat to the U.S. Senate in 2004; and served from January 3, 2005, to November 16, 2008, when he resigned from office, having been elected President; family: married to Michelle; two children: Malia and Sasha; elected as President of the United States on November 4, 2008, and took the oath of office on January 20, 2009.

EXECUTIVE OFFICE OF THE PRESIDENT

1600 Pennsylvania Avenue, NW., 20500

Eisenhower Executive Office Building (EEOB), 17th Street and Pennsylvania Avenue, NW., 20500, phone (202) 456–1414, http://www.whitehouse.gov

The President of the United States.—Barack H. Obama.
Personal Secretary to the President.—Katherine Johnson.
Special Assistant to the President and Personal Aide.—Reginald Love.

OFFICE OF THE VICE PRESIDENT

phone (202) 456–1414

The Vice President.—Joseph R. Biden, Jr.
Chief of Staff to the Vice President.—Ron Klain, EEOB, room 202, 456–2423.
Deputy Chief of Staff to the Vice President.—Alan Hoffman, EEOB, room 202, 456–2423.
Counsel to the Vice President.—Cynthia Hogan, EEOB, room 246, 456–3241.
Director of Communications to the Vice President.—Jay Carney, EEOB, room 284, 456–5249.
Press Secretary to the Vice President.—Elizabeth Alexander, EEOB, room 284, 456–5249.
Assistant to the Vice President for—
Domestic Policy.—Terrell McSweeny, EEOB, room 222, 456–3071.
Economic Policy.—Jared Bernstein, EEOB, room 222, 456–3071.
National Security Advisor.—Tony Blinken, EEOB, room 246, 456–2646.
Chief of Staff to Dr. Jill Biden.—Cathy Russell, EEOB, room 200, 456–6773.
Director of Scheduling to the Vice President.—Elisabeth Hire, EEOB, room 239, 456–6773.
Director of Advance to the Vice President.—Vacant, EEOB, room 241, 456–6773.
Executive Assistants to the Vice President: Nancy Orloff, Michele Smith, West Wing.
Director of Correspondence.—Daniel Griffin, EEOB, room 233, 456–6770.

COUNCIL OF ECONOMIC ADVISERS

725 Seventeenth Street, NW., 20006, phone (202) 395–5084
http://www.whitehouse.gov/cea

Chair.—Christinia D. Roomer.
Chief of Staff.—Karen Anderson.

Members: Vacant.

COUNCIL ON ENVIRONMENTAL QUALITY

730 Jackson Place, NW., 20503, phone (202) 456–6224
http://www.whitehouse.gov/ceq

Chair.—Nancy Sutley.
Chief of Staff.—Jon Carson.
Special Assistants to the Chair.—Tarak Shah, John Thomson.
Executive Assistant to the Chair.—Vacant.
Associate Director for—
Agriculture, Lands and Wildlife.—Michael Boots.
Communications.—Christine Glunz.
Congressional Affairs.—Jessica Maher.
Energy and Transportation.—Jason Bordoff.
International Affairs and Climate Change.—Landon Van Dyke.
Natural Resources.—Terry Breyman.
NEPA Oversight.—Horace Greczmiel.
General Counsel.—Edward ''Ted'' Boling.
Administrative Officer.—Angela Stewart.
Administrative Assistant.—Essence Washington.
Records Clerk.—Elizabeth Moss.

PRESIDENT'S INTELLIGENCE ADVISORY BOARD

phone (202) 456–2352

Executive Director.—Stefanie Osburn.
General Counsel.—Homer Pointer.

NATIONAL SECURITY COUNCIL

phone (202) 456–9491

MEMBERS

The President.—Barack H. Obama.
The Vice President.—Joseph R. Biden, Jr.
The Secretary of State.—Hillary Rodham Clinton.
The Secretary of Defense.—Robert M. Gates.
The Secretary of Energy.—Steven Chu.
The Secretary of Treasury.—Timothy F. Geithner.
The Attorney General.—Eric H. Holder, Jr.
The Secretary of Homeland Security.—Janet Napolitano.
The Representative of the United States of America to the United Nations.—Amb. Susan Rice.
The Assistant to the President and Chief of Staff (Chief of Staff to the President).—Rahm Emanuel.
The Assistant to the President for National Security Affairs.—Gen. James L. Jones, USMC (Ret.).

STATUTORY ADVISERS

Director of National Intelligence.—Dennis C. Blair.
Chairman, Joint Chiefs of Staff.—ADM Mike Mullen.

OFFICE OF ADMINISTRATION

Eisenhower Executive Office Building, phone (202) 456–2861

Director of the Office of Administration.—Cameron Moody.
Deputy Director.—Vacant.

Chief, Office of:
Equal Employment Opportunity.—Clara Patterson.
Finance.—Allyson Laackman.
General Counsel.—Vacant.
Information.—Brook Colangelo.
Operations.—Vacant.
Security.—John Gill.

OFFICE OF MANAGEMENT AND BUDGET

Eisenhower Executive Office Building, phone (202) 395–4840

Director.—Peter R. Orszag.
Deputy Director.—Robert L. Nabors.
Deputy Director for Management.—Vacant.
Executive Associate Director.—Jeff Liebman.
Administrator, Office of:
Federal Procurement Policy.—Lesley Field (acting).
Information and Regulatory Affairs.—Cass Sunstein.
Assistant Director for—
Budget.—Elizabeth Robinson.
Legislative Reference.—James J. Jukes.
Associate Director for—
Communications.—Kenneth Baer.
Economic Policy.—Jeff Liebman.
Education, Income Maintenance and Labor Programs.—Robert Gordon.
General Government Programs.—Xavier Briggs.
Health Programs.—Keith Fontenot.
Legislative Affairs.—Vacant.
National Security Programs.—Steve Kosiak.
Natural Resources, Energy and Science Programs.—Sally Ericsson.
General Counsel.—Preeta Bansal.

OFFICE OF NATIONAL DRUG CONTROL POLICY

750 17th Street, NW., phone (202) 395–6738 or 6695, fax 395–7251

Director.—Edward H. Jurith (acting), room 805, 395–6700.
Deputy Director.—Vacant, room 803, 395–7252.
Chief of Staff.—Mark C. Coomer (acting), room 809, 395–6732.
Deputy Chief of Staff.—Jennifer L. deVallance (acting), room 807, 395–6648.
Deputy Director, Office of:
Demand Reduction.—Vacant, room 609, 395–3036.
State and Local Affairs.—Vacant, room 661, 395–7252.
Supply Reduction.—Vacant, room 713, 395–7225.
Assistant Deputy Director, Office of:
Demand Reduction.—Martha M. Gagné, room 610, 395–4622.
State and Local Affairs.—Mark M. Campbell (acting), room 659, 395–6781.
Supply Reduction.—Patrick M. Ward, room 712, 395–5535.
General Counsel.—Michael K. Gottlieb (acting), room 518, 395–4868.
Director, Counterdrug Technology Assessment Center.—David W. Murray, room 804, 395–6788.
Associate Director, National Youth Anti-drug Media Campaign.—Robert W. Denniston, room 560, 395–4653.
Associate Director, Office of:
Legislative Affairs.—Deborah J. Walker (acting), room 825, 395–5595.
Management and Administration.—Michele C. Marx, room 326, 395–6883.
Planning and Budget.—Jon E. Rice, room 846, 395–6791.
Public Affairs.—Rafael E. Lemaitre (acting), room 842, 395–6649.

OFFICE OF SCIENCE AND TECHNOLOGY POLICY

Eisenhower Executive Office Building, phone (202) 456–7116, fax 456–6021
http://www.ostp.gov

Director.—John P. Holdren.

Associate Director for—
Energy and Environment.—Shere Abbott.
National Security and International Affairs.—Vacant.
Science.—Vacant.
Technology and Chief Technology Officer.—Aneesh Chopra.
Chief of Staff.—Jim Kohlenberger.
Executive Director for National Science and Technology Council.—Christyl Johnson.
Executive Director for President's Council of Advisors on Science and Technology.—Deborah D. Stine.

OFFICE OF THE UNITED STATES TRADE REPRESENTATIVE

600 17th Street, NW., 20508, phone (202) 395–6890
http://www.ustr.gov

United States Trade Representative.—Ronald Kirk.
Deputy United States Trade Representative.—Demetrios Marantis.
Deputy U.S. Trade Representative, Geneva.—Peter Allgeier.
Associate U.S. Trade Representative.—Vacant.
Special Textile Negotiator.—Scott Qusenberry.
Chief Agricultural Negotiator.—Vacant.
General Counsel.—Timothy Reif.
Assistant U.S. Trade Representative for—
Administration.—Fred Ames.
Africa.—Florie Liser.
Agricultural Affairs.—James Murphy.
China Affairs.—Tim Stratford.
Congressional Affairs.—Daniel Sepulveda.
Economic Affairs.—David Walters.
Environment and Natural Resources.—Mark Linscott.
Europe and the Mediterranean.—Chris Wilson.
Industry.—Meredith Broadbent.
Intergovernmental Affairs and Public Liaison.—Lisa Garcia.
Japan, Korea and APEC Affairs.—Wendy Cutler.
Monitoring and Enforcement.—Dan Brinza.
Office of the Americas.—Everett Eissnstat.
Policy Coordination.—Carmen Suro-Bredie.
Public/Media Affairs.—Carol Guthrie.
Services, Investment and Intellectual Property.—Christine Bliss.
South Asian Affairs.—Douglas Hartwick.
Southeast Asia, Pacific and Pharmaceutical Policy.—Barbara Weisel.
Trade and Labor.—Lewis Karesh.
World Trade Organization (WTO) and Multilateral Affairs.—Matt Rohde.

THE WHITE HOUSE OFFICE

CABINET AFFAIRS

Assistant to the President and Cabinet Secretary.—Christopher Lu.
Deputy Assistant to the President and Deputy Cabinet Secretary.—Elizabeth Sears Smith.

CHIEF OF STAFF

Assistant to the President and Chief of Staff.—Rahm Emanuel.
Assistant to the President and Deputy Chief of Staff for Operations.—James Messina.
Assistant to the President and Deputy Chief of Staff for Policy.—Mona Sutphen.
Assistant to the President and Senior Advisor.—Peter Rouse.

COMMUNICATIONS

Assistant to the President and Director of Communications.—Anita B. Dunn.

Assistant to the President and Senior Advisor.—David M. Axelrod.
Assistant to the President and Director of Speechwriting.—Jonathan Favreau.
Deputy Assistant to the President and Deputy Director of Communications.—Daniel Pfeiffer.

DOMESTIC POLICY COUNCIL

Assistant to the President and Director of the Domestic Policy Council.—Melody C. Barnes.
Deputy Assistant to the President and Deputy Director of the Domestic Policy Council.—Heather A. Higginbottom.
Deputy Assistant to the President and Director, Office of Social Innovation and Civic Participation.—Sonal Shah.

FAITH-BASED AND NEIGHBORHOOD PARTNERSHIPS

Special Assistant to the President and Executive Director of the White House Office of Faith-Based and Neighborhood Partnerships.—Joshua P. DuBois.

OFFICE OF ENERGY AND CLIMATE CHANGE

Assistant to the President for Energy and Climate Change.—Carol M. Browner.
Deputy Assistant to the President for Energy and Climate Change.—Heather R. Zichal.

OFFICE OF THE FIRST LADY

Assistant to the President, Chief of Staff to the First Lady and Counsel.—Susan Sher.
Deputy Assistant to the President and Director of Policy and Projects for the First Lady.—Jocelyn Frye.
Special Assistant to the President and White House Social Secretary.—Desiree G. Rogers.

OFFICE OF HEALTH CARE REFORM

Counselor to the President and Director of the White House Office for Health Care Reform.—Nancy-Ann DeParle.

OFFICE OF LEGISLATIVE AFFAIRS

Assistant to the President and Director, Office of Legislative Affairs.—Philip M. Schiliro.
Deputy Assistant to the President for Legislative Affairs.—Lisa M. Konwinski.
Deputy Assistant to the President for Legislative Affairs and House Liaison.—Daniel A. Turton.
Deputy Assistant to the President for Legislative Affairs and Senate Liaison.—Shawn P. Maher.

OFFICE OF MANAGEMENT AND ADMINISTRATION

Assistant to the President for Management and Administration.—Bradley J. Kiley.
Deputy Assistant to the President for Management and Administration.—Henry F. DeSio.
Special Assistant to the President and Director of White House Operations.—Katy A. Kale.

OFFICE OF NATIONAL AIDS POLICY

Director of the Office of National AIDS Policy.—Jeff Crowley.

NATIONAL ECONOMIC COUNCIL

Assistant to the President for Economic Policy and Director of the National Economic Council.—Lawrence Summers.

Special Assistant to the President for Economic Policy and Chief of Staff of the National Economic Council.—Marne L. Levine.

Deputy Assistants to the President for Economic Policy: Diana Farrell, Jason L. Furman.

OFFICE OF NATIONAL SECURITY ADVISOR

National Security Advisor.—James Jones.

Assistant to the President and Deputy National Security Advisor.—Thomas Donilon.

Assistant to the President and Deputy National Security Advisor for Counterterrorism and Homeland Security.—John O. Brennan.

Deputy Assistant to the President and Chief of Staff for National Security Operations.—Mark Lippert.

OFFICE OF POLITICAL AFFAIRS

Assistant to the President and Director of Political Affairs.—Patrick Gaspard.

OFFICE OF PRESIDENTIAL PERSONNEL

Assistant to the President and Director of Presidential Personnel.—Donald H. Gips.

Deputy Assistant to the President and Deputy Director of Presidential Personnel.—Kenneth Williams-Bennett.

Special Assistant to the President and Chief of Staff for Presidential Personnel.—Nancy D. Hogan.

OFFICE OF THE PRESS SECRETARY

Assistant to the President and Press Secretary.—Robert L. Gibbs.

Deputy Assistant to the President and National Security Spokesperson.—Denis R. McDonough.

OFFICE OF PUBLIC ENGAGEMENT AND INTERGOVERNMENTAL AFFAIRS

Senior Advisor and Assistant to the President for Intergovernmental Affairs and Public Engagement.—Valerie Jarrett.

Deputy Assistant to the President and Director of the Office of Public Engagement.—Tina Tchen.

Deputy Assistant to the President and Director of Intergovernmental Affairs.—Cecelia Muñoz.

Special Assistant to the President and Chief of Staff of the Office of Intergovernmental Affairs and Public Engagement.—Michael Strautmanis.

OFFICE OF URBAN AFFAIRS

Deputy Assistant to the President and Director, Office of Urban Affairs.—Adolfo Carrion, Jr.

OFFICE OF SCHEDULING AND ADVANCE

Assistant to the President and Director of Scheduling and Advance.—Alyssa M. Mastromonaco.

Deputy Assistant to the President and Director of Appointments and Scheduling.—Danielle M. Crutchfield.

Deputy Assistant to the President and Director of Advance and Operations.—Emmett Beliveau.

OFFICE OF THE STAFF SECRETARY

Assistant to the President and Staff Secretary.—Elizabeth M. Brown.
Deputy Assistant to the President and Deputy Staff Secretary.—Peter Rundlet.
Special Assistant to the President and Director of Presidential Correspondence.—Mike Kelleher.

WHITE HOUSE COUNSEL

Assistant to the President and Counsel to the President.—Gregory B. Craig.
Deputy Assistant to the President and Principal Deputy Counsel to the President.—Daniel Meltzer.
Deputy Assistant to the President and Deputy Counsel to the President.—Cassandra Q. Butts.
Deputy Assistant to the President and Deputy Counsel to the President.—Mary DeRosa.

PRESIDENT'S COMMISSION ON WHITE HOUSE FELLOWSHIPS

Director.—Cindy Moelis.

WHITE HOUSE MILITARY OFFICE

Director.—George Mulligan (acting).
Deputy Director.—George Mulligan.

DEPARTMENT OF STATE

2201 C Street, NW., 20520, phone (202) 647–4000

HILLARY RODHAM CLINTON, Secretary of State; born in Chicago, IL, October 26, 1947; education: B.A., Wellesley College, 1969; J.D., Yale Law School, 1973; professional: Assistant Professor, University of Arkansas School of Law, 1975; Attorney and Partner, Rose Law Firm, 1976–92; board member, Legal Services Corporation Board, 1978–81; First Lady of Arkansas, 1979–81 and 1983–92; board member, Children's Defense Fund, 1986–92; First Lady of the United States, 1993–2001; author, *It Takes A Village,* 1996; *Living History,* 2000; Senator from New York, 2001–09; committees: Armed Services; Budget; Environment and Public Works; Health, Education, Labor and Pensions; Select Committee on Aging; candidate for president, 2007–08; nominated by President Barack Obama to become the 67th Secretary of State, and was confirmed by the U.S. Senate on January 22, 2009.

OFFICE OF THE SECRETARY

Secretary of State.—Hillary Rodham Clinton, room 7226, 647–9572.
Deputy Secretary.—James B. Steinberg.
Deputy Secretary for Management and Resources.—Jacob J. Lew.
Executive Assistant.—Joseph E. Macmanus, 647–9572.
Chief of Staff.—Cheryl Mills, 647–5548.

AMBASSADOR-AT-LARGE FOR WAR CRIMES ISSUES

Ambassador-at-Large.—John C. ''Clint'' Williamson, room 7419A, 647–5072.
Deputy.—Vacant, 647–5543.

OFFICE OF THE CHIEF OF PROTOCOL

Chief of Protocol.—Vacant, room 1232, 647–4543.
Deputy Chief.—Vacant, 647–4120.

OFFICE OF CIVIL RIGHTS

Director.—John M. Robinson, room 7428, 647–9295.
Deputy Director.—Gregory B. Smith.

OFFICE OF COORDINATOR FOR COUNTERTERRORISM

Coordinator/Ambassador-at-Large.—Vacant, room 2509, 647–9892.
Principal Deputy Coordinator.—Ronald L. Schlicher, 647–8949.

COORDINATOR FOR RECONSTRUCTION AND STABILIZATION

Coordinator.—Amb. John Herbst, 663–0307.
Principal Deputy Coordinator.—Larry Sampler (acting), 663–0803.
Deputy Coordinator.—Johnathan Benton (acting), 663–0856.

EXECUTIVE SECRETARIAT

Special Assistant and Executive Secretary.—Daniel B. Smith., room 7224, 647–5301.
Deputy Executive Secretaries: Lewis Lukens, 647–7457; Kenneth H. Merten, 647–8448; Paul D. Wohlers, 647–5302; Uzra S. Zeya, 647–5302.

OFFICE OF THE INSPECTOR GENERAL

2121 Virginia Avenue, NW., 20037

Inspector General.—Vacant, room 8100, 663–0361.
Deputy Inspector General.—Harold W. Geisel (acting), 663–0361.

BUREAU OF INTELLIGENCE AND RESEARCH

Assistant Secretary.—Vacant, room 6531, 647–9177.
Deputy Assistant Secretaries: Catherine Brown, 647–7825; James Buchanan, 647–9633; John R. Dinger, 647–7826.

OFFICE OF LEGAL ADVISER

The Legal Advisor.—Vacant, room 6423, 647–9598.
Principal Deputy Legal Adviser.—James H. Thessin, 647–8460.
Deputy Legal Advisers: Susan Biniaz, 647–2006; Jonathan B. Schwartz, 647–5036.

BUREAU OF LEGISLATIVE AFFAIRS

Assistant Secretary.—Richard R. Verma, room 7325, 647–4204.
Deputy Assistant Secretary (Global, Regional and Functional).—Michael C. Polt, 647–4204.
Deputy Assistant Secretary (Senate).—Miguel Rodriguez, 647–2645.
Deputy Assistant Secretary (House).—David Adams, 647–2623.

POLICY PLANNING STAFF

Director.—Anne-Marie Slaughter, room 7311, 647–2972.
Principal Deputy Director.—Derick Challet.

BUREAU OF RESOURCE MANAGEMENT

Assistant Secretary/Chief Financial Officer.—Vacant, room 7427, 647–7490.
Deputy Chief Financial Officer.—Christopher Flaggs, 261–8620.

OFFICE OF THE U.S. GLOBAL AIDS COORDINATOR

Coordinator.—Vacant, room SA–29, 663–2304.
Deputy U.S. Global Aids Coordinator/Chief of Staff.—Thomas Walsh, 663–2639.
Assistant Coordinator.—Michele Moloney-Kitts, 663–2704.
Director of Multilateral Outreach.—Margaret Lidstone, 663–2586.

UNDER SECRETARY FOR POLITICAL AFFAIRS

Under Secretary.—Amb. William J. Burns, room 7240, 647–2471.
Executive Assistant.—Daniel A. Russell, 647–1598.

AFRICAN AFFAIRS

Assistant Secretary.—Phillip Carter III (acting), room 6234, 647–4485.
Principal Deputy Assistant Secretaries: Mary Jo Wells, Carl Wycoff, 647–2080.

EAST ASIAN AND PACIFIC AFFAIRS

Assistant Secretary.—Vacant, 647–9596.
Principal Deputy Assistant Secretary.—Glyn Davies, 736–4393.
Deputy Assistant Secretaries: Alex Arvizu, 647–8929; Scott Marciel, 647–6904; John Norris, 647–6910.

EUROPEAN AND EURASIAN AFFAIRS

Assistant Secretary.—Daniel Fried, room 6226, 647–9626.
Principal Deputy Assistant Secretary.—Marcie Ries, 647–5146.
Deputy Assistant Secretaries: Matthew Bryza, 647–5547; Anita Friedt (acting), 647–9903; Judith Garber, 647–6233; Stuart Jones, 647–6415.

NEAR EASTERN AFFAIRS

Assistant Secretary.—Vacant, room 6242, 647–7209.
Principal Deputy Assistant Secretary.—Jeffrey Feltman, 647–7207.
Deputy Assistant Secretaries: David Hale, 647–7170; Bill Hudson (acting), 647–7166; Richard Schmierer, 647–0554; Madelyn Spirnak (acting), 647–7168.

SOUTH AND CENTRAL ASIAN AFFAIRS

Assistant Secretary.—Richard Boucher, room 6254, 736–4325.
Principal Deputy Assistant Secretary.—Patrick Moon, 736–4331.
Deputy Assistant Secretaries: Paul Jones, George Krol, 736–4331; Michael Owen, 647–1114.

WESTERN HEMISPHERE AFFAIRS

Assistant Secretary.—Thomas Shannon, room 6262, 647–5780.
Principal Deputy Assistant Secretary.—Craig Kelly, 647–6754.
Deputy Assistant Secretaries: Roberta Jacobson, 647–8387; Christopher McMullen, 647–8563; David Robinson, 647–7337.

INTERNATIONAL NARCOTICS AND LAW ENFORCEMENT AFFAIRS

Assistant Secretary.—David T. Johnson, room 7333, 647–8464.
Principal Deputy Assistant Secretary.—William J. McGlynn, 647–6642.
Deputy Assistant Secretaries: Charles Snyder, Elizabeth Verville, 647–9822.

INTERNATIONAL ORGANIZATION AFFAIRS

Assistant Secretary.—Esther Brimmer, room 6323, 647–9600.
Principal Deputy Assistant Secretary.—James B. Warlick, 647–9602.
Deputy Assistant Secretaries: Gerald C. Anderson, 647–9604; Donna Roginski (acting), 647–7857.

UNDER SECRETARY FOR ECONOMIC, BUSINESS, AND AGRICULTURAL AFFAIRS

Under Secretary.—Vacant, room 7256, 647–7575.
Executive Assistant.—Douglas Hengel, 647–1498.

ECONOMIC AND BUSINESS AFFAIRS

Assistant Secretary.—Vacant, room 4932/4934, 647–7971.
Principal Deputy Assistant Secretary.—David D. Nelson, 647–9496.
Deputy Assistant Secretaries: John Byerly, 647–4045; William Craft (acting), 647–6324.

UNDER SECRETARY FOR ARMS CONTROL AND INTERNATIONAL SECURITY

Under Secretary.—Vacant, room 7208, 647–1049.
Executive Assistant.—Stephen A. Elliott, 647–1749.

INTERNATIONAL SECURITY AND NONPROLIFERATION

Head.—Eliott Kang, room 7531, 647–5999.

Principal Deputy Assistant Secretary.—Patricia McNerney, 647–6977.

POLITICAL-MILITARY AFFAIRS

Assistant Secretary.—Vacant, room 6212, 647–9022.
Principal Deputy Assistant Secretary.—Frank Ruggiero, 647–9023.
Deputy Assistant Secretary.—Gregory T. Delawie.

VERIFICATION, COMPLIANCE, AND IMPLEMENTATION

Assistant Secretary.—Rose Gottemoeller, room 5950, 647–5315.
Principal Deputy Assistant Secretary.—Vacant.
Deputy Assistant Secretaries.—Richard Davis (acting), 647–9170; Karin Look, 647–5553.

UNDER SECRETARY FOR PUBLIC DIPLOMACY AND PUBLIC AFFAIRS

Under Secretary.—Vacant, room 7261, 647–9199.
Deputy Under Secretary.—Dina Habib Powell.
Executive Assistant.—Daniel B. Smith.

EDUCATIONAL AND CULTURAL AFFAIRS

Assistant Secretary.—Vacant, 203–5118.
Principal Deputy Assistant Secretary.—C. Miller Crouch, 203–5122.
Deputy Assistant Secretaries: Stanley Colvin, 203–7415; Alina Romanowski, 203–8687.

INTERNATIONAL INFORMATION PROGRAMS

Coordinator.—Jeremy Curtin, 453–8358.

PUBLIC AFFAIRS

Assistant Secretary.—Vacant, room 6800, 647–6607.
Deputy Assistant Secretary.—Teresa D. Fynes.
Deputy Spokesman.—Robert A. Wood, 647–9606.

UNDER SECRETARY FOR MANAGEMENT

Under Secretary.—Patrick F. Kennedy, room 7207, 647–1500.
Executive Assistant.—Edward Alford, 647–1501.

ADMINISTRATION

Assistant Secretary.—Vacant, room 6330, 647–1492.
Deputy Assistant Secretaries: Llewellyn Hedgbeth, 663–2215; William Moser (703) 875–6956; Steve Rodriguez, 647–1492.

CONSULAR AFFAIRS

Assistant Secretary.—Janice L. Jacobs, room 6811, 647–9576.
Principal Deputy Assistant Secretary.—Michael D. Kirby, 647–9577.
Deputy Assistant Secretaries: Michele Bond, 647–6541; David Donahue, 647–6947; Brenda Sprague, 647–5366.

DIPLOMATIC SECURITY AND OFFICE OF FOREIGN MISSIONS

Assistant Secretary.—Eric J. Boswell, room 6316, 647–6290.
Principal Deputy Assistant Secretary.—Gregory B. Starr (571) 345–3815.
Deputy Assistant Secretaries: Patrick Donovan, 345–3836; Charlene R. Lamb, 345–3841; Justine Sincavage, 647–3417.

DIRECTOR GENERAL OF THE FOREIGN SERVICE AND DIRECTOR OF HUMAN RESOURCES

Director General.—Harry K. Thomas, Jr., room 6218, 647–9898.
Principal Deputy Assistant Secretary.—Teddy Taylor, 647–9438.
Deputy Assistant Secretaries: Judy Chammas, 647–5942; Linda Taglialatela, 647–5152.

FOREIGN SERVICE INSTITUTE

Director.—Ruth Whiteside, room F2102 (703) 302–6703.
Deputy Director.—Rose Likins (703) 302–6707.

INFORMATION RESOURCE MANAGEMENT

Assistant Secretary.—Susan Swart, 647–2889.
Principal Deputy Assistant Secretary.—Charles Wisecarver, 647–2863.
Deputy Chief Information Officers: Janice Fedak, 647–3184; John Streufert (703) 812–2555.

MEDICAL SERVICES

Assistant Secretary.—Thomas W. Yun, 663–1649.
Deputy Assistant Secretary.—Vacant, 663–1641.

OVERSEAS BUILDING OPERATIONS

Assistant Secretary.—Adam Namm (acting), (703) 875–6351.
Managing Director.—Jay Hicks, 875–6357.
Executive Assistant.—Annette P. Feeley, 875–5036.

UNDER SECRETARY FOR DEMOCRACY AND GLOBAL AFFAIRS

Under Secretary.—Vacant, room 7250, 647–6240.
Executive Assistant.—Jeffrey DeLaurentis, 647–7609.

DEMOCRACY, HUMAN RIGHTS AND LABOR

Assistant Secretary.—Vacant, room 7802, 647–2126.
Principal Deputy Assistant Secretary.—Karen B. Stewart, 647–2590.

OCEANS AND INTERNATIONAL ENVIRONMENTAL AND SCIENTIFIC AFFAIRS

Assistant Secretary.—Vacant, room 7831, 647–1554.
Principal Deputy Assistant Secretary.—Reno L. Harnish (acting), 647–3004.
Deputy Assistant Secretaries: David A. Balton, 647–2396; Jeffrey A. Miotke, 647–8309; Daniel Reifsnyder, 647–2232.

POPULATION, REFUGEES AND MIGRATION

Assistant Secretary.—Vacant, room 5824, 647–5767.
Principal Deputy Assistant Secretary.—Samuel M. Witten, 647–5982.
Deputy Assistant Secretaries: William Fitzgerald, Kelly Ryan, 647–5822.

UNITED STATES PERMANENT REPRESENTATIVE TO THE UNITED NATIONS

U.S. Permanent Representative.—Susan E. Rice, room 6317, 736–7555.
Deputy to the Ambassador.—Erica Barks-Ruggles.

DIRECTOR OF FOREIGN ASSISTANCE

Director of U.S. Foreign Assistance/Administrator of USAID.—Richard L. Greene (acting), room 5932, 647–2527.
Chief of Staff.—Nazanin Ash, 647–2604.

UNITED STATES DIPLOMATIC OFFICES—FOREIGN SERVICE

(C= Consular Office, N= No Embassy or Consular Office)

http://usembassy.state.gov

LIST OF CHIEFS OF MISSION

AFGHANISTAN, ISLAMIC REPUBLIC OF (Kabul).
Hon. Karl W. Eikenberry.
ALBANIA, REPUBLIC OF (Tirana).
Hon. John L. Withers II.
ALGERIA, DEMOCRATIC AND POPULAR REPUBLIC OF (Algiers).
Hon. David D. Pearce.
ANDORRA (Andorra La Vella) (N)
Vacant.
ANGOLA, REPUBLIC OF (Luanda).
Hon. Dan Mozena.
ANTIGUA AND BARBUDA (St. John's) (N).
Vacant.
ARGENTINA (Buenos Aires).
Hon. Earl Anthony Wayne.
ARMENIA, REPUBLIC OF (Yerevan).
Hon. Marie L. Yovanovitch.
AUSTRALIA (Canberra).
Vacant.
AUSTRIA, REPUBLIC OF (Vienna).
Vacant.
AZERBAIJAN, REPUBLIC OF (Baku).
Hon. Anne E. Derse.
BAHAMAS, THE COMMONWEALTH OF THE (Nassau).
Vacant.
BAHRAIN, STATE OF (Manama).
Hon. Joseph Adam Ereli.
BANGLADESH, PEOPLE'S REPUBLIC OF (Dhaka).
Hon. James Francis Moriarty.
BARBADOS (Bridgetown).
Vacant.
BELARUS, REPUBLIC OF (Minsk).
Vacant.
BELGIUM (Brussels).
Vacant.
BELIZE (Belize City).
Vacant.
BENIN, REPUBLIC OF (Cotonou).
Hon. Gayleatha Beatrice Brown.
BOLIVIA, REPUBLIC OF (La Paz).
Vacant.
BOSNIA-HERZEGOVINA (Sarajevo).
Hon. Charles Lewis English.
BOTSWANA, REPUBLIC OF (Gaborone).
Hon. Stephen James Nolan.
BRAZIL, FEDERATIVE REPUBLIC OF (Brasilia).
Hon. Clifford M. Sobel.
BRUNEI DARUSSALAM (Bandar Seri Begawan).
Hon. William Edward Todd.
BULGARIA, REPUBLIC OF (Sofia).
Hon. Nancy E. McEldowney.
BURKINA FASO (Ouagadougou).
Hon. Jeanine E. Jackson.
BURMA, UNION OF (Rangoon).
Mr. Larry M. Dinger.
BURUNDI, REPUBLIC OF (Bujumbura).
Hon. Patricia Newton Moller.
CAMBODIA, KINGDOM OF (Phnom Penh).
Hon. Carol Ann Rodley.
CAMEROON, REPUBLIC OF (Yaounde).
Hon. Janet E. Garvey.
CANADA (Ottawa).
Vacant.
CAPE VERDE, REPUBLIC OF (Praia).
Hon. Marianne Matuzic Myles.
CENTRAL AFRICAN REPUBLIC (Bangui).
Hon. Frederick B. Cook.
CHAD, REPUBLIC OF (N'Djamena).
Hon. Louis John Nigro, Jr.
CHILE, REPUBLIC OF (Santiago).
Hon. Paul E. Simons.
CHINA, PEOPLE'S REPUBLIC OF (Beijing).
Vacant.
COLOMBIA, REPUBLIC OF (Bogota).
Hon. William R. Brownfield.
COMOROS, UNION OF (Moroni) (N).
Hon. R. Niels Marquardt.
CONGO, REPUBLIC OF THE (Brazzaville).
Hon. Alan W. Eatham, Jr.
CONGO, DEMOCRATIC REPUBLIC OF THE (Kinshasa).
Hon. William John Garvelink.
COSTA RICA, REPUBLIC OF (San Jose).
Hon. Peter E. Cianchette.
COTE D'IVOIRE, REPUBLIC OF (Abidjan).
Hon. Wanda L. Nesbitt.
CROATIA, REPUBLIC OF (Zagreb).
Hon. Robert Anthony Bradtke.
CUBA (Havana).
Mr. Jonathan Farrar.
CURACAO (Willemstad).
Mr. Timothy J. Dunn.
CYPRUS, REPUBLIC OF (Nicosia).
Hon. Frank Charles Urbancic.
CZECH REPUBLIC (Prague).
Vacant.
DENMARK (Copenhagen).
Vacant.

DJIBOUTI, REPUBLIC OF (Djibouti).
Hon. James Christopher Swan.
DOMINICAN REPUBLIC (Santo Domingo).
Vacant.
EAST TIMOR, DEMOCRATIC REPUBLIC OF (Dili).
Hon. Hans G. Klemm.
ECUADOR, REPUBLIC OF (Quito).
Hon. Heather M. Hodges.
EGYPT, ARAB REPUBLIC OF (Cairo).
Hon. Margaret Scobey.
EL SALVADOR, REPUBLIC OF (San Salvador).
Vacant.
EQUATORIAL GUINEA, REPUBLIC OF (Malabo) (N).
Vacant.
ERITREA, STATE OF (Asmara).
Hon. Ronald K. McMullen.
ESTONIA, REPUBLIC OF (Tallinn).
Vacant.
ETHIOPIA, FEDERAL DEMOCRATIC REPUBLIC OF (Addis Ababa).
Hon. Donald Y. Yamamoto.
FIJI ISLANDS, REPUBLIC OF THE (Suva).
Hon. C. Steven McGann.
FINLAND, REPUBLIC OF (Helsinki).
Vacant.
FRANCE (Paris).
Vacant.
GABONESE REPUBLIC (Libreville).
Hon. Eunice S. Reddick.
GAMBIA, REPUBLIC OF THE (Banjul).
Hon. Barry Leon Wells.
GEORGIA (Tbilisi).
Hon. John F. Tefft.
GERMANY, FEDERAL REPUBLIC OF (Berlin).
Vacant.
GHANA, REPUBLIC OF (Accra).
Hon. Donald Gene Teitelbaum.
GREECE (Athens).
Hon. Danial V. Speckhard.
GRENADA (St. George) (N).
Vacant.
GUATEMALA, REPUBLIC OF (Guatemala).
Hon. Stephen George McFarland.
GUINEA, REPUBLIC OF (Conakry).
Vacant.
GUINEA-BISSAU, REPUBLIC OF (Bissau) (N).
Hon. Marcia Stephens Bloom Bernicat.
GUYANA, CO-OPERATIVE REPUBLIC OF (Georgetown).
Hon. John Melvin Jones.
HAITI, REPUBLIC OF (Port-au-Prince).
Hon. Janet Ann Sanderson.
HOLY SEE (Vatican City).
Vacant.
HONDURAS, REPUBLIC OF (Tegucigalpa).
Hon. Hugo Llorens.
HONG KONG (Hong Kong) (C).
Mr. Joseph R. Donovan, Jr.
HUNGARY, REPUBLIC OF (Budapest).
Vacant.
ICELAND, REPUBLIC OF (Reykjavik).
Hon. Carol van Voorst.
INDIA (New Delhi).
Vacant.
INDONESIA, REPUBLIC OF (Jakarta).
Hon. Cameron R. Hume.
IRAQ, REPUBLIC OF (Baghdad)
Hon. Christopher R. Hill.
IRELAND (Dublin).
Vacant.
ISRAEL, STATE OF (Tel Aviv).
Hon. James B. Cunningham.
ITALY (Rome).
Vacant.
JAMAICA (Kingston).
Vacant.
JAPAN (Tokyo).
Vacant.
JERUSALEM (C).
Mr. Jacob Walles.
JORDAN, HASHEMITE KINGDOM OF (Amman).
Hon. Robert Stephen Beecroft.
KAZAKHSTAN, REPUBLIC OF (Almaty).
Hon. Richard E. Hoagland.
KENYA, REPUBLIC OF (Nairobi).
Hon. Michael E. Ranneberger.
KIRIBATI, REPUBLIC OF (Tarawa) (N).
Hon. C. Steven McGann.
KOREA, REPUBLIC OF (Seoul).
Hon. D. Kathleen Stephens.
KOSOVO (Pristina).
Hon. Tina S. Kaidanow.
KYRGYZ REPUBLIC (Bishkek).
Hon. Tatiana C. Gfoeller-Volkoff.
KUWAIT, STATE OF (Kuwait City).
Hon. Deborah K. Jones.
LAO PEOPLE'S DEMOCRATIC REPUBLIC (Vientiane).
Hon. Ravic Rolf Huso.
LATVIA, REPUBLIC OF (Riga).
Vacant.
LEBANON, REPUBLIC OF (Beirut).
Hon. Michele J. Sison.
LESOTHO, KINGDOM OF (Maseru).
Hon. Robert B. Nolan.
LIBERIA, REPUBLIC OF (Monrovia).
Hon. Linda Thomas-Greenfield.
LIBYA (Tripoli).
Hon. Gene Allen Cretz.
LIECHTENSTEIN, PRINCIPALITY OF (Vaduz) (N).
Vacant.
LITHUANIA, REPUBLIC OF (Vilnius).
Hon. John A. Cloud, Jr.
LUXEMBOURG, GRAND DUCHY OF (Luxembourg).
Hon. Ann Louise Wagner.
MACEDONIA, REPUBLIC OF (Skopje).
Hon. Philip Thomas Reeker.
MADAGASCAR, REPUBLIC OF (Antananarivo).
Hon. R. Niels Marquardt.
MALAWI, REPUBLIC OF (Lilongwe).
Hon. Peter William Bodde.
MALAYSIA (Kuala Lumpur).
Hon. James R. Keith.

MALDIVES, REPUBLIC OF (Male) (N).
Hon. Robert O. Blake, Jr.
MALI, REPUBLIC OF (Bamako).
Hon. Gillian Arlette Milovanovic.
MALTA, REPUBLIC OF (Valletta).
Vacant.
MARSHALL ISLANDS, REPUBLIC OF THE (Majuro).
Vacant.
MAURITANIA, ISLAMIC REPUBLIC OF (Nouakchott).
Hon. Mark M. Boulware.
MAURITIUS, REPUBLIC OF (Port Louis).
Vacant.
MEXICO (Mexico City).
Vacant.
MICRONESIA, FEDERATED STATES OF (Kolonia).
Hon. Miriam K. Hughes.
MOLDOVA, REPUBLIC OF (Chisinau).
Hon. Asif Chaudhry.
MONACO (Monaco).
Vacant.
MONGOLIA (Ulaanbaatar).
Hon. Mark C. Minton.
MONTENEGRO, REPUBLIC OF (Podgorica).
Hon. Roderick W. Moore.
MOROCCO, KINGDOM OF (Rabat).
Vacant.
MOZAMBIQUE, REPUBLIC OF (Maputo).
Vacant.
NAMIBIA, REPUBLIC OF (Windhoek).
Hon. Gail Dennise Mathieu.
NAURU, REPUBLIC OF (Yaren) (N).
Hon. C. Steven McGann.
NEPAL, KINGDOM OF (Kathmandu).
Hon. Nancy J. Powell.
NETHERLANDS, KINGDOM OF THE (The Hague).
Vacant.
NEW ZEALAND (Wellington).
Vacant.
NICARAGUA, REPUBLIC OF (Managua).
Hon. Robert J. Callahan.
NIGER, REPUBLIC OF (Niamey).
Hon. Bernadette Mary Allen.
NIGERIA, FEDERAL REPUBLIC OF (Abuja).
Hon. Robin Renee Sanders.
NORWAY (Oslo).
Hon. Benson K. Whitney.
OMAN, SULTANATE OF (Muscat).
Hon. Gary A. Grappo.
PAKISTAN, ISLAMIC REPUBLIC OF (Islamabad).
Hon. Anne Woods Patterson.
PANAMA, REPUBLIC OF (Panama).
Hon. Barbara J. Stephenson.
PAPUA NEW GUINEA (Port Moresby).
Hon. Leslie V. Rowe.
PARAGUAY, REPUBLIC OF (Asunción)
Hon. Liliana Ayalde.
PERU, REPUBLIC OF (Lima).
Hon. Peter Michael McKinley.
PHILIPPINES, REPUBLIC OF THE (Manila).
Hon. Kristie A. Kenney.
POLAND, REPUBLIC OF (Warsaw).
Hon. Victor Henderson Ashe.
PORTUGAL, REPUBLIC OF (Lisbon).
Vacant.
QATAR, STATE OF (Doha).
Hon. Joseph Evan LeBaron.
ROMANIA (Bucharest).
Vacant.
RUSSIAN FEDERATION (Moscow).
Hon. John R. Beyrle.
RWANDA, REPUBLIC OF (Kigali).
Hon. W. Stuart Symington.
SAINT KITTS AND NEVIS (Basseterre) (N).
Vacant.
SAINT LUCIA (Castries) (N).
Vacant.
SAINT VINCENT AND THE GRENADINES (Kingstown) (N).
Vacant.
SAMOA (Apia) (N).
Vacant.
SAN MARINO, REPUBLIC OF (San Marino) (N).
Vacant.
SAO TOME AND PRINCIPE, DEMOCRATIC REPUBLIC OF (Sao Tome) (N).
Hon. Eunice S. Reddick.
SAUDI ARABIA, KINGDOM OF (Riyadh).
Vacant.
SENEGAL, REPUBLIC OF (Dakar).
Hon. Marcia Stephens Bloom Bernicat.
SERBIA (Belgrade)
Hon. Cameron Munter.
SEYCHELLES, REPUBLIC OF (Victoria) (N).
Vacant.
SIERRA LEONE, REPUBLIC OF (Freetown).
Hon. June Carter Perry.
SINGAPORE, REPUBLIC OF (Singapore).
Vacant.
SLOVAK REPUBLIC (Bratislava).
Vacant.
SLOVENIA, REPUBLIC OF (Ljubljana).
Vacant.
SOLOMON ISLANDS (Honiara) (N).
Hon. Leslie V. Rowe.
SOUTH AFRICA, REPUBLIC OF (Pretoria).
Vacant.
SPAIN (Madrid).
Vacant.
SRI LANKA, DEMOCRATIC SOCIALIST REPUBLIC OF (Colombo).
Hon. Robert O. Blake, Jr.
SUDAN, REPUBLIC OF THE (Khartoum).
Vacant.
SURINAME, REPUBLIC OF (Paramaribo).
Hon. Lisa Bobbie Schreiber Hughes.
SWAZILAND, KINGDOM OF (Mbabane).
Hon. Maurice S. Parker.
SWEDEN (Stockholm).
Vacant.
SWITZERLAND (Bern).
Vacant.
SYRIAN ARAB REPUBLIC (Damascus).

Vacant.
TAJIKISTAN, REPUBLIC OF (Dushanbe).
Hon. Tracey Ann Jacobson.
TANZANIA, UNITED REPUBLIC OF (Dar es Salaam).
Vacant.
THAILAND, KINGDOM OF (Bangkok).
Hon. Eric G. John.
TOGOLESE REPUBLIC (Lome).
Hon. Patricia McMahon Hawkins.
TONGA, KINGDOM OF (Nuku'alofe) (N).
Hon. C. Steven McGann.
TRINIDAD AND TOBAGO, REPUBLIC OF (Port-of-Spain).
Vacant.
TUNISIA, REPUBLIC OF (Tunis).
Hon. Robert F. Godec.
TURKEY, REPUBLIC OF (Ankara).
Hon. James Franklin Jeffrey.
TURKMENISTAN (Ashgabat).
Vacant.
TUVALU (Funafuti) (N).
Hon. C. Steven McGann.
UGANDA, REPUBLIC OF (Kampala).
Hon. Steven Alan Browning.
UKRAINE (Kyiv).
Hon. William B. Taylor, Jr.
UNITED ARAB EMIRATES (Abu Dhabi).
Hon. Richard G. Olson.
UNITED KINGDOM OF GREAT BRITAIN AND NORTHERN IRELAND (London).
Vacant.
URUGUAY, ORIENTAL REPUBLIC OF (Montevideo).
Vacant.
UZBEKISTAN, REPUBLIC OF (Tashkent).
Hon. Richard Boyce Norland.
VANUATU, REPUBLIC OF (Port Vila) (N).
Hon. Leslie V. Rowe.
VENEZUELA, BOLIVARIAN REPUBLIC OF (Caracas).
Vacant.
VIETNAM, SOCIALIST REPUBLIC OF (Hanoi).
Hon. Michael W. Michalak.
YEMEN, REPUBLIC OF (Sanaa).
Hon. Stephen A. Seche.
ZAMBIA, REPUBLIC OF (Lusaka).
Hon. Donald E. Booth.
ZIMBABWE, REPUBLIC OF (Harare).
Hon. James C. McGee.

UNITED STATES PERMANENT DIPLOMATIC MISSIONS TO INTERNATIONAL ORGANIZATIONS

AFRICAN UNION (Addis Ababa).
Vacant.
EUROPEAN UNION (Brussels).
Vacant.
NORTH ATLANTIC TREATY ORGANIZATION (Brussels).
Hon. Kurt Volker.
ORGANIZATION FOR ECONOMIC COOPERATION AND DEVELOPMENT (Paris).
Vacant.
ORGANIZATION FOR SECURITY AND COOPERATION IN EUROPE (Vienna).
Vacant.
ORGANIZATION OF AMERICAN STATES (Washington, DC).
Hon. Hector Morales, Jr.
UNITED NATIONS (Geneva).
Vacant.
UNITED NATIONS (New York).
Hon. Susan E. Rice.
UNITED NATIONS (Vienna).
Hon. Gregory L. Schulte.

DEPARTMENT OF THE TREASURY

1500 Pennsylvania Avenue, NW., 20220, phone (202) 622–2000, http://www.ustreas.gov

TIMOTHY F. GEITHNER, Secretary of the Treasury; born in New York, NY, August 18, 1961; education: B.A., Dartmouth College, 1983; M.A. in International Economics and East Asian Studies, Johns Hopkins School for Advanced International Studies, 1985; professional: International Economist, Overseas Private Investment Corporation, 1984–85; Research Associate, Kissinger Associates, 1985–88; International Economist, Treasury, 1988–89; Assistant to the U.S. Financial Services Negotiator, Treasury, 1989–90; Assistant Financial Attaché, Treasury, 1990–91; Special Assistant to the Assistant Secretary for International Affairs, Treasury, 1991–92; Special Assistant to the Under Secretary for International Affairs, Treasury, 1992–94; Deputy Assistant Secretary for International Monetary and Financial Policy, Treasury, 1994–97; Senior Deputy Assistant Secretary, International Monetary and Financial Policy, Treasury 1997; Assistant Secretary for International Affairs, Treasury, 1997–98; Under Secretary for International Affairs, Treasury, 1998-2001; Senior Fellow, Council on Foreign Relations, 2001; Director, Policy Development and Review, International Monetary Fund, 2001–03; President and CEO, Federal Reserve Bank of New York, 2003–09; married: Carole; children: Elise and Benjamin; nominated by President Barack Obama to become the 75th Secretary of the Treasury and confirmed by the U.S. Senate on January 26, 2009.

OFFICE OF THE SECRETARY

Secretary of the Treasury.—Timothy F. Geithner, room 3330 (202) 622–1100.
Executive Assistant.—Shirley Gathers, 622–5377.
Confidential Assistant.—Cheryl Matera, 622–0190.

OFFICE OF THE DEPUTY SECRETARY

Deputy Secretary.—Neal S. Wolin, room 3326 (202) 622–1080.
Executive Assistant.—Betty Ann Hunt, 622–2025.
Review Analyst.—Amanda Mendel, 622–1080.

OFFICE OF THE CHIEF OF STAFF

Chief of Staff.—Mark Patterson, room 3408 (202) 622–1906.
Deputy Chief of Staff.—Alastair Fitzpayne, room 3414, 622–5780.
Review Analyst.—Reavie Harvey, 622–0626.
Executive Secretary.—Andrew Mayock, room 3410, 622–6096.
White House Liaison.—Patrick Maloney, room 3420, 622–9469.

OFFICE OF THE GENERAL COUNSEL

General Counsel.—Robert Hoyt, room 3000 (202) 622–0283.
Deputy General Counsel.—Lily Fu, 622–6362.
Staff Assistants: Karen M. Hill, Teresa R. Jones, 622–0283.
Senior Advisor to the General Counsel.—Mike Maher, room 3010, 622–3654.
Assistant General Counsel for—
Banking and Finance.—Roberta McInerney, room 2000, 622–1988.
Enforcement and Intelligence.—Mark Monborne, room 2308, 622–1286.
General Law and Ethics.—Bernard Knight, room 2020, 622–1137.
International Affairs.—Russell L. Munk, room 2316, 622–1899.
Legislation and Litigation.—Tom McGivern, room 2312, 622–2317.
Deputy Assistant General Counsel for—
Banking and Finance.—Peter Bieger, room 2000, 622–1975.
Enforcement and Intelligence.—James Freis, room 2306, 622–0264.

General Law and Ethics.—John Schorn, room 2019, 622–1142.
International Affairs.—Marilyn L. Muench, room 2010, 622–1986.
Chief Counsel, Foreign Assets Control.—Sean Thorton, Annex 3123, 622–9880.
Deputy Chief Counsel.—Matthew Tuchband, Annex 3121, 622–1654.

OFFICE OF THE INSPECTOR GENERAL

Inspector General.—Eric Thorson, room 4436 (202) 622–1090.
Deputy Inspector General.—Dennis S. Schindel.
Counsel to the Inspector General.—Richard Delmar, suite 510, 927–0650.
Assistant Inspector General for—
Audit.—Marla Freedman, suite 600, 927–5400.
Investigations.—Matthew Issman, suite 500, 927–5260.
Management Services.—John Czajkowski, suite 510, 927–5200.
Deputy Assistant Inspector General for—
Audit.—Robert Taylor, suite 600, 927–5400.
Investigations.—P. Brian Crane, suite 500, 927–5260.
Management.—Debra McGruder, suite 510, 927–5229.

OFFICE OF THE UNDER SECRETARY FOR DOMESTIC FINANCE

Under Secretary.—Vacant, room 3312 (202) 622–1703.
Senior Advisor to the Under Secretary.—Vacant.

OFFICE OF THE ASSISTANT SECRETARY FOR FINANCIAL INSTITUTIONS

Assistant Secretary.—Michael Barr, room 2326 (202) 622–2610.
Senior Advisor.—Amias Gerety, 622–8716.
Deputy Assistant Secretary, Office of:
Consumer Protection.—Eric Stein, 622–0488.
Financial Education.—Vacant.
Financial Institutions, Critical Infrastructure Protection and Compliance Policy.—Vacant.
Director, Office of:
Community Adjustment and Investment Program (CAIP).—Louisa Quittman, room 1414, 622–8103.
Financial Institutions Policy.—Mario Ugoletti, room 1418, 622–0715.
Financial Education.—Dubis Correal, room 1413, 622–4848.
Outreach.—Vacant.
Executive Director, Office of:
Community Development Financial Institutions Fund.—Donna Gambrell, 601 13th Street, 2nd floor, 622–4203.
Terrorism Risk Insurance Program.—Jeffrey S. Bragg, 1425 New York Avenue, NW., room 2114, 622–6770.

OFFICE OF THE ASSISTANT SECRETARY FOR FINANCIAL MARKETS

Assistant Secretary.—Karthik Ramanathan (acting), room 2000 (202) 622–2245.
Deputy Assistant Secretary, Office of:
Federal Finance.—Matthew Rutherford, room 2422, 622–1244.
Government Financial Policy.—Matthew Kabaker, 622–1677.
Director, Office of:
Advanced Counterfeit Deterrence.—Reese Fuller, room 1326, 622–1882.
Debt Management.—Karthik Ramanathan, room 2414, 622–6844.
Federal Lending.—Gary Burner, National Press Building, suite 228, 622–2470.
Financial Market Policy.—Heidilynne Schultheiss, room 1404, 622–2692.
Policy and Legislative Review.—Paula Farrell, National Press Building, suite 1148, 622–2450.

OFFICE OF THE FISCAL ASSISTANT SECRETARY

Assistant Secretary.—Richard Gregg (acting), room 2112 (202) 622–0560.
Deputy Assistant Secretary for—
Accounting Policy.—Nancy Fleetwood, room 2104, 622–0550.
Fiscal Operations and Policy.—Gary Grippo, room 2108, 622–0570.

Director, Office of Fiscal Projections.—David Monroe, room 2040, 622–0580.

OFFICE OF THE ASSISTANT SECRETARY FOR FINANCIAL STABILITY

Assistant Secretary.—Vacant.
Senior Advisor.—Rawan Abdelrazek, 622–0240.
Chief Office of:
Compliance Officer.—Paul Wolfteich, 622–6338.
Counsel.—Duane Morse, 622–1192.
Financial Officer.—Jennifer Main, 927–9458.
Investment Officer.—Vacant.
Operating Officer.—Howard Schweitzer, 622–6963.
Risk Officer.—Vacant, 622–8722.
Capital Purchase Program.—Ted Schaffner, 622–6872.
Financial Agent Management.—Gary Grippo (acting), 622–0570.
Homeownership Preservation.—Nancy Fleetwood (acting), 927–4000.

FINANCIAL MANAGEMENT SERVICE

401 14th Street, SW., 20227, phone (202) 874–6740, fax 874–7016

Commissioner.—David A. Lebryk (acting).
Deputy Commissioner.—Margaret Marquette (acting).
Assistant Commissioner for—
Debt Management Services.—Scott Johnson.
Federal Finance.—Sheryl Morrow.
Governmentwide Accounting.—D. James Sturgill.
Information Resources (Chief Information Officer).—John Kopec (acting).
Management (Chief Financial Officer).—David Rebich (acting).
Payments Management.—Rita Bratcher.
Chief Counsel.—Mike Collotta (acting).
Director for Legislative and Public Affairs.—Alvina M. McHale.

BUREAU OF THE PUBLIC DEBT

799 9th Street, NW., 20239, phone (202) 504–3500, fax 504–3630

[Codified under U.S.C. 31, section 306]

Commissioner.—Van Zeck.
Deputy Commissioner.—Anita Shandor (acting).
Executive Director for—
Administrative Resource Center.—Cynthia Springer (304) 480–7227.
Government Securities Regulations Staff.—Lori Santamorena, 504–3632.
Public and Legislative Affairs Staff.—Kim B. Treat, 504–3535.
Assistant Commissioner, Office of:
Financing.—Dara Seaman (acting), 504–3697.
Management Services.—Fred Pyatt, (304) 480–8101.
Public Debt Accounting.—Debra Hines (304) 480–5101.
Securities Operations.—John Swales (304) 480–6516.

OFFICE OF THE UNDER SECRETARY FOR INTERNATIONAL AFFAIRS

Under Secretary.—Lael Brainard, room 3428 MT (202) 622–1270.
Senior Advisor.—Raji Jagadeesan, room 3217, 622–1025.
Staff Assistant.—Paige Gebhardt, room 3213, 622–1193.

OFFICE OF THE ASSISTANT SECRETARY FOR INTERNATIONAL AFFAIRS

Assistant Secretaries: Andy Baukol (acting), room 3212 MT, 622–2129; Mark Sobel (acting), room 3036 MT (202) 622–0168.
Senior Advisor.—Jamie Franco, room 3213 MT, 622–0117.
Staff Assistants: Loretta Fogle, room 3218 MT, 622–0139; Rosemary Harris, room 3034 MT, 622–0168.
Special Assistant for Personnel and Management.—Barbara Geiser, room 5406A MT, 622–0333.

Deputy Assistant Secretary for—
Africa and the Middle East.—Andy Baukol, room 3218A MT, 622–2159.
Asian Nations.—Robert Dohner, room 3218B MT, 622–7222.
Environment and Energy.—William ''Bill'' Pizer, room 3221 MT, 622–0173.
Europe and Eurasia.—Eric Meyer (acting), room 4138A MT, 622–0603.
International Development Finance and Debt.—Karen Mathiasen (acting), room 5313 MT, 622–0070.
International Monetary and Financial Policy.—Mark Sobel, room 3034 MT, 622–0168.
International Trade.—Sharon Yuan, room 3204A MT, 622–6883.
Investment Security.—Mark Jaskowiak, room 3203 MT, 622–0478.
Research and Analysis.—Vacant, room 3213 MT.
Technical Assistance Policy.—W. Larry McDonald, room 3041A MT, 622–5504.
Western Hemisphere.—Nancy Lee, room 3204B MT, 622–2916.
Directors for International Affairs:
Africa (INN).—Dan Peters, room 4456B MT, 622–5280.
Business Office.—Theresa Wagoner, room 6286 Met Square, 622–1196.
Business Office IA Business Administration.—Jennifer Beasley, room 4464 MT, 622–6843.
East Asia (ISA).—Chris Winship, room 4462 MT, 622–0132.
Environment and Energy Policy.—Beth Urbanas, room 1024B MT, 622–2956.
Europe and Eurasia (ICN).—Eric Meyer, room 4138A MT, 622–0603.
Global Economics Group (IMG).—John Weeks, room 5422F MT, 622–9885.
International Banking and Securities Markets (IMB).—William Murden, room 5308 MT, 622–2775.
International Debt Policy (IDD).—John Hurley, room 5417B MT, 622–9124.
International Monetary Policy (IMF).—E. Clay Berry, room 5326 MT, 622–2156.
International Trade (ITT).—Whit Warthin, room 5204A MT, 622–1733.
Investment Security (IFI).—Mark Jaskowiak, room 3203 MT, 622–5052.
Market Room (IMR).—Michael Padroni, room 2313 MT, 622–3665.
Middle East and North Africa (INM).—Francisco Parodi, room 5008 MT, 622–7144.
Multilateral Development Banks (IDB).—Liza Morris (acting), room 5313L MT, 622–6489.
South and Southeast Asia (ISS).—Malachy Nugent, room 4440 MT, 622–4262.
Technical Assistance.—Mike Ruffner, 740 15th Street, NW., 622–2886.
Trade Finance and Investment Negotiations (ITF).—Steven Tvardek, room 5419J MT, 622–1749.
Western Hemisphere (IWH).—Luyen Tran, room 1458A MT, 622–0763.

U.S. BANKS

U.S. Executive Director of:
Inter-American Development Bank (IABD).—San Juan Miguel Rafael.
International Monetary Fund.—Meg Lundsager, (202) 623–7764.
World Bank.—Eli Whitney Debevoise II, 458–0115.

OVERSEAS

U.S. Executive Director of:
African Development Bank and Fund (AFDB) (Tunisia).—Amb. Mimi Alemayehou, 9–011–216–71–102–010.
Asian Development Bank (ADB) (Manila, Philippines).—Curtis Chin, 9–011–632–632–6050.
European Bank for Reconstruction and Development (EBRD).—Kenneth Peel, 9–011–44–207–338–6459.

UNDER SECRETARY FOR TERRORISM AND FINANCIAL INTELLIGENCE

Under Secretary.—Stuart Levey, room 4326 (202) 622–8260.

ASSISTANT SECRETARY FOR TERRORIST FINANCING

Assistant Secretary.—Vacant.
Deputy Assistant Secretary for Terrorist Financing and Financial Crimes.—Daniel Glaser, room 4304, 622–1943.
Director, Office of:

Global Affairs.—Brian Grant, room 4310, 622–0769.
Strategic Policy.—Chip Poncy, room 4308, 622–9761.

ASSISTANT SECRETARY FOR INTELLIGENCE AND ANALYSIS

Assistant Secretary.—Janice B. Gardner, room 4332 (202) 622–1835.
Deputy Assistant Secretary.—Howard Mendelsohn, room 2441, 622–1841.
Deputy Assistant Secretary for Security.—Charles Cavella, room 2523, 622–2585.
Director, Emergency Programs.—Kelly Wolslayer, room 1020, 622–2195.

OFFICE OF FOREIGN ASSETS CONTROL

Director.—Adam J. Szubin, room 2240 (202) 622–2510.

EXECUTIVE OFFICE FOR ASSET FORFEITURE

1341 G Street, NW., Suite 900, 20005, phone (202) 622–9600

Director.—Eric Hampl.

FINANCIAL CRIMES ENFORCEMENT NETWORK (FINCEN)

P.O. Box 39, Vienna, VA 22183, phone (703) 905–3591

Director.—James Freis.

OFFICE OF THE ASSISTANT SECRETARY FOR ECONOMIC POLICY

Assistant Secretary.—Vacant, room 3454, (202) 622–2200.
Senior Advisor to the Assistant Secretary.—Vacant, room 3445D, 622–2734.
Deputy Assistant Secretary for Policy Coordination.—Vacant, room 3449.
Deputy Assistant Secretary for Macroeconomic Analysis.—Vacant, room 3439.
Director, Office of Macroeconomic Analysis.—Ralph Monaco, room 2449, 622–2293.
Deputy Assistant Secretary for Microeconomic Analysis.—Vacant, room 3449, 622–4995.
Director, Office of Microeconomic Analysis.—John Worth, room 4426, 622–2683.

OFFICE OF THE ASSISTANT SECRETARY FOR LEGISLATIVE AFFAIRS

Assistant Secretary.—Vacant, room 3134 (202) 622–1900.
Deputy to the Assistant Secretary.—Vacant, room 3464.
Special Assistant.—Vacant, room 3134.
Deputy Assistant Secretary for—
Appropriations and Management.—Vacant, room 2464.
Banking and Finance.—Damon Munchus, room 3128.
Special Assistant.—Vacant, room 3124.
International Affairs.—Vacant, room 3128.
Special Assistant.—Vacant, room 3124.
Tax and Budget.—David Vandivier, room 3462.
Special Assistant.—Stacy Rolland, room 3124.
Administrative Specialist.—Linda L. Powell, room 3111, 622–0535.
Congressional Inquiry Analyst.—Ora D. Starks, room 3453, 622–0576.
Legislative Analyst.—Gail Harris-Berry, room 3453, 622–4401.

OFFICE OF THE ASSISTANT SECRETARY FOR MANAGEMENT / CHIEF FINANCIAL OFFICER

Assistant Secretary for Management.—Vacant, room 2438 (202) 622–0410.
Deputy Assistant Secretary for Management and Budget.—Vacant, 622–0021.
Deputy Assistant Secretary for Human Resources and Chief Human Capital Officer.—Rochelle Granat, 1500 Pennsylvania Avenue, NW., room 1136, 622–6052.
Deputy Chief Financial Officer.—Al Runnels, room 6253, 622–0750.
Director of:
Accounting and Internal Control.—James R. Lingebach, room 6263, 622–0818.

Asset Management.—Charles Ingram, room 6179, 622–2178.
Budget.—Robert Mahaffie, room 6118, 622–1479.
Conference Events and Meeting Services.—Lucinda Gooch, room 3094, Annex, 622–2071.
Departmental Budget Execution.—Chantale Wong, room 6123, Met Square, 622–5475.
Disclosure Services.—Dale Underwood, room 6200, Annex, 622–0874.
Environmental Safety and Health.—Steven Wallace, room 6001, 622–1712.
Equal Opportunity and Diversity.—Mariam Harvey, room 8139, 622–1160.
Facilities Management.—Polly Dietz, room 1155, 622–7067.
Facilities Support Services.—James Thomas, room 6100, Annex, 622–4080.
Financial Management.—Andy Pavord, room 6069, Met Square, 622–5644.
Human Resource Strategy and Solutions.—Dennis Cannon, room 8121, 622–1109.
Human Resources Operations.—Rhonda Coachman-Steward, room 1458, 927–4800.
Information Services.—Veronica Marco, room 6904, 622–2477.
Printing and Graphics.—Craig Larsen, room 6100, Annex, 622–1409.
Procurement Services.—Ernest Dilworth, room 2154, New York Avenue, 622–1066.
Small and Disadvantaged Business Utilization.—Teresa Lewis, room 6099, Met Square, 622–2826.
Strategic Planning and Performance Management.—Martin Melone, room 6133, Met Square, 622–9316.
Treasury Building.—Polly Dietz, room 1041, 622–7067.
Senior Procurement Executive.—Thomas Sharpe, room 6111, Met Square, 622–1039.
Budget Officer.—Carol Bryant, room 6075, Met Square, 622–7346.
Accounting Officer.—David Legge, room 6070, Met Square, 622–1167.
Facilities Support Services DD.—Rosa Perry, room 6100, Annex, 622–3807.

OFFICE OF THE ASSISTANT SECRETARY FOR PUBLIC AFFAIRS

Assistant Secretary.—Vacant, room 3438 MT (202) 622–2910.
Deputy Assistant Secretary, Public Affairs Operations.—Jenni LeCompte, room 3446 MT, 622–2920.
Deputy Assistant Secretary, Public Affairs.—Andrew Williams, room 3446 MT, 622–2920.
Senior Advisor, Public Affairs.—Molly Buford, room 3020 MT, 622–3431.
Deputy Assistant Secretary/Public Liaison.—Gabrielle Trebat, room 3122 MT, 622–2792.
Review Analyst and Scheduling Coordinator.—Carmen Alvarado, room 3442 MT, 622–7483.
Specialist, Public Affairs/Enforcement Specialist.—Marti Adams, room 3023 MT, 622–2960.
Public Affairs Specialist, Domestic Finance.—Meg Reilly, room 3028 MT, 622–2960.
Speechwriter to the Secretary.—Peter Gosselin, room 3030 MT, 622–0631.
Media Coordinator.—Erika Gudmundson, room 3024 MT, 622–0470.

OFFICE OF THE ASSISTANT SECRETARY FOR TAX POLICY

Assistant Secretary.—Vacant, room 3120 MT, (202) 622–0050.
Deputy Assistant Secretary for—
International Tax Affairs.—Michael Mundaca, 3045 MT, 662–0642.
Tax Analysis.—Vacant, room 3064 MT, 662–0120.
Tax Policy.—Vacant, room 3116 MT, 662–0140.
Tax, Trade and Tariff Policy.—Timothy Skud, room 3104 MT, 622–0220.
Tax Legislative Counsel.—Eric SanJuan (acting), room 3040 MT, 622–1776.
Deputy Tax Legislative Counsel.—John Parcell, room 4224 MT, 622–2578.
International Tax Counsel.—John Harrington, room 3054 MT, 622–0589.
Deputy International Tax Counsel.—Vacant, room 5064 MT.
Benefits Tax Counsel.—William Thomas Reeder, room 3050 MT, 622–1341.
Director, Office of Tax Analysis.—James Mackie, room 4116 MT, 622–1326.
Director, Division of:
Business and International Taxation.—Geraldine A. Gerardi, room 4221 MT, 622–1782.
Economic Modeling and Computer Applications.—Robert Gillette, room 4039 MT, 622–0852.
Individual Taxation.—Vacant, room 4043 MT.
Receipts Forecasting Division.—Scott Jaquette, room 4064 MT, 622–1319.
Revenue Estimating Division.—John McClelland, room 4112 MT, 622–1129.

BUREAU OF ENGRAVING AND PRINTING

14th and C Streets, NW., 20228, phone (202) 874–2000

[Created by act of July 11, 1862; codified under U.S.C. 31, section 303]

Director.—Larry R. Felix.
Deputy Director.—Pamela J. Gardiner, 874–2016.
Chief Counsel.—Kevin Rice, 874–2306.
Associate Directors:
Chief Financial Officer (CFO).—Leonard R. Olijar, 874–2020.
Chief Information Officer (CIO).—Peter O. Johnson, 874–3000.
Associate Director for—
Eastern Currency Facility.—Jon J. Cameron, 874–2032.
Western Currency Facility.—Charlene Williams (817) 847–3802.
Management.—Scott Wilson, 874–2040.
Product and Technology Development.—Judith Diaz-Myers, 874–2008.

OFFICE OF THE COMPTROLLER OF THE CURRENCY

250 E Street, SW., 20219, phone (202) 874–5000

Comptroller.—John C. Dugan, 874–4900.
Chief of Staff/Senior Deputy Comptroller (Public Affairs).—John G. Walsh, 874–4880.
Chief Counsel.—Julie L. Williams, 874–5200.
Director for Congressional Liaison.—John Hardage, 874–4840.
Senior Deputy Comptroller of:
Chief National Bank Examiner.—Timothy W. Long, 874–2870.
International and Economic Affairs.—Mark Levonian, 874–5010.
Large Bank Supervision.—Douglas W. Roeder, 874–4610.
Management.—Thomas R. Bloom, 874–5080.
Midsize/Community Bank Supervision.—Jennifer C. Kelly, 874–5020.
Ombudsman.—Larry Hattix, 874–1530.
Chief Information Officer.—Bajinder Paul, 874–4480.

INTERNAL REVENUE SERVICE

1111 Constitution Avenue, NW., 20224, phone (202) 622–5000

[Created by act of July 1, 1862; codified under U.S.C. 26, section 7802]

Commissioner.—Douglas H. Shulman, 622–9511.
Chief of Staff.—Jonathan Davis, 927–5600.
Deputy Commissioner, Services and Enforcement.—Linda Stiff, 622–6860.
Commissioner of:
Large and Mid-Sized Business.—Frank Ng, 283–8710.
Small Business/Self-Employed.—Chris Wagner, 622–0600.
Tax Exempt and Government Entities.—Steven Miller, 283–2500.
Wage and Investment.—Richard Byrd, (404) 338–7060.
Chief, Criminal Investigation.—Eileen Mayer, 622–3200.
Director, Office of Professional Responsibility.—Carolyn Gray (acting), 927–3397.
Director, Whistleblower Office.—Steve Whitlock, 622–0351.
Deputy Commissioner, Operations Support.—Mark Ernst, 622–4255.
Chief:
Agency-Wide Shared Services.—Dave Grant (acting), 622–7500.
Appeals.—Sarah Hall Ingram, 435–5600.
Communications and Liaison.—Frank Keith, 622–5440.
EEO and Diversity.—William Williams, 622–5400.
Financial Officer.—Alison Doone, 622–6400.
IRS Human Capital Officer.—James Falcone, 622–7676.
Office of Privacy, Information Protection and Data Security.—Deborah Wolf (202) 927–5170.
Technology Officer.—Terence Milholland, 622–6800.
Chief Counsel.—Clarissa Potter (acting), 622–3300.
National Taxpayer Advocate.—Nina E. Olson, 622–6100.

Director, Office of Research, Analysis and Statistics.—Mark Mazur, 874–0100.
Office of Legislative Affairs.—Floyd Williams, 622–3720.

OFFICE OF THRIFT SUPERVISION

1700 G Street, NW., 20552, phone (202) 906–6000, fax 906–5660

[Codified in U.S.C. 12, section 1462a]

Director.—Scott M. Polakoff (acting), 906–6853.
Deputy Director/Chief Operating Officer.—Scott M. Polakoff, 906–6853.
Chief Counsel.—John Bowman, 906–6372.
Managing Director of:
Examinations, Supervision and Consumer Protection.—Timothy T. Ward, 906–5666.
External Affairs.—Barbara Shycoff, 906–7165.
Chief Financial/Information Officer.—Wayne G. Leiss, 906–6101.

INSPECTOR GENERAL FOR TAX ADMINISTRATION (TIGTA)

1125 15th Street, NW., Room 700A, 20005

phone (202) 622–6500, fax 927–0001

Inspector General.—J. Russell George.
Principal Deputy Inspector General.—Joseph Hungate.
Congressional Liaison.—Robert Sperling, 927–7164.
Chief Counsel.—Roderick Fillinger, 622–3139.
Deputy Inspector General for Audit.—Michael R. Phillips, 927–7085.
Assistant Inspector General for—
Compliance and Enforcement Operations.—Margaret Begg, 622–8510.
Management Services and Organizations.—Nancy Nakamura, 622–8500.
Returns Processing and Accounts Services.—Michael McKenney, 622–5916.
Deputy Inspector General for Investigations.—Steven M. Jones, 927–7160.
Assistant Inspectors General for Investigations: —Timothy P. Camus, Michael A. Delgado.
Deputy Assistant Inspector General for Investigations.—Gregory L. Holley, Sr.
Associate Inspector General for Mission Support.—Larry Koskinen, 622–8482.
Chief of Operations.—Jennifer Donnan, (404) 274–8258.
Deputy Inspector General for Inspections and Evaluations.—David Holmgren, 927–7048 .

OFFICE OF THE TREASURER OF THE UNITED STATES

Treasurer.—Vacant, (202) 622–0100.
Senior Advisor.—Vacant.
Senior Writer.—Vacant.

UNITED STATES MINT

801 9th Street, NW., 20002, phone (202) 354–7200, fax 756–6160

Director.—Edmund C. Moy.
Executive Assistant to the Director.—Arnetta Cain.
Deputy Director.—Andrew Brunhart.
Staff Assistant to the Deputy Director.—Vacant.
Chief Counsel.—Dan Shaver (202) 354–7280.
Director, Legislative and Intergovernmental Affairs.—Clifford Northup (202) 354–6700.
Director, Public Affairs.—Becky Bailey (202) 354–7720.
Associate Director for Protection.—Dennis O'Connor (202) 354–7300.
Deputy Associate Director.—Bill R. Bailey (202) 354–7300.
Associate Director/Chief Information Officer.—Vacant.
Deputy Associate Director.—Jay Mahanand (202) 354–7700.
Associate Director/Chief Financial Officer.—Patricia M. Greiner (202) 354–7800.
Deputy Associate Director.—David Motl (202) 354–7800.
Associate Director, Sales and Marketing.—B.B. Craig (202) 354–7500.
Deputy Associate Director.—Rich Peterson (202) 354–7800.
Associate Director, Manufacturing.—Vacant.
Deputy Associate Director.—Vacant.

DEPARTMENT OF DEFENSE

The Pentagon 20301–1155, phone (703) 545–6700

fax 695–3362/693–2161, http://www.defenselink.mil

ROBERT M. GATES, Secretary of Defense; born in Wichita, KS, September 25, 1943; education: B.A., College of William and Mary, 1965; M.A., Indiana University, 1966; Ph.D., Georgetown University, 1974; military service: U.S. Air Force, 1967–69, served as an officer in the Strategic Air Command; professional: intelligence analyst, Central Intelligence Agency (CIA), 1966–74; staff, National Security Council, 1974–79; Director, DCA/DDCI Executive Staff, CIA, 1981–82; Deputy Director for Intelligence, CIA, 1982–86; Chair, National Intelligence Council, 1983–86; Deputy Director of Central Intelligence, CIA, 1986–89; Deputy Assistant to the President for National Security Affairs, CIA, 1989; Assistant to the President and Deputy for National Security Affairs, CIA, 1989–91; Director, CIA, 1991–93; private consultant; author, *From the Shadows: The Ultimate Insider's Story of Five Presidents and How They Won the Cold War,* 1996; interim Dean of the George Bush School of Government and Public Service, Texas A & M University, 1999–2001; President, Texas A & M University, 2002–07; President, National Eagle Scout Association; awards: National Security Medal; Presidential Citizens Medal; National Intelligence Distinguished Service Medal; Distinguished Intelligence Medal; family: married to Becky; two children; nominated by President George W. Bush to become the 22nd Secretary of Defense, and was confirmed by the U.S. Senate on December 6, 2006.

OFFICE OF THE SECRETARY

Pentagon, Room 3E880, 20301–1000, phone (703) 692–7100, fax 697–8339

Secretary of Defense.—Robert M. Gates.

OFFICE OF THE DEPUTY SECRETARY

1010 Defense Pentagon, Room 3E944, 20301–1010, phone (703) 692–7150

Deputy Secretary of Defense.—William J. Lynn.

EXECUTIVE SECRETARIAT

Pentagon, Room 3E718, 20301–1000, phone (703) 692–7120, fax 695–2553

Executive Secretary.—Vacant.

GENERAL COUNSEL

Pentagon, Room 3E833, 20301–1600, phone (703) 695–3341, fax 693–7278

General Counsel.—Jeh Charles Johnson.
Principal Deputy.—Robert S. Taylor (703) 697–7248.

OPERATIONAL TEST AND EVALUATION

Pentagon, Room 3D1067, 20301–1700, phone (703) 697–4813, fax 614–9103

Director.—Dr. Charles McQueary.

INSPECTOR GENERAL

400 Army Navy Drive, Suite 1000, Arlington VA 22202–4704, phone (703) 604–8300 fax 604–8310, hotline 1–800–424–9098, hotline fax 604–8569

Inspector General.—Gordon S. Heddell (acting).

UNDER SECRETARY OF DEFENSE FOR ACQUISITION, TECHNOLOGY AND LOGISTICS

Pentagon, Room 3E1010, 20301, phone (703) 697–7021

Under Secretary.—John J. Young, Jr.
Deputy Under Secretary for—
Advanced Systems and Concepts.—Dr. Charles W. Perkins (acting).
Industrial Policy.—Gary Powell (acting).
Installations and Environment.—Hon. Wayne Arny.
Logistics and Materiel Readiness.—Hon. Phillip J. Bell.
Science and Technology.—Dr. Andre Van Tilborg.
Director, Office of Small Business Program.—Linda Oliver (acting).
Director, Defense Research and Engineering.—Al Shaffer (acting).
Assistant to the Secretary of Defense for Nuclear and Chemical and Biological Defense Programs.—Hon. Frederick S. Celec.

JOINT STRIKE FIGHTER PROGRAM OFFICE

200 12th Street South, Suite 600, Arlington, VA 22202–5402, phone (703) 602–7640, fax 602–7649

Program Executive Officer.—Brig. Gen. David R. Heinz, USMC.

UNDER SECRETARY OF DEFENSE (COMPTROLLER) AND CHIEF FINANCIAL OFFICER

Pentagon, Room 3E770, 20301–1100, phone (703) 695–3237

Under Secretary/Chief Financial Officer.—Robert F. Hale.
Principal Deputy Under Secretary.—Michael J. McCord.

UNDER SECRETARY OF DEFENSE FOR PERSONNEL AND READINESS

Pentagon, Room 3E764, 20301–4000, phone (703) 695–5254

Under Secretary.—Vacant.
Principal Deputy Under Secretary.—Vacant, 697–2121.
Assistant Secretary for—
Health Affairs.—Vacant, 697–2113.
Reserve Affairs.—Vacant, 697–6631.
Deputy Under Secretary for—
Civilian Personnel Policy.—Vacant, 614–9487.
Military Community and Family Policy.—Vacant, 697–7220.
Military Personnel Policy.—Bill Carr, 571–0116.
Plans.—Gail McGinn, 571–0094.
Program Integration.—Jeanne Fites, 614–3970.
Readiness.—Dr. Samuel Kleinman, 693–0466.

UNDER SECRETARY OF DEFENSE FOR POLICY

Pentagon, Room 3E806, 20301–2000, phone (703) 697–7200

Under Secretary.—Hon. Michèle A. Flournoy.
Principal Deputy.—Hon. James N. Miller.
Assistant Secretary of Defense for—
Homeland Defense and America's Security Affairs.—Vacant.
International Security Affairs.—Hon. Alexander R. Vershbow.

Special Operations/Low-Intensity Conflict and Interdependent Capabilities.—Hon. Michael G. Vickers.
Global Strategic Affairs.—Vacant.
Asian and Pacific Security Affairs.—Vacant.

ASSISTANT SECRETARY FOR NETWORKS AND INFORMATION INTEGRATION/CHIEF INFORMATION OFFICER

Pentagon, Room 3E172, 20301–6000, phone (703) 695–0348

Assistant Secretary.—Vacant.
Principal Deputy Assistant Secretary.—Cheryl Roby.

ASSISTANT SECRETARY FOR LEGISLATIVE AFFAIRS

Pentagon, Room 3E970, 20301–1300, phone (703) 697–6210, fax 695–5860

Assistant Secretary.—Christian P. Marrone (acting).
Principal Deputy.—Christian P. Marrone.

ASSISTANT TO THE SECRETARY OF DEFENSE FOR INTELLIGENCE OVERSIGHT

Pentagon, Room 2E1052, 20301–7200, phone (703) 275–6550

Assistant to the Secretary.—William R. Dugan.

ASSISTANT SECRETARY FOR PUBLIC AFFAIRS

Pentagon, Room 2E694, 20301–1400, phone (703) 697–9312, fax 695–4299 public inquiries 697–5737

Assistant Secretary.—Vacant.
Principal Deputy.—Vacant.
Deputy Assistant Secretary.—Bryan Whitman.

ADMINISTRATION AND MANAGEMENT

Pentagon, Room 3A710, 20301–1950, phone (703) 692–7138

Director.—Michael L. Rhodes (acting), room 3A724, 493–7995.
Deputy Director.—Regina F. Meiners (acting), room 3A886, 697–1142.

DEPARTMENT OF DEFENSE FIELD ACTIVITIES

DEFENSE MEDIA ACTIVITY

EFC Plaza, 601 North Fairfax Street, Room 300, Alexandria, VA 22314 phone (703) 428–1200

Director.—Vacant.
Chief of Staff.—COL Michael S. Galloucis.
Director for American Forces Radio and Television Services.—Melvin W. Russell, room 360, (703) 429–0617.

DEPARTMENT OF DEFENSE EDUCATION ACTIVITY

4040 North Fairfax Drive, Arlington, VA 22203

School Information (703) 588–3030

Director.—Dr. Shirley Miles, 588–3200.
Principal Deputy Director and Associate Director for Education.—Charlie Toth, 588–3105.
Associate Director for Finance and Business Operations.—Kevin Kelly, 588–3305.

General Counsel.—Karen Grosso Lambert, 588–3064.

DEPARTMENT OF DEFENSE HUMAN RESOURCES ACTIVITY

4040 Fairfax Drive, Arlington, VA 22209, phone (703) 696–1036

Director.—Vacant.
Deputy Director.—Vacant.
Executive Director.—Sharon Cooper, 696–0909.

TRICARE MANAGEMENT ACTIVITY

5111 Leesburg Pike, Suite 810, Falls Church, VA 22041, phone (703) 681–8707

Director.—Ellen Embrey (acting).
Deputy Director.—RADM Christine Hunter.

DEFENSE PRISONER OF WAR / MISSING PERSONNEL OFFICE

241 18th Street, Suite 800, Arlington, VA 22202, phone (703) 699–1102, fax 602–1890

Director.—Amb. Charles A. Ray.

OFFICE OF ECONOMIC ADJUSTMENT

400 Army Navy Drive, Suite 200, Arlington, VA 22202, phone (703) 604–6020

Director.—Patrick J. O'Brien.
Director of:
Operations.—Ronald Adkins, 604–5141.
Programs.—Dave Larson, 604–5148.
Assistant to Director.—Sehree M. Mickel, 604–5131, fax 604–5843.
Sacramento Regional Manager.—Gary Kuwabara (acting), (916) 557–7365.

WASHINGTON HEADQUARTERS SERVICES

Pentagon, phone (703) 693–7995

Director.—Michael L. Rhodes.
Director for—
Acquisitions and Procurement Office.—Frances Sullivan, 696–4030.
Administrative Services.—Frank Wilson, 601–6100.
Defense Facilities.—Ralph Newton, 697–7241.
Executive Services and Communications.—Craig Glassner, 693–7965.
Financial Management Directorate.—David Zlowe, 699–3350.
Human Resources.—Chris Koehle, 699–1800.
Information Technology.—Mary George, 604–4569.
Pentagon Renovation Program Office.—Sajeel Ahmed, 614–5129.
Planning and Evaluation Office.—Anne O'Connor, 588–8140.
WHS General Counsel.—William ''Bill'' Brazis, 693–7374.

JOINT CHIEFS OF STAFF

OFFICE OF THE CHAIRMAN

Pentagon, Room 2E872, 20318–0001, phone (703) 697–9121

Chairman.—ADM Michael G. Mullen, USN.
Vice Chairman.—GEN James E. Cartwright, USMC, room 2E724, 614–8948.
Assistant to the Chairman, Joint Chiefs of Staff.—Lt. Gen. Paul J. Selva, USAF, room 2E868, 695–4605.

JOINT STAFF

Director.—LTG Stanley McChrystal, USA, room 2E936, 614–5221.
Vice Director.—MG Walter E. Gaskin, USMC, room 2E936, 614–5223.

Director for—

Manpower and Personnel, J–1.—BG Gary S. Patton, USA, room 1E948, 697–6098.

Joint Staff Intelligence, J–2.—MG Michael T. Flynn, USA, room 1E880, 697–9773.

Operations, J–3.—LTG John M. Paxton, USMC, room 2D874, 697–3702.

Logistics, J–4.—LTG Kathleen M. Gainey, USA, room 2E828, 697–7000.

Strategic Plans and Policy, J–5.—VADM James A. Winnefeld, Jr., USN, room 2E996, 695–5618.

Command, Control, Communications and Computer Systems, J–6.—VADM Nancy Brown, USN, room 2D860, 695–6478.

Operational Plans and Joint Force Development, J–7.—BG Michael E. Rounds, USA, room 2B865, 697–9031.

Force Structure, Resources, and Assessment, J–8.—VADM Steven Stanley, USN, room 1E962, 697–8853.

DEFENSE AGENCIES

BALLISTIC MISSILE DEFENSE AGENCY

7100 Defense Pentagon, 20301–7100, phone (703) 695–6344

Director.—LTG Patrick O'Reilly, USA, 695–6344.

Deputy Director.—RDML Joseph Horn, Jr., USN, 695–6330.

Director, Public Affairs.—Richard Lehner, 697–8997.

Director, Legislative Affairs.—Tyler White (acting), 697–8889.

DEFENSE ADVANCED RESEARCH PROJECTS AGENCY

3701 North Fairfax Drive, Arlington, VA 22203, phone (703) 696–2444

Director.—Dr. Robert Leheny (acting), 696–2402.

Deputy Director.—Vacant.

DEFENSE COMMISSARY AGENCY

1300 E Avenue, Fort Lee, VA 23801–1800, phone (804) 734–8718/8330

Director.—Philip E. Sakowitz, Jr., 734–8720.

Chief Operating Officer.—Michael J. Dowling (acting), 734–8330.

WASHINGTON OFFICE

241 18th Street, Suite 302, Arlington, VA 22202–3405, phone (703) 602–0157/2297

Chief.—Daniel W. Sclater.

DEFENSE CONTRACT AUDIT AGENCY

8725 John J. Kingman Road, Suite 2135, Fort Belvoir, VA 22060 phone (703) 767–3200

Director.—April G. Stephenson.

Deputy Director.—Francis P. Summers, Jr., 767–3272.

DEFENSE FINANCE AND ACCOUNTING SERVICE

1851 South Bell Street, Room 920, Arlington, VA 22240 phone (703) 607–2616

Director.—Teresa A. McKay.

Deputy Director.—Richard P. Gustafson.

DEFENSE INFORMATION SYSTEMS AGENCY

P.O. Box 4502, Arlington, VA 22204, phone (703) 607–6020

Director.—LTG Carroll Pollett, USA, room 4222, 607–6001.
Vice Director.—RADM Elizabeth Hight, USN, room 4235, 607–6010.

DEFENSE INTELLIGENCE AGENCY

Pentagon, Room 3E258, 20340–7400, phone (703) 697–5101

Director.—LTG Michael Maples.
Deputy Director.—LeLilia Long.

DEFENSE LEGAL SERVICES AGENCY

Pentagon, Room 3E833, 20301–1600, phone (703) 695–3341, fax 693–7278

Director/General Counsel.—Jeh C. Johnson.
Principal Deputy Director.—Daniel Dell'Orto, 697–7248.

DEFENSE LOGISTICS AGENCY

8725 John J. Kingman Road, Suite 2533, Ft. Belvoir, VA 22060
phone (703) 767–5264

Director.—VADM Alan S. Thompson, SC, USN.
Vice Director.—Maj. Gen. Arthur B. Morrill III, USAF.

DEFENSE SECURITY COOPERATION AGENCY

201 12th Street South, Suite 203, Arlington, VA 22202–5408, phone (703) 604–6604

Director.—VADM Jeffrey A. Wieringa, USN.
Deputy Director.—Beth M. McCormick, 604–6606.

DEFENSE SECURITY SERVICE

1340 Braddock Place, Alexandria, VA 22314–1651, phone (703) 325–5364

Director.—Kathleen Watson.
Chief of Staff.—Wendell Warner.

DEFENSE THREAT REDUCTION AGENCY

8725 John J. Kingman Road, Stop 6201, Ft. Belvoir, VA 22060–6201
phone (703) 767–7594/4941

Director.—MG Randy E. Manner (acting), USA.
Deputy Director.—Vacant.
Chief Legislative Affairs.—Jeff Subko.

NATIONAL GEOSPATIAL—INTELLIGENCE AGENCY

4600 Sangamore Road, Bethesda, MD 20816, phone (301) 227–7400

Director.—VADM Robert B. Murrett, USN.
Deputy Director.—Lloyd B. Rowland.

NATIONAL SECURITY AGENCY/CENTRAL SECURITY SERVICE

Ft. George G. Meade, MD 20755, phone (301) 688–6524

Director.—LTG Keith B. Alexander, USA.

Deputy Director.—John C. Inglis.
Deputy Chief.—Brig. Gen. Noel T. ''Tom'' Jones, USAF.

JOINT SERVICE SCHOOLS

9820 Belvoir Road, Ft. Belvoir, VA 22060, phone (800) 845–7606

DEFENSE ACQUISITION UNIVERSITY

President.—Frank J. Anderson, Jr. (703) 805–3360.
Vice President.—James McMichael (703) 805–4592.
Chief of Staff.—Joseph Johnson (703) 805–2828.

NATIONAL DEFENSE INTELLIGENCE COLLEGE

President.—A. Denis Clift (202) 231–3344.

NATIONAL DEFENSE UNIVERSITY

Fort McNair, Building 62, 300 Fifth Avenue, 20319
phone (202) 685–3912

President.—LTG Frances Wilson, USMC, room 307, 685–3922.
Senior Vice President.— Amb. Richard Roth, room 307A, 685–3923.

INFORMATION RESOURCES MANAGEMENT COLLEGE

Senior Director.— Dr. Robert D. Childs (202) 685–3886.

JOINT FORCES STAFF COLLEGE

7800 Hampton Boulevard, Norfolk, VA 23511–1702, phone (757) 443–6200

Commandant.—BG Katherine P. Kasun, USA, room A202.

INDUSTRIAL COLLEGE OF THE ARMED FORCES

Commandant.—RADM Garry E. Hall, USN, room 200 (202) 685–4337.

NATIONAL WAR COLLEGE

Commandant.—Maj. Gen. Robert Steel, USAF, room 124 (202) 685–4342.

UNIFORMED SERVICES UNIVERSITY OF THE HEALTH SCIENCES

4301 Jones Bridge Road, Bethesda, MD 20814

President.—Charles L. Rice, M.D., room A1019 (301) 295–3013.

DEPARTMENT OF THE AIR FORCE

Pentagon, 1670 Air Force, Washington, DC 20330–1670

phone (703) 697–7376, fax 695–8809

SECRETARY OF THE AIR FORCE

Secretary of the Air Force.—Michael B. Donley, room 4E878.
Confidential Assistant.—Elizabeth C. Owen.
Senior Military Assistant.—Col. Charles H. Porter.
Deputy Military Assistant.—Lt. Col. Ronald E. Jolly.
Military Aid.—Maj. Michael Curry.

SECAF / CSAF EXECUTIVE ACTION GROUP

Chief.—Col. Charles Brown (703) 697–5540.
Deputy Chief.—Lt. Col. Dan Tippett.

UNDER SECRETARY OF THE AIR FORCE

Pentagon, 1670 Air Force, Room 4E858, 20330–1670, phone (703) 697–1361

Under Secretary.—Vacant.
Confidential Assistant.—Vacant.
Senior Military Assistant.—Vacant.
Military Assistant.—Vacant.
Executive Assistant.—TSgt Donald Jones.

CHIEF OF STAFF

Pentagon, 1670 Air Force, Room 4E924, 20330

phone (703) 695–9227

Chief of Staff.—Gen. Norton A. Schwartz.
Executive Officer.—Col. Jon Norman.
Vice Chief of Staff.—Gen. William Fraser, room 4E938, 695–7911.
Assistant Vice Chief of Staff.—Lt. Gen. Frank Klotz, room 4E944, 695–7913.
Director, Operations Group.—Col. Charles Brown, room 4D919, 697–5540.
Chief Master Sergeant of the Air Force.—CMSAF Rodney J. McKinley, room 4E941, 695–0498.

DEPUTY UNDER SECRETARY FOR INTERNATIONAL AFFAIRS

Pentagon, 1080 Air Force Pentagon, Room 4D831, 20330–1080

Rosslyn, 1500 Wilson Boulevard, 8th Floor, Arlington, VA 22209

Deputy Under Secretary.—Bruce S. Lemkin (703) 695–7261.
Senior Executive Officer.—Lt. Col. Kevin Berkompas, 695–7261.
Executive Officer.—Maj. Bradley McAlpine, 693–1941.
Executive Assistant.—Georgia Smothers, 695–7261.
Assistant Deputy.—Maj. Gen. Richard Perraut, 588–8855.
Executive Officers: Lt. Col. Keli Bedics, 588–8833; Lt. Col. Patrick Sullivan, 588–8828.
Executive Assistant.—Linda Barnett, 588–8800.
Director of Policy.—Richard A. Genaille, 588–5560.
Director of Regional Affairs.—Brig. Gen. Lyn Sherlock, 588–8820.

ASSISTANT SECRETARY FOR ACQUISITION

Pentagon, 1060 Air Force, 20330

1500 Wilson Boulevard, Arlington, VA 22209 (Rosslyn)

1745 Jefferson Davis Highway, Suite 307, Arlington, VA 22202

110 Luke Avenue, Suite 200, Bolling AFB, DC 20032–6400

Assistant Secretary.—Sue C. Payton (703) 697–6361.
Senior Military Assistant.—Col. James Haywood, 697–6990.
Military Assistant.—Lt. Col. William McGuffey, 697–6362.

Principal Deputy.—David M. Van Buren, 697–9373.
Military Assistant.—Lt. Col. Paul E. Henderson, 693–9350.

Military Deputy.—Lt. Gen. Mark Shackelford, 697–6363.
Executive Officer.—Maj. Ted Shoepe, 695–7311.

DEPUTY ASSISTANT SECRETARY FOR ACQUISITION INTEGRATION

1500 Wilson Boulevard, Arlington, VA 22209 (Rosslyn)

Deputy Assistant Secretary.—Blaise J. Durante (703) 588–7211.
Associate Deputy Assistant Secretary.—Jeffery R. Shelton, 696–0082.
Executive Officer.—Maj. Pete Jackson, 588–7217.

DEPUTY ASSISTANT SECRETARY FOR CONTRACTING

Deputy Assistant Secretary.—Roger S. Correll (703) 588–7070.
Associate Deputy Assistant Secretary.—Pamela C. Schwenke, 588–7010.
Executive Officer.—Lt. Col. Richard Wells, 588–1004.

DEPUTY ASSISTANT SECRETARY FOR SCIENCE, TECHNOLOGY AND ENGINEERING

Deputy Assistant Secretary.—Terry Jaggers (703) 588–7770.
Associate Deputy Assistant Secretary.—Col. James Collins, 588–7771.
Executive Officer.—Lt. Col. Ed Masterson, 588–7777.

CAPABILITY DIRECTORATE FOR GLOBAL POWER PROGRAMS

Director.—Maj. Gen. Jay H. Lindell (703) 588–7171.
Deputy Director.—Col. Wesley Ballenger, 588–7177.
Executive Officers: Maj. Lori Foringer, 588–7170; Maj. Rich Mott, 588–7172.

CAPABILITY DIRECTORATE FOR GLOBAL REACH PROGRAMS

Director.—Maj. Gen. Randal D. Fullhart (703) 588–7752.
Deputy Director.—Col. Dempsey Hackett, 588–7756.
Executive Officer.—Lt. Col. Jeff Gates, 588–7753.

CAPABILITY DIRECTORATE FOR INFORMATION DOMINANCE

Director.—Martha J. ''Marty'' Evans (703) 588–6346.
Deputy Director.—Col. Andre Gerner, 588–6350.
Executive Officer.—Lt. Col. Chris Lohr, 588–6345.

DIRECTORATE FOR SPECIAL PROGRAMS

Director.—Col. Roger Vincent (703) 588–1631.
Deputy Director.—Col. Gregory Dragoo, 588–1002.
Associate Director.—Ryan Dow, 588–1463.
Executive Officer.—Maj. Fredrick ''Rick'' Hunt, 588–1128.

AIR FORCE PROGRAM EXECUTIVE OFFICERS

Program Executive Officer for—
Aircraft.—Lt. Gen. John Hudson (937) 255–5714.
Combat and Mission Support.—Brig. Gen. Wendy Masiello (703) 588–7190.
Command and Control/Combat Support Systems.—Lt. Gen. Ted Bowlds (781) 478–5102.
Weapons.—Maj. Gen. David Eidsaune (850) 882–5422.
Joint Strike Fighter Program.—Maj. Gen. Charles Davis (703) 602–7640.

DIRECTORATE FOR AIR FORCE RAPID CAPABILITIES

Director.—David E. Hamilton (202) 767–1800.
Deputy and Technical Director.—Randall G. Walden.
Executive Officer.—Richard Brown, 767–3203.

ASSISTANT SECRETARY FOR FINANCIAL MANAGEMENT AND COMPTROLLER OF THE AIR FORCE

Pentagon, 1130 Air Force, 20330

CGN, Air Force Cost Analysis Agency, Crystal Gateway North

1111 Jefferson Davis Highway, Suite 403, Arlington, VA 22202

Assistant Secretary.—John G. Vonglis (acting), room 4E978 (703) 697–1974.
Military Assistant.—Col. Jim Reitzel, 695–0837.
Chief, Enlisted Matters.—CMSgt Bryn LePine, 614–5437.

PRINCIPAL DEPUTY ASSISTANT SECRETARY FOR FINANCIAL MANAGEMENT

Principal Deputy Assistant Secretary.—John G. Vonglis (703) 697–4464.
Military Assistant.—Lt. Col. Manny Maldonado, 695–0829.

DEPUTY ASSISTANT SECRETARY FOR BUDGET

Deputy Assistant Secretary.—Maj. Gen. Larry O. Spencer, room 5D912 (703) 695–1875.
Executive Officer.—Lt. Col. J. R. Weilacher, 695–1876.
Deputy.—Patricia J. Zarodkiewicz, 695–1875.
Director of:
Budget and Appropriations Liaison.—Col. Keith Zuegel, room 5C949, 614–8114.
Budget Investment.—Teri Spoutz, room 5D912, 697–1220.
Budget Management and Execution.—BJ White-Olsen, room 5D912, 695–9737.
Budget Operations and Personnel.—Brig. Gen. David Price, room 5D912, 697–0627.
Budget Programs.—Col. John Pletcher, room 5C950, 614–7883.

DEPUTY ASSISTANT SECRETARY FOR COST AND ECONOMICS

Deputy Assistant Secretary.—Richard K. Hartley, room 5E975 (703) 697–5311.
Associate Deputy Assistant Secretary.—Ranae Woods, 697–5313.
Executive Officer.—Lt. Col. James Bell, 697–5312.
Technical Director for Cost and Economics.—Jay Jordan, CGN, room 403, 604–0400.
Director, Economics and Business Management.—Stephen M. Connair, room 4C843, 693–9347.

DEPUTY ASSISTANT SECRETARY FOR FINANCIAL OPERATIONS

Deputy Assistant Secretary.—Audrey Y. Davis, Pentagon, room 5D739.
Associate Deputy Assistant Secretary.—Vacant.
Military Assistant.—Capt. Jessi Rozman, Pentagon, room 5D739 (703) 614–4180.
Director for—
Accounting Policy and Reporting.—Fred Carr, Andrews AFB, MD (301) 981–9222.
AF Financial Systems Organization.—Rick Staley, Wright-Patterson AFB, OH (937) 257–8447.

Financial Services.—Joan Causey, Ellsworth AFB, SD (605) 385–8696.
Information Systems and Technology.—Vacant.
Process Improvement and Integration.—Josephine Davis, Arlington, VA (703) 588–8544.
Workforce Management.—Wesley Breeding (703) 697–2657.

ASSISTANT SECRETARY FOR INSTALLATIONS, ENVIRONMENT AND LOGISTICS

Assistant Secretary.—Kevin W. Billings (acting), room 4E996 (703) 697–4936.
Executive Officer.—Lt. Col. Heather Buono, 697–4219.
Military Assistant.—Col. Bobbie Griffin, 697–5023.
Confidential Assistant.—Cathy Hudock, 697–4936.

DEPUTY ASSISTANT SECRETARY FOR INSTALLATIONS (SAF/IEI)

Deputy Assistant Secretary.—Kathleen I. Ferguson, room 4B941 (703) 695–3592.
Deputy for Installation Policy.—James P. Holland, (703) 614–6232.
Office Manager.—Pamela L. Coghill, 695–3592.
Director, Strategic Initiatives/Military Assistant.—Lt. Col. Stephen Wood, 695–6456.
Resource Manager.—Everette Dewaine Longus, 697–4391.
Director, Planning and Strategic Development.—Col. Joseph Schwarz, 697–7003.
Director, Installation Programs.—Lt. Col. Brian Weidmann, 695–5730.
Director, Installation and Housing Management.—Lt. Col. Douglas W. Gilpin, 697–1980.
Guam Program Management Office Liaison.—Marriane Serrano, 602–5548.
Air Force Real Property Agency Liaison.—Robert McCann, 697–7244.
Director, Air National Guard and Reserve Affairs.—Col. Peter Tunison, 695–5730.
Director, Asset Management.—Edward Pokora, 693–9328.
Asset Management.—Roy Murray, 614–6230.
Assistant for Privatization Real Estate Support.—Hillary Yarbrough, 697–1113.

BRAC PROGRAM MANAGEMENT OFFICE (SAF/IEI–PMO)

Director.—Col. Joseph Morganti, Crystal Gateway 1, suite 1000, (703) 604–5276.
Director.—Douglas D. McCoy (acting), 604–3646.
Chief, Resources Division.—Wellington Selden, 604–5295.
Information Management.—JJ Cook, 604–5273.
Comm Liaison.—Donna Oscepinski, 604–5264.
Operations Cell: Tim Brennan, 604–5253; Steve Cornish, 604–5256; Greg Keysor, 604–5288; Ray Neall, 604–5359; Robert Niswonger, 601–0181; Geoffrey S. Oliver, 604–5277; George ''Stu'' Pugh, 604–5272.
Communication Director.—Frank T. Smolinsky, 604–5270.
Resources.—Paul Freund, 604–5298; Helen Griffith, 604–5210; Kathy Teter, 602–5438.

DEPUTY ASSISTANT SECRETARY FOR ENVIRONMENT, SAFETY AND OCCUPATIONAL HEALTH (SAF/IEE)

Deputy Assistant Secretary.—Michael F. McGhee (acting), room 4B941, 697–9297.
Executive Secretary.—Sheenia Williams, 697–9297.
Executive Officer.—Lt. Col. Randolph R. Smith, 693–3254.
Director of Safety.—Vance Lineberger, 693–7706.
Director for—
Energy Policy.—Col. Donald Hickman, 693–9534.
Environmental Policy.—Michele Indermark, 614–8458.
Environmental Programs.—Lt. Col. Mark E. Smallwood, 692–9515.
Occupational Health.—Lt. Col. Wade Weismann, 693–9544.
Special Assistant for Energy Policy.—Col. Suzanne Johnson, 693–9339.
Energy Contractors Support: Richard B. Brill II, 697–1016; George Hutchinson, 693–1098; William Noel, 697–1018; Daniel Kowalczyk, 697–1198.

DEPUTY ASSISTANT SECRETARY FOR LOGISTICS (SAF/IEL)

Deputy Assistant Secretary.—Debra K. Walker, room 4B941, 695–3592.
Director of Logistics and Transformation.—Mark Van Gilst, 692–9090.
Chief, Depot Operations and Strategic Planning.—Col. Philip Greco, 693–2185.
Chief, Supply Chain Management.—Deb Inman, 697–1641.

Chief, Weapon System Integration.—Rita Dixon, 614–6240.

AIR FORCE REAL PROPERTY AGENCY

143 Billy Mitchell Boulevard, Suite 1, San Antonio, TX 7822–1858

Director.—Robert ''Bob'' Moore, (210) 925–0936.
Secretary to the Director.—Linda Cosper, 925–0192.
Deputy Director.—Jeffrey Domm, 925–3024.
Secretary to the Deputy Director.—Stephanie Fishel, 925–4380.

ASSISTANT SECRETARY FOR MANPOWER AND RESERVE AFFAIRS

1660 Air Force Pentagon, Room 4E1010, 20330

Assistant Secretary.—Craig W. Duehring (703) 697–2302.
Principal Deputy Assistant.—Ronald Winter (703) 693–9312.
Mobilization Assistant.—Maj. Gen. Keith Meurlin, 614–5978.
Confidential Assistant.—Ruth N. Thornton, 695–6677.
Military Assistant.—Col. Charlene Jefferson, 697–2303.
Executive Officer.—Lt. Col. Richard Alderete, 697–1258.
Superintendent.—TSgt Henry Lopez, 697–5828.

DEPUTY ASSISTANT SECRETARY FOR FORCE MANAGEMENT INTEGRATION

Deputy Assistant Secretary.—Barbara J. Barger (703) 614–4751.
Executive Secretary.—Dottie A. Baltimore, 614–4751.
Assistant Deputy for—
Force Management Integration.—Charlene M. Bradley, 614–4751.
Family Programs.—Linda Stephens-Jones, 693–9574.
Health Affairs.—Carol J. Thompson, 693–9764.
Officer Accessories and Programs.—David A. French, 693–9333.
Force Support Services.—Tamara S. Moes, 693–9765.
Military Force Management.—Thomas E. Booth, 697–7783.
Total Force Integration.—Timothy S. McIsaac, 695–2459.

DEPUTY ASSISTANT SECRETARY FOR RESERVE AFFAIRS

Deputy Assistant Secretary.—Tom Jones, room 5D742 (703) 697–6376.
Executive Secretary.—Stephanie Parry, 697–6375.
Assistant for—
Air Force Reserve Matters.—Col. John Ellsworth, 697–6431.
ANG Matters.—Col. R. Brian Arnold, 697–9504.
Enlisted Matters.—CMSgt Darise Jackson, 697–6429.
Director, AF Auxiliary Programs.—Col. Weston, 693–9512.
IMA to SAF/MRR.—Col. Robert Burton, 693–9511.
Military Executive for Air Reserve Forces Policy Division Committee.—Lt. Col. Laura Hunter, 697–6430.
Special Assistant for Reserve Matters.—Col. Anne Hamilton, 693–9505.

DEPUTY ASSISTANT SECRETARY FOR STRATEGIC DIVERSITY INTEGRATION

Deputy Assistant Secretary.—Rose Gault, room 5E783 (703) 697–6586.
Assistant Deputy Assistant Secretary.—Lori Powell (703) 697–6583.
Executive Secretary.—Karen Sauls (703) 697–6586.

AIR FORCE REVIEW BOARDS AGENCY

Director.—Joe G. Lineberger, AAFB, Building 1535 (240) 857–3137.
Confidential Assistant.—Marilyn Redmond.
Chief, Review Boards Management.—CMSgt Jeffory C. Gabrelcik, 857–3119.

CHIEF OF WARFIGHTING INTEGRATION AND CHIEF INFORMATION OFFICER

1800 Air Force Pentagon, Room 4E1050, 20330

Chief of Warfighting Integration and Chief Information Officer.—LTG William T. Lord (703) 695–6829.
Deputy Chief of Warfighting Integration and Deputy Chief Information Officer.—Daniel F. McMillin, 697–1605.
Director of:
Warfighter Systems Integration and Deployment.—BG William Bender, room 1D857, 695–1835.
Infrastructure Delivery—MG Paul Capasso, room 1D857, 692–4584.
Cyberspace Transformation and Strategy.—BG David Cotton, room 1D857, 697–1326.
Policy and Resources.—Bobby Smart, room 1D857, 695–1839.

DEPUTY CHIEF OF STAFF FOR INTELLIGENCE, SURVEILLANCE AND RECONNAISSANCE

Deputy Chief of Staff.—Lt. Gen. David A. Deptula (703) 695–5613.
Assistant Deputy Chief of Staff.—Maj. Gen. Paul Dettmer.
Executive Officer.—Lt. Col. Karen Rolirad.
Director of:
Analysis and Estimates.—Col. Michael Phillips.
Doctrine, Strategy and Future Development.—Brig. Gen. Dash Jamieson, 614–2144.
Intelligence, Surveillance and Reconnaissance Capabilities.—Maj. Gen. Blair Hansen, 695–6240.
Intelligence, Surveillance and Reconnaissance Innovations.—James Clark, 695–6240.
Resources.—Kenneth Dumm.

DEPUTY CHIEF OF STAFF FOR LOGISTICS, INSTALLATIONS AND MISSION SUPPORT

Pentagon, 1030 Air Force, 20330

Crystal Gateway North, 1111 Jefferson Davis Highway, Arlington, VA 22202 (CGN)

Crystal Gateway 1, 1235 Jefferson Davis Highway, Arlington, VA 22202 (CG1)

Rosslyn, 1500 Wilson Boulevard, Arlington, VA 22209 (ROS)

Deputy Chief of Staff.—LTG Loren M. Reno, Pentagon, room 4E260 (703) 695–3153.
Assistant Deputy.—Michael A. Aimone, Pentagon, room 4E260, 695–6236.
Director of:
Global Combat Support.—MG Duane Jones, Pentagon, room 1E718A, 697–8860.
Transformation.—Grover L. Dunn, Pentagon, room 5E768, 697–6559.
Logistics.—MG Robert McMahon, Pentagon, room 4E278, 695–4900.
Resources Intregation.—BG Art Cameron, Pentagon, room 4A272, 697–2822.
The Civil Engineer.—MG Del Eulberg, Pentagon, room 4C1057, 693–4301.
Security Forces.—BG Mary Hertog, Pentagon, room 5E1040, 693–5401.

DEPUTY CHIEF OF STAFF FOR MANPOWER AND PERSONNEL

Pentagon, 1040 Air Force, Room 4D765, 20330

Deputy Chief of Staff.—LTG Richard Y. Newton III (703) 697–6088.
Assistant Deputy.—Timothy Beyland.
Chief, Personnel Issues Team.—LTC Shawna O'Brien, room 4D765, 695–4212.
Director of:
Air Force General Officer Managemet.—COL Thomas Sharpy, room 4D1054, 697–1181.
Force Development.—Joseph McDade, room 4D950, 695–2144.
Executive Services.—CAPT Phillip Blevins, room 4D765, 697–1125.
Force Management Policy.—BG Darrell Jones, room 4D950A, 695–6770.
Manpower, Organization, and Resources.—BG Sharon Dunber, room 5A328, 692–1601.
Plans and Integration.— Mark Doboga, room 4D1054A, 697–5222.

DEPUTY CHIEF OF STAFF FOR OPERATIONS, PLANS AND REQUIREMENTS

Pentagon, 1630 Air Force, Room 4E1024, 20330

Deputy Chief of Staff.—Lt. Gen. Daniel J. Darnell (703) 697–9991.

Assistant Deputy.—Maj. Gen. Richard E. Webber, 697–9881.
Mobility Assistant.—Brig. Gen. Michael N. Wilson, 697–3087.
Director of:
Operations.—Maj. Gen. Mark Gibson, room 5D756, 695–9067.
Operational Capability Requirements.—Maj. Gen. Stephen Mueller, room 5C889A / 5D756, 695–3018.
Operational Planning, Policy and Strategy.—Maj. Gen. William Rew, room 5D756, 695–9016.
Resource Integration.—Mark Budgeon, room 5E873.

DEPUTY CHIEF OF STAFF FOR STRATEGIC PLANS AND PROGRAMS

Pentagon, 1070 Air Force, Room 4E124, 20330–1070

Deputy Chief of Staff.—LTG Raymond Johns, Jr. (703) 697–9472.
Assistant Deputy Chief of Staff.—Barbara Westgate.
Military Assistant Deputy Chief of Staff.—MG Stanley E. Clarke.
Directorate of Programs.—BG Robert Worley, room 5B279, 697–2038.
Director for Strategic Planning.—BG Mark Ramsay, room 5D1050, 697–3117.

DIRECTORATE OF STUDIES AND ANALYSIS, ASSESSMENTS AND LESSONS LEARNED

Pentagon, 1570 Air Force, 20330

1777 N. Kent Street, 6th and 7th Floors, Rosslyn, VA 22209

Director.—Dr. Jacqueline R. Henningsen, Ph.D., SES (703) 588–6995.
Deputy Director.—Brig. Gen. Earl D. Matthews.
Senior Advisor.—Vacant.
Technical Director.—Vacant.
Chief Analyst.—Col. Cynthia A. Brown.

ADMINISTRATIVE ASSISTANT TO THE SECRETARY

Pentagon, 1720 Air Force, 20330

2221 South Clark Street, Arlington, VA 22202 (CP6)

229 Brookley Avenue, Bolling AFB, Washington, DC 20032 (BAFB1)

3 Brookley Avenue, Box 94, Bolling AFB, Washington, DC 20032 (BAFB2)

Administrative Assistant.—William A. Davidson, Pentagon, room 4E824 (703) 695–9492.
Deputy Administrative Assistant.—Robert E. Corsi, Jr., 695–9492.
Senior Executive Assistant.—Lt. Col. Wendy Wasik, 695–9492.
Executive Assistant.—Maj. Tara Valentine, 695–9492.
Executive Administrator.—Nancy Beeson.
General Manager, Executive Dining Facility.—Alfonso Sisneros, room 4D869, 697–1112.
Director of:
Art Program Office.—Russell Kirk, room 5E271, 697–2858.
Central Adjudication Facility.—Col. Laura Hickman, BAFB1 (202) 767–9236.
Declassification Office.—Linda Smith, CP6, Suite 600, 604–4665.
Departmental Publishing Office.—Jessica Spencer-Gallucci, BAFB2 (202) 404–2380.
Facilities Support Division.—Larry Bickel, room 5D855, 697–8222.
Human Resources and Manpower Division.—Marilynn Jung, room 4D828, 697–5895.
Policy, Plans and Resources Division.—Carolyn Lunsford, room 5D883, 695–4007.
Security, Counterintelligence and Special Programs Oversight Division.—Scott Deacon, room MD779, 693–2013.
Information Protection Division.—Daniel McGarvey, room MC832, 693–0614.

AUDITOR GENERAL

Pentagon, 1120 Air Force, 20330

4170 Hebble Creek Road, Building 280, Room 1, Wright-Patterson AFB, OH 45433 (WPAFB)

5023 Fourth Street, March ARB, CA 95218 (MARB)

1101 Wilson Boulevard, Suite 1010, Arlington, VA 22201 (Rosslyn)

2509 Kennedy Circle, Building 125, Brooks City-Base, TX 78235

Auditor General.—Theodore J. Williams, room 4D836 (703) 614–5626.
Deputy Auditor General and Director of Operations.—Cathy B. Novel, room 4D836 (703) 614–5626.

AIR FORCE AUDIT AGENCY

Assistant Deputy Auditor General.—Michael V. Barbino, Rosslyn (703) 696–7764.
Assistant Auditor General for—
Acquisition and Logistics Audits.—Sharon Puschmann, WPAFB (937) 257–7473.
Financial and Systems Audits.—Judith Simon, MAFB (951) 655–7011.
Support and Personnel Audits.—James W. Salter, Jr., Brooks City-Base (210) 536–1999.

CHIEF OF CHAPLAINS

Bolling AFB, 112 Luke Avenue, Building 5683, Washington, DC 20032

Chief.—Chaplain (Maj. Gen.) Cecil R. Richardson, room 316 (202) 767–1476.
Deputy Chief.—Chaplain (Brig. Gen.) David H. Cyr, room 313, 767–4599.

CHIEF OF SAFETY

Pentagon, 1400 Air Force, Room 4C855, 20330–1400

Chief of Safety/Commander, Air Force Safety Center.—Maj. Gen. Frederick Roggero, (703) 693–7281.
Executive.—Maj. Nikki Nader, 614–3389.
Director, Safety Issues Division.—Col. ET Thompson, 693–3333.

GENERAL COUNSEL

Pentagon, 1740 Air Force, 20330

General Counsel.—Robert T. Maguire (acting), (703) 697–0941.
Principal Deputy.—Vacant.
Military Assistant.—Col. Louis J. Cherry, 697–8418.
Deputy General Counsel for—
Acquisition.—James Hughes, room 5B914, 697–3900.
Contractor Responsibility.—Steven A. Shaw, Ballston, 588–0057.
Dispute Resolution.—Richard Deavel, Rosslyn, 599–2211.
Fiscal, Ethics and Administrative Law.—Cheri Cannon, room 4C934, 693–9291.
International Affairs.—Michael W. Zehner, room 4C756, 697–5196.
National Security and Military Affairs.—W. Kipling Atlee, room 4C948, 695–5663.

AIR FORCE HISTORIAN

1190 Air Force Pentagon, Room 5E823, Washington, DC 20330–1190

Director.—C.R. ''Dick'' Anderegg (703) 697–5600.
Executive Officer.—Maj. Michael Beavin, 697–2289.
Director, Air Force Historical Research Agency, Maxwell AFB, AL.—Dr. Charles O'Connell (334) 953–5342.

INSPECTOR GENERAL

Pentagon, 1140 Air Force, Room 4E1040, 20330–1140

Inspector General.—Lt. Gen. Ronald F. Sams (703) 697–6733.

Deputy Inspector General.—Maj. Gen. Garry C. Dean, 697–4351.
Executive Officer.—Maj. Ryan Sweeney, 697–4787.
Advisor for—
Air National Guard Matters.—Col. Alan Buck, room 5B937, 693–3578.
Reserve Matters.—Col. Ray Joinson, room 5B937, 697–0339.
Director of:
Complaints Resolution Directorate.—Col. John Dowless, room 110, 588–1558.
Inspections.—Vacant, room 110, 588–1531.
Special Investigations.—Col. Kevin Jacobsen, room 5B919, 697–0411.
Senior Officials Inquiries.—Col. Robert McCormick, room 5B937, 693–3579.

JUDGE ADVOCATE GENERAL

Pentagon, 1420 Air Force, 20330

1501 Wilson Boulevard, Suite 810, Arlington, VA 22209 (Rosslyn)

112 Luke Avenue, Suite 343, Bolling AFB, Washington, DC 20032 (BAFB)

Judge Advocate General.—Lt. Gen. Jack L. Rives (703) 614–5732.
Director for—
Civil Law and Litigation.—Col. Peter Seebeck, Rosslyn, room 810, 696–9040.
USAF Judiciary.—Col. Scott Martin, BAFB, room 336 (202) 767–1535.
General Law.—Conrad Von Wald, room 5E279, 614–4075.
International Law.—Col. Mary Perry, room 5C269, 695–9631.

LEGAL OPERATIONS

Commander, Air Force Legal Operations Agency.—Brig. Gen. Richard C. Harding, BAFB, room 336 (202) 404–8758.

LEGAL SERVICES

Commander, Air Force Legal Services Agency.—COL Evan Haberman, BAFB, room 336 (202) 404–8758.

DIRECTORATE OF LEGISLATIVE LIAISON

Pentagon, 1160 Air Force, 20330

Rayburn House Office Building, Room B–322, 20515 (RHOB)

Russell Senate Office Building, Room SR–182, 20510 (RSOB)

Director.—Maj. Gen. Herbert Carlisle, room 4E812 (703) 697–8153.
Deputy Director.—Brig. Gen. Scott Hanson, 697–2650.
Mobilization Assistant to the Director.—Col. Michael LoGrande, 695–2650.
Executive Officer to the Director.—Maj. Catherine Logan, 697–4142.
Executive Officer to the Deputy Director.—Vacant, 697–2650.
Chief of:
Air Operations.—Tom Shubert, room 4B654, 697–1500.
Congressional Inquiries.—Col. Hal Hoxie, room 4B654, 697–3783.
Directors Action Group and Research.—Daniel Sitterly, room 4C689, 695–0182.
House Liaison Office.—Col. Michael Fleck, RHOB (202) 685–4531.
Programs and Legislation.—Col. Tyrone Woodyard, room 4C689, 697–7950.
Senate Liaison Office.—Col. John Dolan, RSOB (202) 685–2573.
Weapons Systems.—Col. Thomas Lawhead, room 4B689, 697–3376.

NATIONAL GUARD BUREAU

1411 Jefferson Davis Highway, Arlington, VA 22202

Chief.—GEN Craig R. McKinley, Pentagon, room 2A726 (703) 614–3087.
Legislative Liaison.—BG James D. Demeritt, JP–1, Crystal City, Suite P400, 607–2770.
Director for—
Air National Guard.—LTG Harry M. Wyatt, Pentagon, room 4C943, 614–8033.

Army National Guard.—MG Raymond Carpenter (acting), Readiness Center, Arlington, VA, 607–7002.
Joint Staff.—MG Peter M. Aylward, JP–1, Crystal City, Suite 12000, 607–2204.

OFFICE OF PUBLIC AFFAIRS

Director.—Col. Les Kodlick (703) 967–6061.
Executive Officer.—Maj. Catie Hague.
Chief of:
Current Operations.—Marcella Adams, room 4C712, 695–0640.
Engagement.—Wendy Varhegyi, 695–9664.
Strategy and Assessment.—Col. Darrell Adams.
Requirements and Development.—Sherry Medders, room 4A120, 697–6701.

AIR FORCE RESERVE

Pentagon, 1150 Air Force, Room 4D762, 20330

Chief, Air Force Reserve/Commander, Air Force Reserve Command.—Lt. Gen. Charles E. Stenner, Jr. (703) 695–9225.
Deputy to Chief of Air Force Reserve.—Brig. Gen. Howard N. Thompson, 614–7307.
Deputy Executive Officer.—Lt. Col. Dennis Burgart, 695–5528.
Executive NCO.—TSgt Raquel Ayuso, 614–7307.

SCIENTIFIC ADVISORY BOARD

1602 California Drive, Suite 251, Andrews AFB, MD 20762

Chair.—John Betz (301) 981–9985.
Vice Chair.—Ann Karagozian.
Military Director.—Lt. Gen. Mark Shackelford (Pentagon 4E962), (703) 695–7311.
Executive Director.—Lt. Col. David Lucia.
Military Assistants: Lt. Col. Ed Ryan, 981–7156; Lt. Col. Rob Ward, 981–7149.
Administration.—TSgt Cindy Winterton, 981–7225.

AIR FORCE SCIENTIST

Pentagon, 1075 Air Force, Room 4E288, 20330

Chief Scientist.—Dr. Werner Dahm (703) 697–7842.
Military Assistant.—Col. Eric Silkowkski.

OFFICE OF SMALL BUSINESS PROGRAMS

Pentagon, 1060 Air Force, 20330–1060

Director.—Ronald A. Poussard (703) 696–1103.

SURGEON GENERAL

Pentagon, 1780 Air Force, Room 4C882, 20330–1780

Bolling AFB, 110 Luke Avenue, Building 5681, Suite 400, Washington, DC 20332–7050

Surgeon General.—Lt. Gen. James G. Roudebush (703) 692–6800.
Executive Officer.—Col. Mike Miller (703) 692–6990.
Deputy Surgeon General.—Maj. Gen. C. Bruce Green (202) 767–4766.
Executive Officer.—Lt. Col. Deb Miesle (202) 767–4759.
Director for—
Congressional and Public Affairs.—Donna Tinsley (202) 767–4774.
Financial Management.—Col. Joanne McPherson (703) 681–6045.
Medical Operations.—Maj. Gen. Thomas Loftus (202) 767–0020.
Force Development.—Maj. Gen. Kimberly Siniscalchi (202) 767–4498.
Strategic Plans and Programs.—Brig. Gen. Patricia Lewis (703) 588–0009.
Modernization.—Brig. Gen. Theresa Casey (703) 681–7055.

Corps Directors for—
Medical.—Col. Arnyce Pock (202) 767–4492.
Biomedical Sciences.—Col. Bonnie Johnson (202) 767–4499.
Nursing.—Col. Donnalee Sykes (202) 767–4462.
Medical Services.—Col. Denise Lew (202) 767–4432.
Dental Corps.—Col. Grant Hartup (202) 767–4385.

DIRECTORATE OF TEST AND EVALUATION

Pentagon, 1650 Air Force, Room 5E839, 20330

Director.—John Manclark (703) 697–4774.
Deputy Director.—David Hamilton.
Executive Officer.—Lt. Col. John M. Brandt, Jr., 697–5067.

AIR FORCE BOARD FOR CORRECTION OF MILITARY RECORDS (AFBCMR)

Executive Director.—Al Walker, AAFB, Building 1535 (240) 857–3502.
Deputy Executive Director.—Phillip Horton.
Chief Examiners: Greg Johnson, O.B. Taylor.
NCOIC, AFBCMR.—MSgt Sylvia Brooks, 857–3502.

AIR FORCE CIVILIAN APPELLATE REVIEW OFFICE

Director.—Rita S. Looney, AAFB, Building 1535 (240) 857–3167.
Assistant Director.—Sharon E. Hanlon, 857–3361.

AIR FORCE PERSONNEL COUNCIL

Director.—Col. Venetia Brown, AAFB Building 1535 (240) 857–3138.
Senior Legal Advisor.—Col. Ferah Ozbek, 857–3535.
Senior Medical Advisor.—Col. August Hein, 857–5774.
Chief, Air Force Discharge Review Board.—Wanda Langley, 857–3504.
Chief, Awards/Decoration/Air Force Reserve Advisor.—Col. Beth Mann, 857–5342.
Executive Secretary/Attorney Advisor on Clemency/Parole Board.—James D. Johnston, 857–5329.
Executive Secretary, DOD Civilian/Military Service Review Board.—James D. Johnston, 857–5329.

ARMY AND AIR FORCE EXCHANGE SERVICE

3911 S. Walton Walker Boulevard, Dallas, TX 75236, phone 1–800–527–6790

Commander.—MG Keith L. Thurgood, USA.
Chief Operating Officer.—Michael P. Howard.

WASHINGTON OFFICE/OFFICE OF THE BOARD OF DIRECTORS

2511 Jefferson Davis Highway, Suite 11600

Arlington, VA 22202–3922, phone (703) 604–7523, DSN 664–7523

Director/Executive Secretary.—Gregg Cox.
Deputy Director/Executive Assistant.—Rick Struss.

DEPARTMENT OF THE ARMY

The Pentagon, Washington, DC 20310, phone (703) 695–2442

OFFICE OF THE SECRETARY

Pentagon, Room 3E700, 20310–0101, phone (703) 695–1717, fax 697–8036

Secretary of the Army.—John M. McHugh.
Executive Officer.—COL Laura Potter, 695–1717.

OFFICE OF THE UNDER SECRETARY

Pentagon, Room 3E700, 20310–0102, phone (703) 695–4311

Under Secretary of the Army.—Vacant.
Executive Officer.—COL Ferdinand Irizarry, 695–4312.

CHIEF OF STAFF

Pentagon, Room 3E672, 20310–0200, phone (703) 697–0900

Chief of Staff.—GEN George W. Casey, Jr.
Vice Chief of Staff—GEN Peter W. Chiarelli, 695–4371.
Director, CSA's Staff Group.—COL Guy Beougher, room 3D654, 693–8371.
Director of Army Staff.—LTG David H. Huntoon, Jr., room 3E663, 695–3542.
Sergeant Major.—SMA Kenneth O. Preston, room 3E677, 695–2150.
Director, Office of:
Army Protocol.—Linda Jacobs, room 3A532, 697–0692.
Executive Communications and Control.—COL Thea Harvell, room 3D664, 695–7552.
Program Analysis and Evaluation.—MG William T. Grisoli, room 3E362, 695–4617.
Test and Evaluation Office.—James C. Cooke, Crystal City, 602–3508.

DEPUTY UNDER SECRETARY OF THE ARMY

101 Army Pentagon, Room 3E650, 20310–0001, phone (703) 697–5075

Deputy Under Secretary.—Thomas E. Kelly III.
Executive Officer.—COL J.B. Burton, 697–5075.
Administrative Assistant.—SSG Nikki King, 695–4392.
Deputy.—Jeffrey White.
Executive Officer.—Mark Von Heeringen.
Executive Assistant.—Carol Hopper.

ASSISTANT SECRETARY FOR ACQUISITION, LOGISTICS AND TECHNOLOGY

103 Army Pentagon, Room 2E532, 20310–0103, phone (703) 693–6154

Assistant Secretary.—Dean G. Popps (acting).
Confidential Assistant.—Vacant.
Chief of Staff.—COL Jonathan Maddux, 695–5749.
Executive Officer.—MAJ Robert M. Collins, 695–6742.
Military Deputy.—LTG N. Ross Thompson, 697–0356.
Secretary to the Military Deputy.—Tracey Beaulieu, 693–3927.
Executive Officer to the Military Deputy.—LTC Torry Brennan, 697–0356.
DASA Acquisition and Systems Management.—BG Mark Brown, 695–3115.
DASA Defense Export and Cooperation.—Keith Webster, 588–8070.

DASA Plans, Programs and Resources.—Tom Mullins, 697–0387.
DASA Policy and Logistics.—Wimpy Pybus, 697–5050.
DASA Procurement.—Edward Harrington, 695–2488.
DASA Science and Technology.—Dr. Thomas H. Killion, 692–1830.
DASA Strategic Communications and Business Transformation.—Mark Rocke, 683–7050.

ASSISTANT SECRETARY FOR CIVIL WORKS

Pentagon, Room 3E446, 20310–0108, phone (703) 697–8986, fax 697–7401

Assistant Secretary.—Hon. John Paul Woodley, Jr.
Executive Officer.—COL Michael F. Pfenning, 697–9809.
Military Assistant.—LTC John S. Hurley, 695–0482.
Deputy Assistant Secretary for—
Management and Budget.—Claudia L. Tornblom, 695–1376.
Policy, Planning and Review.—Douglas Lamont (202) 761–0016.
Policy and Legislation.—Terrence C. Salt, 695–1370.

ASSISTANT SECRETARY FOR FINANCIAL MANAGEMENT AND COMPTROLLER

109 Army Pentagon, Room 3E324, 20310–0109, phone (703) 614–4337

Assistant Secretary.—Vacant.
Military Deputy for Budget.—LTG Edgar E. Stanton, room 3E324, 614–4034.
Military Assistant.—LTC Jill F. Cahill, room 3E324, 614–5548.
Executive Officer.—COL Mark A. McAlister, room 3E324, 614–4292.
Executive Assistant.—Roderick M. Johnson, room 3E324, 614–4337.
Deputy Assistant Secretary for—
Army Budget.—William H. Campbell, room 3E336, 614–1595.
Cost and Economics.—Steve Bagby, room 3E352, 692–1722.
Financial Operations.—John Argodale, room 3A320, 692–7294.

ASSISTANT SECRETARY FOR INSTALLATIONS AND ENVIRONMENT

Pentagon, Room 3E464, 20310–0110, phone (703) 692–9800

Assistant Secretary.—Vacant.
Principal Deputy Assistant Secretary.—Vacant, 692–9802.
Executive Officer.—COL Carl Coffman, 692–9804.
Deputy Assistant Secretary for—
Energy and Partnerships.—Vacant, room 3D453, 692–9890.
Environment, Safety and Occupational Health.—Addison "Tad" Davis, room 3D453, 697–1913.
Installations and Housing.—Joseph F. Calcara, room 3E475, 697–8161.
Strategic Infrastructure.—L. Jerry Hansen, room 3D453, 692–9817.

ASSISTANT SECRETARY FOR MANPOWER AND RESERVE AFFAIRS

Pentagon, Room 2E460, 20310–0111, phone (703) 697–9253

Assistant Secretary.—Thomas R. Lamont.
Principal Deputy Assistant Secretary.—Vacant, room 2E460.
Executive Officer.—LTC John Williams, 697–9253.
Deputy Assistant Secretary for—
EEO and Civil Rights.—Rock Dillard (acting), Crystal City, 604–0582.
Force Management, Manpower/Resources.—Jay Aronowitz (acting), room 2E485, 614–8143.
Medical and Health Affairs.—Vacant, 2E460, 695–2455.
Personnel Oversight.—Lynn Heirakuji, 2E469, 697–2044.
Recruiting and Retention.—Tony Stamilio (acting), 2E482, 697–2631.
Reserve Affairs.—James Doty (acting), 2D484, 614–1648.
Review Boards.—Catherine Mitrano, Crystal City, 607–1438.

ASSISTANT CHIEF OF STAFF FOR INSTALLATION MANAGEMENT

Pentagon, Room 3E474, 20310–0600, phone (703) 693–3233, fax 693–3507

Assistant Chief of Staff.—LTG Robert Wilson.
Deputy Assistant.—Dr. Craig College.

ADMINISTRATIVE ASSISTANT

Pentagon, Room 3E733, 20310–0105, phone (703) 695–2442, fax 697–6194

Administrative Assistant.—Joyce E. Morrow.
Deputy Administrative Assistant.—Larry Stubblefield, Taylor Building, room 13116, 602–5541.
Executive Officer.—Vacant, Pentagon, room 3E733, 695–7444.
Chief, Resource Operations Center.—Gem A. Loranger, Taylor Building, room 13094, 602–7181.
Executive Director for—
U.S. Army Information Technology Agency.—Larry Stubblefield (acting), Taylor Building, room 13116, 602–5541.
U.S. Army Resources and Programs Agency.—Larry Stubblefield, Taylor Building, room 13116, 602–5541 / 6856.
Army Headquarters Services.—Larry Stubblefield, Taylor Building, room 13116, 602–5541.
Army Information Management Support Center.—Gabriele Daniel, Taylor Building, room 9202, 602–2645.
Army Multimedia and Visual Information.—Joseph Hickey (acting), Pentagon, room MG652, 697–1798.
Army Publishing.—Paul Beardsley, Hoffman 1, room 1010, 325–6801.
Consolidated Customer Service Center.—Deb Bouslog, 1671 Nelson Street, Ft. Detrick, MD (301) 619–0417.
Data Center Services (Pentagon).—Gerald Reed, Pentagon, room BF849D, 692–0880.
Defense Telecommunications Services (Washington).—John Maditz, Taylor Building, room 10016, 602–1299.
Equal Employment Opportunity.—Beatrice Bernfeld, Taylor Building, room 8200, 602–7213.
Human Resources Management.—Karen Perkins, Taylor Building, room 8016, 602–2220.
Deputy Executive Director for Enterprise Operations.—Kay Sclater, 1777 North Kent Street, room 4100, 588–8730.
Enterprise Security Service (Pentagon).—Darren King, 1777 North Kent Street, room 8200, 588–8050.
Logistics (Washington).—Fernando Ortiz, Taylor Building, room 10122, 602–7856.
Network Infrastructure Services and Operations (Pentagon).—Virginia Arreguin, Pentagon, room ME882, 614–5761.
Pentagon Chaplain.—COL Daniel Minjares, Pentagon, room 1E443, 692–9377.
Real Estate and Facilities.—Lacy Saunders, Taylor Building, room 13038, 602–6157.
Records Management and Declassification Agency.—Steve Raho, 7701 Telegraph Road, room 102, 428–6462.
Security and Safety.—David Beltz, Taylor Building, room 3056, 602–0306.
Support Services (Washington).—I. Washburn, Pentagon, room BF666A, 692–4857.
Telecommunications Center (Pentagon).—George Krenik, Pentagon, room 2C654, 695–1874.
The Institute of Heraldry.—Charles Mugno, Ft. Belvoir, Building 1466, room S–103, 806–4969.
Executive Transportation.—Andrew Hare, Taylor Building, room 8064, 602–2678.

ARMY RESERVE

Pentagon, Room 2B548, 20310–2400, phone (703) 697–1784

Chief.—LTG Jack C. Stultz.
Deputy Chief.—BG Julia Kraus, 697–1260.
Chief of Staff.—COL Charles Phillips (acting).

AUDITOR GENERAL

3101 Park Center Drive, Alexandria, VA 22302–1596

phone (703) 681–9809, fax 681–4602

Auditor General.—Patrick J. Fitzgerald.

Principal Deputy Auditor General.—Benjamin J. Piccolo, 681–9819.
Executive Officer.—LTC Brenda L. Hickey.
Chief of Staff.—Jackson W. Muller.
General Counsel.—William H. Guinan.
Deputy Auditor General for—
Acquisition and Logistics Audits.—Joseph P. Mizzoni, 681–9583.
Forces and Financial Audits.—Anita F. Bales, 681–9585.
Policy and Operations Management.—Monique Y. Ferrell (acting), 681–9820.

CHIEF INFORMATION OFFICER / G–6

Pentagon, Room 3E608, 20310–0107, phone (703) 695–4366, fax 695–3091

Chief Information Officer.—LTG Jeffrey A. Sorenson.
Deputy Chief Information Officer.—Michael Krieger, 695–6604.
Executive Officer.—COL Nathaniel Smith, 697–5503.
Director of:
Architecture, Operations, Network and Space.—MG Randolph Strong, room 1E148, 602–3842.
Governance, Acquisition and Chief Knowledge Office.—Robert Kazimer, room 7178, Taylor Building, Crystal City, VA, 602–9316.
Chief Integration Office.—BG Stuart M. Dyer, Taylor Building, room 7154, Crystal City, VA, 602–8002.
Chief of Cyber Operations.—BG Steven Smith, room 3E619, 693–1327.
Commander, NETCOM.—MG Susan Lawrence, Ft. Huachuca, AZ (502) 538–6161.

CHIEF OF CHAPLAINS

Pentagon, Room 2A514A, 20310–2700, phone (703) 695–1133, fax 695–9834

Chief of Chaplain.—Chaplain (MG) Douglas L. Carver.
Deputy Chief of Chaplains.—Chaplain (BG) Donald L. Rutherford, 695–1135.

CHIEF OF ENGINEERS

GAO Building, 441 G Street, NW., 20314, phone (202) 761–0001
fax 761–4463

Chief of Engineers/Commanding General for U.S. Army Corps of Engineers.—LTG Robert L. Van Antwerp.
Deputy Commander.—MG Don T. Riley, 761–0002.
Deputy Commanding General for Civil and Emergency Operations.—MG Merdith ''Bo'' Temple, 761–0099.
Director of Civil Works.— Steve Stockton, 761–0100.
Deputy Commanding General for Military and International Operations.—MG Jeffrey J. Dorko, 761–0379.
Director of Military Programs.—J. Joseph Tyler, 761–0382.
Chief of Staff.—COL Stephen L. Hill, 761–0761.

GENERAL COUNSEL

Pentagon, Room 2E724, 20310–0104, phone (703) 693–9235, fax 693–9254

General Counsel.—Vacant.
Principal Deputy General Counsel.—Levator Norsworthy, Jr. (acting).
Executive Officer/Special Counsel.—COL John Kent.
Deputy General Counsel for—
Acquisition.—Levator Norsworthy, Jr., room 3C546, 697–5120.
Civil Works and Environment.—Craig R. Schmauder, room 3D546, 695–3024.
Ethics and Fiscal Law.—Brent Green, room 3C546, 695–5105.
Operations and Personnel.—Stephanie Barna, room 3C546, 695–0562.

INSPECTOR GENERAL

Pentagon, Room 5D561, 20310–1700, phone (703) 695–1500, fax 614–5628

Inspector General.—LTG R. Steven Whitcomb.

Deputy Inspector General.—MG William McCoy.
Executive Officer.—COL Robert Zebrowski, 695–1502.

INTELLIGENCE / G–2

Pentagon, Room 2E408, 20310–1000, phone (703) 695–3033

Deputy Chief of Staff.—LTG Richard Zahner.
Executive Officer.—COL Jim Lee.
Assistant Deputy Chiefs: James Faust, 697–4644; MG Greg Schumacher, 695–3929.
Director, Office of:
Counterintelligence / HUMINT.—Gerry Turnbow, 695–2374.
Foreign Liaison.—COL Scott Denney, 692–1467.
Foreign Intelligence.—COL Paul Seitz, 695–2186.
Information Management.—Lynn Schnurr, 693–7019.
Operations and Plans.—COL Jim Stockmoe, 695–1623.
Resource Integration.—Roxanne Hammond, 695–1233.

THE JUDGE ADVOCATE GENERAL

Pentagon, Room 2B514, 20310–2200, phone (703) 697–5151, fax 693–0600

The Judge Advocate General.—LTG Scott C. Black.
Deputy Judge Advocate General.—MG Daniel V. Wright, 693–5112.
Assistant Judge Advocate General for Military Law and Operations.—BG Malinda E. Dunn, Rosslyn, VA, 588–6734.
Commander, United States Army Legal Services Agency.—BG Clyde J. Tate II, Ballston, VA, 588–6269.
Commander / Commandant, USA The Judge Advocate General's Legal Center and School.—BG Dana K. Chipman, Charlottesville, VA (434) 971–3301.

LEGISLATIVE LIAISON

Pentagon, Room 1E416, 20310–1600, phone (703) 697–6767, fax 614–7599

Chief.—MG Bernard S. Champoux.
Deputy Chief.—BG Ben Hodges, 695–1235.
Principal Deputy.—Joseph Guzowski, 695–1374.
Special Assistant for Legislative Affairs for Intelligence.—Robert J. Winchester, 695–3918.
Executive Officer.—COL Wayne A. Green, room 1E428, 695–3524.
Chief of:
Congressional Activities Division.—Joe Eule, room 1D437, 697–3206.
Congressional Inquiry.—Harry Williams, room 1E423, 697–8381.
House Liaison Division.—COL Chris Hughes, room B325, Rayburn House Office Building, Washington, DC (202) 225–6818.
Investigations and Legislative Division.—COL Holly Cook, room 1E433, 697–0276.
Programs Division.—COL T.C. Williams, room 1E385, 693–8766.
Senate Liaison Division.—COL Marty Schweitzer, room SR183, Senate Russell Office Building, Washington, DC (202) 224–2881.
Support Operations Division.—Debra Billington, room 1E423, 693–9910.

LIAISON OFFICES

Pentagon, Room 2A474, 20310–2200

U.S. Army, Europe (USAREUR): David Dull, Dr. Bryan T. van Sweringen, SFC Ralf S. Vogt (703) 692–6886, fax 614–9714.
U.S. Army Accessions Command.—LTG Benjamin C. Freakley (757) 788–4859.
U.S. Army Forces Command (FORSCOM) / U.S. Army Training and Doctrine Command (TRADOC): LTC Wayne G. Cherry, Jr., Laverne De Sett, SSG Eric Gaulke, Celeste Johnson, SSG Justin Suszek, (703) 697–2552 / 2588, fax 697–5725.
U.S. Army, Pacific (USARPAC).—Robert Ralston (703) 693–4032, fax 693–4036.
U.S. Forces Korea (USFK): Cathy Abell, Harrison J. Parker III, Ronald R. Rollison, Sharon L. Smith (703) 693–4038, fax 695–4576.

LOGISTICS / G–4

Pentagon, Room 1E394, 20310–0500, phone (703) 695–4102, fax 697–3518

Deputy Chief of Staff.—LTG Mitchell H. Stevenson.
Assistant Deputies Chief of Staff.—MG Vincent E. Boles, Sarah H. Finnicum.
Director of:
Corporate Information Office.—Carlos D. Morrison.
Force Projection and Distribution.— John M. Welsh (acting), room 1E384.
Logistics Integration Agency.—Vicky S. Ramdass.
Maintenance.—Christopher J. Lowman.
Operations and Logistics Readiness.—BG Steven M. Anderson, room 1E367.
Resource Integration.—Robert J. Turzak.
Strategy and Integration.—BG Phillip J. Thorpe.
Supply.—Michael W. Brown.

NATIONAL GUARD BUREAU

1636 Defense Pentagon, Washington, DC 20301–1636
phone (703) 614–3087, fax 614–0274

Chief.—GEN Craig R. McKinley.
Director, Joint Staff.—MG Peter Aylward, 607–2204.
Director, Air National Guard.—Lt. Gen. Harry M. Wyatt III, 604–8033.

OPERATIONS AND PLANS / G–3/5/7

Pentagon, Room 2E670, 20310–0400, phone (703) 695–2904

Deputy Chief of Staff.—LTG James D. Thurman.
Assistant Deputy Chiefs of Staff: Mark R. Lewis, 692–7883; MG Robert P. Lennox, 697–5180.

PERSONNEL / G–1

Pentagon, Room 2E446, 20310–0300, phone (703) 697–8060

Deputy Chief of Staff.—LTG Michael D. Rochelle.
Assistant Deputy Chief of Staff.—Karl Schneider, 692–1585.
Assistant Deputy Chief of Staff for Mobilization and Reserve Affairs.—MG Jeffrey L. Arnold, room 1C449, 695–7693.
Director, Office of:
Army Research Institute.—Dr. Michelle Sams, 602–7766.
Civilian Personnel.—Dr. Susan L. Duncan, room 2C453, 695–5701.
Human Resources.—MG John Hawkins, room 2C453, 695–5418.
MANPRINT.—Dr. Michael Drillings, room 2C485, 695–6761.
Military Personnel Management.—BG Gina Farrisee, room 1D429, 695–5871.
Plans, Resources and Operations.—Roy Wallace, room 2B453, 697–5263.

PUBLIC AFFAIRS

Pentagon, Room 1E484, 20310–1500, phone (703) 695–5135, fax 693–8362

Chief.—MG Kevin Bergner.
Deputy Chief.—BG Jeffrey Phillips.
Principal Deputy Chief.—Stephanie Hoehne.
Chief of Staff.—COL James L. Miller.
Executive Officer.—COL Henry Huntley.
Chief of:
Community Relations and Outreach Division.—COL Rivers Johnson.
Media Relations Division.—COL Cathy Abbott.
Plans.—COL Mike Whetston.
Resource Management Division.—Tina Kitts.

SMALL BUSINESS PROGRAMS

Pentagon, Room 3B514, 20310–0106, phone (703) 697–2868, fax 693–3898

Director.—Tracey L. Pinson.

Deputy Director.—Paul L. Gardner.

SURGEON GENERAL

Skyline Place 6, Suite 672, 5109 Leesburg Pike, Falls Church, VA 22041–3258

phone (703) 681–3000, fax 681–3167

Surgeon General.—LTG Eric B. Schoomaker.
Deputy Surgeon General.—MG David A. Rubenstein, 681–3002.

MAJOR ARMY COMMANDS

U.S. ARMY FORCES COMMAND (FORSCOM)

Fort McPherson, GA 30330–1062, phone (404) 464–5054

Commanding General.—GEN Charles C. Campbell.
Executive Officer.—COL Henry Larsen.
Deputy Commanding General for—
Army National Guard.—MG Ronald Chastain, 464–7596.
Chief of Staff.—LTG Joseph F. Peterson, 464–5053.
U.S. Army Reserve.—LTG Jack C. Stultz, Jr., 464–8002.
Command Sergeant Major.—CSM Dennis M. Carey, 464–5055.
Secretary of the General Staff.—COL Darlene S. Freeman, 464–6051.
Operations Center.—COL William Hardy (800) 974–8480.
Liaison Office (Washington, DC).—LTC Wayne Cherry (703) 697–2591.

U.S. ARMY MATERIEL COMMAND (AMC)

9301 Chapek Road, Fort Belvoir, VA 22060–5527

phone (703) 806–9625

Commanding General.—GEN Ann Dunwoody, 806–9626.
Executive Officer.—COL Stephen Lyons, 806–8778.
Deputy Commanding General.—LTG James Pillsbury, 806–9705.
Executive Officer.—COL Brian Lindamood, 806–9701.
Deputy Executive to the Commanding General.—Kathryn Condon, 806–9637.
Executive Officer.—COL Douglas Evans, 806–8100.
Chief of Staff.—COL Dennis Thompson, 806–9709.
Command Sergeant Major.—CSM Jeffrey Mellinger, 806–8257.
Secretary of the General Staff.—MAJ Christine Rice, 806–8116.
Operations Center.—MG Kevin Leonard, 806–9720.
Legislative Liaison.—COL Archie Davis, 806–8120.

U.S. ARMY TRAINING AND DOCTRINE COMMAND (TRADOC)

Fort Monroe, VA 23651–5000

Commanding General.—GEN Martin Dempsey (757) 788–3514.
Executive Officer.—COL Gary Brito, 788–2922.
Deputy Commanding General/Chief of Staff.—LTG David Valcourt, 788–3126.
Executive Officer.—LTC John Machesney, 788–3112.
Assistant Chief of Staff.—COL John Moore, 788–3112.
CG USAAC/DCG (IMT).—LTG Benjamin Freakley, 788–2207.
Executive Officer.—LTC Thomas Kelly, 788–4415.
Command Sergeant Major.—CSM David Bruner, 788–4133.
Secretary of the General Staff.—Fred Batchelor, 788–3563.
Operations Center.—James Lynch, 788–2256.
Liaison Office (Washington, DC).—LTC Wayne Cherry, 697–2588.

DEPARTMENT OF THE NAVY

Pentagon 20350–1000, phone (703) 695–3131

OFFICE OF THE SECRETARY OF THE NAVY

Pentagon, Room 4E686, phone (703) 695–3131

Secretary of the Navy.—BJ Penn (acting).
Confidential Assistant.—Vacant.
Executive Assistant.—CAPT Michael Walley, USN.
Special Assistant.—Michael Griffes.
Administrative Aide.—CDR Gary Mayes, USN, 695–5410.
Personal Aide.—LT Kimberly Thompson, USN.
Special Assistant for Public Affairs.—CAPT Beci Brenton, 697–7491.
Senior Military Assistant.—COL Robert Hedelund, USMC.

OFFICE OF THE UNDER SECRETARY OF THE NAVY

Pentagon, Room 4E720, phone (703) 695–3141

Executive Assistant and Naval Aide.—Vacant.
Military Assistant and Marine Aide.—Vacant.
Administrative Assistant.—YN1 J. Lloyd, USN.
Confidential Assistant.—Vacant.
Assistant for Administration.—E. Roberson, room 4E763, 697–0047.
Facilities and Support Services Division.—W. O'Donnell, room 5A532, 695–2843.
Director of:
Financial Management Division.—D. Nugent, AA/2507, 693–0321.
OPTI.—G. Wyckoff, room AA/4101, 695–6191.
SADBU.—Paulette Widmann (acting) (202) 685–6485.
SHHRO and Special Programs Division.—W. Mann, room AA/2510, 693–0888.
EEO Manager.—D. McCormick, room AA/2052, 693–0202.

GENERAL COUNSEL

Pentagon, Room 4E782
Washington Navy Yard, Building 36, 720 Kennon Street, SE., 20374
phone (703) 614–1994

General Counsel.—Hon. Frank R. Jimenez.
Principal Deputy General Counsel.—Anne Brennan (acting), 614–8733.
Executive Assistant and Special Counsel.—CAPT David F. Hayes, JAGC, USN.
Associate General Counsel for—
Litigation.—T. Ledvina, building 36, 685–6989.
Management.—S. Krasik, room 4E635, 614–8734.
Assistant General Counsel for—
Ethics.—D. LaCroix, room 4D641, 614–7425.
Manpower and Reserve Affairs.—R. Cali, room 4C640, 692–6162.
Research, Development and Acquisition.—Tom Frankfurt, room 4C682, 614–6985.
Military Assistant.—LTC James Duncan, USMC, 692–6164.
Administrative Assistant.—LT Christopher Grocki, USN, room 4E782, 614–4472.

INSPECTOR GENERAL

Washington Navy Yard, 1254 9th Street, SE., Building 172, 20374, phone (202) 433–2000

Inspector General.—VADM Anthony L. Winns.
Deputy Naval Inspector General.—Jill Vines-Loftus.

OFFICE OF INFORMATION

Pentagon, Room 4B463, phone (703) 697–7391

Chief.—RDML Frank Thorp IV.

Deputy Chief.—CAPT Rob Newell.
Executive Assistant.—CDR Dawn Cutler.
Assistant Chief for—
Administration and Resource Management.—William Mason, 692–4747.
Media Operations.—CDR Cappy Surette, 697–5342.
Defense Media Activity (Navy Element).—CAPT Dave Werner (202) 433–5764.
Requirements and Policy.—CAPT Bruce Cole, 695–0911.
Strategic Plans.—CAPT Herman Phillips, 692–4728.

JUDGE ADVOCATE GENERAL

Pentagon, Room 5D834

Washington Navy Yard, 1322 Patterson Avenue, Suite 3000, 20374–5066
phone (703) 614–7420, fax (703) 614–4610

Judge Advocate General.—RADM Bruce E. MacDonald.
Executive Assistant.—CAPT John Hannink.
Deputy Judge Advocate General.—RADM James W. Houck.
Executive Assistant to the Deputy Judge Advocate General.—LCDR Brad Appleman.
Assistant Judge Advocate General for Civil Law.—CAPT Chris Morin, WNY, Building 33, 614–7415, fax 614–9400.
Deputy Assistant Judge Advocate General for—
Administrative Law.—CAPT Chris Morin, 614–7415.
Admiralty.—CDR Robert Hyde (202) 685–5075.
Claims, Investigations and Tort Litigation.—Patricia A. Leonard (202) 685–4600, fax 685–5484.
General Litigation.—Grant Lattin (202) 685–5450, fax 685–5472.
International and Operational Law.—CAPT Patrick J. Neher, 697–9161.
Legal Assistance.—CDR Steve Haycock (202) 685–4642, fax 685–5486.
National Security Litigation and Intelligence Law.—CDR Jane Brill (202) 685–5464, fax 685–5467.
Assistant Judge Advocate General for Military Justice.—COL Peter Collins, USMC, Building 58, 3rd Floor, Washington Navy Yard, 20374–1111 (202) 685–7053, fax 685–7084.
Deputy Assistant Judge Advocate General for Criminal Law.—CDR Christian L. Reismeir, USMC (202) 685–7060, fax 685–7687.
Assistant Judge Advocate General for Operations and Management.—CAPT Mark D. Lawton (202) 685–5190, fax 685–8510.
Deputy Assistant Judge Advocate General for—
Management and Plans.—CAPT Frederick D. Mitchell (202) 685–8372, fax 685–5479.
Military Personnel.—CAPT Robert A. Sanders (202) 685–7254, fax 685–5489.
Reserve and Retired Personnel Programs.—LCDR James T. Mills (202) 685–5216, fax 685–8510.
Special Assistants to the Judge Advocate General—
Command Master Chief.—LNCM Chris Browning (202) 685–5194, fax 685–8510.
Comptroller.—Dennis J. Oppman (202) 685–5274, fax 685–5455.
Inspector General.—Joseph Scranton (202) 685–5192, fax 685–5461.

LEGISLATIVE AFFAIRS

Room 4C549, phone (703) 697–7146, fax 697–1009

Chief.—RADM Michael H. Miller.
Deputy Chief.—CAPT Steve Vahsen.
Executive Assistant.—LCDR Ken Anderson.
Congressional Information and Public Affairs.—CDR Katherine Goode, 695–0395.
Congressional Operations.—Dee Wingfield, 693–5764.
Director for—
House Liaison.—CAPT Joe McClain (202) 225–7808.
Assistant House Liaison.—LCDR Brian Elkowitz (202) 225–3075.
Legislation.—CAPT Jeff Horwitz, 697–2851.
Naval Programs.—Tom Crowley, 693–2919.
Senate Liaison.—CAPT John Nowell (202) 685–6006.
Assistant Senate Liaison.—CDR C.J. Cassidy (202) 685–6007.

ASSISTANT SECRETARY FOR FINANCIAL MANAGEMENT AND COMPTROLLER

Pentagon, Room 4E618, phone (703) 697–2325

Executive Assistant and Naval Aide.—CAPT John E. Roberti.
Military Assistant and Marine Aide.—MAJ Phillip R. Bonincontri, USMC.
Director, Office of:
Budget.—RADM John T. Blake, room 4E348, 697–7105.
Financial Operations.—M. Easton, WNY, 685–6701.

ASSISTANT SECRETARY FOR INSTALLATIONS AND ENVIRONMENT

Pentagon, Room 4E739, phone (703) 693–4530

Assistant Secretary.—Hon. B.J. Penn.
Executive Assistant and Naval Aide.—CAPT Tilghman Payne.
Confidential Assistant.—Jim Howland.
Military Aide.—Vacant.
Assistant General Counsel.—Ronald Borro, 614–1090.
Deputy of:
Environment.—D. Schregardus, 614–5080.
Infrastructure Analysis.—Dennis Biccick, Crystal City, 602–6633.
Installations and Facilities.—Howard Snow, room 4E731, 693–4527.
Safety.—Tom Rollow, 614–5179.

ASSISTANT SECRETARY FOR MANPOWER AND RESERVE AFFAIRS

Pentagon, Room 4E615, phone (703) 697–2180

Assistant Secretary.—Patricia C. Adams (acting), room 4E590, 695–4333.
Executive Assistant and Naval Aide.—CAPT Annie B. Andrews, room 4E590, 695–4537.
Military Assistant and Marine Aide.—COL Robert C. Clements, room 4E590, 697–0975.
Secretary.—Antonio C. Sturgis, room 4E590, 695–4333.
Administrative Officer.—Vacant, 614–8288.
Administrative Chief.—YNC Michael Stokes, room 4E590, 697–2179.
Assistant General Counsel.—Robert Cali, room 4D548, 692–6162.
Deputy Assistant Secretary of:
Civilian Human Resources.—Patricia C. Adams, room 4E590, 695–2633.
Staff Director.—Tia Butler, room 4D548, 571–9032.
Manpower Personnel Policy.—Vacant, 693–7700.
Staff Director.—CAPT Karen Vigneron, room 4D548, 693–0592.
Reserve Affairs.—Vacant, 614–1327.
Staff Director.—CAPT Michael Herman, room 4D548, 695–5302.
Total Force Transformation.—Vacant, 693–7700.
Staff Director.—Margo Shorter, room 4D548, 693–7715.

SECRETARY OF THE NAVY COUNCIL OF REVIEW BOARDS

Washington Navy Yard, 720 Kennon Street, SE., Room 309, 20374–5023

phone (202) 685–6408, fax 685–6610

Director.—COL Mark D. Franklin, USMC.
Counsel.—Roger R. Claussen.
Staff Assistant to Director.—LaVerne C. Queen.
Physical Evaluation Board.—Robert J. Gaines.
Naval Clemency and Parole Board.—COL James Nierle, USMC.
Naval Discharge Review Board.—COL Jeffrey Riehl, USMC, 685–6408.
Combat-Related Special Compensation Board.—Leif Larsen.
Board of Decorations and Medals.—COL James Nierle, USMC.

ASSISTANT SECRETARY FOR RESEARCH, DEVELOPMENT AND ACQUISITION

Pentagon, Room 4E665, phone (703) 695–6315

Assistant Secretary.—Hon. Sean J. Stackley.

Executive Assistant and Naval Aide.—CAPT David Lewis.
Military Assistant and Marine Aide.—COL Floyd Usry.
Principal Military Deputy.—VADM David Architzel.
Executive Assistant and Naval Aide.—CDR Jeff Edler.
Principal Civilian Deputy.—James Thomsen, room 4C681, 614–6430.
Executive Assistant and Naval Aide.—CDR Ellen Evanoff.
Acquisition Career Management.—Carolyn Willis, BF992, 614–0522.
Deputy Assistant Secretary of the Navy for—
Acquisition and Logistics Management.—RADM (Sel) Sean Cream, BF992, 614–9445.
Air Programs.—Tom Laux, room 4C746, 614–7794.
C4I and Space Programs.—Dr. Gary Federici, room BF963, 914–6589.
Expeditionary Warfare Programs.—Roger Smith, room 4C746, 614–4794.
International Programs.—RDML Steve Voetsch, Crystal City, VA, 601–9800.
Management and Budget.—CAPT Francis Tisak (acting), room 4C656, 697–1091.
Ship/Integrated Warfare Systems Programs.—Allison Stiller, room 4C712, 697–1710.

CHIEF INFORMATION OFFICER

Chief Information Officer.—R. Carey, room PT1/2100, 602–1800.

CHIEF OF NAVAL OPERATIONS

Pentagon, Room 4E662, phone (703) 695–0532, fax 693–9408

Chief of Naval Operations.—ADM Gary Roughead.
Vice Chief of Naval Operations.—ADM Patrick Walsh.
Judge Advocate General of the Navy.—VADM Bruce McDonald.
Special Assistant for Inspection Support.—VADM Anthony Winns.
President, Board of Inspection and Survey.—RADM Raymond Klein.
Director, Office of:
Naval Criminal Investigative Service.—Thomas Betro.
Naval Intelligence. —VADM Jack Dorsett.
Naval Nuclear Propulsion Program.—ADM Kirkland Donald.
Navy Staff.—VADM John Harvey.
Chief of:
Chaplains.—VADM Robert Burt.
Information.—RDML Frank Thorp IV.
Legislative Affairs.—RADL Mike Miller.
Naval Education Training.—RADM Gary Jones.
Naval Reserve.—VADM Dirk Debbink.
Commander, Naval Safety Center.—RADM Arthur Johnson.
Deputy for—
Communication Networks.—VADM Harry Harris.
Fleet Readiness and Logistics.—VADM Michael Loose.
Information, Plans, and Strategy.—VADM William Crowder.
Integration of Capabilities and Resources.—VADM Barry McCullough.
Manpower Personnel Education and Training.—VADM Mark E. Ferguson.
Surgeon General of the Navy.—VADM Adam Robinson.
Oceanographer of the Navy.—RADM Dave Gove.

BUREAU OF MEDICINE AND SURGERY

2300 E. Street, NW., 20372–5300, phone (202) 762–3701
fax 762–3750

Chief.—VADM Adam M. Robinson, Jr., MC, USN.

MILITARY SEALIFT COMMAND

914 Charles Morris Court, SE., Washington Navy Yard, 20398–5540

phone (202) 685–5001, fax 685–5020

Commander.—RADM Mark H. Buzby.

NATIONAL NAVAL MEDICAL CENTER

Bethesda, MD 20889, phone (301) 295–5800/5802, fax 295–5336.

Commander.—RDML Matthew L. Nathan.

NAVAL AIR SYSTEMS COMMAND

47123 Buse Road, Building 2272, Patuxent River, MD 20670
phone (301) 757–1487

Commander.—VADM David Venlet.

NAVAL CRIMINAL INVESTIGATIVE SERVICE COMMAND

716 Sicard Street, SE., Suite 2000, 20388, phone (202) 433–8800,
fax 433–9619

Director.—Thomas A. Betro.

NAVAL DISTRICT OF WASHINGTON

1343 Dahlgren Avenue, SE., 20374–5001, phone (202) 433–2777, fax 433–2207

Commandant.—RDML Patrick J. Lorge.
Deputy Commandant.—CAPT Marcus B. Yonehiro.

NAVAL FACILITIES ENGINEERING COMMAND

Washington Navy Yard, 1322 Patterson Avenue, SE., Suite 1000, 20374
phone (202) 685–9499, fax 685–1463

Commander.—RADM Wayne G. Shear.

OFFICE OF NAVAL INTELLIGENCE

4251 Suitland Road, 20395, phone (301) 669–3001, fax 669–3509

Commander.—CAPT J. Todd Ross.

NAVAL SEA SYSTEMS COMMAND

Washington Navy Yard, 1333 Isaac Hull Avenue, SE., Stop 1010, 20376–1010
phone (202) 781–0100

Commander.—VADM Kevin M. McCoy.

NAVAL SUPPLY SYSTEMS COMMAND

Mechanicsburg, PA, phone (717) 605–3433

Commander.—RADM M.J. Lyden.

SPACE AND NAVAL WARFARE SYSTEMS COMMAND SPACE FIELD ACTIVITY

14675 Lee Road, Chantilly, VA 20151, phone (703) 808–4631
fax 808–1448

Commander.—RDML Liz Young.

U.S. NAVAL ACADEMY

Annapolis, MD 21402, phone (410) 293–1000

Superintendent.—VADM Jeffrey L. Fowler, USN, 293–1500.

Commandant of Midshipmen.—CAPT Matthew L. Klunder, USN, 293–7005.

U.S. MARINE CORPS HEADQUARTERS

Pentagon, Room 4E586, phone (703) 614–2500

Commandant.—Gen. J.T. Conway.
Assistant Commandant.—Gen. J.F. Amos.
Aide-de-Camp.—Lt. Col. H.R. Van Opdorp.
Chaplain.—RADM R.F. Burt.
Dental Officer.—CAPT D.L. Taylor.
Fiscal Director of the Marine Corps.—C.E. Cook.
Inspector General of the Marine Corps.—Brig. Gen. K.J. Lee.
Judge Advocate.—Brig. Gen. J.C. Walker.
Legislative Assistant.—Brig. Gen. M.R. Regner.
Medical Officer.—RADM (UH) R.R. Jeffries.
Military Secretary.—Col. G.F. Milburn.
Sergeant Major of the Marine Corps.—Sgt. Maj. C.W. Kent.
Deputy Commandant of Marine Corps for—
Aviation.—Lt. Gen. G.J. Trautman.
Installations and Logistics.—Maj. Gen. E.G. Usher.
Manpower and Reserve Affairs.—Lt. Gen. R.S. Coleman.
Plans, Policies, and Operations.—Lt. Gen. J.F. Dunford.
Public Affairs.—Col. D. Lapan.
Programs and Resources.—Lt. Gen. D.D. Thiessen (703) 614–3435.
Director of:
Intelligence.—Brig. Gen. R.M. Lake.
Marine Corps History and Museums.—Col. (Ret.) J.W. Ripley.

MARINE BARRACKS

Eighth and I Streets, SE., 20390, phone (202) 433–4094

Commanding Officer.—Col. A.H. Smith.

TRAINING AND EDUCATION COMMAND

3300 Russell Road, Quantico, VA 22134, phone (703) 784–3730, fax 784–3724

Commanding General.—Brig. Gen. M.G. Spiese.

DEPARTMENT OF JUSTICE

Robert F. Kennedy Department of Justice Building

950 Pennsylvania Avenue, NW., 20530, phone (202) 514–2000
http://www.usdoj.gov

ERIC H. HOLDER, JR., Attorney General; born in New York City, NY, education: Columbia College, 1973; Columbia Law School, 1976; professional: Department of Justice Criminal Division, 1976–88; Associate Judge of the Superior Court of the District of Columbia, 1988–93; United States Attorney for the District of Columbia, 1993–97; Deputy Attorney General, 1997–2001; partner with law firm of Covington & Burling L.L.P., 2001–09; nominated by President Barack Obama to become the Attorney General of the United States on December 1, 2008 and was confirmed by the U.S. Senate on February 2, 2009.

OFFICE OF THE ATTORNEY GENERAL

RFK Main Justice Building, Room 5111, phone (202) 514–2001

Attorney General.—Eric H. Holder, Jr.

Chief of Staff and Counselor to the Attorney General.—Kevin A. Ohlson, room 5115, 514–3892.

Deputy Chief of Staff and Counselor to the Attorney General.—James Garland, room 5112, 305–8674.

Confidential Assistant to the Attorney General.—Annie Bradley, room 5111, 514–2001.

Counselors to the Attorney General: John Bies, room 5110, 616–7740; Amy Jeffress, room 5116, 305–7378; Aaron Lewis, room 5214, 616–2372; Monty Wilkinson, room 5224, 514–9798.

Counselor to the Attorney for Executive Branch Relations.—Margaret Richardson, room 5119, 514–9665.

Director of Scheduling.—Paige Fitzgerald, room 5131, 514–4195.

OFFICE OF THE DEPUTY ATTORNEY GENERAL

RFK Main Justice Building, Room 4111, phone (202) 514–2101

Deputy Attorney General.—David W. Ogden, room 4111.

Principal Associate Deputy Attorney General.—Kathryn H. Ruemmler, room 4208, 514–2105.

Chief of Staff and Counselor.—Stuart F. Delery, room 4210, 307–2090.

Associate Deputy Attorneys General: Neil H. MacBride, room 4216, 514–5650; David Margolis, room 4113, 514–4945; Lisa Monaco, room 4218, 514–3712; Scott N. Schools, room 4119, 305–7848; Donald B. Verrilli, Jr., room 4114, 514–4680.

Associate Deputy Attorney General and Director, OCDETF.—Stuart Nash, room 4212, 514–8699.

Senior Counsels to the Deputy Attorney General: Jennifer Shasky Calvery, room 4115, 514–0049; Eric R. Columbus, room 4214, 307–2510; Edward N. Siskel, room 4217, 353–8878.

Counsels to the Deputy Attorney General: Jason C. Chipman, room 4220, 353–3030; Chad Golder, room 4121, 305–0091; Stephanie K. Pell, room 4222, 305–8657; Daphna Renan, room 4116, 305–3481; Bradley T. Smith, room 4315, 305–9886.

Special Assistant to the Deputy Attorney General.—Mark E. Michalic, room 4112, 514–0438.

Confidential Assistant to the Deputy Attorney General.—Linda E. Long, room 4111, 514–1904.

OFFICE OF THE ASSOCIATE ATTORNEY GENERAL

RFK Main Justice Building, Room 5706, phone (202) 514–9500

Associate Attorney General.—Thomas J. Perrelli.

Principal Deputy Associate Attorney General.—Joseph R. Guerra.

Deputy Associate Attorneys General: Helaine Greenfeld, room 5722, 616–0038; Samuel Hirsch, room 5732, 616–2728.

Counsel to the Associate Attorney General.—Brian Hauck, room 5730, 353–2811.

Confidential Assistant.—Currie Gunn, room 5708, 305–2636.

OFFICE OF THE SOLICITOR GENERAL

RFK Main Justice Building, Room 5143, phone (202) 514–2201
http://www.usdoj.gov/osg

Solicitor General.—Elena Kagan, room 5143, 514–2201.
Principal Deputy Solicitor General.—Neal K. Katyal, room 5143, 514–2206.
Deputy Solicitors General: Michael R. Dreeben, room 5623, 514–2255; Edwin S. Kneedler, room 5137, 514–3261; Malcolm L. Stewart, room 5137, 514–4218.
Executive Officer.—William J. Dziwura (acting), room 5140, 514–5507.
Supervisory Case Management Specialist.—Emily C. Spadoni, room 5608, 514–2218.
Chief, Research and Publications Section.—Patricia Stanczak-Kraus, room 6634, 514–4459.

ANTITRUST DIVISION

RFK Main Justice Building, 950 Pennsylvania Avenue, NW., 20530
City Center Building, 1401 H Street, NW., 20530 (CCB)
Bicentennial Building, 600 E Street, NW., 20530 (BICN)
Liberty Place Building, 325 Seventh Street, NW., 20530 (LPB)
Patrick Henry Building, 601 D Street, NW., 20530 (PHB)

Assistant Attorney General.—Vacant, room 3109 (202) 514–2401.
Deputy Assistant Attorneys General: Scott M. Hammond, room 3214, 514–3543; Carl Shapiro, room 3117, 514–0731; Vacant, room 3210, 514–1157; Vacant, room 3212, 305–4517; Vacant, room 3121, 514–2408.
Director of:
Criminal Enforcement.—Marc Siegel, room 3217, 514–3543.
Economics Enforcement.—Kenneth Heyer, room 3112, 514–6995.
Operations.—Robert J. Kramer, room 3118, 514–3544.
Freedom of Information Act Officer.—SueAnn Slates (LPB), room 200, 514–2692.
Executive Officer.—Thomas D. King (PHB), room 10150, 514–4005.
Section Chiefs:
Appellate.—Catherine G. O'Sullivan (PHB), room 3222, 514–2413.
Competition Policy.—Robert Majure (acting), (BICN), room 10900, 307–6341.
Economic Litigation.—Norman Familant (BICN), room 10800, 307–6323.
Economic Regulatory.—Daniel O'Brien (BICN), room 10100, 307–6591.
Foreign Commerce.—Edward T. Hand, room 3623, 514–2464.
Legal Policy.—Robert A. Potter, room 3236, 514–2512.
Litigation I.—Mark J. Botti (CCB), room 4000, 307–0827.
Litigation II.—Maribeth Petrizzi (CCB), room 3000, 307–0924.
Litigation III.—John R. Read (LPB), room 300, 616–5935.
National Criminal Enforcement.—Lisa M. Phelan (CCB), room 3700, 307–6694.
Networks and Technology.—James Tierney (BICN), room 9300, 514–5634.
Telecommunications and Media.—Nancy M. Goodman (CCB), room 8000, 514–5621.
Transportation, Energy, and Agriculture.—Donna Kooperstein (LPB), room 500, 307–6351.

FIELD OFFICES

California: Phillip H. Warren, 450 Golden Gate Avenue, Room 10–0101, Box 36046, San Francisco, CA 94102 (415) 436–6660.
Georgia: Nezida S. Davis, Richard B. Russell Building, 75 Spring Street, SW., Suite 1176, Atlanta, GA 30303 (404) 331–7100.
Illinois: Marvin N. Price, Jr., Rookery Building, 209 South LaSalle Street, Suite 600, Chicago, IL 60604 (312) 353–7530.
New York: Ralph T. Giordano, 26 Federal Plaza, Room 3630, New York, NY 10278 (212) 264–0391.
Ohio: Scott M. Watson, Plaza 9 Building, 55 Erieview Plaza, Suite 700, Cleveland, OH 44114 (216) 522–4070.
Pennsylvania: Robert E. Connolly, Curtis Center, One Independence Square West, 7th and Walnut Streets, Suite 650, Philadelphia, PA 19106 (215) 597–7405.
Texas: Duncan S. Currie, Thanksgiving Tower, 1601 Elm Street, Suite 4950, Dallas, TX 75201 (214) 880–9401.

CIVIL DIVISION

RFK Main Justice Building, 950 Pennsylvania Avenue, NW., 20530

20 Massachusetts Avenue, NW., 20530 (20MASS)

1100 L Street, NW., 20530 (L ST)

National Place Building, 1331 Pennsylvania Avenue, NW., 20530 (NATP)

1425 New York Avenue, NW., 20530 (NYAV)

Patrick Henry Building, 601 D Street, NW., 20530 (PHB)

Assistant Attorney General.—Michael F. Hertz (acting), room 3607 (202) 514–7179.
Principal Deputy Assistant Attorney General.—Vacant, room 3605, 353–2793.

APPELLATE STAFF

Deputy Assistant Attorney General.—Vacant, room 3131, 514–1258.
Director.—Robert E. Kopp, room 7519, 514–3311.
Deputy Director.—William Kanter, room 7517, 514–4575.

COMMERCIAL LITIGATION BRANCH

Deputy Assistant Attorney General.—Stuart E. Schiffer, room 3607, 514–3306.
Directors: David M. Cohen (L ST), room 12124, 514–7300; John N. Fargo (L ST), room 11116, 514–7223; Michael F. Hertz (PHB), room 9902, 514–7179; J. Christopher Kohn (L ST), room 10036, 514–7450.
Office of Foreign Litigation.—Robert Hollis (L ST), room 11006, 514–7455.
Deputy Directors: Joyce R. Branda (PHB), room 9904, 307–0231; Jeanne Davidson (L ST), room 12132, 307–0290.
Legal Officer.—Donna C. Maizel, Esq., U.S. Department of Justice, Civil Division European Office, The American Embassy, London, England, PSC 801, Box 42, FPO AE, 09498–4042, 9+011–44–20–7894–0840.
Attorney-in-Charge.—Barbara Williams, Suite 359, 26 Federal Plaza, New York, NY 10278 (212) 264–9240.

CONSUMER LITIGATION

Deputy Assistant Attorney General.—Vacant, room 3127, 514–3045.
Director.—Eugene M. Thirolf (NATP), room 950N, 307–3009.

FEDERAL PROGRAMS BRANCH

Deputy Assistant Attorney General.—Vacant, room 3137, 514–3310.
Directors: Felix Baxter (20MASS), room 7100, 514–4651; Joseph H. Hunt, room 7348, 514–1259; Jennifer D. Rivera (20MASS), room 6100, 514–3671.
Deputy Directors: Vincent M. Garvey (20MASS), room 7346, 514–3449; Sheila M. Lieber (20MASS), room 7102, 514–3786.

IMMIGRATION LITIGATION

Deputy Assistant Attorney General.—Vacant, room 3131, 514–1258.
Director.—Thomas W. Hussey (NATP), room 7026S, 616–4852.
Deputy Directors: Donald E. Keener (NATP), room 7022S, 616–4878; David J. Kline (NATP), room 7006N, 616–4856; David M. McConnell (NATP), room 7260N, 616–4881.

MANAGEMENT PROGRAMS

Director.—Kenneth L. Zwick, room 3140, 514–4552.
Directors, Office of:
Administration.—Shirley Lloyd (L ST), room 9008, 307–0016.
Planning, Budget, and Evaluation.—Linda S. Liner (L ST), room 9042, 307–0034.
Management Information.—Dorothy Bahr (L ST), room 8044, 616–8026.
Litigation Support.—Clarisse Abramidis (L ST), room 9126, 616–5014.
Policy and Management Operations.—Kevin Burket (L ST), room 8128, 616–8073.

TORTS BRANCH

Deputy Assistant Attorney General.—Vacant, room 3127, 514–3045.
Directors: Peter Frost (NYAV), room 10122, 616–4000; Timothy P. Garren (NYAV), room 8122, 616–4171; J. Patrick Glynn (NATP), room 8028S, 616–4200; Phyllis J. Pyles (NATP), room 8098N, 616–4252;
Deputy Directors: JoAnn J. Bordeaux (NATP), room 8024S, 616–4204; Paul F. Figley (NATP), room 8096N, 616–4248.
Attorneys-in-Charge: Robert Underhill, 450 Golden Gate Avenue, 10/6610, Box 36028, San Francisco, CA 94102–3463, FTS: (415) 436–6630; Vacant, Suite 320, 26 Federal Plaza, New York, NY 10278–0140, FTS: (212) 264–0480.

CIVIL RIGHTS DIVISION

RFK Main Justice Building, 950 Pennsylvania Avenue, NW., 20530

1425 New York Avenue, NW., 20035 (NYAV)

601 D Street, NW., 20004 (PHB)

100 Indiana Avenue, NW., 20004 (NALC)

1800 G Street, NW., 20004 (NWB)

http://www.usdoj.gov/crt

Assistant Attorney General.—Loretta King (acting), room 5643 (202) 514–2151.
Principal Deputy Assistant Attorney General.—Vacant, room 5748, 353–9065.
Deputy Assistant Attorneys General: Steven Rosenbaum (acting), room 5742, 514–2151; John Wodatch (acting), room 5637, 514–2151; Vacant, room 5744, 616–1278.
Counsels to the Assistant Attorney General: Olegario Cantos VII, room 5529, 514–8191; John Richmond, room 5642, 305–9750; Karen Stevens (acting), room 5644, 353–8621; Eric Treene, room 5531, 353–8622; Vacant, room 5539, 305–9750; Vacant, room 5637, 514–3845.
Chief of Staff.—Pamela Barron, room 5541, 353–3426.
Section Chiefs:
Appellate.—David K. Flynn, room 3647, 514–2195.
Coordination and Review.—Merrily A. Friedlander (NYAV), room 6001, 307–2222.
Criminal.—Mark Kappelhoff (PHB), room 5102, 514–3204.
Disability Rights.—Renee Wohlenhaus (acting), (NYAV), room 4055, 307–2227.
Educational Opportunities.—Jeremiah Glassman (PHB), room 4002, 514–4092.
Employment Litigation.—John Gadzichowski (acting), (PHB), room 4040, 514–3831.
Housing and Civil Enforcement.—Donna Murphy (acting), (NWB), room 7002, 514–4713.
Special Litigation.—Shanetta Brown Cutler (PHB), room 5114, 514–6255.
Voting.—John K. Tanner (NWB), room 7254, 307–2767.
Deputy Chief, Special Counsel Office.—Katherine Baldwin, room 9030, 514–3896.
Special Counsel for Immigration Related Unfair Employment Practices.—Vacant, room 9032, 616–5528.

OFFICE OF COMMUNITY ORIENTED POLICING SERVICES

1110 Vermont Avenue, NW., 20530

DIRECTOR'S OFFICE

Director.—Timothy Quinn (acting), 10th floor, (202) 616–2888.
Office Manager.—Sharon Baker.
Chief of Staff.—Timothy Quinn.
Deputy Director for—
Management.—Timothy Quinn.
Supervisory Management Analyst.—Laurel Matthews.
Operations.—Robert Phillips.

ADMINISTRATIVE DIVISION

Assistant Director.—Mary Hyland, 4th floor, 616–9418.

Human Capital Manager.—Debbie Brown, 10th floor, 353–0109.

AUDIT DIVISION

Assistant Director.—Cynthia Bowie, 4th floor, 616–3645.

COMMUNICATIONS DIVISION

Assistant Director.—David Buchanan, 11th floor, 514–9079.

GRANTS ADMINISTRATION DIVISION

Assistant Director.—Andy Dorr, 353–9736.
Grant Regional Supervisors:
John Oliphant, 9th floor, 307–3411.
Linda Gist, 5th floor, 514–8091.
Keesha Thompson, 5th floor, 616–1902.
Scott McNichol, 8th floor, 616–9266.

GRANT MONITORING DIVISION

Assistant Director.—Marcia Samuels, 9th floor, 514–8507.

LEGAL DIVISION

General Counsel.—Lani Lee, 12th floor, 514–3750.
Deputy General Counsel.—Charlotte C. Grzebien, 616–2899.
Associate General Counsel.—Jenny Wu, 514–9424.

PROGRAM / POLICY SUPPORT AND EVALUATION

Assistant Director.—Matthew Scheider, 7th floor, 514–2301.

TECHNICAL ASSISTANCE AND TRAINING DIVISION

Assistant Director.—Beverly Alford, 7th floor, 514–2301.

COMMUNITY RELATIONS SERVICE

600 E Street, NW., Suite 6000, 20530, phone (202) 305–2935
fax 305–3009 (BICN)

Director.—Ondray T. Harris.
Deputy Associate Director.—Diane Mitchum.
Attorney Advisor.—George Henderson, 305–2964.
Media Affairs Officer.—Vacant, 305–2966.

REGIONAL DIRECTORS

New England.—Frances Amoroso, 408 Atlantic Avenue, Suite 222, Boston, MA 02110–1032 (617) 424–5715.
Northeast Region.—Reinaldo Rivera, 26 Federal Plaza, Suite 36–118, New York, NY 10278 (212) 264–0700.
Mid-Atlantic Region.—Vacant, Customs House, Second and Chestnut Streets, Suite 208, Philadelphia, PA 19106 (215) 597–2344.
Southeast Region.—Thomas Battles, Citizens Trust Company Bank Building, Suite 900, 75 Piedmont Avenue NE., Atlanta, GA 30303 (404) 331–6883.
Midwest Region.—Jesse Taylor, Xerox Center Building, 55 West Monroe Street, Suite 420, Chicago, IL 60603 (312) 353–4391.

Southwest Region.—Carmelita P. Freeman, Hardwood Center, 1999 Bryan Street, Suite 2050, Dallas, TX 75201 (214) 655–8175.
Central Region.—Pascual Marquez, 1100 Maine Street, Suite 1320, Kansas City, MO 64105 (816) 426–7433.
Rocky Mountain Region.—Philip Arreola, 1244 Speer Boulevard, Suite 650, Denver, CO 80204–3584 (303) 844–2973.
Western Region.—Ron Wakabayashi, 888 South Figueroa Street, Suite 1880, Los Angeles, CA 90017 (213) 894–2941.
Northwest Region.—Rosa Melendez, Federal Office Building, 915 Second Avenue, Suite 1808, Seattle, WA 98174 (206) 220–6700.

CRIMINAL DIVISION

RFK Main Justice Building, 950 Pennsylvania Avenue, NW., 20530
phone (202) 514–2601

Bond Building, 1400 New York Avenue, NW., 20005 (Bond)

1331 F Street, NW., 20004 (F Street)

John C. Keeney Building, 1301 New York Avenue, NW., 20530 (1301 NY)

Patrick Henry Building, 601 D Street, NW., 20530 (PHB)

Assistant Attorney General.—Rita M. Glavin (acting), room 2206, 514–7200.
Chief of Staff.—Mythili Raman (acting), room 2208, 514–2601.
Deputy Assistant Attorneys General: Kenneth A. Blanco, room 2115, 616–3027; David Hennessy (acting), room 2212, 307–0745; John C. Keeney, room 2109, 514–2621; John Morton (acting), room 2113, 353–9827; Bruce C. Swartz, room 2119, 514–2333.
Counselor to the Assistant Attorney General.—Steven E. Fagell, room 2214, 353–3485.
Senior Counsels to the Assistant Attorney General: Stacey Luck, room 2222, 305–0273; Ian McCaleb, room 2228, 514–4389; James Reynolds, room 2313, 616–8664; Richard M. Rogers, room 2110, 307–0030; Jonathan Wroblewski, room 2218, 514–4730.
Executive Officer.—Steve Parent (Bond), room 5100, 514–2641.
Section Chiefs / Office Directors:
Appellate.—Patty M. Stemler, room 1264, 514–2611.
Asset Forfeiture and Money Laundering.—Richard Weber (Bond), suite 10100, 514–1263.
Capital Case Unit.—Margaret P. Griffey (PHB), room 6140, 353–7172.
Child Exploitation and Obscenity.—Andrew G. Oosterbaan (Bond), suite 6000, 514–5780.
Computer Crime and Intellectual Property.—Michael DuBose (1301 NY), suite 600, 514–1026.
Domestic Security.—Teresa McHenry, room 7748, 616–5731.
Enforcement Operations.—Maureen Killion (1301 NY), suite 1200, 514–6809.
Fraud.—Steven Tyrrell (Bond), room 4100, 514–7023.
International Affairs.—Mary Ellen Warlow (1301 NY), suite 900, 514–0000.
International Criminal Investigative Training Assistant Program.—Carr Trevillian IV (F Street), suite 500, 305–8190.
Narcotics and Dangerous Drugs.—Paul M. O'Brien (Bond), room 11100, 514–0917.
Overseas Prosecutorial Development, Assistance and Training.—Carl Alexandre (F Street), room 400, 514–1323.
Organized Crime and Racketeering.—Bruce G. Ohr (1301 NY), suite 700, 514–3595.
Policy and Legislation.—Jonathan Wroblewski, room 7730, 514–4194.
Public Integrity.—William Welch (Bond), suite 12100, 514–1412.
Special Investigations.—Eli M. Rosenbaum (1301 NY), suite 200, 616–2492.

OFFICE OF DISPUTE RESOLUTION

RFK Main Justice Building, Room 5736, phone (202) 616–9471
http://www.usdoj.gov/odr

Director / Senior Counsel.—Joanna M. Jacobs (acting), room 5734, 514–8910.
Dispute Resolution Support Specialist.—Krista van der Horst, room 5736, 616–0666.

DRUG ENFORCEMENT ADMINISTRATION

Lincoln Place-1 (East), 600 Army-Navy Drive, Arlington, VA 22202 (LP–1)
Lincoln Place-2 (West), 700 Army-Navy Drive, Arlington, VA 22202 (LP–2)

Administrator.—Michele M. Leonhart (acting), room W–12060 (202) 307–8000.
Chief of Staff.—Vacant, room 12060, 307–8003.
Deputy Administrator.—Michele M. Leonhart, room W–12058–F, 307–7345.
Equal Employment Opportunity Officer.—Oliver C. Allen, room E–11275, 307–8888.
Executive Assistants: Robert S. Brisolari, room W–12058–E, 307–8770; Christopher D. Evans, room W–12058–C, 307–7998; Vacant, room 12060, 307–8003.
Chief, Congressional and Public Affairs.—Mary Irene Cooper, room W–12228, 307–7363.
Chief, Executive Policy and Strategic Planning.—Kevin D. Whaley, room W–11100, 307–7420.
Section Chiefs:
Congressional Affairs.—Sheldon Shoemaker, room W–12104, 307–4461.
Demand Reduction.—Eric Akers, room W–9049–E, 307–7988.
Information Services.—Donald E. Joseph, room W–12232, 307–7967.
Public Affairs.—Garrison K. Courtney (acting), 307–7979.
Chief Counsel.—Wendy H. Goggin, room W–12142–C, 307–7322.
Deputy Chief Counsel.—Robert C. Gleason, room E–12375, 307–8020.
Chief, Office of Administrative Law Judges.—Mary Ellen Bittner, room E–2129, 307–8188.

FINANCIAL MANAGEMENT DIVISION

Chief Financial Officer.—Frank M. Kalder, room W–12138, 307–7330.
Deputy Assistant Administrators for—
Acquisition Management.—Christinia K. Sisk, room W–5100, 307–7888.
Finance.—John Osterday, room E–7397, 307–7002.
Resource Management.—Charlotte A. Saunders, room E–7399, 307–4800.
Section Chiefs:
Acquisition Management.—Angel Perez, room W–5028, 307–5074.
Controls and Coordination.—Brian Parks, room E–7395, 307–7080.
Evaluations and Planning.—Donna Wilson, room E–850P, 307–7463.
Financial Integrity.—Bradley J. Honkus, room E–7101, 307–7082.
Financial Operations.—Tammy Balas, room E–7165, 307–9933.
Financial Reports.—Sherri Woodle, room E–7297, 307–7040.
Financial Systems.—Daniel G. Gillette, room E–7205, 307–7031.
Organization and Staffing Management.—Donna Ciccolella, room E–7331, 307–7077.
Policy and Transportation.—Beverly Hobbs, room W–5018, 307–7808.
Program Liaison and Analysis.—Brian Horn, room E–7225, 307–7073.
Statistical Services.—James Tauber, room W–6200, 307–8279.

HUMAN RESOURCES DIVISION

Assistant Administrator.—Raymond Pagliarini, room W–12020, 307–4177.
Section Chiefs:
Administrative Management.—Glenda A. Rollins, room W–3058, 307–4701.
Recruitment and Placement.—Margie Aira, room W–3242, 307–4055.
Career Board Executive Secretary.—Karen Marrero, room W–2268, 307–7349.
Chairman, Board of Professional Conduct.—Patrick T. Dunn, room E–9333, 307–8980.
Special Agent-in-Charge, Office of Training.—John R. McCarty, 2500 Investigation Parkway, DEA Academy, Quantico, VA 22135 (703) 632–5010.
Assistant Special Agents-in-Charge:
Domestic Training Section 1.—William Faiella (703) 632–5110.
Domestic Training Section 2.—Robin Dinlocker (703) 632–5310.
International Training Section.—James T. Farnsworth (703) 632–5330.

INSPECTIONS DIVISION

Chief Inspector.—James Kasson, room W–12042A, 307–7358.
Deputy Chief Inspector, Office of:
Inspections.—Kevin M. Foley (acting), room W–4348, 307–8200.
Professional Responsibility.—Karl C. Colder, room W–4176, 307–8235.

Security Programs.—Barbara M. Roach, room W–2340, 307–3465.

INTELLIGENCE DIVISION

Assistant Administrator.—Anthony P. Pacido (acting), room W–12020A, 307–3607.
Special Agent in Charge, El Paso Intelligence Center.—Arthur Doty, Building 11339, SSG Sims Street, El Paso, TX 79908–8098 (915) 760–2011.
Deputy Associate Administrator, Office of Intelligence.—Judith E. Bertini, room W–12020C, 307–3607.
Executive Assistant.—Karen D. Smith, 307–3607.
Special Assistant.—Jeffrey T. Walsh, 307–3607.
Deputy Assistant Administrator, Office of:
Fusion Center.—John Riley (703) 561–7117.
National Security Intelligence.—Doug Poole, 307–7600.
Special Intelligence.—Ava A. Cooper-Davis, Merrifield, VA (703) 561–7111.
Section Chiefs:
Associate National Security.—Barry Zulauf, 307–7769.
Data Management.—Virginia Hoh (703) 561–7671.
Indications/Warnings.—Cheryl Hooper, 307–8541.
Investigative Intelligence.—Lourdes Border, 307–9284.
Investigative Support.—Marilyn Wankel (703) 488–4246.
Management and Production Section.—James A. Curtin, room W–7268, 307–7534.
Operational Support.—Benjamin J. Sanborn, room E–5015, 307–3645.
Policy Liaison.—Pat Lowery, 307–8541.
Requirements/Production.—Thomas Neal, (202) 307–4825.
Strategic Intelligence.—Sallie Castro, 353–9581.
Technical Support.—Gisele Gatjanis (703) 561–7107.

OPERATIONS DIVISION

Chief of Operations.—Thomas G. Harrigan, room W–12050, 307–7340.
Chiefs of:
Enforcement/Administrative Support.—Vacant.
Financial Operations.—John Arvanitis, room W–10190, 307–4379.
Global Enforcement Operations.—Thomas M. Harrigan, room W–11070, 307–7927.
International Programs.—Vacant, room W–11024, 307–4233.
Operations Management.—David Dongilli, room W–11148, 307–4200.
Special Projects.—Frankie Shroyer, 307–7858.
Deputy Assistant Administrator, Office of Diversion Control.—Joseph T. Rannazzisi, room E–6295, 307–7165.
Special Agent in Charge, Aviation Division.—William C. Brown, Ft. Worth, TX (817) 837–2004.
Special Agent in Charge, Special Operations Division.—Derek S. Maltz, Chantilly, VA (703) 488–4205.

OPERATIONAL SUPPORT DIVISION

Assistant Administrator.—Preston Grubbs, room W–12142, 307–4730.
Deputy Assistant Administrator, Office of:
Administration.—Mary E. Colarusso (acting), room W–9088, 307–7708.
Forensic Sciences.—Thomas J. Janovsky, room W–7342, 307–8866.
Information Systems.—Dennis R. McCrary, room E–3105, 307–7454.
Investigative Technology.—Fred Ganem, Lorton, VA (703) 495–6500.
Section Chiefs:
Administrative Operations.—Janet Gates (acting), room W–5100–A, 307–7866.
Concord Program Management.—Millie Tyler, room E–3007, 307–9895.
Facilities and Finance.—William A. Kopitz, room W–5244, 307–7792.
Hazardous Waste Disposal.—John Patrick, room W–7308, 307–8872.
Integration and Management.—Venita Phillips, room E–3206, 307–9892.
Laboratory Operations.—Bradley Campbell, room W–7310, 307–8880.
Laboratory Support.—Richard P. Meyers, room W–7348, 307–8785.
Operations and Support.—Barry Smallwood, room E–4111, 307–9896.
Program Planning and Control Staff.—Maria Hughes, room E–3163, 307–9885.
Software Development.—Ruth Torres, room E–3285, 307–9883.

Surveillance Support.—Albert Laurita, Lorton, VA (703) 495–6736.
Technology Officer.—Mark Shafernich.
Telecommunications/Intercept Support.—Earl W. Hewitt, Lorton, VA (703) 495–6676.
Associate Deputy Assistant Administrator, Office of:
Information Systems.—Julie Jones, room E–3005, 307–5269.
Forensic Sciences: Nelson A. Santos, room W–7344, 307–8866; Steven M. Sottolano, room W–7346, 307–8868.

FIELD OFFICES

Special Agent-in-Charge:

Atlanta Division.—Rodney Benson, Room 800, 75 Spring Street, SW., Atlanta, GA 30303 (404) 893–7100.

Boston Division.—Steven W. Derr, JFK Federal Building, Room E–400, 15 New Sudbury Street, Boston, MA 02203–0402 (617) 557–2100.

Caribbean Division.—Javier Pena, Metro Office Park, Millennium Park Plaza #15, 2nd Street, Suite 710, Guaynabo, PR 00968 (787) 277–4700.

Chicago Division.—Gary G. Olenkiewicz, Suite 1200, John C. Kluczynski Federal Building, 230 South Dearborn Street, Chicago, IL 60604 (312) 353–7875.

Dallas Division.—James L. Capra, 10160 Technology Boulevard East, Dallas, TX 75220 (214) 366–6900.

Denver Division.—Jeffrey D. Sweetin, 115 Inverness Drive East, Englewood, CO 80112–5116 (303) 705–7300.

Detroit Division.—Robert L. Corso, 431 Howard Street, Detroit, MI 48226 (313) 234–4000.

El Paso Division.—Joseph Arabit, 660 Mesa Hills Drive, Suite 2000, El Paso, TX 79912 (915) 832–6000.

Houston Division.—Zoran B. Yankovich, 1433 West Loop South, Suite 600, Houston, TX 77027–9506 (713) 693–3000.

Los Angeles Division.—Timothy J. Landrum, 255 East Temple Street, 20th Floor, Los Angeles, CA 90012 (213) 621–6700.

Miami Division.—Mark Trouville, Phoenix Building, 8400 NW. 53rd Street, Miami, FL 33166 (305) 994–4870.

Newark Division.—Gerald P. McAleer, 80 Mulberry Street, 2nd Floor, Newark, NJ 07102–4206 (973) 776–1100.

New Orleans Division.—Jimmy S. Fox III, 3838 North Causeway Boulevard, Suite 1800, 3 Lakeway Center, Metaire, LA 70002 (504) 840–1100.

New York Division.—John P. Gilbride, 99 10th Avenue, New York, NY 10011 (212) 337–3900.

Philadelphia Division.—Joseph Bryfonski, William J. Green Federal Building, 600 Arch Street, Room 10224, Philadelphia, PA 19106 (215) 861–3474.

Phoenix Division.—Elizabeth W. Kempshall, 3010 North Second Street, Suite 301, Phoenix, AZ 85012 (602) 664–5600.

San Diego Division.—Ralph W. Partridge, 4560 Viewridge Avenue, San Diego, CA 92123–1672 (858) 616–4100.

San Francisco Division.—Anthony D. Williams, 450 Golden Gate Avenue, 14th Floor, San Francisco, CA 94102 (415) 436–7900.

Seattle Division.—Arnold R. Moorin, 400 Second Avenue West, Seattle, WA 98119 (206) 553–5443.

St. Louis Division.—Harry Sommers, 317 South 16th Street, St. Louis, MO 63103 (314) 538–4600.

Washington, DC Division.—Ava Cooper-Davis, 800 K Street, NW., Suite 500, Washington, DC 20001 (202) 305–8500.

OTHER DEA OFFICES

Special Agents-in-Charge:

Arthur A. Doty, El Paso Intelligence Center, Building 11339, SSG Sims Street, El Paso, TX 79908 (915) 760–2000.

William C. Brown, Aviation Operations Division, 2300 Horizon Drive, Fort Worth, TX 76177 (817) 837–2000.

Derek S. Maltz, Special Operations Division, 14560 Avion Parkway, Chantilly, VA 20151 (703) 488–4200.

William Faiella (acting), Office of Training, P.O. Box 1475, Quantico, VA 22134 (703) 632–5000.

FOREIGN OFFICES

Ankara, Turkey: American Embassy Ankara, DEA / Justice, PSC 93, Box 5000, APO AE 09823–5000, 9–011–90–312–468–6136.

Asuncion, Paraguay: DEA / Justice, American Embassy Asuncion, Unit 4740, APO AA 34036, 9–011–595–21–210–738.

Athens, Greece: American Embassy Athens, DEA / Justice, PSC 108, Box 14, APO AE 09842, 9–011–30–210–643–4328.

Bangkok, Thailand: American Embassy, DEA / Justice, Box 49, APO AP 96546–0001, 9–011–662–205–4984.

Beijing, China: American Embassy Beijing, DEA / Justice, PSC 461, Box 50, FPO AP 96521–0002, 9–011–8610–8529–6880.

Belmopan, Belize: American Embassy Belmopan, DEA / Justice, PSC 120, Unit 7405, APO AA 34025, 301–985–9387.

Bern, Switzerland: Department of State, DEA / Justice, 5110 Bern Place, Washington, DC 20521–5110, 9–011–41–31–357–7367.

Bogota, Colombia: American Embassy Bogota, DEA / Justice, Unit 5116, APO AA 34038, 9–011–571–315–2121.

Brasilia, Brazil: DEA / Justice, American Embassy Brasilia, Unit 3500, APO AA 34030, 9–011–55–61–3312–7122.

Bridgetown, Barbados: American Embassy Bridgetown, CMR 1014, DEA / Justice, FPO AA 34055, 9–1–246–227–4171.

Brussels, Belgium: American Embassy Brussels, DEA / Justice, PSC 82, Box 137, APO AE 09710, 9–011–32–2–508–2420.

Buenos Aires, Argentina: DEA / Justice, American Embassy Buenos Aires, Unit 4309, APO AA 34034, 9–011–5411–5777–4696.

Cairo, Egypt: American Embassy Cairo, DEA / Justice, Unit 64900, Box 25, APO AE 09839–4900, 9–011–20–2–2797–2461.

Canberra, Australia: American Embassy Canberra, DEA / Justice, APO AP 96549, 9–011–61–2–6214–5903.

Caracas, Venezuela: American Embassy Caracas, DEA / Justice, Unit 4962, APO AA 34037, 9–011–582–212–975–8380 / 8443 / 8407.

Cartagena, Resident Office: American Embassy, DEA Cartagena, Unit 5141, APO AA 34038, 9–011–575–664–9369.

Chiang-Mai, Resident Office: American Embassy Chiang–Mai, Box C, APO AP 96546, 9–011–66–53–217–285.

Ciudad, Resident Office: U.S. Consulate / Ciudad Juarez Resident Office, P.O. Box 10545, El Paso, TX 79925 9–011–52–656–611–1179.

Cochabamba, Resident Office: Unit 3220, Box 211, APO AA 34032, 9–011–591–4–429–3320.

Copenhagen, Denmark: American Embassy Copenhagen, DEA / Justice, PSC 73, APO AE 09716, 9–011–45–35–42–2680.

Curacao, Netherlands Antilles: American Consulate Curacao, DEA / Justice, Washington, DC 20521, 9–011–5999–461–6985.

Dubai, United Arab Emirates: U.S. Consulate General, DEA / Justice, 6020 Dubai Place, Dulles, VA 20189–6020, 9–011–971–4–311–6220.

Dushanbe, Tajikistan: American Embassy Dushanbe, DEA / Justice, Drug Enforcement Administration, 7090 Dushanbe Place, Dulles, VA 20189–7090, 9–011–992–37–229–2807.

Frankfurt, Resident Office: American Consulate General Frankfurt, DEA / Justice, PSC 115, Box 1017, APO AE 09213–0115, 9–011–49–69–7535–3770.

Freeport, Bahamas Resident Office: GPS, c/o U.S. Embassy, DEA, 5115 Northwest 17th Terrace, Hanger #39A, Ft. Lauderdale, FL 33309, 9–1–242–352–5353 / 5354.

Guadalajara, Resident Office: DEA, Guadalajara Resident Office, P.O. Box 9001, Brownsville, TX 78520, 9–011–52–33–3268–2191.

Guatemala City, Guatemala: American Embassy Guatemala City, DEA / Justice, Unit 3311, APO AA 34024, 9–011–502–331–4389.

Guayaquil, Resident Office: DEA / Justice, American Embassy Guayaquil, Unit 5350, APO AA, 34039, 9–011–593–42–32–3715.

The Hague, Netherlands: American Embassy The Hague, DEA / Justice, Unit 6707, Box 8, APO AE 09715, 9–011–31–70–310–2327.

Hanoi, Vietnam: American Embassy Hanoi, DEA / Justice, PSC 461, Box 400, FPO AP 96521–0002, 9–011–844–850–5011.

Hermosillo, Resident Office: U.S. Consulate—Hermosillo, P.O. Box 1689, Nogales, AZ 85628–1689, 9–011–52–662–289–3550.

Hong Kong, Resident Office: U.S. Consulate General Hong Kong, DEA / Justice, PSC 461, Box 16, FPO AP 96521–0006, 9–011–852–2521–4536.

Islamabad, Pakistan Country Office: DEA / Justice, American Embassy Islamabad, DEA / Justice, Unit 62215, APO AE 09812–2215, 9–011–92–51–208–2918.

Istanbul, Turkey Resident Office: American Consulate General, DEA / Justice, PSC 97, Box 0002, APO AE 09827, 9–011–90–212–335–9179.

Kabul, Afghanistan Country Office: DEA / Justice, American Embassy Kabul, 8160 Kabul Place, Washington, DC 20521–6180, 301–490–1042.

Kingston, Jamaica Country Office: U.S. Embassy Kingston, 142 Old Hope Road, Kingston 6, Jamaica 9–1–876–702–6004.

Kuala Lumpur, Malaysia Country Office: American Embassy Kuala Lumpur, DEA / Justice, APO AP 96535–8152, 9–011–603–2142–1779.

Lagos, Nigeria: Department of State, DEA / Justice, 8300 Lagos Place, Washington, DC 20521–8300, 9–011–234–1–261–9837.

La Paz, Bolivia: American Embassy La Paz, DEA / Justice, Unit 3220, DPO AA 34032, 9–011–591–2–216–8313.

Lima, Peru: American Embassy Lima, DEA / Justice, Unit 3810, APO AA 34031, 9–011–511–618–2475.

London, England: American Embassy London, DEA / Justice, Unit 8400, Box 0008, FPO AE 09498–4008, 9–011–44–207–894–0826.

Madrid, Spain: American Embassy Madrid, DEA / Justice, PSC 61, Box 0014, APO AE 09642, 9–011–34–91–587–2280.

Managua, Nicaragua: DEA, American Embassy Nicaragua, Unit 2700, Box 21, APO AA 34021, 9–011–505–252–7738.

Manila, Philippines: American Embassy Manila, DEA / Justice, PSC 500, Box 11, FPO AP 96515, 9–011–632–301–2084.

Matamoros, Mexico Resident Office: Matamoros DEA, P.O. Box 9004, Brownsville, TX 78501, 9–011–52–868–149–1285.

Mazatlan, Resident Office: DEA, Mazatlan Resident Office, P.O. Box 9006, Brownsville, TX 78520–0906, 9–011–669–982–1775.

Merida, Mexico: U.S. Consulate—Merida, P.O. Box 9003, Brownsville, TX 78520–0903, 9–011–52–999–942–5738.

Mexico City, Mexico: DEA / Justice, U.S. Embassy Mexico City, P.O. Box 9000, Brownsville, TX 78520, 9–011–52–55–5080–2600.

Milan, Resident Office: American Consulate Milan, DEA / Justice, PSC 833, Box 60–M, FPO AE 09624, 9–011–39–02–2903–5422.

Monterrey, Resident Office: U.S. Consulate General, Monterrey Resident Office, P.O. Box 9002, Brownsville, TX 78520–0902, 9–011–5281–8340–1299.

Moscow, Russia: American Embassy Moscow, DEA / Justice, PSC 77, APO AE 09721, 9–011–7–495–728–5218.

Nassau: Nassau Country Office, DEA / Justice, American Embassy Nassau, 3370 Nassau Place, Washington, DC 20520, 9–1–242–322–1700.

New Delhi, India: American Embassy New Delhi, Department of State, 9000 New Delhi Place, Washington, DC 20521, 9–011–91–11–2419–8495.

Nicosia, Cyprus: American Embassy Nicosia, DEA / Justice, PSC 815, Box 1, FPO AE 09836–0001, 9–011–357–22–393–302.

Nuevo Laredo, Mexico: DEA, Nuevo Laredo Resident Office, P.O. Box 3089, Laredo, TX 78044–3089, 9–011–52–867–714–0512.

Ottawa, Canada: American Embassy Ottawa, DEA / Justice, P.O. Box 35, Ogdensburg, New York 13669, 9–1–613–238–5633.

Panama City, Panama: American Embassy Panama, DEA / Justice, Unit 0945, APO AA 34002, 9–011–507–317–5541.

Paramaribo, Suriname: American Embassy Paramaribo, DEA / Justice, 3390 Paramaribo Place, Dulles, VA 20189–3390, 301–985–8693.

Paris, France: American Embassy Paris, DEA / Justice, PSC 116, Box A–224, APO AE 09777, 9–011–33–1–4312–2732.

Peshawar, Pakistan: American Consulate Peshawar, DEA / Justice, Unit 62217, APO AE 09812–2217, 9–011–92–91–584–0424 / 0425.

Port–Au–Prince, Haiti: U.S. Department of State, 3400 Port-au-Prince, DEA, Washington, DC 20521, 9–011–509–2–229–8413.

Port of Spain, Trinidad and Tobago: Department of State DEA / Justice, Port of Spain Country Office, 3410 Port of Spain Place, Washington, DC 20537, 9–1–868–628–8136.

Pretoria, South Africa: American Embassy Pretoria, Department of State, DEA / Justice, Washington, DC 20521–9300, 9–011–2712–362–5008.
Quito, Ecuador: DEA / Justice, American Embassy Quito, Unit 5338, APO AA 34039, 9–011–593–22–231–547.
Rangoon, Burma: American Embassy Rangoon, DEA / Justice, Box B, APO AP 96546, 9–011–95–1–536–509.
Rome, Italy: American Embassy Rome, DEA / Justice, PSC 833, Box 22, FPO AE 09624, 9–011–39–06–4674–2319.
San Jose, Costa Rica: American Embassy San Jose, DEA / Justice, Unit 3440, Box 376, APO AA 34020–0376, 9–011–506–22–20–2433.
San Salvador, El Salvador: American Embassy San Salvador, DEA / Justice, Unit 3130, APO AA 34023, 9–011–503–2278–6005.
Santa Cruz, Resident Office: DEA / Justice, American Embassy, Unit 3913 (Santa Cruz), APO AA 34032, 9–011–591–332–7153.
Santiago, Chile: DEA / Justice, American Embassy Santiago, Unit 3460, Box 136, APO AA 34033–0136, 9–011–56–2–330–3401.
Santo Domingo, Dominican Republic: American Embassy Santo Domingo, DEA / Justice, Unit 3470, APO AA 34041, 9–1–809–687–3754.
Sao Paulo, Resident Office: DEA / Justice, American Embassy Sao Paulo, Unit 3502, APO AA 34030, 301–985–9364.
Seoul, Korea: American Embassy Seoul, DEA / Justice, Unit 15550, APO AP 96205–0001, 9–011–82–2–397–4260.
Singapore: American Embassy Singapore, Unit 4280 Box #30, FPO AP 96507–0030, 9–011–65–6476–9021.
Tashkent: Uzbekistan Country Office, DEA / Justice, 7110 Tashkent Place, Washington, DC 20521, 9–011–998–371–120–8924.
Tegucigalpa, Honduras: American Embassy Tegucigalpa, Tegucigalpa Country Office, Unit 3480, Box 212, APO AA 34022, 301–985–9321.
Tijuana, Resident Office: DEA, Tijuana Resident Office, P.O. 439039, San Diego, CA 92143–9039, 9–011–526–646–22–7452.
Tokyo, Japan: American Embassy Tokyo, DEA / Justice, Unit 45004, Box 224, APO AP 96337–5004, 9–011–81–3–3224–5452.
Trinidad, Bolivia Resident Office: American Embassy La Paz, DEA / Justice, Unit 3220 TRO, DPO AA 34032, 301–985–9398.
Udorn, Thailand Resident Office: American Embassy (Udorn), Box UD, APO AP 96546, 9–011–66–42–247–636.
Vancouver Resident Office: DEA Vancouver, 1574 Gulf Road #1509, Point Roberts, WA 98281, 9–1–604–694–7710.
Vienna, Austria: Vienna Country Office, DEA / Justice, American Embassy, 9900 Vienna Place, Dulles, VA 20189–9900, 9–011–43–1–31339–7551.
Vientiane, Laos: American Embassy Vientiane, DEA / Justice, Unit 8165, Box V, APO AP 96546, 9–011–856–21–219–565.
Warsaw, Poland Country Office: DEA / Justice, American Embassy Warsaw, Unit 5010, Box 27, DPO AE 09730–5010, 9–011–48–22–504–2000.

ENVIRONMENT AND NATURAL RESOURCES DIVISION

RFK Main Justice Building, 950 Pennsylvania Avenue, NW., 20530

601 D Street, NW., 20004 (PHB)

Assistant Attorney General.—John C. Cruden (acting), room 2143 (202) 514–2701.
Principal Deputy Assistant Attorney General.—Vacant, room 2141, 514–3370.
Deputy Assistant Attorneys General: John C. Cruden, room 2611, 514–2718; Eileen Sobeck, room 2607, 514–0943.
Counsels to the Assistant Attorney General: Vacant, room 2129, 514–5243; Vacant, room 2133, 514–4700.
Executive Officer.—Robert L. Bruffy (PHB), room 2038, 616–3147.
Section Chiefs:
Appellate.—James C. Kilbourne (PHB), room 8046, 514–2748.
Environmental Crimes.—Stacey H. Mitchell (PHB), room 2102, 305–0363.
Environmental Defense.—Letitia J. Grishaw (PHB), room 8002, 514–2219.
Environmental Enforcement.—Bruce Gelber (NYAV), room 13063, 514–4624.
General Litigation.—K. Jack Haugrud (PHB), room 3102, 305–0438.
Indian Resources.—Craig Alexander (PHB), room 3016, 514–9080.
Land Acquisition.—Virginia P. Butler (PHB), room 3638, 305–0316.
Policy, Legislation, and Special Litigation.—Pauline M. Milius (PHB), room 8022, 514–2586.

Wildlife and Marine Resources.—Jean E. Williams (PHB), room 3902, 305–0210.

FIELD OFFICES

801 B Street, Suite 504, Anchorage, AK 99501–3657

Trial Attorneys: Regina Belt (907) 271–3456; Dean Dunsmore (907) 271–5452.

501 I Street, Suite 9–700, Sacramento, CA 95814–2322

Trial Attorneys: Stephen Macfarlane (916) 930–2204; Charles Shockey (916) 930–2203.

301 Howard Street, Suite 1050, San Francisco, CA 94105–2001

Trial Attorneys: David Glazer (415) 744–6477; Robert Mullaney (415) 744–6483; Bradley O'Brien (415) 744–6484; Angela O'Connell (415) 744–6485; Judith Rabinowitz (415) 744–6486; Mark Rigau (415) 744–6487.

999 18th Street, Suite 945, North Tower, Denver, CO 80202

Trial Attorneys: David Askman (303) 844–1381; Bruce Bernard (303) 844–1361; Bradley Bridgewater (303) 844–1359; Dave Carson (303) 844–1349; Jerry Ellington (303) 844–1363; Robert Foster (303) 844–1362; Jim Freeman (303) 844–1489; Dave Gehlert (303) 844–1386; Alan Greenberg (303) 844–1366; David Harder (303) 844–1372; Robert Homiak (303) 844–1391; Lee Leininger (303) 844–1364; John Moscato (303) 844–1380; Mark Nitcynski (303) 844–1498; Terry Petrie (303) 844–1369; Daniel Pinkston (303) 844–1804; Susan Schneider (303) 844–1348.

Administrative Officer.—David Jones (303) 844–1807.

161 East Mallard Drive, Suite A, Boise, ID 83706

Trial Attorneys: David Negri (208) 331–5943; Ronald Sutcliffe (208) 334–1211.

One Gateway Center, Suite 6116, Newton Corner, MA 02158

Trial Attorneys: Catherine Fiske (617) 450–0444; Donald Frankel (617) 450–0442.

c/o U.S. Attorney's Office, 105 E. Pine Street, 2nd Floor, Missoula, MT 59802

Trial Attorney.—Robert Anderson (406) 829–3322.

c/o U.S. Attorney's Office, 555 Pleasant Street, Suite 352, Concord, NH 03301

Trial Attorney.— Kristine Tardiff (603) 225–1562, ext. 283.

c/o U.S. Attorney's Office, 201 Third Street, NW., Suite 900, Albuquerque, NM 87102

Trial Attorney.—Andrew Smith (505) 224–1468.

c/o NOAA / DARCNW, 7600 San Point Way, NE., Seattle, WA 98115–0070

Trial Attorneys: Jim Nicholl (206) 526–6616; Mike Zevenbergen (206) 526–6607.

EXECUTIVE OFFICE FOR IMMIGRATION REVIEW (EOIR)

5107 Leesburg Pike, Suite 2600, Falls Church, VA 22041

Director.—Thomas Snow (acting), 2600 SKYT (703) 305–0169.

Deputy Director.—Vacant.
Associate Director/Chief of Staff.—Paula Nasca.
Executive Secretariat.—Terry Samuels.
Assistant Director/General Counsel.—John Blum (acting), 2600 SKYT, 305–0470.
Deputy General Counsel.—Vacant.
Assistant Director of:
Administration.—Lawrence M. D'Elia, 2300 SKYT, 305–1171.
Management Programs.—Frances A. Mooney, 2600 SKYT, 305–0289.
Planning, Analysis and Technology.—Amy Dale, 2600 SKYT, 605–0445.
Chairman, Board of Immigration Appeals.—Juan Osuna, 2400 SKYT, 305–1194.
Chief, Office of the Chief Administrative Hearing Officer.—Michael J. Creppy, 2500 SKYT, 305–0864.
Chief Judge, Office of the Chief Immigration Judge.—Michael C. McGoings (acting), 2500 SKYT, 305–1247.
Deputy Chief Immigration Judge.—Vacant.
Telephone Directory Coordinator.—Annette Thomas, 2300 SKYT, 605–1336.

EXECUTIVE OFFICE FOR UNITED STATES ATTORNEYS (EOUSA)

RFK Main Justice Building, Room 2242, phone (202) 514–2121

Director.—H. Marshall Jarrett, room 2242.
Deputy Director/Chief of Staff.—Terry Derden, room 2242.
Administrative Officer.—Paul Suddes (acting), room 2248, 307–0450.
General Counsel.—Jay Macklin, room 5500, 501 3rd Street, NW., 514–4024.
Director, Office of Legal Education.—Michael Bailie, National Advocacy Center, 1620 Pendleton Street, Columbia, SC 29201 (803) 705–5100.
Assistant Director:
Equal Employment Opportunity Staff.—Rita Sampson, room 524, NPB, 514–3982.
Evaluation and Review Staff.—Chris Barnes, room 8500, BICN, 616–6790.
FOIA and Privacy Act Staff.—Garry Stewart, room 7300, BICN, 616–6757
Assistant Director/Senior Advisor for Management and Operations, District Management and Assistance Program.—David Downs, room 8100, BICN, 616–6600.
Senior Counsel for Strategic Planning and Communications.—Frank Shults, room 2242, 514–2121.
Executive Assistant/Attorney Generals Advisory Committee Liaison.—Judith Beeman, room 2335, 514–4633.
Deputy Director/Counsel to the Director.—Norman Wong, room 2242, 514–2121.
Counsel for Legal Programs.—Dan Villegas, room 7600, BICN, 616–6444.
Assistant Director of:
Financial Litigation Unit.—Laurie Levin, room 7600, BICN, 616–6444.
LECC/Victim Witness.—Vacant.
Programs.—Virginia Howard, room 7600, BICN, 616–6444.
Counsel for Legal Initiatives.—David Smith, room 2256, 353–3035.
Assistant Director, Data Analysis Staff.—Michelle Slusher, room 2000, BICN, 616–6779.
Chief Financial Officer.—Lisa Bevels, room 2200, BICN, 616–6886.
Assistant Director of:
Audits.—Andrew Katsaros, room 2200, BICN.
Budget Execution.—Mary Ellen Kline, room 2200, BICN.
Budget Formulation.—Kevin Fick, room 2200, BICN.
Financial Systems.—Vacant, room 2200, BICN.
Chief Information Officer.—Mark Fleshman, room 2300, BICN, 616–6973.
Assistant Director of:
Case Management Staff.—Joe Welsh, room 7500, BICN, 616–6919.
Information Security Staff.—Ted Shelkey, room 2300, BICN, 616–6973.
Office Automation Staff: Anne Callaghan (acting), room 9100, BICN, 616–6985; Kevin Shaw (acting), room 9100, BICN, 616–1259.
Telecommunications and Technology Development Staff.—Denny Ko, room 6004, BICN, 305–4772.
Chief Operating Officer.—Paul Suddes (acting), room 2248, 307–0450.
Associate Director.—Gail Ratliffe, room 8100, BICN, 616–6876.
Assistant Director of:
Acquisitions Staff.—Janis Harrington, room 5200, BICN, 616–6425.
Employee Assistance Staff.—Ed Neunlist, room 6800, BICN, 353–1722.
Facilities/Support Services Staff.—Ana Indovina, room 5200, BICN, 616–6425.
Personnel Staff.—Jean Dunn, room 8430, BICN, 305–8147.

Security Programs Staff.—Tim George, room 2600, BICN, 616–6878.
Victims Rights Ombudsman.—Marie O'Rourke, room 2521, 616–0003.
Office of Tribal Justice.—Tracy Toulou, room 2229A, 514–8812.

EXECUTIVE OFFICE FOR UNITED STATES TRUSTEES

20 Massachusetts Avenue, NW., 20530, phone (202) 307–1391

http://www.usdoj.gov/ust

Director.—Clifford J. White III, room 8000.
Principal Deputy Director.—Mark A. Redmiles.
Deputy Director.—Vacant.
Associate Director.—Jeffrey M. Miller.
General Counsel.—Ramona Elliott, room 8100, 307–1399.
Chief Information Officer.—Monique K. Bourque, 353–3548.
Assistant Director, Office of:
Administration.—Santal Manos, room 8200, 514–8646.
Research and Planning.—Philip Crewson, room 8310, 616–8932.
Review and Oversight.—Doreen Solomon, room 8338, 305–0222.

U.S. TRUSTEES

Region I:
Room 1184, 10 Causeway Street, Boston, MA 02222–1043 (617) 788–0400.
Suite 303, 537 Congress Street, Portland, ME 04101 (207) 780–3564.
14th Floor, 446 Main Street, Worchester, MA 01608 (508) 793–0555.
Suite 605, 1000 Elm Street, Manchester, NH 03101 (603) 666–7908.
Suite 910, 10 Dorrance Street, Providence, RI 02903 (401) 528–5551.
Region II:
21st floor, 33 Whitehall Street, New York, NY 10004 (212) 510–0500.
Suite 200, 74 Chapel Street, Albany, NY 12207 (518) 434–4553.
Suite 100, 42 Delaware Avenue, Buffalo, NY 14202 (716) 551–5541.
Long Island Federal Courthouse, 560 Federal Plaza, Central Islip, NY 11722–4456 (631) 715–7800.
Suite 302, 150 Court Street, New Haven, CT 06510 (203) 773–2210.
Room 609, 100 State Street, Rochester, NY 14614 (716) 263–5812.
Room 105, 10 Broad Street, Utica, NY 13501 (315) 793–8191.
Suite 4529, 271 Cadman Plaza East, Brooklyn, NY 11201 (718) 422–4960
Region III:
Suite 500, 833 Chestnut Street, Philadelphia, PA 19107 (215) 597–4411.
Suite 2100, One Newark Center, Newark, NJ 07102 (973) 645–3014.
Suite 970, 1001 Liberty Avenue, Pittsburgh, PA 15222 (412) 644–4756.
Suite 1190, 228 Walnut Street, Harrisburg, PA 17101 or P.O. Box 969, Harrisburg, PA 17108 (717) 221–4515.
Suite 2207, 844 King Street, Wilmington, DE 19801 (302) 573–6491.
Region IV:
Suite 953, 1835 Assembly Street, Columbia, SC 29201 (803) 765–5250.
Room 210, 115 S. Union Street, Alexandria, VA 22314 (703) 557–7176.
Room 625, 200 Granby Street, Norfolk, VA 23510 (757) 441–6012.
Room 2025, 300 Virginia Street East, Charleston, WV 25301 (304) 347–3400.
First Campbell Square Building, 210 First Street, SW., Suite 505, Roanoke, VA 24011 (540) 857–2806.
Suite 4304, U.S. Courthouse, 701 East Broad Street, Richmond, VA 23219 (804) 771–2310.
Suite 600, 6305 Ivy Lane, Greenbelt, MD 20770 (301) 344–6216.
Suite 2625, 101 West Lombard Street, Baltimore, MD 21201 (410) 962–4300.
Region V:
Suite 2110, 400 Poydras Street, New Orleans, LA 70130 (504) 589–4018.
Suite 3196, 300 Fannin Street, Shreveport, LA 71101–3099 (318) 676–3456.
Suite 706, 100 West Capitol Street, Jackson, MS 39269 (601) 965–5241.
Region VI:
Room 976, 1100 Commerce Street, Dallas, TX 75242 (214) 767–8967.
Room 300, 110 North College Avenue, Tyler, TX 75702 (903) 590–1450.
Region VII:

Suite 3516, 515 Rusk Avenue, Houston, TX 77002 (713) 718–4650.
Room 230, 903 San Jacinto, Austin, TX 78701 (512) 916–5328.
Suite 533, 615 East Houston Street, San Antonio, TX 78205 (210) 472–4640.
Suite 1107, 606 North Carancahua Street, Corpus Christi, TX 78476 (361) 888–3261.

Region VIII:
Suite 400, 200 Jefferson Avenue, Memphis, TN 38103 (901) 544–3251.
Suite 512, 601 West Broadway, Louisville, KY 40202 (502) 582–6000.
Fourth floor, 31 East 11th Street, Chattanooga, TN 37402 (423) 752–5153.
Room 318, 701 Broadway, Nashville, TN 37203 (615) 736–2254.
Suite 500, 100 East Vine Street, Lexington, KY 40507 (859) 233–2822.

Region IX:
Suite 441, BP Building, 201 Superior Avenue East, Cleveland, OH 44114 (216) 522–7800.
Suite 200, Schaff Building, 170 North High Street, Columbus, OH 43215–2403 (614) 469–7411.
Suite 2030, 36 East Seventh Street, Cincinnati, OH 45202 (513) 684–6988.
Suite 700, 211 West Fort Street, Detroit, MI 48226 (313) 226–7999.
Suite 200R, 125 Ottawa Street, Grand Rapids, MI 49503 (616) 456–2002.

Region X:
Room 1000, 101 West Ohio Street, Indianapolis, IN 46204 (317) 226–6101.
Suite 1100, 401 Main Street, Peoria, IL 61602 (309) 671–7854.
Suite 555, 100 East Wayne Street, South Bend, IN 46601 (574) 236–8105.

Region XI:
Suite 873, 219 S. Dearborn Street, Chicago, IL 60606 (312) 886–5785.
Room 430, 517 East Wisconsin Avenue, Milwaukee, WI 53202 (414) 297–4499.
Suite 304, 780 Regent Street, Madison, WI 53715 (608) 264–5522.

Region XII:
Suite 400, 225 Second Street, SE., Cedar Rapids, IA 52401 (319) 364–2211.
Suite 1015, U.S. Courthouse, 300 S. Fourth Street, Minneapolis, MN 55415 (612) 664–5500.
Room 793, 210 Walnut Street, Des Moines, IA 50309–2108 (515) 284–4982.
Suite 303, 314 South Main Street, Sioux Falls, SD 57102–6321 (605) 330–4450.

Region XIII:
Suite 3440, 400 East 9th Street, Kansas City, MO 64106–1910 (816) 512–1940.
Suite 6353, 111 South 10th Street, St. Louis, MO 63102 (314) 539–2976.
Suite 1200, 200 West Capital Avenue, Little Rock, AR 72201–3344 (501) 324–7357.
Suite 1148, 111 South 18th Plaza, Omaha, NE 68102 (402) 221–4300.

Region XIV:
Suite 204, 230 North First Avenue, Phoenix, AZ 85003 or P.O. Box 36170, Phoenix, AZ 85067 (602) 682–2600.

Region XV:
Suite 600, 402 West Broadway Street, San Diego, CA 92101–8511 (619) 557–5013.
Suite 602, 1132 Bishop Street, Honolulu, HI 96813–2836 (808) 522–8150.

Region XVI:
725 South Figueroa, 26th floor, Los Angeles, CA 90017 (213) 894–6811.
Suite 9041, 411 West Fourth Street, Santa Ana, CA 92701–8000 (714) 338–3401.
Suite 300, 3685 Main Street, Riverside, CA 92501 (909) 276–6990.
Suite 115, 21051 Warner Center Lane, Woodland Hills, CA 91367 (818) 716–8800.

Region XVII:
Suite 700, 235 Pine Street, San Francisco, CA 94104–3401 (415) 705–3300.
Suite 7–500, U.S. Courthouse, 501 I Street, Sacramento, CA 95814–2322 (916) 930–2100.
Suite 1401, 2500 Tulare Street, Fresno, CA 93721 (559) 487–5002.
Suite 690N, 1301 Clay Street, Oakland, CA 94612–5217 (510) 637–3200.
Room 4300, 300 Las Vegas Boulevard South, Las Vegas, NV 89101 (702) 388–6600.
Suite 2129, 300 Booth Street, Reno, NV 89502 (775) 784–5335.
Room 268, 280 South First Street, San Jose, CA 95113 (408) 535–5525.

Region XVIII:
Suite 5103, 700 Stewart Street, Seattle, WA 98101 (206) 553–2000.
Suite 213, 620 Southwest Main Street, Portland, OR 97205 (503) 326–4000.
Suite 220, 720 Park Boulevard, Boise, ID 83712 (208) 334–1300.
Room 593, 920 West Riverside, Spokane, WA 99201 (509) 353–2999.
Suite 204, 301 Central Avenue, Great Falls, MT 59401 (406) 761–8777.
Suite 258, 605 West Fourth Avenue, Anchorage, AK 99501 (907) 271–2600.
Suite 1100, 405 East Eighth Avenue, Eugene, OR 97401 (541) 465–6330.

Region XIX:

Suite 1551, 999 Eighteenth Street, Denver, CO 80202 (303) 312–7230.
Suite 203, 308 West 21st Street, Cheyenne, WY 82001 (307) 772–2790.
Suite 300, 405 South Main Street, Salt Lake City, UT 84111 (801) 524–5734.

Region XX:

Room 500, Epic Center, 301 North Main Street, Wichita, KS 67202 (316) 269–6637.
Suite 112, 421 Gold Street, SW., Albuquerque, NM 87102 (505) 248–6544.
Suite 408, 215 Northwest Dean A. McGee Avenue, Oklahoma City, OK 73102 (405) 231–5950.
Suite 225, 224 South Boulder Avenue, Tulsa, OK 74103 (918) 581–6670.

Region XXI:

Room 362, 75 Spring Street, SW., Atlanta, GA 30303 (404) 331–4437.
Suite 301, 500 Tanca Street, San Juan, PR 00901 (787) 729–7444.
Room 1204, 51 Southwest First Avenue, Miami, FL 33130 (305) 536–7285.
Suite 302, 222 West Oglethorpe Avenue, Savannah, GA 31401 (912) 652–4112.
Suite 1200, 501 East Polk Street, Tampa, FL 33602 (813) 228–2000.
Suite 302, 440 Martin Luther King Boulevard, Macon, GA 31201 (478) 752–3544.
Suite 128, 110 East Park Avenue, Tallahassee, FL 32301 (850) 521–5050.
Suite 620, 135 West Central Boulevard, Orlando, FL 32801 (407) 648–6301.

BUREAU OF ALCOHOL, TOBACCO, FIREARMS, AND EXPLOSIVES (ATF)

99 New York Avenue, NE., 20226

OFFICE OF THE DIRECTOR

Director.—Kenneth Melson (acting), (202) 648–8700.
Deputy Director.—Vacant.

OFFICE OF CHIEF COUNSEL

Chief Counsel.—Stephen R. Rubenstein, 648–7000.
Deputy Chief Counsel.—Teresa Ficaretta.

OFFICE OF ENFORCEMENT PROGRAMS AND SERVICES

Assistant Director.—Carson Carroll, 648–7080.
Deputy Assistant Director.—Audrey Stucko.

OFFICE OF EQUAL OPPORTUNITY

Executive Assistant.—Stacie Brockman, 648–7597.
Deputy Executive Assistant.—Dora Silas, 648–7393.

OFFICE OF FIELD OPERATIONS

Assistant Director.—William J. Hoover, 648–8410.
Deputy Assistant Director for—
Central.—Mark Chait.
East.—Julie Torres.
West.—William McMahon.
Industry Operations.—James A. Zamillo, Sr.

OFFICE OF MANAGEMENT/CFO

Assistant Director/Chief Financial Officer.—Melanie Stinnett, 648–7800.
Deputy Assistant Director.—Vivian Michalic.

OFFICE OF OMBUDSMAN

Ombudsman.—Marianne Ketels, 648–7412.

OFFICE OF PROFESSIONAL RESPONSIBILITY AND SECURITY OPERATIONS

Assistant Director.—Kelvin Crenshaw, 648–7500.
Deputy Assistant Director.—Kenneth Massey.

OFFICE OF PUBLIC AND GOVERNMENTAL AFFAIRS

Assistant Director.—W. Larry Ford, 648–8500.
Deputy Assistant Director.—Arthur Herbert.
Chief of:
Legislative Affairs Division.—Henry Lescault, 648–8510.
Public Affairs Division.—Scott Thomasson, 648–8500.

OFFICE OF SCIENCE AND TECHNOLOGY/CIO

Assistant Director/Chief Information Officer.—W. Larry Bell (acting), 648–8390.
Deputy Assistant Director.—Francis Frande (acting).

OFFICE OF STRATEGIC INTELLIGENCE AND INFORMATION

Assistant Director.—James E. McDermond, 648–7600.
Deputy Assistant Director.—Steve Martin.

OFFICE OF TRAINING AND PROFESSIONAL DEVELOPMENT

Assistant Director.—Mark Logan, 648–8460.
Deputy Assistant Director.—Valerie Goddard.

FEDERAL BUREAU OF INVESTIGATION

J. Edgar Hoover Building, 935 Pennsylvania Avenue, NW., 20535–0001

phone (202) 324–3000, http://www.fbi.gov

Director.—Robert S. Mueller III, 324–3444.
Deputy Director.—John S. Pistole, 324–3315.
Associate Deputy Director.—Timothy Murphy, 324–4180.
Chief of Staff.—W. Lee Rawls, 324–3444.

OFFICE OF THE DIRECTOR/DEPUTY DIRECTOR/ASSOCIATE DEPUTY DIRECTOR

Office of the General Counsel.—Valerie E. Caproni, 324–6829.
Office of Public Affairs.—John Miller, 324–5352.
Office of Congressional Affairs.—Richard Powers, 324–5051.
Office of Professional Responsiblity.—Candice M. Will, 324–8284.
Office of Equal Employment Opportunity Affairs.—Veronica Venture, 324–4128.
Office of the Ombudsman.—Sarah Zeigler, 324–2156.
Inspection Division.—Kevin Perkins, 324–2901.
Facilities and Logistics Services Division.—Patrick G. Findlay, 324–2875.
Finance Division.—Richard Haley II, 324–4104.
Records Management Division.—William L. Hooton, 324–7141.
Security Division.—Roland Corvington, Jr., 324–7112.

OFFICE OF THE CHIEF INFORMATION OFFICER

Chief Information Officer.—Chad Fulgham, 324–6165.
Assistant Director of:
Information Technology Operations Division.—Louis J. Blazy III, 324–4507.
IT Policy and Planning Office.—Carlo Lucchesi, 233–9201.
IT Program Management Office.—John M. Hope, 324–2307.

Office of the Chief Technology Officer.—Jerome W. Israel, 324–5441.

CRIMINAL INVESTIGATIONS BRANCH

Executive Assistant Director.—Thomas Harrington, 324–4880.
Assistant Director of:
Criminal Investigative Division.—Kenneth Kaiser, Jr., 324–4260.
Critical Incident Response Group.—Robert Blecksmith (703) 632–4100.
Cyber Division.—Shawn Henry, 651–3044.
Office of International Operations.—Sean Joyce (acting), 324–5292.
Law Enforcement Coordination Office.—Ronald Ruecker, 324–7126.

HUMAN RESOURCES BRANCH

Executive Assistant Director.—Donald E. Packham, 324–3514.
Assistant Director of:
Human Resources Division.—John Raucci, 324–3000.
Training and Development Division.—Brian Lamkin (703) 632–1100.

NATIONAL SECURITY BRANCH

Executive Assistant Director.—Arthur Cummings, 324–7045.
Assistant Director of:
Counterintelligence Division.—Daniel Cloyd, 324–4614.
Counterterrorism Division.—Michael Heimbach, Jr., 324–2770.
Directorate of Intelligence.—Kevin Favreau, 324–7605.
Weapons of Mass Destruction Directorate.—Dr. Vahid Majidi, 324–4965.

SCIENCE AND TECHNOLOGY BRANCH

Executive Assistant Director.—Louis Grever (202) 324–0805.
Assistant Director of:
Criminal Justice Information Services Division.—Jerome Pender III (304) 625–2700.
Laboratory Division.—D. Christian Hassell (703) 632–7001.
Operational Technology Division.—Marcus C. Thomas (acting), (703) 632–6100.

FIELD DIVISIONS

Albany: 200 McCarty Avenue, Albany, NY 12209 (518) 465–7551.
Albuquerque: 4200 Luecking Park Avenue NE., Albuquerque, NM 87107 (505) 224–2000.
Anchorage: 101 East Sixth Avenue, Anchorage, AK 99501 (907) 258–5322.
Atlanta: 2635 Century Center Parkway, NE., Suite 400, Atlanta, GA 30345 (404) 679–9000.
Baltimore: 2600 Lord Baltimore Avenue, Baltimore, MD 21244 (410) 265–8080.
Birmingham: 1000 18th Street North, Birmingham, AL 35203 (205) 326–6166.
Boston: One Center Plaza, Suite 600, Boston, MA 02108 (617) 742–5533.
Buffalo: One FBI Plaza, Buffalo, NY 14202 (716) 856–7800.
Charlotte: Wachovia Building, 400 South Tryon Street, Suite 900, Charlotte, NC 28285 (704) 377–9200.
Chicago: 2111 West Roosevelt Road, Chicago, IL 60608–1128 (312) 431–1333.
Cincinnati: Federal Office Building, 550 Main Street, Room 9000, Cincinnati, OH 45202 (513) 421–4310.
Cleveland: 1501 Lakeside Avenue, Cleveland, OH 44114 (216) 522–1400.
Columbia: 151 Westpark Boulevard, Columbia, SC 29210 (803) 551–4200.
Dallas: J. Gordon Shanklin Building, One Justice Way, Dallas, TX 75220 (972) 559–5000.
Denver: Federal Office Building, 1961 Stout Street, Room 1823, Denver, CO 80294 (303) 629–7171.
Detroit: P.V. McNamara Federal Office Building, 477 Michigan Avenue, 26th Floor, Detroit, MI 48226 (313) 965–2323.

El Paso: 660 South Mesa Hills Drive, Suite 3000, El Paso, TX 79912 (915) 832–5000.
Honolulu: Kalanianaole Federal Office Building, 300 Ala Moana Boulevard, Room 4–230, Honolulu, HI 96850 (808) 566–4300.
Houston: 2500 East T.C. Jester, Suite 200, Houston, TX 77008 (713) 693–5000.
Indianapolis: Federal Office Building, 575 North Pennsylvania Street, Room 679, Indianapolis, IN 46204 (371) 639–3301.
Jackson: Federal Office Building, 100 West Capitol Street, Suite 1553, Jackson, MS 39269 (601) 948–5000.
Jacksonville: 7820 Arlington Expressway, Suite 200, Jacksonville, FL 32211 (904) 721–1211.
Kansas City: 1300 Summit, Kansas City, MO 64105 (816) 512–8200.
Knoxville: John J. Duncan Federal Office Building, 710 Locust Street, Room 600, Knoxville, TN 37902 (423) 544–0751.
Las Vegas: John Lawrence Bailey Building, 1787 West Lake Mead Boulevard, Las Vegas, NV 89106–2135 (702) 385–1281.
Little Rock: #24 Shackleford West Boulevard, Little Rock, AR 72211 (501) 221–9100.
Los Angeles: Federal Office Building, 11000 Wilshire Boulevard, Suite 1700, Los Angeles, CA 90024 (310) 477–6565.
Louisville: 600 Martin Luther King, Jr. Place, Room 500, Louisville, KY 40202 (502) 583–2941.
Memphis: Eagle Crest Building, 225 North Humphreys Boulevard, Suite 3000, Memphis, TN 38120 (901) 747–4300.
Miami: 16320 Northwest Second Avenue, Miami, FL 33169 (305) 944–9101.
Milwaukee: 330 East Kilbourn Avenue, Suite 600, Milwaukee, WI 53202 (414) 276–4684.
Minneapolis: 111 Washington Avenue South, Suite 100, Minneapolis, MN 55401 (612) 376–3200.
Mobile: 200 North Royal Street, Mobile, AL 36602 (334) 438–3674.
New Haven: 600 State Street, New Haven, CT 06511 (203) 777–6311.
New Orleans: 2901 Leon C. Simon Boulevard, New Orleans, LA 70126 (504) 816–3122.
New York: 26 Federal Plaza, 23rd Floor, New York, NY 10278 (212) 384–1000.
Newark: Claremont Tower Building, 11 Centre Place, Newark, NJ 07102 (973) 792–3000.
Norfolk: 150 Corporate Boulevard, Norfolk, VA 23502 (757) 455–0100.
Oklahoma City: 3301 West Memorial, Oklahoma City, OK 73134 (405) 290–7770.
Omaha: 10755 Burt Street, Omaha, NE 68114 (402) 493–8688.
Philadelphia: William J. Green, Jr., Federal Office Building, 600 Arch Street, Eighth Floor, Philadelphia, PA 19106 (215) 418–4000.
Phoenix: 201 East Indianola Avenue, Suite 400, Phoenix, AZ 85012 (602) 279–5511.
Pittsburgh: Martha Dixon Building, 3311 East Carson Street, Pittsburgh, PA 15203 (412) 432–4000.
Portland: Crown Plaza Building, 1500 Southwest First Avenue, Suite 401, Portland, OR 97201 (503) 224–4181.
Richmond: 1970 East Parham Road, Richmond, VA 23228 (804) 261–1044.
Sacramento: 4500 Orange Grove Avenue, Sacramento, CA 95841 (916) 481–9110.
Salt Lake City: 257 Towers Building, 257 East, 200 South, Suite 1200, Salt Lake City, UT 84111 (801) 579–1400.
San Antonio: 5740 University Heights Boulevard, San Antonio, TX 78249 (210) 225–6741.
San Diego: Federal Office Building, 9797 Aero Drive, San Diego, CA 92123 (858) 565–1255.
San Francisco: 450 Golden Gate Avenue, 13th Floor, San Francisco, CA 64102 (415) 553–7400.
San Juan: U.S. Federal Office Building, 150 Chardon Avenue, Room 526, Hato Rey, PR 00918 (787) 754–6000.
Seattle: 1110 Third Avenue, Seattle, WA 98101 (206) 622–0460.
Springfield: 900 East Linton Avenue, Springfield, IL 62703 (217) 522–9675.
St. Louis: 2222 Market Street, St. Louis, MO 63103 (314) 241–5357.
Tampa: 5525 West Gray Street, Tampa, FL 33609 (813) 273–4566.
Washington, DC: 601 Fourth Street, NW., Washington, DC 20535 (202) 278–3400.

FEDERAL BUREAU OF PRISONS (BOP)

320 First Street, NW., 20534

General Information Number (202) 307–3198

Director.—Harley G. Lappin, room 654, HOLC, 307–3250.
Director, National Institute of Corrections.—Morris L. Thigpen, Sr., 7th floor, 500 FRST, 307–3106.
Assistant Director of:

Administration.—William Dalius, 9th floor, 500 FRST, 307–3230.
Correctional Programs.—Joyce Conley, room 554, HOLC, 307–3226.
General Counsel.—Kathleen M. Kenney, room 958C, HOLC, 307–3062.
Health Services.—Newton Kendig, M.D., room 1054, HOLC, 307–3055.
Human Resources Management.—Whitney LeBlanc, room 754, HOLC, 307–3082.
Industries, Education, and Vocational Training.—Paul Laird, 8th floor, 400 FRST, 305–3501.
Information, Policy and Public Affairs.—Thomas R. Kane, Ph.D., room 641, HOLC, 514–6537.
Regional Director for—
Mid-Atlantic.—Kim White (301) 317–3101.
North Central.—Michael K. Nalley (913) 621–3939.
Northeast.—Scott Dodrill (215) 521–7300.
South Central.—Gerardo Maldonado (214) 224–3389.
Southeast.—Ray Holt (678) 686–1200.
Western.—Robert McFadden (209) 956–9700.
Telephone Directory Coordinator.—Marla Clayton, 307–3250.

OFFICE OF THE FEDERAL DETENTION TRUSTEE

4601 N. Fairfax Drive, Suite 9110, Arlington, VA 22203, phone (202) 353–4601

Trustee.—Stacia A. Hylton.
Deputy Trustee.—David F. Musel.

FOREIGN CLAIMS SETTLEMENT COMMISSION

Bicentennial Building (BICN), 600 E Street, NW., Suite 6002, 20579, phone (202) 616–6975

Chair.—Mauricio J. Tamargo.
Commissioners.—Stephen C. King; Rafael E. Martinez.
Chief Counsel.—Jaleh F. Barrett.
Special Assistant.—Emily B. Hollenberg, 616–6983.
Executive Officer.—Judith H. Lock, 616–6986.

OFFICE OF INFORMATION POLICY

1425 New York Avenue, NW., 20530, phone (202) 514–3642

Director.—Melanie Ann Pustay.
Chief of Staff.—Carmen L. Mallon.
Associate Director.—Janice Galli McLeod.

OFFICE OF THE INSPECTOR GENERAL

RFK Main Justice Building, Room 4706, phone (202) 514–3435

950 Pennsylvania Avenue, NW., 20530

Inspector General.—Glenn A. Fine.
Deputy Inspector General.—Paul K. Martin.
Counselor to the Inspector General.—Cynthia A. Schnedar.
Senior Counsel.—William Blier.
General Counsel.—Gail A. Robinson, RFK, Suite 4726, 616–0646.
Assistant Inspectors General:
Audit.—Caryn Marske (NYAV), Suite 13000, 616–1697.
Evaluations and Inspections.—Mike Gulledge (NYAV), Suite 6100, 616–4620.
Investigations.—Thomas F. McLaughlin (NYAV), Suite 7100, 616–4760.
Management and Planning.—Gregory T. Peters (NYAV), Suite 7000, 616–4550.
Oversight and Review.—Carol F. Ochoa (NYAV), Suite 13000, 616–0645.

REGIONAL AUDIT OFFICES

Atlanta: Ferris B. Polk, Suite 1130, 75 Spring Street, Atlanta, GA 30303 (404) 331–5928.

Chicago: Carol S. Taraszka, Suite 3510, Citicorp Center, 500 West Madison Street, Chicago, IL 60661 (312) 353–1203.

Dallas: Robert J. Kaufman, Room 575, Box 4, 207 South Houston Street, Dallas, TX 75202–4724 (214) 655–5000.

Denver: David M. Sheeren, Suite 1500, Chancery Building, 1120 Lincoln Street, Denver, CO 80203 (303) 864–2000.

Philadelphia: Thomas O. Puerzer, Suite 201, 701 Market Street, Philadelphia, PA 19106 (215) 580–2111.

San Francisco: David J. Gaschke, Suite 201, 1200 Bayhill Drive, San Bruno, CA 94066 (650) 876–9220.

Washington: Troy M. Meyer, 1300 North 17th Street, Suite 3400, Arlington, VA 22209 (202) 616–4688.

Computer Security and Information Technology Audit Office: Norman Hammonds, room 5000 (202) 616–3801.

Financial Statement Audit Office: Marilyn A. Kessinger, 1125 New York Avenue, NW., #13000, Washington, DC 20530 (202) 616–4660.

REGIONAL INVESTIGATIONS OFFICES

Atlanta: Eddie D. Davis, 60 Forsyth Street, SW., Room 8M45, Atlanta, GA 30303 (404) 562–1980.

Boston: Thomas M. Hopkins, U.S. Courthouse, 1 Courthouse Way, Room 9200, Boston, MA 02210 (617) 748–3218.

Chicago: John F. Oleskowicz, P.O. Box 1802, Chicago, IL 60690 (312) 886–7050.

Denver: Norman K. Lau, Suite 1501, 1120 Lincoln Street, Denver, CO 80203 (303) 335–4201.

Dallas: James H. Mahon, 2505 State Highway 360, Room 410, Grand Prairie, TX 75050 (817) 385–5200.

Detroit: Nicholas V. Candela, Suite 1402, 211 West Fort Street, Detroit, MI 48226 (313) 226–4005.

El Paso: Eric Benn, Suite 135, 4050 Rio Bravo, El Paso, TX 79902 (915) 577–0102.

Houston: Carlos Capano, P.O. Box 53509, Houston, TX 77052 (713) 718–4888.

Los Angeles: Kenneth R. Strange, Jr., Suite 655, 330 North Brand Street, Glendale, CA 91203 (818) 543–1172.

McAllen: Wayne D. Beaman, Suite 510, Bentsen Tower, 1701 W. Business Highway 83, McAllen, TX 78501 (956) 618–8145.

Miami: Teresa M. Gulotta Powers, Suite 200, 510 Shotgun Road, Sunrise, FL 33326 (954) 370–8300.

New York: Ralph F. Paige, One Battery Park, 29th floor, New York, NY 10004 (212) 824–3650.

Philadelphia: Kenneth R. Connaughton, Jr., P.O. Box 43508, Philadelphia, PA 19106 (215) 861–8755.

San Francisco: Michael Barranti, Suite 220, 1200 Bayhill Drive, San Bruno, CA 94066 (650) 876–9058.

Seattle: Wayne Hawney, Suite 104, 620 Kirkland Way, Kirkland, WA 98033 (425) 828–3998.

Tucson: Joseph V. Cuffari, 405 West Congress, Room 3600, Tucson, AZ 85701 (520) 620–7389.

Washington: Gene E. Morrison, 1425 New York Avenue, NW., Suite 7100, Washington, DC 20530 (202) 616–4760.

Fraud Detection Office.—David R. Glendinning, room 7100 (202) 353–2975.

INTERPOL—U.S. NATIONAL CENTRAL BUREAU

phone (202) 616–9000

Director.—Martin Renkiewicz, 616–9700.

Deputy Director.—Timothy A. Williams.

Information Technology.—Wayne Towson, 616–3855.

General Counsel.—Kevin Smith, 616–4103.

Assistant Director, Division of:

Administrative Services.—Joanne Fitzgerald, 616–7983.

Alien/Fugitive.—Lydia Blakey, 616–0310.

Drug.—Jose Baeza, 616–3379.

Economic Crimes.—Gary Hyde, 616–5466.

State and Local Liaison.—Michael D. Muth, 616–8272.

Terrorism and Violent Crimes.—Michael Bukovac, 616–7258.

OFFICE OF INTERGOVERNMENTAL AND PUBLIC LIAISON

RFK Main Justice Building, Room 1629, phone (202) 514–3465

Director.—Vacant.
Deputy Director.—Vacant.
Associate Director.—Vacant.

JUSTICE MANAGEMENT DIVISION

RFK Main Justice Building, 950 Pennsylvania Avenue, NW., 20530

Rockville Building, 1151–D Seven Locks Road, Rockville, MD 20854 (ROC)

Bicentennial Building, 600 E Street, NW., 20004 (BICN)

National Place Building, 1331 Pennsylvania Avenue, NW., 20530 (NPB)

20 Massachusetts Avenue, NW., 20530

Patrick Henry Building, 601 D Street, NW., 20530 (PHB)

1425 New York Avenue, NW., 20530

Assistant Attorney General for Administration.—Lee J. Lofthus, room 1111 (202) 514–3101.
Deputy Assistant Attorney General/Policy, Management and Planning.—Michael H. Allen.
Staff Directors for—
Department Ethics Office.—Janice Rodgers, (NPB), room 1150, 514–8196.
General Counsel Office.—Stuart Frisch, General Counsel (NPB), room 520, 514–3452.
Internal Review and Evaluation Office.—Neil Ryder, room 1055 (NPB), 616–5499.
Management and Planning.—David Orr (NPB), room 1400, 307–1800.
Procurement Executive.—Michael H. Allen, room 1111, 514–3101.
Records Management Policy Office.—Jeanette Plante, room 1209 (NPB), 514–3528.
Small and Disadvantaged Business Utilization Office.—David Sutton (NPB), room 1010, 616–0521.
Deputy Assistant Attorney General/Controller.—Jolene Lauria-Sullens, room 1112, 514–1843.
Staff Directors for—
Asset Forfeiture Management.—Candace Olds, room 6400, 20 Massachusetts Avenue, 616–8000.
Budget.—Karin O'Leary, room 7601, 514–4082.
Debt Collection Management.—Kathleen Haggerty (NPB), room 904, 514–5343.
Finance.—Melinda Morgan (BICN), room 4070, 616–5800.
Procurement Services.—James Johnston (NPB), room 1000, 307–2000.
Unified Financial System Project Management Office.—Kay Clarey, room 10100 (PHB), 305–3651.
Deputy Assistant Attorney General, Human Resources/Administration.—Mari Santangelo, room 1112, 514–5501.
Staff Directors for—
Attorney Recruitment and Management Office.—Louis DeFalaise, Suite 5200, 20 Massachusetts Avenue, 514–8900.
Consolidated Executive Office.—Cyntoria Carter, room 7113, 514–5537.
DOJ Executive Secretariat.—Dana Paige, room 4412, 514–2063.
Equal Employment Opportunity.—Vontell Tucker, 1425 New York Avenue, Suite 1000, 616–4800.
Facilities and Administrative Services.—Edward A. Hamilton, (NPB), room 1050, 616–2995.
Library.—Blaine Dessy, room 7535, 514–2133.
Personnel.—Rodney Markham (NPB), room 1110, 514–6788.
Security and Emergency Planning.—James Dunlap, room 6217, 514–2094.
Deputy Assistant Attorney General/Information Resources Management and CIO.—Vance Hitch, room 1310–A, 514–0507.
Staff Directors for—
E-Government Services.—Eric Olson, room 1314, 514–0507.

Enterprise Solutions.—John Murray (PHB), room 4606, 514–0507.
IT Security.—Kevin Deeley (PHB), room 1600, 514–0507.
Operation Services.—Roger Beasley, room 1315, 514–3404.
Policy and Planning.—Kent Holgrewe, room 1310, 514–4292.

OFFICE OF JUSTICE PROGRAMS (OJP)

810 7th Street, NW., 20531

OFFICE OF THE ASSISTANT ATTORNEY GENERAL

Assistant Attorney General.—Laurie O. Robinson (acting), (202) 307–5933.
Deputy Assistant Attorney General.—Beth McGarry, 307–5933.
Manager, Equal Employment Opportunity.—Tonya Yarborough (acting), 353–2562.

BUREAU OF JUSTICE ASSISTANCE

Director.—James Burch III (acting), 616–6500.
Deputy Directors of:
Policy.—James H. Burch II, 307–5910.
Programs.—Eileen Garry, 307–6226.

BUREAU OF JUSTICE STATISTICS

Director.—Michael Sinclair (acting), 307–0765.
Deputy Directors of:
Statistical Collections and Analysis.—Michael Sinclair, 307–0765.
Statistical Planning, Policy and Operations.—Gerard Ramker, 307–0759.

NATIONAL INSTITUTE OF JUSTICE

Director.—Kristina Rose (acting), 307–0466.
Deputy Director of:
Research and Evaluation.—Margaret Zahn (acting), 616–8911.
Science and Technology.—John Morgan, 305–0995.

OFFICE OF JUVENILE JUSTICE AND DELINQUENCY PREVENTION

Administrator.—Jeff Slowikowski (acting), 307–5911.
Deputy Administrator.—Nancy Ayers 353–9427.

OFFICE FOR VICTIMS OF CRIME

Director.—Joye E. Frost (acting), 307–5983.
Deputy Director.—Barbara Walker, 305–2172.

COMMUNITY CAPACITY DEVELOPMENT OFFICE

Director.—Dennis Greenhouse, 616–1152.
Deputy Director.—Denise Viera, 616–1152.

OFFICE OF ADMINISTRATION

Director.—Phillip Merkle, 307–0087.
Deputy Director, Division of:
Acquisition Management.—Eldred Jackson, 514–0696.
Human Resources.—Jennifer McCarthy, 616–0389.
Support Services.—Cornelius Holmes, 305–2140.

OFFICE OF THE CHIEF FINANCIAL OFFICER

Chief Financial Officer.—Marcia Paull, 307–2820.
Deputy Chief Financial Officer.—Leigh Benda, 353–8153.

OFFICE OF THE CHIEF INFORMATION OFFICER

Chief Information Officer.—Walter Iwanow, 305–9071.
Deputy Chief Information Officer.—Angel Santa, 514–9089.

OFFICE FOR CIVIL RIGHTS

Director.—Michael Alston, 307–0690.

OFFICE OF COMMUNICATIONS

Director.—Kim M. Lowry, 305–2388.
Deputy Director.—Summer Duncan, 514–7838.

OFFICE OF THE GENERAL COUNSEL

General Counsel.—Rafael A. Madan, 307–6235.

OFFICE OF LEGAL COUNSEL

RFK Main Justice Building, Room 5218, phone (202) 514–2051

Assistant Attorney General.—Vacant.
Deputy Assistant Attorneys General: Marty Lederman, room 5231, Daniel Koffsky, room 5238, 514–2030.
Principal Deputy Assistant Attorney General.—David Barron, room 5218, 514–4132.
Special Counsels: Paul P. Colborn, room 5240, 514–2048; Rosemary Hart, room 5242, 514–2027.

OFFICE OF LEGAL POLICY

RFK Main Justice Building, Room 4234, phone (202) 514–4601

Assistant Attorney General.—Kevin R. Jones (acting), 616–4604.
Principal Deputy Assistant Attorney General.—Spencer A. Overton, room 4238, 616–9987.
Deputy Assistant Attorneys General: Rajesh De, room 4246, 307–3024; Larry Rothenberg, room 4226, 514–3116; Robyn Thiemann, room 4237, 514–8356.
Chief of Staff.—Paul Almanza, room 4228, 616–2250.

OFFICE OF LEGISLATIVE AFFAIRS

RFK Main Justice Building, Room 1145, phone (202) 514–2141

Assistant Attorney General.—Vacant.
Special Counsel to the Assistant Attorney General.—M. Faith Burton.
Deputy Assistant Attorney General.—Vacant.

NATIONAL DRUG INTELLIGENCE CENTER (NDIC)

319 Washington Street, Johnstown, PA 15901–1622, phone (814) 532–4601

RFK Main Justice Building, Room 1335, 20530, phone (202) 532–4040

Director.—Michael F. Walther (814) 532–4607.
Deputy Director.—Irene S. Hernandez (814) 532–4675.
Chief of Staff.—Steven R. Frank (814) 532–4728.
Chief Counsel.—Kevin M. Walker (814) 532–4660.
Assistant Director for—
Intelligence Division.—Bruce D. Shannon (acting), (814) 532–4613.
Intelligence Support Division.—David J. Mrozowski (814) 532–4926.
Policy and Interagency Affairs.—Joseph E. Donovan (202) 532–4036.
Telephone Directory Coordinator.—Pamela F. Warchola (814) 532–4607.

NATIONAL SECURITY DIVISION

RFK Main Justice Building, Room 7339, phone (202) 514–1057

Assistant Attorney General.—David S. Kris.
Deputy Assistant Attorneys General: Todd Hinnen, Brad Wiegmann.
Chief of Staff.—Brad Wiegmann.
Deputy Chief of Staff.—Donald Vieira.
Senior Counsels to the Assistant Attorney General: James Reynolds, George Z. Toscas.
Counsels to the Assistant Attorney General: Leonard Bailey, Virginia Vander Jagt.
Special Assistant to the Assitant Attorney General.—Vacant.

COUNTERESPIONAGE SECTION

1400 New York Avenue, NW., Room 9418, phone (202) 514–1191

Chief.—John Dion, room 9100, 514–1187.
Deputy Chief.—Steve Pelak.

COUNTERTERRORISM SECTION

Chief.—Michael J. Mullaney (acting), room 2643, 514–0849.
Deputy Chief for—
International Terrorism Unit I.—Sharon Lever.
International Terrorism Unit II.—Jennifer Smith.
Policy, Legislation, and Planning Unit.—Scott Glick.
Terrorist Financing Unit.—Michael Taxay.

OFFICE OF INTELLIGENCE

Counsel for Intelligence Policy.—James A. Baker, room 6150, 514–5600.
Section Chief for—
Litigation.—Nancy Newcomb (acting).
Operations.—Tashina Gauhar.
Oversight.—Mark A. Bradley (acting).

OFFICE OF JUSTICE FOR VICTIMS OF OVERSEAS TERRORISM

1331 Pennsylvania Avenue, NW., Suite 726N, 20004

Director.—Heather Cartwright, 532–4100.

OFFICE OF THE PARDON ATTORNEY

1425 New York Avenue, NW., 20530, phone (202) 616–6070

Pardon Attorney.—Ronald L. Rodgers.
Deputy Pardon Attorney.—Helen M. Bollwerk.

OFFICE OF PROFESSIONAL RESPONSIBILITY

RFK Main Justice Building, Room 3266, phone (202) 514–3365

Counsel.—H. Marshall Jarrett.
Deputy Counsel.—Judith B. Wish.
Associate Counsels: William J. Birney, Paul L. Colby, James G. Duncan, Mary Anne Hoopes.
Senior Assistant Counsels: Neil C. Hurley, Tamara Kessler.
Assistant Counsels: Carolyn Adams, Mary Aubry, Kathleen Brandon, William Causey, Terry Derden, Mark G. Fraase, Greg Gonzalez, Amy Goldfrank, Lyn A. Hardy, Lisa Howard,

Tamara J. Kessler, Frederick C. Leiner, Margaret S. McCarty, Noreen McCarthy, Oliver McDaniel, Ruth Plagenhoef, Trini Ross, John Tavana, Robert Thomson, James Vargasor, Marlene M. Wahowiak, Barbara L. Ward.

PROFESSIONAL RESPONSIBILITY ADVISORY OFFICE

1425 New York Avenue, NW., 20530, phone (202) 514–0458

Director.—Jerri Dunston.
Deputy Director.—Stacy Ludwig.

OFFICE OF PUBLIC AFFAIRS

RFK Main Justice Building, Room 1220, phone (202) 514–2007

Director.—Matthew A. Miller.
Deputy Directors: Tracy Schmaler, Gina M. Talamona.

TAX DIVISION

RFK Main Justice Building, 950 Pennsylvania Avenue, NW., 20530

Judiciary Center Building, 555 Fourth Street, NW., 20001 (JCB)

Maxus Energy Tower, 7717 N. Harwood Street, Suite 400, Dallas, TX 75242 (MAX)

Patrick Henry Building, 601 D Street, NW., 20004 (PHB)

Assistant Attorney General.—John A. DiCicco (acting), room 4141 (202) 514–2901.
Deputy Assistant Attorneys General: Ronald A. Cimino (acting), room 4613 (Main) 514–2915 (Criminal Matters); D. Patrick Mullarkey (acting), room 7804–A (JCB), 307–6533 (Civil Matters); Gilbert S. Rothenberg (acting), room 4333 (Main), 514–3361 (Appellate and Review).
Senior Legislative Counsel.—Eileen M. Shatz, room 4134 (Main), 307–6419.
Civil Trial Section Chiefs:
Central Region.—Seth Heald (JCB), room 8921–B, 514–6502.
Eastern Region.—David A. Hubbert (JCB) room 6126, 307–6426.
Northern Region.—D. Patrick Mullarkey (JCB), room 7804–A, 307–6533.
Southern Region.—Michael Kearns (JCB), room 6243–A, 514–5905.
Southwestern Region.—Louise P. Hytken (MAX), room 4100 (214) 880–9725.
Western Region.—Richard R. Ward (JCB), room 7907–B, 307–6413.
Criminal Enforcement Section Chiefs:
Northern Region.—Rosemary E. Paguni (PHB), room 7334, 514–2323.
Southern Region.—Bruce Salad (PHB), room 7640, 514–5112.
Western Region.—Mitchell J. Ballweg (acting), (PHB), room 7038, 514–5072.
Section Chiefs:
Appellate.—David I. Pincus (acting), room 4333, 514–3361.
Court of Federal Claims.—Steven I. Fraham (JCB), room 8804–A, 307–6440.
Criminal Appeals and Tax Enforcement Policy.—Alan Hechtkopf (PHB), room 7101, 514–3011.
Office of Review.—Deborah Meland (JCB), room 6846, 307–6567.
Executive Officer.—Joseph E. Young (PHB), room 7802, 616–0010.

UNITED STATES MARSHALS SERVICE (USMS)

Washington, DC 20530–1000

[Use (202) for 307 exchange and (703) for 557, 603, 416 and 285 exchanges]

fax (202) 307–5040

Director.—John F. Clark (202) 307–9001.
Chief of Staff.—Sean Fahey, 307–9841.
Associate Director for Administration.—Chris Dudley, 305–9575.
Associate Director for Operations.—Robert J. Finan II, 307–9500.
Chief, Congressional Affairs.—Doug Disrud, 307–5140, fax 307–5228.
Deputy Chief, Congressional Affairs.—Alexis Fooshé, 353–1430, fax 307–5228.

Chief, Public Affairs.—Jeff Carter, 353–1469, fax 307–8729.
Deputy Chief, Public Affairs.—Steve Blando, 307–9344.

EQUAL EMPLOYMENT OPPORTUNITY (EEO)

Chief.—Joann Grady, 307–9048, fax 307–8765.

OFFICE OF THE GENERAL COUNSEL (OGC)

Chief.—Gerald M. Auerbach, 307–9054, fax 307–9456.
Principal Deputy General Counsel.—Lisa Dickinson, 307–9054.

OFFICE OF INSPECTION (OI)

Chief.—Herman Brewer, Jr., 307–9155.

ASSET FORFEITURE DIVISION (AFD)

Assistant Director.—Michael A. Pearson, 307–9221, fax 307–5020.
Deputy Assistant Director.—Eben Morales.

FINANCIAL SERVICES DIVISION (FSD)

Assistant Director.—Edward Dolan, 307–9193, fax 353–8340.
Deputy Assistant Director.—Jim Murphy.

HUMAN RESOURCES DIVISION (HRD)

Assistant Director.—Darla K. Callaghan, 307–9625, fax 307–9461.
Deputy Assistant Director.—Cheryl Jacobs, 353–3253

INFORMATION TECHNOLOGY DIVISION (ITD)

Assistant Director.—Lisa Davis, 307–9677, fax 307–5130.
Deputy Assistant Director.—Judd Nicholson.

MANAGEMENT SUPPORT DIVISION (MSD)

Assistant Director.—Donald Donovan, 307–9011, fax 307–5026.

TRAINING DIVISION

Assistant Director.—Marc A. Farmer, (912) 267–2505.
Deputy Assistant Director.—Vernon Johnson (acting), 267–2731, fax 267–2882.

INVESTIGATIVE OPERATIONS DIVISION (IOD)

Assistant Director.—T. Michael Earp, 307–9195, fax 307–9299.
Deputy Assistant Director.—Geoff Shank, 307–9043.

JUSTICE PRISONER AND ALIEN TRANSPORTATION SYSTEM (JPATS)

Assistant Director.—Scott C. Rolstad, Kansas City, MO (816) 467–1900, fax 467–1980.

JUDICIAL SECURITY DIVISION (JSD)

Assistant Director.—Michael J. Prouot, 307–9500, fax 307–5206.
Judicial Operations, Deputy Assistant Director.—Robert Fagan, 353–3257.
Judicial Services, Deputy Assistant Director.—Steven Conboy, 307–4987.

PRISONER OPERATIONS DIVISION (POD)

Assistant Director.—Candra S. Symonds, 307–5100, fax 307–9234.

TACTICAL OPERATIONS DIVISION (TOD)

Assistant Director.—William Snelson, 307–9100, fax 307–3446.

WITNESS SECURITY DIVISION (WSD)

Assistant Director.—Sylvester E. Jones, 307–9150.
Deputy Assistant Director.—Tom Wight, 307–9150.

U.S. PAROLE COMMISSION

5550 Friendship Boulevard, Suite 420, Chevy Chase, MD 20815, phone (301) 492–5990 fax 492–6694

Chairman.—Edward F. Reilly, Jr.
Vice Chairman.—Cranston J. Mitchell.
Commissioners: Patricia A. Cushwa, Isaac Fulwood, Jr.
Chief of Staff.—Thomas W. Hutchison.
Case Operations Administrator.—Stephen J. Husk.
Case Service Administrator.—Deirdre M. Jackson.
General Counsel.—Rockne J. Chickinell.
Executive Officer.—Judy I. Carter.
Staff Assistant to the Chairman.—Patricia W. Moore.

OFFICE ON VIOLENCE AGAINST WOMEN

800 K Street, NW., Suite 920, 20530

Director.—Catherine Pierce (acting), (202) 307–3876.
Deputy Tribal Director.—Lorraine Edmo, 514–8804.
Senior Policy Advisor.—Anna Martinez, 514–6975.
Special Assistant to the Director.—Ellen Williams, 307–3341.
Associate Directors: Darlene Johnson, 307–6795; Lauren Nassikas, 305–1792; Nadine Neufville, 305–2590; Susan Williams, 616–3851.

DEPARTMENT OF THE INTERIOR

Interior Building, 1849 C Street, NW., 20240, phone (202) 208–3100, http://www.doi.gov

KEN SALAZAR, Secretary of the Interior; born in Alamosa, CO, March 2, 1955; education: J.D., University of Michigan Law School; B.A., Colorado College; professional: United States Senator from Colorado, 2005–09; Attorney General of Colorado, 1999–2005; Executive Director, Colorado Department of Natural Resources, 1990–94; chief legal counsel to Governor Roy Romer, 1987–90; Natural Resources Lawyer, Small Business Owner, Farmer; member, Colorado College Board of Trustees; chair, Conference of Western Attorneys General; chair, National Association of Attorneys General Environment Committee; chair, Colorado Peace Officers Standards and Training Board; chair, Rio Grande Compact Commission; chair, Sangre de Cristo Land Grant Commission; chair, Great Outdoors Colorado; religion: Roman Catholic; married: Hope; children: Melinda and Andrea; granddaughter: Mireya; nominated by President Barack Obama to become the 50th Secretary of the Interior, and was confirmed by the U.S. Senate on January 20, 2009.

OFFICE OF THE SECRETARY

Secretary of the Interior.—Ken Salazar, room 6156, 208–7351.
Special Assistant/Director, Scheduling and Advance.—Joan Padilla, room 6154.
Special Assisant.—Terri Johnson.
Chief of Staff.—Thomas ''Tom'' Strickland, room 6144.
Deputy Chief of Staff.—Renee Stone, room 6140.
Senior Advisor for Economic Recovery.—Chris Henderson, room 6120, 208–7471.
Senior Advisor to the Secretary.—Kenneth ''Ken'' Lane, room 6142.
Director of External and Intergovernmental Affairs.—Ray Rivera, room 6212, 208–1923.
Senior Advisor for Alaska Affairs.—Kim Elton, room 6020, 208–4177.
Counselor to the Secretary.—Steve Black, room 6130, 208–4123.

EXECUTIVE SECRETARIAT

Director.—Fay Iudicello, room 7212, 208–3181.

CONGRESSIONAL AND LEGISLATIVE AFFAIRS

Director.—Christopher Mansour, room 6256, 208–7693.
Deputy Directors: Sarah Bittleman, room 6251; Meghan Conklin, room 6253.
Legislative Counsel.—Chris Salotti, room 6241.

OFFICE OF COMMUNICATIONS

Director.—Betsy Hildebrandt, room 6213, 208–6416.
Deputy Director.—Matt Lee-Ashley.
Press Secretary.—Kendra Barkoff.
New Media Director.—Katelyn Sabochik.
Information Officers: Joan Moody, Frank Quimby, Hugh Vickery.

OFFICE OF THE DEPUTY SECRETARY

Deputy Secretary.—David Hayes, room 6117, 208–6291.
Special Assistant to the Deputy Secretary.—Kat Pustay, room 6116, 208–3744.
Associate Deputy Secretary.—Laura Davis, room 6117, 208–6291.
Science Advisor to the Deputy Secretary.—Kit Batten, room 6118, 208–6291.

ASSISTANT SECRETARY FOR FISH AND WILDLIFE AND PARKS

Assistant Secretary.—Vacant, room 3160 (202) 208–5347.
Principal Deputy Assistant Secretary.—Will Shafroth, room 3159, 208–4416.
Deputy Assistant Secretaries.—Vacant, room 3144, 208–3928; Vacant, room 3159, 208–4416.
Chief of Staff.—Vacant, room 3155, 208–7400.

U.S. FISH AND WILDLIFE SERVICE

Director.—Vacant (202) 208–4717.
Deputy Director.—Rowan Gould, 208–4545.
Chief, Office of Law Enforcement.—Benito Perez, 208–3809.
Assistant Director for External Affairs.—Elizabeth H. Stevens, 208–6541.
Chief, Division of:
Congressional and Legislative Affairs.—Lesli Gray (703) 358–2241.
Conservative Partnerships.—Phil Million (703) 358–1711.
Public Affairs.—Chris Tollefson (703) 358–2222.
Assistant Director for—
Migratory Birds.—Paul Schmidt, 208–1050.
Budget, Planning, and Human Capital.—Denise Sheehan (703) 358–2333.
Business Management and Operations.—Paul Henne (703) 358–1822.
Endangered Species.—Brian Arroyo (acting), 208–4646.
Fisheries and Habitat Conservation.—Gary Frazer, 208–6394.
International Affairs.—Teiko Saito (acting), 208–6393.
Wildlife and Sport Fish Restoration.—Hannibal Bolton, 208–1050.
Chief, National Wildlife Refuge System.—Gregory Siekaniec, 208–5333.
Regional Directors:
Region 1.—Robyn Thorson, Eastside Federal Complex, 911 Northeast 11th Avenue, Portland, OR 97232 (503) 231–6118, fax 872–2716.
Region 2.—Benjamin Tuggle, Room 1306, 500 Gold Avenue, SW., Albuquerque, NM 87103 (505) 248–6845, fax (503) 872–2716.
Region 3.—Thomas Melius, Federal Building, Fort Snelling, Twin Cities, MN 55111 (612) 713–5301, fax 713–5284.
Region 4.—Samuel D. Hamilton, 1875 Century Boulevard, Atlanta, GA 30345 (404) 679–4000, fax 679–4006.
Region 5.—Marvin Moriarty, 300 Westgate Center Drive, Hadley, MA 01035 (413) 253–8300, fax 253–8308.
Region 6.—Stephen Guertin, 134 Union Boulevard #400, Lakewood, CO 80228 (303) 236–7920, fax 236–8295.
Region 7.—Geoff Hasketts, 1011 East Tudor Road, Anchorage, AK 99503 (907) 786–3542, fax 786–3306.
Region 8.—Renne Lohoefener, 2800 Cottage Way, #W2606, Sacramento, CA 95825 (916) 414–6464, fax 414–6484.

NATIONAL PARK SERVICE

Director.—Dan Wenk (acting), room 3113 (202) 208–4621.
Deputy Director for Operations.—Ernest Quintana (acting), room 3112, 208–3818.
Deputy Director for Support Services.—Kate Stevenson (acting), room 3124, 208–3818.
Chief of Staff.—John Piltzecker (acting), room 3120, 208–3818.
Associate Director for—
Cultural Resources.—Jan Matthews, room 3128, 208–7625.
Natural Resources, Stewardship and Science.—Bert Frost, room 3130, 208–3884.
Park Planning, Facilities and Lands.—Steve Whitesell, room 3116, 208–3264.
Partnerships, Interpretation, and Education, Volunteers and Outdoor Recreation.—Christopher Jarvi, room 3129, 208–4829.
Visitor and Resource Protection.—Karen Taylor-Goodrich, room 3124, 565–1020.
Comptroller.—Bruce Sheaffer, room 2711, 208–4566.
Assistant Director for Legislative and Congressional Affairs.—Don Hellman (acting), room 7256, 208–5655.
Chief, Office of Public Affairs.—Dave Barna, room 7012, 208–6843.
Assistant Director, Business Services.—Vic Knox (acting), room 2023, 208–5651.
Chief Information Officer.—Larry Curran, 1201 Eye Street, NW., Washington, DC 20005, 354–1441.
Assistant Director, Workforce Management.—Jerry Simpson, room 3127, 208–5587.

Regional Directors:

Alaska.—Sue Masica, 240 West Fifth Avenue, Room 114, Anchorage, AK 99501 (907) 644–3510, fax 644–3816.

Intermountain.—Mike Snyder, P.O. Box 25287, 12795 West Alameda Parkway, Denver, CO 80225 (303) 969–2500, fax 969–2785.

Midwest.—Dave Given (acting), 601 Riverfront Drive, Omaha, NE 68102 (402) 661–1736, fax 661–1737.

National Capital.—Peggy O'Dell, 1100 Ohio Drive, SW., Washington, DC 20242 (202) 619–7000, fax 619–7220.

Northeast.—Dennis Reidenbach, U.S. Custom House, 200 Chestnut Street, Suite 306, Philadelphia, PA 19106 (215) 597–7013, fax 597–0815.

Southeast.—David Vela, 100 Alabama Street, NW., 1924 Building, Atlanta, GA 30303 (404) 562–3327, fax 562–3216.

Pacific West.—Jon Jarvis, 1111 Jackson Street, Suite 700, Oakland, CA 94607 (510) 817–1304, fax 817–1485.

ASSISTANT SECRETARY FOR INDIAN AFFAIRS

Assistant Secretary.—Vacant.

Principal Deputy Assistant Secretary.—Vacant.

Deputy Assistant Secretary for—

Economic Development.—George Skibine, 219–4066.

Management.—Grayford Payne, 208–7163.

Director of:

Communications.—Nedra Darling, 219–4150.

Congressional Affairs.—Darren Pete, 208–6983.

BUREAU OF INDIAN AFFAIRS

Director.—Jerry Gidner, room 4600 (202) 208–5116.

Deputy Director of:

Field Operations.—Michael Smith.

Law Enforcement.—William ''Pat'' Ragsdale, 208–4853.

Tribal Services.—Vacant.

Trust.—Vicki Forrest, 208–5831.

BUREAU OF INDIAN EDUCATION

Director.—Kevin Skenandore (acting), room 3609 (202) 208–6123.

Chief of Staff.—Spike Big Horn.

ASSISTANT SECRETARY FOR LAND AND MINERALS MANAGEMENT

Assistant Secretary.—Ned Farquhar, room 6614 (202) 208–6734.

Deputy Assistant Secretary.—Ned Farquhar.

Deputy Assistant Secretary.—Vacant.

BUREAU OF LAND MANAGEMENT

Director.—Michale Pool (acting), room 5662 (202) 208–3801.

Deputy Director of:

Operations.—Michael Nedd (acting).

Programs and Policy.—Vacant.

Division Chief, Legislative Affairs and Correspondence.—Patrick Wilkerson, 452–5010.

Deputy Division Chief.—Andrea Nelson.

State Directors:

Alaska.—Tom Lonnie, 222 West Seventh Avenue No. 13, Anchorage, AK 99513 (907) 271–5080, fax 271–4596.

Arizona.—Jim Kenna, One North Central Avenue, Phoenix, AZ 85004 (602) 417–9500, fax 417–9398.

California.—Jim Abbott (acting), 2800 Cottage Way, Suite W1834, Sacramento, CA 95825 (916) 978–4600, fax 978–4699.

Colorado.—Sally Wisely, 2850 Youngfield Street, Lakewood, CO 80215 (303) 239–3700, fax 239–3934.

Eastern States.—Juan Palma, 7450 Boston Boulevard, Springfield, VA 22153 (703) 440–1700, fax 440–1701.

Idaho.—Tom Dyer, 1387 South Vinnell Way, Boise, ID 83709 (208) 373–4000, fax 373–3919.

Montana.—Gene Terland, 5001 Southgate Drive, Billings, MT 59101 (406) 896–5012, fax 896–5004.

Nevada.—Ron Wenker, 1340 Financial Boulevard, Reno, NV 89502 (775) 861–6590, fax 861–6601.

New Mexico.—Linda S.C. Rundell, 1474 Rodeo Road, P.O. Box 27115, Sante Fe, NM 87505 (505) 438–7501, fax 438–7452.

Oregon.—Ed Shepard, 333 S.W. 1st Avenue, P.O. Box 2965, Portland, OR 97204 (503) 808–6024, fax 808–6308.

Utah.—Selma Sierra, 440 West 200 South, Suite 500, P.O. Box 45155, Salt Lake City, UT 84101 (801) 539–4010, fax 539–4013.

Wyoming.—Don Simpson, 5353 Yellowstone Road, P.O. Box 1828, Cheyenne, WY 82003 (307) 775–6001, fax 775–6028.

MINERALS MANAGEMENT SERVICE

Director.—Walter Cruickshank (acting), (202) 208–3500.

Deputy Director.—Walter D. Cruickshank.

Associate Director for—

Administration and Budget.—Robert E. Brown, 208–3220.

Minerals Revenue Management.—Gregory J. Gould, 208–3415.

Offshore Energy and Minerals Management.—Chris C. Oynes, 208–3530.

Policy and Management Improvement.—George F. Triebsch, 208–3398.

Congressional Affairs:

Director.—M. Lyn Herdt, 208–3502, fax 208–3918.

Minerals Revenue Issues.—Anita Gonzales-Evans.

Offshore Minerals Issues.—Julie Fleming.

Outer Continental Shelf Regional Directors:

Alaska.—John T. Goll, 949 East 36th Avenue, Suite 300, Anchorage, AK 99508 (907) 334–5200.

Gulf of Mexico.—Lars T. Herbst, 1201 Elmwood Park Boulevard, New Orleans, LA 70123 (504) 736–2589.

Pacific.—Ellen G. Aronson, 770 Paseo Camarillo, Camarillo, CA 93010 (805) 389–7502.

OFFICE OF SURFACE MINING RECLAMATION AND ENFORCEMENT

Director.—Glenda Owens (acting), room 231 (202) 208–4006.

Deputy Director.—Glenda Owens, 208–2807.

Assistant Director for Finance and Administration.—Ted Woronka, 208–2546.

Congressional Contact.—Peter Mali, 208–2566.

Regional Director for—

Appalachian Coordinating Center.—Thomas D. Shope, Three Parkway Center, Pittsburgh, PA 15220 (412) 937–2828, fax 937–2903.

Mid-Continent Coordinating Center.—Ervin Barchenger, 501 Belle Street, Room 216, Alton, IL 62002 (618) 463–6463, fax 463–6470.

Western Coordinating Center.—Allen Klein, 1999 Broadway, Suite 3320, Denver, CO 80202 (303) 844–1401, fax 844–1522.

ASSISTANT SECRETARY FOR POLICY, MANAGEMENT AND BUDGET

Assistant Secretary.—Vacant, room 5110 (202) 208–1927.

Director, Office of Budget.—Vacant.

Deputy Assistant Secretary for—

Budget and Business Management.—Pamela K. Haze, 208–7966.

Insular Affairs.—Vacant, room 4328, 208–4736.

Law Enforcement and Security.—Larry Parkinson, room 3412, 208–5773.

Human Capitol, Performance, and Partnerships.—Vacant, room 5120, 208–1738.

Policy and Program Management.—Vacant, room 5124, 208–3219.

Deputy Chief, Human Capitol Officer.—Kathleen Wheeler, room 5120, 208–4727.

ASSISTANT SECRETARY FOR WATER AND SCIENCE

Assistant Secretary.—Amy Holley (acting), room 6657 (202) 208–3186.
Principal Deputy Assistant Secretary.—Vacant.
Deputy Assistant Secretary.—Vacant.
Chief of Staff.—Amy Holley, room 6645, 208–6011.

U.S. GEOLOGICAL SURVEY

The National Center, 12201 Sunrise Valley Drive, Reston, VA 20192

phone (703) 648–7411, fax 648–4454

Director.—Suzette M. Kimball (acting).
Deputy Director.—Robert E. Doyle, 648–7412.
Office of:
Administrative Policy and Services.—Karen Baker, 648–7200.
Budget and Performance.—Carla Burzyk, 648–4443.
Communications and Outreach.—Barbara Wainman, 648–5750.
Congressional Liaison Officer.—Timothy J. West, 648–4300.
Human Capital.—Pam Malam, 648–7414.
Public Affairs Officer.—Mike Gauldin, 648–4054.
Associate Directors for—
Biology.—Susan D. Haseltine, 648–4050.
Geography.—Bryant Cramer, 648–7413.
Geology.—Tim Miller, 648–6600.
Geospatial Information and Chief Information Officer.—Kevin Gallagher, 648–5747.
Water.—Matt Larsen, 648–5215.
Regional Director for—
Central Region.—Stanley Ponce, P.O. Box 25046, Denver Federal Center, Building 810, Denver, CO 80225 (303) 202–4740.
Eastern Region.—William Werkheiser, 11649 Leetown Road, Kearneysville, WV 25430 (304) 724–4521.
Western Region.—Anne Kinsinger, 909 First Avenue, Suite 704, Seattle, WA 98104 (206) 220–4578.

BUREAU OF RECLAMATION

Commissioner.—Vacant, room 7654 (202) 513–0501.
Deputy Commissioner for—
External and Intergovernmental Affairs.—Vacant, room 7645, 513–0615.
Operations.—Karl Wirkus.
Policy, Administration, and Budget.—Darryl Beckmann, room 7650, 513–0509.
Chief of Staff.—Kerry Rae, room 7646.
Chief of:
Congressional and Legislative Affairs.—Vacant, room 7643, 513–0565.
Public Affairs.—Daniel J. DuBray, room 7644, 513–0574.
Regional Directors:
Great Plains.—Michael J. Ryan, P.O. Box 36900, Billings, MT 59107 (406) 247–7795, fax 247–7793.
Lower Colorado.—Lorri Gray-Lee, P.O. Box 61470, Boulder City, NV 89006 (702) 293–8000, fax 293–8614.
Mid-Pacific.—Donald Glaser, 2800 Cottage Way, Sacramento, CA 95825 (916) 978–5580, fax 978–5599.
Pacific Northwest.—Bill McDonald, 1150 North Curtis Road, Suite 100, Boise, ID 83706 (208) 378–5127, fax 378–5129.
Upper Colorado.—Larry Walkoviak, 125 South State Street, room 6107, Salt Lake City, UT 84138 (801) 524–3785, fax 524–5499.

OFFICE OF INSPECTOR GENERAL

Inspector General.—Mary Kendall (acting), room 4410 (202) 208–5745.
Deputy Inspector General.—Steve Hardgrove (acting), room 4420.
Associate Inspector General for Whistleblower Protection.—Richard Trinidad, room 4445.
Associate Inspector General for External Affairs.—Kris Kolesnik, room 4427.

OFFICE OF THE SOLICITOR

Solicitor.—Vacant, room 6415 (202) 208–4423.
Deputy Solicitors.—Arthur E. Gary (acting), Lawrence J. Jensen.
Associate Solicitor for—
Administration.—Ed Keable.
General Law.—Vacant.
Indian Affairs.—Edith Blackwell.
Land and Water.—Laura Brown.
Mineral Resources.—Bob Comer.
Counselor to Solicitor for Indian Trust Litigation.—Paul Smyth.
Senior Counsel CADR.—Shayla Simmons.
Designated Agency Ethics Official.—Melinda Loftin, 208–5295.

OFFICE OF THE SPECIAL TRUSTEE FOR AMERICAN INDIANS

Special Trustee.—Donna Erwin (acting), room 5140 (202) 208–4866.

DEPARTMENT OF AGRICULTURE

Jamie L. Whitten Building, 1400 Independence Avenue, SW., 20250

phone (202) 720–3631, http://www.usda.gov

TOM VILSACK, Secretary of Agriculture; education: B.A., Hamilton College; J.D., Albany Law School; professional: Governor, Iowa, 1999–2007; nominated by President Barack Obama to become the 30th Secretary of Agriculture, and was confirmed by the U.S. Senate on January 20, 2009.

OFFICE OF THE SECRETARY

Secretary of Agriculture.—Tom Vilsack, room 200–A (202) 720–3631.
Deputy Secretary.—Kathleen Merrigan.
Chief of Staff.—John Norris.
Deputy Chief of Staff.—Carole Jett.

ASSISTANT SECRETARY FOR ADMINISTRATION

Jamie L. Whitten Building, Room 240–W, phone (202) 720–3291

Assistant Secretary.—Pearlie S. Reed.
Deputy Assistant Secretaries: Robin Heard, Dr. Alma C. Hobbs.
Executive Assistants: Tiffany Brooks, Debbie Hamilton, Shirley Hill.
Confidential Assistants: Greg Diephouse, Roberta S. Jeanquart.

OFFICE OF ADMINISTRATIVE LAW JUDGES

South Agriculture Building, Room 1070–S, phone (202) 720–6383

Chief Administrative Law Judge.—Marc R. Hillson.
Secretary to the Chief Administrative Law Judge.—Diane Green.
Administrative Law Judges: Jill S. Clifton, Peter M. Davenport, Victor W. Palmer, 720–8161.
Hearing Clerk.—Leslie E. Whitfield, 720–4443.

OFFICE OF HUMAN CAPITAL MANAGEMENT

Jamie L. Whitten Building, Room 302–W, phone (202) 720–3585

Director.—Jill Crumpacker.
Secretary.—Valerie Thorne.
Deputy Director.—Vacant.
Division Director for—
Departmental Human Resources and Executive Resources.—Leslie Violette, 720–2101.
Employee Recruitment/Development.—Mary Jo Thompson, 720–0822.
Quality of Work Life.—James Stevens, 720–1046.

OFFICE OF THE JUDICIAL OFFICER

South Agriculture Building, Room 1449–S, phone (202) 720–4764

Judicial Officer.—William G. Jenson.
Attorney.—Stephen Reilly.
Legal Technician.—Gloria Derobertis.

OFFICE OF MANAGEMENT SERVICES

Office of Management Services.—Jeanette Chiari (202) 720–9824.
Secretary.—Trinda Reynolds.
Director of:
Budget Formulation Division.—Patricia Jackson, 720–0253.
Working Capital Fund Division.—Janet Walker, 720–4555.
Director, Information Resources Division.—Judith Dudley, 720–5348.
USDA FOIA Officer.—Rita Morgan, 720–8164.

OFFICE OF OPERATIONS

South Agriculture Building, Room 1456–S, phone (202) 720–3937

Director.—John Crew.
Director, Office of:
Facilities.—Valencia Winstead, 720–2804.
Management Services.—Morris Tate.
Director for—
Beltsville Service Center.—Carlos Casaus (acting), (301) 394–0410.
Mail and Reproduction.—Michele Lambert, 720–8393.
Washington Area Service Center.—Earl Brittingham, 720–2777.

OFFICE OF PROCUREMENT AND PROPERTY MANAGEMENT

Reporters Building, Room 302, phone (202) 720–9448

Director.—Russ Ashworth (acting).
Division Director for—
Procurement Operations.—Michael McFarland, 690–0142.
Procurement Policy.—Todd Repass, 690–1060.
Procurement Systems.—Vacant, 401–1023.
Property Management.—Denise Hayes, 720–7283.
Radiation Safety.—John Jensen (301) 504–2440.

OFFICE OF SECURITY SERVICES

Director.—Russ Ashworth, room S–310 (202) 720–0272.
Division Chief for—
Continuity of Operations Planning.—Leslie Pozanek, 720–2667.
Personnel and Document Security.—Susan Gulbranson, 720–7373.
Physical Security.—Richard Holman, 720–3901.
Director, Office of:
Emergency Programs.—James Redington, 690–3191.
Protective Operations.—Ken Lescallett, 720–6270.

OFFICE OF SMALL AND DISADVANTAGED BUSINESS UTILIZATION

South Agriculture Building, Room 1085–S, phone (202) 720–7117

Director.—Quinton Robinson.
Deputy Director.—Joe Ware.

ASSISTANT SECRETARY FOR CIVIL RIGHTS

Jamie L. Whitten Building, Room 240–W, phone (202) 720–3808

Assistant Secretary.—Joe Leonard, Jr., Ph.D.
Deputy Assistant Secretary.—Mary McNeil.
Associate Assistant Secretary.—Rhonda Davis (acting).

OFFICE OF BUDGET AND PROGRAM ANALYSIS

Jamie L. Whitten Building, Room 101–A, phone (202) 720–3323

Director.—W. Scott Steele.
Associate Director.—Michael L. Young, 720–5303.
Deputy Director for—
Budget, Legislative and Regulatory Systems.—Donald Bice, room 102–E, 720–6667.
Program Analysis.—Christopher Zehren, room 126–W, 720–3396.

OFFICE OF THE CHIEF ECONOMIST

Jamie L. Whitten Building, Room 112–A, phone (202) 720–4164

Chief Economist.—Joseph W. Glauber.
Deputy Chief Economist.—James Hrubovcak, room 112–A, 720–4737.
Chairperson, World Agricultural Outlook Board.—Gerald A. Bange, room 4419–S, 720–6030.
Chief Meteorologist.—Ray Motha, room 4441–S, 720–8651.
Global Change Program Office.—William Hohenstein, room 4407–S, 720–6698.
Office of Energy Policy and New Uses.—Roger Conway, room 4059–S, 401–0461.
Office of Risk Assessment and Cost Benefit Analysis.—James D. Schaub, room 4032–S, 720–8022.
Office of Sustainable Development.—Carol Kramer-LeBlanc, room 112–A, 720–2456.
Supervisory Meteorologist, National Weather Service.—Brad Pugh, room 4443–S, 720–6030.

OFFICE OF THE CHIEF FINANCIAL OFFICER

Jamie L. Whitten Building, Room 143–W, phone (202) 720–5539

Chief Financial Officer.—Jon M. Holladay (acting).
Deputy Chief Financial Officer.—Jon M. Holladay, room 143–W, 720–0727.
Associate Chief Financial Officers for—
Financial Operations.—John Brewer, room 3053–S, 720–9427.
Financial Policy and Planning.—Vacant.
Financial Systems.—Michael Clanton, room 3057–S, 690–3068.
Director, National Finance Center.—Jerry Lohfink, P.O. Box 60000, New Orleans, LA 70160 (504) 426–0120.

OFFICE OF THE CHIEF INFORMATION OFFICER

Jamie L. Whitten Building, Room 414–W, phone (202) 720–8833

Chief Information Officer.—Chris L. Smith (acting).
Deputy Chief Information Officer for Cyber Security and Privacy Information Operations.—Chris L. Smith.
Deputy Chief Information Officer for Policy and Architecture.—Charles McClam, 690–3361.
Associate Chief Information Officer for—
Cyber and Privacy Policy and Oversight.—Mary S. Heard (acting), 720–0492.
Data Center Operations (National Information Technology Center).—Kent Armstrong, 8930 Ward Parkway, Kansas City, MO 64114, (816) 926–6501.
International Security Operations Center.—Chris Lowe (acting), 720–5939.
International Technology Services.—David Shearer, 2150 Centre Avenue, Building A, Fort Collins, CO 80526 (970) 295–5020.
Director for—
E-Learning-AgLearn.—Stan Gray, 694–0006.
Innovations and Operational Architecture.—Owen Unangst, 2150 Centre Avenue, Building A, Fort Collins, CO 80526, (970) 295–5538.
Program Management.—Clif Gonzales, 694–5984.
Resource Management.—Kate Hickman, 720–8109.
Telecommunications Services and Operations.—John Donovan, 720–8695.

OFFICE OF COMMUNICATIONS

Jamie L. Whitten Building, Room 402–A, phone (202) 720–4623

Director.—Chris Mather.
Deputy Director.—Vacant.
Assistant Director.—Larry Quinn.
Press Secretary.—Caleb Weaver.
Center Director for—
Broadcast Media and Technology.—David Black.
Constituent Affairs.—Vacant.
Creative Services.—Carolyn O'Connor.
Information Technology.—Wayne Moore.
Web Services and Distribution.—Amanda Eamich (acting).

OFFICE OF CONGRESSIONAL RELATIONS

Jamie L. Whitten Building, Room 212–A, phone (202) 720–7095

Assistant Secretary.—Vacant.
Deputy Assistant Secretaries: Christine Sarcone (acting); Doug Crandall (acting).
Congressional Liaison for—
Farm and Foreign Agricultural Service.—Vacant.
Food Safety and Food, Nutrition and Consumer Services.—Vacant.
Natural Resources and Environment.—Vacant.
Marketing and Regulatory Programs/Rural Development.—Vacant.
Research, Economics and Education.—Vacant.

EXTERNAL AND INTERGOVERNMENTAL AFFAIRS

Room 216–A, phone (202) 720–6643

Director.—Vacant.
Deputy Director.—Vacant.

NATIVE AMERICAN PROGRAMS

Room 544–A, phone (202) 690–1615

Director.—Dawn Charging.

OFFICE OF THE EXECUTIVE SECRETARIAT

Jamie L. Whitten Building, Room 116–A, phone (202) 720–7100

Director.—Bruce Bundick.
Deputy Director.—Vacant.

GENERAL COUNSEL

Jamie L. Whitten Building, Room 107–W, phone (202) 720–3351

General Counsel.—James Michael Kelly (acting).
Deputy General Counsel.—James Michael Kelly.
Associate General Counsel for—
Civil Rights.—Arlean Leland, 720–1760.
International Affairs, Commodity Programs and Food Assistance Programs.—Ralph Linden, 720–6883.
Legislation, Litigation, General Law.—James Michael Kelly, 720–3351.
Marketing, Regulatory and Food Safety Programs.—John Golden, 720–3155.
Natural Resources.—Thomas Millett, 720–9311.
Rural Development.—David P. Grahn, 720–6187.
Assistant General Counsel, Division of:
Civil Rights Litigation.—Inga Bumbary-Langston, 720–3955.

Community Development.—Paul Loizeaux, 720–4591.
Conservation and Environment.—Stuart L. Shelton, 720–7121.
Food and Nutrition.—Ronald W. Hill, 720–6181.
General Law.—L. Benjamin Young, Jr., 720–5565.
International Affairs and Commodity Programs Division.—Vacant, 720–9246.
Legislation.—Michael J. Knipe, 720–5354.
Litigation.—Brian Sonfield, 720–4733.
Marketing.—Kenneth H. Vail, 720–5935.
Natural Resources.—Thomas Millet, 720–7121.
Regulatory.—Thomas M. Walsh, 720–5550.
Rural Utilities.—Terence M. Brady, 720–2764.
Trade Practices.—Mary K. Hobbie, 720–5293.
Director, Administration and Resource Management.—Charlene Buckner, 720–6324.
Resource Management Specialist.—Robyn Davis, 720–4861.

INSPECTOR GENERAL

Jamie L. Whitten Building, Room 117–W, phone (202) 720–8001, fax 690–1278

Inspector General.—Phyllis K. Fong.
Deputy Inspector General.—Kathleen Tighe, room 117–W, 720–7431.
Assistant Inspector General for—
Audit.—Robert Young, room 403–E, 720–6945.
Investigations.—Karen Ellis, room 507–A, 720–3306.
Management.—Suzanne Murrin, room 5–E, 720–6979.

NATIONAL APPEALS DIVISION

3101 Park Center Drive, Suite 1100, Alexandria, VA 22302

Director.—Roger J. Klurfeld (703) 305–2708.
Deputy Director.—M. Terry Johnson.

UNDER SECRETARY FOR NATURAL RESOURCES AND ENVIRONMENT

Jamie L. Whitten Building, Room 217–E, phone (202) 720–7173

Deputy Under Secretaries.—Dr. Ann M. Bartuska (acting), Hank Kashdan (acting), Doug Lawrence.

FOREST SERVICE

Sydney R. Yates Building, 201 14th Street, SW., 20250, phone (202) 205–1661

Chief.—Abigail Kimbell.
Associate Chief.—Hank Kashdan, 205–1779.
Director for—
International Programs.—Valdis E. Mezainis, 205–1650.
Law Enforcement and Investigations.—David Ferrell (acting), (703) 605–4690.
Legislative Affairs.—Douglas Crandall, 205–1637.

BUSINESS OPERATIONS

Sydney R. Yates Building, Fifth Floor, phone (202) 205–1707

Deputy Chief.—Charles L. Myers.
Associate Deputy Chief.—Jacqueline Myers, 205–1709.
Senior Staff Assistant.—Rita Stevens, 401–4470.
Director for—
Acquisition Management.—Ron Hooper (703) 605–4744.
Budget and Financial Management.—Donna Carmical (505) 563–7103.
Civil Rights.—Debra Muse, 205–0827.
Freedom of Information/Privacy Act.—George Vargas, 205–0444.

Homeland Security.—Arthur Bryant, 205–0942.
Human Resources Management.—Robin Bailey (503) 563–9700.
Information Resources Management.—Vaughn Stokes (505) 563–7978.
Job Corps.—Larry Dawson (303) 236–9939.
Program and Budget Analysis.—Lenise Lago, 205–1088.
Regulatory and Management Services.—Thelma Strong, 205–5102.
Safety and Occupational Health.—Ralph Dorn (703) 605–4482.
Strategic Planning and Assessment.—Ron Ketter (202) 205–0987.

NATIONAL FOREST SYSTEM

Sydney R. Yates Building, Third Floor, phone (202) 205–1523

Deputy Chief.—Joel Holtrop.
Associate Deputy Chief.—Gloria Manning.
Staff Director of:
Ecosystem Management Coordination.—Greg Smith (acting), 205–0895.
Engineering.—Richard Sowa (703) 605–4646.
Forest Management.—Tom Peterson, 205–0893.
Minerals and Geology Management.—Tony Ferguson (703) 605–4545.
Range Management.—Janette Kaiser, 205–0893.
Recreation and Heritage Resources.—Jim Bedwell, 205–0900.
Watershed, Fish, Wildlife, Air and Rare Plants.—Anne Zimmermann, 205–1671.
Wilderness, Wild and Scenic Resources.—Chris Brown, 205–0925.
Lands and Realty Staff.—Greg Smith, 205–1248.

RESEARCH AND DEVELOPMENT

Sydney R. Yates Building, First Floor, phone (202) 205–1665

Deputy Chief.—Ann M. Bartuska, 205–1665.
Associate Deputy Chief.—David A. Cleaves, 205–1702.
Staff Assistants: Daina Apple, 205–1452; Chris Rose, 205–1105.
Special Assistant.—Jennifer Plyler, 205–1751.
Staff Director of:
Environmental Sciences.—Vacant (703) 605–5277.
Forest Management Sciences.—Carlos Rodriguez-Franco (703) 605–5252.
Policy Analysis.—William Lange, 205–1775.
Quantitative Sciences.—Richard W. Guldin (703) 605–4177.
Resource Use Sciences.—Rob Doudrick (703) 605–4880.
Science Quality Services.—John Sebelius (703) 605–5294.

STATE AND PRIVATE FORESTRY

Sydney R. Yates Building, Second Floor, phone (202) 205–1657

Deputy Chief.—James E. Hubbard, 205–1606.
Associate Deputy Chiefs: John Phipps, Robin Thompson.
Staff Assistants: Marilyn Chilton, Debbie Pressman.
Director of:
Conservation Education.—Safiya Samman, 205–5681.
Cooperative Forestry.—Paul Ries, 205–1389.
Fire and Aviation Management.—Tom Harbour, 205–1483.
Forest Health Protection.—Rob Mangold (703) 605–5334.
National Fire Plan.—Rick Prausa, 205–1579.
Office of Tribal Relations.—Fred Clark, 205–1514.
Urban/Community Forestry.—Steve Marshall (acting), 401–4076.

NATURAL RESOURCES CONSERVATION SERVICE

South Building, Room 5105–A, phone (202) 720–7246

Chief.—Dave White.
Associate Chief.—Virginia ''Ginger'' Murphy, 720–4531.
Director, Division of:
Civil Rights.—Joseph Hairston (301) 504–2181.

Legislative.—Kari Cohen (acting), 720–2771.
Public Affairs.—Dianne Guidry 720–3210.

DEPUTY CHIEF FOR FINANCIAL MANAGEMENT

Deputy Chief.—Steve Butler, 720–5904.
Associate Deputy Chief.—Carol Phillips, 690–0432.
Team Leaders:
Accounting Team.—Linda Washington, 205–5415.
Budget Team.—Selena Miller, 205–6134.
Fiscal Team.—Robin Kelly, 205–0113.

DEPUTY CHIEF OF MANAGEMENT

Deputy Chief.—Eloris Speight (acting), (202) 720–7847.
Associate Deputy Chief.—Terrell Erickson (acting).
Ethics Officer.—Ellen Pearson (301) 205–1826.
Director, Division of:
Human Resources Management.—Letitia Toomer (acting), 720–2227.
Information Technology.—Jason Restad, (202) 690–0242.
Management Services.—Juliette White, 720–4102.
National Employee Development Center.—Chris Tippie (817) 509–3242.
Chief Information Officer.—Wendall Oaks, (970) 217–8185.
Supervisory Agency Representative.—Lauren Ruby (301) 504–2176.

DEPUTY CHIEF OF PROGRAMS

Deputy Chief.—Ed Burton (acting), (202) 720–4527.
Associate Deputy Chief.—Andree DuVarney (acting), 702–0134.
Director, Division of:
Conservation Planning and Technical Assistance.—Dan Lawson, 720–1510.
Easement Programs.—John Glover, 720–1854.
Financial Assistance Programs.—Gregory Johnson, 720–1845.
Resource Conservation, Development and Outreach Division.—Anne Dubey, 720–2847.
Team Leader for—
Business Tools Team.—Jon Vrana, 720–9483.
Program Allocations and Management Support Team.—Maggie Rhodes, 690–0547.

DEPUTY CHIEF OF SCIENCE AND TECHNOLOGY

Deputy Chief.—Tony Kramer (acting), (202) 720–4630.
Director, Division of:
Animal Husbandry and Clean Water.—Richard Swenson (301) 504–2196.
Conservation Engineering.—Noller Herbert, 720–2520.
Ecological Sciences.—Michael Hubbs, 720–2587.
Resource Economics and Social Sciences.—Felix Spinelli (acting), 720–2307.

DEPUTY CHIEF OF SOIL SURVEY AND RESOURCE ASSESSMENT

Deputy Chief.—Doug Lawrence (202) 690–4616.
Director, Division of:
International Programs.—Melvin Westbrook (301) 504–2271.
Resources Inventory and Assessment.—Tommie Parham (301) 504–2300.
Soil Survey.—Michael L. Golden, 720–1820.

DEPUTY CHIEF OF STRATEGIC PLANNING AND ACCOUNTABILITY

Deputy Chief.—Lesia Reed (acting), (202) 720–6297.
Director, Division of:
Budget Planning and Analysis.—Raymond ''Gus'' Hughbanks, 720–4533.
Operations Management and Oversight.—Katherine Gugulis, 720–8388.

Strategic and Performance Planning—Patty Lawrence, 690–0467.

UNDER SECRETARY FOR FARM AND FOREIGN AGRICULTURAL SERVICES

Under Secretary.—Vacant.

Deputy Under Secretaries: Carolyn B. Cooksie, (202) 720–3111; Patricia Sheikh, 720–7107; Linda Treese, 720–2542.

FARM SERVICE AGENCY

South Building, Room 3086–S, phone (202) 720–3467

Administrator.—Dennis J. Taitano (acting).

Associate Administrator for—

Operations and Management.—Vacant.

Programs.—James E. Meidinger (acting).

Civil Rights.—Johnny Toles, 410–7197.

Economic and Policy Analysis Staff.—Joy Harwood (acting), room 3741–S, 720–3451.

Legislative Liaison Staff.—Mary Helen Askins, room 3613–S, 720–3865.

Public Affairs Staff.—Kent Poltish, room 3624–S, 720–5237.

Deputy Administrator for Farm Programs.—Candace Thompson (acting), room 3612–S, 720–3175.

Assistant Deputy Administrator.—Lynn Tjeerdsma, 720–2070.

Conservation and Environmental Programs Division.—Robert Stephenson, room 4714–S, 720–6221.

Price Support Division.—Grady Bilberry, room 4095–S, 720–7901.

Production, Emergencies and Compliance Division.—Diane Sharp, room 4754, 720–7641.

Deputy Administrator for Loan Programs.—Carolyn Cooksie, room 3605–S, 720–4671.

Program Development and Economic Enhancement Division.—Bobby Reynolds, room 4919–S, 720–3647.

Loan Making Division.—James Radintz, room 5438–S, 720–1632.

Loan Servicing and Property Management Division.—Veldon Hall, room 5449–S, 720–4572.

Deputy Administrator for Field Operations.—Robert Stephenson (acting), room 3092, 690–2807.

Assistant Deputy Administrator.—John W. Chott, Jr., room 8092, 690–2807.

Operations Review and Analysis Staff.—Thomas McCann, room 2720–S, 690–2532.

Deputy Administrator for Commodity Operations.—Sandra Wood (acting), room 3080–S, 720–3217.

Kansas City Commodity Office.—George Aldaya (816) 926–6301.

Procurement and Donations Division.—Sue King, room 5755, 720–5074.

Warehouse and Inventory Division.—Steve Gill (acting), room 5962–S, 720–2121.

Deputy Administrator for Management.—Phil Short, room 3095–S, 720–3438.

Budget Division.—Dennis Taitano, room 4720–S, 720–3674.

Financial Management Division.—Dennis Taitano, room 4747–S, 720–3674.

Human Resources Division.—Patricia Farmer, room 5200 (L–St), 418–8950.

Information Technology Services Division.—Steve Sanders, room 5768–S, 720–5320.

Management Services Division.—Mary Winters, room 520–PRTL, 720–3438.

FOREIGN AGRICULTURAL SERVICE

South Building, Room 5071, phone (202) 720–3935, fax 690–2159

Administrator.—Michael V. Michener.

Senior Advisors to the Administrator: Jaime Adams, 720–0006; Christine Turner, 690–4267.

Chief of Staff.—Lona Stoll, 690–8064.

Associate Administrators: John D. Brewer, 720–3935; Suzanne Hale (acting), 690–8108.

General Sales Manager.—Patricia Sheikh (acting), 720–4055.

Executive Assistant.—Debra Oliver, 720–3935.

Director of:

Civil Rights Staff.—Carmen Cantor, 720–7061.

Legislative and Public Affairs.—Christopher Church, 720–6830.

Public Affairs and Executive Correspondence.—Sally Klusaritz, 720–4064.

OFFICE OF ADMINISTRATIVE OPERATIONS

Deputy Administrator.—Frank Lee (202) 720–0690.
Senior Advisor.—David Pendlum, 720–1293.
Director, Division of:
Budget.—Scott Redman, 690–4052.
Contracts and Agreements.—Edwin MacLaughlin, 720–0281.
Information Technology.—Bryan Dixon, 690–2936.
Program Management.—William Hawkins, 720–3241.

OFFICE OF CAPACITY BUILDING AND DEVELOPMENT

Deputy Administrator.—Patricia R. Sheikh (202) 720–6887.
Assistant Deputy Administrators: Gary Groves, 690–1791; Ross Kreamer, 690–4056.
Policy Coordination and Planning Staff.—Roger Mireles, 720–1314.
Director, Division of:
Development Resources and Disaster Assistance.—Robert Curtis, 690–1924.
Food Assistance.—Ronald Croushorn, 720–4221.
Trade and Scientific Capacity Building.—Susan Owens, 690–4872.
Trade and Scientific Exchanges.—Lynne Reich, 690–1821.

OFFICE OF COUNTRY AND REGIONAL AFFAIRS

Deputy Administrator.—Jim Higiston (acting), (202) 720–7562.
Assistant Deputy Administrators: Jocelyn Brown, 690–1779; Norval Francis, 720–1134.
Director, Division of:
Africa and Middle East.—Ted MacLaughlin (acting), 720–1326.
Asia.—Cina Radler, 720–3403.
Europe.—Sharynne Nenon, 720–1330.
Western Hemisphere.—Bruce Zanin, 720–5219.

OFFICE OF FOREIGN SERVICE OPERATIONS

Deputy Administrator.—Charles T. Alexander (202) 720–8322.
Assistant Deputy Administrator.—Susan Schayes, 690–4062.
Director for—
Africa and Middle East Area.—Kim Svec, 690–4066.
Asia Area.—Kathleen Wainio, 690–4053.
Europe Area.—David Young, 690–4057.
Planning and Global Resources Staff.—Karen Darden, 720–1346.
Western Hemisphere Area.—Hugh Maginnis, 720–3223.

OFFICE OF GLOBAL ANALYSIS

Deputy Administrator.—Maurice House (202) 720–6301.
Assistant Deputy Administrators: John Nuttall, 690–1198; Patrick Packnett, 720–1590.
Agricultural Economists: Michael Dwyer, 720–3124; Renee Schwartz, 720–9825.
Director, Division of:
Industry and Sector Analysis Division.—Tim Rocke, 690–0292.
International Production Assessment Division.—Tom St. Clair (acting), 720–2974.
Trade and Biofuels Analysis Divsion.—Mike Dwyer, 720–3124.

OFFICE OF NEGOTIATIONS AND AGREEMENTS

Deputy Administrator.—Robert Riemenschnedier (202) 720–6136.
Assistant Deputy Administrators: Brian Grunenfelder, 720–6136; Gregg Young, 720–1324.
Director, Division of:
Monitoring and Enforcement.—Charles Bertsch, 720–6278.
Multilateral Negotiations and Agreements.—Andrew Burst, 720–9519.
Regional and Bilateral Negotiations and Agreements.—Melinda Sallyards, 690–1173.

OFFICE OF SCIENTIFIC AND TECHNICAL AFFAIRS

Deputy Administrator.—J. Lawrence Blum (202) 720–2701.
Assistant Deputy Administrators: Daniel Berman, 720–1286; Robert Macke, 720–4434; Howard Wetzel, 720–8031.
Director, Division of:
Animal.—Clay Hamilton, 720–1353.
International Regulations and Standards.—Cathy McKinnell, 690–0929.
New Technologies and Production Methods.—Merritt Chesley, 720–2579.
Market Access and Bilateral Issues.—Kent Sisson, 720–2579.
Plant.—Steven Shnitzler, 720–0765.
Processed Production and Technical Regulations.—Audrey Talley (acting).

OFFICE OF TRADE PROGRAMS

Deputy Administrator.—Christian Foster (202) 401–0015.
Assistant Deputy Administrators: Quinton Gray, 401–0023; Marcus Lower, 720–2705.
Special Assistant to Deputy.—Daniel Martrinez, 205–9432.
Director, Division of:
Agriculture Marketing Specialist.—Mirna Ferreiro, 720–8557.
Credit Programs.—Mark Rowse, 720–0624.
Executive Assistant.—Ida Cummunings, 720–9516.

RISK MANAGEMENT AGENCY

South Building, Room 6092–S, phone (202) 690–2803

Administrator.—William J. Murphy (acting).
Associate Administrator.—Timothy Witt (acting).
Deputy Administrator for—
Compliance.—Michael Hand, room 4619–S, 720–0642.
Insurance Services.—William Murphy, room 6709–S, 690–4494.
Product Management.—Timothy Witt, Kansas City (816) 926–7394 / 7822.

UNDER SECRETARY FOR RURAL DEVELOPMENT

Jamie L. Whitten Building, phone (202) 720–4581

Under Secretary.—Dallas Tonsager.
Deputy Under Secretaries: —Cheryl L. Coak, Victor Vasquez.
Chief of Staff.—Jim Newby.
Deputy Chief of Staff.—Lana Nesbit.
Director, Legislative and Public Affairs.—Timothy McNeilly, 720–1019.

BUSINESS AND COOPERATIVE PROGRAMS

South Building, Room 5801–S, phone (202) 690–4730

Administrator.—Judith A. Canales.
Associate Administrator.—Curtis A. Wiley, 720–6165.
Oversight / Resource Coordination Staff (OCS).—Nannie Hill-Midgett, 690–4100.
Deputy Administrator for Business Programs.—Pandor H. Hadjy (acting), 720–7287.
Director of:
Business and Industry Division.—Carolyn Parker, 690–4103.
Specialty Lenders Division.—Jody Raskind, 720–0410.
Deputy Administrator for Cooperative Programs.—Leann Oliver, 720–7558.
Assistant Deputy Administrator.—Andy Jermolowizc, 720–8460.
Director of:
Cooperative Development Division.—John H. Wells, 720–3350.
Cooperative Marketing Division.—Thomas H. Stafford, 690–0368.
Cooperative Resources Management Division.—Vacant, 690–1374.

RURAL HOUSING SERVICE

South Building, Room 5014–S, phone (202) 690–1533

Administrator.—James C. Alsop (acting).
Director, Program Support Staff.—Richard A. Davis, 720–9619.
Deputy Administrator for Single Family.—Phillip Stetson (acting), 720–5177.
Director of:
Family Housing Direct Loan Division.—Philip Stetson, 720–1474.
Family Housing Guaranteed Loan Division.—Roger Glendenning, 720–1452.
Deputy Administrator for Multi-Family Housing.—Thomas Hannah, 720–3773.
Deputy Director.—Sue Harris-Green, 720–1606.
Director of:
Direct Loan and Grant Processing Division.—Chadwick Parker, 720–1502.
Multi-Family Housing Portfolio Management Division, Direct Housing.—Stephanie White, 720–1600.

RURAL UTILITIES SERVICE

South Building, Room 5135, phone (202) 720–9540

Administrator.—Jonathan Adelstein.
Deputy Administrator.—Jessica Zufolo.
Assistant Administrator for—
Electric Division.—Nivin Elgohary (acting), room 5165, 720–9505.
Program Accounting and Regulatory Analysis.—Kenneth M. Ackerman, room 5159, 720–9450.
Telecommunications.—David Villano, room 5151, 720–9554.
Water and Environmental Programs.—Jacqueline Ponti-Lazaruk, room 5145, 690–2670.
Director of:
Advanced Services Division.—Vacant, room 2845–S, 690–4493.
Broadband Division.—Kenneth Kuchno, room 2846–S, 690–4673.
Electric Staff Division.—George Shultz, room 1246–S, 720–1900.
Northern Regional Electric Division.—Joseph Badin, room 0243–S, 720–1420.
Northern Area, Telecommunications Program.—Shawn Arner (acting), room 2835–S, 720–1025.
Power Supply Division.—Victor T. Vu, room 270–S, 720–6436.
Southern Regional Electric Division.—Doris Nolte, room 221–S, 720–0848.
Southern Area, Telecommunications Program.—Ken B. Chandler, room 2808–S, 720–0800.
Telecommunications Standards Division.—John Schnell (acting), room 2868–S, 720–8663.
Chief, Portfolio Management Branch.—Steve Saulnier, room 2231–S, 720–9631.
Engineering and Environmental Staff.—Mark Plank, room 2237, 720–1649.

FOOD, NUTRITION, AND CONSUMER SERVICES

1400 Independence Avenue, SW., Room 216–E, Whitten Building, 20250

Under Secretary.—Kevin Concannon, (202) 720–7711.
Deputy Under Secretary.—Janey Thornton.

FOOD AND NUTRITION SERVICE

3101 Park Center Drive, Room 906, Alexandria, VA 22302, (703) 305–2062

OFFICE OF THE ADMINISTRATOR

Administrator.—Julia Paradis.
Deputy Administrator, Supplemental Nutrition Assistance Program.—Lisa Pino (703) 305–2064.
Deputy Administrator, Special Nutrition Programs.—Audrey Rowe, 305–2060.

OFFICE OF RESEARCH AND ANALYSIS

Director.—Steven Carlson, room 1014 (703) 305–2017.

Assistant Director.—Rich Lucas, room 1002, 605–0707.
Division, Director of:
Family Program Staff.—Carol Olander, room 1030, 305–2134.
Special Nutrition Staff.—Jay Hirschman, room 1010, 305–2117.

OFFICE OF COMMUNICATIONS AND GOVERNMENTAL AFFAIRS

Chief Communications Officer.—Susan Siemietkowski (acting), room 926–A (703) 305–2281.
Deputy Director.—Susan Siemietkowski, room 926–B, 305–2281.
Division, Director of:
Controlled Correspondence Officer.—Twanda Rodgers, room 918, 305–2066.
Governmental Affairs.—Robert Beard (acting), room 918, 305–2010.
Public Affairs.—Jean Daniel, room 912, 305–2286.

OFFICE OF MANAGEMENT TECHNOLOGY AND FINANCE

Associate Administrator.—Enrique Gomez, room 906 (703) 305–2064.
Director of Civil Rights.—Lorena Carrasco, room 942, 305–2195.

MANAGEMENT

Deputy Administrator.—Ralph Charlip, room 400 (703) 305–2030.
Division, Director of:
Contracts Management.—Jason Kattman (acting), room 220, 305–2251.
Human Resources.—Frank Curnow, room 404, 305–2326.
Logistics and Facility Management.—Mark Rucker, room 222, 305–2220.

FINANCIAL MANAGEMENT

Deputy Administrator (CFO).—Enrique Gomez (acting), room 712 (703) 305–2046.
Division, Director of:
Accounting.—Rose McClyde, room 724, 305–2850.
Administrative Operations.—Larry Blim, room 716, 305–2240.
Budget.—David Burr, room 708, 305–2172.
Grants and Fiscal Policy.—Lael Lubing, room 732, 305–2048.
Internal Controls, Audits, and Investigations Liaison.—Diane Kriviski, room 732, 305–2493.

INFORMATION TECHNOLOGY

Deputy Administrator.—Jonathan Alboum, room 314 (703) 605–4318.
Information Security Officer.—Brad Nix, room 314, 305–2242.
Division, Director of:
Portfolio Management.—Jacquie Butler, room 314, 605–4318.
Technology.—Rich Platt, room 316, 305–2346.

OFFICE OF PROGRAM SERVICE AND SUPPORT

Associate Administrator.—Tim O'Connor, room 906 (703) 305–2060.
Division, Director of:
Office of Emergency Management and Food Safety.—Brenda Lisi, room 1441, 305–1504.
Office of Strategic Initiatives Partnership and Outreach.—Duke Storen, room 1441, 305–1504.

OFFICE OF SUPPLEMENTAL NUTRITION ASSISTANCE PROGRAM

Associate Administrator.—Jessica Shahin, room 808 (703) 305–2026.
Division, Director of:
Benefit Redemption.—Jeff Cohen, room 408, 305–2434.

Program Accountability and Administration.—Karen Walker, room 816, 305–2413.
Program Development.—Art Foley, room 814, 305–2494.

OFFICE OF SPECIAL NUTRITION PROGRAMS

Associate Administrator.—Ron Vogel, room 628 (703) 305–2052.
Division, Director of:
Child Nutrition.—Cindy Long, room 640, 305–2590.
Food Distribution.—Laura Castro (acting), room 500, 305–2680.
Supplemental Food Program.—Debra Whitford, room 520, 305–2746.

CENTER FOR NUTRITION POLICY AND PROMOTION

Executive Director.—Dr. Raj Anand, room 1034 (703) 305–7600.
Deputy Director.—Robert Post, room 1034, 305–7600.
Division, Director of:
Evidence Analysis Library.—Joanne Spahn, room 1034, 305–2870.
Nutrition Guidance and Analysis.—Carole Davis, room 1034, 605–4265.
Nutrition Marketing and Communication Division.—Jackie Haven, room 1034, 605–4434.
Public Affairs and FNS Liaison.—John Webster, room 1034, 605–4270.

UNDER SECRETARY FOR FOOD SAFETY

Under Secretary.—Ronald F. Hicks (acting), (202) 720–0350.
Deputy Under Secretary.—Vacant.
Confidential Assistant to the Under Secretary.—Vacant.

FOOD SAFETY AND INSPECTION SERVICE

Jamie L. Whitten Building, Room 331–E, phone (202) 720–7025, fax 690–0550

Administrator.—Alfred V. Almanza.
Deputy Administrator.—Bryce Quick, 720–7900.
U.S. Manager for Codex.—Karen Stuck, room 4861–S, 720–2057.

OFFICE OF FIELD OPERATIONS (OFO)

Assistant Administrator.—Dr. Kenneth E. Petersen, room 344–E (202) 720–8803.
Deputy Assistant Administrator.—Judy Riggins, 720–5190.
Executive Associates, Regulatory Operations: Cheryl Hicks, room 3159–S, 690–2709; Dr. William James, room 3153–S, 720–9521; Dr. Armia Tawadrous, room 3161–S, 720–5714.
Director of:
Recall Management Staff.—Dr. Lisa Volk, room 0010–S, 690–6536.

OFFICE OF DATA INTEGRATION AND FOOD PROTECTION (ODIFP)

Assistant Administrator.—Dr. Carol A. Maczka, room 3130–S (202) 720–5643.
Deputy Assistant Administrator.—Dr. Perfecto Santiago, 205–0452.
Director of:
Biosurveillance and Emergency Response Staff.—Mary K. Cutshall, 414 Aero Building, 690–6523.

OFFICE OF INTERNATIONAL AFFAIRS (OIA)

Assistant Administrator.—Dr. Ronald Jones, room 3143–S (202) 720–3473.
Deputy Assistant Administrator.—Vacant, 720–5362.
Director, Import Inspection Division.—Jerry Elliott, room 1–2288B (301) 504–2153.

OFFICE OF MANAGEMENT (OM)

Assistant Administrator.—Anthony Thompson., room 347–E (202) 720–4425.
Deputy Assistant Administrator.—Karen A. Messmore, 720–4744.

OFFICE OF POLICY, PROGRAM AND EMPLOYEE DEVELOPMENT (OPPED)

Assistant Administrator.—Philip Derfler, room 350–E (202) 720–2709.
Deputy Assistant Administrator.—Daniel Engeljohn, 205–0495.

OFFICE OF PROGRAM EVALUATION, ENFORCEMENT AND REVIEW (OPEER)

Assistant Administrator.—William C. ''Bill'' Smith, room 3133–S (202) 720–8609.
Deputy Assistant Administrator.—Dr. Jane Roth, room 3133–S, 720–8609.
Director of:
Compliance and Investigations Division.—Zygmunt Sala, room 300B–CQ, WEC, 418–8874.
Program Evaluation and Improvement Staff.—Matthew Michael, room 3831–S, 720–6735.

OFFICE OF PUBLIC AFFAIRS AND CONSUMER EDUCATION (OPACE)

Assistant Administrator.—Terri Nintemann, room 339–E (202) 720–8217.
Deputy Assistant Administrator.—Robert Tynan, room 3137–S, 720–3884.
Director of:
Congressional and Public Affairs Staff.—Carol Blake, room 1175–S, 720–9891 or 9113.
Executive Correspondence and Issues Management Staff.—Jonathan Theodule, room 1167–S, 690–3882.

OFFICE OF PUBLIC HEALTH SCIENCE (OPHS)

Assistant Administrator.—Dr. David Goldman, room 341–E (202) 720–2644.
Deputy Assistant Administrator.—Dr. Elisabeth Hagen, room 341–E, 205–0293.

OFFICE OF CATFISH INSPECTION PROGRAMS (OCIP)

Assistant Administrator.—William ''Billy'' P. Milton, Jr., room 3162–S, 720–5735.

OFFICE OF OUTREACH, EMPLOYEE EDUCATION AND TRAINING (OOEET)

Assistant Administrator.—Dr. Karlease Kelly, room 4862–S, 205–0194.

UNDER SECRETARY FOR RESEARCH, EDUCATION, AND ECONOMICS

Under Secretary.—Dr. Rajiv J. Shah (202) 720–5923.
Deputy Under Secretary.—Dr. Katherine Smith (acting).
Counselor to the Under Secretary.—Rachael Goldfarb, Esq., 720–8885.
Senior Advisor for Energy and Environment.—Maura O'Neill, 720–4395.
Senior Advisor for International Programs.—Ann Tutwiler, 720–6118.

AGRICULTURAL RESEARCH SERVICE

Administration Building, Room 302–A, phone (202) 720–3656, fax 720–5427

Administrator.—Edward B. Knipling.
Associate Administrator for—
Research Operations.—Antoinette A. Betschart, 720–3658.
Research Programs.—Caird E. Rexroad (301) 504–5084.
Director of:
Budget and Program Management Staff.—Vacant, room 358–A, 720–4421.
Legislative Affairs.—David Kelly, 720–3173.

Information Staff.—Sandy Miller-Hays (301) 504–1638.
Assistant Administrator, Research Operations and Management, Office of Technology Transfer.—Richard J. Brenner (301) 504–6905.
Deputy Administrator, Administrative and Financial Management.—James H. Bradley, 690–2575.
National Agricultural Library.—Vacant (301) 504–5248.
U.S. National Arboretum.—Thomas S. Elias, 245–4539.

AREA OFFICES

Director of:
Beltsville Area.—Joseph Spence, 10300 Baltimore Boulevard, Building 003, Room 223, BARC–West, Beltsville, MD 20705 (301) 504–6078.
North Atlantic Area.—Dariusz Swietlik, 600 East Mermaid Lane, Room 2031, Wyndmoor, PA 19038 (215) 233–6593.
South Atlantic Area.—Darrell Cole, P.O. Box 5677, College Station Road, Room 201, Athens, GA 30605 (706) 546–3311.
Mid South Area.—Edgar King, Jr., 141 Experiment Station Road, Stoneville, MS 38776 (662) 686–5265.
Midwest Area.—Larry Chandler, 1815 North University Street, Room 2004, Peoria, IL 61604–0000 (309) 681–6602.
Pacific West Area.—Andrew Hammond, 800 Buchanan Street, Room 2030, Albany, CA 94710 (510) 559–6060.
Northern Plains Area.—Wilbert H. Blackburn, 2150 Centre Avenue, Building D, Ft. Collins, CO 80525–8119 (970) 492–7057.
Southern Plains Area.—Dan Upchurch, 1001 Holleman Drive East, College Station, TX 77845 (979) 260–9346.

COOPERATIVE STATE RESEARCH, EDUCATION AND EXTENSION SERVICE

Jamie L. Whitten Building, Room 305–A, phone (202) 720–4423, fax 720–8987

Administrator.—Dr. Colien Heffernan.
Associate Administrator.—Ralph A. Otto, 720–7441.
Assistant Administrator/Legislative Liaison.—James Spurling, room 305–A, 720–8187.
Directors, Office of:
Budget.—Tina Buch, room 332–A, 720–2675.
Communications.—Janet Allen, room 4231, 720–2677.
Equal Opportunity Staff.—Curt DeVille, room 1230, 720–2700.
Planning and Accountability.—Robert McDonald, room 1315, 720–5623.
Deputy Administrator for—
Competitive Programs.—Deborah Sheely (acting), room 2334, 401–5024.
Economic and Community Systems.—Frank Boteler, room 4343, 720–7947.
Extramural Programs.—Andrea Brandon, room 2256, 401–6021.
Families, 4–H and Nutrition.—Dan Kugler (acting), room 3231, 401–4555.
Information Systems and Technology Management.—Michel Desbois, room 4122, 401–0117.
Natural Resources and Environment.—Dan Kugler, room 3231, 401–4555.
Science and Education Resources Development.—Frank Boteler (acting), room 4343, 720–7947.

ECONOMIC RESEARCH SERVICE

1800 M Street, NW., 20036–5831, phone (202) 694–5000

Administrator.—Katherine R. Smith (acting), room N4145.
Associate Administrator.—John Kort, room N4150.
Assistant Administrator.—Stephen Crutchfield, room N4149.
Special Assistant to Administrator.—Leslee Lowstutter, room N4151.
Civil Rights Director.—Joyce Key, room N4152.
Division Directors:
Food Economics.—Laurian Unnevehr, room N2168, 694–5400.
Information Services.—Ron Bianchi, room S2032, 694–5100.
Market Trade and Economics.—Sally Thompson, room N5119, 694–5200.

Resource and Rural Economics.—Mary Bohman, room S4182, 694–5500.

NATIONAL AGRICULTURAL STATISTICS SERVICE

South Agriculture Building, Room 5041A–S, phone (202) 720–2707, fax 720–9013

Administrator.—Cynthia Clark.
Associate Administrator.—Joseph T. Reilly, 720–4333.
Deputy Administrator for—
Field Operations.—Marshall L. Dantzler, room 5053, 720–3638.
Programs and Products.—Carol House, room 5029, 690–8141.
Division Directors for—
Census and Survey.—Robert T. Bass, room 6306, 720–4557.
Information Technology.—John P. Nealon, room 5847, 720–2984.
Research and Development.—James M. Harris, Fairfax, (703) 877–8000, ext. 100.
Statistics.—Joseph Prusacki, room 5433, 720–3896.

UNDER SECRETARY FOR MARKETING AND REGULATORY PROGRAMS

Jamie A. Whitten Building, Room 228–W, phone (202) 720–4256, fax 720–5775

Under Secretary.—Vacant.
Deputy Under Secretary.—Vacant.
Special Assistant to the Under Secretary.—Vacant.
Confidential Assistant to the Under Secretary.—Lucas Knowles, 690–2832.

AGRICULTURAL MARKETING SERVICE

South Agriculture Building, Room 3064–S, phone (202) 720–5115, fax 720–8477

Administrator.—Vacant.
Associate Administrator.—David R. Shipman, 720–4276.
Deputy Associate Administrator.—Charles R. Martin, 720–4024.
Deputy Administrator for—
Compliance and Analysis Programs.—Ellen King, room 3507–S, 720–6766.
Cotton and Tobacco Programs.—Darryl Earnest, room 2639–S, 720–3193.
Dairy Programs.—Dana Cole, room 2968–S, 720–4392.
Fruit and Vegetable Programs.—Robert C. Keeney, room 2077–S, 720–4722.
Poultry Programs.—Craig Morse, room 2902–S, 720–5705.
Science and Technology.—Robert L. Epstein, room 1090–S, 720–5231.
Transportation and Marketing.—Barbara C. Robinson, room 1098, 690–1300.
Director, Legislative and Review Staff.—Chris Sarcone, room 2625–S, 720–3203.

ANIMAL AND PLANT HEALTH INSPECTION SERVICE (APHIS)

Jamie L. Whitten Building, Room 312–E, phone (202) 720–3668, fax 720–3054

OFFICE OF THE ADMINISTRATOR

Administrator.—Cindy J. Smith.
Associate Administrator.—Kevin Shea.
Director of Civil Rights Enforcement and Compliance.—Anna P. Grayson, room 1137–S, 720–6312, fax 720–2365.

ANIMAL CARE

4700 River Road, Riverdale, MD 20737, phone (301) 734–4980, fax 734–4328

Deputy Administrator.—Chester Gipson.
Associate Deputy Administrator.—Andrea Morgan.

BIOTECHNOLOGY REGULATORY SERVICES

4700 River Road, Riverdale, MD 20737, phone (301) 734–7324, fax 734–8724

Deputy Administrator.—Michael Gregoire.
Assistant Deputy Administrator.—Sidney Abel, 734–5716.

INTERNATIONAL SERVICES

Jamie L. Whitten Building, Room 324–E, phone (202) 720–7593, fax 690–1484

Deputy Administrator.—Dan Sheesley.
Associate Deputy Administrator.—Eric Hoffman, 720–7021.
Division Directors: Freida Skaggs (301) 734–5214; John Wyss, 734–3779.
Trade Support Team.—John Greifer, room 1128, 720–7677.

LEGISLATIVE AND PUBLIC AFFAIRS

South Building, Room 1147–S, phone (202) 720–2511, fax 720–3982

Deputy Administrator.—Bethany Jones.
Associate Deputy Administrator.—James Ivy.
Assistant Director of:
Public Affairs.—Ed Curlett (301) 734–7799.
Executive Correspondence.—Christina Myers (301) 734–7776.
Freedom of Information.—Lesia Banks (301) 734–8296.

MARKETING AND REGULATORY PROGRAMS BUSINESS SERVICES

Jamie L. Whitten Building, Room 308–E, phone (202) 720–5213, fax 690–0686

Deputy Administrator.—Gregory Parham.
Associate Deputy Administrator.—Joanne Munno.
Division Directors:
Financial Management.—Laura MacKenzie, 720–7865.
Investigative and Enforcement Services.—Alan Christian (301) 734–6491.
Management Services.—Howard Price (301) 734–6502.
MRP Human Resources: Karen Benham, Ellen King, room 1709–S, 720–6377.

PLANT PROTECTION AND QUARANTINE

Jamie L. Whitten Building, Room 302–E, phone (202) 720–5601, fax 690–0472

Deputy Administrator.—Rebecca Bech.
Associate Deputy Administrator.—Paul Eggert, 720–4441.
Assistant to the Deputy Administrator.—John H. Payne, 720–5601.
Director of:
Biocontrol.—Dale Meyerdirk (301) 734–5667.
Center for Plant Health Science and Technology.—Gordon Gordh (919) 513–2400.
Phytosanitary Issues Management.—Cathleen Enright (301) 734–5291.
Resource Management Support.—Terri Burrell (301) 734–7764.
Technical Information Systems.—Allison Young (301) 734–5518.

POLICY AND PROGRAM DEVELOPMENT

4700 River Road, Riverdale, MD 20737, phone (301) 734–5136, fax 734–5899

Deputy Administrator.—Christine Zakarka.
Associate Deputy Administrator.—Shannon Hamm.
Unit Chiefs:
Planning, Evaluation and Monitoring.—Connie Williams, 734–8512.
Policy Analysis and Development.—Janet W. Berls, 734–8667.
Regulatory Analysis and Development.—Cynthia Howard, 734–0682.
Risk Analysis.—Richard Fite, 734–3634.

VETERINARY SERVICES

Jamie L. Whitten Building, Room 317–E, phone (202) 720–5193, fax 690–4171

Deputy Administrator.—John Clifford.
Administrative Assistant.—Paula Lee, 720–5793.
Associate Deputy Administrator for Regional Operations.—Jere Dick, 720–5193.
Assistant Deputy Administrator.—Vacant (301) 734–3754.
Director for—
Emergency Programs.—Randall Crom (301) 734–8073.
Inspection and Compliance.—Steven A. ''Ames'' Karli (515) 232–5785.
National Center of Import and Export.—Gary S. Colgrave (301) 734–4356.
Outreach Liaison.—Joseph Annelli (301) 794–8073.
Policy, Evaluation and Licensing.—Richard E. Hill, Jr. (515) 232–5785.

WILDLIFE SERVICES

South Building, Room 1624, phone (202) 720–2054, fax 690–0053

Deputy Administrator.—William H. Clay.
Assistant Deputy Administrator.—Martin Mendoza.
Director for Operational Support.—Joanne Garrett (301) 734–7921.

GRAIN INSPECTION, PACKERS AND STOCKYARDS ADMINISTRATION

South Building, Room 2055, phone (202) 720–0219, fax 205–9237

Administrator.—Alan Christian (acting), room 2055–S.
Director of:
Budget and Planning Staff.—Patricia Donohue-Galvin, room 2045–S, 720–0231.
Civil Rights Staff.—Eugene Bass, room 0623–S, 720–0218.
Information Technology Staff.—Frieda Achtentuch, room 2446–S, 720–1741.
Management Support Staff.—Albert Conerly, room 1651–S, 720–0234.
Deputy Administrator for Federal Grain Inspection Service.—Randall Jones, room 2063–S, 720–9170.
Director of:
Compliance.—Thomas O'Connor, room 1647–S, 720–8262.
Field Management Division.—John Giler, room 2409–S, 720–0228.
Office of International Affairs.—John Pitchford, room 1629–S, 720–0226.
Technical Services Division.—Donald Kendall, Kansas City, MO (816) 891–0463.
Deputy Administrator for Packers and Stockyards Programs.—Alan Christian, room 2055–S, 720–7051.
Director of:
Business and Economic Analysis Division.—Gary McBryde, room 2430–S, 720–7455.
Policy and Litigation Division.—Brett Offutt, room 2420–S, 720–7363.
Regional Supervisors:
Atlanta, GA.—Elkin Parker (404) 562–5840.
Aurora, CO.—John Barthel (303) 375–4240.
Des Moines, IA.—Jay Johnson (515) 323–2579.

DEPARTMENT OF COMMERCE

Herbert C. Hoover Building

14th Street between Pennsylvania and Constitution Avenues, NW., 20230

phone (202) 482–2000, http://www.doc.gov

GARY LOCKE, Secretary of Commerce; born in Seattle, WA, January 21, 1950; third-generation American with paternal ancestry from Taishan, and Guangdong in China; education: graduated, Franklin High School, Seattle, WA, 1968; B.A., political science, Yale University, 1972; J.D., Boston University School of Law, 1975; professional: Washington State House of Representatives, served as chair of the Appropriations Committee, 1983–94; Chief Executive, King County, becoming the first elected Chinese American, 1994–97; Deputy Prosecuting Attorney, King County; Governor, State of Washington, becoming the first elected Chinese American in U.S. history, 1997–2005; partner in the Seattle Office of International Law Firm Davis Wright Tremaine LLP, co-chaired the firm's China and governmental-relations practice groups; Leader of 10 productive trade missions to Asia, Mexico and Europe, significantly expanding the sale of Washington products and services; married: Mona Lee Locke; three children: Emily Nicole, Dylan James, and Madeline Lee; nominated by President Barack Obama to become the 36th Secretary of Commerce, and was confirmed by the U.S. Senate on March 26, 2009.

OFFICE OF THE SECRETARY

Secretary of Commerce.—Gary Locke, room 5858 (202) 482–2112.
Deputy Secretary.—Vacant, room 5838, 482–8376.
Chief of Staff.—Ellen Moran, room 5858, 482–4246.
Senior Advisor and Deputy Chief of Staff.—Rick Wade, room 5862, 482–4246.
Deputy Chief of Staff.—Jay Reich.
Chief Protocol Officer.—Roger Lau, room 5847, 482–8011.
Director, Office of:
Business Liaison.—Anne Olaimey, room 5062, 482–1360.
Executive Secretariat.—Tene Dolphin, room 5516, 482–3934.
Policy and Strategic Planning.—Travis Sullivan, room 5865, 482–4127.
Public Affairs.—Kevin Griffis, room 5413, 482–4883.
Scheduling and Advance.—Roger Fisk, room 5883, 482–5129.
White House Liaison.—Rick Siger, room 5835, 482–1684.

GENERAL COUNSEL

General Counsel.—Cameron F. Kerry, room 5870 (202) 482–4772.
Deputy General Counsel.—Nicole Lamb-Hale.

ASSISTANT SECRETARY FOR LEGISLATIVE AND INTERGOVERNMENTAL AFFAIRS

Assistant Secretary.—April Boyd, room 5421 (202) 482–3663, fax 482–4420.
Deputy Assistant Secretary.—Daraka Satcher, room 5421, 482–3663.
Director for—
Intergovernmental Affairs.—William Ramos, room 5422, 482–3663, fax 482–4420.
Legislative Affairs.—Courtney Gregoire, room 5422, 482–3663, fax 482–4420.

CHIEF FINANCIAL OFFICER (CFO) AND ASSISTANT SECRETARY FOR ADMINISTRATION

Chief Financial Officer and Assistant Secretary.—Vacant, room 5830 (202) 482–4951, fax 482–3592.
Deputy Assistant Secretary for Administration.—John F. Charles, room 5830.

Deputy Chief Financial Officer/Director for Financial Management.—Lisa Casias, room 6827, 482–1207, fax 482–5070.

Director for—

Acquisition Management.—Helen M. Hurcombe, room 6422, 482–4248, fax 482–1711.

Administrative Services.—Fred Fanning, room 6316, 482–1200, fax 482–8890.

Budget.—Neil Shapiro, room 5820, 482–5969, fax 482–3361.

Civil Rights.—Suzan J. Aramaki, room 6010, 482–0625, fax 482–3364.

Human Resources Management.—Deborah A. Jefferson, room 5001, 482–4807, fax 482–0249.

Management and Organization.—John J. Phelan III, room 5327, 482–3707, fax 482–1423.

Security.—Alfred Broadbent, room 1069, 482–4371, fax 501–6355.

Small and Disadvantaged Business Utilization.—LaJuene Desmukes, room 6411, 482–1472, fax 482–0501.

CHIEF INFORMATION OFFICER

Chief Information Officer.—Suzanne Hilding, room 5029B, (202) 482–4797.

Deputy Chief Information Officer.—Vacant, room 5027.

Office of:

Computer Systems.—Jerry Harper (acting), 5285 Port Royal Road, Room 1030, Springfield, VA 22151 (703) 487–4044.

IT Policy and Planning.—Diana Hynek (acting), room 6612, 482–0266.

IT Security, Infrastructure and Technology.—Earl Neal, room 6895, 482–4708.

Networking and Telecommunications.—Wayne Blackwood, room 6078, 482–3175.

Systems Development and Support.—Izella Dornell (acting), room 5027, 482–1888.

INSPECTOR GENERAL

Inspector General.—Todd J. Zinser, room 7898C, (202) 482–4661.

Deputy Inspector General.—Edward Blansitt, room 7898C, 482–3516.

Chief of Staff.—Lisa Allen, room 7898C, 482–5422.

Counsel to Inspector General.—Wade Green, Jr., room 7892, 482–1577.

Principal Assistant Inspector General Audit and Evaluation.—Judith Gordon, room 7886B, 482–2754.

Assistant Inspector General, Office of:

Auditing.—Brett Baker, room 7886B, 482–2600.

Economic and Statistical Program Assessment.—Ron Prevost, room 7520, 482–3052.

Systems Acquisition and IT Security.—Allen Crawley, room 7876, 482–1855.

Investigations.—Scott Berenberg, room 7087, 482–3860.

ECONOMICS AND STATISTICS ADMINISTRATION

Under Secretary for Economic Affairs.—Rebecca Blank, room 4848, (202) 482–3727.

Chief Counsel.—Roxie Jamison Jones, room 4868A, 482–5394.

Chief Economist.—Vacant, room 4842, 482–3523.

Associate Under Secretary for—

Communications.—Joanne Caldwell (acting), room 4836, 482–2760.

Economic Information Officer.—Jane A. Callen, room 4855, 482–2235.

Management.—James K. White, room 4834, 482–2405.

Director, Office of:

Economic Conditions.—Carl E. Cox, room 4861, 482–4871.

Policy Development.—Jane Molloy, room 4858, 482–5926.

STAT–USA.—Francine Krasowska, room 4886, 482–3429.

Deputy Chief Financial Officer, Finance and Administration.—Joanne Buenzli-Crane, room 4842, 482–3038.

BUREAU OF ECONOMIC ANALYSIS

1441 L Street, NW., 20230, phone (202) 606–9900

Director.—J. Steven Landefeld, room 6006, 606–9600.

Deputy Director.—Rosemary Marcuss, room 6005, 606–9602.

Chief Economist.—Ana Aizcorbe, room 6060, 606–9985.

Chief Information Officer.—Brian Callahan, room 6052, 606–9906.
Chief Statistician.—Dennis J. Fixler, room 6060, 606–9607.
Associate Director for—
Industry.—Brian Moyer, room 6004, 606–9612.
International Economics.—Obie Whichard, room 6062, 606–9604.
National Economic Accounts.—Brent R. Moulton, room 6064, 606–9606.
Regional Economics.—Joel Platt, room 6065, 606–9605.
Division Chiefs:
Administrative Services.—C. Brian Grove, room 3003, 606–9624.
Balance of Payments.—Robert Yuskavage, room 8024, 606–9672.
Communications.—Dorothy Andrake, room 3029, 606–9630.
Current Industry Analysis.—Vacant.
Government.—Pamela Kelly, room 4067, 606–9781.
Industry Benchmark.—Erich Strassner, room 4006, 606–9539.
International Investment.—Obie G. Wichard, room 7006, 606–9890.
National Income and Wealth.—Carol E. Moylan, room 5006, 606–9711.
Regional Economic Analysis.—Ian Mead, room 9018, 606–9661.
Regional Economic Measurement.—Robert L. Brown, room 8066, 606–9246.

THE BUREAU OF THE CENSUS

4600 Silver Hill Road, Suitland, MD 20746

Director.—Thomas Mesenbourg (acting), room 8H002 (301) 763–2135.
Deputy Director and Chief Operating Officer.—Thomas Mesenbourg, room 8H006, 763–2138.
Associate Director for—
Administration and Chief Financial Officer.—Theodore A. Johnson, room 8H144, 763–3464.
Communications.—Steven Jost, room 8H138, 763–2512.
Comptroller.—Andrew H. Moxam, room 2K108, 763–9575.
Decennial Census.—Arnold Jackson, room 8H122, 763–8626.
Demographic Programs.—Howard Hogan, room 8H134, 763–2160.
Economic Programs.—Harvey Monk, room 8H132, 763–2932.
Field Operations.—Marilia Matos, room 8H126, 763–2072.
Information Technology and CIO.—Brian McGrath, room 5K030, 763–2117.
Strategic Planning and Innovation.—Nancy M. Gordon, room 8H128, 763–2126.
Assistant to the Associate Director for Communications.—Burton Reist, room 8H062, 763–3949.
Special Assistant to the Associate Director Information Technology.—Thomas Meerholtz, room 5K030, 763–3774.
Assistant Director for—
Acquisition Division.—Michael L. Palensky, room 3J438, 763–1818.
Decennial Census and American Community Survey.—Daniel Weinberg, room 3H162, 763–5791.
Economic Programs.—Vacant, room 8K108, 763–2932.
Information Technology.—Vacant.
Division and Office Chiefs for—
Administrative and Customer Services.—F. Grailand Hall, room 3J138, 763–1629.
Administrative and Management Systems Division.—James Aikman, room 3K138, 763–3149.
Advisory Committee Office.—Jeri Green, room 8H153, 763–2070.
American Community Survey Office.—Susan Schechter, room 3K276, 763–8050.
Analysis and Executive Support.—Kathleen Styles, room 8H028, 763–3460.
Budget Division.—James Tyler, room 2K122, 763–3903.
Census 2010 Publicity Office.—Tasha Boone (acting), room 8H749, 763–3977.
Center for Economic Studies.—Ron Jarmin, room 2K124, 763–1858.
Company Statistics Division.—Ewen M. Wilson, room 1182, 763–3388.
Computer Services Division.—Jeffery Mayer, Bowie 28, 763–4341.
Congressional Affairs Office.—Vacant, 763–6100.
Customer Liaison and Marketing Services Office.—Barbara Harris, room 8H180, 763–1305.
Data Integration Division.—Vacant.
Decennial Automation Contract Management Office.—Vacant.
Decennial Management Division.—Frank Vitrano, room 3H174, 763–3691.
Decennial Statistical Studies Division.—David Whitford, room 4K276, 763–4035.

Decennial Systems and Contract Management Office.—Vacant, room 3H574, 763–2933.
Demographic Statistical Methods Division.—Ruth Ann Killion, room 7H162, 763–2048.
Demographic Surveys Division.—Cheryl Landman, room 7H128, 763–3773.
Economic Planning and Coordination Division.—Shirin A. Ahmed, room 8K122, 763–2558.
Economic Statistical Methods and Programming Division.—Samuel Jones, room 7K108, 763–2265.
Equal Employment Opportunity Office.—Roy P. Castro, room 3K106, 763–5120.
Field Division.—Brian Monaghan, room 5H128, 763–2011.
Finance Division.—Joan Simms, room 2K106, 763–6803.
Foreign Trade Division.—William Bostic, Jr., room 6K032, 763–2255.
Geography Division.—Timothy Trainor, room 4H174, 763–2131.
Governments Division.—Lisa Blumerman, room 5K156, 763–8050.
Housing and Household Economic Statistics.—David Johnson, room 7H174, 763–6443.
Human Resources Division.—Tyra Dent Smith, room 2J436, 763–5863.
Information Systems Support and Review Office.—John Leidich (acting), room 4K020, 763–5740.
Information Technology Security Office.—Timothy P. Ruland, room 5K124, 763–2869.
International Relations Office.—Carole Popoff, room 8H017, 763–3222.
Manufacturing and Construction.—Thomas Zabelsky, Jr., room 7K154, 763–4593.
National Processing Center.—David Hackbarth (812) 218–3344.
Population.—Enrique Lamas, room 5H174, 763–2071.
Privacy Office.—Mary Frazier, room 8H168, 763–2906.
Public Information Office.—Kenneth C. Meyer, room 8H160, 763–3100.
Security Office.—Harold L. Washington, Jr., room 2J438, 763–1716.
Service Sector Statistics.—Mark E. Wallace, room 2J438, 763–2683.
Statistical Research Division.—Tommy Wright, room 5K108, 763–1702.
Systems Support.—Nora Bea Parker, room 5K032, 763–2999.
Technologies Management Office.—Barbara M. LoPresti, room 5H160, 763–7765.
Telecommunications Office.—Scott Williams, room 4K032, 763–1793.

BUREAU OF INDUSTRY AND SECURITY

Under Secretary.—Daniel O. Hill (acting), room 3892 (202) 482–1427.
Deputy Under Secretary.—Daniel O. Hill.
Chief Counsel.—John Masterson, room 3839, 482–2315.
Office of Congressional and Public Affairs.—Eugene Cottilli (acting), room 3897, 482–0097.
Director, Office of Administration.—Gay Shrum, room 6622, 482–1900.
Chief Information Officer.—Dawn Leaf, room 6092, 482–4848.
Assistant Secretary for Export Administration.—Matthew Borman (acting), room 3886, 482–5491.
Deputy Assistant Secretary.—Matthew Borman.
Operating Committee Chair.—Vacant, room 3889, 482–5485.
Office of:
Exporter Services.—Bernard Kritzer, room 1093, 482–0436.
National Security and Technology Transfer Controls.—Eileen M. Albanese, room 2616, 482–4196.
Nonproliferation and Treaty Compliance.—Alexander Lopes, room 2093, 482–3825.
Strategic Industries and Economic Security.—Michael Vaccaro, room 3878, 482–4506.
Technology Evaluation.—Kevin Kurland, room 3886, 482–2385.
Assistant Secretary for Export Enforcement.—Kevin Delli-Colli (acting), room 3730, 482–3618.
Deputy Assistant Secretary.—Kevin Delli-Colli, room 3721, 482–5914.
Office of:
Antiboycott Compliance.—Edward Weant, room 6098, 482–5914.
Enforcement Analysis.—Glenn Krizay, room 4065, 482–4255.
Export Enforcement.—Tom Madigan, room 4525, 482–2252.

ECONOMIC DEVELOPMENT ADMINISTRATION

Assistant Secretary.—Sandra R. Walters (acting), room 7800 (202) 482–5081.
Deputy Assistant Secretary.—Dennis Alvord (acting).
Chief Counsel.—Barry Bird, room 7005, 482–4687.
Chief Information Officer.—Darice Ahrnsbrak, room 7114, 482–2507.

OFFICE OF EXECUTIVE SECRETARIAT AND EXTERNAL AFFAIRS (OESEA)

Deputy Assistant Secretary.—Brian Borlik (acting), room 7814, (202) 482–2900.
Director, Division of:
Legislative Affairs.—Angela Ewell-Madison (acting), room 7816, 482–2900.
Public Affairs.—Brian Borlik (acting), room 7814, 482–3901.
Executive Secretariat.—Brian Borlik (acting).

OFFICE OF FINANCE AND MANAGEMENT SERVICES

Chief Financial Officer/Chief Administrative Officer.—Sandra R. Walters (202) 482–5892.
Deputy Chief Financial Officer.—Ted Wolfgang, room 7822.
Director, Budget Division.—Errol Stewart.

INTERNATIONAL TRADE ADMINISTRATION

Under Secretary.—Michelle O'Neill (acting), room 3850 (202) 482–2867.
Deputy Under Secretary.—Michelle O'Neill, room 3842, 482–3917.
Chief of Staff.—Theodore Johnston, room 3850, 482–2867.
Legislative and Intergovernmental Affairs.—Erin Mewhirter (acting), room 3424, 482–3015.
Public Affairs.—Vacant, room 3416, 482–3809.

ADMINISTRATION

Director and Chief Financial Officer.—David Robinson, room 3827 (202) 482–5855.
Deputy Chief Financial Officer.—Jim Donahue, room 4112, 482–0210.
Director, Office of:
Human Resources Management.—Ronald Glaser, room 7060, 482–3505.
Organization and Management Support.—Mary Ann McFate, room 4001, 482–5436.
Chief Information Officer.—Renee Macklin, room 4800, 482–3801.

TRADE PROMOTION AND U.S. AND FOREIGN COMMERCIAL SERVICE

Assistant Secretary for Trade Promotion and Director General of the Commercial Service.—Rochelle Lipsitz (acting), room 3802 (202) 482–0725.
Deputy Director General.—Rochelle Lipsitz, room 3802, 482–0725.
Career Development and Assignment.—Rebecca Mann, room 1222, 482–5208.
Deputy Assistant Secretary for—
Domestic Operations.—Vacant, room 3810, 482–4767.
International Operations.—William Zarit, room 3128, 482–6228.
Office of Global Trade Program.—Stacey Silva, room 2810, 482–6220.
Director for—
Africa, Near East and South Asia.—Christian Reed, room 2013, 482–1209.
East Asia and Pacific.—Patrick Santillo, room 3122, 482–0423.
Europe.—Reginald Miller, room 3133, 482–5402.
Western Hemisphere.—Judy Reinke, room 1223, 482–3913.
Trade Promotion Coordinating Committee.—Pat Kirwan, room 3051, 482–5455.

ASSISTANT SECRETARY FOR IMPORT ADMINISTRATION

Assistant Secretary.—Ronald Lorentzen (acting), room 3099 (202) 482–1780.
Deputy Assistant Secretary.—Ronald Lorentzen, room 3099B, 482–1780.
Chief Counsel.—John D. McInerney, room 3622, 482–5589.
Director for—
Office of Accounting.—Neal Halper, room 3087–B, 482–2210.
Office of Policy.—Kelly Parkhill (acting), room 3713, 482–4412.
Statutory Import Programs Staff.—Faye Robinson, room 4100W, 482–1660.
Deputy Assistant Secretary for—
Antidumping Countervailing Duty Operations.—John Anderson (acting), room 3095, 482–5497.
Antidumping Countervailing Duty Policy and Negotiations.—Carole Showers (acting), room 3075, 482–2104.
Textiles and Apparel.—Janet Heinzen (acting), room 3001A, 482–3737.

ASSISTANT SECRETARY FOR MARKET ACCESS AND COMPLIANCE

Assistant Secretary.—Stephen Jacobs (acting), room 3868A (202) 482–3022.
Deputy Assistant Secretary.—Stephen Jacobs (acting), room 3868A, 482–3022.
Deputy Assistant Secretary for—
Asia.—Ira Kasoff (acting), room 2038, 482–4527.
Trade Agreements Compliance.—Skip Jones, room 3043, 482–5767.
Europe.—Jay Burgess (acting), room 3863, 482–5638.
Africa, the Middle East and South Asia.—Holly Vineyard (acting), room 2329, 482–4651.
Western Hemisphere.—Walter Bastian (acting), room 3826, 482–5324.
Director, Office of:
Africa.—Kevin Boyd, room 2037, 482–4227.
APEC (Asian and Asia-Pacific Economic Cooperation) Affairs.—Brenda Fisher, room 2308, 482–5334.
European Country Affairs.—Jay Burgess, room 3319, 482–4915.
Japan.—Nicole Melcher, room 2322, 482–2515.
Latin America and the Caribbean.—John Anderson, room 3203, 482–2436.
Middle East and North Africa.—Cherie Loustanau, room 2031, 482–4442.
Multilateral Affairs.—Steward L. ''Skip'' Jones, Jr., room 3027, 482–2307.
NAFTA Secretariat.—Caratina Alston, room 2061, 482–5438.
North American Free Trade Agreement and Inter-American Affairs.—Andrew Rudman, room 3024, 482–0507.
Russia, Ukraine, and Eurasia.—Jack Brougher, room 3318, 482–1104.

ASSISTANT SECRETARY FOR MANUFACTURING

Assistant Secretary.—Mary Saunders (acting), room 3832 (202) 482–1461.
Deputy Assistant Secretary.—Mary Saunders, room 3832.
Deputy Assistant Secretary for—
Industry Analysis.—Praveen Dixit, room 2814B, 482–5241.
Manufacturing.—Henry Misisco (acting), room 2800A, 482–1872.
Services.—Joel Secundy, room 1128, 482–6908.

PRESIDENT'S EXPORT COUNCIL

[Authorized by Executive Orders 12131, 12534, 12551, 12610, 12692, 12774, 12869, and 12974 (May through September 1995)]

Executive Director, Under Secretary of International Trade.—Vacant, room 3850 (202) 482–1124.
Executive Secretary.—Mark Chittum, room 4043.

MINORITY BUSINESS DEVELOPMENT AGENCY

Director.—Vacant.
Associate Director.—Edith McCloud, room 5092 (202) 482–6224.
Chief of:
Business Development.—Efrain Gonzalez, room 5079, 482–4282.
Financial Management Officer.—Ronald Marin, room 5089, 482–1621.
Legislative, Educational and Intergovernmental Affairs.—Bridget Gonzales, room 5069A, 482–3774.
Chief Counsel.—Jedd Vertman, room 5069, 482–5045.
Chief Information Officer.—Yolanda Whitley, room 5082, 482–3831.
Deputy Chief Information Officer.—Shirley Dean, room 5082, 482–5946.

NATIONAL OCEANIC AND ATMOSPHERIC ADMINISTRATION

Under Secretary for Oceans and Atmosphere.—Jane Lubchenco, Ph.D., room 5128 (202) 482–3436.
Deputy Under Secretary.—Mary M. Glackin, room 5810, 482–4569.
Assistant Secretary/Deputy Administrator.—Vacant, room 5804, 482–3567.
Deputy Assistant Secretary for Oceans and Atmosphere.—Vacant, room 5804, 482–3567.
Deputy Assistant Secretary for International Affairs.—Dr. James Turner, room 6224, 482–6196.

Director, Office of:
Communications.—Scott Smullen (acting), room 6217, 482–6090.
Education.—Louisa Koch, room 6869, 482–3384.
Legislative Affairs.—Brook Davis (acting), room 5221, 482–4981.
Marine and Aviation Operations.—RADM Jonathan W. Bailey, Jr., 8403 Colesville Road, Suite 500, Silver Spring, MD 20910 (301) 713–7600.
Program Analysis and Evaluation.—Steve Austin, room 6121, 482–1050.
Chief of Staff.—Vacant, room 5120, 482–3436.
Chief Financial Officer.—Maureen Wylie, room 6805, 482–0917.
Chief Administrative Officer.—William ''Bill'' Broglie, SSMC4, room 8431 (301) 713–0836, ext. 105.
Chief Information Officer, High Performance Computing and Communications.—Joseph Klimavicz, SSMC3, room 9651 (301) 713–9600.
General Counsel.—Jane Chalmers (acting), room 5814, 482–4080.
Acquisition and Grants.—Mitchell Ross, SSMC1, room 6300.
Decision Coordination and Executive Secretariat.—Kelly L. Quickle, room 5230, 482–2985.
Federal Coordinator for Meteorology.—Samuel P. Williamson, SSMC1, room 1500.
Program Coordination.—Vacant.
Workforce Management.—Eduardo Ribas, SSMC4, room 12520, 713–6300.

NATIONAL MARINE FISHERIES SERVICE

1315 East-West Highway, Silver Spring, MD 20910

Assistant Administrator.—James W. Balsiger, Ph.D. (acting), room 14636, (301) 713–2239.
Deputy Assistant Administrator for—
Operations.—John Oliver, room 14743, 713–2239.
Regulatory Programs.—Samuel Rauch, room 14657, 713–2239.
Director, Office of:
Habitat Conservation.—Patricia Montanio, room 14828, 713–2325.
International Affairs.—Rebecca Lent, Ph.D., room 12659, 713–9090.
Law Enforcement.—Dale Jones, room 415, 427–2300.
Management and Budget.—Gary Reisner, room 14450, 713–2259.
Protected Resources.—Jim Lecky, room 13821, 713–2332.
Science and Technology.—Ned Cyr, Ph.D., room 12450, 713–2367.
Scientific Programs and Chief Science Advisor.—Steven Murawski, Ph.D., room 14659, 713–2239.
Seafood Inspection Program.—Tim Hansen, room 10837, 713–2351.
Sustainable Fisheries.—Alan Risenhoover, room 13362, 713–2334.
Chief Information Officer.—Larry Tyminski, room 3657, 713–2372.

NATIONAL OCEAN SERVICE

Assistant Administrator.—John H. Dunnigan, room 13632 (301) 713–3074.
Deputy Assistant Administrator.—Dr. William Corso, room 13156, 713–3074.
Director, Office of Operational Oceanographic Products and Services.—Michael Szabados, room 6633, 713–2981.
Deputy Director.—Rick Edwing, room 662, 713–2981.
Chief Financial Officer.—Elizabeth Scheffler, room 13430, 713–3056.
Director, Office of:
Coast Survey.—CAPT Steve Barnum, room 6147, 713–2770.
International Programs.—Clement Lewsey, room 10414, 713–3078.
National Centers for Coastal Ocean Science.—Gary C. Matlock, room 8211, 713–3020.
National Geodetic Survey.—David Zilkoski, room 8657, 713–3222.
NOAA Coastal Services.—Margaret A. Davidson (843) 740–1220.
Ocean and Coastal Resource Management.—David Kennety, room 10413, 713–3155.
Response and Restoration.—Ken Barton (acting), room 10102, 713–2989.
Special Projects.—Daniel Farrow, room 9515, 713–3000.

NATIONAL ENVIRONMENTAL SATELLITE, DATA AND INFORMATION SERVICE

Assistant Administrator.—Mary E. Kicza, room 8338 (301) 713–3578.

Deputy Assistant Administrator.—Charles S. Baker, room 8300, 713–2010.
Deputy Assistant Administrator, Systems.—Abigail Harper, room 8338, 713–2005.
Chief Information Officer.—Zachary Goldstein, room 8110, 713–9220.
Chief Financial Officer.—Michael H. Abreu, room 8338, 713–9476.
Deputy Chief Financial Officer.—Cherish Johnson, room 8340, 713–9228.
International and Interagency Affairs Chief.—D. Brent Smith, room 7315, 713–2024.
Director, Office of:
Commercial Remote Sensing Regulatory Affairs.—Jane D'Aguanno, room 8260, 713–3385.
Coastal Ocean Laboratory.—Wayne Wilmot, room 4651, 713–3272.
Environmental Information Services.—Ida Hakkarinen, room 7232, 713–0813.
GOES–R Program.—Gregory A. Mandt, room C100, 286–1355.
Management Operations and Analysis.—Christine Carpino, room 8132, 713–9210.
National Climatic Data Center.—Sharon LeDuc (acting), room 557–C (828) 271–4476.
National Geophysical Data Center.—Christopher Fox, room 1B148 (303) 497–6215.
National Oceanographic Data Center.—Margarita Gregg, room 4820, 713–3270.
National Polar Orbiting Operational Environmental Satellite System Integrated Program Office.—Ed Phillips, room 1450, 713–4705.
Satellite Applications and Research.—Al Powell, room 701, 763–8127.
Satellite Data Processing and Distribution.—Kathleen A. Kelly (acting), room 1605, 817–4435.
Satellite Operations.—Kathleen A. Kelly, room 1605, 817–4000.
Space Commercialization.—Charles S. Baker (acting), room 8300, 713–2010.
Systems Development.—Gary K. Davis, room 3301, 713–0100.

NATIONAL WEATHER SERVICE

Assistant Administrator.—David L. Johnson, room 18150 (301) 713–9095.
Deputy Assistant Administrator.—John E. Jones, Jr., room 18130, 713–0711.
Chief Financial Officer.—Robert J. Byrd, room 18176, 713–0397.
Deputy Chief Financial Officer.—John Potts, room 18212, 713–0718.
Chief Information Officer.—Larry Curran (acting), room 17424, 713–1360.
Director, Office of:
Climate, Water and Weather Services.—Dennis H. McCarthy (acting), room 14348, 713–0700.
Hydrologic Development.—Gary M. Carter, room 8212, 713–1658.
National Centers for Environmental Prediction.—Louis W. Uccellini, room 101, 763–8016.
Operational Systems.—John McNulty, room 16212, 713–0165.
Science and Technology.—Gregory A. Mandt, room 15146, 713–1746.

OCEANIC AND ATMOSPHERIC RESEARCH

Assistant Administrator.—Richard W. Spinrad, Ph.D. (301) 713–2458.
Deputy Assistant Administrator for—
Labs and Cooperative Institutes.—Alexander MacDonald, Ph.D.
Programs and Administration.—Craig McLean.
Director of:
Earth System Research Laboratory.—Alexander MacDonald, Ph.D. (303) 497–6005.
Division of:
Chemical Sciences.—A.R. "Ravi" Ravishankara, Ph.D. (303) 497–3134.
Global Monitoring.—Jim Butler, Ph.D. (303) 497–6074.
Global Systems.—Steve Koch, Ph.D. (303) 497–6818.
Physical Science.—William Neff, Ph.D. (303) 497–6457.
Air Resources Laboratory.—Steven Fine, Ph.D., 713–0295, ext. 136.
Atlantic Oceanographic and Meteorological Laboratory.—Robert Atlas (305) 361–4300.
Geophysical Fluid Dynamics Laboratory.—Ram Ramaswamy, Ph.D. (609) 452–6503.
Great Lakes Environmental Research Laboratory.—Mare Colton, Ph.D. (734) 741–2245.
National Sea Grant College Program.—Leon Cammen, room 11716, 713–2448.
National Severe Storms Laboratory.—James Kimpel, Ph.D. (405) 325–6907.
Pacific Marine Environmental Laboratory.—Eddie N. Bernard, Ph.D. (206) 526–6810.
Director, Office of:
Arctic Research.—John Calder, 713–2518.
Climate Program.—Chester Koblinsky, 427–2334.
Oceanic Exploration and Research.—CAPT Harris Halverson (acting), 713–1010.

PROGRAM, PLANNING AND INTEGRATION

Assistant Administrator.—Laura K. Furgione, room 15628 (301) 713–1632.
Deputy Assistant Administrator.—Paul N. Doremus, room 15629, 713–3318.

UNITED STATES PATENT AND TRADEMARK OFFICE

P.O. Box 1450, 600 Dulany Street, Arlington, VA 22313–1450

phone (571) 272–8600

Under Secretary of Commerce for Intellectual Property and Director of U.S. Patent and Trademark Office.—John J. Doll (acting).
Deputy Under Secretary of Commerce for Intellectual Property and Deputy Director of the U.S. Patent and Trademark Office.—John J. Doll.
Chief of Staff.—Eleanor Meltzer, 272–7690.
Senior Legal Advisor.—Elizabeth Dougherty.
Director of Public Affairs.—Jennifer Rankin Byrne, 272–8400.

COMMISSIONER FOR PATENTS

Commissioner.—Margaret A. Focarino (acting), (571) 272–8800.
Deputy Commissioner for Patent Examination Policy.—Andrew Hirshfeld (acting).
Director, Office of:
Patent Cooperation Treaty Legal Administration.—Charles A. Pearson, 272–3224.
Patent Legal Administration.—Robert A. Clarke, 272–7735.
Deputy Commissioner for Patent Operations.—Margaret A. Focarino.
Assistant Deputy Commissioner for Patent Operations:
Chemical Discipline.—Bruce Kisliuk (TC 1600, 1700, and 2900).
Electrical I Discipline.—James Dwyer (TC 2100 and 2400).
Electrical II Discipline.—Andrew Faile (TC 2600 and 2800).
Mechanical Discipline.—Robert Oberleitner (TC 3600 and 3700).
Patent Examining Group Directors:
Technology Center 1600 (biotechnology and organic chemistry): George Elliott, 272–0600; John LeGuyader, 272–0500; Irem Yucel, 272–0700.
Technology Center 1700/2900 (chemical and materials engineering/design): Jasemine Chambers, 272–2200; Sharon Gibson, 272–1100; Gary Jones, 272–1300; Jacqueline Stone, 272–1200.
Technology Center 2100 (computer architecture and software): Wendy Garber, 272–1400; Andrew Hirshfeld, 272–2168; Nestor Ramirez, 272–4150.
Technology Center 2400 (networking, multiplexing, cable, and security): Timothy Callahan, 272–1740; Jack Harvey, 272–4056; Valencia Martin-Wallace 272–4020.
Technology Center 2600 (communications): Mark R. Powell, 272–4550; Wanda Walker, 272–4750.
Technology Center 2800 (semiconductor, electrical mechanical and physics/optics): John Cabeca, 272–8004; Richard Seidel, 272–2950.
Technology Center 3600 (transportation, construction, electronic commerce, agriculture, national security, and license and review): Wynn Coggins, 272–5350; Katherine Matecki, 272–5250; Fred Schmidt, 272–5150.
Technology Center 3700 (mechanical engineering, manufacturing, and products): Donald Hajec, 272–2975; Robert Olszewski, 272–6788; Karen Young, 272–3750.
Director, Office of:
Central Reexamination Unit.—Gregory Morse, 272–3838.
Data Management (PUBS).—Deborah Stephens (703) 756–1492.
Legal Administration and Petitions (PCT).—Charles Pearson, 272–3224.
Oversees South Tower Operations.—Robert Olszewski (703) 756–1491.
Patent Application Processing (PCT Operations): Kevin Little (acting), (703) 756–1451.
Patent Classification.—Olik Chaudhuri (acting), 272–1855.
Patent Financial Management.—John Buie, 272–6283.
Patent Legal Administration.—Robert A. Clarke, 272–7735.
Patent Processing Services (OIPE).—Thomas Koontz (703) 756–1490.
Patent Training.—Jin Ng, 272–7400.
Patent Quality Assurance.—Paula Hutzell, 272–0531.
Administrator, Office of:
Patent Resources Administration.—John Mielcarek, 272–8110.
Search and Information Resources Administration.—David Talbott, 272–1934.

COMMISSIONER FOR TRADEMARKS

Commissioner.—Lynne Beresford (571) 272–8901.
Deputy Commissioner for Trademark Operations.—Deborah Cohn.
Trademark Examination Law Office Managing Attorneys:
Law Office 101.—Ron Sussman, 272–9696.
Law Office 102.—Karen Strzyz, 272–9419.
Law Office 103.—Michael Hamilton, 272–9278.
Law Office 104.—Chris Doninger, 272–9297.
Law Office 105.—Thomas G. Howell, 272–9302.
Law Office 106.—Mary Sparrow, 272–9332.
Law Office 107.—Leslie Bishop, 272–9445.
Law Office 108.—Andrew Lawrence, 272–9342.
Law Office 109.—Dan Vavonese, 272–9288.
Law Office 110.—Chris Pedersen, 272–9371.
Law Office 111.—Craig Taylor, 272–9395.
Law Office 112.—Angela Wilson, 272–9443.
Law Office 113.—Odette Bonnet, 272–9426.
Law Office 114.—Margaret Le, 272–9456.
Law Office 115.—Thomas Vlcek, 272–9485.
Law Office 116.—Michael Baird, 272–9487.
Law Office 117.—Loretta Beck, 272–9245.
Director, Office of Trademark Program Control.—Betty Andrews, 272–9666.
Deputy Commissioner for Trademark Examination Policy.—Sharon Marsh, 272–8901.
Director, Office of Trademark Quality Review.—Kevin Peska, 272–9658.

ADMINISTRATOR FOR EXTERNAL AFFAIRS

Administrator for External Affair.—John J. Doll (acting), (571) 272–8600.
Director, Office of:
Governmental Affairs.—Jefferson D. Taylor, 272–7300.
Intellectual Property Policy and Enforcement.—Lois Boland, 272–9300.
Dean of Training and Education.—Robert L. Stoll, 272–9300.

CHIEF FINANCIAL OFFICER

Chief Financial Officer.—Mark J. Olechowski (acting), (571) 272–9200.
Deputy Chief Financial Officer.—Michelle Picard (acting).
Senior Financial Manager.—Janice Lambert.
Director of:
Corporate Planning.—Brendan Hourigan (acting), 272–6295.
Finance.—Mark Krieger, 272–6339.
Financial Management Systems.—Gita Zoks, 272–6363.
Procurement.—Katherine Kudrewicz, 272–6575.

CHIEF ADMINISTRATIVE OFFICER

Chief Administrative Officer.—Stephen Smith (571) 272–9600.
Director of:
Corporate Services.—John Hassett, 272–6250.
Civil Rights.—Bismarck Myrick, 272–6315.
Human Resources.—Karen Karlinchak, 272–6200.

OFFICE OF GENERAL COUNSEL

General Counsel.—James A. Toupin (571) 272–7000.
Deputy General Counsel for—
General Law.—William Covey, 272–3000.
Intellectual Property Law and Solicitor.—Raymond Chen, 272–9035.
Chief Administrative Patent Judge, Board of Patent Appeals and Interferences.—Michael R. Fleming, 272–9797.
Vice Chief Administrative Patent Judge.—James T. Moore, 272–9797.
Chief Administrative Trademark Judge, Trademark Trial and Appeal Board.—J. David Sams, 272–4304.

Director, Office of Enrollment and Discipline.—Harry I. Moatz, 272–4097.

CHIEF INFORMATION OFFICER

Chief Information Officer.—John B. Owens II (571) 272–9400.
Chief of Staff.—John S. ''Scott'' Williams, 272–5664.
Deputy Chief Information Officer.—Deborah Diaz, 272–9410.
Chief Technology Officer/Director of Infrastructure Engineering and Operations.—James P. ''Jim'' Flanagan, 272–6908.
Director of:
Administrative Management.—Toby D. Bennett, 272–6205.
Budget and Finance.—Keith M. Vanderbrink, 272–5662.
Program Administration Organization.—Kay Melvin, 272–9025.
Customer Information Services.—Ted L. Parr (703) 756–1267.
Manager, Office of:
Electronic Information Products.—Lyn Donaldson (703) 756–1222.
Public Information Services.—Martha Sneed (703) 756–1236.
Public Records Division.—Ted L. Parr (acting), (703) 756–1267.
Customer Support Services.—Pam H. Kitchens, 272–8987.
Enterprise Systems Services.—Carol R. Eakins, 272–5426.
Director of Organizational Policy and Governance.—Rod W. Turk, 272–1975.
Network and Telecommunications.—James ''Buck'' Buchanan (acting), 272–9449.
Director of Information Management Services.—Chris S. Niedermayer, 272–4877.
Quality Management.—Brain R. Jones, 272–1659.
Systems Development and Maintenance.—David C. Conley, 272–8783.

CHIEF PERFORMANCE IMPROVEMENT OFFICER

Chief Performance Improvement Officer.—Barry K. Hudson (acting), (571) 272–9200.

NATIONAL INSTITUTE OF STANDARDS AND TECHNOLOGY

Director.—Dr. Patrick Gallagher (acting), (301) 975–2300.
Deputy Director.—Dr. Patrick Gallagher..
Chief Scientist.—Dr. Richard Kayser, 975–2300.
Baldrige National Quality Program.—Dr. Harry S. Hertz, 975–2360.
International and Academic Affairs.—Dr. Claire M. Saundry, 975–2386.
NIST/Boulder Laboratories.—Dr. Kent Rochford (303) 497–5285.
Chief of Staff.—Kevin Kimball (acting), 975–3070.
Congressional and Legislative Affairs.—Jim Schufreider, 975–5675.
Program Office.—Dr. Jason Boehm, 975–8678.
Public and Business Affairs.—Gail J. Porter, 975–3392.
Chief Financial Officer.—Todd Grams, 975–5000.
Budget.—Thomas P. Klausing, 975–2669.
Business Systems.—Fred Lehnhoff, 975–2290.
Finance.—Marvin Washington, 975–6897.
Grants and Agreements Management.—Laura Cesario, 975–8006.
Chief Human Capital Officer.—Essex Brown (acting), 975–3002.
Human Resources Management.—Essex Brown, 975–3801.
Management and Organization.—Catherine S. Fletcher, 975–4054.
Safety, Health and Environment.—Rosamond A. Rutledge-Burns, 975–5818.
Civil Rights and Diversity Office.—Mirta-Marie M. Keys, 975–2042.
Chief Information Officer.—Dr. Simon Szykman, 975–6500.
Applications Systems.—L. Dale Little, 975–8982.
Customer Access and Support.—Tim Halton, 975–8920.
Enterprise Systems.—James E. Fowler, 975–6888.
Information Technology Security and Networking.—Robert Glenn, 975–3667.
Telecommunications and CIO Support.—Bruce Rosen, 975–3299.
Chief Facilities Management Officer.—Stella Fiotes, 975–8836.
Administrative Services.—David T. Henry, 975–8994.
Emergency Services.—Dr. Benjamin Overbey, 975–8247.
Engineering, Maintenance and Support Services.—Stephen S. Salber (303) 497–5680.
Plant.—John Bollinger, 975–6900.
Director, Technology Services.—Dr. Belinda L. Collins, 975–4500.
Deputy Director.—Vacant, 975–4510.

Information Services.—Mary-Deirdre Coraggio, 975–5158.
Measurement Services.—Robert L. Watters, Jr., 975–4122.
Standards Services.—Dave Alderman, 975–2396.
Weights and Measures.—Carol Hockert, 975–5507.
Director, Technology Innovation Program.—Marc G. Stanley, 975–2162.
Deputy Director.—Dr. Lorel Wisniewski, 975–5232.
Project Management Office.—Linda Beth Schilling, 975–2887.
Selection Management Office.—Thomas Wiggins, 975–5416.
Director, Hollings Manufacturing Extension Partnership Program.—Roger D. Kilmer, 975–4676.
Deputy Director.—Aimee Dobrzeniecki, 975–8322.
Program Development Office.—Stephen J. Thompson, 975–5042.
Systems Operations Office.—Michael J. Simpson, 975–6147.
Director, Electronics and Electrical Engineering Laboratory.—Dr. Kent Rochford (acting), (303) 497–5285.
Deputy Director.—Dr. James Otthoff, 975–2220.
Electromagnetics.—Dr. Peter Wilson (acting), (303) 497–3406.
Optoelectronics.—Dr. Robert Hickernell (acting), (303) 497–3455.
Quantum Electrical Metrology.—Dr. Michael Kelley (303) 497–4736.
Semiconductor Electronics.—Dr. David G. Seiler, 975–2054.
Director, Center for Nanoscale Science and Technology.—Dr. Robert Celotta, 975–8001.
Director, Manufacturing Engineering Laboratory.—Dr. Howard Harary (acting), 975–3400.
Deputy Director.—Dr. Al Wavering, 975–3401.
Fabrication Technology.—Mark E. Luce, 975–2159.
Intelligent Systems.—Elena Messina, 975–3510.
Manufacturing Metrology.—Kevin K. Jurrens (acting), 975–5486.
Manufacturing Systems Integration.—Vacant, 975–3508.
Precision Engineering.—Dr. Michael Postek, 975–2299.
Director, Chemical Science and Technology Laboratory.—Dr. Willie E. May, 975–8300.
Deputy Director.—Dr. Richard Cavanagh, 975–8301.
Analytical Chemistry.—Dr. Stephen A. Wise, 975–3108.
Biochemical Science.—Dr. Laurie E. Locascio, 975–3130.
Process Measurements.—Dr. James R. Whetstone, 975–2609.
Surface and Microanalysis Science.—Dr. John Small, 975–3900.
Thermophysical Properties.—Dr. Daniel G. Friend (303) 497–5424.
Director, Physical Laboratory.—Dr. Katharine B. Gebbie, 975–4201.
Deputy Director.—Dr. William R. Ott, 975–4202.
Atomic Physics.—Dr. Carl J. Williams, 975–3531.
Electron and Optical Physics.—Dr. Charles W. Clark, 975–3709.
Ionizing Radiation.—Dr. Lisa R. Karam, 975–5561.
Optical Technology.—Dr. Gerald Fraser, 975–3797.
Quantum Physics.—Dr. Steven T. Cundiff (303) 497–7858.
Time and Frequency.—Dr. Thomas R. O'Brian (303) 497–4570.
Director, Materials Science and Engineering Laboratory.—Dr. Eric J. Amis (acting), 975–5658.
Deputy Director.—Dr. Eric J. Amis, 975–6681.
Ceramics.—Dr. Debra L. Kaiser, 975–6119.
Materials Reliability.—Dr. Stephanie Hooker (303) 497–4326.
Metallurgy.—Dr. Frank W. Gayle, 975–6161.
Polymers.—Dr. Eric Lin (acting), 975–6743.
Director, NIST Center for Neutron Research.—Dr. Robert Dimeo (acting), 975–6210.
Director, Building and Fire Research Laboratory.—Dr. S. Shyam-Sunder, 975–5900.
Deputy Director.—Dr. William L. Grosshandler, 975–6850.
Building Environment.—Dr. Hunter Fanney, 975–5864.
Fire Research.—Dr. Anthony Hamins, 975–6598.
Materials and Construction Research.—Dr. Jonathan W. Martin, 975–6707.
Director, Information Technology Laboratory.—Cita M. Furlani, 975–2900.
Deputy Director.—James A. St. Pierre, 975–2900.
Advanced Network Technologies.—Dr. David Su, 975–6194.
Computer Security.—William Curt Barker, 975–8443.
Information Access.—Dr. Martin Herman, 975–4495.
Mathematical and Computational Sciences.—Dr. Ronald F. Boisvert, 975–3800.
Software Diagnostics and Conformance Testing.—Kathleen Roberts, 975–2144.
Statistical Engineering.—Dr. Antonio Possolo (acting), 975–2853.

NATIONAL TECHNICAL INFORMATION SERVICE

5285 Port Royal Road, Springfield, VA 22161

Director.—Ellen Herbst (703) 605–6400.
Deputy Director.—Bruce Borzino, 605–6405.
Administration.—Vicki Buttram, 605–6133.
Business Operations.—Bruce Borzino, 605–6405.
Chief Information Officer.—Keith Sinner, 605–6310.
Customer Relations.—Jon Birdsall, 605–6102.
Finance.—Mary Houff, 605–6611.
Policy.—Steven Needle, 605–6404.

NATIONAL TELECOMMUNICATIONS AND INFORMATION ADMINISTRATION

1401 Constitution Avenue, NW., DC, 20230

Assistant Secretary and Administrator.—Vacant, room 4898 (202) 482–1840.
Deputy Assistant Secretary.—Anna M. Gomez, 482–1840.
Chief of Staff.—Thomas Power.
Senior Advisors: Larry Atlas, Mark G. Seifert (acting).
Advisor.—Angela Simpson.
Advisor, Communications.—Rochelle Cohen.
Special Advisor.—Edward ''Smitty'' Smith.
Chief Counsel.—Kathy Smith.
Communications and Information Infrastructure Assurance.—Daniel Hurley.
Congressional Affairs.—Jim Wasilewski.
Institute for Telecommunication Sciences.—Al Vincent (303) 497–3500.
International Affairs.—Fiona Alexander.
Policy Analysis and Development.—Tim Sloan (acting).
Spectrum Management.—Karl Nebbia.
Telecommunications and Information Applications.—Bernadette McGuire-Rivera.

DEPARTMENT OF LABOR

Frances Perkins Building, Third Street and Constitution Avenue, NW., 20210

phone (202) 693–5000, http://www.dol.gov

HILDA L. SOLIS, Secretary of Labor; education: B.A., California State Polytechnic University, Pomona, 1979; M.P.A., University of Southern California, 1981; professional: White House Office of Hispanic Affairs, 1980–81; Management Analyst, Office of Management and Budget, 1981; California State Assembly, 1992–94; California State Senate, 1994–2000; member of 32nd Congressional District in California, 2001–09; member of Rio Hondo Community College Board of Trustees, 1985; member of California Senate Industrial Relations Committee, 1996; vice chair, of the Helsinki Commission's General Committee on Democracy, Human Rights and Humanitarian Questions, 2007; married: Sam H. Sayyad; recipient of John F. Kennedy Profile in Courage Award, 2000; and other awards for professional accomplishments; nominated by President Barack Obama to become the 25th Secretary of Labor, and was confirmed by the U.S. Senate on February 24, 2009.

OFFICE OF THE SECRETARY

phone (202) 693–6000

Secretary of Labor.—Hilda L. Solis.
Deputy Secretary.—Seth Harris.
Associate Deputy Secretary.—Naomi Walker.
Executive Secretariat Director.—Deborah Greenfield.
Chief of Staff.—Katherine Archuleta.
Director of Advance and Scheduling.—Carolyn Mosley.

OFFICE OF THE 21ST CENTURY WORKFORCE

Director.—Vacant (202) 693–6490.
Deputy Director.—Vacant.
Senior Counsel.—Vacant.

ADMINISTRATIVE LAW JUDGES

Techworld, 800 K Street, NW., Suite 400–N, 20001–8002

Chief Administrative Law Judge.—John M. Vittone (202) 693–7542.
Associate Chief Judges: William S. Colwell, Stephen L. Purcell.

ADMINISTRATIVE REVIEW BOARD

Chairman.—Wayne C. Beyer, room N–5404 (202) 693–6200.

ASSISTANT SECRETARY FOR ADMINISTRATION AND MANAGEMENT

Assistant Secretary.—T. Michael Kerr, room S–2203 (202) 693–4040.
Deputy Assistant Secretary for—
Budget and Performance Planning.—Maureen Walsh.
Operations.—Edward C. Hugler.
Security and Emergency Management.—Kenneth McCreless, room S–1229G, 693–7990.
Special Assistant.—Claudette Brito.
Administrative Officer.—Noelia Fernandez.
Staff Assistant.—Chris Yerxa.

BUSINESS OPERATIONS CENTER

Director.—Al Stewart, room S–1524 (202) 693–4028.
Deputy Director.—John Saracco.
Office of:
Acquisition Management Services.—Valerie Veatch, room S–1519B, 693–7245.
Administrative Services.—Phil Puckett, room S–1521, 693–6650.
Competitive Sourcing.—William Keisler, room S–1519A, 693–4020.
Management Support Services.—Karen Nunley, room S–1519B, 693–7272.
Procurement Services.—Sandra Foster, room S–4307, 693–4586.
Worker Safety and Health Services.—Vacant, room S–1513B, 693–6670.

CENTER FOR PROGRAM PLANNING AND RESULTS

Director.—Richard French, room S–3317 (202) 693–4088.
Office of:
DOL Historian.—Linda Stinson, room N–2445, 693–4085.
Planning.—Mark Davis, 693–7126.
Wirtz Labor Library.—Jean Bowers, room N–2445, 693–6600.

CIVIL RIGHTS CENTER

Director.—Ramos Suris Fernandez, room N–4123 (202) 693–6500.
Staff Assistant.—Danielle White.
Office of:
Compliance Assistance and Planning.—Kevin Malone, 693–6531.
EEO Coordinator of Counselors.—Lillian Winstead, 693–6504.
Enforcement / External.—Julia Mankata Tamakloe (acting), 693–6502.
Enforcement / Internal.—Naomi Berry Perez, 693–6503.
Reasonable Accommodation Hotline.—Dawn Johnson, room N–4123, 693–6569.

DEPARTMENTAL BUDGET CENTER

Director.—Geoff Kenyon, room S–4020 (202) 693–4090.
Deputy Director.—Mark P. Wichlin.
Staff Assistant.—Patricia Smith.
Office of:
Agency Budget Programs.—James Martin, 693–4077.
Budget Policy and Systems.—Sandra Mulcahy, 693–4078.
Financial Management Operations.—Chris Calogero (acting), room S–5526, 693–4087.

EMERGENCY MANAGEMENT CENTER

Director.—Greg Rize, 800 K Street, NW., Suite 450 North, 20001–8002 (202) 693–7555.
Deputy Director.—Pete Podell.

GOVBENEFITS.GOV

Program Manager.—Curtis Turner, room N–4309 (202) 693–4025.

HUMAN RESOURCES CENTER

Director.—Suzy M. Barker, room C–5526 (202) 693–7600.
Deputy Director.—Betty Lopez.
Office of:
Administration and Management Services.—Tracey Schaeffer, C–5515, 693–7773.
Continuous Learning and Career Management.—Kim Green, room N–5464, 693–7630.
Employee and Labor Management Relations.—Carol Qualls, room N–5464, 693–7670.
Executive Resources and Personnel Security.—Andrea Burckman, room C–5508, 693–7800.
Human Resources Consulting and Operations.—Maria McAplin, room C–5516, 693–7690.
Human Resources Policy and Accountability.—Jerome Bonner, room 5464, 693–7720.
Workforce Planning and e-Innovations.—Dennis Sullivan, room C–5516, 693–7740.

Worklife and Benefits Programs.—Brooke Brewer, room N–5454, 693–7610.

INFORMATION TECHNOLOGY CENTER

Director.—Thomas Wiesner, room N–1301 (202) 693–4567.
Deputy Director.—Yann King.
Administrative Officer.—Kathy Fox, 693–4215.
Director, Office of:
Chief Information Officer Programs.—Peter Sullivan, 693–4211.
Systems Development and Integration.—Richard Lewis, 693–4149.
Technical Services.—Hamid Ouyachi, 693–4173.
IT Help Desk.—8 a.m. to 6:30 p.m., room N–1505, 693–4444.

SECURITY CENTER

Director.—Tom Holman, room S–1229G (202) 693–7200.
Deputy Director.—Vacant.

ASSISTANT SECRETARY FOR POLICY

Assistant Secretary.—Vacant, room S–2312 (202) 693–5959.
Deputy Assistant Secretary.—Susan E. Howe.
Chief of Staff.—Vacant.
Staff Assistant.—Vacant.
Senior Policy Advisor.—Mary Beth Maxwell.
Director, Office of:
Compliance Assistance Policy.—Barbara Bingham, 693–5080.
Economic Policy and Analysis.—Ronald Bird, 693–4966.
Regulatory and Programmatic Policy.—Kathleen Franks, 693–5072.

BENEFITS REVIEW BOARD

Chair.—Nancy S. Dolder, room N5101 (202) 693–6300.

BUREAU OF LABOR STATISTICS

Postal Square Building, Suite 4040, 2 Massachusetts Avenue, NE., 20212, phone (202) 691–7800

Commissioner.—Keith Hall.
Deputy Commissioner.—Philip L. Rones, 691–7802.
Associate Commissioner, Office of:
Administration.—Daniel J. Lacey, suite 4060, 691–7777.
Compensation and Working Conditions.—William Wiatrowski, suite 4130, 691–6300.
Employment and Unemployment Statistics.—John M. Galvin, suite 4945, 691–6400.
Field Operations.—Robert A. Gaddie, suite 2935, 691–5800.
Prices and Living Conditions.—Michael Horrigan, suite 3120, 691–6960.
Productivity and Technology.—Michael Harper, suite 2150, 691–5600.
Publications and Special Studies.—Michael Levi, suite 4110, 691–5900.
Survey Methods Research.—John Etinge, suite 1950, 691–7404.
Technology and Survey Processing.—Fernando Burbano, suite 5025, 691–7600.
Assistant Commissioner, Office of:
Compensation Levels and Trends.—Phil Doyle, suite 4130, 691–6200.
Consumer Prices and Price Indexes.—John Layng, suite 3130, 691–6955.
Current Employment Analysis.—Thomas Nardone, suite 4675, 691–6379.
Industrial Prices and Price Indexes.—David Friedman, suite 4170, 691–6307.
Industry Employment Statistics.—Patricia Getz, suite 4840, 691–6521.
Occupational Statistics and Employment Projections.—Dixie Sommers, suite 2135, 691–5701.
Director of:
Survey Processing.—Richard L. Schroeder, suite 5025, 691–6730.
Technology and Computing Services.—Rick Kryger, suite 5025, 691–7562.

BUREAU OF INTERNATIONAL LABOR AFFAIRS

Deputy Under Secretary.—Marcia Eugenio (acting), room C–4325 (202) 693–4849.

Associate Deputy Under Secretary.—Vacant.
Director, Office of:
Child Labor, Forced Labor, and Human Trafficking.—Kevin Willcutts (acting), 693–4832.
International Relations.—Robert Shepard, 693–4808.
Trade and Labor Affairs.—Gregory Schoepfle, 693–4887.

OFFICE OF THE CHIEF FINANCIAL OFFICER

Chief Financial Officer.—Lisa Fiely (acting), room S–4030 (202) 693–6800.
Deputy Chief Financial Officer.—Lisa Fiely.
Associate Deputy CFO for Fiscal Integrity.—Yoko Albayrak.
Associate Deputy CFO for Financial Systems.—John ''Jack'' Blair, room N–2719.
Administrative Officer.—Robert Balin (acting).

OFFICE OF FISCAL INTEGRITY

Division of:
Central Accounting Operations.—Larry Allen, room S–4502.
Client Accounting Services.—Shelia Alexander, room N–5526.
E Travel.—Valerie Hall, room N–2719, 693–6829.
Financial Compliance.—Ellen Waterhouse, room S–4502.
Financial Policy and Analysis.—Richard Zeutenhorst, room S–4030.
Financial Reporting.—Miguel Reyes, room S–4502, 693–6800.

OFFICE OF FINANCIAL SYSTEMS

Division of:
Systems Architecture and Development.—Kenneth Bode, room N–2719, 693–6844.
Quality Assurance and Security.—Vacant, room N–2719, 693–6919.
Payroll Systems Support.—Roy Abreu, room S–4214, 693–4324.
Production Support and System Administration.—Vacant, room N–2719, 693–6900.

OFFICE OF CONGRESSIONAL AND INTERGOVERNMENTAL AFFAIRS

Assistant Secretary.—Brian Kennedy, room S–2006 (202) 693–4601.
Chief of Staff.—Laura MacDonald, room S–2006, 693–4601.
Staff Assistant.—Glenda Manning, room S–2006, 693–4601.
Deputy Assistant Secretary, Congressional.—Vacant, room S–2220, 693–4600.
Deputy Assistant Secretary, Intergovernmental.—Vacant, room S–2006, 693–6400.
Associate Assistant Secretary/Budget and Appropriations.—Teri Bergman, room S–2220, 693–4600.
Senior Legislative Officers:
Employee Benefits.—Michele Evermore, room S–2220, 693–4600.
Employment and Training.—Adri Jayaratne, room S–2220, 693–4600.
Employment Standards.—Charmaine Manansala, room S–2220, 693–4600.
Legislative Officer.—Vacant.
Congressional Research Assistant.—Vacant.
Senior Intergovernmental Officer.—Vacant.
Administrative Officer.—Joycelyn Daniels, room S–1318, 693–4600.

REGIONAL OFFICES (ALL REGIONAL OFFICES ARE VACANT)

Region I, Boston.—Connecticut, Maine, Massachusetts, New Hampshire, Rhode Island, Vermont.
Region II, New York.—New York, New Jersey, Puerto Rico, Virgin Islands.
Region III, Philadelphia.—Pennsylvania, Delaware, District of Columbia, Maryland, Virginia, West Virginia.
Region IV, Atlanta.—Alabama, Georgia, Florida, Kentucky, Mississippi, North Carolina, South Carolina, Tennessee.
Region V, Chicago.—Illinois, Indiana, Michigan, Minnesota, Ohio, Wisconsin.
Region VI, Dallas.—Texas, Arkansas, Louisiana, New Mexico, Oklahoma.
Region VII, Des Moines.—Iowa, Kansas, Nebraska, Missouri.
Region VIII, Denver.—Colorado, Montana, North Dakota, South Dakota, Wyoming.

Region IX, San Francisco.—California, Hawaii, Nevada, Arizona, Guam.
Region X, Seattle.—Alaska, Idaho, Oregon, Washington.

OFFICE OF DISABILITY EMPLOYMENT POLICY

Assistant Secretary.—Vacant, room S–1303, (202) 693–7880, TTY 693–7881.
Deputy Assistant Secretary.—John Davey.
Chief of Staff.—Vacant.
Special Assistant.—Vacant.
Director of Policy Development.—Susan Parker.

EMPLOYEE BENEFITS SECURITY ADMINISTRATION

Assistant Secretary.—Vacant, room S–2524 (202) 693–8300.
Deputy Assistant Secretaries: Michael L. Davis; Alan D. Lebowitz, room N–5677, 693–8315.
Chief of Staff.—Vacant, room S–2524, 693–8300.
Executive Assistant to the Deputy Assistant Secretary.—Becki Marchand, 693–8315.
Confidential Assistant.—Michelle Brown.
Special Assistant.—Christine Donahue.
Director of:
Program, Planning, Evaluation and Management.—Brian C. McDonnell, room N–5668, 693–8480.
Chief Accountant.—Ian Dingwall, room N–5459, 693–8360.
Enforcement.—Virginia Smith, room N–5702, 693–8440.
Exemption Determinations.—Ivan L. Strasfeld, room N–5649, 693–8540.
Information Management.—John Helms, room N–5459, 693–8600.
Program Services.—Sharon Watson, room N–5625, 693–8630.
Regulations and Interpretations.—Robert Doyle, room N–5669, 693–8500.
Policy and Research.—Joseph Piacentini, room N–5718, 693–8410.

EMPLOYEES COMPENSATION APPEALS BOARD

Chairman and Chief Judge.—Alec J. Koromilas, room N–5416 (202) 693–6420.

EMPLOYMENT AND TRAINING ADMINISTRATION

Assistant Secretary.—Jane Oates, room S–2307 (202) 693–2700.
Deputy Assistant Secretary.—Douglas F. Small.
Administrator, Office of:
Apprenticeship.—John Ladd, room N–5306, 693–2796.
Financial and Administrative Management.—Daphne Y. Jefferson, room N–4653, 693–2800.
Foreign Labor Certification.—William B. Carlson, room C–4312, 693–3010.
National Response.—Erica R. Cantor, room N–5422, 693–3500.
Performance and Technology.—John R. Beverly III, room S–5206, 693–3031.
Policy Development and Research.—Thomas M. Dowd, room N–5637, 693–3700.
Regional Operations.—Grace Kilbane (acting), room C–4517, 693–3690.
Workforce Investment.—Gay M. Gilbert, room S–4231, 693–3980.
Workforce Security.—Cheryl Atkinson, room S–4231, 693–3029.

EMPLOYMENT STANDARDS ADMINISTRATION

Assistant Secretary.—Shelby Hallmark (acting), room S–2321 (202) 693–0200.
Deputy Assistant Secretary for Operations.—John Correll.
Special Assistant.—Shawn Hooper.
Administrator, Wage and Hour Program.—John McKeon (acting), 693–0051.
Deputy Administrator.—Vacant.
Deputy Administrator for Operations.—Russell Harris.
Chief of Staff.—Vacant.
Director, Office of:
External Affairs.—Vacant.
Planning and Analysis.—Vacant.

Wage Determinations.—Shirley Ebbesen.
Deputy Assistant Secretary, Office of Federal Contract Compliance Programs.—Lorenzo Harrison (acting), 693–0101.
Deputy Director.—Vacant.
Special Assistant.—Vacant.
Director of Workers' Compensation Programs.—Shelby Hallmark, 693–0031.
Director, Division of:
Coal Mine Worker's Compensation.—James DeMarce.
Energy Employees Occupational Illness Compensation Program.—Rachel Leiton.
Federal Employees Compensation.—Douglas Fitzgerald.
Longshore and Harber Worker's Compensation.—Michael Niss.
Director, Office of Management, Administration and Planning.—Anne Baird-Bridges, 693–0608.
Deputy Director.—Deborah Becker.
Director, Equal Employment Opportunity Unit.—Pamela Gibbs, 693–0300.

OFFICE OF FAITH BASED INITIATIVES

Director.—Jedd Medefind (202) 693–6451.
Deputy Director.—Jacqueline Halbig, 693–4600.

OFFICE OF THE INSPECTOR GENERAL

Inspector General.—Gordon S. Heddell, room S–5502 (202) 693–5100.
Deputy Inspector General.—Daniel R. Petrole.
Chief of Staff.—Dale Wilson.
Assistant Inspector General for—
Audit.—Elliot P. Lewis, room S–5518, 693–5168.
Inspection and Special Investigations.—Asa Cunningham, room S–5021, 693–5211.
Labor Racketeering and Fraud Investigations.—Thomas F. Farrell, room S–5014, 693–7034.
Legal Services.—Howard L. Shapiro, room S–5508, 693–5116.
Management and Policy.—Nancy Ruiz de Gamboa, room S–5028, 693–5191.

MINE SAFETY AND HEALTH ADMINISTRATION

1100 Wilson Boulevard, Arlington, VA 22209–3939, phone (202) 693–9414
fax 693–9401, http://www.msha.gov

Assistant Secretary.—Vacant, room 2322, 693–9414.
Deputy Assistant Secretary for Policy.—Vacant, room 2321.
Deputy Assistant Secretary for Operations.—Michael Davis, room 2324.
Director, Office of:
Accountability.—Pete Montali (acting), room 2326, 693–9604.
Assessments.—Jay P. Mattos, room 2518, 693–9702.
Diversity and Equal Opportunity.—Darlene Farrar-Warren, room 2407, 693–9885.
Employee Safety and Health.—Richard D. Feehan, room 2434, 693–9586.
Program Education and Outreach Services.—Layne Lathram, room 2317, 693–9422.
Program Evaluation and Information Resources.—George M. Fesak, Jr., room 2300, 693–9750.
Standards, Regulations and Variances.—Patricia Silvey, room 2313, 693–9440.
Technical Support.—Linda Zeiler (acting), room 2330, 693–9470.

COAL MINE SAFETY AND HEALTH

Administrator.—Kevin Stricklin, room 2424, 693–9500.
Deputy Administrator.—Charles J. Thomas (acting), room 2426, 693–9503

METAL AND NONMETAL MINE SAFETY AND HEALTH

Administrator.—Felix Quintana, room 2436, 693–9600.
Deputy Administrator.—Neal Merrifield, room 2437, 693–9645.

EDUCATIONAL POLICY AND DEVELOPMENT

Director.—Jeffrey A. Duncan, room 2100, 693–9570.

Deputy Director.—Thomas Kesslar, room 2148, 693–9570.

OCCUPATIONAL SAFETY AND HEALTH ADMINISTRATION

Assistant Secretary.—Vacant, room S–2315 (202) 693–2000.
Deputy Assistant Secretary.—Donald G. Shalhoub.
Chief of Staff.—Vacant.
Director, Office of:
Equal Employment Opportunity.—Catherine Fortune, 693–2150.
Communications.—Jennifer Ashley, 693–1999.
Director of:
Administrative Programs.—Kimberly A. Locey, 693–1600.
Construction.—Richard Fairfax (acting), 693–2100.
Cooperative and State Programs.—Steven Witt, 693–2200.
Enforcement Programs.—Richard Fairfax, 693–2100.
Evaluation and Analysis.—Keith Goddard, 693–2400.
Information Technology.—Cheryle Greenaugh, 693–1818.
Technology Support and Emergency Management.—Tom Galassi, 693–2300.
Standards and Guidance.—Dorothy Dougherty, 693–1950.

OFFICE OF PUBLIC AFFAIRS

Assistant Secretary.—Jaime Zapata (acting), room S–2514 (202) 693–4676.
Deputy Assistant Secretary.—Jaime Zapata.

REGIONAL OFFICES

Region I.—Connecticut, Maine, Massachusetts, New Hampshire, Rhode Island, Vermont.
Public Affairs Director.—John Chavez, JFK Federal Building, Government Center, 25 New Sudbury Street, Room 525–A, Boston, MA 02203 (617) 565–2075.
Region IIA.—New York, Puerto Rico, Virgin Islands.
Regional Representative.—John Chavez, JFK Federal Building, Government Center, 25 New Sudbury Street, Room 525–A, Boston, Massachusetts 02203 (617) 565–2075.
Region IIB.—New Jersey.
Regional Representative.—Leni Uddyback-Fortson, Curtis Center, 170 S. Independence Mall West, Suite 633-East, Philadelphia, PA 19106–3306 (215) 861–5102.
Region III.—Delaware, District of Columbia, Maryland, Pennsylvania, Virginia, West Virginia.
Public Affairs Director.—Leni Uddyback-Fortson, Curtis Center, 170 S. Independence Mall West, Suite 633-East, Philadelphia, PA 19106–3306 (215) 861–5102.
Region IV.—Alabama, Florida, Georgia, Kentucky, Mississippi, North Carolina, South Carolina, Tennessee.
Public Affairs Director.—Mike Wald, Atlanta Federal Center, 61 Forsyth SW, Suite 6B75, Atlanta, GA 30303 (404) 562–2078.
Region V.—Illinois, Indiana, Michigan, Minnesota, Ohio, Wisconsin.
Public Affairs Director.—Bradley Mitchell, Room 3194, 230 South Dearborn Street, Room 3192, Chicago, IL 60604 (312) 353–6976.
Region VI.—Arkansas, Louisiana, New Mexico, Oklahoma, Texas.
Public Affairs Director.—Elzabeth Todd (acting), Room 734, 525 Griffin Street, Dallas, TX 75202 (972) 850–4710.
Region VII.—Iowa, Kansas, Missouri, Nebraska.
Public Affairs Specialist.—Rich Kulczewski, 1999 Broadway, Suite 1640, Denver, CO 80202 (303) 844–1303.
Region VIII.—Colorado, Montana, North Dakota, South Dakota, Utah, Wyoming.
Public Affairs Director.—Rich Kulczewski, 1999 Broadway, Suite 1640, Denver, CO 80202 (303) 844–1303.
Region IX.—Arizona, California, Guam, Hawaii, Nevada.
Public Affairs Director.—Deanne Amaden, Suite 2–650, 90 7th Street, San Francisco, CA 94103–1516 (415) 625–2630.
Region X.—Alaska, Idaho, Oregon, Washington.
Public Affairs Director.—Mike Shimizu, Building B, Room 930, 1111 Third Avenue, Seattle WA, 98101 (206) 553–7620.

OFFICE OF SMALL BUSINESS PROGRAMS

Director.—José A. ''Joe'' Lira, room C2318 (202) 693–6460.

OFFICE OF THE SOLICITOR

Solicitor.—Carol A. DeDeo (acting), room S–2002 (202) 693–5260.
Deputy Solicitor.—Vacant.
Staff Assistant.—Linette Wilson.
Special Assistant.—Vacant.
Deputy Solicitor for—
National Operations.—Carol A. DeDeo, 693–5261.
Regional Operations.—Ronald O. Whiting, 693–5262.

DIVISION OF BLACK LUNG AND LONGSHORE LEGAL SERVICES

Associate Solicitor.—Rae Ellen James, room N–2117 (202) 693–5660.
Deputy Associate Solicitor.—Vacant.
Counsel for—
Administrative Litigation and Legal Advice.—Michael J. Rutledge.
Appellate Litigation.—Patricia M. Nece.
Longshore.—Mark A. Reinhalter.

DIVISION OF CIVIL RIGHTS AND LABOR-MANAGEMENT

Associate Solicitor.—Katherine E. Bissell, room N–2474 (202) 693–5740.
Deputy Associate Solicitor.—Peter J. Constantine.
Counsel for—
Advice and Statutory Programs.—Mark S. Flynn.
Interpretation and Advice.—Suzan Chastain.
Litigation and Regional Coordination.—Beverly I. Dankowitz.
LMRDA Programs.—Sharon E. Hanley.

DIVISION OF EMPLOYMENT AND TRAINING LEGAL SERVICES

Associate Solicitor.—Gary M. Buff, room N–2101 (202) 693–5710.
Deputy Associate Solicitor.—Jonathan H. Waxman, 693–5730.
Counsel for—
Employment and Training Advise.—Robert P. Hines, Michael N. Apfelbaum.
Immigration Programs.—Vacant.
International Affairs and USERRA.—Donald D. Carter, Jr.
Litigation.—Harry L. Sheinfeld.

DIVISION OF FAIR LABOR STANDARDS

Associate Solicitor.—Steven J. Mandel, room N–2716 (202) 693–5555.
Deputy Associate Solicitor.—William C. Lesser.
Counsel for—
Appellate Litigation.—Paul L. Frieden.
Legal Advice.—Lynn McIntosh.
Trial Litigation.—Jonathan M. Kronheim.
Whistleblower Programs.—Ellen R. Edmond.

DIVISION OF FEDERAL EMPLOYEE AND ENERGY WORKERS COMPENSATION

Associate Solicitor.—Jeffrey L. Nesvet, room S–4325 (202) 693–5320.
Deputy Associate Solicitor.—Thomas G. Giblin.
Counsel for—
Claims and Compensation.—Catherine P. Carter.
Energy Employees Compensation.—Sheldon O. Turley, Jr.
Chief, FEÇA Subrogation Unit.—Gertrude B. Gordon.

DIVISION OF MINE SAFETY AND HEALTH

1100 Wilson Boulevard, 22nd Floor, Arlington, VA 22209

Associate Solicitor.—Heidi W. Strassler (acting), room 2222 (202) 693–9333.
Deputy Associate Solicitor.—Heidi W. Strassler.
Counsel for—
Appellate Litigation.—W. Christian Schumann, room 2220.
Standards and Legal Advice.—April E. Nelson, room 2224.
Trial Litigation.—Mark K. Malecki, room 2226.

DIVISION OF OCCUPATIONAL SAFETY AND HEALTH

Associate Solicitor.—Joseph M. Woodward, room S–4004 (202) 693–5452.
Deputy Associate Solicitor.—Ann S. Rosenthal.
Counsel for—
Appellate Litigation: Michael P. Doyle, Charles F. James.
Health Standards.—Ian J. Moar.
Regional Litigation and Legal Advice: Orlando J. Pannocchia, Robert W. Swain.
Safety Standards.—Robert J. Biersner.
Special Litigation.—Kenneth A. Hellman.

DIVISION OF PLAN BENEFITS SECURITY

Associate Solicitor.—Timothy D. Hauser, room N–4611 (202) 693–5600.
Deputy Associate Solicitor.—William Scott.
Counsel for—
Appellate and Special Litigation: Elizabeth Hopkins, Nathaniel I. Spiller.
Fiduciary Litigation.—Risa D. Sandler.
General Litigation.—Leslie Canfield Perlman.
Regulation.—William White Taylor.

HONORS PROGRAM

Director.—Nancy M. Rooney, room N–2700 (202) 693–5260.

OFFICE OF LEGAL COUNSEL

Associate Solicitor.—Robert A. Shapiro, room N–2700 (202) 693–5500.
Counsel for—
Ethics.—Robert M. Sadler, 693–5528.
Legislative Affairs.—Jill M. Otte, 693–5525.

MANAGEMENT AND ADMINISTRATIVE LEGAL SERVICES

Associate Solicitor.—William W. Thompson II, room N–2428 (202) 693–5405.
Counsel for—
Administrative Law.—Ray Mitten, Jr., 693–5405.
Appropriations and Contracts.—Ginger Ackerman, 693–5378.
FOIA/FACA.—Joseph J. Plick, 693–5527.
Chief, Human Resources.—Matthew Green, 693–5324.
Financial Manager.—James Taylor, room N–2427, 693–5412.
IT/IRM Manager.—Cheryl C. Hogans, room N–2414, 693–5368.

VETERANS' EMPLOYMENT AND TRAINING SERVICE

Assistant Secretary.—Vacant, room S–1313 (202) 693–4700.
Deputy Assistant Secretary for Operations and Management.—John McWilliam.
Chief of Staff.—Vacant.
Special Assistant.—Vacant.
Director for—
Agency Management and Budget.—Paul Briggs, 693–4713.
Compliance, Investigations, and Research.—Ruth Samardick, 693–4706.

Government and Legislative Affairs.—Ronald Drach, 693–4749.
Grants and Transition Programs.—Gordon Burke, 693–4707.

REGIONAL OFFICES

Atlanta:
Administrator.—William J. Bolls, Jr. (404) 562–2305.
Boston:
Administrator.—David W. Houle (617) 565–2080.
Chicago / Kansas City:
Administrator.—Heather Higgins (312) 353–0970.
Dallas / Denver:
Administrator.—Lester L. Williams, Jr. (972) 850–4718.
Philadelphia:
Administrator.—Joseph W. Hortiz, Jr. (215) 861–5390.
Seattle / San Francisco:
Administrator.—Christopher D. Still (415) 625–7670.

WOMEN'S BUREAU

Director.—Vacant, room S–3002 (202) 693–6730.
Chief of Staff.—Vacant.
National Office Coordinator.—Karen Furia.
Field Coordinator.—Beverly Lyle (972) 850–4700.
Chief, Office of:
Information and Support Services.—Catherine Breitenbach.
Policy and Programs.—Karen Furia (acting).

DEPARTMENT OF HEALTH AND HUMAN SERVICES

200 Independence Avenue, SW., 20201, http://www.hhs.gov

KATHLEEN G. SEBELIUS, Secretary of Health and Human Services; born in Cincinnati, OH, May 15, 1948; education: B.S., Trinity University, 1970; M.P.A., University of Kansas, 1977; professional: elected Governor of Kansas, 2002 and re-elected, 2006; before tenure as Governor, served as the Kansas State Insurance Commissioner for 8 years; served as a member of the Kansas House of Representatives, 1986–94; married: Gary, a federal magistrate judge; children: two sons, Ned and John; nominated by President Barack Obama to become the 21st Secretary of Health and Human Services, confirmed by the U.S. Senate and sworn in, both on April 28, 2009.

OFFICE OF THE SECRETARY

Secretary of Health and Human Services.—Kathleen G. Sebelius (202) 690–7000.
Executive Assistant to the Secretary.—Lynda M. Gyles.

OFFICE OF THE DEPUTY SECRETARY

Chief of Staff.—Vacant (202) 690–8157.
Deputy Chief of Staff.—Vacant, 690–5400.
Executive Secretary.—Vacant, 690–5627.
Deputy Executive Secretary.—Ashley Files, 401–4273.
Director, Intergovernmental Affairs.—Vacant, 690–6060.
Chair, Departmental Appeals Board.—Constance Tobias, 565–0220.

ASSISTANT SECRETARY FOR ADMINISTRATION AND MANAGEMENT

Assistant Secretary.—Segundo Pereira (acting), (202) 690–7431, fax 401–5207.
Principal Deputy Assistant Secretary.—Segundo Pereira.
Deputy Assistant Secretary for Human Resources.—Antonia Harris, 690–6191.
Executive Officer, Office of the Secretary Executive Office.—Denise Wells, 690–8794.
Deputy Assistant Secretary for—
Acquisition Management and Policy.—Nancy Gunderson (acting), 690–8554.
Business Transformation.—Robert Noonan, 690–5803.
Facilities Management and Policy.—Howard Kelsey, 401–1437.
Director, Office of:
Diversity Management and Equal Employment Opportunity.—Vacant, 205–2821.
Program Support Center.—Paul Bartley, (301) 443–3921.
Small and Disadvantaged Business Utilization.—Debbie Ridgely, 690–7300.

PROGRAM SUPPORT CENTER

5600 Fishers Lane, Rockville, MD 20857

Director.—Paul S. Bartley (301) 443–3921.
Deputy Director.—Terry Hurst, 443–2365.
Federal Operational Health.—Gene Migliaccio, Ph.D., 594–0260.
Financial Management Service.—William McCabe, 443–1478.
Administrative Operations Service.—Michael Tyllas, Ph.D., 443–2516.
Strategic Acquisitions Service.—Christie Goodman, 443–6557.
Information and Systems Management Service.—Terry Hurst, 443–2365.

ASSISTANT SECRETARY FOR LEGISLATION

Assistant Secretary.—Barbara Pisaro Clark (acting), (202) 690–7627.
Deputy Assistant Secretary for—
Congressional Liaison.—Vacant, 690–6786.
Discretionary Health Programs.—Vacant, 690–7627.
Human Services Programs.—Vacant, 690–6311.
Mandatory Health Programs.—Vacant, 690–7450.

ASSISTANT SECRETARY FOR PLANNING AND EVALUATION

Assistant Secretary for Planning and Evaluation.—Vacant.
Principal Deputy Assistant Secretary.—Donald Moulds (acting), (202) 690–7858.
Deputy Assistant Secretary for—
Disability and Long Term Care.—Vacant, 690–6443.
Health Policy.—Vacant, 690–6870.
Human Services Policy.—Vacant, 690–7409.
Science and Data Policy.—Jim Scanlon, 690–7100.

ASSISTANT SECRETARY FOR PUBLIC AFFAIRS

Assistant Secretary.—Vacant (202) 690–7850.
Deputy Assistant Secretary for Media.—Vacant, 690–6343, fax 690–6247.
Director, Division of Freedom of Information/Privacy.—Robert Eckert, 690–7453.

ASSISTANT SECRETARY FOR PREPAREDNESS AND RESPONSE

Assistant Secretary.—RADM W. Craig Vanderwagen (202) 205–2882.
Principal Deputy Assistant Secretary.—Dr. Gerald Parker.
Principal Deputy Director and Director for the Office Biomedical Advanced Research and Development Authority.—Dr. Robin Robinson, 260–1200.
Deputy Assistant Secretary and Director, Office for—
Medicine, Science, and Public Health.—Dr. Mary Mazanec, 205–2882.
Policy and Strategic Planning.—Brian Kamoie, 205–2882.
Preparedness and Emergency Operations.—Dr. Kevin Yeskey, 205–0872.
Director for the Office of Resource Planning and Evaluation.—Jay Petillo, 205–2882.

ASSISTANT SECRETARY FOR RESOURCES AND TECHNOLOGY

Assistant Secretary.—Vacant (202) 690–6396.
Principal Deputy Assistant Secretary.—Richard Turman, 690–6061.
Deputy Assistant Secretary for—
Budget.—Norris Cochran, 690–7393.
Finance.—Shelia Conley, 690–7084.
Grants.—Vacant, 690–6617.
Chief, Information Office.—Michael Carleton, 690–6162.

OFFICE FOR CIVIL RIGHTS

Director.—Robinsue Frohboese (acting), (202) 619–0403.
Principal Deputy Director.—Robinsue Frohboese.
Deputy Director for—
Civil Rights Division.—Tamara L. Miller, J.D. 619–0403.
Health Information Privacy.—Susan McAndrew, J.D. 619–0403.
Management Operations.—Joanne Chiedi, 619–0403.
Toll Free Voice Number (Nationwide)—1–800–368–1019.
Toll Free TDD Number (Nationwide)—1–800–527–7697.

OFFICE OF THE GENERAL COUNSEL

fax [Immediate Office] 690–7998, fax [Admin. Office] 690–5452

General Counsel.—David S. Cade (202) 690–7741.
Deputy General Counsel.—Vacant.
Associate General Counsel for:
Centers for Medicare and Medicaid Division.—Janice Hoffman, 619–0150.
Children, Family and Aging Division.—Robert Keith, 690–8005.
Civil Rights Division.—Edwin Woo, 619–0900.
Ethics Division/Special Counsel for Ethics.—Edgar Swindell, 690–7258.
Food and Drug Division.—Sheldon T. Bradshaw (301) 827–1137.
General Law Division.—Jeffrey Davis, 619–0150.
Legislation Division.—Sondra Steigen Wallace, 690–7773.
Public Health Division.—David Benor (301) 443–2644.

OFFICE OF GLOBAL HEALTH AFFAIRS

Director.—James Kulikowski (acting), (202) 690–6174.

OFFICE OF THE INSPECTOR GENERAL

330 Independence Avenue, SW., 20201

Inspector General.—Daniel R. Levinson (202) 619–3148.
Principal Deputy Inspector General.—Larry J. Goldberg, 619–3148.
Chief Counsel to the Inspector General.—Lewis Morris, 619–0335.
Deputy Inspector General for:
Audit Services.—Joseph Vengrin, 619–3155.
Evaluation and Inspections.—Stuart Wright, 619–0480.
Investigations.—Tim Menke, 619–3210.
Management and Policy.—Sam Shellenberger, 205–5154.
Director, External Affairs.—Claire Barnard, 619–1343.

OFFICE OF MEDICARE HEARINGS AND APPEALS

Chief Administrative Law Judge.—Hon. Judge Perry Rhew (216) 615–4000.
Executive Director.—Maria Price Detherage (703) 235–0689.
Director, Management Operations.—Robert Velasco, 235–0141.

OFFICE OF THE NATIONAL COORDINATOR FOR HEALTH INFORMATION TECHNOLOGY

National Coordinator for Health Information Technology.—David Blumenthal, M.D., M.P.P. (202) 690–7151.

OFFICE OF PUBLIC HEALTH AND SCIENCE

Assistant Secretary for Health.—Howard K. Koh M.D., M.P.H. (202) 690–7694.
Assistant to the Assistant Secretary for Health.—Dinah Bembo (202) 690–7694.
Principal Deputy Assistant Secretary for Health.—Donald Wright, M.D., M.P.H. (202) 690–7694.
The Surgeon General.—Vacant (301) 443–4000.
Deputy Assistant Secretary, Office of:
Disease Prevention and Health Promotion.—Penelope Slade-Sawyer, P.T., M.S.W. (202) 401–6295.
HIV/AIDS Policy.—Christopher Bates, (202) 690–5560.
Minority Health.—Garth Graham, M.D., M.P.H. (240) 453–6179.
Population Affairs.—Evelyn Kappeler (acting), (240) 453–2805.
President's Council on Physical Fitness and Sports.—Sergio Rojas (202) 690–5187.
Research Integrity.—Donald Wright, M.D., M.P.H. (acting), (301) 443–4000.
Women's Health.—Wanda Jones, Ph.D. (202) 690–7650.
Director, Office of:
Commissioned Corps Force Management.—Denise Canton (240) 453–6091.
Human Research Protections.—Jerry Menikoff, M.D., J.D. (240) 453–6900.
National Vaccine Programs.—Bruce Gellin, M.D., M.P.H. (202) 205–5294.
Regional Administrators for—
Region I: CT, ME, MA, NH, RI, VT.—Michael Milner, PA–C (617) 565–4999.
Region II: NJ, NY, PR, VI.—Robert L. Davidson, MSW, M.D., M.S. (212) 742–7036.
Region III: DE, DC, MD, PA, VA, WV.—Dalton G. Paxman, Ph.D. (215) 861–4631.
Region IV: AL, FL, GA, KY, MS, NC, SC, TN.—Clara H. Cobb, M.S., R.N. (404) 562–7894.
Region V: IL, IN, MI, MN, OH, WI.—James Galloway, M.D., FACP, FACC (312) 353–1385.
Region VI: AR, LA, NM, OK, TX.—Epi Elizondo, Ph.D., PA–C (214) 767–3879.
Region VII: IA, KS, MO, NE.—John Babb, R.P.H., M.P.A. (816) 426–3291.
Region VIII: CO, MT, ND, SD, UT, WY.—Zachery Taylor, M.D., M.S. (303) 844–7680.
Region IX: AZ, CA, HI, NV, Guam, American Samoa, CNMI, FSMI, RMI, Palau.—Ronald Banks, M.D., M.P.H. (415) 437–8096.

Region X: AK, ID, OR, WA.—Patrick O'Carroll, M.D., M.P.H., FACPM (206) 615–2469.

ADMINISTRATION ON AGING

1 Massachusetts Avenue, NW., 20001

Assistant Secretaries.—Kathy Greenlee, (202) 401–4541; Edwin L. Walker (acting), 357–3557.
Deputy Assistant Secretary for Policy and Management.—John Wren, 357–3460.
Director for—
Communications.—Carol Crecy, 357–3505.
Executive Secretariat.—Harry Posman, 357–3540.
Evaluation.—Saadia Greenberg, 357–3554.
Planning and Policy Development.—Lori Gerhard, 357–3443.

ADMINISTRATION FOR CHILDREN AND FAMILIES

370 L'Enfant Promenade, SW., 20447

Assistant Secretary.—David Hansell (acting), (202) 401–5180.
Principal Deputy Assistant Secretary.—David Hansell.
Deputy Assistant Secretary for Policy and External Affairs.—Vacant, 401–9200.
Deputy Assistant Secretary for Administration.—Curtis L. Coy, 401–9238.
Senior Advisor to the Assistant Secretary.—Vacant, 401–6947.
Director, Regional Operations Staff.—Diann Dawson, 401–4802.
Commissioner for Administration on:
Children, Youth and Families.—Maiso Bryant (acting), 205–8347.
Developmental Disabilities.—Patricia Morrissey (acting), 690–6590.
Deputy Commissioner, Administration for Native Americans.—Caroline Gray, 401–5590.
Commissioner, Office of Child Support Enforcement.—Vicki Turteski, 401–9369.
Associate Commissioner for—
Children's Bureau.—Vacant, 205–8618.
Family and Youth Services Bureau.—Vacant, 205–8102.
Director, Office of:
Community Services.—Yolanda Butler (acting), 401–9333.
Family Assistance.—Vacant, 401–9275.
Head Start.—Patricia Brown (acting), 205–8573.
Legislative Affairs and Budget.—Madeline Mocko (acting), 401–9223.
Planning, Research and Evaluation.—Noami Goldstein (acting), 401–9220.
Public Affairs.—Pamela Carter (acting), 401–9215.
Refugee Resettlement.—Martha Newton (acting), 401–9246.
Regional Operations.—Diann Dawson (acting), 401–4802.

AGENCY FOR HEALTHCARE RESEARCH AND QUALITY (AHRQ)

Director.—Carolyn Clancy, M.D. (301) 427–1200.
Deputy Director.—Kathleen Kendrick, R.N.

AGENCY FOR TOXIC SUBSTANCES AND DISEASE REGISTRY

1600 Clifton Road, NE., Atlanta, GA 30333

Administrator.—Richard E. Besser, M.D. (acting), (404) 639–7000.
Deputy Administrator.—Anne Schuchat, M.D. (acting).
Assistant Administrator.—Howard Frumkin, M.D., Ph.D., 498–0004.

CENTER FOR FAITH BASED AND COMMUNITY INITIATIVES

Director.—Ben O'Dell (acting), (202) 358–3595.

CENTER FOR DISEASE CONTROL AND PREVENTION

1600 Clifton Road, NE., Atlanta, GA 30333, phone (404) 639–7000

Director.—Richard E. Besser, M.D. (acting).

Deputy Director for—

Policy, Legislation and Communication.—Donald Shriber, J.D., M.P.H. (acting).

Management and Budget.—Bill Nichols, M.P.A. (acting).

Science and Public Health Program.—Anne Schuchat, M.D. (acting).

Chief of:

Operating Officer.—William P. Nichols, M.P.A. (acting).

Public Health Practice.—Dr. Stephanie B. Bailey, M.D., Ph.D.

Science Office.—Dr. Tanja Popovic, M.D., Ph.D.

Chief of Staff.—Joe Henderson (acting).

Staff Offices—

CDC Washington.—Edward L. Hunter, M.A. (acting), (202) 245–0600.

Enterprise Communication.—Donna Garland, B.A., 639–7540.

Dispute Resolution Equal Employment Opportunity.—Gilbert Camacho, M.S. (770) 488–3227.

Strategy and Innovation.—Brad Perkins, M.D., M.B.A., 639–7000.

Workforce and Career Development.—Stephen B. Thacker, M.D., 639–6010.

Coordinating Office for:

Global Health.—Steven Blount, M.P.H., 639–7429.

Terrorism Preparedness and Response.—Daniel M. Sosin, M.D., M.P.H. (acting), 639–3057.

Coordinating Center for Environmental Health and Injury Prevention.—Henry Falk, M.D. (770) 488–0608.

National Center for Environmental Health/Agency for Toxic Substances and Disease Registry.—Howard Frumkin, M.D. (770) 488–0604.

National Center for Injury Prevention and Control.—Ileana Arias, Ph.D. (770) 488–4696.

Coordinating Center for Health Information and Services.—Steve Solomon, M.D., 498–0123.

National Center for Health Marketing.—Jay Bernhardt, Ph.D., 498–0990.

National Center for Health Statistics.—Edward J. Sondik, Ph.D. (301) 458–4500.

National Center for Public Health Informatics.—Leslie Lenert, M.D., M.S., 498–2475.

Coordinating Center for Health Promotion.—Kathleen Toomey, M.D., M.P.H., 498–6700.

National Center for Birth Defects and Developmental Disabilities.—Edwin Trevathan, M.D., M.P.H., 498–3800.

National Center for Chronic Disease Prevention and Health Promotion.—Janet Collins, Ph.D. (770) 488–5401.

Coordinating Center for Infectious Diseases.—Mitch Cohen, M.D., 639–2100.

National Center for Immunization and Respiratory Diseases.—Beth Bell, M.D., M.P.H. (acting), 639–8200.

National Center for Zoonotic, Vector-Borne and Enteric Diseases.—Lonnie King, D.V.M., 639–7380.

National Center for HIV/AIDS, Viral Hepatitis, STD, and TB Prevention.—Kevin Fenton, M.D., 639–8000.

National Center for Preparedness, Detection and Control of Infectious Diseases.—Rima Khabbaz, M.D., 639–3967.

National Institute for Occupational Safety and Health.—Christine Branche, Ph.D. (acting), (202) 245–0625.

CENTERS FOR MEDICARE AND MEDICAID SERVICES

200 Independence Avenue, SW., 20201, phone (202) 690–6726

Administrator.—Charlene Frizzera (acting).

Deputy Administrator.—Michelle Snyder (acting).

Chief Operating Officer.—Charlene Frizzera (410) 786–3151.

Chief, Office of Actuary.—Rick Foster (410) 786–6374.

Director, Center for:

Beneficiary Choices.—Jonathan Blum (202) 690–6726.

Medicaid and State Operations.—Jackie Garner (410) 786–3870.

Medicare Management.—Jonathan Blum (410) 786–4164.

Director, Office of:

Acquisitions and Grants Management.—Rodney Benson (410) 786–8853.

Beneficiary Information Services.—Mary Agnes Laureno (410) 786–6885.

Clinical Standards and Quality.—Barry Straube, M.D. (410) 786–6841.

E-Health Standard & Services.—Tony Trenkle (410) 786–4160.

Equal Opportunity and Civil Rights.—Arlene Austin (410) 786–5110.

External Affairs.—Teresa Nino (202) 401–3135.
Financial Management.—Deborah Taylor (410) 786–5448.
Information Services.—Julie Boughn (410) 786–1800.
Legislation.—Amy Hall (acting), (202) 690–5960.
Operations Management.—Jim Weber (410) 786–1051.
Policy.—Karen Milgate (202) 690–0630.
Research, Development, and Information.—Tim Love (410) 786–0948.
Strategic Operations and Regulatory Support.—Jacqueline White (202) 690–8390.
Regional Administrator for:
Atlanta.—Renard Murray (404) 562–7150.
Boston.—Carol Maloof (617) 565–1188.
Chicago.—Jackie Garner (312) 886–6432.
Dallas.—James Farris, M.D. (214) 767–6427.
Denver.—Jeff Hinson (303) 844–2111.
Kansas City.—Nanette Foster Reilly (816) 426–5233.
New York.—James T. Kerr (212) 616–2205.
Philadelphia.—Nancy O'Connor (215) 861–4140.
San Francisco.—David Sayen (415) 744–3501.
Seattle.—John Hammarlund (206) 615–2306.

FOOD AND DRUG ADMINISTRATION

10903 New Hampshire Avenue, Silver Spring, MD 20993

Commissioner.—Joshua M. Sharfstein, M.D., (acting), (301) 796–5000.
Deputy Commissioner for International and Special Programs.—Murray M. Lumpkin, M.D., 827–5709.
Deputy Commissioner for Operations.—John Dyer, M.P.H., 796–4700.
Deputy Commissioner for Policy.—Randall Lutter, Ph.D., 796–4800.
Chief Counsel.—Michael Landa (acting), 827–1137.
Associate Commissioner for—
External Relations.—Lawrence Bachorik, 827–3330.
Operations.—John Gentile, 796–4729.
Planning.—Malcolm Bertoni, 796–4850.
Regulatory Affairs.—Michael Chappel (acting), 827–3101.
Assistant Commissioner for—
International Programs.—Mary Lou Valdez, 827–4480.
Legislation.—Stephen Mason (acting), 827–0102.
Planning.—Malcolm Bertoni, 796–4850.
Policy.—Jeffrey Shuren, M.D., 796–4830.
Public Affairs.—George Strait, 796–4540.
Special Health Issues.—Theresa A. Toigo, 827–4460.
Women's Health.—Kathleen Uhl, 827–0350.
Director, Center for—
Biologics Evaluation and Research.—Jesse Goodman, M.D., 827–0372.
Devices and Radiological Health.—Daniel Schultz, M.D. (240) 276–3939.
Drug Evaluation and Research.—Janet Woodcock, M.D., 796–5400.
Food Safety and Applied Nutrition.—Stephen Sundlof, D.V.M., Ph.D., 436–1600.
Veterinary Medicine.—Bernadette Dunham, D.V.M., Ph.D. (204) 276–9000.
National Center for Toxicological Research.—William Slikker, Jr., Ph.D. (870) 543–7517.
Director, Office of:
Executive Secretariat.—Dotty Foellmer, 796–4520.
Executive Operations.—L'Tonya Davis, 796–4557.
Equal Opportunity and Diversity Management.—Debra Chew, 827–4840.
Financial Management.—William Collinson, 827–5001.
Orphan Products Development.—Timothy Cote, 827–3666.

HEALTH RESOURCES AND SERVICES ADMINISTRATION

5600 Fishers Lane, Rockville, MD 20857

Administrator.—Mary K. Wakefield, Ph.D, RN (301) 443–2216.
Deputy Administrator.—Marcia K. Brand, 443–2194.
Senior Advisor.—Tina M. Cheatham, 443–2216.
Associate Administrator for—

Clinician Recruitment and Service.—Richard J. Smith III, 594–4130.
Federal Assistance Management.—Rebecca Spitzgo, 443–3524.
Financial Management.—S. Anthony McCann, 443–4244.
Health Information Technology.—Cheryl Austein-Castnoff, 443–0201.
Health Professions.—Diana Espinosa (acting), 443–5794.
Healthcare System.—Joyce Somsak, 443–3300.
HIV/AIDS.—Deborah Parham-Hopson, 443–1993.
Maternal and Child Health.—Peter C. van Dyck, 443–2170.
Performance Review.—Stephen R. Smith, 594–4130.
Primary Health Care.—James Macrae, 594–4110.
Rural Health Policy.—Tom Morris, 443–0835.
Director, Office of:
Center for Quality.—Denise Geolot, 443–0458.
Commissioned Corps Affairs.—Kerry Nesseler, 443–2741.
Communications.—Judy Andrews (acting), 443–3376.
Equal Opportunity and Civil Rights.—M. June Horner, 443–5636.
Information Technology.—Catherine Flickinger, 443–6846.
International Health.—Kerry Nesseler, 443–2741.
Legislation.—Patricia Stroup, 443–1890.
Management.—Wendy Ponton, 443–2053.
Minority Health and Health Disparities.—Tanya Raggio, 443–2964.
Planning and Evaluation.—Lyman Van Nostrand, 443–1891.

INDIAN HEALTH SERVICE

801 Thompson Avenue, Rockville, MD 20852

Director.—Yvette Roubideaux, M.D., M.P.A. (301) 443–1083.
Deputy Director.—Robert McSwain.
Deputy Director of:
Field Operations.—Kathleen Annette, M.D. (acting).
Management Operations.—Randy Grinnell, M.P.H.
Chief Medical Officer.—Susan V. Karol, M.D.
Director of:
Equal Employment Opportunity.—Pauline Bruce, 443–1108.
Legislative Affairs.—Michael Mahsetky, 443–7261.
Public Affairs.—Thomas W. Sweeney, 443–3593.
Tribal Programs.—Ronald Demaray (acting), 443–1104.
Tribal Self-Governance.—Hankie Ortiz, 443–7821.
Urban Indian Health Programs.—Phyllis Wolfe, 443–4680.

NATIONAL INSTITUTES OF HEALTH

9000 Rockville Pike, Bethesda, MD 20892

Director.—Raynard S. Kington (acting), M.D., Ph.D. (301) 496–2433.
Deputy Director.—Lawrence A. Tabak (acting), D.D.S., Ph.D., 496–7322.
Senior Advisor to the Director.—Ruth L. Kirschstein, M.D., 496–7504.
Assistant Director for OD Coordination.—Susan Persons, 496–2433.
Director, Executive Secretariat.—Ann Brewer, R.N., 496–1461.
Director, Office of Federal Adivsory Committee Policy.—Jennifer Spaeth, 496–2123.
Executive Officer, Office of the Director.—LaVerne Y. Stringfield, 594–8231.
Chief Information Officer.—John ''Jack'' F. Jones, Ph.D., 496–5703.
Legal Advisor, Office of the General Counsel.—Barbara M. McGarey, J.D., 496–6043.
Deputy Director for—
Extramural Research.—Sally J. Rockey (acting), Ph.D., 496–1096.
Intramural Research.—Michael M. Gottesman, M.D., 496–1921.
Management.—Colleen Barros, 496–3271.
Director, Division of Program Coordination, Planning, and Strategic Initiatives.—Lana S. Skirboll (acting), 402–9852.
Associate Director for—
Administration.—Diane Frasier (acting), 496–4422.
AIDS Research.—Jack E. Whitescarver, Ph.D., 496–0357.
Behavioral and Social Sciences Research.—Christine Bachrach (acting), Ph.D., 496–9485.
Budget.—John Bartrum, 496–4477.

Communications and Public Liaison.—John T. Burklow, 496–4461.
Disease Prevention.—Barnett S. Kramer, M.D., M.P.H., 496–1508.
Research on Women's Health.—Vivian W. Pinn, M.D., 402–1770.
Research Services.—Alfred C. Johnson, Ph.D., 496–2215.
Science Policy.—Amy Patterson (acting), M.D., 496–2122.

Director, Office of:
Ethics.—Raynard S. Kington, M.D., Ph.D. (acting), 402–6628.
Equal Opportunity and Diversity Management.—Lawrence N. Self, 496–6301.
Financial Management.—Kenneth Stith, 402–8831.
Human Resources.—Chris Major, 496–3592.
Legislative Policy and Analysis.—Roz Gray (acting), 496–3471.
Management Assessment.—Suzanne J. Servis, 496–1873.
Research Facilities Development and Operations.—Daniel Wheeland, 594–0999.
Technology Transfer.—Mark L. Rohrbaugh, Ph.D., J.D., 594–7700.

Directors:
Eunice Kennedy Shriver National Institute of Child Health and Human Development.—Duane F. Alexander, M.D., 496–3454.
Fogarty International Center.—Roger I. Glass, M.D., Ph.D., 496–1415.
National Center on Minority Health and Health Disparities.—John Ruffin, Ph.D., 402–1366.
National Library of Medicine.—Donald A.B. Lindberg, M.D., 496–6221.
Warren Grant Magnuson Clinical Center.—John I. Gallin, M.D., 496–4114.

Director, Center for—
Information Technology.—John "Jack" F. Jones, Ph.D (acting), 496–5703.
Scientific Review.—Antonio Scarpa, M.D., Ph.D., 435–1114.

Director, National Center for—
Complementary and Alternative Medicine.—Josephine P. Briggs, M.D., 435–6826.
Research Resources.—Barbara Alving, M.D., 496–5793.

Director, National Institute on:
Aging.—Richard J. Hodes, M.D., 496–9265.
Alcohol Abuse and Alcoholism.—Kenneth R. Warren, Ph.D. (acting), 443–3885.
Drug Abuse.—Nora D. Volkow, M.D., 443–6480.
Deafness and Other Communication Disorders.—James F. Battey, Jr., M.D., Ph.D., 402–0900.

Director, National Institute of:
Allergy and Infectious Diseases.—Anthony S. Fauci, M.D., 496–2263.
Arthritis and Musculoskeletal and Skin Diseases.—Stephen I. Katz, M.D., Ph.D., 496–4353.
Biomedical Imaging and Bioengineering.—Roderic I. Pettigrew, Ph.D., M.D., 496–8859.
Dental and Craniofacial Research.—Lawrence Tabak, D.D.S., Ph.D., 496–3571.
Diabetes and Digestive and Kidney Diseases.—Griffin P. Rodgers, M.D., M.A.C.P., 496–5877.
Environmental Health Sciences.—Linda S. Birnbaum, Ph.D., D.A.B.T., A.T.S. (919) 541–3201.
General Medical Sciences.—Jeremy M. Berg, Ph.D., 594–2172.
Mental Health.—Thomas Insel, M.D., 443–3673.
Neurological Disorders and Stroke.—Story C. Landis, Ph.D., 496–9746.
Nursing Research.—Patricia A. Grady, Ph.D., R.N., 496–8230.

Director, National:
Cancer Institute.—John E. Niederhuber, M.D., 496–5615.
Eye Institute.—Paul A. Sieving, M.D., Ph.D., 496–2234.
Heart, Lung and Blood Institute.—Elizabeth G. Nabel, M.D., 496–5166.
Human Genome Research Institute.—Alan E. Guttmacher, M.D. (acting), 496–0844.

SUBSTANCE ABUSE AND MENTAL HEALTH SERVICES ADMINISTRATION

1 Choke Cherry Road, Rockville, MD 20857

Administrator.—Eric Broderick, D.D.S., M.P.H. (acting), room 8–1061 (240) 276–2000.
Deputy Administrator.—Kana Enomoto, M.A. (acting), room 8–1059, 276–2000.
Principal Advisor to the Administrator.—Mark A. Weber, room 8–1076, 276–2000.
Policy Planning and Budget.—Daryl Kade, 276–2200.

Director, Center for—
Mental Health Services.—A. Kathryn Power, M.Ed., room 6–1057, 276–1310.
Substance Abuse Prevention.—Frances M. Harding, room 4–1057, 276–2420.
Substance Abuse Treatment.—H. Westley Clark, M.D., J.D., M.P.H., CAS, FASAM, room 5–1015, 276–1660.

Director, Office of:
Applied Studies.—Peter Delany, Ph.D., LCSW–C, room 7–1047, 276–1250.
Communications.—Bradford Stone (acting), room 8–1031, 276–2130.
Policy, Planning and Budget.—Daryl W. Kade, room 8–1083, 276–2200.
Program Services.—Elaine Parry, M.S., room 7–1073, 276–1110.

DEPARTMENT OF HOUSING AND URBAN DEVELOPMENT

Robert C. Weaver Federal Building, 451 Seventh Street, SW., 20410
phone (202) 708–1112, http://www.hud.gov

SHAUN DONOVAN, Democrat, of Washington, DC; born in New York, NY, January 24, 1966; undergraduate and graduate degrees from Harvard University, graduating from Harvard College in 1987, Master of Public Administration from the John F. Kennedy School of Government and a master's in architecture at the Graduate School of Design in 1995. Commissioner of the New York City Department of Housing Preservation and Development (HPD); visiting scholar, New York University; consultant to the Millennial Housing Commission; Deputy Assistant Secretary for Multifamily Housing and acting FHA commissioner (HUD); Community Preservation Corporation (CPC), a non-profit lender and developer of affordable housing. Married to Liza Gilbert; two sons; nominated by President-elect Barack Obama on December 13, 2008; confirmed by the U.S. Senate through unanimous consent on January 22, 2009; sworn-in on January 26.

OFFICE OF THE SECRETARY

Secretary of Housing and Urban Development.—Shaun Donovan, room 10000 (202) 708–0417.
Chief of Staff.—Laurel A. Blatchford, 708–2713.
Deputy Chief of Staff.—Ana Marie Argilagos, 708–1781.
Director, Center for Faith Based and Community Initiatives.—Mark Linton, 708–2404.
Chief Executive Officer.—Marcella Belt, 708–3750.
Administrative Officer.—Marianne C. DeConti, 708–3750.

OFFICE OF THE DEPUTY SECRETARY

Deputy Secretary.—Ron C. Sims, room 10100 (202) 708–0123.
Chief of Staff for the Deputy Secretary.—Maura Brueger.

ASSISTANT SECRETARY FOR ADMINISTRATION

Assistant Secretary.—Vacant, room 6100 (202) 708–0940.
General Deputy Assistant Secretary.—Sharman R. Lancefield (acting).
Executive Secretariat.—Cynthia A. O'Connor, 708–3054.
Deputy Assistant Secretary for—
Budget and Management Support.—Karen S. Jackson, 708–1583.
Human Resource Management.—Sharman R. Lancefield, 708–3946.

ASSISTANT SECRETARY FOR COMMUNITY PLANNING AND DEVELOPMENT

Assistant Secretary.—Mercedes Márquez, room 7100 (202) 708–2690.
General Deputy Assistant Secretary.—Nelson R. Bregon.
Deputy Assistant Secretary for—
Grant Programs.—Vacant.
Operations.—William H. Eargle, Jr., 401–6367.
Special Needs.—Mark Johnston, 708–1590.

ASSISTANT SECRETARY FOR CONGRESSIONAL AND INTERGOVERNMENTAL RELATIONS

Assistant Secretary.—Vacant.

General Deputy Assistant Secretary.—Vacant, room 10120 (202) 708–0005.
Deputy Assistant Secretary for—
Congressional Relations.—Bernard Fulton, 708–0380.
Intergovernmental Relations.—Frank Vaccarella, 708–0005.

ASSISTANT SECRETARY FOR FAIR HOUSING AND EQUAL OPPORTUNITY

Assistant Secretary.—Vacant, room 5100 (202) 708–4252.
General Deputy Assistant Secretary.—Bryan Greene, 708–4211.
Deputy Assistant Secretary for—
Enforcement and Programs.—Cheryl Ziegler, 619–8046.
Operations and Management.—Karen A. Newton, 708–0768.

ASSISTANT SECRETARY FOR HOUSING

Assistant Secretary/Federal Housing Commissioner.—Brian D. Montgomery, room 9100 (202) 708–2601.
General Deputy Assistant Secretary.—Ronald Y. Spraker (acting).
Deputy Assistant Secretary for—
Affordable Housing Preservation.—Theodore Toon, 708–0001.
Finance and Budget.—George Tomchick (acting), 401–8975.
Housing Operations.—Craig T. Clemmensen, 708–1104.
Multifamily Housing.—Vacant, 708–2495.
Regulatory Affairs and Manufactured Housing.—Vacant, 708–6401.
Single Family Housing.—Phillip Murray, 708–3175.

ASSISTANT SECRETARY FOR POLICY DEVELOPMENT AND RESEARCH

Assistant Secretary.—Raphael W. Bostic, room 8100 (202) 708–1600.
General Deputy Assistant Secretary.—Jean Lin Pao.
Deputy Assistant Secretary for—
Economic Affairs.—Kurt G. Usowski, 708–3080.
International Affairs.—John M. Geraghty, 708–0770.
Research, Evaluation, and Monitoring.—Kevin J. Neary, 708–4230.

ASSISTANT SECRETARY FOR PUBLIC AFFAIRS

General Deputy Assistant Secretary.—Neill Coleman, room 10132 (202) 708–0980.
Deputy Assistant Secretary.—Jereon M. Brown.
Press Secretary.—Melanie Roussell.

ASSISTANT SECRETARY FOR PUBLIC AND INDIAN HOUSING

Assistant Secretary.—Vacant, room 4100 (202) 708–0950.
General Deputy Assistant Secretary.—Paula Blunt.
Deputy Assistant Secretary, for—
Field Operations.—Deborah Hernandez, 708–4016.
Native American Programs.—Rodger J. Boyd, 401–7914.
Office of Field Operations.—Deborah Hernandez, 708–4016.
Policy, Programs and Legislative Initiatives.—Bessy Kong, 708–0713.
Public Housing and Voucher Programs.—Milan Ozdinec, 401–8812.
Public Housing Investments.—Dominique Blom, 401–8812.
Real Estate Assessment Center.—J. David Reeves, 475–8906.

ASSISTANT DEPUTY SECRETARY FOR FIELD POLICY AND MANAGEMENT

Assistant Deputy Secretary.—Vacant, room 7106 (202) 708–2426.

GOVERNMENT NATIONAL MORTGAGE ASSOCIATION

President.—Joseph J. Murin (202) 708–0926.

Executive Vice President.—Thomas R. Weakland (acting).
Senior Vice President, Office of:
Finance.—Michael J. Najjum, Jr., 401–2064.
Management Operations.—Cheryl W. Owens, 708–2648.
Mortgage-Backed Securities.—Stephen L. Ledbetter, 708–4141.
Program Operations.—Thomas R. Weakland, 708–2884.
Vice President, Office of Capital Markets.—Kirk D. Freeman, 401–8970.

CHIEF FINANCIAL OFFICER

Chief Financial Officer.—Vacant, room 10234 (202) 708–1946.
Deputy Chief Financial Officer.—Vacant.
Assistant Chief Financial Officer for—
Accounting.—Juanita Galberath, 708–3601.
Budget.—Anthony Scardino.
Financial Management.—Frank Murphy.
Systems.—Gail B. Dise, 708–1757.

CHIEF INFORMATION OFFICER

Chief Information Officer.—Jerry E. Williams, room 4160 (202) 708–0306.
General Deputy Chief Information Officer for—
Business and Information Technology Modernization.—Lynn Allen, 708–0306.
IT Operations.—Mike Milazzo, 708–4562.
Chief Information Security Officer.—Marion Cody, 619–9057.

CHIEF PROCUREMENT OFFICER

Chief Procurement Officer.—Jemine A. Bryon, room 5280 (202) 708–0600.
Deputy Chief Procurement Officer.—Vacant.
Associate Chief Procurement Officer.—David R. Williamson, 708–3477.

GENERAL COUNSEL

General Counsel.—Helen R. Kanovsky, room 10110 (202) 708–2244.
General Deputy General Counsel.—Nestor M. Davidson.
Deputy General Counsel for—
Housing Programs.—John W. Herold, room 10110, 708–2244.
Operations.—Linda M. Cruciani, room 10240, 402–2565.
Associate General Counsel for—
Assisted Housing and Community Development.—Elton J. Lester, room 8162, 708–0212.
Fair Housing.—Estelle D. Franklin, room 10272, 708–0340.
Finance and Regulatory Compliance.—John P. Opitz, room 9256, 708–2203.
Human Resources.—Paula A. Lincoln, room 10164, 708–2864.
Insured Housing.—John J. Daly, room 9226, 708–1274.
Legislation and Regulations.—Camille E. Acevedo, room 10282, 708–1793.
Litigation.—Nancy Christopher, room 10258, 708–0300.
Program Enforcement.—Dane M. Narode, 708–2350.
Deputy Director, Departmental Enforcement Center.—Henry S. Czauski, 708–3554.

INSPECTOR GENERAL

Inspector General.—Kenneth M. Donohue, Sr., room 8256 (202) 708–0430.
Deputy Inspector General.—Michael P. Stephens.
Counsel to the Inspector General, Office of Legal Counsel.—Vacant, 708–1613.
Assistant Inspector General, Office of:
Audit.—James Heist, 708–0364.
Investigation.—John McCarty, 708–0390.
Management and Policy.—Dennis A. Raschka, 708–0006.

OFFICE OF DEPARTMENTAL EQUAL EMPLOYMENT OPPORTUNITY

Director.—Linda Bradford Washington, room 2134 (202) 708–3362.

OFFICE OF DEPARTMENTAL OPERATIONS AND COORDINATION

Director.—Inez Banks-Dubose, room 2124 (202) 708–2806.
Deputy Director.—Joseph F. Smith.

OFFICE OF HEALTHY HOMES AND LEAD HAZARD CONTROL

Director.—Jon L. Gant, room 8236 (202) 708–0310.
Deputy Director.—Mathew Ammon.

SMALL AND DISADVANTAGED BUSINESS UTILIZATION

Director.—Arnette McGill (acting), room 2200 (202) 708–5477.

HUD REGIONAL DIRECTORS

Region I.—Connecticut, Maine, Massachusetts, New Hampshire, Rhode Island, Vermont.
Regional Director.—Vacant, Thomas P. O'Neill, Jr. Federal Building, 10 Causeway Street, Room 301, Boston, MA 02222–1092 (617) 994–8200.
Region II.—New Jersey, New York.
Regional Director.—Sean Moss, 26 Federal Plaza, Suite 3541, New York, NY 10278–0068 (212) 264–8000, ext. 7109.
Region III.—Delaware, District of Columbia, Maryland, Pennsylvania, Virginia, West Virginia.
Regional Director.—Guy Ciarrocchi, The Wanamaker Building, 100 Penn Square East, Philadelphia, PA 19107–3380 (215) 656–0600.
Region IV.—Alabama, Florida, Georgia, Kentucky, Mississippi, North Carolina, Puerto Rico, South Carolina, Tennessee.
Regional Director.—Robert Young, Five Points Plaza, 40 Marietta Street, NW., 2nd Floor, Atlanta, GA 30303–2806 (404) 331–5001.
Region V.—Illinois, Indiana, Michigan, Minnesota, Ohio, Wisconsin.
Regional Director.—Joseph Galvan, Ralph Metcalfe Federal Building, 77 West Jackson Boulevard, Chicago, IL 60604–3507 (312) 353–5680.
Region VI.—Arkansas, Louisiana, New Mexico, Oklahoma, Texas.
Regional Director.—A. Cynthia Leon, 801 Cherry Street, Fort Worth, TX 76113–2905 (817) 978–5540.
Region VII.—Iowa, Kansas, Missouri, Nebraska.
Regional Director.—Macie Houston, Gateway Tower II, 400 State Avenue, Room 200, Kansas City, KS 66101–2406 (913) 551–5462.
Region VIII.—Colorado, Montana, North Dakota, South Dakota, Utah, Wyoming.
Regional Director.—John Carson, 1670 Broadway, Denver, CO 80202–4801 (303) 672–5440.
Region IX.—Arizona, California, Hawaii, Nevada.
Regional Director.—Richard K. Rainey, 600 Harrison Street, 3rd Floor, San Francisco, CA 94107–1300 (415) 489–6400.
Region X.—Alaska, Idaho, Oregon, Washington.
Regional Director.—John Meyers, Seattle Federal Office Building, 909 First Avenue, Suite 200, Seattle, WA 98104–1000 (206) 220–5101.

DEPARTMENT OF TRANSPORTATION

1200 New Jersey Avenue, SE., Washington, DC 20590

phone (202) 366–4000, http://www.dot.gov

RAY LAHOOD, Secretary of Transportation; born in Peoria, IL, December 6, 1945; education: B.A., Bradley University, Peoria, IL; professional: United States Congressman from 1995–2009; member of the House Committees on Transportation and Infrastructure; Veterans Affairs, and Agriculture, Intelligence, and Appropriations; chairman of four Bipartisan Congressional retreats; Chief of Staff to U.S. Congressman Robert Michel, 1983–94; Illinois State Representative from 1982–83; District Administrative Assistant to Congressman Thomas Rails, 1977–82; Bi-State Metropolitan Planning Commission, 1974–77; teacher; director, Rock Island County Youth Services Bureau, 1972–74; family: married to Kathy LaHood; four children: Darin, Amy, Sam, and Sara; nine grandchildren; nominated by President Barack H. Obama to become the 16th Secretary of Transportation, and was confirmed by the U.S. Senate on January 23, 2009.

OFFICE OF THE SECRETARY

[Created by the act of October 15, 1966; codified under U.S.C. 49]

Secretary of Transportation.—Ray LaHood, room W93–317 (202) 366–1111.
  Deputy Secretary.—John D. Porcari, 366–2222.
  Chief of Staff.—Joan DeBoer, 366–1103.
    Deputy Chief of Staff.—Marlise Streitmatter, 366–6800.
  Under Secretary of Transportation for Policy.—Roy Kienitz, 366–1815.
  Director, Office of:
    Civil Rights.—Mary N. Jones (acting), room W78–318, 366–4648.
    Executive Secretariat.—Carol C. Darr, room W93–324, 366–4277.
    Intelligence and Security.—Michael Lowder, room W56–302, 366–6525.
    Small and Disadvantaged Business Utilization.—Brandon Neal, room W56–308, 366–1930.

ASSISTANT SECRETARY FOR ADMINISTRATION

Assistant Secretary.—Linda J. Washington room W80–322 (202) 366–2332.
  Director, Office of:
    Facilities, Information and Asset Management.—George Fields, room W58–334, 366–9284.
    Financial Management.—Marie Petrosino, room W81–306, 366–3967.
    Hearings, Chief Administrative Law Judge.—Judge Ronnie A. Yoder, room E12–356, 366–2142.
    Human Resource Management.—Nancy Mowry, room W81–302, 366–4088.
    Security.—Lee Privett, room W54–336, 366–4677.
    Senior Procurement Executive.—Joanie Newhart, room W83–306, 366–4263.

ASSISTANT SECRETARY FOR AVIATION AND INTERNATIONAL AFFAIRS

Assistant Secretary.—Christa Fornarotto (acting), room W88–300 (202) 366–8822.
  Deputy Assistant Secretaries: Christa Fornarotto, Susan McDermott, room W88–300, 366–4551.
    Director, Office of:
      Aviation Analysis.—Todd Homan, room W86–481, 366–5903.

International Aviation.—Paul Gretch, room W86–406, 366–2423.
International Transportation and Trade.—Bernestine Allen, room W88–306, 366–4398.

ASSISTANT SECRETARY FOR BUDGET AND PROGRAMS

Assistant Secretary/Chief Financial Officer.—Vacant, room W95–330 (202) 366–9191.
Deputy Assistant Secretary.—Lana Hurdle, room W95–316, 366–9192.
Deputy Chief Financial Officer.—Vacant, room W95–302, 366–9192.
Director, Office of:
Budget and Program Performance.—Ellen Heup, room W93–308, 366–4594.
Financial Management.—Laurie Howard, room W93–322, 366–1306.

ASSISTANT SECRETARY FOR GOVERNMENTAL AFFAIRS

Assistant Secretary.—Vacant, room W85–326 (202) 366–4573.
Deputy Assistant Secretaries: Robert Letteney, Joanna Turner.
Associate Directors: Curtis Johnson, Yasmin Yaver.

ASSISTANT SECRETARY FOR TRANSPORTATION POLICY

Assistant Secretary.—David Matsuda (acting), room 10228 (202) 366–0582.
Deputy Assistant Secretaries.—David Matsuda, 336–0301; Elizabeth Osborne, room W82–314, 366–8979; Joel Szabat, room W82–308, 493–2208.

GENERAL COUNSEL

General Counsel.—Rosalind A. Knapp (acting), room W92–300, 366–4713.
Deputy General Counsel.—Rosalind A. Knapp.
Assistant General Counsel for—
Aviation Enforcement and Proceedings.—Samuel Podberesky, room W96–322, 366–9342.
International Law.—Donald H. Horn, room W98–324, 366–2972.
Legislation.—Thomas W. Herlihy, room W96–326, 366–4687.
Litigation.—Paul M. Geier, room W94–310, 366–4731.
Regulation and Enforcement.—Neil K. Eisner, room W96–302, 366–4723.
Operatoins.—Ronald Jackson, room W96–304, 366–4710.

INSPECTOR GENERAL

Inspector General.—Calvin L. Scovel III, room W70–300 (202) 366–1959.
Deputy Inspector General.—David A. Dobbs, 366–6767.
Principal Assistant Inspector General for Auditing and Evaluation.—Ann Calvaresi Barr, room 9217, 366–0500.
Assistant Inspector General for—
Acquisition and Procurement Audits.—Mark Zabarsky, room 9228, 366–1496.
Aviation and Special Program Audits.—Lou Dixon, 366–0500.
Competition and Economic Analysis.—David Tornquist, 366–9682.
Financial and Information Technology Audits.—Rebecca Leng, 366–1496.
Investigations.—Tim Barry, 366–1967.
Legal, Legislative and External Affairs.—Brian A. Dettelbach, 366–8751.
Surface and Maritime Program Audits.—Joe Come, 366–5630.
Deputy Assistant Inspector General for—
Aviation and Special Program Audits.—Matthew Hamption, 366–0500.
Surface and Maritime Program Audits.—Rosalyn Millman, 366–5630.

REGIONAL AUDIT OFFICES

Regional Program Directors:
Tina Nysted, 61 Forsyth Street, SW., Suite 17T60, Atlanta, GA 30303 (404) 562–3854.
Scott Macey, 201 Mission Street, Suite 1750, San Francisco, CA 94105 (415) 744–3090.
Darren Murphy, 915 Second Avenue, Room 644, Seattle, WA 98174 (206) 220–7754.
Earl Hedges, 10 South Howard Street, Suite 4500, Baltimore, MD 21201 (410) 962–3612.

REGIONAL INVESTIGATIONS OFFICES

Special Agents-In-Charge:
Region I.—Ted Doherty, 55 Broadway, Room 1055, Cambridge, MA 02142 (617) 494–2701.
Region II.—Ned E. Schwartz, 201 Varick Street, Room 1161, New York, NY 10014 (212) 337–1250.
Region III.—Kathryn Jones, 409 3rd Street, SW., Room 301, Washington, DC 20024 (202) 260–8580.
Region IV.—John Long, 61 Forsythe Street, SW., Suite 17T60, Atlanta, GA 30303 (404) 562–3850.
Region V.—Michelle McVicker, 200 West Adams Street, Suite 300, Chicago, IL 60606 (312) 353–0106.
Region VI.—Max Smith, 819 Taylor Street, Room 13A42, Fort Worth, TX 76102 (817) 978–3236.
Region IX.—Hank W. Smedley, 201 Mission Street, Suite 1750, San Francisco, CA 94105 (415) 744–3090.

OFFICE OF PUBLIC AFFAIRS

Assistant to the Secretary and Director of Public Affairs.—Jill Zuckman, room W93–310 (202) 366–4570.
Deputy Director.—Maureen Knightly.
Associate Director of Media Relation.—William S. ''Bill'' Adams, 366–5580.
Speech Writing and Research Division.—Amy Bernsteen, room 10413, 366–5580.

FEDERAL AVIATION ADMINISTRATION

800 Independence Avenue, SW., 20591 (202) 267–3484

Administrator.—Lynne A. Osmus (acting), 267–3111.
Chief of Staff.—Jana Murphy.
Senior Counsel to the Administrator.—Vacant, 267–7417.
Executive Assistant to the Administrator.—Sharon Harrison, 267–3111.
Deputy Administrator.—Vacant, 267–8111.
Senior Advisor to the Deputy Administrator.—David Weingart (acting), 267–7417.
Assistant Administrator for Financial Services.—Ramesh K. Punwani, 267–9105.
Deputy Assistant Administrator.—Victoria Wassmer, 267–3882.
Director of Budget.—Carol Rose, 267–8010.
Deputy Director of Budget.—Greg Rasnake.
Director of Financial Controls.—Carl Burrus, 267–7140.
Director of Financial Management.—Allison Ritman, 267–3018.
Assistant Administrator for Civil Rights.—Fanny Rivera, 267–3254.
Deputy Assistant Administrator.—Barbara A. Edwards, 267–3264.
Assistant Administrator for Aviation Policy, Planning and Environment.—Nancy LoBue (acting), 267–3927.
Deputy Assistant Administrator.—Carl Burleson (acting), 267–7954.
Director of:
Aviation Policy and Plans.—Nan Shellabarger, 267–3274.
Environment and Energy.—Carl Burleson, 267–3576.
Chief Counsel.—James W. Whitlow (acting), 267–3222.
Deputy Chief Counsel.—James W. Whitlow, 267–3773.
Assistant Administrator for Government and Industry Affairs.—Mary U. Walsh (acting), 267–3277.
Deputy Assistant Administrator.—Vacant, 267–8211.
Assistant Administrator for Human Resource Management.—Ventris C. Gibson, 267–3456.
Deputy Assistant Administrator.—Darlene Freeman (acting), 267–3850.
Deputy Assistant Administrator for Strategic Labor Relations.—Melvin Harris, 267–3979.
Director of:
Accountability Board.—Maria Fernandez-Greczmiel, 267–3065.
Center for Management and Leadership Development.—Darlene Freeman, 267–3850.
Corporate, Learning and Development.—Paul Meyer (acting), 267–9041.
Labor and Employee Relations.—Melvin Harris, 267–3979.

Personnel.—Angela Porter (acting), 267–3850.

Assistant Administrator for Information Services.—David Bowen (CIO), 493–4570.

Director of Information Systems Security.—Michael F. Brown, 267–7104.

Assistant Administrator for Communications.—Laura J. Brown, 267–3883.

Deputy Assistant Administrator.—Laura J. Brown, 267–3883.

Deputy Assistant Administrator for Corporate Communications.—Gerald Lavey, 267–9499.

Assistant Administrator for International Aviation.—Di Reimold (acting), 385–8900.

Deputy Assistant Director of International Aviation.—Di Reimold.

Asia-Pacific.—Jeri Alles, 011–86–10–8532–1761, x102.

Europe, Africa, and Middle East.—Stephen Creamer 011 (322) 508–2700.

Western Hemisphere.—Dawn Veatch (202) 385–8869.

Assistant Administrator for Regions and Center Operations.—Paula Lewis, 267–7369.

Deputy Assistant Administrator.—Michael A. Crillo, 267–7369.

Regional Administrator for—

Alaskan.—Bob Lewis (acting) (907) 271–5645.

Central.—Joseph Miniace (816) 329–3050.

Eastern.—Carmine Gallo (718) 553–3000.

Great Lakes.—Barry D. Cooper (847) 294–7294.

New England.—Amy Lind Corbett (781) 238–7020.

Northwest Mountain.—Kathryn Vernon (425) 227–2001.

Southern.—Douglas Murphy (404) 305–5000.

Southwest.—Teresa Bruner (817) 222–5001.

Western-Pacific.—William C. Withycombe (310) 725–3550.

Director, Mike Monroney Aeronautical Center.—Lindy Ritz (405) 954–4521.

Assistant Administrator for Security and Hazardous Materials.—Claudio Manno (acting), 267–7211.

Deputy Assistant Administrator.—Claudio Manno, 267–7211.

Director of:

Emergency Operations and Communications.—Chris J. Rocheleau, 267–8075.

Field Operations.—Thomas D. Ryan, 267–7211.

Hazardous Materials.—Christopher Bonanti, 267–9864.

Internal Security.—Bruce Herron, 267–7714.

Chief Operating Officer for Air Traffic Services.—Henry P. Krakowski, 493–5602.

Senior Vice President for—

Acquisition and Business Services.—James H. Washington, 267–7222.

Safety Services.—Robert O. Tarter, 267–3341.

Finance Business Unit.—Eugene D. Juba, 267–3022.

NextGen and Operations Planning Services.—Victoria Cox, 267–7111.

Strategy and Performance Business Unit.—John Pipes, 267–5724.

Operations Business.—Richard L. Day, 267–7224.

Vice President for—

En Route and Oceanic Services.—Richard Duchame (acting), 385–8501.

Service Center.—Walt Cochran (acting), 385–8361.

System Operations Service Unit.—Nancy B. Kalinowski, 267–3666.

Technical Operations Service Unit.—Teri Bristol, 267–3366.

Technical Training.—D. Shawn Clark, 267–8311.

Terminal Service Unit.—Mike Sammartino (acting), 385–8801.

Director of:

Joint Planning Development Office.—Charles Leader, 220–3310.

William J. Hughes Technical Center.—Wilson Felder (609) 485–6641.

Associate Administrator for Airports.—Catherine Lang, 267–9471.

Deputy Associate Administrator.—Randall S. Fiertz (acting), 267–3085.

Director of:

Airport Planning and Programming.—Benito DeLeon, 267–8775.

Airport Safety and Standards.—Michael J. O'Donnell, 267–3053.

Associate Administrator for Commercial Space Transportation.—Dr. George C. Nield, 267–7793.

Deputy Associate Administrator.—James E. VanLaak, 267–7848.

Associate Administrator for Aviation Safety.—Peggy Gilligan, 267–3131.

Deputy Associate Administrator.—John J. Hickey, 267–7804.

Director of:

Accident Investigation.—Hooper Harris, 267–7788.

Air Traffic Oversight.—Tony Ferrante, 267–5202.

Aircraft Certification Service.—Dorenda Baker, 267–8235.

Aviation Safety Analytical Services.—Jay J. Pardee, 267–9179.

Flight Standards Service.—John Allen, 267–8237.

Quality, Integration and Executive.—Tina Amereihn, 493–5717.
Rulemaking.—Pamela Hamilton, 267–9677.
Federal Air Surgeon.—Dr. Fred Tilton, 267–3535.

FEDERAL HIGHWAY ADMINISTRATION

Washington Headquarters, 1200 New Jersey Avenue, SE., 20590–9898

Turner-Fairbank Highway Research Center (TFHRC)

6300 Georgetown Pike, McLean, VA 22201

Administrator.—Vacant (202) 366–0650.
Deputy Administrator.—Vacant, 366–2242.
Associate Administrator/Director of TFHRC.—Michael F. Trentacoste, 493–3259.
Associate Administrator for Administration.—Patricia A. Prosperi, 366–0604.
Executive Director.—Jeffrey F. Paniati, 366–2242.
Chief Counsel.—Karen Hedlund, 366–0740.
Chief Financial Officer.—Elissa K. Konove, 366–2563.
Associate Administrator for—
Civil Rights.—Allen Masuda, 366–0752.
Federal Lands.—John R. Baxter, 366–9472.
Infrastructure.—King W. Gee, 366–0371.
Operations.—Jeffrey A. Lindley, 366–8753.
Policy.—James A. Cheatham (acting), 366–0585.
Public Affairs.—Cathy St. Denis, 366–2244.
Planning, Environment, and Realty.—Gloria M. Shepherd, 366–0116.
Safety.—Joseph S. Toole, 366–2288.

FIELD SERVICES

Organizationally report to Executive Director (HOA–3), Washington, DC

Director of Technical Services.—Amy Lucero, 12300 West Dakota Avenue, Suite 340, Lakewood, CO 80228 (708) 283–3513.
Director of:
Field Services—North.—Joyce A. Curtis, 10 South Howard Street, Baltimore, MD 21201–2819 (410) 962–0739.
Field Services—South.—David C. Gibbs, 61 Forsyth Street, SW., Suite 17T26, Atlanta, GA 30303–3104 (404) 562–3573.
Field Services—West.—Christine M. Johnson, 2520 West 4700 South, Suite 9C, Salt Lake City, UT 84118–1847 (801) 967–5979.

FEDERAL MOTOR CARRIER SAFETY ADMINISTRATION

Administrator.—Vacant, room W60–308 (202) 366–1927.
Deputy Administrator.—Rose A. McMurray (acting).
Chief Safety Officer.—Rose A. McMurray.
Chief Counsel.—David Tochen (acting), 493–0349.
Associate Administrator for Field Operation.—Daniel Hartman, 366–2525.
Director, Office of Communications.—Candice Tolliver, 366–8810.

FIELD OFFICES

Eastern Service Center (CT, DC, DE, MA, MD, ME, NJ, NH, NY, PA, PR, RI, VA, VT, WV).—802 Cromwell Park Drive, Suite N, Glen Burnie, MD 21061 (443) 703–2240.

Midwestern Service Center (IA, IL, IN, KS, MI, MO, MN, NE, OH, WI).—19900 Governors Drive, Suite 210, Olympia Fields, IL 60461 (708) 283–3577.

Southern Service Center (AL, AR, FL, GA, KY, LA, MS, NC, NM, OK, SC, TN, TX).—1800 Century Boulevard, NE., Suite 1700, Atlanta, GA 30345–3220 (404) 327–7400.

Western Service Center (American Samoa, AK, AZ, CA, CO, Guam, HI, ID, Mariana Islands, MT, ND, NV, OR, SD, UT, WA, WY).—Golden Hills Office Centre, 12600 W. Colfax Avenue, Suite B–300, Lakewood, CO 80215 (303) 407–2350.

FEDERAL RAILROAD ADMINISTRATION

1120 Vermont Avenue, NW., 20590, phone (202) 493–6000

http://www.fra.dot.gov

Administrator.—Joseph C. Szabo, room W30–308, 493–6014.
Associate Administrator for—
Finance Management and Administration.—Margaret Reid, room W36–312, 493–6100.
Policy and Program Development.—Timothy Barkley, room W33–320, 493–1305.
Railroad Development.—Mark E. Yachmetz, room W38–316, 493–6381.
Safety.—Jo Strang, room W35–328, 493–6304.
Chief Counsel.—Mark Lindsey, room W31–320, 493–6048.
Director of:
Budget.—Donna Alwine, room W36–308, 493–6455.
Civil Rights.—Calvin Gibson, room W31–302, 493–6010.
Financial Management.—Kimberly Orben, room W36–306, 493–6454.
Public Affairs.—Vacant, room W31–304, 493–6006.

REGIONAL OFFICES (RAILROAD SAFETY)

Region 1 (Northeastern).—Connecticut, Maine, Massachusetts, New Hampshire, New Jersey, New York, Rhode Island, Vermont.
Regional Administrator.—Les Fiorenzo, Room 1077, 55 Broadway, Cambridge, MA 02142 (617) 494–2302.
Region 2 (Eastern).—Delaware, District of Columbia, Maryland, Pennsylvania, Virginia, West Virginia, Ohio.
Regional Administrator.—Les Fiorenzo (acting), 1510 Chester Pike, Baldwin Tower, Suite 660, Crum Lynne, PA 19022 (610) 521–8200.
Region 3 (Southern).—Kentucky, Tennessee, Mississippi, North Carolina, South Carolina, Georgia, Alabama, Florida.
Regional Administrator.—Bonnie Murphy (acting), 61 Forsyth Street, NW., Suite 16T20, Atlanta, GA 30303 (404) 562–3800.
Region 4 (Central).—Minnesota, Illinois, Indiana, Michigan, Wisconsin.
Regional Administrator.—Lawrence Hasvold, 200 W. Adams Street, Chicago, IL 60606 (312) 353–6203.
Region 5 (Southwestern).—Arkansas, Louisiana, New Mexico, Oklahoma, Texas.
Regional Administrator.—Bonnie Murphy, 4100 International Plaza, Suite 450, Ft. Worth, TX 96109 (817) 862–2200.
Region 6 (Midwestern).—Iowa, Missouri, Kansas, Nebraska, Colorado.
Regional Administrator.—Darrell J. Tisor, DOT Building, 901 Locust Street, Suite 464, Kansas City, MO 64106 (816) 329–3840.
Region 7 (Western).—Arizona, California, Nevada, Utah.
Regional Administrator.—Alvin L. Settle, 801 I Street, Suite 466, Sacramento, CA 95814 (916) 498–6540.
Region 8 (Northwestern).—Idaho, Oregon, Wyoming, Montana, North Dakota, South Dakota, Washington, Alaska.
Regional Administrator.—Dave Brooks, 500 Broadway, Murdock Executive Plaza, Suite 240, Vancouver, WA 98660 (360) 696–7536.

FEDERAL TRANSIT ADMINISTRATION

Administrator.—Vacant.
Deputy Administrator.—Matt Welbes (acting).
Chief Counsel.—Vacant, 366–4011.
Director, Office of Civil Rights.—Cheryl Hershey, 366–6161.
Associate Administrator for—
Administration.—Ann Linnertz, 366–4018.
Budget and Policy.—Robert Tuccillo, 366–1691.
Communications and Congressional Affairs.—Vacant, 366–4043.
Planning and Environment.—Susan Borinsky, 366–2360.
Program Management.—Susan Schruth, 366–4020.
Research, Demonstration and Innovation.—Vincent Valdes, 366–3052.

MARITIME ADMINISTRATION

Administrator and Chairman, Maritime Subsidy Board.—Vacant, room W22–318 (202) 366–5823.

Deputy Administrator.—James E. Caponiti (acting), room W22–314, 366–1719.

Secretary, Maritime Administration and Maritime Subsidy Board.—Vacant, 366–5746.

Chief Counsel and Member, Maritime Subsidy Board.—Rand Pixa (acting), room W26–302, 366–5711.

Director, Office of Congressional and Public Affairs.—Vacant, room W22–322, 366–4105.

Public Affairs Officer.—Susan Clark, room W22–324, 366–5067.

Office of Assistant Administrator.—James E. Caponiti, room W28–316, 366–5772.

Director of:

International Activities.—Gregory Hall, room W28–314, 366–2765.

Policy and Plans.—Janice G. Weaver, room W28–312, 366–5482.

Associate Administrator for Budget and Programs/Chief Financial Officer.—David J. Rivait, room W26–306, 493–0476.

Director, Office of:

Accounting.—Jim Chen, room W26–307, 366–5103.

Budget.—James Lampert, room W26–310, 366–1369.

National Security Resource Management.—Jennifer Fallis, room W25–1947, 366–1947.

Resources.—Vacant, room W26–309, 366–5110.

Associate Administrator for Administration.—Taylor E. Jones II, room W21–330, 366–5497.

Director, Office of:

Acquisition.—Vacant, room W28–304, 366–9081.

Management and Information Services.—Richard A. Weaver, room W28–302, 366–2811.

Personnel.—Kim Norris, room W28–311, 366–4141.

Associate Administrator for Environment and Compliance.—Joseph A. Byrne, room W21–326, 366–1931.

Director, Office of:

Environment.—Michael C. Carter, room W28–313, 366–8887.

Safety.—Joseph A. Byrne (acting), room W21–326, 366–1931.

Security.—Owen Doherty, room W23–312, 366–1883.

Associate Administrator for Intermodal System Development.—Keith Lesnick, room W21–320, 366–4721.

Deputy.—Roger V. Bohnert, room W21–324, 366–0720.

Director, Office of:

Deepwater Ports and Offshore Activities.—Yvette Fields, room W21–310, 366–0926.

Gateway Offices.—Roger V. Bohnert, room W21–324, 366–0720.

Infrastructure Development and Congestion Mitigation.—Robert Bouchard, room W21–308, 366–5474.

Marine Highways and Passenger Services.—James D. Pugh, room W21–315, 366–5468.

Shipper and Carrier Outreach.—Richard J. Lolich, room W21–309, 366–0704.

Associate Administrator for National Security.—Kevin M. Tokarski, room W25–330, 366–5400.

Director, Office of:

Emergency Preparedness.—Thomas M.P. Christensen, room W23–304, 366–5909.

Sealift Support.—Jerome D. Davis, room W25–324, 366–6252.

Ship Disposal.—Curt J. Michanczyk, room W23–311, 366–6467.

Ship Operations.—William H. Cahill, room W23–302, 366–1875.

Associate Administrator for Business and Workforce Development.—Jean E. McKeever, room W21–318, 366–5737.

Director, Office of:

Cargo Preference and Domestic Trade.—Thomas W. Harrelson, room W23–314, 366–5515.

Financial Approvals and Marine Insurance.—Edmond J. Fitzgerald, room W23–322, 366–2279.

Chief, Division of:

Business Finance.—Gregory V. Sparkman, room W23–322, 366–1908.

Director, Office of:

Maritime Workforce Development.—Anne Dougherty, room W23–323, 366–5469.

Shipyards and Marine Finance.—Jean E. McKeever (acting), room W21–318, 366–5737.

FIELD ACTIVITIES

Director for:
North Atlantic Region.—Robert F. McKeon, 1 Bowling Green, room 418, New York, NY 10004 (212) 668–3330.
Great Lakes Region.—Floyd Miras, Suite 185, 2860 South River Road, Des Plaines, IL 60018 (847) 905–0122.
Western Region.—John Hummer, Suite 2200, 201 Mission Street, San Francisco, CA 94105 (415) 744–3125.
South Atlantic Region.—M. Nuns Jain, Building 4D, Room 211, 7737 Hampton Boulevard, Norfolk, VA 23505 (757) 441–6393.

U.S. MERCHANT MARINE ACADEMY

Superintendent.—RADM Allen Worley, Kings Point, NY 11024 (516) 773–5000.
Assistant Superintendent for Academic Affairs (Academic Dean).—Shashi N. Kumar.

NATIONAL HIGHWAY TRAFFIC SAFETY ADMINISTRATION

Administrator.—Vacant, room W42–302 (202) 366–1836.
Chief of Staff.—Vacant.
Deputy Administrator.—Ronald L. Medford (acting), 366–1836.
Executive Director, Public Affairs.—Mark Paustenbach, 366–5408.
Director of Legislative Affairs.—Will Otero, 366–2111.
Senior Associate Administrator for—
Policy and Operation.—Gregory Walter, 366–2330.
Traffic Injury Control.—Brian McLaughlin, 366–1755.
Vehicle Safety.—Ronald Medford, 366–9700.
Associate Administrator for—
Communications and Consumer Information.—Susan Gorcowski, 366–9550.
Enforcement.—Daniel C. Smith, 366–2669.
National Center for Statistics and Analysis.—Marilena Amoni, 366–1503.
Planning, Administrative and Financial Management.—Rebecca Pennington, 366–2550.
Regional Operations and Program Delivery.—Marlene Markison, 366–2121.
Research and Program Development.—Jeffrey P. Michael, 366–1755.
Rulemaking.—Stephen R. Kratzke, 366–1810.
Vehicle Safety Research Program.—John Maddox, 366–4862.
Chief Information Officer.—Colleen Coggins, 366–4878.
Director, Office of:
Civil Rights.—Rose Trujillo, 366–0972.
External Affairs.—Vacant, 366–2111.
Legislative Affairs.—Wilfred Otero, 366–2111.
Chief Counsel.—O. Kevin Vincent, 366–9511.
Director, Executive Correspondence.—Gregory Walter, 366–2330.
Supervisor, Executive Correspondence.—Bernadette Millings, 366–5470.

REGIONAL OFFICES

Region 1.—Connecticut, Maine, Massachusetts, New Hampshire, Rhode Island, Vermont.
Regional Administrator.—Philip J. Weiser, Volpe National Transportation Center, 55 Broadway, Kendall Square, Code RTV–8E, Cambridge, MA 02142 (617) 494–3427.
Region 2.—Pennsylvania, New York, New Jersey, Puerto Rico, Virgin Islands.
Regional Administrator.—Thomas M. Louizou, 222 Mamaroneck Avenue, Suite 204, White Plains, NY 10605 (914) 682–6162.
Region 3.—Delaware, District of Columbia, Maryland, Kentucky, North Carolina, Virginia, West Virginia.
Regional Administrator.—Elizabeth Baker, 10 South Howard Street, Suite 6700, Baltimore, MD 21201 (410) 962–0090.
Region 4.—Alabama, Florida, Georgia, South Carolina, Tennessee.
Regional Administrator.—Terrance D. Schiavone, Atlanta Federal Center, 61 Forsyth Street, SW., Suite 17T30, Atlanta, GA 30303–3106 (404) 562–3739.
Region 5.—Illinois, Indiana, Michigan, Minnesota, Ohio, Wisconsin.
Regional Administrator.—Michael Witter, 19900 Governors Drive, Suite 201, Olympia Fields, IL 60461 (708) 503–8892.

Region 6.—Louisiana, Mississippi, New Mexico, Oklahoma, Texas, Indian Nations.
Regional Administrator.—George S. Chakiris, 819 Taylor Street, Room 8A38, Fort Worth, TX 76102–6177 (817) 978–3653.

Region 7.—Arkansas, Iowa, Kansas, Missouri, Nebraska.
Regional Administrator.—Romell Cooks, 901 Locust Street, Room 466, Kansas City, MO 64106 (816) 329–3900.

Region 8.—Colorado, North Dakota, Nevada, South Dakota, Utah, Wyoming.
Regional Administrator.—Bill Watada, 12300 West Dakota Avenue, Suite 140, Lakewood, CO 80228–2583 (720) 963–3100.

Region 9.—American Samoa, Arizona, California, Guam, Mariana Islands, Hawaii.
Regional Administrator.—David Manning, 201 Mission Street, Suite 1600, San Francisco, CA 94105 (415) 744–3089.

Region 10.—Alaska, Idaho, Montana, Oregon, Washington.
Regional Administrator.—John Moffat, Federal Building, 915 Second Avenue, Suite 3140, Seattle, WA 98174 (206) 220–7640.

PIPELINE AND HAZARDOUS MATERIALS SAFETY ADMINISTRATION

Administrator.—Vacant, room E27–300 (202) 366–4433.
Deputy Administrator.—Cynthia Douglass (acting).
Assistant Administrator/Chief Safety Officer.—Cynthia Douglass.
Chief Counsel.—Vacant, 366–4400.
Director, Office of Civil Rights.—Helen E. Hagin, room E27–334, 366–9638.
Chief Financial Officer.—Monica Summitt, 366–4347.
Associate Administrator for—
Governmental, International and Public Affairs.—Vacant, room E27–300, 366–4831.
Hazardous Materials Safety.—Ted Willke, room E21–316, 366–0656.
Management and Administration.—Vacant, 366–4347.
Pipeline Safety.—Jeffrey Wiese, room E22–321, 366–4595.

HAZARDOUS MATERIALS SAFETY OFFICES

Chief of:
Eastern Region.—Colleen D. Abbenhaus, 820 Bear Tavern Road, Suite 306, West Trenton, NJ 08628 (609) 989–2256.
Central Region.—Kevin Boehne, Suite 478, 2350 East Devon Avenue, Des Plaines, IL 60018 (847) 294–8580.
Western Region.—Scott Simmons, 3401 Centre Lake Drive, Suite 550–B, Ontario, CA 91764 (909) 937–3279.
Southern Region.—John Heneghan, 1701 Columbia Avenue, Suite 520, College Park, GA 30337 (404) 305–6120.
Southwest Region.—Billy Hines, 2320 LaBranch Street, room 2100, Houston, TX 77004 (713) 718–3950.

PIPELINE SAFETY OFFICES

Director of:
Eastern Region.—Byron Coy, 820 Bear Tavern Road, Suite 306, West Trenton, NJ 08628 (609) 989–2277.
Central Region.—Ivan A. Huntoon, 901 Locust Street, Room 462, Kansas City, MO 64106 (816) 329–3800.
Western Region.—Chris Hoidal, 12600 West Colfax Avenue, Suite A250, Lakewood, CO 80215 (303) 231–5701.
Southwest Region.—Rodrick M. Seeley, 2320 LaBranch Street, Suite 2100, Houston, TX 77004 (713) 718–3748.
Southern Region.—Linda Daugherty, 61 Forsyth Street, Suite 6T15, Atlanta, GA 30303 (404) 562–3530.

RESEARCH AND INNOVATIVE TECHNOLOGY ADMINISTRATION (RITA)

http://www.rita.dot.gov

Deputy Administrator.—Dr. Steven K. Smith (acting), room E37–312 (202) 366–0145.

Chief Counsel.—Robert A. Monniere (acting), room E35–330, 366–5498.
Chief Financial Officer.—Katherine Montgomery, room E35–324, 366–2577.
Public Affairs Contact, Bureau of Transportation Statistics.—David Smallen, room E36–328, 366–5568.
Director for—
Governmental, International and Public Affairs.—Thomas Bolle (acting), room E36–338, 366–4792.
Intelligent Transportation Systems.—Shelly Row, room E31–304, 366–5719.
Transportation Safety Institute.—John Phillips, room MPB 348B, 6500 South MacArthur Boulevard, Oklahoma City, OK 73169 (405) 954–3153.
Volpe National Transportation Systems Center.—Dr. Richard John (acting), room 1240, 55 Broadway, Kendall Square, Cambridge, MA 02142 (617) 494–2222.

SAINT LAWRENCE SEAWAY DEVELOPMENT CORPORATION-U.S. DOT

Administrator.—Collister Johnson, Jr., room W32–300 (202) 366–0091, fax 366–7147.
Director, Office of:
Budget and Logistics.—Kevin P. O'Malley.
Congressional and Public Relations.—Nancy T. Alcalde.
Trade Development.—Rebecca McGill.

SEAWAY OPERATIONS

180 Andrews Street, P.O. Box 520, Massena, NY 13662–0520

phone (315) 764–3200, fax (315) 764–3235

Associate Administrator.—Salvatore Pisani.
Deputy Associate Administrator.—Carol A. Fenton.
Assistant.—Mary C. Fregoe.
Chief Counsel.—Carrie Mann Lavigne.
Chief Financial Officer.—Marsha Sienkiewicz (acting).
Director, Office of:
Engineering and Maintenance.—Thomas A. Lavigne.
Lock Operations and Marine Services.—Lori K. Curran.

SURFACE TRANSPORTATION BOARD

395 E Street, SW., 20423–0001, phone (202) 245–0245

http://www.stb.dot.gov

Chairman.—Francis P. Mulvey (acting), 245–0210.
Vice Chairman.—Charles D. Nottingham, 245–0200.
Commissioner.—Vacant.
Office of:
Economics, Environmental Analysis, and Administration.—Leland L. Gardner, 245–0291.
General Counsel.—Ellen D. Hanson, 245–0260.
Proceedings.—Rachel D. Campbell, 245–0350.
Public Assistance, Governmental Affairs, and Compliance.—Matthew T. Wallen, 245–0238.
Secretary.—Anne K. Quinlan, 245–0350.

DEPARTMENT OF ENERGY

James Forrestal Building, 1000 Independence Avenue, SW., 20585

phone (202) 586–5000, http://www.doe.gov

STEVEN CHU, Secretary of Energy; born on February 28, 1948, in St. Louis, MO; education: A.B., mathematics; B.S., physics, the University of Rochester, 1970; Ph.D., physics, University of California, Berkley, 1976; honorary degrees from 10 universities; professional: 1997 Nobel Prize in Physics; Director, Lawrence Berkley National Laboratory; professor, University of California, Berkley; professor, Stanford; Bell Labs; organizations: National Academy of Sciences; American Philosophical Society; Chinese Academy of Sciences; Academia Sinica; Korean Academy of Sciences; Technology and numerous other civic and professional organizations; married: Dr. Jean Chu; two children, two stepchildren, and six grandchildren; nominated by President Barack Obama to become the 12th Secretary of Energy, and was confirmed by the U.S. Senate on January 20, 2009.

OFFICE OF THE SECRETARY

Secretary of Energy.—Steven Chu (202) 586–6210.
Deputy Secretary.—Vacant, 586–5500.
Chief of Staff.—Rod O'Connor, 586–9712.
Inspector General.—Gregory H. Friedman, 586–4393.
General Counsel.—Vacant, 586–5281.
Chief Information Officer.—Thomas N. Pyke, Jr., 586–0166.
Chief Human Capital Officer.—Rita Franklin (acting), 586–5610.
Chief Financial Officer.—Steve Isakowitz, 586–4171.
Director, Office of:
Economic Impact and Diversity.—Annie Whately (acting), 586–8383.
Health, Safety and Security.—Glenn S. Podonski, 586–9275.
Hearings and Appeals.—Poli Marmolejos (acting), 287–1566.
Intelligence and Counterintelligence.—Stan Borgia, 586–2610.
Management.—Ingrid Kolb, 586–2550.
Public Affairs.—Dan Leistikow, 586–4940.
Assistant Secretary for—
Congressional and Intergovernmental Affairs.—Vacant, 586–5450.
Policy and International Affairs.—Vacant, 586–5800.
Administrator for Energy Information Administration.—Howard Gruenspecht (acting), 586–4361.

UNDER SECRETARY OF ENERGY

Under Secretary of Energy.—Vacant (202) 586–7700.
Assistant Secretary for—
Energy Efficiency and Renewable Energy.—Vacant, 586–9220.
Environmental Management.—Ines Triay (acting), 586–7709.
Fossil Energy.—Vacant, 586–6660.
Nuclear Energy.—Vacant, 586–6630.
Director, Office of:
Civilian Radioactive Waste Management.—Christopher Kouts, 586–6850.
Electricity Delivery and Energy Reliability.—Pat Hoffman, 586–1411.
Legacy Management.—David Geiser, 586–7550.

UNDER SECRETARY FOR SCIENCE

Under Secretary for Science.—Vacant (202) 586–5430.

NATIONAL NUCLEAR SECURITY ADMINISTRATION

Administrator / Under Secretary of Energy for Nuclear Security.—Thomas D'Agostino (202) 586–5555.
Deputy Administrator for—
Defense Programs.—Vacant, 586–2179.
Defense Nuclear Nonproliferation.—Kenneth Baker, 586–0645.
Naval Reactors.—ADM Kirtland Donald, USN, 781–6174.
Deputy Under Secretary for Counter-terrorism.—Dr. Steven Aoki, 586–4308.
Associate Administrator for—
Defense Nuclear Security.—Bradley Peterson, 586–8900.
Emergency Operations.—RADM Joseph Krol, USN (Ret.), 586–9892.
Infrastructure and Environment.—Thad Konopnicki, 586–7349.

MAJOR FIELD ORGANIZATIONS

OPERATIONS OFFICES

Managers:
Chicago.—Marvin Gunn.
Idaho.—Dennis M. Miotla (acting), (208) 526–5665, fax 526–0542.
Oak Ridge.—D. Booher (865) 576–4444.
Richland.—David A. Brockman (509) 376–7395.
Savannah River.—Jeffrey Allison (803) 725–2405.

SITE OFFICES

Managers:
Livermore.—Alice C. Williams (925) 422–0879.
Nevada.—Stephen A. Mellington (702) 295–3211.

NNSA SERVICE CENTER

Director, Albuquerque.—Karen L. Boardman (505) 845–6050.

FIELD OFFICE

Manager, Golden.—Rita L. Wells (303) 275–4792.

POWER MARKETING ADMINISTRATIONS

Administrator, Power Administration:
Bonneville.—Stephen J. Wright (503) 230–5101, fax 230–4018.
Southeastern Area.—Kenneth Legg (706) 213–3805.
Southwestern Area.—Jon C. Worthington (918) 595–6601.
Western Area.—Timothy J. Meeks (720) 962–7077.

OFFICE OF SCIENTIFIC AND TECHNICAL INFORMATION

Director.—Walter L. Warnick (301) 903–7996, fax 903–8972.

NAVAL REACTORS OFFICES

Manager.—Henry A. Cardinali (518) 395–4690.
Deputy Manager.—Matthew J. Brott (412) 476–7251.

OFFICE OF CIVILIAN RADIOACTIVE WASTE MANAGEMENT

Washington, DC.—Christopher A. Kouts (202) 586–6850.

FOSSIL ENERGY FIELD OFFICES

Director, National Energy Technology Lab.—Carl O. Bauer (304) 285–4511.
Project Manager, Strategic Petroleum Reserve Project Office.—William C. Gibson Jr. (504) 734–4201.

NAVAL PETROLEUM RESERVES

Director, Colorado, Utah, Wyoming (Oil Shale Reserves).—Clarke D. Turner (307) 233–4848.

FEDERAL ENERGY REGULATORY COMMISSION

888 First Street, NE., 20426

Chair.—Jon Wellinghoff (202) 502–6580.
Commissioners:
Suedeen G. Kelly, 502–6501.
Philip D. Moeller, 502–8852.
Marc Spitzer, 502–8366.
Deputy Chief Administrative Law Judge.—Curtis L. Wagner, Jr., 502–8300.
Executive Director.—Thomas R. Herlihy, 502–8300.
General Counsel.—Cynthia Marlette, 502–6000.
Director, Office of:
Administrative Litigation.—Richard Miles, 502–8700.
Electric Reliability.—Joseph McClelland, 502–8600.
Energy Projects.—Jeff Wright, 502–8162.
Enforcement.—Susan Court, 502–8183.
External Affairs.—Pat Schaub (acting), 502–8616.

DEPARTMENT OF EDUCATION

400 Maryland Avenue, SW., 20202

phone (202) 401–3000, fax 401–0596, http://www.ed.gov

ARNE DUNCAN, Secretary of Education; born in Chicago, IL, November 6, 1964; children: Clare and Ryan; education: B.A., Harvard University, *magna cum laude*, 1987; professional: professional basketball player in Australia, 1987–91; Director of Ariel Education Initiative, 1992–98; Deputy Chief of Staff to the Chief Executive Officer of the Chicago Public Schools, 1999–2001; Chief Executive Officer of the Chicago Public Schools, 2001–09; nominated by President Barack Obama to become the 9th Secretary of Education on December 16, 2008; confirmed on January 20, 2009.

OFFICE OF THE SECRETARY

Room 7W301, phone (202) 401–3000, fax 260–7867

Secretary of Education.—Arne Duncan.
Chief of Staff.—Margot Rogers.
Deputy Chief of Staff.—Matt Yale.

OFFICE OF THE DEPUTY SECRETARY

Room 7W308, phone 401–1000

Deputy Secretary.—Vacant.
Chief of Staff.—Vacant.

OFFICE OF THE UNDER SECRETARY

Room 7E307, phone (202) 401–0429

Under Secretary.—Vacant.
Chief of Staff.—Vacant.

OFFICE OF THE CHIEF FINANCIAL OFFICER

LBJ 400 Maryland Avenue, SW., phone (202) 401–0085, fax 401–0006

Chief Financial Officer.—Thomas Skelly (acting), LBJ, room 4E313, 401–0287.
Deputy Chief Financial Officer.—Danny A. Harris, Ph.D., LBJ, room 4E314, 401–0896.
Executive Officer.—Michael Holloway, LBJ, room 4E231, 401–0322.
Director of:
Contracts and Acquisitions Management.—Hugh Hurwitz, PCP, room 7153, 550 12th Street, SW., 20202, 245–6555.
Financial Improvement and Post Audit Operations.—Linda Stracke, UCP, room 21A5, 830 First Street, NE., 377–3301.
Financial Management Operations.—Gary Wood, LBJ, room 4W122, 401–0862.

OFFICE OF THE CHIEF INFORMATION OFFICER

PCP 550 12th Street, SW., phone (202) 245–6400, fax 245–6621

Chief Information Officer.—Danny Harris, PCP, room 9112, 245–0896.

Deputy Chief Information Officer.—Brian Burns, PCP, room 9149, 245–6642.
Executive Officer.—Michael Holloway, LBJ, room 4E231, 401–0322.
Director of:
Financial Systems Services.—Constance Davis, LBJ, room 4E230, 401–3892.
Information Assurance Services.—Vacant, PCP, room 9150, 245–6069.
Information Technology Program Services.—Ken Moore, PCP, room 9168, 245–6908.
Information Technology Services.—Lisa Mendis, PCP, room 9151, 245–6153.

OFFICE OF MANAGEMENT

Room 2W301, phone (202) 401–5848, fax 260–3761

Assistant Secretary.—JoAnn Ryan, room 2W311, 401–5848, fax 260–3761.
Deputy Assistant Secretary.—Vacant.
Chief of Staff.—Donna Butler, room 2W309, 401–8530.
Executive Officer.—David Cogdill, room 2W227, 401–0695, fax 401–3513.
Service Director of:
Equal Employment Opportunity Services.—Vacant.
Facilities and Management Services.—Victoria Bateman, room 2E315, 260–8267, fax 401–0994.
Human Resources Services.—Vacant.
Office of Hearings and Appeals.—Frank J. Furey, L'Enfant Plaza–2134, 619–9701, fax 619–9726.
Regulatory Information Management Services.—Leo Eiden, room 2W226, 401–0544, fax 401–0920.
Security Services.—Winona Varnon, room 2W330, 401–1583, fax 260–3761.

OFFICE FOR CIVIL RIGHTS

550 12th Street, SW., Room 5000, 20202–1100, phone (202) 245–6800, fax 245–6840 or 6844

Assistant Secretary.—Russlynn Ali.
Deputy Assistant Secretary for Enforcement.—Dianne Piché, room 6090, 245–6700.
Confidential Assistant.—Michael Lamb, room 6099, 245–6700.
Director of:
Enforcement, East/Midwest.—Randolph Wills, room 6089, 245–6700.
Enforcement, South/West.—Cynthia Pierre, room 6094, 245–6700.
Deputy Assistant Secretary for Policy.—Vacant.
Program Legal Group.—Sandra Battle, room 6125, 245–6767.
Resource Management Group.—Lester Slayton, room 6117, 245–6700.

OFFICE OF COMMUNICATIONS AND OUTREACH

Room 5E300, phone (202) 401–0404, fax 401–8607

Assistant Secretary.—Peter Cunningham, room 7W101, LBJ, 401–2563.
Press Secretary.—John White, room 7E203, LBJ, 401–8459.
Deputy Assistant Secretaries:
Communication Development.—David Hoff, room 7W103, LBJ, 401–6359.
Communication Services.—John McGrath, room 5E231, LBJ, 401–1309.
External Affairs/Outreach.—Massie Ritsch, room 5E330, LBJ, 260–2671.

OFFICE OF ELEMENTARY AND SECONDARY EDUCATION

Room 3W300, phone (202) 401–0113, fax 205–0303

Assistant Secretary.—Joseph Conaty (acting), room 3W315, 401–0113.
Deputy Assistant Secretary.—Vacant.
Chief of Staff.—Vacant.
Deputy Assistant Secretary for Policy and Strategic Initiatives.—Vacant.
Deputy Assistant Secretary for Management.—Alex Goniprow, room 3W314, 401–9090.
Executive Director, White House Initiative on Educational Excellence for Hispanic Americans.—Glorimar Nosal (acting), room 5E335, 401–0078.

Director of:

Academic Improvement and Teacher Quality Programs.—Joseph Conaty, room 3E314, 260–8228, fax 260–8969.

Impact Aid Programs.—Catherine Schagh, room 3E105, 260–3858, fax 205–0088.

Office of Indian Education.—Cathie Carothers, room 3E121, 205–0687.

Office of Migrant Education.—Lisa Ramirez, room 3E317, 260–1127, fax 205–0089.

School Support and Technology Programs.—Jenelle Leonard, room 3W203, 401–3641.

Student Achievement and School Accountability Programs.—Zollie Stevenson, Jr., room 3W230, 206–0826.

OFFICE OF ENGLISH LANGUAGE ACQUISITION

400 Maryland Avenue, SW., 5C–132, 20202, phone (202) 401–4300, fax 401–8452

Assistant Deputy Secretary and Director.—Richard Smith (acting).

Deputy of Policy.—Vacant.

Chief of Staff.—Richard L. Smith.

OFFICE OF FEDERAL STUDENT AID

830 First Street, NE., 20202, phone (202) 377–3000, fax 275–5000

Chief Operating Officer.—James F. Manning (acting).

Deputy Chief Operating Officer.—James F. Manning.

Ombudsman.—Debra Wiley, room 41I1, 377–3801.

Chief of:

Business Operations Officer.—Sue Szabo, room 83E3, 377–3437.

Communications Officer.—Christopher B. Greene, room 114F1, 377–4003.

Compliance Officer.—Victoria Edwards, room 81K2, 377–4273.

Financial Officer.—Jay Hurt, room 54E1, 377–3453.

Information Officer.—John Fare, room 91J1, 377–3707.

Director, Policy Liaison and Implementation Staff.—Jeff Baker, room 113C1, 377–4009.

Program Manager of Administration Services.—Barbara L. Malebranche, room L113, 377–3126.

General Manager of:

Enterprise Performance Management Services.—Linda Hall (acting), room 94F2, 377–3382.

Student Awareness and Applicant Services.—Jennifer Douglas, room 32E4, 377–3201.

OFFICE OF THE GENERAL COUNSEL

Room 6E301, phone (202) 401–6000, fax 205–2689

General Counsel.—Charles P. Rose.

Senior Counsel.—Robert Wexler.

Chief of Staff.—Robert Wexler (acting).

Executive Officer.—J. Carolyn Adams, 401–8340.

Deputy General Counsel for—

Departmental and Legislative Service.—Vacant.

Postsecondary and Regulatory Service.—Vacant.

Program Service.—Philip Rosenfelt.

OFFICE OF INNOVATION AND IMPROVEMENT

phone (202) 205–4500

Assistant Deputy Secretary.—James Shelton, 401–0479.

Associate Assistant Deputy Secretary.—Margo Anderson.

Chief of Staff.—Vacant.

OFFICE OF INSPECTOR GENERAL

Potomac Center Plaza (PCP), 8th Floor, 20024, phone (202) 245–6900, fax 245–6993

Inspector General.—John P. Higgins, Jr.
Deputy Inspector General.—Mary Mitchelson.
Counsel to the Inspector General.—Mary Mitchelson.
Assistant Inspector General for—
Audit Services.—Helen Lew, 245–7050.
Cyber Audit and Computer Crime Investigations.—Charles E. Coe, 245–7034.

INTERNATIONAL AFFAIRS OFFICE

Room 6W108, phone (202) 401–0430, fax 401–2508

Director.—JoAnne Livingston (acting).
Asia/Pacific, International Education Week.—JoAnne Livingston.
International Visitors, Special Education.—Sambia Shivers-Barclay.
USNEI, Visas and Mobility, Higher Education, Trade, OECD, Europe.—E. Stephen Hunt.
Western Hemisphere, Organization of American States (OAS).—Rafael Nevarez.
Staff Assistant/Official Passports and Visas.—Mone't Peterson-Cox.

INSTITUTE OF EDUCATION SCIENCES

555 New Jersey Avenue, NW., Room 600, 20208, phone (202) 219–1385, fax 219–1466

Director.—Sue Betka (acting), 219–1385.
Deputy Director for—
Administration and Policy.—Sue Betka.
Science.—Anne Riccuiti, 219–2247.
National Center for Education Statistics.—Stuart Kerachsky (acting), 502–7442.
National Center for Education Research.—Lynn Okagaki, 219–2006.
National Center for Education Evaluation and Regional Assistance.—Phoebe Cottingham, 219–2484.
National Center for Special Education Research.—Lynn Okagaki (acting), 219–2006.

OFFICE OF LEGISLATION AND CONGRESSIONAL AFFAIRS

Room 6W301, phone (202) 401–0020, fax 401–1438

Assistant Secretary.—Gabriella Gomez, 401–0020.
Deputy Assistant Secretary.—J. Lloyd Horwich.
Special Assistant.—Jodie Fingland, 401–1043.
Confidential Assistants: Kristen Adams, 260–1446; William Ragland, 401–0029.

OFFICE OF PLANNING, EVALUATION AND POLICY DEVELOPMENT

Room 5E301, phone (202) 401–0831, fax 401–8607

Assistant Secretary.—Carmel Martin, room 5E313.
Deputy Assistant Secretaries: Judy Wurtzel, room 5E311; Emma Vadehra, room 5E327.
Executive Officer.—JoAnn Ryan, room 7E103, 401–3082, fax 205–0723.
Director of:
Budget Service.—Thomas Skelly, room 5W313, 401–0281, fax 401–6139.
Performance Information Management Service.—Ross C. Santy, room 5E309, 401–3554.
Policy and Program Studies Service.—Alan Ginsburg, room 6W230, 401–3132, fax 401–3036.

OFFICE OF POSTSECONDARY EDUCATION

1990 K Street, NW., 20006, phone (202) 502–7750, fax 502–7677

Assistant Secretary.—Dan Madzelan.
Chief of Staff.—Francine Picoult (acting).

Deputy Assistant Secretary for Higher Education Programs.—Vickie Sehray (acting), 502–7555.
Deputy Assistant Secretary for Policy, Planning and Innovation.—Vacant.
Executive Director for—
White House Initiative on Historically Black Colleges and Universities.—Leonard Haynes (acting), suite 6107, 502–7900.
White House Initiative on Tribal Colleges and Universities.—Alan Schiff (acting), room 7010, 219–7040.

OFFICE OF SAFE AND DRUG-FREE SCHOOLS

Room 1E110, phone (202) 245–7896, fax 245–7168

Assistant Deputy Secretary.—Bill Modzeleski (acting), room 10089, 245–7831.
Associate Assistant Deputy Secretary.—Bill Modzeleski.

OFFICE OF SPECIAL EDUCATION AND REHABILITATIVE SERVICES

Potomac Center Plaza (PCP), 550 12th Street, SW., 5th Floor, 20202

phone (202) 245–7468, fax 245–7636

Assistant Secretary.—Andrew J. Pepin (acting).
Executive Administrator.—Andrew J. Pepin, room 5106, 245–7632.
Director of:
National Institute on Disability and Rehabilitation Research.—Ruth Brannon (acting), 245–7640.
Office of Special Education Programs.—Patricia Guard (acting).
Commissioner of the Rehabilitation Services Administration.—Edward Anthony (acting).

OFFICE OF VOCATIONAL AND ADULT EDUCATION

550 12th Street, SW., Room 1100, 20202, phone (202) 245–7700, fax 245–7171

Assistant Secretary.—Vacant.
Chief of Staff.—Vacant.
Deputy Assistant Secretary.—Vacant.
Staff Assistant.—Vacant.

DEPARTMENT OF VETERANS AFFAIRS

Mail should be addressed to 810 Vermont Avenue, NW., Washington, DC 20420
http://www.va.gov

ERIC K. SHINSEKI, Secretary of Veterans Affairs; education: graduated, U.S. Military Academy, West Point, NY, 1965; M.A., Duke University; graduated, National War College; military service: Chief of Staff, U.S. Army, 1999–2003; Vice Chief of Staff, U.S. Army, 1998–99; Commanding General, United States Army, Europe and Seventh Army; Commanding General NATO Land Forces, Central Europe; Commander NATO-led Stabilization Force, Bosnia-Herzegovina; Vietnam War Veteran; military awards: Defense Distinguished Service Medal, Distinguished Service Medal, Legion of Merit (with Oak Leaf Clusters), Bronze Star Medal with "V" Device (with 2 Oak Leaf Clusters), Purple Heart (with Oak Leaf Cluster), Defense Meritorious Service Medal, Meritorious Service Medal (with 2 Oak Leaf Clusters), Air Medal, Parachutist Badge, Ranger Tab, Joint Chiefs of Staff Identification Badge, and Army Staff Identification Badge; married: Patricia; two children; nominated by President Barack Obama to become 7th Secretary of Veterans Affairs, and was confirmed by the U.S. Senate on January 21, 2009.

OFFICE OF THE SECRETARY

Secretary of Veterans Affairs.—Eric K. Shinseki (202) 461–4800.
Deputy Secretary of Veterans Affairs.—W. Scott Gould, 461–4800.
Chief of Staff.—John R. Gingrich, 461–4800.
Deputy Chief of Staff.—Michael Cardarelli, 461–4808.
Senior Advisor to the Secretary.—John Spinelli, 461–4874.
Special Assistant for Veterans Service Organizations Liaison.—Kevin S. Secor, 461–4835.
Executive Secretary.—Kenneth Greenberg, 461–4869.
Director, Center for—
Faith-Based Community Initiative.—Stephen Dillard (acting), 461–7604.
Minority Veterans.—Lucretia McClenney, 461–6191.
Women Veterans.—Irene Trowell-Harris, Ed.D., RN, 461–6193.
Employment Discrimination Complaint Adjudication.—Rafael Torres (acting), 1722 I Street, NW., 461–1650.
Small and Disadvantaged Business Utilization.—Gail Wegner (acting), 801 I Street, NW., 461–4300.

BOARD OF VETERANS' APPEALS

Chairman.—James P. Terry, 811 Vermont Avenue, NW. (202) 461–8001.
Vice Chairman.—Steve Keller.

OFFICE OF GENERAL COUNSEL

General Counsel.—Will A. Gunn (202) 461–4995.
Deputy General Counsel.—John "Jack" Thompson, 461–4995.

OFFICE OF INSPECTOR GENERAL

Inspector General.—George J. Opfer, 801 I Street, NW. (202) 461–4720.
Deputy Inspector General.—Richard J. Griffin.

OFFICE OF ACQUISITIONS, LOGISTICS, AND CONSTRUCTION

Executive Director.—Glenn D. Haggstrom, 811 Vermont Avenue, NW. (202) 461–8007.
Deputy Assistant Secretary.—Jan R. Frye.
Director, Office of Construction and Facilities Management.—Donald H. Orndoff, 811 Vermont Avenue, NW., 461–8009.

ASSISTANT SECRETARY FOR CONGRESSIONAL AND LEGISLATIVE AFFAIRS

Assistant Secretary.—Danny Devine (acting), (202) 461–6491.
Executive Assistant.—Mary Kay Stack, 461–6490.
Deputy Assistant Secretary.—Danny Devine, 461–6490.
Legislative Advisor.—Charles Likel, 461–6491.
Director for—
Congressional and Legislative Affairs.—Len Sistek, 461–6492.
Congressional Liaison.—Patricia Covington, 224–5351 or 225–2280.
Congressional Reports and Correspondence.—Judith Sterne, 461–6493.

ASSISTANT SECRETARY FOR PUBLIC AND INTERGOVERNMENTAL AFFAIRS

Assistant Secretary.—L. Tammy Duckworth (202) 461–7500.
Deputy Assistant Secretary for—
Intergovernmental and International Affairs.—Emily Smith, 461–7400.
Public Affairs.—Vacant.

ASSISTANT SECRETARY FOR POLICY AND PLANNING

Assistant Secretary.—Karen W. Pane (acting), (202) 461–5800.
Principal Deputy Assistant Secretary.—Karen W. Pane, 461–5800.
Deputy Assistant Secretary for—
Planning and Evaluation.—Julie Anderson, 461–4817.
Policy.—Mark Gorenflo, 461–5762.

ASSISTANT SECRETARY FOR OPERATIONS, SECURITY AND PREPAREDNESS

Assistant Secretary.—Jose D. Riojas (202) 461–4980.
Deputy Assistant Secretary for—
Emergency Management.—Kevin Hanretta, 461–4985.
Security and Law Enforcement.—Frederick R. Jackson, 461–6920.

ASSISTANT SECRETARY FOR MANAGEMENT

Assistant Secretary/Chief Financial Officer.—Rita Reed (acting), (202) 461–6600.
Principal Deputy Assistant Secretary.—Rita A. Reed, 461–6703.
Deputy Assistant Secretary for—
Budget.—Daniel A. Tucker, 461–6630.
Finance.—Edward J. Murray, 461–6180.

ASSISTANT SECRETARY FOR INFORMATION AND TECHNOLOGY

Assistant Secretary.—Roger W. Baker (202) 462–6910.
Principal Deputy Assistant Secretary.—Stephen W. Warren, 461–6910.

ASSISTANT SECRETARY FOR HUMAN RESOURCES AND ADMINISTRATION

Assistant Secretary.—John U. Sepúlveda (202) 461–7750.
Principal Deputy Assistant Secretary.—Willie L. Hensley, 461–7750.
Deputy Assistant Secretary for—
Administration.—C.G. ''Deno'' Verenes, 461–5000.
Diversity Management and Inclusion.—Georgia Coffey, 1575 I Street, NW., 461–4131.
Human Resources Management.—Vicki Brooks, 461–7765.
Labor-Management Relations.—Vacant, 461–4119.
Resolution Management.—Rafael Torres, 1575 I Street, NW., 501–2800.

NATIONAL CEMETERY ADMINISTRATION

Under Secretary for Memorial Affairs.—Steve L. Muro (acting), (202) 461–6112.

Deputy Under Secretary.—Steve L. Muro, 461–6013.
Executive Assistant.—George Eisenbach, 461–6014.
Director of:
Communications Management Service.—Dave Schettler, 461–6234.
Construction Management.—Fred Neun, 461–8919.
Field Programs.—Patrick Hallinan, 461–6071.
Finance and Planning.—Ronald Walters, 461–6510.
Management Support Service.—Vacant, 461–6220.
Memorial Programs Service.—Don Murphy (acting), 501–3100.
State Cemetery Grants Service.—Frank Salvas, 461–8947.

VETERANS BENEFITS ADMINISTRATION

Under Secretary.—Adm. Patrick Dunne, 1800 G Street, NW. (202) 461–9300.
Deputy Under Secretary.—Mike Walcoff.
Chief of Staff.—Lois Mittelstaedt.
Associate Deputy Under Secretary for—
Field Operations.—Diana Rubens, 461–9340.
Policy and Program Management.—Vacant, 461–9320.
Management.—Geraldine Breakfield, 461–9412.
Chief Financial Officer.—Jimmy Norris, 461–9900.
Director of:
Education.—Keith M. Wilson, 461–9800.
Employee Development and Training.—Vacant, 461–9867.
Insurance.—Thomas Lastowka (215) 381–3100.
Loan Guaranty.—Mark Bologna, 461–9500.
Vocational Rehabilitation and Employment.—Ruth Fanning, 461–9333.

VETERANS HEALTH ADMINISTRATION

Under Secretary.—Gerald M. Cross, M.D., FAAFP (acting), (202) 461–7000.
Principal Deputy Under Secretary for Health.—Robert A. Petzel, M.D., (acting) 461–7008.
Deputy Under Secretary for Health for Operations and Management.—Joseph A. Williams, Jr., RN, BSN, MPM (acting), 461–7026.
Chief of Staff.—Ann C. Patterson (acting), 461–7016.
Assistant Deputy Under Secretary for—
Health for Clinical and Organizational Support.—Laura O'Grady, RN, MSN, 461–7008.
Health for Policy and Planning.—Patricia Vandenberg, MHA, BSN, 461–7100.
Associate Deputy Under Secretary for Health for Quality and Safety.—William E. Duncan, M.D., Ph.D., MACP, 461–7254.
Medical Inspector.—John Pierce, M.D., 1575 I Street, NW., 501–2000.
Executive Director, Federal Recovery Program.—Karen Guice, M.D., M.P.P., 461–4839.
Chief Officer for—
Academic Affiliations.—Malcolm Cox, M.D., 461–9490.
Business.—Gary M. Baker, 461–1600.
Communications.—Vacant.
Compliance and Business Integrity.—Caitlin O'Brien, 1575 I Street, NW., 501–0364.
Employee Education System.—Joy W. Hunter, 461–4076.
Ethics in Health Care.—Ellen Fox, M.D., 1575 I Street, NW., 501–0364.
Financial.—W. Paul Kearns III, FACHE, FHFMA, CPA, 461–6666.
Health Information.—Craig B. Luigart, 461–5848.
Nursing.—Cathy Rick, RN, CNAA, FACHE, 461–6962.
Patient Care Services.—Madhulika Agarwal, M.D., M.P.H., 461–7590.
Patient Safety.—James P. Bagian, M.D., PE (734) 930–5920.
Procurement and Logistics.—Frederick Downs, Jr., 461–1770.
Public Health and Environmental Hazards.—Lawrence Deyton, MSPH, M.D., 461–7200.
Quality and Performance.—Joseph Francis, M.D., M.P.H. (acting), 1717 H Street, NW., 266–4533.
Readjustment Counseling.—Alfonso R. Batres, Ph.D., M.S.S.W., 461–6525.
Research and Development.—Joel Kupersmith, M.D., 461–1700.
Research Oversight.—J. Thomas Puglisi, Ph.D., CIP, 1717 H Street, NW., 266–4580.

DEPARTMENT OF HOMELAND SECURITY

U.S. Naval Security Station, 3801 Nebraska Avenue, NW., 20393

phone (202) 282–8000

JANET NAPOLITANO, Secretary of Homeland Security; born on November 29, 1957, in New York City, NY; education: graduated from Santa Clara University in 1979, where she won a Truman Scholarship and received her Juris Doctor (J.D.) in 1983 from the University of Virginia School of Law; public service: Prior to joining the Obama Administration, Napolitano was mid-way through her second term as Governor of the State of Arizona. While Governor, Napolitano was the first woman to chair the National Governors Association where she was instrumental in creating the Public Safety Task Force and the Homeland Security Advisors Council. She also chaired the Western Governors Association. Napolitano previously served as the Attorney General of Arizona and the U.S. Attorney for the District of Arizona; nominated by President Barak Obama to become the 3rd Secretary of Homeland Security on December 1, 2008, and was confirmed by the U.S. Senate on January 20, 2009. Janet Napolitano was sworn in January 21, 2009, as the 3rd Secretary of the Department of Homeland Security.

OFFICE OF THE SECRETARY

Secretary of Homeland Security.—Janet Napolitano.
Deputy Secretary of Homeland Security.—Jane Holl Lute.
Chief of Staff for Policy.—Noah Kroloff.
Chief of Staff for Operations.—Jan Lesher.

CITIZENSHIP AND IMMIGRATION SERVICES OMBUDSMAN

Ombudsman.—Richard Flowers (acting).

CIVIL RIGHTS AND CIVIL LIBERTIES

phone (202) 401–1474, Toll Free: 1–866–644–8360

Officer for Civil Rights and Civil Liberties.—Timothy Keefer (acting).

OFFICE OF COUNTERNARCOTICS ENFORCEMENT

Director.—John Leech (acting).

EXECUTIVE SECRETARIAT

Executive Secretary.—Philip McNamara.

OFFICE OF THE FEDERAL COORDINATOR FOR GULF COAST REBUILDING

Federal Coordinator.—Janet Woodka.

OFFICE OF THE GENERAL COUNSEL

General Counsel.—Ivan K. Fong.

OFFICE OF INSPECTOR GENERAL

phone (202) 254–4100

Inspector General.—Richard L. Skinner.
Principal Deputy Inspector General.—James L. Taylor.
Deputy Inspector General for Disaster Assistance Oversight.—Matthew Jadacki.
General Counsel to the Inspector General.—Richard N. Reback.
Assistant Inspector General for—
Administration.—Charles Edwards.
Audits.—Anne Richards.
Information Technology.—Frank Deffer.
Inspections.—Carlton I. Mann.
Investigations.—Thomas Frost.
Director, Congressional and Media Affair.—Marta Metelko.
Executive Assistant to the Inspector General.—Denise S. Johnson.

OFFICE OF INTELLIGENCE AND ANALYSIS

Chief Intelligence Officer.—Bart Johnson (acting).

OFFICE OF LEGISLATIVE AND INTERGOVERNMENTAL AFFAIRS

phone (202) 447–5890

Assistant Secretary.—Chani Wiggins.
Deputy Assistant Secretaries: Nelson Peacock, Sue Ramanathan.

MILITARY ADVISOR'S OFFICE

Senior Military Advisor to the Secretary.—RADM Charlie Ray.

PRIVACY OFFICE

phone (571) 227–3813

Chief Privacy Officer.—Mary Ellen Challahan.

OFFICE OF PUBLIC AFFAIRS

Deputy Assistant Secretary.—Sean Smith.

NATIONAL PROTECTION AND PROGRAMS DIRECTORATE

phone (202) 282–8400

Under Secretary.—Rand Beers.
Deputy Under Secretary.—Philip Reitinger.
Chief of Staff.—Anthony Molet (acting).
Chief Operating Officer.—Dallas Brown.
Assistant Secretary for—
Cybersecurity and Communications.—Gregory Schaffer.
Deputy Infrastructure Protection.—James Snyder.
Intergovernmental Programs.—Juliette Kayyem.
Director for—
Risk Management and Analysis.—Tina Gabbrielli.
United States Visitor and Immigrant Status Indicator Technology.—Robert Mocny.

SCIENCE AND TECHNOLOGY DIRECTORATE

Under Secretary.—Bradley Buswell (acting).
Deputy Under Secretary.—Bradley Buswell.
Chief of Staff.—Vacant.

Division Head of:
Border and Maritime Security Division.—Anh Duong.
Chemical and Biological Division.—Dr. Elizabeth George.
Command, Control, and Interoperability Division.—Dr. David Boyd.
Explosives Division.—James Tuttle.
Human Factors Division.—Dr. Sharla Rausch.
Infrastructure/Geophysical Division.—Chirs Doyle.
Director of:
International Cooperative Programs Office.—Lilia Ramirez.
Test and Evaluation and Standards Division.—Gary Carter.
Interagency and First Responders Programs Division.—Randy Zeller.

MANAGEMENT DIRECTORATE

Under Secretary.—Elaine C. Duke.
Deputy Under Secretary.—Sharie Bourbeau.
Chief Administrative Services Officer.—Donald Bathurst.
Chief Financial Officer.—Peggy Sherry (acting).
Chief Human Capital Officer.—Jeff Neal.
Chief Information Officer.—Margie Graves (acting).
Chief Procurement Officer.—Richard Gunderson (acting).
Chief Security Officer.—Jerry Williams.

OFFICE OF POLICY DIRECTORATE

Assistant Secretary.—David Heyman.
Deputy Assistant Secretary, Office of:
Immigration and Border Security.—Esther Olavarria.
Screening Coordination.—Kathy Kraninger.
Strategic Plans.—Alan Cohn.
Assistant Secretary, Office of:
International Affairs.—Alan Bersin.
Policy Development.—Arif Alikhan.
Private Sector.—Bridger McGaw (acting).
State and Local Law Enforcement.—Ted Sexton.
Director, Office of Immigration Statistics.—Michael Hoefer.
Chair, Homeland Security Advisory Council.—Becca Sharp.

FEDERAL EMERGENCY MANAGEMENT (FEMA) DIRECTORATE

500 C Street, SW., 20472, phone (202) 646–2500

Administrator.—W. Craig Fugate.
Deputy Administrator.—David Garratt (acting).
Director of Louisiana Transitional Recovery Office.—Tony Russell (acting).
Chief of Staff.—Jason McNamara.
Chief Financial Officer.—Norman Dong.
Chief Administrative Services Officer.—Thomas R. McQuillan.
Director Information Technology.—Jeanne Etzel.
Chief Counsel.—David A. Trissell.
Counselor to the Administrator and the Deputy Administrator.—Michael Coen.
Superintendent, Emergency Management Institute.—Dr. Cortez Lawrence.
Superintendent, United States Fire Administration.—Dr. Denis Onieal.
Executive Secretary.—Elizabeth Edge.
Office of:
Equal Rights.—Pauline Campbell.
External Affairs.—Brent Colburn.
Human Capital.—James Vincent (acting).
Intergovernmental Affairs.—Allison Schwartz.
International Affairs.—Carole Cameron (acting).
Legislative Affairs.—Pat Hart.
Policy and Program Analysis.—Robert Farmer (acting).
Assistant Administrators:
Disaster Assistance Directorate.—Elizabeth A. Zimmerman.
Disaster Operations Directorate.—William L. Carwile III.

Management.—Albet Sligh.
Mitigation and Federall Insurance Administrator.—Edward Connor (acting).
National Continuity Programs.—Patricia A. Buckingham (acting).

OFFICE OF OPERATIONS COORDINATION

phone (202) 282–9580

Director.—RAMD John Acton.
Deputy Director.—Robert Cohen.
Chief of Staff.—Mary Kruger.

DOMESTIC NUCLEAR DETECTION OFFICE

phone (202) 254–7320

Director.—Dr. Charles Gallaway (acting).
Assistant Director, Office of:
Mission Management.—Huban Gowadia.
National Technical Nuclear Forensics Center.—William Daitch.
Operations Support.—Jay Manning.
Product Acquisition and Deployment.—Ernest Muenchau.
Systems Architecture.—John Zabko (acting).
Systems Engineering and Evaluation.—Julian Hill.
Transformational Research and Development.—William Hagan.

TRANSPORTATION SECURITY ADMINISTRATION (TSA)

601 South 12th Street, Arlington, VA 22202–4220

Assistant Secretary.—Gale Rossides (acting).
Deputy Assistant Secretary.—Keith Kauffman (acting).
Chief of Staff.—Art Mcias.

UNITED STATES CUSTOMS AND BORDER PROTECTION (CBP)

1300 Pennsylvania Avenue, NW., 20229

Commissioner.—Jayson P. Ahern (acting), (202) 344–1010 / 344–2001.
Chief of Staff.—Marco A. Lopez, 344–1080.
Deputy Chief of Staff.—Anne Marie Stacey, 344–1080 / 344–2001.
Chief Counsel.—Alfonso Robles, 344–2990.
Equal Employment Opportunity.—Franklin C. Jones, 344–1610.
Director, Office of:
Intelligence.—Rodney A. Snyder, 344–1150.
Policy and Planning.—David Pagan (acting), 344–2700.
Secure Border Initiative.—Mark Borkowski, 344–2450.
Chief, Office of Border Patrol.—David V. Aguilar, 344–2050.
Assistant Commissioner, Office of:
CBP Air and Marine.—Michael C. Kostelnik, 344–3950.
Congressional Affairs.—Seth Statler, 344–1760.
Field Operations.—Tom Winkowski, 344–1620.
Finance.—Eugene H. Schied, 344–2300.
Human Resources Management.—Christine Gaugler, 863–6100.
Information and Technology.—Charles A. Armstrong, 344–1680.
Internal Affairs.—James F. Tomsheck, 344–1800.
International Affairs and Trade Relations.—Allen Gina, 344–3000.
International Trade.—Daniel Baldwin, 863–6000.
Public Affairs.—Bob Jacksta (acting), 344–1700.
Training and Development.—Patricia Duffy, 344–1130.

UNITED STATES IMMIGRATION AND CUSTOMS ENFORCEMENT (ICE)

Assistant Secretary.—John Morton (202) 732–3000.
Senior Counselor.—Beth Gibson.

Chief of Staff.—Suzanne Barr.
Principal Legal Advisor.—Peter Vincent, 732–5000.
Policy.—Susan Cullen, 732–4292.
Professional Responsibility.—Timothy Moynihan (acting), 732–8339.
Congressional Relations.—Judy Rogers (acting), 732–4200.
Public Affairs.—Kelly Nantel (acting), 732–4242.
Executive Secretariat and Information Management.—Deborah Neve, 732–6161.
Audit Liaison.—Robert DeAntonio, 732–4284.
Privacy Officer.—Lyn Rahilly, 732–3300.
Deputy Assistant Secretary for Operations.—John Torres, 732–3000.
Chief of Staff.—David Shaw, 732–3000
Federal Protective Service.—Gary Schenkel, 732–8000.
Detention and Removal Operations.—James Hayes, 732–3100.
Intelligence.—Susan Lane, 732–5248.
International Affairs.—Raymond Parmer, 732–0350.
Investigations.—Marcy Forman, 732–5100.
National Firearms and Tactical Training Unit.—Humberto Medina, 732–3937.
National Response.—Sharon Peyus (acting), 732–5303.
Reporting and Operations Center.—David Fisher (acting), 732–5200.
Secure Communities.—David Venturella, 732–3900.
State, Local and Tribal Coordination.—William Riley (acting), 732–5050.
Deputy Assistant Secretary for Management.—Theresa C. Bertucci, 732–3000.
Chief of Staff.—Tammy Meckley, 732–3000.
Acquisition Management.—Ashley Lewis, 732–2600.
Chief:
Diversity Officer.—Deborah Lewis, 732–7700.
Financial Officer.—Alexander Keenan, 732–3075.
Information Officer.—Luke McCormack, 732–2000.
Freedom of Information Act.—Catrina Pavlik Keenan, 732–0300.
Human Capital Officer.—Robert Parsons, 732–7770.
Training and Development.—Charles DeVita, 732–7800.

FEDERAL LAW ENFORCEMENT TRAINING CENTER

1131 Chapel Crossing Road, Glynco, GA 31524

Director.—Connie L. Patrick (912) 267–2070.
Deputy Director.—Ken Keene, 267–2680.
Senior Associate Director, Washington Operations.—John Dooher (202) 233–0260.
Assistant Director/Chief Financial Officer.—Alan Titus, 267–2999.
Assistant Director/Chief Information Officer.—Sandy Peavy, 267–2014.
Assistant Director for—
Adminstration.—Marcus Hill, 267–2231.
Field Training.—Cynthia Atwood, 267–2445.
Training.—Bruce Bowen, 267–3373.
Training Innovation and Management.—Mike Hanneld, 267–2934.

UNITED STATES CITIZENSHIP AND IMMIGRATION SERVICES

20 Massachusetts Avenue, NW., 20529, phone (202) 272–1000

Director.—Vacant.
Deputy Director.—Michael Aytes (acting).
Chief of Staff.—Lauren Kielsmeier.
Chief Information Officer.—Steve Bucher (acting).
Associate Director for—
Domestic Operations Directorate.—Donald Neufeld (acting).
National Security and Records Verification Directorate.—Gregory B. Smith.
Refugee, Asylum and International Operations Directorate.—Lori Scialabba.
Chief, Office of:
Administration.—Nancy Guilliams.
Administrative Appeals.—John F. Grissom.
Chief Counsel.—Dea Carpenter (acting).
Citizenship.—Laura Patching (acting).
Communications.—Christopher Bentley (acting).
Congressional Relations.—James McCament.

Planning, Budget, and Finance/Chief Financial Officer.—Rendell Jones.
Policy and Strategy.—Pearl Chang (acting).

UNITED STATES COAST GUARD

2100 Second Street, SW., 20593, phone (202) 267–2229

Commandant.—ADM Thad W. Allen.
Vice Commandant.—VADM David Pekoske.
Chief of Staff.—RADN John Currier.
Special Assistant to the Chief of Staff.—RDML Thomas F. Atkin.
Chief Administrative Law Judge.—Hon. Joseph N. Ingolia.
Judge Advocate General/Chief Counsel.—RDML William D. Baumgartner.
Deputy Judge Advocate General/Deputy Chief Counsel.—Calvin Lederer.
Director, Office of Governmental and Public Affairs.—RDML Charles D. Michel.
Senior Military Advisor to the Secretary of Homeland Security.—RDML Charles Ray.

UNITED STATES SECRET SERVICE

245 Murray Drive, SW., Building 410, 20223

Director.—Mark Sullivan.
Deputy Director.—Keith Prewitt.
Deputy Assistant Director, Congressional Affairs Program.—Faron Paramore (202) 406–5676, fax 406–5740.

INDEPENDENT AGENCIES, COMMISSIONS, BOARDS

ADVISORY COUNCIL ON HISTORIC PRESERVATION

1100 Pennsylvania Avenue, NW., Suite 803, 20004

phone (202) 606–8503, http://www.achp.gov

[Created by Public Law 89–665, as amended]

Executive Director.—John M. Fowler.
Chairman.—John L. Nau III, Houston, Texas.
Vice Chairman.—Susan Snell Barnes, Aurora, Illinois.
Directors for:
Office of Preservation Initiatives.—Ronald D. Anzalone.
Office of Communications, Education, and Outreach.—Susan A. Glimcher.
Office of Administration.—Ralston Cox.
Office of Federal Agency Programs.—Reid J. Nelson.
Coordinator, Native American Program.—Valerie Hauser.
Expert Members:
Jack Williams, Seattle, Washington.
Ann Alexander Pritzlaff, Denver, Colorado.
Julia A. King, St. Leonard, Maryland.
Citizen Members:
Rhonda Bentz, Arlington, Virginia.
John A. Garcia, Albuquerque, New Mexico.
Mark A. Sadd, Esq., Charleston, West Virginia.
Native American Member.—John L. Berrey, Quapaw, Oklahoma.
Governor.—Hon. Mark Sanford, Columbia, South Carolina.
Mayor.—Hon. William ''Bill'' Haslam, Knoxville, Tennessee.
Architect of the Capitol.—Stephen T. Ayers (acting), AIA.
Secretary, Department of:
Agriculture.—Hon. Thomas J. Vilsack.
Interior.—Hon. Ken Salazar.
Defense.—Dr. Robert Gates.
Transportation.—Hon. Ray LaHood.
Commerce.—Hon. Gary Locke.
Housing and Urban Development.—Hon. Shaun Donovan.
Veterans' Affairs.—Hon. Eric K. Shinseki.
Administrator for—
Environmental Protection Agency.—Hon. Lisa P. Jackson.
General Services Administration.—Paul F. Prouty (acting).
National Trust for Historic Preservation.—J. Clifford Hudson, Chairman, Oklahoma City, Oklahoma.
National Conference of State Historic Preservation Officer.—Ruth Pierpont, President, Waterford, New York.

AFRICAN DEVELOPMENT FOUNDATION

1400 Eye Street, NW., Suite 1000, 20005–2248, phone (202) 673–3916, fax 673–3810

http://www.usadf.gov

[Created by Public Law 96–5331]

BOARD OF DIRECTORS

Chair.—Adm. John Agwunobi.
Vice Chair.—John W. Leslie, Jr.
Private Members: Julius Coles, Morgan Davis.
Public Member.—Vacant.

STAFF

President and CEO.—Lloyd O. Pierson.
General Counsel.—Doris Mason Martin.
Chief Information Officer.—Larry P. Bevan.
Director of:
Financial Management, Strategic Planning, and Evaluation.—William Schuerch.
Management and Administration and Chief Human Capital Officer.—M. Catherine Gates.
Legislative and Public Affairs.—Vacant.
Regional Program Directors, Program and Field Operations: Rama Bah, Thomas Coogan, Christine S. Fowles, Paul Olson.

AMERICAN BATTLE MONUMENTS COMMISSION

Courthouse Plaza II, Suite 500, 2300 Clarendon Boulevard, Arlington, VA 22201–3367

phone (703) 696–6902

[Created by Public Law 105–225]

Chairman.—None appointed as of 6/6/09.
Commissioners: None appointed as of 6/6/09.
Secretary.—Joseph Maxwell Cleland.
Executive Director.—BG William J. Leszczynski, Jr, U.S. Army (Ret.).
Director for—
Engineering and Maintenance.—Thomas R. Sole.
Finance.—Alan Gregory.
Personnel and Administration.—Theodore Gloukoff.
Public Affairs.—Michael G. Conley.

(Note: Public law changed to 105–225, August 1998; H.R. 1085).

AMERICAN NATIONAL RED CROSS

National Headquarters, 2025 E Street, NW., 20006, phone (202) 303–5000

Government Relations and Strategic Partnerships, phone (202) 303–4371, fax 638–3960

HONORARY OFFICERS

Honorary Chair.—Barack H. Obama, President of the United States.

CORPORATE OFFICERS

Chairman.—Bonnie McElveen-Hunter.
President/CEO.—Gail J. McGovern.
General Counsel/Secretary.—Mary S. Elcano.
Chief Financial Officer.—Brian Rhoa.

BOARD OF GOVERNORS

Cesar A. Aristeiguieta
Sanford A. Belden
Paula E. Boggs
Richard M. Fountain
Allan I. Goldberg
James G. Goodwin
Ann F. Kaplan
James W. Keyes
Anna Maria Larsen
Bonnie McElveen-Hunter
Youngme E. Moon
Suzanne Nora Johnson
Richard Patton
Laurence E. Paul
Joseph B. Pereles
Melanie R. Sabelhaus
H. Marshall Schwarz
Steven H. Wunning

ADMINISTRATIVE OFFICERS

President of Humanitarian Services.—Gerald DeFrancisco.
President of Biomedical Services.—Shaun P. Gilmore.
Chief Public Affairs Officer.—Suzanne DeFrancis.
Ombudsman.—Sarah R. Kith.
Chief Audit Executive.—Dale Bateman.
Congressional Affairs—
Senior Vice President for Government Relations and Strategic Partnerships.—Neal Denton.
Senior Director, Congressional Affairs.—Cherae Bishop.
Senior Policy Advisor.—Dawn P. Latham.
Legislative Specialist.—Marin Reynes.

APPALACHIAN REGIONAL COMMISSION

1666 Connecticut Avenue, NW., 20009, phone (202) 884–7660, fax 884–7693

Federal Co-Chair.—Anne B. Pope.
Alternate Federal Co-Chair.—Vacant.
States' Washington Representative.—Cameron Whitman.
Executive Director.—Thomas M. Hunter.
Chief of Staff.—Guy Land.

ARMED FORCES RETIREMENT HOME

3700 North Capitol Street, NW., Box 1303, Washington, DC 20011–8400
phone (202) 730–3077, fax 730–3166

Chief Operating Officer.—Timothy C. Cox.
Chief Financial Officer.—Steven G. McManus.
Chief Information Officer.—Maurice Swinton.

ARMED FORCES RETIREMENT HOME—WASHINGTON

phone (202) 730–3504, fax 730–3127

Director.—David Watkins.

ARMED FORCES RETIREMENT HOME—GULFPORT

1800 Beach Drive, Gulfport, MS 39507

Closed due to Hurricane Katrina.

BOARD OF GOVERNORS OF THE FEDERAL RESERVE SYSTEM

Constitution Avenue and 20th Street, NW., 20551, phone (202) 452–3000

Chairman.—Ben S. Bernanke.
Vice Chair.—Donald L. Kohn.
Members: Elizabeth A. Duke, Daniel K. Tarullo, Kevin M. Warsh.
Assistant to the Board and Division Director.—Michelle A. Smith.
Assistants to the Board: Winthrop P. Hambley, Rosanna Pianalto-Cameron, David W. Skidmore.

Special Assistants to the Board: Laricke D. Blanchard, Brain J. Gross, Robert M. Pribble.

DIVISION OF BANKING SUPERVISION AND REGULATION

Director.—Roger T. Cole.

Deputy Directors: Norah M. Barger, Deborah P. Bailey, Peter J. Purcell.

Associate Directors: Barbara J. Bouchard, Betsy Cross, Jon D. Greenlee, Jack P. Jennings, Arther W. Lindo, David S. Jones, William C. Schneider, William G. Spaniel, Coryann Stefansson, Molly S. Wassom.

Deputy Associate Directors: Kevin M. Bertsch, James A. Embersit.

Assistant Directors: Philip Aquilino, Robert T. Ashman, Lisa DeFerrari, Adrienne Haden, Robert T. Maahs, Rick Naylor, Nina A. Nichols, Dana E. Payne, Nancy J. Perkins, Sabeth I. Siddique.

Advisers: Timothy Clark, Kevin Clarke, Nida Davis, Michael Foley, Charles H. Holm, William F. Treacy, Sarkis D. Yoghourtdgjian.

DIVISION OF CONSUMER AND COMMUNITY AFFAIRS

Director.—Sandra F. Braunstein.

Deputy Director.—Glenn E. Loney.

Associate Counsel and Advisor.—Adrienne D. Hurt.

Associate Directors: Anna Alvarez Boyd, Leonard Chanin, Tonda E. Price.

Assistant Directors: Tim Burniston, Joseph Firchein, Allne Fishbein, Suzanne Killian, James A. Michaels.

Adviser.—Maryann F. Hunter.

DIVISION OF FEDERAL RESERVE BANK OPERATIONS AND PAYMENT SYSTEMS

Director.—Louise L. Roseman.

Deputy Directors: Donald V. Hammond, Jeffrey C. Marquardt.

Senior Associate Director.—Paul W. Bettge.

Associate Directors: Kenneth D. Buckley, Dorothy B. LaChapelle, Jeff J. Stehm.

Deputy Associate Directors: Greg Evans, Susan Foley, Lisa Hoskins.

Assistant Directors: Michael J. Lambert, Michael Stan, Buck Tanis.

DIVISION OF INFORMATION TECHNOLOGY

Director.—Maureen T. Hannan.

Deputy Directors: Geary Cunningham, Wayne Edmondson, Sharon Mowry.

Deputy Associate Directors: Po Kim, Sue Marycz, Ray Romero.

Assistant Directors: Lisa Bell, Glenn Eskow, Kofi Sapong, Raj Yelisetty.

DIVISION OF INTERNATIONAL FINANCE

Director.—Nathan Sheets.

Deputy Directors: Thomas A. Connors, Steven B. Kamin.

Associate Directors: Michael Leahy, Ralph W. Tryon.

Deputy Associate Directors: Trevor Reeve, John H. Rogers.

Assistant Directors: Christopher J. Erceg, Linda S. Kole.

Advisers: Mark S. Carey, Jane T. Haltmaier.

DIVISION OF MONETARY AFFAIRS

Director.—Brian F. Madigan.

Deputy Directors: James Clouse, Deborah J. Danker, William B. English.

Senior Associate Director.—Sherry Edwards.

Associate Directors: Andrew Levin, Bill Nelson.

Deputy Associate Directors: Seth Carpenter, Roberto Perli.

Assistant Director.—Egon Zakrajsek.

Senior Adviser.—Steve Meyer.

DIVISION OF RESEARCH AND STATISTICS

Director.—David J. Stockton.
Deputy Directors: Patrick M. Parkinson, David Wilcox.
Senior Associate Directors: Myron L. Kwast, Lawrence Slifman.
Associate Directors: Nellie Liang, David Reifschneider, Janice Shack-Marquez, William Wascher, Patricia White.
Deputy Assistant Directors: Michael Gibson, S. Wayne Passmore, Dan Sichel, Joyce K. Zickler.
Assistant Directors: Michael S. Cringoli, Karen Dynan, Diana Hancock, Michael Killey, Michael Palumbo, Robin Prgaer, Mary M. West.
Senior Advisers: Glenn B. Canner, Matthew Eichner, Stephen Oliner.

INSPECTOR GENERAL

Inspector General.—Elizabeth A. Coleman.
Assistant Inspector Generals: Anthony J. Castaldo, Laurence A. Froehlich, Andrew Patchan, Jr., Harvey Witherspoon.

LEGAL DIVISION

General Counsel.—Scott G. Alvarez.
Deputy General Counsels: Richard M. Ashton, Kathleen M. O'Day.
Associate General Counsels: Stephanie Martin, Anne E. Misback, Katherine H. Wheatley.
Assistant General Counsels: Kieran J. Fallon, Stephen H. Meyer, Patricia A. Robinson, Cary K. Williams.

MANAGEMENT DIVISION

Director.—Fay Peters.
Deputy Directors: Michael Clark, Donald Spicer.
Senior Associate Directors: Todd A. Glissman, William Mitchell, Billy J. Sauls.
Associate Directors: Christine M. Fields, James Riesz, Marie Savoy.
Deputy Associate Directors: Elaine Boutilier, Charlies O'Malley, Tara Tinsley-Pelitere.
Assistant Directors: Keith Bates, Jeffrey Peirce, Christopher Suma, Theresa Trimble.

OFFICE OF THE SECRETARY

Secretary.—Jennifer J. Johnson.
Deputy Secretary.—Robert deV. Frierson.
Associate Secretary.—Margaret M. Shanks.
Assistant Secretaries: Penelope Beattie, Dorothy Shean.

STAFF DIRECTOR FOR MANAGEMENT

Staff Director.—Stephen R. Malphrus.
Deputy Staff Director.—Charles S. Struckmeyer.
EEO Programs Director.—Sheila Clark.
Senior Adviser.—Lynn S. Fox.

BROADCASTING BOARD OF GOVERNORS

330 Independence Avenue, SW., Suite 3360, 20237

phone (202) 203–4545, fax 203–4568

The Broadcasting Board of Governors oversees the operation of the IBB and provides yearly funding grants approved by Congress to three non-profit grantee corporations, Radio Free Europe/Radio Liberty, Radio Free Asia, and the Middle East Broadcasting Networks.

Chairman.—Vacant.

INTERNATIONAL BROADCASTING BUREAU

[Created by Public Law 103–236]

The International Broadcasting Bureau (IBB) is composed of the Voice of America, and Radio and TV Marti.

Deputy Director, International Broadcasting Bureau.—Danforth Austin (acting), (202) 203–4515, fax 203–4587.
Director of:
Cuba Broadcasting.—Pedro Roig (305) 437–7010, fax 437–7016.
Voice of America.—Danforth Austin (202) 203–4500, fax 203–4513.
President, Radio Free Asia.—Libby Liu (202) 530–4900, fax 721–7460.
President, Radio Free Europe.—Jeffrey Gedmin (acting), (202) 457–6900, fax 457–6992.
President, Middle East Broadcasting Networks.—Brian Conniff (703) 852–9000, fax 991–1250.

GOVERNORS

Joaquin F. Blaya
Blanquita Walsh Cullum
D. Jeffrey Hirschberg
Steven J. Simmons
Hillary Rodham Clinton (ex officio)

STAFF

Executive Director.—Jeffrey Trimble.
Director of:
Management Planning.—Janice Brambilla.
Strategic Planning.—Bruce Sherman.
Chief Financial Officer.—Janet Stormes.
Congressional Coordinator.—Susan Andross.
Executive Assistant.—Armanda Matthews.
Legal Counsel.—Timi Kenealy (acting).
Management and Program Assistant.—Elisabeth Crawford.
Policy and Program Coordinator.—John Giambalvo.
Special Projects Officer.—Oanh Tran.

CENTRAL INTELLIGENCE AGENCY

phone (703) 482–1100

Director.—Leon Panetta.
Deputy Director.—Stephen R. Kappes.
Associate Deputy Director.—Scott White.
General Counsel.—John Rizzo (acting).
Director of:
Intelligence.—Michael J. Morell.
Public Affairs.—Mark Mansfield.
Science and Technology.—Stephanie L. O'Sullivan.
Support.—John P.

COMMISSION OF FINE ARTS

National Building Museum, 401 F Street, NW., Suite 312, 20001–2728
phone (202) 504–2200, fax 504–2195, http://www.cfa.gov

Commissioners:
Earl A. Powell III, Washington, DC., Chair.
Pamela Nelson, Dallas, TX, Vice-Chair.
Diana Balmori, New York, NY.
John Belle, New York, NY.
N. Michael McKinnell, Boston, MA.
Witold Rybczynski, Philadelphia, PA.
Elyn Zimmerman, New York, NY.

Secretary.—Thomas Luebke, AIA.
Assistant Secretary.—Frederick J. Lindstrom.

BOARD OF ARCHITECTURAL CONSULTANTS FOR THE OLD GEORGETOWN ACT

Stephen Vanze, AIA, Chair.
David Cox, FAIA.
Anne Lewis, FAIA.

COMMITTEE FOR PURCHASE FROM PEOPLE WHO ARE BLIND OR SEVERELY DISABLED

1421 Jefferson Davis Highway, Jefferson Plaza 2, Suite 10800
Arlington, VA 22202–3259, phone (703) 603–7740, fax 603–0655

Chairperson.—Andrew D. Houghton.
Vice Chairperson.—James H. Omvig.
Executive Director.—Tina Ballard.
Members:
Perry Edward ''Ed'' Anthony, Department of Education.
Paul Laird, Department of Justice.
Kathleen A. James, Department of the Air Force.
J. Anthony ''Tony'' Poleo, Department of Defense.
Abram Claude, Jr., Private Citizen.
Robert T. Kelly, Jr., Private Citizen.
Andrew D. Houghton and Robert T. Kelly, Jr., private citizens (representing nonprofit agency employees with other severe disabilities).
James H. Omvig and Abram Claude, Jr., private citizens (representing nonprofit agency employees who are blind).

COMMODITY FUTURES TRADING COMMISSION

Three Lafayette Centre, 1155 21st Street, NW., 20581, phone (202) 418–5000
fax 418–5521, http://www.cftc.gov

Chairman.—Gary Gensler, 418–5154.
Chief of Staff.—Eric Juzenas, 418–5076.
Commissioners:
Bart Chilton, 418–5060.
Michael V. Dunn, 418–5070.
Walter L. Lukken, 418–5014.
Jill Sommers, 418–5076.
Executive Director.—Madge A. Bolinger, 418–5160.
General Counsel.—Dan Berkovitz, 418–5361.
Office of the Chief Economist.—Jeff Harris, 418–5563.
Director, Division of:
Clearing and Intermediary Oversight.—Ananda Radhakrishnan, 418–5188.
Enforcement.—Steve Obie (acting), 418–5111.
Market Oversight.—Rick Shilts, 418–5260.
Director, Office of:

External Affairs.—Robert Holifield (acting), 418–5082.
Inspector General.—A. Roy Lavik, 418–5110.
International Affairs.—Jacqueline H. Mesa, 418–5386.
Secretary.—David Stawick, 418–5071.

REGIONAL OFFICES

Chicago: 525 West Monroe Street, Suite 1100, Chicago, IL 60601 (312) 596–0700, fax 596–0716.
Kansas City: Two Emanuel Cleaver II Boulevard, Suite 300, Kansas City, MO 64112, (816) 960–7700, fax 960–7750.
Minneapolis: 510 Grain Exchange Building, 400 South 4th Street, Minneapolis, MN 55415, (612) 370–3255, fax 370–3257.
New York: 140 Broadway, Nineteenth floor, New York, NY 10005 (646) 746–9700, fax 746–9938.

CONSUMER PRODUCT SAFETY COMMISSION

4330 East West Highway, Bethesda, MD 20814, phone (301) 504–7923

fax 504–0124, http://www.cpsc.gov

[Created by Public Law 92–573]

Chairperson.—Thomas H. Moore (acting), 504–7902.
Commissioner.—Nancy Nord, 504–7901.
Executive Director.—Vacant.
Deputy Executive Director.—Vacant.
Director, Office of:
The Secretary.—Todd A. Stevenson, 504–7923.
Congressional Relations.—Vacant.
General Counsel.—Cheryl A. Falvey, 504–7642.

CORPORATION FOR NATIONAL AND COMMUNITY SERVICE

1201 New York Avenue, NW., 20525, phone (202) 606–5000

http://www.cns.gov

[Executive Order 11603, June 30, 1971; codified in 42 U.S.C., section 4951]

Chief Executive Officer.—Nicola O. Goren (acting), 606–6676.
Chief of Staff.—Nicola O. Goren.
Chief Financial Officer.—Bill Anderson (acting), 606–6980.
Inspector General.—Gerald Walpin, 606–9390.
Director of:
AmeriCorps/National Civilian Community Corps.—Mikel Herrington (acting), 606–6706.
AmeriCorps/State and National.—Lois Nembhard (acting), 606–6827.
AmeriCorps/VISTA.—Paul Davis (acting), 606–6608.
Learn and Serve America.—Elson Nash (acting), 606–6834.
National Senior Service Corps.—Angela Roberts (acting), 606–6822.
Office of Government Relations.—Rhoda Glickman, 606–6731.
General Counsel.—Frank Trinity, 606–6677.

DEFENSE NUCLEAR FACILITIES SAFETY BOARD

625 Indiana Avenue, NW., Suite 700, 20004, phone (202) 694–7000

fax 208–6518, http://www.dnfsb.gov

Chairman.—Vacant.
Vice Chairman.—John E. Mansfield.
Members: Joseph F. Bader, Larry W. Brown, Peter S. Winokur.
General Counsel.—Richard A. Azzaro.
General Manager.—Brian Grosner.
Technical Director.—Timothy J. Dwyer.

DELAWARE RIVER BASIN COMMISSION

25 State Police Drive, P.O. Box 7360, West Trenton, NJ 08628–0360

phone (609) 883–9500, fax 883–9522, http://www.drbc.net

[Created by Public Law 87–328]

FEDERAL REPRESENTATIVES

Federal Commissioner.—COL Peter A. DeLuca Commander, U.S. Army Corps of Engineers, North Atlantic Division (718) 765–7000.
First Alternate.—COL Christopher J. Larsen, U.S. Army Corps of Engineers, North Atlantic Division (718) 765–7001.
Second Alternate.—LTC Thomas J. Tickner, District Commander, U.S. Army Corps of Engineers, Philadelphia (215) 656–6502.
Third Alternate.—Henry W. Gruber, P.E., Chief, Basin Planning, U.S. Army Corps of Engineer, Philadelphia (215) 656–6582.

STAFF

Executive Director.—Carol R. Collier, ext. 200.
Deputy Executive Director.—Robert Tudor, ext. 208.
Commission Secretary/Assistant General Counsel.—Pamela M. Bush, Esq., ext. 203.
Communications Manager.—Clarke Rupert, ext. 260.

DELAWARE REPRESENTATIVES

State Commissioner.—Jack A. Markell, Governor (302) 577–3210.
First Alternate.—Collin O'Mara, Secretary, Delaware Department of Natural Resources and Environmental Control (DNREC), (302) 739–9000.
Second Alternate.—Katherine E. Bunting-Howarth, J.D., Ph.D., Director, Division of Water Resources (DNREC), (302) 739–9949.
Third Alternate.—Dr. Harry W. Otto, Senior Science Advisor, Office of the Director, Division of Water Resources (DNREC), (302) 739–9949 (Ret: July 1, 2009).

NEW JERSEY REPRESENTATIVES

State Commissioner.—Jon S. Corzine, Governor (609) 292–6000.
First Alternate.—Mark N. Mauriello, Commissioner, New Jersey Department of Environmental Protection (NJDEP), (609) 292–2885.
Second Alternate.—John S. Watson, Jr., Deputy Commissioner, for Natural Resources (NJDEP), (609) 633–7660.
Third Alternate.—Michele Putman, Director, Division of Water Supply (NJDEP), (609) 292–7219.
Fourth Alternate.—Fred Sickels, Assistant Director of Water Supply Permitting (NJDEP), (609) 292–2957.
Fifth Alternate.—Dr. Joseph A. Miri, Research Scientist, Chief, Office of Water Policy (NJDEP), (609) 292–7219.

NEW YORK REPRESENTATIVES

State Commissioner.—David A. Paterson, Governor (518) 474–8390.
First Alternate.—Alexander B. Grannis, Commissioner, New York State Department of Environmental Conservation (NYSDEC), (518) 402–8540.
Second Alternate.—James G. DeZolt, P.E., Director, Division of Water (NYSDEC), (518) 402–8233.
Third Alternate.—Mark Klotz, P.E., Director, Bureau of Water Resources Management (NYDEC), (518) 402–8086.
Fourth Alternate.—Peter Freehafer, Chesapeake and Delaware Program Coordinator (NYSDEC), (518) 402–8205.

PENNSYLVANIA REPRESENTATIVES

State Commissioner.—Edward G. Rendell, Governor (717) 787–2500.
First Alternate.—Cathy Curran Myers, Special Assistant to the Secretary for Pennsylvania's Recovery, Office of the Secretary, Pennsylvania Department of Environmental Protection (PADEP), (717) 787–7196.
Second Alternate.—John T. Hines (acting), Deputy Secretary, Office of Water Management (PADEP), (717) 783–4693.

Third Alternate.—Susan K. Weaver, P.E., Chief, Water Use Planning Division (PADEP), (717) 772–4048.

ENVIRONMENTAL PROTECTION AGENCY

1200 Pennsylvania Avenue, NW., 20460, phone (202) 564–4700, http://www.epa.gov

Administrator.—Lisa P. Jackson.
Deputy Administrator.—Scott Fulton (acting), 564–4711.
Chief of Staff.—Diane Thompson, 564–6999.
Deputy Chief of Staff.—Ray Spears 564–4715.
Agriculture Counsel.—Larry Elworth, 564–7719.
White House Liaison.—MaryGrace Galston, 564–7960.
Environmental Appeals Board: Scott Fulton, Edward Reich, Kathie Stein, Anna Wolgast, 233–0122.
Associate Administrator for—
Congressional and Intergovernmental Relations.—Joyce Frank (acting), 564–5200.
Homeland Security.—Juan Reyes, 564–2844.
Policy, Economics, and Innovation.—Marcia Mulkey, 564–4332.
Public Affairs.—Allyn Brooks-LaSure, 564–8368.
Director, Office of:
Children's Health Protection.—Ruth McCully, 564–2188.
Civil Rights.—Karen Higginbotham, 564–7272.
Cooperative Environmental Management.—Rafael DeLeon, 233–0090.
Executive Secretariat.—Eric Wachter, 564–7311.
Executive Services.—Diane Bazzle, 564–0444.
Science Advisory Board.—Vanessa Vu, 343–9999.
Small and Disadvantaged Business Utilization.—Jeanette L. Brown, 564–4100.
Director of Management, Office of Administrative Law Judges.—Susan Biro, 564–6255.

ADMINISTRATION AND RESOURCES MANAGEMENT

Assistant Administrator.—Craig Hooks, 564–4600.
Deputy Assistant Administrator.—Susan Hazen, 564–1861.

AIR AND RADIATION

Assistant Administrator.—Gina McCarthy, 564–7404.
Deputy Assistant Administrators: Beth Craig, Barnes Johnson, 564–7400.

ENFORCEMENT AND COMPLIANCE ASSURANCE

Assistant Administrator.—Cynthia Giles, 564–2440.
Principal Deputy Assistant Administrator.—Catherine McCabe.
Deputy Assistant Administrator.—Randy Hill.

OFFICE OF ENVIRONMENTAL INFORMATION

Assistant Administrator.—Linda Travers (acting), 564–6665.
Deputy Assistant Administrator.—Michael Flynn (acting).

CHIEF FINANCIAL OFFICER

Chief Financial Officer.—Maryann Froehlich (acting), 564–1151.
Deputy Chief Financial Officer.—Joshua Baylson (acting).

GENERAL COUNSEL

General Counsel.—Pat Hirsch, 564–8064.
Principal Deputy General Counsel.—Mary Kay Lynch (acting), 564–8064.
Deputy General Counsel.—Kevin McLean (acting), 564–8040.

INSPECTOR GENERAL

Inspector General.—Bill Roderick (acting), 566–0847.

Deputy Inspector General.—Mark Bialek.

INTERNATIONAL AFFAIRS

Assistant Administrator.—Michelle DePass, 564–6600.
Deputy Assistant Administrator.—Kathy Petrucelli (acting).

PREVENTION, PESTICIDES, AND TOXIC SUBSTANCES

Assistant Administrator.—James Jones (acting), 564–2902.
Principal Deputy Assistant Administrator.—Betsy Shaw.

RESEARCH AND DEVELOPMENT

Assistant Administrator.—Lek Kadelis, 564–6620.
Deputy Assistant Administrator of:
Management.—Larry Reiter.
Science.—Kevin Teichman (acting).

SOLID WASTE AND EMERGENCY RESPONSE

Assistant Administrator.—Mathy Stanislaus, 566–0200.
Principal Deputy Assistant Administrator.—Barry Breen.

WATER

Assistant Administrator.—Renee Wynn (acting), 564–5700.
Director of Emergency Management.—Debbie Dietrich.

REGIONAL ADMINISTRATION

Region I, Boston.—Connecticut, Maine, New Hampshire, Rhode Island, Vermont.
Regional Administrator.—Ira Leighton (acting), One Congress Street, Suite 1100, Boston, MA 02114 (617) 918–1010.
Public Affairs.—Nancy Grantham.
Region II, New York City.—New Jersey, New York, Puerto Rico, Virgin Islands.
Regional Administrator.—George Pavlou (acting), 290 Broadway, New York, NY 10007 (212) 637–5000.
Public Affairs.—Bonnie Bellow (212) 637–3660.
Region III, Philadelphia.—Delaware, Washington, DC, Maryland, Pennsylvania, Virginia, West Virginia.
Regional Administrator.—William Early (acting), 1650 Arch Street, Philadelphia, PA 19103–2029 (215) 814–2900.
Public Affairs.—Gail Tindal (215) 814–5100.
Region IV, Atlanta.—Alabama, Florida, Georgia, Kentucky, Mississippi, North Carolina, South Carolina, Tennessee.
Regional Administrator.—Stan Meiburg (acting), 61 Forsyth Street, SW., Atlanta, GA 30303–8960 (404) 562–8357.
Public Affairs.—Carl Terry (404) 562–8327.
Region V, Chicago.—Illinois, Indiana, Michigan, Minnesota, Ohio, Wisconsin.
Regional Administrator.—Bharat Mathur (acting), 77 West Jackson Boulevard, Chicago, IL 60604–3507 (312) 886–3000.
Public Affairs.—Anne Rowan.
Region VI, Dallas.—Arkansas, Louisiana, New Mexico, Oklahoma, Texas.
Regional Administrator.—Lawrence Starfield (acting), Fountain Place, 1445 Ross Avenue, 12th Floor, Suite 1200, Dallas, TX 75202–2733 (214) 665–2100.
Public Affairs.—David W. Gray.
Region VII, Kansas City.—Iowa, Kansas, Missouri, Nebraska.
Regional Administrator.—William Rice (acting), 901 North 5th Street, Kansas City, MO 66101 (913) 551–7006.
Public Affairs.—Rich Hood (913) 551–7305.
Region VIII, Denver.—Colorado, Montana, North Dakota, South Dakota, Utah, Wyoming.
Regional Administrator.—Carol Rushin (acting), 999 18th Street, Suite 300, Denver, CO 80202–2466 (303) 312–6308.

Public Affairs.—Larry Grandison (303) 312–6599.

Region IX, San Francisco.—Arizona, California, Hawaii, Nevada, American Samoa, Guam.

Regional Administrator.—Laura Yoshii (acting), 75 Hawthorne Street, San Francisco, CA 94105 (415) 947–8702.

Public Affairs.—Kathleen Johnson.

Region X, Seattle.—Alaska, Idaho, Oregon, Washington.

Regional Administrator.—Michelle Pirzadeh (acting), 1200 Sixth Avenue, Seattle, WA 98101 (206) 553–1234.

Public Affairs.—Rick Parkin (206) 553–1901.

EQUAL EMPLOYMENT OPPORTUNITY COMMISSION

131 M Street, NE., 20507, phone (202) 663–4900

Chairman.—Stuart J. Ishimaru (acting), suite 6NW08F, 663–4001, fax 663–4110.

Chief Operating Officer.—Vacant.

Deputy Chief Operating Officer.—Richard Roscio, suite 6NW08F, 663–4655.

Confidential Assistant.—Melissa Fenwick, suite 6NW08F, 663–4002.

Special Assistants: Sharon Alexander, suite 6NW08F, 663–4790; Antoinette Eates, suite 6NW08F, 663–4067; Jacinta Ma, suite 6NW08F, 663–4970; Mona Papillon, suite 6NW08F, 663–4649; Daniel Vail, suite 6NW08F, 663–4571.

COMMISSIONERS

Vice Chair.—Christine Griffin (acting), suite 6NE37F, 663–4036, fax 663–7101.

Commissioner.—Constance Barker, suite 6NE25F, 663–4027, fax 663–7121.

General Counsel.—James Lee (acting), 5th floor, 663–7034, fax 663–4196.

Legal Counsel.—Peggy Mastroianni (acting), 5th floor, 663–4327, fax 663–4639.

Director, Office of:

Chief Financial Officer.—Jeffrey Smith, 4th floor, 663–4200, fax 663–7068.

Communications and Legislative Affairs.—Brett Brenner (acting), 6th floor, 663–4191, fax 663–4912.

Equal Opportunity.—Veronica Villalobos, 6th floor, 663–4012, fax 663–7003.

Executive Secretariat/Executive Secretary.—Stephen Llewellyn, 6th floor, 663–4703, fax 663–4114.

Field Operations.—Carlton Hadden, 5th floor, 663–4459, fax 633–7022.

Field Programs.—Nicholas Inzeo, 5th floor, 663–4801, fax 663–7190.

Human Resources.—James Neely (acting), 4th floor, 663–4306, fax 663–4324.

Information Technology.—Kimberly Hancher, 4th floor, 663–4447, fax 663–4451.

Inspector General.—Aletha Brown, 6th floor, 663–4327, fax 663–7204.

Research, Information and Planning.—Deidre Flippen, 4th floor, 663–4853, fax 663–4093.

EXPORT–IMPORT BANK OF THE UNITED STATES

811 Vermont Avenue, NW., 20571, phone (800) 565–EXIM, fax 565–3380

President and Chairman.—Fred Hochberg, room 1215, 565–3500.

Vice President and Vice Chairman.—Vacant.

Directors: Diane Farrell, room 1257, 565–3520; Bijan Kian, room 1209, 565–3540; J. Joseph Grandmaison, room 1235, 565–3530.

Chief Operating Officer/General Counsel.—Vacant, room 947, 565–3229.

Chief Financial Officer.—John Simonson, room 1054, 565–3952.

Chief Information Officer.—Fernanda Young, room 1045, 565–3798.

Senior Vice President of:

Credit Risk Management.—Kenneth Tinsley, room 919, 565–3222.

Congressional Affairs.—Thomas Lopach, room 1261, 565–3216.

Export Finance.—John McAdams, room 1115, 565–3222.

Policy and Planning.—James C. Cruse, room 1243, 565–3761.

Resource Management.—Michael Cushing, room 1017, 565–3561.

Small Business.—John Richter, room 1115, 565–3701.

Vice President of:

Asset Management.—Frances Nwachuku, room 741, 565–3618.

Business Credit.—Pamela Boweres, room 1129, 565–3792.

Communications.—Phil Cogan, room 1264, 565–3203.

Congressional Affairs.—William Hellert, room 1261–A, 565–3233.

Controller.—Joseph Sorbera, room 1053, 565–3241.
Country Risk and Economic Analysis.—William Marsteller, room 701, 565–3739.
Credit Review and Compliance.—Walter Hill, Jr., room 915, 565–3672.
Credit Underwriting.—David Carter, room 919, 565–3667.
Domestic Business Development.—Wayne L. Gardella, room 1137, 565–3787.
Engineering and Environment.—James Mahoney, room 1169, 565–3573.
Office of Industry Sector Development.—C. Michael Forgione, room 1107, 565–3224.
Operation and Data Quality.—Michele Kuester, room 719, 565–3221.
Policy Analysis.—Helen Walsh, room 1238, 565–3768.
Short-Term Trade Finance.—Walter Kosciow, room 1176, 565–3649.
Structured Finance.—Barbara A. O'Boyle, room 1005, 565–3694.
Strategic Initiatives.—Raymond Ellis, room 1123, 565–3674.
Trade Finance and Insurance.—Jeffrey Abramson, room 931, 565–3633.
Transportation.—Robert A. Morin, room 1035, 565–3453.
Transportation Portfolio Management.—Michele Dixey, room 1059, 565–3554.
Treasurer.—David Sena, room 10051, 565–3272.
Directors of:
Administration and Security.—Paul Perez, room 1023, 565–3312.
Contracting Services.—Mark Pitra, room 1023, 565–3388.
Human Resources.—Natasha McCarthy, room 771, 565–3592.
Inspector General.—Michael Tankersley, room 975, 565–3923.

FARM CREDIT ADMINISTRATION

1501 Farm Credit Drive, McLean, VA 22102–5090

phone (703) 883–4000, fax 734–5784

[Reorganization pursuant to Public Law 99–205, December 23, 1985]

Chair.—Leland A. Strom.
Board Members:
Nancy C. Pellett.
Vacant.
Secretary to the Board.—Roland Smith, 883–4009, fax 790–5241.
Chief Operating Officer.—William J. Hoffman, 883–4340, fax 790–5241.
Chief Examiner and Director, Office of Examination.—Thomas G. McKenzie, 883–4160, fax 893–2978.
Director, Office of:
Congressional and Public Affairs.—Michael A. Stokke, 883–4056, fax 790–3260.
General Counsel.—Charles R. Rawls, 883–4020, fax 790–0052.
Inspector General.—Carl Clinefelter, 883–4030, fax 883–4059.
Management Services.—Stephen Smith, 883–4200, fax 883–4151.
Regulatory Policy.—Andrew Jacob, 883–4414, fax 883–4477.
Secondary Market Oversight.—Robert Coleman, 883–4280, fax 883–4478.
Chief Human Capital Officer.—Philip Shebest, 883–4200, fax 893–2608.
Chief Information Officer.—Doug Valcour, 883–4200, fax 883–4151.
Manager, Equal Employment Opportunity.—Jeff McGiboney, 883–4353, fax 883–4351.

FEDERAL COMMUNICATIONS COMMISSION

445 12th Street, SW., 20554, phone (202) 418–0200, http://www.fcc.gov

FCC National Consumer Center: 1–888–225–5322 / 1–888–835–5322 (TTY)

Chairman.—Michael J. Copps (acting), room 8–B115, 418–2000.
Confidential Assistant.—Carolyn Conyers.
Chief of Staff.—Rick Chessen (acting).
Senior Legal Advisor.—Scott Deutchman (acting).
Legal Advisor.— Jennifer Schneider.
Commissioner.—Jonathan S. Adelstien, room 8–A302, 418–2300.
Confidentail Assistant.—Katherine Yocum.
Chief of Staff / Senior Legal Advisor.—Renée Crittendon.
Legal Advisors: Rudy Brioché, Mark Stone.
Commissioner.—Robert McDowell, room 8–C302, 418–2200.
Confidential Assistant.—Brigid Calamis.
Chief of Staff / Senior Legal Advisor.—Angela Giancarlo.

Legal Advisors: Nicholas Alexander, Rosemary Harold.
Commissioner.—Vacant.
Commissioner.—Vacant.

OFFICE OF ADMINISTRATIVE LAW JUDGES

Administrative Law Judge.—Richard L. Sippel, room 1–C768, 418–2280.

OFFICE OF COMMUNICATIONS BUSINESS OPPORTUNITIES

Director.—Carolyn Fleming Williams, room 4–A760, 418–0990.

CONSUMER AND GOVERNMENTAL AFFAIRS BUREAU

Bureau Chief.—Catherine Seidel, room 5–C758, 418–1400.
Chief of Staff.—Pam Slipakoff, room 5–C739.
Deputy Bureau Chief of:
Outreach.—Thomas Wyatt, room 5–C755.
Policy.—Suzanne Tetreault (acting), room 5–C754.
Assistant Bureau Chief, Administration and Management.—Patricia Green, room 5–A848.
Chief, Division of:
Consumer Affairs and Outreach.—Rachel Kazan, room 4–C763.
Consumer Inquiries and Complaints Division.—Jeffrey Tignor (acting), room 5–A847.
Consumer Policy.—Erica McMahon, room 5–A844.
Chief, Office of:
Disability Rights.—Thomas Chandler, room 3–B431.
Intergovernmental Affairs.—Gregory Vadas, room 5–A660.
Infomation Resource Management.—Bill Cline (acting), room CY–B533.
Reference Information Center.—Bill Cline, room CY–B533.

ENFORCEMENT BUREAU

Chief.—Kris Monteith, room 3–C252, 418–1098.
Deputy Bureau Chiefs: Gene Fullano, Dana Schaffer.
Chief, Division of:
Investigations and Hearings.—Hillary DeNigro, room 4–C321, 418–7334.
Market Disputes Resolution.—Alex Starr, room 4–C342, 418–7248.
Spectrum Enforcement.—Kathryn Berthot, room 3–C366, 418–1160.
Telecommunications.—Colleen Heitkamp, room 4–C224, 418–7320.
Director of:
North East Region: Chicago, IL.—G. Michael Moffitt (847) 813–4671.
South Central Region: Kansas City, MO.—Dennis P. ''Denny'' Carlton (816) 316–1243.
Western Region: San Diego, CA.—Rebecca L. Dorch (925) 407–8708.

OFFICE OF ENGINEERING AND TECHNOLOGY

Chief.—Julius Knapp, room 7–C155, 418–2470.

OFFICE OF GENERAL COUNSEL

General Counsel.—P. Michele Ellison (acting), room 8–C757, 418–1700.
Deputy General Counsels: Ajit Pai, Joseph Palmore.
Associate General Counsel.—Jacob Lewis.

OFFICE OF INSPECTOR GENERAL

Inspector General.—David L. Hunt (acting), room 2–C750, 418–0470.

INTERNATIONAL BUREAU

Chief.—John V. Giusti (acting), room 6–C746, 418–0437.

Deputy Chief.—Roderick K. Porter, room 6–C752, 418–0423.
Chief, Division of:
Policy.—James Ball, room 7–A760, 418–0427.
Satellite.—Robert Nelson, room 6–A665, 418–0719.
Strategic Analysis and Negotiations.—Kathryn O'Brien, room 6–A763, 418–0439.

OFFICE OF LEGISLATIVE AFFAIRS

Director.—Michael S. Perko (acting), room 8–C432, 418–1900.

OFFICE OF MANAGING DIRECTOR

Managing Director.—Mary Beth Richards (acting), room 8–C464, 418–0980.
Deputy Managing Directors: Mindy Ginsburg, Joseph Hall.
Secretary.—Marlene Dortch, room TW–B204, 418–0300.
Deputy Secretary.—William F. Caton.
Chief Human Capital Officer.—Bonita Tingley, room 1–A100, 418–0293 (TTY); 418–0150 (Employment Verification).

MEDIA BUREAU

Chief.—Robert H. Ratcliffe (acting), room 3–C740, 418–7200.
Senior Deputy Bureau Chief.—Roy J. Stewart, room 2–C347.
Chief of Staff.—Thomas Horan, room 3–C478.
Chief, Division of:
Audio Services.—Peter H. Doyle, room 2–A360, 418–2700
Engineering.—John Wong, room 2–A838, 418–7012.
Industry Analysis.—Royce Sherlock, room 2–C360, 418–2330.
Policy.—Mary Beth Murphy, room 4–A766, 418–2120.
Video.—Barbara A. Kreisman, room 2–A666, 418–1600.

OFFICE OF MEDIA RELATIONS

Director.—David H. Fiske, room CY–C314, 418–0500.

OFFICE OF STRATEGIC PLANNING AND POLICY ANALYSIS

Chief.—Elizabeth Andrion (acting), room 7–C347, 418–2030.

WIRELESS TELECOMMUNICATIONS BUREAU

Chief.—James Schlichting (acting), room 6–6413, 418–0600.
Deputy Bureau Chiefs: Chris Moore, room 6–6417; Joel Taubenblatt, room 6–6419.
Assistant Bureau Chief for Management.—Carlette Smith, room 6–6422, 418–2466.
Chief, Division of:
Action and Spectrum Access.—Margaret Wiener, room 6–6419, 418–0660.
Broadband.—Blaise Scinto, room 3–C124, 418–BITS.
Mobility.—Roger Noel, room 6–6411, 418–0620.
Spectrum and Competition Policy.—Nese Guendelsberger (acting), room 6–6405, 418–0634.
Spectrum Management Resource and Technology.—Mary Bucher (acting), (Gettysburg), (717) 338–2656.

WIRELINE COMPETITION BUREAU

Chief.—Julie Veach (acting), room 5–C354, 418–1500.
Deputy Bureau Chief.—Donald Stockdale, room 5–C450, 418–1500.

OFFICE OF WORKPLACE DIVERSITY

Director.—Lawerence Schaffner (acting), room 5–B444, 418–1799.

REGIONAL AND FIELD OFFICES
NORTHEAST REGION

Regional Director of:
Chicago: G. Michael Moffitt, Park Ridge Office Center, Room 306, 1550 Northwest Highway, Park Ridge, IL 60068 (847) 813–4671.

FIELD OFFICES—NORTHEAST REGION

Director of:
Boston: Dennis V. Loria, One Batterymarch Park, Quincy, MA 02169 (617) 786–1154.

Columbia: James T. Higgins, 9200 Farm House Lane, Columbia, MD 21046 (301) 725–0019.

Detroit: James A. Bridgewater, 24897 Hathaway Street, Farmington Hills, MI 48335 (248) 471–5661.

New York: Dan Noel, 201 Varick Street, Room 1151, New York, NY 10014 (212) 337–1865.

Philadelphia: Gene J. Stanbro, One Oxford Valley Office Building, Room 404, 2300 East Lincoln Highway, Langhorne, PA 19047 (215) 741–3022.

SOUTH CENTRAL REGION

Regional Director of:
Kansas City: Dennis P. Carlton, 520 NE Colbern Road, Second Floor, Lee's Summit, MO 64086 (816) 316–1243.

FIELD OFFICES—SOUTH CENTRAL REGION

Director of:
Atlanta: Doug Miller, Koger Center, 3575 Koger Boulevard, Suite 320, Duluth, GA 30096 (770) 935–3372.

Dallas: James D. Wells, 9330 LBJ Freeway, Room 1170, Dallas, TX 75243 (214) 575–6361.

Kansas City: Robert C. McKinney, 520 Northeast Colbern Road, Second Floor, Lee's Summit, MO 64086 (816) 316–1248.

New Orleans: Leroy ''Bud'' Hall, 2424 Edenborn Avenue, Room 460, Metarie, LA 70001 (504) 219–8989.

Tampa: Ralph M. Barlow, 2203 North Lois Avenue, Room 1215, Tampa, FL 33607 (813) 348–1741.

WESTERN REGION

Regional Director of:
Denver: Rebecca Dorch, 215 South Wadsworth Boulevard, Suite 303, Lakewood, CO 80226 (303) 407–8708.

FIELD OFFICES—WESTERN REGION

Director of:
Denver: Nikki Shears, 215 South Wadsworth Boulevard, Suite 303, Lakewood, CO 80226 (303) 231–5212.

Los Angeles: Catherine Deaton, Cerritos Corporate Towers, 18000 Studebaker Road, Room 660, Cerritos, CA 90701 (562) 865–0235.

San Diego: William Zears, Interstate Office Park, 4542 Ruffner Street, Room 370, San Diego, CA 92111 (858) 496–5125.

San Francisco: Thomas N. Van Stavern, 5653 Stoneridge Drive, Suite 105, Pleasanton, CA 94588 (925) 416–9777.

Seattle: Kris McGowan, 11410 Northeast 122nd Way, Room 312, Kirkland, WA 98034 (425) 820–6271.

FEDERAL DEPOSIT INSURANCE CORPORATION

550 17th Street, NW., 20429

phone (877) 275–3342, http://www.fdic.gov

Chairman.—Sheila C. Bair.
Senior Advisor to the Chairman for Supervision.—Jason C. Cave, 898–3548.
Deputy to the Chairman for External Affairs.—Paul Nash, 898–6962.
Deputy to the Chairman and Chief Financial Officer.—Steve App, 898–8732.
Vice Chairman.—Martin J. Gruenburg, 898–3888.
Deputy.—Barbara Ryan, 898–3841.
Director.—Thomas J. Curry, 898–3957.
Deputy to the Director.—Lisa K. Roy, 898–3764.
Director (OCC).—John C. Dugan, 874–4900.
Deputy.—William Rowe, 898–6960.
Director (OTS).—John E. Bowman (acting), 906–6327.
Senior Counsel (Special Projects).—Charlotte M. Bahin, 906–6452.
Director, Office of Legislative Affairs.—Eric J. Spitler, 898–3837, fax 898–3745.

FEDERAL ELECTION COMMISSION

999 E Street, NW., 20463

phone (202) 694–1000, Toll Free (800) 424–9530, fax 219–3880, http://www.fec.gov

Chairman.—Steven T. Walther, 694–1055.
Vice Chairman.—Matthew S. Petersen, 694–1011.
Commissioners:
Cynthia L. Bauerly, 694–1020.
Caroline C. Hunter, 694–1045.
Donald F. McGahn II, 694–1050.
Ellen L. Weintraub, 694–1035.
Staff Director.—Robert A. Hickey, 694–1007, fax 219–2338.
Deputy Staff Director for—
Compliance/Chief Compliance Officer.—John D. Gibson, 694–1158.
Information Technology/Chief Information Officer.—Alec Palmer, 694–1250.
Communications/Chief Communications Officer.—Arthur Forster, 694–1681.
Assistant Staff Director for—
Information Division.—Greg Scott 694–1100.
Disclosure.—Patricia Klein Young, 694–1120.
Director for Congressional Affairs.—J. Duane Pugh, 694–1006.
Press Officer.—Judith Ingram, 694–1220.
Director Human Resources.—James J. Wilson, 694–1080.
Administrative Officer.—Aileen Baker, 694–1240.
EEO Director.—Judy McLaughlin (acting), 694–1229.
General Counsel.—Thomasenia P. Duncan, 694–1650.
Deputy General Counsel.—P. Christopher Hughey.
Associate General Counsel for—
Enforcement.—Ann Marie Terzaken.
General Law and Advice.—Lawrence Calvert.
Litigation.—David Kolker.
Policy.—Rosemary C. Smith.
Library Director (Law).—Leta L. Holley.
Chief Financial Offier.—Mary Sprague, 694–1217.
Deputy Chief Financial Officer/Budget Director.—Rich Kodl, 694–1216.
Director of Accounting.—Judy Berning, 694–1230.
Inspector General.—Lynne A. McFarland, 694–1015.
Deputy Inspector General.—Jonathon A. Hatfield.

FEDERAL HOUSING FINANCE AGENCY *

1700 G Street, NW., 4th Floor, 20552

phone (202) 414–3800, fax 414–3823, and

1625 Eye Street, NW., 4th Floor, 20006

phone (202) 408–2500, fax 408–1435, http://www.fhfa.gov

[Created by Housing and Economic Recovery Act of 2008, 122 Stat. 2654, Public Law 110–289—July 30, 2008]

Director.—James B. Lockhart III 414–6923.
Chief Operating Officer and Senior Deputy Director for Housing Mission and Goals.—Edward J. DeMarco.
Deputy Director, Division of:
Federal Home Loan Bank Regulation.—Stephen Cross, 408–2500.
Enterprise Regulation.—Christopher Dickerson, 414–6923.
General Counsel.—Alfred Pollard, 414–6924.
Senior Deputy General Counsel.—Christopher T. Curtis, 408–2500.
Inspector General.—Edward Kelley (acting), (800) 793–7724.
Associate Director for—
Congressional Affairs.—Joanne Hanley, 414–6922.
External Relations.—Peter Brereton, 414–6922.
Senior Associate Director for—
Conservatorship.—Jeff Spohn, 414–3763.
Chief Accountant.—Wanda DeLeo, 343–1830.
Examinations.—John Kerr, 414–8972 / 343–1317.
Monitoring and Analysis.—Anthony G. Cornyn, 408–2500.
Supervisory Policy.—Karen Walter, 408–2500.
Chief, Office of:
Administrative Officer.—David A. Lee, 408–2514.
Economist.—Patrick Lawler, 414–3776.
Financial Officer.—Mark Kinsey, 414–3811.
Human Capital Officer.—Janet Murphy, 408–2810.
Information Officer.—Kevin Winkler, 414–3769.

FEDERAL LABOR RELATIONS AUTHORITY

1400 K Street, NW., 20424–0001, phone (202) 218–7770, fax 482–6635

FLRA Agency Head.—Carol Waller Pope, 218–7900.
Executive Director.—Sonna Stampone (acting), 218–7941.
Director, Policy and Performance Management/Chief Human Capital Offier.—Catherine V. Emerson, 218–7945.
Solicitor.—Rosa Koppel, 218–7999.
Inspector General.—Francine Eichler, 218–7970.
Collaboration and Alternative Dispute Resolution Program.—Andy Pizzi, 218–7933.
Foreign Service Impasse Disputes Panel.—Vacant, 218–7790.
Foreign Service Labor Relations Board.—Carol Waller Pope, 218–7900.

AUTHORITY

Chariman.—Carol Waller Pope, 218–7900.
Chief Counsel.—Susan D. McCluskey.
Member.—Thomas M. Beck, 218–7930.
Chief Counsel.—James Abbott, 218–7930.
Member.—Vacant, 218–7920.
Chief Counsel.—Vacant, 218–218–7930.
Chief, Case Intake and Publication.—Donald Harris, 218–7740.

* The Federal Housing Finance Agency (FHFA) was created on July 30, 2008, when President Bush signed into law the Housing and Economic Recovery Act of 2008. The Act created a world-class, empowered regulator with all of the authorities necessary to oversee vital components of our country's secondary mortgage markets—Fannie Mae, Freddie Mac, and the Federal Home Loan Banks. In addition, this law combined the staffs of the Office of Federal Housing Enterprise Oversight (OFHEO), the Federal Housing Finance Board (FHFB), and the GSE mission office at the Department of Housing and Urban Development (HUD).

GENERAL COUNSEL OF THE FLRA

General Counsel.—Vacant, 218–7910.
Assistant General Counsel for Legal Policy and Advice.—Sarah Whittle Spooner.
Assistant General Counsel for Appeals.—Richard Zorn.

OFFICE OF ADMINISTRATIVE LAW JUDGES

Chief Judge.—Charles Center, 218–7950.

FEDERAL SERVICE IMPASSES PANEL (FSIP)

FSIP Chairman.—Vacant, 218–7790.
Executive Director.—H. Joseph Schimansky, 218–7790.

REGIONAL OFFICES

Regional Directors:
Atlanta.—Richard S. Jones (acting), Marquis Two Tower, Suite 701, 285 Peachtree Center Avenue, Atlanta, GA 30303 (404) 331–5300, fax (404) 331–5280.
Boston.—Philip T. Roberts (acting), 10 Causeway Street, Suite 472, Boston, MA 02222 (617) 565–5100, fax 565–6262.
Chicago.—Peter A. Sutton, 55 West Monroe, Suite 1150, Chicago, IL 60603 (312) 886–3465, fax 886–5977.
Dallas.—James E. Petrucci, 525 Griffin Street, Suite 926, LB 107, Dallas, TX 75202 (214) 767–6266, fax 767–0156.
Denver.—Matthew Jarvinen, 1244 Speer Boulevard, Suite 100, Denver, CO 80204 (303) 844–5224, fax 844–2774.
San Francisco.—Gerald M. Cole, 901 Market Street, Suite 220, San Francisco, CA 94103 (415) 356–5000, fax 356–5017.
Washington, DC.—Robert Hunter, 1400 K Street, NW., Suite 200, Washington, DC 20005 (202) 357–6029, fax (202) 482–6724.

FEDERAL MARITIME COMMISSION

800 North Capitol Street, NW., 20573

phone (202) 523–5725, fax 523–0014

OFFICE OF THE CHAIRMAN

Chairman.—Joseph E. Brennan (acting), room 1000, 523–5723.
Counsel.—Steven D. Najarian.
Commissioner.—Rebecca F. Dye, room 1038, 523–5715.
Counsel.—Edward L. Lee, Jr.
Commissioner.—Vacant, room 1044, 523–5712.
Counsel.—Vacant.
Commissioner.—Vacant, room 1032, 523–5723.
Counsel.—Vacant.
Commissioner.—Vacant, room 1026, 523–5721.
Counsel.—Vacant.

OFFICE OF THE SECRETARY

Secretary.—Karen V. Gregory, room 1046, 523–5725.
Assistant Secretary.—Tanga S. FitzGibbon.
Librarian.—Charlotte C. White, room 1085, 523–5762.
Director, Office of Consumer Affairs and Dispute Resolution.—Ronald D. Murphy, room 1082, 523–5807.

OFFICE OF EQUAL EMPLOYMENT OPPORTUNITY

Director.—Keith I. Gilmore, room 1052, 523–5859.

OFFICE OF THE GENERAL COUNSEL

General Counsel.—Peter J. King, room 1018, 523–5740.
Deputy General Counsel.—Vacant.

OFFICE OF ADMINISTRATIVE LAW JUDGES

Chief Judge.—Clay G. Guthridge, room 1088, 523–5750.

OFFICE OF THE INSPECTOR GENERAL

Inspector General.—Adam R. Trzeciak, room 1054, 523–5863.

OFFICE OF ADMINISTRATION

Director.—Vacant, room 926, 523–5800.
Deputy Director/CIO.—Anthony Haywood.
Director, Office of:
Financial Management.—Karon E. Douglass, room 916, 523–5770.
Human Resources.—Hatsie H. Charbonneau, room 924, 523–5773.
Information Technology.—James M. Woods, room 904, 523–5835.
Management Services.—Michael H. Kilby, room 924, 523–5900.

OFFICE OF OPERATIONS

Director.—Austin L. Schmitt, room 972, 523–0988.
Deputy Director.—Rachel E. Dickon.
Area Representatives:
Houston.—Debra A. Zezima (281) 591–6088.
Los Angeles.—Oliver E. Clark (310) 514–4905.
New Orleans.—Bruce N. Johnson, Sr. (504) 589–6662.
New York: Joseph A. Castellano (718) 553–2223; Emanuel J. Mingione (718) 553–2228.
Seattle.—Michael A. Moneck (206) 553–0221.
South Florida.—Andrew Margolis (954) 963–5362.

BUREAU OF CERTIFICATION AND LICENSING

Director.—Sandra L. Kusumoto, room 970, 523–5787.
Special Assistants: Mary T. Hoang, Jerome Johnson.
Director, Office of:
Passenger Vessels and Information Processing.—Vacant, 523–5818.
Transportation Intermediaries.—Ronald Podlaskowich, 523–5843.

BUREAU OF ENFORCEMENT

Director.—Vern W. Hill, room 900, 523–5783 or 523–5860.
Deputy Director.—George A. Quadrino.

BUREAU OF TRADE ANALYSIS

Director.—Florence A. Carr, room 940, 523–5796.
Deputy Director.—Rebecca A. Fenneman.
Director, Office of:
Agreements.—Jeremiah D. Hospital, 523–5793.
Economics and Competition Analysis.—Roy J. Pearson, 523–5845.
Service Contracts and Tariffs.—Francis G. Kardian, room 940, 523–5856.

FEDERAL MEDIATION AND CONCILIATION SERVICE

2100 K Street, NW., 20427, phone (202) 606–8100, fax 606–4251

[Codified under 29 U.S.C. 172]

Director.—Scot L. Beckenbaugh (acting).
Deputy Director.—Scot L. Beckenbaugh.
Chief of Staff.—Fran L. Leonard, 606–3661.
General Counsel.—Dawn Starr, 606–8090.
Director for—
ADR/International/FMCS Institute.—Michael Stein, 606–8099.
Arbitration Services.—Vella M. Traynham, 606–5111.
Budget and Finance.—Fran L. Leonard, 606–3661.
Grants.—Linda Stubbs, 606–8181.
Human Resources.—Dan Ellerman, 606–5460.
Information Systems and Administrative Services.—Dan W. Funkhouser, 606–5477.
Regional Director (Eastern/Western).—John F. Buettner (216) 520–4805.

FEDERAL MINE SAFETY AND HEALTH REVIEW COMMISSION

601 New Jersey Avenue, NW., Suite 9500, 20001

phone (202) 434–9900, fax 434–9944

[Created by Public Law 95–164]

Chairperson.—Michael F. Duffy, room 9515, 434–9924.
Commissioner.—Robert F. Cohen, Jr., room 9527, 434–9912.
Executive Director.—Lisa M. Boyd, room 9509, 434–9905.
Chief Administrative Law Judge.—Robert J. Lesnick, room 8515, 434–9958.
General Counsel.—Michael McCord, room 9547, 434–9935.

FEDERAL RETIREMENT THRIFT INVESTMENT BOARD

1250 H Street, NW., 20005, phone (202) 942–1600, fax 942–1676

[Authorized by 5 U.S.C. 8472]

Executive Director.—Gregory T. Long, 942–1601.
General Counsel.—Thomas K. Emswiler, 942–1660.
Director, Office of:
Automated Systems.—Mark Hagerty, 942–1610.
External Affairs.—Thomas J. Trabucco, 942–1640.
Finance.—James B. Petrick, 942–1630.
Investments.—Theresa Ray, 942–1630.
Participant Services.—Pamela-Jeanne Moran, 942–1450.
Research and Strategic Planning.—Renee Wilder, 942–1630.

Chairman.—Andrew M. Saul, 942–1660.
Board Members:
Thomas A. Fink.
Alejandro M. Sanchez.
Gordon J. Whiting.
Terrence A. Duffy.

FEDERAL TRADE COMMISSION

600 Pennsylvania Avenue, NW., 20580

phone (202) 326–2222, http://www.ftc.gov

Chairman.—Jonathan Leibowitz, room 338, 326–3400.
Staff Assistant.—June Young, room 340, 326–2105.
Chief of Staff.—Joni Lupovitz, room 344, 326–3743.
Commissioners: Pamela Jones Harbour, room 328, 326–2907; William E. Kovacic, room 538, 326–2150; J. Thomas Rosch, room 528, 326–3651.

Director, Office of:
Competition.—Richard A. Feinstein, room 370, 326–3658.
Congressional Relations.—Jeanne Bumpus, room 404, 326–3680.
Consumer Protection.—David Vladeck, room 470, 326–2234.
Economics.—Joseph Farrell, room 270, 326–2888.
Policy Planning.—Susan S. DeSanti, room 392, 326–2210.
Public Affairs.—Claudia Bourne Farrell (acting), room 421, 326–2181.
Executive Director.—Charles Schneider, room 426, 326–2748.
General Counsel.—Willard K. Tom, room 570, 326–3020.
Secretary.—Donald S. Clark, room 172, 326–2514.
Inspector General.—John Seeba, room 1119NJ, 326–2800.
Chief Administrative Law Judge.—D. Michael Chappell, room 106, 326–3637.

REGIONAL DIRECTORS

East Central Region: Jonathan M. Steiger (acting), Eaton Center, Suite 200, 1111 Superior Avenue, Cleveland, OH 44114 (216) 263–3455.
Midwest Region: C. Steve Baker, 55 East Monroe Street, Suite 1825, Chicago, IL 60603 (312) 960–5634.
Northeast Region: Leonard Gordon, One Bowling Green, Suite 318, New York, NY 10004 (212) 607–2829.
Northwest Region: Robert J. Schroeder, 915 Second Avenue, Suite 2896, Seattle, WA 98174 (206) 220–6350.
Southeast Region: Bradley Elbein, 225 Peachtree Street, NE., Suite 1500, Atlanta, GA 30303 (404) 656–1390.
Southwest Region: Deanya T. Kuckelhan, 1999 Bryan Street, Suite 2150, Dallas, TX 75201 (214) 979–9350.
Western Region—Los Angeles: Jeffrey Klurfeld, 18077 Wilshire Boulevard, Suite 700, Los Angeles, CA 90024–3679 (310) 824–4343.
Western Region—San Francisco: Jeffrey Klurfeld, 901 Market Street, Suite 570, San Francisco, CA 94103 (415) 848–5100.

FOREIGN–TRADE ZONES BOARD

1401 Constitution Avenue, NW., Room 2111, 20230

phone (202) 482–2862, fax 482–0002

Chairman.—Gary Locke, Secretary of Commerce.
Member.—Timothy F. Geithner, Secretary of the Treasury.
Executive Secretary.—Andrew McGilvray.

GENERAL SERVICES ADMINISTRATION

1800 F Street, NW., 20405, phone (202) 501–0800, http://www.gsa.gov

OFFICE OF THE ADMINISTRATOR

Administrator.—Paul F. Prouty (acting).
Deputy Administrator.—Barnaby L. Brasseux (202) 501–1226.
Chief of Staff.—Danielle Germain (202) 501–1216.

CENTRAL OFFICE

OFFICE OF CONGRESSIONAL AND INTERGOVERNMENTAL AFFAIRS

Associate Administrator.—Ralph Conner (acting), 501–0563.
Director of:
Congressional Support Services.—Marcia Herzog.
Legislative Affairs.—Greg Parks.
Senior Advisor for Appropriations.—Michael Gurgo.

OFFICE OF THE CHIEF FINANCIAL OFFICER

Chief Financial Officer.—Kathleen Turco, 501–1721.

Director of:
Budget.—Deborah Schilling, 501–0719.
Controller.—Faye Basden (acting), 219–3617.
Finance.—Douglas Glenn, 501–0562.
Financial Management Systems.—Lynne E. Johnson (acting), 501–3429.

OFFICE OF THE CHIEF HUMAN CAPITAL OFFICER

Chief Human Capital Officer.—Gail T. Lovelace, 501–0398.
Deputy Chief Human Capital Officer.—William A. Kelly, 501–0885.
Associate Administrator for Performance Improvement.—Vince Warrick, 501–1143.

OFFICE OF THE GENERAL COUNSEL

General Counsel.—Lennard S. Loewentritt (acting), 501–2200.
Associate General Counsel for—
General Law.—Eugenia D. Ellison, 501–1460.
Personal Property .—Janet Harney (acting), 501–1156.
Real Property.—Barry Segal, 501–0430.

OFFICE OF THE CHIEF INFORMATION OFFICER

Chief Information Officer.—Casey Coleman, 501–1000.
Director, Office of:
Enterprise Infrastructure.—Philip E. Klokis, 501–3437.
Enterprise Management Services.—Daryle Seckar, 208–5054.
Enterprise Solution.—Teresa D. Sorrenti, 219–3393.

OFFICE OF GOVERNMENTWIDE POLICY

Associate Administrator and Chief Acquisition Officer.—Michael Robertson, 501–8880.
Principal Deputy Associate Administrator.—Stan Kaczmarczyk.
Executive Officer.—Tony Butcher.
Executive Director:
Office of Policy Initiatives.—James L. Dean, 273–3563.
Regulatory Information Service Center.—John C. Thomas, 482–7340.
Deputy Associate Administrator, Office of:
Real Property Management.—Carolyn Austin-Diggs, 501–0856.
Travel, Transportation, and Asset Management.—Rebecca R. Rhodes, 501–1777.
Assistant Deputy Associate Administrator, Office of Technology Strategy.—Keith Thurston, 501–0202.

OFFICE OF CITIZEN SERVICES AND COMMUNICATIONS

Associate Administrator.—David Bethel, 501–0705.

OFFICE OF CIVIL RIGHTS

Associate Administrator.—Madeline Caliendo, 501–0767.

OFFICE OF PERFORMANCE IMPROVEMENT

Associate Administrator.—Steven D. McPeek, 501–1143.

OFFICE OF SMALL BUSINESS UTILIZATION

Associate Administrator.—Mary Parks (acting), 501–1021.

OFFICE OF THE INSPECTOR GENERAL

Inspector General.—Brian D. Miller, 501–0450.
Deputy Inspector General.—Robert C. Erickson, Jr., 501–3105.

Director of Communications and Congressional Affairs.—Dave Farley, 219–1062.
Director, Office of Internal Evaluation and Analysis.—Peter J. Coniglio, 501–0468.
Counsel to the Inspector General.—Richard Levi, 501–1932.
Assistant Inspector General for—
Administration.—Carolyn Presley-Doss, 501–4638.
Auditing.—Theodore R. Stehney, 501–0374.
Investigations.—Gregory G. Rowe, 501–1397.

BOARD OF CONTRACT APPEALS

Chairman.—Stephen M. Daniels (202) 606–8820.
Vice Chairman.—Robert W. Parker, 606–8819.
Chief Counsel.—Margaret S. Pfunder, 606–8787.
Clerk.—Beatrice Jones, 606–8800.

Board Judges, 606–8820: Anthony S. Borwick, Stephen M. Daniels, Jerome Drummond, Beryl Gilmore, Catherine B. Hyatt, H. Chuck Kullberg, R. Anthony McCann, Howard Pollack, Patricia Sheridan, Jeri Somers, Candida Steel, James Stern, Joseph Vergilio, Richard Walters.

NATIONAL SERVICES

FEDERAL ACQUISITION SERVICE

Commissioner.—James A. Williams (703) 605–5400.
Deputy Commissioner.—Tyree Varnado.
Chief Information Officer.—Liz Delnegro (acting), 605–2576.
Controller.—Jon Jordan, 605–5440.
Assistant Commissioner for—
Administration.—Karen Hampel, 605–5574.
Acquisition Management.—Steve Kempf (703) 605–5527.
Assisted Acquisition Services.—Mary Davie, (703) 306–6728.
Customer Accounts and Research.—Gary Feit, 605–5644.
General Supplies and Services.—Joseph Jeu, 605–5511.
Integrated Technology Services.—Ed O'Hare (703) 306–6200.
Strategic Business Planning and Process Improvement.—Amanda Fredriksen (acting), (703) 605–5513.
Travel, Motor Vehicle and Card Services.—Bill Webster (703) 605–5500.

PUBLIC BUILDINGS SERVICE

Commissioner.—Robert Peck (202) 501–1100.
Deputy Commissioner.—Anthony Costa.
Chief of Staff.—Benjamin Kochanski (acting).
Chief Architect.—Leslie Shepherd, 501–1888.
Budget and Financial Management.—Lisa Ward, 501–0658.
PBS Assistant Commissioner for—
Capital Construction.—Leslie Shepherd, 501–1888.
Organizational Resources.—Sean Mildrew, 501–0971.
PBS Deputy Assistant Commissioner, Office of Real Estate Portfolio Management.—David Foley, 501–0638.

REGIONAL OFFICES

National Capital Region: 7th and D Streets, SW., Washington, DC 20407 (202) 708–9100.
Regional Administrator.—Sharon J. Banks (acting).
Regional Commissioner for Federal Acquisition Service.—Alfonso Finley, (202) 708–6100.
Regional Commissioner for Public Buildings Service.—Bart Bush, (202) 708–5891.
Regional Counsel.—Paula DeMuth, (202) 708–5155.
New England Region: Thomas P. O'Neill Federal Building, 10 Causeway Street, Boston, MA 02222 (617) 565–5860.
Regional Administrator.—Glenn Rotondo (acting).
Regional Commissioner for Federal Acquisition Service.—Sharon Wall (617) 565–5721.
Regional Commissioner for Public Buildings Service.—Glenn Rotondo, (617) 565–5694.
Northeast and Caribbean Region: 26 Federal Plaza, New York, NY 10278 (212) 264–2600.

Regional Administrator.—John Scorcia (acting).
Regional Commissioner for Federal Acquisition Service.—Patrick Donovan (acting), (212) 264–4039.
Regional Commissioner for Public Buildings Service.—John Scorcia (212) 264–4282.

Mid-Atlantic Region: The Strawbridge's Building, 20 North Eighth Street, Philadelphia, PA 19107 (215) 446–4900.
Regional Administrator.—Linda C. Chero (acting).
Regional Commissioner for Federal Acquisition Service.—Linda C. Chero.
Regional Commissioner for Public Buildings Service.—Robert Hewell (215) 446–4500.
Regional Counsel.—Robert J. McCall (215) 446–4946.

Southeast Sunbelt Region: 77 Forsyth Street, Suite 600, Atlanta, GA 30303 (404) 331–3200.
Regional Administrator.—Jimmy H. Bridgeman (acting).
Regional Commissioner for Federal Acquisition Service.—William ''Bill'' Sisk (404) 331–5114.
Regional Commissioner for Public Buildings Service.—James Weller (acting), (404) 562–0263.

Great Lakes Region: 230 South Dearborn Street, Chicago, IL 60604 (312) 353–5395.
Regional Administrator.—J. David Hood (acting).
Regional Commissioner for Federal Acquisition Service.—Frank Hoeft.
Regional Commissioner for Public Buildings Service.—Michael Gelber.

Heartland Region: 1500 East Bannister Road, Kansas City, MO 64131 (816) 926–7201.
Regional Administrator.—Michael T. Brinks (acting).
Regional Commissioner for Federal Acquisition Service.—Sharon Henry (acting), (816) 823–1700.
Regional Commissioner for Public Buildings Service.—Mary Ruwwe (816) 926–7231.

Greater Southwest Region: 819 Taylor Street, Fort Worth, TX 76102 (817) 978–2321.
Regional Administrator.—George Prochaska (acting).
Regional Commissioner for Federal Acquisition Service.—George Prochaska (817) 574–2516.
Regional Commissioner for Public Buildings Service.—James Feracci (acting), (817) 978–2522.

Rocky Mountain Region: Building 41, Denver Federal Center, Denver, CO 80225 (303) 236–7329.
Regional Administrator.—Timothy O. Horne (acting).
Regional Commissioner for Federal Acquisition Service.—Timothy O. Horne (303) 236–7197.
Regional Commissioner for Public Buildings Service.—Scott Conner (303) 236–7245.

Pacific Rim Region: 450 Golden Gate Avenue, Room 5–2690, San Francisco, CA 94102 (415) 522–3001.
Regional Administrator.—Jeffrey Neely (acting).
Regional Commissioner for Federal Acquisition Service.—John Boyan (415) 522–2777.
Regional Commissioner for Public Buildings Service.—Mary Filippini (415) 522–3100.

Northwest/Arctic Region: GSA Center, 400 15th Street, SW., Auburn, WA 98001 (253) 931–7000.
Regional Administrator.—Robin G. Graf (acting).
Regional Commissioner for Federal Acquisition Service.—Gary G. Casteel (253) 931–7115.
Regional Commissioner for Public Buildings Service.—Catharine A. Kualii (acting), (253) 931–7200.

HARRY S. TRUMAN SCHOLARSHIP FOUNDATION

712 Jackson Place, NW., 20006

phone (202) 395–4831, fax 395–6995

[Created by Public Law 93–642]

BOARD OF TRUSTEES

President.—Madeleine K. Albright.
Chairman Emeritus.—Elmer B. Staats.
Vice Chairman.—Ike Skelton, Representative from Missouri.
Vice President.—Max Sherman.
General Counsel.—C. Westbrook Murphy.
Members:

W. Todd Akin, Representative from Missouri.
Max Baucus, Senator from Montana.
Christopher S. Bond, Senator from Missouri.
Javaid Anwar, CEO, Quality Care Consultants, LLC.
Hon. Arne Duncan, Secretary of Education.
Hon. Dave Heineman, Governor, State of Nebraska.
Roger Hunt, U.S. District Judge.
John Kidde, Vice President, Ventura Foods.
Hon. John Peyton, Mayor, City of Jacksonville, Florida.
Sharon ''Nyota'' Tucker, Assistant Professor, Albany State University.
Juanita Vasquez-Gardner, Judge, 399th District Court of Texas.

Executive Secretary.—Frederick G. Slabach.
Deputy Executive Secretary.—Tara Yglesias.
Chief Information Officer.—Tonji Wade.
Education Officer.—Ruth Keen.

JAMES MADISON MEMORIAL FELLOWSHIP FOUNDATION

2000 K Street, Suite 303, NW., 20006–1809

phone (202) 653–8700, fax 653–6045

[Created by Public Law 99–591]

BOARD OF TRUSTEES

Members Appointed by the President of the United States:

John Cornyn, Senator from Texas, *Acting Chairman.*
Eric Cantor, Representative from Virginia.
Robert C. Scott, Representative from Virginia.
Steven M. Colloton, U.S. Circuit Judge, U.S. Court of Appeals 8th Circuit, Des Moines, Iowa.
Joseph Manchin III, Governor of West Virginia.
Diarmuid F. O'Scannlain, U.S. Circuit Judge, U.S. Court of Appeals 9th Circuit, Portland, Oregon.
John J. Faso, Attorney, Manatt, Phelps & Phillips, Albany, New York.
Harvey M. Tettlebaum, Partner, Husch Blackwell Sanders LLP, Jefferson City, Missouri.
J.C.A. Stagg, Editor, *The Papers of James Madison*, University of Virginia, Charlottesville, Virginia.
John R. Petrocik, Chair, Department of Political Science, University of Missouri, Columbia, Missouri.
Arne Duncan, U.S. Secretary of Education (ex officio).

Foundation Staff:

President.—Admiral Paul A. Yost, Jr.
Vice President and Director of Programs.—Lewis F. Larsen.
Director of Administration and Finance.—Stephen W. Weiss.
Academic Advisor to the President.—Herman Belz.
Special Assistant / Office Manager.—Norma J. Claytor.
Academic Assistant.—Sheila Osbourne.
Program Analyst.—Elizabeth G. Ray.

INTER-AMERICAN FOUNDATION

901 North Stuart Street, 10th Floor, Arlington, VA 22203, phone (703) 306–4301

Chair, Board of Directors.—John P. Salazar (acting).
Vice Chair, Board of Directors.—Thomas J. Dodd (acting).
President.—Larry L. Palmer.
General Counsel and Senior Vice President.—Jennifer Hodges Reynolds.
Vice President of Operations.—Linda Kolko.
Regional Director for South America and the Caribbean.—Judith Morrison.
Regional Director for Central America and Mexico.—Jill Wheeler.

JOHN F. KENNEDY CENTER FOR THE PERFORMING ARTS

2700 F Street, NW., 20566, phone (202) 416–8000, fax 416–8205

BOARD OF TRUSTEES

Honorary Chairs:

Mrs. Michelle Obama
Mrs. Laura Bush
Secretary Hillary Rodham Clinton
Mrs. George Bush
Mrs. Ronald Reagan
Mrs. Jimmy Carter
Mrs. Gerald R. Ford
Mrs. Lyndon B. Johnson

Officers:

Chairman.—Stephen A. Schwarzman.
President.—Michael M. Kaiser.
Secretary.—Jean Kennedy Smith.
Assistant Secretary.—Ann Stock.
Treasurer.—Roland Betts.
General Counsel.—Maria Kersten.

Members Appointed by the President of the United States:

Wilma E. Bernstein
Nancy Goodman Brinker
Elliott B. Broidy
Betsy DeVos
Edward W. Easton
Judith Ann Eisenberg
Emilo Estefan, Jr.
Donald J. Hall, Jr.
James A. Haslam II
Helen Lee Henderson
Joan E. Hotchkis
Sheldon B. Kamins
James V. Kimsey
Nancy G. Kinder
Herbert V. Kohler, Jr.
C. Michael Kojaian
Carl H. Linder III
Donna G. Marriott
Norman Y. Mineta
Marilyn Carlson Nelson
Robert Frank Pence
William Charles Powers
Jack L. Oliver III
Gabrielle B. Reynolds
Dr. Condoleeza Rice
Joseph E. Robert, Jr.
Duane R. Roberts
David M. Rubenstein
Shirley W. Ryan
Leonard Sands
Stephen A. Schwarzman
Jean Kennedy Smith
Dean A. Spanos
Marc I. Stern
Alexander F. Treadwell
Stephen A. Wynn

Ex Officio Members Designated by Act of Congress:

(Note: The names of Senators and Representatives appear in order of their years of service)

Hillary Rodham Clinton, Secretary of State.
Kathleen Sebelius, Secretary of Health and Human Services.
Arne Duncan, Secretary of Education.
James M. Inhofe, Senator from Oklahoma.
Harry Reid, Senator from Nevada.
Thad Cochran, Senator from Mississippi.
Dianne Feinstein, Senator from California.
James L. Oberstar, Representative from Minnesota.
Patrick J. Kennedy, Representative from Rhode Island.
Nancy Pelosi, Speaker of the U.S. House of Representatives from California.
John A. Boehner, Representative from Ohio.
John L. Mica, Representative from Florida.
Roy Blunt, Representative from Missouri.
Rosa L. DeLauro, Representative from Connecticut.
Adrian M. Fenty, Mayor, District of Columbia.
Wayne Clough, Secretary, Smithsonian Institution.
James H. Billington, Librarian of Congress.
Earl A. Powell III, Chairman, Commission of Fine Arts.
Vacant, Director, National Park Service.
Michelle Rhee, Chancellor, DC Public Schools.

Honorary Trustees:

Buffy Cafritz
Kenneth M. Duberstein
James H. Evans
Alma Gildenhorn
Melvin R. Laird
Leonard L. Silverstein

Senior Counsel.—Robert Barnett.
Founding Chairman.—Roger L. Stevens (deceased).
Chairmen Emeriti: James A. Johnson, James D. Wolfensohn.

LEGAL SERVICES CORPORATION

3333 K Street, NW., 3rd Floor, 20007–3522

phone (202) 295–1500, fax 337–6797

BOARD OF DIRECTORS

Frank B. Strickland, *Chair*
Lillian R. BeVier, *Vice Chair*
Jonann C. Chiles
Thomas A. Fuentes
Herbert S. Garten
David Hall
Michael D. McKay
Thomas R. Meites
Laurie I. Mikva
Bernice Phillips-Jackson
Sarah M. Singleton

President.—Helaine M. Barnett.
Vice President for Programs and Compliance.—Karen Sarjeant.
Vice President, Legal Affairs, General Counsel and Corporate Secretary.—Victor M. Fortuno.
Chief Administrative Officer.—Charles Jeffress.
Inspector General.—Jeffrey E. Schanz.

NATIONAL AERONAUTICS AND SPACE ADMINISTRATION

300 E Street, SW., 20546, phone (202) 358–0000, http://www.nasa.gov

OFFICE OF THE ADMINISTRATOR

Code AA000, Room 9F44, phone 358–1010

Administrator.—Charles F. Bolden, Jr.
Deputy Administrator.—Lori Garver, 358–1020.
Executive Assistants: Kia Burnette, 358–1827; Kathryn Manuel, 358–1020.
Chief of Staff.—Vacant, 358–1827.
White House Liaison.—David Noble, 358–2198.
Chief Health and Medical Officer.—Dr. Richard S. Williams, room 7P13, 358–2390.

AERONAUTICS RESEARCH MISSION DIRECTORATE

Code EA000, Room 6J39–A, phone 358–4600

Associate Administrator.—Jaiwon Shin.
Deputy Associate Administrator.—Vacant.

OFFICE OF THE CHIEF FINANCIAL OFFICER (CFO)

Code 1A000, Room 8E39–A, phone 358–0978

Chief Financial Officer / Chief Acquisition Officer.—Ronald Spoehel.
Deputy Chief Financial Officer.—Terry Bowie, 358–1135.

OFFICE OF DIVERSITY AND EQUAL OPPORTUNITY PROGRAMS

Code LF000, Room 4Y23, phone 358–2167

Assistant Administrator for Equal Opportunity Programs.—Brenda R. Manuel.

EXPLORATION SYSTEMS MISSION DIRECTORATE

Code BA000, Room 2U39, phone 358–1523

Associate Administrator.—Doug Cooke, 358–7246.
Deputy Associate Administrator.—Vacant, 358–1523.
Deputy Associate Administrator for Policy and Plans.—Tom Cremins, 358–1747.

OFFICE OF EXTERNAL RELATIONS

Code ND000, Room 7V39, phone 358–0400

Assistant Administrator.—Michael F. O'Brien.
Deputy Assistant Administrator.—Al Condes.

OFFICE OF THE GENERAL COUNSEL

Code MA000, Room 9V39, phone 358–2450

General Counsel.—Michael Wholley.
Deputy General Counsel.—Vacant.

OFFICE OF HUMAN CAPITAL MANAGEMENT

Code LE000–A, Room 4V84, phone 358–0520

Assistant Administrator.—Tony Dawsey.

OFFICE OF INFRASTRUCTURE AND ADMINISTRATION

Code LD000, Room 4G74, phone 358–2800

Deputy Assistant Administrator.—Olga Dominguez.
Deputy Assistant Administrator for—
Headquarters Operations.—Christopher Jedrey.
Policy.—Jeffrey Parker.

OFFICE OF INSPECTOR GENERAL

Code W, Room 8U79, phone 358–1220

Inspector General.—Vacant.
Deputy Inspector General.—Thomas Howard.

OFFICE OF LEGISLATIVE AFFAIRS

Code NC000, Room 9L39, phone 358–1948

Assistant Administrator.—Vacant.
Deputy Assistant Administrator.—Mary D. Kerwin.

OFFICE OF PROCUREMENT

Code LH000, Room 5G70, phone 358–2090

Assistant Administrator.—Thomas S. Luedtke.

OFFICE OF PUBLIC AFFAIRS

Code NB000, Room 9P39, phone 358–1400

Assistant Administrator.—Robert Jacobs (acting).

SAFETY AND MISSION ASSURANCE

Code GA000, Room 5W21, phone 358–2406

Chief Officer.—Bryan D. O'Connor.
Deputy Chief Officer.—James D. Lloyd.

SCIENCE MISSION DIRECTORATE

Code DA000, room 3C26, phone 358–3889

Associate Administrator.—Edward Weiler.
Deputy Associate Administrator.—Michael Luther, 358–2165.
Deputy Associate Administrator for—
Programs.—Michael R. Luther, 358–0260.
Technology.—George Komar, 358–3000.
Chief Engineer.—Vacant, 358–7245.
Chief Scientist.—Vacant, 358–2470.

OFFICE OF SECURITY AND PROGRAM PROTECTION

Code LG000, Room 9U70, phone 358–2010

Associate Administrator.—David Saleeba.

Deputy Associate Administrator.—Clint Herbert.

OFFICE OF SMALL AND DISADVANTAGED BUSINESS UTILIZATION

Code LI000, Room 5C39, phone 358–2088

Assistant Administrator.—Glenn A. Delgado.

SPACE OPERATIONS MISSION DIRECTORATE

Code CA000, Room 7K39, phone 358–2015

Associate Administrator.—William H. Gerstenmayer.
Deputy Associate Administrator.—Lynn F.H. Cline, 358–1200.
Deputy Associate Administrator for—
Program Integration.—Dr. William Michael Hawes, 358–0104.
Space Shuttle.—William C. Hill, 358–0571.

NASA NATIONAL OFFICES

Air Force Space Command/XPX (NASA): Peterson Air Force Base, CO 80914.
NASA Senior Representative.—Jeffrey Ashby (719) 554–4900.
Ames Research Center: Moffett Field, CA 94035.
Director.—Simon P. Worden (650) 604–5000.
Dryden Flight Research Center: P.O. Box 273, Edwards, CA 93523.
Director.—Kevin L. Petersen (661) 276–3311.
Glenn Research Center at Lewisfield: 21000 Brookpark Road, Cleveland, OH 44135.
Director.—Dr. Woodrow Whitlow (216) 433–4000.
Goddard Institute for Space Studies: Goddard Space Flight Center, 2880 Broadway, New York, NY 10025.
Head.—Dr. James E. Hansen (212) 678–5500.
Goddard Space Flight Center: 8800 Greenbelt Road, Greenbelt, MD 20771.
Director.—Dr. Ed Weiler (301) 286–2000.
Jet Propulsion Laboratory: 4800 Oak Grove Drive, Pasadena, CA 91109.
Director.—Dr. Charles Elachi (818) 354–4321.
Lyndon B. Johnson Space Center: Houston, TX 77058–3696.
Director.—Michael L. Coats (281) 483–0123.
John F. Kennedy Space Center: Kennedy Space Center, FL 32899.
Director.—James W. Kennedy (321) 867–5000.
Langley Research Center: Hampton, VA 23681.
Director.—Lesa Roe (757) 864–1000.
George C. Marshall Space Flight Center: Marshall Space Flight Center, AL 35812.
Director.—David A. King (256) 544–2121.
Michoud Assembly Facility: P.O. Box 29300, New Orleans, LA 70189.
Manager.—John K. White (504) 257–3311.
NASA IV & V Facility: NASA Independent Verification and Validation Facility, 100 University Drive, Fairmont, WV 26554.
Director.—Nelson H. Keeler (304) 367–8200.
NASA Management Office: Jet Propulsion Laboratory, 4800 Oak Grove Drive, Pasadena, CA 91109.
Director.—Dr. Robert A. Parker (818) 354–5359.
John C. Stennis Space Center: Stennis Space Center, MS 39529.
Director.—Dr. Richard Gilbrech (228) 688–2211.
Vandenberg AFB: P.O. Box 425, Lompoc, CA 93438.
Manager.—Ted L. Oglesby (805) 866–5859.
Wallops Flight Facility: Goddard Space Flight Center, Wallops Island, VA 23337.
Director.—John Campbell (757) 824–1000.
White Sands Test Facility: Johnson Space Center, P.O. Drawer MM, Las Cruces, NM 88004.
Manager.—Joseph Fries (505) 524–5771.

NASA OVERSEAS REPRESENTATIVES

Australia: APO AP 96549, 011–61–2–6281–8501.
Europe: U.S. Embassy, Paris, PSC 116 APO AE 09777, 011–33–1–4312–2100.
NASA Representative.—Don Miller.

Japan: U.S. Embassy, Tokyo, Unit 45004, Box 235, APO AP, 96337–5004, 011–81–3–3224–5827.
NASA Representative.—William Jordan.
Russia: U.S. Embassy, Moscow, PSC 77/NASA APO AE 09721, (256) 961–6333.
NASA Representative.—Phillip Cleary.
Spain: PSC No. 61, Box 0037, APO AE 09642, 011–34–91–548–9250.

NATIONAL ARCHIVES AND RECORDS ADMINISTRATION

700 Pennsylvania Avenue, NW., 20408–0001

8601 Adelphi Road, College Park, MD 20740–6001

http://www.nara.gov

[Created by Public Law 98–497]

Archivist of the United States.—Adrienne C. Thomas (acting), (202) 357–5900, fax 357–5901.
Deputy Archivist of the United States.—Adrienne C. Thomas (202) 357–5900 (301) 837–1600, fax 837–3218.
Chief of Staff.—Debra Wall (301) 837–1600, fax 837–3218.
Assistant Archivist, Office of:
Administration.—Adrienne C. Thomas (301) 837–3050, fax 837–3217.
Federal Register.—Raymond A. Mosely (202) 741–6010, fax 741–6012.
Information Services.—Martha Morphy (301) 837–3670, fax 837–3213.
Presidential Libraries.—Sharon Fawcett (301) 837–3250, fax 837–3199.
Records Services, Washington, DC.—Michael J. Kurtz (301) 837–3110, fax 837–1617.
Regional Records Services.—Thomas Mills (301) 837–2950, fax 837–1617.
Executive Director, National Historical Publications and Records Commission.—Kathleen Williams (202) 501–5010, fax 357–5914.
Director for—
Congressional Affairs and Communications Staff.—John O. Hamilton (202) 357–5100, fax 357–5959.
Equal Employment Opportunity and Diversity Programs.—Robert Jew (301) 837–1849, fax 837–0869.
Information Security Oversight Office.—William Bosanko (202) 357–5250, fax 357–5907.
Policy and Planning Staff.—Susan Ashtianie (301) 837–1850, fax 837–0319.
General Counsel.—Gary M. Stern (301) 837–1750, fax 837–0293.
Inspector General.—Paul Brachfeld (301) 837–3000, fax 837–3197.

ADMINISTRATIVE COMMITTEE OF THE FEDERAL REGISTER

800 North Capitol Street, NW., Suite 700, 20002, phone (202) 741–6070

Members:
Adrienne C. Thomas (acting), Archivist of the United States, *Chair*.
Robert Tapella, Public Printer of the United States.
Rosemary Hart, Senior Counsel, Department of Justice.
Secretary.—Raymond A. Mosley, Director of the Federal Register, National Archives and Records Administration.

NATIONAL ARCHIVES TRUST FUND BOARD

phone (301) 837–3550, fax 837–3191

Members:
Adrienne C. Thomas (acting), Archivist of the United States, *Chair*.
Dr. Carole Watons (acting), Chairman, National Endowment for the Humanities.
Kenneth Carfine, Fiscal Assistant Secretary, Department of the Treasury.
Secretary.—Lawrence Post.

NATIONAL HISTORICAL PUBLICATIONS AND RECORDS COMMISSION

700 Pennsylvania Avenue, NW., 20408

phone (202) 357–5010, fax 357–5914

http://www.archives.gov/nhprc

Members:

Adrienne Thomas (acting), Archivist of the United States, Chairman, National Archives and Records Administration.

Barbara Jacobs Rothstein, Director, Federal Judicial Center, Judicial Branch.

Benjamin L. Cardin, Senator of Maryland.

John B. Larson, Representative of Connecticut.

James W. Ceaser, Department of Politics, University of Virginia, Presidential Appointee.

Nancy Davenport, President, Nancy Davenport & Associates, LLC, Presidential Appointee.

Stuart Rochester, Chief Historian, Office of the Secretary, Department of Defense.

Deanna Marcum, Associate Librarian for Library Services, Library of Congress.

Vacant, Department of State.

Raymond Smock, Director, Robert C. Byrd Center for Legislative Studies, Association for Documentary Editing.

J. Kevin Graffagnino, Director, William Clements Library, University of Michigan, American Association for State and Local History.

Stanley N. Katz, Lecturer with the rank of Professor, Director, Center for Arts and Cultural Policy Studies, Woodrow Wilson School, Princeton University, American Historical Association.

Roy H. Tryon, State Archivist and Records Administrator, South Carolina Department of Archives and History, National Association of Government Archives and Records Administrators.

Julie Saville, Professor of History, University of Chicago, Organization of American Historians.

Timothy L. Ericson, Senior Lecturer Emeritus, University of Wisconsin-Milwaukee, Society of American Archivists.

Executive Director.—Kathleen Williams (202) 357–5010.

REGIONAL OFFICES

Central Plains Region: *Regional Director.*—R. Reed Whitaker (816) 268–8031.

Central Plains Region.—400 West Pershing Road, Kansas City, MO 64108 (816) 268–8026.

Great Lakes Region: *Regional Director.*—David E. Kuehl (773) 948–9011.

Chicago.—7358 South Pulaski Road, Chicago, IL 60629 (773) 948–9007.

Dayton.—3150 Springboro Road, Dayton, OH 45439 (937) 425–0605.

Mid Atlantic Region: *Regional Director.*—V. Chapman Smith (215) 606–0102.

Center City Philadelphia.—900 Market Street, Philadelphia, PA, 19107 (215) 606–2100.

Northeast Philadelphia.—14700 Townsend Road, Philadelphia, PA 19154 (215) 305–2000.

Northeast Region: *Regional Director.*—Diane LeBlanc (781) 663–0133.

Boston.—380 Trapelo Road, Waltham, MA 02452–6399 (781) 663–0130.

Pittsfield.—10 Conte Drive, Pittsfield, MA 01201–8230 (413) 236–3600.

New York City.—201 Varick St., New York, NY 10014–4811 (212) 401–1620.

Pacific Alaska Region: *Regional Director.*—Candance Lein Hayes, (206) 336–5142.

Seattle.—6125 Sand Point Way NE, Seattle, WA 98115 (206) 336–5143.

Anchorage.—654 West Third Avenue, Anchorage, AK 99501 (907) 261–7810.

Pacific Region: *Director.*—David Drake (650) 238–3477.

San Francisco.—1000 Commodore Drive, San Bruno, CA 94066 (650) 238–2471.

Rocky Mountain Region: *Regional Director.*—Barbara Voss (303) 407–5701.

Rocky Mountain Region.—Building 48, Denver Federal Center, Denver, CO 80225 (303) 407–5703.

Southeast Region: *Regional Director.*—James McSweeney (770) 968–2505.

Southeast Region.—4712 Southpark Boulevard, Ellenwood, GA 30294.

Southwest Region: *Regional Director.*—Preston Huff (817) 551–2001.

Southwest Region.—501 W. Felix Street, Ft. Worth, TX 76115 (817) 831–5904.

National Personnel Records Center: *Director.*—Ronald L. Hindman (314) 801–0574.

National Personnel Records Center.—9700 Page Avenue, St. Louis, MO 63132 (314) 801–9221.

Presidential Libraries.—Sharon K. Fawcett (301) 837–3250, fax (301) 837–3199.

Director for—

Herbert Hoover Library.—Timothy G. Walch, West Branch, IA 52358–0488 (319) 643–5301.

Franklin D. Roosevelt Library.—Cynthia M. Koch, Hyde Park, NY 12538–1999 (845) 486–7770.
Harry S. Truman Library.—Michael Devine, Independence, MO 64050–1798 (816) 268–8200.
Dwight D. Eisenhower Library.—Karl Weissenbach, Abilene, KS 67410–2900 (785) 263–6700.
John F. Kennedy Library.—Thomas Putnam, Boston, MA 02125–3398 (617) 514–1600.
Lyndon Baines Johnson Library.—Vacant, Austin, TX 78705–5702 (512) 721–0200.
Richard Nixon Library.—Timothy Naftali, Yorba Linda, CA 92886 (714) 983–9121.
Gerald R. Ford Library.—Elaine K. Didier, Ann Arbor, MI 48109–2114 (734) 205–0555.
Gerald R. Ford Museum.—Elaine K. Didier, Grand Rapids, MI 49504–5353 (616) 254–0400.
Jimmy Carter Library.—Jay E. Hakes, Atlanta, GA 30307–1498 (404) 865–7100.
Ronald Reagan Library.—R. Duke Blackwood, Simi Valley, CA 93065–0699 (800) 410–8354.
George Bush Library.—Warren Finch, College Station, TX 77845 (979) 691–4000.
William J. Clinton Library.—Terri Garner, Little Rock, AR 72201 (501) 244–2887.
George W. Bush Library.—Alan Lowe, Lewisville, TX 75057 (972) 353–0500

NATIONAL CAPITAL PLANNING COMMISSION

401 9th Street, NW., North Lobby, Suite 500, 20004, phone (202) 482–7200
fax 482–7272, info@ncpc.gov, http://www.ncpc.gov

APPOINTIVE MEMBERS

Presidential Appointees:
John V. Cogbill III, *Chair.*
Herbert F. Ames.
John W. Hart.
Mayoral Appointees:
Arrington Dixon.
Stacie S. Turner.
Ex Officio Members:
Dr. Robert M. Gates, Secretary of Defense.
First Alternate.—Michael L. Rhodes.
Second Alternate.—Ralph E. Newton.
Third Alternate.—Bradley Provancha.
Ken Salazar, Secretary of the Interior.
First Alternate.—Daniel N. Wenk.
Second Alternate.—Vacant.
Third Alternate.—Peggy O'Dell.
Fourth Alternate.—Peter May.
Paul F. Prouty (acting), Administrator of General Services.
First Alternate.—Vacant.
Second Alternate.—Vacant.
Third Alternate.—Bart Bush.
Fourth Alternate.—Michael S. McGill.
Joseph I. Lieberman, Chairman, Senate Committee on Homeland Security and Governmental Affairs.
Alternate.—Deborah Parkinson.
Edolphus Towns, Chairman, House Committee on Oversight and Government Reform.
First Alternate.—Michael McCarthy.
Second Alternate.—Mark Stephenson.
Third Alternate.—Wm. Miles.
Adrian M. Fenty, Mayor of the District of Columbia.
First Alternate.—Harriet Tregoning.
Second Alternate.—Jennifer Steingasser.
Vincent C. Gray, Chairman, Council of the District of Columbia.
First Alternate.—Robert E. Miller, Esq., NCPC Vice Chairman.
Second Alternate.—Christopher Murray.

EXECUTIVE STAFF

Executive Director.—Marcel C. Acosta, 482–7221.
Chief Operating Officer.—Barry S. Socks, 482–7209.
Senior Planning Advisor.—Christine L. Saum, 482–7245.
Secretariat.—Deborah B. Young, 482–7228.
General Counsel.—Lois Schiffer, 482–7223.
Director, Office of:
Administration.—Charles J. ''Jody'' Rieder, 482–7255.
Intergovernmental Affairs.—Julia A. Koster, 482–7211.
Physical Planning.—William G. Dowd, 482–7240.
Policy and Research.—Michael Sherman, 482–7254.
Public Affairs.—Lisa N. MacSpadden, 482–7263.
Urban Design and Plan Review.—David Levy, 482–7247.

NATIONAL COMMISSION ON LIBRARIES AND INFORMATION SCIENCE

1800 M Street, NW., Suite 350, North Tower 20036–5841

phone (202) 606–9200, fax 606–9203, http://www.nclis.gov

[Created by Public Law 91–345]

Chair.—Beth Fitzsimmons, Ph.D., Ann Arbor, MI.
Vice Chair.—Bridget L. Lamont, Springfield, IL.
Members:
José A. Aponte, San Diego, CA.
Sandra F. Ashworth, Bonners Ferry, ID.
Edward L. Bertorelli, Boston, MA.
James H. Billington, Ph.D., Librarian of Congress, Washington, DC. (Ex-officio)
Serves for the Librarian of Congress:
Deanna Marcum, Ph.D., The Library of Congress, Washington, DC.
Jan Cellucci, Hudson, MA.
Carol L. Diehl, Neenah, WI.
Allison Druin, Ph.D., College Park, MD.
Patricia M. Hines, Mayesville, SC.
Colleen E. Huebner, Ph.D., Seattle, WA.
Stephen M. Kennedy, Concord, NH.
Anne-Imelda Radice, Ph.D., Director, Institute of Museum and Library Services, Washington, DC. (Ex-officio)
Mary H. Perdue, Salisbury, MD.
Diane Rivers, Ph.D., Brimingham, AL.
Herman L. Totten, Ph.D., Denton, TX.
Chairpersons Emeritus:
Charles Benton.
Frederick Burkhardt.
Elinor M. Hashim.
Jerald C. Newman.
Charles E. Reid.

EXECUTIVE STAFF

Director of Operations.—Madeleine C. McCain.
Director, Statistics and Surveys.—Neal K. Kaske.
Special Assistant, Technical.—Kim Miller.
Management Operations Analyst.—Joe Dyer.

NATIONAL COUNCIL ON DISABILITY

1331 F Street, NW., Suite 850, 20004, phone (202) 272–2004, fax 272–2022

Chairperson.—John R. Vaughn, Fort Myers, FL.
Vice Chairperson.—Chad Colley, New Smyrna Beach, FL.
Vice Chairperson.—Patricia Pound, Austin, TX.
Members:

Victoria Ray Carlson, Naperville, IL.
Robert R. Davila, Ph.D., New Market, MD.
Graham Hill, Arlington, VA.
Marylyn Howe, Marshfield Hills, MA.
Kathleen Martinez, Oakland, CA.
Lisa Mattheiss, East Ridge, TN.
Heather Whitestone McCallum, St. Simons Island, GA.
Katherine O. McCary, Midlothian, VA.
Lonnie Moore, Chula Vista, CA.
Anne Rader, McLean, VA.
Linda Wetters, Columbus, OH.
Tony J. Williams, Clyde Hill, WA.

NATIONAL CREDIT UNION ADMINISTRATION

1775 Duke Street, Alexandria, VA 22314–3428, phone (703) 518–6300, fax 518–6319

Chairman.—Michael E. Fryzel.
Vice Chairman.—Rodney E. Hood.
Board Member.—Christiane Gigi Hyland.
Secretary to the Board.—Mary Rupp.
Executive Director.—David Marquis, 518–6320, fax 518–6661.
Deputy Executive Director.—Larry Fazio, 518–6322.
Deputy Director Inspector General.—William DeSarno, 518–6350.
Director, Office of:
Capital Markets and Planning.—Owen Cole, 518–6620, fax 518–6663.
Chief Financial Officer.—Mary Ann Woodson, 518–6570, fax 518–6664.
Chief Information Officer.—Doug Verner, 518–6440, fax 518–6669.
Corporate Credit Unions.—Mark Treichel, 518–6640, fax 518–6665.
EEO.—Chrisanthy Loizos, 518–6325.
Examination and Insurance.—Melinda Love, 518–6360, fax 518–6666.
General Counsel.—Robert M. Fenner, 518–6540, fax 518–6667.
Deputy General Counsel.—Michael McKenna.
Human Resources.—Kathy Sachen-Gute, 518–6510, fax 518–6668.
Public and Congressional Affairs.—John J. McKechnie III, 518–6330.
Small Credit Union Initiatives.—Tawana James, 518–6610.

REGIONAL OFFICES

Director, Office of:
Region I (Albany).—Anthony LaCreta (acting), 9 Washington Square, Washington Avenue Extension, Albany, NY 12205 (518) 862–7400, fax 862–7420.
Region II (National Capital Region).—Marcia Sarrazin (acting), 1775 Duke Street, Suite 4206, Alexandria, VA 22314 (703) 519–4600, fax 519–4620.
Region III (Atlanta).—Alonzo A. Swann III, 7000 Central Parkway, Suite 1600, Atlanta, GA 30328 (678) 443–3000, fax 443–3020.
Region IV (Austin).—Keith Morton, 4807 Spicewood Springs Road, Suite 5200, Austin, TX 78759–8490 (512) 342–5600, fax 342–5620.
Region V (Tempe).—Jane Walters, 1230 West Washington Street, Suite 301, Tempe, AZ 85281 (602) 302–6000, fax 302–6024.
President, Asset Management and Assistance Center (Austin).—Mike Barton, 4807 Spicewood Springs Road, Suite 5100, Austin, TX 78759–8490 (512) 231–7900, fax 231–7920.

NATIONAL FOUNDATION ON THE ARTS AND THE HUMANITIES

Old Post Office Building, 1100 Pennsylvania Avenue, NW., 20506

NATIONAL ENDOWMENT FOR THE ARTS

http://www.arts.gov

Chairman.—Rocco Landesman (202) 682–5001.
Senior Deputy Chairman.—Joan Shigekawa, 682–5415.
Deputy Chairman for—
Grants and Awards.—Bill O'Brien, 682–5441.
Management and Budget.—Laurence Baden, 682–5408.
Director of:
Communication.—Yosi Sargent, 682–5570.

Government Affairs (Congressional/White House/Federal and International Partnerships).—Anita Decker, 682–5434.
Research and Analysis.—Sunil Iyengar, 682–5424.
General Counsel.—Karen Elias (acting), 682–5654.
Inspector General.—Toni Jones, 682–5402.

THE NATIONAL COUNCIL ON THE ARTS

Chairman.—Rocco Landesman.
Council Operations Director.—Michael Faubion (202) 682–5433.

Members:

James K. Ballinger
Miguel Campaneria
Ben Donenberg
JoAnn Falletta
Lee Greenwood
Joan Israelite
Charlotte Kessler
Bret Lott
Jerry Pinkney
Frank Price
Terry Teachout
Karen Lias Wolff

Ex Officio Members:

Robert F. Bennett, Senator
Sheldon Whitehouse, Senator
Patrick J. Tiberi, Representative

NATIONAL ENDOWMENT FOR THE HUMANITIES

phone (202) 606–8400, info@neh.gov, http://www.neh.gov

Chairman.—Carole M. Watson (acting), 606–8310.
Deputy Chairman.—Michael McDonald (acting), 606–8235.
Director, Communications.—Noel Milan (acting), 606–8446.
Director, White House and Congressional Affairs.—Jeremy Bernard, 606–8310.
General Counsel.—Michael McDonald, 606–8322.
Inspector General.—Sheldon L. Bernstein, 606–8350.
Public Information Officer.—Christopher Flynn, 606–8446.
Director, Strategic Planning.—Larry Myers, 606–8428.

NATIONAL COUNCIL ON THE HUMANITIES

Members:

Herman J. Belz
Josiah Bunting III
Jamsheed K. Choksy
Dawn H. Delbanco
Jane Marie "Jamie" Doggett
Jean B. Elshtain
Gary D. Glenn
Allen C. Guelzo
Mary Habeck
Craig Haffner
David Hertz
James D. Hunter
Tamar Jacoby
Harvey Klehr
Iris Cornelia Love
Robert S. Martin
Wilfred M. McClay
Ricardo J. Quinones
Marvin Scott
Marguerite H. Sullivan
Carol M. Swain
Kenneth R. Weinstein
Jay Winik

FEDERAL COUNCIL ON THE ARTS AND THE HUMANITIES

Federal Council Members:

Patrice Walker Powell (acting), Chairman, National Endowment for the Arts.
Carole M. Watson (acting), Chairman, National Endowment for the Humanities.
Arden L. Bement, Jr., Director, National Science Foundation.
Paul F. Prouty (acting), Administrator, General Services Administration.
James H. Billington, Librarian of Congress, Library of Congress.
Hilda Solis, Secretary, Department of Labor.
Gary F. Locke, Secretary, Department of Commerce.
Shaun L.S. Donovan, Secretary, Department of Housing and Urban Development.
Ken Salazar, Secretary, Department of the Interior.
Kathleen Sebelius, Secretary, Department of Health and Human Services.
Earl A. Powell III, Chairman, Commission of Fine Arts.
Raymond H. LaHood, Secretary, Department of Transportation.
Eric K. Shinseki, Secretary, Department of Veterans Affairs.
Earl A. Powell III, Director, National Gallery of Art.
Anne-Imelda M. Radice Ph.D., Director, Institute for Museum and Library Services.

Anne-Imelda M. Radice Ph.D., Chairman, National Museum and Library Services Board.
Nancy Erickson, Secretary of the Senate.
Gerald W. Clough, Secretary, Smithsonian Institution.
Arne Duncan, Secretary, Department of Education.
Fortney Pete Stark, Member, U.S. House of Representatives.
Adrienne Thomas (acting), Archivist of the United States, National Archives and Records Administration.
C. Miller Crouch (acting), Assistant Secretary, Bureau of Educational and Cultural Affairs, Under Secretary for Public Diplomacy and Public Affairs, Department of State.
Anthony Costa (acting), Commissioner, Public Buildings Service, General Services Administration.
Staff Contact.—Alice M. Whelihan, Indemnity Administrator, National Endowment for the Arts, 682–5574.

INSTITUTE OF MUSEUM AND LIBRARY SERVICES

phone (202) 653–4657, fax 653–4625, http://www.imls.gov

[The Institute of Museum and Library Services was created by the Museum and Library Services Act of 1996, Public Law 104–208]

Director.—Anne-Imelda M. Radice, Ph.D., 653–4746.
Chief of Staff.—Kate Fernstrom, 653–4643.
Deputy Director for—
Library Services.—Mary Chute, 653–4700.
Museum Services.—Marsha Semmel, 653–4789.
Policy, Planning, Research and Communications.—Mamie Bittner, 653–4757.
Associate Deputy Director for—
Library Services.—Joyce Ray, Ph.D., 653–4700.
Museum Services.—Mary Estelle Kennelly, 653–4789.
Research and Statistics.—A. Carlos Manjarrez, 653–4671.
State Programs.—Laurie Brooks, 653–4650.
Counsel to the Director.—Schroeder Cherry, Ed.D., 653–4670.
Chief Financial Officer.—Shannon Hensler, 653–4721.
General Counsel.—Nancy Weiss, 653–4787.

NATIONAL MUSEUM AND LIBRARY SERVICES BOARD

Members:
Beverly E. Allen
Katherine M.B. Berger
Karen Brosius
Julia W. Bland
Mary Chute
Nonvoting Member
Jan Cellucci
Gail M. Daly
A. Wilson Greene
William J. Hagenah
Mark Y. Herring
Ioannis N. Miaoulis
Douglas G. Myers
Christina Orr-Cahall
Amy Owen
Sandra Pickett
Jeffrey H. Patchen
Lotsee Patterson
Anne-Imelda M. Radice, Ph.D., Chairperson
Harry Robinson, Jr.
Marsha Semmel
Nonvoting Member
Katina Strauch
Kim Wang

NATIONAL GALLERY OF ART

Sixth Street and Constitution Avenue, NW., 20565

phone (202) 737–4215, http://www.nga.gov

[Under the direction of the Board of Trustees of the National Gallery of Art]

BOARD OF TRUSTEES

General Trustees:
John Wilmerding, Chairman.
Victoria P. Sant, President.
Frederick W. Beinecke.
Mitchell P. Rales.
Sharon Percy Rockefeller.
Trustees Emeriti:
Robert F. Erburu.

John C. Fontaine.
Julian Ganz, Jr.
Alexander M. Laughlin.
David O. Maxwell.
Robert H. Smith.
Ruth Carter Stevenson.
Ex Officio Trustees:
John G. Roberts, Jr., Chief Justice of the United States.
Hillary Rodham Clinton, Secretary of State.
Timothy F. Geithner, Secretary of the Treasury.
G. Wayne Clough, Secretary of the Smithsonian Institution.
Director.—Earl A. Powell III.
Deputy Director.—Franklin Kelly.
Dean, Center for Advanced Study in the Visual Arts.—Elizabeth Cropper.
Administrator.—Darrell Willson.
Treasurer.—James E. Duff.
Secretary-General Counsel.—Elizabeth A. Croog.
Executive Officer, Development and External Affairs.—Joseph J. Krakora.

NATIONAL LABOR RELATIONS BOARD

1099 14th Street, NW., 20570–0001

Personnel Locator (202) 273–1000

Chairman.—Wilma B. Liebman, 273–1770, fax 273–4270.
Chief Counsel.—John Colwell.
Deputy Chief Counsel.—Gary W. Shinners.
Members:
Board Member.—Peter C. Schaumber, 273–1790.
Chief Counsel.—Terence Flynn.
Deputy Chief Counsel.—Robert F. Kane.
Board Member.—Vacant, 273–1070.
Chief Counsel.—James R. Murphy (acting).
Deputy Chief Counsel.—David P. Martin.
Board Member.—Vacant, 273–1740.
Chief Counsel.—Peter Winkler (acting).
Deputy Chief Counsel.—Vacant.
Board Member.—Vacant, 273–1770.
Chief Counsel.—Vacant.
Deputy Chief Counsel.—Kathleen Nixon.
Executive Secretary.—Lester A. Heltzer, 273–1940, fax 273–4270.
Deputy Executive Secretary.—David B. Parker, 272–2000.
Associate Executive Secretaries: Henry S. Breiteneicher, 273–2917; Richard D. Hardick, 273–1935; Margaret H. Rafferty, 273–1937.
Solicitor.—William B. Cowen, 273–2914, fax 273–1962.
Inspector General.—David P. Berry, 273–1960, fax 273–2344.
Director, Representation Appeals.—Lafe E. Solomon, 273–1975, fax 273–1962.
Director, Division of Information.—Vacant, 273–1991, fax 273–1789.
General Counsel.—Ronald E. Meisburg, 273–3700, fax 273–4483.
Deputy General Counsel.—John E. Higgins, Jr.

DIVISION OF JUDGES

Chief Administrative Law Judge.—Robert A. Giannasi, 501–8800, fax 501–8686.
Deputy Chief Administrative Law Judge.—Vacant, 501–8800.
Associate Chief Administrative Law Judges:
Joel P. Biblowitz, 120 West 45th Street, 11th Floor, New York, NY 10036–5503 (212) 944–2943, fax 944–4904.
William N. Cates, 401 West Peachtree Street, NW., Suite 1708, Atlanta, GA 30308–3510 (404) 331–6654, fax 331–2061.
Mary Miller Cracraft, 901 Market Street, Suite 300, San Francisco, CA 94103–1779 (415) 356–5255, fax 356–5254.
Director, Office of Appeals.—Yvonne T. Dixon, 273–3760, 273–4283.
Deputy Director.—Deborah M.P. Yaffe.
Director, Division of Administration.—Gloria J. Joseph, 273–3890, fax 273–2928.

Deputy Director.—Kathleen James.

DIVISION OF OPERATIONS MANAGEMENT

Associate General Counsel.—Richard Siegel, 273–2900, fax 273–4274.
Deputy Associate General Counsel.—Anne Purcell.
Assistant General Counsels: Joseph F. Frankl, 273–2893; Shelley S. Korch, 273–2889; Nelson Levin, 273–2885; James G. Paulsen, 273–2881.
Executive Assistant.—Carole K. Coleman, 273–2901.
Special Counsels: Elizabeth Bach, Joseph M. Davis, Barry F. Smith, 273–2918, fax 273–0864.

DIVISION OF ADVICE

Associate General Counsel.—Barry J. Kearney, 273–3800, fax 273–4275.
Deputy Associate General Counsel.—Ellen A. Farrell.
Assistant General Counsels:
Injunction Litigation Branch.—Judith I. Katz, 273–3812.
Regional Advice Branch.—David Colangelo, 273–3831.
Research and Policy Planning Branch.—Jacqueline A. Young, 273–3825.

DIVISION OF ENFORCEMENT LITIGATION

Associate General Counsel.—John H. Ferguson, 273–2950, fax 273–4244.
Deputy Associate General Counsel.—Margery E. Lieber, 273–2950.
Appellate and Supreme Court Litigation Branch:
Deputy Associate General Counsel.—Linda J. Dreeben, 273–2960.
Assistant General Counsel.—David Haberistreit, 273–0979.
Deputy Assistant General Counsels: Fred Cornell, 273–2993; Margaret Gaines, 273–2984; Howard E. Perlstein, 273–2946.
Special Litigation Branch:
Assistant General Counsel.—Eric G. Moskowitz, 273–2930, fax 273–1799.
Deputy Assistant General Counsel.—Abby P. Simms, 273–2934.
Contempt Litigation and Compliance Branch:
Assistant General Counsel.—Stanley R. Zirkin, 273–3739, fax 273–4244.
Deputy Assistant General Counsels: Daniel F. Collopy, 273–3745; Kenneth J. Shapiro, 273–3741.

NATIONAL MEDIATION BOARD

1301 K Street, NW., Suite 250 East, 20005, phone (202) 692–5000, fax 692–5080

Chairman.—Elizabeth Dougherty, 692–5016.
Board Members: Harry Hoglander, 692–5022; Linda Puchala, 692–5021.
Director, Office of:
Administration.—June D.W. King, 692–5010.
Alternative Dispute Resolution Services.—Daniel Rainey, 692–5051.
Arbitration Services.—Roland Watkins, 692–5055.
Legal Affairs.—Mary L. Johnson, 692–5040.
Mediation Services.—Larry Gibbons, 692–5040.

NATIONAL RESEARCH COUNCIL—NATIONAL ACADEMY OF SCIENCES NATIONAL ACADEMY OF ENGINEERING—INSTITUTE OF MEDICINE

2101 Constitution Avenue, NW., 20418, phone (202) 334–2000

The National Research Council, National Academy of Sciences, National Academy of Engineering, and Institute of Medicine, serves as an independent adviser to the Federal Government on scientific and technical questions of national importance. Although operating under a congressional charter granted the National Academy of Sciences in 1863, the National Research Council and its three parent organizations are private organizations, not agencies of the Federal Government, and receive no appropriations from Congress.

NATIONAL RESEARCH COUNCIL

Chairman.—Ralph Cicerone, President, National Academy of Sciences, 334–2100.
Vice Chairman.—Charles Vest, President, National Academy of Engineering, 334–3200.
Executive Officer.—E. William Colglazier, 334–3000.
Director, Office of Congressional and Government Affairs.—James E. Jensen, 334–1601.

NATIONAL ACADEMY OF SCIENCES

President.—Ralph Cicerone, 334–2100.
Vice President.—Barbara Schaal, Washington University, St. Louis.
Home Secretary.—John I. Brauman, Stanford University.
Foreign Secretary.—M.T. Clegg, University of California, Irvine.
Treasurer.—Jeremiah P. Ostriker, Princeton University.
Executive Officer.—E. William Colglazier, 334–3000.

NATIONAL ACADEMY OF ENGINEERING

President.—Charles Vest, 334–3200.
Chairman.—Irwin M. Jacobs, Qualcomm, Inc.
Vice President.—Maxine Savitz (Ret.), Honeywell, Inc.
Home Secretary.—Thomas Budinger, Lawrence Berkeley National Laboratory.
Foreign Secretary.—George Bugliarello (Ret.), Polytechnic University.
Executive Officer.—Lance Davis, 334–3677.
Treasurer.—''Dan'' Mote, Jr., University of Maryland, President C.D.

INSTITUTE OF MEDICINE

President.—Harvey V. Fineberg, M.D., 334–3300.
Executive Officer.—Judith A. Salerno, 334–2177.

NATIONAL SCIENCE FOUNDATION

4201 Wilson Boulevard, Suite 1245, Arlington, VA 22230

phone (703) 292–5111, http://www.nsf.gov

Director.—Arden L. Bement, Jr.
Deputy Director.—Cora Marrett.
Inspector General.—Christine C. Boesz, 292–7100.
Equal Opportunity Programs.—James H. Lightbourne, 292–8020.
Director, Office of:
Legislative and Public Affairs.—Jeff Nesbit, 292–8070.
Integrative Activities.—W. Lance Haworth, 292–8040.
Polar Programs.—Karl Erb, 292–8030.
General Counsel.—Lawrence Rudolph, 292–8060.
Assistant Director for—
Biological Sciences.—James Collins, 292–8400.
Computer and Information Science and Engineering.—Jeannette M. Wing, 292–8900.
Education and Human Resources.—Wanda E. Ward (acting), 292–8300.
Engineering.—Thomas W. Peterson, 292–8300.
Geosciences.—Tim Killeen, 292–8500.
Mathematical and Physical Sciences.—Tony Chan, 292–8800.
Social, Behavorial, and Economic Sciences.—David W. Lightfoot, 292–8700.
Director, Office of:
Budget, Finance, and Award Management.—Thomas N. Cooley, 292–8200.
Information and Resource Management.—Anthony Arnolie, 292–8100.

NATIONAL SCIENCE BOARD

Chairman.—Steven C. Beering (703) 292–7000.
Vice Chairman.—Patricia D. Galloway.
Executive Officer.—Craig R. Robinson.

MEMBERS

Mark Abbott
Dan E. Arvizu
Barry C. Barish
Steven C. Beering
Camilla Bonbow
Ray M. Bowen
John Bruer
G. Wayne Clough
France A. Cordova
Kelvin K. Droegemier
Patricia Galloway
Jose-Marie Griffiths
Esin Gulari
Louis J. Lanzerotti
Alan I. Leshner
G.P. Peterson
Douglas D. Randall
Arthur K. Reilly
Diane L. Souvaine
Jon C. Strauss
Kathryn D. Sullivan
Thomas Taylor
Richard Thompson

NATIONAL TRANSPORTATION SAFETY BOARD

490 L'Enfant Plaza, SW., 20594, phone (202) 314–6000

Chairman.—Deborah A.P. Hersman, 314–6660.
Vice Chairman.—Christopher A. Hart, 314–6149.
Member.—Robert L. Sumwalt III, 314–6021.
Managing Director.—David Mayer (acting), 314–6318.
General Counsel.—Gary Halbert, 314–6616.
Chief Administrative Law Judge.—William W. Fowler, Jr., 314–6150.
Chief Financial Officer.—Steven Goldberg, 314–6212.
Director, Office of:
Aviation Safety.—Tom Haueter, 314–6302.
Government Affairs.—Vacant.
Highway Safety.—Bruce Magladry, 314–6419.
Marine Safety.—Jack Spencer, 314–6495.
Public Affairs.—Ted Lopatkiewicz, 314–6100.
Railroad, Pipeline and Hazardous Materials Investigations.—Bob Chipkevich, 314–6461.
Research and Engineering.—Joseph Kolly (acting), 314–6502.
Safety Recommendations/Advocacy.—Elaine Weinstein, 314–6171.
Transportation Disaster Assistance.—Sharon Bryson, 314–6185.

NEIGHBORHOOD REINVESTMENT CORPORATION

(Doing business as NeighborWorks America)

1325 G Street, NW., Suite 800, 20005, phone (202) 220–2300, fax 376–2600

BOARD OF DIRECTORS

Chair.—Thomas J. Curry, Director, Federal Deposit Insurance Corporation.
Vice Chair.—Julie L. Williams, First Senior Deputy Comptroller and Chief Counsel, Office of the Comptroller of the Currency.
Members:
Shaun Donovan, Secretary, U.S. Department of Housing and Urban Development.
Elizabeth A. Duke, Member, Board of Governors, Federal Reserve System.
John E. Bowman (acting), Director, Office of Thrift Supervision.
Chief Executive Director.—Kenneth D. Wade, 220–2410.
General Counsel/Secretary.—Jeffrey T. Bryson, 220–2372.
Chief Operating Officer.—Eileen Fitzgerald, 220–2452.
Chief Financial Officer.—Michael Forster, 220–2374.
Director for—
Development and Communications.—Linda Cotton-Perry, 220–2312.
Field Operations.—Robert Burns, 220–2313.
Finance and Administration.—Michael Forster, 223–2374.
Internal Audit.—Frederick Udochi, 220–2409.
Public Policy and Legislative Affairs.—Steven J. Tuminaro, 220–2415.
Training.—Paul Kealey, 220–2375.

NUCLEAR REGULATORY COMMISSION

Washington, DC 20555–0001, phone (301) 415–7000, http//www.nrc.gov

[Authorized by 42 U.S.C. 5801 and U.S.C. 1201]

OFFICE OF THE CHAIRMAN

Chairman.—Gregory B. Jaczko, 415–1820.

Chief of Staff.—Josh Batkin, 415–1750.
Administrative Assistant.—Glenda P. Evans, 415–1820.

COMMISSIONERS

Kristine L. Svinicki—415–1855.
Chief of Staff.—Jeffry Sharkey.
Administrative Assistant.—Janet L. Lepre.

Dale E. Klein—415–1759.
Chief of Staff.—Paul T. Dickman.
Administrative Assistant—Linda S. Herr.

STAFF OFFICES OF THE COMMISSION

Secretary.—Annette L. Vietti-Cook, 415–1969, fax 415–1672.
Chief Financial Officer.—James E. Dyer, 415–7322, fax 415–4236.
Commission Appellate Adjudication.—Brooke D. Poole, 415–2653, fax 415–3200.
Congressional Affairs.—Rebecca L. Schmidt, 415–1776, fax 415–8571.
General Counsel.—Stephen G. Burns, 415–1743, fax 415–3086.
Inspector General.—Hubert T. Bell, 415–5930, fax 415–5091.
International Programs.—Margaret M. Doane, 415–1780, fax 415–2400.
Public Affairs.—Eliot B. Brenner, 415–8200, fax 415–2234.

ADVISORY COMMITTEE ON MEDICAL USES OF ISOTOPES

Chariman.—Leon S. Malmud, M.D.
Committee Coordinator.—Ashley Cockerham, (240) 888–7129.

ADVISORY COMMITTEE ON REACTOR SAFEGUARDS

Chairman.—Mario V. Bonaca.
Executive Director.—Edwin M. Hackett, 415–7360, fax 415–5589.

ATOMIC SAFETY AND LICENSING BOARD PANEL

Chief Administrative Judge.—E. Roy Hawkens, 415–7454, fax 415–5599.

OFFICE OF THE EXECUTIVE DIRECTOR FOR OPERATIONS

Executive Director for Operations.—R. William Borchardt, 415–1700, fax 415–2700.
Deputy Executive Director for—
Corporate Management.—Darren Ash, 415–7443, fax 415–2700.
Materials, Waste, Research, State, Tribal and Compliance Programs.—Martin J. Virgilio, 415–1705, fax 415–2700.
Reactor and Preparedness Programs.—Bruce S. Mallett, 415–1713, fax 415–2700.
Director, Office of:
Administration.—Kathryn O. Greene, 492–3500, fax 492–5400.
Enforcement.—Cynthia Carpenter, 415–2741, fax 415–3431.
Federal and State Materials and Environmental Management Programs.—Charles L. Miller, 415–7197, fax 415–6680.
Human Resources.—James F. McDermott, 492–2076, fax 492–2247.
Information Services.—Thomas M. Boyce, 415–8700, fax 415–4246.
Investigations.—Guy P. Caputo, 415–2373, fax 415–2370.
New Reactors.—Michael R. Johnson, 415–1897, fax 415–2700.
Nuclear Material Safety and Safeguards.—Michael F. Weber, 492–3557, fax 492–3360.
Nuclear Reactor Regulation.—Eric J. Leeds, 415–1270, fax 415–8333.
Nuclear Regulatory Research.—Brian W. Sheron, 251–7900, fax 251–7426.
Nuclear Security and Incident Response.—Roy P. Zimmerman, 415–8003, fax 415–6382.
Small Business and Civil Rights.—Corenthis B. Kelley, 415–7380, fax 415–5953.

REGIONAL OFFICES

Region I: Samuel J. Collins, 475 Allendale Road, King of Prussia, PA 19406 (610) 337–5299, fax 337–5241.
Deputy Regional Administrator.—Marc L. Dapas, 337–5359.
Region II: Luis A. Reyes, 61 Forsyth Street SE, Atlanta, GA 30303 (404) 562–4410, fax 562–4766.
Deputy Regional Administrator.—Victor M. McCree, 562–4411.
Region III: Mark A. Satorius, 2443 Warrensville Road, Suite 210, Lisle, IL 60532 (630) 829–9657, fax 515–1096.
Deputy Regional Administrator.—Cindy Pederson, 829–9658.
Region IV: Elmo E. Collins, Suite 400, 611 Ryan Plaza Drive, Arlington, TX 76011 (817) 860–8225, fax 860–8122.
Deputy Regional Administrator.—Charles Casto, 860–8226.

OCCUPATIONAL SAFETY AND HEALTH REVIEW COMMISSION

1120 20th Street, NW., 20036–3457, phone (202) 606–5100

[Created by Public Law 91–596]

Chairman.—Thomasina V. Rogers, 606–5370.
Chief Counsel and Legal Advisor to the Chairman.—Richard L. Huberman, 606–5370.
Confidential Assistant to the Chairman.—Melik Ahmir-abdul.
Commissioner.—Horace A. Thompson, 606–5374.
Chief Counsel to the Commissioner.—Tressi L. Cordaro.
Confidential Assistant to the Commissioiner.—Romona J. Ely.
Administrative Law Judges:
Patrick B. Augustine, U.S. Customs House, 721 19th Street, Room 407, Denver, CO 80202–2517.
Marvin G. Bober, 1120 20th Street, NW., 9th Floor, Washington, DC 20036–3457.
Sidney Goldstein, U.S. Customs House, 721 19th Street, Room 407, Denver, CO 80202–2517.
Benjamin Loye, U.S. Customs House, 721 19th Street, Room 407, Denver, CO 80202–2517.
Covette Rooney, 1120 20th Street, NW., 9th Floor, Washington, DC 20036–3457.
James R. Rucker, Jr., U.S. Customs House, 721 19th Street, Room 407, Denver, CO 80202–2517.
John Schumacher, 1120 20th Street, NW., 9th Floor, Washington, DC 20036–3457.
Stephen J. Simko, 100 Alabama Street, SW., Building 1924, Room 2R90, Atlanta, GA 30303–3104.
Irving Sommer, 1120 20th Street, NW., 9th Floor, Washington, DC 20036–3457.
Nancy L. Spies, 100 Alabama Street, SW., Building 1924, Room 2R90, Atlanta, GA 30303–3104.
Ken S. Welsch, 100 Alabama Street, SW., Building 1924, Room 2R90, Atlanta, GA 30303–3104.
General Counsel.—Nadine Mancini.
Executive Secretary.—Ray H. Darling, Jr.
Director, Office of Administration.—Richard Loeb.

OFFICE OF GOVERNMENT ETHICS

1201 New York Avenue, NW., Suite 500, 20005, phone (202) 482–9300, fax 482–9238

[Created by Act of October 1, 1989; codified in 5 U.S.C. app., section 401]

Director.—Robert I. Cusick.
Confidential Assistant.—Beverly Johnson.
General Counsel.—Don W. Fox.
Deputy General Counsel.—Walter M. Shaub, Jr.
Deputy Director for—
Administration and Information Management.—Barbara A. Mullen-Roth.
Agency Programs.—Joseph E. Gangloff.
International Assistant and Governance Initiatives.—Jane S. Ley.
Associate Director for—
Education Division.—Matthew S. Cross.
Information Resources Management (CIO).—James T. ''Ty'' Cooper.

Program Review Division.—Dale A. ''Chip'' Christopher.
Program Services Division.—Patricia C. Zemple.

OFFICE OF PERSONNEL MANAGEMENT

Theodore Roosevelt Building, 1900 E Street, NW., 20415–0001

phone (202) 606–1800, http://www.opm.gov

OFFICE OF THE DIRECTOR

Director.—John Berry, 606–1000.
Executive Assistant / Scheduler.—Demetriss Williams.
Counselor to the Director.—Vic Basile.
Senior Advisors to the Director: Jonathan Foley, John O'Brien.
Senior Advisor to the Director / White House Liaison.—Michael A. Grant.
Executive Assistant.—Torlanda Young.
Deputy Director Designate.—Christine Griffin.
Executive Assistant.—Vacant.
Director, Office of the CFC.—Mark W. Lambert.
Chief of Staff / Director of External Affairs.—Elizabeth Montoya.
Senior Executive Assistant.—Blondell Darby-Boone.
Deputy Chiefs of Staff: Justin Johnson, Jennifer I. Mason.
Deputy Chief of Staff / Executive Secretariat.—Richard B. Lowe.
Special Assistant to the Director.—Matthew W. Collier.
White House Fellow.—Ken Robbins.

OFFICE OF THE CHIEF FINANCIAL OFFICER

Chief Financial Officer.—Mark Reger, 606–1918.
Associate Chief Financial Officer, Center for—
Administrative Officer.—Patrice W. Mendonca, 606–2204.
Budget and Performance.—Dan Marella, 606–2368.
Internal Control and Risk Management.—David Cushing, 606–4660.
Financial Systems Management.—Rochelle Bayard, 606–4366.
Financial Services.—Keith Willingham, 606–1606.

OFFICE OF COMMUNICATIONS AND PUBLIC LIAISON

Director.—Sedelta Verble, 606–2402.
Director, Office of:
Administration.—Ray Theirault.
Web Design.—Vivian Mackey.
Speech Writer.—Harry J. Kruglik.
Public Affairs Specialist.—John Marble.
Public Affairs and Congressional Relations Specialist.—Marcus Williams.

OFFICE OF CONGRESSIONAL RELATIONS

Director.—Tania A. Shand, 606–1300.
Deputy Director.—Thomas Richards.
Administrative Officer.—Catherine A. Ford.
Congressional Relations Officer.—N. Malik Walker.
Chief, Legislative Analysis.—Gay Gardner (acting), 606–1424.
Constituent Services, Capitol Hill.—Charlene E. Luskey, B332 Rayburn House Office Building, 225–4955, fax 225–4974.
Constituent Services Representative.—Katie Pennell.

FEDERAL INVESTIGATIVE SERVICES DIVISION

Associate Director.—Kathy L. Dillaman, (724) 794–5612.
Deputy Associate Director for—
Operations.—Kenneth J. Zawodny, Jr.

Services.—Joy S. Fairtile, 606–1042.
External Affairs.—Merton W. Miller, 606–1042.
Assistant Director for Security Programs.—Thomas L. Forman, 606–1042.

HUMAN CAPITAL LEADERSHIP AND MERIT SYSTEM ACCOUNTABILITY DIVISION

Associate Director.—Kevin E. Mahoney, 606–1575.
Deputy Associate Director, Center for—
General Government.—Joseph Kennedy, 606–5181.
Human Capital Strategy and Systems Design.—Sydney Smith-Heimbrock, 606–2762.
Human Resources.—Anita R. Hanson (acting), 606–2773.
Merit System Accountability.—Jeff Sumberg, 606–2786.
National Security.—Ray Decker, 606–2511.
Natural Resources Management.—Anita R. Hanson (acting), 606–2773.
Performance Management Systems and Evaluation.—Patsy Stevens (acting), 606–1574.
Small Agencies.—Linda Datcher (acting), 606–2611.

MODERNIZATION AND HUMAN RESOURCES LINE OF BUSINESS PROGRAM MANAGEMENT OFFICE

Director.—Reginald Brown, 606–1332.
Administration and Finance.—Elizabeth Mautner, 606–1121.
Program Manager:
Enterprise Human Resources Integration (EHRI).—Matthew Perry, 606–1416.
Human Resources Line of Business (HRLOB).—Vacant, 606–1534.
Retirement Systems Modernization (RSM).—Matthew Perry, 606–1416.
Deputy Program Manager, Retirement Systems Modernization (RSM).—Martha Mitchell, 606–4836.
Program Coordinator:
E-Training.—Daniel McKay, 606–1451.
E-Payroll.—Anita Murray, 606–4262.
Shared Services Center Coordinator.—Vacant, 606–4185.

HUMAN RESOURCES PRODUCTS AND SERVICES DIVISION

Associate Director.—Kay T. Ely, 606–0600.
Staff Assistants: Eridani Quiroz, Lorraine Waller.
Senior Advisor.—Eileen Kirwan.
Executive Officer.—Dale A. Anglin.
Deputy Associate Director, Center for Leadership Capacity Services.—Renee L. Roman, 606–2100.
Director of:
Succession Planning Programs.—Leslie Pollack, 606–1040.
Federal Executive Institute.—Kevin L. Marshall, (434) 980–6200.
Eastern Management Development Center.—Charles W. Cranford (304) 879–8000.
Western Management Development Center.—Myhre ''Bud'' Paulson (303) 671–1010.
Deputy Associate Director, Center for Retirement and Insurance Services.—Kathleen M. McGettigan, 606–0462.
Assistant Director for—
Insurance Services Programs.—Lorraine E. Dettman, 606–0745.
Retirement Services Programs.—Joseph E. Donald, Jr., 606–0300.
Deputy Associate Director, Center for Talent Services.—Frank Esquivel, 606–1029.
Assistant Director, HR Consulting Programs.—Kim Bauhs, 606–1029.

OFFICE OF THE GENERAL COUNSEL

General Counsel.—Elaine Kaplan, 606–1700.
Senior Policy Counsel.—Robert H. Shriver III.
Deputy General Counsel.—Kathie Ann Whipple.
Associate General Counsels.—Steven E. Abow, R. Alan Miller.

OFFICE OF THE INSPECTOR GENERAL

Inspector General.—Patrick E. McFarland, 606–1200.

Deputy Inspector General.—Norbert E. Vint.
Executive Assistant.—A. Paulette Berry.
Counsel to the Inspector General.—Timothy C. Watkins, 606–2030.
Assistant Inspector General, Office of:
Audits.—Michael E. Esser.
Investigations.—Michelle B. Schmitz.
Legal Affairs.—J. David Cope, 606–3807.
Management.—Terri H. Fazio, 606–0846.

MANAGEMENT SERVICES DIVISION

Associate Director and Chief Human Capital Officer.—Ronald C. Flom, 606–3207.
Deputy Associate Director, Center for—
Contracting, Facilities and Administrative Services.—Tina B. McGuire, 606–2200.
Human Capital Management Services and Deputy Chief Human Capital Officer.—Mark D. Reinhold, 606–1402.
Information Services and Chief Information Officer.—Janet L. Barnes, 606–2150.
Security and Emergency Actions.—Dean S. Hunter, 606–3130.
Chief, Center for Equal Employment Opportunity.—Lorna S. Lewis, 606–2460.

STRATEGIC HUMAN RESOURCES POLICY DIVISION

Associate Director.—Nancy H. Kichak, 606–6500.
Executive Assistant.—Mekaela Bratcher.
Deputy Associate Director, Center for—
Employee and Family Support Policy.—Dan Green, 606–0770.
Workforce Information and Systems Requirements.—Maureen Higgins, 606–1343.
Learning, Executive Resources and Policy Analysis.—Ana Mazzi (acting), 606–8046.
Pay and Leave Administration.—Jerry Mikowicz, 606–2880.
Performance and Pay Systems.—Chuck Grimes, 606–2838.
Talent and Capacity Policy.—Angela Bailey, 606–8097.
Workforce Relations and Accountability Policy.—Ana Mazzi, 606–2930.
Chief Actuary, Office of the Actuaries.—Steve Niu, 606–0722.

OFFICE OF THE SPECIAL COUNSEL

1730 M Street, NW., Suite 300, 20036–4505, phone (202) 254–2000

[Authorized by 5 U.S.C 1101 and 5 U.S.C 1211]

Special Counsel.—Vacant.
Deputy Special Counsel.—Vacant.
Congressional and Public Affairs Division.—Vacant.
Associate Special Counsel for Legal Counsel and Policy.—Erin McDonnell.
Senior Associate Special Counsel for Investigation and Prosecution.—Leonard Dribinsky.
Associate Special Counsel for Investigation and Prosecution.—William Reukauf.
CFO/Director of Administrative Services.—Roderick Anderson.

THE PEACE CORPS

1111 20th Street, NW., 20526, phone (202) 692–2000

Phone (202) 692–2000, Toll-Free Number (800) 424–8580, http://www.peacecorps.gov

[Created by Public Law 97–113]

OFFICE OF THE DIRECTOR

phone (202) 962–2100, fax 692–2101

Director.—Aaron Williams.
Deputy Director.—Vacant.
Chief of Staff/Chief of Operations.—Kathy Rulon (acting).
Deputy Chief of Staff/Deputy Chief of Operations.—Vacant.
White House Liaison/Senior Advisor to the Director.—Elisa Montoya.
Senior Advisor to the Director.—Maryann Minutillo.

Expert Consultant.—James Cuffe.
Administrative Officer.—Matt Smith.
American Diversity Program Manager.—Shirley Everest.
Director, Office of:
Communications.—Allison Price.
Congressional Relations.—Suzie Carroll (acting).
Press Relations.—Vacant.
Private Sector Initiative.—Barbi Broadus (acting).
Strategic Information, Research and Planning.—Cynthia Threlkeld (acting).
General Counsel.—Carl Sosebee (acting)
Aids Relief Coordinator.—Pam Martin.
Regional Directors of:
Africa Operations.—Lynn Foden (acting).
Europe, Mediterranean and Asia Operations.—David Burgess (acting).
Inter-America and Pacific Operations.—Roger Conrad (acting).
Directors, Office of:
Acquisitions and Contract Management Officer.—Carey Fountain.
Chief Financial Officer Chief.—Thomas Bellamy (acting).
Accounting and Financial Reporting.—Richard Lubarski.
Accounts Receivable and Cash Management.—Alcindor Rosier.
Budget and Analysis Officer.—Mary Koskinen.
Financial Policy and Compliance.—Vacant.
Financial Systems Deputy Officer.—Charles Kemp (acting).
Global Accounts Payable.—Charle Ann Rooney.
Volunteer and PSC Financial Services.—Kari Abood.
Chief Information Officer.—Chris Sarandos (acting).
Application Systems.—Terry Keyfauver.
IT Architecture, Standards, and Practices Chief Architect.—Beth Gray.
IT Planning and Training Chief.—Fletcher Honemond.
IT Security Program Chief Officer.—Timothy Howard.
Operations and Infrastructure.—Steve Moore.
Inspector General.—Kathy Buller.
Management Associate.—Earl Yates.
Administrative Services Chief.—James Pimpedly.
Human Resource Management.—Pat Connelly.
Overseas Building Operations Manager.—Vacant.
Overseas Executive Selection and Support Manager.—Bruce Cohen.
Peace Corps Response.—Heather Schwenk (acting).
Overseas Programming and Training Support.—Howard Anderson (acting).
Field Assistance Support Division Chief.—Howard Anderson.
Knowledge Exchange and Professional Development Chief.—Sally Caldwell.
Safety and Security Associate.—Ed Hobson.
Volunteer Recruitment and Selection Associate.—Rosie Mauk.
Chief of Operations.—Arnaldo Claudio.
Recruitment.—Shari Hubert.
Domestic Programs.—Marjorie Anctil (acting).
University Programs, Office of:
Fellows/USA Program Manager.—Julie Driver.
Master's International Program Manager.—Eric Goldman.
Coverdell World Wise Schools.—Marjorie Anctil.
Operations, Office of:
Placement Manager.—Andrej Kolaja.
Recruitment Support Manager.—Dorothy Sullivan.
Volunteer Support Associate.—Jules Delaune.
Medical Services.—Glenn Egelman.
Special Services.—Richard Pyle (acting).

REGIONAL OFFICES

Atlanta (FL, GA, TN, MS, AL, SC, PR): 100 Alabama Street, Building 1924, Suite 2R70, Atlanta, GA 30303 (404) 562–3451, fax 562–3455.
Manager.—Kenton Ayers.
Public Affairs Specialist.—David Leavitt.
Boston (MA, VT, NH, RI, ME): Tip O'Neill Federal Building, 10 Causeway Street, Suite 450, Boston, MA 02222–1099 (617) 565–5555, fax 565–5539.
Manager.—Erin Mone.

Public Affairs Specialist.—Elizabeth Chamberlain.

Chicago (IL, IN, KY, MI, MO, OH, IA, MN, ND, SD, WI): 55 West Monroe Street, Suite 450, Chicago, IL 60603 (312) 353–4990, fax 353–4192.

Manager.—Kathryn O'Connor (acting).

Public Affairs Specialist.—Casey Lowman.

Dallas (AR, LA, NM, OK, TX, CO, KS, NE, UT, WY): 1100 Commerce Street, Suite 427, Dallas, TX 75242 (214) 253–5400, fax 253–5401.

Manager.—Sharon Sugarek.

Public Affairs Specialist.—Shannon Borders.

Los Angeles (Southern CA, AZ): 2361 Rosecrans Avenue, Suite 155, El Segundo, CA 90245–0916 (310) 356–1100, fax 356–1125.

Manager.—Robert Robinson.

Public Affairs Specialist.—Kate Kuykendall.

New York (NY, NJ, CT, PA): 201 Varick Street, Suite 1025, New York, NY 10014 (212) 352–5440, fax 352–5442.

Manager.—Vincent Wickes.

Public Affairs Specialist.—Molly Jennings Levine.

San Francisco (Northern CA, NV, HI): 1301 Clay Street, Suite 620N, Oakland, CA 94612; (510) 452–8444, fax 452–8441.

Manager.—Janet Allen.

Public Affairs Specialist.—Nathan Sargent.

Seattle (WA, OR, ID, AK, MT): Westlake Building, 1601 5th Avenue, Suite 605, Seattle, WA 98101 (206) 553–5490, fax 553–2343.

Manager.—Eileen N. Conoboy.

Public Affairs Specialist.—Melanie Forthun.

Washington, DC (DC, MD, NC, WV, DE, VA): 1525 Wilson Boulevard, Suite 100, Arlington, VA 22209 (202) 692–1040, fax 692–1041

Manager.—Christopher Gilson.

Public Affairs Specialist.—Stephen Chapman.

PENSION BENEFIT GUARANTY CORPORATION

1200 K Street, 20005–4026, (202) 326–4000

BOARD OF DIRECTORS

Chairman.—Hilda Solis, Secretary of Labor.

Members:

Timothy F. Geithner, Secretary of the Treasury.

Gary Locke, Secretary of Commerce.

OFFICIALS

Director.—Vincent Snowbarger (acting), 326–4010.

Deputy Director.—Vincent Snowbarger.

Chief Officer for—

Finance.—Patricia Kelly, 326–4060.

Insurance Program.—Terrence Deneen, 326–4050.

Management and Human Capital.—Stephen Barber, 326–4180.

Operations.—Richard Macy, 326–4010.

Information.—Patsy Garnett, 326–4010.

Department Director for—

Benefits Administration and Payment.—Bennie Hagans, 326–4050.

Budget and Organizational Performance.—Edgar Bennett, 326–4120.

Communications and Public Affairs.—Jeffrey Speicher (acting), 326–4040.

Contracts and Controls Review.—Martin Boehm, 326–4161.

Facilities and Services.—Patricia Davis, 326–4150.

Financial Operations.—Theodore Winter, 326–4060.

General Counsel.—Judith Starr, 326–4020.

Human Resources.—Arrie Etheridge, 326–4110.

Information Technology Infrastructure Operations.—Kenneth Oliver (acting), 326–4151.

Information Technology and Business Modernization.—Srividhya Shyamsunder, 326–4000.

Insurance Supervision and Compliance.—Joseph House, 326–4020.

Legislative and Regulatory Affairs.—John Hanley, 326–4130.

Policy, Research and Analysis.—David Gustafson, 326–4080.

Procurement.—Arthur Block (acting), 326–4160.
Chief Counsel.—Israel Goldowitz, 326–4020.
Inspector General.—Rebecca Batts, 326–4030.

POSTAL REGULATORY COMMISSION

901 New York Avenue, NW., Suite 200, 20268–0001
phone (202) 789–6800, fax 789–6886

Chairman.—Ruth Y. Goldway, 789–6810.
Vice Chairman.—Nanci E. Langley, 789–6813.
Commissioners:
Mark Acton, 789–6866.
Dan G. Blair, 789–6801.
Tony Hammond, 789–6805.
Chief Administrative Officer and Secretary.—Vacant, 789–6840.
Director, Public Affairs and Government Relations.—Ann Fisher, 789–6803.
General Counsel.—Stephen L. Sharfman, 789–6820.
Office of Accountability and Compliance.—John Waller, 789–6850.

SECURITIES AND EXCHANGE COMMISSION

100 F Street, NE., 20549, phone (202) 551–7500
TTY Relay Service 1–800–877–8339 http://www.sec.gov

THE COMMISSION

Chairman.—Mary L. Schapiro, 551–2100, fax 772–9200.
Chief of Staff.—Didem A. Nisanci.
Deputy Chief of Staff/Counselor to the Chairman.—Kayla J. Gillan.
Senior Advisors to the Chairman: Stephen Cohen, Stephen Devine, Jennifer McHugh.
Counsels: Christy Romero, Matthew Strada, Haimera Workie.
Commissioners:
Kathleen L. Casey, 551–2600, fax 772–9345.
Counsels to the Commissioner: James Burns, Justin Daly, Blaise Brennan.
Elisse Walter, 551–2800, fax 772–9340.
Counsels to the Commissioner: Christian Broadbent, Matt Daigler, Lesli Sheppard.
Luis A. Aguilar, 551–2500, fax 772–9335.
Counsels to the Commissioner: Smeeta Ramarathnam, Zachary May, Sarah Otte.
Troy A. Paredes, 551–2700, fax 772–9330.
Counsels to the Commissioner: Dawn Jessen, Bradley J. Bondi, Scott Kimpel.

OFFICE OF THE SECRETARY

Secretary.—Elizabeth Murphy, 551–5400, fax 772–9324.
Deputy Secretary.—Florence Harmon, 551–5604.
Assistant Secretary.—Jill Peterson, 551–5458.
Assistant Director, Library.—Cindy Plisch, 551–5458.

OFFICE OF THE EXECUTIVE DIRECTOR

Executive Director.—Diego Ruiz, 551–4300, fax 777–1025.
Chief Management Analyst.—Kenneth Johnson.

OFFICE OF INVESTOR EDUCATION AND ADVOCACY

Director.—Mary Head (acting), 551–6500, fax 772–9295.
Deputy Director.—Vacant.
FOIA and Privacy Act Officer.—M. Celia Winter, 551–7900, fax 772–9336.
FOIA/PA Branch Chiefs: Brenda Fuller, Ligia Glass, Frank Henderson.

OFFICE OF EQUAL EMPLOYMENT OPPORTUNITY

Director.—Alta Rodriquez (acting), 551–6040, fax 772–9316.

OFFICE OF THE CHIEF ACCOUNTANT

Chief Accountant.—James Kroeker, 551–5300, fax 772–9253.
Deputy Chief Accountant:
Accounting.—James Kroeker.
International.—Julie Erhardt.
Professional Practice.—Paul Beswick.
Senior Associate Chief Accountants: John Albert, 551–5337; Edmund Bailey, 551–5339; Susan Koski-Grafer, 551–5349; Shelly Luisi, 551–5350; Jenifer Minke-Girard, 551–5351; Josh Jones.
Chief Counsel.—Jeff Minton, 551–5342.

OFFICE OF COMPLIANCE INSPECTIONS AND EXAMINATIONS

Director.—John Walsh (acting), 551–6200, fax 772–9179.
Senior Advisor.—Karen Burgess.
Associate Director/Chief Counsel.—John Walsh, 551–6460.
Associate Directors: Mary Ann Gadziala (Broker/Dealer/Self-Regulatory Organization), 551–6400; Gene Gohlke (Investment Adviser/Investment Company), 551–6300.
Assistant Directors: Louis Becka (Investment Adviser/Investment Company), 551–6300; Tina Barry (Self-Regulatory Organization), 551–6210; Thomas Eidt (Self-Regulatory Organization), 551–6256; Richard Hannibal (Broker/Dealer), 551–6400; Mavis Kelly (Investment Adviser/Investment Company), 551–6300; Helene McGee (Self-Regulatory Organization), 551–6270; A. Duer Meehan (Broker/Dealer), 551–6400.

OFFICE OF ECONOMIC ANALYSIS

Chief Economist.—James Overdahl, 551–6600, fax 772–9290.
Deputy Chief Economist.—Stewart Mayhew, 551–6617.
Assistant Chief Economist.—Cindy Alexander, 551–6602.
Office of:
Litigation Support.—Chyhe Becker, 551–6654.
Markets and Intermediaries.—Amy Decker, 551–6663.

OFFICE OF THE GENERAL COUNSEL

General Counsel.—David Becker, 551–5100, fax 772–9260.
Deputy General Counsel for—
Legal Policy and Administrative Practice.—Alexander Cohen, 551–5160.
Litigation and Adjudication.—Andrew Vollmer, 551–5110.
Principal Assistant General Counsel for Litigation and Adjudication.—Joan Loizeuax.
Assistant General Counsels for Adjudication: Kermit Kennedy, 551–5164; Joan McCarthy, 551–5150.
Solicitor, Appellate Litigation and Bankruptcy.—Jacob Stillman, 551–5130.
Deputy Solicitor, Appellate Litigation and Bankruptcy.—Eric Summergrad, 551–5022.
Special Counsel to the Solicitor.—Allan Capute, 551–5122.
Assistant General Counsels for Appellate Litigation and Bankruptcy: Katharine Gresham, 551–5148; Mark Pennington, 551–5189; Randall Quinn, 551–5198.
Associate General Counsel for Counseling and Regulatory Policy.—Diane Sanger, 551–5002.
Ethics Counsel.—William Lenox, 551–5170.
Principal Associate General Counsel for Legal Policy.—Meridith Mitchell, 551–5184.
Assistant General Counsels for Legal Policy: David Frederickson, 551–5144; Richard Levine, 551–5168; Janice Mitnick, 551–5185; Lori Price, 551–5184.
Assistant General Counsel for Legislation and Financial Services.—Stephen Jung, 551–5162.
Associate General Counsel for Litigation and Administrative Practice.—Richard M. Humes, 551–5140.
Assistant General Counsels for Litigation and Administrative Practice: George Brown, 551–5121, Samuel Forstein, 551–5139; Melinda Hardy, 551–5149; Thomas Karr, 551–5163.

DIVISION OF INVESTMENT MANAGEMENT

Director.—Andrew Donahue, 551–6720, fax 772–9288.

Senior Advisor to the Director.—Vacant, 551–6720.
Associate Director, Chief Counsel.—Douglas J. Scheidt, 551–6701.
Assistant Chief Counsels: David W. Grim (International Issues), 551–6825; Nadya B. Roytblat (Financial Institutions), 551–6825.
Enforcement Liaison.—Barbara Chretien-Dar, 551–6785.
Associate Director, Office of:
Exemptive Applications and Special Projects.—Elizabeth G. Osterman, 551–6746.
Disclosure and Insurance Product Regulation.—Susan Nash, 551–6742.
Legal and Disclosure.—Barry D. Miller, 551–6725.
Regulatory Policy and Investment Adviser Regulation.—Robert E. Plaze, 551–6702.
Assistant Director, Office of:
Disclosure and Review No. 1.—Brent J. Fields, 551–6921.
Disclosure and Review No. 2.—Frank J. Donaty, 551–6925.
Disclosure Regulation.—Mark T. Uyeda, 551–6784.
Enforcement Liaison.—Barbara Chretien-Dar, 551–6785.
Financial Analysis.—Paul B. Goldman, 551–6715.
Insurance Products.—William J. Kotapish, 551–6795.
Investment Adviser Regulation.—Sarah A. Bessin, 551–6787.
Investment Company Regulation No. 1.—Janet M. Grossnickle, 551–6821.
Investment Company Regulation No. 2.—Michael W. Mundt, 551–6821.
Regulatory Policy.—C. Hunter Jones, Penelope W. Saltzman, 551–6792.
Chief Accountant, Office of Chief Accountant.—Richard F. Sennett, 551–6918.

DIVISION OF CORPORATION FINANCE

Director.—Meredith Cross, 551–3100, fax 772–9213.
Deputy Director of:
Disclosure Operations.—Shelley E. Parratt, 551–3130.
Legal and Regulatory.—Brian Breheny, 551–3120.
Associate Directors:
Legal Office.—Paula Dubberly, 551–3180.
Regulatory Policy.—Mauri L. Osheroff, 551–3190.
Chief Accountant.—Wayne Carnall, 551–3400.
Disclosure Operations: Paul Belvin, 551–3150; James Daly, 551–3140; Barry Summer, 551–3160.
Chief Counsel.—Thomas Kim, 551–3520.
Chief, Office of:
CF OIT.—Cecile Peters, 551–3610.
Disclosure Support.—Patti Dennis, 551–3610.
Enforcement Liaison.—Mary Kosterlitz, 551–3420.
International Corporate Finance.—Paul Dudek, 551–3450.
Mergers and Acquisitions.—Michele Anderson, 551–3440.
Rulemaking.—Felicia Kung, 551–3430.
Small Business Policy.—Gerald Laporte, 551–3460.
Assistant Directors: Karen Garnett, 551–3780; Peggy Fisher, 551–3800; Barbara Jacobs, 551–3730; Pamela Long, 551–3760; H. Christopher Owings, 551–3720; Jeffrey Reidler, 551–3710; John Reynolds, 551–3790; Todd Schiffman, 551–3770; H. Roger Schwall, 551–3740; Larry Spirgel, 551–3810; Max Webb, 551–3750.

DIVISION OF ENFORCEMENT

Director.—Robert Khuzami, 551–4500, fax 772–9279.
Senior Advisors: Pauline Calande, 551–4950; Donna Norman, 551–4878.
Deputy Director.—Lorin Reisner, 551–4787.
Associate Director.—Cheryl J. Scarboro, 551–4403.
Chief, Office of Internet Enforcement.—John R. Stark, 551–4892.
Assistant Directors: Josh Felker, 551–4960; Reid Muoio, 551–4488.
Associate Director.—Fredric Firestone, 551–4711.
Assistant Directors: Gregory Faragasso, 551–4734; Gerald Hodgkins, 551–4719; Kenneth Lench, 551–4938.
Associate Director.—Christopher Conte, 551–4834.
Assistant Directors: Charles Cain, 551–4911; Vacant, 551–4484; Timothy England, 551–4959; David Wiederkehr, 551–4628.
Associate Director.—Scott Friestad, 551–4962.
Assistant Directors: David Frohlich, 551–4963; Laura Josephs, 551–5117; Robert Kaplan, 551–4969; John Polise, 551–4981.

Chief, Market Surveillance.—Mark Lineberry, 551–4549.
Associate Director.—Antonia Chion, 551–4842.
Assistant Directors: Kara Brockmeyer, 551–4829; Daniel Chaudoin, 551–4952; Yuri Zelinsky, 551–4769.
Chief Counsel.—Joan E. McKown, 551–4933.
Assistant Chief Counsel.—Charlotte L. Buford, 551–4843.
Chief Litigation Counsel.—Luis Mejia, 551–4481.
Deputy Chief Litigation Counsel.—Mark A. Adler, 551–4402.
Chief Accountant.—Vacant.
Associate Chief Accountants: Regina M. Barrett, 551–4615; Dwayne Brown, 551–4616; David M. Estabrook, 551–4621; Jason Flemmon, 551–4617; Pierron Leef, 551–4620.
Deputy Director, Office of Collections, Distributions and Financial Management.—Lynn Powalski, 551–4927.
Director, Regional Office Operations.—James A. Clarkson, 551–4932.

DIVISION OF MARKET REGULATION

Director.—Erik Sirri, 551–5500, fax 772–9273.
Deputy Director.—Robert L.D. Colby, 551–5770.
Chief of Operations.—Herbert Brooks, 551–5671.
Associate Director, Chief Counsel.—Catherine McGuire, 551–5551.
Deputy Chief Counsel.—Paula Jenson, 551–5581.
Associate Directors:
Broker Dealer Finances.—Michael Macchiaroli, 551–5510.
Market Supervision: Elizabeth King, 551–5600; David Shillman, 551–5685.
Trading Practices and Processing.—James Brigagliano, 551–5700.
Assistant Directors: Katherine England, 551–5611; Kelly Riley, 551–5661; John Roeser, 551–5631; Nancy Sanow, 551–5621; Michael Gaw, 551–5602; Martha Haines (Municipal Finance), 551–5681.
Assistant Directors:
Clearance and Settlement.—Jerry Carpenter, 551–5710.
Enforcement Liaison and Institutional Trading.—Jo Anne Swindler, 551–5750.
Financial Responsibility.—Thomas McGowan, 551–5520.
Market Operations.—Herb Brooks, 551–5670.
Market Watch.—Alton Harvey, 551–5691.
Prudential Supervision and Risk Analysis #1.—Matthew Eichner, 551–5530.

OFFICE OF ADMINISTRATIVE LAW JUDGES

Chief Administrative Law Judge.—Brenda Murray, 551–6030, fax 777–1031.
Administrative Law Judges: Carol Fox Foelak, James Kelly, Robert Mahony.

OFFICE OF INTERNATIONAL AFFAIRS

Director.—Ethiopis Tafara, 551–6690, fax 772–9280.
Deputy Director.—Elizabeth Jacobs.
Assistant Directors: Sherman Boone, 551–6686; Robert Fisher, 551–6652; Susan Yashar, 551–6683.

OFFICE OF LEGISLATIVE AND INTERGOVERNMENTAL AFFAIRS

Director.—William Schulz, 551–2010, fax 772–9250.
Deputy Directors: Timothy Henseler, Julie Z. Davis.

OFFICE OF THE INSPECTOR GENERAL

Inspector General.—David Kotz, 551–6060, fax 772–9265.
Deputy Inspector General.—Noelle Frangipane, 551–6035.

OFFICE OF PUBLIC AFFAIRS

Director.—John Nester, 551–4120, fax 777–1026.
Deputy Director.—John D. Heine, 551–4123.

OFFICE OF FINANCIAL MANAGEMENT

Associate Executive Director.—Kristine Chadwick, 551–7840, fax (703) 914–0172.
Assistant Director for Finance and Accounting.—Zayra Okrak, 551–7856.
Assistant Director for Planning and Budget.—Diane Galvin, 551–7853.

OFFICE OF INFORMATION TECHNOLOGY

Director/Chief Information Officer.—Charles Boucher, 551–8800, fax (703) 914–2621.

OFFICE OF ADMINISTRATIVE SERVICES

Associate Executive Director.—Sharon Sheehan, 551–7400, fax (703) 914–4459.
Assistant Directors:
Procurement, Security, and Publishing.—Beth Blackwood, 551–7408.
Real Property and Facilities Support.—John Branch, 551–8344.

OFFICE OF HUMAN RESOURCES

Associate Executive Director.—Jeffrey Risinger, 551–7500, fax 777–1028.
Chief Counsel for Diversity Initiatives.—Ronald Crawford.
Assistant Directors: Teri Ellison (Center for Talent Management and Employee Programs), 551–4105; Timothy Buckley, 551–7902.

REGIONAL OFFICES

Atlanta Regional Office: 3475 Lenox Road, NE., Suite 1000, Atlanta, GA 30326 (404) 842–7600, fax (404) 842–7633.
Regional Director.—Katherine Addleman, 842–7610.
Associate Director, Enforcement.—Vacant.
Assistant Regional Directors, Enforcement: Stephen Donahue, 842–7618, Madison Loomis, 842–7622.
Associate Director, Examinations.—James Carley, 842–7645.
Assistant Regional Director, Broker/Dealer Examinations.—Howard Dennis, 842–7643.
Associate Regional Directors, Investment Company/Investment Adviser Examinations: Herbert Campbell, 842–7677; Askari Foy, 842–7623.
Regional Trail Counsel.—William Hicks, 842–7675.
Boston Regional Office: 33 Arch Street, 23rd Floor, Boston, MA 02110 (617) 573–8900, fax (617) 573–4590.
Regional Director.—David Bergers, 573–8927.
Associate District Administrator, Enforcement.—John Dugan, 573–8936.
Assistant District Administrators, Enforcement: Sandra Bailey, 573–8976; Martin Healey, 573–8952; Philip Koski, 573–8964.
Associate Regional Director, Examinations.—Lucile Corkery, 573–8932.
Assistant District Administrators, Investment Adviser/Investment Company Examinations: Andrew Caverly, (Broker/Dealer), 573–8922; Michael Garrity (Investment Adviser/Investment Company), 573–8944; Joseph Mick (Investment Adviser/Investment Company), 573–8975; Elizabeth Salini, 573–8931.
Chicago Regional Office: 175 West Jackson Boulevard, Suite 900, Chicago, IL 60604 (312) 353–7390, fax 353–7398.
Regional Director.—Merri Jo Gillette, 353–9338.
Senior Associate Regional Director, Enforcement.—Robert J. Burson, 353–7428.
Associate Regional Director, Enforcement.—Timothy L. Warren, 353–7394.
Associate Regional Directors, Examinations: Jane E. Jarcho, 353–5479; Barbara S. Lorenzen, 353–7436.
Assistant Regional Directors, Enforcement: Peter Chan, 353–7410; Kathryn A. Pyszka, 353–7416; Scott J. Hlavacek, 353–1679; James A. Davidson, 353–5712; Paul A. Montoya, 353–7429; John J. Sikora, 353–7418.
Assistant Regional Directors, Examinations: Doug R. Adams, 353–7402; Maureen Dempsey, 886–1496; Lewis A. Garcia, 353–6888; Daniel R. Gregus, 353–7423; Thomas Kirk, 886–3956; David J. Mueller, 353–7404; Thomas Murphy, 886–8513; Larry P. Perdue, 353–7219.
Denver Regional Office: 1801 California Street, Suite 1500, Denver, CO 80202 (303) 844–1000, fax (303) 844–1010.
Regional Director.—Donald M. Hoerl, 844–1060.

Associate Regional Director.—Vacant.

Assistant Regional Directors, Enforcement: Mary S. Brady, 844–1023; Laura Metcalfe, 844–1092; Amy Norwood, 844–1029.

Associate Regional Director, Office of the Regulator.—Kevin Goodman, 844–1040.

Assistant Regional Director, Broker/Dealer and Transfer Agent Examinations.—Lonnie Morgan, 844–1048.

Assistant Regional Director, Investment Adviser and Company Examinations.—Thomas Piccone, 844–1016.

Fort Worth Regional Office: 801 Cherry Street, Unit #18, Fort Worth, TX 76102 (817) 978–3821, fax 978–2700.

Regional Director.—Rose Romero, 900–2623.

Associate Regional Director, Enforcement.—Stephen Korotash, 978–6490.

Regional Trial Counsel.—Toby Galloway, 978–6447.

Assistant Regional Directors, Enforcement: Kevin Edmundson, 978–1411; David Peavler, 978–6459; Stephen Webster, 978–6459.

Associate Regional Director, Examinations.—Kimberly Garber, 900–2622.

Assistant Regional Director, Broker/Dealer Examinations.—Donna Esau, 900–2612.

Assistant Regional Directors, Investment Company/Investment Adviser Examinations.—David Taylor, 978–1414; Mary Walters, 978–6487.

Los Angeles Regional Office: 5670 Wilshire Boulevard, 11th Floor, Los Angeles, CA 90036 (323) 965–3998, fax 965–3816.

Regional Director.—Rosalind R. Tyson, 965–3893.

Associate Regional Directors, Enforcement: Michele Wein Layne, 965–3850; Andrew G. Petillon, 965–3214.

Senior Assistant Regional Director, Enforcement.—Kelly C. Bowers, 965–3924.

Assistant Regional Directors, Enforcement: Lorraine Echavarria, 695–3914; Finola Halloran Manvelian, 965–3980; Diana Tani, 965–3991.

Associate Regional Director, Regulation.—Martin J. Murphy, 965–3859.

Assistant Regional Directors, Investment Company/Investment Adviser Examinations: David Ito, 965–4509; Michael P. Levitt, 965–2684; Charles T. Liao, 965–2688.

Assistant Regional Directors, Broker/Dealer Examinations: Karol L.K. Pollock, 965–3861; Cindy S. Wong, 965–3927.

Miami Regional Office: 801 Brickell Avenue, Suite 1800, Miami, FL 33131 (305) 982–6300, fax (305) 536–4120.

Regional Director.—Vacant, 982–6332.

Associate Regional Directors:

Enforcement.—Glenn S. Gordon, 536–6360.

Examination.—John C. Mattimore, 982–6357.

Assistant Regional Directors:

Enforcement: Eric R. Busto, 982–6362; Chedly C. Dumornay, 982–6377; Teresa Verges, 982–6384.

Examination: Faye A. Chin, 982–6305; Nicholas A. Monaco, 982–6310.

New York Regional Office: 3 World Financial Center, Suite 400, New York, NY 10281–1022, (212) 336–1100, fax (212) 336–1323.

Regional Director.—George S. Canellos, 336–1020.

Associate Regional Directors, Enforcement: Robert B. Blackburn, 336–1050; Andrew Calamari, 336–0042; David Rosenfeld, 336–0153.

Assistant Regional Directors, Enforcement: Alistaire Bambach, 336–0027; Alison Conn, 336–0052; Robert DeLeonardis (Investigations), 336–0056; Gerald Gross, 336–0085; Ken Joseph, 336–0097; Bruce Karpati, 336–0104; Leslie Kazon, 336–0107; Robert Keyes, 336–0109; David Markowitz, 336–0128; George Stepaniuk, 336–0173; Alex Vasilescu, 336–0178; Sanjay Wadhwa, 336–0181; Scott York, 336–0188.

Associate Regional Director, Investment Adviser/Investment Company Examinations.—Thomas Biolsi, 336–6446.

Assistant Regional Directors: Dawn Blankenship, 336–0197; William Delmage, 336–0495; Joseph Dimaria, 336–0497; Dorothy Eschwie, 336–0502.

Associate Regional Directors, Broker/Dealer: Richard D. Lee, 336–1010; Robert A. Sollazzo, 336–1070.

Assistant Regional Directors, Broker/Dealer Examinations: Richard A. Heapy, 336–0464; Linda Lettieri, 336–0474; John M. Nee, 336–0484; Rosanne R. Smith, 336–0928; Steven Vitulano, 336–0936.

Philadelphia Regional Office: Mellon Independence Center, 701 Market Street, Suite 2000, Philadelphia, PA 19106 (215) 597–3100, fax 597–3194.

Regional Director.—Daniel Hawke, 597–3191.

Associate Regional Director, Regulation.—Joy G. Thompson, 597–6135.

Associate Regional Directors, Enforcement: Elaine C. Greenberg, 597–3107; David Horowitz, 597–2950.

Associate Regional Directors, Enforcement: Paul Hee, 597–8307; Frank Thomas, 597–1048.
Assistant Regional Director, Broker/Dealer Examination.—A. Laurence Ehrhart, 597–2983.
Salt Lake Regional Office: 15 West South Temple Street, Suite 1800, Salt Lake City, UT 84101 (801) 524–5796, fax 524–3558.
Regional Director.—Kenneth D. Israel, 524–6745.
San Francisco Regional Office: 44 Montgomery Street, Suite 2600, San Francisco, CA 94104 (415) 705–2500, fax 705–2501.
Regional Director.—Marc J. Fagel, 705–2449.
Associate Regional Director.—Michael S. Dicke, 705–2458.
Assistant Regional Directors: Edward Haddad (Investment Adviser/Investment Company), 705–2344; Jennet Zundel (Broker/Dealer), 705–2452; Matthew O'Toole (Investment Adviser/Investment Company), 705–2477.
Associate Regional Director, Regulation.—Daryl Hagel, 705–2340.
Assistant Regional Directors, Enforcement: Tracy Davis, 705–2318; Michael S. Dicke 705–2458; Marc J. Fagel, 705–2449; Cary Robnett, 705–2335.

SELECTIVE SERVICE SYSTEM

1515 Wilson Boulevard, 5th Floor, Arlington, VA 22209–2425

phone (703) 605–4100, fax 605–4106, http://www.sss.gov

Director.—Ernest E. Garcia (acting), 605–4010.
Inspector General.—Carlo Verdino, 605–4022.
Director for—
Operations.—Scott Campbell 605–4110.
Resource Management.—Edward A. Blackadar, Jr., 605–4032.
Public and Intergovernmental Affairs.—Richard S. Flahavan, 605–4017, fax 605–4106.
Financial Management.—Carlo Verdino, 605–4022.
Registration Information Office, P.O. Box 94638, Palatine, IL 60094–4638, phone (847) 688–6888, fax (847) 688–2860.

SMALL BUSINESS ADMINISTRATION

409 Third Street, SW., 20416

phone (202) 205–6600, fax 205–7064, http://www.sbaonline.sba.gov

Administrator.—Karen Mills, 205–6605.
Deputy Administrator.—Vacant.
Chief of Staff.—Ana Ma, 205–6605.
Director of Executive Secretariat.—Kim Bradley, 205–6608.
General Counsel.—Sara Lipscomb, 205–6642.
Chief Counsel for Advocacy.—Vacant.
Inspector General.—Peter McClintock (acting), 205–6586.
Chief Financial Officer.—Jonathan Carver, 205–6449.
Director, Community Relations.—Susan Walthall, 205–7180.
Associate Administrator for—
Disaster Assistance.—James Rivera, 205–6734.
Field Operations.—Jess Knox, 205–6808.
Office of Communications and Public Liaison.—Jonathan Swain, 205–6740.
Assistant Administrator for—
Congressional and Legislative Affairs.—Nicholas Coutsos (acting), 205–6700.
Equal Employment Opportunity and Civil Rights Compliance.—Margareth J. Bennett, 205–6750.
Hearings and Appeals.—Delorice Ford, 401–8200.
Associate Administrator for Management and Administration.—Darryl Hairston, 205–6610.
Director, Office of Business Operations.—Denise Wright, 205–6642.
Chief Information Officer.—Robert Naylor (acting), 205–6708.
Chief Human Capital Officer.—Napoleon Avery, 205–6784.
Associate Administrator for—
Capital Access.—Eric Zarnikow, 205–6657.
Entrepreneurship Education.—Ellen Thrasher, 205–6671.
Director, Office of Financial Assistance.—Grady Hedgespeth, 205–6490.
Associate Administrator for—
Investment.—Vacant, 205–6510.
Small Business Development Centers.—Antonio Doss, 205–6766.

Director, Office of:
Surety Guarantees.—Frank Lalumiere, 205–6540.
International Trade.—Luz Hopewell, 205–6720.
Associate Administrator for—
Government Contracting and Business Development.—Joseph Jordan, 205–6459.
Office of Veterans' Business Development.—William Elmore, 205–6773.
Women's Business Ownership.—Ana Harvey, 205–6673.
Director, Office of:
Business Development.—Joseph Loddo, 205–5852.
Government Contracting.—Dean Koppel (acting), 205–6460.
Office of:
Size Standard.—Khem J. Sharma, 205–6618.
Technology.—Edsel Brown, 205–6450.

SMITHSONIAN INSTITUTION

Smithsonian Institution Building—The Castle (SIB), 1000 Jefferson Drive, SW., 20560

phone (202) 633–1000, http://www.smithsonian.org

The Smithsonian Institution is an independent trust instrumentality created in accordance with the terms of the will of James Smithson of England who in 1826 bequeathed his property to the United States of America ''to found at Washington under the name of the Smithsonian Institution an establishment for the increase and diffusion of knowledge among men.'' Congress pledged the faith of the United States to carry out the trust in 1836 (Act of July 1, 1836, C. 252, 5 Stat. 64), and established the Institution in its present form in 1846 (August 10, 1846, C. 178, 9 Stat. 102), entrusting the management of the institution to its independent Board of Regents.

THE BOARD OF REGENTS

ex officio

Chief Justice of the United States.—John G. Roberts, Jr., Chancellor.
Vice President of the United States.—Joseph R. Biden, Jr.

Appointed by the President of the Senate
Hon. Thad Cochran
Hon. Christopher J. Dodd
Hon. Patrick J. Leahy

Appointed by the Speaker of the House
Hon. Sam Johnson
Hon. Doris O. Matsui
Hon. Xavier Becerra

Appointed by Joint Resolution of Congress

Anne d'Harnoncourt
Phillip Frost
Shirley Ann Jackson
Robert Kogod
David Rubenstein
Dr. Patty Stonesifer
Alan G. Spoon
Roger Sant
Vacant.

Chief of Staff to the Regents.—John K. Lapiana, 633–5230.

OFFICE OF THE SECRETARY

Secretary.—Dr. G. Wayne Clough, 633–1846.
Chief of Staff.—Patricia Bartlett, 633–1869.
Inspector General.—Sprightley Ryan, 633–7050.
General Counsel.—Judith Leonard, 633–5099.
Director of:
Communications and Public Affairs.—Evelyn Lieberman, 633–5190.
External Affairs.—Virginia Clark, 633–5021.
Government Relations.—Nell Payne, 633–5125.
Policy and Analysis.—Carole M.P. Neves, 633–5585.

OFFICE OF THE UNDER SECRETARY FOR FINANCE AND ADMINISTRATION

Under Secretary.—Alison McNally, 633–5240.

Director of:

Accessibility Program.—Elizabeth Ziebarth, 633–2946.

Exhibits, The Arts and Industries Building and the International Gallery.—Ellen Dorn, 633–7421.

Special Events and Protocol.—Nicole L. Krakora, 633–2020.

Director, Office of:

Equal Employment and Minority Affairs.—Era Marshall, 633–6414.

Exhibits Central.—Michael Headley, 633–4514.

Facilities Engineering and Operations.—Bruce Kendall, 633–1873.

Human Resources.—James Douglas, 633–6301.

Chief, Office of:

Finance.—Alice Maroni, 633–7120.

Information Technology.—Anne Speyer, 633–1688.

Ombudsman.—Chandra Heilman, 633–2010.

OFFICE OF THE UNDER SECRETARY FOR HISTORY, ART, AND CULTURE

Under Secretary.—Dr. Richard Kurin, 633–5240.

Director of:

Anacostia Community Museum.—Camille Akeju, 633–4839.

Archives of American Art.—John Smith, 275–1874.

Asian Pacific American Program.—Franklin Odo, 786–2963.

Center for Folklife Programs and Cultural Heritage.—Dan Sheehy (acting), 633–6440.

Cooper Hewitt, National Design Museum.—Caroline Baumann (acting), (212) 849–8370.

Freer and Sackler Galleries.—Julian Raby, 633–0456.

Hirshhorn Museum and Sculpture Garden.—Richard Koshalek, 633–2824.

National Museum of African American History and Culture.—Lonnie Bunch, 633–4751.

National Museum of African Art.—Dr. Johnnetta Cole, 633–4610.

National Museum of American History.—Brent Glass, 633–3435.

National Museum of the American Indian.—Kevin Glover, 633–6700.

National Portrait Gallery.—Martin Sullivan, 275–1740.

National Postal Museum.—Allen Kane, 633–5500.

Smithsonian Affiliations Program.—Harold Closter, 633–5321.

Smithsonian American Art Museum.—Elizabeth Broun, 275–1515.

Smithsonian Associates Program.—Barbara Tuceling, 633–8880.

Smithsonian Center for Education and Museum Studies.—Stephanie L. Norby, 633–5297.

Smithsonian Latino Center.—Eduardo Diaz, 633–1240.

Smithsonian Institution Archives.—Anne Van Camp, 633–5908.

Smithsonian Institution Libraries.—Nancy Gwinn, 633–2240.

Smithsonian Institution Traveling Exhibition Service.—Anna Cohn, 633–3136.

Smithsonian Photography Initiative.—Merry Foresta, 633–2928.

OFFICE OF THE UNDER SECRETARY FOR SCIENCE

Under Secretary.—Dr. Eva Pell, 633–5127.

Director of:

International Relations.—Francine Berkowitz, 633–4795.

National Air and Space Museum.—Jack Dailey, 633–2350.

National Museum of Natural History.—Dr. Cristián Samper, 633–2664.

National Science Resources Center.—Sally Goetz Shuler, 633–2972.

National Zoological Park.—Dr. Stephen Monfort (acting), 633–4442.

Office of Research and Training Services.—Catherine Harris, 633–7070.

Smithsonian Astrophysical Observatory.—Charles Alcock (617) 495–7100.

Smithsonian Environmental Research Center.—Anson Hines (443) 482–2208.

Smithsonian Museum Conservation Institute.—Robert Koestler (301) 238–1205.

Smithsonian Tropical Research Institute.—Eldredge Bermingham, 011–507–212–8110.

SMITHSONIAN ENTERPRISES

President.—Tom Ott, 633–5169.

Publisher, Smithsonian Magazine.—Kerry Bianchi, 633–6090.

Editor, Smithsonian Magazine.—Carey Winfrey, 633–6072.

SOCIAL SECURITY ADMINISTRATION

Altmeyer Building, 6401 Security Boulevard, Baltimore, MD 21235 (ALTMB)

Annex Building, 6401 Security Boulevard, Baltimore, MD 21235 (ANXB)

East High Rise Building, 6401 Security Boulevard, Baltimore, MD 21235 (EHRB)

Gwynn Oak Building, 1710 Gwynn Oak Avenue, Baltimore, MD 21207 (GWOB)

International Trade Commission Building, 500 E Street, SW., Washington, DC 20254 (ITCB)

Meadows East Building, 6401 Security Boulevard, Baltimore, MD 21235 (ME)

Metro West Tower Building, 300 North Greene Street, Baltimore, MD 21201 (MWTB)

National Computer Center, 6201 Security Boulevard, Baltimore, MD 21235 (NCC)

One Skyline Tower, 5107 Leesburg Pike, Falls Church, VA 22041 (SKY)

Operations Building, 6401 Security Boulevard, Baltimore, MD 21235 (OPRB)

Rolling Road Commerce Center, 2709 Rolling Road, Baltimore, MD 21244 (RRCC)

Security West Tower, 1500 Woodlawn Drive, Baltimore, MD 21241 (SWTB)

West High Rise Building, 6401 Security Boulevard, Baltimore, MD 21235 (WHRB)

http://www.socialsecurity.gov

OFFICE OF THE COMMISSIONER

Commissioner.—Michael J. Astrue, ALTMB, suite 900 (410) 965–3120 or ITCB, room 850 (202) 358–6000.

Deputy Commissioner.—Vacant, ALTMB, suite 960 (410) 965–9000 or ITCB, room 874 (202) 358–6000.

Chief of Staff.—Margaret J. Tittel (acting), ALTMB, suite 900 (410) 965–9050 or ITCB, room 858 (202) 358–6000.

Deputy Chief of Staff.—Michael Gallagher (acting), ALTMB, suite 900 (410) 965–3148.

Executive Counselor to the Commissioner.—James A. Winn, ALTMB, suite 960 (410) 966–8323.

Executive Secretary.—Robin Kaplan, ALTMB, suite 900 (410) 965–3462.

Special Advisor for Health Information Technology.—James Borland, ALTMB, room 935 (410) 965–3269.

Associate Commissioner, Office of International Programs.—Diane K. Braunstein (acting), OPRB, room 3700 (410) 597–1649.

OFFICE OF THE CHIEF ACTUARY

Chief Actuary.—Stephen C. Goss, ALTMB, room 700 (410) 965–3000.

Deputy Chief Actuary for—

Long Range.—Alice H. Wade, ALTMB, room 700 (410) 965–3002.

Short Range.—Eli N. Donkar, ALTMB, room 760 (410) 965–3004.

OFFICE OF THE CHIEF INFORMATION OFFICER

Chief Information Officer.—Franklin Baitman, ALTMB, room 500 (410) 966–5738.

Deputy Chief Information Officer.—Gregory C. Pace, ALTMB, room 500 (410) 965–3494.

Associate Chief Information Officer for—

Information Technology Investment Management.—Lester P. Diamond, ALTMB, room 348 (410) 965–3429.

Information Strategy, Security and Assurance.—Karen Palm (acting), ALTMB, room 500 (410) 965–5523.

Chief Information Security Officer.—John T. Smith, ALTMB, room 342 (410) 966–1155.

OFFICE OF COMMUNICATIONS

Deputy Commissioner.—James Courtney, ALTMB, room 460 (410) 965–1720, or ITCB, room 866 (202) 358–6131.

Assistant Deputy Commissioner.—Philip A. Gambino, ALTMB, room 460 (410) 965–1720.
Associate Commissioner, Office of:
Communication, Planning, and Technology.—Thomas J. Tobin, ANXB, room 3165 (410) 965–4029.
External Affairs.—Cheri A. Parlaman, ANXB, room 3505 (410) 965–1804.
Public Inquiries.—Sheryll T. Ziporkin, OPI Windsor Park (410) 965–5330.
Press Officer.—Mark R. Lassiter, ALTMB, room 440 (410) 965–8904.

OFFICE OF DISABILITY ADJUDICATION AND REVIEW

Deputy Commissioner.—David V. Foster, SKY, suite 1600 (703) 605–8200, or ALTMB, room 560 (410) 965–6006.
Assistant Deputy Commissioner.—Ronald T. Raborg, SKY, suite 1600 (703) 605–8200, or ALTMB, room 560 (410) 965–5200.
Executive Director, Office of Appellate Operations.—Patricia A. Jonas, SKY, suite 1400 (703) 605–7100.
Associate Commissioner, Office of Management.—Eileen C. McDaniel, SKY, suite 1700 (703) 605–8700.
Chief Administrative Law Judge.—Frank A. Cristaudo, SKY, suite 1608 (703) 605–8500.
Executive Coordinator for—
Automation and Strategic Management Information.—Judith C. Kautsch, SKY, suite 1604 (703) 605–8910.
Budget Analysis and Finance.—Elizabeth M. Reich, SKY, suite 1600 (703) 605–8396.
Materiel Resources.—James Bentley, SKY, suite 1600 (703) 605–8454.
Regional Chief Administrative Law Judges:
Atlanta.—Ollie L. Garmon, 61 Forsyth Street, SW., Suite 20T10, Atlanta, GA 30303 (404) 562–1182.
Boston.—Carol Sax, One Bowdoin Square, 10th Floor, Boston, MA 02114 (617) 720–0438.
Chicago.—Paul C. Lillios, 200 West Adams Street, Suite 2901, Chicago, IL 60606 (312) 886–5252.
Dallas.—Joan Parks Saunders, 1301 Young Street, Suite 460, Dallas, TX 75202 (214) 767–9401.
Denver.—Marsha R. Stroup, 1244 North Speer Boulevard, Suite 600, Denver, CO 80204 (303) 844–6100.
Kansas City.—John H. Fraze, 1100 Main Street, Suite 1700, Kansas City, MO 64105 (888) 238–7975.
New York.—Mark Sochaczewsky, 26 Federal Plaza, Room 34–116, New York, NY 10278 (212) 264–4036.
Philadelphia.—Jasper J. Bede, 300 Spring Garden Street, 4th Floor, Philadelphia, PA 19123 (215) 597–4100.
San Francisco.—JoAnn L. Anderson (acting), 555 Battery Street, 5th Floor, San Francisco, CA 94111 (415) 705–2000.
Seattle.—David J. DeLaittre, 701 5th Avenue, Suite 2900 M / S 904, Seattle, WA 98104 (206) 615–2236.

OFFICE OF RETIREMENT AND DISABILITY POLICY

Deputy Commissioner.—David A. Rust, ALTMB, room 100 (410) 965–0100.
Assistant Deputy Commissioner.—Marianna LaCanfora, ALTMB, room 100 (410) 965–5514.
Associate Commissioner, Office of:
Income Security Programs.—JoEllen Felice, ALTMB, room 252 (410) 965–5641.
Disability Programs.—Art Spencer (acting), OPRB, room 3515 (410) 966–5766.
Employment Support Programs.—Dan O'Brien (acting), OPRB, room 2607 (410) 597–1632.
Program Development and Research.—Richard Balkus, ALTMB, room 128 (410) 966–7918.
Medical and Vocational Expertise.—Robert E. Emrich, Jr., SWTB, room 6190 (410) 966–4800.
Research, Evaluation and Statistics.—Manuel de la Puente, ITCB, room 828 (202) 358–6020.
Retirement Policy.—Jason Fichtner, ITCB, room 858 (202) 358–6053.
Executive Director, Notice Improvement and Authentication.—Alan Lane, WHRB, room 1126 (410) 965–4331.
Director, PolicyNet and Program Support.—John Chlumsky, RRCC, room 1740 (410) 965–2860.

OFFICE OF BUDGET, FINANCE AND MANAGEMENT

Deputy Commissioner.—Mary Glenn-Croft, ALTMB, room 800 (410) 965–2910.
Assistant Deputy Commissioner.—Stephanie Hall (acting), ALTMB, room 800 (410) 965–9704.
Associate Commissioner, Office of:
Acquisition and Grants.—Dianne L. Rose, 7111 Security Boulevard (rear entrance), room 120 (410) 965–9455.
Budget.—Bonnie Kind, WHRB, room 2126 (410) 965–3501.
Facilities Management.—Betsy Bake, OPRB, room 2710 (410) 965–9308.
Financial Policy and Operations.—Ronald T. Sayers, EHRB, room 200 (410) 965–3403.
Publications and Logistics Management.—Gary G. Arnold, ANXB, room 1540 (410) 965–4272.
Director, Office of Strategic Services.—Chris Molander, WHRB, room 4200 (410) 965–7401.

OFFICE OF THE GENERAL COUNSEL

General Counsel.—David F. Black, ALTMB, room 600 (410) 965–0600.
Deputy General Counsel.—Thomas W. Crawley, ALTMB, room 600 (410) 965–3414.
Associate General Counsel for—
General Law.—Tina M. Waddell, ALTMB, room 600 (410) 965–5288.
Program Law.—Gwen Jones Kelley, ALTMB, room 628 (410) 965–0495.
Public Disclosure.—Jonathan R. Cantor, 1500 Dunleavy Building (410) 966–4206.
Regional Chief Counsel for—
Atlanta.—Mary Ann Sloan, Atlanta Federal Center, 61 Forsyth Street, SW., Suite 20T45, Atlanta, GA 30303 (404) 562–1010.
Boston.—Robert J. Triba, JFK Federal Building, Room 625, Boston, MA 02203 (617) 565–2380.
Chicago.—Donna L. Calvert, 200 West Adams Street, 30th Floor, Chicago, IL 60606 (312) 353–8201.
Dallas.—Mike McGaughran, 1301 Young Street, Room A–702, Dallas, TX 75202–5433 (214) 767–4660.
Denver.—Deana R. Erti-Lombardi, Federal Office Building, 1961 Stout Street, Suite 1001A, Denver, CO 80294 (303) 844–0013.
Kansas City.—Kristi A. Schmidt, Federal Office Building, 601 East 12th Street, Room 965, Kansas City, MO 64106 (816) 936–5756.
New York.—Stephen P. Conte (acting), 26 Federal Plaza, Suite 3904, New York, NY 12078 (212) 264–3650, ext. 218.
Philadelphia.—Eric P. Kressman (acting), 300 Spring Garden Street, 6th Floor, Philadelphia, PA 19123 (215) 597–1847.
San Francisco.—Lucille Gonzales-Meis, 333 Market Street, Suite 1500, San Francisco, CA 94105 (415) 977–8971.
Seattle.—David Morado, 701 Fifth Avenue, Suite 2900, M/S 901, Seattle, WA 98104 (206) 615–2539.

OFFICE OF HUMAN RESOURCES

Deputy Commissioner.—Dr. Reginald F. Wells, ALTMB, room 200 (410) 965–1900.
Assistant Deputy Commissioner.—Donna L. Siegel, ALTMB, room 200 (410) 965–7642.
Associate Commissioner for—
Civil Rights and Equal Opportunity.—A. Jacy Thurmond, ANXB, room 2571 (410) 965–3318.
Labor Management and Employee Relations.—Milton R. Beever, ANXB, room 2170 (410) 965–5772.
Office of:
Learning.—Steven Patrick, EHRB, room 100 (410) 965–0709.
Personnel.—Fred Glueckstein, ANXB, room 4170 (410) 966–9958.
Director of:
Executive and Special Services.—Bonnie L. Doyle, ANXB, room 2510 (410) 965–4463.
Human Capital Planning.—Linda Walk, ALTMB, room 570 (410) 965–8171.

OFFICE OF THE INSPECTOR GENERAL

Inspector General.—Patrick P. O'Carroll, ALTMB, suite 300 (410) 966–8385.

Deputy Inspector General.—James A. Kissko, ALTMB, suite 300 (410) 966–8385.
Counsel to the Inspector General.—Jonathan L. Lasher, 3–ME–1 (410) 965–7178.
Assistant Inspector General for—
Audit.—Steven L. Schaeffer, 3–ME–2 (410) 965–9701.
External Relations.—Wade V. Walters IV, 3–ME–4 (410) 594–2176.
Investigations.—Richard A. Rohde, 3–ME–3 (410) 966–2436.
Technology and Resource Management.—Michael D. Robinson, 2–ME–4 (410) 965–8240.

OFFICE OF LEGISLATIVE AND REGULATORY AFFAIRS

Deputy Commissioner.—Angela Jones Arnett (acting), ITCB, room 818 (202) 358–6030, or ALTMB, room 152 (410) 965–2386.
Assistant Deputy Commissioner.—Angela Jones Arnett, ITCB, room 818 (202) 358–6030, or ALTMB, room 152 (410) 965–2386.
Associate Commissioner for—
Legislative Development.—Thomas M. Parrott, ALTMB, room 146 (410) 965–3735.
Legislative Operations.—Sean P. Brune, ALTMB, room 150 (410) 966–8088.
Regulations.—Dean S. Landis, WHRB, room 4400 (410) 965–0520.
Congressional Affairs.—Vacant.
Director for—
Congressional Constituent Relations.—Sharon A. Wilson, WHRB, room 3202 (410) 965–3531.
Disability Insurance.—John Brzostowski, WHRB, room 3216 (410) 965–1472.
Immigration, Data Exchange and Enumeration.—Kitty Chilcoat, WHRB, room 3223 (410) 966–5482.
Retirement and Survivors Insurance Benefits.—Timothy J. Kelley, WHRB, room 3210 (410) 965–3293.
Supplemental Security Income and Health.—Erik Hansen, WHRB, room 3227 (410) 965–3112.

OFFICE OF OPERATIONS

Deputy Commissioner.—Linda S. McMahon, WHRB, room 1204 (410) 965–3143.
Assistant Deputy Commissioner.—Roger P. McDonnell, WHRB, room 1204 (410) 965–4292.
Associate Commissioner, Office of:
Automation Support.—DeBorah V. Russell, ANXB, room 4705 (410) 965–1345.
Central Operations.—Carolyn L. Simmons, SWTB, room 7000 (410) 966–7000.
Disability Determinations.—Ruby D. Burrell, ANXB, room 3570 (410) 965–1250.
Electronic Services.—Jo M. Armstrong, ANXB, room 3840 (410) 965–7166.
Public Service and Operations Support.—N. Mark Blatchford, WHRB, room 1224 (410) 965–4844.
Telephone Services.—Roy Snyder, ANXB, room 4845 (410) 965–1111.
Regional Commissioner for—
Atlanta.—Paul D. Barnes, 61 Forsyth Street, Suite 23T30, Atlanta, GA 30303 (404) 562–5600.
Boston.—Manuel J. Vaz, JFK Federal Building, Room 1900, Boston, MA 02203 (617) 565–2870.
Chicago.—James F. Martin, Harold Washington Social Security Center, 600 West Madison Street, Chicago, IL 60661 (312) 575–4000.
Dallas.—Ramona Schuenemeyer, 1301 Young Street, Suite 130, Dallas, TX 75202–5433 (214) 767–4207.
Denver.—Nancy A. Berryhill, Federal Office Building, 1961 Stout Street, Room 325, Denver, CO 80294 (303) 844–2388.
Kansas City.—Michael Grochowski, Federal Office Building, 601 East 12th Street, Room 436, Kansas City, MO 64106 (816) 936–5700.
New York.—Beatrice Disman, 26 Federal Plaza, Room 40–102, New York, NY 10278 (212) 264–3915.
Philadelphia.—Laurie Watkins, P.O. Box 8788, 300 Spring Garden Street, Philadelphia, PA 19123 (215) 597–5157.
San Francisco.—Peter D. Spencer, 1221 Nevin Avenue, Richmond, CA 94801 (510) 970–8400.
Seattle.—Don Schoening, 701 5th Avenue, Seattle, WA 98104–7075 (206) 615–3762.

OFFICE OF SYSTEMS

Deputy Commissioner.—William E. Gray, ALTMB, room 400 (410) 965–7747.

Assistant Deputy Commissioner.—Jerry L. Berson, ALTMB, room 400 (410) 965–6124.

Associate Commissioner, Office of:

Applications and Supplemental Security Income Systems.—Peter V. Herrera, Jr., OPRB, room 2100 (410) 965–0413.

Disability Systems.—Vacant, OPRB, room 3610 (410) 966–8193.

Earnings, Enumeration and Administrative Systems.—John Simermeyer, OPRB, room 3100 (410) 965–5789.

Enterprise Support, Architecture and Engineering.—Thomas G. Grzymski, OPRB, room 4100 (410) 965–7626.

Retirement and Survivors Insurance Systems.—William B. Zielinski, OPRB, room 4700 (410) 966–4966.

Systems Electronic Services.—Steve A. Kautsch, OPRB, room 3003 (410) 965–3513.

Telecommunications and Systems Operations.—Phillip H. Becker, Jr., NCC, room 550 (410) 965–1500.

OFFICE OF QUALITY PERFORMANCE

Deputy Commissioner.—G. Kelly Croft, ALTMB, room 860 (410) 965–7481.

Assistant Deputy Commissioner.—Glenn E. Sklar, ALTMB, room 860 (410) 965–6247.

Associate Commissioner, Office of:

Quality Improvement.—Daryl X. Wise, EHRB, room 4138 (410) 965–4557.

Quality Review.—Martin Hansen, EHRB, room 6145 (410) 965–5328.

Quality Data Management.—Pamela A. Mazerski, EHRB, room 5141 (410) 965–2161.

Field Directors—

Atlanta.—Robert L. Raines, 61 Forsyth Street, SW., Suite 21T60, Atlanta, GA 30303 (404) 562–5676.

Baltimore.—Patricia A. Biggers, Oak Meadows, Room 261 (410) 966–9230.

Boston.—Christine D. Tebbetts, 99 High Street, Suite 400, Boston, MA 02110 (617) 695–6631.

Chicago.—Mary T. Byrns, 600 West Madison Street, 5th Floor, Chicago, IL 60661 (312) 575–6002.

Dallas.—Ethyl A. Mymbs, 1301 Young Street, Room 300, Dallas, TX 75202 (214) 767–3448.

Denver.—Ronald R. Miller, 1961 Stout Street, FOB Room 126, Denver, CO 80294 (303) 844–2601.

Kansas City.—Daryl A. Gray, 601 East 12th Street, Room 1200 South, Kansas City, MO 64106 (816) 936–5151.

New York.—Vera Bostick-Borden, 26 Federal Plaza, Room 39–100, New York, NY 10278 (212) 264–2827.

Philadelphia.—Gail B. Davis, 300 Spring Garden, 2nd Floor East, Philadelphia, PA 19123 (215) 597–2978.

San Francisco.—Michael A. Gerber, 1221 Nevin Avenue, 4th Floor, Richmond, CA 94801 (510) 970–4625.

Seattle.—Rubie J. Toney, 701 5th Avenue, Suite 2900, Seattle, WA 98104 (206) 615–2146.

STATE JUSTICE INSTITUTE

1650 King Street, Suite 600, Alexandria, VA 22314, phone (703) 684–6100

http://www.sji.gov

BOARD OF DIRECTORS

Chairman.—Robert A. Miller.

Vice Chairman.—Joseph F. Baca.

Secretary.—Sandra A. O'Connor.

Executive Committee Member.—Keith McNamara.

Members:

Terrence B. Adamson
Robert N. Baldwin
Sophia H. Hall
Tommy Jewell
Arthur A. McGiverin

Officers:
Executive Director.—Janice Munsterman.
Deputy Director.—Jonathan Mattiello.

SUSQUEHANNA RIVER BASIN COMMISSION

COMMISSIONERS AND ALTERNATES

Federal Government.—COL David E. Anderson (Commissioner); COL Peter A. DeLuca (Alternate); COL Christopher J. Larsen (Alternate).
New York.—James M. Tierney (Commissioner); Kenneth P. Lynch (Alternate); Peter Freehafer (2nd Alternate).
Pennsylvania.—Vacant (Commissioner); Cathleen C. Myers (Alternate); John Hines (2nd Alternate); Sue Weaver (3rd Alternate).
Maryland.—Dr. Robert Summers (Commissioner); Herbert Sachs (Alternate).

STAFF

1721 North Front Street, Harrisburg, PA 17102, phone (717) 238–0423

srbc@srbc.net, http://www.srbc.net

Executive Director.—Paul O. Swartz.
Deputy Director.—Thomas W. Beauduy.
Chief Administrative Officer.—Duane A. Friends.
Secretary to the Commission.—Stephanie L. Richardson.
Chief, Watershed Assessment and Protection.—David W. Heicher.
Chief, Water Resources Management.—Michael G. Brownell.
Director of Communications.—Susan S. Obleski.

TENNESSEE VALLEY AUTHORITY

One Massachusetts Avenue, NW., Suite 300, 20444, phone (202) 898–2999

Knoxville, TN 37902, phone (865) 632–2101

Chattanooga, TN 37401, phone (423) 751–0011

Muscle Shoals, AL 35660, phone (202) 386–2601

BOARD OF DIRECTORS

Chairman.—Mike Duncan (865) 632–4000 (Knoxville).
Directors: Dennis Bottorff (Knoxville), Tom Gilliland (Knoxville), Willliam Graves (Knoxville), Bill Sansom (Knoxville) Howard Thrailkill (Knoxville).
President/Chief Operating Officer.—Tom D. Kilgore (865) 632–2366 (Knoxville).
Chief Financial Officer.—Kim Greene (865) 632–4049 (Knoxville).
Chief Nuclear Officer.—Preston Swafford (423) 751–8682 (Chattanooga).
Chief Operating Officer.—Bill McCollum (423) 751–6016 (Chattanooga).

CORPORATE VICE PRESIDENTS

Vice Presidents:
Chief Administrative Officer/Executive Vice President.—John E. Long, Jr. (865) 632–6307 (Knoxville).
Communications.—David Mould (865) 632–2370 (Knoxville).
Customer Resources.—Kenneth R. Breeden (615) 232–6011 (Nashville).
Enironment, Policy.—Anda Ray (865) 632–4131 (Knoxville).
General Counsel.—Maureen Dunn (865) 632–4131 (Knoxville).
Government Relations.—Emily Reynolds (615) 232–6669 (Nashville).
Human Resources.—Phillip L. Reynolds (423) 751–3185 (Chattanooga).
Inspector General.—Richard W. Moore (865) 621–4120 (Knoxville).

CHIEF OPERATING OFFICER ORGANIZATION

Power Supply and Fuels.—Van M. Wardlaw (423) 751–3907 (Chattanooga).
Fossil Power Group.—John McCormick (423) 751–3013 (Chattanooga).
Power System Operations.—Rob Manning (423) 751–6000 (Chattanooga).
River System Operations.—Janet Herrin (865) 632–6770 (Knoxville).

WASHINGTON OFFICE

phone (202) 898–2999, fax 898–2998

Government Relations Director.—Justin Maierhofer.

U.S. ADVISORY COMMISSION ON PUBLIC DIPLOMACY

2200 C Street, NW., SA–5, C2E15, 20520–0582

phone (202) 203–7880, fax 203–7886

[Created by Executive Order 12048 and Public Law 96–60]

Chair.—William J. Hybl.
Members: Amb. Elizabeth Bagley, Amb. Penne Korth Peacock, Amb. Lyndon Olson, Jr., Lezlee Westine, Jay T. Snyder.
Executive Director.—Carl Chan.
Administrative Officer.—Jamice Clayton.

U.S. AGENCY FOR INTERNATIONAL DEVELOPMENT

1300 Pennsylvania Avenue, NW., 20523, phone (202) 712–0000

http://www.usaid.gov

Administrator.—Alonzo Fulgham (acting), room 6.09, 712–4040, fax 216–3797.
Deputy Administrator.—Vacant.
Counselor.—James Michel (acting), room 6.08, 712–5010.
Chief Operating Officer.—Susan Fine (acting), room 6.09–042, 712–1577.
Executive Secretary.—Connie Turner (acting), room 6.08–36, 712–0700.
Assistant Administrator for—
Africa.—Earl Gast (acting), room 4.08, 712–0500.
Asia.—Margot Ellis (acting), room 4.09, 712–0200.
Democracy, Conflict and Humanitarian Assistance.—Jon Brause (acting), room 8.05, 712–0100.
Economic Growth, Agriculture, and Trade.—Michael Yates (acting), room 3.09, 712–0670.
Europe and Eurasia.—Gene George (acting), room 5.06, 712–0260.
Global Health.—Gloria Steele (acting), room 3.06, 712–4120.
Latin America and the Caribbean.—Janet Ballantyne (acting), room 5.09, 712–4800.
Legislative and Public Affairs.—Vacant, room 6.10, 712–4300.
Management.—Drew Luten (acting), room 6.09, 712–1200.
Middle East.—George Laudato (acting), room 4.09, 712–0300.
Director, Office of:
Development Partners.—Karen Turner, room 6.07, 712–0900.
Equal Opportunity Resources.—Jessalyn L. Pendarvis, room 2.09, 712–1110.
Security.—Randy Streufert, room 2.06, 712–0990.
Small and Disadvantaged Business Utilization.—Mauricio Vera, room 5.08, 712–1500.
General Counsel.—Arnold Haiman (acting), room 6.06, 712–0900.
Inspector General.—Donald Gambatesa, room 6.06, 712–1150.

U.S. COMMISSION ON CIVIL RIGHTS

624 Ninth Street, NW., 20425, phone (202) 376–7700, fax 376–7672

(Codified in 42 U.S.C., section 1975)

Chairperson.—Gerald A. Reynolds.
Vice Chairperson.—Abigail Thernstrom.
Commissioners: Todd Gaziano, Gail Heriot, Peter N. Kirsanow, Arlan D. Melendez, Ashley L. Taylor, Jr., Michael Yaki.
Staff Director.—Martin Dannenfelser.

U.S. ELECTION ASSISTANCE COMMISSION

1225 New York Avenue, NW., Suite 1100, Washington, DC 20005

phone (202) 566–3100, (866) 747–1471, fax 566–3127, http://www.eac.gov

[Created by Public Law 107–252]

Commission Chair.—Gineen Bresso Beach, 566–3100.
Vice Chair.—Gracia M. Hillman.
Commissioner.—Donetta L. Davidson.
Commissioner.—Vacant.

OFFICE OF THE EXECUTIVE DIRECTOR

Executive Director.—Thomas R. ''Tom'' Wilkey (202) 566–3100.
Chief Operating Officer.—Alice P. Miller.
Chief Financial Officer.—Annette Lafferty.

OFFICE OF COMMUNICATIONS AND CONGRESSIONAL AFFAIRS

Director of Communications.—Jeannie Layson (202) 566–3103.

OFFICE OF THE GENERAL COUNSEL

General Counsel.—Vacant (202) 566–3100.

OFFICE OF THE INSPECTOR GENERAL

Inspector General.—Curtis Crider (202) 566–3125.

U.S. HOLOCAUST MEMORIAL COUNCIL

The United States Holocaust Memorial Museum

100 Raoul Wallenberg Place, SW., 20024, phones (202) 488–0400 / (202) 314–7881 fax 488–2690

Officials:
Chair.—Fred S. Zeidman, Houston, TX.
Vice Chair.—Joel M. Geiderman, Los Angeles, CA.
Director.—Sara J. Bloomfield, Washington, DC.

Members:
Debra Abrams, Boca Raton, FL.
Elliott Abrams, Great Falls, VA.
Miriam Adelson, Las Vegas, NV.
James M. Abroms, Birmingham, AL.
Sheldon G. Adelson, Las Vegas, NV.
Ivan E. Becker, Princeton, NJ.
Dottie Bennett, Falls Church, VA.
Frank R. Berman, Edina, MN.
Tom A. Bernstein, New York, NY.
Norman R. Bobins, Chicago, IL.
Joshua B. Bolten, Bethesda, MD.
Joseph M. Brodecki, Potomac, MD.
Alan I. Casden, Beverly Hills, CA.
Michael Chertoff, Potomac, MD.
Bruce L. Bilalosky, Los Angeles, CA.
Marek J. Chodakiewicz, Washington, DC.
Carol B. Cohen, Highland Park, IL.
Debra Lerner Cohen, Washington, DC.
William J. Danhof, Lansing, MI.
Sam M. Devinki, Kansas City, MO.
Michael David Epstein, Rockville, MD.
Donald Etra, Los Angeles, CA.
Itchko Ezratti, Sunrise, FL.
David M. Flaum, Rochester, NY.
Marilyn R. Fox, Clayton, MO.
Michael J. Gerson, Arlington, VA.
Howard L. Ganek, New York, NY.
Tony B. Gelbart, Boca Raton, FL.
JoAnne T. Ginsberg, Washington, DC.
Constance B. Girard-diCarlo, Philadelphia, PA.
Zvi Y. Gitelman, Ann Arbor, MI.
Marc Goldman, Boca Raton, FL.
Sanford L. Gottesman, Austin, TX.
Cheryl F. Halpern, Livingston, NJ.
J. David Heller, Cleveland, OH.
Andrew S. Hochberg, Northbrook, IL.
Norman Hascoe, Greenwich, CT (deceased).
Phyllis G. Heideman, Bethesda, MD.
Arlene Herson, Boca Raton, FL.

Rebbetzin Esther Jungreis, New York, NY.
Alice A. Kelikian, Cambridge, MA.
Amy Kaslow, Potomac, MD.
Ezra Katz, Coconut Grove, FL.
Edward I. Koch, New York, NY.
Howard Konar, West Henrietta, NY.
Douglas R. Korn, New York, NY.
M. Ronald Krongold, Coral Gables, FL.
Michael I. Lebovitz, Chattanooga, TN.
Elena N. Lefkowitz, New York, NY.
Norma Lerner, Hunting Valley, OH.
William S. Levine, Phoenix, AZ.
Steven M. Levy, New York, NY.
Hadassah F. Lieberman, Washington, DC.
Marcia P. McCraw, Seattle, WA.
Kenneth B. Mehlman, Washington, DC.
Mervin G. Morris, Menlo Park, CA.
Michael A. Morris, Atlanta, GA.
Michael B. Mukasey, New York, NY.
Marvin A. Pomerantz, West Des Moines, IA (deceased).
Dennis Prager, Glendale, CA.
Pierre-Richard Prosper, Salt Lake City, UT.
Alan N. Rechtschaffen, New York, NY.
Harry Reicher, Philadelphia, PA.
J. Philip Rosen, New York, NY.
Jack Rosen, New York, NY.
Alvin H. Rosenfeld, Bloomington, IN.
Eric F. Ross, South Orange, NJ.
Richard S. Sambol, Toms River, NJ.
Mickey Shapiro, Farmington Hills, MI.
Florence Shapiro, Plano, TX.
Daniel R. Silva, Washington, DC.
Jay Stein, Jacksonville, FL.
Ronald G. Steinhart, Dallas, TX.
Nechama Tec, Stamford, CT.
Merryl H. Tisch, New York, NY.
Sonia Weitz, Peabody, MA.
William F. Weld, New York, NY.
Elie Wiesel, Boston, MA.
Jeffrey S. Wilpon, Flushing, NY.
Bradley D. Wine, Bethesda, MD.
Judith Yudof, Oakland, CA.

Former Chairs:
Irving Greenberg, 2000–2002.
Miles Lerman (deceased), 1993–2000.
Harvey M. Meyerhoff, 1987–1993.
Elie Wiesel, 1980–1986.

Former Vice Chairs:
Ruth B. Mandel, 1993–2005.
William J. Lowenberg, 1986–1993.
Mark E. Talisman, 1980–1986.

Congressional Members:

Senate:
Russell D. Feingold, from Wisconsin.
Orrin G. Hatch, from Utah.
BERNARD SANDERS, from Vermont.
Frank R. Lautenberg, from Nevada.

House of Representatives:
Eric Cantor, from Virginia.
Steven C. LaTourette, from Ohio.
Henry A. Waxman, from California.

Ex Officio Members:
U.S. Department of:
Education.—Philip H. Rosenfelt.
Interior—Jane M. Lyder.
State.—J. Christian Kennedy.

Council Staff:
General Counsel.—Gerard Leval.
Secretary of the Council.—Jane M. Rizer Miller.

U.S. INSTITUTE OF PEACE

1200 17th Street NW., Suite 200, 20036

phone (202) 457–1700, fax 429–6063

BOARD OF DIRECTORS

Public Members:
Chairman.—J. Robinson West.
Vice Chairman.—George E. Moose.
Members:
Anne H. Cahn
Chester A. Crocker
Kerry Kennedy
Ikram U. Khan
Stephen D. Krasner
Jeremy A. Rabkin
Judy Van Rest
Nancy Zirkin
Ex Officio:
Department of Defense.—Dr. James N. Miller (Secretary's Designate).
Department of State.—Hillary Rodham Clinton.
National Defense University.—Vice Admiral Ann E. Rondeau.
United States Institute of Peace.—Richard H. Solomon.
Officials:
President.—Richard H. Solomon.
Executive Vice President.—Tara Sonenshine.
Chief Financial Officer.—Michael Graham.

Vice President for—
Center for—
Conflict Analysis and Prevention.—Abiodun Williams.
Mediation and Conflict Resolution.—David Smock.
Post-Conflict Peace and Stability Operations.—William Taylor.
Centers of Innovation.—Daniel P. Serwer.
Domestic Programs, Education and Training Center.—Pamela Aall.
Grants and Fellowships Programs.—Steven Heydemann.
Headquarters Project.—Charles E. Nelson.
International Programs, Education and Training Center.—Michael Lekson.
Associate Vice President for—
Grant Program.—Kathleen Kuehnast.
Jennings Randolph Fellowship Program.—Chantal De Jonge Oudraat.
Media, Conflict, and Peacebuilding Center of Innovation.—Sheldon Himelfarb.
Religion and Peacemaking Center of Innovation.—David Smock.
Rule of Law Center of Innovation.—Colette Rausch (acting).
Science, Technology, and Peacebuilding Center of Innovation.—Sheldon Himelfarb.
Sustainable Economies Center of Innovation.—Raymond Gilpin.
Director of:
Congressional Relations.—Laurie Schultz Helm.
Public Affairs and Communication.—Lauren Sucher.
Publications.—Valerie Norville.

U.S. INTERNATIONAL TRADE COMMISSION

500 E Street, SW., 20436

phone (202) 205–2000, fax 205–2798, http://www.usitc.gov

COMMISSIONERS

Chairman.—Shara L. Aranoff, Democrat, Maryland.
Vice Chairman.—Daniel R. Pearson, Republican, Minnesota.
Commissioners:
Charlotte R. Lane, Republican, West Virginia.
Deanna Tanner Okun, Republican, Idaho.
Dean A. Pinkert, Democrat, Virginia.
Irving A. Williamson, Democrat, New York.
Congressional Relations Officer.—Dominic Bianchi, 205–3151.
Secretary.—Marilyn R. Abbott, 205–2799.
Administrative Law Judges: Charles E. Bullock, 205–2681; Carl C. Chameski, 708–4051; Theodore Essex, 205–2692; James E. Gildea, 205–1801; Robert K. Rogers, Jr., 205–3352.
General Counsel.—James M. Lyons, 205–3101.
Inspector General.—Vacant.
Chief Information Officer.—Stephen A. McLaughlin, 205–3131.
Director, Office of:
Administration.—Stephen A. McLaughlin, 205–3131.
Economics.—Robert B. Koopman, 205–3216.
Equal Employment Opportunity.—Jacqueline A. Waters, 205–2240.
External Relations.—Lyn M. Schlitt, 205–3141.
Facilities Management.—Jonathan Brown, 205–2745.
Finance.—Patricia Katsouros, 205–2682.
Human Resources.—Cynthia Roscoe, 205–2651.
Industries.—Karen Laney-Cummings, 205–3296.
Investigations.—John Ascienzo (acting).
Operations.—Robert A. Rogowsky, 205–2230.
Tariff Affairs and Trade Agreements.—David Beck, 205–2603.
Unfair Import Investigations.—Lynn I. Levine, 205–2561.

U.S. MERIT SYSTEMS PROTECTION BOARD

1615 M Street, NW., 20419

phone (202) 653–7220, toll-free (800) 209–8960, fax 653–7130

[Created by Public Law 95–454]

Chairman.—Neil Anthony Gordon McPhie.

Vice Chairman.—Mary M. Rose.
Member.—Vacant.
Chief of Staff.—Tracey Watkins.
General Counsel.—B. Chad Bungard.
Appeals Counsel.—Lynore Carnes.

REGIONAL OFFICES

Regional Directors:

Atlanta Regional Office: Covering Alabama, Florida, Georgia, Mississippi, South Carolina, Tennessee.—Thomas J. Lamphear, 10th Floor, 401 West Peachtree Street NW, Atlanta, GA 30308 (404) 730–2755, fax 730–2767.

Central Regional Office: Covering Illinois, Iowa, Kansas City, Kansas, Kentucky, Indiana, Michigan, Minnesota, Missouri, Ohio, Wisconsin.—Martin Baumgaertner, 31st Floor, 230 South Dearborn Street, Chicago, IL 60604 (312) 353–2923, fax 886–4231.

Dallas Regional Office: Covering Arkansas, Louisiana, Oklahoma, Texas.—Sharon Jackson, Chief Administrative Judge, Room 620, 1100 Commerce Street, Dallas, TX 75242 (214) 767–0555, fax 767–0102.

Northeastern Regional Office: Covering Connecticut, Delaware, Maryland (except Montgomery and Prince Georges counties), Massachusetts, New Hampshire, New Jersey (except the counties of Bergen, Essex, Hudson, and Union), Pennsylvania, Rhode Island, Vermont, West Virginia.—William L. Boulden, 1601 Market Street, Suite 1700, Philadelphia, PA 19103 (215) 597–9960, fax 597–3456.

New York Field Office: Covering New York, Puerto Rico, Virgin Islands, the following counties in New Jersey: Bergen, Essex, Hudson, Union.—Arthur Joseph, Chief Administrative Judge, Room 3137–A, 26 Federal Plaza, New York, NY 10278 (212) 264–9372, fax 264–1417.

Western Regional Office: Covering Alaska, California, Hawaii, Idaho, Nevada, Oregon, Washington, and Pacific Overseas.—Amy Dunning, 201 Mission Street, Suite 2310, San Francisco, CA 94105–1831 (415) 904–6772, fax 904–0580.

Denver Field Office: Covering Arizona, Colorado, Kansas (except Kansas City), Montana, Nebraska, New Mexico, North Dakota, South Dakota, Utah, Wyoming.—Vacant, Chief Administrative Judge, 165 South Union Boulevard, Suite 318, Lakewood, CO 80228 (303) 969–5101, fax 969–5109.

Washington Regional Office: Covering Washington, DC, Maryland (counties of Montgomery and Prince Georges), North Carolina, Virginia, all overseas areas not otherwise covered.—Jeremiah Cassidy, Chief Administrative Judge, 1811 Diagonal Road, Suite 205, Alexandria, VA 22314 (703) 756–6250, fax 756–7112.

U.S. OVERSEAS PRIVATE INVESTMENT CORPORATION

1100 New York Avenue, NW., 20527, phone (202) 336–8400

President.—Dr. Lawrence Spinelli (acting).
Chief of Staff.—John Moran.
Deputy Chief of Staff.—Jacqueline Strasser.
Chief of Administrative Services.—John Moran (acting).
Vice President and General Counsel.—Robert O'Sullivan (acting).
Vice President and Chief Financial Officer.—Jacqueline Strasser (acting).
Vice President for—
External Affairs.—Dr. Lawrence Spinelli (acting).
Insurance.—Rod Morris.
Investment Funds.—Barbara Day (acting).
Investment Policy.—Dr. Berta Heybey (acting).
Small and Medium Enterprise Finance.—James Polan.
Structured Finance.—Robert B. Drumheller.
Director, Economic Impact Analysis Group.—Dr. Berta Heybey.
Special Assistant for Congressional and Intergovernmental Affairs.—James W. Morrison, 336–8417.

BOARD OF DIRECTORS

Government Directors:
Alonzo L. Fulgham (acting), Administrator, U.S. Agency for International Development.
Demetrios Marantis, Deputy U.S. Trade Representative.

Private Sector Directors:

Samuel E. Ebbesen (General, USA, Ret.), President and Chief Executive Officer, Virgin Island Telephone Corporation, St. Thomas, Virgin Islands.
Christopher J. Hanley, General Secretary-Treasurer, International Union of Operating Engineers, Washington, DC.
Diane Ingels Moss, President and Owner, Cartera Investment Corporation, Dallas, Texas.
Diane M. Ruebling, President, The Ruebling Group, Scottsdale, Arizona/Longville, Minnesota.
C. William Swank, Retired Executive Vice President, Ohio Farm Bureau Federation, Westerville, Ohio.
Sanford L. Gottesman, President, The Gottesman Company, Austin, Texas.
Patrick J. Durkin, Managing Director, JFitzbibbons LLC, New York, New York.

Staff:

Board Counsel.—Robert O'Sullivan (acting).
Corporate Secretary.—Connie M. Downs, 336–8438.

U.S. POSTAL SERVICE

475 L'Enfant Plaza, SW., 20260–0010, phone (202) 268–2000

BOARD OF GOVERNORS

Chairman.—Carolyn Lewis Gallagher.
Vice Chairman.—Louis J. Giuliano.
Postmaster General/CEO.—John E. Potter.
Deputy Postmaster General/Chief Operating Officer.—Patrick R. Donahoe.

MEMBERS

Mickey D. Barnett
James H. Bilbray
Alan C. Kessler
James C. Miller
Thurgood Marshall, Jr.

OFFICERS OF THE BOARD OF GOVERNORS

Secretary to the Board of Governors.—Julie S. Moore.

OFFICERS OF THE POSTAL SERVICE

Postmaster General, Chief Executive Officer.—John E. Potter, 268–2550.
Deputy Postmaster General/Chief Operating Officer.—Patrick R. Donahoe, 268–4842.
Chief Financial Officer and Executive Vice President.—Joseph Corbett, 268–5272.
Chief Human Resources Officer and Executive Vice President.—Anthony J. Vegliante, 268–7852.
Chief Postal Inspector.—William R. Gilligan, 268–5615.
Senior Vice President of:
Customer Relations.—Stephen M. Kearney, 268–2244.
General Counsel.—Mary Anne Gibbons, 268–2950.
Government Relations and Public Policy.—Marie Therese Dominguez, 268–2506.
Intelligent Mail and Address Quality.—Thomas G. Day, 268–6200.
Operations.—Steven J. Forte, 268–5100.
Senior Vice President/Managing Director of Global Business.—Pranab Shah, 268–2131.
Vice President of:
Corporate Communication.—Mitzi R. Betman, 268—2143.
Consumer Advocate.—Delores J. Killette, 268–2281.
Controller.—Vincent H. DeVito, 268–8201.
Delivery and Post Office Operations.—Linda J. Welch, 268–6500.
Employee Development and Diversity.—Susan M. LaChance, 268–6566.
Employee Resource Management.—Deborah Giannoni-Jackson, 268–3783.
Engineering.—David E. Williams (703) 280–7001.
Facilities.—Tom A. Samra (703) 526–2727.
Network Operations.—Jordan M. Small, 268–6258.
Pricing.—Maura Robinson, 268–7319.

Sales.—Susan M. Plonkey (703) 292–8800.
Supply Management.—Susan M. Brownell, 268–4040.
Judicial Officer.—William A. Campbell.
Senior Vice President, Strategy and Transition.—Marc D. McCrery.
Senior Vice President of:
Business Mail Entry and Payment Technologies.—Pritha Mehra.
Sustainability.—Samuel M. Pulcrano.

President, Mailing and Shipping Services.—Robert F. Bernstock.
Vice President of:
Ground Shipping.—James P. Cochrane.
Retail Products and Services.—Timothy C. Healy.
Expedited Shipping.—Gary C. Reblin.

Chief Information Officer and Executive Vice President.—Ross Philo.
Vice President of:
Information Technology Operations.—George W. Wright.
Labor Relations.—Douglas A. Tulino.
Finance and Planning.—Stephen J. Masse.

U.S. RAILROAD RETIREMENT BOARD

844 North Rush Street, Chicago, IL 60611, phone (312) 751–4777, fax 751–7154

Office of Legislative Affairs, 1310 G Street, NW., Suite 500, 20005

phone (202) 272–7742, fax 272–7728, e-mail: ola@rrb.gov

http://www.rrb.gov

Chairman—Michael S. Schwartz (312) 751–4900, fax 751–7193.
Assistant to the Chairman.—Nancy S. Pittman.
Counsel to the Chairman.—Stephen W. Seiple.
Labor Member.—V.M. Speakman, Jr., 751–4905, fax 751–7194.
Assistants to the Labor Member: James C. Boehner, Geraldine L. Clark, Michael J. Collins.
Counsel to the Labor Member.—Thomas W. Sadler.
Management Member.—Jerome F. Kever, 751–4910, fax 751–7189.
Assistant to the Management Member.—Joseph M. Waechter.
Counsel to the Management Member.—Robert M. Perbohner.
Attorney-Advisor to the Management Member.—Ann L. Chaney.
Inspector General.—Martin J. Dickman, 751–4690, fax 751–4342.
General Counsel.—Steven A. Bartholow, 751–4935, fax 751–7102.
Assistant General Counsel.—Marguerite P. Dadabo, 751–4945, fax 751–7102.
Secretary to the Board.—Beatrice E. Ezerski, 751–4920, fax 751–4923.
Director of:
Assessment and Training.—Catherine A. Leyser, 751–4757, fax 751–7190.
Equal Opportunity.—Lynn E. Cousins, 751–4925, fax 751–7179.
Field Service.—Martha M. Barringer, 751–4515, fax 751–3360.
Hearings and Appeals.—Karl T. Blank, 751–4941, fax 751–7159.
Human Resources.—Keith B. Earley, 751–4392, fax 751–7164.
Legislative Affairs.—Margaret A. Lindsley (202) 272–7742, fax 272–7728.
Operations.—Robert J. Duda, 751–4698, fax 751–7157.
Policy and Systems.—Ronald Russo, 751–4984, fax 751–4650.
Programs.—Dorothy A. Isherwood, 751–4980, fax 751–4333.
Supervisor of:
Acquisition Management.—Paul T. Ahern, 751–7130, fax 751–4923.
Congressional Inquiry.—Carl D. Mende, 751–4970, fax 751–7154.
Public Affairs.—Anita J. Rogers, 751–4737, fax 751–7154.
Chief of:
Actuary.—Frank J. Buzzi, 751–4915, fax 751–7129.
Benefit and Employment Analysis.—Marla L. Huddleston, 751–4779, fax 751–7129.
Finance.—Kenneth P. Boehne, 751–4930, fax 751–4931.
Information.—Terri S. Morgan, 751–4851, fax 751–7169.
Resource Management Center.—Janet M. Hallman, 751–4543, fax 751–7161.
Librarian.—Katherine Tsang, 751–4926, fax 751–4924.
SEO/Director of Administration.—Henry M. Valiulis, 751–4990, fax 751–7197.

U.S. SENTENCING COMMISSION

One Columbus Circle, NE., Suite 2–500, South Lobby, 20002–8002
phone (202) 502–4500, fax 502–4699

Chair.—Ricardo H. Hinojosa.
Vice Chairs: William B. Carr, Jr., Ruben Castillo, William K. Sessions III.
Commissioners: Dabney L. Friedrich, Beryl A. Howell.
Commissioners, ex officio: Isaac Fulwood, Jr., Jonathan J. Wroblewski.
Staff Director.—Judith W. Sheon, 502–4510.
General Counsel.—Kenneth P. Cohen, 502–4520.
Director of:
Administration.—Susan Brazel, 502–4610.
Research and Data Collection.—Glenn R. Schmitt, 502–4530.
Director and Chief Counsel of Office of Training.—Pamela G. Montgomery, 502–4540.
Public Affairs Officer.—Michael Courlander, 502–4597.
Legislative and Governmental Affairs.—Lisa A. Rich, 502–4519.

U.S. TRADE AND DEVELOPMENT AGENCY

1000 Wilson Boulevard, Suite 1600, Arlington, VA 22209, phone (703) 875–4357

Director.—Leocadia I. Zak (acting).
Deputy Director.—Leocadia I. Zak.
Chief of Staff.—Thomas R. Hardy.
Administrative Officer.—Carolyn Hum.
Communications and Policy Advisor.—Donna Thiessen.
Congressional Relations Advisor.—Amy Lorenzini Wren.
Contracting Officer.—Vacant.
Economist/Evaluation Officer.—David Denny.
Financial Manager.—Noreen St. Louis.
General Counsel.—James A. Wilderotter.
Grants Administrator.—Patricia Daughetee.
Policy and Planning Director.—Geoffrey Jackson.
Resource Advisor.—Micheal Hillier.
Regional Director for—
East Asia.—Geoffrey Jackson.
Europe and Eurasia.—Daniel D. Stein.
Latin America and the Caribbean.—Nathan Younge.
Middle East and North Africa.—Carl B. Kress.
South and Southeast Asia.—Henry Steingass.
Sub-Saharan Africa.—Paul Marin.

WASHINGTON METROPOLITAN AREA TRANSIT AUTHORITY

600 Fifth Street, NW., 20001, phone (202) 637–1234

General Manager.—John B. Catoe.
General Counsel.—Carol A. O'Keeffe.
Chief Financial Officer.—Carol D. Kissal.
Chief Operating Officer for—
Bus Service.—Milo Victoria.
Rail Service.—Dave Kubicek.
Assistant General Manager for—
Corporate Communications.—Sara P. Wilson.
System Safety and Environmental Management.—Alexa Dupigny-Samuels.
Director, Office of:
Policy and Government Relations.—Sarah A. Kline.
Public Relations.—Lisa Farbstein.
Chief, Transit Police Department.—Michael Taborn.

WASHINGTON NATIONAL MONUMENT SOCIETY

[Organized 1833; chartered 1859; amended by Acts of August 2, 1876, October, 1888]

President Ex Officio.—Barack H. Obama, President of the United States.
First Vice President.—James W. Symington, 1666 K Street, NW., Suite 500, Washington, DC 20006–2107 (202) 778–2107.

Treasurer.—Henry Ravenel, Jr.
Secretary.—Steve Lorenzetti, Superintendent (acting), National Mall and Memorial Parks, 900 Ohio Drive, SW., Washington, DC 20024–2000, 485–9875.

Members:

Christopher Addison
Vincent C. Burke, Jr.
Robert W. Duemling
Gilbert M. Grosvenor
Potter Stewart
C. Boyden Gray
John D.H. Kane
John A. Washington

Member Emeritus:

Harry F. Byrd, Jr.

WOODROW WILSON INTERNATIONAL CENTER FOR SCHOLARS

One Woodrow Wilson Plaza 1300 Pennsylvania Avenue, NW., 20004–3027

phone (202) 691–4000, fax 691–4001

(Under the direction of the Board of Trustees of Woodrow Wilson International Center for Scholars)

Director/President.—Lee H. Hamilton, 691–4202.
Deputy Director.—Michael Van Dusen, 691–4055.
Executive Assistant to the President.—Nora Coulter.
Director for—
Administrative Management and Human Resources.—Leslie Johnson.
Financial Management.—John Dysland.

Board of Trustees:
Chairman.—Joseph B. Gildenhorn.
Vice Chairman.—Sander R. Gerber.

Private Members:

Charles E. Cobb, Jr.
Robin Cook
Charles L. Glazer
Carlos M. Gutierrez
Susan Hutchison
Barry S. Jackson
Ignacio E. Sanchez

Public Members:

Hillary Rodham Clinton, Secretary of State.
Arne Duncan, Secretary of Education.
Kathleen Sebelius, Secretary of Health and Human Services.
James Leach, Chairman of the National Endowment for the Humanities.
G. Wayne Clough, Secretary of the Smithsonian Institution.
James H. Billington, Librarian of Congress.
Adrienne Thomas, Archivist of the United States.

Designated Appointee of the President of the United States from within the Federal Government.—Vacant.

JUDICIARY

SUPREME COURT OF THE UNITED STATES

One First Street, NE., 20543, phone (202) 479–3000

JOHN G. ROBERTS, JR., Chief Justice of the United States, was born in Buffalo, NY, January 27, 1955. He married Jane Marie Sullivan in 1996 and they have two children, Josephine and John. He received an A.B. from Harvard College in 1976 and a J.D. from Harvard Law School in 1979. He served as a law clerk for Judge Henry J. Friendly of the United States Court of Appeals for the Second Circuit from 1979–80 and as a law clerk for then Associate Justice William H. Rehnquist of the Supreme Court of the United States during the 1980 term. He was Special Assistant to the Attorney General, U.S. Department of Justice from 1981–82, Associate Counsel to President Ronald Reagan, White House Counsel's Office from 1982–86, and Principal Deputy Solicitor General, U.S. Department of Justice from 1989–93. From 1986–89 and 1993–2003, he practiced law in Washington, DC; He was appointed to the United States Court of Appeals for the District of Columbia Circuit in 2003; nominated Chief Justice of the Supreme Court of the United States by President George W. Bush on September 5, 2005; sworn in on September 29, 2005.

JOHN PAUL STEVENS, Associate Justice, was born in Chicago, IL, April 20, 1920. He married Maryan Mulholland, and has four children, John Joseph (deceased), Kathryn, Elizabeth Jane, and Susan Roberta. He received an A.B. from the University of Chicago, and a J.D. from Northwestern University School of Law. He served in the United States Navy from 1942–45, and was a law clerk to Justice Wiley Rutledge of the Supreme Court of the United States during the 1947 term. He was admitted to law practice in Illinois in 1949. He was Associate Counsel to the Subcommittee on the Study of Monopoly Power of the Judiciary Committee of the U.S. House of Representatives, 1951–52, and a member of the Attorney General's National Committee to Study Antitrust Law, 1953–55. He was Second Vice President of the Chicago Bar Association in 1970. From 1970–75, he served as a Judge of the United States Court of Appeals for the Seventh Circuit; nominated to the Supreme Court December 1, 1975, by President Ford; confirmed by the Senate December 17, 1975; sworn in on December 19, 1975.

ANTONIN SCALIA, Associate Justice, was born in Trenton, NJ, March 11, 1936. He married Maureen McCarthy and has nine children, Ann Forrest, Eugene, John Francis, Catherine Elisabeth, Mary Clare, Paul David, Matthew, Christopher James, and Margaret Jane. He received his A.B. from Georgetown University and the University of Fribourg, Switzerland, and his LL.B. from Harvard Law School, and was a Sheldon Fellow of Harvard University from 1960–61. He was in private practice in Cleveland, OH from 1961–67, a Professor of Law at the University of Virginia from 1967–71, and a Professor of Law at the University of Chicago from 1977–82, and a Visiting Professor of Law at Georgetown University and Stanford University. He was chairman of the American Bar Association's Section of Administrative Law., 1981–82, and its Conference of Section Chairmen, 1982–83. He served the Federal Government as General Counsel of the Office of Telecommunications Policy from 1971–72, Chairman of the Administrative Conference of the United States from 1972–74, and Assistant Attorney General for the Office of Legal Counsel from 1974–77. He was appointed Judge of the United States Court of Appeals for the District of Columbia Circuit in 1982; appointed by President Reagan as Associate Justice of the U.S. Supreme Court; sworn in on September 26, 1986.

ANTHONY M. KENNEDY, Associate Justice, was born in Sacramento, CA, July 23, 1936. He married Mary Davis and has three children. He received his B.A. from Stanford University and the London School of Economics, and his LL.B. from Harvard Law School.

He was in private practice in San Francisco, CA from 1961–63, as well as in Sacramento, CA from 1963–75. From 1965 to 1988, he was a Professor of Constitutional Law at the McGeorge School of Law, University of the Pacific. He has served in numerous positions during his career, including a member of the California Army National Guard in 1961, the board of the Federal Judicial Center from 1987–88, and two committees of the Judicial Conference of the United States: the Advisory Panel on Financial Disclosure Reports and Judicial Activities, subsequently renamed the Advisory Committee on Codes of Conduct, from 1979–87, and the Committee on Pacific Territories from 1979–90, which he chaired from 1982–90. He was appointed to the United States Court of Appeals for the Ninth Circuit in 1975; nominated by President Reagan as Associate Justice of the U.S. Supreme Court; sworn in on February 18, 1988.

CLARENCE THOMAS, Associate Justice, was born in the Pin Point community of Georgia near Savannah June 23, 1948. He married Virginia Lamp in 1987 and has one child, Jamal Adeen, by a previous marriage. He attended Conception Seminary and received an A.B., *cum laude,* from Holy Cross College, and a J.D. from Yale Law School in 1974. He was admitted to law practice in Missouri in 1974, and served as an Assistant Attorney General of Missouri from 1974–77, an attorney with the Monsanto Company from 1977–79, and Legislative Assistant to Senator John Danforth from 1979–81. From 1981–82, he served as Assistant Secretary for Civil Rights, U.S. Department of Education, and as Chairman of the U.S. Equal Employment Opportunity Commission from 1982–90. He became a Judge of the United States Court of Appeals for the District of Columbia Circuit in 1990; nominated by President George H.W. Bush as Associate Justice of the U.S. Supreme Court; took the constitutional oath on October 18, 1991 and the judicial oath on October 23, 1991.

RUTH BADER GINSBURG, Associate Justice, was born in Brooklyn, NY, March 15, 1933. She married Martin D. Ginsburg in 1954, and has a daughter, Jane, and a son, James. She received her B.A. from Cornell University, attended Harvard Law School, and received her LL.B. from Columbia Law School. She served as a law clerk to the Honorable Edmund L. Palmieri, Judge of the United States District Court for the Southern District of New York, from 1959–61. From 1961–63, she was a research associate and then associate director of the Columbia Law School Project on International Procedure. She was a Professor of Law at Rutgers University School of Law from 1963–72, and Columbia Law School from 1972–80, and a fellow at the Center for Advanced Study in the Behavioral Sciences in Stanford, CA from 1977–78. In 1971, she was instrumental in launching the Women's Rights Project of the American Civil Liberties Union, and served as the ACLU's General Counsel from 1973–80, and on the National Board of Directors from 1974–80. She was appointed a Judge of the United States Court of Appeals for the District of Columbia Circuit in 1980; nominated Associate Justice by President Clinton, June 14, 1993, confirmed by the Senate, August 3, 1993, and sworn in August 10, 1993.

STEPHEN G. BREYER, Associate Justice, was born in San Francisco, CA, August 15, 1938. He married Joanna Hare in 1967, and has three children, Chloe, Nell, and Michael. He received an A.B. from Stanford University, a B.A. from Magdalen College, Oxford, and an LL.B. from Harvard Law School. He served as a law clerk to Justice Arthur Goldberg of the Supreme Court of the United States during the 1964 term, as a Special Assistant to the Assistant U.S. Attorney General for Antitrust, 1965–67, as an Assistant Special Prosecutor of the Watergate Special Prosecution Force, 1973, as Special Counsel of the U.S. Senate Judiciary Committee, 1974–75, and as Chief Counsel of the committee, 1979–80. He was an Assistant Professor, Professor of Law, and Lecturer at Harvard Law School, 1967–94, a Professor at the Harvard University Kennedy School of Government, 1977–80, and a Visiting Professor at the College of Law, Sydney, Australia and at the University of Rome. From 1980–90, he served as a Judge of the United States Court of Appeals for the First Circuit, and as its Chief Judge, 1990–94. He also served as a member of the Judicial Conference of the United States, 1990–94, and of the United States Sentencing Commission, 1985–89; nominated Associate Justice by President Clinton May 13, 1994, confirmed by the Senate July 29, 1994, and sworn in on August 3, 1994.

SAMUEL ANTHONY ALITO, Jr., Associate Justice, was born in Trenton, NJ, April 1, 1950. He married Martha-Ann Bomgardner in 1985, and has two children, Philip and Laura. He served as a law clerk for Leonard I. Garth of the United States Court of Appeals for the Third Circuit from 1976–77. He was Assistant U.S. Attorney, District of New Jersey, 1977–81, Assistant to the Solicitor General, U.S. Department of Justice, 1981–85, Deputy Assistant Attorney General, U.S. Department of Justice, 1985–87, and U.S. Attorney, District of New Jersey, 1987–90. He was appointed to the United States Court of Appeals for the Third Circuit in 1990; nominated Associate Justice of the U.S. Supreme Court by President George W. Bush on October 31, 2005; sworn in on January 31, 2006.

SONIA SOTOMAYOR, Associate Justice of the United States Supreme Court, was born in Bronx, NY, June 25, 1954. She earned a B.A. in 1976 from Princeton University, graduating *summa cum laude* and receiving the university's highest academic honor. In 1979, she earned a J.D. from Yale Law School where she served as an editor of the *Yale Law Journal.* She served as Assistant District Attorney in the New York County District Attorney's Office from 1979–84. She then litigated international commercial matters in New York City at Pavia & Harcourt, where she served as an associate and then partner from 1984–92. In 1991, President George H.W. Bush nominated her to the U.S. District Court Southern District of New York, and she served in that role from 1992–98. She served as a judge on the United States Court of Appeals for the Second Circuit from 1998–2009. President Barack Obama nominated her as an Associate Justice of the Supreme Court on May 26, 2009, and she was sworn in on August 8, 2009.

Officers of the Supreme Court

Clerk.—William K. Suter.
Librarian.—Judith Gaskell.
Marshal.—Pamela Talkin.
Reporter of Decisions.—Frank D. Wagner.
Counsel.—Scott Harris.
Curator.—Catherine Fitts.
Public Information Officer.—Kathleen L. Arberg.
Director of Data Systems.—Donna Clement.
Counselor to the Chief Justice.—Jeffrey P. Minear.

UNITED STATES COURTS OF APPEALS

First Judicial Circuit (Districts of Maine, Massachusetts, New Hampshire, Puerto Rico, and Rhode Island).—*Chief Judge:* Sandra L. Lynch. *Circuit Judges:* Michael Boudin, Juan R. Torruella; Kermit V. Lipez; Jeffrey R. Howard. *Senior Circuit Judges:* Bruce M. Selya; Norman H. Stahl. *Circuit Executive:* Gary H. Wente (617) 748–9613. *Clerk:* Richard C. Donovan (617) 748–9057, John Joseph Moakley U.S. Courthouse, One Courthouse Way, Suite 2500, Boston, MA 02210.

Second Judicial Circuit (Districts of Connecticut, New York, and Vermont).—*Chief Judge:* Dennis Jacobs. *Circuit Judges:* John M. Walker, Jr.; Guido Calabresi; José A. Cabranes; Rosemary S. Pooler; Chester J. Straub; Robert D. Sack; Sonia Sotomayor; Robert A. Katzmann; Barrington D. Parker, Jr.; Reena Raggi. *Senior Circuit Judges:* Wilfred Feinberg; James L. Oakes; Thomas J. Meskill; Jon O. Newman; Richard J. Cardamone; Ralph K. Winter; Roger J. Miner; Joseph M. McLaughlin; Amalya L. Kearse; Pierre N. Leval. *Circuit Executive:* Karen Greve Milton (212) 857–8700. *Clerk:* Tom Asreen (acting), (212) 857–8500, Thurgood Marshall United States Courthouse, 40 Foley Square, New York, NY 10007–1581.

Third Judicial Circuit (Districts of Delaware, New Jersey, Pennsylvania, and Virgin Islands).—*Chief Judge:* Anthony J. Scirica. *Circuit Judges:* Dolores K. Sloviter; Theodore A. McKee; Marjorie O. Rendell; Maryanne Trump Barry; Thomas L. Ambro; Julio M. Fuentes; D. Brooks Smith; D. Michael Fisher; Michael A. Chagares; Kent A. Jordan. *Senior Circuit Judges:* Ruggero J. Aldisert; Joseph F. Weis, Jr.; Leonard I. Garth; Walter K. Stapleton; Morton I. Greenberg; Robert E. Cowen; Richard L. Nygaard; Jane R. Roth; Franklin S. Van Antwerpen. *Circuit Executive:* Toby D. Slawsky (215) 597–0718. *Clerk:* Marcia M. Waldron (215) 597–2995, U.S. Courthouse, 601 Market Street, Philadelphia, PA 19106.

Fourth Judicial Circuit (Districts of Maryland, North Carolina, South Carolina, Virginia, and West Virginia).—*Chief Judge:* William W. Wilkins. *Circuit Judges:* H. Emory Widener, Jr.; Paul V. Niemeyer; J. Harvie Wilkinson III; Karen J. Williams; M. Blane Michael; Diana Gribbon Motz; William B. Traxler, Jr.; Robert B. King; Roger L. Gregory; Dennis W. Shedd; Allyson K. Duncan. *Senior Circuit Judge:* Clyde H. Hamilton. *Circuit Executive:* Samuel W. Phillips (804) 916–2184. *Clerk:* Patricia S. Connor (804) 916–2700, Lewis F. Powell, Jr. U.S. Courthouse Annex, 1100 E. Main Street, Richmond, VA 23219.

Fifth Judicial Circuit (Districts of Louisiana, Mississippi, and Texas).—*Chief Judge:* Edith H. Jones. *Circuit Judges:* E. Grady Jolly; W. Eugene Davis; Jerry E. Smith; Jacques L. Wiener, Jr.; Rhesa H. Barksdale; Emilio M. Garza; Harold R. DeMoss, Jr.; Fortunato P. Benavides; Carl E. Stewart; James L. Dennis; Edith Brown Clement; Edward C. Prado; Carolyn Dineen King. *Senior Circuit Judges:* Thomas M. Reavley; Will Garwood; Patrick E. Higginbotham; John M. Duhé, Jr. *Circuit Executive:* Gregory A. Nussel (504) 310–7777. *Clerk:* Charles R. Fulbruge III (504) 310–7700, John Minor Wisdom, U.S. Court of Appeals Building, 600 Camp Street, New Orleans, LA 70130–3425.

Sixth Judicial Circuit (Districts of Kentucky, Michigan, Ohio, and Tennessee).—*Chief Judge:* Danny J. Boggs; *Circuit Judges:* Boyce F. Martin, Jr.; Alice M. Batchelder; Martha Craig Daughtrey; Karen Nelson Moore; R. Guy Cole, Jr.; Eric Lee Clay; Ronald Lee Gilman; Julie Smith Gibbons; John M. Rogers; Jeffrey S. Sutton; Deborah L. Cook; David McKeague; Richard Allen Griffin. *Senior Circuit Judges:* Damon J. Keith; Gilbert S. Merritt; Cornelia G. Kennedy; Ralph B. Guy, Jr.; James L. Ryan; Alan E. Norris; Richard F. Suhrheinrich; Eugene E. Siler, Jr. *Circuit Executive:* James A. Higgins (513) 564–7200. *Clerk:* Leonard Green (513) 564–7000, Potter Stewart U.S. Courthouse, 100 E. Fifth Street, Cincinnati, OH 45202.

Seventh Judicial Circuit (Districts of Illinois, Indiana, and Wisconsin).—*Chief Judge:* Frank H. Easterbrook. *Circuit Judges:* Richard A. Posner; Joel M. Flaum; Kenneth F. Ripple; Daniel A. Manion; Michael S. Kanne; Ilana Diamond Rovner; Diane P. Wood; Terence T. Evans; Ann Claire Williams; Diane S. Sykes. *Senior Circuit Judges:* Thomas E. Fairchild; William J. Bauer; Richard D. Cudahy; John L. Coffey. *Circuit Executive:* Collins T. Fitzpatrick (312) 435–5803. *Clerk:* Gino J. Agnello (312) 435–5850, 2722 U.S. Courthouse, 219 S. Dearborn Street, Chicago, IL 60604.

Eighth Judicial Circuit (Districts of Arkansas, Iowa, Minnesota, Missouri, Nebraska, North Dakota, and South Dakota).—*Chief Judge:* James B. Loken. *Circuit Judges:* Pasco M. Bowman II; Roger L. Wollman; Morris S. Arnold; Diana E. Murphy; Kermit E. Bye; William Jay Riley; Michael J. Melloy; Lavenski R. Smith; Steven M. Colloton; Raymond W. Gruender; Duane Benton; Bobby E. Shepherd. *Senior Circuit Judges:* Donald P. Lay; Myron H. Bright; John R. Gibson; Pasco M. Bowman II; Frank J. Magill; C. Arlen Beam; David R. Hansen; Morris S. Arnold. *Circuit Executive:* Millie Adams (314) 244–2600. *Clerk:* Michael E. Gans (314) 244–2400, 111 S. Tenth Street, Suite 24.327, St. Louis, MO 63102.

Ninth Judicial Circuit (Districts of Alaska, Arizona, Central California, Eastern California, Northern California, Southern California, Guam, Hawaii, Idaho, Montana, Nevada, Northern Mariana Islands, Oregon, Eastern Washington and Western Washington).—*Chief Judge:* Mary M. Schroeder. *Circuit Judges:* Harry Pregerson; Stephen Reinhardt; Alex Kozinski; Diarmuid F. O'Scannlain; Pamela Ann Rymer; Andrew J. Kleinfeld; Michael Daly Hawkins; Sidney R. Thomas; Barry G. Silverman; Susan P. Graber; M. Margaret McKeown; Kim McLane Wardlaw; William A. Fletcher; Raymond C. Fisher; Ronald M. Gould; Richard A. Paez; Marsha S. Berzon; Richard C. Tallman; Johnnie B. Rawlinson; Richard R. Clifton; Jay S. Bybee; Consuelo M. Callahan; Carlos T. Bea. *Senior Circuit Judges:* James R. Browning; Alfred T. Goodwin; J. Clifford Wallace; Joseph Tyree Sneed III; Procter Hug, Jr.; Otto R. Skopil, Jr.; Betty Binns Fletcher; Jerome Farris; Authur L. Alarcon; Warren J. Ferguson; Dorothy W. Nelson; William C. Canby, Jr.; Robert Boochever; Robert R. Beezer; Cynthia Holcomb Hall; Melvin Brunetti; John T. Noonan, Jr.; David R. Thompson; Edward Leavy; Stephen Trott; Ferdinand F. Fernandez; Thomas G. Nelson; A. Wallace Tashima. *Circuit Executive:* Gregory B. Walters (415) 556–2000. *Clerk:* Cathy A. Catterson (415) 556–9800, P.O. Box 193939, San Francisco, CA 94119–3939.

Tenth Judicial Circuit (Districts of Colorado, Kansas, New Mexico, Oklahoma, Utah, and Wyoming).—*Chief Judge:* Deanell Reece Tacha. *Circuit Judges:* Paul J. Kelly, Jr.; Robert H. Henry; Mary Beck Briscoe; Carlos F. Lucero; Michael R. Murphy; Harris L Hartz; Terrence L. O'Brien; Michael W. McConnell; Timothy M. Tymkovich; Neil M. Gorsuch; Jerome A. Holmes. *Senior Circuit Judges:* William J. Holloway, Jr.; Robert H. McWilliams; Monroe G. McKay; Stephanie K. Seymour; John C. Porfilio; Stephen H. Anderson; Bobby R. Baldock; Wade Brorby; David M. Ebel. *Circuit Executive:* David Tighe (303) 844–2067. *Clerk:* Betsy Shumaker (303) 844–3157, Byron White United States Courthouse, 1823 Stout Street, Denver, CO 80257.

Eleventh Judicial Circuit (Districts of Alabama, Florida, and Georgia).—*Chief Judge:* J.L. Edmondson. *Circuit Judges:* Gerald Bard Tjoflat; R. Lanier Anderson III; Stanley F. Birch, Jr.; Joel F. Dubina; Susan Harrell Black; Edward E. Carnes; Rosemary Barkett; Frank Mays Hull; Stanley Marcus; Charles Reginald Wilson; William H. Pryor Jr. *Senior Circuit Judges:* John C. Godbold; James C. Hill; Peter T. Fay; Phyllis A. Kravitch; Emmett Ripley Cox. *Circuit Executive:* Norman E. Zoller (404) 335–6535. *Clerk:* Thomas K. Kahn (404) 335–6100, 56 Forsyth Street, NW., Atlanta, GA 30303.

UNITED STATES COURT OF APPEALS

FOR THE DISTRICT OF COLUMBIA CIRCUIT

333 Constitution Avenue, NW., 20001, phone (202) 216–7300

DAVID BRYAN SENTELLE, chief circuit judge, born in Canton, NC, February 12, 1943; son of Horace and Maude Sentelle; married to Jane LaRue Oldham; daughters: Sharon, Reagan, and Rebecca; B.A., University of North Carolina at Chapel Hill, 1965; J.D. with honors, Uni-versity of North Carolina School of Law, 1968; associate, Uzzell and Dumont, Charlotte, 1968–79; Assistant U.S. Attorney, Charlotte, 1970–74; North Carolina State District Judge, 1974–77; partner, Tucker, Hicks, Sentelle, Moon and Hodge, Charlotte, 1977–85; U.S. District Judge for the Western District of North Carolina, 1985–87; appointed to the U.S. Court of Appeals by President Reagan in October 1987; assumed the position of Chief Judge on February 11, 2008.

DOUGLAS HOWARD GINSBURG, circuit judge; born in Chicago, IL, May 25, 1946; diploma, Latin School of Chicago, 1963; B.S., Cornell University, 1970 (Phi Kappa Phi, Ives Award); J.D., University of Chicago, 1973 (Mecham Prize Scholarship 1970–73, Casper Platt Award, 1973, Order of Coif, Articles and Book Rev. Ed., 40 U. Chi. L. Rev.); bar admissions: Illinois (1973), Massachusetts (1982), U.S. Supreme Court (1984), U.S. Court of Appeals for the Ninth Circuit (1986); member: Mont Pelerin Society, American Economic Association, American Law and Economics Association, Honor Society of Phi Kappa Phi, American Bar Association, Antitrust Section, Council, 1985–86 (ex officio), judicial liaison (2000–03 and 20009–12); advisory boards: Competition Policy International; Harvard Journal of Law and Public Policy; Journal of Competition Law and Economics; Law and Economics Center, George Mason University School of Law; Supreme Court Economic Review; University of Chicago Law Review; Board of Directors: Foundation for Research in Economics and the Environment, 1991–2004; Rappahannock County Conservation Alliance, 1998–2004; Rappahannock Association for Arts and Community, 1997–99; Committees: Judicial Conference of the United States, 2002–08, Budget Committee, 1997–2001, Committee on Judicial Resources, 1987–96; Boston University Law School, Visiting Committee, 1994–97; University of Chicago Law School, Visiting Committee, 1985–88; law clerk to: Judge Carl McGowan, U.S. Court of Appeals for the District of Columbia Circuit, 1973–74; Associate Justice Thurgood Marshall, U.S. Supreme Court, 1974–75; previous positions: assistant professor, Harvard University Law School, 1975–81; Professor 1981–83; Deputy Assistant Attorney General, Antitrust Division, U.S. Department of Justice, 1983–84; Administrator for Information and Regulatory Affairs, Executive Office of the President, Office of Management and Budget, 1984–85; Assistant Attorney General, Antitrust Division, U.S. Department of Justice, 1985–86; lecturer in law, Columbia University, New York City, 1987–88; lecturer in law, Harvard University, Cambridge, MA, 1988–89; distinguished professor of law, George Mason University, Arlington, VA, 1988–present; senior lecturer, University of Chicago Law School, 1990–present; lecturer on law, New York Law School, 2005–09; appointed to U.S. Court of Appeals for the District of Columbia Circuit by President Reagan on October 14, 1986, taking the oath of office on November 10, 1986, Chief Judge, 2001–08.

KAREN LECRAFT HENDERSON, circuit judge. [Biographical information not supplied, per Judge Henderson's request.]

JUDITH W. ROGERS, circuit judge; born in New York, NY; A.B. (with honors), Radcliffe College, 1961; Phi Beta Kappa honors member; LL.B., Harvard Law School, 1964; LL.M., University of Virginia School of Law, 1988; law clerk, D.C. Juvenile Court, 1964–65; assistant U.S. Attorney for the District of Columbia, 1965–68; trial attorney, San Francisco Neighborhood Legal Assistance Foundation, 1968–69; Attorney, U.S. Department of Justice, Office of the Associate Deputy Attorney General and Criminal Division, 1969–71; General Counsel, Congressional Commission on the Organization of the D.C. Government, 1971–72; legislative assistant to D.C. Mayor Walter E. Washington, 1972–79; Corporation Counsel for the District of Columbia, 1979–83; trustee, Radcliffe College, 1982–90; member of Visiting Committee to Harvard Law School, 1984–90; appointed by President Reagan to the District of Columbia Court of Appeals as an Associate Judge on September 15, 1983; served as Chief Judge, November 1, 1988 to March 17, 1994; appointed by President Clinton to the U.S. Court of Appeals for the District of Columbia Circuit on March 18, 1994, and entered on duty March 21, 1994; member of Executive Committee, Conference of Chief Justices, 1993–94; member, U.S. Judicial Conference Committee on the Codes of Conduct, 1998–2004.

DAVID S. TATEL, circuit judge; born in Washington, DC, March 16, 1942; son of Molly and Dr. Howard Tatel (deceased); married to the former Edith Bassichis, 1965; children: Rebecca, Stephanie, Joshua, and Emily; grandchildren: Olivia, Maya, Olin, Reuben, Rae, and Cameron; B.A., University of Michigan, 1963; J.D., University of Chicago Law School, 1966; instructor, University of Michigan Law School, 1966–67; associate, Sidley and Austin, 1967–69, 1970–72; director, Chicago Lawyers' Committee for Civil Rights Under Law, 1969–70; director, National Lawyers' Committee for Civil Rights Under Law, 1972–74; director, Office for Civil Rights, U.S. Department of Health, Education and Welfare, 1977–79; associate and partner, Hogan and Hartson, 1974–77, 1979–94; lecturer, Stanford University Law School, 1991–92; board of directors, Spencer Foundation, 1987–97 (chair, 1990–97); board of directors, National Board for Professional Teaching Standards, 1997–2000; National Lawyers' Committee for Civil Rights Under Law, co-chair, 1989–91; chair, Carnegie Foundation for the Advancement of Teaching; member of the American Philosophical Society, the National Academy of Education, and the National Academy of Sciences Committee on Science, Technology and Law; admitted to practice law in Illinois in 1966 and the District Columbia in 1970; appointed to the U.S. Court of Appeals for the District of Columbia Circuit by President Clinton on October 7, 1994, and entered on duty October 11, 1994.

MERRICK BRIAN GARLAND, circuit judge; born in Chicago, IL, 1952; A.B., Harvard University, 1974, *summa cum laude,* Phi Beta Kappa, Paul Revere Frothingham and Richard Perkins Parker Award; J.D., Harvard Law School, 1977, *magna cum laude,* articles editor, Harvard Law Review; law clerk to Judge Henry J. Friendly, U.S. Court of Appeals for the 2d Circuit, 1977–78; law clerk to Justice William J. Brennan, Jr., U.S. Supreme Court, 1978–79; Special Assistant to the Attorney General, 1979–81; associate then partner, Arnold and Porter, Washington, DC, 1981–89; Assistant U.S. Attorney, Washington, DC, 1989–92; partner, Arnold and Porter, 1992–93; Deputy Assistant Attorney General, Criminal Division, U.S. Department of Justice, 1993–94; Principal Associate Deputy Attorney General, 1994–97; Lecturer on Law, Harvard Law School, 1985–86; Associate Independent Counsel, 1987–88. Edmund J. Randolph Award, U.S. Department of Justice, 1997. Admitted to the bars of the District of Columbia; U.S. District Court; Court of Appeals, District of Columbia Circuit; U.S. Courts of Appeals for the 4th, 9th, and 10th Circuits; and U.S. Supreme Court. Author: *Antitrust and State Action*, 96 Yale Law Journal 486 (1987); *Antitrust and Federalism,* 96 Yale Law Journal 1291 (1987); *Deregulation and Judicial Review,* 98 Harvard Law Review 505 (1985); co-chair, Administrative Law Section, District of Columbia Bar, 1991–94; President, Board of Overseers, Harvard University, 2009–10, member, 2003–09; American Law Institute; U.S. Judiciary Conference Committee on Judicial Security, 2008–present, Committee on the Judicial Branch, 2001–05; appointed to the U.S. Court of Appeals for the District of Columbia Circuit on April 9, 1997.

JANICE ROGERS BROWN, circuit judge; born in Greenville, AL; B.A., California State University, 1974; J.D., University of California School of Law, 1977; LL.M., University of Virginia School of Law, 2004; Deputy Legislative Counsel, Legislative Counsel Bureau, 1977–79; Deputy Attorney General, California Department of Justice, 1979–87; Deputy Secretary and General Counsel, California Business, Transportation, and Housing Agency, 1987–90; Senior Associate, Nielsen, Merksamer, Parinello, Mueller and Naylor, 1990–91; Legal Affairs Secretary for Governor Pete Wilson, 1991–94; Associate Justice, California Court of Appeals for the Third District, 1994–96; Associate Justice, California Supreme Court, 1996–2005; appointed to the U.S. Court of Appeals for the District of Columbia Circuit by President George W. Bush on February 14, 2005 and sworn in on July 1, 2005.

THOMAS B. GRIFFITH, circuit judge; born in Yokohama, Japan, July 5, 1954; B.A., Brigham Young University, 1978; J.D., University of Virginia School of Law, 1985; editor, Virginia Law Review; associate, Robinson, Bradshaw and Hinson, Charlotte, NC, 1985–89; associate and then a partner, Wiley, Rein and Fielding, Washington, DC, 1989–95 and 1999–2000; Senate Legal Counsel of the United States, 1995–99; Assistant to the President and General Counsel, Brigham Young University, Provo, UT, 2000–05; member, Executive Committee of the American Bar Association's Central European and Eurasian Law Initiative; appointed to the United States Court of Appeals for the District of Columbia Circuit on June 14, 2005 and sworn in on June 29, 2005.

BRETT M. KAVANAUGH, circuit judge; born in Washington, DC, February 12, 1965; son of Edward and Martha Kavanaugh; married to Ashley Estes; two daughters; B.A., *cum laude*, Yale College, 1987; J.D., Yale Law School, 1990; law clerk to Judge Walter Stapleton of the U.S. Court of Appeals for the Third Circuit, 1990–91; law clerk for Judge Alex Kozinski of the U.S. Court of Appeals for the Ninth Circuit, 1991–92; attorney, Office of the Solicitor General of the United States, 1992–93; law clerk to Associate Justice Anthony Kennedy of the U.S. Supreme Court, 1993–94; Associate Counsel, Office of Independent Counsel, 1994–97; partner, Kirkland & Ellis LLP, 1997–98, 1999–2001; Associate Counsel and then Senior Associate Counsel to President George W. Bush, 2001–03; Assistant to the President and Staff Secretary to President Bush, 2003–06; Adjunct Professor of Law, Georgetown University Law Center, 2007; Lecturer on Law, Harvard Law School, 2008–09; appointed to the U.S. Court of Appeals for the District of Columbia Circuit on May 30, 2006.

SENIOR CIRCUIT JUDGES

HARRY T. EDWARDS, senior circuit judge; born in New York, NY, November 3, 1940; son of George H. Edwards and Arline (Ross) Lyle; married to Pamela Carrington Edwards; children: Brent and Michelle; B.S., Cornell University, 1962; J.D. (with distinction), University of Michigan Law School, 1965; associate with Seyfarth, Shaw, Fairweather and Geraldson, 1965–70; professor of law, University of Michigan, 1970–75 and 1977–80; professor of law, Harvard University, 1975–77; visiting professor of law, Free University of Brussels, 1974; arbitrator of labor/management disputes, 1970–80; vice president, National Academy of Arbitrators, 1978–80; member (1977–79) and chairman (1979–80), National Railroad Passenger Corporation (Amtrak); Executive Committee of the Association of American Law Schools, 1979–80; public member of the Administrative Conference of the United States, 1976–80; International Women's Year Commission, 1976–77; American Bar Association Commission of Law and the Economy; co-author of four books: *Labor Relations Law in the Public Sector, The Lawyer as a Negotiator, Higher Education and the Law*, and *Collective Bargaining and Labor Arbitration*; recent book, Edwards & Ellliot, *Federal Standards of Review*, was published by Thomson West, 2007; recipient of the Judge William B. Groat Alumni Award, 1978, given by Cornell University; the Society of American Law Teachers Award (for ''distinguished contributions to teaching and public service''); the Whitney North Seymour Medal presented by the American Arbitration Association for outstanding contributions to the use of arbitration; Recipient of the 2004 Robert J. Kutak Award, presented by the American Bar Association Selection of Legal Education and Admission to the Bar ''to a person who meets the highest standards of professional responsibility and demonstrates substantial achievement toward increased understanding between legal education and the active practice of law'', and several Honorary Doctor of Laws degrees; teaches law on a part-time basis; has recently taught at Duke, Georgetown, Michigan, and Harvard Law Schools, and is presently teaching courses at N.Y.U.; A.B.A.; co-chair of the Forensics Science Committee established by the National Academy of Sciences, 2006–09; appointed to the U.S. Court of Appeals, February 20, 1980; served as chief judge September 15, 1994 to July 16, 2001.

LAURENCE HIRSCH SILBERMAN, senior circuit judge; recipient of the Presidential Medal of Freedom, June 19, 2008; born in York, PA, October 12, 1935; son of William Silberman and Anna (Hirsch); married to Rosalie G. Gaull on April 28, 1957 (Deceased), married Patricia Winn on January 5, 2008; children: Robert Stephen Silberman, Katherine DeBoer Balaban, and Anne Gaull Otis; B.A., Dartmouth College, 1957; LL.B., Harvard Law School, 1961; admitted to Hawaii bar, 1962; District of Columbia bar, 1973; associate, Moore, Torkildson and Rice, 1961–64; partner (Moore, Silberman and Schulze), Honolulu, 1964–67; attorney, National Labor Relations Board, Office of General Counsel, Appellate Division, 1967–69; Solicitor, Department of Labor, 1969–70; Under Secretary of Labor, 1970–73; partner, Steptoe and Johnson, 1973–74; Deputy Attorney General of the United States, 1974–75; Ambassador to Yugoslavia, 1975–77; President's Special Envoy on ILO Affairs, 1976; senior fellow, American Enterprise Institute, 1977–78; visiting fellow, 1978–85; managing partner, Morrison and Foerster, 1978–79 and 1983–85; executive vice president, Crocker National Bank, 1979–83; lecturer, University of Hawaii, 1962–63; board of directors, Commission on Present Danger, 1978–85, Institute for Educational Affairs, New York, NY, 1981–85, member: General Advisory Committee on Arms Control and Disarmament, 1981–85; Defense Policy Board, 1981–85; vice chairman, State Department's Commission on Security and Economic Assistance, 1983–84; American Bar Association (Labor Law Committee, 1965–72, Corporations and Banking Committee, 1973, Law and National Security Advisory Committee, 1981–85); Hawaii Bar Association Ethics Committee, 1965–67; Council on Foreign Relations, 1977–present; Judicial Conference Committee on Court Administration and Case Management,

1994; Adjunct Professor of Law (Administrative Law) Georgetown Law Center, 1987–94; 1997; Adjunct Professor of Law, New York University Law School, 1995–96; Distinguished Visitor From the Judiciary, Georgetown on The Intelligence Capabilities of the United States Regarding Weapons of Mass Destruction, 2004–05; appointed to the U.S. Court of Appeals for the District of Columbia Circuit by President Reagan on October 28, 1985.

STEPHEN F. WILLIAMS, senior circuit judge; born in New York, NY, September 23, 1936; son of Charles Dickerman Williams and Virginia (Fain); married to Faith Morrow, 1966; children: Susan, Geoffrey, Sarah, Timothy, and Nicholas; B.A., Yale, 1958, J.D., Harvard Law School, 1961; U.S. Army Reserves, 1961–62; associate, Debevoise, Plimpton, Lyons and Gates, 1962–66; Assistant U.S. Attorney, Southern District of New York, 1966–69; associate professor and professor of law, University of Colorado School of Law, 1969–86; visiting professor of law, UCLA, 1975–76; visiting professor of law and fellow in law and economics, University Chicago Law School, 1979–80; visiting George W. Hutchison Professor of Energy Law, SMU, 1983–84; consultant to: Administrative Conference of the United States, 1974–76; Federal Trade Commission on energy-related issues, 1983–85; member, American Law Institute; appointed to the U.S. Court of Appeals for the District of Columbia Circuit by President Reagan, June 16, 1986.

A. RAYMOND RANDOLPH, senior circuit judge; born in Riverside, NJ, November 1, 1943; son of Arthur Raymond Randolph, Sr. and Marile (Kelly); two children: John Trevor and Cynthia Lee Randolph; married to Eileen Janette O'Connor, May 18, 1984. B.S., Drexel University, 1966; J.D., University of Pennsylvania Law School, 1969, *summa cum laude;* managing editor, University of Pennsylvania Law Review; Order of the Coif. Admitted to Supreme Court of the United States; Supreme Court of California; District of Columbia Court of Appeals; U.S. Courts of Appeals for the First, Second, Fourth, Fifth, Sixth, Seventh, Ninth, Eleventh, and District of Columbia Circuits. Memberships: American Law Institute. Law clerk to Judge Henry J. Friendly, U.S. Court of Appeals for the Second Circuit, 1969–70; Assistant to the Solicitor General, 1970–73; adjunct professor of law, Georgetown University Law Center, 1974–78; George Mason School of Law, 1992; Deputy Solicitor General, 1975–77; Special Counsel, Committee on Standards of Official Conduct, House of Representatives, 1979–80; special assistant attorney general, State of Montana (honorary), 1983–July 1990; special assistant attorney general, State of New Mexico, 1985–July 1990; special assistant attorney general, State of Utah, 1986–July 1990; advisory panel, Federal Courts Study Committee, 1989–July 1990; partner, Pepper, Hamilton and Scheetz, 1987–July 1990; chairman, Committee on Codes of Conduct, U.S. Judicial Conference, 1995–98; distinguished professor of law, George Mason Law School, 1999–present; recipient, Distinguished Alumnus Award, University of Pennsylvania Law School, 2002; appointed to the U.S. Court of Appeals for the District of Columbia Circuit by President George H.W. Bush on July 16, 1990, and took oath of office on July 20, 1990.

OFFICERS OF THE UNITED STATES COURT OF APPEALS FOR THE DISTRICT OF COLUMBIA CIRCUIT

Circuit Executive.—Jill C. Sayenga (202) 216–7340.
Clerk.—Mark J. Langer, 216–7000.
Chief Deputy Clerk.—Marilyn R. Sargent, 216–7000.
Chief, Legal Division.—Martha Tomich, 216–7500.

UNITED STATES COURT OF APPEALS

FEDERAL CIRCUIT

717 Madison Place, NW., 20439, phone (202) 633–6550

PAUL R. MICHEL, chief circuit judge; born in Philadelphia, PA, February 3, 1941; son of Lincoln M. and Dorothy Michel; educated in public schools in Wayne and Radnor, PA; B.A., Williams College, 1963; J.D., University of Virginia Law School, 1966; married Brooke England, 2004; adult children, Sarah Elizabeth and Margaret Kelley; Second Lieutenant, U.S. Army Reserve, 1966–72; admitted to practice: Pennsylvania (1967), U.S. District Court (1968), U.S. Circuit Court (1969), and U.S. Supreme Court (1969); Assistant District Attorney, Philadelphia, PA, 1967–71; Deputy District Attorney for Investigations, 1972–74; Assistant Watergate Special Prosecutor, 1974–75; assistant counsel, Senate Intelligence Committee, 1975–76; deputy chief, Public Integrity Section, Criminal Division, U.S. Department of Justice, 1976–78; ''Koreagate'' prosecutor, 1976–78; Associate Deputy Attorney General, 1978–81; Acting Deputy Attorney General, Dec. 1979–Feb. 1980; counsel and administrative assistant to Senator Arlen Specter, 1981–88; nominated December 19, 1987 by President Ronald Reagan to be circuit judge, U.S. Court of Appeals for the Federal Circuit, confirmed by Senate on February 29, 1988, and assumed duties of the office on March 8, 1988; member of the Judicial Conference of the United States, 2004–present; elevated to the position of Chief Judge on December 25, 2004.

PAULINE NEWMAN, circuit judge; born in New York, NY, June 20, 1927; daughter of Maxwell H. and Rosella G. Newman; B.A., Vassar College, 1947; M.A. in pure science, Columbia University, 1948; Ph.D. degree in chemistry, Yale University, 1952; LL.B., New York University School of Law, 1958; Doctor of Laws (honorary), Franklin Pierce School of Law, 1991; admitted to the New York bar in 1958 and to the Pennsylvania bar in 1979; worked as research scientist for the American Cyanamid Co. from 1951–54; worked for the FMC Corp. from 1954–84 as patent attorney and house counsel and, since 1969, as director of the Patent, Trademark, and Licensing Department; on leave from FMC Corp. worked for the United Nations Educational, Scientific and Cultural Organization as a science policy specialist in the Department of Natural Sciences, 1961–62; offices in scientific and professional organizations include: member of Council of the Patent, Trademark and Copyright Section of the American Bar Association, 1982–84; board of directors of the American Patent Law Association, 1981–84; vice president of the United States Trademark Association, 1978–79, and member of the board of directors, 1975–76, 1977–79; board of governors of the New York Patent Law Association, 1970–74; president of the Pacific Industrial Property Association, 1978–80; executive committee of the International Patent and Trademark Association, 1982–84; board of directors: the American Chemical Society, 1973–75, 1976–78, 1979–81; American Institute of Chemists, 1960–66, 1970–76; Research Corp., 1982–84; member: board of trustees of Philadelphia College of Pharmacy and Science, 1983–84; patent policy board of State University of New York, 1983–84; national board of Medical College of Pennsylvania, 1975–84; governmental committees include: State Department Advisory Committee on International Intellectual Property, 1974–84; advisory committee to the Domestic Policy Review of Industrial Innovation, 1978–79; special advisory committee on Patent Office Procedure and Practice, 1972–74; member of the U.S. Delegation to the Diplomatic Conference on the Revision of the Paris Convention for the Protection of Industrial Property, 1982–84; awarded Wilbur Cross Medal of Yale University Graduate School, 1989, the Jefferson Medal of the New Jersey Intellectual Property Law Association, 1988; the Eli Whitney Award of the Connecticut Patent Law Association, 1999; Lifetime Achievement Award; Managing Intellectual Property, 2008; AIPLA Present's Outstanding Service Award, 2007; Outstanding Public Service Award; New York Intellectual Property Law Association, 2005; Lifetime Achievement Award; Sedona Conference, 2006; the Award for Outstanding Contributions in the Intellectual Property Field of the Pacific Industrial Property Association, 1987; Vanderbilt Medal of New York University School of Law, 1995; Vasser College Distinguished Achievement Award, 2002; Distinguished Professor of Law, George Mason University School of Law (adjunct faculty); Council on Foreign Relations; appointed judge of the U.S. Court of Appeals for the Federal Circuit by President Reagan and entered upon duties of that office on May 7, 1984.

HALDANE ROBERT MAYER, circuit judge; born in Buffalo, NY, February 21, 1941; educated in the public schools of Lockport, NY; B.S., U.S. Military Academy, West Point, NY, 1963; J.D., Marshall-Wythe School of Law, The College of William and Mary in Virginia, 1971; editor-in-chief, *William and Mary Law Review,* Omicron Delta Kappa; admitted to practice in Virginia and the District of Columbia; board of directors, William and Mary Law School Association, 1979–85; served in the U.S. Army, 1963–75, in the Infantry and the Judge Advocate General's Corps; awarded the Bronze Star Medal, Meritorious Service Medal, Army Commendation Medal with Oak Leaf Cluster, Combat Infantryman Badge, Parachutist Badge, Ranger Tab, Ranger Combat Badge (RVN), Campaign and Service Ribbons; resigned from Regular Army and was commissioned in the U.S. Army Reserve, currently Lieutenant Colonel, retired; law clerk for Judge John D. Butzner, Jr., U.S. Court of Appeals for the Fourth Circuit, 1971–72; private practice with McGuire, Woods and Battle in Charlottesville, VA, 1975–77; adjunct professor, University of Virginia School of Law, 1975–77, 1992–94, George Washington University National Law Center, 1992–96; Special Assistant to the Chief Justice of the United States, Warren E. Burger, 1977–80; private practice with Baker and McKenzie in Washington, DC, 1980–81; Deputy and Acting Special Counsel (by designation of the President), 1981–82; appointed by President Reagan to the U.S. Claims Court, 1982; appointed by President Reagan to the U.S. Court of Appeals for the Federal Circuit, June 15, 1987; assumed duties of the office, June 19, 1987; elevated to the position of Chief Judge on December 25, 1997; relinquished that position on December 24, 2004, after having held it for seven years; Judicial Conference of the U.S. Committee on the International Appellate Judges Conference, 1988–91, Committee on Judicial Resources, 1990–97 and 2007–present; member of the Judicial Conference of the United States, 1997–2004.

ALAN D. LOURIE, circuit judge; born in Boston, MA, January 13, 1935; son of Joseph Lourie and Rose; educated in public schools in Brookline, MA; A.B., Harvard University, 1956; M.S., University of Wisconsin, 1958; Ph.D., University of Pennsylvania, 1965; J.D., Temple University, 1970; married; two children; four grandchildren; employed at Monsanto Company (chemist, 1957–59); Wyeth Laboratories (chemist, literature scientist, patent liaison specialist, 1959–64); SmithKline Beecham Corporation, (Patent Agent, 1964–70; assistant director, Corporate Patents, 1970–76; director, Corporate Patents, 1976–77; vice president, Corporate Patents and Trademarks and Associate General Counsel, 1977–90); vice chairman of the Industry Functional Advisory Committee on Intellectual Property Rights for Trade Policy Matters (IFAC 3) for the Department of Commerce and the Office of the U.S. Trade Representative, 1987–90; Treasurer of the Association of Corporate Patent Counsel, 1987–89; President of the Philadelphia Patent Law Association, 1984–85; member of the board of directors of the American Intellectual Property Law Association (formerly American Patent Law Association), 1982–85; member of the U.S. delegation to the Diplomatic Conference on the Revision of the Paris Convention for the Protection of Industrial Property, October–November 1982, March 1984; chairman of the Patent Committee of the Law Section of the Pharmaceutical Manufacturers Association, 1980–85; member of the Judicial Conference Committee on Financial Disclosure, 1990–98; member of the Judicial Conference Committee on Codes of Conduct, 2005; member of the American Bar Association, the American Chemical Society, the Cosmos Club, and the Harvard Club of Washington; recipient of the Jefferson Medal of the New Jersey Intellectual Property Law Association for outstanding contributions to intellectual property law, 1998; recipient of the first Distinguished Intellectual Property Professional Award of the Intellectual Property Owners Education Foundation, 2008; admitted to: Supreme Court of Pennsylvania, U.S. District Court for the Eastern District of Pennsylvania, U.S. Court of Appeals for the Third Circuit, U.S. Court of Appeals for the Federal Circuit, U.S. Supreme Court; nominated January 25, 1990, by President George H.W. Bush to be circuit judge, U.S. Court of Appeals for the Federal Circuit, confirmed by the Senate on April 5, 1990, and assumed duties of the office on April 11, 1990.

RANDALL R. RADER, circuit judge; born in Hastings, NE, April 21, 1949; son of Raymond A. and Gloria R. Rader; B.A., Brigham Young University, 1971–74, (*magna cum laude*), Phi Beta Kappa; J.D., George Washington University Law Center, 1974–78; legislative assistant to Representative Virginia Smith; legislative director, counsel, House Committee on Ways and Means to Representative Philip M. Crane, 1978–81; General Counsel, Chief Counsel, Subcommittee on the Constitution, 1981–86; Minority Chief Counsel, Staff Director, Subcommittee on Patents, Trademarks and Copyrights, Senate Committee on Judiciary, 1987–88; Judge, U.S. Claims Court, 1988–90, nominated by President Ronald Reagan; recipient:

Outstanding Young Federal Lawyer Award by Federal Bar Association, 1983; Jefferson Medal Award, 2003; bar member: District of Columbia, 1978; Supreme Court of the United States, 1984; nominated to the U.S Court of Appeals for the Federal Circuit by President George H.W. Bush on June 12, 1990; confirmed by Senate August 3, 1990, sworn in August 14, 1990.

ALVIN A. SCHALL, circuit judge; born in New York City, NY, April 4, 1944; son of Gordon W. Schall and Helen D. Schall; preparatory education: St. Paul's School, Concord, NH, 1956–62, graduated *cum laude*; higher education: B.A., Princeton University, 1962–66; J.D., Tulane Law School, 1966–69; married to the former Sharon Frances LeBlanc, children: Amanda and Anthony; associate with the law firm of Shearman and Sterling in New York City, 1969–73; Assistant United States Attorney, Office of the United States Attorney for the Eastern District of New York, 1973–78; Chief of the Appeals Division, 1977–78; Trial Attorney, Senior Trial Counsel, Civil Division, United States Department of Justice, Washington, DC, 1978–87; member of the Washington, DC law firm of Perlman and Partners, 1987–88; Assistant to the Attorney General of the United States, 1988–92; author, *Federal Contract Disputes and Forums, Chapter 9 in Construction Litigation: Strategies and Techniques,* published by John Wiley and Sons (Wiley Law Publications), 1989; bar memberships: State of New York (1970), U.S. District Courts for the Eastern and Southern Districts of New York (1973), U.S. Court of Appeals for the Second Circuit (1974), U.S. Court of Federal Claims, formerly the U.S. Claims Court (1978), District of Columbia (1980), U.S. Court of Appeals for the Federal Circuit (1982), Supreme Court of the United States (1989), U.S. Court of Appeals for the District of Columbia Circuit (1991), and United States District Court for the District of Columbia (1991); appointed U.S. Court of Appeals for the Federal Circuit by President George H.W. Bush on August 17, 1992, sworn in on August 19, 1992.

WILLIAM CURTIS BRYSON, circuit judge; born in Houston, TX, August 19, 1945; A.B., Harvard University, 1969; J.D., University of Texas School of Law, 1973; married with two children; law clerk to Hon. Henry J. Friendly, circuit judge, U.S. Court of Appeals for the Second Circuit, 1973–74, and Hon. Thurgood Marshall, associate justice, U.S. Supreme Court, 1974–75; associate, Miller, Cassidy, Larroca and Lewin, Washington, DC, 1975–78; Department of Justice, Criminal Division, 1979–86, Office of Solicitor General, 1978–79 and 1986–94; Office of the Associate Attorney General, 1994; nominated in June 1994 by President Clinton to be circuit judge, U.S. Court of Appeals for the Federal Circuit, and assumed duties of the office on October 7, 1994.

ARTHUR J. GAJARSA, circuit judge; born in Norcia (Pro. Perugia), Italy, March 1, 1941; married to Melanie Gajarsa; five children; Rensselaer Polytechnic Institute, Troy, NY, 1958–62, B.S.E.E., Bausch and Lomb Medal, 1958, Benjamin Franklin Award, 1958; Catholic University of America, Washington, DC, 1968; M.A. in economics, graduate studies; J.D., Georgetown University Law Center, Washington, DC, 1967; patent examiner, U.S. Patent Office, Department of Commerce, 1962–63; patent adviser, U.S. Air Force, Department of Defense, 1963–64; patent adviser, Cushman, Darby and Cushman, 1964–67; law clerk to Judge Joseph McGarraghy, U.S. District Court for the District of Columbia, Washington, DC, 1967–68; attorney, Office of General Counsel, Aetna Life and Casualty Co., 1968–69; special counsel and assistant to the Commissioner of Indian Affairs, Bureau of Indian Affairs, Department of Interior, 1969–71; associate, Duncan and Brown, 1971–72; partner, Gajarsa, Liss and Sterenbuch, 1972–78; partner, Garjarsa, Liss and Conroy, 1978–80; partner, Wender, Murase and White, 1980–86; partner and officer, Joseph Gajarsa, McDermott and Reiner, P.C., 1987–97; registered patent agent, registered patent attorney, 1963; admitted to the D.C. bar, U.S. District Court for the District of Columbia, and U.S. Court of Appeals for the District of Columbia, 1968; Connecticut State Bar, 1969; U.S. Supreme Court, 1971; Superior Court for D.C., Court of Appeals for D.C., 1972; U.S. Courts of Appeals for the Ninth and Federal Circuits, 1974; U.S. District Court for the Northern District of New York, 1980; awards: Sun and Balance Medal, Rensselaer Polytechnic Institute, 1990; Gigi Pieri Award, Camp Hale Association, Boston, MA, 1992; Rensselaer Key Alumni Award, 1992; 125th Anniversary Medal, Georgetown University Law Center, 1995; Order of Commendatore, Republic of Italy, 1995; Alumni Fellow Award, Rensselaer Alumni Association, 1996; Board of Directors, National Italian American Foundation, 1976–97, serving as general counsel, 1976–89, president, 1989–92, and vice chair, 1993–96; Rensselaer Neuman Foundation, trustee, 1973-present; Foundation for Improving Understanding of the Arts, trustee, 1982–96; Outward Bound, U.S.A., trustee, 1987–2002; John Carroll Society, Board of Governors, 1992–96; Rensselaer Polytechnic Institute, trustee, 1994-present; Georgetown University, regent, 1995–2001; Georgetown University Board of Directors, 2001–present; member: Federal, American, Federal Circuit, and D.C. Bar Associations; American Judicature Association; nominated for appointment to the U.S. Court of Appeals for the Federal Circuit on April 18, 1996 by President Clinton; confirmed by the Senate on July 31, 1997; entered service September 12, 1997.

RICHARD LINN, circuit judge; Polytechnic Preparatory County Day School, Brooklyn, NY, Bachelor of Electrical Engineering degree, Rensselaer Polytechnic Institute; J.D., Georgetown University Law Center; served as patent examiner at the U.S. Patent and Trademark Office, 1965–68; member of the founding Board of Governors of the Virginia State Bar Section on Patent, Trademark and Copyright Law, chairman, 1975; member of the American Intellectual Property Law Association; the Virginia Bar Intellectual Property Law Section; and the Federal Circuit Bar Association; admitted to the Virginia bar in 1969, the District of Columbia bar in 1970, and the New York bar in 1994; admitted to practice before the U.S. Supreme Court, the U.S. Courts of Appeals for the Fourth, Sixth, District of Columbia, and Federal Circuits, and the U.S. District Courts for the Eastern District of Virginia and the District of Columbia; partner, Marks and Murase, L.L.P., 1977–97, and member of the Executive Committee, 1987–97; partner, Foley and Lardner, 1997–99, Practice Group Leader, Electronics Practice Group, and Intellectual Property Department, 1997–99; recipient, Rensselaer Alumni Association Fellows Award for 2000; adjunct professor of law and professional lecturer, George Washington University Law School, 2001–03; member, Advisory Board of the George Washington University Law School, 2001–present; Master, Giles S. Rich American Inn of Court, 2000–present, president, 2004–05; member, Richard Linn American Inn of Court, 2007–present; visiting member, Hon. William C. Conner American Inn of Court, 2008–present; nominated to be Circuit Judge by President Clinton on September 28, 1999, and confirmed by the Senate on November 19, 1999; assumed duties of the office on January 1, 2000.

TIMOTHY B. DYK, circuit judge; A.B., Harvard College (*cum laude*), 1958; LL.B. (*magna cum laude*), Harvard Law School, 1961; law clerk to Justices Reed and Burton (retired), 1961–62; law clerk to Chief Justice Warren, 1962–63; special assistant to Assistant Attorney General, Louis F. Oberdorfer, 1963–64; associate and partner, Wilmer, Cutler & Pickering, 1964–90; partner, and chair, of Issues & Appeals Practice area (until nomination) with Jones, Day, Reavis and Pogue, 1990–2000; and Adjunct Professor at Yale, University of Virginia and Georgetown Law Schools; nominated for appointment to the U.S. Court of Appeals for the Federal Circuit on April 1, 1998 by President Clinton; confirmed by the Senate on May 24, 2000; entered on duty June 9, 2000.

SHARON PROST, circuit judge; born in Newburyport, MA; daughter of Zyskind and Ester Prost; two sons, Matthew and Jeffrey; educated in Hartford, CT; B.S., Cornell University, 1973; M.B.A., George Washington University, 1975; J.D., Washington College of Law, American University, 1979; admitted to practice in Washington, DC, 1979; LL.M., George Washington University School of Law, 1984; Labor Relations Specialist, U.S. Civil Service Commission, 1973–76; Labor Relations Specialist/Auditor, U.S. General Accounting Office, 1976–79; Trial Attorney, Federal Labor Relations Authority, 1979–82; Chief Counsel's Office, Department of Treasury, 1982–84; Assistant Solicitor, Associate Solicitor, and then Acting Solicitor, National Labor Relations Board, 1984–89; Adjunct Professor of Labor Law, George Mason University School of Law, 1986–87; Chief Labor Counsel, Senate Labor Committee—minority, 1989–93; Chief Counsel, Senate Judiciary Committee—minority, 1993–95; Deputy Chief Counsel, Senate Judiciary Committee—majority, 1995–2001; Chief Counsel, Senate Judiciary Committee—majority, 2001; appointed by President George W. Bush to the U.S. Court of Appeals for the Federal Circuit, September 21, 2001; assumed duties of the office on October 3, 2001.

KIMBERLY H. MOORE, circuit judge; born in Baltimore, MD; married to Matthew J. Moore; four children; B.S.E.E., Massachusetts Institute of Technology, 1990; M.S., Massachusetts Institute of Technology, 1991; J.D. (*cum laude*), Georgetown University Law Center, 1994; Electrical Engineer, Naval Surface Warfare Center, 1988–92; Associate, Kirkland & Ellis, 1994–95; Judicial Clerk, Hon. Glenn L. Archer, Jr., Chief Judge, United States Court of Appeals for the Federal Circuit, 1995–97; Assistant Professor of Law, Chicago-Kent College of Law, 1997–99; Associate Director of the Intellectual Property Law Program, Chicago-Kent College of Law, 1998–99; Assistant Professor of Law, University of Maryland School of Law, 1999–2000; Associate Professor of Law, George Mason University School of Law, 2000–04; Professor of Law, George Mason University School of Law, 2004–06; nominated to the United States Court of Appeals for the Federal Circuit by President George W. Bush on May 18, 2006; confirmed by the Senate on September 5, 2006 and assumed the duties of office on September 8, 2006.

SENIOR CIRCUIT JUDGES

DANIEL M. FRIEDMAN, senior circuit judge; born in New York, NY, February 8, 1916; son of Henry M. and Julia (Freedman) Friedman; attended the Ethical Culture Schools in New York City; A.B., Columbia College, 1937; LL.B., Columbia Law School, 1940; married to Leah L. Lipson (deceased), January 16, 1955; married to Elizabeth M. Ellis (deceased), October 18, 1975; admitted to New York bar, 1941; private practice, New York, NY, 1940–42; legal staff, Securities and Exchange Commission, 1942, 1946–51; served in the U.S. Army, 1942–46; Appellate Section, Antitrust Division, U.S. Department of Justice, 1951–59; assistant to the Solicitor General, 1959–62; second assistant to the Solicitor General, 1962–68; First Deputy Solicitor General, 1968–78; Acting Solicitor General, January–March 1977; nominated by President Carter as chief judge of the U.S. Court of Claims, March 22, 1978; confirmed by the Senate, May 17, 1978, and assumed duties of the office on May 24, 1978; as of October 1, 1982, continued in office as judge of the U.S. Court of Appeals for the Federal Circuit, pursuant to section 165, Federal Courts Improvement Act of 1982, Public Law 97–164, 96 Stat. 50.

GLENN LEROY ARCHER, JR., senior circuit judge; born in Densmore, KS, March 21, 1929; son of Glenn L. and Ruth Agnes Archer; educated in Kansas public schools; B.A., Yale University, 1951; J.D., with honors, George Washington University Law School, 1954; married to Carole Joan Thomas; children: Susan, Sharon, Glenn III, and Thomas; First Lieutenant, Judge Advocate General's Office, U.S. Air Force, 1954–56; associate (1956–60) and partner (1960–81), Hamel, Park, McCabe and Saunders, Washington, DC; nominated in 1981 by President Ronald Reagan to be Assistant Attorney General for the Tax Division, U.S. Department of Justice, and served in that position from December 1981 to December 1985; nominated in October 1985 by President Reagan to be circuit judge, U.S. Court of Appeals for the Federal Circuit; took the oath of office as a Circuit Judge in December 1985; elevated to the position of Chief Judge on March 18, 1994, served in that capacity until December 24, 1997; took senior status beginning December 25, 1997.

S. JAY PLAGER, senior circuit judge; born May 16, 1931; son of A.L. and Clara Plager; three children; educated public schools, Long Branch, NJ; A.B., University of North Carolina, 1952; J.D., University of Florida, with high honors, 1958; LL.M., Columbia University, 1961; Phi Beta Kappa, Phi Kappa Phi, Order of the Coif, Holloway Fellow, University of North Carolina; Editor-in-Chief, University of Florida Law Review; Charles Evans Hughes Fellow, Columbia University; commissioned, Ensign U.S. Navy, 1952; active duty Korean conflict; honorable discharge as Commander, USNR, 1971; professor, Faculty of Law, University of Florida, 1958–64; University of Illinois, 1964–77; Indiana University School of Law, Bloomington, 1977–89; visiting research professor of law, University of Wisconsin, 1967–68; visiting fellow, Trinity College and visiting professor, Cambridge University, 1980; visiting scholar, Stanford University Law School, 1984–85; dean, Indiana University School of Law, Bloomington, 1977–84; counselor to the Under Secretary, U.S. Department of Health and Human Services, 1986–87; Associate Director, Office of Management and Budget; Executive Office of the President of the United States, 1987–88; Administrator, Office of Information and Regulatory Affairs; Office of Management and Budget; Executive Office of the President of the United States, 1988–89; appointed by President George H.W. Bush to the U.S. Court of Appeals for the Federal Circuit in November 1989; assumed senior status November 2000.

RAYMOND C. CLEVENGER III, senior circuit judge; born in Topeka, KS, August 27, 1937; son of R. Charles and Mary Margaret Clevenger; educated in the public schools in Topeka, Kansas, and at Phillips Academy, Andover, MA; B.A., Yale University, 1959; LL.B., Yale University, 1966; law clerk to Justice White, October term, 1966; practice of law at Wilmer, Cutler and Pickering, Washington, DC, 1967–90; nominated to the U.S. Court of Appeals for the Federal Circuit by President George H.W. Bush on January 24, 1990, confirmed on April 27, 1990 and assumed duties on May 3, 1990.

OFFICERS OF THE UNITED STATES COURT OF APPEALS FOR THE FEDERAL CIRCUIT

Circuit Executive and Clerk of Court.—Jan Horbaly (202) 312–5520.
Senior Technical Assistant.—Melvin L. Halpern, 312–3484.
Senior Staff Attorney.—J. Douglas Steere, 312–3490.
Circuit Librarian.—Patricia M. McDermott, 312–5500.

Information Technology Office.—Mona Harrington, 312–3474.
Administrative Services Office.—Dale Bosley, 312–5517.
Chief Deputy Clerk for Operations.—Pamela Twiford, 312–5522.

UNITED STATES DISTRICT COURT FOR THE DISTRICT OF COLUMBIA

E. Barrett Prettyman U.S. Courthouse, 333 Constitution Avenue, NW., Room 4106, 20001
phone (202) 354–3320, fax 354–3412

ROYCE C. LAMBERTH, chief judge; born in San Antonio, TX, July 16, 1943; son of Nell Elizabeth Synder and Larimore S. Lamberth, Sr.; South San Antonio High School, 1961; B.A., University of Texas at Austin, 1966; LL.B., University of Texas School of Law, 1967; permanent president, class of 1967, University of Texas School of Law; U.S. Army (Captain, Judge Advocate General's Corps, 1968–74; Vietnam Service Medal, Air Medal, Bronze Star with Oak Leaf Cluster, Meritorious Service Medal with Oak Leaf Cluster); assistant U.S. attorney, District of Columbia, 1974–87 (chief, civil division, 1978–87); President's Reorganization Project, Federal Legal Representation Study, 1978–79; honorary faculty, Army Judge Advocate General's School, 1976; Attorney General's Special Commendation Award; Attorney General's John Marshall Award, 1982; vice chairman, Armed Services and Veterans Affairs Committee, Section on Administrative Law, American Bar Association, 1979–82, chairman, 1983–84; chairman, Professional Ethics Committee, 1989–91; co-chairman, Committee of Article III Judges, Judiciary Section 1989–present; chairman, Federal Litigation Section, 1986–87; chairman, Federal Rules Committee, 1985–86; deputy chairman, Council of the Federal Lawyer, 1980–83; chairman, Career Service Committee, Federal Bar Association, 1978–80; appointed judge, U.S. District Court for the District of Columbia by President Reagan, November 16, 1987; appointed by Chief Justice Rehnquist to be Presiding Judge of the United States Foreign Intelligence Surveillance Court, May 1995–2002.

PAUL L. FRIEDMAN, judge; born in Buffalo, NY, February 20, 1944; son of Cecil A. and Charlotte Wagner Friedman; B.A. (political science), Cornell University, 1965; J.D., *cum laude,* School of Law, State University of New York at Buffalo, 1968; admitted to the bars of the District of Columbia, New York, U.S. Supreme Court, and U.S. Courts of Appeals for the D.C., Federal, Fourth, Fifth, Sixth, Seventh, Ninth and Eleventh Circuits; Law Clerk to Judge Aubrey E. Robinson, Jr., U.S. district court for the District of Columbia, 1968–69; Law Clerk to Judge Roger Robb, U.S. Court of Appeals for the District of Columbia Circuit, 1969–70; Assistant U.S. Attorney for the District of Columbia, 1970–74; assistant to the Solicitor General of the United States, 1974–76; associate independent counsel, Iran-Contra investigation, 1987–88, private law practice, White and Case (partner, 1979–94; associate, 1976–79); member: American Bar Association, Commission on Multidisciplinary Practice (1998–2000), District of Columbia bar (president, 1986–87), American Law Institute (1984) and ALI Council, 1998, American Academy of Appellate Lawyers, Bar Association of the District of Columbia, Women's Bar Association of the District of Columbia, Washington Bar Association, Hispanic Bar Association, Assistant United States Attorneys Association of the District of Columbia (president, 1976–77), Civil Justice Reform Act Advisory Group (chair, 1991–94), District of Columbia Judicial Nomination Commission (member, 1990–94; chair, 1992–94), Advisory Committee on Procedures, U.S. Court of Appeals for the D.C. Circuit (1982–88), Grievance Committee; U.S. District Court for the District of Columbia (member, 1981–87; chair, 1983–85); fellow, American College of Trial Lawyers; fellow, American Bar Foundation; board of directors: Frederick B. Abramson Memorial Foundation (president, 1991–94), Washington Area Lawyers for the Arts (1988–92), Washington Legal Clinic for the Homeless (member, 1987–92; vice-president 1988–91), Stuart Stiller Memorial Foundation (1980–94), American Judicature Society (1990–94), District of Columbia Public Defender Service (1989–92); member: Cosmos Club, Lawyers Club of Washington; appointed judge, U.S. District Court for the District of Columbia by President Clinton, June 16, 1994, and took oath of office August 1, 1994; U.S. Judicial Conference Advisory Committee on Federal Criminal Rules.

RICARDO M. URBINA, judge; born of an Honduran father and Puerto Rican mother in Manhattan, NY; B.A., Georgetown University, 1967; J.D., Georgetown Law Center, 1970; staff attorney, D.C. Public Defender Service, 1970–72; after a period of private practice with an emphasis on commercial litigation, joined the faculty of Howard University School of Law, during which time he maintained a private practice; directed the university's criminal justice clinic and taught criminal law, criminal procedure and torts, 1974–81; voted Professor of the Year by the Howard Law School student body, 1978; nominated to the D.C. Superior

Court by President Carter, 1980; appointed to the bench as President Reagan's first presidential judicial appointment and the first Hispanic judge in the history of the District of Columbia, 1981; during his thirteen years on the Superior Court, Judge Urbina served as Chief Presiding Judge of the Family Division for three years and chaired the committee that drafted the Child Support Guidelines later adopted as the District of Columbia's child support law; managed a criminal calendar (1989–90) that consisted exclusively of first degree murder, rape and child molestation cases; designated by the Chief Judge to handle a special calendar consisting of complex civil litigation; twice recognized by the United States Department of Health and Human Services for his work with children and families; selected one of the Washingtonians of the Year by *Washington Magazine,* 1986; received Hugh Johnson Memorial Award for his many contributions to ". . . the creation of harmony among diverse elements of the community and the bar by D.C. Hispanic Bar Association;" received the Hispanic National Bar Association's 1993 award for demonstrated commitment to the "Preservation of Civil and Constitutional Rights of All Americans", and the 1995 NBC-Hispanic Magazine National VIDA Award in recognition of lifetime community service; adjunct professor at the George Washington University Law School since 1993; served as a visiting instructor of trial advocacy at the Harvard Law School, 1996–97; Latino Civil Rights Center presented him with the Justice Award in 1999; conferred Distinguished Adjunct Teacher Award by George Washington University Law School in 2001 and in 2005 has been awarded the David Seidlson Chair for Trial Advocacy; appointment by President Clinton to the U.S. District Court for the District of Columbia in 1994 made him the first Latino ever appointed to the federal bench in Washington, DC.

EMMET G. SULLIVAN, judge; born in Washington, DC; graduated McKinley High School, 1964; B.A., Howard University, 1968; J.D., Howard University Law School, 1971; law clerk to Judge James A. Washington, Jr.; joined the law firm of Houston and Gardner, 1973–80, became a partner; thereafter was a partner with Houston, Sullivan and Gardner; board of directors of the D.C. Law Students in Court Program; D.C. Judicial Conference Voluntary Arbitration Committee; Nominating Committee of the Bar Association of the District of Columbia; U.S. District Court Committee on Grievances; adjunct professor at Howard University School of Law; member: National Bar Association, Washington Bar Association, Bar Association of the District of Columbia; appointed by President Reagan to the Superior Court of the District of Columbia as an associate judge, 1984; deputy presiding judge and presiding judge of the probate and tax division; chairperson of the rules committees for the probate and tax divisions; member: Court Rules Committee and the Jury Plan Committee; appointed by President George H.W. Bush to serve as an associate judge of the District of Columbia Court of Appeals, 1991; chairperson for the nineteenth annual judicial conference of the District of Columbia, 1994 (the Conference theme was "Rejuvenating Juvenile Justice—Responses to the Problems of Juvenile Violence in the District of Columbia"); appointed by chief judge Wagner to chair the "Task Force on Families and Violence for the District of Columbia Courts"; nominated to the U.S. District Court by President Clinton on March 22, 1994; and confirmed by the U.S. Senate on June 15, 1994; appointed by Chief Justice Rehnquist to serve on the Federal Judicial Conference Committee on Criminal Law, 1998; District of Columbia Judicial Disabilities and Tenure Commission, 1996–2001; presently serving on the District of Columbia Judicial Nomination Commission; first person in the District of Columbia to have been appointed to three judicial positions by three different U.S. Presidents.

COLLEEN KOLLAR-KOTELLY, judge; born in New York, NY; daughter of Konstantine and Irene Kollar; attended bilingual schools in Mexico, Ecuador and Venezuela, and Georgetown Visitation Preparatory School in Washington, DC; received B.A. degree in English at Catholic University (Delta Epsilon Honor Society); received J.D. at Catholic University's Columbus School of Law (Moot Court Board of Governors); law clerk to Hon. Catherine B. Kelly, District of Columbia Court of Appeals, 1968–69; attorney, United States Department of Justice, Criminal Division, Appellate Section, 1969–72; chief legal counsel, Saint Elizabeths Hospital, Department of Health and Human Services, 1972–84; received Saint Elizabeths Hospital Certificate of Appreciation, 1981; Meritorious Achievement Award from Alcohol, Drug Abuse and Mental Health Administration (ADAMHA), Department of Health and Human Services, 1981; appointed judge, Superior Court of the District of Columbia by President Reagan, October 3, 1984, took oath of office October 21, 1984; served as Deputy Presiding Judge, Criminal Division, January 1996–April 1997; received Achievement Recognition Award, Hispanic Heritage CORO Awards Celebration, 1996; appointed judge, U.S. District Court for the District of Columbia by President Clinton on March 26, 1997, took oath of office May 12, 1997; appointed by Chief Justice Rehnquist to serve on the Financial Disclosure Committee, 2000–2002; Presiding Judge of the United States Foreign Intelligence Surveillance Court, 2002–present.

HENRY H. KENNEDY, Jr., judge; born in Columbia, SC, February 22, 1948; son of Henry and Rachel Kennedy; A.B., Princeton University, 1970; J.D., Harvard University, 1973; admitted to the bar of the District of Columbia, 1973; Reavis, Pogue, Neal and Rose, 1972 and 1973; Assistant United States Attorney for the District of Columbia, 1973–76; United States Magistrate for the District of Columbia, April 1976–79; appointed Judge, Superior Court of the District of Columbia, by President Carter, December 17, 1979; member: American Bar Foundation; District of Columbia Bar; Washington Bar Association; Bar Association of the District of Columbia; American Law Institute; member: The Barristers; Sigma Pi Phi; Epsilon Boule; Trustee, Princeton University; appointed judge, United States District Court for the District of Columbia, by President Clinton on September 18, 1997.

RICHARD W. ROBERTS, judge; born in New York, NY; son of Beverly N. Roberts and Angeline T. Roberts; graduate of the High School of Music and Art, 1970; A.B. Vassar College, 1974; M.I.A. School for International Training, 1978; J.D., Columbia Law School, 1978; Honors Program trial attorney, Criminal Section, Civil Rights Division, U.S. Department of Justice, Washington, DC, 1978–82; Associate, Covington and Burling, Washington, DC, 1982–86; Assistant U.S. Attorney, Southern District of NY, 1986–88; Assistant U.S. Attorney, 1988–93, then Principal Assistant U.S. Attorney, District of Columbia, 1993–95; Chief, Criminal Section, Civil Rights Division, U.S. Department of Justice, Washington, DC, 1995–98; adjunct professor of trial practice, Georgetown University Law Center, Washington, DC, 1983–84; Guest faculty, Harvard Law School, Trial Advocacy Workshop, 1984–present; admitted to bars of NY (1979) and DC (1983); U.S. District Court for District of Columbia, 1983; U.S. Court of Appeals for the D.C. Circuit, 1984; U.S. Supreme Court, 1985; U.S. District Court for the Southern District of NY and U.S. Court of Appeals for the Second Circuit, 1986; past or present member or officer of National Black Prosecutors Association; Washington Bar Association; National Conference of Black Lawyers; Department of Justice Association of Black Attorneys; Department of Justice Association of Hispanic Employees for Advancement and Development; DC Bar, Committee on Professionalism and Public Understanding About the Law; American Bar Association Criminal Justice Section Committees on Continuing Legal Education, and Race and Racism in the Criminal Justice System; ABA Task Force on the Judiciary; DC Circuit Judicial Conference Arrangements Committee; D.C. Judicial Conference Planning Committee; Edward Bennett Williams Inn of Court, Washington, DC, master; board of directors, Alumnae and Alumni of Vassar College; African American Alumni of Vassar College; Vassar Club of Washington, DC; Concerned Black Men, Inc., Washington DC Chapter; Sigma Pi Phi, Epsilon Boule; Council on Foreign Relations; DC Coalition Against Drugs and Violence; Murch Elementary School Restructuring Team; nominated as U.S. District Judge for the District of Columbia by President Clinton on January 27, 1998 and confirmed by the Senate on June 5, 1998; took oath of office on July 31, 1998.

ELLEN SEGAL HUVELLE, judge; born in Boston, MA, June 3, 1948; daughter of Robert M. Segal, Esq. and Sharlee Segal; B.A., Wellesley College, 1970; Masters in City Planning, Yale University, 1972; J.D., *magna cum laude*, Boston College Law School, 1975 (Order of the Coif; Articles Editor of the law review); law clerk to Chief Justice Edward F. Hennessey, Massachusetts Supreme Judicial Court, 1975–76; associate, Williams & Connolly, 1976–84; partner, Williams & Connolly, 1984–90; associate judge, Superior Court of the District of Columbia, 1990–99; member: American Bar Association, District of Columbia Bar, Women's Bar Association; Fellow of the American Bar Foundation; Master in the Edward Bennett Williams Inn of Court and member of the Inn's Executive Committee; instructor of Trial Advocacy at the University of Virginia Law School; member of Visiting Faculty at Harvard Law School's Trial Advocacy Workshop; Boston College Law School Board of Overseers; appointed judge, U.S. District Court for the District of Columbia by President Clinton in October 1999, and took oath of office on February 25, 2000.

REGGIE B. WALTON, judge; born in Donora, PA, February 8, 1949; son of the late Theodore and Ruth (Garard) Walton; B.A., West Virginia State College, 1971; J.D., American University, Washington College of Law, 1974; admitted to the bars of the Supreme Court of Pennsylvania, 1974; United States District Court for the Eastern District of Pennsylvania, 1975; District of Columbia Court of Appeals, 1976; United States Court of Appeals for the District of Columbia Circuit, 1977; Supreme Court of the United States, 1980; United States District Court for the District of Columbia; Staff Attorney, Defender Association of Philadelphia, 1974–76; Assistant United States Attorney for the District of Columbia, 1976–80; Chief, Career Criminal Unit, Assistant United States Attorney for the District of Columbia, 1979–80; Executive Assistant United States Attorney for the District of Columbia, 1980–81; Associate Judge, Superior Court of the District of Columbia, 1981–89; Deputy Presiding Judge of the Criminal Division, Superior Court of the District of Columbia, 1986–89; Associate Director, Office of National Drug Control Policy, Executive Office of the President, 1989–

91; Senior White House Advisor for Crime, The White House, 1991; Associate Judge, Superior Court of the District of Columbia, 1991–2001; Presiding Judge of the Domestic Violence Unit, Superior Court of the District of Columbia, 2000; Presiding Judge of the Family Division, Superior Court of the District of Columbia, 2001; Instructor: National Judicial College, Reno, Nevada, 1999–present; Harvard University Law School, Trial Advocacy Workshop, 1994–present; National Institute of Trial Advocacy, Georgetown University Law School, 1983–present; Co-author, Pretrial Drug Testing—an Essential component of the National Drug Control Strategy, Brigham Young University Law Journal of Public Law (1991); Distinguished Alumnus Award, American University, Washington College of Law (1991); The William H. Hastie Award, The Judicial Council of the National Bar Association (1993); Commissioned as a Kentucky Colonel by the Governor (1990, 1991); Governor's Proclamation declaring April 9, 1991, Judge Reggie B. Walton Day in the State of Louisiana; The West Virginia State College National Alumni Association James R. Waddy Meritorious Service Award (1990); Secretary's Award, United States Department of Veterans Affairs (1990); Outstanding Alumnus Award, Ringgold High School (1987); Director's Award for Superior Performance as an Assistant United States Attorney (1980); Profiled in book entitled "Black Judges on Justice: Prospectives From The Bench" by Linn Washington (1995); appointed district judge, United States District Court for the District of Columbia by President George W. Bush, September 24, 2001, and took oath of office October 29, 2001; appointed by President Bush in June of 2004 to serve as the Chairperson of the National Prison Rape Reduction Commission, a two-year commission created by the United States Congress that is tasked with the mission of identifying methods to curb the incidents of prison rape.

JOHN D. BATES, judge; born in Elizabeth, NJ, October 11, 1946; son of Richard D. and Sarah (Deacon) Bates; B.A., Wesleyan University, 1968; J.D., University of Maryland School of Law, 1976; U.S. Army (1968–71, 1st Lt., Vietnam Service Medal, Bronze Star); law clerk to Hon. Roszel Thomsen, U.S. District Court for the District of Maryland, 1976–77; Assistant U.S. Attorney, District of Columbia, 1980–97 (Chief, Civil Division, 1987–97); Director's Award for Superior Performance (1983); Attorney General's Special commendation Award (1986); Deputy Independent Counsel, Whitewater Investigation, 1995–97; private practice of law, Miller & Chevalier (partner, 1998–2001), Chair of Government Contracts Litigation Department and member of Executive Committee), Steptoe & Johnson (associate, 1977–80); District of Columbia Circuit Advisory Committee for Procedures, 1989–93; Civil Justice Reform Committee of the U.S. District Court for the District of Columbia, 1996–2001; Treasurer, D.C. Bar, 1992–93; Publications Committee, D.C. Bar (1991–97, Chair 1994–97); D.C. Bar Special Committee on Government Lawyers, 1990–91; D.C. Bar Task Force on Civility in the Profession, 1994–96; D.C. Bar Committee on Examination of Rule 49, 1995–96; Chairman, Litigation Section, Federal Bar Association, 1986–89; Board of Directors, Washington Lawyers Committee for Civil Rights and Urban Affairs, 1999–2001; appointed to the U.S. District Court for the District of Columbia in December, 2001.

RICHARD J. LEON, judge; born in South Natick, MA, December 3, 1949; son of Silvano B. Leon and Rita (O'Rorke) Leon; A.B., Holy Cross College, 1971, J.D., *cum laude,* Suffolk Law School, 1974; LL.M. Harvard Law School, 1981; Law Clerk to Chief Justice McLaughlin and the Associate Justices, Superior Court of Massachusetts, 1974–75; Law Clerk to Hon. Thomas F. Kelleher, Supreme Court of Rhode Island, 1975–76; admitted to bar, Rhode Island, 1975 and District of Columbia, 1991; Special Assistant U.S. Attorney, Southern District of New York, 1977–78; Assistant Professor of Law, St. John's Law School, New York, 1979–83; Senior Trial Attorney, Criminal Section, Tax Division, U.S. Department of Justice, 1983–87; Deputy Chief Minority Counsel, U.S. House Select "Iran-Contra" Committee, 1987–88; Deputy Assistant U.S. Attorney General, Environment Division, 1988–89; Partner, Baker & Hostetler, Washington, DC, 1989–99; Commissioner, The White House Fellows Commission, 1990–92; Chief Minority Counsel, U.S. House Foreign Affairs Committee "October Suprise" Task Force, 1992–93; Special Counsel, U.S. House Banking Committee "Whitewater" Investigation, 1994; Special Counsel, U.S. House Ethics Reform Task Force, 1997; Adjunct Professor, Georgetown University Law Center, 1997–present; Partner, Vorys, Sater, Seymour and Pease, Washington, DC, 1999–2002; Commissioner, Judicial Review Commission on Foreign Asset Control, 2000–01; Master, Edward Bennett Williams Inn of Court; appointed U.S. District Judge for the District of Columbia by President George W. Bush on February 19, 2002; took oath of office on March 20, 2002.

ROSEMARY M. COLLYER, judge; born in White Plains, NY, November 19, 1945; daughter of Thomas C. and Alice Henry Mayers; educated in parochial and public schools in Stamford, Connecticut; B.A., Trinity College, Washington, DC, 1968; J.D., University of Denver College of Law, 1977; practiced with Sherman & Howard, Denver, Colorado, 1977–81; Chairman, Federal Mine Safety and Health Review Commission, 1981–84 by appointment of President

Reagan with Senate confirmation; General Counsel, National Labor Relations Board, 1984–89 by appointment of President Reagan with Senate confirmation; private practice with Crowell & Moring LLP, Washington, DC 1989–2003; member and chairman of the firm's Management Committee; appointed U.S. District Judge for the District of Columbia by President George W. Bush and took oath of office on January 2, 2003.

SENIOR JUDGES

LOUIS FALK OBERDORFER, senior judge; born in Birmingham, AL, February 21, 1919; son of A. Leo and Stella Falk Oberdorfer; A.B., Dartmouth College, 1939; LL.B., Yale Law School, 1946 (editor in chief, Yale Law Journal, 1941); admitted to the bar of Alabama, 1947, District of Columbia, 1949; U.S. Army, rising from private to captain, 1941–45; law clerk to Justice Hugo L. Black, 1946–47; attorney, Paul Weiss, Wharton, Garrison, 1947–51; partner, Wilmer, Cutler and Pickering, and predecessor firms, 1951–61 and 1965–77; Assistant Attorney General, Tax Division, U.S. Department of Justice, 1961–65; president, District of Columbia Bar, 1977; transition chief executive officer, Legal Services Corp., 1975; co-chairman, Lawyers' Committee for Civil Rights Under Law, 1967–69; member, Advisory Committee on Federal Rules of Civil Procedure, 1963–84; visiting lecturer, Yale Law School, 1966, 1971; adjunct professor, Georgetown Law Center, 1993–present; appointed judge of the U.S. District Court for the District of Columbia by President Carter on October 11, 1977, and took oath of office on November 1, 1977; senior status July 31, 1992.

GLADYS KESSLER, senior judge; born in New York, NY, January 22, 1938; B.A., Cornell University, 1959; LL.B. Harvard Law School, 1962; member: American Judicature Society (board of directors, 1985–89); National Center for State Courts (board of directors, 1984–87); National Association of Women Judges (president, 1983–84); Women Judges' Fund for Justice, (president, 1980–82); Fellows of the American Bar Foundation; President's Council of Cornell Women; American Law Institute; American Bar Association—committees: Alternative Dispute Resolution, Bioethics and AIDS; Executive Committee, Conference of Federal Trial Judges; private law practice—partner, Roisman, Kessler and Cashdan, 1969–77; associate judge, Superior Court of the District of Columbia, 1977–94; court administrative activities: District of Columbia Courts Joint Committee on Judicial Administration, 1989–94; Domestic Violence Coordinating Council (chairperson, 1993–94); Multi-Door Dispute Resolution Program (supervising judge, 1985–90); family division, D.C. Superior Court (presiding judge, 1981–85); Einshac Institute Board of Directors; U.S. Judicial Conference Committee on Court Administration and Court Management; Frederick B. Abramson Memorial Foundation Board of Directors; Our Place Board of Directors; Vice Chair, District of Columbia Judicial Disabilities and Tenure Commission; appointed judge, U.S. District Court for the District of Columbia by President Clinton, June 16, 1994, and took oath of office, July 18, 1994.

THOMAS F. HOGAN, senior judge; born in Washington, DC, May 31, 1938; son of Adm. Bartholomew W. (MC) (USN) Surgeon Gen., USN, 1956–62, and Grace (Gloninger) Hogan; Georgetown Preparatory School, 1956; A.B., Georgetown University (classical), 1960; master's program, American and English literature, George Washington University, 1960–62; J.D., Georgetown University, 1965–66; Honorary Degree, Doctor of Laws, Georgetown University Law Center, May 1999; St. Thomas More Fellow, Georgetown University Law Center, 1965–66; American Jurisprudence Award: Corporation Law; member, bars of the District of Columbia and Maryland; law clerk to Hon. William B. Jones, U.S. District Court for the District of Columbia, 1966–67; counsel, Federal Commission on Reform of Federal Criminal Laws, 1967–68; private practice of law in the District of Columbia and Maryland, 1968–82; adjunct professor of law, Potomac School of Law, 1977–79; adjunct professor of law, Georgetown University Law Center, 1986–88; public member, officer evaluation board, U.S. Foreign Service, 1973; member: American Bar Association, State Chairman, Maryland Drug Abuse Education Program, Young Lawyers Section (1970–73), District of Columbia Bar Association, Bar Association of the District of Columbia, Maryland State Bar Association, Montgomery County Bar Association, National Institute for Trial Advocacy, Defense Research Institute, The Barristers, The Lawyers Club; chairman, board of directors, Christ Child Institute for Emotionally Ill Children, 1971–74; served on many committees; USDC Executive Committee; Conference Committee on Administration of Federal Magistrates System, 1988–91; chairman, Inter-Circuit Assignment Committee, 1990–present; appointed judge of the U.S. District Court for the District of Columbia by President Reagan on October 4, 1982; Chief Judge June 19, 2001; member: Judicial Conference of the United States 2001–present; Executive Committee of the Judicial Conference, July 2001–present.

JAMES ROBERTSON, senior judge; born in Cleveland, OH, May 18, 1938; son of Frederick Irving and Doris (Byars) Robertson; educated at Western Reserve Academy, Hudson, OH; A.B., Princeton University, 1959 (Woodrow Wilson School); served as an officer in the U.S. Navy, on destroyers and in the Office of Naval Intelligence, 1959–64; LL.B., George Washington University, 1965 (editor-in-chief, George Washington Law Review); admitted to the bar of the District of Columbia, 1966; associate, Wilmer, Cutler and Pickering, 1965–69; chief counsel, litigation office, Lawyers' Committee for Civil Rights Under Law, Jackson, MS, 1969–70; executive director, Lawyers' Committee for Civil Rights Under Law, Washington, DC, 1971–72; partner, Wilmer, Cutler and Pickering, 1973–94; co-chair, Lawyers' Committee for Civil Rights Under Law, 1985–87; president, Southern Africa Legal Services and Legal Education Project, Inc., 1989–94; president, District of Columbia bar, 1991–92; fellow, American College of Trial Lawyers; fellow, American Bar Foundation; member, American Law Institute; appointed U.S. District Judge for the District of Columbia by President Clinton on October 11, 1994 and took oath of office on December 31, 1994; member, Judicial Conference Committee on Information Technology, 1996–present, chair, 2002–present; member, Foreign Intelligence Surveillance Court, 2001–present.

Officers of the United States District Court for the District of Columbia

United States Magistrate Judges: Deborah A. Robinson; Alan Kay; John M. Facciola.
Clerk of Court.—Nancy Mayer-Whittington.
Administrative Assistant to the Chief Judge.—Sheldon L. Snook.
Bankruptcy Judge.—S. Martin Teel, Jr.

UNITED STATES COURT OF INTERNATIONAL TRADE

One Federal Plaza, New York, NY 10278–0001, phone (212) 264–2800

JANE A. RESTANI, chief judge; born in San Francisco, CA, 1948; parents: Emilia C. and Roy J. Restani; husband: Ira Bloom; B.A., University of California at Berkeley, 1969; J.D., University of California at Davis, 1973; law review staff writer, 1971–72; articles editor, 1972–73; member, Order of the Coif; elected to Phi Kappa Phi Honor Society; admitted to the bar of the Supreme Court of the State of California, 1973; joined the civil division of the Department of Justice under the Attorney General's Honor Program in 1973 as a trial attorney; assistant chief commercial litigation section, civil division, 1976–80; director, commercial litigation branch, civil division, 1980–83; recipient of the John Marshall Award of outstanding legal achievement in 1983; Judicial Improvements Committee (now Committee on Court Administration and Case Management) of the Judicial Conference of the United States from 1987–94; Judicial Conference Advisory Committee on the Federal Rules of Bankruptcy Procedure, and liaison to the Advisory Committee on the Federal Rules of Civil Procedure, 1994–96; ABA Standing Committee on Customs Laws, 1990–93; and the Board of Directors, New York State Association of Women Judges, 1992–present; nominated to the United States Court of International Trade on November 2, 1983 by President Reagan; entered upon the duties of that office on November 25, 1983; elevated to Chief Judge on November 1, 2003.

GREGORY W. CARMAN, judge; born in Farmingdale, Long Island, NY; son of Nassau County District Court Judge Willis B. and Marjorie Sosa Carman; B.A., St. Lawrence University, Canton, NY, 1958; J.D., St. John's University School of Law (honors program), 1961; University of Virginia Law School, JAG (with honors), 1962; admitted to New York bar 1961; practiced law with firm of Carman, Callahan & Sabino, Farmingdale, NY; admitted to practice: U.S. Court of Military Appeals 1962, U.S. District Courts, Eastern and Southern Districts of New York 1965, Second Circuit Court of Appeals 1966, Supreme Court of the United States 1967, U.S. Court of Appeals, District of Columbia 1982; Councilman Town of Oyster Bay 1972–80; member U.S. House of Representatives, 97th Congress; member Banking, Finance and Urban Affairs Committee and Select Committee on Aging; member International Trade, Investment, and Monetary Policy Subcommittee; U.S. Congressional Delegate to International I.M.F. Conference; nominated by President Reagan, confirmed and appointed Judge of the U.S. Court of International Trade, March 2, 1983; Acting Chief Judge 1991; Chief Judge 1996–2003; Statutory Member, Judicial Conference of United States; member Executive Committee, Judicial Branch Committee, and Subcommittees on Long Range Planning, Benefits, Civic Education, and Seminars; Captain, U.S. Army, 1958–64; awarded Army Commendation Medal for Meritorious Service 1964; Member Rotary International 1964–present; named Paul Harris Fellow of The Rotary Foundation of Rotary International; member Holland Society, and recipient of its 1999 Gold Medal for Distinguished Achievement in Jurisprudence; member Federal Bar Association, American Bar Association, Fellow of American Bar Foundation, member New York State Bar Association, member and former chair New York State Bar Association's Committee on Courts and the Community, and recipient of its 1996 Special Recognition Award; Doctor of Laws, honoris causa, Nova Southeastern University, 1999; Distinguished Jurist in Residence, Touro College Law Center, 2000; Doctor of Laws, honoris causa, St. John's University, 2002; Inaugural Lecturer, DiCarlo U.S. Court of International Trade Lecture, John Marshall Law School 2003; Distinguished Alumni Citation, St. Lawrence University 2003; Italian Board of Guardians Public Service Award 2003; director and member Respect For Law Alliance Inc.; Executive Committee member and past president Theodore Roosevelt American Inn of Court; past president Protestant Lawyers Association of Long Island; member Vestry, St. Thomas's Episcopal Church, Farmingdale, NY; married to Nancy Endruschat (deceased); children: Gregory Wright, Jr., John Frederick, James Matthew, and Mira Catherine; married to Judith L. Dennehy.

DONALD C. POGUE, judge; graduated *magna cum laude*, Phi Beta Kappa from Dartmouth College; did graduate work at the University of Essex, England; J.D., Yale Law School and a Masters of Philosophy, Yale University; married 1971; served as judge in Connecticut's Superior Court; appointed to the bench in 1994; served as chairman of Connecticut's Commission on Hospitals and Health Care; practiced law in Hartford for 15 years; lectured on labor law at the University of Connecticut School of Law; assisted in teaching the Harvard Law School's program on negotiations and dispute resolution for lawyers; chaired the Connecticut Bar Association's Labor and Employment Law Section; appointed a Judge of the United States Court of International Trade in 1995; chair of the Court's Long Range Planning Committee, and of its Budget Committee; member of the Judicial Conference's Committee on the Administrative Office; serviced by designation in the 2d, 3d, 5th, 9th, 11th and Federal Circuits and in the D.C. and New York Southern district courts.

EVAN J. WALLACH, judge; born in Superior, AZ, November 11, 1949; son of Albert A. and Sara F. Wallach; married to Katherine Colleen Tobin, 1992; graduate of Acalanes High School, Lafayette, CA, 1967; attended Diablo Valley Junior College, Pleasant Hill, CA, 1967–68; news editor, Viking Reporter; member Alfa Gamma Sigma, National Junior College Honor Society, member, Junior Varsity Wrestling Team; enlisted United States Army, January, 1969, PVT–SGT, served as Reconnaissance Sergeant 8th Engineer Bn., 1st Calvary Division (Air Mobile), Republic of Vietnam, 1970–71, Bronze Star Medal, Air Medal, Valorous Unit Citation, Good Conduct Medal; attended University of Arizona, 1971–73, graduated B.A., Journalism (high honors), Phi Beta Kappa, Phi Kappa Phi, Kappa Tau Alfa, Rufenacht French Language Prize, Douglas Martin Journalism Scholarship; attended University of California, Berkeley, 1973–76, graduated J.D., 1976, research assistant to Prof. Melvin Eisenberg, member of University of California Honor Society; Associate (1976–82) and Partner (1983–95) Lionel Sawyer and Collins, Las Vegas, NV with emphasis on media representation; attended Cambridge University, Cambridge, England, LL.B. (international law) (honors), 1981, member Hughes Hall College Rowing Club, Cambridge University Tennis Club; elected, Honorary Fellow Hughes Hall College, 2008–present; General Counsel and Public Policy Advisor to U.S. Senator Harry Reid (D) of Nevada, 1987–88; served CAPT–MAJ Nevada Army National Guard, 1989–95; served as Attorney / Advisor, International Affairs Division; Office of the Judge Advocate General of the Army, February–June, 1991–92; Meritorious Service Medal (oak leaf cluster); Nevada Medal of Merit; General Counsel, Nevada Democratic Party, 1978–80, 1982–86; General Counsel, Reid for Congress campaign, 1982, 1984; Reid for Senate campaign, 1986, 1992; General Counsel, Bryan for Senate campaign, 1988; Nevada State Director, Mondale for President campaign, 1984; State Director, Nevada and Arizona Gore for President campaign, 1988; General Counsel Nevada Assembly Democratic Caucus, 1990–95; General Counsel, Society for Professional Journalists, 1988–95; General Counsel, Nevada Press Association, 1989–95; awarded American Bar Association Liberty Bell Award, 1993; Nevada State Press Association President's Award, 1994; Clark County School Librarians Intellectual Freedom Award, 1995; Law of War, Adjunct Professor, New York Law School, 1997–present; Brooklyn Law School 2000–present; member, Nevada Bar Association, 1977; U.S. District Court, District of Nevada, 1977; District of Columbia, 1988; Ninth Circuit Court of Appeals, 1989; American Law Institute and ALI Adviser on Principles of World Trade Law: National Treatment; author, *Legal Handbook for Nevada Reporters* (1994); Comparison of British and American Defense Based Prior Restraint, *ICLQ* (1984); Treatment of Crude Oil As A War Munition, *ICLQ* (1992); Three Ways Nevada Unconstitutionally Chills The Media; Nevada Lawyer (1994); Co-Editor, *Nevada Civil Practice Handbook* (1993); Extradition to the Rwandan War Crimes Tribunal: Is Another Treaty Required, *USCLA Journal of International Law and Foreign Affairs* (Spring / Summer, 1998); The Procedural and Evidentiary Rules of the Post World War II War Crimes Trials: Did They Provide An Outline For International Criminal Procedure? *Columbia Journal of Translational Law* (Spring, 1999); Webmaster, International Law of War Association, lawofwar.org; Afghanistan, Yamashita and Uchiyama: Does the Sauce Suit the Gander? *The Army Lawyer* (June 2003); The Logical Nexus Between the Decision to Deny Application of the Third Geneva Convention to the Taliban and Al Queda and the Mistreatment of Prisoners of War in Abu Ghraib, *Case Western Reserve Journal of International Law 541* (2004); Drop by Drop: Forgetting the History of Water Torture in U.S. Courts, *Columbia Journal of Transnational Law* (2007). Command Responsiblity, co-author of *Chapter in Bassouni,* International Criminal Law (3rd Ed.) (2008).

JUDITH M. BARZILAY, judge; born in Russell, KS, January 3, 1944; husband, Sal (Doron) Barzilay; children, Ilan and Michael; parents, Arthur and Hilda Morgenstern; B.A., Wichita State University, 1965; M.L.S., Rutgers University School of Library and Information Science, 1971; J.D., Rutgers University School of Law, 1981, Moot Court Board, 1980–81; trial attorney, U.S. Department of Justice (International Trade Field Office), 1983–86; litigation associate, Siegel, Mandell and Davidson, New York, NY, 1986–88; Sony Corporation of America, 1988–98; customs and international trade counsel, 1988–89; vice-president for import and export operations, 1989–96; vice-president for government affairs, 1996–98; executive board of the American Association of Exporters and Importers, 1993–98; appointed by Treasury Secretary Robert Rubin to the Advisory Committee on Commercial Operations of the United

States Customs Service, 1995–98; nominated for appointment on January 27, 1998 by President Clinton; sworn in as judge June 3, 1998.

DELISSA A. RIDGWAY, judge; born in Kirksville, MO, June 28, 1955; B.A. (honors), University of Missouri-Columbia, 1975; graduate work, University of Missouri-Columbia, 1975–76; J.D., Northeastern University School of Law, 1979; Shaw Pittman Potts & Trowbridge (Washington, DC), 1979–94; Chair, Foreign Claims Settlement Commission of the U.S., 1994–98; Adjunct Professor of Law, Cornell Law School, 1999–present; Adjunct Professor of Law, Washington College of Law/The American University, 1992–94; District of Columbia bar, Secretary, 1991–92; Board of Governors, 1992–98; President, Women's Bar Association, 1992–93; American Bar Association, Commission on Women in the Profession, 2002–09; Federal Bar Association, National Council, 1993–2002, 2003–05; Government Relations Committee, 1996–2008, Public Relations Committee Chair, 1998–99; Executive Committee, National Conference of Federal Trial Judges, 2004–present; chair, National Conference of Federal Trial Judges, 2009–10; Founding Member of Board, D.C. Conference on Opportunities for Minorities in the Legal Profession, 1992–93; Chair, D.C. Bar Summit on Women in the Legal Profession, 1995–98; Fellow, American Bar Foundation; Member, American Law Institute; Fellow, Federal Bar Foundation; Earl W. Kintner Award of the Federal Bar Association (2000); Woman Lawyer of the Year, Washington, DC (2001); Distinguished Visiting Scholar-in-Residence, University of Missouri-Columbia (2003); sworn in as a judge to the U.S. Court of International Trade in May 1998.

RICHARD K. EATON, judge; born in Walton, NY; married to Susan Henshaw Jones; two children: Alice and Elizabeth; attended Walton public schools; B.A., Ithaca College, J.D., Union University Albany Law School, 1974; professional experience: Eaton and Eaton, partner; Mudge Rose Guthrie Alexander & Ferdon, New York, NY, associate and partner; Stroock & Stroock & Lavan, partner served on the staff of Senator Daniel Patrick Moynihan; confirmed by the United States Senate to the U.S. Court of International Trade on October 22, 1999.

TIMOTHY C. STANCEU, judge; born in Canton, OH; A.B., Colgate University, 1973; J.D., Georgetown University Law Center, 1979; appointed to the U.S. Court of International Trade by President George W. Bush and began serving on April 15, 2003; prior to appointment, private practice for thirteen years in Washington, DC, with the law firm Hogan & Hartson, L.L.P., during which he represented clients in a variety of matters involving customs and international trade law; Deputy Director, Office of Trade and Tariff Affairs, U.S. Department of the Treasury; where his responsibilities involved the regulatory and enforcement matters of the U.S. Customs Service and other agencies; Special Assistant to the Assistant Secretary of the Office of Enforcement, U.S. Department of the Treasury; Program Analyst and Environmental Protection Specialist, U.S. Environmental Protection Agency, where he concentrated on the development and review of regulations on various environmental subjects.

LEO M. GORDON, judge; graduate of Newark Academy in Livingston, NJ; University of North Carolina—Chapel Hill, Phi Beta Kappa, 1973; J.D., Emory University School of Law, 1977; member of the Bars of New Jersey, Georgia and the District of Columbia; Assistant Counsel at the Subcommittee on Monopolies and Commercial Law, Committee on the Judiciary, U.S. House of Representatives, 1977–78; in that capacity, Judge Gordon was the principal attorney responsible for the Customs Courts Act of 1980 that created the U.S. Court of International Trade; for the past 25 years of his career, Judge Gordon was on the staff at the Court, serving first as Assistant Clerk from 1981–99, and then Clerk of the Court from 1999–2006; appointed to the U.S. Court of International Trade in March 2006.

SENIOR JUDGES

THOMAS J. AQUILINO, Jr., senior judge; born in Mount Kisco, NY, December 7, 1939; son of Thomas J. and Virginia B. (Doughty) Aquilino; married to Edith Berndt Aquilino; children: Christopher Thomas, Philip Andrew, Alexander Berndt; attended Cornell University, 1957–59; B.A., Drew University, 1959–60, 1961–62; University of Munich, Germany, 1960–61; Free University of Berlin, Germany, 1965–66; J.D., Rutgers University School of Law, 1966–69; research assistant, Prof. L.F.E. Goldie (Resources for the Future—Ford Foundation), 1967–69; administrator, Northern Region, 1969 Jessup International Law Moot Court Competition; served in the U.S. Army, 1962–65; law clerk, Hon. John M. Cannella, U.S. District Court for the Southern District of New York, 1969–71; attorney with Davis Polk & Wardwell, New York, NY, 1971–85; admitted to practice New York, U.S. Supreme Court, U.S. Courts of Appeals for Second and Third Circuits, U.S. Court of International Trade, U.S. Court of Claims, U.S. District Courts for Eastern, Southern and Northern Districts of New York,

Interstate Commerce Commission; adjunct professor of law, Benjamin N. Cardozo School of Law, 1984–95; Mem., Drew University Board of Visitors, 1997–present; appointed to the U.S. Court of International Trade by President Reagan on February 22, 1985; confirmed by U.S. Senate, April 3, 1985.

NICHOLAS TSOUCALAS, senior judge; born in New York, NY, August 24, 1926; one of five children of George M. and Maria (Monogenis) Tsoucalas; married to Catherine Aravantinos; two daughters: Stephanie and Georgia; five grandchildren; B.S., Kent State University, 1949; LL.B., New York Law School, 1951; attended New York University Law School; entered U.S. Navy, 1944–46; served in the American and European Theaters of War on board the USS *Oden,* the USS *Monticello* and USS *Europa;* reentered Navy, 1951–52 and served on the carrier, USS *Wasp;* admitted to New York bar, 1953; appointed Assistant U.S. Attorney for the Southern District of New York, 1955–59; appointed in 1959 as supervisor of 1960 census for the 17th and 18th Congressional Districts; appointed chairman, Board of Commissioners of Appraisal; appointed judge of Criminal Court of the City of New York, 1968; designated acting Supreme Court Justice, Kings and Queens Counties, 1975–82; resumed service as judge of the Criminal Court of the City of New York until June 1986; former chairman: Committee on Juvenile Delinquency, Federal Bar Association, and the Subcommittee on Public Order and Responsibility of the American Citizenship Committee of the New York County Lawyers' Association; member of the American Bar Association, New York State Bar Association; founder of Eastern Orthodox Lawyers' Association; former president: Greek-American Lawyers' Association, and Board of Directors of Greek Orthodox Church of ''Evangelismos'', St. John's Theologos Society, and Parthenon Foundation; member, Order of Ahepa, Parthenon Lodge, F.A.M.; appointed judge of the U.S. Court of International Trade by President Reagan on September 9, 1985, and confirmed by U.S. Senate on June 6, 1986; assumed senior status on September 30, 1996.

R. KENTON MUSGRAVE, senior judge; born in Clearwater, FL, September 7, 1927; married May 7, 1949 to former Ruth Shippen Hoppe, of Atlanta, GA; three children: Laura Marie Musgrave (deceased), Ruth Shippen Musgrave, Esq., and Forest Kenton Musgrave; attended Augusta Academy (Virginia); B.A., University of Washington, 1948; editorial staff, Journal of International Law, Emory University; J.D., with distinction, Emory University, 1953; assistant general counsel, Lockheed Aircraft and Lockheed International, 1953–62; vice president and general counsel, Mattel, Inc., 1963–71; director, Ringling Bros. and Barnum and Bailey Combined Shows, Inc., 1968–72; commissioner, BSA (Atlanta), 1952–55; partner, Musgrave, Welbourn and Fertman, 1972–75; assistant general counsel, Pacific Enterprises, 1975–81; vice president, general counsel and secretary, Vivitar Corporation, 1981–85; vice president and director, Santa Barbara Applied Research Corp., 1982–87; trustee, Morris Animal Foundation, 1981–94; director Emeritus, Pet Protection Society, 1981–present; director, Dolphins of Shark Bay (Australia) Foundation, 1985–present; trustee, The Dian Fossey Gorilla Fund, 1987–present; trustee, The Ocean Conservancy, 2000–present; vice president and director, South Bay Social Services Group, 1963–70; director, Palos Verdes Community Arts Association, 1973–79; member, Governor of Florida's Council of 100, 1970–73; director, Orlando Bank and Trust, 1970–73; counsel, League of Women Voters, 1964–66; member, State Bar of Georgia, 1953–present; State Bar of California, 1962–present; Los Angeles County Bar Association, 1962–87 and chairman, Corporate Law Departments Section, 1965–66; admitted to practice before the U.S. Supreme Court, 1962; Supreme Court of Georgia, 1953; California Supreme Court, 1962; U.S. Customs Court, 1967; U.S. Court of International Trade, 1980; nominated to the U.S. Court of International Trade by President Reagan on July 1, 1987; confirmed by the Senate on November 9, and took oath of office on November 13, 1987.

RICHARD W. GOLDBERG, senior judge; born in Fargo, ND, September 23, 1927; married; two children, a daughter and a son; J.D., University of Miami, 1952; served on active duty as an Air Force Judge Advocate, 1953–56; admitted to Washington, DC bar, Florida bar and North Dakota bar; from 1959 to 1983, owned and operated a regional grain processing firm in North Dakota; served as State Senator from North Dakota for eight years; taught military law for the Army and Air Force ROTC at North Dakota State University; was vice-chairman of the board of Minneapolis Grain Exchange; joined the Reagan administration in 1983 in Washington at the U.S. Department of Agriculture; served as Deputy Under Secretary for International Affairs and Commodity Programs and later as Acting Under Secretary; in 1990 joined the Washington, DC law firm of Anderson, Hibey and Blair; appointed judge of the U.S. Court of International Trade in 1991; assumed senior status in 2001.

Officers of the United States Court of International Trade

Clerk.—Tina Potuto Kimble (212) 264–2814.

UNITED STATES COURT OF FEDERAL CLAIMS

Lafayette Square, 717 Madison Place, NW., 20005, phone (202) 219–9657

EDWARD J. DAMICH, chief judge; born in Pittsburgh, PA, June 19, 1948; son of John and Josephine (Lovrencic) Damich; A.B., St. Stephen's College, 1970; J.D., Catholic University, 1976; professor of law at Delaware School of Law of Widener University, 1976–84; served as a Law and Economics Fellow at Columbia University School of Law, where he earned his L.L.M. in 1983 and his J.S.D. in 1991; professor of law at George Mason University, 1984–98; appointed by President George H.W. Bush to be a Commissioner of the Copyright Royalty Tribunal, 1992–93; Chief Intellectual Property Counsel for the Senate Judiciary Committee, 1995–98; admitted to the Bars of the District of Columbia and Pennsylvania; member of the District of Columbia Bar Association, Pennsylvania Bar Association, American Bar Association, Supreme Court of the United States, the Federal Circuit and *Association litteraire et artistique internationale;* president of the National Federation of Croatian Americans, 1994–95; appointed by President Clinton as judge, U.S. Court of Federal Claims, October 22, 1998; appointed by President George W. Bush as chief judge, U.S. Court of Federal Claims, May 13, 2002; at present Judge Damich is an adjunct professor of law at the Georgetown University Law Center.

LAWRENCE M. BASKIR, judge; born in Brooklyn, NY, January 10, 1938; married to Marna Tucker, two children; A.B., *magna cum laude*, Princeton University; Woodrow Wilson School of Public and International Affairs, 1959; LL.B., Harvard Law School, 1962; Principal Deputy General Counsel, Department of the Army, 1994–98; private practice and Editor-In-Chief, Military Law Reporter, 1981–94; Legislative Director to Senator Bill Bradley, 1979–81; Deputy Assistant Secretary (Legislation), Office of the Secretary, Department of the Treasury, 1977–79; Director, Vietnam Offender Study; Faculty Fellow, University of Notre Dame Law School, 1975–77; Director, Presidential (Ford) Clemancy Board, White House, 1974–75; Chief Counsel, Subcommittees on Constitutional Rights and Separation of Powers, Senate Judiciary Committee, Senator Sam J. Ervin, Chairman, 1967–74; publications include *Chance and Circumstances: The Draft, the War and the Vietnam Generation*; consultant to Information Intelligence Committees, U.S. Congress; Adjunct Professor and Lecturer, Georgetown, Notre Dame, Catholic Law Schools, and American University; appointed judge of the U.S. Court of Federal Claims on October 22, 1998; chief judge, July 11, 2000 to May 10, 2002.

CHRISTINE ODELL COOK "O.C." MILLER, judge; born in Oakland, CA, August 26, 1944; married to Dennis F. Miller; B.A., Stanford University, 1966; J.D., University of Utah College of Law, 1969; Comment Editor, Utah Law Review; member, Utah Chapter Order of the Coif; Clerk to Chief Judge David T. Lewis, U.S. Court of Appeals for the 10th Circuit; trial attorney, Civil Division, U.S. Department of Justice; trial attorney, Federal Trade Commission, Bureau of Consumer Protection; Hogan and Hartson, litigation section; Pension Benefit Guaranty Corporation, Special Counsel; U.S. Railway Association, Assistant General Counsel; Shack and Kimball P.C., litigation; member of the Bars of the State of California and District of Columbia; member of the University Club and the Cosmos Club; appointed to the U.S. Court of Federal Claims by President Reagan on December 10, 1982, and confirmed as Christine Cook Nettsheim; reappointed by President Clinton on February 4, 1998.

MARIAN BLANK HORN, judge; born in New York, NY, 1943; daughter of Werner P. and Mady R. Blank; married to Robert Jack Horn; three daughters; attended Fieldston School, New York, NY, Barnard College, Columbia University and Fordham University School of Law; admitted to practice U.S. Supreme Court, 1973, Federal and State courts in New York, 1970, and Washington, DC, 1973; assistant district attorney, Deputy Chief Appeals Bureau, Bronx County, NY, 1969–72; attorney, Arent, Fox, Kintner, Plotkin and Kahn, 1972–73; adjunct professor of law, Washington College of Law, American University, 1973–76; litigation attorney, Federal Energy Administration, 1975–76; senior attorney, Office of General

Counsel, Strategic Petroleum Reserve Branch, Department of Energy, 1976–79; deputy assistant general counsel for procurement and financial incentives, Department of Energy, 1979–81; deputy associate solicitor, Division of Surface Mining, Department of the Interior, 1981–83; associate solicitor, Division of General Law, Department of the Interior, 1983–85; principal deputy solicitor and acting solicitor, Department of Interior, 1985–86; adjunct professor of law, George Washington University National Law Center, 1991–present; Woodrow Wilson Visiting Fellow, 1994; assumed duties of judge, U.S. Court of Federal Claims in 1986 and confirmed for a second term in 2003.

LYNN J. BUSH, judge; born in Little Rock, AR, December 30, 1948; daughter of John E. Bush III and Alice (Saville) Bush; one son, Brian Bush Ferguson; B.A., Antioch College, 1970, Thomas J. Watson Fellow; J.D., Georgetown University Law Center, 1976; admitted to the Arkansas Bar in 1976 and to the District of Columbia Bar in 1977; trial attorney, Commercial Litigation Branch, Civil Division, U.S. Department of Justice, 1976–87; senior trial attorney, Naval Facilities Engineering Command, Department of the Navy, 1987–89; counsel, Engineering Field Activity Chesapeake, Naval Facilities Engineering Command, Department of the Navy, 1989–96; administrative judge, U.S. Department of Housing and Urban Development Board of Contract Appeals, 1996–98; nominated by President Clinton to the U.S. Court of Federal Claims, June 22, 1998; and assumed duties of the office on October 26, 1998.

NANCY B. FIRESTONE, judge; born in Manchester, NH, October 17, 1951; B.A., Washington University, 1973; J.D., University of Missouri, Kansas City, 1977; one child: Amanda Leigh; attorney, Appellate Section and Environmental Enforcement Section, U.S. Department of Justice, Washington, DC, 1977–84; Assistant Chief, Policy Legislation and Special Litigation, Environment and Natural Resources Division, Department of Justice, Washington, DC, 1984–85; Deputy Chief, Environmental Enforcement Section, Department of Justice, Washington, DC, 1985–89; Associate Deputy Administrator, Environmental Protection Agency, Washington, DC, 1989–92; Judge, Environmental Appeals Board, Environmental Protection Agency, Washington, DC, 1992–95; Deputy Assistant Attorney General, Environment and Natural Resources Division, Department of Justice, Washington, DC, 1995–98; Adjunct Professor, Georgetown University Law Center, 1985–present; appointed to the U.S. Court of Federal Claims by President Clinton on October 22, 1998.

EMILY CLARK HEWITT, judge; born in Baltimore, MD, May 26, 1944; educated at the Roland Park Country School, Baltimore, MD, 1949–62; A.B., Cornell University, 1966; M. Phil., Union Theological Seminary, 1975; J.D. c.l., Harvard Law School, 1978; ordained minister in the Episcopal Church (diaconate, 1972; priesthood, 1974); member, Bar of the Supreme Judicial Court of The Commonwealth of Massachusetts, 1978; administrator, Cornell / Hofstra Upward Bound Program, 1967–69; lecturer, Union Theological Seminary, 1972–73 and 1974–75; assistant professor, Andover Newton Theological School, 1973–75; private practice of law, Hill & Barlow, 1978–93; council member, Real Property Section, Massachusetts Bar Association, 1983–86; member, Executive Committee and chair, Practice Standards Committee, Massachusetts Conveyancers Association, 1990–92; General Counsel, U.S. General Services Administration, 1993–98; member, Administrative Conference of the United States, 1993–95; member, President's Interagency Council on Women, 1995–98; appointed to the U.S. Court of Federal Claims on October 22, 1998; entered duty on November 10, 1998.

FRANCIS M. ALLEGRA, judge; born in Cleveland, OH, October 14, 1957; married to Regina Allegra; one child (Domenic); B.A., Borromeo College of Ohio, 1978; J.D., Cleveland State University, 1981; judicial clerk to Chief Trial Judge Philip R. Miller, U.S. Court of Claims, 1981–82; associate, Squire, Sanders & Dempsey (Cleveland), 1982–84; line attorney, Appellate Section, then 1984–89, Counselor to the Assistant Attorney General, both with Tax Division, U.S. Department of Justice; Counselor to the Associate Attorney General (1994) then Deputy Associate Attorney General (1994–98), U.S. Department of Justice; appointed to the U.S. Court of Federal Claims on October 22, 1998.

LAWRENCE J. BLOCK, judge, born in New York City, March 15, 1951; son of Jerome Block and Eve Silver; B.A., *magna cum laude,* New York University, 1973; J.D., The John Marshall Law School, 1981; law clerk for Hon. Roger J. Miner, United States District Court Judge for Northern District of New York, 1981–83; Associate, New York office of Skadden, Arps, Slate, Meagher and Flom, 1983–86; Attorney, Commercial Litigation Branch, U.S. Department of Justice, 1986; Senior Attorney-Advisor, Office of Legal Policy and Policy Development, U.S. Department of Justice, 1987–90; adjunct professor, George Mason University School of Law, 1990–91; acting general counsel for legal policy and deputy assistant general counsel for legal policy, U.S. Department of Energy, 1990–94; senior counsel, Senate

Judiciary Committee, 1994–02; admitted to the bar of Connecticut; admitted to practice in the U.S. Supreme Court, 1982, the United States District Court for the northern district of New York, 1982, the U.S. Court of Appeals for the Eleventh Circuit, 1985, the United States District Court for the Eastern District of New York, 1985; appointed by President George W. Bush on October 3, 2002, to a 15-years term as judge, U.S. Court of Federal Claims.

SUSAN G. BRADEN, judge, born in Youngstown, OH, November 8, 1948; married to Thomas M. Susman; daughter (Daily); B.A., Case Western Reserve University, 1970; J.D., Case Western Reserve University School of Law, 1973; post graduate study Harvard Law School, Summer, 1979; private practice, 1985–2003 (1997–2003 Baker & McKenzie); Federal Trade Commission: Special Counsel to Chairman, 1984–85, Senior Attorney Advisor to Commissioner and Acting Chairman, 1980–83; U.S. Department of Justice, Antitrust Division, Senior Trial Attorney, Energy Section, 1978–80; Cleveland Field Office, 1973–78; Special Assistant Attorney General for the State of Alabama, 1990; Consultant to the Administrative Conference of the United States, 1984–85; 2000 Co-Chair, Lawyers for Bush-Cheney; General Counsel Presidential Debate for Dole-Kemp Campaign, 1996; Counsel to RNC Platform, 1996; Coordinator for Regulatory Reform and Antitrust Policy, Dole Presidential Campaign, 1995–96; National Steering Committee, Lawyers for Bush-Quayle, 1992; Assistant General Counsel, Republican National Convention, 1988, 1992, 1996, 2000; elected At-Large Member, D.C. Republican National Committee, 2000–02; member of the American Bar Association (Council Member, Section on Administrative Law and Regulatory Practice, 1996–99), Federal Circuit Bar Association, District of Columbia Bar Association, Computer Law Bar Association; admitted to the Supreme Court of Ohio, 1973, U.S. District Court for the District of Columbia, 1980, U.S. Supreme Court, 1980; U.S. Court of Appeals for the District of Columbia, 1992; U.S. Court of Appeals for the Second Circuit, 1993, U.S. Court of Appeals for the Federal Circuit, 2001; appointed to the U.S. Court of Federal Claims by President George W. Bush on July 14, 2003.

CHARLES F. LETTOW, judge, born in Iowa Falls, IA, February 10, 1941; son of Carl F. and Catherine Lettow; B.S.Ch.E., Iowa State University, 1962; LL.B., Stanford University, 1968, Order of the Coif; M.A., Brown University, 2001; Note Editor, Stanford Law Review; married to B. Sue Lettow; children: Renee Burnett, Carl Frederick II, John Stangland, and Paul Vorbeck; served U.S. Army, 1963–65; law clerk to Judge Ben C. Duniway, U.S. Court of Appeals for the Ninth Circuit, 1968–69, and Chief Justice Warren E. Burger, Supreme Court of the United States, 1969–70; counsel, Council on Environmental Quality, Executive Office of the President, 1970–73; associate (1973–76) and partner (1976–2003), Cleary, Gottlieb, Steen & Hamilton, Washington, DC; admitted to practice before the U.S. Supreme Court, the U.S. Courts of Appeals for the D.C., Second, Third, Fourth, Fifth, Sixth, Eighth, Ninth, Tenth, and Federal Circuits, the U.S. District Courts for the District of Columbia, the Northern District of California, and the District of Maryland, and the U.S. Court of Federal Claims; member: American Law Institute, the American Bar Association, the D.C. Bar, the California State Bar, the Iowa State Bar Association, and the Maryland State Bar; nominated by President George W. Bush to the U.S. Court of Federal Claims in 2001 and confirmed and took office in 2003.

MARY ELLEN COSTER WILLIAMS, judge; born in Flushing, NY, April 3, 1953; married to Mark Calhoun Williams; son: Justin; daughter: Jacquelyn; B.A. *summa cum laude* (Greek and Latin); M.A. (Latin), Catholic University, 1974; J.D. Duke University; Editorial Board, *Duke Law Journal,* 1976–77; admitted to the District of Columbia Bar; Associate, Fulbright and Jaworski, 1977–79; Associate, Schnader, Harrison, Segal and Lewis, 1979–83; Assistant U.S. Attorney, Civil Division, District of Columbia, 1983–87; Partner—Janis, Schuelke, and Wechsler, 1987–89; Administrative Judge, General Services Board of Contract Appeals March 1989–July 2003; Secretary, District of Columbia Bar, 1988–89; Fellow, American Bar Foundation, Elected, 1985; Board of Directors, Bar Association of District of Columbia, 1985–88; Chairman, Young Lawyers Section, Bar Association of District of Columbia, 1985–86; Chair, Public Contract Law Section of American Bar Association, 2002–03, Chair-Elect, Vice-Chair, Secretary, Council, 1995–2002; Delegate, Section of Public Contract Law, ABA House of Delegates 2003–04; Lecturer, Government Contract Law, 1989–present; appointed to the U.S. Court of Federal Claims on July 21, 2003.

VICTOR JOHN WOLSKI, judge; born in New Brunswick, NJ, November 14, 1962; son of Vito and Eugenia Wolski; B.A., B.S., University of Pennsylvania, 1984; J.D., University of Virginia School of Law, 1991; married to Lisa Wolski, June 3, 2000; admitted to Supreme Court of the United States, 1995; California Supreme Court, 1992; Washington Supreme Court, 1994; Oregon Supreme Court, 1996; District of Columbia Court of Appeals, 2001;

U.S. Court of Appeals for the Ninth Circuit, 1993; U.S. Court of Appeals for the Federal Circuit, 2001; U.S. District Court for the Eastern District of California, 1993; U.S. District Court for the Northern District of California, 1995; U.S. Court of Federal Claims, 2001; U.S. District Court for the District of Columbia, 2002; research assistant, Center for Strategic and International Studies, 1984–85; research associate, Institute for Political Economy, 1985–88; Confidential Assistant and Speechwriter to the Secretary, U.S. Dept. of Agriculture, 1988; paralegal specialist, Office of the General Counsel, U.S. Dept. of Energy, 1989; law clerk to Judge Vaughn R. Walker, U.S. District Court for the Northern District of California, 1991–92; attorney, Pacific Legal Foundation, 1992–97; General Counsel, Sacramento County Republican Central Committee, 1995–97; Counsel to Senator Connie Mack, Vice-Chairman of the Joint Economic Committee, U.S. Congress, 1997–98; General Counsel and Chief Tax Adviser, Joint Economic Committee, U.S. Congress, 1999–2000; associate, Cooper, Carvin & Rosenthal, 2000–01; associate, Cooper & Kirk, 2001–03; nominated by President George W. Bush to the U.S. Court of Federal Claims on September 12, 2002, renominated January 7, 2003, and confirmed by U.S. Senate on July 9, 2003.

THOMAS C. WHEELER, judge; born in Chicago, IL, March 18, 1948; married; two grown children; B.A., Gettysburg College, 1970; J.D., Georgetown University Law School, 1973; private practice in Washington, DC, 1973–2005; associate and partner, Pettit & Martin until 1995; partner, Piper & Marbury (later Piper Marbury Rudnick & Wolfe, and then DLA Piper Rudnick Gray Cary); member of the District of Columbia Bar; American Bar Association's Public Contracts and Litigation Sections; appointed to the U.S. Court of Federal Claims on October 24, 2005.

MARGARET M. SWEENEY, judge; born in Baltimore, MD; B.A. in history, Notre Dame of Maryland, 1977; J.D., Delaware Law School, 1981; Delaware Family Court Master, 1981–83; litigation associate, Fedorko, Gilbert, & Lanctot, Morrisville, PA, 1983–85; law clerk to Hon. Loren A. Smith, Chief Judge of the U.S. Court of Federal Claims, 1985–87; Trial Attorney in the General Litigation Section of the Environment and Natural Resources Division of the United States Department of Justice, 1987–99; President, U.S. Court of Federal Claims Bar Association, 1999; Attorney Advisor, United States Department of Justice Office of Intelligence Policy and Review, 1999–2003; Special Master, U.S. Court of Federal Claims, 2003–05; member of the bars of the Supreme Court of Pennsylvania and the District of Columbia Court of Appeals; appointed to the U.S. Court of Federal Claims by President George W. Bush on October 24, 2005, and entered duty on December 14, 2005.

SENIOR JUDGES

THOMAS J. LYDON, senior judge; born in Portland, ME, June 3, 1927; educated in the parochial and public schools in Portland; B.A., University of Maine, 1948–52; LL.B. (1952–55) and LL.M. (1956–57), Georgetown University Law Center; trial attorney, Civil Division, Department of Justice, 1955–67; Chief, Court of Claims Section, Civil Division, 1967–72; trial commissioner (trial judge), U.S. Court of Claims, 1972 to September 30, 1982; judge, U.S. Claims Court, October 1, 1982–July 31, 1987; senior judge, August 1, 1987–present.

JAMES F. MEROW, senior judge; born in Salamanca, NY, March 16, 1932; educated in the public schools of Little Valley, NY and Alexandria, VA; A.B. (with distinction), The George Washington University, 1953; J.D. (with distinction), The George Washington University Law School, 1956; member: Phi Beta Kappa, Order of the Coif, Omicron Delta Kappa; married; officer, U.S. Army Judge Advocate General's Corps, 1956–59; trial attorney-branch director, Civil Division, U.S. Department of Justice, 1959–78; trial judge, U.S. Court of Claims, 1978–82; member of Virginia State Bar, District of Columbia Bar, American Bar Association, and Federal Bar Association; judge, U.S. Court of Federal Claims since October 1, 1982 and reappointed by President Reagan to a 15-year term commencing August 5, 1983.

REGINALD W. GIBSON, senior judge; born in Lynchburg, VA, July 31, 1927; son of McCoy and Julia Gibson; son, Reginald S. Gibson, Jr.; educated in the public schools of Washington, DC; served in the U.S. Army, 1946–47; B.S., Virginia Union University, 1952; Wharton Graduate School of Business Administration, University of Pennsylvania, 1952–53; LL.B., Howard University School of Law, 1956; admitted to the District of Columbia Bar in 1957 and to the Illinois Bar in 1972; Internal Revenue agent, Internal Revenue Service, Washington, DC, 1957–61; trial attorney, tax division, criminal section, Department of Justice, Washington, DC, 1961–71; senior and later general tax attorney, International Harvester Co.,

Chicago, IL, 1971–82; judge, U.S. Court of Federal Claims, December 15, 1982–August 15, 1995; senior status, August 15, 1995–present.

JOHN PAUL WIESE, senior judge; born in Brooklyn, NY, April 19, 1934; son of Gustav and Margaret Wiese; B.A., *cum laude*, Hobart College, 1962, Phi Beta Kappa; LL.B., University of Virginia School of Law, 1965; married to Alice Mary Donoghue, June, 1961; one son, John Patrick; served U.S. Army, 1957–59; law clerk: U.S. Court of Claims, trial division, 1965–66, and Judge Linton M. Collins, U.S. Court of Claims, appellate division, 1966–67; private practice in District of Columbia, 1967–74 (specializing in government contract litigation); trial judge, U.S. Court of Claims, 1974–82; admitted to bar of the District of Columbia, 1966; admitted to practice in the U.S. Supreme Court, the U.S. Court of Appeals for the Federal Circuit, the U.S. Court of Federal Claims; member: District of Columbia Bar Association and American Bar Association; designated in Federal Courts Improvement Act of 1982 as judge, U.S. Court of Federal Claims and reappointed by President Reagan to 15-year term on October 14, 1986.

ROBERT J. YOCK, senior judge; born in St. James, MN, January 11, 1938; son of Dr. William J. and Erma Yock; B.A. St. Olaf College, 1959; J.D., University of Michigan Law School, 1962; married to Carla M. Moen, June 13, 1964; children: Signe Kara and Torunn Ingrid; admitted to the Minnesota Supreme Court in 1962; Court of Military Appeals, 1964; U.S. Supreme Court, 1965; U.S. District Court for the District of Minnesota, 1966; U.S. District Court for the District of Columbia, 1972; U.S. Court of Claims, 1979; and U.S. Court of Federal Claims, 1982; member: Minnesota State Bar Association, and District of Columbia Bar Association; served in the U.S. Navy, Judge Advocate General's Corps, 1962–66; private practice, St. Paul, MN, 1966–69; entered Government service as chief counsel to the National Archives and Record Services of the General Services Administration, 1969–70; executive assistant and legal advisor to the Administrator of General Services, 1970–72; assistant general counsel at GSA, 1972–77; trial judge, U.S. Court of Claims, 1977–82; designated by Public Law 97–164 as judge, U.S. Court of Federal Claims, 1982–83; renominated by President Reagan as judge, U.S. Court of Federal Claims, June 20, 1983, confirmed by U.S. Senate, August 4, 1983, reappointed to 15-year term, August 5, 1983.

LAWRENCE S. MARGOLIS, senior judge; born in Philadelphia, PA, March 13, 1935; son of Reuben and Mollie Margolis; B.A., Central High School, Philadelphia, PA; B.S. in mechanical engineering from the Drexel Institute of Technology (now Drexel University), 1957; J.D., George Washington University Law School, 1961; married to Doris May Rosenberg, January 30, 1960; children: Mary Aleta and Paul Oliver; admitted to the District of Columbia Bar; patent examiner, U.S. Patent Office, 1957–62; patent counsel, Naval Ordnance Laboratory, White Oak, MD, 1962–63; assistant corporation counsel for the District of Columbia, 1963–66; attorney, criminal division, U.S. Department of Justice and special assistant U.S. attorney for District of Columbia, 1966–68; assistant U.S. attorney for the District of Columbia, 1968–71; appointed U.S. magistrate for District of Columbia in 1971; reappointed for a second 8-year term in 1979 and served until December, 1982 when appointed a judge, U.S. Court of Federal Claims; chairman, U.S. Court of Federal Claims: Security Committee, Building Committee, and Alternative Dispute Resolution Committee; chairman, American Bar Association, judicial administration division, 1980–81; chairman, National Conference of Special Court Judges, 1977–78; board of directors, Bar Association of the District of Columbia, 1970–72; editor: DC Bar Journal, 1966–73, Young Lawyers Newspaper editor, 1965–66; executive council, Young Lawyers Section, 1968–69; board of editors, The Judges' Journal and The District Lawyer; president, George Washington University National Law Association, 1983–84; president, George Washington Law Association, District of Columbia Chapter, 1975–76; board of governors, George Washington University General Alumni Association, 1978–85; fellow, Institute of Judicial Administration, 1993–present; member, District of Columbia Judicial Conference; former member, board of directors, National Council of U.S. Magistrates; former president, Federal Bar Toastmasters; former technical editor, Federal Bar Journal; faculty, Federal Judicial Center; trustee, Drexel University, 1983–91; member, Rotary Club; Board of Managers, Central High (Philadelphia, PA); president, Washington, DC, Rotary Club, 1988–89, District governor, 1991–92; American Bar Association Judicial Administration Division Award for distinguished service as chairman for 1980–81; Drexel University and George Washington University Distinguished Alumni Achievement Awards; Drexel University 100 (one of top 100 graduates); Center for Public Resources Alternative Dispute Resolution Achievement Award, 1987; George Washington University Community Service Award; nominated by President Ronald Reagan as a judge on the U.S. Court of Federal Claims on September 27, 1982, confirmed by the Senate and received Commission on December 10, 1982, took oath of office on December 15, 1982.

LOREN ALLAN SMITH, senior judge; born in Chicago, IL, December 22, 1944; son of Alvin D. and Selma (Halpern) Smith; B.A., Northwestern University, 1966; J.D., Northwestern University School of Law, 1969; married; admitted to the Bars of the Illinois Supreme Court; the Court of Military Appeals; the U.S. Court of Appeals, District of Columbia Circuit; the U.S. Court of Appeals for the Federal Circuit; the U.S. Supreme Court; the U.S. Court of Federal Claims; honorary member: The University Club; consultant, Sidley and Austin Chicago, 1972–73; general attorney, Federal Communications Commission, 1973; assistant to the Special Counsel to the President, 1973–74; Special Assistant U.S. Attorney, District of Columbia, 1974–75; chief counsel, Reagan for President campaigns, 1976 and 1980; professor, Delaware Law School, 1976–84; distinguished lecturer at Columbus School of Law, The Catholic University of America and distinguished adjunct professor at George Mason University School of Law; deputy director, Executive Branch Management Office of Presidential Transition, 1980–81; Chairman, Administrative Conference of the Unites States, 1981–85; served as a member of the President's Cabinet Councils on Legal Policy and on Management and Administration; appointed to the U.S. Court of Federal Claims on July 11, 1985; entered on duty September 12, 1985; served as chief judge from January 14, 1986, until July 11, 2000.

ERIC G. BRUGGINK, senior judge; born in Kalidjati, Indonesia, September 11, 1949; naturalized U.S. citizen, 1961; married to Melinda Harris Bruggink; sons: John and David; B.A., *cum laude* (sociology), Auburn University, AL, 1971; M.A. (speech), 1972; J.D., University of Alabama, 1975; Hugo Black Scholar and Note and Comments Editor of Alabama Law Review; member, Alabama State Bar and District of Columbia Bar; served as law clerk to chief judge Frank H. McFadden, Northern District of Alabama, 1975–76; associate, Hardwick, Hause and Segrest, Dothan, AL, 1976–77; assistant director, Alabama Law Institute, 1977–79; director, Office of Energy and Environmental Law, 1977–79; associate, Steiner, Crum and Baker, Montgomery, AL, 1979–82; Director, Office of Appeals Counsel, Merit Systems Protection Board, 1982–86; appointed to the U.S. Court of Federal Claims on April 15, 1986.

BOHDAN A. FUTEY, senior judge; born in Ukraine, June 28, 1939; B.A., Western Reserve University, 1962; M.A., 1964; J.D., Cleveland Marshall Law School, 1968; married to the former Myra Fur; three children: Andrew, Lidia, and Daria; partner, Futey and Rakowsky, 1968–72; chief assistant police prosecutor, city of Cleveland, 1972–74; executive assistant to the mayor of Cleveland, 1974–75; partner, Bazarko, Futey and Oryshkewych, 1975–84; chairman, U.S. Foreign Claims Settlement Commission, May 1984–87; member: District of Columbia Bar Association, the Ukrainian American Bar Association; actively involved with Democratization and Rule of Law programs organized by the Judicial Conference of the United States, the Department of State, and the American Bar Association in Ukraine and Russia; has participated in judicial exchange programs, seminars, and workshops and has been a consultant to the working group on Ukraine's Constitution and Ukrainian Parliament; advisor to the International Foundation for Election Systems (IFES) and the International Republican Institutes (IRI) democracy programs for Ukraine; served as an official observer during the parliamentary and presidential elections in 1994 and 1998 and conducted briefings on Ukraine's election law for international observers; has lectured on Constitutional Law at the Ukrainian Free University in Munich and Passau University, Germany; also at Kyiv State University and Lviv University in Ukraine; nominated judge of the U.S. Court of Federal Claims on January 30, 1987, and entered on duty, May 29, 1987.

ROBERT HAYNE HODGES, Jr., senior judge; born in Columbia, SC, September 11, 1944, son of Robert Hayne and Mary (Lawton) Hodges; educated in the public schools of Columbia, SC; attended Wofford College, Spartanburg, SC; B.S., University of South Carolina, 1966; J.D., University of South Carolina Law School, 1969; married to Ruth Nicholson (Lady) Hodges, August 23, 1963; three children; appointed to the U.S. Court of Federal Claims on March 12, 1990.

UNITED STATES TAX COURT

400 Second Street, NW., 20217, phone (202) 521–0700

JOHN O. COLVIN, chief judge; born in Ohio, 1946; A.B., University of Missouri, 1968; J.D., 1971; LL.M., Taxation, Georgetown University Law Center, 1978; admitted to practice law in Missouri (1971) and District of Columbia (1974); Office of the Chief Counsel, U.S. Coast Guard, Washington, DC, 1971–75; served as Tax Counsel, Senator Bob Packwood, 1975–84; Chief Counsel (1985–87), and Chief Minority Counsel (1987–88), U.S. Senate Finance Committee; Federal Bar Association and recipient of the FBA Tax Section's Liles Award; Adjunct Professor of Law, Georgetown University Law Center and recipient of Charles Fahy Distinguished Adjunct Professor Award; appointed by President Reagan as Judge, United States Tax Court, on September 1, 1988, for a term ending August 31, 2003; reappointed on August 12, 2004, for a term ending August 11, 2019; elected as Chief Judge for a two-year term effective June 1, 2006, and June 1, 2008.

MARY ANN COHEN, judge; born in New Mexico, 1943; attended public schools in Los Angeles, CA; B.S., University of California, at Los Angeles, 1964; J.D., University of Southern California School of Law, 1967; practiced law in Los Angeles, member in law firm of Abbott & Cohen; American Bar Association, Section of Taxation, and Continuing Legal Education Activities; received Dana Latham Memorial Award from Los Angeles County Bar Association Taxation Section, 1997; Jules Ritholz Memorial Merit Award from ABA Tax Section Committee on Civil and Criminal Tax Penalties, 1999; Bruce I. Hochman Award from the UCLA Tax Controversy Program, 2007; and Joanne M. Garvey Award from California Bar Taxation Section, 2008; appointed by President Reagan as Judge, United States Tax Court, on September 24, 1982, for a term ending September 23, 1997; served as Chief Judge from June 1, 1996 to September 23, 1997; reappointed on November 7, 1997, for a term ending November 6, 2012, and served again as Chief Judge from November 7, 1997 to May 31, 2000.

THOMAS B. WELLS, judge; born in Ohio, 1945; B.S., Miami University, Oxford, OH, 1967; J.D., Emory University Law School, Atlanta, GA, 1973; LL.M., Taxation, New York University Law School, New York, 1978; Supply Corps Officer, U.S. Naval Reserve, active duty 1967–70, Morocco and Vietnam, received Joint Service Commendation Medal; admitted to practice law in Georgia; member of law firm of Graham and Wells, P.C.; County Attorney for Toombs County, GA; City Attorney, Vidalia, GA, until 1977; member of law firm of Hurt, Richardson, Garner, Todd and Cadenhead, Atlanta, until 1981; law firm of Shearer and Wells, P.C. until 1986; member of American Bar Association, Section of Taxation; State Bar of Georgia, member of Board of Governors; Board of Editors, Georgia State Bar Journal; member, Atlanta Bar Association; Editor of the *Atlanta Lawyer;* active in various tax organizations, such as Atlanta Tax Forum (presently, Honorary Member); Director, Atlanta Estate Planning Council; Director, North Atlanta Tax Council; American College of Tax Counsel, Honorary Fellow; Emory Law Alumni Association's Distinguished Alumnus Award, 2001; Life Member, National Eagle Scout Association, Eagle Scout, 1960; member: Vidalia Kiwanis Club (President); recipient, Distinguished President Award; appointed by President Reagan as Judge, United States Tax Court, on October 13, 1986, for a term ending October 12, 2001; reappointed by President George W. Bush on October 10, 2001, for a term ending October 9, 2016; served as Chief Judge from September 24, 1997 to November 6, 1997, and from June 1, 2000 to May 31, 2004.

JAMES S. HALPERN, judge; born in New York, 1945; Hackley School, Terrytown, NY, 1963; B.S., Wharton School, University of Pennsylvania, 1967; J.D., University of Pennsylvania Law School, 1972; LL.M., Taxation, New York University Law School, 1975; Associate Attorney, Mudge, Rose, Guthrie and Alexander, New York City, 1972–74; assistant professor of law, Washington and Lee University, 1975–76; assistant professor of law, St. John's University, New York City, 1976–78; visiting professor, Law School, New York University, 1978–79; associate attorney, Roberts and Holland, New York City, 1979–80; Principal Technical Advisor, Assistant Commissioner (Technical) and Associate Chief Counsel (Technical), Internal Revenue Service, Washington, DC, 1980–83; partner, Baker and Hostetler, Washington, DC, 1983–90; Adjunct Professor, Law School, George Washington University, Washington, DC, 1984–present; Colonel, U.S. Army Reserve (retired); appointed by President George H.W. Bush as Judge, United States Tax Court, on July 3, 1990, for a term ending July 2, 2005; reappointed on November 2, 2005, for a term ending November 1, 2020.

MAURICE B. FOLEY, judge; born in Illinois, 1960; B.A., Swarthmore College; J.D., Boalt Hall School of Law at the University of California at Berkeley; LL.M., Georgetown University Law Center; attorney for the Legislation and Regulations Division of the Internal Revenue Service, Tax Counsel for the United States Senate Committee on Finance; Deputy Tax Legislative Counsel in the U.S. Treasury's Office of Tax Policy; appointed by President Clinton as Judge, United States Tax Court, on April 9, 1995, for a term ending April 8, 2010.

JUAN F. VASQUEZ, judge; born in San Antonio, Texas, 1948; attended Fox Tech High School; A.D. (Data Processing), San Antonio Junior College; B.B.A. (Accounting), University of Texas, Austin, 1972; attended State University of New York, Buffalo in 1st year law school, 1975; J.D., University of Houston Law Center, 1977; LL.M., Taxation, New York University Law School of Law, 1978; Certified Public Accountant , Certificate from Texas, 1976; admitted to State Bar of Texas, 1977; admitted to the United States Tax Court, 1978; certified in Tax Law by Texas Board of Legal Specialization, 1984; admitted to the United States District Court, Southern District of Texas, 1982, Western District of Texas, 1985 and United States Court of Appeals for the Fifth Circuit, 1982; and the Supreme Court of the United States of America, 1996; private practice of tax law, in San Antonio, TX, 1987–April 1995; partner, Leighton, Hood and Vasquez, in San Antonio, TX, 1982–87; Trial Attorney, Office of Chief Counsel, Internal Revenue Service, Houston, TX, 1978–82; accountant, Coopers and Lybrand, Los Angeles, CA, 1972–74; member of American Bar Association, Tax Section; Texas State Bar, Tax and Probate Section; Fellow of Texas and San Antonio Bar Foundations; College of State Bar of Texas; National Hispanic Bar Association and Hispanic Bar Association of the District of Columbia; Mexican American Bar Association (MABA) of San Antonio (Treasurer); Houston MABA; Texas MABA (Treasurer); National Association of Hispanic CPA's San Antonio Chapter (founding member); member of Greater Austin Tax Litigation Association; served on Austin Internal Revenue Service District Director's Practitioner Liaison Committee, 1990–91 (chairman, 1991); appointed by President Clinton as Judge, United States Tax Court, on May 1, 1995, for a term ending April 30, 2010.

JOSEPH H. GALE, judge; born in Virginia, 1953; A.B., Philosophy, Princeton University, 1976; J.D., University of Virginia School of Law, Dillard Fellow, 1980; practiced law as an Associate Attorney, Dewey Ballantine, Washington, DC, and New York, 1980–83; Dickstein, Shapiro and Morin, Washington, DC, 1983–85; served as Tax Legislative Counsel for Senator Daniel Patrick Moynihan (D–NY), 1985–88; Administrative Assistant and Tax Legislative Counsel, 1989; Chief Counsel, 1990–93; Chief Tax Counsel, Committee on Finance, U.S. Senate, 1993–95; minority Chief Tax Counsel, Senate Finance Committee, January 1995–July 1995; minority Staff Director and Chief Counsel, Senate Finance Committee, July 1995–January 1996; admitted to District of Columbia Bar; member of American Bar Association, Section of Taxation; appointed by President Clinton as Judge, United States Tax Court, February 6, 1996, for a term ending February 5, 2011.

MICHAEL B. THORNTON, judge; born in Mississippi, 1954; B.S. in Accounting, *summa cum laude*, University of Southern Mississippi, 1976; M.S. in Accounting, 1997; M.A. in English Literature, University of Tennessee, 1979; J.D. (with distinction), Duke University School of Law, 1982; Order of the Coif, Duke Law Journal Editorial Board; admitted to District of Columbia Bar, 1982; served as Law Clerk to the Honorable Charles Clark, Chief Judge, U.S. Court of Appeals for the Fifth Circuit, 1983–84; practiced law as an Associate Attorney, Sutherland, Asbill and Brennan, Washington, DC, 1982–83 and summer 1981; Miller and Chevalier, Chartered, Washington, DC, 1985–88; served as Tax Counsel, U.S. House Committee on Ways and Means, 1988–93; Chief Minority Tax Counsel, U.S. House Committee on Ways and Means, January 1995; Attorney-Adviser, U.S. Treasury Department, February–April 1995; Deputy Tax Legislative Counsel in the Office of Tax Policy, United States Treasury Department, April 1995–February 1998; recipient of Treasury Secretary's Annual Award, U.S. Department of the Treasury, 1997; Meritorious Service Award, U.S. Department of the Treasury, 1998; appointed by President Clinton as Judge, United States Tax Court, on March 8, 1998, for a term ending March 7, 2013.

L. PAIGE MARVEL, judge; born in Maryland, 1949; B.A., *magna cum laude,* College of Notre Dame, 1971; J.D. with honors, University of Maryland School of Law, Baltimore, MD, 1974; Order of the Coif; member, Maryland Law Review and Moot Court Board; Garbis & Schwait, P.A., associate (1974–76) and shareholder (1976–85); shareholder, Garbis, Marvel & Junghans, P.A., 1985–86; shareholder, Melnicove, Kaufman, Weiner, Smouse & Garbis, P.A., 1986–88; partner, Venabel, Baetjer & Howard L.L.P., 1988–98; member, American Bar Association, Section of Taxation, Vice-Chair, Committee Operations, 1993–95; Council Director 1989–92; Chair, Court Procedure Committee, 1985–87; Maryland State Bar Association, Board of Governors, 1988–90, and 1996–98; Chair, Taxation Section 1982–83; Federal Bar Association, Section of Taxation, Section Council, 1984–90; Fellow, American Bar Foundation; Fellow, Maryland Bar Foundation; Fellow and former Regent, American College of Tax Counsel, 1996–98; member, American Law Institute; Advisor, ALI Restatement of Law Third-The Law Governing Lawyers 1988–98; University of Maryland Law School Board of Visitors, 1995–2001; Loyola / Notre Dame Library, Inc. Board of Trustees, 1996–2003; Advisory Committee, University of Baltimore Graduate Tax Program, 1986–present; Co-editor, Procedure Department, The Journal of Taxation, 1990–98; member, Commissioner's Review Panel on IRS Integrity, 1989–91; member and Chair, Procedure Subcommittee, Commission to Revise the Annotated Code of Maryland (Tax Provisions), 1981–87; member, Advisory Commission to the Maryland State Department of Economic and Community Development, 1978–81; recipient, President's Medal, College of Nortre Dame, 2006; Jules Ritholz Award, ABA Tax Section's Civil and Criminal Tax Penalties Comm., 2004; First Annual Tax Excellence Award, Maryland State Bar Association Tax Section, 2002; named one of Maryland's Top 100 Women, 1998; recipient, ABA Tax Section's Distinguished Service Award, 1995; recipient, MSBA Distinguished Service Award, 1982–83; listed in Best Lawyers in America, 1991–98; *Who's Who in the East;* author of various articles and book chapters on tax and tax litigation topics; appointed by President Clinton as Judge, United States Tax Court, on April 6, 1998, for a term ending April 5, 2013.

JOSEPH ROBERT GOEKE, judge; born in Kentucky, 1950; B.S., *cum laude*, Xavier University, 1972; J.D., University of Kentucky College of Law, 1975 (Order of the Coif); admitted to Illinois and Kentucky Bar, U.S. District Court for the Northern District of Illinois (Trial Bar), U.S. Court of Federal Claims; Trial Attorney, Chief Counsel's Office, Internal Revenue Service, New Orleans, LA, 1975–80; Senior Trial Attorney, Chief Counsel's Office, Internal Revenue Service, Cincinnati, OH, 1980–85; Special International Trial Attorney, Chief Counsel's Office, Internal Revenue Service, Cincinnati, OH, 1985–88; partner, Law Firm of Mayer, Brown, Rowe and Maw, Chicago, IL, 1988–2003; appointed by President George W. Bush as Judge, United States Tax Court, on April 22, 2003, for a term ending April 21, 2018.

ROBERT A. WHERRY, Jr., judge; born in Virginia, 1944; B.S., and J.D., University of Colorado; LL.M., Taxation, New York University Law School; fellow and former Regent of the American College of Tax Counsel and former chairman of the Taxation Section of the Colorado Bar Association; served as chairman of the Small-Business Tax Committee of the Colorado Association of Commerce and Industry, as president of the Greater Denver Tax Counsel Association, is a past chairman of the Administrative Practice Committee of the American Bar Association Tax Section, a member of the Council, and a member of the Advisory Committee of the American Bar Association Section of Dispute Resolution; listed in *The Best Lawyers in America* (in tax litigation); his articles have appeared in ALI-ABA publications, The Colorado Lawyer, Tax Notes, and State Tax Notes; former Colorado correspondent for State Tax Notes and has spoken at numerous tax institutes, including the University of Denver Tax Institute, Tulane University Tax Institute, and American Bar Association Tax Section programs; was an instructor in Tax Court litigation for the National Institute for Trial Advocacy; appointed by President George W. Bush as Judge, United States Tax Court, on April 23, 2003, for a term ending April 22, 2018.

DIANE L. KROUPA, judge; born in South Dakota, 1955; B.S.F.S., Georgetown University School of Foreign Service, 1978; J.D., University of South Dakota Law School, 1981; practiced tax law at Faegre & Benson, LLP in Minneapolis, MN; Minnesota Tax Court Judge, 1995–2001 (Chief Judge, 1998–2001); attorney-advisor, Legislation and Regulations Division, Office of Chief Counsel, 1981–84, and served as attorney-advisor to Judge Joel Gerber, United States Tax Court, 1984–85; admitted to practice law in South Dakota (1981), District of Columbia (1985) and Minnesota (1986); member: American Bar Association (Tax Section), Minnesota State Bar Association (Tax Section), National Association of Women Judges (1995–present), American Judicature Society (1995–present); Distinguished Service Award Recipient (2001), Minnesota State Bar Association (Tax Section); Volunteer of the Year Award, Junior

League of Minneapolis (1993); Community Volunteer of the Year, Minnesota State Bar Association (1998); appointed by President George W. Bush as Judge, United States Tax Court, on June 13, 2003, for a term ending June 12, 2018.

MARK V. HOLMES, judge; born in New York, 1960; B.A., Harvard College, 1979; J.D., University of Chicago Law School, 1983; admitted to New York and District of Columbia Bars; U.S. Supreme Court; DC, Second, Fifth and Ninth Circuits; Southern and Eastern Districts of New York, Court of Federal Claims; practiced in New York as an Associate, Cahill Gordon & Reindel, 1983–85; Sullivan & Cromwell, 1987–91; served as Clerk to the Hon. Alex Kozinski, Ninth Circuit, 1985–87; and in Washington as Counsel to Commissioners, United States International Trade Commission, 1991–96; Counsel, Miller & Chevalier, 1996–2001; Deputy Assistant Attorney General, Tax Division, 2001–03; member, American Bar Association (Litigation and Tax Sections); appointed by President George W. Bush as Judge, United States Tax Court, on June 30, 2003, for a term ending June 29, 2018.

HARRY A. HAINES, judge; born in Montana, 1939; B.A., St. Olaf College, 1961; J.D., University of Montana Law School, 1964; LL.M., Taxation, New York University Law School, 1966; admitted to Montana Bar and U.S. District Court, Montana, 1964; practiced law in Missoula, MT, as a partner, Law Firm of Worden, Thane & Haines, 1966–2003; Adjunct Professor, Law School, University of Montana, 1967–91; appointed by President George W. Bush as Judge, United States Tax Court, on April 22, 2003 for a term ending April 21, 2018.

DAVID GUSTAFSON, judge; born in Greenville, SC, in 1956; B.A. *summa cum laude,* Bob Jones University, 1978; Duke University School of Law, J.D. with distinction, 1981; Order of the Coif, 1981; Executive Editor of the *Duke Law Journal,* 1980–81; admitted to the District of Columbia Bar, 1981; Associate at the law firm of Sutherland, Asbill and Brennan, in Washington, DC, 1981–83; Trial Attorney, 1983–89, Assistant Chief, 1989–2005, and Chief, 2005–2008 in the Court of Federal Claims Section of the Tax Division in the U.S. Department of Justice, and Coordinator of Tax Shelter Litigation for the entire Tax Division, 2002–2006; Tax Division Outstanding Attorney Awards, 1985, 1989, 1997, and 2001–2005; Federal Bar Association's Younger Attorney Award, 1991. President of the Court of Federal Claims Bar Association, 2001; appointed by President George W. Bush as Judge, United States Tax Court, on July 29, 2008, for a term ending July 29, 2023.

RICHARD T. MORRISON, judge; born in Hutchinson, Kansas 1967. B.A., B.S., University of Kansas, 1989; visiting student at Mansfield College, Oxford University, 1987–88; J.D., University of Chicago Law School, 1993; M.A., University of Chicago, 1994; Clerk to Judge Jerry E. Smith, United States Court of Appeals for the Fifth Circuit, 1993–94; Associate, Baker & McKenzie, Chicago, IL, 1994–96; Associate, Mayer Brown & Platt, Chicago, IL, 1996–2001; Deputy Assistant Attorney General for Review and Appellate Matters, Tax Division, United States Department of Justice, from 2001–2008 (except for term as Acting Assistant Attorney General, from July 2007 to January 2008); nominated by President George W. Bush as Judge, United States Tax Court, on November 15, 2007; confirmed by Senate, July 7, 2008.

ELIZABETH CREWSON PARIS, judge; born in Oklahoma, 1958; B.S., University of Tulsa, 1980; J.D., University of Tulsa College of Law, 1987; LL.M., Taxation, University of Denver College of Law, 1993; admitted to the Supreme Court of Oklahoma and U.S. District Court for the District of Oklahoma, 1988; U.S. Tax Court, U.S. Court of Federal Claims, U.S. Court of Appeals for the Tenth Circuit, 1993; Supreme Court of Colorado, 1994; former partner, Brumbley, Bishop, and Paris, 1992; Senior associate, McKenna and Cueno, 1994; Tax Partner, Reinhart, Boerner, Van Deuren, Norris and Rieselbach, 1998; Tax Counsel to the United States Senate Finance Committee, 2000–20008; member of the American Bar Association, Section of Taxation and Real Property and Probate Sections; formerly served as vice chair to both Agriculture and Entity Selection Committees; member of Colorado and Oklahoma Bar Associations; recognized as Distinguished Alumnus by the University of Tulsa School of Law; author of numerous tax, estate planning, real property agriculture articles and chapters; former Adjunct Professor, Georgetown University Law Center, LL.M. Taxation Program, and University of Tulsa College of Law; appointed by President George W. Bush as Judge, United States Tax Court, on July 30, 2008, for a term ending July 29, 2023.

SENIOR JUDGES

HOWARD A. DAWSON, Jr., senior judge; born in Arkansas, 1922; Woodrow Wilson High School, Washington, DC, 1940; B.S. in Commerce, University of North Carolina, 1946; J.D. with honors, George Washington University School of Law, 1949; President, Case Club; Secretary-Treasurer, Student Bar Association; private practice of law, Washington, DC, 1949–50; served with the United States Treasury Department, Internal Revenue Service, as follows: Attorney, Civil Division, Office of Chief Counsel, 1950–53; Civil Advisory Counsel, Atlanta Region, 1953–57; Regional Counsel, Atlanta Region, 1958; Personal Assistant to Chief Counsel, 1958–59, Assistant Chief Counsel (Administration), 1959–62; U.S. Army Finance Corps, 1943–45; two years in European Theater; Captain, Finance Corps, U.S. Army Reserve (Retired); member of District of Columbia Bar (1949), Georgia Bar (1958), American Bar Association (Section of Taxation), Federal Bar Association, Chi Psi, Delta Theta Phi, George Washington University Law Alumni Association; appointed by President Kennedy as Judge, Tax Court of the United States, on August 21, 1962, for a term ending June 1, 1970; reappointed on June 2, 1970, for a term ending June 1, 1985; served as Chief Judge of the Tax Court from July 1, 1973, to June 30, 1977, and again from July 1, 1983, to June 1, 1985; retired on June 2, 1985; David Brennan Distinguished Professor of Law, University of Akron Law School, Spring Term, 1986; Professor and Director, Graduate Tax Program, University of Baltimore Law School, 1986–89; Distinguished Visiting Professor of Law, University of San Diego, Winter 1991; recalled as Senior Judge to perform judicial duties 1990–present.

ARTHUR L. NIMS III, senior judge; born in Oklahoma, 1923; attended public schools, Macon, GA, and Deerfield Academy, Deerfield, MA; B.A., Williams College; LL.B., University of Georgia Law School; LL.M., Taxation, New York University Law School; served as an officer, lieutenant (jg.), U.S. Naval Reserve, on active duty in the Pacific Theater during World War II; admitted to Georgia Bar, 1949; practiced law in Macon, GA, 1949–51; Special Attorney, Office of the District Counsel, Internal Revenue Service, New York, 1951–54; attorney, Legislation and Regulations Division, Chief Counsel's Office, Washington, DC, 1954–55; admitted to New Jersey Bar, 1955; partner in the law firm of McCarter and English, Newark, NJ, 1961–79; Secretary, Section of Taxation, American Bar Association, 1977–79; Chairman, Section of Taxation, New Jersey State Bar Association, 1969–71; member, American Law Institute; American College of Tax Counsel; received Kellogg Award for Lifetime Achievement from Williams College; received Tax Society of New York University Award for lifetime achievement; appointed by President Carter as Judge, United States Tax Court, on June 29, 1979, for a term ending June 28, 1994; served as Chief Judge of the Tax Court from June 1, 1988 to May 31, 1992; recalled on June 1, 1992, as Senior Judge to perform judicial duties from that date to the present.

JULIAN I. JACOBS, senior judge; born in Maryland, 1937; B.A., University of Maryland, 1958; LL.B., University of Maryland Law School, 1960; LL.M., Taxation, Georgetown Law Center, 1965; admitted to Maryland Bar, 1960; attorney, Internal Revenue Service, Washington, DC, 1961–65, and Buffalo, NY, in Regional Counsel's Office, 1965–67; entered private practice of law in Baltimore, MD, 1967; associate (1972–74) and partner (1974–84) in the Law Firm of Gordon, Feinblatt, Rothman, Hoffberger and Hollander; Chairman, study commission to improve the quality of the Maryland Tax Court, 1978; member, study groups to consider changes in the Maryland tax laws; Commissioner on a commission to reorganize and recodify article of Maryland law dealing with taxation, 1980; Lecturer, Tax Seminars and Professional programs; Chairman, Section of Taxation, Maryland State Bar Association; Adjunct Professor of Law, Graduate Tax Program, University of Baltimore School of Law, 1991–93; Adjunct Professor of Law, Graduate Tax Program, University of San Diego School of Law, 2001; Adjunct Professor of Law, Graduate Tax Program, University of Denver School of Law, 2001–present; appointed by President Reagan as Judge, United States Tax Court, on March 30, 1984, for a term ending March 29, 1999; recalled on March 30, 1999, as Senior Judge to perform judicial duties from that date to the present.

HERBERT L. CHABOT, senior judge; born in New York, 1931; Stuyvesant High School, 1948; B.A., *cum laude*, C.C.N.Y., 1952; LL.B., Columbia University, 1957; LL.M. in Taxation, Georgetown University, 1964; served in United States Army, 2 years, and Army Reserves (civil affairs units), for 8 years; served on Legal Staff, American Jewish Congress, 1957–61; attorney-adviser to Judge Russell E. Train, 1961–65; Congressional Joint Committee on Taxation, 1965–78; elected Delegate, Maryland Constitutional Convention, 1967–68; adjunct professor, National Law Center, George Washington University, 1974–83; member of American Bar Association, Tax Section, and Federal Bar Association; appointed by President Carter as Judge, United States Tax Court, on April 3, 1978, for a term ending April 2, 1993;

served as Senior Judge on recall performing judicial duties until reappointed on October 20, 1993, for a term ending October 19, 2008; retired on June 30, 2001, but recalled on July 1, 2001, as Senior Judge to perform judicial duties to the present time.

ROBERT PAUL RUWE, senior judge; born in Ohio, 1941; Roger Bacon High School, St. Bernard, OH, 1959; Xavier University, Cincinnati, OH, 1963; J.D., Salmon P. Chase College of Law (graduated first in class), 1970; admitted to Ohio Bar, 1970; Special Agent, Intelligence Division, Internal Revenue Service, 1963–70; joined Office of Chief Counsel, Internal Revenue Service in 1970, and held the following positions: Trial Attorney (Indianapolis), Director, Criminal Tax Division, Deputy Associate Chief Counsel (Litigation), and Director, Tax Litigation Division; appointed by President Reagan as Judge, United States Tax Court, on November 20, 1987, for a term ending November 19, 2002; recalled on November 20, 2002, as Senior Judge to perform judicial duties from that date to the present.

LAURENCE J. WHALEN, senior judge; born in Pennsylvania, 1944; A.B., Georgetown University, 1967; J.D., Georgetown University Law Center, 1970; LL.M., 1971; admitted to District of Columbia and Oklahoma Bars; Special Assistant to the Assistant Attorney General, Tax Division, Department of Justice, 1971–72; trial attorney, Tax Division, 1971–75; private law practice in Washington, DC, with Hamel and Park (now Hopkins, Sutter, Hamel and Park), 1977–84; also in Oklahoma City, OK, with Crowe and Dunlevy, 1984–87; member of Oklahoma Bar Association, District of Columbia Bar Association, and American Bar Association, appointed by President Reagan as Judge, United States Tax Court, on November 23, 1987, for a term ending November 22, 2002; recalled on November 23, 2002, as Senior Judge to perform judicial duties from that date to the present.

RENATO BEGHE, senior judge; born in Illinois, 1933; A.B., University of Chicago, 1951; J.D., University of Chicago, 1954; Phi Beta Kappa, Order of the Coif, co-managing editor of Law Review, Phi Gamma Delta; admitted New York Bar, 1955; practiced law with Carter, Ledyard and Milburn, New York City (associate 1954–65; partner 1965–83) and Morgan, Lewis and Bockius, New York City, 1983–89; bar associations: Association of the Bar of City of New York, nonresident member, Taxation Committee (1962–65), Art Law Committee (1979–83), Chairman (1980–83), Special Committee on Lawyer's Role in Tax Practice (1981–83), Committee on Taxation of International Transactions (1990); New York State Bar Association, nonresident member, Tax Section Chairman (1977–78), Co-Chairman, Joint Practice Committee of Lawyers and Accountants (1989–90); American Bar Association, Tax Section; International Bar Association, Business Section Committee N (Taxation), Judge's Forum, Human Rights Institute; International Fiscal Association; member, American Law Institute, Income Tax Advisory Group (1981–89), and American College of Tax Counsel (since 1981); former member, America-Italy Society, Inc; member, Honorable Order of Kentucky Colonels; appointed by President George H.W. Bush as Judge, United States Tax Court, on March 26, 1991, for a term ending March 25, 2006; retired on February 28, 2003, but continues to perform judicial duties as a Senior Judge on recall.

JOEL GERBER, senior judge; born in Illinois, 1940; B.S., business administration, Roosevelt University, 1962; J.D., DePaul University, 1965; LL.M., Taxation, Boston University Law School, 1968; admitted to the Illinois Bar, 1965; Georgia Bar, 1974; Tennessee Bar, 1978; served with U.S. Treasury Department, Internal Revenue Service, as trial attorney, Boston, MA, 1965–72; senior trial attorney, Atlanta, GA, 1972–76; District Counsel, Nashville, TN, 1976–80; Deputy Chief Counsel, Washington, DC, 1980–84; Acting Chief Counsel, May 1983–March 1984; recipient of a Presidential Meritorious Rank Award, 1983; Secretary of the Treasury's Exceptional Service Award, 1984; Lecturer in Law, Vanderbilt University, 1976–80; appointed by President Reagan as Judge, United States Tax Court, on June 18, 1984, for a term ending June 17, 1999; served as Senior Judge on recall performing judicial duties until reappointed on December 15, 2000, for a term ending December 14, 2015; served as Chief Judge from June 1, 2004, to May 31, 2006; assumed senior status on June 1, 2006.

CAROLYN P. CHIECHI, senior judge; born in New Jersey, 1943; B.S. (*magna cum laude,* Class Rank: 1), Georgetown University, 1965; J.D., 1969 (Class Rank: 9); LL.M., Taxation, 1971; Doctor of Laws, Honoris Causa, 2000; practiced with law firm of Sutherland, Asbill & Brennan, Washington, DC and Atlanta, GA (partner, 1976–92; associate, 1971–76); served as attorney-adviser to Judge Leo H. Irwin, United States Tax Court, 1969–71; member, District of Columbia Bar, 1969–present (member, Taxation Section, 1973–99; member, Taxation Section Steering Committee, 1980–82, Chairperson, 1981–82; member, Tax

Audits and Litigation Committee, 1986–92, Chairperson, 1987–88); member, American Bar Association, 1969–present (member, Section of Taxation, 1969–present; member, Committee on Court Procedure, 1991–present; member, Litigation Sectiton, 1995–2000; member, Judicial Division, 1997–2000); Federal Bar Association, 1969–present (member, Section of Taxation, 1969–present; member, Judiciary Division, 1992–present); Fellow, American College of Tax Counsel; Fellow, American Bar Foundation; member, Women's Bar Association of the District of Columbia, 1992–present; Board of Governors, Georgetown University Alumni Association, 1994–97, 1997–2000; Board of Regents, Georgetown University, 1988–94, 1995–2001; National Law Alumni Board, Georgetown University, 1986–93; Board of Directors, Stuart Stiller Memorial Foundation, 1986–99; American Judicature Society, 1994–present; one of several recipients of the first Georgetown University Law Alumni Awards (1994); one of several recipients of the first Georgetown University Law Center Alumnae Achievement Awards (1998); admitted to Who's Who in American Law, Who's Who of American Women, and Who's Who in America; appointed by President George H.W. Bush as Judge, United States Tax Court, on October 1, 1992, for a term ending September 30, 2007.

STEPHEN J. SWIFT, senior judge; born in Utah, 1943; Menlo Atherton High School, Atherton, CA, 1961; B.S., Brigham Young University, Political Science, 1967; J.D., George Washington University Law School, 1970; Attorney, U.S. Department of Justice, Tax Division, 1970–74; Assistant U.S. Attorney, Tax Division, U.S. Attorney's Office, San Francisco, CA, 1974–77; Vice President and Senior Tax Counsel, Tax Department, Bank of America N.T. and S.A., San Francisco, CA, 1977–83; adjunct professor, Graduate Tax Programs, Golden Gate University and University of Baltimore; member of California Bar, District of Columbia Bar, and American Bar Association, Section of Taxation; appointed by President Reagan as Judge, United States Tax Court, on August 16, 1983, for a term ending August 15, 1998; served as Senior Judge on recall performing judicial duties until reappointed by President Clinton on December 1, 2000, for a term ending November 30, 2015.

DAVID LARO, senior judge; born in Michigan, 1942; B.A., University of Michigan, 1964; J.D., University of Illinois Law School, 1967; LL.M., Taxation, New York University Law School, 1970; admitted to Michigan Bar and United States District Court (Eastern District), 1968; former partner of law firm of Winegarden, Booth, Shedd, and Laro, 1970–75; member of law firm of Laro and Borgeson, 1975–86; member, David Laro, Attorney at Law, P.C., 1986–92; counsel to Dykema Gossett, Ann Arbor, MI, 1989–90; president and chief executive officer of Durakon Industries, Inc., 1989–91; Chairman, Board of Durakon Industries, Inc., 1991–92; Chairman, Board of Republic Bank, 1986–92; Vice Chairman and Co-Founder of Republic Bancorp, Inc., 1986–92; Regent, University of Michigan Board of Regents, 1975–81; member, Michigan State Board of Education, 1982–83; Chairman, Michigan State Tenure Commission, 1972–75; Commissioner, Civil Service Commission, Flint, MI, 1984–85; Commissioner of Police, Flint, 1972–74; member, Political Leadership Program, Institute of Public Policy and Social Research; member, Ann Arbor Art Association Board of Directors; member, Holocaust Foundation (Ann Arbor); adjunct professor of law, Georgetown University Law School; instructor, National Institute for Trial Advocacy; visiting professor, University of San Diego Law School; member, National Advisory Committee for New York University Law School; at the request of the American Bar Association and the Central Eastern European Law Initiative, contributed written comments on the Draft Laws of Ukraine and Uzbekistan and on the creation of specialized courts in Eastern Europe; as a consultant for Harvard University (Harvard Institute for International Development), and Georgia State University, lectured in Moscow to Russian judges on the subject of tax reform and litigation procedures in May 1997 and December 1998; commentator for the American Bar Association's Central and East European Law Initiative on the draft laws of Uzbekistan, Kazakhstan, Slovakia, Ukraine, and Republic of Macedonia; lectured to Judges and tax officials in Azerbaijan on tax reform; appointed by President George H.W. Bush as Judge, United States Tax Court, on November 2, 1992, for a term ending November 1, 2007.

SPECIAL TRIAL JUDGES OF THE COURT

Robert N. Armen, Jr.; Lewis R. Carluzzo; John F. Dean; Stanley J. Goldberg; Peter J. Panuthos (chief special trial judge).

Officers of the Court

Clerk.—Robert R. Di Trolio, 521–4600.
Budget and Accounting Officer.—Joseph Hardy.
Librarian.—Elsa Silverman.
Reporter.—Sheila Murphy.

UNITED STATES COURT OF APPEALS FOR THE ARMED FORCES [1]

450 E Street, NW., 20442–0001, phone 761–1448, fax 761–4672

ANDREW S. EFFRON, chief judge; born in Stamford, CT, September 18, 1948; A.B., Harvard College, 1970; J.D., Harvard Law School, 1975; The Judge Advocate General's School, U.S. Army, 1976, 1983; legislative aide to the late Representative William A. Steiger, 1970–76 (two years full-time, the balance between school semesters); judge advocate, Office of the Staff Judge Advocate, Fort McClellan, Alabama, 1976–77; attorney-adviser, Office of the General Counsel, Department of Defense, 1977–87; Counsel, General Counsel, and Minority Counsel, Committee on Armed Services, U.S. Senate, 1987–96; nominated by President Clinton to serve on the U.S. Court of Appeals for the Armed Forces, June 21, 1996; confirmed by the Senate, July 12, 1996; took office on August 1, 1996.

JAMES E. BAKER, associate judge; born in New Haven, CT, March 25, 1960; education: BA., Yale University, 1982; J.D., Yale Law School, 1990; Attorney, Department of State, 1990–93; Counsel, President's Foreign Intelligence Advisory Board / Intelligence Oversight Board, 1993–94; Deputy Legal Advisor, National Security Counsel, 1994–97; Special Assistant to the President and Legal Advisor, National Security Counsel, 1997–2000; military service: U.S. Marine Corps and U.S. Marine Corp Reserve; nominated by President Clinton to serve on the U.S. Court of Appeals for the Armed Forces; began service on September 19, 2000.

CHARLES E. ERDMANN, associate judge; born in Great Falls, MT, June 26, 1946; B.A., Montana State University, 1972; J.D., University of Montana Law School, 1975; Air Force Judge Advocate Staff Officers Course, 1981; Air Command and Staff College, 1992; Air War College, 1994; Military Service: U.S. Marine Corps, 1967–70; Air National Guard, 1981–2002 (retired as a Colonel); Assistant Montana Attorney General, 1975–76; Chief Counsel, Montana State Auditor's Office, 1976–78; Chief Staff Attorney, Montana Attorney General's Office, Antitrust Bureau; Bureau Chief, Montana Medicaid Fraud Bureau, 1980–82; General Counsel, Montana School Boards Association, 1982–86; private practice of law, 1986–95; Associate Justice, Montana Supreme Court, 1995–97; Office of High Representative of Bosnia and Herzegovina, Judicial Reform Coordinator, 1998–99; Office of High Representative of Bosnia and Herzegovina, Head of Human Rights and Rule of Law Department, 1999; Chairman and Chief Judge, Bosnian Election Court, 2000–01; Judicial Reform and International Law Consultant, 2001–2002; appointed by President George W. Bush to serve on the U.S. Court of Appeals for the Armed Forces on October 9, 2002, commenced service on October 15, 2002.

SCOTT W. STUCKY, associate judge; born in Hutchinson, KS, January 11, 1948; B.A. (*summa cum laude*), Wichita State University, 1970; J.D., Harvard Law School, 1973; M.A., Trinity University, 1980; LL.M. with highest honors, George Washington University, 1983; Federal Executive Institute, 1988; Harvard Program for Senior Officials in National Security, 1990; National War College, 1993; admitted to bar, Kansas and District of Columbia; U.S. Air Force, judge advocate, 1973–78; U.S. Air Force Reserve, 1982–2003 (retired as colonel); married to Jean Elsie Seibert of Oxon Hill, MD, August 18, 1973; children: Mary-Clare, Joseph; private law practice, Washington, DC, 1978–82; branch chief, U.S. Nuclear Regulatory Commission, 1982–83; legislative counsel and principal legislative counsel, U.S. Air Force, 1983–96; General Counsel, Committee on Armed Services, U.S. Senate, 1996–2001 and 2003–06; Minority Counsel, 2001–03; National Commander-in-Chief, Military Order of the Loyal Legion of the United States, 1993–95; Board of Directors, Adoption Service Information Agency, 1998–2002 and 2004–07; Board of Directors, Omicron Delta Kappa Society, 2006–present; member, Federal Bar Association (Pentagon Chapter), Judge Advocates Association,

[1] Prior to October 5, 1994, United States Court of Military Appeals.

The District of Columbia Bar; OPM LEGIS Fellow, office of Senator John Warner (R–VA), 1986–87; member and panel chairman, Air Force Board for Correction of Military records, 1989–96; nominated by President George W. Bush to serve on the U.S. Court of Appeals for the Armed Forces on November 15, 2006; confirmed by the Senate, December 9, 2006; began service on December 20, 2006.

MARGARET A. RYAN, associate judge; born in Chicago, IL, May 23, 1964; B.A. (*cum laude*), Knox College; J.D. (*summa cum laude*), University of Notre Dame Law School; recipient of the William T. Kirby Legal Writing Award and the Colonel William J. Hoynes Award for Outstanding Scholarship; active duty in the U.S. Marine Corps, 1986–99, serving as a communications officer, staff officer, company commander, platoon commander and operations officer in units within the II and III Marine Expeditionary Forces and as a judge advocate in Okinawa, Japan, and Quantico, VA; also served as Aide de Camp to General Charles C. Krulak, the 31st Commandant of the Marine Corps; law clerk to the Honorable J. Michael Luttig, U.S. Court of Appeals for the Fourth Circuit, and law clerk to the Honorable Clarence Thomas, Associate Justice of the Supreme Court of the United States; litigation partner at the law firm of Bartlik Beck Herman Palenchar & Scott LLP and partner in litigation and appellate practices at the law firm Wiley Rein Fielding LLP; nominated by President George W. Bush to serve on the U.S. Court of Appeals for the Armed Forces on November 15, 2006; confirmed by the Senate on December 9, 2006; began service on December 20, 2006.

SENIOR JUDGES

WILLIAM HORACE DARDEN, senior judge; born in Union Point, GA, May 16, 1923; son of William W. and Sara (Newsom) Darden; B.B.A., University of Georgia, 1946; LL.B., University of Georgia, 1948; admitted to bar of Georgia and to practice before the Georgia Supreme Court, 1948; active duty in U.S. Navy from July 1, 1943 to July 3, 1946, when released to inactive duty as lieutenant (jg.); married to Mary Parrish Viccellio of Chatham, VA, December 31, 1949; children: Sara Newsom, Martha Hardy, William H., Jr., Daniel Hobson; secretary to U.S. Senator Richard B. Russell, 1948–51; chief clerk of U.S. Senate Committee on Armed Services, 1951–53; professional staff member and later chief of staff, U.S. Senate Committee on Armed Services, February 1953 to November 1968; received recess appointment as judge of the U.S. Court of Military Appeals from President Johnson on November 5, 1968, to succeed the late Judge Paul J. Kilday; took oath of office on November 13, 1968; nominated by President Johnson for the unexpired part of the term of the late Judge Paul J. Kilday ending May 1, 1976; confirmed by Senate on January 14, 1969; designated chief judge by President Nixon on June 23, 1971; resigned December 29, 1973; elected to become senior judge on February 11, 1974.

WALTER THOMPSON COX III, senior judge; born in Anderson, SC, August 13, 1942; son of Walter T. Cox and Mary Johnson Cox; married to Vicki Grubbs of Anderson, SC, February 8, 1963; children: Lisa and Walter; B.S., Clemson University, 1964; J.D. (*cum laude*), University of South Carolina School of Law, 1967; graduated Defense Language Institute (German), 1969; graduated basic course, the Judge Advocate General's School, Charlottesville, VA, 1967; studied procurement law at that same school, 1968; active duty, U.S. Army judge advocate general's corps, 1964–72 (1964–67, excess leave to U.S.C. Law School); private law practice, 1973–78; elected resident judge, 10th Judicial Circuit, South Carolina, 1978–84; also served as acting associate justice of South Carolina supreme court, on the judicial council, on the circuit court advisory committee, and as a hearing officer of the judicial standards commission; member: bar of the Supreme Court of the United States; bar of the U.S. Court of Military Appeals; South Carolina Bar Association; Anderson County Bar Association; the American Bar Association; the South Carolina Trial Lawyers Association; the Federal Bar Association; and the Bar Association of the District of Columbia; has served as a member of the House of Delegates of the South Carolina Bar, and the Board of Commissioners on Grievances and Discipline; nominated by President Reagan, as judge of U.S. Court of Military Appeals, June 28, 1984, for a term of 15 years; confirmed by the Senate, July 26, 1984; sworn-in and officially assumed his duties on September 6, 1984; retired on September 30, 1999 and immediately assumed status of senior judge on October 1, 1999 and returned to full active service until September 19, 2000.

EUGENE R. SULLIVAN, senior judge; born in St. Louis, MO, August 2, 1941; son of Raymond V. and Rosemary K. Sullivan; married to Lis U. Johansen of Ribe, Denmark, June 18, 1966; children: Kim A. and Eugene R. II; B.S., U.S. Military Academy, West Point, 1964; J.D., Georgetown Law Center, Washington, DC, 1971; active duty with the

U.S. Army, 1964–69; service included duty with the 3rd Armored Division in Germany, and the 4th Infantry Division in Vietnam; R&D assignments with the Army Aviation Systems Command; one year as an instructor at the Army Ranger School, Ft. Benning, GA; decorations include: Bronze Star, Air Medal, Army Commendation Medal, Ranger and Parachutist Badges, Air Force Exceptional Civilian Service Medal; following graduation from law school, clerked with U.S. Court of Appeals (8th Circuit), St. Louis, 1971–72; private law practice, Washington, DC, 1972–74; assistant special counsel, White House, 1974; trial attorney, U.S. Department of Justice, 1974–82; deputy general counsel, Department of the Air Force, 1982–84; general counsel of the Department of Air Force, 1984–86; Governor of Wake Island, 1984–86; presently serves on the Board of Governors for the West Point Society of the District of Columbia; the American Cancer Society (Montgomery County Chapter); nominated by President Reagan, as judge, U.S. Court of Military Appeals on February 25, 1986, and confirmed by the Senate on May 20, 1986, and assumed his office on May 27, 1986; President George H.W. Bush named him the chief judge of the U.S. Court of Military Appeals, effective October 1, 1990, a position he held for five years; he retired on September 30, 2001 and immediately assumed status of senior judge and returned to full active service until Sept. 30, 2002.

H.F. "SPARKY" GIERKE, senior judge; born in Williston, ND, March 13, 1943; son of Herman F. Gierke, Jr., and Mary Kelly Gierke; children: Todd, Scott, Craig, and Michelle; B.A., University of North Dakota, 1964; J.D., University of North Dakota, 1966; graduated basic course, the Judge Advocate General's School, Charlottesville, VA, 1967; graduated military judge course, the Judge Advocate General's School, Charlottesville, VA, 1969; active duty, U.S. Army judge advocate general's corps, 1967–71; private practice of law, 1971–83; served as a justice of the North Dakota supreme court from October 1, 1983 until appointment to U.S. Court of Military Appeals; admitted to the North Dakota Bar, 1966; admitted to practice law before all North Dakota Courts, U.S. District Court for the District of North Dakota, U.S. District Court for the Southern District of Georgia, U.S. Court of Military Appeals, and U.S. Supreme Court; served as president of the State Bar Association of North Dakota in 1982–83; served as president of the North Dakota State's Attorneys Association in 1979–80; served on the board of governors of the North Dakota Trial Lawyers Association from 1977–83; served on the board of governors of the North Dakota State Bar Association from 1977–79 and from 1981–84; served as vice chairman and later chairman of the North Dakota Judicial Conference from June 1989 until November 1991; fellow of the American Bar Foundation and the American College of Probate Counsel; member of the American Bar Association, American Judicature Society, Association of Trial Lawyers of America, Blue Key National Honor Fraternity, Kappa Sigma Social Fraternity, University of North Dakota President's Club; in 1984, received the Governor's Award from Governor Allen I. Olson for outstanding service to the State of North Dakota; in 1988 and again in 1991, awarded the North Dakota National Leadership Award of Excellence by Governor George A. Sinner; in 1989, selected as the Man of the Year by the Delta Mu Chapter of the Kappa Sigma Fraternity and as Outstanding Greek Alumnus of the University of North Dakota; also awarded the University of North Dakota Sioux Award (UND's alumni association's highest honor); in 1983–84, served as the first Vietnam era state commander of the North Dakota American Legion; in 1988–89, served as the first Vietnam era national commander of the American Legion; nominated by President George H.W. Bush, October 1, 1991; confirmed by the Senate, November 14, 1991; sworn-in and assumed office on the U.S. Court of Military Appeals, November 20, 1991; on October 1, 2004, he became the Chief Judge until his retirement on September 30, 2006.

SUSAN J. CRAWFORD, senior judge; born in Pittsburgh, PA, April 22, 1947; daughter of William E. and Joan B. Crawford; married to Roger W. Higgins of Geneva, NY, September 8, 1979; one child, Kelley S. Higgins; B.A., Bucknell University, Pennsylvania, 1969; J.D. (*cum laude*), Dean's Award, Arthur McClean Founder's Award, New England School of Law, Boston, MA, 1977; history teacher and coach of women's athletics, Radnor High School, Pennsylvania, 1969–74; associate, Burnett and Eiswert, Oakland, MD, 1977–79; Assistant State's Attorney, Garrett County, Maryland, 1978–80; partner, Burnett, Eiswert and Crasford, 1979–81; instructor, Garrett County Community College, 1979–81; deputy general counsel, 1981–83, and general counsel, Department of the Army, 1983–89; special counsel to Secretary of Defense, 1989; inspector general, Department of Defense, 1989–91; member: bar of the Supreme Court of the United States; bar of the U.S. Court of Military Appeals, Maryland Bar Association, District of Columbia Bar Association, American Bar Association, Federal Bar Association, and the Edward Bennett Williams American Inn of Court; member: board of trustees, 1989–present, and Corporation, 1992–present, of New England School of Law; board of trustees, 1988–present, Bucknell University; nominated by President Bush as judge, U.S. Court of Military Appeals, February 19, 1991, for a term of 15 years; confirmed by the Senate on November 14, 1991, sworn in and officially assumed her duties on November 19, 1991; on October 1, 1999, she became the Chief Judge for a term of five years.

Officers of the U.S. Court of Appeals for the Armed Forces

Clerk of the Court.—William A. DeCicco.
Chief Deputy Clerk of the Court.—David A. Anderson.
Deputy Clerk for Opinions.—Patricia Mariani.
Court Executive.—Keith Roberts.
Librarian.—Agnes Kiang.

UNITED STATES COURT OF APPEALS FOR VETERANS CLAIMS

625 Indiana Avenue, NW., 20004, phone (202) 501–5970

WILLIAM P. GREENE, Jr., chief judge; born in Bluefield, WV, July 27, 1943, to William and Dorothy Greene; married to Madeline Sinkford of Bluefield, WV; two children; B.A., political science, West Virginia State College, 1965; J.D., Howard University, Washington, DC, 1968; active duty in the United States Army Judge Advocate General's Corps following graduation from law school; as Judge Advocate, completed military education at the Basic, Advanced, and Military Judges' courses at the Judge Advocate General's School, the Army Command and General Staff College, Fort Leavenworth, KS, and the Army War College, Carlisle Barracks, PA; served as the Chief Prosecutor, Fort Knox, KY, 1969–70, and Chief Defense Counsel, Army Command, Hawaii, 1970–73; Army chief recruiter for lawyers, 1974–77; Department Chair, Criminal Law Division, the Judge Advocate General's School, Charlottesville, VA, 1981–84; Deputy Staff Judge Advocate, Third Infantry Division, Germany 1977–80; Staff Judge Advocate, Second Infantry Division, Korea 1984–85; following graduation from the United States Army War College, selected to serve as the Staff Judge Advocate of the United States Military Academy at West Point, NY, 1986–90, followed by another selection as Staff Judge Advocate at Fort Leavenworth, KS; retired from the United States Army as Colonel, 1993, receiving several awards during this service, including three Legions of Merit, three Meritorious Service Medals, and two Army Commendation Medals; appointed by the Attorney General of the United States as an Immigration Judge, Department of Justice, presiding over immigration cases in Maryland and Pennsylvania, June 1993—November 1997; nominated for appointment by President Clinton May 16, 1997; confirmed by the U.S. Senate November 7, 1997; sworn in November 24, 1997.

BRUCE E. KASOLD, judge; born in New York, 1951; B.S., United States Military Academy, 1973; J.D., *cum laude*, University of Florida, 1979; LL.M., Georgetown University, 1982; Honors Graduate, the Judge Advocate General's School Graduate Program, 1984; admitted to the bars of the U.S. Supreme Court, the Florida Supreme Court, the District of Columbia Court of Appeals; member: Florida Bar, District of Columbia Bar, the Federal Bar Association, Order of the Coif; retired from the U.S. Army, Lieutenant Colonel, Air Defense Artillery and Judge Advocate General's Corp, 1994; commercial litigation attorney, Holland & Knight Law Firm, 1994–95; Chief Counsel, U.S. Senate Committee on Rules and Administration, 1995–98; Chief Counsel, Secretary of the Senate and Senate Sergeant at Arms, 1998–2003; appointed by President George W. Bush to the U.S. Court of Appeals for Veterans Claims on December 13, 2003; sworn in December 31, 2003.

LAWRENCE B. HAGEL, judge; born in Washington, IN, 1947; B.S., United States Naval Academy, 1969; J.D., University of the Pacific McGeorge School of Law, 1976; LL.M. (Labor Law, with highest honors) The National Law Center, George Washington University, 1983; admitted to the bars of the U.S. Supreme Court, the United States Court of Appeals for the Fourth, Ninth, Tenth, D.C. and Federal Circuits, U.S. Court of Appeals for the Armed Forces, U.S. Court of Appeals for Veterans Claims, Supreme Court of the States of Iowa and California and the District of Columbia; commissioned in the U.S. Marine Corps, second lieutenant, infantry officer 1969–72 service in Vietnam and Puerto Rico; Marine Corps judge advocate 1973–90, assignments concentrated in criminal and civil litigation; Deputy General Counsel and General Counsel, Paralyzed Veterans of America, 1990–2003; appointed by President George W. Bush in December 2003, to the U.S. Court of Appeals for Veterns Claims; confirmed by the U.S. Senate to the Court of Appeals on December 9, 2003; sworn in January 2, 2004.

WILLIAM A. MOORMAN, judge; born in Chicago, IL, January 23, 1945; B.A., University of Illinois at Champaign-Urbana, 1967; J.D., University of Illinois College of Law, 1970; commissioned in the United States Air Force, second lieutenant, Reserve Officers Training Corps, 1970; entered active duty, 1971; Judge Advocate General's Corps, 1972–2002, serving as the senior attorney at every level of command, culminating his active military service with his appointment as the Judge Advocate General of the United States Air Force; military decorations include the Superior Service Medal with oak leaf cluster, the Legion of Merit with oak leaf cluster, the Joint Meritorious Service Medal, and the Meritorious Service Medal with four oak leaf clusters; retired from the Air Force in April 2002, in the grade of Major General; Counselor to the General Counsel, Department of Veterans Affairs, 2002; Assistant to the Secretary for Regulation Policy and Management, Department of Veterans Affairs, 2003; appointed by President George W. Bush as Acting Assistant Secretary of Management for the Department of Veterans Affairs, August 2004; author: ''Executive Privilege and the Freedom of Information Act: Sufficient Protection for Aircraft Mishap Reports?'', 21 Air Force Law Review 581 (1979); ''Cross-Examination Techniques,'' 27 Air Force Law Review 105 (1987); ''Fifty Years of Military Justice: Does the UCMJ Need To Be Changed?'', 48 Air Force Law Review 185 (2000); ''Humanitarian Intervention and International Law in the Case of Kosovo,'' 36 New England Law Review 775 (2002); ''Serving Our Veterans Through Clearer Rules,'' 56 Administrative Law Review 207 (2004); recipient: Albert M. Kuhfeld Outstanding Young Judge Advocate of the Air Force Award 1979, Stuart R. Reichart Outstanding Senior Attorney of the Air Force Award 1992, University of Illinois College of Law Distinguished Alumnus Award 2001, Department of Veterans Affairs Exceptional Service Award 2004; nominated for appointment to the U.S. Court of Appeals for Veterans Claims on September 21, 2004, by President George W. Bush; confirmed by the U.S. Senate November 20, 2004; sworn in December 16, 2004.

ALAN G. LANCE, Sr., judge; born in McComb, OH, April 27, 1949; B.A. in english and history, distinguished military graduate, South Dakota State University, 1971; commissioned U.S. Army, June 1971; graduated University of Toledo School of Law and Law Review, 1973; admitted to the U.S. Supreme Court, U.S. Court of Military Appeals, State of Ohio, State of Idaho; commissioned U.S. Army, Judge Advocate Generals Corps, 1974 and served as Claims Officer, defense counsel, Chief of Defense Counsel, Legal Assistance Officer, Administrative Law Officer and in the absence of a military Judge, military Magistrate for the 172nd Infantry Brigade (Alaska) 1974–77; Army Commendation Medal 1977; served as the Command Judge Advocate, Corpus Christi Army Depot, 1977–78; engaged in private practice of law, Ada County, Idaho, 1978–94; elected to the Idaho House of Representatives, 1990, and served as Majority Caucus chairman, 1992–94; elected as Idaho Attorney General (31st) in 1994 and 1998; Distinguished Alumnus Award, University of Toledo School of Law, 2002; inducted into the Ohio Veterans Hall of Fame, November 2004; nominated as a Judge of the United States Court of Appeals for Veterans Claims by President George W. Bush; confirmed by the U.S. Senate to the Court of Appeals for Veterans Claims, November 2004 and sworn in on December 17, 2004.

ROBERT N. DAVIS, judge; born in Kewanee, IL, September 20, 1953; graduated from Davenport Central High School, Davenport, IA, 1971; B.A., University of Hartford, 1975; J.D. Georgetown University Law Center, 1978; admitted to the bars of the U.S. Supreme Court, the Ninth Circuit Court of Appeals; the State of Virginia; and the State of Iowa; career record 1978–83 appellate attorney with the Commodity Futures Trading Commission; 1983–88 attorney with the United States Department of Education, Business and Administrative law division of the Office of General Counsel; 1983 Governmental exchange program with the United States Attorneys office, District of Columbia; Special Assistant United States Attorney; 1988–2001 Professor of Law, University of Mississippi School of Law; 2001–05 Professor of Law, Stetson University College of Law; Published extensively in the areas of constitutional law, administrative law, national security law and sports law. Founder and Faculty Editor-in-Chief, Journal of National Security Law, arbitrator/mediator with the American Arbitration Association and the United States Postal Service. Gubernatorial appointment to the National Conference of Commissioners on Uniform State Laws 1993–2000. Joined the United States Navy Reserve Intelligence Program in 1988. Presidential recall to active duty in 1999, Bosnia and 2001 for the Global War on Terrorism. Military decorations include Joint Service Commendation Medal, Joint Service Achievement Medal, Navy Achievement Medal, NATO Medal, Armed Forces Expeditionary Medal, Armed Forces Reserve Medal with ''M'' device, Overseas Service Ribbon, National Defense Ribbon, Joint Meritorious Unit Award, and Global War on Terrorism Medal. Nominated for appointment by President George W. Bush on March 23, 2003; confirmed by the United States Senate on November 21, 2004; Commissioned on December 4, 2004 as a Judge, United States Court of Appeals for Veterans Claims.

MARY J. SCHOELEN, judge; born in Rota, Spain; B.A., political science, University of California at Irvine, 1990; J.D., George Washington University Law School, 1993; admitted to the State Bar of California; law clerk for the National Veterans Legal Services Project, 1992–93; legal intern to the U.S. Senate Committee on Veterans' Affairs, 1994; staff attorney for Vietnam Veterans of America's Veterans Benefits Program, 1994–97; Minority Counsel, U.S. Senate Committee on Veterans' Affairs, 1997–2001; Minority General Counsel, March

2001–June 2001; Deputy Staff Director, Benefits Programs / General Counsel, June 2001–03; Minority Deputy Staff Director, Benefits Programs / General Counsel, 2003–04; nominated by President George W. Bush; appointed a Judge of the United States Court of Appeals for Veterans Claims; confirmed by the U.S. Senate to the United States Court of Appeals for Veterans Claims on November 20, 2004; sworn in December 20, 2004.

OFFICERS OF THE U.S. COURT OF VETERANS APPEALS

Clerk of the Court.—Norman Y. Herring, 501–5970.
Chief Deputy Clerk Operations Manager.—Anne P. Stygles.
Counsel to the Clerk.—Cary P. Sklar.
Senior Staff Attorney (Central Legal Staff).—Cynthia Brandon-Arnold.
Deputy Executive Officer.—Robert J. Bieber.
Librarian.—Allison Mays.

JUDICIAL PANEL ON MULTIDISTRICT LITIGATION

Thurgood Marshall Federal Judiciary Building, Room G–255, North Lobby, One Columbus Circle, NE., 20002, phone (202) 502–2800, fax 502–2888

(National jurisdiction to centralize related cases pending in multiple circuits and districts under 28 U.S.C. §§ 1407 & 2112)

Chairman.—John G. Heyburn II, U.S. District Judge, Western District of Kentucky.
Judges:
Robert L. Miller, Jr., Chief Judge, U.S. District Court, Northern District of Indiana.
Kathryn H. Vratil, U.S. District Judge, District of Kansas.
David R. Hansen, Senior U.S. Court of Appeals Judge, Eighth Circuit.
W. Royal Furgeson, Jr., U.S. District Judge, Northern District of Texas.
Frank C. Damrell, Jr., Senior U.S. District Judge, Eastern District of California.
Executive Attorney.—Robert A. Cahn.
Clerk.—Jeffery N. Lüthi.

ADMINISTRATIVE OFFICE OF THE U.S. COURTS

Thurgood Marshall Federal Judiciary Building

One Columbus Circle, NE., 20544, phone (202) 502–2600

Director.—James C. Duff, 502–3000.
Deputy Director.—Jill C. Sayenga, 502–3015.
Chief, Office of:
Audit.—Jeff Larioni, 502–1000.
Long-Range Planning.—Brian Lynch, 502–1300.
Management, Planning and Assessment.—Cathy A. McCarthy, 502–1300.
Associate Director and General Counsel.—William R. Burchill, Jr., 502–1100.
Deputy General Counsel.—Robert K. Loesche.
Assistant Director, Judicial Conference Executive Secretariat.—Laura C. Minor, 502–2400.
Deputy Assistant Directors: Jeffrey A. Hennemuth, Wendy Jennis.
Assistant Director, Legislative Affairs.—Cordia A. Strom, 502–1700.
Deputy Assistant Director.—Daniel A. Cunningham.
Chief, Judicial Impact Office.—Richard A. Jaffe.
Assistant Director, Public Affairs.—David A. Sellers, 502–2600.
Assistant Director, Office of Court Administration.—Noel J. Augustyn, 502–1500.
Deputy Assistant Director.—Glen K. Palman.
Chief of:
Appellate Court and Circuit Administration Division.—Gary Bowden, 502–1520.
Bankruptcy Court Administration Division.—Glen K. Palman, 502–1540.
Court Administration Policy Staff.—Abel J. Mattos, 502–1560.
District Court Administration Division.—Robert Lowney, 502–1570.
Public Access and Records Management Division.—Michel M. Ishakian, 502–1500.
Technology Division.—Gary L. Bockweg, 502–2500.
Assistant Director, Office of Defender Services.—Ted Lidz, 502–3030.
Deputy Assistant Director.—Steven G. Asin.
Chief of:
Information Technology Division.—George M. Drakulich.
Legal, Policy and Training Division.—Richard A. Wolff.
Program Budget, Operations and Assessment Division.—Steven G. Asin (acting).
Assistant Director, Office of Facilities and Security.—Ross Eisenman, 502–1200.
Deputy Assistant Director.—William J. Lehman.
Chief of:
Court Security Office.—Edward M. Templeman, 502–1280.
Judiciary Emergency Preparedness Office.—William J. Lehman.
Security and Facilities Policy Staff.—Melanie F. Gilbert.
Space and Facilities Division.—Debra L. Worley.
Assistant Director, Office of Finance and Budget.—George H. Schafer, 502–2000.
Deputy Assistant Director.—Michael N. Milby.
Chief of:
Accounting and Financial Systems Division.—Charles S. Glenn, 502–2200.
Budget Division.—James R. Baugher, 502–2100.
Financial Liaison and Analysis Office.—Penny Jacobs Fleming, 502–2028.
Assistant Director, Office of Human Resources.—Charlotte G. Peddicord, 502–1170.
Deputy Assistant Director.—Nancy E. Ward.
Chief of:
Benefits Division.—Cynthia Roth, 502–1160.
Business Technology Optimization Division.—Christopher D. Mays, 502–3210.
Court Personnel Management Division.—Nancy E. Ward (acting), 502–3100.
Fair Employment Practices Office.—Trudi M. Morrison, 502–1380.
Judges Compensation and Retirement Services Office.—Carol S. Sefren, 502–1380.
Policy and Strategic Initiatives Office.—Harvey L. Jones, 502–3185.
Assistant Director for Information Technology.—Howard J. Grandier, 502–2300.

Deputy Assistant Director.—Joseph R. Peters, Jr.
Chief Technology Officer.—Richard D. Fennell.
Chief of:
IT Applications Development Office.—Ann E. Haun (acting), 502–2730.
IT Infrastructure Management Division.—Craig W. Jenkins, 502–2640.
IT Policy Staff.—Terry A. Cain, 502–3300.
IT Project Coordination Office.—Robert D. Morse, 502–2377.
IT Security Office.—Robert N. Sinsheimer, 502–2350.
IT Systems Deployment and Support Division.—Ann E. Haun, 502–2700.
Assistant Director for Internal Services.—Doreen Bydume, 502–4200.
Chief of:
AO Administrative Services Division.—Iris Guerra, 502–1220.
AO Information and Technology Services Division.—John C. Chang, 502–2830.
AO Personnel Division.—Cheri Thompson Reid, 502–3800.
AO Procurement Management Division.—William Roeder, 502–1330.
Assistant Director for Judges Programs.—Peter G. McCabe, 502–1800.
Deputy Assistant Director.—R. Townsend Robinson, 502–1800.
Chief of:
Article III Judges Division.—Margaret A. Irving, 502–1860.
Bankruptcy Judges Division.—Francis F. Szczebak, 502–1900.
Magistrate Judges Division.—Thomas C. Hnatowski, 502–1830.
Rules Committee Support Office.—John K. Rabiej, 502–1820.
Statistics Division.—Steven R. Schlesinger, 502–1440.
Assistant Director, Office of Probation and Pretrial Services.—John M. Hughes, 502–1600.
Deputy Assistant Director.—Matthew G. Rowland.
Chief of:
Criminal Law Policy Staff.—James C. Oleson.
Programs Administration Division.—Nancy Beatty Gregoire.
Special Projects Office.—Nancy Lee Bradshaw.
Technology Division.—Nicholas B. DiSabatino.

FEDERAL JUDICIAL CENTER

One Columbus Circle, NE., 20002–8003, phone (202) 502–4000

Director.—Judge Barbara J. Rothstein, 502–4160, fax 502–4099.
Deputy Director.—John S. Cooke, 502–4164, fax 502–4099.
Director of:
Communications, Policy and Design Office.—Sylvan A. Sobel, 502–4250, fax 502–4077.
Education Division.—Bruce M. Clarke, 502–4257, fax 502–4299.
Federal Judicial History Office.—Bruce A. Ragsdale, 502–4181, fax 502–4077.
International Judicial Relations Office.—Mira Gur-Arie, 502–4191, fax 502–4099.
Research Division.—James B. Eaglin, 502–4070, fax 502–4199.
Systems Innovation and Development Office.—Ted Coleman, 502–4223, fax 502–4288.

DISTRICT OF COLUMBIA COURTS

H. Carl Moultrie I Courthouse, 500 Indiana Avenue, NW., 20001
phone (202) 879–1010

Executive Officer.—Anne B. Wicks, 879–1700.
Deputy Executive Officer.—Cheryl R. Bailey, 879–1700; fax 879–4829.
Director, Legislative, Intergovernmental and Public Affairs.—Leah Gurowitz, 879–1700.

DISTRICT OF COLUMBIA COURT OF APPEALS

phone (202) 879–1010

Chief Judge.—Eric T. Washington.

Associate Judges:
Kathryn A. Oberly.
Vanessa Ruiz.
Inez Smith Reid.
Stephen H. Glickman.
Noël Anketell Kramer.
John R. Fisher.
Anna Blackburne-Rigsby.
Phyllis D. Thompson.

Senior Judges:
Theodore R. Newman.
William C. Pryor.
Annice M. Wagner.
John W. Kern III.
James A. Belson.
Warren R. King.
John M. Ferren.
Frank Q. Nebeker.
John M. Steadman.
John A. Terry.
Frank E. Schwelb.
Michael W. Farrell.

Clerk.—Garland Pinkston, Jr., 879–2725.
Chief Deputy Clerk.—Joy A. Chapper, 879–2722.
Administration Director.—John Dyson, 879–2738.
Admissions Director.—Jacqueline Smith, 879–2714.
Public Office Operations Director.—Terry Lambert, 879–2702.
Senior Staff Attorney.—Rosanna M. Mason, 879–2718.

SUPERIOR COURT OF THE DISTRICT OF COLUMBIA

phone (202) 879–1010

Chief Judge.—Lee F. Satterfield.
Associate Judges:
Geoffrey M. Alprin.
Jennifer Anderson.
Judith Bartnoff.
John H. Bayly, Jr.
Ronna L. Beck.
James E. Boasberg.
Patricia A. Broderick.
A. Franklin Burgess, Jr.
Zoe Bush.
Jerry S. Byrd.
John M. Campbell.
Russell F. Canan.
Erik P. Christian.
Kaye K. Christian.
Jeanette Clark.
Natalia M. Combs Greene.
Laura A. Cordero.
Harold L. Cushenberry, Jr.
Linda Kay Davis.
Rafael Diaz.
Herbert B. Dixon, Jr.
Stephanie Duncan-Peters.
Gerald I. Fisher.
Wendell P. Gardner, Jr.
Brook Hedge.
Brian Holeman.
Craig Iscoe.
Gregory Jackson.
William M. Jackson.
John Ramsey Johnson.
Anita Josey-Herring.
Ann O'Regan Keary.
Neal E. Kravitz.
Lynn Lebowitz.
Cheryl M. Long.
José M. López.
Judith N. Macaluso.
Juliet McKenna.
Zinora Mitchell-Rankin.
Robert E. Morin.
Thomas J. Motley.
John M. Mott.
Hiram E. Puig-Lugo.
Michael L. Rankin.
Judith E. Retchin.
Robert I. Richter.
Robert R. Rigsby.
Maurice A. Ross.
Michael Ryan.
Fern Flanagan Saddler.
Lee F. Satterfield.
Mary A. Gooden Terrell.
Linda D. Turner.
Odessa F. Vincent.
Frederick H. Weisberg.
Rhonda Reid-Winston.
Melvin R. Wright.
Joan Zeldon.

Magistrate Judges:
Janet Albert.
Diane Brenneman.
Julie Breslow.
Evelyn B. Coburn.
Carol Ann Dalton.
J. Dennis Doyle.
Diana Harris Epps.
Tara Fentress.
Joan Goldfrank.
Ronald A. Goodbread.
S. Pamela Gray.
Andrea L. Harnett.

Karen Howze.
Noel Johnson.
Milton C. Lee.
Michael McCarthy.
John McCabe.
Aida L. Melendez.
William W. Nooter.
Richard H. Ringell.
Mary Grace Rook.
Frederick Sullivan.
Elizabeth Carroll Wingo.

Senior Judges:

Mary Ellen Abrecht.
Bruce D. Beaudin.
Leonard Braman.
Arthur L. Burnett, Sr.
Frederick Dorsey.
Stephen F. Eilperin.
George Herbert Goodrich.
Henry F. Greene.
Eugene N. Hamilton.
John R. Hess.
Richard A. Levie.
Bruce S. Mencher.
Stephen G. Milliken.
J. Gregory Mize.
Truman A. Morrison III.
Tim Murphy.
Nan R. Shuker.
Robert S. Tignor.
Fred B. Ugast.
Paul R. Webber III.
Ronald P. Wertheim.
Susan R. Winfield.
Peter H. Wolf.
Patricia A. Wynn.

Clerk of the Court.—Duane B. Delaney, 879–1400.

GOVERNMENT OF THE DISTRICT OF COLUMBIA

John A. Wilson Building, 1350 Pennsylvania Avenue, NW., 20004

phone (202) 724–8000

[All area codes within this section are (202)]

COUNCIL OF THE DISTRICT OF COLUMBIA

Council Chairman (at Large).—Vincent C. Gray, Suite 504, 724–8032.
Chairman Pro Tempore.—Jack Evans.
Council Members (at Large):
David A. Catania, Suite 404, 724–7772.
Phil Mendelson, Suite 402, 724–8064.
Kwame R. Brown, Suite 506, 724–8174.
Michael A. Brown, Suite 406, 724–8105.
Council Members:
Jim Graham, Ward 1, Suite 105, 724–8181.
Jack Evans, Ward 2, Suite 106, 724–8058.
Mary M. Cheh, Ward 3, Suite 108, 724–8062.
Muriel Bowser, Ward 4, Suite 110, 724–8052.
Harry Thomas, Jr., Ward 5, Suite 107, 724–8028.
Thomas Wells, Ward 6, Suite 408, 724–8072.
Yvette M. Alexander, Ward 7, Suite 400, 724–8068.
Marion Barry, Ward 8, Suite 102, 724–8045.
Council Officers:
Secretary to the Council.—Cynthia Brock-Smith, Suite 5, 724–8080.
Budget Director.—Eric Goulet, Suite 508, 724–8139.
General Counsel.—Brian K. Flowers, Suite 4, 724–8026.
Policy Analysis Director.—Susan Banta, Suite 11, 654–6183.
D.C. Auditor.—Deborah K . Nichols, 717 14th Street, NW., 727–3600.

EXECUTIVE OFFICE OF THE MAYOR

Suite 327, phone (202) 727–6300, fax 727–8127

Mayor of the District of Columbia.—Adrian M. Fenty.
Executive Assistant to the Mayor.—Glenis McKoy.
Chief of Staff.—Carrie S. Kohns.
Deputy Chief of Staff.—Sara Lasner.
Special Assistants to the Chief of Staff.—Tiffany Crowe, Ashley Marshall.
Executive Assistant to the Chief of Staff.—Natalie Stake.
Deputy Mayor for—
Education.—Victor Reinoso.
Planning and Economic Development.—Valerie Santos, suite 317, 727–6365, fax 727–6307.
Secretary of the District of Columbia.—Stephanie D. Scott, Ph.D., suite 419, 727–6306, fax 727–3582.
General Counsel.—Andrew "Chip" Richardson III, suite 327, 727–1597, fax 727–8127.
Inspector General.—Charles J. Willoughby, Esq., 717 14th Street, NW., 5th Floor, 20020, 727–2540, fax 727–9846.
Director of:
Communications.—Mafara Hobson, suite 327, 727–5011, fax 727–8127.
Mayor's Office of Community Relations and Services.—Sarah Latterner, suite 211, 442–8150, fax 727–9846.
Policy and Legislative Affairs.—Bridget Davis, suite 511, 727–6979, fax 727–3765.
Scheduling.—Sandy Castor, suite 327, 727–4043, fax 727–8127.

OFFICE OF THE CITY ADMINISTRATOR

Suite 533, phone (202) 478–9200, fax (202) 535–1224

City Administrator/Deputy Mayor.—Neil Albert.
Executive Assistant to City Administrator.—Xzaquoinett Warrick.

COMMISSIONS

Arts and Humanities, 410 8th Street, NW., 5th Floor, 20004, 724–5613, fax 727–4135.
Executive Director.—Gloria Nauden.
Chairperson.—Dorothy McSweeny.

Judicial Disabilities and Tenure, 515 5th Street, NW., Suite 312, 20001, 727–1363, fax 727–9718.
Executive Director.—Cathaee Hudgins.
Chairperson.—William P. Lightfoot.

Judicial Nominations, 616 H Street, NW., Suite 623, 20001, 879–0478, fax 737–9126.
Executive Director.—Peggy Smith.

Serve DC, 441 4th Street, NW., Suite 1140 North, 20001, 727–7925, fax 727–9198.
Executive Director.—Amy Ward.

Washington Metropolitan Area Transit, 1828 L Street, NW., 20036, 331–1671, fax 653–2179.
Executive Director.—Bill Morrow.

DEPARTMENTS

Child and Family Services Agency, 400 6th Street, SW., 5th Floor, 20024, 442–6000, fax 442–6498.
Director.—Dr. Roque Gerald.

Consumer and Regulatory Affairs, 941 North Capitol Street, NE., 20002, 442–4400, fax 442–9445.
Director.—Linda Argo.

Corrections, 1923 Vermont Avenue, NW., Room 207N, 20001, 673–7316, fax 671–0169.
Director.—Devon Brown.

Environment, 2000 14th Street, NW., 20009, 673–6700, fax 673–6725.
Director.—George Hawkins.

Employment Services, 609 H Street, NE., 20002, 724–7000, fax 673–6993.
Director.—Joe Walsh.

Fire and Emergency Medical Services, 1923 Vermont Avenue, NW., Suite 201, 20001, 673–3331, fax 673–3188.
Fire Chief.—Dennis L. Rubin.

Health, 825 North Capitol Street, NE., 20002, 671–5000, fax 442–4788.
Director.—Dr. Pierre Vigilance, M.D., M.P.A., FACPE.

Housing and Community Development, 801 North Capitol Street, NE., 8th floor, 20002, 442–7200, fax 442–8391.
Director.—Leila Edmonds.

Human Services, 64 New York Avenue, NE., 6th floor, 20002, 671–4200, fax 671–4325.
Director.—Clarence Carter.

Insurance, Securities and Banking, 810 1st Street, NE., Suite 701, 20002, 727–8000, fax 535–1196.
Commissioner.—Thomas E. Hampton.

Mental Health, 77 P Street, NE., 4th Floor, 20002, phone 673–7440, fax 673–3433.
Director.—Stephen T. Baron, LCSW–C.

Metropolitan Police, 300 Indiana Avenue, NW., 20001, phone 311 or (202) 737–4404 if calling from outside DC, fax 727–9524.

Police Chief.—Cathy L. Lanier.

Motor Vehicles, 301 C Street, NW., 20001, 727–5000, fax 727–4653.
Director.—Lucinda M. Babers.

Parks and Recreation, 3149 16th Street, NW., 20010, 673–7647, fax 673–6694.
Director.—Dr. Ximena Hartsock.

Public Works, 2000 14th Street, NW., 6th Floor, 20009, 673–6833, fax 671–0642.
Director.—William O. Howland, Jr.

Small and Local Business Development, 441 4th Street, NW., Suite 970 North, 20001, 727–3900, fax 724–3786.
Director.—Lee Smith.

Transportation, 2000 14th Street, NW., 6th Floor, 20009, 673–6813, fax 671–0642.
Director.—Gabe Klein.

Youth Rehabilitation Services, 1000 Mt. Olivet Road, NE., 20002, 576–8175, fax 576–8457.
Director.—Vincent N. Schiraldi.

OFFICES

Administrative Hearings, 825 North Capitol Street, NE., Suite 4150, 20002, 442–9091.
Chief Judge.—Tyrone T. Butler.

Aging, 441 Fourth Street, NW., Suite 900 South, 20001, 724–5622, fax 724–4979.
Director.—Clarence Brown.

Asian and Pacific Islander Affairs, 441 4th Street, NW., Suite 805 South, 20001, 727–3120, fax 727–9655.
Executive Director.—Soohyun ''Julie'' Koo.

Attorney General, 1350 Pennsylvania Avenue, NW., Suite 409, 20004, 727–3400, fax 724–6590.
Attorney General.—Peter Nickles (acting).

Boards and Commissions, 441 4th Street, NW., Suite 530 South, 20001, 727–1372, fax 727–2359.
Director.—Bridgett Davis.

Cable Television and Telecommunications, 3007 Tilden Street, NW., Pod P, 20008, 671–0066, fax 332–7020.
Acting Director.—Eric E. Richardson.

Chief Financial Officer, 1350 Pennsylvania Avenue, NW., Suite 203, 20004, 727–2476, fax 727–1643.
Chief Financial Officer.—Natwar M. Gandhi.

Chief Medical Examiner, 1910 Massachusetts Avenue, SE., Building 27, 20003, 698–9000, fax 698–9100.
Chief Medical Examiner.—Dr. Marie-Lydie Pierre-Louis.

Chief Technology Officer, 441 4th Street, NW., Suite 930 South, 20001, 727–2277, fax 727–6857.
Chief Technology Officer.—Chris Wiley.

Communications Office, 1350 Pennsylvania Avenue, NW., Suite 533, 20004, 727–5011, fax 727–9561.
Director.—Mafara Hobson.

Community Relations and Services, 1350 Pennsylvania Avenue, NW., Suite 211, 20004, 442–8150, fax 727–5931.
Director.—Sarah Latterner.

Contracting and Procurement, 441 4th Street, NW., Suite 700 South, 20001, 727–0252, fax 727–9385.
Chief Procurement Officer.—David Gragan.

Emergency Management Agency, 2720 Martin Luther King, Jr. Avenue, SE., 20032, 727–6161, fax 673–2290.
Director.—Darrell Darnell.

Employee Appeals, 717 14th Street, NW., 3rd Floor, 20005, 727–0004, fax 727–5631.

Executive Director.—Warren Cruise, Esq.

Finance and Resource Management, 441 4th Street, NW., Suite 890 North, 20001, 727–0333, fax 727–0659.
Director of Finance Operations.—Mohamed Mohamed.

Human Resources, 441 4th Street, NW., Suite 300 South, 20001, 442–9600, fax 727–6827.
Director.—Brender L. Gregory.

Human Rights, 441 4th Street, NW., Suite 570N, 20001, 727–4559, fax 727–9589.
Director.—Gustavo F. Velasquez.

Labor-Management Programs, 441 4th Street, NW., Suite 1150 North, 20001, 727–4999, fax 724–7713.
Director.—Ronald S. Flowers.

Labor Relations and Collective Bargaining, 441 4th Street, NW., Suite 820 North, 20001, 724–4953, fax 727–6887.
Director.—Natasha Campbell.

Latino Affairs, 2000 14th Street, NW., 2nd Floor, 20009, 671–2825, fax 673–4557.
Director.—Mercedes Lemp.

Lesbian, Gay, Bisexual and Transgender Affairs, 1350 Pennsylvania Avenue, NW., Suite 211, 20004, 442–8150, fax 727–5931.
Director.—Chris Dyer.

Mayor's Office of Community Relations and Services, 1350 Pennsylvania Avenue, NW., Suite 211, 20004, 442–8150, fax 727–5445.
Director.—Sarah Latterner.

Motion Picture and Television Development, 441 4th Street, NW., Suite 760 North, 20001, 727–6608, fax 727–3246.
Director.—Kathy Hollinger.

Partnerships and Grants Development, 441 4th Street, NW., Suite 1130 North, 20001, 727–8900, fax 727–1652.
Director.—Lafayette Barnes.

Planning, 801 North Capitol Street, NE., Suite 4000, 20002, 442–7600, fax 442–7638.
Director.—Harriet Tregoning.

Policy and Legislative Affairs, 1350 Pennsylvania Avenue, NW., Suite 511, 20004, 727–6979, fax 727–3765.
Deputy Chief of Staff.—Bridgett Davis.

Property Management, 441 4th Street, NW., Suite 1100 South, 20001, 724–4400, fax 727–9877.
Director.—Robin Eve Jasper.

Risk Management, 441 4th Street, NW., Suite 800 South, 20001, 727–8600, fax 727–8319.
Director.—Kelly Valentine.

State Education, 441 4th Street, NW., Suite 350 North, 20001, 727–6436, fax 727–2019.
State Education Officer.—Kerri Briggs.

Unified Communications, 2720 Martin Luther King Jr. Avenue, SE., 20032, 730–0524, fax 730–0513.
Director.—Janice Quintana.

Veterans Affairs, 441 4th Street, NW., Suite 570 South, 20001, 724–5454, fax 727–7117.
Director.—Timothy Smith.

Victim Services, 1350 Pennsylvania Avenue, NW., Suite 407, 20004, 727–3934, fax 727–1617.
Director.—Melissa Hook.

Zoning, 441 4th Street, NW., Suite 210, 20001, 727–6311, fax 727–6072.
Director.—Jerrily R. Kress, FAIA.

INDEPENDENT AGENCIES

Advisory Neighborhood Commissions, 1350 Pennsylvania Avenue, NW., Suite 8, 20004, 727–9945, fax 727–0289.

Executive Director.—Gottlieb Simon.

Alcoholic Beverage Regulation Administration, 941 North Capitol Street, NE., Suite 7200, 20002, 442–4423, fax 727–9685.
Director.—Fred Moosally.

Board of Elections and Ethics, 441 4th Street, NW., Suite 250 North, 20001, 727–2525, fax 347–2648.
Chairperson of the Board.—Teri Stroud.

Criminal Justice Coordinating Council, 441 4th Street, NW., Suite 727 North, 20001, 442–9283, fax 442–4922.
Executive Director.—Nancy Ware.

District of Columbia Court of Appeals, 500 Indiana Avenue, NW., Room 6000, 20001, 879–2701, fax 626–8840.
Chief Judge.—Eric T. Washington.

District of Columbia Housing Authority, 1133 North Capitol Street, NE., 20001, 535–1500, fax 535–1740.
Executive Director.—Michael P. Kelly.

District of Columbia Public Defender Service, 633 Indiana Avenue, NW., 20001, 628–1200, fax 824–2378.
Director.—Avis Buchanan.

District of Columbia Public Library, 901 G Street, NW., Suite 400, 20001, 727–1101, fax 727–1129.
Director.—Ginnie Cooper.

District of Columbia Public Schools, 825 North Capitol Street, NW., Suite 9026, 20002, 442–4226, fax 442–5026.
Superintendent.—Michelle Rhee.

District of Columbia Retirement Board, 900 7th Street, NW., 2nd Floor, 20001, 343–3200, fax 566–5000.
Executive Director.—Constance Donovan (acting).

District of Columbia Sentencing Commission, 441 4th Street, NW., Suite 830 South, 20001, 727–8822, fax 727–7929.
Executive Director.—Kim S. Hunt.

District of Columbia Sports and Entertainment Commission, 2400 East Capitol Street, SE., 20003, 547–9077, fax 547–7460.
Chief Executive Officer.—Erik Moses.

District Lottery and Charitable Games Control Board, 2101 Martin Luther King Jr. Avenue, SE., 20020, 645–8000, fax 645–7914.
Executive Director.—Jeanette A. Michael.

Housing Finance Agency, 815 Florida Avenue, NW., 20001, 777–1600, fax 986–6705.
Executive Director.—Harry D. Sewell.

Metropolitan Washington Council of Governments, 777 North Capitol Street, NE., 20002, 962–3200, fax 962–3201.
Executive Director.—Dave Robertson.

People's Counsel, 1133 15th Street, NW., Suite 500, 20005, 727–3071, fax 727–1014.
People's Counsel.—Elizabeth A. Noel, Esq.

Police Complaints, 1400 I Street, NW., Suite 700, 20005, 727–3838, fax 727–9182.
Executive Director.—Philip K. Eure.

Public Charter School Board, 1436 U Street, NW., Suite 401, 20009, 328–2660, fax 328–2661.
Executive Director.—Josephine Baker.

Public Employee Relations Board, 717 14th Street, NW., 11th Floor, 20005, 727–1822, fax 727–9116.
Executive Director.—Julio Castillo.

Public Service Commission, 1333 H Street, NW., Suite 200W, 20005, 626–5100, fax 393–1389.
Chairperson.—Agnes A. Yates.

Superior Court of the District of Columbia, H. Carl Moultrie I Courthouse, 500 Indiana Avenue, NW., 20001, 879–1010.

Chief Judge.—Rufus G. King III.

Taxicab Commission, 2041 Martin Luther King Jr. Avenue, SE., Suite 204, 20020, 645–6009, fax 889–3604.
Chairperson.—Doreen Thompson.

Washington Convention Center Authority, 801 Mount Vernon Place, NW., 20001, 249–3012, fax 249–3133.
CEO/General Manager.—Greg O'Dell.

Washington, DC Convention and Tourism Corporation, 1212 New York Avenue, NW., Suite 600, 20005, 904–0616 or 249–3012, fax 789–7037.
President/CEO.—William A. Hanbury.

Water and Sewer Authority, 5000 Overlook Avenue, SW., 20032, 787–2000, fax 787–2210.
Chairperson.—Glenn S. Gerstell.

Workforce Investment Council, 609 H Street, NE., Suite 521, 20002, 698–5826, fax 724–1334.
Chairperson.—Barbara B. Lang.

OTHER

Board of Real Property Assessments and Appeals, 441 4th Street, NW., Suite 430, 20001, 727–6860, fax 727–0392.
Director.—Paul Strauss.

Contract Appeals Board, 717 14th Street, NW., Suite 430, 20005, 727–6597, fax 727–3993.
Chief Administrative Judge.—Jonathan D. Zischkau.

Justice Grants Administration, 1350 Pennsylvania Avenue, NW., Suite 327A, 20004, 727–6239, fax 727–1617.
Director.—Josh Weber.

Rehabilitation Services Administration, 810 First Street, NE., 20002, 442–8663, fax 442–8742.
Administrator.—Elizabeth B. Parker.

DISTRICT OF COLUMBIA POST OFFICE LOCATIONS

900 Brentwood Road, NE., 20066–9998, General Information (202) 636–1200

Postmaster.—Delores D. Killett.

CLASSIFIED STATIONS

Station	Phone	Location/Zip Code
Anacostia	523–2119	2650 Naylor Rd., SE., 20020
Ben Franklin	523–2386	1200 Pennsylvania Ave., NW., 20044
B.F. Carriers	636–2289	900 Brentwood Rd., NE., 20004
Benning	523–2391	3937–½ Minnesota Ave., NE., 20019
Bolling AFB	767–4419	Bldg. 10, Brookley Avenue, 20332
Brightwood	726–8119	6323 Georgia Ave., NW., 20
Brookland	523–2126	3401 12th St., NE., 20017
Calvert	523–2908	2336 Wisconsin Ave., NW., 20007
Cleveland Park	523–2396	3430 Connecticut Ave. NW., 20008
Columbia Heights	523–2192	6510 Chillum Pl., NW., 20010
Congress Heights	523–2122	400 Southern Ave., SE., 20032
Customs House	523–2195	3178 Bladensburg Rd., NE., 20018
Dulles	(703) 471–9497	Dulles International Airport, 20041
Farragut	523–2507	1145 19th St., NW., 20033
Fort Davis	842–4964	3843 Pennsylvania Ave., SE., 20020
Fort McNair	523–2144	300 A. St., SW., 20319

CLASSIFIED STATIONS—CONTINUED

Station	Phone	Location / Zip Code
Frederick Douglass	842–4959	Alabama Ave., SE., 20020
Friendship	523–2153 / 2130	4005 Wisconsin Ave., NW., 20016
Georgetown	523–2406	1215 31st St., NW., 20007
Government Mail	523–2138 / 2139	3300 V Street, NE., 20018–9998
Headsville	357–3029	Smithsonian Institute, 20560
Kalorama	523–2906	2300 18th St., NW., 20009
Lamond Riggs	523–2041	6200 North Capitol St., NW., 20
LeDroit Park	483–0973	416 Florida Ave., NW., 20001
L'Enfant Plaza	523–2014	458 L'Enfant Plaza, SW., 20026
Main Office Window	636–2130	Curseen / Morris P & DC, 900 Brentwood Rd., NE., 20066–9998
Martin L. King, Jr	523–2001	1400 L St., NW., 20043
McPherson	523–2394	1750 Pennsylvania Ave., NW, 20038
Mid City	....	Temporarily Closed
NASA	358–0235 / 0199	600 Independence Ave., SW., 20546
National Capitol	523–2368	2 Massachusetts Ave., NE., 20002
Naval Research Lab	767–3426	4565 Overlook Ave., 20390
Navy Annex	(703) 920–0815	1668 D Street, 20335
Northeast	388–5216	1563 Maryland Ave., NE., 20002
Northwest	523–2570	5632 Connecticut Ave., NW., 20015
Palisades	842–2291	5136 MacArthur Blvd., NW., 20016
Pavilion Postique	523–2571	1100 Pennsylvania Ave., NW., 20004
Pentagon	(703) 695–6835	Concourse Pentagon (Army-20301 / 20310; Air Force-20330; Navy-20350)
Petworth	523–2681	4211 9th St., NW., 20
Postal Square	523–2022	2 Massachusetts Ave., NW., 20002
Randle	584–6807	2341 Pennsylvania Ave., SE., 20023
River Terrace	523–2884	3621 Benning Rd., NE., 20019
Southeast	523–2174	327 7th St., SE., 20003
Southwest	523–2597	45 L St., SW., 20024
State Department	523–2574	2201 C St., NW., 20520
T Street	232–6301	1915 14th St., NW., 20009
Tech World	523–2019	800 K St., NW., 20001
Temple Heights	523–2563	1921 Florida Ave., NW., 20009
Twentieth Street	523–2411	2001 M St., NW., 20036
U.S. Naval	433–2216	940 M St., SE., 20374
V Street	636–2272 / 2273	Section 2, Curseen / Morris P & DC, 900 Brentwood Rd., NE., 20002–9998
Walter Reed	782–3768	6800 Georgia Ave., NW., 20012
Ward Place	523–5109	2121 Ward Pl., NW., 20037
Washington Square	523–2632	1050 Connecticut Ave., NW., 20035
Watergate	965–4598	2512 Virginia Ave., NW., 20037
Woodridge	523–2195	2211 Rhode Island Ave., NE., 20018

INTERNATIONAL ORGANIZATIONS

EUROPEAN SPACE AGENCY (E.S.A.)

Headquarters: 8–10 Rue Mario Nikis, 75738 Paris Cedex 15, France
phone 011–33–1–5369–7654, fax 011–33–1–5369–7560

Chairman of the Council.—Per Tegnér.
Director General.—Jean-Jacques Dordain.
Member Countries:

Austria	Greece	Portugal
Belgium	Ireland	Spain
Denmark	Italy	Sweden
Finland	Luxembourg	Switzerland
France	Netherlands	United Kingdom
Germany	Norway	Czech Republic

Cooperative Agreement.—Canada.

European Space Operations Center (E.S.O.C.), Robert-Bosch-Str. 5, D–64293 Darmstadt, Germany, phone 011–49–6151–900, fax 011–49–6151–90495.

European Space Research and Technology Center (E.S.T.E.C.), Keplerlaan 1, NL–2201, AZ Noordwijk, ZH, The Netherlands, phone 011–31–71–565–6565, Telex: 844–39098, fax 011–31–71–565–6040.

European Space Research Institute (E.S.R.I.N.), Via Galileo Galilei, Casella Postale 64, 00044 Frascati, Italy, phone 011–39–6–94–18–01, fax 011–39–6–9418–0280.

Washington Office (E.S.A.), 955 L'Enfant Plaza, SW., Suite 7800, 20024.
Head of Office.—Dieckmann Andreas (202) 488–4158, fax 488–4930, *Diekmann.andreas@esa.int.*

INTER-AMERICAN DEFENSE BOARD

2600 16th Street, NW., 20441, phone (202) 939–6041, fax 387–2880

Chairman.—Lt. Gen. José Roberto Machado e Silva, Air Force, Brazil.
Vice Chairman.—GB Mario Ferro Rendon, Army, Guatemala.
Secretary.—CF Paulo César Bittencourt Ferreira, Navy, Brazil.
Director General.—GB Ancil W. Antoine, Army, Trinidad and Tobago.
Deputy Secretary for—
Administration.—COL Pedro Pimentel, Army, Chile.
Conference.—Col. Luiz Cláudio Moreira Novaes, Air Force, Brazil.

CHIEFS OF DELEGATION

Antigua and Barbuda.—COL Trevor Thomas, Defense Forces.
Argentina.—Minister Francisco Julian Licastro, Civilian.
Barbados.—LTC Clyde Parris, Army.
Belize.—COL Stephen Heusner, Defense Forces.
Boliva.—Vacant.
Brazil.—Maj. Gen. Átila Maia da Rocha, Air Force.
Canada.—MG Doug Langton, Canadian Forces.
Chile.—GB Juan Biskupovic Moya, Army.
Colombia.—Maj. Gen. Eduardo Behar Benitez, Air Force.
Dominican Republic.—MG Andres Apolinar Disla, Army.
Ecuador.—COL Juan Villegas Aldaz, Army.

El Salvador.—COL Victor Manuel Bolaños, Army.
Guatemala.—Col. Julio Cesar Lopez, Air Force.
Guyana.—COL Mark Anthony Philips, Army.
Haiti.—Minister Counselor Charles Leon, Civilian.
Honduras.—Contalmirante Jose Eduardo Espinal (suspended), Navy.
Jamaica.—COL Anthony Anderson, Defense Forces.
Mexico.—GB Juan A. Cordero, Army.
Nicaragua.—COL Ronald Torres, Army.
Panama.—Comisionado Jaime Ruiz, Civilian.
Paraguay.—COL Adalberto Garcete, Army.
Peru.—Almirante Carlos Gamarra, Navy.
Suriname.—COL Glenn Sedney, Army.
Trinidad and Tobago.—COL Ronald Maunday, Army.
United States.—Maj. Gen. Darren McDew, Air Force.
Uruguay.—Contralmirante Federico Lebel, Navy.
Venezuela.—Primer Secretario Carlos Alberto Rodriguez Torrealba, Civilian.

INTER-AMERICAN DEFENSE COLLEGE

Director.—RADM Moira Flanders, Navy, USA.
Vice Director.—MG Jorge Raul Larrea, Army, Peru.
Chief of Studies.—GB Roberto Efrain Rodriguez, Army, Guatemala.

INTER-AMERICAN DEVELOPMENT BANK

1300 New York Avenue, NW., 20577, phone (202) 623–1000

http://www.iadb.org

OFFICERS

President.—Luis Alberto Moreno (Colombia).
Chief, Office of the President.—Luis Giorgio.
Executive Vice President.—Daniel M. Zelikow (United States).
Chief Advisor.—Robert N. Kaplan.
Director, Office of Evaluation and Oversight.—Stephen A. Quick.
Research and Chief Economist.—Eduardo Lora, a.i.
Executive Auditor.—Alan N. Siegfried.
External Relations Advisor.—Jorge de Lama.
Ombudsperson.—Dóris Campos-Infantino.
Secretary.—German Quintana.
Advisor, Office of Outreach and Partnerships.—Bernardo Guillamon.
Advisor, Office of Risk Management.—Fernando Yñigo.
Manager, Office of Strategic Planning and Development Effectiveness.—Luis Estanislao Echebarria.
Chief, Office of Institutional Integrity.—Roberto de Michele, a.i.
Vice President for Countries.—Roberto Vellutini.
Country Manager, Office of:
Department Andean Group.—Alicia Ritchie.
Department Caribbean.—Dora Currea.
Department Central America, Mexico, Panama and Dominican Republic.—Gina Montiel.
Department Southern Cone.—Carlos Hurtado Lopez.
Vice President for Sectors and Knowledge.—Santiago Levy.
Manger of:
Infrastructure and Environment Sector.—José Agustin Aguerre, a.i.
Institutional Capacity and Finance Sector.—Mario Marcel.
Knowledge and Learning.—Graciela Schamis.
Social Sector.—Kei Kawabata.
Trade and Integration.—Antoni Estevadeordal.
Vice President for Finance and Administration.—Manuel Rapoport.
Manager of:
Budget and Administrative Services.—John Hauge.
Finance Department.—Edward Bartholomew.
Human Resources.—Guillermo Miranda.
Information Technology.—Simon Gauthier.

Legal Department.—James Spinner.

Vice President for Private Sector and Non-Sovereign Guaranteed Operations.—Steven Piug.

Manager of:

Office of the Multilateral Investment Fund.—Julie Katzman.

Opportunities for the Majority Sector.—Luiz Ros.

Structured and Corporate Financing Department.—Hans Schulz.

BOARD OF EXECUTIVE DIRECTORS

Argentina and Haiti.—Eugenio Diaz-Bonilla.

Alternate.—Martin Bes.

Austria, Denmark, Finland, France, Norway, Spain, and Sweden.—Marc Olivier Strauss-Kahn.

Alternate.—Elisabeth Anna Gruber.

Bahamas, Barbados, Guyana, Jamaica, Trinidad and Tobago.—Winston Alfred Cox.

Alternate.—Richard Bernal.

Belgium, Germany, Israel, Italy, The Netherlands, and Switzerland.—Hans Hammann.

Alternate.—Francesca Manno.

Belize, Costa Rica, El Salvador, Guatemala, Honduras, and Nicaragua.—Manuel Coronel.

Alternate.—Carmen Maria Madriz.

Bolivia, Paraguay, and Uruguay.—Luis Hernando Larrazabal.

Alternate.—Marcelo Bisogno.

Brazil, and Suriname.—Jose Carlos Miranda.

Alternate.—Sergio Portugal.

Canada.—Vinita Watson.

Alternate.—Peter Cameron.

Chile and Ecuador.—Alejandro Foxley.

Alternate.—Xavier Eduardo Santillan.

Colombia and Ecuador.—Luis G. Echeverri.

Croatia, Japan, Portugal, Slovenia, and United Kingdom.—Yasusuke Tsukagoshi.

Alternate.—Stewart Shaw Mills.

Dominican Republic and Mexico.—Cecilia Ramos Avila.

Alternate.—Roberto B. Saladín.

Panama and Venezuela.—Adina Bastidas.

Alternate.—Fernando Eleta.

Peru and Colombia.—Veronica Zavala.

Alternate.—Luis Guillermo Echeverri.

United States of America.—Miguel Rafael San Juan.

INTER-AMERICAN TROPICAL TUNA COMMISSION

8604 La Jolla Shores Drive, La Jolla, CA 92037–1508
phone (858) 546–7100, fax 546–7133, http://www.iattc.org

Director.—Guillermo A. Compeán.

Deputy Director.—Brian S. Hallman.

Commissioners:

Colombia:

Carlos Alberto Robles, Ministerio de Agricultura y Desarrollo Rural, Av. Jiménez 7–65, Bogotá, Colombia (57–1) 334–1199 ext. 310, fax 282–8388; email: carlos.robles@minagricultura.gov.co.

José Alfredo Ramos González, Ministerio de Comercio Industria y Turismo, Calle 28 #13A–15 piso 6°, Bogotá, Colombia (57–1) 606–7530, fax 606–7534; email: aramos@mincomercio.gov.co.

Vladimir Puentes, Ministerio de Ambiente, Vivienda y Desarrollo Territorial, Calle 37 No. 8–40 Piso 4, Bogotá, Colombia (57–1) 332–3400 ext. 2490, fax 332–3457; email: vpuentes@minambiente.gov.co.

Yadir Salazar Mejía, Ministerio de Relaciones Exteriores, Calle 10 No. 5–51 Palacio de San Carlos, Bogotá, Colombia (57–1) 381–4265, fax 381–4747; email: yadir.salazar@cancilleria.gov.co.

Costa Rica:

Asdrúbal Vásquez, Ministerio de Agricultura y Ganadería, Calle 16-Av. 6, Cartago, 549–7050, Costa Rica (506) 2234–1498, fax 2253–4321; email: vazqueza1@ice.co.cr.

Bernal A. Chavarría V., Ministerio de Agricultura y Ganadería, Sabana Sur, 400 Sur, San José, 1000, Costa Rica (506) 2290–8808, fax 2232–4651; email: bchavarria@bcvabogados.com.

Luís Dobles Ramírez, Instituto Costarricense de Pesca y Acuicultura, Ave. 10, San José, 1000, Costa Rica (506) 2248–1130, fax 2248–1196; email: ludora@ice.co.cr.

Ecuador:

Guillermo Morán, Ministerio de Agricultura, Ganadería, Acuacultura y Pesca, Av. 3 y Calle 12, Manta, Manabí, Ecuador (593–5) 262–7911, fax 262–7930; email: guillermo.moran@pesca.gov.ec.

Luís Torres Navarrete, Subsecretaría de Recursos Pesqueros, Víctor Rendón 1006, Lorenzo Garaicoa, Guayaquil, Guayas, Ecuador (593–4) 256–0993, fax 230–0636; email: probecuador@gye.satnet.net.

Ramón Montaño, Subsecretaría de Recursos Pesqueros, Av. 3, Calle 12, Manta, Ecuador (593–5) 262–7930, fax 262–7911; email: rmontaño@pesca.gov.ec.

El Salvador:

José Emilio Suadi, Ministerio de Agricultura y Ganadería, Final 1a. Av. Norte y Av. Manuel Gallardo, Santa Tecla, El Salvador (503) 228–9302, fax 228–1938, email jsuadi@mag.gob.sv.

Manuel Calvo García-Benavides, Calvo Pesca, Ed. Gran Plaza, Local 103, Col. San Benito, San Salvador, El Salvador (503) 2244–4848, fax 2444–8850; email: mane.calvo@calvo.es.

Sonia M. Salaverría, Cendepesca, 1a. Avenida Norte y Avenida Manuel Gallardo, Santa Tecla, El Salvador (503) 2228–0034, fax 2228–0074; email: ssalaverría@mag.gob.sv.

España:

Fernando Curcio, Secretaría General de Pesca Marítima, José Ortega y Gasset, 57, Madrid, 28006 Spain (34–91) 347–6030, fax 347–6032; email: drpesmar@mapya.es.

Rafael Centenera, Secretaría General de Relaciones Pesqueras Internacionales, C. Ortega y Gasset, 57, Madrid, 28006 Spain (34–91) 347–6040, fax 347–6042; email: acuintpm@mpa.es.

Samuel Juarez, Embajada de España, 2375 Pennsylvania Ave., NW., Washington, DC 20037, USA (202) 728–2339, fax 728–2320; email: juarez@mapausa.org.

France:

Christiane Laurent-Monpetit, Ministere de l'Intérieur, de l'Outre-Mer et des Collectivites T., 27, rue Oudinot Paris, 75358 F SPO7, France (33–1) 5369–2466, fax 5369–2065; email: christiane.laurent-monpetit@outre_mer.gouv.fr.

Jonathan Lemeunier, Minitere de l'Agriculture et de la Peche, Direction des Peches Maritimes, Secretariat d'Etat a la Mer, 3 Place Fontenoy, Paris, 75007 France (33–1) 4955–8236, fax 4955–8200; email: jonathan.lemeunieer@agriculture.gouv.fr.

Marie-Sophie Dufau-Richet, Secretariat d'etat a la Mer, 16 Boulevard Raspail, Paris, 75700 France (33–1) 5363–4153, fax 5363–4178; email: Marie.sophie.dufau_richeti@pm.gouv.fr

Michel Sallenave, Haut Commissariat de la République Française en Polynésie, 43 Avenue Bruat. BP 115 Papeete, 98713 French Polynesia (689) 468–517, fax 468–600; email: michel.sallenave@polynesie-francaise.pref.gouv.fr.

Guatemala:

Hugo Alsina Lagos, Ministerio de Agricultura, Ganadería y Alimentación, 3er Nivel, Edificio la Ceiba, Carretera al Pacífico, Km 22 B., Villanueva, Guatemala (502) 6640–9320, fax 6640–9321; email: hugo.alsina@maga.gob.gt.

Bryslie Siomara Cifuentes Velasco, Ministerio de Agricultura, Ganadería y Alimentación, Km. 22 Carretera al Pacífico, Edificio La Ceiba, 3er. Nivel, Guatemala, Guatemala (502) 6640–9320, fax 6640–9321; email: bcifuentes@maga.gob.gt.

Manuel de Jesús Ixquiac Cabrera, Ministerio de Agricultura, Ganadería y Alimentación, Km. 22 Carretera al Pacífico, Eificio La Ceiba, 3er. Nivel, Guatemala City, Guatemala (502) 6640–9320, fax 6640–9321; email: unipesca04@yahoo.com.mx.

Rómulo Dimas Gramajo Lima, Ministerio de Agricultura, Ganadería y Alimentación, 7a. Ave. 12–90 Zona 13 2 Nivel, Villa Nueva, Guatemala (502) 2413–7026, fax 2413–7027, email rgramajo@maga.gob.gt.

Japan:

Masahiro Ishikawa, Federation of Japan Tuna Fisheries Cooperative Associations, 2–3–22 Kudankita Chiyoda-Ku, Tokyo, 102, Japan (81–3) 3264–6167, fax 3234–7455; email: section1@intldiv.Japantuna.or.jp.

Shingo Ota, Fisheries Agency of Japan, 1–2–1 Kasumigaseki, Chiyoda-Ku, Tokyo, 100–8907 Japan (81–3) 3591–1086, fax 3502–0571; email: shingo_oota@nm.maff.go.jp.

Yutaka Aoki, Ministry of Foreign Affairs, 2–2–1 Kasumigaseki, Chiyoda-ku, Tokyo 100–8919 Japan (81–3) 5501–8000, fax 5501–8332; email: yutaka.aoki@mofa.go.jp.

Korea:

Chiguk Ahn, Ministry for Food, Agriculture, Forestry and Fisheries, 88, Gwanmun-ro, Gwacheon-si, Gyeonggi-do, 427–719 Republic of Korea (82–2) 500–2414, fax 503–9174; email: chiguka62@yahoo.com.

Il Jeong Jeong, Ministry for Food, Agriculture, Forestry and Fisheries, 88, Gwanmun-do, Gwacheon-si, Gyeonggi-do, 427–719 Republic of Korea (82–2) 500–2422, fax 503–9174; email: icdmomaf@chol.com.

Jeongseok Park, Ministry for Food, Agriculture, Forestry and Fisheries, Government Complex Gwacheon, Jungang-dong 1, Gwacheon, Gyeonggi-do, Republic of Korea (82–2) 500–2426, fax 503–9174; email: jspark2@mifaff.go.kr.

México:

Ramón Corral, Comisión Nacional de Acuicultura y Pesca, Avenida Municipio Libre 377, piso 4–A, Colegio Santa Cruz Atoyac, Delegación Benito, México, DF 03310, Mexico (52–55) 9183–1000, fax 9183–1000; email: rcorrala@conapesca.gob.mx.

Mario Aguilar, Comisión Nacional de Acuicultura y Pesca, 1666 K Street, NW., 12th floor, Washington, DC 20006, USA (202) 293–8138, fax 887–6970; email: mariogaguilars@aol.com.

Michel Dreyfus, Instituto Nacional de la Pesca, Km 97.5 carretera Tijuana-Ensenada, Ensenada, B.C. 22890, México (52–646) 174–6085, fax 174–6135; email: dreyfus@cicese.mx.

Miguel A. Cisneros, Instituto Nacional de la Pesca, Pitágoras #1320, Piso 8vo. Col. Sta Cruz Atoyac, México, D.F. 03310, Mexico (52–55) 3781–9501, fax 3626–8421; email: miguel.cisneros@inapesca.sagarpa.gob.mx.

Nicaragua:

Armando Segura, Cámara de la Pesca de Nicaragua, Camino de Oriente B–2, Managua, Nicaragua (505) 2278–7091, fax 2278–2427; email: capenic@ibw.com.ni.

Danilo Rosales Pichardo, Instituto Nicaragüense de la Pesca y Acuicultura, Del Busto José Martí 5c al Este Barrio Largaespada Managua, Nicaragua (505) 2251–0487, fax 2248–7149; email: drosales@inpesca.gob.ni.

Julio César Guevara Q., INATUN, Balboa Ancón, Panamá City, 0843–02264 Panama (507) 204–4672, fax 204–4651; email: cpesca@gfextun.com.

Steadman Fagoth, Instituto Nicaragüense de la Pesca y Acuicultura, Del Busto Jose Marti, 5 cuadras al Este, Bo. Largaespada Managua, Nicaragua (505) 248–7149; email: sfagoth@mific.gob.ni.

Panamá:

Carlos Eduardo Icaza Epperson, Asociación Panameña de la Industria del Atún, Calle 50, Edif. Plaza 50, Piso 2, Ofic. 1, Panamá City, Panama (507) 393–0600, fax 393–0601; email: apiapanama@cableonda.net.

George Novey, ARAP/Autoridad de los Recursos Acuáticos de Panamá, Altos de Curundu, Calle Manuel Melo, Edificio 571 Panamá City, 0816–01611, Panama (507) 507–0765, fax 507–0754; email: gnovey@yahoo.com.

Ramón González, ARAP/Autoridad de los Recursos Acuáticos de Panamá, Edificio El Paso Elevado, Vía Transismica Panamá City, 0819–05850, Panama (507) 511–6018 ext. 207; email: dgordenación@arap.gob.pa.

María Patricia Díaz, FIPESCA, Corozal, Zona Libre de Proceso, Edif. 319, Panamá City, Panama (507) 317–3861, fax 317–3862; email: latintuna@yahoo.com.

Perú:

Alfonso Miranda, Ministerio de la Producción, Calle Uno Oeste Nro.060 Urbanización Corpac-San Isidro, Lima 27, Peru (51–1) 616–2208, fax 616–2222–703; email: amiranda@produce.gob.pe.

Doris Sotomayor Yalan, Ministerio de Relaciones Exteriores, Jr. Ucayali N° 318-Jr. Lampa N° 535, Lima, Peru (51–1) 311–2658; email: dsotomayor@rree.gob.pe.

Gladys Cárdenas, Instituto del Mar del Perú, Esquina de Gamarra y General Valle s/n Chucuito-Callao, Lima, Peru (51–1) 4200–144, fax 420–0144; email: gcardenas@imarpe.gob.pe.

Jorge Vértiz Calderón, Ministerio de Producción Pesquería, Calle 1 Oeste #60, Urb. Córpac, San Isidro, Lima 27, Peru (51–1) 224–3423, fax 224–2381; email: jvertiz2produce.gob.pe.

USA:

Patrick Rose, U.S. Commissioner to IATTC, P.O. Box 7242, Rancho Santa Fe, CA, 92067, USA (858) 756–2733, fax 756–5850; email: pat.socal@yahoo.com.

Robert C. Fletcher, Sport Fishing Association of California, 1084 Bangor St., San Diego, CA, 92106, USA (619) 226–6455, fax 226–0175; email: dart@sacemup.org.

Rodney McInnis, NOAA/National Marine Fisheries Service, 501 West Ocean Blvd., Suite 4200, Long Beach, CA, 90802, USA (562) 980–4005, fax 980–4018; email: rod.mcinnis@noaa.gov.

Vanuatu:

Christophe Emelee, Vanuatu Government Agent International Fisheries, P.O. Box 1640 Socapore Area, Lini Hwy,Port Vila, Vanuatu (678) 25887, fax 25608; email: tunafishing@vanuatu.com.vu.

Dimitri Malvirlani, Vanuatu Maritime Authority, Marine Quay, P.O. Box 320, Port-Vila, Vanuatu (678) 23128, fax 22949; email: vma@vanuatu.com.vn.

Laurent Parente, Vanuatu International Maritime Organization, P.O. Box 1435, Port Vila, Vanuatu (336) 9951–1207; email: laurentparente-vanuatu-imo@hotmail.com.

Roy M. Joy, Embassy of Vanuatu, Avenue de Tervueren 380 Chemin de Ronde, Brusels, 1150, Belgium (32–2) 771–7494, fax 771–7494; email: rjoy@vanuatuembassy.net.

Venezuela:

Alvin Delgado Martínez, Fundatun-PNOV, Av. Ppal. EL dique Edif. San Pablo, PH, Cumaná, Sucre, 6101, Venezuela (58–293) 433–0431, fax 433–0431; email: fundatunpnov@yahoo.com.

Gilberto Giménez, Instituto Socialista de la Pesca y Acuicultura, Av. Principal el Bosque, entre Sta. Lucía y Sta. Isabel, Torre Credicard, piso 9, Caracas, Venezuela (58–212) 461–9225, fax 574–3587; email: ori@insopesca.gob.ve.

Nancy Tablante, Instituto Socialista de la Pesca y Acuicultura, Av. Principal El Bosque, entre Avds. Sta. Isabel ySta. Lucía, Torre Credicard, piso 9, Caracas, DC, Venezuela (58–212) 953–9972, fax 571–4889; email: ori@inapesca.gov.ve, heralica@cantv.net.

INTERNATIONAL BOUNDARY AND WATER COMMISSION, UNITED STATES AND MEXICO

UNITED STATES SECTION

The Commons, Building C, Suite 100, 4171 North Mesa, El Paso, TX 79902–1441

phone (915) 832–4100, fax 832–4190, http://www.ibwc.state.gov

Commissioner.—Cornelius Williams ''Bill'' Ruth, 832–4101.
Secretary.—Adolfo Mata, 832–4105.
Principal Engineers: John Merino, 832–4749; Alfredo Riera, 832–4160.
Human Resources Director.—Kevin Petz, 832–4114.
General Counsel/Legal Advisor.—Pamela Barber, 832–4109.

MEXICAN SECTION

Avenida Universidad, No. 2180, Zona de El Chamizal, A.P. 1612–D, C.P. 32310,

Ciudad Juarez, Chihuahua, Mexico

P.O. Box 10525, El Paso, TX 79995.

phone 011–52–16–13–7311 or 011–52–16–13–7363 (Mexico)

Commissioner.—Roberto F. Salmon Castello.
Secretary.—Jose de Jesus Luevano Grano.
Principal Engineers: Gilberto Elizalde Hernandez, L. Antonio Rascon Mendoza.

INTERNATIONAL BOUNDARY COMMISSION, UNITED STATES AND CANADA

UNITED STATES SECTION

2401 Pennsylvania Avenue, NW., Suite 475, 20037, phone (202) 736–9100

Commissioner.—Kyle Hipsley (acting).
Deputy Commissioner.—Kyle Hipsley.
Administrative Officer.—Tracy Morris.

CANADIAN SECTION

615 Booth Street, Room 555, Ottawa, ON, Canada K1A 0E9, phone (613) 995–4341

Commissioner.—Peter Sullivan.
Deputy Commissioner.—Al Arseneault.

INTERNATIONAL COTTON ADVISORY COMMITTEE

Headquarters: 1629 K Street, NW., Suite 702, 20006, secretariat@icac.org phone (202) 463–6660, fax 463–6950

(Permanent Secretariat of the Organization)

MEMBER COUNTRIES

Argentina
Australia
Belgium
Brazil
Burkina Faso
Cameroon
Chad
China (Taiwan)
Colombia
Côte d'Ivoire
Egypt
Finland
France
Germany
Greece
India
Iran
Israel
Italy
Kazakhstan
Kenya
Korea, Republic of
Mali
Netherlands
Nigeria
Pakistan
Poland
Russia
South Africa
Spain
Sudan
Switzerland
Syria
Tanzania
Togo
Turkey
Uganda
United States
Uzbekistan
Zambia
Zimbabwe

Executive Director.—Terry P. Townsend.
Statistician.—Armelle Gruere.
Economists: Andrei Guitchounts, Alejandro Plastina.
Head of Technical Information Section.—M. Rafiq Chaudhry.

INTERNATIONAL JOINT COMMISSION, UNITED STATES AND CANADA

UNITED STATES SECTION

2401 Pennsylvania Avenue, NW., Suite 400, 20440

phone (202) 736–9000, fax 254–4564, http://www.ijc.org

Chair.—Irene B. Brooks.
Commissioners: Allen I. Olson, Sam Speck.
Secretary.—Charles A. Lawson.
Legal Advisor.—Susan Daniel.
Engineering Advisor.—Mark Colosimo.
Public Information Officer.—Frank Bevacqua.
Ecologist.—Vacant.

CANADIAN SECTION

234 Laurier Avenue West, Ottawa, Ontario Canada K1P 6K6
phone (613) 995–2984, fax 993–5583

Chairman.—Rt. Hon. Herb Gray.
Commissioners: Pierre Trépanier, Lyle Knott.
Secretary.—Murray Clamen.
Legal Advisor.—Gavin Murphy.
Engineering Advisor.—Paul Pilon.
Senior Environmental Advisor.—Joel Weiner.

GREAT LAKES REGIONAL OFFICE

Eighth Floor, 100 Ouellette Avenue, Windsor, Ontario Canada N9A 6T3
phone (519) 257–6700 (Canada), (313) 226–2170 (U.S.)

Director.—John Gannon (acting).
Public Affairs Officer.—Vacant.

INTERNATIONAL LABOR ORGANIZATION

Headquarters: Geneva, Switzerland, http://www.ilo.org

Washington Office, 1828 L Street, NW., Suite 600, 20036

phone (202) 653–7652, fax 653–7687, washington@ilo.org

Liaison Office with the United Nations

220 East 42nd Street, Suite 3101, New York, NY 10017–5806

International Labor Office (Permanent Secretariat of the Organization)
Headquarters Geneva:
Director-General.—Juan Somavia.
Washington:
Director.—Vacant.
Special Assistant to the Director.—Marina Colby.

INTERNATIONAL MONETARY FUND

700 19th Street, NW., 20431, phone (202) 623–7000

http://www.imf.org

MANAGEMENT AND SENIOR OFFICERS

Managing Director.—Dominique Strauss-Kahn.
First Deputy Managing Director.—John Lipsky.
Deputy Managing Directors: Takatoshi Kato, Murilo Portugal.
Economic Counselor.—Olivier Blanchard.
IMF Institute Director.—Leslie Lipschitz.
Legal Department General Counsel.—Sean Hagan.
Departmental Directors:
African.—Antoinette Sayeh.
Asia and Pacific.—Anoop Singh.
Budget and Planning.—Siddharth Tiwari.
European.—Marek Belka.
External Relations.—Caroline Atkinson.
Finance.—Andrew Tweedie.
Fiscal Affairs.—Carlo Cottarelli.
Internal Audit and Inspection.—Barry Potter.
Middle Eastern.—Masood Ahmed.
Monetary and Capital Markets.—Jose Vinals.
Policy Development and Review.—Reza Moghadam.
Research.—Olivier Blanchard.
Secretary.—Russell Kinkaid.
Statistics.—Adelheid Burgi-Schmelz.
Technology and General Services.—Frank Harnischfeger.
Western Hemisphere.—Nicolas Eyzaguirre.
Director, Regional Office for Asia and the Pacific.—Akira Ariyoshi.
Director, Europe Offices.—Emmanuel van der Meensbrugghe.
Director and Special Representative to the United Nations.—Elliott Harris.

EXECUTIVE DIRECTORS AND ALTERNATES

Executive Directors:
Abdallah S. Alazzaz, represents Saudi Arabia.

Alternate.—Ahmed Al Nassar.
Ambroise Fayolle, represents France.
Alternate.—Benoit Claveranne.
Jens Henriksson, represents Denmark, Estonia, Finland, Iceland, Latvia, Lithuania, Norway, Sweden.
Alternate.—Jarle Bergo.
Ramon Guzman, represents Costa Rica, El Salvador, Guatemala, Honduras, Mexico, Nicaragua, Spain, Venezuela (Republica Bolivariana de).
Alternate.—Alfonso Guerra.
Michael Horgan, represents Antigua and Barbuda, the Bahamas, Barbados, Belize, Canada, Dominica, Grenada, Ireland, Jamaica, St. Kitts and Nevis, St. Lucia, St. Vincent and the Grenadines.
Alternate.—Stephen O'Sullivan.
Samuel Itam, represents Angola, Botswana, Burundi, Eritrea, Ethiopia, Gambia, Kenya, Lesotho, Malawi, Mozambique, Namibia, Nigeria, Sierra Leone, South Africa, Sudan, Swaziland, Tanzania, Uganda, Zambia, Zimbabwe.
Alternate.—Moeketsi Majoro.
Adarsh Kishore, represents Bangladesh, Bhutan, India, Sri Lanka.
Alternate.—K.G.D.D. Dheerasinghe.
Duangmanee Vongpradhip, represents Brunei Darussalam, Cambodia, Fiji, Indonesia, Lao People's Democratic Republic, Malaysia, Myanmar, Nepal, Singapore, Thailand, Tonga, Vietnam.
Alternate.—Adrian Chua.
Thomas Moser, represents Azerbaijan, Kyrgyz Republic, Poland, Switzerland, Tajikistan, Turkmenistan, Uzbekistan, Serbia.
Alternate.—Katarzyna Zajdel-Kurowska.
Paulo Nogueira Batista, Jr., represents Brazil, Colombia, Dominican Republic, Ecuador, Guyana, Haiti, Panama, Suriname, Trinidad and Tobago.
Alternate.—María Ines Agudelo.
Willy Kiekens, represents Austria, Belarus, Belgium, Czech Republic, Hungary, Kazakhstan, Luxembourg, Slovak Republic, Slovenia, Turkey.
Alternate.—Johann Prader.
Laurean W. Rutayisire, represents Benin, Burkina Faso, Cameroon, Cape Verde, Central African Republic, Chad, Comoros, Congo (Democratic Republic of), Congo (Republic of), Côte d'Ivoire, Djibouti, Equatorial Guinea, Gabon, Guinea, Guinea-Bissau, Madagascar, Mali, Mauritania, Mauritius, Niger, Rwanda, São Tomé and Principe, Senegal, Togo.
Alternate.—Kossi Assimaidou.
Arrigo Sadun, represents Albania, Greece, Italy, Malta, Portugal, San Marino.
Alternate.—Miranda Xafa.
Meg Lundsager, represents United States.
Alternate.—Daniel Heath.
Daisuke Kotegawa, represents Japan.
Alternate.—Hiromi Yamaoka.
Jafar Mojarrad, represents Afghanistan (Islamic State of), Algeria, Ghana, Iran (Islamic Republic of), Morocco, Pakistan, Tunisia.
Alternate.—Mohammed Daïri.
Pablo Pereira, represents Argentina, Bolivia, Chile, Paraguay, Peru, Uruguay.
Alternate.—David Vogel.
Klaus D. Stein, represents Germany.
Alternate.—Stephan von Stenglin.
A. Shakour Shaalan, represents Bahrain, Egypt, Iraq, Jordan, Kuwait, Lebanon, Libya Arab, Jamahiriya, Maldives, Oman, Qatar, Syrian Arab Republic, United Arab Emirates, Yemen (Republic of).
Alternate.—Sami Geadah.
Aleksei V. Mozhin, represents Russian Federation.
Alternate.—Andrei Lushin.
Hi-Su Lee, represents Australia, Kiribati, Korea, Marshall Islands, Micronesia (Federated States of), Mongolia, New Zealand, Palau, Papua New Guinea, Philippines, Samoa, Seychelles, Solomon Islands, Vanuatu.
Alternate.—Christopher Y. Legg.
Age F.P. Bakker, represents Armenia, Bosnia and Herzegovina, Bulgaria, Croatia, Cyprus, Georgia, Israel, Macedonia (former Yugoslav Republic of), Moldova, Montenegro Republic, Netherlands, Romania, Ukraine.
Alternate.—Yuriy G. Yakusha.
Jianxiong He, represents China.
Alternate.—Zhengxin Zhang.

Alex Gibbs, represents United Kingdom.
Alternate.—Susanna Moorehead.

INTERNATIONAL ORGANIZATION FOR MIGRATION

Headquarters: 17 Route Des Morillons (P.O. Box 71), CH1211, Geneva 19, Switzerland

Washington Mission: 1752 N Street, NW., Suite 700, 20036, phone (202) 862–1826

New York Mission: 122 East 42nd Street, Suite 1610, New York, NY 10168–1610 phone (212) 681–7000

HEADQUARTERS

Director General.—William Lacy Swing (United States).
Deputy Director General.—Laura Thompson (Costa Rica).
Washington Regional Representative.—Richard E. Scott (United States).
New York Chief of Mission.—Michael Gray (United States).
Permanent Observer to the United Nations.—Luca Dall'Oglio (Italy).

MEMBER STATES

Afghanistan
Albania
Algeria
Angola
Argentina
Armenia
Australia
Austria
Azerbaijan
Bahamas
Bangladesh
Belarus
Belgium
Belize
Benin
Bolivia
Bosnia and Herzegovina
Brazil
Bulgaria
Burkina Faso
Burundi
Cambodia
Cameroon
Canada
Cape Verde
Chile
Colombia
Congo
Costa Rica
Côte d'Ivoire
Croatia
Cyprus
Czech Republic
Democratic Republic of the Congo
Denmark
Dominican Republic
Ecuador
Egypt
El Salvador
Estonia
Finland
France
Gabon
Gambia
Georgia
Germany
Ghana
Greece
Guatemala
Guinea
Guinea-Bissau
Haiti
Honduras
Hungary
India
Iran, Islamic Republic of
Ireland
Israel
Italy
Jamaica
Japan
Jordan
Kazakhstan
Kenya
Kyrgyzstan
Latvia
Liberia
Libyan Arab Jamahiriya
Lithuania
Luxembourg
Madagascar
Mali
Malta
Mauritania
Mexico
Mongolia
Montenegro
Morocco
Namibia
Nepal
Netherlands
New Zealand
Nicaragua
Nigeria
Niger (the)
Norway
Pakistan
Panama
Paraguay
Peru
Philippines
Poland
Portugal
Republic of Korea
Republic of Mauritius
Republic of Moldova
Romania
Rwanda
Senegal
Serbia
Sierra Leone
Slovakia
Slovenia
Somalia
South Africa
Spain
Sri Lanka
Sudan
Sweden
Switzerland
Tajikistan
Thailand
Togo
Trinidad and Tobago
Tunisia
Turkey
Uganda
Ukraine

United Kingdom of Great Britain and Northern Ireland
United Republic of Tanzania
United States of America
Uruguay
Venezuela, Bolivarian Republic of
Vietnam
Yemen
Zambia
Zimbabwe

STATES WITH OBSERVER STATUS

Bahrain
Bhutan
China
Cuba
Ethiopia
Guyana
Holy See
Indonesia
Mozambique
Namibia
Papua New Guinea
Qatar
Russian Federation
San Marino
Sao Tomé and Principe
The former Yugoslav Republic of Macedonia
Turkmenistan

IOM OVERSEAS LIAISON AND OPERATIONAL OFFICES

Afghanistan, Herat, Kabul
Albania, Tirana
Angola, Luanda
Argentina, Buenos Aires *
Armenia, Yerevan
Australia, Canberra *
Austria, Wien *
Azerbaijan, Baku
Bangladesh, Dhaka *
Belarus, Minsk
Belgium / Luxembourg, Bruxelles *
Bolivia, La Paz
Bosnia and Herzegovina, Sarajevo
Bulgaria, Sofia
Cambodia, Phnom Penh
Cameroun, Yaoundé
Canada, Ottawa, Ontario
Chile, Santiago de Chile
China, Hong Kong
Colombia, Santafé de Bogotá
Congo, Brazzaville
Congo, (Democratic Republic of), Gombe, Kinshasa
Costa Rica, San José *
Cote D'Ivoire, Abidjan
Croatia, Zagreb
Czech Republic, Praha
Dominican Republic, Santo Domingo
Ecuador, Quito
Egypt, Cairo *
El Salvador, San Salvador
Estonia, Tallinn
Ethiopia, Addis Ababa
Finland, Helsinki *
France, Paris
Gambia, Banjul
Georgia, Tbilisi
Germany, Berlin, Nuremberg
Ghana, Accra North
Greece, Athens
Guatemala, Ciudad de Guatemala
Guinea, Conakry
Guinea-Bissau, Guinea Bissau
Haita, Port au Prince
Honduras, Tegucigalpa
Hungary, Budapest *
India, Hyderabad
Indonesia, Jakarta, Banda Aceh, Mataram Kupang, Situbondo, Yogkakarta, Nias
Iran, Tehran
Iraq, Amman
Ireland, Dublin
Italy, Roma *
Jamaica, Kingston
Japan, Tokyo
Jordan, Amman
Kazakhstan, Almaty
Kenya, Nairobi *
Korea (Republic of), Seoul
Kosovo, Pristina
Kuwait, Kuwait City
Kyrgyzstan, Bishkek City
Lao, Vientiane
Latvia, Riga
Lebanon, Beirut
Liberia, Monrovia
Libya Arab Jamhiriya, Tripoli
Lithuania, Vilnius
Mali, Bamako
Malta, Valletta
Mauritania, Nouakchott
Mauritius, Port Louis
Mexico, Mexico DF
Moldova, (Republic of) Chisinau
Montenegro, Podgorica
Morocco, Rabat
Mozambique, Maputo
Myanmar, Yangon
Nauru (Republic of), Central Pacific
Nepal, Kathmandu
Netherlands, Den Haag
Nicaragua, Managua
Niger, Niamey
Nigeria, Abuja
Norway, Oslo
Pakistan, Islamabad *
Panama, Panama
Papua New Guinea, Manus
Peru, Lima *
Philippines, Metro Manila *
Poland, Warszawa
Portugal, Lisboa
Romania, Bucharest
Russia, Moscow
Saudi Arabia, Riyadh
Senegal, Dakar *
Serbia, Belgrade
Sierra Leone, Freetown
Slovak Republic, Bratislava
Slovenia, Ljubljana
Somalia, Somaliland
South Africa, Pretoria *
Spain, Madrid
Sri Lanka, Colombo
Sudan, Khartoum
Switzerland, Bern
Syrian Arab Republic, Damascus
Tajikistan, Dushanbe
Tanzania, Dar es Salaam
Thailand, Bangkok *
The Former Yogoslav Republic of Macedonia, Skopje
Timor Leste, Dili
Trinidad and Tobago, Port of Spain
Tunisia, Tunis
Turkey, Ankara
Turkmenistan, Ashgabad
Uganda, Kampala
Ukraine, Kyiv
United Kingdom, London
United States of America, Washington *, New York *, Los Angeles, Miami,
Uruguay, Montevideo
Uzbekistan, Tashkent
Venezuela, Caracas
Vietnam, Hanoi, Ho Chi Minh City
Yemen, Yemen
Zambia, Lusaka
Zimbabwe, Harare

INTERNATIONAL PACIFIC HALIBUT COMMISSION, UNITED STATES AND CANADA

Headquarters: University of Washington, Seattle, WA 98195

phone (206) 634–1838, fax 632–2983

Mailing address: P.O. Box 95009, Seattle WA 98145–2009

American Commissioners:

Ralph G. Hoard, 4019 21st Avenue W., Seattle, WA 98199, (206) 282–0988, fax 281–0329.

Phillip Lestenkof, P.O. Box 288, St. Paul Island, AK 99660, (907) 546–2597.

Dr. Jim Balsiger, National Marine Fisheries Service, P.O. Box 21668, Juneau, AK 99802, (907) 586–7221, fax 586–7249.

Canadian Commissioners:

Dr. Laura Richards, Pacific Biological Station, 3190 Hammond Bay Road, Nanaimo, B.C., Canada V9T 6N7, (250) 729–8369, fax 756–7053.

Larry Johnson, Huu-ay-aht First Nations, 3483 3rd Avenue, Port Alberni, B.C., Canada V9Y 4E4 (250) 723–0100.

Gary Robinson, 7055 Vivian Drive, Vancouver, B.C., Canada V5S 2V2 (604) 321–8244, fax 321–8264.

Director and Secretary (ex officio).—Dr. Bruce M. Leaman, P.O. Box 95009, Seattle, WA 98145–2009.

ORGANIZATION OF AMERICAN STATES

17th Street and Constitution Avenue, NW., 20006
phone (202) 458–3000, fax 458–3967

PERMANENT MISSIONS TO THE OAS

Antigua and Barbuda.—Ambassador Deborah Mae-Lovell, Permanent Representative, 3216 New Mexico Avenue, NW., 20016, phone 362–5122 / 5166 / 5211, fax 362–5225.

Argentina.—Ambassador Rodolfo Gil, Permanent Representative, 1816 Corcoran Street, NW., 20009, phone 387–4142 / 4146 / 4170, fax 328–1591.

The Bahamas.—Ambassador Cornelius A. Smith, Permanent Representative, 2220 Massachusetts Avenue, NW., 20008, phone 319–2660 to 2667, fax 319–2668.

Barbados.—Ambassador John E. Beale, Permanent Representative, 2144 Wyoming Avenue, NW., 20008, phone 939–9200 / 9201 / 9202, fax 332–7467.

Belize.—Ambassador Nestor Mendez, Permanent Representative, 2535 Massachusetts Avenue, NW., 20008–3098, phone 332–9636, ext. 228, fax 332–6888.

Bolivia.—Ambassador Jose Enrique Pinelo, Permanent Representative, 1929 19th Street, NW., 20009, phone 785–0218 / 0219 / 0224, fax 296–0563.

Brazil.—Ambassador Ruy Casaes, Permanent Representative, 2600 Virginia Avenue, NW., Suite 412, 20037, phone 333–4224 / 4225 / 4226, fax 333–6610.

Canada.—Ambassador Graeme C. Clark, Permanent Representative, 501 Pennsylvania Avenue, NW., 20001, phone 682–1768, Ext. 7724, fax 682–7624.

Chile.—Ambassador Pedro Oyarce, Permanent Representative, 2000 L Street, NW., Suite 720, 20036, phone 887–5475 / 5476 / 5477, fax 775–0713.

Colombia.—Ambassador Luis Alfonso Hoyos, Permanent Representative, 1609 22nd Street, NW., 20008, phone 332–8003 / 8004, fax 234–9781.

Costa Rica.—Ambassador Jose Enrique Castillo, Permanent Representative, 2112 S Street, NW., Suite 300, 20008, phone 234–9280 / 9281, fax 986–2274.

Dominica.—Ambassador Judith Ann Rolle, Interim Representative, 3216 New Mexico Avenue, NW., 20016, phone 364–6781, fax 364–6791.

Dominican Republic.—Ambassador Virgilio Alcantara, Permanent Representative, 1715 22nd Street, NW., 20008, phone 332–9142 / 0616 / 0772, fax 232–5038.

Ecuador.—Agustin Fornell, Interim Representative, 2535 15th Street, NW., 20009, phone 234–1494 / 1692 / 8053, fax 667–3482.

---

* Mission with Regional Functions.

El Salvador.—Ambassador Luis Menendez, Interim Representative, 1400 16th Street, NW., 20036, phone 595–7546 / 7545, fax 232–4806.
Grenada.—Ambassador Denis G. Antoine, Permanent Representative, 1701 New Hampshire Avenue, NW., 20009, phone 265–2561, fax 265–2468.
Guatemala.—Ambassador Jorge Skinner-Klee, Permanent Representative, 1507 22nd Street, NW., 20037, phone 833–4015 / 4016 / 4017, fax 833–4011.
Guyana.—Ambassador Bayney R. Karran, Permanent Representative, 2490 Tracy Place, NW., 20008, phone 265–6900 / 6901, fax 232–1297.
Haiti.—Ambassador Duly Brutus, Permanent Representative, 2311 Massachusetts Avenue, NW., 20008, phone 332–4090 / 4096, fax 518–8742.
Jamaica.—Ambassador Anthony Johnson, Permanent Representative, 1520 New Hampshire Avenue, NW., 20036, phone 986–0121 / 0123 / 452–0660, fax 452–9395.
Mexico.—Ambassador Gustavo Albin, Permanent Representative, 2440 Massachusetts Avenue, NW., 20008, phone 332–3663 / 3664 / 3984, fax 234–0602.
Nicaragua.— Ambassador Denis Ronaldo Moncada Colindres, Permanent Representative, 1627 New Hampshire Avenue, NW., 20009, phone 332–1643 / 1644 / 939–6536, fax 745–0710.
Panama.—Ambassador Guillermo Cochez, Permanent Representative, 2201 Wisconsin Avenue, NW., Suite 240, 20007, phone 965–4826 / 4819, fax 965–4836.
Paraguay.—Ambassador Manuel Maria Cáceres, Permanent Representative, 2022 Connecticut Avenue, NW., 20008, phone 232–8020 / 8021 / 8022, fax 244–3005.
Peru.—Ambassador Maria Zavala Valladares, Permanent Representative, 1901 Pennsylvania Avenue, NW., Suite 402, 20006, phone 232–2281 / 2282 / 1973, fax 466–3068.
Saint Kitts and Nevis.—Ambassador Dr. Izben C. Williams, Permanent Representative, 3216 New Mexico Avenue, NW., 20016, phone 686–2636, fax 686–5740.
Saint Lucia.—Ambassador Michael Louis, Permanent Representative, 3216 New Mexico Avenue, NW., 20016, phone 364–6792 to 6795, fax 364–6723.
Saint Vincent and The Grenadines.— Ambassador La Celia A. Prince, Permanent Representative, 3216 New Mexico Avenue, NW., 20016, phone 364–6730, fax 364–6736.
Suriname.—Ambassador Jacques R.C. Kross, Permanent Representative, 4301 Connecticut Avenue, NW., Suite 462, 20008, phone 244–7488 / 7590 / 7591 / 7592, fax 244–5878.
Trinidad and Tobago.—Ambassador Glenda Morean-Phillip, Permanent Representative, 1708 Massachusetts Avenue, NW., 20036–1903, phone 467–6490, fax 785–3130.
United States of America.—W. Lewis Amselem, Interim Representative, WHA / USOAS Bureau of Western Hemisphere Affairs, Department of State, Room 5914, 20520–6258, phone 647–9376, fax 647–0911 / 6973.
Uruguay.—Ambassador María del Luján Flores, Permanent Representative, 2801 New Mexico Avenue, NW., Suite 1210, 20007, phone 333–0588 / 0687, fax 337–3758.
Venezuela.—Ambassador Roy Chaderton Matos, Permanent Representative, 1099 30th Street, NW., Second Floor, 20007, phone 342–5837 / 5838 / 5839 / 5840 / 5841, fax 625–5657.

GENERAL SECRETARIAT

Secretary General.—José Miguel Insulza, 458–3000.
Chief of Staff to the Secretary General.—Ricardo Domínguez, 458–3705.
Assistant Secretary General.—Albert R. Ramdin, 458–6046, fax 458–3011.
Chief of Staff to the Assistant Secretary General.—Sherry Tross, 458–3497.
Executive Secretary for—
Integral Development.—Alfonso Quiónez, 458–3510.
Inter-American Commission on Human Rights.—Santiago A. Canton, 458–6002.
Under Secretary for—
Administration and Finance.—Frank Almaguer, 458–3436.
Multidimensional Security.—Alexandre Addor-Neto, 458–6010.
Political Affairs.—Victor Rico, 458–3589.
Director, Department of:
External Relations.—Adam Blackwell, 458–3151.
Legal Services.—Jean Michel Arrighi, 458–3407.
Press and Communications.—Alvaro Briones (acting), 458–6829.
Director, Summits Secretariat.—David Morris, 458–3127.

ORGANIZATION FOR ECONOMIC CO-OPERATION AND DEVELOPMENT

Headquarters: 2 rue André-Pascal, 75775 Paris CEDEX 16, France
phone (331) 4524–8200, fax 4524–8500

Secretary-General.—Angel Gurria.

Deputy Secretaries General: Mari Amano, Aart Jan de Geus, Pier Carlo Padoan.

Member Countries:

Australia	Hungary	Norway
Austria	Iceland	Poland
Belgium	Ireland	Portugal
Canada	Italy	Slovak Republic
Czech Republic	Japan	Spain
Denmark	Korea	Sweden
Finland	Luxembourg	Switzerland
France	Mexico	Turkey
Germany	Netherlands	United Kingdom
Greece	New Zealand	United States

OECD WASHINGTON CENTER

2001 L Street, NW., Suite 650, 20036, phone (202) 785–6323, fax 785–0350

http://www.oecdwash.org

Head of Center.—Jill A. Schuker.

PAN AMERICAN HEALTH ORGANIZATION (PAHO) REGIONAL OFFICE OF THE WORLD HEALTH ORGANIZATION

525 23rd Street, NW., 20037, phone (202) 974–3000
fax 974–3663

Director.—Dr. Mirta Roses Periago, 974–3408.
Deputy Director.—Dr. Jon Adrus, 974–3178.
Assistant Director.—Dr. Socorro Gross-Galiano, 974–3404.
Director of Administration.—Michael A. Boorstein, 974–3412.

PAHO / WHO FIELD OFFICES

OPS / WHO OFICINAS DE LOS REPRESENTANTES EN LOS PAISES

Office of the Eastern Caribbean Coordinator. Barbados and Eastern Caribbean Countries (Antigua and Barbuda, Barbados, Dominica, Grenada, St. Kitts and Nevis, Saint Lucia, St. Vincent and the Grenadines. Eastern Caribbean: Anguilla, British Virgin Islands, Montserrat).—Dr. Gina Watson, P.O. Box 508, Dayralls and Navy Garden Roads, Christ Church, Bridgetown, Barbados, phone (246) 426–3860 / 435–9263, fax 228–5402, email: ECC@ecc.paho.org, http://www.cpc.paho.org.

Caribbean Program Coordinator. (French Antilles: Guadaloupe, Martinique, St. Martin and St. Bartholomew, French Guiana).—Dr. Bernadette Theodore-Gandi, P.O. Box 508, Dayralls and Navy Garden Roads, Christ Church, Bridgetown, Barbados, phone (246) 426–3860 / 3865 / 427–9434, fax 436–9779, email: email@cpc.paho.org, http://www.cpc.paho.org.

PAHO / WHO Representatives:

Argentina.—Dr. José Antonio Pagés, Marcelo T. de Alvear 684, 4o. piso, 1058 Buenos Aires, Argentina, phone (54–11) 4319–4200, fax 4319–4201, e-mail: info@ops.org.ar, http://www.ops.org.ar.

Bahamas (Turks and Caicos).—Dr. Merle Lewis, Union Court, Elizabeth Avenue, P.O. Box N 4833, Nassau, Bahamas, phone (242) 326–7299 / 356–4730, fax 326–7012, e-mail: email@bah.paho.org.

Belize.—Dr. Beverly Barnett, 4792 Coney Drive, Coney Drive Business Plaza, 3rd Floor, P.O. Box 1834, Belize City, Belize, phone (501–2) 2448–85 / 2339–46, fax 2309–17, e-mail: admin@blz.paho.org, http://www.blz.paho.org.

Bolivia.—Dr. Christian Darras, Calle Víctor Sanjines 2678, Edificio Torre Barcelona, pisos 1, 6 y 7, Zona Sopocachi, Casillas Postales 9790 y 2504, La Paz, Bolivia, phone (591–2) 2412–465 / 313, fax 2412–598, e-mail: pwrbol@bol.ops-oms.org, http://www.ops.org.bo.

Brazil.—Mr. Diego Victoria, Setor de Embaixadas Norte, Lote 19, 70800–400, Brasília, Caixa Postal 08–729, 70312–970, Brasilia, D.F., Brasil, phone (55–61)3251–9595 / 9549 / 9500, fax 3251–9591, e-mail: email@bra.ops–oms.org, http://www.opas.org.br/.

Chile.—Dr. Rubén Torres, Avenida Providencia No. 1017, Piso 4 y 5, Casilla 9459, Santiago, Chile, phone (56–2)437–4600 / 4605, fax 264–9311, e-mail: email@chi.ops–oms.org, http://www.chi.ops-oms.org.

Colombia.—Dr. Roberto Sempértegui, a.i, Carrera 7 No. 74–21, Piso 9, Edificio Seguros Aurora, Apartado Aéreo 253367, Santa Fe de Bogotá, D.C., Colombia, phone (57–1) 314–4141 / 254–7050, fax 254–7070, e-mail: ops–col@latino.net.co, http://www.col.ops-oms.org/.

Costa Rica.—Dr. Federico Hernández Pimentel, a.i., Calle 16, Avenida 6 y 8, Distrito Hospital, Apartado 3745, San Jose, Costa Rica, phone (506) 2258–5810 / 257–6034, fax 2258–5830, e-mail: email@cor.ops–oms.org, http://www.cor.ops–oms.org.

Cuba.—Dra. Lea Guido, Calle 4 No. 407, entre 17 y 19 Vedado, Apartado Postal 68, La Habana, Cuba C.P. 10400, phone (53–7) 831–8944 / 837–5808, fax 833–2075 / 866–2075, e-mail: pwr@cub.ops–oms.org or cruzmari@cub.ops–oms.org, http://www.cub.ops–oms.org.

Dominican Republic.—Dr. Ana Cristina Nogueira, Edificio OPS / OMS, y Defensa Civil, Calle Pepillo Salcedo–Recta Final, Plaza de la Salud, Ensanche La Fe, Apartado Postal 1464, Santo Domingo, Republica Dominicana, phone (809) 562–1519 / 544–3241, fax 544–0322, e-mail: email@dor.ops–oms.org, http://www.dor.ops–oms.org.

Ecuador.—Dr. Celia Riera a.i., Av. Amazonas 2889 y Mariana de Jesus, Quito, Ecuador, phone (593–2) 2460–330 / 296 / 215, fax 2460–325, e-mail: email@ecu.ops-oms.org, http://www.opsecu.org.ec.

El Salvador.—Dr. Priscilla Rivas-Loria, 73 Avenida Sur No. 135, Colonia Escalón, Apartado Postal 1072, Sucursal Centro, San Salvador, El Salvador, phone (503) 2298–3491 / 0021 / 2279–1650, fax 2298–1168, e-mail: email@els.ops-oms.org, http://www.ops.org.sv/.

Guatemala.—Dr. Pier Paolo Balladelli, Edificio Etisa, Plaza España, 7ª Avenida 12–23, Zona 9, Apartado Postal 383, Guatemala, Guatemala, phone (011–502) 2332–2032 / 2334–3803 / 2331–0583, fax 2334–3804, http://www.ops.org.gt.

Guyana.—Dr. Kathleen Israel, Lot 8 Brickdam Stabroek, P.O. Box 10969, Georgetown, Guyana, phone (592) 225–3000 / 227–5150 / 5158 / 5159 / 6371 / 223–6372, fax 226–6654 / 227–4205, e-mail: email@guy.paho.org.

Haiti.—Dr. Henriette Chamouillet, No. 295 Avenue John Brown, Boite Postale 1330, Port-au-Prince, Haiti, phone (509) 2245–7675, fax 245–6917, e-mail: email@hai.ops-oms.org.

Honduras.—Dr. Lilian Reneau-Vernon, Edificio Imperial, 6o.y 7o.piso, Avenida Republica de Panama, Frente a la Casa de Naciones Unidas, Apartado Postal 728, Tegucigalpa MDC, Honduras, phone (504) 221–6091 / 6102, fax 221–6103, e-mail: pwr@hon.ops–oms.org, http://www.paho-who.hn.

Jamaica (Bermuda and Cayman).—Dr. Ernest Pate, Old Oceana Building, 7th Floor, 2–4 King Street, P.O. Box 384, Cross Roads, Kingston 5, Jamaica, phone (876) 967–4626 / 4691 / 5198 / 922–4630 / 4424, fax 967–5189, e-mail: email@jam.ops-oms.org.

Mexico.—Dr. Philippe Lamy, Edificio Torre Prisma, Horacio Nº 1855, 3er. Piso, Of. 305, (Blvd. Manuel Avila Camacho No. 191), Colonia Los Morales, Polanco, Apartado Postal 06–601, Mexico D.F., 11510, Mexico, phone (52–55) 5089–0880 / 0870, fax 5395–5681, e-mail: e-mail@mex.ops-oms.org, http://www.mex.ops–oms.org.

Nicaragua.—Dr. Jorge Luis Prosperi, Complejo Nacional de Salud, Camino a la Sabana, Apartado Postal 1309, Managua, Nicaragua, phone (505) 2289–4200 / 4800, fax 2289–4999, e-mail: email@nic.ops-oms.org, http://www.ops.org.ni.

Panama.—Dr. Joaquín Molina Leza, Ministerio de Salud de Panama, Ancon, Avenida Gorgas, Edificio 261, 2o piso, Apartado Postal 0843–3441, Panama, Republica de Panama, phone (507) 262–0030 / 1996, fax 262–4052, e-mail: email@pan.ops–oms.org, http://ops-oms.org.pa.

Paraguay.—Dr. Rubén Figueroa, Edificio ''Faro del Rio'' Mcal Lopez 957 Esq. Estados Unidos, Casilla de Correo 839, Asunción, Paraguay, phone (595–21) 450–495 / 496 / 497 / 499 / 499–864, fax 450–498, e-mail: email@par.ops–oms.org, http://www.par.ops-oms.org.

Peru.—Dr. Manuel Peña, Los Pinos 251, Urbanizaciõn Camacho, La Molina, Lima 27, Peru, phone (51–1) 319–5700 / 5781, fax 437–3640, e-mail: email@per.ops-oms.org, http://www.per.ops.oms.org.

Puerto Rico.—Dr. Raúl Castellanos Bran, P.O. Box 70184, San Juan, Puerto Rico 00936, phone (787) 274–7608, fax 250–6547 / 767–8341.

Suriname.—Dr. Stephen Simon, Burenstraat #33 (PPS Building), P.O. Box 1863, Paramaribo, Suriname, phone (597) 471–676 / 425–355, fax 471–568, e-mail: email@sur.paho.org.

Trinidad and Tobago.—Dr. Carol Boyd-Scobie, 49 Jerningham Avenue, P.O. Box 898, Port-of-Spain, Trinidad, phone (868) 624–7524 / 4376 / 5642 / 5928 / 625–4492, fax 624–5643, email: email@trt.paho.org.

United States-Mexico Border.—Dr. Maria Teresa Cerqueira, 5400 Suncrest Drive, Suite C–4, El Paso, TX 79912, United States of America, phone (915) 845–5950, fax 845–4361, email: email@fep.paho.org, http://www.fep.paho.org/.

Uruguay.—Dr. Jose Fernando Dora, Avenida Brasil 2697, Aptos. 5, 6 y 8, 2do. Piso, Casilla de Correo 1821, 11300, Montevideo, Uruguay, phone (598–2) 707–3589 / 3590, fax 707–3530, e-mail: pwr@uru.ops-oms.org, http://www.ops.org.uy/.

Venezuela (Netherlands Antilles).—Dr. Jorge Jenkins, Avenida Sexta entre 5a y 6a, Apartado 6722, Carmelitas, Transversal, Altamira, Caracas 1010, Venezuela, phone (58–212) 206–5022 / 5000 / 0403, fax 261–6069, e-mail: email@ven.ops-oms.org, http://www.ops-oms.org.ve/.

CENTERS

Caribbean Epidemiology Center (CAREC).—Dr. Jose Campione, 16–18 Jamaica Boulevard, Federation Park, P.O. Box 164, Port–of–Spain, Trinidad, phone (1–868) 622–4261 / 4262 / 3168 / 3277, fax 622–2792, e-mail: email@carec.ops-oms.org.

Caribbean Food and Nutrition Institute (CFNI).—Dr. Fitzroy J. Henry, University of the West Indies, P.O. Box 140–Mona, Kingston 7, Jamaica, phone (1–876), 927–1540 / 1541 / 1927, fax 927–2657, e-mail: e-mail@cfni.paho.org.

Institute of Nutrition of Central America and Panama (INCAP).—Dr. Jose Adan Montes, Carretera Roosevelt, Zona 11, Apartado Postal 1188, Guatemala, Guatemala, phone (502) 2471–5655 / 0148 / 2473–6518, fax 2473–6529, e-mail: email@incap.ops-oms.org, Biblioteca Virtual en Salud: http://www.incap.bvssan.org.gt.

Latin American and Caribbean Center on Health Sciences Information (BIREME).—Mr. Abel Laerte Packer, Rua Botucatu 862, Vila Clementino, Caixa Postal 20381, CEP.04023–062, Sao Paulo, SP, Brasil, phone (55–11) 5576–9800 / 5572–3226, fax 575–8868 / 5549–2590, e-mail: email@bireme.ops-oms.org.

Latin American Center for Perinatology and Human Development (CLAP).—Dr. Ricardo Fescina, Hospital de Clinicas, Piso 16, Casilla de Correo 627, Montevideo, Uruguay, phone (598–2) 487–2929 / 2930 / 2931 / 2933, fax 487–2593, e-mail: postmaster@clap.ops–oms.org.

Pan American Center for Sanitary Engineering and Environmental Sciences (CEPIS).—Dr. Mauricio Pardon Ojeda, Calle Los Pinos 251, Urbanizacion Camacho, Casilla Postal 4337, Lima 100, Peru, phone (51–1) 319–5700 / 5785, fax 437–3640, e-mail: cepis@cepis.ops-oms.org.

Pan American Foot-and-Mouth Disease Center (PANAFTOSA).—Dr. Ottorino Cosivi, Avenida Presidente Kennedy 7778, (Antiga Estrada Rio-Petropolis), São Bento, Duque de Caxias, CEP 25040–000, Caixa Postal 589, 20001 Rio de Janeiro, Brasil, phone (55–21) 3661–9000 / 9005 / 9002, fax 3661–9001, e-mail: panaftosa@panaftosa.pos-oms.org.

PERMANENT JOINT BOARD ON DEFENSE, CANADA–UNITED STATES

CANADIAN SECTION

National Defence Headquarters, MG George R. Pearkes Building, Ottawa, ON Canada K1A OK2, phone (613) 992–4423

Members:

Military Policy.—MG Michael Ward, Director General International Security Policy.
Defence Policy.—COL Al Stephenson, Director, Western Hemisphere Policy.
Foreign Affairs.—Shelley Whiting, Director of the Defence and Security Relations Division.
Privy Council.—BG Christian Rousseau, Director of Operations, Defence / International Security.
CANADACOM.—BG J.P.P.J. Lacroix, Chief of Staff, Canada Command.
NORAD.—MG Pierre Forgues, Director J3.
Public Safety.—Vacant.
Military Secretary.—CDR Steve Thompson, Directorate of Western Hemisphere Policy.
Political Secretary.—Michael Vonk, Directorate of Continental Defence Relations.

UNITED STATES SECTION

JCS, J–5, Western Hemisphere Directorate, Pentagon, Room 2E773, 20318

phone (703) 695–4477

Members:

Military Policy (Joint Staff).—MG George Smith, room 2E773, 695–4477.
Defense Policy (OSD).—Dr. Frank Mora, room 5D435, 697–3915.
State Department.—Ned Nolan, room 3917, State Department (202) 647–2273.
National Security Council.—Kevin O'Reilly (202) 456–9139.
USNORTHCOM.—Maj. Gen. Chris Miller (719) 554–1429.
NORAD.—Vacant.

DHS.—RDML Charlie Ray (202) 282–8155.
Military Secretary.—CDR Larry Kistler, 695–4477.
Political Secretary.—Eric Lundberg, room 3917, State Department (202) 647–2475.

SECRETARIAT OF THE PACIFIC COMMUNITY

B.P. D5, 98848 Noumea Cedex, New Caledonia, phone (687) 26.20.00, fax 26.38.18
E-mail: spc@spc.int, http://www.spc.int

Director-General.—Dr. Jimmie Rodgers.
Senior Deputy Director General, Suva.—Fekitamoeloa Utoikamanu.
Deputy Director General, Noumea.—Richard Mann.
Director of Corporate Services.—Leslie Walker.
Director of the Marine Resource Division.—Michael Batty.
Head of the Planning Unit.—Vacant.

U.S. Contact: Bureau of East Asian and Pacific Affairs, Office of Australia, New Zealand and Pacific Island Affairs, Department of State, Washington, DC 20520, phone (202) 736–4741, fax 647–0118

Countries and Territories Covered by the SPC:

American Samoa
Australia
Cook Islands
Federated States of Micronesia
Fiji
France
French Polynesia
Guam
Kiribati
Marshall Islands
Nauru
New Caledonia
New Zealand
Niue
Northern Mariana Islands
Palau
Papua New Guinea
Pitcairn Islands
Samoa
Solomon Islands
Tokelau
Tonga
Tuvalu
United States
Vanuatu
Wallis and Futuna

UNITED NATIONS

GENERAL ASSEMBLY

The General Assembly is composed of all 192 United Nations Member States.

SECURITY COUNCIL

The Security Council has 15 members. The United Nations Charter designates five States as permanent members, and the General Assembly elects 10 other members for two-year terms. The term of office for each non-permanent member of the Council ends on 31 December of the year indicated in parentheses next to its name.

The five permanent members of the Security Council are China, France, Russian Federation, United Kingdom and the United States.

The 10 non-permanent members of the Council in 2007 are Austria (2010), Japan (2010), Uganda (2010), Burkina Faso (2009), Libyan Arab Jamahiriya (2009), Vietnam (2009), Costa Rica (2009), Mexico (2010), Croatia (2009), Turkey (2010).

ECONOMIC AND SOCIAL COUNCIL

The Economic and Social Council has 54 members, elected for three-year terms by the General Assembly. The term of office for each member expires on 31 December of the year indicated in parentheses next to its name. Voting in the Council is by simple majority; each member has one vote. In 2005, the Council is composed of the following 54 States:

Algeria (2009)
Barbados (2009)
Belarus (2009)
Bolivia (2009)
Brazil (2010)
Cameroon (2010)
Canada (2009)
Cape Verde (2009)
China (2010)
Congo (2010)
Côte d'Ivoire (2011)
El Salvador (2009)
Estonia (2011)
France (2011)
Germany (2011)
Greece (2011)
Guatemala (2011)
Guinea-Bissau (2011)
India (2011)
Indonesia (2009)
Iraq (2009)
Japan (2011)
Kazakhstan (2009)
Liechtenstein (2011)
Luxembourg (2009)
Malawi (2009)
Malaysia (2010)
Mauritius (2011)
Moldova (2010)
Morocco (2011)
Mozambique (2010)
Namibia (2011)
Netherlands (2009)
New Zealand (2010)
Niger (2010)
Norway (2010)
Pakistan (2010)
Peru (2011)
Philippines (2009)
Poland (2010)
Portugal (2011)
Republic of Korea (2010)
Romania (2009)
Russian Federation (2010)
Saint Kitts and Nevis (2011)
Saint Lucia (2010)
Saudi Arabia (2011)
Somalia (2009)
Sudan (2009)
Sweden (2010)
United States of America (2009)
Uruguay (2010)
Venezuela (Bolivarian Republic of) (2011)
United Kingdom of Great Britain and Northern Ireland (2010)

TRUSTEESHIP COUNCIL

The Trusteeship Council has five members: China, France, Russian Federation, United Kingdom and the United States. With the independence of Palau, the last remaining United Nations trust territory, the Council formerly suspended operation on 1 November 1994. By a resolution adopted on that day, the Council amended its rules of procedure to drop the obligation to meet annually and agreed to meet as occasion required—by its decision or the decision of its President, or at the request of a majority of its members or the General Assembly or the Security Council.

INTERNATIONAL COURT OF JUSTICE

The International Court of Justice has 15 members, elected by both the General Assembly and the Security Council. Judges hold nine-year terms.

The current composition of the court is as follows: President Hisashi Owada (Japan); Vice-President Peter Tomka (Slovakia). Judges: Shi Jiuyong (China), Abdul G. Koroma (Sierra Leone), Awn Shawkat Al-Khasawneh (Jordan), Thomas Buergenthal (United States of America), Bruno Simma (Germany), Ronny Abraham (France), Kenneth Keith (New Zealand), Bernardo Sepúlveda-Amor (Mexico), Mohamed Bennouna (Morocco), Leonid Skotnikov (Russian Federatión), Antônio A. Cançado Trindade (Brazil), Abdulqawi Ahmed Yusuf (Somalia), Christopher Greenwood (United Kingdom of Great Britain and Northern Ireland).

The Registrar of the Court is Mr. Philippe Couvreur (Belgium).

UNITED NATIONS SECRETARIAT

One United Nations Plaza, New York, NY 10017, (212) 963-1234, http://www.un.org.

Secretary General.—Ban Ki-moon (Republic of Korea).
Deputy Secretary.—Dr. Asha Rose Migiro (Tanzania).

EXECUTIVE OFFICE OF THE SECRETARY-GENERAL

Chief of Staff.—Vijay Nambiar (India).

Assistant Secretary-General for Policy Planning.—Robert C. Orr (United States).
Spokesman.—Michele Montas.

OFFICE OF INTERNAL OVERSIGHT SERVICES

Under-Secretary-General.—Inga-Britt Ahlenius (Sweden).

OFFICE OF LEGAL AFFAIRS

Under-Secretary-General and Legal Counsel.— Patricia O'Brien.
Assistant Secretary General.—Peter Taksoe-Jensen.

DEPARTMENT OF POLITICAL AFFAIRS

Under-Secretary-General.—B. Lynn Pascoe (United States).
Assistant Secretary-General.—Haile Menkerios.
Assistant Secretary-General.—Oscar Fernandez-Taranco.

DEPARTMENT FOR DISARMAMENT AFFAIRS

Under-Secretary-General.—Sergio de Queiroz Duarte.

DEPARTMENT OF PEACE-KEEPING OPERATIONS

Under-Secretary-General.— Alain Le Roy.
Assistant Secretary-General.— Edmond Mulet.
Assistant Secretary-General.— Dimitry Titov.
Military Adviser.—Chikadibia Obiakor.

OFFICE FOR THE COORDINATION OF HUMANITARIAN AFFAIRS

Under-Secretary-General, Emergency Relief Coordinator.—John Holmes (United Kingdom).
Assistant Secretary General/Deputy Emergency Relief Coordinator.—Catherine Bragg.

DEPARTMENT OF ECONOMIC AND SOCIAL AFFAIRS

Under-Secretary-General.—Zukang Sha..
Assistant Secretary-General.—Kwame Sundaram Jomo.
Assistant Secretary-General.—Rachel N. Mayanja.
Assistant Secretary-General.—Thomas Stelzer.

DEPARTMENT OF GENERAL ASSEMBLY AND CONFERENCE MANAGEMENT

Under-Secretary-General.—Shaaban M. Shaaban.
Assistant Secretary-General.—Franz Baumann.

DEPARTMENT OF PUBLIC INFORMATION

Under-Secretary-General.—Kiyotaka Akasaka (Japan).

DEPARTMENT OF MANAGEMENT

Under-Secretary-General.—Angela Kane.
Assistant Secretary-General, Controller.—Jun Yamazaki.
Officer-in-Charge, Human Resources Management.—Catherine Pollard.
Officer-in-Charge, Central Support Services.—Warren Sach.

OFFICE OF THE SPECIAL REPRESENTATIVE OF THE SECRETARY-GENERAL FOR CHILDREN AND ARMED CONFLICT

Under-Secretary-General.—Radhika Coomaraswamy (Sri Lanka).

UNITED NATIONS FUND FOR INTERNATIONAL PARTNERSHIPS

Executive Director.—Amir A. Dossal (United Kingdom).

UNITED NATIONS AT GENEVA (UNOG)

Palais des Nations, 1211 Geneva 10, Switzerland, phone (41–22) 917–1234.
Director-General of UNOG/Assistant Secretary-General.—Sergei A. Ordzhonikidze (Russian Federation).

UNITED NATIONS AT VIENNA (UNOV)

Vienna International Centre, P.O. Box 500, A–1400 Vienna, Austria, phone (43–1) 21345.
Director-General.—Antonio Maria Costa (Italy).

UNITED NATIONS INFORMATION CENTRE

1775 K Street, NW., Suite 400, Washington, DC 20006

phone: (202) 331–8670, fax: (202) 331–9191, email: unicdc@unicwash.org

http://www.unicwash.org

Director.—William Davis (United States).

REGIONAL ECONOMIC COMMISSIONS

Economic Commission for Africa (ECA), Africa Hall, P.O. Box 3001, Addis Ababa Ethiopia, phone (251–1) 51–72–00, fax (251–1) 51–44–16.
Executive Secretary.—Abdoulie Jannah (Gambia).
Economic Commission for Europe (ECE) Palais des Nations, 1211 Geneva 10, Switzerland, phone (41–22) 917–2893.
Executive Secretary.—Ján Kubiš.
Economic Commission for Latin America and the Caribbean (ECLAC), Casilla 179–D, Santiago, Chile, phone (56–2) 210–2000, fax (56–2) 208–0252.
Executive Secretary.—Alicia Barcena.
Economic and Social Commission for Asia and the Pacific (ESCAP), United Nations Building, Rejdamnern Avenue, Bangkok, Thailand, phone (66–2) 288–1234, fax (66–2) 288–1000.
Executive Secretary.—Noeleen Heyzer.
Economic and Social Commission for Western Asia (ESCWA), P.O. Box 11–8575, Riad El-Solh Square, Beirut, Lebanon, phone 9611–981301, fax 9611–981510.
Executive Secretary.—Bader Omar Al-Dafa.
Regional Commissions, New York Office, (ECE, ESCAP, ECLAC, ECA, ESCWA), fax 963–1500.
Officer-in-Charge.—Amr Nour.
Social Affairs Officer.—Daniela Simioni.
Documentation.—Nilima Silver.

FUNDS, PROGRAMMES, AND BODIES OF THE UNITED NATIONS

Advisory Committee on Administrative and Budgetary Questions (ACABQ), One United Nations Plaza, New York, NY 10017, phone (212) 963–7456.
Chairman.—Shari Klugman.

Office of the High Commissioner for Human Rights, Palais des Nations, 8–14 Avenue de la Paix, 1211 Geneva 10, Switzerland, phone (41–22) 917–1234.
High Commissioner for Human Rights.—Navanethem Pillay.

International Civil Service Commission (ICSC), One United Nations Plaza, New York, NY 10017, phone (212) 963–8464.

Chairman.—Kingston Rhodes (Sierra Leone).

Joint Inspection Unit (JIU), Palais des Nations, 1211 Geneva 10, Switzerland, phone (41–22) 917–1234.
Chairman.—Gérard Biraud (France).

Panel of External Auditors of the UN, Specialized Agencies and International Atomic Energy Agency, One United Nations Plaza, New York, NY 10017, phone (212) 963–5623.
Chairman.—Swatantra Anand Goolsarran.

United Nations Human Settlements Programme (UN-HABITAT), UN Office at Nairobi, P.O. Box 30030, Nairobi, Kenya, phone (254–2) 621–1234.
Executive Director.—Anna Kajumulo Tibaijuka (UR of Tanzania).

United Nations Children's Fund (UNICEF), UNICEF House, 3 UN Plaza, New York, NY 10017, phone (212) 326–7000.
Executive Director.—Ann Veneman (USA).

United Nations Conference on Trade and Development (UNCTAD), Palais des Nations, 8–14 Avenue de la Paix, 1211 Geneva 10, Switzerland, phone (41–22) 917–1234.
Officer-in-Charge.—Supachai Panitchpakdi.

United Nations Development Fund for Women (UNIFEM), 304 East 45th Street, Sixth Floor, New York, NY 10017, phone (212) 906–6400.
Director.—Inés Alberdi.

United Nations Development Programme (UNDP), 1 United Nations Plaza, New York, NY 10017, phone (212) 906–5000.
Administrator.—Kemal Dervis (Turkey).

United Nations Development Programme (UNDP), Liaison Office, 1775 K Street, NW., Suite 420, Washington, DC 20006, phone (202) 331–9130.
Director.—Frederick S. Tipson (USA).

United Nations Environment Programme (UNEP), P.O. Box 30552, Nairobi, Kenya, phone (254–2) 621–1234.
Executive Director.—Achim Steiner.

United Nations High Commissioner for Refugees (UNHCR), Case Postale 2500, CH–1211 Geneve 2 Depot, Switzerland, phone (41–22) 739– 8111.
High Commissioner.—Antonio Guterres (Portugal).

United Nations High Commissioner for Refugees (UNHCR), Regional Office for the United States and the Caribbean, 1775 K Street, NW., Third Floor, Washington, DC 20006, phone (202) 296–5191.
Regional Representative.—Michel Gaubaudan.

United Nations Institute for Disarmament Research (UNIDIR), Palais des Nations, 1211 Geneva 10, Switzerland, phone (41–22) 917–4292.
Director.—Patricia Lewis (United Kingdom).

United Nations Institute for Training and Research (UNITAR), Palais des Nations, 1211 Geneva 10, Switzerland, phone (41–22) 798–5850.
Executive Director.—Carlos Lopes (Guinea Bissau).

United Nations International Drug Control Programme (UNODC), P.O. Box 500, A–1400 Vienna, Austria, phone (43–1) 21345 ext. 4251.
Executive Director.—Antonio Maria Costa (Italy).

United Nations International Research and Training Institute for the Advancement of Women (INSTRAW), P.O. Box 21747, Santo Domingo, Dominican Republic, phone (1–809) 685–2111.
Director.—Carmen Moreno (Mexico).

United Nations Interregional Crime and Justice Research Institute (UNICRI), Viale Maestri del Lavoro, 10, 10127 Turin, Italy, phone (39–11) 6537–111.
Director.—Sandro Calvani (Italy).

United Nations Office for Project Services (UNOPS), P.O. Box 2695, 2100 Copenhagen, Denmark, phone (45–3) 546–7500.
Executive Director.—Jan Mattson (Sweden).

United Nations Population Fund (UNFPA), 220 East 42nd Street, New York, NY 10017, phone (212) 297–5000.
Executive Director.—Thoraya Ahmed Obaid (Saudi Arabia).

United Nations Relief and Works Agency for Palestine Refugees in the Near East (UNRWA), Headquarters Amman, P.O. Box 140157, Amman 11814, Jordan, phone (+ 962 6) 580–8100. Headquarters Gaza, P.O. Box 61, Gaza City, or P.O. Box 338, Ashqelon, phone (+ 972 8) 288–7333.
Commissioner-General.—Karen Konig Abuzayd (USA).

United Nations Research Institute for Social Development (UNRISD), Palais des Nations, 1211 Geneva 10, Switzerland, phone (41–22) 917–3020.
Deputy Director (Officer in Charge).—Peter Utting (Australia).

United Nations Volunteers Programme (UNV), Postfach 260111, D–53153 Bonn, Germany, phone (49–228) 815–2000.
Executive Coordinator.—Flavia Pansieri (Italy).

World Food Programme (WFP), Via C.G.Viola 68, Parco dei Medici, 00148 Rome, Italy, phone (39–6) 65131.
Executive Director.—Josette Sheeran (USA).

United Nations University (UNU), 5–53–70 Jingumae, Shibuya-ku, Tokyo 150–8925, Japan, phone (81–3) 5467–1212.
Rector.—Konrad Osterwalder (Switzerland).

SPECIALIZED AGENCIES

Food and Agriculture Organization (FAO), Viale delle Terme di Caracalla, 00153 Rome, Italy, phone (39–6) 57051.
Director–General.—Jacques Diouf (Senegal).

Food and Agriculture Organization, Liaison Office for North America, Suite 500, 2175 K Street, NW., Washington, DC 20037, phone (1–202) 653–2400.
Director.—Daniel J. Gustafson.

International Civil Aviation Organization (ICAO), 999 University Street, Montréal, Quebec H3C 5H7, Canada, phone (1–514) 954–8219.
Secretary-General.—Raymond Benjamin (France).

International Fund for Agricultural Development (IFAD), Via Paolo di Dono, 44, 00142 Rome, Italy, phone (39–6) 54591.
President.—Kanayo F. Nwanze (Nigeria).

External Affairs Department, IFAD North American Liaison Office, 1775 K Street, NW., Suite 410, Washington, DC 20006, phone (1–202) 331–9099.
Director.—Cheryl Morden (USA).

International Labour Organization (ILO), 4, Routes des Morillons, CH–1211 Geneva 22, Switzerland, phone (41–22) 799–6111.
Director-General.—Juan Somavia (Chile).

ILO Washington Branch Office, 1828 L Street, NW., Suite 600, Washington, DC 20036, phone (1–202) 653–7652.
Officer in Charge.—Marina Colby.

International Maritime Organization (IMO), 4 Albert Embankment, London SE1 7SR, United Kingdom, phone (44–20) 7735–7611.
Secretary-General.—Efthimios Mitropoulos (Greece).

International Monetary Fund (IMF), 700 19th Street, NW., Washington, DC 20431, phone (1–202) 623–7000.
Managing Director.—Dominique Strauss-Kahn (France).

International Telecommunications Union (ITU), Palais des Nations, 1211 Geneva 20, Switzerland, phone (41–22) 730–5111.
Secretary-General.—Hamadoun Touré (Mali).

United Nations Educational, Scientific and Cultural Organization (UNESCO), 7 Place de Fontenoy, 75732 Paris 07 SP, France, phone (33–1) 4568–1000.
Director-General.—Koichiro Matsuura (Japan).

United Nations Industrial Development Organization (UNIDO), Vienna International Centre, Wagramerstr. 5, P.O. Box 300, A–1400 Vienna, Austria, phone (43–1) 26026–0.
Director-General.—Kandeh Yumkella (Sierra Leone).

Universal Postal Union (UPU), International Bureau, Case Postale, 3000 Berne 15, Switzerland, phone (41–31) 350–3111.

Director–General.—Edouard Dayan (France).

World Bank Group, 1818 H Street, NW., Washington, DC 20433, phone (1–202) 473–1000.
President.—Robert B. Zoellick (USA).

World Health Organization (WHO), 20 Avenue Appia, 1211 Geneva 27, Switzerland, phone (41–22) 791–2111.
Director-General.—Margaret Chan (China).

World Health Organization Liaison Office, 1889 F Street, NW., Room 369, Washington, DC 20006, phone (1–202) 974–3324.
Special Adviser to the Director–General.—Michael Riggs (USA).

World Intellectual Property Organization (WIPO), 34, chemin des Colombettes, CH–1211 Geneva 20, Switzerland, phone (41–22) 338–9111.
Director General.—Francis Gurry (Australia).

World Meteorological Organization (WMO), 7bis, avenue de la Paix, Case Postale 2300, CH 1211 Geneva 2, Switzerland, phone (41–22) 730–8111.
Secretary-General.—Michel Jarraud (France).

RELATED BODY

International Atomic Energy Agency (IAEA), P.O. Box 100, Wagramer Strasse 5, A–1400 Vienna, Austria, phone (431) 2600–0.
Director General.—Mohamed Elbaradei (Egypt).
(The IAEA is an independent intergovernmental organization under the aegis of the UN).

SPECIAL AND PERSONAL REPRESENTATIVES AND ENVOYS OF THE SECRETARY-GENERAL

AFRICA

African Region:
Special Adviser to the Secretary-General on Africa and High Representative for the Least Developed Countries, Landlocked Developing Countries and Small Island Developing States.—Cheick Sidi Diarra (Mali).

Burundi:
Executive Representative of the Secretary-General for Burundi and Head of the UN Integrated Office in Burundi.—Youssef Mahmoud (Tunisia).

Central African Republic:
Special Representative of the Secretary–General and Head of the United Nations Peacebuilding Office in the Central African Republic.—Sahle-Work Zewde (Ethiopia).

Central African Republic and Chad:
Special Representative of the Secretary–General and Head of the United Nations Mission in the Central African Republic and Chad Principal.—Jose Victor Da Silva Angelo (Portugul).
Deputy Special Representative of the Secretary-General for the United Nations Mission in the Central African Republic and Chad.—Rima Salah (Jordan).

Cóte d'Ivoire:
Special Representative of the Secretary–General for Cóte d'Ivoire.—Choi Young-Jin (Republic of Korea).
Principal Deputy Special Representative of the Secretary-General.—Abou Moussa (Chad).
Deputy Special Representative of the Secretary-General for Humanitarian Coordination, Recovery and Reconstruction.—Georg Charpentier (Finland).

Democratic Republic of the Congo:
Special Representative of the Secretary-General for the Democratic Republic of the Congo.—Alan Doss (United Kingdom of Great Britain and Northern Ireland).
Deputy Special Representative of the Secretary-General for the Democratic Republic of the Congo.—Ross Mountain (New Zealand).
Deputy Special Representative of the Secretary-General for the Democratic Republic of the Congo.—Leila Zerrougui (Algeria)

Equatorial Guinea and Gabon:
Special Adviser to the Secretary-General and Mediator in the border dispute between Equatorial Guinea and Gabon.—Nicolas Michel (Switzerland).

Great Lakes Region:

Special Representative of the Secretary-General for the Great Lakes Region.—Olusegun Obasanjo (Nigeria).

Guinea-Bissau:

Representative of the Secretary-General and Head of UNOGBIS.—Joseph Mutaboba (Rwanda).

Horn of Africa:

Special Envoy.—Kjell Magne Bondevik (Norway).

Liberia:

Special Representative.—Ellen Margareth Loj (Denmark).

Deputy Special Representative for Recover and Good Governance.—Moustapha Soumaré (Mali).

Deputy Special Representative for Rule of Law.—Henrietta Joy Abena Nyarko Mensa-Bonsu (Ghana).

Sierra Leone:

Executive Representative for United Nations Integrated Peacebuilding Office in Sierra Leone (UNIPSIL).—Michael von der Schulenburg (Germany).

Somalia:

Special Representative.—Ahmedou Ould-Abdallah (Mauritania).

Sudan:

Special Representative.—Ashraf Jehangir Qazi (Pakistan).

Deputy Special Representative.—Vacant.

Deputy Special Representative and the UN Resident Coordinator and Humanitarian Coordinator.—Ameerah Haq (Bangladesh.)

Sudan / Darfur:

Joint Special Representative for the African Union and the United Nations Hybrid Operations in Darfur.—Henry Anyidoho (Ghana).

Deputy Joint AU-UN Special Representative for Operations and Management.—Mohamed Yonis (Somalia).

West Africa:

Special Representative.—Said Djinnit (Algeria).

Western Sahara:

Special Representative.—Hany Abdel-Aziz (Egypt).

Personal Envoy.—Christopher Ross (United States).

THE AMERICAS

Latin American Region:

Special Adviser.—Diego Cordovez (Ecuador).

Haiti:

Special Representative.—Hédi Annabi (Tunisia).

Principal Deputy Special Representative.—Luiz Carlos da Costa (Brazil).

Deputy Special Representative and Humanitarian Coordinator, Resident Coordinator and Resident Representative for UNDP.—Joel Boutroue (France).

Special Envoy.—William J. Clinton (United States).

Deputy Special Envoy.—Paul Farmer (United States).

ASIA AND THE PACIFIC

Afghanistan:

Special Representative.—Kai Eide (Norway).

Deputy Special Representative for Relief, Recovery and Reconstruction; UN Resident Coordinator and the UN Humanitarian Coordinator in Afghanistan.—Robert Watkins (Canada).

Deputy Special Representative for Political Issues.—Wolfgang Weisbrod-Weber, temporary (Germany).

Central Asia:

Special Representative and Head of the UN Regional Centre for Preventive Diplomacy for Central Asia.—Miroslav Jenca (Slovakia).

Nepal:

Representative.—Karin Landgren (Sweden).

Pakistan:

Special Envoy for Assistance.—Jean-Maurice Ripert (France).

Timor Leste:

Special Representative.—Atul Khare (India).

Deputy Special Representative for Governance Support, Development and Humanitarian Coordination.—Finn Reske-Nielsen (Denmark)

Deputy Special Representative for Security Sector Support and Rule of Law.—Takahisa Kawakami (Japan).

EUROPE

Cyprus:

Special Representative.—Taye-Brook Zerihoun (Ethiopia).

Former Yugoslav Republic of Macedonia-Greece:

Personal Envoy.—Matthew Nimetz (United States).

Georgia:

Special Representative.—Johan Verbeke (Belgium).

Kosovo:

Special Representative.—Lamberto Zannier (Italy).

Deputy Special Representative for Reconstruction (European Union).—Paul Acda (United Kingdom).

MIDDLE EAST

Middle East:

Special Coordinator for the Middle East Peace Process.—Robert H. Serry (Nertherlands).

Deputy Special Coordinator for the Middle East Peace Process.—Max Gaylard.

Special Envoy for the Implementation of Security Council Resolution 1559.—Terje Roed-Larsen (Norway).

Iraq:

Special Representative.—Ad Melkert (Netherlands).

Deputy Special Representative for Political Affairs.—Andrew Gilmore (UK).

Deputy Special Representative for Humanitarian, Reconstruction and Development Affairs.—Christine McNab (Sweden).

Iraq (International Compact):

Special Adviser on International Compact with Iraq and Other Issues.—Ibrahim Gambari (Nigeria).

Iraq / Kuwait:

Secretary-General's High-level Coordinator for compliance by Iraq with its obligations regarding the repatriation or return of all Kuwaiti and third country nationals or their remains, as well as the return of all Kuwaiti property, including archives seized by Iraq.—Gennady P. Tarasov (Russian Federation).

Lebanon:

Special Coordinator of the Secretary-General for Lebanon.—Michael C. Williams (United Kingdom).

OTHER HIGH LEVEL APPOINTMENTS

Alliance of Civilizations:

High Representative.—Jorge Sampaio (Portugal).

Children and Armed Conflict:

Special Representative.—Radhika Coomaraswamy (Sri Lanka).

Climate Change:

Special Envoys on Climate Change: Gro Harlem Brundtland (Norway), Ricardo Lagos Escobar (Chile), Festus Mogae (Botswana), Srgjan Kerim (former Yugoslav Republic of Macedonia).

Commonwealth of Independent States (CIS):

Special Envoy.—Yuli Vorontsov (Russian Federation).

Conference on Disarmament:

Personal Representative.—Sergei A. Ordzhonikidze (Russian Federation).

Disaster Reduction:

Special Representative.—Margareta Wahlstrom (Sweden).

Financing for Development:
Special Adviser.—Phillipe Douste-Blazy (France).

Gender Issues and Advancement of Women:
Special Adviser.—Rachel N. Mayanja (Uganda).

Global Compact:
Special Adviser.—Klaus M. Leisinger (United States).

HIV / AIDS in Africa:
Special Envoy.—Elizabeth Mataka (Botswana).

HIV / AIDS in Asia:
Special Envoy.—Nafis Sadik (Pakistan).

HIV / AIDS in the Caribbean Region:
Special Envoy.—George Alleyne (Barbados).

HIV / AIDS in Eastern Europe:
Vacant.

Human Rights:
Special Representative.—Margaret Sekaggya (Uganda).

Human Rights and the Business Community:
Special Representative.—John Ruggie (United States).

Human Rights in Cambodia:
Special Representative.—Yash Ghai (Kenya).

Malaria:
Special Envoy.—Ray Chambers (United States).

Migration:
Special Representative.—Peter Sutherland (Ireland).

Internally Displaced Persons:
Representative.—Walter Kalin (Switzerland).

Least Developed Countries, Landlocked Developing Countries, and Small Island Developing States:
Special Adviser.—Cheick Sidi Diarra (Mali), (Also Special Adviser to the Secretary General on Africa).

Millennium Development Goals:
Special Adviser.—Jeffrey D. Sachs (United States).
Executive Coordinator.—Eveline Herfkens (Netherlands).

Prevention of Genocide:
Special Advisor.—Francis Deng (Sudan).

Sport for Development and Peace:
Special Adviser.—Wilfried Lemke (Germany).

Tuberculosis:
Special Representative.—Jorge Sampaio (Portugal).

United Nations International School (UNIS):
Special Representative.—Silvia Fuhrman (United States).

Violence Against Children:
Special Representative.—Marta Santos Pais (Portugal).

World Summit on Information Society:
Special Adviser.—Nitin Desai (India).

WORLD BANK GROUP

The World Bank Group comprises five organizations: the International Bank for Reconstruction and Development (IBRD), the International Development Association (IDA), the International Finance Corporation (IFC), the Multilateral Investment Guarantee Agency (MIGA) and the International Centre for the Settlement of Investment Disputes (ICSID).

Headquarters: 1818 H Street, NW., 20433, (202) 473–1000

INTERNATIONAL BANK FOR RECONSTRUCTION AND DEVELOPMENT

President.—Robert Zoellick.
Managing Directors: Graeme Wheeler, Ngozi N. Okonjo-Iweala, Juan Jose Daboub.
Special Adviser to the MDs.—Danny Leipziger.

Senior Vice President and General Counsel.—Anne-Marie Leroy.
Senior Vice President, Development Economics, and Chief Economist.—Justin Yifu Lin.
Vice President and Head, Human Development Network.—Joy Phumaphi.
Chief Financial Officer.—Vincenzo La Via.
Vice President and Chief Information Officer and Head, Information Solutions Network.—Shelley B. Leibowitz.
Vice President and Controller.—Charles McDonough.
Vice President and Corporate Secretary.—Kristalina Georgieva.
Vice President and Treasurer.—Kenneth G. Lay
Vice President of:
Africa.—Obiageli Katryn Ezekwesili.
East Asia and Pacific.—James W. Adams.
South Asia.—Isabel Guerrero.
Vice President and Network Head Sustainable Development Network.—Katherine Sierra.
Senior Vice President External Affairs.—Marwan Muasher.
North American Affairs (External Affairs) Special Representative.—Matthew Niemeyer.
Europe (External Affairs) Special Representative.—Cyrill Muller.
UN External Affairs, Special Representative.—Ferid Belhaj.
Japan-External Affairs, Special Representative.—Kazu Tanigushi.
Human Resources.—Hasan A. Tuluy.
Latin America and the Caribbean.—Pamela Cox.
Middle East and North Africa.—Shamshad Akhtar.
Vice President and Network Head, Operations Policy and Country Services.—Jeffrey Gutman.
Vice President and Network Head Poverty Reduction and Economic Management Network.—Otaviano Canuto.
Vice President and Network Head Financial and Private Sector Development (World Bank and IFC).—Penelope Brook (acting).
Resource Mobilization and Cofinancing.—Geoffrey B. Lamb.
Strategy, Finance and Risk Management.—John Herlihy.
Vice President, World Bank Institute.—Sanjay Pradhan.
Director-General, Independent Evaluation.—Vinod Thomas.
Vice President, Corporate Finance and Risk Management.—Fayezul Choudhury.
Vice President, Concessional Finance and Global Partnerships.—Axel Van Trotsenburg.
Vice President, Institutional Integrity.—Leonard McCarthy.

OTHER WORLD BANK OFFICES

London: New Zealand House, 15th Floor, Haymarket, London SW1Y 4TE, England.
Geneva: 3, Chemin Louis Dunant, CP 66, CH 1211, Geneva 10, Switzerland.
Paris: 66, Avenue d'Iena, 75116 Paris, France.
Brussels: 10, rue Montoyer, B–1000 Brussels, Belgium.
Tokyo: Fukoku Seimei Building, 10th Floor, 2–2–2 Uchisawai-cho, Chiyoda-Ku, Tokyo 100, Japan.
Sydney: c/o South Pacific Project Facility, 89 York Street, Level 8, GPO Box 1612, Sydney, NSW 2000, Australia.
Frankfurt: Bockenheimer Landstrasse 109, 60325 Frankfurt am Main, Germany.

BOARD OF EXECUTIVE DIRECTORS

Bahrain, Egypt (Arab Republic of), Iraq, Jordan, Kuwait, Lebanon, Libya, Maldives, Oman, Qatar, Syrian Arab Republic, United Arab Emirates, Yemen (Republic of).
Executive Director.—Merza H. Hasan.
Alternate.—Ayman Alkaffas.
Saudi Arabia.
Executive Director.—Abdulrahman M. Almofadhi.
Alternate.—Abdulhamid Alkhalifa.
Austria, Belarus, Belgium, Czech Republic, Hungary, Kazakhstan,
Luxembourg, Slovak Republic, Slovenia, Turkey.
Executive Director.—Konstantin Huber (Austria).
Alternate.—Gino Alzetta (Belgium).
Australia, Cambodia, Kiribati, Korea (Republic of), Marshall Islands, Micronesia (Federated States of), Mongolia, New Zealand, Palau, Papua New Guinea, Samoa, Solomon Islands, Vanuatu.

Executive Director.—James Hagan.
Alternate.—Do Hyeong Kim.
Albania, Greece, Italy, Malta, Portugal, San Marino, Timor-Leste.
Executive Director.—Giovanni Majnoni.
Alternate.—Nuno Mota Pinto.
United States.
Executive Director.—E. Whitney Debevoise.
Brazil, Colombia, Dominican Republic, Ecuador, Haiti, Panama, Philippines, Suriname, Trinidad and Tobago.
Executive Director.—Carolina Renteria.
Alternate.—Rogerio Studart.
Germany.
Executive Director.—Michael Hofmann.
Alternate.—Ruediger Von Kleist.
Afghanistan, Algeria, Ghana, Iran (Islamic Republic of), Morocco, Pakistan, Tunisia.
Executive Director.—Sid Ahmed Dib.
Alternate.—Javed Talat.
France.
Executive Director.—Ambroise Fayolle.
Alternate.—Frederick Jeske-Schonhoven.
Benin, Burkina Faso, Cameroon, Cape Verde, Central African Republic, Chad, Comoros, Congo (Democratic Republic of), Congo (Republic of), Cote d'lvoire, Djibouti, Equatorial Guinea, Gabon, Guinea, Guinea-Bissau, Madagascar, Mali, Mauritania, Mauritius, Niger, Rwanda, Sao Tome and Principe, Senegal, Togo.
Executive Director.—Louis Philippe Ong Seng.
Alternate.—Agapito Mendes Dias.
Brunei Darussalam, Fiji, Indonesia, Lao People's Democratic Republic, Malaysia, Myanmar, Nepal, Singapore, Thailand, Tonga, Vietnam.
Executive Director.—Sun Vithespongse.
Alternate.—Irfa Ampri.
Denmark, Estonia, Finland, Iceland, Latvia, Lithuania, Norway, Sweden.
Executive Director.—Svein Aass.
Alternate.—Jens Haarlov.
Russian Federation.
Executive Director.—Alexey G. Kvasov.
Alternate.—Eugene Miagkov.
Costa Rica, El Salvador, Guatemala, Honduras, Mexico, Nicaragua, Spain, Venezuela (Republica Bolivariana de).
Executive Director.—Jose A. Rojas.
Alternate.—Marta Garcia Jauregui.
Antigua and Barbuda, Bahamas (The), Barbados, Belize, Canada, Dominica, Grenada, Guyana, Ireland, Jamaica, St. Kitts and Nevis, St. Lucia, St. Vincent and the Grenadines.
Executive Director.—Sammy Watson.
Alternate.—Ishmael Lightbourne.
Armenia, Bosnia and Herzegovina, Bulgaria, Croatia, Cyprus, Georgia, Israel, Macedonia (former Yugoslav Republic of), Moldova, Netherlands, Romania, Ukraine.
Executive Director.—Rudolf Treffers.
Alternate.—Claudis Doltu.
Japan.
Executive Director.—Toru Shikibu.
Alternate.—Masato Kanda.
Argentina, Bolivia, Chile, Paraguay, Peru, Uruguay.
Executive Director.—Dante Contreras.
Alternate.—Felix Alberto Camarasa.
United Kingdom.
Executive Director.—Susanna Moorehead.
Alternate.—Stewart James.
Angola, Botswana, Burundi, Eritrea, Ethiopia, Gambia (The), Kenya, Lesotho, Liberia, Malawi, Mozambique, Namibia, Nigeria, Seychelles, Sierra Leone, South Africa, Sudan, Swaziland, Tanzania, Uganda, Zambia, Zimbabwe.
Executive Director.—Toga McIntosh.
Alternate.—Hassan Ahmed.
Bangladesh, Bhutan, India, Sri Lanka.
Executive Director.—Pulok Chatterji.
Alternate.—Kazi M. Aminul Islam.
Azerbaijan, Serbia and Montenegro, Kyrgyz Republic, Poland, Switzerland, Tajikistan, Turkmenistan, Uzbekistan, Yugoslavia (Fed. Rep. of), Switzerland, Yemen, Republic of.

Executive Director.—Michel Mordasini.
Alternate.—Michal Krupinski.
China.
Executive Director.—Jianyi Zou.
Alternate.—Yingming Yang.

INTERNATIONAL DEVELOPMENT ASSOCIATION

[The officers, executive directors, and alternates are the same as those of the International Bank for Reconstruction and Development.]

INTERNATIONAL FINANCE CORPORATION

President.—Robert Zoellick.
Executive Vice President.—Lars Thunell.
Vice President and Corporate Secretary.— Kristalina Georgieva.
Vice President:
Finance and Treasurer.—Nina Shapiro.
Human Resources and Administration.—Dorothy H. Berry.
Vice President, Risk Management.—Michel G. Maila.
Private Sector Development / Chief Economist.—Penelope Brook (acting).
Director-General, Independent Evaluation.—Vinod Thomas.
Chief Information Officer and Corporate Business Informatics.—William Piatt.
Compliance Advisor / Ombudsman (IFC / MIGA).—Meg Taylor.
Vice President and General Counsel.—Rachel Robbins.
Director, Corporate Relations Unit Manager.—Bruce Moats.
Director, Office of:
Agribusiness.—Jean-Paul Pinard.
Controller's and Budgeting.—Christian Grossman.
Corporate Portfolio and Risk Management.—Marc A. Babin.
Credit Review.—Francisco Tourreilles.
Environment and Social Development.—Rachel Kyte.
Financial Operations.—Avil Hofman.
Global Financial Markets.—Jyrki Koskelo.
Global Information and Communications Technologies.—Mohsen A. Khalil.
Global Manufacturing and Services.—Dimitris Tsitsiragos.
Health and Education.—Guy M. Ellena.
Infrastructure.—Rashad-Rudolf Kaldany.
Municipal Fund.—Declan J. Duff.
Oil, Gas, Mining and Chemicals.—Peter van der Veen.
Operations Evaluation Group.—Marvin Taylor-Dormond.
Private Equity and Investment Funds.—Haydee Celaya.
Risk Management and Financial Policy.—Lakashmi Shyam-Sunder.
Special Operations.—Maria Da Graca Dominguez.
Trust Funds.—Mwaghazi Mwachofi.
Central and Eastern Europe.—Jerome Sooklal.
East Asia and Pacific.—Richard Ranken.
Latin America and Caribbean.—Atul Mehta.
Middle East and North Africa.—Michael Essex.
South Asia.—Paolo Martelli.
Southern Europe and Central Asia.—Shabbaz Mavaddat.
Sub-Saharan Africa.—Thierry Tanoh.

MULTILATERAL INVESTMENT GUARANTEE AGENCY

President.—Robert Zoellick.
Executive Vice President.—Izumi Kobayashi.
Vice President and General Counsel, Legal Affairs and Claims Group.—Peter Cleary.
Compliance Advisor / Ombudsman (IFC/ICC & MIGA).—Meg Taylor.
Chief Operating Officer.—James P. Bond.
Director of:
External Outreach and Partners Group.—Moina Varkie.

Operations Group.— Edith Quintrell.

Director and Chief Economist, Economics and Policy Group.—Frank Lysy.

Director and Chief Financial Officer, Finance and Risk Management Group.—Kevin Lu.

FOREIGN DIPLOMATIC OFFICES IN THE UNITED STATES

AFGHANISTAN

Embassy of Afghanistan
2341 Wyoming Avenue, NW., Washington, DC 20008
phone (202) 483–6410, fax 483–6488
His Excellency Said Tayeb Jawad
Ambassador E. and P.
Consular Offices:
California, Los Angeles
New York, New York

AFRICAN UNION

Delegaton of the African Union Mission
1919 Pennsylvania Avenue, NW., Suite 7001, Washington, DC 20006
Embassy of the African Union
phone (202) 293–8006, fax 429–7130
Her Excellency Amina Salum Ali
Ambassador (Head of Delegation)

ALBANIA

Embassy of the Republic of Albania
2100 S Street, NW., Washington, DC 20008
phone (202) 223–4942, fax 628–7342
His Excellency Aleksander Sallabanda
Ambassador E. and P.
Consular Offices:
Connecticut, Greenwich
Florida, Ft. Lauderdale
Georgia, Avondale Estates
Louisiana, New Orleans
Michigan, West Bloomfield
New York, New York
North Carolina, Pinehurst
Ohio, Cleveland
Texas, Houston

ALGERIA

Embassy of the Democratic Republic of Algeria
2118 Kalorama Road, NW., Washington, DC 20008
phone (202) 265–2800, fax 667–2174
His Excellency Abdallah Baali
Ambassador E. and P.

ANDORRA

Embassy of Andorra
Two United Nations Plaza, 27th Floor, New York, NY 10017
phone (212) 750–8064, fax 750–6630
Mr. Andreu Jordi Tomas
First Secretary (Charge D'Affaires, A.I.)

ANGOLA

Embassy of the Republic of Angola
2100–2108 16th Street, NW., Washington, DC 20009
phone (202) 785–1156, fax 785–1258
Her Excellency Josefina Pitra Diakité
Ambassador E. and P.
Consular Offices:
New York, New York
Texas, Houston

ANTIGUA AND BARBUDA

Embassy of Antigua and Barbuda
3216 New Mexico Avenue, NW., Washington, DC 20016
phone (202) 362–5122, fax 362–5225
Her Excellency Deborah Mae Lovell
Ambassador E. and P. / Consul General
Consular Offices:
Florida, Miami
New York, New York

ARGENTINA

Embassy of the Argentine Republic
1600 New Hampshire Avenue, NW., Washington, DC 20009
phone (202) 238–6400, fax 332–3171
His Excellency Hector Marcos Timerman
Ambassador E. and P.
Consular Offices:
California, Los Angeles
Florida, Miami
Georgia, Atlanta
Illinois, Chicago
New York, New York
Texas, Houston

ARMENIA

Embassy of the Republic of Armenia
2225 R Street, NW., Washington, DC 20008
phone (202) 319–1976, fax 319–2982
His Excellency Tatoul Markarian
Ambassador E. and P.
Consular Office: California, Los Angeles

AUSTRALIA

Embassy of Australia

1601 Massachusetts Avenue, NW., Washington, DC 20036
phone (202) 797–3000, fax 797–3168
His Excellency Dennis James Richardson
Ambassador E. and P.
Consular Offices:
- California:
  - Los Angeles
  - San Francisco
- Colorado, Denver
- Florida, Miami
- Georgia, Atlanta
- Hawaii, Honolulu
- Illinois, Chicago
- Massachusetts, Boston
- New York, New York
- Texas, Houston
- Trust Territories of the Pacific Islands:
  - Kolonia, Micronesia
  - Pago Pago
- Washington, Seattle

AUSTRIA

Embassy of Austria
3524 International Court, NW., Washington, DC 20008–3035
phone (202) 895–6700, fax 895–6750
Her Excellency Dr. Christian Prosl
Ambassador E. and P.
Consular Offices:
- Alaska, Anchorage
- Arizona, Scottsdale
- California:
  - Los Angeles
  - San Francisco
- Colorado, Denver
- Florida:
  - Miami
  - Orlando
- Georgia, Atlanta
- Hawaii, Honolulu
- Illinois, Chicago
- Louisiana, New Orleans
- Massachusetts, Boston
- Michigan, Detroit
- Minnesota, St. Paul
- Missouri:
  - Kansas City
  - St. Louis
- Nevada, Las Vegas
- New York:
  - Buffalo
  - New York
- North Carolina, Charlotte
- Ohio, Columbus
- Oregon, Portland
- Pennsylvania, Pittsburgh
- Puerto Rico, San Juan
- Texas, Houston
- Utah, Salt Lake City
- Virgin Islands, St. Thomas
- Virginia, Richmond
- Washington, Seattle
- Wisconsin, Milwaukee

AZERBAIJAN

Embassy of the Republic of Azerbaijan
2741 34th Street, NW., Washington, DC 20008
phone (202) 337–3500, fax 337–5911
His Excellency Yashar Aliyev
Ambassador E. and P.
Consular Office: California, Los Angeles

BAHAMAS

Embassy of the Commonwealth of The Bahamas
2220 Massachusetts Avenue, NW., Washington, DC 20008
phone (202) 319–2660, fax 319–2668
His Excellency Cornelius Alvin Smith
Ambassador E. and P.
Consular Offices:
- Florida, Miami
- Georgia, Fairburn
- New York, New York

BAHRAIN

Embassy of the Kingdom of Bahrain
3502 International Drive, NW., Washington, DC 20008
phone (202) 342–0741, fax 362–2192
Her Excellency Huda Ezra Ebrahim Nonoo
Ambassador E. and P.
Consular Offices:
- California, San Diego
- New York, New York

BANGLADESH

Embassy of the People's Republic of Bangladesh
3510 International Drive, NW., Washington, DC 20008
phone (202) 244–0183, fax 244–5366
His Excellency M. Humayun Kabir
Ambassador E. and P.
Consular Offices:
- California, Los Angeles
- Hawaii, Honolulu
- Louisiana, New Orleans
- New York, New York
- Texas, Houston

BARBADOS

Embassy of Barbados
2144 Wyoming Avenue, NW., Washington, DC 20008
phone (202) 939–9200, fax 332–7467
His Excellency John Ernest Beale
Ambassador E. and P.

Consular Offices:
- California, San Francisco
- Colorado, Denver
- Florida, Miami
- Georgia, Atlanta
- Illinois, Chicago
- Kentucky, Louisville
- Louisiana, New Orleans
- Massachusetts, Boston
- Michigan, Detroit
- New York, New York
- Ohio, Toledo
- Oregon, Portland
- Texas, Sugar Land

BELARUS

Embassy of the Republic of Belarus
1619 New Hampshire Avenue, NW., Washington, DC 20009
phone (202) 986–1604, fax 986–1805
His Excellency Mikhail Khvostov
Ambassador E. and P.
Consular Office: New York, New York

BELGIUM

Embassy of Belgium
3330 Garfield Street, NW., Washington, DC 20008
phone (202) 333–6900, fax 333–3079
His Excellency Jan Jozef Matthysen
Ambassador E. and P. / Consul General
Consular Offices:
- Alaska, Anchorage
- Arizona, Phoenix
- California:
  - Los Angeles
  - San Diego
  - San Francisco
- Colorado, Denver
- Florida, Miami
- Georgia, Atlanta
- Hawaii, Honolulu
- Illinois:
  - Chicago
  - Moline
- Kansas, Kansas City
- Kentucky, Louisville
- Louisiana, New Orleans
- Maryland, Baltimore
- Massachusetts, Boston
- Michigan, Bloomfield
- Minnesota, St. Paul
- Missouri, St. Louis
- New York, New York
- Ohio, Cincinnati
- Oregon, Portland
- Pennsylvania:
  - Philadelphia
  - Pittsburgh
- Puerto Rico, San Juan
- Texas:
  - Fort Worth
  - Houston
  - San Antonio
- Utah, Salt Lake City
- Virginia, Norfolk
- Washington, Seattle
- Wisconsin, Milwaukee

BELIZE

Embassy of Belize
2535 Massachusetts Avenue, NW., Washington, DC 20008
phone (202) 332–9636, fax 332–6888
His Excellency Nestor E. Mendez
Ambassador E. and P.
Consular Offices:
- California:
  - Los Angeles:
  - San Francisco
- Florida, Miami
- Illinois:
  - Belleville
  - Chicago
- Louisiana, New Orleans
- Michigan, Detroit
- Nevada, Las Vegas
- North Carolina, Wilmington
- Ohio, Dayton
- Puerto Rico, San Juan
- Texas:
  - Dallas
  - Houston

BENIN

Embassy of the Republic of Benin
2124 Kalorama Road, NW., Washington, DC 20008
phone (202) 232–6656, fax 265–1996
His Excellency Segbe Cyrille Oguin
Ambassador E. and P.
Consular Office: California, Los Angeles

BHUTAN

Consular Office: New York, New York

BOLIVIA

Embassy of the Republic of Bolivia
3014 Massachusetts Avenue, NW., Washington, DC 20008
phone (202) 483–4410, fax 328–3712
Ms. Erika Angela Duenas Loayza
Minister / Counselor (Charge D'Affaires, A.I.)
Consular Offices:
- Alabama, Mobile
- California:
  - Los Angeles
  - San Francisco
- Florida, Miami

Georgia, Atlanta
Illinois, Chicago
Massachusetts, Boston
Minnesota, Minneapolis
New York, New York
Oklahoma, Oklahoma City
Puerto Rico, San Juan
Texas:
Dallas
Houston
Washington, Seattle

BOSNIA AND HERZEGOVINA

Embassy of Bosnia and Herzegovina
2109 E Street, NW., Washington, DC 20037
phone (202) 337–1500, fax 337–1502
Her Excellency Mitar Kujundzic
Ambassador E. and P.
Consular Offices:
Illinois, Chicago
New York, New York

BOTSWANA

Embassy of the Republic of Botswana
1531–1533 New Hampshire Avenue, NW., Washington, DC 20036
phone (202) 244–4990, fax 244–4164
His Excellency Lapologang Caesar Lekoa
Ambassador E. and P.
Consular Offices:
California:
Los Angeles
San Francisco
Georgia, Atlanta
Texas, Houston

BRAZIL

Brazilian Embassy
3006 Massachusetts Avenue, NW., Washington, DC 20008
phone (202) 238–2700, fax 238–2827
His Excellency Antonio de Aguiar Patriota
Ambassador E. and P.
Consular Offices:
Alabama, Birmingham
Arizona, Scottsdale
California:
Los Angeles
San Diego
San Francisco
Florida, Miami
Georgia, Atlanta
Hawaii, Honolulu
Illinois, Chicago
Kentucky, Convington
Louisiana, New Orleans
Massachusetts, Boston
New York, New York
Tennessee, Memphis
Trust Territories of the Pacific Islands, Hong Kong
Texas, Houston
Utah, Salt Lake City
Virginia, Norfolk

BRUNEI

Embassy of the State of Brunei Darussalam
3520 International Court, NW., Washington, DC 20008
phone (202) 237–1838, fax 885–0560
Ms. Angela Oi Foong Shim
Minister / Counselor (Charge D'Affaires, A.I.)

BULGARIA

Embassy of the Republic of Bulgaria
1621 22nd Street, NW., Washington, DC 20008
phone (202) 387–0174, fax 234–7973
His Excellency Latchezar Yordanov Petkov
Ambassador E. and P.
Consular Offices:
California:
Los Angeles
Sacramento
Florida, Boca Raton
Illinois, Chicago
Maryland, Baltimore
Nevada, Las Vegas
New York, New York
Pennsylvania, Media

BURKINA FASO

Embassy of Burkina Faso
2340 Massachusetts Avenue, NW., Washington, DC 20008
phone (202) 332–5577, fax 667–1882
His Excellency Paramanga Ernest Yonli
Ambassador E. and P.
Consular Offices:
California, Los Angeles
Louisiana, New Orleans

BURMA

Embassy of the Union of Burma
2300 S Street, NW., Washington, DC 20008
phone (202) 332–3344, fax 332–4351
Mr. Myint Lwin
Minister / Counselor (Charge D'Affaires, A.I.)
Consular Office: New York, New York

BURUNDI

Embassy of the Republic of Burundi
2233 Wisconsin Avenue, NW., Suite 212, Washington, DC 20007
phone (202) 342–2574, fax 342–2578
His Excellency Celestin Niyongabo
Ambassador E. and P.
Consular Office: California, Los Angeles

CAMBODIA

Royal Embassy of Cambodia
4530 16th Street, NW., Washington, DC 20011
phone (202) 726–7742, fax 726–8381
His Excellency Heng Hem
Ambassador E. and P.
Consular Office: Washington, Seattle

CAMEROON

Embassy of the Republic of Cameroon
2349 Massachusetts Avenue, NW., Washington, DC 20008
phone (202) 265–8790, fax 387–3826
His Excellency Bienvenu Joseph C. Foe Atangana
Ambassador E. and P.
Consular Offices:
- California, San Francisco
- Texas, Houston

CANADA

Embassy of Canada
501 Pennsylvania Avenue, NW., Washington, DC 20001
phone (202) 682–1740, fax 682–7726
His Excellency Michael H. Wilson
Ambassador E. and P.
Consular Offices:
- Alaska, Anchorage
- Arizona:
  - Phoenix
  - Tucson
- California:
  - Los Angeles
  - San Diego
  - San Francisco
  - San Jose
- Colorado, Denver
- Florida:
  - Miami
  - Tampa
- Georgia, Atlanta
- Illinois, Chicago
- Iowa, Muscatine
- Louisiana, New Orleans
- Maine, Portland
- Massachusetts, Boston
- Michigan, Detroit
- Minnesota, Minneapolis
- Missouri, St. Louis
- Montana, Nashua
- Nebraska, Omaha
- New Jersey, Princeton
- New York:
  - Buffalo
  - New York
- North Carolina:
  - Huntersville
  - Raleigh
- Ohio, Cleveland
- Oregon, Portland
- Pennsylvania:
  - Philadelphia
  - Pittsburgh
- Puerto Rico, San Juan
- Tennessee, Memphis
- Texas:
  - Dallas
  - Houston
  - San Antonio
- Utah, Bountiful
- Virginia, Richmond
- Washington, Seattle

CAPE VERDE

Embassy of the Republic of Cape Verde
3415 Massachusetts Avenue, NW., Washington, DC 20007
phone (202) 965–6820, fax 965–1207
Her Excellency Maria De Fatima Da Veiga
Ambassador E. and P.
Consular Office: Massachusetts, Boston

CENTRAL AFRICAN REPUBLIC

Embassy of Central African Republic
1618 22nd Street, NW., Washington, DC 20008
phone (202) 483–7800, fax 332–9893
His Excellency Emmanuel Touaboy
Ambassador E. and P.
Consular Offices:
- California, Los Angeles
- New York, New York

CHAD

Embassy of the Republic of Chad
2002 R Street, NW., Washington, DC 20009
phone (202) 462–4009, fax 265–1937
His Excellency Bechir Mahamoud Adam
Ambassador E. and P.

CHILE

Embassy of the Republic of Chile
1732 Massachusetts Avenue, NW., Washington, DC 20036
phone (202) 785–1746, fax 887–5579
His Excellency Jose Mario Goni Carrasco
Ambassador E. and P.
Consular Offices:
- California:
  - Los Angeles
  - San Diego
  - San Francisco
  - Santa Clara
- Florida, Miami
- Georgia, Atlanta
- Hawaii, Honolulu
- Illinois, Chicago

Louisiana, New Orleans
Massachusetts, Boston
Missouri, Kansas City
Nevada, Las Vegas
New York, New York
Pennsylvania, Philadelphia
Puerto Rico, San Juan
South Carolina, Charleston
Texas:
Dallas
Houston
Utah, Provo
Washington, Olympia

CHINA

Embassy of the People's Republic of China
2300 Connecticut Avenue, NW., Washington, DC 20008
phone (202) 495–2000, fax 495–2138
His Excellency Wen Zhong Zhou
Ambassador E. and P.
Consular Offices:
California:
Los Angeles
San Francisco
Illinois, Chicago
New York, New York
Texas, Houston

COLOMBIA

Embassy of Colombia
2118 Leroy Place, NW., Washington, DC 20008
phone (202) 387–8338, fax 232–8643
Her Excellency Maria Carolina Barco Isakson
Ambassador E. and P.
Consular Offices:
California:
Beverly Hills
San Francisco
Florida, Miami
Georgia, Atlanta
Illinois, Chicago
Louisiana, New Orleans
Massachusetts, Boston
New York, New York
Puerto Rico, San Juan
Texas, Houston

COMOROS

Embassy of the Union of Comoros
866 United Nations Plaza, Suite 418, New York, NY 10017
phone (212) 750–1637, fax 750–1657
His Excellency Mohamed Toihiri
Ambassador E. and P.

CONGO, DEMOCRATIC REPUBLIC OF

Embassy of the Democratic Republic of Congo
1726 M Street, NW., Suite 601, Washington, DC 20036
phone (202) 234–7690, fax 234–2609
Her Excellency Faida Mitifu
Ambassador E. and P.
Consular Office: New York, New York

CONGO, REPUBLIC OF

Embassy of the Republic of the Congo
4891 Colorado Avenue, NW., Washington, DC 20011
phone (202) 726–5500, fax 726–1860
His Excellency Serge Mombouli
Ambassador E. and P.
Consular Office: Louisiana, New Orleans

COSTA RICA

Embassy of Costa Rica
2114 S Street, NW., Washington, DC 20008
phone (202) 234–2945, fax 265–4795
His Excellency Luis Diego Escalante Vargas
Ambassador E. and P.
Consular Offices:
Arizona, Tucson
California:
Los Angeles
San Francisco
Colorado, Denver
Florida, Miami
Georgia, Atlanta
Illinois, Chicago
Louisiana, New Orleans
Massachusetts, Boston
Minnesota, Minneapolis
New York, New York
Puerto Rico, San Juan
Texas:
Austin
Dallas
Houston

CÔTE D'IVOIRE

Embassy of the Republic of Côte d'Ivoire
2424 Massachusetts Avenue, NW., Washington, DC 20008
phone (202) 797–0300, fax 462–9444
His Excellency Yao Charles Koffi
Ambassador E. and P.
Consular Offices:
California:
Los Angeles
San Francisco
Connecticut, Stamford
Florida, Orlando
Michigan, Detroit
Texas, Houston

CROATIA

Embassy of the Republic of Croatia
2343 Massachusetts Avenue, NW., Washington, DC 20008
phone (202) 588–5899, fax 588–8936
His Excellency Kolinda Grabar Kitarovic
Ambassador E. and P.
Consular Offices:
- California, Los Angeles
- Illinois, Chicago
- Kansas, Kansas City
- Louisiana, New Orleans
- New York, New York
- Pennsylvania, Pittsburgh
- Washington, Seattle

CYPRUS

Embassy of the Republic of Cyprus
2211 R Street, NW., Washington, DC 20008
phone (202) 462–5772, fax 483–6710
His Excellency Andreas S. Kakouris
Ambassador E. and P.
Consular Offices:
- Arizona, Phoenix
- California:
  - Los Angeles
  - San Francisco
- Georgia, Atlanta
- Illinois, Chicago
- Louisiana, New Orleans
- Massachusetts, Boston
- Michigan, Detroit
- New York, New York
- North Carolina, Jacksonville
- Oregon, Portland
- Texas, Houston
- Washington, Seattle

CZECH REPUBLIC

Embassy of the Czech Republic
3900 Spring of Freedom Street, NW., Washington, DC 20008
phone (202) 274–9100, fax 966–8540
His Excellency Petr Kolar
Ambassador E. and P.
Consular Offices:
- Alaska, Anchorage
- California:
  - Los Angeles
  - San Francisco
- Florida, Ft. Lauderdale
- Georgia, Atlanta
- Illinois, Chicago
- Louisiana, New Orleans
- Massachusetts, Wellesley
- Minnesota, St. Paul
- Missouri, Kansas City
- New York:
  - Buffalo
  - New York
- Oregon, Portland
- Pennsylvania:
  - Philadelphia
  - Pittsburgh
- Puerto Rico, San Juan
- Texas, Houston

DENMARK

Royal Danish Embassy
3200 Whitehaven Street, NW., Washington, DC 20008
phone (202) 234–4300, fax 328–1470
His Excellency Friis Arne Petersen
Ambassador E. and P.
Consular Offices:
- Alabama, Mobile
- Alaska, Anchorage
- Arizona, Scottsdale
- California:
  - San Diego
  - San Francisco
  - Studio City
- Colorado, Denver
- Florida:
  - Hollywood
  - Jacksonville
  - Tampa
- Georgia:
  - Atlanta
  - Macon
- Hawaii, Honolulu
- Illinois, Chicago
- Indiana, Indianapolis
- Iowa, Des Moines
- Louisiana, New Orleans
- Maryland, Baltimore
- Massachusetts, Boston
- Michigan, Detroit
- Minnesota, Minneapolis
- Missouri:
  - Kansas City
  - St. Louis
- Nebraska, Omaha
- New York, New York
- Ohio, Cleveland
- Oklahoma, Oklahoma City
- Oregon, Portland
- Pennsylvania:
  - Philadelphia
  - Pittsburgh
- Puerto Rico, San Juan
- South Carolina, Charleston
- Tennessee, Nashville
- Texas:
  - Dallas
  - Houston

Utah, Salt Lake City
Virgin Islands, St. Thomas
Virginia, Norfolk
Washington, Seattle
Wisconsin, Milwaukee

DJIBOUTI

Embassy of the Republic of Djibouti
1156 15th Street, NW., Suite 515, Washington, DC 20005
phone (202) 331–0270, fax 331–0302
His Excellency Roble Olhaye
Ambassador E. and P.

DOMINICA

Embassy of the Commonwealth of Dominica
3216 New Mexico Avenue, NW., Washington, DC 20016
phone (202) 364–6781, fax 364–6791
Ms. Judith Anne Rolle
Third Secretary (Charge D'Affaires, A.I.)
Consular Office: New York, New York

DOMINICAN REPUBLIC

Embassy of the Dominican Republic
1715 22nd Street, NW., Washington, DC 20008
phone (202) 332–6280, fax 265–8057
His Excellency Roberto Bernardo Saladin Selin
Ambassador E. and P.
Consular Offices:
California, Sun Valley
Florida, Miami
Illinois, Chicago
Louisiana, New Orleans
Massachusetts, Boston
New York, New York
Puerto Rico:
Mayaguez
San Juan

ECUADOR

Embassy of Ecuador
2535 15th Street, NW., Washington, DC 20009
phone (202) 234–7200, fax 667–3482
His Excellency Luis Beningo Gallegos Chiriboga
Ambassador E. and P.
Consular Offices:
California:
Los Angeles
San Francisco
Florida:
Miami
Tampa
Georgia, Atlanta
Illinois, Chicago
Louisiana, New Orleans
Massachusetts, Boston
Minnesota, Eden Prairie
Nevada, Las Vegas
New Jersey, Newark
New York, New York
Puerto Rico, San Juan
Texas:
Dallas
Houston

EGYPT

Embassy of the Arab Republic of Egypt
3521 International Court, NW., Washington, DC 20008
phone (202) 895–5400, fax 244–4319
His Excellency Sameh Hassan Shoukry
Ambassador E. and P.
Consular Offices:
California, San Francisco
Illinois, Chicago
New York, New York
Texas, Houston

EL SALVADOR

Embassy of El Salvador
1400 16th Street, NW., Suite 100, Washington, DC 20036
phone (202) 265–9671, fax 232–3763
Consular Offices:
Arizona:
Nogales
Phoenix
California:
Chula Vista
Costa Mesa
Los Angeles
Oakland
San Francisco
Santa Ana
Florida, Miami
Georgia, Duluth
Illinois, Chicago
Louisiana, New Orleans
Massachusetts, Boston
Missouri:
Kansas City
St. Louis
Nevada, Las Vegas
New Jersey, Elizabeth
New York, New York
Pennsylvania, Philadelphia
Puerto Rico, Bayamon
Texas:
Dallas
Houston
Utah, Salt Lake City
Virginia, Woodbridge

EQUATORIAL GUINEA

Embassy of the Republic of Equatorial Guinea

2020 16th Street, NW., Washington, DC 20009
phone (202) 518–5700, fax 518–5252
Her Excellency Purificacion Angue Ondo
Ambassador E. and P.

ERITREA

Embassy of the State of Eritrea
1708 New Hampshire Avenue, NW., Washington, DC 20009
phone (202) 319–1991, fax 319–1304
His Excellency Ghirmai Ghebremariam
Ambassador E. and P.
Consular Office: California, Oakland

ESTONIA

Embassy of Estonia
2131 Massachusetts Avenue, NW., Washington, DC 20008
phone (202) 588–0101, fax 588–0108
His Excellency Vaino Reinart
Ambassador E. and P.
Consular Offices:
- California:
  - Los Angeles
  - San Francisco
- Illinois, Chicago
- New Hampshire, Portsmouth
- New York, New York

ETHIOPIA

Embassy of Ethiopia
3506 International Drive, NW., Washington, DC 20008
phone (202) 364–1200, fax 686–9551
His Excellency Dr. Samuel Assefa Lemma
Ambassador E. and P.
Consular Offices:
- California, Los Angeles
- New York, New York
- Texas, Houston
- Washington, Seattle

EUROPEAN UNION

Delegation of the European Commission
2300 M Street, NW., Washington, DC 20037
phone (202) 862–9500, fax 429–1766
His Excellency John Bruton
Ambassador (Head of Delegation)

FIJI

Embassy of the Republic of the Fiji Islands
2000 M Street, NW., Suite 710, Washington, DC 20036
phone (202) 466–8320, fax 466–8325
His Excellency Winston Thompson
Ambassador E. and P.
Consular Offices:
- California:
  - El Segundo
  - San Francisco
- Oregon, Portland
- Texas, Dallas

FINLAND

Embassy of Finland
3301 Massachusetts Avenue, NW., Washington, DC 20008
phone (202) 298–5800, fax 298–6030
His Excellency Pekka Lintu
Ambassador E. and P.
Consular Offices:
- Alabama, Birmingham
- Alaska, Anchorage
- Arizona, Phoenix
- California:
  - Los Angeles
  - Portola Valley
  - San Diego
- Colorado, Denver
- Connecticut, Norwich
- Florida:
  - Lake Worth
  - Miami
- Georgia, Atlanta
- Hawaii, Honolulu
- Illinois, Chicago
- Louisiana, New Orleans
- Maryland, Baltimore
- Massachusetts, Boston
- Michigan:
  - Farmington
  - Marquette
- Minnesota:
  - Minneapolis
  - Virginia
- New Jersey, Newark
- New Mexico, Albequerque
- New York, New York
- Oregon, Portland
- Puerto Rico, San Juan
- Texas:
  - Dallas
  - Houston
- Virginia, Norfolk
- Washington, Seattle

FRANCE

Embassy of France
4101 Reservoir Road, NW., Washington, DC 20007
phone (202) 944–6000, fax 944–6166
His Excellency Pierre Nicolas Vimont
Ambassador E. and P.
Consular Offices:
- Alabama, Auburn University
- Alaska, Anchorage

Arizona, Phoenix
Arkansas, Little Rock
California:
  Los Angeles
  Sacramento
  San Diego
  San Francisco
  San Jose
Colorado, Denver
Connecticut, Hartford
Florida:
  Clearwater
  Miami
  Orlando
Georgia:
  Atlanta
  Savannah
Guam, Tamuning
Hawaii, Honolulu
Idaho, Boise
Illinois, Chicago
Indiana, Indianapolis
Iowa, Indianola
Kentucky, Louisville
Louisiana
  Lafayette
  New Orleans
Maine, Portland
Massachusetts, Boston
Michigan, Detriot
Minnesota, Minneapolis
Mississippi, Jackson
Missouri:
  Kansas City
  Saint Louis
Montana, Missoula
Nevada, Las Vegas
New Hampshire, Manchester
New Jersey, Princeton
New Mexico, Albequerque
New York:
  Buffalo
  New York
North Carolina, Charlotte
Ohio:
  Cincinnati
  Cleveland
Oklahoma, Oklahoma City
Oregon, Portland
Pennsylvania:
  Philadelphia
  Pittsburgh
Puerto Rico, San Juan
Rhode Island, Providence
South Carolina, Columbia
Tennessee, Memphis
Texas:
  Austin
  Dallas
  Houston
  San Antonio
Utah, Salt Lake City
Vermont, Essex Junction
Virgin Islands, St. Thomas
Virginia, Norfolk
Washington, Seattle
Wyoming, Dubois

GABON

Embassy of the Gabonese Republic
2034 20th Street, NW., Suite 200, Washington, DC 20009
phone (202) 797–1000, fax 332–0668
His Excellency Carlos Victor Boungou
Ambassador E. and P.
Consular Office: New York, New York

GAMBIA

Embassy of The Gambia
1424 K Street, NW., Suite 600, Washington, DC 20005
phone (202) 785–1379, fax 785–1430
Her Excellency Neneh MacDouall Gaye
Ambassador E. and P.
Consular Offices:
  California, Los Angeles
  Florida, Miami

GEORGIA

Embassy of the Republic of Georgia
2209 Massachusetts Avenue, NW., Washington, DC 20008
phone (202) 387–2390, fax 393–4537
His Excellency Vasil Sikharulidze
Ambassador E. and P.
Consular Offices:
  Alabama, Mobile
  California, Orange
  Massachusetts, Boston
  New York, New York
  Puerto Rico, San Juan
  Texas, Houston

GERMANY, FEDERAL REPUBLIC OF

Embassy of the Federal Republic of Germany
4645 Reservoir Road, NW., Washington, DC 20007
phone (202) 298–4000, fax 298–4249
His Excellency Dr. Klaus Scharioth
Ambassador E. and P.
Consular Offices:
  Alabama, Birmingham
  Alaska, Anchorage
  Arizona, Phoenix

California:
Carlsbad
Los Angeles
San Francisco
Colorado, Denver
Florida:
Miami
Naples
Georgia, Atlanta
Illinois, Chicago
Indiana, Indianapolis
Iowa, Indianola
Kansas, Kansas City
Kentucky, Louisville
Louisiana, New Orleans
Maine, Portland
Massachusetts, Boston
Michigan, Auburn Hills
Minnesota, Minneapolis
Nevada, Las Vegas
Mississippi, Jackson
Missouri, St. Louis
New Mexico, Albequerque
New York:
Buffalo
New York
North Carolina, Charlotte
Ohio:
Cincinnati
Cleveland
Oklahoma, Oklahoma City
Oregon, Portland
Pennsylvania:
Philadelphia
Pittsburgh
South Carolina, Greer
Tennessee, Nashville
Texas:
Corpus Christi
Dallas
Houston
San Antonio
Trust Territories of the Pacific Islands:
Manila, Philippines
Wellington, New Zealand
Utah, Salt Lake City
Virginia, Virginia Beach
Washington, Spokane

GHANA

Embassy of Ghana
3512 International Drive, NW., Washington, DC 20008
phone (202) 686–4520, fax 686–4527
His Excellency Dr. Kwame Bawuah-Edusei
Ambassador E. and P.
Consular Offices:
New York, New York
Texas, Houston

GREECE

Embassy of Greece
2217 Massachusetts Avenue, NW., Washington, DC 20008
phone (202) 939–1300, fax 939–1324
His Excellency Vassilis Kaskarelis
Ambassador E. and P.
Consular Offices:
California:
Los Angeles
San Francisco
Florida, Tampa
Georgia, Atlanta
Illinois, Chicago
Louisiana, New Orleans
Massachusetts, Boston
New York, New York
Texas, Houston

GRENADA

Embassy of Grenada
1701 New Hampshire Avenue, NW., Washington, DC 20009
phone (202) 265–2561, fax 265–2468
Her Excellency Gillian Margaret Susan Bristol
Ambassador E. and P.
Consular Offices:
California, Pomona
Florida, Ft. Lauderdale
Illinois, Chicago
Michigan, Northville
New York, New York

GUATEMALA

Embassy of Guatemala
2220 R Street, NW., Washington, DC 20008
phone (202) 745–4952, fax 745–1908
His Excellency Francisco Villagran De Leon
Ambassador E. and P.
Consular Offices:
Alabama, Montgomery
Arizona, Phoenix
California:
Los Angeles
San Diego
San Francisco
Colorado, Denver
Florida:
Ft. Lauderdale
Jupiter
Miami
Georgia, Atlanta
Illinois, Chicago

Louisiana:
Lafayette
New Orleans
Minnesota, Minneapolis
Missouri, Kansas City
Nevada, North Las Vegas
New York, New York
North Carolina, Charlotte
Oregon, Portland
Pennsylvania, Philadelphia
Puerto Rico, San Juan
Rhode Island, Providence
Tennessee, Memphis
Texas:
Houston
San Antonio
Washington, Seattle

GUINEA

Embassy of the Republic of Guinea
2112 Leroy Place, NW., Washington, DC 20008
phone (202) 986–4300, fax 986–3800
His Excellency Mory Karamoko Kaba
Ambassador E. and P.
Consular Offices:
Florida, Jacksonville
Ohio, Cleveland
Pennsylvania, Philadelphia

GUINEA-BISSAU

Embassy of the Republic of Guinea-Bissau
P.O. Box 33813, Washington, DC 20033
phone (301) 947–3958
Mr. Henrique Adriano Da Silva
Minister-Counselor

GUYANA

Embassy of Guyana
2490 Tracy Place, NW., Washington, DC 20008
phone (202) 265–6900, fax 232–1297
His Excellency Bayney Karran
Ambassador E. and P.
Consular Offices:
California, Los Angeles
Florida, Miami
New York, New York
Texas, Houston

HAITI

Embassy of the Republic of Haiti
2311 Massachusetts Avenue, NW., Washington, DC 20008
phone (202) 332–4090, fax 745–7215
His Excellency Raymond Alcide Joseph
Ambassador E. and P.
Consular Offices:
California, San Francisco
Colorado, Denver
Florida:
Miami
Orlando
Georgia, Atlanta
Illinois, Chicago
Indiana, Evansville
Louisiana, New Orleans
Massachusetts, Boston
Michigan, Detroit
Missouri, St. Louis
New Jersey, Trenton
New York, New York
Ohio, Cleveland
Pennsylvania:
Philadelphia
Pottsville
Puerto Rico, San Juan
Texas, Houston

HOLY SEE

Apostolic Nunciature
3339 Massachusetts Avenue, NW., Washington, DC 20008
phone (202) 333–7121, fax 337–4036
His Excellency Pietro Sambi
Apostolic Nuncio

HONDURAS

Embassy of Honduras
3007 Tilden Street, NW., Suite 4–M, Washington, DC 20008
phone (202) 966–2604, fax 966–9751
His Excellency Roberto Flores Bermudez
Ambassador E. and P.
Consular Offices:
Arizona, Phoenix
California:
Los Angeles
San Diego
San Francisco
Florida:
Jacksonville
Miami
Georgia, Atlanta
Hawaii, Honolulu
Illinois, Chicago
Louisiana:
Baton Rouge
New Orleans
Maryland, Baltimore
Massachusetts, Boston
Minnesota, Minneapolis
Missouri, St. Louis
Nevada, Reno
New York, New York
Texas, Houston

HUNGARY

Embassy of the Republic of Hungary
3910 Shoemaker Street, NW., Washington, DC 20008
phone (202) 362–6730, fax 966–8135
His Excellency Dr. Ferenc Somogyi
Ambassador E. and P.
Consular Offices:
- California:
  - Los Angeles
  - San Francisco
- Colorado, Denver
- Florida, Miami
- Georgia, Morrow
- Hawaii, Honolulu
- Illinois, Chicago
- Louisiana, New Orleans
- Massachusetts, Boston
- Missouri, St. Louis
- New York, New York
- Ohio, Cleveland
- Puerto Rico, Mayaguez
- Texas, Houston
- Washington, Seattle

ICELAND

Embassy of Iceland
1156 15th Street, NW., Suite 1200, Washington, DC 20005
phone (202) 265–6653, fax 265–6656
His Excellency Hjalmar W. Hannesson
Ambassador E. and P.
Consular Offices:
- Alaska, Anchorage
- Arizona, Phoenix
- California:
  - Los Angeles
  - San Diego
  - San Francisco
- Colorado, Englewood
- Florida:
  - Orlando
  - Plantation
  - Tallahassee
- Georgia, Atlanta
- Illinois, Chicago
- Kentucky, Louisville
- Louisiana, New Orleans
- Massachusetts, Boston
- Michigan, Detroit
- Minnesota, Minneapolis
- Missouri, Grandview
- New York, New York
- North Dakota, Grand Fork
- Oregon, Portland
- Pennsylvania, Harrisburg
- Puerto Rico, San Juan
- South Carolina, Charleston
- Texas:
  - Dallas
  - Houston
- Utah, Salt Lake City
- Virginia, Norfolk
- Washington, Seattle
- Wisconsin, Madison

INDIA

Embassy of India
2107 Massachusetts Avenue, NW., Washington, DC 20008
phone (202) 939–7000, fax 483–3972
Her Excellency Meera Shankar
Ambassador E. and P.
Consular Offices:
- California, San Francisco
- Georgia, Atlanta
- Hawaii, Honolulu
- Illinois, Chicago
- Louisiana, New Orleans
- New York, New York
- Texas, Houston

INDONESIA

Embassy of the Republic of Indonesia
2020 Massachusetts Avenue, NW., Washington, DC 20036
phone (202) 775–5200, fax 775–5365
His Excellency Sudjadnan Parnohadiningrat
Ambassador E. and P.
Consular Offices:
- California:
  - Los Angeles
  - San Francisco
- Hawaii, Honolulu
- Illinois, Chicago
- New York, New York
- Texas, Houston

IRAN

See Pakistan

IRAQ

Embassy of the Republic of Iraq
3421 Massachusetts Avenue, NW., Washington, DC 20007
phone (202) 742–1600, fax 462–5066
His Excellency Samir Shakir Mahmood Sumaida'ie
Ambassador E. and P.

IRELAND

Embassy of Ireland
2234 Massachusetts Avenue, NW., Washington, DC 20008
phone (202) 462–3939, fax 232–5993
His Excellency Michael Collins

Ambassador E. and P.
Consular Offices:
California:
Los Angeles
San Francisco
Florida, Naples
Georgia, Atlanta
Illinois, Chicago
Massachusetts, Boston
Missouri, St. Louis
Nevada, Reno
New York, New York
Texas, Houston

ISRAEL

Embassy of Israel
3514 International Drive, NW., Washington, DC 20008
phone (202) 364–5500, fax 364–5607
His Excellency Michael Scott Oren
Ambassador E. and P.
Consular Offices:
California:
Los Angeles
San Francisco
Florida, Miami
Georgia, Atlanta
Illinois, Chicago
Massachusetts, Boston
New York, New York
Pennsylvania, Philadelphia
Texas, Houston

ITALY

Embassy of Italy
3000 Whitehaven Street, NW., Washington, DC 20008
phone (202) 612–4400, fax 518–2151
His Excellency Giovanni Castellaneta
Ambassador E. and P.
Consular Offices:
Alaska, Anchorage
Arizona, Phoenix
California:
Fresno
Los Angeles
Sacramento
San Francisco
San Jose
Colorado, Denver
Connecticut, Hartford
Florida:
Miami
Orlando
Sarasota
Georgia:
Atlanta
Savannah
Hawaii, Honolulu
Illinois, Chicago
Indiana, Indianapolis
Kansas, Kansas City
Louisiana, New Orleans
Maryland, Baltimore
Massachusetts:
Boston
Worcester
Michigan, Detroit
Minnesota, St. Paul
Missouri, St. Louis
New Jersey:
Newark
Trenton
New York:
Buffalo
Mineola
Mt. Vernon
New York
Rochester
Ohio, Cleveland
Oregon, Portland
Pennsylvania:
Philadelphia
Pittsburgh
Puerto Rico, San Juan
Rhode Island, Providence
South Carolina, Charleston
Texas:
Dallas
Houston
Utah, Salt Lake City
Virginia, Norfolk
Washington, Seattle

JAMAICA

Embassy of Jamaica
1520 New Hampshire Avenue, NW., Washington, DC 20036
phone (202) 452–0660, fax 452–0081
His Excellency Anthony Smith Johnson
Ambassador E. and P.
Consular Offices:
California:
Los Angeles
San Francisco
Florida, Miami
Georgia, Atlanta
Illinois, Chicago
Massachusetts, Boston
New Hampshire, Manchester
New York, New York
Pennsylvania, Philadelphia
Texas:
Dallas
Houston

Virginia, Richmond
Washington, Seattle

JAPAN

Embassy of Japan
2520 Massachusetts Avenue, NW., Washington, DC 20008
phone (202) 238–6700, fax 328–2187
His Excellency Ichiro Fujisaki
Ambassador E. and P.
Consular Offices:
Alabama, Birmingham
Alaska, Anchorage
Arizona, Tempe
California:
Los Angeles
San Diego
San Francisco
Colorado, Denver
Connecticut, Simsbury
Florida, Miami
Georgia, Atlanta
Guam, Agana
Hawaii:
Hilo
Honolulu
Illinois, Chicago
Indiana, Indianapolis
Kansas, Shawnee Mission
Kentucky, Lexington
Louisiana, New Orleans
Massachusetts, Boston
Michigan, Detroit
Minnesota, Minneapolis
Missouri, St. Louis
Nebraska, Omaha
Nevada, Las Vegas
New York:
Buffalo
New York
North Carolina, High Point
Oklahoma, Oklahoma City
Oregon, Portland
Pennsylvania, Philadelphia
Puerto Rico, San Juan
Tennessee, Nashville
Texas:
Dallas
Houston
Trust Territories of the Pacific Islands:
Mariana Islands
Pago Pago
Washington, Seattle
Wyoming, Casper

JORDAN

Embassy of the Hashemite Kingdom of Jordan
3504 International Drive, NW., Washington, DC 20008
phone (202) 966–2664, fax 966–3110
His Royal Highness Prince Zeid Raad Zeid Al Hussein
Ambassador E. and P.
Consular Offices:
California, San Francisco
Illinois, Chicago
Michigan, Detroit

KAZAKHSTAN

Embassy of the Republic of Kazakhstan
1401 16th Street, NW., Washington, DC 20036
phone (202) 232–5488, fax 232–5845
His Excellency Erlan A. Idrissov
Ambassador E. and P.
Consular Office: New York, New York

KENYA

Embassy of the Republic of Kenya
2249 R Street, NW., Washington, DC 20008
phone (202) 387–6101, fax 462–3829
His Excellency Peter N.R.O. Ogego
Ambassador E. and P.
Consular Offices:
California, Los Angeles
New York, New York

KIRIBATI

Consular Office: Hawaii, Honolulu

KOREA

Embassy of the Republic of Korea
2450 Massachusetts Avenue, NW., Washington, DC 20008
phone (202) 939–5600, fax 387–0250
His Excellency Duck Soo Han
Ambassador E. and P.
Consular Offices:
Alaska, Anchorage
California:
Los Angeles
San Francisco
Florida, Miami
Georgia, Atlanta
Guam, Agana
Hawaii, Honolulu
Illinois, Chicago
Louisiana, New Orleans
Massachusetts, Boston
Michigan, Detroit
Montana, Helena
New York, New York
Oklahoma, Oklahoma City
Oregon, Beaverton
Pennsylvania, Philadelphia
Puerto Rico, San Juan

South Carolina, Columbia
Texas:
Dallas
Houston
Washington, Seattle

KOSOVO REPUBLIC

Embassy of the Republic of Kosovo
900 19th Street, NW., Suite 400, Washington, DC 20006
phone (202) 380–3581, fax 380–3628
Mr. Avni Spahiu
Charge D'Affaires Ad Interim

KUWAIT

Embassy of the State of Kuwait
2940 Tilden Street, NW., Washington, DC 20008
phone (202) 966–0702, fax 966–0517
His Excellency Sheikh Salem Abdullah Al Jaber Al-Sabah
Ambassador E. and P.
Consular Office: California, Los Angeles

KYRGYZSTAN

Embassy of the Kyrgyz Republic
1001 Pennsylvania Avenue, NW., Suite 600, Washington, DC 20004
phone (202) 338–5141, fax 338–5139
Her Excellency Zamira Beksultanovna Sydykova
Ambassador E. and P.
Consular Offices:
California:
Buellton
Los Angeles
Montana, Helena
New Jersey, South Plainfield
New York, New York
Texas, Houston
Utah, Orem

LAOS

Embassy of the Lao People's Democratic Republic
2222 S Street, NW., Washington, DC 20008
phone (202) 332–6416, fax 332–4923
His Excellency Phiane Philakone
Ambassador E. and P.

LATVIA

Embassy of Latvia
2306 Massachusetts Avenue, NW., Washington, DC 20008
phone (202) 328–2840, fax 328–2860
Mr. Maris Selga
Charge d'Affaires
Consular Offices:
California:
Costa Mesa
Los Angeles
Connecticut, Greenwich
Florida, Ft. Lauderdale
New York:
Buffalo
New York
Ohio, Cincinnati
Texas, Houston

LEBANON

Embassy of Lebanon
2560 28th Street, NW., Washington, DC 20008
phone (202) 939–6300, fax 939–6324
His Excellency Antoine Chedid
Ambassador E. and P.
Consular Offices:
California:
Los Angeles
San Diego
Florida, Miami
Massachusetts, Boston
Michigan, Detroit
New York, New York
North Carolina, Raleigh
Texas, Houston

LESOTHO

Embassy of the Kingdom of Lesotho
2511 Massachusetts Avenue, NW., Washington, DC 20008
phone (202) 797–5533, fax 234–6815
His Excellency David Mohlomi Rantekoa
Ambassador E. and P.
Consular Offices:
Louisiana, New Orleans
Texas, Austin

LIBERIA

Embassy of the Republic of Liberia
5201 16th Street, NW., Washington, DC 20011
phone (202) 723–0437, fax 723–0436
His Excellency Milton Nathaniel Barnes
Ambassador E. and P.
Consular Offices:
California:
Los Angeles
San Francisco
Florida, Tampa
Georgia, Atlanta
Illinois, Chicago
Louisiana, New Orleans
Michigan, Detroit
New York, New York
Pennsylvania, Philadelphia

LIBYA

Embassy of the Libyan Arab Jamahiriya
2600 Virginia Avenue, NW., Suite 705, Washington, DC 20037

phone (202) 944–9601, fax 944–9606
His Excellency Ali Suleiman Aujali
Ambassador E. and P.

LIECHTENSTEIN

Embassy of the Principality of Liechtenstein
888 17th Street, NW., Suite 1250, Washington, DC 20006
phone (202) 331–0590, fax 331–3221
Her Excellency Claudia Fritsche
Ambassador E. and P.
Consular Offices:
- California, Los Angeles
- Georgia, Macon

LITHUANIA

Embassy of the Republic of Lithuania
2622 16th Street, NW., Washington, DC 20009
phone (202) 234–5860, fax 328–0466
His Excellency Audrius Bruzga
Ambassador E. and P.
Consular Offices:
- Arizona, Phoenix
- California:
  - Lafayette
  - Los Angeles
- Florida:
  - Palm Beach
  - St. Petersburg
- Georgia, Marietta
- Illinois, Chicago
- Michigan:
  - Detroit
  - Lansing
- Minnesota, Stillwater
- New Hampshire, Manchester
- New Jersey, Mendham
- New York:
  - New York
  - Webster
- Ohio, Cleveland
- Oregon, Portland
- Texas, Houston
- Washington, Seattle

LUXEMBOURG

Embassy of Grand Duchy of Luxembourg
2200 Massachusetts Avenue, NW., Washington, DC 20008
phone (202) 265–4171, fax 328–8270
His Excellency Jean Paul Ernest Senninger
Ambassador E. and P.
Consular Offices:
- California:
  - San Francisco
  - Woodland Hills
- Georgia, Atlanta
- Illinois, Chicago
- Indiana, Indianapolis
- Louisiana, New Orleans
- Massachusetts, Boston
- Michigan, Detroit
- Minnesota, Edina
- Missouri, Kansas City
- New York, New York
- Ohio, Cleveland
- Oregon, Portland
- Texas, Ft. Worth
- Washington, Seattle

MACEDONIA

Embassy of the Republic of Macedonia
1101 30th Street, NW., Suite 302, Washington, DC 20007
phone (202) 667–0501, fax 667–2131
His Excellency Zoran Jolevski
Ambassador E. and P.
Consular Offices:
- Michigan, Southfield
- Florida, Naples
- New Jersey, Clifton

MADAGASCAR

Embassy of the Republic of Madagascar
2374 Massachusetts Avenue, NW., Washington, DC 20008
phone (202) 265–5525, fax 265–3034
His Excellency Jocelyn Bertin Radifera
Ambassador E. and P.
Consular Offices:
- California, San Diego
- New York, New York
- Pennsylvania, Philadelphia

MALAWI

Embassy of Malawi
1156 15th Street, NW., Suite 320, Washington, DC 20005
phone (202) 721–0270, fax 721–0288
His Excellency Hawa Olga Ndilowe
Ambassador E. and P.

MALAYSIA

Embassy of Malaysia
3516 International Court, NW., Washington, DC 20008
phone (202) 572–9700, fax 572–9882
Mr. Ilango Karuppannan
Minister / Counselor (Charge D'Affaires, A.I.)
Consular Offices:
- California, Los Angeles
- Hawaii, Honolulu
- New York, New York
- Oregon, Portland
- Texas, Houston

MALDIVES

Embassy of the Republic of Maldives
800 2nd Avenue, Suite 400E, New York, NY 10017
phone (212) 599–6195, fax 661–6405
His Excellency Ahmed Khaleel
Charge D'Affaires Ad Interim

MALI

Embassy of the Republic of Mali
2130 R Street, NW., Washington, DC 20008
phone (202) 332–2249, fax 332–6603
His Excellency Abdoulaye Diop
Ambassador E. and P.
Consular Offices:
- Florida, Ft. Lauderdale
- Georgia, Atlanta
- Louisiana, New Orleans
- Massachusetts, Boston
- New Mexico, Albuquerque

MALTA

Embassy of Malta
2017 Connecticut Avenue, NW., Washington, DC 20008
phone (202) 462–3611, fax 387–5470
His Excellency Mark Anthony Miceli Farrugia
Ambassador E. and P.
Consular Offices:
- California:
  - Los Angeles
  - San Francisco
- Florida, Ft. Lauderdale
- Louisiana, Metairie
- Massachusetts, Bellmont
- Michigan, Detroit
- Minnesota, St. Paul
- New York, New York
- Pennsylvania, Philadelphia
- Tennessee, Kingsport
- Texas:
  - Austin
  - Dallas
  - Houston
- Washington, Seattle

MARSHALL ISLANDS

Embassy of the Republic of the Marshall Islands
2433 Massachusetts Avenue, NW., 1st Floor, Washington, DC 20008
phone (202) 234–5414, fax 232–3236
His Excellency Banny de Brum
Ambassador E. and P.
Consular Offices:
- Guam, Agana
- Hawaii, Honolulu

MAURITANIA

Embassy of the Islamic Republic of Mauritania
2129 Leroy Place, NW., Washington, DC 20008
phone (202) 232–5700, fax 319–2623
His Excellency Ibrahima Dia
Ambassador E. and P.

MAURITIUS

Embassy of the Republic of Mauritius
4301 Connecticut Avenue, NW., Suite 441, Washington, DC 20008
phone (202) 244–1491, fax 966–0983
His Excellency Keerteecoomar Ruhee
Ambassador E. and P.
Consular Offices:
- Arizona, Sun City
- California:
  - Los Angeles
  - San Francisco

MEXICO

Embassy of Mexico
1911 Pennsylvania Avenue, NW., Washington, DC 20006
phone (202) 728–1600, fax 728–1698
His Excellency Arturo Sarukhan Casamitjana
Ambassador E. and P.
Consular Offices:
- Alaska, Anchorage
- Arizona:
  - Douglas
  - Nogales
  - Phoenix
  - Tucson
  - Yuma
- Arkansas, Little Rock
- California:
  - Calexico
  - Fresno
  - Los Angeles
  - Oxnard
  - Sacramento
  - Salinas
  - San Bernardino
  - San Diego
  - San Francisco
  - San Jose
  - Santa Ana
- Colorado, Denver
- Florida:
  - Jacksonville
  - Miami
  - Orlando
- Georgia, Atlanta
- Hawaii, Honolulu
- Illinois, Chicago
- Indiana, Indianapolis
- Massachusetts, Boston
- Michigan, Detroit
- Minnesota, St. Paul

Missouri, Kansas City
Nebraska, Omaha
Nevada, Las Vegas
New Mexico, Albuquerque
New York, New York
North Carolina:
Charlotte
Raleigh
Oregon, Portland
Pennsylvania, Philadelphia
Puerto Rico, San Juan
Texas:
Austin
Brownsville
Corpus Christi
Dallas
Del Rio
Eagle Pass
El Paso
Houston
Laredo
McAllen
Midland
San Antonio
Utah, Salt Lake City
Virginia, Richmond
Washington, Seattle
Wisconsin, Madison

MICRONESIA

Embassy of the Federated States of Micronesia
1725 N Street, NW., Washington, DC 20036
phone (202) 223–4383, fax 223–4391
His Excellency Yosiwo P. George
Ambassador E. and P.
Consular Offices:
Guam, Tamuning
Hawaii, Honolulu

MOLDOVA

Embassy of the Republic of Moldova
2101 S Street, NW., Washington, DC 20008
phone (202) 667–1130, fax 667–1204
His Excellency Nicolae Chirtoaca
Ambassador E. and P.
Consular Offices:
New York, New York
North Carolina, Hickory
Pennsylvania, Philadelphia
Virginia, Norfolk

MONACO

Embassy of Monoco
3400 International Drive, NW., Suite 2K–100, Washington, DC 20008
phone (202) 234–1530, fax 244–7656
His Excellency Gilles Alexandre Noghes
Ambassador E. and P.
Consular Offices:
California:
Los Angeles
San Francisco
Florida, Miami
Illinois, Chicago
Massachusetts, Boston
New York, New York
Texas, Dallas

MONGOLIA

Embassy of Mongolia
2833 M Street, NW., Washington, DC 20007
phone (202) 333–7117, fax 298–9227
His Excellency Bekhbat Khasbazar
Ambassador E. and P.
Consular Offices:
California:
Canoga Park
San Francisco
Colorado, Denver
Georgia, Atlanta
Illinois, Chicago
New Jersey, Plainfield
New York, New York
Texas, Houston
Utah, Springfield

MONTENEGRO

Embassy of the Republic of Montenegro
1610 New Hampshire Avenue, NW., Washington, DC 20009
phone (202) 234–6108, fax 234–6109
His Excellency Miodrag Vlahovic
Ambassador E. and P.
Consular Office: New York, New York

MOROCCO

Embassy of the Kingdom of Morocco
1601 21st Street, NW., Washington, DC 20009
phone (202) 462–7980, fax 265–0161
His Excellency Aziz Mekouar
Ambassador E. and P.
Consular Offices:
California, Los Angeles
Hawaii, Honolulu
Kansas, Kansas City
Massachusetts, Cambridge
New York, New York

MOZAMBIQUE

Embassy of the Republic of Mozambique
1990 M Street, NW., Suite 570, Washington, DC 20036
phone (202) 293–7146, fax 835–0245
His Excellency Armando Alexandre Panguene
Ambassador E. and P.

NAMIBIA

Embassy of the Republic of Namibia
1605 New Hampshire Avenue, NW., Washington, DC 20009
phone (202) 986–0540, fax 986–0443
His Excellency Patrick Nandago
Ambassador E. and P.
Consular Offices:
- Michigan, Detroit
- Florida, Orlando
- Texas, Houston

NAURU

Embassy of the Republic of Nauru
800 Second Avenue, New York, NY 10017
phone (212) 937–0074, fax 937–0079
Her Excellency Marlene Inemwin Moses
Ambassador E. and P.
Consular Offices:
- Guam, Agana
- Hawaii, Honolulu
- Trust Territories of the Pacific Islands:
  - Pago Pago

NEPAL

Embassy of Nepal
2131 Leroy Place, NW., Washington, DC 20008
phone (202) 667–4550, fax 667–5534
Mr. Kali Prasad Pokhrel
Minister / Counselor (Charge D'Affaires, A.I.)
Consular Offices:
- California:
  - Los Angeles
  - San Francisco
- Illinois, Chicago
- Massachusetts, Boston
- New York, New York
- Ohio, Cleveland

NETHERLANDS

Royal Netherlands Embassy
4200 Linnean Avenue, NW., Washington, DC 20008
phone (202) 244–5300, fax 362–3430
His Excellency Regina Veronica Maria Bos Jones
Ambassador E. and P.
Consular Offices:
- Arizona, Phoenix
- California:
  - Los Angeles
  - San Francisco
- Colorado, Denver
- Florida:
  - Jacksonville
  - Miami
- Georgia, Atlanta
- Hawaii, Honolulu
- Illinois, Chicago
- Louisiana, New Orleans
- Massachusetts, Boston
- Michigan:
  - Detroit
  - Grand Rapids
- Minnesota, Minneapolis
- Missouri:
  - Kansas City
  - St. Louis
- New York, New York
- North Carolina, Raleigh
- Ohio, Cleveland
- Oregon, Portland
- Pennsylvania, Philadelphia
- Puerto Rico, Rio Piedras
- Texas, Houston
- Trust Territories of the Pacific Islands:
  - Manila, Phillipines
- Utah, Salt Lake City
- Washington, Bellevue

NEW ZEALAND

Embassy of New Zealand
37 Observatory Circle, NW., Washington, DC 20008
phone (202) 328–4800, fax 667–5227
His Excellency Roy Neil Ferguson
Ambassador E. and P.
Consular Offices:
- California:
  - Sacramento
  - San Diego
  - San Francisco
  - Santa Monica
- Georgia, Atlanta
- Guam, Tamuning
- Hawaii, Honolulu
- Illinois, Chicago
- New Hampshire, Boston
- New York, New York
- Texas, Houston
- Trust Territories of the Pacific Islands:
  - Pago Pago
- Utah, Salt Lake City
- Washington, Seattle

NICARAGUA

Embassy of the Republic of Nicaragua
1627 New Hampshire Avenue, NW., Washington, DC 20009
phone (202) 939–6570, fax 939–6545
Mr. Alcides J. Montiel Barillas
Minister / Counselor (Charge D'Affaires, A.I.)
Consular Offices:
- California:
  - Los Angeles
  - San Francisco
- Colorado, Denver

Florida, Miami
Georgia, Atlanta
Louisiana, Metairie
Massachusetts, Springfield
Missouri, St. Louis
New York, New York
North Carolina, Charlotte
Oklahoma, Tulsa
Pennsylvania:
  Philadelphia
  Pittsburgh
Puerto Rico, San Juan
Texas, Houston

NIGER

Embassy of the Republic of Niger
2204 R Street, NW., Washington, DC 20008
phone (202) 483–4224, fax 483–3169
Her Excellency Aminata Maiga Djibrilla
Ambassador E. and P.

NIGERIA

Embassy of the Federal Republic of Nigeria
3519 International Court, NW., Washington, DC 20008
phone (202) 986–8400, fax 362–6541
Mr. Baba Gana Wakil
Minister (Charge D'Affaires, A.I.)
Consular Offices:
  Georgia, Atlanta
  New York, New York

NORWAY

Royal Norwegian Embassy
2720 34th Street, NW., Washington, DC 20008
phone (202) 333–6000, fax 337–0870
His Excellency Wegger Christian Strommen
Ambassador E. and P.
Consular Offices:
  Alabama, Mobile
  Alaska, Anchorage
  Arizona, Glendale
  California:
    Los Angeles
    San Diego
    San Francisco
  Colorado, Denver
  Florida:
    Jacksonville
    Miami
    Pensacola
    Tampa
  Georgia, Atlanta
  Hawaii, Honolulu
  Illinois, Chicago
  Iowa, Des Moines
  Louisiana, New Orleans
  Massachusetts, Boston
  Michigan, Detroit
  Minnesota, Minneapolis
  Montana, Billings
  Nebraska, Omaha
  New York, New York
  North Dakota, Fargo
  Oklahoma, Tulsa
  Oregon, Portland
  Pennsylvania, Philadelphia
  Puerto Rico:
    Ponce
    San Juan
  South Carolina, Charleston
  South Dakota, Sioux Falls
  Texas:
    Dallas
    Houston
  Utah, Salt Lake City
  Virginia, Norfolk
  Washington, Seattle
  Wisconsin, Madison

OMAN

Embassy of the Sultanate of Oman
2535 Belmont Road, NW., Washington, DC 20008
phone (202) 387–1980, fax 745–4933
Her Excellency Hunaina Sultan Ahmed al-Mughairy
Ambassador E. and P.
Consular Office: California, Los Angeles

PAKISTAN

Embassy of Pakistan
3517 International Court, NW., Washington, DC 20008
phone (202) 243–6500, fax 686–1544
His Excellency Husain Haqqani
Ambassador E. and P.
Consular Offices:
  California:
    Los Angeles
    Sunnyvale
  Illinois, Chicago
  Maine, Portland
  Massachusetts, Boston
  New York, New York
  Texas, Houston

PALAU

Embassy of the Republic of Palau
1700 Pennsylvania Avenue, NW., Suite 400, Washington, DC 20006
phone (202) 452–6814, fax 452–6281
His Excellency Hersey Kyota
Ambassador E. and P.
Consular Offices:
  California, LaCanada Flintridge
  Guam, Tamuning
  Hawaii, Honolulu

PANAMA

Embassy of the Republic of Panama
2862 McGill Terrace, NW., Washington, DC 20008
phone (202) 483–1407, fax 483–8416
His Excellency Federico A. Humbert Arias
Ambassador E. and P.
Consular Offices:
  California:
    San Diego
    San Francisco
  Florida:
    Miami
    Tampa
  Georgia, Atlanta
  Hawaii, Honolulu
  Louisiana, New Orleans
  New York, New York
  Pennsylvania, Philadelphia
  Puerto Rico, San Juan
  Texas, Houston

PAPUA NEW GUINEA

Embassy of Papua New Guinea
1779 Massachusetts Avenue, NW., Suite 805, Washington, DC 20036
phone (202) 745–3680, fax 745–3679
His Excellency Evan Jeremy Paki
Ambassador E. and P.
Consular Offices:
  California, Los Angeles
  Texas, Houston

PARAGUAY

Embassy of Paraguay
2400 Massachusetts Avenue, NW., Washington, DC 20008
phone (202) 483–6960, fax 234–4508
His Excellency James Spalding Hellmers
Ambassador E. and P.
Consular Offices:
  California, Los Angeles
  Florida, Miami
  Kansas, Kansas City
  Michigan, Detroit
  New York, New York
  Puerto Rico, San Juan
  Texas:
    Bellaire
    Fort Worth

PERU

Embassy of Peru
1700 Massachusetts Avenue, NW., Washington, DC 20036
phone (202) 833–9860, fax 659–8124
His Excellency Luis Miguel Valdivieso Montano
Ambassador E. and P.
Consular Offices:
  Arizona, Mesa
  California:
    Los Angeles
    Sacramento
    San Francisco
  Colorado, Denver
  Connecticut, Hartford
  Florida:
    Miami
    Tampa
  Georgia, Atlanta
  Hawaii, Honolulu
  Illinois, Chicago
  Louisiana, New Orleans
  Massachusetts, Boston
  Missouri, St. Louis
  New Jersey, Paterson
  New York, New York
  Oklahoma, Tulsa
  Texas:
    Dallas
    Houston
  Washington, Seattle

PHILIPPINES

Embassy of the Republic of the Philippines
1600 Massachusetts Avenue, NW., Washington, DC 20036
phone (202) 467–9300, fax 467–9417
His Excellency Willy C. Gaa
Ambassador E. and P.
Consular Offices:
  California:
    Los Angeles
    San Francisco
  Florida, North Miami
  Georgia, Atlanta
  Guam, Tamuning
  Hawaii, Honolulu
  Illinois, Chicago
  Louisiana, New Orleans
  New York, New York
  Trust Territories of the Pacific Islands:
    Mariana Islands

POLAND

Embassy of the Republic of Poland
2640 16th Street, NW., Washington, DC 20009
phone (202) 234–3800, fax 328–6271
His Excellency Robert Ryszard Kupiecki
Ambassador E. and P.
Consular Offices:
  Alaska, Anchorage
  California, Los Angeles
  Colorado, Longmont
  Florida, Miami
  Hawaii, Honolulu

Illinois, Chicago
Massachusetts, Boston
Missouri, St. Louis
New York, New York
Ohio, Oxford
Oregon, Portland
Pennsylvania, Pittsburgh
Puerto Rico, San Juan
Texas, Houston

PORTUGAL

Embassy of Portugal
2012 Massachusetts Avenue, NW., Washington, DC 20036
phone (202) 328–8610, fax 462–3726
His Excellency João de Vallera
Ambassador E. and P.
Consular Offices:
California:
Los Angeles
San Francisco
Tulare
Connecticut, Waterbury
Florida, Miami
Hawaii, Honolulu
Illinois, Chicago
Louisiana, New Orleans
Massachusetts:
Boston
New Bedford
New Jersey, Newark
New York, New York
Puerto Rico, San Juan
Rhode Island, Providence
Texas, Houston

QATAR

Embassy of the State of Qatar
2555 M Street, NW., Suite 200, Washington, DC 20037
phone (202) 274–1600, fax 237–0061
His Excellency Ali Bin Fahad Faleh Al-Hajri
Ambassador E. and P.
Consular Office: Texas, Houston

ROMANIA

Embassy of Romania
1607 23rd Street, NW., Washington, DC 20008
phone (202) 332–4846, fax 232–4748
His Excellency Adrian Cosmin Vierita
Ambassador E. and P.
Consular Offices:
California:
Los Angeles
San Francisco
Florida, Hollywood
Illinois, Chicago
Indiana, Indianapolis
Louisiana, New Orleans
Massachusetts, Boston
Michigan, Detroit
Minnesota, Minneapolis
Nevada, Las Vegas
New York, New York
Ohio, Cleveland
Oklahoma, Norman
Oregon, Portland
Pennsylvania, Philadelphia
Texas:
Dallas
Houston
Utah, Salt Lake City
Virginia, Norfolk

RUSSIA

Embassy of the Russian Federation
2650 Wisconsin Avenue, NW., Washington, DC 20007
phone (202) 298–5700, fax 298–5735
His Excellency Sergey Ivanovich Kislyak
Ambassador E. and P.
Consular Offices:
Alaska, Anchorage
California, San Francisco
Colorado, Denver
Florida, Pinellas Park
Hawaii, Honolulu
Minnesota, Minneapolis
New York, New York
Puerto Rico, San Juan
Texas, Houston
Utah, Salt Lake City
Washington, Seattle

RWANDA

Embassy of the Republic of Rwanda
1714 New Hampshire Avenue, NW., Washington, DC 20009
phone (202) 232–2882, fax 232–4544
His Excellency James Kimonyo
Ambassador E. and P.
Consular Offices:
California, San Francisco
Illinois, Geneva

SAMOA

Embassy of the Independent State of Samoa
800 2nd Avenue, 4th Floor, New York, NY 10017
phone (212) 599–6196, fax 599–0797
His Excellency Ali'ioaiga Feturi Elisaia
Ambassador E. and P.
Consular Offices:
American Samoa, Pago Pago
California, Torrance

SAN MARINO

Embassy of Republic of San Marino
2650 Virginia Avenue, NW., Washington, DC 20037
phone (202) 250–1535
His Excellency Paolo Rondelli
Ambassador E. and P.
Consular Offices:
- Hawaii, Honolulu
- Michigan, Detroit
- New York, New York

SAO TOME AND PRINCIPE

Embassy of Sao Tome and Principe
1211 Connecticut Avenue, NW., Suite 300, Washington, DC 20036
phone (202) 775–2075, fax 775–2077
His Excellency Ovidio Pequeno
Ambassador E. and P.
Consular Offices:
- Georgia, Atlanta
- Illinois, Chicago

SAUDI ARABIA

Royal Embassy of Saudi Arabia
601 New Hampshire Avenue, NW., Washington, DC 20037
phone (202) 342–3800, fax 944–3113
His Excellency Adel bin Ahmed Al-Jubeir
Ambassador E. and P.
Consular Offices:
- California, Los Angeles
- New York, New York
- Texas, Houston

SENEGAL

Embassy of the Republic of Senegal
2112 Wyoming Avenue, NW., Washington, DC 20008
phone (202) 234–0540, fax 332–6315
His Excellency Dr. Amadou Lamine Ba
Ambassador E. and P.
Consular Offices:
- Florida, Miami
- Georgia, Atlanta
- Louisiana, New Orleans
- Massachusetts, Boston
- New York, New York
- Texas, Houston

SERBIA

Embassy of the Republic of Serbia
2134 Kalorama Road, NW., Washington, DC 20008
phone (202) 332–0333, fax 332–3933
His Excellency Vladimir Petrovic
Ambassador E. and P.
Consular Offices:
- Colorado, Denver
- Illinois, Chicago
- Louisiana, Metairie
- New York, New York
- Ohio, Cleveland
- Wyoming, Cheyenne

SEYCHELLES

Embassy of the Republic of Seychelles
800 2nd Avenue, Suite 400C, New York, NY 10017
phone (212) 972–1785, fax 972–1786
His Excellency Ronald Jean Jumeau
Ambassador E. and P.
Consular Offices:
- Alaska, Anchorage
- Washington, Seattle

SIERRA LEONE

Embassy of Sierra Leone
1701 19th Street, NW., Washington, DC 20009
phone (202) 939–9261, fax 483–1793
His Excellency Bockari Kortu Stevens
Ambassador E. and P.

SINGAPORE

Embassy of the Republic of Singapore
3501 International Place, NW., Washington, DC 20008
phone (202) 537–3100, fax 537–0876
Her Excellency Heng Chee Chan
Ambassador E. and P.
Consular Offices:
- California, San Francisco
- Florida, Miami
- Illinois, Chicago
- New York, New York
- Texas, Houston

SLOVAK REPUBLIC

Embassy of the Slovak Republic
3523 International Court, NW., Washington, DC 20008
phone (202) 237–1054, fax 237–6438
His Excellency Peter Burian
Ambassador E. and P.
Consular Offices:
- California:
  - Los Angeles
  - San Francisco
- Colorado, Denver
- Florida, Ft. Lauderdale
- Illinois, Chicago
- Indiana, Indianapolis
- Massachusetts, Weston
- Michigan, Detroit
- Minnesota, Minneapolis
- Missouri, Kansas City
- Nevada, Las Vegas

New York, New York
Ohio, Cleveland
Pennsylvania, Pittsburgh
Washington, Bainbridge Island

SLOVENIA

Embassy of the Republic of Slovenia
1525 New Hampshire Avenue, NW., Washington, DC 20036
phone (202) 332–9332, fax 667–4563
His Excellency Roman Kirn
Ambassador E. and P.
Consular Offices:
California, San Francisco
Colorado, Denver
Florida, Palm Beach
Georgia, Atlanta
Hawaii, Honolulu
Kansas, Mission Hills
New York, New York
Ohio, Cleveland
Tennessee, Knoxville
Texas, Houston

SOLOMON ISLANDS

Embassy of the Solomon Islands
800 2nd Avenue, Suite 400L, New York, NY 10017
phone (212) 599–6192, fax 661–8925
His Excellency Collin D. Beck
Ambassador E. and P.

SOUTH AFRICA

Embassy of the Republic of South Africa
3051 Massachusetts Avenue, NW., Washington, DC 20008
phone (202) 232–4400, fax 265–1607
His Excellency Welile Augustine Witness Nhlapo
Ambassador E. and P.
Consular Offices:
Alabama, Mobile
California, Los Angeles
Illinois, Chicago
New York, New York
Utah, Salt Lake City

SPAIN

Embassy of Spain
2375 Pennsylvania Avenue, NW., Washington, DC 20037
phone (202) 452–0100, fax 833–5670
His Excellency Jorge Dezcallar De Mazarredo
Ambassador E. and P.
Consular Offices:
Alaska, Anchorage
Arizona, Phoenix
California:
Los Angeles
San Diego
San Francisco
Colorado, Englewood
Florida:
Miami
Orlando
Pensacola
Saint Augustine
Tampa
Georgia, Atlanta
Hawaii, Honolulu
Idaho, Boise
Illinois, Chicago
Louisiana, New Orleans
Massachusetts, Boston
Michigan, Ann Arbor
Minnesota, St. Paul
Missouri:
Kansas City
St. Louis
New Jersey, Newark
New Mexico:
Albuquerque
Santa Fe
New York, New York
North Carolina, Durham
Ohio:
Cleveland
Cincinnati
Pennsylvania, Philadelphia
Puerto Rico, San Juan
Texas:
Corpus Christi
Dallas
El Paso
Houston
San Antonio
Utah, Salt Lake City
Washington, Seattle

SRI LANKA

Embassy of the Democratic Socialist Republic of Sri Lanka
2148 Wyoming Avenue, NW., Washington, DC 20008
phone (202) 483–4025, fax 232–7181
His Excellency Jaliya Chitran Wickramasuriya
Ambassador E. and P.
Consular Offices:
Arizona, Phoenix
California, Los Angeles
Georgia, Atlanta
Hawaii, Honolulu
Illinois, Chicago
Louisiana, New Orleans
Massachusetts, Boston
New Jersey, Newark
New Mexico, Santa Fe
New York, New York

ST. KITTS AND NEVIS

Embassy of St. Kitts and Nevis
3216 New Mexico Avenue, NW., Washington, DC 20016
phone (202) 686–2636, fax 686–5740
His Excellency Dr. Izben Cordinal Williams
Ambassador E. and P.
Consular Offices:
- California, Los Angeles
- Florida, Miami
- Georgia, Atlanta
- New York, New York
- Texas, Dallas
- Virgin Islands, St. Thomas

ST. LUCIA

Embassy of St. Lucia
3216 New Mexico Avenue, NW., Washington, DC 20016
phone (202) 364–6792, fax 364–6723
His Excellency Dr. Michael Louis
Ambassador E. and P.
Consular Offices:
- California, Los Angeles
- Florida, Miami
- New York, New York
- Virgin Islands, St. Croix

ST. VINCENT AND THE GRENADINES

Embassy of St. Vincent and the Grenadines
3216 New Mexico Avenue, NW., Washington, DC 20016
phone (202) 364–6730, fax 364–6736
Her Excellency La Celia A. Prince
Ambassador E. and P.
Consular Offices:
- California, Los Angeles
- Louisiana, New Orleans
- New York, New York

SUDAN

Embassy of the Republic of the Sudan
2210 Massachusetts Avenue, NW., Washington, DC 20008
phone (202) 338–8565, fax 667–2406
ambassador Akec Khoc Aciew Khoc
Charge D'Affaires Ad Interim

SURINAME

Embassy of the Republic of Suriname
4301 Connecticut Avenue, NW., Suite 460, Washington, DC 20008
phone (202) 244–7488, fax 244–5878
His Excellency Jacques Ruben Constantijn Kross
Ambassador E. and P.
Consular Offices:
- Florida, Miami
- Louisiana, New Orleans

SWAZILAND

Embassy of the Kingdom of Swaziland
1712 New Hampshire Avenue, NW., Washington, DC 20009
phone (202) 234–5002, fax 234–8254
His Excellency Ephraim Mandlenkosi M. Hlophe
Ambassador E. and P.

SWEDEN

Embassy of Sweden
2900 K Street, NW., Washington, DC 20007
phone (202) 467–2600, fax 467–2699
His Excellency Sven Jonas Hafstroem
Ambassador E. and P.
Consular Offices:
- Alaska, Anchorage
- Arizona, Phoenix
- California:
  - Los Angeles
  - San Diego
  - San Francisco
- Colorado, Denver
- Florida:
  - Ft. Lauderdale
  - Tampa
- Georgia, Atlanta
- Hawaii, Honolulu
- Illinois, Chicago
- Kansas, Merriam
- Louisiana, New Orleans
- Massachusetts, Boston
- Michigan, Ann Arbor
- Minnesota, Minneapolis
- Missouri, St. Louis
- Nebraska, Omaha
- Nevada, Las Vegas
- New York:
  - Jamestown
  - New York
- North Carolina, Raleigh
- Ohio, Cleveland
- Oregon, Portland
- Pennsylvania, Philadelphia
- Puerto Rico, San Juan
- Texas:
  - Dallas
  - Houston
- Utah, Salt Lake City
- Virgin Islands, St. Thomas
- Virginia, Norfolk
- Washington, Seattle
- Wisconsin, Milwaukee

SWITZERLAND

Embassy of Switzerland

2900 Cathedral Avenue, NW., Washington, DC 20008
phone (202) 745–7900, fax 387–2564
His Excellency Urs Johann Ziswiler
Ambassador E. and P.
Consular Offices:
- Arizona, Paradise Valley
- California:
  - Los Angeles
  - San Francisco
- Colorado, Boulder
- Florida:
  - Miami
  - Orlando
- Georgia, Atlanta
- Hawaii, Honolulu
- Illinois, Chicago
- Indiana, Indianapolis
- Louisiana, New Orleans
- Massachusetts, Boston
- Michigan, Detroit
- Minnesota, Minneapollis
- Missouri, Kansas City
- New York:
  - New York
  - Williamsville
- North Carolina, Charlotte
- Ohio, Cleveland
- Pennsylvnaia:
  - Philadelphia
  - Pittsburgh
- Puerto Rico, San Juan
- South Carolina, Spartanburg
- Texas:
  - Dallas
  - Houston
- Trust Territories of the Pacific Islands:
  - Pago Pago
- Utah, Salt Lake City
- Washington, Mercer Island

SYRIA

Embassy of the Syrian Arab Republic
2215 Wyoming Avenue, NW., Washington, DC 20008
phone (202) 232–6313, fax 234–9548
His Excellency Dr. Imad Moustapha
Ambassador E. and P.
Consular Offices:
- California, Los Angeles
- Michigan, Detroit
- Texas, Houston

TAJIKISTAN

Embassy of the Republic of Tajikistan
1005 New Hampshire Avenue, NW., Washington, DC 20037
phone (202) 223–6090, fax 223–6091
His Excellency Abdujabbor Shirinov
Ambassador E. and P.

TANZANIA

Embassy of the United Republic of Tanzania
2139 R Street, NW., Washington, DC 20008
phone (202) 939–6125, fax 797–7408
His Excellency Ombeni Yohana Sefue
Ambassador E. and P.
Consular Offices:
- Florida, Boca Raton
- Georgia, Atlanta
- Illinois, St. Louis

THAILAND

Embassy of Thailand
1024 Wisconsin Avenue, NW., Washington, DC 20007
phone (202) 944–3600, fax 944–3611
His Excellency Don Pramudwinai
Ambassador E. and P.
Consular Offices:
- Alabama, Montgomery
- California, Los Angeles
- Colorado, Denver
- Florida, Coral Gables
- Georgia, Atlanta
- Hawaii, Honolulu
- Illinois, Chicago
- Kansas, Kansas City
- Louisiana, New Orleans
- Massachusetts, Boston
- New York, New York
- Oklahoma, Broken Arrow
- Oregon, Portland
- Puerto Rico, Hato Rey
- Texas:
  - Dallas
  - El Paso
  - Houston

TIMOR LESTE

Embassy of the Democratic Republic of Timor Leste
4201 Connecticut Avenue, NW., Suite 504, Washington, DC 20008
phone (202) 966–3202, fax 966–3205
Mr. Jorge Trindade Neves De Camoes
Counselor (Charge D'Affaires, A.I.)

TOGO

Embassy of the Republic of Togo
2208 Massachusetts Avenue, NW., Washington, DC 20008
phone (202) 234–4212, fax 232–3190
His Excellency Edawe Limbiye Kadangha Bariki
Ambassador E. and P.
Consular Offices: Florida, Miami

TONGA

Embassy of the Kingdom of Tonga
250 East 51st Street, New York, NY 10022
phone (917) 369–1025, fax 369–1024
Her Excellency Fekitamoeloa Tupoupai Utoikamanu
Ambassador E. and P.
Consular Offices:
  California, San Francisco
  Hawaii, Honolulu

TRINIDAD AND TOBAGO

Embassy of the Republic of Trinidad and Tobago
1708 Massachusetts Avenue, NW., Washington, DC 20036
phone (202) 467–6490, fax 785–3130
Her Excellency Glenda Patricia Morean Phillip
Ambassador E. and P.
Consular Offices:
  Florida, Miami
  New York, New York
  Puerto Rico, San Juan
  Texas, Houston

TUNISIA

Embassy of Tunisia
1515 Massachusetts Avenue, NW., Washington, DC 20005
phone (202) 862–1850, fax 862–1858
His Excellency Habib Mansour
Ambassador E. and P.
Consular Offices:
  California, San Francisco
  Florida, Miami
  New York, New York
  Texas:
    Dallas
    Houston

TURKEY

Embassy of the Republic of Turkey
2525 Massachusetts Avenue, NW., Washington, DC 20008
phone (202) 612–6700, fax 612–6744
His Excellency Nabi Şensoy
Ambassador E. and P.
Consular Offices:
  California:
    Los Angeles
    Oakland
  Georgia, Atlanta
  Illinois, Chicago
  Maryland, Baltimore
  Massachusetts, Boston
  Michigan, Farmington
  Mississippi, Jackson
  Missouri, Kansas City
  New York, New York
  Texas, Houston
  Washington, Seattle

TURKMENISTAN

Embassy of Turkmenistan
2207 Massachusetts Avenue, NW., Washington, DC 20008
phone (202) 588–1500, fax 588–0697
His Excellency Meret Bairamovich Orazov
Ambassador E. and P.

UGANDA

Embassy of the Republic of Uganda
5911 16th Street, NW., Washington, DC 20011
phone (202) 726–0416, fax 726–1727
His Excellency Perezi Karukubiro Kamunanwire
Ambassador E. and P.
Consular Offices:
  California, Los Angeles
  Florida, Jupiter
  Washington, Gig Harbor

UKRAINE

Embassy of Ukraine
3350 M Street, NW., Washington, DC 20007
phone (202) 349–2920, fax 333–0817
His Excellency Oleh Shamshur
Ambassador E. and P.
Consular Offices:
  California, San Francisco
  Illinois, Chicago
  Michigan, Detroit
  New York, New York
  Ohio, Cleveland
  Texas, Houston

UNITED ARAB EMIRATES

Embassy of the United Arab Emirates
3522 International Court, NW., Washington, DC 20008
phone (202) 243–2400, fax 243–2432
His Excellency Yousif Mana Saeed Alotaiba
Ambassador E. and P.

UNITED KINGDOM

British Embassy
3100 Massachusetts Avenue, NW., Washington, DC 20008
phone (202) 588–6500, fax 588–7870
His Excellency Sir Nigel Elton Sheinwald
Ambassador E. and P.
Consular Offices:
  Alaska, Anchorage
  Arizona, Phoenix
  California:
    Los Angeles
    San Diego
    San Francisco

San Jose
Colorado, Denver
Florida:
Miami
Orlando
Georgia, Atlanta
Illinois, Chicago
Indiana, Indianapolis
Kansas, Kansas City
Louisiana, New Orleans
Massachusetts, Boston
Michigan, Detroit
Minnesota, Minneapolis
Nevada, Las Vegas
New York, New York
North Carolina, Charlotte
Ohio, Cleveland
Oklahoma, Tulsa
Oregon, Portland
Pennsylvania:
Philadelphia
Pittsburgh
Puerto Rico, San Juan
Tennessee, Nashville
Texas:
Dallas
Houston
San Antonio
Trust Territories of the Pacific Islands:
Nuku'alofa, Tonga
Utah, Salt Lake City
Washington, Bellevue
Wisconsin, Madison

URUGUAY

Embassy of Uruguay
1913 I Street, NW., Washington, DC 20006
phone (202) 331–1313, fax 331–8142
His Excellency Carlos Alberto Gianelli
Ambassador E. and P.
Consular Offices:
California:
Los Angeles
San Francisco
Florida, Miami
Illinois, Chicago
Louisiana, New Orleans
Nevada, Reno
New York, New York
Puerto Rico, San Juan
Texas, Houston
Utah, Salt Lake City

UZBEKISTAN

Embassy of the Republic of Uzbekistan
1746 Massachusetts Avenue, NW., Washington, DC 20036
phone (202) 293–6803, fax 293–6804
His Excellency Abdulaziz Khafizovich Kamilov
Ambassador E. and P.
Consular Offices:
Colorado, Denver
Georgia, Greensboro
New York, New York
Washington, Seattle

VANUATU

Consular Office: Northern Mariana Islands, Saipan

VENEZUELA

Embassy of the Bolivarian Republic of Venezuela
1099 30th Street, NW., Washington, DC 20007
phone (202) 342–2214, fax 342–6820
His Excellency Bernardo Alvarez Herrera
Ambassador E. and P.
Consular Offices:
California, San Francisco
Florida, Miami
Illinois, Chicago
Louisiana, New Orleans
Massachusetts, Boston
New York, New York
Puerto Rico, San Juan
Texas, Houston

VIETNAM

Embassy of Vietnam
1233 20th Street, NW., Suite 400, Washington, DC 20036
phone (202) 861–0737, fax 861–0917
His Excellency Phung Cong Le
Ambassador E. and P.
Consular Office: California, San Francisco

YEMEN

Embassy of the Republic of Yemen
2319 Wyoming Avenue, NW., Washington, DC 20008
phone (202) 965–4760, fax 337–2017
His Excellency Abdulwahab A. Al-Hajjri
Ambassador E. and P.
Consular Offices:
California, San Francisco
Michigan, Detroit

ZAMBIA

Embassy of the Republic of Zambia
2419 Massachusetts Avenue, NW., Washington, DC 20008
phone (202) 265–9717, fax 332–0826
Her Excellency Dr. Inonge Mbikusita Lewanika
Ambassador E. and P.

ZIMBABWE

Embassy of the Republic of Zimbabwe
1608 New Hampshire Avenue, NW., Washington, DC 20009

phone (202) 332–7100, fax 483–9326
His Excellency Dr. Machivenyika T. Mapuranga
Ambassador E. and P.

The following is a list of countries with which diplomatic relations have been severed:

After each country, in parenthesis, is the name of the country's protecting power in the United States.

CUBA (Switzerland)
IRAN (Pakistan)

PRESS GALLERIES*

SENATE PRESS GALLERY

The Capitol, Room S–316, phone 224–0241

Director.—S. Joseph Keenan
Deputy Director.—Joan McKinney
Media Coordinators:
Elizabeth Crowley
Amy H. Gross
Wendy A. Oscarson-Kirchner
James D. Saris

HOUSE PRESS GALLERY

The Capitol, Room H–315, phone 225–3945

Superintendent.—Jerry L. Gallegos
Deputy Superintendent.—Justin J. Supon
Assistant Superintendents:
Ric Andersen
Molly Cain
Drew Cannon
Laura Reed

STANDING COMMITTEE OF CORRESPONDENTS

Maureen Groppe, Gannett Washington Bureau, Chair
Laura Litvan, Bloomberg News, Secretary
Alan K. Ota, Congressional Quarterly
Richard Cowan, New York Times
Andrew Taylor, Reuters
Lisa Mascaro, Las Vegas Sun

RULES GOVERNING PRESS GALLERIES

1. Administration of the press galleries shall be vested in a Standing Committee of Correspondents elected by accredited members of the galleries. The Committee shall consist of five persons elected to serve for terms of two years. Provided, however, that at the election in January 1951, the three candidates receiving the highest number of votes shall serve for two years and the remaining two for one year. Thereafter, three members shall be elected in odd-numbered years and two in even-numbered years. Elections shall be held in January. The Committee shall elect its own chairman and secretary. Vacancies on the Committee shall be filled by special election to be called by the Standing Committee.

2. Persons desiring admission to the press galleries of Congress shall make application in accordance with Rule VI of the House of Representatives, subject to the direction and control of the Speaker and Rule 33 of the Senate, which rules shall be interpreted and administered by the Standing Committee of Correspondents, subject to the review and an approval by the Senate Committee on Rules and Administration.

3. The Standing Committee of Correspondents shall limit membership in the press galleries to bone fide correspondents of repute in their profession, under such rules as the Standing Committee of Correspondents shall prescribe.

*Information is based on data furnished and edited by each respective gallery.

4. An applicant for press credentials through the Daily Press Galleries must establish to the satisfaction of the Standing Committee of Correspondents that he or she is a full-time, paid correspondent who requires on-site access to congressional members and staff. Correspondents must be employed by a news organization:

(a) with General Publication periodicals mailing privileges under U.S. Postal Service rules, and which publishes daily; or

(b) whose principal business is the daily dissemination of original news and opinion of interest to a broad segment of the public, and which has published continuously for 18 months.

The applicant must reside in the Washington, D.C. area, and must not be engaged in any lobbying or paid advocacy, advertising, publicity or promotion work for any individual, political party, corporation, organization, or agency of the U.S. government, or in prosecuting any claim before Congress or any federal government department, and will not do so while a member of the Daily Press Galleries.

Applicants' publications must be editorially independent of any institution, foundation or interest group that lobbies the federal government, or that is not principally a general news organization.

Failure to provide information to the Standing Committee for this determination, or misrepresenting information, can result in the denial or revocation of credentials.

5. Members of the families of correspondents are not entitled to the privileges of the galleries.

6. The Standing Committee of Correspondents shall propose no changes in the these rules except upon petition in writing signed by not less than 100 accredited members of the galleries. The above rules have been approved by the Committee on Rules and Administration.

NANCY PELOSI,
Speaker of the House of Representatives.

CHARLES E. SCHUMER,
Chair, Senate Committee on Rules and Administration.

MEMBERS ENTITLED TO ADMISSION

PRESS GALLERIES

Abdullah, Halimah: McClatchy Newspapers
Abel, Allen: National Post
Abrams, James: Associated Press
Abrams, Sandra: Reuters
Abruzzese, Sarah: Washington Times
Achenbach, Joel: Washington Post
Ackerman, Andrew: Bond Buyer
Adair, William: St. Petersburg Times
Adams, Christopher: McClatchy Newspapers
Adams, Rebecca: Congressional Quarterly
Adams, Richard: London Guardian
Adamy, Janet: Wall Street Journal
Adcock, Beryl: McClatchy Newspapers
Adler, Joseph: American Banker
Adofo, Adjoa: Congressional Quarterly
Aemisegger, Celine: EFE News Services
Agres, Theodore: Washington Times
Ahearn, David: Defense Daily
Ahlrich, Alan: Congressional Quarterly
Ahn, Sung Joong: Korea Times
Akers, Mary Ann: Washington Post
Akinwande, Ifedayo: Congressional Quarterly
Alamiri, Yasmeen: Saudi Press Agency
Alandete, David: El Pais
Alberta, Timothy: Wall Street Journal
Alberts, Sheldon: Canwest News Service
Alexander, Charles: Reuters
Ali, Syed: Congressional Quarterly
Allen, Amanda: Congressional Quarterly
Allen, JoAnne: Reuters
Allen, Jonathan: Congressional Quarterly
Allen, Kent: Congressional Quarterly
Allen, Ross: Argus Media
Allen, Victoria: Reuters
Allison, Wes: St. Petersburg Times
Alonso-Zaldivar, Ricardo: Associated Press
Alpert, Bruce: New Orleans Times-Picayune
Al-Sowayel, Naila: Saudi Press Agency
Alvarez, Marina: Los Angeles Times
Ammann, Beat: Neue Zuercher Zeitung
Anderson, Andre: McClatchy Newspapers
Anderson, Joanna: Congressional Quarterly
Anderson, Mark: Dow Jones Newswires
Andrews, Edmund: New York Times
Angle, Martha: Congressional Quarterly
Anstey, Christopher: Bloomberg News
Antonen, Mel: USA Today
Anyz, Daniel: Hospodarske Noving Daily
Appelbaum, Binyamin: Washington Post
Apuzzo, Matt: Associated Press
Argetsinger, Amy: Washington Post
Arimoto, Takashi: Sankei Shimbun
Arita, Tsukasa: Kyodo News
Armstrong, Andrew: Congressional Quarterly
Arnold, John Jay: Associated Press
Ashburn, Emma: Asahi Shimbun
Asher, James: McClatchy Newspapers
Asher, Julie: Catholic News Service
Ashizuka, Tomoko: Nikkei
Aslam, Abid: Inter Press Service
Asseo, Laurie: Bloomberg News
Attias, Melissa: Congressional Quarterly
Aukofer, Frank: Artists & Writers Syndicate
Aversa, Jeannine: Associated Press
Awaji, Ai: Jiji Press
Ayuso Determeyer, Sylvia: German Press Agency-DPA
Azpiazu, Maria: EFE News Services
Babaeva, Svetlana: RIA Novosti
Babcock, Charles: Bloomberg News
Babington, Charles: Associated Press
Bacon, Jr., Perry: Washington Post
Baert, Patrick: Agence France-Presse
Baker, Peter: New York Times
Baldor, Lolita: Associated Press
Baldwin, Thomas: London Times
Ball, Michael: Argus Media
Balz, Daniel: Washington Post
Banales, Jorge: EFE News Services
Banks, Adelle: Religion News Service
Baquet, Dean: New York Times
Barakat, Matthew: Associated Press
Barker, James: Congressional Quarterly
Barker, Jeffrey: Baltimore Sun
Barkley, Tom: Dow Jones Newswires
Barnes, Julian: Los Angeles Times
Barnes, Robert: Washington Post
Baron, Ana: Clarin
Barrera, Ruben: Notimex Mexican News Agency
Barrett, Barbara: McClatchy Newspapers
Barrett, Devlin: Associated Press
Barrett, Terrence: Bloomberg News
Bartash, Jeffrey: MarketWatch
Bartscht, Jill: Washington Post
Bartz, Diane: Reuters
Bashir, Mustafa: Saudi Press Agency
Bater, Jeffrey: Dow Jones Newswires
Baumann, David: Congressional Quarterly
Baygents, Ronald: Kuwait News Agency
Bayle, Juan Cañete: El Periodico
Baylis, Jamie: Congressional Quarterly

MEMBERS ENTITLED TO ADMISSION—Continued

Bazar, Emily: USA Today
Bazinet, Kenneth: New York Daily News
Beary, Brian: Europolitics
Beattie, Alan: Financial Times
Beattie, Jeff: Energy Daily
Beatty, Andrew: Agence France-Presse
Becker, Bernard: New York Times
Beckner, Steven: Market News International
Bell, Peter: Congress Daily
Bellantoni, Christina: Washington Times
Bello, Marisol: USA Today
Bendavid, Naftali: Wall Street Journal
Bender, Adam: Communications Daily
Bender, Bryan: Boston Globe
Benenson, Robert: Congressional Quarterly
Benesova, Dagmar: World Business Press
Benjamin, Matthew: Bloomberg News
Benkelman, Susan: Congressional Quarterly
Benoit, Daphne: Agence France-Presse
Benson, Clea: Congressional Quarterly
Berley, Max: Bloomberg News
Berry, Deborah: Gannett News Service
Berry, John: Bloomberg News
Bettelheim, Adriel: Congressional Quarterly
Bicknell, Arwen Adams: Congressional Quarterly
Bicknell, John: Congressional Quarterly
Biddle, Joanna: Agence France-Presse
Bilski, Christina: Nikkei
Birnbaum, Jeffrey: Washington Times
Birnbaum, Michael: Washington Post
Biskupic, Joan: USA Today
Bivins, Larry: Gannett News Service
Bjerga, Alan: Bloomberg News
Blackledge, Brett: Associated Press
Blackstone, Brian: Dow Jones Newswires
Bland, Melissa: Reuters
Blinch, Russell: Reuters
Bliss, Jeffrey: Bloomberg News
Blum, Justin: Bloomberg News
Blumenthal, Les: McClatchy Newspapers
Boadle, Anthony: Reuters
Bohan, Caren: Reuters
Bold, Michael: McClatchy Newspapers
Boles, Corey: Dow Jones Newswires
Bolstad, Erika: McClatchy Newspapers
Borak, Donna: Associated Press
Borenstein, Seth: Associated Press
Bostick, Romaine: Bloomberg News
Bourge, Christian: Washington Times
Bouza, Teresa: EFE News Services
Bowen, Joel: Congressional Quarterly
Bowman, Curtis Lee: Scripps Howard News Service
Boyd, Robert: McClatchy Newspapers
Boyer, David: Philadelphia Inquirer
Brady, Erik: USA Today
Braithwaite, Tom: Financial Times
Brandmaier, Frank: German Press Agency-DPA
Branson, Louise: USA Today
Brasher, Philip: Des Moines Register
Brauchli, Marcus: Washington Post
Braun, Stephen: Associated Press
Bravin, Jess: Wall Street Journal
Bridis, Ted: Associated Press
Brinsley, John: Bloomberg News
Broder, David: Washington Post
Broder, John: New York Times
Broder, Jonathan: Congressional Quarterly
Brodie, Michael: LRP Publications
Brodmann, Ronald: Congressional Quarterly
Brooks, David: New York Times
Brooks, David: La Jornada
Brown, David: Washington Post
Brown, DeNeen: Washington Post
Brune, Thomas: Newsday
Buddhavarapu, Bhagyashree: Singapore Straits Times
Bull, Alister: Reuters
Bumiller, Elisabeth: New York Times
Burger, Timothy: Bloomberg News
Burgess, Jeff: New York Times
Burke, Daniel: Religion News Service
Burns, Judith: Dow Jones Newswires
Burns, Robert: Associated Press
Burr, Thomas: Salt Lake Tribune
Burt, Andy: Bloomberg News
Buskirk, Howard: Communications Daily
Bussey, John: Wall Street Journal
Butler, Desmond: Associated Press
Cadei, Emily: Congressional Quarterly
Cadiz, Antonieta: La Opinion
Calmes, Jackie: New York Times
Calvo-Platero, Mario: Il Sole 24 Ore
Camia, Catalina: USA Today
Campo, Marcello: ANSA Italian News Agency
Canellos, Peter: Boston Globe
Canham, Matt: Salt Lake Tribune
Caño, Antonio: El Pais
Cantu, Leslie: Communications Daily
Capaccio, Anthony: Bloomberg News
Caplan, Abby: Argus Media
Cappiello, Dana: Associated Press
Carmichael, Lachlan: Agence France-Presse
Carney, Dan: USA Today
Carney, David: Tech Law Journal
Carney, Timothy: Washington Examiner
Carpenter, Amanda: Washington Times
Carroll, James: Congressional Quarterly
Carroll, James: Louisville Courier Journal
Carter, Sara: Washington Times
Cartwright, Linda: Congressional Quarterly
Casabona, Elizabeth: Fairchild News Service
Cass, Connie: Associated Press
Cassata, Donna: Associated Press
Casteel, Chris: Oklahoman
Cermak, Christopher: German Press Agency-DPA

MEMBERS ENTITLED TO ADMISSION—Continued

Chadbourn, Margaret: Bloomberg News
Chaddock, Gail: Christian Science Monitor
Chamberlain, Kenneth: Congress Daily
Chan, Sammie: Gannett News Service
Chandler, Michael: Washington Post
Chandra, Shobhana: Bloomberg News
Chandrasekaran, Rajiv: Washington Post
Chang, Tsung-Chih: United Daily News
Chaplain, Myriam: Agence France-Presse
Charles, Deborah: Reuters
Chebium, Raju: Gannett News Service
Chen, Edwin: Bloomberg News
Chen, Kathy: Wall Street Journal
Chen, Shawn: Associated Press
Chew, Cassie: Wall Street Journal
Chiantaretto, Mariuccia: Il Giornale
Chikazawa, Moriyasu: Kyodo News
Chinni, Dante: Christian Science Monitor
Chipman, Kimberly: Bloomberg News
Cho, David: Washington Post
Cho, Nam: Segye Times
Choate, Patricia: Scripps Howard News Service
Choi, Hyung Du: Munwha Ilbo
Chong, Christina Young: Korea Times
Christensen, Mike: Congressional Quarterly
Christian, Molly: Argus Media
Christie, Rebecca: Bloomberg News
Chu, Keith: Western Communications
Chun, Young Sik: Munwha Ilbo
Chwallek, Gabriele: German Press Agency-DPA
Cillizza, Chris: Washington Post
Cindemir, Mehmet: Hurriyet
Clampitt, Brian: Asahi Shimbun
Clark, Colin: Military.com
Clark, Lesley: Miami Herald
Clarke, David: Congressional Quarterly
Clearwater, Cindy: Reuters
Clerico, Luciano: ANSA Italian News Agency
Clymer, Adam: New York Times
Cocco, Marie: Washington Post Writer's Group
Codrea, George: Congressional Quarterly
Cohen, Sarah: Washington Post
Cohn, Peter: Congress Daily
Coile, Zachary: San Francisco Chronicle
Cole, August: Wall Street Journal
Coleman, Michael: Albuquerque Journal
Collins, Michael: Scripps Howard News Service
Collinson, Stephen: Agence France-Presse
Colvin, Ross: Reuters
Condon, Stephanie: CNET News.com
Condon, Jr., George: Congress Daily
Conery, Ben: Washington Times
Conkey, Christopher: Wall Street Journal
Conlon, Charles: Congressional Quarterly
Connealy, Erin: Asahi Shimbun
Conners, Maureen: Congressional Quarterly
Connolly, Catherine: Washington Post
Conrad, Dennis: Associated Press
Conway, Neal: Congressional Quarterly
Cook, David: Christian Science Monitor
Cooke, Anthony: Dow Jones Newswires
Coomes, Jessica: Congressional Quarterly
Cooney, Jessica Benton: Congressional Quarterly
Cooper, Helene: New York Times
Cooper, Kent: Political Money Line
Cooper, Richard: Los Angeles Times
Cooper, Sonya: Bloomberg News
Copeland, Libby: Washington Post
Copeland, Peter: Scripps Howard News Service
Corbett, Rebecca: New York Times
Corbett Dooren, Jennifer: Dow Jones Newswires
Corbin, Kenneth: Internetnews.com
Corchado, Alfredo: Dallas Morning News
Cornwell, Susan: Reuters
Cowan, Richard: Reuters
Craig, Tim: Washington Post
Cranford, John: Congressional Quarterly
Crawley, John: Reuters
Crites, Alice: Washington Post
Crittenden, Michael: Dow Jones Newswires
Crutsinger, Martin: Associated Press
Cunningham, Sarah: Reuters
Curl, Joseph: Washington Times
Curran, Timothy: Washington Post
Cushman, Jr., John: New York Times
da Costa, Mario Navarro: ABIM
Daly, Matthew: Associated Press
Daniel, Douglass: Associated Press
Daniels, Alex: Arkansas Democrat-Gazette
Dann, Carey: Congress Daily
Dao, James: New York Times
Davenport, Coral: Congressional Quarterly
Davenport, J. Christian: Washington Post
Davidson, Joe: Washington Post
Davidson, Julie: LRP Publications
Davidson, Kate: Congressional Quarterly
Davidson, Paul: USA Today
Davidz, Elizabeth: Associated Press
Davies, Anne: Sydney Morning Herald
Davies, Frank: San Jose Mercury News
Davis, Aaron: Washington Post
Davis, David: Congressional Quarterly
Davis, Julie: Associated Press
Davis, Robert: Wall Street Journal
Davis, Susan: Wall Street Journal
DeBard, Amanda: Washington Times
Debusmann, Bernd: Reuters
Decamme, Guillaume: Agence France-Presse
Dechter, Gadi: Bloomberg News
Decker, Brett: Washington Times
Decker, Susan: Bloomberg News
DeFrank, Thomas: New York Daily News
Deguchi, Tomohiro: Kyodo News
Del Giudice, Vincent: Bloomberg News

MEMBERS ENTITLED TO ADMISSION—Continued

Del Riccio, Cristiano: ANSA Italian News Agency
Delgado, Jose: El Nuevo Dia
DeLuce, Daniel: Agence France-Presse
DeMarco, Edward: Bloomberg News
Demirjian, Karoun: Congressional Quarterly
Dennis, Brady: Washington Post
Deparle, Jason: New York Times
Dermody, William: USA Today
Deshimaru, Sachiko: Nikkei
Desmond, Harold: Reuters
Dessouky, Dean: Saudi Press Agency
Diaz, Kevin: Minneapolis Star Tribune
Diaz-Briseno, Jose: Reforma Newspaper
Dick, Jason: Congress Daily
Dickerson, Christine: IFR Markets
Dickson, David: Washington Times
Dickson, Virgil: Communications Daily
Dilanian, Ken: USA Today
Dinan, Stephen: Washington Times
Dineen, John: Congressional Quarterly
Dixon, Kim: Reuters
Dlouhy, Jennifer: Hearst Newspapers
Dobbyn, Timothy: Reuters
Dodge, Catherine: Bloomberg News
Doering, Christopher: Reuters
Doggett, Tom: Reuters
Dolan, Christopher: Washington Times
Dolinger, David Allen: Wall Street Journal
Dombey, Daniel: Financial Times
Dominello, Amy: Media General News Service
Donmoyer, Ryan: Bloomberg News
Donnelly, John: Congressional Quarterly
Dorell, Oren: USA Today
Dorning, Mike: Chicago Tribune
Douglas, William: McClatchy Newspapers
Dowd, Maureen: New York Times
Downing, James: Restructuring Today
Doyle, Leonard: London Independent
Doyle, Michael: McClatchy Newspapers
Drajem, Mark: Bloomberg News
Drake, Bruce: Congressional Quarterly
Drawbaugh, Kevin: Reuters
Dreazen, Yochi: Wall Street Journal
Drinkard, Jim: Associated Press
Drobnyk, Josh: Allentown Morning Call
Drummond, Bob: Bloomberg News
Dufour, Jeff: Washington Examiner
Duggan, Loren: Congressional Quarterly
Duggan, Paul: Washington Post
Duin, Julia: Washington Times
Dumain, Emma: Congressional Quarterly
Dunham, Richard: Houston Chronicle
Dunham, Will: Reuters
Dunphy, Harry: Associated Press
Dutton, Audrey: Bond Buyer
Dvorak, Petula: Washington Post
Dwyer, Paula: New York Times
Earle, Geoff: New York Post
Eaton, Sabrina: Cleveland Plain Dealer
Eckert, Paul: Reuters
Eckert, Toby: Congressional Quarterly
Eckstrom, Kevin: Religion News Service
Edmonds, Jr., Ronald: Associated Press
Edney, Anna: Congress Daily
Eggen, Daniel: Washington Post
Eichelberger, Curtis: Bloomberg News
Eilperin, Juliet: Washington Post
Eisler, Peter: USA Today
Eisman, Dale: Virginian-Pilot
El Hamti, Maribel: EFE News Services
El Nasser, Haya: USA Today
Elboghdady, Dina: Washington Post
Elkins, Donald: Associated Press
Ellicott, Val: Gannett News Service
Elliott, Geoff: Australian
Elliott, Philip: Associated Press
Ellis, Kristi: Fairchild News Service
Elsibai, Nadine: Bloomberg News
Emerling, Gary: Washington Times
Enoch, Daniel: Bloomberg News
Epstein, Edward: Congressional Quarterly
Espo, David: Associated Press
Ethridge, Emily: Congressional Quarterly
Evans, Ben: Associated Press
Eversley, Melanie: USA Today
Faen, Wang: Xinhua News Agency
Fahrenthold, David: Washington Post
Faler, Brian: Bloomberg News
Fallis, David: Washington Post
Farah, Samer: Reuters
Farhi, Paul: Washington Post
Farnam, Timothy: Wall Street Journal
Farrell, John Aloysius: GlobalPost
Favole, Jared: Dow Jones Newswires
Fears, Darryl: Washington Post
Fein, Geoff: Defense Daily
Feld, Karen: Capital Connections
Feldman, Carole: Associated Press
Feldmann, Linda: Christian Science Monitor
Felker, Edward: Washington Times
Feller, Ben: Associated Press
Felsenthal, Mark: Reuters
Fendrich, Howard: Associated Press
Ferrari, Francisco: Agence France-Presse
Ferraro, Thomas: Reuters
Ferrechio, Susan: Washington Examiner
Ferrer, Sandra: Agence France-Presse
Fessenden, Helen: Congress Daily
Fetterman, Mindy: USA Today
Fields, Gary: Wall Street Journal
Fingerhut, Eric: Jewish Telegraphic Agency
Finn, Peter: Washington Post
Fireman, Ken: Bloomberg News
Fisher, Marc: Washington Post

MEMBERS ENTITLED TO ADMISSION—Continued

Fitzgerald, Alison: Bloomberg News
Flaherty, Anne: Associated Press
Flaherty, Mary Pat: Washington Post
Flanders, Gwen: USA Today
Flattau, Edward: Global Horizons Syndicate
Fletcher, Michael: Washington Post
Flitter, Emily: American Banker
Ford, Matt: Associated Press
Forsythe, Michael: Bloomberg News
Fournier, Ron: Associated Press
Fowler, Daniel: Congressional Quarterly
Fowler, Maria: Gannett News Service
Fox, Margaret: Reuters
Fox, Michael: Congress Daily
Fram, Alan: Associated Press
Frank, Thomas: USA Today
Fraze, Barbara: Catholic News Service
Freedman, Dan: Hearst Newspapers
Freeman, Sholnn: Washington Post
Freking, Kevin: Associated Press
Friedman, Daniel: Congress Daily
Friedman, Robert: Scripps Howard News Service
Fritze, John: USA Today
Frommer, Frederic: Associated Press
Fry, Jamey: Congressional Quarterly
Fudo, Takashi: Jiji Press
Fuhrig, Frank: German Press Agency-DPA
Fullerton, Jane: Arkansas Democrat-Gazette
Funk, Lynne: Bond Buyer
Furlow, Robert: Associated Press
Furukawa, Masakazu: Tokyo Chunichi Shimbun
Galan, Frederic: Agence France-Presse
Gallagher, Brian: USA Today
Gallu, Joshua: Bloomberg News
Gamboa, Suzanne: Associated Press
Gambrell, Kathy: Congress Daily
Gaouette, Nicole: Bloomberg News
Gardiner, Andrew: USA Today
Gardner, Amy: Washington Post
Gates-Davis, Marilyn: Congressional Quarterly
Gaul, Gilbert: Washington Post
Gaynair, Gillian: Associated Press
Gearan, Anne: Associated Press
Gehrke, Robert: Salt Lake Tribune
Gensheimer, Lydia: Congressional Quarterly
Geracimos, Ann: Washington Times
Gerhart, Ann: Washington Post
Ghosh-Siminoff, Sasha: Congressional Quarterly
Gibson, William: South Florida Sun-Sentinel
Gienger, Viola: Bloomberg News
Gilbert, Craig: Milwaukee Journal Sentinel
Gillman, Todd: Dallas Morning News
Gillum, Jack: USA Today
Giroux, Gregory: Congressional Quarterly
Glass, Pamela: Le Mauricien
Glass, Robert: Associated Press
Glod, Maria: Washington Post
Goad, Ben: Riverside Press-Enterprise
Goldbacher, Raymond: USA Today
Goldberg, Jonathan: Congressional Quarterly
Golden, Rodrek: Reuters
Goldenberg, Suzanne: London Guardian
Goldfarb, Zachary: Washington Post
Goldman, Julianna: Bloomberg News
Goldschlag, William: New York Daily News
Goldschmidt, Jim: McClatchy Newspapers
Goldsmith, Reese: Congressional Quarterly
Goldstein, Amy: Washington Post
Goldstein, Avram: Bloomberg News
Goldstein, Daniel: Platts News Service
Goldstein, David: Kansas City Star
Golle, Vince: Bloomberg News
Goller, Howard Scot: Reuters
Gomez, Alan: USA Today
Gomez, Sergio: El Tiempo
Gomez, Shawn: Associated Press
Gomlak, Norman: Congressional Quarterly
Gonzalez, Francisco: EFE News Services
Goode, Darren: Congress Daily
Goodman, Adrianne: New York Times
Goodridge, Elizabeth: New York Times
Gorcester, Andrew: Jiji Press
Gordon, Greg: McClatchy Newspapers
Gordon, Marcy: Associated Press
Gorman, Siobhan: Wall Street Journal
Goto, Shihoko: Congress Daily
Gowen, Annie: Washington Post
Graham-Silverman, Adam: Congressional Quarterly
Grancharov, Givco: Argus Media
Gray, Andrew: Reuters
Greenberg, Brigitte: Bloomberg News
Greene, Robert: Bloomberg News
Greiling Keane, Angela: Bloomberg News
Greve, Frank: McClatchy Newspapers
Grier, Peter: Christian Science Monitor
Griffith, Stephanie: Agence France-Presse
Grim, Ryan: Huffington Post
Grimaldi, James: Washington Post
Groppe, Maureen: Gannett News Service
Gruenwald, Juliana: Congress Daily
Guenther, Markus: Westdeutsche Allgemeine
Guevara, Tomas: El Diario de Hoy
Guggenheim, Ken: Associated Press
Guha, Krishna: Financial Times
Guihaire, Edouard: Agence France-Presse
Gulino, Denny: Market News International
Gutman, Roy: McClatchy Newspapers
Ha, Taewon: Korea Dong-A Ilbo
Haberkorn, Jennifer: Washington Times
Hackett, Laurel: Scripps Howard News Service
Hagenbaugh, Barbara: USA Today
Hager, George: USA Today
Hall, Kevin: McClatchy Newspapers
Hall, Mimi: USA Today

MEMBERS ENTITLED TO ADMISSION—Continued

Hallock, Kimberly: Congressional Quarterly
Hallow, Ralph: Washington Times
Hamalainen, Aloysia: St. Louis Post-Dispatch
Hamann, Carlos: Agence France-Presse
Hamburger, Thomas: Los Angeles Times
Hampton, Olivia: Agence France-Presse
Hananel, Sam: Associated Press
Hannett, Thomas: Congressional Quarterly
Hargrove, Thomas: Scripps Howard News Service
Harland, Janis: New York Times
Harper, Jennifer: Washington Times
Harris, Charles: Yomiuri Shimbun
Harris, Gardiner: New York Times
Harris, Hamil: Washington Post
Hart, Dan: Bloomberg News
Hart, Kim: Washington Post
Hartnagel, Nancy: Catholic News Service
Hartson, Merrill: Associated Press
Hatch, David: Congress Daily
Hawkings, David: Congressional Quarterly
Hayakawa, Toshiyuki: Sekai Nippo
Haygood, Wil: Washington Post
Hazar, Hasan: Turkiye Daily
Healy, James: USA Today
Healy, Robert: Congressional Quarterly
Heath, Brad: USA Today
Heavey, Susan: Reuters
Hebert, H. Josef: Associated Press
Hedgpeth, Dana: Washington Post
Hefling, Kimberly: Associated Press
Heilprin, John: Associated Press
Heller, Marc: Watertown Daily Times
Hendel, Caitlin: Congressional Quarterly
Henderson, Gregory: Associated Press
Hendrickx, Frank: Netherlands Press Association
Hendrie, Paul: Congressional Quarterly
Henriksson, Karin: Svenska Dagbladet
Henry, John: Associated Press
Hernandez, Jose: El Universal
Hernandez, Raymond: New York Times
Herrmann, Frank: Rheinische Post
Herszenhorn, David: New York Times
Hess, David: Congress Daily
Hess, Pamela: Associated Press
Hesse, Monica: Washington Post
Higgins, David: Congressional Quarterly
Higgins, Sean: Investor's Business Daily
Higuchi, Takuya: Jiji Press
Hill, Charlotte: Agence France-Presse
Hill, Patricia: Washington Times
Hillyer, Quin: Washington Times
Hilsenrath, Jon: Wall Street Journal
Hinton, Earl: Associated Press
Hitt, Greg: Wall Street Journal
Hoffecker, Leslie: Congressional Quarterly
Hoffman, Lisa: Scripps Howard News Service
Hogberg, David: Investor's Business Daily
Holland, Jesse: Associated Press
Holland, Steve: Reuters
Holly, Christopher: Energy Daily
Holzer, Jessica: Dow Jones Newswires
Holzer, Linda: USA Today
Homan, Timothy: Bloomberg News
Homma, Keiichi: Yomiuri Shimbun
Hon, Chua Chin: Singapore Straits Times
Hong, Liu: Xinhua News Agency
Honore, Hugues: Agence France-Presse
Hook, Janet: Los Angeles Times
Hopkins, Cheyenne: American Banker
Hortobagyi, Monica: USA Today
Horwich, Lee: USA Today
Hoskinson, Charles: Congressional Quarterly
Hossain, Farhana: New York Times
Hotakainen, Rob: McClatchy Newspapers
House, Billy: Congress Daily
Hoy, Anne: Congressional Quarterly
Hsu, Spencer: Washington Post
Hu, Fang: Xinhua News Agency
Hudson, Audrey: Washington Times
Hughes, Darrell: Dow Jones Newswires
Hughes, John: Bloomberg News
Hughes, Siobhan: Dow Jones Newswires
Hughey, Ann: Bloomberg News
Hui, Ju: China Youth Daily
Hull, Anne: Washington Post
Hulse, Carl: New York Times
Hultman, Tamela: AllAfrica.com
Hume, Lynn: Bond Buyer
Hunley, Jonathan: News and Messenger
Hunt, Albert: Bloomberg News
Hunt, Kasie: Congress Daily
Hunt, Terence: Associated Press
Hunter, Kathleen: Congressional Quarterly
Hurley, Lawrence: Los Angeles Daily Journal
Hurley, Liam: Saudi Press Agency
Hurst, Steven: Associated Press
Hurt, Charles: New York Post
Hussain, Abdul-Hussain: Al Rai
Hussein, Sara: Agence France-Presse
Hwang, Jae Hoon: Yonhap News Agency
Hyde, Justin: Detroit Free Press
Hyong, Hwang Doo: Yonhap News Agency
Iafolla, Robert: Los Angeles Daily Journal
Ignatiou, Michail: Ethnos Greece
Ikeda, Nestor: Associated Press
Irons, John: Congressional Quarterly
Irwin, Walton Neil: Washington Post
Issenberg, Sasha: Boston Globe
Itkowitz, Colby: Congressional Quarterly
Ito, Hiroshi: Asahi Shimbun
Ito, Kosuke: Jiji Press
Ivanovich, David: Argus Media
Ives-Halperin, Benton: Congressional Quarterly
Iwamoto, Masako: Nikkei

MEMBERS ENTITLED TO ADMISSION—Continued

Iwata, Nakahiro: Tokyo Chunichi Shimbun
Jackler, Rosalind: USA Today
Jackman, Thomas: Washington Post
Jackson, David: USA Today
Jackson, Henry: Associated Press
Jackson, Herbert: Bergen Record
Jackson-Randall, Maya: Dow Jones Newswires
Jakes, Lara: Associated Press
Jalonick, Mary Clare: Associated Press
James, Frank: Chicago Tribune
Jamrisko, Michelle: Kyodo News
Jansen, Bart: Congressional Quarterly
Jehl, Douglas: New York Times
Jelinek, Pauline: Associated Press
Jenkins, Chris: Washington Post
Jennings, Angel: Wall Street Journal
Jensen, Kristin: Bloomberg News
Jessen, Kory: Associated Press
Jha, Lalit: India Press Trust
Jha, Shweta: Congressional Quarterly
Jiang, Guopeng: Xinhua News Agency
Johnson, Annie: Congressional Quarterly
Johnson, Carrie: Washington Post
Johnson, Fawn: Dow Jones Newswires
Johnson, Kevin: USA Today
Johnson, Matthew: Congressional Quarterly
Johnston, David: New York Times
Johnston, Nicholas: Bloomberg News
Jones, David: Washington Times
Jones, Kerry: Congressional Quarterly
Jordan, Alethea: Gannett Washington Bureau
Jordan, Bryant: Military.com
Jordan, Charles: Congress Daily
Joshi, Jitendra: Agence France-Presse
Jourdier, Marc: Agence France-Presse
Joy, Patricia: Congressional Quarterly
Junius, Dennis: Associated Press
Justsen, Klaus: Jyllands-Posten
Kaiser, Emily: Reuters
Kaiser, Robert: Washington Post
Kajita, Takehito: Kyodo News
Kalish, Brian: Dow Jones Newswires
Kamalick, Joseph: ICIS News
Kamen, Al: Washington Post
Kampeas, Ron: Jewish Telegraphic Agency
Kane, Paul: Washington Post
Kang, Cecilia: Washington Post
Kaper, Stacy Lynn: American Banker
Kapochunas, Rachel: Congressional Quarterly
Karam, Joyce: Al-Hayat
Karey, Gerald: Platts News Service
Karush, Sarah: Associated Press
Kasperowicz, Pete: IFR Markets
Kastner, Kevin: Market News International
Kato, Takefumi: Jiji Press
Kato, Yoichi: Asahi Shimbun
Katsuda, Toshihiko: Asahi Shimbun
Katz, Ian: Bloomberg News
Keating, Dan: Washington Post
Keefe, Bob: Atlanta Journal Constitution
Keefe, Stephen: Nikkei
Kelley, Matthew: USA Today
Kellman Blazar, Laurie: Associated Press
Kelly, Dennis: USA Today
Kelly, Erin: Gannett News Service
Kemper, Bob: Congress Daily
Kendall, Brent: Dow Jones Newswires
Kercheval, Nancy: Bloomberg News
Kerr, Jennifer: Associated Press
Kerry, Frances: Reuters
Kertes, Noella: Congressional Quarterly
Kessler, Glenn: Washington Post
Khaledi, Kayvon: Congressional Quarterly
Kiefer, Francine: Christian Science Monitor
Kiely, Eugene: USA Today
Kiely, Kathy: USA Today
Kilian, Martin: Tages Anzeiger
Kim, Angela: Congressional Quarterly
Kim, Anne: Congressional Quarterly
Kim, Eun: Gannett News Service
Kim, Hong Yeol: Korea Economic Daily
Kim, Jae Hong: Yonhap News Agency
Kim, Jin Ho: Kyunghyang Shinmun
Kim, Jungwook: Joongang Ilbo
Kim, Kyun Mi: Seoul Shinmun
Kim, Myung Ho: Kukmin Daily
Kimura, Kazuhiro: Kyodo News
King, Ledyard: Gannett News Service
King, Llewellyn: Energy Daily
King, Peter: Congressional Quarterly
King, Jr., Neil: Wall Street Journal
Kipling, Bogdan: Kipling News Service
Kirchhoff, Suzanne: USA Today
Kirk, Jim: Bloomberg News
Kirkpatrick, David: New York Times
Kirsanov, Dmitry: Itar-Tass News Agency
Kishi, Masayuki: Hokkaido Shimbun
Kishida, Yoshiki: Jiji Press
Kittross, David: LRP Publications
Kivlan, Terence: Congress Daily
Klimek, Eric: Associated Press
Kluever, Reymer: Sueddeutsche Zeitung
Klug, Foster: Associated Press
Kniazkov, Maxim: Agence France-Presse
Knott, Alex: Congressional Quarterly
Knowlton, Brian: International Herald Tribune
Knox, Olivier: Agence France-Presse
Kobayashi, Toshiya: Akahata
Koch, Wendy: USA Today
Kodjak-Fitzgerald, Alison: Bloomberg News
Koh, Seung Il: Yonhap News Agency
Komarow, Steven: Associated Press
Komatsu, Kenichi: Mainichi Shimbun
Komori, Yoshihisa: Sankei Shimbun

MEMBERS ENTITLED TO ADMISSION—Continued

Konjevoda, Jerry: IFR Markets
Kopecki, Dawn: Bloomberg News
Korade, Matthew: Congressional Quarterly
Koring, Paul: Toronto Globe and Mail
Kornblut, Anne: Washington Post
Kotecki, Emily: Washington Post
Kramer, Reed: AllAfrica.com
Kranish, Michael: Boston Globe
Krawzak, Paul: Congressional Quarterly
Kreisher, Otto: Congress Daily
Krieger, Hilary Leila: Jerusalem Post
Kroepsch, Adrianne: Congressional Quarterly
Kuhnhenn, Jim: Associated Press
Kuk, Kiyon: Segye Times
Kumar, Arun: Indo-Asian News Service
Kumar, Dinesh: Communications Daily
Kunkle, Fredrick: Washington Post
Kuno, Shuko: Jiji Press
Kurose, Yoshinari: Yomiuri Shimbun
Kurtz, Howard: Washington Post
Kusano, Kazuhiko: Mainichi Shimbun
Kwon, Taeho: Hankyoreh Daily
La Franchi, Howard: Christian Science Monitor
Labaton, Stephen: New York Times
Labbe, Theola: Washington Post
Labriny, Azeddine: Saudi Press Agency
Lakashmanan, Indira: Bloomberg News
Lake, Eli: Washington Times
Lambert, Lisa: Reuters
Lambrecht, William: St. Louis Post-Dispatch
Lambro, Donald: Washington Times
Landay, Jonathan: McClatchy Newspapers
Landers, James: Dallas Morning News
Landers, Peter: Wall Street Journal
Landler, Mark: New York Times
Lane, Charles: Washington Post
Lane, Kamala: Associated Press
Langan, Michael: Agence France-Presse
Langley, Monica: Wall Street Journal
Lanham, Yuko: Asahi Shimbun
Lanman, Scott: Bloomberg News
Lanteaume, Sylvie: Agence France-Presse
Lardner, Richard: Associated Press
Laris, Michael: Washington Post
Larkin, Catherine: Bloomberg News
Lawder, David: Reuters
Lawrence, Jill: USA Today
Layton, Lyndsey: Washington Post
Leah, Carliner: Congressional Quarterly
Leahy, Michael: Washington Post
Leary, Alex: St. Petersburg Times
Lebling, Madonna: Washington Post
Lee, Byonghan: Korea Times
Lee, Chang-Yul: Korea Times
Lee, Do Woon: Seoul Shinmun
Lee, Ha Won: Chosun Ilbo
Lee, Jong Kook: Korea Times
Lee, Keehong: Korea Dong-A Ilbo
Lee, Matthew: Associated Press
Lee, Sang Il: Joongang Ilbo
Leeds, Charles: Los Angeles Times-Washington Post News Service
Lefkow, David Christopher: Agence France-Presse
Lehmann, Chris: Congressional Quarterly
Leibovich, Mark: New York Times
Leiby, Richard: Washington Post
Leinwand, Donna: USA Today
Leissner, Janet: Associated Press
Lengell, Sean: Washington Times
Leocha, Charles: Tripso.com
Leonatti, Andrew: Congress Daily
Leonhardt, David: New York Times
Lesnes, Corine: Le Monde
Lesparre, Michael: Votes in Congress Service
Lester, William: Associated Press
Leubsdorf, Carl: Dallas Morning News
Lever, Robert: Agence France-Presse
Levey, Noam: Los Angeles Times
Levin, Adam: Congressional Quarterly
Levin, Alan: USA Today
Levinson, Nathan: Congressional Quarterly
Lewis, Charles: Hearst Newspapers
Lewis, Finlay: Congressional Quarterly
Lewis, Neil: New York Times
Li, Jing: China News Service
Li, Zhenyu: China Press
Lichtblau, Eric: New York Times
Liebert, Larry: Bloomberg News
Lightman, David: McClatchy Newspapers
Lin, Betty: World Journal
Lindell, Cecile: Daily Deal
Lindeman, Eric: Energy Daily
Lipari, James: Associated Press
Liptak, Adam: New York Times
Lipton, Eric: New York Times
Litvan, Laura: Bloomberg News
Liu, Kuen-yuan: Central News Agency
Liu, Lina: Xinhua News Agency
Liu, Ping: China Times
Lizama, Orlando: EFE News Services
Lloyd, Janice: USA Today
Lobe, James: Inter Press Service
Lobianco, Tom: Washington Times
Lobsenz, George: Energy Daily
Locker, Ray: USA Today
Lockhead, Carolyn: San Francisco Chronicle
Lomax, Simon: Bloomberg News
Lopez, Jose: Notimex Mexican News Agency
Lorber, Sarah Jane: New York Times
Lott, John: Washington Times
Loubette, Celine: Agence France-Presse
Loven, Jennifer: Associated Press
Lovenheim, Sarah: Washington Post
Lowe, Christian: Military.com
Lowy, Joan: Associated Press

MEMBERS ENTITLED TO ADMISSION—Continued

Lozano, Laurent: Agence France-Presse
Lubold, Gordon: Christian Science Monitor
Luce, Edward: Financial Times
Luft, Kerry: Tribune Company
Lynch, David: USA Today
Lynch, Sarah: Dow Jones Newswires
Lytle, Tamara: Freelance
Macaron, Joe: Kuwait News Agency
Macaskill, Ewen: London Guardian
MacGillis, Alec: Washington Post
Mack, Kristen: Washington Post
Magner, Mike: Congress Daily
Mahabir, Karen: Associated Press
Maher, Aya: Asahi Shimbun
Make, Jonathan: Communications Daily
Malandain, Lucile: Agence France-Presse
Malenic, Maria: Defense Daily
Maler, Sandra: Reuters
Mann, Jason: Congress Daily
Mann, William: Associated Press
Mann, Windsor: Washington Times
Manning, Stephen: Associated Press
Mannion, James: Agence France-Presse
Mansfield, Matthew: Argus Media
Mantell, Ruth: MarketWatch
Mao, Li: Science & Technology Daily
Marcus, Aliza: Bloomberg News
Marcus, Ruth: Washington Post
Marenco, Julio Ernesto: La Prensa Grafica of El Salvador
Margasak, Lawrence: Associated Press
Margetta, Robert James: Congressional Quarterly
Marimow, Anne: Washington Post
Marino, Marie: Gannett News Service
Marklein, Mary Beth: USA Today
Markon, Jerome: Washington Post
Marrero, Diana: Milwaukee Journal Sentinel
Marsh, Julia: Yomiuri Shimbun
Marshall, Stephen: USA Today
Martin, Gary: San Antonio Express-News
Marutani, Hiroshi: Nikkei
Mascaro, Lisa: Las Vegas Sun
Mason, Jeff: Reuters
Mathes, Michael: Agence France-Presse
Mathews, Mark: Orlando Sentinel
Matthews, Robert Guy: Wall Street Journal
Matthews, William: Congressional Quarterly
Mattingly, Phil: Congressional Quarterly
Maynard, Michael: MarketWatch
Mazzetti, Mark: New York Times
McAuliff, Michael: New York Daily News
McCabe, Scott: Washington Examiner
McCarthy, Meghan: Congressional Quarterly
McCarthy, Mike: German Press Agency-DPA
McCarty, Courtney: Congressional Quarterly
McCarty, Mark: Medical Device Daily
McCaslin, John: Washington Times
McConnell, William: Daily Deal
McCormick, John: Chicago Tribune
McCoy, J. J.: Restructuring Today
McCutcheon, Chuck: Congressional Quarterly
McDermott, Ryan: Communications Daily
McDonald, Greg: Congressional Quarterly
McElhatton, Jr., James: Washington Times
McFeatters, Dale: Scripps Howard News Service
McGaughy, Lauren: Asahi Shimbun
McGreal, Chris: London Guardian
McKeever, Amy: Mainichi Shimbun
McKendry, Ian: Market News International
McKinnon, John: Wall Street Journal
McLean, Demian: Bloomberg News
McManus, Doyle: Los Angeles Times
McNeil, Margaret: MarketWatch
McPike, Erin: Congress Daily
McQuillan, Mark: Bloomberg News
McQuillen, William: Bloomberg News
Meadows, Clifford: New York Times
Meckler, Laura: Wall Street Journal
Meek, James: New York Daily News
Meinert, Peer: German Press Agency-DPA
Mekay, Emad: America In Arabic News Agency
Mekay, Emad: Inter Press Service
Melvin, Jasmin: Reuters
Memmott, Mark: USA Today
Memoli, Michael: Real Clear Politics
Mercer, Marsha: Mercer Media
Merida, Kevin: Washington Post
Merle, Renae: Washington Post
Meszoly, Robin: Bloomberg News
Metzler, Natasha: Associated Press
Meyer, Joshua: Los Angeles Times
Michaels, David: Dallas Morning News
Michaels, Jim: USA Today
Michalski, Patty: USA Today
Middleton, Chris: Bloomberg News
Miga, Andrew: Associated Press
Mikes, Zoltan: World Business Press
Mikkelsen, Randall: Reuters
Milbank, Dana: Washington Post
Miller, Greg: Los Angeles Times
Miller, Kristie: La Salle News Tribune
Miller, Mark: TVNewsday.com
Miller, Reuben: Merger Market of Financial Times
Miller, Richard: Bloomberg News
Miller, Steven: Washington Times
Miller, William: Washington Post
Milligan, Susan: Boston Globe
Millikin, David: Agence France-Presse
Mills, Betty: Griffin-Larrabee News Service
Miniter, Richard: Washington Times
Miroff, Nick: Washington Post
Mitchell, Joshua: Dow Jones Newswires
Miyazaki, Takeo: Yomiuri Shimbun
Mochizuki, Hirotsugu: Asahi Shimbun
Mohammed, Arshad: Reuters

MEMBERS ENTITLED TO ADMISSION—Continued

Molotsky, Irvin: Congress Daily
Moltz, David: Inside Higher Ed
Monge, Yolanda: El Pais
Montet, Virginie: Agence France-Presse
Montgomery, David: Washington Post
Montgomery, Lori: Washington Post
Morales, Armando: La Razon
Moran, Tessa: IFR Markets
Morello, Carol: Washington Post
Morgan, David: Reuters
Morris, Damiko: Associated Press
Morris, David: Congress Daily
Morse, Dan: Washington Post
Morton, Joseph: Omaha World-Herald
Moses, Rebekah: Asahi Shimbun
Moss, Daniel: Bloomberg News
Mott, Gregory: Bloomberg News
Mozgovaya, Natasha: Haaretz Daily
Mufson, Steven: Washington Post
Mulligan, John: Providence Journal
Mullins, Brody: Wall Street Journal
Mummolo, Jonathan: Washington Post
Mundy, Alicia: Wall Street Journal
Munoz-Acebes, Cesar: EFE News Services
Murayama, Yusuke: Asahi Shimbun
Murphy, Kathleen: Congressional Quarterly
Murray, Brendan: Bloomberg News
Murray, William: Oil Daily
Murti, Bhattiprolu: Dow Jones Newswires
Muscat, Sabine: Financial Times Deutschland
Mussenden, Sean: Media General News Service
Muth, Chaz: Catholic News Service
Mutikani, Lucia: Reuters
Myers, Jim: Tulsa World
Myers, Michael: Myers News Service
Mykkanen, Pekka: Helsingin Sanomat
Nagourney, Adam: New York Times
Nahmias, Melinda: Congressional Quarterly
Nail, Dawson: Communications Daily
Najor, Pamela: Argus Media
Nakamura, David: Washington Post
Nakashima, Ellen: Washington Post
Nakaya, Yuji: Kyodo News
Nasaw, Daniel: London Guardian
Nather, David: Congressional Quarterly
Nayar, Krishnan: Calcutta Telegraph
N'Diaye, Yali: Market News International
Neergaard, Lauran: Associated Press
Neubauer, Chuck: Washington Times
Neuman, Johanna: Los Angeles Times
Newhall, Marissa: Washington Post
Newman, Christopher: Argus Media
Nicholas, Peter: Los Angeles Times
Nichols, Hans: Bloomberg News
Niedowski, Erika: Abu Dhabi National
Nielsen, David: Scripps Howard News Service
Niles, Ryan: Wall Street Journal
Nishimura, Hiroshi: Akahata
Nishina, Michi: Kyodo News
Nixon, Ron: New York Times
Njuguna, Wangui: LRP Publications
Nkansah, E. Roy: Congressional Quarterly
Noel, Essex: Reuters
Noone, Dennis: Gannett Washington Bureau
Norington, Brad: Australian
Norman, Jane: Congressional Quarterly
Northey, Hannah: Argus Media
Norton, C. JoAnne: Bloomberg News
Norton, Emily: Congressional Quarterly
Noyes, Andrew: Congress Daily
Nutting, Brian: Congressional Quarterly
Nutting, Rex: MarketWatch
Nylen, Leah: Congressional Quarterly
O'Brien, Nancy: Catholic News Service
O'Connell, James: Bloomberg News
O'Connor, Sarah: Financial Times
Odion-Esence, Brai: Market News International
Odle, John Robert: Kyodo News
Ogata, Toshihiko: Asahi Shimbun
Ogawa, Satoshi: Yomiuri Shimbun
Ogle, Alexander: Agence France-Presse
Ohji, Tomoko: Mainichi Shimbun
Ohlemacher, Stephen: Associated Press
Ohlsson, Erik: Dagens Nyheter
Ohsumi, Ryu: Nikkei
Oikawa, Masaya: Mainichi Shimbun
Oishi, Itaru: Nikkei
Okada, Akihiro: Yomiuri Shimbun
Okamuto, Michiro: Yomiuri Shimbun
O'Keefe, Edward: Washington Post
Olchowy, Mark: Associated Press
Oliphant, James: Chicago Tribune
Olson, Elizabeth: New York Times
O'Neil, Anne: Argus Media
O'Reilly II, Joseph: Bloomberg News
Orndorff, Mary: Birmingham News
Orol, Ronald: MarketWatch
Orr, J. Scott: Newark Star-Ledger
Ostermann, Dietmar: Frankfurter Rundschau
Ota, Alan: Congressional Quarterly
Ourlian, Robert: Los Angeles Times
Overberg, Paul: USA Today
Ozyurt, Ahu: Milliyet
Pace, David: Associated Press
Page, Clarence: Chicago Tribune
Page, Susan: USA Today
Pakhomov, Alexander: Itar-Tass News Agency
Palank, Jacqueline: Dow Jones Newswires
Paletta, Damian: Wall Street Journal
Paley, Amit: Washington Post
Palmer, Avery: Congressional Quarterly
Palmer, Doug: Reuters
Palomo, Elvira: EFE News Services
Papantoniou, Lambros: Eleftheros Typos

MEMBERS ENTITLED TO ADMISSION—Continued

Parisi, Christina: Congressional Quarterly
Parisse, Emmanuel: Agence France-Presse
Park, Jungbin: Yonhap News Agency
Park, Kwang Duk: Korea Times
Park, Sang Hyun: Yonhap News Agency
Parker, Ashley: New York Times
Parker, Kathleen: Washington Post Writer's Group
Parks, Daniel: Congressional Quarterly
Parsons, Christi: Chicago Tribune
Passenheim, Antje: German Press Agency-DPA
Patel, Yogettaben: Dow Jones Newswires
Patrick, Richard: USA Today
Pattison, Mark: Catholic News Service
Pear, Robert: New York Times
Pearlstein, Steven: Washington Post
Peck, Louis: Congress Daily
Pelofsky, Jeremy: Reuters
Pena, Maria: EFE News Services
Perez, Anthony J.: USA Today
Perez, Evan: Wall Street Journal
Perine, Keith: Congressional Quarterly
Perkins, Mary: Yomiuri Shimbun
Perrone, Matthew: Associated Press
Pershing, Ben: Washington Post
Peterson, Molly: Bloomberg News
Phelps, Timothy: Los Angeles Times
Phillips, Kathleen: New York Times
Phillips, Lauren: Congressional Quarterly
Phillips, Michael: Wall Street Journal
Philpott, Thomas: Military Update
Pianin, Eric: Washington Post
Picani, Silvia: La Nacion
Pickard-Cambridge, Claire: Argus Media
Picket, Kerry: Washington Times
Pickler, Nedra: Associated Press
Pincus, Walter: Washington Post
Pine, Art: Congress Daily
Pitney, Nico: Huffington Post
Piper, Greg: Communications Daily
Piven, Benjamin: Yomiuri Shimbun
Pleming, Sue: Reuters
Plocek, Joseph: Market News International
Plungis, Jeff: Bloomberg News
Poirier, John: Reuters
Ponnudurai, Parameswaran: Agence France-Presse
Pope, Charles: Oregonian
Posner, Michael: Congress Daily
Potter, Mitchell: Toronto Star
Povich, Elaine: Congress Daily
Powell, Stewart: Hearst Newspapers
Power, Stephen: Wall Street Journal
Poyraxlar, Elcin: Cumhuriyet
Preciphs, Joi: Bloomberg News
Price, Deborah: Detroit News
Priest, Dana: Washington Post
Pruitt, Claude: USA Today
Przybyla, Heidi: Bloomberg News
Puente, Maria: USA Today
Pugh, Anthony: McClatchy Newspapers
Pulizzi, Henry: Dow Jones Newswires
Purce, Melinda: Associated Press
Purger, Tibor: Magyar Szo
Putman, Eileen: Associated Press
Puzzanghera, James: Los Angeles Times
Qiang, Zou: China Legal Daily
Qianliang, Yu: Xinhua News Agency
Quaid, Libby: Associated Press
Quinn, Andrew: Reuters
Raasch, Charles: Gannett News Service
Radnofsky, Louise: Wall Street Journal
Raimon, Marcelo: ANSA Italian News Agency
Rajagopalan, Sethuraman: Pioneer-India
Rajghatta, Chidanand: Times of India
Ramadan, Wafik: L'Orient-Le Jour
Ramaswamy, Anindita: German Press Agency-DPA
Rampton, Roberta: Reuters
Rankin, Robert: McClatchy Newspapers
Rascoe, Ayesha: Reuters
Rastello, Sandrine: Bloomberg News
Ratnam, Gopal: Bloomberg News
Raum, Thomas: Associated Press
Ray, Eric: Congressional Quarterly
Ray, Rachel: London Daily Telegraph
Raymond, Anthony: Political Money Line
Raymond, Jill: Congressional Quarterly
Reber, Paticia: German Press Agency-DPA
Recio, Maria: Fort Worth Star-Telegram
Redden, Elizabeth: Inside Higher Ed
Reddy, Sudeep: Wall Street Journal
Rehmann, Marc: Congressional Quarterly
Rehrmann, Laura: Gannett News Service
Reichard, John: Congressional Quarterly
Reid, Timothy: London Times
Reilly, Sean: Mobile Register
Rein, Lisa: Washington Post
Ren, Haijun: Xinhua News Agency
Retter, Daphne: New York Post
Reynolds, David: Dow Jones Newswires
Reynolds, Maura: Los Angeles Times
Reynolds Lewis, Katherine: Freelance
Ricci, Andrea: Reuters
Rice, Charles: Merger Market of Financial Times
Richardson, Betty: Congressional Quarterly
Richert, Catharine: Congressional Quarterly
Richey, Warren: Christian Science Monitor
Richter, Paul: Los Angeles Times
Richwine, Lisa: Reuters
Rickett, Keith: Associated Press
Rickman, Jonathan: Energy Daily
Riddell, Kelly: Bloomberg News
Riechmann-Kepler, Deb: Associated Press
Riley, Kim: LRP Publications
Riley, Lauren: Saudi Press Agency
Riley, Michael: Denver Post

MEMBERS ENTITLED TO ADMISSION—Continued

Riley, Michael: Congressional Quarterly
Risen, James: New York Times
Riskind, Jonathan: Columbus Dispatch
Rizzo, Katherine: Congressional Quarterly
Robb, Gregory: MarketWatch
Robbins, James: Washington Times
Roberts, Roxanne: Washington Post
Robinson, Eugene: Washington Post
Robinson, James: Los Angeles Times
Robinson, John: Defense Daily
Rogin, Joshua: Congressional Quarterly
Rohner, Mark: Bloomberg News
Roig, Carlos: USA Today
Roig-Franzia, Manuel: Washington Post
Romano, Lois: Washington Post
Roosevelt, Ann: Defense Daily
Rose, Matthew: Wall Street Journal
Rosen, James: McClatchy Newspapers
Rosenberg, Elizabeth: Argus Media
Rosenkrantz, Holly: Bloomberg News
Ross, Sonya: Associated Press
Roth, Bennett: Congressional Quarterly
Rowland, Kara: Washington Times
Rowley, James: Bloomberg News
Ruane, Michael: Washington Post
Rubin, Richard: Congressional Quarterly
Rucker, Patrick: Reuters
Rucker, Philip: Washington Post
Ruf, Renzo: Der Bund
Rugaber, Chris: Associated Press
Rulon Herman, Malia: Gannett Washington Bureau
Runningen, Roger: Bloomberg News
Rutenberg, Jim: New York Times
Rutherford, Emelie: Defense Daily
Ryan, Kiki: Washington Examiner
Ryan, Timothy: Reuters
Ryu, Jae-Hoon: Hankyoreh Daily
Sacks, Stephen: Tokyo Chunichi Shimbun
Sadeqi, Sherouq: Kuwait News Agency
Sadowski, Dennis: Catholic News Service
Saito, Nobuhiro: Mainichi Shimbun
Salant, Jonathan: Bloomberg News
Salcedo, Michele: Associated Press
Samukawa, Akira: Kyodo News
Sanchez, Humberto: Congress Daily
Sands, David: Washington Times
Sands, Ken: Congressional Quarterly
Sanger, David: New York Times
Sanner, Ann: Associated Press
Santini, Jean-Louis: Agence France-Presse
Saslow, Eli: Washington Post
Satter, Andrew: Congressional Quarterly
Savage, Charlie: New York Times
Savage, David: Los Angeles Times
Scally, William: William Scally Reports
Scannell, Kara: Wall Street Journal
Schatz, Amy: Wall Street Journal
Schatz, Joseph: Congressional Quarterly
Scheuble, Kristy: Bloomberg News
Schlesinger, Jacob: Wall Street Journal
Schlisserman, Courtney: Bloomberg News
Schmick, William: Bloomberg News
Schmid, Randolph: Associated Press
Schmidt, Robert: Bloomberg News
Schmitt, Eric: New York Times
Schneider, Andrew: Seattle Post-Intelligencer
Scholtes, Jennifer: Congressional Quarterly
Schoof, Renee: McClatchy Newspapers
Schouten, Fredreka: USA Today
Schroeder, Peter: Bond Buyer
Schroeder, Robert: MarketWatch
Schulte, Brigid: Washington Post
Schwed, Craig: Gannett News Service
Schweid, Barry: Associated Press
Scott, Heather: Market News International
Scully, Megan: Congress Daily
Seeley, Tina: Bloomberg News
Seib, Gerald: Wall Street Journal
Seibel, Mark: McClatchy Newspapers
Seper, Jerry: Washington Times
Sevastopulo, Demetri: Financial Times
Shackelford, Lucy: Washington Post
Shalal-Esa, Andrea: Reuters
Shane, Scott: New York Times
Shanker, Thomas: New York Times
Shapira, Ian: Washington Post
Shaw, John: Market News International
Shear, Michael: Washington Post
Sheikh, Nezar: Saudi Press Agency
Shepardson, David: Detroit News
Sheridan, Kerry Colleen: Agence France-Presse
Sheridan, Mary Beth: Washington Post
Sherman, Mark: LRP Publications
Sherman, Mark: Associated Press
Sherman, Paul: CapitalBeat.com
Sherzai, Magan: Agence France-Presse
Shields, Gerard: Baton Rouge Advocate
Shields, Mark: Creators Syndicate
Shields, Todd: Bloomberg News
Shimada, Akihiro: Tokyo Chunichi Shimbun
Shuppy, Anne: Congressional Quarterly
Sia, Richard: Congress Daily
Sichelman, Lew: United Media
Siddons, Andrew: Yomiuri Shimbun
Sidorov, Dmitry: Kommersant
Sidoti, Elizabeth: Associated Press
Silva, Mark: Chicago Tribune
Silvassy, Kathleen: Congressional Quarterly
Simmons, Christine: Associated Press
Simmons, Deborah: Washington Times
Simon, Neil: Media General News Service
Simon, Richard: Los Angeles Times
Simpson, Cameron: Wall Street Journal
Sisk, Richard: New York Daily News

MEMBERS ENTITLED TO ADMISSION—Continued

Sisto, Carrie: Argus Media
Sitov, Andrei: Itar-Tass News Agency
Skarzenski, Ronald: New York Times
Skorneck, Carolyn: Associated Press
Skotzko, Stacey: Congressional Quarterly
Slater, James: Agence France-Presse
Sloan, Steven: American Banker
Smith, Donna: Reuters
Smith, Elliot Blair: Bloomberg News
Smith, Jeffrey: Washington Post
Smith, Sylvia: Fort Wayne Journal Gazette
Smith, Veronica: Agence France-Presse
Smolkin, Rachel: USA Today
Snider, Michael: USA Today
Sniffen, Michael: Associated Press
Sobczyk, Joseph: Bloomberg News
Soga, Ian: Bloomberg News
Solomon, Deborah: Wall Street Journal
Solomon, John: Washington Times
Solomon, Jonathan: Wall Street Journal
Somashekhar, Sandhya: Washington Post
Somerville, Glenn: Reuters
Southall, Ashley: New York Times
Sowdwer-Staley, Megan: Congressional Quarterly
Spang, Thomas: Berliner Zeitung
Spangler, Todd: Detroit Free Press
Sparks, Sarah: LRP Publications
Spence, Matthew: London Times
Spence, Tony: Catholic News Service
Spencer, Samuel: Restructuring Today
Spiegel, Peter: Wall Street Journal
Spieler, Matthew: Congressional Quarterly
Spillius, Alexander: London Daily Telegraph
St. George, Donna: Washington Post
Stanek, Steven: Abu Dhabi National
Starks, Tim: Congressional Quarterly
Stein, Robert: Washington Post
Stempleman, Neil: Reuters
Stephens, Joe: Washington Post
Stern, Christopher: Bloomberg News
Stern, Seth: Congressional Quarterly
Sternberg, Steve: USA Today
Sternberg, William: USA Today
Sternstein, Aliya: Congressional Quarterly
Stevenson, Richard: New York Times
Stewart, Bruce Scott: Sankei Shimbun
Stewart, Nikita: Washington Post
Stockman, Farah: Boston Globe
Stohr, Greg: Bloomberg News
Stolberg, Sheryl: New York Times
Stone, Andrea: USA Today
Storey, David: Reuters
Stoughton, Stephenie: Associated Press
Stout, David: New York Times
Straus, Miriam: Congressional Quarterly
Stripling, John: ICIS News
Strobel, Warren: McClatchy Newspapers
Strohm, Chris: Congress Daily
Strong, Thomas: Associated Press
Stuever, Hank: Washington Post
Sturgeon, William: Tokyo Chunichi Shimbun
Sugimoto, Ichiro: Kyodo News
Sugita, Hiroki: Kyodo News
Sullivan, Andy: Reuters
Sullivan, Bartholomew: Scripps Howard News Service
Sullivan, Eileen: Associated Press
Sun, Lena: Washington Post
Superville, Darlene: Associated Press
Surzhanskiy, Andrey: Itar-Tass News Agency
Susami, Fumitaka: Kyodo News
Swann, Christopher: Bloomberg News
Swarns, Rachel: New York Times
Sweeney, Jeanne: LRP Publications
Sweet, Lynn: Chicago Sun-Times
Swindell, Bill: Congress Daily
Syeed, Nafeesa: Associated Press
Symes, Frances: Congressional Quarterly
Tachino, Junji: Asahi Shimbun
Tackett, Michael: Bloomberg News
Taillefer, Pierre: Agence France-Presse
Takahashi, Hiroyuki: Jiji Press
Takei, Toru: Kyodo News
Talev, Margaret: McClatchy Newspapers
Talley, Ian: Dow Jones Newswires
Tandon, Shaun: Agence France-Presse
Tankersley, James: Chicago Tribune
Tanzi, Alex: Bloomberg News
Tate, Curtis: McClatchy Newspapers
Tavara, Santiago: Notimex Mexican News Agency
Taylor, Andrew: Associated Press
Taylor, Marisa: McClatchy Newspapers
Teitelbaum, Michael: Congressional Quarterly
Temple-West, Patrick: Bond Buyer
Tessler, Joelle: Associated Press
Tetreault, Stephan: Stephens Media Group
Theimer, Sharon: Associated Press
Theobald, William: Gannett News Service
Thibodeaux, Sarah: Congressional Quarterly
Thibodeaux, Troy: Associated Press
Thiruvengadam, Meena: Dow Jones Newswires
Thomas, Helen: Hearst Newspapers
Thomas, Ken: Associated Press
Thomas, Richard: Votes In Congress Service
Thomasson, Dan: Scripps Howard News Service
Thomma, Steven: McClatchy Newspapers
Thompson, Cheryl: Washington Post
Thompson, Krissah: Washington Post
Thompson, Marilyn: Washington Post
Thompson, Robert: Washington Post
Tilove, Jonathan: New Orleans Times-Picayune
Tobe, Hajime: Kyodo News
Tokito, Mineko: Yomiuri Shimbun
Toles, Tom: Washington Post
Toloui-Semnani, Neda: Congressional Quarterly

MEMBERS ENTITLED TO ADMISSION—Continued

Tomasky, Michael: London Guardian
Tomkin, Robert: Congressional Quarterly
Tompson, Trevor: Associated Press
Toppo, Gregory: USA Today
Torobin, Jeremy: Bloomberg News
Torres, Carlos: Bloomberg News
Torres, Craig: Bloomberg News
Torry, Jack: Columbus Dispatch
Torry, Saundra: USA Today
Tranausky, Todd: Argus Media
Trankovits, Laszlo: German Press Agency-DPA
Trejos, Nancy: Washington Post
Trescott, Jacqueline: Washington Post
Trottman, Melanie: Wall Street Journal
Trowbridge, Gordon: Detroit News
Trygstad, Kyle: Real Clear Politics
Tsao, Nadia Y.F.: Liberty Times
Tucker, Boyd Neely: Washington Post
Tumgoren, Serdar: Congressional Quarterly
Tumulty, Brian: Gannett News Service
Tunks, Larry: Congressional Quarterly
Turley, Melissa: LRP Publications
Turque, Bill: Washington Post
Tyson, Ann Scott: Washington Post
Tyson, James: Bloomberg News
Ukai, Satoshi: Asahi Shimbun
Urano, Eri: Tokyo Chunichi Shimbun
Urban, Peter: Connecticut Post
Urdaneta, Diego: Agence France-Presse
Uy, Erin: LRP Publications
Vadala, Gregory: Congressional Quarterly
Val Mitjavila, Eusebio: La Vanguardia
Valentino, Paolo: Corriere Della Sera
Valery, Chantal: Agence France-Presse
Van Nostrand, Jim: McClatchy Newspapers
Vanden Brook, Tom: USA Today
Vanderbilt, Sarah: Congressional Quarterly
Vanderhaar, William: Associated Press
Vargas, Jose Antonio: Washington Post
Vargas, Theresa: Washington Post
Varsalona, Devin: Congressional Quarterly
Vaughan, Martin: Dow Jones Newswires
Veigle, Anne: Communications Daily
Vekshin, Alison: Bloomberg News
Venkannaiah, Krishna: Hindustan Times
Vergano, Dan: USA Today
Vicini, James: Reuters
Vidal Liy, Macarena: EFE News Services
Vineys, Kevin: Associated Press
Vogel, Stephen: Washington Post
Vogt, Christophe: Agence France-Presse
Volpe, Paul: Washington Post
Von Marschall, Christoph: Der Tagesspiegel
Vorman, Julie: Reuters
Wagman, Robert: Newspaper Enterprise
Wagner, Daniel: Associated Press
Wagner, John: Washington Post
Waitz, Nancy: Reuters
Walcott, John: McClatchy Newspapers
Wald, Matthew: New York Times
Walker, Emily: Medpagetoday.com
Wallbank, Derek: Congressional Quarterly
Wallsten, Peter: Los Angeles Times
Walters, Anne: German Press Agency-DPA
Wang, Herman: Chattanooga Times Free Press
Wang, Stephanie: Asahi Shimbun
Wang, Yu-Ting: Communications Daily
Wangsness, Lisa: Boston Globe
Ward, Andrew: Financial Times
Ward, Jon: Washington Times
Warminsky, Joseph: Congressional Quarterly
Warner, Judith: New York Times
Warren, Timothy: Washington Times
Warrick, Joby: Washington Post
Watanabe, Hiroo: Sankei Shimbun
Watson, Traci: USA Today
Watters, Susan: Fairchild News Service
Wayne, Alexander: Congressional Quarterly
Wayne, Leslie: New York Times
Webber, Caitlin: Congressional Quarterly
Weekes, Jr., Michael: Reuters
Wehrman, Jessica: Dayton Daily News
Wei, Jing: Xinhua News Agency
Wei, Wang: Xinhua News Agency
Weiner, Mark: Syracuse Post-Standard
Weinstein, Matthew: Congressional Quarterly
Weir, Kytja: Washington Examiner
Weisman, Jonathan: Wall Street Journal
Weiss, Eric: Washington Post
Weiss, Miles Geoffrey: Bloomberg News
Welch, James: USA Today
Wellisz, Chris: Bloomberg News
Wells, Letitia: McClatchy Newspapers
Wells, Robert: Dow Jones Newswires
Werner, Erica: Associated Press
Wessel, David: Wall Street Journal
West, Paul: Baltimore Sun
Westbrook, Jesse: Bloomberg News
Westley, Brian: Associated Press
Wetzstein, Cheryl: Washington Times
Weyl, Ben: Congressional Quarterly
White, Dina: Chicago Tribune
White, Gordon: Washington Telecommunications Services
White, Joseph: Wall Street Journal
White, Josh: Washington Post
White, Keith: Congress Daily
White, Jr., Joseph: Associated Press
Whitesides, John: Reuters
Whitmire, Guy: Congressional Quarterly
Whitten, Daniel: Bloomberg News
Whoriskey, Peter: Washington Post
Wilkison, David: Associated Press
Williams, Jr., Joseph: Boston Globe
Williamson, Elizabeth: Wall Street Journal

MEMBERS ENTITLED TO ADMISSION—Continued

Willis, Robert: Bloomberg News
Wilson, George: Congress Daily
Wilson, Patricia: Reuters
Wilson, Scott: Washington Post
Winicour, Daniel: Congressional Quarterly
Winski, Joe: Bloomberg News
Wirzbicki, Alan: Boston Globe
Witcover, Jules: Tribune Media Services
Witkowski, Nancy Benac: Associated Press
Woellert, Lorraine: Bloomberg News
Wolf, Daniel: Scripps Howard News Service
Wolf, Jim: Reuters
Wolf, Richard: USA Today
Wolfe, Frank: LRP Publications
Wolfe, Kathryn: Congressional Quarterly
Woo, Yee Ling: Congressional Quarterly
Wood, David: Baltimore Sun
Woodward, Bob: Washington Post
Woodward, Calvin: Associated Press
Wu, Qing Cai: China News Service
Wuetherich, Peter: Agence France-Presse
Wutkowski, Karey: Reuters
Wynn, Randall: Congressional Quarterly
Xian, Wen: China People's Daily
Xiangwen, Ge: Xinhua News Agency
Xiao-Jing, Du: China Press
Xiong, Min: 21st Century Business Herald
Xuejiang, Li: China People's Daily
Yada, Toshihiko: Yomiuri Shimbun
Yamada, Tetsuro: Yomiuri Shimbun
Yamamoto, Hideya: Sankei Shimbun
Yamour, Heather: Kuwait News Agency
Yan, Feng: Xinhua News Agency
Yancey, Matthew: Associated Press
Yang, Liming: China Youth Daily
Yang, Quinchuan: Xinhua News Agency
Yano, Kimiko: Kyodo News
Yasunaga, Tatsuro: Kyodo News
Yaukey, John: Gannett News Service
Yen, Hope: Associated Press
Yoder, Eric: Washington Post
Yoest, Patrick: Dow Jones Newswires
Yoneyama, Yusuke: Nikkei
Yoon, Kyongho: Maeil Business Newspaper
York, Byron: Washington Examiner
Yost, Pete: Associated Press
Young, Donna: BioWorld Today
Young, Kerry: Congressional Quarterly
Young, Mark: Media General News Service
Younglai, Rachelle: Reuters
Youssef, Nancy: McClatchy Newspapers
Yu, Donghui: China Press
Zabarenko, Deborah: Reuters
Zacharia, Janine: Bloomberg News
Zagaroli, Lisa: McClatchy Newspapers
Zajac, Andrew: Chicago Tribune
Zak, Dan: Washington Post
Zakaria, Tabassum: Reuters
Zamora Barcelo, Jordi: Agence France-Presse
Zapor, Patricia: Catholic News Service
Zeitvogel, Karin: Agence France-Presse
Zeleny, Jeff: New York Times
Zeller,. Shawn: Congressional Quarterly
Zhang, Jane: Wall Street Journal
Zhao, Yi: Xinhua News Agency
Zhu, Xingfu: Shanghai Wenhui Daily
Zibel, Alan: Associated Press
Ziener, Markus: Handelsblatt
Zimmerman, Carol: Catholic News Service
Zitner, Aaron: Los Angeles Times
Zlodorev, Dmitri: Itar-Tass News Agency
Zongker, Brett: Associated Press
Zoroya, Gregg: USA Today
Zoupaniotis, Apostolos: Cyprus News Agency
Zremski, Jerry: Buffalo News
Zwelling, Michael: Restructuring Today

NEWSPAPERS REPRESENTED IN PRESS GALLERIES

House Gallery 225–3945, 225–6722   Senate Gallery 224–0241

21ST CENTURY BUSINESS HERALD—(202) 431–1526; 1706 Euclid Street, NW., Washington, DC 20009: Min Xiong.

ABIM—(703) 243–2104; 1344 Merrie Ridge Road, McLean, VA 22101: Mario Navarro da Costa.

ABU DHABI NATIONAL—(202) 662–7086; 1081 National Press Building, Washington, DC 20045: Erika Niedowski, Steven Stanek.

AGENCE FRANCE-PRESSE—(202) 414–0541; 1500 K Street, NW., Suite 600, Washington, DC 20036: Patrick Baert, Andrew Beatty, Daphne Benoit, Joanna Biddle, Lachlan Carmichael, Myriam Chaplain, Stephen Collinson, Guillaume Decamme, Daniel DeLuce, Francisco Ferrari, Sandra Ferrer, Frederic Galan, Stephanie Griffith, Edouard Guihaire, Carlos Hamann, Olivia Hampton, Charlotte Hill, Hugues Honore, Sara Hussein, Jitendra Joshi, Marc Jourdier, Maxim Kniazkov, Olivier Knox, Michael Langan, Sylvie Lanteaume, David Christopher Lefkow, Robert Lever, Celine Loubette, Laurent Lozano, Lucile Malandain, James Mannion, Michael Mathes, David Millikin, Virginie Montet, Alexander Ogle, Emmanuel Parisse, Parameswaran Ponnudurai, Jean-Louis Santini, Kerry Colleen Sheridan, Magan Sherzai, James Slater, Veronica Smith, Pierre Taillefer, Shaun Tandon, Diego Urdaneta, Chantal Valery, Christophe Vogt, Peter Wuetherich, Jordi Zamora Barcelo, Karin Zeitvogel.

AKAHATA—(202) 393–5238; 978 National Press Building, Washington, DC 20045: Toshiya Kobayashi Hiroshi Nishimura.

AL RAI—(202) 561–9154; 1210 Massachusetts Avenue, Washington, DC 20005: Abdul-Hussain Hussain.

ALBUQUERQUE JOURNAL—(202) 662–7488; 1111 National Press Building, Washington, DC 20045: Michael Coleman.

AL-HAYAT—(202) 783–5544; 1185 National Press Building, Washington, DC 20045: Joyce Karam.

ALLAFRICA.COM—(202) 546–0777; 920 M Street, SE., Washington, DC 20003: Tamela Hultman, Reed Kramer.

ALLENTOWN MORNING CALL—(202) 824–8216; 1025 F Street, NW., Washington, DC 20004: Josh Drobnyk.

AMERICA IN ARABIC NEWS AGENCY—(202) 372–5919; 1293 National Press Building, Washington, DC 20045: Emad Mekay.

AMERICAN BANKER—(202) 434–0317; 4401 Wilson Boulevard, Arlington, VA 20005: Joseph Adler, Emily Flitter, Cheyenne Hopkins, Stacy Lynn Kaper, Steven Sloan.

ANSA ITALIAN NEWS AGENCY—(202) 628–3317; 1285 National Press Building, Washington, DC 20045: Marcello Campo, Luciano Clerico, Cristiano Del Riccio, Marcelo Raimon.

ARGUS MEDIA—(202) 775–0240; 1012 14th Street, Suite 1500, Washington, DC 20005: Ross Allen, Michael Ball, Abby Caplan, Molly Christian, Givco Grancharov, David Ivanovich, Matthew Mansfield, Pamela Najor, Christopher Newman, Hannah Northey, Anne O'Neil, Claire Pickard-Cambridge, Elizabeth Rosenberg, Carrie Sisto, Todd Tranausky.

ARKANSAS DEMOCRAT-GAZETTE—(202) 662–7690; 1190 National Press Building, Washington, DC 20045: Alex Daniels, Jane Fullerton.

ARTISTS & WRITERS SYNDICATE—(703) 820–4232; 6325 Beachway Drive, Falls Church, VA 22044: Frank Aukofer.

ASAHI SHIMBUN—(202) 783–1000; 1022 National Press Building, Washington, DC 20045: Emma Ashburn, Brian Clampitt, Erin Connealy, Hiroshi Ito, Yoichi Kato, Toshihiko Katsuda, Yuko Lanham, Aya Maher, Lauren McGaughy, Hirotsugu Mochizuki, Rebekah Moses, Yusuke Murayama, Toshihiko Ogata, Junji Tachino, Satoshi Ukai, Stephanie Wang.

ASSOCIATED PRESS—(202) 641–9400; 1100 13th Street, NW., Suite 700, Washington, DC 20005: James Abrams, Ricardo Alonso-Zaldivar, Matt Apuzzo, John Jay Arnold, Jeannine Aversa, Charles Babington, Lolita Baldor, Matthew Barakat, Devlin Barrett, Brett Blackledge, Donna Borak, Seth Borenstein, Stephen Braun, Ted Bridis, Robert Burns, Desmond Butler, Dana Cappiello, Connie Cass, Donna Cassata, Shawn Chen, Dennis Conrad, Martin Crutsinger, Matthew Daly, Douglass Daniel, Elizabeth Davidz, Julie Davis, Jim Drinkard, Harry Dunphy, Ronald Edmonds, Jr., Donald Elkins, Philip Elliott, David Espo, Ben Evans, Carole Feldman, Ben Feller, Howard Fendrich, Anne Flaherty, Matt Ford, Ron Fournier, Alan Fram, Kevin Freking, Frederic Frommer, Robert Furlow, Suzanne Gamboa, Gillian Gaynair, Anne Gearan, Robert Glass, Shawn Gomez, Marcy Gordon, Ken Guggenheim, Sam Hananel, Merrill Hartson, H. Josef Hebert, Kimberly Hefling, John Heilprin, Gregory Henderson, John Henry, Pamela Hess, Earl Hinton, Jesse Holland, Terence Hunt, Steven Hurst, Nestor Ikeda, Henry Jackson, Lara Jakes, Mary Clare Jalonick, Pauline Jelinek, Kory Jessen, Dennis Junius, Sarah Karush, Laurie Kellman Blazar, Jennifer Kerr, Eric Klimek, Foster Klug, Steven Komarow, Jim Kuhnhenn,

NEWSPAPERS REPRESENTED—Continued

Kamala Lane, Richard Lardner, Matthew Lee, Janet Leissner, William Lester, James Lipari, Jennifer Loven, Joan Lowy, Karen Mahabir, William Mann, Stephen Manning, Lawrence Margasak, Natasha Metzler, Andrew Miga, Damiko Morris, Lauran Neergaard, Stephen Ohlemacher, Mark Olchowy, David Pace, Matthew Perrone, Nedra Pickler, Melinda Purce, Eileen Putman, Libby Quaid, Thomas Raum, Keith Rickett, Deb Riechmann-Kepler, Sonya Ross, Chris Rugaber, Michele Salcedo, Ann Sanner, Randolph Schmid, Barry Schweid, Mark Sherman, Elizabeth Sidoti, Christine Simmons, Carolyn Skorneck, Michael Sniffen, Stephenie Stoughton, Thomas Strong, Eileen Sullivan, Darlene Superville, Nafeesa Syeed, Andrew Taylor, Joelle Tessler, Sharon Theimer, Troy Thibodeaux, Ken Thomas, Trevor Tompson, William Vanderhaar, Kevin Vineys, Daniel Wagner, Erica Werner, Brian Westley, Joseph White, Jr., David Wilkison, Nancy Benac Witkowski, Calvin Woodward, Matthew Yancey, Hope Yen, Pete Yost, Alan Zibel, Brett Zongker.

ATLANTA JOURNAL CONSTITUTION—(202) 887–8380; 400 North Capitol Street, NW., Suite 750, Washington, DC 20001: Bob Keefe.

AUSTRALIAN—(202) 628–7079; 446 National Press Building, Washington, DC 20045: Geoff Elliott, Brad Norington.

BALTIMORE SUN—(202) 824–8410; 1090 Vermont Avenue, NW., Washington, DC 20005: Jeffrey Barker, Paul West, David Wood.

BATON ROUGE ADVOCATE—(202) 554–0458; S–316 U.S. Capitol, Washington, DC 20510: Gerard Shields.

BERGEN RECORD—(202) 249–2160; 1701 16th Street, NW., Washington, DC 20008: Herbert Jackson.

BERLINER ZEITUNG—(301) 762–9661; 1717 Sunrise Drive, Rockville, MD 20854: Dietmar Ostermann.

BIOWORLD TODAY—(202) 739–9556; 1725 K Street, NW., Suite 700, Washington, DC 20006: Donna Young.

BIRMINGHAM NEWS—(202) 744–5574; 700 12th Street, NW., Washington, DC 20005: Mary Orndorff.

BLOOMBERG NEWS—(202) 624–1800; 1399 New York Avenue, 11th Floor, Washington, DC 20005: Christopher Anstey, Laurie Asseo, Charles Babcock, Terrence Barrett, Matthew Benjamin, Max Berley, John Berry, Alan Bjerga, Jeffrey Bliss, Justin Blum, Romaine Bostick, John Brinsley, Timothy Burger, Andy Burt, Anthony Capaccio, Margaret Chadbourn, Shobhana Chandra, Edwin Chen, Kimberly Chipman, Rebecca Christie, Sonya Cooper, Gadi Dechter, Susan Decker, Vincent Del Giudice, Edward DeMarco, Catherine Dodge, Ryan Donmoyer, Mark Drajem, Bob Drummond, Curtis Eichelberger, Nadine Elsibai, Daniel Enoch, Brian Faler, Ken Fireman, Alison Fitzgerald, Michael Forsythe, Joshua Gallu, Nicole Gaouette, Viola Gienger, Julianna Goldman, Avram Goldstein, Vince Golle, Brigitte Greenberg, Robert Greene, Angela Greiling Keane, Dan Hart, Timothy Homan, John Hughes, Ann Hughey, Albert Hunt, Kristin Jensen, Nicholas Johnston, Ian Katz, Nancy Kercheval, Jim Kirk, Alison Kodjak-Fitzgerald, Dawn Kopecki, Indira Lakashmanan, Scott Lanman, Catherine Larkin, Larry Liebert, Laura Litvan, Simon Lomax, Aliza Marcus, Demian McLean, Mark McQuillan, William McQuillen, Robin Meszoly, Chris Middleton, Richard Miller, Daniel Moss, Gregory Mott, Brendan Murray, Hans Nichols, C. JoAnne Norton, James O'Connell, Joseph O'Reilly II, Molly Peterson, Jeff Plungis, Joi Preciphs, Heidi Przybyla, Sandrine Rastello, Gopal Ratnam, Kelly Riddell, Mark Rohner, Holly Rosenkrantz, James Rowley, Roger Runningen, Jonathan Salant, Kristy Scheuble, Courtney Schlisserman, William Schmick, Robert Schmidt, Tina Seeley, Todd Shields, Elliot Blair Smith, Joseph Sobczyk, Ian Soga, Christopher Stern, Greg Stohr, Christopher Swann, Michael Tackett, Alex Tanzi, Jeremy Torobin, Carlos Torres, Craig Torres, James Tyson, Alison Vekshin, Miles Geoffrey Weiss, Chris Wellisz, Jesse Westbrook, Daniel Whitten, Robert Willis, Joe Winski, Lorraine Woellert, Janine Zacharia.

BOND BUYER—(202) 434–0300; 4401 Wilson Boulevard, Suite 910, Arlington, VA 22203: Andrew Ackerman, Audrey Dutton, Lynne Funk, Lynn Hume, Peter Schroeder, Patrick Temple-West.

BOSTON GLOBE—(202) 857–5050; 1130 Connecticut Avenue, Suite 520, Washington, DC 20036: Bryan Bender, Peter Canellos, Sasha Issenberg, Michael Kranish, Susan Milligan, Farah Stockman, Lisa Wangsness, Joseph Williams, Jr., Alan Wirzbicki.

BUFFALO NEWS—(202) 737–3188; 841 National Press Building, Washington, DC 20045: Jerry Zremski.

CALCUTTA TELEGRAPH—(301) 654–6008; 5500 Friendship Boulevard Suite, Suite 1217, Chevy Chase, MD 20815: Krishnan Nayar.

CANWEST NEWS SERVICE—(202) 662–7576; 1206 National Press Building, Washington, DC 20045: Sheldon Alberts.

CAPITAL CONNECTIONS—(202) 337–2044; 1698 32nd Street, NW., Washington, DC 20007: Karen Feld.

CAPITALBEAT.COM—(202) 546–8903; 325 Pennsylvania Avenue SE., Suite 250, Washington, DC 20003: Paul Sherman.

CATHOLIC NEWS SERVICE—(202) 541–3275; 3211 Fourth Street, NE., Washington, DC 20017: Julie Asher, Barbara Fraze, Nancy Hartnagel, Chaz Muth, Nancy O'Brien, Mark Pattison, Dennis Sadowski, Tony Spence, Patricia Zapor, Carol Zimmerman.

CENTRAL NEWS AGENCY—(703) 207–0223; 1173 National Press Building, Washington, DC 20045: Kuen-yuan Liu.

CHATTANOOGA TIMES FREE PRESS—(202) 468–3182; 3722 Van Ness Street, NW., Washington, DC 20016: Herman Wang.

NEWSPAPERS REPRESENTED—Continued

CHICAGO SUN-TIMES—(202) 662–8808; 1206 National Press Building, Washington, DC 20045: Lynn Sweet.

TRIBUNE—(202) 824–8200; 1025 F Street, NW., Suite 700, Washington, DC 20004: Mike Dorning, Frank James, John McCormick, James Oliphant, Clarence Page, Christi Parsons, Mark Silva, James Tankersley, Dina White, Andrew Zajac.

CHINA LEGAL DAILY—(571) 331–1916; 2111 Jefferson Davis Highway, Apartment 1109, Arlington, VA 22202: Zou Qiang.

CHINA NEWS SERVICE—(571) 315–1266; 2200 North Westmoreland Street, Suite 503, Arlington, VA 22213: Jing Li, Qing Cai Wu.

CHINA PEOPLE'S DAILY—(703) 648–1298; 2506 Falls Mere Court, Falls Church, VA 22202: Wen Xian, Li Xuejiang.

CHINA PRESS—(703) 289–6651; 4100 Massachusetts Avenue, NW., Apartment 119, Washington, DC 20016: Zhenyu Li, Du Xiao-Jing, Donghui Yu.

CHINA TIMES—(202) 347–5670; 952 National Press Building, Washington, DC 20045: Ping Liu.

CHINA YOUTH DAILY—(202) 344–5416; 1600 South Eads Street, Apartment 805N, Arlington, VA 22202: Ju Hui, Liming Yang.

CHOSUN ILBO—(202) 783–4236; 1291 National Press Building, Washington, DC 20045: Ha Won Lee.

CHRISTIAN SCIENCE MONITOR—(202) 481–6650; 910 16th Street, Suite 200, Washington, DC 20006: Gail Chaddock, Dante Chinni, David Cook, Linda Feldmann, Peter Grier, Francine Kiefer, Howard La Franchi, Gordon Lubold, Warren Richey.

CLARIN—(202) 737–4850; 988 National Press Building, Washington, DC 20045: Ana Baron.

CLEVELAND PLAIN DEALER—(202) 638–1366; 930 National Press Building, Washington, DC 20045: Sabrina Eaton.

CNET NEWS.COM—(202) 686–1202; 4501 Connecticut Avenue, NW., Suite 422, Washington, DC 20008: Stephanie Condon.

COLUMBUS DISPATCH—(202) 824–6766; 400 North Capitol Street, Suite 750, Washington, DC 20001: Jonathan Riskind, Jack Torry (202) 824–6765.

COMMUNICATIONS DAILY—(202) 872–9200; 2115 Ward Court, NW., Washington, DC 20037: Adam Bender, Howard Buskirk, Leslie Cantu, Virgil Dickson, Dinesh Kumar, Jonathan Make, Ryan McDermott, Dawson Nail, Greg Piper, Anne Veigle, Yu-Ting Wang.

CONGRESS DAILY—(202) 739–8400; 600 New Hampshire Avenue, NW., Washington, DC 20037: Peter Bell, Kenneth Chamberlain, Peter Cohn, George Condon Jr., Carey Dann, Jason Dick, Anna Edney, Helen Fessenden, Michael Fox, Daniel Friedman, Kathy Gambrell, Darren Goode, Shihoko Goto, Juliana Gruenwald, David Hatch, David Hess, Billy House, Kasie Hunt, Charles Jordan, Bob Kemper, Terence Kivlan, Otto Kreisher, Andrew Leonatti, Mike Magner, Jason Mann, .Erin McPike, Irvin Molotsky, David Morris, Andrew Noyes, Louis Peck, Art Pine, Michael Posner, Elaine Povich, Humberto Sanchez, Megan Scully, Richard Sia, Chris Strohm, Bill Swindell, Keith White, George Wilson.

CONGRESSIONAL QUARTERLY—(202) 419–8515; 1255 22nd Street, NW., Washington, DC 20037: Rebecca Adams, Adjoa Adofo, Alan Ahlrich, Ifedayo Akinwande, Syed Ali, Kent Allen, Amanda Allen, Jonathan Allen, Joanna Anderson, Martha Angle, Andrew Armstrong, Melissa Attias, James Barker, David Baumann, Jamie Baylis, Robert Benenson, Susan Benkelman, Clea Benson, Adriel Bettelheim, Arwen Adams Bicknell, John Bicknell, Joel Bowen, Jonathan Broder, Ronald Brodmann, Emily Cadei, James Carroll, Linda Cartwright, Mike Christensen, David Clarke, George Codrea, Charles Conlon, Maureen Conners, Neal Conway, Jessica Coomes, Jessica Benton Cooney, John Cranford, Coral Davenport, Kate Davidson, David Davis, Karoun Demirjian, John Dineen, John Donnelly, Bruce Drake, Loren Duggan, Emma Dumain, Toby Eckert, Edward Epstein, Emily Ethridge, Daniel Fowler, Jamey Fry, Marilyn Gates-Davis, Lydia Gensheimer, Sasha Ghosh-Siminoff, Gregory Giroux, Jonathan Goldberg, Reese Goldsmith, Norman Gomlak, Adam Graham-Silverman, Kimberly Hallock, Thomas Hannett, David Hawkings, Robert Healy, Caitlin Hendel, Paul Hendrie, David Higgins, Leslie Hoffecker, Charles Hoskinson, Anne Hoy, Kathleen Hunter, John Irons, Colby Itkowitz, Benton Ives-Halperin, Bart Jansen, Shweta Jha, Matthew Johnson, Annie Johnson, Kerry Jones, Patricia Joy, Rachel Kapochunas, Noella Kertes, Kayvon Khaledi, Anne Kim, Angela Kim, Peter King, Alex Knott, Matthew Korade, Paul Krawzak, Adrianne Kroepsch, Carliner Leah, Chris Lehmann, Adam Levin, Nathan Levinson, Finlay Lewis, Robert James Margetta, William Matthews, Phil Mattingly, Meghan McCarthy, Courtney McCarty, Chuck McCutcheon, Greg McDonald, Kathleen Murphy, Melinda Nahmias, David Nather, E. Roy Nkansah, Jane Norman, Emily Norton, Brian Nutting, Leah Nylen, Alan Ota, Avery Palmer, Christina Parisi, Daniel Parks, Keith Perine, Lauren Phillips, Eric Ray, Jill Raymond, Marc Rehmann, John Reichard, Betty Richardson, Catharine Richert, Michael Riley, Katherine Rizzo, Joshua Rogin, Bennett Roth, Richard Rubin, Ken Sands, Andrew Satter, Joseph Schatz, Jennifer Scholtes, Anne Shuppy, Kathleen Silvassy, Stacey Skotzko, Megan Sowdwer-Staley, Matthew Spieler, Tim Starks, Seth Stern, Aliya Sternstein, Miriam Straus, Frances Symes, Michael Teitelbaum, Sarah Thibodeaux, Neda Toloui-Semnani, Robert Tomkin, Serdar Tumgoren, Larry Tunks, Gregory Vadala, Sarah Vanderbilt, Devin Varsalona, Derek Wallbank, Joseph Warminsky, Alexander Wayne, Caitlin Webber, Matthew Weinstein, Ben Weyl, Guy Whitmire, Daniel Winicour, Kathryn Wolfe, Yee Ling Woo, Randall Wynn, Kerry Young, Shawn Zeller.

NEWSPAPERS REPRESENTED—Continued

CONNECTICUT POST—(202) 662–8927; 1255 National Press Building, Washington, DC 20045: Peter Urban.

CORRIERE DELLA SERA—(202) 383–2788; 700 12th Street, NW., Suite 1000, Washington, DC 20005: Paolo Valentino.

CREATORS SYNDICATE—(202) 662–1255; 5777 West Century Boulevard, Suite 700, Los Angeles CA 90045: Mark Shields.

CUMHURIYET—(202) 758–3222; 603 A Street, SE., Washington, DC 20003: Elcin Poyraxlar.

CYPRUS NEWS AGENCY—(646) 286–9640; 1125 6th Street, NE., Washington, DC 20002: Apostolos Zoupaniotis.

DAGENS NYHETER—(202) 429–0134; 1001 Connecticut Avenue, NW., Suite 428, Washington, DC 20036: Erik Ohlsson.

DAILY DEAL—(202) 429–2991; 1775 K Street, Suite 590, Washington, DC 20006: Cecile Lindell, William McConnell.

DALLAS MORNING NEWS—(202) 661–8410; 1325 G Street, Suite 250, Washington, DC 20005: Alfredo Corchado, Todd Gillman, James Landers, Carl Leubsdorf, David Michaels.

DAYTON DAILY NEWS—(202) 887–8328; 400 North Capitol Street, NW., Washington, DC 20001: Jessica Wehrman.

DEFENSE DAILY—(703) 522–5655; 1500 Wilson Boulevard, Suite 515, Arlington, VA 22209: David Ahearn, Geoff Fein, Maria Malenic, John Robinson, Ann Roosevelt, Emelie Rutherford.

DENVER POST—(202) 662–8907; 1255 National Press Building, Washington, DC 20010: Michael Riley.

DER BUND—(202) 403–7115; 31 Kennedy Street, NW., Apartment 202, Washington, DC 20011: Renzo Ruf.

DER TAGESSPIEGEL—(202) 686–3547; 3200 Patterson Street, NW., Washington, DC 20015: Christoph Von Marschall.

DES MOINES REGISTER—(202) 906–8138; 1100 New York Avenue, Washington, DC 20005: Philip Brasher.

DETROIT FREE PRESS—(202) 906–8204; 1100 New York Avenue, Suite 200E, Washington, DC 20005: Justin Hyde, Todd Spangler.

DETROIT NEWS—1255 National Press Building, Washington, DC 20045: Deborah Price (202) 906–8205, David Shepardson (202) 662–8378, Gordon Trowbridge (202) 662–8378.

DOW JONES NEWSWIRES—(202) 862–9200; 1025 Connecticut Avenue, Suite 800, Washington, DC 20036: Mark Anderson, Tom Barkley, Jeffrey Bater, Brian Blackstone, Corey Boles, Judith Burns, Anthony Cooke, Jennifer Corbett Dooren, Michael Crittenden, Jared Favole, Jessica Holzer, Darrell Hughes, Siobhan Hughes, Maya Jackson-Randall, Fawn Johnson, Brian Kalish, Brent Kendall, Sarah Lynch, Joshua Mitchell, Bhattiprolu Murti, Jacqueline Palank, Yogettaben Patel, Henry Pulizzi, David Reynolds, Ian Talley, Meena Thiruvengadam, Martin Vaughan, Robert Wells, Patrick Yoest.

EFE NEWS SERVICES—(202) 745–7692; 1220 National Press Building, Washingon, DC 20045: Celine Aemisegger, Maria Azpiazu, Jorge Banales, Teresa Bouza, Maribel El Hamti, Francisco Gonzalez, Orlando Lizama, Cesar Munoz-Acebes, Elvira Palomo, Maria Pena, Macarena Vidal Liy.

EL DIARIO DE HOY—(571) 278–1321; 603 South Adams Street, Arlington, VA 22204: Tomas Guevara.

EL NUEVO DIA—(202) 662–7360; 960d National Press Building, Washington, DC 20045: Jose Delgado.

EL PAIS—(202) 638–7604; 1134 National Press Building, Washington, DC 20045: David Alandete, 20045: Antonio Caño, Yolanda Monge.

EL PERIODICO DE CATALUNYA—(202) 352–4153; 6406 Ruffin Road, Chevy Chase, MD 20815: Juan Cañete Bayle.

EL TIEMPO—(202) 607–5929; 1102 National Press Building, Washington, DC 20045: Sergio Gomez.

EL UNIVERSAL—(202) 262–6656; 1193 National Press Building, Washington, DC 20045: Jose Hernandez.

ELEFTHEROS TYPOS—(202) 675–0697; 784 National Press Building, Washington, DC 20045: Lambros Papantoniou.

ENERGY DAILY—(703) 358–9201; 1500 Wilson Boulevard, Suite 515, Arlington, VA 22209: Jeff Beattie, Christopher Holly, Llewellyn King, Eric Lindeman, George Lobsenz, Jonathan Rickman.

ETHNOS GREECE—(202) 361–7843; 1133 14th Street, NW., Suite 507, Washington, DC 20005: Michail Ignatiou.

EUROPOLITICS—(202) 758–8462; 1200 5th Street, #203, Washington, DC 20001: Brian Beary.

FAIRCHILD NEWS SERVICE—(202) 496–4975; 1050 17th Street, NW., Suite 600, Washington, DC 20036: Elizabeth Casabona, Kristi Ellis, Susan Watters.

FINANCIAL TIMES—(202) 289–5474; 1023 15th Street, NW., Washington, DC 20005: Alan Beattie, Tom Braithwaite, Daniel Dombey, Krishna Guha, Edward Luce, Sarah O'Connor, Demetri Sevastopulo, Andrew Ward.

FINANCIAL TIMES DEUTSCHLAND—(202) 588–9411; 1023 15th Street, NW., Suite 700, Washington, DC 20005: Sabine Muscat.

FORT WAYNE JOURNAL GAZETTE—(202) 879–6710; 551 National Press Building, Washington, DC 20045: Sylvia Smith.

FORT WORTH STAR-TELEGRAM—(202) 383–6103; 700 12th Street, NW., Suite 1000, Washington, DC 20005: Maria Recio.

NEWSPAPERS REPRESENTED—Continued

FRANKFURTER RUNDSCHAU—(301) 762–9661; 1717 Sunrise Drive, Rockville, MD 20854: Dietmar Ostermann.

FREELANCE—(202) 824–8255; 1025 F Street, NW., Suite 700, Washington, DC 20004: Tamara Lytle.

FREELANCE—(301) 767–9830; 8307 Rising Ridgeway, Bethesda, MD 20817: Katherine Reynolds Lewis.

GANNETT WASHINGTON BUREAU—(202) 906–8100; 1100 New York Avenue, Washington, DC 20005: Deborah Berry, Larry Bivins, Sammie Chan, Raju Chebium, Val Ellicott, Maria Fowler, Maureen Groppe, Alethea Jordan, Erin Kelly, Eun Kim, Ledyard King, Marie Marino, Dennis Noone, Charles Raasch, Laura Rehrmann, Malia Rulon Herman, Craig Schwed, William Theobald, Brian Tumulty, John Yaukey.

GERMAN PRESS AGENCY-DPA—(202) 662–1220; 1112 National Press Building, Washington, DC 20045: Sylvia Ayuso Determeyer, Frank Brandmaier, Christopher Cermak, Gabriele Chwallek, Frank Fuhrig, Mike McCarthy, Peer Meinert, Antje Passenheim, Anindita Ramaswamy, Paticia Reber, Laszlo Trankovits, Anne Walters.

GLOBAL HORIZONS SYNDICATE—(202) 966–8636; 1330 New Hampshire Avenue, NW., Washington, DC 20036: Edward Flattau.

GLOBALPOST—(202) 468–6100; 10004 Frederick Avenue, Kensington, MD 20895: John Aloysius Farrell.

GRIFFIN-LARRABEE NEWS SERVICE—(202) 548–6343; 2404 Davis Avenue, Alexandria, VA 22302: Betty Mills.

HAARETZ DAILY—(240) 669–8790; 204 Congressional Lane, Rockville, MD 20852: Natasha Mozgovaya.

HANDELSBLATT—(202) 244–0238; 3823 Fessenden Street, NW., Washington, DC 20016: Markus Ziener.

HANKYOREH DAILY—(202) 347–7411; 821 National Press Building, Washington, DC 20045: Taeho Kwon, Jae-Hoon Ryu.

HEARST NEWSPAPERS—(202) 263–6400; 1700 12th Street, NW., Suite 1000, Washington, DC 20006: Jennifer Dlouhy, Dan Freedman, Charles Lewis, Stewart Powell, Helen Thomas.

HELSINGIN SANOMAT—(301) 907–0080; 5009 Del Ray Avenue, Bethesda, MD 20814: Pekka Mykkanen.

HINDUSTAN TIMES—(202) 731–7937; 4000 Massachusetts Avenue, NW., #716, Washington, DC 20016: Krishna Venkannaiah.

HOKKAIDO SHIMBUN—(202) 783–6033; 1012 National Press Building, Washington, DC 20045: Masayuki Kishi.

HOSPODARSKE NOVING DAILY—(202) 344–7730; 4933 Crescent Street, Bethesda, MD 20816: Daniel Anyz.

HOUSTON CHRONICLE—(202) 263–6511; 1850 K Street, NW., Suite 1000, Washington, DC 20006: Richard Dunham.

HUFFINGTON POST—(202) 885–9947; 1704 R Street, NW., Washington, DC 20009: Ryan Grim, Nico Pitney.

HURRIYET—(301) 564–6691; 16 Grove Ridge Court, Rockville, MD 20852: Mehmet Cindemir.

ICIS NEWS—333 North Fairfax Street, Suite 301, Alexandria, VA 22314: Joseph Kamalick (202) 776–1352, John Stripling (202) 659–9208.

IFR MARKETS—1100 13th Street, NW., Suite 200, Washington, DC 20005: Christine Dickerson (202) 772–0950, Pete Kasperowicz (202) 772–0959, Jerry Konjevoda (202) 772–0950, Tessa Moran (292) 772–0954.

II GIORNALE—(202) 237–1019; 2841 Arizona Terrace, Washington, DC 20016: Mariuccia Chiantaretto.

II SOLE 24 ORE—(202) 362–3871; 5051 Overlook Road, NW., Washington, DC 20016: Mario Calvo-Platero.

INDIA PRESS TRUST—(301) 564–2963; 10500 Rockville Pike, Suite 1217, North Bethesda, MD 20852: Lalit Jha.

INDO-ASIAN NEWS SERVICE—(301) 412–9234; 4801 Kenmore Avenue, Apartment 910, Alexandria, VA 22304: Arun Kumar.

INSIDE HIGHER ED—(202) 659–9208; 1320 18th Street, NW., 5th Floor, Washington, DC 20036: David Moltz, Elizabeth Redden.

INTER PRESS SERVICE—(202) 662–7160; 1293 National Press Building, Washington, DC 20045: Abid Aslam, James Lobe, Emad Mekay.

INTERNATIONAL HERALD TRIBUNE—(202) 862–0357; 1627 I Street, NW., Washington, DC 20006: Brian Knowlton.

INTERNETNEWS.COM—(202) 506–7743; 2800 Quebec Street, NW., Apartment 823, Washington, DC 20001: Kenneth Corbin.

INVESTOR'S BUSINESS DAILY—(202) 728–2152; 1001 Connecticut Avenue, Suite 415, Washington, DC 20036: Sean Higgins, David Hogberg.

ITAR-TASS NEWS AGENCY—(202) 662–7080; 1004 National Press Building, Washington, DC 20045: Dmitry Kirsanov, Alexander Pakhomov, Andrei Sitov, Andrey Surzhanskiy, Dmitri Zlodorev.

JERUSALEM POST—(202) 758–0862; 1706 Q Street, NW., #3, Washington, DC 20009: Hilary Leila Krieger.

JEWISH TELEGRAPHIC AGENCY—(202) 737–0935; 1025 Vermont Avenue, NW., #504, Washington, DC 20005: Eric Fingerhut, Ron Kampeas.

NEWSPAPERS REPRESENTED—Continued

JIJI PRESS—(202) 783–4330; 550 National Press Building, Washington, DC 20045: Ai Awaji, Takashi Fudo, Andrew Gorcester, Takuya Higuchi, Kosuke Ito, Takefumi Kato, Yoshiki Kishida, Shuko Kuno, Hiroyuki Takahashi.

JOONGANG ILBO—(202) 347–0122; 839 National Press Building, Washington, DC 20045: Jungwook Kim, Sang Il Lee.

JYLLANDS-POSTEN—(301) 320–9079; 6405 Little Leigh Court, Cabin John, MD 20818: Klaus Justsen.

KANSAS CITY STAR—(202) 383–6001; 700 12th Street, NW., Suite 1000, Washington, DC 20005: David Goldstein.

KIPLING NEWS SERVICE—(301) 929–0760; 12611 Farnell Drive, Silver Spring, MD 20906: Bogdan Kipling.

KOMMERSANT—(202) 248–8191; 3700 Massachusetts Avenue, NW., Suite 317, Washington, DC 20016: Dmitry Sidorov.

KOREA DONG-A ILBO—(202) 347–4097; 974 National Press Building, Washington, DC 20045: Taewon Ha (202) 347–4097, Keehong Lee.

KOREA ECONOMIC DAILY—(703) 850–3396; 8108 Meadow Springs Court, Vienna, VA 22182: Hong Yeol Kim.

KOREA TIMES—(703) 941–8002; 7601 Little River Turnpike, Third Floor, Annandale, VA 22003: Sung Joong Ahn, Christina Young Chong, Chang-Yul Lee, Byonghan Lee, Jong Kook Lee, Kwang Duk Park.

KUKMIN DAILY—(202) 637–0567; 909 National Press Building, Washington, DC 20045: Myung Ho Kim.

KUWAIT NEWS AGENCY—(202) 347–5554; 906 National Press Building, Washington, DC 20045: Ronald Baygents, Joe Macaron, Sherouq Sadeqi, Heather Yamour.

KYODO NEWS—(202) 347–5767; 400 National Press Building, Washington, DC 20045: Tsukasa Arita, Moriyasu Chikazawa, Tomohiro Deguchi, Michelle Jamrisko, Takehito Kajita, Kazuhiro Kimura, Yuji Nakaya, Michi Nishina, John Robert Odle, Akira Samukawa, Ichiro Sugimoto, Hiroki Sugita, Fumitaka Susami, Toru Takei, Hajime Tobe, Kimiko Yano, Tatsuro Yasunaga.

KYUNGHYANG SHINMUN—(703) 272–3884; 4101 Cathedral Avenue, NW., Suite 811, Washington, DC 20016: Jin Ho Kim.

LA JORNADA—(202) 547–5852; 2708 4th Street, NE., Washington, DC 20003: David Brooks.

LA NACION—(202) 628–7907; 1193 National Press Building, Washington, DC 20045: Silvia Picani.

LA OPINION—(410) 710–8415; 110 West 39th Street, NW., Apartment 616, Baltimore, MD 21210: Antonieta Cadiz.

LA PRENSA GRAFICA OF EL SALVADOR—(202) 758–2632; 300 Hamilton Street, NW., Washington, DC 20011: Julio Ernesto Marenco.

LA RAZON—(703) 379–0095; 4922 South Chesterfield Road, Arlington, VA 22206: Armando Morales.

LA SALLE NEWS TRIBUNE—(703) 509–7890; 209 Pennsylvania Avenue, SE., Washington, DC 20003: Kristie Miller.

LA VANGUARDIA—(301) 229–1695; 6812 Algonquin Avenue, Bethesda, MD 20817: Eusebio Val Mitjavila.

LAS VEGAS SUN—(202) 662–7436; 1290 National Press Building, Washington, DC 20045: Lisa Mascaro.

LE MAURICIEN—(301) 728–7442; 1084 Pipestem Place, Potomac, MD 20854: Pamela Glass.

LE MONDE—(202) 248–9075; 3841 Harrison Street, NW., Washington, DC 20005: Corine Lesnes.

LIBERTY TIMES—(202) 879–6765; 1294 National Press Building, Washington, DC 20045: Nadia Y.F. Tsao.

LONDON DAILY TELEGRAPH—(202) 393–5197; 1310 G Street, NW., Suite 750, Washington, DC 20005: Rachel Ray, Alexander Spillius.

LONDON GUARDIAN—(202) 223–2486; 1730 Rhode Island Avenue, NW., #502, Washington, DC 20036: Richard Adams, Suzanne Goldenberg, Ewen Macaskill, Chris McGreal, Daniel Nasaw, Michael Tomasky.

LONDON INDEPENDENT—(202) 288–7109; 2963 Albemarle Street, NW., Washington, DC 20008: Leonard Doyle.

LONDON TIMES—(202) 347–7659; 446 National Press Building, Washington, DC 20045: Thomas Baldwin, Timothy Reid, Matthew Spence.

L'ORIENT-LE JOUR—(202) 342–1213; 1045 31st Street, #404, Washington, DC 20007: Wafik Ramadan.

LOS ANGELES DAILY JOURNAL—(202) 484–8255; 963 National Press Building, Washington, DC 20045: Lawrence Hurley.

LOS ANGELES DAILY JOURNAL—(202) 942–9700; 601 Pennsylvania Avenue, NW., Suite 900, Washington, DC 20004: Robert Iafolla.

LOS ANGELES TIMES—(202) 824–8300; 1090 Vermont Avenue, NW., Suite 1000, Washington, DC 20005: Marina Alvarez, Julian Barnes, Richard Cooper, Thomas Hamburger, Janet Hook, Noam Levey, Doyle McManus, Joshua Meyer, Greg Miller, Johanna Neuman, Peter Nicholas, Robert Ourlian, Timothy Phelps, James Puzzanghera, Maura Reynolds, Paul Richter, James Robinson, David Savage, Richard Simon, Peter Wallsten, Aaron Zitner.

LOS ANGELES TIMES-WASHINGTON POST NEWS SERVICE—(202) 334–6175; 1150 15th Street, NW., Washington, DC 20071: Charles Leeds.

NEWSPAPERS REPRESENTED—Continued

LOUISVILLE COURIER JOURNAL—(202) 906–8141; 1100 New York Avenue, NW., Washington, DC 20005: James Carroll.

LRP PUBLICATIONS—(561) 622–6520; 360 Hiatt Drive, Palm Beach Gardens, FL 33418: Michael Brodie, Julie Davidson, David Kittross, Wangui Njuguna, Kim Riley, Mark Sherman, Sarah Sparks, Jeanne Sweeney, Melissa Turley, Erin Uy, Frank Wolfe.

MAEIL BUSINESS NEWSPAPER—(202) 637–0567; 909 National Press Building, Washington, DC 20045: Kyongho Yoon.

MAGYAR SZO—(202) 904–4433; 1775 Massachusetts Avenue, Suite 326, Washington, DC 20036: Tibor Purger.

MAINICHI SHIMBUN—(202) 737–2817; 340 National Press Building, Washington, DC 20045: Kenichi Komatsu, Kazuhiko Kusano, Amy McKeever, Tomoko Ohji, Masaya Oikawa, Nobuhiro Saito.

MARKET NEWS INTERNATIONAL—(202) 371–2121; 552 National Press Building, Washington, DC 20045: Steven Beckner, Denny Gulino, Kevin Kastner, Ian McKendry, Yali N'Diaye, Brai Odion-Esence, Joseph Plocek, Heather Scott, John Shaw.

MARKETWATCH—(202) 824–0566; 1240 National Press Building, Washington, DC 20045: Jeffrey Bartash, Ruth Mantell, Michael Maynard, Margaret McNeil, Rex Nutting, Ronald Orol, Gregory Robb, Robert Schroeder.

McCLATCHY NEWSPAPERS—700 12th Street, NW., Suite 1000, Washington, DC 20005: Halimah Abdullah (202) 383–6055, Christopher Adams (202) 383–6071, Beryl Adcock (202) 383–6056, Andre Anderson (202) 383–6071, James Asher (202) 383–6053, Barbara Barrett (202) 383–0012, Les Blumenthal (202) 365–0008, Michael Bold (202) 383–0017, Erika Bolstad (202) 383–3765, Robert Boyd (202) 383–6007, William Douglas (202) 383–6026, Michael Doyle (202) 383–0006, Jim Goldschmidt (202) 383–6086, Greg Gordon (202) 383–0010, Frank Greve (202) 383–6003, Roy Gutman (202) 383–6030, Kevin Hall (202) 383–6038, Rob Hotakainen (202) 383–0009, Jonathan Landay (202) 383–6012, David Lightman (202) 383–6101, Anthony Pugh (202) 383–6013, Robert Rankin (202) 383–6017, James Rosen (202) 383–0014, Renee Schoof (202) 383–6004, Mark Seibel (202) 383–6027, Warren Strobel (202) 383–6033, Margaret Talev (805) 218–1073, Curtis Tate (202) 363–3018, Marisa Taylor (202) 383–6164, Steven Thomma (202) 383–6042, Jim Van Nostrand (202) 383–6006, John Walcott (202) 383–6002, Letitia Wells (202) 383–6032, Nancy Youssef (202) 662–6000, Lisa Zagaroli (202) 662–4380.

MEDICAL DEVICE DAILY—(202) 719–7814; 4301 Connecticut Avenue, NW., Washington, DC 20008: Mark McCarty.

MEDPAGETODAY.COM—(734) 754–6977; 2101 16th Street, NW., Apartment 816, Washington, DC 20009: Emily Walker.

MERCER MEDIA—(703) 684–1724; 409 South Pitt Street, Alexandria, VA 22314: Marsha Mercer.

MERGER MARKET OF FINANCIAL TIMES—(202) 434–1070; 1012 K Street, NW., Suite 915, Washington, DC 20005: Reuben Miller, Charles Rice.

MIAMI HERALD—(202) 383–6054; 700 12th Street, NW., Suite 1000, Washington, DC 20005: Lesley Clark.

MILITARY UPDATE—(703) 830–6863; P.O. Box 231111, Centreville, VA 20120: Thomas Philpott.

MILITARY.COM—(202) 299–0704; 2355 Ashmead Place, NW., Washington, DC 20009: Colin Clark.

MILITARY.COM—611 Pennsylvania Avenue, SE., Suite 405, Washington, DC 20003: Bryant Jordan (540) 785-9176, Christian Lowe (202) 544–2495.

MILLIYET—(202) 248–3215; 3700 Massachusetts Avenue, NW., Apartment 533, Washington, DC 20016: Ahu Ozyurt.

MILWAUKEE JOURNAL SENTINEL—(202) 662–7290; 940 National Press Building, Washington, DC 20045: Craig Gilbert, Diana Marrero.

MINNEAPOLIS STAR TRIBUNE—(202) 408–2753; 1090 Vermont Avenue, NW., Suite 1000, Washington, DC 20005: Kevin Diaz.

MOBILE REGISTER—(202) 316–4596; 700 12th Street, NW., Suite 1000, Washington, DC 20005: Sean Reilly.

MUNWHA ILBO—(202) 662–7342; 909 National Press Building, Washington, DC 20045: Hyung Du Choi, Young Sik Chun.

MYERS NEWS SERVICE—(202) 479–1130; 8213 Taunton Place, Springfield, VA 22152: Michael Myers.

NATIONAL POST—(202) 662–7576; 17811 Shotley Bridge Place, Olney, MD 20832: Allen Abel.

NETHERLANDS PRESS ASSOCIATION—(703) 272–7499; 520 Woodland Court, NW., Vienna, VA 22180: Frank Hendrickx.

NEUE ZUERCHER ZEITUNG—(202) 237–5602; 3808 Woodley Road, NW., Washington, DC 20016: Beat Ammann.

NEW ORLEANS TIMES-PICAYUNE—(202) 383–7861; 700 12th Street, NW., Suite 1000, Washington, DC 20001: Bruce Alpert, Jonathan Tilove.

NEW YORK DAILY NEWS—(202) 467–6670; 1050 Thomas Jefferson Street, NW., Second Floor, Washington, DC 20007: Kenneth Bazinet, Thomas DeFrank, William Goldschlag, Michael McAuliff, James Meek, Richard Sisk.

NEWSPAPERS REPRESENTED—Continued

NEW YORK POST—(202) 393–1787; 1114 National Press Building, Washington, DC 20045: Geoff Earle, Charles Hurt, Daphne Retter.

NEW YORK TIMES—(202) 862–0300; 1627 I Street, NW., Suite 700, Washington, DC 20006: Edmund Andrews, Peter Baker, Dean Baquet, Bernard Becker, John Broder, David Brooks, Elisabeth Bumiller, Jeff Burgess, Jackie Calmes, Adam Clymer, Helene Cooper, Rebecca Corbett, John Cushman, Jr., James Dao, Jason Deparle, Maureen Dowd, Paula Dwyer, Adrianne Goodman, Elizabeth Goodridge, Janis Harland, Gardiner Harris, Raymond Hernandez, David Herszenhorn, Farhana Hossain, Carl Hulse, Douglas Jehl, David Johnston, David Kirkpatrick, Stephen Labaton, Mark Landler, Mark Leibovich, David Leonhardt, Neil Lewis, Eric Lichtblau, Adam Liptak, Eric Lipton, Sarah Jane Lorber, Mark Mazzetti, Clifford Meadows, Adam Nagourney, Ron Nixon, Elizabeth Olson, Ashley Parker, Robert Pear, Kathleen Phillips, James Risen, Jim Rutenberg, David Sanger, Charlie Savage, Eric Schmitt, Scott Shane, Thomas Shanker, Ronald Skarzenski, Ashley Southall, Richard Stevenson, Sheryl Stolberg, David Stout, Rachel Swarns, Matthew Wald, Judith Warner, Leslie Wayne, Jeff Zeleny.

NEWARK STAR-LEDGER—(202) 255–6719; 2529 West Meredith Drive, Vienna, VA 22181: J. Scott Orr.

NEWS AND MESSENGER—(703) 369–5738; 14010 Smoketown Road, Woodbridge, VA 22192: Jonathan Hunley.

NEWSDAY—(202) 408–2715; 1090 Vermont Avenue, NW., Washington, DC 20005: Thomas Brune.

NEWSPAPER ENTERPRISE—(301) 320–5559; 6008 Osceola Road, Bethesda, MD 20816: Robert Wagman.

NIKKEI—(202) 393–1388; 815 Connecticut Avenue, Suite 310, Washington, DC 20006: Tomoko Ashizuka, Christina Bilski, Sachiko Deshimaru, Masako Iwamoto, Stephen Keefe, Hiroshi Marutani, Ryu Ohsumi, Itaru Oishi, Yusuke Yoneyama.

NOTIMEX MEXICAN NEWS AGENCY—(202) 347–5227; 975 National Press Building, Washington, DC 20045: Ruben Barrera, Jose Lopez, Santiago Tavara.

OIL DAILY—(202) 662–0723; 1411 K Street, NW., #608, Washington, DC 20005: William Murray.

OKLAHOMAN—(202) 662–7543; 914 National Press Building, Washington, DC 20045: Chris Casteel.

OMAHA WORLD-HERALD—(202) 997–9787; 1009 National Press Building, Washington, DC 20045: Joseph Morton.

OREGONIAN—(202) 731–5152; P.O. Box 6285, Washington, DC 20013: Charles Pope.

ORLANDO SENTINEL—(202) 824–8222; 1025 F Street, NW., Suite 700, Washington, DC 20004: Mark Mathews.

PHILADELPHIA INQUIRER—(856) 912–9922; 1301 North Courthouse Road, #601, Arlington, VA 22201: David Boyer.

PIONEER—(INDIA)—(703) 876–6149; 2731 Pleasantdale Road, #203, Vienna, VA 22180: Sethuraman Rajagopalan.

PLATTS NEWS SERVICE—(202) 383–2250; 1200 G Street, NW., Washington, DC 20005: Daniel Goldstein, Gerald Karey.

POLITICAL MONEY LINE—(202) 237–2500; P.O. Box 6285, Washington, DC 20015: Kent Cooper, Anthony Raymond.

PROVIDENCE JOURNAL—(202) 661–8423; 1325 G Street, NW., Washington, DC 20005: John Mulligan.

REAL CLEAR POLITICS—(202) 725–7343; 320 D Street, NE., #3, Washington, DC 20008: Michael Memoli, Kyle Trygstad.

REFORMA NEWSPAPER—(202) 341–3255; 1009 New Hampshire Avenue, Suite 7, Washington, DC 20037: Jose Diaz-Briseno.

RELIGION NEWS SERVICE—(202) 383–7863; 1930 18th Street, NW., Washington, DC 20009: Adelle Banks, Daniel Burke, Kevin Eckstrom.

RESTRUCTURING TODAY—(202) 351–6880; 4418 MacArthur Boulevard, Suite 202, Washington, DC 20007: James Downing, J. J. McCoy, Samuel Spencer, Michael Zwelling.

REUTERS—(202) 898–8300; 1333 H Street, Suite 500, Washington, DC 20005: Sandra Abrams, Charles Alexander, JoAnne Allen, Victoria Allen, Diane Bartz, Melissa Bland, Russell Blinch, Anthony Boadle, Caren Bohan, Alister Bull, Deborah Charles, Cindy Clearwater, Ross Colvin, Susan Cornwell, Richard Cowan, John Crawley, Sarah Cunningham, Bernd Debusmann, Harold Desmond, Kim Dixon, Timothy Dobbyn, Christopher Doering, Tom Doggett, Kevin Drawbaugh, Will Dunham, Paul Eckert, Samer Farah, Mark Felsenthal, Thomas Ferraro, Margaret Fox, Rodrek Golden, Howard Scot Goller, Andrew Gray, Susan Heavey, Steve Holland, Emily Kaiser, Frances Kerry, Lisa Lambert, David Lawder, Sandra Maler, Jeff Mason, Jasmin Melvin, Randall Mikkelsen, Arshad Mohammed, David Morgan, Lucia Mutikani, Essex Noel, Doug Palmer, Jeremy Pelofsky, Sue Pleming, John Poirier, Andrew Quinn, Roberta Rampton, Ayesha Rascoe, Andrea Ricci, Lisa Richwine, Patrick Rucker, Timothy Ryan, Andrea Shalal-Esa, Donna Smith, Glenn Somerville, Neil Stempleman, David Storey, Andy Sullivan, James Vicini, Julie Vorman, Nancy Waitz, Michael Weekes Jr., John Whitesides, Patricia Wilson, Jim Wolf, Karey Wutkowski, Rachelle Younglai, Deborah Zabarenko, Tabassum Zakaria.

RHEINISCHE POST—(202) 966–2303; 5810 Chevy Chase Parkway, NW., Washington, DC 20015: Frank Herrmann.

RIA NOVOSTI—(202) 386–1687; 1706 18th Street, NW., Washington, DC 20008: Svetlana Babaeva.

NEWSPAPERS REPRESENTED—Continued

RIVERSIDE PRESS-ENTERPRISE—(202) 661–8422; 1325 G Street, Suite 250, Washington, DC 20005: Ben Goad.

SALT LAKE TRIBUNE—(202) 662–8732; 1255 National Press Building, Washington, DC 20045: Thomas Burr, Matt Canham, Robert Gehrke.

SAN ANTONIO EXPRESS-NEWS—(202) 263–6451; 700 12th Street, NW., Suite 1000, Washington, DC 20006: Gary Martin.

SAN FRANCISCO CHRONICLE—(202) 263–6573; 700 12th Street, NW., Suite 1000, Washington, DC 20006: Zachary Coile, Carolyn Lockhead.

SAN JOSE MERCURY NEWS—(202) 662–8921; 1255 National Press Building, Washington, DC 20045: Frank Davies.

SANKEI SHIMBUN—(202) 347–2842; 330 National Press Building, Washington, DC 20045: Takashi Arimoto, Yoshihisa Komori (202) 347–2603, Bruce Scott Stewart, Hiroo Watanabe, Hideya Yamamoto.

SAUDI PRESS AGENCY—(202) 944–3890; 601 New Hampshire Avenue, NW., Washington, DC 20037: Yasmeen Alamiri, Naila Al-Sowayel, Mustafa Bashir, Dean Dessouky, Liam Hurley, Azeddine Labriny, Lauren Riley, Nezar Sheikh.

SCIENCE & TECHNOLOGY DAILY—(703) 255–1171; 9770 Oleander Avenue, Vienna, VA 22181: Li Mao.

SCRIPPS HOWARD NEWS SERVICE—(202) 408–1484; 1090 Vermont Avenue, Suite 1000, Washington, DC 20005: Curtis Lee Bowman, Patricia Choate, Michael Collins, Peter Copeland, Robert Friedman, Laurel Hackett, Thomas Hargrove, Lisa Hoffman, Dale McFeatters, David Nielsen, Bartholomew Sullivan, Dan Thomasson, Daniel Wolf.

SEATTLE POST-INTELLIGENCER—(202) 422–2313; 700 12th Street, NW., Suite 1000, Washington, DC 20006+666666666: Andrew Schneider.

SEGYE TIMES—(703) 627–7081; 909 National Press Building, Washington, DC 20045: Nam Cho, Kiyon Kuk.

SEKAI NIPPO—(202) 898–8292; 1133 19th Street, NW., 8th Floor, Washington, DC 20036: Toshiyuki Hayakawa.

SEOUL SHINMUN—(202) 393–4061; 905 National Press Building, Washington, DC 20045: Kyun Mi Kim (202) 393–4061, Do Woon Lee.

SHANGHAI WENHUI DAILY—(703) 521–2371; 1600 South Eads Street, Suite 1134N, Arlington, VA 22202: Xingfu Zhu.

SINGAPORE STRAITS TIMES—(202) 662–8728; 916 National Press Building, NW., Washington, DC 20045: Bhagyashree Buddhavarapu, Chua Chin Hon.

SOUTH FLORIDA SUN-SENTINEL—(202) 824–8256; 1090 Vermont Avenue, NW., Suite 1000, Washington, DC 20005: William Gibson.

ST. LOUIS POST-DISPATCH—(202) 298–6880; 1025 Connecticut Avenue, Suite 1102, Washington, DC 20036: Aloysia Hamalainen, William Lambrecht.

ST. PETERSBURG TIMES—(202) 463–0577; 1100 Connecticut Avenue, #1300, Washington, DC 20036: William Adair, Wes Allison, Alex Leary.

STEPHENS MEDIA GROUP—(202) 783–1760; 1100 G Street, NW., Suite 535, Washington, DC 20001: Stephan Tetreault.

SUEDDEUTSCHE ZEITUNG—(301) 229–3736; 7017 Hopewood Street, Bethesda, MD 20817: Reymer Kluever.

SVENSKA DAGBLADET—(202) 362–8253; 3601 Connecticut Avenue, #622, Washington, DC 20008: Karin Henriksson.

SYDNEY MORNING HERALD—(202) 737–6360; 1310 G Street, #750, Washington, DC 20005: Anne Davies.

SYRACUSE POST-STANDARD—(202) 383–7818; 3900 Fairfax Drive, Suite 1321, Arlington, VA 22203: Mark Weiner.

TAGES ANZEIGER—(202) 332–8575; 2026 16th Street, NW., #5, Washington, DC 20009: Martin Kilian.

TECH LAW JOURNAL—(202) 364–8882; 3034 Newark Street, NW., Washington, DC 20008: David Carney.

TIMES OF INDIA—(301) 495–9548; 7505 Akfred Drive, Silver Spring, MD 20910: Chidanand Rajghatta.

TOKYO CHUNICHI SHIMBUN—(202) 783–9479; 1012 National Press Building, Washington, DC 20045: Masakazu Furukawa, Nakahiro Iwata, Stephen Sacks, Akihiro Shimada, William Sturgeon, Eri Urano.

TORONTO GLOBE AND MAIL—(202) 662–7167; 2000 M Street, Suite 330, Washington, DC 20036: Paul Koring.

TORONTO STAR—(202) 662–7390; 982 National Press Building, Washington, DC 20045: Mitchell Potter.

TRIBUNE COMPANY—(202) 824–8340; 1025 F Street, NW., Suite 700, Washington, DC 20004: Kerry Luft.

TRIBUNE MEDIA SERVICES—(202) 298–8359; 3042 Q Street, NW., Washington, DC 20007: Jules Witcover.

TRIPSO.COM—(617) 569–1966; 7062 Solomon Seal Court, Springfield, VA 22152: Charles Leocha.

TULSA WORLD—(202) 484–1424; 1417 North Inglewood Street, Arlington, VA 22205: Jim Myers.

NEWSPAPERS REPRESENTED—Continued

TURKIYE DAILY—(202) 253–3289; 6 Marketree Court, Montgomery Village, MD 20886: Hasan Hazar.

TVNEWSDAY.COM—(301) 773–0058; 2425: Valley Way, Cheverly, MD 20785: Mark Miller.

UNITED DAILY NEWS—(202) 737–6426; 835 National Press Building, Washington, DC 20045: Tsung-Chih Chang.

UNITED MEDIA—(301) 494–0430; 3330 Blue Heron Drive North, Chesapeake Beach, MD 20732: Lew Sichelman.

USA TODAY—(202) 906–8100; 1100 New York Avenue, Suite 200E, Washington, DC 20037: Mel Antonen, Emily Bazar, Marisol Bello, Joan Biskupic, Erik Brady, Louise Branson, Catalina Camia, Dan Carney, Paul Davidson, William Dermody, Ken Dilanian, Oren Dorell, Peter Eisler, Haya El Nasser, Melanie Eversley, Mindy Fetterman, Gwen Flanders, Thomas Frank, John Fritze, Brian Gallagher, Andrew Gardiner, Jack Gillum, Raymond Goldbacher, Alan Gomez, Barbara Hagenbaugh, George Hager, Mimi Hall, James Healy, Brad Heath, Linda Holzer, Monica Hortobagyi, Lee Horwich, Rosalind Jackler, David Jackson, Kevin Johnson, Matthew Kelley, Dennis Kelly, Kathy Kiely, Eugene Kiely, Suzanne Kirchhoff, Wendy Koch, Jill Lawrence, Donna Leinwand, Alan Levin, Janice Lloyd, Ray Locker, David Lynch, Mary Beth Marklein, Stephen Marshall, Mark Memmott, Jim Michaels, Patty Michalski, Paul Overberg, Susan Page, Richard Patrick, Anthony J. Perez, Claude Pruitt, Maria Puente, Carlos Roig, Fredreka Schouten, Rachel Smolkin, Michael Snider, William Sternberg, Steve Sternberg, Andrea Stone, Gregory Toppo, Saundra Torry, Tom Vanden Brook, Dan Vergano, Traci Watson, James Welch, Richard Wolf, Gregg Zoroya.

VIRGINIAN-PILOT—(703) 913–9872; 7802 Glenister Drive, Springfield, VA 22152: Dale Eisman.

VOTES IN CONGRESS SERVICE—(202) 667–9760; 1822 Corcoran Street, NW., Washington, DC 20009: Michael Lesparre, Richard Thomas.

WALL STREET, JOURNAL—(202) 862–9200; 1025 Connecticut Avenue, NW., Suite 800, Washington, DC 20036: Janet Adamy, Timothy Alberta, Naftali Bendavid, Jess Bravin, John Bussey, Kathy Chen, Cassie Chew, August Cole, Christopher Conkey, Robert Davis, Susan Davis, David Allen Dolinger, Yochi Dreazen, Timothy Farnam, Gary Fields, Siobhan Gorman, Jon Hilsenrath, Greg Hitt, Angel Jennings, Neil King, Jr., Peter Landers, Monica Langley, Robert Guy Matthews, John McKinnon, Laura Meckler, Brody Mullins, Alicia Mundy, Ryan Niles, Damian Paletta, Evan Perez, Michael Phillips, Stephen Power, Louise Radnofsky, Sudeep Reddy, Matthew Rose, Kara Scannell, Amy Schatz, Jacob Schlesinger, Gerald Seib, Cameron Simpson, Deborah Solomon, Jonathan Solomon, Peter Spiegel, Melanie Trottman, Jonathan Weisman, David Wessel, Joseph White, Elizabeth Williamson, Jane Zhang.

WASHINGTON EXAMINER—(202) 903–2000; 1015 15th Street, NW., Suite 500, Washington, DC 20005: Timothy Carney, Jeff Dufour, Susan Ferrechio, Scott McCabe, Kiki Ryan, Kytja Weir, Byron York.

WASHINGTON POST—(202) 334–6000; 1150 15th Street, NW., Washington, DC 20071: Joel Achenbach, Mary Ann Akers, Binyamin Appelbaum, Amy Argetsinger, Perry Bacon, Jr., Daniel Balz, Robert Barnes, Jill Bartscht, Michael Birnbaum, Marcus Brauchli, David Broder, DeNeen Brown, David Brown, Michael Chandler, Rajiv Chandrasekaran, David Cho, Chris Cillizza, Sarah Cohen, Catherine Connolly, Libby Copeland, Tim Craig, Alice Crites, Timothy Curran, J. Christian Davenport, Joe Davidson, Aaron Davis, Brady Dennis, Paul Duggan, Petula Dvorak, Daniel Eggen, Juliet Eilperin, Dina Elboghdady, David Fahrenthold, David Fallis, Paul Farhi, Darryl Fears, Peter Finn, Marc Fisher, Mary Pat Flaherty, Michael Fletcher, Sholnn Freeman, Amy Gardner, Gilbert Gaul, Ann Gerhart, Maria Glod, Zachary Goldfarb, Amy Goldstein, Annie Gowen, James Grimaldi, Hamil Harris, Kim Hart, Wil Haygood, Dana Hedgpeth, Monica Hesse, Spencer Hsu, Anne Hull, Walton Neil Irwin, Thomas Jackman, Chris Jenkins, Carrie Johnson, Robert Kaiser, Al Kamen, Paul Kane, Cecilia Kang, Dan Keating, Glenn Kessler, Anne Kornblut, Emily Kotecki, Fredrick Kunkle, Howard Kurtz, Theola Labbe, Charles Lane, Michael Laris, Lyndsey Layton, Michael Leahy, Madonna Lebling, Richard Leiby, Sarah Lovenheim, Alec MacGillis, Kristen Mack, Ruth Marcus, Anne Marimow, Jerome Markon, Kevin Merida, Renae Merle, Dana Milbank, William Miller, Nick Miroff, David Montgomery, Lori Montgomery, Carol Morello, Dan Morse, Steven Mufson, Jonathan Mummolo, David Nakamura, Ellen Nakashima, Marissa Newhall, Edward O'Keefe, Amit Paley, Steven Pearlstein, Ben Pershing, Eric Pianin, Walter Pincus, Dana Priest, Lisa Rein, Roxanne Roberts, Eugene Robinson, Manuel Roig-Franzia, Lois Romano, Michael Ruane, Philip Rucker, Eli Saslow, Brigid Schulte, Lucy Shackelford, Ian Shapira, Michael Shear, Mary Beth Sheridan, Jeffrey Smith, Sandhya Somashekhar, Donna St. George, Robert Stein, Joe Stephens, Nikita Stewart, Hank Stuever, Lena Sun, Cheryl Thompson, Marilyn Thompson, Robert Thompson, Krissah Thompson, Tom Toles, Nancy Trejos, Jacqueline Trescott, Boyd Neely Tucker, Bill Turque, Ann Scott Tyson, Jose Antonio Vargas, Theresa Vargas, Stephen Vogel, Paul Volpe, John Wagner, Joby Warrick, Eric Weiss, Josh White, Peter Whoriskey, Scott Wilson, Bob Woodward, Eric Yoder, Dan Zak.

WASHINGTON POST WRITER'S GROUP—(202) 334–7375; 1150 15th Street, NW., Washington, DC 20071: Marie Cocco, Kathleen Parker.

WASHINGTON TELECOMMUNICATIONS SERVICES—(804) 776–7947; 1006 Harrison Circle, Alexandria, VA 22304: Gordon White.

WASHINGTON TIMES—(202) 636–3000; 3600 New York Avenue, NE., Washington, DC 20002: Sarah Abruzzese, Theodore Agres, Christina Bellantoni, Jeffrey Birnbaum, Christian Bourge, Amanda Carpenter,

NEWSPAPERS REPRESENTED—Continued

Sara Carter, Ben Conery, Joseph Curl, Amanda DeBard, Brett Decker, David Dickson, Stephen Dinan, Christopher Dolan, Julia Duin, Gary Emerling, Edward Felker, Ann Geracimos, Jennifer Haberkorn, Ralph Hallow, Jennifer Harper, Patricia Hill, Quin Hillyer, Audrey Hudson, David Jones, Eli Lake, Donald Lambro, Sean Lengell, Tom Lobianco, John Lott, Windsor Mann, John McCaslin, James McElhatton, Jr., Steven Miller, Richard Miniter, Chuck Neubauer, Kerry Picket, James Robbins, Kara Rowland, David Sands, Jerry Seper, Deborah Simmons, John Solomon, Jon Ward, Timothy Warren, Cheryl Wetzstein.

WATERTOWN DAILY TIMES—(202) 662–7085; 930 National Press Building, Washington, DC 20045: Marc Heller.

WESTDEUTSCHE ALLGEMEINE—(202) 363–7791; 4611 47th Street, NW., Washington, DC 20016: Markus Guenther.

WESTERN COMMUNICATIONS—(202) 662–7456; 920 National Press Building, Washington, DC 20045: Keith Chu.

WILLIAM SCALLY REPORTS—(202) 362–2382; 2918 Legation Street, NW., Washington, DC 20015: William Scally.

WORLD BUSINESS PRESS—(646) 784–9776; 4706 Commons Drive, A–303, Annandale, VA 22003: Dagmar Benesova, Zoltan Mikes.

WORLD JOURNAL—(202) 215–1718; 835 National Press Building, Washington, DC 20045: Betty Lin.

XINHUA NEWS AGENCY—(202) 661–8181; 1201 National Press Building, Washington, DC 20045: Wang Faen, Liu Hong, Fang Hu, Guopeng Jiang, Lina Liu, Yu Qianliang, Haijun Ren, Jing Wei, Wang Wei, Ge Xiangwen, Feng Yan, Quinchuan Yang, Yi Zhao.

YOMIURI SHIMBUN—(202) 783–0363; 802 National Press Building, Washington, DC 20045: Charles Harris, Keiichi Homma, Yoshinari Kurose, Julia Marsh, Takeo Miyazaki, Satoshi Ogawa, Akihiro Okada, Michiro Okamuto, Mary Perkins, Benjamin Piven, Andrew Siddons, Mineko Tokito, Toshihiko Yada, Tetsuro Yamada.

YONHAP NEWS AGENCY—(202) 783–5539; 1299 National Press Building, Washington, DC 20045: Jae Hoon Hwang, Hwang Doo Hyong, Jae Hong Kim, Seung Il Koh, Jungbin Park, Sang Hyun Park.

PRESS PHOTOGRAPHERS' GALLERY*

The Capitol, Room S–317, 224–6548

www.senate.gov/galleries/photo

Director.—Jeffrey S. Kent.
Deputy Director.—Mark A. Abraham.
Assistant Director.—Tricia Munro.

STANDING COMMITTEE OF PRESS PHOTOGRAPHERS

Scott Applewhite, Associated Press, *Chair*
Dennis Brack, Black Star, *Secretary-Treasurer*
Jim Bourg, Reuters
Khue Bui, Newsweek
Stephen Crowley, New York Times
Win McNamee, Getty Images

RULES GOVERNING PRESS PHOTOGRAPHERS' GALLERY

1. (a) Administration of the Press Photographers' Gallery is vested in a Standing Committee of Press Photographers consisting of six persons elected by accredited members of the Gallery. The Committee shall be composed of one member each from Associated Press Photos; Reuters News Pictures or AFP Photos; magazine media; local newspapers; agency or freelance member; and one at-large member. The at-large member may be, but need not be, selected from media otherwise represented on the Committee; however no organization may have more than one representative on the Committee.

(b) Elections shall be held as early as practicable in each year, and in no case later than March 31. A vacancy in the membership of the Committee occurring prior to the expiration of a term shall be filled by a special election called for that purpose by the Committee.

(c) The Standing Committee of the Press Photographers' Gallery shall propose no change or changes in these rules except upon petition in writing signed by not less than 25 accredited members of the gallery.

2. Persons desiring admission to the Press Photographers' Gallery of the Senate shall make application in accordance with Rule 33 of the Senate, which rule shall be interpreted and administered by the Standing Committee of Press Photographers subject to the review and approval of the Senate Committee on Rules and Administration.

3. The Standing Committee of Press photographers shall limit membership in the photographers' gallery to bona fide news photographers of repute in their profession and Heads of Photographic Bureaus under such rules as the Standing Committee of Press Photographers shall prescribe.

4. Provided, however, that the Standing Committee of Press Photographers shall admit to the gallery no person who does not establish to the satisfaction of the Committee all of the following:

(a) That any member is not engaged in paid publicity or promotion work or in prosecuting any claim before Congress or before any department of the Government, and will not become so engaged while a member of the gallery.

*Information is based on data furnished and edited by each respective gallery.

(b) That he or she is not engaged in any lobbying activity and will not become so engaged while a member of the gallery.

The above rules have been approved by the Committee on Rules and Administration.

NANCY PELOSI,
Speaker, House of Representatives.

CHARLES E. SCHUMER,
Chair, Senate Committee on Rules and Administration.

MEMBERS ENTITLED FOR ADMISSION

PRESS PHOTOGRAPHERS' GALLERY

Ake, David: Associated Press Photos
Alvarez, Miguel: La Prensa Grafica of El Salvador
Applewhite, J. Scott: Associated Press Photos
Archambault, Charles: U.S. News & World Report
Arrossi, Eddie: Freelance
Ashley, Douglas: Suburban Communications Corp.
Augustino, Jocelyn: Freelance
Auth, Bill: Freelance
Barouh, Stan: 1105 Media
Barrett, Steve: Freelance
Barrick, Matthew: Freelance
Beale, John: Pittsburgh Post Gazette
Beiser, H. Darr: USA / Today
Berg, Lisa: Freelance
Biddle, Susan: Washington Post
Bingham, Mary ''Molly'': Freelance
Binks, Porter: Sports Illustrated
Bivera, Johnny: Freelance
Blass, Eileen: USA / Today
Bloom, Richard: Freelance
Bochatey, Terry: Reuters News Pictures
Boitano, Stephen: Freelance
Bourg, Jim: Reuters News Pictures
Bowe, Christy: Image Catcher News
Brack, William: Black Star
Brack, Abby: Freelance
Bridges, George: McClatchy Tribune
Brier, Joe: Freelance
Brown, Robert: Richmond Times Dispatch
Brown, Thomas: Army Times
Bruce, Andrea: Washington Post
Bui, Khue: Newsweek
Burke, Lauren: Freelance
Calvert, Mary: Washington Times
Cameron, Gary: Reuters News Pictures
Carioti, Richard: Washington Post
Cavanaugh, Matthew: European Pressphoto Agency
Cedeno, Ken: Freelance
Ceneta, Manuel: Associated Press Photos
Chikwendiu, Jahi: Washington Post
Clark, Bill: Roll Call
Clark, Kevin: Washington Post
Clement, Richard: Freelance
Cohen, Marshall: Bigmarsh News Photos
Connor, Kristopher: Freelance
Connor, Michael: Washington Times
Conrad, Fred: The New York Times
Coppage, Gary: Photo Press International
Council, Andrew: Freelance
Crowley, Stephen: The New York Times
Curtis, Rob: Army Times
Cutraro, Andrew: Freelance
Davidson, Linda: Washington Post
Devorah, Carrie: Freelance
Dharapak, Charles: Associated Press Photos
Dietsch, Kevin: United Press International
DiPasquale, Jill: Army Times
Dougherty, Sean: USA / Today
Douliery, Olivier: Abaca USA
Downing, Lawrence: Reuters News Pictures
Drenner, Dennis: Freelance
Du Cille, Michel: Washington Post
Eddins, Jr. Joseph: Washington Times
Edmonds, Ronald: Associated Press Photos
Eile, Evan: USA / Today
Elswick, Jon: Associated Press Photos
Ernst, Jonathan: Freelance
Esquivel, Robert: Herald Standard
Etheridge, Susan: The New York Times
Fabiano, Gary: Sipa Press
Falk, Steven: The Philadelphia Daily News
Falkenberg, Katie: Washington Times
Ferrell, Scott: CQ Weekly
Fitz-Patrick, Bill: Abaca USA
Franco, Angel: The New York Times
Frako, Jeff: Gannett
Freilich, Jon: Freelance
Fremson, Ruth: The New York Times
Frey, Katherine: Washington Post
Gail, Carl: Washington Post
Gainer, Denny: USA / Today
Gamarra, Ruben: Notimex
Gandhi, Pareshkumar: Rediff.com / India Abroad Pub.
Garcia, Mannie: Freelance
Gatty, Michael: Periodical News Service
Geissinger, Michael: Freelance
Ghanbari, Haraz: Associated Press Photos
Gilbert, Patrice: Freelance
Glenn, Alexis: United Press International
Glenn, Larry: Freelance
Golden, Melissa: Freelance
Graham, Douglas: Roll Call
Gripas, Yuri: Freelance
Gruber, Jack: USA / Today
Guerrucci, Aude: Polaris Images
Hambach, Eva: Agence France-Presse
Hamburg, Harry: Freelance
Haring, Paul: Catholic News Service
Harrington, John: Black Star
Heisler, Todd: The New York Times
Helber, Stephen: Associated Press Photos

MEMBERS ENTITLED FOR ADMISSION—Continued

Henry, Dennis: European Pressphoto Agency
Herbert, Gerald: Associated Press Photos
Hershorn, Gary: Reuters News Pictures
Hoffman, Brendan: Freelance
Holloway, David: Freelance
Holt, Victor: Washington Informer
Hubbard, Garrett: USA / Today
Hutchens, Jeff: Freelance
Joseph, Marvin: Washington Post
Kahn, Nikki: Washington Post
Kamm, Nicholas: Agence France-Presse
Kang, Hyungwon: Reuters News Pictures
Katz, Martin: Fairfax County Times
Kelly, Ryan: CQ Weekly
Kemper, Gary: European Pressphoto Agency
Keres, Preston: Washington Post
Kidd, David: Governing
Kittner, Sam: Freelance
Kleponis, Chris: Freelance
Kossoff, Leslie: Freelance
Kraft, Brooks: Time Magazine
Lamarque, Kevin: Reuters News Pictures
Lamkey, Jr., Rod: Washington Times
LaVor, Martin: Freelance
Lawidjaja, Rudy: Freelance
Lee, David: Freelance
Lessig, Alan: Army Times
Lipski, Richard: Washington Post
Loeb, Saul: Agence France-Presse
LoScalzo, Jim: Freelance
Ludidon, Amanda: Freelance
Lukasova, Veronika: Freelance
Lynch, M. Patricia: Frontiers News Magazine
MacMillan, Jeffrey: Freelance
Maddaloni, Chris: Army Times
Magana, Jose: Freelance
Mahaskey, M. Scott: Army Times
Mallin, Jay: Freelance
Malonson, Jacqueline: Freelance
Mara, Melina: Washington Post
Markel, Brad: Capri
Marks, Donovan: Freelance
Martin, Jacquelyn: Associated Press Photos
Martineau, Gerald: Washington Post
Martinez Monsivais, Pablo: Associated Press Photos
Mataquin, Oscar: Freelance
Mathieson Greg: MAI Photo Agency
McCrehin, Jud: USA / Today
McDonnell, John: Washington Post
McNamee, Win: Getty Images
Miller, Elisa: New York Daily News
Mills, Douglas: The New York Times
Morigi, Paul: Freelance
Morris, Christopher: Time Magazine
Mount, Bonnie: Washington Post
Muhammad, Ozier: The New York Times
Naji-Allah, Khalid: Freelance
Newton, Jonathan: Washington Post
Ngan, Mandel: Agence France-Presse
Nipp, Lisa: Freelance
O'Leary, William: Washington Post
Ommanney, Charles: Newsweek
Otfinowski, Danuta: Freelance
Palu, Louie: Zuma Press
Panagos, Dimitrios: Greek American News Agency
Parcell, James: Washington Post
Patterson, Kathryn: USA / Today
Perkins, Lucien: Washington Post
Petros, Bill: Freelance
Piggott, Rhyne: USA / Today
Poleski, David: Freelance
Powers, Christopher: Education Week
Powers, Carol: Freelance
Premack Jay: Freelance
Purcell, Steve: Freelance
Raab, Susana: Freelance
Radzinschi, Diego: Legal Times
Raedle, Joe: Getty Images
Raimondo, Lois: Washington Post
Rasmussen, Andy: Oregonian
Reed, Jason: Reuters News Pictures
Reinhard, Rick: Impact Digitals
Reynolds, Michael: European Pressphoto Agency
Ricardel, Vincent: Freelance
Richards, Paul: Agence France-Presse
Riecken, Astrid: Washington Times
Riley, Molly: Reuters News Pictures
Roberts, Joshua: Freelance
Robinson, Scott: Freelance
Sachs, Ronald: Consolidated News Pictures
Salisbury, Barbara: Washington Times
Samperton, Kyle: Freelance
Sandkuhler, Lauren: National Journal
Sandys, Toni: Washington Post
Savoia, Stephon: Associated Press Photos
Schaeffer, Sandra: MAI Photo Agency
Schmallz, Julia: USA / Today
Schwartz, Michael: The Politico
Scott, Andrew: USA / Today
Semiatin, Morris: Freelance
Shell, Mary: Time Magazine
Shelley, Allison: Washington Times
Silverman, Joseph: Washington Times
Sloan, Tim: Agence France-Presse
Smialowski, Brendan: Freelance
Somodevilla, Kenneth: Getty Images
Squires, Derek: Tax Analysts
Suanes, Rafael: Freelance
Sweets, Fredric: St. Louis American
Sykes, Jack: Professional Pilot Magazine
Sypher, Mark: Freelance
Takeda, Yasushi: Shukan Shincho, Shinchosha Co.
Temchine, Michael: Freelance
Theiler, Michael: Freelance

MEMBERS ENTITLED FOR ADMISSION—Continued

Thew, Shawn: European Pressphoto Agency
Thomas, Ronald: Freelance
Thomas, Ricardo: The Detroit News
Thresher, James: Washington Post
Trippett, Robert: Freelance
Van Riper, Frank: WashingtonPost.com
Varias, Stelios: Reuters News Pictures
Vemmer, Sheila: Army Times
Visser, Robert: Photopress Washington
Voisin, Sarah: Washington Post
Voss, Stephen: Freelance
Vucci, Evan: Associated Press Photos
Walker, Harry: McClatchy Tribune
Walker, Diana: Time Magazine
Walsh, Susan: Associated Press Photos
Watkins, Jr., Frederick: Freelance
Watson, James: Agence France-Presse
Wells, Jonathan: Sipa Press
Westcott, Jay: Freelance
Whitesell, Gregory: Freelance
Williams, Tom: Roll Call
Williamson, Michael: Washington Post
Wilson, Alex: Washington Times
Wilson, Mark: Getty Images
Winters, Damon: The New York Times
Wolf, Lloyd: Freelance
Wolf, Kevin: Freelance
Wollenberg, Roger: United Press International
Wong, Alex: Getty Images
Woodward, Tracy: Washington Post
Yim, Heesoon: Hana
Young, Jim: Reuters News Pictures
Zhang, Yan: Xinhua News Agency
Ziffer, Steve: Freelance

SERVICES REPRESENTED

(Service and telephone number, office address, and name of representative)

ABACA USA—(212) 224–8460; 28–30 West 36th Street, Suite 1004, New York, NY 10018: Douliery, Olivier; Fitz-Patrick, Bill.

AGENCE FRANCE PRESSE—(202) 414–0521; 1500 K Street, NW., Suite 600, Washington, DC 20005: Vincent, Almavy; Karen Blier-Schmeets, Karen; Kamm, Nicholas; Loeb, Saul; Mgan, Mandel; Richards, Paul; Sloan, Tim; Watson, James.

ARMY TIMES PUBLISHING—(703) 750–8699; 6883 Commercial Drive, Springfield, VA 22159: Brown, Thomas; Curtis, Rob; DiPasquale, Jill; Lessig, Alan; Maddaloni, Chris; Mahaskey, M. Scott; Vemmer, Shelia.

ASSOCIATED PRESS PHOTOS—(202) 641–9510; 1100 K Street, NW., Suite 700, Washington, DC 20005: Ake, David; Associated Press Photos (main contact); Applewhite, Scott J.; Ceneta, Manuel B.; Castoto, Susan; Dharapak, Charles; Deitz, James; Edmonds, Ronald; Elswick, Jon; Ghanbari, Haraz; Helber, Stephen; Herbert, Gerald; Lizik, Ron; Mark, Leighton; Martin, Jacquelyn; Martinez Monsivais, Pablo; Partlow, Wayne; Savoia, Stephen; Walsh, Susan; Vucci, Evan.

BIGMARSH NEWS PHOTOS—(202) 364–8332; 5131 52nd Street, NW., Washington, DC 20016: Cohen, Marshall.

BLACK STAR—(703) 547–1176; 7704 Tauxemont Road, Alexandria, VA 22308: Brack, William; Harrington, John.

CAPRI—(717) 757–2962; 485 Sundale Drive York, PA 17402: Markel, Brad.

CATHOLIC NEWS SERVICE—(202) 541–3250; 3211 Fourth Street, NE., Washington, DC 20017: Haring, Paul.

CONSOLIDATED NEWS PICTURES—(202) 543–3203; 10305 Leslie Street, Silver Spring, MD 20902–4857: Sachs, Ronald.

CQ WEEKLY—(202) 822–1431; 1414 22nd Street, NW., Washington, DC 20037: Ferrell, Scott; Kelly, Ryan.

EDUCATION WEEK—(301) 280–3100; 6935 Arlington Road, Suite 100, Bethesda, MD 20814: Powers, Christopher.

EUROPEAN PRESS PHOTO—(202) 347–4694; 1252 National Press Building, 529 14th Street, NW., Washington, DC 20045: Cavanaugh, Matthew; Henry, Dennis; Kemper, Gary; Reynolds, Michael; Thew, Shawn.

FAIRFAX COUNTY TIMES—1760 Reston Parkway, Suite 411, Reston, VA 20190: Katz, Martin.

FRONTIERS NEWS MAGAZINE—(301) 229–0635; P.O. Box 634, Glen Echo, MD 20812: Lynch, M. Patricia.

GANNETT—(703) 854–5800; 7950 Jones Branch Drive, McLean, VA 22107: Franco, Jeff.

GOVERNING—1100 Connecticut Avenue, NW., Washington, DC 20036: Kidd, David.

GETTY IMAGES—(646) 613–3703; National Press Building, 529 14th Street, NW., Washington, DC 20045: McNamee, Win; Somodevilla, Kenneth; Wilson, Mark; Wong, Alex.

GREEK AMERICAN NEWS AGENCY—(516) 931–2333; 107 Frederick Avenue, Babylon, NY 11702: Panagos, Dimitrios.

HANA—(202) 262–4541; 11311 Park Drive, Fairfax, VA 22030: Yim, Heesoon.

HERALD STANDARD—(724) 439–7500; 8118 East Church Street, Uniontown, PA 15401: Esquivel, Robert.

IMAGECATCHER NEWS—4911 Hampden Lane, Apt #3, Bethesda, MD 20814: Bowe, Christy.

IMPACT DIGITALS—(212) 614 8406; 171 Thompson Street, #9, New York, NY 10012: Reinhard, Rick.

LA PRENSA GRAFICA OF EL SALVADOR—San Salvador, El Salvador: Alvarez, Miguel A.

LEGAL TIMES—(202) 457–0686; 1730 M Street, NW., Suite 802, Washington, DC 20036: Radzinschi, Diego.

MAI PHOTO AGENCY—(703) 968–0030; 6601 Ashmere Lane, Centreville, VA 20120: Mathieson, Greg; Schaeffer, Sandra.

McCLATCHY TRIBUNE—(202) 383–6142; 700 12th Street, Suite 1000, Washington, DC 20005: Bridges, George; Walker, Harry E.

NATIONAL JOURNAL—(202) 739–8400; 600 New Hampshire Avenue, Washington, DC 20037: Sandkuhler, Lauren.

NEW YORK DAILY NEWS—(202) 739–8400; 450 West 33rd Street, New York, NY 10001: Miller, Elisa.

NEWSWEEK—(202) 626–2085; 1750 Pennsylvania Avenue, NW., Suite 1220, Washington, DC 20006: Bui, Khue; Ommanney, Charles.

SERVICES REPRESENTED—Continued

NOTIMEX—(202) 347–5227; 529 14th Street, NW., Suite 975, Washington, DC 20045: Gamarra, Ruben F.

OREGONIAN—(503) 221–8370; 1320 Southwest Broadway Portland, OR 97201: Rasmussen, Randy L.

PERIODICAL NEWS SERVICE—9206 Vollmerhausen Road, Jessup, MD 20794: Gatty, Michael; Gatty, Mary Anne.

PHOTOPRESS WASHINGTON—(202) 234–8787; 4051 34th Street, Mount Rainer, MD 20712: Visser, Robert.

PHOTOPRESS INTERNATIONAL—(540) 286–1045; P.O. Box 190, Goldvein, VA 22720: Coppage, Gary.

PITTSBURG POST GAZETTE—National Press Building, 529 14th Street, Washington, DC 20045: Beale, John.

POLARIS IMAGES—259 West 30th Street, 13th Floor, New York, NY 10001: Guerrucci, Aude.

PROFESSIONAL PILOT MAGAZINE—3014 Colvin Street, Alexandria, VA 22314: Sykes, Jack.

REDIFF.COM / INDIA ABROAD PUB.—(646) 432–6054; 43 West 24th Street, 2nd Floor, New York, NY 10010: Gandhi, Pareshkumar.

REUTERS NEWS PICTURES—(202) 898–8333; 1333 H Street, NW., Suite 500, Washington, DC 20005: Bochatey, Terry; Bourg, Jim; Cameron, Gary A.; Downing, Lawrence; Hershorn, Gary; Kang, Hyungwon; Lamarque, Kevin; Reed, Jason; Riley, Molly; Rubenstein, Larry; Varias, Stelios; Young, Jim.

RICHMOND TIMES DISPATCH—(804) 649–6496; 300 East Franklin Street, Richmond, VA 23219: Brown, Robert.

ROLL CALL—(202) 824–6800; 50 F Street, NW., 7th Floor, Washington, DC 20001: Clark, Bill; Graham, Douglas; Williams, Tom.

SHUKAN SHINCHO, SHINCHOSHA CO.—(703) 243–1569; 2001 North Adams Street, #715, Arlington, VA 22201: Takeda, Yasushi.

SIPA PRESS—(212) 463–0150; 307 7th Avenue, Suite 807, New York, NY 10010: Fabiano, Gary; Wells, Jonathan.

SPORTS ILLUSTRATED—(212) 522–3325; 1271 Avenue of the Americas, Room 1970, New York, NY 10020: Binks, Porter.

LOUIS AMERICAN—(314) 533–8000; 4242 Lindell Street, Louis, MO 63108: Sweets, Fredric.

TAX ANALYSTS—(703) 533–4400; 400 Maple Avenue, Suite 400, Falls Church, VA 22046: Squires, Derek.

THE DETROIT NEWS—(312) 222–2030; 615 West Lafayette Avenue, Photo Department, Detroit, MI 48226: Thomas, Ricardo.

THE HILL—(202) 628–8525; 733 15th Street, Washington, DC 20005: Nash, Greg.

THE NEW YORK TIMES—(202) 862–0300; 1627 Eye Street, NW., Washington, DC 20006: Conrad, Fred; Crowley, Stephen; Etheridge, Susan; Franco, Angel; Fremson, Ruth; Heisler, Todd; Mills, Douglas; Muhammad, Ozier; Winters, Damon.

THE POLITICO—(703) 647–7694: 1100 Wilson Boulevard, 6th Floor, Arlington, VA 22209: Schwarrtz, Michael; Shinkle, John.

THE PHILADELPHIA DAILY NEWS—400 North Broad Street, Philadelphia, PA 19130: Falk, Stephen.

WASHINGTON INFORMER—(202) 561–4100; 3117 Martin L. King Avenue, SE., Washington, DC 20032: Holt, Victor.

WASHINGTON POST—(202) 334–7380; 1150 15th Street, NW., Washington, DC 20071: Biddle, Susan; Bruce, Andrea; Carioti, Richard; Chikwendiu, Jahi; Clark, Kevin; Davidson, Linda; Du Cille, Michel; Frey, Katherine; Gail, Carl; Hillian, Vanessa; Joseph, Marvin; Kahn, Nikki; Keres, Preston; Lindsey, Debra; Lipski, Richard; Maltby, Melissa; Mara, Melina; Martineau, Gerald; McDonnell, John; Mount, Bonnie; Nakashima, Giuliana; Newton, Jonathan; O'Leary, William; Parcell, James; Perkins, Lucien; Raimondo, Lois; Sandys, Toni; Saunders, Ray; Thresher, James; Voisin, Sarah; Williamson, Michael; Woodward, Tracy.

WASHINGTON TIMES—(202) 636–3000; 3600 New York Avenue, NE., Washington, DC 20002: Calvert, Mary; Connor, Michael; Eddins, Jr., Joseph; Falkenberg, Katie; Lamkey, Jr., Rod; Reicken, Astrid; Salisbury, Barbara; Shelley, Allison; Silverman, Joseph; Wilson, Alex; Van Riper, Frank.

TIME MAGAZINE—(202) 861–4062; 555 12th Street, NW., Suite 600, Washington, DC 20004: Kraft, Brooks; Morris, Christopher; Shell, Mary; Vega, Leslie; Walker, Diana.

U.S. NEWS & WORLD REPORT—(202) 955–2210; 1050 Thomas Jefferson Street, NW., Washington, DC 20007: Archambault, Charles.

UNITED PRESS INTERNATIONAL—(202) 898–8071; 1133 19th Street, NW., Suite 800, Washington, DC 20036: Benic, Patrick; Deitsch, Kevin; Glenn, Alexis; Wollenberg, Roger.

USA / TODAY—(703) 854–5216; 7950 Jones Branch Road, McLean, VA 22107: Beiser, H. Darr; Blass, Eileen; Cochran, Mick; Daugherty, Sean; Eile, Evan; Gainer, Denny; Hubbard, Garrett; McCrehin, Jud; Patterson, Kathryn; Piggott, Rhyne; Schmallz, Julia; Scott, Andrew.

ZUMA PRESS—34189 Pacific Coast Highway, Dana Point, CA 92629: Palu, Louie.

XINHUA—(703) 875–0082; 1740 14th Street, Arlington, VA 22209: Zhang, Yan.

WHITE HOUSE NEWS PHOTOGRAPHERS' ASSOCIATION

P.O. Box 7119 Ben Franklin Station, Washington, DC 20044–7119

www.whnpa.org

OFFICERS

John Harrington, Freelance, *President*
Paul Morse, Freelance, *Vice President*
Ronald Sachs, Consolidated News Photos, *Secretary*
Jonathan Elswick, Associated Press, *Treasurer*

EXECUTIVE BOARD

Toni Sandys (Washington Post)
Matthew Cavanaugh (EPA)
Allison Shelley (Washington Times)
Ed Eaves (NBC News)
Charles MacDonald, (National Geographic Channel)
Fletcher Johnson, (ABC News)
Chip Somodevilla, Contest Chair (Getty Images)
Pege Gilgannon, Contest Chair, Television (WJLA–TV)
Pierre Kattar, Contest Chair, New Media (washingtonpost.com)
Jamie Rose, Contest Chair, Student (Freelance)
Leighton Mark, Education Chair (Associated Press)

MEMBERS REPRESENTED

Adlerblum, Robin: CBS News
Ake, J. David: Associated Press
Alberter, Jr., William: CNN
Allen, Tom: Washington Post (Ret.)
Allen, Michael: ABC News
Andrews, Philip: Roll Call
Andrews, Scott: Canon
Applewhite, J. Scott: Associated Press
Archambault, Charles: U.S. News & World Report
Arrington, Clyde: ABC News
Ashley, Douglas: Suburban Newspapers & ABC TV
Assaf, Christopher: Baltimore Sun
Atherton, James:
Auth, William: Freelance
Bacheler, Peter: Freelance
Bahler, Barry: Department of Homeland Security
Bahruth, William:
Baker, David: ITN
Ballard, Karen: Freelance
Barrick, Matthew: Caring Magazine
Baysden III, Earl: WTTG–TV
Beiser, H. Darr: USA Today
Benic, Patrick: UPI
Bennett, Ronald T.: Executive Branch
Bennett, Brian: Time
Berglie, James: Zuma Press
Biddle, Susan: Washington Post
Binks, Porter: Sports Illustrated
Bivera, Johnny: Freelance
Blaylock, Kenneth:
Bodnar, John: CNN
Bourg, James: Reuters
Bowe, Christy: ImageCatcher News
Bracco II, Dominic: Freelance
Brack, Dennis: Black Star
Brandon, Alex: Associated Press
Bridges, George: Knight Ridder / Tribune
Bridgham, Kenneth:
Brier, Joseph: Freelance
Brown, Stephen:
Brown, Thomas: Army Times
Brown, Sr., Henry: ABC
Bruce, Andrea: Washington Post
Bryan, Beverly:
Buell, Hal: AP (Ret.)

MEMBERS REPRESENTED—Continued

Bui, Khue: Freelance
Burgess, Robert: Freelance
Burke, Jr., William C.: Page One Photography
Burnett, David: Contact Press Images
Calvert, Mary: Washington Times
Carioti, Ricky: Washington Post
Cassetta, Guido: Freelance
Castoro, Susan: Associated Press
Cavanaugh, Matthew: EPA
Cedeno, Ken: Freelance
Ceneta, Manuel: Associated Press
Chang Crandall, Jennifer: Washingtonpost.com
Chikwendiu, Jahi: Washington Post
Cirace, Robert: CNN (Ret.)
Cirone, Joseph: Responsive Media
Clark, Bill: Roll Call
Clark, Kevin: Washington Post
Clarkson, Rich: Rich Clarkson & Associaties
Cochran, Michael: USA Today
Cohen, Marshall: Big Marsh News Photos
Cohen, Stuart: Freelance
Colburn, James: Freelance
Collins, Maxine: BBC TV
Conger, Dean:
Connor, Michael: Washington Times
Cook, Stephen: Washingtonpost.com
Cook, Dennis: Associated Press (Ret.)
Costello II, Thomas: Asbury Park Press
Couig, Caroline: Discovery Communications
Crane, Arnold: The LaVor Group
Crawford, Walter: WJLA–TV
Crowley, Stephen: The New York Times
Curran, Patrick: WTTG–TV
Curtis, Rob: Army Times Publishing
Curtiss, Cathaleen: AOL
Cutraro, Andrew: Aurora Photos
Daniell, Parker: Freelance
Daugherty, Bob: Associated Press (Ret.)
Davidson, Linda: Washington Post
Davis, Amy: Baltimore Sun
de la Cruz, Benedict: Washingtonpost.com
Dennehey, Paul:
Desfor, Max:
Devorah, Carrie: Freelance
Dharapak, Charles: Associated Press
DiBartolo, Melissa: Nikon
Dietsch, Kevin: UPI
Dietz, Jim: AP
Dillon, Tim:
Doane, Martin: WJLA–TV
Donaldson, Nancy: New York Times
Dorwin, Harold: Smithsonian Institution
Douliery, Oliver: ABACA Press
Downing, Larry: Reuters
Drapkin, Arnold: TIME Magazine
Dryden, Valerie: Freelance for: Bloomberg news, NYT
duCille, Michel: Washington Post
Dukehart, Coburn: NPR Digital News
Dukehart, Jr., Thomas: WUSA–TV
Duley, Jim: Penn Camera
Dunmire, John: WTTG–TV (Ret.)
Eaves, Ed: NBC News
Eddins, Joseph: Washington Times
Edmonds, Ron: Associated Press
Eisert, Sandra: Freelance Consultant
Elbert II, Joseph: Washington Post
Elovich, Dyan: Washingtonpost.com
Elswick, Jonathan: Associated Press
Elvington, Glenn: ABC News
Ernst, Jonathan: Freelance
Eroglu, Levent: Australian Broadcasting Corp.
Ewan, Julia: Washington Post
Ewing, David: Freelance
Fabiano, Gary: Freelance
Falk, Steven: Philadelphia Daily News
Falkenberg, Katie: Washington Times
Feld, Ric: Associated Press
Feldman, Roy: Freelance
Feldman, Randy: Viewpoint Communications Inc.
Ferron, Karl: Baltimore Sun
Fielman, Sheldon: NBC News
Figueroa, Noreen:
Fine, Paul: Fine Films
Fine, Holly: Fine Films
Fitz-Patrick, Bill: Freelance
Folwell, Frank: Freelance
Fookes, Gary: Freelance (Ret.)
Ford, Nancy: IFPO / American International News
Forte, BJ: WTTG–TV
Foss, Philip: Speed Graphic
Foster, H. William: Freelance
Frame, John: WTTG–TV
Freeman, Roland: Freelance
Freeman, Barry: ABC News
Frey, Katherine: Washington Post
Fridrich, George: Brighter Images Productions, LLC
Fulton, Bradley: CTV
Gail, C. Mark: Washington Post
Garcia, Alexandra: WPNI
Garcia, Mannie: Freelance
Geiger, Ken: National Geographic
Geissinger, Michael: Freelance
Ghanbari, Haraz: Associated Press
Giebel, Edward: ABC News Freelance
Gilgannon, Pege: WJLA
Gilka, Robert:
Gilkey, David: NPR
Glenn, Alexis: UPI
Gmiter, Bernard: ABC News, Freelance (Ret.)
Golden, Melissa: Freelance
Goodman, Jeffrey: NBC / Freelance
Goulait, Bert: Freelance
Gould - Phillips, Carol: Current Viewpoint
Goyal, Raghubir: Asia Today & India Globe / ATN News

MEMBERS REPRESENTED—Continued

Graham, Douglas: Roll Call
Grant, Kelli: Pixways Inc.
Green, Barnaby: Sky News
Greenblatt, William: UPI
Gripas, Yuri: Reuters
Guerrucci, Aude: Polaris
Gundy, Dorry: BBC News
Gupta, Avi: U.S. News & World Report
Guzy, Carol: Washington Post
Hakuta, Michael: Wash. Post Newsweek Interactive
Halstead, Dirck: The Digital Journalist
Hamburg, Harry: (Ret.)
Haring, Paul: Catholic News Service
Harnick, Andrew: Washington Examiner
Harrington, John: Freelance
Harrity, Chick: Whimsy Works
Heffner, Michael: AOL
Heikes, Darryl: Freelance
Heilemann, Tami: Department of Interior
Heiner, Steve: Nikon
Henderson, Gregory: Associated Press
Herbert, Gerald: Associated Press
Hershorn, Gary: Reuters
Hill, Robb: Freelance
Hillian, Vanessa: Washington Post (Ret.)
Hinds, Hugh: WRC / NBC
Hoffman, Brendan: Freelance
Hoiland, Harald:
Holloway, David: Freelance
Holt, Victor: Washington Informer
Hopkins, Brian: WJLA–TV
Horan, Michael: WTTG–TV
Hubbard, Garrett: USA Today
Hutchens, Jeff: Freelance
Ing, Lance: WTTG–TV
Jackson, Lawrence: Associated Press
Johnson, Fletcher: ABC
Johnson, Kenneth: ABC–TV
Johnston, Frank: Washington Post
Jones, Nelson: WTTG–TV
Joseph, Marvin: Washington Post
Kahn, Nikki: Washington Post
Kang, Hyungwon: Reuters News Pictures
Kapustin, Doug: Baltimore Sun
Kattar, Pierre: Washingtonpost.com
Kawajiri, Chiaki: Baltimore Sun
Kelly, Colin: Army Times
Kennedy, Thomas: Washington Post Newsweek Interactive
Kennedy, Charles: Knight Ridder / Tribune
Kennerly, David: Eagles Roar Inc.
Keres, Preston: Washington Post
Kittner, Sam: Freelance
Kleber, David:
Koenig III, Paul:
Koppelman, Mitch: Reuters Television
Korab, Alexandra: AOL
Kossoff, Leslie: LK Photos
Kraft, Brooks: Time Magazine
Lamarque, Kevin: Reuters
Lambert, H.M.:
Lamkey, Jr., Rod: Washington Times
Larsen, Gregory: Freelance
Lavies, Bianca: Freelance
LaVor, Marty: Freelance
Lawrence, Jeffrey:
Lee, David: Freelance
Lee, Erik: WTTG–TV
Lessig, Alan: Army Times
Levy, Glenn Ann: Freelance
Levy, John:
Lindquist, Heather: Freelance / SIPA
Lipski, Richard: Washington Post
Lizik, Ronald: Associated Press
Lockhart, June:
Lockley, Peter: The Washington Times
Loeb, Saul: AFP
Lopossey, Monica: Baltimore Sun
LoScalzo, James: U.S. News & World Report
Love, Diane: Tribal Cultures Productions
Lynaugh, Mike: Freelance
Lynch, Elizabeth: National Journal
Lyons, Paul: NET (Ret.)
MacDonald, Jim: Canadian TV Network
MacDonald, Charles: National Geographic Channel
MacMillan, Jeffrey: U.S. News & World Report, Freelance
Maddaloni, Christopher: Roll Call
Maggiolo, Vito: CNN
Mallin, Jay: Freelance
Mann, Donna:
Manolova, Yanina:
Mara, Melina: Washington Post
Mark, Leighton: Associated Press
Marks, Donovan: Washington National Cathedral
Martin, Jacquelin: AP
Martin, Jr., James: ABC News
Martineau, Gerald: Washington Post
Martinez Monsivais, Pablo: Associated Press
Mason, Thomas: WTTG–TV
Mathieson, Greg: MAI Photo News Agency, Inc.
Mazariegos, Mark: CBS News
Maze, Stephanie: Maze Productions Inc. / Moonstone Press, LLC
Mazer Field, Joni: Freelance
Mazzatenta, O.: Freelance
McAlpine, Chase: 6515 Belcrest Road, APT 208C
McCarthy III, Edward: Hudson Valley Black Press
McDermott, Richard: NBC Universal
McDonnell, John: Washington Post
McGinnis, Lowell: Roll Call / Contract
McKay, Richard: Cox Newspapers
McKee, Staci: WashingtonPost.com
McKenna, William: BBC World News America
McKiernan, Scott: Zuma Press
McNamee, Win: Getty Images

MEMBERS REPRESENTED—Continued

McNamee, Wallace: Freelance
McNay, James: Senior Editor Kobre Guide
Miller, Elisa: Freelance
Mills, Doug: New York Times
Mole, Robert: NBC
Morris, Larry: Washington Post (Ret.)
Morris, Peter: CNN
Morse, Paul: Freelance
Moulton, Paul:
Murano, Daniel: Washingtonpost.com
Murphy, John: Freelance
Murtaugh, Peter: Murtaugh Productions, LLC
Natoli, Sharon: Freelance
Nelson, Andrew: Christian Science Monitor
Newton, Jonathan: Washington Post
Nikpour, Javad: Ace Photo / Freelance
Nolan, David: Nolan & Company
Norling, Richard: Freelance
O'Keefe, Dennis: Freelance
O'Leary, William: Washington Post
Oates, Walter:
Ommanney, Charles: Newsweek
Ortez, George: (Ret.) since 1980
Palu, Louie: Zuma Press
Panzer, Chester: NBC–WRC
Parcell, James: Washington Post (Ret.)
Parikh, Chhayal: U.S. News & World Report
Partlow, Wayne: Associated Press
Pearson, Robert: Bob Pearson Photography
Pekala, Bill: Nikon
Pergola, Nichoals:
Perkins, Lucian: Freelance
Petros, Bill: Freelance
Pinczuk, Murray: Freelance
Poggi, Jennifer: U.S. News & World Report
Poole, John: NPR
Popper, Andrew: Business Week
Potasznik, David: Point of View Production Services Inc.
Powell, Jr., William: NBC (Ret.)
Powers, Carol: Freelance
Premack, Jay: Freelance
Proser, Michael: ABC–News
Rabbage, Mark: BBC TV
Raimondo, Lois: Washington Post
Raker, Lester: ABC News
Rane, Andrea: Freelance
Reed, Jason: Reuters
Reeder, Robert:
Rensberger, Scott: Freelance
Ribeiro, Luiz: The New York Post
Richards, Paul: AFP
Riecken, Astrid: Washington Times
Riley, Molly: Reuters
Roberts, Joshua: Freelance
Robinson, Sr., Clyde:
Rose, Jamie: Freelance
Rossman, Megan: WPNI
Roth, Jr., Johnie: NBC (Ret.)
Russek II, Ronald: UPI
Sachs, Ronald: Consolidated News Photos
Salisbury, Barbara: Washington Times / Insight Magazine
Sandys, Toni: Washington Post
Sardari, Kaveh: Sardi Group, Inc.
Saunders, Ray: Washington Post
Schauble, Justin: Persistent Video Productions
Schmick, Paul: Freelance (Ret.)
Schneider, Jack: NBC–TV
Scicchitano, Carmine: NBC
Semiatin, Morris: Morris Semiatin-Photographer
Shea, Nicole: AARP
Shefte, Whitney: Washingtonpost.com
Shelley, Allison: Washington Times
Shirmohammadi, Abbas: Panoramic Visions
Shlemon, Christopher: Independent TV News
Sikes, Laura: Freelance
Silverman, Joe: Washington Times
Simons, Beth: ABC News
Sisco, Paul: (Ret.)
Skeans, Jr., Ronald: BBC
Sloan, Tim: AFP
Smialowski, Brendan: Freelance
Smith, Dayna:
Smith, Jason: WTTG–TV
Sommer, Emilie: Freelance
Somodevilla, Kenneth: Getty
Souza, Peter: Ohio University
Stearns, Stan: Freelance
Stein, Norman: Ascent Media Systems and Technology Services
Stein III, Arthur: Freelance
Stoddard, Mark: Freelance
Stoklas, George: Embassy Camera (Ret.)
Suban, Mark: NIKON
Swain, Bethany Anne: CNN
Swann, Dierdre: Washingtonpost.com
Sweetapple, Daniel: Australian Broadcasting Corp.
Swenson, Gordon: ABC (Ret.)
Swiatkowski, Edward:
Sykes, Jack: Professional Pilot Magazine
Temchine, Michael: Freelance
Tessmer, Joseph: Freelance
Thalman, Mark: Across the Pond Productions
Thomas, Margaret:
Thomas, Ronald: Office Cable Television & Telecommunications
Thresher, James: Washington Post
Tiffen, Steve: The Tiffen Company
Tinsley, Jeff: Smithsonian Institution (Ret.)
Tolbert IV, George Dalton: Freelance (Ret.) U.S. Senate
Trippett, Robert: World Picture News
Tripplaar, Kristoffer: Freelance
Tsuboi, Kazuo: World Photo Press
Usher, Chris: Freelance

MEMBERS REPRESENTED—Continued

Valeri, Charlene: National Geographic
Van Riper, Frank: Goodman / Van Riper Photography
Vemmer, Shelia: Army Times
Vennell, Vicki: ABC News
Vicario, Virginia: ABC News
Voisin, Sarah: Washington Post
Voss, Stephen: Freelance
Vucci, Evan: Associated Press
Walker, Diana: Time Magazine
Wallace, Jim: Smithsonian Institution
Walsh, Susan: Associated Press
Walz, Mark: CNN
Ward, Fred: Black Star
Watrud, Donald: WTTG–TV
Watson, James: AFP
Weik, David: ABC Television News (Ret.)
Wells, Jim: Freelance
Welther, Fred:
Wiegman, Jr., Dave: (Ret.) NBC
Wilkes, Douglas: WTTG–TV
Williams, Milton: Freelance
Williams, Robert: NBC News
Williams, Thomas: Roll Call Newspaper
Williamson, Michael: Washington Post
Wilson, Jim: New York Times Photo
Wilson, Mark: Getty Images
Witcher, Troy: Washington Times / Insight Magazine
Witte, Joel: WTTG–TV
Wollenberg, Roger: United Press International
Wong, Alex: Getty Images
Woodward, Tracy: Washington Post
Wray, Eric: ABC News
Yokota, Victoria: Freelance
Young, Jim: Reuters
Young, Bruce: The Evans-McCan Group
Young, Jennifer: The Evans-McCan Group
Zervos, Stratis: Freelance-Zervos Video Productions, LLC
Zhang, Yan: XINHUA News Agency
Ziccardi, Marc: PNY Technologies, Inc.
Vineys, Kevin: Associated Press

RADIO AND TELEVISION CORRESPONDENTS' GALLERIES*

SENATE RADIO AND TELEVISION GALLERY

The Capitol, Room S–325, 224–6421

Director.—Michael Mastrian
Deputy Director.—Jane Ruyle
Senior Media Relations Coordinators: Michael Lawrence, Erin Yeatman
Media Relations Coordinators: Chris Bois, Arlen Salazar

HOUSE RADIO AND TELEVISION GALLERY

The Capitol, Room H–321, 225–5214

Director.—Olga Ramirez Kornacki
Deputy Director.—Andy Elias
Assistant for Administrative Operations Manager.—Gail Davis
Media Logistics Coordinators: Helen DeBarge, Anthony Kellaher, Kimberly Oates

EXECUTIVE COMMITTEE OF THE RADIO AND TELEVISION CORRESPONDENTS' GALLERIES

Linda Scott, The Newshour with Jim Lehrer, *Chair*
Peter Slen, C–SPAN, *Vice Chair*
Linda Kenyon, SRN News, *Treasurer*
Jeffrey Ballou, Aljazeera
Jill Jackson, CBS News
Dave McConnell, WTOP Radio
Chad Pergram, Fox News

RULES GOVERNING RADIO AND TELEVISION CORRESPONDENTS' GALLERIES

1. Persons desiring admission to the Radio and Television Galleries of Congress shall make application to the Speaker, as required by Rule 34 of the House of Representatives, as amended, and to the Committee on Rules and Administration of the Senate, as required by Rule 33, as amended, for the regulation of the Senate wing of the Capitol. Applicants shall state in writing the names of all radio stations, television stations, systems, or news-gathering organizations by which they are employed and what other occupation or employment they may have, if any. Applicants shall further declare that they are not engaged in the prosecution of claims or the promotion of legislation pending before Congress, the Departments, or the independent agencies, and that they will not become so employed without resigning from the galleries. They shall further declare that they are not employed in any legislative or executive department or independent agency of the Government, or by any foreign govern-

*Information is based on data furnished and edited by each respective gallery.

ment or representative thereof; that they are not engaged in any lobbying activities; that they do not and will not, directly or indirectly, furnish special information to any organization, individual, or group of individuals for the influencing of prices on any commodity or stock exchange; that they will not do so during the time they retain membership in the galleries. Holders of visitors' cards who may be allowed temporary admission to the galleries must conform to all the restrictions of this paragraph.

2. It shall be a prerequisite to membership that the radio station, television station, system, or news-gathering agency which the applicant represents shall certify in writing to the Radio and Television Correspondents' Galleries that the applicant conforms to the foregoing regulations.

3. The applications required by the above rule shall be authenticated in a manner that shall be satisfactory to the Executive Committee of the Radio and Television Correspondents' Galleries who shall see that the occupation of the galleries is confined to bona fide news gatherers and/or reporters of reputable standing in their business who represent radio stations, television stations, systems, or news-gathering agencies engaged primarily in serving radio stations, television stations, or systems. It shall be the duty of the Executive Committee of the Radio and Television Correspondents' Galleries to report, at its discretion, violation of the privileges of the galleries to the Speaker or to the Senate Committee on Rules and Administration, and pending action thereon, the offending individual may be suspended.

4. Persons engaged in other occupations, whose chief attention is not given to—or more than one-half of their earned income is not derived from—the gathering or reporting of news for radio stations, television stations, systems, or news-gathering agencies primarily serving radio stations or systems, shall not be entitled to admission to the Radio and Television Galleries. The Radio and Television Correspondents' List in the Congressional Directory shall be a list only of persons whose chief attention is given to or more than one-half of their earned income is derived from the gathering and reporting of news for radio stations, television stations, and systems engaged in the daily dissemination of news, and of representatives of news-gathering agencies engaged in the daily service of news to such radio stations, television stations, or systems.

5. Members of the families of correspondents are not entitled to the privileges of the galleries.

6. The Radio and Television Galleries shall be under the control of the Executive Committee of the Radio and Television Correspondents' Galleries, subject to the approval and supervision of the Speaker of the House of Representatives and the Senate Committee on Rules and Administration.

Approved.

NANCY PELOSI,
Speaker, House of Representatives.

CHARLES E. SCHUMER,
Chair, Senate Committee on Rules and Administration.

MEMBERS ENTITLED TO ADMISSION

RADIO AND TELEVISION CORRESPONDENTS' GALLERIES

Abbott, Stacey: National Public Radio
Abdalla, Hebah: Aljazeera International
Abdallah, Khalil: CNN
Abdalwahab, Yamen: Al Arabiya TV
Abdel-Aziz, Amr: AP–Broadcast
Abdulgawad, Atef: AP–Broadcast
Abe, Takaaki: Nippon TV Network
Abed, Nader: Middle East Television Network (Alhurra)
Abell, Jeff: Sinclair Broadcast Group
Abeshouse, Bob: Aljazeera International
Aboud, Abdushakur: Voice of America
Abraha, Zeresnaey: Aljazeera International
Abramson, Larry: National Public Radio
Abtar, Rana: Middle East Television Network (Alhurra)
Abu-Hamdyia, Reema: Russia Today Television
Abukasem, Hassan: Radio Free Asia
Aburahma, Eyad: Aljazeera Satellite Channel (Peninsula)
Acharya, Niharika: Voice of America
Ackerman, Tom: Aljazeera International
Acosta, Jim: CNN
Adams, Brian: Reuters Radio & TV
Adams, Douglas A.: NBC News
Adams, Katy: WTTG–Fox Television
Adams, Marc: BBC
Addison, Quentin: Metro Teleproductions
Adlerblum, Robin: CBS News
Advani, Reena: National Public Radio
Aervitz, Irina: Federal News Service
Ahearn, Brian Marshall: East Coast Television
Ahlers, Mike: CNN
Ahmad, Asad: Voice of America
Ahmed, Ali: AP–Broadcast
Ahmed, Lukman: BBC
Ahmed, M. Anis: Voice of America
Aich, Atirath: Aljazeera International
Aiello, Jr., Augustine ''Bud'': National Public Radio
Aisida, Christopher: NBC News
Aitken, Cynthia: AP–Broadcast
Akahori, Yuichi: Nippon TV Network
Alami, Mohammed: Aljazeera Satellite Channel (Peninsula)
Albano, Thomas: CBS News
Alberter, William: CNN
Alcazar, Carlos: Hispanic Communications Network
Alcazar, Obdulia: Hispanic Communications Network
Alexander, Blayne: NBC News
Alexander, Clinton N.: CBS News
Alexander, Kenneth: C-SPAN
Alexander, Robert: WJLA–TV / Newschannel 8
Alfa, Nadine: Reuters Radio & TV
Alford, Kelly: Middle East Television Network (Alhurra)
Ali, Ahmed M.: FEDNET
Aliaga, Julio: WZDC–TV
Alimchandani, Manish: Voice of America
Aliyarova Horowitz, Dilshad: Voice of America
Allahyari, Gholamreza: Voice of America
Allard, John William: ABC News
Allard, Marc: BBC
Alldredge, Thomas: C–SPAN
Allen, Darrell: Voice of America
Allen, Keith: Reuters Radio & TV
Allison, Lynn Quarles: WETA
Almanza, Armando: Ventana Productions
Almeleh, John: Pacifica Radio
Alnwick, Melanie: WTTG–Fox Television
Alrawi, Khaldoun: AP–Broadcast
Alvey, Jay: WRC–TV / NBC–4
Amirault-Michel, Theresa: C–SPAN
Amkas, Karlina: Voice of America
Ammerman, Stuart: CBS News
Amparo, Raquel Divina: WTTG–Fox Television
Anastasi, Patrick: NBC News
Anderson, Carl: Diversified Communications, Inc. (DCI)
Anderson, Charles: WETA
Anderson, Chinita: National Public Radio
Anderson, Patrick: Swiss Broadcasting
Andrews, Wyatt: CBS News
Ang, Sarita: Voice of America
Angelini, Mark: Belo Capital Bureau
Angle, James L.: Fox News
Angrand, Salome: Medill News Service
Anna, Ubeda: Spanish Public Television (TVE)
Anthony, Karyn: CBS News
Antonie, Victor: Reuters Radio & TV
Anyse, Alana: Fox News
Aoun, Larissa: Middle East Television Network (Alhurra)
Apte, Aunshuman: Voice of America
Aragon, Carlos O.: WPWC–AM (Radio Fiesta)
Arcega, Milandro: Voice of America
Archer, Nelson: CNN
Archuleta, Eddie: CBS News
Archuleta, John: CBS News
Arena, Bruno: Diversified Communications, Inc. (DCI)
Arensberg, Chloe: CBS News

MEMBERS ENTITLED TO ADMISSION—Continued

Arenstein, Howard: CBS News
Arestad, Anders: C–SPAN
Arioka, Kaori: NHK–Japan Broadcasting Corporation
Armfield, Robert: Fox News
Armstrong, Patricia M.: ABC News
Armstrong, Thomas Ayres: ABC News
Armwood, Adrian: CBS News
Arnold, Howard Clayton: WTTG–Fox Television
Arreaga, Marco Vinicio: CNN
Artesona, Eva: TV3–Televisio De Catalunya
Arthy, Sally: Sky News
Ary, Haider: Voice of America
Aryankalavil, Babu: Middle East Television Network (Alhurra)
Asaoka, Motoyasu: TV Tokyo
Asher, Julie: TF1–French TV
Assmann, Karin: Spiegel German TV
Assuras, Thalia: CBS News
Atai, Shahin: C–SPAN
Atif, Muhammad: Voice of America
Atkinson, Emily: CNN
Attawia, Moaz: American Press and TV Services (APTVS)
Attkisson, Sharyl: CBS News
Aubrey, Allison: National Public Radio
Augenstein, Neal: WTOP Radio
Augustus, Shannon: C–SPAN
Auster, Bruce: National Public Radio
Austin, Jonathan: CTV Canadian TV
Austin, Kenneth: NBC News
Ausura, Bret: NBC News
Avary, Max: Radio Free Asia
Avloshenko, Maxim: Russia Today Television
Avrutine, Matthew: CNN
Awada, Mohamad: AP–Broadcast
Aynte, Abdirahman: BBC
Azais, Jean Pascal: Spanish Public Television (TVE)
Azizzada, Abdul Ahad: Voice of America
Azzam, Heni: Aljazeera Satellite Channel (Peninsula)
Baader, Johann Tobias: German TV ARD
Baber, Christine: Mobile Video Services, LTD.
Bacheler, David: CNN
Bachenheimeri, Stephan: Deutsche Welle TV
Baghi, Baubak: Aljazeera Satellite Channel (Peninsula)
Bagnall, Thomas: Voice of America
Bagnato, Barry: CBS News
Baier, Bret: Fox News
Bailor, Michelle: C–SPAN
Bajoghli, Ramin: Voice of America
Baker, Cissy: Tribune Broadcasting
Baker, Dai: Independent Television News (ITN)
Baker, Les: Fox News
Baker, Sarah E.: CNN
Balinovic, Daniel: Reuters Radio & TV
Ballasy, Nicholas: CNSNEWS.COM
Ballou, Jeff: Aljazeera International
Balsamo, James: Diversified Communications, Inc. (DCI)
Ban, Hyeonju: Seoul Broadcasting System (SBS)
Banaszak, Brendan: National Public Radio
Banerjee, Sreya: Reuters Radio & TV
Banhawy, Fahd: American Press and TV Services (APTVS)
Banjanovic, Almir: CNN
Banks, Erik: CNN
Banks, James: Eurovision Americas, Inc.
Banks, Josh: Fox News
Banks, Mark: ABC News
Banks, Morris: CBS News
Bannigan, Mike: Fox Business Network
Banville, Lee: The Newshour with Jim Lehrer
Barba, Patricia Yolanda: C–SPAN
Barbour, Lantz: Eye-To-Eye Video
Barnard, Bob: WTTG–Fox Television
Barnd, Jeff: Sinclair Broadcast Group
Barnes, Audrey: WUSA-TV
Barnes, Chris: Fox News Radio
Barnes, David: Community TV of PG's
Barnes, Peter: Fox Business Network
Barnett, Christopher: Environment & Energy Publishing, LLC
Barnett, James: CNN
Baroody, Emaile: AP–Broadcast
Barr, Bruce: CBS News
Barreda, Eric: NHK–Japan Broadcasting Corporation
Barrett, C. Wesley: Hearst–Argyle Television
Barrett, Kathryn: ABC News
Barrett, Natasha: WJLA–TV / Newschannel 8
Barrett, Ted: CNN
Barreyre, Christophe: TF1–French TV
Barshak, Valery: Aljazeera International
Bartlett, Scott: NHK–Japan Broadcasting Corporation
Bartlett, Stephen: CNN
Barton, Tomoko: Fuji TV Japan
Basch, Michelle: WTOP Radio
Bascom, Jon: Bloomberg Radio & TV
Bash, Dana: CNN
Basinger, Stuart: Fox News
Baskerville, Kia: CBS News
Bassas, Antoni: TV3–Televisio De Catalunya
Bastien, Andrew: Aljazeera International
Bate, Dana: Nightly Business Report
Batten, Rodney: NBC News
Baumel, Susan: Voyage Productions
Bautista, Mark: WJLA–TV / Newschannel 8
Bawa, Malini: Fox News
Baydalov, Pavel: Channel One Russian TV
Baylor, Demetra: Aljazeera International
Bays, James: Aljazeera International
Baysden III, Earl T.: WTTG–Fox Television
Beahn, James: WTTG–Fox Television

MEMBERS ENTITLED TO ADMISSION—Continued

Beal, Kate: WTOP Radio
Beale, Jonathan: BBC
Beall, Gary: NBC News
Beatty, Laura: Al Arabiya TV
Bebic, Damir: Voice of America
Beck, Katie: BBC
Becker, Bruce: Fox Business Network
Becker, Chris: Fox News
Becker, Farrel: CBS News
Becker, Frank: WJLA–TV / Newschannel 8
Bediako, Regina: NHK–Japan Broadcasting Corporation
Beemsterboer, Nicole: National Public Radio
Bejarano, Mark: National Public Radio
Belcher, Christopher: BBC
Bell, Alfred: NBC News
Bell, Brad: WJLA–TV / Newschannel 8
Bell, Reginald Joey: NBC News
Bellard, Joseph: Bloomberg Radio & TV
Bellis, Michael: NBC News
Belter, Stephen Lowell: C–SPAN
Bena, John: CNN
Bender, Bob: ABC News
Bender, Jason: C–SPAN
Benetato, Michael: NBC News
Benitez, Barbara: Aljazeera International
Benjamin, Brian: ABC News
Bennett, Justin: NBC News
Bennett, Mark R.: CBS News
Bennett, Shepard: SRN News (SALEM)
Bensen, Jackie: WRC–TV / NBC–4
Benson, Miles: Link TV
Benson, Pamela S.: CNN
Bentz, Leslie Ann: CNN
Bentz, Thomas: CNN
Berenstein, Erica E.: Agence France Presse (AFP–TV)
Bergel, Jenni: National Public Radio
Berger, Judson: Fox News
Bergmann, Christina: Deutsche Welle TV
Berko, Art: Viewpoint Communications
Berman, David: CNN
Bernardini, Laura: CNN
Bernier, Marc: Talk Radio News Service
Bernius, Andrew: C–SPAN
Bertelli, Mara: Swiss Broadcasting
Berti, Barbara: CNN
Best, Tanisha: NBC News
Betsill, Brett: C–SPAN
Bevington, Ben: BBC
Beyer, Kevin: Diversified Communications, Inc. (DCI)
Beyer, William: WTTG–Fox Television
Bezdrob, Shayla: Fox News
Bharania, Anoopam: Reuters Radio & TV
Bhatia, Varuna: Fox News
Bickel, Charles: East Coast Television
Biddle, Michael: C–SPAN
Biggs, Mark: Aljazeera International
Bintrim, Tim R.: NBC News
Bird, Charles: Irish Radio & TV (RTE)
Bishara, Marwan: Aljazeera International
Bistis, George: Voice of America
Bivens, Laquasha: CNN
Bjoergaas, Tove: Norwegian Broadcasting
Black, Phillip M.: ABC News
Blackburn, Regina: NBC News
Blackman, Jay: NBC News
Blackman, John: NBC News
Blackwill, Sarah: NBC News
Blakley, Jonathan: National Public Radio
Blanchet, Sharon: BBC
Blanco, Hugo: AP–Broadcast
Blanco, Iscar: Voice of America
Blandburg, Victor: Irish Radio & TV (RTE)
Blitzer, Wolf: CNN
Block, Deborah: Voice of America
Block, Melissa: CNN
Block, Melissa: National Public Radio
Blooston, Victoria: NBC News
Blount, Jeffrey: NBC News
Blythe, Andrew: Eurovision Americas, Inc.
Bo, Teresa: Aljazeera International
Bock, Nicolas: Canadian Broadcasting Corporation (CBC)
Bodlander, Gerald: AP–Broadcast
Bodnar, John: CNN
Bohannon, Garrett: Eurovision Americas, Inc.
Bohannon, Joseph: NBC News
Bohn, Kevin: CNN
Bohrman, David: CNN
Boland, Siobhan: C–SPAN
Bolduan, Katherine: CNN
Bonamigo, Bruno: Canadian Broadcasting Corporation (CBC)
Bonds, Howard: Aljazeera International
Booker, Brakkton: National Public Radio
Bookhultz, Bruce: WJLA–TV / Newschannel 8
Boone, Dannie: C–SPAN
Borger, Gloria: CNN
Borniger, Herta: German TV ARD
Bortner, Christopher: CNN
Bosch, Anna: Spanish Public Television (TVE)
Bosch van Rosenthal, Eelco: NOS DUTCH PUBLIC RADIO & TV (VRT)
Bosland, Katie MacLean: ABC News
Bost, Mark: WUSA–TV
Boswell, Craig: Fox News
Boughton, Bryan: Fox News
Bouleau, Gilles: TF1–French TV
Bowen, Timothy: WETA
Bowman, Michael: Voice of America
Bowman, Quinn: The Newshour with Jim Lehrer
Bowman, Tom: National Public Radio
Bowser, Betty Ann: The Newshour with Jim Lehrer
Boyd, Wayne F.: ABC News

MEMBERS ENTITLED TO ADMISSION—Continued

Brablec, Radek: National Public Radio
Bradley Hagerty, Barbara: National Public Radio
Bragale, Charles: WRC–TV / NBC–4
Bragg, Jennifer: Aljazeera International
Bramson, Robert E.: ABC News
Branche, Glennwood: ABC News
Brandt, John: Fox News
Brandus, Paul: Talk Radio News Service
Branigan, Pat J.: The Washington Bureau
Bransford, Fletcher: Fox News
Brasch, Darci: WTOP Radio
Braun, Joshua: CNN
Brawner, Greta: C–SPAN
Bream, Shannon: Fox News
Breiterman, Charles: ABC News
Brevner, Michael: CNN
Brewer, Katherine: Australian Broadcasting Corporation
Brewton, Fashela: NBC News
Brickley, Adam: CNSNEWS.COM
Brieger, Annette: German TV ARD
Bright, Whitney: NBC News
Brinkley, Danielle: To The Contrary (Persephone Productions)
Briski, Natasa: PRO Plus
Britch, Ray: CNN
Britt, Lanna: Fox News
Brittain, Becky: CNN
Brock, Alan Matthew: WJLA–TV / Newschannel 8
Brockman, Joshua: National Public Radio
Brody, David: CBN News
Broffman, Craig A.: CNN
Broleman, Michael: NBC Newschannel
Bronstein, Scott: CNN
Brookes, Adam: BBC
Brooks, Kurt: WUSA–TV
Brooks, Sam: ABC News
Broom, Jr., William Wescott: WUSA–TV
Brower, Brooke: NBC News
Brown, Adam: NBC News
Brown, Christopher: Talk Radio News Service
Brown, Dana: Hearst–Argyle Television
Brown, Daniel: WTTG–Fox Television
Brown, Daryl: WTTG–Fox Television
Brown, Edgar: Fox News
Brown, Gavin: Morningside Partners, LLC
Brown, Henry M.: ABC News
Brown, Jeffrey: The Newshour with Jim Lehrer
Brown, Jerome: Voice of America
Brown, Joel L.: CBS News
Brown, Kathy: Radio One
Brown, Kristi: CBS News
Brown, Malcolm: Feature Story News
Brown, Matt: CN8 The Comcast Network
Brown, Pamela: WJLA–TV / Newschannel 8
Brown, Paul: C–SPAN
Brown, Paul: National Public Radio
Brown, Randall: NBC News
Brown, Sarah: Aljazeera International
Brown, Tracy Ann: AP–Broadcast
Browne, Kari: BBC
Bruce, Andrea: CBS News
Bruna, Gaby: WASHINGTONPOST.COM
Bruns, David: AP–Broadcast
Bryant, Aubrey: WUSA–TV
Bryce, Alison Kairns: National Public Radio
Brzezinski, Mika: NBC News
Bua, Jon-Christopher: Sky News
Buchanan, Marisa: NBC News
Buck, Melanie: CNN
Buckhorn, Burke: CNN
Buckland, Carol: CNN
Buckley, Julia Redpath: National Public Radio
Buehler, Paul: WTTG–Fox Television
Buel, Meredith: Voice of America
Bullard, Larry: WRC–TV / NBC–4
Bullard Harmon, Susan: CBS News
Bullock, Peter: Reuters Radio & TV
Bullock, Tom: National Public Radio
Bundock, Susan J.: C–SPAN
Burch, Brian: CNN
Burdick, Leslie: C–SPAN
Burgarella, Hunter: CNN
Burgdorf, Louis: NBC News
Burke, James: C–SPAN
Burke, Michael C.: Voice of America
Burketh, Ivan: National Public Radio
Burkowske, Andrew: Reuters Radio & TV
Burlij, Terence: The Newshour with Jim Lehrer
Burnett, Gordon: Radio Free Asia
Burns, Alison: Cox Broadcasting
Burton, Alex: Aljazeera International
Burton, Matthew W.: ABC News
Bushman, Monica: America Abroad Media
Bustamante, Antonio: Televisa News Network (ECO)
Butcher, Robert E: National Public Radio
Butler, James M.: Diversified Communications, Inc. (DCI)
Butler, Norman Anthony: NBC News
Butler, Shannan: CNN
Byrne, Joseph: Talk Radio News Service
Byrnes, Dennis: National Public Radio
C. W. Hsu, Roger: Voice of America
Cabral, Juan E.: CNN
Cacas, Max: Federal News Radio AM 1050
Cadoret, Remi: TF1–French TV
Cahill Murphy, Kathy: C–SPAN
Caifa, Karin: CNN
Calder, William: CBS News
Caldwell, Leigh Ann: Free Speech Radio News
Caldwell, Traci: NBC News
Calfat, Marcel: Canadian Broadcasting Corporation (CBC)
Calo-Christian, Nancy: C–SPAN
Camarda, Tim: Viewpoint Communications

MEMBERS ENTITLED TO ADMISSION—Continued

Cameron, Carl: Fox News
Cameron, Scott: National Public Radio
Campbell, Barbara: National Public Radio
Campbell, Christopher: Aljazeera Satellite Channel (Peninsula)
Campbell, Colin: ATN Productions, LTD.
Campbell, Karen: Community TV of PG's
Cancelleri, Heidi: East Coast Television
Candia, Kirsten: German TV ZDF
Canizales, Cesar Alberto: Fox News
Caperton, Katherine: XM Satellite Radio
Caplan, Craig: C–SPAN
Capra, Anthony: NBC News
Capuchinho, Marcelo: TV Globo International
Caravello, David: CBS News
Carberry, Sean: America Abroad Media
Cardarelli, John: C–SPAN
Carey, Julie: WRC–TV / NBC–4
Carlson, Brett: Dispatch Broadcast Group
Carlson, Brett: NBC Newschannel
Carlson, Christopher: ABC News
Carlson, Steve: Fox News
Carlsson, Leif: Swedish Broadcasting
Carlsson, Lisa: Swedish Broadcasting
Carner, John: Eurovision Americas, Inc.
Carney, Keith: FEDNET
Caronello, Sophie: Bloomberg Radio & TV
Carpeaux, Emily: Feature Story News
Carpel, Michael: Fox News
Carpio, Erick: WZDC–TV
Carr, Martin: WETA
Carrick, Kenneth: C–SPAN
Carrillo, Silvio: Aljazeera International
Carroll, Alfred G.: East Coast Television
Carroll, Patricia: CNN
Carson, Charles: WTTG–Fox Television
Carter, Brianne: WJLA–TV / Newschannel 8
Carter, Christopher: CNN
Carter, Dave: WRC–TV / NBC–4
Carter, Jr., Walter: Fox News
Casanas, Juan: Fox News
Casey, Libby: Alaska Public Radio Network
Casey, Sean: WRC–TV / NBC–4
Cassano, Joseph Angelo: East Coast Television
Cassidy, David: Belo Capital Bureau
Castiel, Carol: Voice of America
Catanza, Damian Ross: Fox Business Network
Cates, Ann: Marketwatch
Catherine, Carl Cyril: ABC News
Catrett, David Keith: CNN
Causey, Mike: Federal News Radio AM 1050
Cavin, Anthony: CBS News
Cawley, Kevin: Aljazeera International
Cecil, Brenda: Deutsche Welle TV
Centanni, Steve: Fox News
Cetta, Denise: CBS News
Chaboudez, Patrick: Swiss Broadcasting
Chace, Zoe: National Public Radio
Chaggaris, Steven: CBS News
Chandler, Matthew: Aljazeera International
Chang, Ailsa: National Public Radio
Chang, Darzen: WETA
Chang, Min: New Tang Dynasty TV
Chang, Peggy: Voice of America
Changuris, Zeke: WJLA–TV / Newschannel 8
Channell, Warren: CNN
Chapin, Edith: CNN
Chapman, Irwin: Bloomberg Radio & TV
Chapman, Maria: Aljazeera International
Chapman, Michael W.: CNSNEWS.COM
Chappell, Jill: CNN
Charpa, Silvia: German Broadcasting Systems–ARD
Chase, David: Cox Broadcasting
Chattman, Tanya: C–SPAN
Chavez, Roby: WTTG–Fox Television
Chaytor, David: WUSA–TV
Chell, Lindsay: CBS News
Chen, Yi Qiu: Hong Kong Phoenix Satellite Television
Chenevey, Steve: WTTG–Fox Television
Cherkaoui, Adil: Middle East Television Network (Alhurra)
Cherkuru, Kavitha: Aljazeera International
Chernenkoff, Kelly: Fox News
Cherouny, Robert: Aljazeera International
Cherquis, Gustavo: WZDC–TV
Chevez, Carlos: National Public Radio
Chicca, Trish: CNN
Chick, Jane S.: CBS News
Chimes, Art: Voice of America
Ching, Nike: Voice of America
Chinn, Lisa: ABC News
Chinn Lucie, Surae: WUSA–TV
Chirinos, Carlos: BBC
Cho, Eunjung: Voice of America
Cho, Soo Hyun: MBC–TV Korea (Munhwa)
Chophel, Lobsang: Radio Free Asia
Chrisinger, Travis Renee: ABC News
Christian, George: CBS News
Chung, E-Ting: CTI–TV (Taiwan)
Cilberti, David: CNN
Cinque, Vicente: TV Globo International
Claar, Matthew: C–SPAN
Clark, James: C–SPAN
Clark, Stephen: Fox News
Clark, Theodore E.: National Public Radio
Clary, Gregory: CNN
Clemann, William: WUSA–TV
Clemons, Bobby: CNN
Cline, Betsy: NBC News
Clugston, Gregory: SRN News (Salem)
Clune, Sarah: The Newshour with Jim Lehrer
Cockerham, Richard: Fox News
Cocklin, Anne: ABC News
Cocklin, Stephen: ABC News
Coffey-Lambert, Claudia: WTTG–Fox Television

MEMBERS ENTITLED TO ADMISSION—Continued

Coffman, Mary: Medill News Service
Cofske, Harvey: Irish Radio & TV (RTE)
Cohen, Josh: C–SPAN
Cole, Bryan: Fox News
Coleman, Steven: AP–Broadcast
Coleman, Thomas: CBS News
Coles, David: The Newshour with Jim Lehrer
Colimore, Eric: Fox News
Coll, Dennis: National Public Radio
Collender, Howard: Mobile Video Services, LTD.
Collingwood, Eloise: C–SPAN
Collins, Bruce D.: C–SPAN
Collins, Maxine: BBC
Collins, Michael: Voice of America
Collins, Pat: WRC–TV / NBC–4
Collins, Sr. Russell W.: East Coast Television
Colson, Allison: CNN
Colton, Michael: Canadian Broadcasting Corporation (CBC)
Combs, Cody: CNN
Compton, Woodrow: CNN
Conan, Neal: National Public Radio
Concaugh, Jr., Joseph: Diversified Communications, Inc. (DCI)
Coney, Carol: CBS News
Conlin, Sheila: NBC Newschannel
Conneen, Mike: WJLA–TV / Newschannel 8
Conner, Eric: Fox News
Connolly, Camille: CBS News
Connolly, Kevin: BBC
Connor, Brendan: Aljazeera International
Connors, Ben: Aljazeera International
Connors, Erin: ATN Productions, LTD.
Conover, William: C–SPAN
Conroy, Margaret: NBC News
Contreras, Glenda: Telemundo Network
Contreras, Jorge: Univision
Conway, Zoe: BBC
Cook, Court: WJLA–TV / Newschannel 8
Cook, James L.: C–SPAN
Cook, Peter: Bloomberg Radio & TV
Cooke, David M.: Diversified Communications, Inc. (DCI)
Cooke, Joe: ABC News
Coomarasamy, James: BBC
Cooper, Caroline: HD Net
Cooper, John: CBS News
Cooper, Rebecca J.: WJLA–TV / Newschannel 8
Corcoran, Patricia: WTTG–Fox Television
Cordes, Nancy: CBS News
Corner, Cleve: C–SPAN
Cornish-Emery, Audie: National Public Radio
Correa, Pedro: Telemundo Network
Correro, Michael: Aljazeera International
Cortez, William Fernando Pinzon: Telesur
Costantini, Bob: CNN
Costello, Amanda Elizabeth: CNN
Costello, Thomas: NBC News
Cote, Timothy: ABC News
Cotterman, Christina: Fox News
Coudoux, Sylvain: NHK–Japan Broadcasting Corporation
Coulter, Pam: ABC News
Courson, Paul: CNN
Cousins, Bria C.: CNBC
Cover, Matthew: CNSNEWS.COM
Cowman, Chris: East Coast Television
Coyte, Benjamin: CNN
Craca, Thomas: CBS News
Craig, John: Diversified Communications, Inc. (DCI)
Craig, John: East Coast Television
Crandall, Jennifer Chang: WASHINGTONPOST.COM
Cratty, Carol A.: CNN
Cravedi, Dennis: C–SPAN
Craven, William C.: National Public Radio
Crawford, James: CNN
Crawford, Walter: WJLA–TV / Newschannel 8
Crawford Greenburg, Jan: ABC News
Crawley, Plummer: CNBC
Creswell, Kelly: WJLA–TV / Newschannel 8
Cridland, Jeffrey: WUSA–TV
Crosariol, Paul Michael: Diversified Communications, Inc. (DCI)
Crosswhite-Chigbue, Karla: CNN
Crowley, Candy: CNN
Crowley, Dennis: United News and Information
Crudele, Bethany: CNN
Crum, John: CBS News
Crupi, Nick: Voice of America
Crutchfield, Curtis: Community TV of PG's
Cruz, Danny: Federal News Service
Csonka, Judit: Hungarian News TV
Cuddy, Matthew: CNBC
Culbertson, Danielle: Aljazeera International
Culhane, Patricia: NBC News
Cullen, Michael: National Public Radio
Cullum, James W.: Talk Radio News Service
Cunha, John: CNN
Cunningham, Anthony: Reuters Radio & TV
Curran, Patrick J.: WTTG–Fox Television
Currier, Liam: C–SPAN
Curtis, Alexander: C–SPAN
Curtis, Jodie: Fox News
Czaplinski, Michael: National Public Radio
Czzowitz, Greg: C–SPAN
Dahiya, Nishant: National Public Radio
Dahl, Heather: Feature Story News
Dalbah, Mohammad: Aljazeera Satellite Channel (Peninsula)
Dalmasy, Patricia: Voice of America
Daly, Corbett B.: Thomson Reuters
Daly, John: CBS News
Damdul, Dorjee: Radio Free Asia
Danielewicz, Joe: Fox News

MEMBERS ENTITLED TO ADMISSION—Continued

Daniels, Pete: C–SPAN
d'Annibale, Thomas J.: ABC News
Dao, Thao: Radio Free Asia
Dargakis, Minas: Voice of America
Daschle, Kelly: AP–Broadcast
d'Auchamp, Elisabeth: Danish Broadcasting Corporation
Dauchess, Matthew: C–SPAN
Daugherty, Jeffery: Voice of America
Davenport, Anne: The Newshour with Jim Lehrer
Davie, Bianca: AP–Broadcast
Davieaud, Helene: TF1–French TV
Davis, Clinton: WTTG–Fox Television
Davis, Jennifer: Fox News
Davis, Marcus: CNN
Davis, Mitch: Fox News Radio
Davis, Patrick A.: CNN
Davis, Rebecca: National Public Radio
Davis, Tanya: C–SPAN
Davoudi, Rima: Aljazeera International
Davydov, Allan: Radio Free Europe
Day, Kara: CNN
De Chalvron, Alain: France 2 Television
de Franceschi, Jela: Voice of America
de Guise, Louis: Canadian Broadcasting Corporation (CBC)
De La Cruz, Benedict: WASHINGTONPOST.COM
De La Torre, Gloria Vanessa: Caracol Television
de Nies, Yunji Elisabeth: ABC News
de Schaetzen, Emilie: Eurovision Americas, Inc.
de Sola, David: CNN
de Vega, Carlos: CNN
Dean, Erika: National Public Radio
Debre, Guillaume: TF1–French TV
DeCherd, Chris: Voice of America
Decker, Jonathan: Reuters Radio & TV
DeFrank, Debra: Fox News
Dehghanpour, Siamak: Voice of America
del Pino, Javier: Cadena Ser
Delargy, Christine: CBS News
Delfour, Stephane H.: Agence France Presse (AFP–TV)
D'Elia, Bartholomew Joseph: CBS News
Delta, Monica Cecilia: Univision
DeMar, Brian: National Public Radio
DeMarco, Lauren: WTTG–Fox Television
Demarest, Sarah: NBC News
DeMark, Michael Angelo: Adventure Hill ENG
DeMark, Michael: Fox News
Demas, William: Diversified Communications, Inc. (DCI)
Dennert, Mary Pat: Fox News
Deputy, William: National Public Radio
DePuyt, Bruce: WJLA–TV / Newschannel 8
Deroche, Sylvie: Swiss Broadcasting
Derville, Claire: Canal Plus French TV
Desgrosseilliers, Kate: C–SPAN
DeSimone, Bridget: The Newshour with Jim Lehrer
Desjardins, Lisa: CNN
Dessert, Tristan: TF1–French TV
Detrow, Jon: AP–Broadcast
Deveson, Max: BBC
DeVito, Andrea: Fox News
Dhindsa, Gurvir: WTTG–Fox Television
Dhue, Stephanie: Nightly Business Report
Diakides, Anastasia: CNN
Diamond, Aaron: France 2 Television
Diarra, Fatou: BBC
Diaz, Juan Carlos: Telemundo Network
Dickerson, Villinda: Aljazeera International
Diggs, Bridget: C–SPAN
Dillon, H. Estel: NBC Newschannel
Dills, Geoff: Independent Television News (ITN)
Dimmler, Erika: CNN
Dimsdale, John: Marketplace Radio
Dineen, Dawn: Morningside Partners, LLC
Disselkamp, Henry: ABC News
Dittmer, Bryan: ABC News
Divaris, Oliver: German TV ZDF
Dixon Gumm, Penny: Voice of America
Dixson, Charles H.: CBS News
Diylan, Jani: Voice of America
Djordjevic, Bratislav: Voice of America
Doane, Martin C.: WJLA–TV / Newschannel 8
Dobbins, Colin: CNN
Dobhal, Deepak: Voice of America
Doebele, Constance: C–SPAN
Doell, Michelle: C–SPAN
Doherty, Brian: Fox News
Doherty, Peter M.: ABC News
Dolce, Stephen: CNN
Dolma, Rigdhen: Radio Free Asia
Donaghy, Nina: Fox News
Donahue, Edward: AP–Broadcast
Donald, William: Eye–To–Eye Video
Donelan, Jennifer: WJLA–TV / Newschannel 8
Donnison, Jon: BBC
Donovan, Beth: National Public Radio
Donovan, Brian: ABC News
Donovan, Christopher: NBC News
Dorcil, Cherubin: Voice of America
Dore, Margaret: Fox News
Dorning, Courtney: National Public Radio
Dorobek, Chris: Federal News Radio AM 1050
Dougherty, Danny: STATELINE.ORG
Dougherty, Jill: CNN
Dougherty, Mark: WUSA–TV
Dougherty, Martin: CNN
Dougherty, Paul G.: ABC News
Douglas, Dianna: National Public Radio
Dowlatshahi, Tala: Talk Radio News Service
Downey, Truval: The Newshour with Jim Lehrer
Doyle Belvedere, Jessica: WUSA–TV
Dozier, Kimberly: CBS News
Dress, Marc: Metro Teleproductions

MEMBERS ENTITLED TO ADMISSION—Continued

Drosjack, Melissa: Fox News
Dubinsky, Inna: Voice of America
Dubroff, Richard: C–SPAN
Duckham, Justin: Talk Radio News Service
Duffy, Brian: National Public Radio
Dukehart, Coburn: National Public Radio
Dumpe, Megan: Fox News
Dunaway, John: CNN
Duncan, Michael J: Potomac Radio News
Duncan, Victoria: NBC News
Dunkin, John: ABC News
Dunlavey, Thomas: CNN
Dunlop, William: Eurovision Americas, Inc.
Dunn, Katia: National Public Radio
Dunn, Lauren: WRC–TV / NBC–4
Dunston, Andre: WJLA–TV / Newschannel 8
Dupree, Jamie: Cox Broadcasting
Durand, Lucho: Aljazeera International
Durham, Deborah: Univision
Durham, Lisa: CNN
Durham, Timothy: Aljazeera International
Durkin, Edward: WRC–TV / NBC–4
Durnin, Gordon: Aljazeera International
Dutton, Beth: Fox News
Dyball, Kenneth: C–SPAN
Dyer, Lois: CBS News
Eades, Jr., Paul: C–SPAN
Eagle, William: Voice of America
Eaton, Hugh: National Public Radio
Eaves, James: NBC News
Eborn, Katrice: C–SPAN
Ebrahim, Margaret: HD Net
Echevarria, Pedro L.: C–SPAN
Echeverria, Jamillah: WZDC–TV
Echols, Jerry: Fox News
Eck, Christina: German Press Agency
Eckert, Barton: WTOP Radio
Eckert, Jessica: Army Times Publishing Company
Edmondson, William: Fox News
Edson, Rich: Fox Business Network
Edwards, Brian: CBN News
Edwards, Camille: WRC–TV / NBC–4
Ehrenberg, Richard: ABC News
Eiras, Arlene: Reuters Radio & TV
Eisenbarth, Ronald: C–SPAN
Eisenhuth, Alfred Scott: NBC News
Eizeldin, Sam T.: American Press and TV Services (APTVS)
El Masry, Faiza: Voice of America
El Murr, Jessy: BBC
El Sewaify, Mirona Mohamed: AP–Broadcast
Eldridge, James W.: Fox News
Eldridge, Michael: Washington Bureau News Service
Element, Lee Ann: Aljazeera International
Elfa, Albert: TV3–Televisio De Catalunya
Elgin, John: Middle East Television Network (Alhurra)
El-Hamalawy, Mahmoud: Aljazeera Satellite Channel (Peninsula)
Elhassani, Camille: Aljazeera International
Elizondo, Gabriel: Aljazeera International
Elkins, Brenda: Aljazeera International
Ellard, Nancy: NBC Newschannel
Ellenwood, Gary: C–SPAN
Elliott, Angel: BET Nightly News
Elliott-Taylor, Debbie: National Public Radio
Ellis, Neal: National Public Radio
Elving, Ronals: National Public Radio
Elvington, Daniel Glenn: ABC News
Emanuel, Mike: Fox News
Enciu, Edward: C–SPAN
Endo, Sandra: CNN
Engel, Seth: C–SPAN
Engelke, Anja: German TV ARD
Engler, Per Anders: Swedish Broadcasting
Ensign, Ernie: WJLA–TV / Newschannel 8
Epatko, Larisa: The Newshour with Jim Lehrer
Epstein, Steve: Fox News
Erbe, Bonnie: To The Contrary (Persephone Productions)
Ernst, Charlotte: TV2–Denmark
Ernst, Manuel: German TV ZDF
Eroglu, Levent: Australian Broadcasting Corporation
Espinosa, Ken D.: UPI.com
Espinoza, Cholene: Talk Radio News Service
Esquivel, Patricia: C–SPAN
Evans, Kendall A.: ABC News
Evans, Laura: WTTG–Fox Television
Everly, Thomas: Ventana Productions
Evstatieva, Monika: National Public Radio
Fabian, Kathleen: CNN
Fabic, Greg: C–SPAN
Facsar, Fanny: German TV ZDF
Faerber, Fritz: AP–Broadcast
Fagen, Joel: Fox News
Fahrendorff, Claus: Danish Broadcasting Corporation
Fain, Dustin: Diversified Communications, Inc. (DCI)
Faison, Al: Reuters Radio & TV
Fakhry, Ghida: Aljazeera International
Falls, John: CBS News
Fancher, Diane: STATELINE.ORG
Fang, Sabrina: Dispatch Broadcast Group
Fant, Barbara: NBC News
Fantacone, John L.: CBS News
Farid, Mahtab: USI NEWS
Farkas, Daniel: Middle East Television Network (Alhurra)
Farkas, Mark: C–SPAN
Farley, Tim: XM Satellite Radio
Farmer, Scott: East Coast Television
Farnum, Douglas: NBC News
Farrell, Kate: BBC
Fasman, Jonathan Elie: The Economist

MEMBERS ENTITLED TO ADMISSION—Continued

Fattahi, Kambiz: BBC
Fay, Mary Beth: NBC News
Feather, Rich: Ventana Productions
Feeney III, Joseph A.: WTTG–Fox Television
Feeney, Susan: National Public Radio
Fehr, Stephen C.: STATELINE.ORG
Feist, Sam: CNN
Feldman, Randy: Viewpoint Communications
Fendley, Gail: Religion & Ethics Newsweekly
Fendrick, Anne-Marie: NHK–Japan Broadcasting Corporation
Fennell, Dionne: Aljazeera International
Ferder, Bruce: Voice of America
Ferrero, Diana: Aljazeera International
Ferrigno, Tony: WJLA–TV / Newschannel 8
Ferrise, Patrick William: XM Satellite Radio
Fessler, Pam: National Public Radio
Fetzer, Robert: Diversified Communications, Inc. (DCI)
Fiegel, Eric James: CNN
Field, Andy: ABC News
Fielman, Sheldon: NBC News
Fierro, Juan Martinez: Cope Radio (Spain)
Figura, John: CBS News
Filburn, Sean: Belo Capital Bureau
Fils, Dyane: Eurovision Americas, Inc.
Finamore, Charles: ABC News
Finch, Mark: Fox News
Fingar, Craig: CNN
Finkel, Ben: Viewpoint Communications
Finland, Alexander: Fox News
Finney, Richard: Radio Free Asia
Fischer, Elizabeth: NBC News
Fishel, Justin: Fox News
Fisher, Harold Thomas: WHUR
Fisher, Kristen: WUSA–TV
Fitzgerald, Tom: WTTG–Fox Television
Fixel, Taryn: CNN
Flaherty, Lindsay: Mobile Video Services, LTD.
Flanagan, Danielle: WUSA–TV
Flannery, Amy: Diversified Communications, Inc. (DCI)
Fleeson, Richard: C–SPAN
Fleming, Bon: Nippon TV Network
Flintoff, Corey: National Public Radio
Flores, Cesar: BT Video Productions
Flynn, Michael: WUSA–TV
Flynn, Michael Francis: WRC–TV / NBC–4
Fodrea, Linda: Fox News
Fogarty, Kevin: Reuters Radio & TV
Forcucci, Michael: WJLA–TV / Newschannel 8
Ford, Michael: Diversified Communications, Inc. (DCI)
Ford, Sam: WJLA–TV / Newschannel 8
Foreman, Thomas: CNN
Forman, David: NBC News
Fornoff, Matthias: German TV ZDF
Forrest, Kerri: CBS News
Forsyth, Robert: WJLA–TV / Newschannel 8
Forsythe, Jonathan Putnam: WASHINGTONPOST.COM
Forte, B.J.: WTTG–Fox Television
Foster, Carl: C–SPAN
Foster, Scott: NBC News
Foster, Tom: Fox News
Foster Mathewson, Lesli: WUSA–TV
Foty, Tom: CBS News
Foukara, Abderrahim: Aljazeera Satellite Channel (Peninsula)
Foundas, John: WTTG–Fox Television
Fournelis, Yianis: WTTG–Fox Television
Fowler, Maria: Gannett News Service
Fowlin, Joy: To The Contrary (Persephone Productions)
Fox, David: ABC News
Fox, Jason Erik: Reuters Radio & TV
Fox, Michael: Aljazeera Satellite Channel (Peninsula)
Fox, Peggy: WUSA–TV
Fox, Peter: Reuters Radio & TV
Frado, John: CBS News
Frail, Marie: Reuters Radio & TV
Frame, John: WTTG–Fox Television
Frankel, Bruce: TF1–French TV
Franklin, Delroy: ATN Productions, LTD.
Frazier, William: C–SPAN
Frei, Matt: BBC
French, Michael A.: WTTG–Fox Television
French, Patrick: CBS News
Friar, David J.: AP–Broadcast
Fridrich, George: NBC News
Frieden, Terry: CNN
Friedman, Dave: Fox News
Friedman, Matthew: AP–Broadcast
Friend-Daniel, Kenya: CNN
Frost, Adrian Lee: Talk Radio News Service
Frost, Lovisa: Talk Radio News Service
Fry, Jim: Voice of America
Fuchs, Joanne: CNBC
Fullwood, Adrian: AP–Broadcast
Fulton, Bradley: CTV Canadian TV
Fung, Kenneth: Need To Know News
Fuquen, Luis: C–SPAN
Furlow, Tony: CBS News
Furman, Hal E.: CBS News
Fuss, Brian: CBS News
Fuss, Robert J.: CBS News
Futrowsky, David: Fox News
Fyanes, Jo Ann Marie: ABC News
Gabriel, Monica: CNSNEWS.COM
Gacka, Monica: Fox News
Gaeng, Timothy: Eye–To–Eye Video
Gaetano, Lawrence: NBC News
Gaffney, Dennis: NBC News
Gaffney, Matthew: WTTG–Fox Television
Gaffney, Patricia Ann: CNN

MEMBERS ENTITLED TO ADMISSION—Continued

Gafner, Randall: Dispatch Broadcast Group
Gailey, Gretchen: Fox News
Galdabini, Christian: Fox News
Galey, Melinda Mizell: Fox News
Galindo, Fadia: CNSNEWS.COM
Galindo, Michael: BT Video Productions
Gallacher, Andy: BBC
Gallagher, John: C–SPAN
Gallagher, Joseph: Voice of America
Gallasch, Hillery D.: German TV ARD
Gallo, Dan: Fox News
Gamble, Hadley: Fox News
Gangel, Jamie: NBC News
Gao, Jun: China Central TV Bureau
Garber, Scott: CNN
Garcez, Bruno: BBC
Garcia, Alexandra: WASHINGTONPOST.COM
Garcia, Gina: CBS News
Garcia, Guillermo: Reuters Radio & TV
Garcia, Joe: Fox News
Garcia, Jon D.: ABC News
Gardella, Richard: NBC News
Garg, Maya: Aljazeera International
Garifo, Stephen: WUSA–TV
Garlikov, Lydia: CNN
Garlock, John: C–SPAN
Garner, Dave: WTOP Radio
Garner, Jean: Aljazeera International
Garraty, Timothy C.: CNN
Garrett, Major: Fox News
Garsd, Jasmine: National Public Radio
Garvin, Keith: WRC–TV / NBC–4
Gary, Garney: C–SPAN
Gaskin, Keith: NBC News
Gasparello, Linda: White House Chronicle
Gassot, Philippe: ARTE TV
Gauntt, Tiffany: Fox News
Gauss, Martina: German TV ZDF
Gauthier, Arthur R.: ABC News
Gavasheli, Mindia Mikhailovich: Russia Today Television
Gebhardt, William: NBC News
Geewax, Marilyn: National Public Radio
Geldon, Ben: Bloomberg Radio & TV
Geleschun, Uwe: German TV ARD
Gelles, David: NBC News
Gelman, Micah: AP–Broadcast
Gembara, Deborah: Reuters Radio & TV
Gentilo, Richard: AP–Broadcast
Gentry, Pamela: BET Nightly News
Gentry, Robert: TV Asahi
George, John: WETA
George, Maurice: CNN
George, Pavithra: Reuters Radio & TV
Gergely, Valer: Voice of America
Gerrard, Ian: Federal News Service
Gersh, Darren: Nightly Business Report
Getter, Thomas: Radio One
Gewargis, Natalie V.: ABC News
Geyelin, Philip: CBS News
Ghanem, Pierre: Al Arabiya TV
Ghattas, Kim: BBC
Giammetta, Max: WTTG–Fox Television
Gibbons, Gene: STATELINE.ORG
Gibbons, Sarah: Eurovision Americas, Inc.
Gibson, Jake: Fox News
Gibson, Jenna: Fox News
Gibson, Sheri Lynn: NBC Newschannel
Giebel, Edward Adam: ABC News
Gieras, Cladia Melissa: WPWC–AM (Radio Fiesta)
Gilardoni, Diego: Swiss Broadcasting
Gilbert, Sarah: BBC
Gilgannon, Pege: WJLA–TV / Newschannel 8
Gilkey, David: National Public Radio
Gillette, David: WETA
Gilliam, Dirk: CBS News
Gillis, Gary: Fox News
Gilman, Jeff: WTTG–Fox Television
Gilmore, John: CNN
Gimbel, Tara: ABC News
Ginebra, Nelson: NBC Newschannel
Ginsburg, Benson: CBS News
Girouard, April: Fox News
Giusto, Thomas M.: ABC News
Gjelten, Tom: National Public Radio
Glass, Evan: CNN
Glassman, Matt: WRC–TV / NBC–4
Gleason, Norma: C–SPAN
Gleaton, Oji: WJLA–TV / Newschannel 8
Glennon, John: Fox News
Glinton, Sonari: National Public Radio
Glynn, William: NBC Newschannel
Gmiter, Bernard: ABC News
Goddard, Andre: CNN
Goddard, Meghan: Bloomberg Radio & TV
Godinez, Hector: WZDC–TV
Godsick, Andrew L.: NBC Newschannel
Goggans, Stephanie: CNN
Gold, Lawrence: AP–Broadcast
Gold, Peter: Fuji TV Japan
Goldfein, Michael: Belo Capital Bureau
Goldman, David: Community TV of PG's
Goldman, Jeff Scott: CBS News
Goldstein, Jessica: National Public Radio
Goler, Wendell: Fox News
Gomes, Karina: Aljazeera International
Gomez, Ruben: Federal News Radio AM 1050
Gomez, Serafin: Fox News
Gonsar, Dhondup: Radio Free Asia
Gonyea, Don: National Public Radio
Gonzalez, Antonio R.: ABC News
Gonzalez, Carlos: WTTG–Fox Television
Gonzalez, John: WJLA–TV / Newschannel 8
Gonzalez, Julio: Hispanic Communications Network
Goodall, Sam: CBS News

MEMBERS ENTITLED TO ADMISSION—Continued

Goodknight, Charles A: WRC–TV / NBC–4
Goodman, Jeffrey: NBC News
Gorbutt, Richard: WUSA–TV
Gordemer, Barry: National Public Radio
Gordon, Herbert: WRC–TV / NBC–4
Gordon, Stuart: ABC News
Gorman, James W.: AP–Broadcast
Gorsky, Edward: NBC News
Gottlieb, Brian: BBC
Gould, Robert: C–SPAN
Gourley, Meghan: BBC
Gousha, Elizabeth: CNN
Gracey, David: CNN
Gradison, Robin: ABC News
Graham, Fred: Court TV
Gram, Steffen William: Danish Broadcasting Corporation
Gramlich, John P.: STATELINE.ORG
Granda, Marco: Venezuela TV
Grange, Pierre: TF1–French TV
Granitz, Peter: Capitol News Connection (CNC)
Grant, Neva: National Public Radio
Grappe, Marjolaine: France 2 Television
Grasso, Neil: CBS News
Graves, Lindsay: NBC News
Gray, James: CNN
Gray, Melissa: National Public Radio
Gray, Sean: Aljazeera International
Gray, Tim: C–SPAN
Graydon, James: CNN
Grayson, Gisele: National Public Radio
Greeley, Brendan Harrison: The Economist
Green, Barnaby: Sky News
Green, Jessie J.: WTOP Radio
Green, Molette Eileen: WHUR
Green, Travis: National Public Radio
Greenaway, Steve: American Press and TV Services (APTVS)
Greenback, William: Voice of America
Greenbaum, Adam: NBC Newschannel
Greenbaum, Adam: Voice of America
Greenberg, Sarah: NBC News
Greenblatt, Larry: Viewpoint Communications
Greene, James M.: NBC News
Greene, Thomas: CNN
Greenfieldboyce, Nell: National Public Radio
Greenleaf, Devin: Aljazeera International
Greenspan, Samuel: Free Speech Radio News
Greenwood, John K.: Danish Broadcasting Corporation
Gregory, David: NBC News
Greiner, Nicholas P.: ABC News
Gremaud, Seth: UPI.com
Grether, Nicole: AP–Broadcast
Griffin, Jennifer: Fox News
Griffin, Kevin R.: WETA
Griffith, Brandis: WJLA–TV / Newschannel 8
Griffitts, William: Mobile Video Services, LTD.
Griggs, Kendall: WJLA–TV / Newschannel 8
Grigsby, Lee: Eurovision Americas, Inc.
Groome, Marsha: NBC News
Gross, Andrew F.: NBC News
Gross, David: CBS News
Gross, Josh: CBS News
Gross, Jr., Eddie S.: CNN
Groth, Annette: Norwegian Broadcasting
Groussain, Caroline: Agence France Presse (AFP–TV)
Grzech, Cherie: Fox News
Guastadisegni, Richard: WJLA–TV / Newschannel 8
Guerouani, Fayrouz: AP–Broadcast
Guest, Frank: Federal News Service
Guise, Gregory: WUSA–TV
Gunja, Arwa: National Public Radio
Gura, David: National Public Radio
Gural, Kathleen: East Coast Television
Gursky, Gregg L.: Fox News
Gusovsky, Dina: Russia Today Television
Gustafson, David: The Newshour with Jim Lehrer
Guthrie, Savannah: NBC News
Gutmann, Hanna: Washington Radio and Press Service
Guzman, Armando: Azteca America
Guzman, Roberto: Azteca America
Gwadz, Joel: CBS News
Gyal, Palden: Radio Free Asia
Gyldensted, Cathrine: Danish Broadcasting Corporation
Gypson, Katherine: America Abroad Media
Ha, Gwen: Radio Free Asia
Haan, Mike: CNN
Haas, Brian: ABC News
Habbick, Alan: Canadian Broadcasting Corporation (CBC)
Haberl, Emma: Fox News
Habermann, Claudette: National Public Radio
Haberstick, Fred: Fox News
Habib, Elias: Al Arabiya TV
Hackel, Clifford: CNN
Hackett, Steve: WJLA–TV / Newschannel 8
Hadad, Norman: WJLA–TV / Newschannel 8
Haddad, Karim: Aljazeera International
Haefeli, Brian: Fox News
Hafiz, Jihan Fahema: American Press and TV Services (APTVS)
Hager, Mary: CBS News
Hager, Nathan: WTOP Radio
Hagerty, Michael: WJLA–TV / Newschannel 8
Haggerty, Patrick: This Week in Agribusiness (RFD–TV)
Hahn, Jay: Eurovision Americas, Inc.
Hahn, Stephen: ABC News
Haidari, Mohamed-Ali: Middle East Television Network (Alhurra)
Haider, Roquia: Voice of America
Haim, Laura: Canal Plus French TV

MEMBERS ENTITLED TO ADMISSION—Continued

Hakel, Peter: WJLA–TV / Newschannel 8
Hakuta, Michael Akira: WASHINGTONPOST.COM
Haley, Ron: Fox News
Halkett, Kimberly: Aljazeera International
Hall, Richard: C–SPAN
Haller, Sylvia: NBC News
Halloran, Liz: National Public Radio
Hamberg, Steven: Viewpoint Communications
Hamby, Peter: CNN
Hamilton, Christopher: Middle East Television Network (Alhurra)
Hamilton, James: Aljazeera International
Hamilton, Valerie: German TV ARD
Hamrick, Mark: AP–Broadcast
Han, Carol: Cox Broadcasting
Handel, Sarah: National Public Radio
Handelsman, Steve: NBC Newschannel
Handleman, Michelle: CBS News
Handly, Jim: WRC–TV / NBC–4
Haning, Evan: WTOP Radio
Hanley, Patricia: Religion & Ethics Newsweekly
Hanneman, Kirk: Federal News Service
Hansen, Eric: C–SPAN
Hanson, Chris: C–SPAN
Hanson, David: NBC News
Harding, Alison: CNN
Harding, Claus L.: Diversified Communications, Inc. (DCI)
Harding, Jillian: CNN
Hardy, Arthur: CBS News
Harima, Takushi: Tokyo Broadcasting System
Harkness, Stephen: C–SPAN
Harlan, Jeremy: CNN
Harleston, Robb: C–SPAN
Harmon, Predi-Reko: CBS News
Harper, Steve: Eurovision Americas, Inc.
Harris, Lanese: CNN
Harris, Leon: WJLA–TV / Newschannel 8
Harris, Richard: National Public Radio
Harris, Roy: Diversified Communications, Inc. (DCI)
Hartfield, Elizabeth: CBS News
Hartge, John: CBS News
Hartman, Brian Robert: ABC News
Hartman, Rome: BBC
Hartung, Kaylee: CBS News
Hartzenbusch, Lara: BBC
Harvey, Alan: NBC News
Harvey, Kinsey: C–SPAN
Harwood, John: CNBC
Haselton, Brennan: WTOP Radio
Hash, James: WUSA–TV
Hass, Thomas: Eurovision Americas, Inc.
Hassan, Alegra: CBN News
Hassan, Sara: Aljazeera International
Hastings Wotring, Melanie: WJLA–TV / Newschannel 8
Hatton, Laura: New Tang Dynasty TV
Hattori, Ayumi: TV Asahi
Hatuqa, Dalia: Aljazeera Satellite Channel (Peninsula)
Hawke, Anne: National Public Radio
Hawkins, Shonty: WUSA–TV
Hay, Sally: Aljazeera International
Hayden, Marylynn: Aljazeera International
Hayes, Bryan: Capitol News Connection (CNC)
Hayes, Monique: The Newshour with Jim Lehrer
Hayes, Samantha: CNN
Hayley, Harold P.: Aljazeera International
Haynes, Maurice: C–SPAN
Hays, Guerin: CNN
Haywood, Barry: ABC News
Hazelton, Jennifer: Fox News
He, Yun: China Central TV Bureau
Healey, Sean: German TV ZDF
Hecht, Barry: Diversified Communications, Inc. (DCI)
Heffley, William: C–SPAN
Heina, Martin: Fox News
Heiner, Stephen: Middle East Television Network (Alhurra)
Held, Amy: WTOP Radio
Helm, Ronald G.: CNN
Helman, Jonathan: CNN
Henao, Liliana: WZDC–TV
Henderson, Ross: Aljazeera International
Hendin, Robert: CBS News
Hendren, John Edward: ABC News
Hendren, Karen: Reuters Radio & TV
Hendricks, Mark: CBN News
Henn, Stephen: Marketplace Radio
Henneberg, Mary Janne: Fox News
Henrehan, John: WTTG–Fox Television
Henry, Ed: CNN
Henry, Jonelle P.: C–SPAN
Henry, Tanu: BET Nightly News
Herbas, Francis: Fox News
Herbst, Henry: Federal News Service
Herrera, Esequiel: ABC News
Herrera, Ruben: German TV ZDF
Herridge, Catherine: Fox News
Herrod, Michael: Independent Television News (ITN)
Hester, Deirdre: CBS News
Heyman, Leslye: C–SPAN
Hibbitts, Mi Jeong Y.: Voice of America
Hickman, Stacy: Fox News
Hidaka, Masano: Diversified Communications, Inc. (DCI)
Hidaka, Yoshiki: Diversified Communications, Inc. (DCI)
Higgins, Ricardo: NBC News
Higgins, Ricardo: WRC–TV / NBC–4
Highland, Dan: Hearst–Argyle Television
Hill, Benjamin F.: CNN

MEMBERS ENTITLED TO ADMISSION—Continued

Hill, Dallas: C–SPAN
Hill, Lee: National Public Radio
Hill, Martin: Fox News
Hinds, Hugh: WRC–TV / NBC–4
Hinkle, Melisse Paige: UPI.com
Hirano, Ayuko: Nippon TV Network
Hirzel, Conrad: CNN
Ho, King Man: Radio Free Asia
Hoch, Maureen: The Newshour with Jim Lehrer
Hochman, Jordana: National Public Radio
Hoder, Shawn: WJLA–TV / Newschannel 8
Hodge, Darnley: CNBC
Hoessler, Christof: German TV ARD
Hoffman, Jessica: The Newshour with Jim Lehrer
Hoffmaster, Bob: C–SPAN
Holden, Michael: C–SPAN
Holland, John: NBC News
Holland, Sarah B.: CNN
Hollenbeck, Paul: BT Video Productions
Holman, Kwame: The Newshour with Jim Lehrer
Holmes, Horace: WJLA–TV / Newschannel 8
Holmes, LA: Fox News
Holter, Peggy: Aljazeera International
Holtschneider, Joseph: Mobile Video Services, LTD.
Holtzman, Geoff: Talk Radio News Service
Honhadze, Myroslava: Voice of America
Hoodbhoy, Nafisa: Voice of America
Hooley, Gemma: National Public Radio
Hoover, Toni: CBS News
Hopkins, Adrienne Moira: Fox News
Hopkins, Brian: WJLA–TV / Newschannel 8
Hopper, Dave: BBC
Hopper, Douglas: National Public Radio
Horan, Michael: WTTG–Fox Television
Horcajuelo, Inigo: Spanish Public Television (TVE)
Horie, Tomoko: Nippon TV Network
Hormuth, Tom: WJLA–TV / Newschannel 8
Horn, Charles: Viewpoint Communications
Horsley, Scott William: National Public Radio
Hosford, Matthew Alan: ABC News
Hotep, Amon: ABC News
Hou, Lijun: China Central TV Bureau
House, Jeremy: SRN News (Salem)
Houston, Karen Gray: WTTG–Fox Television
Hovell, Bret: ABC News
Hovell, Dean: ABC News
Howard, Cory R.: Fox News
Howard, James: National Public Radio
Howell, George: C–SPAN
Hoye, Matthew: CNN
Hristova, Rozalia: BBC
Hsieh, Yi-Pe: C–SPAN
Hsiung, Ya Hwa: Voice of America
Hssani, Nasser: Aljazeera Satellite Channel (Peninsula)
Hsu, Andrea: National Public Radio
Htike Oo, Thein: Voice of America
Htun, Kyaw Min: Radio Free Asia
Hubbard, Marge: CBS News
Huckeby, Paul: Fox News
Hudson, Adam: Fox News
Huebler, Ryan: WTTG–Fox Television
Huesch, Johanna: German TV ARD
Huff, Dan: AP–Broadcast
Huff, Priscilla: Feature Story News
Hughes, James: NBC News
Hughes, Megan: Cox Broadcasting
Hume, Brit: Fox News
Humeau, Thierry: Aljazeera International
Hung, Shirley: CNN
Hunn, Johney Burke: National Public Radio
Hunt, Al: Bloomberg Radio & TV
Hunter, Paul: Canadian Broadcasting Corporation (CBC)
Hunter, Ryan: WUSA–TV
Huq, Ahsanul: Voice of America
Hurley, Charles: CNN
Hurley, Karina: Hispanic Communications Network
Hurt, James: NBC Newschannel
Hurtado, Eugenia Viviana: ABC News
Hussain, Iftikhar: Voice of America
Hussain, Samira: Canadian Broadcasting Corporation (CBC)
Hussein, Mohammed: BBC
Hutcherson, Trudy: Aljazeera International
Hutchins, Argin: National Public Radio
Hutchinson, Heather: WRC–TV / NBC–4
Hyater, John: WETA
Hyatt, George: NBC News
Hyman, Mark: Sinclair Broadcast Group
Ibrahim, Homam: Aljazeera International
Ifill, Gwen: The Newshour with Jim Lehrer
Ii, Tadayoshi: TV Asahi
Ikonomi, Ilir: Voice of America
Ing, Lance: WTTG–Fox Television
Ingle, Cynthia: C–SPAN
Ingle, Julian: Aljazeera International
Ingram, Julian: Community TV of PG's
Inoue, Nami: Tokyo Broadcasting System
Inoue, Yusuke: TV Asahi
Inskeep, Steve: National Public Radio
Irvine, John: Independent Television News (ITN)
Irving, Terry: CNN
Irwin, Sarah: Reuters Radio & TV
Isaac, Denise: WZDC–TV
Isaac, Monique: East Coast Television
Isham, Christopher: CBS News
Jackson, Craig: CNN
Jackson, Jill: CBS News
Jackson, Katharine: Reuters Radio & TV
Jackson, Robert: National Public Radio
Jackson, Roberta: C–SPAN
Jackson, Ryan: Aljazeera International
Jackson, Samuel: WJLA–TV / Newschannel 8
Jackson-Han, Sarah: Radio Free Asia
Jacobi, Steve: CBN News

MEMBERS ENTITLED TO ADMISSION—Continued

Jacobs, Adia: CNN
Jacobson, Murrey: The Newshour with Jim Lehrer
Jaeger, Kevin: WJLA–TV / Newschannel 8
Jaffe, Gary: Voice of America
Jaffe, Matthew: ABC News
Jafri, Syed: Voice of America
James, Frank: National Public Radio
James, Karen: CNBC
James, Thomas: WUSA–TV
Jamison, Dennis: CBS News
Jamshidi, Kaveh: Voice of America
Jang, Myeong Hwa: Radio Free Asia
Janney, Oliver: CNN
Jansen, Lesa: CNN
Japaridze, NuNu: CNN
Jarboe, Brian: National Public Radio
Jarvis, Julie: NBC Newschannel
Jaskot, Sheila: C–SPAN
Jeannet, Francois: Swiss Broadcasting
Jeffrey, Terence: CNSNEWS.COM
Jeffries, Katherine: C–SPAN
Jenkins, David: CNN
Jenkins, Gene: CBN News
Jenkins, Keith: National Public Radio
Jenkins, William G.: Fox News
Jennings, Alicia: NBC News
Jennings, Claude: SRN News (Salem)
Jennings, Lori: Bloomberg Radio & TV
Jeong, Inseok: Korean Broadcasting Systems
Jermin, Ede: WRC–TV / NBC–4
Jesenicnik, Vlasta: RTV Slovenija
Jessup, John: CBN News
Jia, Elizabeth Yi Chao: WUSA–TV
Jibai, Wafaa: BBC
Jimenez, Martin: Fox Business Network
Jing, Hui: New Tang Dynasty TV
Joehnk, Astrid: German Public Radio (ARD)
Johnke, Tracy: Marketwatch
Johns, Joseph: CNN
Johnsen, Kyle: CNN
Johnson, Bruce: WUSA–TV
Johnson, Douglas: Voice of America
Johnson, Fletcher: ABC News
Johnson, Irene: WJLA–TV / Newschannel 8
Johnson, Jennifer: NBC Newschannel
Johnson, Kenneth: ABC News
Johnson, Kevin: Cox Broadcasting
Johnson, Kia: Reuters Radio & TV
Johnson, Paul: Global TV Canada
Johnson, Rich: Fox News Radio
Johnson, Rolanda: German TV ZDF
Johnson, Sasha: CNN
Johnson, Stephanie: WTTG–Fox Television
Johnson, Tiane: To The Contrary (Persephone Productions)
Johnson-Wilson, Latraniecesa: C–SPAN
Johnston, Derek Leon: ABC News
Johnston, Jeffrey: CBS News
Johnston, Michael: Cox Broadcasting
Jonas, Megan: C–SPAN
Joneidi, Majid: BBC
Jones, Alex: CNN
Jones, Alvin: C–SPAN
Jones, Andrew: BBC
Jones, Andrew: C–SPAN
Jones, Athena: NBC News
Jones, Chelsea: Fox News
Jones, Chelsea: National Public Radio
Jones, Gwyneth: NBC News
Jones, Jenine: Aljazeera International
Jones, Kimberly: National Public Radio
Jones, Lyrone Steven: WTTG–Fox Television
Jones, Nelson: WTTG–Fox Television
Jones, S. Dawn: Talk Radio News Service
Jones, Torrance: Fox News
Jones, Victoria: Talk Radio News Service
Joost, Nathalie: Fox News
Jordan, Rosiland: Aljazeera International
Joseph, Akilah N.: ABC News
Josipovic, Sasa: Aljazeera International
Joslyn, James: WJLA–TV / Newschannel 8
Joy, Richard: Ventana Productions
Joya, Steve E.: ABC News
Joyce, Christopher: National Public Radio
Joyce, Daniel: Bloomberg Radio & TV
Joyner, Arcelious: Middle East Television Network (Alhurra)
Jubar, Muriel: Aljazeera International
Judge, Michael C.: CNN
Juma, Mamatjan: Radio Free Asia
Jung, Ahreum: Radio Free Asia
Jung, Mark: Seoul Broadcasting System (SBS)
Jung, Sung Min: Seoul Broadcasting System (SBS)
Kabbaj, Hakim: AP–Broadcast
Kafanov, Lucy: Feature Story News
Kalbasi, Bahman: BBC
Kalbfleisch, Catherine: Aljazeera International
Kallaugher, Kevin: The Economist
Kamilindi, Thomas: Voice of America
Kane, Heather: Aljazeera International
Kane, James F.: ABC News
Kanneth, Polson: ABC News
Kaplan, Bill: Metro Teleproductions
Kapp, Bonney Lea: CNN
Kapp, Bonney: Fox News
Kara-Murza, Vladimir: RTVI / ECHO–TV
Karl, Jonathan: ABC News
Karson, Danielle: Marketplace Radio
Kastan, Klaus: German Public Radio (ARD)
Katkov, Mark: CBS News
Kato, Atsuchi: NHK–Japan Broadcasting Corporation
Kattar, Pierre: WASHINGTONPOST.COM
Katz, Barry: C–SPAN
Katz, Craig: CBS News
Kaufman, Rebecca: Aljazeera International

MEMBERS ENTITLED TO ADMISSION—Continued

Kavanaugh, John M.: NBC News
Kay, Kathy: BBC
Kaye, Matthew: The Berns Bureau, Inc.
Kearney, Ali: Aljazeera International
Kearns, Kara: NBC News
Keator, John C.: National Public Radio
Keedy, Matthew: CBN News
Kehoe, Steven: C–SPAN
Keilar, Brianna: CNN
Keith, Tamara: National Public Radio
Kelemen, Michele: National Public Radio
Kell, Laura: Voice of America
Kellerman, Mike: American Press and TV Services (APTVS)
Kelley, Alice: German TV ZDF
Kelley, Bridget: National Public Radio
Kelley, Colleen: Fox News
Kelley, Jon: C–SPAN
Kelley, Pamela: CNN
Kelly, Carol Anne Clark: National Public Radio
Kelly, Colin Francis: Army Times Publishing Company
Kelly, Mary Louise: National Public Radio
Kelly, Terence: Diversified Communications, Inc. (DCI)
Kennedy, Robert: C–SPAN
Kennedy, Suzanne: WJLA–TV / Newschannel 8
Kenney, Colleen: WTTG–Fox Television
Kenny, Christopher: CNN
Kenny, Justin: Reuters Radio & TV
Kenworthy, Alison: WJLA–TV / Newschannel 8
Kenworthy, Zachary: Fox News
Kenyon, Linda: SRN News (Salem)
Kerchner, Eric C.: ABC News
Kerley, David P.: ABC News
Kerpen, Mati: WJLA–TV / Newschannel 8
Kerr, Roxane: C–SPAN
Kerr, Ryan: Fox News
Kessler, Jonathan L.: ABC News
Ketcham, Lew: C–SPAN
Kettlewell, Christian: AP–Broadcast
Keyes, Allison: National Public Radio
Keyes, Charley: CNN
Khader, Ibrahim: Aljazeera Satellite Channel (Peninsula)
Khalaf, Lina: Aljazeera International
Khalaf, Lina: Aljazeera Satellite Channel (Peninsula)
Khalaf, Mysa: Aljazeera Satellite Channel (Peninsula)
Khallash, Affra: ATN Productions, LTD.
Khallash, Taleb: ATN Productions, LTD.
Khallash, Zina: ATN Productions, LTD.
Khan, Huma: ABC News
Khan, Ilyas: Voice of America
Khan, Riz: Aljazeera International
Khananayev, Grigory: Fox News
Kharel, Ram C.: Sagarmatha Television
Khin, May: Radio Free Asia
Khyzhnyak, Nataliya: BBC
Kidd, Sally F.: Hearst–Argyle Television
Kieffer, Vivian: Radio Free Asia
Kiendl, Robert: German Broadcasting Systems–ARD
Kiernan, Ryan: NBC News
Kilaru, Vandana: CNN
Killion, Nikole: Hearst–Argyle Television
Kim, Annabel: MBC–TV Korea (Munhwa)
Kim, Jin Kuk: Radio Free Asia
Kim, Keunsam: Voice of America
Kim, Sang Chul: MBC–TV Korea (Munhwa)
Kimmel, Denise: CTV Canadian TV
King, Caitlin: AP–Broadcast
King, Colleen: NBC News
King, John: CNN
King, Kevin: C–SPAN
King, Kevin G.: WUSA–TV
King Lilleston, Kristi: WTOP Radio
Kinlaw, Worth: CNN
Kinney, George P.: CNN
Kinney, Jeff: CNN
Kinney, Laura: Hearst–Argyle Television
Kinney, Michael: WJLA–TV / Newschannel 8
Kirby, Michael: FEDNET
Kirk, Beverly: WJLA–TV / Newschannel 8
Kirkland, Pamela: XM Satellite Radio
Kirn-Slaboszewicz, Mia: Aljazeera International
Kitanovska, Lilica: Voice of America
Klayman, Elliot: Eye–To–Eye Video
Klein, Erin: Voice of America
Klein, Kent: Voice of America
Klein, Richard G.: ABC News
Klein, Rob: Metro Teleproductions
Klenk, Ann: NBC News
Klinger, Carol: National Public Radio
Klopp, Felicitas: German TV ARD
Knapp, Timothy: Mobile Video Services, LTD.
Knezek, Paul: Eurovision Americas, Inc.
Knighton, David: C–SPAN
Knoller, Mark: CBS News
Knott, John: ABC News
Kodaka, Nami: NHK–Japan Broadcasting Corporation
Kohno, Kenji: NHK–Japan Broadcasting Corporation
Kokufuda, Kaoru: Tokyo Broadcasting System
Komatsu, Yoshiyuki: TV Asahi
Kono, Torao: NHK–Japan Broadcasting Corporation
Koolhof, Vanessa M.: WJLA–TV / Newschannel 8
Korff, Jay: WJLA–TV / Newschannel 8
Kornely, Michael: Voice of America
Kornely, Sharon: Medill News Service
Kornitzer, David: Federal News Service
Kornreich, Lauren: CNN
Kos, Martin: BT Video Productions
Koslow, Marc: NBC News

MEMBERS ENTITLED TO ADMISSION—Continued

Kosnar, Michael: NBC News
Koster, Susan: Voice of America
Kotke, Wolfgang: Deutsche Welle TV
Kotke, Wolfgang: German TV ZDF
Kotuby, Stephanie: CNN
Kovach, Robert S.: CNN
Kozel, Sandy: AP–Broadcast
Krantz, Laura: National Public Radio
Kraus, Laura: CBN News
Kreinbihl, Mary: Fox Business Network
Kreindler, Virginia Coyne: NBC Newschannel
Kreuz, Greta: WJLA–TV / Newschannel 8
Kroll, Donald Eugene: ABC News
Kross, Kathryn: Bloomberg Radio & TV
Kube, Courtney: NBC News
Kubota, Suzanne: Federal News Radio AM 1050
Kuczynski, Ronald: CNN
Kuhn, Eric: CNN
Kulkarni, Rohit: Voice of America
Kupper, Carmen: German TV ZDF
Kurcias, Martin R.: National Public Radio
Kyaw, Nay Rein: Radio Free Asia
Kyaw, Zaw Moe: Radio Free Asia
LaBella, Michael: Nightly Business Report
Labott, Elise: CNN
Laboy, Felix: C–SPAN
Lacey, Donna: Fox News
LaFollette, Marianna: Fox News
Laidman, Daniel Aaron: National Public Radio
Lamb, Brian: C–SPAN
Lambert, Brandon: Fuji TV Japan
Lambidakis, Stephanie: CBS News
Lamonica, Ely: Voyage Productions
Landay, Woodrow: Australian Broadcasting Corporation
Landers, Kim: Australian Broadcasting Corporation
Landphair, Ted: Voice of America
Landy, John: BBC
Lane, Christopher: WETA
Langen, Janne: Finnish Broadcasting Company (YLE)
Langfitt, Frank: National Public Radio
Langguth, Dana: Aljazeera International
Langley, Kevin: National Public Radio
Lanningham, Kyle: Swedish Broadcasting
Lanza, Jessica: Middle East Television Network (Alhurra)
Lanzara, Catherine: WJLA–TV / Newschannel 8
Lapidus, Faith: Voice of America
Larade, Darren: C–SPAN
Larsen, Greg: CBS News
Laslo, Matt: Capitol News Connection (CNC)
Latendresse, Richard: GROUPE TVA
Latremoliere, France: NBC News
Laughlin, Ara: Community TV of PG's
Laughlin, James: CBN News
Laurin, Caroline: Canadian Broadcasting Corporation (CBC)
Lavallee, Michael: Tokyo Broadcasting System
Laville, Molly: C–SPAN
Law, Katie: BBC
Lawn, Connie: Audio Video News
Lawrence, Chris: CNN
Lawrence, John: Ventana Productions
Lawson, Sam: CNBC
Lawton, Kim: Religion & Ethics Newsweekly
Layne, B. Christopher: WRC–TV / NBC–4
Lazar, Robert: C–SPAN
Lazernic, Ira: C–SPAN
Lazo, Larry: CNN
Le, Viet: National Public Radio
Le Du, Donaig: Radio France Internationale
Leake, Myron: CNN
Leamy, Elisabeth: ABC News
Lebedeva, Natasha: NBC News
LeCroy, Philip: Fox News
Lee, Andrea: Canadian Broadcasting Corporation (CBC)
Lee, Charles Rusty N.: East Coast Television
Lee, Donald A.: CBS News
Lee, Edward: WETA
Lee, Erik: WTTG–Fox Television
Lee, Jessica: CNSNEWS.COM
Lee, Jin Seo: Radio Free Asia
Lee, Kyu: Radio Free Asia
Lee, Soo Kyung: Radio Free Asia
Legget, Dennis: Aljazeera International
Lehrer, Jim: The Newshour with Jim Lehrer
Leidelmeyer, Ronald: WRC–TV / NBC–4
Leiken, Katherine: German TV ZDF
Leist, Elizabeth: NBC News
Leister, Meaghan: Fox News
Lendzian, Kay: German TV ZDF
Lent, David: Fox News
Lentz, Rudiger: Deutsche Welle TV
Leong, Dexter: CBS News
Leong, Ming: WJLA–TV / Newschannel 8
Leshan, Bruce: WUSA–TV
Lester, Paul: WUSA–TV
Levi, Michelle: CBS News
Levin, Rachel: Aljazeera International
Levine, Adam: CNN
Levine, Joanne: Aljazeera International
Levine, Michael: Fox News
Lewis, Avi: Aljazeera International
Lewis, Edward: Fox News
Lewis, Elliott: Hearst–Argyle Television
Lewis, Jerry S.: WETA
Lewis, John B.: WJLA–TV / Newschannel 8
Lewis, Nelson: Fox News
Lewnes, Lisa: Reuters Radio & TV
Lewnes, Pericles: Middle East Television Network (Alhurra)
Li, Denise: CBS News
Li, Qinghao: China Central TV Bureau
Li, Wo Tak: Radio Free Asia

MEMBERS ENTITLED TO ADMISSION—Continued

Liasson, Mara: National Public Radio
Libert, Tara: TV2–Denmark
Liberto, Jennifer: CNN
Libretto, John: NBC News
Licht, Christopher: NBC News
Lielischkies, Udo: German TV ARD
Lien, Arthur: NBC News
Lien, Jonathan: CBS News
Liffiton, Bruce: CBS News
Likowski, Alex: WJLA–TV / Newschannel 8
Lilling, Dave: Metro Teleproductions
Lim, Jae-Hak: Radio Free Asia
Lim, Lister: Aljazeera International
Lin, Chuan: New Tang Dynasty TV
Lin, Dongwei: China Central TV Bureau
Lincoln, Diane: The Newshour with Jim Lehrer
Lindberg, Lyle: Voice of America
Lindblom, Mark: C–SPAN
Linden, Louis: Diversified Communications, Inc. (DCI)
Lindsey, Melvin A.: ABC News
Lingner, Tilman: Swiss Broadcasting
Linker, Ron: NOS Dutch Public Radio & TV (VRT)
Lipes, Joshua: Radio Free Asia
Liss, Sharon Kehnemui: Fox News
Lissit, Arleen: CBS News
Little, Craig: WTTG–Fox Television
Little, Walter: Bloomberg Radio & TV
Littleton, Philip: CNN
Litzinger, Sam: CBS News
Liu, Enming: Voice of America
Liu, Libo: Voice of America
Liu, Zhengzhu: Hong Kong Phoenix Satellite Television
Livingston, Scott: Sinclair Broadcast Group
Livingston, Stephanie: Fox News
Lloyd, Robert: East Coast Television
Lobel, Aaron: America Abroad Media
Lobodjinski, Keith: Need To Know News
Lockhart, Kathleen: NBC News
Lodoe, Kalden: Radio Free Asia
Loebach, Joseph W.: NBC News
Loeschke, Paul: C–SPAN
Logan, Christopher: WJLA–TV / Newschannel 8
Logan, Lara: CBS News
Logan, Russell: C–SPAN
Londres, Eduardo: Bloomberg Radio & TV
Long, Culver: Reuters Radio & TV
Long, James V.: NBC News
Longmire, Jennifer: National Public Radio
Loper, Catherine: Fox News
Lopez, Edwing: Azteca America
Lopez, Juan Carlos: CNN
Lopez, Lesley: Eurovision Americas, Inc.
Lopez, Myra B.: AP–Broadcast
Lopez-Isa, Anthony: WTTG–Fox Television
Lora, Edwin: CNN
Lora, Willie A.: CNN
Lord, Bill: WJLA–TV / Newschannel 8
Lorek, Stanley: ABC News
Lormand, John: SRN News (Salem)
Losey, Andrew: CNN
Loucks, William: Canadian Broadcasting Corporation (CBC)
Lowman, Wayne: Fox News
Luangkhot, Viengsay: Radio Free Asia
Lucas, Dave: WJLA–TV / Newschannel 8
Lucas, Fred: CNSNEWS.COM
Lucas, Mary Grace: CNN
Lucchini, Maria Rosa: WFDC–TV Univision
Ludden, Jennifer: National Public Radio
Ludwin, James: AP–Broadcast
Luhn, Laurie: Fox News
Lukas, Jayne: Global TV Canada
Lund, Susan: National Public Radio
Lurch, Jr., David L.: NBC News
Lutt, Howard: CNN
Lutterbeck, Deborah: Reuters Radio & TV
Lutz, Ellsworth M.: ABC News
Luzader, Doug: Fox News
Luzquinos, Julio: Ventana Productions
Ly, Sherri: WTTG–Fox Television
Lyders, Caroline: WJLA–TV / Newschannel 8
Lynds, Stacia: Fox News
Lynn, Gary: NBC News
Lyon, Michael: Fox News
Lyons, Theodore: East Coast Television
Mabry, Krystal Michelle: CNN
MacDonald, James: CTV Canadian TV
MacDonald, Neil: Canadian Broadcasting Corporation (CBC)
MacFarlane, Scott: Cox Broadcasting
Macholz, Wolfgang: German TV ZDF
Mackaye, Amanda: CBS News
MacNeil, Lachlan Murdoch: ABC News
Maddux, Catherine: Voice of America
Madeeha, Anwar: Voice of America
Madorma, Tracey: Fox News
Maer, Peter: CBS News
Mager, Dickon: Sky News
Magleby, Marie: CNSNEWS.COM
Magnuson, Eric: WTTG–Fox Television
Maher, Heather: Radio Free Europe
Jchrowitz, Mike: Fox News Radio
Makelainen, Mika: Finnish Broadcasting Company (YLE)
Makharadze, George: Aljazeera International
Makori, Vincent: Voice of America
Malbon, Joy: CTV Canadian TV
Malik, Mansoor: Voice of America
Malone, Freddie: NBC News
Malone, James: Voice of America
Malone, Junius: NBC News
Malone, Rodney: NBC News
Maltas, Michael: CNN
Manatt, Dan: Talk Radio News Service

MEMBERS ENTITLED TO ADMISSION—Continued

Mandelson, Adam: Eurovision Americas, Inc.
Mann, Jon: WJLA–TV / Newschannel 8
Mannos, Sofia: AP–Broadcast
Manogue, Michael: ABC News
Manresa, Elizabeth: CNN
Mansour, Fadi: Aljazeera Satellite Channel (Peninsula)
Marantz, Michael: WTTG–Fox Television
Marchione, Mark Anthony: CNN
Marchitto, Tom: National Public Radio
Marcus, Gale: ABC News
Marder, Jennifer: The Newshour with Jim Lehrer
Maric, Goran: Aljazeera International
Marks, Carole: Talk Radio News Service
Marks, Simon: Feature Story News
Marno, Joseph: Aljazeera International
Marno, Mike: Aljazeera International
Maroney, Sean: Voice of America
Marquis, Melissa: National Public Radio
Marrapodi, Eric Christian: CNN
Marriott, Mai: CBS News
Marriott, Marc: CBS News
Marriott, Michael: CBS News
Marshall, Allison: CN8 The Comcast Network
Marshall, Kelly: CNN
Marshall, Nancy: Marketplace Radio
Marshall, Steve: CBS News
Martin, David: AP–Broadcast
Martin, David: CBS News
Martin, Michel: National Public Radio
Martin, Rachel Elizabeth: ABC News
Martin, Sam: C–SPAN
Martin, Wisdom: WTTG–Fox Television
Martin Ewing, Samara: WUSA–TV
Martin, Jr., James: ABC News
Martinez, Luis: ABC News
Martinez, Sandra: Aljazeera International
Martino, Jeffrey: WETA
Mason, Tabetha: Aljazeera International
Mastis, Lindsey Janiece: WUSA–TV
Mastrian, Michael J.: Radio TV Gallery
Masuda, Tsuyoshi: NHK–Japan Broadcasting Corporation
Mathieu, Joe: XM Satellite Radio
Matkosky, Tim: Cox Broadcasting
Matthews, Chris: NBC News
Matthews, Claude: NBC News
Matthews, Katrina: Federal News Radio AM 1050
Matthews, Lisa N.: AP–Broadcast
Matthews, Paul: CNN
Matthews, Ronald H.: CBS News
Matthews, Valerie: C–SPAN
Matzka, Jeffrey Alan: SRN News (Salem)
Mauro, Craig: Aljazeera International
Maxwell, Darraine: ABC News
May, Tim: Fox News
Mayhew, Linda Carol: Diversified Communications, Inc. (DCI)
Mazariegos, Mark: CBS News
Mazyck, Robin: CBN News
McCabe, Valerie: NHK–Japan Broadcasting Corporation
McCalister, Sharon: National Public Radio
McCann, Michael: C–SPAN
McCann, Sean: C–SPAN
McCarty, D. Jay: CBS News
McCarty, D. Page: CBS News
McCash, Douglas: German TV ZDF
McCaughan, Timothy: CNN
McClam, Kevin: Fox News
McCleery, Kathleen: The Newshour with Jim Lehrer
McClellan, Max: CBS News
McCloskey, George: Fox News
McClure, Tipp K.: Reuters Radio & TV
McConnaughey, Brian: FEDNET
McConnell, Alison: Need To Know News
McConnell, Dave: WTOP Radio
McConnell, Dugald: CNN
McCown, Gregory: ABC News
McCrary, Scott: CBS News
McCullough, Christopher Colin: Link TV
McDermott, Michele Marie: ABC News
McDermott, Richard: NBC Newschannel
McDevitt, Rebecca: WJLA–TV / Newschannel 8
McDonald, Mark: Capitol News Connection (CNC)
McDonald, Natashka Patricia: WTOP Radio
McDougall, Ian: Reuters Radio & TV
McEachin, Johnny: NBC News
McFadden, Kerith: CNN
McFadden, Samuel James: WTTG–Fox Television
McFarland, Patty: NBC News
McGarrity, Gerard: C–SPAN
McGarvy, Sean: WTTG–Fox Television
McGinn, Anne: Fox News
McGinty, Derek: WUSA–TV
McGlinchy, Jim: CBS News
McGrath, Megan: WRC–TV / NBC–4
McGrath, Patrick: WTTG–Fox Television
McGreevy, Allen: BBC
McGuire, Ellen: NBC News
McGuire, Lorna: WTTG–Fox Television
McGuire, Michael: CBS News
McHenry, Brittany: WJLA–TV / Newschannel 8
McHenry, Jr., Robert: ABC News
McIntosh, Denise: CNN
McKelway, Douglas: WJLA–TV / Newschannel 8
McKenna, Duncan: NBC News
McKenna, William: BBC
McKinley, Robert: CBS News
McKinney, Paul: Aljazeera International
McKnight, William Charles: CNN
McKnight, William: WUSA–TV
McLaughlin, Ross: WJLA–TV / Newschannel 8
McLellan, Daniel: CBS News
McManamon, Erin T.: Hearst–Argyle Television
McManus, Eleanor Spektor: CNN

MEMBERS ENTITLED TO ADMISSION—Continued

McManus, Kevin Anthony: Global TV Canada
McManus, Michael: HD News
McManus, Nicole: NBC Newschannel
McMichael IV, Samuel J.: CNN
McMullan, Michael: CNN
McNair, Erik T.: ABC News
McNair, Romaine Desaree: WHUR
McNary, Kirstin: Fox News Radio
McNeely-Johnson, Helena: National Public Radio
McWhinney, David: Aljazeera International
Meadows, Mark: Need To Know News
Means, Jeffrey: Voice of America
Mears, Carroll Ann: NBC News
Mears, William: CNN
Medvee, Dennis: National Public Radio
Meech, James: CNN
Meehan, Brian: Bloomberg Radio & TV
Meghani, Sagar: AP–Broadcast
Mehrpore, Abdu: Voice of America
Meier, Markus: N–TV German News Channel
Mejia, Douglas: WZDC–TV
Melendy, David R.: AP–Broadcast
Melhem, Omar: Al Arabiya TV
Melhem, Richard: Al Arabiya TV
Melia, Mike: The Newshour with Jim Lehrer
Melick, Rob: Fox News
Melton, James: Metro Teleproductions
Meltzer, Erik Stephen: New Tang Dynasty TV
Meluza, Lourdes: Univision
Melvin, Craig: WRC–TV / NBC–4
Memmott, Mark: National Public Radio
Men, Kimseng: Voice of America
Mena, Alexia V.: CNN
Mendelson, Beth: Voice of America
Mendoza, Natalia: TF1–French TV
Mengel, Trenton: AP–Broadcast
Meraz, Gregorio: Televisa News Network (ECO)
Merena, Michael: National Public Radio
Mergener, Tara: CBS News
Merideth, Lila: AP–Broadcast
Merobshoev, Seeno: C–SPAN
Meserve, Jeanne: CNN
Messer, Christopher: Aljazeera Satellite Channel (Peninsula)
Metlin, Philip: WTTG–Fox Television
Metzger, Justin: C–SPAN
Metzger, Rochelle: Community TV of PG's
Meucci, Jason Robert: CNN
Meyer, Dick: National Public Radio
Meyer, Kerry: Diversified Communications, Inc. (DCI)
Michael, Yukiko: Nippon TV Network
Michaud, Robert: Aljazeera International
Mihmandarli, Bulut: Voice of America
Miklaszewski, James: NBC News
Milam, Greg: Sky News
Milenic, Alexander: WTTG–Fox Television
Miles, Jon: Aljazeera International
Milford, Robert H.: Mobile Video Services, LTD.
Millar, Christopher: NBC News
Miller, Andrew Peter: C–SPAN
Miller, Annette: The Newshour with Jim Lehrer
Miller, Avery: ABC News
Miller, Bridget: CNSNEWS.COM
Miller, Elizabeth: BBC
Miller, Eric: Aljazeera International
Miller, Jason: Federal News Radio AM 1050
Miller, Josh: WJLA–TV / Newschannel 8
Miller, Karen: Free Speech Radio News
Miller, Michael: Fox News
Miller, Mitchell: WTOP Radio
Miller, Paul Keith: CNN
Miller, Richard F.: Talk Radio News Service
Miller, Sunlen Mari: ABC News
Miller, Tim: Middle East Television Network (Alhurra)
Mills, Chris: Fox Business Network
Mills, Joe: National Public Radio
Mills, Kate: C–SPAN
Milne, Claudia: BBC
Milstein, Jeff: America Abroad Media
Minkovski, Alyona: Russia Today Television
Minner, Richard: NBC News
Minor, Jon: FEDNET
Minoso, Guillermo: National Public Radio
Minott, Gloria: WPFW–FM
Mitchell, Andrea: NBC News
Mitchell, Carrie: Federal News Service
Mitnick, Steven: NBC News
Miyake, Yuko: TV Tokyo
Moeller, Burke: Reuters Radio & TV
Mohan, Sabina: NBC News
Mohen, Peter: CNN
Mokhtari, Mohamed: Middle East Television Network (Alhurra)
Molinares-Hess, Ione Indira: CNN
Molineaux, Diana: Radio Marti
Monack, David: C–SPAN
Monange, Arielle: France 2 Television
Monroe, Carol Taylor: CBN News
Montague, William: Norwegian Broadcasting
Montanaro, Domenico: NBC News
Monte, John: NBC News
Montenegro, Lori: Telemundo Network
Montero, Adrian Moya: ATN Productions, LTD.
Montero, Luisa Fernanda: Hispanic Communications Network
Monthei, Matthew: Aljazeera International
Montoro, Victor R.: C–SPAN
Mooar, Brian: NBC Newschannel
Moody, Kate: Feature Story News
Mooney, Alex: CNN
Moore, Dennis: Fox Business Network
Moore, Garrette: C–SPAN
Moore, Jacob: CBN News
Moore, Linwood: C–SPAN

MEMBERS ENTITLED TO ADMISSION—Continued

Moore, Terrence: Metro Networks
Moore, W. Harrison: Middle East Television Network (Alhurra)
Moorhead, Jeremy: CNN
Moorman, Jeffrey Roger: Diversified Communications, Inc. (DCI)
Mora, Edwin: CNSNEWS.COM
Morales, Isabel: Hispanic Communications Network
Morales, Victor: Voice of America
Morehouse, Brittany Catherine: WUSA–TV
Morgan, Donald: CBS News
Morgan, Keith B.: ABC News
Morgan, Marcia: National Public Radio
Morgan, Nancy Gerstman: WETA
Moroney, Tom: Bloomberg Radio & TV
Morris, Amy: Federal News Radio AM 1050
Morris, Holly: WTTG–Fox Television
Morris, Peter: CNN
Morris, Sarah: BBC
Morrisette, Roland: Bloomberg Radio & TV
Morrissey, John: AP–Broadcast
Morse, Richard: Fox News
Morton, Dan: C–SPAN
Mortreux, Vincent: TF1–French TV
Moses, Lester: NBC News
Mosettig, Michael: The Newshour with Jim Lehrer
Mosley, Matthew: Fuji TV Japan
Moubray, Virginia: CNN
Mount, George M.: CNN
Moussa, Widiane: Independent Television News (ITN)
Moya, Anna Parachkevova: ATN Productions, LTD.
Mozaffari, Shaheen: NBC News
Mueller, Jens: German TV ARD
Mueller, John: Middle East Television Network (Alhurra)
Mueller-Thum, Sabine: German Broadcasting Systems–ARD
Muhammad, Alverda: National Scene News
Muhammad, Askia: National Scene News
Muhammad, Seleena M.: Fox News
Muir, Robert: Reuters Radio & TV
Munford, Corey: Radio Free Asia
Munoz, Luis: Middle East Television Network (Alhurra)
Munoz, Luis: Radio MARTI
Muratani, Tateki: Fuji TV Japan
Murphy, Frederick: NBC News
Murphy, John: CBS News
Murphy, Richard: WTTG–Fox Television
Murphy, Terry: C–SPAN
Murray, Elizabeth: Fox News
Murray, Mark: NBC News
Murray, Matthew: WRC–TV / NBC–4
Murray, Megan: Fox News
Murray, Timothy K.: Ventana Productions
Murry, Rosetta: CNN
Mursa, Alexander: Russia Today Television
Murtaugh, Peter: BBC
Murugesan, Vidya: NBC News
Musa, Imad: Aljazeera International
Musha, Jilili: Radio Free Asia
Muskat, Steven: Dispatch Broadcast Group
Muturi, Muthoni: National Public Radio
Myers, Lisa: NBC News
Myrick, Yetta: C–SPAN
Nadler, Gary: ABC News
Naidoo, Anand: Aljazeera International
Naing, Ingjin: Radio Free Asia
Najjar, Ruqaiyah: BET Nightly News
Namgyal, Tseten: Radio Free Asia
Napier, Genvieve: Aljazeera International
Napier, Joyce: Canadian Broadcasting Corporation (CBC)
Narahari, Priya: Eurovision Americas, Inc.
Nardi, William: WRC–TV / NBC–4
Nash, Renee Jacqueline: WHUR
Nason, Andrew: C–SPAN
Nathan, Caroline: The Newshour with Jim Lehrer
Nathan, Nancy: NBC News
Natsui, Yuki: TV Asahi
Nawaz, Amna: NBC News
Naylor, Brian: National Public Radio
Neal, Jason: NBC News
Neapolitan, Michael: Mobile Video Services, LTD.
Neefus, Chris: CNSNEWS.COM
Neel, Joe R.: National Public Radio
Neidenberg, Jennifer: CNN
Nelson, Christopher: National Public Radio
Nelson, Donna: NBC News
Nelson, James: Fox News
Nelson, Joseph: Washington Bureau News Service
Nelson, Marie: National Public Radio
Nelson, Suzanne: CNN
Neubauer, Kristin: Reuters Radio & TV
Neville, Shaun: Hearst–Argyle Television
Nevins, Elizabeth: NBC News
Newberry, Tom: NBC Newschannel
Nguyen, Anh: Fox News
Nguyen, Hoai: Radio Free Asia
Ni, Chia-Hui: TVBS
Nicci, Nicholette: CNN
Nicholas, Eric: Bloomberg Radio & TV
Nickerson, Dewayne: CBS News
Nicolaidis, Virginia: CNN
Niiler, Eric: Capitol News Connection (CNC)
Nikuradze, David: Rustavi 2 Broadcasting Company
Nisbet-Smith, Robert: Sky News
Nishigaki, Soichiro: Fuji TV Japan
Niu, Haifeng: China Central TV Bureau
Nixon, Adam: Middle East Television Network (Alhurra)
Nocciolo, Ernest G.: CNN
Noguchi, Yuki: National Public Radio
Noh, Jung Min: Radio Free Asia
Nolen, John: CBS News

MEMBERS ENTITLED TO ADMISSION—Continued

Noonan, Heidi: Fox News
Noonan, Terence James: WUSA–TV
Noor, Matiullah Abid: Voice of America
Norins, Jamie: Diversified Communications, Inc. (DCI)
Norland, Dean E.: ABC News
Norling, Richard A.: ABC News
Norma, Montenegro: WFDC–TV Univision
Norris, Christopher Charles: Diversified Communications, Inc. (DCI)
Norris, Donna: C–SPAN
Norris, James: Middle East Television Network (Alhurra)
Norris, Jane: Federal News Radio AM 1050
Norris, Michele: National Public Radio
Northam, Jackie: National Public Radio
Nowak, Christopher: CNN
Nunez, Jorge: WFDC–TV Univision
Nurenberg, Gary Keith: WUSA–TV
Nurre, Bridget: NBC News
Nyberg, Carina: Federal News Service
Nyrop, Siri E.: Voice of America
Nyunt Oo, Thar: Voice of America
Oakley, Angela Ann: WTTG–Fox Television
O'Banion, Beverly: CNN
O'Berry, D. Kerry: Fox News
Oberti, Ralf: Aljazeera International
Oblinger, Anne: CNN
O'Brien, David: NBC News
O'Brien, Jane: BBC
Och, Phillip Andrew: Fox News
O'Connell, Benjamin: C–SPAN
O'Connell, Mike: NBC Newschannel
O'Day, Andrew: Marketwatch
Odom, Quillie: Fox News
O'Donnell, Kelly: NBC News
O'Donnell, Norah: NBC News
O'Donnell, Patrick: Eye–To–Eye Video
O'Gara, Patrick M.: Hearst–Argyle Television
Offermann, Claudia: German TV ZDF
Ogasawara, Kazuya: TV Asahi
Ogulnik, John: Swiss Broadcasting
Oikonomou, Konstantinos: Aljazeera International
Oinounou, Mosheh: Fox News
Okorn, Peter: Aljazeera International
Olaya, Daniel: Hispanic Communications Network
O'Leary, Lizzie: Bloomberg Radio & TV
Olick, Diana: CNBC
Oliger, Brian: WTOP Radio
Olmsted, Alan: C–SPAN
Olson, Anna: Nightly Business Report
Orchard, Mark: Aljazeera International
O'Regan, Michael: WRC–TV / NBC–4
Orgel, Paul: C–SPAN
Orr, Bob: CBS News
Osborne, Kyle: WJLA–TV / Newschannel 8
O'Shea, Jr., Daniel J.: ABC News
Oszancak, Hakan: AP–Broadcast
Ota, Kanako: TV Tokyo
O'Toole, Timothy James: Diversified Communications, Inc. (DCI)
Otth, John: CNN
Ouafi, Mohamed Said: AP–Broadcast
Outen, Gwen: National Public Radio
Overby, Peter: National Public Radio
Overton, Heather: C–SPAN
Overton, Kathi: East Coast Television
Oyebanjo, Nike: C–SPAN
Ozug, Matt: America Abroad Media
Pace, Julie: AP–Broadcast
Pacheco, Antonio: WETA
Padilla-Cirino, Mercy: Hispanic Communications Network
Pagan, Louis: AP–Broadcast
Page, David: CBN News
Palacios, Glenn: Aljazeera International
Palca, Joe: National Public Radio
Palmeri, Tara: CNN
Panov, Alexander: RTVi / ECHO–TV
Panzer, Chester: WRC–TV / NBC–4
Papinashvili, Aleksandre: Rustavi 2 Broadcasting Company
Parabaniuk, Julia: Voice of America
Park, Jung-Woo: Radio Free Asia
Park, Kathy: WJLA–TV / Newschannel 8
Parker, Andre: CNN
Parker, Beth: WTTG–Fox Television
Parker, Eric: Federal News Service
Parker, Glenn: Aljazeera International
Parker, Julie: WJLA–TV / Newschannel 8
Parker, Robert Geoffrey: CNN
Parker, Sarah Elizabeth: CNN
Parkinson, John R.: ABC News
Parkinson, Malik C.: ATN Productions, LTD.
Parks, Chris: CNN
Parsell, Robert: Voice of America
Parshall, Janet: SRN News (Salem)
Pastre, Dominique: Fox News
Patrick, Dan: WJLA–TV / Newschannel 8
Patruznick, Michael: C–SPAN
Patsalos, Connie: NBC News
Patsko, Daniel: ABC News
Patterson, Ashley: Belo Capital Bureau
Patterson, Jay E.: ABC News
Paulert, Ruediger: German TV ARD
Pauls, Hartmut: German TV ZDF
Paxton, Bradford S.: Fox News
Payne, Aaron C.: CNN
Payne, Nathan: CNN
Payne, Scott: AP–Broadcast
Payton, Strader: TV Tokyo
Paz Vergara, Miguel: CBN News
Peaches, Sandra: Community TV of PG's
Peacock, Grant: Fox News
Peaks, Gershon: Reuters Radio & TV
Pearson, Hampton: CNBC

MEMBERS ENTITLED TO ADMISSION—Continued

Pearson, Matt: Free Speech Radio News
Pearson, Vincent: National Public Radio
Peltier, Yves: Canadian Broadcasting Corporation (CBC)
Pena, Ana Sarai: Telesur
Penaloza, Marisa: National Public Radio
Pennell, Elizabeth: Morningside Partners, LLC
Pennybacker, Gail: WJLA–TV / Newschannel 8
Perez, Nitza: Telesur
Pergram, Chad: Fox News
Perkins, Anthony D.: WTTG–Fox Television
Perkins, Douglas W.: NBC News
Perkins, Vernon: C–SPAN
Perron, Marilisa: CBS News
Perry, Christina: C–SPAN
Perry, Herbert: CBS News
Perry, Michelle: NBC News
Perry, Jr., Timothy: The Newshour with Jim Lehrer
Peslis, Chris: Fox News
Peterson, Gordon: WJLA–TV / Newschannel 8
Peterson, James: CBS News
Peterson, Karen: WUSA–TV
Peterson, Rebecca: CBS News
Peterson, Robert: CBS News
Petraitis, Gerald: AP–Broadcast
Petras, William: NBC News
Pettigrew, Chris: WJLA–TV / Newschannel 8
Pettit, Debra: NBC News
Peyton, Michael: CBS News
Pham, Jacqueline: Fox News
Pham, Than: Radio Free Asia
Philippon, Alan: CNN
Phillips, Sean: National Public Radio
Phillips, Steven: Reuters Radio & TV
Phimphachanh, Manichanh: Radio Free Asia
Pick, Lauren: Fox News
Pigott III, Bernard: Fox News Radio
Pillon, Annette: ABC News
Pimble, William: CBS News
Pinczuk, Murray: NHK–Japan Broadcasting Corporation
Pineda, Juan: Ventana Productions
Pinzon, Wingel: Telemundo Network
Piper, Jeff: WRC–TV / NBC–4
Pitocco, Nickolas: C–SPAN
Pittman, Tom: WTTG–Fox Television
Pizarro, Fernando: Univision
Placie, Jordan: CNN
Plante, Gilles: Canadian Broadcasting Corporation (CBC)
Plante, William: CBS News
Plater, Christopher: WJLA–TV / Newschannel 8
Pliszak, Richard K.: ABC News
Plotkin, Mark: WTOP Radio
Poch, Reasey: Voice of America
Poduch, Shelby: NBC News
Poley, Michael: CNN
Policastro, Jacqueline: Lilly Broadcasting
Pollock, Zoe: The Newshour with Jim Lehrer
Polmer, Brendan: CNN
Poole, Michael: Eye–To–Eye Video
Pope, Lindsey: CNN
Popovici, Andrei: RTVi / ECHO–TV
Popp, Chris: CNN
Porsella, Claude L.: Radio France Internationale
Porteous, James: Aljazeera International
Porter, Almon: C–SPAN
Porter, Christina: C–SPAN
Porter, Taylor: C–SPAN
Portnoy, Steven A.: ABC News
Postovit, David: Hearst–Argyle Television
Potisk, Steve: Marketwatch
Potts, Charlotte: German TV ZDF
Potts, Tracie: NBC Newschannel
Poulin, Hugues: Canadian Broadcasting Corporation (CBC)
Poulou, Penelope: Voice of America
Pourziaiee, Mehrnoosh: BBC
Powell, Brian William: Radio Free Asia
Powell, Dennis: ABC News
Powell, Lee: AP–Broadcast
Pozniak, Stephen: WJLA–TV / Newschannel 8
Prah, Pamela M.: STATELINE.ORG
Pratapas, Lauren Marie: CNN
Preloh, Anne: C–SPAN
Press, Robert: Bloomberg Radio & TV
Presutti, Carolyn: Voice of America
Price, Matthew: BBC
Primmer, Ryan: Reuters Radio & TV
Privitera, Alessandro: N24 German TV
Probst, Eva: German TV ARD
Pronko, Tony: C–SPAN
Publicover, Robert: WTOP Radio
Pugliese, Pat: CNBC
Pyon, Changsop: Radio Free Asia
Pyzyk, Katie: Fox News
Queen, Shegoftah: Voice of America
Quijano, Elaine: CNN
Quinn, Diana: CBS News
Quinn, Jason: Ventana Productions
Quinn, John: Voice of America
Quinn, Mary: ABC News
Quinn, Saul: Ventana Productions
Quinnette, John: NBC News
Quinones, Manuel: Capitol News Connection (CNC)
Quinonez, Omar A.: ABC News
Qureshi, Sophia: Aljazeera International
Rabbage, Mark: BBC
Rabin, Carrie: CBS News
Rabin, Mark: CNN
Rabkin, Job: Independent Television News (ITN)
Racki, Jason: Fox Business Network
Rad, Ali: Fox News
Radelat, Carmen: NBC News
Radia, Kirit M.: ABC News
Radu, Bogdan: CNN

MEMBERS ENTITLED TO ADMISSION—Continued

Rady, Meaghan: NBC News
Raffaele, Robert: Voice of America
Rager, Bryan: Reuters Radio & TV
Rahman, Omar: AP–Broadcast
Raine, John Patrick: Aljazeera International
Rainey, Brian: Fox News
Rakes, Allison: CBS News
Ramchandani, Lavina: Hearst–Argyle Television
Ramienski, Dorothy: Federal News Radio AM 1050
Ramirez, Edwin: CNN
Ramirez, Fabiana: Religion & Ethics Newsweekly
Ramirez, Roselena: Telesur
Ramos, Rosario: UPI.com
Rampietti, Alessandro: Aljazeera International
Rampy, R. Grant: Tribune Broadcasting
Randev, Sonia: Community TV of PG's
Randle, Jim: Voice of America
Raney, Adam: Aljazeera International
Raphel, Paul: WTTG–Fox Television
Rathner, Jeffrey: WETA
Ratner, Ellen: Talk Radio News Service
Ratner, Victor: ABC News
Rattansi, Shihab: Aljazeera International
Raval, Adi: BBC
Raval, Nikhil: C–SPAN
Raviv, Daniel: CBS News
Ray, Alonzo: NBC News
Ray, Branden: CNN
Reap, Patrick: CNN
Redding, William: ABC News
Redman, Justine: CNN
Reeder, Louis R.: Environment & Energy Publishing, LLC
Reese, Howard: The Newshour with Jim Lehrer
Reeve, Richard: WJLA–TV / Newschannel 8
Reeves, Alea: Aljazeera International
Reeves, Austin: WTTG–Fox Television
Refo, Jacqueline Nicole: WASHINGTONPOST.COM
Reid, Charles: CBS News
Reilly, Robert: C–SPAN
Reinsel, Ed: Fox News
Remillard, Michele: Fox News
Remme, Klaus: Deutscheland Radio
Renaud, Jean: CNN
Renken, David: Fox News
Rensberger, Scott: TV2–Denmark
Resnick, Jon: AP–Broadcast
Rettenmaier, Daniela: German TV ARD
Reuter, Cynthia: C–SPAN
Reyes, Elaine: WTTG–Fox Television
Reyes, Malissa: WJLA–TV / Newschannel 8
Reyes, Victor: Telemundo Network
Reynolds, Andrew: National Public Radio
Reynolds, Catherine C.: Cox Broadcasting
Reynolds, Douglas: ABC News
Reynolds, Judy: Religion & Ethics Newsweekly
Reynolds, Robert: Aljazeera International
Rhee, Hoin: MBC–TV Korea (Munhwa)
Rhodes, Charles Chedester: WASHINGTONPOST.COM
Rhodes, Elizabeth: Fox News
Ricalde, Katheryn C.: Fox News
Ricciuti, Leah Marie: ABC News
Rice, Ben: WJLA–TV / Newschannel 8
Rice, Jack: Talk Radio News Service
Richard, Sylvain: Canadian Broadcasting Corporation (CBC)
Rickard, Michael: WTTG–Fox Television
Riddick, Marquita: Aljazeera International
Ridolfi, Sarah Santer: Fox News
Riess, Steffanie: German TV ZDF
Riggs, James: CNN
Riggs, Tyrone W.: ABC News
Rigney, Paul: C–SPAN
Riha, Anne Marie: Fox News
Riley, Charles Ramsden: CNN
Riner, Corbett: Fox News
Rios, Delia: C–SPAN
Rios-Hernandez, Raul: CNN
Riskin, Igor: Channel One Russian TV
Ritchie, Thomas: AP–Broadcast
Roach, Kevin: AP–Broadcast
Roane Skehan, Andrea: WUSA–TV
Robbins, Diana Claudia: German TV ARD
Robbins, Francisco: CBS News
Robbins, Michael: Fox News
Robbins, Sarah: BBC
Robert, Olivier: Eye–To–Eye Video
Roberts, Corinne: ABC News
Roberts, Jean Pierre: Eurovision Americas, Inc.
Roberts, John: CNN
Roberts, Nathan: WTOP Radio
Roberts, Susan: CBS News
Robertson, Greg: CNN
Robertson, Tamara: Fox News
Robinson, Courtney: WJLA–TV / Newschannel 8
Robinson, Daniel: Voice of America
Robinson, David: CNN
Robinson, Margaret: The Newshour with Jim Lehrer
Robinson, Querry: NBC News
Robinson, Veronica: WTOP Radio
Roca, Xavier: TV3–Televisio De Catalunya
Rocha, Juan: Ventana Productions
Rocha, Samuel: Reuters Radio & TV
Rockler, Julia: The Washington Bureau
Rocque, Tiffany: C–SPAN
Rodeffer, Mark: C–SPAN
Rodgers, William: Voice of America
Rodriguez, Eduardo: AP–Broadcast
Rodriguez, Janet: CNN
Rodriguez, Martine: C–SPAN
Rohrbeck, Douglas: Fox News
Rojas, Carlos A.: ABC News
Rokus, Brian: CNN
Roland, Abu Bakr: ABC News

MEMBERS ENTITLED TO ADMISSION—Continued

Roller, Richard L.: ABC News
Rollins, Bonnie: NBC Newschannel
Romilly, George: ABC News
Roof, Peter: NBC Newschannel
Rose, Art: WTOP Radio
Rose, Francis: Federal News Radio AM 1050
Rose, Jeff: WJLA–TV / Newschannel 8
Rose, Joe: WJLA–TV / Newschannel 8
Rose, Raymond: NBC News
Roselli, H. Michael: CNN
Rosen, James: Fox News
Rosen, Nancy: To The Contrary (Persephone Productions)
Rosen, Rachel: CNN
Rosenbaum, Jill: CBS News
Rosenberg, Andrew: National Public Radio
Rosenberg, Gary: ABC News
Rosenberg, Howard: CBS News
Rosenberg, Jeffrey: National Public Radio
Rosewicz, Barbara: STATELINE.ORG
Rosgaard, Jessica: CNN
Ross, Adrienne: Fox News
Ross, Caley: Fox News
Ross, Jane: Reuters Radio & TV
Ross, Lee: Fox News
Ross, Mary Katherine: CNN
Rossel, Maria Luisa: W Radio
Rossetti-Meyer, Misa: Diversified Communications, Inc. (DCI)
Roth, Linda: CNN
Roth, Theodore: ABC News
Rouleau, Marie-Paul: Canadian Broadcasting Corporation (CBC)
Rovner, Julie: National Public Radio
Rowe, Hildrun: German TV ZDF
Rowe, Tom: Reuters Radio & TV
Royce, Lindy: CNN
Roycraft, David: WUSA–TV
Royster, Meredith: WTTG–Fox Television
Ruby, Tracy: C–SPAN
Rudd, Michael: WJLA–TV / Newschannel 8
Rudin, Ken: National Public Radio
Ruff, David: CNN
Ruff, Jennifer: C–SPAN
Ruffini, Christina: CBS News
Ruggiero, Diane: CNN
Rullo, Madeline: NBC News
Rushing, Ian William: CBN News
Rushing, Joshua: Aljazeera International
Russel, Kimberly: Voice of America
Russell, Eugene: WTTG–Fox Television
Russert, Luke: NBC News
Rust, Emily: CNN
Ruttenberg, Roee: Aljazeera International
Ruzaliev, Odil: Voice of America
Ryan, Fred: WJLA–TV / Newschannel 8
Ryan, Jason: ABC News
Ryan, Kate: WTOP Radio
Ryan, Marty: Fox News
Rydell, Kate: CBS News
Ryntjes, Daniel: Feature Story News
Rysak, F. David: WTTG–Fox Television
Sachs, Rob: National Public Radio
Sachtleben, Doug: SRN News (Salem)
Sacks, Howard: NBC News
Sadighi, Nader: Radio Free Europe
Saffelle, Jeffery Lynn: Diversified Communications, Inc. (DCI)
Sagalyn, Daniel: The Newshour with Jim Lehrer
Saine-Spang, Cynthia: Voice of America
Sakurai, Reiko: NHK–Japan Broadcasting Corporation
Salam, Najiba: Voice of America
Salan, Jennifer: Aljazeera International
Salas, Pedro: CNN
Salazar, Marcela: Univision
Salih, Balen: Voice of America
Salim, Yuni: Voice of America
Salkoff, Brooke Hart: NBC Newschannel
Sallstrom, Royce: CBN News
Saloomey, Kristen: Aljazeera International
Sam, Borin: Radio Free Asia
Samaniego, Manny: Aljazeera International
Sammon, Bill: Fox News
Sampaio, Frederico: C–SPAN
Sampy, David: East Coast Television
Sampy, David: Independent Television News (ITN)
Samuels, Rebecca: NBC News
Sanchez, Claudio: National Public Radio
Sanchez, George D.: ABC News
Sanchez, Marcelo: WZDC–TV
Sanchez, Pablo: Univision
Sandell, Clayton: ABC News
Sanders, Molly: C–SPAN
Sanders-Smith, Sherry: C–SPAN
Sandiford, Michelle: C–SPAN
Sanfuentes, Jose Antoine: NBC News
Sano, Jun: Fuji TV Japan
Santa-Rita, Joad Jose: Voice of America
Santo, Vincent: CNN
Santos, Jose G.: CNN
Sanvido, Colleen: NBC News
Sarfo-Kantanka, Johnson: C–SPAN
Sargent, Mark: WTTG–Fox Television
Sarhan, Hanaan: Aljazeera International
Sarkar, Kabiruddin: Voice of America
Sarralde, Andrea: WZDC–TV
Sartorius, Scott: NBC News
Satchell, David: WUSA–TV
Sato, Keiichi: Nippon TV Network
Satterfield, John T.: ABC News
Savage, Craig: Fox News
Savchenko, Yulia: BBC
Savio, Gabriella: Diversified Communications, Inc. (DCI)
Savoy, Gregory: Reuters Radio & TV

MEMBERS ENTITLED TO ADMISSION—Continued

Sawan, Arwa: American Press and TV Services (APTVS)
Sawyer, Bill: WJLA–TV / Newschannel 8
Scanlan, William: C–SPAN
Scanlon, Jason: Fox News
Scarpelli, Leah: National Public Radio
Schaff, Michael: CBN News
Schall, Fred: WTTG–Fox Television
Schank, Lindsey Arent: Bloomberg Radio & TV
Schantz, Douglas N.: CNN
Schantz, Kristy: CN8 The Comcast Network
Scharf, Jason: Eurovision Americas, Inc.
Schayer, Cara: Fox News
Scheid, Harry: FEDNET
Schell, Barbara: Aljazeera International
Scherer, Klaus: German TV ARD
Scheuer, John: C–SPAN
Schiavone, Louise: ABC News
Schieffer, Bob: CBS News
Schiff, Brian: Voice of America
Schlegel, Barry C.: CNN
Schlenker, Aungthu: Radio Free Asia
Schloemer, Peter: German TV ZDF
Schmickler, Marion: German TV ARD
Schmidt, Emily: WJLA–TV / Newschannel 8
Schneider, Jr., Edward: Voice of America
Schneider, Fred: CBS News
Schneider, James: WETA
Schneider, William: CNN
Schoenmann, Donald: Eye–To–Eye Video
Scholfield, Piers: BBC
Scholl, Christopher: CBS News
Scholtyssyk, Lars: Deutsche Welle TV
Schott, Sonia: Radio VALERA Venezuela
Schreiber, Joe: Viewpoint Communications
Schrock, Matthew J.: Medill News Service
Schulter, Jonathan M.: CNSNEWS.COM
Schultze, Emily: CNN
Schuster, Henry: CBS News
Schuster, Paul: BBC
Schwager, Milena: BBC
Schwandt, Kimberly: Fox News
Schwartz, Matthew S.: Talk Radio News Service
Schweiger, Ellen: C–SPAN
Sciammacco, Sara: Capitol News Connection (CNC)
Scicchitano, Carmine: NBC News
Scott, Christopher Eric: CN8 The Comcast Network
Scott, Harry: Radio Free Asia
Scott, Linda: The Newshour with Jim Lehrer
Scriabine, Raisa: Link TV
Scritchfield, Andrew: NBC News
Scruggs, Wesley: NBC News
Scully, Steven: C–SPAN
Seabrook, Andrea: National Public Radio
Seabrook, Willliam: WETA
Seaby, Gregory: WJLA–TV / Newschannel 8
Sears, Carl: NBC News
Seeholzer, Bjoern Tony: East Coast Television
Seem, Thomas H.: CBS News
Sefia, Stephanie: Aljazeera International
Segraves, Mark: WTOP Radio
Seidman, Joel: NBC News
Seifert, Jan Philipp: German TV ZDF
Selma, Reginald G.: CNN
Selsky, Lauren: NBC News
Sennett, John Gordon: ATN Productions, LTD.
Seo, Ja Ryen: Korean Broadcasting Systems
Serhan, Ali: AP–Broadcast
Serna, Adriana Ahmad: CMI TV (Colombia)
Serper, Noelle: Religion & Ethics Newsweekly
Seymour, Allison: WTTG–Fox Television
Seymour, William Nicoll: WJLA–TV / Newschannel 8
Shaffir, Gregory: CBS News
Shakhov, Dmytro: RTVi / ECHO–TV
Shalhoup, Joseph: NBC News
Shan, Zijun: Radio Free Asia
Shannon, Dennis: CBS News
Shannon, Holly: WJLA–TV / Newschannel 8
Shannon, Michael Patrick: ABC News
Shapiro, Adam: Fox Business Network
Shapiro, Ari: National Public Radio
Shapiro, Joseph: National Public Radio
Sharief, Islam: Aljazeera International
Sharma, B. K.: WJLA–TV / Newschannel 8
Sharp, Adam: C–SPAN
Sharpe, Bob: BBC
Shaughnessy, Lawrence: CNN
Shaw, Cathy: National Public Radio
Shaw, Joseph: Hearst–Argyle Television
Shaw, LaQuoya D.: UPI.com
Sheehan, Kathleen: Federal News Service
Shefte, Whitney: WASHINGTONPOST.COM
Shekinskaya, Nargiz: RTVi / ECHO–TV
Shelton, Steve: Fox News
Shen, Jianing: China Central TV Bureau
Shepherd, Shawna: CNN
Sherman, Emily: CNN
Sherwood, Ian: BBC
Sherwood, Tom: WRC–TV / NBC–4
Shi, Wei: New Tang Dynasty TV
Shields, Daniel: Fox News Radio
Shiels, Molly: CNN
Shipman, Claire: ABC News
Shirwani, Motabar: Voice of America
Shively, Caroline: Fox News
Shlemon, Chris: Independent Television News (ITN)
Shoffner, Harry: BBC
Shogren, ElizaBeth: National Public Radio
Shoji, Shin: NHK–Japan Broadcasting Corporation
Shon, Robert: WTTG–Fox Television
Shott, Dave: Fox News
Shoup, Anna: The Newshour with Jim Lehrer
Shukran, Halai: C–SPAN
Shull, Roger: Reuters Radio & TV
Sicuranza (Kelley), Daniela: Fox News

MEMBERS ENTITLED TO ADMISSION—Continued

Sides, James: NHK–Japan Broadcasting Corporation
Siegel, Robert C.: National Public Radio
Siegfriedt, Anita: Fox News
Sierra, Joann Lucia: CNN
Silberbrandt, Allan: TV2–Denmark
Silberner, Joanne: National Public Radio
Sills, Cecil John: NBC Newschannel
Silman III, Jimmie: WUSA–TV
Silva Llancaleo, Juan: CNN
Silva-Pinto, Luis Fernando: TV Globo International
Silver, David: NBC News
Silver, Diane: The Newshour with Jim Lehrer
Silver, Janet E.: Australian Broadcasting Corporation
Silverberg, Hank: WTOP Radio
Silverman, Art: National Public Radio
Silverman, Rachel: Feature Story News
Silverstein, Matthew: Fox News
Simeone, Ronald: NBC News
Simmons, Gregory: Fox News
Simmons, Sarah: WTTG–Fox Television
Simms, Jeffery: CNN
Simon, Jeff: CNN
Simons, John: Aljazeera International
Simpson, Cynne: WJLA–TV / Newschannel 8
Simpson, Mariam: Aljazeera International
Sims, Colin: Aljazeera International
Sina, Ralph: German TV ARD
Sinderbrand, Rebecca: CNN
Singer, Lauren: NBC News
Singeri, Sonam Lhamo: Radio Free Asia
Sit, David: The Newshour with Jim Lehrer
Skeans, Ron: BBC
Skehan, Michael: East Coast Television
Skene, Mathieu: Aljazeera International
Skirble, Rosanne: Voice of America
Skokowski, Christopher: FEDNET
Skomal, Paul: Fox News
Slack, Mary Beth: Need To Know News
Slafka, Kristi: CNN
Slansky, Heike: German TV ZDF
Slattery, Julie: Bloomberg Radio & TV
Slen, Peter: C–SPAN
Slewka, Stephanie: German TV ZDF
Slie, Charles: NBC News
Sloane, Ward C.: CBS News
Slobogin, Kathy: CNN
Smith, Alison: Canadian Broadcasting Corporation (CBC)
Smith, Anthony Grey: Diversified Communications, Inc. (DCI)
Smith, Christie: NBC Newschannel
Smith, Cindy: ABC News
Smith, Cynthia L.: Fox News
Smith, Douglas: East Coast Television
Smith, Graham: National Public Radio
Smith, James E.: ABC News
Smith, Jason H.: WTTG–Fox Television
Smith, Lindley: C–SPAN
Smith, Mark S.: AP–Broadcast
Smith, Michael: WETA
Smith, Phillip: Aljazeera International
Smith, Sarah: Independent Television News (ITN)
Smith, Skip: CNN
Smith, William: Belo Capital Bureau
Smith-Spark, Laura: BBC
Sneed, Kimberly: NBC News
Snyder, Tanya: Capitol News Connection (CNC)
Soe, Khin Maung: Radio Free Asia
Soh, June: Voice of America
Sok, Pov: Voice of America
Sokolova, Elena: Russian State TV and Radio (RTR)
Solano, Roxana: WZDC–TV
Solari, Benjamin Southwick: Federal News Service
Solimani-Lezhnev, Andrey: Russian State TV and Radio (RTR)
Solodovnikov, Mikhail: Russian State TV and Radio (RTR)
Solorzano, Gilbert: NBC News
Som, Sattana: Radio Free Asia
Sonnheim, Jon: Cox Broadcasting
Sorensen, Eric D.: Global TV Canada
Sorenson, Ben: C–SPAN
Soucy, Peggy: Eurovision Americas, Inc.
Soudah, Gus: Aljazeera International
Sozio, George A.: ABC News
Spear, Anita Brikmanis: WUSA–TV
Speck, Alan: C–SPAN
Spector, Teresa: Fox News
Speights, Eric: ABC News
Speiser, Matthew: CNN
Spence, Robert: C–SPAN
Spencer, Darcy: WRC–TV / NBC–4
Sperry, Todd: CNN
Spevak, Joe: WTTG–Fox Television
Spicer, Nick: Aljazeera International
Spiegler, Theodore: CBS News
Spinelli, Paul: Sinclair Broadcast Group
Spiro, David: Reuters Radio & TV
Spoerry, Philip Scott: CNN
Sprankle, James: Fox News
Srivastava, Amish: Voice of America
St. John, Jonathan: Fox Business Network
Stack, Andrew Michael: WUSA–TV
Stahl, Steven: CNN
Stakelbeck, Erick: CBN News
Stalnaker, Kurt: National Public Radio
Stamberg, Susan: National Public Radio
Stanford, Dave: CBS News
Stang, Tim: Bloomberg Radio & TV
Staniar, Britton: Bloomberg Radio & TV
Stanitz, Emily: Bloomberg Radio & TV
Stanke, Donald E.: WTTG–Fox Television
Stark, Lisa: ABC News
Starling, Alison: WJLA–TV / Newschannel 8

MEMBERS ENTITLED TO ADMISSION—Continued

Starnes, Todd: Fox News Radio
Starr, Barbara: CNN
Starr, Penny: CNSNEWS.COM
Staton, Thomas M.: ABC News
Statter, David: WUSA–TV
Stay, Daniel J.: Fox News
Stead, Scott: CNN
Stebbins, William: Aljazeera International
Steele, Andrew: BBC
Stefany, Steve: ABC News
Steinhauser, Lesley Creegan: Irish Radio & TV (RTE)
Steinhauser, Paul: CNN
Stemple, Lexi: Fox News
Stencil, Meredith: CBS News
Stenner, Andrew: Fox News
Stephanopoulos, George: ABC News
Sterling, Vaughn: CNN
Stevens, Seneca: Fox News
Stevenson, James: Voice of America
Stevenson, Louis: WTTG–Fox Television
Stewart, Andrew: SRN News (Salem)
Stewart, Martina: CNN
Stewart, Philip: WJLA–TV / Newschannel 8
Stewart, Robin Anthony: Ventana Productions
Stix, Gabriel: CBS News
Stoddard, Mark S.: ABC News
Stoddard, Rick: C–SPAN
Stok, Silvester: RTV Slovenija
Stone, Carolyn: CNN
Stone, Emily: WTTG–Fox Television
Stone, Evie: National Public Radio
Stout, Matthew: Fox News
Stoutzenberger, Tim: CNN
Strachan, Jason: CNN
Strand, Paul: CBN News
Straub, Terry: Diversified Communications, Inc. (DCI)
Streeter, James: NBC News
Streitfeld, Rachel: CNN
Strickland, Kenneth: NBC News
Strickler, Laura: CBS News
Stringer, Ashley: CNBC
Stringer, James: BBC
Strothe, Stephen: N24 German TV
Stumpo, Donald: WRC–TV / NBC–4
Styles, Julian: CNN
Suarez, Fernando J.: CNN
Suarez, Rafael: The Newshour with Jim Lehrer
Suddeth, James: Fox News
Suddeth, Rick: Fox News
Sughroue, Jon: NBC News
Suiters, Kimberly: WRC–TV / NBC–4
Sullivan, Laura: National Public Radio
Sullivan, Robert: NBC News
Sullivan, Sean: NHK–Japan Broadcasting Corporation
Sullivan, Virginia L.: National Public Radio
Summers, Elizabeth: The Newshour with Jim Lehrer
Summers, Patrick: Fox News
Sumrell, John: WTTG–Fox Television
Sung, Chinling: Hong Kong Phoenix Satellite Television
Sung, In Hyun: Korean Broadcasting Systems
Suo, Paul: Hong Kong Phoenix Satellite Television
Sutherland, JJ: National Public Radio
Sutherland, Leigh: NBC News
Suto, Ena: TV Asahi
Svolopoulos, Christina: Fox News
Swagler, Craig: CBS News
Swain, Bethany: CNN
Swain, Susan: C–SPAN
Swain, Todd: Mobile Video Services, LTD.
Swan, Sean: Independent Television News (ITN)
Swanier, Sherrell: CNN
Swann, Michael: WRC–TV / NBC–4
Sweeney, Charles: CNN
Sweeney, Robert: WRC–TV / NBC–4
Sweetapple, Dan: Australian Broadcasting Corporation
Sylvester, John: Fox News Radio
Sylvester, Lisa: CNN
Symanski, Mary: C–SPAN
Symons, Devin Clarke: Nippon TV Network
Syrjanen, Janne: Aljazeera International
Szypulski, Tom: Aljazeera International
Tabaar, Mohammed: BBC
Tahir, Ahmad: Voice of America
Tait, Ted: BBC
Takagane, Yuka: NHK–Japan Broadcasting Corporation
Takagi, Masaru: NHK–Japan Broadcasting Corporation
Takagi, Yosuke: NHK–Japan Broadcasting Corporation
Takao, Jun: NHK–Japan Broadcasting Corporation
Takar, Nafees: Voice of America
Takezaki, Tomoyasu: Nippon TV Network
Takruri, Dena: Aljazeera Satellite Channel (Peninsula)
Tamboli, Jay: Talk Radio News Service
Tamerlani, George: Reuters Radio & TV
Tang, Shiding: China Central TV Bureau
Tanner, Scott: Radio One
Tansomboon, Chamroen: Voice of America
Tapper, Jake: ABC News
Tashdjian, Kevork: Voice of America
Tashi, Yeshi: Radio Free Asia
Tasillo, Mary Ellen: Fox News
Tate, Deborah: Voice of America
Tate, Tiffany: BET Nightly News
Tatton, Abbi: CNN
Taylor, Audrey: ABC News
Taylor, Dan: CNN
Taylor, Eric Scott: ABC News
Taylor, John: WRC–TV / NBC–4

MEMBERS ENTITLED TO ADMISSION—Continued

Taylor, Michael: Aljazeera International
Taylor, Russell J.: C–SPAN
Teboe, Mark: Aljazeera International
Teeples, Joseph: C–SPAN
Tejerina, Pilar: Aljazeera International
Temin, Thomas R.: Federal News Radio AM 1050
Tendencia, Editha: Eurovision Americas, Inc.
Tennent, Gerald W.: National Public Radio
Teply, Marcus: German TV ZDF
Teranishi, Kenji: Nippon TV Network
Terry, David: SRN News (Salem)
Tevault, Neil David: National Public Radio
Thai, Xuan: CNN
Thalman, Mark: Ventana Productions
Theall, David J.: CNN
Thein, Kyaw K.: Voice of America
Thery, Samara: The Newshour with Jim Lehrer
Thoman, Eric: C–SPAN
Thomas, Christopher: Community TV of PG's
Thomas, Evelyn: CBS News
Thomas, Gary: Voice of America
Thomas, Joseph: Mobile Video Services, LTD.
Thomas, Michael: East Coast Television
Thomas, Philippa: BBC
Thomas, Sharahn: National Public Radio
Thomas, Shari: ABC News
Thomas, Will: WTTG–Fox Television
Thomas III, James B.: CNN
Thompson, Jerry: CNN
Thompson, Joseph: ABC News
Thompson, Lisa: CNN
Thompson, Ron: Radio One
Thompson, Shaleem: Reuters Radio & TV
Thompson Anderson, Laetitia: WTTG–Fox Television
Thorne, C. Patrick: Washington Bureau News Service
Thornton, Ronald: NBC News
Thorp, Frank: CBS News
Thuman, Autria: Fox News
Thuman, Scott: WJLA–TV / Newschannel 8
Tiller, Arthur: C–SPAN
Tillery, Richard: The Washington Bureau
Tillery, Rick Craig: The Washington Bureau
Tillman, Thomas E.: CBS News
Tilman, Brandon: C–SPAN
Timmermann, Michael: WJLA–TV / Newschannel 8
Tin, Annie: C–SPAN
Tipper, William: CNN
Todd, Brian: CNN
Todd, Chuck: NBC News
Todd, Deborah: CBS News
Toman, George: NBC News
Toman, George: NBC Newschannel
Toms, Sarah Fiona: Reuters Radio & TV
Topgyal, Benpa: Radio Free Asia
Torlone, Lauren: Fox News
Torpey, Robert: Fox News
Totenberg, Nina: National Public Radio
Toulouse, Anne: Radio France Internationale
Tovarek, Steve: CNN
Toya, Mitsuhiro: Tokyo Broadcasting System
Trainor, Thomas: Eurovision Americas, Inc.
Trammell, Michael: WUSA–TV
Trauzzi, Monica: Environment & Energy Publishing, LLC
Travers, Karen Lynn: ABC News
Traynham, Peter C.: CBS News
Traynham, Robert: CN8 The Comcast Network
Triay, Andres P.: CBS News
Trull, Armando Ernesto: WUSA–TV
Trunov, Denis Mikhaylovich: Russia Today Television
Tschida, Stephen: WJLA–TV / Newschannel 8
Tsou, Chris: Ventana Productions
Tsugawa, Takafumi: Tokyo Broadcasting System
Tuan, Shih-Yuan: TVBS
Tucker, Elke: German TV ZDF
Tully, Andrew: Radio Free Europe
Tuohey, Kenneth: CNN
Turner, Catherine: Aljazeera International
Turner, Chris: CNN
Turner, Patricia: Fox News
Turner, Renee: NBC News
Turnham, Steve: CNN
Tuss, Adam: WTOP Radio
Tuszynski, Tom: Al Arabiya TV
Tutman, Dan D.: CBS News
Tyler, Brett: CNN
Tyler, Lamonte Bryant: Fox News
Tyler, Thomas Joseph: Diversified Communications, Inc. (DCI)
Uchimiya, Ellen: Fox News
Udenans, Vija: ABC News
Uenuma, Francine Izumi: WASHINGTONPOST.COM
Uhl, Kim: CNN
Uhls, Anna Rachel: WASHINGTONPOST.COM
Ulaby, Neda: National Public Radio
Ulbrich, Sabine: N24 German TV
Ulery, Brad: AP–Broadcast
Uliano, Richard J.: CNN
Ulloa, Melinda: Reuters Radio & TV
Ulloa, Victor: CBS News
Umeh, Maureen: WTTG–Fox Television
Umrani, Anthony R.: CNN
Unger, Barry: Voice of America
Upadhyay, Brajesh: BBC
Uprety, Sharmila: Sagarmatha Television
Urbina, Luis: WRC–TV / NBC–4
Ure, Laurie: CNN
Ureta, Juan: NBC News
Uribe, Juvenal: Morningside Partners, LLC
Urquhart, Jonathan: BBC
Ury, Faryl: AP–Broadcast
Vail, Patrick: Washington Bureau News Service

MEMBERS ENTITLED TO ADMISSION—Continued

Vakili, Mohammad Reza: Radio Free Europe
Van Cleave, Kristopher: WJLA–TV / Newschannel 8
Van de Mark, Ellen: NBC News
van der Laan, Nanette: Independent Television News (ITN)
Van Horn, Allan: NBC News
Van Susteren, Greta: Fox News
Van Winkle, Saadia: Community TV of PG's
Vance, Denise: AP–Broadcast
Vance, Lauren: WUSA–TV
Vancini, Larry: Hearst–Argyle Television
VanderVeen, Jacob: Mobile Video Services, LTD.
VanderVeen, Lawrence: Mobile Video Services, LTD.
Vanderveen, Paul: WETA
Vanestsyan, Aram: Voice of America
Vann, Araxie: Voice of America
Vasa, Sampath: WETA
Vaughan, Scott: Reuters Radio & TV
Vaughn, Mike: WJLA–TV / Newschannel 8
Vega, Fernando: Fox News
Vennell, Vicki A.: ABC News
Venuto, Anthony: East Coast Television
Verducci, Kara: Fox News
Verdugo, Adam: NBC News
Vestal, Christine: STATELINE.ORG
Vicario, Virginia A.: ABC News
Vicary, Lauren: NBC News
Vidushi, Vidushi: Voice of America
Viers, Dana: CNN
Vila, Xavier: Catalunya Radio
Vilen, Paula Hannele: Finnish Broadcasting Company (YLE)
Villamizar, Monica: Aljazeera International
Villavicencio, Monica: America Abroad Media
Villone Garcia, Patricia: Community TV of PG's
Vinson, Bryce: Fox News
Viqueira, Michael: NBC News
Virji, Anar: Aljazeera International
Visioli, Todd: Fox News
Visley, Andrew G.: AP–Broadcast
Vitorovich, Susan: NBC News
Vizcarra, Mario: Univision
Vlahos, Kelley Beaucar: Fox News
Vo, Vina: Aljazeera International
Vock, Daniel: STATELINE.ORG
Voegeli, Peter: Swiss Broadcasting
Vogel, Erin: Fox News
Vohar, Den: AP–Broadcast
Volk Harper, Kristin: UPI.com
Volkov, Dmitri: NTV–Russia Broadcasting Company
Volskiy, Anton: NTV–Russia Broadcasting Company
von Bonsdorff, Juri Tomas: Finnish Broadcasting Company (YLE)
von Trotha, Dorothea: German TV ZDF
Voth, Charles: WETA
Vu, Pauline: STATELINE.ORG
Vu, Tu H.: CNN
Vukmer, David: NBC News
Vurnis, Ambrose: WRC–TV / NBC–4
Wagner, Paul: WTTG–Fox Television
Wait, Kevin: National Public Radio
Waldon, Michael: AP–Broadcast
Wali, Kurban: Radio Free Asia
Walker, Bill: WJLA–TV / Newschannel 8
Walker, Jackie Lyn: ABC News
Walker, John: Voice of America
Walker, Sebastian: Aljazeera International
Walker, Teshima: National Public Radio
Walker, Tom: Dispatch Broadcast Group
Walker, William: CBS News
Wallace, Chris: Fox News
Wallace, John L.: Fox News
Wallace, Roger: Fox Business Network
Wallace, Zelda: Cox Broadcasting
Walsh, Carly: Aljazeera International
Walsh, Deirdre: CNN
Walsh, Mary Frances: ABC News
Walsh, Mary: CBS News
Walter, Christopher: CNN
Walton, Doreen: BBC
Walton-James, Vickie: National Public Radio
Walz, Mark: CNN
Wang, Jin: Aljazeera International
Wang, Taofeng: Hong Kong Phoenix Satellite Television
Waqfi, Wajd: Aljazeera Satellite Channel (Peninsula)
Ward, Derrick: WRC–TV / NBC–4
Warmerdam, Sander: NOS DUTCH Public Radio & TV (VRT)
Warner, Craig: CBS News
Warner, Margaret: The Newshour with Jim Lehrer
Warner, Tarik: WRC–TV / NBC–4
Warrick, David: CBS News
Washburn, Kevin: C–SPAN
Washington, Erick: CBS News
Washington, Ervin: Nightly Business Report
Washington Anderson, Robert: WJLA–TV / Newschannel 8
Waters, Hunter: CNN
Watkins, Duane: WTTG–Fox Television
Watrel, Jane: WRC–TV / NBC–4
Watrud, Don: WTTG–Fox Television
Watson, Carline: National Public Radio
Watson, Monica: Morningside Partners, LLC
Watson, Owen: BBC
Watson, Walter: National Public Radio
Watts, Andrew: National Public Radio
Watts, Michael: CNN
Wayne, Amanda: Fox News
Weakly, David: NBC News
Weaver, Justin Michael: ABC News
Webb, David: WJLA–TV / Newschannel 8

MEMBERS ENTITLED TO ADMISSION—Continued

Webb, Justin: BBC
Webb, Tracey: CNN
Webster, Aaron: Fox News
Webster, Aaron: Middle East Television Network (Alhurra)
Weeks, Linton Weeks: National Public Radio
Wehinger, Amy: Fox News
Weidenbosch, Glenn E.: ABC News
Weinberg, Ali: NBC News
Weinberg, Ilana: America Abroad Media
Weinbloom, Hank: Fox News Radio
Weiner, Dawn: Fox News Radio
Weiner, Eric: Tokyo Broadcasting System
Weinfeld, Michael: AP–Broadcast
Weinstein, Jessica: Fox News
Weinstein, Richard: C–SPAN
Weisbrod, Eric: CNN
Weiss, Brian: Bloomberg Radio & TV
Welch, Joanna: XM Satellite Radio
Wellen, Alex: CNN
Weller, George D.: ABC News
Welna, David: National Public Radio
Werdel, Paul: Aljazeera International
Werschkul, Benjamin: The New York Times On The Web
Wertheimer, Linda: National Public Radio
Whitaker, Mark: NBC News
White, Douglas: ABC News
White, Edward: CNN
White, Jordan: Federal News Service
White, Kenneth: CNN
White, Mark: CBS News
Whiteside, John P.: ABC News
Whitley, John H.: CBS News
Whitley, Walter: Fox News
Whitney, Hannah: Washington Bureau News Service
Whitney, Jonathan: BBC
Whitney, Michael: Washington Bureau News Service
Whittemore, Megan: Fox News
Whittington, Christopher: NBC News
Widmer, Christopher: CBS News
Wiedenbauer, Heidi: Cox Broadcasting
Wiesen, Stefan: German TV ZDF
Wiggins, Christopher: NBC Newschannel
Wik, Snorre: Aljazeera International
Wilde, Winston: NBC News
Wildman, Jim: National Public Radio
Wilk, Wendy: Hearst–Argyle Television
Wilkes, Douglas H.: WTTG–Fox Television
Wilkins, Tracee: WRC–TV / NBC–4
Wilkinson, Wendla: NBC News
Williams, Abigail: NBC News
Williams, Armstrong: Sinclair Broadcast Group
Williams, Candace: Voice of America
Williams, Christopher Anthony: America Abroad Media
Williams, Colleen: Fox News
Williams, David: Fox News
Williams, Jeffrey L.: Cox Broadcasting
Williams, John: Fox News
Williams, Juan: National Public Radio
Williams, Keith: WUSA–TV
Williams, Kenneth E.: CBS News
Williams, Kevin: NBC News
Williams, Louis Pete: NBC News
Williams, Michele: Radio One
Williams, Robert T.: NBC News
Williams, Steven: WTTG–Fox Television
Williams-Kief, Brendan: WRC–TV / NBC–4
Williamson, Christopher: NBC News
Willingham, Kimberly: Fox News
Willingham, Val: CNN
Willis, Anne Marie: Fox News
Wilp, Christian: N–TV German News Channel
Wilson, Brenda: National Public Radio
Wilson, Brian: Fox News
Wilson, Christopher: NBC News
Wilson, George: Radio One
Wilson, Kristin: NBC News
Wilson, Mark: CBS News
Wilson, Simon: BBC
Wilson, Stephanie: WUSA–TV
Wilson, Toni: ABC News
Wilson, Vanessa: NBC News
Winder, Robert: Aljazeera International
Windham, Ronald: Tribune Broadcasting
Winick, Todd James (TJ): ABC News
Winkler, Alice: National Public Radio
Winn, Thomas Pete: CNSNEWS.COM
Winslow, David: AP–Broadcast
Winslow, Linda: The Newshour with Jim Lehrer
Winterhalter, Ruthann: C–SPAN
Winters, Ronald: ABC News
Wishon, Jennifer Ann: CBN News
Wisniewski, Erica: The Hill
Witte, Joel: WTTG–Fox Television
Witten, Robert: NBC News
Wittstock, Melinda: Capitol News Connection (CNC)
Wlach, Jennifer Lauren: HD Net
Wolf, Zachary B.: ABC News
Wolfe, Lisa: Federal News Radio AM 1050
Wolfson, Charles: CBS News
Wolfson, Scott: WTTG–Fox Television
Wolfson-Stevenson, Paula: Voice of America
Won, Il Hee: Seoul Broadcasting System (SBS)
Wood, Audrey: CBS News
Wood, Christopher: C–SPAN
Wood, Elisha Michelle: ABC News
Wood, Greg: BBC
Wood, Winston: Voice of America
Woodruff, Judy: The Newshour with Jim Lehrer
Wordock, Colleen: Bloomberg Radio & TV
Wordock, John: Marketwatch

MEMBERS ENTITLED TO ADMISSION—Continued

Workman, Paul Thomas: CTV Canadian TV
Wray, Taylor Curtice: Federal News Service
Wright, Dale: WJLA–TV / Newschannel 8
Wright, David J.: ABC News
Wright, James: Aljazeera International
Wright, Kelly: Fox News
Wright, Tracey Marie: Global TV Canada
Wrona, Marcin Wojciech: TVN Poland
Wu, Hanying: China Central TV Bureau
Wu, Ruonian: New Tang Dynasty TV
Wulff, John: ABC News
Wynne Johnson, Elizabeth: Capitol News Connection (CNC)
Wyszogrodzki, Marcin: TVN Poland
Xavier, Wilkins: Aljazeera International
Xiang, Dong: New Tang Dynasty TV
Xie, Jiao Christine: Hong Kong Phoenix Satellite Television
Xie, Yanmei: Capitol News Connection (CNC)
Xu, Jinglu: New Tang Dynasty TV
Xu, Susie: CNN
Xue, Bin: New Tang Dynasty TV
Yager, Joshua: CBS News
Yaklyvich, Brian: CNN
Yam, Raymond: Voice of America
Yamada, Mio: NHK–Japan Broadcasting Corporation
Yamada, Nancy M.: WUSA–TV
Yancy, Shawn: WTTG–Fox Television
Yang, Carter: CBS News
Yang, Chunfang: New Tang Dynasty TV
Yang, Eun: WRC–TV / NBC–4
Yang, Fuqing: China Central TV Bureau
Yang, John: NBC News
Yang, Sungwon: Radio Free Asia
Yarborough, Rick: WTTG–Fox Television
Yarmuth, Floyd: CNN
Yates, H. William: CBS News
Ydstie, John: National Public Radio
Yellin, Jessica: CNN
Yeung, Richard: NBC News
Yianopoulos, Karen: Middle East Television Network (Alhurra)
Yin, Chunsheng: China Central TV Bureau
Yoon, Robert: CNN
Young, Jeffrey: Living on Earth
Young, Jeremy: Aljazeera International
Young, Melissa A.: ABC News
Young, Rick: FRONTLINE (PBS)
Young, Robert Latimer: C–SPAN
Young, Saundra: CNN
Young, Jr., Jerome: CBN News
Younis, Omar: Reuters Radio & TV
Yu, Annie: WTTG–Fox Television
Yu, John: New Tang Dynasty TV
Yungfleisch, Patrick: Morningside Partners, LLC
Zaidi, Huma: NBC News
Zairi, Said: FEDNET
Zajko, Robert: Diversified Communications, Inc. (DCI)
Zanatta, Dennis: TV Globo International
Zang, Guohua: CTI–TV (Taiwan)
Zann, Julie Gardner: Middle East Television Network (Alhurra)
Zariquiey, Juan Pablo: WZDC–TV
Zayed, Nahedah: Aljazeera International
Zderic, Srdjan: Aljazeera International
Zechar, David: ABC News
Zeffler, Marcus: BBC
Zeledon, Franklin: Morningside Partners, LLC
Zeliger, Robert: The Newshour with Jim Lehrer
Zerivitz, Brad: Feature Story News
Zervos, Stratis: ABC News
Zhodzishsky, Ilya: Russia Today Television
Zhu, Hua: China Central TV Bureau
Zibel, Eve: Fox News
Ziegler, Albrecht: German Public Radio (ARD)
Ziegler, Julia: Federal News Radio AM 1050
Zimmerman, Douglas: Environment & Energy Publishing, LLC
Zmidzinski, Andy: WJLA–TV / Newschannel 8
Zoric, Iva: BBC
Zosso, ElizaBeth: Middle East Television Network (Alhurra)

NETWORKS, STATIONS, AND SERVICES REPRESENTED

Senate Gallery 224–6421 House Gallery 225–5214

ABC NEWS—(202) 222-7206; 1717 DeSales Street, NW., Washington, DC 20036: Jane Aylor, Kimberly Berryman (202) 222–7208, Loretta Marbury.

ADVENTURE HILL ENG—(703) 644–6909; 9216 Capricorn Court, Burke, VA 22015: Michael Angelo DeMark.

AGENCE FRANCE PRESSE (AFP–TV)—(202) 372–7206; 1500 K Street, NW., Washington, DC 20005: Erica Berenstein, Stephane Delfour (202) 413–2612.

AL ARABIYA TV—(202) 355–6626; National Press Building, 529 14th Street, NW., Suite 530, Washington, DC 20045: Richard Melhem.

ALASKA PUBLIC RADIO NETWORK—(202) 488–1961; 810 East Ninth Avenue, Anchorage, AL 99501: Libby Casey.

ALJAZEERA INTERNATIONAL—(202) 397–2469; 1627 K Street, NW., Suite 4006, Washington, DC 20006: Jeffrey Ballou, William Stebbins (496–4500).

ALJAZEERA SATELLITE CHANNEL (PENINSULA)—(202) 327–8200; 1627 K Street, NW., Suite 200, Washington, DC 20006: Abderrahim Foukara, Dianne McNair (202) 327–8201.

AMERICA ABROAD MEDIA—(202) 457–8050; 1020 19th Street, NW., Suite 650, Washington, DC 20036: Sean Carberry.

AMERICAN PRESS AND TV SERVICES (APTVS)—(202) 903–0271; 1919 M Street, NW., Washington, DC 20036: Sam Eizeldin.

AP–BROADCAST—(202) 736–1172; 1825 K Street, Washington, DC 20006: Ed Tobias, Denise Vance.

ARMY TIMES PUBLISHING COMPANY—(703) 750–8196; 6883 Commercial Drive, Springfield, VA 22159: Alan Lessig.

ARTE TV—(202) 297–3651; 2000 M Street, NW., Washington, DC 20036: Philippe Gassot.

ATN PRODUCTIONS, LTD.—(202) 898–8270; 1510 H Street, NW., 7th Floor, Washington, DC 20005: Affra Khallash.

AUDIO VIDEO NEWS—(703) 354–6795; 3622 Stanford Circle, Falls Church, VA 22041: Connie Lawn.

AUSTRALIAN BROADCASTING CORPORATION—(202) 626–5161; 2000 M Street, NW., Suite 660, Washington, DC 20036: Janet Silver.

AZTECA AMERICA—(202) 419–6134; 400 North Capitol Street, NW., Suite 361, Washington, DC 20001: Armando Guzman.

BBC—(202) 253–4960; 2000 M Street, NW., #800, Washington, DC 20009: Sofia Diarra, Sarah Gilbert (202) 352–2721.

BELO CAPITAL BUREAU—(202) 661–8471; 1325 C Street, NW., Suite 250, Washington, DC 20005: Al Banegas, Ashley Patterson.

BET NIGHTLY NEWS—(202) 841–5435; 400 North Capitol Street, NW., Suite 361, Washington, DC 20001: Tiffany Tate.

BLOOMBERG RADIO & TV—(202) 624–1933; 1399 NY Avenue, NW., 11th Floor, Washington, DC 20005: Sonya Cooper, Joe Winski.

BT VIDEO PRODUCTIONS—(301) 370–0808; 7117 Wolftree Lane, Rockville, MD 20852: Paul Hollenbeck.

CADENA SER—(301) 656–1556; 4520 Cumberland Avenue, Chevy Chase, MD 20815: Javier del Pino.

CANADIAN BROADCASTING CORPORATION (CBC)—(202) 383–2905; National Press Building, 529 14th Street, NW., Suite 500, Washington, DC 20045: Genevieve Ast.

CANAL PLUS FRENCH TV—(202) 641–9289; 1100 13 Street, NW., Suite 400, Washington, DC 20001: Laura Haim.

CAPITOL NEWS CONNECTION (CNC)—(202) 631–2436; 110 Maryland Avenue, NE., Washington, DC 20002: Martin Howe, Eric Niiler (498–5483).

CARACOL TELEVISION—(517) 303–1949; 529 14th Street, NW., 8th Floor, Washington, DC 20045: Gloria DeLaTorre.

CATALUNYA RADIO—(301) 845–2358; 311 Fallsworth Place, Walkersville, MD 21793: Xavier Vila.

CBN NEWS—(202) 467–2526; 1919 M Street, NW., Suite 100, Washington, DC 20036: Laura Kraus, Michael ''Anthony'' Schaff (202) 833–2707.

CBN NEWS—(202) 457–4430; 2020 M Street, NW., Washington, DC 20036: Karyn Anthony.

CHANNEL ONE RUSSIAN TV—(202) 744–5330: Igor Riskin.

CHINA CENTRAL TV BUREAU—(301) 530–2932; 2000 M Street, NW., Suite 880, Washington, DC 20036: Jun Gao.

CMI TV (COLOMBIA)—(703) 655–0775: Adriana Ahmad Serna.

NETWORKS, STATIONS, AND SERVICES REPRESENTED—Continued

CN8 THE COMCAST NETWORK—(202) 719–9201; 101 Constitution Avenue, NW., Suite L–150, Washington, DC 20001: Robert Traynham.

CNBC—(202) 776–7405; 1025 Conneticut Avenue, NW., Washington, DC 20836: Matthew Cuddy.

CNN—(202) 898–7911; 820 1st Street, NE., Washington, DC 20002: Kelly Marshall, Emily Rust (202) 515–2279.

CNSNEWS.COM—(703) 683–7045; 325 South Patrick Street, Alexandria, VA 22314: Michael Chapman.

COMMUNITY TV OF PG'S—(301) 464–4560; 9475 Lottsford Road, Largo, MD 20774: Curtis Crutchfield.

COPE RADIO (SPAIN)—(202) 686–1982; 4904 Bett Road, NW., Washington, DC 20016: Juan Martinez Fierro.

COURT TV—(212) 973–7948; 400 North Capitol Street, NW., #366, Washington, DC 20001: Tom Donahue.

COX BROADCASTING—(202) 777–7000; 400 North Capitol Street, NW., #750, Washington, DC 20001: Heidi Wiedenbaum.

C–SPAN—(202) 626–7966; 400 North Capitol Street, NW., #650, Washington, DC 20001: Michelle Doell, Terence Murphy (202) 737–3220.

CTI–TV (TAIWAN)—(202) 331–9110; 1825 K Street, NW., Suite 710, Washington, DC 20006: Guohua Zang.

CTV CANADIAN TV—(202) 466–3595; 2000 M Street, NW., Suite #330, Washington, DC 20036: Thomas Clark, Denise Kimmel.

DANISH BROADCASTING CORPORATION—(202) 785–1460; 3643 Jenifer Street, NW., Washington, DC 20015: Grethe Winther.

DEUTSCHE WELLE TV—(202) 460–9727; 2000 M Street, NW., Suite 335, Washington, DC 20036: Hillery Gallasch, Rudiger Lentz (703) 981–2215.

DEUTSCHELAND RADIO—(301) 765–0211: Klaus Remme.

DISPATCH BROADCAST GROUP—(202) 737–4630; 400 North Capitol Street, Suite 850, Washington, DC 20001: Tom Walker.

DIVERSIFIED COMMUNICATIONS, INC. (DCI)—(202) 470–5147; 2000 M Street, NW., 3rd Floor, Washington, DC 20036: Jamie Norins, Terry Straub (202) 775–4300.

EAST COAST TELEVISION—(202) 419–6161; 1919 M Street, NW., Suite UM, Washington, DC 20036: Chris Cowman, Mike Skehan (202) 775–0894.

ENVIRONMENT & ENERGY PUBLISHING, LLC—(202) 628–6500; 122 C Street, NW., Suite 722, Washington, DC 20001: Kevin Braun.

EUROVISION AMERICAS, INC.—(202) 293–9371; 2000 M Street, NW., Suite 300, Washington, DC 20036: William Dunlop.

EYE–TO–EYE VIDEO—(301) 907–7464; 4614 Chevy Chase Boulevard, Chevy Chase, MD 20815: Elliot Klayman.

FEATURE STORY NEWS—(202) 296–9012; 1730 Rhode Island Avenue, Suite 405, Washington, DC 20036: Priscilla Huff, Simon Marks.

FEDERAL NEWS RADIO AM 1050—(202) 895–5137: Lisa Wolfe.

FEDERAL NEWS SERVICE—(202) 216–2813; 1000 Vermont Avenue, NW., Washington, DC 20005: Kirk Hannemon, Carrie Mitchell (202) 216–2807.

FEDNET—(202) 393–7300; 50 F Street, NW., Suite 1C, Washington, DC 20001: Keith Carney.

FINNISH BROADCASTING COMPANY (YLE)—(202) 785–1460: Grethe Winther.

FOX BUSINESS NETWORK—(202) 715–1687; 400 North Capitol Street, NW., Washington, DC 20001: Mary Kreinbihl.

FOX NEWS—(202) 824–6345; 400 North Capitol Street, NW., Washington, DC 20001: Fred Haberstick.

FOX NEWS RADIO—(917) 846–5533; 5353 Cassons Neck Road, Cambridge, MD 21613: Mitch Davis, Dawn Weiner (212) 301–3958.

FRANCE 2 TELEVISION—(202) 833–1818; 2000 M Street, NW., Suite 320, Washington, DC 20036: Stephanie Cheval, Alain de Chalvron, Marjolaine Grappe (202) 320–5055.

FREE SPEECH RADIO NEWS—(202) 588–0999; 2390 Champlain Street, NW., Washington, DC 20009: Leigh Ann Caldwell.

FRONTLINE (PBS)—(617) 300–5386: Lisa Sullivan.

FUJI TV JAPAN—(202) 347–1600; 529 14th Street, NW., Suite 330, Washington, DC 20045: Peter Gold.

GANNETT NEWS SERVICE—(202) 906–8125; 1100 New York Avenue, Washington, DC 20005: Maria Fowler.

GERMAN BROADCASTING SYSTEMS-ARD—(202) 944–5290: Jens Borchers, Silvia Charpa.

GERMAN PRESS AGENCY—(202) 662–1220; 969 National Press Building, Washington, DC 20045: Laszlo Trankovits.

GERMAN PUBLIC RADIO (ARD)—(202) 362–3889; 3132 M Street, NW., Washington, DC 20007: Astrid Joehnk.

GERMAN TV ARD—(202) 298–6535; 3132 M Street, NW., Washington, DC 20007: Gabriela Eaglesome.

GERMAN TV ZDF—(202) 333–3909; 1077 31st Street, NW., Washington, DC 20007: Kirsten Candia, Matthias Fornoff, Rolanda Johnson (301) 537–6351.

NETWORKS, STATIONS, AND SERVICES REPRESENTED—Continued

GLOBAL TV CANADA—(202) 824–0426; 400 North Capitol Street, NW., #850, Washington, DC 20001: Eric Sorensen.

GROUPE TVA—(202) 822–4588; 1620 I Street, NW., Suite 1000, Washington, DC 20006: Richard Latendresse.

HD NET—(202) 664–4841; 1021 North Garfield Street, Suite 445, Arlington, VA 22201: Jennifer Wlach.

HD NEWS—(516) 803–9608; 2000 M Street, NW., Suite 340, Washington, DC 20036: Chris Long, Michael McManus (202) 470–5137.

HEARST-ARGYLE TELEVISION—(202) 457–0220; 1825 K Street, NW., #720, Washington, DC 20006: Shaun Neville, Wendy Wilk.

HISPANIC COMMUNICATIONS NETWORK—(202) 360–4089; 1126 16th Street, NW., 3rd Floor, Washington, DC 20036: Carlos Alcazar, Mercy Padilla (202) 360–4112.

HONG KONG PHOENIX SATELLITE TELEVISION—(202) 420–5510; 1100 13th Street, NW., Suite 400, Washington, DC 20005: Zhengshu Liu.

HUNGARIAN NEWS TV—(202) 746–6086; 318 South Fairfax Street, Alexandria, VA 22314: Judit Csonka.

INDEPENDENT TELEVISION NEWS (ITN)—(202) 429–9080; 400 North Capitol Street, NW., #899, Washington, DC 20008: Ian Glover-James, Michael Herrod.

IRISH RADIO & TV (RTE)—(202) 467–5933; 1750 16th Street, NW., #53, Washington, DC 20009: Robert Shortt, Lesley Steinhauser.

KOREAN BROADCASTING SYSTEMS—(202) 662–7345: Jei Choon Yun.

LILLY BROADCASTING—(202) 669–6280; 1220 Peach Street, Erie, PA 16501: Jacqueline Policastro.

LINK TV—(202) 255–5594: Miles Benson.

LIVING ON EARTH—(202) 554–0644: Jeff Young.

MARKETPLACE RADIO—(202) 789–5948; 1333 M Street, NW., West Tower, #600, Washington, DC 20005: John Dimsdale.

MARKETWATCH—(202) 824–0566; 529 14th Street, NW., #1240, Washington, DC 20045: Rex Nutting, John Wordock (202) 824–0574.

MBC–TV KOREA (MUNHWA)—(202) 347–0078; 529 14th Street, NW., #1131, Washington, DC 20045: Annabel Kim, Jaihong Kwon.

MEDILL NEWS SERVICE—(202) 661–0104; 1325 G Street, NW., #730, Washington, DC 20005: Mary Coffman, Sharon Kornely (202) 661–0106.

METRO NETWORKS—(301) 628–2766; 8403 Colesville Road, #1500, Silver Spring, MD 20910: Terry Moore, Rachel Roberts-Crowson (302) 628–2700.

METRO TELEPRODUCTIONS—(301) 608–9077; 1400 East West Hihgway, Suite 628, Silver Spring MD 20910: Dave Lilling.

MIDDLE EAST TELEVISION NETWORK (ALHURRA)—(202) 852–9338; 7600–D Boston Boulevard, Springfield, VA 22153: Harrison Moore.

MOBILE VIDEO SERVICES, LTD.—(202) 331–8882; 1620 I Street, NW., #1000, Washington, DC 20006: Christine Baber, Lawrence Vander Veen.

MORNINGSIDE PARTNERS, LLC—(202) 365–4801; 4200 Forbes Road, Suite 200, Lanham, MD 20706: Dawn Dineen.

N24 GERMAN TV—(202) 331–9400: Stephan Strothe.

NATIONAL PUBLIC RADIO—(202) 513–2000; 635 Massachussetts Avenue, NW., Washington, DC 20001: William Craven.

NATIONAL SCENE NEWS—(202) 298–9519; 1718 M Street, NW., #333, Washington, DC 20036: Askia Muhammad.

NBC NEWS—(202) 885–4200; 4001 Nebraska Avenue, NW., Washington, DC 20016: Sharon Spurrier.

NBC NEWSCHANNEL—(202) 783–2615; 400 North Capitol Street, Suite 850, Washington, DC 20001: Jay Hurt.

NEED TO KNOW NEWS—(202) 506–1705; 440 South LaSalle Street, #1208, Chicago, IL 60605: Noel Nedli, Mary Beth Slack (202) 393–1225.

NEW TANG DYNASTY TV—(301) 515–5422; 229 W 28th Street, Suite 1200, New York, NY 10001: Dong Xiang.

NHK–JAPAN BROADCASTING CORPORATION—(202) 828–5180; 2030 M Street, NW., Suite 706, Washington, DC 20036: Yoshio Nishikawa.

NIGHTLY BUSINESS REPORT—(202) 682–9029; 1325 G Street, NW., #1005, Washington, DC 20005: Darren Gersh.

NIPPON TV NETWORK—(202) 638–0890; 529 14th Street, NW., #1036, Washington, DC 20045: Keiichi Sato.

NORWEGIAN BROADCASTING—(202) 785–1460; 2000 M Street, NW., #890, Washington, DC 20036: Grethe Winther.

NOS DUTCH PUBLIC RADIO & TV (VRT)—(202) 466–8793; 2000 M Street, NW., #365, Washington, DC 20036: Sander Warmerdam.

N–TV GERMAN NEWS CHANNEL—(202) 420–5530; 1100 13th Street, NW., Suite 400, Washington, DC 20005: Christian Wilp.

NETWORKS, STATIONS, AND SERVICES REPRESENTED—Continued

NTV–RUSSIA BROADCASTING COMPANY—(202) 420–5540; 1100 13th Street, NW., Suite 400, Washington, DC 20005: Anton Volskiy.

PACIFICA RADIO—(202) 588–0999; 2390 Champlain Street, NW., Washington, DC 20009: Verna Avery-Brown.

POTOMAC RADIO NEWS—(202) 244–2781; P.O. Box 32244, Washington, DC 20007: Michael Duncan.

PRO PLUS—(202) 297–0562; 3700 Massachusetts Avenue, NW., #428, Washington, DC 20016: Natasa Briski.

RADIO FRANCE INTERNATIONALE—(202) 249–2997; 3700 Massachusetts Avenue, NW., #538, Washington, DC 20016: Donaig Le Du, Anne Toulouse (202) 714–9816.

RADIO FREE ASIA—(202) 721–7443; 2025 M Street, NW., Suite 300, Washington, DC 20036: Richard Finney.

RADIO FREE EUROPE—(202) 457–6950; 1201 Connecticut Avenue, NW., Washington, DC 20036: Andrew Tully.

RADIO MARTI—(305) 437–7178; 4201 NW 77th Avenue, Miami, FL 33166: Clara Dominguez.

RADIO ONE—(301) 429–2673; 5900 Princess Garden Pkwy 7th Floor, Lanham, MD 20706: Ronald Thompson.

RADIO VALERA VENEZUELA—(202) 528–6540; 529 14th Street, NW., 8th Floor, Washington, DC 20045: Sonia Schott.

RELIGION & ETHICS NEWSWEEKLY—(202) 216–4400; 1333 H Street, NW., 6th Floor, Washington, DC 20005: Arnold Labaton, Judy Reynolds (202) 216–2388.

REUTERS RADIO & TV—(202) 310–6475; 1333 H Street, NW., 6th Floor, Washington, DC 20005: George Tamerlani.

RTV SLOVENIJA—(202) 364–2624: Vlasta Jesenicnik.

RTVI / ECHO–TV—(202) 742–6576; 1001 Pennsylvania Avenue, NW., Suite 6310, Washington, DC 20004: Vladimir Kara-Murza.

RUSSIA TODAY TELEVISION—(202) 775–2305; 1825 K Street, NW., Suite 710, Washington, DC 20006: Mindia Gavasheli.

RUSSIAN STATE TV AND RADIO (RTR)—(202) 460–6830; 2000 N Street, NW., Suite 810, Washington, DC 20007: Solodovnikov Mikhail.

RUSTAVI 2 BROADCASTING COMPANY—(202) 957–4496; 6301 Steveson Avenue, #414, Alexandria, VA 22304: David Nikuradze.

SAGARMATHA TELEVISION—(703) 646–5110; 9655 Hawkshead Drive, Lorton, VA 22079: Ram Kharel.

SEOUL BROADCASTING SYSTEM (SBS)—(202) 637–9850; 529 14th Street, NW., #979, Washington, DC 20045: Kyung Youl Shin.

SINCLAIR BROADCAST GROUP—(202) 293–1092; 10706 Beaver Dam Road, Cockeysville, MD 21030: Paul Spinelli.

SKY NEWS—(202) 824–6583; 400 North Capitol Street, NW., #550, Washington, DC 20001: Sally Arthy, Andoun Wilson (202) 824–6580.

SPANISH PUBLIC TELEVISION (TVE)—(202) 785–1813; 2000 M Street, NW., #325, Washington, DC 20036: Anna Ubeda.

SPIEGEL GERMAN TV—(202) 347–1735; 1202 National Press Building, Washington, DC 20045: Karin Assman.

SRN NEWS (SALEM)—(703) 528–6213; 1901 North Moore Street, #201, Arlington, VA 22209: Ken Lormand.

STATELINE.ORG—(202) 419–4464; 1615 L Street, NW., Washington, DC 20016: Barbara Rosewicz, Joshua Brockman (202) 419–4497, Gene Gibbons.

SWEDISH BROADCASTING—(202) 785–1460; 2000 M Street, NW., Suite 890, Washington, DC 20036: Grethe Winther.

SWISS BROADCASTING—(202) 429–9668; 2000 M Street, NW., Suite 370, Washington, DC 20036: Sylvie Deroche.

TALK RADIO NEWS SERVICE—(202) 510–6340; 236 Massachusetts Avenue, NE., Suite 306, Washington, DC 20002: Lovisa Frost, Ellen Ratner (202) 337–5322, Jay Tamboli (202) 510–6337.

TELEMUNDO NETWORK—(202) 737–7830; 400 North Capitol Street, NW., Suite 850, Washington, DC 20001: Guillermo Martinez, Lori Montenegro.

TELESUR—(202) 739–1750; 1825 K Street, NW., Suite 710, Washington, DC 20006: Roselena Ramirez.

TELEVISA NEWS NETWORK (ECO)—(202) 347–0407; 1825 K Street, NW., Suite 710–G, Washington, DC 20006: Gregorio Meraz.

TF1–FRENCH TV—(202) 223–3642; 2000 M Street, NW., Suite 870, Washington, DC 20036: Julie Asher, Gilles Bouleau.

THE BERNS BUREAU, INC.—(202) 314–5165: Matt Kaye.

THE ECONOMIST—(202) 429–0896; 1730 Rhode Island Avenue, NW., Suite 1210, Washington, DC 20036: Brendan Greeley.

THE HILL—(202) 628–8510; 1625 K Street, NE., Suite 900, Washington, DC 20006: Sheila Casey.

THE NEW YORK TIMES ON THE WEB—(202) 862–0361; 1627 I Street, NW., #1700, Washington, DC 20006: Benjamin Werschkul,

NETWORKS, STATIONS, AND SERVICES REPRESENTED—Continued

THE NEWSHOUR WITH JIM LEHRER—(703) 998–2157; 3620 South 27th Street, Arlington, VA 22206: Monique Hayes, Judy Willis (703) 998–2137.

THE WASHINGTON BUREAU—(202) 347–6396; 400 North Capitol Street, NW., #775, Washington, DC 20001: Richard Tillery.

THIS WEEK IN AGRIBUSINESS (RFD–TV)—(301) 942–1996; 9915 Hillridge Drive, Kensington, MD 20895: Orion Samuelson.

THOMSON REUTERS—(202) 772–0962; 1100 13th Street, NW., Suite 200, Washington, DC 20005: Corbett Daly.

TO THE CONTRARY (PERSEPHONE PRODUCTIONS)—(202) 973–2066; 1819 L Street, NW., 7th Floor, Washington, DC 20036: Joy Fowlin.

TOKYO BROADCASTING SYSTEM—(202) 393–3800; 1088 National Press Building, Washington, DC 20045: Katsumi Hino, Michael Lavallee.

TRIBUNE BROADCASTING—(202) 468–2757; 1025 F Street, NW., #700, Washington, DC 20004: Dina White.

TV ASAHI—(202) 347–2933; 529 14th Street, NW., #1280, Washington, DC 20045: Tadayoshi II, Ena Suto.

TV GLOBO INTERNATIONAL—(202) 429–2525; 2141 Wisconsin Avenue, NW., Suite L, Washington, DC 20007: Loius Fernando Silva.

TV TOKYO—(202) 638–0441; 1333 H Street, NW., 5th Floor, Washington, DC 20005: Motoyasu Asaoka.

TV2–DENMARK—(202) 828–4555; 2000 M Street, NW., Suite 375, Washington, DC 20036: Charlotte Ernst.

TV3–TELEVISIO DE CATALUNYA—(202) 785–0580; 2000 M Street, NW., Suite 830, Washington, DC 20036: Albert Elfa.

TVBS—(202) 812–2821: Jessica Ni.

TVN POLAND—(202) 215–5052; 7429 Chummley Court, Falls Church, VA 22043: Marcin Wrona.

UNITED NEWS AND INFORMATION—(202) 783–2002; 529 14th Street, NW., Suite 1057D, Washington, DC 20045: Sharon Gotkin.

UNIVISION—(202) 682–6160; 101 Constitution Avenue, NW., Suite 810E, Washington, DC 20001: Deborah Durham. UPI.com—(202) 441–0630; 1133 19th Street, NW., Suite 800, Washington, DC 20036: Kristin Volk Harper.

USI NEWS—(202) 494–1809; 10500 Rockville Pike, #1520, Rockville, MD 20852: Mahtab Farid.

VENEZUELA TV—(202) 642–1242: Marco Granda.

VENTANA PRODUCTIONS—(202) 785–5112; 1825 K Street, NW., #501, Washington, DC 20006: Armando Almanza, Grace I-Tang.

VIEWPOINT COMMUNICATIONS—(301) 565–1650; 8607 2nd Avenue, Suite 400, Silver Spring, MD 20910: Larry Greenblatt.

VOICE OF AMERICA—(202) 382–5130; 330 Independence Avenue, SW., Washington, DC 20237: Darrell Allen, Joan Butler (202) 203–4025, Michelle Mitchel (202) 382–5422.

VOYAGE PRODUCTIONS—(202) 296–2389; 565 Pennsylvania Avenue, NW., #302, Washington, DC 20001: Susan Baumel.

W RADIO—(202) 494–4092; 4301 Massachussetts Avenue, NW., #A114, Washington, DC 20016: Maria Luisa Rossel.

WASHINGTON BUREAU NEWS SERVICE—(202) 255–8685; 7425 Savan Point Way, Columbia, MD 21045: Michael Whitney.

WASHINGTON RADIO AND PRESS SERVICE—(301) 580–9134; 6702 Pawtucket Road, Bethesda, MD 20817: Hanna Gutmann.

WASHINGTONPOST.COM—(703) 469–2638: Tom Kennedy, Charles Rhodes (703) 469–2597.

WETA—(703) 998–2660; 2775 South Quincy Street, Arlington, VA 22206: Megan Adair, Christopher Lane.

WFDC–TV UNIVISION—(202) 522–8643; 101 Constitution Avenue, NW., Suite L–100, Washington, DC 20001: Ernesto Clavijo, Maria Rosa Lucchini (301) 385–6301, Norma Montenegro (202) 522–8640.

WHITE HOUSE CHRONICLE—(202) 662–9745; 1042 Wisconsin Avenue, NW., Washington, DC 20007: Linda Gasparello.

WHUR—(202) 253–4331; 529 Bryant Street, NW., Washington, DC 20059: Renee Nash.

WJLA–TV / NEWSCHANNEL 8—(703) 236–9421; 1100 Wilson Boulevard, Arlington, VA 22209: Ming Leong, Bill Lord (703) 236–9480.

WPFW–FM—(202) 588–0999; 2390 Champlain Street, NW., Washington, DC 20009: Gloria Minott, Robert West.

WPWC–AM (RADIO FIESTA)—(703) 494–0100: Carlos Aragon.

WRC–TV/NBC–4—(202) 885–4111; 4001 Nebraska Avenue, NW., #6, Washington, DC 20016: Vickie Burns, Ede Jermin (202) 885–4270.

WTOP RADIO—(202) 895–5060; 3400 Idaho Avenue, NW., Washington, DC 20016: Mike McMearty, Mitchell Miller (202) 895–5272.

WTTG–FOX TELEVISION—(202) 895–3130; 5151 Wisconsin Avenue, NW., Washington, DC 20016: Rich Murphy.

NETWORKS, STATIONS, AND SERVICES REPRESENTED—Continued

WUSA–TV—(202) 895–5551; 4100 Wisconsin Avenue, NW., Washington, DC 20016: Samara Martin Ewing.

WZDC–TV—(703) 820–8333: Julio Aliaga, Jamillah Echeverria.

XM SATELLITE RADIO—(202) 412–9430: Joe Mathews.

PERIODICAL PRESS GALLERIES*

HOUSE PERIODICAL PRESS GALLERY

The Capitol, H–304, 225–2941

Director.—Robert M. Zatkowski.
Assistant Directors: Gerald Rupert, Jr., Robert L. Stallings.

SENATE PERIODICAL PRESS GALLERY

The Capitol, S–320, 224–0265

Director.—Edward V. Pesce.
Assistant Directors: Justin Wilson, Shawna Blair.

EXECUTIVE COMMITTEE OF CORRESPONDENTS

Richard E. Cohen, National Journal
Jay Newton-Small, Time Magazine
Lauren Whittington, Roll Call
Heather Rothman, BNA News
Meg Shreve, Tax Notes
Steve LeVine, Business Week
Paul Bedard, U.S. News & World Report

RULES GOVERNING PERIODICAL PRESS GALLERIES

1. Persons eligible for admission to the Periodical Press Galleries must be bona fide resident correspondents of reputable standing, giving their chief attention to the gathering and reporting of news. They shall state in writing the names of their employers and their additional sources of earned income; and they shall declare that, while a member of the Galleries, they will not act as an agent in the prosecution of claims, and will not become engaged or assist, directly or indirectly, in any lobbying, promotion, advertising, or publicity activity intended to influence legislation or any other action of the Congress, nor any matter before any independent agency, or any department or other instrumentality of the Executive Branch; and that they will not act as an agent for, or be employed by the Federal, or any State, local or foreign government or representatives thereof; and that they will not, directly or indirectly, furnish special or "insider" information intended to influence prices or for the purpose of trading on any commodity or stock exchange; and that they will not become employed, directly or indirectly, by any stock exchange, board of trade or other organization or member thereof, or brokerage house or broker engaged in the buying and selling of any security or commodity. Applications shall be submitted to the Executive Committee of the Periodical Correspondents' Association and shall be authenticated in a manner satisfactory to the Executive Committee.

2. Applicants must be employed by periodicals that regularly publish a substantial volume of news material of either general, economic, industrial, technical, cultural, or trade character. The periodical must require such Washington coverage on a continuing basis and must be owned and operated independently of any government, industry, institution, association, or lobbying organization. Applicants must also be employed by a periodical that is published for profit and is supported chiefly by advertising or by subscription, or by a periodical meeting the conditions in this paragraph but published by a nonprofit organization that, first, operates independently of any government, industry, or institution and, second, does not engage, directly or indirectly, in any lobbying or other activity intended to influence any matter before Congress or before any independent agency or any department or other instrumentality of the Executive Branch. House organs are not eligible.

*Information is based on data furnished and edited by each respective gallery.

3. Members of the families of correspondents are not entitled to the privileges of the galleries.

4. The Executive Committee may issue temporary credentials permitting the privileges of the galleries to individuals who meet the rules of eligibility but who may be on short-term assignment or temporarily residing in Washington.

5. Under the authority of Rule 6 of the House of Representatives and of Rule 33 of the Senate, the Periodical Galleries shall be under the control of the Executive Committee, subject to the approval and supervision of the Speaker of the House of Representatives and the Senate Committee on Rules and Administration. It shall be the duty of the Executive Committee, at its discretion, to report violations of the privileges of the galleries to the Speaker or the Senate Committee on Rules and Administration, and pending action thereon, the offending correspondent may be suspended. The committee shall be elected at the start of each Congress by members of the Periodical Correspondents' Association and shall consist of seven members with no more than one member from any one publishing organization. The committee shall elect its own officers and a majority of the committee may fill vacancies on the committee. The list in the Congressional Directory shall be a list only of members of the Periodical Correspondents' Association.

NANCY PELOSI,
Speaker, House of Representatives.

CHARLES E. SCHUMER,
Chair, Senate Committee on Rules and Administration.

MEMBERS ENTITLED TO ADMISSION

PERIODICAL PRESS GALLERIES

Aarons, Dakarai I.: Education Week
Abramson, Julie L.: National Journal Group, National Journal
Abse, Nathan: Federal Employees News Digest
Ackley, Kate: Roll Call Group, Roll Call
Adler, Ben M.: Politico
Ainsley, Laura: CD Publications
Alarkon, Walter P.: The Hill
Albergo, Paul F.: BNA News
Alexis, Alexei: BNA News
Allen, Michael P.: Politico
Allen, Jared L.: The Hill
Amber, Michelle: BNA News
Ambinder, Marc J.: National Journal Group, Atlantic Monthly
Ambrosio, Patrick: BNA News
Anderson, Sarah E.: Exchange Monitor Publications
Anselmo, Joseph: McGraw-Hill Co., Aviation Week
Antonides, David Scott: Tax Notes
Aplin, Donald G.: BNA News
Apokis, Dimitrios: Investor's World
Aquino, John T.: BNA News
Arnoult, Sandra: Penton Media Inc.
Ashburn, Elyse: Chronicle of Higher Education
Ashton, Jerome C.: BNA News
Ashworth, Jerry: Thompson Publishing Group
Asker, James R.: McGraw-Hill Co., Aviation Week
Assam, Cecelia M.: BNA News
Atkins, Pamela S.: BNA News
Atlas, Stephen Terry: U.S. News & World Report
Atwood, John Filar: CCH Inc.
August, Melissa A.: Time Inc., Time Magazine
Aulino, Margaret: BNA News
Ault, Alicia: International Medical News Group
Ayers, Cameron S.: Thompson Publishing Group
Ayers, Carl: UCG
Babbin, Jed L.: Human Events
Baer, Susan: Washingtonian
Baghdadi, Ramsey: FDC Reports
Bailey, Holly: Newsweek
Bain, Ben S.: 1105 Government Information Group, Federal Computer Week
Baker, Samuel U.: Inside Washington Publishers
Bancroft, John: Inside Mortgage Finance
Barak, Sarah: Thompson Publishing Group
Barash, Martina S.: BNA News
Barbagallo, Paul J.: Telecommunications Reports
Barbash, Fred: Politico
Barbic, Kari: Weekly Standard
Barnes, Fred W.: Weekly Standard
Barnes, James A.: National Journal Group, National Journal
Barone, Michael D.: U.S. News & World Report
Barr, Sarah M.: BNA News
Barry, John A.: Newsweek
Barry, Theresa: Washington Business Information
Bartholet, Jeffrey I.: Newsweek
Basken, Paul A.: Chronicle of Higher Education
Bass, Geremy C.: Inside Mortgage Finance
Bass, Carla D.: McGraw-Hill Co.
Basu, Sandra L.: U.S. Medicine
Baumann, Jeannie: BNA News
Bazelon, Emily: Slate
Beam, Jacob Christopher: Slate
Beaven, Lara W.: Inside Washington Publishers
Bedard, Paul: U.S. News & World Report
Behr, Peter B.: Environment & Energy Publishing
Beizer, Douglas: 1105 Government Information Group, Washington Technology
Belian, David P.: Washington Business Information
Belton, Beth M.: Kiplinger Washington Editors
Belz, Emily C.: World Magazine
Bendery, Jennifer L.: Roll Call Group, Roll Call
Benjamin, Mark: Salon
Bennett, John T.: Army Times Publishing Co.
Bennett, Alison: BNA News
Benton, Nicholas F.: Falls Church News Press
Ben-Yosef, Andrea L.: BNA News
Berger, Brian: Space News
Berger, Mary: Washington Trade Daily
Berger, James R.: Washington Trade Daily
Berke, Kenneth H.: Federal Publications, Government Contractor
Berlin, Joshua L.: FDC Reports
Berman, Dan: Environment & Energy Publishing
Berman-Gorvine, Martin J.: Washington Business Information
Besser, James David: New York Jewish Week
Bhambhani, Dipka: McGraw-Hill Co., Aviation Week
Bialecki, Marissa R.: Thompson Publishing Group
Biggs, Alicia E.: BNA News
Billings, Deborah D.: BNA News
Billings, Erin P.: Roll Call Group, Roll Call
Billitteri, Thomas J.: CQ Researcher
Bivins, Amy E.: BNA News
Blake, Aaron: The Hill
Blank, Peter L.: Kiplinger Washington Editors
Blumenstyk, Goldie: Chronicle of Higher Education
Bodenner, Chris P.: National Journal Group, The Hotline

MEMBERS ENTITLED TO ADMISSION, PERIODICAL PRESS GALLERIES—Continued

Boessenkool, Antonie L.: Army Times Publishing Co.
Bogardus, Kevin J.: The Hill
Bolen, Cheryl: BNA News
Bolton, Alexander: The Hill
Bomster, Mark W.: Education Week
Bondioli, Sara E.: Roll Call Group, Roll Call
Bontrager, Eric: Environment & Energy Publishing
Borchersen-Keto, Sarah A.: CCH Inc.
Bouve, Andrew D.S.: Slate
Boyd, John D.: Journal of Commerce
Boyle, Katherine V.: Environment & Energy Publishing
Boyles, William R.: Health Market Survey
Boyles, Virginia M.: Health Market Survey
Bracken, Leonard: BNA News
Bradley, David M.: Natural Gas Intelligence
Brady, Matthew: National Underwriter
Brady, Jessica L.: Roll Call Group, Roll Call
Brand, Chad X.: Roll Call Group, Gallery Watch
Brandolph, David B.: BNA News
Brannen, Kate O.: Inside Washington Publishers
Braun, Kevin D.: Environment & Energy Publishing
Bravender, Robin L.: Environment & Energy Publishing
Breech, Laura E.: Tax Notes
Bresnahan, John: Politico
Brevetti, Rossella E.: BNA News
Brinton, S. Turner: Space News
Briscoe, Daren: Newsweek
Bristow, Melissa S.: Kiplinger Washington Editors
Britt, Angela L.: BNA News
Brodsky, Robert G.: National Journal Group, Government Executive
Brooks, George A.: Inside Mortgage Finance
Brotherton, Elizabeth: Roll Call Group, Roll Call
Brown, David L.: National Law Journal
Brown, Janet M.: Press Associates
Brown, Simon A.: Tax Notes
Brown, Jill: Atlantic Information Services
Brownstein, Ronald J.: National Journal Group, National Journal
Brownstein, Andrew D.: Thompson Publishing Group
Bruce, R. Christian: BNA News
Bruno, Michael: McGraw-Hill Co., Aviation Week
Bruno, Debra A.: Roll Call Group, Roll Call
Brush, Silla A.: The Hill
Bryant, Sue: BNA News
Buchta, Cheryl: McGraw-Hill Co., Aviation Week
Buckley, Elizabeth: Food Chemical News
Budoff Brown, Carrie D.: Politico
Buhl, John M.: Tax Notes
Bullock, Lorinda M.: International Medical News Group
Buntin, John: Governing
Burkhart, Lori: Public Utilities Fortnightly
Burnham, Michael P.: Environment & Energy Publishing
Burns, Alexander I.: Politico
Busetti, Max S.: Thompson Publishing Group
Butchock, Steve: Medical Devices Report
Butler, Amy: McGraw-Hill Co., Aviation Week
Byerrum, Ellen: BNA News
Bylander, Jessica E.: FDC Reports
Byrne, James S.: CD Publications
Byus, Jonathan: 1105 Government Information Group, Government Computer News
Cahlink, George F.: Roll Call Group, Congress Now
Cain, Derrick: BNA News
Calabresi, Massimo T.: Time Inc., Time Magazine
Calderone, Michael L.: Politico
Caldwell, Christopher: Weekly Standard
Callahan, Madelyn R.: BNA News
Cano, Craig: McGraw-Hill Co.
Carbine, Michael E.: Atlantic Information Services
Cardman, Michael: Thompson Publishing Group
Carey, John A.: McGraw-Hill Co., Business Week
Carlile, Amy V.: Environment & Energy Publishing
Carlson, Jeffrey E.: CCH Inc.
Carlstrom, Gregg L.: Army Times Publishing Co.
Carney, Timothy P.: Evans-Novak Political Report
Carney, Eliza Newlin: National Journal Group, National Journal
Carr, Jennifer: Tax Notes
Carter, Charlene A.: Roll Call Group, Congress Now
Caruso, Lisa: National Journal Group, National Journal
Casey, Winter: National Journal Group, National Journal
Cash, Catherine: McGraw-Hill Co.
Cassidy, William B.: Journal of Commerce
Castelli, Elise: Army Times Publishing Co.
Castelli, Christopher: Inside Washington Publishers
Cavallaro, Gina: Army Times Publishing Co.
Cavanagh, Sean: Education Week
Cavanaugh, Amy L.: Washington Blade
Cavas, Christopher: Army Times Publishing Co.
Cecala, Guy David: Inside Mortgage Finance
Cech, Scott J.: Education Week
Censer, Marjorie J.: Inside Washington Publishers
Chappell, Kevin U.: Jet/Ebony
Chavanne, Bettina H.: McGraw-Hill Co., Aviation Week
Chemnick, Jean M.: McGraw-Hill Co.
Cherry, Sheila: BNA News
Chi, Tina M.: BNA News
Chibbaro, Jr., Louis M.: Washington Blade
Childers, Andrew J.: BNA News
Choma, Russell M.: BNA News
Chronister, Gregory: Education Week
Ciampoli, Paul G.: McGraw-Hill Co.
Cinquegrani, Gayle C.: BNA News
Clapp, Stephen: Food Chemical News
Clark, Charles S.: Tax Notes

MEMBERS ENTITLED TO ADMISSION, PERIODICAL PRESS GALLERIES—Continued

Clark, Timothy: National Journal Group, Government Executive
Clarke, David Paul: Inside Washington Publishers
Clarke, Conor J.: National Journal Group, Atlantic Monthly
Clemmitt, Marcia: CQ Researcher
Clift, Eleanor: Newsweek
Coder, Jeremiah G.: Tax Notes
Coffin, James B.: Public Lands News
Cogan, Marin E.: New Republic
Cohen, Janey: BNA News
Cohen, Richard E.: National Journal Group, National Journal
Cohen, Andrea R.: Roll Call Group, Roll Call
Cohn, Laura S.: Kiplinger Washington Editors
Cole, Torie D.: CCH Inc.
Coller, Andrea L.: Politico
Collins, Brian: National Mortgage News
Collins, Eve: Atlantic Information Services
Comer, John Matthew: Environment & Energy Publishing
Compart, Andrew W.: McGraw-Hill Co., Aviation Week
Conant, Eve K.: Newsweek
Connolly, Katie M.: Newsweek
Conroy, Declan: Setanta Publishing, Food Protection Report
Continetti, Matthew: Weekly Standard
Cook, Steven: BNA News
Cook, Robert C.: BNA News
Cook, Jr., Charles E.: Cook Political Report
Cooper, Stephen K.: CCH Inc.
Cooper, Rebecca A.: Exchange Monitor Publications
Corbett, Warren: Set-Aside Alert
Cordner, Christine T.: McGraw-Hill Co.
Corley, Matilda Monroe: BNA News
Cottle, M. Michelle: New Republic
Coughlin, Brett G.: Inside Washington Publishers
Cowden, Richard H.: BNA News
Cox, Matthew: Army Times Publishing Co.
Cox, Bowman D.: FDC Reports
Coyle, Marcia: National Law Journal
Crabtree, Susan: The Hill
Craft, Kevin R.: National Journal Group National Journal
Craver, Martha L.: Kiplinger Washington Editors
Crawford, Elizabeth R.: FDC Reports
Crider, Richard: Thompson Publishing Group
Crook, Clive: National Journal Group, Nationaljournal.com
Cruickshank, Paula L.: CCH Inc.
Cullen, Richard T.: Politico
Cummings, Jeanne M.: Politico
Curran, John P.: Telecommunications Reports
Currie, Duncan M.: National Review
Cusack, Robert: The Hill
Daigneau, Elizabeth: Governing
D'Aprile, Shane: Politics Magazine
Darby, Seyward L.: New Republic
Darcey, Susan W.: FDC Reports
Davies, Stephen A.: Endangered Species & Wetlands Report
Davis, Michelle R.: Education Week
Davis, Jeffrey J.: Transportation Weekly
Davis, Steve: Atlantic Information Services
Davis, S. Diane: BNA News
Davis, Bronwyn L.: BNA News
Davis, Charles R.: Inside Washington Publishers
Davis, Molly M.: Inside Washington Publishers
Davis, Jill R.: National Journal Group, Government Executive
Day, Jeff: BNA News
DeBonis, Mike: Washington City Paper
Deigh, Gloria: BNA News
Dela Rosa, Darrell D.: CQ Researcher
DeLeon, Carrie R.: Telecommunications Reports
Dembeck, Chet E.: CD Publications
Dennis, Steven T.: Roll Call Group, Roll Call
Deslauriers, Jacqueline C.: Research Institute of America Group
Deutermann, Elizabeth A.: Thompson Publishing Group
Devernoe, Tanya: BNA News
Diamond, Phyllis: BNA News
Dickerson, John F.: Slate
Diegmueller, Karen: Education Week
DiGuglielmo, Joey: Washington Blade
DiMascio, Jennifer: Politico
Dindino, Carrie A.: National Journal Group, The Hotline
Dinnage, Russell: Environment & Energy Publishing
DiSciullo, Joseph: Tax Notes
Ditta, Sara A.: Inside Washington Publishers
Doan, Michael F.: Kiplinger Washington Editors
DoBias, Matthew: Crain Communications
Dobson, Jon: FDC Reports
Doi, Ayako: Japan Digest
Dolley, Steven D.: McGraw-Hill Co.
Dombroski, Cathy H.: FDC Reports
Domone, Dana J.: BNA News
Donlan, Thomas G.: Barron's
Doolan, Kelley: McGraw-Hill Co.
Douillard-Proulx, Rachelle M.: National Journal Group, The Hotline
Doyle, Kenneth P.: BNA News
Doyle, John M.: McGraw-Hill Co., Aviation Week
Draper, Robert L.: GQ Magazine
Drew, Elizabeth: New York Review of Books
Dreyfuss, Robert C.: Rolling Stone
Drucker, David M.: Roll Call Group, Roll Call
Duarte, Nicole A.: Tax Notes
Dube, Lawrence E.: BNA News
Duffy, Jennifer: Cook Political Report
Duffy, Thomas Patrick: Inside Washington Publishers
Duffy, Michael W.: Time Inc., Time Magazine

MEMBERS ENTITLED TO ADMISSION, PERIODICAL PRESS GALLERIES—Continued

Duncan, Alexander M.: McGraw-Hill Co.
Durrett, LaTasha S.: Research Institute of America Group
Dutra, Antonio: BNA News
Eastland, Katherine L.: Weekly Standard
Eastland, Terry: Weekly Standard
Easton, Nina J.: Time Inc., Fortune Magazine
Edmondson, Thomas: BNA News
Edmonson, Robert G.: Journal of Commerce
Edney, Hazel Trice: Afro American Newspapers
Edwards, Dean R.: Falls Church News Press
Edwards, Lynne: U.S. News & World Report
Edwards, Jewel W.: BNA News
Edwards, Thomas J.: CD Publications
Edwards, Charles J.: Thompson Publishing Group
Ege, Konrad: Freitag
Eggerton, John S.: Reed Business Information, Broadcasting & Cable
Eglovitch, Joanne S.: FDC Reports
Eisele, Albert: The Hill
Eisenhower, Karl J.: National Journal Group, Nationaljournal.com
Eisenstein, Michael: BNA News
Eisler, Benjamin R.: New Republic
Eisler, Kim: Washingtonian
Eleveld, Karen Kerry L.: Advocate
Elfin, Dana: BNA News
Elliott, Amy S.: Tax Notes
Ellis, Isobel: National Journal Group, National Journal
Elmore, Wesley: Tax Notes
Emeigh, Jr., Geoffrey: BNA News
Enayat, Maryam: Thompson Publishing Group
Engan, Luke P.: Inside Washington Publishers
Englund, William A.: National Journal Group, National Journal
Ephron, Dan: Newsweek
Epstein, Keith: McGraw-Hill Co., Business Week
Ericksen, Charles A.: Hispanic Link News Service
Esquivel, J. Jesus: Proceso
Evans, Jeffrey: International Medical News Group
Evans, Larry E.: BNA News
Evans, Laura O.: UCG
Ewing, Philip T.: Army Times Publishing Co.
Ezzard, Catherine Sullivan: BNA News
Fabian, Thecla R.: BNA News
Faerstein, Ian D.: National Journal Group, The Hotline
Fain, Paul A.: Chronicle of Higher Education
Fairbanks, Eve R.: New Republic
Falk, Leora M.: BNA News
Falvella-Garraty, Susan M.: Irish Echo
Fanshel, Fran: UCG
Fasman, Jon: Economist
Fath, Meredith: Tax Notes
Feltman, Peter E.: CCH Inc.
Ferguson, Andrew: Weekly Standard
Ferguson, Brett: BNA News
Ferullo, Michael: BNA News
Fialka, John J.: Environment & Energy Publishing
Fickling, Amy: McGraw-Hill Co.
Fiegl, Charles: UCG
Field, Kelly: Chronicle of Higher Education
Findlay, Christie E.: Politics Magazine
Fineman, Howard: Newsweek
Finet, J.P.: BNA News
Fiorino, Frances: McGraw-Hill Co., Aviation Week
Fischer, Karin: Chronicle of Higher Education
Fitzpatrick, Erika: Congressional Digest
Fleet, Leslie G.: BNA News
Flint, Perry A.: Penton Media Inc.
Flynn, Joan Marie: Thompson Publishing Group
Foer, Franklin L.: New Republic
Forbes, Sean I.: BNA News
Fordney, Jason L.: McGraw-Hill Co.
Fotos, Christopher P.: McGraw-Hill Co., Aviation Week
Fourney, Susan: National Journal Group, Government Executive
France, Stephen: BNA News
Francis, Laura: BNA News
Francis, Theo: McGraw-Hill Co., Business Week
Frandsen, Jon C.: Kiplinger Washington Editors
Franklin, Mary Beth: Kiplinger Washington Editors
Frates, Chris: Politico
Freda, Diane: BNA News
Freddoso, David A.: National Review
Freedberg, Jr., Sydney J.: National Journal Group, National Journal
Freedland, Seth M.: Inside Washington Publishers
Frerking, Elizabeth M.: Politico
Frieden, Joyce: International Medical News Group
Friedl, Kevin E.: National Journal Group, Nationaljournal.com
Friedman, Lisa F.: Environment & Energy Publishing
Friel, Brian: National Journal Group, National Journal
Frojo, Renee L.: Washington Business Information
Frumkin, Kimberly B.: Kiplinger Washington Editors
Fulghum, David: McGraw-Hill Co., Aviation Week
Galentine, Elizabeth R.: Employee Benefit Advisor
Gallagher, John: Journal of Commerce
Gannon, John: BNA News
Gantz, Rachel: UCG
Garber, Kent D.: U.S. News & World Report
Gardner, Rebecca: International Medical News Group
Gardner, Lauren M.: BNA News
Garland, Susan B.: Kiplinger Washington Editors
Garner, W. Lynn: BNA News
Gartrell, Peter T.: McGraw-Hill Co.
Gavant, Kelli L.: Thompson Publishing Group
Gay, Patrice L.: Tax Notes
Gdowski, Jessica C.: UCG

MEMBERS ENTITLED TO ADMISSION, PERIODICAL PRESS GALLERIES—Continued

Geisel, Jerome M.: Crain Communications
Geman, Ben: Environment & Energy Publishing
Gerecht, Michael: CD Publications
Gerstein, Joshua A.: Politico
Gerth, Linda: New Republic
Getter, Lisa: UCG
Gettinger, Steve: National Journal Group, National Journal
Gettlin, Robert H.: National Journal Group, National Journal
Gewertz, Catherine: Education Week
Ghosh, Aparisim: Time Inc., Time Magazine
Giaccino, Linda A.: CD Publications
Gilbert, Lorraine S.: BNA News
Gilbert, Mary M.: National Journal Group, Nationaljournal.com
Gilcrest, Laura H.: McGraw-Hill Co.
Gilston, Samuel M.: Gilston-Kalin Communications
Gizzi, John: Human Events
Glass, Andrew J.: Politico
Glenn, David G.: Chronicle of Higher Education
Gloger, Katja: Stern
Gnaedinger, Charles: Tax Notes
Goehausen, Hilary A.: CCH Inc.
Goindi, Geeta: Express India
Goldberg, Jeffrey: New Yorker
Goldberg, Paul: The Cancer Letter
Goldberg, Kirsten: The Cancer Letter
Goldfarb, Samuel D.: Tax Notes
Goldman, Ted: Roll Call Group, Roll Call
Goldwasser, Joan: Kiplinger Washington Editors
Goldwyn, Brant: CCH Inc.
Golub, Barbra: Atlantic Information Services
Gonzales, Nathan: Rothenberg Political Report
Good, Christopher E.: National Journal Group, Atlantic Monthly
Goodin, Emily L.: The Hill
Goodin, Emily: National Journal Group, The Hotline
Goodman, Joshua: Governing
Goodman, Sara E.: Environment & Energy Publishing
Goodwine, Velma: Research Institute of America Group
Gordon, Meryl: Elle
Gordon, Rebekah S.: Inside Washington Publishers
Gordy, Cynthia D.: Time Inc., Essence Magazine
Gotsch, Ted: Telecommunications Reports
Gottlieb, Matthew P.: National Journal Group, The Hotline
Gough, Robert: UCG
Gould, Joseph M.: Inside Washington Publishers
Goulder, Robert: Tax Notes
Goyal, Raghubir: Asia Today
Graff, Garrett: Washingtonian
Green, Joshua: National Journal Group, Atlantic Monthly
Green, Charles A.: National Journal Group, National Journal
Greenblatt, Alan: Governing
Greenhalgh, Keiron: McGraw-Hill Co.
Gregg, Diana I.: BNA News
Gregorits, Angela: BNA News
Grena Manley, Mary Ann: BNA News
Grimaldi, Christine H.: BNA News
Grindley, Lucas M.: National Journal Group, Nationaljournal.com
Gross, Grant J.: IDG News Service
Grover, Elizabeth A.: BNA News
Gruber, Peter: Focus
Gruber, Amelia M.: National Journal Group, Government Executive
Gruenberg, Mark J.: Press Associates
Guarino, Douglas: Inside Washington Publishers
Guay, Thomas A.: Progressive Business Publications
Guest, Robert: Economist
Guido, Daniel W.: McGraw-Hill Co.
Gurdon, Hugo: The Hill
Gutman, James H.: Atlantic Information Services
Gvozdas, Susan E.: Army Times Publishing Co.
Haas, Joseph A.: FDC Reports
Haddad, Tammy M.: Newsweek
Hadley, Richard D.: UCG
Hagstrom, Jerry: National Journal Group, National Journal
Hair, Connie L.: Human Events
Hall, Holly: Chronicle of Higher Education
Halonen, Douglas J.: Crain Communications
Ham, Mary Katherine: Weekly Standard
Hamme, Nathan S.: Falls Church News Press
Hammon, Jamie R.: FDC Reports
Hand, Eric K.: Nature
Haniffa, Aziz: India Abroad
Hanner, Kenneth W.: Human Events
Hansard, Sara: Crain Communications
Hansen, Brian: McGraw-Hill Co.
Hanson, Melinda: BNA News
Hanson, Clayton A.: Roll Call Group, Gallery Watch
Harbrecht, Douglas A.: Kiplinger Washington Editors
Harder, Amy A.: National Journal Group, Nationaljournal.com
Harman, Thomas: CD Publications
Harrington, William J.: Inside Washington Publishers
Harris, Joann Christine: Tax Notes
Harris, Shane: National Journal Group, National Journal
Harrison, David: BNA News
Harrison, Tom: McGraw-Hill Co.
Hart, James T.: Thompson Publishing Group
Haseley, Donna L.: Inside Washington Publishers
Hausmann, Helen D.: McGraw-Hill Co.
Hayes, Christopher L.: Nation
Hayes, Stephen F.: Weekly Standard
Hayes, Peter S.: BNA News

MEMBERS ENTITLED TO ADMISSION, PERIODICAL PRESS GALLERIES—Continued

Healy, Amber M.: Food Chemical News
Hebel, Sara: Chronicle of Higher Education
Heckathorn, Mark E.: Thompson Publishing Group
Heflin, Jay S.: Roll Call Group, Congress Now
Hegland, Corine: National Journal Group, National Journal
Hegstad, Maria A.: Inside Washington Publishers
Heil, Emily A.: Roll Call Group, Roll Call
Hellman, Gregory S.: BNA News
Hellman, Gregory S.: Inside Washington Publishers
Helminski, Edward L.: Exchange Monitor Publications
Heltman, John H.: Inside Washington Publishers
Hemingway, Mark W.: National Review
Hench, Stephanie M.: Tax Notes
Henderson, Nia-Malika A.: Politico
Hendrie, Caroline: Education Week
Hennig, Jutta: Inside Washington Publishers
Henry, Patricia M.: BNA News
Herbert, David G.: National Journal Group, Nationaljournal.com
Hernandez, Luis: Thompson Publishing Group
Hess, Ryan E.: MII Publications
Heydt, Marci K.: UCG
Hicks, Travis: Thompson Publishing Group
Hill, Keith M.: BNA News
Hill, Richard: BNA News
Hillman, G. Robert: Politico
Hirsh, Michael P.: Newsweek
Hiruo, Elaine: McGraw-Hill Co.
Ho, Soyoung: Research Institute of America Group
Hobbs, Susan R.: BNA News
Hobbs, M. Nielsen: FDC Reports
Hoff, David: Education Week
Hoffman, Michael R.: Army Times Publishing Co.
Hoffman, Rebecca E.: BNA News
Hoffman, William S.: Thompson Publishing Group
Hoffman, Donald B.: Thompson Publishing Group
Hofmann, Mark A.: Crain Communications
Hogan, Monica J.: FDC Reports
Holland, William: McGraw-Hill Co.
Hollis, Christopher E.: Washington Business Information
Holmes, Gwendolyn C.: BNA News
Holmes, Allan T.: National Journal Group, Government Executive
Hooper, Molly K.: The Hill
Hoover, Eric: Chronicle of Higher Education
Hoover, Kent: Washington Business Journal
Horowitz, Jay: BNA News
Horwood, Rachel Jane: Economist
Hosenball, Mark J.: Newsweek
Houghton, Mary J.: FDC Reports
Howell, Katie J.: Environment & Energy Publishing
Huang, Grant G.: UCG
Huffman, Jason A.: Food Chemical News
Humes, James E.: National Journal Group, National Journal
Humphrey, Shonda: Tax Notes
Hunter, Pamela E.: McGraw-Hill Co.
Hyland, Terence: BNA News
Hylton, William S.: GQ Magazine
Hynes, Casey E.: Roll Call Group, Roll Call
Iannotta, Rebecca D.: Space News
Iannotta, Ben J.: Army Times Publishing Co.
Ichniowski, Thomas F.: McGraw-Hill Co.
Idaszak, Jerome: Kiplinger Washington Editors
Iekel, John F.: Thompson Publishing Group
Ingram, David H.: National Law Journal
Ip, Gregory W.: Economist
Isenstadt, Alex: Politico
Isikoff, Michael: Newsweek
Jackman, Francis L.: McGraw-Hill Co., Aviation Week
Jackson, Valarie N.: McGraw-Hill Co.
Jackson, Jr., David Randall: Tax Notes
Jacobs, Jeremy P.: The Hill
Jacobson, Todd K.: Exchange Monitor Publications
Jacobson, Louis A.: National Journal Group, National Journal
Jaffe, Harry S.: Washingtonian
James, Betty: Federal Publications, Government Contractor
Jaworski, Thomas: Tax Notes
Jeffrey, Jeff T.: National Law Journal
Jenkins, Linda: Human Events
Jenks, Paul H.: Roll Call Group, Gallery Watch
Joe, Michael H.: Tax Notes
Johansen, Alison: BNA News
Johnson, Bridget C.: The Hill
Johnson, Chris C.: Washington Blade
Johnson, Alisa: BNA News
Johnson, Lyrica: Federal Publications, Government Contractor
Johnson, Jenny L.: Inside Washington Publishers
Johnson, Regina: McGraw-Hill Co.
Johnson, Wendy: UCG
Jones, Joyce: Black Enterprise
Jones, Danielle D.: Politico
Jones, Henry B.: Tax Notes
Jones, Elizabeth: Washington Business Information
Jones, George G.: CCH Inc.
Jonson, Nick: McGraw-Hill Co.
Joseph, Cameron E.: National Journal Group, National Journal
Joslyn, Heather: Chronicle of Higher Education
Jost, Kenneth W.: CQ Researcher
Jowers, Karen Grigg: Army Times Publishing Co.
Joyce, Stephen: BNA News
Judis, John B.: New Republic
Juliano, Nicholas P.: Inside Washington Publishers
Kady II, Martin J.: Politico
Kahn, Debra: Environment & Energy Publishing
Kamens, Jessie K.: BNA News
Kaplan, Karen H.: Nature
Kaplan, Hugh B.: BNA News

MEMBERS ENTITLED TO ADMISSION, PERIODICAL PRESS GALLERIES—Continued

Kaplun, Alex: Environment & Energy Publishing
Karem, Brian: Montgomery County Sentinel
Karp, Aaron E.: Penton Media Inc.
Karrs, Emily J.: National Review
Kash, Wyatt: 1105 Government Information Group, Government Computer News
Katel, Peter: CQ Researcher
Katkin, Brian A.: National Law Journal
Kauffman, Tim: Army Times Publishing Co.
Kaufman, Bruce S.: BNA News
Kaufmann, Gregory R.: Nation
Kavanagh, Susan: CCH Inc.
Kavruck, Deborah A.: Washington Counseletter
Kelderman, Eric: Chronicle of Higher Education
Keller, Gail S.: BNA News
Kelly, Patrice Wingert: Newsweek
Kelly, Catherine A.: FDC Reports
Kelly, Spencer: UCG
Kennedy, Kelly: Army Times Publishing Co.
Kennedy, Laura W.: Kiplinger Washington Editors
Kennedy, Hugh: UCG
Kersten, Denise M.: Washingtonian
Kessler, Ronald B.: Newsmax
Khan, Altaf U.: BNA News
Khan, Alyah: Inside Washington Publishers
Khimm, Suzy: New Republic
King, Maureen: Telecommunications Reports
Kingsbury, Alex: U.S. News & World Report
Kingsley, Kim: Politico
Kinney, Jeff: BNA News
Kirby, Paul S.: Telecommunications Reports
Kirchick, James R.: New Republic
Kirkland, John R.: BNA News
Kirkland, Joel: McGraw-Hill Co.
Kitfield, James: National Journal Group, National Journal
Kitto, Kristofer E.: The Hill
Kizer, Jean E.: Thompson Publishing Group
Klamper, Amy E.: Space News
Kleba, Heather L.: Governing
Klein, Alyson: Education Week
Klesta, Michael: Roll Call Group, Roll Call
Klimko, Frank: CD Publications
Klingst, Martin E.: Die Zeit
Koch, Kathy: CQ Researcher
Koffler, Keith F.: Roll Call Group, Roll Call
Kondracke, Morton M.: Roll Call Group, Roll Call
Koons, Jennifer J.: Environment & Energy Publishing
Kosova, Weston: Newsweek
Koss, Geof M.: Roll Call Group, Congress Now
Kosterlitz, Julie A.: National Journal Group, National Journal
Koszczuk, Jaculine M.: National Journal Group, National Journal
Kovski, Alan D.: BNA News
Kraft, Scott: UCG
Kramer, Linda: Glamour Magazine
Kraushaar, Josh P.: Politico
Krieger, Zvika: New Republic
Kriz Hobson, Margaret E.: National Journal Group, National Journal
Kroh, Eric L.: Tax Notes
Kubetin, Sally: International Medical News Group
Kubetin, W. Randy: BNA News
Kucinich, Jacqueline F.: Roll Call Group, Roll Call
Kuckro, Rod: McGraw-Hill Co.
Kumar Sen, Ashish: Outlook Magazine
Kurtz, Josh: Roll Call Group, Roll Call
Kuypers-Denlinger, Corinne: UCG
LaBrecque, Louis C.: BNA News
Lacey, Anthony: Inside Washington Publishers
Laffler, Mary Jo: FDC Reports
LaGrone, Samuel R.: Army Times Publishing Co.
Lamb, Kelsey R.: Roll Call Group, Gallery Watch
Lambert, Kevin C.: BNA News
Lamoreaux, Denise: Thompson Publishing Group
Lamothe, Daniel G.: Army Times Publishing Co.
Langel, Stephen J.: Roll Call Group, Congress Now
Lankford, Kimberly: Kiplinger Washington Editors
Larsen, Kathy Carolin: McGraw-Hill Co.
Last, Jonathan V.: Weekly Standard
Leaman, Emily B.: Washingtonian
Learner, Neal R.: Atlantic Information Services
Leatherman, Jacquelyn D.: CCH Inc.
Leber, Jessica E.: Environment & Energy Publishing
Lee, Carol E.: Politico
Lee, Steve K.: BNA News
Leeuwenburgh, Todd H.: Thompson Publishing Group
Lehmann, Evan W.: Environment & Energy Publishing
Lehr, Katherine V.: National Journal Group, The Hotline
Leopold, George H.: CMP Media Inc.
Lepage, Michael G.: Roll Call Group, Gallery Watch
Lerer, Lisa R.: Politico
Lesniewski, Niels P.: Roll Call Group, Gallery Watch
Levin, Joshua: Slate
LeVine, Steven: McGraw-Hill Co., Business Week
Li, Zengxin: Caijing Magazine
Liang, John: Inside Washington Publishers
Libit, Daniel J.: Politico
Limpert, John: Washingtonian
Lindeman, Ralph: BNA News
Lindsay, Drew: Washingtonian
Ling, Katherine C.: Environment & Energy Publishing
Linnane, Jacqueline: Roll Call Group, Gallery Watch
Lipka, Sara: Chronicle of Higher Education
Lipowicz, Alice: 1105 Government Information Group, Washington Technology
Lithwick, Dahlia Hannah: Slate

MEMBERS ENTITLED TO ADMISSION, PERIODICAL PRESS GALLERIES—Continued

Littleton, Julia A.: Environment & Energy Publishing
Lizza, Ryan C.: New Yorker
Loewenberg, Samuel R.: Politico
Long, Karen S.: UCG
Lorenzo, Aaron E.: BNA News
Losey, Stephen: Army Times Publishing Co.
Lotven, Amy L.: Inside Washington Publishers
Loveless, William E.: McGraw-Hill Co.
Lovell, Aaron J.: Inside Washington Publishers
Lovley, Erika M.: Politico
Lowe, Paul D.: Aviation International News
Lowther, William: Mail on Sunday
Lubell, Jennifer: Crain Communications
Luccioli, Colleen M.: Environment & Energy Publishing
Lucey, Eric J.: Thompson Publishing Group
Lunney, Kellie: National Journal Group, Government Executive
Luntz, Taryn: Environment & Energy Publishing
Lustig, Joe: Thompson Publishing Group
Lynsen, Joshua J.: Washington Blade
Maas, Angela K.: Atlantic Information Services
Macabrey, Jean-Marie C.: Environment & Energy Publishing
MacDonald, Neil A.: Technology Commercialization
Macy, Daniel J.: Thompson Publishing Group
Madden, Mike R.: Salon
Maggs, John J.: National Journal Group, National Journal
Magill, Barbara: Thompson Publishing Group
Mahtesian, Charles G.: Politico
Maine, Amanda: CCH Inc.
Maixner, Edward: Kiplinger Washington Editors
Malloy, Eileen: BNA News
Manasevit, Max: Thompson Publishing Group
Mandel, Jennifer A.: Environment & Energy Publishing
Mandell, Dara S.: Jewish Press
Manickavasagam, Malini: BNA News
Manzo, Kathleen K.: Education Week
Marcucci, Carl: Radio Business Report Inc., Radio Business Report
Mark, Roy S.: Eweek
Mark, David F.: Politico
Marre, Klaus: The Hill
Marron, Jessica: McGraw-Hill Co.
Marshall, Christa L.N.: Environment & Energy Publishing
Martin, Jonathan L.: Politico
Martinez, Gebe: Politico
Martinez, Barbara E.: Politico
Martinson, Erica L.: Inside Washington Publishers
Masterson, Kathryn E.: Chronicle of Higher Education
Mathews, James C.: McGraw-Hill Co., Aviation Week
Matthews, Sidney William: Army Times Publishing Co.
Mauro, Antony E.: National Law Journal
Maxwell, Lesli A.: Education Week
Mayer, Jane: New Yorker
Maze, Richard: Army Times Publishing Co.
Mazumdar, Anandashankar: BNA News
McAlvanah, Nora J.: National Journal Group, The Hotline
McArdle, John: Roll Call Group, Roll Call
McAuley, David: BNA News
McBeth Laping, Karen: McGraw-Hill Co.
McCaffery, Gregory: BNA News
McCarter, Ernest Mickey L.: HS Today
McClenahen, John: Penton Media Inc.
McCleskey, Ellen E.: BNA News
McConnell, Beth Ann: Sedgwick Publishing Co.
McCord, Quinn T.: National Journal Group, The Hotline
McCormack, Richard: Manufacturing & Technology News
McCormack, John M.: Weekly Standard
McCormally, Kevin: Kiplinger Washington Editors
McCracken, Rebecca P.: BNA News
McCullough, Amy C.: Army Times Publishing Co.
McDermott, Kevin B.: UCG
McGarry, Brendan W.: Army Times Publishing Co.
McGeehon, Dale: Thompson Publishing Group
McGolrick, Susan J.: BNA News
McGovern, Kathryn A.: Thompson Publishing Group
McGowan, Kevin P.: BNA News
McGrane, Victoria G.: Politico
McInerney, Susan M.: BNA News
McIntosh, Toby: BNA News
McKenna, Ted: PR Week
McKinney, Amber: BNA News
McLeary, Paul J.: McGraw-Hill Co., Aviation Week
McMichael, William H.: Army Times Publishing Co.
McMorris-Santoro, Evan: National Journal Group, The Hotline
McMurtrie, Elizabeth: Chronicle of Higher Education
McNamara, Meghan: Exchange Monitor Publications
McNeil, Michele: Education Week
McQuilken, Marisa S.: National Law Journal
McSherry, Alison B.: Roll Call Group, Roll Call
McTague, James: Barron's
Mechcatie, Elizabeth: International Medical News Group
Medford, Clayton P.: Inside Washington Publishers
Meinecke, Elisabeth C.: Human Events
Melillo, Wendy: Adweek Magazine
Mercurio, John C.: National Journal Group, The Hotline
Merrion, Paul Robert: Crain Communications
Messenger, Robert G.: Weekly Standard

MEMBERS ENTITLED TO ADMISSION, PERIODICAL PRESS GALLERIES—Continued

Meyers, David B.: Roll Call Group, Roll Call
Mezo, Ingrid M.J.: FDC Reports
Michels, Jennifer L.: McGraw-Hill Co., Aviation Week
Miller, John J.: National Review
Miller, Reed J.: FDC Reports
Miller, Sean J.: National Journal Group, The Hotline
Miller, Tricia L.: Roll Call Group, Roll Call
Miller, Margaret H.: Thompson Publishing Group
Mills, Jim L.: The Hill
Mitchell, Charles F.: Roll Call Group, Roll Call
Moehrle, Patrick E.: Thompson Publishing Group
Mokhiber, Russell: Corporate Crime Reporter
Mola, Roger Andrew: Aviation International News
Monastersky, Richard A.: Nature
Moncrief, JoAnne P.: National Journal Group, National Journal
Moody, Brittany Elyse: McGraw-Hill Co., Aviation Week
Moore, Michael D.: BNA News
Moore, Miles David: Crain Communications
Moragne, Lenora: Black Congressional Monitor
Morales, Cecilio: MII Publications
Morello, Lauren: Environment & Energy Publishing
Morin, Christopher Scott: Thompson Publishing Group
Morring, Jr., Frank: McGraw-Hill Co., Aviation Week
Morris, Jefferson F.: McGraw-Hill Co., Aviation Week
Morris, Ryan: National Journal Group, National Journal
Morris, Jodie: National Journal Group, National Journal
Morrissey, James A.: Textile World
Morton, Peter G.: Financial Post
Mosquera, Mary: 1105 Government Information Group, Federal Computer Week
Mulero, Eugene: Roll Call Group, Congress Now
Mulkern, Anne C.: Environment & Energy Publishing
Mullen, Lindsey E.: Thompson Publishing Group
Mulrine, Anna: U.S. News & World Report
Mumford, Christine M.: BNA News
Munoz, German: News Bites
Munoz, Carlo: Inside Washington Publishers
Munro, Neil P.: National Journal Group, National Journal
Muolo, Paul A.: National Mortgage News
Muradian, Vago: Army Times Publishing Co.
Murdoch, Joyce M.: National Journal Group, National Journal
Murray, Matthew: Roll Call Group, Roll Call
Mutcherson-Ridley, Joyce: CCH Inc.
Myers, Dee Dee: Vanity Fair
Myers, Cathleen R.: BNA News
Nagesh, Gautham V.: National Journal Group, Government Executive
Napoli, Denise E.: International Medical News Group
Nartker, Michael: Exchange Monitor Publications
Naseef, Kate M.: BNA News
Natter, Aryeh J.: BNA News
Naylor, Sean D.: Army Times Publishing Co.
Neal, Rebecca K.: Army Times Publishing Co.
Nealy, Michelle J.: Diverse: Issues in Higher Education
Needham, Vicki A.: Roll Call Group, Congress Now
Nelson, Ryan: FDC Reports
Nettles, Meredith K.: National Journal Group, The Hotline
Neumann, Daniel: Inside Washington Publishers
Newell, Ashley C.: Tax Notes
Newell, Elizabeth A.: National Journal Group, Government Executive
Newkumet, Christopher J.: McGraw-Hill Co.
Newman, Michael: Slate
Newmyer, Arthur: Roll Call Group, Roll Call
Newton-Small, Jay: Time Inc., Time Magazine
Nichols, William D.: Politico
Nichols, Timieka: 1105 Government Information Group, Federal Computer Week
Nicholson, Jonathan: BNA News
Noah, Timothy Robert: Slate
Noe, Holly C.: National Journal Group, The Hotline
Novack, Janet: Forbes
Oberdorfer, Carol: BNA News
Oberle, Sean F.: Oberle Communications, Product Safety Letter
Obey, Douglas: Inside Washington Publishers
O'Brien, Michael P.: The Hill
O'Brien, Maura E.: National Journal Group, The Hotline
O'Connor, Patrick M.: Politico
Oczypok, Katherine M.: The Hill
Oddis, Michelle E.: Human Events
Ognanovich, Nancy: BNA News
Olsen, Florence E.: BNA News
Omestad, Thomas E.: U.S. News & World Report
Onley, Gloria R.: BNA News
Orchowski, Margaret: Hispanic Outlook in Higher Education
Orrick, Sarah M.: Congressional Digest
Orth, Maureen: Vanity Fair
Ortman, Emily M.: Roll Call Group, Roll Call
Osborn, Kris J.: Army Times Publishing Co.
Ostroff, Jim: Kiplinger Washington Editors
O'Toole, Charles C.: Tax Notes
O'Toole, Thomas: BNA News
Otteman, Scott A.: Inside Washington Publishers
Packer-Tursman, Judith L.: Atlantic Information Services
Page, Paul: Journal of Commerce
Pak, Janne Kum Cha C.: USA Journal
Palazzolo, Joseph R.: National Law Journal
Palmer, Anna A.: Roll Call Group, Roll Call

MEMBERS ENTITLED TO ADMISSION, PERIODICAL PRESS GALLERIES—Continued

Parillo, Kristen A.: Tax Notes
Parker, Susan T.: Natural Gas Intelligence
Parker, Laura J.: Vanity Fair
Parker, Stuart H.: Inside Washington Publishers
Parker, Alexander M.: National Journal Group, Government Executive
Parnes, Amie M.: Politico
Parrish, Molly R.: Letter Publications
Paschal, Mack Arthur: BNA News
Patrick, Steven: BNA News
Patterson, James B.: Thompson Publishing Group
Patton, Zachary L.: Governing
Patton, Oliver B.: Heavy Duty Trucking
Payne, Marissa C.: Exchange Monitor Publications
Pazanowski, Bernard J.: BNA News
Pazanowski, Mary Anne: BNA News
Peake, Daniel P.: Roll Call Group, Gallery Watch
Pearl, Larry: Food Chemical News
Pecquet, Julian J.: Inside Washington Publishers
Pekow, Charles: Community College Week
Perelman, Isabella O.: BNA News
Perlman, Ellen: Governing
Perriello, Anthony M.: BNA News
Perry, Suzanne: Chronicle of Higher Education
Peters, Katherine M.: National Journal Group, Government Executive
Peterson, Denise: FDC Reports
Peterson, Zachary M.: Inside Washington Publishers
Pethokoukis, James M.: U.S. News & World Report
Pettingell, Dolia E.: Poder
Pexton, Patrick: National Journal Group, National Journal
Piemonte, Philip M.: Federal Employees News Digest
Pierce, Emily: Roll Call Group, Roll Call
Pimley, Ward: BNA News
Pitts, Edward: World Magazine
Plank, Kendra Casey: BNA News
Plotz, David: Slate
Plumer, Bradford T.: New Republic
Pluviose, David: Diverse: Issues in Higher Education
Pollard, Nathan A.: BNA News
Ponnuru, Ramesh: National Review
Poppy, Daniel F.: FDC Reports
Postal, Arthur D.: National Underwriter
Poulson, Theresa: National Journal Group, Nationaljournal.com
Pound, Edward T.: National Journal Group, National Journal
Powers, Martha C.: Mid-Atlantic Research
Preston, Caroline S.: Chronicle of Higher Education
Price, Pat: Tax Notes
Prince, Zenith O.: Afro American Newspapers
Pritchard, William R.: BNA News
Prochnay, William W.: Vanity Fair
Pryde, Joan A.: Kiplinger Washington Editors
Pueschel, Matt: U.S. Medicine
Purdum, Todd S.: Vanity Fair
Putrich, Gayle S.: Army Times Publishing Co.
Quirk, Matthew F.: National Journal Group, Atlantic Monthly
Radford, Bruce W.: Public Utilities Fortnightly
Rahim, Saqib: Environment & Energy Publishing
Raju, Manu K.: Politico
Ramirez Esparza, Eddy G.: U.S. News & World Report
Rapp, David R.: 1105 Government Information Group, Federal Computer Week
Rash, Wayne: Eweek
Rayasam, Renuka: Kiplinger Washington Editors
Reed, John T.: Inside Washington Publishers
Rees, John: Mid-Atlantic Research
Reis, Patrick C.: Environment & Energy Publishing
Reishus, Mark: Thompson Publishing Group
Ressler, Thomas: Inside Mortgage Finance
Restivo, Julie C.: Roll Call Group, Gallery Watch
Restuccia, Andrew M.: Inside Washington Publishers
Richards, Ashley A.: Inside Washington Publishers
Richardson, Nathaline: BNA News
Richman, Sheldon B.: BNA News
Rizzuto, Pat: BNA News
Roach, Ronald: Diverse: Issues in Higher Education
Robelen, Erik: Education Week
Roberts, Edward S.: Credit Union Journal
Roberts, Victoria: BNA News
Robinson, Thomas S.: Mass Transit Lawyer
Roeder, Linda: BNA News
Rogers, Robert L.: National Law Journal
Rogers, David E.: Politico
Rohde, Peter: Kiplinger Washington Editors
Rohrer, S. Scott: National Journal Group, National Journal
Roland, Neil D.: Crain Communications
Rolfsen, Bruce: Army Times Publishing Co.
Roque, Ashley N.: Roll Call Group, Congress Now
Rose, Phil A.: Professional Pilot Magazine
Rose, Michael F.: BNA News
Rosen, Jeffrey M.: New Republic
Rosenberg, Alyssa B.: National Journal Group, Government Executive
Rothenberg, Stuart: Rothenberg Political Report
Rothman, Heather M.: BNA News
Rothstein, Betsy: The Hill
Rowley, Dorothy M.: Afro American Newspapers
Roy, Daniel J.: BNA News
Rudd, Jr., Terrence: International Medical News Group
Ruel-Sabatier, Patrick M.: Le Point
Ruggeri, Amanda E.: U.S. News & World Report
Rushing, J. Taylor: The Hill
Russo, Eugene I.: Nature
Ryan, Jr., Frederick J.: Politico
Saenz, Cheryl L.: BNA News
Sahd, Timothy J.: National Journal Group, The Hotline

MEMBERS ENTITLED TO ADMISSION, PERIODICAL PRESS GALLERIES—Continued

Saiyid, Amena H.: McGraw-Hill Co.
Sala, Susan J.: BNA News
Saletan, William B.: Slate
Salzano, Carlo J.: Waterways Journal
Sammon, Richard: Kiplinger Washington Editors
Samuels, Christina: Education Week
Samuelsohn, Darren: Environment & Energy Publishing
Samuelson, Robert J.: Newsweek
Samuelson, Ruth D.: Washington City Paper
Sander, Elizabeth Libby C.: Chronicle of Higher Education
Sandler, Michael A.: The Hill
Sands, Derek O.: McGraw-Hill Co.
Sangillo, Gregg Thomas: National Journal Group, National Journal
Sartipzadeh, Saied Ali: BNA News
Sasseen, Jane A.: McGraw-Hill Co., Business Week
Sault, Samantha K.: Weekly Standard
Savage, Luiza C.: Maclean's
Savener, Matthew J.: Roll Call Group, Roll Call
Savoie, Andy: McGraw-Hill Co., Aviation Week
Sawchuk, Stephen A.: Education Week
Scarcella, Michael A.: National Law Journal
Scheiber, Noam J.: New Republic
Scheid, Brian J.: Inside Washington Publishers
Scherer, Michael B.: Time Inc., Time Magazine
Scherman, Bob: Satellite Business News
Schieken, William: Federal Publications, Government Contractor
Schiff, Daniel A.: FDC Reports
Schlesinger, Robert EK: U.S. News & World Report
Schlosser Chandraseraran, Julie: Time Inc., Fortune Magazine
Schmidt, Peter: Chronicle of Higher Education
Schneider, Martin A.: Exchange Monitor Publications
Schneider, Andrew C.: Kiplinger Washington Editors
Schoeff, Jr., Mark: Crain Communications
Schoenberg, Tom: National Law Journal
Schofield, Adrian: McGraw-Hill Co., Aviation Week
Schomisch, Jeffrey: Thompson Publishing Group
Schorr, Burt: UCG
Schroeder, Anne C.: Politico
Schubert, Charlotte M.: Nature
Schuff, Sally: Farm Progress News
Schuh, Kristen M.: Inside Mortgage Finance
Schwab, Nicole E.: U.S. News & World Report
Schwartz, David H.: BNA News
Scoblic, J. Peter: New Republic
Scorza, John Forrest: Thompson Publishing Group
Scott, Dean T.: BNA News
Scutro, Andrew M.: Army Times Publishing Co.
Seiden, Daniel I.: BNA News
Selingo, Jeffrey: Chronicle of Higher Education
Sellers, Malorie A.: National Journal Group, National Journal
Serafini, Marilyn Werber: National Journal Group, National Journal
Setze, Karen Jeanne: Tax Notes
Sevidaz, Jay A.: Journal of Commerce
Sfiligoj, Mark L.: Kiplinger Washington Editors
Shafer, Jack: Slate
Shannon, Darren J.: McGraw-Hill Co., Aviation Week
Shapiro, Walter: Salon
Shappell, Brian M.: CD Publications
Sharpe, Stephanie: McGraw-Hill Co.
Sheedy, Rachel L.: Kiplinger Washington Editors
Sheets, Andy: Tax Notes
Sheikh, Fawzia: Inside Washington Publishers
Shepard, Steven G.: National Journal Group, The Hotline
Sheppard, Doug: Tax Notes
Shoop, Thomas J.: National Journal Group, Government Executive
Shreve, Margaret: Tax Notes
Silva, Jeffrey S.: Crain Communications
Simendinger, Alexis A.: National Journal Group, National Journal
Simmons, Quintin: Tax Notes
Simon, Roger M.: Politico
Simpson, Jason M.: Inside Washington Publishers
Singer, Paul B.: Roll Call Group, Roll Call
Skalka, Jennifer C.: National Journal Group, The Hotline
Skiba, Katherine M.: U.S. News & World Report
Slaninka, R. Josephj: Montgomery County Sentinel
Slattery, Sandra: Federal Publications, Government Contractor
Slaughter, David A.: Thompson Publishing Group
Smallen, Jill: National Journal Group, National Journal
Smalley, Suzanne M.: Newsweek
Smee, Bill D.: Slate
Smith, Jasper B.: Tax Notes
Smith, Lauren M.: FDC Reports
Smith, Jennifer C.: Inside Washington Publishers
Smith, Katie: Roll Call Group, Roll Call
Snider, Adam: BNA News
Snow, Nicholas J.: Oil & Gas Journal
Snyder, Katharine: Mine Safety and Health News
Snyder, Jim: The Hill
Sobieraj, Sandra: Time Inc., People Magazine
Solomon, Goody L.: News Bites
Soraghan, Mike: The Hill
Southern, E. Richard: Federal Publications, Government Contractor
Spence, Charles F.: General Aviation News
Spencer, Patricia S.: BNA News
Spicer, Malcolm E.: FDC Reports
Spiering, Charlie R.: Evans-Novak Political Report
Splete, Heidi: International Medical News Group
Spotswood, Stephen: U.S. Medicine
Sprague, John: Budget & Program

MEMBERS ENTITLED TO ADMISSION, PERIODICAL PRESS GALLERIES—Continued

Stam, John H.: BNA News
Stanton, Lynn E.: Telecommunications Reports
Stanton, John: Roll Call Group, Roll Call
Starobin, Paul J.: National Journal Group National Journal
Steinberg, Julie A.: BNA News
Steinberg, Aaron: UCG
Steingart, Gabor I.: Der Spiegel
Steinke, Scott A.: FDC Reports
Steis, Ellen Beswick: Natural Gas Intelligence
Steis, Alexander Beswick: Natural Gas Intelligence
Stencel, Mark: Governing
Stern, Jonathan D.: UCG
Sternstein, Aliya E.: National Journal Group, Government Executive
Stevenson, Margaret K.: FDC Reports
Stewart, David D.: Tax Notes
Stimson, James A.: BNA News
Stimson, Leslie P.: NewBay Media
Stoddard, Alexandra B.: The Hill
Stokeld, Frederick W.: Tax Notes
Stone, Daniel E.: Newsweek
Stone, Peter H.: National Journal Group, National Journal
Straub, Noelle C.: Environment & Energy Publishing
Straus, Brian A.: Penton Media Inc.
Strawbridge, James O.: Inside Washington Publishers
Strong, Jonathan A.: Inside Washington Publishers
Sturges, Peyton Mackay: BNA News
Sullivan, Martin A.: Tax Notes
Sullivan, John H.: BNA News
Sullivan, Monica C.: National Journal Group, National Journal
Sullivan, Amy E.: Time Inc., Time Magazine
Supiano, Beckie: Chronicle of Higher Education
Sutter, Susan M.: Scrip World Pharmaceutical News
Sutton, Eileen C.: BNA News
Swanson, Ian B.: The Hill
Sweeney, Ray: CD Publications
Sweeting, Paul: Reed Business Information, Reed Business Information
Swisher, Larry: BNA News
Swope, Christopher: Governing
Tacconelli, Gail: Newsweek
Talwani, Sanjay: NewBay Media
Tan, Michelle: Army Times Publishing Co.
Taulbee, Pamela D.: FDC Reports
Taylor, Ronald A.: BNA News
Taylor, Phil A.: Environment & Energy Publishing
Taylor, Dan P.: Inside Washington Publishers
Taylor, Jessica L.: National Journal Group, National Journal
Taylor, Vincent E.: UCG
Taylor II, B.J.: Atlantic Information Services
Taylor, Jr., Stuart: National Journal Group, National Journal
Tegtmeier, Lee Ann: McGraw-Hill Co., Aviation Week
Temple, Amanda N.: Roll Call Group, Gallery Watch
Terzian, Philip: Weekly Standard
Teske, Steven: BNA News
Thibodeau, Patrick: IDG Communications
Thompson, Mark J.: Time Inc., Time Magazine
Thorn, Judith: BNA News
Thorndike, Joseph: Tax Notes
Thrush, Glenn H.: Politico
Tice, James S.: Army Times Publishing Co.
Tiernan, Tom: McGraw-Hill Co.
Tilghman, Andrew S.: Army Times Publishing Co.
Timmerman, Kenneth R.: Newsmax
Tinkelman, Joseph A.: BNA News
Tiron, Roxana: The Hill
Todaro, Jane B.: McGraw-Hill Co., Business Week
Toeplitz, Shira R.: Roll Call Group, Roll Call
Tollefson, Jeff S.: Nature
Topor, Eric D.: BNA News
Torres, Katherine: Penton Media Inc.
Tosh, Dennis A.: Thompson Publishing Group
Trick, Randy J.: Exchange Monitor Publications
Triplett, Michael R.: BNA News
Tsigas, Maria: UCG
Tsui, Amy: BNA News
Tucker, Miriam E.: International Medical News Group
Tucker, Charlotte E.: BNA News
Tumulty, Karen: Time Inc., Time Magazine
Tuttle, Steve: Newsweek
Twachtman, Gregory: FDC Reports
Unnikrishnan, Madhu: McGraw-Hill Co., Aviation Week
Upholt, Boyce M.: Politics Magazine
Vaida, Bara: National Journal Group, National Journal
Valverde, Janice A.: BNA News
Vample, Gwendolyn: Thompson Publishing Group
Vance, Kevin G.: Weekly Standard
Veis, Gregory P.: New Republic
Verespej, Michael: Crain Communications
Viadero, Debra: Education Week
Victor, Kirk: National Journal Group, National Journal
Vissiere, Helene: Le Point
Vogel, Kenneth P.: Politico
Von Zeppelin, Cristina L.: Forbes
Voorhees, Joshua M.: Environment & Energy Publishing
Wachter, Kerri: International Medical News Group
Wadman, Meredith: Nature
Wakeman, Nick: 1105 Government Information Group, Washington Technology
Waldrop, M. Mitchell: Nature
Walker, Karen J.: Army Times Publishing Co.
Walker, Chandra: CCH Inc.

MEMBERS ENTITLED TO ADMISSION, PERIODICAL PRESS GALLERIES—Continued

Walker, Christopher C.: FDC Reports
Walsh, Mark: Education Week
Walsh, Elsa: New Yorker
Walsh, Kenneth T.: U.S. News & World Report
Walsh, Gertrude: 1105 Government Information Group, Government Computer News
Walter, Amy: National Journal Group, The Hotline
Walthall, Janet C.: BNA News
Ware, Patricia: BNA News
Washington, Kimi J.: CD Publications
Washington, Debbie: Inside Washington Publishers
Wasley, Paula E.: Chronicle of Higher Education
Wasserman, David N.: Cook Political Report
Wasson, Erik L.: Inside Washington Publishers
Watkins, Steve: Army Times Publishing Co.
Weber, Rick: Inside Washington Publishers
Webster, James C.: Webster Communications
Wechsler, Jill: Pharmaceutical Executive
Wegner, Mark A.: Roll Call Group, Gallery Watch
Weigelt, Matthew: 1105 Government Information Group, Federal Computer Week
Weil, Jenny: McGraw-Hill Co.
Weiner, Joann M.: Tax Notes
Weisgerber, Marcus: Inside Washington Publishers
Weisskopf, Michael: Time Inc., Time Magazine
Weissmann, Jordan H.: National Law Journal
Weixel, Nathaniel L.: BNA News
Welch, Jake: National Journal Group, National Journal
Werble, Cole P.: FDC Reports
Whieldon, Esther: McGraw-Hill Co.
White, Nicola M.: Tax Notes
White, Rodney A.: McGraw-Hill Co.
White, Andrew A.: Thompson Publishing Group
White III, Frank: BNA News
Whitelaw, Kevin: U.S. News & World Report
Whitney, Blake K.: Roll Call Group, Roll Call
Whittington, Lauren: Roll Call Group, Roll Call
Wieser, Eric: McGraw-Hill Co.
Wilczek, Yin: BNA News
Wildstrom, Stephen H.: McGraw-Hill Co., Business Week
Wilhelm, Ian L.: Chronicle of Higher Education
Wilkerson, John S.: Inside Washington Publishers
Wilkie, Christina W.: The Hill
Willen, Mark: Kiplinger Washington Editors
Willenson, Kim: Japan Digest
Williams, Grant: Chronicle of Higher Education
Williams, Jeffrey: Satellite Business News
Williams, Risa D.: Tax Notes
Williams, Eileen J.: BNA News
Williams, Mark A.: BNA News
Williams, Michelle N.: National Journal Group, Nationaljournal.com
Wills, Nicholas J.: Washington Business Information
Wilson, Christopher E.: Slate
Wilson, Reid H.: The Hill
Wilson, Stanley E.: Institutional Investor
Windsor, Joseph K.: Federal Publications, Government Contractor
Winebrenner, Jane A.: BNA News
Wingfield, Brian R.: Forbes
Winston, Catherine Kate A.: Inside Washington Publishers
Winter, Allison A.: Environment & Energy Publishing
Witt, Elder: Governing
Witze, Alexandra: Nature
Wolverton, Bradley: Chronicle of Higher Education
Wood, Graeme C.A.: National Journal Group, Atlantic Monthly
Woods, Randall O.: McGraw-Hill Co.
Wooldridge, Adrian: Economist
Wright, Charlotte: McGraw-Hill Co.
Wright, Jr., James: Afro American Newspapers
Wyand, Michael W.: BNA News
Yachnin, Jennifer: Roll Call Group, Roll Call
Yager, Christopher J.: The Hill
Yaksick, Jr., George L.: CCH Inc.
Yamazaki, Kazutami: Washington Watch
Yehle, Emily J.: Roll Call Group, Roll Call
Yerkey, Gary G.: BNA News
Yin, Sandra: UCG
Yingling, Jennifer: The Hill
Yochelson, Mindy: BNA News
Yohannan, Suzanne M.: Inside Washington Publishers
Yordanova-Kline, Milena: McGraw-Hill Co.
York, Kelli G.: Thompson Publishing Group
Young, Sam: Tax Notes
Young, Jeffrey: The Hill
Youngman, Sam A.: The Hill
Yuill, Barbara: BNA News
Zaman, Gulnar: Tax Notes
Zaneski, Cyril ''Cy'' T.: Environment & Energy Publishing
Zehr, Mary Ann: Education Week
Zimmermann, Eric M.: The Hill
Zumbrun, Joshua H.: Forbes
Zung, Robert Te-Kang: BNA News
Zurcher, Anthony W.: Congressional Digest

PERIODICALS REPRESENTED IN PRESS GALLERIES

House Gallery 225–2941, Senate Gallery 224–0265

ADVOCATE—(310) 806–4288; 811 Quincy Street, NW., #401, Washington, DC 20010: Karen ''Kerry'' L. Eleveld.

ADWEEK MAGAZINE—(202) 833–8184; 910 17th Street, NW., Suite 215, Washington, DC 20005: Wendy Melillo.

AFRO AMERICAN NEWSPAPERS—(202) 332–0080; 1917 Benning Road, NE., Washington, DC 20002: Hazel Trice Edney, Zenith O. Prince, Dorothy M. Rowley, James Wright, Jr.

ARMY TIMES PUBLISHING CO.—(703) 750–9000; 6883 Commercial Drive, Springfield, VA 22159: John T. Bennett, Antonie L. Boessenkool, Gregg L. Carlstrom, Elise Castelli, Gina Cavallaro, Christopher Cavas, Matthew Cox, Philip T. Ewing, Susan E. Gvozdas, Michael R. Hoffman, Ben J. Iannotta, Karen Grigg Jowers, Tim Kauffman, Kelly Kennedy, Samuel R. LaGrone, Daniel G. Lamothe, Stephen Losey, Sidney William Matthews, Richard Maze, Amy C. McCullough, Brendan W. McGarry, William H. McMichael, Vago Muradian, Sean D. Naylor, Rebecca K. Neal, Kris J. Osborn, Gayle S. Putrich, Bruce Rolfsen, Andrew M. Scutro, Michelle Tan, James S. Tice, Andrew S. Tilghman, Karen J. Walker, Steve Watkins.

ASIA TODAY—(703) 978–1906; 27025 McPhearson Square Washington, DC 20038: Raghubir Goyal.

ATLANTIC INFORMATION SERVICES—(202) 775–9008; 1100 17th Street, NW., Suite 300, Washington, DC 20036: Jill Brown, Michael E. Carbine, Eve Collins, Steve Davis, Barbra Golub, James H. Gutman, Neal R. Learner, Angela K. Maas, Judith L. Packer-Tursman, B.J. Taylor II.

AVIATION INTERNATIONAL NEWS—(301) 230–4520; 5605 Alderbrook Court, #T6, Rockville, MD 20851: Paul D. Lowe, Roger Andrew Mola.

BARRON'S—(202) 862–6606; 1025 Connecticut Avenue, NW., Suite 800, Washington, DC 20036: Thomas G. Donlan, James McTague.

BLACK CONGRESSIONAL MONITOR—(202) 488–8879; P.O. Box 75035, Washington, DC 20024: Lenora Moragne.

BLACK ENTERPRISE—(202) 544–3143; 1220 Orren Street, NE., Washington, DC 20002: Joyce Jones.

BNA NEWS—(703) 341–3000; 1801 South Bell Street, Arlington, VA 22202: Paul F. Albergo, Alexei Alexis, Michelle Amber, Patrick Ambrosio, Donald G. Aplin, John T. Aquino, Jerome C. Ashton, Cecelia M. Assam, Pamela S. Atkins, Margaret Aulino, Martina S. Barash, Sarah M. Barr, Jeannie Baumann, Alison Bennett, Andrea L. Ben-Yosef, Alicia E. Biggs, Deborah D. Billings, Amy E. Bivins, Cheryl Bolen, Leonard Bracken, David B. Brandolph, Rossella E. Brevetti, Angela L. Britt, R. Christian Bruce, Sue Bryant, Ellen Byerrum, Derrick Cain, Madelyn R. Callahan, Sheila Cherry, Tina M. Chi, Andrew J. Childers, Russell M. Choma, Gayle C. Cinquegrani, Janey Cohen, Steven Cook, Robert C. Cook, Matilda Monroe Corley, Richard H. Cowden, S. Diane Davis, Bronwyn L. Davis, Jeff Day, Gloria Deigh, Tanya Devernoe, Phyllis Diamond, Dana J. Domone, Kenneth P. Doyle, Lawrence E. Dube, Antonio Dutra, Thomas Edmondson, Jewel W. Edwards, Michael Eisenstein, Dana Elfin, Geoffrey Emeigh, Jr., Larry E. Evans, Catherine Sullivan Ezzard, Thecla R. Fabian, Leora M. Falk, Brett Ferguson, Michael Ferullo, J.P. Finet, Leslie G. Fleet, Sean I. Forbes, Stephen France, Laura Francis, Diane Freda, John Gannon, Lauren M. Gardner, W. Lynn Garner, Lorraine S. Gilbert, Diana I. Gregg, Angela Gregorits, Mary Ann Grena Manley, Christine H. Grimaldi, Elizabeth A. Grover, Melinda Hanson, David Harrison, Peter S. Hayes, Gregory S. Hellman, Patricia M. Henry, Keith M. Hill, Richard Hill, Susan R. Hobbs, Rebecca E. Hoffman, Gwendolyn C. Holmes, Jay Horowitz, Terence Hyland, Alison Johansen, Alisa Johnson, Stephen Joyce, Jessie K. Kamens, Hugh B. Kaplan, Bruce S. Kaufman, Gail S. Keller, Altaf U. Khan, Jeff Kinney, John R. Kirkland, Alan D. Kovski, W. Randy Kubetin, Louis C. LaBrecque, Kevin C. Lambert, Steve K. Lee, Ralph Lindeman, Aaron E. Lorenzo, Eileen Malloy, Malini Manickavasagam, Anandashankar Mazumdar, David McAuley, Gregory McCaffery, Ellen E. McCleskey, Rebecca P. McCracken, Susan J. McGolrick, Kevin P. McGowan, Susan M. McInerney, Toby McIntosh, Amber McKinney, Michael D. Moore, Christine M. Mumford, Cathleen R. Myers, Kate M. Naseef, Aryeh J. Natter, Jonathan Nicholson, Carol Oberdorfer, Nancy Ognanovich, Florence E. Olsen, Gloria R. Onley, Thomas O'Toole, Mack Arthur Paschal, Steven Patrick, Bernard J. Pazanowski, Mary Anne Pazanowski, Isabella O. Perelman, Anthony M. Perriello, Ward Pimley, Kendra Casey Plank, Nathan A. Pollard, William R. Pritchard, Nathaline Richardson, Sheldon B. Richman, Pat Rizzuto, Victoria Roberts, Linda Roeder, Michael F. Rose, Heather M. Rothman, Daniel J. Roy, Cheryl L. Saenz, Susan J. Sala, Saied Ali Sartipzadeh, David H. Schwartz, Dean T. Scott, Daniel I. Seiden, Adam Snider, Patricia S. Spencer, John H. Stam, Julie A. Steinberg, James A. Stimson, Peyton Mackay Sturges, John H. Sullivan, Eileen C. Sutton, Larry Swisher, Ronald A. Taylor, Steven Teske, Judith Thorn, Joseph A. Tinkelman, Eric D. Topor, Michael R. Triplett, Amy Tsui, Charlotte E. Tucker, Janice A. Valverde, Janet C. Walthall, Patricia Ware, Nathaniel L. Weixel, Frank White III, Yin Wilczek, Eileen J. Williams, Mark A. Williams, Jane A. Winebrenner, Michael W. Wyand, Gary G. Yerkey, Mindy Yochelson,.Barbara Yuill, Robert Te-Kang Zung.

BUDGET & PROGRAM—(202) 628–3860; P.O. Box 6269, Washington, DC 20015: John Sprague.

CAIJING MAGAZINE—(202) 294–6261; 800 4th Street, SW., S–124, Washington, DC 20024: Zengxin Li.

PERIODICALS REPRESENTED IN PRESS GALLERIES—Continued

CCH INC.—(202) 842–7355; 1015 15th Street, NW., Suite 1000, Washington, DC 20005: John Filar Atwood, Sarah A. Borchersen–Keto, Jeffrey E. Carlson, Torie D. Cole, Stephen K. Cooper, Paula L. Cruickshank, Peter E. Feltman, Hilary A. Goehausen, Brant Goldwyn, George G. Jones, Susan Kavanagh, Jacquelyn D. Leatherman, Amanda Maine, Joyce Mutcherson-Ridley, Chandra Walker, George L. Yaksick, Jr.

CD PUBLICATIONS—(301) 588–6380; 8204 Fenton Street, Silver Spring, MD 20910: Laura Ainsley, James S. Byrne, Chet E. Dembeck, Thomas J. Edwards, Michael Gerecht, Linda A. Giaccino, Thomas Harman, Frank Klimko, Brian M. Shappell, Ray Sweeney, Kimi J. Washington.

CHRONICLE OF HIGHER EDUCATION—(202) 466–1000; 1255 23rd Street, NW., Suite 700, Washington, DC 20037: Elyse Ashburn, Paul A. Basken, Goldie Blumenstyk, Paul A. Fain, Kelly Field, Karin Fischer, David G. Glenn, Holly Hall, Sara Hebel, Eric Hoover, Heather Joslyn, Eric Kelderman, Sara Lipka, Kathryn E. Masterson, Elizabeth McMurtrie, Suzanne Perry, Caroline S. Preston, Elizabeth ''Libby'' C. Sander, Peter Schmidt, Jeffrey Selingo, Beckie Supiano, Paula E. Wasley, Ian L. Wilhelm, Grant Williams, Bradley Wolverton.

CMP MEDIA INC.—(202) 746–0611; 1639 York Mills Lane, Reston, VA 20194: George H. Leopold.

COMMUNITY COLLEGE WEEK—(301) 493–6926; 5225 Pooks Hill Road, #1118 N, Washington, DC 20814: Charles Pekow.

CONGRESSIONAL DIGEST—(301) 634–3113; 605 10th Street, NE., Washington, DC 20002: Erika Fitzpatrick, Sarah M. Orrick, Anthony W. Zurcher.

COOK POLITICAL REPORT—(202) 739–8525; 600 New Hamsphire Avenue, NW., Washington, DC 20037: Charles E. Cook, Jr., Jennifer Duffy, David N. Wasserman.

CORPORATE CRIME REPORTER—(202) 737–1680; 1209 National Press Building, Washington, DC 20045: Russell Mokhiber.

CQ RESEARCHER—(202) 729–1800; 2300 North Street, NW., Suite 800, Washington, DC 20037: Thomas J. Billitteri, Marcia Clemmitt, Darrell D. Dela Rosa, Kenneth W. Jost, Peter Katel, Kathy Koch.

CRAIN COMMUNICATIONS—(202) 662–7200; 814 National Press Building, Washington, DC 20045: Matthew DoBias, Jerome M. Geisel, Douglas J. Halonen, Sara Hansard, Mark A. Hofmann, Jennifer Lubell, Paul Robert Merrion, Miles David Moore, Neil D. Roland, Mark Schoeff, Jr., Jeffrey S. Silva, Michael Verespej.

CREDIT UNION JOURNAL—(202) 434–0334; 1325 G Street, NW., Suite 910, Washington, DC 20005: Edward S. Roberts.

DER SPIEGEL—(202) 347–5222; 1202 National Press Building, Washington, DC 20045: Gabor I. Steingart.

DIE ZEIT—(202) 492–6076; 940 National Press Building, Washington, DC 20045: Martin E. Klingst.

DIVERSE: ISSUES IN HIGHER EDUCATION—(703) 385–2980; 10520 Warwick Avenue, Suite B–8, Fairfax, VA 22030: Michelle J. Nealy, David Pluviose, Ronald Roach.

ECONOMIST—(202) 429–0890; 1730 Rhode Island Avenue, NW., Suite 1210, Washington, DC 20036: Jon Fasman, Robert Guest, Rachel Jane Horwood, Gregory W. Ip, Adrian Wooldridge.

EDUCATION WEEK—(301) 280–3100; 6935 Arlington Road, Suite 100, Bethesda, MD 20814: Dakarai I. Aarons, Mark W. Bomster, Sean Cavanagh, Scott J. Cech, Gregory Chronister, Michelle R. Davis, Karen Diegmueller, Catherine Gewertz, Caroline Hendrie, David Hoff, Alyson Klein, Kathleen K. Manzo, Lesli A. Maxwell, Michele McNeil, Erik Robelen, Christina Samuels, Stephen A. Sawchuk, Debra Viadero, Mark Walsh, Mary Ann Zehr.

ELLE—(202) 462–2957; 3133 Connecticut Avenue, NW., Suite 315, Washington, DC 20008: Meryl Gordon.

EMPLOYEE BENEFIT ADVISOR—(202) 504–1110; 1325 G Street, NW., Suite 900, Washington, DC 20005: Elizabeth R. Galentine.

ENDANGERED SPECIES & WETLANDS REPORT—(301) 891–3791; 6717 Poplar Avenue, Takoma Park, MD 20912: Stephen A. Davies.

ENVIRONMENT & ENERGY PUBLISHING—(202) 628–6500; 122 C Street, NW., Suite 722, Washington, DC 20001: Peter B. Behr, Dan Berman, Eric Bontrager, Katherine V. Boyle, Kevin D. Braun, Robin L. Bravender, Michael P. Burnham, Amy V. Carlile, John Matthew Comer, Russell Dinnage, John J. Fialka, Lisa F. Friedman, Ben Geman, Sara E. Goodman, Katie J. Howell, Debra Kahn, Alex Kaplun, Jennifer J. Koons, Jessica E. Leber, Evan W. Lehmann, Katherine C. Ling, Julia A. Littleton, Colleen M. Luccioli, Taryn Luntz, Jean-Marie C. Macabrey, Jennifer A. Mandel, Christa L.N. Marshall, Lauren Morello, Anne C. Mulkern, Saqib Rahim, Patrick C. Reis, Darren Samuelsohn, Noelle C. Straub, Phil A. Taylor, Joshua M. Voorhees, Allison A. Winter, Cyril ''Cy'' T. Zaneski.

EVANS-NOVAK POLITICAL REPORT—(202) 393–4340; 1750 Pennsylvania Avenue, NW., Suite 1203, Washington, DC 20006: Timothy P. Carney, Charlie R. Spiering.

EWEEK—(703) 425–9231; 11711 Amkin Drive, Clifton, VA 20009: Roy S. Mark, Wayne Rash.

EXCHANGE MONITOR PUBLICATIONS—(202) 296–2814; 4455 Connecticut Avenue, NW., Suite A700, Washington, DC 20008: Sarah E. Anderson, Rebecca A. Cooper, Edward L. Helminski, Todd K. Jacobson, Meghan McNamara, Michael Nartker, Marissa C. Payne, Martin A. Schneider, Randy J. Trick.

EXPRESS INDIA—(703) 599–6623; 1541 Wellingham Court, Vienna, VA 22182: Geeta Goindi.

FALLS CHURCH NEWS PRESS—(703) 532–3267; 450 West Broad, Street, #321, Falls Church VA 22046: Nicholas F. Benton, Dean R. Edwards, Nathan S. Hamme.

PERIODICALS REPRESENTED IN PRESS GALLERIES—Continued

FARM PROGRESS NEWS—(202) 484–0744; 520 North Street, SW., Suite S–514, Washington, DC 20024: Sally Schuff.

FEDERAL EMPLOYEES NEWS DIGEST—(703) 707–1888; 610 Herndon Parkway, Suite 400, Herndon, VA 20710: Nathan Abse, Philip M. Piemonte.

FEDERAL PUBLICATIONS GOVERNMENT CONTRACTOR—(800) 328–9378; 1100 Thirteenth Street, NW., Suite 200, Washington, DC 20005: Kenneth H. Berke, Betty James, Lyrica Johnson, William Schieken, Sandra Slattery, E. Richard Southern, Joseph K. Windsor.

FDC REPORTS—(240) 221–4500; 5635 Fishers Lane, Suite 6000, Rockville, MD 20852: Ramsey Baghdadi, Joshua L. Berlin, Jessica E. Bylander, Bowman D. Cox, Elizabeth R. Crawford, Susan W. Darcey, Jon Dobson, Cathy H. Dombroski, Joanne S. Eglovitch, Joseph A. Haas, Jamie R. Hammon, M. Nielsen Hobbs, Monica J. Hogan, Mary J. Houghton, Catherine A. Kelly, Mary Jo Laffler, Ingrid MJ Mezo, Reed J. Miller, Ryan Nelson, Denise Peterson, Daniel F. Poppy, Daniel A. Schiff, Lauren M. Smith, Malcolm E. Spicer, Scott A. Steinke, Margaret K. Stevenson, Pamela D. Taulbee, Gregory Twachtman, Christopher C. Walker, Cole P. Werble.

FINANCIAL POST—(202) 842–1190; 6300 Dahlonega Road, Bethesda, MD 20816: Peter G. Morton.

FOCUS—(301) 581–0999; 8515 Rosewood Drive, Bethesda, MD 20814: Peter Gruber.

FOOD CHEMICAL NEWS—(703) 527–1680; 2200 Clarendon Boulevard, Suite 1401, Arlington, VA 22201: Elizabeth Buckley, Stephen Clapp, Amber M. Healy, Jason A. Huffman, Larry Pearl.

FORBES—(202) 785–1480; 1101 17th Street, NW., Suite 409, Washington, DC 20036: Janet Novack, Cristina L. Von Zeppelin, Brian R. Wingfield, Joshua H. Zumbrun.

FREITAG—(301) 699–3908; 4506 32nd Street, Mt. Rainier, MD 20712: Konrad Ege.

GENERAL AVIATION NEWS—(301) 330–2715; 1915 Windjammer Way, Gaithersburg, MD 20879: Charles F. Spence.

GILSTON-KALIN COMMUNICATIONS—(301) 570–4544; 4816 Sweetbirch Drive, Rockville, MD 20853: Samuel M. Gilston.

GLAMOUR MAGAZINE—(703) 317–4949; 6100 Edgewood Terrace, Alexandria, VA 22307: Linda Kramer.

GOVERNING—(202) 862–8802; 1100 Connecticut Avenue, NW., Suite 1300, Washington, DC 20036: John Buntin, Elizabeth Daigneau, Joshua Goodman, Alan Greenblatt, Heather L. Kleba, Zachary L. Patton, Ellen Perlman, Mark Stencel, Christopher Swope, Elder Witt.

GQ MAGAZINE—(202) 905–0463; 63 Shifflett Road, Free Union, VA 22940: Robert L. Draper, William S. Hylton.

HEALTH MARKET SURVEY—(202) 362–5408; 3767 Oliver Street, NW., Washington, DC 20015: William R. Boyles, Virginia M. Boyles.

HEAVY DUTY TRUCKING—(703) 683–9935; 320 Mansion Drive, Alexandria, VA 22302: Oliver B. Patton.

HISPANIC LINK NEWS SERVICE—(202) 234–0280; 1420 North Street, NW., Suite 101, Washington, DC 20005: Charles A. Ericksen.

HISPANIC OUTLOOK IN HIGHER EDUCATION—(202) 966–1147 x100; 3505 Rodman Street, NW., Washington, DC 20008: Margaret Orchowski.

HS TODAY—(202) 537–5174; P.O. Box 5843, Washington, DC 20016: Ernest ''Mickey'' L. McCarter.

HUMAN EVENTS—(202) 216–0600; One Massachusetts Avenue, NW., Washington, DC 20001: Jed L. Babbin, John Gizzi, Connie L. Hair, Kenneth W. Hanner, Linda Jenkins, Elisabeth C. Meinecke, Michelle E. Oddis.

IDG COMMUNICATIONS—(202) 333–2448; 2630 Adams Mill Road, NW., Apt. 304, Washington, DC 20009: Patrick Thibodeau.

IDG NEWS SERVICE—(202) 595–9882; 906 Phillip Powers Drive, Laurel, MD 20707: Grant J. Gross.

INDIA ABROAD,—(703) 383–6744; 5026 Huntwood Manor Drive, Fairfax, VA 22030: Aziz Haniffa.

INSIDE MORTGAGE FINANCE—(301) 951–1240; 7910 Woodmont Avenue, Suite 1000, Bethesda, MD 20814: John Bancroft, Geremy C. Bass, George A. Brooks, Guy David Cecala, Thomas Ressler, Kristen M. Schuh.

INSIDE WASHINGTON PUBLISHERS—(703) 416–8500; 1919 South Eads Street, #201, Arlington, VA 22202: Samuel U. Baker, Lara W. Beaven, Kate O. Brannen, Christopher Castelli, Marjorie J. Censer, David Paul Clarke, Brett G. Coughlin, Charles R. Davis, Molly M. Davis, Sara A. Ditta, Thomas Patrick Duffy, Luke P. Engan, Seth M. Freedland, Rebekah S. Gordon, Joseph M. Gould, Douglas Guarino, William J. Harrington, Donna L. Haseley, Maria A. Hegstad, Gregory S. Hellman, John H. Heltman, Jutta Hennig, Jenny L. Johnson, Nicholas P. Juliano, Alyah Khan, Anthony Lacey, John Liang, Amy L. Lotven, Aaron J. Lovell, Erica L. Martinson, Clayton P. Medford, Carlo Munoz, Daniel Neumann, Douglas Obey, Scott A. Otteman, Stuart H. Parker, Julian J. Pecquet, Zachary M. Peterson, John T. Reed, Andrew M. Restuccia, Ashley A. Richards, Brian J. Scheid, Fawzia Sheikh, Jason M. Simpson, Jennifer C. Smith, James O. Strawbridge, Jonathan A. Strong, Dan P. Taylor, Debbie Washington, Erik L. Wasson, Rick Weber, Marcus Weisgerber, John S. Wilkerson, Catherine ''Kate'' A. Winston, Suzanne M. Yohannan.

INSTITUTIONAL INVESTOR—(202) 393–0728; 1319 F Street, NW., Suite 805, Washington, DC 20004: Stanley E. Wilson.

PERIODICALS REPRESENTED IN PRESS GALLERIES—Continued

INTERNATIONAL MEDICAL NEWS GROUP—(240) 221–4500; 5635 Fishers Lane, Suite 6000, Rockville, MD 20852: Alicia Ault, Lorinda M. Bullock, Jeffrey Evans, Joyce Frieden, Rebecca Gardner, Sally Kubetin, Elizabeth Mechcatie, Denise E. Napoli, Terrence Rudd, Jr., Heidi Splete, Miriam E. Tucker, Kerri Wachter.

INVESTOR'S WORLD—(202) 664–2827; 4807 Falstone Avenue, Chevy Chase, MD 20815: Dimitrios Apokis.

IRISH ECHO—(202) 870–7404; 9534 Fernwood Road, Bethesda, MD 20817: Susan M. Falvella-Garraty.

JAPAN DIGEST—(703) 931–2500; 3424 Barger Drive, Falls Church, VA 22044: Ayako Doi, Kim Willenson.

JET/EBONY—(202) 393–5860; 1750 Pennsylvania Avenue, NW., Suite 1201, Washington, DC 20006: Kevin U. Chappell.

JEWISH PRESS—(917) 703–1312; 1725 20th Street, NW., #F1, Washington, DC 20009: Dara S. Mandell.

JOURNAL OF COMMERCE—(202) 355–1150; 1270 National Press Building, Washington, DC 20045: John D. Boyd, William B. Cassidy, Robert G. Edmonson, John Gallagher, Paul Page, Jay A. Sevidaz.

KIPLINGER WASHINGTON EDITORS—(202) 887–6400; 1729 H Street, NW., Washington, DC 20006: Beth M. Belton, Peter L. Blank, Melissa S. Bristow, Laura S. Cohn, Martha L. Craver, Michael F. Doan, Jon C. Frandsen, Mary Beth Franklin, Kimberly B. Frumkin, Susan B. Garland, Joan Goldwasser, Douglas A. Harbrecht, Jerome Idaszak, Laura W. Kennedy, Kimberly Lankford, Edward Maixner, Kevin McCormally, Jim Ostroff, Joan A. Pryde, Renuka Rayasam, Peter Rohde, Richard Sammon, Andrew C. Schneider, Mark L. Sfiligoj, Rachel L. Sheedy, Mark Willen.

LE POINT—(202) 549–5070; 4542 28th Street, NW., Washington, DC 20008: Patrick M. Ruel-Sabatier, Helene Vissiere.

LETTER PUBLICATIONS—(301) 779–2036; 7831 Woodmont Avenue, #386 Bethesda, MD 20814: Molly R. Parrish.

McGRAW-HILL CO.—(202) 383–2000; 1200 G Street, NW., Suite 1000, Washington, DC 20005: Carla D. Bass, Dipka Bhambhani, Cheryl Buchta, Craig Cano, Catherine Cash, Jean M. Chemnick, Paul G. Ciampoli, Christine T. Cordner, Steven D. Dolley, Kelley Doolan, Alexander M. Duncan, Amy Fickling, Jason L. Fordney, Peter T. Gartrell, Laura H. Gilcrest, Keiron Greenhalgh, Daniel W. Guido, Brian Hansen, Tom Harrison, Helen D. Hausmann, Elaine Hiruo, William Holland, Pamela E. Hunter, Thomas F. Ichniowski, Valarie N. Jackson, Regina Johnson, Nick Jonson, Joel Kirkland, Rod Kuckro, Kathy Carolin Larsen, William E. Loveless, Jessica Marron, Karen McBeth Laping, Christopher J. Newkumet, Amena H. Saiyid, Derek O. Sands, Stephanie Sharpe, Tom Tiernan, Jenny Weil, Esther Whieldon, Rodney A. White, Eric Wieser, Randall O. Woods, Charlotte Wright, Milena Yordanova–Kline.

McGRAW-HILL CO., AVIATION WEEK—(202) 383–2350; 1200 G Street, NW., Suite 900, Washington, DC 20005: Joseph Anselmo, James R. Asker, Michael Bruno, Amy Butler, Bettina H. Chavanne, Andrew W. Compart, John M. Doyle, Frances Fiorino, Christopher P. Fotos, David Fulghum, Francis L. Jackman, James C. Mathews, Paul J. McLeary, Jennifer L. Michels, Brittany Elyse Moody, Frank Morring, Jr., Jefferson F. Morris, Andy Savoie, Adrian Schofield, Darren J. Shannon, Lee Ann Tegtmeier, Madhu Unnikrishnan.

McGRAW-HILL CO., Business Week—(202) 383–2100; 1200 G Street, NW., Suite 1100, Washington, DC 20005: John A. Carey, Keith Epstein, Theo Francis, Steven LeVine, Jane A. Sasseen, Jane B. Todaro, Stephen H. Wildstrom.

MACLEAN'S—(202) 362–1658; 1111 11th Street, NW., Suite 301, Washington, DC 20001: Luiza C. Savage.

MAIL ON SUNDAY—(202) 547–7980; 510 Constitution Avenue, NE., Washington, DC 20002: William Lowther.

MANUFACTURING & TECHNOLOGY NEWS—(703) 750–2664; P.O. Box 36, Annandale, VA 22003: Richard McCormack.

MASS TRANSIT LAWYER—(703) 548–5177; P.O. Box 320308, Alexandria, VA 22320: Thomas S. Robinson.

MEDICAL DEVICES REPORT—(703) 361–6472; 7643 Bland Drive, Manassas, VA 20109: Steve Butchock.

MID-ATLANTIC RESEARCH—(800) 227–7140; 2805 St. Paul Street, Baltimore, MD 21218: Martha C. Powers, John Rees.

MII PUBLICATIONS—(202) 347–4822 x105; 1800 I Street, NW., Suite 301, Washington, DC 20006: Ryan E. Hess, Cecilio Morales.

MINE SAFETY AND HEALTH NEWS—(703) 217–8270; 5935 4th Street, North Arlington, VA 22203: Katharine Snyder.

MONTGOMERY COUNTY SENTINEL—(301) 838–0788; 22 West Jefferson Street, Suite 309, Rockville, MD 20850: Brian Karem, R. Josephj Slaninka.

NATION—(202) 546–2239; 110 Maryland Avenue, Suite 308, Washington, DC 20002: Christopher L. Hayes, Gregory R. Kaufmann.

NATIONAL LAW JOURNAL—(202) 457–0686; 1730 M Street, NW., Suite 800, Washington, DC 20036: David L. Brown, Marcia Coyle, David H. Ingram, Jeff T. Jeffrey, Brian A. Katkin, Antony E. Mauro, Marisa S. McQuilken, Joseph R. Palazzolo, Robert L. Rogers, Michael A. Scarcella, Tom Schoenberg, Jordan H. Weissmann.

PERIODICALS REPRESENTED IN PRESS GALLERIES—Continued

NATIONAL MORTGAGE NEWS—(202) 434–0323; 1325 G Street, NW., Suite 900, Washington, DC 20005: Brian Collins, Paul A. Muolo.

NATIONAL JOURNAL GROUP, ATLANTIC MONTHLY—(202) 266–7000; 600 New Hampshire Avenue, NW., Washington, DC 20037: Marc J. Ambinder, Conor J. Clarke, Christopher E. Good, Joshua Green, Matthew F. Quirk, Graeme C.A. Wood, Robert G. Brodsky.

NATIONAL JOURNAL GROUP, GOVERNMENT EXECUTIVE—(202) 739–8400; 600 New Hampshire Avenue, NW., Washington, DC 20037: Timothy Clark, Jill R. Davis, Susan Fourney, Amelia M. Gruber, Allan T. Holmes, Kellie Lunney, Gautham V. Nagesh, Elizabeth A. Newell, Alexander M. Parker, Katherine M. Peters, Alyssa B. Rosenberg, Thomas J. Shoop, Aliya E. Sternstein.

NATIONAL JOURNAL GROUP, NATIONAL JOURNAL—(202) 739–8400; 600 New Hampshire Avenue, NW., Washington, DC 20037: Julie L. Abramson, James A. Barnes, Ronald J. Brownstein, Eliza Newlin Carney, Lisa Caruso, Winter Casey, Richard E. Cohen, Kevin R. Craft, Isobel Ellis, William A. Englund, Sydney J. Freedberg, Jr., Brian Friel, Steve Gettinger, Robert H. Gettlin, Charles A. Green, Jerry Hagstrom, Shane Harris, Corine Hegland, James E. Humes, Louis A. Jacobson, Cameron E. Joseph, James Kitfield, Julie A. Kosterlitz, Jaculine M. Koszczuk, Margaret E. Kriz Hobson, John J. Maggs, JoAnne P. Moncrief, Ryan Morris, Jodie Morris, Neil P. Munro, Joyce M. Murdoch, Patrick Pexton, Edward T. Pound, S. Scott Rohrer, Gregg Thomas Sangillo, Malorie A. Sellers, Marilyn Werber Serafini, Alexis A. Simendinger, Jill Smallen, Paul J. Starobin, Peter H. Stone, Monica C. Sullivan, Jessica L. Taylor, Stuart Taylor, Jr., Bara Vaida, Kirk Victor, Jake Welch.

NATIONAL JOURNAL GROUP, NATIONALJOURNAL.COM—(202) 739–8400; 600 New Hampshire Avenue, NW., Washington, DC 20037: Clive Crook, Karl J. Eisenhower, Kevin E. Friedl, Mary M. Gilbert, Lucas M. Grindley, Amy A. Harder, David G. Herbert, Theresa Poulson, Michelle N. Williams.

NATIONAL JOURNAL GROUP, THE HOTLINE—(202) 739–8400; 600 New Hampshire Avenue, NW., Washington, DC 20037: Chris P. Bodenner, Carrie A. Dindino, Rachelle M. Douillard-Proulx, Ian D. Faerstein, Emily Goodin, Matthew P. Gottlieb, Katherine V. Lehr, Nora J. McAlvanah, Quinn T. McCord, Evan McMorris-Santoro, John C. Mercurio, Sean J. Miller, Meredith K. Nettles, Holly C. Noe, Maura E. O'Brien, Timothy J. Sahd, Steven G. Shepard, Jennifer C. Skalka, Amy Walter.

NATIONAL REVIEW—(202) 543–9226; 233 Pennsylvania Avenue, SE., 3rd Floor, Washington, DC 20003: Duncan M. Currie, David A. Freddoso, Mark W. Hemingway, Emily J. Karrs, John J. Miller, Ramesh Ponnuru.

NATIONAL UNDERWRITER—(202) 728–0506; 1301 Connecticut Avenue, NW., Washington, DC 20036: Matthew Brady, Arthur D. Postal.

NATURAL GAS INTELLIGENCE—(703) 318–8848; 22648 Glenn Drive, Suite 305, Sterling VA 20164: David M. Bradley, Susan T. Parker, Ellen Beswick Steis, Alexander Beswick Steis.

NATURE—(202) 737–2355; 968 National Press Building, Washington, DC 20045: Eric K. Hand, Karen H. Kaplan, Richard A. Monastersky, Eugene I. Russo, Charlotte M. Schubert, Jeff S. Tollefson, Meredith Wadman, M. Mitchell Waldrop, Alexandra Witze.

NEW REPUBLIC—(202) 508–4444; 1331 H Street, NW., Suite 700, Washington, DC 20005: Marin E. Cogan, M. Michelle Cottle, Seyward L. Darby, Benjamin R. Eisler, Eve R. Fairbanks, Franklin L. Foer, Linda Gerth, John B. Judis, Suzy Khimm, James R. Kirchick, Zvika Krieger, Bradford T. Plumer, Jeffrey M. Rosen, Noam J. Scheiber, J. Peter Scoblic, Gregory P. Veis.

NEW YORK JEWISH WEEK—(703) 978–4724; 8713 Braeburn Drive, Annandale, VA 22203: James David Besser.

NEW YORK REVIEW OF BOOKS—(202) 244–1092; 5018 Eskridge Terrace, NW., Washington, DC 20016: Elizabeth Drew.

NEW YORKER—(202) 955–0964; 1730 Rhode Island Avenue, NW., Suite 603, Washington, DC 20036: Jeffrey Goldberg, Ryan C. Lizza, Jane Mayer, Elsa Walsh.

NEWBAY MEDIA—(703) 852–4600; 5285 Shawnee Road, Suite 100, Alexandria, VA 22312: Leslie P. Stimson, Sanjay Talwani.

NEWS BITES—(202) 723–2477; 1712 Taylor Street, NW., Washington, DC 20011: German Munoz, Goody L. Solomon.

NEWSMAX—(301) 279–5818; 2516 Stratton Drive, Potomac, MD 20854: Ronald B. Kessler, Kenneth R. Timmerman.

NEWSWEEK—(202) 626–2000; 1750 Pennsylvania Avenue, NW., Suite 1220, Washington, DC 20006: Holly Bailey, John A. Barry, Jeffrey I. Bartholet, Daren Briscoe, Eleanor Clift, Eve K. Conant, Katie M. Connolly, Dan Ephron, Howard Fineman, Tammy M. Haddad, Michael P. Hirsh, Mark J. Hosenball, Michael Isikoff, Patrice Wingert Kelly, Weston Kosova, Robert J. Samuelson, Suzanne M. Smalley, Daniel E. Stone, Gail Tacconelli, Steve Tuttle.

OBERLE COMMUNICATIONS PRODUCT SAFETY LETTER—(301) 229–1027; 4907 Bayard Boulevard, Bethesda, MD 20816: Sean F. Oberle.

OIL & GAS JOURNAL—(703) 532–1588; 7013 Jefferson Avenue, Falls Church, VA 22042: Nicholas J. Snow.

OUTLOOK MAGAZINE—(202) 659–4398; 2400 Virginia Avenue, NW., Apt. C721, Washington, DC 20037: Ashish Kumar Sen.

PERIODICALS REPRESENTED IN PRESS GALLERIES—Continued

PENTON MEDIA INC.—(301) 650–2420; 8380 Colesville Road, Suite 700, Silver Spring, MD 20910: Sandra Arnoult, Perry A. Flint, Aaron E. Karp, John McClenahen, Brian A. Straus, Katherine Torres.

PHARMACEUTICAL EXECUTIVE—(301) 656–4634; 7715 Rocton Avenue, Chevy Chase, MD 20815: Jill Wechsler.

PODER—(703) 707–0236; 2300 Davius Lane, Reston, VA 20191: Dolia E. Pettingell.

POLITICO—(202) 289–1155; 1100 Wilson Boulevard, 6th Floor, Arlington, VA 22209: Ben M. Adler, Michael P. Allen, Fred Barbash, John Bresnahan, Carrie D. Budoff Brown, Alexander I. Burns, Michael L. Calderone, Andrea L. Coller, Richard T. Cullen, Jeanne M. Cummings, Jennifer DiMascio, Chris Frates, Elizabeth M. Frerking, Joshua A. Gerstein, Andrew J. Glass, Nia-Malika A. Henderson, G. Robert Hillman, Alex Isenstadt, Danielle D. Jones, Martin J. Kady II, Kim Kingsley, Josh P. Kraushaar, Carol E. Lee, Lisa R. Lerer, Daniel J. Libit, Samuel R. Loewenberg, Erika M. Lovley, Charles G. Mahtesian, David F. Mark, Jonathan L. Martin, Gebe Martinez, Barbara E. Martinez, Victoria G. McGrane, William D. Nichols, Patrick M. O'Connor, Amie M. Parnes, Manu K. Raju, David E. Rogers, Frederick J. Ryan, Jr., Anne C. Schroeder, Roger M. Simon, Glenn H. Thrush, Kenneth P. Vogel.

POLITICS MAGAZINE—(703) 778–4025; 1655 North Fort Myer Drive, Suite 825, Arlington, VA 22209: Shane D'Aprile, Christie E. Findlay, Boyce M. Upholt.

PR WEEK—(202) 248–6626; 2501 Porter Street, NW., #820, Washington, DC 20008: Ted McKenna.

PRESS ASSOCIATES—(202) 898–4825; 2605 P Street, NW., Suite A, Washington, DC 20007: Janet M. Brown, Mark J. Gruenberg.

PROCESO—(202) 737–1538; 1253 National Press Building, Washington, DC 20045: J. Jesus Esquivel.

PROFESSIONAL PILOT MAGAZINE—(703) 370–0606; 30 South Quaker Lane, Suite 300, Alexandria, VA 22314: Phil A. Rose.

PROGRESSIVE BUSINESS PUBLICATIONS—(410) 349–8200; 1528 Circle Drive, Annapolis, MD 21409: Thomas A. Guay.

PUBLIC LANDS NEWS—(703) 553–0552; 133 South Buchanan Street, Arlington, VA 22204: James B. Coffin.

PUBLIC UTILITIES FORTNIGHTLY—(703) 847–7720; 8229 Boone Boulevard, Suite 400, Vienna, VA 22182: Lori Burkhart, Bruce W. Radford.

RADIO BUSINESS REPORT INC., RADIO BUSINESS REPORT—(646) 746–6400; 4402 Boxwood Drive, Montclair, VA 22025: Carl Marcucci.

REED BUSINESS INFORMATION, BROADCASTING & CABLE—(646) 746–6400; 8015 Hatteras Lane, Springfield, VA 22151: John S. Eggerton, Paul Sweeting.

RESEARCH INSTITUTE OF AMERICA GROUP—(202) 842–1240; 1275 K Street, NW., Suite 875, Washington, DC 20005: Jacqueline C. Deslauriers, LaTasha S. Durrett, Velma Goodwine, Soyoung Ho.

ROLL CALL GROUP, CONGRESS NOW—(202) 824–6800; 50 F Street, NW., Suite 700, Washington, DC 20001: George F. Cahlink, Charlene A. Carter, Jay S. Heflin, Geof M. Koss, Stephen J. Langel, Eugene Mulero, Vicki A. Needham, Ashley N. Roque.

ROLL CALL GROUP, GALLERY WATCH—(202) 824–6800; 50 F Street, NW., Suite 700, Washington, DC 20001: Chad X. Brand, Clayton A. Hanson, Paul H. Jenks, Kelsey R. Lamb, Michael G. Lepage, Niels P. Lesniewski, Jacqueline Linnane, Daniel P. Peake, Julie C. Restivo, Amanda N. Temple, Mark A. Wegner.

ROLL CALL GROUP, ROLL CALL—(202) 824–6800; 50 F Street, NW., Suite 700, Washington, DC 20001: Kate Ackley, Jennifer L. Bendery, Erin P. Billings, Sara E. Bondioli, Jessica L. Brady, Elizabeth Brotherton, Debra A. Bruno, Andrea R. Cohen, Steven T. Dennis, David M. Drucker, Ted Goldman, Emily A. Heil, Casey E. Hynes, Michael Klesta, Keith F. Koffler, Morton M. Kondracke, Jacqueline F. Kucinich, Josh Kurtz, John McArdle, Alison B. McSherry, David B. Meyers, Tricia L. Miller, Charles F. Mitchell, Matthew Murray, Arthur Newmyer, Emily M. Ortman, Anna A. Palmer, Emily Pierce, Matthew J. Savener, Paul B. Singer, Katie Smith, John Stanton, Shira R. Toeplitz, Blake K. Whitney, Lauren Whittington, Jennifer Yachnin, Emily J. Yehle.

ROLLING STONE—(703) 619–0275; 2200 Lakeshire Drive, Alexandria, VA 22308: Robert C. Dreyfuss.

ROTHENBERG POLITICAL REPORT—(202) 546–2822; 50 F Street, NW., 7th Floor, Washington, DC 20001: Nathan Gonzales, Stuart Rothenberg.

SALON—(202) 333–5695; 3417½ M Street, NW., Washington, DC 20007: Mark Benjamin, Mike R. Madden, Walter Shapiro.

SATELLITE BUSINESS NEWS—(202) 785–0505; 5505 Connecticut Avenue, NW., #281, Washington, DC 20015: Bob Scherman, Jeffrey Williams.

SCRIP WORLD PHARMACEUTICAL NEWS—(703) 527–1680 x112; 2200 Clarendon Boulevard, Suite 1401, Arlington, VA 22201: Susan M. Sutter.

SEDGWICK PUBLISHING CO.—(301) 229–1197; 5713 Overlea Road, Bethesda, MD 20816: Beth Ann McConnell.

SET-ASIDE ALERT—(301) 229–5561; 7720 Wisconsin Avenue, #213, Bethesda, MD 20814: Warren Corbett.

PERIODICALS REPRESENTED IN PRESS GALLERIES—Continued

SETANTA PUBLISHING FOOD PROTECTION REPORT—(703) 548–3146; P.O. Box 25277, Alexandria, VA 22313: Declan Conroy.

SLATE—(202) 261–1310; 1350 Connecticut Avenue, Suite 400, Washington, DC 20036: Emily Bazelon, Jacob Christopher Beam, Andrew D.S. Bouve, John F. Dickerson, Joshua Levin, Dahlia Hannah Lithwick, Michael Newman, Timothy Robert Noah, David Plotz, William B. Saletan, Jack Shafer, Bill D. Smee, Christopher E. Wilson.

SPACE NEWS—(703) 658–8400; 6883 Commerce Drive, Springfield, VA 22159: Brian Berger, S. Turner Brinton, Rebecca D. Iannotta, Amy E. Klamper.

STERN—(240) 535–6573; 7017 Hopewood Street, Bethesda, MD 20817: Katja Gloger.

TAX NOTES—(703) 533–4400; 400 South Maple Avenue, Suite 400, Falls Church, VA 22046: David Scott Antonides, Laura E. Breech, Simon A. Brown, John M. Buhl, Jennifer Carr, Charles S. Clark, Jeremiah G. Coder, Joseph DiSciullo, Nicole A. Duarte, Amy S. Elliott, Wesley Elmore, Meredith Fath, Patrice L. Gay, Charles Gnaedinger, Samuel D. Goldfarb, Robert Goulder, Joann Christine Harris, Stephanie M. Hench, Shonda Humphrey, David Randall Jackson, Jr., Thomas Jaworski, Michael H. Joe, Henry B. Jones, Eric L. Kroh, Ashley C. Newell, Charles C. O'Toole, Kristen A. Parillo, Pat Price, Karen Jeanne Setze, Andy Sheets, Doug Sheppard, Margaret Shreve, Quintin Simmons, Jasper B. Smith, David D. Stewart, Frederick W. Stokeld, Martin A. Sullivan, Joseph Thorndike, Joann M. Weiner, Nicola M. White, Risa D. Williams, Sam Young, Gulnar Zaman.

TECHNOLOGY COMMERCIALIZATION—(703) 522–6648; P.O. Box 100595, Arlington, VA 22210: Neil A. MacDonald.

TELECOMMUNICATIONS REPORTS—(202) 842–8923; 1015 15th Street, NW., 10th Floor, Washington, DC 20005: Paul J. Barbagallo, John P. Curran, Carrie R. DeLeon, Ted Gotsch, Maureen King, Paul S. Kirby, Lynn E. Stanton.

TEXTILE WORLD—(703) 421–5283; 20911 Royal Villa Terrace, Potomac Falls, VA 20165: James A. Morrissey.

THE CANCER LETTER—(202) 362–1809; 3821 Woodley Road, NW., Washington, DC 20016: Paul Goldberg, Kirsten Goldberg.

THE HILL—(202) 628–8500; 1625 K Street, NW., Suite 900, Washington, DC 20006: Walter P. Alarkon, Jared L. Allen, Aaron Blake, Kevin J. Bogardus, Alexander Bolton, Silla A. Brush, Susan Crabtree, Robert Cusack, Albert Eisele, Emily L. Goodin, Hugo Gurdon, Molly K. Hooper, Jeremy P. Jacobs, Bridget C. Johnson, Kristofer E. Kitto, Klaus Marre, Jim L. Mills, Michael P. O'Brien, Katherine M. Oczypok, Betsy Rothstein, J. Taylor Rushing, Michael A. Sandler, Jim Snyder, Mike Soraghan, Alexandra B. Stoddard, Ian B. Swanson, Roxana Tiron, Christina W. Wilkie, Reid H. Wilson, Christopher J. Yager, Jennifer Yingling, Jeffrey Young, Sam A. Youngman, Eric M. Zimmermann.

THOMPSON PUBLISHING GROUP—(202) 872–4000; 805 15th Street, NW., 3rd Floor, Washington, DC 20005: Jerry Ashworth, Cameron S. Ayers, Sarah Barak, Marissa R. Bialecki, Andrew D. Brownstein, Max S. Busetti, Michael Cardman, Richard Crider, Elizabeth A. Deutermann, Charles J. Edwards, Maryam Enayat, Joan Marie Flynn, Kelli L. Gavant, James T. Hart, Mark E. Heckathorn, Luis Hernandez, Travis Hicks, William S. Hoffman, Donald B. Hoffman, John F. Iekel, Jean E. Kizer, Denise Lamoreaux, Todd H. Leeuwenburgh, Eric J. Lucey, Joe Lustig, Daniel J. Macy, Barbara Magill, Max Manasevit, Dale McGeehon, Kathryn A. McGovern, Margaret H. Miller, Patrick E. Moehrle, Christopher Scott Morin, Lindsey E. Mullen, James B. Patterson, Mark Reishus, Jeffrey Schomisch, John Forrest Scorza, David A. Slaughter, Dennis A. Tosh, Gwendolyn Vample, Andrew A. White, Kelli G. York.

TIME INC., ESSENCE MAGAZINE—(202) 861–4000; 1130 Connecticut Avenue, NW., Washington, DC 20036: Cynthia D. Gordy, Nina J. Easton, Julie Schlosser Chandraseraran.

TIME INC., PEOPLE MAGAZINE—(202) 861–4000; 1130 Connecticut Avenue, NW., Washington, DC 20036: Sandra Sobieraj.

TIME INC., TIME MAGAZINE—(202) 861–4000; 1130 Connecticut Avenue, NW., Washington, DC 20036: Melissa A. August, Massimo T. Calabresi, Michael W. Duffy, Aparisim Ghosh, Jay Newton-Small, Michael B. Scherer, Amy E. Sullivan, Mark J. Thompson, Karen Tumulty, Michael Weisskopf.

TRANSPORTATION WEEKLY—(703) 371–1226; 2301 North Stafford Street, Arlington, VA 22207: Jeffrey J. Davis.

U.S. MEDICINE—(202) 463–6000; 1004 17th Street, NW., Suite 1101, Washington, DC 20036: Sandra L. Basu, Matt Pueschel, Stephen Spotswood.

U.S. NEWS & WORLD REPORT—(202) 955–2000; 1050 Thomas Jefferson Street, NW., Washington, DC 20007: Stephen Terry Atlas, Michael D. Barone, Paul Bedard, Lynne Edwards, Kent D. Garber, Alex Kingsbury, Anna Mulrine, Thomas E. Omestad, James M. Pethokoukis, Eddy G. Ramirez Esparza, Amanda E. Ruggeri, Robert E.K. Schlesinger, Nicole E. Schwab, Katherine M. Skiba, Kenneth T. Walsh, Kevin Whitelaw.

UCG—(301) 287–2700; 9737 Washington Boulevard, Suite 100, Gaithersburg, MD 20878: Carl Ayers, Laura O. Evans, Fran Fanshel, Charles Fiegl, Rachel Gantz, Jessica C. Gdowski, Lisa Getter, Robert Gough, Richard D. Hadley, Marci K. Heydt, Grant G. Huang, Wendy Johnson, Spencer Kelly, Hugh Kennedy, Scott Kraft, Corinne Kuypers-Denlinger, Karen S. Long, Kevin B. McDermott, Burt Schorr, Aaron Steinberg, Jonathan D. Stern, Vincent E. Taylor, Maria Tsigas, Sandra Yin.

PERIODICALS REPRESENTED IN PRESS GALLERIES—Continued

USA JOURNAL—(202) 714–7330; P.O. Box 714, Washington, DC 20044: Janne Kum Cha C. Pak.

VANITY FAIR—(202) 244–3424; 5146 Klingle Street, NW., Washington, DC 20016: Dee Dee Myers, Maureen Orth, Laura J. Parker, William W. Prochnay, Todd S. Purdum.

WASHINGTON BLADE—(202) 661–8075; 529 14th Street, NW., Suite 545, Washington, DC 20045: Amy L. Cavanaugh, Louis M. Chibbaro, Jr., Joey DiGuglielmo, Chris C. Johnson, Joshua J. Lynsen.

WASHINGTON BUSINESS INFORMATION—(703) 538–7600; 300 North Washington Street, Suite 200, Falls Church, VA 22046: Theresa Barry, David P. Belian, Martin J. Berman-Gorvine, Renee L. Frojo, Christopher E. Hollis, Elizabeth Jones, Nicholas J. Wills.

WASHINGTON BUSINESS JOURNAL—(703) 258–0845; 1555 Wilson Boulevard, Suite 400, Arlington, VA 22209: Kent Hoover.

WASHINGTON CITY PAPER—(202) 332–2100; 2390 Champlain Street, NW., Washington, DC 20009: Mike DeBonis, Ruth D. Samuelson.

WASHINGTON COUNSELETTER—(202) 244–6709; 5712 26th Street, NW., Washington, DC 20015: Deborah A. Kavruck.

WASHINGTON TRADE DAILY—(301) 946–0817; P.O. Box 1802, Wheaton, MD 20915: Mary Berger, James R. Berger.

WASHINGTON WATCH—(301) 263–9023; 5923 Onondaga Road, Bethesda, MD 20816: Kazutami Yamazaki.

WASHINGTONIAN—(202) 296–3600; 1828 L Street, NW., Suite 200, Washington, DC 20036: Susan Baer, Kim Eisler, Garrett Graff, Harry S. Jaffe, Denise M. Kersten, Emily B. Leaman, John Limpert, Drew Lindsay.

WATERWAYS JOURNAL—(703) 524–2490; 5220 North Carlin Springs Road, Arlington, VA 22203: Carlo J. Salzano.

WEBSTER COMMUNICATIONS—(703) 525–4013; 3835 North 9th Street, Suite 401W, Arlington, VA 22203: James C. Webster.

WEEKLY STANDARD—(202) 293–4900; 1150 17th Street, NW., Suite 505, Washington, DC 20036: Kari Barbic, Fred W. Barnes, Christopher Caldwell, Matthew Continetti, Katherine L. Eastland, Terry Eastland, Andrew Ferguson, Mary Katherine Ham, Stephen F. Hayes, Jonathan V. Last, John M. McCormack, Robert G. Messenger, Samantha K. Sault, Philip Terzian, Kevin G. Vance.

WORLD MAGAZINE—(202) 445–0454; 1300 East Capitol Street, NE., Washington, DC 20003: Emily C. Belz, Edward Pitts.

1105 GOVERNMENT INFORMATION GROUP, FEDERAL COMPUTER WEEK—(703) 876–5110; 3141 Fairview Park Drive, Suite 777, Falls Church, VA 22042: Ben S. Bain, Mary Mosquera, Timieka Nichols, David R. Rapp, Matthew Weigelt.

1105 GOVERNMENT INFORMATION GROUP, GOVERNMENT COMPUTER NEWS—(703) 876–5110; 3141 Fairview Park Drive, Suite 777, Falls Church, VA 22042: Jonathan Byus, Wyatt Kash, Gertrude Walsh.

1105 GOVERNMENT INFORMATION GROUP, WASHINGTON TECHNOLOGY—(703) 876–5110; 3141 Fairview Park Drive, Suite 777, Falls Church, VA 22042: Douglas Beizer, Alice Lipowicz, Nick Wakeman.

CONGRESSIONAL DISTRICT MAPS

ALABAMA—Congressional Districts—(7 Districts)

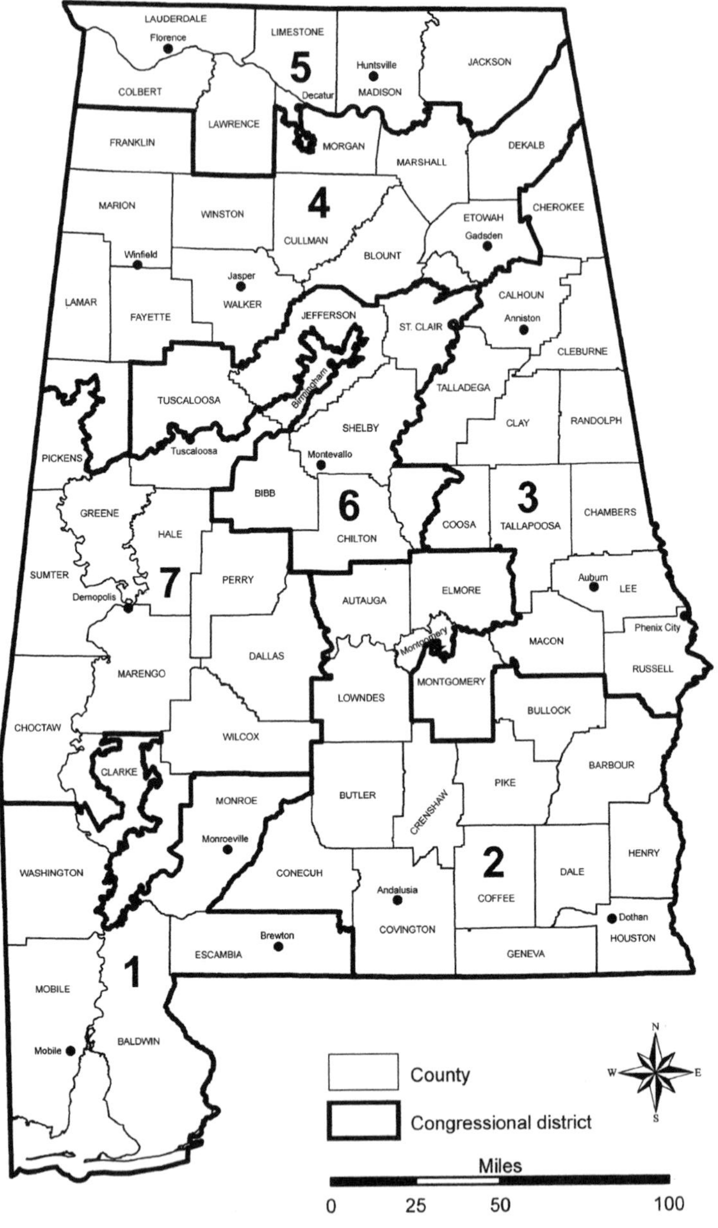

ALASKA—Congressional District—(1 District At Large)

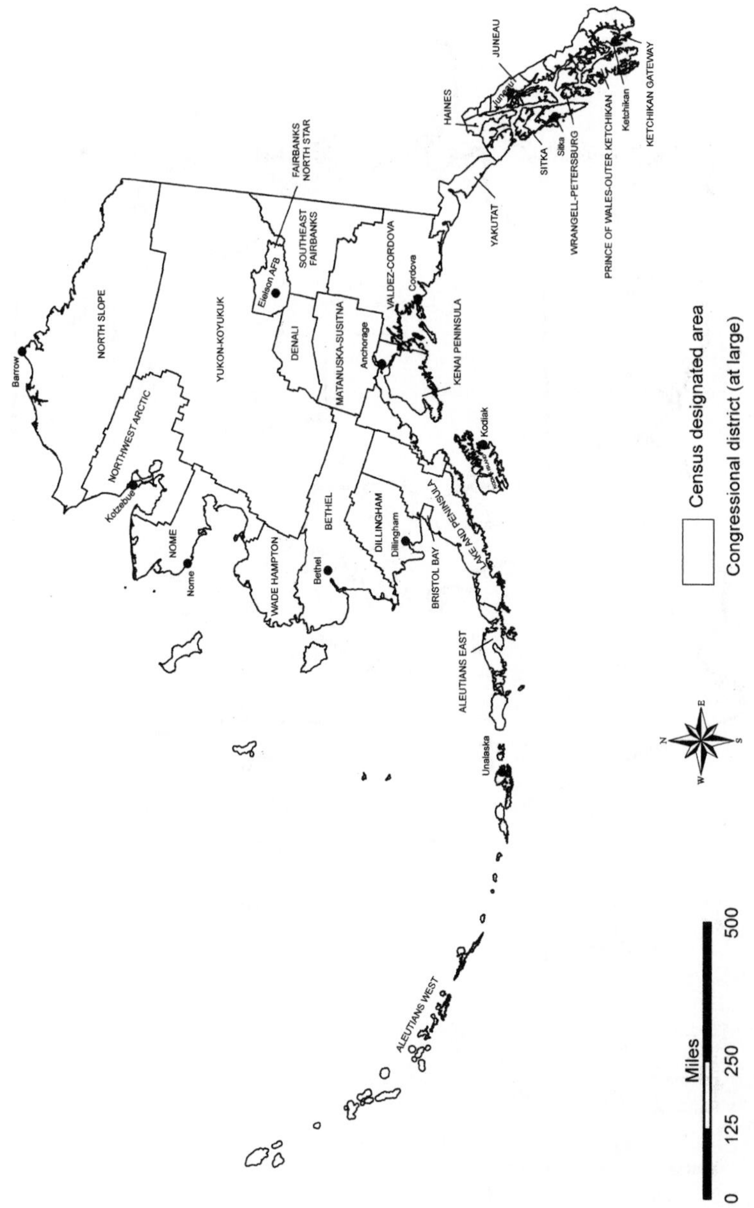

ARIZONA—Congressional Districts—(8 Districts)

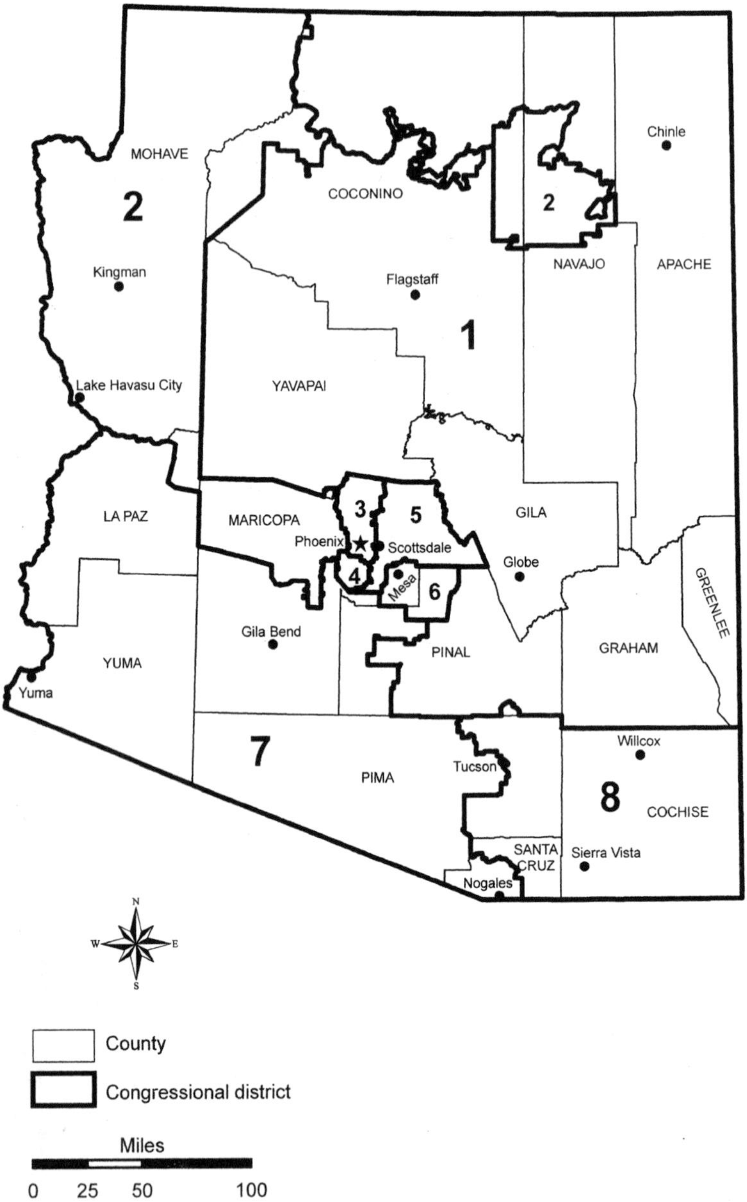

ARKANSAS—Congressional Districts—(4 Districts)

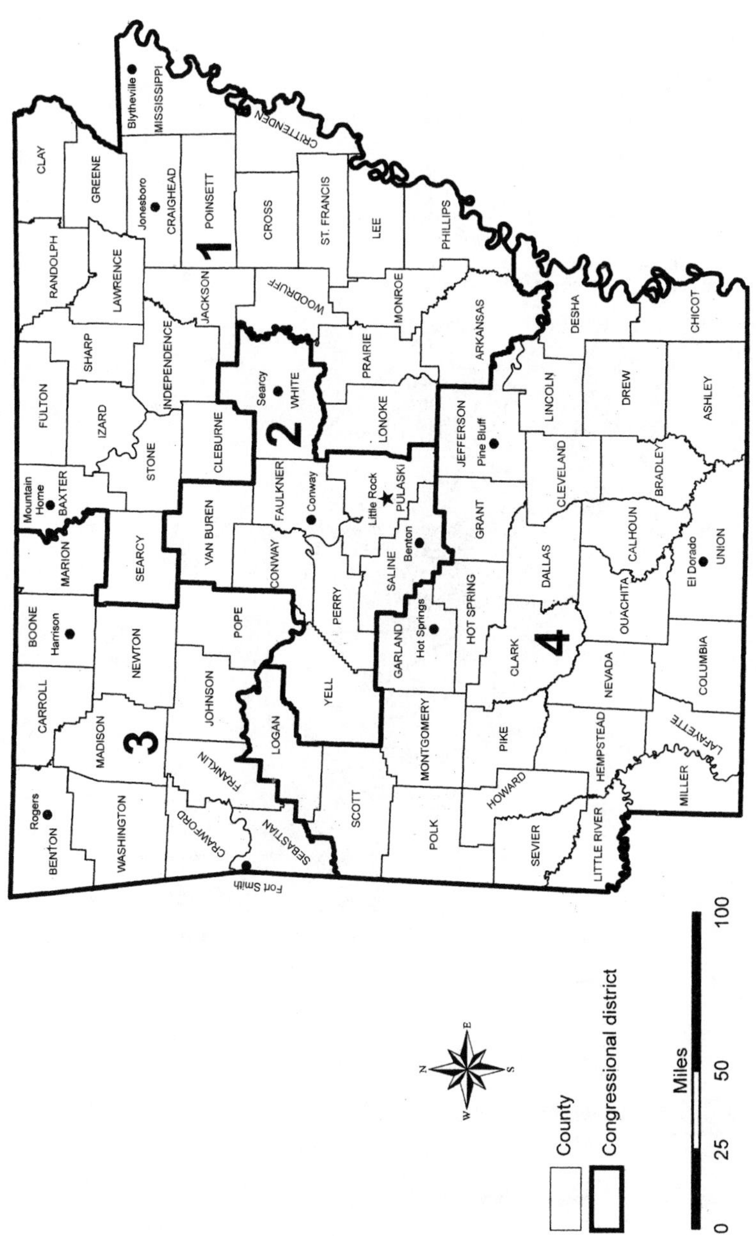

CALIFORNIA—Congressional Districts—(53 Districts)

COLORADO—Congressional Districts—(7 Districts)

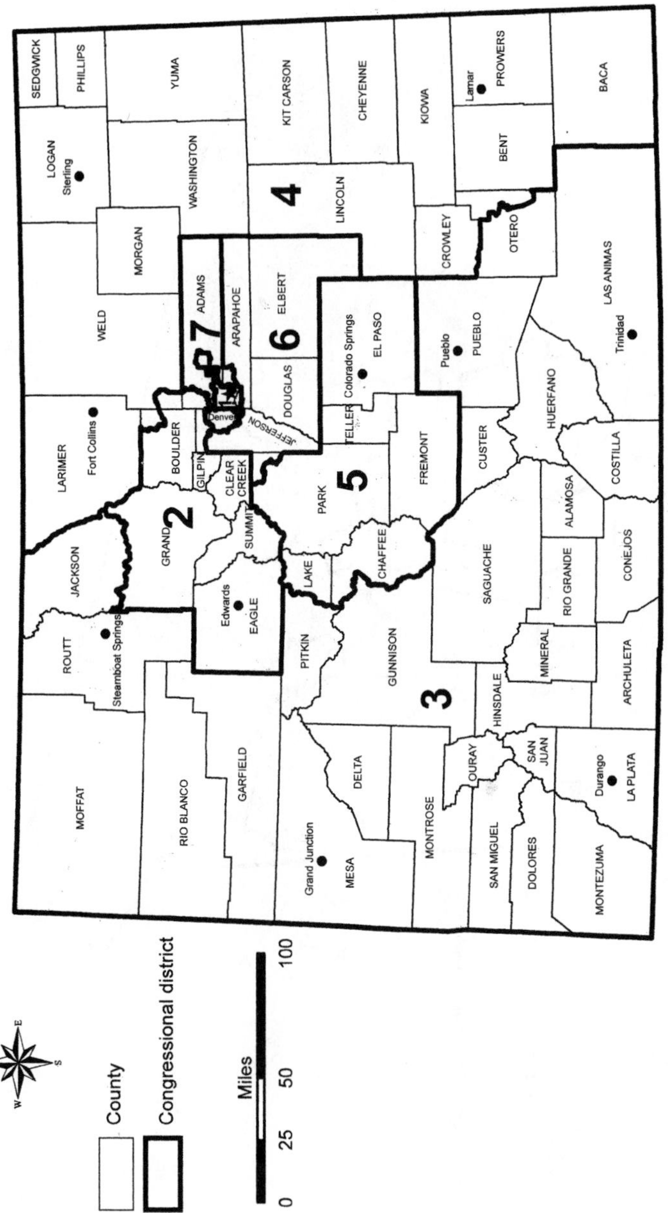

CONNECTICUT—Congressional Districts—(5 Districts)

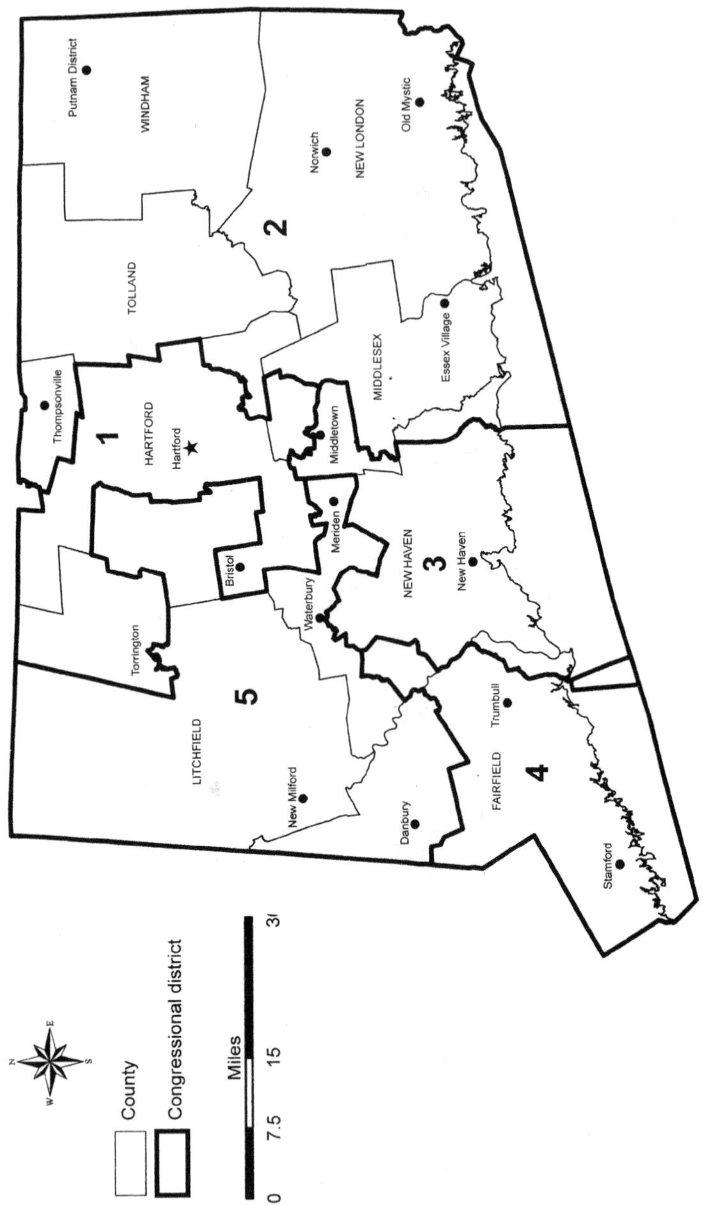

DELAWARE—Congressional District—(1 District At Large)

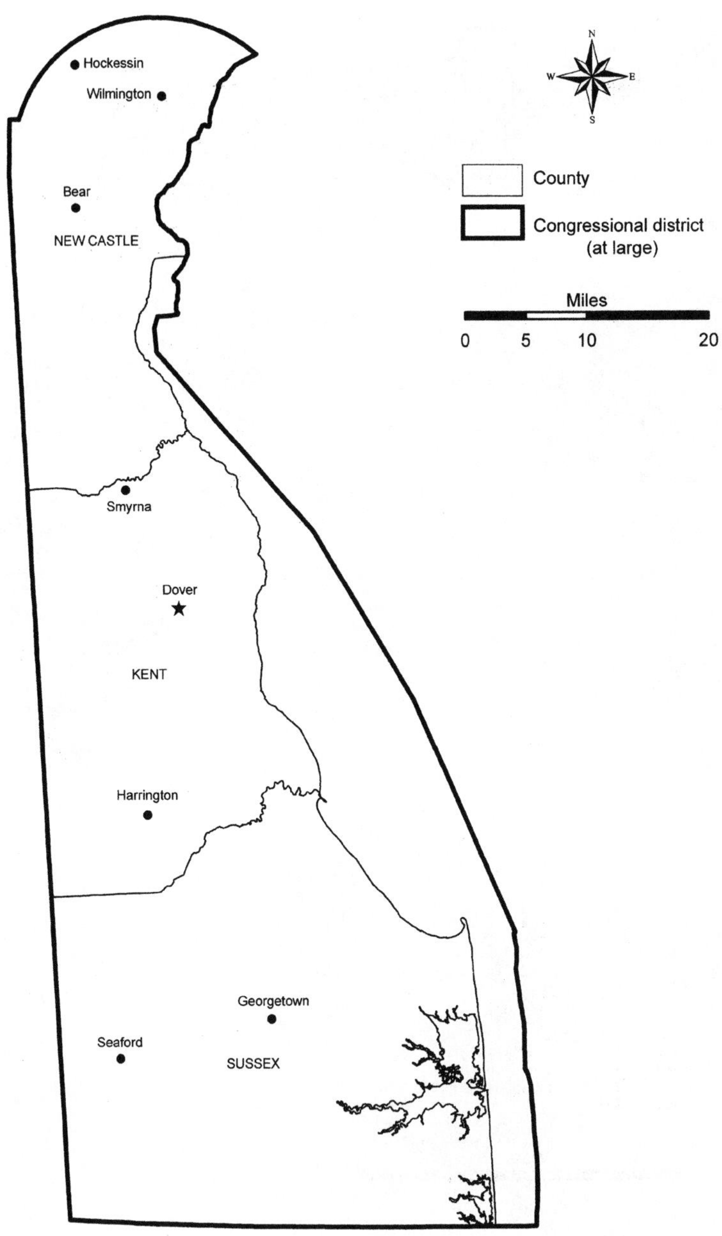

FLORIDA—Congressional Districts—(25 Districts)

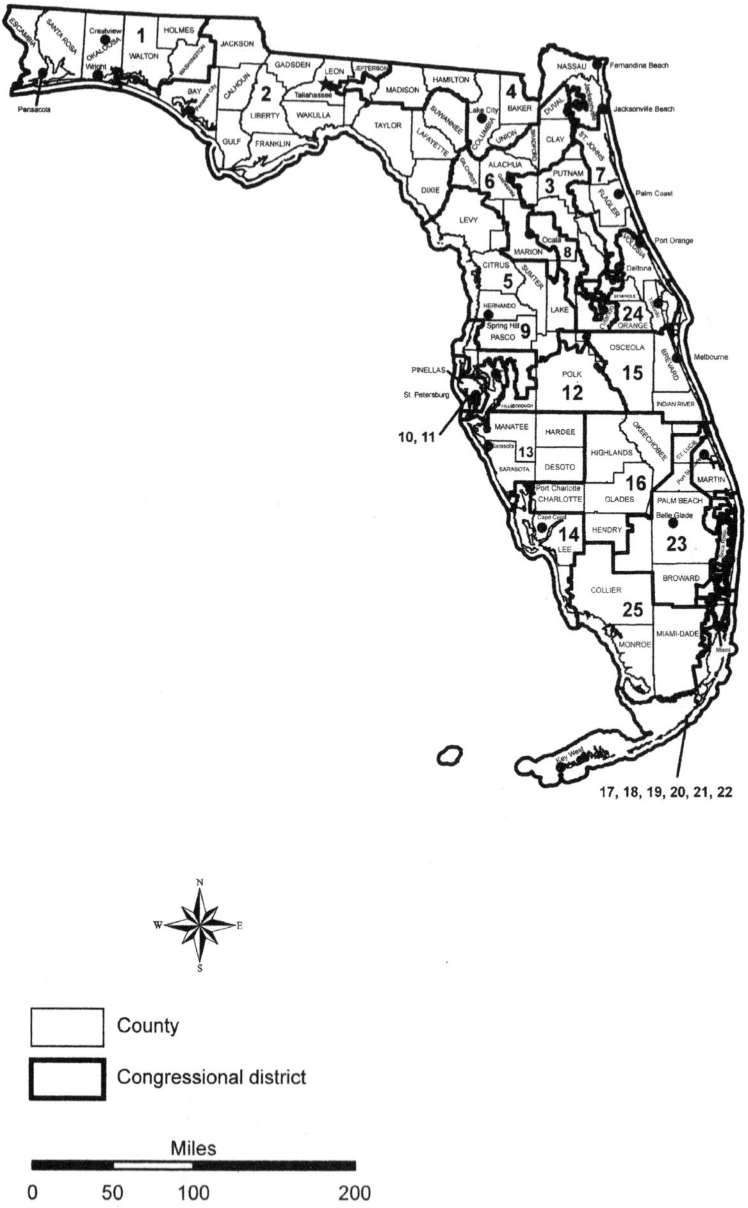

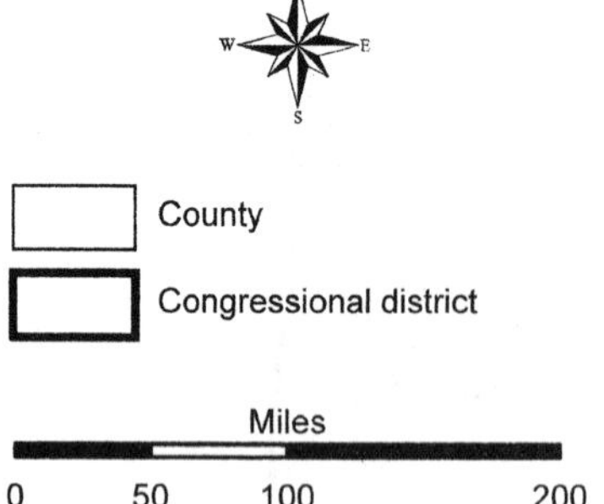

GEORGIA—Congressional Districts—(13 Districts)

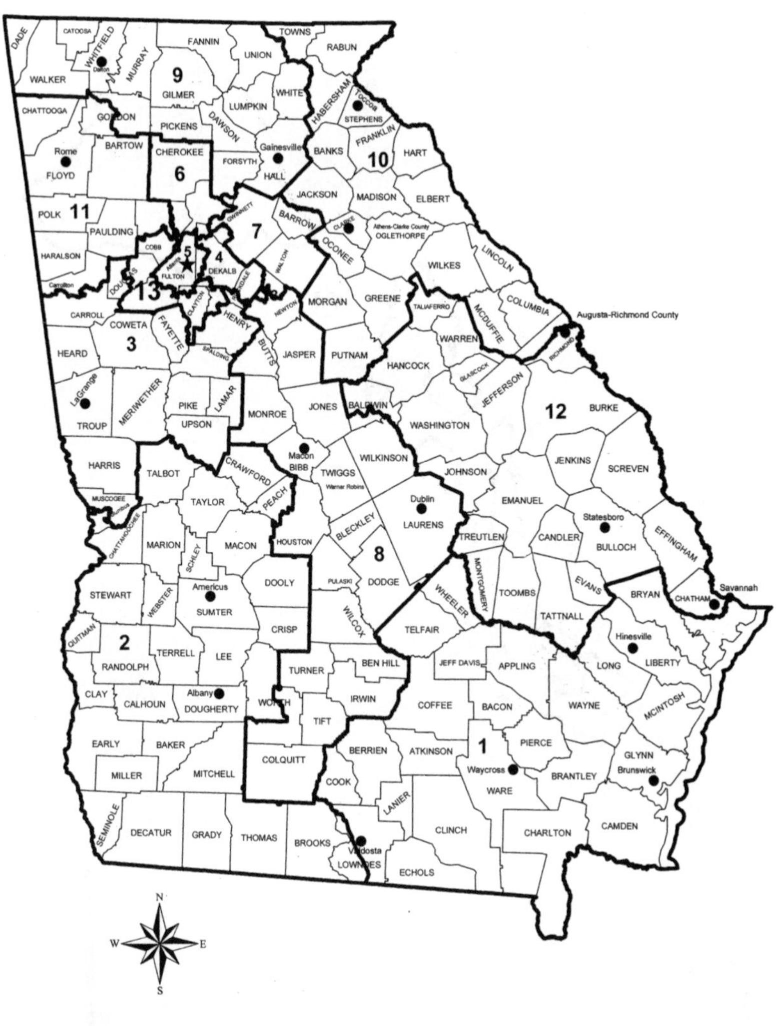

County

Congressional district
Effective May 06, 2005

Miles
0 25 50 100

HAWAII—Congressional Districts—(2 Districts)

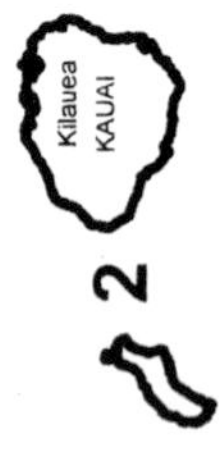

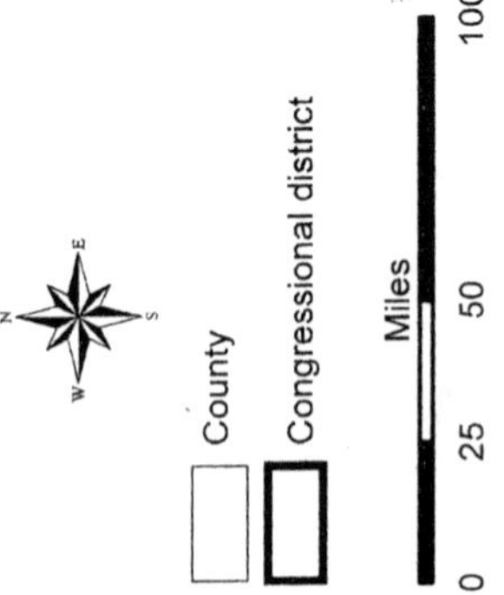

IDAHO—Congressional Districts—(2 Districts)

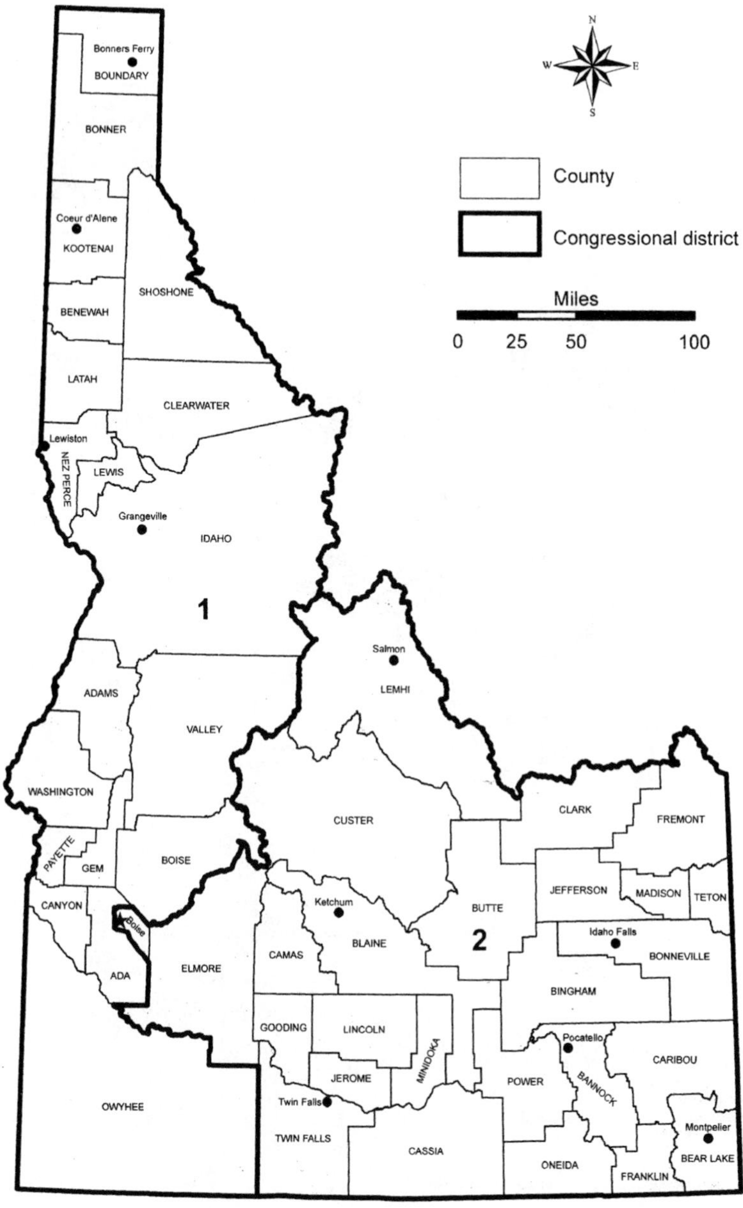

ILLINOIS—Congressional Districts—(19 Districts)

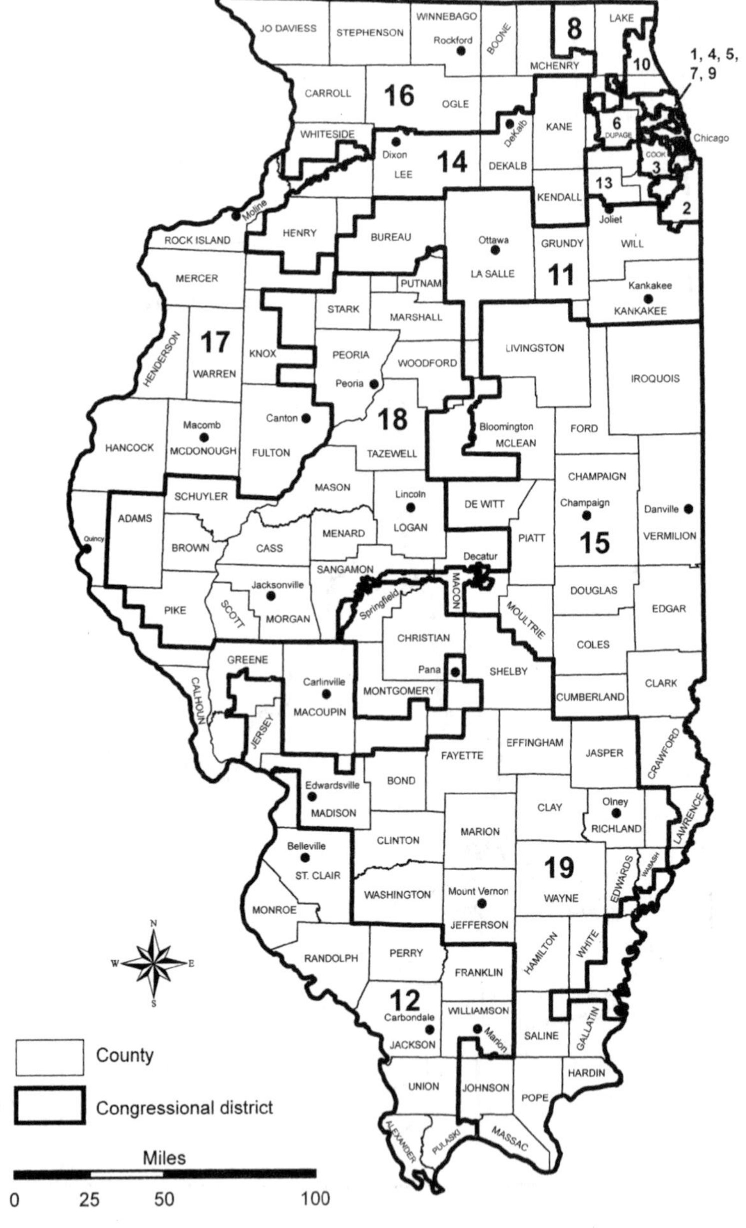

INDIANA—Congressional Districts—(9 Districts)

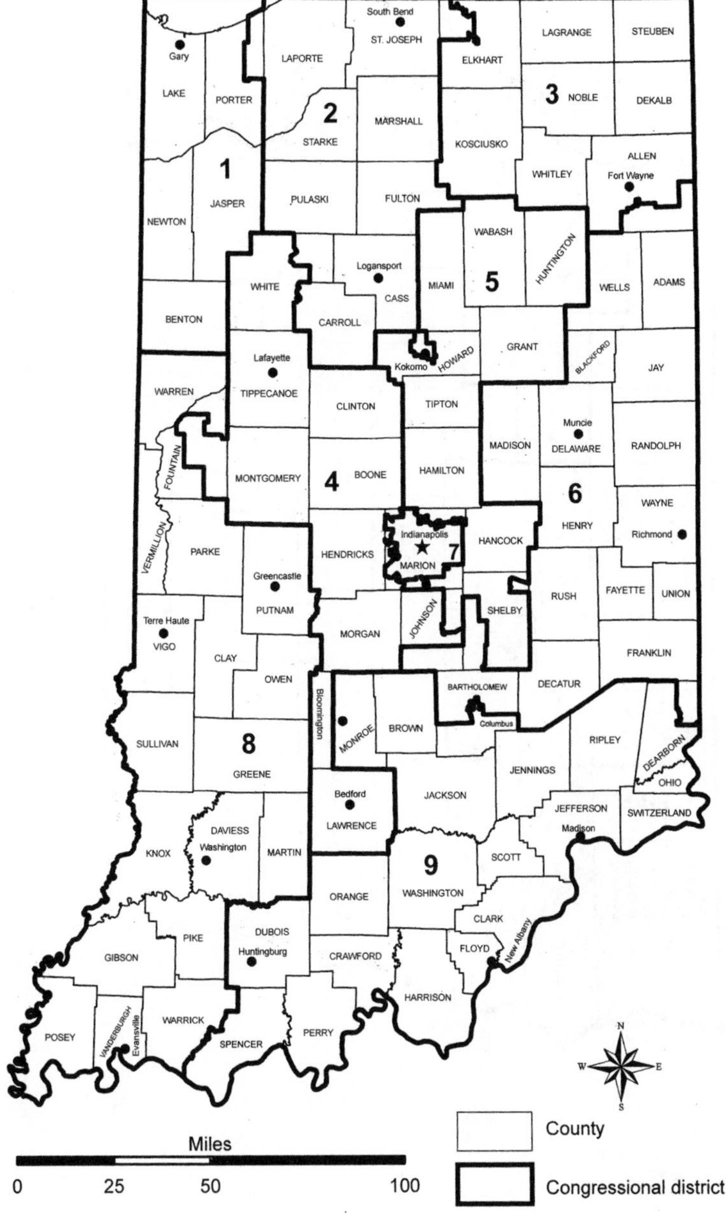

IOWA—Congressional Districts—(5 Districts)

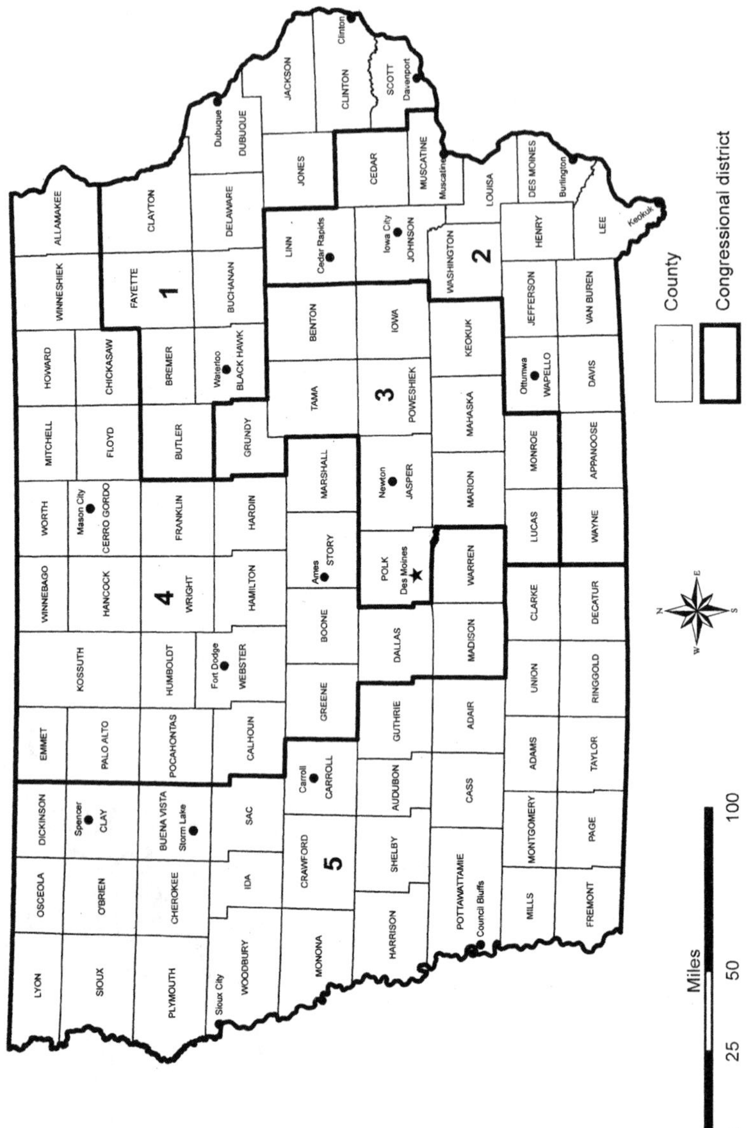

KANSAS—Congressional Districts—(4 Districts)

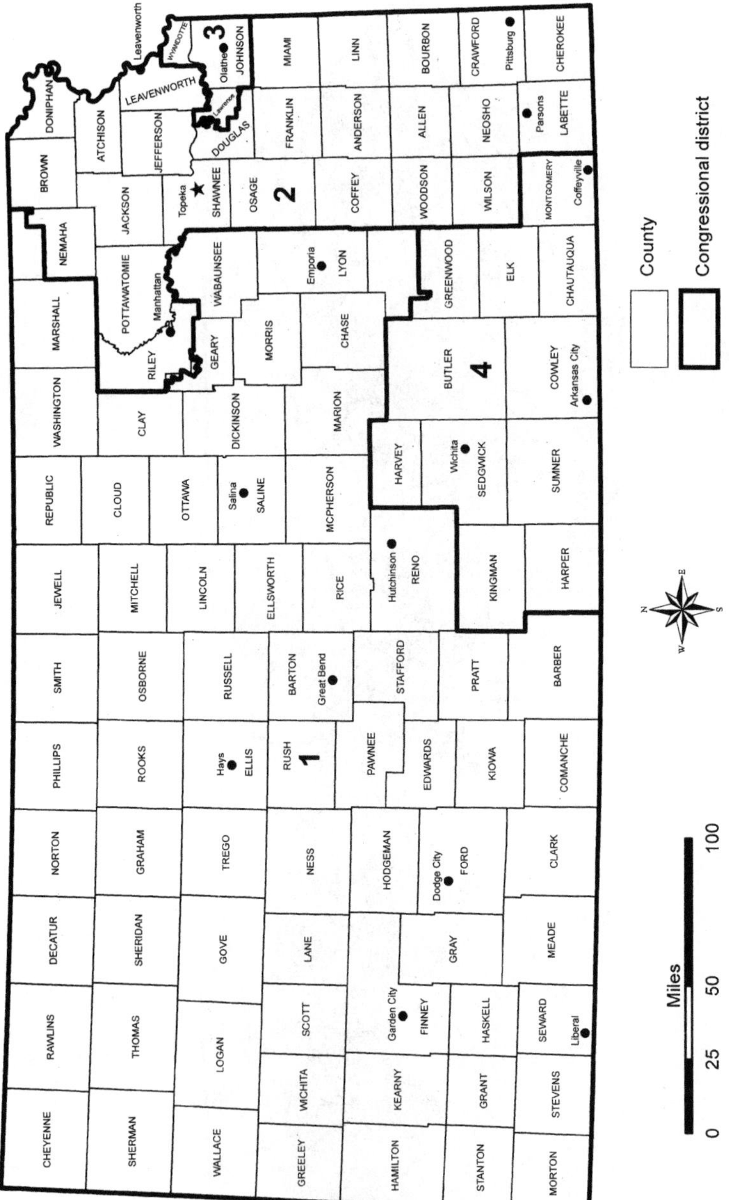

KENTUCKY—Congressional Districts—(6 Districts)

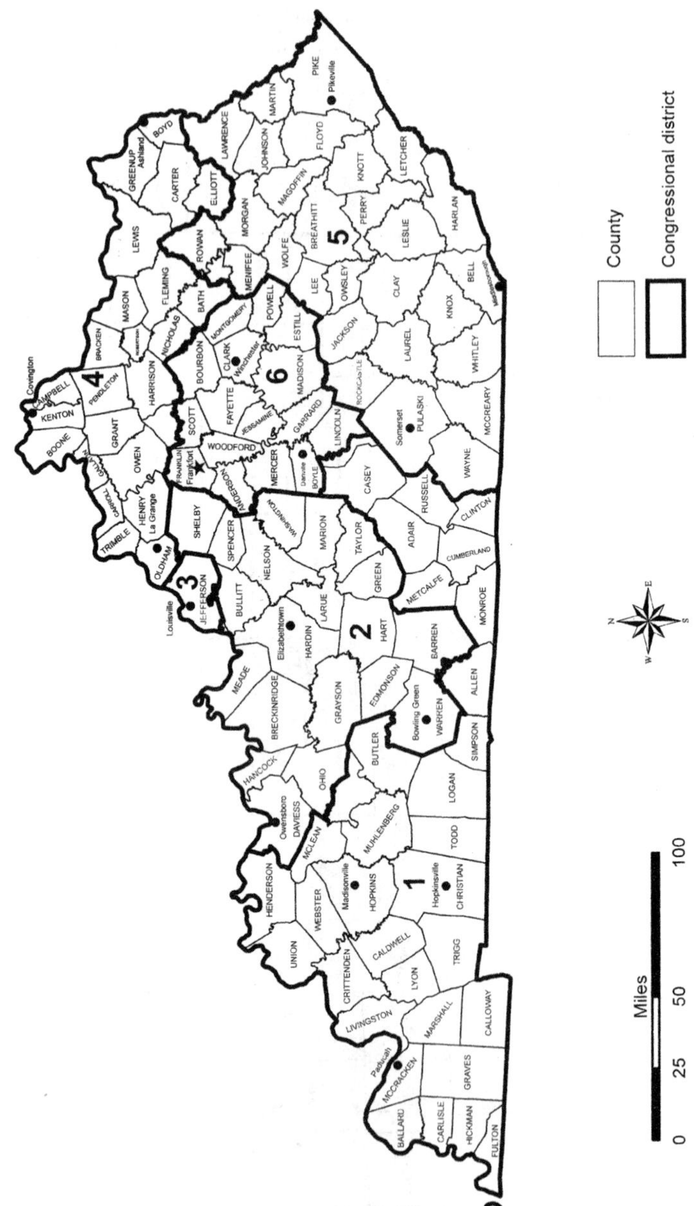

LOUISIANA—Congressional Districts—(7 Districts)

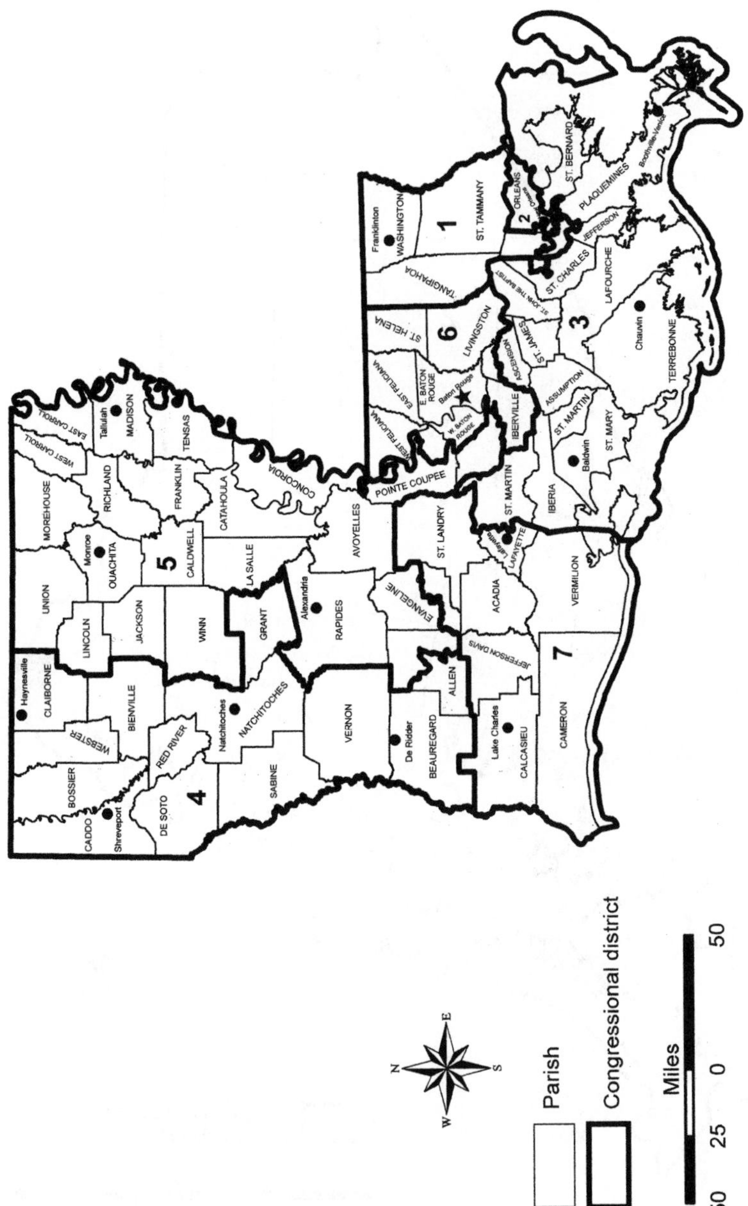

MAINE—Congressional Districts—(2 Districts)

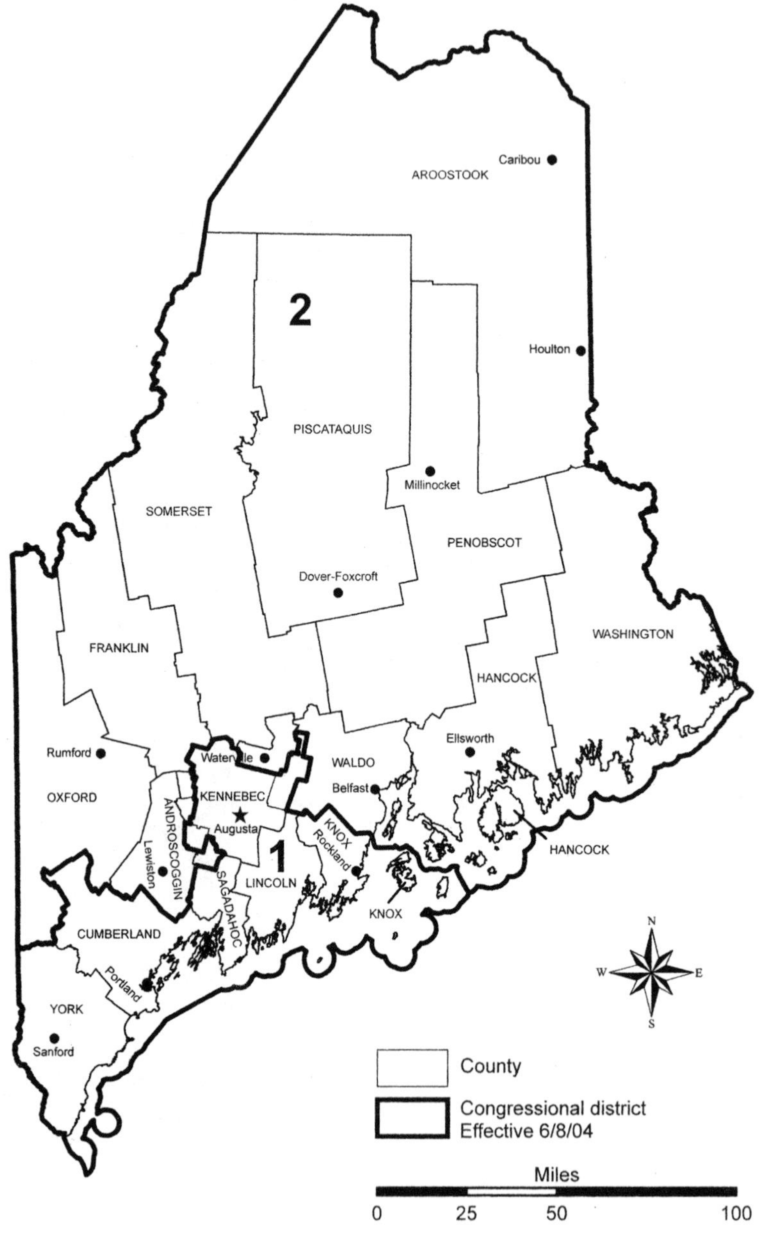

MARYLAND—Congressional Districts—(8 Districts)

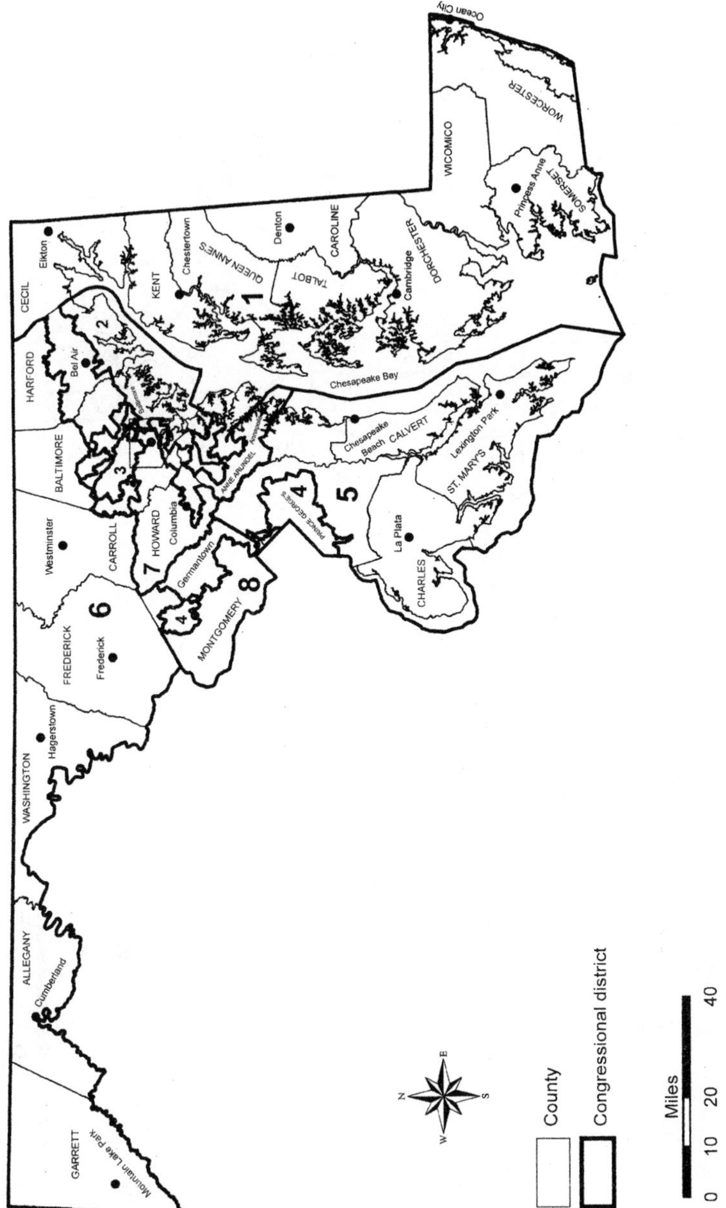

MASSACHUSETTS—Congressional Districts—(10 Districts)

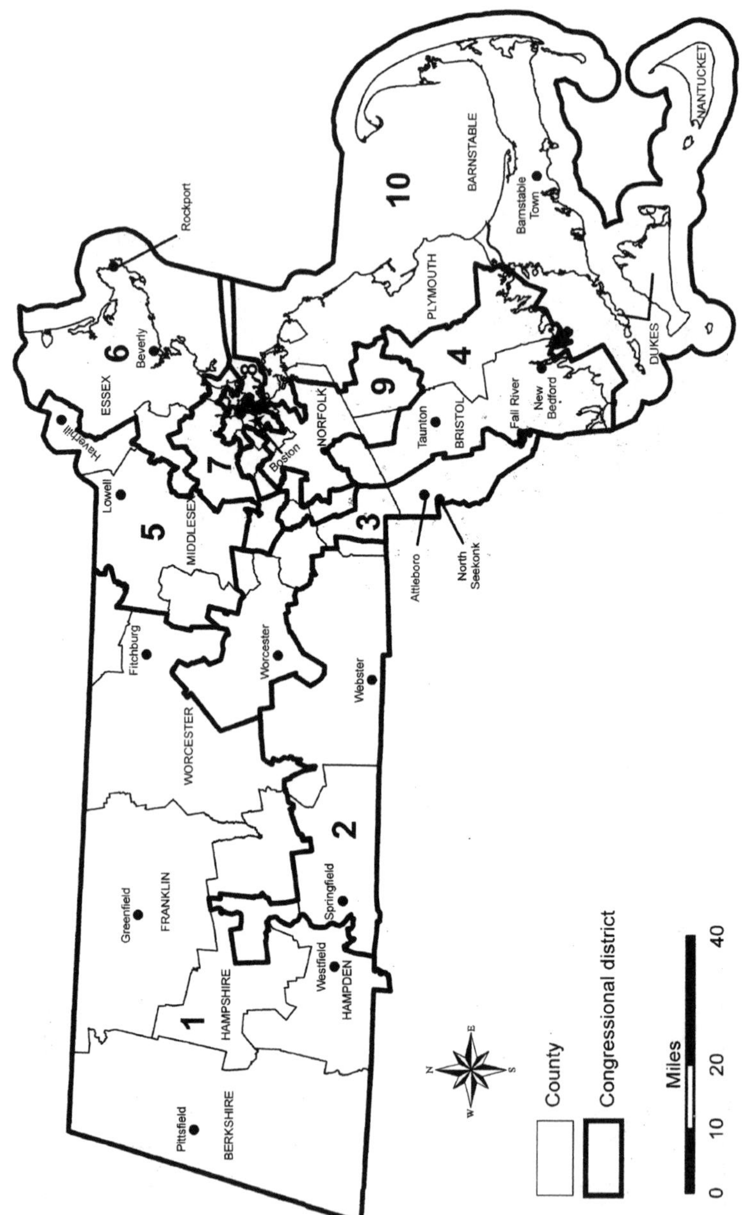

MICHIGAN—Congressional Districts—(15 Districts)

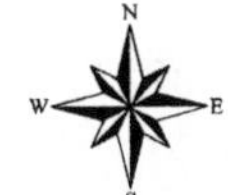

County

Congressional district

Miles

0 25 50 100

MINNESOTA—Congressional Districts—(8 Districts)

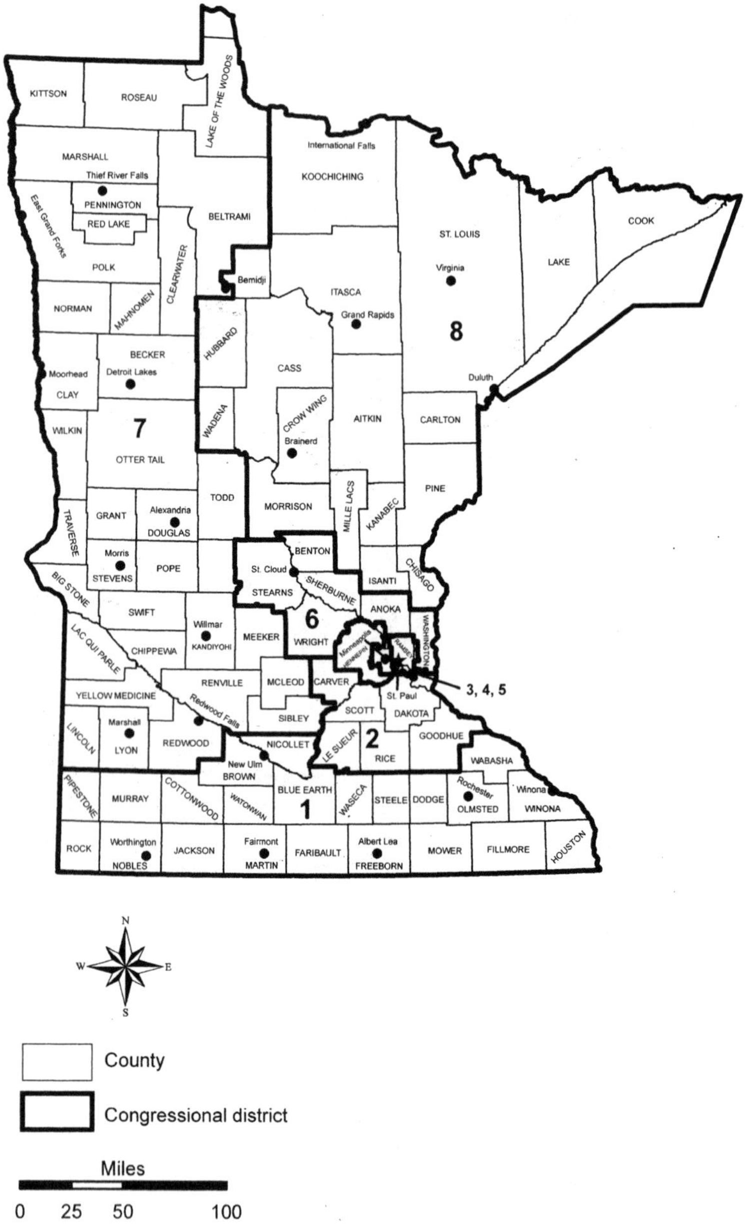

County

Congressional district

Miles

0 25 50 100

MISSISSIPPI—Congressional Districts—(4 Districts)

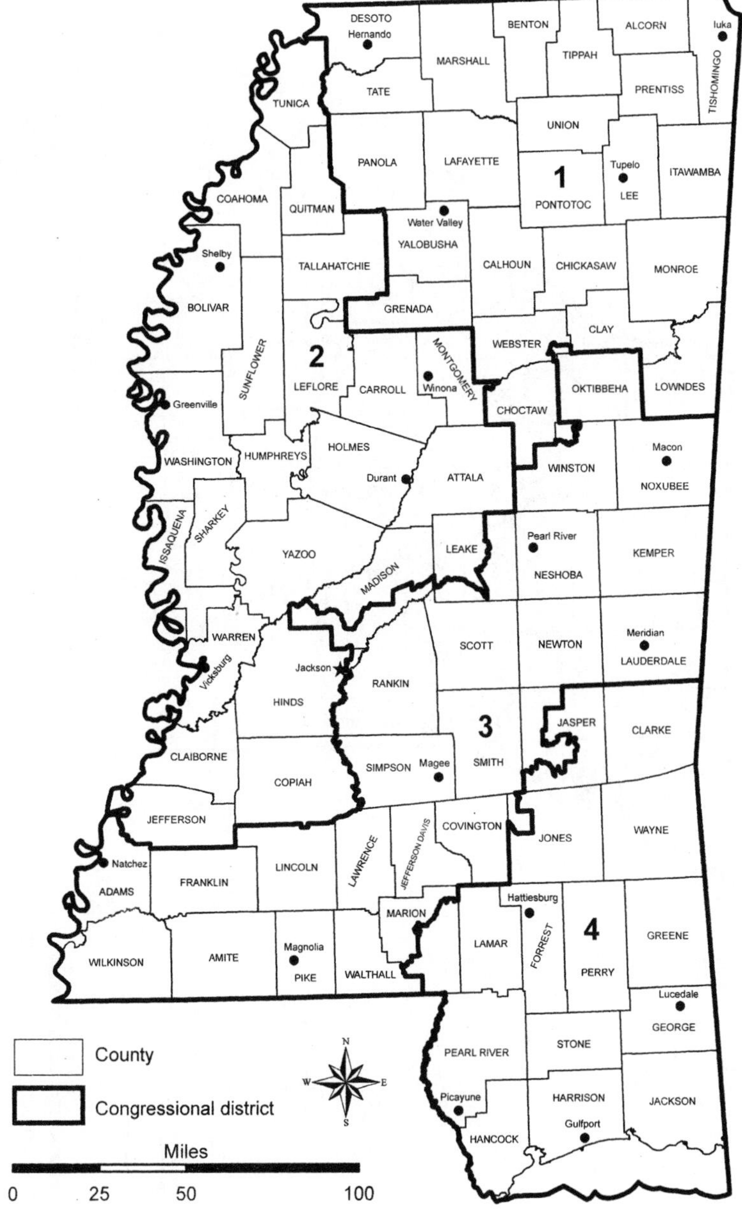

MISSOURI—Congressional Districts—(9 Districts)

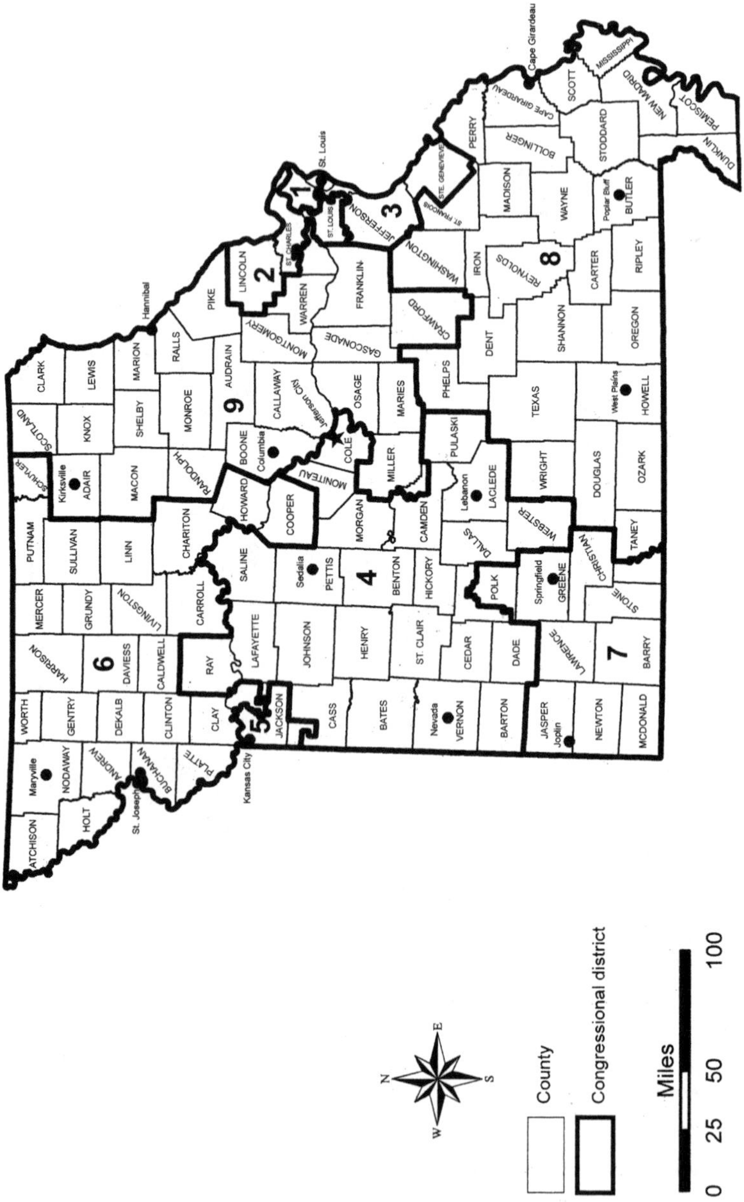

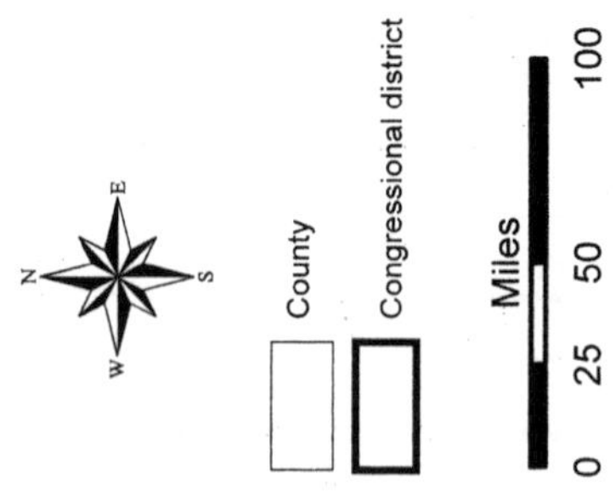

MONTANA—Congressional District—(1 District At Large)

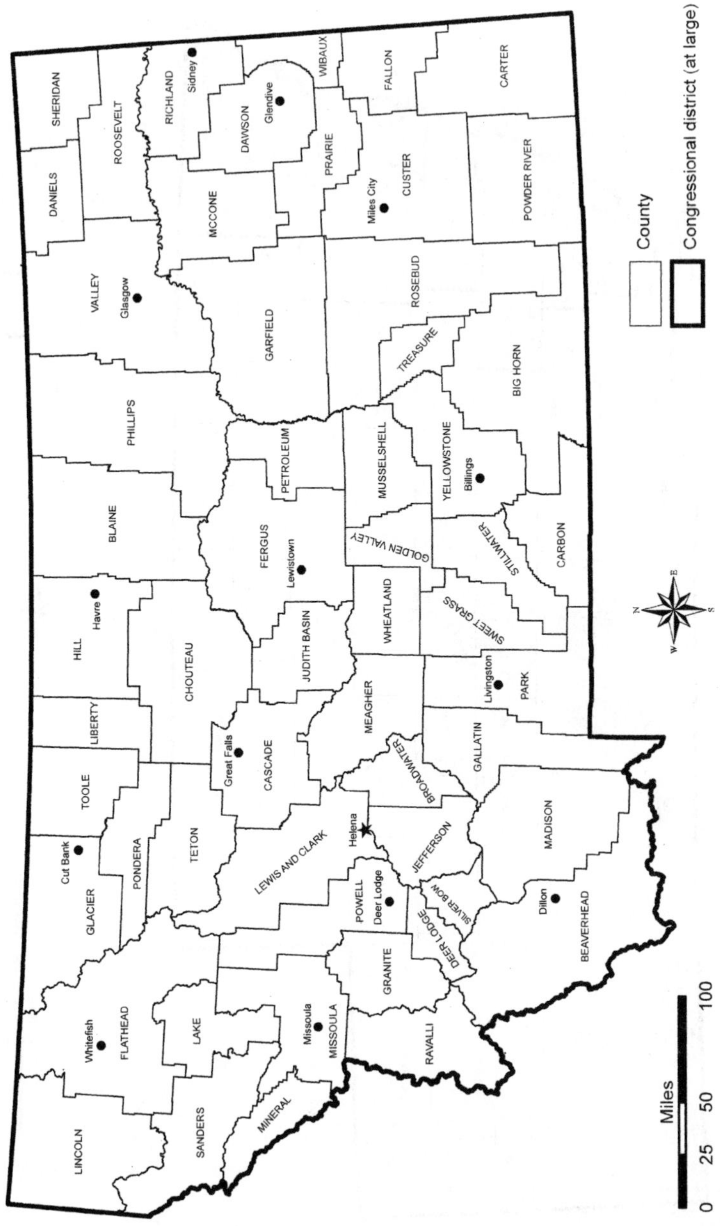

NEBRASKA—Congressional Districts—(3 Districts)

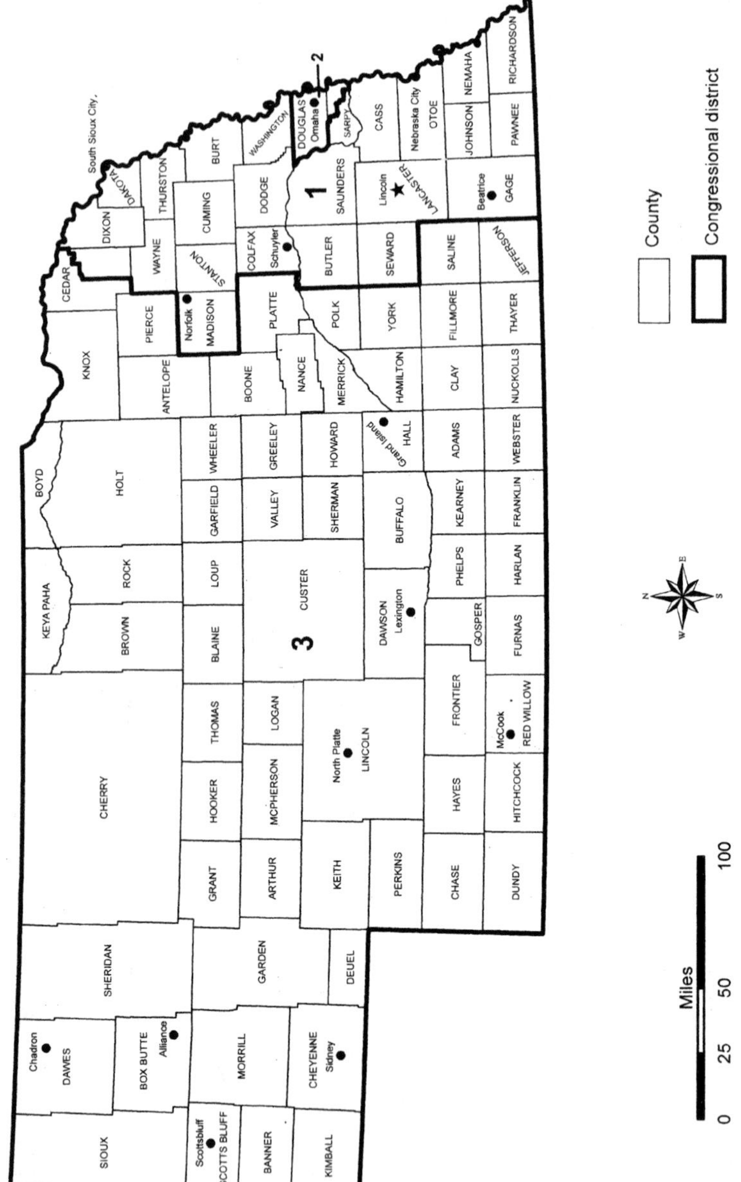

NEVADA—Congressional Districts—(3 Districts)

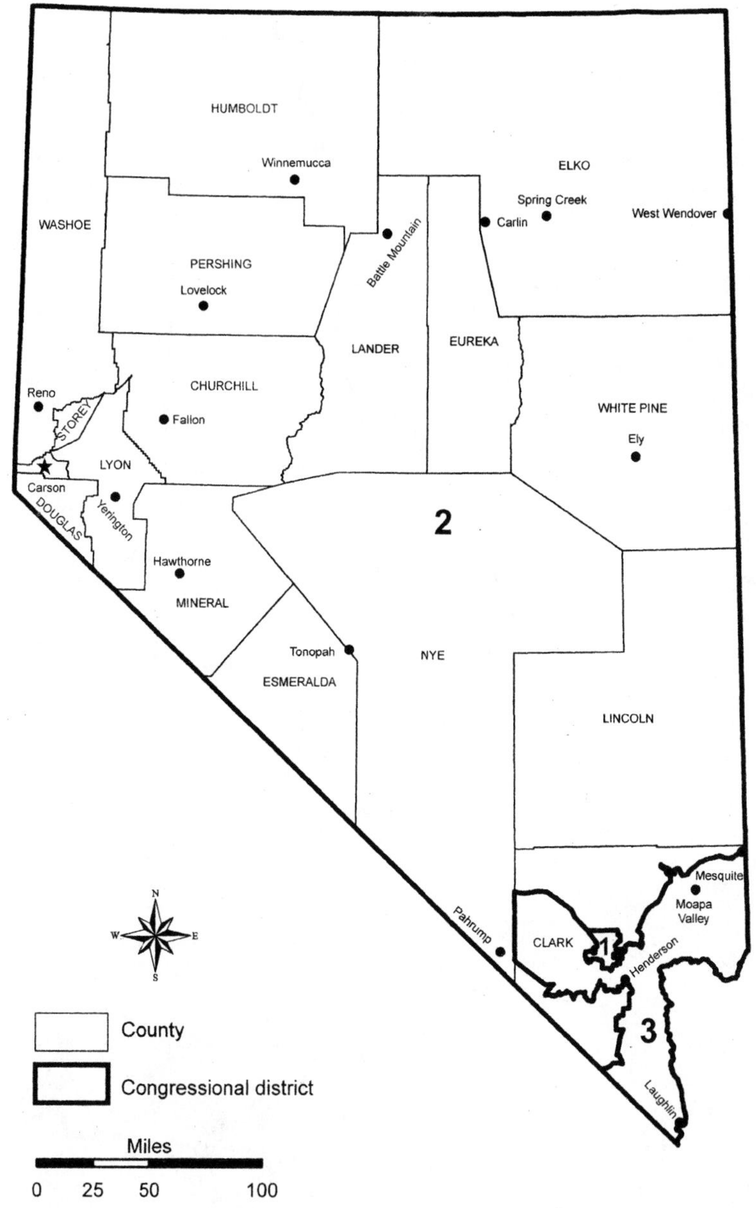

NEW HAMPSHIRE—Congressional Districts—(2 Districts)

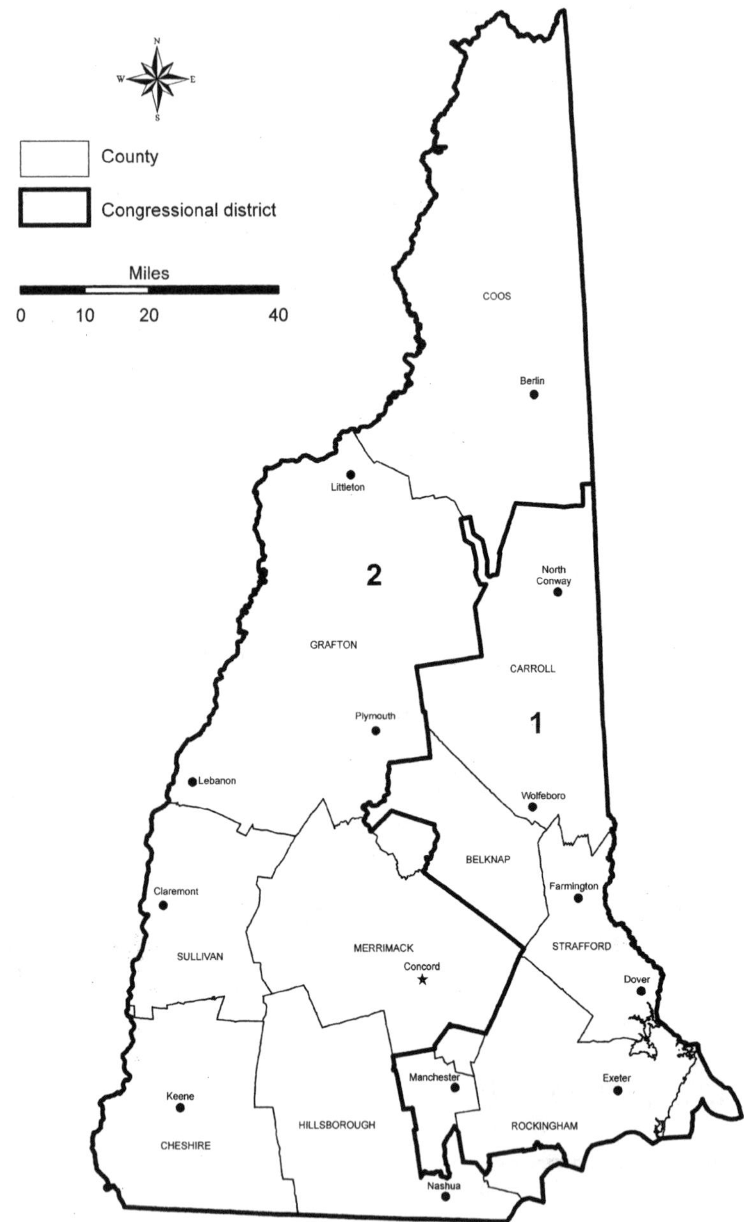

NEW JERSEY—Congressional Districts—(13 Districts)

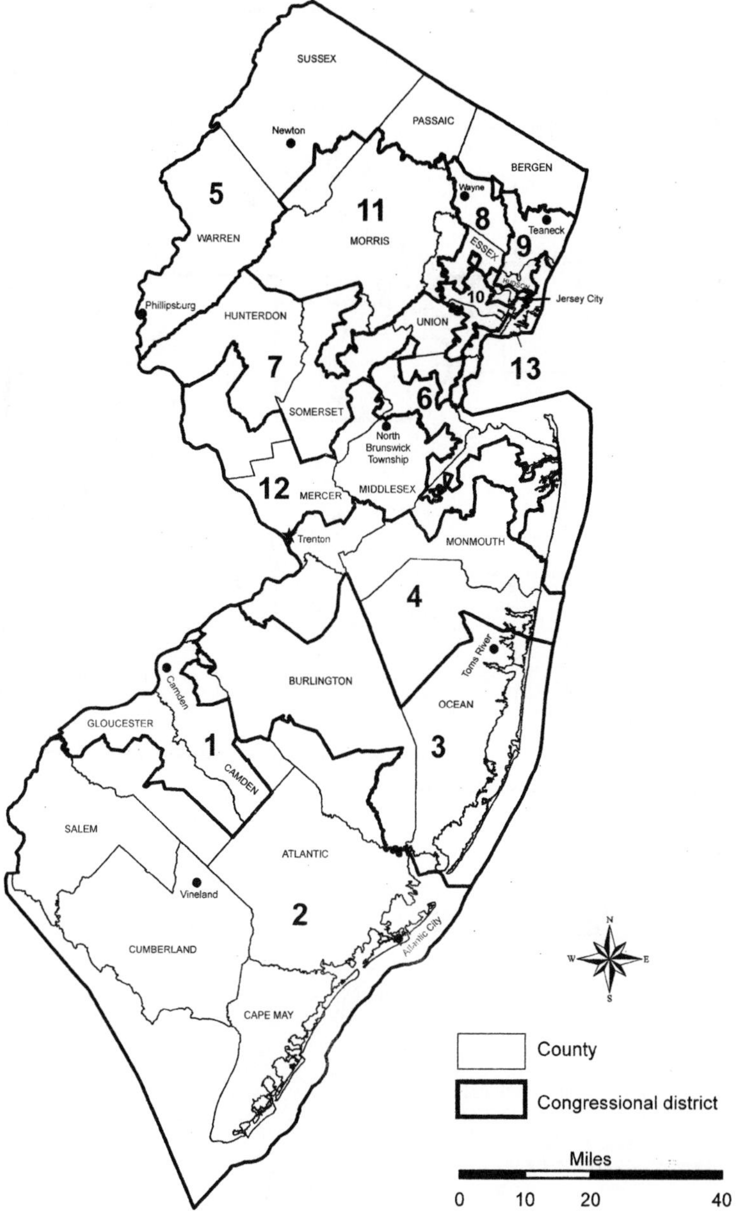

NEW MEXICO—Congressional Districts—(3 Districts)

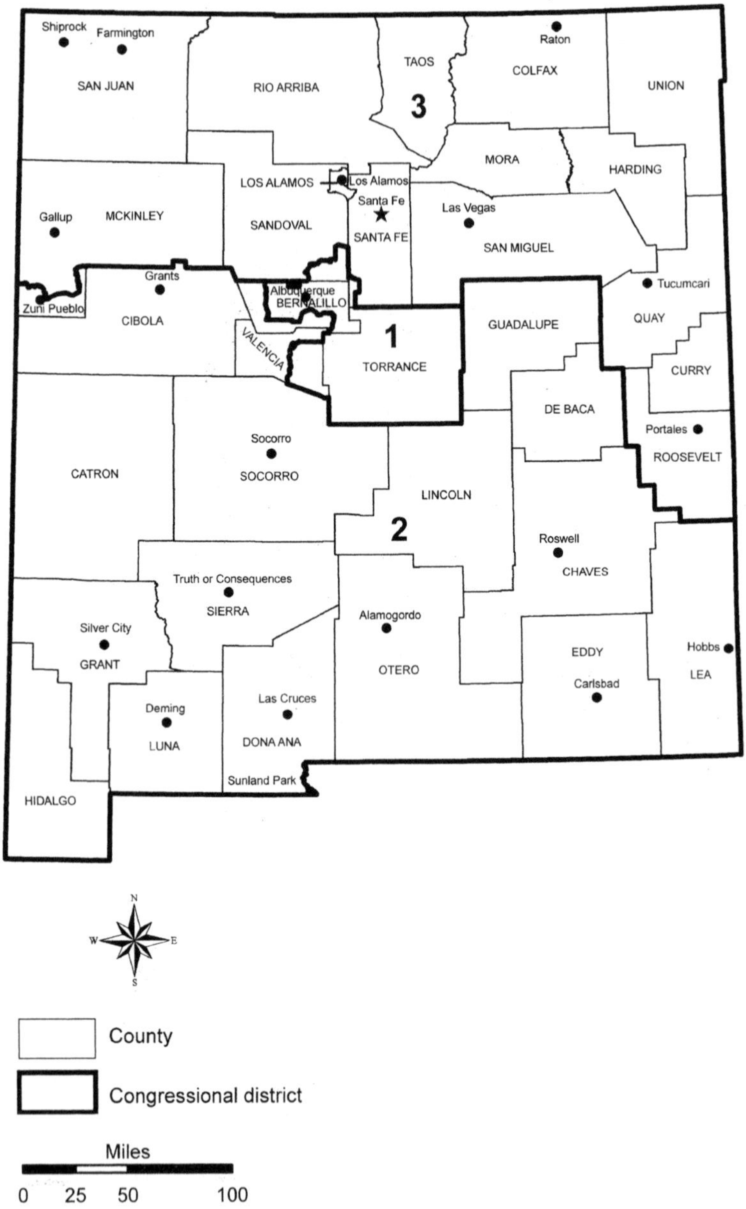

Shiprock
Farmington
SAN JUAN
RIO ARRIBA
TAOS
3
Raton
COLFAX
UNION
MORA
HARDING
LOS ALAMOS
Los Alamos
Santa Fe
SANTA FE
Gallup
MCKINLEY
SANDOVAL
Las Vegas
SAN MIGUEL
Grants
Zuni Pueblo
CIBOLA
Albuquerque
BERNALILLO
Tucumcari
QUAY
VALENCIA
1
TORRANCE
GUADALUPE
CURRY
DE BACA
Portales
ROOSEVELT
CATRON
Socorro
SOCORRO
LINCOLN
2
Roswell
CHAVES
Truth or Consequences
SIERRA
Alamogordo
OTERO
Silver City
GRANT
EDDY
Carlsbad
Hobbs
LEA
Deming
LUNA
Las Cruces
DONA ANA
Sunland Park
HIDALGO

County

Congressional district

Miles

0 25 50 100

NEW YORK—Congressional Districts—(29 Districts)

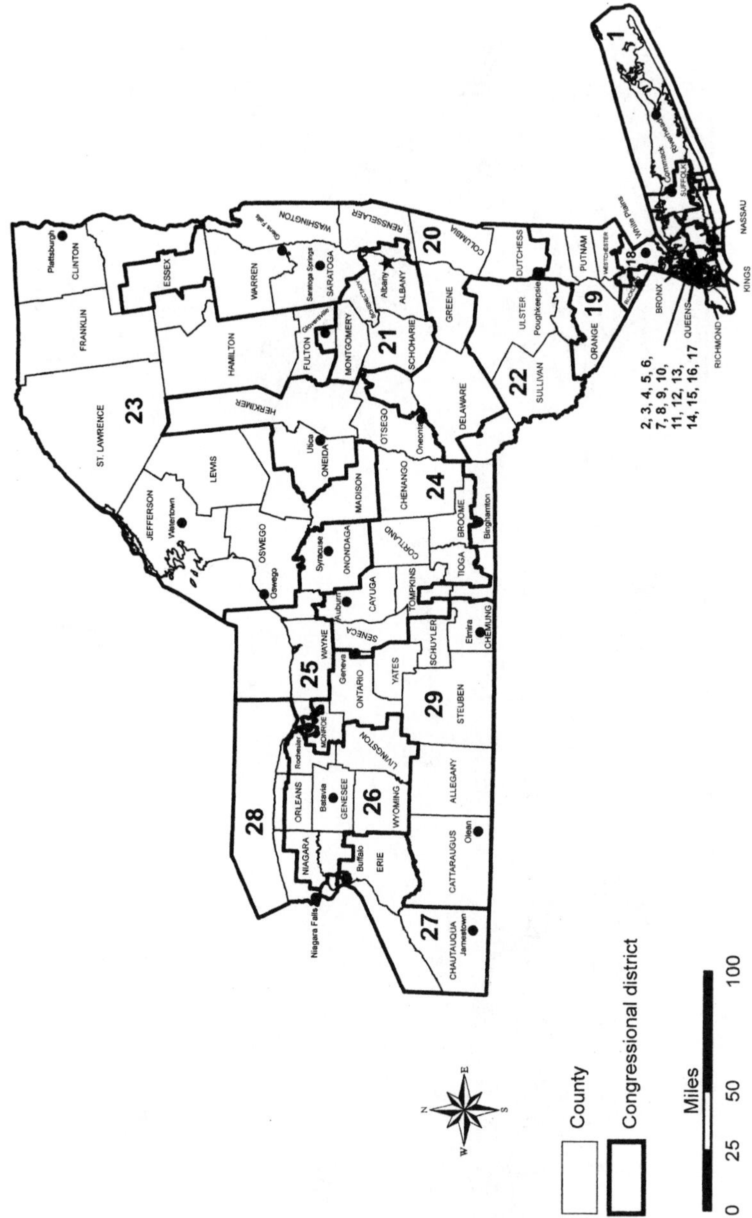

NORTH CAROLINA—Congressional Districts—(13 Districts)

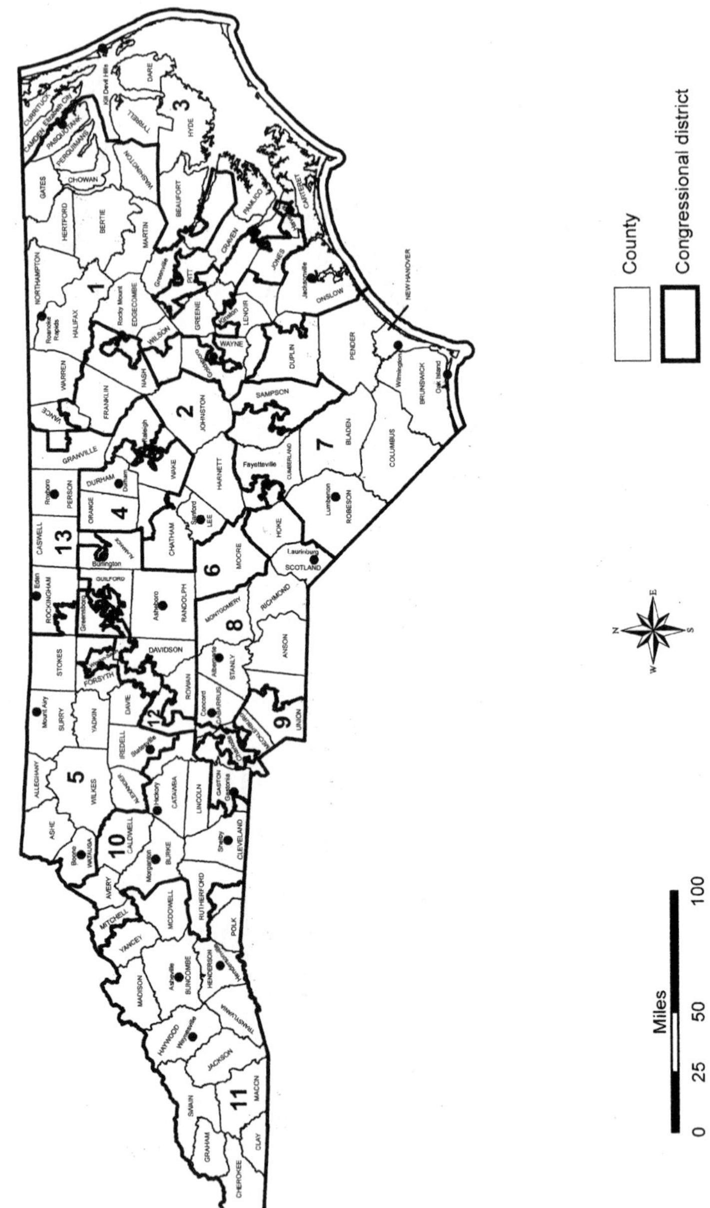

NORTH DAKOTA—Congressional District—(1 District At Large)

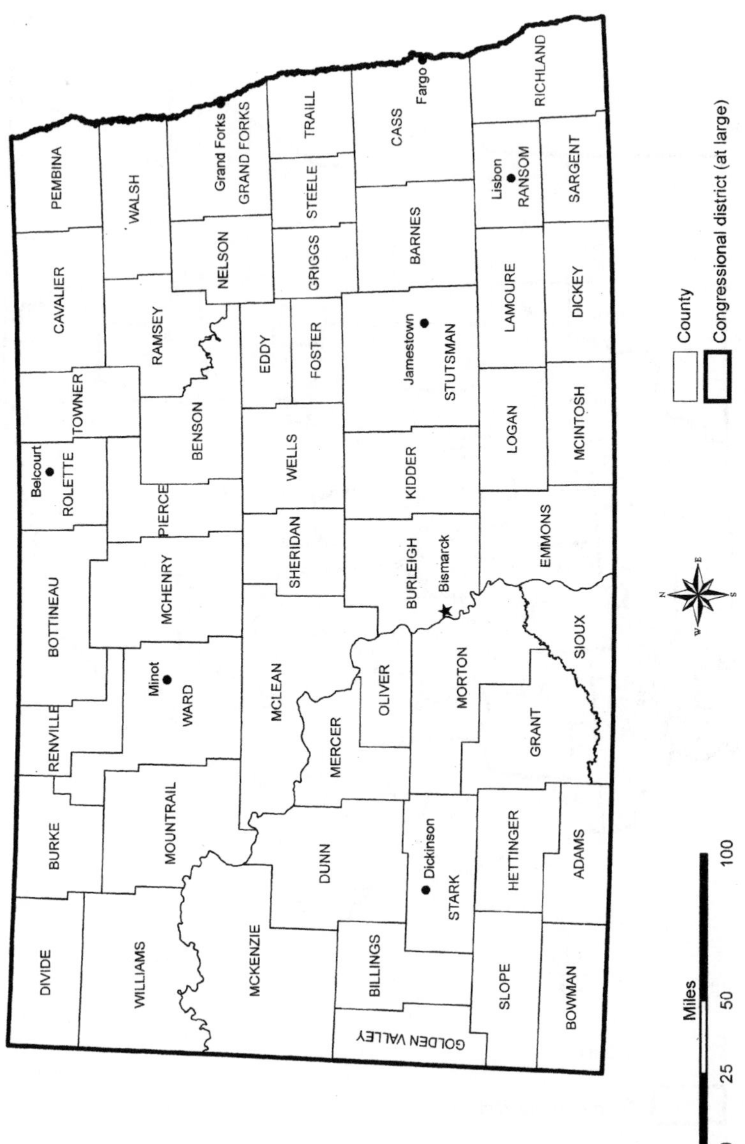

OHIO—Congressional Districts—(18 Districts)

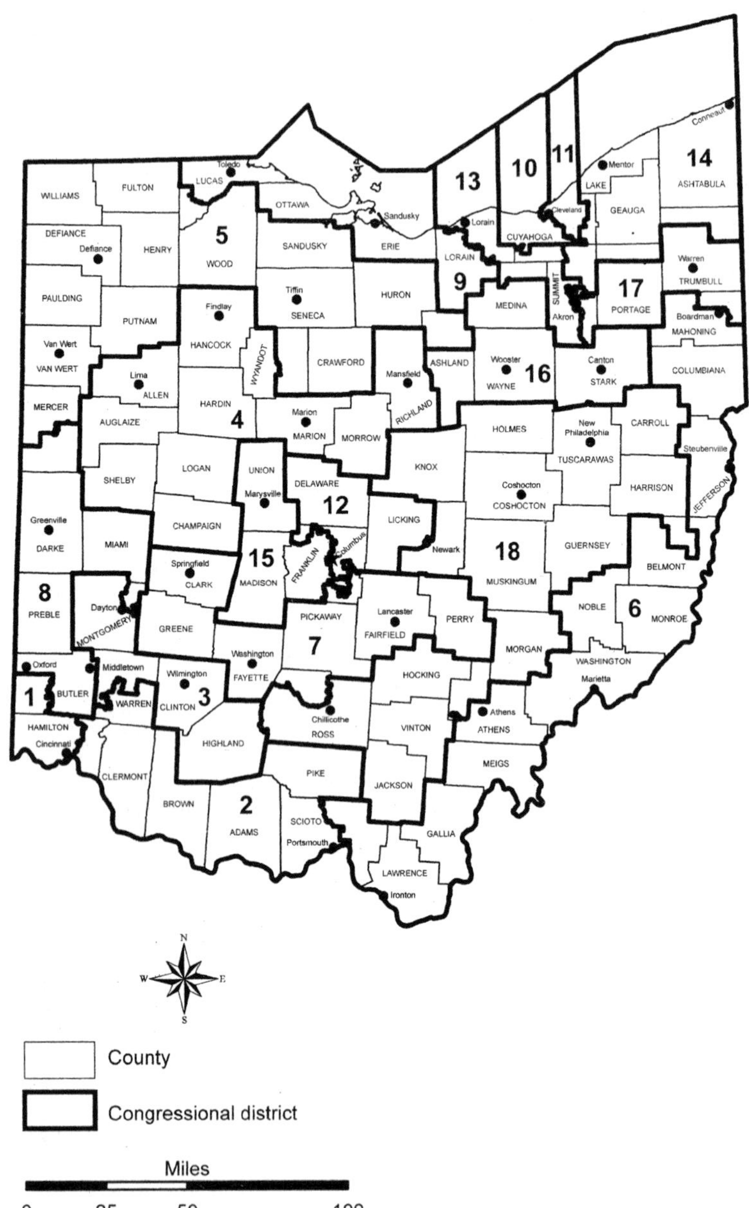

OKLAHOMA—Congressional Districts—(5 Districts)

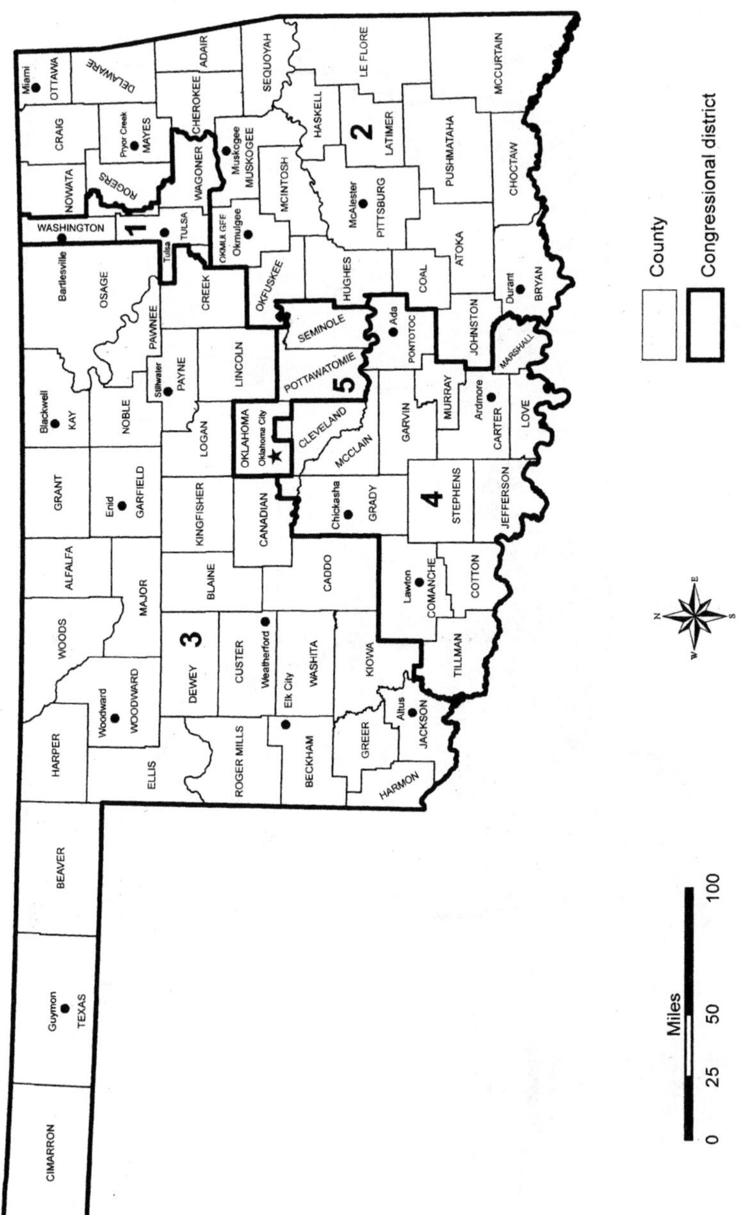

OREGON—Congressional Districts—(5 Districts)

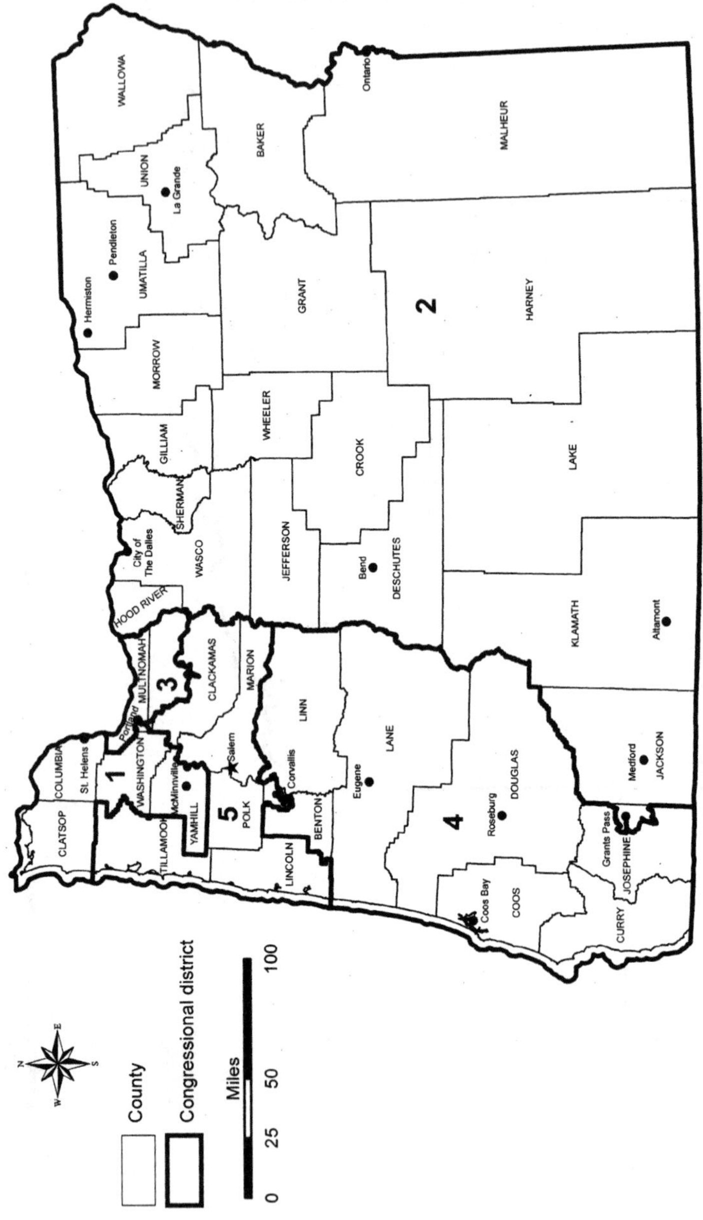

PENNSYLVANIA—Congressional Districts—(19 Districts)

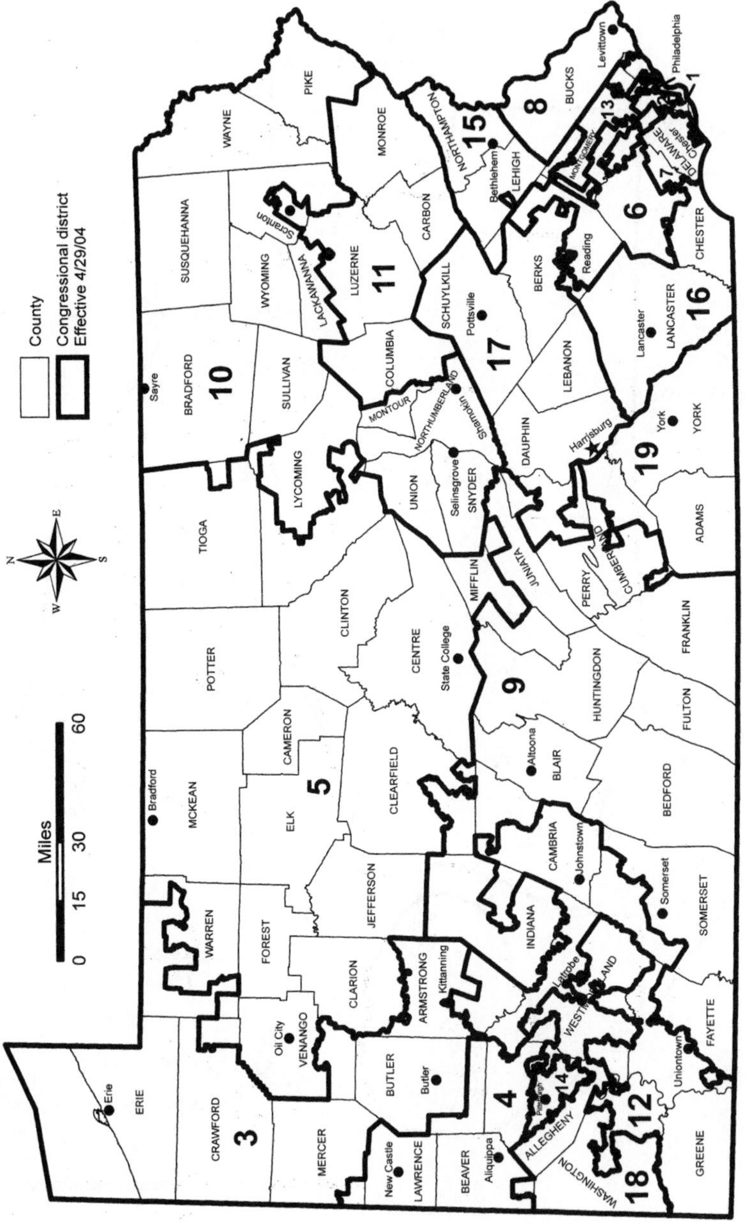

RHODE ISLAND—Congressional Districts—(2 Districts)

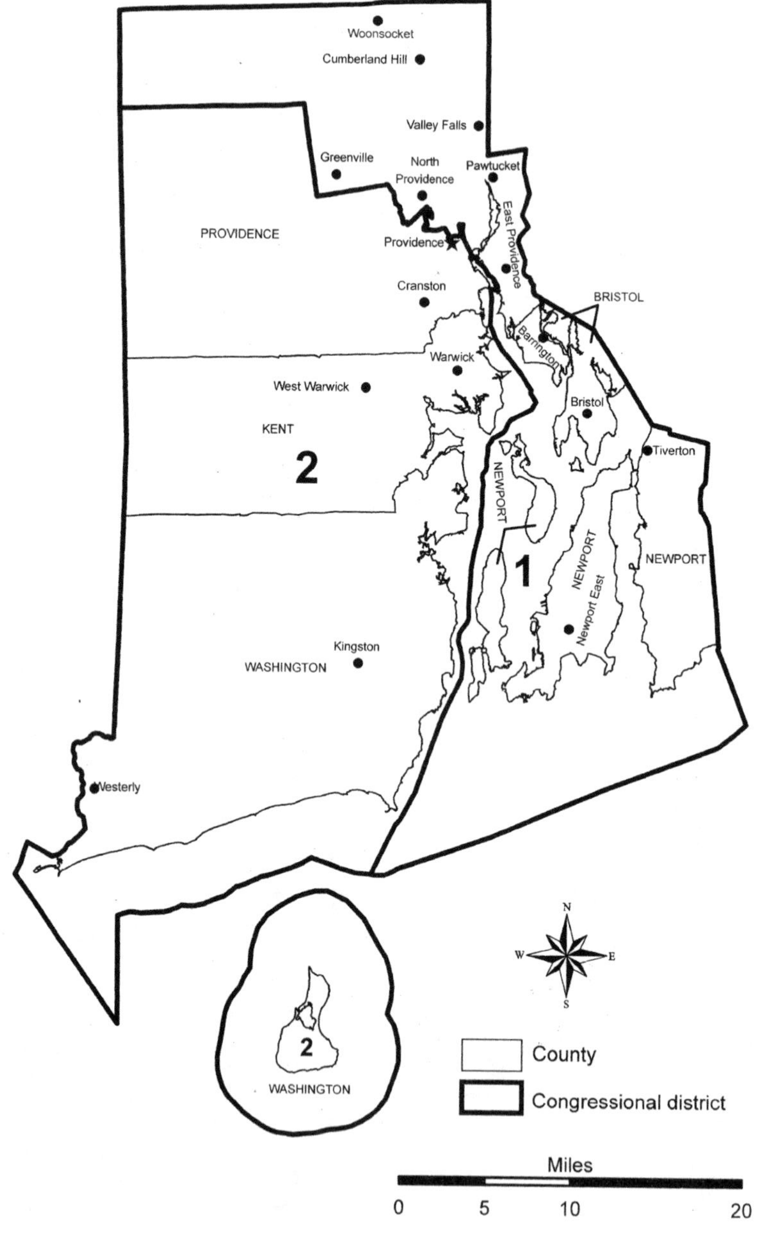

SOUTH CAROLINA—Congressional Districts—(6 Districts)

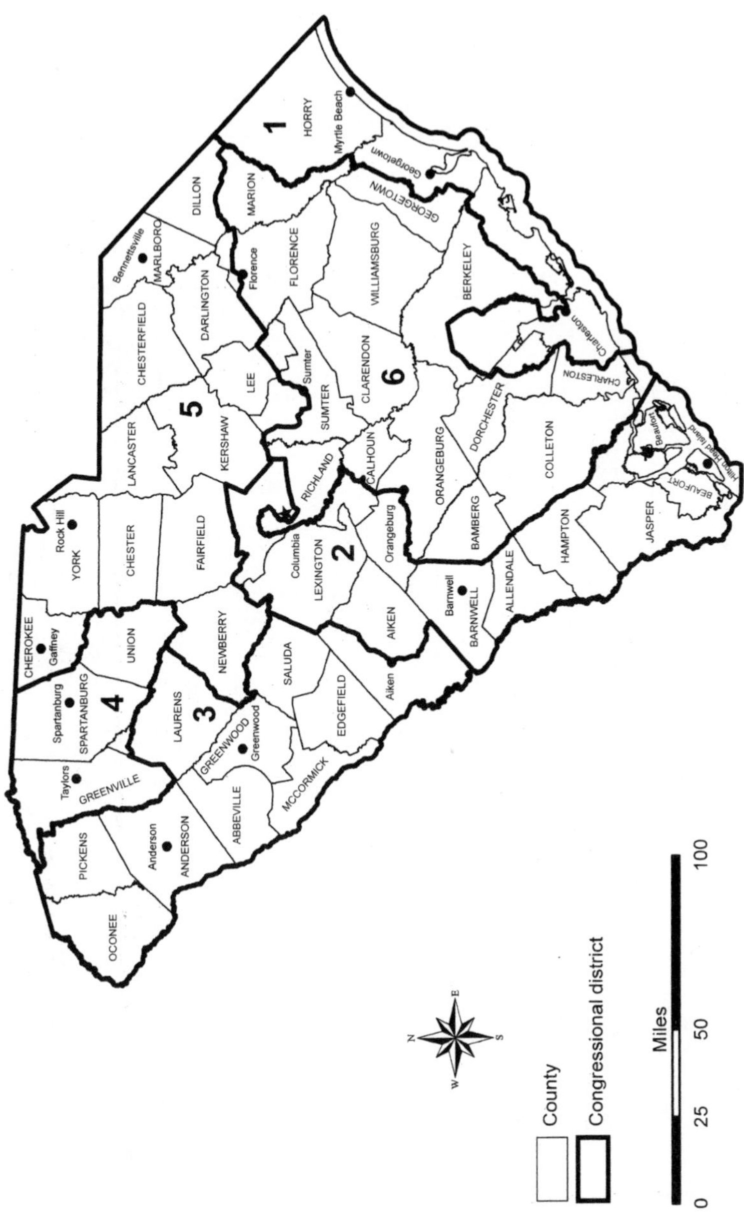

SOUTH DAKOTA—Congressional District—(1 District At Large)

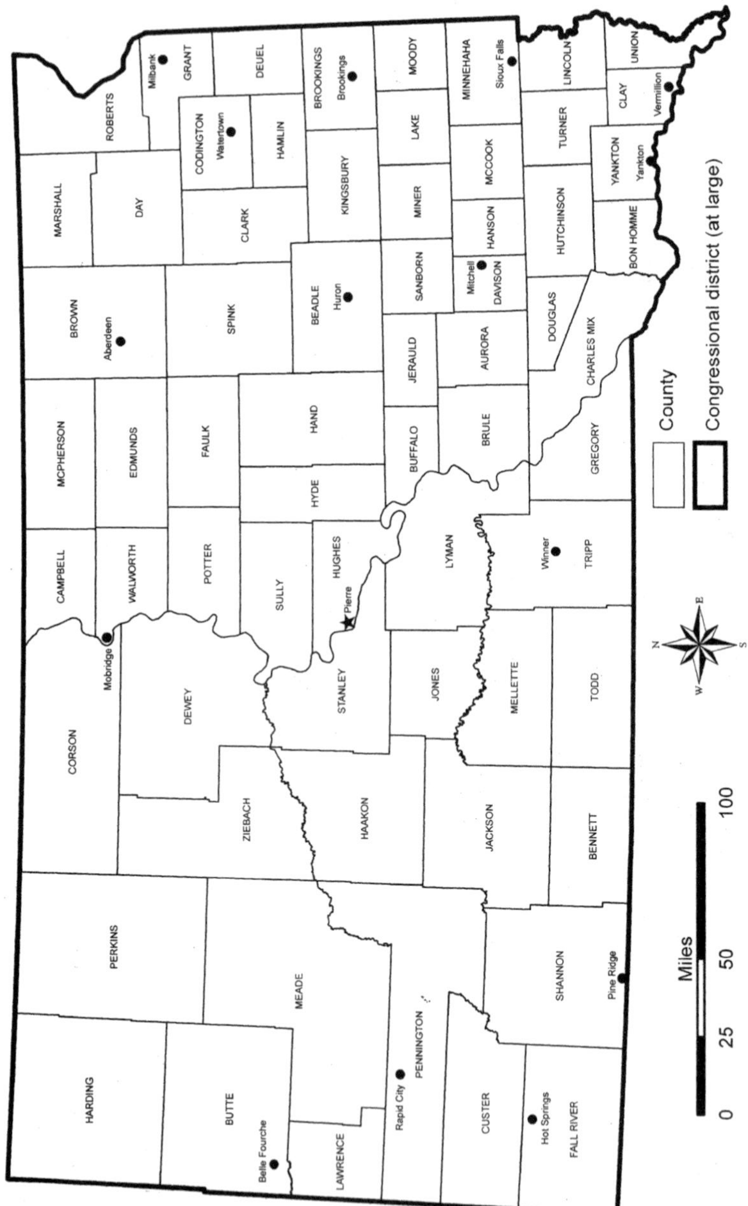

TENNESSEE—Congressional Districts—(9 Districts)

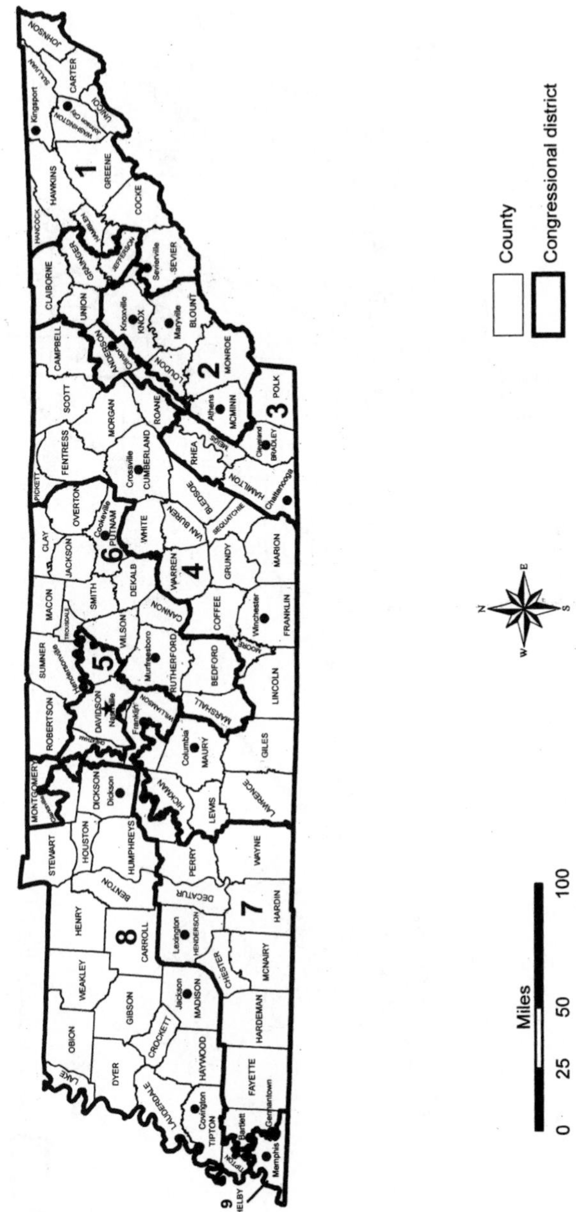

TEXAS—Congressional Districts—(32 Districts)

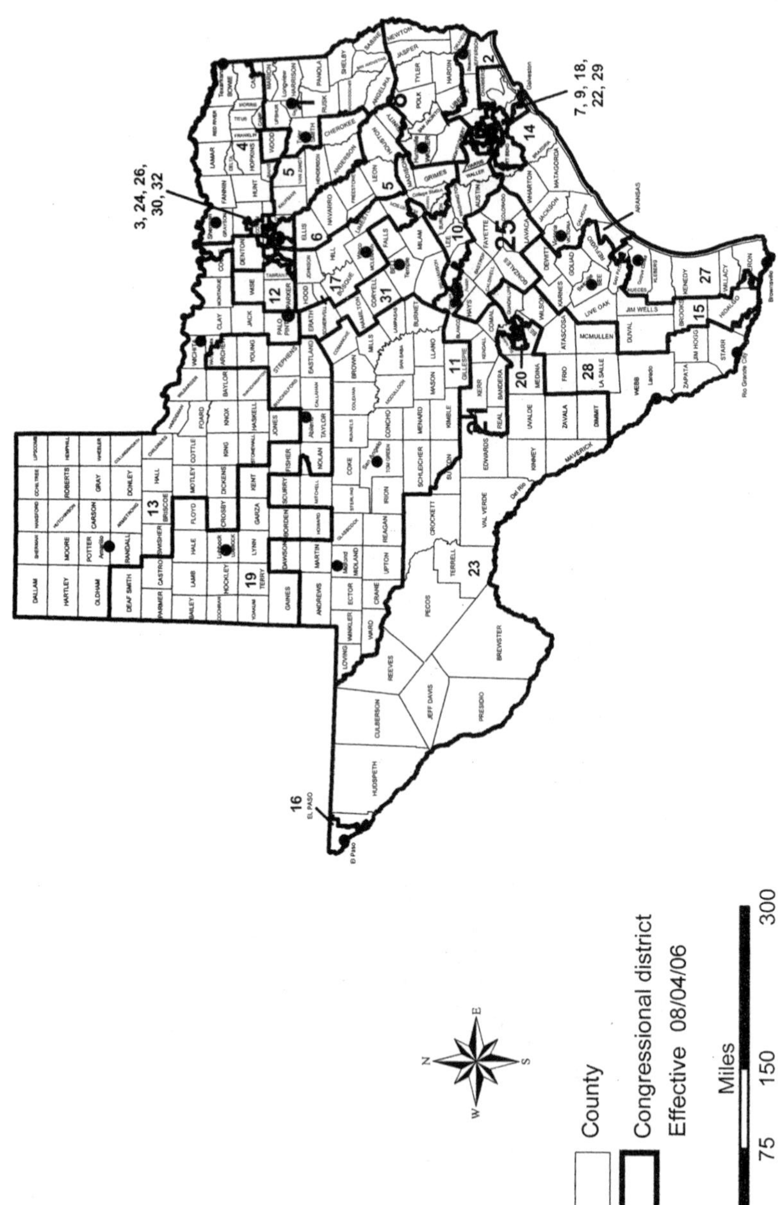

UTAH—Congressional Districts—(3 Districts)

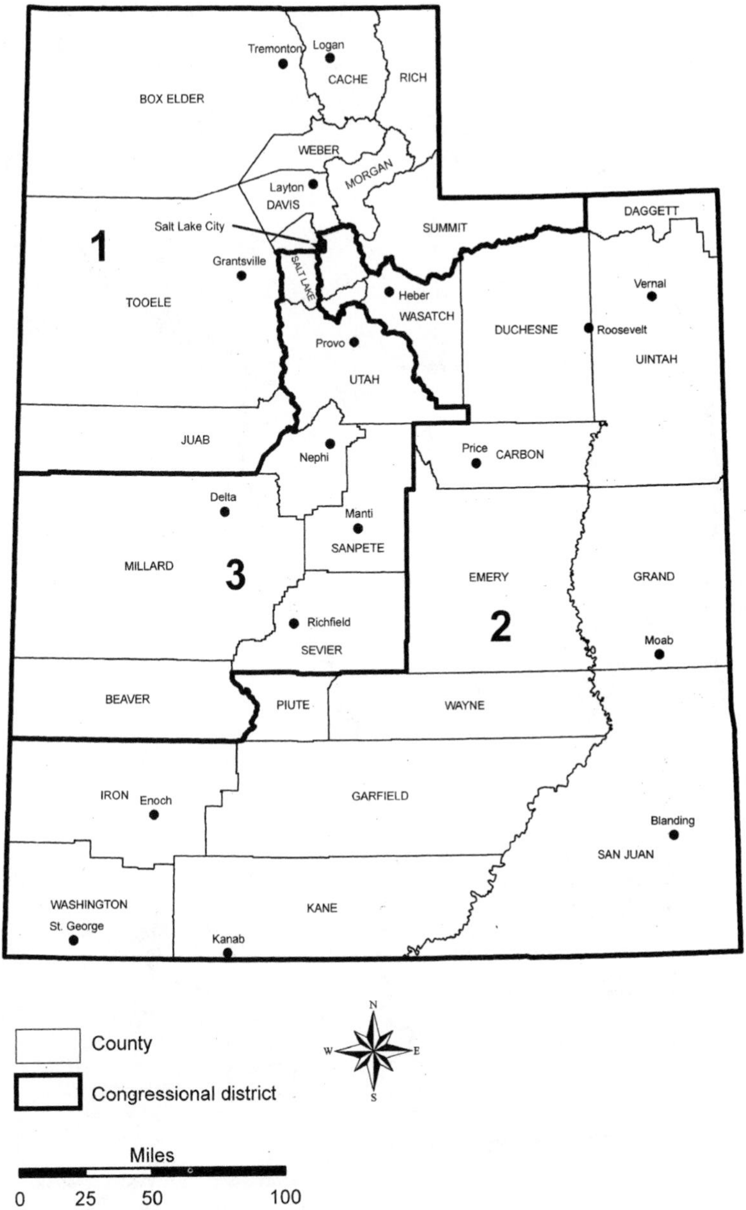

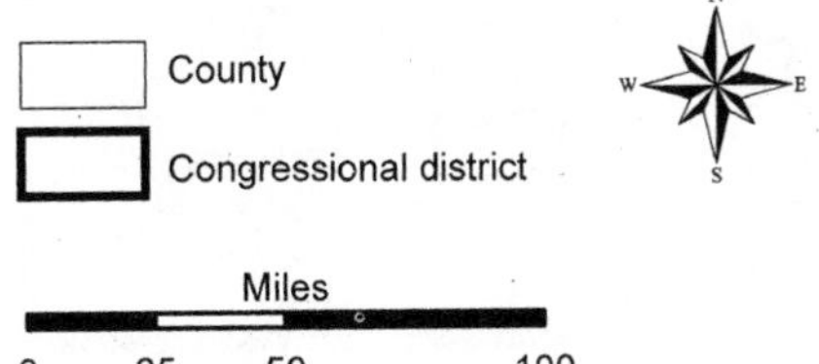

VERMONT—Congressional District—(1 District At Large)

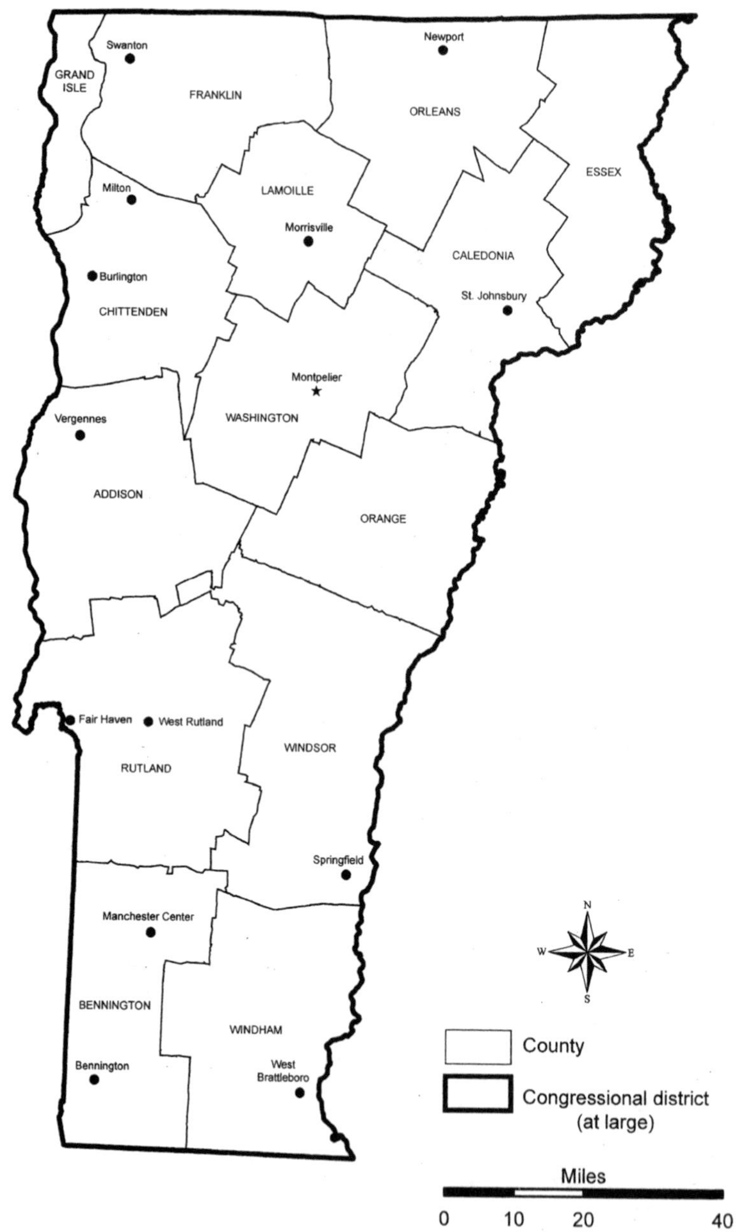

VIRGINIA—Congressional Districts—(11 Districts)

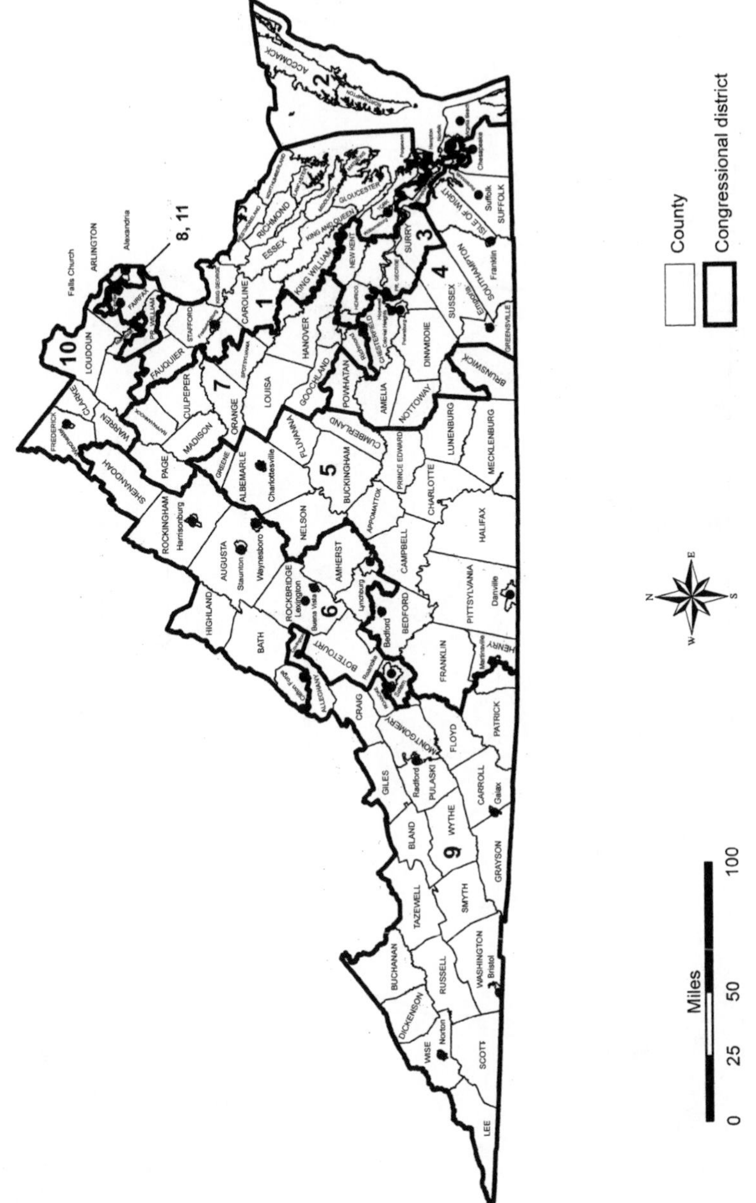

WASHINGTON—Congressional Districts—(9 Districts)

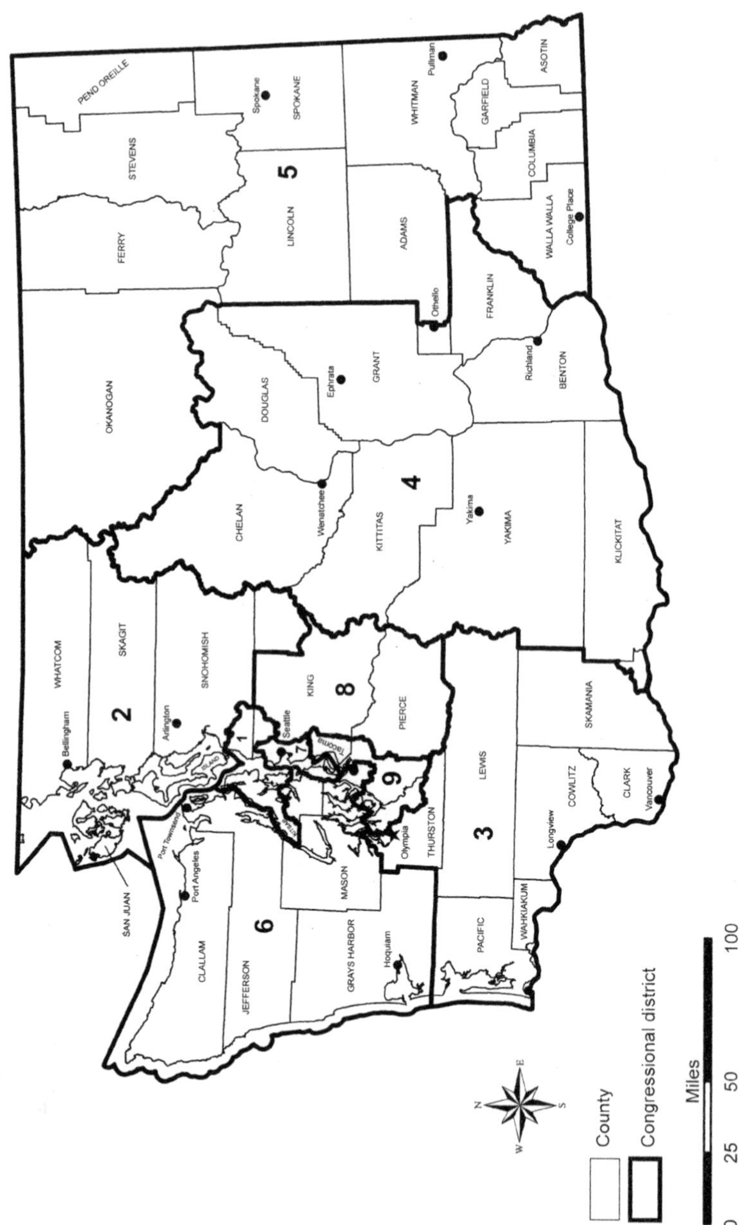

WEST VIRGINIA—Congressional Districts—(3 Districts)

County

Congressional district

Miles

0 25 50 100

WISCONSIN—Congressional Districts—(8 Districts)

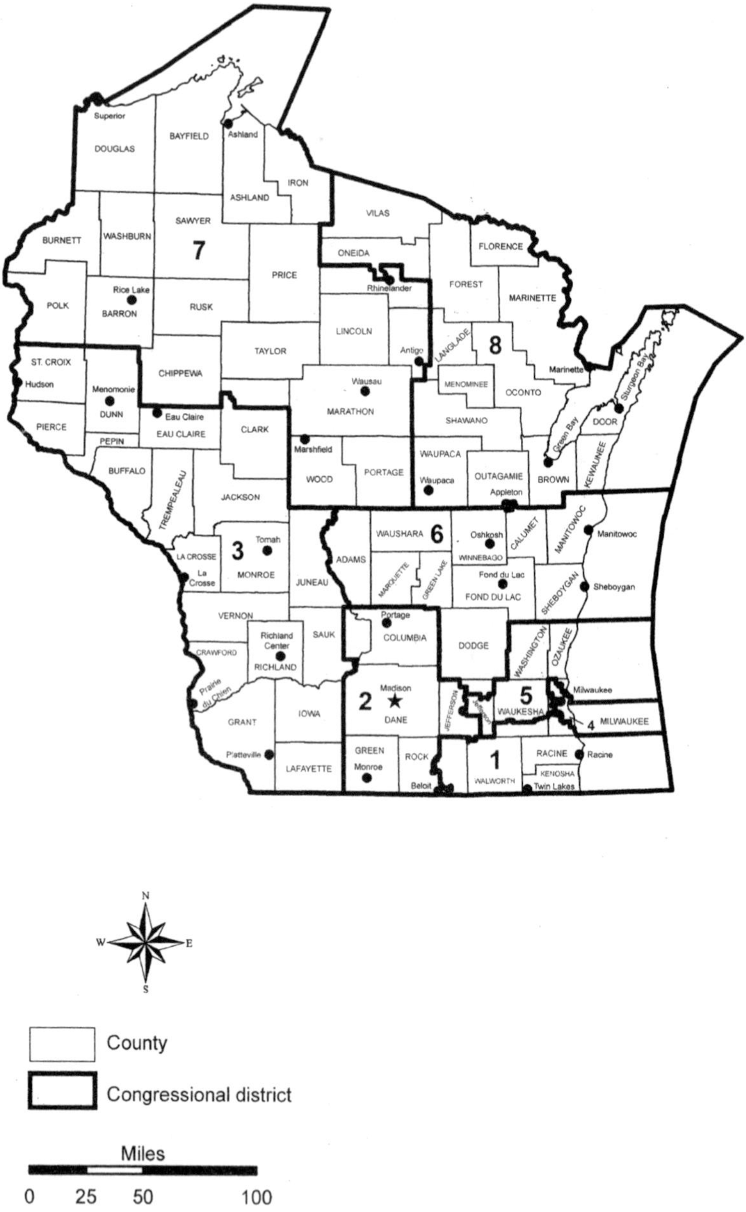

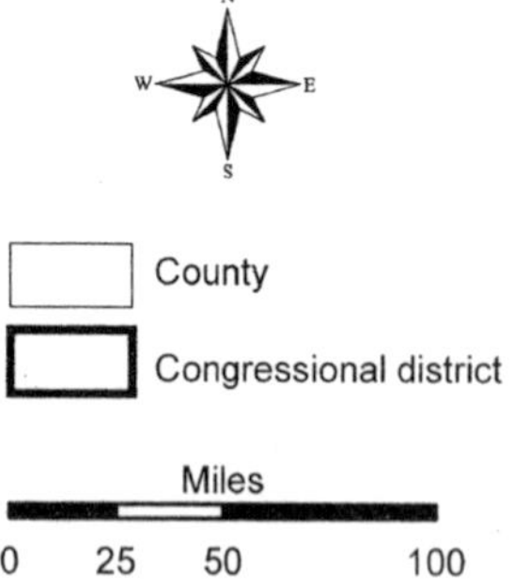

WYOMING—Congressional District—(1 District At Large)

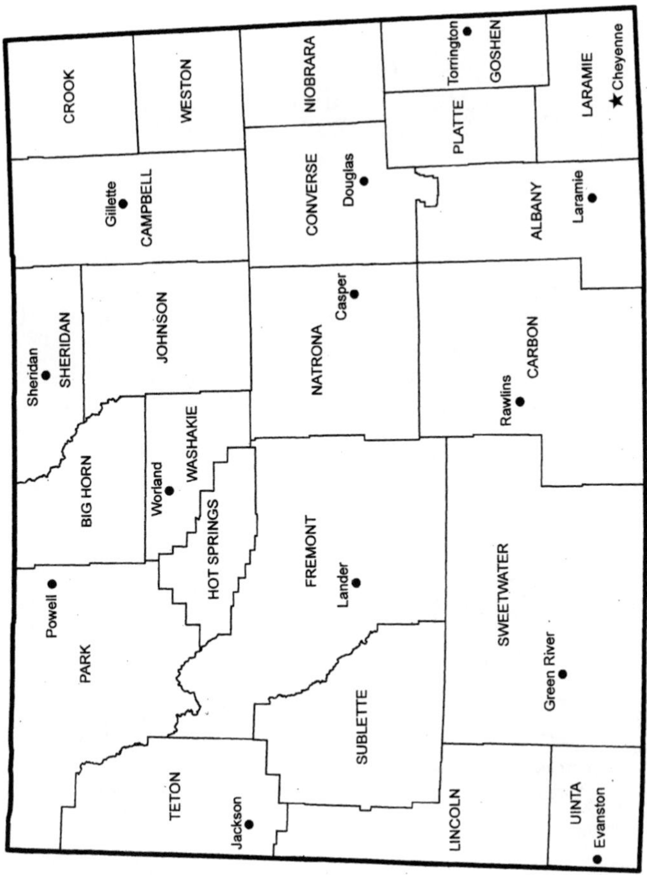

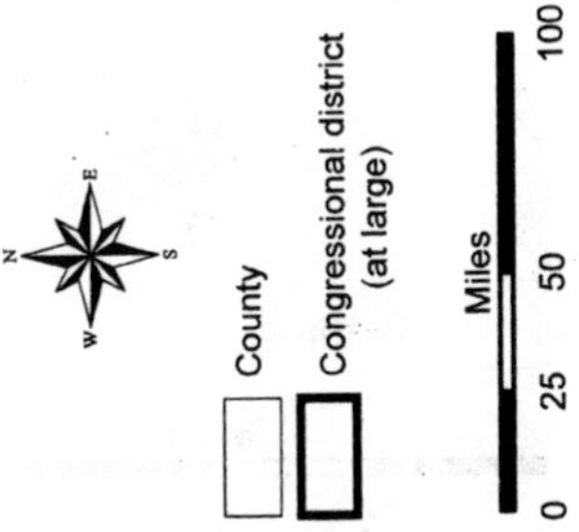

AMERICAN SAMOA—(1 Delegate At Large)

SWAINS ISLAND

MANU'A

ROSE ISLAND

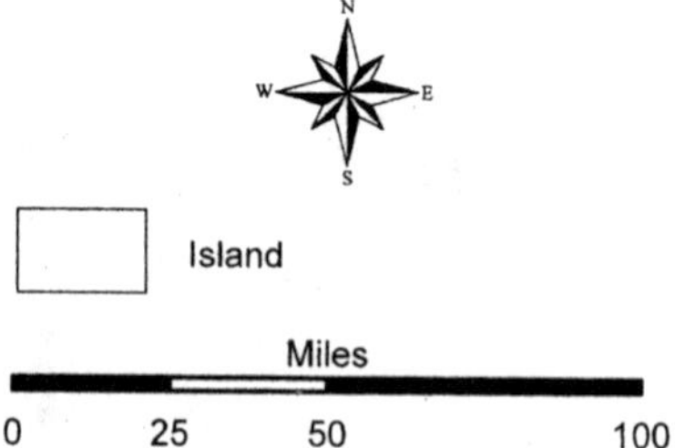

DISTRICT OF COLUMBIA—(1 Delegate At Large)

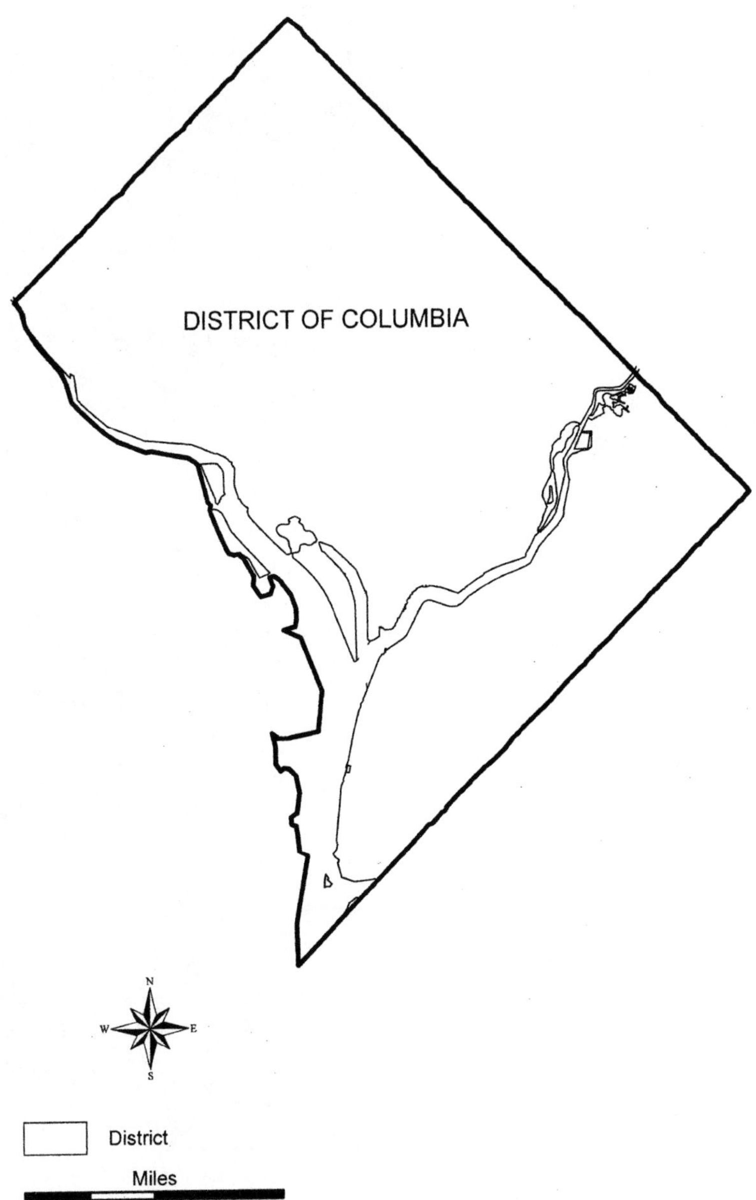

GUAM—(1 Delegate At Large)

PUERTO RICO—(1 Resident Commissioner At Large)

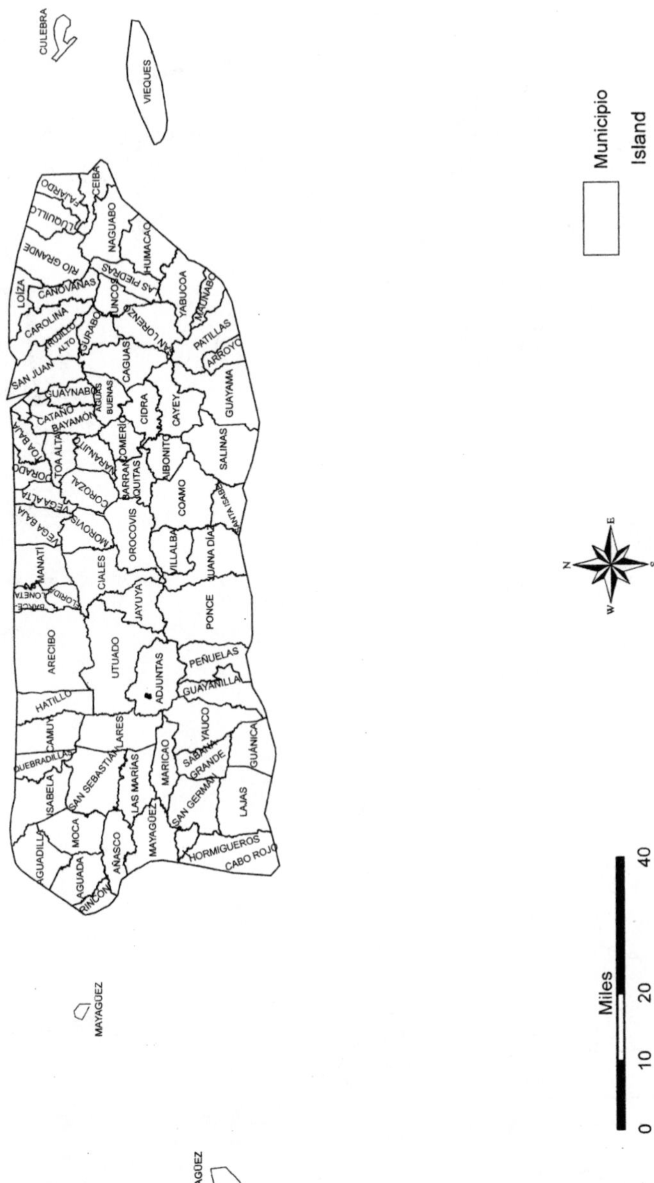

THE VIRGIN ISLANDS OF THE UNITED STATES—(1 Delegate At Large)

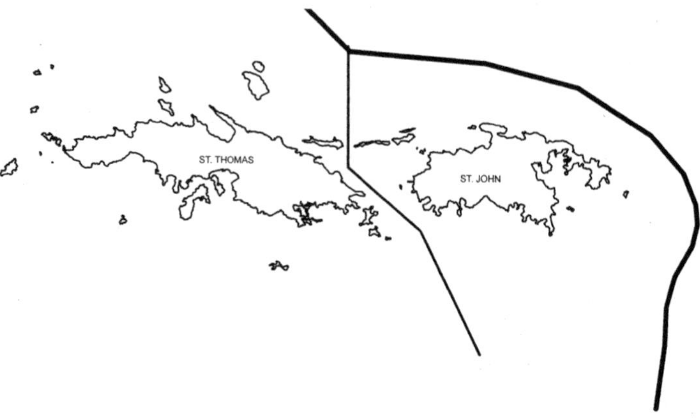

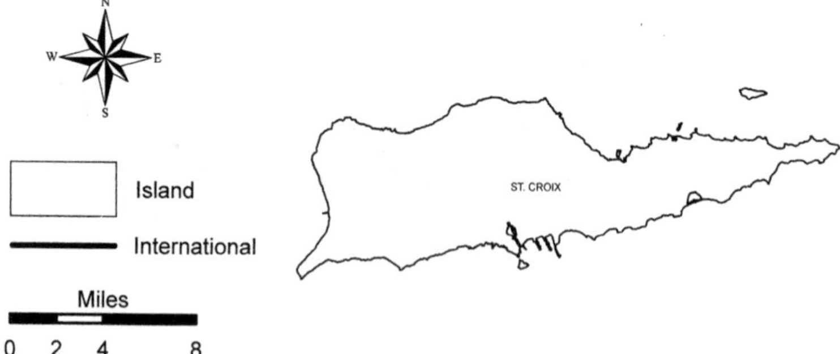

NAME INDEX

C

I

O

W

X

Y